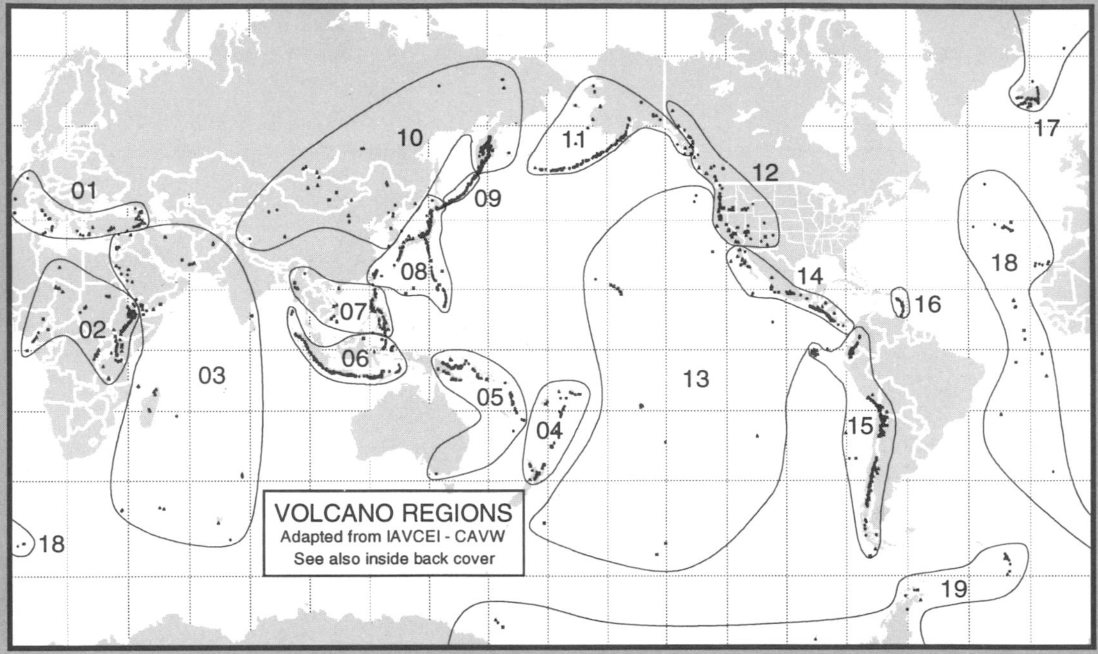

CODE BEFORE DATE (p. 15 - 18)

Code	Meaning	Count
–	BC date	1124
?	eruption itself uncertain	810
@	eruption locality uncertain	59
X	discredited eruption	156
A	anthropology	30
C	carbon-14 (uncorrected)	773
D	dendrochronology (tree ring)	19
F	fission track	3
G	carbon-14 (corrected)	126
H	hydration rind - glass	10
I	ice core	54
K	K-Ar	9
L	lichenometry	2
M	magnetism	29
R	Ar-Ar	4
S	SOFAR (hydrophonic)	37
T	tephrochronology	501
U	thermoluminescence	3
V	varve count	19

CODE AFTER DATE (UNCERTAINTY) (p. 15)

Code		Years	Days	Code		Years	Days	
a	=	± 1	± 1	*o*	=	± 18	± 25	
b	=	2	2	*p*	=	20	30	(1 mo)
c	=	3	3	*q*	=	25	45	
d	=	4	4	*r*	=	30	60	(2 mo)
e	=	± 5	± 5	*s*	=	40	75	
f	=	6	6	*t*	=	± 50	± 90	(3 mo)
g	=	7	7	*u*	=	75	120	
h	=	8	8	*v*	=	100	150	
i	=	9	9	*w*	=	150	180	(6 mo)
j	=	± 10	± 10	*x*	=	200	270	
k	=	12	12	*y*	=	± 300	± 365	(1 yr)
m	=	14	15	*z*	=	500	545	
n	=	16	20	*	=	1000	730	(2 yr)

> = eruption after date listed
< = eruption before date listed
? = date uncertain (no data)

EXAMPLES:

1731<	=	before 1731
1731a	=	between 1730 & 1732
1731 1105d	=	between Nov 1 & 9
1750 t	=	18th century
1790 j	=	late 18th century
1778 02 ?	=	February (?) 1778

ABBREVIATIONS

CAVW = Catalog of Active Volcanoes of the World
IAVCEI = International Association of Volcanology and Chemistry of the Earth's Interior
SEAN = Scientific Event Alert Network
GVN = Global Volcanism Network

METRIC CONVERSIONS

m = meter (3.28 feet)
km = kilometer (0.6214 miles)
km^3 = cubic kilometers (0.24 cubic miles)

VOLUME (p. 25)

Vol volume of lava erupted (left column)
L / T volume of tephra (right column)
7/- = 10^7 m^3 lava, no recorded tephra volume
-/9 = 10^9 m^3 tephra, no recorded lava volume
7/8 = 10^7 m^3 lava, 10^8 m^3 tephra

VOLCANOES OF THE WORLD

INTRODUCTION 34 pages describing tabulated data headings, procedures used, noteworthy examples, data use cautions, and relationsh of volcanism in space and time.

DIRECTORY 1511 volcanoes believed active in last 10,000 years. Arranged geographically by region (see map opposite), with locations heights, types, known eruptive histories, and behavioral characteristics. Detailed maps, and summaries of history, geography, and tectonics, introduce each region.

FATALITIES & EVACUATIONS 414 fatal events summarized and (for the past 19 years) 101 evacuations tabulated.

CHRONOLOGY 7886 eruptions from 8000 BC through 1993 AD. Arranged chronologically, with durations, explosive magnitudes, and volume of products (when known). Drawings and photographs illustrate the processes and features covered in the book.

GAZETTEER 10,400 cross-referenced volcano names, synonyms, and feature names. A name index.

REFERENCES 2041 source citations for more detailed information, arranged chronologically by region.

WORLD MAP Volcano locations and subregion numbering scheme that provides the basic cross-referencing device used throughout the book (inside back cover).

Abbreviations and codes used in data tables, together with their frequency of occurrence, follow:

VOLCANO TYPE (p. 10, fig. 5)

Caldera(s)	83
Cinder cone(s)	87
Complex volcano(es)	54
Compound volcano	13
Cone(s)	8
Crater rows	5
Explosion crater(s)	7
Fissure vent(s)	21
Fumarole field(s)	13
Hydrothermal field	6
Lava cone	2
Lava dome(s)	40
Maar(s)	15
Pumice cone(s)	4
Pyroclastic cone(s)	35
Pyroclastic shield	3
Scoria cone(s)	10
Shield volcano(es)	164
Somma volcano(es)	6
Stratovolcano(es)	699
Subglacial volcano	6
Submarine volcano(es)	105
Tuff cone(s) & tuff ring(s)	13
Unknown	32
Volcanic complex	2
Volcanic field	92

VOLCANO STATUS (p. 12)

Documented eruptions	
Historical	539
Dating methods	
Radiocarbon	106
Tephrochronology	33
Anthropology	22
Hydrophonic	7
Dendrochronology	4
Ar-Ar	2
Hydration Rind	1
Ice Core	1
K-Ar	1
Lichenometry	1
Magnetism	1
Varve Count	1
Geologic evidence	
Holocene	530
Holocene?	108
Fumarolic	65
Hot Springs	5
Seismicity	4
Others	
Uncertain	57
Pleistocene-thermal	23
Not a Volcano	14

ERUPTIVE CHARACTERISTICS (p. 20 - 22)

		Number	%	CAVW *
PLACE	**Central** crater eruption	4440	56.3	○
	Flank (excentric) **vent**	757	9.6	
	Radial fissure eruption	574	7.3	
	Regional fissure eruption	295	3.7	=
WATER	**Submarine** eruption	289	3.7	
	New island formation	95	1.2	
	Subglacial eruption	104	1.3	
	Crater lake eruption	323	4.1	
TEPHRA	**Explosive** (normal explosions)	5547	70.3	↑
	Pyroclastic flows	763	9.7	→
	Phreatic explosions	838	10.6	
	Fumarolic activity	19	0.2	
LAVA	**Lava** flow(s)	1999	25.3	⇒
	Lava lake eruption	93	1.2	
	Dome extrusion	374	4.7	
	Spine extrusion	20	0.3	
DAMAGE	**Fatalities**	330	4.2	†
	Damage (land, property, etc)	847	10.7	
	Mudflows (lahars)	489	6.2	
	Tsunami (giant sea waves)	62	0.8	

x = recorded – = not recorded
* symbol used in CAVW Catalogs

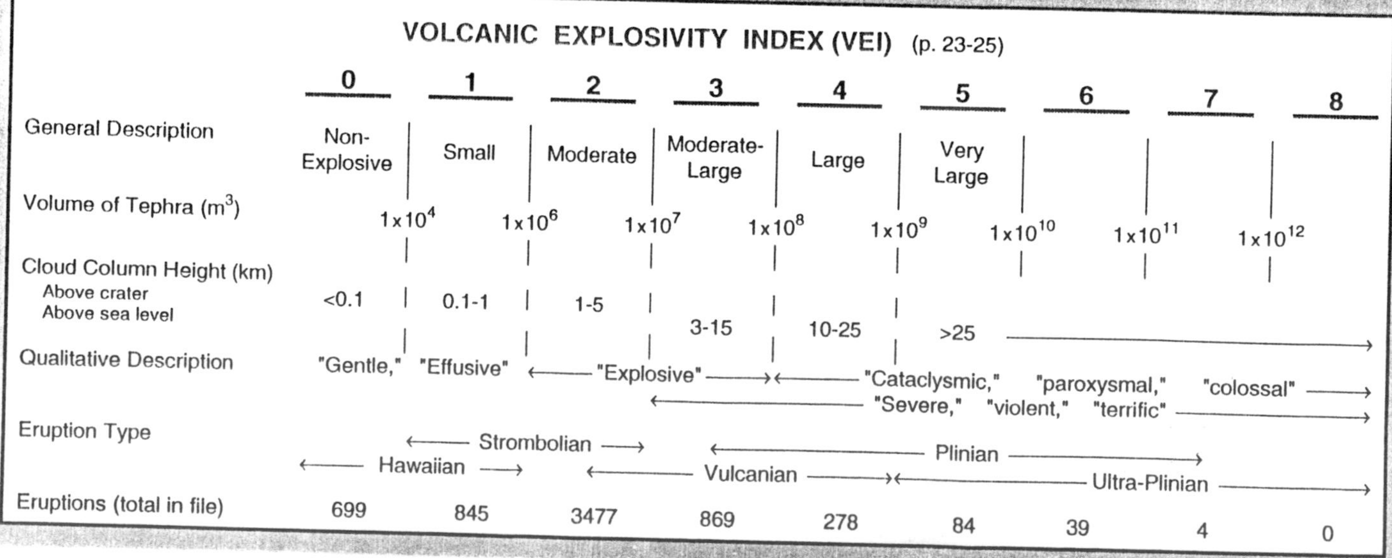

VOLCANIC EXPLOSIVITY INDEX (VEI) (p. 23-25)

	0	1	2	3	4	5	6	7	8
General Description	Non-Explosive	Small	Moderate	Moderate-Large	Large	Very Large			
Volume of Tephra (m^3)		1×10^4	1×10^6	1×10^7	1×10^8	1×10^9	1×10^{10}	1×10^{11}	1×10^{12}
Cloud Column Height (km) Above crater / Above sea level	<0.1	0.1-1	1-5	3-15	10-25	>25 →			
Qualitative Description	"Gentle,"	"Effusive"	←"Explosive"→		←"Cataclysmic," "paroxysmal," "colossal" → / ←"Severe," "violent," "terrific" →				
Eruption Type	← Hawaiian →	← Strombolian →	← Vulcanian →		← Plinian → / ← Ultra-Plinian →				
Eruptions (total in file)	699	845	3477	869	278	84	39	4	0

Volcanoes of the World

Front Cover

Vigorous explosive and effusive activity in October, 1822 from the central cone of Vesuvius. Viewed across the Bay of Naples by an unknown artist. This eruption marked the paroxysmal conclusion of an eruptive period that began in 1796. From the collection of Maurice & Katia Krafft.

Back Cover

1831 eruption forming the ephemeral Graham Island in a submarine volcanic field SW of Sicily. July 13 strombolian eruptions from several vents, painted by Camillo de Vito. This eruption captured the popular imagination of the time; another painting of this event is shown in Fig. 15 (p. 193). From the collection of Maurice & Katia Krafft.

Volcanoes of the World

SECOND EDITION

A Regional Directory, Gazetteer, and Chronology of Volcanism During the Last 10,000 Years

Tom Simkin & Lee Siebert
Smithsonian Institution, Global Volcanism Program

with the collaboration of
Russell Blong, Jonathan Dehn, Christopher Newhall,
Roland Pool, and Thomas C. Stein

Published in association with 

the Smithsonian Institution

Library of Congress Catalog Card Number 93-77813

First published by Geoscience Press in 1994.

Publisher's Cataloging in Publication
(Prepared by Quality Books Inc.)
Simkin, Tom.
Volcanoes of the world / Tom Simkin and Lee Siebert
p. cm.
ISBN 0-945005-12-1
1. Volcanoes.
I. Siebert, Lee. II. Title.
QE522.S55 1993 551.2'1
QBI93-20626

Published by

Geoscience Press
PO Box 42948, Tucson AZ 85733-2948
Phone (602) 326-9595

In association with

Smithsonian Institution, Global Volcanism Program
NHB Stop 119
Washington DC 20560

Manufactured in the United States of America

Contents

Preface

Volcanoes and their processes cover an enormous spectrum: from inconspicuous fissures to majestic peaks and from mild steaming to terrifying paroxysms. To understand volcanism – an essential step towards either combating its dangers or utilizing its resources – we must gauge its full breadth and attempt to wrestle its elements into some kind of framework. This book is one of many efforts toward that end.

Volcanology, more than most disciplines, depends upon history. The range of behavior is broad enough, and the intervals between events are long enough, that we must mine the contemporary and historical records to learn the dynamic aspects – times, speeds, sequences – that are difficult or impossible to obtain for prehistoric eruptions. Well-documented examples from the past can be enormously helpful in interpreting a volcanic crisis, and understanding the processes of the present is a long-established geological key for unlocking secrets of the past.

For 26 years our group at the Smithsonian has been aggressively seeking descriptions of ongoing volcanism around the world, trying to ensure that the right questions are asked while the answers are still available, integrating data from diverse sources, and sharing this information with a broadening community interested in volcanism. We quickly learned that basic volcanological information is widely scattered, making it difficult to answer the first questions asked when confronted by a newly active volcano (where is it? what is its history? who has studied it?). Consequently, we started a database in 1971, when that word was still young, and early database history is recounted below in the preface to its first product, our 1981 book. The 13 years since that book have brought many new eruptions, additional studies of older eruptions, reviews of our data by regional specialists, and a gratifying response from readers all over the world suggesting changes and additions to improve upon the first edition.

Results of these changes include a net addition of 2322 eruptions (less than one-fifth of them postdating the first edition) and over 170 "new" volcanoes active in the last 10,000 years. References have nearly tripled in this edition and the number of names and synonyms listed in the Gazetteer has doubled. We believe that quality has increased along with quantity, but must emphasize – as we do throughout the following text – that the record of volcanism remains far from complete.

In addition to the acknowledgements below, in the first edition's preface, it is a pleasure to thank the many people who have contributed to the current volume during the past 13 years.

A long-term collaboration with Chris Newhall, of the U.S. Geological Survey, began prior to our first edition and has continued through the long gestation period of the second. He reviewed the complete first edition and, along with Dan Shackelford, provided us with detailed notes on virtually every page. We thank them both for their large efforts and the improvements they have brought to the current edition. In the table below, we list some of the many people who have contributed to full regions or parts of regions (using the numbering scheme shown on both inside covers). The use of italics singles out the friends who have reviewed large segments (in some cases all) of their region's entries. We regret not being able to list all of the many readers who have sent reprints or otherwise alerted us to problems with individual entries in our first edition.

01 *Jörg Keller, Jean Tanguy, Roberto Scandone, Claudia Principe, Jean Feraud, Guy Camus*, Romolo Romano, Vicente Araña, J-M Mallarach, James Mellaart, Oskar Ermann, Frank Clover.

02 *Giday Woldegabriel, Celia Nyamweru, Pierre Vincent, Martin Smith*, Peter Dunkley, Craig Feibel.

03 *Laurent Stieltjes, Guy Camus*, Graeme Wheller, JP Poirer, Reginald Briggs, Alta Walker.

04 *John Latter, Bruce Houghton, Jim Cole*, Paul Taylor.

05 *Wally Johnson*, Chris McKee, Malcolm Sheard.

06 *George De Neve, Tom Casadevall*, Eddie Effendi, Liek Pardyanto, Kaswanda, Haroun Said, Nanang Rahardja, David Sussman, Chris Newhall and Roy Torley, Pierre Vetch.

07 *Chris Newhall, Olimpio Peña, John Wolfe, Toti Corpuz.*

08 *Toshio Higashino, Masaki Takahashi*, Yosihiro Sawada, Dick Moore, Toki Tiba, Hiroki Kamata.

09 Genrich Steinberg, Andre Tsvetkov, Ed Erlich.

10 *Ed Erlich, Jim Whitford-Stark, Vera Ponamareva*, Yuri Doubik, Oleg Volynets, Sergei Rasskazov, Ming Zhang, Jiaqi Liu, Jim Gill, Alexander Belousov, William Kidd, Geoff Wadge.

11 *Chris Nye*, Tom Miller, Steve McNutt, John Reeder, Klaus Jacob.

12 *Cathy Hickson*, Neil Church.

13 *Jack Lockwood*, Tom Wright, Jacques Talandier, Hans Barsczus.

14 *Jaime Incer, Larry Feldman, Jorge Barquero, Guillermo Alvarado, Mike Carr, Bill Rose*, Jim Luhr, Steve Nelson, Mark Defant, Antonio Rivera, Jim Reynolds, Sam Bonis, Alfredo MacKenney, Dick Stoiber.

15 *Hugo Moreno, Pete Hall, Bernardo Beate*, Maria Eugenia Petit-Breuilh, Shan de Silva, Moyra Gardeweg, BA Klinck, Steve Porter, John Guest, Tui De Roy, Cindy Stine.

16 *Alan Smith and Keith Rowley*, Haraldur Sigurdsson, Philippe Bouysse, John Shepherd.

17 *Sigurdur Steinthorsson*, Pall Imsland.

18 *Dick Moore, Paco Pérez and Klaus Mehl.*

19 Wes LeMasurier, Phil Kyle.

We have benefited from funding supplied by the U.S. Geological Survey (Volcano Hazards Program), Department of Energy (Geothermal Program), and NASA (Volcano-Climate Interaction Program), and we thank these organizations for their support. Our greatest support, though, has come directly from the U.S. Congress, in the form of line-item funding to the Smithsonian for our Global Volcanism Program. While augmenting our existing global activities, the new program linked naturally to our research on individual volcanoes and our museum collection of volcanological specimens. Starting 10 years ago, this valuable support has: (1) enhanced our eruption reporting; (2) helped establish a permanent archive for maps, photographs, and documents; and (3) enabled our several computer-intensive operations to reach self-sufficiency. This opportune funding allowed us to buy personal computers and software in the early days of the desktop, hire a computer specialist, and free ourselves from the antiquated mainframe system that housed our database through the mid 1980s. Readers comparing the mainframe-generated tables of our first edition with the desktop-generated tables of this edition will recognize the value of modern niceties such as lowercase letters and multiple fonts. These advances have not been without pain, as will be clear to anyone who has lost an electronic file or succumbed to a frozen cursor, but we think the end result has been worth it.

Our first computer specialist, Jon Dehn, helped us select and install the Pick Operating System for our database, programmed the interface between the two, and generated our Directory format from Pick. His successor, Tom Stein, took us to independence, with a final, nervous download from the mainframe in 1988. Tom also designed our Chronology format from Pick, and led us into both computer graphics and Ventura desktop publishing. Roland Pool brought these advances together, added Gazetteer and References formats, produced the maps, and integrated the layout of this book. Additional computer assistance in the late days of book production has been welcomed from Ed Venzke (Fatality/Evacuation table and other layouts) and Genyong Peng (text figures and maps) of our GVN (eruption reporting) group, and earlier help on programming and maps was supplied by interns Scott Chaney and Pavan Khoobchandani. Dan Cole, of our museum's GIS center, and Ken McCormick of the Smithsonian's main computer center also provided help with the regional maps. We thank all these individuals for their valuable assistance, and Pick Systems for their software support.

Additional Smithsonian colleagues have helped make the book a reality. First among these is Ellen Thurnau, whose cheerful efficiency has solved (if not prevented) a host of administrative problems in the last 7 years. A succession of archivists – Elizabeth Nielsen, Courtenay Wilkerson, and Julia Lewis – have organized resources on which we all draw, and our SEAN/GVN colleagues through the years have sought out the new eruption information that helps build our record. This group has included David Squires, Lindsay McClelland, Elizabeth Nielsen, Marge Summers, Lisa Wainger, Katherine Duncker Romanak, David Lescinsky, and our current staff of Ed Venzke, Rick Wunderman, and Genyong Peng. Additional short-term employees and interns have also contributed to the monthly Bulletins. McClelland, who compiled early data in the pre-Siebert years and then led SEAN/GVN for 17 years (and 198 Bulletins), deserves special thanks. Translation assistance has come from Virginia Wong, Boris Behncke, Cheerie Magalit, Gene Jarosewich, and Joe Nelen, in addition to several already named under the region headings above. In the final stages of book completion, Rick Wunderman helped with illustration selection, and intern Justin Mog with References and Gazetteer.

Curatorial colleagues in the Museum's Petrology and Volcanology Division – Bill Melson, Dick Fiske, Jim Luhr, and Sorena Sorensen – have contributed advice, photographs, and encouragement. Jim Luhr has also reviewed the full text, as have more distant colleagues Chris Newhall and (with interference from the Rabaul eruption) Wally Johnson. Chris, Wally, John Latter, Bob Smith, and Grant Heiken have given us thoughtful, helpful counsel on the database through most of its life. Russell Blong instigated, and contributed importantly to, the Fatality table of pp. 165-175. Visiting historian Howard Plotkin helpfully reviewed the Directory text.

We also owe thanks to the publishers who have granted permission to reprint illustrations and, particularly, to the families of Maurice and Katia Krafft both for facilitating access to their magnificent collections and for permission to use several illustrations. Maurice and Katia contributed substantively to this book by their reports and published work, and they were scheduled to review several sections at the time of their tragic deaths. The welcome addition of their illustrations here is a small measure of the large contributions they made to volcanology.

Finally, we ask for your help and offer some in return. Please continue to send us reprints, copies of old documents, maps, photographs, specimens, and (kind) comments on how we can improve our record of your favorite volcano. This kind of feedback is surely the best way to build the better record of global volcanism that will benefit us all. On more than one harried occasion in the past we have failed to respond adequately, and we apologize to those we have neglected, but we have valued every communication received. Please keep the information flowing and we will do our best to incorporate it accurately in our database as it grows. In return, we expect to be able to be more responsive to data requests. For years we have made available on floppy disk an ASCII file of our basic geographic information on each volcano, including date of most recent known eruption (in broad age categories). Now that we have completed our top priority of several years (this book, a long-established form of communication that demands of the user absolutely no computer literacy), we are turning our attention to comparable export files of the more complicated chronologic elements of our database. Early in 1995 we expect to have available both eruption and reference files that can be relationally linked to our (geographic) volcano file. The burgeoning field of electronic information transfer offers great opportunities for interactive access to these data files and to another that we recently began building for petrologic and geochemical data. We ask you to write to us, stating your needs and anticipated uses, and we will do our best to meet your request (we have resisted the temptation to establish the price of export data files as either a documented Holocene volcano or dated eruption not already known to us). In any case, we hope for substantive feedback from many readers to help build a better information base for the future.

Preface to First Edition

Volcanoes provide some of the more awesome and spectacular examples of natural change on our dynamic planet. New material is added to the earth's surface by volcanoes, resources such as geothermal power are produced by volcanoes, and human lives are sometimes changed by volcanoes. The record of global volcanism, however, is fragmentary and scattered. Many volcanoes are remote from human habitation, and the historic record, when compared with the long intervals between many eruptions, is often too short to aid in predicting future volcanic activity. Predictions are needed, though, and the better volcanologic understanding on which they must be based depends, in turn, on accurate locations, chronologies, and descriptions of recent volcanism. Drawing on the efforts of many volcanologists, geologists, and historians, we have compiled data on global volcanism using a computer format that allows rapid retrieval, manipulation, and updating of information. We present here computer-generated tables of these data, designed to provide useful geographic, historic, and volcanologic information on the world's volcanoes condensed into a single reference volume.

We must emphasize at the start, however, that the tables presented here are incomplete. For example, most global volcanism takes place on the sea floor, yet only a small number of submarine eruptions are documented in the scientific literature. Volcanoes that could erupt tomorrow may be missing from our lists because of insufficient historic record (or geologic investigation), and there are still many parts of the world where moderate eruptive activity passes unnoticed or unrecorded. Furthermore, accounts of volcanic activity are widely scattered and we have no doubt missed reports that should have been included.

Nevertheless, to our knowledge this is the first chronologic summary of global volcanism published in English, the first comprehensive one-volume regional directory in English in over a hundred years, and the first cross-referenced Gazetteer of volcano names ever attempted. We hope that this volume will be useful, but that readers will keep constantly in mind the incomplete and subjective nature of the record on which most of it is based. With the help of readers who call our attention to additions and corrections, we expect to update the computer file and produce subsequent editions that are closer to being complete.

This project began in 1971 when Barbara Radovich, working as a Smithsonian student intern under the direction of W.G. Melson, outlined the basic framework of the data file. Many in the Department of Mineral Sciences participated in the initial entry of data from the Catalog of Active Volcanoes (CAVW), the Smithsonian Center for Short-Lived Phenomena, and independent data sets kindly supplied by John Latter, Bob Decker, and Fred Mauk. As the data file grew, and standards developed, early entries were rechecked, revised, and supplemented by additional data from the literature. In late 1979, we began the important additions of unpublished Volcanic Explosivity Index (VEI) assessments by C.G. Newhall and S. Self, and an independent compilation by John Latter.

Within the Smithsonian, the project has been supported by the Department of Mineral Sciences (under the successive chairmanships of Brian Mason, Bill Melson, and Dan Appleman) and the Automatic Data Processing Program (under Jim Mello and Gary Gautier). Since 1979 we have received valuable support from the Volcano Hazards Program of the U.S. Geological Survey, and Chris Newhall's VEI work was largely supported by NASA Grant NSG5145.

Many Smithsonian co-workers have contributed to the data file and this publication. We particularly want to thank Mary McGuigan (for typing countless drafts), Geneva McClain and Edna Montford (for years of keypunching), Cindy Hilmoe (for drafting the map, with the assistance of computer plotting by the World Data Center-A), Ken McCormick (for computer graphics), Peter Kauslick (for bibliographic programming), Kim Clark (for assisting David Bridge with data file programming), Gene Jarosewich and Joe Nelen (for translating), our Museum Library staff (for tracking down obscure references), and Kathy Auer and Daphne Ross (for literature review and a multitude of other tasks).

Many volcanologists around the world have kindly reviewed portions of the data file. Among them are: A. Almohandis (Middle East), R.J. Blong (Australia), O. Gonzalez-Ferran (Chile), M.L. Hall (Ecuador), J. Keller (Mediterranean), P.R. Kyle (Antartica), T.P. Miller (Alaska), P.A. Mohr and C.A. Wood (Ethiopia), H-U. Schmincke (Canary Is.), S. Self (Azores and VEI), A. Sudradjat and P.A. Jezek (Indonesia), S. Thorarinsson and S. Jakobsson (Iceland). The manuscript has benefited from reviews by R.L. Smith, R.J. Blong, and S.A. End.

We owe a large debt to previous compilers – the many groups of workers cited on p. 1-2 – and the many volcanologists of the world. These workers, who know their local volcanoes better than we can ever know them, have shared the results of their work through the scientific literature and thus contributed to the better documentation of global volcanism that we all seek.

Volcanoes of the World

Introduction

This introductory text discusses the column headings of our data tables (printed here in bold letters, e.g., **Status**), the standardized data elements used in the tables (again bold letters, but within quotation marks, e.g., "**Historical**"), and the guidelines that we have followed in building the data file. Use of all capital letters identifies the main data tables of the book, and text section titles, with page numbers (e.g., DIRECTORY, PREVIOUS SUMMARIES, p. 1).

We have attempted to leaven this introduction with some of the more interesting examples from the volcanological record, and summary statistics that might help readers searching for a specific type of information. The reader should have access to a relatively recent volcanology textbook,[1] but we have included brief explanations of some subjects, such as age-dating techniques, essential to our tables yet not covered in most volcanology texts, and illustrations have been added to show processes and their effects. We conclude with some comments on the nature of the historical record and cautions on use of the data set.

PREVIOUS SUMMARIES

Volcano lists are not new. The geographer Varenius (Bernhard Varen) published a list in 1650 that was short (Table 1) but was notable for containing representatives of most major volcanic regions known today.[2] Scrope's work in the last century established the major volcanic belts and a succession of European publications, culminating in Sapper's monumental catalog, added systematic eruption data (including indicators of eruption magnitude) while doubling the number of recognized volcanoes. Since 1917 the major growth has been geological rather than historical, as field investigations have recognized more and more volcanoes with obviously recent, but usually not historical, activity. In the years following World War II, the volcanological community developed the Catalog series described below and, in the 1960s, regular reporting of volcanic activity around the world. In more recent years, increased interest in the effects of volcanic eruptions on climate has prompted the compilation of eruption lists.[3] Table 1 provides a general indication of the growth of global volcanic data,[4] but close comparisons should not be made because different compilers have used different definitions of both "volcano" and "eruption."

REFERENCE[5]	DATE	PAGES **	VOLCANOES WITH DATED ERUPTIONS	ALL "RECENT" VOLCANOES	DATED ERUPTIONS
Varenius	1650	3	21	27	5
Scrope-I	1825	16	150	194	86
Daubeny-I	1826	466	33	73	130
von Hoff	1841	406+470	52	341	56
Daubeny-II	1848	743	85	247	275
Landgrebe	1855	499+450	133	320	269
Scrope-II	1862	171	191	217	214
Fuchs	1865	82	270	672	
Humboldt	1869	237	225	407	?
Mercalli	1907	90	231	415	
Schneider	1911	176	298	367	1440
Sapper	1917	297	430		2039
CAVW	1951-75	2139	441 (527*)	714 (890*)	3542 (4029*)
Katsui (ed.)	1971	160	527	829	
Macdonald	1972	20	516	735	
Gushchenko	1979	474	609	933	5150
Smithsonian-I	1981	76	627	1343	5564
Smithsonian-II	1994	125	805	1511	7886

*CAVW data have been adjusted with 1981 data from our file for the two regions (Alaska and Iceland) not yet covered by CAVW volumes.

**Page totals are for the volcano data alone, not the full reference.

Table 1. Compilations of global volcanic data.

At the May 1922 meeting of the International Union of Geodesy and Geophysics (IUGG) in Rome, a group of volcanologists (later to become the International Association of Volcanology and Chemistry of the Earth's Interior, or IAVCEI) recognized the value of a volcano catalog compiled by regional specialists using a standard format. However, international collaboration was slowed during those troubled years and it was not until after World War II that a format was accepted. The first volume of the *Catalog of Active Volcanoes of the World* (hereinafter *CAVW*) was published in 1951, and the current set of 22 volumes has been an important reference source for all volcanologists as well as the initial source of information for our data file. Volumes for Alaska and Iceland[6] will soon complete the first editions of the *CAVW*. We have retained the regional numbering system of the *CAVW*, where possible, and have also used many other organizational elements of the *CAVW* as the basic format for our computer file, but we have not attempted to "computerize" the full *CAVW*. Although seriously dated, the catalogs remain a valuable source for maps, photographs, early bibliographies, and the petrochemistry of eruptive products.

By 1960, nearly half of the regional *CAVW* volumes had been published, but new eruptions were quickly making the earlier volumes out of date. To deal with this problem, the catalog organizers met at the IUGG meeting in Helsinki that year and decided upon a *Bulletin of*

Volcanic Eruptions to cover global volcanism on an annual basis. These bulletins, produced by the Volcanological Society of Japan since 1960 and now published in the IAVCEI journal *Bulletin of Volcanology*, are based on thorough enquiries to individual volcanologists around the world and normally appear several years after the eruptions that they report. In an effort to gain faster reporting of volcanic (and other) natural events, the Smithsonian Center for Short-Lived Phenomena was founded in 1968. Individual event cards were produced shortly after learning of an event, and a worldwide network of correspondents was developed. In 1975, the Smithsonian Institution ceased supporting the Center for Short-Lived Phenomena, moved its essential employees (and correspondent lists) from Massachusetts to the National Museum of Natural History in Washington, DC, and used them as the nucleus of the new Scientific Event Alert Network (SEAN). This Smithsonian successor to the Center for Short-Lived Phenomena was marked by much closer working relationships with Smithsonian scientists, and a substantially revised emphasis on the types of events being reported. From October of 1975 through 1989, a monthly *SEAN Bulletin* was published for its correspondents, and the first 10 years of reporting was reorganized and indexed in book form.[7] By the end of 1989, SEAN had nearly ceased reporting of non-volcanological events, and its name was changed to Global Volcanism Network (GVN) to better identify its work. Monthly reporting has continued unchanged, but under the name of the *GVN Bulletin*. Since 1977 the Smithsonian has summarized these monthly reports in *Geotimes*, the monthly journal of the American Geological Institute, and (since 1986) in the IAVCEI journal *Bulletin of Volcanology* (itself the subject of a name change, from *Bulletin Volcanologique*, in 1986). The Smithsonian *Bulletin* is available by subscription through the American Geophysical Union (AGU), and is posted on internet and a variety of electronic bulletin boards.[8]

SOURCES

The above sources – the *Catalog of Active Volcanoes*, the *Bulletin of Volcanic Eruptions*, and the Smithsonian *SEAN-GVN Bulletin* – have been the basic building blocks of our data file. In addition, several other global compilations have been helpful: among them are IAVCEI data sheets of post-Miocene volcanoes (1975-80); Gustav Hantke's papers covering the period 1937-1959; *Volcano Letter* reports from 1926-55; Newhall and Dzurisin's caldera monograph; and the independent compilations of Gushchenko and Latter.[9] We have added information new to us and attempted to cover name (or grouping) differences in our GAZETTEER. A number of volcanoes from these compilations have not been included here, however, either because we have evidence against activity within the last 10,000 years or because we were unable to find sufficiently strong evidence for activity in that time (see discussion of Status below). Specific volcano or eruption descriptions from the scientific literature have been incorporated and these, plus broader global summaries such as those mentioned above, are listed in the REFERENCES at the end of this volume.[10] Our search of the literature is by no means complete, but we have received invaluable assistance from the reviewers acknowledged in the Preface, and the many readers of our first edition who have kindly called specific papers to our attention and otherwise improved our database.

YEARS COVERED

We have accepted all volcanoes likely to have been active in Holocene, or Recent, time – the geologic terms for postglacial or post-Pleistocene time. Most (but not all) compilers of the *CAVW* limited their coverage to historical time, but we extended our coverage to allow more equal treatment for regions where the historical record spans only a few hundred years. A longer record is particularly important for such regions, because volcanic repose periods many hundreds of years long are not uncommon (note and compare, for example, the written histories of Italian volcanoes Ischia and Vesuvius on p. 38-39), and major eruptions may be separated by thousands of years (note the radiocarbon records of Mount Rainier and Mount St. Helens on p. 121). In addition to providing the possibility of several thousands of years of volcanic history, postglacial time is often a convenient limit of volcanic history in higher latitudes where evidence of Pleistocene glaciation is clear. The Pleistocene/Holocene boundary was defined as 10,000 years BP (before present) at the 1969 INQUA Congress.[11] More recent work with precise tree-ring chronologies has confirmed the 10,000 ^{14}C year boundary[12] and we use it as the time period covered by our data file. Note, however, that conversion of radiocarbon dates (measured in years BP from 1950) to calendar years results in some dates earlier than 8000 BC, and we have included these dates.

Although only 13% of the eruptions listed in this work are older than 2,000 years, they form an important and rapidly growing part of our file. Between the first and second editions of this book, the number of BC dates increased by 268% compared to 35% for the AD dates. Careful field and laboratory studies are developing detailed histories of individual volcanoes, and we have entered more than 1300 pre-Holocene volcanoes in our file. Smith and Luedke[13] pointed out that terrestrial volcanoes may he intermittently active over 10 million years; studies of the ocean floor suggest that individual volcanoes may remain active for 20 million years;[14] and the IAVCEI data sheet project set a post-Miocene (approximately 12 million years) limit in order to capture all volcanoes that might still be active. Therefore, our present limit of 10,000 years does not include all active volcanoes, but it is a convenient starting point for those that have erupted in postglacial time.

Because of this limit and the lack of widespread prehistoric dating of recent volcanism, half of the volcanoes listed here have no dated eruption. Most of this group are listed because they show clear evidence of eruption(s) within the last few thousand years (e.g., uneroded volcanic ash cones, eruptive products overlying young glacial debris, young unvegetated lava flows in regions where revegetation should be rapid). However, we have also followed the compilers of the *CAVW* in including volcanoes now in the fumarolic stage of development. These features are areas in which volcanic gases or fumes issue from the ground: signs that may mean either a pause between eruptions or the last gasps of a volcano that has not erupted for many thousands of years.

Mud volcanoes, which reach diameters of 2 km in Alaska,[15] have been included by some volcanological compilers but excluded by us. Some mud-volcano eruptions, such as the 1951 California event that distributed fine debris over 6 km from the source,[16] take place in hot springs, but their cause has no direct relation to new volcanic magma, and most mud volcanoes, in fact, result from methane generation in thick sequences of Cenozoic sediments distant from regions of true volcanism.[17]

Finally, we have included volcanoes for which Holocene activity is only uncertain. At some volcanoes it has not been possible to determine whether eruptive activity ceased in the very latest Pleistocene, or the early Holocene, but we have attempted to make that uncertainty clear under both **Status** and date headings.

MAPS and REGIONAL NUMBERING SCHEME

World maps on the inside covers introduce the regional numbering scheme used throughout the book – for both sequencing and cross-referencing – and each region is introduced in the DIRECTORY by detailed maps showing relative positions of individual volcanoes. These maps serve as visual indexes to the volume. The numbering system, developed by the *CAVW* in the late 1930s and used in all catalogs, is geographic and hierarchical. The first two numerals identify region, the next two identify subregion, and the last two or three (after the hyphen) identify individual volcanoes in that subregion. Original *CAVW* volcano numbers have been retained, where possible, to aid cross-referencing, but this has required, for the many volcanoes added since *CAVW* publication, the interpolating of 3-digit volcano numbers between 2-digit-plus-equal-sign *CAVW* numbers. This potentially confusing practice is discussed below (p. 11), but readers are alerted to it here at the start. Our DIRECTORY (p. 37-163) is sequenced by volcano numbers (see first two numerals in black marginal tabs and full, bold numbers in mid-page) for easy location from map, GAZETTEER, or CHRONOLOGY. In a general way, the regional numbers proceed eastward from Europe through the Indian Ocean to New Zealand, then circle back clockwise around the Pacific margin, ending with the Atlantic and Antarctic regions.

We have assigned new subregion numbers where the *CAVW* has no listings, and have renumbered subregions in some areas such us the western United States and Canada (where work of recent decades has increased the number of recognized volcanoes from the 12 listed in the 1960 *Catalog* to the 90 listed here). We have also expanded several regions to cover volcanoes not listed by the *CAVW*. For example; region 05 (Melanesia) now includes Holocene volcanism in Australia, region 10 includes newly recognized Holocene centers in Mainland Asia, region 13 (Hawaii) has been widened to include most of the Pacific Ocean (not already included by the *CAVW* in other regions), and region 17 (Iceland) has been expanded to include the Arctic Ocean. Substantial renumbering has been done since our first edition, particularly in Iceland and New Zealand where work with regional specialists has provided simplification based on the concept of volcano systems. A more detailed discussion of this, and other aspects of volcano numbers, follows on p. 11.

Red symbols give some indication of each volcano's activity status as well as location. For the detailed maps in the DIRECTORY, the 389 volcanoes with known eruptions during this century are shown by solid triangles; those with earlier AD eruptions (231) by partially filled triangles; and those with BC or undated Holocene eruptions (689) by open triangles. For this latter group (often identified by uneroded, youthful cones or fresh, unvegetated lava flows), the lack of dated eruptions generally reflects a weak historical record rather than a lack of geologically recent volcanism. The final group, the 202 locations marked by very small red triangles, represent distinctly less certain activity during the last 10,000 years. These include questionable submarine eruptions and other accounts of doubtful reliability, plus the fumarolic fields that are included in the *CAVW* as evidence of late-stage volcanic development. This group is made up of volcanoes in the "**Uncertain**" and "**Holocene?**" status groups (including those for which the only dated eruptions are questionable), and those for which our volcano **TYPE** designation is no more than a thermal feature (such as fumarolic field or hydrothermal region). On the inside back cover map, volcanoes with dated eruptions are treated differently: those dated historically are shown by one symbol, and those dated by other techniques by another.

For the regional maps, we chose volcano symbol categories (increasingly long time periods since the last known eruption) because unusually long periods of volcanic quiet are often ended by unusually violent eruptions, and this symbol convention helps identify volcanoes that have been apparently quiet for long periods. Volcanoes are also quiet, of course, when they are dead, and there is no simple means of distinguishing between dormant and recently extinct volcanoes.

The maps introducing each region in the DIRECTORY are designed to show relative positions of every volcano at a level of detail not possible in the world map. In addition to volcano information in red, political boundaries are shown and capital cities are named for volcano nations. Cities with populations exceeding 1 million,[18] plus selected smaller cities, are also named for reference purposes. Major drainages are shown, but we had difficulties with the GIS database for these, and in the end decided to include imperfect representation of major rivers rather than none at all. Names are entered for all volcanoes with: ≥10 dated eruptions; eruption(s) with VEI ≥4 or producing ≥1 km^3 of lava; fatal eruptions or recent evacuations; discussion in this text; or other noteworthy characteristics. Volcanoes in regions other than the one being introduced are shown by lighter red triangles (without age distinctions).

Readers wishing a larger world map of volcanoes might be interested in that produced by the U.S. Geological Survey in collaboration with the Smithsonian and the U.S. Naval Research Lab (see inside back cover map caption and end notes[19] for more details). This wall map uses the same volcano symbols used in the detailed DIRECTORY maps here, but shows physiography, tectonic features, seismicity, and impact craters as well.

Our volcano data also appear on a more detailed set of maps published by the Circum-Pacific Map Project. Three map series – Plate Tectonics, Geodynamics, & Hazards – contain a variety of tectonic, age, and seismic data, as well as most of the volcanoes listed here. Five overlapping maps cover the Pacific Basin (including margins, West Indies, Indonesia, and all of Antarctica) at a scale of 1:10 million. These maps have been published since 1981, and the quadrant maps have been followed by a one-map summary at a scale of 1:20 million.[20]

Data Table Summaries

The formats for the 5 data tables that make up most of this book are summarized below. The codes and abbreviations used in the tables are summarized on the inside front cover for easy reference. Additional introductory text (to p. 26) discusses the data in more detail under the column headings used in the tables.

DIRECTORY

This section, the largest in the book, is basically a condensed and updated version of the *CAVW*, but with its time frame expanded to 10,000 years. We have compressed the geographic data, morphology, activity status, and known eruptive history of 1,511 volcanoes into 125 pages of tables. Such an attempt suffers from a very uneven historical record, inconsistent use of important terms ("volcano," "eruption"), and the many uncertainties of reducing subjective, human accounts to a rigid, tabular format. It must be recognized as an inescapably incomplete record, but it should prove useful as a summary and guide to the literature for all readers interested in volcanism. As we found after publishing the first edition, such readers can supply additions and corrections that can in turn be incorporated to provide more accurate and complete editions of this work in the future.

Maps introducing each region are described 5 paragraphs above. Each region is also introduced by a few words about its history, tectonic setting, geography, and noteworthy volcanological features.[21] These introductions are not an attempt to summarize the history and geography of the world, but to provide context for the records that follow. Differences between regions are often large, and the aim of these brief introductions is to increase appreciation for the strengths and weaknesses of each regional data set.

The DIRECTORY consists of a single line of information for each volcano and another for each known eruption. The basic geographical and geological data for each volcano are arranged in columns on a single line and the volcanoes are sequenced regionally by volcano number (see maps and discussion of numbering system on p. 11). Under each volcano, dated eruptions are summarized, each on a single line, including the book's only coverage of eruptive characteristics, and these lines are arranged chronologically. The DIRECTORY thus provides a concise summary of the known eruptive history for each volcano and region. Discussion of the conventions used and information shown will follow under the main sections VOLCANO DATA and ERUPTION DATA (p. 6-26).

FATALITIES and EVACUATIONS

The subject of volcanic hazards has received increased attention in the past decade, with several major treatments having been published since the first edition of this book.[22] Because of widespread interest in the subject, we include here an extended table of all fatal eruptions known to us. These tragic events carry important lessons to everyone who is (or should be) concerned with volcanoes, and their sobering toll gives these lessons a power not found in more theoretical treatments.

Recent interactions between aircraft and volcanic ash emphasize the fact that hazards are not restricted to people living near volcanoes, or even to those hazards described in the table. In 1982 a jumbo jet flying from Singapore to Australia encountered ash over Java's Galunggung volcano, lost power in all 4 engines, and glided silently for an agonizing 13 minutes before the engines were successfully restarted at low altitude. A similar incident over Redoubt, in Alaska, resulted in $80 million damage to the aircraft in 1989. The sparse population of volcanic regions such as Alaska, Kamchatka, and the Kuriles does not immunize them from volcanic hazard, because their explosive volcanoes directly threaten heavily traveled great-circle air routes over the north Pacific. And if aircraft do not come to volcanoes, eruptive clouds occasionally come to aircraft. By 19 September 1992 an ash cloud erupted days earlier from Alaska's Mt. Spurr had drifted 5,000 km to northern Ohio (among the busiest airspaces in the world) and diversions around this very visible cloud resulted in untold costs of rerouting delays. By mid-1994, more than 80 damaging interactions between aircraft and ash had been recognized.[23]

The fatality table is arranged in the sequence of the preceding DIRECTORY, with volcano name (and number) followed by entries for each fatal eruption, carrying date (**YEAR M-Dy**), number of **Deaths**, proportion that can be assigned to principal **Agents** or causes, and **Remarks**, a free-form description of the event. For cross-referencing to other parts of the book, both volcano number and eruption **Start date** are shown. More detailed description of table elements appears in a box immediately preceding the table (p. 163).[24]

Our main purpose has been to present the realities of fatal eruptions as a powerful and effective lesson. For many years the American Alpine Club has published an annual pamphlet that simply describes the serious climbing accidents of the preceding year. That little booklet has been required reading for many mountaineers, and a wonderfully effective primer on climbing safety. We have the same hope for this table.

A fatality table, however, places unfair emphasis on the negative side of volcano hazard work. Increased understanding of, and attention to, volcanic hazards in recent decades has resulted in many successful evacuations and the saving of thousands of lives. Therefore, we follow the table with a shorter listing of known evacuations as well as fatalities since 1975. This covers the time period of regular Smithsonian reporting by SEAN and GVN.[25]

CHRONOLOGY

This section arranges all 7,886 eruptions in a chronological sequence by **START** date **(YEAR M-Dy)**, displaying all volcanism known to have taken place in each year. The record begins with a few eruptions older than 8000 BC (because of the 10,000 BP radiocarbon years as discussed above) and ends with the last day of 1993. For any given year, those eruptions known to be continuing from the previous year are listed first (sequenced by volcano number).[26] These are followed by eruptions known only to have taken place sometime during the year (also sequenced by volcano number), and finally by eruptions starting in a known month or day. However, attention must be paid, particularly with older dates, to the uncertainty code (p. 15) and to the uncorrected radiocarbon dates (p. 17). An eruption listed simply as "seventeenth century" will be shown only <u>once</u> as "1650 t" (1650 ± 50 years), and radiocarbon dates preceeded by "C" may be as much as 900 years off of the true calendar date.

When the date of an eruption's end is known, we have displayed the **Duration** (in days), but for the 7% of all eruptions exceeding 999 days we have simply listed "**>3yr.**" **VOLCANO NAME** is then listed, followed by **Subregion** name (truncated after some longer names). **NUMBER** allows cross-reference to map or directory, for additional information, and both **VEI** and volume data (**Vol/LT**) indicate eruption size. When more than one VEI is assigned for an eruption, as for a paroxysmal explosion following the listed start date, they appear separately in chronologic sequence. Thus the catastrophic eruption of Tambora appears on 5 April 1815, but the eruption's start is also entered in 1812, and its continuing lower-level activity is noted for 1813 and 1814. The recent eruption of Mount St. Helens is listed in 1980 for its 27 March start, its 18 May paroxysmal eruption, and 5 subsequent events that produced ash cloud heights of 13 km or more.

Art work and photographs are interspersed through the CHRONOLOGY to show the processes and features treated in the book. Their sequence attempts to convey a sense of history, as a reminder that our record of volcanism is largely a human record and, as such, is subject to the many frailties of history.

GAZETTEER

Volcano names are commonly confused by synonyms, official geographic name changes, subsidiary feature names, and the grouping of nearby features in different ways. We have attempted to reduce this confusion by listing alphabetically all 10,400 names in our file, stating their relationship to the 1,511 volcano names used here, and listing volcano number for cross-reference. Morphologic type of each primary volcano is listed with each mention of it (see detailed description of TYPE below), and under its main entry (bolded **NAME** and **NUMBER**) we further identify the primary volcano by listing its total number of dated eruptions, its year of most recent eruption,[27] and its status. Such information can be helpful when choosing between several features with similar names or synonyms (there are, for example, 5 "Ploskys" in Kamchatka, and separate "Pan de Azucars" in Alaska, Colombia, Ecuador, and the Canary Islands).

Many volcanoes carry words such as "Mount", "Cerro", or "Volcan" before the proper name by which they are uniquely known, and the use of such modifiers is often uncertain or confusing (e.g., "Mount Lassen", "Lassen Peak", or "Lassen Volcanic center"?). Therefore we have placed frequently used modifiers, with comma, behind the proper name (e.g., "Darwin, Volcan"), with appropriate cross-references in the GAZETTEER.

We have tended to group nearby volcanic vents under one VOLCANO entry, following the model of Kilauea, Hawaii (where eruptions 50 km from the volcano center are clearly linked to it) rather than that of the Canary Islands (where the *CAVW* lists vents separated by only a few kilometers as distinct "volcanoes"). This tendency toward grouping is likely to continue as understanding of regional volcanism increases. In Iceland, for example, the 70 volcanoes of our first edition have been reduced to 33, based on the concept of "volcanic systems" linked by detailed petrologic and tectonic characteristics.[28] Such changes enhance the value of a gazetteer tying together various volcanic features and the names by which they have been known.

We have not, however, assigned names to unnamed volcanoes based on nearby geographic features. This means that 82 volcanoes are listed under "unnamed" (47 of them submarine), but their positions can be determined from geographic coordinates and more detailed geographic locations are entered in our data file for most.

Note also the guide on p. 253 introducing the GAZETTEER. Here we have pointed out some common alternative spellings that greatly reduce the number of synonyms that we need to list in the GAZETTEER.

REFERENCES

The final set of tables making up this publication is a listing of the source documents used in our compilation. These 2,041 references are arranged by region, and chronologically within each region. The regions are in the same *CAVW* sequence used here in volcano numbering, map, and directory.

This scheme should enable the reader to find references on a specific volcano, group, or eruption, but close attention must be paid to the *CAVW* series and the "global" references listed at the start. For each region, the *CAVW* and other major regional summaries are marked by a star to the left of the citation and the regional title is underlined. In general, eruptions subsequent to the *CAVW* date can he found in the references by Hantke (to 1959), the Volcanological Society of Japan (since 1960), and the Smithsonian Institution (since 1968). The other references listed under "global" have been searched for volcanological data not found elsewhere, and the coverage of additional regional references is clear from their titles in most cases. For some we have added clarification in square brackets. References used for each volcano and eruption are entered with the appropriate data in our data file, but we have not attempted to cross-reference all sources in the tabular summaries presented here. Some references are listed because we have added data for a single eruption, but we may not have exhaustively searched the full reference for other possible additions to our file.

While these listings provide a helpful guide to the literature for each region, they do not form a definitive bibliography. These are simply the references we have used in entering the data presented here. If, for example, a detailed eruption description is published 5 years after the event, but its petrologic and other data carry nothing to change the original data entered at the time from preliminary sources, then we would not necessarily have added it to our reference list. We must also admit that we do not see all the available literature, and our coverage is particularly weak in non-English journals. We invite readers to help us correct this by sending references of papers (reprints or copies if possible) that are missing in our listings here.[8]

More detailed discussion of individual data elements, and how we have dealt with them, follows. Most section titles are keyed to the headings of the tables described briefly above, and data headings appear in bold-faced letters in the text.

Volcano Data

One of the most difficult problems of standardization has been the varying usage of the word "volcano." Definitions of "volcano" range from individual vents, measured in meters, through volcanic edifices measured in kilometers or tens of kilometers, to volcanic fields measured in hundreds of kilometers. In a compilation such as this one, the disadvantage of the narrowest definition is not so much the multiplicity of names introduced, as the dismembering of a single volcanic plumbing system's history into apparently unrelated separate records. The interiors of ancient volcanoes, now eroded and exposed for geologic study, show us that most subsurface magma chambers – the suppliers of lavas to overlying volcanoes – are at least several kilometers in diameter. We also know that many contemporary volcanoes grow by additions from countless flank vents as well as activity at a central crater (Figure 29). Consequently, we have tended to group closely spaced "volcanoes" such as the historical vents of the Canary Islands (many listed as separate volcanoes in the *CAVW*) by the major volcanic edifice on which they are found. The names of historical vents are retained under the **Area of activity** heading and are alphabetically listed in the GAZETTEER. Volcanoes listed here are rarely closer than 10 km to their nearest neighbor, and are commonly separated by at least 20 km.[29]

Another problem is simply the identification of volcanoes. Prominent, steaming cones are easy to recognize, but water, ice, erosion, collapse processes, or dense vegetation can mask very dangerous volcanoes. Lake Taupo, in the center of New Zealand's North Island, is beautifully tranquil, with no obvious features alerting nongeologists to its particularly violent history. In the Alaskan summer of 1975, two volcanologists traced an ever-thickening ash layer to a vent now covered by the Hayes Glacier, and a "new" volcano was added to the NE end of the Aleutian arc.[30] Also in Alaska, 5 decades passed before the true source of this century's largest eruption was recognized: Subsurface magma connections led to prominent collapse of Mount Katmai in 1912, and this was assumed to be the eruption's source until careful fieldwork showed it to be Katmai's inconspicuous neighbor, Novarupta.[31] These examples illustrate why the listings below must be recognized as incomplete.

Inclusion in this compilation may depend on thoroughness of mapping – quite variable through the world's volcanic regions – and the most dangerous volcanoes may be those not yet recognized by compilers.

VOLCANO NAME

Within each volcanic region, the **VOLCANO NAME** appears first on the left side of the page. With few exceptions, we have used the names listed by the compilers of the *CAVW*, the contributors to the IAVCEI post-Miocene data sheets, and individual volcanologists reporting on additional volcanoes. We have preferred broader island names, locatable on standard maps, rather than crater names locally used to identify the full island volcano, and we have dropped modifiers, such as "Mount," when they seemed unnecessary. For Japanese volcanoes we have listed the more widely used Hepburn style of spelling, but no longer follow this (as in our first edition) with the *CAVW* name in square brackets, although all *CAVW* names appear alphabetically as synonyms in the GAZETTEER. We have used square brackets, however, to indicate alternative names that are widely encountered in the literature (e.g. "Cerro Azul [Quizapu]" in Chile). Readers familiar with older spellings of Indonesian names will note that newer official names are used here with the older names appearing as synonyms in the GAZETTEER. In the new names TJ, DJ, J and OE appear as C, J, Y, and U, respectively. We have excluded special characters from other languages that would strain our already-overburdened computers.

A few names have also been changed from the *CAVW* to reflect the broader time coverage of this compilation. Historically active features that are clearly part of a larger feature active in Holocene time have been listed under the larger feature. For example, the *CAVW* lists volcano number 0603-31= as Bromo; however, Bromo is but one of several youthful features in Tengger caldera, so we have used the caldera name for 0603-31= and indicated Bromo both as the area of historical activity in the DIRECTORY and as a subsidiary feature in the GAZETTEER. An extension of the time coverage problem is the grouping problem mentioned above. Amboy, a solitary cinder cone 200 km east of Los Angeles, is entered as a single volcano, and so is the Michoacan-Guanajuato Field, made up of nearly 1,000 cinder cones dotting a 200 x 200 km area in Mexico.[32] Clearly not all "volcanoes" are equal, and caution must be used in any serious counting of them.[33]

SUBREGION

A more general geographic location appears in parentheses after the volcano name in all tables. This normally consists of the **Subregion** designated by the *CAVW* compilers (and identified by the third and fourth digits of the *CAVW* volcano number system continued here – see map on inside back cover), but we have added a more general location name where useful for identification. And not all of these locations are fully displayed – some subregion names have necessarily been abbreviated following unusually long volcano names. Some truncation results from the combination of space constraints and the use of proportionally spaced type.

In the DIRECTORY – where formal subregions are often clear from the regional sequence – we have often substituted a more specific location, such as island name, after the volcano name.

LATITUDE and LONGITUDE

Geographic coordinates are listed in decimal parts of a degree. This facilitates both computer manipulation of data and rapid estimation of distances between points (one degree of latitude being equal to 111 km). To retain some indication of the accuracy of original locations, when converting from minutes and seconds we have listed 3 digits to the right of the decimal point only where seconds were originally specified. We list 2 digits if only degrees and minutes were given in the original (e.g., 71° 41' = 71.68° whereas 71° 41' 01" = 71.684°). Readers should also beware of obviously generalized locations such as X.00° or Y.50°. When different references give different positions for the same volcano, we include each (with references) in the computer data file, attempt to determine which is most reliable, and list that location here. For some regions, where our growing archive of topographic maps permits, we have obtained more precise locations than given in older sources. Newly obtained maps for the Kuriles and Kamchatka, for example, have permitted correction of deliberately mislocated volcano positions that were a cold war artifact. An asterisk (*) following the **LAT**itude entry warns the reader that the location is the centerpoint of a broad volcanic field. The absence of an asterisk, however, does not mean that the coordinates given match the eruption site. Tens of kilometers may separate eruptive centers of a single volcano, particularly in large caldera complexes and rift settings.

Distribution of the world's volcanoes with respect to **LAT**itude has gained wide interest because of the relationship between large volcanic eruptions and climate. Major explosive eruptions drive volcanic ash and gas tens of kilometers into the stratosphere where, because fine ash and aerosol particles settle slowly and are not washed out by rain, they may be distributed around the globe by stratospheric circulation. For months or years before settling back to Earth, then, this layer of volcanic aerosol acts as a solar radiation filter, lowering temperatures on the Earth below it. The extent to which this process has affected global climate in the past is a matter of considerable scientific debate,[34] but the fact that individual eruptions can affect climate is established (the catastrophic eruption of Indonesia's Tambora in 1815, for example, contributed to a lowering of global temperatures that brought June snow-storms to New England and widespread crop failure to northern latitudes).[35] The Earth's rotation strongly influences stratospheric circulation patterns and therefore any concentration of the world's volcanoes by latitude is important in assessing their effect on global climate.

Figure 1 shows the distribution of the world's known volcanoes by latitude. Two thirds of the volcanoes are in the northern hemisphere and only 19% are between 10°S and the South Pole. The northern hemisphere concentration reflects the fact that two-thirds of the world's land area is also north of the equator, but nevertheless indicates the greater vulnerability of the northern hemisphere to volcanically induced climate change.

The most northerly volcano in our list is an unnamed submarine volcano in the Arctic Ocean only 192 km from the North Pole. Three eruptions have been attributed to this site. The next most northerly volcano, on Jan Mayen island and 2104 km from the pole, has been recently quite active with vigorous eruptions in 1970 and early 1985.

The southernmost historically active volcano is Mount Erebus, 1387 km from the South Pole on Ross Island, Antarctica. This volcano was erupting violently when first seen by Ross, in 1841, and is active today with a molten lava lake that has been circulating in its summit crater since at least 1972. The many young cinder cones of the Royal Society Range, 80 km closer to the pole are probably Holocene, and local ash layers have been found in glaciers, but no eruptions have been dated.

No significant concentration of volcanoes by **LONG**-itude is obvious, but over 1000 volcanoes (or two-thirds of those listed) lie around the Pacific Ocean margin forming the well known "Ring of Fire."[37] Linear belts of volcanoes are a striking feature of the planet (see inside cover maps) and they reflect, in most cases, convergence of the major tectonic plates that make up the Earth's outer shell.

These vast plates, moving at speeds of only a few centimeters per year, form a shifting jig-saw puzzle with the major earthquake and volcano belts marking the unrest at plate boundaries.[38] Where plates converge, with the thinner plate normally being thrust down under the thicker, a line of volcanoes grows above (and as a result of) the under-thrusting. Because this type of volcanism is normally both explosive and near (if not on) land, we have a reasonably complete listing of these eruptions (approximately 85% of this file). The spreading apart of major plates, however, is characterized by the relatively nonexplosive outpouring of fluid lava and commonly takes place one or more kilometers below the surface of the ocean. Consequently we have a very

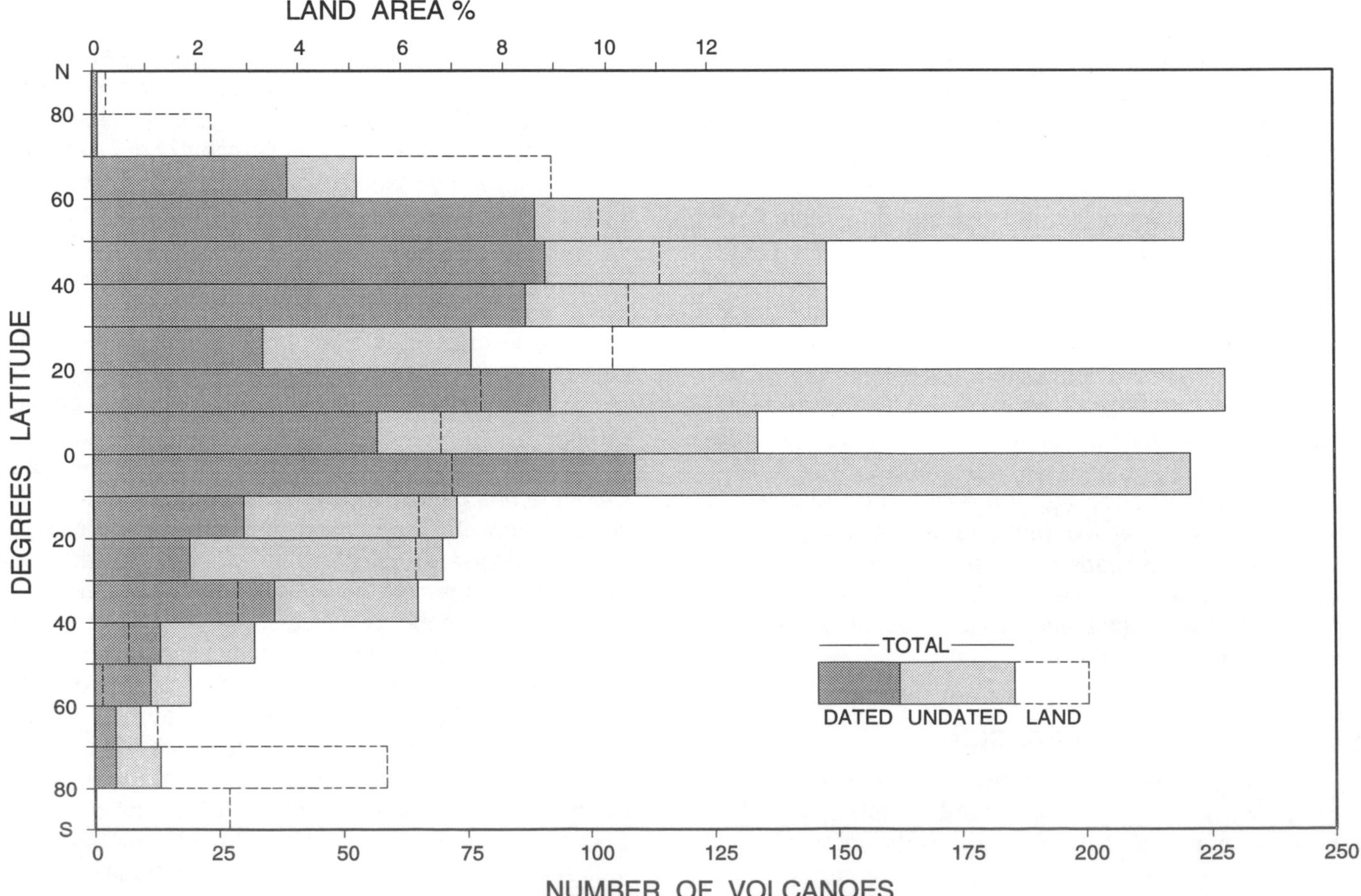

Figure 1. Distribution of known volcanoes per 10 degrees of latitude. Thin dashed line shows the percentage of land area per 10 degrees.[36]

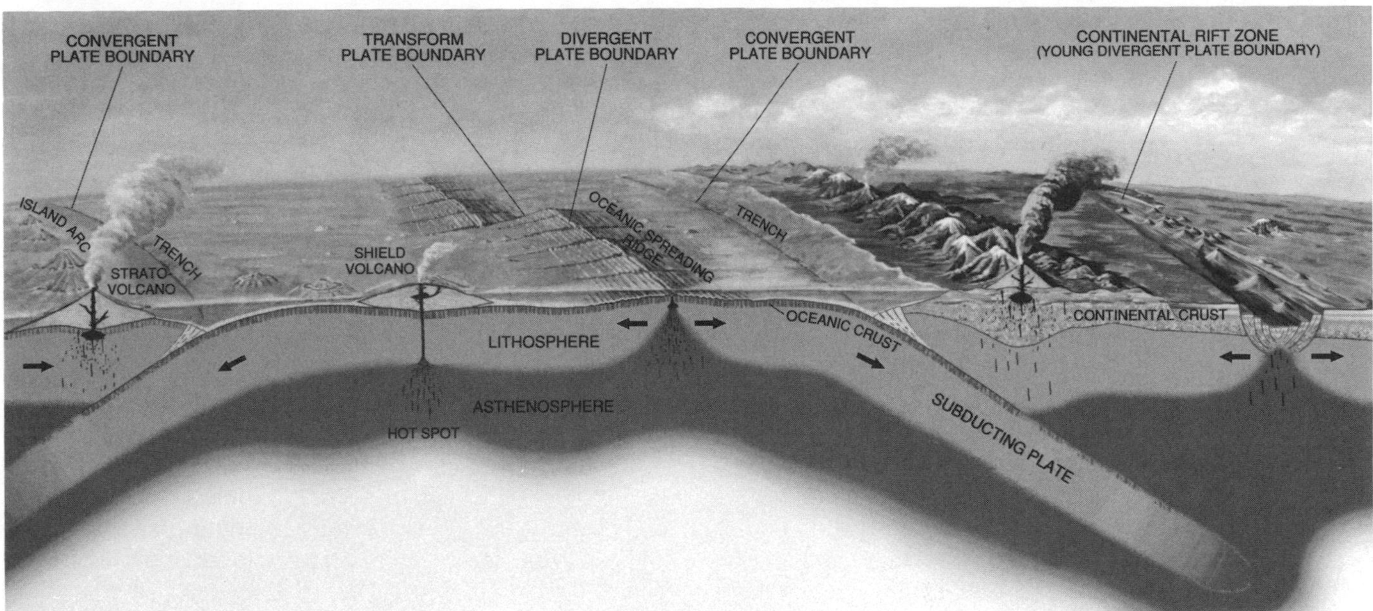

Figure 2. Plate Tectonics: schematic cross-section illustrating processes. Artist José F. Vigil.[19]

incomplete record of this important type of volcanism. Rift volcanism forms only 5% of our eruption file (Figure 3) and is dominated by those few regions, such as East Africa and Iceland, where the spreading apart of plates takes place above sea level. The remainder of our file – less than a tenth of the total – represents volcanism within major plates rather than at their boundaries. This takes place when deep "hot spots" penetrate the overlying crust and old volcanic products are carried slowly away from the volcanic center by the moving plate. Although our record of intraplate volcanism is probably better than that for the volcanism of spreading ocean ridges, we no doubt miss many examples, particularly from the sea floor.

ELEVATION

ELEVation of each volcano's highest point is listed in meters above or below sea level. Elevation for the same volcano may differ because of different surveying techniques or because of volcanological changes (e.g. the 400 m change in Mount St. Helens' summit height in 1980). As with latitude and longitude, when separate values for the same feature appear in different references we list both (with reference) in the computer file and display here the one that seems to be most reliable. When unable to resolve a difference any other way, we normally display the more recent figure. Most elevations, both in the *CAVW* and original references, are given in meters, but when we have had to convert from other units we have attempted to retain a measure of the original's accuracy by rounding the conversion to the same number of significant figures as in the original. Thus a 2,600 ft elevation, apparently rounded to the nearest 100 ft, is listed here as 790 m rather than the 792 m figure that is the exact metric equivalent (but implies more accuracy than in the original measurement).

The height of a volcano above its regional base is of more volcanological interest than its absolute elevation above sea level, but it is unavailable for 39% of the listed volcanoes and is often a highly subjective measurement, particularly in the case of oceanic volcanoes. With neighboring volcanoes, for example, it is often impossible to state what proportion of each summit elevation is the result of its own plumbing system, and how much is contributed by its neighbor (or a now-buried, older volcano). When it is listed by the *CAVW* or other sources, we have entered this figure into our data bank but have not displayed it in this publication.

Less than 4% of the listed volcanoes, most of them submarine, have **ELEV**ations unknown to us. Submarine volcano elevations (or depths) are particularly unreliable because changes are often rapid, dramatic, and unrecorded. We normally list the most recent elevation

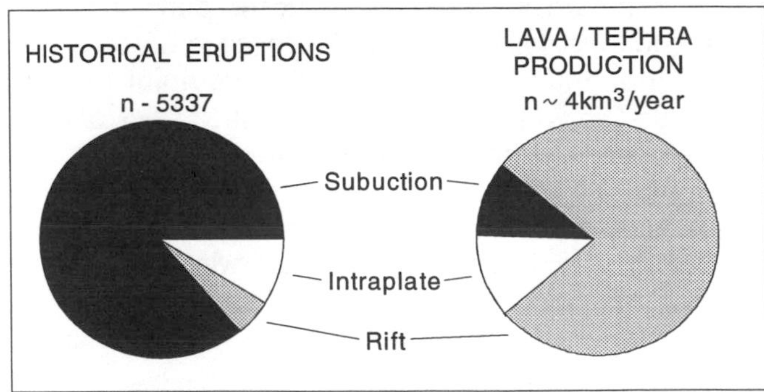

Figure 3. Pie diagrams contrasting the volcanism that we see with that we don't. Left diagram shows proportion of documented historical eruptions from subduction zones (black), mid-ocean ridges (stipple), and hotspot settings (white). Right diagram shows proportion of annual magma budget in the same settings (with same symbols).[39]

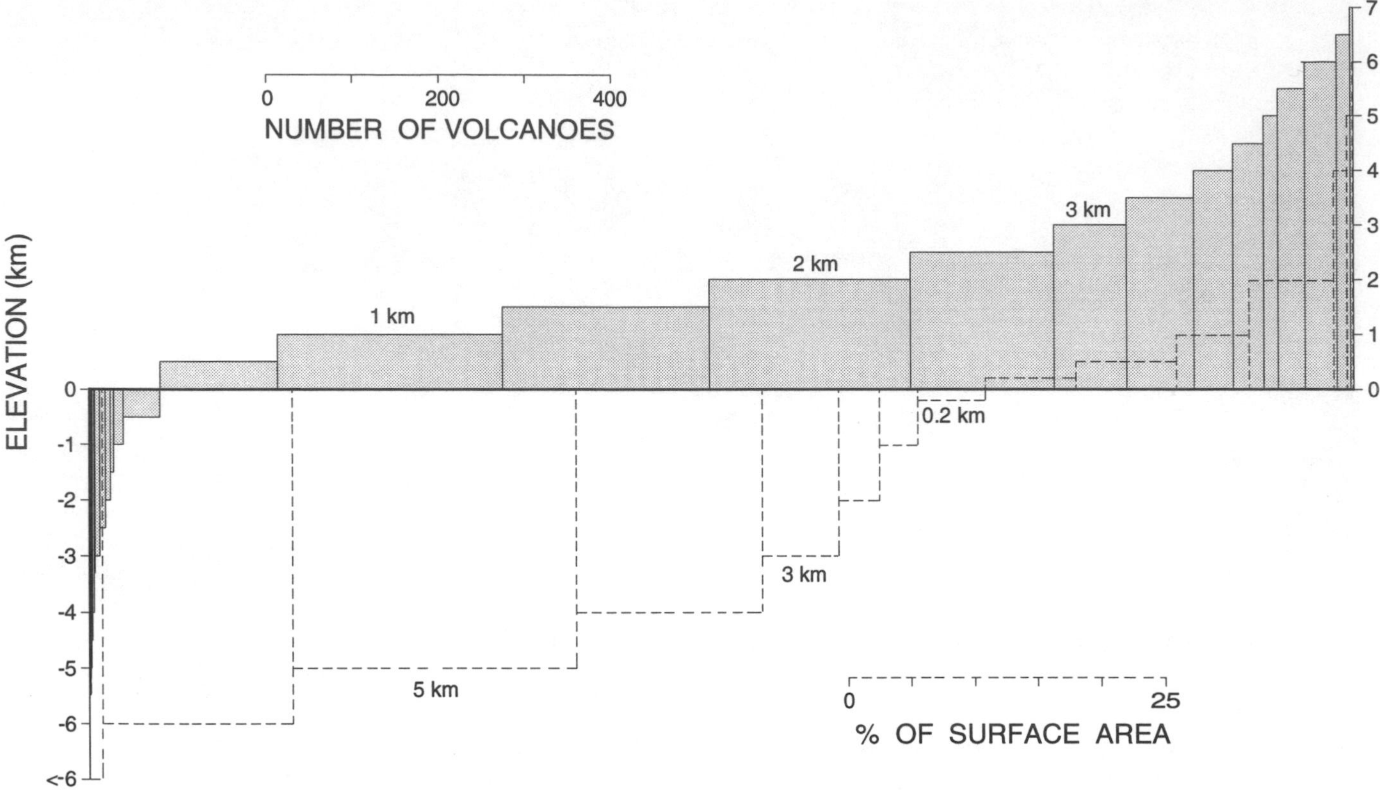

Figure 4. Distribution of known volcanoes by elevation. Addition of the many unknown volcanoes of the sea floor would greatly alter this distribution, as shown by the dashed lines giving percentages of Earth's surface area within various depths and elevations.[40]

when several are given, but caution should be used with *all* submarine volcano elevations.

Roughly 30% of the volcanoes in our list are within 1,000 m of sea level, 62% are within 2,000 m and 79% are within 3,000 m of sea level (Figure 4). Only 88 volcanoes, or 6% of our file, have elevations above 5,000 m (16,400 ft): 88% of these are in the South American Andes and nearly two-thirds of the total are in that chain's central segment (15-28°S).

The highest volcano with historical eruptions is Llullaillaco (volcano number 1505-11=) in the northern Chilean Andes. Its elevation is 6,739 m and three eruptions were recorded there in the second half of the last century. Active fumaroles, however, mark the summit crater of Nevado Ojos del Salado, 267 km to the south of, and 148 m higher than, Llullaillaco. The youthful nature of Nevado Ojos del Salado suggests that its lack of historical eruptions stems only from its remote location, and it is rightfully the world's highest volcano. The only higher mountain in the Americas, Argentina's Aconcagua at 7,021 m, was listed as active by Darwin during the voyage of the *Beagle*, but Chilean colleagues[41] tell us that the mountain is not a volcano and its height results from imbricate thrust faulting.

The deepest submarine volcano in our list has less significance because the record is so poor. Seawater not only hides eruptions from view, but its weight also provides enormous pressure on the deep-sea floor, inhibiting (and often prohibiting) the explosive release of volcanic gases that frequently calls attention to shallow submarine eruptions. A few historical reports, however, give some credence to explosive volcanism on the deep-sea floor: 1955 activity at 4000 m near Hawaii (1302-10=), 1865 activity at 4200 m west of the Azores (1801-04=), uncertain 1852 activity at 5300 m in the central mid-Atlantic (1805-04=), and an 1850 event at about 6000 m depth off Taiwan. Non-explosive volcanism regularly takes place at great depths on the ocean floor, as shown by photography of fresh volcanic features at depths of 5 km in the Cayman Trough, Caribbean Sea,[42] but our record of it is exceedingly scanty.

TYPE (MORPHOLOGY)

Volcanoes come in a variety of shapes and sizes. Under the heading of **TYPE**, we have attempted to characterize the morphology of each volcano. Several features may be entered into our computer in descending order of size, but only an abbreviated version of the major feature is printed in the DIRECTORY and GAZETTEER. If, for example, a stratovolcano contains a caldera that is itself filled by lava domes and pyroclastic cones, this will typically be abbreviated only as "**Stratovolc**" in the DIRECTORY and GAZETTEER. We have followed the *CAVW* entry in most cases, and inspection of the table of types (on inside front cover) will show that little attempt has been made to standardize usage. Figure 5 illustrates the main profiles shown, but the reader should consult a volcanological textbook[43] for further description (and recognize that different volcanologists have used different terms for the same features). Interest in the landforms of other planets has prompted a more quantitative approach to the morphology of Earth's volcanoes.[44] Lacking a standardized nomenclature, however, we have generally listed the volcano types as given in the various sources used in our compilation. Therefore, this data element is not suitable for a search for all examples of a given volcano type (a tuff cone, for example, might be listed under "**Cone**," "**Pyrocl cone**," "**Tuff cone**," "**Maar**," or possibly "**Expl crater**" or "**Pumice cone**," and would not be listed at all in the DIRECTORY if it is a subsidiary feature of a larger volcanic landform). The element does, however, provide helpful information about the size and shape of each volcano listed.

NUMBER

The volcano number consists of a 4-digit number identifying region and subregion, followed (after a hyphen) by a 2 or 3-digit individual volcano number. This scheme follows that of the *CAVW* and has already been discussed above under **MAPS and REGIONAL NUMBERING SCHEME** (p. 3). The DIRECTORY is sequenced by volcano **NUMBER**, and the number is repeated as the basic cross-referencing device in the CHRONOLOGY and GAZETTEER sections as well. We have followed the exact *CAVW* numbering where possible, and volcanoes bearing numbers identical to those used by the *CAVW* carry an "=" symbol at the end of the number to facilitate reference to the *CAVW* for fuller descriptions. When we have added a volcano between those already numbered, we have added a third numeral. Thus Lipari, between Stromboli (0101-04=) and Vulcano (0101-05-), is given the number 0101-041 rather than the next available two-digit number at the end of the Italian subregion. This scheme permits natural geographic sequencing of volcanoes while retaining original *CAVW* numbering. Letters have been added at the end of a very few individual volcano numbers to designate volcanoes thought likely to be interconnected yet sufficiently separated that one cannot be clearly designated a subfeature of another. The grouping is shown by using the same volcano number in each case, with letters at the end of each individual number in the group. When adding numbers in regions not previously numbered by the *CAVW*, and when renumbering in regions such as the Canary Islands and the western United States, we have used only two numerals for the individual volcano number but have designated the fact that it cannot be found under this number in the *CAVW* by adding a "–" in the last place. Crater Lake, for example, is numbered 1202-16- here, but was not included in the *CAVW*.[45]

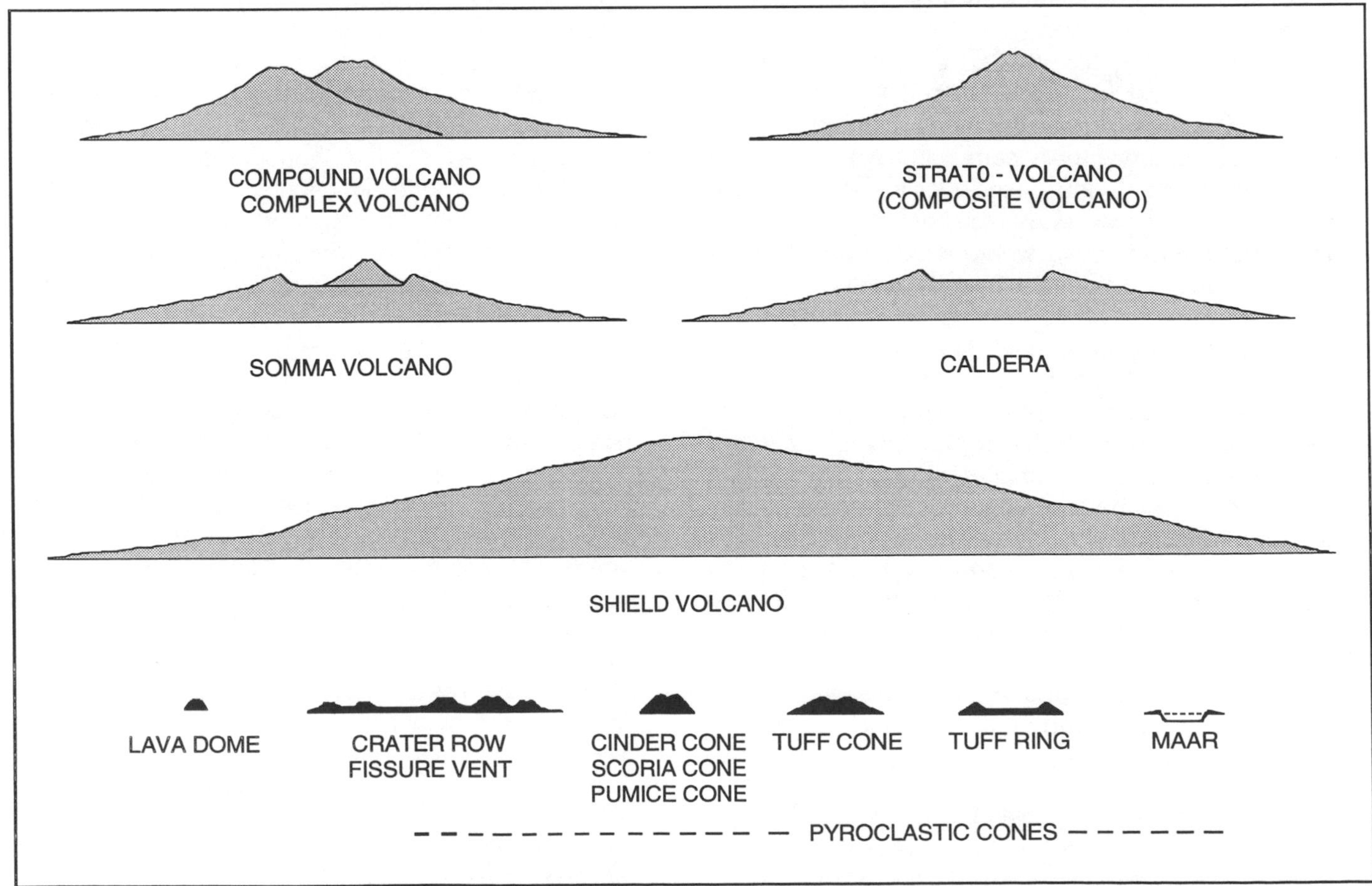

Figure 5. Types of volcanoes. Schematic profiles are vertically exaggerated by 2:1 (shaded) and 4:1 (dark) from the data of Pike.[44] Relative sizes are only approximate, as dimensions vary within each group. Figures 12-31, in the CHRONOLOGY section, illustrate these features as well.

STATUS

This element states, essentially, the most persuasive reason for including each volcano in this compilation. A "**historical**" eruption, documented during or shortly after observation, is the best evidence for inclusion. We list 539 volcanoes with historical eruptions, the criterion used by many people terming a volcano "active." However, we have tried to provide more even coverage of the globe's volcanoes, many of which carry no written record until 80 centuries after the first historically documented eruption in our file (Central Turkey, in 6200 BC, see Figure 12). To do this we have included 183 volcanoes[46] with dated eruptions during the last 10,000 years, as determined by techniques, such as "**Radiocarbon**" dating. For volcanoes with different eruptions dated by different techniques, we have entered under **Status** the technique that seemed to confirm Holocene activity most certainly. These techniques are listed on the inside front cover and summarized below under DATING TECHNIQUES (p. 15). We should mention, however, that the "**Anthropology**" status covers volcanoes with undated (but recent) activity described in native legends as well as activity dated by buried artifacts.

The remaining **Status** categories cover the many volcanoes (52% of our file) for which Holocene eruptions have not been dated, but are either likely or possible. These status categories will be discussed in approximate order of decreasing certainty.

First in certainty for undated eruptions comes the variety of general evidence lumped together under "**Holocene**" status. These locations, although without dated products, are virtually certain to have been active in postglacial time. Evidence includes volcanic products overlying latest Pleistocene glacial debris, youthful volcanic landforms in areas where erosion should have been pronounced in many thousands of years, and vegetation patterns that would have been far richer if the volcanic substrates were more than a few thousand (or hundred) years old. We have included in this category volcanoes mapped by original authors simply as "Holocene" or "postglacial." Some subjectivity is involved in this assignment, and the compiler is dependent upon the field experience of the original author. Many early investigators, unaware of slow erosion rates in arid regions, described lava flows as "extremely fresh, probably erupted within the last few hundred or few thousand years," but later radiometric dating has shown them to be Pleistocene or even older. We have generally required strong evidence for entry under this category, but 529 volcanoes bear "**Holocene**" status in our file, and another 108 (with distinctly less certainty)[47] are identified as "**Holocene?**".

Many volcanoes with obviously recent, but undated, eruptions are still visibly hot, as evidenced by surface thermal features. For 70 volcanic locations, or 5% of our file, one or more of the following thermal features are displayed in the **Status** category. "**Fumarolic**" locations are those characterized by steam and volcanic gas, or fume, reaching the surface. Temperatures are near the boiling point of water and a substantial supply of groundwater is necessary. In our 1981 edition, we used the word "**Solfataric**" for **Status** when sulfur dominated the volcanic gases, but we have since encountered inconsistencies with this usage[48] and have combined it with "**Fumarolic**" here. When the volume of water is large compared to steam and gas, however, the words "**Hot springs**" are used.[49] A "**Fumarolic**" or "**Hot springs**" status is assigned, however, only where we have seen no explicit evidence for Holocene *eruptive* activity.

Less certain is our **Status** category, "**Uncertain**", used for 57 volcanoes: with possible Holocene activity, but with sufficiently questionable documentation that we wanted to draw attention to that uncertainty. These entries include mariner's equivocal reports of submarine volcanism and volcanoes known only by uncertain reports of historical activity (with no other evidence of Holocene eruptions). The nature of this uncertainty is normally described in the free-form "remarks" category of our computer data file, but cannot be displayed in the tabular formats presented here.

One additional element must also be mentioned here as uncertain. We have followed the *CAVW* in including some thermal features, such as fumarolic fields, despite absence of other evidence for their Holocene volcanism. In fact, some areas, such as the Valles and Long Valley calderas in the western United States, show good evidence precluding eruptions in the last 10,000 years (but equally good evidence of still-molten magma below the surface). For 19 such volcanoes the word "**Pleistocene**" precedes the appropriate thermal feature listed above. For another 4, the designation "**Pleistocene-Geysers**" is used to identify uncommon variations of hot springs from which steam and water are periodically erupted. Although many thermal features require only a high local heat flow and groundwater, we have not included such features unless they are clearly related to volcanism.

Finally, we should comment on the "youthful" volcanoes that we have <u>not</u> included in the file. A volcano mapped as "Quaternary" would not be entered unless more specific Holocene age data were available. When a group of volcanoes is listed in a region of "Pleistocene-Holocene volcanism," we have entered only those for which Holocene evidence is available. Volcanoes listed as Holocene, or "active", in previous compilations, but later found to be Pleistocene or older, have also been excluded. For a few "volcanoes," well established in the literature (such as the *CAVW*, or our first edition) but later found to be misidentifications, we have entered "**Not a Volcano**" under **Status**. These have not been entered in any volcano totals and do not appear on our map, but we thought it best to include them in the DIRECTORY and GAZETTEER to avoid confusion when making comparisons with earlier lists.

In summary, the **Status** category conveys the following hierarchical progression from high to low certainty of

Holocene volcanism: (1) "**Historical,**" (2) dated eruptions based on a spectrum of techniques from "**Hydrophonic**" through "**Radiocarbon**" to "**Anthropology,**" which is transitional to (3) "**Holocene,**" (4) thermal features such as "**Fumarolic**", (5) "**Holocene?**", (6) "**Uncertain,**" and (7) thermal features preceded by the word "**Pleistocene-.**" Any entry can (and probably does) carry evidence to be found under lower levels of this hierarchy, but we have entered the highest **Status** category indicated by the data known to us. Furthermore, the **Status** listed is that of the *most recent eruptive* activity. A major Pleistocene center with only a single Holocene flank vent, for example, would have a "**Holocene**" status.

Eruption Data

The arrival of volcanic products at the Earth's surface is termed an eruption. Some definitions of the word include purely gaseous expulsions but we confine the term to events that involve the explosive ejection of fragmental material, the effusion of liquid lava, or both. This fragmental material may be old as well as new; the explosive interaction of volcanically generated heat and near-surface water can cause dramatic eruptions without any fresh volcanic material reaching the surface. Furthermore, some eruptions are over in minutes, others go on for centuries, and still others, in Scrope's words[50] of 1862, "exhibit an infinite variety of phases intermediate between the extremes of vivacity and sluggishness."

Added to this variety of eruptive types and durations is another "infinite variety" of monitoring quality – from volcanoes rich with sensing instruments and trained observers to remote volcanoes that are often hidden by clouds from their highly infrequent visitors. These variations cause problems for compilers (particularly when using a tabular computer format devoid of the subjective words with which we commonly express variations) and render true standardization impossible on a global scale.

A common problem through much of the historical record is the popular tendency to describe a volcano as "smoking" or "steaming." The full spectrum of steam venting ranges from normal fumarolic emission (with steam clouds many hundreds of meters above the volcano under some meteorological conditions) to very large steam columns that can rapidly rise to more than 10 km above the vent. We have ignored small clouds identified only as steam (Figure 30), but entered the large events, such as the spectacular steam columns that rose 10-14 km from Alaska's Trident and Redoubt volcanoes in 1967-68.[52] We have, however, placed a question mark before the date to indicate uncertainty of large steam emissions with questionable ash content. We have also used the question mark in this way to mark volcanoes noted simply as "smoking," since this description might refer to either ash eruptions or steam emission. There has been no uniformity in treatment of such reports by previous compilers, and it is certain that an unknown number of simple steam clouds have entered the historical record as "eruptions."[53] In recent decades, at least one-third (and as many as three-fourths) of a

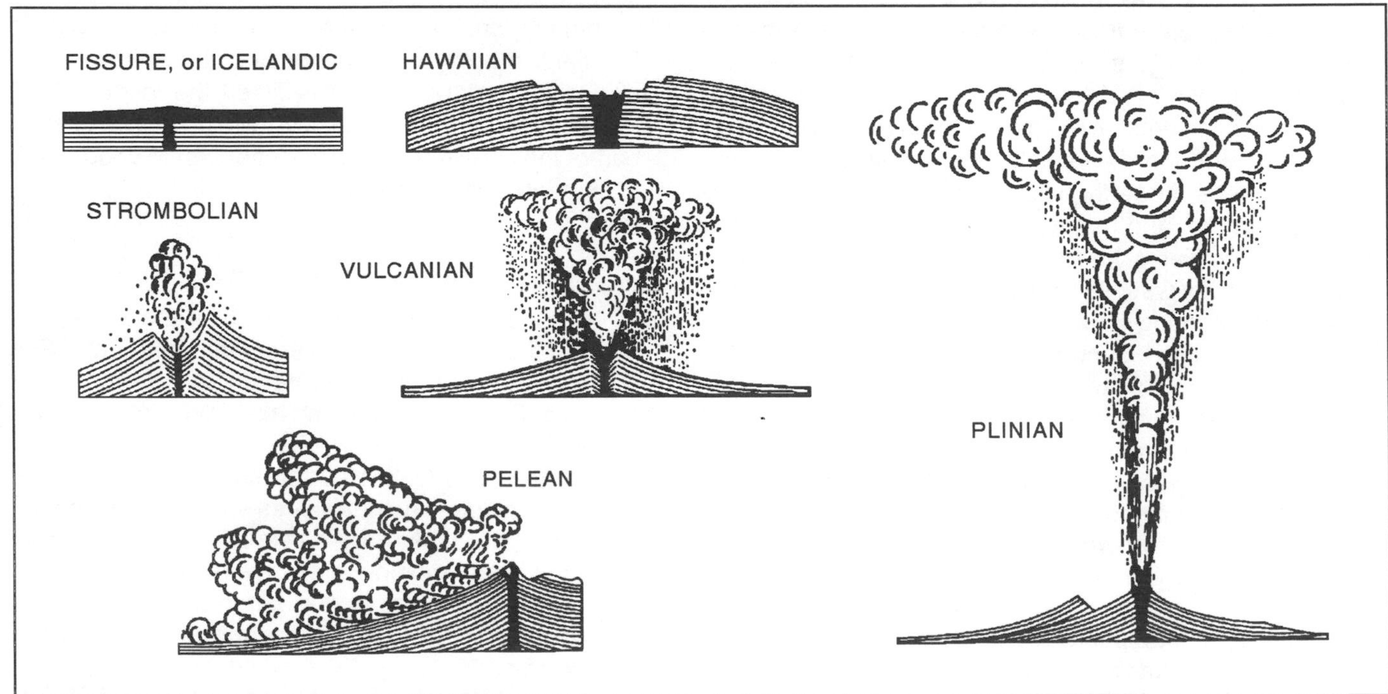

Figure 6. Types of eruptions: schematic cross-sections after Holmes.[51] The great range in explosivity depends upon many factors, particularly the magma's gas content and its viscosity (influencing the manner in which gas escapes the liquid).

year's uncertain eruptions are submarine, and many result from reports of discolored water observed during reconnaissance flights over the waters south of Japan.

Although some false eruptions have entered the historical record without the confirmation of solid volcanic products, many more true eruptions have been altogether missed simply because nobody was present to document them. This is easy to understand for remote volcanoes or the distant past, but eruptions can be missed even today on well-monitored volcanoes. In 1982, volcanologists on Kilauea, probably the world's best instrumented volcano, recognized a tiny deposit of fresh scoria (<3 m^3) that had not been present at this rarely visited East Rift site two years earlier.[54] The eruption has been tied to a seismic swarm recorded on the rainy night of 10-11 March, 1980. Larger eruptions have been recognized after-the-fact in the Galápagos Islands, at least two since tour boats began regular operation in late 1969, and even larger eruptions have no doubt been missed in more remote regions. In recent decades, however, atmospheric monitoring has advanced so well that any moderately large sulfur-producing eruption is soon recognized. In early 1982, laser imaging radar (LIDAR) stations around the world reported a new volcanic aerosol layer, and spectacular "volcanic" sunsets were being observed. The responsible volcano was not known, and the aerosol layer was dubbed "the mystery cloud", but retrospective work with SO_2-sensing satellite images later showed the source to have been Zaire's Nyamuragira. The eruption had been recognized and studied (Figure 23), but its remarkable gas component was surprising.[7]

Eruptions are particularly easy to miss when, as in the 1980 Kilauea example, they take place during a period of frequent <u>in</u>trusive activity. Following a major earthquake in 1975, and continuing through 1981, scientists at the Hawaiian Volcano Observatory documented 15 episodes of intrusion – when magma moved laterally below the surface – and only two significant surface eruptions. The rift earthquake made room available below the surface, and magma filled it before returning to the more familiar style of eruptions in 1983. Similar intrusive activity was well documented in Iceland during an episode of rifting covering the same years, and offering a fascinating example of spreading processes at major plate boundaries. Here repeated cycles of inflation at Krafla were punctuated by brief episodes of rifting, with magma generally moving laterally below the surface. This pattern suggests that plate divergence takes place during intense episodes of several meters separation over a few years, followed by perhaps 100 years of quiet, rather than steady-state separation of a few centimeters per year.[55]

Well-studied eruptions are commonly recognized as having distinct phases of activity, often including quiet periods lasting for days or months between more vigorous bursts of activity that are clearly part of a single, long eruptive period. Untrained observers, however, commonly report these bursts of activity as separate eruptions and these, in turn are difficult to distinguish in the historical record from the observations of travelers witnessing an ongoing remote eruption at separate times. A 1970s review of well-studied, longer eruptions showed us that quiet periods are commonly measured in days and weeks but rarely exceed 3 months. We also looked at the intervals between eruptions of each individual volcano in our file, finding a disproportionately large number in the 0-to-3 month range. Most of these apparently closely spaced eruptions have not been studied, but we believe that careful volcanological investigation would group most of them as phases in longer eruptions. Accordingly, in order to simplify our file, we have arbitrarily treated an eruption following its predecessor by less than 3 months as a phase of the earlier eruption, unless careful work has shown it to be distinct. All phase data remain in our file, but only the start and stop dates are systematically shown in this publication. However, major explosions during the lifetime of an eruption (if assigned a specific VEI – see discussion below) are shown in our CHRONOLOGY table. All eruptions with separate phase data – either designated by original authors or resulting from our grouping of events less than 3 months apart – are marked in the DIRECTORY by a "+" symbol in the **P** (for **P**hase) column between **Start** and **Stop** dates.

AREA OF ACTIVITY

For the simple volcano with central summit vent, we have normally not specified the location of eruptions from that vent other than to place an "x" in the first **Eruptive Characteristic** (designated by **Central**, for eruption location, and present for 54% of the eruptions in our file). For flank eruptions, however, and those from named subsidiary features, we have listed the location under **Area of activity** where possible. We have also used this part of the DIRECTORY to call attention to uncertainties in eruption location (see below).

DATES: START and STOP

For each of the 7,886 eruptions in the file we have entered the **Start** date by year, month, and day (**YEAR M-Dy**), where known. Some ancient eruptions are known only to the century and many only to the year. Of the eruptions in our file, 57% are known to the month and 45% to the day. Only 10% are known to the hour, and 6% to the minute, but these times are not displayed here. All dates (and times) are local, as used in virtually all volcanological reporting, but conversions to Greenwich, or Universal, time are in our data bank. BC dates are indicated by a "-" before the year and appear chronologically in all tables.

Readers should be cautioned that the DIRECTORY does not list the dates of paroxysmal eruptions occurring after the start of eruptive activity. These dates are, however, listed in the CHRONOLOGY and (as detailed below under VEI) an "*" symbol in the **VEI** column of the DIRECTORY indicates the existence of an additional event, between the start and stop dates shown, that can be found in the CHRONOLOGY. As detailed above (under ERUPTION DATA) a "+" in the **P** column between **Start** and **Stop** dates in the DIRECTORY indicates the existence of phase data available in the data file but not displayed here.

The end of an eruption is usually less dramatic than its start, and the commonly gradual decline in eruptive activity makes precise "stop dates" difficult to determine. Other eruptions, not recognized until well after they ended, are entered only with an approximate start date. These factors combine to explain the absence of a listed stop date for 59% of the eruptions in our file.

UNCERTAINTIES

Uncertainties of time, place, and event surround an unfortunately large proportion of the volcanological literature. When the eruption's location is uncertain, as when a mariner's report fails to specify which of an island's several volcanoes was erupting, we have listed it with the most likely volcano but prefaced the date with the commercial "at" sign ("@") to indicate location uncertainty. Only 60 of the eruptions (<1%) carry this uncertainty, and we briefly describe the problem under the **Area of Activity** heading. When the existence of the eruption itself is uncertain, however, as with questionable submarine eruption reports, or subaerial activity that may have been nothing more than increased fumarolic emission, we place a question mark ("**?**") before the date (10% of the file). When the eruption is certain but the date is not, one way of indicating the uncertainty is by a question mark after the date (4% of the file), but this is entered only when no further information exists on the extent of the uncertainty.

Date uncertainty is expressed in several ways. When the eruption is known only to year or month (57% of the file), we simply leave the following columns blank. But when the size of the uncertainty is known (11% of the file) we indicate this by a letter code (Table 2). This code allows us to deal with eruption dates known only as falling between two observations ("after May 10 but before May 24" becomes **0517g**, or May 17 ± 7), more general ranges ("17th century" becomes **1650 t** or 1650 ± 50), or specific analytical uncertainties (a corrected radiocarbon date of "1750 BC ± 150" becomes G**-1750w**). When original sources list an uncertainty not exactly matched by our letter code, we use the closest available letter.

If we have been unable to determine the type of uncertainty intended by the original reporter, we have placed a question mark after the date. An undated ash layer sandwiched between two layers of known age is assigned an age midway between the two, and preceded by a "**T**", indicating that the age is determined by tephrochronology. Such dates may have a greater uncertainty than that listed, however, because the two dated layers may themselves have dating uncertainties of substantial (but unknown) size.

Also following some dates is the "greater than" (>) or "less than" (<) symbol. The most common use of the ">" symbol is in designating "**stop date**" for the 105 eruptions believed to be continuing at the time of the report used in our compilation. The "<" symbol is also used for eruptive products known only to be younger than a dated object or horizon, such as lava flows covering earthen dams constructed 800-1200 BC in Yemen (this date, for Jabal Hylan, becomes A**-1200>**). The "<" symbol is used when it is the *date* that is younger than the *eruption* (but it is the only date available and is generally believed to be close to the true start date). Examples are observation dates for "new" volcanic features when earlier, pre-eruption observation dates are not known. We have used these symbols as little as possible, but felt it better to include such "maximum" or "minimum" dates, with appropriate symbols, than to ignore them. The "<" symbol, though, should be used more often than the historical record permits: many older dates listed by us under **Start**, for example, may have been reports by travelers witnessing an eruption that had been underway for some time.

	Years	Days		Years	Days
a =	± 1	± 1	*o* =	± 18	± 25
b =	2	2	*p* =	20	30 (1 mo)
c =	3	3	*q* =	25	45
d =	4	4	*r* =	30	60 (2 mo)
e =	± 5	± 5	*s* =	40	75
f =	6	6	*t* =	± 50	± 90 (3 mo)
g =	7	7	*u* =	75	120
h =	8	8	*v* =	100	150
i =	9	9	*w* =	150	180 (6 mo)
j =	± 10	± 10	*x* =	200	270
k =	12	12	*y* =	± 300	± 365 (1 yr)
m =	14	15	*z* =	500	545
n =	16	20	* =	1000	730 (2 yr)

Table 2. Uncertainty codes following Year (& M-Dy).

DATING TECHNIQUES

Some "historical" eruptions are known only to the century, but most of the large uncertainties (157 eruptions, or 3% of the file, are known to only ± 100 years or more) are the result of dating techniques. When a date is not historical, but results from a dating technique, that technique is shown by a letter code immediately preceding the start year. This code is listed on the inside front cover, and the techniques are briefly described below, in a general but not rigorous order of decreasing accuracy.

S = SOFAR, or submarine "**Hydrophone**" detection. Explosive eruptions on the sea floor send out shock waves through the water in much the same way that earthquakes send shock waves through Earth's solid crust. The velocities are slower, about 5300 km /hr, but these waves travel for long distances through the SOFAR channel (a layer of water within 1200 m of the surface) and their arrival times at submarine hydrophones can be used to locate the eruption in the same way that seismologists locate earthquake epicenters. Study of hydrophone records from observed submarine eruptions has shown features characteristic of volcanism, and when these features appear on records from more remote parts of the sea floor they have been used to locate and to date (often to the hour and minute) volcanism that would otherwise have been completely missed. Many of the eruptions carrying this designation in our file were reported between 1966 and 1974 by investigators who have not continued their monitoring.[56] In 1993, however, declassification of military monitoring systems has resulted in documentation of a significant sea-floor eruption 420 km off the coast of Washington state[57] – later confirmed by a variety of oceanographic evidence – and this technique should tell us much about sea floor volcanism in the future.

Although the quiet, nonexplosive effusion of lava that typifies most seafloor volcanism is difficult to detect by hydrophones, earthquake swarms commonly accompany these more gentle eruptions in places such as Hawaii and Iceland, and such swarms from submerged seamounts have been interpreted as submarine eruptions. We have entered 3 volcanoes (one off of Hawaii and two near Tahiti) because of earthquake swarms (**Status** entered as "**Seismicity**") and the fresh glass dredged from their submerged summits. However, the earthquake swarms might represent magma movement without eruption, so we have preceded these dates with a question mark rather than a symbol representing the "seismic" dating technique.

D = "DENDROCHRONOLOGY." The annual character of tree rings was recognized by the ancient Greeks, and use of tree rings to reconstruct the past goes back at least to Leonardo.[58] Dendrochronology has been used in volcanology both for indirect evidence of climate change from huge eruptions and for more direct reconstruction of nearby events.

The eruption of Sunset Crater, in northern Arizona, so stunted the growth of local trees that its record was clearly left in their annual growth rings, and careful counting of these rings has dated the eruption at 1065 AD.[59] Similar tree-ring dating of nearby, affected trees has established eruption dates elsewhere,[60] and interest is strong in the proxy record of eruptions large enough to have influenced global climate. Distant but long-lived trees bear frost rings from known historical eruptions, and the hope is strong that tree-ring chronologies will help establish a detailed record of the planet's largest eruptions.[61]

Other paleobotanical techniques can also be useful to volcanology. The famous eruption resulting in Oregon's Crater Lake, for example, is dated only to ± 50 years (nearly 6,000 years ago), but careful study of pollen associated with its volcanic ash in a far-away Montana bog showed that the eruption began in the autumn and apparently continued for at least 3 years.[62] Analysis of annual layers in Irish peat bogs is revealing detailed records (including fine particles of volcanic ash) from Icelandic eruptions, and leaf impressions under Japanese ash layers are dating prehistoric eruptions to the exact season of the year.[63] In New Zealand, insect remains preserved by the famous Taupo eruption of the second century AD have shown that the eruption took place in the early afternoon.[64] The application of biology to eruptive deposits holds great promise for unraveling the recent histories of many volcanoes.

V = "VARVE COUNT." Seasonal changes affect the sediment accumulation in many small lakes, particularly where the spring melting of ice provides an annual layer of coarse sandy particles to the lake floor in alternation with the finer clay deposited through the rest of the year. These layers, or varves, can later be counted to establish the date for a layer of volcanic ash in their midst. Like tree rings, these annual layers provide very accurate dates under ideal conditions and careful work, but uncertainty increases with age and nonideal conditions. Only two dates in the file carry stated uncertainties, and they are ± 50 and ± 300.[65] The sediments of Turkey's Lake Van provide a remarkable record – 16 eruptions since 8104 BC – of nearby Nemrut volcano, but uncertainties are not listed.[66]

I = "ICE CORE." The far-traveled aerosol of major eruptions (see pp. 7, 24) eventually settles to the Earth's surface, leaving a chemical trace in glaciers and ice caps that grow by annual accumulation of snow. Cores through these annual layers then provide an important record of past volcanism that can extend, as with the new cores from Greenland, over 250,000 years.[67] Whereas tree ring studies give an unequivocal link to volcanism only if close to the source, strongly acidic layers are formed in the ice of both polar regions by major historical eruptions, and similar, even stronger, layers in prehistoric portions of the core point clearly to volcanism with global distribution as the cause. This gives the exciting potential of establishing a complete chronology of large, sulfur-producing eruptions, but the difficulty lies in determining which volcano was responsible for a specific acidic layer.

Aerosols move swiftly around the globe but their spread to the north and south is relatively slow. Thus an eruption from high northern latitudes (Iceland, Alaska, Kamchatka) leaves a relatively large volcanic deposit on Greenland, whereas a comparable one from low latitudes leaves a much smaller record, and one from the southern hemisphere may leave none at all. Small volcanic ash particles have been found in some cores, allowing petrological corelation with an individual volcano,[68] but substantial uncertainty surrounds the identification of most eruptive sources. Added to this problem is the danger of misinterpreting the completeness of volcanism's recent historical record. Very large eruptions may well have been missed only a few hundred years ago in some parts of the world, so the matching of acidity spikes with poorly constrained dates from the volcanic record needs caution. Although this technique holds great promise, we have entered only 8 ice core dates in the DIRECTORY (3 from Antarctica, 4 from Iceland, and one from Melanesia). In the CHRONOLOGY, however, we list several (51) dates of major eruptions for which the source is unknown. These dates are chronologically well constrained and unequivocally volcanic; the entry at 1259 AD, for example, is based on acidity spikes in cores from both polar regions[69] and is regarded as the largest eruption of the millennium. Continued research should permit greatly increased use of this technique in building the prehistoric volcanological record.

A = "ANTHROPOLOGY." About half of these 30 dates are native legend, or "traditional" dates. Some are entered without an uncertainty code (e.g., Bedouin legends of a 640 AD Arabian eruption), while other uncertainties range from ± 5 to ± 50 years (the "11th century" eruption in Mexico's Michoacan field), but all should be treated with some caution, recognizing the human ability to misremember an undocumented date. Some "**Anthropology**" dates come from buried artifacts and others from dated structures (temples, dams) affected by an eruption.[70] An eruption date in the Galápagos Islands is based on marmalade pots. The pots were stashed by English buccaneers in 1683, and fragments were later found by Heyerdahl[71] in a lava flow recognized as "young" by Darwin during his historic visit of 1835. The eruption is therefore dated here as "A 1759u", or midway between 1683 and 1835, ± 76 years. Other dates have been obtained by anthropologists but entered directly in our file under the dating technique used (commonly ^{14}C).

L = "LICHENOMETRY." The slow but rather regular growth rate of lichens on a lava flow surface has been used to date two eruptions on Penguin Island, Antarctica.[72] The technique is useful for establishing relative ages on young lava flows, but absolute ages require accurate baseline growth rates, under comparable conditions of climate and substrate, that are rarely available over more than a century.

M = "MAGNETISM." When lava cools from its molten state, it often retains an accurate "memory" of the Earth's magnetic field at that time. Secular variation, or historical wander of the Earth's magnetic poles, has been large enough that careful study of a lava's magnetic "memory" may reveal its approximate date of cooling. The number of dates in our file based on this technique have increased dramatically from the 2 in our 1981 book to 29 here. Most carry uncertainties in the ± 25-150-year range. The accuracy of the technique decreases greatly for events older than a few thousand years, and the oldest eruption dated by magnetics – Oregon's Mount Bachelor around 5800 BC – carries a ± 750-year uncertainty.[73]

C = "^{14}C," or <u>un</u>corrected radiocarbon. Over 90% of all prehistoric dates in our file result from this technique, at least indirectly, and 773 carry the designation "**C**", up 239% from the number in our 1981 book. The technique is based upon the late 1940s discovery that living trees and other organic matter contain minute amounts of carbon's radioactive isotope (of atomic weight 14). When the organism dies, its radioactive carbon is no longer replenished and the proportion of ^{14}C in its carbon begins to decrease by radioactive decay. Because this decay rate is accurately known, careful laboratory measurement of the ^{14}C/^{12}C ratio in prehistoric wood can accurately date that wood's death. Although the half-life of ^{14}C is about 5,730 years, and its initial concentration is only one part in a trillion (10^{12}) parts of ^{12}C, ages to 40,000 years are measured routinely.[74]

Radiocarbon dates are normally expressed in years BP ("before present"), and we have followed the standard convention of treating 1950 as "present" (unless otherwise stated) in converting to eruption year dates. Some uncertainty in radiocarbon dates is guaranteed by analytical error and the fact that the ^{14}C decay rate is known only to within ± 30 years. Most authors combine these and other factors in a single uncertainty, or "±" value, after each radiocarbon date presented. We then accept the author's reported date and attach the appropriate uncertainty code upon entry to our file,[75] but see discussion in the next paragraphs for important cautions against mistaking these dates for calendar dates. Uncertainties for uncalibrated radiocarbon dates listed here range from ± 10 to ± 1,835 years, but 70% are between ± 100 and ± 300 years. The youngest radiocarbon dates are for Pagan, in the Marianas, and Canada's Iskut-Unuk River Cone Group (both around 1800 AD). Over 400 radiocarbon dates in this compilation would have been "**historical**" if they had taken place in southern Italy where the written record extends to 1500 BC.

G = "^{14}C", or corrected radiocarbon. Careful radiocarbon dating has been done on selected portions of long-lived bristlecone pine trees that can be independently dated by tree-ring techniques. This work shows generally close agreement (<100-150 years) between the two methods for the last 2,500 years, but they then diverge until "true" tree-ring dates exceed radiocarbon dates by 700-900 years for the last 4,000 years of the Holocene. The reason for this divergence is apparent variation in past content of atmospheric radiocarbon. For many years there was substantial disagreement between different laboratories, but a common calibration program for correcting raw radiocarbon dates was published last year and has gained wide acceptance.[76] When a corrected date is available we have proceeded it by the letter "**G**" (which can be thought of, mnemonically, as a slightly altered "**C**"). However, we have not attempted to correct the uncorrected dates of other workers (over 86% of our radiocarbon dates). Many published dates are not accompanied with all the information required[77] for an accurate correction, and we have chosen not to risk confusing the situation by publishing incorrect dates not reported by original authors. The mixing of uncorrected dates with a growing number of calender dates can, however, be very misleading to readers who do not pay attention to the letter code in front of prehistoric dates,[78] particularly those in the BC part of the CHRONOLOGY. In 1981, uncorrected radiocarbon dates so dominated the first 7,500 years of the CHRONOLOGY that we could emphasize their good *relative* sequence, and state that the distinction with the *absolute* time scale was less significant for the remaining 96% of CHRONOLOGY entries (the difference being small between corrected and uncorrected radiocarbon dates in the last 2,500 years). Now, however, the increased accuracy of other techniques makes it imperative that readers be aware of the significant age difference between "**C**" and "**G**" dates: to 100-150 years during the last 2,500 years rising to 900 years in the early Holocene.

U = "THERMOLUMINESCENCE" dating depends on the effects of radioactive decay (like "**F**") rather than direct counts of isotopic ratios (like "**C**", "**G**", "**K**", and "**R**"). Some electrons emitted during decay are trapped in crystal defects, and laboratory heating frees them, producing light in the process. The amount of light depends, in part, on the age of the crystal. This technique is much used by archeologists, and is represented here by 3 dates from the Chaine des Puy in central France. Uncertainties are not given by the authors, but they prefer the thermoluminescence dates to older ^{14}C dates carrying uncertainties of ± 300-350 years.[79]

T = "TEPHROCHRONOLOGY." Aristotle used the Greek word for ash, "tephra," in describing an eruption on the island of Vulcano. Because modern volcanologists define "ash" as particles smaller than 2 mm in diameter, a broader term is useful for describing material of *all* sizes explosively ejected by volcanoes. In 1944, Sigurdur Thorarinsson proposed the word "tephra" for this purpose[80] and it is widely accepted today. Tephra from large explosive eruptions may be distributed over enormous distances, forming a distinctive layer that later proves useful as a "marker" horizon dating associated layers of sediment. Careful mapping of layers throughout a volcanic area can develop a *relative* sequence of overlapping ash layers. When some of these ash layers are dated, either historically or by some other technique, then dates can be assigned to the intervening layers in this relative sequence. The technique is a broad one, embracing a variety of field geologic and stratigraphic methods,[80] and we have used this designation to cover prehistoric eruptions for which our source specified no technique (as, for example, a date placed midway between two radiocarbon-dated eruptions). Uncertainties are commonly large, ranging from ± 10 to ± 3,000, with a median around ± 500 years.

H = "HYDRATION RIND." Obsidian flows were molten liquids with unusually high viscosity inhibiting nucleation and growth of the crystals that make up most volcanic rocks. The resulting glass is unstable and gradually decomposes by the addition of moisture from the atmosphere. The thickness of the hydration rind on an obsidian flow surface is proportional to the time that it has been exposed to the atmosphere, and this thickness has been used to date 10 flows in our file, mainly from Oregon's Newberry Caldera and California's Mono Craters.[81] Uncertainties are large for this technique, ranging from ± 360 to ± 1740 years for the dates included here, and hydration rates are affected by regional climatic variations. No new dates by this technique have been added since our 1981 book.

K = "K-Ar", or Potassium-Argon, is one of the most widely used methods of geochronometry. Like radiocarbon dating, it depends upon the relative proportions of parent (^{40}K) to daughter (^{40}Ar) isotopes, and the well-established half-life of that constant decay. It has been used to date rocks approaching the age of the Earth (4.5 x 10^9 years), but is rarely used on materials younger than 100,000 years.[82] Of the 9 K-Ar dates listed here, none is younger than 1000 BC and all but one are from Italy. Uncertainties given in the original reports range from ± 600 to ± 2,000 years.

R = "ARGON-ARGON" ($^{40}Ar/^{39}Ar$) dating was first developed in the late 1980s. It is similar in many ways to K/Ar dating, but offers greater precision and requires much smaller amounts of material. During stepwise heating, a spectrum of apparent ages is shown by changing isotopic ratios (reflecting contamination) until reaching a plateau representing the crystal's true age. The technique is particularly useful for relatively young materials, and is bringing new order to geologic time scales over the past few tens of millions of years. Only 4 dates using this technique are listed here; all from Kenya in the 6th to 8th millennium BC, but with uncertainties in the ± 2,000-4,000 year range.[83]

F = "FISSION TRACK." This technique depends upon the natural spontaneous fission decay of uranium. The resulting heavy fission particles leave minute damage tracks in volcanic glass that can be revealed by chemical etching of a cut and polished surface. The number of tracks per unit area, counted microscopically, is proportional to the age of the glass (for any given uranium content) and can therefore provide eruption ages. Although the technique is capable of better accuracy, one (of only 3) fission track age included here – 1000 BP from Canada's Mount Edziza[84] – carries the largest uncertainty in the file: ± 6000 years!

X = "DISCREDITED ERUPTION." This is not a dating technique, but identifies events that – although once established in the volcanological literature, such as the *CAVW* – have since been discredited. These are included in none of our totals, but great effort is often invested in proving a reported eruption to be false, and we thought it better to retain these 156 "non-events" – in a form that allows easy identification (and removal) – rather than have them appear to readers of earlier compilations as mistaken omissions. A discredited eruption appears in the DIRECTORY but not in the CHRONOLOGY.

DURATION

Duration information exists for only 41% of the eruptions in our file. Its quality suffers from the above-mentioned difficulty of recognizing the gradual end of an eruption that may have begun quite dramatically. But it suffers even more from inconsistent definition of the word "eruption," as discussed above (p. 13). At Stromboli, for example, references to volcanism go back at least 2,400 years, but the record is clearly uneven. Although it appears that Stromboli has been characterized by essentially continuous mild volcanism for most of that period, we have followed the *CAVW* in entering the first known paroxysmal activity (1558 AD) and the more explosive events since then. We have also indicated the persistent, low-level activity by starting the record with a 0450 BC eruption continuing to the present. Therefore the resulting durations show a series of shorter events with median duration of 18 days (mean = 52 days) along with a single duration of 2,400 years! With these cautions in mind, however, it is interesting to examine the distribution of known eruption durations.

Of the 3,211 eruptions in our file with duration data, 9% ended in less than a day and 16% within 2 days.[85] A total of 24% ended within a week, 30% within two weeks, 43% within a month, and 53% within two months. Only 17% exceeded one year, 7% exceeded three years, and 0.5% exceeded 30 years. The median duration is 7 weeks. Again demonstrating the unremarkable nature of most eruption endings, only 12% of durations are accurately known to the day, 55% carry uncertainties of ± 1 day, 63% ≤1 week, and 89% ≤1 month.

Eruptive activity is rarely distributed evenly throughout the full duration, and an eruption's paroxysmal phase may come at any time. Several prominent eruptions, such as Krakatau 1883 and Mount St. Helens 1980 culminated months after lower level activity began, but it is a mistake to assume that days, weeks, or months are

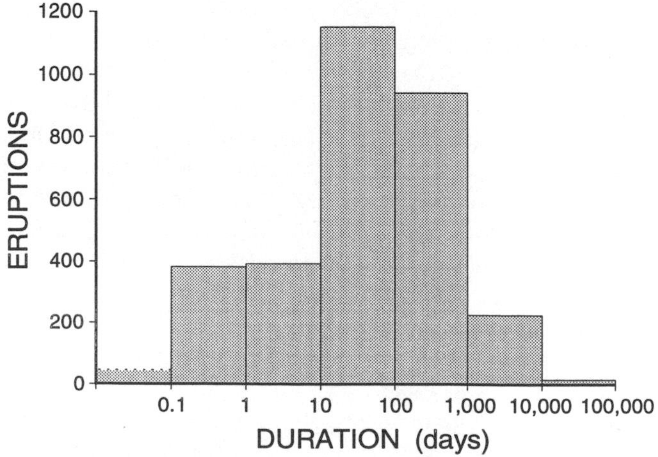

Figure 7. Histogram of 3,211 eruption durations: those for which stop (as well as start) date is known. The data for ≤0.1 days (2½ hours) are dashed because relatively few durations listed as ≤1 day carry sufficient time information to be more specific. Median duration is 7 weeks.

Date	Durations			Duration uncertainty	
	number	per decade	as % of historical eruptions	% ≤1 day	median
8000 BC – 1500 AD	53	0.1	17	30	± 20 days
1500 AD – 1900 AD	1041	26.0	43	44	± 5 days
1900 AD – 1968 AD	1317	193.7	66	55	± 1 day
1968 AD – 1994 AD	789	493.1	97	64	± 1 day

Table 3. Duration data through time.

available to prepare for an eruption's paroxysmal phase. Several major eruptions (e.g. Tarawera 1886, Bandaisan 1888, Hekla 1947, Sheveluch 1964, Usu 1977) reached their climax within an *hour* of their start.[86] Precursory unrest – at least that perceptible to uninstrumented observers – is also often too short to provide a helpful warning of impending eruption. Careful, instrumental monitoring is the best defense against eruption surprises.[87]

An eruption's stop date is a useful indicator of reporting quality (Table 3). Prior to 1500 AD, stop dates (and thus durations) were known from only 53 eruptions (17% of those historically documented in that time period), and their median uncertainty was ± 20 days. Since 1968, durations are known from 97% of the eruptions and their median uncertainty is ± 1 day. Table 3 also shows additional data bounded by dates of 1500 AD (western explorations, printing press), 1900 AD (radio, telegraphy, aircraft) and 1968 (start of regular Smithsonian reporting). Eruptions described accurately enough to include a stop date have increased dramatically, both in number per decade and as a percentage of known eruptions. Over this same time, uncertainties surrounding these stop dates have decreased concomitantly.

Although several very brief explosive eruptions have been recorded,[88] the shortest major eruption known to us is the fatal event in 1977 when the long-lived molten lava lake of Nyiragongo, Zaire, drained in less than one hour, flooding the outer flanks with 20 million cubic meters of exceptionally fluid lava that moved downslope at speeds reaching 60 km /hr.[89] Such short eruptions must be balanced against the above-mentioned 2,400 year activity of Stromboli, but there are others, such as the continuing eruption of Yasur (active in Vanuatu since it was first discovered by Captain Cook in 1774), that may have been even longer.[90]

A good indication of a new eruption's likely duration would seem to be the previous history of that volcano, but the record is rarely extensive enough, and even the better records often defy simple generalization. On Hawaii's Kilauea, for example, 1 out of every 4 eruptions ends in 2 days or less, 11 of them lasting less than 24 hours; yet Kilauea also has 3 of the longest eruptions in our file (43, 27, and 17 years) with a fourth possibly in the making (the East Rift activity that began in January of 1983 continuing at the time of this writing).

Perhaps the most sobering lessons about eruption duration (and about the wide range of behavior in a single eruption) come from Indonesia's Tambora in 1815. Over three full years of mild eruptive activity there preceded a dramatic eruption, with cloud height estimated at 33 km. Such paroxysmal explosions end many eruptions, and reasonable people might then have concluded that the eruption had ended. But they would have been wrong. After that lull of 5 days came history's largest explosive eruption: The culminating blast reached heights estimated at 44 km, caused three days of total darkness 500 km from the volcano, and ultimately resulted in 92,000 fatalities.[91] Predicting an eruption's end is no easier than predicting its beginning.

ERUPTIVE CHARACTERISTICS

In our DIRECTORY, we have indicated the presence, when known, of 20 characteristics selected by the originators of the *CAVW* and shown throughout these volumes, generally by the symbols reproduced here in the inside front cover guide to our abbreviations. Our data file contains a larger list of characteristics and we have modified some of the older *CAVW* entries, but we have not yet systematically revised the full file and we therefore present here only the basic 20 characteristics that have been reasonably well standardized. Our compressed format is designed to provide a swift summary of the behavior common to a particular volcano or region, but also to allow a systematic search for eruptions of a particular type. No such search can be complete, however, because most of the eruptions in the file were neither documented adequately at the time, nor studied sufficiently since, to enable us to list all characteristics with confidence. Many eruptions have no characteristics listed at all, and many more carry only a single entry, such as "normal explosions," despite the likelihood of other characteristics having accompanied them. Positive identification of a particular characteristic is indicated by an "x" in that column, uncertainty is shown by a "?", and negative (absence of information as well as absence of that characteristic) by a "-".

The first 4 characteristics describe where the eruption took place (see also discussion of **Area of Activity** on p. 14). **Central crater** is entered for 56% of the eruptions listed here; Japan's Aso has the most central crater eruptions in the file with 151, followed by Italy's Etna with 135. **Flank vent**, or parasitic crater (see Figure 14), eruptions have been noted for 204 volcanoes, and Piton de la Fournaise, on the Indian Ocean island of Reunion, leads the list with 47 such eruptions. Some volcanoes, such as Alaska's Trident and Chile's Cerro Azul (Quizapu), have recorded eruptions from parasitic craters only. **Radial fissure** eruptions are listed for 105 volcanoes. Hawaii's Mauna Loa leads the list with 82 radial eruptions, but Etna (79), Fournaise (43, see Figure 26), and Kilauea (45) have frequent eruptions of this type. Although eruptions also take place from fissures circumferential to the volcano, they were not among the symbols chosen for *CAVW* and are not designated here. **Regional fissure** eruptions are entered for only 78 volcanoes. One third of these are in Iceland, where eruptions fill new linear fissures resulting from the spreading of the Atlantic Ocean (Figure 18). Icelandic eruptions, led by Hekla (30), Vatnafjoll (26), Krafla (23), and Bardarbunga (11) make up 58% of the regional fissure eruptions in the file.

The next 4 characteristics deal with eruptions interacting with water. **Submarine** eruptions are the most common, with 289 eruptions from 93 locations, but these recorded events are only a small fraction of all submarine eruptions (see p. 9-10 and 16). Kavachi, in the Solomon Islands has 25 known submarine eruptions since 1938. Seawater unquestionably complicates eruption reporting. An Icelandic volcanologist once balanced simultaneous telephone calls concerning a nearby submarine eruption.[92] One was from a policeman in a mainland phonebooth looking out at the eruption column and describing its red interior. The other was from an airplane pilot circling the site and declaring emphatically that there was no eruption. Apparently a confluence of currents had caused a waterspout-like cloud and sunset glint gave it a red glow. Some skepticism is called for in dealing with ocean eruption reports, and we have recently eliminated from our listings an 1853 submarine event 55 km off the coast of California. This was entered in the *CAVW* on the basis of high water spouting and shoal soundings, but the ocean floor bedrock is 15 million years old and the shoals are frequented by whales. We have also rejected submarine eruption events such as the shock waves and sulfurous smells reported from a Soviet ship[93] in the middle of the Gulf of Alaska in 1964, on the day of the famous Good Friday earthquake, one of this century's largest.

A specific type of submarine eruption – **New island**, or Island Building – was added to the original *CAVW* list of characteristics in 1953. These events have special importance for biologists interested in colonization, as on Iceland's new island of Surtsey, formed from 1963 to 1967. We record 95 new islands, but the fact that they are from only 39 locations shows that many of the islands were short-lived; eroded by the sea soon after they were formed, only to be followed by other islands built by later eruptions (Figure 15). The famous Greek island of Santorini had 7 island-forming eruptions between 197 BC and 1866 AD (Figure 16), and Kavachi has built itself above sea-level at least 9 times since 1950. We have used this symbol for eruptions forming islands in caldera lakes (e.g., Taal, Askja) as well as the open ocean, but the former are identified by the absence of an "x" in the column for submarine eruptions. **Subglacial** eruptions represent a special interaction with water. Most are not recorded, but in Iceland the sudden release of water from such eruptions forms tremendous floods ("jökulhlaups" or glacier bursts) with flow rates that have exceeded those of the Amazon River. These are marked by a "J" rather than an "x" in the **Mudflow** column (see below). Of the 104 known subglacial eruptions, 86 were in Iceland, with Grimsvötn (40), Bardarbunga (19), and Katla (17) accounting for most. Only a third of the 21 volcanoes that have produced subglacial eruptions are from Iceland. Most are in high latitudes, but one is from Ecuador's Antisana, just 55 km from the equator, and 6 more are from other Andean volcanoes.

Crater lake eruptions are recorded from 55 volcanoes (Figure 22). Water and hot magma make an explosive combination, and a summit crater lake on an active volcano places these two components in dangerous proximity. Lake water adds to the danger by contributing, in an eruption, to mudflows that can devastate the volcano's outer slopes and beyond. The Costa Rican volcano Poás has had at least 38 crater lake eruptions, with one (in 1910) reportedly shooting a fountain of water 4 km in the air. Ruapehu, in New Zealand, has recorded the most crater lake eruptions (48), with Aso (46) close behind, but the most devastating has been Java's Kelut, where extensive efforts to drain the lake have successfully reduced its danger after 10 fatal eruptions claimed many thousands of lives. A very few of the 323 eruptions bearing this symbol are from regional rather than summit lakes, but these should be clear from the initial "place" characteristic.

The next 3 characteristics deal with explosive volcanism. **Explosive** eruptions (or "normal explosions" in the original *CAVW* terminology) is the single most common characteristic, appearing in 70% of all eruptions[94] (Figures 15, 23, & 24). Around 150 volcanoes have recorded 10 or more explosive eruptions and Etna leads the list with 173 in the past 8000 years. Aso has recorded 151 since 553 AD. **Pyroclastic flows** are hot glowing avalanches that can move down slopes at hurricane speeds, devastating all living things in their paths (Figures 25 & 13). They are recorded from 237 volcanoes and 763 eruptions. Java's Merapi has had pyroclastic flows in 31 of its 66 historical eruptions since 1548 AD, and 11 of these 31 have been fatal. The famous West Indian volcano Mont Pelée has had more pyroclastic flow eruptions dated (51): only 3 have been in historical time, but that of 1902 destroyed 28,000 lives in only a few minutes (Figure 21). The term nuée ardente has been used in the *CAVW*, and by us (in the first edition), to cover a variety of pyroclastic-flow phenomena, including pyroclastic surges and Merapi-type dome collapse flows. Our current use of the term pyroclastic flow covers the same broad range.

Phreatic explosions result from the mixing of cold water and hot rock (Figure 15). The products of these explosions contain only fragmented older rock, but the source of the heat is normally near-surface magma, and this may appear in the products as small proportions of fresh glass. As the proportion of fresh material increases to dominance, either in a different phase of the eruption or in a different eruption, the words "phreatic" or "phreato-magmatic" no longer apply. We list this characteristic for 838 eruptions from 237 volcanoes, but usage of the term is variable and most explosions are too poorly studied to know their phreatic component. Thus the presence of an "x" in the **Explosive** column does not necessarily imply a magmatic eruption. Nevertheless, phreatic eruptions are commonly associated with the "water" characteristics discussed two paragraphs above, and the expected relationship with crater lake eruptions is particularly clear. The 13 volcanoes with the greatest number of phreatic explosions (35% of the total) also account for nearly half of all crater lake eruptions.

Fumarolic events – dramatic steaming, or fuming like that shown in Figure 30 – are treated differently here than in the *CAVW* (where the word "Solfataric" is used: see discussion p. 12). We have excluded over 100 events listed by the *CAVW* as solely fumarolic, and, although almost all eruptions have associated fumarolic activity, we do not record this. The 19 events from 14 volcanoes marked here as **Fumarolic** mostly represent cases in which distant observations of apparent eruptions carried cautionary phrases such as "possibly only fumarolic activity", or different sources disagreed on whether an "eruption" emitted any solid material. For these we have placed a "?" in front of the eruption date and identified the nature of the uncertainty by an "x" in this column. In unusual circumstances molten sulfur is emitted from volcanic vents, and interest in these unusual events increased with the 1979 discovery of sulfur eruptions on Io, a moon of Jupiter. We have used the "fumarolic" characteristic column to mark such eruptions of sulfur at Krakatau, Binuluan, Kirishima, Shiretoko-Iwo-Zan, Ebeko, and Poás.

The next 4 characteristics deal with the eruption of fluid lava, the most common being **Lava flows** (Figures 26, 27, & 17). Lava flows occurred in only 25% of the listed eruptions, but nearly half of the volcanoes with dated eruptions have dated flows, and of course a much higher proportion have prehistoric flows. Lava flows are the dominant eruptive product around the global rift system, where new material is being added to the crust, and within the deep ocean basins, but they are overwhelmingly dominated by explosive eruption products near continental margins where crustal material is being consumed. Of the 805 volcanoes with dated eruptions, 93 have had lava flows with all eruptions and 448 have had them with none. The leading producers are Etna (128 recorded eruptions with lava flows), Fournaise (128), and Mauna Loa (109). **Lava lakes** are a particularly spectacular type of lava flow, forming molten lakes over submerged vents that may keep them circulating colorfully for tens of years. Lava lakes are known from 31 volcanoes, with Kilauea accounting for a third of the 93 recorded lava lake eruptions (Figure 27). The Nyiragongo lake (0203-03=) also provided useful information during its 49 year existence, and lava lakes were still active at Erta Ale (0201-08=), Masaya (1404-10=), and Erebus (1900-02=) in 1994. We have followed the *CAVW* in applying this symbol also to eruptions that ponded lava in pre-existing pit craters or calderas. Drilling through the crusts of such lakes as they solidified has provided valuable data on the cooling history and fractionation of magma.[95] Lava **Domes** form when lava is too viscous and too limited in volume to spill substantially over the rim of its crater and move down slope as a lava flow (contrast Figures 27 & 17). These steep-sided viscous masses are commonly extruded after the explosive discharge of more gas-rich magma, and may grow to make up much of the volcanic edifice. The upper 800 m of California's Lassen Peak, for example, is a dome with a basal diameter of about 2.5 km, but most are smaller and some (such as those recently active at Japan's Usu volcano) grow largely below the surface, uplifting the ground above. Santiaguito dome, on Volcán Santa Mariá, Guatemala, began growing in 1922 and continues active today. We list 374 dome-forming eruptions from 135 volcanoes, led by Merapi, with 32, Bezymianny, on the Kamchatka Peninsula, with 31 (since 1955), and Mount St. Helens, with 15. **Spines** are a minor (but spectacular) subdivision of domes, forming when a slender column of nearly solid lava is thrust upward from the top of a growing dome. After the tragic 1902 eruption at Mont Pelée, a celebrated spine was thrust 311 m high (at rates to 25 m /day) before it crumbled (Figure 21). We list 20 spine-forming eruptions from 14 volcanoes, but many smaller spines have been produced during the 374 dome-forming eruptions in the file.

The final group of 4 characteristics deals with the effects of eruptions on humans. **Fatal**ities are recorded for 330 eruptions from 145 volcanoes; not a large percentage of either total, but some eruptions have been calamitous and these have not been evenly distributed in either space or time.[96] Indonesia's Kelut and Merapi, Japan's Asama, and the Philippines' Mayon have had 14, 11, 14, and 12 fatal eruptions,respectively. These three nations – among the most densely populated in the world – have 47% of the world's fatal volcanoes and 61% of history's fatal eruptions. These countries now have vigorous volcano hazard programs working to reduce such proportions in the future, and their recent successes are shown in the table on p. 177. In the 130 years prior to 1903 the world's population doubled and over 200,000 deaths resulted from volcanism, most of them in 5 major eruptions with death tolls exceeding 10,000. After 1902, and its three Caribbean disasters, the world's population had again doubled by the mid 1960s, but volcanism had claimed less than 16,000 lives. In the first edition of this book, we suggested that one reason for this dramatic reduction was increased monitoring and understanding of volcanoes, but another was simply good luck. That luck ran out, and in the years since 1981 more than 28,000 lives have been lost to volcanoes. Population densities continue to increase exponentially in many volcanic regions and we must increase monitoring and understanding at an even faster rate if we are to avoid even greater volcanic disasters.

Damage to property or other human infrastructures[97] has been recorded for 847 eruptions from 248 volcanoes. As with the fatality data, there is a strong association with population density, and the 3 most destructive volcanoes are Etna (Figure 14), Aso, and Merapi (with 61, 31, and 21 eruptions, respectively). **Mudflows**, or lahars, are a major cause of this destruction. Mudflows form in several different ways, but many large explosive volcanoes bring together their three essential components of: steep slopes, extensive ash deposits, and abundant water (in crater lakes, swiftly melted ice, or the rains commonly associated with both mountain peaks and eruptions). These often combine to form dense mudflows sweeping down slope with enormous momentum that can carry them for tens of kilometers across flat arable land beyond the foot of the volcano (Figure 31). Volcanic mudflows are reported from 489 eruptions and 160 volcanoes, with 27 having come from Cotopaxi in the Ecuadorian Andes. Pyroclastic flows from its 1877 eruption swiftly melted the perennial ice at its 5,897 m summit and soon turned the vast, fertile inter-Andean valley below into a roiling sea of mud, moving at speeds averaging 70 km /hr. The 1985 eruption of Nevado del Ruiz, destroying the town of Armero and 22,000 lives, and the 1991 mudflows from Pinatubo – continuing today in the Philippines – are more recent examples. Mudflows directly associated with glacier bursts, or Jökulhlaups (see above), are identified in the DIRECTORY by a J, rather than the x used to indicate other characteristics.

Tsunami are long-period sea waves (often mistakenly called tidal waves) that travel at speeds up to 800 km /hour and may build to devastating heights upon approaching land. They form when huge masses of water are suddenly displaced, either by earthquake or by eruption. One of the most powerful eruptions of recent centuries, at Krakatau in 1883, produced lethal waves with each major explosion, killing more than 34,000 Javans and Sumatrans. The largest wave, an estimated 15 m high in the open ocean, reached heights to 40 m on the heavily populated coast, carrying a steamship 2½ km inland and stranding it 24 m above sea level (Figure 20). This tsunami immediately followed the largest explosion, heard 4,653 km away, that hurled ash into the stratosphere. The even larger eruption of Santorini, in the 17th century BC, is likewise thought to have produced major tsunami affecting the eastern Mediterranean (perhaps contributing to flood legends and the end of the Minoan civilization). Many tsunami result when large parts of the seafloor are displaced by tectonic earthquakes, some of which may also trigger eruptions. We list tsunami from 42 volcanoes and 62 eruptions, with the largest number from Italy's Stromboli and Taal in the Philippine Islands (5 each). Taal is in a large lake, rather than an ocean, and damaging waves have accompanied 5 historical eruptions, all of them fatal. The Japanese word "Tsunami" means "long wave in the harbor" and has the same form for singular and plural.

VOLCANIC EXPLOSIVITY INDEX (VEI)

The reported size, or "bigness," of historical eruptions depends very much on both the experience and vantage point of the observer. Volcanology, unfortunately, has no instrumentally determined magnitude scale, like that used successfully by seismologists for earthquakes, and it is easy to understand why one observer's "major" eruption might be another's "moderate," or even "small" event. However, there are several size measurements that can aid quantitative ranking of eruptions, such as height of eruptive cloud, volume of eruptive products, distances to which objects of a particular size were thrown, and explosive energy coupled into the air wave (measured by recording barographs). Walker[98] has provided a thoughtful discussion of the various measures of "bigness" and both the Volcanological Society of Japan and the Smithsonian's SEAN/GVN have been attempting to gather the quantitative data needed from contemporary eruptions. However, these data exist for an unfortunately small proportion of contemporary eruptions and that proportion decreases dramatically as one goes back in the historical record. To meet the need for a meaningful magnitude measure that can be easily applied to the past, Newhall and Self [99] have integrated quantitative data with the subjective descriptions of observers. The result is the Volcanic Explosivity Index (VEI), and we have used this wherever possible for the past 15 years.[100]

The VEI has some similarities to the Richter magnitude scale for earthquakes. It is a simple 0-to-8 index of increasing explosivity, each interval representing an increase around a factor of ten. The VEI combines total volume of explosive products, eruptive cloud height, descriptive terms, and other measures (Table 4). Note that there is some intentional overlap in criteria for VEI assignment and a combination of data is used whenever possible. Attention is paid to the records of nearby volcanoes in estimating VEI for poorly described eruptions, and a correction has been made for the fact that only the relatively important eruption records survive in the early history of most regions. Eruptions before a certain date – generally 1700 AD for most regions but different in some (1000 AD for Iceland, Europe, and Japan; 1500 for parts of Central America and Mexico; and 1800 AD for Tonga-Samoa, Melanesia, and Kamchatka) depending on regional history – have had some VEI values increased by 1 unit and these upgraded values are indicated in our tables by an up-arrow (e.g. 3↑).

Eruptions that were definitely explosive, but carry no other descriptive information in their record, have been assigned a default VEI of 2, leading to a disproportionate number of eruptions bearing this VEI. And the counterpart of VEI upgrading described above is the downgrading (by one VEI unit) for those eruptions in which substantial tephra volumes were accumulated over long periods of time and/or much of that volume was in near-vent cone construction. Parícutin, the volcano born in a Mexican cornfield, is a good example: it produced 1.3 km^3 of tephra, but over a 9-year eruption, and is consequently assigned a VEI of 4. The VEI emphasizes explosivity, and eruptions that produce their tephra over a

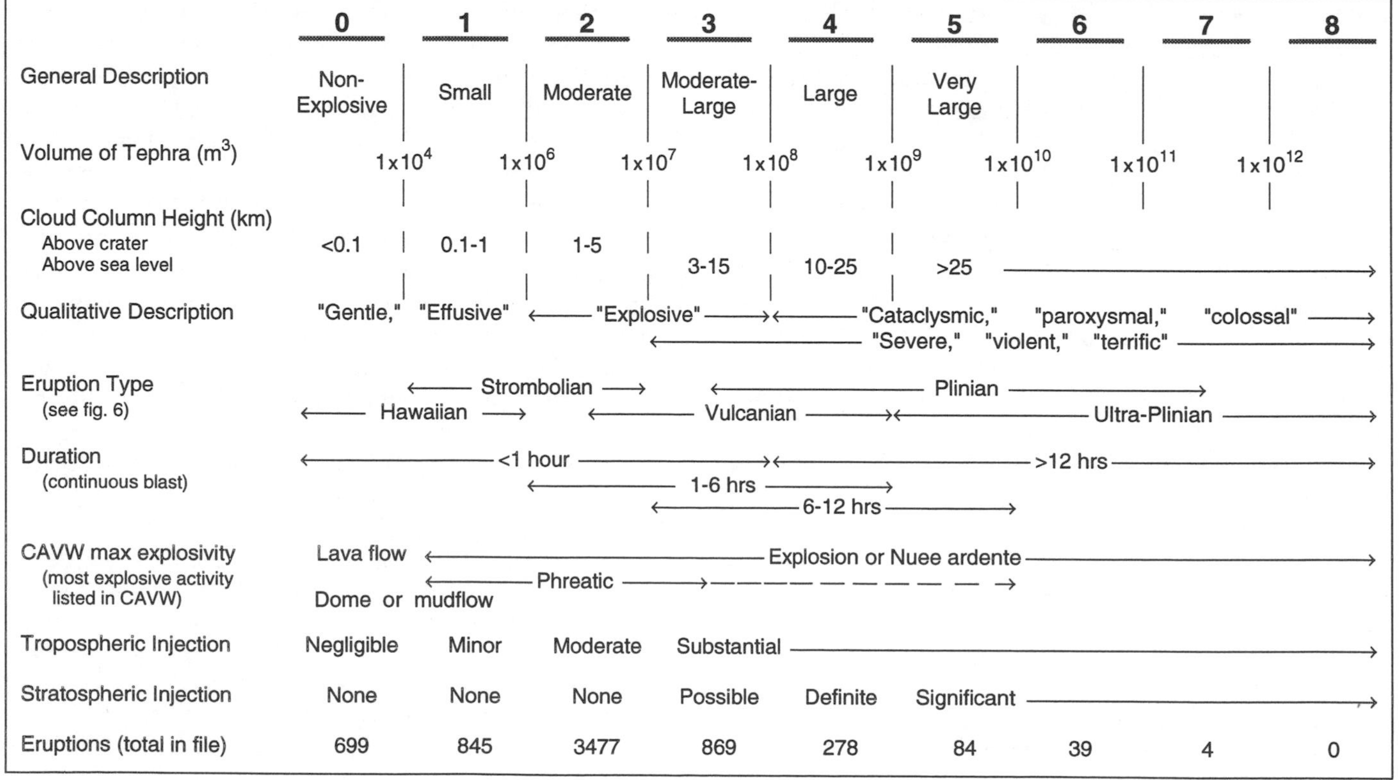

	0	1	2	3	4	5	6	7	8
General Description	Non-Explosive	Small	Moderate	Moderate-Large	Large	Very Large			
Volume of Tephra (m^3)		1×10^4	1×10^6	1×10^7	1×10^8	1×10^9	1×10^{10}	1×10^{11}	1×10^{12}
Cloud Column Height (km) Above crater	<0.1	0.1-1	1-5						
Above sea level				3-15	10-25	>25 ⟶			
Qualitative Description	"Gentle,"	"Effusive"	⟵ "Explosive" ⟶		⟵ "Cataclysmic,"	"paroxysmal,"		"colossal" ⟶	
				⟵ "Severe,"	"violent,"	"terrific" ⟶			
Eruption Type (see fig. 6)		⟵ Strombolian ⟶		⟵ Plinian ⟶					
	⟵ Hawaiian ⟶		⟵ Vulcanian ⟶			⟵ Ultra-Plinian ⟶			
Duration (continuous blast)	⟵ <1 hour ⟶				⟵ >12 hrs ⟶				
			⟵ 1-6 hrs ⟶						
				⟵ 6-12 hrs ⟶					
CAVW max explosivity (most explosive activity listed in CAVW)	Lava flow	⟵ Explosion or Nuee ardente ⟶							
		⟵ Phreatic ⟶ – – – – – – – – →							
	Dome or mudflow								
Tropospheric Injection	Negligible	Minor	Moderate	Substantial ⟶					
Stratospheric Injection	None	None	None	Possible	Definite	Significant ⟶			
Eruptions (total in file)	699	845	3477	869	278	84	39	4	0

Table 4. Volcanic Explosivity Index (VEI) criteria. [99]

long period normally have less impact than those producing an equivalent volume in a shorter, more violent lifetime. Recent observations at Redoubt and Pinatubo volcanoes have shown that, although pyroclastic flows are emplaced along the surface, elutriating ash clouds can produce ash columns comparable to those of large, vertically directed explosions. Pyroclastic-flow deposit volumes are thus included with tephra-fall volumes as indicators of eruption magnitude.

The VEI was developed, in fact, to aid studies of climatic impact from volcanism. It was developed by volcanologists as a purely volcanological measure of eruption bigness, in order to avoid the circularity of using climatic effects to measure eruptions and then using that measure to confirm the influence of volcanism on climate. It has proved to be a helpful approximation of bigness, particularly useful in allowing assignments based on skimpy information from the historical record, but it had barely been introduced when it quickly showed its limitations as a measure of climatic influence. The 1982 eruption of Mexico's El Chichón, although very close to the 1980 eruption of Mount St. Helens by VEI measures, produced a dramatically larger aerosol cloud. Because of the many sophisticated tools available in the 1980s for monitoring the atmosphere and stratosphere, it was soon recognized that the critical difference between these two events was that El Chichón contributed roughly 10 times the SO_2 that St. Helens did to higher altitudes. SO_2 reacts with stratospheric H_2O to produce an aerosol of H_2SO_4, and it is this fine mist, distributed as a broad stratospheric layer, that acts as a shield to solar radiation, thereby cooling the Earth's surface below. The lesson of these two eruptions showed that eruptive volume, cloud height, and the other eruption descriptors of the VEI provide an inadequate measure of climatic impact. What is needed is the incorporation of an eruption's SO_2 production into its magnitude, but that is proving difficult to do. While SO_2 can be measured in contemporary eruptions,[101] it is difficult to assess for the past, so we have retained the VEI here as the most useful measure available for eruptions through the full Holocene record.

A "*" following a VEI unit indicates that there are two or more VEI assignments for that eruption, as in the common example of a short, paroxysmal eruption accompanied by lower level activity over months or years. In the DIRECTORY, the "*" follows the maximum VEI recorded between the indicated start and stop dates, and alerts the reader to the fact that more information on the eruption can be found in the CHRONOLOGY section between these dates. In the CHRONOLOGY, an *italicized line* warns the reader that this event is part of a longer eruption: that preceding, and possibly succeeding, VEI data may be found in the CHRONOLOGY between the start and stop dates listed in the DIRECTORY. VEI data on paroxysmal phases is entered mainly for the large, well-studied eruptions and the data used to establish VEIs for separate eruptive phases are not available for many eruptions in our file. We show multiple VEI information for only 4% of the eruptions listed here. As described above in the CHRONOLOGY introduction, italics are used in that table to identify lesser entries; for continuing year or multiple VEI eruptions, only the single largest event is listed in normal type while italics indicate other entries. When the level of activity differs significantly from year to year (in a continuing eruption), the VEI assigned to that year is entered as a separate line and no *Cont* inuing year entry appears.[102]

A "**?**" accompanies those VEI's that were particularly difficult to assign, and those that are based on purely circumstantial evidence. For example, a VEI of 1? might have been assigned to an undescribed eruption because a nearby contemporaneous eruption received sufficient historical comment to confidently assign a VEI of 2. When there was simply no evidence on which to base a VEI, this column has normally been left empty (20% of the eruptions in our file).

A "**+**" following a VEI indicates an eruption volume in the upper third of the range for that particular VEI designation. It shows those eruptions known to be larger than most others sharing the same VEI numeral, but its absence does not necessarily indicate a relatively small event. The designation is used only for VEIs ≥4 and volume data permit adding it to only 22 events, but it is helpful to identify the obviously larger events in volume ranges that span a full order of magnitude.

Bold type is used in both DIRECTORY and CHRONOLOGY listings to emphasize VEIs of 5 and above. We have also used letters in the VEI column to identify eruptions known to have been large (probably VEI ≥4) but lacking the reported data necessary to assign a specific VEI. Eruptions associated with caldera collapse are normally large, and those for which we have been unable to assign a VEI are here indicated by a bold "**C**" in the VEI column. The same is true for plinian deposits and, in the absence of more quantitative data, we have marked such eruptions with "**P**" in the VEI column.[103] Finally, as mentioned above under DATING TECHNIQUES, we have entered in the CHRONOLOGY some of the largest eruptions known only from ice core research. These are marked by an "**I**" before the date and "Source unknown" message under "**VOLCANO NAME**."[104]

No Holocene eruption has been assigned a VEI of 8 and only four eruptions – Tambora 1815, Baitoushan ca. 1050, Kikai ca. 4350 BC, and Crater Lake ca. 4895 BC – carry a VEI of 7. VEI's of 5 or more have been assigned to 127 eruptions from 81 volcanoes; New Zealand, with a relatively small number of volcanoes but a well-developed tephrochronologic record, leads the list with 9% of these eruptions. Taupo alone has had 4 eruptions warranting a VEI greater than 4, and the youngest of these (ca. 180 AD) is thought by Walker[98] to be the most powerful eruption known (80% of its products – or 20 km^3 of tephra – having been distributed farther than 220 km from its source). At least 404 eruptions carry a VEI of 4 or more. Iceland's Hekla dominates the 170 volcanoes on this list with 13 major eruptions (9 of them – from 1104 to 1947 AD – within its extraordinarily well-studied historical record). Fully half of the volcanoes for which we have VEI data have had "large" eruptions in the VEI range 3-7. Magnitude and frequency of eruptions is discussed in more detail below (p. 29).

One further limitation of the VEI must be mentioned. Radar measurements of eruption-cloud heights, such as those made following the May 18 paroxysm at St. Helens in 1980, have shown that rather small events can reach quite high altitudes, and these observations have been supported by grain-size measurements and the modeling of eruption dynamics.[105] The upper limits of cloud height used in the original VEI designations (Table 4) are too low, with the result that some VEIs assigned on the basis of cloud height are one (or even two) units higher than they would have been on the basis of tephra volume. When both measures are known, volume is used to assign VEI, but for many events in recent decades only cloud height is available. This means that some VEIs, particularly in the 3-4 range, are higher than they should be. The VEI structure has not been revised, though, and we have not undertaken the large job of rechecking VEI assignments based on cloud height. Instead, we use the VEI as a helpful guide to size for 80% of known Holocene eruptions. It should not be used to indicate size of effusive, lava-producing eruptions, its limitations in assessing climatic impact have been discussed above, and some assignments are no doubt off by one or even two units. However, no alternative measure can be applied to more than a small proportion of Holocene events. If used with reasonable caution, VEI is a valuable indicator of eruptive magnitude.

VOLUME OF PRODUCTS (Vol L / T)

Accurate measurement of eruptive volumes requires careful field work and is often subject to unresolvable uncertainties. The many difficulties of making accurate measurements have, unfortunately, inhibited the reporting of even rough estimates, and we have volume information for only 16% of the eruptions in our file. Volume estimates can be made, however, thousands of years after the eruption, and the number of these estimates is increasing rapidly as volcanologists piece together the Holocene histories of important volcanoes. We have volume data from 289 volcanoes, but nearly a third of the volumes are from 8 vigorous, well studied volcanoes: Etna (113), Kilauea (55), Oshima (43), Fournaise (41), Nyamuragira (40), Hekla (33), Mauna Loa (32), and Merapi (32).

Although full volume data, including references, are entered in the data file, only the order of magnitude is displayed here. Thus a lava volume of 1,300,000 cubic meters, or 1.3×10^6 m^3, appears in the appropriate "L / T" column simply as "6." This means that an eruption volume may be nearly 10 times larger than the exponent shown, but there is such large initial uncertainty in most eruptive volumes that we preferred to display – in the limited space available – at least this order-of-magnitude estimate as a crude indication of both eruption size and the availability of volume estimates. In some cases the original source lists only order of magnitude data.[106]

Volumes of 10^9 m^3 (1 km^3) or larger are emphasized in the DIRECTORY and CHRONOLOGY by use of **bold** type. VEIs of 5 and above have received this treatment (see above), so doing the same for non-explosive, effusive eruptions assures that all events likely to have produced a cubic kilometer of material are emphasized by **bold** type in the VEI or Volume columns on the right-hand side of our tables.

The measurements needed to determine volume are difficult to make in the field. Thick deposits often hide their true thickness, and thin, distal deposits are by nature ephemeral (although often comprising a significant proportion of the total volume). Much ash falls in the sea, where measurements are difficult, costly, and often rendered inaccurate by marine processes such as bioturbation. In addition to these uncertainties, tephra volumes are generally listed without correction for three important factors: (a) vesicularity (the void space occupied by air bubbles, or vesicles, in pumiceous material); (b) the extraneous fragments of older rock included accidentally in the deposit; or (c) compaction of ash layers with time. The tephra volume displayed, therefore, may be substantially larger than the volume of new magma emitted.

The volume figures listed here vary widely in size. Iceland accounts for both the smallest and largest historical lava volumes known; from the 26 m^3 of magma extruded from a Krafla borehole[107] in 1977 to the 12.3 km^3 of lava from Lakagigar[108] in 1783 (Figure 18). The largest historical lava flows, however, are dwarfed by some in the prehistoric, geologic record. Fifteen million years ago, single flows measuring 700 km^3 flooded 1,000 km^2 areas of the northwestern United States in only a few days.[109] The same is true of large explosive eruptions. Tephra from history's largest eruption – Tambora 1815 – exceeded 100 km^3, but only 74,000 years earlier another Indonesian volcano, Toba, erupted 2,800 km^3 of rhyolitic magma.[110] Two million years ago a Yellowstone eruption produced 2,500 km^3 of magma in devastating ash flows, the like of which have (fortunately) never been seen in history.[111] A much more recent eruption from Yellowstone, 0.66 million years ago (Ma), was nearly as large, and numerous Oligocene eruptions in the western U.S. were even larger.[112]

Volume data are available for only 1244 eruptions in our file, and a far smaller proportion of all eruptions – unrecorded as well as recorded – in Holocene time. This fact should caution against misuse of volume data, and the reader should also be cautioned about a possibly confusing convention that we have used for volume data in the CHRONOLOGY section. The volume data for the whole eruption has been repeated when a continuing eruption is repeated in a following year or years. These repetitions are clear because the line is italicized (see also discussion in VEI section above), and we have deleted some repeated volumes that we know are inapplicable (such as the early volumes for the Tambora eruption that began in 1812 but produced its major tephra volume in April of 1815). For most eruptions, however, we have not been able to apportion the volume in successive years, and we have thought it better to repeat the total (with cautionary italics) than to assign it arbitrarily to the eruption's start date.

Historical Record: Trends and Cautions

The value of the recent volcanological record is obvious to geologists. The events of the present provide some of our best clues in interpreting the volcanic products of the past few billion years of Earth history. Eyewitness accounts, photographs, and instrumental documentation all build a picture of the processes, rates, and interrelationships of events that cannot be found from the products alone (and yet are essential to understanding volcanism). In studying a particular eruption, the accounts of similar historical eruptions can provide valuable guides; in investigating a specific type of volcanic process or product the historical record gives a useful dynamic context; and in assessing the likelihood of future activity at a particular volcano the historical behavior of similar (but better documented) volcanoes is often helpful. The tables that follow are designed to assist such studies at the same time that they provide answers for the more common questions concerning volcanism around a particular place or time.

The limitations of the volcanological record are not as obvious, however, and require continued emphasis to caution anyone brash enough to mistake the record for the reality. Perhaps the best illustration of the record's limitations come from the data themselves. In Figure 8, the last 600 years of apparent global volcanism are shown by the number of volcanoes known to have been active each year. The nearly exponential increase through recent centuries suggests either that the planet will soon be overwhelmed by volcanic activity or that the reporting of volcanism has been improving dramatically over time. The striking growth of global population has spread potential reporters over much of the Earth, and technological advances have facilitated information transfer. Reporting of other natural events, such as tornadoes or fireballs, has no doubt increased similarly. Earthquake reporting with its dependence on instruments, has increased at an even more rapid rate in recent years, yet seismologists do not suggest that earthquakes are more common in this century simply because more of them are being recorded.

Another indicator of the growth of the volcanic record is the increase in number of historically active volcanoes around the world (Figure 8). If a list of such volcanoes had been continuously kept, it would, at the time of Christ, have contained only the names of 9 Mediterranean volcanoes and West Africa's Mount Cameroon. In the next ten centuries the list would have grown by only 30 names, 18 of them Japanese. Newly settled Iceland soon added 7 volcanoes to help swell the list to 63 by 1400 AD, where Figure 8 begins. The list has continued to grow, with several important volcanic regions such as New Zealand, Alaska, and Hawaii being unrepresented until the last 250 years. Only in the present century has the *rate* of growth declined significantly. This continuing growth in the number of known volcanoes would be even more dramatic were it not for recent work in regions like New Zealand and Iceland. Here careful investigation of nearby centers has recognized individual features that are genetically linked in the same "volcano system", and combining them has actually <u>de</u>creased the number of known volcanoes in these regions.

By 1510 AD, historical eruptions had been recorded from 70 volcanoes and the number had grown by only about 1 per decade through the 15th century.[113] Following that year, though, "new" volcanoes were added to the (retrospective) world list at a rate averaging 5 per decade through the 16th century. This increase was accompanied by a larger and more rapid increase in the number of volcanoes active: from 4-9 per decade in the century before 1510 to an average of 22 per decade through the remainder of the 16th century. These increases resulted in part from the great Spanish/Portuguese marine explorations – the Age of Discovery – around the end of the 15th century, when Columbus, Balboa, Vasco da Gama, Magellan, and others opened Latin America and much of the western Pacific to European record-keeping. But perhaps equally important was the development, and widespread distribution of the printing press in the late 15th century, markedly increasing the likelihood that new volcanological records would survive.

Through the 17th and into the early 18th century, the list of new volcanoes was increasing more rapidly than the list of reported eruptions. Most continents had been outlined by 1700, though, and in the 18th century global trade flourished, the Industrial Revolution was under way, and the reporting of new eruptions swiftly dominated the discovery of new volcanoes. By the middle of the 19th century, the major communications advances of the Industrial Revolution (e.g., daily newspapers, the telegraph) were established, the young science of geology was flourishing (with journals reporting eruptions), and the shape of the world was cartographically known. Since that time, both the reporting of volcanism and the discovery of new volcanoes have continued to increase, but neither has dominated the other, with a remarkably constant 26-34% of known volcanoes erupting in each of the last 15 decades.

The last 200 years, with humans distributed over most of the globe and relatively efficient communication lines in use, would thus seem to be the best part of the

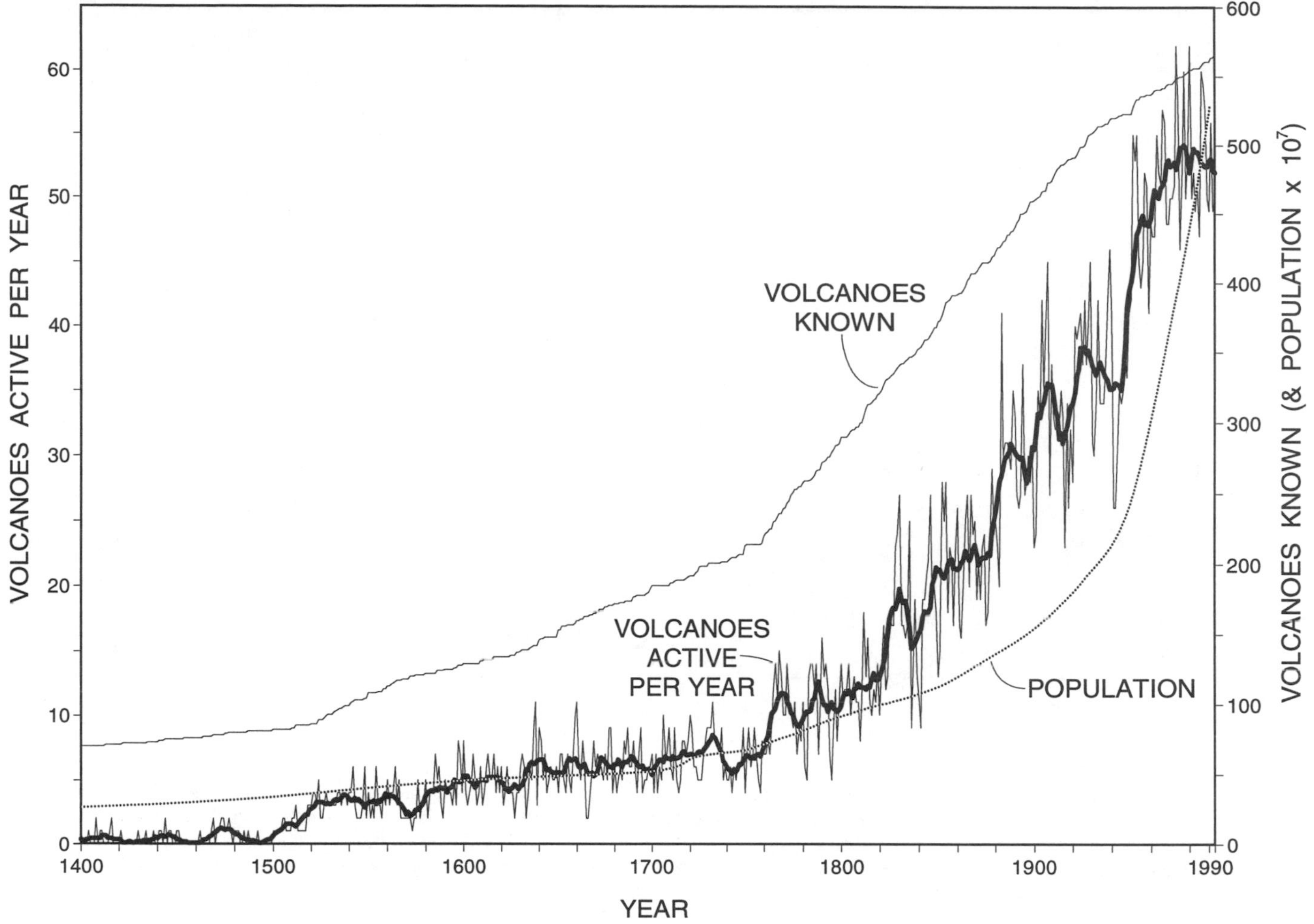

Figure 8. 600 years of volcano reporting. Total number of volcanoes erupting per year (thin line) and 10-year running mean of same data (thick line). Eruption dates with an uncertainty >1 year have not been included in this total, nor have uncertain eruptions (those preceded by a ? mark in the tables that follow). A volcano with more than one eruption recorded in a year is counted only once. "Volcanoes known" is the total number that have had an historically recorded eruption by any given year. "Population" is the world's estimated human population.[114]

record to search for episodic, or cyclical, trends in global volcanism. Examination of the geologic record for many regions shows major periods of Earth history in which volcanic products are clearly concentrated,[115] and it is natural to look for episodes of increased volcanism in the more detailed recent record. Even in the last 200 years, however, we find historical trends in reporting overshadowing any real trends in volcanism.

Figure 9 shows the detailed record of volcanism over the last 200 years. The overall trend of increased reporting, so dominant in Figure 8, is evident, but we notice that the two most prominent drops below that rising trend correspond precisely with the two world wars of this century. In times of great international instability, the people (and presses) that might otherwise have reported natural phenomena were simply preoccupied with other things. In the years 1941-45, for example, the number of volcanoes reported active in the western Pacific and Indonesia dropped by nearly one-third from the preceding 5 years, while regions less affected by the war showed little change. With more observers in more unusual areas during World War II, it seems likely that more eruptions than normal were actually witnessed, but it is easy to appreciate why many of these eruptions were never recorded in the scientific literature.[116]

Great economic crises, like wars, might also be expected to interfere with the reporting of natural events. While it may seem presumptuous to relate one of the most precipitous drops in reported volcanism to the stock market collapse of 1929, the effect of the ensuing Great Depression was widespread and devastating. Historian Rene Albrecht-Carrie[117] concluded that "By the early 1930's, every major advanced economy – except that of Russia – was in deep trouble, marked by a drastic fall in production and by widespread unemployment." From the late l920's to the early 1930's, every volcanic region in the world – except those of Russia, Melanesia, and the West Indies[118] – showed a drop in the number of volcanoes reported active.

Because reporting of volcanism depends on humans, it seems reasonable to expect that widespread preoccupation with war or economic depression has at times decreased reporting effectiveness, resulting in apparent drops in global volcanism. For the same reason,

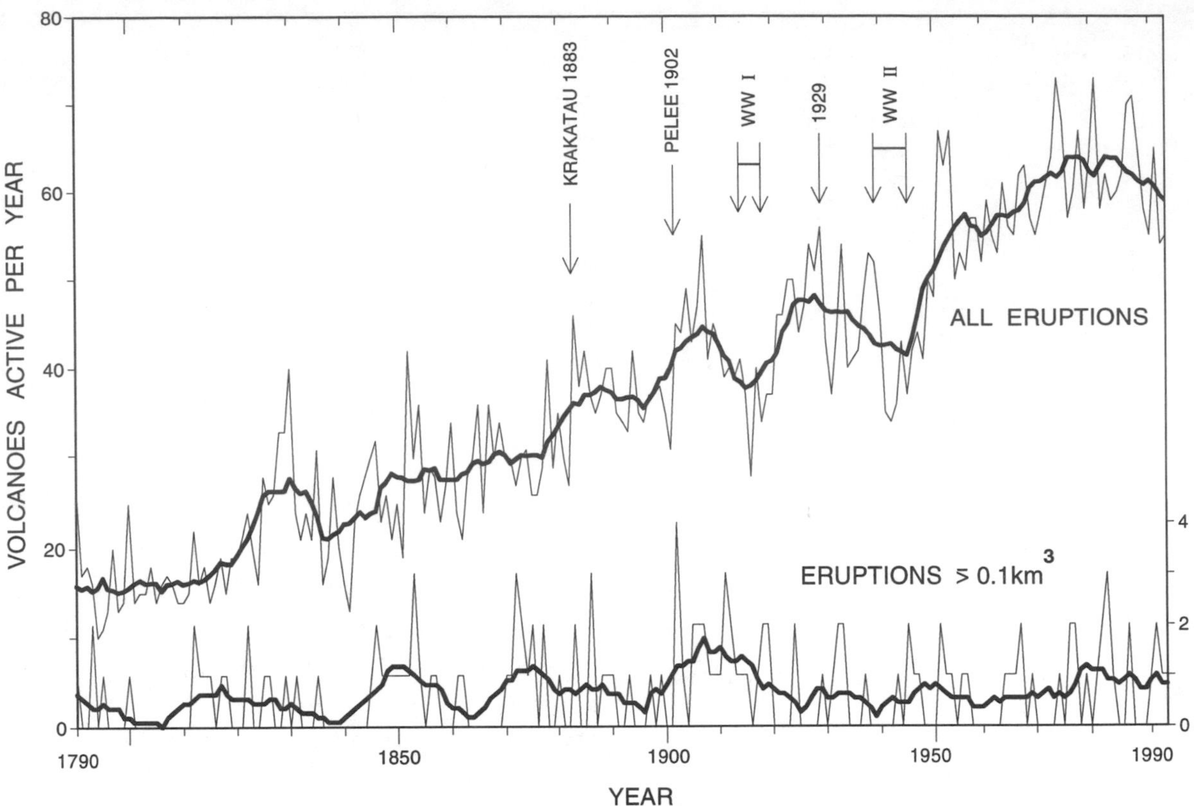

Figure 9. Last 200 years of volcano reporting. Total number of volcanoes erupting per year (thin upper line) and 10-year running mean of same data (thick upper line). These numbers are generally 5-10% higher than those for the same year in Figure 8 because these include uncertain eruptions[119] (preceded by ? in DIRECTORY and CHRONOLOGY). Lower lines show only the annual number of volcanoes producing large eruptions (≥0.1 km^3 of tephra or VEI ≥4) and scale is enlarged (on right axis). Thick lower line again shows 10-year running mean.

it seems reasonable to expect that times of increased global sensitivity to volcanism would result in increased reporting effectiveness, with more people reporting more events (and editors being more inclined to publish eruption reports). Such times of increased sensitivity to volcanism naturally follow major, widely publicized eruptions, and the newsworthiness of an eruption depends, in turn, more on its location and human impact than on its size. The 1980 eruption of Mount St. Helens, for example, generated enormous media attention, while the remarkably similar 1956 eruption of Bezymianny, in which no lives were lost and ash fell mainly on the sparsely populated Kamchatka Peninsula, was hardly noticed by the world press.[120] Two of the most notorious eruptions of recent centuries were at Krakatau in 1883 (over 36,000 victims) and Mont Pelée in 1902 (about 29,000 victims).[121] They received widespread global publicity for years afterwards and the resulting increased sensitivity to volcanism may be at least partially responsible for the relatively high level of reported volcanism for 5-to-7 years after each eruption (Figure 9).

In the first edition of this book we wrote: "With the media attention devoted to the 1980 eruption of Mount St. Helens, we should expect to see another 'peak' of volcanism in the early 1980s". This obviously did not happen. The frequency of volcanism has remained remarkably constant through the past 3 decades and the reason, we like to think, may be that we are finally approaching reasonably comprehensive reporting of global volcanism. In 1960, the Volcanological Society of Japan began a program of systematic annual summaries, and in 1968 the Smithsonian initiated the global network of correspondents that continues to publish monthly reports on volcanism.[8]

This leaves peaks in the late 1820s and early 1950s (Figure 9) as the most prominent changes in apparent volcanism that have no obvious relationship with historic events likely to influence eruption reporting either positively or negatively. In fact, these peaks may be explained by unusual reporting patterns of just a few people in Alaska and Indonesia.

During the first 7 years of the 1820s, an average of 2½ Alaskan volcanoes were reported active each year, and the average was lower in the 7 years following 1831. In the years between, however, the average jumped to 10 per year, and all but one were in the Aleutians. Those 4 years were those covered by the Lutke expedition's exploration of the Aleutians and their 1834-36 reports.[122] In 1950, Coats[123] remarked on this example of reporting variations influencing the historical record of a seldom-visited region like the Aleutians.

Reporting in Alaska had not improved greatly after WW-II, but the years 1951-53 averaged over 8 volcanoes per year active, in contrast to an average of 2.8 for the other 37 years of the first 4 decades following WW-II. The years 1951-53 also happened to be peak years for the U.S. Geological Survey's volcanological program in Alaska and the only years in which USGS personnel contributed regular reports to the *Volcano Letter*, our prime source for Alaskan volcano data during these years. The USGS Alaska volcano program ended in 1954, but resumed strongly in the late 1980s, with the opening of the Alaska Volcano Observatory. In the past 8 years, an average of 5 volcanoes per year have been reported active.

A similar pattern marked reporting in Indonesia after WW-II. Volcanological interest ran high with the 1951 publication of Neumann van Padang's Catalog for this active region, the first volume in the *CAVW* series, and in 1953 another compilation (by DeNeve) supplemented the *CAVW*. However, the number of active volcanoes dropped from 13 in 1953 to 2 in 1954 and remained low through that difficult decade in Indonesia, rising again to around 10 per year in the mid 1960s after the rejuvenation of the Volcanological Survey. Thus, a period of unusually low reporting in this one vigorous volcanic belt contributes substantially to isolating the two apparent peaks of volcanism on either side of it (in the early 1950's and mid 1960's).

Thus all major trends in our recent volcanological record can be reasonably explained by socioeconomic and exploration influences. However, the best evidence that these trends are apparent rather than real comes from the record of large eruptions alone. At the base of Figure 9 we plot the data for eruptions producing more than 0.1 km^3 of tephra, using the same conventions as the plot of *all* eruptions above it (but at an expanded vertical scale). These are the large eruptions of VEI ≥4 to which words such as "violent", "plinian", and even "cataclysmic" are applied. Their effects are far reaching and they are the eruptions that are not likely to have been missed in the recent record. Their constancy over the past 120 years tells us that the wide variation in the overlying record of all eruptions is solely the variation in smaller events that *are* more likely to be missed.

ERUPTION MAGNITUDE and FREQUENCY

The data of Figure 9 show us that the larger eruptions (VEI ≥4) have taken place at a reasonably constant rate of nearly 1 per year for most of the last 200 years, and that *all* eruptions have averaged about 60 per year for the last 20-30 years. These data reinforce our intuition that, like earthquakes, the frequency of eruptions decreases with increasing size: There are a lot of small ones, fewer medium-sized ones, and not so many large ones. Furthermore, the data, and the historical argument marshalled above, suggest that the record for small eruptions is good for only a few recent decades, whereas the record for larger events is good for more than a century. To explore these relationships quantitatively, we have borrowed from the seismologists' magnitude-frequency plots, using the VEI as our best measure of magnitude. In Figure 10, the number of eruptions at each VEI increment is shown for various time intervals in the recent past: 30, 200, 1000, and 2 million years. These intervals were chosen in the hope that they are long enough to be representative yet short enough to have reasonably accurate reporting. The results are encouraging.

Another way of interpreting this plot is that subaerial eruptions producing at least 10^6 m^3 of tephra (VEI 2) take place at an average rate of once every few weeks somewhere on Earth. Those producing ≥10^7 m^3, like the VEI 3 Ruiz event that generated such fatal mudflows in 1985, take place several times a year. Eruptions the size of St. Helens 1980 (10^9 m^3, or 1 km^3 and VEI 5) occur perhaps once a decade, and those like Krakatau 1883 (>10 km^3) on the order of once a century. The historical record, however, fails to prepare us for the much larger eruptions of the past. The above-mentioned Toba eruption, only 74,000 years ago in Indonesia, produced nearly 10,000

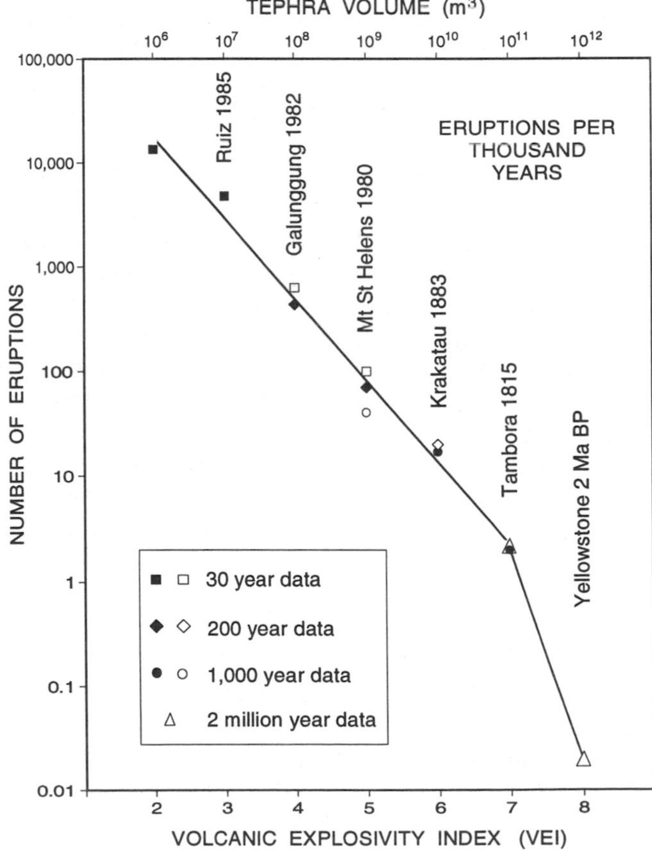

Figure 10. Magnitude and frequency of Holocene eruptions. Total number of eruptions during various intervals (going back in time from 1 January 1994) for each VEI class and normalized to "per 1000 years". Eruptions of low explosivity (VEI 0 and 1) are not shown, and a logarithmic scale is used to allow resolution of the lower frequencies found with the larger eruptions. Tephra volumes corresponding to each VEI class are shown at top (see Table 4). Best-fit line is determined by an exponential regression model for VEI 2-7 using data points that are filled.[124] Data points from Decker[125] for VEI 7 and 8 are shown by open triangles. Well-known eruptions are labeled to illustrate each VEI class.

times more magma (2800 km^3) than the St. Helens eruption,[110] and even larger eruptions are known from the older geologic record.

There are, however, no known eruptions of VEI 9, or 10^4 km^3 of tephra, and magma chambers of such dimensions are virtually unknown in the geologic record. Therefore, simple extrapolation of the Holocene record in Figure 10 is not warranted beyond VEI 7, and that value is based on only two data points over a long millennia. The shape of the magnitude-frequency relationship at this end is unclear, but Decker has attempted to improve it by plotting data from Newhall & Dzurisin's compilation of caldera unrest during the last 2 million years.[125] The data set is incomplete, as the authors themselves are quick to acknowledge, and Decker is forced to make some large assumptions, but his extension is probably closer to the truth than extrapolation of the historical data. Decker's calculations suggest 22 VEI 7 events every 10,000 years and 2 VEI 8 events every 100,000 years. An example of a VEI 8 eruption is the above-mentioned[111] Yellowstone event about 2 million years ago, producing 2,500 km^3 of ash that was distributed over at least a 16-state area (including Los Angeles, Tucson, El Paso, and Des Moines). Compacted thicknesses of 0.2 m have been measured at distances of 1500 km from the source,[126] and its impact must have been profound.

It is useful, however, to look at the known effect of large historical eruptions in the context of Figure 10. The 1980 eruption of Mount St. Helens (VEI 5, or 1/decade) was a *local* catastrophe with devastation over hundreds of km^2. The 1883 eruption of Krakatau (VEI 6, or 1/century) was a *regional* catastrophe, with 36,000 dead, one as far away as India. Another order of magnitude larger, the 1815 eruption of Tambora (VEI 7, or 1-2/millennium) caused global cooling, with summer snowstorms and crop failures on the opposite side of the globe.[35] A New England farmer in 1816 would be justified in calling it a global catastrophe. The effects of a VEI 8 event, such as Yellowstone 2 Ma, must have been *global* by any definition.

EPISODICITY and PERIODICITY

None of the historical discussion above excludes the probability that real fluctuations are present in the recent volcanic record. Fluctuations are to be expected in a random distribution, but the record contains some intriguing episodic concentrations of volcanism. The famous 1902 eruption of Mount Pelée was preceded only one day earlier, by an equally explosive eruption on St. Vincent, 165 km to the south and much too far to consider subsurface plumbing connections. These were followed 5 months later by an even larger eruption of Guatemala's Santa María, 3260 km to the west on the opposite side of the Caribbean Plate. In no other year have three explosive eruptions of this magnitude been recorded, and it is tempting to link them to plate tectonic movement.[127] Within an 8 month period in 1974, 5 of the 7 historically active volcanoes in the western Bismarck arc erupted, several for the first time in this century.[128] On an even shorter time scale, Darwin[129] noted simultaneous eruptions of several Andean volcanoes (and the Juan Fernandez islands) around the time of the great 1835 earthquake that he experienced in Chile. Furthermore, fortnightly earth tide cycles clearly have influenced the timing of some eruptions[130] and cycles of activity have been shown for many volcanoes.[131]

Although episodic volcanism has clearly been demonstrated on a local, and even regional scale, evidence of global synchroneity is lacking and certainly none has been found in our own work with this Holocene data set. Going much further back in time, and concentrating on the Cordillera of western North America, Armstrong and Ward assessed a huge data set with great care. They concluded that "although magmatism is always locally episodic, the episodes blur into a continuum of magmatic activity when the whole Cordilleran region is viewed during later Cenozoic time."[132] Statistical approaches have been applied with seeming success, only to be contradicted by other workers using different approaches and different data sets.[133] Large-scale magmatic episodicity is difficult to confirm, given the inherently incomplete nature of the geologic record, and demonstrating periodicity in these episodes is, inescapably, even more difficult.[134]

Plate tectonics, major earthquakes, tides, glacial unloading, and no doubt other factors affect volcanism in ways that are only just beginning to be appreciated. However, we have stressed the historical factors that have influenced the *reporting* of volcanism in order to emphasize the many frailties of the historical record. Users of the data tabulated in this book should keep these historical factors in mind, and remember that chronological records of deep-sea rift eruptions – volumetrically the dominant form of global volcanism (Figure 3) – are virtually unknown.

Conclusions

The record of large explosive eruptions is now being extended back beyond the Holocene by several important new techniques. Ice cores, with unequivocal acidic layers marking fallout of far-traveled volcanic aerosols, and accurate dendrochronology records of nearby as well as distant environmental effects, are now being correlated, and differences being resolved. The resulting chronology, when strengthened by data from other ice sheets and trees, supplemented by tephrochronology, promises a vastly improved record of major Holocene eruptions throughout the globe. The large-eruption end of Figure 10's magnitude-frequency relationship – so difficult to assess from a short and incomplete historical record – may soon be filled in with some confidence.

New techniques, plus heightened awareness of volcanic hazards, are contributing to a rapid increase in volcanological data that is independent of the historical record. Painstaking field mapping; accurate dating of prehistoric events; modern petrologic analysis of volcanic products, laboratory experiments at the high temperatures and pressures of volcano interiors; theoretical modeling of eruptive processes utilizing interdisciplinary approaches: all are needed, along with the chronological record, to understand the history and hazards of active volcanoes. It is the chronological record, though, that teaches the hard lesson that a volcano's long repose is more likely to be a cause for concern than reassurance. Differentiation processes act slowly in a magma chamber deep below a seemingly quiet volcano – steadily concentrating volatiles in increasingly siliceous liquid – on a time scale that dwarfs human memory and most record-keeping. In Figure 11 we have shown, for each VEI class, the interval ranges since the last eruption, in order to illustrate the fact that long periods of quiet commonly precede the more explosive eruptions. This illustration would be even more dramatic if pre-eruption intervals were known for more of the large explosive events. Some of the most calamitous eruptions of recent decades have been from volcanoes with no previously known historical volcanism (Table 5). Drawing on the geologic record of several well-studied older volcanoes, R.L. Smith has shown[135] that gigantic ash-flow eruptions (fortunately not yet known in the historical record) may follow quiet intervals measured in millions of years.

Year	Volcano	First historical?	Deaths
1991	Cerro Hudson (Chile)	no	0
1991	Pinatubo (Philippines)	yes	800
1982	El Chichón (Mexico)	yes	2,000
1980	Mount St. Helens (USA)	no	57
1956	Bezymianny (Kamchatka)	yes	0
1932	Cerro Azul/Quizapu (Chile)	no	0
1912	Novarupta/Katmai (Alaska)	yes	2
1907	Ksudach (Kamchatka)	yes	0
1902	Santa María (Guatemala)	yes	>5,000
1886	Tarawera (New Zealand)	yes	>150
1883	Krakatau (Indonesia)	no	36,417
1875	Askja (Iceland)	yes	0
1854	Sheveluch (Kamchatka)	yes	0
1835	Cosiguina (Nicaragua)	yes	5-10
1822	Galunggung (Indonesia)	yes	4,011
1815	Tambora (Indonesia)	yes	92,000

Table 5. Largest Explosive Eruptions of the 19th & 20th Centuries.[136]

Clearly we must extend the record back beyond the 10,000 years covered in this volume if we are to include all volcanoes that might erupt next year, and clearly much work needs to be done in refining the global volcanological record for even the past few centuries. This compilation is a step in that direction, though, and we close, as we did in 1981, with the hope that the continuing assistance of many workers from many disciplines will result in more thorough compilations in the years ahead.

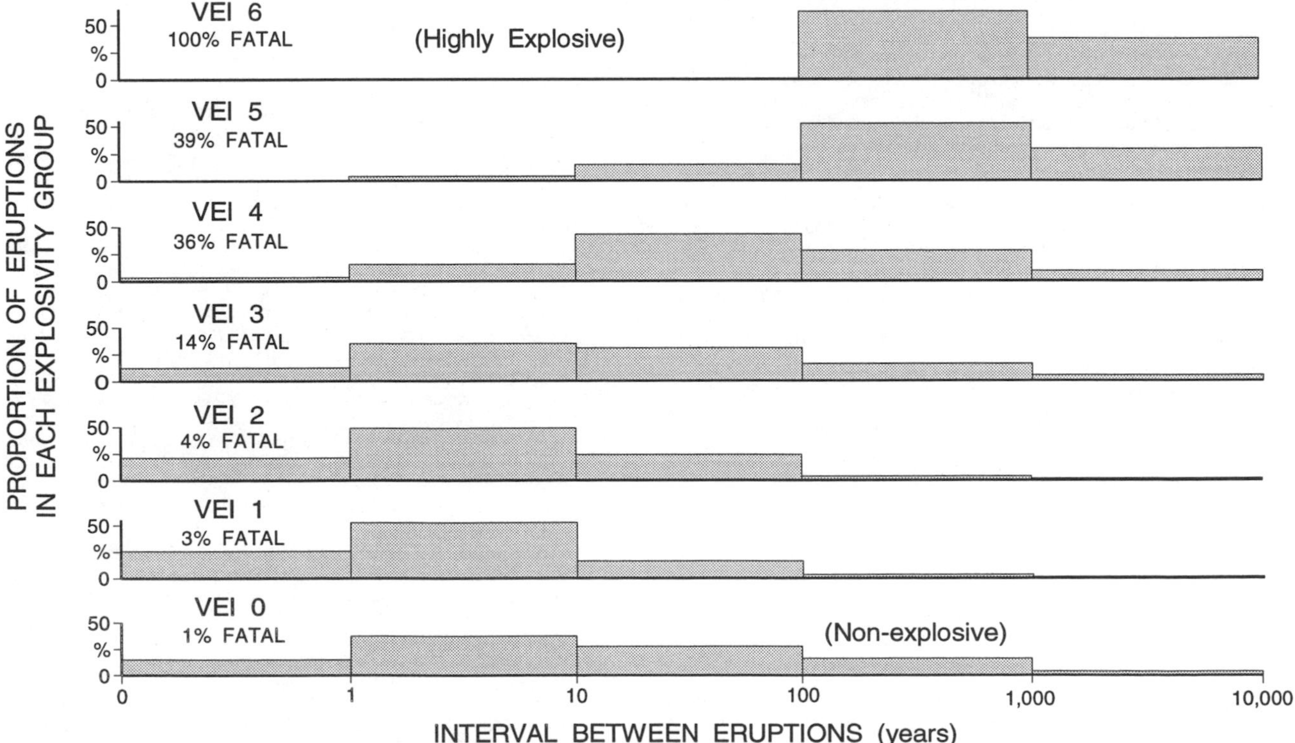

Figure 11. Explosivity and time intervals between eruptions. For each VEI unit, eruptions are grouped by time interval from start of previous eruption. The number of eruptions in VEI groups 0 to 6 are, respectively: 446, 677, 2991, 692, 230, 48, 16. For each group, the percentage of historical eruptions that have been fatal is also shown to emphasize the danger of large explosive eruptions from volcanoes that have appeared to be quiet for hundreds to thousands of years.

Notes

** marks sections of REFERENCES (p. 305-349) in which full citation is found. See beginning of REFERENCES section for list of abbreviations.

1. For example: (**A**) Macdonald 1972 ***Global***. (**B**) Williams H, McBirney A R 1979, *Volcanology.* San Francisco: Freeman Cooper, 397 p. (**C**) Decker R W & B B 1991, *Mountains of Fire.* Cambridge: Cambridge Univ Press, 198 p. (**D**) Marti J, Aranya V 1993, *La Volcanologia Actual.* Madrid: Consejo Superior de Investigationes Cientificas, 578 p. (**E**) Francis P 1993, *Volcanoes: a Planetary Perspective.* Oxford: Oxford Univ Press, 443 p. See also note 94.

2. Pliny's great *Natural History,* finished two years before his death in the famous 79 AD eruption of Vesuvius, mentions as volcanoes: Etna, Lipari, and centers in East Africa, Turkey, and the Middle East.

3. For example, Lamb 1970, Latter 1975, and others cited under ***Global***, including the first edition of this book.

4. An excellent treatment of the history of volcanology through these years is: Krafft M 1993, *Volcanoes: Fire from the Earth* [English translation]: New York: Harry N Abrams, 207 p.

5. (**A**) Varen B 1650, *Geographia Generalis, in qua Affectiones Generales tell Uris Explicantur.* Amstelodami Apud L Elzevirium, 786 p. (**B**) Daubeny C 1826, *A Description of Active and Extinct Volcanoes.* London: Phillips, 467 p. (**C**) von Hoff K E A 1841, *Chronik der Erdbeben und Vulcan-Ausbruche.* Gotha: Justus Perthes, 405 p. (**D**) Daubeny C 1848, *A Description of Active and Extinct Volcanoes* (2nd ed). London: R & J E Taylor, 743 p. (**E**) Landgrebe G 1855, *Naturgeschichte der Vulcane.* Gotha: Justus Perthes, 499 & 450 p in two parts. (**F**) Fuchs C W C 1865, *Die Vulkanischen Erscheinungen der Erde.* Heidelberg: C F Winter'sche Verlagshandlung, 582 p. (**G**) Mercalli G 1907, *Vulcani Attivi della Terra.* Milan: Ulrico Hoepli, 421 p. (**H**) Schneider 1911 ***1402***. (**I**) CAVW 1951-75 ***starred REFERENCES for each region***. (**J**) Other citations appear under ***Global***.

6. (**A**) Miller *et al.* in review ***1100*** (**B**) Steinthorsson *et al.* in preparation ***1700***

7. McClelland *et al.* 1989 ***Global***

8. *GVN Bulletin* subscriptions from: American Geophysical Union (2000 Florida Avenue NW, Washington DC 20009, phone 202/462-6900). Annual subscription price is $20 to U.S. addresses and $32 to all other countries. An electronic version of the *Bulletin* is posted on the VOLCANO listserv (volcano@asuacad.bitnet; contact Jonathan Fink, Arizona State University, jon.fink@asu.edu). Text and figures are also available via Internet Gopher (nmnhgoph.si.edu). GVN (and other parts of our volcano group) can be contacted at: MRC 129, National Museum of Natural History, Smithsonian Institution, Washington DC 20560, phone 202/357-1511, fax 202/357-2476. E-mail reaches GVN through Internet (mnhms017@sivm.si.edu), and PINET (volcano).

9. See ***Global***

10. When a secondary compiler has sent us information with no firmer source than undocumented communication from another secondary compiler, we have not included the information in our file (but have attempted to confirm or deny it from more direct sources).

11. Fairbridge R W 1968, "Holocene, postglacial or Recent epoch." *In:* Fairbridge R W (ed), *Encyclopedia of Geomorphology.* Encyclopedia of Earth Sciences Series, Stroudsburg, Pennsylvania: Dowden, Hutchinson & Ross, 3: 525-36.

12. Becker B, Kromer B, Trimborn P 1991, A stable-isotope tree-ring timescale of the Late Glacial/Holocene boundary. *Nature,* 353: 647-49. See also Harland W B, Armstrong R L, Cox A V, Craig L E, Smith A G, Smith D G 1989, *A Geologic Time Scale 1989.* Cambridge: Cambridge Univ Press, 263 p.

13. Smith R L, Luedke R G 1984, Potentially active volcanic lineaments and loci in western conterminous United States. P. 96-109, *In:* Boyd F R (ed) *Explosive Volcanism: Inception, Evolution, and Hazards.* Washington, DC: Natl Acad, 176 p.

14. Menard H W 1969, Growth of drifting volcanoes. *Jour Geophys Res,* 74: 4827-37.

15. Reitsema R H 1979, Gases of mud volcanoes in the Copper River Basin, Alaska. *Geochim Cosmochim Acta,* 43: 183-88.

16. White D E 1955, Violent mud-volcano eruption of Lake City Hot Springs, Northeastern California. *Geol Soc Amer Bull,* 66: 1109-30.

17. Hedberg H D 1974, Relation of methane generation to undercompacted shales, shale diapirs, and mud volcanoes. *Amer Assoc Petroleum Geol Bull,* 58: 661-73.

18. United Nations 1993, *World Urbanization Prospects*: the 1992 version. New York: Publ ST/ESA/SER.A/136

19. *This dynamic planet; a world map of volcanoes, earthquakes, impact craters and plate tectonics*; by Simkin T, Unger J D, Tilling R I, Vogt P R, Spall H; second edition available from U.S. Geological Survey, Map Distribution, Box 25256, Federal Center, Denver, CO 80225 (1-800-USA-MAPS)

20. The Circum-Pacific Map Project is based at MS 952, U.S. Geological Survey, 345 Middlefield Road, Menlo Park, CA 94025. The maps are available from USGS Map Distribution (see note 19 above).

21. Many references were used in preparing these regional introductions; the following were particularly helpful: (**A**) Fernandez-Armesto F (ed) 1991, *Atlas of World Exploration.* London: Times Books, 285 p. (**B**) Schnauble J (ed) 1993, *The SBS World Guide.* Melbourne, Australia: The Text Publ Co, 611 p. (**C**) Wright J W (ed) 1993, *The Universal Almanac, 1994.* Kansas City: Universal Press Syndicate Co., 716 p. (**D**) Trager J 1992, *The People's Chronology.* New York: Henry Holt, 1237 p. (**E**) *Webster's New Geographical Dictionary,* 1988, Springfield, Mass: Merriam-Webster, 1376 p.

22. (**A**) Blong 1984 ***global***. (**B**) Latter (ed) 1989 ***global***. (**C**) UNDRO 1985, *Volcanic Emergency Management.* New York: United Nations, 86 p. (**D**) *Proceedings Kagoshima International Conference on Volcanoes 1988,* 932 p. (**E**) Tilling R I (ed) 1989, *Volcanic Hazards.* Washington, DC: Amer Geophys Union, 123 p.

23. (**A**) Casadevall T J 1994, personal communication. (**B**) see also Casadevall T J (ed) 1994, Proceedings volume, the first international symposium on volcanic ash and aviation safety. *U S Geol Surv Bull,* in press. (**C**) Casadevall T J, Krohn M D 1994, Effects of the 1992 Mount Spurr eruptions on airports and aviation operations in the United States and Canada. *U S Geol Surv Bull,* in press.

24. As with other parts of the book, we have not attempted to cite every source of information presented in the FATALITY table. This is a luxury we have not been able to indulge adequately anywhere in the book. We have, however, tried to mention major sources in a form that will permit interested readers to find them in the REFERENCES.

25. This is an expansion of table 6 on p. 33 of McClelland *et al.* 1989 ***Global***.

26. We have not, however, followed this practice for the probably continuing activity of Stromboli (0101-04=) between its first record 2,400 years ago and the start of its detailed history in 1558 AD. Yearly repetition of this one entry in our CHRONOLOGY would add 10 pages to the length of this book.

27. Both these eruption figures exclude questionable eruptions.

28. (**A**) Jakobsson 1979 ***1700***. (**B**) Steinthorsson *et al.*, in preparation. ***1700***. (**C**) See also comments by Smith & Luedke (note 13 above) on volcanic systems.

29. Vogt P R 1974, Volcanic spacing, fractures, and the thickness of the lithosphere. *Earth Planet Sci Lett,* 21: 235-52.

30. Miller T P, Smith R L 1976, "New" volcanoes in the Aleutian arc. *U S Geol Surv Circ 733,* p.11.

31. Curtis G H 1968 ***1101***

32. Hasanaka & Carmichael 1985 ***1400*** (and reproduced in Luhr & Simkin 1993 ***1400***)

33. G P Scrope, upon completing one of the earliest volcano counts in 1825 ("upwards of 170", globally), wrote ". . . but the accounts that have been collected of some are very vague; and . . . it is obvious that many which have been long extinct are of course liable to be again restored to activity by the combination of influential circumstances." By the time of his second edition, 132 years ago, he was predating two of the most important messages that we have sought to emphasize here: "All such enumerations must, however, be considered as approximative merely, and much below the truth. First, because, while a very large proportion of the earth's subaerial surface is still unknown or imperfectly explored, it is highly probable that through that far larger area which is subaqueous--being indeed fully three-fourths of the whole--many volcanic vents exist which have not yet raised an eruptive orifice visibly above the surface of the ocean. Secondly, because the intervals of quiescence which occur between eruptions of a volcano are occasionally of such long duration that all accounts of any occurrence of the kind are liable to be lost or forgotten, and the eruptive character of its site consequently ignored until a fresh outbreak proclaims the continued activity of the subterranean focus." Both references under ***Global***.

34. (**A**) Rampino, Self, & Fairbridge 1979 ***Global***. (**B**) Bryson R A, Goodman B M 1980, Volcanic activity and climatic changes. *Science,* 207: 1041-44. (**C**) See also more recent summaries by Rampino M R, Self S, Stothers R B 1988, Volcanic winters. *Annual Rev Earth Planet Sci,* 16: 73-99. (**D**) Sigurdsson H, Laj P 1992, Atmospheric effects of volcanic eruptions. *In:* Nierenberg W A (ed), *Encyclopedia Earth Systems Science,* San Diego: Academic Press, 1: 183-99. (**E**) Robock A 1991, The volcanic contribution to climate change of the past 100 years. *In:* Schlesinger M E (ed), *Greenhouse-Gas-Induced Climatic Change.* Amsterdam: Elsevier, p. 429-41. (**F**) Simarski L T 1992, *Volcanism and Climate Change.* Washington, DC: Amer Geophys Union Spec Rep, 27 p.

35. (**A**) Harington C R (ed) 1992, *The Year Without a Summer: World Climate in 1816.* Ottawa: Canadian Museum of Nature, 578 p. (**B**) Stommel H & E, 1983, *Volcano Weather.* Newport, RI: Seven Seas Press, 177 p.

36. Kossinna E 1933, Die Erdoberflache. *In:* Gutenberg B (ed), *Handbuch der Geophysik,* 2: 869-954, Berlin: Borntraeger.

37. For this sum we have excluded from the circum-Pacific area the Sunda Arc (subregions 0601-0604) resulting from subduction of Indian Ocean crust NE under the Eurasian Plate. Also excluded are inland subregions (0705, 1001-1007, 1104, 1204-1210) and oceanic groups lying within the marginal "ring" (1503, 1506, and all of region 13).

38. See general introductions such as: (**A**) Cox A, Hart R B 1986, *Plate Tectonics: How it Works.* Palo Alto, Calif: Blackwell Scientific Publications, 392 p. (**B**) Wyllie P J 1976, *The Way the Earth Works.* New York: John Wiley, 296 p. (**C**) Sullivan W 1991, *Continents in Motion*, 2nd ed. New York: American Institute of Physics, 430 p. (**D**) Kious W J, Tilling R I, in press, *Plate tectonics: the dynamic earth.* U S Geol Surv, 56 p. (**E**) and note 19 above.

39. Crisp J 1984, Rates of magma emplacement and volcanic output. *Jour Volc Geotherm Res*, 20: 177-211. An earlier estimate of magma budgets was made by Nakamura K 1974, Preliminary estimate of global volcanic production rate. P. 273-86, *In*: Colp J, Furimoto A (eds) *Utilization of Volcanic Energy*, Hilo: Univ. Hawaii & Sandia Corp.

40. Depth data from Menard H W, Smith S M 1966, Hypsometry of ocean basin provinces. *Jour Geophys Res*, 71: 4305-25. Elevation data from Kossinna (note 36).

41. M Gardeweg, O Gonzales-Ferran, H Moreno-Roa

42. Ballard R D 1976, Window on Earth's interior. *Natl Geog*, 150: 228-249

43. See books cited in note 1 (above) or others emphasizing morphology such as (**A**) Cotton C A 1969, *Volcanoes as Landscape Forms*, 2nd ed. New York: Hafner, 416 p. (**B**) or Ollier C D 1969, *Volcanoes.* Cambridge: M.I.T. Press, 177 p.

44. E.g., Pike R J 1978, Volcanoes on the inner planets: some preliminary comparisons of gross topography. *Proc 9th Lunar Planet Sci Conf*, p. 3239-73.

45. Only 12 volcanoes were included in the *CAVW* for the western U.S.

46. Double the number in the first edition

47. This group includes locations for which equally reliable sources disagree over the existence of Holocene volcanism. Also included are those for which uncertainty is expressed by the original author (e.g., "perhaps Holocene age"), and line straddlers (e.g., "late Pleistocene or early Holocene").

48. N H Fisher, in the introduction to his 1957 *CAVW* Melanesia catalog ***0500***, described difficulty in distinguishing between "fumarolic" and "solfataric" on the basis of temperature or gases, but felt that the former indicated a higher degree of activity and closer association with magma. Other workers have noted strong fluctuation in sulfur production through time. We believe that usage has been too inconsistent to merit retaining the two terms. "Solfatara" is the name of a tuff ring at Campi Flegrei that erupted in 1198.

49. In 1981 we included 3 deep-sea sites with this status. These sea-floor springs, which reached temperatures of 350°C, were on oceanic rift zones at the divergence of lithospheric plates. As marine exploration has continued, however, these hot springs are found to be common, and we now restrict our inclusion of deep-sea centers to those with dated eruptive activity.

50. P. 14, in Scrope 1862 ***Global***

51. Holmes A 1965, *Principles of Physical Geology*, 2nd ed. London: Nelson, 1288 p. (diagram on p 305).

52. Volcanological Society of Japan 1970, *Bull Volc Eruptions*, no 10.

53. Miller *et al.*, in review ***1100***

54. Banks N 1982, personal communication; see also Peterson & Moore 1987, p. 167 ***1302***.

55. McClelland *et al.* 1989 ***Global***, and see also references under ***1300*** and ***1700***.

56. (**A**) Kibblewhite 1966 ***0401***. (**B**) Norris & Johnson 1969 ***0804***. (**C**) Sigurdsson & Shepherd 1974 ***1600***.

57. Smithsonian Institution 1993, Juan de Fuca Ridge at 46.5°N. *Global Volc Network Bull*, 18(7): 2-3. See also 13 abstracts in symposium on this eruption, Amer Geophys Union Fall Meeting, 1993. *EOS* 74(43): 619-20.

58. Baillie M G L 1982, *Tree-ring Dating and Archaeology.* Chicago: Univ Chicago Press, 274 p.

59. Smiley 1958 ***1209***

60. See Yamaguchi 1983-93 ***1201***. The accuracy of the date depends upon the accuracy of the tree-ring time scale developed for that region (see Fritts H C 1977, *Tree Rings and Climate.* New York: New York Academic Press, 562 p)

61. LaMarche V C, Hirschboeck K K 1984, Frost rings as records of major volcanic eruptions. *Nature*, 307: 121-26.

62. Mehringer *et al.* 1977 ***1201***

63. (**A**) Pilcher J R, Hall V A 1992, Toward a tephrochronology for the Holocene of the north of Ireland. *The Holocene*, 2,3: 255-59. (**B**) Hayakawa *et al.* 1994 ***0803***

64. Lowe D 1993, personal communication.

65. In our 1981 book, we cited varve dates of ± 1-3 years for 19th century eruptions in Alaska, but these have not been confirmed. The ± 50 and ± 300 dates are from (**A**) Scott 1977 ***1201***, and (**B**) Porter 1973 ***1302***

66. Degans *et al.* 1984 ***0103***

67. (**A**) Hammer C U 1977, Past volcanism revealed by Greenland Ice Sheet impurities. *Nature*, 270: 482-85. (**B**) Hammer C H, Clausen H B, Dansgaard W 1980, Greenland ice sheet evidence of post-glacial volcanism and its climatic impact. *Nature*, 288: 230-35. (**C**) and other citations ***end of REFERENCES***.

68. Palais J M, Kirchner S, Delmas R J 1990, Identification of some global volcanic horizons by major element analysis of fine ash in Antarctic ice. *Ann Glaciol*, 14: 216-20.

69. (**A**) Langway C C, Clausen H B, Hammer C U 1988, An interhemispheric volcanic time-marker in ice cores from Greenland and Antarctica. *Ann Glaciol*, 10: 102-08. (**B**) Palais J M, Germani M S, Zielinski G A 1992. Inter-hemispheric transport of volcanic ash from a 1259 AD volcanic eruption to the Greenland and Antarctic ice sheets. *Geophys Res Lett*, 19: 801-04.

70. The Michoacan reference is from (**A**) Yarza de De la Torre 1971 ***1401*** and others (including 0200 AD burned temple and 1200 BC dam flow) are from (**B**) Neumann van Padang 1963 ***0301*** (*CAVW* for Arabia).

71. Heyerdahl T 1963, Archeology in the Galápagos Islands. *Occ Pap Calif Acad Sci*, 44: 45-51.

72. Birkenmajer 1979 ***1900***

73. Scott & Gardner 1992 ***1201***

74. This technique is described by Taylor R E 1987, *Radiocarbon Dating: an Archeological Perspective.* Orlando: Academic Press, 212 p. Another helpful reference, including other techniques described here, is by Michael H N, Ralph E K 1971, *Dating Techniques for Archeologists.* Cambridge: M.I.T. Press, 227 p.

75. We also include in our file, when possible, the material dated and its relationship to the eruption.

76. See Stuiver M, Reimer P J 1993, Extended ^{14}C database and revised CALIB 3.0 ^{14}C age calibration program. *Radiocarbon* 35: 215-31 (and other papers in this 244 p. issue devoted to calibration).

77. Information such as laboratory precision, relation of dated material to eruption, number of independent dates, contamination of sample, etc.

78. See, for example, Southon J R, Brown T A, in press; The GISP2 ice core record of volcanism since 7000 B.C.; Science Discussion of paper by Zielinski *et al.* *** see end of REFERENCES***.

79. de Goer *et al.* 1991 ***0100***

80. (**A**) Thorarinsson S 1974, "The terms 'Tephra' and 'Tephrochronology'." p. xvii-xviii, *In*: (**B**) Westgate J A, Gold C M (eds), *World Bibliography and Index of Quaternary Tephrochronology.* Calgary: Univ Alberta, 528 p. This full reference provides a valuable introduction to the field of tephrochronology, as does (**C**) Self S, Sparks R S J (eds) 1981, *Tephra Studies.* Dordrecht: Reidel, 481 p.

81. Friedman 1968, 1977 ***1201, 1203***

82. Dalrymple G B, Lanphere M A 1969, *Potassium-Argon Dating: Principles, Techniques, and Applications to Geochronology.* San Francisco: W.H. Freeman, 240 p.

83. Dunkley *et al.* 1993 ***0202***

84. Aumento & Souther 1973 ***1200***

85. These figures are significantly larger than in our 1981 book, reflecting the relative shortness of the (more than 1000) durations added to the file since then. In 1981 we noted that 9% of our 2,139 durations ended within 2 days, and that same figure now applies to those ending in less than one day. Longer periods were: 19, 25, 40, and 52% for (respectively) a week, 2 weeks, a month, and 2 months. Conversely lower percentages marked the longer durations, with 21, 10, and <1% for those exceeding 1, 3, and 30 years.

86. Simkin T, Siebert L 1984. Explosive eruptions in space and time: durations, intervals, and a comparison of the world's volcanic belts. P. 110-21, *In*: Boyd F R (ed), *Explosive Volcanism: Inception, Evolution, and Hazards.* Washington, DC: Natl Acad, 176 p.

87. Ewart J W, Swanson D A (eds) 1992, Monitoring volcanoes: techniques and strategies used by the staff of the Cascades Volcano Observatory, 1980-90. *US Geol Surv Bull 1966*, 204 & 223 pp.

88. For example, the minutes-long Krafla borehole eruption described under VOLUMES (p. 23 and note 107).

89. Krafft 1990, reported velocities of 15-60 km /hr, substantially less than the 100 km /hr of Tazieff 1976-77, based on the escape of many villagers in the lava's path (***0201 for both***).

90. In addition to Stromboli and Yasur, another 13 volcanoes have been erupting through the past 19 years (the reporting span of SEAN/GVN) and are likely to remain active for some time. They are: Erta ale, Ethiopia; Manam, Langila, and Bagana, Papua New Guinea; Semeru and Dukono, Indonesia; Suwanose-jima and Sakura-jima, Japan; Santa Maria and Pacaya, Guatemala; Arenal, Costa Rica; Sangay, Ecuador; and Erebus, Antarctica.

91. Sigurdsson & Carey 1989 ***0604***

92. Grönvold K 1984, personal communication.

93. Gushchencko 1979 ***Global***

94. Study of this important type of volcanism has advanced greatly in recent decades. Authoritative guides are: (**A**) Fisher R V, Schmincke H-U 1984, *Pyroclastic Rocks.* Berlin: Springer-Verlag, 472 p., and (**B**) Heiken G, Wohletz K 1985. *Volcanic Ash.* Berkeley: Univ Calif Press, 245 p.

95. Peck D L, Wright T L, Decker R W 1979, The lava lakes of Kilauea. *Sci Amer,* 241: 114-28. See also Wright T L, Peck D L, Shaw H R 1976, Kilauea lava lakes: natural laboratories for study of cooling, crystallization, and differentiation of basaltic magma. *Amer Geophys Union Monograph,* 19: 375-90.

96. See also FATALITIES & EVACUATIONS tables on p. 165-177.

97. Our definition is broader than *CAVW*'s "Destruction of arable land", and includes damage to roads, bridges, and buildings.

98. Walker 1980 ***0401***

99. Newhall C G, Self S 1982, The volcanic explosivity index (VEI): an estimate of explosive magnitude for historical volcanism. *Jour Geophys Res (Oceans & Atmospheres),* 87: 1231-38. This scheme builds on an earlier scale introduced in Japan: Tsuya 1955 ***0803***

100. These data were generously shared with us in 1979 by Chris Newhall. We added VEI's for an additional ca. 1500 eruptions from our files, resolved differences in consultation with Newhall, and incorporated the VEI in our 1981 book and here.

101. See, for example, Bluth G J S, Doiron S D, Schnetzler C C, Krueger A J, Walter L S 1992, Global tracking of the SO_2 clouds from the June, 1991 Mount Pinatubo eruptions. *Geophys Res Lett,* 19: 151-55.

102. E.g. Arenal in March 1987, February 1988, and since has a VEI of 2 whereas its earlier, continuing years are assigned a VEI of 1.

103. When both caldera collapse and plinian deposits are known, the letter "**C**" takes precedence, but in neither case can these designations be used as a comprehensive listing of such characteristics. Most such events have reported data permitting a VEI assignment in this column, and for others we may simply have missed noting the existence of the characteristic.

104. These 45 dates are largely from the Zielinski *et al.* report on the GISP2 core from Greenland ***see end of REFERENCES***. They represent SO_4^{2-} residuals ≥90 ppb, a figure chosen (somewhat arbitrarily) to include some historical low-latitude events with VEI ≥4 while excluding high-latitude events of VEI ≤3 from Iceland and Alaska. Several dates from the last 1000 years are marked with "SP" (South Pole) and are from the work of Delmas *et al.* 1992 ***also see end of REFERENCES***. These are sulfate levels >200 ng/g (not directly comparable to the GISP2 measurements). This limit was chosen because several historical eruptions as close to GISP2 as to the South Pole failed to exceed the 90 ppb cutoff used there, and were in the 100-190 ng/g range at the South Pole.

105. Sigurdsson H 1991, The intensities and magnitudes of volcanic eruptions. *Earthquakes and Volcanoes,* 22(3): 142-6

106. Volumes for 62 eruptions have been entered from Sapper 1917 ***Global*** and are only rough estimates involving no field investigation. We have, however, compared Sapper's estimates with those made during subsequent field studies. Half of his estimates (made to an order of magnitude) were correct and the others were never off by more than one order of magnitude. We have entered the more modern data where they exist, but retained Sapper's estimates elsewhere. In the few cases when he gave a volume to two orders of magnitude, we have entered the midpoint, with a large corresponding uncertainty that covers both orders of magnitude.

107. Larsen *et al.* 1979 ***1700***

108. Thorarinsson 1969 ***1700***

109. Swanson D A, Wright T L 1978, "Bedrock geology of the Northern Columbia Plateau and adjacent areas." P. 37-58, *In:* Baker V R, Nummadal D (eds), T*he Channeled Scabland.* Washington, DC: NASA.

110. (**A**) Chesner & Rose 1991 ***0601***, but see also (**B**) Ninkovich D, Sparks R S J, Ledbetter M T 1978, The exceptional magnitude and intensity of the Toba eruption, Sumatra: an example of the use of deep-sea tephra layers as a geological tool. *Bull Volc,* 41: 286-98.

111. Christiansen 1984 ***1505***

112. G A Izett 1992, personal communication. See also note 126.

113. In our 1981 edition, we treated the number of erupting volcanoes as a percentage of the number of volcanoes known at that time over the past 600 years. We called the resulting normalized curve the Reporting Index: the number of volcanoes active in a decade as a percentage of the total known at the start of that decade, and plotted as a 5 decade running average. We found that this index, which shows the same pattern with 1994 data, divides the last 600 years into 3 main plateaus during which reported volcanism maintained a roughly constant relationship to the number of known volcanoes despite increases in both. The breaks separating these plateaus come early in the 16th century and the latter half of the 18th century. We think that these breaks represent historical rather than volcanological changes, as discussed here, but we found that the Reporting Index was widely mistaken as a measure of the quality of reporting, with each plateau thought to represent comparably reliable reporting through that time period. Therefore, we have not retained the index here, but discuss the historical factors likely to have affected volcanological reporting.

114. Data from (**A**) McEvedy C, Jones R 1978, *Atlas of World Population History.* Harmondsworth: Penguin Books, 368 p. (to 1750 AD), and (**B**) Population Reference Bureau, Washington, D.C. (since 1750).

115. E.g., (**A**) Kennett J P 1981, Marine tephrochronology. *In:* C Emiliani (ed), *The Sea: The Oceanic Lithosphere.* New York: John Wiley, 7: 1373-1435. (**B**) Kennett J P, McBirney A R, Thunnell R C 1977, Episodes of Cenozoic volcanism in the circum-Pacific region. *Jour Volc Geotherm Res,* 2: 145-63. (**C**) Vogt P R 1979, Global magmatic episodes: new evidence and implications for the "steady state" mid-oceanic ridge. *Geology,* 7: 93-98.

116. *Zeitschrift für Vulkanologie,* for example, ceased publication in 1938 and *Bulletin Volcanologique* halted from 1940 to 1948. *The Volcano Letter* (1925-1955, reprinted 1987 ***Global***), which carried reports on global volcanism both before and after WW-II, contains only one non-Hawaiian report in the years 1941-45; its average number of pages per year dropped to 17 during this same period, in contrast to 52 before (1935-40) and 26 after (1946-55).

117. Albrecht-Carrie R 1972, p 1051, *In:* Garraty J A, Gay P (eds), *The Columbia History of the World.* New York: Harper & Row, 1237 p.

118. Only one eruption was reported during this time interval in Antarctica, where the effects of the Great Depression would not be large. In region 03, a single eruption was reported each year throughout the period 1926-33.

119. We thought it useful to show trends both with and without the uncertain eruptions. The numbers differ by 5-10% but general trends discussed here are the same in both. In the past two decades, however, the discolored water observations discussed on p. 14 have increased to make up a significant proportion of these events. The presence or absence of such events in a given year depends on whether aerial reconnaissance flights were reported that year.

120. A more recent example is the contrast between the 1991 eruptions of Mt. Pinatubo and Cerro Hudson. The first was front page news because of its fatalities, its effects on nearby military bases in the Philippines, and its sheer size. But the second, only 2 months later in southern Chile, was also very large, yet created barely a ripple of interest in the international news.

121. The eruption of Soufriere St. Vincent, only 165 km S and one day earlier, added 1680 victims. Santa María, on the opposite side of the Caribbean and 5 months later, added more than 4500 additional victims, making this easily the worst year of this century for volcano fatalities.

122. Lutke's around-the-world expedition featured the Aleutians, and the expedition reports included accounts of a surveyor who made year-around observations in the central Aleutians in 1829-32 (Meyers, in preparation, ***1100***)

123. Coats 1950 ***1101***

124. This plot differs slightly from that published in *Annual Reviews* (note 134, below) in that it is not cumulative ("the number of events at this VEI level or higher") and because more recent data are used.

125. (**A**) Decker R W 1990, How often does a Minoan eruption occur? *In:* Hardy D A (ed) *Thera and the Aegean World III* 2: 444-52. London: Thera Foundation. (**B**) Newhall & Dzurisin 1988 ***Global***

126. Izett G A, Wilcox R E 1982, Map showing localities and inferred distributions of the Huckelberry Ridge, Mesa Falls, and Lava Creek ash beds (Pearlette family ash beds) of Pliocene and Pleistocene age in the western United States and southern Canada. *U S Geol Surv Misc Invest Ser Map,* I-1325.

127. Rose 1972 ***1402***

128. Cooke *et al.* 1976 ***0500***

129. Darwin C 1840, On the connexion of certain volcanic phenomena in South America; and on the formation of mountain chains and volcanos, as the effect of the same power by which continents are elevated. *Trans Geol Soc London,* 5(2nd series): 601-31.

130. E.g. (**A**) Mauk F J, Johnston M J S 1973, On the triggering of volcanic eruptions by earth tides. *Jour Geophys Res,* 78: 3356-3362. (**B**) Dzurisin D 1980, Influence of fortnightly earth tides at Kilauea volcano, Hawaii. *Geophys Res Lett,* 7: 925-928.

131. E.g. (**A**) Newhall 1979 ***0703***. (**B**) Luhr J F, Carmichael I S E 1990, Petrologic monitoring of cyclical eruptive activity at Volcan Colima, Mexico. *Jour Volc Geotherm Res,* 42: 235-60. (**C**) Scandone *et al.* 1993 ***0101***

132. Armstrong R L, Ward P 1991, Evolving geographic patterns of Cenozoic magmatism in the North American Cordillera: the temporal and spatial association of magmatism and metamorphic core complexes. *Jour Geophys Res,* 96: 13,201-24 (see p. 13,203).

133. Gudmundsson & Saemundsson, 1980 ***1701***, for example, have analyzed the eruptions of Iceland from 1550 to 1978 and found neither statistical clustering nor periodicity, although Bjornsson *et al,* 1977 ***1703*** called attention to a ca. 100-year periodicity for the recently active Krafla region, and Thorlaksson found non-random behavior in two Icelandic volcanoes (Thorlaksson J E 1967, A probability model of volcanoes and the probability of eruptions of Hekla and Krafla. *Bull Volc,* 31: 97-106)

134. Additional discussion of these questions can be found in Simkin T 1993, Terrestrial volcanism in space and time. *Annual Rev Earth Planet Sci,* 21: 427-52. See also references in notes 7 and 86 for comparisons of different volcanic belts using volcanological parameters from our database.

135. Figure 12 in: Smith R L 1979, Ash-flow magmatism. *Geol Soc Amer Spec Pap,* 180: 5-27., and see also note 13.

136. Events of VEI ≥5 since 1800 AD. Fatality data include deaths from indirect effects, and FATALITIES table (p. 165-177) carries more information.

Directory of Volcanoes

Bandai volcano, Japan, 1888 (Sekiya and Kikuchi, 1889)

Europe to Caucasus (01)

This region was appropriately placed first by the *CAVW* organizers in their numbering sequence: It is marked by traditions of record-keeping that go back thousands of years and by generations of historians devoted to mining those records. It is often called "The Cradle of Western Civilization", but it is also very much the cradle of volcanology. The earliest known documentation of volcanism is an Anatolian wall painting of a nearby cinder cone eruption around 6200 BC (Fig. 12, p. 180); the vigorous record of Etna goes back to 1500 BC; and the catastrophic eruption of Vesuvius in 79 AD, with the burial of Pompeii, continues to serve today as an object lesson in volcanism. The region has given us the first documented "new mountain", Monte Nuovo, in 1538, the first "new island" at Santorini in 197 BC, and the word "volcano" itself (derived from Vulcan, the Roman god of fire). The mid-18th century work of Guettard and Desmarest on pre-historic volcanoes of central France, and Hutton's work on older volcanics in Scotland taught the world that contemporary processes explain the volcanic landforms and rocks of the past. Regular documentation of volcanism began with Vesuvius: Hamilton's systematic observations from 1766 through 1794, the world's first volcano observatory in 1845, and Palmieri's seismographic monitoring of the 1872 eruption. In 1879, Fouqué's monograph on Santorini explained the fundamentals of caldera collapse 4 years before the Krakatau eruption – on the other side of the globe – gave the world a dramatic example of the process. And the continuing vigor of both volcanism and volcanology in this important region adds to our understanding of volcanoes every year.

This region's eruptive record is easily the longest of any. Roughly half of its 52 volcanoes have dated eruptions and more than half of these begin with BC events. Many of these were dated by radiocarbon or other techniques, but a remarkably large number were documented by humans. By 500 AD – 85% of the way through the Holocene – 61 eruptions had been historically documented in the world and 57 of them were from region 01.

The volcanism of this broad region, stretching from Spain to the Caucasus, is largely the result of convergence between the Eurasian Plate and the northward-moving African Plate. The geology is diverse and complex, with microplates defying easy tectonic generalizations. However, subduction under the Greek islands (Hellenic arc) and southern Italy (Calabrian arc) explains the region's principal volcanic centers.

The combined human population of all volcano-bearing nations in this region approaches 400 million, the most populous of *CAVW* regions (unless all of China is included in region 10).

Region 01 accounts for 11% (224) of eruptions known to have produced lava flows, most being from Etna's remarkable 3500 year history. The region also produces high proportions of the world's known radial fissure and submarine eruptions. It has the largest proportion (8%) of volcanoes with lava domes as their primary feature. Attention to the ancient record is shown by the variety of unusual dating techniques used (>80% of all dates from K-Ar and varves, 3 from

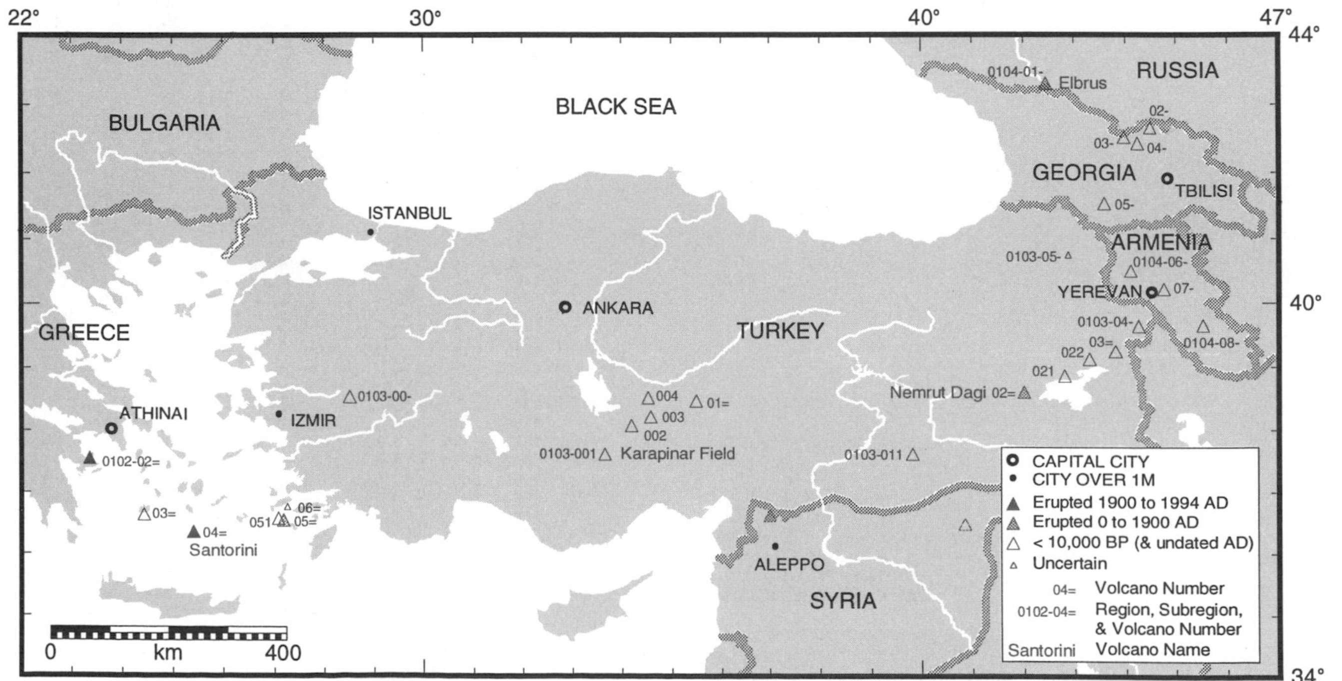

thermoluminescence, and one from fission tracks). The region also has the largest number (26) of discredited eruptions.

Since the first edition of our book, we have renumbered some volcanoes in this region. We grouped 3 Holocene centers of western Europe under subregion 0100, placing them before Italy and providing a regular geographic progression to the east (these centers appeared *after* Turkey and the Caucasus in the 1981 book). Furthermore, we moved the volcanoes of Iran into Region 03, as discussed below under that region's introduction. The map on the inside back cover serves as a graphic guide to subregion numbering.

VOLCANO NAME (Subregion) ...... / ERUPTION — Area of Activity	**LAT**	**LONG**	**ELEV** (m)	**TYPE**	**NUMBER**	**Status** / Start **Year**	Start M-Dy	P	Stop **Year**	Stop M-Dy	ERUPTIVE CHARACTERISTICS: Central / Flank vent / Radial fiss / Regional*	Submarine / New island / Subglacial / Crater lake	Explosive / Pyro flow / Phreatic / Fumarolic	Lava flow / Lava lake / Dome / Spine	Fatal / Damage / Mudflow / Tsunami	**VEI**	Vol L/T
EUROPE - W																	
WEST EIFEL VOLC FIELD (Germany)	**50.17 N***	**6.85 E**	**600**	**Maars**	**0100-01-**	**Radiocarbon**											
Strohn, Pulvermaar						C **-8300**y	....		....	....	----	----	x---	----	----		
Ulmener Maar........................						C **-7050***	....		....	....	----	----	x---	----	----		
CHAINE DES PUYS (France)	**45.50 N***	**2.75 E**	**1464**	**Cinder cones**	**0100-02-**	**Radiocarbon**											
Western Puy de Dome.................						C **-7840**x	....		....	....	----	----	x---	--x-	----		
Puy Mey...........................						U **-7740**?	....		....	....	----	----	x---	x---	----		
(Taphanel tephra)....................						C **-7020**v	....		....	....	----	----	x---	----	----		
Puys Chopine, Vasset, Cratere Kilian						C **-6550**?	....		....	....	----	----	xx--	--x-	----		
Puy de Pariou........................						U **-6250**?	....		....	....	----	----	xxx-	xx--	----		
Puy de Lassolas, Puy de la Vache........						C **-6020**w	....		....	....	----	----	x---	x---	----		
Puy de Come, Puy Montchier............						U **-5760**?	....		....	....	----	----	x---	----	----		
Montcineyre, Estivadoux, Pavin..........						C **-4040**w	....		....	....	----	----	xx--	x---	----		-/7
OLOT VOLC FIELD (Spain).........	**42.17 N**	**2.53 E**	**893**	**Pyrocl cones**	**0100-03-**	**Holocene?**											
ITALY																	
COLLI EUGANEI GROUP (Italy)	45.32 N	11.75 E	600		0101-00-	Not a Volcano											
LARDERELLO (Italy)..............	**43.25 N**	**10.87 E**	**500**	**Expl craters**	**0101-001**	**Historical**											
Lago Vecchienna						**1282**<	....		....	....	x---	---x	x-x-	----	-x--	3?	
AMIATA (Italy)	**42.90 N**	**11.63 E**	**1738**	**Lava domes**	**0101-002**	**Pleistocene-Fumarolic**											
VULSINI (Italy)	**42.60 N**	**11.93 E**	**800**	**Caldera**	**0101-003**	**Historical**											
						-0104	....		....	....	----	----	----	----	----		
ALBANO, MONTE (Italy)	**41.73 N**	**12.70 E**	**949**	**Caldera**	**0101-004**	**Holocene?**											
(no historical eruptions)						X -0540	....		....	....	----	----	----	----	----		
(no historical eruptions)						X -0114	....		....	....	----	----	----	----	----		
CAMPI FLEGREI (Italy)	**40.827 N**	**14.139 E**	**458**	**Caldera**	**0101-01=**	**Historical**											
Agnano.............................						T **-8050***	....		....	....	x---	----	xx--	----	----	4	-/8
Baia						C **-6450**?	....		....	....	x---	----	x---	----	----	3	
Pisani						T **-6050**?	....		....	....	x---	----	x---	----	----	3	
Fondi di Baia						A **-3120**u	....		....	....	x---	----	x---	----	----	3	
Cigliano						T **-2950**?	....		....	....	x---	----	xx--	----	----	4	-/8
Agnano-Monte Santangelo..............						T **-2850**?	....		....	....	x---	----	xx--	----	----		
Astroni						T **-2750**?	....		....	....	x---	----	xx--	----	----	3	
Agnano Monte Spina						C **-2450**?	....		....	....	x---	----	xx--	----	----	4	-/8
Monte Olibano-Accedemia..............						K **-1950***	....		....	....	x---	----	x---	--x-	----	2	7/-
Solfatara............................						T **-1900**?	....		....	....	x---	----	x---	----	----	3	-/7
Averno						T **-1850**?	....		....	....	x---	----	xx--	----	----	4	-/8
Astroni						C **-1750**?	....		....	....	x---	----	xx--	x---	----	3?	
Monte Senga						T **-1700**?	....		....	....	x---	----	xx--	----	----	3	-/7
Solfatara............................						**1198**	....		....	....	x---	----	--x-	----	-x--	1	
Monte Nuovo						**1538**	0929	+	**1538**	1006	x---	----	xxx-	xx--	xx--	3	-/7
VESUVIUS (Italy)	**40.821 N**	**14.426 E**	**1281**	**Complx volc**	**0101-02=**	**Historical**											
						C **-5960**v	....		....	....	x---	----	xx--	----	--x-	**5**	**-/9**
						C **-3580**?	....		....	....	x---	----	x---	----	--x-		
						C **-1740**w	....		....	....	x---	----	xx--	----	-xx-	**5**	**-/9**
(same as 3690 BP Avellino eruption)......						X -1150t	....		....	....	----	----	----	----	----		
						A **-0800**<	....		....	....	x---	----	x---	----	----	3	
						A **-0600**<	....		....	....	x---	----	x---	----	----	3	
						0079	0824	+	**0079**	0828a	x---	----	xx--	----	xxxx	**6**	**-/10**
						0172	....		....	....	x---	----	x---	----	----	2	
						0203	....		....	....	x---	----	x---	----	----	3	
						0222	....		**0235**	....	x---	----	x---	----	----	2	
						0379	....		**0395**	....	x---	----	x---	----	----	2	
						0472	1105		**0472**	1106?	x-?-	----	xx--	?---	-xx-	4	-/8
						0505	1109		....	....	x---	----	----	?---	----		
						0512	0708		....	....	x---	----	x---	----	-x--	4?	
						0536	....		....	....	x---	----	x---	----	----	2	
						0685	02 ?		**0685**	03 ?	x---	----	x---	x---	-?--	3	
						0787	....		....	....	x---	----	x---	x---	??--	3	
						0968	1201p		....	....	x---	----	x---	x---	-?--	3	
						? **0991**	....		....	....	x---	----	x---	----	----	3	
						? **0999**	....		....	....	x---	----	?---	----	----	3	
						1007	....		....	....	x---	----	x---	----	----	3	
						1037	0127		....	....	x---	----	x---	x---	----	3	
						1049	....		....	....	x---	----	----	x---	----	1	
						1073e	....		....	....	x-x-	----	x---	x---	----	3	
						1139	0601		**1139**	0609	x---	----	x---	x---	----	3	
						? **1150**	....		....	....	x---	----	x---	----	----		
						? **1270**	....		....	....	x---	----	x---	----	----		
						? **1347**	....		....	....	x---	----	x---	----	----		
						1500	....		....	....	x---	----	--x-	----	----	2	
Summit, SW and S flanks...............						**1631**	1215		**1632**	0131?	x-x-	----	xx--	?---	xxxx	4	-/8
						1637	0701	+	**1652**	1231	x---	----	x---	----	--x-	2*	
						1654	0225	+	**1680**	0328	x---	----	x---	?---	-xx-	3*	
						1682	0812	+	**1682**	0822	x---	----	x---	x---	x---	3	
						1685	1003	+	**1694**	0429	x---	----	x---	x---	-x--	3*	
						1696	0731	+	**1698**	0715	x---	----	x---	x---	-xx-	3*	
						1701	0701	+	**1704**	0523	x---	----	x---	x---	----	2	
Summit and SW flank..................						**1706**	0720		**1707**	0822	x-x-	----	x---	x---	-xx-	3*	
Summit, upper east and south flanks......						**1712**	0205	+	**1723**	0708	x-x-	----	x---	x---	-x--	3*	
						1724	0904	+	**1730**	0401?	x---	----	x---	x---	----	3*	
Summit and SW flank..................						**1732**	1225		**1737**	0604	x-x-	----	x---	x---	xxx-	3*	
Summit, upper SE, E and lower S flank....						**1744**	1101	+	**1761**	0106	x-x-	----	x---	x---	-x--	3*	
Summit, upper SW, SE, S and N flanks....						**1764**	0701?	+	**1767**	1027	x-x-	----	x---	x---	-x--	3*	7/-

VOLCANO NAME (Subregion) / ERUPTION —	LAT	LONG	ELEV (m)	TYPE	NUMBER	Area of Activity	Status / Start Year	Start M-Dy	P	Stop Year	Stop M-Dy	Central / Flank vent / Radial fiss / Regional*	Submarine / New island / Subglacial / Crater lake	Explosive / Pyro flow / Phreatic / Fumarolic	Lava flow / Lava lake / Dome / Spine	Fatal / Damage / Mudflow / Tsunami	VEI	Vol L/T
VESUVIUS (Italy) *continued*.........						Summit, N, NE, SE and E flanks	**1770**	0215	+	**1779**	1004?	x-x-	----	x---	x---	xxx-	3*	7/-
						Summit and SW flank (550-300 m)	**1783**	0818	+	**1794**	0705	x-x-	----	x---	x---	xxx-	3*	7/8
						Summit, upper SW and east flanks	**1796**	0115	+	**1822**	1116	x-x-	----	x---	x---	xxx-	3*	-/8
						Summit, upper E and S flanks	**1824**	0702	+	**1834**	0902	x-x-	----	x---	x---	-xx-	3*	
						Summit, upper east and west flanks	**1835**	0101	+	**1839**	0103	x-x-	----	x---	x---	----	3*	7/-
						Summit, upper N and E flanks	**1841**	0920	+	**1850**	0216	x-x-	----	x---	x---	-x--	2*	
						Summit and upper N flank	**1854**	1214	+	**1855**	0527	x-x-	----	x---	x---	-x--	3*	7/-
						Summit and SW flank (300-225 m)	**1855**	1219	+	**1861**	1231	x-x-	----	x---	x---	-x--	3*	7/-
						Summit and upper SE flank	**1864**	0210	+	**1868**	1126	x-x-	----	x---	x---	----	2*	6/-
						Summit and upper NW and SW flanks.....	**1870**	1201	+	**1872**	0430	x-x-	----	x---	x---	xx--	3*	7/7
						Summit, upper SE, SSE, NW, NNW flanks .	**1875**	1218	+	**1906**	0422	x-x-	----	xx--	x---	xxx-	4*	8/8
						Summit and upper flanks	**1913**	0705	+	**1944**	0404	x-x-	----	x---	x---	xx--	3*	8/7
ISCHIA (Italy)	**40.73 N**	**13.898 E**	**789**	**Complx volc**	**0101-03=**		**Historical**											
						Selva del Napolitano, Piedmonte	K **-7550***	....		....	....	x---	----	----	--x-	----		
						Zaro, Marecocco	K **-4050***	....		....	....	x---	----	x---	x-x-	----		
						Submarine SE flank (Secca d'Ischia)......	A **-3500?**	....		....	....	-x--	x---	xx--	----	----		
						Cantariello	K **-3050***	....		....	....	x---	----	x---	x---	----		
						Punta della Cannuccia	T **-2700***	....		....	....	x---	----	x---	----	----		
						Costa Sparaina........................	K **-2350***	....		....	....	x---	----	x---	--x-	----		
						Castiglione	A **-0750**t	....		....	....	x---	----	----	x---	-x--		
						Costa del Lenzuolo....................	T **-0700**u	....		....	....	x---	----	xx--	----	----		
							-0500?	....		....	....	x---	----	----	----	----		
						Bosco dei Conti and Fondo Ferraro ?	**-0470?**	....		....	....	x---	----	x---	--x-	----		
							? **-0350?**	....		....	....	x---	----	x---	----	---x		
						Porto d'Ischia	**-0250**t	....		....	....	x---	----	x---	x---	----		
						Rotaro I.............................	**-0091**	....		....	....	x---	----	x---	x---	----		
							-0006p	....		....	....	x---	----	----	----	----		
						Rotaro II	**0069**	....		....	....	----	----	x---	--x-	----		
						Montangnone-Maschiata, Posta Lubrano ..	**0080**a	....		....	....	x---	----	x---	--x-	----		
						Rotaro II and Monte Trippodi ?...........	**0145?**	....		....	....	x---	----	x---	--x-	----		
						Vateliero, Molara-Cava Nocelle, Rotar.....	**0295**j	....		....	....	x---	----	x---	x---	----		
						Arso	1302	0118		**1302**	03	x---	----	x---	x---	xx--		
STROMBOLI (Aeolian Is)...........	**38.789 N**	**15.213 E**	**926**	**Stratovolc**	**0101-04=**		**Historical**											
							-0450<	....		**1993**>	....	x---	----	x---	----	----	2	
							1558<	....		....	....	x---	----	x---	----	----	2	
						Summit and west flank	**1768**	....		....	....	x-x-	----	x---	x---	----	2	
							1770	....		....	....	--x-	x---	----	----	----	2	
							1778	0301		**1778**	0302	x---	----	x---	----	----	2	
							1822	1022		....	....	x---	----	x---	----	----	3	
							1833	....		....	....	x---	----	x---	----	----	2	
							1850	....		....	....	x---	----	x---	----	----	2	
							1855	1003		....	....	x---	----	x---	----	----	2	
							1856	07		....	....	x---	----	x---	----	----	2	
							1865	0126e		**1865**	0205d	x---	----	x---	----	----	2	
							1874	06		....	....	x---	----	x---	----	----	2	
							1879	0205		....	....	x---	----	x---	----	----	2	
							1879	0603		**1879**	0608	x---	----	x---	----	----	2	
							1881	1015		**1881**	1018	x---	----	x---	----	----	2	
							1882	1117		**1882**	1130	x-x-	----	x---	----	----	3	
							1885	0301		**1885**	0310	x---	----	x---	----	----	2	
							1888	1024		**1889**	0626	x---	----	x---	x---	----	2	4/-
							1891	0624	+	**1891**	0831	x---	----	x---	x---	----	3	4/-
							1892	1105		....	....	x---	----	x---	----	----	2	
							1893	0130		....	....	x---	----	x---	----	----	2	
							1893	1111		....	....	x---	----	x---	----	----	2	
							1895	0329		....	....	x---	----	x---	----	----	2	
							1896	0713		....	....	x---	----	x---	----	----	2	
							1897	0717		....	....	x---	----	x---	----	----	2	
							1898	0824		....	....	x---	----	x---	----	----	2	
							1900	0804		**1900**	0822	x---	----	x---	----	----	2	
							1900	1019		....	....	x---	----	x---	----	----	2	
							1903	0101	+	**1903**	06	x---	----	x---	x---	----	2	4/-
							1903	1111		**1903**	1118	x---	----	x---	x---	----	2	
							1905	0407		**1905**	0416	x---	----	x---	----	----	2	
							1906	0411		....	....	x---	----	x---	----	----	2	
							1906	0715		....	....	x---	----	x---	----	----	2	
							1907	0111	+	**1907**	0529	x---	----	x---	x---	----	3*	
							1912	0722		**1912**	0825	x---	----	x---	----	----	2	
							1915	0618	+	**1915**	1126	x---	----	x---	x---	----	2	5/-
							1916	0620		**1916**	0704	x---	----	x---	x---	----	2	4/-
							1919	0522		....	....	x---	----	x---	----	xx-x	3	
							1921	0604		**1921**	0622	x---	----	x---	x---	----	2	3/-
							1930	0203		**1930**	0206	x---	----	x---	x---	----	2	
							1930	0911	+	**1930**	1202	x---	----	x---	x---	xx-x	3*	3/-
							1934	0202		**1934**	0202	x---	----	x---	----	----	2	
							1934	0821		....	....	x---	----	x---	----	----	2	
							1935	0225		**1935**	0227	x---	----	----	x---	----	1	3/-
							1935	0721		....	....	x---	----	----	x---	----	0	
							1936	0131		....	....	x---	----	x---	x---	----	2	
							1937	0106		**1937**	0121	x---	----	x---	----	----	2	
							1937	1114?		....	....	x---	----	x---	x---	----	2	2/-
							1938	0111	+	**1938**	0127	x---	----	----	x---	----	1	4/-
							1938	0505		**1938**	0518	x---	----	----	x---	----	1	
							1938	1105	+	**1939**	0608	x---	----	x---	x---	----	2*	4/-
							1941	0822		....	....	x---	----	x---	x---	----	2	3/-
							1943	1203	+	**1944**	02	x---	----	x---	x---	----	2*	
							1944	0820	+	**1944**	1026e	x---	----	xx--	x---	---x	2*	2/-
							1949	0606		**1949**	0609	x---	----	x---	x---	----	2	3/-
							1950	1020		**1950**	1023	x---	----	x---	x---	----	2	3/-
							1951	0411		....	....	x---	----	x---	x---	----	2	
							1952	0607		**1952**	0617	x---	----	----	x---	----	2	3/-
							1954	0201		**1954**	0313	x---	----	xx--	x---	---x	2	4/-
						Summit and submarine NW flank.........	**1954**	1206		**1955**	05 ?	x-x-	xx--	x---	x---	----	2*	4/-
							1956	0101		**1956**	0316	x---	----	----	x---	----	0	4/-
							1959	0519		....	....	----	----	x---	----	---x	2	

VOLCANO NAME (Subregion) / ERUPTION — Area of Activity	LAT	LONG	ELEV (m)	TYPE	NUMBER	Status / Start Year	Start M-Dy	P	Stop Year	Stop M-Dy	Central / Flank vent / Radial fiss / Regional*	Submarine / New island / Subglacial / Crater lake	Explosive / Pyro flow / Phreatic / Fumarolic	Lava flow / Lava lake / Dome / Spine	Fatal / Damage / Mudflow / Tsunami	VEI	Vol L/T
STROMBOLI (Aeolian Is) *continued*						**1966**	0409		**1966**	0412	x---	----	x---	x---	----	2	
						1967	0419		**1967**	0813	x---	----	----	x---	----	0	3/-
						1971	0331		**1971**	0501	x---	----	x---	x---	----	2	
						1975	1104	+	**1975**	1124	x---	----	x---	x---	----	1	4/5
						1985	1206		**1986**	0425	x-x-	----	xxx-	x---	x---	2	6/4
LIPARI (Aeolian Is)................	**38.48 N**	**14.95 E**	**602**	**Stratovolc**	**0101-041**	**Historical**											
Gabellotto-Fiume Bianco						F **-7900***	....		....	....	x---	----	xx--	x-x-	----		
Pelato (Forgia Vecchia, Rocche Rossi)						**0729**	....		....	....	x---	----	xx--	x-x-	----		
VULCANO (Aeolian Is).............	**38.404 N**	**14.962 E**	**500**	**Stratovolc**	**0101-05=**	**Historical**											
Fossa						K **-3550***	....		....	....	x---	----	----	x---	----	0	
Fossa						K **-2650***	....		....	....	x---	----	----	x---	----	0	
Fossa						**-0475**?	....		....	....	x---	----	x---	----	----		
Fossa						**-0360**j	....		....	....	x---	----	x---	----	----	3?	
Fossa						**-0300**	....		....	....	x---	----	x---	----	----	3	
						-0215	....		....	....	----	x---	----	----	----		
Vulcanello I..........................						**-0183**	....		....	....	-x--	xx--	x---	----	----	4	
Between Vulcano and Panarea						**-0126**	06		....	....	----	xx--	----	----	---x		
Vulcanello...........................						**-0091**	....		....	....	-x--	----	x---	----	----	3?	
(no 43 BC eruption: Stothers 1893)						X -0043	....		....	....	----	----	----	----	----		
Vulcanello ?						**-0024**e	....		....	....	-x--	----	----	----	----		
Vulcanello...........................						**-0010**j	....		....	....	-x--	----	----	x---	----		
Fossa						**0050**t	....		....	....	x---	----	x---	----	----		
Fossa						**0144**	....		....	....	x---	----	?---	?---	----		
Fossa and Vulcanello III................						**0526**?	....		....	....	xx--	----	x---	----	----	3	
Fossa						**0729**	....		....	....	x---	----	x---	----	----		
						0925q	....		....	....	----	----	x---	----	----	3?	
Vulcanello ?						**1250**t	....		....	....	-?--	----	----	----	----		
						1444	0204		....	....	----	?---	x---	----	----	3	
Vulcanello III.........................						**1550**	....		....	....	-x--	----	x---	----	----	3	
						1618	....		....	....	----	----	x---	----	----		
						1626	03		**1626**	04	----	----	x---	----	----	3	
						1631	....		....	....	----	----	x---	----	----		
Fossa						**1651**	....		....	....	x---	----	x---	----	----		
Fossa						**1688**	....		....	....	x---	----	x---	----	----		
Forgia Vecchia II and Fossa.............						**1727**	....		....	....	xx--	----	xxx-	----	--x-	3	
Fossa						**1731**	....		**1739**	....	x---	----	x---	x---	--x-	3*	
Fossa						**1771**	0217		**1771**	05	x---	----	x---	----	----	3	
Fossa						? **1775**	....		....	....	x---	----	?---	----	----		
Fossa						**1780**	....		....	....	x---	----	x---	----	----	2	
Fossa						? **1786**	....		....	....	x---	----	x---	----	----	3	
Fossa						? **1812**	....		....	....	x---	----	?---	----	----	1?	
Fossa						? **1822**	....		?**1823**	....	x---	----	?---	----	----	2?	
Fossa						? **1831**	....		....	....	x---	----	?---	----	----	1?	
Fossa						**1873**	09	+	**1879**	....	x---	----	x---	----	----	3*	
Fossa						**1886**	0105d		....	....	x---	----	x---	----	----	3	
Fossa						**1888**	0802		**1890**	0322	x---	----	xx--	----	-xx-	3*	
5 km east of Vulcanello						? **1892**	1214		....	....	----	?---	----	----	----	0	
(smoke clouds not due to eruption)						X 1968	0711		....	....	----	----	----	----	----		
ETNA (Sicily)	**37.734 N**	**15.004 E**	**3350**	**Shield**	**0101-06=**	**Historical**											
						C **-6190**x	....		....	....	----	----	x---	----	----		
						C **-5150**w	....		....	....	----	----	x---	----	----		
						C **-4150**w	....		....	....	----	----	x---	----	----		
						C **-3510**w	....		....	....	----	----	x-x-	----	--x-		
						C **-3050**w	....		....	....	----	----	x---	----	----		
						C **-2330**v	....		....	....	----	----	x---	----	----		
						-1500t	....		....	....	--?-	----	x---	x---	-x?-	**5?**	
(confused with ca. 1500 BC eruption)						X -1470	....		....	....	----	----	----	----	----		
						? **-0735**	....		....	....	----	----	----	----	----		
South ?, Mt. Mompilieri ?						**-0695**b	....		....	....	--x-	----	x---	x---	-x--		
						? **-0565**	....		....	....	----	----	----	----	----		
South flank ?						**-0479**	08		**-0476**?	....	--x-	----	x---	x---	-x--		
South flank						**-0425**	0315m		**-0424**?	....	--x-	----	?---	x---	-x--		
East flank (700 m?)						**-0396**?	0715q		....	....	--x-	----	x---	x---	-x--		
						-0350?	....		....	....	?---	----	x---	x---	----		
						-0141	1231y		....	....	?---	----	x---	x---	x---		
						-0135	....		....	....	--?-	----	x---	x---	----		
						-0126	06 <		....	....	x-?-	----	x---	x---	----		
South flank, summit						**-0122**	....		....	....	x-x-	----	x---	x---	----	4?	
						? **-0061**	....		....	....	?---	----	x---	----	----		
						? **-0056**	....		....	....	----	----	----	----	----		
West flank and summit ?						**-0049**	....		....	....	?-x-	----	x---	x---	----		
						-0044	03 ?		....	....	x-?-	----	x---	x---	-x--	3?	
East side ?						**-0036**	0715q		....	....	x-?-	----	x---	x---	----		
						-0032	1231y		....	....	----	----	----	----	----		
						? **-0010**?	....		....	....	x---	----	?---	?---	----		
						0010j	....		....	....	x---	----	x---	----	----		
						0039a	....		....	....	x---	----	x---	----	----		
(description of Etna, not eruption)						X 0050	....		....	....	----	----	----	----	----		
(incorrect eruption report: Stothers & Rampino)						X 0072	....		....	....	----	----	----	----	----		
						0080?	....		....	....	x---	----	x---	?---	----		
(no 165 AD eruption: Stothers & Rampino 1983)						X 0165	....		....	....	----	----	----	----	----		
South flank..........................						**0252**?	0201		**0252**?	0209	x-x-	----	?---	x---	-x--	3?	
(incorrectly interpreted as eruption)						X 0400	....		....	....	----	----	----	----	----		
(incorrectly interpreted as eruption)						X 0410	....		....	....	----	----	----	----	----		
						0417?	....		....	....	----	----	x---	----	----		
(no specific eruptions AD 500-560)						X 0500	....		....	....	----	----	----	----	----		
(no specific eruptions AD 500-560)						X 0560	....		....	....	----	----	----	----	----		
(incorrect reference to eruption)..........						X 0604	....		....	....	----	----	----	----	----		
						? **0644**	....		....	....	----	----	----	----	----		
South flank (1200 m, S of Mt. Sona)						**0812**?	....		....	....	--x-	----	x---	x---	----		8/5
						? **0814**	....		....	....	----	----	----	----	----		
						? **0859**	....		....	....	----	----	----	----	----		
						? **0911**	....		....	....	----	----	----	----	----		
						? **1004**	....		....	....	----	----	----	----	----		
						? **1044**	....		....	....	----	----	----	----	----		
WSW flank (1500 m) ?						**1063**a	....		....	....	--?-	----	x---	x---	----		

VOLCANO NAME (Subregion) ...... LAT / ERUPTION —	LONG ELEV (m) TYPE NUMBER / Area of Activity	Status	Start Year	Start M-Dy	P	Stop Year	Stop M-Dy	Central / Flank vent / Radial fiss / Regional*	Submarine / New island / Subglacial / Crater lake	Explosive / Pyro flow / Phreatic / Fumarolic	Lava flow / Lava lake / Dome / Spine	Fatal / Damage / Mudflow / Tsunami	VEI	Vol L/T
ETNA (Sicily) *continued*			**1157**	....		....	....	----	----	----	----	----	2?	
			1160	....		....	....	----	----	----	----	----	2?	
			1164	....		....	....	----	----	----	----	----	2?	
	(tectonic earthquake, eruption doubtful)....	?	**1169**	0204		....	....	--?-	----	?---	?---	----		
	(probably confused with 1169 events)	X	1175	....		....	....	----	----	----	----	----		
			1194	....		....	....	----	----	----	----	----	2?	
			1222	....		....	....	----	----	----	----	----	2?	
			1250	....		....	....	----	----	----	----	----	2?	
	East flank (Valle del Bove)..............		**1284**	....		**1285**	01 ?	--x-	----	----	x---	----		
	(confused with 1329 eruption: Tanguy 1981)	X	1321	....		X1328	....	----	----	----	----	----		
	East (Mt. Lepre ?, Valle del Bove)		**1329**	0628		**1329**	0715	--x-	----	x---	x---	----	2	
	SE flank		**1329**	0715		**1329**	0804d	x-x-	----	x---	x---	?x--	3?	7/6
			1333	....		....	....	?---	----	x---	?---	----	2	
	(confused with 1329 eruption: Tanguy 1981)	X	1334	....		....	....	----	----	----	----	----		
			1350	....		....	....	x---	----	x---	----	----	2	
	SSE (370 m), Mts. Pomiciari, Arsi		**1381**?	0806		....	....	--x-	----	?---	x---	-x--	2	7/6
	Summit, south flank (N of Mt. Arso)		**1408**	1108		**1408**	1120	x-x-	----	x---	x---	-x--	3	
	South (N of Mt. Arso and 950 m)		**1444**	....		....	....	x-x-	----	x---	x---	-x--	2	
	East (Valle del Bove, 1630 or 1825 m).....		**1446**	0925		....	....	--x-	----	----	x---	----	1	
			1447	0921		....	....	x---	----	x---	x---	----	1	
	(no 1470 eruption: Tanguy 1981).........	X	1470	....		....	....	----	----	----	x---	----		
			1494?	....		....	....	x---	----	?---	?---	----	1	
	(no activity recorded 1494-1533)	X	1533	....		....	....	----	----	----	----	----		
	(probably same as 1536 eruption)	X	1535	....		....	....	----	----	----	----	----		
	Summit, S, N & W flanks (1400-2500 m) ...		**1536**	0322		**1536**	0430?	x-x-	----	x---	x---	xxx-	3	7/5
	Summit, south flank (1800-1500 m)		**1537**	03	+	**1537**	07	x-x-	----	x---	x---	-x--	2	7/6
			1540	07		....	....	x---	----	x---	----	----	1	
			1541	07 ?		....	....	x---	----	x---	----	----	2	
	(no 1550 eruption: Tanguy 1981).........	X	1550	....		....	....	----	----	----	----	----		
		?	**1554**	....		....	....	x---	----	----	----	----	2	
	NE flank		**1566**	1101		....	....	x-x-	----	x---	x---	-x--	2	7/5
	(doubtful, confused with 1579 ?)	X	1578	....		....	....	----	----	----	----	----		
	SE flank		**1579**	0909?		**1580**?	....	--x-	----	x---	x---	-x--		
	SW flank ?		**1595**?	....		....	....	--x-	----	x---	x---	----	3	8/7
	Central Crater (SW and S slope)		**1603**	07		**1610**	....	x---	----	x---	x---	----	2	
	SW flank (2250-1950 m)?		**1607**	0628		....	....	--x-	----	x---	x---	----	2	7/6
	(confused with 1607 eruption)	X	1609	07		....	....	----	----	----	----	----		
	SW flank (2800?-1700 m)		**1610**	0206	+	**1610**	0815	x-x-	----	x---	x---	-x--	2	7/-
	NNW flank (2550 m)..................		**1614**	0701?		**1624**	....	x-x-	----	x---	x---	-x--	2	**9**/6
		?	**1633**	0221		....	....	?-?-	----	?---	?---	----		
	SE, SSE (1770 m), Little Mt. Pecorara.....		**1634**	1219	+	**1638**	0427	x-x-	----	x---	x---	-x--	1	8/5
	(1640 is error for 1643 eruption)..........	X	1640	....		....	....	----	----	----	----	----		
	North flank (2100-1275 m)		**1643**	0220		....	....	--x-	----	----	x---	----	1	
	NNE (2000 m, 1800 m), Mt. Nero.........		**1646**	1120		**1647**	0117	--x-	----	x---	x---	-x--	2	8/7
	West (2500-2125 m), east (900 m)?		**1651**	0116		**1653**	....	x-x-	----	x---	x---	-x--	1	8/5
			1654	....		**1656**?	....	x---	----	x---	x---	----	1	
	South flank (800 m, Mt. Rossi)...........		**1669**	0311		**1669**	0715	x-x-	----	x---	x---	-x--	3*	8/7
	East flank (Valle del Bove, 2900 m)		**1682**	0901		....	....	?-x-	----	?---	x---	----	2	
	East slope of Central Crater.............		**1688**	....		....	....	x---	----	x---	x---	----	1	
	East flank (Valle del Bove, 1800 m)		**1689**	0314		....	....	x-x-	----	x---	x---	-x--	1	7/-
	(tectonic earthquake, eruption doubtful)....	?	**1693**	0109		....	....	x---	----	?---	?---	----		
			1693	12		**1694**	11	x---	----	x---	----	----	3*	
	East flank (Valle del Bove, 2000 m)		**1702**	0308		**1702**	0508	x-x-	----	x---	x---	-x--	1	7/-
	Central Crater (SW slope)		**1723**	1122		**1724**	0510?	x---	----	x---	x---	-x--	2	
	Central Crater (West slope)		**1732**	1209		**1733**	0126e	x---	----	x---	x---	-x--	2	
	Central Crater.......................		**1735**	1004	+	**1736**	09	x---	----	x---	x---	----	2	
	Central Crater.......................		**1744**	07		**1745**	09	x---	----	x---	----	----	2	
	Central Crater.......................		**1747**	09		**1749**	03	x---	----	x---	x---	----	2	
	Central Crater.......................		**1752**	....	+	**1758**	....	x---	----	x---	x---	----	2	
	East flank (Valle del Bove, 1750 m)		**1755**	0309		**1755**	0315	x-x-	----	x---	x---	-xx-	3	6/-
	Central Crater, south flank (3000 m)		**1758**	1103?	+	**1759**	02	x---	----	x---	x---	----	2*	
	West flank (1600 m, 1700 m, Mt. Nuovo)...		**1763**	0206		**1763**	0310?	--x-	----	x---	x---	-x--	2	7/7
	South flank (2500 m, Montagnola)		**1763**	0618		**1763**	0910	--x-	----	x---	x---	-x--	3	8/7
	NW flank (2600 m?)		**1764**	....		**1765**	....	--x-	----	----	x---	----	0	
	South flank (2100-1950 m).............		**1766**	0427		**1766**	1106	x-x-	----	x-?-	x---	-x--	2	7/6
	Central Crater.......................		**1767**	0502		....	....	x---	----	x---	----	----		
	Central Crater.......................	?	**1770**	0528a		....	....	x---	----	?---	----	----		
	Central Crater.......................		**1776**	....		....	....	x---	----	x---	----	----		
	Summit, S & SSW flanks (2300-1500 m) ...		**1780**	0420	+	**1780**	06	x-x-	----	x---	x---	-x--	2*	7/3
	Central Crater.......................		**1781**	0331p	+	**1781**	0510	x---	----	x---	x---	----	2	
	Central Crater.......................		**1787**	0604d	+	**1787**	0811>	x---	----	x---	x---	-x--	4*	
	Central Crater.......................		**1791**	02		**1791**	09	x---	----	x---	----	----	2	
	Central Crater, west slope		**1792**	03	+	**1792**	0524	x---	----	x---	x---	----	2	
	Summit, SE flank (2600-1900 m)		**1792**	0525		**1793**	0526e	x-x-	----	x-x-	x---	-x--	3	7/5
	Central Crater.......................		**1797**	....		**1801**	....	x---	----	x---	x---	----	2	
	East flank (Valle del Bove, 1800 m)		**1802**	1115		**1802**	1117	x-x-	----	x---	x---	----	2	6/-
			1803	....	+	**1809**	11 ?	x---	----	x---	x---	----	2	
	North (3000 m), NE (1300 m), ...		**1809**	0327		**1809**	0409	x-x-	----	x---	x---	-x--	2	7/6
	Central Crater.......................		**1810**	1226e		....	....	x---	----	x---	----	----	1	
	East (Valle del Bove 3000-2000 m)		**1811**	1027		**1812**	05	x-x-	----	x---	x---	----	2	7/6
	Offshore from Aci-Castello	?	**1816**	0306		....	....	----	?---	----	----	----	0	
	East (Valle del Bove 2850-2400 m)		**1819**	0527		**1819**	0801	x-x-	----	x---	x---	----	3	7/7
	Central Crater.......................		**1822**	0621		....	....	x---	----	x---	----	----	1?	
	Central Crater.......................		**1827**	1010		**1827**	1014	x---	----	x---	----	----	1?	
	Central Crater.......................		**1828**	0802	+	**1832**	1027	x---	----	x---	x---	----	2*	
	SE (2900 m), NW (2200 m), W (1700 m)...		**1832**	1031		**1832**	1122	--x-	----	x---	x---	xx--	2	7/6
	Central Crater.......................		**1833**	03		....	....	x---	----	x---	x---	----	2	
	Central Crater.......................		**1838**	0708	+	**1839**	02	x---	----	x---	x---	----	2	
	Central Crater (south & east slopes)		**1842**	1118	+	**1842**	1229?	x---	----	x---	x---	----	2	
	West flank (2375-1900 m)		**1843**	1117		**1843**	1128	x-x-	----	x---	x---	xx--	2	7/6
	East (Valle del Bove 1950-1700 m)		**1852**	0820	+	**1853**	0527	x-x-	----	x---	x---	-x--	2	8/6
	Central Crater.......................		**1857**	0906		....	....	x---	----	x---	----	----	1?	
	Central Crater.......................		**1863**	0501	+	**1863**	0728c	x---	----	x---	x---	----	2	
	Central Crater.......................		**1864**	0805d	+	**1864**	0919	x---	----	x---	x---	----	2	
	NE flank (1825-1625 m, Mt. Sartorius).....		**1865**	0130	+	**1865**	0628	x-x-	----	x---	x---	-x--	2	8/6
	Central Crater.......................		**1868**	1126	+	**1868**	1208	x---	----	x---	----	----	3	

VOLCANO NAME (Subregion) LAT LONG ELEV (m) TYPE NUMBER	ERUPTION — Area of Activity	Status	Start Year	Start M-Dy	P	Stop Year	Stop M-Dy	ERUPTIVE CHARACTERISTICS: Central / Flank vent / Radial fiss / Regional*	Submarine / New island / Subglacial / Crater lake	Explosive / Pyro flow / Phreatic / Fumarolic	Lava flow / Lava lake / Dome / Spine	Fatal / Damage / Mudflow / Tsunami	VEI	Vol L/T
ETNA (Sicily) *continued*	East flank (W wall of Valle del Bove)		**1869**	0926		**1869**	0926	--x-	----	----	x---	----	0	6/-
	Central Crater		**1874**	05		**1874**	0829	x---	----	x---	----	----	2	
	North flank (2800-2030 m)		**1874**	0829		**1874**	0831	--x-	----	x---	x---	----	2	6/6
	Central Crater		**1878**	1223	+	**1883**	0331>	x-x-	----	x---	x---	-x--	2	
	SSW (2650-2300 m), NNE (2400-1690 m)		**1879**	0526		**1879**	0607	--x-	----	x---	x---	-x--	3	7/7
	South flank (1200-950 m, Mt. Leone)		**1883**	0322		**1883**	0324	--x-	----	x---	x---	----	2	4/5
	Central Crater		**1884**	....		**1885**	....	x---	----	x---	----	----	1	
	South flank (1500-1300 m)		**1886**	0518	+	**1886**	0607	x-x-	----	x---	x---	-x--	3	7/6
	Central Crater		**1891**	0823		....	....	x---	----	x---	?---	----	1?	
	Central Crater		**1892**	0620		**1892**	0630	x---	----	x---	----	----	1	
	South flank (2025-1800 m)		**1892**	0708	+	**1892**	1229	x-x-	----	x---	x---	-x--	2	8/6
	Central Crater		**1893**	0426		**1898**	06	x---	----	x---	x---	----	2	
	Central Crater		**1899**	0719		**1899**	0805	x---	----	x---	----	----	3	
			1899	1115		**1907**	08	x---	----	x---	x---	----	1	
	SE flank (Valle del Bove 2500-2275 m)		**1908**	0429		**1908**	0430	x-x-	----	x---	x---	----	2	6/5
	Central Crater		**1908**	0520		**1909**	0928	x---	----	x---	----	----	1	
	South flank (2350-1950 m, Mt. Ricco)		**1910**	0323		**1910**	0418	x-x-	----	x---	x---	-x--	2	7/5
	Central Crater		**1910**	1227		**1911**	0217	x---	----	x---	x---	----	2	
	(collapse of NE Crater: no eruption)	X	**1911**	0527		....	....	----	----	----	----	----		
	Central Crater, NE Crater		**1911**	08		....	....	x---	----	x---	----	----	1	
	NE flank (2550-1650 m)		**1911**	0910		**1911**	0922	x-x-	----	x---	x---	-x--	1	7/6
	Central Crater		**1912**	0804		**1912**	08	x---	----	x---	x---	----	3	
	Central Crater, NE Crater		**1913**	1113		**1917**	03	x---	----	x---	x---	----	2	
	NE Crater, Central Crater		**1917**	0624	+	**1917**	0705d	x---	----	x---	----	-x--	2	
	NE Crater, Central Crater		**1918**	03	+	**1918**	11	x---	----	x---	x---	----	1	
	NW flank (3100-1900 m)		**1918**	1129?		**1918**	1130?	--x-	----	x---	x---	----	1?	6/-
	Central Crater, NE Crater		**1919**	0315	+	**1923**	0610?	x---	----	x---	x---	----	2	
	NE flank (2500-1800 m)		**1923**	0617		**1923**	0718	x-x-	----	x---	x---	-x--	2	7/5
	Central Crater		**1923**	1009		**1924**	....	x---	----	x---	----	----	1	
	NE Crater		**1924**	1227		**1925**	02	x---	----	x---	----	----	1	
	NE Crater		**1926**	0102		**1926**	06	x---	----	x---	----	----	1	
	Central Crater		**1928**	0731		**1928**	0820	x---	----	x---	----	----	1	
	East flank (2600, 2300-1400, 1200 m)		**1928**	1102		**1928**	1120	x-x-	----	x---	x---	xx--	1	7/6
	NE Crater		**1929**	0802		....	....	x---	----	x---	----	----	1	
	NE Crater		**1930**	1101		....	....	x---	----	x---	----	----	1	
	Central Crater, NE Crater		**1931**	0726e		**1933**	09	x---	----	x---	----	----	2	
	NE Crater		**1934**	0105		**1934**	0107	x---	----	x---	----	----	1	
	Central Crater, NE Crater		**1935**	0707	+	**1939**	12	x---	----	x---	x---	----	2	
	Central Crater, NE Crater		**1940**	0316	+	**1942**	0628?	x---	----	x---	x---	-x--	3	
	SW flank (2780-2240 m)		**1942**	0630	+	**1942**	0705	x-x-	----	x---	x---	----	2	6/5
	NE Crater		**1942**	0919	+	**1944**	0915	x---	----	x---	----	----	1	
	NE Crater		**1945**	0605d		**1945**	10	x---	----	x---	----	----	1	
	NE Crater		**1946**	02		**1946**	10	x---	----	x---	----	----	1	
	NE Crater, Central Crater		**1947**	0129		**1947**	0224	x---	----	x---	----	----	2	
	NE flank (3050, 2350, 2300, 2225 m)		**1947**	0224		**1947**	0310	--x-	----	x---	x---	-x--	1	6/4
	South (3200 m), NW (3150, 2425-1900 m)		**1949**	1202	+	**1950**	01	x-x-	----	x-x-	x---	-x--	2	6/5
	East flank (2820-2250 m)		**1950**	1125		**1951**	1202	--x-	----	x-x-	x---	-x--	2	8/6
	NE Crater		**1951**	0921		**1952**	0530	x---	----	x---	----	----	1	
		?	**1953**	0730		....	....	----	----	x---	----	----	2	
	NE Crater, Central Crater		**1955**	0405	+	**1956**	0407	x---	----	x---	x---	----	2*	6/-
	NE Crater		**1957**	0205	+	**1957**	0507	x---	----	x---	x---	----	2	6/7
	NE Crater		**1957**	0825		**1958**	0503	x---	----	x---	x---	----	2	
	NE Crater, Central Crater		**1958**	11		**1958**	12	x---	----	x---	----	----	1	
	Central Crater		**1959**	0323		**1959**	0425e	x---	----	x---	----	----	1	
	Central and NE Craters, NNE (3100 m)		**1959**	1017	+	**1964**	1231	x-x-	----	x---	x---	-x--	3*	
	NE Crater, Central Crater		**1966**	0110		**1971**	....	x---	----	x---	x---	----	2	
	SE flank (2550 m)		**1968**	0107		**1968**	0504	--x-	----	----	x---	----	0	
	SE flank (3000 m), east (2700-1800 m)		**1971**	0405	+	**1971**	0612	x-xx	----	x---	x---	-x--	2	7/6
	Central Crater		**1971**	0919		**1979**	03 ?	x---	----	x---	----	----	2	
	West flank (1670 m and 1650 m)		**1974**	0130	+	**1974**	0329	--x-	----	x---	x---	-x--	2	6/6
	NE Crater		**1974**	0929	+	**1978**	0329	x---	----	x---	x---	----	2	7/-
	North flank (2625 m)		**1975**	0224		**1975**	0829	--x-	----	x---	x---	----	1	6/-
	SE flank (3000-2575 m)		**1978**	0429		**1978**	0605	--x-	----	x---	x---	----	2	7/-
	SE Crater, SE, ENE flank (3000-2300 m)		**1978**	0824		**1978**	0830	--x-	----	x---	x---	----	2	6/-
	SE Crater, SE flank (2600-1675 m)		**1978**	1118		**1978**	1129	x-x-	----	x---	x---	----	2	6/-
	Central Crater		**1979**	0705d	+	**1992**	1203	x---	----	x-x-	----	xx--	2*	
	SE Crater, SE, E and NE flanks		**1979**	0716	+	**1979**	0809	x-x-	----	x---	x---	-x--	2	6/-
	SE Crater		**1980**	0111		**1980**	09	x---	----	x---	----	----	2	
	NE Crater		**1980**	0708	+	**1980**	0926	x---	----	x---	x---	----	3*	6/-
	NE Crater		**1981**	0126e	+	**1981**	0305d	x---	----	x---	x---	----	2	6/-
	NNW flank (2250-1120 m)		**1981**	0317		**1981**	0323	--x-	----	x---	x---	-x--	1	7/5
	NE Crater		**1981**	1126		**1981**	1126	x---	----	x---	----	----	2	
	South flank (2250-2450 m)		**1983**	0328		**1983**	0806	--x-	----	x-x-	x---	-x--	1	8/5
	SE Crater		**1984**	0427?		**1984**	1018	x---	----	x---	x---	----	2	7/-
	NE Crater		**1984**	0720	+	**1986**	0924	x---	----	x---	x---	-x--	2*	5/6
	SE Crater, south flank (2620-2150 m)		**1985**	0308	+	**1985**	0713	x-x-	----	x-x-	x---	-xx-	2	7/-
	SE Crater and SE flank (2750 m)		**1985**	1219	+	**1985**	1231	x-x-	----	x---	x---	----	2	6/-
	Valle del Bove (2900-2200 m)		**1986**	1030		**1987**	0227	--x-	----	x---	x---	----	2	7/6
	NE and SE Craters		**1987**	0308h	+	**1987**	0516	x---	----	x-x-	----	x---	2*	
	SE Crater		**1988**	1004		**1989**	0630	x---	----	x---	x---	----	1	
	SE Crater and SE and NE flanks		**1989**	0911	+	**1989**	1009	x-x-	----	x---	xx--	-x--	2	7/-
	SE and NE Craters		**1989**	1216		**1990**	04	x---	----	x---	x---	----	1	
	NE and SE Craters		**1990**	10		**1992**	0422	x---	----	x---	----	----	1	
	SE flank (3000 and 2400-2100 m)		**1991**	1214		**1993**	0330	--x-	----	x---	x---	-x--	2	8/-
	NE Crater		**1993**	0203		**1993**	0203	x---	----	x-x-	----	----	1	
	Central Crater, NE Crater		**1993**	0803		**1993**	1005d	x---	----	x---	----	----	1	
CAMPI FLEGREI MAR SICILIA (Italy). **37.10 N* 12.70 E -8 Subm volcs 0101-07=**		**Historical**												
			-0253k	....		....	....	----	x---	----	----	----		
	Guila Ferdinandeo		**1632**	....		....	....	----	x---	----	----	----	0	
	Guila Ferdinandeo	?	**1701**	....		....	....	----	xx--	----	----	----	2	
	Guila Ferdinandeo (Graham Island)		**1831**	0628>		**1831**	08	----	xx--	x---	----	----	3*	-/8
	Pinne		**1846**	1004		**1846**	1005	----	x---	----	----	----	2	
	Guila Ferdinandeo		**1863**	0812		....	....	----	xx--	----	----	----	2	
	Pinne		**1867**	....		....	....	----	x---	----	----	----	0	
	Pinne		**1911**	0930		....	....	----	x---	----	----	----	2	

VOLCANO NAME (Subregion) / ERUPTION — Area of Activity	LAT	LONG	ELEV (m)	TYPE	NUMBER	Status / Start Year	Start M-Dy	P	Stop Year	Stop M-Dy	ERUPTIVE CHARACTERISTICS (Central, Flank vent, Radial fiss, Regional* / Submarine, New island, Subglacial, Crater lake / Explosive, Pyro flow, Phreatic, Fumarolic / Lava flow, Lava lake, Dome, Spine / Fatal, Damage, Mudflow, Tsunami)	VEI	Vol L/T
PANTELLERIA (Italy)	**36.77 N**	**12.02 E**	**836**	**Shield**	**0101-071**	**Historical**							
Cuddia di Mida, Valenza						K **-7050?**	....		....	....	x--- ---- x--- x--- ----		
Cuddia Patite ?						C **-6130**u	....		....	....	x--- ---- x--- ---- ----		
Punta Tracino						C **-5610**v	....		....	....	-x-- ---- x--- ---- ----		
Cuddia Randazzo						C **-3635**y	....		....	....	x--- ---- x--- x--- ----		
Hingeline vent system						C **-1080**y	....		....	....	x--- ---- x--- ---- ----		
Foerstner (4 km NNW of Pantelleria)						**1891**	1017		**1891**	1025	---x x--- x--- ---- ----	1	
South of Pantelleria						? **1891**	12		....	....	---- ?--- ---- ---- ----		

GREECE

VOLCANO NAME (Subregion) / ERUPTION — Area of Activity	LAT	LONG	ELEV (m)	TYPE	NUMBER	Status / Start Year	Start M-Dy	P	Stop Year	Stop M-Dy	ERUPTIVE CHARACTERISTICS	VEI	Vol L/T
SUSAKI (Greece)	37.935 N	23.073 E	180		0102-01=	Not a Volcano							
METHANA (Greece)	**37.615 N**	**23.336 E**	**760**	**Lava domes**	**0102-02=**	**Historical**							
Kameno Vouno						**-0258**o	....		....	....	---- ---- x--- x-x- ----	3	7/-
						? **1922**	08		....	....	---- ---- ?--- ---- ----		
MILOS (Greece)	**36.699 N**	**24.439 E**	**751**	**Stratovolcs**	**0102-03=**	**Holocene**							
SANTORINI (Greece)	**36.404 N**	**25.396 E**	**564**	**Shields**	**0102-04=**	**Historical**							
						G **-1650**t	....		....	....	x--x x--- xxx- ---- xxxx	6	-/10
Hiera Island						**-0197**	....		....	....	x--x xx-- x--- --x- ----	3	
(eruption took place in 46 A.D.)						X 0019	....		....	....	---- ---- ---- ---- ----		
Thia Island						**0046**	....		**0047**	....	x--x xx-- x--- x-x- ---x	3	
NE side of Thia Island						**0726**	....		....	....	x--x xx-- x--- x-x- ----	3	7/-
Mikri Kameni						**1570**	....		**1573**	....	x--x xx-- x--- x-x- ----	3	7/-
Colombo Bank (6.5 km NE of Thera)						**1650**	0927		**1650**	1206	-x-x xx-- x--- x--- xx-x	4?	-/8
Nea Kameni						**1707**	0523		**1711**	0911	x--x xx-- x--- x-x- ----	3	8/-
Georgios, Afroessa and Reka domes						**1866**	0126		**1870**	1015	x--x xx-- x--- x-x- ----	2	8/-
Nea Kameni (Dafni, Naftilos)						**1925**	0811	+	**1928**	0317	x--x x--- xxx- x-x- ?---	2*	8/-
Nea Kameni (Triton, Ktenas, Fouque)						**1939**	0820	+	**1941**	0702a	x--x x--- x-x- x-x- ----	2	7/-
Nea Kameni (Liatsikas dome)						**1950**	0110		**1950**	0202	x--x ---- x-x- x-x- ----	2	6/-
NISYROS (Greece)	**36.58 N**	**27.18 E**	**698**	**Stratovolc**	**0102-05=**	**Historical**							
						? **1422**	....		....	....	---- ---- ?-?- ?--- ----	2	
						1871	....		....	....	x--- ---- x-x- ---- -x--	2	
						1873	0911		**1873**	0926	x--- ---- x-x- ---- ----	2	
						1888	0925d		....	....	---- ---- --x- ---- ----	2	
YALI (Greece)	**36.63 N**	**27.10 E**	**176**	**Lava domes**	**0102-051**	**Holocene**							
KOS (Greece)	**36.829 N**	**27.257 E**	**430**	**Fumarole flds**	**0102-06=**	**Pleistocene-Fumarolic**							

TURKEY

VOLCANO NAME (Subregion) / ERUPTION — Area of Activity	LAT	LONG	ELEV (m)	TYPE	NUMBER	Status / Start Year	Start M-Dy	P	Stop Year	Stop M-Dy	ERUPTIVE CHARACTERISTICS	VEI	Vol L/T
KULA (Turkey-W)	**38.58 N***	**28.52 E**	**750**	**Cinder cones**	**0103-00-**	**Holocene**							
KARAPINAR FIELD (Turkey-C)	**37.67 N***	**33.65 E**	**1302**	**Cinder cones**	**0103-001**	**Holocene**							
(more likely Karapinar than Hasan Dagi)						**@-6200>**	....		....	....	x?-- ---- x--- ?--- ----		
HASAN DAGI (Turkey-C)	**38.13 N**	**34.17 E**	**3253**	**Stratovolc**	**0103-002**	**Holocene**							
GOLLU DAG (Turkey-C)	**38.25 N**	**34.57 E**	**2143**	**Lava dome**	**0103-003**	**Holocene**							
ACIGOL-NEVSEHIR (Turkey-C)	**38.57 N***	**34.52 E**	**1689**	**Maars**	**0103-004**	**Holocene**							
ERCIYES DAGI (Turkey-C)	**38.52 N**	**35.48 E**	**3916**	**Stratovolc**	**0103-01=**	**Holocene**							
						? **0253<**	....		....	....	-x-- ---- ?--- ---- ----		
KARACALIDAG (Turkey-E)	**37.67 N**	**39.83 E**	**1957**	**Shield**	**0103-011**	**Holocene**							
NEMRUT DAGI (Turkey-E)	**38.65 N**	**42.02 E**	**3050**	**Stratovolc**	**0103-02=**	**Historical**							
						V **-7769?**	....		....	....	---- ---- x--- ---- ----		
						V **-7579?**	....		....	....	---- ---- x--- ---- ----		
						V **-7087?**	....		....	....	---- ---- x--- ---- ----		
						V **-6471?**	....		....	....	---- ---- x--- ---- ----		
						V **-6213?**	....		....	....	---- ---- x--- ---- ----		
						V **-5745?**	....		....	....	---- ---- x--- ---- ----		
						V **-5320?**	....		....	....	---- ---- x--- ---- ----		
						V **-5152?**	....		....	....	---- ---- x--- ---- ----		
						V **-5085?**	....		....	....	---- ---- x--- ---- ----		
						V **-4849?**	....		....	....	---- ---- x--- ---- ----		
						V **-4615?**	....		....	....	---- ---- x--- ---- ----		
						V **-4321?**	....		....	....	---- ---- x--- ---- ----		
						V **-1662?**	....		....	....	---- ---- x--- ---- ----		
						V **-1396?**	....		....	....	---- ---- x--- ---- ----		
						V **-0531?**	....		....	....	---- ---- x--- ---- ----		
						V **1402?**	....		....	....	---- ---- x--- ---- ----		
North flank (Nemrut Boynu)						**1441**	....		....	....	--x- ---- x--- x--- ----		
SUPHAN DAGI (Turkey-E)	**38.92 N**	**42.82 E**	**4434**	**Stratovolc**	**0103-021**	**Holocene**							
GIREKOL (Turkey-E)	**39.17 N**	**43.33 E**		**Unknown**	**0103-022**	**Holocene**							
TENDURUK DAGI (Turkey-E)	**39.33 N**	**43.83 E**	**3584**	**Shield**	**0103-03=**	**Holocene**							
ARARAT, MT. (Turkey-E)	**39.70 N**	**44.28 E**	**5165**	**Stratovolc**	**0103-04-**	**Holocene**							
KARS PLATEAU (Turkey-E)	**40.75 N***	**42.90 E**	**3000**	**Volc field**	**0103-05-**	**Holocene?**							
						? **1450**t	....		....	....	---- ---- ---- ---- ----	2?	
						? **1959**	07		....	....	x--- ---- --?- ---- ----	2	

CAUCASUS & ARMENIA

VOLCANO NAME (Subregion) / ERUPTION — Area of Activity	LAT	LONG	ELEV (m)	TYPE	NUMBER	Status / Start Year	Start M-Dy	P	Stop Year	Stop M-Dy	ERUPTIVE CHARACTERISTICS	VEI	Vol L/T
ELBRUS (Russia-SW)	**43.33 N**	**42.45 E**	**5633**	**Stratovolc**	**0104-01-**	**Tephrochronology**							
						T **0050**t	....		....	....	---- ---- x--- x--- ----		
KASBEK (Georgia)	**42.70 N**	**44.50 E**	**5050**	**Stratovolc**	**0104-02-**	**Tephrochronology**							
						C **-4000**t	....		....	....	---- ---- ---- x--- ----		
						T **-0750**t	....		....	....	---- ---- ---- ---- ----		
KABARGIN OTH GROUP (Georgia)	**42.55 N***	**44.00 E**	**3650**	**Cinder cones**	**0104-03-**	**Holocene**							
UNNAMED (Georgia)	**42.45 N***	**44.25 E**	**3750**	**Cinder cones**	**0104-04-**	**Holocene**							
UNNAMED (Georgia)	**41.55 N***	**43.60 E**	**3400**	**cones**	**0104-05-**	**Holocene**							
ARAGATS (Armenia)	**40.55 N**	**44.12 E**	**4090**	**Stratovolc**	**0104-06-**	**Holocene**							
AGMAGAN-KARADAG (Armenia)	**40.275 N***	**44.75 E**	**3560**	**Volc field**	**0104-07-**	**Holocene**							
DAR-ALAGES (Armenia)	**39.70 N***	**45.542 E**	**3329**	**Unknown**	**0104-08-**	**Holocene**							

Africa & Red Sea (02)

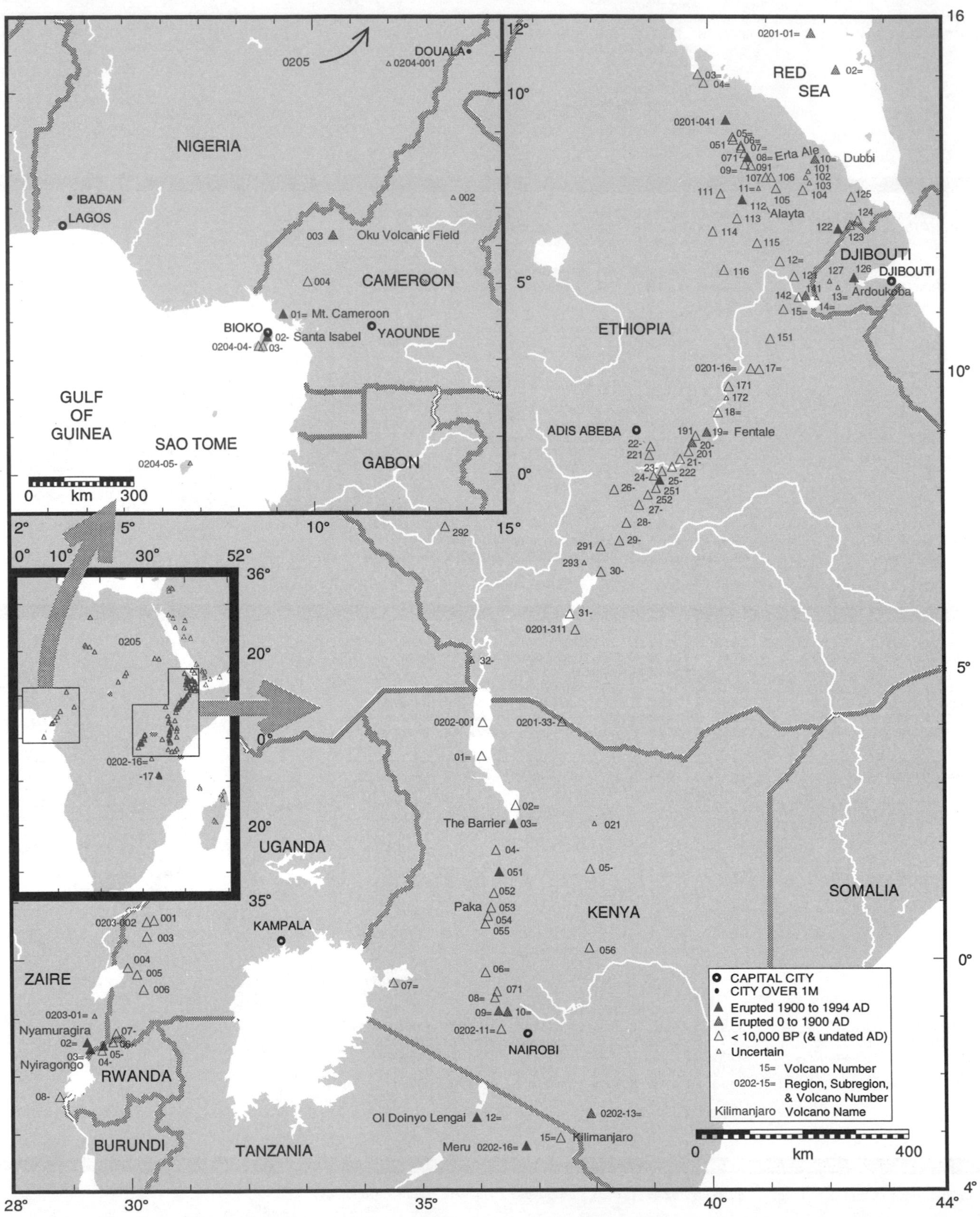

Africa is the only region other than the Mediterranean with an historically dated BC eruption (at Mt Cameroon, observed by a passing Carthaginian navigator in the 5th century BC). By the 15th century AD, however, when Portuguese exploration of Africa had begun and Vasco de Gama sailed to India via the Cape of Good Hope, only 2 more eruptions had been recorded, both from Ethiopia. In the next 3 ⅔ centuries, another 20 some eruptions were recorded, but the main historical record of the continent began with the opening of the Suez Canal at the end of 1869, and the heyday of African exploration that followed. Four-fifths of the region's 136 historical eruptions are since 1870.

Most African volcanoes result from hotspots, the rifting in E Africa, or a combination of the two. The East African rift, one of the world's most dramatic extensional structures, has produced the continent's highest and lowest volcanoes, ranging from massive Kilimanjaro to vents in Ethiopia's Danakil Depression that lie below sea level. Two neighboring volcanoes in Zaire's Virunga National Park, Nyamuragira and Nyiragongo, are responsible for nearly two-fifths of Africa's historical eruptions.

Africa has the highest percentage of volcanoes that are undated but known to be Holocene, reflecting the early stage of detailed geologic studies. The continent has the most volcanic centers with pyroclastic cones and fissure vents (as primary features), many of which lie within the East African Rift. It also has many shields, but the most common edifice type, as with 13 other regions, is the stratovolcano (cinder cones are more abundant in many areas, but are commonly grouped as a single volcanic field). The continent, however, has recorded relatively few large (VEI ≥4) eruptions in the Holocene (and 3 of these 4 were BC). Africa leads the world in lava lake production, with 9% of its eruptions – all at Nyiragongo and Erta Ale – having exhibited this uncommon characteristic.

VOLCANO NAME (Subregion) / ERUPTION — Area of Activity	LAT	LONG	ELEV (m)	TYPE	NUMBER	Status / Start Year	Start M-Dy	P	Stop Year	Stop M-Dy	Central, Flank vent, Radial fiss, Regional*	Submarine, New island, Subglacial, Crater lake	Explosive, Pyro flow, Phreatic, Fumarolic	Lava flow, Lava lake, Dome, Spine	Fatal, Damage, Mudflow, Tsunami	VEI	Vol L/T
ETHIOPIA & RED SEA																	
TEYR, DJEBEL (Red Sea)	15.70 N	41.742 E	244	Stratovolc	0201-01=	Historical											
						1750t	....		....	....	----	----	x---	----	----	2	
						1833	1231y		....	....	----	----	x---	----	----	2	
						1863	....		....	....	----	----	?---	----	----	2	
						1883	....		....	....	----	----	?---	----	----	2	
ZUBAYR, JEBEL (Red Sea)	15.08 N	42.17 E	191	Shield	0201-02=	Historical											
Saddle Island						1824	....		....	....	----	----	x---	----	----	2	
Saddle Island						? 1846	0814		....	....	----	----	?--?	----	----	2	
JALUA (Ethiopia)	15.042 N	39.82 E	713	Stratovolc	0201-03=	Holocene											
ALID (Ethiopia)	14.88 N	39.92 E	904	Stratovolc	0201-04=	Holocene											
DALLOL (Ethiopia)	14.242 N	40.30 E	-48	Expl crater	0201-041	Historical											
						1926	....		....	....	----	----	--x-	----	----	1	
GADA ALE (Ethiopia)	13.975 N	40.408 E	287	Stratovolc	0201-05=	Holocene											
CATHERINE (Ethiopia)	13.92 N	40.42 E	100	Tuff ring	0201-051	Holocene											
ALU (Ethiopia)	13.82 N	40.55 E	429	Fissure vents	0201-06=	Holocene											
DALAFFILLA (Ethiopia)	13.792 N	40.55 E	613	Stratovolc	0201-07=	Holocene											
BORALE ALE (Ethiopia)	13.725 N	40.60 E	668	Stratovolc	0201-071	Holocene											
ERTA ALE (Ethiopia)	13.60 N	40.67 E	613	Shield	0201-08=	Historical											
						? 1873	....		....	....	----	----	?---	----	----	2	
						? 1903	....		....	....	----	----	?---	----	----	2	
						? 1904	1101r		....	....	----	----	?---	----	----	2	
						1906	05		....	....	x---	----	?---	?x--	----	0	
						1940	....		....	....	x---	----	----	-x--	----	0	
						1960	01		....	....	x-x-	----	----	x---	----	0	
						1967<	....		1993>	....	x---	----	----	xx--	----	0	
ALE BAGU (Ethiopia)	13.52 N	40.63 E	1031	Stratovolc	0201-09=	Holocene											
HAYLI GUBBI (Ethiopia)	13.50 N	40.72 E	521	Shield	0201-091	Holocene											
DUBBI (Ethiopia)	13.58 N	41.808 E	1625	Stratovolc	0201-10=	Historical											
						1400	0715q		....	....	x---	----	x---	x---	----		
						1861	0508		1861	09 ?	x---	----	x---	x---	xx--	3	
						? 1863	....		....	....	----	----	?---	----	----	2	
						? 1900?	....		....	....	----	----	----	x---	----		
NABRO (Ethiopia)	13.37 N	41.70 E	2218	Stratovolc	0201-101	Holocene?											
MALLAHLE (Ethiopia)	13.27 N	41.65 E	1875	Stratovolc	0201-102	Holocene?											
SORKALE (Ethiopia)	13.18 N	41.725 E	1611	Stratovolc	0201-103	Holocene?											
ASAVYO (Ethiopia)	13.07 N	41.60 E	1200	Shield	0201-104	Holocene											
MAT ALA (Ethiopia)	13.10 N	41.15 E	523	Shield	0201-105	Holocene											
TAT ALI (Ethiopia)	13.28 N	41.07 E	700	Shield	0201-106	Holocene											
BORAWLI (Ethiopia)	13.30 N	40.98 E	812	Stratovolc	0201-107	Holocene											
AFDERA (Ethiopia)	13.08 N	40.85 E	1295	Stratovolc	0201-11=	Holocene?											
MA ALALTA (Ethiopia)	13.02 N	40.20 E	1815	Stratovolc	0201-111	Holocene											
ALAYTA (Ethiopia)	12.88 N	40.57 E	1501	Shield	0201-112	Historical											
						1907	06		1907	0804>	---x	----	x---	x---	xx--	2	
						1915	....		....	....	----	----	x---	----	----		
DABBAHU (Ethiopia)	12.60 N	40.48 E	1442	Stratovolc	0201-113	Holocene											
DABBAYRA (Ethiopia)	12.38 N	40.07 E	1302	Shield	0201-114	Holocene											
HARARO MANDA (Ethiopia)	12.17 N	40.82 E	600	Fissure vents	0201-115	Holocene											
GROPPO (Ethiopia)	11.73 N	40.25 E	930	Stratovolc	0201-116	Holocene											
KURUB (Ethiopia)	11.88 N	41.208 E	625	Stratovolc	0201-12=	Holocene											
BORAWLI COMPLEX (Ethiopia)	11.63 N	41.45 E	875	Lava domes	0201-121	Holocene											
MANDA-INAKIR (Ethiopia)	12.38 N	42.20 E	600	Fissure vents	0201-122	Historical											
Kammourta						1928	1231y		....	....	---x	----	x---	x---	----		
MOUSA ALLI (Ethiopia)	12.47 N	42.40 E	2028	Stratovolc	0201-123	Holocene											
GUFA (Ethiopia)	12.55 N*	42.53 E	600	Volc field	0201-124	Holocene											
ASSAB VOLC FIELD (Ethiopia)	12.95 N*	42.43 E	987	Volc field	0201-125	Holocene											
ARDOUKOBA (Djibouti)	11.58 N*	42.47 E	298	Fissure vents	0201-126	Historical											
						1978	1107		1978	1114	---x	----	x---	xx--	----	1	7/-
TIHO (Djibouti)	11.53 N	42.05 E	500	Fumarole fld	0201-127	Pleistocene-Fumarolic											
GARBES (Djibouti)	11.42 N	42.20 E	1000	Fumarole fld	0201-13=	Pleistocene-Fumarolic											
BOINA (Djibouti)	11.25 N	41.83 E	300	Fumarole fld	0201-14=	Pleistocene-Fumarolic											
DAMA ALI (Ethiopia)	11.28 N	41.63 E	1068	Shield	0201-141	Holocene											
						@ 1631	0214?		....	....	----	----	x---	----	----		
ASMARA (Ethiopia)	11.27 N	41.52 E	500	Pyrocl cone	0201-142	Holocene											
GABILLEMA (Ethiopia)	11.08 N	41.27 E	1459	Stratovolc	0201-15=	Holocene											
YANGUDI (Ethiopia)	10.58 N	41.042 E	1383	Complx volc	0201-151	Holocene											
AYELU (Ethiopia)	10.082 N	40.702 E	2145	Stratovolc	0201-16=	Holocene											
						? 1928	....		....	....	----	----	?---	----	----	2	
ADWA (Ethiopia)	10.070 N	40.840 E	1733	Stratovolc	0201-17=	Holocene											
						? 1828	....		....	....	----	----	?---	----	----	2	
						? 1928	....		....	....	----	----	?---	----	----	2	
HERTALI (Ethiopia)	9.78 N	40.33 E	900	Fissure vent	0201-171	Holocene											
LIADO HAYK FIELD (Ethiopia)	9.57 N*	40.28 E	878	Maars	0201-172	Holocene?											
DOFEN (Ethiopia)	9.35 N	40.13 E	1151	Stratovolc	0201-18=	Holocene											
FENTALE (Ethiopia)	8.975 N	39.93 E	2007	Stratovolc	0201-19=	Historical											
						1250t	....		....	....	----	----	----	x---	-x--		
Caldera floor and SW flank						1820?	....		....	....	---x	----	----	x---	----	0	
BERU (Ethiopia)	8.95 N	39.75 E	1100	Unknown	0201-191	Holocene											

VOLCANO NAME (Subregion) / ERUPTION — Area of Activity	LAT	LONG	ELEV (m)	TYPE	NUMBER	Status / Start Year	Start M-Dy	P	Stop Year	Stop M-Dy	Central / Flank vent / Radial fiss / Regional*	Submarine / New island / Subglacial / Crater lake	Explosive / Pyro flow / Phreatic / Fumarolic	Lava flow / Lava lake / Dome / Spine	Fatal / Damage / Mudflow / Tsunami	VEI	Vol L/T
KONE (Ethiopia)	**8.80 N**	**39.692 E**	**1619**	**Calderas**	**0201-20-**	**Historical**											
East caldera margin						**1820**j	....		....	....	x---	----	x---	x---	----	1	
UNNAMED (Ethiopia)	**8.70 N***	**39.63 E**	**1300**	**Pyrocl cones**	**0201-201**	**Holocene**											
BOSET-BERICHA (Ethiopia)	**8.558 N**	**39.475 E**	**2447**	**Stratovolcs**	**0201-21-**	**Holocene**											
BISHOFTU FIELD (Ethiopia)	**8.78 N***	**38.98 E**	**1850**	**Fissure vents**	**0201-22-**	**Holocene**											
UNNAMED (Ethiopia)	**8.62 N***	**38.95 E**	**1800**	**Fissure vents**	**0201-221**	**Holocene**											
SODORE (Ethiopia)	**8.43 N***	**39.35 E**	**1765**	**Pyrocl cones**	**0201-222**	**Holocene**											
GEDAMSA Caldera (Ethiopia)	**8.35 N**	**39.18 E**	**1984**	**Caldera**	**0201-23-**	**Holocene**											
BORA-BERICCIO COMPLEX (")	**8.27 N**	**39.03 E**	**2285**	**Pumice cones**	**0201-24-**	**Holocene**											
TULLU MOJE (Ethiopia)	**8.158 N**	**39.13 E**	**2349**	**Pumice cone**	**0201-25-**	**Anthropology**											
Giano						A **1775**q	....		....	....	----	----	----	----	----		
Wonji fault belt, SE of Lake Koka						**1900**?	....		....	....	---x	----	x---	x---	-x--		
UNNAMED (Ethiopia)	**8.07 N***	**39.07 E**	**1800**	**Fissure vents**	**0201-251**	**Holocene**											
UNNAMED (Ethiopia)	**7.95 N***	**38.93 E**	**1889**	**Fissure vents**	**0201-252**	**Holocene**											
BUTAJIRI-SILTI FIELD (Ethiopia)	**8.05 N***	**38.35 E**	**2281**	**Fissure vents**	**0201-26-**	**Holocene**											
ALUTU (Ethiopia)	**7.77 N**	**38.78 E**	**2335**	**Stratovolc**	**0201-27-**	**Holocene**											
SHALA (Ethiopia)	**7.47 N**	**38.55 E**	**2075**	**Stratovolc**	**0201-28-**	**Holocene**											
CORBETTI Caldera (Ethiopia)	**7.18 N**	**38.43 E**	**2320**	**Caldera**	**0201-29-**	**Holocene**											
(fumarolic activity only)						X 1957	....		X1964	....	----	----	---x	----	----		
BILATE RIVER FIELD (Ethiopia)	**7.07 N***	**38.10 E**	**1700**	**Volc field**	**0201-291**	**Holocene**											
TEPI (Ethiopia)	**7.42 N***	**35.43 E**	**2728**	**Shield**	**0201-292**	**Holocene**											
HOBICHA Caldera (Ethiopia)	**6.78 N**	**37.83 E**	**1800**	**Caldera**	**0201-293**	**Holocene?**											
CHIRACHA (Ethiopia)	**6.65 N**	**38.12 E**	**1650**	**Stratovolc**	**0201-30-**	**Holocene**											
TOSA SUCHA (Ethiopia)	**5.92 N***	**37.57 E**	**1650**	**Cinder cones**	**0201-31-**	**Holocene**											
UNNAMED (Ethiopia)	**5.65 N***	**37.67 E**	**1200**	**Cinder cones**	**0201-311**	**Holocene**											
KORATH RANGE (Ethiopia)	**5.10 N***	**35.88 E**	**912**	**Tuff cones**	**0201-32-**	**Holocene?**											
MEGA BASALT FIELD (Ethiopia/Kenya)	**4.08 N***	**37.42 E**	**1067**	**Pyrocl cones**	**0201-33-**	**Holocene**											

AFRICA - KENYA TO ZAIRE

VOLCANO NAME (Subregion) / ERUPTION — Area of Activity	LAT	LONG	ELEV (m)	TYPE	NUMBER	Status / Start Year	Start M-Dy	P	Stop Year	Stop M-Dy	Central / Flank vent / Radial fiss / Regional*	Submarine / New island / Subglacial / Crater lake	Explosive / Pyro flow / Phreatic / Fumarolic	Lava flow / Lava lake / Dome / Spine	Fatal / Damage / Mudflow / Tsunami	VEI	Vol L/T
NORTH ISLAND (Kenya)	**4.07 N**	**36.05 E**	**520**	**Tuff cones**	**0202-001**	**Holocene**											
CENTRAL ISLAND (Kenya)	**3.50 N**	**36.042 E**	**550**	**Stratovolc**	**0202-01=**	**Holocene**											
East side of Central Island						? **1974**	0722?		?**1974**	0727a	----	----	--?x	----	----		
SOUTH ISLAND (Kenya)	**2.63 N**	**36.600 E**	**700**	**Stratovolc**	**0202-02=**	**Historical**											
						1888	....		....	....	x---	----	x---	----	----		
MARSABIT (Kenya)	**2.32 N**	**37.97 E**	**1707**	**Shield**	**0202-021**	**Holocene?**											
BARRIER, THE (Kenya)	**2.32 N**	**36.57 E**	**1032**	**Shield**	**0202-03=**	**Historical**											
North flank (Teleki's Volcano)						M **1030**w	....		....	....	-x--	----	----	x---	----	0	
North flank (Teleki's Volcano)						M **1050**w	....		....	....	-x--	----	----	x---	----	0	
North flank (Teleki's Volcano)						M **1090**t	....		....	....	-x--	----	----	x---	----	0	
North flank (Teleki's Volcano)						**1871**c	....		....	....	-x--	----	x---	x---	----	2	
North flank (Teleki's Volcano)						**1888**	....		....	....	-xx-	----	----	x---	----	0	
North flank (Teleki's Volcano)						**1895**	....		....	....	-x--	----	x---	x---	----	2	
North flank (Teleki) and Likaiyu						**1897**	05 <		....	....	xx--	----	x---	----	----	2?	
Andrew's or Teleki's Volcanoes						? **1906**	....		....	....	-x--	----	----	----	----		
Andrew's or Teleki's Volcanoes						**1917**	....		....	....	-x--	----	x---	----	----	2	
South flank (Andrew's Volcano)						? **1920**c	....		....	....	-x--	----	?---	----	----		
North flank (Teleki)						**1921**	1231y		....	....	-x--	----	x---	x---	----	2	
NAMARUNU (Kenya)	**1.90 N**	**36.27 E**	**817**	**Shield**	**0202-04-**	**Tephrochronology**											
Lower eastern flanks						T **-6550***	....		....	....	-x--	----	?---	?---	----		
SEGERERUA PLATEAU (Kenya)	**1.57 N***	**37.90 E**	**699**	**Pyrocl cones**	**0202-05-**	**Holocene**											
EMURUANGOGOLAK (Kenya)	**1.50 N**	**36.33 E**	**1328**	**Shield**	**0202-051**	**Radiocarbon**											
North flank						C **-8050***	....		....	....	-x--	----	----	x---	----		
North flank						T **-6550***	....		....	....	-x--	----	x---	x---	----		
North flank						M **1115**w	....		....	....	-x--	----	----	x---	----	0	
NE flank						M **1160**w	....		....	....	-x--	----	----	x---	----	0	
NE flank						M **1230**w	....		....	....	-x--	----	----	x---	----	0	
NE flank						M **1300**w	....		....	....	-x--	----	----	x---	----	0	
South caldera rim						C **1700**v	....		....	....	x---	----	----	x---	----	0	
South caldera rim						M **1910**t	....		....	....	x---	----	----	x---	----	0	
SILALI (Kenya)	**1.15 N**	**36.23 E**	**1528**	**Shield**	**0202-052**	**Ar/Ar**											
Upper east flank						R **-7050***	....		....	....	-x--	----	----	x-x-	----		
Eastern part of caldera						R **-6050***	....		....	....	x---	----	----	x---	----		
Upper east flank						R **-5050***	....		....	....	-x--	----	----	x-x-	----		
PAKA (Kenya)	**0.92 N**	**36.18 E**	**1697**	**Shield**	**0202-053**	**Ar/Ar**											
						R **-6050***	....		....	....	x---	----	xx--	----	--x-	C	
KOROSI (Kenya)	**0.77 N**	**36.12 E**	**1446**	**Shield**	**0202-054**	**Holocene**											
OL KOKWE (Kenya)	**0.63 N**	**36.08 E**	**1130**	**Shield**	**0202-055**	**Holocene**											
NYAMBENI HILLS (Kenya)	**0.23 N**	**37.87 E**	**750**	**Shield**	**0202-056**	**Holocene**											
MENENGAI (Kenya)	**0.20 S**	**36.07 E**	**2278**	**Shield**	**0202-06=**	**Tephrochronology**											
						T **-7350***	....		....	....	x---	----	x-x-	----	----		
HOMA MOUNTAIN (Kenya)	**0.38 S**	**34.50 E**	**1751**	**Complx volc**	**0202-07=**	**Holocene**											
ELMENTEITA BADLANDS (Kenya)	**0.52 S***	**36.27 E**	**2126**	**Pyrocl cones**	**0202-071**	**Holocene**											
EBURRU, OL DOINYO (Kenya)	**0.63 S**	**36.23 E**	**2856**	**Complx volc**	**0202-08=**	**Holocene**											
OLKARIA (Kenya)	**0.904 S***	**36.292 E**	**2434**	**Pumice cones**	**0202-09=**	**Radiocarbon**											
Olubutot						C **1770**t	....		....	....	--x-	----	xx--	x---	----		
LONGONOT (Kenya)	**0.92 S**	**36.45 E**	**2776**	**Shield**	**0202-10=**	**Anthropology**											
						C **-7200**v	....		....	....	----	----	x---	----	----		
						C **-1330**v	....		....	....	----	----	x---	----	----		
Northern flank						A **1863**e	....		....	....	-x--	----	----	?---	----	0	7/-
SUSWA (Kenya)	**1.175 S**	**36.35 E**	**2356**	**Shield**	**0202-11=**	**Holocene**											
LENGAI, OL DOINYO (Tanzania)	**2.751 S**	**35.902 E**	**2890**	**Stratovolc**	**0202-12=**	**Historical**											
						T **-1550***	....		....	....	----	----	x---	----	----		
						T **-0050?**	....		....	....	----	----	x---	----	----		
						T **0700?**	....		....	....	----	----	x---	----	----		
						T **1350?**	....		....	....	----	----	x---	----	----		
North Crater						**1880**	12		....	....	x---	----	x---	----	----	2	
North Crater						**1882**	....		**1883**	....	x---	----	----	----	----	2	
(fumarolic activity only)						X 1894	....		....	....	----	----	---x	----	----		
(fumarolic activity only)						X 1904	....		....	....	x---	----	---x	----	----		
North Crater						**1914**	0815x		**1915**	....	x---	----	----	x---	----	0	
North Crater						**1916**	1201p		**1917**	06	x---	----	x---	x---	-x--	3*	
North Crater						**1921**	02		....	....	x---	----	x---	----	--x-	2	
North Crater						**1926**	....		....	....	x---	----	x---	----	----	2	

VOLCANO NAME (Subregion) / ERUPTION — Area of Activity	LAT	LONG	ELEV (m)	TYPE	NUMBER	Status / Start Year	Start M-Dy	P	Stop Year	Stop M-Dy	Central / Flank vent / Radial fiss / Regional*	Submarine / New island / Subglacial / Crater lake	Explosive / Pyro flow / Phreatic / Fumarolic	Lava flow / Lava lake / Dome / Spine	Fatal / Damage / Mudflow / Tsunami	VEI	Vol L/T
LENGAI, OL DOINYO *continued*																	
North Crater						**1940**	0724	+	**1941**	02	x---	----	x-x-	----	-xx-	3*	
North Crater						**1954**	0726e		**1954**	09	x---	----	x---	----	----	2	
North Crater						**1955**	0119		**1955**	0120	x---	----	x---	----	----	2	
North Crater						**1958**	0206<		....	....	x---	----	x---	?---	----	1	
North Crater						**1960**	03 <	+	**1966**	1128p	x---	----	x---	x---	-x--	3*	
North Crater						**1967**	0708		**1967**	0904	x---	----	x---	----	----	3	
						? **1969**	07 ?		....	....	x---	----	?---	----	----		
(1974 eruption report incorrect)						X 1974	08		X1974	09	----	----	----	----	----		
North Crater						**1983**	0101		**1993>**	....	x---	----	x---	xx--	----	2*	
CHYULU HILLS (Kenya)	**2.68**	**S* 37.88**	**E 2188**	**Volc field**	**0202-13=**	**Anthropology**											
Umani						C **1470**x	....		....	....	----	----	----	x---	----		
Shaitani and Chaimu						A **1855**e	....		....	....	x---	----	x---	x---	----	2	
KILIMANJARO (Tanzania)	**3.07**	**S 37.35**	**E 5895**	**Stratovolc**	**0202-15=**	**Holocene**											
MERU (Tanzania)	**3.25**	**S 36.75**	**E 4565**	**Stratovolc**	**0202-16=**	**Historical**											
Meru caldera						C **-5850**?	....		....	....	x---	----	x---	----	--x-	C	
Dome NW of Ash Cone						**1878**a	....		....	....	x---	----	x---	x---	----	2	
Dome NW of Ash Cone						**1886**?	....		....	....	x---	----	----	x---	----	0	
Ash Cone						**1910**	1026	+	**1910**	1222	x---	----	x---	----	----	2	
IGWISI HILLS (Tanzania)	**4.87**	**S* 31.92**	**E**	**Tuff cones**	**0202-161**	**Holocene**											
UNNAMED (Tanzania)	**8.63**	**S 33.57**	**E**	**Pyrocl cone**	**0202-162**	**Holocene**											
SW USANGU BASIN (Tanzania)	**8.75**	**S* 33.80**	**E 2179**	**Volc field**	**0202-163**	**Holocene**											
NGOZI (Tanzania)	**8.97**	**S 33.57**	**E 2622**	**Caldera**	**0202-164**	**Holocene**											
IZUMBWE-MPOLI (Tanzania)	**8.93**	**S 33.40**	**E 1568**	**Pyrocl cones**	**0202-165**	**Holocene**											
RUNGWE (Tanzania)	**9.13**	**S 33.67**	**E 2961**	**Stratovolc**	**0202-166**	**Holocene**											
KIEYO (Tanzania)	**9.23**	**S 33.78**	**E 2175**	**Stratovolc**	**0202-17=**	**Historical**											
Sarabwe and Fiteko						**1800**?	....		....	....	x---	----	x---	x---	xx--	2	
RUSEKERE (Uganda)	**0.73**	**N 30.38**	**E 1615**	**Tuff cones**	**0203-001**	**Holocene**											
FORT PORTAL FIELD (Uganda)	**0.70**	**N* 30.25**	**E 1524**	**Tuff cones**	**0203-002**	**Holocene**											
KYATWA VOLC FIELD (Uganda)	**0.45**	**N* 30.25**	**E 1430**	**Tuff cones**	**0203-003**	**Holocene**											
KATWE-KIKORONGO FIELD (")	**0.08**	**S* 29.92**	**E 1067**	**Tuff cones**	**0203-004**	**Holocene**											
BUNYARUGURU FIELD (Uganda)	**0.20**	**S* 30.08**	**E 1554**	**Expl craters**	**0203-005**	**Holocene**											
KATUNGA (Uganda)	**0.47**	**S 30.18**	**E 1707**	**Tuff cone**	**0203-006**	**Holocene**											
MAY-YA-MOTO (Zaire)	**0.93**	**S 29.33**	**E 950**	**Fumarole fld**	**0203-01=**	**Fumarolic**											
NYAMURAGIRA (Zaire)	**1.408**	**S 29.20**	**E 3058**	**Shield**	**0203-02=**	**Historical**											
						G **1550**v	....		....	....	x?--	----	----	?---	----		
						1865	....		....	....	----	----	----	----	----		
North flank						**1882**	....		....	....	-x--	----	----	----	----		
						1894	06		....	....	x---	----	x---	x---	----	2	
						1896	....		....	....	----	----	x---	----	----	1	
NNW fissure zone						**1899**	02		....	....	-xx-	----	x---	x---	----	1	
East flank (Singiro)						**1901**	....		....	....	-x--	----	x---	x---	----	2	7/6
SSE fissure zone						**1902**	0422?		....	....	-xx-	----	----	x---	----	0	
SW flank (Nahimbi)						**1904**	04		**1904**	0516?	-x--	----	x---	x---	----	2	7/7
East flank (Kanamaharagi)						**1905**	0722		**1905**	0925>	-x--	----	x---	x---	----	2	7/7
Summit caldera						? **1906**	....		....	....	x---	----	x---	----	----	1	
Summit caldera						**1907**	04		**1907**	05	x---	----	x---	----	----	1	
Summit caldera						**1907**	1107		**1907**	1205	x---	----	x---	----	----	3	
Summit caldera						**1908**	....		....	....	x---	----	?---	----	----		
Summit caldera						**1909**	05		**1909**	05	x---	----	?-?-	----	----	1?	
SW flank (Rumoka), and summit						**1912**	1203	+	**1913**	04	xx--	----	x---	x---	xx--	3	7/7
SSW flank (Lake Kivu)						**1920**	....		....	....	--x-	---x	?---	----	----	0	
Caldera						**1921**	....		**1938**	0117c	x---	----	x---	xx--	----	0	8/-
Summit, SE and SW flanks (Tshambene)						**1938**	0128		**1940**	0625e	xxx-	----	x-x-	xx--	-x-x	1	8/-
SW flank (Gituro, Muhuboli), N flank						**1948**	0301		**1948**	0715e	-xx-	----	x---	xx--	----	2	7/7
SW flank (Gituro)						**1951**	0725		**1951**	0728	-x--	----	x---	----	----	1	-/4
NNW fissure zone (Shabubembe-Ndakaza)						**1951**	1116		**1952**	0116	xxx-	----	x---	xx--	----	2	7/5
SSE fissure zone (Mihaga)						**1954**	0221		**1954**	0528	-xx-	----	x---	x---	----	1	7/6
Summit caldera and NNW fissure zone						**1956**	1117		**1956**	1118	x-x-	----	x---	x---	----	1	5/4
Summit caldera and SSE fissure zone						**1957**	1228		....	....	x-x-	----	----	x---	----	0	6/-
North flank (Kitsimbanyi), NNW rift						**1958**	0807	+	**1958**	1121	-xx-	----	x---	x---	----	2	7/6
North flank (Gakararanga)						**1967**	0423		**1967**	0509	-xx-	----	x---	x---	----	2	7/7
WNW flank (Rugarama)						**1971**	0324		**1971**	0505d	-x--	----	x---	x---	-x--	3	7/7
SSW flank (Murara and Harakandi)						**1976**	1223	+	**1977**	0615e	-xx-	----	x---	xx--	----	1	7/7
North flank (Gasenyi)						**1980**	0130		**1980**	0224	-xx-	----	x---	x---	-x--	3	7/7
SE flank (Rugarambiro)						**1981**	1225		**1982**	0114	-xx-	----	x---	x---	-x--	3	7/7
NW flank (Kivandimwe)						**1984**	0223		**1984**	0314	-xx-	----	x---	x---	-x--	2	7/7
South flank (near Kitazungurwa)						**1986**	0716		**1986**	0820	-x-x	----	x---	xx--	-x--	2	7/7
North Flank (Gafuranindi)						**1987**	1230		**1988**	0104	--x-	----	x---	x---	----	1	6/6
Summit, SE and East flank						**1989**	0424	+	**1989**	0815e	xxx-	----	x---	x---	----	3	7/7
NE flank (Mikombe)						**1991**	0920		**1993**	0208	--x-	----	x---	x---	-x--	3*	
NYIRAGONGO (Zaire)	**1.52**	**S 29.25**	**E 3469**	**Stratovolc**	**0203-03=**	**Historical**											
Southern pit						**1884**	....		....	....	x---	----	x---	----	----	1	
(probably Nyiragongo)						@ **1891**<	....		....	....	x---	----	----	----	----		
						1894	....		....	....	x---	----	----	-x--	----	1	
						1898	....		....	....	x---	----	----	----	----	1	
						1899	....		....	....	x---	----	x---	----	----	1	
						1900	....		....	....	x---	----	x---	----	----	1	
						1901	....		....	....	x---	----	x---	----	----	1	
						1902	....		....	....	x---	----	----	----	----	1	
						1905	....		....	....	x---	----	----	-x--	----	1	
						1906	....		....	....	x---	----	----	----	----	1	
Southern craters						? **1908**	1201p		....	....	?---	----	----	----	----		
Southern pit						**1911**	08		**1911**	10	x---	----	----	----	----	1	
						1918	....		....	....	x---	----	----	-x--	----	1	
						1920	....		**1921**	....	x---	----	x---	----	----	1	
						1927	03		**1977**	0110	x---	----	----	xx--	----	1	
North, south, and west flanks						**1977**	0110		**1977**	0110	x-x-	----	x---	x---	xx--	1	7/4
						1982	0621		**1982**	1017m	x---	----	--x-	xx--	----	1	7/-
KARISIMBI (Zaire/Rwanda)	**1.50**	**S 29.45**	**E 4507**	**Stratovolc**	**0203-04-**	**Holocene**											
VISOKE (Zaire/Rwanda)	**1.47**	**S 29.492**	**E 3711**	**Stratovolc**	**0203-05-**	**Historical**											
						@ **1891**	....		....	....	----	----	----	----	----		
11 km north of summit (Mugogo)						**1957**	0801		**1957**	0803	-x--	----	x---	x---	----	1	5/5
MUHAVURA (Uganda/Rwanda)	**1.38**	**S 29.67**	**E 4127**	**Stratovolc**	**0203-06-**	**Holocene**											
BUFUMBIRA (Uganda)	**1.23**	**S* 29.72**	**E 2440**	**Cinder cones**	**0203-07-**	**Holocene**											
TSHIBINDA (Zaire)	**2.32**	**S* 28.75**	**E 1460**	**Cinder cones**	**0203-08-**	**Holocene**											

VOLCANO NAME (Subregion) / ERUPTION — Area of Activity	LAT	LONG	ELEV (m)	TYPE	NUMBER	Status / Start Year	Start M-Dy	P	Stop Year	Stop M-Dy	Central / Flank vent / Radial fiss / Regional*	Submarine / New island / Subglacial / Crater lake	Explosive / Pyro flow / Phreatic / Fumarolic	Lava flow / Lava lake / Dome / Spine	Fatal / Damage / Mudflow / Tsunami	VEI	Vol L/T
AFRICA - W & N																	
BIU PLATEAU (Nigeria)	**10.75 N***	**12.00 E**		**Volc field**	**0204-001**	**Holocene?**											
NGAOUNDERE PLATEAU (Cameroon)	**7.25 N***	**13.67 E**		**Volc field**	**0204-002**	**Holocene?**											
OKU VOLC FIELD (Cameroon)	**6.25 N***	**10.50 E**	**3011**	**Maars**	**0204-003**	**Radiocarbon**											
Lake Nyos						C **1550**v	....		....	....	x---	----	xxx-	----	----	3	-/7
Lake Nyos						? **1986**	0821		?**1986**	1230?	----	---?	--?-	----	xx--		
MANENGOUBA (Cameroon)	**5.03 N**	**9.83 E**	**2411**	**Stratovolc**	**0204-004**	**Holocene**											
CAMEROON, MT. (Cameroon)	**4.203 N**	**9.170 E**	**4095**	**Stratovolc**	**0204-01=**	**Historical**											
						-0450t	....		....	....	----	----	?---	?---	-?--	3	
						1650t	....		....	....	----	----	?---	----	----	3↑	
South flank (2600 m)						**1807**h	....		....	....	-x--	----	x---	x---	----	3	
						1825j	....		....	....	----	----	?---	----	----	2	
Near Fako						**1838**	1231y		....	....	----	----	x---	x---	----	2	
West flank						**1852**	....		....	....	-x--	----	x---	x---	----	2	
						1865	....		....	....	x---	----	x---	----	----	2	
						1866	01 ?		....	....	----	----	?---	----	----	2	
SW flank (2250 m) and NW flank						**1868**	....		....	....	-x--	----	x---	----	----	2	
						1871	....		....	....	----	----	?---	----	----	2	
NE flank (Okoli Craters)						**1909**	0428		**1909**	06 ?	-x--	----	x---	x---	----	2	
Mateer (W, 3300 m), Waldau (SW flank)						**1922**	0203	+	**1922**	0824	-x--	----	x---	x---	-x--	2	7/-
Near Fako						**1925**	....		....	....	x---	----	----	----	----		
						1954	0628		**1954**	0726	x---	----	x-x-	x---	----	2	
NE flank (1500 m)						**1959**	0123		**1959**	0319	-x--	----	x---	x---	-x--	2	
SW flank (2500 m)						**1982**	1016		**1982**	1112	--x-	----	x---	x---	-xx-	2	7/5
SANTA ISABEL (Bioko)	**3.58 N***	**8.75 E**	**3007**	**Shield**	**0204-02-**	**Historical**											
SE flank						**1898**?	....		....	....	-x--	----	----	----	----		
SE flank, near Bahu						**1903**	....		....	....	-x--	----	----	----	----		
SE flank						**1923**	....		....	....	-x--	----	----	----	----		
SAN JOAQUIN (Bioko)	**3.35 N***	**8.63 E**	**2009**	**Shield**	**0204-03-**	**Holocene**											
SAN CARLOS (Bioko)	**3.35 N***	**8.52 E**	**2260**	**Shield**	**0204-04-**	**Holocene**											
SAO TOME (Africa-W)	**0.32 N***	**6.72 E**	**2024**	**Shield**	**0204-05-**	**Holocene?**											
HARUJ (Libya)	**27.25 N***	**17.50 E**	**1200**	**Scoria cones**	**0205-00-**	**Holocene**											
TOH, TARSO (Chad)	**21.33 N***	**16.33 E**	**2000**	**Volc field**	**0205-001**	**Holocene**											
TOUSSIDE, TARSO (Chad)	**21.03 N**	**16.45 E**	**3265**	**Stratovolc**	**0205-01=**	**Holocene**											
VOON, TARSO (Chad)	**20.92 N**	**17.28 E**	**3100**	**Stratovolc**	**0205-02=**	**Fumarolic**											
KOUSSI, EMI (Chad)	**19.80 N**	**18.53 E**	**3415**	**Stratovolc**	**0205-021**	**Holocene**											
MARRA, JEBEL (Sudan)	**12.95 N**	**24.27 E**	**3042**	**Volc field**	**0205-03-**	**Radiocarbon**											
Deriba caldera						G **-2000**?	....		....	....	x---	----	x---	----	----	C	
KUTUM VOLC FIELD (Sudan)	**14.50 N***	**25.80 E**		**Scoria cones**	**0205-04-**	**Holocene?**											
MEIDOB VOLC FIELD (Sudan)	**15.13 N***	**26.17 E**	**1000**	**Scoria cones**	**0205-05-**	**Holocene**											
BAYUDA VOLC FIELD (Sudan)	**18.33 N***	**32.75 E**		**Cinder cones**	**0205-06-**	**Radiocarbon**											
						C **0850**t	....		....	....	----	----	----	x---	----		
UMM MARAFIEB, JEBEL (Sudan)	**18.20 N***	**33.80 E**		**Scoria cones**	**0205-07-**	**Holocene?**											

Mid-East & Indian Ocean (03)

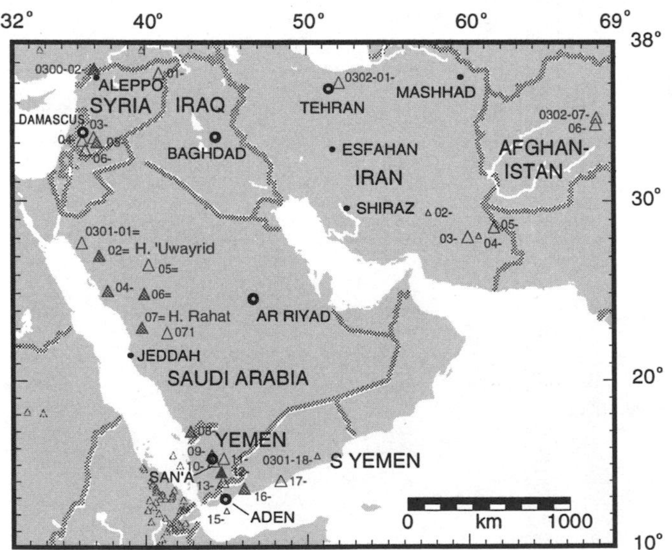

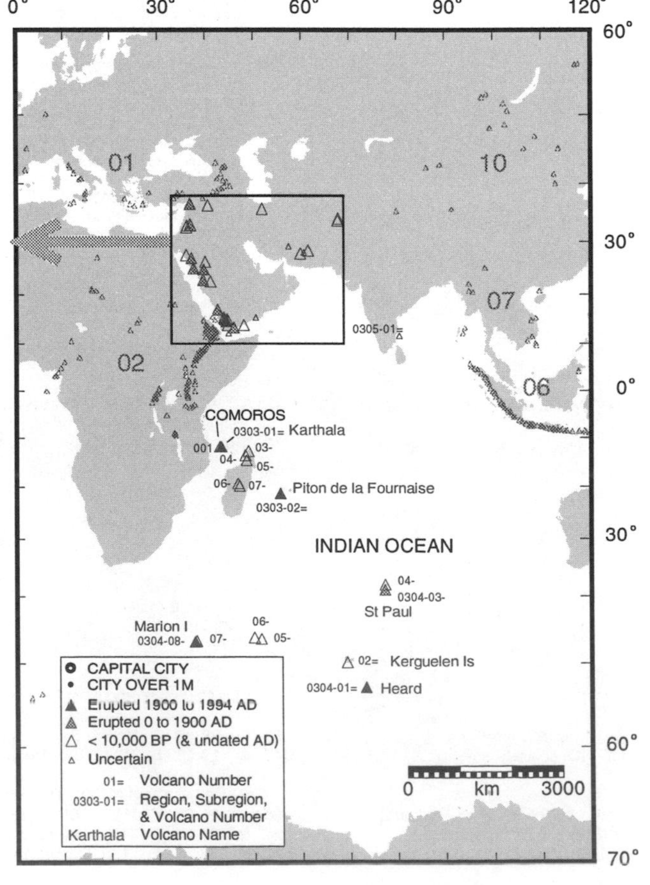

This region is a mixture of island hotspot volcanoes (in the Indian Ocean) and continental, rift-influenced volcanoes (from Saudi Arabia and Syria to western Afghanistan). The Comoros Islands and Reunion dominate the eruption record (93% of dated events) in contrast to the Middle Eastern volcanoes that dominate volcano listings (>60% of the region), population, and land area (both 99%).

The early historical record extends back to the 5th century AD. The region's earliest recorded eruption, a 9 km-long lava flow, bears the date 0500 AD (±100) and, like the next 7, was from the Middle East, where the new religion of Islam unified Arabia in the 7th century. The first reported eruption of the region's most active volcano, Piton de la Fournaise on the island of Reunion, was not until the 17th century, and by then half of the 14 historically active volcanoes in the region had recorded their first known eruptions. All were from the Middle East, with the exception of an account written in the 10th to 12th centuries describing a summit eruption on Grand Comore island. In the last few centuries, though, the Indian Ocean has dominated the volcanic record of the region.

Reunion was known to the Arabs and visited by the Portuguese in the early 1500s. The first of its 153 known eruptions was in 1640, and France claimed the island around 1662. It has been French virtually continuously since then. Settlers moved in from 1715, and 600,000 people now live on the 2510 km^2 island. A modern volcano observatory was established there in 1980.

The Comoros were controlled by Moslem Sultans until acquired by the French in the latter half of the last century. After the early eruption mentioned above (1050 AD ±150) no further reports are known until the early 19th century. The Comoros became a French overseas territory in 1947 and declared independence in 1975.

Madagascar's first settlers are believed to have arrived in the 5th century, but no historical eruptions are known from their youthful volcanoes. The French settled in 1626, and the island became a colony in 1896. The independent Malagasy Republic was declared in 1960, but ended in a 1972 coup, and the island is again called Madagascar.

The Kerguelen Archipelago was first visited in 1772 and has been occupied since 1950 by a small research station staff. Uninhabited neighboring islands St. Paul and Amsterdam are also Overseas Territories of France. The glacier-covered and unoccupied island of Heard is owned by Australia, and Marion Island belongs to South Africa. A small research station is maintained on Marion.

Fully 98% of region 03's dated eruptions have been historically documented, a proportion exceeded only by Indonesia. This region and Antarctica are distinguished by having no known eruptions of substantial size (VEI ≥4 or ≥1 km^3 of lava).

Iran's volcanoes have been moved from Region 01 to this region since our 1981 first edition, along with the recently recognized volcanoes of Afghanistan. Iran was not included in the original *CAVW* regions and clearly caused a problem for the *CAVW* editors (it was published as a separate appendix to the "Turkey and Caucasus" volume, 2 years after publication of the "Arabia and the Indian Ocean" volume). In 1981 we placed the volcanoes of Syria (not covered by *CAVW*) in region 03 because of the unbroken connection of young, eastern Mediterranean volcanics with the Arabian volcanoes. Following recognition of Holocene centers in Afghanistan, we think it makes geographic and geologic sense to include them with Iran in a broad "Middle East" grouping extending east from the Mediterranean and south into the Indian Ocean.

03

VOLCANO NAME (Subregion) / ERUPTION — Area of Activity	LAT	LONG	ELEV (m)	TYPE	NUMBER	Status / Start Year	Start M-Dy	P	Stop Year	Stop M-Dy	ERUPTIVE CHARACTERISTICS (Central, Flank vent, Radial fiss, Regional* / Submarine, New island, Subglacial, Crater lake / Explosive, Pyro flow, Phreatic, Fumarolic / Lava flow, Lava lake, Dome, Spine / Fatal, Damage, Mudflow, Tsunami)	VEI	Vol L/T
SYRIA													
SHARAT KOVAKAB (Syria)	36.53 N*	40.85 E	534	Volc field	0300-01-	Holocene							
UNNAMED (Syria)	36.67 N	37.00 E		Unknown	0300-02-	Historical							
						1222	....		....	....	---- ---- ---- x--- ----	0?	
UNNAMED (Syria)	33.308 N*	36.925 E	945	Volc field	0300-03-	Holocene							
UNNAMED (Syria)	33.15 N*	36.258 E	1197	Volc field	0300-04-	Holocene							
ES SAFA (Syria)	33.08 N*	37.15 E		Volc field	0300-05-	Historical							
Jabal Druse						1850j	....		....	....	---- ---- ---- -x-- ----	0	
UNNAMED (Syria)	32.658 N*	36.425 E	1436	Volc field	0300-06-	Holocene							
ARABIA													
RAHAH, HARRAT AR (Saudi Arabia)	27.80 N*	36.17 E	1660	Volc field	0301-01=	Anthropology							
'UWAYRID, HARRAT (Saudi Arabia)	27.08 N*	37.25 E	1900	Volc field	0301-02=	Anthropology							
Hala-'l-Bedr, Hala-'l-'Ishqua or both						A 0640?	....		....	....	---- ---- x--- x--- xx--	2?	
LUNAYYIR, HARRAT (Saudi Arabia)	25.17 N*	37.75 E	1370	Volc field	0301-04-	Historical							
						1000<	....		....	....	---- ---- ---- x--- ----		
ITHNAYN, HARRAT (Saudi Arabia)	26.58 N*	40.20 E	1625	Volc field	0301-05=	Holocene							
KHAYBAR, HARRAT (Saudi Arabia)	25.00 N*	39.92 E	2093	Volc field	0301-06=	Historical							
Harrat Lali						0650t	....		....	....	---- ---- ?--- ?--- ----	2?	
RAHAT, HARRAT (Saudi Arabia)	23.08 N*	39.78 E	1744	Volc field	0301-07=	Historical							
West of Madinah						0641	....		....	....	---x ---- x--- ---- ----	2	
Fissure 20 km SE of Madinah						1256	0605		1256	0727?	---x ---- x--- x--- ----	3	8/-
Near Madinah						? 1292	....		....	....	---- ---- ---- ?--- ----		
KISHB, HARRAT (Saudi Arabia)	22.80 N*	41.38 E	1475	Volc field	0301-071	Holocene							
YAR, JABAL (Saudi Arabia)	17.05 N*	42.83 E	305	Volc field	0301-08-	Historical							
						1810j	....		....	....	---- ---- ?--- ?--- ----	2	
ARHAB, HARRA OF (Yemen)	15.63 N*	44.08 E	3100	Volc field	0301-09-	Historical							
East flank of Jabal Zebib						A 0200>	....		....	....	-x-- ---- x--- x--- -x--	2?	
South flank of Kaulet Hattab						0500v	....		....	....	-x-- ---- ---- x--- -x--	0	
MARHA, JABAL EL- (Yemen)	15.28 N	44.22 E	2650	Tuff cone	0301-10-	Holocene							
HAYLAN, JABAL (Yemen)	15.43 N*	44.78 E	1550	Volc field	0301-11-	Anthropology							
West of Sirwan						A -1200>	....		....	....	---- ---- ---- x--- ----	0?	
DHAMAR, HARRAS OF (Yemen)	14.57 N*	44.67 E	3500	Volc field	0301-12-	Historical							
Near the town of Dhamar						1937	....		....	....	---- ---- ?--- ---- ----	2	
HAMMAN DEMT, JABAL (Yemen)	14.05 N	44.75 E		Cone	0301-13-	Anthropology							
NAR, JABAL AN (Yemen)	13.33 N	43.73 E			0301-14-	Not a Volcano							
UNNAMED (Gulf of Aden)	12.25 N	45.00 E		Submarine	0301-15-	Uncertain							
SAWAD, HARRA ES- (South Yemen)	13.58 N*	46.12 E	1737	Volc field	0301-16-	Historical							
						1253	....		....	....	---- ---- ?--- ---- ----	3	
BAL HAF, HARRA OF (South Yemen)	14.05 N*	48.33 E	233	Volc field	0301-17-	Holocene							
BIR BORHUT (South Yemen)	15.55 N*	50.63 E		Volc field	0301-18-	Holocene?							
						? 0950?	....		....	....	---- ---- ?--- ?--- ----		
ORMUS ISLANDS (Oman-E of)	26.00 N	56.50 E			0301-19-	Not a Volcano							
(earthquake uplift?, not eruption)						X 1945	12		....	....	---- ---- ---- ---- ----		
IRAN & AFGHANISTAN													
DAMAVAND (Iran-N)	35.951 N	52.109 E	5670	Stratovolc	0302-01-	Holocene							
QAL'EH HASAN ALI (Iran-SE)	29.40 N*	57.57 E		Maars	0302-02-	Holocene?							
BAZMAN (Iran-SE)	28.07 N	60.00 E	3490	Stratovolc	0302-03-	Fumarolic							
UNNAMED (Iran-SE)	28.17 N*	60.67 E		Volc field	0302-04-	Holocene?							
TAFTAN (Iran-SE)	28.60 N	61.60 E	4050	Stratovolc	0302-05-	Holocene							
(unconfirmed press reports)						? 1993	0425		....	....	---- ---- ---- ?--- ----		
DACHT-I-NAVAR GROUP (Afghan.)	33.95 N*	67.92 E	3800	Lava domes	0302-06-	Holocene							
VAKAK GROUP (Afghanistan)	34.25 N*	67.97 E	3190	Volc field	0302-07-	Holocene							

VOLCANO NAME (Subregion) / ERUPTION — Area of Activity	LAT	LONG	ELEV (m)	TYPE	NUMBER	Status		Start Year	Start M-Dy	P	Stop Year	Stop M-Dy	Central vent / Flank vent / Radial fiss / Regional*	Submarine / New island / Subglacial / Crater lake	Explosive / Pyro flow / Phreatic / Fumarolic	Lava flow / Lava lake / Dome / Spine	Fatal / Damage / Mudflow / Tsunami	VEI	Vol L/T
INDIAN OCEAN																			
GRILLE, LA (Indian O.-W)	**11.47 S**	**43.33 E**	**1087**	**Shield**	**0303-001**	**Holocene**													
KARTHALA (Indian O.-W)	**11.75 S**	**43.38 E**	**2361**	**Shield**	**0303-01=**	**Historical**													
								1050w	....		....	....	----	----	?---	?---	----		
								1808	....		....	....	----	----	----	----	----		
								1814	1231y		....	....	----	----	----	----	----		
								1821	1231y		....	....	----	----	----	----	----		
								1828	05		....	....	-x--	----	x---	----	----	2?	
								1830	....		....	....	-?--	----	x---	----	----	2?	
Summit caldera ?								**1833**	....		....	....	?---	----	----	----	----		
SE flank								**1848**	....		....	....	--x-	----	----	x---	----	0	
West-SW flank (400 m)								**1850**?	....		....	....	--x-	----	----	x---	----	0	
SE flank								**1855**	0701p		....	....	-xx-	----	x---	x---	-x--	2	
SE flank (Badjini Massif) & summit								**1857**	....		....	....	x-x-	----	x---	x---	----	2	
Upper NE flank (2200 m)								**1858**	....		....	....	-xx-	----	x---	x---	----	2	
NW flank (Diboini Plateau fissures)								**1859**	....		....	....	--x-	----	x---	x---	----	2	
SE flank (Badjini Massif, 1200 m)								**1860**	1229		....	....	--x-	----	----	x---	----	0	
(date perhaps confused with 1860)							?	**1862**	....		....	....	-x--	----	x---	x---	----	2	
								1865	....		....	....	-?--	----	?---	----	----	2?	
NW flank (Diboini Plateau)								**1872**	....		....	....	-xx-	----	x---	x---	----	2	
SE flank (Badjini Massif)								**1876**	....		....	....	-xx-	----	----	x---	-x--	0	
SE flank (Badjini Massif)								**1880**	....		....	....	--x-	----	x---	x---	----	2	
SE flank								**1883**	03		**1884**	....	-xx-	----	x---	x---	xx--	2	
North flank (1300 m)								**1904**	0225		**1904**	04	--x-	----	x---	x---	xx--	2	
North flank (1300 m)								**1910**	03		**1910**	03	--x-	----	x---	----	----	1	
NE flank, Changomeni, NE Chahale								**1918**	0811	+	**1918**	0826	x-x-	----	x-x-	x---	----	3*	
								1928b	....		....	....	x---	----	----	----	----	1?	
Cheminee Nord (Changomeni)								**1948**	0422	+	**1948**	0616	x?--	----	x---	-x--	----	2	
Chahale crater								**1952**	0210?		**1952**	0212	x---	---x	x---	----	----	2	
Chahale crater								**1956**	0601?		....	....	x---	----	?---	?---	----	2?	
Between Changomeni & Chahale Craters								**1965**	0712		**1965**	0712	x---	----	x---	xx--	----	2?	5/-
North end of summit crater								**1972**	0908		**1972**	1005	x---	----	x---	xx--	----	1	6/-
SW flank								**1977**	0405		**1977**	0410	--x-	----	x---	x---	-x--	1	6/5
Choungou-Chahale Crater								**1991**	0711		**1991**	0711	x---	----	x-x-	----	----	2	
FOURNAISE, PITON DE LA (Reunion)	**21.229 S**	**55.713 E**	**2631**	**Shield**	**0303-02=**	**Historical**													
								1640	....		....	....	----	----	x---	x---	----	2	
								1649	....		....	....	----	----	x---	x---	----	2	
								1669	....		....	....	----	----	x---	x---	----	2	
								1671	....		....	....	----	----	x---	x---	----	2	
								1672	....		....	....	----	----	x---	x---	----	2	
								1703<	....		**1705**	....	----	----	----	x---	----	0	
NE rift zone								**1708**	04		**1708**	04	--x-	----	----	x---	----	0	7/-
								1709	....		....	....	----	----	?---	x---	----	2	
								1721	06		....	....	----	----	x---	----	----	2	
L'Enclos and NE rift zone								**1733**?	....		....	....	--x-	----	----	x---	-x--	0	
								1734	0101		**1734**	0306	----	----	----	x---	----	2	
								1734	12		**1734**	12	----	----	----	x---	----	2	
								1751	06		**1751**	06	----	----	x---	x---	----	2	
								1753	....		....	....	----	----	--x-	x---	----	2	
								1759	....		....	....	----	----	----	----	----		
								1760	1215		**1760**	1229	----	----	x-x-	----	----	2	
								1766	03	+	**1766**	0526e	x---	----	x-x-	?-x-	----	2	
Formica Leo								**1768**	....		....	....	-x--	----	x---	x---	----	2	
								1771	....		....	....	----	----	?---	----	----		
								1772	02		....	....	x---	----	x---	----	----	2	
								1772	1118		....	....	x---	----	x---	x---	----	2	
SE rift zone								**1774**	....		....	....	--x-	----	----	x---	-x--	0	7/-
								1775	....		....	....	----	----	x---	x---	----	2	
SE rift zone (Piton Takamaka)								**1776**	....		....	....	--x-	----	----	x---	-x--	0	6/-
								1784	....		**1785**	....	x---	----	x---	----	----	2	
								1786	0605?	+	**1786**	0804>	----	----	x---	x---	----	2	
Bory								**1787**	0614		**1787**	0801	x?--	----	x---	x---	----	2	7/-
								1789	06		**1789**	07	----	----	----	x---	----	2	
Dolomieu, Mamelon Central								**1791**	0605d		**1791**	0727?	x---	----	x-x-	x-x-	----	2*	7/-
								1792	1219?		....	....	----	----	----	x---	----	0	
								1794	01		**1794**	01	----	----	----	x---	----	0	
								1795	....		....	....	----	----	----	?---	----		
								1797?	....		....	....	----	----	----	x---	----	0	
SE rift zone								**1800**	1102		**1800**	1108	--x-	----	----	x---	----	0	7/-
								1801	1027	+	**1802**	0428g	x---	----	x-x-	x---	----	2	
								1802	12		....	....	x---	----	----	x---	----	2	
								1807	0323	+	**1807**	0613	xx--	----	x---	x---	----	2	
								1809	0717		**1809**	0808	x---	----	x---	----	----	2	
								1810	1120	+	**1810**	1128	x---	----	x---	----	----	2	
Summit and above Piton de Crac								**1812**	0805d	+	**1812**	12	xx--	----	x-x-	x---	----	2	
								1813	0926	+	**1813**	1126	x---	----	x---	x---	----	2	
								1814	0910	+	**1814**	1013	x---	----	x---	x---	----	2	
								1815	0121		**1815**	0127	x---	----	x---	----	----	2	
Summit and Plaine des Osmondes								**1815**	0815		**1815**	0816	xx--	----	x---	x---	----	2	
								1816	1215		....	....	xx--	----	----	x---	----	0	
								1817	01		**1817**	04	x---	----	----	----	----	0	
NW rift zone								**1820**	01		**1820**	02	--x-	----	x---	x---	----	2	
								1821	0227		**1821**	0410	x---	----	x-x-	x---	----	2	
								1824	02		....	....	----	----	----	x---	----	0	
								1824	12		....	....	----	----	----	x---	----	0	
Cratere Faujas								**1830**	10		....	....	-x--	----	----	x---	----	0	
L'Enclos and NE rift zone								**1832**	03		....	....	--x-	----	----	x---	----	0	
								1842	04		....	....	----	----	----	x---	----	0	
								1843	....		....	....	----	----	----	x---	----	0	
Summit and Piton de Crac								**1844**	0319		**1844**	0511	x-x-	----	x---	x---	----	2	
								1844	12		....	....	----	----	x---	x---	----	2	
								1845	....		....	....	----	----	----	x---	----	0	
								1846	....		....	....	----	----	----	x---	----	0	
								1847	....		....	....	----	----	----	x---	----	0	
								1848	....		....	....	----	----	----	x---	----	0	
								1849	....		....	....	----	----	----	x---	----	0	
								1850	1103		**1850**	1112	----	----	----	x---	----	0	

VOLCANO NAME (Subregion) ...... **LAT** **LONG** **ELEV (m)** **TYPE** **NUMBER** **Status**

FOURNAISE, PITON DE LA *continued*

ERUPTION — Area of Activity		Start Year	Start M-Dy	P	Stop Year	Stop M-Dy	Central / Flank vent / Radial fiss / Regional*	Submarine / New island / Subglacial / Crater lake	Explosive / Pyro flow / Phreatic / Fumarolic	Lava flow / Lava lake / Dome / Spine	Fatal / Damage / Mudflow / Tsunami	VEI	Vol L/T
Bruland, l'Enclos Velain		**1851**	....		....	....	x---	----	----	-x--	----	0	
Brulant		**1852**	....		....	....	x---	----	----	-x--	----	0	
		1858	1103		**1859**	01	x---	----	x---	x---	-x--	2	7/-
		1859	0508	+	**1859**	0523>	x---	----	x---	x---	----	2	
Dolomieu and l'Enclos		**1860**	0122	+	**1860**	0320	x-x-	----	x-x-	x---	----	2	-/5
Brulant		**1861**	0319		**1861**	0319	x---	----	x---	----	----	2	
		1863	1220		**1864**	0129	x---	----	----	x---	-x--	0	
		1865	0205		**1865**	0210	x---	----	x---	x---	----	2	
		1868	03		....	....	----	----	----	x---	-x--	0	
		1869?	....		....	....	----	----	----	?---	----	2?	
	?	**1870**	0201p		....	....	----	----	----	?---	----	0	
		1871	0621		**1871**	0705	x---	----	----	x---	----	0	
	?	**1872**	0201p		....	....	----	----	----	?---	----	0	
		1874	0201p		....	....	----	----	----	----	----		
		1874	0629	+	**1874**	1107>	x---	----	x-x-	x---	----	2	
		1875	1126	+	**1875**	1211?	----	----	----	x---	----	0	
		1876	1211		**1876**	1211?	----	----	----	?---	----		
		1878	0314		**1878**	0330	-x--	----	----	x---	----	0	
	?	**1882**	....		....	....	----	----	----	?---	----	0	
		1884	0204		**1884**	0205	----	----	----	x---	----	0	
Grandes Pentes and summit		**1889**	06	+	**1889**	0811>	xx--	----	x---	x---	-x--	2	
Summit, Grandes Pentes		**1890**	02	+	**1891**	0204	xx--	----	x-x-	x---	-x--	2	
		1894	08		....	....	----	----	----	x---	-x--	2	
		1897	0105d		**1897**	0124	--x-	----	----	x---	----	0	
		1898	0114		**1898**	0120	----	----	----	x---	----	2	
		1898	1126		....	....	x---	----	x---	x---	----	2	
		1899	0213	+	**1899**	0718>	xxx-	----	x---	x---	-x--	2	
East of Dolomieu		**1900**	0511		**1900**	0530	-x--	----	----	x---	----	0	
East of Dolomieu		**1901**	0221		**1901**	0225	-x--	----	----	x---	----	2	
NE flank (above Piton de Crac)		**1901**	0704		**1901**	0706	-x--	----	x---	x---	----	2	
		1902	0813		**1902**	0818	x-x-	----	x---	x---	----	2	
		1903?	....		....	....	----	----	----	x---	----	0	
NE flank (above Piton de Crac)		**1904**	0819	+	**1904**	1017	-x--	----	x---	x---	----	2	
		1905	0215		**1905**	0216	x---	----	x-x-	x---	----	2	
		1907	1129		**1907**	1205d	-x--	----	----	x---	----	0	
	?	**1908**	....		....	....	----	----	----	?---	----	0	
East of Cratere Faujas		**1909**	04		....	....	-x--	----	x---	x---	----	2	
		1910	1116		**1910**	1212	-x--	----	x---	x---	----	2	
		1913	0710		**1913**	0803	--x-	----	x---	x---	----	2	
Summit, N and NE of Crater Velain		**1915**	0722	+	**1915**	1121	xx--	----	x---	x---	----	2	
NE flank (above Piton de Crac)		**1917**	0429		**1917**	0429	-x--	----	----	x---	----	0	
		1920	0628	+	**1920**	1018	-x--	----	----	x---	----	0	
		1921	1127		**1921**	1203	xx--	----	?---	x---	----	2	
		1924	0519		**1924**	0523>	----	----	----	x---	----	0	
		1924	0903		**1924**	0913	x---	----	?---	x---	----	2	
		1925	1230	+	**1926**	0420	?-x-	----	x---	x---	----	2	
North flank		**1926**	0918	+	**1927**	0615	--x-	----	----	x---	----	2	
		1929	1223		**1929**	1231	xx--	----	x---	x---	----	2	
		1930	0523		**1930**	0524	x---	----	----	x---	----	0	
Summit, NE flank (Cratere Haug)		**1931**	0122	+	**1931**	0826e	xxx-	----	x---	x---	-x--	2	8/-
		1932	11		**1932**	11	----	----	----	----	----		
Dolomieu, upper and SE flanks		**1933**	0607	+	**1934**	0401	xx--	----	x---	x---	----	2	
		1935?	....		....	....	----	----	x---	----	----	2	
Near 1933 crater		**1936**	09		....	....	--x-	----	----	x---	----	0	
Bory, flanks of Bory and Dolomieu		**1937**	0813	+	**1937**	1125	x-x-	----	x---	x---	----	2	6/-
		1938	0725		**1938**	0729	-x--	----	x---	x---	----	1	
ESE and SW flanks, Dolomieu		**1938**	1207	+	**1939**	0115	xxx-	----	x---	x---	-x--	2	7/-
		1941?	....		....	....	----	----	x---	----	----	1	
Bory, rim of Dolomieu		**1942**	1005		**1942**	1025	x-x-	----	x---	x---	----	2	6/-
SE of Dolomieu, lower Grandes Pentes		**1943**	0330?		**1943**	0526e	-xx-	----	x---	x---	-x--	2	7/-
		1944	0411		**1944**	0501	-x--	----	x---	x---	----	2	
SE flank near Nez Coupe du Tremblet		**1945**	0415		**1945**	0506	xx--	----	x---	x---	----	2	6/-
Dolomieu crater and upper flanks		**1946**	0618		**1946**	0705	xx--	----	x---	x---	----	2	6/-
Dolomieu, Grand Brule		**1947**?	....		....	....	x-x-	----	x---	x---	----	2	
South flank (le Chateau Fort)		**1948**	0214		**1948**	0308	-x--	----	x---	x---	----	2	6/-
	?	**1949**	10		....	....	-?--	----	?---	?---	----	2	
South flank (2080 m)		**1950**	0225		**1950**	0402	-xx-	----	x---	x---	----	2	6/-
SE of Bory		**1950**	0830		**1950**	0905	-x--	----	x---	?---	----	2	
North part of Grand Brule	?	**1951**	06		....	....	-x--	----	----	x---	----	0	
		1951	0910		**1951**	0920	-x--	----	x---	----	----	1	
NE flank near north rim (1500 m)		**1952**	0519		**1952**	0720	-x--	----	x---	x---	----	2	6/-
South, NW & N flanks, Dolomieu, Bory		**1953**	0313	+	**1953**	0708	-xx-	----	x---	x---	----	2	7/-
		1954	01		**1954**	12	-x--	----	----	----	----		
Dolomieu, Bory, S, SE & ESE flanks		**1955**	0706	+	**1957**	0316	xxx-	----	x---	x-x-	-x--	2*	7/-
Bory, N of Bory, NE of Dolomieu		**1957**	0902	+	**1957**	1116	xxx-	----	x---	x---	----	2	6/-
Dolomieu		**1958**	0530	+	**1958**	0920	xx--	----	x---	x---	----	2	
Bory		**1959**	0311	+	**1959**	0806	x---	----	x---	x---	----	2	6/-
Bory, south flank (2030 m)		**1960**	0111	+	**1960**	0310	xxx-	----	x---	x---	----	2	6/-
NE flank (east of Cratere Picard)		**1961**	0405		**1961**	0425	-x--	----	----	x---	-x--	0	7/-
Dolomieu, upper east flank (2410 m)		**1963**	1107		**1963**	1121	x-x-	----	x---	----	----	2	-/7
Dolomieu, upper east and NE flanks		**1964**	0430		**1964**	0508	x-x-	----	x---	x---	----	2	
East flank (1930 m)		**1964**	1221		**1965**	0215	-xx-	----	x---	x---	----	2?	7/-
SE flank (Cratere Maillard, 2400 m)		**1966**	0315		**1966**	0515	--x-	----	x---	x---	----	2?	7/-
South, ENE, north and SE of Dolomieu		**1972**	0609	+	**1972**	1210	-xx-	----	x---	xx--	----	2	7/5
		1973	0108		**1973**	0116	----	----	----	x---	----	0	
Dolomieu (SSW wall)		**1973**	0510	+	**1973**	0905	x---	----	x---	x---	----	2	5/-
Dolomieu and SE flank (1320-2350 m)		**1975**	1104	+	**1976**	0406	-xx-	----	x---	xx--	-x--	1	7/5
North of Dolomieu (2250-2330 m)		**1976**	1102		**1976**	1104	--x-	----	x---	x---	----	1	5/4
NE and SE of Dolomieu, NE rift zone		**1977**	0324	+	**1977**	0416	--x-	----	x---	x---	-x--	0	6/-
ENE flank (2050-2200 m, 1850-1920 m)		**1977**	1024		**1977**	1117	-xx-	----	x---	x---	----	1	7/-
SE, SW and N flanks, Dolomieu & Bory		**1979**	0528	+	**1979**	0714	x-x-	----	x---	x---	----	1	5/-
Bory, SW, N & NW of Dolomieu		**1981**	0203	+	**1981**	0505	x-x-	----	x-x-	xx--	----	2	7/-
SSW flank of Dolomieu (2110-2300 m)		**1983**	1204	+	**1984**	0218	--x-	----	x---	x---	----	2	7/-
Dolomieu and flanks, SE rift zone		**1985**	0614	+	**1988**	1229	xxx-	----	x-x-	xx--	-x--	1	8/-
Dolomieu and SE flank		**1990**	0118	+	**1990**	0508	x-x-	----	----	x---	----	0	6/-
Dolomieu and upper east flank		**1991**	0719		**1991**	0720	--x-	----	----	x---	----	0	
Dolomieu and upper SE flank		**1992**	0827		**1992**	0923	--x-	----	----	x---	----	1	

AMBRE-BOBAOMBY (Madagascar).. **12.48 S* 49.10 E 1475 Volc field 0303-03- Holocene**

VOLCANO NAME (Subregion) / ERUPTION — Area of Activity	LAT	LONG	ELEV (m)	TYPE	NUMBER	Status / Start Year	Start M-Dy	P	Stop Year	Stop M-Dy	Central / Flank vent / Radial fiss / Regional	Submarine / New island / Subglacial / Crater lake	Explosive / Pyro flow / Phreatic / Fumarolic	Lava flow / Lava lake / Dome / Spine	Fatal / Damage / Mudflow / Tsunami	VEI	Vol L/T
NOSY-BE (Madagascar)	**13.32 S***	**48.48 E**	**214**	**Cinder cones**	**0303-04-**	**Holocene**											
ANKAIZINA FIELD (Madagascar)	**14.30 S***	**48.67 E**	**2878**	**Cinder cones**	**0303-05-**	**Holocene**											
ITASY VOLC FIELD (Madagascar)	**19.00 S***	**46.77 E**	**1800**	**Scoria cones**	**0303-06-**	**Radiocarbon**											
						C **-7130**v	....		....	....	----	----	x---	----	----		
						C **-6050**<	....		....	....	----	----	----	x---	----		
ANKARATRA FIELD (Madagascar)	**19.40 S***	**47.20 E**	**2644**	**Cinder cones**	**0303-07-**	**Holocene**											
HEARD (Indian O.-S)	**53.106 S**	**73.513 E**	**2745**	**Stratovolc**	**0304-01=**	**Historical**											
						? **1881**	0602		....	....	-x--	--x-	?--?	----	----	2	
Mawson Peak						**1910**	03		**1910**	04	x---	--x-	x---	----	----	2	
Mawson Peak						**1950**	0124		**1952**	0312?	x---	--x-	x---	x---	----	2	
Mawson Peak						**1953**	0820		**1953**	1118	x---	--x-	x---	----	----	2	
Mawson Peak						**1954**	0413?		**1954**	0613?	x---	--x-	x---	?---	----	2	
Mawson Peak						**1985**	0114		**1987**	01 ?	x---	--x-	x---	xx--	----	2?	
Mawson Peak						? **1992**	0117		?**1992**	0118	x---	----	?---	----	----		
Mawson Peak						**1992**	0529?		....	....	x---	----	----	----	----	0	
Mawson Peak						**1993**	0102m		....	....	x---	----	x---	x---	----	2?	
KERGUELEN ISLANDS (Indian O.-S)	**49.58 S**	**69.50 E**	**1840**	**Stratovolcs**	**0304-02=**	**Holocene**											
ST. PAUL (Indian O.-S)	**38.72 S**	**77.53 E**	**268**	**Stratovolc**	**0304-03=**	**Historical**											
SW flank (near Cape West)						**1793**	....		....	....	-x--	----	x---	----	----	2	
AMSTERDAM ISLAND (Indian O.-S)	**37.83 S**	**77.52 E**	**881**	**Stratovolc**	**0304-04-**	**Holocene**											
POSSESSION, ILE DE LA (")	**46.42 S**	**51.63 E**	**934**	**Stratovolc**	**0304-05-**	**Holocene**											
COCHONS, ILE AUX (Indian O.-S)	**46.10 S**	**50.23 E**	**775**	**Stratovolc**	**0304-06-**	**Holocene**											
PRINCE EDWARD ISLAND (")	**46.63 S**	**37.95 E**	**672**	**Shield**	**0304-07-**	**Holocene**											
MARION ISLAND (Indian O.-S)	**46.90 S**	**37.75 E**	**1230**	**Shields**	**0304-08-**	**Historical**											
E-W fissure from summit to W coast						**1980**	09 ?		....	....	-xx-	--x-	x---	x---	----	1	6/-
UNNAMED (Indian O.-E)	**11.75 N**	**80.75 E**		**Submarine ?**	**0305-01=**	**Uncertain**											
						? **1757**	....		....	....	----	??--	----	----	----	0	

New Zealand to Fiji (O4)

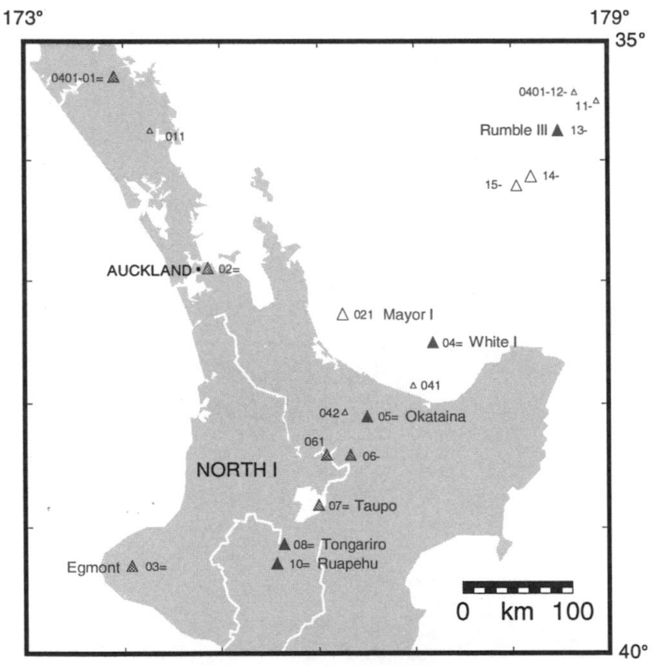

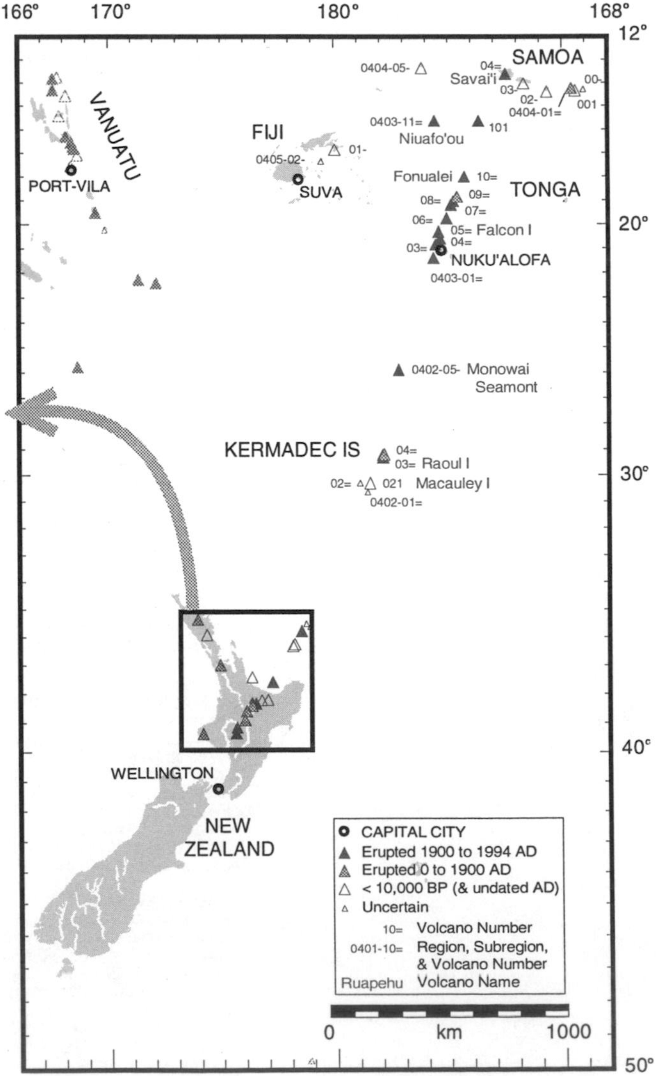

After the Indian Ocean, the *CAVW* regions begin a long clockwise circuit around the Pacific Rim starting with New Zealand. The Pacific's "Ring of Fire" has produced 66% of the world's Holocene volcanoes and 65% of its dated eruptions, largely by subduction of the huge Pacific plate and several smaller plates. The region introduced here is geographically small but volcanologically important. Its total land area is 292,000 km^2 (the size of Arizona) and its population is 4.4 million (the size of greater Philadelphia). New Zealand makes up 92% of the land area and 77% of the population.

Estimates of Maori arrival in New Zealand range from 800 AD to 1350 AD, and the first European to sight the islands was probably Tasman in 1642. Written records, however, were not kept until whalers started to land in the 1790s and detailed record-keeping began with the missionaries in the late 1810s. The earliest historically-dated eruption was at White Island in 1826. The first permanent settlement (Wellington) and the Maori treaty (ceding sovereignty to England) came in 1840. The Kermadec Islands, totaling 34 km^2 in area, were annexed to New Zealand in 1887, and a small research station is maintained there.

New Zealand contains the world's strongest concentration of youthful rhyolitic volcanoes, and voluminous ignimbrite sheets blanket much of North Island. Associated caldera formation places this region at the top of the list, along with Indonesia, of volcanoes with caldera as the primary morphologic feature. A strong emphasis on tephrochronology has documented the Quaternary volcanic history of this active island in unusual detail: No other region has a higher proportion (74%) of its large eruptions in the BC age range. In collaboration with New Zealand colleagues, we have reorganized the North Island volcanoes in an effort to achieve a closer genetic identification of each center (see introduction). This has resulted in a net reduction in volcano numbers for this region since our 1981 book.

The Kingdom of Tonga is an archipelago of two parallel island belts: that to the east is low, fertile, coralline, and well populated, while that to the west is young, volcanic, and ranges from steep cones to ephemeral islands. The unbroken line of subduction, from NZ through the Kermadecs and Tonga, ends abruptly and the trench swings west toward the remarkable, donut-shaped island of Niuafo'ou, a basaltic shield volcano with a large, lake-filled caldera. European contact with Tonga began in the 17th century and Captain Cook named them the Friendly Isles in 1773; the first recorded eruption was in the next year.

The Samoan islands are formed by a hotspot to the NE of the Tonga-Kermadec-NZ subduction zone, and are volcanically distinct from their neighbors. They were invaded by Fijians in the early 13th century, but may well have been settled thousands of years earlier. European contact was first made by the Dutch in 1722, but detailed record keeping began with the arrival of missionaries from London in 1830. The 1725 eruption of Savai'i, covering 190 km^2 with 2 km^3 of lava, was the first historical volcanism in region 04. In 1900 the islands were divided, with the smaller western islands going to the US and the larger, more populated, and more volcanic western islands going to Germany. New Zealand annexed Western Samoa and administered it from 1914 to 1962, when it became independent.

The two Holocene centers of Fiji form small islands NE and E of the two largest islands that support 90% of the population. The archipelago was populated for thousands of years by Polynesians, but the Dutch began European exploration in 1643, and it became a British crown colony in 1874 before achieving independence in 1970. Although not in the *CAVW* for Region 04, Fiji was added by us in 1981 upon recognition of its Holocene volcanism.

Much of the region north of New Zealand's North Island is made up of seamounts and small islands, including 16 submarine volcanoes. The region has the largest number of eruptions dated by SOFAR technology, or underwater sound. No other region has a higher proportion of eruptions building new islands (21%, all in Tonga and the Kermadecs) or producing pyroclastic flows (27%, mostly on New Zealand's North Island).

04

VOLCANO NAME (Subregion) / ERUPTION — Area of Activity	LAT	LONG	ELEV (m)	TYPE	NUMBER	Status	Start Year	Start M-Dy	P	Stop Year	Stop M-Dy	ERUPTIVE CHARACTERISTICS: Central / Flank vent / Radial fiss / Regional*	Submarine / New island / Subglacial / Crater lake	Explosive / Pyro flow / Phreatic / Fumarolic	Lava flow / Lava lake / Dome / Spine	Fatal / Damage / Mudflow / Tsunami	VEI	Vol L/T
NEW ZEALAND																		
KAIKOHE-BAY OF ISLANDS (N Zeal)	**35.30**	**S*173.90 E**	**388**	**Volc field**	**0401-01=**	**Radiocarbon**												
Te Puke						C	**0400y**	....		....	....	xx-x	----	x---	x---	----		
WHANGAREI (New Zealand)	**35.75**	**S*174.27 E**	**397**	**Cinder cones**	**0401-011**	**Holocene?**												
AUCKLAND FIELD (New Zealand)	**36.90**	**S*174.87 E**	**260**	**Volc field**	**0401-02=**	**Radiocarbon**												
Rangitoto						C	**1350?**	....		....	....	x---	----	x---	x---	----		9/-
MAYOR ISLAND (New Zealand)	**37.28**	**S 176.25 E**	**355**	**Shield**	**0401-021**	**Radiocarbon**												
SE caldera rim						C	**-6050u**	....		....	....	x---	----	x---	x---	----		
South end of caldera, Taratimi Bay						C	**-4390x**	....		....	....	xxx-	x---	xxx-	----	----	5	-/9
EGMONT (New Zealand)	**39.30**	**S 174.07 E**	**2518**	**Stratovolc**	**0401-03=**	**Radiocarbon**												
						T	**-6050?**	....		....	....	x---	----	xx--	x---	----		
						C	**-5020u**	....		....	....	x---	----	x---	----	--x-		
						T	**-3050?**	....		....	....	----	----	x---	----	----		
						T	**-2750?**	....		....	....	----	----	x---	----	----		
						T	**-2650?**	....		....	....	----	----	x---	----	----		
						C	**-2540w**	....		....	....	----	----	x---	----	----		
						T	**-2310y**	....		....	....	----	----	x---	----	----		
Fanthams Peak						T	**-1350w**	....		....	....	-x--	----	x---	----	----		
Southern Beehive						T	**-1250?**	....		....	....	-x--	----	----	--x-	----		
						C	**-1160w**	....		....	....	----	----	x---	----	----		
						C	**-0040u**	....		....	....	x---	----	xx--	--x-	----		
						C	**0520w**	....		....	....	----	----	xx--	----	----		
						T	**0550?**	....		....	....	----	----	x---	----	----		
						C	**1400t**	....		....	....	x---	----	xx--	----	----		
						C	**1480t**	....		....	....	----	----	x---	----	----		
						C	**1500r**	....		....	....	x---	----	xx--	--x-	-x--		
						D	**1655?**	....		....	....	x---	----	xx--	----	-x--		
						D	**1755?**	....		....	....	x---	----	x---	----	----		
WHITE ISLAND (New Zealand)	**37.52**	**S 177.18 E**	**321**	**Stratovolcs**	**0401-04=**	**Historical**												
							1826	1201		....	....	x---	----	x---	----	----	2	
							1836b	....		....	....	x---	----	?---	----	----	2	
						?	**1856h**	....		....	....	x---	----	?---	----	----	2	
						?	**1885**	01		....	....	x---	----	?---	----	----	2	
West end of crater							**1885**	10		....	....	x---	----	x-x-	----	----	2	
						?	**1886**	0610		?**1886**	0615	x---	----	?---	----	----	2	
							1886	0916	+	**1886**	12 ?	x---	----	x---	----	----	2	
						?	**1908**	1128		?**1908**	1206	x---	----	?---	----	----	2	
							1909	0513		....	....	x---	----	x---	----	----	2	
(landslide without eruption)						X	1914	0910?		....	....	x---	----	----	----	xxx-		
NW end of crater (Lot's Wife vent)							**1922**	....		....	....	x---	----	x---	----	----	2	
North end of crater (Schuberts Fairy?)							**1924**	....		....	....	x---	----	x---	----	----	2	
Little Donald vent							**1926**	0203		....	....	x---	----	x---	----	----	2	
Between Big Donald and Lot's Wife)							**1928**	0901		**1928**	0903a	x---	----	x---	----	----	1	
							1930	0316		....	....	x---	----	x---	----	----	2	
Foot of crater ridge (1933 crater)							**1933**	0402		....	....	x---	----	x---	----	----	3	
Noisy Nellie Crater							**1947**	01 <		....	....	x---	----	x---	----	----	2	
							1955	01		....	....	x---	----	x---	----	----	2	
							1957	1211		....	....	x---	----	x---	----	----	2	
Noisy Nellie and 1933 craters							**1958**	12		....	....	x---	----	x---	----	----	1	
Noisy Nellie Crater							**1959**	1214		**1959**	1220	x---	----	x---	----	----	2	
Big John Crater							**1962**	1215		....	....	x---	----	x---	----	----	3	
Gilliver Crater							**1966**	1113	+	**1967**	03	x---	----	xxx-	----	----	3	
Rudolf vent (back wall of 1933 crater							**1968**	0127		**1969**	02	x---	----	x---	----	----	3*	
Rudolf vent							**1969**	08		**1969**	09	x---	----	x---	----	----	2	
Rudolf vent							**1970**	0630p		....	....	x---	----	x---	----	----	2	
Noisy Nellie Crater							**1971**	0409c		....	....	x---	----	x-x-	----	----	2	
South of Rudolf (1971 crater)							**1971**	0719		**1971**	0720	x---	----	x-x-	----	----	2	

VOLCANO NAME (Subregion) / ERUPTION — Area of Activity	LAT	LONG	ELEV (m)	TYPE	NUMBER	Status / Start Year	Start M-Dy	P	Stop Year	Stop M-Dy	ERUPTIVE CHARACTERISTICS (Central, Flank vent, Radial fiss, Regional* / Submarine, New island, Subglacial, Crater lake / Explosive, Pyro flow, Phreatic, Fumarolic / Lava flow, Lava lake, Dome, Spine / Fatal, Damage, Mudflow, Tsunami)	VEI	Vol L/T
WHITE ISLAND *continued*													
SE of Donald Mound						1974	0908j		....	....	x--- ---- --x- ---- ----	2	
Christmas, Gibrus, and 1978 craters						1976	1218		1981	1025q	x--- ---- xxx- ---- ----	3*	-/7
(incorrect report of eruption)						X 1982	0701		....	....	---- ---- ---- ---- ----		
North margin of 1978 crater complex						1983	1226e		1984	0212e	x--- ---- x--- ---- ----	2	
Congress and numerous other craters						1986	0201?		1993>	....	x--- ---- x-x- ---- ----	3*	
WHALE ISLAND (New Zealand)	**37.858 S**	**176.98 E**	**348**	**Complx volc**	**0401-041**	**Pleistocene-Fumarolic**							
ROTORUA (New Zealand)	**38.08 S**	**176.27 E**	**757**	**Caldera**	**0401-042**	**Pleistocene-Geysers**							
OKATAINA (New Zealand)	**38.12 S**	**176.50 E**	**1111**	**Lava domes**	**0401-05=**	**Historical**							
West Rerewhakaaitu fissures						T -8050?	....		....	....	---x ---- --x- ---- ----		
Rotoma caldera, Tuahu, Kawerau						C -6580j	....		....	....	---x ---- xxx- x-x- ----	6	9/10
Mt. Edgecumbe						T -5550?	....		....	....	---x ---- ---- x-x- ----	0	
Haroharo (Te Horoa & other domes)						C -5300p	....		....	....	---x ---- xx-- x-x- ----	5	10/9
Haroharo (Makatiti and other domes)						C -2880p	....		....	....	---x ---- xx-- x-x- ----	6	9/10
Haroharo (Rotokawau to Rotoatua)						C -1490u	....		....	....	--x- ---- x--- ---- ----	4+	8/8
Mt. Edgecumbe						T -0300?	....		....	....	---x ---- ---- x-x- ----	0	9/-
Te Kopia thermal area						T 0180?	....		....	....	---x ---- --x- ---- ----		
Tarawera (Kaharoa eruption)						C 1180p	....		....	....	---x ---- xxx- --x- --x-	5	9/9
Tarawera (Wahanga-Waimangu fissure)						1886	0610	+	1886	08	---x ---- xxx- ---- xx--	5	-/9
Waimangu (Echo Crater)						1896	....		....	....	---- ---? --x- ---- ----	1?	
Waimangu Geyser						1900	01		1904	1101	---- ---- --x- ---- x---	1	
Waimangu (Echo Crater)						1905	0218		1905	0223	---- ---- --x- ---- ----	1	
Waimangu (Echo Crater)						1905	0617		1905	0617	---- ---- --x- ---- ----	1	
Waimangu (NW of Fairy Crater)						1906	0221		1906	0221	---- ---- --x- ---- ----	1	
Waimangu (Echo Crater)						1908	1001		1908	1001	---- ---- --x- ---- ----	1	
Waimangu (Echo Crater)						1910	0724		1910	0725	---- ---- --x- ---- ----	1	
Waimangu (Echo Crater)						1912	04		....	....	---- ---- --x- ---- ----	1	
Waimangu (Echo Crater)						1913	0127		1913	0127	---- ---- --x- ---- ----	1	
Waimangu (NW of Fairy Crater)						1914	0128		1914	02	---- ---- --x- ---- ----	1	
Waimangu (Echo Crater and NW of Fairy)						1915	0204	+	1915	0413	---- ---- --x- ---- ----	1	
Waimangu (Echo Crater)						1915	1105	+	1915	1109	---- ---- --x- ---- ----	1	
Waimangu (Echo Crater)						1917	0324	+	1917	0404	---- ---- -?x- ---- xx--	1	
Waimangu (Echo Crater)						1918	....		1920	....	---- ---x --x- ---- ----	1	
Waimangu (Echo Crater)						1924	....		....	....	---- ---x --x- ---- ----	1	
Rotomahana						1926	1117		1926	1118	---- ---x --x- ---- ----	1	
Rotomahana						1951	06		....	....	---- ---x --x- ---- ----	1	
Waimangu (Echo Crater)						1973	0222		1973	0222	---x ---x --x- ---- ----	1	-/3
REPOROA (New Zealand)	**38.42 S**	**176.33 E**	**592**	**Caldera**	**0401-06-**	**Tephrochronology**							
Waiotapu thermal area						T 1180?	....		....	....	---x ---- --x- ---- ----		
MAROA (New Zealand)	**38.42 S**	**176.08 E**	**1156**	**Calderas**	**0401-061**	**Tephrochronology**							
Orakeikorako						T -7050?	....		....	....	---x ---- --x- ---- ----		
Orakeikorako						T 0180?	....		....	....	---x ---- --x- ---- ----		
TAUPO (New Zealand)	**38.82 S**	**176.00 E**	**760**	**Caldera**	**0401-07=**	**Radiocarbon**							
East-central Lake Taupo						G -9850?	....		....	....	---x ---x xx-- ?--- ----	5	-/9
4 km west of Te Kohaiakahu Point						G -9450?	....		....	....	x--- ---x x--- ?--- ----	4+	-/8
Acacia Bay lava dome						G -9430?	....		....	....	---x ---- x--- --x- ----	4	7/8
Central and east-central Lake Taupo						G -8000?	....		....	....	x--- ---- xx-- ---- ----	5	-/9
SE Lake Taupo (Motutaiko Island)						G -5100?	....		....	....	x--- ---x x--- --x- ----	3	8/7
East-central Lake Taupo						G -4700?	....		....	....	x--- ---x x--- ?--- ----	4	-/8
4 km WNW of Te Kohaiakahu Point						G -4100?	....		....	....	x--- ---x x--- ?--- ----	4	-/8
						G -4000?	....		....	....	x--- ---x x--- ?--- ----	3	-/7
						G -3450?	....		....	....	x--- ---x x--- ?--- ----	3	-/7
4 km NW of Te Kohaiaikahu Point						G -3400?	....		....	....	x--- ---x x--- ?--- ----	4	
2 km west of Te Kohaiakahu Point						T -3350?	....		....	....	x--- ---x x--- ?--- ----	3	-/7
5 km NW of Te Kohaiakahu Point						G -3300?	....		....	....	x--- ---- x--- ?--- ----	4	-/8
5 km NW of Te Kohaiakahu Point						G -2900?	....		....	....	x--- ---x x--- ?--- ----	4	-/8
N Lake Taupo, 2 km S of Te Tuhi Point						G -2850?	....		....	....	x--- ---- x--- ?--- ----	3	-/7
						T -2800?	....		....	....	x--- ---- x--- ?--- ----	3	-/7
3 km NW of Te Kohaiakahu Point						G -2600?	....		....	....	x--- ---- x--- ?--- ----	4	-/8
S Lake Taupo, 3 km SW of Motutaiko I.						G -2500?	....		....	....	x--- ---x x--- ---- ----	3	-/7
East Lake Taupo (Horomatangi Reefs?)						G -1600?	....		....	....	x--- ---- xx-- ---- ----	**6**	**-/10**
4 km west of Te Kohaiakahu Point						G -1250?	....		....	....	x--- ---x x--- ?--- ----	3	-/7
5 km NE of Motutaiko Island						G -0900?	....		....	....	x--- ---x x--- ?--- ----	4	-/8
4 km NW of Te Kohaiakahu Point						G -0850?	....		....	....	x--- ---x x--- ?--- ----	4+	-/8
Ouaha Hills						T -0800?	....		....	....	x--- ---- x--- x--- ----	2	7/6
4 km NW of Te Kohaiakahu Point						G -0200?	....		....	....	x--- ---x x--- ?--- ----	4+	-/8
East Lake Taupo (Horomatangi Reefs)						G 0180?	0115q		....	....	x--- ---x xx-- ---- --x-	**6+**	**-/10**
East Lake Taupo (Horomatangi Reefs)						T 0210?	....		....	....	x--- ---x ---- --x- ----	0	8/-
TONGARIRO (New Zealand)	**39.13 S**	**175.642 E**	**1978**	**Stratovolcs**	**0401-08=**	**Historical**							
North Crater, Blue Lake						C -7750x	....		....	....	x--- ---- x--- ---- ----	5	-/9
Ngauruhoe and Red Crater						C -0550x	....		....	....	xx-- ---- x--- ---- ----		-/9
Upper Te Mari Craters						T 1500t	....		....	....	-x-- ---- ---- x--- ----		
Ngauruhoe						1839	02		1839	03	x--- ---- x--- ---- ----	1?	
Ngauruhoe						1841	....		....	....	x--- ---- x--- ---- ----	2	
Ngauruhoe						1844	10	+	1845	01	x--- ---- x--- ---- ----	2	
SSE flank (Red Crater)						1855	....		....	....	-x-- ---- x--- ---- ----	2	
Ngauruhoe						1857	02		1857	03	x--- ---- x--- ---- ----	2	
SSE flank (Red Crater)						1859	0421		....	....	-x-- ---- --x- ---- ----	1?	
Ngauruhoe						1862	01		....	....	x--- ---- x--- ---- ----	2	
Ngauruhoe						1863	....		1864	04	x--- ---- x--- ---- ----	2	
Ngauruhoe						1864	12		1865	01	x--- ---- x--- ---- ----	2	
NE flank (Upper Te Mari Crater)						1869	....		....	....	-x-- ---- x--- ---- ----	2	
Ngauruhoe						1869	08		....	....	x--- ---- x--- ---- ----	2	
Ngauruhoe (northwest sub-crater)						1870	04		1870	08	x--- ---- x--- x--- ----	2	
Ngauruhoe						? 1875	1001t		....	....	x--- ---- ?--- ---- ----	2	
Ngauruhoe (northwest sub-crater)						1878	0901u		....	....	x--- ---- x--- ---- ----	2	
Ngauruhoe						1881	0706		....	....	x--- ---- x--- ---- ----	2	
Ngauruhoe (south sub-crater)						1883	0425e		....	....	x--- ---- x--- ---- ----	2	
SSE flank (Red Crater)						1885a	....		1887	....	-x-- ---- --x- ---- ----	1	
NE flank (upper Te Mari Crater)						1886	06		....	....	-x-- ---- x--- ---- ----	2	
SSE flank (Red Crater)						? 1890	03		....	....	-x-- ---- --?- ---- ----	1	

VOLCANO NAME (Subregion) …… LAT / ERUPTION —	LONG ELEV (m) TYPE NUMBER / Area of Activity	Status / Start Year	Start M-Dy	P	Stop Year	Stop M-Dy	Central, Flank vent, Radial fiss, Regional*	Submarine, New island, Subglacial, Crater lake	Explosive, Pyro flow, Phreatic, Fumarolic	Lava flow, Lava lake, Dome, Spine	Fatal, Damage, Mudflow, Tsunami	VEI	Vol L/T
TONGARIRO (New Zealand) *continued*	Ngauruhoe	1892	02		1892	03	x---	----	x---	----	----	2	
	Ngauruhoe	1892	11		1892	12	x---	----	x---	----	----	2	
	NE flank (upper Te Mari Crater)	1892	1130		....	....	-x--	----	xx--	----	-x--	2	
	NE flank (upper Te Mari Crater)	1896	11		1896	1226e	-x--	----	x---	----	----	2	
	Ngauruhoe	1897	....		....	....	x---	----	x---	----	----	2	
	Ngauruhoe	1898	01		....	....	x---	----	x---	----	----	2	
	Ngauruhoe	1904	1122		....	....	x---	----	x---	----	----	2	
	Ngauruhoe	1905	....		....	....	x---	----	x---	----	----	2	
	Ngauruhoe	1906	03		....	....	x---	----	x---	----	----	2	
	Ngauruhoe (south sub-crater)	1907	02	+	1907	05	x---	----	x---	----	----	2	
	Ngauruhoe	1907	11		....	....	x---	----	x---	----	----	2	
	Ngauruhoe	1909	03	+	1909	07	x---	----	x---	----	----	2	
	Ngauruhoe	1910	01		....	....	x---	----	x---	----	----	2	
	Ngauruhoe	1910	10	+	1911	01	x---	----	x---	----	----	2	
	Ngauruhoe	1913	01		....	....	x---	----	x---	----	----	2	
	Ngauruhoe	1913	05		....	....	x---	----	x---	----	----	2	
	Ngauruhoe	1914	09		1914	10	x---	----	x---	----	----	2	
	Ngauruhoe	1917	10		1917	11	x---	----	x---	----	----	2	
	Ngauruhoe	1924	0109		1924	0130	x---	----	x---	----	----	2	
	Ngauruhoe	1924	0522		....	....	x---	----	x---	----	----	2	
	Ngauruhoe	1924	10		1924	11	x---	----	x---	----	----	2	
	Ngauruhoe	1925	11		1925	12	x---	----	x---	----	----	2	
	Ngauruhoe and Red Crater	1926	0416		1926	06	xx--	----	x---	----	----	2	
	Ngauruhoe	1926	1221		1926	1230?	x---	----	x---	----	----	2	
	North flank (Ketetahi)	? 1927	....		....	....	-x--	----	--?-	----	----	1?	
	Ngauruhoe	1928	0303		....	....	x---	----	x---	----	----	2	
	Ngauruhoe	1928	07		....	....	x---	----	x---	----	----	2	
	Ngauruhoe	1931	02	+	1931	05	x---	----	x---	----	----	2	
	Ngauruhoe	1934	06		....	....	x---	----	x---	----	----	2	
	Ngauruhoe	1934	12	+	1935	02	x---	----	x---	----	----	2	
	Ngauruhoe	1937	01		....	....	x---	----	x---	----	----	2	
	Ngauruhoe	1939	08		....	....	x---	----	x---	----	----	2	
	Ngauruhoe	1940	09		1940	10	x---	----	x---	----	----	2	
	Ngauruhoe	1948	0430		1948	05	x---	----	x---	----	----	2	
	Ngauruhoe	1948	09		....	....	x---	----	x---	----	----	2	
	Ngauruhoe (south sub-crater)	1949	0209		1949	0303	x---	----	xx--	x-x-	----	2	5/-
	Ngauruhoe	1950	0616		....	....	x---	----	x---	----	----	2	
	Ngauruhoe	1951	05		....	....	x---	----	x---	----	----	2	
	Ngauruhoe (south sub-crater)	1952	1129		1953	07	x---	----	x---	----	----	2	
	Ngauruhoe (south sub-crater)	1954	0513		1955	0621	x---	----	xx--	x---	----	3	6/-
	Ngauruhoe (south sub-crater)	1956	0111		1956	0211	x---	----	x---	----	----	2	
	Ngauruhoe	1958	1105		1958	1118?	x---	----	x---	----	----	2	
	Ngauruhoe	1959	0601		....	....	x---	----	x---	----	----	2	
	Ngauruhoe	1962	0524		....	....	x---	----	x---	----	----	2	
	Ngauruhoe	1968	0818		....	....	x---	----	x---	----	----	2	
	Ngauruhoe	1969	0121		....	....	x---	----	x---	----	----	2	
	Ngauruhoe	1972	0319		1972	0606	x---	----	x-x-	----	----	2	
	Ngauruhoe	1972	1122	+	1974	0819	x---	----	xx--	----	----	3*	
	Ngauruhoe	1975	0212	+	1975	0223	x---	----	xx--	----	--x-	3	-/6
	Ngauruhoe	1976	0823		1976	0828	x---	----	x---	----	----	1	
	Ngauruhoe	1977	0704		1977	0704	x---	----	x---	----	----	1	
RUAPEHU (New Zealand) .... 39.28 S	175.57 E 2797 Stratovolc 0401-10=	Historical											
	Upper north flank (Pinnacle Ridge)	C -7840<	....		....	....	-x--	----	x---	----	----	4	-/8
	NE flank (Tama Lakes area)	T -7750?	....		....	....	-x--	----	x---	----	----		
	North flank (Whakapapanui Gorge area)	C -7590v	....		....	....	-x--	----	?---	--x-	----		
	NE flank (Whakapapa)	T -5550*	....		....	....	-x--	----	x---	x---	----		
		1861	0213	+	1861	0516>	x---	----	x-?-	--x-	-xx-	2	
		1889	0501		....	....	x---	---x	--x-	----	--x-	2	
		1895	0310		1895	0314>	x---	---x	x-x-	----	--x-	2	
		1903	....		....	....	x---	---x	x-x-	----	--x-	2	
		1906	0315		....	....	x---	---x	x-x-	----	----	2	
		1918	0629		....	....	x---	---x	--x-	----	----	2	
		1921	10		....	....	x---	---x	--x-	----	----	2	
		1925	0122		....	....	x---	---x	--x-	----	-xx-	2	
		1934	0811		....	....	x---	---x	--x-	----	----	2	
		1934	12	+	1935	02	x---	---x	--x-	----	----	2	
		1936	0509?		1936	0513	x---	---x	x-x-	----	----	2	
		1940	04		....	....	x---	---x	--x-	----	----	2	
		1942	0810		....	....	x---	---x	--x-	----	----	2	
		1944	10		....	....	x---	---x	--x-	----	----	2	
		1945	0308	+	1945	12	x---	---x	x-x-	--x-	----	3*	7/-
		1946	04	+	1946	06	x---	---x	x-x-	----	----	2	
		1946	1121	+	1947	0531	x---	---x	x-x-	----	----	1	
		1948	0501		....	....	x---	---x	--x-	----	----	1	
		1950	0626		1950	0626	x---	---x	--x-	----	----	1	
		1951	0319		....	....	x---	---x	--x-	----	----	1	
		1952	07		....	....	x---	---x	--x-	----	----	1	
		1956	1118		1956	1118	x---	---x	--x-	----	----	1	
		1959	0521	+	1959	0831	x---	---x	?-x-	----	----	1	
		1966	0404	+	1966	0927	x---	---x	x-x-	x---	----	1	
		1967	0722	+	1967	1004?	x---	---x	?-x-	----	----	1	
		1968	0407	+	1968	0610	x---	---x	--x-	----	--x-	2*	
		1969	0622		1969	0622	x---	---x	xxx-	----	-xx-	2	
		1970	0916		1970	0916	x---	---x	x---	----	----	1	
		1971	0403	+	1971	11	x---	---x	x-x-	----	--x-	2*	-/6
		1972	1022	+	1973	0104	x---	---x	--x-	----	----	1	
		1973	1031	+	1974	1118o	x---	---x	--x-	----	----	1	
		1975	0424	+	1975	0427	x---	---x	xxx-	----	-xx-	2	
		1975	1017<		1975	1017<	x---	---x	--x-	----	----	1	
		1976	0406		1976	0406	x---	---x	--x-	----	----	1	
		1976	11		1976	11	x---	---x	x-x-	----	----	1	
		1977	07	+	1979	0117	x---	---x	xx--	----	--x-	2*	-/5
		1979	0630	+	1979	0715	x---	---x	--x-	----	----	1	
		1979	1205		1980	0415	x---	---x	x-x-	----	----	1	

VOLCANO NAME (Subregion) / ERUPTION — Area of Activity	LAT	LONG	ELEV (m)	TYPE	NUMBER	Status / Start Year	Start M-Dy	P	Stop Year	Stop M-Dy	ERUPTIVE CHARACTERISTICS (Central, Flank vent, Radial fiss, Regional* / Submarine, New island, Subglacial, Crater lake / Explosive, Pyro flow, Phreatic, Fumarolic / Lava flow, Lava lake, Dome, Spine / Fatal, Damage, Mudflow, Tsunami)	VEI	Vol L/T
RUAPEHU (New Zealand) *continued*						**1980**	1018		**1980**	1103	x--- ---x x-x- ---- ----	1	
						1981	1025?		**1982**	04	x--- ---x x-x- ---- ----	1	
						1985	0521<		**1985**	0609?	x--- ---x --x- ---- ----	1	
						1986	0208		**1986**	0209?	x--- ---x --x- ---- ----	1	
						1987	0824	+	**1987**	0830	x--- ---x --x- ---- ----	1	
						1988	0320		**1988**	0525c	x--- ---x --x- ---- ----	1	
						1988	1208	+	**1989**	0305?	x--- ---x x-x- ---- --x-	1	
						1989	0701		**1989**	0920?	x--- ---x --x- ---- ----	1	
						1990	0107		**1990**	0131	x--- ---x --x- ---- ----	1	
						1990	0617	+	?**1990**	0908<	x--- ---x --x- ---- ----	0	
						? **1991**	0705?		?**1991**	0714?	x--- ---x --?- ---- ----	1	
						1992	0208		**1992**	0306	x--- ---x --x- ---- ----	1	
RUMBLE I (New Zealand)	**35.50 S**	**178.875 E**	**-1100**	**Submarine**	**0401-11-**	**Uncertain**							
RUMBLE II (New Zealand)..........	**35.43 S**	**178.65 E**	**-880**	**Submarine**	**0401-12-**	**Uncertain**							
RUMBLE III (New Zealand)	**35.745 S**	**178.478 E**	**-140**	**Submarine**	**0401-13-**	**Hydrophonic**							
						S **1958**	0709		S**1962**	....	---- x--- ---- ---- ----	0	
						S **1963**	01		S**1966**	12 >	---- x--- ---- ---- ----	0	
						S **1970**	....		....	....	---- x--- ---- ---- ----	0	
						S **1973**	1015		S**1973**	1017	---- x--- ---- ---- ----	0	
						S **1986**	0615		S**1986**	0805?	---- x--- ---- ---- ----	0	
RUMBLE IV (New Zealand)	**36.22 S**	**178.05 E**	**-450**	**Submarine**	**0401-14-**	**Fumarolic**							
(Rumble III activity, not Rumble IV)						X 1966	04		X1966	12 >	---- ---- ---- ---- ----		
RUMBLE V (New Zealand)	**36.139 S**	**178.197 E**	**-700**	**Submarine**	**0401-15-**	**Fumarolic**							

KERMADECS

VOLCANO NAME (Subregion) / ERUPTION — Area of Activity	LAT	LONG	ELEV (m)	TYPE	NUMBER	Status / Start Year	Start M-Dy	P	Stop Year	Stop M-Dy	ERUPTIVE CHARACTERISTICS	VEI	Vol L/T
CURTIS ISLAND (Kermadec Is)	**30.542 S**	**178.561 W**	**137**	**Submarine**	**0402-01=**	**Uncertain**							
(steaming not caused by an eruption)						X 1899	....		....	....	---- ---- ---- ---- ----		
						? **1936**	0618		?**1936**	12	---- ?--- ---- ---- ----		
BRIMSTONE ISLAND (Kermadec Is) .	**30.23 S**	**178.92 W**	**-2000**	**Submarine ?**	**0402-02=**	**Uncertain**							
						? **1825**	0906		....	....	---- ??-- ---- ---- ----		
MACAULEY ISLAND (Kermadec Is) ..	**30.20 S**	**178.47 W**	**238**	**Caldera**	**0402-021**	**Holocene**							
RAOUL ISLAND (Kermadec Is)......	**29.27 S**	**177.92 W**	**516**	**Stratovolc**	**0402-03=**	**Historical**							
SE part of Raoul caldera						C **-2000**v	....		....	....	x--- ---- xx-- ---- ----	4	-/8
SW part of Raoul caldera...............						C **-1350**w	....		....	....	x--- ---- xx-- ---- ----	4	-/8
Denham Bay caldera						C **-0210**u	....		....	....	x--- ---- xx-- ---- ----	**6**	**-/10**
						T **-0050?**	....		....	....	---- ---- x--- ---- ----	3?	-/7
North flank of Moumoukai volcano........						T **0300**x	....		....	....	-x-- ---- xx-- ---- ----	4	-/8
South part of Raoul Caldera.............						T **0600**x	....		....	....	x--- ---- x--- ---- ----	4	-/8
Green Lake Pumice Crater..............						C **0700**v	....		....	....	x--- ---- x--- ---- ----	4	-/8
Pukekohu Crater						T **0775**u	....		....	....	x--- ---- --x- ---- ----	3	-/7
Expedition Crater						T **1000**x	....		....	....	x--- ---- --x- ---- ----	4	-/8
Rangitahua Crater						C **1630**t	....		....	....	x--- ---- x-x- ---- ----	4	-/8
Denham Bay?, Tui Lake Crater						C **1720**t	....		....	....	x--- x--- x--- ---- ----	4	-/8
Denham Bay and Smith Crater						**1814**	0309		....	....	x--- xx-- x-x- ---- ----	3	-/7
Denham Bay, Green Lake						**1870**	0620d		**1870**	1003	x--- xx-- x-x- ---- ----	3	-/7
(post-1870 eruption unsubstantiated)......						X 1872	0201r		....	....	---- ---- ---- ---- ----		
West side of Green Lake, Denham Bay....						**1964**	1121	+	**1965**	0425?	---x x--- xxx- ---- ----	2	
UNNAMED (Kermadec Is)	**29.18 S**	**177.87 W**	**-560**	**Submarine**	**0402-04=**	**Historical**							
8 km NNE of Raoul Island						**1886**	03		....	....	---- x--- x--- ---- ----	0	
7 km NNE of Raoul Island						? **1987**	0325		?**1987**	0325	---- ?--- ---- ---- ----	0	
MONOWAI SEAMOUNT (Kermadec-N	**25.888 S**	**177.188 W**	**-100**	**Submarine**	**0402-05-**	**Historical**							
						? **1944**	....		....	....	---- ?--- ---- ---- ----	0	
						S **1977**	04		S**1977**	04	---- x--- ---- ---- ----	0	
						1977	1017		**1979**	0419>	---- x--- ---- ---- ----	0	
						S **1980**	01		S**1980**	01	---- x--- ---- ---- ----	0	
						S **1982**	05		S**1982**	05	---- x--- ---- ---- ----	0	
						S **1986**	06		S**1986**	06	---- x--- ---- ---- ----	0	
						S **1988**	0908		S**1988**	0908	---- x--- ---- x--- ----	0	
						S **1990**	0530	+	S**1991**	0325	---- x--- ---- ---- ----	0	

TONGA

VOLCANO NAME (Subregion) / ERUPTION — Area of Activity	LAT	LONG	ELEV (m)	TYPE	NUMBER	Status / Start Year	Start M-Dy	P	Stop Year	Stop M-Dy	ERUPTIVE CHARACTERISTICS	VEI	Vol L/T
UNNAMED (Tonga Is)	**21.38 S**	**175.65 W**	**-500**	**Submarine**	**0403-01=**	**Historical**							
						1907	07		....	....	---- x--- ---- ---- ----	0	
						1932	1201p		....	....	---- x--- ---- ---- ----	0	
UNNAMED (Tonga Is)	21.07 S	175.33 W			0403-02=	Not a Volcano							
(date of depth sounding, not eruption)						X 1943	....		....	....	---- ---- ---- ---- ----		
UNNAMED (Tonga Is)	**20.85 S**	**175.53 W**	**-13**	**Submarine**	**0403-03=**	**Historical**							
						1911	08		....	....	---- x--- ---- ---- ----	0	
						1923	0701		....	....	---- x--- ---- ---- ----	0	
UNNAMED (Tonga Is)	**20.57 S**	**175.38 W**		**Submarine**	**0403-04=**	**Historical**							
						1912	0429		....	....	---- x--- x--- ---- ----	2	
						1937	....		....	....	---- x--- x--- ---- ----	2	
1 km SSE of Hunga Ha'apai.............						**1988**	0601		**1988**	0603>	---- x--- x--- ---- ----	0	
FALCON ISLAND (Tonga Is)........	**20.32 S**	**175.42 W**	**145**	**Submarine**	**0403-05=**	**Historical**							
						? **1781**	....		....	....	---- ?--- ---- ---- ----	0	
						? **1865**	....		....	....	---- ?--- ---- ---- ----	0	
						1877	....		....	....	---- x--- x--- ---- ----	2	
						1885	1011?		**1886**	....	---- xx-- x--- ---- ----	3	-/8
						1894	12		....	....	---- xx-- x--- ---- ----	2	
						1921	11		....	....	---- xx-- x--- ---- ----	2	
						1927	1004		....	....	x--- xx-- x--- ---- ----	2	
						1928	05		....	....	---- x--- x--- ---- ----	2?	
						1933	04		....	....	---- ---- x--- ---- ----	2	

VOLCANO NAME (Subregion) / ERUPTION — Area of Activity	LAT	LONG	ELEV (m)	TYPE	NUMBER	Status / Start Year	Start M-Dy	P	Stop Year	Stop M-Dy	ERUPTIVE CHARACTERISTICS (Central, Flank vent, Radial fiss, Regional* / Submarine, New island, Subglacial, Crater lake / Explosive, Pyro flow, Phreatic, Fumarolic / Lava flow, Lava lake, Dome, Spine / Fatal, Damage, Mudflow, Tsunami)	VEI	Vol L/T
FALCON ISLAND (Tonga Is) *continued*						**1936**	06		....	....	x--- ---- x--- ---- ----	2	
						@ 1970	0103		....	....	---- x--- ---- ---- ----	0	
TOFUA (Tonga Is)	**19.75 S**	**175.07 W**	**512**	**Caldera**	**0403-06=**	**Historical**							
						1774	06		....	....	x--- ---- x--- ---- ----	2	
						1792	....		....	....	x--- ---- ---- x--- ----	0	
						1854	....		....	....	x--- ---- x--- ---- ----	2	
						1885	10 <		....	....	x--- ---- x--- ---- ----	2	
West Crater ?						**1906**	01		**1906**	02	xx-- ---- x--- x--- ----	2	
West Crater ?						**1906**	12		....	....	xx-- ---- x--- x--- ----	2	
West Crater, ...						**1958**	1231u		....	....	x--- ---- x--- ---- ----	2	
METIS SHOAL (Tonga Is)	**19.18 S**	**174.87 W**	**-4**	**Submarine**	**0403-07=**	**Historical**							
						1851	....		....	....	---- x--- ---- ---- ----	0	
						1852	....		....	....	---- x--- ---- ---- ----	0	
						1858	....		....	....	---- xx-- x--- ---- ----	2	
						1878	....		....	....	---- ---- x--- ---- ----	2	
						1886	....		....	....	---- ---- x--- ---- ----	2	
						1894	....		....	....	---- ---- ---- ---- ----	2	
						1967	1211<		**1968**	01	---- xx-- x-x- ---- ----	2	
						1979	0510<		**1979**	0721>	---- xx-- x--- ---- ----	2	
HOME REEF (Tonga Is)............	**18.992 S**	**174.775 W**	**-2**	**Submarine**	**0403-08=**	**Historical**							
						1852	....		....	....	---- xx-- x--- ---- ----	2	
						? **1857**	....		....	....	---- ??-- ---- ---- ----	2	
						1984	0301		**1984**	0305	---- xx-- x--- ---- ----	3?	
LATE (Tonga Is)..................	**18.806 S**	**174.65 W**	**518**	**Stratovolc**	**0403-09=**	**Historical**							
East side crater, ...						**1790**	....		....	....	-x-- ---- ---- x--- ----	2	
East side crater, ...						**1854**	....		....	....	-x-- ---- x--- x--- ----	2	
FONUALEI (Tonga Is)	**18.02 S**	**174.325 W**	**200**	**Stratovolc**	**0403-10=**	**Historical**							
						1791	....		....	....	x--- ---- x--- ---- ----	2	
						1846	10		....	....	x--- ---- x--- x--- ----	4?	7/8
						1847	0709		**1847**	0713?	x--- ---- x--- x--- -x--	3?	
						1906	03		....	....	---- ---- ---- ---- ----		
Summit, west and SE sides						**1939**	06		....	....	xx ? x x	2	
North-central part of the island...........						**1951**	0821		....	....	x--- ---- x--- x--- ----	2	
						1957	06		....	....	---- ---- ---- ---- ----		
						? **1974**	0216		....	....	---- ---- --?x ---- ----	2	
CURACOA (Tonga Is)	**15.62 S**	**173.67 W**	**-33**	**Submarine**	**0403-101**	**Historical**							
6.4 km SW of Curacoa Reef.............						**1973**	0711		**1973**	0716	---- x--- x--- ---- ----	3	
13 km north of Tafahi						**1979**	0514		....	....	---- x--- ---- ---- ----	1	
NIUAFO'OU (Tonga Is)	**15.60 S**	**175.63 W**	**260**	**Shield**	**0403-11=**	**Historical**							
South end of caldera ?						**1814**	....		....	....	x--- ---x x-x- x--- -x--	2	
(probably confused with 1853 eruption)						X 1840	....		....	....	---- ---- ---- ?--- ----		
SW caldera rim (Ahau village area)						**1853**	0624		**1853**	0624?	-x-- ---- ---- x--- xx--	0	
SSW flank..............................						**1867**	0412		....	....	-x-- ---- x--- x--- -x--	1	
NE side of caldera						**1886**	0831		**1886**	0918?	x--- ---x x-x- ---- -xx-	4?	-/8
						1887	....		....	....	---- ---- x--- ---- ----	2	
West side, near Alele 'Uta village.........						**1912**	1015e		....	....	-x-- ---- x--- x--- -x--	2	
West flank.............................						**1929**	0725		**1929**	0726	-x-- ---- x--- x--- -x--	2	
South flank						**1935**	1207	+	**1936**	02 ?	-x-- ---- x-x- x--- -x--	2	
SW flank...............................						**1943**	0926		**1943**	1016p	-x-- ---- x-x- x--- -x--	2	
North flank						**1946**	0909		**1946**	0917	-x-- ---- x--- x--- -x--	2	
						? **1947**	01		....	....	---- ---- ---- ---- ----		
						? **1959**	....		....	....	---- ---- ---- ---- ----		
NE part of caldera lake (Vai Lahi)						**1985**	0321		**1985**	0322	x--- ---x x--- ---- ----	0	-/2

SAMOA & W

VOLCANO NAME (Subregion) / ERUPTION — Area of Activity	LAT	LONG	ELEV (m)	TYPE	NUMBER	Status / Start Year	Start M-Dy	P	Stop Year	Stop M-Dy	ERUPTIVE CHARACTERISTICS	VEI	Vol L/T
UNNAMED (American Samoa)	**14.23 S**	**169.07 W**	**-650**	**Submarine**	**0404-00-**	**Uncertain**							
(source of SOFAR eruption signal?)						? **1973**	07		....	....	---- x--- ---- ---- ----		
TA'U (American Samoa)	**14.23 S**	**169.454 W**	**931**	**Shield**	**0404-001**	**Holocene**							
OFU-OLOSEGA (American Samoa) ..	**14.175 S**	**169.618 W**	**639**	**Shields**	**0404-01=**	**Historical**							
Submarine vent 3 km SE of Olosega						**1866**	0912		**1866**	1115e	---x x--- x--- ---- ----	2	
TUTUILA (American Samoa)	**14.295 S**	**170.70 W**	**653**	**Tuff cones**	**0404-02-**	**Holocene**							
UPOLU (Western Samoa)	**13.935 S**	**171.72 W**	**1100**	**Shield**	**0404-03-**	**Holocene**							
SAVAI'I (Western Samoa)	**13.612 S**	**172.525 W**	**1858**	**Shield**	**0404-04=**	**Historical**							
Mauga Afi (west-central Toasivi ridge).....						**1725s**	....		....	....	x-x- ---- x--- x--- -x--	2	9/-
Mata Ole Afi (1649 m)						**1902**	1030		**1902**	1117d	x-x- ---- x--- x--- ----	1	
Matavanu (north flank 402 m)						**1905**	0804		**1911**	11	-xx- ---- x--- xx-- -x-x	2	9/6
WALLIS ISLANDS (Samoa-W of)	**13.30 S**	**176.17 W**	**143**	**Shields**	**0404-05-**	**Holocene**							

FIJI

VOLCANO NAME (Subregion) / ERUPTION — Area of Activity	LAT	LONG	ELEV (m)	TYPE	NUMBER	Status / Start Year	Start M-Dy	P	Stop Year	Stop M-Dy	ERUPTIVE CHARACTERISTICS	VEI	Vol L/T
TAVEUNI (Fiji Is-SW Pacific)	**16.82 S**	**179.97 W**	**1241**	**Shield**	**0405-01-**	**Radiocarbon**							
South end of Taveuni						C **-0100**w	....		....	....	--x- ---- x--- ---- -x--	2	
KORO (Fiji Is-SW Pacific)...........	**17.32 S**	**179.40 E**	**522**	**Cinder cones**	**0405-02-**	**Holocene?**							

Melanesia & Australia (05)

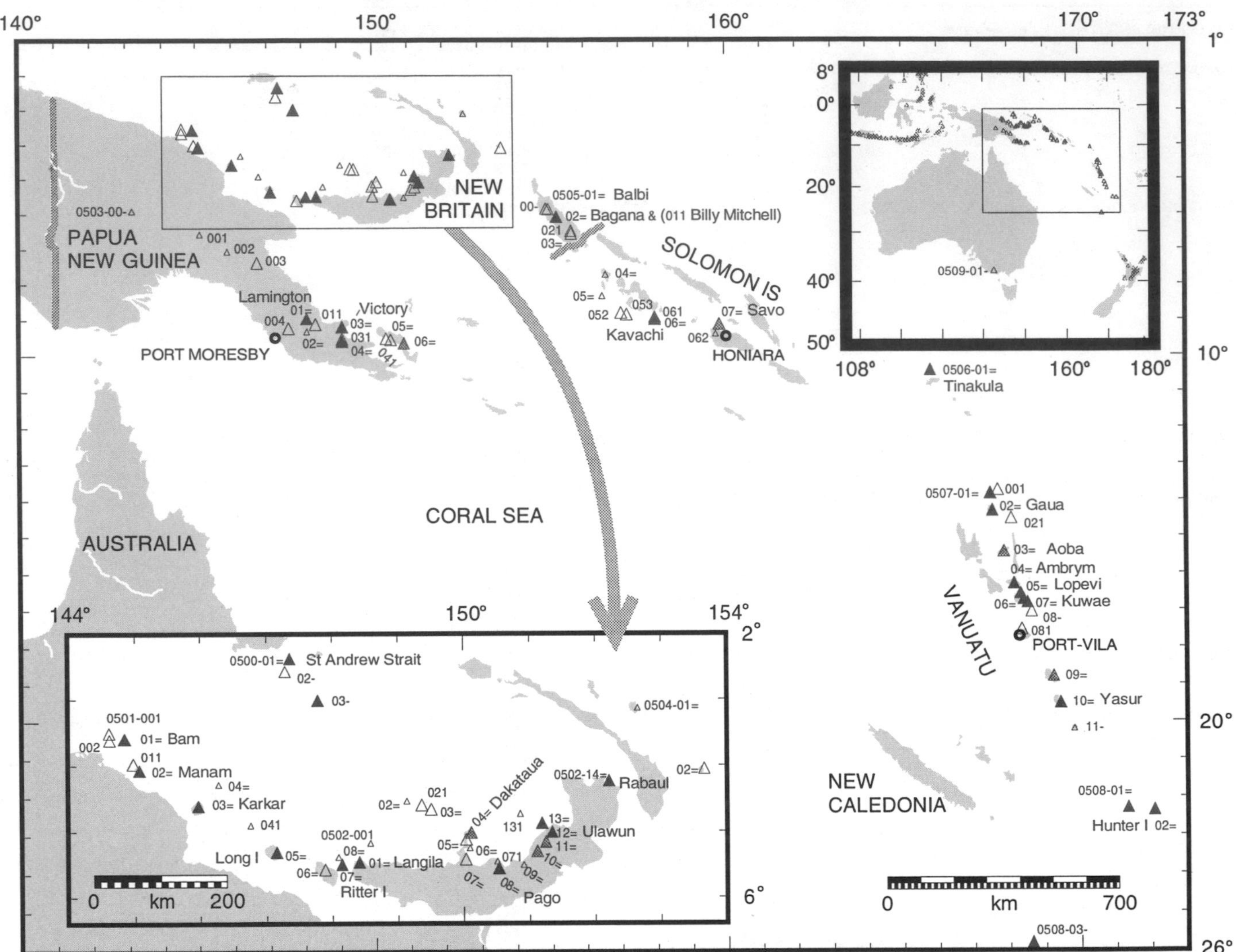

The islands of Melanesia have been inhabited for at least 3,000 years, but the first western contact was with sailors from Spain and Portugal who landed on New Guinea around 1526 AD. The Solomon Islands were discovered by westerners in 1568, when the region's first historical eruption was recorded on Savo. The New Hebrides (now Vanuatu) were discovered by Spaniards in 1606, a year after the Dutch sighted northernmost Australia. But it was not until Cook's historic voyage of 1770 that Australia's east coast was discovered, and its substantial settling did not begin until 1788. In 1884, Germany took possession of the northern part of New Guinea, and 3 days later Britain declared the southern section a protectorate, followed by outright annexation in 1888. Of all historically documented eruptions now known from Melanesia, three-fourths have been recorded in this century.

In 1906 this British territory was transferred to newly independent Australia, who took control of the northern portion of New Guinea as well during World War I (WW-I). With the exception of Japanese occupation in 1942-45, this situation prevailed until self-government was declared in 1973 and full independence came to Papua New Guinea (PNG) two years later. The Solomon Islands had only sporadic contact with the west until Britain established a protectorate in the 1890s; the islands gained independence in 1978. Captain Cook extensively explored the islands to the south in 1774, naming them the New Hebrides. Both France and Britain formed trading posts and missions in the last century, formalizing an Anglo-French Condominium in 1906, but the islands remained isolated despite considerable attention during WW-II. The Republic of Vanuatu was declared in 1980.

South of New Britain lies an oceanic trench that parallels its arcuate coast. Nearing the Solomons, the trench swings SE'ly, then down along the Vanuatu chain before turning east again and ending below Hunter Island. This trench system marks the subduction of oceanic crust – the Solomon and Coral Seas – moving N, NE, and E under the volcanic islands formed by this process. Tectonic complications in the form of two short oceanic spreading centers affect nearby volcanoes: One extends from SE New Guinea eastward to Kavachi, and the other runs broadly east-west below the Admiralty Islands at the north end of the region.

Melanesia matches the Atlantic Ocean for the region with the highest proportion (5%) of its eruptions being submarine, and it has the largest absolute number of island-building eruptions (22, nearly half of them from Kavachi). The region's combined land area equals that of California, but many areas are sparsely settled and its population is only slightly greater than that of Los Angeles.

The magnificent natural harbor of Rabaul, formed by a major eruption and collapse in the 6th century, was the capital of PNG from 1910 through 1941, and site of a 1937 eruption that killed 441 people. This event led to the founding, in the same year, of one of the world's pre-eminent volcano centers, the Rabaul Volcanological Observatory (RVO), operated by the Geological Survey of Papua New Guinea. RVO covers all the volcanoes of PNG, and its work has been particularly valuable in major eruptions such as Lamington in 1951, only a year after RVO resumed operations following WW-II. RVO has been among the most faithful and reliable reporters of regional volcanism: in the first 10 years of SEAN, region 05 was second only to Japan in number of reports, with 262 from 20 volcanoes, and has been first in several subsequent years. As this book goes to press, however, the town of Rabaul is under 75 cm of ash from a late September eruption that is continuing at lower levels.

OFFSHORE NEW GUINEA & ADMIRALTY ISLANDS

VOLCANO NAME (Subregion)	LAT	LONG	ELEV (m)	TYPE	NUMBER	Status	ERUPTION — Area of Activity	Start Year	Start M-Dy	P	Stop Year	Stop M-Dy	Central / Flank vent / Radial fiss / Regional*	Submarine / New island / Subglacial / Crater lake	Explosive / Pyro flow / Phreatic / Fumarolic	Lava flow / Lava lake / Dome / Spine	Fatal / Damage / Mudflow / Tsunami	VEI	Vol L/T
ST. ANDREW STRAIT (Admiralty Is)	**2.38 S**	**147.35 E**	**270**	**Complx volc**	**0500-01=**	**Historical**													
							Lou Island (Bedal volcano)	C **-0240**v	....		....	....	x---	----	xx--	----	----		
							Lou Island (Bedal volcano)	C **0350**?	....		....	....	x---	----	x---	----	xx--		
							Tuluman	**1883**	0328		....	....	----	x---	x---	----	----	2	
							Tuluman	**1953**	0627	+	**1957**	0128	----	xx--	x---	x-x-	-x-x	2*	8/-
BALUAN (Admiralty Is-SW Pac)	**2.57 S**	**147.28 E**	**254**	**Stratovolc**	**0500-02-**	**Holocene?**													
								? **1931**	....		....	....	----	?---	----	----	----	0	
UNNAMED (Admiralty Is-SW Pac)	**3.03 S**	**147.78 E**	**-1300**	**Submarine**	**0500-03-**	**Hydrophonic**													
								S **1972**	0108	+	S**1972**	0112	----	x---	----	----	----	0	
BLUP BLUP (New Guinea-NE of)	**3.508 S**	**144.62 E**	**402**	**Stratovolc**	**0501-001**	**Holocene**													
							(Manam erupted in 1616, not Blup Blup)	X 1616	....		....	....	----	----	----	----	----		
							(eruption report not valid)	X 1830	....		....	....	----	----	----	----	----		
KADOVAR (New Guinea-NE of)	**3.62 S**	**144.62 E**	**365**	**Stratovolc**	**0501-002**	**Holocene**													
							(Manam erupted in 1616, not Kadovar)	X 1616	....		....	....	----	----	----	----	----		
								? **1700**	04		....	....	----	----	----	----	----		
BAM (New Guinea-NE of)	**3.60 S**	**144.85 E**	**685**	**Stratovolc**	**0501-01=**	**Historical**													
							(eruption from Manam, not Bam)	X 1616	....		....	....	----	----	----	----	----		
							(1700 activity at Kadovar, not Bam)	X 1700	04		....	....	----	----	----	----	----		
							(eruption between 1868 and 1875)	X 1868	....		....	....	----	----	----	----	----		
								1872d	....		....	....	x---	----	x---	----	-x--	3	
								1874	0520		....	....	x---	----	x---	----	----	2	
								1877	1113		....	....	x---	----	x---	----	----	3	
								? **1883**	03		....	....	----	----	----	----	----		
							(date of Finsch observation was May 1885).	X 1884	....		....	....	----	----	----	----	----		
								? **1885**	0520		....	....	----	----	----	----	----		
								? **1888**	....		....	....	----	----	----	----	----		
								? **1897**	....		?**1898**	....	----	----	----	----	----		
								1907	11		....	....	x---	----	x---	----	----	2	
								1908	0712		....	....	x---	----	x---	----	----	2	
								1909	0419		**1909**	0913	x---	----	x---	----	----	2	
								1913	....		....	....	x---	----	?---	----	----		
								? **1920**b	....		....	....	x---	----	----	----	----		
								1924	....		....	....	x---	----	x---	----	-x--	2	
								? **1936**	07		?**1939**	04	x---	----	----	----	----		
							(1941 & 1942 eruptions not verified)	X 1941	....		X1942	....	----	----	----	----	----		
								1944	....		....	....	x---	----	x---	----	----	2	
							(this eruption took place in 1947)	X 1946	1201p		....	....	----	----	----	----	----		
								1947	0313s		....	....	x---	----	x---	----	----	2	
								1954	0803	+	**1957**	0102	x---	----	x---	----	-x--	2*	
								1957	1026		**1957**	1026	x---	----	x---	----	----	1	
								1958	0311j		**1958**	0419?	x---	----	x---	----	----	2	
								1958	0905		**1958**	0910	x---	----	x---	----	----	2	
								1959	0402	+	**1959**	1031	x---	----	x---	----	----	2	
								1960	0428		**1960**	0706	x---	----	x---	----	----	2	
BOISA (New Guinea-NE of)	**3.994 S**	**144.963 E**	**240**	**Stratovolc**	**0501-011**	**Holocene?**													
MANAM (New Guinea-NE of)	**4.10 S**	**145.061 E**	**1807**	**Stratovolc**	**0501-02=**	**Historical**													
								1616	0706		....	....	x---	----	x---	----	----	2?	
							(eruption in 1643, not 1642)	**1643**	0421		....	....	x---	----	x---	----	----	2	
							South Crater	**1700**	0402		....	....	x---	----	?---	----	----		
								1830	....		....	....	x---	----	x---	----	----	2	
							South Crater	**1877**	1029		**1877**	1113>	x---	----	x---	----	----	2	
								? **1884**	....		....	....	----	----	----	----	----		
								1885	05		....	....	x---	----	x---	----	----		
								1887	06		**1895**	....	x---	----	x?--	x---	----	2	
							Main Crater, South Crater	**1899**a	....		....	....	x---	----	x---	x---	x---	2?	
								? **1901**	....		?**1902**	....	x---	----	?---	----	?---		
								1904	0430p		....	....	----	----	----	----	----		
								1904	1026		**1904**	1027	x---	----	x?--	?---	-x--	3?	
								? **1907**	....		....	....	----	----	----	----	----		
								1909	....		**1914**?	....	x---	----	x---	x---	----	2	
								1917	....		....	....	x---	----	x---	----	----	2	
							South Crater, Main Crater	**1919**	0811		....	....	x---	----	xx--	?---	-x--	4	
								1920	1205?		**1921**	03	x---	----	xxx-	?---	-x--	2	
								1922	....		....	....	x---	----	x---	----	----	3?	
								? **1923**	....		....	....	----	----	----	----	----	2?	
								? **1924**	....		....	....	----	----	----	----	----	2?	
								1925	....		....	....	x---	----	x---	----	----	2?	
								1926	03		**1928**	0301p	x---	----	x---	----	----	2	
								1932	....		**1934**	....	x---	----	x---	----	----	2	
							Main Crater, South Crater	**1936**	09	+	**1939**	....	x---	----	xx--	x---	----	3*	
							South Crater	**1946**	1201p		**1947**	09	x---	----	x---	x---	----	3	7/-
								1953	04		**1953**	08	x---	----	x---	----	----	2	
								1954	05		**1954**	06	x---	----	x---	----	----	2	
							South Crater, Main Crater	**1956**	1208	+	**1958**	08	x---	----	xx--	x---	-xx-	3*	7/7
							South Crater	**1959**	06		**1959**	07	x---	----	x---	----	----	2	
							Main Crater, South Crater	**1959**	12	+	**1960**	12 >	x---	----	xx--	x---	----	2	6/-
							South Crater	**1961**	07		**1961**	09	x---	----	x---	x---	----	2	
							South Crater	**1962**	04		....	....	x		x---	x---	----	2	
							South Crater	**1963**	02		**1963**	05 >	x---	----	x---	x---	----	2	
							South Crater	**1963**	1126	+	**1964**	04	x---	----	xx--	x---	----	2*	6/-
							South Crater	**1965**	....		**1966**	0125>	x---	----	xx--	x---	----	2	6/-
							South Crater, Main Crater	**1974**	0304?		**1993**>	....	x---	----	xx--	x---	-x--	3*	7/-
KARKAR (New Guinea-NE of)	**4.649 S**	**145.964 E**	**1839**	**Stratovolc**	**0501-03=**	**Historical**													
								C **-7140**w	....		....	....	x---	----	xx--	----	--x-	**C**	
								C **-0870**u	....		....	....	x---	----	x?--	----	--x-		
								C **0520**v	....		....	....	x---	----	xx--	----	----	**C**	
								C **0730**?	....		....	....	x---	----	xx--	----	----	**P**	
							South flank (Patilo Cone)	C **1065**x	....		....	....	-x--	----	x---	----	----		
								1643	0420		....	....	x---	----	x---	----	----	3↑	
								? **1830**	....		....	....	----	----	?---	----	----		
								1885	....		....	....	x---	----	x---	----	----	2?	
								1895	0617		**1895**	08	x---	----	x---	x---	xx--	2	7/-
							Ulumam	? **1962**?	....		....	....	x---	----	?---	----	----	2?	
							Bagiai	**1974**	0214	+	**1974**	0808	x---	----	x---	x---	----	2	7/-

VOLCANO NAME (Subregion) / ERUPTION — Area of Activity	LAT	LONG	ELEV (m)	TYPE	NUMBER	Status / Start Year	Start M-Dy	P	Stop Year	Stop M-Dy	Central / Flank vent / Radial fiss / Regional*	Submarine / New island / Subglacial / Crater lake	Explosive / Pyro flow / Phreatic / Fumarolic	Lava flow / Lava lake / Dome / Spine	Fatal / Damage / Mudflow / Tsunami	VEI	Vol L/T
KARKAR (New Guinea-NE of) *continued*																	
Bagiai						**1974**	1230?	+	**1975**	0626	x---	----	x---	x---	----	2	6/-
SE foot of Bagiai						**1979**	0112?	+	**1979**	0809	x---	---x	xxx-	----	x-x-	2*	-/7
						? **1980**	0107		?**1980**	0117	x---	----	?---	----	----	1	
UNNAMED (New Guinea-NE of)	**4.311 S**	**146.256 E**	**-2000**	**Submarine ?**	**0501-04=**	**Uncertain**											
(correct date is 1944, not 1945)						? **1944**	....		....	....	----	?---	----	----	----	0	
						? **1951**	1124		....	....	----	?---	----	----	----	0	
YOMBA (New Guinea-NE of)	**4.92 S**	**146.75 E**		**Unknown**	**0501-041**	**Uncertain**											
LONG ISLAND (New Guinea-NE of)	**5.358 S**	**147.12 E**	**1280**	**Complx volc**	**0501-05=**	**Historical**											
						C **-2040**v	....		....	....	x---	----	xx--	----	----	**6**	**-/10**
						C **1660**p	....		....	....	x---	----	xx--	----	xxx-	**6**	**-/10**
Lake Wisdom						**1933**	....		....	....	x---	---x	----	----	----		
Lake Wisdom						**1938**	....		....	....	x---	---x	----	----	----		
Motmot						**1943**	....		....	....	x---	---x	x---	----	----		
Motmot						**1953**	0508		**1954**	0107	x---	---x	x-x-	----	----	3	
Motmot						**1955**	0605		**1955**	0613	x---	---x	x---	----	----	3	
Motmot						? **1961**	....		....	....	x---	----	?--x	----	----		
Motmot						**1968**	0316		**1968**	0612	x---	---x	x---	----	----	2	
Motmot						**1973**	04	+	**1974**	0228	x---	----	x-x-	x---	----	2	
Motmot						**1976**	0102u		....	....	x---	----	x---	----	----	1	
N or NE of Motmot?						**1993**	1105d		....	....	x---	---x	----	----	----	0	
UMBOI (New Guinea-NE of)	**5.589 S**	**147.875 E**	**1548**	**Complx volc**	**0501-06=**	**Holocene**											
RITTER ISLAND (New Guinea-NE of)	**5.52 S**	**148.121 E**	**140**	**Stratovolc**	**0501-07=**	**Historical**											
						1700	0324		....	....	x---	----	x?--	----	----	3↑	
						1793	0629		....	....	x---	----	x?--	----	----	2	
						? **1848**	0413		?**1848**	0710?	x---	----	----	----	----		
						? **1878**	1231p		....	....	x---	----	----	----	----		
						? **1885**	0113?		....	....	x---	----	----	----	----		
(probably Ritter or Langila: Cooke)						@ **1887**	0202		@**1887**	0205	----	----	x---	----	----	2	
						1888	0313		**1888**	0313	x---	----	x-x-	----	xx-x	2?	
West of Ritter Island						**1972**	1009		**1972**	1009	x---	x---	x---	----	---x	1	
600-900 m west of Ritter Is.						**1974**	1017		**1974**	1017	x---	x---	x---	----	---x	1	
SAKAR (New Guinea-NE of)	**5.414 S**	**148.094 E**	**992**	**Stratovolc**	**0501-08=**	**Holocene?**											
NEW BRITAIN																	
UNNAMED (New Britain-N of)	**5.20 S**	**148.57 E**		**Submarine ?**	**0502-001**	**Uncertain**											
						? **1983**	0615		?**1983**	0616	----	?---	----	----	----		
LANGILA (New Britain)	**5.525 S**	**148.42 E**	**1330**	**Complx volc**	**0502-01=**	**Historical**											
Crater 2						**1878**	....		....	....	x---	----	x---	x---	----	2	
						1884	....		....	....	----	----	x---	----	----	2	
						1890	....		....	....	----	----	----	x---	----	0	
North Crater (crater 1)						**1900**	....		....	....	x---	----	x---	----	----	2	
NE Crater (crater 2)						**1907**	....		....	....	x---	----	x---	----	----	2	
Crater 2						? **1942**e	....		....	....	x---	----	x---	----	----	1?	
Crater 2						**1954**	0518		**1954**	1113	x---	----	x---	----	----	3	
Crater 2						**1955**	0215		**1955**	0217	x---	----	x---	----	----	2	
Crater 2						**1955**	0601		**1955**	0616	x---	----	x---	----	----	2	
Crater 2						**1956**	0325		**1956**	0331	x---	----	x---	----	----	2	
Crater 2						**1958**	0421	+	**1958**	0604d	x---	----	x---	----	----	2	
Crater 3, Crater 2						**1960**	1219	+	**1961**	0925e	xx--	----	x---	x---	----	2	4/-
Crater 2, Crater 3						**1962**	03	+	**1963**	0811	xx--	----	x---	----	----	2	
Crater 2, Crater 3						**1964**	1204d	+	**1966**	0923c	xx--	----	x---	----	----	2	
Crater 2, Crater 3						**1967**	0119	+	**1968**	06	xx--	----	x---	x---	----	2	4/-
Crater 2 or 3						**1969**	0929		**1969**	0929	x---	----	x---	----	----	2	
Crater 2						**1970**	0520	+	**1970**	0922	x---	----	x---	----	----	2	
Crater 2						**1971**	0126e	+	**1972**	0705d	x---	----	x---	----	----	2	
Crater 3, Crater 2						**1973**	0224d	+	**1993**>	....	xx--	----	xxx-	x-x-	----	3*	7/-
NARAGE (New Britain)	**4.55 S**	**149.125 E**	**307**	**Stratovolc**	**0502-02=**	**Pleistocene-Geysers**											
MUNDUA (New Britain)	**4.63 S**	**149.35 E**	**179**	**Complx volc**	**0502-021**	**Holocene**											
GAROVE (New Britain)	**4.692 S**	**149.50 E**	**368**	**Stratovolc**	**0502-03=**	**Holocene**											
DAKATAUA (New Britain)	**5.056 S**	**150.108 E**	**400**	**Caldera**	**0502-04=**	**Anthropology**											
						C **0800**t	....		....	....	x---	----	xx--	----	----	**C**	
Makalia						A **1895**e	....		....	....	x---	----	x---	x---	xx--	2	
BOLA (New Britain)	**5.15 S**	**150.03 E**	**1155**	**Stratovolc**	**0502-05=**	**Holocene**											
GARUA HARBOUR (New Britain)	**5.269 S***	**150.088 E**	**565**	**Volc field**	**0502-06=**	**Holocene?**											
GARBUNA GROUP (New Britain)	**5.45 S**	**150.03 E**	**564**	**Stratovolcs**	**0502-07=**	**Holocene**											
LOLO (New Britain)	**5.47 S**	**150.50 E**	**805**	**Stratovolc**	**0502-071**	**Holocene?**											
PAGO (New Britain)	**5.58 S**	**150.52 E**	**742**	**Caldera**	**0502-08=**	**Historical**											
Witori						C **-7510**w	....		....	....	----	----	x---	----	----		
Witori						C **-3650**?	....		....	....	x---	----	x---	----	----		
Witori						C **-1350**?	....		....	....	x---	----	x---	----	----	**6?**	**-/10**
Witori						C **-0640**y	....		....	....	x---	----	xx--	----	----		
Witori						C **0420**v	....		....	....	x---	----	x---	----	----		
Witori						C **0750**?	....		....	....	x---	----	x---	----	----		
(same as 1911-1918 eruption)						X 1900?	....		....	....	----	----	----	----	----		
						1911	....		**1918**	05 ?	x---	----	x---	x---	-x--	3	
						1920b	....		....	....	x---	----	----	x---	----	0	8/-
						1933	07 ?		**1933**	08 ?	x---	----	x---	----	----	2	
WALO (New Britain)	**5.53 S**	**150.90 E**	**15**	**Hrdrothrm fld**	**0502-09=**	**Hot Springs**											
HARGY (New Britain)	**5.33 S**	**151.10 E**	**1148**	**Stratovolc**	**0502-10=**	**Radiocarbon**											
Galloseulo						C **-5050**?	....		....	....	x---	----	x---	x---	----		
Galloseulo						C **0950**?	....		....	....	x---	----	x---	----	----		
BAMUS (New Britain)	**5.20 S**	**151.23 E**	**2248**	**Stratovolc**	**0502-11=**	**Anthropology**											
						C **-0345**u	....		....	....	----	----	xx--	----	----		
						C **-0270**t	....		....	....	----	----	xx--	----	----		
						C **1645**t	....		....	....	----	----	xx--	----	----		
						1886h	....		....	....	x---	----	xx--	--?-	----	3?	
ULAWUN (New Britain)	**5.05 S**	**151.33 E**	**2334**	**Stratovolc**	**0502-12=**	**Historical**											
						1700	0311		....	....	x---	----	x---	----	----	2	
						1878	....		....	....	x---	----	x---	----	----	2	
						1898	....		....	....	x---	----	xx--	----	----	3	
(no confirmed eruption in 1912)						X 1912	....		....	....	----	----	----	----	----		
						1915	04		....	....	x---	----	x---	----	-x--	3	
						1918	0721?		....	....	x---	----	x---	----	----	2	
						1919	0528?		....	....	x---	----	x---	----	----	2	

VOLCANO NAME (Subregion) / ERUPTION — Area of Activity	LAT	LONG	ELEV (m)	TYPE	NUMBER	Status / Start Year	Start M-Dy	P	Stop Year	Stop M-Dy	Central / Flank vent / Radial fiss / Regional*	Submarine / New island / Subglacial / Crater lake	Explosive / Pyro flow / Phreatic / Fumarolic	Lava flow / Lava lake / Dome / Spine	Fatal / Damage / Mudflow / Tsunami	VEI	Vol L/T
ULAWUN (New Britain) *continued*						**1927**	07		**1927**	0917>	x---	----	x---	----	----	2	
						? **1937**	05		....	....	----	----	?---	----	----		
						1941	0126		**1941**	0126	x---	----	x---	----	----	2	
						? **1951**	....		....	....	----	----	?---	----	----		
						1958	0201r		....	....	x---	----	x---	----	----	2	
						1960	0729c		**1962**	11	x---	----	x---	----	----	2	
						1963	0317		**1963**	0502?	x---	----	x---	----	----	2	
						1967	0122		**1967**	1228	x---	----	x---	----	-x--	2	
						1970	0115		**1970**	0211	x-x-	----	xx--	x---	----	3	6/6
						1973	1004		**1973**	1019	x---	----	xx--	x---	----	2	7/6
Summit, lower east flank						**1978**	0507		**1978**	0514	x-x-	----	xx--	x---	-x--	3	6/7
						1980	1006		**1980**	1007	x---	----	xx--	----	-x--	3	-/7
						1983	1106	+	**1984**	0313	x---	----	--x-	----	----	1	
						1984	0823	+	**1984**	0911	x---	----	x-x-	----	----	1	
						1984	1230		**1985**	0127	x---	----	x---	x-x-	----	1	5/-
						1985	1117		**1985**	1122	x---	----	xx--	x---	----	3*	6/6
						1989	0101	+	**1989**	12 ?	x---	----	x-x-	----	----	2	
						1993	0112		**1993**	0131	x---	----	x-?-	-?--	----	2	
LOLOBAU (New Britain)	**4.92 S**	**151.158 E**	**858**	**Caldera**	**0502-13=**	**Historical**											
Hulu						C **1100r**	....		....	....	x---	----	x---	----	----	4	-/8
East flank (Sili, Malo), Hulu ?						**1904**	0809		**1905**	1018>	xx--	----	x---	x---	----	**P***	
						? **1908**	....		....	....	----	----	----	----	----		
East flank (Sili)						**1911**	....		?**1912**	....	-xx-	----	x---	x---	----	4	8/8
UNNAMED (New Britain-N of)	**4.75 S**	**150.85 E**		**Submarine ?**	**0502-131**	**Uncertain**											
						? **1951**	....		....	....	----	?---	----	----	----	0	
						? **1970**	0602		?**1970**	0613	----	?---	----	----	----	0	
RABAUL (New Britain).............	**4.271 S**	**152.203 E**	**688**	**Pyrocl shield**	**0502-14=**	**Historical**											
						C **-1550u**	....		....	....	x---	----	xx--	----	----	5	-/9
						C **0540v**	....		....	....	x---	----	xx--	----	----	**6**	**-/10**
Kombiu.............................						M **0650?**	....		....	....	-x--	----	----	x---	----	0	
Tavurvur ?						**1767**	0910		....	....	x---	----	x---	----	----	2	
Tavurvur............................						**1791**	0522		....	....	x---	----	x---	----	----	2?	
Sulfur Creek..........................						**1850?**	....		....	....	x---	----	x-x-	----	xx--	2	
Vulcan Island and Tavurvur						**1878**	0130?	+	**1878**	0226b	x---	xx--	x-x-	----	xx-x	3	-/8
Vulcan and Tavurvur						**1937**	0529		**1937**	0602	xx--	xx--	xxx-	----	xxxx	4?	-/8
Tavurvur............................						**1940**	0204d		**1940**	0518	x---	---x	--x-	----	----	1	
Tavurvur............................						**1941**	0606		**1942**	0331p	x---	----	x---	x---	-x--	2	
Tavurvur............................						**1943**	1124		**1943**	1223>	x---	----	x---	----	----	2	

NEW GUINEA & D'ENTRECASTEAUX ISLANDS

VOLCANO NAME (Subregion) / ERUPTION — Area of Activity	LAT	LONG	ELEV (m)	TYPE	NUMBER	Status / Start Year	Start M-Dy	P	Stop Year	Stop M-Dy	Central / Flank vent / Radial fiss / Regional*	Submarine / New island / Subglacial / Crater lake	Explosive / Pyro flow / Phreatic / Fumarolic	Lava flow / Lava lake / Dome / Spine	Fatal / Damage / Mudflow / Tsunami	VEI	Vol L/T
DOMA PEAKS (New Guinea)	**5.90 S**	**143.15 E**	**3568**	**Stratovolc**	**0503-00-**	**Holocene?**											
CRATER MOUNTAIN (New Guinea) ..	**6.58 S**	**145.08 E**	**3233**	**Stratovolc**	**0503-001**	**Holocene?**											
YELIA (New Guinea)	**7.05 S**	**145.858 E**	**3384**	**Stratovolc**	**0503-002**	**Holocene?**											
KORANGA (New Guinea)	**7.33 S**	**146.708 E**		**Expl crater**	**0503-003**	**Holocene**											
MADILOGO (New Guinea)..........	**9.20 S**	**147.57 E**	**850**	**Pyrocl cone**	**0503-004**	**Holocene**											
LAMINGTON (New Guinea).........	**8.95 S**	**148.15 E**	**1680**	**Stratovolc**	**0503-01=**	**Historical**											
						C **-5980y**	....		....	....	----	----	x---	----	----		
						C **-4850y**	....		....	....	----	----	x---	----	----		
						1951	0117	+	**1956**	....	x---	----	xx--	--xx	xxx-	4*	8/-
HYDROGRAPHERS RANGE (")	**9.00 S**	**148.37 E**	**1915**	**Stratovolc**	**0503-011**	**Holocene**											
MUSA RIVER (New Guinea)	**9.308 S**	**148.13 E**	**808**	**Hydrothrm fld**	**0503-02=**	**Hot Springs**											
MANAGLASE PLATEAU (")	**9.08 S**	***148.33 E**	**1342**	**Volc field**	**0503-021**	**Anthropology**											
VICTORY (New Guinea)...........	**9.20 S**	**149.07 E**	**1925**	**Stratovolc**	**0503-03=**	**Historical**											
						? **1810j**	....		....	....	----	----	----	----	----	2?	
						1890?	....		**1935**e	....	x---	----	xx--	--x-	xx--	2	
SESSAGARA (New Guinea)	**9.48 S**	***149.13 E**	**370**	**Unknown**	**0503-031**	**Holocene**											
WAIOWA (New Guinea)............	**9.57 S**	**149.075 E**	**640**	**Pyrocl cone**	**0503-04=**	**Historical**											
(eruption began in 1943, not 1942)						**1943**	0918	+	**1944**	0831	xx--	----	xxx-	----	--x-	3*	
GOODENOUGH (D'Entrecasteaux Is) .	**9.48 S**	***150.35 E**	**220**	**Volc field**	**0503-041**	**Holocene**											
IAMELELE (D'Entrecasteaux Is)	**9.52 S**	**150.53 E**	**200**	**Lava domes**	**0503-05=**	**Holocene**											
DAWSON STRAIT GROUP (")	**9.62 S**	***150.88 E**	**500**	**Volc field**	**0503-06=**	**Hydration Rind**											
Oiau						H **1350?**	....		....	....	----	----	----	----	----		

NEW IRELAND & BOUGAINVILLE

VOLCANO NAME (Subregion) / ERUPTION — Area of Activity	LAT	LONG	ELEV (m)	TYPE	NUMBER	Status / Start Year	Start M-Dy	P	Stop Year	Stop M-Dy	Central / Flank vent / Radial fiss / Regional*	Submarine / New island / Subglacial / Crater lake	Explosive / Pyro flow / Phreatic / Fumarolic	Lava flow / Lava lake / Dome / Spine	Fatal / Damage / Mudflow / Tsunami	VEI	Vol L/T
LIHIR (New Ireland-SW Pac)	**3.125 S**	**152.642 E**	**700**	**Volc complx**	**0504-01=**	**Holocene**											
AMBITLE (New Ireland-SW Pac).....	**4.08 S**	**153.65 E**	**450**	**Stratovolc**	**0504-02=**	**Radiocarbon**											
East side of caldera						C **-0350v**	....		....	....	x---	----	x---	----	----		
TORE (Bougainville-SW Pac)........	**5.83 S**	**154.93 E**	**2200**	**Lava cone**	**0505-00-**	**Holocene**											
BALBI (Bougainville-SW Pac)	**5.83 S**	**154.98 E**	**2715**	**Stratovolc**	**0505-01=**	**Holocene**											
Crater B ?...........................						? **1825q**	....		....	....	x---	----	x---	----	x---		
BILLY MITCHELL (Bougainville)	**6.092 S**	**155.225 E**	**1544**	**Pyrocl shield**	**0505-011**	**Radiocarbon**											
						C **1030q**	....		....	....	x---	----	x---	----	----	**5+**	**-/9**
						C **1580p**	....		....	....	x---	----	xx--	----	----	**6**	**-/10**
BAGANA (Bougainville-SW Pac).....	**6.140 S**	**155.195 E**	**1750**	**Lava cone**	**0505-02=**	**Historical**											
						1842	0315		....	....	x---	----	----	x---	----	1	
						1865c	....		**1883**	....	----	----	x---	----	----	2	
						1883	1231p		....	....	x---	----	x---	----	x---	3	
						1894	....		**1895**	....	x---	----	xx--	x---	----	2	
						1897	0516?		....	....	x---	----	x---	----	----	2	
						1899	....		....	....	----	----	----	----	----		
						1908	0715		....	....	x---	----	?---	?---	----	2?	
						? **1909**	07		....	....	----	----	----	----	----		
						1937	0907		....	....	x---	----	x---	----	----	3	
						1938	0515		....	....	x---	----	xx--	----	----	3	
						1939	0130?		....	....	x---	----	x---	x---	----	2	
						1943	0407<		....	....	x---	----	----	x---	----	1	
						1945	....		**1947**	....	x---	----	x---	x---	----	2	
						1948	1201p	+	**1951**	1201p	x---	----	xx--	x-x-	----	3*	
						1952	0229		**1952**	10	x---	----	xx--	x-x-	----	4	
						1953	06		**1953**	09	x---	----	xx--	----	----	3*	
						1956	....		....	....	x---	----	x---	----	----	2	
						1959?	....		**1960**	05	x---	----	x---	x---	----	2	
						1961	0726		....	....	x---	----	x---	----	----	2	
						1962	0215	+	**1963**	....	x---	----	x---	x---	----	2	

VOLCANO NAME (Subregion) / ERUPTION — Area of Activity	LAT	LONG	ELEV (m)	TYPE	NUMBER	Status	Start Year	Start M-Dy	P	Stop Year	Stop M-Dy	Central / Flank vent / Radial fiss / Regional*	Submarine / New island / Subglacial / Crater lake	Explosive / Pyro flow / Phreatic / Fumarolic	Lava flow / Lava lake / Dome / Spine	Fatal / Damage / Mudflow / Tsunami	VEI	Vol L/T
BAGANA (Bougainville) *continued*							**1964**	0424		**1965**	....	x---	----	x-x-	x---	----	2	
							1966	0320		**1967**	1130	x---	----	xx--	x-x-	----	3*	
							1968	08		**1968**	08	x---	----	x---	----	----	2	
							1970	0521m	+	**1971**	08 >	x---	----	x---	x---	----	2	
							1972	....		**1993>**	....	x---	----	xx--	x-x-	----	2*	6/-
TAKUAN GROUP (Bougainville)	**6.442 S**	**155.608 E**	**2210**	**Volc complx**	**0505-021**	**Holocene**												
LOLORU (Bougainville-SW Pac)	**6.52 S**	**155.62 E**	**1887**	**Pyrocl shield**	**0505-03=**	**Radiocarbon**												
							C **-6950?**	....		....	....	x---	----	x---	----	----		
							C **-4150?**	....		....	....	x---	----	xx--	----	----		
							C **-3150?**	....		....	....	x---	----	xx--	----	----		
							C **-2150?**	....		....	....	x---	----	xx--	----	----		
							C **-1260y**	....		....	....	x---	----	xx--	----	----		
							C **-1050?**	....		....	....	x---	----	x---	----	----		

SOLOMON ISLANDS & SANTA CRUZ

VOLCANO NAME (Subregion) / ERUPTION — Area of Activity	LAT	LONG	ELEV (m)	TYPE	NUMBER	Status	Start Year	Start M-Dy	P	Stop Year	Stop M-Dy	Central / Flank vent / Radial fiss / Regional*	Submarine / New island / Subglacial / Crater lake	Explosive / Pyro flow / Phreatic / Fumarolic	Lava flow / Lava lake / Dome / Spine	Fatal / Damage / Mudflow / Tsunami	VEI	Vol L/T
NONDA (Vella Lavella I)	**7.67 S**	**156.60 E**	**760**	**Stratovolc**	**0505-04=**	**Pleistocene-Fumarolic**												
SIMBO (Solomon Is-SW Pac)	**8.292 S**	**156.52 E**	**335**	**Stratovolc**	**0505-05=**	**Uncertain**												
COOK (Solomon Is-SW Pac)	8.415 S	157.10 E	-1300		0505-051	Not a Volcano												
(no volcano at this location)							X 1964	0525		X1964	0614?	----	----	----	----	----		
KANA KEOKI (Solomon Is-SW Pac)	**8.75 S**	**157.03 E**	**-700**	**Submarine**	**0505-052**	**Holocene**												
COLEMAN SEAMOUNT (Solomon Is)	**8.83 S**	**157.17 E**		**Submarine**	**0505-053**	**Holocene**												
KAVACHI (Solomon Is-SW Pac)	**9.02 S**	**157.95 E**	**-20**	**Submarine**	**0505-06=**	**Historical**												
							1939	0430?		....	....	----	x---	x---	----	----	2	
							1942?	....		....	....	----	x---	----	----	----	1	
							1950	1201p		....	....	----	x---	x---	----	----	2	
							1951	1201p		....	....	----	x---	x---	----	---x	2	
							1952	0416		**1953**	0131?	----	xx--	x---	x---	----	2	
							1957	0208		....	....	----	x---	--x-	----	----	0	
							1958	1121		**1958**	1202?	----	x?--	----	?---	----	0	
							1961	0328<		....	....	----	xx--	x---	x---	----	2	
							1962	01		**1962**	02	----	x---	x---	----	----	2	
(eruption Dec. 14, 1963, not 1961)							**1963**	1214		**1964**	0131?	----	xx--	--x-	x---	----	2*	
							1965	1211		**1965**	1213	----	xx--	--x-	x---	----	2	
							1966	0319		**1966**	0322>	----	x---	x-x-	----	----	2	
							1969	1028	+	**1970**	0206	----	xx--	x---	x---	----	2	
							1972	1024		....	....	----	x---	----	----	----	0	
							1974	1112		**1974**	1212?	----	x---	----	----	----	1	
							1975	08		....	....	----	x---	x---	----	----	1	
							1976	0824		**1976**	1013	----	xx--	x---	x---	----	1	
							1977	0222		....	....	----	x---	x---	----	----	1	
							1977	0717?		**1977**	0722	----	x---	x---	----	----	1	
							1978	0621		**1978**	0722f	----	xx--	x---	x---	----	2	
							1980	1007		**1981**	0225	----	x---	x---	----	----	1	
							? **1981**	0915e		....	....	----	?---	----	----	----	0	
							1982	0407		**1982**	0602a	----	x---	x---	----	----	2	
							1985	1209		**1986**	0228c	----	x---	x---	----	----	1	
							1986	0705		**1986**	0723	----	xx--	x-x-	----	----	1	
							1991	0504<		**1991**	0617c	----	xx--	x---	----	----	2	
UNNAMED (Solomon Is-SW Pac)	**8.92 S**	**158.03 E**	**-240**	**Submarine**	**0505-061**	**Holocene**												
GALLEGO (Solomon Is-SW Pac)	**9.35 S**	***159.73 E**	**1000**	**Volc field**	**0505-062**	**Holocene?**												
SAVO (Solomon Is-SW Pac)	**9.13 S**	**159.82 E**	**510**	**Stratovolc**	**0505-07=**	**Historical**												
							1568	....		....	....	x---	----	xx--	----	?---	3	
							1835e	....		**1847**?	....	x---	----	xx--	----	x---	3?	
TINAKULA (Santa Cruz Is-SW Pac)	**10.38 S**	**165.80 E**	**851**	**Stratovolc**	**0506-01=**	**Historical**												
							C **-1050?**	....		....	....	----	----	x---	----	----		
							1595	....		....	....	x---	----	x---	x---	----	3↑	
							1768	08		....	....	----	----	x---	----	----	2	
							1797	....		....	....	----	----	x---	----	----	1?	
							1840?	....		....	....	x---	----	xx--	----	xx--	3?	
							1855	08		....	....	x---	----	x---	----	----	2	
							1857	08		....	....	----	----	x---	----	----	2	
							1869	03		....	....	----	----	x---	----	----	2	
							1871	....		....	....	----	----	x---	x---	----	2?	
							1886	....		....	....	----	----	----	----	----		
							1909	08		....	....	----	----	x---	x---	----	2	
							1951	1023		**1951**	1127p	x---	----	x---	x---	----	3	
							? **1955**	08		?**1955**	1015r	----	----	--?-	----	----	2?	
Upper NW flank							**1965**	1123	+	**1966**	0611	-x--	----	x-x-	x---	---x	3*	
Upper and lower NW flanks							**1971**	0906		**1971**	1211	-x--	----	xx--	x---	-x-x	2	
Upper NW flank							**1984**	0603<		**1985**	0613>	-x--	----	x---	----	----	2	

VANUATU & S

VOLCANO NAME (Subregion) / ERUPTION — Area of Activity	LAT	LONG	ELEV (m)	TYPE	NUMBER	Status	Start Year	Start M-Dy	P	Stop Year	Stop M-Dy	Central / Flank vent / Radial fiss / Regional*	Submarine / New island / Subglacial / Crater lake	Explosive / Pyro flow / Phreatic / Fumarolic	Lava flow / Lava lake / Dome / Spine	Fatal / Damage / Mudflow / Tsunami	VEI	Vol L/T
MOTLAV (Vanuatu-SW Pacific)	**13.67 S**	**167.67 E**	**411**	**Stratovolc**	**0507-001**	**Holocene**												
SORETIMEAT (Vanua Lava I)	**13.80 S**	**167.47 E**	**921**	**Complx volc**	**0507-01=**	**Historical**												
(eruption ca. 1860, not ca. 1856)							**1860?**	....		....	....	x---	----	x---	----	----	2?	
(eruption ca. 1865, not ca. 1861)							**1865?**	....		....	....	x---	----	x---	----	----	2	
NW flank							**1965**	0809		**1966**	....	-x--	----	x-x-	----	----	2	
GAUA (Santa Maria I)	**14.27 S**	**167.50 E**	**797**	**Stratovolc**	**0507-02=**	**Historical**												
Mt. Garat							? **1962**	07 <		....	....	x---	----	?---	----	----		
Mt. Garat (upper SE flank)							**1963**	0915e		**1963**	1109>	x---	----	x---	----	----	2	
Mt. Garat							**1965**	0927		**1965**	0930>	x---	----	x---	----	----	3	
Mt. Garat							**1966**	....		....	....	x---	----	x---	----	----	2	
Mt. Garat							**1967**	07		....	....	x---	----	x---	----	----	2	
Mt. Garat (upper SE flank)							**1968**	....		**1968**	1201p	x---	----	x---	----	----	2	
Mt. Garat							**1969**	0922		....	....	x---	----	x---	----	----	2	
Mt. Garat (upper SE flank)							**1971**	0512		**1971**	0513	x---	----	x---	----	----	2	
Mt. Garat (upper SE flank)							**1973**	1009	+	**1974**	0121	x---	----	x---	----	----	2*	
Mt. Garat							**1976**	0115e		....	....	x---	----	x---	----	----	2	
Mt. Garat							**1977**	0413		**1977**	0413	x---	----	x---	----	----	2	
Mt. Garat							**1980**	....		....	....	x---	----	--?-	----	----	1?	
Mt. Garat							**1981**	0709		**1981**	0709	x---	----	?-?-	----	----	1?	
Mt. Garat							**1982**	0418		**1982**	0418	x---	----	x-?-	----	----	2	
MERE LAVA (Vanuatu-SW Pacific)	**14.45 S**	**168.05 E**	**1028**	**Stratovolc**	**0507-021**	**Holocene**												
							? **1606**	....		....	....	----	----	----	----	----		

VOLCANO NAME (Subregion) / ERUPTION — Area of Activity	LAT	LONG	ELEV (m)	TYPE	NUMBER	Status / Start Year	Start M-Dy	P	Stop Year	Stop M-Dy	Central, Flank vent, Radial fiss, Regional* / Submarine, New island, Subglacial, Crater lake / Explosive, Pyro flow, Phreatic, Fumarolic / Lava flow, Lava lake, Dome, Spine / Fatal, Damage, Mudflow, Tsunami	VEI	Vol L/T
AOBA (Vanuatu-SW Pacific)	15.40 S	167.83 E	1496	Shield	0507-03=	Anthropology							
Lakes Vui and Manaro Ngoru						C 1590t	....		....	....	x--- ---- x--- ---- ----		
Lake Vui and upper west flank						A 1670?	....		....	....	xxx- ---- x-x- x--- xx--	2?	
SE side of Lake Manaro Lakua						A 1870?	....		....	....	x--- ---- x-x- ---- xxx-	2?	
AMBRYM (Vanuatu-SW Pacific)	16.25 S	168.12 E	1334	Stratovolc	0507-04=	Historical							
						C 0050v	....		....	....	x--- ---- xx-- x--- ----	6+	-/10
						1774	....		....	....	---- ---- x--- ---- ----	2	
West flank						1820?	....		....	....	--x- ---- ---- x--- -x--		
						1863	....		1864	....	x--- ---- x--- x--- ----	2	
						? 1870	....		....	....	---- ---- ?--- ---- ----		
						1871	....		....	....	---- ---- x--- ---- ----	2	
Marum						1883	....		....	....	x--- ---- x--- ---- ----	2	
Marum and/or Benbow						1884	....		....	....	x--- ---- ?--- ---- ----	2?	
						1886	07		....	....	x--- ---- x--- ---- ----	2	
SE flank (6 km from SE Point), Marum						1888	0224d		1888	04 ?	xx-- ---- x--- x--- ----	2	
Benbow and west flank						1894	1015		1895	0210>	x-x- ---- x--- x--- xx--	3	
						1898	0326		....	....	---- ---- ?--- ---- ----	1?	
						1908	....		....	....	---- ---- ?--- ---- ----	2?	
						? 1909	0628		....	....	---- ---- ?--- ---- ----		
Base of Marum						1910	....		....	....	x--- ---- ---- x--- ----	0?	
Marum ?, west flank ?						1912	....		....	....	x?-- ?--- ?--- ---- ----		
Benbow, west flank, Marum						1913	1014		1914	....	xxx- ---- x--- x--- xx--	3*	
Marum, crater at southeast point						1915	1020		....	....	xx-- ---- x--- ---- ----	2	
Benbow, west flank, Marum						1929	0628	+	1929	0701	xxx- x--- x--- x--- -x--	2	
Benbow						1935	09	+	1936	01	x--- ---- x--- -x-- ----	2	
Benbow and west flank						1937	0327		1937	04	x-x- ---- x--- x--- ----	2	
Benbow, Marum ?						1938	....		....	....	x--- ---- x--- ---- ----	2	
NW flank of Benbow						1942	0606		....	....	x-x- ---- x--- x--- ----	2	
Benbow						1950	1206		1951	1125e	x--- ---- x--- ---- -xx-	4*	-/8
Benbow						1952	0810		1952	1226e	x--- ---- x--- ---- -x--	2	
Benbow, Mbuelesu, S flank of Benbow						1953	05		1953	1013?	xx-- ---- x--- -x-- ----	2	
Benbow						1954	....		....	....	x--- ---- x--- ---- ----	2	
Benbow						1955	....		....	....	x--- ---- x--- x--- ----	2	
Benbow, Marum						1957	0826e		1957	10	x--- ---- x--- ---- ----	1?	
Benbow and Marum						1958	1118		....	....	x--- ---- ?--- ---- ----	2?	
Marum						1959	04		....	....	x--- ---- x--- ---- ----	2	
Mbuelesu, Benbow, near Marum						1960	0917		....	....	xx-- ---- ?--- -x-- ----	1?	
Benbow, Marum, south of Marum						1961	0815		1963	0403	xx-- ---- x--- -x-- ----	3*	
Benbow, Marum						1963	0830		1963	0923>	x--- ---- x--- ---- ----	2	
Marum, Benbow						1964	02 ?		1966	09 >	xx-- ---- x--- -x-- ----	2	
Marum, Benbow, Mbuelesu						1967	07		1970	0829	x--- ---- x--- -x-- -x--	2	
Marum, Benbow						1971	0203		1971	1105	x--- ---- x--- -x-- ----	2	
Benbow, Marum						1972	0415		1972	0815	x--- ---- x--- x--- -x--	3*	
Benbow, Mbuelesu, Marum						1973	0415e		1976	1014	xx-- ---- x--- -x-- ----	3*	
						1977	0120e		1977	0128?	x--- ---- x--- ---- -x--	2	
						1977	08		1977	0930	x--- ---- x--- ---- ----	2	
Benbow						1979	0126e		1979	0218?	x--- ---- x--- ---- -x--	2	
Benbow, Marum						1979	0606		1979	09 ?	x--- ---- x--- ---- ----	2	
Marum						1980	0516	+	1980	0818	x--- ---- x--- ---- ----	3*	
Benbow, Marum						1981	0220		1981	0930	x--- ---- x-x- x--- -x--	2	
Marum						1983	....		....	....	x--- ---- x--- ---- ----	2	
						1984	....		1986	0308>	x--- ---- x--- ---- ----	2	
New cone 3 km east of Marum						1986	1113		1986	1119?	x--- ---- x--- x--- ----	2	
Benbow, Mbwelesu, Marum, Niri Taten						1988	0212?	+	1988	0823	xx-- ---- x--- xx-- ----	3	6/-
Marum, Benbow, Niri Mbwelesu Taten						1989	0424		1989	1223	xx-- ---- x--- xx-- -?--	2	
Mbwelesu, Niri Mbwelesu, Niri Taten						1990	09 <		1991	07 >	x--- ---- x--- ---- ----	2	
LOPEVI (Vanuatu-SW Pacific)	16.507 S	168.346 E	1413	Stratovolc	0507-05=	Historical							
						1863	....		....	....	x--- ---- x?-- ---- ----	2	
						1864	0609		....	....	x--- ---- xx-- ---- ----	3	
						1874	....		....	....	---- ---- ---- ---- ----	2	
						1884	....		....	....	---- ---- ---- ---- ----		
						? 1892	10		....	....	---- ---- ---- ---- ----		
						1893	....		....	....	---- ---- ---- ---- ----	2	
						? 1898	....		....	....	x--- ---- ---- ---- ----		
						1908	....		....	....	?--- ---- ---- x--- ----	2	
						1922	0628		1922	0701	---- ---- ?--- ---- ----	2	
						1933	....		....	....	---- ---- ---- ---- ----		
NW and SE flanks						1939	0202		....	....	-xx- ---- x--- x--- -x--	2	
NW and/or SW flanks						1939	1101		....	....	-xx- ---- xx-- x--- -x--	2	
NW flank (640 m)						1960	0710		1960	09	-xx- ---- xx-- x--- -x--	3	
NW flank						1962	07		....	....	-xx- ---- ---- x--- ----	0	
Summit, NW, north, east and SE flanks						1963	0707	+	1965	....	xxx- ---- xx-- x--- -x--	3*	
Summit and northwest flank						1967	0127		1969	0331	xxx- ---- x--- x--- ----	3*	
Summit, northwest and east flanks						1970	0509		1972	0807	xxx- ---- x--- x--- ----	2*	
Summit and northwest flank						1974	01		1974	1007	x?-- ---- x-?- ---- ----	2	
Summit and northwest flank						1975	0306c	+	1975	0623	xx-- ---- x--- ---- ----	2	
						1976	0501	+	1976	0905	x--- ---- x--- ---- ----	1	
Summit and northwest flank						1978	1122	+	1979	03	xx-- ---- x--- x--- ----	2*	
NW flank						1979	0702	+	1979	0912	-x-- ---- x--- ---- ----	2	
Summit, NW and SE flanks						1980	0415	+	1980	0820	xx-- ---- x--- x--- -x--	3	
						1982	1024		1982	1025	x--- ---- x--- ---- ----	2	
EAST EPI (Vanuatu-SW Pacific)	16.68 S	168.37 E	-34	Caldera	0507-06=	Historical							
						1920	0122		....	....	---- xx-- ---- ---- ----	2	
Epib and other vents						1953	0212		1953	0219	x--- xx-- x--- ---- ----	3	
						? 1953	11		....	....	---- ?--- ---- ---- ----	0	
						1958	09 ?		1958	11 ?	---- x--- x--- ---- ----	2?	
						1960	07 ?		....	....	---- x--- ---- ---- ----	0	
						? 1971	1028		?1971	1115?	---- ?--- ---- ---- ----	0	
						? 1972	0515e		?1972	0625e	---- ?--- ---- ---- ----	0	
						? 1973	0505d		?1973	1026e	---- ?--- ---- ---- ----	0	
Epia and Epib						? 1974	11		?1974	11	x--- ?--- ---- ---- ----	0	
South flank of Epib						1979e	....		....	....	-x-- x--- ---- ---- ----	0	
						? 1988	08		....	....	---- ?--- ---- ---- ----	0	
KUTALI, TAVANI (Vanuatu-SW Pac)	16.73 S	168.28 E	833	Stratovolcs	0507-061	Holocene?							
TAVAI RURO (Vanuatu-SW Pacific)	16.80 S	168.43 E	554	Stratovolc	0507-062	Holocene?							
KUWAE (Vanuatu-SW Pacific)	16.829 S	168.536 E	-2	Caldera	0507-07=	Historical							
						I 1452j	....		....	....	x--- ---- xx-- ---- xx--	6	-/10

VOLCANO NAME (Subregion) / ERUPTION	LAT	LONG	ELEV (m)	TYPE	NUMBER	Status / Area of Activity	Start Year	Start M-Dy	P	Stop Year	Stop M-Dy	Central / Flank vent / Radial fiss / Regional*	Submarine / New island / Subglacial / Crater lake	Explosive / Pyro flow / Phreatic / Fumarolic	Lava flow / Lava lake / Dome / Spine	Fatal / Damage / Mudflow / Tsunami	VEI	Vol L/T
KUWAE (Vanuatu-SW Pacific) *continued*						Karua	**1897**	....		**1901**	....	x---	xx--	----	----	----	2	
						Karua	**1923**	....		**1925**	....	x---	xx--	----	----	----	2?	
						Karua	**1948**	0922		**1948**	0929	x---	xx--	x---	----	----	2	
						Karua	**1949**	04		....	....	x---	x---	x---	----	----	3	
						Karua	**1949**	10		**1949**	12	x---	xx--	----	----	----	3	
						Karua	**1952**	1003		....	....	x---	x---	x---	----	----	1	
						Karua	**1953**	0212		....	....	x---	x---	----	----	----	1?	
						Karua	**1958**	1007?		**1958**	1218	x---	x---	x---	----	----	2*	
						Karua	**1959**	0918?		**1959**	0920?	x---	xx--	----	----	----	2	
						Karua	? **1970**	0912		?**1970**	0920	x---	?---	----	----	----	0	
						Karua	**1971**	0222		**1971**	0222	x---	xx--	x---	----	----	2	
						Karua	? **1972**	0305e		?**1972**	0515e	x---	?---	----	----	----	0	
						Karua	? **1973**	0505d		?**1973**	10	x---	?---	----	----	----	0	
						Karua	**1974**	0204d		**1974**	09 ?	x---	xx--	----	----	----	0	
						Karua	? **1977**	0201		....	....	x---	?---	----	----	----	0	
						Karua	? **1979**	09		....	....	x---	?---	----	----	----	0	
						Karua	? **1980**	0820		....	....	x---	?---	----	----	----	0	
UNNAMED (Vanuatu-SW Pacific)	**16.992 S**	**168.592 E**	**216**	**Stratovolcs**	**0507-08-**	**Holocene**												
NORTH VATE (Vanuatu-SW Pacific)	**17.45 S**	**168.33 E**	**594**	**Stratovolcs**	**0507-081**	**Holocene**												
TRAITOR'S HEAD (Erromango I)	**18.75 S**	**169.23 E**	**837**	**Stratovolc**	**0507-09=**	**Historical**												
						NE flank submarine vent	**1881**	....		....	....	-x--	x---	----	----	----	0	
						Four submarine vents N of Erromango	? **1959**	....		....	....	----	?---	----	----	----		
YASUR (Tanna I)	**19.52 S**	**169.425 E**	**361**	**Stratovolc**	**0507-10=**	**Historical**												
							C **0850**y	....		....	....	x---	----	x---	----	----		
							C **1150**?	....		....	....	x---	----	x---	----	----		
							1774<	....	+	**1993**>	....	x---	----	x-x-	-x--	-x-x	3*	
ANEITYUM (Vanuatu-SW Pacific)	**20.20 S**	**169.83 E**	**852**	**Stratovolcs**	**0507-11-**	**Holocene?**												
MATTHEW ISLAND (SW Pacific)	**22.33 S**	**171.32 E**	**177**	**Stratovolc**	**0508-01=**	**Historical**												
							? **1828**	01		....	....	----	----	----	----	----		
						West-Matthew	**1949**<	....		....	....	x---	xx--	x---	x---	----	2	
						West-Matthew (October 1954, not 1953)	**1954**	10 ?		....	....	x---	----	?---	----	----	2	
						West-Matthew	**1956**b	....		....	....	x-x-	----	----	----	----	0?	
							? **1966**	08		....	....	----	----	?---	----	----		
							? **1976**	1127		....	....	x---	----	--?-	----	----	1?	
HUNTER ISLAND (SW Pacific)	**22.40 S**	**172.05 E**	**297**	**Stratovolc**	**0508-02=**	**Historical**												
							? **1797**	....		....	....	----	----	----	----	----		
							1835	....		....	....	----	----	----	x---	----		
							1841	0315		....	....	----	----	x---	----	----		
							? **1892**	....		....	....	----	----	----	----	----		
						East side	**1895**	1124		....	....	-x--	----	x---	x---	----		
							1903	....		....	....	----	----	----	----	----		
						(eruption report not valid)	X 1983	0309<		....	....	----	----	----	----	----		
UNNAMED (SW Pacific)	**25.78 S**	**168.63 E**	**-2400**	**Submarine**	**0508-03-**	**Hydrophonic**												
						Norfolk Island Ridge	S **1963**	0911		S**1964**	....	----	x---	x---	----	----	0	
AUSTRALIA																		
NEWER VOLCANICS PROV (Aust)	**37.77 S***	**142.50 E**	**1011**	**Shields**	**0509-01-**	**Radiocarbon**												
						Red Rock	C **-5850**?	....		....	....	x---	----	x---	----	----		
						Mt. Napier	C **-5290**<	....		....	....	x---	----	----	x---	----		
						Mt. Schank	F **-3000**z	....		....	....	x--x	----	x-x-	x---	----		
						Mt. Gambier	C **-2900**w	....		....	....	x---	----	x-x-	x---	----		

Indonesia & Andaman Islands (06)

Indonesia consists of more than 13,000 islands, spread over an area approximating that of the conterminous United States. Its population of nearly 200 million is three-fourths of the US's, but with only one-fifth of the land area.

Although Chinese records show a Krakatau eruption in the 3rd century AD, and some 17 additional historical eruptions are reported from Kelut as well as Krakatau through the 15th century, uncertainty surrounds many of them. Europeans first began to document eruptions in 1512 (Sangeang Api and Gunungapi Wetar), about the time Portugal gained control of the Mollucan clove trade. The Dutch East India Company controlled the islands from 1602 through 1780, followed by the Dutch government. Britain took temporary control of the islands in the early 19th century, but the Dutch returned and unrest marked much of the century. The disastrous Krakatau eruption of 1883 was followed by several devastating eruptions on other islands and in 1920 a Volcano Survey was established by the government, leading to much improved volcano monitoring and reporting. The islands were occupied by Japan from early 1942, and WW-II was followed by a 4 year war of independence, with sovereignty gained at the end of 1949. The Volcanological Survey of Indonesia (VSI) now operates a network of 64 volcano observatories continuously monitoring 59 volcanoes.

The great sweep of the Sunda Arc, over 3000 km from NW Sumatra to the Banda Sea, results from the subduction of Indian Ocean crust beneath the Asian Plate. This arc includes 76% of the region's volcanoes, but those on either end are tectonically more complex. To the NNW, the basaltic volcanism of the Andaman Islands results from short spreading centers, and to the east the Banda Arc reflects Pacific Ocean crust subducted westward. North of this arc, tectonic complexity increases, with converging plate fragments forming multiple subduction zones, mainly oriented N-S, that in turn produce the Sulawesi-Sangihe volcanoes on the west and Halmahera on the east of the collision zone.

Indonesia leads the world in many volcano statistics. It has the largest number of historically active volcanoes (76), its total of 1171 dated eruptions is only narrowly exceeded by Japan's 1274, and these two regions have combined to produce ⅓ of the known explosive eruptions. Indonesia has suffered the highest numbers of eruptions producing fatalities, damage to arable land, mudflows, tsunamis, domes, and pyroclastic flows (104, 186, 84, 13, 76, and 96, respectively). In the first 5 of these, Indonesia also leads other regions in the global *proportion* of eruptions with each characteristic. In recent years, however, the VSI has compiled an enviable record of evacuating populations before eruption disasters occur. As shown by the table on p. 176, Indonesia has had many more evacuations recently than any other nation, with 17 numbering in the thousands, and fatalities have been avoided in all but a few eruptions.

Four-fifths of Indonesian volcanoes with dated eruptions have erupted in this century, and history shows the danger of volcanoes that have not erupted in recent centuries. Relatively few stratigraphic studies of older volcanic deposits have been completed in Indonesia, and only 0.5% of known Indonesian eruptions have been dated by other than historical techniques, emphasizing the need for more study of the prehistoric record in this region.

Indonesia was the subject of the first *CAVW* in 1951, authored in Holland by Meir Neumann van Padang, who had grown up in Indonesia and worked there as a geologist. He went on to spearhead the *CAVW* series, authoring or co-authoring 6 catalogs and overseeing publication of 21 before retiring, at the age of 73, in 1967.

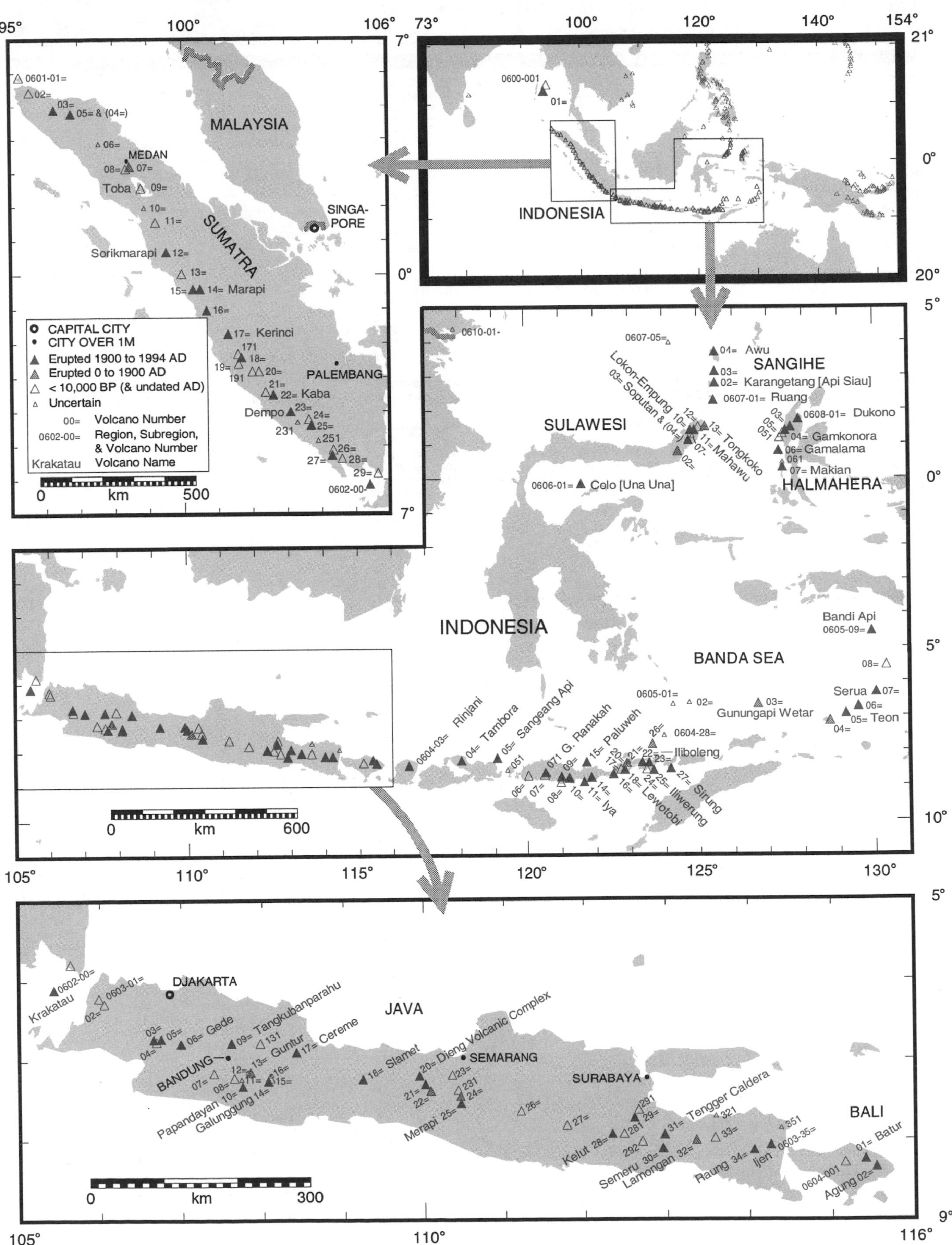
MALAYSIA
SUMATRA
MEDAN
Toba
Sorikmarapi
Marapi
Kerinci
Kaba
Dempo
PALEMBANG
SINGA-PORE
CAPITAL CITY
CITY OVER 1M
Erupted 1900 to 1994 AD
Erupted 0 to 1900 AD
< 10,000 BP (& undated AD)
Uncertain
00= Volcano Number
0602-00= Region, Subregion, & Volcano Number
Krakatau Volcano Name
0 km 500
INDONESIA
SULAWESI
SANGIHE
Awu
Karangetang [Api Siau]
Ruang
Lokon-Empung
Soputan
Tongkoko
Mahawu
Colo [Una Una]
Dukono
Gamkonora
Gamalama
Makian
HALMAHERA
BANDA SEA
Bandi Api
Serua
Teon
Gunungapi Wetar
Iliboleng
Rinjani
Tambora
Sangeang Api
G. Ranakah
Paluweh
Lewotobi
Iliwerung
Sirung
Iya
0 km 600
JAVA
DJAKARTA
Krakatau
Gede
Tangkubanparahu
Cereme
BANDUNG
Guntur
Papandayan
Galunggung
Slamet
Dieng Volcanic Complex
SEMARANG
Merapi
SURABAYA
Kelut
Semeru
Lamongan
Tengger Caldera
Raung
Ijen
BALI
Batur
Agung
0 km 300
06

VOLCANO NAME (Subregion) / ERUPTION — Area of Activity	LAT	LONG	ELEV (m)	TYPE	NUMBER	Status / Start Year	Start M-Dy	P	Stop Year	Stop M-Dy	ERUPTIVE CHARACTERISTICS (Central, Flank vent, Radial fiss, Regional* / Submarine, New island, Subglacial, Crater lake / Explosive, Pyro flow, Phreatic, Fumarolic / Lava flow, Lava lake, Dome, Spine / Fatal, Damage, Mudflow, Tsunami)	VEI	Vol L/T
SUMATRA & ANDAMAN ISLANDS													
NARCONDUM (Andaman Is-Ind O) . . .	**13.43 N**	**94.25 E**	**710**	**Stratovolc**	**0600-001**	**Holocene**							
BARREN ISLAND (Andaman Is-Ind O)	**12.292 N**	**93.875 E**	**305**	**Stratovolc**	**0600-01=**	**Historical**							
(eruption May 12, 1787, not 1783)						**1787**	0512		....	....	x--- ---- ?--- ---- ----	2	
						1789	0324		....	....	x--- ---- x--- ---- ----	2	
						1795	1220		**1795**	1221>	x--- ---- x--- ---- ----	2	
						1803	11		**1804**	0131>	x--- ---- x--- x--- ----	2	
						? **1852**	....		....	....	?--- ---- ?--- ---- ----	2	
NE flank						**1991**	0406<		**1991**	1031g	xx-- ---- x--- x--- -x--	2	
PULAU WEH (Sumatra).	**5.88 N**	**95.33 E**	**584**	**Stratovolc**	**0601-01=**	**Fumarolic**							
SEULAWAH AGAM (Sumatra)	**5.425 N**	**95.60 E**	**1726**	**Stratovolc**	**0601-02=**	**Holocene**							
						? **1510j**	....		....	....	-?-- ---- ?--- ---- ----	2	
Van Heutsz Crater						? **1839**	0112		?**1839**	0113	-x-- ---- x--- ---- ----	2	
PEUET SAGUE (Sumatra).	**4.925 N**	**96.33 E**	**2780**	**Complx volc**	**0601-03=**	**Historical**							
						1918	....		**1921**	....	x--- ---- xx-- --x- ----	2	
GEUREUDONG, BUR NI (Sumatra) . .	**4.82 N**	**96.80 E**	**2590**	**Stratovolc**	**0601-04=**	**Fumarolic**							
TELONG, BUR NI (Sumatra)	**4.77 N**	**96.808 E**	**2624**	**Stratovolc**	**0601-05=**	**Historical**							
						1837	0925e		....	....	x--- ---- x--- ---- ----	2	
						1839	0112		**1839**	0113	x--- ---- x--- ---- ----	2	
						1856	0414		....	....	x--- ---- x--- ---- ----	2	
						1919	12		....	....	x--- ---- x--- ---- ----	2	
						1924	1207		....	....	---- ---- ---- ---- ----	2	
						1937	....		....	....	---- ---- ---- ---- ----		
GAYOLESTEN (Sumatra)	**3.87 N**	**97.60 E**	**1500**	**Fumarole fld**	**0601-06=**	**Fumarolic**							
SIBAYAK (Sumatra).	**3.208 N**	**98.47 E**	**2212**	**Stratovolc**	**0601-07=**	**Historical**							
						1881	....		....	....	---- ---- x--- ---- ----		
SINABUNG (Sumatra)	**3.17 N**	**98.392 E**	**2460**	**Stratovolc**	**0601-08=**	**Fumarolic**							
						? **1881**	....		....	....	---- ---- x--- ---- ----		
TOBA (Sumatra).	**2.58 N**	**98.83 E**	**2157**	**Caldera**	**0601-09=**	**Holocene**							
HELATOBA-TARUTUNG (Sumatra) . .	**2.03 N**	**98.93 E**	**1100**	**Fumarole fld**	**0601-10=**	**Fumarolic**							
BUAL BUALI (Sumatra).	**1.57 N**	**99.25 E**	**1819**	**Stratovolc**	**0601-11=**	**Fumarolic**							
SORIKMARAPI (Sumatra)	**0.687 N**	**99.537 E**	**2145**	**Stratovolc**	**0601-12=**	**Historical**							
						1829?	....		....	....	x--- ---- x-x- ---- ----	2	
						1879	....		....	....	x--- ---- --x- ---- ----	2	
Summit and east flank (Jurang Siunik).						**1892**	0521		....	....	xx-- ---- --x- ---- xxx-	2	
East flank (Sibanggor Julu)						**1893**	0104		**1893**	0104	-x-- ---- --x- ---- ----	2	
						1917	0520		**1917**	0520	x--- ---- x-x- ---- ----	2	
						1970	....		....	....	---- ---- x--- ---- ----	2	
						1986	0705		**1986**	0714	x--- ---- x-x- ---- ----	1	-/2
TALAKMAU (Sumatra)	**0.079 N**	**99.982 E**	**2912**	**Complx volc**	**0601-13=**	**Holocene**							
						? **1937**	0908		....	....	x--- ---- ---- ---- ----	1	
MARAPI (Sumatra).	**0.380 S**	**100.471 E**	**2891**	**Complx volc**	**0601-14=**	**Historical**							
						1770	....		....	....	x--- ---- x--- ---- ----	2	
						1807	....		....	....	x--- ---- x--- ---- ----	2	
						1822	0723		**1822**	0731	x--- ---- x--- x--- -x--	2	
						1833	....		**1834**	....	x--- ---- x--- ---- ----	2?	
						1845	1116		**1845**	1118	x--- ---- x--- ---- ----	2?	
						1854	0829>		....	....	x--- ---- x--- ---- ----	2	
						1855	1002		**1856**	01	x--- ---- x--- ---- ----	2	
						1861	04		....	....	x--- ---- x--- ---- ----	2?	
						1863	0523		....	....	x--- ---- x--- ---- ----	2?	
						1871	0424		....	....	x--- ---- x--- ---- ----	2?	
						1871	0924		....	....	x--- ---- x--- ---- ----	2?	
						1876	0404		....	....	x--- ---- x--- ---- ----	2?	
						1876	08		**1877**	06	x--- ---- x--- ---- ----	2?	
						1883	0625	+	**1883**	0827	x--- ---- --x- ---- ----	1	
						1883	12		**1883**	12	x--- ---- x--- ---- ----	1	
						1885	1112		....	....	x--- ---- x--- ---- ----	2?	
						1886	0331		**1886**	0503	x--- ---- x--- ---- ----	2	
						1888	0219		**1888**	0319	x--- ---- x--- ---- ----	2?	
						1889	0327		**1889**	0417?	x--- ---- x--- ---- ----	2?	
						1904	0418		**1904**	0418	x--- ---- x--- ---- ----	1	
						1905	1101		....	....	x--- ---- x--- ---- ----	2?	
						1907	1217		**1908**	09	x--- ---- x--- ---- ----	2?	
						1910	....		....	....	x--- ---- x--- ---- ----	2?	
						1911	1102		....	....	x--- ---- x--- ---- ----	2?	
						1913	0623		**1913**	0731	x--- ---- x--- ---- ----	2?	
						1914	0701		....	....	x--- ---- x--- ---- ----	2?	
						1915	12		....	....	x--- ---- x--- ---- ----	2?	
						1916	0505	+	**1916**	0707	x--- ---- x--- ---- ----	1	
						1917	0616	+	**1917**	0916	x--- ---- x--- ---- ----	2?	
						1918	0308		**1918**	0310	x--- ---- x--- ---- ----	2?	
						1918	0815e		**1918**	0815e	x--- ---- x--- ---- ----	2?	
						1919	0228		**1919**	0301	x--- ---- x--- ---- ----	2?	
						1925	04 ?		....	....	x--- ---- ---- x--- ----	0	
Kepundan Bongsu						**1927**	0205	+	**1927**	0803	x--- ---- x--- ---- ----	2	
Kepundan Bongsu						**1929**	0622		**1929**	0622	x--- ---- x--- ---- ----	2	
						1930	0409<	+	**1930**	1207	x--- ---- x--- x-?- ----	2*	
						1932	....		....	....	x--- ---- ?--- ---- ----	2?	
Kepundan Kuniang, Kepundan Jinggo.						**1943e**	....		....	....	x--- ---- x--- ---- ----		
Kepundan Bongsu						**1949**	0429		**1949**	0430	x--- ---- x--- ---- ----	2	
						1949	1015e		**1949**	1022e	x--- ---- x--- ---- ----	2	
Kepundan Bongsu, Kuniang, Jinggo						**1950**	0927		**1952**	0614	x--- ---- x--- ---- ----	2*	
Kepundan Bongsu, B and C Craters						**1954**	08		**1957**	12 >	---- ---- x--- ---- ----	2?	
						1958	0623		**1958**	0623?	x--- ---- x--- ---- ----	1	
						1958	1017	+	**1958**	1025	x--- ---- x--- ---- ----	1	
B and C Craters, Kebun Bungo						**1966**	03	+	**1966**	06	x--- ---- x--- ---- ----	1	
Crater C, Bungsu Crater.						**1967**	04	+	**1967**	07	x--- ---- x--- ---- ----	1	
Craters B and C						? **1968**	12		?**1968**	12	x--- ---- --?- ---- ----	1	
Bungo, Bongsu, Tuo, B and C Craters.						**1970**	0726e	+	**1971**	0820	x--- ---- x-?- ---- ----	2	
Verbeek Crater.						**1973**	0724		**1973**	0724	x--- ---- x--- ---- ----	2	
Verbeek Crater, B and C Craters						**1975**	01		**1979**	0911	x--- ---- x-x- ---- xxx-	2*	
						1980	0329		....	....	x--- ---- x--- ---- ----	1	

VOLCANO NAME (Subregion) / ERUPTION — Area of Activity	LAT	LONG	ELEV (m)	TYPE	NUMBER	Status	Start Year	Start M-Dy	P	Stop Year	Stop M-Dy	ERUPTIVE CHARACTERISTICS (Central, Flank vent, Radial fiss, Regional* / Submarine, New island, Subglacial, Crater lake / Explosive, Pyro flow, Phreatic, Fumarolic / Lava flow, Lava lake, Dome, Spine / Fatal, Damage, Mudflow, Tsunami)	VEI	Vol L/T
MARAPI (Sumatra) *continued*							**1982**	0310<		**1982**	05	x--- ---- x--- ---- ----	1	
							1982	12		**1982**	12	x--- ---- x--- ---- ----	1	
Kepundan Tuo and Kepundan Verbeek....							**1983**	....		....	....	x--- ---- x--- ---- ----	1	
Kepundan Tuo, Kepundan B							**1984**	1115		**1984**	1115	x--- ---- --x- ---- ----	1	
Verbeek Crater........................							**1987**	0115		**1993>**	....	x--- ---- x--- --x- x---	2	6/-
TANDIKAT (Sumatra)	**0.433 S**	**100.317 E**	**2438**	**Stratovolc**	**0601-15=**	**Historical**								
Summit crater and upper NE flank........							**1889**	0219		**1889**	1204	xx-- ---- x-x- ---- ----	1	
							1914	0531		....	....	x--- ---- x--- ---- ----	1	
							1924	04		**1924**	04 ?	x--- ---- x-x- ---- ----	1	
TALANG (Sumatra)	**0.978 S**	**100.679 E**	**2896**	**Stratovolc**	**0601-16=**	**Historical**								
							1833	10		....	....	-x-- ---- x--- ---- ----	2	
							1843	1021		....	....	-x-- ---- x--- ---- ----	2	
							1845	0422		....	....	-x-- ---- x--- ---- ----	2	
							1876?	....		....	....	-x-- ---- x--- ---- ----	2	
							1963	....		....	....	---- ---- ---- ---- ----	2	
NE slope (200 m below summit)							**1967**	1010	+	**1967**	1010	--x- ---- ?-?- ---- ----	1	
							1968	0114		**1968**	0114?	--x- ---- x--- ---- ----	1	
							1968	09		**1968**	10	--x- ---- x--- ---- ----	2	
NE flank (Pajang Crater)							? **1986**	0716		?**1986**	1013	-x-- ---- --x- ---- ----	1	
KERINCI (Sumatra)	**1.692 S**	**101.27 E**	**3805**	**Stratovolc**	**0601-17=**	**Historical**								
							1838	....		....	....	x--- ---- x--- ---- ----	2	
							1842	....		....	....	x--- ---- x--- ---- ----	2	
							1874?	....		....	....	x--- ---- x--- ---- ----	2?	
							1878	1211		....	....	x--- ---- --x- ---- ----	2	
							1887	0323		**1887**	0330	x--- ---- --x- ---- ----	2?	
							1908	10		?**1909**	....	x--- ---- x-?- ---- ----	2	
							1921	05		**1921**	06	x--- ---- x--- ---- ----	2	
							1923	09		**1923**	09	x--- ---- --?- ---- ----	1	
							1936	0429		**1936**	0429	x--- ---- x-x- ---- ----	2	
							1936	0830		**1936**	0830	x--- ---- x-x- ---- ----	2	
							1937	0908		....	....	x--- ---x --x- ---- ----	2	
							1938	0119		**1938**	0318	x--- ---- --x- ---- ----	2	
							1952	01		**1952**	06	x--- ---- x--- ---- ----	2	
							1960	07		....	....	x--- ---- x--- ---- ----	2	
							1963	07		....	....	x--- ---- x--- ---- ----	2	
							1964	0708		**1964**	0708?	x--- ---- x--- ---- ----	2	
							1966	0609		**1966**	0630>	x--- ---- x--- ---- ----	2	
							1967	1102		....	....	x--- ---- x--- ---- ----	2	
							1968	0203		**1968**	0318	x--- ---- x--- ---- ----	2	
							1969	....		**1970**	....	x--- ---- x--- ---- ----	2	
							? **1971**	06		?**1971**	06	x--- ---- --x- ---- ----	1?	
HUTAPANJANG (Sumatra)	**2.27 S**	**101.60 E**		**Stratovolc**	**0601-171**	**Holocene**								
SUMBING (Sumatra)	**2.42 S**	**101.73 E**	**2508**	**Stratovolc**	**0601-18=**	**Historical**								
							1909	0603		**1909**	07	x--- ---- x--- ---- ----	2	
							1921	0523		**1921**	0603	-x-- ---- x--- ---- ----	2	
KUNYIT (Sumatra)	**2.592 S**	**101.63 E**	**2151**	**Stratovolc**	**0601-19=**	**Fumarolic**								
PENDAN (Sumatra)	**2.82 S**	**102.02 E**		**Unknown**	**0601-191**	**Holocene**								
BELIRANG-BERITI (Sumatra).......	**2.82 S**	**102.18 E**	**1958**	**Compnd volc**	**0601-20=**	**Fumarolic**								
LUMUTDAUN, BUKIT (Sumatra).....	**3.38 S**	**102.37 E**	**2467**	**Stratovolc**	**0601-21=**	**Fumarolic**								
KABA (Sumatra)	**3.52 S**	**102.62 E**	**1952**	**Stratovolc**	**0601-22=**	**Historical**								
							1833	1124		**1833**	1125	x--- ---x x--- ---- xxx-	2	
							1834	11		....	....	x--- ---- x--- ---- -x--	2	
							1853	11		....	....	x--- ---- x--- ---- -xx-	2	
Kaba Baru ? and Kaba Vogelsang........							**1868**	10		**1869**	....	?x-- ---- x--- ---- ----	2	
Kaba Volgelsang and Kaba Baru.........							**1873**	....		**1892**	1101p	xx-- ---- x--- ?--- ----	2	
Kaba Baru							**1907**	....		....	....	x--- ---- x--- ---- ----	2	
							? **1918**	0809		....	....	x--- ---- --?- ---- ----	2?	
Kaba Baru, Kaba Lama							**1939**	1119		**1941**	0314	x--- ---- x-x- ---- ----	2	
Kaba Vogelsang......................							**1950**	03		**1951**	04	-x-- ---- x--- ---- ----	1*	
							1952	0401		**1952**	0428	x--- ---- x--- ---- ----	2	
							1956	0322		**1956**	0328	x--- ---- x--- ---- ----	2	
DEMPO (Sumatra)	**4.03 S**	**103.13 E**	**3173**	**Stratovolc**	**0601-23=**	**Historical**								
							1817	1231y		....	....	x--- ---- x--- ---- ----	2	
							1839?	....		....	....	x--- ---- x--- ---- ----	2	
							1853	0101		....	....	x--- ---- x--- ---- ----	2	
							1879	0518		....	....	x--- ---- x--- ---- ----	2	
							1880	05		....	....	x--- ---- --x- ---- ----	2	
							1881	0216		....	....	x--- ---- x--- ---- ----	2	
							1881	12		**1881**	12	x--- ---- x--- ---- ----	2	
							1884	06		**1884**	07	x--- ---- x--- ---- ----	2	
							1895	0702	+	**1895**	0930	x--- ---- x--- ---- ----	2	
							1900	0604		**1900**	0604	x--- ---- x--- ---- ----	2	
							1900	1026		**1900**	1027	x--- ---- x--- ---- ----	2	
							1905	....		....	....	x--- ---x --x- ---- ----	0	
							1908	0216		**1908**	0217	x--- ---- x-?- ---- ----	2	
							1921	04		**1921**	04	x--- ---x --x- ---- ----	1	
							1923	0519?		**1923**	0519?	x--- ---x --x- ---- ----	1	
							1926	0422		**1926**	0424	x--- ---x --x- ---- ----	2	
							1934	0124	+	**1934**	0425	x--- ---- x--- ---- -x--	2	
							1936	1126		**1936**	1127	x--- ---- x--- ---- ----	2	
							1939	0718	+	**1939**	0730	x--- ---x x-x- ---- -x--	2	
							1939	1219		**1940**	0221	x--- ---x x-x- ---- -xx-	2*	
							1940	07		....	....	x--- ---- x--- ---- ----	2	
							1964	0214		**1964**	0214	x--- ---- x--- ---- ----	2	
							1973	0124		**1973**	0125	x--- ---- x-x- ---- ----	2	
							1974	0226		**1974**	1020	x--- ---- x-?- ---- -x--	2	
PATAH (Sumatra)	**4.27 S**	**103.30 E**	**2817**	**Unknown**	**0601-231**	**Uncertain**								
LUMUT BALAI, BUKIT (Sumatra)....	**4.22 S**	**103.62 E**	**2055**	**Stratovolc ?**	**0601-24=**	**Fumarolic**								
BESAR, GUNUNG (Sumatra)	**4.43 S**	**103.67 E**	**1899**	**Stratovolc ?**	**0601-25=**	**Historical**								
Marga Bayur (Gemurah Ilahan)							**1940**	04		....	....	-x-- ---- --x- ---- ----	1	
RANAU (Sumatra)	**4.83 S**	**103.92 E**	**1881**	**Caldera**	**0601-251**	**Holocene?**								
							? **1887**	1007	+	?**1888**	0120	---- ---? ---- ---- ----		
							? **1903**	1209		?**1903**	1209	---- ---? ---- ---- ----		
SEKINCAU BELIRANG (Sumatra) ...	**5.12 S**	**104.32 E**	**1719**	**Caldera**	**0601-26=**	**Fumarolic**								

VOLCANO NAME (Subregion) / ERUPTION — Area of Activity	LAT	LONG	ELEV (m)	TYPE	NUMBER	Status / Start Year	Start M-Dy	P	Stop Year	Stop M-Dy	Central / Flank vent / Radial fiss / Regional	Submarine / New island / Subglacial / Crater lake	Explosive / Pyro flow / Phreatic / Fumarolic	Lava flow / Lava lake / Dome / Spine	Fatal / Damage / Mudflow / Tsunami	VEI	Vol L/T
SUOH (Sumatra)	**5.25 S**	**104.27 E**	**1000**	**Maars**	**0601-27=**	**Historical**											
Pematang Bata						**1933**	0710		**1933**	0805	x---	----	-xx-	----	----	4	-/8
HULUBELU (Sumatra)	**5.35 S**	**104.60 E**	**1040**	**Caldera**	**0601-28=**	**Fumarolic**											
RAJABASA (Sumatra)	**5.78 S**	**105.625 E**	**1281**	**Stratovolc**	**0601-29=**	**Fumarolic**											
KRAKATAU																	
KRAKATAU (Indonesia)	**6.102 S**	**105.423 E**	**813**	**Caldera**	**0602-00=**	**Historical**											
						0250t	....		....	....	x---	----	x---	----	----		
						0416	....		....	....	x---	----	x---	----	xx-x	C	
						0850t	....		....	....	----	----	----	----	----		
						0950t	....		....	....	----	----	----	----	----		
						1050t	....		....	....	----	----	----	----	----		
						1150t	....		....	....	----	----	----	----	----		
						1350t	....		....	....	----	----	----	----	----		
						1550t	....		....	....	----	----	----	----	----		
Perbuwatan						**1680**	05		**1681**	1119>	x---	----	x---	x---	----	3	-/8
Krakatau Island (Perbuwatan, Danan)						**1883**	0520	+	**1883**	1021?	x---	x---	xx-x	----	xxxx	6*	-/10
Anak Krakatau						**1927**	1229	+	**1930**	0815	x--x	xx--	xxx-	----	----	2*	
Anak Krakatau						**1931**	0923	+	**1932**	0217	xx--	---x	x---	----	----	2	
Anak Krakatau						**1932**	1114	+	**1934**	0609	x---	---x	x---	----	----	3*	
Anak Krakatau						**1935**	0104	+	**1935**	0712	x---	x--x	x-x-	----	----	2	
Anak Krakatau						**1936**	1013		**1936**	11	x---	?---	x---	----	----	1	
Anak Krakatau						**1937**	0806	+	**1937**	1123	x---	---x	x---	----	----	2	
Anak Krakatau						**1938**	0704	+	**1940**	0702	x---	x--x	x-x-	----	----	3*	
Anak Krakatau						**1941**	0128		**1941**	0212	x---	---x	x---	----	----	2	
Anak Krakatau						**1942**	0129		**1942**	0130	x---	---x	x---	----	----	2	
Anak Krakatau						**1943**	....		....	....	x---	---?	?---	----	----	2	
Anak Krakatau						**1944**	....		....	....	x---	---?	?---	----	----	2	
Anak Krakatau						**1945**	....		....	....	x---	---?	?---	----	----	2	
Anak Krakatau						**1946**	0725		**1946**	0725	x---	---x	x---	----	----	1	
Anak Krakatau						**1946**	1226e	+	**1947**	0807>	x---	---x	x---	----	----	2	
Anak Krakatau						**1949**	0512		....	....	x---	---x	x---	----	----	2	
Anak Krakatau						**1950**	0703		**1950**	0707	x---	---x	x---	----	----	2	
Anak Krakatau						**1952**	1010		**1952**	1011	x---	---x	x---	----	----	2	
Anak Krakatau						**1953**	0317		**1953**	0501?	x---	---x	x---	----	----	2	
Anak Krakatau						**1953**	0921	+	**1953**	1125	x---	---x	x---	----	----	2	
Anak Krakatau						**1955**	0211		....	....	x---	----	x---	----	----	2	
Anak Krakatau						**1958**	1002	+	**1959**	0625d	x---	---x	x---	----	----	2	
Anak Krakatau						**1959**	12		**1963**	....	x---	---x	x---	x---	----	2	6/-
Anak Krakatau						**1965?**	....		....	....	x---	----	x-x-	?---	----	1?	
Anak Krakatau						? **1969**	....		....	....	----	----	----	----	----	2?	
Anak Krakatau						**1972**	0610c	+	**1973**	0701p	xx--	----	x---	x---	----	2	6/-
Anak Krakatau						**1975**	0327		**1975**	1026e	x---	----	x---	x---	----	2	6/-
Anak Krakatau						**1978**	0710		**1978**	11	x---	----	x---	----	----	1	-/4
Anak Krakatau						**1979**	0715e	+	**1979**	11	x---	----	x---	x---	----	2	4/-
Anak Krakatau						**1980**	0315e	+	**1980**	12	x---	----	x---	x---	----	2	5/-
Anak Krakatau						**1981**	0424	+	**1981**	1020	x---	----	x---	----	----	1	
Anak Krakatau (S flank 1960-81 cone)						**1988**	0214e		**1988**	04 ?	xx--	----	x---	x---	----	2	5/-
Anak Krakatau						**1992**	1107		**1993**	10	x---	----	x---	x---	x---	1	6/-
JAVA																	
DANAU COMPLEX (Java-W)	**6.20 S**	**105.97 E**	**1778**	**Caldera**	**0603-01=**	**Holocene**											
KARANG (Java-W)	**6.27 S**	**106.042 E**	**1778**	**Stratovolc**	**0603-02=**	**Fumarolic**											
KIARABERES-GAGAK (Java-W)	**6.73 S**	**106.65 E**	**1511**	**Stratovolc**	**0603-03=**	**Historical**											
Kawah Cibodas						**1923**	06		....	....	----	----	--x-	----	----	1	
Cibeureum West						**1929**	....		....	....	----	----	--x-	----	----	1	
Kawah Cibodas						**1935**	0531p		....	....	----	----	--x-	----	----	1	
Cipanas Parabakti						**1936**	1026		**1936**	1028	----	----	--x-	----	----	1	
Kawah Parabakti						**1938**	12		....	....	----	----	--x-	----	----	1	
Kawah Parabakti						**1939**	0406<		....	....	----	----	--x-	----	----	1	
PERBAKTI (Java-W)	**6.75 S**	**106.68 E**	**1699**	**Stratovolc**	**0603-04=**	**Fumarolic**											
SALAK (Java-W)	**6.72 S**	**106.73 E**	**2211**	**Stratovolc**	**0603-05=**	**Historical**											
Salak 3						? **1699**	0105		....	....	x---	----	?---	----	-xx-		
Kawah Ratu						**1780**	....		....	....	-x--	----	x---	----	----	2	
Kawah Ratu						**1902**	....		**1903**	....	-x--	----	--x-	----	----	2	
Kawah Ratu						**1919**	....		....	....	-x--	----	--x-	----	----	2	
Kawah Cikaluwung Putri						**1935**	02		....	....	-x--	----	--x-	----	----	2	
Kawah Cikaluwung Putri						**1938**	0131e		....	....	-x--	----	--x-	----	----	2	
GEDE (Java-W)	**6.78 S**	**106.98 E**	**2958**	**Stratovolc**	**0603-06=**	**Historical**											
						1747	....		**1748**	....	x---	----	x---	?---	----	3	
						1761	....		....	....	x---	----	x---	----	----	2	
						1832	0829		**1832**	0829	x---	----	x---	----	----	3	
						1840	1112	+	**1840**	1211	x---	----	xx--	----	-x--	3*	
						1843	0728		....	....	x---	----	x---	----	----	2	
						1845	0123	+	**1845**	0305	x---	----	x---	----	----	2	
						1847	1017		**1847**	1018	x---	----	x---	----	----	2	
						1848	0508		....	....	x---	----	x---	----	----	2	
						1852	0528		**1852**	0528	x---	----	x---	----	-x--	2	
						1853	0314		**1853**	0314	x---	----	x---	----	----	3?	
						1866	0918		....	....	x---	----	x---	----	----	2	
						1870	08	+	**1870**	1003	x---	----	x---	----	----	2	
						1886	0610		**1886**	0816	x---	----	x---	----	----	2	
						1887	1022		**1887**	1022	x---	----	x---	----	----	2	
						? **1889**	0508<		....	....	x---	----	----	----	----	1	
						1891	....		....	....	x---	----	x---	----	----	2	
						1899	0501		**1899**	0514	x---	----	x---	----	----	2	
						1909	0502		**1909**	0502	x---	----	x---	----	----	1	
Kawah Ratu?, Kawah Lanang						**1947**	0902	+	**1948**	0128	x---	----	x-x-	----	----	2	-/5
Kawah Leutik (Kawah Ratu)						**1948**	1115	+	**1949**	0205	x---	----	x---	----	----	2	-/5
						? **1955**	0721		?**1955**	0802	x---	----	--x-	----	----	1	
						1956	0428		**1956**	0428	x---	----	x---	----	----	2?	
						1957	0313		**1957**	0313	x---	----	x---	----	----	2	
PATUHA (Java-W)	**7.15 S**	**107.37 E**	**2434**	**Stratovolc**	**0603-07=**	**Holocene**											
WAYANG-WINDU (Java-W)	**7.208 S**	**107.63 E**	**2182**	**Stratovolc**	**0603-08=**	**Fumarolic**											
TANGKUBANPARAHU (Java-W)	**6.77 S**	**107.60 E**	**2084**	**Stratovolc**	**0603-09=**	**Historical**											
						1826	1011		**1826**	1011	x---	----	--?-	----	----	2	

VOLCANO NAME (Subregion) / ERUPTION — Area of Activity	LAT	LONG	ELEV (m)	TYPE	NUMBER	Status	Start Year	Start M-Dy	P	Stop Year	Stop M-Dy	Central / Flank vent / Radial fiss / Regional*	Submarine / New island / Subglacial / Crater lake	Explosive / Pyro flow / Phreatic / Fumarolic	Lava flow / Lava lake / Dome / Spine	Fatal / Damage / Mudflow / Tsunami	VEI	Vol L/T
TANGKUBANPARAHU (Java-W) *continued*																		
Kawah Ratu and Kawah Domas							**1829**	0401		**1829**	0404?	x---	----	x-x-	----	----	2	
							1842	....		....	....	x---	----	--?-	----	----		
Kawah Ratu B							**1846**	0527		....	....	x---	----	x?--	----	xxx-	2	
Kawah Baru							**1896**	0522		**1896**	0523	x---	----	x-x-	----	----	2	
Kawah Ratu B							**1910**	0407		**1910**	05	x---	----	x-x-	----	----	2	
Kawah Ecoma							**1926**	0301		**1926**	0709	x---	----	x-x-	----	----	1?	
Kawah Ecoma							**1929**	0520		**1929**	0520	x---	----	--x-	----	----	0	
Kawah Ecoma							**1952**	0704?		**1952**	0711	x---	----	x-x-	----	----	1	
Kawah Baru							**1957**	01		**1957**	01	x---	----	--x-	----	----	1	
							1961	0716	+	**1961**	0801	x---	----	--x-	----	----	1	
							1965	02		**1965**	03	x---	----	--x-	----	----	1	
							1965	10		**1965**	10	x---	----	--x-	----	----	1	
Kawah Ecoma							**1967**	07	+	**1967**	07	x---	----	--x-	----	----	1	
Kawah Ecoma							**1969**	0720		**1969**	1021	x---	----	x-x-	----	----	1	
Kawah Ratu							**1983**	0914		....	....	x---	----	x-x-	----	----	1	
Kawah Baru							? **1985**	1115		?**1985**	1115	x---	----	--x-	----	----	1	
PAPANDAYAN (Java-W)	**7.32 S**	**107.73 E**	**2665**	**Stratovolc**	**0603-10=**	**Historical**												
							1772	0812		**1772**	0812	x---	----	x-x-	----	xx--	3	
Kawah Baru, Kawah Nangklak							**1923**	0311		**1925**	0309	x---	----	x-x-	----	x---	1	
							1942	0815		**1942**	0816	x---	----	--?-	----	----	1?	
KAWAHMANUK (Java-W)	**7.23 S**	**107.72 E**	**2608**	**Fumarole fld**	**0603-11=**	**Fumarolic**												
KAWAHKAMOJANG (Java-W)	**7.125 S**	**107.80 E**	**1730**	**Fumarole fld**	**0603-12=**	**Fumarolic**												
GUNTUR (Java-W)	**7.13 S**	**107.83 E**	**2249**	**Complx volc**	**0603-13=**	**Historical**												
							1690	....		....	....	x---	----	x---	----	xx--	3	
							1777	....		....	....	----	----	----	----	----	2?	
							1780	....		....	....	x---	----	x---	x---	----	2	
							1800	....		....	....	----	----	----	x---	?-?-		
							1803	0403		**1803**	0415	x---	----	x---	----	----	2	
							1807	0901		**1807**	0906	x---	----	x---	----	----	2	
							1809	0509		....	....	x---	----	x---	----	----	2	
							1815	0815		....	....	x---	----	x---	----	----	2	
							1816	0921		....	....	x---	----	x---	----	----	2	
							1818	1021		**1818**	1024	x---	----	x---	----	----	2	
							1825	0614		**1825**	0615	x---	----	x---	----	-x--	2	
							1827	0513		....	....	x---	----	x---	----	----	2	
							1828	0514	+	**1828**	0708	x---	----	x---	----	----	2	
							1829	....		....	....	x---	----	x---	----	xx--	2	
							1832	0116		....	....	x---	----	x---	----	----	2	
							1832	0808		**1832**	0813	x---	----	x---	----	----	2	
							1833	0901		....	....	x---	----	x---	----	----	2	
							1834	12		**1835**	01	x---	----	x---	----	-x--	2	
							1836	1011		....	....	x---	----	x---	----	----	2	
							1840	0520		**1840**	0524	x---	----	x---	x---	----	2	
							1841	1114		**1841**	1114	x---	----	x---	----	-x--	2	
							1843	0104		**1843**	0104	x---	----	x---	----	----	3	-/6
							1843	1126		**1843**	1126	x---	----	x---	----	-?--	2?	
							1847	1016	+	**1847**	1028	x---	----	x---	----	----	2	
							? **1885**	0118		....	....	----	----	----	----	----		
							? **1887**	....		....	....	----	----	----	----	----		
TAMPOMAS (Java-W)	**6.77 S**	**107.95 E**	**1684**	**Stratovolc**	**0603-131**	**Holocene**												
GALUNGGUNG (Java-W)	**7.25 S**	**108.05 E**	**2168**	**Stratovolc**	**0603-14=**	**Historical**												
							1822	1008		**1822**	1201p	x---	----	xx--	--x-	xxx-	5	-/9
							1894	1017		**1894**	12	x---	----	xx--	----	-xx-	3	-/7
Gunung Jadi							**1918**	0717		**1918**	0730	x---	----	x---	--x-	----	1	7/-
New crater at Gunung Jadi location							**1982**	0405	+	**1983**	0108	x---	----	xx--	x---	xxx-	4*	-/8
							1984	0109		**1984**	0131?	x---	----	x-x-	----	----	1	
TALAGABODAS (Java-W)	**7.208 S**	**108.07 E**	**1020**	**Stratovolc**	**0603-15=**	**Fumarolic**												
KAWAHKARAHA (Java-W)	**7.17 S**	**108.08 E**	**1155**	**Fumarole fld**	**0603-16=**	**Fumarolic**												
							? **1861**	05		....	....	x---	----	--?-	----	----		
CEREME (Java-W)	**6.892 S**	**108.40 E**	**3078**	**Stratovolc**	**0603-17=**	**Historical**												
							1698	0203		....	....	?---	----	x---	----	xxx-	3	
							1772	0811		**1772**	0812	x---	----	x---	----	----	2	
							1775	0104		....	....	?---	----	?---	----	----	2	
							1805	04		....	....	x---	----	x---	----	----	2	
Floor and north wall of East Crater							**1937**	0624		**1938**	0107	x-x-	----	x-x-	----	----	2	
							1951	0301		**1951**	0302	----	----	x---	----	----	2?	
SLAMET (Java-C)	**7.242 S**	**109.208 E**	**3432**	**Stratovolc**	**0603-18=**	**Historical**												
							1772	0811		**1772**	0812	x---	----	x---	----	----	2	
							1825	10		....	....	x---	----	x---	----	----	2	
							1835	09		**1835**	09	x---	----	x---	----	----	2	
							1849	1201		....	....	x---	----	x---	----	----	2	
							1860	0319		**1860**	0411	x---	----	x---	----	----	2	
							1875	0529<		**1875**	0604d	x---	----	x---	----	----	2	
							1875	1102b		**1875**	1226e	x---	----	x---	----	----	2	
							1885	0321		**1885**	0330	x---	----	x---	----	----	2	
							1890	0806	+	**1890**	0829	x---	----	x---	----	----	2	
							1904	0714		**1904**	0809	x---	----	x---	----	----	2	
							1923	0602		**1923**	0602	x---	----	x---	----	----	2	
							1926	1123a		**1926**	1130	x---	----	x---	----	----	2	
							1927	0227		**1927**	0227	x---	----	x---	----	----	2	
							1928	0320	+	**1928**	0512	x-x-	----	x---	----	----	2	
							1929	0606	+	**1929**	0615	x---	----	x---	----	----	2	
							1930	0402	+	**1930**	0413	x---	----	x---	----	----	2	
							1932	0701	+	**1932**	0910	x---	----	x---	----	----	2	
							1933	0512		**1933**	0513	x---	----	x---	----	----	1?	
							? **1934**	....		....	....	----	----	----	----	----		
							1937	....		....	....	x---	----	----	----	----		
							1939	0329	+	**1939**	0715	x---	----	x---	----	----	2	
							1939	1204		**1939**	1204	x---	----	x---	----	----	2	
							1940	0315	+	**1940**	0415	x---	----	x---	----	----	2	
							? **1943**	0318		....	....	x---	----	----	----	----		
							1943	1002		**1944**	0105	x---	----	x---	----	----	2	
							1944	0509		**1944**	1030	x---	----	x---	----	----	2	
							1948	1114		**1948**	1215	x---	----	x---	----	----	2	
							1951	0211		....	....	x---	----	x---	----	----	2	
							1951	0626		**1952**	0101	x---	----	x---	----	----	2	
							1953	08		**1953**	10	x---	----	x---	----	----	2	

VOLCANO NAME (Subregion) / ERUPTION — Area of Activity	LAT	LONG	ELEV (m)	TYPE	NUMBER	Status / Start Year	Start M-Dy	P	Stop Year	Stop M-Dy	Central / Flank vent / Radial fiss / Regional*	Submarine / New island / Subglacial / Crater lake	Explosive / Pyro flow / Phreatic / Fumarolic	Lava flow / Lava lake / Dome / Spine	Fatal / Damage / Mudflow / Tsunami	VEI	Vol L/T
SLAMET (Java-C) *continued*						**1955**	1112		**1955**	1220?	x---	----	x---	----	----	2	
						1957	0208		**1957**	0208	x---	----	x---	----	----	2	
						1958	0417		**1958**	0507	x---	----	x---	----	----	2	
						1958	0913		**1958**	1105d	x---	----	x---	----	----	2	
						1960	12		**1961**	01	x---	----	x---	----	----	2	
						1966	....		....	....	x---	----	x---	----	----	2	
						1967	0507	+	**1967**	07	x---	----	x---	----	----	2	
						1969	0623		**1969**	08	x---	----	x---	----	----	2	
						1973	08		....	....	x---	----	----	x---	----	1?	
						? **1974**	0529		?**1974**	0529	x---	----	----	----	----	2	
						1988	0712		**1988**	0713	x---	----	x---	----	----	1	
						1989	0712		**1989**	0713	x---	----	x---	----	----	1	
DIENG VOLC COMPLEX (Java-C) ...	**7.20 S***	**109.92 E**	**2565**	**Complx volc**	**0603-20=**	**Historical**											
Sikunang						C **-6590**w	....		....	....	x---	----	----	x---	----	0	
Sikidang-Siterus						C **-0500**u	....		....	....	----	----	--x-	----	----		
						C **-0050**v	....		....	....	x---	----	----	x---	----	0	
						C **1195**v	....		....	....	x---	----	--x-	----	----		
Pakuwaja						**1375**u	....		....	....	x---	----	x---	----	----	3↑	
(perhaps confused with 1786 eruption)						? **1776**	....		....	....	----	----	--?-	----	----		
Butak Petarangan (Butak)						**1786**	....		....	....	x---	----	x-x-	----	xx--	2	
Pakuwaja						**1825**	....		....	....	x---	----	x-x-	----	----	2	
Pakuwaja						**1826**	1011		**1826**	1015	x---	----	x-x-	----	x---	2	
Pakuwaja						**1847**	1204		....	....	x---	----	x-x-	----	x---	2	
Sikidang						**1883**	1226e		**1884**	0318	----	----	--x-	----	----	1*	
Butak Petarangan (Timbang)						**1928**	0513		....	....	-x--	----	--x-	----	xxx-	2	
Butak Petarangan.						**1939**	1013		**1939**	1015	-x-x	----	--x-	----	xxx-	1?	
Sileri						**1943**	1103		....	....	----	----	--x-	----	----	1	
Sileri						**1944**	1204		....	....	x---	----	x-x-	----	xx--	2	
						? **1952**	07		....	....	----	----	----	----	----	1?	
						1953	0324		**1953**	0325	----	----	x---	----	----	2	
Candradimuka area						**1954**	1206		**1954**	1206	----	----	--x-	----	----	0	
Sileri						**1956**	0602		**1956**	0602	----	----	--x-	----	----	1	
Sileri						**1964**	1213		**1964**	1213	----	----	x-x-	----	x---	1	
Sinila and Sigluduk.						**1979**	0220		**1979**	0220	-x--	----	--x-	----	xxx-	1	-/5
Sikidang						**1981**	....		....	....	----	----	--x-	----	----	1?	
Sileri						**1986**	0806		**1986**	0806	x---	---x	--x-	----	----	1	
						1993	0123		**1993**	0123?	x---	----	--x-	----	----	1	
SUNDORO (Java-C).	**7.30 S**	**109.992 E**	**3151**	**Stratovolc**	**0603-21=**	**Historical**											
						1806?	....		....	....	x---	----	x---	----	----	2	
						1818	....		....	....	x---	----	x---	----	----	2	
Summit, NW and NE flanks						**1882**	0401		**1882**	0407	xx--	----	x---	----	----	2	
						1883	08 ?		....	....	x---	----	x---	----	----	2	
						1887	1113		**1887**	1114	x---	----	x---	----	----	2	
						1902	0501		**1902**	0525	x---	----	--x-	----	----	1	
NE and SW slopes, 2850-2980m, ...						**1903**	1017	+	**1903**	1022	-x--	----	x---	----	----	2	
Summit crater K5						**1906**	0922	+	**1906**	1220	x-x-	----	x---	----	----	2	
						1971	1029		**1971**	1109	x---	----	--x-	----	----	2	
SUMBING (Java-C)	**7.38 S**	**110.058 E**	**3371**	**Stratovolc**	**0603-22=**	**Historical**											
						1730?	....		....	....	x---	----	----	x---	----	1	
UNGARAN (Java-C).	**7.18 S**	**110.33 E**	**2050**	**Stratovolc**	**0603-23=**	**Holocene**											
TELOMOYO (Java-C)	**7.37 S**	**110.40 E**	**1894**	**Stratovolc**	**0603-231**	**Holocene**											
MERBABU (Java-C).	**7.45 S**	**110.43 E**	**3145**	**Stratovolc**	**0603-24=**	**Historical**											
						1560	....		....	....	----	----	x---	----	----		
						? **1570**	....		....	....	----	----	----	----	----		
(1586 eruption not from Merbabu)						X 1586	....		....	....	x---	----	x---	----	----		
						1797	....		....	....	x---	----	x---	----	----	2	
MERAPI (Java-C).	**7.542 S**	**110.442 E**	**2911**	**Stratovolc**	**0603-25=**	**Historical**											
						C **-0050**?	....		....	....	x---	----	xx--	----	----		
						G **0825**x	....		....	....	x---	----	xx--	----	----		
(eruption ^{14}C dated 100-300 yrs earlier)						X 1006	....		....	....	----	----	----	----	----		
						1548	....		....	....	x---	----	x?--	----	----	3↑	
						1554	....		....	....	x---	----	x?--	----	----	3↑	
						1560	....		....	....	x---	----	x?--	----	----	3↑	
						1584	....		....	....	x---	----	x---	----	----	3↑	
						1587	....		....	....	x---	----	xx--	----	xxx-	3↑	
						1658	....		....	....	x---	----	x---	----	----	3↑	
						1663	1231y		....	....	x---	----	x---	----	----	3↑	
						1672	0804		....	....	x---	----	xx--	----	xxx-	3	
						1677	....		....	....	x---	----	x---	----	----	3↑	
						1678	0819		....	....	x---	----	x---	----	----	3↑	
						1745	....		....	....	x---	----	x---	----	----	2	
						1752	....		....	....	x---	----	x---	----	----	2	
						1755	....		....	....	x---	----	x---	----	----	2	
						1768	0819		....	....	x---	----	x---	----	----	2	
						1786	0717		....	....	----	----	----	--x-	----	1	
						1797	....		....	....	----	----	----	--x-	----	1	
						1807	....		....	....	x---	----	x---	----	----	2	
						1810	....		....	....	----	----	----	--x-	----	1	
						1812	....		**1813**	....	----	----	----	--x-	----	1	
						1820	....		**1822**	....	----	----	----	--x-	----	1	7/-
						1822	1227		**1823**	0406	x---	----	xx--	--x-	xxx-	3	8/7
						1828	1218		**1828**	1219	x---	----	x---	----	----	2	
						1832	1225		**1835**	....	x---	----	xx--	x-x-	xx?-	3	7/7
						1837	0810		**1838**	06	x---	----	xx--	x-x-	----	3	7/7
						1840	01		....	....	?---	----	?---	----	----	2	
						1846	0406		....	....	x---	----	x---	----	----	2	
						1846	0902		**1847**	10	x---	----	xx--	x-x-	-xx-	3	
						? **1848**	0108		....	....	?---	----	?---	----	----		
						1849	0426		....	....	x---	----	xx--	----	-x--	2	-/6
						1849	0914		**1849**	0924	x---	----	xx--	----	-x--	3	-/7
						? **1854**	09		....	....	x---	----	----	----	----		
						1862	....		**1864**	0526	x---	----	xx--	x-x-	----	2*	7/6
						1865	1024		**1867**	....	x?--	----	x?--	x-x-	-x--	2	7/7
						1869	0528		**1869**	12 ?	x---	----	xx--	x-x-	-x--	2	7/-
						1872	0415	+	**1872**	0421	x---	----	xx--	----	xx--	4	-/8
						1872	1103		**1873**	01 ?	x---	----	x---	----	----	2	

VOLCANO NAME (Subregion) / ERUPTION — Area of Activity	LAT	LONG	ELEV (m)	TYPE	NUMBER	Status	Start Year	Start M-Dy	P	Stop Year	Stop M-Dy	Central, Flank vent, Radial fiss, Regional*	Submarine, New island, Subglacial, Crater lake	Explosive, Pyro flow, Phreatic, Fumarolic	Lava flow, Lava lake, Dome, Spine	Fatal, Damage, Mudflow, Tsunami	VEI	Vol L/T
MERAPI (Java-C) *continued*							**1878**	....		**1879**	0620	x---	----	x---	x---	----	2	
							1883	0725		**1884**	11	x---	----	----	--x-	----	1	
						?	**1885**	0224d		....	....	x---	----	--?-	----	----	1	
							1888	0818		**1888**	1220	x---	----	xx--	--x-	-xx-	3	
							1889	07		....	....	x---	----	--?-	----	----	1	
							1891	0825		**1891**	12 ?	x---	----	x---	----	----	1	
							1893	10		....	....	x---	----	----	----	----	1	
							1894	0127		**1894**	0202	x---	----	x---	--x-	-x--	2	-/6
							1897	....		....	....	x---	----	xx--	----	----	3	
							1902	0203		**1902**	0203	x---	----	x---	--x-	----	1	
							1902	12	+	**1904**	0620e	x---	----	xx--	x-x-	xx--	2*	-/6
							1905	01		**1905**	0601	x---	----	xx--	x-x-	----	2	-/6
							1906	0201e	+	**1907**	0217	x---	----	xx--	x-x-	----	2*	-/6
							1908	....		....	....	x---	----	----	--x-	----	1?	
							1909	0201		**1913**	05	x---	----	x---	--x-	----	2	7/-
							1915	0328		**1915**	0515	x---	----	x---	--x-	----	2	
							1918	....		....	....	----	----	----	----	----		
							1920	0725		**1921**	02	x---	----	xx--	--x-	xx--	3*	-/6
							1922	0218	+	**1922**	0808	x---	----	x---	--x-	----	2	6/-
							1923	....		....	....	----	----	----	----	----		
							1924	0911		**1924**	0913a	x---	----	xx--	----	----	1	
							1930	1125		**1931**	10	x-x-	----	xx--	x-x-	xxx-	3*	7/6
							1933	1001		**1935**	04	x---	----	xx--	x-x-	----	3	7/6
							1939	1213	+	**1940**	09	x---	----	xx--	--x-	----	2*	6/-
Batang							**1942**	0530	+	**1943**	1026e	x---	----	xx--	x-x-	-x--	3*	6/6
							1944	....		**1945**	....	x---	----	?x--	--?-	----	2	
							1948	0929		**1949**	....	x---	----	x---	x---	----	2	
							1953	0302	+	**1958**	12	x---	----	xxx-	--x-	xxx-	3*	
							1961	0413	+	**1961**	0508	x---	----	xx--	x---	xx--	2	
SW slope (2600 m)							**1967**	0112	+	**1969**	06	xx--	----	xx--	x-x-	xxx-	3*	7/7
							1971	01		**1971**	0726	x---	----	-x--	----	----	1	
							1972	1006		**1990**	....	x---	----	xx--	x-x-	-xx-	3*	
NW of 1984 lava dome							**1992**	0120		**1993**	12 >	x---	----	xx--	--x-	-x--	2	7/-
LAWU (Java-C)	**7.625 S**	**111.192 E**	**3265**	**Stratovolc**	**0603-26=**	**Holocene**												
WILIS (Java-C)	**7.808 S**	**111.758 E**	**2563**	**Stratovolc**	**0603-27=**	**Holocene**												
KELUT (Java-E)	**7.93 S**	**112.308 E**	**1731**	**Stratovolc**	**0603-28=**	**Historical**												
							1000	....		....	....	x---	---x	x---	----	-??-	3	
							1311	....		....	....	x---	---x	x---	----	???-	3	
							1334	....		....	....	x---	---x	x---	----	xxx-	3	
							1376	....		....	....	x---	---x	x---	--x-	x---	3↑	
							1385	....		....	....	x---	---x	x---	----	xxx-	3↑	
							1395	....		....	....	x---	---x	x---	----	-??-	3↑	
							1411	....		....	....	x---	---x	x---	----	-??-	3↑	
							1450	....		....	....	x---	---x	----	----	----	3↑	
							1451	....		....	....	x---	---x	x---	----	-??-	3↑	
							1462	....		....	....	x---	---x	x---	----	-??-	3↑	
							1481	....		....	....	x---	---x	x---	----	-??-	3↑	
							1548	....		....	....	x---	---x	x---	----	-xx-	3↑	
							1586	....		....	....	x---	---x	x---	----	xxx-	**5?**	**-/9**
							1641	....		....	....	x---	---x	x---	----	-??-	4?	-/8
							1716	0720		....	....	x---	---x	x---	----	xxx-	2	
							1752	0501		....	....	x---	---x	x---	----	-??-	2	
							1771	0110		....	....	x---	---x	x---	----	-??-	2	
							1776	....		....	....	x---	---x	x---	----	-??-	2	
							1785	....		....	....	x---	---x	x---	----	-??-	2	
							1811	0605		....	....	x---	---x	x---	----	-??-	2	
							1825	....		....	....	x---	---x	x---	----	xxx-	2	
							1826	1011	+	**1826**	1025	x---	---x	xx--	----	xxx-	4?	-/8
							1835	....		....	....	x---	---x	x---	----	-xx-	2	
							1848	0516		....	....	x---	---x	xx--	----	xx--	3	
							1851	0124		....	....	x---	---x	x---	----	-??-	2	
							1864	0104		**1864**	0104	x---	---x	x---	----	xxx-	2	
(breach of crater wall: no eruption)						X	1875	0129		....	....	----	----	----	----	xxx-		
							1901	0522		**1901**	0523	x---	---x	xx--	----	xxx-	3	-/6
							1919	0519		**1919**	0520	x---	---x	xx--	----	xxx-	4	-/8
							1920	1206		**1920**	1212	x---	---x	x---	--x-	----	2	5/-
							1951	0831		**1951**	0831	x---	---x	xx--	----	xxx-	3	
							1966	0426		**1966**	0427	x---	---x	xx--	----	xxx-	4	-/7
							1967	0218		**1967**	0218	x---	----	--x-	----	----	1	
Crater floor at foot of Kelut Peak							**1967**	1211		**1967**	1211	x---	----	--x-	----	----	1	
							1990	0210	+	**1990**	0217?	x---	---x	xxx-	----	xxx-	4	-/8
KAWI-BUTAK (Java-E)	**7.92 S**	**112.45 E**	**2651**	**Stratovolcs**	**0603-281**	**Holocene**												
ARJUNO-WELIRANG (Java-E)	**7.725 S**	**112.58 E**	**3339**	**Stratovolc**	**0603-29=**	**Historical**												
NW flank (Kawah Plupuh)							**1952**	0815e		....	....	-x--	----	--?-	----	--x-	0	
Welirang						?	**1991**	0913		....	....	x---	----	?---	----	----		
PENANGGUNGAN (Java-E)	**7.62 S**	**112.63 E**	**1653**	**Stratovolc**	**0603-291**	**Holocene**												
						?	**0200?**	....		....	....	----	----	----	----	----		
MALANG PLAIN (Java-E)	**8.02 S***	**112.68 E**	**680**	**Maars**	**0603-292**	**Holocene**												
SEMERU (Java-E)	**8.108 S**	**112.92 E**	**3676**	**Stratovolc**	**0603-30=**	**Historical**												
							1818	1108		....	....	x---	----	x---	x---	----	2	
							1829	02		....	....	x---	----	x---	----	----	2	
							1830	1215		**1830**	1216	x---	----	x---	----	----	2	
							1832	0418		....	....	x---	----	x---	?---	----	2	
							1836	0803		**1836**	0805	x---	----	x---	----	----	2	
							1838	07	+	**1838**	1018	x---	----	x---	----	----	2	
							1842	01		**1842**	03	x---	----	x---	----	----	2	
							1844	0925		**1844**	0927	x---	----	x---	x---	----	2	
							1845	01		**1845**	07	x---	----	x---	x---	----	2	
							1848	02		....	....	x---	----	x---	----	----	2	
							1848	0804		....	....	x---	----	x---	x---	----	2	
							1851	01		....	....	x---	----	x---	----	----	2	
							1856	0910		....	....	x---	----	x---	x---	----	2	
							1857	0813		**1857**	09	x---	----	x---	----	----	2	
							1860	04	+	**1860**	06	x---	----	x---	----	-x--	2	
(eruption probably from Lamongan)						X	1864	0702		....	....	----	----	----	----	----		
							1865	0415e		....	....	x---	----	x---	?---	----	2	

VOLCANO NAME (Subregion) ...... LAT LONG ELEV (m) TYPE NUMBER / ERUPTION — Area of Activity	Status Start Year	Start M-Dy	P	Stop Year	Stop M-Dy	Central / Flank vent / Radial fiss / Regional	Submarine / New island / Subglacial / Crater lake	Explosive / Pyro flow / Phreatic / Fumarolic	Lava flow / Lava lake / Dome / Spine	Fatal / Damage / Mudflow / Tsunami	VEI	Vol L/T
SEMERU (Java-E) *continued*	**1867**	0415e		**1867**	05	x---	----	x---	----	----	2	
	1872	1023		**1872**	1023	x---	----	x---	----	----	2	
	1877	04		....	....	x---	----	x---	----	----	2	
	1877	09		....	....	x---	----	x---	----	----	2	
	1878	....		....	....	x---	----	x---	x---	----	2	
	1879	....		....	....	x---	----	x---	----	----	2	
	1884	1210?	+	**1885**	09	x---	----	xx--	x---	xxx-	2	
	1886	0125	+	**1886**	0826e	x---	----	x---	----	----	2	
	1887	02		**1887**	03	x---	----	x---	----	----	2	
	1887	0910		**1887**	1011	x---	----	x---	x---	----	2	
	1888	02	+	**1888**	10	x---	----	?x--	----	----	2	
	1889	01	+	**1891**	0531>	x---	----	x---	x---	----	2*	
	1892	03		**1892**	04	x---	----	x---	----	----	2	
	1893	01	+	**1893**	05	x---	----	x---	----	----	2	
	1893	1211	+	**1894**	02	x---	----	x---	----	----	2*	
	1895	0522	+	**1895**	1001	x---	----	xx--	x---	-xx-	2	
	1896	05		**1896**	06	x---	----	x---	----	----	2	
	1897	0101		**1897**	0103	x---	----	x---	x---	----	2	
	1898	0223		....	....	x---	----	x---	x---	----	2	
	1899	0117	+	**1899**	0331?	x---	----	x---	----	----	2	
	1899	0811		....	....	x---	----	x---	----	----	2	
	1899	12		....	....	x---	----	x---	----	----	2	
	1900	0329		**1900**	0411>	x---	----	x---	x---	----	2	
	1901	0129		**1901**	0130>	x---	----	x---	----	----	2	
	1903	0326		**1903**	06	x---	----	x---	----	----	2	
	1904	0102		**1904**	0116	x---	----	x---	----	----	2	
	1905	0804		....	....	x---	----	x---	----	----	2	
	1907	0107		**1907**	0110	x---	----	x---	----	----	2	
	1907	0709<		....	....	x---	----	x---	----	----	2	
	1908	01		**1908**	12	x---	----	x---	----	----	2	
	1909	09	+	**1910**	0322	x---	----	xx--	----	-x--	2*	
	1910	1116	+	**1911**	02	x---	----	x---	----	----	2	
	1911	1108		**1911**	12	x---	----	xx--	x---	-xx-	3*	
	1912	0828		....	....	x---	----	x---	----	----	2	
Jonggring Seloko	**1913**	0623		**1913**	0626?	x---	----	x---	----	-xx-	2	
ESE flank (1400-1775 m)	**1941**	0921		**1942**	02	--x-	----	x---	x---	-x--	2	7/-
Jonggring Seloko	**1945**	0612		**1945**	0618	x---	----	x---	----	----	2	
Jonggring Seloko	**1946**	02		**1946**	05	x---	----	xxx-	----	xxx-	2	
Jonggring Seloko	**1946**	1029	+	**1947**	06	x---	----	xx--	--x-	-xx-	2	
Jonggring Seloko	**1950**	0828		**1964**	12	x---	----	xx--	x-x-	-xx-	2*	
Jonggring Seloko	**1967**	0831		**1993>**	....	x---	----	xxx-	x-x-	xxx-	3*	
TENGGER Caldera (Java-E) .... **7.942 S 112.95 E 2329 Stratovolc 0603-31=**	**Historical**											
(all historical eruptions from Bromo).......	? **1767**	....		....	....	x---	----	----	----	----		
	? **1775**	....		....	....	x---	----	----	----	----		
	1804	09		....	....	x---	----	x---	----	----	2	
	1815	0405		**1815**	0417>	x---	----	x---	----	----	2	
	1820	....		....	....	x---	----	?-?-	----	----	2	
	1822	1228		**1823**	0105d	x---	----	x---	----	----	2	
	1825	1105		**1825**	1108	x---	----	x---	----	----	2	
	1829	1105		**1829**	1111	x---	----	x---	----	-x--	2	
	1830	0303		....	....	x---	----	x---	----	----	2	
	1830	1215		**1830**	1216	x---	----	x---	----	----	2	
	1835	....		....	....	x---	----	x---	----	----	2	
	1842	0124		**1842**	06	x---	---x	x---	----	----	2	
	1843	01		....	....	x---	----	x---	----	----	2	
	1844	1109		....	....	x---	----	x---	----	----	2	
	@ **1856**	0910		....	....	x---	----	x---	----	----	2	
	1857	....		....	....	x---	----	x---	----	----	2	
	1858	0304		....	....	x---	----	x---	----	----	2	
	1858	1018		....	....	x---	----	x---	----	----	2	
	1859	0130		**1859**	0304d	x---	----	x---	----	----	2	
	1860	0612		**1860**	0614	x---	----	x---	----	----	2	
	1865	04		**1865**	05	x---	----	x---	----	----	2	
	1865	1201		**1865**	1218	x---	----	x---	----	----	2	
	1866	07		....	....	x---	----	x---	----	----	2	
	1867	1213	+	**1868**	0112	x---	----	x---	----	----	2	
	1877	0424?		....	....	x---	----	x---	----	----	2	
	1885	06 ?		....	....	x---	----	x---	----	----	2	
	1885	1031		**1886**	0110	x---	----	x---	----	-x--	2	
	1886	0415	+	**1886**	0426	x---	----	x---	----	----	2	
(all historical eruptions from Bromo).......	**1886**	1111		**1887**	0125	x---	----	x---	----	----	2	
	? **1888**	0227		....	....	x---	----	--x-	----	----	2	
	1890	05		**1890**	09	x---	----	x---	----	----	2	
	1893	0113	+	**1893**	0327	x---	----	x---	----	----	2	
	1896	....		....	....	x---	----	x---	----	----	2	
	1906	0925	+	**1907**	0518	x---	----	x---	----	----	2	
	1907	0828		....	....	x---	----	x---	----	----	2	
	1907	1214	+	**1908**	0213	x---	----	x---	----	----	2	
	1909	0112		**1909**	0114	x---	----	x---	----	----	2	
	1910	0118		**1910**	0121	x---	----	x---	----	----	2	
	1915	11	+	**1916**	06	x---	----	x---	----	-x--	3	
	1921	06	+	**1921**	1017	x---	----	x---	----	----	2	
	1922	0205	+	**1922**	0620	x---	----	x---	----	----	2	
	1928	0315e		**1928**	07	x---	----	x---	----	----	2	
	1928	1216		....	....	x---	----	x---	----	----	2	
	1929	0807		**1929**	0908	x---	----	x---	----	----	2	
	1930	0530		**1930**	07	x---	----	x---	----	----	2	
	1935	07		....	....	x---	----	x---	----	----	2	
	1939	0624		**1939**	07	x---	----	x---	----	----	2	
	1940	0425	+	**1940**	0703>	x---	----	x---	----	----	2	
	1948	0215		**1948**	0425	x---	----	x---	----	-x--	3	
	1950	0527	+	**1950**	08	x---	----	x---	----	----	2	
	1955	1229		**1955**	1230	x---	----	x---	----	----	2	
	1956	06		**1956**	07 ?	x---	----	x---	----	----	2	
	1972	0126		**1972**	03	x---	----	x---	----	-x--	2	
	1980	0605a		**1980**	0920	x---	----	x-x-	---?	----	2	
(all historical eruptions from Bromo).......	? **1983**	0415e	+	?**1983**	0628a	x---	----	--?-	----	----	1	

VOLCANO NAME (Subregion)	LAT	LONG	ELEV (m)	TYPE	NUMBER	Status	ERUPTION — Area of Activity	Start Year	Start M-Dy	P	Stop Year	Stop M-Dy	Central / Flank vent / Radial fiss / Regional*	Submarine / New island / Subglacial / Crater lake	Explosive / Pyro flow / Phreatic / Fumarolic	Lava flow / Lava lake / Dome / Spine	Fatal / Damage / Mudflow / Tsunami	VEI	Vol L/T
TENGGER Caldera (Java-E) *continued*							(all historical eruptions from Bromo)	**1983**	1221		**1983**	1221	x---	----	x---	----	----	1	
								1984	0521		**1984**	0531	x---	----	x---	----	----	1	
LAMONGAN (Java-E)	**8.00 S**	**113.342 E**	**1651**	**Stratovolc**	**0603-32=**	**Historical**													
								1799	....		....	....	x---	----	x---	----	----	2	
								1806	05		....	....	x---	----	x---	----	----	2	
								1808	1208		....	....	x---	----	x---	----	----	2	
								1817	....		....	....	x---	----	x---	----	----	2	
								1818	1008		....	....	x---	----	x---	----	----	2	
								1821	1215e		**1822**	0105	xx--	----	x---	x---	----	2	
								1824	0101?		**1824**	0131?	x---	----	x---	----	----	2	
								1826	....		....	....	x---	----	x---	----	----	2	
								1829	01		**1829**	02	x---	----	x---	x---	----	2	
								1830	02		**1830**	03	x---	----	x---	x---	----	2	
								1838	0704		**1838**	0706	x---	----	x---	----	----	2	
								1838	1018		....	....	x---	----	x---	----	----	2	
								1841	0716	+	**1842**	08	x---	----	x---	----	----	2	
								1843	08	+	**1844**	09	x---	----	x---	?---	xx--	2	
								1847	0326	+	**1847**	0626	xx--	----	x---	x---	----	2	
								1847	0925		....	....	xx--	----	x---	x---	----	2	
							Summit and north flank	**1849**	06	+	**1849**	09	xx--	----	x---	x---	----	2	
								1856	0301		**1856**	0614	x---	----	x---	----	----	2	
								1859	0227		**1859**	03	x---	----	x---	----	-x--	2	
								1861	....		....	....	x---	----	x---	----	----	2	
								1864	0609		**1864**	07	x---	----	x---	x---	----	2	
							Summit and south slope	**1869**	0406		**1869**	0504	xx--	----	x---	x---	-x--	2	
								1869	0912		....	....	x---	----	x---	x---	xx--	2	
								1870	0302		**1870**	0305	x---	----	x---	----	----	2	
							Summit and SW flank	**1870**	0818	+	**1871**	0205a	xx--	----	x---	----	----	2	
								1872	0815		**1872**	0918	x---	----	x---	----	----	2	
								1874	0520	+	**1874**	0821	x---	----	x---	----	----	2	
								1877	0424?	+	**1877**	0512?	xx--	----	x---	x---	-x--	3*	
								1883	0413		**1883**	0504a	xx--	----	x---	x---	-x--	2	7/-
								1884	0106	+	**1884**	0623	x---	----	x---	----	----	2	
								1885	0311	+	**1886**	1015e	x---	----	x---	x---	-x--	2	
								1887	0703a		**1887**	0709	x---	----	x---	----	----	2	
								1887	11	+	**1888**	0227	x---	----	x---	----	----	2	
								1888	09		**1888**	1006	x---	----	x---	----	----	2	
								1889	0907		**1889**	11	x---	----	x---	----	----	2	
								1890	0323h		**1890**	05	x---	----	x---	----	----	2	
								1890	0905d	+	**1891**	01 >	x---	----	x---	?---	----	2	
								1891	0925e		**1891**	1005d	x---	----	x---	x---	----	2	
								1893	1118		....	....	x---	----	x---	----	-xx-	2	
								1896	0905		**1896**	0919>	x---	----	x---	----	----	?	
							SW flank 400 m (Mt. Anyar)	**1898**	0205		**1898**	0215	-x--	----	x---	x---	-x--	2	
								? **1953**	0404		?**1953**	06	x---	----	----	----	----	2?	
LURUS (Java-E)	**7.70 S**	**113.58 E**	**539**	**Complx volc**	**0603-321**	**Holocene?**													
IYANG-ARGAPURA (Java-E)	**7.97 S**	**113.57 E**	**3088**	**Complx volc**	**0603-33=**	**Holocene**													
RAUNG (Java-E)	**8.125 S**	**114.042 E**	**3332**	**Stratovolc**	**0603-34=**	**Historical**													
							(may be same as 1593 eruption)	? **1586**	....		....	....	x---	---x	x---	----	xx--	3	
								1593	....		....	....	x---	---x	x---	----	xx--	5?	-/9
								1597	0117		**1597**	0202>	x---	---x	x---	----	xx--	3	
								1638	....		....	....	x---	---x	x---	----	xxx-	4?	-/8
								1730	....		....	....	x---	---x	x---	----	xxx-	3?	-/8
								1793f	....		....	....	x---	----	x---	----	----	2	
								1804d	....		....	....	x---	----	x---	----	----	2	
								1812	....		**1814**?	....	x---	----	x---	----	----	2	
								1815	1231y		....	....	x---	----	x---	----	----	2	
								1817	0116		**1817**	0210?	x---	---x	x---	----	xxx-	4?	-/8
								1838	....		....	....	x---	---x	x---	----	-xx-	2	
								1849	1201p		....	....	x---	----	----	----	----		
								1859	1214		....	....	x---	----	x---	----	----	2	
								1860	09 <		....	....	x---	----	x---	----	----	2	
								1864	0702		**1864**	12	x---	----	x---	----	----	2	
								1881	....		....	....	x---	----	?---	----	----		
								1885	0621		**1885**	0622	x---	----	x---	----	----	2	
								1890	07		**1890**	0915b	x---	----	x---	----	----	2	
								1896	08		....	....	x---	----	x---	----	----	2	
								1897	04		....	....	x---	----	x---	----	----	2	
								1902	0216		**1902**	0227>	x---	----	x---	x---	----	2	
								1903	1128	+	**1904**	01	x---	----	x---	----	----	2	
								1913	0510	+	**1913**	12	x---	----	x---	----	----	2	
								1915	05		....	....	x---	----	x---	----	----	2	
								1916	11		**1916**	12	x---	----	x---	----	----	2	
								1917	0222		....	....	x---	----	x---	----	----	2	
							1913 cone	**1921**	0214d		**1921**	04	x---	----	x---	x---	----	2	
								1924	02 <		....	....	x---	----	x---	x---	----	2	
								? **1924**	0820		....	....	x---	----	----	----	----	2?	
							Central cone and NW crater wall	**1927**	0802	+	**1928**	03 ?	x---	----	x---	----	----	2	
								1928	11		....	....	x---	----	x---	----	----	2	
								1929	0427r		....	....	x---	----	x---	----	----	2	
								1933	1121		**1933**	1206	x---	----	x---	----	----	2	
								1936	0822	+	**1936**	1211	x---	----	x---	----	----	2	
								1937	1027	+	**1937**	1127	x---	----	x---	----	----	2	
								1938	0813	+	**1939**	0110>	x---	----	x---	----	----	2	
								1940	....		....	....	?---	----	?---	----	----	2	
								1941	1213		....	....	x---	----	x---	----	----	2	
								1943	0317		**1943**	0618	x---	----	x---	----	----	2	
								1944	0630	+	**1945**	0419	x---	----	x---	?---	----	2	
								1953	0131		**1953**	0415e	x---	----	x---	x---	-x--	3	8/-
								1955	0118		**1955**	0118	x---	----	x---	----	----	2?	
								1956	0213		**1956**	0325	x---	----	x---	----	----	3*	
								1971	0914		**1971**	0914	x---	----	--x-	----	----	1	
								1973	05		**1973**	10	x---	----	x---	----	----	1	
								1974	0615		**1974**	0717?	x---	----	x---	----	----	2	
								1975	03		**1975**	05	x---	----	x-x-	----	----	1	
								1976	0607		**1976**	1121	x---	----	x---	----	----	2	
								1977	0609		**1977**	0630	x---	----	xx--	----	----	2	
								1978	01		**1979**	12 >	x---	----	x-?-	----	----	1	

VOLCANO NAME (Subregion) / ERUPTION — Area of Activity	LAT	LONG	ELEV (m)	TYPE	NUMBER	Status / Start Year	Start M-Dy	P	Stop Year	Stop M-Dy	Central / Flank vent / Radial fiss / Regional*	Submarine / New island / Subglacial / Crater lake	Explosive / Pyro flow / Phreatic / Fumarolic	Lava flow / Lava lake / Dome / Spine	Fatal / Damage / Mudflow / Tsunami	VEI	Vol L/T
RAUNG (Java-E) *continued*						**1982**	0718		**1982**	0720	x---	----	x---	----	-x--	3	
						1985	0823		**1985**	1228	x---	----	x---	----	----	2	
						1987	....		**1989**	0728c	x---	----	x---	----	----	1	
						1990	01 <		**1990**	12 >	x---	----	x---	----	----	2	
						1991	0910		**1991**	1003>	x---	----	x---	----	----	2	
						1993	0401t		....	....	x---	----	x---	----	----	1	
IJEN (Java-E)	**8.058 S**	**114.242 E**	**2386**	**Stratovolcs**	**0603-35=**	**Historical**											
						1796	....		....	....	x---	---x	--x-	----	--x-	2	
						1817	0115e		**1817**	0218?	x---	---x	x---	----	xxx-	2*	
						1917	0225		**1917**	0314	x---	---x	--x-	----	----	1	
						1936	1105		**1936**	1125	x---	---x	--x-	----	--x-	2	
						1952	0422		**1952**	0424a	x---	---x	x-x-	----	----	1	
						1993	0703		**1993**	0801	x---	---x	--x-	----	----	1	
BALURAN (Java-E)	**7.85 S**	**114.37 E**	**1247**	**Stratovolc**	**0603-351**	**Holocene?**											
LESSER SUNDA ISLANDS																	
BRATAN (Bali)	**8.28 S**	**115.13 E**	**2276**	**Caldera**	**0604-001**	**Holocene**											
BATUR (Bali)	**8.242 S**	**115.375 E**	**1717**	**Caldera**	**0604-01=**	**Historical**											
						1804	....		....	....	x---	----	x---	----	----	2	
						1821	0316		....	....	x---	----	x---	----	----	2	
						1849	....		....	....	x---	----	x---	x---	----	2	
Batur I						**1854**	0428		....	....	x---	----	x---	----	----	1?	
SE flank of Batur I						**1888**	0530		**1888**	0531	x-x-	----	x---	x---	----	2	
						1897	....		....	....	x---	----	x---	----	----	2	
West flank						**1904**	....		....	....	-x--	----	x---	x---	----	2	
Batur I and SW flank (Batur II)						**1905**	....		....	....	xx--	----	x---	x---	-x--	2	
SW flank (Batur II)						**1921**	0129		**1921**	0417	x---	----	x---	x---	----	2	
						1922	0830		....	....	x---	----	x---	----	----	2	
Batur II						**1923**	....		....	....	x---	----	x---	----	----	2	
Batur II						**1924**	03		**1924**	03 ?	x---	----	x---	----	----	2	
Batur II						**1925**	0105d		**1925**	0105d	x---	----	x---	----	----	2	
SW flank below Batur III						**1926**	0802		**1926**	0921	-xx-	----	x---	xx--	-x--	2	7/6
SW, W flanks (near Batur III, Butus)						**1963**	0905	+	**1964**	0510	-xx-	----	x---	x---	-x--	2	7/5
SW flank (near Batur III)						**1965**	0818		**1965**	12	-x--	----	x---	?---	-x--	1	
SW flank (west of 1965 vent)						**1966**	0428		....	....	-x--	----	x---	----	----	1	
SW flank (Batur III)						**1968**	0123	+	**1968**	0215	-x--	----	x---	x---	----	2	6/-
SW flank (1963 vent)						**1970**	0105d		**1970**	0115	-x--	----	x---	----	----	1	
						1971	0311		**1971**	06	x---	----	x---	----	----	1	
Batur III						**1972**	0119	+	**1972**	03	x---	----	x---	----	----	2	
						1973	....		....	....	----	----	----	----	----		
Batur III						**1974**	0312	+	**1974**	04	x---	----	x---	x---	----	2	
AGUNG (Bali)	**8.342 S**	**115.508 E**	**3142**	**Stratovolc**	**0604-02=**	**Historical**											
						1808	....		....	....	x---	----	x---	----	----	2	
						? **1821**	0316		....	....	x---	----	x---	----	----	2	
						1843	....		....	....	x---	----	x---	----	----	2	
						1963	0219		**1964**	0126	x---	----	xx--	x---	xxx-	4*	8/8
RINJANI (Lombok I)	**8.42 S**	**116.47 E**	**3726**	**Stratovolc**	**0604-03=**	**Historical**											
Gunung Barujari						**1847**	0910		**1847**	0912	x---	----	x---	----	----	2	
Gunung Barujari						**1884**	0808		**1884**	0810a	x---	----	x---	----	----	2	
Gunung Barujari						**1900**	1130		**1900**	1202	x---	----	x---	x---	----	2	
Gunung Barujari						**1901**	0601		**1901**	0602	x---	----	x---	----	----	2	
Gunung Barujari						**1906**	0429		....	....	x---	----	x---	----	----	1?	
Gunung Barujari						**1909**	1130		**1909**	1202	x---	----	x---	----	--x-	2	
Gunung Barujari (Segara Munjar)						**1915**	1104		....	....	x---	----	x---	----	----	2	
Rinjani summit						? **1941**	0530		....	....	x---	----	----	----	----		
NW flank of Barujari (Rombongan)						**1944**	1225		**1945**	0101?	xx--	---x	x---	x-x-	-x--	2	7/-
NW flank of Gunung Barujari						**1949**	....		**1950**	....	xx--	----	----	x---	----	0	
Gunung Barujari						**1953**	1015q		....	....	x---	----	----	----	----	0?	
Gunung Barujari						**1965**	09		....	....	-x--	----	----	?---	----	0	
East side of Barujari (2250 m)						**1966**	0328	+	**1966**	0808	x---	----	x---	x---	----	1	6/4
TAMBORA (Sumbawa I)	**8.25 S**	**118.00 E**	**2850**	**Stratovolc**	**0604-04=**	**Historical**											
						C **-3910**x	....		....	....	x---	----	xx--	----	----		
						C **-3050**?	....		....	....	x---	----	xx--	----	----		
						C **0740**w	....		....	....	x---	----	x---	----	----		
						1812	....	+	**1815**	0715?	x---	----	xx--	----	xx-x	7*	-/11
						1819	08		....	....	x---	----	x---	----	----	2	
SW part of caldera (Doro Afi Toi)						**1880**r	....		....	....	x---	----	x---	x-x-	----	2	
NE part of caldera floor						**1967**p	....		....	....	x---	----	----	x---	----	0	
SANGEANG API (Lesser Sunda Is)	**8.18 S**	**119.058 E**	**1949**	**Complx volc**	**0604-05=**	**Historical**											
						1512	....		....	....	x---	----	x---	----	----	3↑	
						1715	....		....	....	x---	----	x---	----	----	2	
						1821	0323		....	....	x---	----	x---	----	----	2	
						1860	0911		**1860**	10	x---	----	x---	----	----	2	
Doro Api						**1911**	0213		**1911**	0302	x---	----	x---	x---	----	2	
						1912	04		....	....	x---	----	x---	----	----	2	
						1927	....		....	....	x---	----	x---	----	----	2	
Doro Api						**1953**	0319		**1953**	0515>	x---	----	x---	x---	--x-	3	
						1954	0426		....	....	x---	----	x---	----	----	2	
						1954	1104		....	....	x---	----	x---	----	----	2	
						1955	....		....	....	x---	----	--x-	----	----	1	
						1956	12		....	....	x---	----	--x-	----	----	1	
						1957	....		....	....	x---	----	--x-	----	----	1	
						1958	....		....	....	x---	----	x---	----	----	1?	
Doro Api						**1964**	0129		**1965**	1201p	x---	----	x---	x-x-	----	2	6/-
						1966	0228		**1966**	11	x---	----	x---	----	----	2	
Doro Api						**1985**	0730		**1988**	02	x---	----	xx--	x---	--x-	3*	7/-
GILIBANTA (Lesser Sunda Is)	**8.52 S**	**119.35 E**		**Submarine ?**	**0604-051**	**Uncertain**											
						? **1957**	0808		?**1957**	0809	----	----	----	----	----		
SANO, WAI (Flores I)	**8.68 S**	**120.025 E**	**903**	**Caldera**	**0604-06=**	**Fumarolic**											
POCO LEOK (Flores I)	**8.68 S**	**120.48 E**	**1675**	**Unknown**	**0604-07=**	**Fumarolic**											
RANAKAH, GUNUNG (Flores I)	**8.62 S**	**120.52 E**	**2100**	**Lava domes**	**0604-071**	**Historical**											
Anak Ranakah						**1987**	1228		**1989**	04 >	-x--	----	xx--	x--x	----	3*	7/6
Anak Ranakah						**1991**	03 <		....	....	x---	----	x---	----	----	1	
INIERIE (Flores I)	**8.875 S**	**120.95 E**	**2245**	**Stratovolc**	**0604-08=**	**Fumarolic**											

VOLCANO NAME (Subregion) / ERUPTION — Area of Activity	LAT	LONG	ELEV (m)	TYPE	NUMBER	Status	Start Year	Start M-Dy	P	Stop Year	Stop M-Dy	Central, Flank vent, Radial fiss, Regional* / Submarine, New island, Subglacial, Crater lake / Explosive, Pyro flow, Phreatic, Fumarolic / Lava flow, Lava lake, Dome, Spine / Fatal, Damage, Mudflow, Tsunami	VEI	Vol L/T
INIELIKA (Flores I)	**8.73 S**	**120.98 E**	**1559**	**Complx volc**	**0604-09=**	**Historical**								
							1905	11		**1905**	11	x--- ---- x-x- ---- -x--	2	
EBULOBO (Flores I)	**8.808 S**	**121.18 E**	**2124**	**Stratovolc**	**0604-10=**	**Historical**								
							1830	....		....	....	x--- ---- x--- x--- ----	2	
							1888	....		....	....	x--- ---- x--- ---- ----	2	
							1910	0410		....	....	x--- ---- x--- ---- ----	2	
							1924	11		....	....	x--- ---- xx-- ---- ----	2	
							1938	05		**1938**	06	---- ---- ---- ---- ----		
							1941	0823h		....	....	x--- ---- ---- x--- ----	0?	
							1969	0227		....	....	x--- ---- x--- ---- ----	2?	
IYA (Flores I)	**8.88 S**	**121.63 E**	**637**	**Stratovolc**	**0604-11=**	**Historical**								
							1671?	....		....	....	x--- ---- x--- ---- ----	3↑	
							1844	05		....	....	x--- ---- x--- ---- ----	2	
							1867	01		....	....	x--- ---- x--- ---- ----	2	
							1868	0504		....	....	x--- ---- x--- ---- ----	2	
							1871	0901		....	....	x--- ---- x--- ---- ----	2	
							1882	....		....	....	x--- ---- x--- ---- ----	2	
							? **1888**	12		....	....	---- ---- ---- ---- ----		
							1953	0904		**1953**	0905	---- ---- x--- ---- ----	2?	
Crater II (upper SW flank)							**1969**	0127		**1969**	0130	-x-- ---- xx-- ---- xx--	3	
							? **1971**	06		?**1971**	06	x--- ---- --?- ---- ----	1	
SUKARIA CALDERA (Flores I)	**8.792 S**	**121.77 E**	**1500**	**Caldera**	**0604-12=**	**Fumarolic**								
NDETE NAPU (Flores I)	**8.72 S**	**121.78 E**	**750**	**Fumarole fld**	**0604-13=**	**Fumarolic**								
KELIMUTU (Flores I)	**8.758 S**	**121.83 E**	**1640**	**Complx volc**	**0604-14=**	**Historical**								
							1865e	....		....	....	---- ---- --?- ---- ----	2	
							1938	05		**1938**	06	---- ---- --x- ---- ----	2	
Tiwu Nua Muri							**1968**	0603	+	**1968**	0729	x--- ---x x-x- ---- ----	1	
PALUWEH (Lesser Sunda Is)	**8.32 S**	**121.708 E**	**875**	**Stratovolc**	**0604-15=**	**Historical**								
							1650t	....		....	....	x--- ---- x--- ---- ----	3	
Rokatenda							**1928**	0804	+	**1928**	0925	x--- ---- x--- --x- xx-x	3	6/7
Rokatenda (1928 crater)							**1963**	1231	+	**1966**	0316	x--- ---- xx-- x-x- xx--	2*	7/-
Rokatenda							**1972**	1022	+	**1973**	0116	x--- ---- x--- ---- -x--	3*	
							1973	1027		**1973**	1028	x--- ---- x--- ---- ----	2	
Rokatenda							**1980**	1105		**1981**	09	x--- ---- xx-- --x- -x--	2	6/-
Rokatenda (west side of lava dome)							**1984**	0509	+	**1984**	0521	x--- ---- x--- ---- ----	2	
Rokatenda (west side of lava dome)							**1985**	0203		**1985**	0203	x--- ---- x--- ---- ----	1	
EGON (Flores I)	**8.67 S**	**122.45 E**	**1703**	**Stratovolc**	**0604-16=**	**Historical**								
							? **1888**	....		?**1892**	....	x--- ---- ---- ---- ----	2	
							1907	0928		....	....	x--- ---- ?--- ---- ----	2	
ILIMUDA (Flores I)	**8.478 S**	**122.671 E**	**1100**	**Stratovolc**	**0604-17=**	**Fumarolic**								
LEWOTOBI (Flores I)	**8.53 S**	**122.775 E**	**1703**	**Stratovolcs**	**0604-18=**	**Historical**								
Lewotobi Lakilaki							**1675q**	....		....	....	x--- ---- x--- x--- ----	3↑	
Lewotobi Lakilaki							? **1859**	07		....	....	---- ---- ---- ---- ----		
Lewotobi Lakilaki							**1861**	0504	+	**1861**	0518	x--- ---- x--- ---- ----	2	
Lewotobi Lakilaki							**1865**	0504		....	....	x--- ---- x--- ---- ----	2	
Lewotobi Lakilaki							**1868**	0713<		....	....	x--- ---- x--- ---- ----	2	
Lewotobi Lakilaki							**1868**	1215		....	....	x--- ---- x--- ---- ----	2	
Lewotobi Lakilaki							**1869**	0707		**1869**	0727	x--- ---- x--- ---- xx--	2	
Lewotobi Lakilaki							**1889**	....		....	....	x--- ---- x--- ---- ----	2	
Lewotobi Lakilaki							**1907**	0928	+	**1907**	1030	x--- ---- x--- x--- xx--	3	
Lewotobi Lakilaki							**1909**	0108		**1910**	0526	x--- ---- x--- x--- ----	2	
Lewotobi Lakilaki							**1914**	0629		....	....	x--- ---- x--- x--- ----	2	
Lewotobi Perempuan							**1921**	0101	+	**1921**	1220	x--- ---- x--- --x- ----	2	5/-
Lewotobi Lakilaki							**1932**	0523		**1933**	1226e	x--- ---- xx-- x-xx ----	3	5/-
Lewetobi Perempuan							**1935**	12		**1935**	1225>	x--- ---- x--- ---- ----	2	
Lewotobi Lakilaki							**1939**	1217		**1940**	0421	x--- ---- x--- ---- ----	2	
Lewotobi Lakilaki							**1968**	1128	+	**1969**	0202	x--- ---- x--- ---- ----	2	
Lewotobi Lakilaki							**1970**	....		....	....	x--- ---- x--- ---- ----	2	
Lewotobi Lakilaki							**1971**	01		....	....	x--- ---- x--- ---- ----	2	
Lewotabi Lakilaki							**1990**	0128		**1990**	06	x--- ---- x--- ---- ----	1	
Lewotobi Lakilaki							**1991**	0511		**1991**	12 ?	x--- ---- x--- ---- ----	1	
LEREBOLENG (Flores I)	**8.358 S**	**122.842 E**	**1117**	**Complx volc**	**0604-20=**	**Historical**								
Burak (Kawah XXIV)							**1873**	....		....	....	x--- ---- x--- ---- ----	2	
Burak (Kawah XXVI)							**1876**	....		....	....	x--- ---- x--- ---- ----	2	
Burak (Kawah XXVII)							**1881**	0316		....	....	x--- ---- x--- ---- ----	2	
RIANG KOTANG (Flores I)	**8.30 S**	**122.892 E**	**200**	**Fumarole fld**	**0604-21=**	**Fumarolic**								
ILIBOLENG (Adonara I)	**8.342 S**	**123.258 E**	**1659**	**Stratovolc**	**0604-22=**	**Historical**								
							1885	09		**1885**	10	x--- ---- x--- ---- ----	2	
							1888	....		....	....	x--- ---- x--- x--- ----	2	
							1904	....		....	....	x--- ---- x--- x--- ----	2	
							1909	1109		....	....	x--- ---- x--- ---- ----	2	
							1925	....		....	....	x--- ---- x--- ---- ----	2	
							1927	....		....	....	x--- ---- ?--- ---- ----	2	
							1944	08		**1944**	10	x--- ---- x--- ---- ----	2	
							1948	0429		....	....	x--- ---- x--- ---- ----	2	
							1949	0204		....	....	x--- ---- x--- ---- ----	2	
							1949	0612		....	....	x--- ---- x--- ---- ----	2	
							1950	03		**1950**	08 ?	x--- ---- x--- ---- ----	2	
							1951	....		....	....	---- ---- x--- ---- ----	2?	
							1973	04		**1974**	04	x--- ---- x--- ---- -x--	2	
							1982	1117		**1982**	1117	x--- ---- x--- ---- ----	2	
							1983	0511	+	**1984**	0413	x--- ---- x--- ---- ----	2*	
							1986	0528	+	**1986**	1124	x--- ---- x--- ---- ----	1	
							1987	1002		**1987**	1002	x--- ---- x--- ---- ----	2	
							1991	0508		**1991**	0630>	---- ---- x--- ---- ----	1	
							1991	1103		**1991**	1115	x--- ---- x--- ---- ----	1	
							1993	06 ?		**1993**	07	x--- ---- x--- ---- ----	1?	
LEWOTOLO (Lomblen I)	**8.272 S**	**123.505 E**	**1423**	**Stratovolc**	**0604-23=**	**Historical**								
							1660	....		....	....	x--- ---- x--- ---- ----	3↑	
							1819	....		....	....	x--- ---- x--- ---- ----	2	
							1849	1006		....	....	x--- ---- x--- ---- ----	2	
K2 crater							**1852**	1005		**1852**	1006	x--- ---- x--- ---- -x--	2	
							1864	....		....	....	x--- ---- x--- ---- ----	2	
							1899	0602		....	....	x--- ---- x--- ---- ----	2	

VOLCANO NAME (Subregion) / ERUPTION — Area of Activity	LAT	LONG	ELEV (m)	TYPE	NUMBER	Status / Start Year	Start M-Dy	P	Stop Year	Stop M-Dy	Central vent / Flank vent / Radial fiss. / Regional*	Submarine / New island / Subglacial / Crater lake	Explosive / Pyro flow / Phreatic / Fumarolic	Lava flow / Lava lake / Dome / Spine	Fatal / Damage / Mudflow / Tsunami	VEI	Vol L/T
LEWOTOLO (Lomblen I) *continued*						**1920**	....		....	....	x---	----	x---	----	----	2	
						1951	1215		....	....	----	----	----	----	----	2	
ILILABALEKAN (Lomblen I)	**8.53 S**	**123.42 E**	**1018**	**Stratovolc**	**0604-24=**	**Fumarolic**											
ILIWERUNG (Lomblen I)	**8.540 S**	**123.590 E**	**1018**	**Complx volc**	**0604-25=**	**Historical**											
Iliwerung (Iliadowajo)						**1870**	....		....	....	x---	----	x---	--x-	x---	3	
Iliwerung						**1910**	....		....	....	x---	----	?---	----	----	2	
Iliwerung............................						**1928**	....		....	....	x---	----	x---	--x-	----	2	7/-
						? **1941**	0605		....	....	----	----	----	----	----		
East flank (Iligripe)						**1948**	0407		**1948**	1126	xxx-	----	xx--	--x-	xx--	2	6/6
						1949	0409		**1949**	0429	x---	----	xx--	----	----	2	
						1950	0910		**1950**	1002	x---	----	xx--	x---	-x--	2	
						1951	1112		**1951**	1116	x---	----	xx--	----	-x--	2	
						1952	0324		....	....	x---	----	x---	----	----	1	
Hobal (submarine vent on SE flank).......						**1973**	1205		**1974**	0822	-x--	xx--	x---	----	x--x	2*	
Hobal (submarine vent on SE flank).......						**1983**	0817		**1983**	0818	-x--	x---	x---	----	x--x	1	
Hobal (submarine vent on SE flank).......						**1993**	0915		**1993**	0919	-x--	x---	x---	----	----	2	
TARA, BATU (Komba I)............	**7.792 S**	**123.579 E**	**748**	**Stratovolc**	**0604-26=**	**Historical**											
						1847	....	+	**1852**	0831>	x---	----	x---	x---	----	2	
SIRUNG (Pantar I)	**8.510 S**	**124.148 E**	**862**	**Complx volc**	**0604-27=**	**Historical**											
						? **1852**	....		....	....	x---	----	--?-	----	----	2	
						? **1899**	03		?**1899**	04	x---	----	--?-	----	----	2	
						? **1927**	....		....	....	x---	---?	--?-	----	----	2	
						1934	0614		**1934**	0715e	x---	----	x-x-	----	----	2	
						1947	04		**1947**	05	x---	----	--x-	----	----	2	
						1953	06		....	....	----	----	----	----	xx--		
						1960	0313		....	....	----	----	----	----	----	2?	
						1964	0208		**1964**	1005>	x---	---x	x-x-	----	----	1	
						1965	0507		**1965**	0518	x---	----	x-x-	----	----	1	
						1965	1102		**1965**	1102	x---	----	x-?-	----	----	1	
						1970	....		....	....	----	----	----	----	----	2?	
YERSEY (Wetar I)	**7.53 S**	**123.95 E**	**-3800**	**Submarine ?**	**0604-28=**	**Uncertain**											

BANDA SEA

VOLCANO NAME (Subregion) / ERUPTION — Area of Activity	LAT	LONG	ELEV (m)	TYPE	NUMBER	Status / Start Year	Start M-Dy	P	Stop Year	Stop M-Dy	Central vent / Flank vent / Radial fiss. / Regional*	Submarine / New island / Subglacial / Crater lake	Explosive / Pyro flow / Phreatic / Fumarolic	Lava flow / Lava lake / Dome / Spine	Fatal / Damage / Mudflow / Tsunami	VEI	Vol L/T
EMPEROR OF CHINA (Banda Sea) ..	**6.62 S**	**124.22 E**	**-2850**	**Submarine ?**	**0605-01=**	**Uncertain**											
						? **1893**<	....		....	....	----	?---	?---	----	----	1?	
						? **1927**	0301p		....	....	----	?---	?---	----	----	2	
NIEUWERKERK (Banda Sea)	**6.60 S**	**124.675 E**	**-2285**	**Submarine ?**	**0605-02=**	**Uncertain**											
						? **1893**<	....		....	....	----	?---	?---	----	----	1?	
						? **1925**	0924		....	....	----	?---	?---	----	----	2	
						? **1927**	0301p		....	....	----	?---	?---	----	----	2	
GUNUNGAPI WETAR (Banda Sea) ..	**6.642 S**	**126.65 E**	**282**	**Stratovolc**	**0605-03=**	**Historical**											
						1512	....		....	....	x---	----	?---	?---	----	3↑	
						1699	....		....	....	x---	----	x---	----	----	3↑	
WURLALI (Damar I)...............	**7.125 S**	**128.675 E**	**868**	**Stratovolc**	**0605-04=**	**Historical**											
						1892	0603		**1892**	0605	x---	----	x---	----	----	2	
TEON (Banda Sea)................	**6.92 S**	**129.125 E**	**655**	**Stratovolc**	**0605-05=**	**Historical**											
						1659	1111		....	....	?---	----	?---	----	----	3↑	
						1660	02		....	....	x---	----	xx--	----	xx--	4?	-/8
						1663	0118		....	....	x---	----	x---	----	----	3↑	
						1693	....		....	....	x---	----	x---	----	----	3↑	
						1904	0603		....	....	x---	----	x---	----	----	2	
NILA (Banda Sea)	**6.73 S**	**129.50 E**	**781**	**Stratovolc**	**0605-06=**	**Historical**											
						1903	1208		....	....	x---	----	--x-	----	----	2	
SE flank						**1932**	0313		....	....	x-x-	----	x-x-	----	----	2	
						1964	03		**1964**	03	----	----	--?-	----	----	1?	
East flank						**1968**	0507	+	**1968**	06	-x-x	----	--x-	----	----	1	
SERUA (Banda Sea)	**6.30 S**	**130.00 E**	**641**	**Stratovolc**	**0605-07=**	**Historical**											
						1683	....		....	....	x---	----	x---	----	----	3↑	
						1687	0615		....	....	x---	----	x---	----	----	3↑	
(perhaps same as 1693 eruption)						? **1692**	0604?		....	....	?---	----	?---	----	----		
						1693	0604		**1693**	07	x---	----	x---	xx--	xx--	4?	-/8
						1694	....		....	....	x---	----	x---	----	----	3↑	
						1844	08		**1844**	09	x---	----	x---	x---	----	2	
						? **1845**	....		....	....	?---	----	?---	----	----	2	
						1846	09 ?		....	....	?---	----	?---	----	----	2	
						1858	....		....	....	x---	----	x---	----	-x--	2	
						1859	....		....	....	x---	----	x---	?---	----	2	
						1919	11		....	....	x---	----	x---	?---	----	2	
Summit and south flank						**1921**	0918		....	....	xx--	----	x---	?---	----	2	
MANUK (Banda Sea)..............	**5.53 S**	**130.292 E**	**282**	**Stratovolc**	**0605-08=**	**Fumarolic**											
BANDA API (Banda Sea)...........	**4.525 S**	**129.871 E**	**640**	**Caldera**	**0605-09=**	**Historical**											
						1586	0417		....	....	x---	----	x---	----	----	3↑	
						1598	....		**1602**	....	x---	----	x---	----	xx--	3	
						1609	....		....	....	x---	----	x---	----	----	3↑	
						1615	0316		**1615**	04 ?	x---	----	x---	----	xx--	3	
						1632	1216		....	....	x---	----	x---	----	----	3↑	
						1635	1118		....	....	x---	----	x---	----	----	1?	
						1683	....		....	....	x-x-	----	x---	----	----	3	
						1690	....		**1696**	0522	x---	----	x---	----	x---	3*	
						1712	05		**1712**	12	x---	----	x---	----	----	2	
						1722	....		....	....	x---	----	x---	----	----	2	
						1749	....		....	....	x---	----	x---	----	----	2	
						1762	....		....	....	x---	----	x---	----	----	2	
						1765	0419		**1766**	10	x---	----	x---	----	----	2	
						1773	0206		....	....	x---	----	x---	----	----	2	
						1775	....		....	....	?---	----	?---	----	----	2	
						1778	....		....	....	?---	----	?---	----	----	2	
						1816	1011		**1816**	12	x---	----	x---	----	----	2	
Summit, south and NNW flanks						**1820**	0611		**1820**	0808	x-x-	----	x---	x---	-x--	2	
North side...........................						**1824**	0422	+	**1824**	0628	xx--	----	x---	x---	----	2	
						1825?	....		**1831**	....	x---	----	x---	----	----	1	
						? **1835**	10		....	....	----	----	----	----	----		
						? **1855**	1229		?**1855**	1230	----	----	----	----	----		
						1890	1123		**1890**	1123	x---	----	x---	----	----	2	

VOLCANO NAME (Subregion) ERUPTION — Area of Activity	LAT	LONG	ELEV (m)	TYPE	NUMBER	Status Start Year	Start M-Dy	P	Stop Year	Stop M-Dy	Central / Flank vent / Radial fiss / Regional*	Submarine / New island / Subglacial / Crater lake	Explosive / Pyro flow / Phreatic / Fumarolic	Lava flow / Lava lake / Dome / Spine	Fatal / Damage / Mudflow / Tsunami	VEI	Vol L/T
BANDA API (Banda Sea) *continued* .. Summit and north flank						1901	0518		....	....	xx--	----	x---	x---	-x--	2	
						? 1902	0320		....	....	x---	----	----	----	----		
Summit, north and south flanks						1988	0509		1988	0517	xxx-	x---	xxx-	x---	xxx-	3?	6/-
SULAWESI																	
COLO [UNA UNA] (Sulawesi)	0.17 S	121.608 E	507	Stratovolc	0606-01=	Historical											
Gunung Colo						1898	0502		1900?	....	x---	---?	x---	----	-xx-	3?	-/7
Gunung Colo						1938j	....		....	....	x---	----	--x-	----	----	1	
Gunung Colo						1983	0718	+	1983	12	x---	----	xxx-	----	-x--	4*	
AMBANG (Sulawesi)	0.75 N	124.42 E	1795	Complx volc	0606-02=	Historical											
						1845e	....		....	....	----	----	----	----	----		
SOPUTAN (Sulawesi)	1.108 N	124.725 E	1784	Stratovolc	0606-03=	Historical											
						1785	1231y		....	....	x---	----	x---	----	----	2	
						1819	....		....	....	x---	----	x---	----	----	2	
						1833?	....		....	....	x---	----	x---	----	----	2	
						1845	0208		....	....	x---	----	x---	----	---x	2	
						1890	....		....	....	?---	----	?---	----	----	2	
						1901	0204		....	....	-x--	----	x-x-	----	----	2	
NE flank (Aesuput)						1906	0617		1906	09	-x--	----	x---	x---	----	2	
NE flank (Aesuput)						1907	0605		1907	0625?	-x--	----	x---	----	----	2	
NE flank (Aesuput)						1908	06		1909	06	-x--	----	x---	x---	----	2	
NE flank (Aesuput)						1910	1115q		....	....	-x--	----	x---	x---	----	2	
NE flank (Aesuput)						1911	11		1912	04	-x--	----	x---	x---	----	2	
NE flank (Aesuput)						1913	04		1913	07	-x--	----	x---	----	----	2	
NE flank (Aesuput Weru)						1915	04		1915	06	-x--	----	----	x-x-	----	2	6/-
NE flank (Aesuput)						1917	11		....	....	-x--	----	x---	----	----	2	
NE flank (Aesuput)						1923	1127		1924	0118	-x--	----	x---	x---	----	2*	7/-
NE flank (Aesuput)						1947	0822		1947	0827	-x--	----	x---	----	----	2	
NE flank (Aesuput)						1953	11		....	....	-x--	----	?---	----	----	2	
Kawah Soputan						1966	0521	+	1967	11	x---	----	xx--	x-x-	-xx-	3*	7/-
						1968	07		1968	08	x---	----	-x--	--x-	----	1	
						1970	02		1970	0526e	x---	----	x---	----	----	2	
						1971	0519		1971	0519	x---	----	--?-	----	----	1	
						1973	0106	+	1973	0527	x---	----	x---	----	----	2	
						1982	0826	+	1982	1110	x---	----	x---	----	-x--	3	-/6
						1984	0524	+	1984	0831	x---	----	x---	----	-x--	3*	-/7
						1985	0519		1985	0520	x---	----	x---	----	-x--	2	-/6
						1989	0422		1989	0423	x---	----	x---	----	-x--	2	
						1991	0522		1991	06	x---	----	x---	x-x-	----	1	6/-
						1991	1012		1993	06 >	x---	----	x---	x-x-	----	1?	7/-
SEMPU (Sulawesi)	1.142 N	124.73 E	1549	Caldera	0606-04=	Fumarolic											
						? 1819	....		....	....	----	----	----	----	----		
TONDANO CALDERA (Sulawesi)	1.23 N	124.83 E	1202	Caldera	0606-07-	Fumarolic											
LOKON-EMPUNG (Sulawesi)	1.358 N	124.792 E	1580	Stratovolc	0606-10=	Historical											
Empung						1375q	....		....	....	x---	----	x---	----	----	3↑	
Empung						1775q	....		....	....	x---	----	x---	----	xx--	3	
Tompaluan						1829	03		....	....	-x--	----	x---	----	----	2	
Tompaluan						1893	0329		1894	0814>	-x--	----	x---	----	----	2	
Tompaluan						1930	08		....	....	-x--	----	x-x-	----	----	2	
Tompaluan						1942	0903		....	....	-x--	----	x---	----	----	2	
Tompaluan						1949	0914		....	....	-x--	----	--x-	----	----	1	
Tompaluan						1951	0702		1953	03	-x--	----	x---	--x-	-x--	3*	
Tompaluan						1958	0219		1959	1223	-x--	----	x?--	--x-	-x--	2	
Tompaluan						1961	0519		1961	12	-x--	----	x---	----	----	2	
Tompaluan						1962	04		1962	11	-x--	----	--x-	----	----	1	
Tompaluan						1963	1217		1964	04	-x--	----	x---	----	----	2	
Tompaluan						1965	0710		1965	0710	-x--	----	x---	----	----	1	
Tompaluan						1966	0924	+	1966	0930?	-x--	----	x---	----	----	2	
Tompaluan						1969	1127		1970	1226e	-x--	---x	xx--	----	-xx-	2	
Tompaluan						1971	0511		1971	1026e	-x--	----	x---	--x-	----	2	2/-
Tompaluan						1973	0915		1974	12	-x--	----	x---	----	----	1	
Tompaluan						1975	11 <		1980	....	-x--	----	x?--	--x-	----	2*	4/-
Tompaluan						? 1984	0605d		?1984	11	-x--	----	--?-	----	----	1	
Tompaluan						1986	0322		1987	0513	-x--	---x	x-x-	----	-xx-	2	
Tompaluan						1988	0421		1988	0501	-x--	----	x---	----	----	1	
Tompaluan						1991	0517		1992	01	-x--	----	xx--	x---	xx--	2*	5/-
MAHAWU (Sulawesi)	1.358 N	124.858 E	1324	Stratovolc	0606-11=	Historical											
						1788<	....		....	....	x---	----	x---	----	----		
						1789	....		....	....	x---	----	x---	----	-?--	2	
						1846	....		....	....	-x--	----	--x-	----	----	2	
						1904	1004<		....	....	x---	----	x---	----	--x-	2	
						1952	....		....	....	----	----	----	----	----	2?	
						1958	0712		1958	0729	x---	----	x-x-	----	xxx-	2?	
						1977	1116		....	....	x---	---x	--x-	----	----	0	
KLABAT (Sulawesi)	1.47 N	125.03 E	1995	Stratovolc	0606-12=	Fumarolic											
TONGKOKO (Sulawesi)	1.52 N	125.20 E	1149	Stratovolc	0606-13=	Historical											
						1680	....		....	....	x---	----	x---	----	-x--	5?	-/9
						1683	....		....	....	x---	----	x---	----	----	3↑	
						1694	....		....	....	x---	----	x---	----	----	3?	
Summit and east flank (Batu Angus)						1801	....		....	....	xx--	---x	x---	x-x-	-x--	2	6/-
Batu Angus Baru						1821	....		....	....	-x--	----	----	x---	----	0	
Batu Angus						1843	....		1846	....	-x--	----	x---	----	----	2	
Batu Angus						1880	....		....	....	-x--	----	----	x-x-	----	1	
SANGIHE ISLANDS																	
RUANG (Sangihe Is)	2.28 N	125.425 E	725	Stratovolc	0607-01=	Historical											
(eruption in 1808, not 1810 or 1811)						1808	....		....	....	x---	----	xx--	----	-x--	2	
						1836?	0422		1836?	0424	x---	----	x---	----	----	2	
						1840	....		....	....	x---	----	xx--	----	----	2	
						1856	09		....	....	x---	----	x---	--x-	----	1	
						1870	0827		1870	0828	x---	----	x---	----	xx--	3?	
						1871	0302		1871	0314	x---	----	xx--	----	xx-x	2	
						1874	1115		....	....	x---	----	xx--	----	-x--	2	
						1889	06		....	....	x---	----	----	--x-	----	1	
						1904	0422		1905	0527	x---	----	xx--	x-x-	-xx-	3?	6/-

VOLCANO NAME (Subregion) / ERUPTION — Area of Activity	LAT	LONG	ELEV (m)	TYPE	NUMBER	Status / Start Year	Start M-Dy	P	Stop Year	Stop M-Dy	Central / Flank vent / Radial fiss / Regional	Submarine / New island / Subglacial / Crater lake	Explosive / Pyro flow / Phreatic / Fumarolic	Lava flow / Lava lake / Dome / Spine	Fatal / Damage / Mudflow / Tsunami	VEI	Vol L/T
RUANG (Sangihe Is) *continued*						**1914**	0529		**1915**	0228p	x---	----	xx--	x---	----	2	
(increased fumarolic activity only)						X 1918	02		....	....	----	----	---x	----	----		
(increased fumarolic activity only)						X 1940	04		....	....	----	----	---x	----	----		
(no eruption in 1946: NVP 1959)						X 1946	1013		X1946	1015	----	----	----	----	----		
						1949	0105	+	**1949**	0119>	x---	----	x---	x-x-	----	2	
KARANGETANG [API SIAU] (Siau I)	**2.78 N**	**125.48 E**	**1784**	**Stratovolc**	**0607-02=**	**Historical**											
						1675	....		....	....	x---	----	x---	----	----	3↑	
						1712	0116		....	....	x---	----	x---	----	----	2	
						1825	....		....	....	x---	----	x---	----	----	2	
						1864	0606		....	....	x---	----	x---	----	----	2	
Crater II?						**1883**	0825		**1883**	0826	x---	----	x---	----	----	2	
Crater III						**1886**	0425		**1886**	0619>	x---	----	x---	----	----	2	
						1887	0527		**1887**	0527	x---	----	x---	----	----	2	
						1892	0614?		....	....	x---	----	x---	----	--x-	2	
						1899	....		....	....	x---	----	x---	----	----	2	
						1900	....		....	....	x---	----	x---	----	----	2	
						1905	0521		**1905**	0522	x---	----	x---	----	----	2	
Crater V						**1921**	03		....	....	x---	----	x---	----	----	2	
Crater IV						**1922**	0504		**1922**	1213	x---	----	x---	x---	----	2	
						1924	05		....	....	x---	----	x---	----	----	2	
						1926	10		....	....	x---	----	x---	----	----	2	
Crater IV						**1930**	0204		**1930**	0206	x---	----	x---	----	----	2	
						1930	11 ?		....	....	x---	----	x---	----	----	2	
						1935	0831		....	....	x---	----	x---	----	----	2	
						1940	0301		**1940**	0309	x---	----	x---	----	----	2	
						1940	0620	+	**1940**	0823	x---	----	x---	----	xx--	2	
						1941	1030		**1941**	1030	x---	----	x---	----	-x--	2	
						1947	0209		**1947**	0209	x---	----	x---	----	----	2	
						1947	1201	+	**1947**	1221	x---	----	x---	----	----	2	
						1948	12		....	....	x---	----	x---	----	----	2	
						1949	0914		....	....	x---	----	x---	----	----	2	
Craters I, II and III						**1952**	02		**1952**	0630	x---	----	x---	----	-x--	2	
						1953	....		....	....	x---	----	x---	----	----	2	
						1961	0228		**1961**	04	x---	----	x---	----	----	2	-/6
						1961	1009		**1961**	1019>	x---	----	x---	----	----	2	-/6
						1962	0129		**1963**	12	x---	----	x---	----	-xx-	2	
						1965	0405d		**1967**	06	x---	----	x---	?---	----	2	
						1967	1129		**1967**	1202	x---	----	x---	----	----	2	
						1970	1127		**1971**	03	x---	----	xx--	x-x-	----	2	
						1972	01	+	**1976**	0405	x---	----	x-x-	x-x-	xxx-	3*	
South flank (1100 m) and summit						**1976**	0915	+	**1977**	09	xx--	----	xx--	x---	xx--	2	7/-
						1978	0222	+	**1978**	1218	x---	----	x---	----	----	1	
NNW flank, 1300 m (Kawah Maralebule)						**1979**	0531		**1979**	0531	-x--	----	x---	----	----	1	
						1980	0324		**1980**	0913	x---	----	x---	----	----	1	
						1982	....		....	....	x---	----	?---	----	----	1	
Summit and SW flank (1443 m)						**1983**	05	+	**1988**	1231>	xx--	----	xxx-	x---	-x--	3*	4/-
						1989	07		**1989**	07	----	----	x---	----	----	1	
						1991	0702<		**1993**	08	x---	----	xx--	x-x-	xx--	1	6/6
BANUA WUHU (Sangihe Is)	**3.138 N**	**125.491 E**	**-5**	**Submarine**	**0607-03=**	**Historical**											
						1835	0423		**1835**	0426	x---	xx--	x---	x-x-	----	2	6/-
						1889	0906		**1899**	0909	x---	xx--	x---	--x-	---x	2	
						1895	07		**1895**	1226e	x---	x---	x---	----	----	2	
						1904	0417		**1904**	0418	x---	xx--	x---	----	----	2	
						1904	0827		....	....	x---	x---	x---	----	----	2	
						1918	0718	+	**1919**	1201p	x---	xx--	x---	--x-	-x-x	3*	
						? **1968**	0905		?**1968**	0909d	----	?---	----	----	----	0	
AWU (Sangihe Is)	**3.67 N**	**125.50 E**	**1320**	**Stratovolc**	**0607-04=**	**Historical**											
						1640	12		**1641**	0104	x---	----	x-x-	----	--x-	5*	-/9
						1646e	....		....	....	x---	----	--x-	----	----	2?	
						1711	1210		**1711**	1216	x---	---x	xxx-	----	xxx-	3	
						1812	0806		**1812**	0808	x---	----	xx--	----	xxx-	4?	-/8
						1856	0302	+	**1856**	0317	x---	----	xx--	----	xxxx	3?	-/8
						1875	08		**1875**	08	x---	----	--x-	----	----	2	
						1883	0825		**1883**	0826	x---	----	x---	----	----	2	
						1885	0818		....	....	x---	----	--x-	----	----	2	
						1892	0607		**1892**	0612?	x---	----	xx--	----	xxxx	3	
						1893	....		....	....	x---	----	--x-	----	----	2	
						1913	0314		**1913**	0314	x---	----	x-x-	----	----	2	
						1921	02		**1921**	1001t	x---	---x	--?-	--x-	----	0	
						1922	0620		**1922**	09	x---	---x	--?-	--x-	----	0	
						1930	12		**1931**	12	x---	---x	--x-	--x-	----	2*	6/-
						1966	0812	+	**1966**	10	x---	---x	xx--	----	xxx-	4	
						? **1968**	08		?**1968**	09	----	----	----	----	----	2	
SE part of summit crater						**1992**	0407i		....	....	x---	----	--x-	----	----	1	
UNNAMED (Sangihe Is)	**3.97 N**	**124.17 E**	**-5000**	**Submarine ?**	**0607-05=**	**Uncertain**											
						? **1922**	0201p		....	....	----	?---	----	----	----	0	
						? **1955**	0213		....	....	----	?---	?---	----	----	0	

HALMAHERA

VOLCANO NAME (Subregion) / ERUPTION — Area of Activity	LAT	LONG	ELEV (m)	TYPE	NUMBER	Status / Start Year	Start M-Dy	P	Stop Year	Stop M-Dy	Central / Flank vent / Radial fiss / Regional	Submarine / New island / Subglacial / Crater lake	Explosive / Pyro flow / Phreatic / Fumarolic	Lava flow / Lava lake / Dome / Spine	Fatal / Damage / Mudflow / Tsunami	VEI	Vol L/T
DUKONO (Halmahera)	**1.70 N**	**127.87 E**	**1087**	**Complx volc**	**0608-01=**	**Historical**											
						1550	1120n		....	....	x---	----	x---	x---	xx--	3	-/8
East flank of Tolo						**1719w**	....		....	....	-x--	----	----	x---	----		
						1868?	....		....	....	x---	----	x---	----	-?--	2	
						1901	....		....	....	x---	----	x---	----	----	2	
Malupang Magiwe and Malupang Warirang.						**1933**	0813		**1993>**	....	x---	----	x---	x---	-xx-	3*	
IBU (Halmahera)	**1.48 N**	**127.63 E**	**1325**	**Stratovolc**	**0608-03=**	**Historical**											
						1911	0830		**1911**	0901	x---	----	x---	----	----	2	
GAMKONORA (Halmahera)	**1.375 N**	**127.52 E**	**1635**	**Stratovolc**	**0608-04=**	**Historical**											
						1564	1231y		....	....	x---	----	x---	x---	xx--	3↑	
						1673	0520		....	....	x---	----	x---	----	xx-x	5?	-/9
						1885e	....		....	....	x---	----	x---	----	----	2	
						1911	....		....	....	----	----	----	----	----	2?	
						1917	1018		**1917**	1018	x---	----	x---	----	----	2	
						1926	06		....	....	x---	----	x---	----	----	1?	
						1949	....		....	....	x---	----	x---	----	----	2	
						1950	10		....	....	x---	----	----	----	----	2	

VOLCANO NAME (Subregion) / ERUPTION — Area of Activity	LAT	LONG	ELEV (m)	TYPE	NUMBER	Status / Start Year	Start M-Dy	P	Stop Year	Stop M-Dy	Central / Flank vent / Radial fiss / Regional*	Submarine / New island / Subglacial / Crater lake	Explosive / Pyro flow / Phreatic / Fumarolic	Lava flow / Lava lake / Dome / Spine	Fatal / Damage / Mudflow / Tsunami	VEI	Vol L/T
GAMKONORA (Halmahera) *continued*						**1951**	....		....	....	----	----	x---	----	----	2	
						1952	0716		**1952**	0905d	x---	----	x---	----	----	2	
						1981	0304	+	**1981**	0725	x---	----	x-x-	----	----	1	-/5
						1987	0413		**1987**	0426	x---	----	x---	----	----	1	
TODOKO-RANU (Halmahera)	**1.30 N**	**127.43 E**	**979**	**Calderas**	**0608-05=**	**Fumarolic**											
JAILOLO (Halmahera)	**1.17 N**	**127.32 E**	**1130**	**Stratovolc**	**0608-051**	**Holocene**											
GAMALAMA (Halmahera)	**0.80 N**	**127.325 E**	**1715**	**Stratovolcs**	**0608-06=**	**Historical**											
						1538	....		....	....	x---	----	x---	----	----	3↑	
						1561	1231y		....	....	xx--	---?	x---	----	--x-	2	
						1605	05		....	....	x---	----	x---	----	----	2	
						1608	0718		**1608**	0719	x---	----	x---	----	-x--	3	
						1635	0329		....	....	x---	----	x---	----	----	2	
						? **1643**	0615		....	....	?---	----	?---	----	----	2	
						1648	0615		**1648**	0618	x---	----	x---	?---	----	2	
						1653	1231y		....	....	x---	----	x---	----	-?--	3↑	
						1659	06		....	....	x---	----	x---	----	----	2	
(earthquake: eruption at Gamkonora)						X 1673	0812		....	....	----	----	----	----	----		
						1676	1231y		....	....	x---	----	x---	----	----	2	
						1686	09 ?		**1686**	1013>	x---	----	x---	----	----	2	
						1687	0510		**1687**	0511	x---	----	x---	----	----	3↑	
						1737	0310		**1737**	0313	x---	----	x---	x---	----	2	
						1739	....		....	....	x---	----	x---	?---	----	2	
North flank						**1763**	....		....	....	-x--	----	----	x---	----	2	7/-
						1770	0706	+	**1770**	1209	xx--	----	x---	----	-x--	3	
						1771	0828	+	**1772**	1009	x---	----	x---	----	xx--	3	
						1773	0202	+	**1773**	0207	x---	----	x---	----	----	2	
						1773	1021	+	**1774**	0122	x---	----	x---	----	xx--	2	
Summit and NW flank (100 m)						**1775**	0820	+	**1775**	1106	xx--	----	xx--	----	xx--	3*	
						1811	0201	+	**1811**	05	x---	----	x---	?---	----	2	
						1812	0907		**1812**	0907	x---	----	x---	----	----	2	
						1814	1127		**1814**	1128	x---	----	x---	----	----	2	
						? **1821**	0822		....	....	x---	----	----	----	----	1	
						1831	0527	+	**1831**	0627	x---	----	x?--	----	----	2	
						1833	0615		....	....	x---	----	x---	----	----	2	
						1835	0104		....	....	x---	----	x---	----	----	2	
						1838	0226	+	**1838**	05	x---	----	x---	----	x---	2	
						1839	0129	+	**1839**	0326	x---	----	x---	?---	----	2*	
						1840	0202	+	**1840**	0929	x---	----	x---	----	-xx-	3	
						? **1841**	0330	+	?**1841**	1120	x---	----	----	----	----	1	
						1842	1006	+	**1842**	1231	x---	----	x---	----	----	1	
						1843	0410	+	**1843**	0527	x---	----	x?--	?---	----	2	
						? **1844**	0324		?**1844**	1114	x---	----	----	----	----	1	
						? **1845**	0423		?**1845**	0903	x---	----	----	----	----	1	
						1846	0519		**1846**	0519	x---	----	x---	----	-x--	2	
						1847	0207		**1847**	0207	x---	----	x---	?---	----	2	
						1847	0907		**1847**	0907	x---	----	----	----	----		
						1849	1127	+	**1850**	1119	x---	----	x---	----	----	2	
						? **1858**	11		?**1859**	09	x---	----	----	----	----	1	
						? **1860**	06		....	....	x---	----	----	----	----	1	
						1862	0715	+	**1862**	10	x---	----	x---	?---	--x-	2	
						? **1863**	0501?		?**1863**	06 ?	x---	----	----	----	----	2	
						1864	0120	+	**1864**	0217	x---	----	x---	----	----	2	
						? **1864**	0604d		?**1864**	0625e	x---	----	----	----	----	1	
						1864	1227		**1865**	0102	x---	----	x---	?---	----	2	
						1868	0313		**1868**	0313	x---	----	x---	----	----	1	
						1868	1113	+	**1869**	0210	x---	----	x---	----	----	2	
						1871	0807	+	**1871**	0925	x---	----	x---	?---	x---	2	
						1884	05		**1884**	05	x---	----	x---	----	--x-	2	
						? **1884**	1208		?**1884**	1209?	x---	----	--?-	----	----	1	
						1895	1219		**1895**	1219	x---	----	x---	----	----	1	
						? **1896**	0803		?**1896**	0804?	x---	----	x---	----	----	1	
						1897	0907		**1897**	0924	x---	----	x---	----	--x-	1	
						1898	0514		**1898**	0528?	x---	----	x---	----	----	2	
						? **1900**	05		?**1900**	0604d	x---	----	x---	----	----	1	
						1907	1117		**1907**	1120	x---	----	x---	x---	--x-	2	
						1911	0902		**1911**	0906	x---	----	x---	----	----	1	
						1918	08		**1918**	0904	x---	----	x---	----	----	1	
						1923	0413	+	**1923**	0506	x---	----	x---	----	----	2	
						1932	1110		**1932**	1113	x---	----	x---	----	----	2	
						1933	1112		....	....	x---	----	x---	----	----	2	
						1938	0908		**1938**	0908	x---	----	x---	----	----	2	
East flank						**1962**	1231		**1963**	0102?	-x--	----	x-x-	----	x---	2	
						1980	0904		**1980**	0923	x---	----	x---	----	-x--	2	-/6
						1983	0809	+	**1983**	0812	x---	----	x---	----	-x--	3	
						1988	0212		**1988**	03 ?	x---	----	x---	----	----	2	
						1990	0425		**1990**	0426	x---	----	x?--	----	-x--	3?	
						? **1991**	0615		?**1991**	0615	x---	----	--?-	----	----	1?	
						1993	0506		**1993**	0521	x---	----	xx--	----	----	2	
MOTIR (Halmahera)	**0.45 N**	**127.40 E**	**690**	**Stratovolc**	**0608-061**	**Uncertain**											
MAKIAN (Halmahera)	**0.32 N**	**127.40 E**	**1357**	**Stratovolc**	**0608-07=**	**Historical**											
						1550<	....		....	....	x---	----	x---	?---	-x-?	3↑	
						1646	0719		**1646**	0721	x-x-	----	x---	----	xx--	4?	-/8
						1760	0922	+	**1761**	0430>	x---	----	x---	----	xx--	4?	-/8
						? **1854**	0618		?**1854**	0618	x---	----	----	----	----	1	
						? **1860**	....		....	....	----	----	?---	----	----		
						1861	1228		**1862**	10	x---	----	xxx-	?---	xxx-	4?	-/8
						1863	0825		**1863**	0831	x---	----	--x-	----	----	1	
						1864	10		**1864**	10	x---	----	--x-	----	----	1	
						1890	0620	+	**1890**	0630	x---	----	x---	?---	xx--	2	
						1988	0729		**1988**	0805	x---	----	xx--	--x-	-x--	3	
UMSINI (New Guinea-W)	1.18 S	134.00 E	2665		0609-01=	Not a Volcano											

BORNEO

VOLCANO NAME (Subregion)	LAT	LONG	ELEV (m)	TYPE	NUMBER	Status
BOMBALAI (Borneo)	**4.40 N**	**117.88 E**	**531**	**Cone**	**0610-01-**	**Holocene?**

Philippines & SE Asia (07)

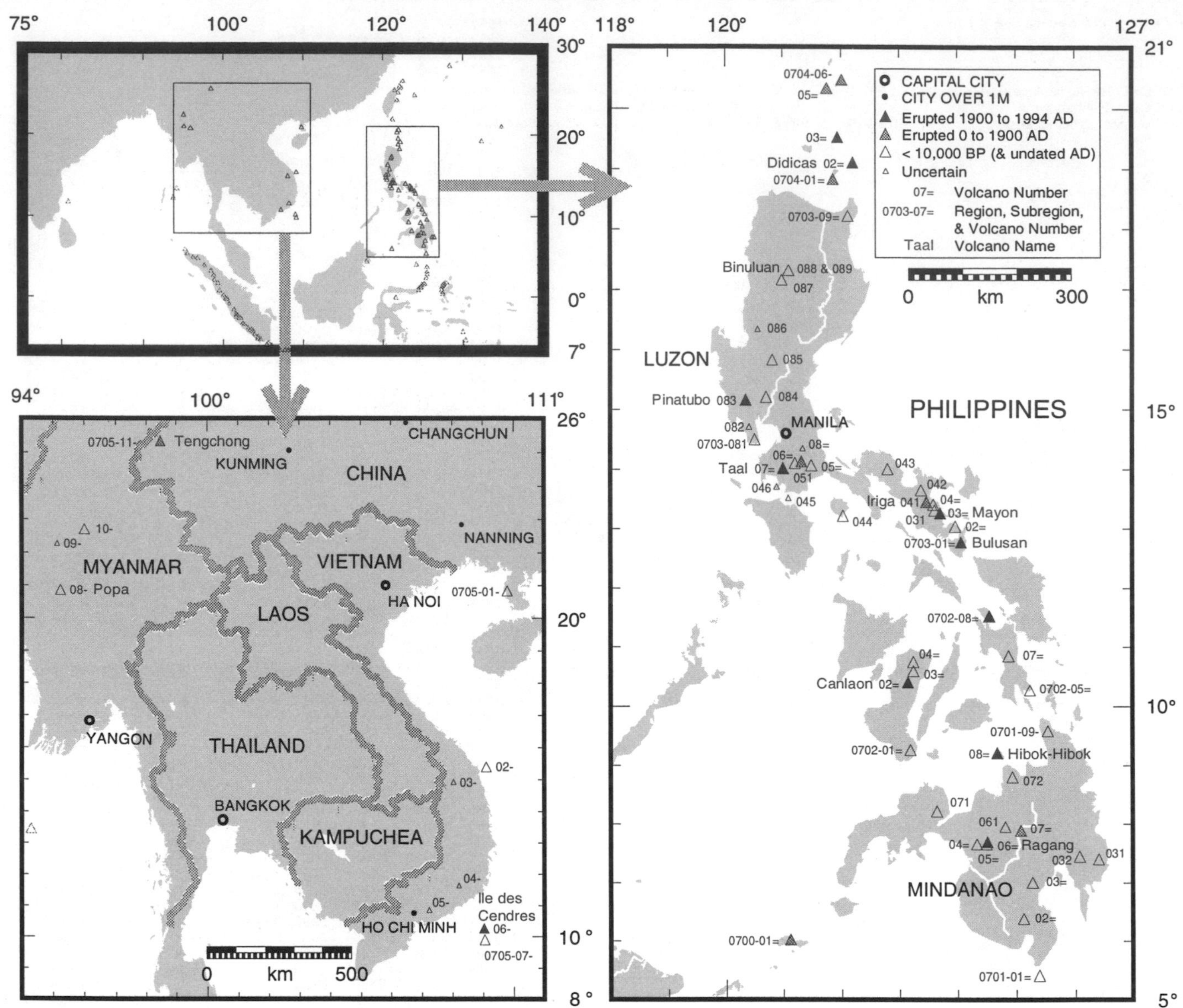

After Magellan's death there in 1521, the Philippines were re-claimed for Spain by Lopez de Legazpi in 1564. The first historical eruption occured 8 years later, at Taal. The islands gained independence from Spain in mid-1898, but were soon occupied by the US and, from 1942 through 1944, by Japan. True independence did not come until 1946. Both the population (nearly 70 million) and land area of the Philippines approximate those of Italy.

Although Indonesia leads the world in both the number and the global proportion of eruptions in each of the last 4 eruptive characteristics listed in our DIRECTORY, the Philippines show substantially higher figures when each is considered as a percentage of the region's total number of eruptions. Fully 13% of Philippine eruptions have resulted in fatalities, and 22% in damage, with the notable Taal and Mayon volcanoes having particularly high human impact. As with Indonesia, though, this record reflects the many years prior to the development of a strong government agency charged with the study of volcanism. PHIVOLCS now maintains a modern monitoring program on most of the islands' volcanoes, and the evacuation table on p. 176 testifies to their effectiveness in dealing with recent eruptions.

Mudflows are also frequently associated with Philippine eruptions, and remain a hazard long after the eruption ceases. Heavy rains in this typhoon-plagued archipelago regularly redistribute new volcanic tephra to surrounding lowlands. Secondary mudflows following the 1991 Pinatubo eruption have been especially devastating (see Fig. 31, p. 251). Tsunamis have accompanied 4% of eruptions in the Philippines, a proportion that is not itself high but one that exceeds all other regions.

The tectonics of the Philippines are not simple, but most volcanoes result from convergence of the Philippine Sea Plate and the Eurasian Plate. In the south the former is subducted westward under the latter, but in the north the opposite pattern prevails. Region 07 has a high proportion of recognized but undated Holocene volcanoes: Two-thirds of the region's 64 volcanoes are undated, and only Africa (with three-fourths) exceeds that proportion.

Burma, only recently recognized as an area of Holocene volcanism, became part of the British Empire in 1886 after several wars. The British withdrew in WW-II and granted independence in 1948. Unrest has followed, and the country's 1988 name change to Myanmar has been widely but not universally accepted.

Vietnam, the other mainland part of Region 07 with several Holocene volcanoes, is also known for recent unrest. It was a province of China from the 1st century BC to 939 AD, and missionary work, particularly by the French, began in the 17th century. French troops captured Saigon in 1859, the rest of Cochin-China (South Vietnam) within 8 years, and North Vietnam by 1887. After Japanese occupation during WW-II, nationalist forces defeated the French in 1954 and the US in 1975. The *CAVW* originally designated region 07 as Philippines only, but Cochin-China was added upon publication of the catalog in 1954, and our expansion to SE Asia followed recognition of Holocene volcanism in Myanmar and SE China.

VOLCANO NAME (Subregion) / ERUPTION — Area of Activity	LAT	LONG	ELEV (m)	TYPE	NUMBER	Status	Start Year	Start M-Dy	P	Stop Year	Stop M-Dy	Central / Flank vent / Radial fiss / Regional*	Submarine / New island / Subglacial / Crater lake	Explosive / Pyro flow / Phreatic / Fumarolic	Lava flow / Lava lake / Dome / Spine	Fatal / Damage / Mudflow / Tsunami	VEI	Vol L/T
PHILIPPINES - S																		
BUD DAJO (Sulu Is-Philippines)	5.95 N	121.07 E	440	Pyrocl cones	0700-01=	Historical												
							1641	0104		....	....	----	----	?---	----	-x--	2?	
							1897	0921		....	....	----	?---	----	----	---x	0	
BALUT (Mindanao-Philippines)	5.40 N	125.375 E	852	Stratovolc	0701-01=	Holocene												
MATUTUM (Mindanao)	6.37 N	125.108 E	2293	Stratovolc	0701-02=	Holocene												
APO (Mindanao)	6.987 N	125.273 E	2954	Stratovolc	0701-03=	Fumarolic												
LEONARD RANGE (Mindanao)	7.393 N	126.397 E	800	Stratovolc	0701-031	Holocene												
UNNAMED (Mindanao)	7.443 N	126.073 E	1300	Unknown	0701-032	Hot Springs												
MAKATURING (Mindanao)	7.647 N	124.32 E	1940	Stratovolc	0701-04=	Holocene												
LATUKAN (Mindanao)	7.65 N	124.47 E	2158	Stratovolc	0701-05=	Holocene												
RAGANG (Mindanao)	7.67 N	124.50 E	2815	Stratovolc	0701-06=	Historical												
							1765	....		....	....	x---	----	?---	----	----	2	
							1834	....		....	....	x---	----	x---	----	----	2	
							1840	0120		**1840**	0405	x---	----	x---	----	----	2	
							1856	1101		....	....	x---	----	x---	----	----	2	
							1858	0218		....	....	x---	----	x---	----	----	2	
							1865	....		....	....	x---	----	x---	----	----	2	
							1871	1208<		....	....	x---	----	x---	----	----	2	
							1873	0116		**1873**	04	x---	----	x---	----	??--	2	
							1915	....		....	....	x---	----	x---	----	----	2	
KALATUNGAN (Mindanao)	7.95 N	124.80 E	2824	Stratovolc	0701-061	Holocene												
CALAYO (Mindanao)	7.877 N	125.068 E	646	Tuff cone	0701-07=	Historical												
							1886	1231y		....	....	----	----	--?-	----	----	2	
MALINDANG (Mindanao)	8.22 N	123.63 E	2435	Stratovolc	0701-071	Holocene												
BALATOCAN (Mindanao)	8.80 N	124.92 E	2300	Compnd volc	0701-072	Fumarolic												
HIBOK-HIBOK (Camiguin)	9.203 N	124.673 E	1332	Stratovolc	0701-08=	Historical												
							1827	....		....	....	?---	---?	?---	----	-xx-	2	
							1862	....		....	....	?---	---?	?---	----	-xx-	2	
Lower northwest flank (Mt. Vulcan)							**1871**	0430		**1875**	....	-x--	----	x---	--x-	xx--	2	8/-
(solfataric activity only)							X 1897	....		....	....	----	----	--?-	----	-x?-		
(solfataric activity only)							X 1902	0727		....	....	----	----	--?-	----	-x?-		
Upper northeast flank							**1948**	0901		**1953**	07	-x--	----	xx--	x-x-	xxx-	3*	
PACO (Mindanao)	9.593 N	125.520 E	524	Compnd volc	0701-09-	Fumarolic												
PHILIPPINES - CENTRAL																		
MAGASO (Negros)	9.258 N	123.175 E	1904	Stratovolc	0702-01=	Holocene												
CANLAON (Negros)	10.412 N	123.132 E	2435	Stratovolc	0702-02=	Historical												
							1866	....		....	....	x---	----	x---	----	----	2	
							1893	07		....	....	x---	----	x---	----	----	2	
							1894	05		**1894**	06	x---	----	x---	----	----	2	
							1902	0131		....	....	x---	----	x---	x---	----	2	
							1904	....		....	....	x---	----	x---	----	----	2	
							1905	1106	+	**1906**	0116>	x---	----	x---	----	----	2	
							1927	....		....	....	----	----	----	----	----		
							1932	12		**1933**	01	----	----	----	----	----		
							1969	1010	+	**1969**	1029	x---	----	x-x-	----	--x-	2	
(no 1970 eruption: Pena 1982, p.c.)							X 1970	0605	+	X1970	0824	x---	----	x---	----	----		
							1978	0627		**1978**	0902	x---	----	x-x-	----	----	2	
							1985	0313		**1985**	0314	x---	----	x-x-	----	----	1	
							1985	1005		**1985**	1007?	x---	----	x---	----	----	1	
							1986	0603	+	**1986**	0818	x---	----	x---	----	----	2	-/5
							1987	0330?		**1987**	0507	x---	----	x---	----	----	1	
							1988	0621	+	**1988**	0702	x---	----	x-x-	----	----	1	
							1989	1025		**1989**	1213>	x---	----	x-x-	----	----	2	
							1992	0108		**1992**	0108	x---	----	x---	----	----	1	
							1992	0610		**1992**	0610	x---	----	x---	----	----	2	
							1993	0825		**1993**	0903	x---	----	x-x-	----	----	2	
MANDALAGAN (Negros)	10.615 N	123.22 E	1879	Stratovolc	0702-03=	Holocene												
SILAY (Negros)	10.77 N	123.23 E	1535	Stratovolc	0702-04=	Holocene												
CABALIAN (Leyte)	10.287 N	125.22 E	945	Stratovolc	0702-05=	Holocene												
MAHAGNOA (Leyte)	10.872 N	124.853 E	800	Stratovolc	0702-07=	Fumarolic												
							? **1895**	....		....	....	----	----	----	----	----		
BILIRAN (Philippines-C)	11.523 N	124.534 E	1187	Compnd volc	0702-08=	Historical												
							1939	0904		....	....	-x--	----	x-x-	----	----		
PHILIPPINES - N																		
BULUSAN (Luzon-Philippines)	12.770 N	124.05 E	1565	Stratovolc	0703-01=	Historical												
							? **1852**	....		....	....	----	----	----	----	----		
							1886	....		....	....	?---	----	?---	----	----	2	
							1889	....		....	....	----	----	----	----	----		
							1892	....		....	....	?---	----	?---	----	----	2	
							1894	....		....	....	?---	----	?---	----	----	2	
							1916	0118		**1916**	0122	x---	----	x-x-	----	----	2	
							1918	10	+	**1922**	05	x---	----	x?--	x-?-	----	2	
							1928	06		....	....	x---	----	x---	----	----	2	
							1933	1225		....	....	x---	----	x---	----	-x-x	2	
							1978	0729	+	**1978**	0814	x---	----	x-x-	----	-x--	2	-/5
							1979	1227		**1980**	0928	x-x-	----	x-x-	----	----	3*	
							1981	0409		**1981**	0427	x---	----	x-x-	----	----	3	
							1983	0625	+	**1983**	0629	x---	----	x-x-	----	----	2	
							1988	0220	+	**1988**	0308	x---	----	x-x-	----	--x-	2	-/4
POCDOL MOUNTAINS (Luzon)	13.05 N	123.958 E	1102	Compnd volc	0703-02=	Holocene												
MAYON (Luzon)	13.257 N	123.685 E	2462	Stratovolc	0703-03=	Historical												
							C **-3100y**	....		....	....	----	----	----	----	----		
							C **0470u**	....		....	....	x---	----	xx--	----	----		
							1616	0219		**1616**	0223	x---	----	xx--	x---	--x-	3	
							1766	0720		**1766**	0725	x---	----	xx--	x---	xxx-	3	

07

VOLCANO NAME (Subregion)	LAT	LONG	ELEV (m)	TYPE	NUMBER	ERUPTION — Area of Activity	Status	Start Year	Start M-Dy	P	Stop Year	Stop M-Dy	Central / Flank vent / Radial fiss / Regional*	Submarine / New island / Subglacial / Crater lake	Explosive / Pyro flow / Phreatic / Fumarolic	Lava flow / Lava lake / Dome / Spine	Fatal / Damage / Mudflow / Tsunami	VEI	Vol L/T
MAYON (Luzon) *continued*.						(may be confused with 1766 lahar date)	X	1767	1024		....	....	----	----	----	----	----		
								1800	1030		**1800**	1031	x---	----	xx--	----	xx--	2	
							?	**1811**	1005		?**1811**	1006	x---	----	x?--	----	----	2	
								1814	0201		**1814**	0215>	xx--	----	xx--	----	xxx-	4	-/8
								1827	0627		**1828**	0228	x---	----	x---	----	-xx-	2	
								1834	....		**1835**	05	x---	----	xx--	?---	--x-	3*	
								1839	....		....	....	x---	----	x---	----	----	2	
								1845	0120a		**1845**	0130a	x---	----	xx--	----	-xx-	3	
								1846	0511		....	....	x---	----	x---	----	----	3	
								1851	0526		**1851**	06	x---	----	x---	----	----	1	
								1853	0713	+	**1853**	0826	x---	----	xx--	----	xxx-	3	
								1855	0322		....	....	x---	----	x---	x---	----	2	
								1857	....		....	....	x---	----	x---	----	----	2	
								1858	01		**1858**	12	x---	----	xx--	x--?	xxx-	2	
								1859	....		....	....	x---	----	?---	---?	----		
								1860	....		....	....	x---	----	?---	----	----		
								1861	....		....	....	x---	----	x---	----	----	1	
								1862	....		....	....	x---	----	x---	----	--x-	2	
							?	**1863**	0530		....	....	----	----	----	----	----		
								1868	1217		....	....	x---	----	x---	----	--x-	2	
								1871	1208		**1872**	01	x---	----	xx--	----	xx--	3	
								1872	0905		**1872**	0909	x---	----	x---	x---	----	1	
								1873	0620		**1873**	0722	x---	----	x---	----	----	2	
								1876	04 ?		....	....	x---	----	x---	----	----		
								1876	1126		**1876**	1126	x---	----	x---	----	----	1	
						Summit and south and SW flanks		**1881**	0706		**1882**	08	x-x-	----	xx--	x---	--x-	3	
								1885	1121		**1885**	1202	x---	----	x---	x---	----	2	
								1886	0708		**1887**	0310	x---	----	xx--	x---	xxx-	3*	
								1888	1215		....	....	x---	----	x---	----	----	1	
								1890	0910		**1890**	0930	x---	----	x---	x---	----	2	
								1891	1003	+	**1892**	0229	x---	----	xx--	x---	-?--	2	
								1893	1003	+	**1893**	1031	x---	----	x---	x---	--x-	1	
						Summit and east flank		**1895**	0720	+	**1895**	1126	x-x-	----	x---	x---	--x-	2	
								1896	0831		**1896**	0927	x---	----	x---	x---	--x-	2	
								1897	0523<	+	**1897**	0723	x---	----	xx--	x---	xxx-	4*	-/7
								1900	0301		**1900**	0306	x---	----	x---	x---	--x-	2	
							?	**1902**	....		....	....	x---	----	x---	----	--x-	1	
								1928	01 ?	+	**1928**	0826e	x---	----	xx--	x---	xxx-	3*	7/7
								1938	0605		....	....	x---	----	xx--	x---	xxx-	2	-/6
								1939	....		....	....	x---	----	x---	----	----	1	
								1941	0913		....	....	x---	----	x---	----	----	1	
								1943	....		....	....	x---	----	x---	----	----	1	
								1947	0107		**1947**	02	x---	----	xx--	x---	xxx-	2	
								1968	0421		**1968**	0520	x---	----	xx--	x---	xxx-	3	7/7
								1978	0307	+	**1978**	09 ?	x---	----	x---	x---	----	2*	7/-
								1984	0909	+	**1984**	1006	x---	----	xx--	x---	?xx-	3*	7/7
								1993	0202	+	**1993**	0402?	x---	----	xx--	x---	xxx-	2?	7/6
MASARAGA (Luzon)	**13.32 N**	**123.60 E**	**1328**	**Stratovolc**	**0703-031**		**Holocene**												
MALINAO (Luzon)	**13.422 N**	**123.597 E**	**1548**	**Stratovolc**	**0703-04=**		**Fumarolic**												
						(small geothermal area explosion)	X	1980	0729		X1980	0729	-x--	----	--x-	----	-x--		
IRIGA (Luzon)	**13.457 N**	**123.457 E**	**1196**	**Stratovolc**	**0703-041**		**Historical**												
								1628?	....		....	....	x---	----	xxx-	----	xx?-	2	
ISAROG (Luzon)	**13.658 N**	**123.37 E**	**1966**	**Stratovolc**	**0703-042**		**Holocene**												
LABO (Luzon)	**14.02 N**	**122.792 E**	**1544**	**Compnd volc**	**0703-043**		**Holocene**												
MALINDIG (Marinduque I)	**13.240 N**	**122.018 E**	**1157**	**Stratovolc ?**	**0703-044**		**Hot Springs**												
DAGIT-DAGITAN (Verde I)	**13.530 N**	**121.078 E**	**364**	**Stratovolc**	**0703-045**		**Pleistocene-Fumarolic**												
PANAY (Luzon)	**13.723 N**	**120.893 E**	**501**	**Stratovolc**	**0703-046**		**Pleistocene-Fumarolic**												
BANAHAW (Luzon)	**14.07 N**	**121.48 E**	**2177**	**Complx volc**	**0703-05=**		**Holocene**												
						Banahao	?	**1730**	....		....	....	x---	----	?---	----	-xx-		
LAGUNA VOLC FIELD (Luzon)	**14.12 N**	***121.30 E**	**654**	**Scoria cones**	**0703-051**		**Anthropology**												
						Sampaloc Lake	A	**1350**v	....		....	....	x---	----	x---	----	----		
MAQUILING (Luzon)	**14.13 N**	**121.20 E**	**1090**	**Stratovolc**	**0703-06=**		**Holocene**												
TAAL (Luzon)	**14.002 N**	**120.993 E**	**400**	**Stratovolc**	**0703-07=**		**Historical**												
								1572	....		....	....	----	----	x---	----	-x--	3	
								1591	....		....	....	----	----	x---	----	----	3↑	
								1608c	....		....	....	----	----	?---	----	----	2?	
								1634	....		....	....	----	----	?---	----	----	3↑	
								1635	....		....	....	----	----	?---	----	----	3↑	
								1641	....		....	....	----	----	x---	----	----	3	
								1645	....		....	....	----	----	?---	----	----	3↑	
						Binintiang Malaki		**1707**	....		....	....	-x--	----	x---	----	----	2	
						Binintiang Munti		**1709**	....		....	....	-x--	----	x---	----	-x--	2	
								1715	....		....	....	-x--	----	x---	----	-x--	2	
						Calauit (SE flank)		**1716**	0924		**1716**	0927	--x-	---x	x---	----	?x-x	4?	
						Binintiang Munti		**1729**	....		....	....	-x--	----	x---	----	----	2	
						Pira-Piraso (NE flank)		**1731**	....		....	....	-x--	-x-x	x---	----	----	2	
								1749	0811?		**1749**	09	xx?-	---x	x---	----	?x-x	3	-/8
						Summit crater and SE flank		**1754**	0515	+	**1754**	1204	xxx-	----	x---	----	xx-x	4*	-/8
								1790	....		....	....	x---	----	?---	----	----	2	
								1808	02		**1808**	04	x---	----	x---	----	-x--	2	
								1825	....		....	....	x---	----	?---	----	----	2	
								1842	....		....	....	x---	----	?---	----	----	2	
								1873	....		....	....	x---	----	?---	----	-?--	2	
								1874	0719		....	....	x---	----	x---	----	xx--	2	
								1878	1112		**1878**	1115	x---	----	x---	----	----	2	
							?	**1885**	....		....	....	----	----	----	----	----		
								1903	04		....	....	x---	----	x---	----	----	2	
						Base of south wall of main crater		**1904**	04		**1904**	0715e	x---	----	--x-	----	----	1	
								1911	0127		**1911**	0208	x---	----	xxx-	----	xx-x	4*	-/8
						SW flank (near Mt. Tabaro)		**1965**	0928		**1965**	0930	-x--	-x-x	xxx-	----	xx-x	4	-/7
						SW flank (near Mt. Tabaro)		**1966**	0705	+	**1966**	0804	-x--	---x	x-x-	----	----	3*	
						SW flank (near Mt. Tabaro)		**1967**	0816		**1967**	0819	-x--	-x-x	x-x-	----	----	1	
						SW flank (near Mt. Tabaro)		**1968**	0131	+	**1968**	0402	-xx-	---x	x-x-	x---	----	2	

VOLCANO NAME (Subregion) / ERUPTION — Area of Activity	LAT	LONG	ELEV (m)	TYPE	NUMBER	Status / Start Year	Start M-Dy	P	Stop Year	Stop M-Dy	Central, Flank vent, Radial fiss, Regional*	Submarine, New island, Subglacial, Crater lake	Explosive, Pyro flow, Phreatic, Fumarolic	Lava flow, Lava lake, Dome, Spine	Fatal, Damage, Mudflow, Tsunami	VEI	Vol L/T
TAAL (Luzon) *continued* — SW flank (near Mt. Tabaro)						**1969**	1029	+	**1969**	1210	-x--	----	x-x-	x---	----	2	6/6
SW flank (near Mt. Tabaro)						**1970**	1109		**1970**	1113	--x-	----	x-x-	----	----	1	
SW flank (near Mt. Tabaro)						**1976**	0903	+	**1976**	1017	-x--	----	x-x-	----	-x--	2	-/6
SW flank (near Mt. Tabaro)						**1977**	1003	+	**1977**	1112?	-x--	----	x-x-	----	----	2	
JALAJALA (Luzon)	14.35 N	121.33 E	743	Fumarole fld	0703-08=	Fumarolic											
MARIVELES (Luzon)	14.50 N	120.50 E	1420	Stratovolc	0703-081	Radiocarbon											
						C -2050?	....		....	....	----	----	----	----	----		
NATIB (Luzon)	14.705 N	120.40 E	1287	Stratovolc	0703-082	Holocene?											
PINATUBO (Luzon)	15.13 N	120.35 E	1600	Stratovolc	0703-083	Historical											
						C -6100w	....		....	....	----	----	xx--	----	----		
						C -0380v	....		....	....	----	----	xx--	----	----		
						C 1315v	....		....	....	----	----	x---	----	--x-		
Lower north flank and summit						**1991**	0402	+	**1991**	0902	xx--	----	xxx-	--x-	xxx-	6*	-/10
Center of caldera lake						**1992**	0705d		**1992**	1030	x---	---x	x-x-	--x-	x-x-	1	
ARAYAT (Luzon)	15.20 N	120.742 E	1026	Stratovolc	0703-084	Holocene											
AMORONG (Luzon)	15.828 N	120.805 E	376	Unknown	0703-085	Fumarolic											
SANTO TOMAS (Luzon)	16.33 N	120.55 E	2260	Stratovolc	0703-086	Uncertain											
PATOC (Luzon)	17.147 N	120.980 E	1865	Stratovolc	0703-087	Fumarolic											
BINULUAN (Luzon)	17.308 N	121.093 E	2329	Compnd volc	0703-088	Fumarolic											
						? 1952	....		....	....	----	----	--?x	----	x-x-	1?	
AMBALATUNGAN GROUP (Luzon)	17.32 N	121.10 E		Compnd volc	0703-089	Fumarolic											
CAGUA (Luzon)	18.222 N	122.123 E	1133	Stratovolc	0703-09=	Holocene											
						? 1860	10		....	....	?---	----	?---	----	----	2	

N OF LUZON

VOLCANO NAME (Subregion) / ERUPTION — Area of Activity	LAT	LONG	ELEV (m)	TYPE	NUMBER	Status / Start Year	Start M-Dy	P	Stop Year	Stop M-Dy	Central, Flank vent, Radial fiss, Regional*	Submarine, New island, Subglacial, Crater lake	Explosive, Pyro flow, Phreatic, Fumarolic	Lava flow, Lava lake, Dome, Spine	Fatal, Damage, Mudflow, Tsunami	VEI	Vol L/T
CAMIGUIN DE BABUYANES	18.83 N	121.860 E	712	Stratovolc	0704-01=	Historical											
SW flank						1857<	....		....	....	-x--	??--	--x-	----	----	2	
DIDICAS (Luzon-N of)	19.077 N	122.202 E	244	Compnd volc	0704-02=	Historical											
						1773	10		....	....	----	?---	----	----	----	0?	
						1856	0930p		1860	10 ?	----	xx--	----	--xx	----	2*	8/-
						? 1900	....		....	....	----	?---	---?	----	----		
						1952	0316<		1953?	....	-x--	xx--	x---	x-x-	----	2	8/-
North side						1969	0321		1969	06	-x--	----	x-x-	----	x--x	2	
NNE side						1978	0106		1978	0109	-x--	----	x---	----	----	2	
BABUYAN CLARO (Luzon-N of)	19.523 N	121.940 E	1180	Stratovolcs	0704-03=	Historical											
Smith volcano						1652?	....		....	....	-x--	----	x---	----	----	3↑	
Babuyan Claro						1831	....		....	....	x---	----	x---	----	-x--	4?	-/8
Babuyan Claro						1860	....		....	....	x---	----	x---	----	----	2	
Smith volcano						1907	....		....	....	-x--	----	--x-	----	----	2	
Babuyan Claro						? 1913	....		....	....	x---	----	--??	----	----	2	
Smith volcano						1917	....		....	....	-?--	----	?---	----	----	2	
Smith volcano						1918	0517		1918	0519	-x--	----	x---	----	----	2	
Smith volcano						1919	05		....	....	-?--	----	?---	----	----	2	
Smith volcano						1924	....		....	....	-x--	----	x---	----	----	2	
UNNAMED (Luzon-N of)	20.33 N	121.75 E	-24	Submarine	0704-05=	Historical											
						1773	10		....	....	----	?---	----	----	----	0	
						1850	....		....	....	----	?---	----	----	----	0	
						1854	0115		....	....	----	?---	----	----	----	0	
IRAYA (Luzon-N of)	20.469 N	122.010 E	1009	Stratovolc	0704-06-	Historical											
						C 0250x	....		....	....	----	----	x---	----	----		
						C 0470t	....		....	....	x---	----	xx--	----	----		
						1464	....		....	....	----	----	----	----	----		

SE ASIA (INDOCHINA)

VOLCANO NAME (Subregion) / ERUPTION — Area of Activity	LAT	LONG	ELEV (m)	TYPE	NUMBER	Status / Start Year	Start M-Dy	P	Stop Year	Stop M-Dy	Central, Flank vent, Radial fiss, Regional*	Submarine, New island, Subglacial, Crater lake	Explosive, Pyro flow, Phreatic, Fumarolic	Lava flow, Lava lake, Dome, Spine	Fatal, Damage, Mudflow, Tsunami	VEI	Vol L/T
LEIZHOU BANDAO (China-SE)	20.83 N*	109.78 E	259	Volc field	0705-01-	Holocene											
CU-LAO RE GROUP (Vietnam)	15.38 N*	109.12 E	181	Cones	0705-02-	Holocene											
TOROENG PRONG (Vietnam)	14.93 N	108.00 E	800	Unknown	0705-03-	Holocene?											
HAUT DONG NAI (Vietnam)	11.60 N*	108.20 E	1000	Volc field	0705-04-	Holocene?											
BAS DONG NAI (Vietnam)	10.80 N*	107.20 E	392	Volc field	0705-05-	Holocene?											
CENDRES, ILE DES (Vietnam-E of)	10.158 N	109.014 E	-20	Subm volcs	0705-06-	Historical											
						1923	0302		1923	0513	xx--	xx--	x---	x---	----	2	-/8
VETERAN (Vietnam-E of)	9.83 N	109.05 E		Submarine	0705-07-	Fumarolic											
						? 1880?	....		....	....	----	?---	----	----	----	0	
						? 1928	....		....	....	----	?---	---?	----	----	0	
POPA (Myanmar)	20.87 N	95.23 E	1518	Stratovolc	0705-08-	Anthropology											
						A -0442	....		....	....	----	----	----	----	----		
LOWER CHINDWIN (Myanmar)	22.28 N*	95.10 E	385	Volc field	0705-09-	Holocene?											
SINGU PLATEAU (Myanmar)	22.70 N*	95.98 E	507	Fissure vents	0705-10-	Holocene											
TENGCHONG (China-S)	25.32 N*	98.47 E	2865	Pyrocl cones	0705-11-	Historical											
Dayingshan						1609	....		....	....	x---	---?	x---	----	?x--		

Japan, Taiwan, & Marianas (08)

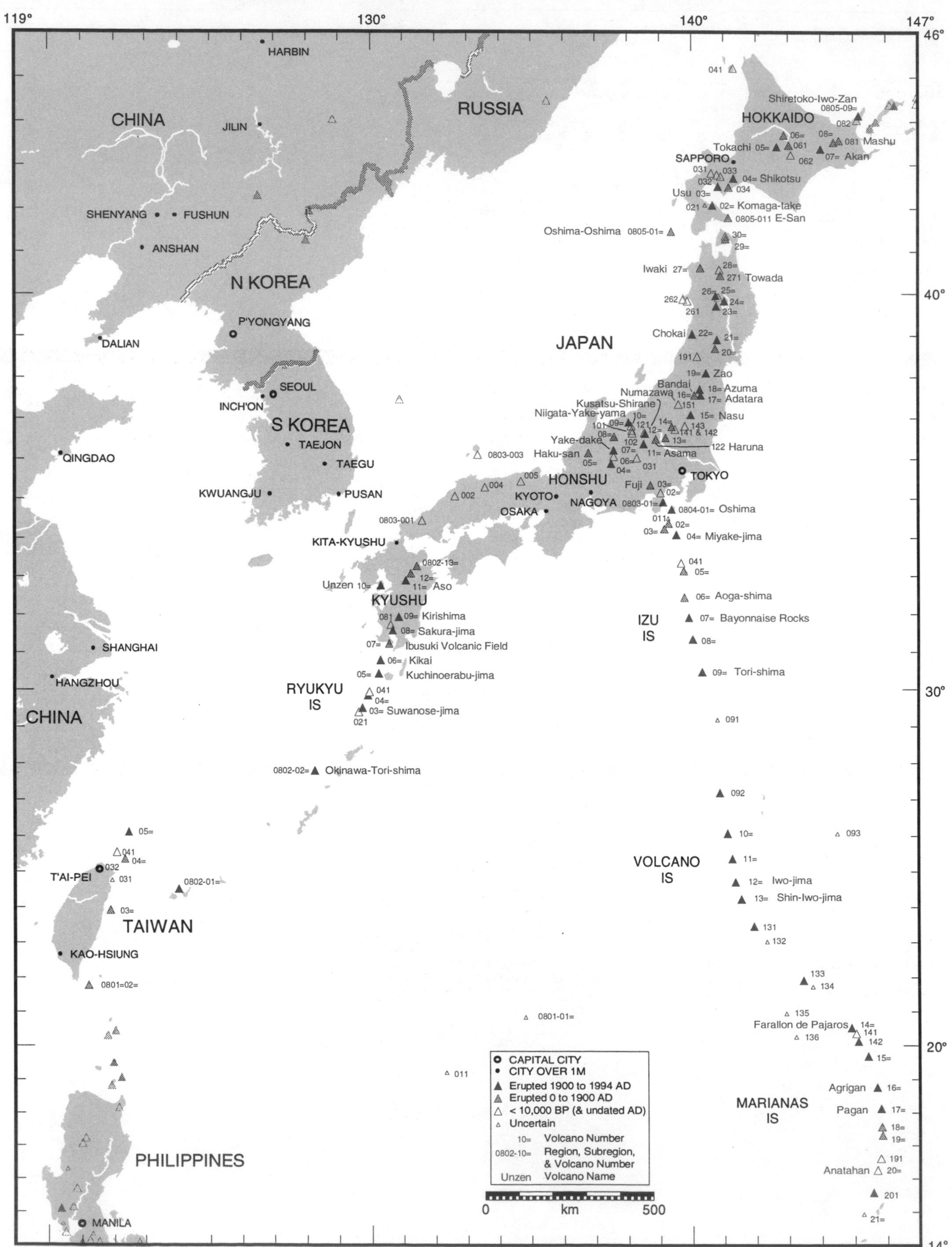
119°
130°
140°
147°
46°
40°
30°
20°
14°
HARBIN
CHINA
JILIN
RUSSIA
SHENYANG
FUSHUN
ANSHAN
N KOREA
P'YONGYANG
DALIAN
SEOUL
INCH'ON
S KOREA
TAEJON
TAEGU
KWUANGJU
PUSAN
QINGDAO
SHANGHAI
HANGZHOU
CHINA
JAPAN
HOKKAIDO
041
Shiretoko-Iwo-Zan
0805-09=
082
06=
08=
081 Mashu
Tokachi 05=
061
062
07= Akan
SAPPORO
031
033
032
04= Shikotsu
034
Usu 03=
021
02= Komaga-take
0805-011 E-San
Oshima-Oshima 0805-01=
30=
29=
Iwaki 27=
28=
271 Towada
26=
25=
262
24=
261
23=
Chokai 22=
21=
20=
191
19= Zao
Bandai
Numazawa
18= Azuma
16=
17= Adatara
Kusatsu-Shirane
151
Niigata-Yake-yama
15= Nasu
10=
101
09=
121
14=
143
12=
141 & 142
08=
102
13=
Yake-dake
07=
122 Haruna
11= Asama
Haku-san
06=
05=
04=
031
0803-003
TOKYO
HONSHU
005
004
002
KYOTO
Fuji
03=
02=
NAGOYA
0803-01=
OSAKA
0804-01= Oshima
011
02=
03=
04= Miyake-jima
0803-001
KITA-KYUSHU
0802-13=
12=
Unzen 10=
11= Aso
KYUSHU
081
09= Kirishima
08= Sakura-jima
07=
Ibusuki Volcanic Field
06= Kikai
05=
Kuchinoerabu-jima
041
05=
06= Aoga-shima
IZU IS
07= Bayonnaise Rocks
08=
09= Tori-shima
RYUKYU IS
041
04=
03= Suwanose-jima
021
091
0802-02= Okinawa-Tori-shima
092
05=
10=
093
041
04=
T'AI-PEI
032
031
0802-01=
11=
VOLCANO IS
12= Iwo-jima
13= Shin-Iwo-jima
03=
TAIWAN
KAO-HSIUNG
131
132
0801=02=
133
134
135
0801-01=
Farallon de Pajaros
14=
141
136
142
15=
011
Agrigan 16=
MARIANAS IS
Pagan 17=
18=
19=
191
Anatahan 20=
201
21=
PHILIPPINES
MANILA
CAPITAL CITY
CITY OVER 1M
Erupted 1900 to 1994 AD
Erupted 0 to 1900 AD
< 10,000 BP (& undated AD)
Uncertain
10= Volcano Number
0802-10= Region, Subregion, & Volcano Number
Unzen Volcano Name
0 km 500

Human settlement of Japan can be traced for tens of thousands of years, and an unbroken line of emperors from 660 BC. Japan's first documented historical eruption was from Aso, its most prolific volcano, in 553 AD, the year after Buddhism was introduced from Korea. A fixed capital was first established in 710. By the time of Japan's largest historical eruption (Towada, 915 AD), 17 Japanese volcanoes had been documented in eruption, more than the rest of the world combined (including 10 in Europe). It was not until 1626, however, that history recorded an eruption from Japan's northern island of Hokkaido, and it was not formally made part of Japan until 1868. A feudal system had dominated all of Japan from 1192, but in 1868, 14 years after the nation was first opened to western trade, the Emperor Meiji overcame shogun power.

To the south, the Mariana Islands were populated from 1500 BC and explored by Spaniards in the 15th century AD, but the islands did not come under Spanish colonial rule until 1668. The first historical eruption was documented the following year. The northern volcanic islands were sold to Germany in 1898, occupied by Japan between the two World Wars, and named a Trust Territory by the UN in 1947 administered by the US. The islands became a self-governing US commonwealth in 1975. Region 08's total land area approximates California's, but its population is 4 times as large, and the Marianas constitute only 0.1% of each.

Japan's long history and careful attention to tephrochronology have produced an unusually detailed and balanced record of Holocene volcanism. One result of this work is that this region now leads all others in the total number of dated eruptions (1274) and number of volcanoes with dated eruptions (94).

Several regions in which tephrochronology is emphasized, such as New Zealand and the Mediterranean, show a high proportion of their large eruptions (VEI ≥4) more than 2000 years ago. In contrast, regions such as Latin America, Indonesia, and the Philippines, show them concentrated in the last 200 years of historical records. Japan, however, (along with Kamchatka, Iceland, and Alaska) shows a balanced temporal distribution of large eruptions, reflecting *both* tephrochronology emphasis and vigorous explosive volcanism during recent centuries.

The volcanoes of this region are unusually explosive, and include Kikai, which produced one of the Earth's largest Holocene explosive eruptions about 6300 radiocarbon years ago. No other region has documented more large explosive eruptions (VEI ≥4), or approaches its total of 41 AD eruptions of this magnitude. Pyroclastic flows have accompanied a record 28% of its eruptions, including the current Unzen eruption.

Most volcanoes in this region result from subduction of westward-moving oceanic crust under the Asian Plate. In the Izu-Marianas chain, however, the crust to the west is also oceanic, forming more basaltic island arcs (but with volcanoes that are far more explosive than oceanic hotspot volcanoes).

Region 08 has the largest number of submarine volcanoes, mostly extending down the Izu-Marianas arc, and the largest number of reported submarine eruptions. The many reports of water discoloration over submarine vents have also contributed to this region's record number (180) of eruptions preceded by a question mark, indicating uncertainty that the eruption actually took place. In nearly equal proportions, Regions 08, 06, and 04 account for nearly three-fourths of the eruptions that have built oceanic islands. Region 08 has also recorded the largest number of phreatic eruptions (232), nearly double those of the closest contender.

VOLCANO NAME (Subregion) / ERUPTION — Area of Activity	LAT	LONG	ELEV (m)	TYPE	NUMBER	Status / Start Year	Start M-Dy	P	Stop Year	Stop M-Dy	ERUPTIVE CHARACTERISTICS (Central, Flank vent, Radial fiss, Regional* / Submarine, New island, Subglacial, Crater lake / Explosive, Pyro flow, Phreatic, Fumarolic / Lava flow, Lava lake, Dome, Spine / Fatal, Damage, Mudflow, Tsunami)	VEI	Vol L/T
TAIWAN & RYUKYU ISLANDS													
UNNAMED (Taiwan-E of)	20.93 N	134.75 E	-6000	Submarine ?	0801-01=	Uncertain							
						? 1850	....		....	....	---- ?--- ---- ---- ----	0	
(incorrect Lat-Long, see 0801-02=)						X 1854	0115		....	....	---- ?--- ---- ---- ----		
UNNAMED (Taiwan-E of)	19.17 N	132.25 E	-10	Submarine	0801-011	Uncertain							
						? 1955	10		....	....	---- ?--- ---- ---- ----	0	
UNNAMED (Taiwan-E of)	21.83 N	121.18 E	-115	Submarine	0801-02=	Historical							
						1854	0115		....	....	---- x--- ---- ---- ----	0	
UNNAMED (Taiwan-E of)	24.00 N	121.83 E		Submarine	0801-03=	Historical							
						1853	1029		1854	01	---- x--- ---- ---- ----	2?	
KUEI-SHAN-TAO (Taiwan)	24.85 N	121.92 E	401	Stratovolc	0801-031	Pleistocene-Fumarolic							
DATUN GROUP (Taiwan)	25.17 N	121.52 E	1130	Stratovolc	0801-032	Pleistocene-Fumarolic							
UNNAMED (Taiwan-N of)	25.42 N	122.33 E	-100	Submarine	0801-04=	Historical							
						1867	....		....	....	---- x--- ---- ---- ----	0	
PENG-CHIA-HSU (Taiwan-N of)	25.63 N	122.07 E	129	Stratovolc	0801-041	Pleistocene-Fumarolic							
ZENGYU (Taiwan-N of)	26.18 N	122.458 E	-418	Submarine	0801-05=	Historical							
						1916	0418		?1927	0601	---- x--- ---- ---- ----	0	
IRIOMOTE-JIMA (Ryukyu Is)	24.558 N	124.00 E	-200	Submarine	0802-01=	Historical							
(eruption October 31, 1924, not 1925)						1924	1031		....	....	---- x--- x--- ---- ----	4?	-/9
OKINAWA-TORI-SHIMA (Ryukyu Is)	27.85 N	128.25 E	217	Complx volc	0802-02=	Historical							
						1664	....		....	....	---- ?--- ---- ---- xx-x		
Iwo-dake						1796	11		....	....	x--- ---- x--- ---- ----	2	
						1829	1201		1829	1216	---- ---- --?- ---- ----	1?	
						1855	0228m		....	....	---- ---- x--- ---- ----	2	
						1868	0228m		....	....	---- ---- x--- ---- ----	1	
						1903	0315e		1903	0826e	x--- ---- x--- ---- ----	2	
Iwo-dake						1959	0608		1959	07	x--- ---- x--x ---- ----	2	
						1967	1125e		....	....	x--- ---- --?- ---- ----	1	
						1968	0718		1968	0718	x--- ---- x-x- ---- ----	1	
AKUSEKI-JIMA (Ryukyu Is)	29.45 N	129.60 E	586	Stratovolc	0802-021	Holocene							
SUWANOSE-JIMA (Ryukyu Is)	29.53 N	129.72 E	799	Stratovolc	0802-03=	Historical							
						T 1600?	....		....	....	---- ---- x--- ---- ----	4+	
Southwestern summit crater						1813	....		....	....	x--- ---- x--- x--- ----	4	
						1877	....		....	....	---- ---- x--- ---- ----	4	
Northeastern summit crater (On-take)						1884	....		....	....	x--- ---- x--- x--- ----	1	
On-take						1885	01		1885	05	x--- ---- x--- ---- ----	2?	
On-take						1889	1002		1889	1013	x--- ---- x--- ---- ----	4	
						? 1914	0321		....	....	x--- ---- ---- ---- ----		
						? 1915	07		?1915	09	x--- ---- ?--- ---- ----	2?	
						1921	1208	+	1922	0126	x--- ---- ---- ---- ----	2?	
On-take						1925	0513		....	....	x--- ---- x--- ---- ----	2?	
On-take						1934	0111		....	....	x--- ---- x--- ---- ----	2?	
On-take						1938	0311		1938	0311	x--- ---- x--- ---- ----	2?	
On-take						1940	1129		....	....	x--- ---- x--- ---- ----	2?	
On-take						1949	10		1993>	....	x--- ---- x--- ---- -x--	2*	
NAKANO-SHIMA (Ryukyu Is)	29.85 N	129.87 E	979	Stratovolcs	0802-04=	Historical							
On-take						1914	01		....	....	x--- ---- --x- ---- ----	1	
On-take						? 1949	10		....	....	x--- ---- ---- ---- ----	1?	
KUCHINO-SHIMA (Ryukyu Is)	29.97 N	129.93 E	627	Stratovolcs	0802-041	Holocene							
KUCHINOERABU-JIMA (Ryukyu Is)	30.43 N	130.22 E	649	Stratovolcs	0802-05=	Historical							
Shin-dake						1840<	....		....	....	x--- ---- ---- ---- ----	2?	

VOLCANO NAME (Subregion)	LAT / LONG / ELEV (m) / TYPE / NUMBER / Status — ERUPTION: Area of Activity		Start Year	Start M-Dy	P	Stop Year	Stop M-Dy	Central / Flank vent / Radial fiss / Regional*	Submarine / New island / Subglacial / Crater lake	Explosive / Pyro flow / Phreatic / Fumarolic	Lava flow / Lava lake / Dome / Spine	Fatal / Damage / Mudflow / Tsunami	VEI	Vol L/T
KUCHINOERABU-JIMA (Ryukyu Is) *continued*	Shin-dake		**1841**	0523	+	**1841**	0801	x---	----	x---	----	xx--	2*	
	Shin-dake	?	**1906**	....		?**1907**	....	----	----	----	----	----		
	Shin-dake		**1914**	0105		....	....	x---	----	--?x	----	----	2?	
	SW flank of Shin-dake		**1931**	0402	+	**1931**	0622	-x--	----	x-x-	----	-x--	3?	
	Shin-dake	?	**1932**	0723		?**1932**	0723	x---	----	?---	----	----	1?	
	Shin-dake		**1933**	1223		**1934**	0112	x---	----	x---	----	xx--	4*	
	Shin-dake		**1945**	1103		**1945**	1103	x---	----	x-x-	----	----	2	
	Shin-dake		**1966**	1122		**1966**	1122	x---	----	--x-	----	----	2	
	Shin-dake		**1968**	1221	+	**1969**	0310	x---	----	x-x-	----	----	3*	
	Shin-dake		**1972**	0902		**1972**	0902	x---	----	--x-	----	----	2	
	Shin-dake		**1973**	1105	+	**1973**	1119	x---	----	x-x-	----	----	2	
	Shin-dake		**1974**	0603		**1974**	0603	x---	----	x-x-	----	----	1	
	Shin-dake		**1976**	0402		**1976**	0402	x---	----	x-x-	----	----	2	
	East side of Shin-dake		**1980**	0928		**1980**	0928	x---	----	x-x-	----	----	2	-/6
KIKAI (Ryukyu Is)	**30.78 N 130.28 E 717 Caldera 0802-06= Historical**													
	Kikai Caldera	C	**-4350?**	....		....	....	x---	----	xx--	----	xx--	7	-/11
	Tokara-Iwo-jima	T	**0500?**	....		....	....	x---	----	x---	x---	----	3	
	Tokara-Iwo-jima	T	**0700?**	....		....	....	x---	----	x---	x---	----	3	
	Tokara-Iwo-jima	?	**1914**	0213		....	....	----	----	----	----	----		
	2 km east of Tokara-Iwo-Jima		**1934**	0919	+	**1935**	08	x---	xx--	x---	x---	----	2*	
	Iwo-dake		**1988**	0118		**1988**	0118	x---	----	x-x-	----	----	1	

KYUSHU

VOLCANO NAME (Subregion)	LAT / LONG / ELEV (m) / TYPE / NUMBER / Status — ERUPTION: Area of Activity		Start Year	Start M-Dy	P	Stop Year	Stop M-Dy	Central / Flank vent / Radial fiss / Regional*	Submarine / New island / Subglacial / Crater lake	Explosive / Pyro flow / Phreatic / Fumarolic	Lava flow / Lava lake / Dome / Spine	Fatal / Damage / Mudflow / Tsunami	VEI	Vol L/T
IBUSUKI VOLC FIELD (Kyushu)	**31.22 N*130.57 E 922 Calderas 0802-07= Historical**													
	Unagi, Narikawa and Yamakawa maars	T	**-5050?**	....		....	....	x---	----	x---	----	----		
	Ikeda-ko caldera	C	**-2690u**	....		....	....	x---	----	xx--	----	----	5	-/9
	Kaimon	T	**-2010?**	....		....	....	----	----	x---	----	-x--	4	-/8
	Kaimon	T	**-1780?**	....		....	....	----	----	x---	----	----	4	-/8
	Kaimon	T	**-1610?**	....		....	....	----	----	x---	----	----	3	-/7
	Nabeshima-dake	T	**-1550?**	....		....	....	x---	----	----	--x-	----		
	Kaimon	T	**-1500?**	....		....	....	----	----	x---	----	----	4	-/8
	Mizunashi, Kagami, Ikezoko maars	T	**-1450?**	....		....	....	x---	----	x---	----	----		
	Kaimon	T	**-0700?**	....		....	....	----	----	x---	x---	----	2	7/6
	Kaimon	T	**-0650?**	....		....	....	----	----	x---	----	----	4	-/8
	Kaimon	T	**-0270?**	....		....	....	----	----	x---	----	----	4	-/8
	Kaimon	T	**-0080?**	....		....	....	----	----	x---	----	----	4	-/8
	Kaimon	T	**0030?**	....		....	....	----	----	x---	----	----	3	-/7
	Kaimon	T	**0130?**	....		....	....	----	----	x---	x---	----	4	7/8
	Kaimon	T	**0150?**	....		....	....	----	----	x---	----	----	4	-/8
	Kaimon	T	**0270?**	....		....	....	----	----	x---	----	----	3	-/7
	Kaimon	T	**0550?**	....		....	....	----	----	x---	----	----	2	-/6
	Kaimon	T	**0600?**	....		....	....	----	----	x---	x---	----	4	8/8
	Kaimon	T	**0660?**	....		....	....	----	----	xx--	----	----	4+	
	Kaimon	T	**0720?**	....		....	....	----	----	x---	----	----	4	-/8
	Kaimon	T	**0770?**	....		....	....	----	----	x---	----	----	4	-/8
	Kaimon	?	**0860**	04		....	....	----	----	?---	----	----	2?	
	Kaimon	?	**0866**	05		....	....	----	----	?---	----	----	2?	
	Kaimon		**0874**	0329		**0874**	07 ?	x---	----	x---	----	-x--	4	
	Kaimon	?	**0882**	11		....	....	----	----	?---	----	----	2?	
	Kaimon		**0885**	0829		**0885**	0928	----	----	x---	x---	-x--	4	
	Kaimon	?	**1615**	0807?		....	....	----	----	?---	----	----		
SAKURA-JIMA (Kyushu)	**31.58 N 130.67 E 1117 Stratovolc 0802-08= Historical**													
	Kita-dake	C	**-7750?**	....		....	....	x---	----	x---	----	----		
	Kita-dake	C	**-7150?**	....		....	....	x---	----	x---	----	----	4	
	Kita-dake	C	**-6350?**	....		....	....	x---	----	x---	----	----		
	Kita-dake	C	**-5950?**	....		....	....	x---	----	x---	----	----		
	Kita-dake	C	**-5400?**	....		....	....	x---	----	x---	----	----		
	Kita-dake	C	**-4800?**	....		....	....	x---	----	x---	----	----		
	Kita-dake	C	**-3550z**	....		....	....	x---	----	x---	----	----	4	
	Kita-dake	C	**-2900?**	....		....	....	x---	----	x---	----	----	4	
	Minami-dake	C	**-0650?**	....		....	....	x---	----	x---	----	----		
			0708	....		....	....	----	xx--	?---	----	----	3↑	
		?	**0712**	....		....	....	----	----	?---	----	----	3?	
			0716	....		**0718**	....	----	xx--	?---	----	----	3↑	
	East flank (Nabe-yama)		**0764**	01		....	....	-x--	----	xxx-	x---	xx--	4	
			0766	0720		....	....	----	xx--	x---	----	x---	3↑	
			0778	....		....	....	----	x---	----	----	----	0?	
	Minami-dake		**1468**	....		....	....	x---	----	x---	----	----	2	
	NE and SW flanks, summit crater		**1471**	1103		**1476**	1008>	xxx-	----	xx--	x---	xx--	5*	8/9
	Minami-dake		**1478**	0923		....	....	x---	----	x---	----	-x--	2?	
	Minami-dake		**1642**	0406		....	....	x---	----	x---	----	----	2?	
		?	**1670**	0601		....	....	----	----	----	----	----	2?	
	Minami-dake		**1678**	0301		....	....	x---	----	x---	----	----	2?	
	Minami-dake		**1706**	01		....	....	x---	----	x---	----	----	2?	
	Minami-dake		**1742**	0406		....	....	x---	----	x---	----	----	2?	
	Minami-dake summit, west flank?		**1749**	09		....	....	x?--	----	x---	?---	----	2	
	Minami-dake		**1756**	0909		....	....	x---	----	x---	----	----	2	
	(earthquake, but not eruption)	X	1766	0605		....	....	----	----	----	----	----		
	NE flank, off NE coast, south flank		**1779**	1108	+	**1781**	05	-xx-	xx--	xx--	x---	xxxx	4*	9/8
	NE flank (offshore)		**1782**	0118		....	....	----	x---	----	----	----	2?	
			1783	0903		....	....	-x--	----	x---	----	----	3	
			1785	1120		....	....	-x--	----	x---	----	----	2	
	Minami-dake		**1790**	0729		....	....	x---	----	x---	----	----	2	
	Minami-dake		**1791**	0911		....	....	x---	----	x---	----	----	2	
	Minami-dake		**1792**	....		....	....	x---	----	x---	----	----	2?	
	Minami-dake		**1794**	....		....	....	x---	----	x---	----	----	2	
	Minami-dake		**1797**	....		....	....	x---	----	x---	----	----	2	
	Minami-dake		**1799**	0327		....	....	x---	----	x---	----	----	2	
	Minami-dake		**1860**	....		....	....	x---	----	x---	----	----	1	
	Minami-dake	?	**1899**	0924		?**1899**	0925	x---	----	----	----	----	1?	
	West, east and SE flanks		**1914**	0112	+	**1915**	05	-xx-	----	xx--	x---	xx--	4	9/8
	Minami-dake		**1935**	0920		**1935**	0924	x---	----	x---	----	----	1	
	Minami-dake		**1938**	0225	+	**1938**	0331	x---	----	x-?-	----	----	2	
	East flank of Minami-dake (750 m)		**1939**	1026		**1939**	1112?	-x--	----	xx--	----	----	2	-/5
	Minami-dake and east flank (750 m)		**1940**	0424	+	**1940**	0709	xx--	----	x---	----	----	2	
	East flank of Minami-dake (750 m)		**1941**	0428	+	**1941**	0826	-x--	----	x---	----	----	2	
	East flank of Minami-dake (750 m)		**1942**	0716		**1942**	0716	-x--	----	x---	----	----	1	

VOLCANO NAME (Subregion) / ERUPTION — Area of Activity	LAT	LONG	ELEV (m)	TYPE	NUMBER	Status	Start Year	Start M-Dy	P	Stop Year	Stop M-Dy	Central / Flank vent / Radial fiss / Regional*	Submarine / New island / Subglacial / Crater lake	Explosive / Pyro flow / Phreatic / Fumarolic	Lava flow / Lava lake / Dome / Spine	Fatal / Damage / Mudflow / Tsunami	VEI	Vol L/T
SAKURA-JIMA (Kyushu) *continued...*																		
East flank of Minami-dake (750 m)							**1946**	01	+	**1946**	11	-x--	----	x---	x---	xxx-	2	8/7
East flank of Minami-dake (750 m)							**1948**	0727		**1948**	0727	-x--	----	x---	----	----	1	
Minami-dake							**1950**	0629		**1950**	0909	x---	----	x-x-	----	----	1	
Minami-dake						?	**1954**	11		?**1954**	12	x---	----	--?-	----	----	1?	
Minami-dake							**1955**	1013		**1993**>	....	x---	----	xxx-	-x--	xxx-	3*	
SUMIYOSHI-IKE (Kyushu)	**31.768 N**	**130.594 E**	**100**	**Maars**	**0802-081**	**Radiocarbon**												
Sumiyoshi-ike						C	**-5050**?	....		....	....	x---	----	x-x-	----	----	2	-/6
Yonemaru						C	**-4550**?	....		....	....	x---	----	xxx-	----	----	3	-/7
KIRISHIMA (Kyushu)	**31.93 N**	**130.87 E**	**1700**	**Shield**	**0802-09=**	**Historical**												
Shinmoe-dake						T	**-7050***	....		....	....	x---	----	x---	----	----	3	-/7
Old Takachiho						T	**-5700***	....		....	....	x---	----	x---	----	----	3	-/7
Old Takachiho						C	**-4350**?	....		....	....	x---	----	x---	x---	----	4	-/8
Takachiho-mine						T	**-3550**?	....		....	....	x---	----	x---	----	----	3	-/7
Takachiho-mine						T	**-3050**?	....		....	....	x---	----	x---	----	----	3	-/7
Shinmoe-dake						C	**-2050**?	....		....	....	x---	----	x---	----	----	3	-/7
Mi-ike						T	**-1050**?	....		....	....	x---	----	xx--	----	----	4	
Ohachi						T	**-0550**?	....		....	....	x---	----	x---	----	----	3	-/7
Ohachi						T	**-0050**?	....		....	....	x---	----	x---	----	----	3	
Ohachi						T	**0100**z	....		....	....	x---	----	x---	x---	----	3	-/7
Ohachi							**0742**	1228		....	....	x---	----	x---	----	----	3	
Ohachi							**0788**	0418		....	....	x---	----	xx--	x---	-x--	4	-/8
Ohachi							**0837**	....		**0839**?	....	x---	----	x---	----	----	3	
							0843	....		**0848**	....	x---	----	x---	----	----	2?	
							0857	....		....	....	x---	----	x---	----	----	2?	
							0858	....		....	....	x---	----	x---	----	----	2?	
							0945	....		....	....	x---	----	x---	----	----	2?	
							1112	0309		....	....	x---	----	x---	----	-x--	2?	
							1113	0227		....	....	x---	----	x---	----	-x--	2?	
							1167	....		....	....	x---	----	x---	----	----	2?	
						?	**1175**	01 ?		....	....	----	----	x---	----	----	2?	
							1184	0207		....	....	x---	----	x---	----	----	2?	
Ohachi							**1235**	0125		....	....	x---	----	x---	----	-x--	2?	
							1381	....		....	....	----	----	x---	----	----	2?	
							1524	....		....	....	x---	----	x---	----	----	2?	
							1554	....		....	....	x---	----	x---	----	----	2?	
							1566	0506		....	....	x---	----	?---	----	----	2?	
							1566	1031		....	....	x---	----	x---	----	x---	3	
							1574	02		....	....	x---	----	x---	----	----	2?	
							1576	....		**1578**	....	x---	----	x---	----	----	2?	
							1585	11 ?		....	....	x---	----	x---	----	----	2?	
							1587	0524		....	....	x---	----	x---	----	----	2?	
							1588	0407		....	....	x---	----	x---	----	----	2?	
							1595	....		....	....	----	----	x---	----	----	2?	
						?	**1596**	....		....	....	----	----	x---	----	----	2?	
							1598	....		**1600**	....	----	----	x---	----	----	2?	
							1613	....		**1614**	....	----	----	x---	----	----	2?	
							1615	....		**1618**	....	----	----	x---	----	----	2?	
							1620	....		....	....	----	----	x---	----	----	2?	
							1628	1026		....	....	x---	----	x---	----	----	2?	
Shinmoe-dake							**1637**	....		**1638**	....	x---	----	x---	----	----	2?	
Ohachi							**1659**	02		**1661**	....	x---	----	x---	----	----	2?	
Ohachi							**1662**	09		**1664**	....	x---	----	x---	----	----	2?	
Ohachi						?	**1667**	....		....	....	x---	----	x---	----	----		
Ohachi							**1677**	....		....	....	x---	----	x---	----	----	2?	
Ohachi							**1678**	0229		....	....	x---	----	x---	----	----	2?	
Ohachi							**1690**	....		....	....	x---	----	x---	----	----	2?	
Ohachi							**1706**	0128		....	....	x---	----	x---	----	-x--	2	
Shinmoe-dake							**1716**	0311		....	....	x---	---x	x-x-	----	--x-	3	-/7
Shinmoe-dake							**1716**	1109	+	**1717**	0213	x---	----	xx--	----	xxx-	3*	-/8
Shinmoe-dake							**1717**	0919		....	....	x---	----	xx--	----	----	3	-/7
Shinmoe-dake							**1719**	....		....	....	x---	----	x---	----	----	2	
Iwo-yama (NW flank of Karakuni-dake)							**1768**	....		....	....	-x--	----	----	x-x-	----	0	
Ohachi							**1769**	....		....	....	x---	----	x---	----	----	2	
Shinmoe-dake							**1771**	....		**1772**	....	x---	----	xx--	xx--	----	2	-/6
Shinmoe-dake							**1822**	0112		....	....	x---	---x	xx--	----	--x-	2	-/6
Shinmoe-dake							**1832**	0420		....	....	x---	----	x---	----	----	2	
Ohachi							**1880**	09		....	....	x---	----	x---	----	----	2	
Ohachi							**1887**	05		....	....	x---	----	x---	----	----	2?	
Ohachi							**1888**	0221	+	**1888**	0509	x---	----	x---	----	----	2	
Ohachi							**1889**	1210	+	**1889**	1218	x---	----	x---	----	----	2	
Ohachi							**1891**	0619?		....	....	x---	----	x---	----	----	2?	
Ohachi							**1891**	1110		**1891**	1120?	x---	----	x---	----	----	2	
Ohachi							**1894**	0225		**1894**	0228?	x---	----	x---	----	----	2	
Ohachi							**1895**	0716	+	**1896**	0626	x---	----	x---	----	x---	2	
Ohachi							**1896**	1221		....	....	x---	----	x---	----	----	2	
Ohachi							**1897**	0503	+	**1897**	0904	x---	----	x---	----	----	2	
Ohachi							**1898**	0208	+	**1898**	0311	x---	----	x---	----	----	2	
Ohachi							**1898**	1226		**1898**	1230	x---	----	x---	----	----	2	
Ohachi							**1899**	0728	+	**1900**	0216	x---	----	x---	----	x---	2	
Ohachi							**1903**	0829	+	**1903**	1125	x---	----	x---	----	----	2	
Ohachi							**1913**	1108	+	**1914**	0108	x---	----	x---	----	----	2	
Ohachi							**1914**	1108		....	....	x---	----	x---	----	----		
Ohachi							**1923**	07		**1923**	07	x---	----	x---	----	x---	2	
(Shinmoe crater lake gas emission)						X	1934	....		....	....	----	----	---x	----	----		
Karakuni-dake ?						?	**1946**	04		....	....	x---	----	?---	----	----	2	
Shinmoe-dake							**1959**	0213		**1959**	0217	x-x-	---x	x-x-	----	--x-	2	-/6
North foot, near Tearai hot springs							**1971**	0805		**1971**	0805	x---	----	x-x-	----	----	1	
Shinmoe-dake							**1979**	0216r		....	....	x---	----	--xx	----	----	1	
Shinmoe-dake							**1992**	0128		**1992**	0128	x---	----	x-x-	----	----	1	-/2
UNZEN (Kyushu)	**32.75 N**	**130.30 E**	**1359**	**Complx volc**	**0802-10=**	**Historical**												
						?	**0860**	....		....	....	----	----	----	----	----		
(eruption occurred in 1663, not 1657)						X	1657	....		....	....	----	----	----	----	----		
Fugen-dake (Tsukumo-jima Pond)							**1663**	04		**1663**	05	x---	----	x---	----	----	2?	
NE flank of Fugen-dake (1200 m)							**1663**	1211		**1663**	1227>	-x--	----	?---	x---	----	2?	6/-
						?	**1690**	....		?**1692**	....	----	----	?---	----	----		
Fugen-dake (summit, NNE), Mayu-yama							**1792**	0210	+	**1792**	0722	xx--	----	x---	x---	xxxx	2	8/-
Fugen-dake						?	**1798**	1113		?**1798**	12	----	----	?---	----	----		
East flank and summit of Fugen-dake							**1990**	1117	+	**1993**	12 >	x---	----	xxx-	--x-	xxx-	1	8/6

VOLCANO NAME (Subregion) ...... LAT LONG ELEV (m) TYPE NUMBER Status

ASO (Kyushu).................... **32.88 N 131.10 E 1592 Caldera 0802-11= Historical**

ERUPTION — Area of Activity		Start Year	Start M-Dy	P	Stop Year	Stop M-Dy	Central / Flank vent / Radial fiss / Regional*	Submarine / New island / Subglacial / Crater lake	Explosive / Pyro flow / Phreatic / Fumarolic	Lava flow / Lava lake / Dome / Spine	Fatal / Damage / Mudflow / Tsunami	VEI	Vol L/T
Kishima-dake........................	T	**-0050?**	....		....	....	x---	----	x---	x---	----	4	
Ojo-dake............................	T	**0100?**	....		....	....	x---	----	x---	x---	----	4	
Kometsuka...........................	T	**0210?**	....		....	....	x---	----	x---	x---	----	3	
(all historical eruptions from Naka-dake) ...		**0553**	....		....	....	x---	----	x---	----	----	3↑	
	?	**0796**	08		....	....	x---	---?	----	----	----	0?	
		0864	1109		....	....	x---	---x	x---	----	--x-	3?	
		0867	0620?		....	....	x---	----	x---	----	----	2	
	?	**0986**	0902		....	....	x---	---x	?---	----	----	2?	
		1229	....		....	....	x---	----	x---	----	----	2	
		1239	0208		....	....	x---	----	x---	----	----	2	
		1240	....		....	....	x---	---x	x---	----	----	2	
		1265	1201?		....	....	x---	----	x---	----	----	2	
		1269	08		....	....	x---	---x	x---	----	----	2	
		1271	0105		....	....	x---	---x	x---	----	----	2	
		1272	04		....	....	x---	---x	x---	----	--?-	2	
		1272	1129		....	....	x---	----	x---	----	----	2	
		1273	08		....	....	x---	----	x---	----	----	2	
		1274	....		....	....	x---	---x	x---	----	-x--	2	
		1281	07		**1281**	08	x---	---x	x---	----	----	2	
		1286	0830		....	....	x---	---x	x---	----	----	2	
		1305	0502		....	....	x---	---x	x---	----	----	2	
		1324	0907		....	....	x---	---x	x---	----	----	2	
		1331	04		**1331**	04	x---	----	x---	----	----	2	
		1331	12		**1333**	06	x---	---x	x---	----	?x--	2	
		1335	0207	+	**1335**	0326	x---	---x	x---	----	-x--	2	
		1340	0203		**1340**	0225	x---	---x	x---	----	-x--	2	
		1343	....		....	....	x---	----	x---	----	----	2	
		1346	....		....	....	x---	----	x---	----	----	2	
		1369	....		....	....	x---	----	x---	----	----	2	
		1375	1220	+	**1376**	0131	x---	---x	x---	----	--?-	2	
		1376	0620		....	....	x---	----	x---	----	----	2	
		1377	0506		....	....	x---	---x	x---	----	-xx-	2	
		1387	0619		....	....	x---	---x	x---	----	----	2	
	?	**1388**	1016		....	....	x---	---x	?---	----	----	2	
	?	**1390**	....		....	....	x---	----	----	----	-x--	2?	
		1434	0510		**1434**	0518	x---	---x	x---	----	--x-	2	
		1438	0109		**1438**	0218	x---	---x	x---	----	----	2	
		1473	0516	+	**1474**	0415q	x---	---x	x---	----	-x--	2	
		1485	0105		....	....	x---	---x	x---	----	x---	2	
		1505	02		....	....	x---	----	x---	----	----	2	
		1506	0406		....	....	x---	----	x---	----	----	2	
		1522	0215		....	....	x---	---x	x---	----	----	2	
		1533	0717		....	....	x---	---x	x---	----	--x-	2	
		1542	0429		....	....	x---	----	x---	----	----	2	
		1558	....		**1559**	....	x---	----	x---	----	-x--	2	
		1562	03		....	....	x---	----	x---	----	----	2	
	?	**1563**	0503		....	....	x---	----	?---	----	----	2?	
		1564	12		....	....	x---	----	x---	----	----	2	
		1576	1115		....	....	x---	----	x---	----	-?--	2	
(all historical eruptions from Naka-dake) ...		**1582**	0217		....	....	x---	----	x---	----	----	2	
		1583	1214		....	....	x---	---x	x---	----	-x?-	2	
		1584	08		....	....	x---	----	x---	----	-x--	2	
		1587	....		....	....	x---	---x	x---	----	----	2	
		1592	....		....	....	x---	----	x---	----	----	2	
		1598	12		**1599**	....	x---	----	x---	----	----	2	
		1611	....		....	....	x---	----	x---	----	----	2	
		1612	0812		....	....	x---	----	x---	----	----	2	
		1613	0808		....	....	x---	---x	x---	----	----	2	
		1620	0603		....	....	x---	---x	x---	----	----	2	
		1631	12		....	....	x---	---x	x---	----	--?-	2	
		1637	0929		**1637**	1005	x---	----	x---	----	----	2	
		1649	07		**1649**	08	x---	----	x---	----	----	2	
		1668	02		....	....	x---	----	x---	----	----	2	
		1668	08		**1669**	....	x---	---x	x---	----	----	2	
		1671	....		....	....	x---	----	x---	----	----	2	
		1675	0216		....	....	x---	----	x---	----	----	2	
		1683	06		....	....	x---	----	--?-	----	----	2	
		1691	04		**1691**	08	x---	----	x---	----	----	2	
	?	**1708**	0917		....	....	x---	---?	?---	----	----	2	
		1709	0213		....	....	x---	---x	x---	----	----	2	
	?	**1753**	....		**?1754**	....	x---	----	?---	----	----	2?	
		1765	01 ?		**1765**	10 ?	x---	----	x---	----	-xx-	3?	
		1772	....		**1780**	....	x---	----	x---	----	-x--	2	
		1781	....		**1788**	....	x---	----	x---	----	----	1	
		1804	0905		....	....	x---	---x	x---	----	----	2	
		1806	06 ?		**1806**	10 ?	x---	----	x---	----	-xx-	2	
		1814	....		....	....	x---	----	x---	----	----	2	
		1815	0210		**1815**	10	x---	----	x---	----	-x--	2	
		1816	0609		**1816**	0706	x---	----	x---	----	x---	2	
		1826	1003	+	**1826**	1122	x---	----	x---	----	-x--	2	
		1827	05		....	....	x---	----	x---	----	-x--	2	
		1827	1112		**1828**	01	x---	----	x---	----	x---	2	
		1828	06 <		....	....	x---	----	x---	----	-x--	2	
		1829	06		....	....	x---	----	x---	----	----	2	
		1830	0216		**1830**	03	x---	----	x---	----	-x--	2	
		1830	0811		**1832**	08	x---	---x	x---	----	-x--	2	
		1835	0501		....	....	x---	----	x---	----	----	2	
		1837	1008		....	....	x---	----	x---	----	----	2	
		1838	0304		....	....	x---	----	x---	----	----	2	
		1854	0226		....	....	x---	---x	x---	----	x---	2	
		1856	0318		**1856**	0613	x---	----	x---	----	----	2	
		1872	1201	+	**1873**	0608	x---	---x	x---	----	xx?-	3*	
		1874	0207		....	....	x---	----	x---	----	----	2	
		1884	0321	+	**1884**	06	x---	----	x---	----	----	2	
		1894	0306	+	**1894**	0830	x---	----	x---	----	----	2	
		1897	0224d		....	....	x---	----	x---	----	----	2	
(all historical eruptions from Naka-dake) ...		**1898**	08 ?		**1899**	....	x---	----	x---	----	----	2	

VOLCANO NAME (Subregion) / ERUPTION — Area of Activity	LAT	LONG	ELEV (m)	TYPE	NUMBER	Status / Start Year	Start M-Dy	P	Stop Year	Stop M-Dy	Central / Flank vent / Radial fiss / Regional*	Submarine / New island / Subglacial / Crater lake	Explosive / Pyro flow / Phreatic / Fumarolic	Lava flow / Lava lake / Dome / Spine	Fatal / Damage / Mudflow / Tsunami	VEI	Vol L/T
ASO (Kyushu) *continued*		(all historical eruptions from Naka-dake) ...				**1906**	0607		....	....	x---	----	x---	----	----	3	
						1907	1212		....	....	x---	----	x---	----	----	2	
						1908	0117		**1908**	0129?	x---	----	x---	----	----	2	
						1909	04		....	....	x---	----	x---	----	----	2	
						1910	0403		....	....	x---	----	?---	----	----	2	
						1911	....		**1912**	....	x---	----	x---	----	----	2	
						1914	0113		....	....	x---	----	x---	----	----	2	
						1916	0419		....	....	x---	----	x---	----	----	2	
						1918	0116		....	....	x---	----	x-x-	----	----	2	
						1919	04		**1919**	05	x---	----	x---	----	----	2	
						1920	....		....	....	x---	----	x---	----	----	2	
						1923	01		**1923**	0917	x---	----	x---	----	----	2	
						1925	0106		....	....	x---	----	x---	----	----	2	
						1926	0921		**1928**	0113	x---	----	x---	----	-x--	2	
						1928	0906	+	**1929**	1023	x---	----	x---	----	-x--	2	
						1930	0903		**1930**	0906	x---	----	x---	----	----	2	
						? **1931**	1018		....	....	x---	----	--?-	----	----	1?	
						1932	06	+	**1933**	0928	x---	---x	x---	----	-x--	2	
						1934	0716		....	....	x---	----	x---	----	----	2	
						1935	0107	+	**1935**	1008	x---	----	x---	----	----	2	
						1936	0205		**1936**	0205	x---	----	x---	----	----	2	
						1936	0808		**1936**	0814	x---	----	x---	----	----	2	
						1937	0113		**1937**	0113	x---	----	x---	----	----	2	
						1937	0507		**1937**	0513	x---	----	x---	----	----	2	
						1938	....	+	**1939**	0811	x---	----	x---	----	----	2	
						1940	0420	+	**1941**	0808	x---	----	x---	----	-x--	2	
						? **1942**	0608		?**1942**	0622	x---	----	----	----	----	1?	
						1943	0621		**1943**	0624	x---	----	x---	----	----	2	
						1943	1209		**1944**	02	x---	----	x---	----	----	2	
						1945	0916		**1945**	0919	x---	----	x---	----	----	2	
						1946	0429	+	**1946**	0624	x---	----	x---	----	----	2	
						1946	1230		**1946**	1230	x---	----	x---	----	----	2	
						1947	0526	+	**1947**	09	x---	----	x---	----	-x--	2	
						1948	0409	+	**1948**	12	x---	----	x---	----	----	1	
						1949	1226		**1949**	0415	x---	----	x---	----	----	2	
						1950	11		**1951**	01	x---	----	x---	----	----	2	
						1951	0504		**1951**	08	x---	----	x---	----	----	2	
						? **1952**	....		....	....	x---	----	----	----	----		
						1953	0427	+	**1953**	0730	x---	----	x---	----	xx--	2	
						1953	12		**1953**	12	x---	----	x---	----	----	1	
						1954	0526		**1954**	0526	x---	----	x---	----	----	1	
						1955	0725		**1955**	0728	x---	----	x---	----	----	1	
						1956	0103?		**1956**	0113	x---	----	x---	----	----	2	
						1956	08		....	....	x---	----	x---	----	----	2	
		(all historical eruptions from Naka-dake)				**1956**	1221		**1956**	1221	x---	----	x---	----	----	1	
						1957	0412		**1957**	0412	x---	----	x---	----	----	1	
						1957	10	+	**1958**	12	x---	----	x---	----	xx--	2*	-/5
						1959	07	+	**1957**	1002	x---	----	x---	----	----	1	
						1960	01		**1960**	0409	x---	----	x---	----	----	2	
						1960	09	+	**1962**	11	x---	----	x-x-	----	----	1	
						1963	0421	+	**1963**	07	x---	----	x---	----	----	1	
						1963	1110	+	**1964**	01	x---	----	x---	----	----	2	
						1964	0514		**1964**	0514	x---	----	x---	----	----	1	
						1964	10	+	**1966**	12	x---	---x	x-x-	----	-x--	2*	
						1967	05	+	**1969**	12	x---	---x	x---	----	----	1	
						1970	0421	+	**1972**	09	x---	---x	x---	----	----	2	
						1973	01	+	**1975**	06	x---	----	x---	----	-x--	2	
						1975	10		**1976**	0113	x---	----	x---	----	----	1	
						1977	0411		**1978**	08	x---	---x	x---	----	-x--	2	
						1979	02	+	**1980**	0308	x---	---x	x-x-	----	xx--	2*	
						1980	0924		**1980**	0924	x---	---x	x-x-	----	----	1	
						1981	0615		**1981**	0615	x---	---x	x-x-	----	----	1	
						1983	07		**1983**	10	x---	---x	--x-	----	----	1	
						1984	0413c	+	**1985**	0624	x---	---x	x-x-	----	----	1	
						1988	0526e		**1988**	0526e	x---	---x	--x-	----	----	1	
						1988	1228		**1988**	1228	x---	----	x-x-	----	----	1	
						1989	0405	+	**1991**	0209	x---	---x	xxx-	----	-x--	2*	
						1992	0423		**1993**	03 ?	x---	---x	x-x-	----	----	2*	
KUJU GROUP (Kyushu)	**33.08**	**N 131.25 E**	**1788**	**Stratovolcs**	**0802-12=**	**Historical**											
						1662?	0126?		....	....	x---	----	x---	----	----	3	
						1675	06 ?		....	....	----	----	?---	----	----	3↑	
TSURUMI (Kyushu)	**33.28**	**N 131.43 E**	**1374**	**Lava domes**	**0802-13=**	**Historical**											
Yufu-dake						T **0200y**	....		....	....	x---	----	xx--	--x-	----	4	
						0771	....		....	....	x---	----	----	--x-	----	0	
						0867	0304		**0867**	0504m	x---	---?	x---	----	-x--	3	

HONSHU

VOLCANO NAME (Subregion) / ERUPTION — Area of Activity	LAT	LONG	ELEV (m)	TYPE	NUMBER	Status / Start Year	Start M-Dy	P	Stop Year	Stop M-Dy	Central / Flank vent / Radial fiss / Regional*	Submarine / New island / Subglacial / Crater lake	Explosive / Pyro flow / Phreatic / Fumarolic	Lava flow / Lava lake / Dome / Spine	Fatal / Damage / Mudflow / Tsunami	VEI	Vol L/T
ABU (Honshu)	**34.50**	**N 131.60 E**	**571**	**Shields**	**0803-001**	**Holocene**											
SANBE (Honshu)	**35.13**	**N 132.62 E**	**1126**	**Caldera**	**0803-002**	**Radiocarbon**											
						C **-1650?**	....		....	....	----	----	xx--	----	----	4?	
OKI-DOGO (Honshu-W of)	**36.17**	**N 133.33 E**	**151**	**Shield**	**0803-003**	**Anthropology**											
DAISEN (Honshu)	**35.37**	**N 133.55 E**	**1731**	**Stratovolc**	**0803-004**	**Holocene**											
KANNABE (Honshu)	**35.50**	**N 134.68 E**	**460**	**Shield**	**0803-005**	**Holocene**											
IZU-TOBU (Honshu)...............	**34.92**	**N 139.12 E**	**1406**	**Pyrocl cones**	**0803-01=**	**Historical**											
Akakubo						T **-8050?**	....		....	....	xx--	----	x---	x---	----	3	6/7
Omuro-yama						T **-3050?**	....		....	....	xx--	----	x---	x-x-	----	4	8/8
Kawagodaira						C **-1090x**	....		....	....	x---	----	xx--	x-x-	----	4+	8/8
Iwanoyama-Izuzan						T **-0050?**	....		....	....	x--x	----	x---	--x-	----	3	8/8
3.6 km NE of Teishi-jima						? **1930**	0301p		....	....	----	?---	----	----	----		
Teishi-kaikyu (4 km NE of Ito City)........						**1989**	0713		**1989**	0713	----	x---	--x-	----	----	1	-/5
HAKONE (Honshu)	**35.22**	**N 139.02 E**	**1438**	**Complx volc**	**0803-02=**	**Radiocarbon**											
NW side of Kami-yama.................						C **-1150v**	....		....	....	x---	----	--x-	----	----		
NW side of Kami-yama.................						C **-0950v**	....		....	....	x---	----	xx--	--xx	----		
FUJI (Honshu)	**35.35**	**N 138.73 E**	**3776**	**Stratovolc**	**0803-03=**	**Historical**											
South flank? (Mishima).................						C **-8540>**	....		....	....	-x--	----	----	x---	----		9/-
						C **-7820x**	....		....	....	x---	----	x---	----	----		

VOLCANO NAME (Subregion) / ERUPTION — Area of Activity	LAT	LONG	ELEV (m)	TYPE	NUMBER	Status / Start Year	Start M-Dy	P	Stop Year	Stop M-Dy	Central, Flank vent, Radial fiss, Regional / Submarine, New island, Subglacial, Crater lake / Explosive, Pyro flow, Phreatic, Fumarolic / Lava flow, Lava lake, Dome, Spine / Fatal, Damage, Mudflow, Tsunami	VEI	Vol L/T
FUJI (Honshu) *continued*						C **-7530y**	....		....	....	x--- ---- x--- ---- ----		
						C **-7305z**	....		....	....	x--- ---- ---- x--- ----		
						C **-6580<**	....		....	....	x--- ---- ---- x--- ----		
						C **-6240y**	....		....	....	x--- ---- x--- ---- ----		
						T **-6050?**	....		....	....	---- ---- ---- x--- ----		
						C **-5540x**	....		....	....	x--- ---- x--- ---- ----		
						C **-5070x**	....		....	....	x--- ---- x--- ---- ----		
						T **-4730z**	....		....	....	x--- ---- x--- ---- ----		
						T **-4115y**	....		....	....	x--- ---- x--- ---- ----		
						C **-3690v**	....		....	....	x--- ---- x--- ---- ----		
						C **-3050?**	....		....	....	x--- ---- x--- ---- ----		
						T **-2800y**	....		....	....	x--- ---- x--- ---- ----		
						T **-2550?**	....		....	....	---- ---- ---- x--- ----		
						C **-2450z**	....		....	....	x--- ---- x--- ---- ----		
						C **-2050?**	....		....	....	---- ---- xx-- ---- ----		
						C **-1850w**	....		....	....	---- ---- xx-- ---- ----		
						T **-1200v**	....		....	....	x--- ---- x--- ---- ----		
						T **-1050?**	....		....	....	x--- ---- x--- ---- ----	5	-/9
NW flank (Omuro-yama)						T **-0950?**	....		....	....	-x-- ---- x--- x--- ----	4+	-/8
Upper SE flank						C **-0930>**	....		....	....	-x-- ---- x--- ---- ----	5	-/9
						C **-0540u**	....		....	....	x--- ---- xx-- ---- ----		
Summit and east flank?						C **-0520x**	....		....	....	xx-- ---- x--- ---- ----		
						C **-0350**	....		....	....	x--- ---- x--- ---- ----		
						T **-0185v**	....		....	....	x--- ---- x--- ---- ----		
South flank						C **-0095w**	....		....	....	-x-- ---- x--- x--- ----		
NW flank (Futatsuzuka)						T **0050?**	....		....	....	-x-- ---- x--- ---- ----	2	
NW flank (Ohira-yama)						T **0100?**	....		....	....	-x-- ---- x--- ---- ----	2	
NW flank (Sajiki-yama)						T **0200?**	....		....	....	-x-- ---- x--- ---- ----	2	
NE flank (Hinokimarubi)						T **0220?**	....		....	....	-x-- ---- x--- x--- ----	2	
SE flank						C **0240w**	....		....	....	-x-- ---- x?-- ---- --?-		
NW flank (Kita-Koriike)						T **0250?**	....		....	....	-x-- ---- x--- ---- ----	2	
NW flank (Oniwa-Okuniwa)						T **0300?**	....		....	....	-xx- ---- x--- x--- ----	1	
SE flank (Kurotsuka)						C **0350y**	....		....	....	-x-- ---- x--- x--- ----	3	
SSE flank (Obuchi Craters)						C **0365x**	....		....	....	-x-- ---- x--- x--- ----		
SE flank (Akatsuka)						T **0400?**	....		....	....	-x-- ---- x--- x--- ----	2	
SE flank (Kita-Kansu-yama)						C **0470v**	....		....	....	-x-- ---- x--- ---- ----	3?	
SE flank (Makuiwa, Nishi-Futatsuzuka)						C **0520v**	....		....	....	-x-- ---- x--- x--- ----	2	
South flank (Takabachi)						T **0530?**	....		....	....	-x-- ---- x--- x--- ----	3	
NW flank (Kori-ike, Hakudairyuo)						C **0720v**	....		....	....	-x-- ---- x--- x--- ----	2	
						0781	0804		....	....	---- ---- x--- ---- ----	3	
Summit and NW flank (Tenjin-yama)						**0800**	0415		**0800**	0519	xx-- ---- x--- x--- -x--	4	
NE flank (Takamarubi ?)						**0802**	0206		....	....	-x-- ---- x--- x--- -x--	2?	
						0826	....		....	....	---- ---- ?--- ---- ----	2?	
NW flank (Koriana)						**0830**	....		....	....	--x- ---- x--- x--- ----	2	
NW flank (Nagao-yama)						**0864**	06		**0865**	....	-x-- ---- x--- x--- -x--	3	8/-
						0870	....		....	....	x--- ---- x--- ---- ----	2?	
North flank (Kenmarubi I)						**0932**	1119		....	....	--x- ---- x--- x--- -x--	2?	
North flank (Kenmarubi II?)						**0937**	12		....	....	--x- ---- ---- x--- ----	0	
NE flank						? **0952**	03 ?		....	....	-x-- ---- ---- ---- ----		
						? **0993**	09 ?		....	....	---- ---- ---- ---- ----		
South flank ?						**0999**	03		....	....	-x-- ---- ?--- ?--- ----	2?	
North flank						? **1017**	....		....	....	-x-- ---- ---- ---- ----		
Summit, SSE flank (Nishi-Asakizuka)						**1033**	0125		....	....	xx-- ---- x--- x--- ----	2	
						1083	0325		....	....	---- ---- ---- ---- ----	2?	
						? **1427**	0707		....	....	---- ---- ?--- ---- ----		
						1511	....		....	....	---- ---- ---- x--- ----	2?	
						1560	....		....	....	---- ---- ---- ---- ----	2?	
(possibly confused with 1707 eruption)						? **1627**	....		....	....	---- ---- ---- ---- ----		
						1700	....		....	....	---- ---- ---- ---- ----	2?	
SE flank (Hoei Craters)						**1707**	1216	+	**1708**	0224?	-x-- ---- x--- ---- -xx-	5	-/9
						? **1709**	0116		....	....	---- ---- ?--- ---- ----		
TATESHINA (Honshu)	**36.10**	**N 138.30**	**E 2530**	**Stratovolcs**	**0803-031**	**Holocene**							
ON-TAKE (Honshu)	**35.90**	**N 137.48**	**E 3063**	**Complx volc**	**0803-04=**	**Historical**							
200 m SW of Kengamine						**1979**	1028		**1980**	0425	x--- ---- xxx- ---- -x--	1	
HAKU-SAN (Honshu)	**36.15**	**N 136.78**	**E 2702**	**Stratovolc**	**0803-05=**	**Historical**							
						T **-7550z**	....		....	....	x--- ---- x--- ---- ----		
						C **-7050?**	....		....	....	x--- ---- x-x- ---- ----		
						C **-6950?**	....		....	....	x--- ---- x-x- ---- ----		
						C **-6850?**	....		....	....	x--- ---- x-x- ---- ----		
						C **-4850?**	....		....	....	x--- ---- x-x- ---- ----		
						C **-4150?**	....		....	....	x--- ---- x-x- ---- ----		
						C **-2950?**	....		....	....	x--- ---- x-x- ---- ----		
						C **-2250?**	....		....	....	x--- ---- x-x- ---- ----		
						C **-2050?**	....		....	....	x--- ---- x-x- ---- ----		
						C **-1450?**	....		....	....	x--- ---- x-x- ---- ----		
Kengamine lava dome						C **-0350?**	....		....	....	x--- ---- x-x- x-x- ----		
						C **-0050?**	....		....	....	x--- ---- x-x- ---- ----		
						C **0150?**	....		....	....	x--- ---- x-x- ---- ----		
						C **0450?**	....		....	....	x--- ---- x-x- ---- ----		
						0706	09 ?		....	....	x--- ---- x-x- ---- ----		
						? **0853**	....		....	....	---- ---- ?--- ---- ----		
						? **0859**	....		....	....	---- ---- ?--- ---- ----		
						? **0900?**	....		....	....	---- ---- ?--- ---- ----		
Midoriga-ike						**1042**	....		....	....	x--- ---- --x- ---- -x--	3?	
						1177	0518		....	....	x--- ---- ?-x- ---- ----	3?	
(fire at summit shrine, no eruption)						X 1239	....		....	....	---- ---- ---- ---- ----		
						C **1250v**	....		....	....	x--- ---- x-x- ---- ----		
						1547	0304		**1547**	10 ?	x--- ---- x-x- ---- -x--	3	
						1548	....		....	....	x--- ---- ?-x- ---- ----	3?	
SW of Midoriga-ike						**1554**	04		**1556**	....	x--- ---- xxx- ---- -x--	3	
Jigoku-no-oana						**1579**	0927a		....	....	x--- ---x x-x- ---- -xx-	3	
						1582	....		....	....	x--- ---- x--- ---- ----	2	
						1640	07		....	....	x--- ---- x--- ---- ----	3?	
						1658	10 ?		....	....	x--- ---- x--- ---- ----	2?	
Midoriga-ike						**1659**	0421		**1659**	07 ?	x--- ---- x-x- ---- ----	2?	
NORIKURA (Honshu)	**36.12**	**N 137.55**	**E 3026**	**Stratovolcs**	**0803-06=**	**Holocene**							
YAKE-DAKE (Honshu)	**36.22**	**N 137.58**	**E 2455**	**Stratovolc**	**0803-07=**	**Historical**							
						T -0050?	....		....	....	---- ---- xx-- x--- ----	4	

VOLCANO NAME (Subregion)	LAT	LONG	ELEV (m)	TYPE	NUMBER	ERUPTION — Area of Activity	Status / Start Year	Start M-Dy	P	Stop Year	Stop M-Dy	Central / Flank vent / Radial fiss / Regional*	Submarine / New island / Subglacial / Crater lake	Explosive / Pyro flow / Phreatic / Fumarolic	Lava flow / Lava lake / Dome / Spine	Fatal / Damage / Mudflow / Tsunami	VEI	Vol L/T
YAKE-DAKE (Honshu) *continued*							@ **0686**	....		....	....	----	----	x---	----	----		
							1585	12 ?		....	....	-?--	----	--?-	----	-xx-	3↑	
						Summit crater (Shoga-ike)	**1907**	1208	+	**1909**	0601	x---	----	x-x-	----	----	2	
						Summit crater (Shoga-ike)	**1910**	1111		**1910**	1130	x---	----	x-x-	----	----	2	
						New summit crater (Inkyo-ko)	**1911**	0506		**1911**	0822	x---	----	x-x-	----	----	2	
							1912	0211		**1912**	0508	----	----	x-x-	----	----	2	
							1913	0901		....	....	----	----	x-x-	----	----	2	
						1911 summit crater, SE flank (Taisho)	**1915**	0606	+	**1915**	0716	x-x-	----	x-x-	----	-xx-	2	
						Taisho Crater	**1916**	0317		**1916**	0412	--x-	----	x-x-	----	----	2	
						Taisho Crater	**1917**	....		....	....	--x-	----	--x-	----	----	1	
						Taisho crater	**1918**	....		....	....	--x-	----	--x-	----	----	1	
						NW flank (Kurodani Crater)	**1919**	11		....	....	-x--	----	--x-	----	----	2	
							1920	....		....	....	----	----	--x-	----	----		
							1921	....		....	....	----	----	--x-	----	----		
							1922	....		....	....	----	----	--x-	----	----		
							1923	0626		....	....	----	----	--x-	----	----	2	
						Summit (Inkyo-ko), NW flank (Kurodani)	**1924**	1116	+	**1926**	0127	xx--	----	x-x-	----	----	2	
							1927	0123	+	**1927**	0429	----	----	x-x-	----	----	2	
							1927	1215		**1927**	1215	----	----	x-x-	----	----	2	
							1929	0417		**1929**	0419	----	----	x-x-	----	----	2	
							1930	0313		**1930**	0511	----	----	--x-	----	----	2	
							1931	0326		**1931**	0624	----	----	x-x-	----	-x--	2	
							1932	0206		....	....	----	----	--x-	----	----	2	
							1935	0911		**1935**	0912	----	----	--x-	----	----	2	
							1939	0604		....	....	----	----	--x-	----	----	2	
						North flank (Kurodani and Nakao-toge)	**1962**	0617	+	**1963**	0629	--x-	----	x-x-	----	-xx-	1	-/5
TATE-YAMA (Honshu)	**36.57**	**N 137.60**	**E 2621**	**Stratovolc**	**0803-08=**		**Historical**											
						Jigoku-dani	T **-2550***	....		....	....	x---	----	--x-	----	----		
						Jigoku-dani	T **-1000>**	....		....	....	x---	----	--x-	----	----		
						Jigoku-dani	**1839**	0610		....	....	x---	----	x-x-	----	----	2	
							? **1858**	0408		....	....	----	----	--?-	----	----		
NIIGATA-YAKE-YAMA (Honshu)	**36.92**	**N 138.03**	**E 2400**	**Lava dome**	**0803-09=**		**Historical**											
							T **-1300y**	....		....	....	x---	----	----	--x-	----		
							T **-0050?**	....		....	....	----	----	xx--	----	----	3	
							0887	....		....	....	x---	----	xx--	x---	-xx-	4	
							? **0989**	....		....	....	----	----	----	----	----		
							1361	....		....	....	x---	----	xx--	----	-xx-	3	
							1773	....		....	....	x---	----	xx--	----	-xx-	3	
						NW flank	**1852**	1101		....	....	-x--	----	--x-	----	----	2	
						NW flank	**1854**	....		....	....	-x--	----	--?-	----	----		
						NE-SW fissures, both sides of summit	**1949**	0205		**1949**	0913	--x-	----	x-x-	----	--x-	2	
							1962	0314		....	....	x---	----	--x-	----	----	1	
							1963	0710	+	**1963**	0930	--x-	----	--x-	----	----	1	
						WNW and NNE side of lava dome	**1974**	0728		**1974**	0728	--x-	----	xxx-	----	xxx-	2	-/5
							1983	0415		**1983**	0415	x---	----	x-x-	----	----	1	
							1987	0425e		....	....	----	----	x-?-	----	----	1?	
						Upper East flank	**1989**	0419	+	**1989**	0426	-x--	----	x-x-	----	----	1	
MYOKO (Honshu)	**36.88**	**N 138.12**	**E 2446**	**Stratovolc**	**0803-10=**		**Radiocarbon**											
							C **-3930x**	....		....	....	x---	----	xx--	----	----		
							C **-2760w**	....		....	....	x---	----	xx--	----	----		
KUROHIME (Honshu)	**36.80**	**N 138.13**	**E 2053**	**Stratovolc**	**0803-101**		**Holocene**											
IIZUNA (Honshu)	**36.73**	**N 138.13**	**E 1917**	**Stratovolc**	**0803-102**		**Holocene**											
ASAMA (Honshu)	**36.40**	**N 138.53**	**E 2560**	**Complx volc**	**0803-11=**		**Historical**											
							C **-3450?**	....		....	....	x---	----	x---	----	----	3	
							A **-2550z**	....		....	....	x---	----	x---	----	----	4	
							A **0350j**	1115m		....	....	x---	----	xx--	x---	-x--	4	
							0685	04		....	....	x---	----	x---	----	----	3	
							0887	....		....	....	x---	----	?---	----	----	3↑	
							1108	0905		**1108**	10	x---	----	xx--	x---	----	**5**	**-/9**
							1281	0703		....	....	x---	----	xx--	----	----	3	
							? **1427**	0707		....	....	x---	----	?---	----	----		
							1518	....		....	....	x---	----	?---	----	----		
							1527	05		....	....	x---	----	x---	----	----	2	
							1528	....		....	....	x---	----	x---	----	----	2	
							1532	0114		....	....	x---	----	x---	----	-xx-	3	
							1590	0415q		....	....	x---	----	x---	----	----	2?	
							1591	0415q		**1591**	1129?	x---	----	x---	----	----	3*	
							? **1595**	0601		....	....	x---	----	?---	----	----		
							1596	0501		**1596**	0505	x---	----	x---	----	x---	2?	
							1596	0819		....	....	x---	----	x---	----	x---	2	
							1597	0417		....	....	x---	----	x---	----	----	2	
							1598	0513		....	....	x---	----	x---	----	x---	2	
							1600	0114		**1600**	0128?	x---	----	x---	----	----	3?	
							1604	....		....	....	x---	----	?---	----	----	2	
							1605	12		....	....	x---	----	x---	----	----	2	
							1609	04		....	....	x---	----	x---	----	----	2	
							1644	0220		....	....	x---	----	x---	----	----	2	
							1645	0224	+	**1645**	0521	x---	----	x---	----	----	2	
							1647	0218	+	**1647**	0325	x---	----	x---	----	----	2	
							1648	0322		....	....	x---	----	x---	----	----	2	
							1648	0829		....	....	x---	----	x---	----	----	2	
							1649	0817		**1649**	0818	x---	----	x---	----	----	2	
							? **1650**	0702		....	....	x---	----	?---	----	----		
							1651	0412		....	....	x---	----	x---	----	----	2	
							1652	0412		....	....	x---	----	x---	----	----	2	
							1653	1231y		....	....	x---	----	?---	----	----	2	
							1655	1125		....	....	x---	----	x---	----	----	2	
							1656	1210		....	....	x---	----	x---	----	----	2	
							1657	1125		....	....	x---	----	x---	----	----	2	
							1658	0724		....	....	x---	----	x---	----	----	2	
							1659	0724		....	....	x---	----	x---	----	----	2	
							1660	0408		....	....	x---	----	x---	----	----	2	
							1661	0414	+	**1661**	0427	x---	----	x---	----	----	2	
							1661	1021		....	....	x---	----	x---	----	----	2	
							1669	0405	+	**1669**	0415	x---	----	x---	----	----	2	
							1703	....		....	....	x---	----	x---	----	----	2	
							1704	0205		**1704**	0209	x---	----	x---	----	----	2	

VOLCANO NAME (Subregion) ...... LAT LONG ELEV (m) TYPE NUMBER / ERUPTION — Area of Activity	Status	Start Year	Start M-Dy	P	Stop Year	Stop M-Dy	Central / Flank vent / Radial fiss / Regional*	Submarine / New island / Subglacial / Crater lake	Explosive / Pyro flow / Phreatic / Fumarolic	Lava flow / Lava lake / Dome / Spine	Fatal / Damage / Mudflow / Tsunami	VEI	Vol L/T
ASAMA (Honshu) *continued*		**1706**	1120		....	....	x---	----	x---	----	----	2	
		1708	1229		**1709**	0108	x---	----	x---	----	----	2	
		1710	0413		....	....	x---	----	x---	----	----	2	
		1711	0413		....	....	x---	----	x---	----	----	2	
		1717	0923		....	....	x---	----	x---	----	----	2	
		1718	0926		....	....	x---	----	x---	----	----	2	
	@	**1719**	0610		@**1719**	0611	----	----	x---	----	----		
		1720	0606		....	....	x---	----	x---	----	----	2	
		1721	0622		....	....	x---	----	x---	----	x---	1	
		1722	1118?		**1722**	1204?	x---	----	x---	----	----	2	
		1723	0205		....	....	x---	----	x---	----	----	2	
		1723	0820		....	....	x---	----	x---	----	----	2	
		1728	1110		....	....	x---	----	x---	----	----	2	
		1729	02		....	....	x---	----	x---	----	----	2	
		1729	11 ?		....	....	x---	----	x---	----	----	2	
		1731	....		....	....	x---	----	x---	----	----	2	
		1732	0730		....	....	x---	----	x---	----	----	2	
		1733	0730		....	....	x---	----	x---	----	----	2	
		1754	0807	+	**1754**	0819	x---	----	x---	----	----	2	
		1755	0705		**1755**	0806	x---	----	x---	----	----	2	
		1762	04		....	....	x---	----	x---	----	----	2	
	@	**1769**	0806		....	....	----	----	x---	----	----		
		1776	0905		....	....	x---	----	x---	----	----	2	
		1777	....		....	....	x---	----	x---	----	----	2	
	?	**1779**	09 ?		....	....	----	----	x---	----	----		
		1783	0509	+	**1783**	0805	x---	----	xx--	x---	xxx-	4*	8/8
		1803	0704		....	....	x---	----	x---	----	?---	2	
		1803	1107		**1803**	1121	x---	----	x---	----	?---	2	
		1815	0228		....	....	x---	----	x---	----	----	3	
		1869	05	+	**1869**	10	x---	----	x---	----	----	2	
		1875	0614		....	....	x---	----	x---	----	----	2	
	?	**1878**	....		....	....	x---	----	x---	----	----	2	
		1879	0927		**1879**	0928	x---	----	x---	----	----	2	
		1889	1224		....	....	x---	----	x---	----	----	2	
		1894	0406		**1894**	0614	x---	----	x---	----	----	2	
		1899	0311		....	....	x---	----	x---	----	----	2	
		1899	0710		**1899**	0807	x---	----	x---	----	----	2	
		1900	0122	+	**1901**	10	x---	----	x---	----	x---	2	
		1902	0207		**1902**	0207	x---	----	x---	----	----	2	
		1902	0805		**1902**	0805	x---	----	x---	----	----	2	
		1903	0528		**1903**	0630	x---	----	x---	----	----	2	
		1904	0804		**1904**	0804	x---	----	x---	----	----	2	
	?	**1905**	....		....	....	----	----	?---	----	----		
		1906	0406		**1906**	0406	x---	----	x---	----	----	2	
		1907	0118	+	**1907**	0328	x---	----	x---	----	----	2	
		1907	0824		**1907**	0824	x---	----	x---	----	----	2	
		1908	0213		**1908**	0219	x---	----	x---	----	----	2	
		1908	0805	+	**1908**	0923	x---	----	x---	----	----	2	
		1909	0129	+	**1914**	0624	x---	----	x---	----	xx--	2	
		1914	1112		**1914**	1216	x---	----	x---	----	----	2	
		1915	0513		**1915**	0827	x---	----	x---	----	----	1	
		1916	0512		**1916**	1002	x---	----	x---	----	----	1	
		1917	0503		**1917**	0731	x---	----	x---	----	----	1	
	?	**1918**	....		....	....	?---	----	?---	----	----		
		1919	0314	+	**1919**	0827	x---	----	x---	----	----	2	
		1920	1210	+	**1921**	0629	x---	----	x---	----	----	2	
		1922	0114		**1922**	04	x---	----	x---	----	----	2	
		1924	0907		**1924**	0929	x---	----	x---	----	----	2	
		1927	03	+	**1928**	0725	x---	----	x---	----	----	2	
		1929	0122	+	**1929**	0405	x---	----	x---	----	----	2	
		1929	0918	+	**1929**	1115	x---	----	x---	----	----	2	
		1930	0418	+	**1930**	10	x---	----	x---	----	x---	2	
		1931	03	+	**1932**	0903	x---	----	x---	----	xx--	3*	
		1933	0109		**1933**	0803	x---	----	x---	----	----	2	
		1934	0109		**1934**	0211	x---	----	x---	----	----	2	
		1934	06		**1934**	06	x---	----	x---	----	----	2	
		1935	01	+	**1937**	07	x---	----	x?--	----	x---	3*	
		1938	03	+	**1942**	12	x---	----	x---	----	x---	2	
		1944	06	+	**1945**	11	x---	----	x---	----	----	2	
		1946	10		**1946**	10	x---	----	x---	----	----	2	
E corner of crater bottom		**1947**	06	+	**1947**	0814	x---	----	x---	----	xx--	2	
		1949	03	+	**1949**	10	x---	----	x---	----	----	2	
		1950	0923	+	**1951**	06	x---	----	x---	----	xx--	2	
		1952	01		**1952**	01	x---	----	x---	----	----	2	
		1952	0609		**1952**	0609	x---	----	x---	----	----	2	
		1953	1227	+	**1955**	0802	x---	----	x---	----	----	3*	
(no eruption in December 1955)..........	X	1955	12		....	....	----	----	----	----	----		
		1958	1003	+	**1959**	0826e	x---	----	xx--	----	-x--	2*	-/5
		1961	0818		**1961**	1116	x---	----	xx--	----	xx--	2	-/4
		1965	0523		**1965**	0523	x---	----	x---	----	----	2	
		1973	0201		**1973**	0524	x---	----	xx--	----	----	2	
		1982	0426		**1982**	0426	x---	----	xxx-	----	-x--	2	
		1982	1002		**1982**	1002	x---	----	x---	----	----	1	
		1983	0408		**1983**	0408	x---	----	x---	----	----	2	
		1990	0720		**1990**	0720	x---	----	x---	----	----	2	
KUSATSU-SHIRANE (Honshu)...... **36.62 N 138.55 E 2176 Stratovolcs 0803-12=**	**Historical**												
	C	**-6270**x	....		....	....	----	----	x-x-	----	----		
Shirane............................	C	**-5050**?	....		....	....	x---	----	x---	x---	----		
Shirane............................	C	**-2900**w	....		....	....	x---	----	x-x-	----	----	2	-/6
Moto-Shirane	C	**-1120**w	....		....	....	x---	----	x-x-	x---	----		
	C	**1470**w	....		....	....	----	----	x-x-	----	----		
Yu-gama...........................		**1805**	....		....	....	x---	----	x-?-	----	----	2	
Yu-gama, NE end of Kara-gama		**1882**	0806		**1882**	0816>	x---	---x	x-x-	----	--x-	2	
Yu-gama and NE part of Yu-gama........		**1897**	0708		**1897**	0816	x---	---x	x-x-	----	----	2	
NE part of Yu-gama		**1900**	1001		**1900**	1001	x---	----	--x-	----	----	1	
North side of Yumi-ike		**1902**	0715		**1902**	12	x---	----	x-x-	----	----	2	
	?	**1903**	....		....	....	----	----	----	----	----		
Yu-gama...........................		**1905**	10		**1905**	10	x---	---x	--xx	----	----	2	

VOLCANO NAME (Subregion) / ERUPTION —	LAT	LONG	ELEV (m)	TYPE	NUMBER	Status / Area of Activity		Start Year	Start M-Dy	P	Stop Year	Stop M-Dy	Central / Flank vent / Radial fiss / Regional*	Submarine / New island / Subglacial / Crater lake	Explosive / Pyro flow / Phreatic / Fumarolic	Lava flow / Lava lake / Dome / Spine	Fatal / Damage / Mudflow / Tsunami	VEI	Vol L/T
KUSATSU-SHIRANE (Honshu) *continued*						Northern part of Yu-gama		**1925**	0122?		**1925**	0130	x---	----	x-x-	----	----	2	
						North part of Yu-gama and S outer rim		**1927**	1229		**1927**	1231	x---	----	x-x-	----	----	2	
						NE part of Yu-gama, SE outer rim		**1932**	1001		**1932**	11	x---	----	--x-	----	xxx-	3*	-/4
							?	**1933**	....		....	....	----	----	----	----	----		
								1934	....		....	....	x---	----	x-x-	----	----	2	
						Yu-gama		**1937**	1127	+	**1937**	1231	x---	----	x-x-	----	----	2	
							?	**1938**	0717		....	....	x---	----	----	----	----		
						Yu-gama		**1939**	02		**1939**	0501	x---	----	x-x-	----	----	2	
						Fissure east and south of Yu-gama		**1942**	0202		....	....	x---	----	x-x-	----	----	1	
								1958	....		....	....	x---	----	x-x-	----	----	1	
						NE corner of Mizu-gama Crater		**1976**	0302		**1976**	0302	x---	----	x-x-	----	----	2	
						Kara-gama, Yu-gama		**1982**	1026	+	**1982**	1229	x---	---x	x-x-	----	----	1	
						Yu-gama, Kara-gama		**1983**	0726	+	**1983**	1221	x---	----	x-x-	----	----	1	
						NW part of Yu-gama	?	**1989**	0106		?**1989**	0106	x---	---x	x-x-	----	----	1	
SHIGA (Honshu)	**36.70 N**	**138.52 E**	**2036**	**Shields**	**0803-121**	**Holocene**													
HARUNA (Honshu)	**36.47 N**	**138.88 E**	**1449**	**Stratovolc**	**0803-122**	**Anthropology**													
						Futatsu-dake	T	**0450**t	....		....	....	x---	----	x---	----	----	3	-/7
						Futatsu-dake	A	**0520**j	0601p		....	....	x---	----	xx--	----	-xx-	4+	-/8
						Futatsu-dake	A	**0550**j	0601p		....	....	x---	----	xx--	--x-	-xx-	**5**	8/9
AKAGI (Honshu)	**36.53 N**	**139.18 E**	**1828**	**Stratovolc**	**0803-13=**	**Historical**													
								1251	0518		....	....	----	----	----	----	----	3?	
							?	**1938**	0716<		....	....	----	----	----	----	----		
HIUCHI (Honshu)	**36.95 N**	**139.28 E**	**2346**	**Stratovolc**	**0803-131**	**Holocene**													
NIKKO-SHIRANE (Honshu)	**36.80 N**	**139.38 E**	**2578**	**Shield**	**0803-14=**	**Historical**													
						Shirane-san		**1625**	....		....	....	----	----	--?-	----	----	3	
						Shirane-san		**1649**	....		....	....	x---	----	x-x-	----	----	3	
						Shirane-san	?	**1871**	04		....	....	----	----	----	----	----		
						Shirane-san (SW side)		**1872**	0514		....	....	-x--	----	--x-	----	----	2	
						Shirane-san		**1873**	0312		....	....	----	----	--x-	----	----	2	
						Shirane-san (west flank)		**1889**	1204		....	....	-x--	----	x-x-	----	----	2	
NANTAI (Honshu)	**36.77 N**	**139.50 E**	**2484**	**Stratovolc**	**0803-141**	**Holocene**													
OMANAGO GROUP (Honshu)	**36.78 N**	**139.50 E**	**2375**	**Lava domes**	**0803-142**	**Holocene**													
TAKAHARA (Honshu)	**36.90 N**	**139.78 E**	**1795**	**Stratovolc**	**0803-143**	**Holocene**													
NASU (Honshu)	**37.12 N**	**139.97 E**	**1917**	**Stratovolcs**	**0803-15=**	**Historical**													
						Chausu-dake	T	**-8050**?	....		....	....	----	----	----	x---	----		
							C	**-4050**?	....		....	....	----	----	xx--	----	----		
						Chausu-dake		**1397**	0217		....	....	x---	----	x-?-	----	-x--	3	
						Chausu-dake		**1404**	0211		....	....	x---	----	x---	----	----	3	
						Chausu-dake		**1408**	0224		....	....	x---	----	x---	----	----	3	
						Chausu-dake		**1410**	0305		....	....	x---	----	x---	----	xx--	2	
						Chausu-dake		**1846**	08		....	....	x---	----	?---	----	----	2	
						Chausu-dake		**1881**	0701		....	....	x---	----	x---	----	-x--	2?	
						Chausu-dake		**1953**	1024		**1953**	1029	x---	----	x-x-	----	----	1	
						Chausu-dake (50 m north of 1953 vent)		**1960**	1010?		....	....	x---	----	x-x-	----	----	1	
						Chausu-dake	?	**1963**	0710		?**1963**	0711	x---	----	--?-	----	----	1	
						Chausu-dake (west side)		**1963**	1120		**1963**	1121	x---	----	x-x-	----	----	1	
NUMAZAWA (Honshu)	**37.43 N**	**139.58 E**	**1100**	**Shield**	**0803-151**	**Radiocarbon**													
							C	**-3040**?	....		....	....	x---	----	xx--	----	----	**5?**	**-/9**
BANDAI (Honshu)	**37.60 N**	**140.08 E**	**1819**	**Stratovolc**	**0803-16=**	**Historical**													
								0806	....		....	....	x---	----	--?-	----	--?-	3	
							?	**1611**	....		....	....	x---	----	--?-	----	--x-		
							?	**1719**<	....		....	....	x---	----	----	----	----		
						Mt. Hanzawa (Bandai foothills)	?	**1767**n	....		....	....	-x--	----	--?-	----	--?-		
								1787<	....		....	....	x---	----	--?-	----	----	2?	
						Numano-taira		**1808**?	....		....	....	x---	----	--?-	----	--x-	2	
						Kobandai		**1888**	0715		**1888**	0715	x---	----	xxx-	----	xxx-	4	-/8
ADATARA (Honshu)	**37.62 N**	**140.28 E**	**1718**	**Stratovolcs**	**0803-17=**	**Historical**													
							?	**1813**	0110		....	....	----	----	----	----	----		
						Numano-taira		**1899**	0824	+	**1899**	1112	x---	----	x---	----	-x--	2	
						Numano-taira		**1900**	0717		**1900**	0717	x---	----	xx?-	----	xx--	2	-/6
AZUMA (Honshu)	**37.73 N**	**140.25 E**	**2024**	**Stratovolcs**	**0803-18=**	**Historical**													
						Issaikyo	?	**1331**	....		....	....	----	----	--?-	----	----		
						Issaikyo	?	**1711**?	....		....	....	----	----	----	----	----		
						Issaikyo (Oana)		**1800**?	....		....	....	-x--	----	--?-	----	----		
						Issaikyo (Oana)	?	**1844**	....		....	....	-x--	----	--x-	----	----	1?	
						Issaikyo (west of Oana)		**1893**	0519		**1893**	0713	-x--	----	x-x-	----	x---	2	
						Issaikyo		**1894**	0316	+	**1894**	0412	----	----	x-?-	----	----	2	
						Issaikyo		**1895**	0308	+	**1895**	0919	----	----	x-x-	----	-x--	2	
						Issaikyo (just S & SW of Oana)	?	**1896**	0905		?**1896**	0919	-x--	----	?-?-	----	----	2	
						Issaikyo		**1914**	....		....	....	----	----	--?-	----	----	1	
						Issaikyo (Oana and NW of Oana)		**1950**	0210	+	**1950**	0219	-x--	----	x-x-	----	----	1	
						Issaikyo		**1952**	0618		....	....	----	----	--x-	----	----	1	
						Issaikyo (Oana)		**1977**	1207		**1977**	1207	-x--	----	x-x-	----	----	1	
ZAO (Honshu)	**38.15 N**	**140.45 E**	**1841**	**Complx volc**	**0803-19=**	**Historical**													
						Okama	?	**0773**	11 ?		....	....	x---	----	----	----	----		
						Okama		**0884**	....		....	....	x---	----	?---	----	----	2?	
						Okama		**1183**	0528		....	....	x---	---x	?---	----	----	2?	
						Okama		**1227**	10 ?		....	....	x---	----	x-?-	----	-x--	3	
						Okama		**1230**	1129		....	....	x---	----	x---	----	----	2?	
						Okama	?	**1331**	....		?**1333**	....	x---	----	--?-	----	----	2?	
						Okama	?	**1350**?	....		....	....	x---	----	--?-	----	----	2?	
						Okama		**1620**	....		....	....	x---	---x	?---	----	----	2?	
						Okama		**1623**	01 ?		**1624**	1125	x---	---x	x---	----	----	3*	
						Okama		**1630**	....		....	....	x---	----	?---	----	----	2?	
						Okama		**1641**	....		....	....	x---	----	?---	----	----	2?	
						Okama		**1668**	....		....	....	x---	----	?---	----	----	2?	
						Okama		**1669**	....		....	....	x---	----	x---	----	-x--	3	
						Okama		**1670**	0426		**1670**	0813>	x---	----	x-x-	----	----	2*	
						Okama		**1694**	0529		**1694**	0830?	x---	---x	?-x-	----	-xx-	2	
						SE side of Okama		**1794**	0922		**1794**	12 >	x---	---x	x-?-	----	-x--	2	
						Okama		**1796**	0324		....	....	x---	---x	--?-	----	----	2	
						Okama		**1804**	05 ?		....	....	x---	---x	--?-	----	----	2	
						Okama		**1806**	0712		....	....	x---	----	--?-	----	----	2	
						Okama		**1809**	0612		**1809**	1229	x---	---x	x-?-	----	-?x-	2	
						Okama		**1821**	0127		**1821**	0501	x---	---x	x---	----	--x-	2*	
						Okama		**1830**	....		....	....	x---	---x	--?-	----	----	2	

VOLCANO NAME (Subregion) / ERUPTION —	LAT	LONG	ELEV (m)	TYPE	NUMBER	Status / Area of Activity	Start Year	Start M-Dy	P	Stop Year	Stop M-Dy	Central, Flank vent, Radial fiss, Regional*	Submarine, New island, Subglacial, Crater lake	Explosive, Pyro flow, Phreatic, Fumarolic	Lava flow, Lava lake, Dome, Spine	Fatal, Damage, Mudflow, Tsunami	VEI	Vol L/T
ZAO (Honshu) *continued*						Okama	**1831**	1122		....	....	x---	---x	--?-	----	--?-	2	
						Okama	**1833**	....		....	....	x---	---x	x-?-	----	----	2	
						Okama	**1867**	1021		....	....	x---	---x	--?-	----	x?x-	2	
						Okama	**1873**	08		**1873**	09	x---	----	--?-	----	----	1?	
						Okama	? **1890**	....		....	....	x---	----	--?-	----	----	1?	
						Okama	**1894**	0703		**1894**	0703	x---	---x	x-?-	----	----	2?	
						Okama	**1895**	0215	+	**1895**	0322	x---	---x	x-?-	----	--x-	2	
						Okama	**1895**	0822	+	**1895**	0927	x---	---x	--?-	----	-xx-	2	
						Okama	**1896**	0308		**1896**	0308	x---	----	x-x-	----	----	1	
						Okama	**1896**	0901?		....	....	x---	---x	--?-	----	----	1?	
						Okama	? **1897**	0114		?**1897**	0114	x---	----	--?-	----	----	1?	
						Okama	**1905**	....		....	....	x---	----	--?-	----	----	1?	
						(1906 report of eruption in 1905)	X 1906	....		....	....	----	----	----	----	----		
						Okama	? **1927**	....		....	....	x---	----	--?-	----	----	1?	
						Okama	? **1939**	07		....	....	x---	---x	--?-	----	--x-	1?	
						Okama	**1940**	0518		**1940**	0518	x---	---x	x-x-	----	----	1	
HIJIORI (Honshu)	**38.60**	**N 140.18 E**	**516**	**Caldera**	**0803-191**	**Radiocarbon**												
							C **-8300***	....		....	....	x---	----	xx--	----	----	**5**	
NARUGO (Honshu)	**38.73**	**N 140.73 E**	**462**	**Lava domes**	**0803-20=**	**Historical**												
							0837	0527		....	....	----	----	x---	----	--?-	1	
KURIKOMA (Honshu)	**38.95**	**N 140.78 E**	**1628**	**Stratovolc**	**0803-21=**	**Historical**												
						Tsurugi-yama	**1726**j	....		....	....	x---	----	--?-	----	----	1?	
							1744	0203		....	....	x---	----	--?-	----	----	2	
							? **1783**	....		....	....	x---	----	--?-	----	-x--		
							1944	1120		**1944**	12	x---	----	--x-	----	-xx-	1	
						SE of Tsurugiyama	**1946**	1124		....	....	x---	----	--x-	----	--x-	2	
							1950	0115		....	....	x---	----	--x-	----	----	2	
CHOKAI (Honshu)	**39.08**	**N 140.03 E**	**2230**	**Stratovolcs**	**0803-22=**	**Historical**												
							C **-0650**?	....		....	....	x---	----	--x-	----	----		
							0573	03 ?		....	....	----	----	x---	----	----		
							0577	1201p		**0578**	0715q	----	----	x---	x---	----		
							? **0610**o	....		....	....	----	----	?---	----	----		
							0711c	....		....	....	----	----	--?-	----	----		
							? **0717**	07		....	....	----	----	x---	----	----		
							0804	....		**0806**	....	x---	----	?---	----	----		
							0817g	....		....	....	----	----	?---	----	----		
							0829e	....		....	....	----	----	x---	----	--x-		
							0839	1014		....	....	----	----	?---	----	----		
							0856	....		....	....	----	----	----	----	----		
							0857	05		....	....	----	----	----	----	----		
							0861	05		....	....	----	----	?---	----	----	3	
							0871	0505		....	....	x---	----	x---	----	--x-	3	
							? **0884**	0726		?**0884**	08	----	----	?---	----	----		
							0915	0823		**0915**	0901	----	----	x---	----	-x--	3	
							0939	0515		....	....	----	----	?---	----	----		
							0948	1231y		....	....	----	----	----	----	----		
							? **0999**	....		....	....	----	----	----	----	----		
							? **1477**	....		....	....	----	----	?---	----	----		
							? **1560**	....		....	....	----	----	?---	----	----		
							1659	04		**1663**a	....	----	----	?---	----	----		
							1735	....		....	....	----	----	x---	----	----	2	
							1738	1231y		....	....	x---	----	x---	----	----	2	
						Small crater at foot of Kojin-yama	**1740**	06 ?		**1741**	10 ?	x---	----	x---	----	-x--	2?	
							1764	....		....	....	x---	----	x---	----	----	2	
						Shinzan (foot of Kojin-yama)	**1800**	12		**1804**	07 ?	x---	----	x---	--x-	x-x-	2*	7/-
						Near Shinzan and Shichiko-zan	**1821**	0523		....	....	x---	----	--?-	----	----	2?	
							1834	0709		**1834**	07	x---	----	x---	----	--?-	2?	
						E side of Shinzan, W of Kojin-yama	**1974**	0301	+	**1974**	0430	x---	----	x-x-	----	--x-	1	-/5
AKITA-KOMAGA-TAKE (Honshu)	**39.75**	**N 140.80 E**	**1637**	**Stratovolcs**	**0803-23=**	**Historical**												
							? **0807**	....		....	....	----	----	?---	----	----		
							T **1100**?	....		....	....	----	----	x---	----	----	2	
							1890	12		**1891**	01	x---	----	x---	----	----	2	
						Yoko-dake	? **1902**	....		....	....	-x--	----	--?-	----	----		
						Ishibora (south flank of Medake)	**1932**	0702		**1932**	0724	--x-	----	x-x-	----	--x-	2	
						Medake	**1970**	0918		**1971**	0126	xx--	----	x---	x---	----	1	6/5
IWATE (Honshu)	**39.85**	**N 141.00 E**	**2041**	**Complx volc**	**0803-24=**	**Historical**												
							1686	0323		**1686**	0326	-x--	----	x---	x---	-xx-	3?	
							1687	0414		**1687**	07	----	----	x---	----	----	3	
							1689	0622		....	....	----	----	x---	----	----	3	
						NE flank of Yakushi-dake	**1719**	02 ?		....	....	-x--	----	x---	x---	----	2	7/-
							1731	1226		**1732**	10 ?	----	----	x---	----	----	2	
						(earthquake swarm, not eruption)	X 1823	....		....	....	----	----	----	----	----		
						W side of Onigajo caldera (Ojigoku)	**1919**	07		**1919**	07	x---	----	x-x-	----	----	1	
						(increased smoke emission)	X 1934	07		X1934	09	----	----	---x	----	----		
HACHIMANTAI (Honshu)	**39.95**	**N 140.85 E**	**1614**	**Stratovolc**	**0803-25=**	**Holocene**												
AKITA-YAKE-YAMA (Honshu)	**39.97**	**N 140.77 E**	**1366**	**Complx volc**	**0803-26=**	**Historical**												
							? **0807**	1101		....	....	----	----	x---	----	----		
							? **1678**	0222		....	....	----	----	?---	----	----		
							1867	....		....	....	x---	----	--?-	----	----		
							1887	....		....	....	x---	----	--x-	----	----	2	
							1890	0923		....	....	x---	----	x-x-	----	----	2	
							1929	09		....	....	x---	----	x-x-	----	----	2	
						Kare-numa	**1948**	....		....	....	x---	----	--x-	----	----	1?	
						Kare-numa	**1949**	0830		**1949**	0831	x---	----	x-x-	----	--x-	2	
						Kare-numa	**1951**	02		....	....	x---	----	--x-	----	----	1?	
							1957	....		....	....	x---	----	--x-	----	--x-	1	
KANPU (Honshu)	**39.93**	**N 139.88 E**	**355**	**Lava dome**	**0803-261**	**Holocene**												
							? **1810**	0914		?**1810**	0926	----	----	--?-	----	----	1?	
MEGATA (Honshu)	**39.95**	**N 139.73 E**	**291**	**Maars**	**0803-262**	**Tephrochronology**												
							T **-7050**?	....		....	....	x---	----	xx--	----	----		
							T **-2050**?	....		....	....	x---	----	xx--	----	-x--		
IWAKI (Honshu)	**40.65**	**N 140.30 E**	**1625**	**Stratovolc**	**0803-27=**	**Historical**												
							1597	01		....	....	x---	----	--x-	----	----	2	
							1597	0613		....	....	x---	----	--x-	----	--x-	2	
						Torinoumi	**1600**	0222		....	....	x---	---x	--x-	----	--x-	2	
						Torinoumi	**1600**	0723		**1600**	0725	x---	---x	--x-	----	-xx-	2	

VOLCANO NAME (Subregion)	LAT	LONG	ELEV (m)	TYPE	NUMBER	ERUPTION — Area of Activity	Status / Start Year	Start M-Dy	P	Stop Year	Stop M-Dy	Central / Flank vent / Radial fiss / Regional*	Submarine / New island / Subglacial / Crater lake	Explosive / Pyro flow / Phreatic / Fumarolic	Lava flow / Lava lake / Dome / Spine	Fatal / Damage / Mudflow / Tsunami	VEI	Vol L/T
IWAKI (Honshu) *continued*						Torinoumi	**1604**	0207		....	....	x---	---x	--x-	----	--x-	3?	
							1605	0410		....	....	x---	----	--x-	----	----	2?	
							1618	0131		....	....	x---	----	x-?-	----	----	2	
							? **1672**	0712		?**1672**	0728	x---	----	--?-	----	----	2?	
							? **1694**	0619		....	....	x---	----	--?-	----	----	2?	
							? **1709**	0423		....	....	x---	----	--?-	----	----	2?	
							? **1769**	....		....	....	----	----	--?-	----	----		
						South flank	? **1782**	0412		....	....	-x--	----	--?-	----	----		
							1782	1201p		**1783**	0312	x---	----	--x-	----	----	2	
							? **1783**	1203		....	....	x---	----	--?-	----	----		
							1790	1009		....	....	x---	----	x-x-	----	----	2	
							1793	0402		....	....	x---	----	--x-	----	----	2	
							1794	0403		....	....	x---	----	--x-	----	----	2	
							1800	0511		....	....	x---	----	--?-	----	----	2	
							1807	0331		....	....	x---	----	--?-	----	----	2	
							1833	0411		....	....	x---	----	--?-	----	----	2	
						Summit and south flank?	**1844**	0407		....	....	x?--	----	--x-	----	----	2	
							1845	0404		....	....	x---	----	--x-	----	----	2	
							1848	0118		....	....	x---	----	--x-	----	----	2	
							1856	0520		....	....	x---	----	--?-	----	----	2	
							1863	0323		....	....	x---	----	--x-	----	----	1	
TOWADA (Honshu)	**40.47 N**	**140.92 E**	**1159**	**Stratovolc**	**0803-271**		**Historical**											
						Goshikiiwa	T **-7550**?	....		....	....	x---	----	x---	----	----	5	-/9
						Goshikiiwa	C **-6650**y	....		....	....	x---	----	x---	----	----	**5?**	-/9
						Goshikiiwa	T **-5050**?	....		....	....	x---	----	x---	----	----	4	-/8
						Goshikiiwa	T **-4050**?	....		....	....	x---	----	x---	----	----	3	-/8
						Goshikiiwa (Nakanoumi)	C **-3440**w	....		....	....	x---	----	xx--	----	----	**5+**	-/9
						Nakanoumi	T **-1050**?	....		....	....	x---	---x	x---	----	----	**4+**	-/8
						Goshikiiwa (NE rim Nakanoumi crater)	**0915**	0817?		....	....	x---	----	xx--	x-x-	-xx-	5	8/9
HAKKODA GROUP (Honshu)	**40.65 N**	**140.88 E**	**1585**	**Stratovolcs**	**0803-28=**		**Holocene**											
OSORE-YAMA (Honshu)	**41.32 N**	**141.08 E**	**879**	**Stratovolc**	**0803-29=**		**Historical**											
							1787<	....		....	....	----	----	----	----	----		
MUTSU-HIUCHI-DAKE (Honshu)	**41.43 N**	**141.07 E**	**781**	**Stratovolc**	**0803-30-**		**Fumarolic**											

IZU & VOLCANO ISLANDS

VOLCANO NAME (Subregion)	LAT	LONG	ELEV (m)	TYPE	NUMBER	ERUPTION — Area of Activity	Status / Start Year	Start M-Dy	P	Stop Year	Stop M-Dy	Central / Flank vent / Radial fiss / Regional*	Submarine / New island / Subglacial / Crater lake	Explosive / Pyro flow / Phreatic / Fumarolic	Lava flow / Lava lake / Dome / Spine	Fatal / Damage / Mudflow / Tsunami	VEI	Vol L/T
OSHIMA (Izu Is-Japan)	**34.73 N**	**139.38 E**	**758**	**Stratovolc**	**0804-01=**		**Historical**											
							T **-0050**?	....		....	....	----	----	x---	----	----	3	
							T **0100**?	....		....	....	----	----	x---	----	----	3	
							T **0200**?	....		....	....	----	----	x---	----	----	3	
							T **0300**?	....		....	....	----	----	x---	----	----	3	
							T **0400**?	....		....	....	----	----	x---	----	----	3	
							T **0500**?	....		....	....	----	----	x---	----	----	3	
						Summit and east flank	**0605**	....		....	....	xx-x	----	x-x-	x---	--x-	3?	7/8
							0630	....		....	....	----	----	x---	x---	----	3	
							0654	....		....	....	x---	----	x-x-	x---	----	3	8/7
							? **0680**	....		....	....	----	----	----	----	----		
							? **0681**	0326		....	....	----	----	----	----	----		
							0684?	1129		....	....	-?--	----	----	x---	----		
						Summit and north and south flanks	**0751**	....		....	....	xx--	----	x---	x---	----	4	8/8
							? **0854**	0914		....	....	----	----	?---	----	----		
						Summit and SE tip of island	**0886**	0629		....	....	xx--	----	x-x-	x---	----	3	8/7
							0936	....		....	....	x---	----	x---	?---	----	4	8/8
						Summit and south flank	**1112**	1118		**1112**	1226e	xx--	----	x---	x---	----	4	8/8
							1267	....		....	....	x---	----	x---	x---	----	4	8/8
							1338	....		....	....	----	----	x---	x---	----	2	
							1415	0521		....	....	----	----	----	?---	----		
							1416	0902		**1416**	12	----	----	?---	----	----	3?	
							1421	0514		....	....	----	----	x---	x---	----	2	
							1442	08		....	....	x--x	----	x---	x---	----	4	8/8
							1527	....		....	....	----	----	x---	x---	----	3	
						Summit and south flank	**1552**	1007	+	**1552**	1015	x-x-	----	x---	x---	----	4	8/8
							1588	....		....	....	----	----	x---	x---	----	3	
							1600	....		**1601**	....	----	----	?---	----	----	2	
							1612	....		**1613**	....	----	----	?---	----	----	2	
							1636	....		**1638**	04 ?	x---	----	x---	x---	----	3	
							1684	0331	+	**1690**	....	x---	----	x---	x---	-x--	3	7/8
							1695	0412		....	....	----	----	?---	----	----		
						Mihara-yama summit & flanks, NE flank	**1777**	0831	+	**1779**	....	xx--	----	x---	x---	----	3*	8/8
						Mihara-yama	**1783**	....		**1786**	....	x---	----	x---	----	-x--	2	
						Mihara-yama	**1789**	....		....	....	x---	----	x---	----	xx--	2	
						Mihara-yama	**1792**	....		....	....	x---	----	----	----	----	2	
						Mihara-yama	**1803**	0926		**1803**	1114>	x---	----	x---	----	----	2	
						Mihara-yama	**1822**	....		**1824**	....	x---	----	x---	----	----	2	
						Mihara-yama	**1827**	....		....	....	x---	----	?---	----	----		
						Mihara-yama	**1837**	....		**1838**	....	x---	----	x---	x---	----	3	
						Mihara-yama	**1846**	....		....	....	x---	----	x---	----	----	2	
						Mihara-yama	? **1868**	1231y		....	....	x---	----	----	----	----		
						Mihara-yama	**1870**	....		....	....	x---	----	x---	----	----	2	
						Mihara-yama	**1876**	1227		**1877**	0205	x---	----	x---	x---	----	2	6/6
						Mihara-yama	**1910**	12		....	....	x---	----	x---	----	----	1	-/4
						Mihara-yama	**1912**	0223		**1913**	0125	x---	----	x---	x---	----	1	7/5
						Mihara-yama	**1914**	0515		**1914**	0526	x---	----	x---	x---	----	2	7/6
						Mihara-yama	**1915**	1010		**1915**	1025?	x---	----	x---	----	----	2	
						Mihara-yama	**1919**	0518	+	**1919**	1223	x---	----	----	x---	----	0	
						Mihara-yama	? **1920**	....		....	....	x---	----	----	?---	----		
						Mihara-yama	**1922**	1208		**1923**	0130	x---	----	x-x-	x---	----	1	6/5
						Mihara-yama	**1928**	0807		**1928**	0808	x---	----	x---	----	----	2	
						Mihara-yama	**1933**	1014		**1933**	11	x---	----	----	x---	----	0	5/-
						Mihara-yama	**1934**	0415		**1934**	0425?	x---	----	----	x---	----	0	
						Mihara-yama	? **1934**	09		....	....	x---	----	----	?---	----		
						Mihara-yama	**1935**	0426		**1935**	0506?	x---	----	----	x---	----	0	
						Mihara-yama	**1937**	0717		**1937**	08	x---	----	----	x---	----	0	
						Mihara-yama	**1938**	0811		**1938**	0811	x---	----	x---	x---	----	1	5/-
						Mihara-yama	**1939**	02		**1939**	02	x---	----	x---	----	----	1?	
						Mihara-yama	**1939**	0901	+	**1939**	0916	x---	----	x---	x---	----	1	5/-
						Mihara-yama	**1940**	0818		**1940**	0819	x---	----	x---	----	----	1	5/5
						Mihara-yama, south rim	**1950**	0716	+	**1951**	0628	x---	----	x---	xx--	----	2	7/6

VOLCANO NAME (Subregion) / ERUPTION — Area of Activity	LAT	LONG	ELEV (m)	TYPE	NUMBER	Status / Start Year	Start M-Dy	P	Stop Year	Stop M-Dy	Central / Flank vent / Radial fiss / Regional*	Submarine / New island / Subglacial / Crater lake	Explosive / Pyro flow / Phreatic / Fumarolic	Lava flow / Lava lake / Dome / Spine	Fatal / Damage / Mudflow / Tsunami	VEI	Vol L/T
OSHIMA (Izu Is-Japan) *continued*																	
Mihara-yama						**1953**	1005	+	**1954**	0208	x---	----	x---	x---	x---	1	5/4
Mihara-yama						**1956**	0103		**1956**	0106	x---	----	x---	----	----	1	
Mihara-yama						? **1956**	0825		?**1956**	0826	x---	----	----	----	----	1?	
Mihara-yama						**1957**	08		**1957**	12	x---	----	x---	----	x---	2	
Mihara-yama						**1958**	0417	+	**1958**	0613	x---	----	x---	----	----	2	
Mihara-yama						**1959**	01		**1959**	01	x---	----	x---	----	----	1	
Mihara-yama						**1959**	10	+	**1960**	11	x---	----	x---	----	----	1	
Mihara-yama						? **1961**	....		....	....	x---	----	----	----	----		
Mihara-yama						**1962**	01	+	**1965**	05	x---	----	x-x-	----	----	1	
Mihara-yama						**1965**	1125		**1966**	0613	x---	----	x---	----	----	1	
Mihara-yama						**1967**	05		**1967**	08	x---	----	x---	----	----	1	
Mihara-yama						**1968**	0119		**1968**	0119	x---	----	x---	----	----	1	
Mihara-yama						**1968**	0728		**1968**	0728	x---	----	x---	----	----	1	
Mihara-yama						**1969**	0119	+	**1969**	07	x---	----	x---	----	----	1	
Mihara-yama						**1970**	0126		**1970**	0131	x---	----	x---	----	----	1	
Mihara-yama						**1970**	0630	+	**1970**	1112	x---	----	x---	----	----	1	
Mihara-yama						**1971**	0405		**1971**	0405	x---	----	x---	----	----	1	
Mihara-yama						**1974**	0228	+	**1974**	0620	x---	----	x---	----	----	2	
Mihara-yama, N part and NW of caldera						**1986**	1115	+	**1986**	1218	x-x-	----	x---	xx--	-x--	3*	7/7
Mihara-yama						**1987**	1116	+	**1988**	0127	x---	----	x-x-	----	-x--	3*	-/4
Mihara-yama (1987 summit crater)						**1990**	1004		**1990**	1004	x---	----	x-x-	----	----	2	
TO-SHIMA (Izu Is-Japan)	**34.52**	**N 139.28 E**	**508**	**Stratovolc**	**0804-011**	**Holocene?**											
NII-JIMA (Izu Is-Japan)	**34.37**	**N 139.27 E**	**432**	**Lava domes**	**0804-02=**	**Historical**											
Achi-yama						**0840**	....		....	....	x---	----	xx--	--x-	----	3	
Mukai-yama						**0886**	0703		....	....	x---	x---	xx--	--x-	----	4	8/-
KOZU-SHIMA (Izu Is-Japan)	**34.22**	**N 139.15 E**	**574**	**Lava domes**	**0804-03=**	**Historical**											
						0832	....		....	....	----	----	----	x---	----		
Tenjo-san						**0838**	0802		....	....	x---	----	xx--	x-x-	----	4	
MIYAKE-JIMA (Izu Is-Japan)	**34.08**	**N 139.53 E**	**815**	**Stratovolc**	**0804-04=**	**Historical**											
						T **-1050?**	....		....	....	x---	----	x---	----	----	C	
Yaema Crater						C **-0210v**	....		....	....	-x--	----	xx--	----	----		
Tairoike Crater						T **0150x**	....		....	....	-x--	----	x---	----	----		
						C **0350v**	....		....	....	----	----	x---	----	----		
						T **0500?**	....		....	....	----	----	x---	----	----	2	
Mi-ike						T **0860?**	....		....	....	----	----	xx--	x---	----	3	
						1085	....		....	....	----	----	x---	----	----	2	
						1154	11		....	....	----	----	?---	----	----	3	
Oyama						**1469**	1224		....	....	x-x-	----	x---	x---	----	3	
						1535	03		....	....	--x-	----	x---	?---	----	2	
						1595	1122		....	....	--x-	----	x---	----	--?-	2	
SW flank (SE of Ako, Kuwanoki-daira?)						**1643**	0331		**1643**	04	-xx-	----	x---	x---	-x--	3	
						1709	0423		....	....	----	----	----	----	----		
SW flank (Kuwanoki-daira)						**1712**	0204		**1714**	....	-xx-	x---	x---	x---	-xx-	2	-/8
Oyama, SSW flank (Shinmio)						**1763**	0817		**1769**	....	xxx-	----	x---	x---	-x--	2	
Summit and NE flank?						**1811**	0127		**1811**	0128	x-x-	----	x---	x---	----	2	
West flank (east and SE of Ako)						**1835**	1111		....	....	-xx-	----	x---	x---	-x--	2	
NNE flank (560 m)						**1874**	0703		**1874**	0717?	--x-	----	x---	x---	xx--	3	
Oyama, NE flank						**1940**	0712	+	**1940**	0805	x-x-	----	x---	x---	xx--	2	6/6
NE flank						**1962**	0824		**1962**	0827	-xx-	----	x---	x---	-x--	2	6/6
SW flank (4.5 km long NE-SW fissure)						**1983**	1003		**1983**	1004	-xx-	----	xxx-	x---	-x--	3	6/6
KUROSE HOLE (Izu Is-Japan)	**33.40**	**N 139.68 E**	**-107**	**Submarine**	**0804-041**	**Holocene**											
HACHIJO-JIMA (Izu Is-Japan)	**33.13**	**N 139.77 E**	**854**	**Stratovolcs**	**0804-05=**	**Historical**											
Nishi-yama						T **-7050***	....		....	....	x---	xx--	x-x-	----	----		
S flank of Higashi-yama (Myohoji)						T **-2550z**	....		....	....	-x--	----	x---	----	----		
North flank of Higashi-yama						T **-2050?**	....		....	....	-x--	----	x---	----	----		
Nishi-yama						**1487**	1207		....	....	x---	----	x---	----	----	2	
Nishi-yama						**1518**	02		**1523**	....	x---	----	x---	----	----	2	
Nishi-yama						**1605**	1027		....	....	x---	----	x---	----	-x--	2	
Submarine flank						**1606**	0123		....	....	-x--	xx--	x---	----	----	2	
						? **1707**	....		....	....	----	----	?---	----	----	2	
AOGA-SHIMA (Izu Is-Japan)	**32.45**	**N 139.77 E**	**423**	**Stratovolc**	**0804-06=**	**Historical**											
						C **-0970z**	....		....	....	x---	----	xx--	----	----		
SE flank						T **-0750y**	....		....	....	-x--	----	x---	x---	----		
SE flank (Kintagaura)						C **-0430x**	....		....	....	-x--	----	x---	----	----		
						1652	....		....	....	x---	----	x-?-	----	----	3	
						1670	....		**1680**	....	x---	---x	x---	----	----	2	
Center, SW part of Ikenosawa crater						**1780**	0727	+	**1785**	05 ?	x---	---x	x---	x---	xxx-	3*	6/7
BAYONNAISE ROCKS (Izu Is-Japan)	**31.92**	**N 139.92 E**	**10**	**Submarine**	**0804-07=**	**Historical**											
14 km north of Bayonnaise Rocks						**1896**	....		....	....	----	xx--	----	----	----	2	
9-15 km SE of Bayonnaise Rocks						**1906**	0407		**1906**	0414	----	x---	x---	----	----	1	
11 km east, 19 km NE, 4 km SW						**1915**	02	+	**1915**	07	----	x---	x---	----	---x	0	
9 km east of Bayonnaise Rocks						**1934**	05		....	....	----	x---	----	----	----	0	
Island at 31.95 N 140.02 E						**1946**	0204d		....	....	----	xx--	----	--xx	----	2	7/-
Myojin-sho						**1952**	0916		**1953**	10	----	xx--	xx--	--xx	x--x	2	7/-
Myojin-sho						**1954**	1104		**1954**	1105	----	x---	----	----	----	0	
4 km north of Bayonnaise Rocks						**1955**	0625		....	....	----	x---	----	----	----	0	
						1957	0502		....	....	----	x---	----	----	----	0	
						1958	....		....	....	----	x---	----	----	----	0	
						1959	....		....	....	----	x---	----	----	----	0	
Myojin-sho						**1960**	0721		....	....	----	x---	----	----	----	2	
Myojin-sho						**1970**	0129		**1970**	06	----	x---	x---	----	----	2	
						? **1971**	0318		....	....	----	?---	----	----	----	0	
Myojin-sho						? **1979**	0713		....	....	----	?---	----	----	----	0	
Myojin-sho						? **1980**	1115		?**1980**	1226>	----	?---	----	----	----	0	
Myojin-sho						? **1983**	0512		....	....	----	?---	----	----	----	0	
Myojin-sho						? **1986**	1024		?**1986**	1024	----	?---	----	----	----	0	
Myojin-sho						? **1987**	1021		?**1987**	1021	----	?---	----	----	----	0	
Myojin-sho						? **1988**	0318		?**1988**	0319	----	?---	----	----	----	0	
SMITH ROCK (Izu Is-Japan)	**31.32**	**N 140.05 E**	**136**	**Submarine**	**0804-08=**	**Historical**											
31.58 N 140.25 E						**1672?**	....		....	....	----	x---	----	----	----	0	
31.00 N 139.03 E						@ **1869**	0506		....	....	----	x---	----	----	----	0	
18 km SW of Smith Rock						**1870**	....		....	....	----	xx--	----	----	----	1?	
100 km SE of Aoga-shima						**1870**	05		....	....	----	xx--	----	----	----	2	
31.50 N 139.50 E (approx.)						@ **1871**	....		....	....	----	x---	----	----	----	0	
31.28 N 139.92 E						? **1873**	....		....	....	----	?---	----	----	----	0	
Just west of Smith Rock						**1916**	0621		....	....	----	x---	----	----	----	0	

VOLCANO NAME (Subregion) / ERUPTION — Area of Activity	LAT	LONG	ELEV (m)	TYPE	NUMBER	Status / Start Year	Start M-Dy	P	Stop Year	Stop M-Dy	Central / Flank vent / Radial fiss / Regional	Submarine / New island / Subglacial / Crater lake	Explosive / Pyro flow / Phreatic / Fumarolic	Lava flow / Lava lake / Dome / Spine	Fatal / Damage / Mudflow / Tsunami	VEI	Vol L/T
TORI-SHIMA (Izu Is-Japan)	**30.48**	**N 140.32 E**	**403**	**Stratovolc**	**0804-09=**	**Historical**											
						1871	04		....	....	----	x---	----	----	----	0	
Komochi-yama, N & SW offshore flanks						**1902**	0807		**1902**	0824	xx--	x---	x-x-	x---	xx--	3	-/7
North side of 1902 crater (Iwo-yama)						**1939**	0817		**1939**	1226e	x---	----	x---	x---	x---	2	7/-
						S **1965**	1113		**1965**	1205d	----	x---	----	----	----	0	
9 km south of Torishima						**1975**	1002		....	....	----	x---	----	----	----	2	
OMACHI SEAMOUNT (Izu Is-Japan)	**29.22**	**N 140.80 E**	**-1700**	**Submarine**	**0804-091**	**Uncertain**											
29.30 N 140.80 E						? **1975**	0910		....	....	----	?---	----	----	----	0	
NISHINO-SHIMA (Volcano Is-Japan)	**27.243**	**N 140.877 E**	**52**	**Caldera**	**0804-092**	**Historical**											
East of Nishino-shima						**1973**	0412	+	**1974**	0505d	----	xx--	x---	x---	----	2	
						? **1975**	....		....	....	----	?---	----	----	----	0	
6.5 km NW of Nishino-shima						? **1978**	1116		....	....	----	?---	----	----	----	0	
South, east, and west sides						? **1980**	0707		....	....	----	?---	----	----	----	0	
						? **1982**	04		?**1982**	04	----	?---	----	----	----	0	
						? **1985**	1202		?**1985**	1202	----	?---	----	----	----	0	
UNNAMED (Volcano Is-Japan)	**26.13**	**N 144.48 E**	**-3200**	**Submarine ?**	**0804-093**	**Uncertain**											
						? **1974**	03		....	....	----	?---	----	----	----	0	
KAITOKU SEAMOUNT (Volcano Is)	**26.122**	**N 141.102 E**	**-10**	**Submarine**	**0804-10=**	**Historical**											
						1543	....		....	....	----	x---	----	----	----	0	
						1984	0308	+	**1984**	0326	----	x---	x---	----	----	0	
KITA-IWO-JIMA (Volcano Is-Japan)	**25.43**	**N 141.23 E**	**792**	**Stratovolc**	**0804-11=**	**Historical**											
						1780	....		....	....	----	x---	----	----	----	0	
						1880	....		**1889**	....	----	x---	x---	----	----	0	
						1930	....		**1945**	....	----	x---	x---	----	----	2?	
						? **1953**	05		....	....	----	?---	----	----	----	0	
IWO-JIMA (Volcano Is-Japan)	**24.75**	**N 141.33 E**	**161**	**Caldera**	**0804-12=**	**Historical**											
West side (Asodai)						**1922**	07		....	....	x---	----	--x-	----	----	1	
NW flank near coast						**1930?**	....		....	....	----	----	--x-	----	----	1	
North and west flanks near coast						**1943a**	....		....	....	----	----	--x-	----	----	1	
Chidoriga-hara						**1957**	0328		**1957**	0328	----	----	--x-	----	----	1	
West side (Asodai)						**1967**	1223		**1967**	1223	x---	----	--x-	----	----	1	
West side (Asodai)						? **1969**	0112		?**1969**	0121	x---	----	--??	----	----	1	
NW of Iwo-jima (24.88 N 141.50 E)						? **1974**	01		....	....	----	?---	----	----	----	0	
West side (Asodai)						**1976**	....		....	....	x---	----	--x-	----	----	1	
West side (Asodai)						**1978**	1211		**1978**	1211	x---	----	--x-	----	----	1	
Kitanohara						**1980**	0313		**1980**	0313	x---	----	--x-	----	----	1	
NW side (Idoga-hama beach)						**1982**	0309		**1982**	0310	x---	----	--x-	----	----	1	
West side (Asodai)						**1982**	1128		**1982**	1129	x---	----	--x-	----	----	1	
SHIN-IWO-JIMA (Volcano Is-Japan)	**24.28**	**N 141.52 E**	**-14**	**Submarine**	**0804-13=**	**Historical**											
Shin-Iwo-jima						**1904**	1114		**1905**	0516	----	xx--	x---	----	----	3	8/8
Shin-Iwo-jima						**1914**	0113		**1914**	0821>	----	xx--	x---	----	----	3	-/9
Fukutoku-okanoba						? **1950**	02		?**1950**	02	----	?---	----	----	----	0	
Fukutoku-okanoba						? **1952**	06		?**1952**	06	----	?---	----	----	----	0	
Fukutoku-okanoba						? **1953**	12		?**1953**	12	----	?---	----	----	----	0	
Fukutoku-okanoba						? **1954**	0204d		....	....	----	?---	----	----	----	0	
Fukutoku-okanoba						? **1955**	04		?**1955**	04	----	?---	----	----	----	0	
Fukutoku-okanoba						? **1956**	04		?**1956**	05	----	?---	----	----	----	0	
Fukutoku-okanoba						? **1958**	07		?**1958**	10	----	?---	----	----	----	0	
Fukutoku-okanoba						? **1959**	07		?**1959**	10	----	?---	----	----	----	0	
Fukutoku-okanoba						? **1960**	07		?**1960**	09	----	?---	----	----	----	0	
Fukutoku-okanoba						? **1962**	07	+	?**1962**	12	----	?---	----	----	----	0	
Fukutoku-okanoba						? **1963**	1027		....	....	----	?---	----	----	----	0	
Fukutoku-okanoba						? **1967**	07		?**1967**	07	----	?---	----	----	----	0	
Fukutoku-okanoba						? **1968**	02		?**1968**	02	----	?---	----	----	----	0	
Fukutoku-okanoba						? **1968**	0814		....	....	----	?---	----	----	----	0	
Fukutoku-okanoba						? **1972**	10		?**1972**	10	----	?---	----	----	----	0	
3.8 km NNE Minami-Iwo-jima						**1973**	1218		**1974**	0216	----	x---	x---	----	----	2*	
Fukutoku-okanoba (24.28 N 141.50 E)						**1974**	1224	+	?**1975**	1113	----	xx--	----	----	----	2	
Fukutoku-okanoba						? **1976**	08	+	?**1985**	1223	----	?---	----	----	----	0	
Fukutoku-okanoba						**1986**	0118		**1986**	0121	----	xx--	x---	----	----	2	
Fukutoku-okanoba						**1987**	0714		**1987**	0817?	----	x---	x---	----	----	0	
Fukutoku-okanoba						? **1987**	09		?**1991**	0206	----	?---	----	----	----	0	
Fukutoku-okanoba						? **1991**	0930		?**1991**	1018	----	?---	----	----	----	0	
Fukutoku-okanoba						**1992**	1110		**1992**	1118?	----	x---	x---	----	----	1	
Fukutoku-okanoba						? **1993**	02		?**1993**	09	----	?---	----	----	----	0	
MINAMI-HIYOSHI (Volcano Is-Japan)	**23.507**	**N 141.905 E**	**-30**	**Submarine**	**0804-131**	**Historical**											
23.50 N 141.92 E						**1975**	0825		....	....	----	x---	----	----	----	0	
						? **1976**	02		....	....	----	?---	----	----	----	0	
Hiyoshi-okinoba (also 23.48 N 141.67)						? **1976**	12	+	?**1977**	0328	----	?---	----	----	----	0	
						? **1978**	0126?		?**1978**	0324	----	?---	----	----	----	0	
						? **1992**	0212		?**1992**	0304	----	?---	----	----	----	0	
NIKKO (Volcano Is-Japan)	**23.075**	**N 142.308 E**	**-391**	**Submarine**	**0804-132**	**Uncertain**											
						? **1979**	0712		....	....	----	?---	----	----	----	0	
FUKUJIN (Volcano Is-Japan)	**21.925**	**N 143.442 E**	**-217**	**Submarine**	**0804-133**	**Historical**											
						1951	0715q		**1951**	1015q	----	x---	x---	----	----	0	
						? **1952**	....		....	....	----	?---	----	----	----	0	
						? **1958**	08		?**1958**	09	----	?---	----	----	----	0	
						? **1959**	08		?**1959**	10	----	?---	----	----	----	0	
						1968	09		....	....	----	x---	----	----	----	0	
21.93 N 143.46 E						**1973**	0927		**1974**	0305	----	x---	x---	----	----	1	
21.95 N 143.45 E						? **1976**	0802		?**1977**	0421	----	?---	----	----	----	0	
						? **1977**	1014		?**1978**	0324	----	x---	----	----	----	0	
						? **1978**	0824		?**1978**	0825	----	?---	----	----	----	0	
						? **1979**	0426		?**1980**	0512	----	?---	----	----	----	0	
						? **1981**	0107		?**1981**	0108	----	?---	----	----	----	0	
						? **1982**	0112		?**1982**	0316	----	?---	----	----	----	0	
						? **1982**	1215		....	....	----	?---	----	----	----	0	
KASUGA SEAMOUNT (Volcano Is)	**21.77**	**N 143.72 E**	**-558**	**Submarine**	**0804-134**	**Uncertain**											
21.78 N 143.71 E						? **1975**	11		....	....	----	?---	----	----	----	0	

MARIANA ISLANDS

VOLCANO NAME (Subregion) / ERUPTION — Area of Activity	LAT	LONG	ELEV (m)	TYPE	NUMBER	Status / Start Year	Start M-Dy	P	Stop Year	Stop M-Dy	Central / Flank vent / Radial fiss / Regional	Submarine / New island / Subglacial / Crater lake	Explosive / Pyro flow / Phreatic / Fumarolic	Lava flow / Lava lake / Dome / Spine	Fatal / Damage / Mudflow / Tsunami	VEI	Vol L/T
UNNAMED (Mariana Is-C Pac)	**21.00**	**N 142.90 E**		**Submarine ?**	**0804-135**	**Uncertain**											
						? **1975**	0910		....	....	----	?---	----	----	----	0	
UNNAMED (Mariana Is-C Pac)	**20.30**	**N 143.20 E**		**Submarine ?**	**0804-136**	**Uncertain**											
						? **1975**	0910		....	....	----	?---	----	----	----	0	

VOLCANO NAME (Subregion)	LAT	LONG	ELEV (m)	TYPE	NUMBER	Status / ERUPTION — Area of Activity	Start Year	Start M-Dy	P	Stop Year	Stop M-Dy	Central, Flank vent, Radial fiss, Regional* / Submarine, New island, Subglacial, Crater lake / Explosive, Pyro flow, Phreatic, Fumarolic / Lava flow, Lava lake, Dome, Spine / Fatal, Damage, Mudflow, Tsunami	VEI	Vol L/T
FARALLON DE PAJAROS (Marianas)	20.53	N 144.90	E 360	Stratovolc	0804-14=	Historical								
						SW side	1864	0107		....	....	-x-- ---- x--- ---- ----	2	
						(publication date of 1864 eruption)	X 1865	....		....	....	---- ---- ---- ---- ----		
						Summit, northeast side	1874?	....		1876	0103	xx-- ---- x--- x--- ----	2	
						Summit, east side	1900?	....		1901	05	xx-- ---- x--- x--- ----	2	
						North side ?	1912	....		....	....	-?-- ---- x--- ?--- ----	2	
							1925	....		....	....	---- ---- x--- ---- ----	2	
							1928	1215e		....	....	---- ---- x--- ---- ----	2?	
						Summit, east side ?	1932	0907		1932	1007	x?-- ---- x--- x--- ----	2	
						Immediately south of Uracas	1934	0715q		....	....	-x-- x--- x--- ---- ----	0	
							1936	0415q		....	....	x--- ---- x--- ---- ----	2	
						East side ?	1939	....		....	....	-?-- ---- x--- ?--- ----	2	
							1941	0328		....	....	x--- ---- x--- x--- ----		
						Summit, south side	1943	....		....	....	xx-- ---- x--- x--- ----	2	
						North side	1947	01 ?		....	....	-x-- ---- ---- x--- ----	0?	
							1951	08		....	....	x--- ---- x--- ---- ----	2	
						Summit, east side	1952	1026e		1953	0415	xx-- ---- x--- x--- ----	2	
						SW of Uracas (20.4 N, 144.8 E)	S 1967	0327		S1967	0410	---- x--- ---- ---- ----	0	
AHYI (Mariana Is-C Pac)	20.43	N 145.03	E -70	Submarine	0804-141	Uncertain								
							? 1979	1115		....	....	x--- ?--- ---- ---- ----	0	
SUPPLY REEF (Mariana Is-C Pac)	20.13	N 145.10	E -8	Submarine	0804-142	Hydrophonic								
						NW of Supply Reef (20.24 N, 145.02 E)	S 1969	0311		S1969	0313	---- x--- ---- ---- ----	0	
						25 km? NW of Supply Reef	? 1985	0902		....	....	---- ?--- ---- ---- ----	0	
						NW of Supply Reef (ca. 20.3 N 144.9E)	S 1989	0921	+	S1989	1227	---- x--- ---- ---- ----	0	
ASUNCION (Mariana Is-C Pac)	19.67	N 145.40	E 857	Stratovolc	0804-15=	Historical								
							? 1690j	....		....	....	---- ---- ---- ---- ----		
							? 1775j	....		....	....	---- ---- ?--- ---- ----	2	
						(same as 1775j eruption: Corwin)	X 1786	....		....	....	---- ---- ---- ---- ----		
						(no specific reference to 1819 activity)	X 1819	....		....	....	---- ---- ---- ---- ----		
						(steaming only, no eruption)	X 1901	....		....	....	---- ---- ---x ---- ----		
						Upper SE and west flanks	1906	....		....	....	-x-- ---- x--- x--- ----	2	
							? 1924	....		....	....	--x- ---- -?-- ---- --?-	2?	
AGRIGAN (Mariana Is-C Pac)	18.77	N 145.67	E 965	Stratovolc	0804-16=	Historical								
							1917	0409		....	....	x--- ---- x--- ---- -x--	4	
PAGAN (Mariana Is-C Pac)	18.13	N 145.80	E 570	Stratovolcs	0804-17=	Historical								
						North Pagan	C 1350v	....		....	....	---- ---- xx-- ---- ----		
						North Pagan	C 1580t	....		....	....	---- ---- xx-- ---- ----		
						North Pagan	1669	....		....	....	---- ---- x--- ?--- ----		
						North Pagan (west flank maar)	C 1800t	....		....	....	x--- ---- xx-- ---- ----		
						North Pagan	1825e	....		....	....	---- ---- x--- ---- ----	2?	
						South Pagan	1864	....		....	....	---- ---- x--- ---- ----	1?	
						North pagan	1873?	....		....	....	x--- ---- x--- x--- ----	3?	
						North Pagan	1909	....		....	....	x--- ---- x--- ---- ----	2	
						North Pagan	1917	....		....	....	x--- ---- x--- ---- ----	2	
						North Pagan	1923	02 ?	+	1923	0326e	x--- ---- x--- x--- ----	3*	
							1925	02	+	1925	0505	x--- ---- x--- x--- ----	2	
						South Pagan, cone within caldera	? 1929	....		?1930	....	x--- ---- ?--? ---- ----		
						("eruption" actually a grassfire)	X 1966	0523		....	....			
						North Pagan (summit and north flank)	1981	0515		1985	0501>	xxx- ---- xx-- x--- -x--	4*	7/8
						North Pagan	1987	0904		1987	0904	x--- ---- x--- ---- ----	1	
						North Pagan	? 1988	0216		....	....	x--- ---- ?--- ---- ----		
						North Pagan	1988	0824	+	1988	1012	x--- ---- x--- ---- ----	2	
						North Pagan	1992	0413		1992	0413	x--- ---- x--- ---- ----	1?	
						North Pagan	1993	0115e		1993	07 >	x--- ---- x--- ---- --x-	2	
ALAMAGAN (Mariana Is-C Pac)	17.60	N 145.83	E 744	Stratovolc	0804-18=	Radiocarbon								
							C 0540u	....		....	....	---- ---- xx-- ---- ----		
							C 0875v	....		....	....	---- ---- xx-- ---- ----		
							? 1864	01		....	....	x--- ---- ?--- ---- ----		
							? 1887	1129		....	....	---- ---- ?--? ---- ----		
GUGUAN (Mariana Is-C Pac)	17.32	N 145.85	E 287	Stratovolc	0804-19=	Historical								
						(solfataric activity only)	X 1819	....		....	....	---- ---- ---x ---- ----		
							1883a	....		....	....	x--- ---- xx-- x--- ----	2?	
						(solfataric activity only)	X 1901	....		....	....	---- ---- ---x ---- ----		
SARIGAN (Mariana Is-C Pac)	16.708	N 145.78	E 538	Stratovolc	0804-191	Holocene								
ANATAHAN (Mariana Is-C Pac)	16.35	N 145.67	E 788	Stratovolc	0804-20=	Holocene								
RUBY (Mariana Is-C Pac)	15.62	N 145.57	E -230	Submarine	0804-201	Hydrophonic								
							S 1966	0421g		S1966	05	---- x--- ---- ---- ----	0	
ESMERALDA BANK (Mariana Is)	15.00	N 145.25	E -43	Submarine	0804-21=	Fumarolic								
							? 1944	0820j		....	....	---- ?--- ---? ---- ----	0	
							? 1964	0414		....	....	---- ?--- ---- ---- ----	2	
							? 1970a	....		....	....	---- ?--- ---- ---- ----	0	
							? 1975	0426		?1975	0429	---- ?--- ---- ---- ----	0	
							? 1982	0406		....	....	---- ?--- ---- ---- ----	0	
							? 1987	0526		....	....	---- ?--- ---- ---- ----	0	

HOKKAIDO

VOLCANO NAME (Subregion)	LAT	LONG	ELEV (m)	TYPE	NUMBER	Status / ERUPTION — Area of Activity	Start Year	Start M-Dy	P	Stop Year	Stop M-Dy	Activity	VEI	Vol L/T
OSHIMA-OSHIMA (Hokkaido-Japan)	41.50	N 139.37	E 737	Stratovolc	0805-01=	Historical								
						Nishi-yama	C -0800v	....		....	....	x--- ---- x--- ---- ----		
						Nishi-yama	C 0250w	....		....	....	x--- ---- x--- ---- ----		
						Nishi-yama	1741	0818?		1742	05	x?-- ---- x--- x--- xx-x	4*	
						Nishi-yama	1759	0819		....	....	x--- ---- x--- ---- ----	2	
						Nishi-yama	? 1786	....		....	....	x--- ---- ---- ---- ----	2?	
						Nishi-yama	1790	01 ?		....	....	x--- ---- x--- ---- ----	2	
E-SAN (Hokkaido-Japan)	41.80	N 141.17	E 618	Stratovolc	0805-011	Historical								
							1846	1118		....	....	x--- ---- --x- ---- xxx-	1	
							1874	....		....	....	---- ---- ---- ---- ----		
KOMAGA-TAKE (Hokkaido)	42.07	N 140.68	E 1140	Stratovolc	0805-02=	Historical								
							T -4050?	....		....	....	x--- ---- xx-- ---- ----		
							T -1050?	....		....	....	x--- ---- xx-- ---- ----		
							1640	0731		1640	1009	x--- ---- xxx- ---- xxxx	5	-/9
							1694	0704		1694	0706	x--- ---- xx-- ---- ----	4	-/8
							? 1710	0627		....	....	---- ---- ---- ---- ----		
							1765	....		....	....	x--- ---- --x- ---- ----	2	
							1784	0208		....	....	x--- ---- --x- ---- ----	2	

VOLCANO NAME (Subregion)	LAT	LONG	ELEV (m)	TYPE	NUMBER	Status / ERUPTION — Area of Activity	Start Year	Start M-Dy	P	Stop Year	Stop M-Dy	Central, Flank vent, Radial fiss, Regional*	Submarine, New island, Subglacial, Crater lake	Explosive, Pyro flow, Phreatic, Fumarolic	Lava flow, Lava lake, Dome, Spine	Fatal, Damage, Mudflow, Tsunami	VEI	Vol L/T
KOMAGA-TAKE (Hokkaido) *continued*						Ansei Crater	1856	0925		....	....	x---	----	xx--	--x-	xx--	4	-/8
						NW side of 1856 (Ansei) crater	1888	0414		....	....	x---	----	--x-	----	----	2	
						South of Ansei Crater	1905	0819		1905	0930	x---	----	--x-	----	-xx-	2	
						SE of Ansei Crater	1919	0617		1919	0726	x---	----	x-x-	----	----	2	
							1922	0522		....	....	x---	----	--x-	----	----	2	
							1923	0227	+	1923	0315	x---	----	--x-	----	----	2	
							1924	0731		....	....	x---	----	x-x-	----	----	2	
							? 1928	0328		....	....	----	----	--?-	----	----		
						SE and NE of Ansei Crater	1929	0617	+	1929	0906	x---	----	xx--	----	xxx-	4	-/8
						(fumarolic activity only)	X 1935	0708		....	....	----	----	---x	----	----		
							? 1935	1015		?1935	1015	x---	----	--?-	----	----		
							1937	0317		1937	0319	x---	----	x-x-	----	----	1	
						NW-SE 1.6 km fissure	1942	1116		1942	1118	x---	----	x-x-	----	--x-	3	-/6
NIGORIGAWA (Hokkaido)	42.12 N	140.45 E	356	Hydrothrm fld	0805-021	Pleistocene-Fumarolic												
USU (Hokkaido)	42.53 N	140.83 E	731	Stratovolc	0805-03=	Historical												
							T -5550z	....		....	....	x---	----	x---	----	----	3?	
							? 1611	10		....	....	----	----	?---	----	----		
							1626	0519		1626	07 ?	----	----	?---	----	----		
							1638	0725		....	....	----	----	x---	----	----		
						Ko-Usu ?	1663	0816		1663	0905d	x---	----	xxx-	--?-	xx--	5	7/9
						Ko-Usu ?	1769	0123		....	....	x---	----	xx--	--?-	-x--	4	-/8
						Foot of Ko-Usu dome, Ogari-yama	1822	0312	+	1822	07	x---	----	xx--	--x-	xxx-	4	-/8
						O-Usu	1853	0422	+	1853	05 >	x---	----	xx--	--x-	----	4	8/8
						North flank (Meiji-Shinzan)	1910	0725	+	1910	11	--x-	----	x---	--x-	xxx-	2	-/6
						East flank (Showa-Shinzan)	1944	0623	+	1945	09	-x--	----	xxx-	--x-	xxx-	2	7/6
						Usu-Shinzan	1977	0807	+	1982	03	x---	----	x-x-	--x-	xxx-	3*	-/7
IWAONUPURI (Hokkaido)	42.88 N	140.63 E	1154	Stratovolcs	0805-031	Holocene												
YOTEI (Hokkaido)	42.83 N	140.82 E	1893	Stratovolc	0805-032	Radiocarbon												
							C -5050?	....		....	....	----	----	----	----	----		
SHIRIBETSU (Hokkaido)	42.767 N	140.916 E	1107	Stratovolc ?	0805-033	Holocene												
KUTTARA (Hokkaido)	42.50 N	141.18 E	581	Stratovolc	0805-034	Tephrochronology												
						West flank (Jigoku-dani)	T 1820v	....		....	....	-x--	----	--x-	----	----	1	-/5
SHIKOTSU (Hokkaido)	42.70 N	141.333 E	1320	Caldera	0805-04=	Historical												
						Tarumai	C -6950?	....		....	....	x---	----	x---	----	----	5	
						Tarumai	C -0800y	....		....	....	x---	----	x---	----	----	5	
						Eniwa volcano (east side of summit)	C -0110v	....		....	....	x---	----	x---	----	----	2	
						Tarumai	1667	0923		....	....	x---	----	xx--	----	----	5	-/9
						Tarumai	1739	0819		1739	0831	x---	----	xx--	----	----	5	
						Tarumai	1804	....		1817	....	x---	----	xx--	----	-x--	3	-/7
						Tarumai	1867	0908		....	....	x---	----	x---	--?-	----	2	
						Tarumai	? 1871	1225		?1871	1228	x---	----	x---	----	----	2	
						Tarumai	1874	0208		1874	0216	x---	----	x---	----	----	3*	-/7
						Tarumai	1883	1007		1883	1105	x---	----	x---	----	----	2	
						Tarumai	1885	0104		....	....	x---	----	x---	----	----	2	
						Tarumai	1886	0413		1886	0428	x---	----	x---	----	----	2	
						Tarumai	1887	0903		1887	1008	x---	----	x---	----	----	2	
						Tarumai	1894	0208		1894	0208	x---	----	x---	----	----	2	
						Tarumai	1894	0817		1894	0817	x---	----	x---	----	----	2	
						Tarumai	1909	0111		1909	0422	x---	----	x---	--x-	----	3*	7/-
						Tarumai (east-west summit fissure)	1917	0430		1917	0512	x-x-	----	x---	----	----	2	
						Tarumai	1918	0613		1918	0731	x---	----	x---	----	----	1	
						Tarumai	1919	0504		1919	0504	x---	----	x---	----	----	2	
						Tarumai	1920	0717		1920	0723	x---	----	x---	----	----	1	
						Tarumai	1921	0706		1921	0706	x---	----	x---	----	----	1	
						Tarumai	1923	02		1923	0823	x---	----	x---	----	----	1	
						Tarumai	1926	1019		1926	1030	x---	----	x---	----	----	2	
						Tarumai	1928	0107		1928	0107	x---	----	x---	----	----	2	
						Tarumai	1928	0906	+	1929	0210	x---	----	x---	----	----	1	
						Tarumai	1931	1011		1931	1024	x---	----	x---	----	----	1	
						Tarumai (east-west summit fissure)	1933	1201		1933	1214	x-x-	----	x---	----	----	2	
						Tarumai	1936	0419		1936	0419	x---	----	x---	----	----	1	
						Tarumai	1936	1115		1936	1126	x---	----	x---	----	----	1	
						Tarumai	1944	0702		1944	0702	x---	----	x-x-	----	----	1	
						Tarumai	1951	0129		1951	0129	x---	----	x---	----	----	2	
						Tarumai	1951	0728		1951	0728	x---	----	x---	----	--x-	2	
						Tarumai	1953	0914?		1953	0914?	x---	----	x-x-	----	----	1	
						Tarumai	1954	0502		1954	0502	x---	----	x---	----	--x-	1	
						Tarumai	1954	1119	+	1955	0214	x---	----	x---	----	----	1	
						Tarumai (SE foot of summit dome)	1978	0514		1978	0517	x---	----	xxx-	----	----	1	-/4
						Tarumai (SE foot of summit dome)	1978	1212		1979	0511	x---	----	x-x-	----	----	1	
						Tarumai	1981	0227<		....	....	x---	----	--x-	----	----	0	-/2
RISHIRI (Hokkaido)	45.18 N	141.25 E	1719	Stratovolc	0805-041	Radiocarbon												
							C -3250>	....		....	....	----	----	x---	----	----		
TOKACHI (Hokkaido)	43.42 N	142.68 E	2077	Stratovolcs	0805-05=	Historical												
						Ground Crater	C -0240?	....		....	....	x---	----	xx--	----	----		
						Maru-yama	C 1670?	....		....	....	x---	----	x---	x---	----	2?	
							1857	....		....	....	x---	----	x---	----	----	2	
						Lower part of Maru-yama?	1887	06		....	....	-x--	----	x-?-	----	----	2	
						Maru-yama (Yunuma)	1889	....		....	....	x---	----	?---	----	----	2	
						Shin-funkako	1925	1120	+	1927	09	x---	----	xxx-	----	xxx-	3*	
						Shin-funkako	1928	01	+	1928	0523	x---	----	x-x-	----	----	1	
						Shin-funkako	1928	1204		1928	1225	x---	----	--x-	----	----	1	
							1931	0516		1931	0516	----	----	x-x-	----	----	1	
						NE of Shin-funkako (Showa Crater)	1952	0817		....	....	x---	----	--x-	----	----		
						NE of Shin-funkako (Showa Crater)	1954	09		1954	09	x---	----	--x-	----	----	1	
						NE of Shin-funkako (Showa Crater)	1956	06 ?		1956	06 ?	x---	----	--x-	----	----	1	
						NE of Shin-funkako (Showa Crater)	1957	0820		1957	0820	x---	----	--x-	----	----	1	
						NE of Shin-funkako (Showa Crater)	1958	1004		1958	1004	x---	----	--x-	----	----	1	
						NE of Shin-funkako (Showa Crater)	1959	0815e	+	1959	1125	x---	----	--x-	----	----	1	
						NW of Kami-Horokamettoku-yama	1961	08		1961	08	x---	----	--x-	----	----	1	
						South of Shin-funkako	1962	0629		1962	09	x---	----	x---	----	xx--	3	-/7
						East wall of 1962 crater	1985	0619		1985	0620	x---	----	x-x-	----	----	1	
						1962 Crater	1988	1216	+	1989	05	x---	----	xxx-	----	--x-	2	-/5
DAISETSU (Hokkaido)	43.68 N	142.88 E	2290	Stratovolcs	0805-06=	Tephrochronology												
						Asahi-dake	T 1400t	....		....	....	x-x-	----	x---	----	----	2	

VOLCANO NAME (Subregion) / ERUPTION — Area of Activity	LAT	LONG	ELEV (m)	TYPE	NUMBER	Status / Start Year	Start M-Dy	P	Stop Year	Stop M-Dy	Central / Flank vent / Radial fiss. / Regional*	Submarine / New island / Subglacial / Crater lake	Explosive / Pyro flow / Phreatic / Fumarolic	Lava flow / Lava lake / Dome / Spine	Fatal / Damage / Mudflow / Tsunami	VEI	Vol L/T
NIPESOTSU-UPEPESANKE (")	**43.45**	**N 143.03**	**E 2013**	**Lava domes**	**0805-061**	**Historical**											
Maru-yama						T **1000?**	....		....	....	----	----	x---	----	----	2	
Maru-yama (No. 1 crater)						**1898**	....		....	....	x-x-	----	--x-	----	----	2	
SHIKARIBETSU GROUP (Hokkaido)	**43.28**	**N 143.08**	**E 1430**	**Lava domes**	**0805-062**	**Holocene**											
AKAN (Hokkaido)	**43.38**	**N 144.02**	**E 1499**	**Caldera**	**0805-07=**	**Historical**											
Me-Akan						**1800<**	....		....	....	x---	----	x---	----	----	1	
Me-Akan						**1808?**	....		....	....	----	----	--?-	----	----		
Me-Akan						? **1927**	04		?**1927**	05	x---	----	--?-	----	----	1	
Me-Akan (NE foot)						? **1951**	0731		?**1952**	03	-x--	----	--?-	----	----	1	
Me-Akan (Nakamachineshiri)						**1954**	0107?	+	**1954**	0413	x---	----	x-x-	----	----	1*	
Me-Akan (Ponmachineshiri)						**1955**	1119		**1955**	1119	x---	----	x-x-	----	----	1	-/4
Me-Akan (Ponmachineshiri)						**1956**	0318		**1956**	1031	x---	----	x-x-	----	----	1	-/5
Me-Akan (Ponmachineshiri)						**1957**	0226	+	**1957**	0905	x---	----	x-x-	----	----	1	
Me-Akan (Ponmachineshiri)						**1958**	0223		**1958**	0223	x---	----	x-x-	----	----	1	
Me-Akan (Nakamachineshiri)						**1959**	0515e		**1959**	10	x---	----	--x-	----	----	1	
Me-Akan (Ponmachineshiri)						**1960**	09		**1960**	09	x---	----	--x-	----	----	1	
Me-Akan (Nakamachineshiri)						**1962**	0428		**1962**	0428	x---	----	--x-	----	----	1	
Me-Akan (Nakamachineshiri)						**1964**	0618?		**1964**	0704?	x---	----	--x-	----	----	1	
Me-Akan (Nakamachineshiri)						**1965**	0515e		**1965**	0515e	x---	----	--x-	----	----	1	
Me-Akan (Nakamachineshiri)						**1966**	0615e		**1966**	0615e	x---	----	--x-	----	----	1	
Me-Akan (SE rim of Ponmachineshir)						**1988**	0105?	+	**1988**	0218?	x---	----	x-x-	----	----	1	
KUTCHARO (Hokkaido)	**43.55**	**N 144.43**	**E 1000**	**Caldera**	**0805-08=**	**Tephrochronology**											
Atosanupuri						T **1000?**	....		....	....	x---	----	----	--x-	----	0	
MASHU (Hokkaido)	**43.57**	**N 144.57**	**E 855**	**Caldera**	**0805-081**	**Radiocarbon**											
						C **-5820**x	....		....	....	----	----	x---	----	----		
						C **-4875**x	....		....	....	x---	----	xx--	----	----	**6**	**-/10**
Kamuinupuri						H **-2200>**	....		....	....	-x--	----	x---	----	----		
Kamuinupuri						C **0175**v	....		....	....	-x--	----	x---	----	----		
Kamuinupuri						C **0970**v	....		....	....	-x--	----	x---	----	----	**5**	
RAUSU (Hokkaido)	**44.073**	**N 145.125**	**E 1660**	**Stratovolc**	**0805-082**	**Holocene**											
SHIRETOKO-IWO-ZAN (Hokkaido)	**44.13**	**N 145.17**	**E 1563**	**Stratovolc**	**0805-09=**	**Historical**											
						? **1857?**	....		....	....	----	----	--?-	----	----		
NW flank						**1876**	0923		**1876**	0926	-x--	----	--x-	----	----	2	
						? **1880**	1124		?**1880**	1126	----	----	--?-	----	----		
NW flank						**1889**	0809		**1889**	0825	-x--	----	--xx	----	----	2?	
NW flank						**1890**	0615		....	....	-x--	----	--xx	----	----	1	
NW flank						**1936**	0201		**1936**	1031	-x--	----	--xx	----	----	1	

Kuriles, Kamchatka, & Mainland Asia (09 & 10)

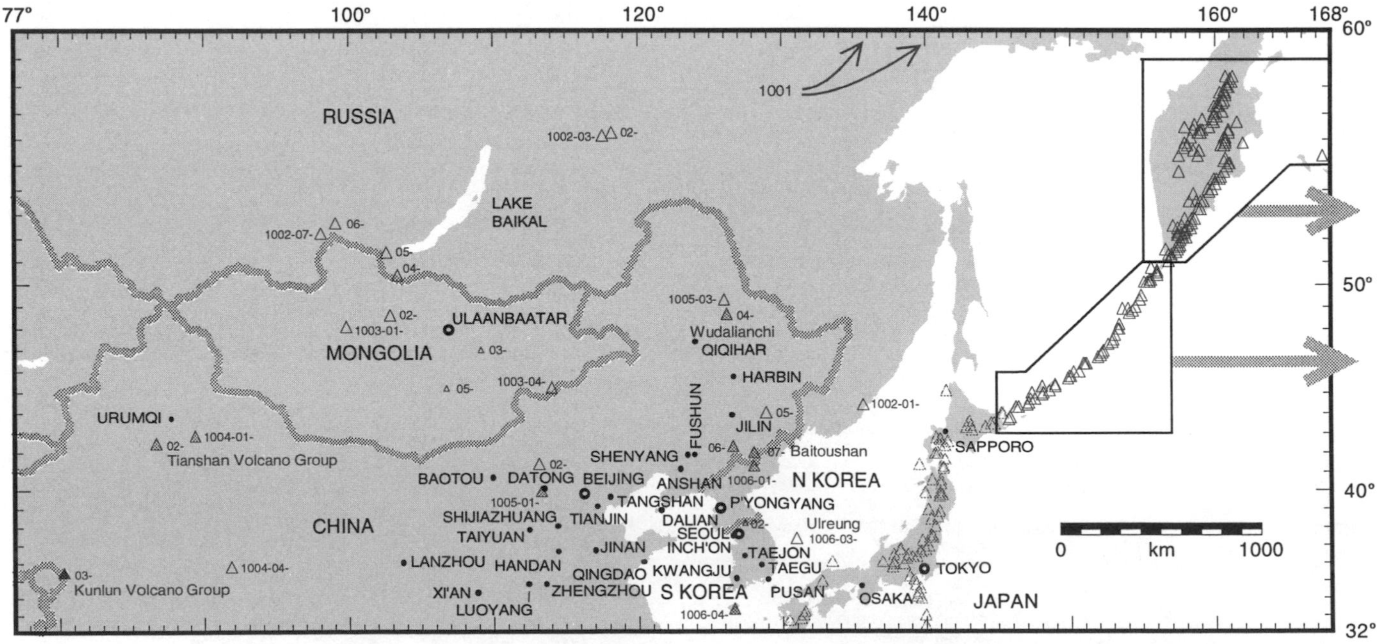

These regions are combined here, since most of their volcanoes form a continuous arc with a shared history and tectonic setting. Actually, the *CAVW* organizers should probably have combined these at the start as Region 09 and used 10 for the volcanoes of mainland Asia, but few if any inland volcanoes were recognized at the time. The original *CAVW* grouping was "Kamchatka and Manchuria", but by the time of publication (1958) this had been widened to "Kamchatka and continental areas of Asia". Nevertheless, only 5 mainland volcanoes were listed in that catalog, as opposed to 30 here; an increase exceeded only by the gains in Region 12 (Western US and Canada).

Russian explorers reached Siberia's Pacific coast in 1637, and the Kamchatka Peninsula by 1697, also the year of its first eruption report (on Kliuchevskoi, the region's most vigorous volcano). Two other Kamchatkan volcanoes are known to have erupted in the 17th century, Mutnovsky and Koshelev, but the first historical eruptions from the Kurile Islands were early in the 18th. Peter the Great's epic exploring expedition, led by Vitus Bering from 1733 to 1742, mapped the east coast of Kamchatka, and La Perouse explored the Kuriles by sea in 1787. The Kuriles have been contested by Japan and Russia, and Japan held the islands from 1875 to the end of WW-II. Heavy colonization of Kamchatka began early in the 19th century, and in 1904 the Trans-Siberian Railroad opened, linking Europe to Vladivostok (and China). Of Kamchatka's 607 historically documented eruptions, 95% have been in the last two centuries (and 71% in the 20th).

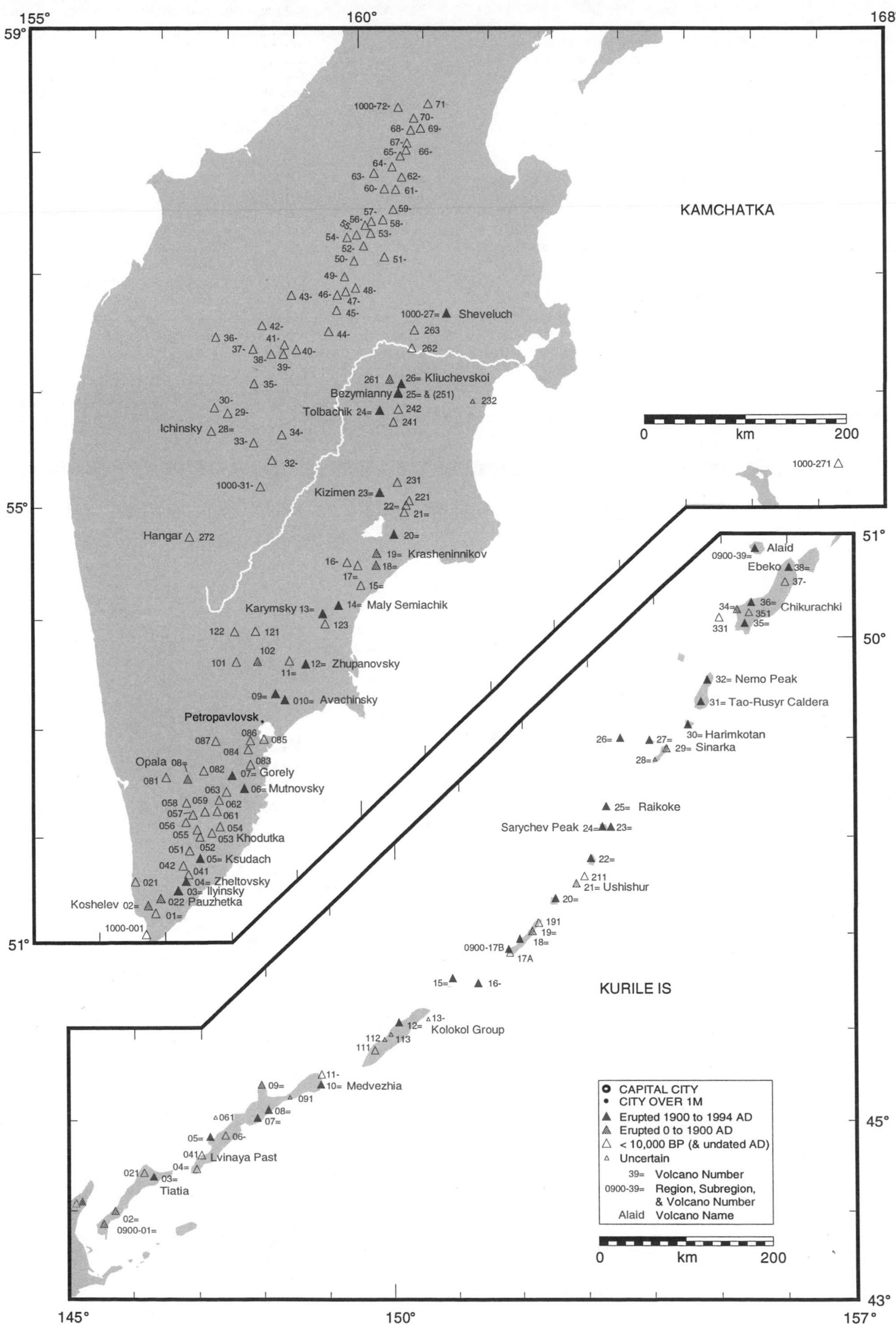
155°
160°
168°
59°
55°
51°
KAMCHATKA
1000-72- △ 71
70-
68- 69-
67-
65- 66-
64-
63- 62-
60- 61-
57- 59-
56- 58-
55-
54- 53-
52-
50- 51-
49-
43- 46- 48-
47-
45-
1000-27= Sheveluch
42-
36- 41- 44-
263
37- 40-
38-
39-
262
261 26= Kliuchevskoi
35-
Bezymianny 25= & (251)
30-
29-
232
Tolbachik 24= 242
241
Ichinsky 28=
34-
33-
32-
1000-31-
231
Kizimen 23=
221
22-
21=
Hangar 272
20=
19= Krasheninnikov
16- 18=
17=
15=
Karymsky 13= 14= Maly Semiachik
123
122 121
102
101 12= Zhupanovsky
11=
09= 010= Avachinsky
Petropavlovsk
086
087 085
084
083
Opala 08=
082 07= Gorely
081
063 06= Mutnovsky
058 059 062
057 061
056 054
055 053 Khodutka
051 052
05= Ksudach
042
041
021 04= Zheltovsky
03= Ilyinsky
Koshelev 02= 022 Pauzhetka
01=
1000-001
0 km 200
1000-271
51°
50°
45°
43°
145°
150°
157°
0900-39= Alaid
Ebeko 38=
37-
34= 36=
351 Chikurachki
331 35=
32= Nemo Peak
31= Tao-Rusyr Caldera
30= Harimkotan
26= 27=
29= Sinarka
28=
25= Raikoke
Sarychev Peak 24= 23=
22=
211
21= Ushishur
20=
191
19=
18=
0900-17B
17A
15= 16-
KURILE IS
13-
12= Kolokol Group
112 113
111
11-
09= 10= Medvezhia
091
061 08=
07=
05= 06-
041 Lvinaya Past
04=
021 03=
Tiatia
02=
0900-01=
CAPITAL CITY
CITY OVER 1M
Erupted 1900 to 1994 AD
Erupted 0 to 1900 AD
< 10,000 BP (& undated AD)
Uncertain
39= Volcano Number
0900-39= Region, Subregion, & Volcano Number
Alaid Volcano Name
0 km 200

As with the rest of the NW Pacific, subduction of the Pacific Plate has produced the vigorous explosive volcanism of the Kurile-Kamchatka arc, but tensional volcanism dominates the mainland part of the region. The Baikal rift, for example, includes young basaltic cinder cones as well as the world's deepest lake.

The contrast between Kamchatka and the mainland remains strong in the timing of historical volcanism, with that on the Asian mainland having begun early but been infrequent in recent centuries. Six volcanoes had erupted by 1697, the year of the first historical Kamchatkan eruption (the first being the Tianshan Group in the 1st century AD, followed by Datong in the 5th century). None of these was known to us at the time of our first edition, and we are hopeful that more work with the detailed chronicles of mainland Asia will further illuminate the volcanic history of this region. One of the world's largest Holocene eruptions, only recently receiving volcanological attention, took place at Baitoushan on the China/Korea border, in the 11th century AD. Mainland Asia's most recent eruptions are Wudalianchi, in 1719-21, and the Kunlun group in 1951.

The Kuriles and Kamchatka are sparsely populated and among the 4 smallest *CAVW* regions. The Kamchatka peninsula holds 454,800 people (63% in the city of Petropavlovsk) and the Kuriles 29,800 (83% in the 3 southern islands of Kunishir, Iturup, and Urup). The addition of mainland Asia, however, makes region 10 easily the most heavily populated, and (with the possible exception of Antarctica) the largest.

Regular monitoring of Kamchatkan volcanoes began in 1935 when the Kamchatka Volcanological Station was founded in Petropavlovsk. This grew into the Institute of Volcanology, the largest in the world, and was split into the IV and the Institute for Volcanic Geology and Geophysics in 1991. Observation of Kurile volcanoes is largely done by the Institute of Volcanology and Geodynamics in Sakhalin.

Region 10 has "grown" more than any other region since the 1981 book, with major efforts on both Kamchatka and mainland Asia resulting in a 64% increase in total number of Holocene volcanoes. The region now has the largest number of undated Holocene volcanoes (105), and is second only to South America in total number of Holocene volcanoes (194). Kamchatka easily leads the world in the number of eruptions (247) dated by tephrochronology and/or radiocarbon, and in the number of big (VEI ≥4) BC eruptions (19). No other region has a higher proportion of eruptions characterized as explosive (86%). Kamchatka also has the largest number of shield volcanoes (48), mostly in the Sredinny Range on the peninsula's western side, and very nearly as many volcanoes consisting primarily of cinder cones (17) as region 12 (below).

VOLCANO NAME (Subregion) / ERUPTION — Area of Activity	LAT	LONG	ELEV (m)	TYPE	NUMBER	Status / Start Year	Start M-Dy	P	Stop Year	Stop M-Dy	Central / Flank vent / Radial fiss / Regional*	Submarine / New island / Subglacial / Crater lake	Explosive / Pyro flow / Phreatic / Fumarolic	Lava flow / Lava lake / Dome / Spine	Fatal / Damage / Mudflow / Tsunami	VEI	Vol L/T
KURILES																	
GOLOVNIN (Kunashir I)	**43.85 N**	**145.53 E**	**541**	**Caldera**	**0900-01=**	**Historical**											
Eastern explosion crater						**1848**	....		....	....	x---	----	x---	----	----	1	
MENDELEEV (Kunashir I)	**43.98 N**	**145.70 E**	**887**	**Stratovolc**	**0900-02=**	**Historical**											
West side of central cone						C **-2250?**	....		....	....	x---	----	xx--	--x-	----		
NE solfatara field						**1880**	....		....	....	-x--	----	--x-	----	----	1	
						? **1900**	....		....	....	----	----	----	----	----	2?	
SMIRNOV (Kunashir I)	**44.43 N**	**146.13 E**	**1189**	**Stratovolc**	**0900-021**	**Holocene**											
TIATIA (Kunashir I)	**44.358 N**	**146.27 E**	**1819**	**Stratovolc**	**0900-03=**	**Historical**											
						1812	08		....	....	----	----	x---	----	----	2	
NNW and SSE flanks						**1973**	0714		**1973**	0728	-x--	----	x---	x---	----	4	-/8
(steam-gas columns: no solid ejecta)						X 1974	....		X1975	....	----	----	----	----	----		
						1978	0720		....	....	----	----	--x-	----	----	2	
						1981	0610	+	**1981**	0625	??--	----	x---	----	----	2?	
						? **1982**	0210		?**1982**	0214	x---	----	--?-	----	----	1	
BERUTARUBE (Iturup I)	**44.47 N**	**146.93 E**	**1220**	**Stratovolc**	**0900-04=**	**Holocene**											
(probably only fumarolic activity)						? **1812**	....		....	....	----	----	?--?	----	----	1	
LVINAYA PAST (Iturup I)	**44.62 N**	**147.00 E**	**528**	**Stratovolc**	**0900-041**	**Radiocarbon**											
						C **-7480**t	....		....	....	x---	----	xx--	----	----	**6+**	**-/10**
ATSONUPURI (Iturup I)	**44.804 N**	**147.13 E**	**1205**	**Stratovolc**	**0900-05=**	**Historical**											
						1812	0905d		....	....	----	----	x---	----	----	1	
						1932	....		....	....	----	----	?---	----	----	2	
BOGATYR RIDGE (Iturup I)	**44.83 N**	**147.37 E**	**1634**	**Stratovolc**	**0900-06-**	**Holocene**											
UNNAMED (Iturup-NW of)	**45.03 N**	**147.208 E**	**-930**	**Submarine**	**0900-061**	**Uncertain**											
17.5 km NW of Iturup Island						? **1967**	0426		....	....	----	?---	----	----	----		
GROZNY GROUP (Iturup I)	**45.02 N**	**147.87 E**	**1211**	**Complx vols**	**0900-07=**	**Historical**											
Ivan Grozny						**1968**	02		**1968**	02	x---	----	x---	----	----	1	
Ivan Grozny						**1970**	....		....	....	x---	----	x---	----	----	1	
Ivan Grozny						**1973**	01		**1973**	01	x---	----	x---	----	----	1	
Ivan Grozny (N flank of central dome)						**1973**	0516		**1973**	0517	-x--	----	x---	----	----	2?	
Ivan Grozny						**1989**	0503		**1989**	0805d	x---	----	x---	----	--x-	2	
BARANSKY (Iturup I)	**45.10 N**	**148.02 E**	**1132**	**Stratovolc**	**0900-08=**	**Historical**											
						C **1460**r	....		....	....	----	----	----	----	----		
						C **1570**r	....		....	....	----	----	----	----	----		
						1951	0715q		....	....	----	----	x---	----	----	1	
CHIRIP (Iturup I)	**45.38 N**	**147.92 E**	**1589**	**Stratovolcs**	**0900-09=**	**Historical**											
						1843	....		....	....	----	----	x---	----	----	2?	
SE of Bogdan Khmelinitskii summit						**1860**?	....		....	....	-x--	----	x---	----	----	1	
GOLETS-TORNYI GROUP (Iturup I)	**45.25 N**	**148.35 E**	**442**	**Pyrocl cones**	**0900-091**	**Holocene?**											
MEDVEZHIA (Iturup I)	**45.38 N**	**148.83 E**	**1124**	**Somma volc**	**0900-10=**	**Historical**											
Kudriavy						**1778**	1231y		....	....	x---	----	x---	----	----	2	
Kudriavy						**1883**	05		**1883**	06	x---	----	x---	x---	----	2	
Kudriavy						? **1946**	....		....	....	----	----	--?-	----	----	2	
Kudriavy						**1958**	....		....	....	----	----	x---	----	----	1	
DEMON (Iturup I)	**45.50 N**	**148.85 E**	**1205**	**Stratovolc**	**0900-11-**	**Holocene**											
IVAO GROUP (Urup I)	**45.77 N**	**149.68 E**	**1426**	**Cinder cones**	**0900-111**	**Holocene**											
RUDAKOV (Urup I)	**45.88 N**	**149.83 E**	**542**	**Stratovolc**	**0900-112**	**Holocene?**											
TRI SESTRY (Urup I)	**45.93 N**	**149.92 E**	**998**	**Stratovolc**	**0900-113**	**Holocene?**											
KOLOKOL GROUP (Urup I)	**46.042 N**	**150.05 E**	**1328**	**Somma volcs**	**0900-12=**	**Historical**											
						1780j	....		....	....	----	----	----	----	----	2?	
Berg						**1845**	....		**1846**	....	----	----	x---	----	----	2	
Berg ?						**1894**	0725		**1894**	0726	----	----	x---	----	----	2	
Trezubetz						**1924**	0313		....	....	-x--	----	x---	----	----	2?	
Berg						**1940**f	....		....	....	x---	----	----	--x-	----		7/-
Berg						**1946**	0415q		....	....	----	----	x---	----	----	2	
Berg						**1952**	0115q		....	....	x---	----	x---	----	----	2	
Berg						**1970**	02		**1970**	03	-x--	----	x---	----	----	3	
Berg (northern part of lava dome)						**1973**	0725		**1973**	0726?	x---	----	x---	----	----	1	
UNNAMED (Urup-E of)	**46.10 N**	**150.50 E**	**-100**	**Submarine ?**	**0900-13-**	**Uncertain**											
7.7 km E of Urup Island						? **1978**	0331		....	....	----	?---	----	----	----	0	
CHIRPOI (Kurile Is)	**46.525 N**	**150.875 E**	**742**	**Caldera**	**0900-15=**	**Historical**											
Cherny						**1712**	1231y		....	....	----	----	x---	----	----	4?	

VOLCANO NAME (Subregion) / ERUPTION	LAT	LONG	ELEV (m)	TYPE	NUMBER	Status / Area of Activity	Start Year	Start M-Dy	P	Stop Year	Stop M-Dy	Central / Flank vent / Radial fiss / Regional*	Submarine / New island / Subglacial / Crater lake	Explosive / Pyro flow / Phreatic / Fumarolic	Lava flow / Lava lake / Dome / Spine	Fatal / Damage / Mudflow / Tsunami	VEI	Vol L/T
CHIRPOI (Kurile Is) *continued*						Snow	**1790**p	....		....	....	----	----	x---	x---	----		
						Snow	**1811**	0611		....	....	----	----	x---	----	----	2	
						Snow (or Cherny)	**1854**	0624		....	....	----	----	x---	----	----	2	
						Cherny	**1857**	07		....	....	----	----	x---	----	----	3	
						Snow	**1879**	05		**1879**	06	----	----	x---	x---	----	2	
						Snow	**1960**	1020		....	....	----	----	x---	----	----	2?	
						Snow	**1982**	1122		....	....	x---	----	?---	----	----	2	
UNNAMED (Kurile Is)	**46.47**	**N 151.28 E**	**-502**	**Submarine**	**0900-16-**	**Hydrophonic**												
							S **1972**	0429		S**1972**	0430	----	x---	----	----	----	0	
MILNE (Simushir I)	**46.82**	**N 151.78 E**	**1540**	**Somma volc**	**0900-17A**	**Holocene**												
GORIASCHAIA SOPKA (Simushir I)	**46.83**	**N 151.75 E**	**891**	**Stratovolc**	**0900-17B**	**Historical**												
							1842	06		....	....	----	----	x---	----	----	3?	
							1849	....		....	....	----	----	x---	----	----	2	
							1881	09		....	....	----	----	x---	x---	----	2	
							1883	0415q		....	....	----	----	----	--?-	----	1	7/-
							1914	0604		**1914**	0604	x---	----	x---	----	----	2	
							? **1944**	....		....	....	----	----	?---	----	----	2	
ZAVARITZKI CALDERA (Simushir I)	**46.925**	**N 151.95 E**	**624**	**Caldera**	**0900-18=**	**Historical**												
						North end of caldera lake	**1923**h	....		....	....	x---	----	x---	--x-	----	1	
						North end of caldera lake	**1957**	1112		**1957**	1201	----	---x	x---	x-x-	--x-	3*	
PREVO PEAK (Simushir I)	**47.02**	**N 152.12 E**	**1360**	**Stratovolc**	**0900-19=**	**Historical**												
							1765e	....		....	....	----	----	xx--	----	-x--	3↑	
							1825q	....		....	....	----	----	x---	----	----	2	
URATAMAN (Simushir I)	**47.12**	**N 152.23 E**	**678**	**Somma volc**	**0900-191**	**Holocene**												
KETOI (Kurile Is)	**47.35**	**N 152.475 E**	**1172**	**Stratovolc**	**0900-20=**	**Historical**												
						Pallas Peak	**1843**	07		**1846**	....	----	----	x---	x---	----	2	
						Pallas Peak	**1924**	....		....	....	----	----	x---	----	----	2	
						Pallas Peak	**1960**	0927		....	....	----	----	x---	----	----	2	
USHISHUR (Kurile Is)	**47.52**	**N 152.80 E**	**401**	**Caldera**	**0900-21=**	**Historical**												
							C **-7450**t	....		....	....	x---	----	x---	----	----	**C**	
						SE caldera wall	**1710**j	....		....	....	x---	----	--x-	----	----	1	
						Center of caldera bay	**1769**>	....		....	....	x---	x---	x---	--x-	----		7/-
						SE caldera wall	**1884**	07		....	....	x---	----	--x-	----	----	1	
SREDNII (Ushishur-NW of)	**47.60**	**N 152.92 E**	**36**	**Submarine**	**0900-211**	**Holocene**												
							? **1880**?	0712		?**1880**?	0712	----	x---	----	----	----	0	
RASSHUA (Kurile Is)	**47.77**	**N 153.02 E**	**956**	**Stratovolc**	**0900-22=**	**Historical**												
						Eastern cone ?	**1846**	....		....	....	x---	----	x---	----	----	3	
							1957	10		....	....	----	----	--x-	----	----	1	
UNNAMED (Matua-E of)	**48.08**	**N 153.33 E**	**-150**	**Submarine**	**0900-23=**	**Historical**												
						Near Toporkovyi islet	**1924**	0215		....	....	----	x---	----	----	----	0	
SARYCHEV PEAK (Matua I)	**48.092**	**N 153.20 E**	**1496**	**Stratovolc**	**0900-24=**	**Historical**												
							1765e	....		....	....	----	----	x---	----	----	2?	
							1805	....		....	....	----	----	----	----	----		
							1879	0115q		....	....	----	----	----	x---	----	0	
							1923	0117		**1923**	0122	----	----	x---	----	----	2	
							1927	....		....	....	----	----	----	----	----	2?	
							1928	0214		....	....	----	----	x---	----	----	2	
							1930	0213		**1930**	0213	----	----	x?--	----	----	3	
							? **1932**?	....		....	....	x---	----	?---	----	----		
							1946	1109		**1946**	1119	x---	----	xx--	x---	----	4	
							1954	08		**1954**	10	----	----	x---	--x-	----	2	
							1960	0830		**1960**	0830	x---	----	x---	----	----	3	
							1965	1209		**1965**	1209	x---	----	x---	----	----	2	
							1976	0923	+	**1976**	1002	x---	----	x---	x---	----	2	6/-
							1986	09 ?		....	....	x---	----	x---	x---	----		
							1989	0113		**1989**	0114	x---	----	x---	----	----	1?	
RAIKOKE (Kurile Is)	**48.292**	**N 153.25 E**	**551**	**Stratovolc**	**0900-25=**	**Historical**												
							1765e	....		....	....	----	----	x---	----	----	2	
							1778	....		....	....	x---	----	x---	----	xx--	4↑	
							1924	0215		....	....	x---	----	x---	----	----	4	
CHIRINKOTAN (Kurile Is)	**48.98**	**N 153.48 E**	**724**	**Stratovolc**	**0900-26=**	**Historical**												
							? **1760**?	....		....	....	----	----	?---	----	----	2	
						North foot of inner summit cone	**1884**f	....		....	....	x---	----	----	x---	----	0	
							1900j	....		....	....	x---	----	x---	----	----		
						Floor of summit explosion crater	**1955**?	....		....	....	x---	----	x---	x---	----	2?	
							1979	04		**1980**	1010	x---	----	x---	x---	----	2	
							1986	1011		**1986**	1012	x---	----	x-x-	----	----	1	
EKARMA (Kurile Is)	**48.958**	**N 153.93 E**	**1170**	**Stratovolc**	**0900-27=**	**Historical**												
						Summit dome	**1767**	....		**1769**	....	x---	----	x---	--x-	----	2	
							1980	0524		....	....	----	----	x---	----	----	1	
KUNTOMINTAR (Shiashkotan I)	**48.77**	**N 154.02 E**	**828**	**Hydrothrm fld**	**0900-28=**	**Pleistocene-Fumarolic**												
						(no Holocene eruptions: see Sinarka)	X 1872	....		....	....	----	----	----	----	----		
SINARKA (Shiashkotan I)	**48.875**	**N 154.175 E**	**934**	**Stratovolc**	**0900-29=**	**Historical**												
							1725q	....		....	....	----	----	----	----	----	2?	
							1846	....		....	....	----	----	x---	----	----	3	
							1855	....		....	....	----	----	x---	----	----	2	
							1872	....		**1878**	....	x---	----	xx--	x-x-	-x--	4	7/-
HARIMKOTAN (Kurile Is)	**49.12**	**N 154.508 E**	**1145**	**Stratovolc**	**0900-30=**	**Historical**												
						Severgin	**1713**	....		....	....	----	----	x---	----	----	3↑	
						Severgin	**1846**	....		....	....	----	----	x---	----	----	2	
						Severgin	**1848**	....		....	....	----	----	x---	----	----	2	
						Severgin	**1883**	....		....	....	----	----	x---	----	----	3	
						Severgin	**1931**	09		....	....	----	----	x---	----	----	1	
						Severgin	**1933**	0108	+	**1933**	0414>	x---	----	xx--	x-x-	xx-x	3	8/-
TAO-RUSYR CALDERA (Onekotan I)	**49.35**	**N 154.70 E**	**1325**	**Stratovolc**	**0900-31=**	**Historical**												
						Tao-Rusyr	C **-5550**u	....		....	....	x---	----	xx--	----	----	**6**	-/10
						Krenitzyn Peak (east flank)	**1952**	1112		**1952**	1119	-x--	---x	x---	--x-	----	3	7/-
NEMO PEAK (Onekotan I)	**49.57**	**N 154.808 E**	**1018**	**Caldera**	**0900-32=**	**Historical**												
							T **-8050**?	....		....	....	x---	----	x---	x---	----		
							T **-7050**?	....		....	....	x---	----	x---	x---	----		
							T **-5550**?	....		....	....	x---	----	x---	x---	----		
							T **-3050**?	....		....	....	x---	----	x---	x---	----		

VOLCANO NAME (Subregion) / ERUPTION — Area of Activity	LAT	LONG	ELEV (m)	TYPE	NUMBER	Status / Start Year	Start M-Dy	P	Stop Year	Stop M-Dy	Central, Flank vent, Radial fiss, Regional* / Submarine, New island, Subglacial, Crater lake / Explosive, Pyro flow, Phreatic, Fumarolic / Lava flow, Lava lake, Dome, Spine / Fatal, Damage, Mudflow, Tsunami	VEI	Vol L/T
NEMO PEAK (Onekotan I) *continued*						T **-1850?**	....		....	....	x--- ---- x--- x--- ----		
						T **-0550v**	....		....	....	x--- ---- x--- x--- ----		
						T **0750?**	....		....	....	x--- ---- x--- x--- ----		
						T **1350?**	....		....	....	x--- ---- ---- --x- ----		
(eruption from Nemo, not Asyrmintar)						**1710j**	....		....	....	x--- ---- x-x- ---- ----	2	
						1906	....		....	....	x--- ---- x-x- --?- ----	2	
SE flank						? **1932?**	....		....	....	-x-- ---- ?--- ---- ----		
(eruption from Nemo, not Asyrmintar)						**1938**	0812		....	....	---- ---- x--- ---- ----	2	
ASYRMINTAR (Onekotan I)	49.60 N	154.90 E	570		0900-33=	Not a Volcano							
SHIRINKI (Kurile Is)	**50.20 N**	**154.98 E**	**761**	**Stratovolc**	**0900-331**	**Holocene**							
FUSS PEAK (Paramushir I)	**50.27 N**	**155.25 E**	**1772**	**Stratovolc**	**0900-34=**	**Historical**							
						1854	0705		....	....	---- ---- x--- ---- ----	3	
KARPINSKY GROUP (Paramushir I)	**50.13 N**	**155.37 E**	**1345**	**Cones**	**0900-35=**	**Historical**							
East side of Karpinsky Ridge						**1952**	1105		....	....	x--- ---- x--- ---- ----	1	
LOMONOSOV GROUP (Paramushir I)	**50.25 N**	**155.43 E**	**1681**	**Cinder cones**	**0900-351**	**Holocene**							
CHIKURACHKI (Paramushir I)	**50.325 N**	**155.458 E**	**1816**	**Stratovolcs**	**0900-36=**	**Historical**							
Tatarinov						T **1690j**	....		....	....	-x-- ---- x--- ---- ----	4	
						1853	12		**1859**	....	x--- ---- x?-- x--- ----	5?	-/9
						? **1933**	0415q		....	....	x--- ---- ?--- ---- ----		
						1957	05		....	....	x--- ---- x--- ---- ----	2	
						1958	0526		**1958**	0527	x--- ---- x--- ---- ----	2	
						1961	0502	+	**1961**	0810	x--- ---- x--- ---- --x-	1	
						1964	0201		**1964**	02	x--- ---- x--- ---- --x-	2	
						1967	0906		**1967**	0920	x--- ---- x--- ---- ----	2	
						1973	0810		**1973**	0928	x--- ---- x--- ---- ----	2	-/6
						1986	1118		**1986**	1207	x--- ---- xxx- x--- --x-	4*	7/8
VERNADSKII RIDGE (Paramushir I)	**50.55 N**	**155.97 E**	**1183**	**Cinder cones**	**0900-37-**	**Holocene**							
EBEKO (Paramushir I)	**50.68 N**	**156.02 E**	**1156**	**Somma volc**	**0900-38=**	**Historical**							
						1793	....		....	....	---- ---- x--- ---- ----	2	
						1859	0927		....	....	---- ---- x--- ---- ----	3	
Sredniy crater						**1934**	1004		**1935**	1015q	x-x- ---- x--x ---- ----	2	-/5
North wall of east amphitheater						**1963**	03		....	....	-x-- ---- --x- ---- ----	1	
						1965	....		**1966**	08	---- ---- --x- ---- ----	1	
Northern crater						**1967**	0208	+	**1967**	04	x--- ---x x-xx ---- ----	1	-/4
Northern crater						**1969**	....		....	....	x--- ---- --x- ---- ----	1	
Northern crater						**1971**	....		....	....	x--- ---- --x- ---- ----	1	
Northern crater						**1987**	1014		**1988**	01	x--- ---x x-x- ---- ----	1	-/4
Northern crater and upper east flank						**1989**	0202		**1990**	0415e	xx-- ---- x-x- ---- ----	2	-/6
Northern crater						**1991**	01		**1991**	01	x--- ---- x-x- ---- ----	1	
ALAID (Kurile Is)	**50.858 N**	**155.55 E**	**2339**	**Stratovolc**	**0900-39=**	**Historical**							
						1790	....		**1793**	....	x--- ---- x--- ---- ----	4*	
						1854	0627		....	....	x--- ---- x--- ---- ----	3	
						1860	0707		**1860**	0709	x--- ---- x--- ---- ----	3	
						1894	....		....	....	x--- ---- x--- ---- ----	2	
East submarine flank (Taketomi)						**1933**	1113		**1934**	08	-x-- xx-- x--- x--- ----	2	
NW foot						**1972**	0618	+	**1972**	0911	-xx- ---- x--- x--- ----	3	7/8
						? **1973**	....		....	....	-x-- ---- --?- ---- ----		
						1981	0427	+	**1981**	0605	x--- ---- x--- ---- -xx-	4*	-/8
						1981	1125		....	....	x--- ---- x--- ---- ----	2	
						1982	0329		**1982**	0329	x--- ---- x--- ---- ----	2	
						1986	0525		**1986**	0528c	x--- ---- x-x- ---- ----	2?	

KAMCHATKA

VOLCANO NAME (Subregion) / ERUPTION — Area of Activity	LAT	LONG	ELEV (m)	TYPE	NUMBER	Status / Start Year	Start M-Dy	P	Stop Year	Stop M-Dy	Central, Flank vent, Radial fiss, Regional* / Submarine, New island, Subglacial, Crater lake / Explosive, Pyro flow, Phreatic, Fumarolic / Lava flow, Lava lake, Dome, Spine / Fatal, Damage, Mudflow, Tsunami	VEI	Vol L/T
MASHKOVTSEV (Kamchatka)	**51.10 N**	**156.72 E**	**503**	**Stratovolc**	**1000-001**	**Holocene**							
KAMBALNY (Kamchatka)	**51.30 N**	**156.87 E**	**2156**	**Stratovolc**	**1000-01=**	**Holocene**							
KOSHELEV (Kamchatka)	**51.357 N**	**156.75 E**	**1812**	**Stratovolc**	**1000-02=**	**Historical**							
SE flank						**1690j**	....		....	....	-x-- ---- x--- ---- ----	3↑	
UNNAMED (Kamchatka)	**51.60 N**	**156.55 E**	**298**	**Cinder cone**	**1000-021**	**Holocene**							
PAUZHETKA (Kamchatka)	**51.43 N**	**156.93 E**	**1331**	**Calderas**	**1000-022**	**Radiocarbon**							
						C **-7545t**	....		....	....	---- ---- x--- ---- ----		
Kurile Lake						C **-6220w**	....		....	....	x--- ---- xx-- ---- ----	**6**	**-/10**
Diky Greben						T **-3950v**	....		....	....	x--- ---- x--- x-x- ----		
Diky Greben						T **-3050?**	....		....	....	x--- ---- x--- ---- ----		
Diky Greben						T **0200y**	....		....	....	x--- ---- x--- x-x- ----		**10/-**
ILYINSKY (Kamchatka)	**51.490 N**	**157.20 E**	**1578**	**Stratovolc**	**1000-03=**	**Historical**							
						T **-6050?**	....		....	....	x--- ---- x--- ---- ----	**C**	
						T **0200y**	....		....	....	-x-- ---- ---- x-x- ----		
NE flank						**1901**	....		....	....	-x-- ---- x-x- x--- ----	3	
ZHELTOVSKY (Kamchatka)	**51.57 N**	**157.323 E**	**1953**	**Stratovolc**	**1000-04=**	**Historical**							
						T **-7050***	....		....	....	x--- ---- xx-- ---- ----	**5**	**-/9**
						T **-6050?**	....		....	....	x--- ---- x--- x--- ----		
						C **-3050?**	....		....	....	---- ---- x--- ---- ----		
						? **1823e**	....		....	....	---- ---- ---- ---- ----		
						1923	0211		**1923**	04	x--- ---- x--- x--- ----	3	
						1972	03		....	....	x--- ---- --x- ---- ----		
KELL (Kamchatka)	**51.65 N**	**157.35 E**	**900**	**Stratovolc**	**1000-041**	**Holocene**							
BELEN'KAYA (Kamchatka)	**51.75 N**	**157.27 E**	**892**	**Stratovolc**	**1000-042**	**Holocene**							
KSUDACH (Kamchatka)	**51.80 N**	**157.53 E**	**1079**	**Shield**	**1000-05=**	**Historical**							
Ksudach III caldera						C **-6850t**	....		....	....	x--- ---- xx-- ---- ----	**C**	
						T **-5850?**	....		....	....	---- ---- x--- ---- ----		
						C **-5350z**	....		....	....	---- ---- xx-- ---- ----		
Ksudach IV caldera						C **-4100t**	....		....	....	x--- ---- xx-- ---- ----	**C**	
						T **-3850?**	....		....	....	---- ---- x--- ---- ----		
						T **-2850y**	....		....	....	---- ---- x--- ---- ----		
						T **-1650?**	....		....	....	x--- ---- xx-- ---- ----		
						C **-0450v**	....		....	....	x--- ---- x--- ---- ----	4	-/8
						C **-0150?**	....		....	....	---- ---- x--- ---- ----		
Ksudach V caldera						C **0155v**	....		....	....	x--- ---- xx-- ---- ----	6	-/10
Stubel						C **0350?**	....		....	....	x--- ---- x--- --?- ----	2	-/6
Stubel						C **0900t**	....		....	....	x--- ---- xx-- ---- ----	5	-/9
Stubel						C **1655v**	....		....	....	x--- ---- x--- ---- --x-	4	-/8
Stubel						**1907**	0328?		....	....	x--- ---- xx-- ---- ----	5	-/9
OZERNOY (Kamchatka)	**51.88 N**	**157.38 E**	**562**	**Shield**	**1000-051**	**Holocene**							
PLOSKY VOLC GROUP (Kamchatka)	**52.02 N***	**157.53 E**	**681**	**Volc field**	**1000-052**	**Holocene**							

VOLCANO NAME (Subregion) / ERUPTION — Area of Activity	LAT	LONG	ELEV (m)	TYPE	NUMBER	Status / Start Year	Start M-Dy	P	Stop Year	Stop M-Dy	Central / Flank vent / Radial fiss / Regional*	Submarine / New island / Subglacial / Crater lake	Explosive / Pyro flow / Phreatic / Fumarolic	Lava flow / Lava lake / Dome / Spine	Fatal / Damage / Mudflow / Tsunami	VEI	Vol L/T
KHODUTKA (Kamchatka)	52.063 N	157.703 E	2090	Stratovolcs	1000-053	Radiocarbon											
NW flank of Priemysh volcano						T -1050<	....		....	....	-x--	----	x---	----	----	4+	-/8
WNW flank (Khodutkinsky maar)						C -0850?	....		....	....	-x--	----	xx--	x-x-	----		7/-
						T -0300y	....		....	....	x---	----	----	x---	----	0	
PIRATKOVSKY (Kamchatka)	52.113 N	157.849 E	1322	Stratovolc	1000-054	Holocene											
OLKOVIY (Kamchatka)	52.077 N	157.477 E	636	Shield	1000-055	Holocene											
OSTANETS (Kamchatka)	52.154 N	157.322 E	719	Shields	1000-056	Holocene											
OTDELNIY (Kamchatka)	52.220 N	157.428 E	791	Shields	1000-057	Holocene											
UNNAMED (Kamchatka)	52.33 N*	157.33 E	638	Pyrocl cones	1000-058	Holocene											
TUNDROVIY (Kamchatka)	52.25 N	157.60 E	739	Shields	1000-059	Holocene											
MUTNOVSKY (Kamchatka)	52.453 N	158.195 E	2322	Complx volc	1000-06=	Historical											
						T -7550?	....		....	....	----	----	x---	----	----	2	-/6
						T -6000?	....		....	....	----	----	x-x-	----	----	2	-/6
						T -5900?	....		....	....	----	----	x-x-	----	----	2	-/6
						T -5800?	....		....	....	----	----	x-x-	----	----	2	-/6
						T -5450?	....		....	....	----	----	x-x-	----	----	2	-/6
						T -5350?	....		....	....	----	----	x-x-	----	----	2	-/6
						T -5250?	....		....	....	----	----	x-x-	----	----	2	-/6
						T -5050?	....		....	....	----	----	x---	----	----	3	-/7
						T -5000?	....		....	....	----	----	x-x-	----	----	2	-/6
						T -4700?	....		....	....	----	----	x-x-	----	----	2	-/6
						T -4650?	....		....	....	----	----	x-x-	----	----	2	-/6
						T -4550?	....		....	....	----	----	x---	----	----	2	-/6
						T -4050?	....		....	....	----	----	x-x-	----	----	2	-/6
						T -3650?	....		....	....	----	----	x-x-	----	----	2	-/6
						T -2900?	....		....	....	----	----	x-x-	----	----	2	-/6
						T -2150?	....		....	....	----	----	x-x-	----	----	3	-/7
						T -2050?	....		....	....	----	----	x-x-	----	----	2	-/6
						T -0450?	....		....	....	----	----	x-x-	----	----	2	-/6
						T -0200?	....		....	....	----	----	x-x-	----	----	2	-/6
						T -0100?	....		....	....	----	----	x-x-	----	----	2	-/6
						T 0050?	....		....	....	----	----	x-x-	----	----	2	-/6
						T 0250?	....		....	....	----	----	x-x-	----	----	2	-/6
						T 0750?	....		....	....	----	----	x-x-	----	----	3	-/7
						T 0950?	....		....	....	----	----	x-x-	----	----	2	-/6
						T 1300?	....		....	....	----	----	x-x-	----	----	2	-/6
						1650t	....		....	....	x---	----	x---	----	----	2	
						1750t	....		....	....	x---	----	x---	----	----	2	
						1848	....		....	....	x---	----	x---	----	----	3	-/7
						1852	03		....	....	x---	----	x---	----	----	2	
						1853	01		....	....	x---	----	x---	----	----	2	
						1853	1218	+	1854	03	x---	----	x---	----	----	2	
						1898	04		1898	0715q	x---	----	x-x-	----	----	2	-/6
						1904	0402	+	1904	0626>	x---	----	x-x-	x---	----	2	
						1916	0715e		....	....	x---	----	x---	----	----	2	
						1916	12		....	....	x---	----	x---	----	----	2	
						1917	0705d		....	....	x---	----	x---	----	----	3?	
						1927	01		1927	02	x---	----	x-x-	----	----	2	
						1928	0125		1928	02	x---	----	x-x-	----	----	2	
						1929	02		....	....	x---	----	x-x-	----	----	2	
						1938	11		....	....	x---	----	x---	----	----	2	
						1939	05		....	....	x---	----	x---	----	----	2	
						1945	0623		....	....	x---	----	x---	----	----	2	
West wall of SW crater						1960	12		1961	01	x---	----	x---	----	----	2	-/6
GOLAYA (Kamchatka)	52.263 N	157.787 E	858	Stratovolc	1000-061	Holocene											
ASACHA (Kamchatka)	52.355 N	157.827 E	1910	Complx volc	1000-062	Holocene											
VISOKIY (Kamchatka)	52.43 N	157.93 E	1234	Stratovolc	1000-063	Holocene											
GORELY (Kamchatka)	52.558 N	158.03 E	1829	Caldera	1000-07=	Historical											
						T -7250?	....		....	....	x---	----	x---	----	----	2	
						T -5950?	....		....	....	x---	----	x---	x---	----	3	-/7
						T -5650?	....		....	....	x---	----	x---	x---	----	3	-/7
						T -5500?	....		....	....	x---	----	x---	x---	----	3	-/7
						T -5450?	....		....	....	x---	----	x---	x---	----	3	-/7
						T -5300?	....		....	....	x---	----	x---	----	----	2	
						T -5150?	....		....	....	x---	----	x---	x---	----	3	-/7
						T -4950?	....		....	....	x---	----	x---	----	----	2	
						T -4750?	....		....	....	x---	----	x---	x---	----	3	-/7
						T -4700?	....		....	....	x---	----	x---	----	----	2	
						T -4650?	....		....	....	x---	----	x---	x---	----	3	-/7
						T -4600?	....		....	....	x---	----	x---	----	----	2	
						T -4500?	....		....	....	x---	----	x---	----	----	2	
						T -4450?	....		....	....	x---	----	x---	----	----	2	-/6
						T -4350?	....		....	....	x---	----	x---	x---	----	3	-/7
						T -4150?	....		....	....	x---	----	x---	----	----	2	-/6
						T -3950?	....		....	....	x---	----	x---	----	----	2	-/6
						T -3900?	....		....	....	x---	----	x---	----	----	2	
						T -3450?	....		....	....	-x--	----	x---	----	----	3	-/7
						T -2750?	....		....	....	-x--	----	x---	x---	----	2	-/6
						T -2450?	....		....	....	-x--	----	x---	x---	----	3	-/7
						T -2250?	....		....	....	----	----	x---	----	----	2	-/6
						T -2200?	....		....	....	----	----	x---	----	----	2	
						T -2050?	....		....	....	----	----	x---	----	----	2	-/6
						T -2000?	....		....	....	----	----	x---	----	----	2	-/6
						T -0350?	....		....	....	----	----	x---	x---	----	3	-/7
						T 0050?	....		....	....	----	----	x---	----	----	3	-/7
						T 0200?	....		....	....	----	----	x---	----	----	3	-/7
						T 0250?	....		....	....	----	----	x---	----	----	3	-/7
						T 0550?	....		....	....	----	----	x---	----	----	3	-/7
						T 1025q	....		....	....	----	----	x---	----	----	3	-/7
						T 1325q	....		....	....	----	----	x-x-	----	----	2?	
						T 1750t	....		....	....	----	----	x-x-	----	----	2?	
						? 1821	....		....	....	----	----	----	----	----		
						1828	06		....	....	x---	----	x---	----	----	3	-/7
						1832	02		....	....	x---	----	x---	----	----	3	-/7
						? 1855	04		....	....	x---	----	?--?	----	----	2?	
						1869	....		....	....	x---	----	x---	----	----	2	
						1929	0901		1930	04	x---	----	x---	----	----	3	-/7
						1930	09		1931	0117	x---	----	x---	----	----	3	-/7

VOLCANO NAME (Subregion) / ERUPTION — Area of Activity	LAT	LONG	ELEV (m)	TYPE	NUMBER	Status / Start Year	Start M-Dy	P	Stop Year	Stop M-Dy	Central / Flank vent / Radial fiss / Regional*	Submarine / New island / Subglacial / Crater lake	Explosive / Pyro flow / Phreatic / Fumarolic	Lava flow / Lava lake / Dome / Spine	Fatal / Damage / Mudflow / Tsunami	VEI	Vol L/T
GORELY (Kamchatka) *continued*						**1931**	05		**1931**	0715q	x---	----	x---	----	----	2	
						? **1932**	....		....	....	----	----	----	----	----		
						1947	12		....	....	x---	----	x---	----	----	2	
						1961	01		....	....	x---	----	x---	----	----	2	
						1980	0615e	+	**1981**	0703	x---	----	xxx-	----	----	3*	-/7
						1984	0804	+	**1986**	0921?	x---	---x	x-x-	----	----	2	
OPALA (Kamchatka)	**52.543 N**	**157.335 E**	**2475**	**Caldera**	**1000-08=**	**Radiocarbon**											
SE flank (Barany Amphitheater)						G **0430?**	....		....	....	-x--	----	xx--	--x-	----	**5+**	**8/9**
(no evidence for summit eruption)						X 1776	1023		....	....	----	----	----	----	----		
(no evidence for summit eruption)						X 1827	....		....	....	----	----	----	----	----		
(no evidence for S flank eruption)						X 1854	....		....	....	----	----	----	----	----		
(no evidence for S flank eruption)						X 1894	....		....	....	----	----	----	----	----		
UNNAMED (Kamchatka)	**52.57 N***	**157.02 E**	**610**	**Cinder cone**	**1000-081**	**Holocene**											
TOLMACHEV DOL (Kamchatka)	**52.63 N***	**157.58 E**	**1021**	**Cinder cones**	**1000-082**	**Holocene**											
VILYUCHIK (Kamchatka)	**52.68 N**	**158.30 E**	**2173**	**Stratovolc**	**1000-083**	**Tephrochronology**											
						T **-5550***	....		....	....	----	----	x---	x---	----		
BARKHATNAYA SOPKA (Kamchatka)	**52.823 N**	**158.27 E**	**870**	**Lava domes**	**1000-084**	**Tephrochronology**											
						T **-3550>**	....		....	....	x---	----	x---	----	----		
UNNAMED (Kamchatka)	**52.92 N**	**158.52 E**	**450**	**Shields**	**1000-085**	**Holocene**											
UNNAMED (Kamchatka)	**52.88 N**	**158.30 E**	**700**	**Shields**	**1000-086**	**Holocene**											
BOLSHE-BANNAYA (Kamchatka)	**52.90 N**	**157.78 E**	**1200**	**Lava domes**	**1000-087**	**Holocene**											
KORYAKSKY (Kamchatka)	**53.320 N**	**158.688 E**	**3456**	**Stratovolc**	**1000-09=**	**Historical**											
						1895	1015q		**1896**	....	----	----	x---	x---	----	2	
						1926	03 ?		....	....	----	----	x-?-	----	----	1?	
Summit and upper NW flank (3000 m)						**1956**	12		**1957**	06	x-x-	----	xx--	----	----	3*	
AVACHINSKY (Kamchatka)	**53.255 N**	**158.830 E**	**2741**	**Stratovolc**	**1000-10=**	**Historical**											
						T **-8050>**	....		....	....	----	----	x---	----	----		
						T **-6050?**	....		....	....	----	----	x---	----	----		
						T **-4700?**	....		....	....	----	----	x---	----	----		
						G **-4400?**	....		....	....	x---	----	xx--	----	----	**5**	**-/9**
						T **-2900?**	....		....	....	----	----	x---	----	----		
						T **-2200?**	....		....	....	----	----	x---	----	----		
						T **-1700?**	....		....	....	----	----	x---	----	----		
						G **-1500?**	....		....	....	----	----	xx--	----	----	**5**	**-/9**
						T **-1300?**	....		....	....	----	----	x---	----	----		
						T **0100?**	....		....	....	----	----	x---	----	----		
						T **0400?**	....		....	....	----	----	x---	----	----		
						T **0700?**	....		....	....	----	----	x---	----	----		
						T **0900?**	....		....	....	----	----	x---	----	----		
						T **1100?**	....		....	....	----	----	x---	----	----		
						T **1200?**	....		....	....	----	----	x---	----	----		
						C **1400?**	....		....	....	x---	----	x---	----	----		
						C **1550?**	....		....	....	x---	----	x---	----	----		
						1737	08	+	**1737**	1017>	x-x-	----	x---	x---	---x	3	-/7
						1772	....		....	....	----	----	x---	----	----	2	
						1779	0615		**1779**	0616	x---	----	x---	----	----	3	-/7
						? **1789**	....		....	....	----	----	----	----	----		
						1827	0627		**1827**	0629	x---	----	x---	x---	--x-	2	
						1828	0417		....	....	----	----	x---	----	----	2	
						? **1837**	....		....	....	----	----	----	----	----		
						1855	0528		**1855**	09	x---	----	x---	----	----	2	
						1878	....		....	....	x---	----	x---	----	----	2	
						1881	....		....	....	x---	----	x---	----	----	2	
						1894	10		**1895**	02	x---	----	xx--	----	----	2	
						1901	0707		**1901**	0713	x---	----	x---	x---	----	2	
						1909	08		....	....	x---	----	x---	x---	----	2	
						? **1910**	....		....	....	----	----	----	----	----		
						1926	0328	+	**1926**	0405	x---	----	xx--	x---	--x-	2	
						? **1927**	....		....	....	----	----	----	----	----		
						1938	0306	+	**1938**	0328>	x---	----	x---	x---	--x-	2	
						1938	0904	+	**1938**	1201>	x---	----	x---	x---	--x-	2	
						1945	0225		**1945**	0226	x---	----	x---	----	--x-	4	-/8
						1991	0113		**1991**	0130	x---	----	x---	x-x-	--x-	3	
UNNAMED (Kamchatka)	**53.63 N**	**158.10 E**	**200**	**Cinder cones**	**1000-101**	**Holocene**											
VEER (Kamchatka)	**53.63 N**	**158.42 E**	**350**	**Cinder cones**	**1000-102**	**Historical**											
Korenevski Ridge						**1856**	....		....	....	----	----	?---	x---	----	0?	
DZENZURSKY (Kamchatka)	**53.637 N**	**158.922 E**	**2155**	**Compnd volc**	**1000-11=**	**Holocene**											
(fumarolic activity only)						X 1923	02		....	....	----	----	---x	----	----		
(fumarolic activity only)						X 1957	0128		X1957	0311	----	----	---x	----	----		
ZHUPANOVSKY (Kamchatka)	**53.590 N**	**159.147 E**	**2958**	**Compnd volc**	**1000-12=**	**Historical**											
						T **-5050?**	....		....	....	----	----	x---	----	----		
						T **-3050?**	....		....	....	----	----	x---	----	----		
						C **-0220t**	....		....	....	----	----	xx--	----	----		
						T **-0050?**	....		....	....	----	----	x---	----	----		
						T **1000z**	....		....	....	----	----	x---	----	----		
						1776	10		....	....	x---	----	x---	----	----	2	
						1882	....		....	....	x---	----	x---	----	----	2	
						1925	....		....	....	x---	----	x---	----	----	2	
						1929	....		....	....	x---	----	x---	----	----	2	
						1940	01		**1940**	02	x---	----	x---	----	----	2	
Middle crater, east crater						**1956**	1227		**1957**	06	x---	----	x---	----	----	2	
						1959	....		....	....	x---	----	x---	----	----	2	
ZAVARITSKY (Kamchatka)	**53.905 N**	**158.385 E**	**1567**	**Stratovolc**	**1000-121**	**Holocene**											
BAKENIN (Kamchatka)	**53.905 N**	**158.07 E**	**2277**	**Caldera**	**1000-122**	**Holocene**											
AKADEMIA NAUK (Kamchatka)	**53.98 N**	**159.45 E**	**1180**	**Stratovolcs**	**1000-123**	**Holocene**											
KARYMSKY (Kamchatka)	**54.05 N**	**159.43 E**	**1486**	**Stratovolc**	**1000-13=**	**Historical**											
Karymsky Caldera						C **-5700t**	....		....	....	x---	----	xx--	x---	----	**6?**	**-/10**
						G **-4150?**	....		....	....	x---	----	x---	----	----		
						G **-3450?**	....		....	....	----	----	x---	x---	----		
						G **-3150?**	....		....	....	----	----	x---	x---	----	3	-/7
						G **-2350?**	....		....	....	----	----	x---	x---	----		
						G **-2250?**	....		....	....	----	----	x---	x---	----	4	-/8
						G **-2050?**	....		....	....	----	----	x---	----	----		
						G **-1400?**	....		....	....	----	----	x---	x---	----		
						G **-1050?**	....		....	....	----	----	x---	x---	----		
						G **-0850?**	....		....	....	----	----	x---	----	----		

VOLCANO NAME (Subregion) / ERUPTION — Area of Activity	LAT	LONG	ELEV (m)	TYPE	NUMBER	Status / Start Year	Start M-Dy	P	Stop Year	Stop M-Dy	Central / Flank vent / Radial fiss / Regional*	Submarine / New island / Subglacial / Crater lake	Explosive / Pyro flow / Phreatic / Fumarolic	Lava flow / Lava lake / Dome / Spine	Fatal / Damage / Mudflow / Tsunami	VEI	Vol L/T
KARYMSKY (Kamchatka) *continued*						G **0950?**	....		....	....	----	----	x---	----	----		
						G **1050?**	....		....	....	----	----	x---	----	----		
						G **1150?**	....		....	....	----	----	x---	----	----		
						G **1450?**	....		....	....	----	----	x---	x---	----		
						C **1690**v	....		....	....	----	----	x---	x---	----		
						1771	....		....	....	x---	----	x---	----	----	2	
						1830	....		....	....	x---	----	x---	----	----	2	
						1852	....		....	....	x---	----	x---	----	----	2	
						1854	09		....	....	x---	----	x---	----	----	2	
						1908	....		....	....	x---	----	x---	----	----	2	
						1911	....		....	....	x---	----	x---	----	----	2	
						1912	01		....	....	x---	----	x---	----	----	2	
						1915	....		....	....	x---	----	x---	----	----	2	
						1921	09		....	....	x---	----	x---	----	----	2	
						1923	02		....	....	x---	----	x---	----	----	2	
						1925	07		....	....	x---	----	x---	----	----	2	
						1929	....		....	....	x---	----	x---	----	----	2	
						1932	06		....	....	x---	----	x---	----	----	2	
						1933	09		**1933**	10	x---	----	x---	----	----	2	
						1934	11	+	**1935**	02	x---	----	x---	x---	----	2	8/-
						1938	10		....	....	----	----	--x-	----	----	2	
						1940	....		....	....	x---	----	x---	----	----	2	
						1943	0201p		....	....	x---	----	x---	----	----	2	
						1945	09		....	....	x---	----	x---	x---	----	2	
						1946	04		....	....	x---	----	x---	----	----	2	
						1946	09		**1946**	10	x---	----	x---	----	----	2	
						1947	04		....	....	x---	----	x---	----	----	2	
						1952	11		....	....	x---	----	x---	----	----	2	
						1953	....		....	....	----	----	x---	----	----	2	
						1955	....		....	....	x---	----	x---	----	----	2	
						1956	03	+	**1957**	02	x---	----	x---	----	----	1	
						1960	04	+	**1964**	12	x---	----	x---	x---	----	3*	6/7
						1965	0515e	+	**1967**	02	x---	----	x---	x---	----	3	
						1967	11		**1967**	11	x---	----	x---	----	----	1	
						1970	0511	+	**1982**	1011	x---	----	xx--	x-x-	--x-	3	7/7
(fumarolic activity only in 1985)						X 1985	0503?		....	....	----	----	----	----	----		
MALY SEMIACHIK (Kamchatka)	**54.13**	**N 159.67**	**E 1560**	**Caldera**	**1000-14=**	**Historical**											
Meso-Semiachik						C **-7550?**	....		....	....	x---	----	x---	x---	----		
Meso-Semiachik east flank (Vostochny)						C **-6950?**	....		....	....	-x--	----	----	x---	----		
Ceno-Semiachik						G **-6150?**	....		....	....	x---	----	x---	x---	----		
Ceno-Semiachik						G **-5850?**	....		....	....	x---	----	x---	----	----		
Ceno-Semiachik						G **-5750?**	....		....	....	x---	----	x---	----	----		
Ceno-Semiachik						G **-5450?**	....		....	....	x---	----	x---	----	----		
Ceno-Semiachik						G **-5050?**	....		....	....	x---	----	x---	----	----		
Ceno-Semiachik						G **-4650?**	....		....	....	x---	----	x---	x---	----		
Ceno-Semiachik flank (Yushny Cone)						G **-4500**t	....		....	....	-x--	----	----	x---	----		
Ceno-Semiachik flank (Obmanuvshy)						G **-3500**t	....		....	....	-x--	----	----	x---	----		
Ceno-Semiachik (Crater IV)						G **-2450?**	....		....	....	x---	----	xx--	----	----		
Ceno-Semiachik						G **-2250?**	....		....	....	x---	----	x---	----	----		
Ceno-Semiachik (SW flank)						G **-1800**t	....		....	....	--x-	----	x---	x---	----		
Ceno-Semiachik						G **-0850?**	....		....	....	x---	----	x---	xx--	----		
Ceno-Semiachik						G **-0650?**	....		....	....	x---	----	x---	----	----		
Ceno-Semiachik						G **-0550?**	....		....	....	x---	----	x---	----	----		
Ceno-Semiachik (Crater V)						G **1400**t	....		....	....	x---	----	x---	xx--	----		
Ceno-Semiachik (Crater VI--Troitsky)						G **1550?**	....		....	....	x---	----	x---	----	----	4	-/8
Ceno-Semiachik (Troitsky Crater)						**1804**	....		....	....	x---	----	x-x-	----	----	3	
Ceno-Semiachik (Troitsky Crater)						**1851**	09		....	....	x---	----	--x-	----	----	2	
Ceno-Semiachik (Troitsky Crater)						**1852**	0415q	+	**1852**	07	x---	----	--x-	----	----	2	
Ceno-Semiachik (Toitsky Crater)						**1945**	09 ?		**1946**	0415q	x---	----	?-x-	----	----	2	
Ceno-Semiachik (Toitsky Crater)						**1952**	1205d		....	....	x---	----	--x-	----	----	2	
BOLSHOI SEMIACHIK (Kamchatka)	**54.32**	**N 160.02**	**E 1720**	**Stratovolcs**	**1000-15=**	**Radiocarbon**											
Ivanov lava dome						C **-6800**y	....		....	....	x---	----	----	--x-	----		
Korona and Yezh lava domes						G **-4450?**	....		....	....	x---	----	----	--x-	----		
TAUNSHITS (Kamchatka)	**54.53**	**N 159.80**	**E 2353**	**Stratovolc**	**1000-16-**	**Radiocarbon**											
						C **-5800**t	....		....	....	x---	----	xx--	--x-	----		
						C **-0550?**	....		....	....	x---	----	xx--	x-x-	----		
UZON (Kamchatka)	**54.50**	**N 159.97**	**E 1617**	**Calderas**	**1000-17=**	**Radiocarbon**											
N part of caldera (Lake Dal'ny maar)						C **-5700**t	....		....	....	x---	----	x---	----	----		
KIKHPINYCH (Kamchatka)	**54.487**	**N 160.253**	**E 1552**	**Stratovolcs**	**1000-18=**	**Radiocarbon**											
Zapadny						G **-2850?**	....		....	....	x---	----	x---	x---	----	3	-/7
Zapadny						G **-2775**q	....		....	....	x---	----	x---	x---	----	4	8/8
East side of Zapadny, Savich Cone						G **0550?**	....		....	....	xx--	---?	x---	x---	--x-	3	7/7
Savich Cone						C **0650?**	....		....	....	x---	----	x---	----	----		
Savich Cone						T **0825**q	....		....	....	x---	----	x---	x---	----		
Savich Cone						C **0900**t	....		....	....	x---	----	x---	----	----	3?	-/8
Savich Cone and north flank						C **1350?**	....		....	....	xx--	----	x---	x---	----	4	8/8
East flank of Savich (Krab Cone)						T **1550?**	....		....	....	-x--	----	----	x---	----		7/-
KRASHENINNIKOV (Kamchatka)	**54.593**	**N 160.273**	**E 1856**	**Caldera**	**1000-19=**	**Radiocarbon**											
Southern Cone & S outer flank fissure						C **-8050?**	....		....	....	x-x-	----	x---	x---	----		
Southern Cone & S outer flank fissure						C **-7250?**	....		....	....	x-x-	----	x-x-	x---	----		
Southern Cone summit, outer SW flank						C **-6550?**	....		....	....	x-x-	----	x---	x---	----		
Southern Cone summit and flank						C **-6350?**	....		....	....	x-x-	----	x---	x---	----		
Northern outer flank fissure						C **-6250?**	....		....	....	--x-	----	x---	x---	----		
Southern Cone summit and flank						C **-6000**t	....		....	....	x-x-	----	x---	x---	----	4	**9**/8
Southern Cone summit and west flank						C **-5800**t	....		....	....	x-x-	----	x---	x---	----	4	7/8
Southern Cone						C **-5450?**	....		....	....	x---	----	x---	----	----		
Northern outer flank fissure						G **-5250?**	....		....	....	--x-	----	x---	x---	----		
Southern Cone						C **-5050?**	....		....	....	x---	----	x---	----	----		
Southern Cone						C **-4850?**	....		....	....	x---	----	x---	----	----		
Northern Cone						G **-4450?**	....		....	....	x---	----	x---	----	----		
Northern Cone & N outer flank fissure						G **-3550?**	....		....	....	x-x-	----	x-x-	x---	----		
Northern Cone						G **-3250?**	....		....	....	x---	----	x---	----	----		
Northern Cone & N outer flank fissure						G **-2950?**	....		....	....	x-x-	----	x-x-	x---	----		
Northern Cone						G **-2250?**	....		....	....	x---	----	x---	----	----		
Northern Cone						G **-1650?**	....		....	....	x---	----	x---	----	----		
N (Zametny) & S (Duga) flank fissures						G **-1350?**	....		....	....	--x-	----	x---	x---	----	3	8/7
Northern Cone						G **-1150?**	....		....	....	x---	----	x---	x---	----		

VOLCANO NAME (Subregion) / ERUPTION —	Area of Activity	LAT	LONG	ELEV (m)	TYPE	NUMBER	Status / Start Year	Start M-Dy	P	Stop Year	Stop M-Dy	Central / Flank vent / Radial fiss / Regional	Submarine / New island / Subglacial / Crater lake	Explosive / Pyro flow / Phreatic / Fumarolic	Lava flow / Lava lake / Dome / Spine	Fatal / Damage / Mudflow / Tsunami	VEI	Vol L/T
KRASHENINNIKOV (Kamchatka) *continued*	Northern Cone						G **-1050?**	....		....	....	x---	----	x---	x---	----		
	Northern Cone						G **-1000t**	....		....	....	x---	----	x---	----	----	3	-/7
	Northern Cone and Southern Cone flank						G **-0850?**	....		....	....	x-x-	----	x---	x---	----		7/-
	Northern Cone and Southern Cone flank						G **-0650?**	....		....	....	x-x-	----	x---	x---	----		
	Northern Cone						G **-0350?**	....		....	....	x---	----	x---	----	----		
	Northern Cone						G **-0250?**	....		....	....	x---	----	x---	----	----		
	Northern Cone						G **-0150?**	....		....	....	x---	----	x---	----	----	C	
	NW flank and central Northern Cone						T **0650?**	....		....	....	x-x-	----	x---	x-x-	----	2	-/6
	Central N Cone, SE flank of S Cone						G **0750?**	....		....	....	x-x-	----	x---	x---	----	3	-/7
	Northern Cone						G **0850?**	....		....	....	x---	----	x---	----	----		
	SW flank of Southern Cone						T **1350?**	....		....	....	--x-	----	----	x---	----	0	7/-
	Northern Cone (Pauk) & SW of S Cone						T **1550?**	....		....	....	x-x-	----	x---	x---	----		7/-
KRONOTSKY (Kamchatka)		**54.753 N**	**160.527 E**	**3528**	**Stratovolc**	**1000-20=**	**Historical**											
							T **-0050?**	....		....	....	----	----	x---	----	----		
	South flank (3150 m)						**1922**	11		....	....	-x--	----	--x-	----	----	2	
	Summit and/or south flank (3150 m)						**1923**	02		....	....	??--	----	?-x-	----	----	2	
GAMCHEN (Kamchatka)		**54.973 N**	**160.702 E**	**2576**	**Complx volc**	**1000-21=**	**Holocene**											
KOMAROV (Kamchatka)		**55.032 N**	**160.720 E**	**2070**	**Stratovolc**	**1000-22=**	**Holocene**											
KOLKHOZHNY (Kamchatka)		**55.07 N**	**160.77 E**	**2161**	**Stratovolc**	**1000-221**	**Holocene**											
KIZIMEN (Kamchatka)		**55.130 N**	**160.32 E**	**2485**	**Stratovolc**	**1000-23=**	**Historical**											
							T **-7800y**	....		....	....	x---	----	x---	x-x-	----	5	-/9
							T **-5300y**	....		....	....	x---	----	x---	--x-	----	5	-/9
							T **-0950?**	....		....	....	x---	----	x---	x-x-	----		
							T **-0050?**	....		....	....	x---	----	x---	x-x-	----		
							1927	12		**1928**	01	----	----	x-x-	----	----	2	
IULT (Kamchatka)		**55.230 N**	**160.587 E**	**1857**	**Stratovolc**	**1000-231**	**Holocene**											
UNNAMED (Kamchatka)		**55.92 N***	**161.75 E**		**Cinder cones**	**1000-232**	**Holocene?**											
TOLBACHIK (Kamchatka)		**55.830 N**	**160.330 E**	**3682**	**Shield**	**1000-24=**	**Historical**											
	SW flank (Lesnaya)						C **-6050?**	....		....	....	x-x-	----	x---	x---	----		
	SW flank (Bubochka)						T **-5650?**	....		....	....	-xx-	----	x---	x---	----		
	SW flank						T **-5600?**	....		....	....	--x-	----	x---	x---	----		
	SW flank and NE flank						T **-5450?**	....		....	....	--x-	----	x---	x---	----		
	Plosky Tolbachik Caldera						T **-5050?**	....		....	....	x---	----	?---	?---	----		
	SW flank (Kruglenky)						T **-2050?**	....		....	....	-xx-	----	x---	x---	----	3	8/7
	SW flank (Mokhnataya)						T **-1750?**	....		....	....	-xx-	----	x---	x---	----	3	
	SW flank (Istochniky)						T **-1650?**	....		....	....	-xx-	----	x---	x---	----		
	SW flank (Serga, Starichky)						T **-0800?**	....		....	....	-xx-	----	x---	x---	----		
	SW flank (Tsepochka, Malishi)						T **-0750?**	....		....	....	-xx-	----	x---	x---	----		
	SW flank (Buraya)						T **-0700?**	....		....	....	-xx-	----	x---	x---	----		
	SW flank (Kust)						T **-0200?**	....		....	....	-xx-	----	x---	x---	----		
	SW flank (Sosed, Malenky)						T **-0100?**	....		....	....	-xx-	----	x---	x---	----		
	SW flank (Maguskin)						T **0000?**	....		....	....	-xx-	----	x---	x---	----		
	SW flank (Mt. 1004, Pra-Visokaya)						T **0050?**	....		....	....	-xx-	----	x---	x---	----	4	8/8
	SW flank (Zapretny)						T **0150?**	....		....	....	x-x-	----	x---	x---	----		
	SW flank (Poteryanny, Yupiter)						T **0250?**	....		....	....	-xx-	----	x---	x---	----		
	SW flank (Zasipannie)						T **0350?**	....		....	....	-xx-	----	x---	x---	----		
	SW flank (Pelmen, Lagerny)						T **0400?**	....		....	....	-xx-	----	x---	x---	----	4	8/8
	SW flank (Dvoinoy, Nedostupny, Dalny)						T **0450?**	....		....	....	-xx-	----	x---	x---	----	3	**9**/7
	SW flank (Kamenistaya)						T **0550?**	....		....	....	-xx-	----	x---	x---	----	3	**9**/7
	SW flank (Peschanie Gorky)						T **0900?**	....		....	....	-xx-	----	x---	x---	----	4	**9/9**
	SW flank (Alaid)						T **0950?**	....		....	....	-xx-	----	x---	x---	----	4	8/8
	SW flank (Kleshnya, Rastaschenny)						T **1000?**	....		....	....	-xx-	----	x---	x---	----	4	**9**/8
	SW flank (Visokaya, Treschina)						T **1050?**	....		....	....	-xx-	----	x---	x---	----	3	**9**/7
	SW flank (Zvezda)						T **1550?**	....		....	....	-xx-	----	x---	x---	----	2	8/6
							? **1699a**	....		....	....	x---	----	?---	----	----	2?	
							1739	0201p		....	....	x---	----	x---	----	----	2?	
							1740	12		....	....	x---	----	x---	x---	----	2	
							1769	0215q		**1769**	1015q	x---	----	x---	----	----	2	
							1788	....		....	....	x---	----	x---	----	----	2	
							1789	....		....	....	x---	----	x---	----	----	2	
							1790	....		....	....	x---	----	x---	----	----	2	
							1793	....		....	....	x---	----	x---	----	----	2	
							1904	....		....	....	x---	----	x---	x---	----	2	
							1931	0304		**1932**	....	x---	----	x---	----	----	2	
							1936	0813<		**1937**	0302	x---	----	x---	----	----	2*	
							1939	0925		**1939**	0927	x---	----	x---	----	----	2	
							1940	02	+	**1940**	04	x---	----	x---	----	----	2	
	Summit, SW flank (1950 m)						**1940**	11	+	**1941**	0715q	xx--	----	x---	x---	----	3*	7/7
							1947	01		....	....	--x-	----	x---	----	----	2?	
							1954	0221	+	**1954**	0613	x---	----	x---	----	----	2	
							1955	0107		**1955**	0209	----	----	x-?-	----	----	2	
							1955	1006	+	**1955**	1208	----	----	x-?-	----	----	2	
							1956	0928	+	**1957**	1128	x---	----	x---	----	----	2	
							1958	0713<		....	....	x---	----	x---	----	----	2?	
							1959	....		**1960**	....	x---	----	x---	----	----	2	
							1961	0324		**1962**	0216>	x---	----	x---	----	----	2	
							1962	08		**1963**	....	x---	----	x---	----	----	1	
							1964	03	+	**1964**	0424>	x---	----	x---	-x--	----	2	
							1965	....		....	....	x---	----	x---	----	----	1	
							1966	0415q		....	....	x---	----	x---	----	----	2	
							1967	03		**1967**	05	x---	----	x---	----	----	2	
							1967	10		**1967**	11	x---	----	x---	----	----	2	
							1968	....		**1969**	....	x---	----	--x-	----	----	1	
							1970	01		**1970**	04	x---	----	x---	----	----	1	
							1970	1201p		....	....	x---	----	x---	----	----	2	
							? **1971**	01		?**1974**	12	x---	----	x-x-	----	----	1?	
	South flank (18 and 28 km from summit)						**1975**	0628	+	**1976**	1210	xx-x	----	x---	x---	----	4*	**9**/8
UDINA (Kamchatka)		**55.755 N**	**160.527 E**	**2923**	**Stratovolcs**	**1000-241**	**Holocene**											
ZIMINA (Kamchatka)		**55.862 N**	**160.603 E**	**3081**	**Stratovolcs**	**1000-242**	**Holocene**											
BEZYMIANNY (Kamchatka)		**55.978 N**	**160.587 E**	**2882**	**Stratovolc**	**1000-25=**	**Historical**											
	Pra-Bezymianny						T **-7050***	....		....	....	x---	----	x---	----	----		
	Pra-Bezymianny						T **-5050?**	....		....	....	x---	----	x---	----	----		
							T **-3050z**	....		....	....	x---	----	x---	x-x-	----		
	Expeditsii and Exstrusivny Greben						T **-1550z**	....		....	....	-x--	----	----	--x-	----		
							T **-1350?**	....		....	....	x---	----	x---	x-x-	----		
							G **-0450?**	....		....	....	----	----	x---	----	----	4	-/8
							T **0050?**	....		....	....	----	----	x---	----	----		

VOLCANO NAME (Subregion) / ERUPTION	LAT	LONG	ELEV (m)	TYPE	NUMBER	Area of Activity	Status	Start Year	Start M-Dy	P	Stop Year	Stop M-Dy	Central / Flank vent / Radial fiss / Regional*	Submarine / New island / Subglacial / Crater lake	Explosive / Pyro flow / Phreatic / Fumarolic	Lava flow / Lava lake / Dome / Spine	Fatal / Damage / Mudflow / Tsunami	VEI	Vol L/T
BEZYMIANNY (Kamchatka) *continued*							T	**0150?**	....		....	....	----	----	x---	x---	----		
							T	**0250?**	....		....	....	----	----	x---	x---	----		8/-
							T	**0600?**	....		....	....	----	----	x---	----	----		
						East summit region (Razrushenny dome) ..	T	**0700t**	....		....	....	x?--	----	xx--	--x-	----	4?	-/8
							T	**0850?**	....		....	....	----	----	x---	x---	----		
						Summit region and western flank.........	T	**0950?**	....		....	....	xx--	----	xx--	x---	----	4?	-/8
								1955	1022	+	**1957**	0301	x---	----	xx--	--x-	--xx	5*	-/9
								1957	0731		**1957**	0731	x---	----	x---	----	----	2	
								1958	01	+	**1958**	0214	x---	----	x---	--x-	----	1	
								1958	0521		....	....	x---	----	x---	--x-	----	1	
								1958	1228	+	**1959**	0330	x---	----	x---	--x-	----	2*	
								1959	1015		**1959**	1104?	x---	----	x---	--x-	----	1	-/4
								1960	0413		**1960**	0414	x---	----	xx--	--x-	----	2	-/6
								1961	0325		**1961**	0326	x---	----	xx--	--x-	--x-	3	-/6
								1961	0521		**1961**	0606	x---	----	xx--	----	----	2	
								1961	1018	+	**1961**	1215	x---	----	x---	--x-	----	3	
								1962	1021		**1962**	1106	x---	----	x---	--x-	----	2	
								1963	05	+	**1963**	09 ?	x---	----	-x--	--x-	----	1	
								1964	0625	+	**1964**	0920	x---	----	-x--	--x-	----	2	6/-
								1964	1225		**1964**	1226	x---	----	-x--	--x-	----	1	
								1965	0309	+	**1970**	03	x---	----	xx--	x-xx	--x-	3*	7/7
								1971	03		**1974**	12 >	x---	----	xx--	--xx	----	3*	
								1976	0325		....	....	x---	----	xx--	x-x-	--x-	2	
								1977	0325		....	....	x---	----	xx--	x-x-	--x-	3	5/7
								1978	0908p		....	....	x---	----	x---	----	--x-	2	
								1979	0211		....	....	x---	----	xx--	x---	----	3	5/7
								1979	0918		....	....	x---	----	xx--	x---	----	2	5/6
								1980	0418		**1980**	0419	x---	----	xx--	x-x-	--x-	3	5/7
								1980	0821		**1980**	0827d	x---	----	xx--	x---	----	2	5/-
								1981	0612		**1983**	0522	x---	----	xxx-	x-xx	--x-	3*	6/7
								1984	0205		**1984**	12	x---	----	xx--	x-x-	----	3*	-/7
								1985	0612	+	**1985**	1214	x---	----	xx--	x-x-	-x--	3*	-/7
								1986	0326e		**1986**	0629	x---	----	xx--	x-x-	----	2*	6/5
								1986	1209		**1988**	0726e	x---	----	xx--	x-x-	----	3*	
								1989	0801		**1989**	0804	x---	----	xx--	x-x-	----	2	
								1990	0129	+	**1990**	1203>	x---	----	xx--	x-x-	----	3*	
								1991	04		**1991**	1129	x---	----	x---	x-x-	----	2*	
								1992	0312		**1992**	0316a	x---	----	x---	x-x-	----	2	
								1993	1021		**1993**	1118?	x---	----	xx--	--x-	----	3	
KAMEN (Kamchatka)..............	**56.02 N**	**160.593 E**	**4585**	**Stratovolc**	**1000-251**		**Holocene**												
KLIUCHEVSKOI (Kamchatka).......	**56.057 N**	**160.638 E**	**4835**	**Stratovolc**	**1000-26=**		**Historical**												
							T	**-5050?**	....		....	....	x---	----	x---	----	----		
							T	**-1050?**	....		....	....	-x--	----	x---	----	----		
							C	**0550?**	....		....	....	-x--	----	x---	----	----		
								1697	....		**1698**	....	x---	----	x---	----	----	3↑	
								1720	....		**1721**	....	x---	----	x---	----	----	2	
								1727	....		**1731**	....	x---	----	x---	x---	----	2	
								1737	0925?		**1737**	1104?	x---	----	x---	x---	----	2	
								1740	....		....	....	----	----	----	----	----		
								1762	....		....	....	x---	----	x---	----	x---	2	
								1767	....		....	....	x---	----	x---	----	----	2	
								1770	05		....	....	x---	----	x---	----	----	2	
								1772	....		....	....	x---	----	x---	----	----	2	
								1785	11		....	....	x---	----	x---	----	----	2	
								1787	09		....	....	----	----	?---	----	----	2?	
								1788	02		....	....	x---	----	x---	----	----	2	
								1788	08		....	....	x---	----	x---	----	----	2	
								1789	1201	+	**1790**	02	x---	----	x---	----	----	2	
								1791	04		....	....	x---	----	x---	----	----	2	
								1791	08		....	....	x---	----	x---	----	----	2	
								1807	0201p		....	....	x---	----	x---	----	----	2	
								1812	09		....	....	x---	----	x---	----	----	2	
								1813	02		....	....	x---	----	x---	----	----	2	
								1819	....		?**1822**	....	x---	----	x---	x---	----	2*	
								1829	0909		....	....	x-x-	----	x---	x---	----	4?	7/8
								1840	....		....	....	x---	----	x---	----	----	2	
								1848	....		....	....	x---	----	x---	----	----	2	
								1852	02		**1852**	03	x---	----	x---	----	----	2	
								1852	08		....	....	x---	----	x---	----	----	2	
								1853	10		**1854**	0217	x---	----	x---	----	----	2	
								1865	09		....	....	x---	----	x---	----	----	2	
								1877	....		....	....	x---	----	x---	----	----	2	
								1878	09		....	....	x---	----	x---	----	----	2	
								1879	....		....	....	x---	----	x---	----	----	2	
								1882	09		....	....	x---	----	x---	----	----	2	
								1883	07		**1883**	08	x---	----	x---	----	----	2	
								1890	04		....	....	x---	----	x---	----	----	2	
								1896	12		**1897**	11	x---	----	x---	x---	----	2	
								1898	0220		....	....	x---	----	x---	x---	----	2	
								1904	0131p	+	**1904**	0614>	x---	----	x---	x---	----	2	
						Summit and east flank		**1907**	08		....	....	xx--	----	x---	x---	----	2	
								1909	06		....	....	x---	----	x---	----	----	2	
								1910	08		....	....	x---	----	x---	----	----	2	
								1911	11		....	....	x---	----	x---	----	----	2	
								1913	01		....	....	-x--	----	x---	----	----	2	
								1915	01		....	....	-x--	----	x---	----	----	2	
								1922	05		....	....	x---	----	x---	----	----	2	
								1923	08	+	**1923**	09	x---	----	x---	----	----	2	
								1925	0404	+	**1925**	1010	x---	----	x---	----	----	2	
								1926	0323		**1926**	0407	x---	----	x---	----	----	2	
								1929	06	+	**1929**	09	x---	----	x---	----	----	2	
								1931	0325		**1931**	0327	x---	----	x---	----	----	4	
								1931	08		**1931**	09	x---	----	x---	----	----	2	
						NE flank (Kirgurich, Tuyla, Biokos)........		**1932**	0125	+	**1932**	1226e	-x--	----	x---	x---	----	2	7/6
								1935	0421		**1936**	1104>	x---	----	x---	----	----	3*	
						Summit, east flank (Bilyukai)		**1937**	0403	+	**1939**	03	xxx-	----	x---	x---	----	3*	8/7
								1944	1209		**1945**	0120>	x-x-	----	x---	x---	----	4*	-/8

VOLCANO NAME (Subregion) / ERUPTION	LAT	LONG	ELEV (m)	TYPE	NUMBER	Status	Area of Activity	Start Year	Start M-Dy	P	Stop Year	Stop M-Dy	Central / Flank vent / Radial fiss / Regional*	Submarine / New island / Subglacial / Crater lake	Explosive / Pyro flow / Phreatic / Fumarolic	Lava flow / Lava lake / Dome / Spine	Fatal / Damage / Mudflow / Tsunami	VEI	Vol L/T
KLIUCHEVSKOI (Kamchatka) *continued*							SE flank (Yubileinoye, 1000-1450 m)......	**1945**	0619		**1945**	0707	--x-	----	x---	x---	----	3	7/7
							SE flank (Apakhonchich, ca. 1600 m)	**1946**	1023		**1946**	1122?	-xx-	----	x-x-	x---	----	2	7/5
								1948	08		....	....	----	----	x---	----	----	2?	
								1949	05		....	....	x---	----	x---	----	----	2	
							Summit, NE flank (Bylinkina, 950 m)	**1951**	1119		**1951**	1130	xxx-	----	x---	x---	----	2	7/6
							Summit, NE flank (Belyankin Crater)	**1953**	0607	+	**1953**	0625	xxx-	----	x---	x---	----	2	7/6
								1954	0528		**1954**	09	x-x-	----	x---	----	----	2	
							Summit and SE flank (1500 m)	**1956**	01	+	**1956**	0802	xxx-	----	x---	x---	----	2*	6/-
								1957	....		....	....	x---	----	x---	----	----	1	
							East part of summit crater	**1958**	0518	+	**1958**	0818>	x---	----	x---	----	----	1	
								1959	0103		....	....	x---	----	x---	----	----	1	
								1960	12	+	**1963**	0322>	x---	----	x---	----	----	3*	-/6
								1963	1113		**1964**	12 ?	x---	----	x---	----	----	1	
							Summit, NE flank (Piip Crater)...........	**1965**	08	+	**1966**	1226	x-x-	----	x---	x---	----	3*	8/7
								1967	....		....	....	x---	----	x---	----	----	1	
								1968	0703		**1968**	0703	x---	----	x?--	----	----	3	
								1969	09		**1969**	12	x---	----	x---	----	----	2	
								1970	0526	+	**1970**	1227	x---	----	x---	----	----	2	
								1971	06		**1971**	07	x---	----	x---	----	----	1	
								1971	11		**1973**	12	x---	----	x-x-	----	----	1	
							Summit and SW flank (3400-3600 m)	**1974**	0408	+	**1974**	12 ?	x-x-	----	x---	x---	----	3*	7/6
							Summit, NE flank (1700 m)	**1977**	0802	+	**1980**	0312	x-x-	----	x---	x---	x---	3*	5/7
								1981	0125		**1981**	0804?	x---	----	x---	----	----	1	
								? **1981**	1221		....	....	----	----	----	----	----		
								1982	0324		**1982**	0502	x---	----	x-?-	----	----	1	
							Summit and east flank (2875 m)	**1982**	1007	+	**1983**	0627	x-x-	--x-	x-x-	x---	x-x-	2*	7/-
								1984	0310	+	**1985**	0128	x---	----	x-x-	x---	--x-	3*	
							Summit and NW flank (3100 m)..........	**1985**	0816	+	**1986**	0121	x-x-	----	x-x-	x---	--x-	3*	
								1986	0608	+	**1986**	0711	x---	----	x---	x---	--x-	2	
							Summit, SE, SW, NE and east flanks	**1986**	1127	+	**1990**	09	x-x-	----	xx--	x---	--x-	3*	7/-
								1991	0408		**1991**	0624?	x---	----	x---	----	----	2	
								1992	0125		**1992**	0514?	x---	----	x---	----	----	2	
								1993	0315e		**1993**	1021?	x---	----	x---	----	----	2	
USHKOVSKY (Kamchatka)	**56.105 N**	**160.470 E**	**3943**	**Compnd volc**	**1000-261**	**Historical**													
							Lavovy Shish cone group...............	C **-6900**w	....		....	....	-x--	----	x---	----	----		
								1890	04		....	....	x---	----	x---	----	----	2?	
ZARECHNY (Kamchatka)	**56.38 N**	**160.83 E**	**760**	**Somma volc**	**1000-262**	**Holocene**													
UNNAMED (Kamchatka)	**56.53 N**	***160.87 E**	**200**	**Cinder cones**	**1000-263**	**Holocene**													
SHEVELUCH (Kamchatka)	**56.653 N**	**161.360 E**	**3283**	**Stratovolc**	**1000-27=**	**Historical**													
								T **-7150**v	....		....	....	----	----	x---	----	----		
								C **-6750**?	....		....	....	----	----	x---	----	----		
								C **-6050**?	....		....	....	----	----	x---	----	----		
							(Sh6 tephra is from Hangar volcano)	X -5050?	....		....	....	----	----	----	----	----		
								T **-2050**?	....		....	....	----	----	x---	----	----		
								T **-1550**?	....		....	....	----	----	x---	----	----		
								T **-1350**?	....		....	....	----	----	x---	----	----		
								C **-1100**x	....		....	....	----	----	x---	----	----		
								C **-0600**t	....		....	....	----	----	x---	----	----		
							(Sh4 tephra is from Ksudach volcano).....	X -0050?	....		....	....	----	----	----	----	----		
								C **0500**t	....		....	....	----	----	xx--	----	----	**5**	-/9
								C **1000**t	....		....	....	----	----	x---	----	----	**5**	-/9
								C **1690**?	....		....	....	----	----	x---	----	----		
							(only fumarolic activity 18th century)	X 1793	....		....	....	----	----	---x	----	----		
								1854	0218		....	....	x---	----	xx--	--x-	-xx-	**5**	-/9
								1879	....		**1883**	....	x---	----	x---	--x-	----	2	
								1897	....		**1898**	....	x---	----	x---	--x-	----	2	
								1905	....		....	....	----	----	----	----	----		
								1928	0127		**1929**	0415q	x---	----	----	--x-	----	1	
								1930	0201p		....	....	----	----	x---	----	----	1	
							Suelich	**1944**	1105		**1950**	0406	x---	----	xx--	--xx	----	2	8/-
							Molodoy Sheveluch summit domes	**1964**	1112		**1964**	1112	x---	----	xx--	----	--x-	4+	-/8
							Center of 1964 crater.................	**1980**	0823		**1981**	1201p	x---	----	xx--	--xx	--x-	1	7/-
								1984	0317	+	**1984**	0906	x---	----	x-x-	----	--x-	2?	
								1985	0526	+	**1985**	1025	x---	----	x-x-	----	----	2	
								1986	0328		**1988**	0227	x---	----	xxx-	----	--x-	3*	
								1988	1207		**1988**	1207	x---	----	xxx-	----	----	2?	
								1989	0407	+	**1989**	0626	x---	----	x-x-	----	--x-	2	
								1990	0129		**1990**	0804	x---	----	xxx-	----	--x-	3*	
								1991	0408		**1991**	0509?	x---	----	x---	----	----	3	
								1993	0318		**1993**	10 ?	x---	----	xx--	--xx	--x-	3*	

Kamchatka - E of & W

VOLCANO NAME (Subregion) / ERUPTION	LAT	LONG	ELEV (m)	TYPE	NUMBER	Status	Area of Activity	Start Year	Start M-Dy	P	Stop Year	Stop M-Dy	Central / Flank vent / Radial fiss / Regional*	Submarine / New island / Subglacial / Crater lake	Explosive / Pyro flow / Phreatic / Fumarolic	Lava flow / Lava lake / Dome / Spine	Fatal / Damage / Mudflow / Tsunami	VEI	Vol L/T
PIIP (Kamchatka-E of)	**55.42 N**	**167.33 E**	**-300**	**Submarine**	**1000-271**	**Tephrochronology**													
								T **-5050**?	....		....	....	----	x---	x---	----	----		
HANGAR (Kamchatka-W)	**54.75 N**	**157.38 E**	**2000**	**Stratovolc**	**1000-272**	**Radiocarbon**													
								C **-5040**u	....		....	....	x---	----	xx--	----	----	**5**	-/9
ICHINSKY (Kamchatka-W)..........	**55.68 N**	**157.73 E**	**3621**	**Stratovolc**	**1000-28=**	**Holocene**													
MALY PAYALPAN (Kamchatka-W)...	**55.82 N**	**157.98 E**	**1802**	**Shields**	**1000-29-**	**Holocene**													
BOLSHOY PAYALPAN (")	**55.88 N**	**157.78 E**	**1906**	**Shields**	**1000-30-**	**Holocene**													
PLOSKY (Kamchatka-W)...........	**55.20 N**	**158.47 E**	**1236**	**Shield**	**1000-31-**	**Holocene**													
AKHTANG (Kamchatka-W)	**55.43 N**	**158.65 E**	**1956**	**Shield**	**1000-32-**	**Holocene**													
KOZYREVSKY (Kamchatka-W)......	**55.58 N**	**158.38 E**	**2016**	**Shield**	**1000-33-**	**Holocene**													
ROMANOVKA (Kamchatka-W)	**55.65 N**	**158.80 E**	**1442**	**Stratovolc**	**1000-34-**	**Holocene**													
UKSICHAN (Kamchatka-W).........	**56.08 N**	**158.38 E**	**1692**	**Shield**	**1000-35-**	**Holocene**													
BOLSHOY-KEKUKNAYSKY (")	**56.47 N**	**157.80 E**	**1401**	**Shields**	**1000-36-**	**Holocene**													
KULKEV (Kamchatka-W)...........	**56.37 N**	**158.37 E**	**915**	**Shield**	**1000-37-**	**Holocene**													
GEODESISTOY (Kamchatka-W)	**56.33 N**	**158.67 E**	**1170**	**Shield**	**1000-38-**	**Holocene**													
ANAUN (Kamchatka-W)............	**56.32 N**	**158.83 E**	**1828**	**Stratovolc**	**1000-39-**	**Holocene**													
KRAINY (Kamchatka-W)	**56.37 N**	**159.03 E**	**1554**	**Shield**	**1000-40-**	**Holocene**													
KEKURNY (Kamchatka-W)	**56.40 N**	**158.85 E**	**1377**	**Shields**	**1000-41-**	**Holocene**													
EGGELLA (Kamchatka-W)	**56.57 N**	**158.52 E**	**1046**	**Shield**	**1000-42-**	**Holocene**													
UNNAMED (Kamchatka-W)	**56.82 N**	**158.95 E**	**1185**	**Shield**	**1000-43-**	**Holocene**													

VOLCANO NAME (Subregion) / ERUPTION — Area of Activity	LAT	LONG	ELEV (m)	TYPE	NUMBER	Status / Start Year	Start M-Dy	P	Stop Year	Stop M-Dy	Central / Flank vent / Radial fiss / Regional*	Submarine / New island / Subglacial / Crater lake	Explosive / Pyro flow / Phreatic / Fumarolic	Lava flow / Lava lake / Dome / Spine	Fatal / Damage / Mudflow / Tsunami	VEI	Vol L/T
VERKHOVOY (Kamchatka-W)	56.52 N	159.53 E	1400	Shield	1000-44-	Holocene											
ALNEY-CHASHAKONDZHA (*)	56.70 N	159.65 E	2598	Stratovolc	1000-45-	Holocene											
CHERNY (Kamchatka-W)	56.82 N	159.67 E	1778	Stratovolc	1000-46-	Holocene											
POGRANYCHNY (Kamchatka-W)	56.85 N	159.80 E	1427	Shields	1000-47-	Holocene											
ZAOZERNY (Kamchatka-W)	56.88 N	159.95 E	1349	Shields	1000-48-	Holocene											
BLIZNETS (Kamchatka-W)	56.97 N	159.78 E	1244	Stratovolc	1000-49-	Holocene											
KEBENEY (Kamchatka-W)	57.10 N	159.93 E	1527	Shield	1000-50-	Holocene											
FEDOTYCH (Kamchatka-W)	57.13 N	160.40 E	965	Shield	1000-51-	Holocene											
SEDANKINSKY (Kamchatka-W)	57.23 N	160.08 E	1241	Shield	1000-52-	Holocene											
GORNY INSTITUTE (Kamchatka-W)	57.33 N	160.20 E	2125	Stratovolc	1000-53-	Holocene											
LEUTONGEY (Kamchatka-W)	57.30 N	159.83 E	1333	Shield	1000-54-	Holocene											
TUZOVSKY (Kamchatka-W)	57.32 N	159.97 E	1533	Shields	1000-55-	Holocene											
TITILA (Kamchatka-W)	57.40 N	160.10 E	1559	Shield	1000-56-	Holocene											
MEZHDUSOPOCHNY (Kamchatka-W)	57.43 N	160.20 E	1641	Shield	1000-57-	Holocene											
SHISHEL (Kamchatka-W)	57.45 N	160.37 E	2525	Shield	1000-58-	Holocene											
ELOVSKY (Kamchatka-W)	57.53 N	160.53 E	1381	Shields	1000-59-	Holocene											
ALNGEY (Kamchatka-W)	57.70 N	160.40 E	1853	Stratovolc	1000-60-	Holocene											
UKA (Kamchatka-W)	57.70 N	160.58 E	1643	Shield	1000-61-	Holocene											
KAILENEY (Kamchatka-W)	57.80 N	160.67 E	1582	Shield	1000-62-	Holocene											
PLOSKY (Kamchatka-W)	57.83 N	160.25 E	1255	Shield	1000-63-	Holocene											
BELY (Kamchatka-W)	57.88 N	160.53 E	2080	Shields	1000-64-	Holocene											
ATLASOVA (Kamchatka-W)	57.97 N	160.65 E	1764	Shields	1000-65-	Holocene											
SNEZHNIY (Kamchatka-W)	58.02 N	160.75 E	2169	Shield	1000-66-	Holocene											
IKTUNUP (Kamchatka-W)	58.08 N	160.77 E	2300	Shields	1000-67-	Holocene											
OSTRY (Kamchatka-W)	58.18 N	160.82 E	2552	Stratovolcs	1000-68-	Holocene											
SNEGOVOY (Kamchatka-W)	58.20 N	160.97 E	2169	Shield	1000-69-	Holocene											
SEVERNY (Kamchatka-W)	58.28 N	160.87 E	1936	Shield	1000-70-	Holocene											
IETTUNUP (Kamchatka-W)	58.40 N	161.08 E	1340	Shields	1000-71-	Holocene											
VOYAMPOLSKY (Kamchatka-W)	58.37 N	160.62 E	1225	Shields	1000-72-	Holocene											

MAINLAND ASIA

VOLCANO NAME (Subregion) / ERUPTION — Area of Activity	LAT	LONG	ELEV (m)	TYPE	NUMBER	Status / Start Year	Start M-Dy	P	Stop Year	Stop M-Dy	Central / Flank vent / Radial fiss / Regional*	Submarine / New island / Subglacial / Crater lake	Explosive / Pyro flow / Phreatic / Fumarolic	Lava flow / Lava lake / Dome / Spine	Fatal / Damage / Mudflow / Tsunami	VEI	Vol L/T
ALUCHIN GROUP (Russia-NE)	66.12 N*	165.63 E	1000	Cones	1001-01-	Holocene											
ANJUISKY (Russia-NE)	67.17 N	165.20 E	1050	Complx volc	1001-02-	Tephrochronology											
Aniusk						T 1500x	....		....	....	x---	----	x---	x---	----	3↑	8/-
BALAGAN-TAS (Russia-NE)	66.43 N	143.73 E	993	Cinder cone	1001-03-	Historical											
						1775e	....		....	....	----	----	x---	----	----	2	
SOUTHERN SIKHOTE-ALIN (Russia)	44.50 N*	135.50 E		Volc field	1002-01-	Holocene											
NE UDOKAN PLATEAU (Russia-SE)	56.33 N*	118.07 E	2180	Volc field	1002-02-	Holocene											
UDOKAN VOLC FIELD (Russia-SE)	56.18 N	117.47 E	1980	Shields	1002-03-	Radiocarbon											
Sini						C -7290v	....		....	....	---x	----	----	x---	----	0	
Chepe						C -0150u	....		....	....	----	----	x---	----	----		
DGIDA BASIN (Russia-SE)	50.52 N*	103.25 E	1500	Cinder cones	1002-04-	Holocene											
TUNKIN DEPRESSION (Russia-SE)	51.50 N*	102.50 E	1200	Volc field	1002-05-	Holocene											
OKA VOLC FIELD (Russia-SE)	52.70 N*	98.98 E	2077	Cinder cones	1002-06-	Holocene											
ULUG-ARGINSKY (Russia-SE)	52.33 N	98.00 E	1800	Cinder cone	1002-07-	Holocene											
TARYATU-CHULUTU (Mongolia)	48.17 N*	99.70 E	2400	Volc field	1003-01-	Holocene											
KHANUY GOL (Mongolia)	48.67 N*	102.75 E	1886	Volc field	1003-02-	Holocene											
BUS-OBO (Mongolia)	47.12 N	109.08 E	1162	Cinder cone	1003-03-	Holocene?											
DARIGANGA VOLC FIELD (Mongolia)	45.33 N*	114.00 E	1778	Cinder cones	1003-04-	Holocene											
MIDDLE GOBI (Mongolia)	45.28 N*	106.70 E	1120	Cinder cones	1003-05-	Holocene?											
TURFAN (China-W)	42.90 N	89.25 E		Cone	1004-01-	Historical											
						1120w	....		....	....	x---	----	x---	----	----		
TIANSHAN VOLC GROUP (China-W)	42.50 N*	86.50 E		Volc field	1004-02-	Historical											
Pechan						0050t	....		....	....	----	----	?---	----	----		
Pechan						0650t	....		....	....	----	----	?---	----	----		
KUNLUN VOLC GROUP (China-W)	35.52 N*	80.20 E	5808	Pyrocl cones	1004-03-	Historical											
Ka-er-daxi						1951	0527		....	....	----	----	x---	----	----	2	
UNNAMED (China-W)	35.85 N*	91.70 E	5400	Volc field	1004-04-	Holocene											
(plume probably of meteorological origin)						X 1973	0716?		....	....	----	----	----	----	----		
DATONG (China-E)	40.00 N*	113.28 E	1882	Cinder cones	1005-01-	Historical											
						0450t	....		....	....	----	----	x---	----	----		
HONGGEERTU (China-E)	41.47 N*	113.00 E	1700	Cinder cones	1005-02-	Holocene											
KELUO GROUP (China-E)	49.37 N*	125.92 E	670	Pyrocl cones	1005-03-	Holocene											
WUDALIANCHI (China-E)	48.72 N*	126.12 E	597	Volc field	1005-04-	Historical											
Laoheishan and Huoshaoshan						1719	....		1721	....	x-x-	----	x-x-	x---	----	3	9/8
JINGPOHU (China-E)	44.08 N*	128.83 E	500	Volc field	1005-05-	Radiocarbon											
						C -3460v	....		....	....	----	----	----	x---	----		
LONGGANG GROUP (China-E)	42.33 N*	126.50 E	1000	Cinder cones	1005-06-	Radiocarbon											
						C 1750?	....		....	....	----	----	----	----	----		
BAITOUSHAN (China/Korea)	41.98 N	128.08 E	2744	Stratovolc	1005-07-	Historical											
						T -1120*	....		....	....	x---	----	xx--	----	----		
						G 1050j	....		....	....	x---	----	xx--	----	--x-	7	-/11
						1413	....		....	....	----	----	----	----	----		
						1597	1006		....	....	----	----	x---	----	----		
						1668	....		....	....	----	----	----	----	----		
						1702	....		....	....	----	----	??--	?---	----		
XIANJINDAO (Korea)	41.33 N	128.00 E		Unknown	1006-01-	Historical											
						1597	1008		....	....	----	----	x---	----	-x--		
CH'UGA-RYONG (Korea)	38.33 N	127.33 E	452	Shield	1006-02-	Holocene?											
ULREUNG (Korea)	37.50 N	130.87 E	984	Stratovolc	1006-03-	Radiocarbon											
						C -7350?	....		....	....	----	----	xx--	----	----	6	-/10
HALLA (Korea)	33.37 N	126.53 E	1950	Shield	1006-04-	Historical											
						1002	....		....	....	-x--	----	x---	----	----		
						1007	....		....	....	-x--	----	x---	----	----		

Alaska (11)

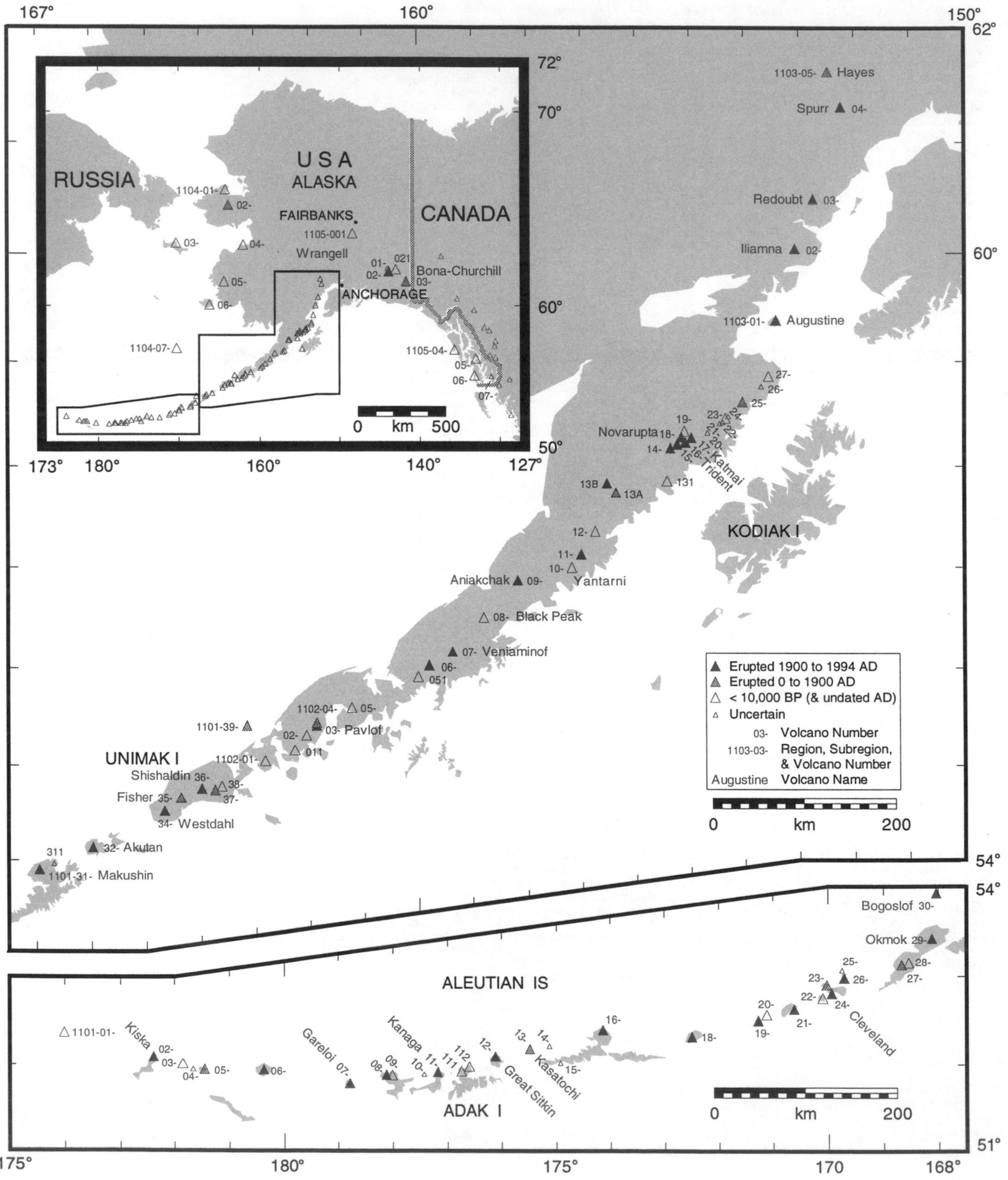

RUSSIA
USA
ALASKA
CANADA
FAIRBANKS
ANCHORAGE
Wrangell
Bona-Churchill
KODIAK I
UNIMAK I
ALEUTIAN IS
ADAK I
Hayes
Spurr
Redoubt
Iliamna
Augustine
Novarupta
Katmai
Trident
Aniakchak
Yantarni
Black Peak
Veniaminof
Pavlof
Shishaldin
Fisher
Westdahl
Akutan
Makushin
Bogoslof
Okmok
Cleveland
Kasatochi
Great Sitkin
Kanaga
Gareloi
Kiska
Erupted 1900 to 1994 AD
Erupted 0 to 1900 AD
< 10,000 BP (& undated AD)
Uncertain
03- Volcano Number
1103-03- Region, Subregion, & Volcano Number
Augustine Volcano Name
0 km 200
0 km 500

The 2500-km-long Aleutian arc is a chain of large calc-alkaline strato-volcanoes and impressive calderas. It is responsible for nearly all the historical volcanism of Alaska. The Wrangell Mountains, to the east, include some of world's largest andesitic shield volcanoes, and basaltic lava fields are scattered throughout the western interior and southeastern panhandle of Alaska.

Western record keeping began in 1741 when Vitus Bering (see introduction to Regions 09 & 10, above) landed in Alaska, but these commonly cloud-covered volcanoes were only occasionally documented in the following decades. Eruption reporting began with Kasatochi in 1760; 4 more had erupted by 1768 and there has been a steady increase since. The first government of Russian America was set up near Sitka in 1799, and in 1867 the US bought Alaska from Russia for $7.2 million. Gold was discovered in 1896, and the population of this vast region had grown substantially by 1912, when the major eruption of Novarupta/Katmai, the world's largest in this century, brought widespread attention to Alaska's many volcanoes. Recognition of their significance during WW-II led to a major USGS mapping program in the Aleutians during the early 1950s, bringing a quantum jump to understanding of these volcanoes. In 1959 Alaska entered the US as our 49th state, ranking first in area, 49th in population, and first in volcanism, with 43 of the nation's 53 historically active volcanoes.

Alaska has the world's largest proportion of stratovolcanoes, although South America and Indonesia have larger totals. Only Indonesia, Japan, and South America have had more volcanoes erupt in this century. Most volcanoes lie in sparsely populated areas, however, and only two Alaskan eruptions have caused fatalities. Weather in the Aleutian arc is notoriously bad, and eruptions take place even today without being observed.

Alaska is one of the two regions assigned by the *CAVW* organizers that is not yet covered in the *CAVW* series, but that catalog is at last in press and its authors have kindly shared it with us. This, the work of Tom Miller and colleagues at the newly established (1988) Alaska Volcano Observatory, and two other book-length treatments of Alaskan volcanoes (starred under REFERENCES - 1100) bring excellent modern coverage to this important volcanic group. These authors have not all followed the *CAVW* numbering of clockwise progression around the Pacific rim, but naming has been reasonably consistent throughout.

VOLCANO NAME (Subregion) / ERUPTION — Area of Activity	LAT	LONG	ELEV (m)	TYPE	NUMBER	Status / Start Year	Start M-Dy	P	Stop Year	Stop M-Dy	ERUPTIVE CHARACTERISTICS: Central / Flank vent / Radial fiss / Regional*	Submarine / New island / Subglacial / Crater lake	Explosive / Pyro flow / Phreatic / Fumarolic	Lava flow / Lava lake / Dome / Spine	Fatal / Damage / Mudflow / Tsunami	VEI	Vol L/T
ALEUTIAN ISLANDS																	
BULDIR (Aleutian Is)	**52.37 N**	**175.98 E**	**656**	**Stratovolc**	**1101-01-**	**Holocene**											
KISKA (Aleutian Is)	**52.10 N**	**177.60 E**	**1220**	**Stratovolc**	**1101-02-**	**Historical**											
						? **1907**	....		....	....	----	----	----	----	----	2?	
						? **1927**	....		....	....	----	----	----	----	----	2?	
North flank (Sirus Point)						**1962**	0124		....	....	-x--	----	x---	x---	----	3	
						1964	0318		....	....	----	----	----	x---	----	0	
						1969	0911		**1969**	0916	----	----	x---	x---	----	2?	
						? **1987**	0415		....	....	----	----	?---	----	----		
Upper NW? flank						**1990**	0601		**1990**	0601?	-x--	----	x-x-	----	----	2	
SEGULA (Aleutian Is)	**52.02 N**	**178.13 E**	**1153**	**Stratovolc**	**1101-03-**	**Holocene**											
DAVIDOF (Aleutian Is)	**51.97 N**	**178.33 E**	**328**	**Stratovolc**	**1101-04-**	**Holocene?**											
LITTLE SITKIN (Aleutian Is)	**51.95 N**	**178.53 E**	**1188**	**Stratovolc**	**1101-05-**	**Historical**											
						1776	....		....	....	----	----	x---	----	----	1?	
Summit and west flank						**1828**	....		?**1830**	....	x-x-	----	----	x---	----		
SEMISOPOCHNOI (Aleutian Is)	**51.95 N**	**179.62 E**	**1221**	**Stratovolc**	**1101-06-**	**Historical**											
Cerberus						? **1772**	....		....	....	x---	----	----	----	----		
Cerberus						? **1790**	....		....	....	x---	----	----	----	----		
Cerberus						? **1792**	....		....	....	x---	----	----	----	----		
Cerberus						? **1830**	....		....	....	x---	----	----	----	----		
Cerberus						**1873**	....		....	....	x---	----	----	----	----		
Sugarloaf ?						**1987**	0413		....	....	-?--	----	x---	----	----	2?	
GARELOI (Aleutian Is)	**51.78 N**	**178.80 W**	**1573**	**Stratovolc**	**1101-07-**	**Historical**											
						? **1760**	....		....	....	----	----	----	----	----		
						1790	....		....	....	----	----	x---	----	----	2	
						1791	....		....	....	----	----	x---	----	----	2	
						1792	....		....	....	----	----	x---	x---	----	2	
						? **1828**	....		?**1829**	....	----	----	----	----	----	2?	
						1873	....		....	....	----	----	----	----	----	2?	
						1922	....		....	....	----	----	x---	----	----	3	
						? **1927**	....		....	....	----	----	----	----	----		
SE flank fissure (near summit to sea)						**1929**	04		**1930**	....	--x-	----	x-x-	x---	-x--	3	
						1950	....		**1951**	....	----	----	x-x-	----	----	1	
						1952	0117		....	....	----	----	x---	----	----	2?	
						1980	0807		**1980**	0917	x---	----	x---	----	----	3?	
						1982	0115		**1982**	0115	x---	----	x---	----	----	3	
						1987	0904		....	....	x---	----	-?--	?---	----	1?	
						1989	0817		....	....	x---	----	x---	----	----	1	
TANAGA (Aleutian Is)	**51.88 N**	**178.13 W**	**1806**	**Stratovolcs**	**1101-08-**	**Historical**											
						1763	....		**1770**	....	----	----	----	----	----		
						? **1791**	0607		....	....	----	----	----	----	----		
						1829	....		....	....	----	----	x---	----	----		
						1914	....		....	....	----	----	----	x---	----	0	
TAKAWANGHA (Tanaga I)	**51.87 N**	**178.02 W**	**1449**	**Stratovolc**	**1101-09-**	**Holocene**											
BOBROF (Aleutian Is)	**51.90 N**	**177.43 W**	**738**	**Stratovolc**	**1101-10-**	**Holocene?**											
KANAGA (Aleutian Is)	**51.92 N**	**177.17 W**	**1307**	**Stratovolc**	**1101-11-**	**Historical**											
						1763	....		....	....	----	----	----	----	----		
						1768	....		....	....	----	----	----	----	----		
						1783	....		**1787**?	....	----	----	----	----	----		
						? **1790**	....		....	....	----	----	----	----	----		
						? **1791**	....		....	....	----	----	----	----	----		
						? **1827**	....		....	....	----	----	----	----	----		
						? **1829**	....		....	....	----	----	----	----	----		
Upper south flank ?						**1904**	....		....	....	--x-	----	----	x---	----	0	
Summit, upper SW flank						**1906**	05		....	....	x-x-	----	----	x---	----		
						1933	....		....	....	----	----	----	----	----		
						1942	....		....	....	----	----	----	----	----	1	
MOFFETT (Adak I)	**51.93 N**	**176.75 W**	**1196**	**Stratovolc**	**1101-111**	**Holocene**											
ADAGDAK (Adak I)	**51.98 N**	**176.60 W**	**645**	**Stratovolc**	**1101-112**	**Holocene**											
GREAT SITKIN (Aleutian Is)	**52.08 N**	**176.13 W**	**1740**	**Stratovolc**	**1101-12-**	**Historical**											
						? **1760**	....		....	....	----	----	----	----	----		
						? **1784**	....		....	....	----	----	----	----	----		
						1792	0526e		....	....	----	----	x---	----	----		
						? **1828**	....		....	....	----	----	----	----	----		
						? **1829**	....		....	....	----	----	----	----	----		
						? **1904**	....		....	....	----	----	----	----	----		

VOLCANO NAME (Subregion) / ERUPTION — Area of Activity	LAT	LONG	ELEV (m)	TYPE	NUMBER	Status / Start Year	Start M-Dy	P	Stop Year	Stop M-Dy	Central / Flank vent / Radial fiss / Regional*	Submarine / New island / Subglacial / Crater lake	Explosive / Pyro flow / Phreatic / Fumarolic	Lava flow / Lava lake / Dome / Spine	Fatal / Damage / Mudflow / Tsunami	VEI	Vol L/T
GREAT SITKIN (Aleutian Is) *continued*						1933	11		....	....	----	----	x---	----	----	2	
						1945	03		....	....	x---	----	x---	x-x-	----	2	7/-
						? 1946	0814		....	....	x---	----	----	----	----		
						1949	1230		1950	0107	----	----	x---	----	----	1	-/4
						1950	1105		1950	1129	----	----	x---	----	----		
(steam plumes without ash emission)						X 1953	0511		X1953	0514	----	----	----	----	----		
						1974	0219		1974	09	x---	----	x---	x-x-	----	2	7/-
						? 1987	0318		....	....	?---	----	----	----	----		
KASATOCHI (Aleutian Is)	52.18	N 175.50	W 314	Stratovolc	1101-13-	Historical											
						1760	....		....	....	----	----	----	?---	----	0	
						? 1827	....		....	....	----	----	----	----	----		
						? 1828	....		....	....	----	----	----	----	----		
						? 1899?	....		....	....	x---	----	?---	----	----		
KONIUJI (Aleutian Is)	52.22	N 175.13	W 272	Stratovolc	1101-14-	Uncertain											
SERGIEF (Atka I)	52.03	N 174.93	W 560	Stratovolc	1101-15-	Uncertain											
ATKA (Atka I)	52.38	N 174.15	W 1533	Stratovolcs	1101-16-	Historical											
Sarichef or more probably Kliuchev						1812	....		....	....	?---	----	x---	----	----	3?	
Korovin						? 1829	....		?1830	....	----	----	----	----	----		
Korovin						? 1844	....		....	....	----	----	----	----	----		
Korovin						1907	....		....	....	x---	----	x---	----	----		
Korovin						? 1951	....		....	....	----	----	----	----	----		
Korovin						? 1953	....		?1954	....	----	----	----	----	----		
Korovin						1973	0825b		....	....	x-x-	----	----	x---	----	0	
Korovin						? 1976	....		....	....	----	----	----	----	----		
Korovin						? 1986	0523		....	....	x---	----	x-x-	----	----	1	
Korovin and Mt. Kliuchev flanks ?						1987	0304?		1987	0318	x?--	----	x---	----	----	2*	
UNNAMED (Amlia-N of)	52.25	N 173.55	W		1101-17-	Not a Volcano											
(SOFAR eruption site not confirmed)						X 1966	07		X1967	08	----	----	----	----	----		
SEGUAM (Aleutian Is)	52.32	N 172.52	W 1054	Stratovolcs	1101-18-	Historical											
						1786	....		1790	....	----	----	----	----	----		
						? 1827	....		....	....	----	----	----	----	----		
						1891	12		....	....	----	----	x---	----	----	2	
						1892	0415q		....	....	----	----	x---	----	----	3	
						1902	....		....	....	----	----	x---	----	----	3	
						? 1927	....		....	....	----	----	----	----	----		
Pyre Peak (2.5 km SE of summit)						1977	0306		1977	0308?	--x-	----	x---	x---	----	1	
Pyre Peak (1.5 km south of summit)						1992	1227		1992	1230	--x-	----	x---	----	----	1	
Near Pyre Peak						1993	0528		1993	0831>	-x--	----	x---	x---	----	2	
AMUKTA (Aleutian Is)	52.50	N 171.25	W 1066	Stratovolc	1101-19-	Historical											
						? 1770	....		....	....	----	----	----	----	----		
						1786	06		1791	....	----	----	x---	----	----	3↑	-/8
						? 1876	....		....	....	----	----	----	----	----		
						1878	....		....	....	----	----	----	----	----		
						1963	0213		....	....	xxx-	----	x---	x---	----	3	
						1987	0904?		....	....	x---	----	x---	----	----	1	
CHAGULAK (Aleutian Is)	52.57	N 171.13	W 1142	Stratovolc	1101-20-	Holocene											
YUNASKA (Aleutian Is)	52.63	N 170.63	W 550	Shield	1101-21-	Historical											
						? 1817	....		....	....	----	----	----	----	----		
						1824	....		....	....	----	----	x---	----	----	3	
						1830	....		....	....	----	----	x---	----	----	2	
						? 1873	....		....	....	----	----	----	----	----	2?	
						? 1929	....		....	....	----	----	----	----	----		
						1937	1103		1937	1104	----	----	x---	?---	----	3	
HERBERT (Aleutian Is)	52.75	N 170.12	W 1290	Stratovolc	1101-22-	Holocene											
CARLISLE (Aleutian Is)	52.90	N 170.05	W 1620	Stratovolc	1101-23-	Historical											
						1774	....		....	....	----	----	----	----	----		
						1828	....		....	....	----	----	----	----	----		
						? 1838	....		....	....	----	----	----	----	----		
						? 1987	1116		....	....	x---	----	--?-	----	----		
CLEVELAND (Chuginadak I)	52.82	N 169.95	W 1730	Stratovolc	1101-24-	Historical											
						1893	....		....	....	----	----	----	----	----		
						1897	....		....	....	----	----	----	----	----		
						? 1929	03		....	....	----	----	----	----	----		
						1932	0101		....	....	----	----	x---	----	----		
						1938	....		....	....	----	----	----	----	----		
						1944	0610		1944	0612	x---	----	x---	x---	x-?-	3	
						? 1951	1101		?1951	12	----	----	?---	----	----		
						? 1953	0625		....	....	x---	----	x---	----	----		
						? 1975	09		....	....	----	----	----	----	----		
						1984	0712		1984	0712	x---	----	x---	----	----	1	
						? 1985	1210		....	....	x---	----	--?-	----	----	1	
						1986	0428		1986	0527>	x---	----	x---	x---	----	2	
						1987	0619		1987	0828	x---	----	x---	x---	----	3*	
						? 1989	1025c		....	....	x---	----	----	?---	----	0	
ULIAGA (Aleutian Is)	53.07	N 169.77	W 888	Stratovolc	1101-25-	Holocene?											
KAGAMIL (Aleutian Is)	52.97	N 169.72	W 893	Stratovolc	1101-26-	Historical											
						1929	12		....	....	----	----	----	----	----		
VSEVIDOF (Umnak I)	53.13	N 168.68	W 2149	Stratovolc	1101-27-	Historical											
						? 1784	....		....	....	x---	----	----	----	----		
						? 1790	0530		....	....	x---	----	----	----	----		
						1817	....		....	....	----	----	----	----	----	3?	
SW end of Umnak Island						1830	....		....	....	----	----	----	----	----		
West flank fissure ?						1878	....		....	....	--?-	----	x---	?---	----	2	
						? 1880	....		....	....	x---	----	----	----	----		
West flank fissure						? 1957	0311		?1957	0312	--?-	----	x-x-	----	----	2	
RECHESCHNOI (Umnak I)	53.15	N 168.55	W 1984	Stratovolc	1101-28-	Holocene											
OKMOK (Umnak I)	53.42	N 168.13	W 1073	Stratovolc	1101-29-	Historical											
						C -6310z	....		....	....	x---	----	xx--	----	----	6?	-/10
						C -0450x	....		....	....	x---	----	xx--	----	----	6?	-/10
						1805	....		....	....	x---	----	----	?---	----		
						1817	0301		1820	....	x---	----	x?--	----	-x--	3	
						1824	....		1830	....	x---	----	----	?---	----		
						1878	....		....	....	x---	----	x---	----	---x	2?	
						1899	....		....	....	x---	----	x---	----	----	3	
						1931	0321	+	1931	0513>	x---	----	x---	?---	----	2	

VOLCANO NAME (Subregion) ...... ERUPTION —	LAT	LONG	ELEV (m)	TYPE	NUMBER	Area of Activity	Status / Start Year	Start M-Dy	P	Stop Year	Stop M-Dy	Central / Flank vent / Radial fiss / Regional*	Submarine / New island / Subglacial / Crater lake	Explosive / Pyro flow / Phreatic / Fumarolic	Lava flow / Lava lake / Dome / Spine	Fatal / Damage / Mudflow / Tsunami	VEI	Vol L/T
OKMOK (Umnak I) *continued*							? **1936**	....		....	....	x---	----	----	----	----		
							1938	....		....	....	x---	----	----	x---	----		
							1943	06		....	....	x---	----	x---	----	----	1	
						SW corner of caldera (Cone A)	**1945**	0604	+	**1945**	12	x---	----	x---	x---	----	2	7/-
						SW corner of caldera (Cone A)	**1958**	0814		**1958**	0825j	x---	----	x---	x---	----	3	8/-
						SW corner of caldera (Cone A)	**1960**	1015q		**1961**	0415q	x---	----	x---	----	----	3	-/7
						SW corner of caldera (Cone A)	**1981**	0324		**1981**	0324	x---	----	x---	----	----	3?	
						SW corner of caldera (Cone A)	**1983**	0708		**1983**	0708	x---	----	x---	----	----	2	
						SW corner of caldera (Cone A)	**1986**	1118	+	**1988**	0226	xx--	----	x---	----	----	2*	
BOGOSLOF (Aleutian Is)...........	**53.93**	**N 168.03**	**W 101**	**Submarine**	**1101-30-**		**Historical**											
						Old Bogoslof (Castle Rock)	**1796**	05		**1804**	....	----	xx--	x---	x-x-	----	3*	7/8
						Old Bogoslof (Castle Rock)	**1806**	....	+	**1823**	....	----	----	x---	x-x-	----	2*	7/-
						New Bogoslof (Grewingk)...............	**1883**	0927<	+	**1895**b	....	----	xx--	x---	--x-	----	3*	7/-
						Metcalf Peak, McCullough Peak	**1906**	0301p	+	**1907**	0901	----	xx--	x---	--xx	----	3*	6/8
						Metcalf Peak..........................	? **1908**	0115q		....	....	----	----	x---	----	----		
						Tahoma Peak........................	**1909**	09		**1910**	0919	----	xx--	x---	--x-	----	2*	
						Tahoma Peak........................	? **1913**	07		....	....	----	----	----	----	----		
						Between New and Old Bogoslof..........	**1926**	07		**1928**	....	----	xx--	x---	--x-	----	2	6/-
						1926-1927 dome	**1931**	1031		....	....	----	----	x---	x---	----	1	
							? **1951**	0921		....	....	----	?---	----	----	----	0	
						North tip of island (NE of 1927 dome)	**1992**	0706		**1992**	0726e	----	----	x---	--x-	----	3	
MAKUSHIN (Unalaska I)	**53.90**	**N 166.93**	**W 2036**	**Stratovolc**	**1101-31-**		**Historical**											
							C **-4165***	....		....	....	x---	----	xx--	----	----	5	-/9
							1768	....		**1769**	....	----	----	x---	----	----	3*	
							? **1790**	0607		....	....	----	----	----	----	----		
							? **1792**	0214		....	....	----	----	----	----	----		
							1802	....		....	....	----	----	x---	----	----	3	
							? **1818**	....		....	....	----	----	----	----	----		
							1826	06	+?	**1838**	....	----	----	x---	----	----	3	
							? **1844**a	....		....	....	----	----	----	----	----		
							1865	....		....	....	----	----	----	----	----		
							? **1867**	....		....	....	----	----	----	----	----		
							1883	....		....	....	----	----	x---	----	----	2	
							1907	....		....	....	----	----	----	----	----		
							? **1912**	....		....	....	----	----	----	----	----		
							1926	1230		....	....	----	----	x---	----	----	2	
							1938	10		....	....	----	----	x---	----	----	2	
							1951	1220		....	....	----	----	x-x-	----	----	1	
							? **1952**	....		....	....	----	----	----	----	----		
						SE side of summit	**1980**	0501s		....	....	x---	----	x-x-	----	----	1	
						(strong steam plume: no ash detected)	X 1986	0428		....	....	----	----	---x	----	----		
							1987	0302		**1987**	0302	x---	----	x-?-	----	----	1	
TABLE TOP-WIDE BAY (Unalaska I) .	**53.98**	**N*166.67**	**W 800**	**Cinder cones**	**1101-311**		**Holocene?**											
AKUTAN (Aleutian Is)	**54.13**	**N 165.97**	**W 1303**	**Stratovolc**	**1101-32-**		**Historical**											
							C **-3250**x	....		....	....	x---	----	xx--	----	----	5	-/9
							? **1790**	....		....	....	----	----	----	----	----		
							? **1828**	....		....	....	----	----	----	----	----		
							? **1838**	....		....	....	----	----	----	----	----		
							? **1845**	....		....	....	----	----	----	----	----		
							1848	0305d		....	....	----	----	x---	----	----	2	
						NW flank (Lava Point)	**1852**	....		....	....	-x--	----	x---	x---	----		
							1865	....		....	....	----	----	----	----	----		
							1867	....		....	....	----	----	----	----	----		
							1883	....		....	....	----	----	x---	----	----	2	
							1887	....		....	....	----	----	----	x---	----	0	
							1892	0923		....	....	----	----	x---	----	----	1	
							1896	....		....	....	----	----	----	----	----		
							1907	....		....	....	----	----	----	----	----		
							1908	0222		....	....	----	----	----	x---	----	0	
							1911	....		....	....	x---	----	x---	----	----	2	
							1912	....		....	....	----	----	----	----	----		
							1927	....		**1928**	....	----	----	x---	----	----	2	
							1929	05 ?		....	....	x---	----	x---	x---	--x-	2	
							1931	05	+	**1931**	08	x---	----	x---	----	----	2	
							1946	12		**1947**	01	x---	----	x---	x---	----	2	
							1948	0429		**1948**	0807>	x---	----	x---	----	----	2	
							1951	10		....	....	----	----	x---	----	----	2	
							1953	....		....	....	----	----	x---	----	----		
							1962	1105d		....	....	x---	----	x---	----	----	2	
							1972	09 ?		**1973**	05 >	x---	----	x---	----	----	2?	
						West flank ?	**1974**	0211<		....	....	-?--	----	x---	x---	----	2	
							1976	1015q		**1977**	0509>	x---	----	x---	----	----	2	
							1978	0925e		**1978**	10	x---	----	x---	x---	----	2	
							1980	0703<		**1980**	0708?	x---	----	x---	?---	----	2	
							1982	1005d		**1983**	05	x---	----	x---	----	----	2	
							1986	0318		**1986**	0630	x---	----	x---	----	----	2	
							1987	0131	+	**1987**	0624	x---	----	x---	----	----	2	
							1988	0326		**1988**	0720	x---	----	x---	----	----	2	
							1989	0227		**1989**	0328<	x---	----	x---	----	----	2	
							1990	0126e		**1990**	0126e	x---	----	x---	----	----	2	
							1990	0906		**1990**	1001	x---	----	x---	----	----	2	
							1991	0915		**1991**	1029a	x---	----	x---	----	----	2	
							1992	0308		**1992**	0531	x---	----	x---	----	----	2	
							1992	1218		....	....	x---	----	x---	----	----	1	
WESTDAHL (Unimak I)	**54.52**	**N 164.65**	**W 1654**	**Stratovolc**	**1101-34-**		**Historical**											
						Pogromni or Westdahl	**1795**	....		....	....	----	----	x---	----	--x-	4	-/9
						Pogromni or Westdahl	**1796**	....		....	....	----	----	----	x---	--x-	0	
						Pogromni or Westdahl	**1820**	....		....	....	----	----	x---	----	----	2	
						Pogromni or Westdahl	**1827**	....		**1830**	....	----	----	x---	----	----	2	
							1964	0310	+	**1964**	0416	-x--	----	x---	x---	----	2	
						South of Westdahl Peak (1450 m)	**1978**	0204		**1978**	0209	x---	--x-	x---	----	-xx-	3	
							? **1979**	0208		?**1979**	0209	----	----	?---	----	----	3?	
						ENE flank (1560-760 m)................	**1991**	1129		**1992**	0115?	--x-	--x-	x---	x---	--x-	3	
FISHER (Unimak I)................	**54.67**	**N 164.35**	**W 1094**	**Stratovolc**	**1101-35-**		**Historical**											
							C **-7170**y	....		....	....	x---	----	xx--	----	----	**6?**	**-/10**
							1795<	....		....	....	----	----	?---	----	----		

VOLCANO NAME (Subregion) / ERUPTION — Area of Activity	LAT	LONG	ELEV (m)	TYPE	NUMBER	Status / Start Year	Start M-Dy	P	Stop Year	Stop M-Dy	Central, Flank vent, Radial fiss, Regional*	Submarine, New island, Subglacial, Crater lake	Explosive, Pyro flow, Phreatic, Fumarolic	Lava flow, Lava lake, Dome, Spine	Fatal, Damage, Mudflow, Tsunami	VEI	Vol L/T
FISHER (Unimak I) *continued*						**1826**	1011		**1827**	01 ?	----	----	x---	----	----	3	
						1830	08		....	....	----	----	x---	----	----	2	
SHISHALDIN (Unimak I)	**54.75**	**N 163.97**	**W 2857**	**Stratovolc**	**1101-36-**	**Historical**											
						? **1775**	....		?**1778**	....	----	----	----	----	----		
						? **1790**	....		....	....	----	----	----	----	----		
						1824	....		....	....	----	----	x---	x---	----	3	
						1825	....		....	....	----	----	----	----	----	2	
						1826	....		....	....	-x--	----	----	x---	----	0	
						1827	....		**1829**	....	----	----	----	----	----	2	
						1830	11		**1830**	12	----	----	x---	x---	----	3	
						1838	....		....	....	----	----	x---	----	----	2	
						1842	....		....	....	----	----	x---	x---	----	2	
						? **1865**	....		....	....	----	----	----	----	----		
						? **1880**	....		?**1881**	....	----	----	----	----	----		
						1883	....		....	....	----	----	x---	----	----	2	
						? **1897**	....		....	....	----	----	----	----	----		
						1898	....		....	....	----	----	x---	x---	----	2	
						? **1899**	....		....	....	----	----	----	----	----		
						1901	....		....	....	----	----	----	----	----		
						? **1912**	....		....	....	----	----	----	----	----		
						1922	1015q		....	....	----	----	x---	x---	--x-	2	
						1925	....		....	....	----	----	----	----	----		
						1927	....		....	....	----	----	----	----	----		
						1928	08		....	....	----	----	x---	----	----	2	
Summit and north flank						**1929**	0528		**1929**	0623>	xx--	----	x---	x---	----	2	
						1932	0201	+	**1932**	0521	x---	----	x---	x---	--x-	2	
						1946	08	+	**1947**	01	----	----	x---	----	----	2	
						1948	....		....	....	----	----	x---	----	----	2	
						1951	04		**1951**	1005d	x---	----	x---	----	----	2	
						1953	1004c		....	....	----	----	x---	----	----	2	
						1955	....		....	....	----	----	x---	----	----		
						1963	1228		....	....	----	----	x---	----	----	2	
						1967	0128		....	....	----	----	x-x-	----	----	2	
						1975	0913		**1975**	1026e	x---	----	x---	?---	--?-	2	
						1976	0406		**1976**	0928	x---	----	x---	----	--?-	2*	
						1978	0208		**1978**	0209?	x---	----	x---	----	----	2	
						1979	02		....	....	x---	----	x---	----	----	2	
						? **1981**	0925		....	....	----	----	?---	----	----		
						1986	0319		**1987**	0215?	x---	----	x-x-	----	----	2	
						1993	1028		....	....	x---	----	x---	----	----	2	
ISANOTSKI (Unimak I)	**54.75**	**N 163.73**	**W 2446**	**Stratovolc**	**1101-37-**	**Historical**											
						@ **1795**	....		....	....	----	----	x---	----	----	3↑	
						@ **1825**	0310		....	....	----	----	x---	----	--x-	4	-/8
						1830	11		....	....	----	----	?---	----	----	2?	
						@ **1831**	03		@**1831**	0506a	----	----	----	x---	----		
						? **1845**	....		....	....	----	----	----	----	----		
ROUNDTOP (Unimak I)	**54.80**	**N 163.60**	**W 1871**	**Stratovolc**	**1101-38-**	**Holocene**											
AMAK (Aleutian Is)	**55.42**	**N 163.15**	**W 513**	**Stratovolc**	**1101-39-**	**Historical**											
						T **-2550z**	....		....	....	----	----	----	x---	----		
						1700	....		**1710**	....	x---	----	----	x---	----		
						1796	....		....	....	x---	----	----	x---	----		

ALASKA - PENINSULA & SW

VOLCANO NAME (Subregion) / ERUPTION — Area of Activity	LAT	LONG	ELEV (m)	TYPE	NUMBER	Status / Start Year	Start M-Dy	P	Stop Year	Stop M-Dy	Central, Flank vent, Radial fiss, Regional*	Submarine, New island, Subglacial, Crater lake	Explosive, Pyro flow, Phreatic, Fumarolic	Lava flow, Lava lake, Dome, Spine	Fatal, Damage, Mudflow, Tsunami	VEI	Vol L/T
FROSTY (Alaska Peninsula)	**55.07**	**N 162.82**	**W 1920**	**Stratovolcs**	**1102-01-**	**Holocene**											
DUTTON (Alaska Peninsula)	**55.18**	**N 162.27**	**W 1473**	**Stratovolc**	**1102-011**	**Holocene**											
EMMONS LAKE (Alaska Peninsula)	**55.33**	**N 162.07**	**W 1465**	**Caldera**	**1102-02-**	**Holocene**											
PAVLOF (Alaska Peninsula)	**55.42**	**N 161.90**	**W 2519**	**Stratovolc**	**1102-03-**	**Historical**											
						1790	....		....	....	----	----	x---	----	----	2	
						1817	....		....	....	----	----	x---	----	----	2	
						1825	....		....	....	----	----	?---	----	----	2?	
						? **1838**	....		....	....	----	----	----	----	----		
(eruption in August 1845, not 1844)						**1845**	0812		....	....	----	----	x---	----	----	2	
						1846	08		**1846**	08	x?--	----	x---	x---	----	2	
Upper north flank						? **1852**	....		....	....	x---	----	----	----	----		
						@ **1866**	0314		....	....	----	----	x---	----	----	2	
						1880	....		....	....	----	----	----	----	----		
						1886	....		....	....	x---	----	----	----	----	2?	
						1892	....		....	....	x---	----	x---	----	----	2?	
						1894	....		....	....	x---	----	x---	----	----	2?	
						1901	....		....	....	----	----	x---	----	----	2?	
Summit and north flank fissure						**1906**	....	+	**1911**	1207?	x-x-	----	x?--	x---	----	3*	
						1914	0706		....	....	----	----	x---	----	----	2	
						1917	10		....	....	----	----	x---	----	----	2	
						1922	1224		**1923**	0228r	x---	----	x---	----	----	2	
						1924	0117		....	....	x---	----	x---	----	----	2	
						1929	03		**1931**	08	x---	----	x---	----	----	2*	
						1936	....		**1948**	05 ?	x---	----	x---	x---	----	3*	
Upper NE or NNE flank						**1950**	0731		**1951**	05	x---	----	x---	----	----	2	
Upper NE or NNE flank						**1951**	10	+	**1952**	03 ?	x---	----	x---	----	----	2	
Upper NE or NNE flank						**1953**	1125		....	....	x---	----	----	----	----		
Upper NNE flank						**1958**	0517		**1958**	0828	x---	----	x---	x---	----	2	
Upper NE or NNE flank						**1960**?	....		**1963**	06 ?	x---	----	x---	----	----	2	
Upper NE or NNE flank						**1966**	0315		....	....	x---	----	x---	?---	----	2	
Upper NE flank						**1973**	1112		**1973**	1113	x---	----	-?--	?---	----	2	-/6
						S **1974**	0312?		S**1974**	0314?	x---	----	x---	----	----	2?	
						1974	0901<	+	**1975**	0106	x---	----	x---	----	--?-	3*	
						1975	0913		**1977**	03 >	x---	----	x---	?---	--?-	2*	
						1980	0706a		....	....	x---	----	x---	----	----	1	
Upper NNE flank						**1980**	1108		**1980**	1113	x---	----	x---	x---	----	3*	-/6
						1981	0330		**1981**	0528	x---	----	x---	----	----	1	
Upper NNE flank (100 m below summit)						**1981**	0925		**1981**	0927	x---	----	x---	x---	----	3	6/7
						? **1982**	0715q		....	....	x---	----	--??	----	----		
						1983	0711		**1983**	0718	x---	----	x---	----	----		
Upper NNE flank						**1983**	1114		**1983**	1218	x---	----	x---	x---	----	3	-/7
NNE & SE summit vents, NE & SE flanks						**1986**	0416		**1988**	0813	xx--	----	xx--	x---	--x-	3*	6/-
						1990	0305		**1990**	0305	x---	----	?-?-	----	----	2?	

VOLCANO NAME (Subregion) / ERUPTION — Area of Activity	LAT	LONG	ELEV (m)	TYPE	NUMBER	Status / Start Year	Start M-Dy	P	Stop Year	Stop M-Dy	Central, Flank vent, Radial fiss, Regional / Submarine, New island, Subglacial, Crater lake / Explosive, Pyro flow, Phreatic, Fumarolic / Lava flow, Lava lake, Dome, Spine / Fatal, Damage, Mudflow, Tsunami	VEI	Vol L/T
PAVLOF SISTER (Alaska Peninsula)	55.45 N	161.87 W	2142	Stratovolc	1102-04-	Historical							
						1762	....		1786	....	---- ---- x--- ---- ----	4*	-/8
DANA (Alaska Peninsula)	55.62 N	161.22 W	1354	Stratovolc	1102-05-	Radiocarbon							
						C-1890?	....		....	....	---- ---- xx-- ---- ----	5	-/9
UNNAMED (Alaska Peninsula)	55.93 N	160.00 W	1555	Cinder cones	1102-051	Holocene							
KUPREANOF (Alaska Peninsula)	56.02 N	159.80 W	1895	Stratovolc	1102-06-	Historical							
SSW flank (1575 m)						1987	0310		1987	0310	-x-- ---- x-?- ---- ----	1	
VENIAMINOF (Alaska Peninsula)	56.17 N	159.38 W	2507	Stratovolc	1102-07-	Historical							
						C-1750?	....		....	....	x--- ---- xx-- ---- ----	6	-/10
						? 1830	....		?1838	....	---- ---- ---- ---- ----	2	
Western intra-caldera cone						1838	0804		1839	04	x--- ---- x--- ---- ----	3	
Western intra-caldera cone						? 1852	....		....	....	x--- ---- ---- ---- ----		
Western intra-caldera cone						1874	0715q		....	....	x--- ---- x--- ---- ----	2?	
Western intra-caldera cone						1892	0828		1892	0830	x--- ---- x--- ---- ----	3	
Western intra-caldera cone						1930	06		....	....	x--- ---- x--- ---- ----	2	
Western intra-caldera cone						1939	0523		1939	0626?	x--- ---- x--- ---- ----	3	
Western intra-caldera cone						1939	11		....	....	x--- ---- x--- ---- ----	2	
Western intra-caldera cone						1944	0328		....	....	x--- ---- x--- ---- ----	2	
Western intra-caldera cone						1956	03		1956	0523	x--- ---- x--- ---- ----	3*	
Western intra-caldera cone						1983	0602		1984	0417	x--- ---- x--- x--- ----	3	7/-
Western intra-caldera cone						1984	1129		1984	1206?	x--- ---- x--- ---- ----	2	
Western intra-caldera cone						1987	0319		1987	0319	x--- ---- x-x- ---- ----	1	
Western intra-caldera cone						1993	0730		1993	1231>	x--- ---- x--- x--- ----	2	
BLACK PEAK (Alaska Peninsula)	56.53 N	158.80 W	1032	Stratovolc	1102-08-	Radiocarbon							
						T-2920z	....		....	....	x--- ---- xx-- ---- ----	6	-/10
ANIAKCHAK (Alaska Peninsula)	56.88 N	158.17 W	1341	Caldera	1102-09-	Historical							
						T-5250*	....		....	....	x--- ---- xx-- ---- ----	6?	-/10
						C-1480j	....		....	....	x--- ---- xx-- ---- ----	6?	-/10
North caldera wall (Half Cone)						C 1450?	....		....	....	x--- ---- x--- ---- ----	5?	-/9
Fissures cutting Vent Mountain						1931	0501		1931	0520>	x-RX- ---- x--- x-x- ----	3*	
						? 1942	....		....	....	---- ---- ---- ---- ----		
						? 1951	0625		?1951	0625	---- ---- ?--- ---- ----		
YANTARNI (Alaska Peninsula)	57.02 N	157.18 W	1336	Stratovolc	1102-10-	Tephrochronology							
						T-0800z	....		....	....	x--- ---- x?-- --x- ----	5	8/9
CHIGINAGAK (Alaska Peninsula)	57.13 N	157.00 W	2075	Stratovolc	1102-11-	Historical							
						? 1852	....		....	....	---- ---- ---- ---- ----		
						? 1929	12		....	....	---- ---- ---- ---- ----		
(ash eruption in July 1971, not 1972)						1971	07		1971	07	---- ---- x--- ---- ----		
KIALAGVIK (Alaska Peninsula)	57.38 N	156.75 W	1575	Stratovolc	1102-12-	Holocene							
UGASHIK-PEULIK (Alaska Peninsula)	57.75 N	156.37 W	1474	Stratovolc	1102-13A	Historical							
Peulik						1814	....		....	....	x--- ---- x--- ---- ----	3	
Peulik						? 1852	....		....	....	---- ---- ---- ---- ----		
UKINREK MAARS (Alaska Peninsula)	57.83 N	156.52 W	91	Maars	1102-13B	Historical							
						1977	0330		1977	0409	---- ---- xxx- -xx- ----	3	5/7
UNNAMED (Alaska Peninsula)	57.87 N	155.42 W	300	Lava dome	1102-131	Holocene							
MARTIN (Alaska Peninsula)	58.17 N	155.35 W	1860	Stratovolc	1102-14-	Historical							
(Kukak Bay ashfall probably from Martin)						@ 1951	0722		....	....	---- ---- x--- ---- ----		
(probably Martin, possibly Mageik)						@ 1953	0217		....	....	---- ---- x--- ---- ----		
MAGEIK (Alaska Peninsula)	58.20 N	155.25 W	2165	Stratovolc	1102-15-	Historical							
						1927	0826e		....	....	---- ---- x--- ---- ----	2	
						? 1929	0819	+	?1929	12	---- ---- x--- ---- ----	2	
						1936	0704		1936	0705	---- ---- x--- ---- ----	3	
						? 1946	....		....	....	---- ---- ?--- ---- ----	3	
TRIDENT (Alaska Peninsula)	58.23 N	155.08 W	1864	Stratovolc	1102-16-	Historical							
						1913	09		....	....	---- ---- ---- ---- ----	1	
						1949	06		....	....	---- ---- ---- ---- ----		
(ash eruption, attributed to Trident)						@ 1950	0702	+	@1950	0818	---- ---- x--- ---- ----	2?	
SW flank (1100 m)						1953	0215		1954	1005?	-x-- ---- x--- x-x- ----	3	8/7
(ash eruption, attributed to Trident)						@ 1956	0908		@1956	0909	---- ---- x--- ---- ----	2	
SW flank						1957	....	+	1960	0810?	-x-- ---- x--- x--- ----	2	
SW flank (1100 m)						1961	0630?		....	....	-x-- ---- x--- ---- ----	2	
SW flank						1962	0609		1962	0609	-x-- ---- x--- ---- ----	3	
SW flank						1963	0401		1963	0403	-x-- ---- x--- ---- --x-	3	
SW flank						1963	1017		1963	1117?	-x-- ---- x--- ---- ----	3	
SW flank						1964	0531		....	....	-x-- ---- x--- ---- ----	3?	
SW flank						1966?	....		....	....	-x-- ---- ---- --x- ----		
SW flank						1967	0905	+	1968	0225	-x-- ---- x--- --x- ----	3*	
SW flank						1968	1113		1968	1113	-x-- ---- x--- ---- ----	3	
SW flank						1974	0715q		1975	0115w	-x-- ---- x--- --x- ----	3	
KATMAI (Alaska Peninsula)	58.27 N	154.98 W	2047	Stratovolc	1102-17-	Historical							
						1912	0606		1912	0721>	x--- ---- x-x- ?--- ----	3	-/7
(eruption report not valid: Hildreth 1983)						X 1914	07		....	....	---- ---- ---- ---- ----		
(eruption report not valid: Hildreth 1983)						X 1920	0309		....	....	---- ---- ---- ---- ----		
(eruption report not valid: Hildreth 1983)						X 1921	1127		....	....	---- ---- ---- ---- ----		
(eruption report not valid: Hildreth 1983)						X 1929	12		....	....	---- ---- ---- ---- ----		
(eruption report not valid: Hildreth 1983)						X 1931	0508		X1931	07	---- ---- ---- ---- ----		
NOVARUPTA (Alaska Peninsula)	58.270 N	155.160 W	841	Caldera	1102-18-	Historical							
						1912	0606	+	1912	10 ?	x--- ---- xxx- ---- xxx-	6	7/10
(eruption report not valid: Hildreth 1983)						X 1949	0519		....	....	---- ---- ---- ---- ----		
(eruption report not valid: Hildreth 1983)						X 1950	0705d		....	....	---- ---- ---- ---- ----		
GRIGGS (Alaska Peninsula)	58.35 N	155.10 W	2317	Stratovolc	1102-19-	Holocene							
SNOWY (Alaska Peninsula)	58.33 N	154.68 W	2161	Stratovolc	1102-20-	Fumarolic							
DENISON (Alaska Peninsula)	58.42 N	154.45 W	2318	Stratovolc	1102-21-	Uncertain							
STELLER (Alaska Peninsula)	58.43 N	154.40 W	2272	Unknown	1102-22-	Uncertain							
KUKAK (Alaska Peninsula)	58.47 N	154.35 W	2040	Stratovolc	1102-23-	Fumarolic							
DEVILS DESK (Alaska Peninsula)	58.48 N	154.30 W	1954	Stratovolc	1102-24-	Uncertain							
KAGUYAK (Alaska Peninsula)	58.62 N	154.05 W	901	Stratovolc	1102-25-	Holocene							
						C 0325?	....		....	....	x--- ---- xx-- ---- ----	6	-/10
FOURPEAKED (Alaska Peninsula)	58.77 N	153.68 W	2104	Stratovolc	1102-26-	Uncertain							
DOUGLAS (Alaska Peninsula)	58.87 N	153.55 W	2140	Stratovolc	1102-27-	Fumarolic							
AUGUSTINE (Alaska-SW)	59.37 N	153.42 W	1252	Lava domes	1103-01-	Historical							
						C 0230x	....		....	....	x--- ---- x--- ---- ----		

VOLCANO NAME (Subregion)	LAT	LONG	ELEV (m)	TYPE	NUMBER	ERUPTION — Area of Activity	Status / Start Year	Start M-Dy	P	Stop Year	Stop M-Dy	Central / Flank vent / Radial fiss / Regional*	Submarine / New island / Subglacial / Crater lake	Explosive / Pyro flow / Phreatic / Fumarolic	Lava flow / Lava lake / Dome / Spine	Fatal / Damage / Mudflow / Tsunami	VEI	Vol L/T
AUGUSTINE (Alaska-SW) *continued*							C **0505**x	....		....	....	x---	----	x---	----	----		
							C **0885**w	....		....	....	x---	----	x---	----	----		
							C **1200**u	....		....	....	x---	----	x---	----	----		
							G **1540**v	....		....	....	x---	----	xx--	--?-	---?	4?	
							T **1650**v	....		....	....	x---	----	??--	----	----		
							1812	....		....	....	x---	----	xx--	--x-	----	3?	
							1883	1006		**1884**?	....	x---	----	xx--	x-x-	-xxx	4	8/8
						(no 1902 eruption: Johnston 1979)	X 1902	....		....	....	----	----	----	----	----		
							? **1908**	....		....	....	----	----	----	----	----		
							1935	0313		**1935**	0818	x---	----	xx--	--x-	--x-	3*	
							1963	1011	+	**1964**	0819	x---	----	xx--	--x-	--x-	2*	7/6
							1971	1007		**1971**	1008	x---	----	x---	----	----	1	
							1976	0122?	+	**1977**	0514?	x---	----	xx--	--x-	-xx-	4*	7/8
							1986	0327	+	**1986**	0831	x---	----	xx--	x-xx	-xx-	4?	-/8
ILIAMNA (Alaska-SW)	**60.03**	**N 153.08**	**W 3053**	**Stratovolc**	**1103-02-**		**Historical**											
							? **1768**	....		....	....	----	----	----	----	----		
							1778	....		**1779**	....	----	----	x---	----	----		
							? **1786**	....		....	....	----	----	----	----	----		
							? **1793**	....		....	....	----	----	----	----	----		
							? **1843**	....		....	....	----	----	x---	----	----		
							1867	....		....	....	----	----	x---	----	----	2	
							1876	....		....	....	----	----	x---	----	----	3	
							? **1933**	0505		....	....	----	----	----	----	----		
							? **1947**	06		....	....	----	----	----	----	----		
							? **1952**	....		....	....	----	----	----	----	----		
							1953	0301		....	....	----	----	x---	----	----	2	
						(steam plume, not eruption: Johnston 1979)	X 1978	1107		X1978	1107	x---	----	---x	----	----		
						(steam plumes, not an eruption)..........	X 1987	0319		X1987	0502	x---	----	---x	----	----		
REDOUBT (Alaska-SW)............	**60.48**	**N 152.75**	**W 3108**	**Stratovolc**	**1103-03-**		**Historical**											
							C **-5780**w	....		....	....	----	----	x---	----	----		
							T **-4550**y	....		....	....	----	----	x---	----	----		
							C **-2890**u	....		....	....	----	----	x---	----	----		
							C **-1550**w	....		....	....	x---	----	x---	----	--x-		
							T **-1075**w	....		....	....	----	----	x?--	----	--x-		
							T **-0205**x	....		....	....	----	----	x?--	----	--x-		
							C **0110**t	....		....	....	----	----	x?--	----	--x-		
							T **1550**t	....		....	....	----	----	x---	----	----		
							T **1600**t	....		....	....	----	----	x---	----	----		
							? **1778**	....		....	....	----	----	----	----	----		
							? **1819**	....		....	....	----	----	----	----	----		
							1902	0118		....	....	----	----	x---	----	----	3	
							? **1933**	0525		....	....	----	----	?---	----	----		
						North end of summit crater (2300 m)	? **1965**	0129		?**1965**	02	x---	----	?---	----	----		
						North end of summit crater (2300 m)	**1966**	0124		**1966**	0220	x---	----	x-x-	----	--J-	3*	
						North end of summit crater (2300 m)	**1966**	1007	+	**1967**	0115	x---	----	x---	----	----	3*	
						North end of summit crater (2300 m)	**1967**	1206	+	**1968**	0428>	x---	----	x---	--x-	----	3*	
						North end of summit crater (2470 m)	**1989**	1214	+	**1990**	0605d	x---	----	xxx-	--x-	-xx-	3*	7/-
SPURR (Alaska-SW)	**61.30**	**N 152.25**	**W 3374**	**Stratovolc**	**1103-04-**		**Historical**											
						Mt. Spurr central dome/cone complex	C **-5110**v	....		....	....	x---	----	x---	----	----		
						South flank (Crater Peak)...............	T **-4050**?	....		....	....	-x--	----	x---	----	----		
						Mt. Spurr central lava/cone complex	C **-3250**?	....		....	....	x---	----	x---	----	----		
							T **1650**t	....		....	....	----	----	x---	----	----		
						South flank (Crater Peak)...............	**1953**	0709	+	**1953**	0716	-x--	----	x-x-	----	--x-	4	
						(fumarolic activity only).................	X 1954	....		....	....	----	----	---x	----	----		
						South flank (Crater Peak)...............	**1992**	0627	+	**1992**	0917	-x--	---x	xx--	----	--x-	4*	-/7
HAYES (Alaska-SW)	**61.62**	**N 152.48**	**W 2788**	**Stratovolc**	**1103-05-**		**Radiocarbon**											
							T **-1850**?	....		....	....	----	----	x---	----	----		
							T **-1550**?	....		....	....	----	----	x---	----	----	**5**	
							T **1200**y	....		....	....	----	----	x---	----	----		

ALASKA - W, E, & SE

VOLCANO NAME (Subregion)	LAT	LONG	ELEV (m)	TYPE	NUMBER	ERUPTION — Area of Activity	Status / Start Year	Start M-Dy	P	Stop Year	Stop M-Dy	Central / Flank vent / Radial fiss / Regional*	Submarine / New island / Subglacial / Crater lake	Explosive / Pyro flow / Phreatic / Fumarolic	Lava flow / Lava lake / Dome / Spine	Fatal / Damage / Mudflow / Tsunami	VEI	Vol L/T
ESPENBERG (Alaska-W)	**66.35**	**N*164.33**	**W 243**	**Volc field**	**1104-01-**		**Tephrochronology**											
						Devil Mountain Lakes..................	T **-5050**?	....		....	....	x---	----	x---	----	----		
IMURUK LAKE (Alaska-W)	**65.60**	**N 163.92**	**W 610**	**Shields**	**1104-02-**		**Radiocarbon**											
						Lost Jim Cone	C **0295**?	....		....	....	x---	----	x---	x---	----		
KOOKOOLIGIT MOUNTAINS (")	**63.60**	**N 170.43**	**W 673**	**Shield**	**1104-03-**		**Holocene**											
ST. MICHAEL (Alaska-W)	**63.45**	**N*162.12**	**W 715**	**Cinder cones**	**1104-04-**		**Anthropology**											
INGAKSLUGWAT HILLS (Alaska-W) .	**61.43**	**N*164.47**	**W 190**	**Cinder cones**	**1104-05-**		**Holocene**											
NUNIVAK ISLAND (Alaska-W)	**60.02**	**N 166.33**	**W 511**	**Shield**	**1104-06-**		**Holocene**											
ST. PAUL ISLAND (Alaska-W)	**57.18**	**N*170.30**	**W 203**	**Cinder cones**	**1104-07-**		**Holocene**											
BUZZARD CREEK (Alaska-E).......	**64.07**	**N 148.42**	**W 830**	**Tuff rings**	**1105-001**		**Radiocarbon**											
							C **-1050**?	....		....	....	x---	----	x---	----	----	2	-/6
SANFORD (Alaska-E)	**62.22**	**N 144.13**	**W 4949**	**Shield**	**1105-01-**		**Holocene?**											
WRANGELL (Alaska-E)............	**62.00**	**N 144.02**	**W 4317**	**Shield**	**1105-02-**		**Historical**											
							C **0190**x	....		....	....	x---	----	xx--	----	----	**C?**	
							1819	....		....	....	----	----	----	----	----	2	
							1884	....		**1885**	....	x---	----	----	----	----	2	
							1899	0903		....	....	x---	----	x-x-	----	----	2	
							1902	....		....	....	x---	----	x-x-	----	----	2	
							? **1907**	0401<		....	....	x---	----	----	----	----		
GORDON (Alaska-E)	**62.13**	**N 143.08**	**W 2755**	**Cinder cones**	**1105-021**		**Holocene**											
BONA-CHURCHILL (Alaska-E)......	**61.38**	**N 141.75**	**W 5005**	**Stratovolcs**	**1105-03-**		**Radiocarbon**											
						Mt. Churchill	C **0065**x	....		....	....	x---	----	x---	----	----	**6**	**-/10**
						Mt. Churchill	C **0700**x	....		....	....	x---	----	x---	----	----	**6**	**-/10**
EDGECUMBE (Alaska-SE)	**57.05**	**N 135.75**	**W 976**	**Stratovolcs**	**1105-04-**		**Radiocarbon**											
							C **-7215**w	....		....	....	----	----	x---	----	--x-		
							C **-3810**u	....		....	....	----	----	x---	----	----		
							C **-2220**v	....		....	....	----	----	x---	----	----		
DUNCAN CANAL (Alaska-SE)	**56.50**	**N*133.10**	**W 15**	**Unknown**	**1105-05-**		**Holocene**											
TLEVAK STRAIT-SUEMEZ IS. (")....	**55.25**	**N*133.30**	**W 50**	**Volc field**	**1105-06-**		**Holocene**											
REVILLAGIGEDO ISLAND (").......	**55.32**	**N*131.05**	**W 500**	**Cinder cones**	**1105-07-**		**Holocene?**											

Canada & Western USA (12)

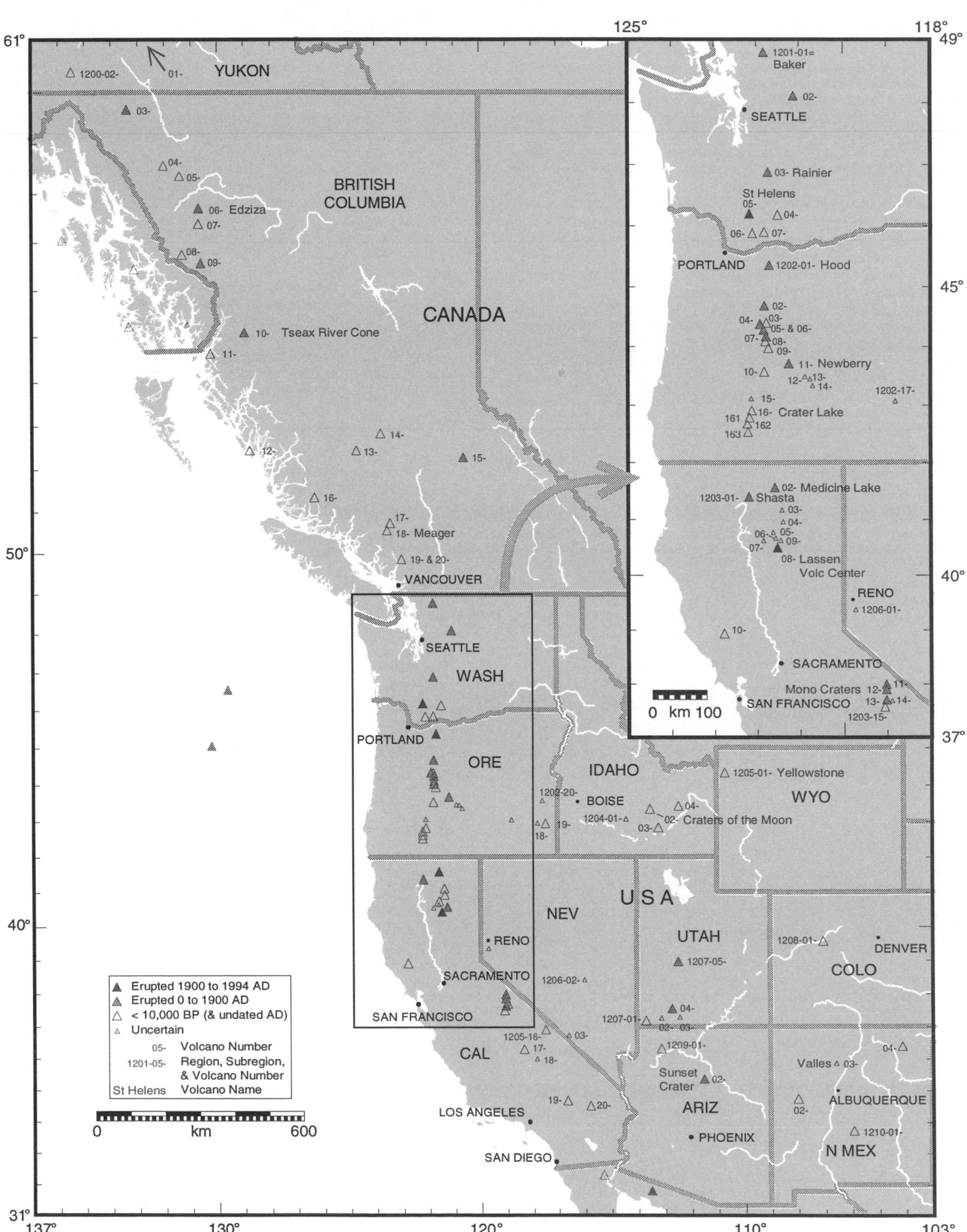

12

This region was originally titled "USA" by the organizers of the *CAVW*, but we added Canada (as subregion 1200) in our first edition. If we add the US volcanoes here (subregions 1201-1210) to those of Alaska and Hawaii, we find 53 historically active volcanoes, placing the US third (behind Indonesia and Japan, and narrowly ahead of Russia's 52) in this dubious national ranking. If the Commonwealth of the Northern Marianas Islands is included, the number of historically active volcanoes rises to 60, and approaches Japan's total of 63.

Volcanoes of region 12 occupy tectonic environments ranging from the subduction volcanism that dominates the Cascade Range to the extensional tectonics controlling vast regions of the western interior, giving region 12 the largest number (and percent) of volcanoes consisting primarily of cinder cone fields.

Only Mount St. Helens and Lassen volcanoes in this region have had unequivocal eruptions in this century whereas 34 have earlier dated eruptions, a lower ratio than any other region and a striking contrast to a region like Indonesia where 83% of its dated eruptions were in this century. Globally, only 20% of dated eruptions are pre-historic, but this proportion is 79% in region 12, testifying to the strong attention paid to the recent geologic record. Region 12 has the largest number of Holocene eruptions dated by radiocarbon (126), by dendrochronology (10), and by magnetics (10).

Native American legends describe eruptions of Sunset Crater, Arizona, now dated to 1064-65 AD, and Canadian Indian legends record a British Columbian eruption in the 18th century. After the historic voyages of Columbus, Spain dominated exploration of North America in the 16th century, with the Grand Canyon first viewed by western eyes in 1540 and the Oregon coast only 4 years later. Permanent inland settlement of Santa Fe came in 1609, only 2 years after the first settlement on the east coast by the British. The founding of the Massachusetts Bay Colony in 1630 started the great emigration to eastern North America. Exploration of the west was slow, though, and it was not until the 1770s that Captain Cook closed the gap between Spaniards working north along the coast and Russians moving toward them from the far northwest. Cook brought publicity to the Pacific coast, and by the end of the century ships from 6 nations were busily trading furs along seacoasts that 20 years earlier had not been seen by Europeans. The first documented eruption in the region was California's Shasta, in 1786. By that year every other region in the world, except Antarctica, had documented at least one historical eruption, and over half of region 01's current list of historical volcanism had been recorded.

In the latter half of the 18th century, while the US was gaining independence in the east, the Rocky Mountains were being explored by the British and French. In 1805 Lewis and Clark sighted the Pacific, and the first historical eruptions of Mount St. Helens were witnessed by settlers in the 1830s. In 1841 the first wagon train reached the Oregon Territories, and in 1848 gold was discovered in California. It was not until the end of the Civil War, though, that westward emigration exploded: the first transcontinental railroad was completed in 1869, and by 1890 the US Census Bureau Director declared that the American frontier was at an end. The US Geological Survey was founded in 1879 and from 1926 through 1931 operated a volcano observatory at Lassen, following that volcano's 1914-17 eruption. The second Cascade eruption of the century, at Mount St. Helens, brought the founding of the Cascades Volcano Observatory in 1980.

VOLCANO NAME (Subregion) / ERUPTION — Area of Activity	LAT	LONG	ELEV (m)	TYPE	NUMBER	Status	Start Year	Start M-Dy	P	Stop Year	Stop M-Dy	ERUPTIVE CHARACTERISTICS (Central, Flank vent, Radial fiss, Regional* / Submarine, New island, Subglacial, Crater lake / Explosive, Pyro flow, Phreatic, Fumarolic / Lava flow, Lava lake, Dome, Spine / Fatal, Damage, Mudflow, Tsunami)	VEI	Vol L/T
CANADA														
FORT SELKIRK (Canada-Yukon)	**62.93**	**N∗137.38**	**W 1239**	**Volc field**	**1200-01-**	**Holocene**								
ALLIGATOR LAKE (Canada-Yukon). .	**60.42**	**N∗135.42**	**W 2217**	**Volc field**	**1200-02-**	**Holocene**								
RUBY MOUNTAIN (Canada-B.C.)....	**59.68**	**N 133.32**	**W 1523**	**Cinder cones**	**1200-03-**	**Historical**								
							1898	1108		....	....	x--- ---- x--- ---- ----	2?	
HEART PEAKS (Canada-B.C.)	**58.60**	**N 131.97**	**W 2012**	**Shield**	**1200-04-**	**Holocene**								
LEVEL MOUNTAIN (Canada-B.C.) ...	**58.42**	**N 131.35**	**W 2190**	**Shield**	**1200-05-**	**Holocene**								
EDZIZA (Canada-B.C.)............	**57.72**	**N 130.63**	**W 2786**	**Stratovolc**	**1200-06-**	**Radiocarbon**								
North flank?							C **-6515**x	....		....	....	-?-- ---- ---- x--- ----		
							T **-0750**v	....		....	....	-x-- ---- ---- x--- ----		
NNE flank (Williams Cone).............							C **0610**w	....		....	....	-x-- ---- x--- x--- ----		
SW flank of Ice Peak							F **0950**∗	....		....	....	-x-- ---- x--- x--- ----	3	-/7
SPECTRUM RANGE (Canada-B.C.) . .	**57.43**	**N 130.68**	**W 2430**	**Shield**	**1200-07-**	**Holocene**								
HOODOO MOUNTAIN (Canada-B.C.).	**56.78**	**N 131.28**	**W 1820**	**Subglacial**	**1200-08-**	**Holocene**								
ISKUT-UNUK RIVER CONES (B.C.) . .	**56.58**	**N∗130.55**	**W 1880**	**Cinder cones**	**1200-09-**	**Radiocarbon**								
Iskut River							C **-6830**w	....		....	....	x--- ---- x--- x--- ----		
Iskut River							C **-4700**y	....		....	....	x--- ---- ---- x--- ----		
Iskut River							C **-3450**w	....		....	....	x--- ---- ---- x--- ----		
Iskut River							C **-1830**y	....		....	....	x--- ---- ---- x--- ----		
Iskut River							C **-0615**w	....		....	....	x--- ---- x--- x--- ----		
Lava Fork							C **1590**t	....		....	....	x--- ---- ---- x--- ----		
Lava Fork							C **1800?**	....		....	....	x--- ---- ---- x--- ----		
Lava Fork							? **1904**	....		....	....	x--- ---- ?--- ---- ----		
TSEAX RIVER CONE (Canada-B.C.) .	**55.12**	**N 128.90**	**W 609**	**Pyrocl cone**	**1200-10-**	**Radiocarbon**								
							C **1325**u	....		....	....	x--- ---- x--- x--- ----		
							C **1730**w	....		....	....	x--- ---- x--- x--- xx--		8/-
CROW LAGOON (Canada-B.C.)	**54.70**	**N 130.23**	**W 335**	**Pyrocl cone**	**1200-11-**	**Holocene**								
MILBANKE SOUND GROUP (B.C.) . .	**52.50**	**N∗128.73**	**W 335**	**Cinder cones**	**1200-12-**	**Holocene**								
SATAH MOUNTAIN (Canada-B.C.)...	**52.47**	**N∗124.70**	**W 1921**	**Volc field**	**1200-13-**	**Holocene**								
NAZKO (Canada-B.C.).............	**52.90**	**N 123.73**	**W 1230**	**Cinder cones**	**1200-14-**	**Radiocarbon**								
							C **-5215**v	....		....	....	x--- ---- x--- x--- ----		
WELLS GRAY-CLEARWATER (B.C.).	**52.33**	**N∗120.57**	**W 2015**	**Cinder cones**	**1200-15-**	**Dendrochronology**								
Dragon Cone							C **-5650?**	....		....	....	x--- ---- x--- x--- ----		
Kostal Cone							D **1550?**	....		....	....	x--- ---- x--- x--- ----		
SILVERTHRONE (Canada-B.C.)	**51.43**	**N 126.30**	**W 3160**	**Caldera**	**1200-16-**	**Holocene**								
BRIDGE RIVER CONES (Canada-B.C)	**50.80**	**N∗123.40**	**W 2500**	**Volc field**	**1200-17-**	**Holocene**								
MEAGER (Canada-B.C.)	**50.63**	**N 123.50**	**W 2680**	**Complx volc**	**1200-18-**	**Radiocarbon**								
NE flank (Bridge River vent)............							C **-0400**t	....		....	....	-x-- ---- xx-- x-x- ----	**5?**	
GARIBALDI LAKE (Canada-B.C.)....	**49.92**	**N∗123.03**	**W 2316**	**Volc field**	**1200-19-**	**Holocene**								
GARIBALDI, MT. (Canada-B.C.)	**49.85**	**N 123.00**	**W 2678**	**Stratovolc**	**1200-20-**	**Radiocarbon**								
SE flank (Opal Cone)							C **-8055**z	....		....	....	-x-- ---- x--- x--- ----	3?	**9/7**
USA - W COAST STATES														
BAKER (US-Washington)	**48.786**	**N 121.82**	**W 3285**	**Stratovolc**	**1201-01=**	**Historical**								
Sherman Crater							C **-6750**∗	....		....	....	x--- ---- xx-- x--- --x-		
South flank (Schreibers Meadow Cone)....							T **-6525**∗	....		....	....	-x-- ---- ---- x--- --x-		
							T **-1300**∗	....		....	....	x--- ---- x--- ---- ----	4	-/8
Sherman Crater							**1792**	....		....	....	x--- ---- x--- ---- ----	2	
Sherman Crater							**1820?**	....		....	....	x--- ---- x--- ---- ----	2	
Sherman Crater							**1843**	....		....	....	x--- ---- x--- ---- ----	2	
(possibly confused with 1843 eruption							? **1846**	....		....	....	x--- ---- ?--- ---- ----		
Sherman Crater							? **1850**	03		....	....	x--- ---- ---- ---- ----		
Sherman Crater							**1852**	1201p		**1853**	01 ?	x--- ---- ?--- ---- --?-	2	

VOLCANO NAME (Subregion)	LAT	LONG	ELEV (m)	TYPE	NUMBER	ERUPTION — Area of Activity	Status Start Year	Start M-Dy	P	Stop Year	Stop M-Dy	Central Flank vent Radial fiss Regional*	Submarine New island Subglacial Crater lake	Explosive Pyro flow Phreatic Fumarolic	Lava flow Lava lake Dome Spine	Fatal Damage Mudflow Tsunami	VEI	Vol L/T
BAKER (US-Washington) *continued*						Sherman Crater	**1854**	....		....	....	x---	----	x---	----	----	2	
						Sherman Crater	? **1856**	....		....	....	x---	----	----	----	----		
						Sherman Crater	**1858**	....		....	....	x---	----	x---	----	----	2	
						Sherman Crater	**1859**	11		**1860**	0426?	x---	----	x---	----	----	2	
						Sherman Crater	? **1860**	12		....	....	x---	----	----	----	----		
						Sherman Crater	**1863**	07		....	....	x---	----	x---	----	----	2	
						Sherman Crater	? **1865**	....		....	....	x---	----	----	----	----		
						Sherman Crater	? **1867**	03		....	....	x---	----	----	----	----		
						Sherman Crater	? **1869**	06		....	....	x---	----	----	----	----		
						Sherman Crater	**1870**	....		....	....	x---	----	x---	----	----	2	
						Sherman Crater	**1880**	0907		**1880**	1127	x---	----	x---	----	----	2	
						Sherman Crater	? **1884**	....		....	....	x---	----	----	----	----		
GLACIER PEAK (US-Washington)	**48.112 N**	**121.113 W**	**3213**	**Stratovolc**	**1201-02-**		**Tephrochronology**											
						(White Chuck Cone is Pleistocene)	X -7350*	....		....	....	----	----	----	----	----		
							C **-3550?**	....		....	....	x---	----	xx--	--x-	--x-		
							C **-3150?**	....		....	....	x---	----	xx--	--x-	--x-		
							C **-0850?**	....		....	....	x---	----	x-?-	--?-	--x-		
							C **0200t**	....		....	....	x---	----	xx--	--x-	--x-	4+	-/8
							C **0900t**	....		....	....	x---	----	xx--	--x-	--x-	3?	-/8
							? **1300y**	....		....	....	----	----	?---	----	--x-		
							T **1700v**	....		....	....	x---	----	x---	----	--x-	2	
RAINIER (US-Washington)	**46.87 N**	**121.758 W**	**4392**	**Stratovolc**	**1201-03-**		**Dendrochronology**											
							C **-6800<**	....		....	....	----	----	x---	----	----	3	-/7
							G **-5400?**	....		....	....	----	----	x---	----	----	2	-/6
							G **-5300?**	....		....	....	----	----	x---	----	----	3	-/7
							G **-4900?**	....		....	....	----	----	x---	----	----	3	-/7
							G **-4400?**	....		....	....	----	----	x---	----	----	2	-/6
							G **-4200?**	....		....	....	----	----	x---	----	----	3	-/7
							G **-3800?**	....		....	....	----	----	x---	----	--?-	3	-/7
							G **-3600?**	....		....	....	----	----	x---	----	----	2	-/6
							G **-3400?**	....		....	....	----	----	x---	----	----	3	-/7
							G **-0520x**	....		....	....	----	----	xx--	----	----		
							G **-0300?**	....		....	....	----	----	x---	----	----	4	-/8
							D **1825?**	....		....	....	----	----	x---	----	----	2	-/6
							? **1843**	....		....	....	x---	----	?---	----	----	2	
							? **1854**	....		....	....	x---	----	?---	----	----	2	
							? **1858**	....		....	....	x---	----	?---	----	----	2	
							? **1870**	....		....	....	x---	----	?---	----	----	2	
							? **1879**	....		....	....	x---	----	?---	----	----	2	
							? **1882**	....		....	....	x---	----	?---	----	----	2	
							? **1894**	1121		?**1894**	1224	x---	----	?---	----	----		
ADAMS (US-Washington)	**46.206 N**	**121.490 W**	**3742**	**Stratovolc**	**1201-04-**		**Tephrochronology**											
						King Mtn fissure (south flank)	T **-7535***	....		....	....	---x	----	x---	----	----		
ST. HELENS (US-Washington)	**46.20 N**	**122.18 W**	**2549**	**Stratovolc**	**1201-05-**		**Historical**											
							G **-2335?**	....		....	....	----	----	xx--	--x-	--x-	5	-/9
							G **-1855?**	....		....	....	----	----	xx--	--x-	--x-	6	-/10
							G **-1675?**	....		....	....	----	----	xx--	----	----	5	-/9
							G **-1610?**	....		....	....	----	----	xx--	--x-	--x-		
							G **-1185?**	....		....	....	----	----	xx--	--x-	--x-		
							G **-1100?**	....		....	....	----	----	xx--	--x-	--x-		
							G **-1010?**	....		....	....	----	----	xx--	--x-	--x-		
							G **-0800?**	....		....	....	----	----	xx--	--x-	--x-		
							G **-0530?**	....		....	....	----	----	xx--	--x-	--x-	4?	-/8
							G **-0275?**	....		....	....	----	----	xx--	x---	----		
							T **-0250?**	....		....	....	----	----	x---	x---	--x-		
						NNE flank (Dogs Head)	G **-0220?**	....		....	....	-x--	----	xx--	--x-	----		
							G **-0095?**	....		....	....	----	----	xx--	----	----		
						SW flank	C **0060y**	....		....	....	-x--	----	----	x---	----	0	
						Lower east flank (East Dome)	G **0185?**	....		....	....	-x--	----	x---	--x-	----		
							T **0230?**	....		....	....	----	----	----	x---	----		
							G **0275?**	....		....	....	----	----	x---	x---	----		
							G **0420?**	....		....	....	x---	----	x---	----	--x-		
						NE flank (Sugar Bowl)	C **0775y**	....		....	....	-x--	----	xx--	--x-	--x-		
						Dome at or near summit	D **1480**	0115u		....	....	x---	----	xx--	--x-	--x-	5+	-/9
							D **1482**	0115u		....	....	x---	----	x---	----	----	5	
							D **1525q**	....		....	....	x---	----	xx--	x---	--x-		
						Pre-1980 summit dome	G **1610s**	....		....	....	x---	----	xx--	--x-	--x-		8/-
						North flank (Goat Rocks area)	D **1800**	0115u		....	....	-x--	----	x---	x---	--x-	5	-/9
						North Flank (Goat Rocks area)	**1831**	08		....	....	-x--	----	x---	?-?-	----	3	
						North flank (Goat Rocks area)	**1835**	03 ?		....	....	-x--	----	x---	?-?-	----	2	
						North flank (Goat Rocks)	**1842**	1122		**1845**	0918?	-x--	----	xx--	--x-	----	3	-/7
						North flank (Goat Rocks)	**1847**	0326		**1847**	0330	-x--	----	x---	--?-	----	2	
							1848	0401<		....	....	----	----	?---	----	----	2?	
						North flank	? **1849**	....		....	....	-x--	----	?---	----	----	2?	
						North flank	**1850**	03		**1850**	05 ?	-x--	----	x---	----	----	2?	
						North flank	**1853**	0315e		**1853**	08 ?	-x--	----	x---	----	----	2?	
						North flank	**1854**	02		**1854**	04	-x--	----	x---	----	----	2	
							1857	04		....	....	----	----	x---	----	----	2	
							? **1898**	0405		....	....	----	----	----	----	----		
							? **1903**	0915		....	....	----	----	--?-	----	----		
							? **1921**	0318		....	....	----	----	----	----	----		
						Summit and north flank	**1980**	0327	+	**1986**	1028c	xx--	--x-	xxx-	--xx	xxx-	5*	7/9
						North side of lava dome	**1989**	1207	+	1990	0106	x---	----	x-x-	----	----	2*	
						North side of lava dome	**1990**	1105	+	**1991**	0214	x---	----	xxx-	----	--x-	3?	
WEST CRATER (US-Washington)	**45.88 N**	***122.08 W**	**914**	**Volc field**	**1201-06-**		**Radiocarbon**											
						West Crater	C **-3050?**	....		....	....	---x	----	x---	x---	----		
INDIAN HEAVEN (US-Washington)	**45.93 N**	**121.82 W**	**1513**	**Shields**	**1201-07-**		**Radiocarbon**											
						Big Lava Bed	C **-6250v**	....		....	....	---x	----	x---	x---	----		8/-
HOOD (US-Oregon)	**45.374 N**	**121.694 W**	**3426**	**Stratovolc**	**1202-01-**		**Historical**											
						NE flank (SSW of Parkdale)	C **-4940w**	....		....	....	-x--	----	x---	x---	----	2	
						Upper SW flank (Crater Rock)	C **0300x**	....		....	....	-x--	----	xx--	----	--x-		
						Upper SW flank (Crater Rock)	C **0510w**	....		....	....	-x--	----	xx--	----	----		
						Upper SW flank (Crater Rock)	C **1390w**	....		....	....	-x--	----	x---	----	--x-		
						Upper SW flank (Crater Rock)	D **1765e**	....		....	....	-x--	----	xx--	--x-	--x-		
						Upper SW flank (Crater Rock)	D **1795e**	....		....	....	-x--	----	x---	--x-	--x-		
						Upper SW flank (Crater Rock)	D **1800?**	....		....	....	-x--	----	xx--	--x-	--x-		

VOLCANO NAME (Subregion) / ERUPTION — Area of Activity	LAT	LONG	ELEV (m)	TYPE	NUMBER	Status / Start Year	Start M-Dy	P	Stop Year	Stop M-Dy	Central / Flank vent / Radial fiss / Regional	Submarine / New island / Subglacial / Crater lake	Explosive / Pyro flow / Phreatic / Fumarolic	Lava flow / Lava lake / Dome / Spine	Fatal / Damage / Mudflow / Tsunami	VEI	Vol L/T
HOOD (US-Oregon) *continued*						? **1853**	....		....	....	----	----	?---	----	----		
						? **1854**	08		....	....	----	----	----	----	----		
						1859	0815		**1859**	0817	----	----	x---	----	----	2	
						1865	0921		**1866**	01 ?	----	----	x---	----	----	2	
						? **1869**	....		....	....	----	----	----	----	----		
Crater Rock						? **1907**	0828		....	....	-x--	----	--?-	----	----		
JEFFERSON (US-Oregon)	**44.692 N**	**121.80 W**	**3199**	**Stratovolc**	**1202-02-**	**Varve Count**											
SSE of Jefferson (Forked Butte)						V **-4500t**	....		....	....	-x--	----	x---	x---	----		
S of Jefferson (South Cinder Peak)						V **0950?**	....		....	....	-x--	----	x---	x---	----		
BLUE LAKE CRATER (US-Oregon)	**44.42 N**	**121.77 W**	**1230**	**Maar**	**1202-03-**	**Radiocarbon**											
						C **-1490y**	....		....	....	----	----	x---	----	----		
SAND MOUNTAIN FIELD (Oregon)	**44.38 N***	**121.93 W**	**1664**	**Cinder cones**	**1202-04-**	**Radiocarbon**											
Nash Crater and other cones						C **-1900?**	....		....	....	---x	----	x---	x---	----	2?	
North and south of Sand Mountain						C **-1490?**	....		....	....	---x	----	x---	----	----	2?	
North Sand Mtn and other cones						C **-1040?**	....		....	....	---x	----	x---	x---	----	2?	
Lost Lake Cones						C **0000w**	....		....	....	---x	----	x---	x---	----	2?	
WASHINGTON (US-Oregon)	**44.332 N**	**121.837 W**	**2376**	**Shield**	**1202-05-**	**Radiocarbon**											
NE flank fissure, 4 km from summit						C **0620?**	....		....	....	---x	----	x---	----	----	1	
BELKNAP (US-Oregon)	**44.285 N**	**121.841 W**	**2095**	**Shields**	**1202-06-**	**Radiocarbon**											
Little Belknap						C **-0935?**	....		....	....	-x--	----	----	x---	----	0	
SW of Belknap (Twin Craters)						C **-0650?**	....		....	....	---x	----	x---	x---	----	2?	
South Belknap						C **0175?**	....		....	....	-x--	----	x---	x---	----	2?	
Belknap Crater						C **0360w**	....		....	....	x---	----	----	x---	----	0	
Belknap Crater						C **0455?**	....		....	....	xx--	----	x---	x---	----	2?	
NORTH SISTER FIELD (US-Oregon)	**44.17 N**	**121.77 W**	**3074**	**Complx volc**	**1202-07-**	**Radiocarbon**											
Sims Butte						T **-7350***	....		....	....	-x--	----	x---	x---	----	2?	
Yapoah Cone						T **-0800?**	....		....	....	---x	----	x---	x---	----	2?	
Four-in-One Cone						C **-0030w**	....		....	....	---x	----	x---	x---	----	2?	
Collier Cone						C **0350v**	....		....	....	-x--	----	x---	x---	----	2?	8/-
SOUTH SISTER (US-Oregon)	**44.10 N**	**121.77 W**	**3157**	**Complx volc**	**1202-08-**	**Radiocarbon**											
SW flank (Rock Mesa)						C **-0350?**	....		....	....	-x--	----	xx--	x-x-	--x-	4	8/8
North & south flanks (Devils Hill)						C **-0050?**	....		....	....	-x-x	----	xx--	x-x-	--x-	3	8/7
						? **1853**	07		....	....	x---	----	?---	----	----		
BACHELOR (US-Oregon)	**43.979 N**	**121.688 W**	**2763**	**Stratovolc**	**1202-09-**	**Tephrochronology**											
North flank (Egan Cone)						M **-5800***	....		....	....	-x--	----	x---	x---	----		
DAVIS LAKE (US-Oregon)	**43.57 N***	**121.82 W**	**2163**	**Volc field**	**1202-10-**	**Radiocarbon**											
S flank of Hamner Butte (Black Rock)						C **-2790?**	....		....	....	-x--	----	x---	x---	----		
NEWBERRY VOLCANO (US-Oregon)	**43.722 N**	**121.229 W**	**2434**	**Shield**	**1202-11-**	**Radiocarbon**											
South and east caldera rim						T **-7050***	....		....	....	x---	----	x---	x-x-	----		
Center, N & S caldera, upper SE flank						H **-4450?**	....		....	....	x---	----	x---	x---	----		
NW rift zone (Lava Cast Forest)						C **-4315y**	....		....	....	--x-	----	----	x---	----	0	
NW rift zone (Lava Butte)						C **-4210u**	....		....	....	--x-	----	x---	x---	----	3	8/7
East Lake fissure, south flank						C **-4135v**	....		....	....	--x-	----	----	x---	----		
NW rift zone (Forest Road flow)						C **-4010v**	....		....	....	--x-	----	----	x---	----	0	
NW rift zone (Sugarpine Butte)						C **-3920v**	....		....	....	--x-	----	x---	x---	----		
NW rift zone (Lava Cascade flow)						C **-3850w**	....		....	....	--x-	----	----	x---	----	0	
South of East Lake						H **-1450?**	....		....	....	x---	----	x---	x---	----		
South caldera wall						C **0315y**	....		....	....	x---	----	x---	----	----	4	-/8
S caldera wall (Big Obsidian Flow)						C **0620x**	....		....	....	x---	----	xx--	x---	----	3	8/7
DEVILS GARDEN (US-Oregon)	**43.512 N***	**120.861 W**	**1698**	**Volc field**	**1202-12-**	**Holocene?**											
SQUAW RIDGE FIELD (US-Oregon)	**43.472 N***	**120.754 W**	**1711**	**Volc field**	**1202-13-**	**Holocene?**											
FOUR CRATERS LAVA FIELD (")	**43.361 N***	**120.669 W**	**1501**	**Volc field**	**1202-14-**	**Holocene?**											
CINNAMON BUTTE (US-Oregon)	**43.116 N***	**122.108 W**	**1956**	**Cinder cones**	**1202-15-**	**Holocene?**											
CRATER LAKE (US-Oregon)	**42.93 N**	**122.12 W**	**2487**	**Caldera**	**1202-16-**	**Radiocarbon**											
North flank (Llao Rock)						C **-5065t**	....		....	....	-x--	----	x---	x---	----	**6**	**8/10**
Mt. Mazama summit and flank vents						C **-4895t**	1015q		....	....	xx--	----	xx--	x---	----	**7**	**8/11**
Wizard Island						M **-4750?**	....		....	....	x---	----	x---	x---	----		
WNW of Wizard Island						T **-2050?**	....		....	....	x---	----	----	--x-	----		
GOOSENEST (US-Oregon)	**42.788 N**	**122.154 W**	**2213**	**Shield**	**1202-161**	**Holocene**											
BIG BUNCHGRASS (US-Oregon)	**42.703 N**	**122.194 W**	**2024**	**Pyrocl cone**	**1202-162**	**Holocene**											
IMAGINATION PEAK (US-Oregon)	**42.552 N**	**122.201 W**	**1986**	**Pyrocl cone**	**1202-163**	**Holocene**											
DIAMOND CRATERS (US-Oregon)	**43.10 N***	**118.75 W**	**1435**	**Volc field**	**1202-17-**	**Holocene?**											
SADDLE BUTTE (US-Oregon)	**43.00 N***	**117.80 W**	**1700**	**Volc field**	**1202-18-**	**Holocene?**											
JORDAN CRATERS (US-Oregon)	**43.03 N***	**117.42 W**	**1473**	**Volc field**	**1202-19-**	**Holocene**											
JACKIES BUTTE (US-Oregon)	**43.606 N***	**117.589 W**	**1420**	**Volc field**	**1202-20-**	**Holocene?**											
SHASTA (US-California)	**41.42 N**	**122.20 W**	**4317**	**Stratovolc**	**1203-01-**	**Historical**											
						T **-8050?**	....		....	....	x---	----	xx--	----	----		
						C **-7750?**	....		....	....	x---	----	xx--	----	--x-		
Summit, S flank, and Shastina						C **-7650v**	....		....	....	xx--	----	xx--	x---	----	4	-/8
Shastina and Black Butte						C **-7415y**	....		....	....	-x--	----	xx--	--x-	----		
Summit, north and west flanks						T **-7350?**	....		....	....	xx--	----	----	x---	----	0	
						T **-7050?**	....		....	....	x---	----	x---	x---	----		
						T **-6650?**	....		....	....	x---	----	xx--	----	--x-		
						C **-6050?**	....		....	....	x---	----	x?--	----	--x-		
						C **-4050?**	....		....	....	x---	----	xx--	----	--x-		
						T **-3050***	....		....	....	x---	----	----	x---	----	0	
						C **-2550?**	....		....	....	x---	----	x---	----	--x-		
						C **-2050?**	....		....	....	x---	----	x---	----	--x-		
						C **-1150?**	....		....	....	x---	----	x---	----	--x-		
						C **-0850?**	....		....	....	x---	----	xx--	----	--x-		
						C **-0650***	....		....	....	x---	----	xx--	----	--x-		
						T **-0550z**	....		....	....	x---	----	xx--	x-x-	----		
						C **-0150?**	....		....	....	x---	----	xx--	----	----		
						T **0050?**	....		....	....	x---	----	----	x---	----	0	
						C **0150?**	....		....	....	x---	----	xx--	----	--?-		
						C **0850?**	....		....	....	x---	----	xx--	----	----		
						C **1200?**	....		....	....	x---	----	x---	----	--x-		
						C **1250?**	....		....	....	x---	----	xx--	----	----		
						1786	....		....	....	x---	----	xx--	----	--x-	3	
MEDICINE LAKE (US-California)	**41.58 N**	**121.57 W**	**2412**	**Shield**	**1203-02-**	**Radiocarbon**											
SE caldera rim						C **-2405v**	....		....	....	x--x	----	x---	x---	----		7/-
Lower north flank (Black Crater)						C **-1075t**	....		....	....	-x-x	----	----	x---	----	0	6/-
SE flank (Burnt Lava flow)						C **-0780v**	....		....	....	-x-x	----	x---	x---	----		8/-

VOLCANO NAME (Subregion) / ERUPTION — Area of Activity	LAT	LONG	ELEV (m)	TYPE	NUMBER	Status / Start Year	Start M-Dy	P	Stop Year	Stop M-Dy	Central / Flank vent / Radial fiss / Regional*	Submarine / New island / Subglacial / Crater lake	Explosive / Pyro flow / Phreatic / Fumarolic	Lava flow / Lava lake / Dome / Spine	Fatal / Damage / Mudflow / Tsunami	VEI	Vol L/T
MEDICINE LAKE (US-California) *continued*																	
NW caldera floor (Medicine lava flow)						M-**0050?**	....		....	....	x---	----	----	x---	----	0	7/-
NE caldera rim (Mt. Hoffman area)						M **0720?**	....		....	....	x--x	----	x---	x---	----		8/-
North flank (Callahan lava flow)						M **0800?**	....		....	....	-x-x	----	x---	x---	----		8/-
SW flank (Paint Pot Crater)						T **0825**q	....		....	....	-x-x	----	x---	x---	----		7/-
SW flank (Little Glass Mountain)						C **0885**v	....		....	....	-x-x	----	x---	x-x-	----	3	8/7
Upper east flank (Glass Mountain)						M **1075**q	....		....	....	-x-x	----	x---	x-x-	----	3?	**9/7**
East flank (Glass Mountain ?)						? **1910**	01		....	....	-?--	----	--?-	----	----	1?	
BRUSHY BUTTE (US-California)	**41.178**	**N 121.443**	**W 1174**	**Shield**	**1203-03-**	**Holocene?**											
BIG CAVE (US-California)	**40.955**	**N 121.365**	**W 1259**	**Shield**	**1203-04-**	**Holocene?**											
TWIN BUTTES (US-California)	**40.78**	**N*121.60**	**W 1631**	**Cinder cones**	**1203-05-**	**Holocene?**											
TUMBLE BUTTES (US-California)	**40.68**	**N*121.55**	**W 2191**	**Cinder cones**	**1203-06-**	**Holocene?**											
POTATO BUTTE (US-California)	**40.63**	**N*121.43**	**W 1532**	**Shields**	**1203-07-**	**Holocene?**											
LASSEN VOLC CENTER (US-Calif)	**40.492**	**N 121.508**	**W 3187**	**Stratovolc**	**1203-08-**	**Historical**											
Chaos Crags						G **0800**y	....		....	....	-x--	----	xx--	--x-	----		
Chaos Crags						G **0880**y	....		....	....	-x--	----	xx--	--x-	----		
Chaos Crags						G **0980**y	....		....	....	-x--	----	xx--	--x-	----		
Cinder Cone						C **1635**w	....		....	....	-x--	----	x---	x---	----	3?	
Chaos Crags						? **1650?**	....		....	....	-x--	----	--?-	--?-	----		
(Cinder Cone eruptions predate 1850)						X 1850	08		X1851	....	----	----	----	----	----		
Lassen Peak						**1914**	0530		**1917**	0629	x---	----	xxx-	x-x-	-xx-	3*	
EAGLE LAKE FIELD (US-California)	**40.63**	**N*121.83**	**W 1652**	**Fissure vents**	**1203-09-**	**Holocene?**											
CLEAR LAKE (US-California)	**38.97**	**N*122.77**	**W 1439**	**Volc field**	**1203-10-**	**Holocene**											
MONO LAKE VOLC FIELD (US-Calif).	**38.00**	**N*119.03**	**W 2121**	**Cinder cones**	**1203-11-**	**Tephrochronology**											
						T **0350**v	....		....	....	----	---x	----	x---	----		
Paoha Island						H **1150**x	....		....	....	----	----	----	--x-	----		
Negit Island						T **1550**y	....		....	....	----	----	----	x---	----		
Paoha Island						T **1785**u	....		....	....	----	----	----	--x-	----		
(South Mono Lake, uncorroborated)						? **1890**	0823?		?**1890**	0823?	----	----	--?-	----	----		
MONO CRATERS (US-California)	**37.88**	**N 119.00**	**W 2796**	**Lava domes**	**1203-12-**	**Radiocarbon**											
Punchbowl						H **-6750***	....		....	....	----	----	----	--x-	----		
Crater north of Punchbowl						H **-3850***	....		....	....	----	----	----	----	----		
Central Mono Craters						H **-0700***	....		....	....	----	----	----	--x-	----		
South Coulee?						G **0010**x	....		....	....	----	----	x---	----	----		
South Coulee?						G **0315**x	....		....	....	----	----	x---	----	----		
Southern Mono Craters						C **0440**v	....		....	....	----	----	xx--	----	----		
NW Coulee and Pumice Pit dome						C **0490**v	....		....	....	----	----	xx--	x-x-	----		
South Coulee						T **0700?**	....		....	....	----	----	xx--	x-x-	----		8/-
Northern Mono Craters?						G **0810**y	....		....	....	----	----	xx--	----	----	4	-/8
Dome on NW edge of NW Coulee						H **1000**x	....		....	....	----	----	x---	--x-	----		
Panum Crater and nearby vents						G **1345**p	....		....	....	----	----	xx--	x-x-	----	4	8/8
INYO CRATERS (US-California)	**37.692**	**N 119.02**	**W 2629**	**Lava domes**	**1203-13-**	**Radiocarbon**											
North of Deadman Creek						H **-4050?**	....		....	....	----	----	----	--x-	----		7/-
Wilson Butte						C **0595**u	....		....	....	----	----	xx--	--x-	----	4?	7/7
S Deadman, Obsidian Flow, Glass Creek						C **1350**t	....		....	....	----	----	xxx-	--x-	----	4	8/8
LONG VALLEY (US-California)	**37.70**	**N 118.87**	**W 3390**	**Caldera**	**1203-14-**	**Pleistocene-Fumarolic**											
RED CONES (US-California)	**37.58**	**N 119.05**	**W 2748**	**Cinder cones**	**1203-15-**	**Holocene**											
UBEHEBE CRATERS (US-Calif)	**37.02**	**N 117.45**	**W 752**	**Maars**	**1203-16-**	**Holocene**											
GOLDEN TROUT CREEK (US-Calif).	**36.358**	**N*118.32**	**W 2886**	**Volc field**	**1203-17-**	**Tephrochronology**											
Groundhog Crater						T **-5550***	....		....	....	----	----	----	x---	----		
COSO VOLC FIELD (US-California)	**36.03**	**N*117.82**	**W 2400**	**Lava domes**	**1203-18-**	**Pleistocene-Hot Springs**											
LAVIC LAKE (US-California)	**34.75**	**N*116.625**	**W 1495**	**Volc field**	**1203-19-**	**Holocene**											
AMBOY (US-California)	**34.55**	**N 115.78**	**W 288**	**Cinder cone**	**1203-20-**	**Holocene**											
UNNAMED (US-Calif-SW of)	32.50	N 119.13	W		1203-21-	Not a Volcano											
(invalid submarine eruption report)						X 1853?	....		....	....	----	----	----	----	----		

USA - WESTERN INTERIOR

VOLCANO NAME (Subregion) / ERUPTION — Area of Activity	LAT	LONG	ELEV (m)	TYPE	NUMBER	Status / Start Year	Start M-Dy	P	Stop Year	Stop M-Dy	Central / Flank vent / Radial fiss / Regional*	Submarine / New island / Subglacial / Crater lake	Explosive / Pyro flow / Phreatic / Fumarolic	Lava flow / Lava lake / Dome / Spine	Fatal / Damage / Mudflow / Tsunami	VEI	Vol L/T
SHOSHONE LAVA FIELD (US-Idaho)	**43.07**	**N*114.43**	**W 1525**	**Cinder cones**	**1204-01-**	**Holocene?**											
CRATERS OF THE MOON (US-Idaho)	**43.42**	**N*113.50**	**W 2005**	**Cinder cones**	**1204-02-**	**Radiocarbon**											
NW of Echo Crater						C **-5890**w	....		....	....	---x	----	----	x---	----	0	9/-
Grassy Cone						C **-5465**w	....		....	....	---x	----	----	x---	----	0	9/-
Silent Cone						C **-4600**v	....		....	....	---x	----	----	x---	----	0	9/-
Sentinel Cone						T **-4250?**	....		....	....	---x	----	----	x---	----	0	8/-
Big Cinder Butte and vents to the SE						C **-4070**t	....		....	....	---x	----	----	x---	----	0	9/-
Black Top Butte						C **-2560**v	....		....	....	---x	----	----	x---	----	0	9/-
Vermillion Chasm to Minidoka-Larkspur						C **-1675**w	....		....	....	---x	----	----	x---	----	0	9/-
North Crater						M **-0350?**	....		....	....	---x	----	----	x---	----	0	8/-
Big Craters, Trench Mortar Flat						C **-0255**q	....		....	....	---x	----	----	x---	----	0	7/-
South of Big Craters, near Broken Top						C **-0126**t	....		....	....	---x	----	----	x---	----	0	9/-
WAPI LAVA FIELD (US-Idaho)	**42.88**	**N*113.22**	**W 1604**	**Shield**	**1204-03-**	**Radiocarbon**											
Kings Bowl Rift, Wapi Lava Field						T **-0300?**	....		....	....	---x	----	--x-	x---	----	2?	9/-
HELL'S HALF ACRE (US-Idaho)	**43.50**	**N*112.45**	**W 1631**	**Shield**	**1204-04-**	**Radiocarbon**											
						C **-2150**x	....		....	....	---x	----	----	x---	----	0	
YELLOWSTONE (US-Wyoming)	**44.43**	**N 110.67**	**W 2805**	**Calderas**	**1205-01-**	**Tephrochronolgy**											
Mary Bay (Yellowstone Lake)						T **-7410***	....		....	....	x---	----	--x-	----	----		
STEAMBOAT SPRINGS (US-Nevada)	**39.375**	**N 119.72**	**W 1415**	**Lava domes**	**1206-01-**	**Pleistocene-Fumarolic**											
LUNAR CRATER FIELD (US-Nevada)	**38.48**	**N*115.97**	**W 2255**	**Cinder cones**	**1206-02-**	**Holocene?**											
CRATER FLAT (US-Nevada)	**36.77**	**N*116.55**	**W 1128**	**Volc field**	**1206-03-**	**Holocene?**											
SANTA CLARA (US-Utah)	**37.257**	**N*113.625**	**W 1465**	**Volc field**	**1207-01-**	**Holocene**											
KOLOB (US-Utah)	**37.33**	**N*113.12**	**W 2727**	**Volc field**	**1207-02-**	**Holocene?**											
BALD KNOLL (US-Utah)	**37.328**	**N 112.408**	**W 2135**	**Cinder cones**	**1207-03-**	**Holocene?**											
MARKAGUNT PLATEAU (US-Utah)	**37.58**	**N*112.67**	**W 2840**	**Volc field**	**1207-04-**	**Dendrochronology**											
						D **1050**<	....		....	....	----	----	----	x---	----		
BLACK ROCK DESERT (US-Utah)	**38.97**	**N*112.50**	**W 1800**	**Volc field**	**1207-05-**	**Radiocarbon**											
Ice Springs Craters						C **1290**w	....		....	....	x---	----	x---	x---	----		
DOTSERO (US-Colorado)	**39.65**	**N 107.03**	**W 2250**	**Expl crater**	**1208-01-**	**Radiocarbon**											
						C **-2200**y	....		....	....	x---	----	x---	x---	--x-	2?	
UINKARET FIELD (US-Arizona)	**36.38**	**N*113.13**	**W 1555**	**Volc field**	**1209-01-**	**Holocene**											
SUNSET CRATER (US-Arizona)	**35.37**	**N*111.50**	**W 2447**	**Cinder cone**	**1209-02-**	**Dendrochronology**											
Sunset Crater, vent 512						D **1065**	0214v		....	....	x--x	----	x---	x---	-x--		

VOLCANO NAME (Subregion) / ERUPTION — Area of Activity	LAT	LONG	ELEV (m)	TYPE	NUMBER	Status / Start Year	Start M-Dy	P	Stop Year	Stop M-Dy	Central, Flank vent, Radial fiss, Regional*	Submarine, New island, Subglacial, Crater lake	Explosive, Pyro flow, Phreatic, Fumarolic	Lava flow, Lava lake, Dome, Spine	Fatal, Damage, Mudflow, Tsunami	VEI	Vol L/T
SUNSET CRATER (US-Arizona) *continued*																	
SE fissure (Gyp Crater, vent 512)						M **1100?**	....		....	....	---x	----	x---	----	----		
West flank of and SE of Sunset Crater.....						M **1180?**	....		....	....	---x	----	x---	x---	----		
Sunset Crater, W and E flanks...........						M **1220?**	....		....	....	x--x	----	x---	x---	----		
CARRIZOZO (US-New Mexico)......	**33.78**	**N 105.93**	**W 1731**	**Cinder cone**	**1210-01-**	**Holocene**											
ZUNI-BANDERA (US-New Mexico)...	**34.80**	**N∗108.00**	**W 2550**	**Volc field**	**1210-02-**	**Anthropology**											
Bandera Crater.......................						G **-9150y**	....		....	....	----	----	x---	x---	----		
McCartys flow.........................						G **-1115y**	....		....	....	----	----	x---	x---	----	0	9/-
VALLES CALDERA (US-New Mexico)	**35.87**	**N 106.57**	**W 3430**	**Caldera**	**1210-03-**	**Pleistocene-Fumarolic**											
RATON-CLAYTON (US-New Mexico).	**36.42**	**N∗104.08**	**W 3350**	**Volc field**	**1210-04-**	**Tephrochronology**											
Capulin Mountain.....................						T **-5300∗**	....		....	....	x---	----	x---	x---	----		

Hawaii & Pacific Ocean (13)

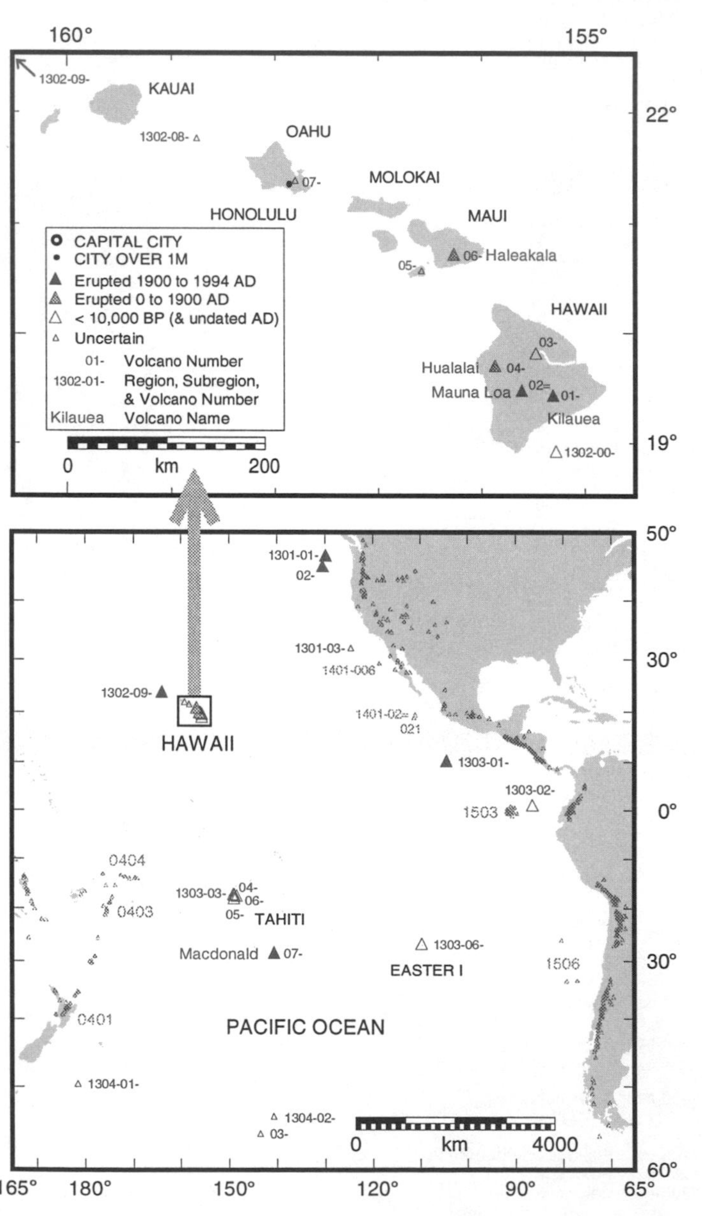

Dominated by the fluid lavas of Hawaii, this region leads the world in eruptions producing lava flows, lava lakes, and radial fissure eruptions (in percentages of both its own total eruptions and those of each characteristic). The region is unusually homogeneous in its products, with virtually all eruptions consisting of basalt, from hotspot (Hawaii, Tahiti, Macdonald, Easter), ocean ridge crest, or fracture zone settings.

Only regions 02, 03, and 19 have produced fewer large explosive eruptions (VEI ≥4). This region has the highest proportion of both shields (33) and submarine volcanoes (58), and these would be higher if island groups like the Galapagos and Revillagigedos had been placed here rather than with their nearest mainland neighbors in the *CAVW*. Because of the careful work on Hawaiian eruptive pre-histories, this region has the second highest number of eruptions dated by radiocarbon: 113, or 43% of its total eruption dates.

Region 13 covered only "Hawaii" upon publication of the 1955 *CAVW* (third in the 22-volume series and – at 9 pages per volcano – the most detailed). By the time of our 1981 book, it was clear that there was Holocene activity elsewhere in the Pacific and, in keeping with the original *CAVW* designations for both Atlantic and Indian oceans, we expanded this region to cover the full ocean basin not already covered by other catalogs (e.g. Galapagos, Chilean, and Mexican islands). The result is the largest region in the book, but the smallest total land area.

Easter Island was first discovered in 1722, and Tahiti in 1767, 11 years before Captain Cook first sighted Hawaii, the most visibly volcanic part of the region. American missionaries arrived in Honolulu in 1820, and the Wilkes Expedition, with 27-yr-old J.D. Dana, arrived in Hawaii in 1840. In 1874, US troops landed in the islands, and in 1893 the Kingdom of Hawaii was overthrown by US Marines. Hawaii was annexed in 1898, ceded itself to the US as the Republic of Hawaii two years later, and became the 50th US state in 1959. In 1911, American volcanologists Perret & Shepherd started the first continuous monitoring of Kilauea, and the Hawaiian Volcano Observatory (HVO) was founded in the next year under the direction of the redoubtable Thomas Jaggar. In 1925 the Observatory came under the administration of the US Geological Survey, and the same year marked the first issue of *Volcano Letter*, an irregular periodical that carried news and volcano commentary from around the world until publication ceased in 1955. HVO has pioneered many approaches to monitoring of active volcanoes, and been instrumental in advancing understanding of ocean island volcanism.

VOLCANO NAME (Subregion) / ERUPTION — Area of Activity	LAT	LONG	ELEV (m)	TYPE	NUMBER	Status / Start Year	Start M-Dy	P	Stop Year	Stop M-Dy	ERUPTIVE CHARACTERISTICS: Central, Flank vent, Radial fiss, Regional*	Submarine, New island, Subglacial, Crater lake	Explosive, Pyro flow, Phreatic, Fumarolic	Lava flow, Lava lake, Dome, Spine	Fatal, Damage, Mudflow, Tsunami	VEI	Vol L/T
PACIFIC - NE																	
UNNAMED (Pacific-NE)............	**46.52**	**N 129.58**	**W-2400**	**Submarine**	**1301-01-**	**Historical**											
Coaxial segment, Juan de Fuca Ridge						**1993**	0626		**1993**	0704?	---x	x---	----	x---	----	0	
UNNAMED (Pacific-NE)............	**45.03**	**N 130.20**	**W-2300**	**Submarine**	**1301-02-**	**Historical**											
Southern Juan de Fuca Ridge						**1986**	08 ?		....	....	---x	x---	----	x---	----	0	7/-
UNNAMED (Pacific-NE)............	**31.75**	**N 124.25**	**W-2533**	**Submarine ?**	**1301-03-**	**Uncertain**											
400 km SW of Pt. Conception, Calif.						? **1972**	1007		....	....	----	?---	----	----	----	0	

VOLCANO NAME (Subregion) … LAT LONG ELEV (m) TYPE NUMBER / ERUPTION — Area of Activity	Status / Start Year	Start M-Dy	P	Stop Year	Stop M-Dy	Central, Flank vent, Radial fiss, Regional*	Submarine, New island, Subglacial, Crater lake	Explosive, Pyro flow, Phreatic, Fumarolic	Lava flow, Lava lake, Dome, Spine	Fatal, Damage, Mudflow, Tsunami	VEI	Vol L/T
HAWAII												
LOIHI SEAMOUNT (Hawaiian Is)..... 18.92 N 155.27 W -980 Submarine 1302-00-	**Seismicity**											
	? **1971**	0917		?**1972**	09	----	?---	----	----	----	0	
	? **1975**	0824?		?**1975**	11	----	?---	----	----	----	0	
	? **1984**	1111		?**1985**	0121	----	?---	----	----	----	0	
	? **1986**	0920		?**1986**	0920	----	?---	----	----	----	0	
KILAUEA (Hawaii)................ 19.425 N 155.292 W 1222 Shield 1302-01-	**Historical**											
SW rift zone	C **-4650?**	....		....	....	--x-	----	----	x---	----	0	
SW rift zone	C **-2850?**	....		....	....	--x-	----	----	x---	----	0	
	T **-2200z**	....		....	....	----	----	x---	----	----		
SW rift zone	C **-1650?**	....		....	....	--x-	----	----	x---	----	0	
SW rift zone	C **-1550?**	....		....	....	--x-	----	----	x---	----	0	
	M **-0850?**	....		....	....	x---	----	----	x---	----		
East rift zone	C **-0410v**	....		....	....	--x-	----	----	x---	----	0	
Summit, East and SW rift zones	C **-0200t**	....		....	....	x-x-	----	----	x---	----	0	
Kilauea summit (Powers Caldera)	C **-0150?**	....		....	....	x---	----	xxx-	----	----	4	-/8
Kilauea summit (Powers Caldera)	M **0150y**	....		....	....	x---	----	----	x---	----	0	
Lower east rift zone	M **0450<**	....		....	....	--x-	----	----	x---	----	0	
East (near Kaipu) and SW rift zones	C **0680u**	....		....	....	--x-	----	x---	x---	----	1?	
Summit ? (Kipuka Nene flows)	M **0850?**	....		....	....	x---	----	----	x---	----	0	
Lower east rift zone (NE of lilewa)	C **1050u**	....		....	....	--x-	----	x---	x---	----	1?	
Kilauea summit (Powers Caldera)	M **1325w**	....		....	....	x---	----	----	x---	----	0	
Lower east rift zone (near Puu Kaliu)	C **1460t**	....		....	....	--x-	----	----	x---	----	0	
Lower east rift zone (near Kehena)	C **1510t**	....		....	....	--x-	----	----	x---	----	0	
Lower east rift zone (Puu Honuaula)	C **1610t**	....		....	....	--x-	----	x---	x---	----	1?	
Kilauea summit (Ai-laau vent)	C **1615?**	....		....	....	x---	----	----	x---	----	0	
Kilauea summit (Observatory vent)	T **1650t**	....		....	....	x---	----	----	x---	----	0	
Upper east rift zone (Kokoolau)	M **1700q**	....		....	....	--x-	----	----	x---	----	0	
East rift zone (Heiheiahulu, 520 m)	**1750?**	....		....	....	--x-	----	----	x---	----	0	7/-
Lower east rift zone (230-375 m)	**1790?**	....		....	....	--x-	----	----	x---	----	0	7/-
Kilauea Caldera	**1790**	11 ?		....	....	x---	----	xxx-	----	x---	4	-/8
Kilauea Caldera	**1820?**	....		....	....	x---	----	x---	x---	----	2	
SW rift zone (Great Crack, 75-580 m)	**1823**	02		**1823**	07	--x-	----	--x-	x---	xx--	0	7/-
Halemaumau	**1823**	08 <	+	**1894**	1206	x---	----	----	xx--	----	0*	
East rim of caldera (Byron's Ledge)	**1832**	0114		....	....	x---	----	----	x---	----	0	
East rift zone (230-950 m)	**1840**	0530		**1840**	0625	--x-	----	----	xx--	-x--	0	8/-
SW rift zone (775 m)	**1868**	0402?		....	....	--x-	----	x---	x---	----	1?	5/-
East rift zone (-20? m)	**1884**	0122		**1884**	0122	--x-	x---	----	?---	----	0	
Halemaumau	**1896**	0103		**1896**	0128	x---	----	----	-x--	----	0	
Halemaumau	**1896**	0711		**1896**	0925e	x---	----	----	-x--	----	0	
Halemaumau	**1897**	0624		**1897**	0627	x---	----	----	?---	----	0	
Halemaumau	**1902**	0214<		**1902**	02	x---	----	----	x---	----	0	
Halemaumau	**1902**	0603	+	**1903**	0305e	x---	----	----	-x--	----	0	
Halemaumau	**1903**	1125		**1904**	0110	x---	----	----	-x--	----	0	
Halemaumau	**1905**	0222	+	**1906**	04	x---	----	----	-x--	----	0	
Halemaumau	**1906**	1202	+	**1924**	02	x---	----	----	-x--	----	0	
Kilauea Caldera	**1918**	0223		**1918**	0309	x---	----	----	x---	----	0	5/-
Kilauea Caldera	**1919**	0207		**1919**	1128	x---	----	----	x---	----	0	7/-
SW rift zone (Mauna Iki, 915 m)	**1919**	1221		**1920**	0730	--x-	----	----	x---	----	0	7/-
Kilauea Caldera	**1921**	0318		**1921**	0325	x---	----	----	x---	----	0	6/-
East rift zone, Makaopuhi, Napau	**1922**	0528		**1922**	0530	-xx-	----	----	x---	----	0	6/-
East rift zone (915 m)	**1923**	0825		**1923**	0825	--x-	----	----	x---	----	0	5/-
Kilauea Caldera	**1924**	0510		**1924**	0527	x---	?---	x-x-	----	x---	2	-/5
Halemaumau	**1924**	0719		**1924**	0729	x---	----	----	x---	----	0	5/-
Halemaumau	**1927**	0707		**1927**	0720	x---	----	----	xx--	----	0	6/-
(1927 lava squeezed out by rockfall)	X 1928	0111		X1928	0111	x---	----	----	----	----		
Halemaumau	**1929**	0220		**1929**	0221	x---	----	----	xx--	----	0	6/-
Halemaumau	**1929**	0725		**1929**	0728	x---	----	----	xx--	----	0	6/-
Halemaumau	**1930**	1119		**1930**	1207	x---	----	----	xx--	----	0	6/-
Halemaumau	**1931**	1223		**1932**	0105	x---	----	----	xx--	----	0	6/-
Halemaumau	**1934**	0906		**1934**	1008	x---	----	----	xx--	----	0	6/-
Halemaumau	**1952**	0627		**1952**	1110	x---	----	x---	xx--	----	0	7/-
Halemaumau	**1954**	0531		**1954**	0603	x---	----	x---	xx--	----	0	6/-
Lower east rift zone (50-400 m)	**1955**	0228	+	**1955**	0526	--x-	----	x-x-	x---	-x--	0	7/-
Kilauea Iki	**1959**	1114		**1959**	1219	x---	----	x---	xx--	----	2	7/6
East rift zone (near Kapoho, 30 m)	**1960**	0113		**1960**	0219	x-x-	----	x-x-	x---	-x--	2	8/-
Halemaumau	**1961**	0224		**1961**	0224	x---	----	----	x---	----	1	5/-
Halemaumau	**1961**	0303		**1961**	0325	x---	----	----	x---	----	1	5/-
Halemaumau	**1961**	0710		**1961**	0717	x---	----	----	x---	----	1	7/-
East rift zone (395-790 m)	**1961**	0922		**1961**	0924	--x-	----	----	x---	----	1	6/-
East rift zone (945-990 m)	**1962**	1207		**1962**	1209	-xx-	----	----	xx--	----	0	5/-
East rift zone (825-960 m)	**1963**	0821		**1963**	0823	-xx-	----	----	xx--	----	0	4/-
East rift zone (700-840 m)	**1963**	1005		**1963**	1006	--x-	----	----	xx--	----	0	6/-
East rift zone (700-915 m)	**1965**	0305		**1965**	0315	-xx-	----	----	xx--	----	0	7/-
East rift zone (915-960 m)	**1965**	1224		**1965**	1225	--x-	----	----	x---	----	0	5/-
Halemaumau	**1967**	1105		**1968**	0713	x---	----	----	x---	----	0	7/-
East rift zone (580-885 m)	**1968**	0822		**1968**	0826	--x-	----	----	xx--	----	0	4/-
East rift zone (730-915 m)	**1968**	1007		**1968**	1022	--x-	----	----	x---	----	0	6/-
East rift zone (885-945 m)	**1969**	0222		**1969**	0228	--x-	----	----	x---	----	0	7/-
East rift zone (Mauna Ulu, 960 m)	**1969**	0524	+	**1974**	0722	-xx-	----	x---	xx--	----	0	8/-
Kilauea Caldera	**1971**	0814		**1971**	0814	x---	----	----	x---	----	0	7/-
Halemaumau and upper SW rift zone	**1971**	0924		**1971**	0929	x-x-	----	----	x---	-x--	0	6/-
East rift zone, Pauahi, Hiiaka	**1973**	0505	+	**1973**	0505	--x-	----	----	x---	----	0	6/-
East rift zone, Pauahi	**1973**	1110		**1973**	1209	-xx-	----	----	xx--	----	0	6/-
Kilauea Caldera, Keanakakoi	**1974**	0719		**1974**	0722	xxx-	----	----	x---	----	0	7/-
Kilauea Caldera	**1974**	0919		**1974**	0919	x---	----	----	x---	----	0	7/-
SW rift zone (1095 m)	**1974**	1231		**1974**	1231	--x-	----	----	x---	----	0	7/-
Kilauea Caldera, Halemaumau	**1975**	1129		**1975**	1129	x-BX-	----	----	x---	----	0	5/-
East rift zone (near Kalalua Crater)	**1977**	0913	+	**1977**	1001	--x-	----	----	x---	----	0	7/-
East rift zone (Pauahi Crater)	**1979**	1116		**1979**	1117	--x-	----	----	x---	----	0	5/-
East rift zone (near Mauna Ulu)	**1980**	0311		**1980**	0311	--x-	----	----	x---	----	0	0/-
Kilauea Caldera (NE of Halemaumau)	**1982**	0430		**1982**	0501	x-BX-	----	----	x---	----	0	5/-
Kilauea Caldera (SSE of Halemaumau)	**1982**	0925		**1982**	0926	x---	----	----	x---	----	0	6/-
East rift zone (Puu O'o, Kupaianaha)	**1983**	0103	+	**1993**>	....	--x-	----	x---	xx--	xx--	1*	8/-
MAUNA LOA (Hawaii)............. 19.475 N 155.608 W 4170 Shield 1302-02=	**Historical**											
NE rift zone	C **-8050?**	....		....	....	--x-	----	----	x---	----	0	

13

VOLCANO NAME (Subregion) ...... LAT LONG ELEV (m) TYPE NUMBER / ERUPTION —	Area of Activity	Status	Start Year	Start M-Dy	P	Stop Year	Stop M-Dy	Central / Flank vent / Radial fiss / Regional*	Submarine / New island / Subglacial / Crater lake	Explosive / Pyro flow / Phreatic / Fumarolic	Lava flow / Lava lake / Dome / Spine	Fatal / Damage / Mudflow / Tsunami	VEI	Vol L/T
MAUNA LOA (Hawaii) *continued*.....	NE rift zone	C	**-7850?**	....		....	....	--x-	----	----	x---	----	0	
	NE rift zone	C	**-7550?**	....		....	....	--x-	----	----	x---	----	0	
	SW rift zone	C	**-7350?**	....		....	....	--x-	----	----	x---	----	0	
	NE and SW rift zones	C	**-7150?**	....		....	....	--x-	----	----	x---	----	0	
	NE rift zone	C	**-6650?**	....		....	....	--x-	----	----	x---	----	0	
	Mokuaweoweo	C	**-6550?**	....		....	....	x---	----	----	x---	----	0	
	NE rift zone	C	**-6250?**	....		....	....	--x-	----	----	x---	----	0	
	NE and SW rift zones	C	**-5850?**	....		....	....	--x-	----	----	x---	----	0	
	SW rift zone	C	**-5650?**	....		....	....	--x-	----	----	x---	----	0	
	SW rift zone	C	**-5350?**	....		....	....	--x-	----	----	x---	----	0	
	SW rift zone	C	**-4250?**	....		....	....	--x-	----	----	x---	----	0	
	NE rift zone	C	**-3750?**	....		....	....	--x-	----	----	x---	----	0	
	NE rift zone	C	**-3350?**	....		....	....	--x-	----	----	x---	----	0	
	SW rift zone	C	**-3250?**	....		....	....	--x-	----	----	x---	----	0	
	NE and SW rift zones	C	**-2750?**	....		....	....	--x-	----	----	x---	----	0	
	Mokuaweoweo	C	**-2350?**	....		....	....	x---	----	----	x---	----	0	
	NE rift zone	C	**-2250?**	....		....	....	--x-	----	----	x---	----	0	
	NE rift zone	C	**-2150?**	....		....	....	--x-	----	----	x---	----	0	
	Mokuaweoweo	C	**-2050?**	....		....	....	x---	----	----	x---	----	0	
	SW rift zone	C	**-2000?**	....		....	....	--x-	----	----	x---	----	0	
	SW rift zone	C	**-1900?**	....		....	....	--x-	----	----	x---	----	0	
	NW and SW rift zones	C	**-1800?**	....		....	....	--x-	----	----	x---	----	0	
	NE rift zone	C	**-1750?**	....		....	....	--x-	----	----	x---	----	0	
	SW rift zone	C	**-1700?**	....		....	....	--x-	----	----	x---	----	0	
	NE and SW rift zones	C	**-1650?**	....		....	....	--x-	----	----	x---	----	0	
	Mokuaweoweo and NE rift zone	C	**-1300?**	....		....	....	x-x-	----	----	x---	----	0	
	Mokuaweoweo	C	**-0950?**	....		....	....	x---	----	----	x---	----	0	
	NE rift zone	C	**-0600?**	....		....	....	--x-	----	----	x---	----	0	
	SW rift zone	C	**-0500?**	....		....	....	--x-	----	----	x---	----	0	
	SW rift zone	C	**-0400?**	....		....	....	--x-	----	----	x---	----	0	
	NE rift zone	C	**-0300?**	....		....	....	--x-	----	----	x---	----	0	
	NE rift zone	C	**-0200?**	....		....	....	--x-	----	----	x---	----	0	
	SE rift zone	C	**-0080?**	....		....	....	--x-	----	----	x---	----	0	
	Mokuaweoweo	C	**-0060?**	....		....	....	x---	----	----	x---	----	0	
	NE and SW rift zones	C	**-0030?**	....		....	....	--x-	----	----	x---	----	0	
	NE rift zone	C	**0050?**	....		....	....	--x-	----	----	x---	----	0	
	SE rift zone	C	**0100?**	....		....	....	--x-	----	----	x---	----	0	
	SE rift zone	C	**0150?**	....		....	....	--x-	----	----	x---	----	0	
	Mokuaweoweo	C	**0200?**	....		....	....	x---	----	----	x---	----	0	
	NE rift zone	C	**0300?**	....		....	....	--x-	----	----	x---	----	0	
	Mokuaweoweo	C	**0350?**	....		....	....	x---	----	----	x---	----	0	
	NE rift zone	C	**0450?**	....		....	....	--x-	----	----	x---	----	0	
	Mokuaweoweo	C	**0480?**	....		....	....	x---	----	----	x---	----	0	
	Mokuaweoweo	C	**0550?**	....		....	....	x---	----	----	x---	----	0	
	Mokuaweoweo	C	**0600?**	....		....	....	x---	----	----	x---	----	0	
	NE rift zone	C	**0630?**	....		....	....	--x-	----	----	x---	----	0	
	Mokuaweoweo	C	**0680?**	....		....	....	x---	----	----	x---	----	0	
	Mokuaweoweo	C	**0810?**	....		....	....	x---	----	----	x---	----	0	
	Mokuaweoweo and northwest flank	C	**0830?**	....		....	....	x-x-	----	----	x---	----	0	
	NE rift zone	C	**0940?**	....		....	....	--x-	----	----	x---	----	0	
	NE rift zone	C	**1040?**	....		....	....	--x-	----	----	x---	----	0	
	NE rift zone	C	**1070?**	....		....	....	--x-	----	----	x---	----	0	
	SW rift zone	C	**1130?**	....		....	....	--x-	----	----	x---	----	0	
	NE rift zone	C	**1170?**	....		....	....	--x-	----	----	x---	----	0	
	NE rift zone and Mokuaweoweo	C	**1190?**	....		....	....	--x-	----	----	x---	----	0	
	SW rift zone	C	**1310?**	....		....	....	--x-	----	----	x---	----	0	
	NE rift zone	C	**1360?**	....		....	....	--x-	----	----	x---	----	0	
	NE rift zone and Mokuaweoweo	C	**1370?**	....		....	....	x-x-	----	----	x---	----	0	
	NE rift zone	C	**1390?**	....		....	....	--x-	----	----	x---	----	0	
	NE rift zone and NW flank	C	**1440?**	....		....	....	--x-	----	----	x---	----	0	
	NE rift zone	C	**1470?**	....		....	....	--x-	----	----	x---	----	0	
	NE rift zone	C	**1500?**	....		....	....	--x-	----	----	x---	----	0	
	NE rift zone	C	**1510?**	....		....	....	--x-	----	----	x---	----	0	
	NE rift zone	C	**1540?**	....		....	....	--x-	----	----	x---	----	0	
	NE rift zone	C	**1640?**	....		....	....	--x-	----	----	x---	----	0	
	NE rift zone	C	**1650?**	....		....	....	--x-	----	----	x---	----	0	
	NW flank	C	**1680?**	....		....	....	--x-	----	----	x---	----	0	
	NE rift zone	C	**1685?**	....		....	....	--x-	----	----	x---	----	0	
	NE rift zone	C	**1730?**	....		....	....	--x-	----	----	x---	----	0	
	North flank (2380 m) and SW rift zone		**1750?**	....		....	....	--x-	----	----	x---	----	0	
	Mokuaweoweo and adjacent vents		**1832**	0620		**1832**	0715g	x-x-	----	----	x---	----	0	7/-
	North flank, Mokuaweoweo and NE rift		**1843**	0109		**1843**	0410?	x-x-	----	----	x---	----	0	8/-
	Mokuaweoweo		**1849**	05		....	....	x---	----	----	x---	----	0	7/-
	Mokuaweoweo and SW rift zone		**1851**	0808		**1851**	0811a	x-x-	----	----	x---	----	0	7/-
	NE rift zone (2560 m) and Mokuaweoweo		**1852**	0217	+	**1852**	0311?	x-x-	----	x---	x---	----	2	8/-
	NE rift zone (3200 m) and Mokuaweoweo		**1855**	0811		**1856**	11	--x-	----	x---	x---	----	1	8/-
	North flank (2800 m) and Mokuaweoweo		**1859**	0123		**1859**	1125	--x-	----	----	x---	-x--	1	8/-
	Mokuaweoweo		**1865**	1230		**1866**	0429?	x---	----	----	x---	----	0	7/-
	SW rift zone (1000 m) and Mokuaweoweo		**1868**	0327	+	**1868**	0422	x-x-	----	x---	x---	xx-x	2*	8/-
	Mokuaweoweo	?	**1870**	0101?		?**1870**	0115?	x---	----	----	?---	----	0	
	Mokuaweoweo		**1871**	0810		**1871**	0830?	x---	----	----	x---	----	0	7/-
	Mokuaweoweo		**1872**	0809		**1872**	09	x---	----	----	x---	----	1	
	Mokuaweoweo		**1873**	0106		**1873**	0107?	x---	----	----	x---	----	0	
	Mokuaweoweo		**1873**	0420		**1874**	1019?	x---	----	----	x---	----	1	
	Mokuaweoweo		**1875**	0110		**1875**	0209?	x---	----	----	x---	----	0	
	Mokuaweoweo		**1875**	0811		**1875**	0818?	x---	----	----	x---	----	0	
	Mokuaweoweo		**1876**	0213		**1876**	0214?	x---	----	----	x---	----	0	
	Mokuaweoweo, submarine west flank		**1877**	0214	+	**1877**	0224	x-x-	x---	----	x---	----	0	6/-
	Mokuaweoweo		**1879**	0309		**1879**	0309?	x---	----	----	x---	----	0	6/-
	Mokuaweoweo		**1880**	0501		**1880**	0506	x---	----	----	x---	----	1	7/-
	NE rift zone (3170 m)		**1880**	1105		**1881**	0810	--x-	----	x---	x---	-x--	1	8/-
	SW rift zone (1740 m) and Mokuaweoweo		**1887**	0116		**1887**	0128?	x-x-	----	----	x---	-x--	0	8/-
	Mokuaweoweo		**1892**	1130		**1892**	1203	x---	----	----	x---	----	0	7/-
	Mokuaweoweo		**1896**	0421		**1896**	0506	x---	----	----	x---	----	0	7/-
	NE rift zone (3260 m) and Mokuaweoweo		**1899**	0701	+	**1899**	0723	x-x-	----	x---	x---	----	1	7/-
	Mokuaweoweo		**1903**	0901	+	**1903**	1207?	x---	----	----	x---	----	0	7/-
	SW rift zone (1890 m) and Mokuaweoweo		**1907**	0109		**1907**	0124>	x-x-	----	----	x---	-x--	0	8/-
	Mokuaweoweo		**1914**	1125		**1915**	0111	x---	----	----	x---	----	0	7/-
	SW rift zone (3000 and 2250 m)		**1916**	0519		**1916**	0530	--x-	----	----	x---	-x--	0	7/-

VOLCANO NAME (Subregion) / ERUPTION —	LAT	LONG	ELEV (m)	TYPE	NUMBER	Status / Area of Activity	Start Year	Start M-Dy	P	Stop Year	Stop M-Dy	Central, Flank vent, Radial fiss, Regional*	Submarine, New island, Subglacial, Crater lake	Explosive, Pyro flow, Phreatic, Fumarolic	Lava flow, Lava lake, Dome, Spine	Fatal, Damage, Mudflow, Tsunami	VEI	Vol L/T
MAUNA LOA (Hawaii) *continued*						SW rift zone (3450 and 2350 m)	**1919**	0926	+	**1919**	1105?	--x-	----	----	x---	-x--	0	8/-
						SW rift (2320 m)	**1926**	0410	+	**1926**	0428?	--x-	----	----	x---	-x--	0	8/-
						Mokuaweoweo	**1933**	1202		**1933**	1218	x-x-	----	----	x---	----	0	8/-
						NE rift zone (3690 m) and Mokuaweoweo	**1935**	1121		**1936**	0102	x-x-	----	----	x---	-x--	0	7/-
						Mokuaweoweo and southwest rift zone	**1940**	0407		**1940**	0818	x-x-	----	x---	x---	----	0	8/-
						NE rift zone (2800 m) and Mokuaweoweo	**1942**	0426		**1942**	0510	x-x-	----	x---	x---	----	0	8/-
						Mokuaweoweo and southwest rift	**1949**	0106		**1949**	0531	x-x-	----	x---	x---	----	0	8/-
						SW rift (2440 m)	**1950**	0601		**1950**	0623	--x-	----	x---	x---	-x--	0	8/-
						Mokuaweoweo and NE and SW rift zones,	**1975**	0705		**1975**	0706	x-x-	----	----	x---	----	0	7/-
						Mokuaweoweo, SW and NE rift zones	**1984**	0325		**1984**	0415	x-x-	----	----	x---	----	0	8/-
MAUNA KEA (Hawaii)	**19.82**	**N 155.47**	**W 4206**	**Shield**	**1302-03-**	**Radiocarbon**												
						South rift zone	G **-3400?**	....		....	....	-xx-	----	x---	x---	----		
						South rift zone (3500-3600 m?)	V **-1650y**	....		....	....	--x-	----	x---	----	----		
HUALALAI (Hawaii)	**19.692**	**N 155.87**	**W 2523**	**Shield**	**1302-04-**	**Historical**												
							C **-7540x**	....		....	....	----	----	----	x---	----	0	
						Cone 60 m north of Hainoa Crater	C **-6820x**	....		....	....	x---	----	----	x---	----	0	
						SE rift zone (1.6 km SE of Hainoa)	C **-4410v**	....		....	....	--x-	----	----	x---	----	0	
							C **-2770u**	....		....	....	----	----	----	x---	----	0	
						NW rift zone (1 km W of Hainoa Crater	C **-2440u**	....		....	....	--x-	----	----	x---	----	0	
						NW rift zone (0.3 km NW of Hainoa)	C **-2040u**	....		....	....	--x-	----	----	x---	----	0	
							C **-1650x**	....		....	....	----	----	----	x---	----	0	
						NW rift zone (0.7 km NW of Luamakami)	C **-1150u**	....		....	....	--x-	----	----	x---	----	0	
							C **-1080x**	....		....	....	----	----	----	x---	----	0	
						North rift zone (700 m ENE of Hainoa)	C **-0720u**	....		....	....	--x-	----	----	x---	----	0	
						North rift zone (3 km NE of Hainoa)	C **-0440t**	....		....	....	--x-	----	----	x---	----	0	
						NW rift zone (Luamakami)	C **-0400u**	....		....	....	--x-	----	----	x---	----	0	
						SE flank (1 km west of Waha Pehe)	C **-0350u**	....		....	....	-x--	----	----	x---	----	0	
						North rift zone (1130-1830 m)	C **-0080u**	....		....	....	--x-	----	----	x---	----	0	8/-
						SSE rift zone (4.5 km NW of Waha Pele	C **0770x**	....		....	....	--x-	----	----	x---	----	1	8/-
						NW rift zone (2 km NW of Luamakami)	C **0920t**	....		....	....	--x-	----	----	x---	----	0	
						SSE rift zone (3 km NE of Waha Pele)	C **1050v**	....		....	....	--x-	----	----	x---	----	1	8/-
						NW rift zone (Puu Alauawa, Nahaha)	T **1150?**	....		....	....	--x-	----	----	x---	----	0	
						SSE rift zone (Waha Pele)	C **1240w**	....		....	....	--x-	----	--x-	x---	----	2	8/-
						NW rift zone (Luamakami)	C **1650t**	....		....	....	--x-	----	--x-	x---	----	1	
						NW rift zone	**1800**	....		**1801**	....	--x-	----	----	x---	xx--	0	8/-
KAHOOLAWE (Maui-S of)	**20.57**	**N 156.57**	**W 450**	**Shield**	**1302-05-**	**Holocene?**												
HALEAKALA (Maui)	**20.708**	**N 156.25**	**W 3055**	**Shield**	**1302-06-**	**Historical**												
						East rift zone	C **-7450y**	....		....	....	--x-	----	----	x---	----		
						SW rift zone	C **-6700v**	....		....	....	--x-	----	----	x---	----		
						SW rift zone	C **-2120v**	....		....	....	--x-	----	----	x---	----		
						SW rift zone	C **-1950t**	....		....	....	--x-	----	----	x---	----		
							C **-0580t**	....		....	....	----	----	x---	----	----		
						SW rift zone	C **1030u**	....		....	....	--x-	----	----	x---	----		
						SW rift zone (Kamahina flow)	C **1060w**	....		....	....	--x-	----	----	x---	----		
						SW rift zone (Keonehunehune)	C **1300w**	....		....	....	--x-	----	----	x---	----		
						SW rift zone (Makua Flow)	C **1360v**	....		....	....	--x-	----	----	x---	----		
						East rift zone	C **1460u**	....		....	....	--x-	----	----	x---	----		
						SW rift zone (180-360 m)	**1790d**	....		....	....	--x-	----	----	x---	----	0	8/-
KOOLAU (Oahu)	**21.37**	**N 157.80**	**W 941**	**Shield**	**1302-07-**	**Holocene?**												
UNNAMED (Oahu-NW of)	**21.75**	**N 158.75**	**W-3000**	**Submarine**	**1302-08-**	**Uncertain**												
							? **1956**	0522		?**1956**	0523	----	?---	?---	----	----	0	
UNNAMED (Necker-NE of)	**23.58**	**N 163.83**	**W-4000**	**Submarine**	**1302-09-**	**Historical**												
						90 km NE of Necker Island	**1955**	0820		**1955**	0822?	----	x---	x---	----	---x	0	
PACIFIC - E & S																		
UNNAMED (Pacific-E)	**9.82**	**N 104.30**	**W-2500**	**Submarine**	**1303-01-**	**Historical**												
						East Pacific Rise (9.8 deg N)	**1991**	03 <		....	....	----	x---	----	x---	----	0	
GALAPAGOS RIFT (Pacific-E)	**0.792**	**N 86.15**	**W-2500**	**Submarine**	**1303-02-**	**Holocene**												
						Galapagos Rift (Clambake vent area)	? **1972**	0629a		....	....	----	?---	----	----	----		
TEAHITIA (Society Is-C Pac)	**17.57**	**S 148.85**	**W-1600**	**Submarine**	**1303-03-**	**Seismicity**												
							? **1982**	0316		?**1982**	0519	----	?---	----	----	----	0	
							? **1983**	0712		?**1983**	0726	----	?---	----	----	----	0	
							? **1983**	1218	+	?**1984**	0714	----	?---	----	----	----	0	
							? **1985**	0110		?**1985**	0125	----	?---	----	----	----	0	
ROCARD (Society Is-C Pac)	**17.642**	**S 148.60**	**W-2100**	**Submarine**	**1303-04-**	**Seismicity**												
							? **1966**	0309		?**1966**	0320	----	x---	----	----	----	0	
							? **1971**	0906		....	....	----	x---	----	----	----	0	
							? **1972**	0704		?**1972**	0719	----	x---	----	----	----	0	
MOUA PIHAA (Society Is-C Pac)	**18.32**	**S 148.67**	**W -180**	**Submarine**	**1303-05-**	**Seismicity**												
							? **1969**	0422		?**1969**	0429	----	x---	----	----	----	0	
							? **1970**	0621		?**1970**	0623	----	x---	----	----	----	0	
MEHETIA (Society Is-C Pac)	**17.87**	**S 148.07**	**W 435**	**Stratovolc**	**1303-06-**	**Anthropology**												
						SE of Mehetia (-1700 m?)	? **1981**	0305	+	?**1981**	12	----	?---	----	----	----	0	
MACDONALD (Austral Is-C Pac)	**28.98**	**S 140.25**	**W -50**	**Submarine**	**1303-07-**	**Hydrophonic**												
						(pumice rafts in South Pacific)	@ **1928**	....		....	....	----	x---	x---	----	----	0?	
						(pumice rafts in South Pacific)	@ **1936**	....		....	....	----	x---	x---	----	----	0?	
							S **1967**	0529		S**1967**	0529	----	x---	----	----	----	0	
							S **1977**	1210		S**1977**	1215	----	x---	----	----	----	0	
							S **1979**	0930		S**1979**	0930	----	x---	----	----	----	0	
							S **1980**	0212		S**1980**	0213	----	x---	----	----	----	0	
							S **1980**	1110	+	S**1981**	0215	----	x---	----	----	----	0	
							S **1982**	0301	+	S**1982**	0606	----	x---	----	----	----	0	
							S **1983**	0314	+	S**1983**	0521	----	x---	----	----	----	0	
							S **1983**	1027	+	S**1984**	0103	----	x---	----	----	----	0	
							S **1986**	0516	+	S**1986**	0802	----	x---	----	----	----	0	
							1987	0604	+	**1989**	0128>	----	x---	x---	----	----	0	
EASTER ISLAND (Pacific-C)	**27.12**	**S 109.45**	**W 530**	**Shields**	**1303-08-**	**Holocene**												
ANTIPODES ISLAND (Pacific-S)	**49.68**	**S 178.77**	**E 402**	**Pyrocl cones**	**1304-01-**	**Holocene?**												
UNNAMED (Pacific-S)	**53.90**	**S 140.30**	**W-1000**	**Submarine**	**1304-02-**	**Uncertain**												
						Seamount by Pacific-Antarctic Ridge?	? **1991**	0311		?**1991**	0319	----	?---	----	----	----	0	
UNNAMED (Pacific-S)	**55.97**	**S 143.17**	**W**	**Submarine**	**1304-03-**	**Uncertain**												
						Udinstev Fracture Zone	? **1990**	1029		?**1990**	1119	----	?---	----	----	----	0	

Mexico & Central America (14)

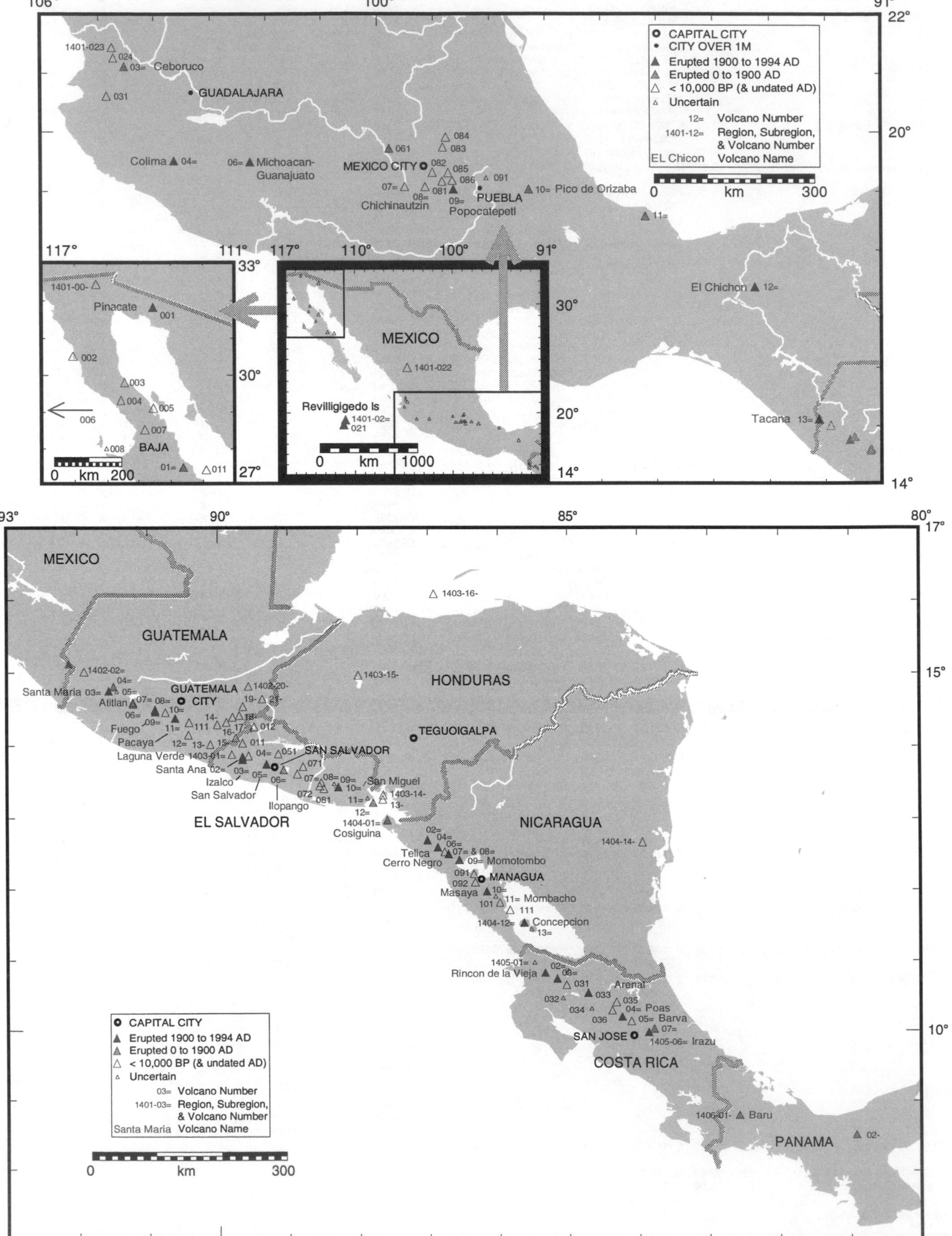

This region was designated "Central America" by *CAVW* organizers, despite the fact that Mexico is in North America. Mexico dominates the region, with 75% of the population and 80% of the land area, and the region's total population ranks it 6th among *CAVW* groups. The Holocene volcanoes of this region, combined with those of South America and the Canary Islands, total 318, meaning that Spanish is spoken around more volcanoes than any other language.

Mexico's early civilizations built the largest city in the Americas and pyramids larger than Egypt's in the second century AD. In 700 AD the Mayans were flourishing from Yucatan to the Pacific, but this civilization fell 200 years later. To the north, though, in the fertile central valley of Mexico, the Toltecs were building the most highly developed pre-Columbian civilization in Latin America. From the mid-12th century the Aztecs dominated, and the first documented new world eruption (Popocatepetl, in 1345) was recorded in the Aztec codices. A population as large as 15 million was present in 1519, when Cortez and 600 conquistadores landed, but within two years the Spaniards had killed the Aztec king and captured their principal city. The spread of the Spanish empire over the region was swift, and most early documentation of volcanism was by Catholic priests.

To the south, Columbus had made the first European landfall on the Caribbean coast of Costa Rica in 1502, and Balboa first sighted the Pacific, at Panama, in 1513. The Kingdom of Guatemala (so known since 1549) was the political heart of Spanish rule in Central America, and had its largest population. Guatemala declared independence from Spain in 1821, along with the other Central American countries. The region has not been free of political unrest, and the quality of volcano reporting has varied in space and time.

Volcanism has had important impacts on the region. As was learned with the 1982 eruption of El Chichon (and the even larger ca. 260 AD eruption of Ilopango, in El Salvador), the region produces large explosive eruptions. Only South America and Japan have had more VEI ≥4 eruptions in the last 200 years, and only Indonesia has suffered more volcanic death tolls exceeding one thousand (see FATALITIES).

Reflecting the strong archeological interest in the two regions, this region narrowly edges Region 01 for the largest number of eruptions dated archeologically (6 and 5 dates, respectively). Two of the world's best examples of the formation of "new volcanoes" took place in central Mexico, when the Jorullo and Paricutin cinder cones were added to the Michoacan-Guanajuato volcanic field in 1759 and 1943 (Fig. 24, p. 231). The explosive eruption of Guatemala's Santa Maria volcano in 1902 was one of the world's largest 20th-century eruptions.

Most active volcanoes in region 14 occur in belts produced by subduction of Pacific oceanic crust beneath the southern edge of the North American Plate and the western edge of the Caribbean Plate. Large stratovolcanoes and silicic calderas are found here, but the region also contains many basaltic volcanic fields, particularly in the central valley of Mexico and along the Guatemala-El Salvador border. A few other active volcanoes in northern Mexico are related to extensional tectonics of the Basin and Range Province, which split the Baja California peninsula from the mainland.

In the years 1975-1985, only Japan, Indonesia, and Melanesia reported more volcanism than this region, and SEAN/GVN *Bulletins* in following years have often carried more reports from this region than from any other (including a record 73 reports from a record 21 volcanoes in 1991).

Honduras was not included in the *CAVW* but, upon learning of its inland Holocene volcanism, we added two volcanoes to the end of region 14 in our 1981 book. More recently, though, Honduran volcanoes of Holocene age have been recognized along the main volcanic front of Central America. Rather than break the geographic sequence, we have renumbered the Honduran volcanoes at the end of subregion 1402, so that the newly recognized volcanoes at the front follow immediately after their Salvadorian neighbors. The two volcanoes from the interior of Honduras then follow before resuming with subregion 1403 at the Nicaraguan volcanic front.

VOLCANO NAME (Subregion) ...... / ERUPTION — Area of Activity	**LAT**	**LONG**	**ELEV (m)**	**TYPE**	**NUMBER**	**Status** / Start Year	Start M-Dy	P	Stop Year	Stop M-Dy	Central / Flank vent / Radial fiss / Regional*	Submarine / New island / Subglacial / Crater lake	Explosive / Pyro flow / Phreatic / Fumarolic	Lava flow / Lava lake / Dome / Spine	Fatal / Damage / Mudflow / Tsunami	**VEI**	Vol L/T
MEXICO - NW																	
PRIETO, CERRO (Mexico-NW)	**32.418 N**	**115.305 W**	**410**	**Cinder cone**	**1401-00-**	**Holocene**											
PINACATE PEAKS (Mexico-NW)	**31.773 N***	**113.498 W**	**1200**	**Cinder cones**	**1401-001**	**Historical**											
						1928	0609		....	....	x---	----	x---	----	----	2?	
						1934	1231		**1935**	0102?	x---	----	x---	----	----	2?	
SAN QUINTIN VOLC FIELD (Baja) ...	**30.468 N***	**115.996 W**	**267**	**Cinder cones**	**1401-002**	**Holocene**											
SAN LUIS GONZAGA, ISLA (Baja)...	**29.814 N**	**114.384 W**	**160**	**Expl craters**	**1401-003**	**Holocene**											
JARAQUAY VOLC FIELD (Baja).....	**29.33 N***	**114.50 W**	**960**	**Cinder cones**	**1401-004**	**Holocene**											
CORONADO (Mexico-Baja Calif).....	**29.08 N**	**113.513 W**	**460**	**Stratovolc**	**1401-005**	**Fumarolic**											
GUADELUPE (Baja-W of)	**29.07 N**	**118.28 W**	**1100**	**Shield**	**1401-006**	**Holocene**											
SAN BORJA VOLC FIELD (Baja)	**28.50 N***	**113.75 W**		**Cinder cones**	**1401-007**	**Holocene**											
UNNAMED (Mexico-Baja Calif)	**28.00 N**	**115.00 W**		**Submarine ?**	**1401-008**	**Uncertain**											
						? **1953**	0720		....	....	----	?---	----	----	----	0	
TRES VIRGENES (Mexico-Baja Calif) .	**27.470 N**	**112.591 W**	**1940**	**Stratovolc**	**1401-01=**	**Historical**											
						1746	0525m		....	....	x---	----	----	----	----		
						? **1857**	....		....	....	?---	----	----	----	----		
TORTUGA, ISLA (Mexico-Baja Calif) .	**27.392 N**	**111.858 W**	**310**	**Shield**	**1401-011**	**Holocene**											
MEXICAN ISLANDS																	
BARCENA (Mexico-Is).............	**19.30 N**	**110.82 W**	**332**	**Cinder cones**	**1401-02=**	**Historical**											
South end of Isla San Benedicto						**1952**	0801	+	**1953**	0224d	x-x-	----	xx--	x-x-	----	3	7/8
SOCORRO (Mexico-Is)	**18.78 N**	**110.95 W**	**1050**	**Shield**	**1401-021**	**Historical**											
						? **1848**	....		....	....	----	----	----	----	----	2?	
						? **1896**	....		....	....	----	----	----	----	----	2?	
						1905	....		....	....	----	----	--?-	----	----	2?	
West of Lomas Coloradas						**1951**	0522		**1951**	0522	-x--	----	--?-	----	----	2?	
Submarine vent 3 km W of Punta Tosca ...						**1993**	0129		**1993**	0217?	-x--	x---	----	----	----	0	
MEXICO - CENTRAL BELT & DURANGO																	
DURANGO VOLC FIELD (Mexico) ...	**24.15 N***	**104.45 W**	**2075**	**Cinder cones**	**1401-022**	**Holocene**											
SANGANGUEY (Mexico)...........	**21.45 N**	**104.73 W**	**2353**	**Stratovolc**	**1401-023**	**Holocene**											
						? **1742**	....		....	....	----	----	----	----	----		
TEPETILTIC, VOLCAN (Mexico).....	**21.27 N**	**104.70 W**	**2020**	**Stratovolc**	**1401-024**	**Holocene**											
CEBORUCO, VOLCAN (Mexico).....	**21.125 N**	**104.50 W**	**2164**	**Stratovolc**	**1401-03=**	**Historical**											
						C **0950?**	....		....	....	x---	----	xx--	----	----	5	-/9
						1542	....		....	....	?---	----	----	?---	----		
						1567	....		....	....	?---	----	----	?---	----		
West flank..........................						**1870**	0221		**1875**	....	-x--	----	x?--	x-x-	-x--	3	9/8
MASCOTA VOLC FIELD (Mexico) ...	**20.62 N***	**104.83 W**	**2540**	**Shields**	**1401-031**	**Holocene**											
COLIMA VOLC COMPLEX (Mexico)..	**19.514 N**	**103.62 W**	**4100**	**Stratovolc**	**1401-04=**	**Historical**											
						C **-7690z**	....		....	....	x---	----	x---	----	----		
						C **-7420z**	....		....	....	x---	----	xx--	----	----		
Colima Cone Group (La Erita)						T **-5050?**	....		....	....	-x--	----	x---	x---	----	3	-/7
Colima Cone Group (Comal Grande)......						T **-4550?**	....		....	....	-x--	----	x---	x---	----	3	-/7

VOLCANO NAME (Subregion) / ERUPTION —	LAT	LONG	ELEV (m)	TYPE	NUMBER	Area of Activity	Status / Start Year	Start M-Dy	P	Stop Year	Stop M-Dy	Central / Flank vent / Radial fiss / Regional*	Submarine / New island / Subglacial / Crater lake	Explosive / Pyro flow / Phreatic / Fumarolic	Lava flow / Lava lake / Dome / Spine	Fatal / Damage / Mudflow / Tsunami	VEI	Vol L/T
COLIMA VOLC COMPLEX (Mexico) *continued*						Colima Cone Group (Comal Chico)	T **-4050?**	....		....	....	-x--	----	x---	----	----	3	-/7
							C **-3030t**	....		....	....	x---	----	xx--	----	----		
						Colima Cone Group (Telcampana)	T **-2950?**	....		....	....	-x--	----	xx--	x---	----	3	-/7
							C **-2370w**	....		....	....	x---	----	xx--	----	--x-	4?	-/8
							C **-1890u**	....		....	....	x---	----	x---	----	----		
						Colima Cone Group (Apaxtepec)	T **0450?**	....		....	....	-x--	----	x---	x---	----	3?	7/6
							C **0725v**	....		....	....	x---	----	xx--	----	----		
							C **1000v**	....		....	....	x---	----	xx--	----	----		
							1560	....		....	....	----	----	?---	----	----	2	
							1576	....		....	....	x---	----	xx--	----	xx--	3	
							1585	0110		....	....	x---	----	xx--	----	----	4	
							1590	0114		....	....	x---	----	xx--	----	----	3	
							1606	1125	+	**1606**	1213>	x---	----	xx--	----	-x--	4	
							1611	0415	+	**1613**	....	x---	----	xx--	----	----	3	
							1622	0608		**1622**	0609	x---	----	xx--	----	----	4	
							1690	....		....	....	x---	----	xx--	----	----	3	
							1743	1022		....	....	x---	----	?---	----	----	2	
							1749	....		....	....	x---	----	?---	----	----	2	
							1770	....		....	....	x---	----	xx--	----	----	2	
							1771	....		....	....	x---	----	xx--	----	----	3	
							1795	....		....	....	x---	----	x---	x---	----	2	
							1804	....		....	....	----	----	?---	----	----	2	
							1806	0325>	+	**1809**	....	x---	----	xx--	----	----	2?	
							1818	0215		**1818**	0531	x---	----	xx--	x---	xx--	4	
							1819	....		....	....	x---	----	x---	----	----	1	
							1866	0304		**1868**	....	x---	----	----	--x-	----	0	
						El Volcancito	**1869**	0612		....	....	xx--	----	x-x-	x---	----	3	8/-
						El Volcancito	**1870**	....		**1871**	....	-x--	----	----	x---	----	0	
						El Volcancito and main crater	**1872**	0226	+	**1873**	0314	xx--	----	xx--	x---	-x--	3	
						El Volcancito	**1874**	0612		....	....	-x--	----	x---	x---	----	1	
						El Volcancito	**1875**	....		**1878**	....	-x--	----	x---	x---	----	1	
							1879	1223	+	**1880**	0430	x---	----	xx--	x---	----	1	
							1881	0323?		**1881**	0412	x---	----	xx--	x---	----	2	
							1882	....		**1884**	....	x---	----	x---	----	----	1	
							1885	1226	+	**1886**	10	x---	----	xx--	x---	-x--	3*	
							1889	0809	+	**1890**	0216	x---	----	xx--	x---	----	4*	
							1890	1118		....	....	x---	----	xx--	----	----	3	
							1891	07	+	**1892**	06	x---	----	xx--	----	----	2	
							1893	1204	+	**1902**	....	x---	----	xx--	x---	----	2*	
							1903	0215	+	**1903**	0314	x---	----	xx--	x---	----	3	
							1904	....		**1906**	....	x---	----	??--	?-?-	----	1?	
							1908	1218	+	**1909**	0305	x---	----	xx--	x---	----	3	
							1913	0120	+	**1931**	....	x---	----	xx--	--x-	-x--	4?	-/8
							? **1941**	0415		?**1941**	04	x---	----	xx--	----	-x--	3?	
							1957	0514		**1959**	....	x---	----	--x-	--x-	----	1	
							1960	....		**1962**	....	x---	----	x---	x-x-	----	1	7/-
							1963	....		**1964**	....	x---	----	-x--	--x-	----	1	
							1965	11	+	**1970**	....	x---	----	xx--	--x-	----	1	
							? **1973**	0130		....	....	x---	----	x---	--x-	----	1	
							1975	11		**1976**	0620	x---	----	-x--	x-x-	----	2	8/-
							1977	12		**1982**	06	x---	----	xx--	x-x-	----	1	5/-
							? **1983**	0211		?**1983**	0215	x---	----	x---	x-x-	----	1?	
							1985	....		**1986**	0105d	x---	----	x---	----	----	1	
						East side of lava dome	**1987**	0702		**1987**	0702	x---	----	-xx-	----	----	1	
							1988	11 <		**1990**	....	x---	----	x---	--x-	----	1	
							1991	0301		**1991**	10	x---	----	xx--	x-x-	-xx-	2	
MICHOACAN-GUANAJUATO (")	**19.48**	**N*102.25**	**W 3170**	**Cinder cones**	**1401-06=**		**Historical**											
						Hoyo El Huanillo	C **-7345y**	....		....	....	x---	----	x---	----	----	3	-/7
						Cerro La Taza	C **-6480y**	....		....	....	x---	----	x---	x---	----	3	-/7
						Cerro El Metate	C **-2750x**	....		....	....	x---	----	x---	x---	----	3	-/7
						Valle de Santiago (La Alberca)	A **-2050?**	....		....	....	x---	----	xxx-	----	----		
						Cerro El Jabali	C **-1880w**	....		....	....	x---	----	x---	x---	----	3	
						Valle de Santiago	A **1050t**	....		....	....	x---	----	x---	----	----		
						Jorullo	**1759**	0929		**1774**	....	xx-x	----	xxx-	x---	-xx-	4*	8/9
						Paricutin	**1943**	0220	+	**1952**	0225	xx-x	----	x---	x---	-x--	4	8/9
JOCOTITLAN (Mexico)	**19.724 N**	**99.757**	**W 3950**	**Stratovolc**	**1401-061**		**Radiocarbon**											
							C **-7740u**	....		....	....	x---	----	xx--	----	----		
							C **1270u**	....		....	....	x---	----	xx--	----	----		
HOLOTEPEC (Mexico)	**19.08**	**N* 99.48**	**W 3000**	**Volc field**	**1401-07-**		**Radiocarbon**											
						Cerro Tetepetl	C **-6560w**	....		....	....	x---	----	----	x---	----		
						Tres Cruces	C **-6490>**	....		....	....	x---	----	x---	----	----	4	-/8
CHICHINAUTZIN (Mexico)	**19.08**	**N* 99.13**	**W 3930**	**Volc field**	**1401-08=**		**Radiocarbon**											
						Pelado	C **-2120<**	....		....	....	----	----	----	x---	----		
						Xitle	C **-0085x**	....		....	....	----	----	x---	x---	-x--	2?	9/-
TENAYO GROUP (Mexico)	**19.17**	**N* 98.82**	**W 3080**	**Cinder cones**	**1401-081**		**Holocene**											
SANTA CATARINA RANGE (Mexico)	**19.32**	**N* 99.00**	**W 2734**	**Volc field**	**1401-082**		**Anthropology**											
GORDO, CERRO (Mexico)	**19.75 N**	**98.808**	**W 3046**	**Cinder cone**	**1401-083**		**Holocene**											
PITOS, SIERRA DE LAS (Mexico)	**19.923 N**	**98.747**	**W 3000**	**Unknown**	**1401-084**		**Holocene**											
PAPAYO (Mexico)	**19.308 N**	**98.70**	**W 3600**	**Lava dome**	**1401-085**		**Holocene**											
IZTACCIHUATL (Mexico)	**19.179 N**	**98.642**	**W 5230**	**Stratovolc**	**1401-086**		**Holocene**											
POPOCATEPETL (Mexico)	**19.023 N**	**98.622**	**W 5465**	**Stratovolcs**	**1401-09=**		**Historical**											
						Volcan El Fraile	C **-7690z**	....		....	....	----	----	xx--	----	----	**P**	
						Volcan El Fraile	T **-6250z**	....		....	....	x---	----	x---	----	----		
						Volcan El Fraile	C **-3030t**	....		....	....	x---	----	xx--	----	----		
						Volcan El Fraile	C **-2370u**	....		....	....	x---	----	xx--	----	----		
						Volcan El Fraile	C **-1890u**	....		....	....	x---	----	x---	----	----		
							C **0725v**	....		....	....	x---	----	xx--	----	----		
							C **0985t**	....		....	....	x---	----	x---	----	----		
							T **1000t**	....		....	....	x---	----	xx--	----	----		
							1345	....		**1347**	....	x---	----	?---	----	----	2?	
							1354	....		....	....	x---	----	?---	----	----	2?	
							1363	....		....	....	x---	----	?---	----	----	2?	
							1488	....		....	....	x---	----	?---	----	----	2?	
							1504	....		....	....	x---	----	?---	----	----	2?	
							? **1509**	....		....	....	----	----	----	----	----		
							? **1512**	....		....	....	----	----	----	----	----	2?	
							1518	....		....	....	x---	----	?---	----	----	2?	

VOLCANO NAME (Subregion)	LAT	LONG	ELEV (m)	TYPE	NUMBER	Status / ERUPTION — Area of Activity	Start Year	Start M-Dy	P	Stop Year	Stop M-Dy	Central, Flank vent, Radial fiss, Regional*	Submarine, New island, Subglacial, Crater lake	Explosive, Pyro flow, Phreatic, Fumarolic	Lava flow, Lava lake, Dome, Spine	Fatal, Damage, Mudflow, Tsunami	VEI	Vol L/T
POPOCATEPETL (Mexico) *continued*							1519	09		1523?	....	x---	----	x---	----	----	3?	
							1528	....		....	....	x---	----	?---	----	----	2?	
							1530	....		....	....	x---	----	x---	----	----	2	
							1539	....		1540	....	x---	----	x---	----	----	2	
							1542	....		....	....	x---	----	?---	----	----	2	
							1548	....		....	....	x---	----	?---	----	----	2	
							1571	....		....	....	x---	----	?---	----	----	2	
							1580	....		....	....	x---	----	?---	----	----	2?	
							1590	....		....	....	x---	----	?---	----	----	2?	
							1592	....		1594	....	x---	----	?---	----	----	2	
							1642	....		....	....	x---	----	?---	----	----	2	
							1663	....		1667	....	x---	----	x---	----	----	2	
							1697	....		....	....	x---	----	?---	----	----	2	
							1720	....		....	....	x---	----	?---	----	----	3	
							1802	....		1804	....	x---	----	?---	----	----	1	
							1827	....		1834	....	x---	----	?---	----	----	1?	
							1852	....		....	....	x---	----	?---	----	----	1?	
							1920	06 ?		1922	....	x---	----	x-x-	--x-	----	1	
							1923	1127		1924	0307	x---	----	x---	----	----	1	
							1933	0123		....	....	x---	----	x---	----	----	1	
							1942	....		1943	....	x---	----	x-x-	----	----	1	
							1947	01		1947	02	x---	----	x-x-	----	----	1	
MALINCHE, LA (Mexico)	19.23 N	98.03 W	4420	Stratovolc	1401-091	Holocene?												
ORIZABA, PICO DE (Mexico)	19.030 N	97.268 W	5610	Stratovolc	1401-10=	Historical												
							C -7450w	....		....	....	x---	----	xx--	x---	----	3	-/7
							C -6760u	....		....	....	x---	----	xx--	--x-	----	4	-/8
							C -6670w	....		....	....	x---	----	xx--	--x-	----	3	-/7
							C -6520w	....		....	....	x---	----	xx--	----	----		
							C -6350u	....		....	....	x---	----	xx--	--x-	----	3	-/7
							C -6220u	....		....	....	x---	----	xx--	--x-	----	3	-/7
							T -6050?	....		....	....	x---	----	x---	----	----	P	
							C -5070v	....		....	....	x---	----	xx--	----	----		
							C -4690y	....		....	....	x---	----	xx--	--x-	----	3	-/7
							C -4250v	....		....	....	x---	----	xx--	--x-	----	3	-/7
							C -2710v	....		....	....	x---	----	x---	--x-	----		
							C -2110v	....		....	....	x---	----	x---	----	----	P	
							C -1500u	....		....	....	x---	----	x---	----	----	P	
							C -1450v	....		....	....	x---	----	----	x---	----	0	8/-
							C 0090v	....		....	....	x---	----	x---	x-x-	----	3	7/7
							C 1260t	....		....	....	x---	----	x---	----	----	P	
							1537	....		....	....	x---	----	----	x---	----	0	
							1545	....		?1565	....	x---	----	x---	x---	----	2	8/-
							1566	....		....	....	x---	----	x---	x---	----	2	
							1569	....		....	....	x---	----	x---	----	----	2	
							1613	....		....	....	x---	----	----	x---	----		
							1630	....		....	....	x---	----	x---	----	----	2	
							1687	....		....	....	x---	----	x---	----	----	2	
SAN MARTIN, VOLCAN DE (Mexico)	18.572 N	95.169 W	1650	Shield	1401-11=	Historical												
						South flank	T -2575*	....		....	....	-x--	----	x---	----	----		
						South flank (Cerro Mono Blanco)	C -1320y	....		....	....	-x--	----	x---	----	-x--		
						South flank	T -0150y	....		....	....	-x--	----	x---	----	----		
						South flank (Cerro Puntiagudo)	C 0115x	....		....	....	-x--	----	x---	x---	----		
						South flank	T 0375u	....		....	....	-x--	----	x---	----	----		
						South flank	T 0500t	....		....	....	-x--	----	x---	----	----		
						SE flank	1664	0115?		....	....	-x--	----	x---	x---	----	3	
						Cinder cones within summit crater	1793	0302	+	1793	12	x---	----	x---	x---	----	4	-/8
							1794	05		1796	....	x---	----	x---	----	----	2?	
							? 1797	....		?1805	....	----	----	----	----	----	2?	
							? 1838	....		....	....	----	----	----	----	----		
							? 1932	1231y		....	....	----	----	----	----	----		

MEXICO - S

VOLCANO NAME (Subregion)	LAT	LONG	ELEV (m)	TYPE	NUMBER	Status / ERUPTION — Area of Activity	Start Year	Start M-Dy	P	Stop Year	Stop M-Dy	Central, Flank vent, Radial fiss, Regional*	Submarine, New island, Subglacial, Crater lake	Explosive, Pyro flow, Phreatic, Fumarolic	Lava flow, Lava lake, Dome, Spine	Fatal, Damage, Mudflow, Tsunami	VEI	Vol L/T
CHICHON, EL (Mexico-Chiapas)	17.360 N	93.228 W	1060	Lava domes	1401-12=	Historical												
							C 0270w	....		....	....	x---	----	xx--	----	----		
							C 0700u	....		....	....	x---	----	xx--	----	----	P	
							C 1350u	....		....	....	x---	----	xx--	--?-	----	P	
							A 1850?	....		....	....	x---	----	x---	----	----		
							1982	0328	+	1982	0911	x---	----	xxx-	----	xxx-	5*	-/9
TACANA (Mexico/Guatemala)	15.130 N	92.113 W	4110	Stratovolc	1401-13=	Historical												
						SW side	? 1855	0112		....	....	--x-	----	?-?-	----	----	1	
						SW side	1878	....		....	....	--x-	----	x-x-	----	----	1	
						SW flank	1949	1222		1950	01	-x--	----	x-xx	----	----	1	
						NE flank (3600 m)	1986	0508		1986	0508	-x--	----	--x-	----	----	1	

GUATEMALA

VOLCANO NAME (Subregion)	LAT	LONG	ELEV (m)	TYPE	NUMBER	Status / ERUPTION — Area of Activity	Start Year	Start M-Dy	P	Stop Year	Stop M-Dy	Central, Flank vent, Radial fiss, Regional*	Submarine, New island, Subglacial, Crater lake	Explosive, Pyro flow, Phreatic, Fumarolic	Lava flow, Lava lake, Dome, Spine	Fatal, Damage, Mudflow, Tsunami	VEI	Vol L/T
TAJUMULCO (Guatemala)	15.034 N	91.903 W	4220	Stratovolc	1402-02=	Holocene												
							? 1821	....		....	....	----	----	?---	----	----	2	
							? 1863	....		....	....	x---	----	?---	----	----	2	
SANTA MARIA (Guatemala)	14.756 N	91.552 W	3772	Stratovolc	1402-03=	Historical												
						SW flank	1902	1024	+	1902	1112	-x--	----	x-x-	----	xxx-	6?	-/10
						SW flank (east end of 1902 crater)	1903	....		1913	....	-x--	---x	x-x-	----	----	2	
						SW flank (Santiaguito)	1922	0622	+	1993>	....	-x--	----	xxx-	x-xx	xxx-	3*	8/8
ALMOLONGA (Guatemala)	14.82 N	91.48 W	3197	Stratovolc	1402-04=	Historical												
						Cerro Quemado	G 0800t	....		....	....	x---	----	xx--	--x-	--x-	3	7/7
						Cerro Quemado	1765	1024		1765	1025	-x--	----	x---	x---	-x--	2	
						(1785 date refers to 1765 eruption)	X 1785	....		....	....	----	----	----	----	----		
						East flank of Cerro Quemado	1818	0116		1818	0619>	-x--	----	x---	x---	-x--	2	
						(fumarolic activity only: Sapper)	X 1823	....		....	....	----	----	---x	----	----		
						(earthquake, not eruption: Sapper)	X 1891	....		....	....	----	----	----	----	----		
TZANJUYUB, VOLCAN DE (")	14.75 N	91.43 W	3542	Stratovolc	1402-05=	Pleistocene-Fumarolic												
ATITLAN (Guatemala)	14.583 N	91.186 W	3535	Stratovolc	1402-06=	Historical												
							1469	....		....	....	----	----	x---	----	----	3↑	
							1505?	....		....	....	----	----	x---	----	--?-	3?	
							1579?	....		1581	1231p	----	----	x---	----	----	2	

VOLCANO NAME (Subregion) / ERUPTION — Area of Activity	LAT	LONG	ELEV (m)	TYPE	NUMBER	Status / Start Year	Start M-Dy	P	Stop Year	Stop M-Dy	Central / Flank vent / Radial fiss / Regional*	Submarine / New island / Subglacial / Crater lake	Explosive / Pyro flow / Phreatic / Fumarolic	Lava flow / Lava lake / Dome / Spine	Fatal / Damage / Mudflow / Tsunami	VEI	Vol L/T
ATITLAN (Guatemala) *continued*						**1663**	....		....	....	----	----	x---	----	--x-	2	
(possibly eruption of Fuego volcano)						@ **1717**	0829		@**1721**	....	----	----	----	----	----		
						1826	11		....	....	----	----	x---	----	----	2	
						1827	0327		....	....	----	----	x---	----	----	2	
						1827	0901	+	**1828**	01 ?	----	----	x---	x---	-x--	3	
						1833	....		....	....	----	----	x---	----	-x--	2	
						1837	06		....	....	----	----	x---	----	----	2	
						1843	07		....	....	x---	----	x---	?---	----	2	
						? **1852**	....		....	....	----	----	?---	----	----	2?	
						1853	0503		....	....	----	----	x---	----	-?--	3	
						? **1856**	....		....	....	----	----	?---	----	----	2	
TOLIMAN (Guatemala)	**14.613 N**	**91.189 W**	**3158**	**Stratovolc**	**1402-07=**	**Holocene**											
ACATENANGO (Guatemala)	**14.501 N**	**90.876 W**	**3976**	**Stratovolc**	**1402-08=**	**Historical**											
						A **0000v**	....		....	....	----	----	x---	----	----		
						A **1450t**	....		....	....	----	----	x---	----	----		
North slope of Pico Mayor						**1924**	1218		**1925**	0607	--x-	----	x---	----	----	3*	
Pico Mayor						**1926**	08		**1927**	0519	x---	----	x-x-	----	----	2*	
Pico Mayor-Yepocapa saddle						**1972**	1112		**1972**	12	-?x-	----	x-x-	----	----	1	
FUEGO (Guatemala)	**14.473 N**	**90.880 W**	**3763**	**Stratovolc**	**1402-09=**	**Historical**											
						1524	0430p		**1524**	0715q	----	----	x---	----	----	2	
(possibly only earthquakes)						? **1526**	....		....	....	----	----	?---	----	----	2	
						1531	1231p		....	....	----	----	x---	----	----	2	
(possibly an eruption of Atitlan)						@ **1541**	....		....	....	----	----	?---	----	----		
						1542	0114		....	....	----	----	----	----	----		
						1551	....		**1552**	0331>	----	----	x---	----	----	2	
(possibly only an earthquake)						? **1557**	0115		....	....	----	----	?---	----	----		
(possibly same as 1557 event)						? **1559**	0116		....	....	----	----	?---	----	----		
(possibly only earthquakes)						? **1565**	....		....	....	----	----	?---	----	----	2	
(possibly same as 1581 eruption)						? **1571**	1225		....	....	----	----	x---	----	----		
(possibly only earthquakes)						? **1575**	....		....	....	----	----	?---	----	----	2	
(possibly only an earthquake)						? **1576**	....		....	....	----	----	?---	----	----	2	
(possibly only earthquakes)						? **1577**	....		....	....	----	----	?---	----	----	2	
						1581	1205		**1582**	0115	x---	----	x---	x---	-x--	4*	-/8
						1585	0115		**1585**	07	----	----	x---	----	----	2	
						1586	0603b		**1586**	12	x---	----	x---	x---	----	2	
						1587	0724		....	....	----	----	x---	----	----	2	
						1614	....		....	....	----	----	x---	----	----	2	
						1617	....		....	....	----	----	x---	----	-x--	3	
						1620	....		....	....	----	----	x---	----	----	2	
						1623	01		....	....	----	----	x---	----	----	2	
						1629	....		**1632**	....	----	----	x---	----	----	2	
(possibly only earthquakes)						? **1679**	....		....	....	----	----	?---	----	----		
(pumice seen off Guatemala coast)						@ **1685**	09		....	....	----	----	x---	----	----	2	
						1686	....		....	....	----	----	x---	----	----	2	
(possibly only an earthquake)						? **1689**	....		....	....	----	----	?---	----	----	2	
						1699	....		....	....	----	----	x---	----	----	2	
						1702	0804		....	....	----	----	x---	----	----	2	
						1705	0131		**1705**	0202	----	----	x---	----	--?-	2	
						1706	1004		....	....	----	----	x---	----	----	2	
(possibly same as 1710 eruption)						? **1709**	1014		....	....	----	----	----	?---	----		
						1710	1014		....	....	----	----	x---	----	----	2	
						1717	0827		**1717**	1226e	----	----	x---	----	-x--	4?	-/8
						1730	09		....	....	----	----	x---	----	----	2	
						1732	05		....	....	----	----	x---	----	----	2	
						1737	0827		**1737**	0924	-x--	----	x---	----	----	4?	-/8
(possibly only an earthquake)						? **1751**	....		....	....	----	----	?---	----	----	2	
(possibly only an earthquake)						? **1765**	....		....	....	----	----	?---	----	----	2	
(possibly only earthquakes)						? **1773**	....		....	....	----	----	?---	----	----	2	
						1799	....		....	....	----	----	x---	----	----	3	-/7
						1826	....		....	....	x---	----	x---	----	----	2	
						1829	....		....	....	----	----	x---	?---	----	2	
						? **1850**	....		....	....	----	----	?---	----	----	2	
						? **1852**	....		....	....	----	----	?---	?---	----	2	
						1855	0929		**1855**	0930	----	----	x---	----	----	2	
						1856	0109		**1856**	0307	----	----	x---	x---	----	2	
						1856	0929		**1856**	0930	----	----	x---	x---	----	2	
						1857	0115		**1857**	0217	x---	----	x---	x---	----	4?	-/8
						1857	0917		....	....	----	----	x---	x---	----	2	
						1860	0818		**1860**	0923	x---	----	x---	x---	-x--	2	
						? **1861**	1121		....	....	----	----	?---	----	----	2	
						? **1867**	....		....	....	----	----	?---	----	----	2	
						1880	0628		**1880**	0820	----	----	x---	x---	----	4?	-/8
						1896	0110		....	....	----	----	x---	----	----	2?	
						1932	0121		**1932**	0122	x---	----	xx--	----	----	4	-/8
						1944	1201p		....	....	----	----	x---	----	----	2	
						1947	....		....	....	----	----	x---	----	----	2	
						1949	11		....	....	----	----	x---	----	----	2	
						1953	0409		**1953**	0413	x---	----	x---	x-x-	----	3	
						1955	0726e		....	....	x---	----	x---	x--x	----	1	
						1957	0219		**1957**	0221>	x---	----	xx--	----	----	3	-/7
						1962	0804	+	**1962**	1109	x---	----	x---	----	--x-	3*	6/7
						1963	0928		**1963**	0930	x---	----	xx--	x---	xxx-	3	-/6
						1966	0207	+	**1966**	0501	x---	----	xx--	x---	----	3*	
						1966	0812		**1966**	0813	x---	----	x---	----	----	3	-/6
						1967	0422		**1967**	0424	x---	----	x---	----	----	2	-/6
						1971	0914		**1971**	0915	x---	----	xx--	----	xxx-	3	-/7
						1973	0223	+	**1973**	0323	x---	----	xx--	----	----	2	-/6
						1974	1010	+	**1974**	1204	x---	----	xx--	----	xx--	4*	-/8
						1975	0528	+	**1975**	1021	x---	----	xx--	----	----	2	
						1977	0303	+	**1977**	0419	x---	----	x---	----	----	1	-/4
						1977	0911		**1979**	0808	x---	----	xx--	x-x-	----	2	-/6
						1987	0105d		**1987**	02 ?	x---	----	x---	----	----	1	
AGUA (Guatemala)	**14.465 N**	**90.743 W**	**3760**	**Stratovolc**	**1402-10=**	**Holocene**											
PACAYA (Guatemala)	**14.381 N**	**90.601 W**	**2552**	**Complx volc**	**1402-11=**	**Historical**											
						T **0750***	....		....	....	x---	----	xx--	----	----		
Cerro Chino						**1565**	08 ?		....	....	-x--	----	x---	x---	-x--	3	
						1623?	....		....	....	----	----	x---	----	-x--	3	

VOLCANO NAME (Subregion) / ERUPTION — Area of Activity	LAT	LONG	ELEV (m)	TYPE	NUMBER	Status / Start Year	Start M-Dy	P	Stop Year	Stop M-Dy	Central, Flank vent, Radial fiss, Regional*	Submarine, New island, Subglacial, Crater lake	Explosive, Pyro flow, Phreatic, Fumarolic	Lava flow, Lava lake, Dome, Spine	Fatal, Damage, Mudflow, Tsunami	VEI	Vol L/T
PACAYA (Guatemala) *continued*						**1651**	0218		**1651**	0413	-x--	----	x---	x---	----	2	
						1655	07		....	....	----	----	x---	----	----	2	
						1664	....		....	....	----	----	x---	----	----	3	
						1668	08		**1669**	0629	----	----	x---	----	----	2	
						1671	08		....	....	----	----	x---	----	----	2	
						1674	07		....	....	----	----	x---	----	----	2	
(possibly same as 1674 eruption)						? **1677**	07		....	....	----	----	?---	----	----		
						1678	08 ?		....	....	----	----	x---	----	----	2	
						1687	0326		**1687**	0327	----	----	x---	----	----	2	
						1690	....		....	....	----	----	x---	----	----	2?	
						1693	....		....	....	----	----	?---	----	----	2?	
						1699	0629		....	....	----	----	?---	----	----	2?	
						? **1717**	....		....	....	----	----	?---	----	----		
						? **1760**	....		....	....	----	----	?---	----	----		
Cerro Chino (SW flank and summit).......						**1775**	0701		**1775**	0723>	-x--	----	x---	x---	----	3	7/7
						1805	....		....	....	----	----	x---	----	----	2	
						? **1830**	....		....	....	----	----	?---	----	----		
Cerro Chino						**1846**	02		....	....	-x--	----	x---	----	----	2	
						1885	12		....	....	----	----	x---	----	----	2	
South flank (Cachajinas vent)						**1961**	0311		**1961**	0415?	-xx-	----	x---	x---	-x--	2	6/-
MacKenney Crater and flank vents						**1965**	0704	+	**1989**	0310	xxx-	----	xx--	xx--	-x--	3*	
MacKenney Crater and flank vents						**1990**	0104?		**1993>**	....	x-x-	----	xx--	x---	-x--	3*	
CUILAPA-BARBARENA (Guatemala)	**14.33 N***	**90.40 W**	**1454**	**Volc field**	**1402-111**	**Holocene**											
TECUAMBURRO (Guatemala)	**14.156 N**	**90.407 W**	**1845**	**Stratovolc**	**1402-12=**	**Radiocarbon**											
NW flank (Ixpaco Crater)						C **-0960**u	....		....	....	-x--	----	--x-	----	----		
MOYUTA (Guatemala).............	**14.03 N**	**90.10 W**	**1662**	**Stratovolc**	**1402-13-**	**Hot Springs**											
FLORES, VOLCAN DE (Guatemala)..	**14.30 N***	**90.00 W**	**1600**	**Volc field**	**1402-14-**	**Holocene**											
CHINGO VOLC FIELD (Guatemala) ..	**14.12 N***	**89.73 W**	**1775**	**Stratovolc**	**1402-15-**	**Holocene**											
SANTIAGO, CERRO (Guatemala)....	**14.33 N***	**89.87 W**	**1192**	**Volc field**	**1402-16-**	**Holocene**											
SUCHITAN VOLC FIELD (Guatemala)	**14.40 N***	**89.78 W**	**2042**	**Stratovolcs**	**1402-17-**	**Holocene**											
(probably Atitlan eruption)						? **1469**	....		....	....	----	----	----	----	----		
IXTEPEQUE, VOLCAN (Guatemala)..	**14.42 N***	**89.68 W**	**1292**	**Lava domes**	**1402-18-**	**Holocene**											
IPALA VOLC FIELD (Guatemala)	**14.55 N***	**89.63 W**	**1650**	**Stratovolc**	**1402-19-**	**Holocene**											
CHIQUIMULA FIELD (Guatemala) ...	**14.83 N***	**89.55 W**	**1192**	**Cinder cones**	**1402-20-**	**Holocene**											
QUEZALTEPEQUE (Guatemala).....	**14.65 N**	**89.35 W**	**1200**	**Unknown**	**1402-21-**	**Holocene**											

EL SALVADOR & HONDURAS

VOLCANO NAME (Subregion) / ERUPTION — Area of Activity	LAT	LONG	ELEV (m)	TYPE	NUMBER	Status / Start Year	Start M-Dy	P	Stop Year	Stop M-Dy	Central, Flank vent, Radial fiss, Regional*	Submarine, New island, Subglacial, Crater lake	Explosive, Pyro flow, Phreatic, Fumarolic	Lava flow, Lava lake, Dome, Spine	Fatal, Damage, Mudflow, Tsunami	VEI	Vol L/T
VERDE, LAGUNA (El Salvador)	**13.891 N**	**89.786 W**	**1829**	**Stratovolcs**	**1403-01=**	**Holocene**											
SINGUIL, CERRO (El Salvador)	**14.05 N***	**89.63 W**	**958**	**Cinder cone**	**1403-011**	**Holocene**											
SAN DIEGO (El Salvador)	**14.27 N***	**89.47 W**	**860**	**Volc field**	**1403-012**	**Holocene**											
SANTA ANA (El Salvador)..........	**13.853 N**	**89.630 W**	**2365**	**Stratovolc**	**1403-02=**	**Historical**											
						? **1520**	....		....	....	----	----	?---	----	----		
						1521	1231y		....	....	----	----	x---	----	-x--	3	
						1524	0430p		....	....	----	----	x---	----	----	3	
						1570?	....		....	....	----	----	x---	----	----		
						1576	....		....	....	----	----	x---	----	----	3	
						? **1621**	....		....	....	----	----	----	----	----		
(doubtful San Marcelino eruption)						X 1650t	....		....	....	--?-	----	----	?---	-?--		
SE flank (San Marcelino)						**1722**	0312		....	....	-xx-	----	x---	x---	-x--	2	
						1734	06 <		....	....	----	----	x---	----	-x--	2?	
						1874	....		....	....	----	----	x---	----	-x--	3	
						? **1878**	....		....	....	----	----	?---	----	----	2	
						1879	0201p		....	....	----	----	x---	----	----	2	
NW flank (Mala Cara)..................						**1880**	03		....	....	-x--	----	x---	----	-x--	3	
						? **1882**	....		....	....	----	----	----	----	----		
						1884	0309		**1884**	0310	----	----	x---	----	----	2	
						1904	0112		**1904**	0126?	----	----	x---	----	----	2	
						1920	11		....	....	----	----	?---	----	----	2	
IZALCO (El Salvador).............	**13.813 N**	**89.633 W**	**1950**	**Stratovolc**	**1403-03=**	**Historical**											
(fumarolic activity prior to 1770)..........						X 1636	....		....	....	----	----	---x	----	----		
						1770	0223		....	....	----	----	x---	x---	----	2	
						1772?	....		....	....	----	----	x---	----	----	2	
						1783	07 ?		....	....	--?-	----	----	x---	----	0	
						1793	0329		**1793**	09	----	----	x---	x---	----	2	
						1798	04		....	....	x---	----	x---	?---	----	2	
						1802	....		**1803**	....	----	----	x---	x---	----	2	
						1805	....		**1807**	....	----	----	x---	----	----	2	
						1817	....		....	....	----	----	x---	----	----	2	
						1825	....		....	....	----	----	x---	x---	----	2	
						1836	....		....	....	----	----	x---	----	----	2	
						1838	....		**1840**	....	x---	----	x---	x---	----	2	
						1842	....		....	....	----	----	x---	----	----	2	
						1844	06		**1844**	10	----	----	x---	x---	----	2	
						1850	....		....	....	x---	----	x---	----	----	2	
						1854	0513		**1854**	0608	----	----	x---	x---	----	2	
Summit and south flank						**1856**	0524	+	**1856**	0901a	x-x-	----	x---	x---	-x--	2	
						1857	0215		**1857**	0219>	x---	----	x---	x---	----	2	
						1858	0206		**1859**	07	----	----	x---	?---	----	2	
						1859	1208		**1860**	0122	----	----	----	x---	----	0	
						1863	....		....	....	----	----	----	x---	----	0	
Summit and NE flank						**1864**	0515b		**1865**	0615e	xx--	----	x---	x---	----	2	
						1866	0427		**1866**	0815e	----	----	x---	----	----	2	
						1867	04		**1867**	08	----	----	x---	----	----	2	
						1868	0216		**1868**	0217	----	----	?---	----	----	2	
Summit and east flank						**1869**	0301?	+	**1869**	0618>	xxx-	----	xx--	x---	-x--	2	
(possibly confused with May 19, 1869)						? **1870**	0519		....	....	----	----	----	?---	----	2?	
						1872	12	+	**1873**	0319>	----	----	x---	----	----	2	
						? **1874**	....		?**1875**	....	----	----	----	----	----		
						1878	....		....	....	----	----	----	----	----		
						1879	1225		**1880**	03	----	----	x---	----	----	2	
						1881	0101		....	....	----	----	----	x---	----	0	
						1882	0712		....	....	----	----	x---	----	----	2	
						1883	0905d		**1883**	1113	-x--	----	x---	----	----	2	
						1884	0309		**1884**	0310	-x--	----	x---	x---	----	2	
						1885	....		....	....	-x--	----	x---	x---	----	2	
						1887	....		**1889**	....	----	----	x---	----	----	2	

VOLCANO NAME (Subregion)	LAT	LONG	ELEV (m)	TYPE	NUMBER	Status	ERUPTION — Area of Activity	Start Year	Start M-Dy	P	Stop Year	Stop M-Dy	Central / Flank vent / Radial fiss / Regional*	Submarine / New island / Subglacial / Crater lake	Explosive / Pyro flow / Phreatic / Fumarolic	Lava flow / Lava lake / Dome / Spine	Fatal / Damage / Mudflow / Tsunami	VEI	Vol L/T
IZALCO (El Salvador) *continued*							Summit and upper east flank	**1890**	0326e		**1890**	0420	xxx-	----	x---	x---	----	0	
								1891	....		**1898**	07	----	----	x---	x---	----	2	
								1899	1231		**1900**	03	----	----	x---	----	----	2	
							Summit and NE flank	**1902**	0510		**1902**	1230	xxx-	----	x---	x---	----	2	
							Summit and east flank	**1903**	11	+	**1905**	03	xx--	----	x---	----	----	2	
							Summit and NE flank	**1912**	0116		**1916**	0126	xxx-	----	x---	x---	----	2	
							SE flank	**1920**	1029		**1921**	0410	-x--	----	x---	x---	----	2	
								1924	03		....	....	----	----	x---	----	----	2	
								1925	1226		**1927**	01	----	----	xx--	x---	xx--	3*	
								1927	....		**1928**?	....	----	----	x---	----	----	2	
							Outer slope of eastern summit crater	**1930**	04		....	....	--x-	----	----	x---	----	0	
								1931	0331t		....	....	----	----	x?--	----	----	2	
								1933	1130	+	**1934**	0112>	----	----	x---	x---	----	2	
								1937?	....		**1938**?	....	----	----	x---	x---	----	2?	
							Summit and SSE flank	**1939**	02	+	**1948**	02	xx--	----	x---	x---	----	2	
							Summit, SW and NE flanks	**1948**	1104	+	**1957**	1201p	xx--	----	xx--	x---	----	3*	
							SSE flank	**1966**	1028		**1966**	11	-x--	----	----	x---	----	0	5/-
COATEPEQUE Caldera (El Salv)	**13.87 N**	**89.55 W**	**746**	**Caldera**	**1403-041**	**Holocene**													
SAN SALVADOR (El Salvador)	**13.736 N**	**89.286 W**	**1893**	**Stratovolc**	**1403-05=**	**Historical**													
							(same as A.D. 260 Ilopango eruption)	X -1043y	....		....	....	----	----	----	----	----		
							NW flank (Laguna Caldera)	C **0590**v	....		....	....	-xx-	----	x---	----	xx--		
							Boqueron	A **1050**y	....		....	....	x---	---x	x---	----	----		
							North flank ?	**1572**b	....		....	....	-x--	----	x---	x---	----	3?	
							NW flank (El Playon)	**1658**	1103		....	....	-xx-	----	x---	x---	-x--	3	7/-
							NW flank (El Playon)	**1671**	08 ?		....	....	-x--	----	x---	----	----	2?	
							El Playon ?	? **1806**	....		....	....	-x--	----	----	?---	----	0	
							Boqueron summit and north flank	**1917**	0607		**1917**	11	xxx-	---x	x---	x---	xx--	3	
GUAZAPA (El Salvador)	**13.90 N**	**89.12 W**	**1438**	**Stratovolc**	**1403-051**	**Holocene**													
ILOPANGO (El Salvador)	**13.672 N**	**89.053 W**	**450**	**Caldera**	**1403-06=**	**Historical**													
							Ilopango	C **0260**v	....		....	....	x---	----	xx--	----	xx--	**6**	**-/10**
							Islas Quemadas	**1879**	1231		**1880**	0326e	x---	---x	x---	--x-	-x--	3*	8/-
SAN VICENTE (El Salvador)	**13.623 N**	**88.852 W**	**2000**	**Stratovolc**	**1403-07=**	**Fumarolic**													
APASTEPEQUE FIELD (El Salv)	**13.72 N***	**88.77 W**	**700**	**Volc field**	**1403-071**	**Holocene**													
TABURETE (El Salvador)	**13.45 N**	**88.53 W**	**1172**	**Stratovolc**	**1403-072**	**Holocene**													
TECAPA (El Salvador)	**13.497 N**	**88.503 W**	**1592**	**Stratovolc**	**1403-08=**	**Fumarolic**													
								? **1878**	1002		....	....	----	----	----	----	----		
USULUTAN (El Salvador)	**13.42 N**	**88.47 W**	**1450**	**Stratovolc**	**1403-081**	**Holocene**													
CHINAMECA (El Salvador)	**13.48 N**	**88.32 W**	**1228**	**Stratovolc**	**1403-09=**	**Fumarolic**													
SAN MIGUEL (El Salvador)	**13.431 N**	**88.272 W**	**2130**	**Stratovolc**	**1403-10=**	**Historical**													
							(eruption 70-80 years before 1586)	**1510**e	....		....	....	x---	----	x?--	?---	----		
							SE flank ?	**1699**	....		....	....	-xx-	----	x---	x---	----	2	
								1762	....		....	....	----	----	?---	x---	----	2	
								1769	....		....	....	----	----	?---	x---	----	2	
							Summit, north and south flanks	**1787**	0921		**1787**	0923	xxx-	----	x---	x---	-x--	2	
								? **1798**?	....		....	....	----	----	?---	----	----	2	
								? **1811**	....		....	....	----	----	?---	----	----	2	
							SSE flank (near Los Perolitos)	**1819**	0718		....	....	--x-	----	x---	x---	-x--	2	
							NNW (1120 m) and upper east flanks	**1844**	0725	+	**1848**	....	-xx-	----	x---	x---	----	2	
								? **1854**	....		....	....	----	----	?---	----	----	2?	
							SSE flank ?	**1855**	12		....	....	-xx-	----	x---	x---	----	2	
								1857	11		....	....	----	----	x---	x---	----	2?	
								1862	01		....	....	----	----	x---	----	----	2	
							SW flank	**1867**	1214		**1868**	0216>	-xx-	----	x---	x---	-x--	2	
								1882	1205d		....	....	----	----	x---	----	----	2	
								1884	0125		**1884**	0128a	x---	----	x---	x---	----	2	
								1890	....		**1891**	....	x---	----	x---	----	----	2	
								1919	1210		**1920**	01	----	----	x---	----	----	2	
								1920	0814		**1925**	....	----	----	x---	----	----	2	
								1929	08		....	....	x---	----	x---	----	----	2	
								1930	0126e		....	....	x---	----	x---	----	----	2	
								1931	03		**1931**	06	x---	----	x---	----	----	2	
								? **1936**?	....		....	....	----	----	?---	----	----	2	
								1939	05		**1939**	07	----	----	x---	----	----	2	
								1954	1021		**1954**	1021	----	----	--x-	----	----	2	
								1964	1023		**1964**	11	x---	----	x---	----	-x--	2	
								1966	0222		....	....	----	----	x---	----	----	2	
								1966	07		....	....	----	----	x---	----	----	2	
								1967	0105		....	....	x---	----	x---	----	-?--	2	
								1970	0330		**1970**	0405	x---	----	x---	----	-x--	1	-/4
								1976	1202	+	**1977**	0301	x---	----	x---	?---	-x--	1	6/-
								1985	11		**1986**	02 >	x---	----	x-x-	----	----	1	
CONCHAGUA (El Salvador)	**13.277 N**	**87.853 W**	**1250**	**Stratovolc**	**1403-11=**	**Uncertain**													
CONCHAGUITA (El Salvador)	**13.22 N**	**87.765 W**	**550**	**Stratovolc**	**1403-12=**	**Historical**													
								1892	1012?		**1892**	1031?	x---	----	x---	----	----	1?	
TIGRE, ISLA EL (Honduras)	**13.27 N**	**87.63 W**	**760**	**Stratovolc**	**1403-13-**	**Holocene**													
ZACATE GRANDE, ISLA (Honduras)	**13.33 N**	**87.63 W**	**600**	**Stratovolc**	**1403-14-**	**Holocene**													
YOJOA, LAKE (Honduras)	**14.98 N***	**87.98 W**	**1090**	**Volc field**	**1403-15-**	**Holocene**													
UTILA ISLAND (Honduras)	**16.10 N***	**86.90 W**	**90**	**Pyrocl cones**	**1403-16-**	**Holocene**													

NICARAGUA

VOLCANO NAME (Subregion)	LAT	LONG	ELEV (m)	TYPE	NUMBER	Status	ERUPTION — Area of Activity	Start Year	Start M-Dy	P	Stop Year	Stop M-Dy	Central / Flank vent / Radial fiss / Regional*	Submarine / New island / Subglacial / Crater lake	Explosive / Pyro flow / Phreatic / Fumarolic	Lava flow / Lava lake / Dome / Spine	Fatal / Damage / Mudflow / Tsunami	VEI	Vol L/T
COSIGUINA (Nicaragua)	**12.98 N**	**87.57 W**	**859**	**Stratovolc**	**1404-01=**	**Historical**													
								C **1500**?	....		....	....	----	----	xx--	----	--x-		
								? **1609**	....		....	....	----	----	?---	----	----		
								1709?	....		....	....	----	----	x?--	----	--?-		
								1809	0328		**1809**	0331a	----	----	x---	----	----	2?	
								1835	0120	+	**1835**	0125?	x---	----	xx--	x---	xx--	**5**	**-/9**
								1852	12		....	....	x---	----	x---	----	----	2?	
								1859	0825		....	....	----	----	x---	----	----		
SAN CRISTOBAL (Nicaragua)	**12.702 N**	**87.004 W**	**1745**	**Stratovolc**	**1404-02=**	**Historical**													
								1528a	....		....	....	x---	----	x---	----	----	3	
								? **1613**	....		....	....	----	----	?---	----	----		
								1680	....		....	....	----	----	x---	----	----	2?	
								1684	07		....	....	x---	----	x---	----	----	2	
								1685	08		....	....	x---	----	x---	----	----	2	
								1971	0503		**1971**	0705d	x---	----	x-x-	----	----	1	

VOLCANO NAME (Subregion) / ERUPTION — Area of Activity	LAT	LONG	ELEV (m)	TYPE	NUMBER	Status	Start Year	Start M-Dy	P	Stop Year	Stop M-Dy	Central / Flank vent / Radial fiss / Regional*	Submarine / New island / Subglacial / Crater lake	Explosive / Pyro flow / Phreatic / Fumarolic	Lava flow / Lava lake / Dome / Spine	Fatal / Damage / Mudflow / Tsunami	VEI	Vol L/T
SAN CRISTOBAL (Nicaragua) *continued*							**1976**	0309	+	**1976**	0316	x---	----	x---	----	----	1	
							1976	0829		**1976**	0829	x---	----	x---	----	----	1	
							1977	1016		**1977**	1016	x---	----	x---	----	----	2	
						?	**1985**	0902		....	....	x---	----	--?-	----	----		
						?	**1987**	11		....	....	----	----	?---	----	----		
TELICA (Nicaragua)	**12.603 N**	**86.845 W**	**1010**	**Stratovolcs**	**1404-04=**	**Historical**												
							1527?	....		....	....	----	----	x---	----	-x--	3?	
							1529	....		....	....	x---	----	x---	----	----	3	
							1613	....		....	....	----	----	x---	----	----	2?	
							1685	08		....	....	x---	----	x---	----	----	2	
						?	**1743**	04		....	....	----	----	?---	----	----	2?	
							1765	....		....	....	----	----	x---	----	----	2	
							1791	0124		....	....	----	----	----	----	----		
(confused with Cerro Negro eruption)						X	1850	....		....	....	----	----	----	----	----		
							1907	11		....	....	----	----	x---	----	----	2	
						?	**1918**	....		....	....	----	----	----	----	----		
							1927	08		**1927**	11	x---	----	x---	----	----	2	
							1928	....		....	....	----	----	x---	----	----	2	
							1929	01		**1929**	01	x---	----	x---	----	----	1?	
							1934	01		....	....	x---	----	x---	----	----	2	
							1937	11		**1938**	08	x---	----	x---	----	-x--	2	
							1939	01		**1939**	06	x---	----	x---	----	----	2	
							1939	11		**1939**	11	x---	----	x---	----	----	2	
							1940	06		**1940**	10	x---	----	x---	----	----	2	
						?	**1941**	....		....	....	----	----	?---	----	----		
							1943	12	+	**1944**	04	x---	----	x---	----	-x--	2	
							1946	04		**1946**	08	x---	----	x---	----	-x--	2	
							1948	....		**1949**	11	x---	----	x---	----	-x--	2	
							1951	0715q		**1951**	1015e	x---	----	x---	----	----	2	
							1962	01		**1962**	01	x---	----	x---	----	----	1	
							1965	0116		**1965**	0128	x---	----	x---	----	-x--	1	
							1966	06		**1966**	06	x---	----	x---	----	----	1	
							1969	0211		**1971**	12 >	x---	----	x---	-x--	-x--	2	
							1975	05		**1976**	03	x---	----	----	-x--	----	0	
							1976	1103	+	**1978**	01 >	x---	----	x-x-	----	----	1	
							1981	02 ?		....	....	x---	----	x---	----	----	1	
							1981	1125e		**1982**	0302	x---	----	x---	----	-x--	2*	
Vent in NE corner of crater							**1987**	11		**1987**	11	x---	----	x---	----	----	1	
ROTA (Nicaragua)	**12.55 N**	**86.75 W**	**836**	**Shield**	**1404-06-**	**Holocene**												
NEGRO, CERRO (Nicaragua)	**12.506 N**	**86.702 W**	**675**	**Cinder cones**	**1404-07=**	**Historical**												
							1850	0413	+	**1850**	0527>	x---	----	x---	x---	-x--	2	
							1867	1114		**1867**	1130	--x-	----	x---	x---	----	2	
							1899	1122		**1899**	1129a	----	----	x---	----	-x--	2	
							1914	10		**1914**	11	x---	----	x---	----	-xx-	2	
							1919	0620		**1919**	0630	----	----	x---	----	----	2	
Summit and upper north flank							**1923**	1023		**1923**	12	x-x-	----	x---	x---	----	2	
							1929	0210		**1929**	03	-xx-	----	x---	x---	----	2	
							1947	0712		**1947**	0725	xx--	----	x---	x---	-x--	2	
							1948	0331		....	....	x---	----	x---	----	----	2	
							1949	06		**1949**	06	x---	----	x---	----	----	2	
							1950	1121		**1951**	12	x---	----	x---	x---	----	2	
							1954	02		**1954**	02	x---	----	x---	----	----	2?	
Summit and east flank							**1957**	0904		**1957**	0924	xx--	----	x---	x---	-x--	2	
							1960	0928		**1960**	1226e	x-x-	----	x---	x---	-x--	2	
							1961	1025		....	....	--x-	----	x---	x---	----	2	
							1962	0321		**1962**	04 ?	x---	----	x---	----	----	2	
							1963	03		....	....	x---	----	x---	----	----	1	
							1964	....		....	....	----	----	----	----	----	2?	
Summit and south flank							**1968**	1023		**1968**	1215	xx--	----	x---	x---	-x--	3	-/7
							1969	1219		**1969**	1229	x---	----	x---	----	----	1	
Summit and east flank							**1971**	0203		**1971**	0214	xx--	----	x---	----	-x--	3	-/7
							1992	0409		**1992**	0414	x---	----	x---	----	-x--	3	-/7
PILAS, LAS (Nicaragua)	**12.495 N**	**86.688 W**	**1050**	**Complx volc**	**1404-08=**	**Historical**												
						@	**1528**	....		....	....	----	----	----	----	----		
El Hoyo							**1952**	1023		**1952**	12	---x	----	x-x-	----	----	1	
El Hoyo							**1954**	1029		**1954**	1031	x---	----	x-x-	----	----	2	
MOMOTOMBO (Nicaragua)	**12.423 N**	**86.540 W**	**1258**	**Stratovolc**	**1404-09=**	**Historical**												
						C	**-2550**y	....		....	....	x---	----	----	x---	----		
						C	**-0800**t	....		....	....	x---	----	xx--	----	----	4+	-/8
						C	**1100**t	....		....	....	x---	----	x---	----	----		
							1524	....		....	....	x---	----	x---	----	----	3	-/7
							1578	02		....	....	x---	----	x---	----	----	2	
							1605	....		**1606**	....	x---	----	x---	----	-xx-	4	-/8
(eruption more likely in 1605-1606)						?	**1609**	....		....	....	----	----	?---	----	-??-		
							1736	....		....	....	x---	----	x---	----	----	2?	
							1764	....		....	....	x---	----	x---	----	----	2	
							1849	....		....	....	x---	----	x---	----	----	2	
							1852	....		....	....	x---	----	?---	----	----	2	
							1854	02		**1854**	03	x---	----	x---	----	----	2	
							1858	....		**1866**	....	x---	----	x---	----	----	2	
							1870	....		....	....	x---	----	x---	----	----	2?	
							1878	1014?		....	....	x---	----	x---	----	----	2	
							1882	0909		....	....	x---	----	x---	----	----	2?	
							1886	0519		**1887?**	....	x---	----	x---	x---	-x--	2	
							1902	0331p		....	....	x---	----	x---	----	----	2?	
							1905	0116		**1905**	0121	x---	----	x---	x---	----	2	-/6
APOYEQUE (Nicaragua)	**12.242 N**	**86.342 W**	**420**	**Stratovolc**	**1404-091**	**Anthropology**												
NEJAPA-TICOMO (Nicaragua)	**12.12 N**	**86.32 W**	**220**	**Fissure vent**	**1404-092**	**Holocene**												
MASAYA (Nicaragua)	**11.984 N**	**86.161 W**	**635**	**Caldera**	**1404-10=**	**Historical**												
West side of caldera						T	**-4550?**	....		....	....	x---	----	x---	----	----	5	-/9
Nindiri							**1524**	....		**1544?**	....	x---	----	----	-x--	----	0	
Nindiri							**1551**	....		....	....	x---	----	----	-x--	----	0	
Nindiri							**1570**	....		....	....	x---	----	----	-x--	----	0	
Nindiri						?	**1586**	....		....	....	x---	----	----	-?--	----	0	
Nindiri						?	**1613**	....		....	....	x---	----	----	-?--	----	0	
Nindiri							**1670**	....		....	....	x---	----	x---	x---	----	3	
North side of Old Masaya Crater							**1772**	0316		**1772**	0325?	x-x-	----	x---	x---	-x--	2	

VOLCANO NAME (Subregion)	LAT	LONG	ELEV (m)	TYPE	NUMBER	ERUPTION — Area of Activity	Status / Start Year	Start M-Dy	P	Stop Year	Stop M-Dy	Central / Flank vent / Radial fiss / Regional	Submarine / New island / Subglacial / Crater lake	Explosive / Pyro flow / Phreatic / Fumarolic	Lava flow / Lava lake / Dome / Spine	Fatal / Damage / Mudflow / Tsunami	VEI	Vol L/T
MASAYA (Nicaragua) *continued*						(confused with 1772 eruption)	X 1775	....		....	....	----	----	----	----	----		
						Between Masaya and Nindiri Craters......	**1852**	07		....	....	x-x-	----	x---	x---	----	2	
						Santiago...........................	**1853**	0409?		**1853**	0915>	x---	----	x-x-	----	----	1?	
						Santiago or San Pedro.................	**1856**	12		**1857**	01	x---	----	x---	----	----	2	
							? **1858**	04		....	....	x---	----	?---	----	----		
						Santiago, San Pedro	**1858**	1110	+	**1859**	0327	x---	----	x---	----	----	2	
						Santiago...........................	**1902**	0715		**1903**	11	x---	----	x---	----	-x--	2	
						Santiago...........................	**1904**	05		**1904**	06	x---	----	x---	----	----	2	
						Santiago and near El Pelon	**1906**	0102	+	**1906**	0109>	x-x-	----	x---	----	-x--	2	
						Santiago...........................	**1913**	0712		....	....	x---	----	?---	-x--	----	1?	
						Santiago...........................	**1919**	....		**1924**	....	x---	----	x---	----	-x--	2	
						Santiago...........................	**1946**	06		**1947?**	....	x---	----	x---	-x--	----	1*	
						Santiago...........................	**1965**	1010?		**1985>**	....	x---	----	x---	xx--	-x--	1*	
						Santiago...........................	**1987**	0215		**1987**	0215	x---	----	x-x-	----	----	1	
						Santiago...........................	**1989**	0220		**1989**	0602?	x---	----	x---	xx--	----	1	
						Santiago...........................	**1993**	0616		**1993**	10 >	x---	----	x---	-x--	----	1	
APOYO (Nicaragua)...............	**11.92 N**	**86.03 W**	**468**	**Caldera**	**1404-101**		**Uncertain**											
MOMBACHO (Nicaragua)	**11.826 N**	**85.968 W**	**1345**	**Stratovolc**	**1404-11=**		**Fumarolic**											
						(uncertain eruption in 1570, not 1560)	? **1570**	....		....	....	x---	----	?---	----	xx--		
						(confused with 1850 Cerro Negro eruption) .	X 1850	....		....	....	----	----	----	----	----		
ZAPATERA ISLAND (Nicaragua)	**11.73 N**	**85.82 W**	**625**	**Stratovolc**	**1404-111**		**Holocene**											
CONCEPCION (Nicaragua)	**11.538 N**	**85.623 W**	**1610**	**Stratovolc**	**1404-12=**		**Historical**											
							? **1800t**	....		....	....	x---	----	?---	----	----	2	
							1883	0405d		**1883**	0630	x---	----	x---	x---	-x--	2	
							1884	....		**1886**	....	x---	----	x---	----	----	2	
							1891	04		**1891**	04	x---	----	x---	----	----	2	
							1902	....		....	....	x---	----	x---	----	-x--	2	
							1907	09		**1910**	....	x-x-	----	x---	x---	----	2	
							1918	01		**1919**	07	x---	----	x---	----	----	2	
							1921	....		**1926**	05	x-x-	----	x---	x---	-x--	2	
							1928	01		**1928**	01	x---	----	x---	----	----	2	
							1929	08		**1929**	10	x---	----	x---	----	----	2	
							1935	02		**1935**	02	x---	----	x---	----	-x--	2	
							1944	04		**1945**	12	x-x-	----	x---	x---	-x--	2	
							1948	....		**1950**	....	x---	----	x---	----	----	2	
							1951	07		**1955**	05	x---	----	x---	----	-x--	2	
							1957	0327		**1957**	0408	x-x-	----	x---	x---	-x--	2	
							1961	1128		**1961**	12	x---	----	x---	----	----	2	
							1962	06		**1962**	06	x---	----	x---	----	----	2	
							1963	0509		....	....	x---	----	x---	----	----	2	
							1973	1224		**1974**	0112	x---	----	x---	----	----	2	
							1977	0404		**1977**	0503	x---	----	x---	----	----	2	
							1978	0330<		**1978**	05 >	x---	----	x---	----	----	2	
							1982	0115e		**1982**	0214e	x---	----	x-x-	----	----	2	
							1983	0316		**1983**	0325	x---	----	x---	----	----	2	
							1984	12		**1985**	0102	x---	----	x-x-	----	-x--	2*	
							1985	1202a	+	**1986**	0420?	x---	----	x---	----	----	1	
MADERA, LA (Nicaragua)..........	**11.446 N**	**85.515 W**	**1394**	**Stratovolc**	**1404-13-**		**Holocene?**											
BLUE, VOLCAN (Nicaragua)........	**12.68 N***	**83.92 W**	**150**	**Cinder cones**	**1404-14-**		**Holocene**											

COSTA RICA & PANAMA

VOLCANO NAME (Subregion)	LAT	LONG	ELEV (m)	TYPE	NUMBER	ERUPTION — Area of Activity	Status / Start Year	Start M-Dy	P	Stop Year	Stop M-Dy	Central / Flank vent / Radial fiss / Regional	Submarine / New island / Subglacial / Crater lake	Explosive / Pyro flow / Phreatic / Fumarolic	Lava flow / Lava lake / Dome / Spine	Fatal / Damage / Mudflow / Tsunami	VEI	Vol L/T
OROSI (Costa Rica)...............	**10.980 N**	**85.473 W**	**1659**	**Stratovolcs**	**1405-01=**		**Uncertain**											
RINCON DE LA VIEJA (Costa Rica) ..	**10.830 N**	**85.324 W**	**1916**	**Complx volc**	**1405-02=**		**Historical**											
							C **-1540v**	....		....	....	x---	----	x---	----	----	4	-/8
							? **1529**	....		....	....	----	----	----	----	----		
							1765	....		....	....	----	----	----	----	----		
						(more likely Rincon Vieja than Orosi)......	@ **1844**	05		....	....	x---	----	x---	----	----	2	
						(more likely Rincon Vieja than Orosi)......	@ **1849**	....		....	....	x---	----	x---	----	----	2	
							? **1851**	....		....	....	----	----	----	----	----		
						(more likely Rincon Vieja than Orosi)......	**1853**	....		**1854**	....	x---	----	x---	----	----	2	
							1860	....		....	....	x---	----	x---	----	----	2	
							1861	....		**1863**	08	x---	----	x---	----	----	2	
							? **1902**	0622		....	....	----	----	?---	----	----	2?	
							1912	0614		....	....	x---	----	x---	----	----	2	
							? **1917**	....		....	....	----	----	?---	----	----		
							1922	0411<		**1922**	0604	x---	----	x---	----	----	2?	
							1966	1129		**1967**	12	x---	----	x-x-	----	-x--	3*	
							1969	0422		**1969**	05	x---	----	x---	----	----	2	
							1969	0920		**1969**	1016	x---	----	x---	----	----	2	
							1970	0814		**1970**	0815	x---	----	x---	----	----	1	
							1983	0206	+	**1983**	0221	x---	---x	x-x-	----	--x-	1	
							1984	0331		**1984**	04	x---	---x	x-x-	----	--x-	1	
							1985	1015q		**1986**	0201p	x---	---x	x-x-	----	----	1	
							1986	1231		**1986**	1231	x---	---x	--x-	----	----	1	
							1987	0401		**1987**	0401	x---	---x	--x-	----	-xx-	1	
							1991	0506		**1991**	0508	x---	---x	x-x-	----	-xx-	1	
							1991	0829		**1991**	0829	x---	---x	x-x-	----	----	1	
							1992	01 ?		**1992**	0326?	x---	---x	--x-	----	----	1	
							? **1992**	08		**?1992**	08	x---	---?	--?-	----	----		
MIRAVALLES (Costa Rica)	**10.748 N**	**85.153 W**	**2028**	**Stratovolc**	**1405-03=**		**Historical**											
							T **-5050?**	....		....	....	----	----	x---	----	----		
						Upper SE flank.......................	**1946**	0914		**1946**	0914	-x--	----	x-x-	----	----	1	
TENORIO GROUP (Costa Rica)	**10.673 N**	**85.015 W**	**1916**	**Stratovolcs**	**1405-031**		**Holocene**											
ANUNCIACION, CERRO (Costa Rica)	**10.472 N**	**85.07 W**	**402**	**Pyrocl cone**	**1405-032**		**Holocene?**											
ARENAL (Costa Rica)	**10.463 N**	**84.703 W**	**1657**	**Stratovolc**	**1405-033**		**Historical**											
						Cerro Chato	C **-3190v**	....		....	....	x---	----	xx--	----	----		
						Cerro Chato	C **-1550v**	....		....	....	x---	----	x---	----	----		
							C **-0900w**	....		....	....	x---	----	x---	----	----		
							C **-0220u**	....		....	....	----	----	x---	----	----		
							C **1080t**	....		....	....	x---	----	xx--	----	----		
							C **1525p**	....		....	....	x---	----	xx--	x---	----	4	7/8
							T **1750t**	....		....	....	x-x-	----	----	x---	----		
						West flank and summit.................	**1968**	0729	+	**1993>**	....	xxx-	----	xxx-	x---	xxx-	3*	7/7
POCO SOL, LAGUNA (Costa Rica) ..	**10.320 N**	**84.660 W**	**789**	**Expl crater ?**	**1405-034**		**Uncertain**											
AGUAS ZARCAS GROUP (")	**10.420 N**	**84.310 W**	**621**	**Pyrocl cones**	**1405-035**		**Holocene**											
PLATANAR, CERRO (Costa Rica) ...	**10.30 N**	**84.366 W**	**2183**	**Stratovolcs**	**1405-036**		**Holocene**											

VOLCANO NAME (Subregion) / ERUPTION — Area of Activity	LAT	LONG	ELEV (m)	TYPE	NUMBER	Status / Start Year	Start M-Dy	P	Stop Year	Stop M-Dy	Central / Flank vent / Radial fiss / Regional*	Submarine / New island / Subglacial / Crater lake	Explosive / Pyro flow / Phreatic / Fumarolic	Lava flow / Lava lake / Dome / Spine	Fatal / Damage / Mudflow / Tsunami	VEI	Vol L/T
POAS (Costa Rica)	**10.20 N**	**84.233 W**	**2708**	**Stratovolc**	**1405-04=**	**Historical**											
Botos Cone						C **-5590**v	....		....	....	x---	----	x---	----	----		
North flank (Cerro Congo)						C **-3190**v	....		....	....	-x--	----	xx--	----	----		
						1828	....		....	....	x---	---x	x-x-	----	----	1	
						1834	....		....	....	x---	---x	x-x-	----	-x--	2	
(possibly confused with 1834 eruption)						? **1838**	....		....	....	----	----	?---	----	----	2?	
						1860	....		....	....	x---	---x	--x-	----	----	1	
						? **1879**	....		....	....	----	----	--?-	----	----	1	
						1880	....		....	....	x---	---x	x-x-	----	-x--	1	
						1888	01		**1891**	....	x---	---x	--x-	----	----	1	
						1895	....		....	....	x---	---x	--x-	----	----	1	
						1898	1229		**1906**	0412>	x---	---x	x-x-	----	----	1*	
						1907	1231y		....	....	x---	---x	x-x-	----	----	1	
						1910	0125		**1910**	02	x---	---x	x-x-	----	----	2	-/5
						1910	0912		**1910**	1014	x---	---x	--x-	----	----	1	
						1914	0530		....	....	x---	---x	x-x-	----	----	2	
						1914	1008		**1915**	0515>	x---	---x	x-x-	----	----	2	
						1925	....		....	....	x---	---x	--x-	----	----	1	
						1929	....		....	....	x---	---x	--x-	----	----	1	
						1941	....		**1946**	....	x---	---x	--x-	----	----	1	
						1946	1104d		....	....	x---	---x	--x-	----	----	1	
						1948	....		**1951**	....	x---	---x	--x-	----	----	1	
						1952	0323		**1957**	1225	x---	---x	xxx-	x---	----	2*	
						1958	....		**1961**	0703?	x---	---x	x-x-	----	----	2*	
						1963	0523	+	**1963**	0702>	x---	---x	x-x-	----	----	2	
						1964	1225		**1965**	03	x---	---x	x-xx	----	----	2	
						1967	0101		....	....	x---	---x	x-x-	----	----	1	
						1969	0503	+	**1969**	0603	x---	---x	--x-	----	----	2	
						1970	07		....	....	x---	---x	--x-	----	----	1	
						1972	0209		**1973**	0908	x---	---x	x-x-	----	----	2*	
						1974	0911	+	**1975**	02	x---	---x	--x-	----	----	2	
						1976	0621	+	**1976**	11	x---	---x	x-x-	----	----	2	
						1977	05		**1977**	07 ?	x---	---x	x-x-	----	----	1	
						1977	1218	+	**1978**	0526e	x---	---x	x-x-	----	----	2	
						1978	0922		**1978**	12	x---	---x	x-xx	----	----	1	
						1979	0908		**1980**	01	x---	---x	x-x-	----	----	1	
						1980	0911		**1980**	0911	x---	---x	x-x-	----	----	1	
						1980	1226		**1980**	1226	x---	---x	x-x-	----	----	1	
						1981	03		**1981**	05	x---	----	--x-	----	----	1	
						1987	06		**1990**	06	x---	---x	x-xx	----	-x--	2*	
						1991	0306		**1991**	0526e	x---	---x	--x-	----	----	1	
						1991	09		**1991**	09	x---	---x	--x-	----	----	0	
						1992	02		**1992**	03	x---	---x	--x-	----	-x--	1	
						1992	10		**1993**	09	x---	---x	--x-	----	----	0	
BARVA (Costa Rica)	**10.135 N**	**84.10 W**	**2906**	**Complx volc**	**1405-05=**	**Tephrochronology**											
						T **-6050***	....		....	....	----	----	x---	----	----	P	
						? **1867**	03		....	....	----	----	?---	----	----		
IRAZU (Costa Rica)	**9.979 N**	**83.853 W**	**3432**	**Stratovolc**	**1405-06=**	**Historical**											
Diego del Haya Crater						**1723**	0216		**1723**	1211	x---	----	x---	----	-xx-	3?	
Diego del Haya Crater						**1726**	05		....	....	x---	----	x---	----	----	2	
						1775?	....		....	....	x---	----	x---	----	----	2?	
						1821	05		....	....	x---	----	x---	----	----	2	
						1822	0507		....	....	x---	----	x---	----	----	2	
						1823	....		....	....	x---	----	x---	----	----	2?	
						? **1826**	....		....	....	----	----	x---	----	----		
						1842	....		....	....	x---	----	x---	----	----	2	
						1844	05		....	....	x---	----	x---	----	----	2	
						1847	0518		....	....	x---	----	x---	----	----	2	
						1875e	....		....	....	x---	----	x---	----	----	2	
						? **1882**	....		....	....	----	----	?--x	----	----	2	
						1883	0103		....	....	x---	----	x---	----	----	2	
						1889	0228		....	....	x---	----	x---	----	----	2	
						1894	....		....	....	----	----	----	----	----		
						1899	....		....	....	----	----	----	----	----		
						1909	....		....	....	----	----	x---	----	----	2	
						1910	....		....	....	----	----	----	----	----		
						1914	0221		....	....	x---	----	x---	----	----	2	
						1917	0927		**1921**	....	x---	----	x-x-	----	-x--	3*	
						1924	03		**1924**	04	x---	----	x---	----	----	2	
						1928	0214		**1928**	0526e	x---	----	x---	----	----	2	
						1930	10		....	....	x---	----	x---	----	----	2	
						1933	0322?		**1933**	0725	x---	----	x---	----	-x--	2*	-/6
						1939	0618		**1940**	....	x---	----	x---	----	-x--	2	
(fumarolic activity, no eruption)						X 1962	0809		....	....	x---	----	---x	----	----		
						1963	0313		**1965**	0213	x---	----	x-x-	--x-	xxx-	3*	
(increased steaming: no eruption)						X 1967	0807		....	....	----	----	---x	----	----		
(increased steaming: no eruption)						X 1974	0302		X1974	0307	----	----	---x	----	----		
TURRIALBA (Costa Rica)	**10.03 N**	**83.77 W**	**3340**	**Stratovolc**	**1405-07=**	**Historical**											
						C **-6300**y	....		....	....	x---	----	xx--	----	----		
						C **-0025**t	....		....	....	x---	----	xx--	----	----		
						? **1723**	....		....	....	x---	----	?---	----	----	1	
						? **1847**	....		....	....	x---	----	----	----	----		
						1853	....		....	....	x---	----	x---	----	----	2	
						1855	05		....	....	x---	----	x---	----	----	2	
						? **1861**	....		....	....	x---	----	----	----	----		
Central and SW summit craters						**1864**	0916		**1865**	03	x---	----	xxx-	----	----	2*	
Central and SW summit craters						**1866**	01		**1866**	0508	x---	----	xxx-	----	--x-	3	-/7
BARU (Panama)	**8.80 N**	**82.558 W**	**3477**	**Complx volc**	**1406-01-**	**Historical**											
						C **0600**u	....		....	....	----	----	x---	----	-x--		
(not an eruption)						X 1210w	....		....	....	----	----	----	----	----		
						1550?	....		....	....	----	----	----	----	----		
YEGUADA, LA (Panama)	**8.523 N**	**80.910 W**	**1297**	**Stratovolc**	**1406-02-**	**Radiocarbon**											
						C **1615**v	....		....	....	----	----	x---	x---	----		

South America (15)

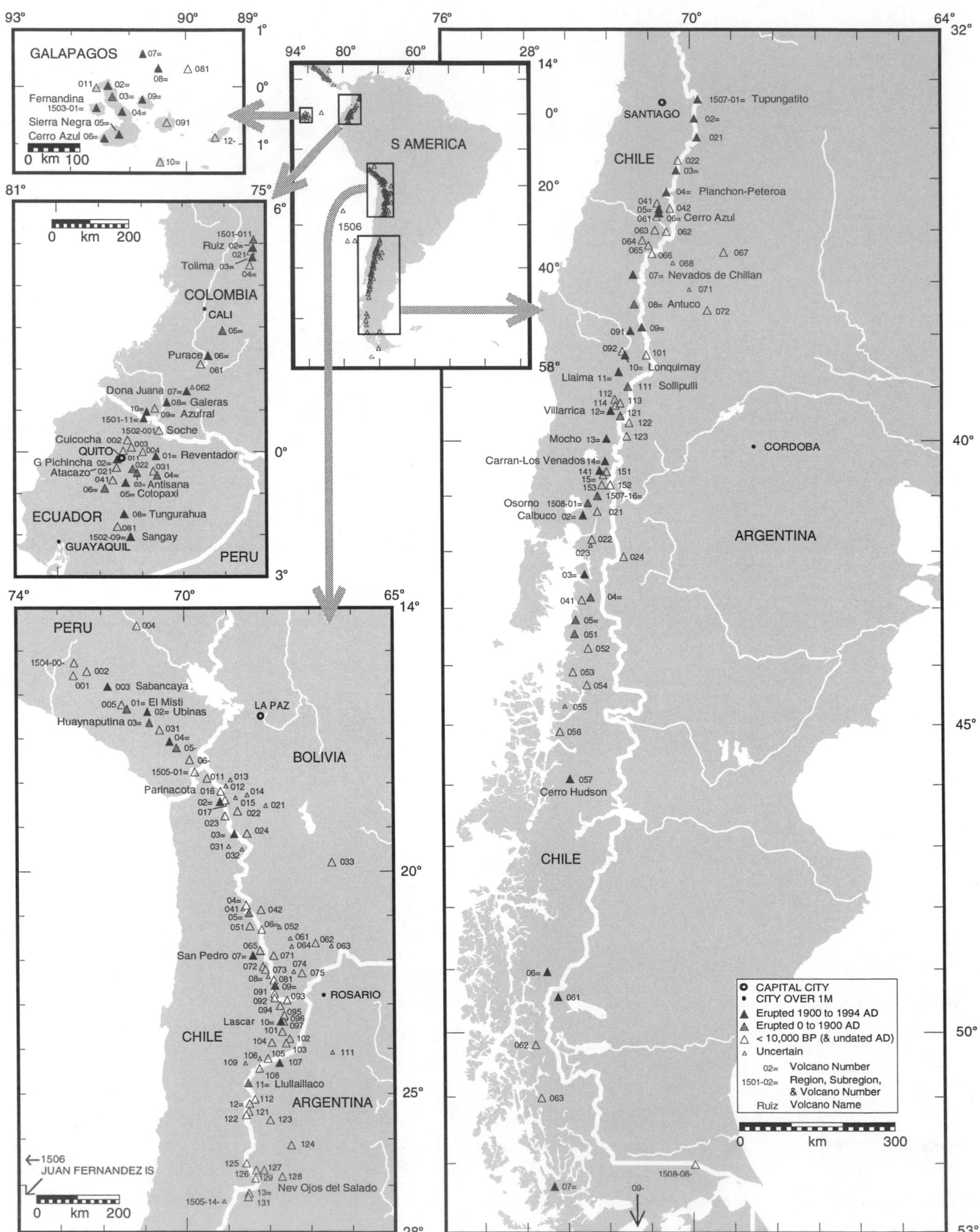
GALAPAGOS
07=
08=
081
011
02=
Fernandina
1503-01=
03=
09=
04=
Sierra Negra 05=
091
Cerro Azul 06=
12-
10=
0 km 100
S AMERICA
1506
0 km 200
1501-011
Ruiz 02=
021
Tolima 03=
04=
COLOMBIA
CALI
05=
Purace 06=
061
Dona Juana 07=
062
08= Galeras
10=
09= Azufral
1501-11=
1502-001 Soche
Cuicocha 002
003
QUITO
004
01= Reventador
011
G Pichincha 02=
022
Atacazo 021
031
041
04=
06=
03= Antisana
05= Cotopaxi
ECUADOR
08= Tungurahua
081
1502-09= Sangay
GUAYAQUIL
PERU
PERU
004
1504-00-
002
001
003 Sabancaya
005
01= El Misti
02= Ubinas
LA PAZ
Huaynaputina 03=
031
04=
05-
06-
BOLIVIA
1505-01=
011
013
Parinacota 016
012
014
02=
015
021
017
022
023
03=
024
031
032
033
04=
041
042
05=
051
06=
052
061
064
062
063
065
San Pedro 07=
071
072
073
074
075
08=
081
09=
ROSARIO
091
093
092
094
095
Lascar 10=
096
097
101
CHILE
104
102
103
111
106
105
109
107
108
11= Llullaillaco
12=
112
ARGENTINA
121
122
123
124
←1506
JUAN FERNANDEZ IS
125
127
126
129
128
13=
Nev Ojos del Salado
1505-14-
131
0 km 200
SANTIAGO
1507-01= Tupungatito
02=
021
CHILE
022
03=
04= Planchon-Peteroa
041
05=
042
061
06= Cerro Azul
063
062
064
065
066
067
068
07= Nevados de Chillan
071
08= Antuco
072
091
09=
092
101
10= Lonquimay
Llaima 11=
111 Sollipulli
112
114
113
Villarrica 12=
121
122
Mocho 13=
123
CORDOBA
Carran-Los Venados 14=
141
151
15=
153
152
1507-16=
Osorno 1508-01=
Calbuco 02=
021
022
023
ARGENTINA
024
03=
041
04=
05=
051
052
053
054
055
056
057
Cerro Hudson
CHILE
06=
061
062
063
1508-08-
07=
09-
CAPITAL CITY
CITY OVER 1M
Erupted 1900 to 1994 AD
Erupted 0 to 1900 AD
< 10,000 BP (& undated AD)
Uncertain
02= Volcano Number
1501-02= Region, Subregion, & Volcano Number
Ruiz Volcano Name
0 km 300

One of the largest of the *CAVW* regions, South America spans the greatest length of any continental volcanic region. Subduction of the eastern Pacific's Nazca Plate beneath South America has produced one of the Earth's highest mountain ranges, and its highest volcano, Nevados Ojos del Salado. Three distinct volcanic belts (see map) are separated by volcanically inactive gaps, where subduction is at such a shallow angle that magma is not generated by the process. South America's first *CAVW* covered the oceanic islands of Ecuador and Chile (in 1962). It was followed one year later by "The Chilean continent" and, in 1966, by "Colombia, Ecuador, & Peru".

South America leads all other regions in population of volcanoes, with 204: it has the largest number of undated "Holocene" volcanoes (112) and is second only to Japan in the number of volcanoes with dated eruptions. The human population, however, totals less than 90 million, or approximately that of Mexico. Colombia accounts for 37% of the population and Argentina for 37% of the land area. Chile has the region's largest number of historically active volcanoes, with 36 (ranking it 5th among nations, behind Russia's 52 and ahead of Iceland's 18). Ecuador, the region's smallest in terms of population and area, is next with 16.

When South America was discovered by Columbus, on his 3rd voyage in 1498, the Inca civilization was large and highly developed, but no records survive of the Andean volcanism that they no doubt witnessed. In 1524, Pizarro started his first voyage along the Pacific coast and within 10 years Atahualpa was executed and the Inca conquered by Spain. Travel overland was slow and difficult, so the Spaniards sailed south, launching their exploration of the Andes from Peru and what is now Ecuador. A result of this pattern is that 27 16th century eruptions are known from Peru northward, while 3 are known south of Peru (and only 8 more in the 17th century). In southern Chile, where the population is sparse and the mountains remote, only 2 (of 24) volcanoes have recorded eruptions before the early 1800s.

The region's first historically documented eruption was at El Misti, sometime between 1438 and 1471, and the next two were from mainland Ecuador in the early 1530s. The Galapagos Islands were discovered in 1535, but their early visitors were largely pirates, and they were still uninhabited when the first scientific mission arrived in 1790. The first eruption was recorded near the end of that century and the first resident settled in 1807. The Chilean islands were discovered by Juan Fernandez in 1574, but no eruptions were recorded by their only early resident, Robinson Crusoe, during his 1704-09 visit: it remained for Charles Darwin to document the first (and only) certain eruption there in 1835.

South America is dominated by large, often glacier-clad, stratovolcanoes (122, more than any other region), and matches Japan in having the most documented VEI ≥4 eruptions in the past 200 years. It has had 15% of the world's mudflow-producing eruptions, including the tragic one at Colombia's Ruiz volcano in 1985. Reflecting the many volcanoes remote from human observers, this region has the largest proportion of eruptions (17%) prefixed by the commercial "at" symbol (@) indicating uncertainty about which of several neighboring volcanoes was actually erupting.

VOLCANO NAME (Subregion) / ERUPTION — Area of Activity	LAT	LONG	ELEV (m)	TYPE	NUMBER	Status / Start Year	Start M-Dy	P	Stop Year	Stop M-Dy	Central / Flank vent / Radial fiss / Regional	Submarine / New island / Subglacial / Crater lake	Explosive / Pyro flow / Phreatic / Fumarolic	Lava flow / Lava lake / Dome / Spine	Fatal / Damage / Mudflow / Tsunami	VEI	Vol L/T
COLOMBIA																	
MESA NEVADA DE HERVEO (Col.)	5.30 N	75.47 W			1501-01=	Not a Volcano											
BRAVO, CERRO (Colombia)	**5.092 N**	**75.30 W**	**4000**	**Stratovolc**	**1501-011**	**Radiocarbon**											
						C **-4280**w	....		....	....	x---	----	x---	----	----	4	-/9
						C **-1310**w	....		....	....	x---	----	x---	----	----	4	-/9
						T **-1050**x	....		....	....	x---	----	x---	----	----	4	-/8
						C **-0725**u	....		....	....	x---	----	xx--	--x-	----	4	-/8
						C **0750**w	....		....	....	x---	----	xx--	--x-	----	4	-/8
						C **1050**u	....		....	....	x---	----	xx--	--x-	----	4	-/8
						C **1325**u	....		....	....	x---	----	x---	----	----	4	-/8
						T **1720**w	....		....	....	x---	----	xx--	--x-	----	4	-/8
RUIZ (Colombia)	**4.895 N**	**75.323 W**	**5321**	**Stratovolc**	**1501-02=**	**Historical**											
Arenas Crater						T **-6660**<	....		....	....	x---	----	xx--	----	--x-		
ENE flank ? (Alto la Piramide ?)						C **-1245**w	....		....	....	-?--	----	xxx-	--?-	--x-		
Arenas Crater						T **-0850**?	....		....	....	x---	----	xx--	----	--x-	4	-/8
Arenas Crater						C **-0200**v	....		....	....	x---	----	x---	----	----	4	-/8
West flank (La Olleta)						C **0350**y	....		....	....	-x--	----	x---	----	----	3	-/7
Arenas Crater						C **0675**t	....		....	....	x---	----	xx--	----	--x-	3	-/7
Arenas Crater						C **1350**?	....		....	....	x---	----	x---	----	--x-	4	-/8
						? **1541**	....		....	....	----	----	--?-	----	----		
Arenas Crater?						**1570**	....		....	....	x---	----	x---	----	----		
Arenas Crater						**1595**	0309<		....	....	x---	--x-	xx--	----	xxx-	4*	-/8
Near Arenas Crater						**1623**	....		....	....	x---	----	?-?-	----	----	1?	
						1805	0314		....	....	??--	----	x-?-	----	----	2	
						? **1826**	....		....	....	----	----	--?-	----	----	2?	
						1828	06		....	....	??--	----	--x-	----	----	2	
						1829	0618		....	....	??--	----	x-?-	----	----	2	
						1831	....		....	....	??--	----	x-?-	----	----	2	
						? **1833**	....		....	....	??--	----	--??	----	----	2?	
Arenas and La Olleta(?) craters						**1845**	0219		....	....	x?--	--?-	xxx-	----	xxx-	3	-/7
						1916	....		....	....	----	----	x-x-	----	----	2	
Arenas Crater						**1984**	1222	+	**1985**	0319?	x---	----	x-x-	----	----	1	
Arenas Crater						**1985**	0911	+	**1991**	07	x---	----	xxx-	----	xxx-	3*	-/7
SANTA ISABEL (Colombia)	**4.82 N**	**75.37 W**	**4950**	**Shield**	**1501-021**	**Radiocarbon**											
						C **-2800**v	....		....	....	----	----	----	x---	----		
TOLIMA (Colombia)	**4.67 N**	**75.33 W**	**5200**	**Stratovolc**	**1501-03=**	**Historical**											
						T **-6200***	....		....	....	----	----	x---	----	----		
						C **-1650**v	....		....	....	----	----	x---	----	----	**P**	
						1822	11		....	....	----	----	x---	----	----	2	
						1825	0302		....	....	----	----	x---	----	----	2	
						1826	05	+	**1826**	0617>	----	----	x---	----	----	2	
						1943	03		....	....	----	----	x---	----	----	2	
MACHIN, CERRO (Colombia)	**4.48 N**	**75.40 W**	**2650**	**Stratovolc**	**1501-04=**	**Tephrochronology**											
						T **-1250**v	....		....	....	----	----	xx--	----	----		
HUILA (Colombia)	**2.92 N**	**76.05 W**	**5365**	**Stratovolc**	**1501-05=**	**Historical**											
						1555e	....		....	....	----	----	x---	----	----		
PURACE (Colombia)	**2.32 N**	**76.40 W**	**4650**	**Stratovolcs**	**1501-06=**	**Historical**											
						C **-0160**t	....		....	....	x---	----	xx--	----	----		
						1816	....		....	....	----	----	----	----	----		
						1827	1118		....	....	x---	----	x---	x---	----	2	
						1835	0123		....	....	x---	----	x---	----	----	2	
						1840	....		....	....	x---	----	x---	----	----	2?	
						1847	1027		**1852**	....	x---	----	x---	----	-x--	3*	
						1860i	....		....	....	x---	----	x---	----	----	2?	
						1869	1004		**1869**	11	x---	----	xx--	----	--x-	3?	
						1870	10		....	....	x---	----	x---	----	----	2	
						1878	0831		....	....	x---	----	x---	----	----	2	
						1881	....		....	....	x---	----	x---	----	----	2	

VOLCANO NAME (Subregion) / ERUPTION — Area of Activity	LAT	LONG	ELEV (m)	TYPE	NUMBER	Status / Start Year	Start M-Dy	P	Stop Year	Stop M-Dy	Central / Flank vent / Radial fiss / Regional*	Submarine / New island / Subglacial / Crater lake	Explosive / Pyro flow / Phreatic / Fumarolic	Lava flow / Lava lake / Dome / Spine	Fatal / Damage / Mudflow / Tsunami	VEI	Vol L/T
PURACE (Colombia) *continued*						**1885**	0525		....	....	x---	----	x---	----	xx--	3	
						1899	....		....	....	x---	----	x---	----	----	2	
						1902?	....		....	....	x---	----	x---	----	----	2	
						1906	....		....	....	x---	----	x---	----	----	2	
						1924	....		....	....	x---	----	x---	----	----	2	
						1925	1012		**1925**	1105	x---	----	x---	----	----	2	
						1926	08		**1926**	09	x---	----	x---	----	----	2	
						1927	....		....	....	x---	----	x---	----	----	2	
						1946	03		**1946**	04	x---	----	x---	----	----	2	
						1947	0427		....	....	x---	----	x---	----	----	2	
						1949	0526		**1949**	0611	x---	----	x---	----	x---	2	
						1956<	....		....	....	x---	----	x---	----	----	2	
						1957	....		....	....	----	----	----	----	----	2?	
						1977	0319		**1977**	0328?	x---	----	x---	----	----	2	
SOTARA (Colombia)	**2.12 N**	**76.58 W**	**4400**	**Stratovolc ?**	**1501-061**	**Holocene**											
PETACAS (Colombia)	**1.57 N**	**76.78 W**	**4054**	**Lava dome**	**1501-062**	**Holocene?**											
DONA JUANA (Colombia)..........	**1.47 N**	**76.92 W**	**4150**	**Stratovolc**	**1501-07=**	**Historical**											
Northeastern caldera						C **-2550**w	....		....	....	x---	----	xx--	--x-	----	C	
						1897	1101		**1906**	....	x---	----	xx--	--x-	x-x-	4*	
GALERAS (Colombia)	**1.22 N**	**77.37 W**	**4276**	**Complx volc**	**1501-08=**	**Historical**											
						C **-2570**u	....		....	....	x---	----	xx--	----	--x-	3	-/6
						C **-2075**y	....		....	....	x---	----	xx--	----	----	2	-/6
						C **-0980**x	....		....	....	x---	----	xx--	----	----	2	-/6
						C **-0410**v	....		....	....	x---	----	xx--	----	--x-	2	-/6
						C **0810**x	....		....	....	x---	----	xx--	----	--x-	2	-/6
						1535	....		....	....	x---	----	x---	----	----	3↑	
						1580	1207		**1580**	1207	x---	----	x---	?---	----	4	
(eruption December 7, 1580)						X 1590	1207		....		----	----	----	----	----		
						1616	0704		**1616**	0704	x---	----	x---	?---	----	3↑	
						1670	....		**1736**	....	x---	----	x---	----	----	2*	
						1754	....		**1756**	....	x---	----	x---	----	----	2	
						1796	11		**1801**	....	x---	----	x---	x---	----	2	
						1823	0617		**1823**	0624	x---	----	x---	x---	----	2	
						1828	1024	+	**1834**	03	x---	----	x---	?---	----	3*	
						1836	....		....	....	x---	----	x---	----	----	2	
						1865	1002		**1870**	....	x---	----	xx--	x---	--x-	3*	7/6
						1889	0703		....	....	x---	----	x---	x---	----	2	
						1891	....		....	....	x---	----	x---	?---	----	2	
						1923	1208		....	....	x---	----	x---	----	----	2	
						1924	10		**1927**	....	x---	----	x---	x-x-	----	3*	
						? **1930**	0417		....	....	x---	----	?---	----	----		
						1932	1010		....	....	x---	----	x---	----	----	2	
						? **1933**	....		....	....	x---	----	?---	----	----		
						1936	0209		**1936**	0827?	x---	----	xx--	?---	----	2	
						? **1947**	0715		....	....	x---	----	?---	----	----	2?	
						1950	0112	+	**1950**	0905	x---	----	x---	----	----	2	
						? **1973**	05		....	....	x---	----	x---	----	----	2	
						1974	....		**1983>**	....	x---	----	x---	----	----	1?	
						1989	0219		**1989**	0509	x---	----	xxx-	----	----	2	-/5
						1990	0107	+	**1992**	0716	x---	----	x?x-	----	-xx-	2*	
						1993	0114	+	**1993**	0607>	x---	----	x---	----	xx--	2	-/6
AZUFRAL, VOLCAN (Colombia).....	**1.08 N**	**77.68 W**	**4070**	**Stratovolc**	**1501-09=**	**Radiocarbon**											
						C **-2095**v	....		....	....	x---	----	xx--	--x-	----		
						C **-1850?**	....		....	....	x---	----	x---	--x-	----		
						C **-1650**w	....		....	....	x---	----	xx--	--x-	----		
						C **-0930?**	....		....	....	x---	----	x---	----	----	P	
CUMBAL (Colombia)	**0.98 N**	**77.88 W**	**4764**	**Stratovolc**	**1501-10=**	**Historical**											
						1877	12		....	....	x---	----	x---	----	----	2	
						1926	1220		**1926**	1221	x---	----	x---	----	----	2	
NEGRO DE MAYASQUER, CERRO (*)	**0.828 N**	**77.964 W**	**4445**	**Stratovolc**	**1501-11=**	**Holocene?**											
(eruption possibly from Reventador)						@ **1936**	0717		....	....	?---	----	?---	----	----	2	

ECUADOR

VOLCANO NAME (Subregion) / ERUPTION — Area of Activity	LAT	LONG	ELEV (m)	TYPE	NUMBER	Status / Start Year	Start M-Dy	P	Stop Year	Stop M-Dy	Central / Flank vent / Radial fiss / Regional*	Submarine / New island / Subglacial / Crater lake	Explosive / Pyro flow / Phreatic / Fumarolic	Lava flow / Lava lake / Dome / Spine	Fatal / Damage / Mudflow / Tsunami	VEI	Vol L/T
SOCHE (Ecuador)	**0.552 N**	**77.580 W**	**3955**	**Stratovolc**	**1502-001**	**Radiocarbon**											
						C **-7720**r	....		....	....	x---	----	xx--	--x-	----	**5?**	
CUICOCHA (Ecuador)	**0.308 N**	**78.364 W**	**3246**	**Caldera**	**1502-002**	**Radiocarbon**											
						C **-1150**w	....		....	....	x---	----	xxx-	----	-x--	**5**	**-/9**
						C **-0950?**	....		....	....	x---	----	xx--	--x-	----		
MOJANDA (Ecuador)..............	**0.13 N**	**78.27 W**	**4294**	**Stratovolc**	**1502-003**	**Radiocarbon**											
						C **-1450**w	....		....	....	----	----	xxx-	----	----	2	
CAYAMBE (Ecuador)..............	**0.029 N**	**77.986 W**	**5790**	**Compnd volc**	**1502-004**	**Holocene**											
REVENTADOR (Ecuador)	**0.078 S**	**77.656 W**	**3562**	**Stratovolc**	**1502-01=**	**Historical**											
						1541	04		....	....	x---	----	x---	----	----	3↑	
						1590	....		....	....	x---	----	x---	----	----	3↑	
						1691	....		....	....	x---	----	x---	----	----	3↑	
						@ **1748<**	....		....	....	x---	----	x---	----	----	2?	
						1797	01		....	....	x---	----	x---	----	----	3	
						@ **1802**	04 ?		@**1802**	05 ?	x---	----	x---	----	----	2	
						1843<	....		....	....	x---	----	x---	----	----		
						1843	1207		....	....	x---	----	x---	----	----	3	
						1844	....		....	....	x---	----	x---	----	----	3	
						1856	1212		**1856**	1213	x---	----	x---	----	----	3	
						1871	0130		....	....	x---	----	x---	----	----	2	
						1894	....		....	....	x---	----	x---	----	----	3	
						1898	0408		**1906**	....	x---	----	xx--	----	----	3	
						1912	02		**1912**	03	x---	----	x---	----	----	3	
						1926	0105d		**1926**	05	x---	----	x---	----	----	3	
						1929	....		....	....	x---	----	x---	----	----	3	
						1936	0827		....	....	x---	----	x---	----	----	3	
						1944	0224		**1944**	0301	x---	----	x---	x---	--x-	3	
						1955	....		....	....	x---	----	x---	----	----	2	
						1958	11		....	....	x---	----	x---	----	----	3	
						1960	06		....	....	x---	----	x---	----	----	3	

VOLCANO NAME (Subregion) / ERUPTION — Area of Activity	LAT	LONG	ELEV (m)	TYPE	NUMBER	Status / Start Year	Start M-Dy	P	Stop Year	Stop M-Dy	Central / Flank vent / Radial fiss / Regional*	Submarine / New island / Subglacial / Crater lake	Explosive / Pyro flow / Phreatic / Fumarolic	Lava flow / Lava lake / Dome / Spine	Fatal / Damage / Mudflow / Tsunami	VEI	Vol L/T
REVENTADOR (Ecuador) *continued*						**1972**	07		**1972**	09	x---	----	x---	x---	--x-	2	7/-
						1973	11		**1974**	07	x---	----	x---	x---	--x-	3*	6/-
						1976	0104		**1976**	05	x---	----	xx--	x---	----	2	7/-
PULULAGUA (Ecuador)	**0.038 N**	**78.463 W**	**3356**	**Caldera**	**1502-011**	**Radiocarbon**											
						C **-0680**w	....		....	....	----	----	xx--	----	----		
						C **-0445**w	....		....	....	x---	----	xx--	--x-	-x--	**C**	
GUAGUA PICHINCHA (Ecuador)	**0.171 S**	**78.598 W**	**4784**	**Stratovolc**	**1502-02=**	**Historical**											
						C **-7000**?	....		....	....	x---	----	x---	--x-	----		
						C **-6650**?	....		....	....	x---	----	xx--	----	----		
						C **-6400**?	....		....	....	x---	----	xx--	--x-	----		
						C **-6300**?	....		....	....	x---	----	xx--	--x-	----		
						C **-6200**?	....		....	....	x---	----	xx--	----	----		
						T **-4850***	....		....	....	x---	----	x---	----	----		
						C **-3500**?	....		....	....	x---	----	x---	----	----		
						T **-2000***	....		....	....	x---	----	x---	----	--x-		
						C **0550**?	....		....	....	x---	----	xx--	----	----		
						C **0970**?	....		....	....	x---	----	xx--	----	----	**P**	
						? **1533**	....		....	....	x---	----	x-?-	----	----	2	
						? **1534**	....		....	....	x---	----	x-?-	----	----	2	
						? **1535**	....		....	....	x---	----	x-?-	----	----	2	
						? **1538**	....		....	....	x---	----	x-?-	----	----	3↑	
						? **1539**	....		....	....	x---	----	x-?-	----	----	2	
						? **1560**	....		....	....	x---	----	x-?-	----	----	2	
						1566	1017	+	**1566**	1116	x---	----	xx--	----	-x--	3↑	
						1575	0908		....	....	x---	----	xx--	----	----	2	
(perhaps confused with 1575 eruption)						? **1577**	....		....	....	x---	----	?---	----	----	2	
						? **1580**	....		....	....	x---	----	x-?-	----	----	2	
						1582	0605		**1598**	....	x---	----	x---	----	----	3*	
						1660	1027		**1660**	1128	x---	----	xx--	--x-	-xx-	4	-/8
						1830	....		....	....	x---	----	x-x-	----	----	2	
						1831	....		....	....	x---	----	x-x-	----	----	3	
						1868	0319		**1868**	0322	x---	----	x-x-	----	----	2	
						1868	08		....	....	x---	----	x-x-	----	----	2	
						1869	03		....	....	x---	----	x-x-	----	----	2	
						1869	0722	+	**1869**	0824	x---	----	x-x-	----	----	2	
						1881	0310		....	....	x---	----	x-x-	----	----	2	
NE side of 1660 lava dome						**1981**	0831e		**1982**	11 ?	x---	----	x-x-	----	----	1*	-/4
NE side of 1660 lava dome						**1985**	05		**1985**	06	x---	----	--x-	----	----	1	
NE side of 1660 lava dome						**1990**	0416		**1990**	0510	x---	----	--x-	----	----	1	
NE side of 1660 lava dome						**1993**	0309		**1993**	0312	x---	----	x-x-	----	x---	1	
ATACAZO (Ecuador)	**0.353 S**	**78.617 W**	**4463**	**Stratovolc**	**1502-021**	**Radiocarbon**											
Ninahuilca						C **-0420**u	....		....	....	x---	----	xx--	--x-	----	**P**	
CHACANA (Ecuador)	**0.375 S**	**78.25 W**	**4643**	**Caldera**	**1502-022**	**Historical**											
						T **-8050**?	....		....	....	x---	----	x---	----	----		
						C **-1580**j	....		....	....	x---	----	x---	----	----		
SW flank						**1760**	....		....	....	-x--	----	x---	x---	-x--	0	9/-
NE flank						**1773**	....		....	....	---x	----	----	x---	-x--	0	8/-
ANTISANA (Ecuador)	**0.481 S**	**78.141 W**	**5753**	**Stratovolc**	**1502-03=**	**Historical**											
(eruption possibly from Reventador)						@ **1590**?	....		....	....	----	----	x---	----	----	2?	
						? **1728**	....		....	....	-x--	----	----	x---	----	0	
NNE side of summit						**1801**	....		**1802**	05 >	x---	--x-	x---	x-?-	----	2	
PAN DE AZUCAR (Ecuador)	**0.43 S**	**77.72 W**	**3482**	**Stratovolc**	**1502-031**	**Holocene**											
SUMACO (Ecuador)	**0.538 S**	**77.626 W**	**3990**	**Stratovolc**	**1502-04=**	**Historical**											
						? **1650**t	....		....	....	x---	----	x---	----	----	3?	
						1895r	....		....	....	x---	----	x---	----	----	2?	
						? **1933**	02		....	....	x---	----	x---	----	----	2	
ILINIZA (Ecuador)	**0.659 S**	**78.714 W**	**5248**	**Stratovolc**	**1502-041**	**Holocene**											
COTOPAXI (Ecuador)	**0.677 S**	**78.436 W**	**5911**	**Stratovolc**	**1502-05=**	**Historical**											
						C **-0455**w	....		....	....	x---	----	xx--	----	xxx-		
(Cotopaxi ashfall?; source unknown)						? **1532**	1115		....	....	x---	----	x---	?---	-x?-	3	
(Cotopaxi ashfall?: source unknown)						? **1533**	10		?**1533**	11	x---	----	x---	x---	--x-	2	
						1534	06		**1534**	07	x---	----	x---	----	--x-	4	
						1698	....		....	....	x---	----	x---	----	xxx-	3?	
						1738	....		....	....	x---	----	x---	x---	--x-	2	
						1740	....		**1741**	....	x---	----	x---	----	----	2	
						1742	0615		**1742**	07	x---	----	x---	x---	xxx-	3?	
						1742	1209		....	....	x-x-	----	xx--	x---	xxx-	3?	
						1743	04		....	....	x---	----	x---	x---	-xx-	2	
						1743	0927		**1743**	1004	x---	----	x---	x---	--x-	2	
						1744	05		**1744**	12	x---	----	xx--	----	-xx-	4*	7/8
						1746	02		....	....	x---	----	x---	----	----	2	
						1747	....		**1749**	....	x---	----	x---	----	----	2	
						1750	0902a		**1750**	0904a	x---	----	x---	----	----	2	
						1766	0210		....	....	x---	----	x---	x---	-xx-	3	
						1768	0404		....	....	x---	----	x---	x---	xxx-	4	7/8
						1803	0104		**1803**	0105	x---	----	x---	x---	-xx-	3	
						1844	....		....	....	x---	----	x---	----	----	2	
						1845	04		....	....	x---	----	x---	----	----	2	
						1850	....		....	....	x---	----	x---	x---	--x-	2	
						1851	06		....	....	x---	----	x---	----	----	2	
						1852	....		....	....	x---	----	x---	----	----	2	
						1853	0913		**1853**	0915	x---	----	x---	x---	--x-	3	7/-
						1854	0403		....	....	x---	----	x---	x---	--x-	2	
						1854	0914		....	....	x---	----	x---	x---	--x-	2	
						1855	11		....	....	x---	----	x---	x---	--x-	2	
						1856	05		....	....	x---	----	x---	x---	--x-	2	
						1856	10		**1856**	12	x---	----	x---	x---	--x-	2	
						1857	....		....	....	x---	----	x---	----	----	2	
						1858	11		**1858**	12	x---	----	x---	x---	--x-	2	
						1859	....		....	....	x---	----	x---	----	----	2	
						1860	....		**1862**	....	x---	----	x---	----	----	2	
						1863	....		....	....	x---	----	x---	x---	--x-	2	
						1866	0921		**1866**	0926	x---	----	x---	x---	----	2	

VOLCANO NAME (Subregion) / ERUPTION — Area of Activity	LAT	LONG	ELEV (m)	TYPE	NUMBER	Status	Start Year	Start M-Dy	P	Stop Year	Stop M-Dy	Central / Flank vent / Radial fiss / Regional*	Submarine / New island / Subglacial / Crater lake	Explosive / Pyro flow / Phreatic / Fumarolic	Lava flow / Lava lake / Dome / Spine	Fatal / Damage / Mudflow / Tsunami	VEI	Vol L/T
COTOPAXI (Ecuador) *continued*							**1867**	....		....	....	x---	----	x---	----	----	2	
							1868	0815		**1868**	0816	x---	----	x---	----	----	2	
							1869	07		**1869**	08	x---	----	x---	----	----	3	
							1870	....		**1876**	....	x---	----	x---	----	----	2	
							1877	01		**1877**	0902	x---	----	xx--	x---	xxx-	4*	7/8
							1878	0823		**1878**	0824	x---	----	xx--	----	----	2	
							1879	0226		**1879**	0619	x---	----	x---	x---	----	2	
							1880	02		**1880**	07	x---	----	x---	x---	--x-	3*	
							1882	01		**1882**	03	x---	----	x---	----	----	2	
							1883	08		....	....	x---	----	x---	x---	--x-	2	
							1883	12		....	....	x---	----	x---	x---	--x-	2	
							1885	0723		....	....	x---	----	x---	x---	--x-	2	
							1886	01		....	....	x---	----	x---	----	----	2	
							1895	....		....	....	x---	----	x---	----	----	2	
							1903	0926	+	**1904**	12	x---	----	x---	x---	--x-	3*	
							1905	....		....	....	x---	----	x---	----	----	2	
							1906	0821	+	**1906**	0919	x---	----	x---	----	----	2	
							1907	06		....	....	x---	----	x---	----	----	2	
							1908	....		**1914**	....	x---	----	x---	----	----	1	
							1922	....		....	....	x---	----	x---	----	----	2	
							1926	....		....	....	x---	----	x---	----	----	2	
							1931	....		....	....	x---	----	x---	----	----	2	
							1939	0202		....	....	x---	----	x---	----	----	2	
							1940	....		....	....	x---	----	x---	----	----	2	
(press reports not confirmed)							? **1942**	0217		?**1942**	0219	x---	----	x---	x---	-x--	3?	
QUILOTOA (Ecuador)	**0.85 S**	**78.90 W**	**3914**	**Caldera**	**1502-06=**	**Radiocarbon**												
							C **1050**w	....		....	....	x---	----	xx--	----	-x--		
(confused with 1660 Pichincha eruption)							X 1660	1128		....	....	----	----	----	----	----		
							? **1725**	....		....	....	x---	---x	?---	----	----	2	
							? **1740**	12		....	....	x---	---x	?---	----	-x--	2	
							? **1759**	....		....	....	x---	---x	?---	----	----	2	
							? **1797**	0204		....	....	x---	---x	----	----	----		
LLANGANATE (Ecuador)	1.22 S	78.25 W			1502-07=	Not a Volcano												
TUNGURAHUA (Ecuador)	**1.467 S**	**78.442 W**	**5023**	**Stratovolc**	**1502-08=**	**Historical**												
							C **-1005**v	....		....	....	x---	----	xx--	----	--x-		
							C **-0265**v	....		....	....	x---	----	xx--	----	----		
							C **0765**x	....		....	....	x---	----	xx--	----	----	3?	-/7
(eruption possibly from Cotopaxi)							@ **1534**	02		....	....	x---	----	x---	----	----	3↑	
							? **1557**	....		....	....	x---	----	?---	----	----	2	
							? **1640**	....		....	....	x---	----	?---	----	----	2	
							1641	....		....	....	x---	----	xx--	----	-x--	3?	
							? **1644**	....		....	....	x---	----	?---	----	----	2	
							? **1646**	....		....	....	x---	----	?---	----	----	2	
							? **1757**	....		....	....	x---	----	?---	----	----	2	
(eruption began in 1773, not 1772)							**1773**	0204	+	**1773**	07 ?	x---	----	xx--	x---	-xx-	3*	
							1776	0103		....	....	x---	----	x-x-	----	----	2	
							? **1777**	....		....	....	x---	----	?---	?---	----	2	
							? **1781**	....		....	....	x---	----	----	?---	----	2	
							1857	0910		....	....	x---	----	x---	----	----	2?	
							? **1885**	01		?**1885**	1016	x---	----	?---	----	----	2?	
							1886	0111	+	**1888**a	....	x---	----	xx--	x---	xxx-	4	
							? **1900**	....		....	....	x---	----	?---	----	----	2?	
							1916	0303	+	**1925**	1201p	x---	----	xxx-	x---	-xx-	4*	
							1944	....		....	....	x---	----	x---	----	----	2	
TULABUG (Ecuador)	**1.780 S***	**78.613 W**	**3336**	**Scoria cones**	**1502-081**	**Holocene**												
SANGAY (Ecuador)	**2.03 S**	**78.33 W**	**5230**	**Stratovolc**	**1502-09=**	**Historical**												
							1628	10		....	....	----	----	x---	----	-x--	3↑	
							1728	0930p	+	**1916**<	....	x---	----	xx--	x-x-	----	3*	
							1934	0808	+	**1993**>	....	xx--	----	xx--	x---	x---	3*	
GALAPAGOS ISLANDS																		
FERNANDINA (Galapagos)	**0.37 S**	**91.55 W**	**1495**	**Shield**	**1503-01=**	**Historical**												
South flank							**1813**	0714<		....	....	-x-?	----	--?-	----	----	2	
							1814	07		**1814**	08	-?-?	----	?---	?---	----	2	
(western Galapagos)							@ **1817**<	....		....	....	-?--	----	x---	x---	----	2	
							1819	....		....	....	-?--	----	x---	x---	----	2	
East summit and SE flank							**1825**	0214		**1825**	10 >	---x	----	?---	x---	----	3	
East flank							**1846**	11		....	....	-?-?	----	----	x---	----	0	
							1888	....		....	....	----	----	----	----	----	1	
							1926	....		....	....	----	----	----	----	----		
South flank near Punta Mangle							**1927**	1213<		....	....	-x--	----	----	x---	----	0	
							1937	03		**1937**	04	-?--	----	----	?---	----	0	
SE, SW and west caldera rim							**1958**	09 ?		**1958**	1230>	--x-	----	----	xx--	----	2	7/-
SE flank							**1961**	0321a		**1961**	09	x-x-	----	x---	x---	----	2	
SE flank							**1968**	0521		**1968**	0523a	-x--	----	x---	x---	----	2	
West caldera wall							**1968**	0611		**1968**	0704<	x---	----	xxx-	x----	----	4	-/8
SE caldera bench							**1972**	0604q		....	....	x---	----	x---	x---	----	0	
ESE caldera wall							**1973**	1209		**1973**	1216a	x---	----	x---	x---	----	2	
SE caldera bench							**1977**	0323		**1977**	0327	x---	----	x---	x---	----	1	
NW caldera bench							**1978**	0808		**1978**	0826	x---	----	x---	x---	----	2	6/-
South caldera rim							**1981**	0801x		....	....	x---	----	----	x---	----	0	
NW corner of caldera							**1984**	0330		....	....	x---	----	x---	x---	----	1	
East caldera wall							**1988**	0914		**1988**	0916	x---	----	x-x-	x---	----	2?	6/-
Base of ESE and NE caldera wall							**1991**	0419		**1991**	0424	x---	----	x---	x---	----	2?	
ECUADOR, VOLCAN (Isabela I)	**0.02 S**	**91.546 W**	**790**	**Shield**	**1503-011**	**Holocene**												
WOLF, VOLCAN (Isabela I)	**0.02 N**	**91.35 W**	**1710**	**Shield**	**1503-02=**	**Historical**												
							1797	08		....	....	----	----	----	----	----		
							1800	0821		**1800**	0821	?---	----	x---	----	----	2?	
ESE flank							**1925**	0411		**1926**	0326>	-x--	----	----	x---	----	1	
							1933	....		....	....	-x--	----	----	?---	----	0	
							1935	02		....	....	----	----	----	----	----		
							1938	....		....	....	-x--	----	----	----	----		
SE flank (1200 m)							**1948**	0124		**1948**	0131>	-x--	----	x---	?---	----	2	
SE flank (610 m)							**1963**	0304		**1963**	0316>	-x--	----	----	x---	----	0	

VOLCANO NAME (Subregion) / ERUPTION — Area of Activity	LAT	LONG	ELEV (m)	TYPE	NUMBER	Status / Start Year	Start M-Dy	P	Stop Year	Stop M-Dy	ERUPTIVE CHARACTERISTICS (Central, Flank vent, Radial fiss, Regional* / Submarine, New island, Subglacial, Crater lake / Explosive, Pyro flow, Phreatic, Fumarolic / Lava flow, Lava lake, Dome, Spine / Fatal, Damage, Mudflow, Tsunami)	VEI	Vol L/T
WOLF, VOLCAN (Isabela I) *continued*						? 1973	1025		?1973	1029	---- ---- ---- ---- ----		
Caldera and SE flank (875 m)						**1982**	0828		**1982**	0906?	x-x- ---- x--- x--- ----	1	
DARWIN, VOLCAN (Isabela I)	**0.18 S**	**91.28 W**	**1330**	**Shield**	**1503-03=**	**Holocene**							
(more likely Darwin than Wolf or Alcedo)						@ 1813	0606		@1813	0607?	---- ---- x--- ---- ----	2?	
ALCEDO, VOLCAN (Isabela I)	**0.43 S**	**91.12 W**	**1130**	**Shield**	**1503-04=**	**Historical**							
SE flank near Cartago Bay						**1953g**	....		....	....	-x-- ---- ---- x--- ----	0	
(eruption more likely at Sierra Negra)						X 1954	1109		....	....	---- ---- ---- ---- ----		
NEGRA, SIERRA (Isabela I)	**0.83 S**	**91.17 W**	**1490**	**Shield**	**1503-05=**	**Historical**							
(south end of Isabela Island)						@ **1813**	0713		....	....	---- ---- x--- ---- ----	2?	
(Isabela Island)						@ **1817**	....		....	....	-x-- ---- ---- ---- ----		
(Isabela Island)						@ **1844**	....		....	....	---- ---- ---- x--- ----	0	
(Isabela Island)						@ **1860**	....		....	....	---- ---- x--- ---- ----	2	
						1911	1231y		....	....	---- ---- ---- ---- ----		
						1948	08		**1949**	02 ?	?--- ---- x--- ?--- ----	2	
Volcan Chico area & NW caldera rim						**1953**	0827		**1954**	01	---- ---- x--- x--- ----	3?	
Upper NNE flank						@ **1954**	1109		....	....	-x-- ---- x-x- x--- ----	2	
(Isabela Island)						@ **1957**	....		....	....	---- ---- ---- ---- ----		
Volcan Chico area & NW caldera rim						**1963**	0413		**1963**	05	---- ---- x--- x--- ----	2	
Volcan Chico						**1979**	1113		**1980**	0114>	---- ---- x--- x--- -x--	3	
AZUL, CERRO (Isabela I)	**0.90 S**	**91.42 W**	**1690**	**Shield**	**1503-06=**	**Historical**							
						1932	....		....	....	---- ---- ---- ---- ----	1?	
East flank (Cerro de Las Animas)						**1940**	....		....	....	-x-- ---- ---- x--- ----	0	
Caldera ring fracture						**1943**	0413b		**1943**	0511?	---- ---- x--- x--- x---	3	
						1948	0630p		....	....	---- ---- ---- x--- ----	0	
						1949?	....		....	....	x--x ---- ---- x--- ----	0	
						1951	....		....	....	---- ---- ---- ---- ----		
East flank						**1959**	0629		**1959**	0731?	---x ---- ---- x--- ----	2?	
North flank?						? **1968**	0612		....	....	---- ---- ?--- ---- ----		
East flank and summit						**1979**	0129		**1979**	0304>	xxx- ---- x--- x--- ----	2?	
PINTA (Galapagos)	**0.58 N**	**90.75 W**	**780**	**Shield**	**1503-07=**	**Historical**							
						1928	....		....	....	?--- ---- ---- ---- ----		
MARCHENA (Galapagos)	**0.33 N**	**90.47 W**	**343**	**Shield**	**1503-08=**	**Historical**							
West to SW caldera rim						**1991**	0925		**1991**	11 ?	x--- ---- x--- x--- ----	2	
GENOVESA (Galapagos)	**0.32 N**	**89.958 W**	**64**	**Shield**	**1503-081**	**Holocene**							
SANTIAGO (Galapagos)	**0.22 S**	**90.77 W**	**920**	**Shield**	**1503-09=**	**Historical**							
West flank (James Bay)						A **1759u**	....		....	....	-?-- ---- ---- x--- ----		
SE flank (Sullivan Bay?)						**1897**	....		....	....	-?-? ---- ---- x--- ----	0	
SE flank						**1904**	....		**1906**	1215q	-?-- ---- ---- ?--- ----	0	
SANTA CRUZ (Galapagos)	**0.62 S**	**90.33 W**	**864**	**Shield**	**1503-091**	**Holocene**							
FLOREANA (Galapagos)	**1.30 S**	**90.45 W**	**640**	**Shield**	**1503-10=**	**Holocene**							
(more likely Sierra Negra eruption)						X 1813	07		....	....	---- ---- ---- ---- ----		
SAN CRISTOBAL (Galapagos)	**0.88 S**	**89.50 W**	**759**	**Shield**	**1503-12-**	**Holocene**							

PERU

VOLCANO NAME (Subregion) / ERUPTION — Area of Activity	LAT	LONG	ELEV (m)	TYPE	NUMBER	Status / Start Year	Start M-Dy	P	Stop Year	Stop M-Dy	ERUPTIVE CHARACTERISTICS	VEI	Vol L/T
FIRURA, NEVADOS (Peru)	**15.23 S**	**72.63 W**	**5498**	**Stratovolcs**	**1504-00-**	**Holocene**							
COROPUNA (Peru)	**15.52 S**	**72.65 W**	**6377**	**Stratovolc**	**1504-001**	**Holocene**							
ANDAHUA VALLEY (Peru)	**15.42 S***	**72.33 W**	**4713**	**Cinder cones**	**1504-002**	**Holocene**							
						? **1913**	0306		....	....	---- ---- ---- ---- ----		
SABANCAYA (Peru)	**15.78 S**	**71.85 W**	**5967**	**Stratovolcs**	**1504-003**	**Historical**							
						1750	....		....	....	---- ---- ?--- ---- ----		
						1784	07		....	....	---- ---- ?--- ---- -x--		
						1986	12		....	....	x--- ---- x-?- ---- ----	1	
						1988	0622		....	....	x--- ---- x-x- ---- ----	1	
						1990	0528		**1992**	02 >	x--- ---- x--- ---- -xx-	3*	
QUIMSACHATA (Peru)	**14.37 S**	**71.17 W**	**3923**	**Lava dome**	**1504-004**	**Holocene**							
CHACHANI, NEVADO (Peru)	**16.191 S**	**71.530 W**	**6057**	**Stratovolc**	**1504-005**	**Holocene**							
MISTI, EL (Peru)	**16.294 S**	**71.409 W**	**5822**	**Stratovolc**	**1504-01=**	**Historical**							
						1454n	....		....	....	x--- ---- x--- ---- -x--	3↑	
						? **1542**	....		....	....	---- ---- ?--- ---- ----	2	
						? **1599**	....		....	....	---- ---- ?--- ---- ----	2	
						1677	....		....	....	---- ---- x--- ---- ----	2	
						1784	....		....	....	---- ---- x--- ---- ----	2	
						1787	....		....	....	---- ---- x--- ---- ----	2	
						? **1826**	....		....	....	---- ---- ?--? ---- ----	2	
						? **1830**	08		....	....	---- ---- ?--- ---- ----	2	
						? **1831**	08		....	....	x--- ---- ---- ---- ----		
						? **1869**	09		....	....	---- ---- ?--- ---- ----	2	
						? **1870**	03		....	....	---- ---- ?--- ---- ----	2	
UBINAS (Peru)	**16.355 S**	**70.903 W**	**5672**	**Stratovolc**	**1504-02=**	**Historical**							
						1550t	....		....	....	---- ---- x--- ---- ----	3?	
						1600	....		....	....	---- ---- ---- ---- ----	2?	
						1662	....		....	....	---- ---- ---- ---- ----	3?	
						1677	....		....	....	x--- ---- x--- ---- ----	2	
						1784	....		....	....	x--- ---- x--- ---- ----	2	
						? **1826**	....		....	....	---- ---- ---- ---- ----		
						1830	....		....	....	x--- ---- x--- ---- ----	2	
						1862	....		....	....	x--- ---- x--- ---- ----	2	
						1865	....		....	....	x--- ---- x--- ---- ----	2	
						1867	0524		**1867**	0528	x--- ---- x--- ---- ----	2	
						1869	10		....	....	x--- ---- x--- ---- ----	2	
						1906	10		....	....	x--- ---- x--- ---- ----	2	
						1907	....		....	....	x--- ---- x--- ---- ----	2	
						1937	06		....	....	x--- ---- x--- ---- -x--	2	
						1951	0723h		**1951**	07	x--- ---- x--- ---- ----	2	
						1956	05		**1956**	1021	x--- ---- x--- ---- -x--	2	
						1969	06		....	....	---- ---- x--x ---- -x--	2?	
HUAYNAPUTINA (Peru)	**16.608 S**	**70.85 W**	**4850**	**Stratovolc ?**	**1504-03=**	**Historical**							
						1600	0219		**1600**	10 ?	x--- ---- xx-- ---- xxx-	6?	-/10
						1667	....		....	....	---- ---- x--- ---- ----	2?	
TICSANI (Peru)	**16.755 S**	**70.595 W**	**5408**	**Stratovolc**	**1504-031**	**Holocene**							

VOLCANO NAME (Subregion) / ERUPTION — Area of Activity	LAT	LONG	ELEV (m)	TYPE	NUMBER	Status / Start Year	Start M-Dy	P	Stop Year	Stop M-Dy	Central, Flank vent, Radial fiss, Regional*	Submarine, New island, Subglacial, Crater lake	Explosive, Pyro flow, Phreatic, Fumarolic	Lava flow, Lava lake, Dome, Spine	Fatal, Damage, Mudflow, Tsunami	VEI	Vol L/T
TUTUPACA (Peru)	**17.025 S**	**70.358 W**	**5815**	**Stratovolc**	**1504-04=**	**Historical**											
						1780	....		....	....	----	----	x---	----	----	2	
						1802	0330		**1802**	07	----	----	x---	----	----	3	
						1862	04		**1862**	05	----	----	x---	----	----	2	
						1902	06	+	**1902**	11	----	----	x---	----	----	2	
YUCAMANE (Peru)	**17.18 S**	**70.20 W**	**5550**	**Stratovolc**	**1504-05-**	**Historical**											
						1787	....		....	....	----	----	----	----	----		
CASIRI, NEVADOS (Peru)	**17.47 S**	**69.82 W**	**5650**	**Stratovolc**	**1504-06-**	**Holocene**											

CHILE - N, BOLIVIA, & ARGENTINA

VOLCANO NAME (Subregion) / ERUPTION — Area of Activity	LAT	LONG	ELEV (m)	TYPE	NUMBER	Status / Start Year	Start M-Dy	P	Stop Year	Stop M-Dy	Central, Flank vent, Radial fiss, Regional*	Submarine, New island, Subglacial, Crater lake	Explosive, Pyro flow, Phreatic, Fumarolic	Lava flow, Lava lake, Dome, Spine	Fatal, Damage, Mudflow, Tsunami	VEI	Vol L/T
TACORA (Chile-N)	**17.72 S**	**69.77 W**	**5980**	**Stratovolc**	**1505-01=**	**Fumarolic**											
						? **1930**	....		....	....	----	----	----	----	----		
						? **1937**	0805		....	....	----	----	?---	----	----		
LEXONE (Chile-N)	**17.87 S**	**69.48 W**	**5340**	**Lava domes**	**1505-011**	**Holocene**											
PATILLA PATA (Bolivia)	**18.05 S**	**69.03 W**	**5300**	**Stratovolc**	**1505-012**	**Holocene?**											
ANALLAJSI, NEVADO (Bolivia)	**17.92 S**	**68.92 W**	**5750**	**Stratovolc**	**1505-013**	**Holocene?**											
MACIZO DE LARANCAGUA (Bolivia)	**18.25 S**	**68.53 W**	**5520**	**Stratovolc**	**1505-014**	**Holocene?**											
MACIZO DE PACUNI (Bolivia)	**18.32 S**	**68.80 W**	**5400**	**Stratovolc**	**1505-015**	**Holocene?**											
PARINACOTA (Chile/Bolivia)	**18.17 S**	**69.15 W**	**6348**	**Stratovolc**	**1505-016**	**Holocene**											
ACOTANGO (Chile/Bolivia)	**18.37 S**	**69.05 W**	**6052**	**Stratovolcs**	**1505-017**	**Holocene**											
GUALLATIRI (Chile-N)	**18.42 S**	**69.17 W**	**6071**	**Stratovolc**	**1505-02=**	**Historical**											
						1825q	....		....	....	x---	----	x---	----	----	2?	
						? **1908**	....		....	....	----	----	----	----	----		
						1913	....		....	....	x---	----	x---	----	----	2	
						1959	0715e		....	....	x---	----	x---	----	----	2	
						1960	1202		....	....	----	--x-	x---	----	----	2	
						? **1985**	1201		....	....	----	----	--?-	----	----		
COLLUMA, CERRO (Bolivia)	**18.50 S**	**68.07 W**	**3876**	**Maar**	**1505-021**	**Holocene?**											
SACABAYA, VOLCAN DE (Bolivia)	**18.62 S**	**68.75 W**	**4215**	**Cinder cone**	**1505-022**	**Holocene**											
ARINTICA, VOLCAN (Chile-N)	**18.73 S**	**69.05 W**	**5597**	**Stratovolc**	**1505-023**	**Holocene**											
TATA SABAYA (Bolivia)	**19.13 S**	**68.53 W**	**5430**	**Stratovolc**	**1505-024**	**Holocene**											
ISLUGA (Chile-N)	**19.15 S**	**68.83 W**	**5050**	**Stratovolc**	**1505-03=**	**Historical**											
						1863	08		....	....	x---	----	----	----	----	1?	
						1868	....		....	....	----	----	----	----	----	2?	
						1869	08		....	....	x---	----	----	----	----	2	
						1877	....		....	....	----	----	----	----	----	2?	
						1878	02		....	....	x---	----	----	x---	-x--	2	
						1885	....		....	....	----	----	----	----	----	1?	
						1913	....		....	....	----	----	x---	----	----	1?	
						? **1960**	....		....	....	----	----	----	----	----	2?	
PUCHULDIZA (Chile-N)	**19.42 S**	**68.97 W**	**4500**	**Hydrothrm fld**	**1505-031**	**Pleistocene-Geysers**											
PINA, CERRO (Chile-N)	**19.492 S**	**68.65 W**	**4037**	**Unknown**	**1505-032**	**Holocene?**											
NUEVO MUNDO (Bolivia)	**19.78 S**	**66.48 W**	**5438**	**Lava domes**	**1505-033**	**Holocene**											
IRRUPUTUNCU (Chile/Bolivia)	**20.73 S**	**68.55 W**	**5163**	**Stratovolc**	**1505-04=**	**Holocene**											
(unconfirmed press reports)						? **1989**	12		....	....	----	----	----	----	----		
UNNAMED (Chile-N)	**20.83 S**	**68.63 W**	**4200**	**Pumice cone**	**1505-041**	**Holocene?**											
PAMPA LUXSAR (Bolivia)	**20.85 S***	**68.20 W**	**5543**	**Volc field**	**1505-042**	**Holocene**											
OLCA-PARUMA (Chile/Bolivia)	**20.93 S**	**68.48 W**	**5407**	**Stratovolcs**	**1505-05=**	**Historical**											
						1865	....		**1867**	....	----	----	----	----	----		
AUCANQUILCHA, CERRO (Chile-N)	**21.22 S**	**68.47 W**	**6176**	**Stratovolc**	**1505-051**	**Holocene**											
SAN AGUSTIN, CERRO (Bolivia)	**21.25 S**	**67.75 W**	**4980**	**Stratovolc**	**1505-052**	**Holocene?**											
OLLAGUE (Chile/Bolivia)	**21.30 S**	**68.18 W**	**5868**	**Stratovolc**	**1505-06=**	**Holocene**											
						? **1903**	1208		....	....	----	----	----	----	----		
YUMIA, CERRO (Bolivia)	**21.50 S**	**67.50 W**	**4050**	**Cone**	**1505-061**	**Holocene?**											
ESCALA (Bolivia)	**21.60 S**	**66.88 W**	**4000**	**Lava dome**	**1505-062**	**Holocene**											
SANTA ISABEL, CERRO (Bolivia)	**21.67 S**	**66.50 W**	**5100**	**Stratovolc**	**1505-063**	**Holocene?**											
MOIRO, CERRO (Bolivia)	**21.68 S**	**67.47 W**	**4250**	**Scoria cone**	**1505-064**	**Holocene?**											
AZUFRE, CERRO DEL (Chile-N)	**21.78 S**	**68.23 W**	**5486**	**Stratovolc**	**1505-065**	**Holocene**											
SAN PEDRO (Chile-N)	**21.88 S**	**68.40 W**	**6145**	**Stratovolcs**	**1505-07=**	**Historical**											
						? **1870**	....		....	....	----	----	----	----	----		
						1877?	....		....	....	x---	----	----	----	----	2	
						1891?	....		....	....	x---	----	----	----	----	2	
						1901	0525		**1901**	08	x---	----	----	----	-x--	2	
						1911	09		....	....	----	----	x---	----	----	2	
						? **1916**	....		....	....	----	----	----	----	----		
						? **1917**	....		....	....	----	----	----	----	----		
						? **1923**	....		....	....	----	----	----	----	----		
						1938	02		....	....	----	----	x---	----	----	2	
						? **1960**	1202		....	....	----	----	?--?	----	----	2	
CHASCON, CERRO (Bolivia)	**21.88 S**	**67.90 W**	**5125**	**Lava dome**	**1505-071**	**Holocene**											
CHAO (Chile-N)	**22.12 S**	**68.15 W**	**5100**	**Lava dome**	**1505-072**	**Holocene**											
TOCONCE, CERRO (Chile-N)	**22.20 S**	**68.10 W**	**5435**	**Stratovolc**	**1505-073**	**Holocene**											
QUETENA (Bolivia)	**22.25 S**	**67.42 W**	**5730**	**Fissure vent**	**1505-074**	**Holocene?**											
UTURUNCO (Bolivia)	**22.27 S**	**67.22 W**	**6008**	**Stratovolc**	**1505-075**	**Holocene**											
TATIO (Chile-N)	**22.35 S**	**68.03 W**	**4280**	**Hydrothrm fld**	**1505-08=**	**Pleistocene-Geysers**											
TOCORPURI, CERROS DE (Chile/Bol)	**22.43 S**	**67.90 W**	**5808**	**Stratovolc**	**1505-081**	**Holocene**											
PUTANA (Chile-N)	**22.57 S**	**67.87 W**	**5890**	**Stratovolc**	**1505-09=**	**Historical**											
						1810j	....		....	....	----	----	----	----	----		
						1972	....		....	....	----	----	----	----	----		
SAIRECABUR (Chile/Bolivia)	**22.73 S**	**67.88 W**	**5971**	**Stratovolcs**	**1505-091**	**Holocene**											
LICANCABUR (Chile/Bolivia)	**22.83 S**	**67.88 W**	**5916**	**Stratovolc**	**1505-092**	**Holocene**											
GUAYAQUES (Chile/Bolivia)	**22.88 S**	**67.58 W**	**5598**	**Lava domes**	**1505-093**	**Holocene**											
PURICO COMPLEX (Chile-N)	**23.00 S**	**67.75 W**	**5703**	**Stratovolcs**	**1505-094**	**Holocene**											
COLACHI (Chile-N)	**23.23 S**	**67.65 W**	**5631**	**Stratovolc**	**1505-095**	**Holocene**											
ACAMARCHI (Chile-N)	**23.30 S**	**67.62 W**	**6046**	**Stratovolc**	**1505-096**	**Holocene?**											
OVERO, CERRO (Chile-N)	**23.35 S**	**67.67 W**	**4555**	**Maar**	**1505-097**	**Holocene**											
LASCAR (Chile-N)	**23.37 S**	**67.73 W**	**5592**	**Stratovolcs**	**1505-10=**	**Historical**											
Lascar II						C -7050?	....		....	....	x---	----	xx--	----	----		
						1848	....		....	....	x---	----	x---	----	----	2	
						? **1853**	....		....	....	----	----	----	----	----	2?	

VOLCANO NAME (Subregion) / ERUPTION — Area of Activity	LAT	LONG	ELEV (m)	TYPE	NUMBER	Status / Start Year	Start M-Dy	P	Stop Year	Stop M-Dy	Central / Flank vent / Radial fiss / Regional*	Submarine / New island / Subglacial / Crater lake	Explosive / Pyro flow / Phreatic / Fumarolic	Lava flow / Lava lake / Dome / Spine	Fatal / Damage / Mudflow / Tsunami	VEI	Vol L/T
LASCAR (Chile-N) *continued*						**1854**	0120		**1854**	0130	----	----	x---	----	----	1	
						1858	04		**1858**	12	----	----	x---	----	----	2?	
						1875	....		....	....	x---	----	x---	----	----	2	
						1883	....		**1885**	....	----	----	x-?-	----	----	2	
						1898	....		....	....	----	----	x---	----	----	2	
						1902	....		....	....	----	----	x---	----	----	2?	
						1933	1009		**1933**	12	x---	----	x---	----	----	2	
						1940	....		....	....	----	----	x---	----	----	2	
East summit crater....................						**1951**	11		**1952**	0219	x---	----	x---	----	----	2?	
						1954	06		**1954**	07	----	----	----	----	----	2?	
						1959	11	+	**1968**	0131>	x---	----	x-x-	----	----	2*	
						1969	0516		....	....	----	----	----	----	----		
						1972	....		....	....	----	----	x---	----	----	2?	
						1974	07		**1974**	09	x---	----	x---	----	----	1	
Western crater of east summit cone.......						? **1985**	03 ?		?**1985**	07 ?	x---	----	----	-?--	----	0	
Western crater of east summit cone.......						**1986**	0914		**1986**	0916	x---	----	x---	----	----	3*	-/7
Western crater of east summit cone.......						**1987**	11 ?		**1989**	11	x---	----	x-x-	--x-	----	2*	6/-
East summit cone....................						**1990**	0220	+	**1990**	0406	x---	----	x---	----	----	3	
						1990	1124		....	....	----	----	x---	----	----	1	
						1991	1021		**1992**	0523?	x---	----	x---	--x-	----	2	-/6
Western crater of east summit cone.......						**1993**	0130	+	**1993**	0508	x---	----	xxx-	--x-	-x--	4*	6/8
						1993	1217		....	....	x---	----	x---	----	----	2	
CHILIQUES (Chile-N)..............	**23.58**	**S 67.70**	**W 5778**	**Stratovolc**	**1505-101**	**Holocene**											
CORDON DE PUNTAS NEGRAS ("). .	**23.75**	**S 67.53**	**W 5852**	**Stratovolcs**	**1505-102**	**Holocene**											
CORDON CHALVIRI (Chile-N)	**23.85**	**S 67.62**	**W 5623**	**Stratovolcs**	**1505-103**	**Holocene**											
TUJLE, CERRO (Chile-N)	**23.83**	**S 67.95**	**W 3550**	**Maar**	**1505-104**	**Holocene**											
PULAR (Chile-N)	**24.18**	**S 68.05**	**W 6233**	**Stratovolcs**	**1505-105**	**Holocene**											
						? **1990**	0424		?**1990**	0424	----	----	?---	----	----	1?	
NEGRILLAR, EL (Chile-N)..........	**24.18**	**S* 68.25**	**W 3500**	**Pyrocl cones**	**1505-106**	**Holocene?**											
ARACAR (Argentina)..............	**24.27**	**S 67.77**	**W 6082**	**Stratovolc**	**1505-107**	**Historical**											
						1993	0328		....	....	x---	----	x-x-	----	----	2	
SOCOMPA (Chile/Argentina)........	**24.40**	**S 68.25**	**W 6051**	**Stratovolc**	**1505-108**	**Radiocarbon**											
						C **-5250?**	....		....	....	x---	----	xx--	----	----		
NEGRILLAR, LA (Chile-N)..........	**24.28**	**S 68.60**	**W 4109**	**Pyrocl cones**	**1505-109**	**Holocene?**											
LLULLAILLACO (Chile/Argentina) ...	**24.72**	**S 68.53**	**W 6739**	**Stratovolc**	**1505-11=**	**Historical**											
						1854	0210		....	....	----	----	x---	----	----	2	
						1868	09		....	....	--x-	----	----	?---	----	0	
						1877	05		....	....	----	----	x---	----	----	2	
TUZGLE, CERRO (Argentina)	**24.05**	**S 66.48**	**W 5550**	**Stratovolc**	**1505-111**	**Holocene?**											
ESCORIAL, CERRO (Chile/Argentina)	**25.08**	**S 68.37**	**W 5447**	**Stratovolc**	**1505-112**	**Holocene**											
LASTARRIA (Chile/Argentina).......	**25.17**	**S 68.50**	**W 5697**	**Stratovolc**	**1505-12=**	**Holocene**											
CORDON DEL AZUFRE (Chile/Arg.). .	**25.33**	**S 68.52**	**W 5463**	**Complx volc**	**1505-121**	**Holocene**											
BAYO, CERRO (Chile/Argentina)	**25.42**	**S 68.58**	**W 5401**	**Complx volc**	**1505-122**	**Holocene**											
ANTOFALLA, VOLCAN (Argentina) . .	**25.53**	**S 68.00**	**W 6100**	**Stratovolc**	**1505-123**	**Fumarolic**											
						? **1901**	....		....	....	----	----	----	----	----		
						? **1911**	....		....	....	----	----	----	----	----		
ANTOFAGASTA DE LA SIERRA ("). .	**26.08**	**S* 67.50**	**W 4000**	**Scoria cones**	**1505-124**	**Holocene**											
NEVADA, SIERRA (Chile/Argentina). .	**26.48**	**S* 68.58**	**W 6127**	**Volc field**	**1505-125**	**Holocene**											
CONDOR, CERRO EL (Argentina) ...	**26.62**	**S 68.35**	**W 6532**	**Stratovolc**	**1505-126**	**Holocene**											
PEINADO (Argentina).............	**26.62**	**S 68.15**	**W 5740**	**Stratovolc**	**1505-127**	**Holocene**											
ROBLEDO (Argentina).............	**26.77**	**S 67.72**	**W 4400**	**Caldera**	**1505-128**	**Holocene**											
FALSO AZUFRE (Chile/Argentina) ...	**26.80**	**S 68.37**	**W 5890**	**Complx volc**	**1505-129**	**Holocene**											
OJOS DEL SALADO, NEVADOS ("). .	**27.12**	**S 68.53**	**W 6887**	**Stratovolc**	**1505-13=**	**Holocene**											
TIPAS (Argentina)	**27.20**	**S 68.55**	**W 6660**	**Complx volc**	**1505-131**	**Holocene**											
COPIAPO (Chile-N)	**27.30**	**S 69.13**	**W 6052**	**Stratovolc**	**1505-14-**	**Uncertain**											

CHILE - ISLANDS

VOLCANO NAME (Subregion) / ERUPTION — Area of Activity	LAT	LONG	ELEV (m)	TYPE	NUMBER	Status / Start Year	Start M-Dy	P	Stop Year	Stop M-Dy	Central / Flank vent / Radial fiss / Regional*	Submarine / New island / Subglacial / Crater lake	Explosive / Pyro flow / Phreatic / Fumarolic	Lava flow / Lava lake / Dome / Spine	Fatal / Damage / Mudflow / Tsunami	VEI	Vol L/T
SAN FELIX (Chile-Is)..............	**26.27**	**S 80.12**	**W 183**	**Shield**	**1506-01=**	**Holocene**											
ROBINSON CRUSOE (Chile-Is)	**33.658**	**S 78.85**	**W 922**	**Shields**	**1506-02=**	**Historical**											
						? **1743**	....		....	....	----	----	----	----	----		
1.6 km north of Punta Bacalao...........						**1835**	0220		**1835**	0221	-x--	x---	x---	----	-x-x	1?	
UNNAMED (Chile-Is)	**33.62**	**S 76.83**	**W -642**	**Submarine**	**1506-04=**	**Uncertain**											
						? **1839**	0212		?**1839**	0213	----	??--	----	----	----		

CHILE-C & ARGENTINA

VOLCANO NAME (Subregion) / ERUPTION — Area of Activity	LAT	LONG	ELEV (m)	TYPE	NUMBER	Status / Start Year	Start M-Dy	P	Stop Year	Stop M-Dy	Central / Flank vent / Radial fiss / Regional*	Submarine / New island / Subglacial / Crater lake	Explosive / Pyro flow / Phreatic / Fumarolic	Lava flow / Lava lake / Dome / Spine	Fatal / Damage / Mudflow / Tsunami	VEI	Vol L/T
TUPUNGATITO (Chile/Argentina)	**33.40**	**S 69.80**	**W 6000**	**Stratovolc**	**1507-01=**	**Historical**											
						@ **1829**	....		....	....	?---	----	----	----	----	2	
						? **1835**	....		....	....	----	----	?---	----	----	2	
						1861	....		....	....	----	----	?---	----	----	2	
						? **1881**	....		....	....	----	----	----	----	----		
						1889	....		**1890**	....	----	----	x---	----	----	2	
						1897	01	+	**1897**	0412>	----	----	x---	----	----	2	
						1901	04		....	....	----	----	x---	----	----	2	
						1907	0215		....	....	----	----	x---	----	----	2	
						1925	....		....	....	----	----	x---	----	----	2	
						1946	....		**1947**	....	----	----	----	----	----	2	
						1958	01		....	....	x---	----	----	----	----	2	
						1959	0326e		....	....	x---	----	x---	----	----	2	
						1959	1016		....	....	----	----	x---	----	----	2	
						1960	0715e		....	....	x---	----	----	x---	----	2	
						1961	0505d	+	**1961**	08 >	x---	----	x---	----	----	2	
						1964	0803	+	**1964**	0919>	x---	----	x---	----	----	2	
						1968	....		....	....	----	----	----	----	----		
SW crater..........................						**1980**	0110		**1980**	0111	x---	----	x---	----	----	2	
NW craters.........................						**1986**	0120		**1986**	0120	x---	----	x-x-	----	----	1	
SAN JOSE (Chile-C)	**33.782**	**S 69.897**	**W 5856**	**Stratovolc**	**1507-02=**	**Historical**											
						1822	1119		**1838**	....	x---	----	x---	----	----	2	
						1881	....		....	....	x---	----	x---	----	----	2	
						1889	....		**1890**	....	----	----	x---	----	----	2	
						1895	....		**1897**	....	----	----	x---	----	----	2	

VOLCANO NAME (Subregion) / ERUPTION — Area of Activity	LAT	LONG	ELEV (m)	TYPE	NUMBER	Status / Start Year	Start M-Dy	P	Stop Year	Stop M-Dy	Central Flank vent Radial fiss Regional*	Submarine New island Subglacial Crater lake	Explosive Pyro flow Phreatic Fumarolic	Lava flow Lava lake Dome Spine	Fatal Damage Mudflow Tsunami	VEI	Vol L/T
SAN JOSE (Chile-C) *continued* — (fumarolic activity only)						X 1931	....		....	....	x---	----	---x	----	----		
(fumarolic activity only)						X 1941	....		....	....	x---	----	---x	----	----		
						1959	....		....	....	----	----	x---	----	----	2	
						1960	....		....	....	----	----	x---	----	----	2	
MAIPO (Chile/Argentina)	**34.161 S**	**69.833 W**	**5264**	**Caldera**	**1507-021**	**Historical**											
						? **1822**	....		....	....	----	----	----	----	----		
						1826	0301		....	....	----	----	x---	----	----		
						1905	1028?		....	....	----	----	----	----	----		
						1912	....		....	....	----	----	?---	----	----		
PALOMO (Chile-C)	**34.608 S**	**70.295 W**	**4860**	**Stratovolc**	**1507-022**	**Holocene**											
TINGUIRIRICA (Chile-C)	**34.814 S**	**70.352 W**	**4280**	**Stratovolc**	**1507-03=**	**Historical**											
						1917	....		....	....	----	----	--?-	----	----	1?	
PLANCHON-PETEROA (Chile-C)	**35.240 S**	**70.570 W**	**4107**	**Calderas**	**1507-04=**	**Historical**											
Peteroa						**1660**	....		....	....	----	----	----	----	----	3↑	
Peteroa (2 km S of Planchon summit)						**1762**	1203		....	....	x---	----	x---	----	----	4	
Peteroa						**1835**	....		....	....	x---	----	----	----	----	2	
Peteroa						**1837**	02		....	....	x---	----	----	x---	--x-	2	
						? **1842**	....		....	....	----	----	----	----	----		
Peteroa						**1860**	....		....	....	x---	----	x---	----	----	2	
						? **1869**	....		....	....	----	----	----	----	----		
						? **1872**	....		....	....	----	----	----	----	----		
Peteroa						**1878**	....		....	....	x---	----	----	----	----	2	
Peteroa (SE of 1762 crater)						**1889**	09		**1894**?	....	x---	----	x---	----	----	2	
Petoroa (south of 1889-94 crater)						**1937**	04		**1937**	0505d	x---	----	x---	x---	----	2	
Peteroa						**1938**	09		**1938**	10	x---	----	?-x-	----	----	2	
Petoroa (1889-94 crater)						**1959**	1106		....	....	x---	----	x---	----	----	1	
Petoroa (1889-94 crater)						**1960**	0710		....	....	x---	----	x---	----	----	1	
Peteroa						**1962**	01		....	....	x---	----	x---	----	----	1	
Peteroa (1889-94 crater)						**1967**	....		....	....	x---	----	--?-	----	----		
Peteroa						**1991**	0209		**1991**	0302b	x---	---x	x---	----	----	2	
MONDACA (Chile-C)	**35.464 S**	**70.800 W**	**2048**	**Lava dome**	**1507-041**	**Holocene**											
CALABOZOS (Chile-C)	**35.558 S**	**70.496 W**	**3508**	**Caldera**	**1507-042**	**Holocene**											
DESCABEZADO GRANDE (Chile-C)	**35.58 S**	**70.75 W**	**3953**	**Stratovolc**	**1507-05=**	**Historical**											
Upper NNE slope						**1932**	0605e		**1933**	....	-x--	----	x-x-	----	----	3	
AZUL, CERRO [QUIZAPU] (Chile-C)	**35.653 S**	**70.761 W**	**3788**	**Stratovolc**	**1507-06=**	**Historical**											
Quizapu						**1846**	1126		**1853**?	....	--x-	----	x---	x---	----	2	**9/-**
Quizapu						? **1903**	01		....	....	-x--	----	--?-	----	----	2?	
Quizapu						**1906**	....		....	....	-x--	----	x-x-	----	----	2	
Quizapu						**1907**	0728		....	....	-x--	----	x-x-	----	----	2	
Quizapu						**1912**	02		....	....	-x--	----	x-x-	----	----	2	
Quizapu						? **1913**	0115q		....	....	-x--	----	--?-	----	----	2?	
Quizapu						**1914**	0908		....	....	-x--	----	x-x-	----	----	3	
Quizapu						**1916**	....	+	**1932**	0421	-x--	----	xxx-	----	-x--	**5***	**-/9**
Quizapu						**1933**	....		**1938**	0725?	-x--	----	x---	----	----	2	
Quizapu						**1949**	0415e		....	....	-x--	----	x-x-	----	----	2?	
Quizapu						**1967**	....		....	....	-x--	----	x-x-	----	----	2?	
HORNITOS, LOS (Chile-C)	**35.725 S**	**70.808 W**	**2000**	**Cinder cones**	**1507-061**	**Holocene**											
MAULE, LAGUNA DEL (Chile-C)	**36.02 S***	**70.58 W**	**3092**	**Stratovolcs**	**1507-062**	**Holocene**											
SAN PEDRO-PELLADO (Chile-C)	**35.989 S**	**70.849 W**	**3621**	**Stratovolcs**	**1507-063**	**Holocene**											
LONGAVI, NEVADO DE (Chile-C)	**36.193 S**	**71.161 W**	**3242**	**Stratovolc**	**1507-064**	**Holocene**											
BLANCA, LOMA (Chile-C)	**36.286 S**	**71.009 W**	**2268**	**Stratovolc**	**1507-065**	**Holocene**											
RESAGO, VOLCAN (Chile-C)	**36.45 S**	**70.92 W**	**1550**	**Cinder cone**	**1507-066**	**Holocene**											
PAYUN MATRU, CERRO (Argentina)	**36.42 S**	**69.20 W**	**3691**	**Shield**	**1507-067**	**Holocene**											
DOMUYO, VOLCAN (Argentina)	**36.63 S**	**70.42 W**	**4709**	**Stratovolc**	**1507-068**	**Holocene?**											
CHILLAN, NEVADOS DE (Chile-C)	**36.863 S**	**71.377 W**	**3212**	**Stratovolc**	**1507-07=**	**Historical**											
Volcan Viejo						**1650**t	....		....	....	----	----	x---	----	----	3?	
Volcan Viejo						**1750**	....		**1751**	....	----	----	?---	----	----	3↑	
(north of Antuco)						@ **1752**	0130		....	....	----	----	----	----	----	2?	
W flank of Cerro Blanco (Cerro Negro)						**1861**	06		**1862**	12	-x--	----	x---	x---	--x-	3	
West flank of Cerro Blanco						**1864**	....		**1865**	....	-x--	----	x---	----	--x-	3	
						1872	....		....	....	----	----	----	----	----		
						1877	....		....	....	----	----	----	----	----		
						1883	....		....	....	----	----	x---	----	----	2?	
Volcan Viejo						**1891**	....		....	....	----	----	x---	----	----	2	
Volcan Viejo						**1898**	....		....	....	----	----	x---	----	----	2	
Volcan Nuevo						**1906**	0806		**1906**	12	-x--	----	x---	----	----	2	
Volcan Nuevo						**1923**	....		....	....	-x--	----	x---	----	----		
Volcan Nuevo						**1929**	....		....	....	-x--	----	x---	----	----	2?	
Volcan Nuevo						**1934**	0117		....	....	----	----	x---	----	----	2?	
Volcan Nuevo						**1945**	....		....	....	-x--	----	x---	----	----		
Volcan Nuevo						**1946**	....		**1947**	....	----	----	x---	----	----	2?	
Volcan Nuevo						**1965**	....		....	....	-x--	----	?---	----	----		
Volcan Nuevo						**1972**	....		....	....	-x--	----	----	----	----		
SE flank of Volcan Nuevo						**1973**	07		**1987**>	....	-x--	----	xx--	x-x-	----	2*	5/-
TROMEN (Argentina)	**37.142 S**	**70.03 W**	**3978**	**Stratovolc**	**1507-071**	**Holocene**											
						? **1822**	....		....	....	----	----	----	----	----		
PUESTO CORTADERAS (Argentina)	**37.55 S**	**69.62 W**	**970**	**Pyrocl cone**	**1507-072**	**Holocene**											
ANTUCO (Chile-C)	**37.406 S**	**71.349 W**	**2979**	**Stratovolc**	**1507-08=**	**Historical**											
						C **-7750**?	....		....	....	x---	----	--x-	----	----		
						1750j	....		....	....	----	----	x---	----	----	2	
						1752	0131		**1752**	0201	x---	----	x---	----	----	3?	
						1806	....		....	....	----	----	----	----	----		
						1820	....		....	....	x---	----	----	----	----	2	
						1828	....		....	....	x---	----	x---	x---	----	1	
						1839	....		....	....	x---	----	----	----	----	2	
						1845	....		....	....	----	----	x---	----	----	2	
						1848	....		....	....	----	----	x---	----	----	2	
NE flank fissure and summit						**1852**	11		**1853**	01	xxx-	----	x---	x---	----	3*	7/-
						1861	....		....	....	x---	----	----	x---	----	0	
						1862	....		....	....	----	----	----	----	----		
						1863	....		....	....	----	----	x---	----	----	2	
						1869	....		....	....	----	----	x---	----	----	2	
(fumarolic activity only)						X 1929	....		....	....	----	----	---x	----	----		
(fumarolic activity only)						X 1972	....		....	....	----	----	---x	----	----		

VOLCANO NAME (Subregion) / ERUPTION — Area of Activity	LAT	LONG	ELEV (m)	TYPE	NUMBER	Status / Start Year	Start M-Dy	P	Stop Year	Stop M-Dy	Central, Flank vent, Radial fiss, Regional*	Submarine, New island, Subglacial, Crater lake	Explosive, Pyro flow, Phreatic, Fumarolic	Lava flow, Lava lake, Dome, Spine	Fatal, Damage, Mudflow, Tsunami	VEI	Vol L/T
COPAHUE (Chile/Argentina)	**37.85 S**	**71.17 W**	**2965**	**Stratovolc**	**1507-09=**	**Historical**											
						1750?	....		....	....	----	----	x---	----	----	2	
						? **1759?**	....		....	....	----	----	?--?	----	----		
						1867?	....		....	....	----	----	?---	----	----	2?	
						1937	....		....	....	----	----	?---	----	----	2?	
						1961	....		....	....	----	----	x---	----	----	2	
Del Agrio crater						**1992**	0722		**1992**	1001	x---	---x	x-x-	----	--J-	2	
CALLAQUI (Chile-C)	**37.92 S**	**71.45 W**	**3164**	**Stratovolc**	**1507-091**	**Historical**											
						1751	1231		....	....	----	----	x---	----	----	2	
						? **1864**	10		....	....	----	----	?--?	----	----		
(eruption from Quetrupillan)						X **1872**	....		....	....	----	----	----	----	----		
						? **1937**	0918		....	....	----	----	----	----	----		
						1980	10		**1980**	10	x---	----	x-x-	----	----	1	
TOLGUACA (Chile-C)	**38.310 S**	**71.645 W**	**2806**	**Stratovolc**	**1507-092**	**Holocene**											
LONQUIMAY (Chile-C)	**38.377 S**	**71.58 W**	**2865**	**Stratovolc**	**1507-10=**	**Historical**											
						1853	02		....	....	x---	----	x---	x---	----	3	
NE flank						**1887**	0602	+	**1890**	01	--x-	----	x---	x---	----	3*	8/-
						1933	0104		....	....	----	----	x---	x---	----	2	
						? **1940**	02		....	....	----	----	?--?	----	----		
NE flank (Navidad Crater)						**1988**	1225		**1990**	0124a	-xx-	----	x---	xx--	xx--	3*	8/8
CHAPULUL, CERRO (Chile-C)	**38.37 S**	**71.08 W**	**2143**	**Cinder cone**	**1507-101**	**Holocene**											
LLAIMA (Chile-C)	**38.692 S**	**71.729 W**	**3125**	**Stratovolc**	**1507-11=**	**Historical**											
						C **-7410**y	....		....	....	----	----	x---	----	----		
						C **-6880**u	....		....	....	----	----	x---	----	----	5	-/9
						C **-5290**x	....		....	....	----	----	xx--	----	----		
						1640	02		....	....	----	----	x---	?---	--x-	4	
						1751	1218		**1752**	....	x---	----	x---	x---	----	2	
						1759	12		....	....	----	----	x---	----	----	2	
						1822	....		....	....	----	----	x---	----	----	2	
						1852	....		**1853**	....	x---	----	x---	----	----	2	
						1862	....		....	....	x---	----	x---	----	----	2	
						1864	....		....	....	x---	----	x---	----	----	3	
						1866	....		....	....	x---	----	x---	----	----	2	
						1869	04		....	....	----	----	----	----	----	2?	
						1872	0606		....	....	x---	----	x---	x---	--x-	2	
						? **1874**	....		....	....	----	----	----	----	----		
						1875	....		**1876**	....	x---	----	x---	x---	-xx-	2	
						1877	0116		**1877**	0624	----	----	x---	x---	----	2	
						1883	....		....	....	----	----	x---	----	----	2	
						1887	0116		**1887**	0624	x---	----	x---	x---	----	2	
						1889	0420		**1889**	07	----	----	x---	----	----	2	
						1892	....		....	....	----	----	x---	----	----	2	
						1893	12	+	**1894**	12	----	----	x---	----	----	2	
						1895	....		**1896**	....	x---	----	x---	x---	--x-	2	
						1903	0512		**1903**	0514	??--	----	x---	x---	----	2	
						1907	....		**1908**	03	----	----	x---	x---	----	2	
						1912	....		....	....	?---	----	x---	----	----	2	
						1914	0703		....	....	----	----	x---	x---	----	2	
						1917	0204		....	....	?---	----	x---	----	----	2	
						1922	1024		....	....	----	----	x---	----	----	2	
SE crater and summit crater						**1927**	1005	+	**1927**	1205	xxx-	----	x---	x---	--x-	2	
						1929	12		....	....	----	----	x---	x---	----	2	
						1930	0706		**1930**	0820	x---	----	x---	x---	----	2	
						1932	0302		**1932**	0302	x---	----	x---	?---	--?-	2?	
						1932	1231		**1933**	0105	x---	----	x---	x---	--x-	3	
						1937	0209?		**1937**	1102	x---	----	x---	x---	xxx-	2	
						1938	12		....	....	x---	----	x---	----	----	1	
						1941	0623		....	....	x---	----	x---	----	----	2	
						1942	0609		**1942**	11	----	----	x---	----	----	2	
						1944	....		....	....	----	----	x---	----	----	2	
						1945	0331		**1945**	0403	----	----	x?--	x---	--x-	3	
						1946	0723		....	....	----	----	x---	x---	--x-	2	
						1949	09		....	....	----	----	x---	x---	----	2	
Summit and SE crater						**1955**	1022	+	**1957**	11	xx--	----	x---	x---	-xx-	3*	
						? **1960**	....		....	....	----	----	----	----	----		
						1964	....		....	....	----	----	x---	x---	----	2	
						1971	1201p		**1972**	0312	----	----	x---	----	----	2	
						1979	1015		**1979**	1128	x---	----	x---	x---	--x-	2	
						1984	0420		**1984**	1126	x---	----	x---	----	--x-	2	
						1990	0225		**1990**	1125	x---	----	x---	----	--?-	1	
						1992	0823		**1992**	0902	x---	----	x-x-	----	----	1	
SOLLIPULLI (Chile-C)	**38.97 S**	**71.52 W**	**2282**	**Caldera**	**1507-111**	**Radiocarbon**											
SW caldera rim (Alpehue crater)						C **-0920**u	....		....	....	-x--	----	xx--	----	--x-	5+	-/9
North flank (Redondo, Chufquen)						C **1240**t	....		....	....	-x--	----	x---	x---	----		
CABURGUA (Chile-C)	**39.20 S**	**71.83 W**	**995**	**Cinder cones**	**1507-112**	**Tephrochronology**											
						T **-5050***			....	....	---x	----	x---	----	----		
REDONDO, CERRO (Chile-C)	**39.27 S**	**71.70 W**	**1496**	**Cinder cones**	**1507-113**	**Tephrochronology**											
						T **-5050***	....		....	....	----	----	x---	----	----		
HUELEMOLLE (Chile-C)	**39.30 S**	**71.82 W**	**810**	**Cinder cones**	**1507-114**	**Tephrochronology**											
						T **-5050***	....		....	....	---x	----	x---	----	----		
VILLARRICA (Chile-C)	**39.42 S**	**71.93 W**	**2847**	**Stratovolc**	**1507-12=**	**Historical**											
						C **-6690?**	....		....	....	----	----	x---	----	----		
						C **-3730?**	....		....	....	----	----	xx--	----	----		
						T **-2985**z	....		....	....	----	----	----	x---	----	0	
						C **-2240?**	....		....	....	----	----	xx--	----	----		
						C **-2140?**	....		....	....	----	----	xx--	----	----		
						T **-1975**w	....		....	....	----	----	----	x---	----	0	
						C **-1810**x	....		....	....	----	----	xx--	----	----	5	
						C **-1080?**	....		....	....	----	----	xx--	----	----		
						C **-0670?**	....		....	....	----	----	xx--	----	----		
						C **0110?**	....		....	....	----	----	----	x---	----	0	
						C **0330?**	....		....	....	----	----	xx--	----	----		
						1558	....		....	....	----	----	x---	----	-x?-	2	

VOLCANO NAME (Subregion) / ERUPTION — Area of Activity	LAT	LONG	ELEV (m)	TYPE	NUMBER	Status	Start Year	Start M-Dy	P	Stop Year	Stop M-Dy	Central / Flank vent / Radial fiss / Regional*	Submarine / New island / Subglacial / Crater lake	Explosive / Pyro flow / Phreatic / Fumarolic	Lava flow / Lava lake / Dome / Spine	Fatal / Damage / Mudflow / Tsunami	VEI	Vol L/T
VILLARRICA (Chile-C) *continued*							1562	....		....	....	----	----	x---	----	----	2	
(earthquake, not eruption)						X	1575	....		....	....	----	----	----	----	xx--		
							1594	....		....	....	----	----	x---	----	----	1	
							1640	0203		....	....	----	----	x---	x---	--x-	3	
						?	1647	0513		....	....	----	----	?---	?---	----	1?	
						?	1657	0315		....	....	----	----	?---	----	----	1?	
							1688	....		....	....	----	----	x---	----	--?-	2	
							1716	....		....	....	----	----	x---	?---	----	1	
							1730	0708		....	....	----	----	x---	----	----	2	
							1737	1224		....	....	----	----	x---	----	----	2	
							1742	....		....	....	----	----	x---	----	----	2	
							1745	....		....	....	----	----	x---	----	----	2	
							1751	1214		....	....	----	----	x---	x---	----	1	
							1759	12		....	....	----	----	x---	----	----	1	
							1777	....		....	....	----	----	x---	----	----	1	
							1780	....		....	....	----	----	?---	----	----	2?	
							1787	....		....	....	----	----	x---	x---	----	1	
							1790	....		....	....	----	----	x---	----	----	2	
							1792	....		....	....	----	----	x---	----	----	2	
							1796	....		....	....	----	----	x---	----	----	2	
							1799	....		....	....	----	----	x---	----	----	2	
							1801	....		....	....	----	----	x---	----	----	2	
							1806	....		....	....	----	----	x---	----	----	2?	
							1815	....		1818	....	----	----	x---	----	----	2	
							1822	1119		....	....	x---	----	x---	----	----	2	
							1832	1224		....	....	----	----	x---	----	----	2	
							1837	1107		1837	1121	----	----	x---	----	----	2	
						?	1852	....		....	....	----	----	----	----	----		
							1853	11		....	....	----	----	x---	x---	----	2	
							1859	0519		1860	0412	----	----	x---	----	----	2	
							1864	10		....	....	----	----	x---	----	----	2	
						?	1867	....		?1868	....	----	----	----	----	----		
							1869	0204		1860	0224d	x---	----	x---	----	----	2	
							1874	04		....	....	x---	----	x---	?---	----	1?	
							1875	1117		1876	....	----	----	x---	----	----	2?	
							1877	0512		....	....	----	----	x---	----	----	2	
							1879	0202		....	....	----	----	x---	----	----	2	
							1883	....		....	....	----	----	x---	----	----	2	
							1893	....		1894?	....	----	----	x---	----	----	2	
							1897	....		1898?	....	----	----	x---	?---	----	2	
							1904	....		....	....	----	----	x---	----	--x-	2	
							1906	0422		....	....	----	----	x---	----	----	1?	
							1907	0510		1907	0526	----	----	x---	----	----	2	
							1908	1031	+	1908	1221?	x---	----	x---	x---	--x-	2	
							1909	0819		....	....	----	----	x---	?---	--x-	2	
						?	1910	....		....	....	----	----	----	----	----		
(1913 eruption report discredited)						X	1913	....		....	....	----	----	----	----	----		
							1915	....		1918?	....	----	----	x---	----	----	1?	
						?	1919	....		....	....	----	----	----	----	----		
							1920	1210		1929	1213	x---	----	x---	x---	--x-	2	
							1921	1210		....	....	----	----	x---	x---	----	2	
							1929	1227		....	....	----	----	x---	----	----	1	
							1933	0105		....	....	----	----	x---	----	----	2	
							1935	....		....	....	----	----	x---	----	----	1?	
							1938	0211		....	....	----	----	x---	----	----	1?	
							1948	1009		1949	0203	x---	----	x---	x---	xxx-	3*	
						?	1950	....		....	....	----	----	----	----	----		
							1958	1106		1959	1221	----	----	x---	----	----	1	
						?	1960	....		?1961	....	----	----	x---	----	----	2?	
							1963	0225?		1963	0921>	x---	----	x---	x---	xxx-	2	
							1964	0302		1964	0303	x---	----	x---	x---	xxx-	2	
							1971	1029	+	1972	0110	x-x-	--x-	x---	x---	xxx-	2	7/-
							1977	0126		1977	0130	----	----	x---	----	----	1	
							1980	0620<		1908	0924	x---	----	xx--	----	----	1	
							1983	1014		1983	1016	x---	----	xx--	----	----	1	
							1984	0811	+	1985	1118	x---	----	x---	x---	-xx-	2	6/-
							1991	0830	+	1991	0917	x---	----	x-x-	----	----	2	
							1992	0911		1992	12 >	x---	----	x-x-	----	----	1	
QUETRUPILLAN (Chile-C)	39.50 S	71.70 W	2360	Caldera	1507-121	Historical												
							1872	0606		....	....	----	----	--x-	----	----	2?	
LANIN (Chile/Argentina)............	39.633 S	71.500 W	3747	Stratovolc	1507-122	Holocene												
HUANQUIHUE GROUP (Argentina) ..	39.87 S	71.55 W	1300	Pyrocl cone	1507-123	Holocene												
MOCHO-CHOSHUENCO (Chile-C) ...	39.928 S	72.027 W	2422	Stratovolc	1507-13=	Historical												
						T	-7700*	....		....	....	----	----	x---	----	----	P	
El Mocho							1864	1101		1864	1103a	----	----	xx--	----	----	2	
El Mocho							1937	0616		....	....	----	----	?---	----	--?-		
CARRAN-LOS VENADOS (Chile-C) ..	40.35 S*	72.07 W	1114	Pyrocl cones	1507-14=	Historical												
Rininahue Maar							1907	0409		1907	0424>	x---	----	x---	x---	-xx-	3	
Carran Maar.........................							1955	0727	+	1955	1112	x---	----	x---	----	xx--	4	-/8
Mirador..............................							1979	0414		1979	0520	x---	----	x---	x---	----	2	6/6
CORDON CAULLE (Chile-C)........	40.52 S	72.20 W	1798	Fissure vents	1507-141	Historical												
							1893?	....		....	....	---x	----	----	----	----		
						?	1905	....		....	....	----	----	----	----	----		
Cordon Caulle-Cordillera Nevada							1921	1213		1922	02	---x	----	x---	x---	----	3?	8/-
							1929	0107		....	....	---x	----	x---	----	----	2?	
							1934	0306		....	....	---x	----	x---	----	----	2?	
SE end of fissure system							1960	0524		1960	0625e	--x-	----	x---	x---	----	3	8/7
PUYEHUE (Chile-C)...............	40.590 S	72.117 W	2236	Stratovolc	1507-15=	Holocene												
MENCHECA (Chile-C).............	40.534 S	72.038 W	1840	Stratovolc	1507-151	Holocene												
PANTOJA, CERRO (Chile-C)	40.77 S	71.95 W	2112	Stratovolc	1507-152	Holocene												
ANTILLANCA GROUP (Chile-C).....	40.771 S	72.153 W	1990	Stratovolcs	1507-153	Holocene												
PUNTIGUIDO-CORDON CENIZOS (")	40.969 S	72.264 W	2493	Stratovolc	1507-16-	Historical												
Cordon Cenizos							1850	....		....	....	-x--	----	x---	----	----		
						?	1930	....		....	....	----	----	----	----	----		

VOLCANO NAME (Subregion) / ERUPTION — Area of Activity	LAT	LONG	ELEV (m)	TYPE	NUMBER	Status / Start Year	Start M-Dy	P	Stop Year	Stop M-Dy	Central, Flank vent, Radial fiss, Regional*	Submarine, New island, Subglacial, Crater lake	Explosive, Pyro flow, Phreatic, Fumarolic	Lava flow, Lava lake, Dome, Spine	Fatal, Damage, Mudflow, Tsunami	VEI	Vol L/T
CHILE - S & ARGENTINA																	
OSORNO (Chile-S)	**41.10 S**	**72.493 W**	**2652**	**Stratovolc**	**1508-01=**	**Historical**											
						? **1575**	....		....	....	----	----	----	----	----		
						? **1640**	....		....	....	----	----	----	----	----		
						? **1644**	....		....	....	----	----	----	----	----		
						1719	....		....	....	x---	----	----	----	----	2	
						1765m	....		....	....	x---	----	x---	----	----	1	
SE base						**1790**	0309		**1791**	1226e	-x--	----	x---	x---	--x-	2	
SSW side						**1834**	1129	+	**1835**	0224d	-x--	----	x---	x---	----	3?	
						1837	1107		....	....	?---	----	?---	----	----	2	
(some sources list ca. 1850 date)						**1851**	....		....	....	----	----	x---	----	----	2?	
(fumarolic activity only)						X 1852	....		....	....	----	----	---x	----	----		
						1855	....		....	....	----	----	x---	----	----	2?	
						1869	....		....	....	----	----	x---	----	----	2	
CALBUCO (Chile-S)	**41.326 S**	**72.614 W**	**2003**	**Stratovolc**	**1508-02=**	**Historical**											
(steam observed from Osorno: Moreno)						X 1837	....		X1838	....	----	----	----	----	----		
						1893	0107		**1894**	0116>	x---	----	x---	?---	-xx-	4	
						1895	....		....	....	----	----	----	----	----		
						1906	....		....	....	----	----	x---	----	----	2	
						1907	0422		....	....	----	----	----	----	----	2?	
						1909	03		....	....	----	----	x---	----	----	2	
						1911	....		**1912**	....	----	----	x---	----	----	2	
						1917	04		....	....	x---	----	x---	x-x-	-xx-	3?	
						1929	0106		**1929**	0106	x---	----	xx--	x---	-xx-	3?	
						1961	0201	+	**1961**	0315e	x---	--x-	x-x-	x---	-xx-	3	
CAYUTE-LA VIGUERIA (Chile-S)	**41.25 S***	**72.27 W**	**506**	**Pyrocl cones**	**1508-021**	**Holocene**											
YATE, MT. (Chile-S)	**41.755 S**	**72.396 W**	**2187**	**Stratovolc**	**1508-022**	**Holocene**											
HORNOPIREN, VOLCAN (Chile-S)	**41.874 S**	**72.431 W**	**1572**	**Stratovolc**	**1508-023**	**Holocene?**											
VOLCANICO, CERRO (Argentina)	**42.07 S**	**71.65 W**		**Cinder cone**	**1508-024**	**Holocene**											
HUEQUI (Chile-S)	**42.377 S**	**72.578 W**	**1318**	**Stratovolc**	**1508-03=**	**Historical**											
						1890	....		....	....	----	----	x---	----	----	2	
						1893	....		....	....	x---	----	----	?---	----	0	
						1896	....		....	....	----	----	x---	----	----	2	
						1906	....		**1907**	....	----	----	x---	----	----	2	
						1920?	....		....	....	----	----	x---	----	----	2	
MINCHINMAVIDA (Chile-S)	**42.78 S**	**72.43 W**	**2404**	**Stratovolc**	**1508-04=**	**Historical**											
						1742	....		....	....	----	----	----	----	----	2	
						1834	11		....	....	----	----	----	----	----		
						1835	0220		**1835**	0315e	-x--	----	----	x---	----	2	
CHAITEN (Chile-S)	**42.833 S**	**72.646 W**	**962**	**Caldera**	**1508-041**	**Holocene**											
CORCOVADO (Chile-S)	**43.18 S**	**72.80 W**	**2300**	**Stratovolc**	**1508-05=**	**Historical**											
						1834	11		....	....	-x--	----	----	----	----	2	
						1835	1111		....	....	-x--	----	x---	----	----	2	
YANTELES, CERRO (Chile-S)	**43.42 S**	**72.83 W**	**2050**	**Stratovolc**	**1508-051**	**Historical**											
						1835	0220		....	....	-x--	----	x---	----	----	2	
PALENA VOLC GROUP (Chile-S)	**43.68 S**	**72.50 W**		**Cinder cones**	**1508-052**	**Holocene**											
MELIMOYU (Chile-S)	**44.08 S**	**72.88 W**	**2400**	**Stratovolc**	**1508-053**	**Holocene**											
PUYUHUAPI (Chile-S)	**44.30 S**	**72.53 W**	**255**	**Cinder cones**	**1508-054**	**Holocene**											
MENTOLAT (Chile-S)	**44.67 S**	**73.08 W**	**1660**	**Stratovolc**	**1508-055**	**Holocene?**											
MACA (Chile-S)	**45.10 S**	**73.20 W**	**3078**	**Stratovolc**	**1508-056**	**Holocene**											
HUDSON, CERRO (Chile-S)	**45.90 S**	**72.97 W**	**1905**	**Stratovolc**	**1508-057**	**Historical**											
						C **-5020**w	....		....	....	----	----	x---	----	----		
						C **-3390**>	....		....	....	----	----	x---	----	----		
						C **-2880**?	....		....	....	----	----	x---	----	----		
						1891	....		....	....	----	----	?---	----	----		
NW part of caldera						**1971**	0812		**1971**	0918>	x---	--?-	x---	?---	xxJ-	3	
NW caldera rim and SW caldera floor						**1991**	0808	+	**1991**	1027	x-x-	--x-	xx--	x---	-xJ-	5*	-/9
LAUTARO (Chile-S)	**49.02 S**	**73.55 W**	**3380**	**Stratovolc ?**	**1508-06=**	**Historical**											
						? **1878**	0118		....	....	----	----	?---	----	----	1	
(between lakes San Martin and Viedma)						@ **1879**	....		....	....	----	----	----	----	----		
						1945	0115q		....	....	----	----	?---	----	----	1	
						1960	0120		....	....	----	----	x---	----	----	1	
(aerial observation, possibly Lautaro)						@ **1961**	10		....	....	----	----	----	----	----	2	
VIEDMA, VOLCAN (Argentina)	**49.358 S**	**73.28 W**	**1300**	**Subglacial**	**1508-061**	**Historical**											
						1988	1115q		....	....	----	--x-	x---	----	--x-		
AGUILERA (Chile-S)	**50.17 S**	**73.83 W**		**Stratovolc ?**	**1508-062**	**Radiocarbon**											
						C **-1395**?	....		....	....	----	----	x---	----	----		
RECLUS (Chile-S)	**50.98 S**	**73.70 W**		**Stratovolc ?**	**1508-063**	**Radiocarbon**											
						T **-1830**>	....		....	....	----	----	x---	----	----		
BURNEY, MONTE (Chile-S)	**52.33 S**	**73.40 W**	**1758**	**Stratovolc**	**1508-07=**	**Historical**											
						T **-1050**z	....		....	....	----	----	x---	----	----		
						1910	03		....	....	----	----	?---	----	----	2	
PALEI-AIKE VOLC FIELD (Chile/Arg)	**52.00 S***	**70.00 W**	**250**	**Cinder cones**	**1508-08-**	**Anthropology**											
						A **-5550***	....		....	....	----	----	x---	x---	----		
COOK, ISLA (Chile-S)	**54.95 S**	**70.27 W**	**150**	**Lava domes**	**1508-09-**	**Holocene**											

West Indies (16)

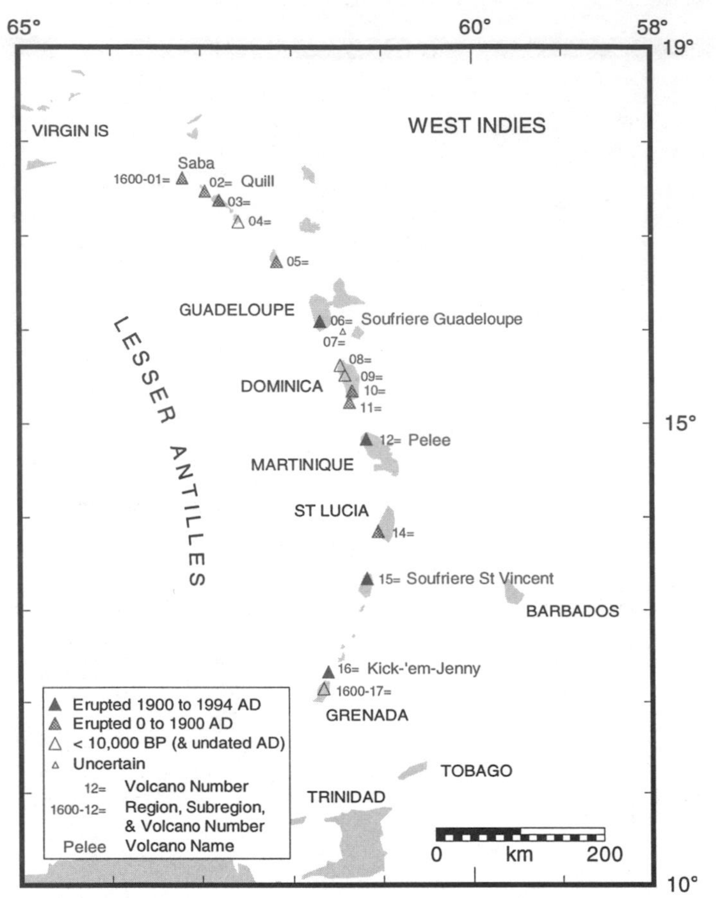

Of the broad region known as the West Indies, only the Lesser Antilles, an arc of small islands formed by subduction of oceanic crust moving westward from the Mid-Atlantic Ridge, are volcanically active, forming the smallest of the *CAVW* regions.

The northern islands were discovered by Columbus on his second voyage, in 1493, and other islands on his third in 1498, but they were passed over by settlers preferring the Greater Antilles to the west. It was not until the 1630s and the sugar trade that Europeans started to settle in the islands. On Saba they chose grassy flatlands that were apparently the newly vegetated tops of very recent valley-filling pyroclastic-flow deposits. And on Martinique settlers noticed that Mont Pelee was suspiciously bare of vegetation. The first historical eruption, though, was on Guadeloupe around 1690. Ownership of islands shifted among the French, British, and Dutch, with Carib indians showing fierce resistance to colonization on some islands. Several islands retain formal ties to Europe, whereas others have achieved independence in recent decades. Monitoring of the volcanoes is by the Seismic Research Unit of the University of the West Indies, principally by seismic data telemetered to their base in Trinidad, and by French observatories in Guadeloupe and Martinique.

This region has the lowest number of volcanoes (17), and smallest area of affected nations. A high proportion of its eruptions (14%, second to Region 12's 19%) have produced domes (Fig. 22, p. 223), and no other region has had a lower proportion of its eruptions produce lava flows (4 of 123, or 3%). Stratovolcanoes dominate (71%) in the West Indies to a degree matched only by Alaska.

Many detailed tephra studies, largely by British and French volcanologists, have produced a regional high of 66% radiocarbon eruption dates. Only 33 historical dates have been recorded in the West Indies and, like the Western United States, three-fourths of its eruptions are dated by non-historical techniques.

VOLCANO NAME (Subregion) / ERUPTION — Area of Activity	LAT	LONG	ELEV (m)	TYPE	NUMBER	Status / Start Year	Start M-Dy	P	Stop Year	Stop M-Dy	Central / Flank vent / Radial fiss / Regional*	Submarine / New island / Subglacial / Crater lake	Explosive / Pyro flow / Phreatic / Fumarolic	Lava flow / Lava lake / Dome / Spine	Fatal / Damage / Mudflow / Tsunami	VEI	Vol L/T
WEST INDIES																	
SABA (W Indies)	**17.63 N**	**63.23 W**	**887**	**Stratovolc**	**1600-01=**	**Historical**											
SW flank						**1636<**	....		....	....	-x--	----	xx--	--??	----		
QUILL, THE (St. Eustatius)	**17.48 N**	**62.95 W**	**601**	**Stratovolc**	**1600-02=**	**Radiocarbon**											
						C **-5990?**	....		....	....	x---	----	xx--	----	----	**P**	
						C **-5860?**	....		....	....	x---	----	xx--	----	----		
						C **0400?**	....		....	....	x---	----	xx--	----	----		
LIAMUIGA (St. Kitts)	**17.37 N**	**62.80 W**	**1156**	**Stratovolc**	**1600-03=**	**Radiocarbon**											
						C **-2320**w	....		....	....	x---	----	xx--	----	--x-	**P**	
						C **-1710**v	....		....	....	x---	----	x---	----	----	**P**	
						C **-0115**v	....		....	....	x---	----	xx--	----	----		
						C **0150**x	....		....	....	x---	----	xxx-	----	----	**P**	
						? **1692**	....		....	....	x---	----	--??	----	----		
						? **1843**	0208		....	....	x---	----	--??	----	----		
NEVIS PEAK (Nevis)	**17.15 N**	**62.58 W**	**985**	**Stratovolc**	**1600-04=**	**Holocene**											
SOUFRIERE HILLS (Montserrat)	**16.72 N**	**62.18 W**	**915**	**Stratovolc**	**1600-05=**	**Radiocarbon**											
Castle Peak						C **1630**t	....		....	....	x---	----	xx--	----	----		
SOUFRIERE GUADELOUPE (W Ind)	**16.05 N**	**61.67 W**	**1467**	**Stratovolc**	**1600-06=**	**Historical**											
						C **-6550?**	....		....	....	----	----	xx--	----	--x-		
						C **-5750?**	....		....	....	----	----	xx--	----	--x-		
South flank (Gros Fougas)						C **-2550?**	....		....	....	-x--	----	xx--	x-x-	----		
						? **-2050?**	....		....	....	----	----	?---	----	----		
						C **-1550?**	....		....	....	----	----	xx--	----	--x-		
Morne Amic						G **-1380?**	....		....	....	x---	----	xx--	--x-	----	3?	
						? **-0950?**	....		....	....	----	----	?---	----	--x-		
Morne Amic ?						C **-0650?**	....		....	....	?---	----	xx--	--x-	--x-	3?	
South flank (Morne Lenglet)						C **-0580>**	....		....	....	-x--	----	x---	x---	----	2	
La Citerne and L'Eschelle cones ?						C **0250**x	....		....	....	-?--	----	x-x-	----	--x-		
						C **1300?**	....		....	....	x---	----	xx--	----	----	3?	
						C **1400?**	....		....	....	----	----	xx--	----	----	**P**	
La Soufriere						G **1440**v	....		....	....	x---	----	xx--	--x-	----	**P**	8/-
Gouffre Dupuy, Gouffre Tarissan						**1690?**	....		....	....	x---	----	--x-	----	----	3↑	
North side of summit dome						**1696**	....		....	....	x---	----	--x-	----	----	3↑	
NW side of summit dome						**1797**	0929		**1797**	1002	x-x-	----	x-x-	----	--x-	2	
NW side of summit dome						**1798**	0426		**1799**	01	x-x-	----	x?x-	----	--x-	2	
						1809	06		**1812**	05	x---	----	--x-	----	----	1	
NW side of summit dome						**1837**	1203		**1838**	0212	x---	----	x-x-	----	--x-	2	
SE side summit dome						**1903**	....		....	....	x---	----	--x-	----	----	2	
ESE side, Napoleon Crater						**1956**	1020		**1956**	1024	x-x-	----	x-x-	----	----	1	-/4
SE side of summit (Gouffre Tarissan)						**1976**	0708	+	**1977**	0301	x-x-	----	x-x-	----	-xx-	2	-/5

VOLCANO NAME (Subregion) / ERUPTION — Area of Activity	LAT	LONG	ELEV (m)	TYPE	NUMBER	Status / Start Year	Start M-Dy	P	Stop Year	Stop M-Dy	Central, Flank vent, Radial fiss, Regional* / Submarine, New island, Subglacial, Crater lake / Explosive, Pyro flow, Phreatic, Fumarolic / Lava flow, Lava lake, Dome, Spine / Fatal, Damage, Mudflow, Tsunami	VEI	Vol L/T
UNNAMED (Guadeloupe-SE of)	15.97 N	61.43 W	-45	Submarine	1600-07=	Pleistocene							
(submarine geyser or karst collapse)						X 1843	0217		X1843	0217	---- ---- ---? ---- ----		
DIABLE, MORNE AU (Dominica)	15.62 N	61.45 W	861	Stratovolc	1600-08=	Fumarolic							
DIABLOTINS, MORNE (Dominica)	15.50 N	61.42 W	1430	Stratovolc	1600-09=	Fumarolic							
MICOTRIN (Dominica)	15.33 N	61.33 W	1387	Lava domes	1600-10=	Historical							
NE of Watt Mtn (Valley of Desolation)						1880	0104		1880	0104	---- ---- x-x- ---- --x-	2?	
PATATES, MORNE (Dominica)	15.22 N	61.37 W	960	Stratovolc	1600-11=	Radiocarbon							
Morne Patates dome						C 1500v	....		....	....	x--- ---- xx-- ---- ----		
PELEE (Martinique)	14.82 N	61.17 W	1397	Stratovolc	1600-12=	Historical							
						C -7225?	....		....	....	x--- ---- xx-- ---- ----	P	
Vent slightly south of present summit						C -6445?	....		....	....	x--- ---- xx-- --x- ----		
						C -6090z	....		....	....	x--- ---- xx-- ---- ----	P	
						C -5795?	....		....	....	x--- ---- xx-- ---- ----		
Vent slightly south of present summit						C -5440?	....		....	....	x--- ---- xx-- ---- ----	P	
						C -4680?	....		....	....	x--- ---- xx-- ---- ----	P	
						C -3820?	....		....	....	x--- ---- xx-- ---- ----	P	
						C -3700?	....		....	....	x--- ---- xx-- --x- ----		
						T -3495x	....		....	....	x--- ---- xx-- ---- ----	P	
						C -3290?	....		....	....	x--- ---- xx-- ---- ----		
						C -3245?	....		....	....	x--- ---- xx-- --x- ----		
Vent slightly south of present summit						C -3150w	....		....	....	x--- ---- xx-- --x- ----		
						C -3015?	....		....	....	x--- ---- xx-- --x- ----		
						C -2660t	....		....	....	x--- ---- xx-- ---- ----		
						C -2560?	....		....	....	x--- ---- xx-- --x- ----		
						C -2460?	....		....	....	x--- ---- xx-- ---- ----		
						C -2425?	....		....	....	x--- ---- xx-- ---- ----	P	
						C -2360?	....		....	....	x--- ---- xx-- --x- ----		
						C -2275?	....		....	....	x--- ---- xx-- ---- ----		
						C -2110v	....		....	....	x--- ---- xx-- ---- ----		
						C -2025?	....		....	....	x--- ---- xx-- ---- ----		
						C -1760r	....		....	....	x--- ---- xx-- ---- ----		
						C -1180p	....		....	....	x--- ---- xx-- ---- ----		
						C -0800t	....		....	....	x--- ---- xx-- ---- ----		
						C -0725?	....		....	....	x--- ---- xx-- ---- ----		
						C -0615?	....		....	....	x--- ---- xx-- ---- ----		
						C -0600?	....		....	....	x--- ---- xx-- ---- ----		
						C -0540j	....		....	....	x--- ---- xx-- --x- ----		
						C -0495?	....		....	....	x--- ---- xx-- ---- ----		
						C -0440?	....		....	....	x--- ---- xx-- ---- ----	P	
						C -0310?	....		....	....	x--- ---- xx-- ---- ----		
						C -0195?	....		....	....	x--- ---- xx-- ---- ----	P	
						C -0065?	....		....	....	x--- ---- xx-- ---- ----	4	-/8
						C 0050?	....		....	....	x--- ---- xx-- ---- ----	P	
						C 0125?	....		....	....	x--- ---- xx-- ---- ----	P	
						C 0220u	....		....	....	x--- ---- xx-- --x- ----		
						C 0280p	....		....	....	x--- ---- xx-- ---- ----	4	-/8
						C 0300?	....		....	....	x--- ---- xx-- ---- ----	P	
						C 0445?	....		....	....	x--- ---- xx-- ---- ----	P	
						C 0645?	....		....	....	x--- ---- xx-- ---- ----		
						C 0720?	....		....	....	x--- ---- xx-- ---- ----		
						C 0810p	....		....	....	x--- ---- xx-- ---- ----	P	
						C 0910?	....		....	....	x--- ---- xx-- ---- ----		
						C 1185?	....		....	....	x--- ---- xx-- ---- ----		
						C 1260p	....		....	....	x--- ---- xx-- ---- ----		
						C 1300t	....		....	....	x--- ---- xx-- ---- ----	4	-/8
						C 1370?	....		....	....	x--- ---- xx-- ---- ----		
						C 1460p	....		....	....	x--- ---- xx-- ---- ----		
						1635<	....		....	....	x--- ---- xx-- --?- ----		
Upper Riviere Claire valley						1792	0122		....	....	-x-- ---- --x- ---- --x-	2	
Upper Riviere Claire valley						1851	0805		1852	....	-x-- ---- x-x- ---- --x-	2	
Riviere Blanche and summit crater						1902	0423	+	1905	1005	xx-- ---x xxx- --xx xxxx	4*	8/8
						1929	0916	+	1932	1201p	x--- ---- xx-- --xx -xx-	3*	
HODDER'S VOLCANO (W Indies)	14.03 N	61.07 W			1600-13=	Not a Volcano							
(no volcano at this location)						X 1902	0509		....	....	---- ---- ---- ---- ----		
QUALIBOU (St. Lucia)	13.83 N	61.05 W	777	Caldera	1600-14=	Historical							
Sulphur Springs area						1766	....		....	....	x--- ---- --x- ---- ----	1	
SOUFRIERE ST. VINCENT (W Indies)	13.33 N	61.18 W	1220	Stratovolc	1600-15=	Historical							
						C -2380v	....		....	....	x--- ---- xx-- x--- --x-		
						C -2310v	....		....	....	x--- ---- xx-- ---- ----		
						C -2200w	....		....	....	x--- ---- xx-- ---- ----		
						C -2135t	....		....	....	x--- ---- xx-- ---- --x-		
						C -2020u	....		....	....	x--- ---- xx-- ---- ----		
						C -1600u	....		....	....	x--- ---- xx-- ---- ----		
						C -0750v	....		....	....	x--- ---- xx-- ---- ----		
						C -0530u	....		....	....	x--- ---- xx-- ---- ----		
						C 0905u	....		....	....	x--- ---- xx-- ---- ----		
						C 1325u	....		....	....	x--- ---- xx-- ---- ----		
						C 1395u	....		....	....	x--- ---- xx-- ---- ----		
						C 1480w	....		....	....	x--- ---- xx-- ---- ----		
						C 1550t	....		....	....	x--- ---- xx-- ---- ----		
						C 1640t	....		....	....	x--- ---- xx-- ---- ----		
						1718	0326		1718	0329	x--- ---- x?-- ---- ----	3?	
						1784	03 <		....	....	x--- ---- ---x --?- ----	0	
Old summit crater & new NE rim crater						1812	0427	+	1812	0609?	xx-- ---x xx-- ---- xxx-	4	-/8
						1814	0109		1814	0109	x--- ---x --x- ---- ----	1?	
						? 1880	....		....	....	x--- ---x ---- ?--- ----	0	
						1902	0506	+	1903	0330	x--- ---x xxx- ---- xxxx	4*	-/8
						1971	1004f		1972	0320	x--- ---x ---- x-x- ----	0	7/-
						1979	0413	+	1979	1026e	x--- ---x xxx- --x- -xx-	3	7/7
KICK-'EM-JENNY (Grenada-N of)	12.30 N	61.63 W	-160	Submarine	1600-16=	Historical							
						1939	0724		1939	0724	---- x--- x--- ---- ----	1	
						S 1943	1005		S1943	1006	---- x--- ---- ---- ----	0	
						S 1953	1030		S1953	1030	---- x--- ---- ---- ----	0	
						S 1965	1025		S1965	1025	---- x--- ---- ---- ----	0	
						S 1966	0505	+	S1966	0806	---- x--- ---- ---- ----	0	
						S 1972	0705		S1972	0705	---- x--- ---- ---- ----	0	

VOLCANO NAME (Subregion)	LAT	LONG	ELEV (m)	TYPE	NUMBER	Status	Start Year	Start M-Dy	P	Stop Year	Stop M-Dy	Central / Flank vent / Radial fiss / Regional* — Submarine / New island / Subglacial / Crater lake — Explosive / Pyro flow / Phreatic / Fumarolic — Lava flow / Lava lake / Dome / Spine — Fatal / Damage / Mudflow / Tsunami	VEI	Vol L/T
ERUPTION — Area of Activity														
KICK-'EM-JENNY (Grenada-N of) *continued*							**1974**	0905		**1974**	0906	---- x--- ---- ---- ---- ----	0	
						S	**1977**	0114		S**1977**	0114	---- x--- ---- ---- ---- ----	0	
						S	**1988**	1229		S**1988**	1230	---- x--- xx-- ---- ---- ----	0	
						S	**1990**	0326		S**1990**	0328	---- x--- ---- ---- ---- ----	0	
ST. CATHERINE (Grenada).........	12.15 N	61.67 W	840	Stratovolc	1600-17=	Holocene								

Iceland & Arctic Ocean (17)

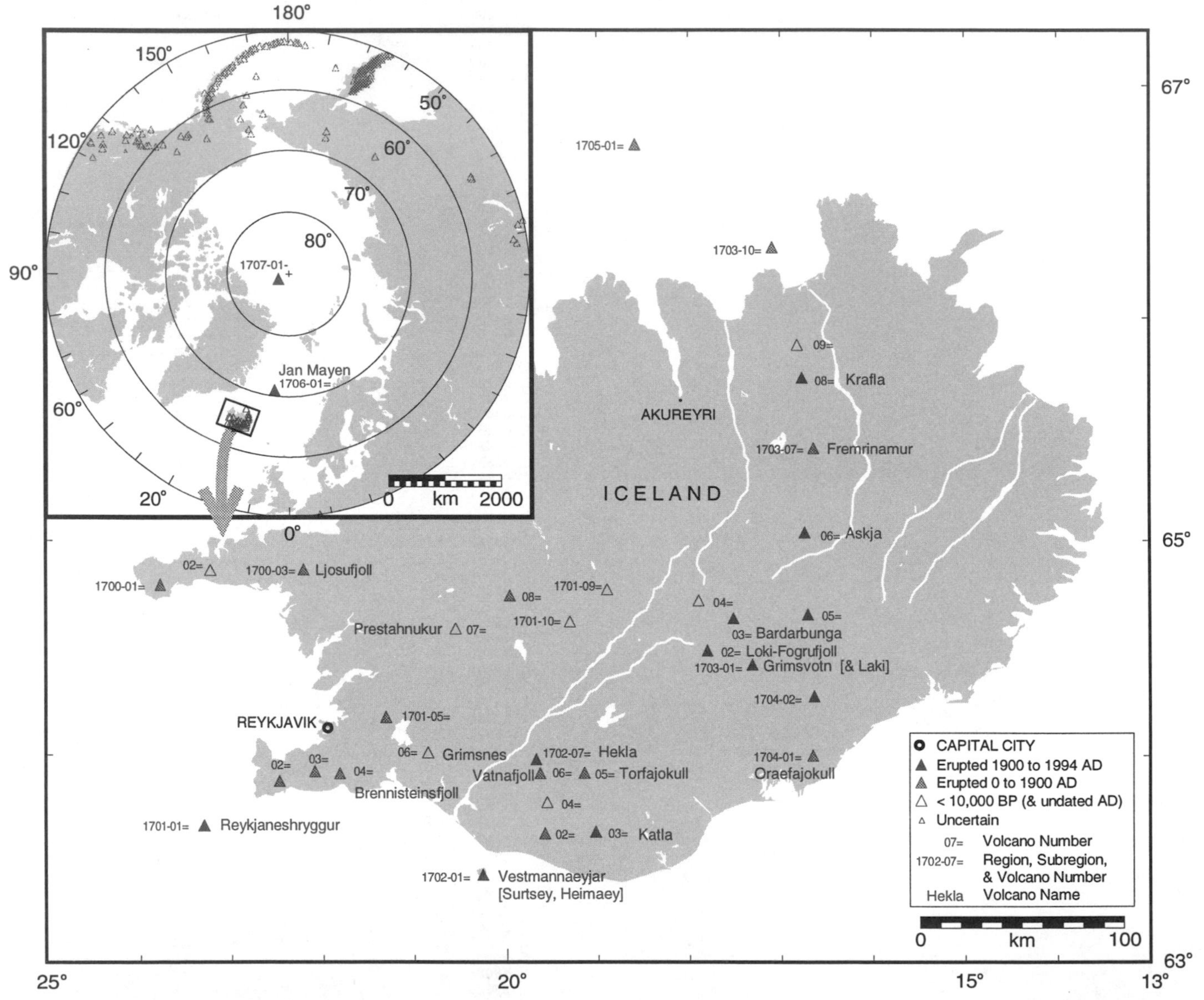

Iceland has the land area of Virginia with 4% of its population. Iceland's population of 0.26 million ranks it above only the Kuriles and Antarctica, among *CAVW* regions, but it enjoys the highest literacy rate (100%) of any nation in the world, and its close interaction with volcanoes makes it indeed a nation of volcanologists.

Iceland has the highest proportion of Holocene volcanoes that bear dated eruptions (86%), and this follows largely from work initiated by Iceland's pioneer of tephrochronology, Sigurdur Thorarinsson. Iceland leads all regions with 35% of eruptions having been dated by this approach, and in the number of volcanoes owing their Holocene status to tephrochronology.

First settled by Vikings in the 9th century AD, Iceland established its own parliament in 930 and recorded its first historical eruption only a few years later. After a golden age of literature in the 12th and 13th centuries, natural history reporting reached a low around the 15th century (only 5 historical eruptions recorded, as opposed to 11 in the 13th and 15 in the 17th centuries). In the years 1707-09 a third of the population died from smallpox, and the 1783-4 Laki eruption killed a fifth of the remaining population by famine. Iceland gained sovereignty from Denmark in 1918 and complete independence in 1944.

Iceland is noted for subglacial and regional fissure eruptions, having produced 83% and 59% (respectively) of the world's total for each type. Fissure eruptions dominate because Iceland combines a hotspot setting with one of the few places where the oceanic rift system emerges above sea level (Fig. 18, p. 203). This setting has brought widespread attention to the region's volcanoes from many geophysical sub-disciplines.

Following the 1974-84 eruptions at Krafla, Iceland's only recent volcanism has been a brief 1991 eruption of Hekla and some uncertain subglacial activity at Loki-Fogrufjoll.

Since our 1981 book, reorganization by volcano systems (described above, under "Volcano Name") has resulted in a substantial drop in number of volcanoes (from 71 to 35), but more meaningful grouping of genetically related surface features. This has come about through the *CAVW* efforts of Sigurdur Steinthorsson and colleagues at the University of Iceland and the Nordic Volcano Institute. Over the time interval since 1981, increased work on the prehistoric record of Iceland has doubled the number of dated Holocene eruptions. Another change since 1981 is expansion of the region to include the full Arctic Ocean. The *CAVW* organizers did not recognize arctic volcanism and assigned no region numbers beyond 19. The somewhat suspect submarine activity from one area 200 km from the North Pole does not really merit a full region of its own, as we gave it in 1981, so we have expanded region 17 beyond Jan Mayen to include the full Arctic Ocean, including Pleistocene volcanism on Spitsbergen.

VOLCANO NAME (Subregion) / ERUPTION — Area of Activity	LAT	LONG	ELEV (m)	TYPE	NUMBER	Status / Start Year	Start M-Dy	P	Stop Year	Stop M-Dy	ERUPTIVE CHARACTERISTICS (Central, Flank vent, Radial fiss, Regional* / Submarine, New island, Subglacial, Crater lake / Explosive, Pyro flow, Phreatic, Fumarolic / Lava flow, Lava lake, Dome, Spine / Fatal, Damage, Mudflow, Tsunami)	VEI	Vol L/T
ICELAND - W													
SNAEFELLSJOKULL (Iceland-W)	64.80 N	23.78 W	1448	Stratovolc	1700-01=	Radiocarbon							
						T -6050*	....		....	....	x--- ---- x--- ---- ----		
East flank (Budaklettur)						T -4550*	....		....	....	---x ---- x--- x--- ----	2	
West flank (Ondverdarnesholar)						T -4050*	....		....	....	-x-- ---- ---- x--- ----	0	
SE flank (Dagverdarahraun)						C -2970y	....		....	....	-x-- ---- ---- x--- ----	0	
NE flank (800 m)						C -2400x	....		....	....	-x-- ---- x--- x--- ----	2?	8/-
South flank (Thufuhraun)						C -2270y	....		....	....	-x-- ---- ---- x--- ----	0	
						C -2010v	....		....	....	x--- ---- x--- ---- ----		
NW flank (Raudholar)						C -1000z	....		....	....	-x-- ---- x--- x--- ----	2	8/-
						C 0200w	....		....	....	x--- ---- x--- ?--- ----		8/-
LYSUHOLL (Iceland-W)	64.87 N*	23.25 W	540	Pyrocl cones	1700-02=	Holocene							
LJOSUFJOLL (Iceland-W)	64.87 N*	22.23 W	988	Fissure vents	1700-03=	Anthropology							
Eldborg						T -7050*	....		....	....	---x ---- x--- x--- ----	2	9/-
Krothraunskula, Raudakula, Graakula						T -2050?	....		....	....	---x ---- x--- x--- ----	3?	
Grabrok						C -1750w	....		....	....	---x ---- x--- x--- ----	2	
Ytri and Stori Raudamelskula						C -0665v	....		....	....	---x ---- x--- x--- ----	2	8/-
Raudhalsar						A 0960j	....		....	....	---x ---- --x- x--- -x--	2	8/-
ICELAND - SW													
REYKJANESHRYGGUR (Iceland-SW)	63.67 N*	23.33 W	80	Subm volcs	1701-01=	Historical							
						T -3800y	....		....	....	---- x--- x--- ---- ----		
Off Ongulbrjotsnef coast						T -1800y	....		....	....	---- x--- x--- ---- ----		
Near Eldey						T 0920?	....		....	....	---- x--- x--- ---- ----		
						1179<	....		....	....	---- x--- x--- ---- ----	2	
Eldey						1211	0831p		....	....	---- xx-- x--- ---- ----	2	
						1223	....		....	....	---- x--- x--- ---- ----	2	
						1231	....		....	....	---- x?-- x--- ---- ----	3	
						1238	....		....	....	---- x--- ---- ---- ----	0	
						1240	....		....	....	---- x--- ---- ---- ----	0	
Geirfuglasker-Eldey area						1422	....		....	....	---- xx-- x--- ---- ----	2	
Near Eldeyjar Islands						1583	0715q		....	....	---- x--- ---- ---- ----	2?	
Nyey						1783	0501<		1783	0815r	---x xx-- x--- ---- ----	3↑	
Eldeyjarbodi						1830	0313?		1831	03 ?	---x x?-- x--- ---- ----	3	
Geirfugladrangur						1879	0530?		1879	0615e	---- x--- x--- ---- ----	1	
NW of Eldey						? 1884	0726		....	....	---- ??-- ---- ---- ----	2?	
NE of Eldey						1926	0605d		....	....	---- x--- ---- ---- ----	0	
Eldeyjarbodi						1966	....		....	....	---- x--- ---- ---- ----	0	
Eldeyjarbodi						1970?	....		....	....	---- x--- ---- ---- ----	0	
REYKJANES (Iceland-SW)	63.88 N*	22.50 W	230	Crater rows	1701-02=	Historical							
Stampar						T -1800y	....		....	....	---x ---- x--- x--- ----	2	
Sundhnukar						C -0400v	....		....	....	---x ---- x--- x--- ----	2	8/-
Lambagja						C -0200?	....		....	....	---x ---- ---- x--- ----	0	
Stampar						1211	....		....	....	---x ---- x--- x--- ----	2	7/-
Arnarsetur, Eldvorp, Illahraun						1226	0715q		1227?	....	---x x--- x--- x--- ----	3?	8/-
(no 1661 eruption at Grindavik)						X 1661	12		....	....	---- ---- ---- ---- ----		
KRISUVIK (Iceland-SW)	63.93 N*	22.10 W	379	Crater rows	1701-03=	Historical							
Burfell						C -5290w	....		....	....	---x ---- x--- x--- ----	2	8/-
Sandfellskofagigir						C -1060u	....		....	....	---x ---- ---- x--- ----	0	7/-
Obrinnisholar						C -0190u	....		....	....	---x ---- x--- x--- ----	2	8/-
Melholl, Afstapahraun						T 0900?	....		....	....	---x ---- x--- x--- ----	2	8/-
Gvendarselsgigar						C 1075u	....		....	....	---x ---- ---- x--- ----	0	7/-
Ogmundargigar						T 1100t	....		....	....	---x ---- x--- x--- -x--	1	8/-
Kapellugigar						1151	....		....	....	---x ---- x--- x--- ----	0	8/-
Mavahlidargigir						1188	....		....	....	---x ---- x--- x--- ----	0	
Tradarfjoll						T 1340?	....		....	....	---x ---- x--- x--- ----	2	
BRENNISTEINSFJOLL (Iceland-SW)	63.92 N*	21.83 W	626	Crater rows	1701-04=	Historical							
Leitin						C -2660u	....		....	....	---x ---- ---- x--- ----	0	9/-
Eldborg a Brennisteinsfjollum						C -1040u	....		....	....	---x ---- x--- x--- ----	2	8/-
Tvibollar						C 0875t	....		....	....	---x ---- x--- x--- ----	2	8/-
Kista (Breiddalshraun)						C 0910u	....		....	....	---x ---- x--- x--- ----	2	7/-
Eldborg at Lambafell						1000?	0625d		....	....	---x ---- ---- x--- ----	0	8/-
Rjupnadyngjur						1188?	....		....	....	---x ---- ---- x--- ----	0	8/-
Kongsfell						T 1200?	....		....	....	---x ---- x--- x--- ----	2	
Grafeldur (Selvogshraun)						1341a	....		....	....	---x ---- x--- x--- ----	2	8/-
HENGILL (Iceland-SW)	64.18 N*	21.33 W	803	Crater rows	1701-05=	Radiocarbon							
SSW of Hengill						C -7290w	....		....	....	---x ---- ---- x--- ----		8/-
Eldborgir						C -7180y	....		....	....	---x ---- ---- x--- ----	0	
Stangarhals						T -5550z	....		....	....	---x ---- ---- x--- ----	0	
Hveradalahraun, Hagavikurhraun						G -3800t	....		....	....	---x ---- x--- x--- ----	2	8/-
Thjofahraun						T -3550z	....		....	....	---x ---- ---- x--- ----	0	
Eldborg undir Meitlum						C -0075u	....		....	....	---x ---- x--- x--- ----	2	8/-
Nesjahraun, Sandey						C 0070u	....		....	....	---x ---- x-x- x--- ----	2	
Reykjafellsgigir, Skardsmyrarhraun						C 0090v	....		....	....	---x ---- x--- x--- ----	2	8/-
GRIMSNES (Iceland-SW)	64.03 N*	20.87 W	214	Crater rows	1701-06=	Radiocarbon							
Selholl South						T -4500?	....		....	....	---x ---- ---- x--- ----	0	
Selholl North						T -4450?	....		....	....	---x ---- x--- x--- ----	2?	
Kerholar, Seydisholar, Tjarnarholar						C -4270w	....		....	....	---x ---- x--- x--- ----	3	9/7
Borgaholl						T -4050?	....		....	....	---x ---- ---- x--- ----	0	
Alftarholl						T -4000?	....		....	....	---x ---- x--- x--- ----	2?	
Kolgrafarholl						T -3900?	....		....	....	---x ---- ---- x--- ----	0	
Raudholar						T -3750?	....		....	....	---x ---- ---- x--- ----	0	

VOLCANO NAME (Subregion) / ERUPTION —	LAT	LONG	ELEV (m)	TYPE	NUMBER	Status / Area of Activity	Start Year	Start M-Dy	P	Stop Year	Stop M-Dy	Central / Flank vent / Radial fiss / Regional*	Submarine / New island / Subglacial / Crater lake	Explosive / Pyro flow / Phreatic / Fumarolic	Lava flow / Lava lake / Dome / Spine	Fatal / Damage / Mudflow / Tsunami	VEI	Vol L/T
GRIMSNES (Iceland-SW) *continued*						Borgarholar	T **-3650**?	....		....	....	---x	----	----	x---	----	0	
						Kalfsholar	T **-3500**?	....		....	....	---x	----	x---	x---	----	2?	
PRESTAHNUKUR (Iceland-SW)	**64.60**	**N* 20.58**	**W 1390**	**Subglacial**	**1701-07=**	**Radiocarbon**												
						Skjaldbreidur	C **-7550**z	....		....	....	x---	----	----	x---	----	0	**10/-**
LANGJOKULL (Iceland-SW)	**64.75**	**N 19.98**	**W 1360**	**Stratovolc**	**1701-08=**	**Radiocarbon**												
						Hallmundahraun	T **0925**q	....		....	....	---x	----	----	x---	----	0	
HOFSJOKULL (Iceland-SW)	**64.78**	**N 18.92**	**W 1782**	**Subglacial**	**1701-09=**	**Holocene**												
KERLINGARFJOLL (Iceland-SW)	**64.63**	**N 19.32**	**W 1488**	**Stratovolc**	**1701-10=**	**Holocene**												
ICELAND - S																		
VESTMANNAEYJAR (Iceland-S)	**63.43**	**N* 20.28**	**W 279**	**Submarine**	**1702-01=**	**Historical**												
						Alsey, Brandur, Sudurey, Hellisey	T **-6050**?	....		....	....	----	xx--	x---	----	----		
						Heimaey (Saefell, Helgafell)	C **-3450**<	....		....	....	----	x---	xx--	x---	----	3	
						SW of Heimaey ?	**1637**	10		**1638**	0228r	----	x---	x---	----	----		
						South or SE of Hellisey	**1896**	09		....	....	----	x---	----	----	----		
						Surtsey	**1963**	1108	+	**1967**	0605	---x	xx--	xx--	x---	----	3*	8/8
						Heimaey (Eldfell)	**1973**	0123		**1973**	0628	---x	x---	x-x-	x---	xx--	3	8/7
EYJAFJOLL (Iceland-S)	**63.63**	**N 19.62**	**W 1666**	**Stratovolc**	**1702-02=**	**Historical**												
							1821	1219		**1823**	0101	x---	--x-	x---	----	--J-	3*	-/8
KATLA (Iceland-S)	**63.63**	**N 19.05**	**W 1512**	**Subglacial**	**1702-03=**	**Historical**												
						Eldgja fissure system	T **-5050**?	....		....	....	---x	----	----	x---	----		
							A **0915**n	....		....	....	----	--?-	x---	----	-xJ-		
						Eldgja fissure system	I **0934**b	....		....	....	---x	----	x---	x---	-x--	4	**9/9**
							0950?	....		....	....	----	--?-	----	x---	-x--	1	
							T **1000**?	....		....	....	----	--x-	x---	----	--J-	4	
							1177b	....		....	....	----	--x-	x---	----	-xJ-	2	
							1245	....		....	....	----	--x-	x---	----	--J-	2	
							1262	....		....	....	----	--x-	x---	----	?-J-	3	
							1311	0118		....	....	----	--x-	x---	----	xxJ-	4?	-/8
						SW of Kotlugja	**1357**c	....		....	....	----	--x-	x---	----	-xJ-	4	-/8
							1416	....		....	....	----	--x-	x---	----	--J-	4?	-/8
							T **1490**?	....		....	....	----	--x-	x---	----	-xJ-	4+	-/8
							1580	0811		....	....	----	--x-	x---	----	-xJ-	3	-/7
							1612	1012		....	....	----	--x-	x---	----	--J-	2	
							1625	0902		**1625**	0914	----	--x-	x---	----	-xJ-	4	-/8
							1660	1103		**1661**	....	----	--x-	x---	----	-x--	4	-/8
							1721	0511		**1721**	1015q	----	--x-	x---	----	-x--	4+	-/8
							1755	1017		**1756**	0213	----	--x-	x---	----	xx--	4+	-/8
							1823	0626		**1823**	0723	----	--x-	x---	----	----	3	-/7
							1860	0508		**1860**	0527	----	--x-	x---	----	----	3	-/7
							1918	1012		**1918**	1104	----	--x-	x---	----	-xJ-	4	-/8
							? **1955**	0625		....	....	----	--?-	----	----	----	1	
TINDFJALLAJOKULL (Iceland-S)	**63.78**	**N 19.57**	**W 1463**	**Stratovolc**	**1702-04=**	**Holocene**												
TORFAJOKULL (Iceland-S)	**63.92**	**N 19.17**	**W 1259**	**Stratovolc**	**1702-05=**	**Historical**												
						W side of caldera (Slettahraun)	T **-6050***	....		....	....	---x	----	----	x---	----		7/-
						Hrafntinnusker and Domadalshraun	T **-5050***	....		....	....	---x	----	----	x---	----		8/-
						W of caldera (Laufafell domes)	T **-4850***	....		....	....	---x	----	----	x---	----		7/-
						N of caldera (Haolduhraun)	T **-4550**z	....		....	....	---x	----	----	x---	----		7/-
						W side of caldera (Markafljot domes)	T **-1550**z	....		....	....	---x	----	----	x---	----		7/-
						N of caldera (Domadalshraun)	T **-1150**v	....		....	....	---x	----	----	x---	----		7/-
						N of caldera (Domadalshraun)	T **0150**v	....		....	....	---x	----	x---	x---	----	3	7/7
						W side of caldera (Hrafntinnuhraun)	T **0900**?	....		....	....	---x	----	x---	x---	----	3	8/7
						W side of caldera (Hrafntinnuhraun)	T **1170**?	....		....	....	---x	----	x---	----	----		
						N of caldera (Namshraun, Laugahraun)	**1477**	03		....	....	---x	----	x---	x---	----	2?	7/-
VATNAFJOLL (Iceland-S)	**63.92**	**N* 19.67**	**W 1235**	**Fissure vents**	**1702-06=**	**Tephrochronology**												
						Vatnafjallahraun	T **-5050***	....		....	....	---x	----	x---	x---	----		
						Raudolduhraun	T **-4950***	....		....	....	---x	----	x---	x---	----		
						West of Laufafell	T **-4750***	....		....	....	---x	----	----	x---	----		
							T **-4550***	....		....	....	---x	----	x---	x---	----		
						Lambadalshraun	T **-4350***	....		....	....	---x	----	x---	x---	----		
						Grasleysisfjallahraun	T **-4150***	....		....	....	---x	----	x---	x---	----		
							T **-3950***	....		....	....	---x	----	----	x---	----		
							T **-3750***	....		....	....	---x	----	----	x---	----		
							T **-3450***	....		....	....	---x	----	x---	x---	----		
						Grafellshraun	T **-3350***	....		....	....	---x	----	x---	x---	----		
						Trollaskogshraun	T **-2950**z	....		....	....	---x	----	----	x---	----		
							T **-2750***	....		....	....	---x	----	x---	x---	----		
						Reynnisfellshraun	T **-2450***	....		....	....	---x	----	----	x---	----		
							T **-1850**z	....		....	....	---x	----	x---	x---	----		
							T **-1650***	....		....	....	---x	----	x---	x---	----		
							T **-1350***	....		....	....	---x	----	x---	x---	----		
							T **-1250***	....		....	....	---x	----	----	x---	----		
						Hraunhalsshraun	T **-1150***	....		....	....	---x	----	----	x---	----		
							T **-0850***	....		....	....	---x	----	x---	x---	----		
							T **-0750**z	....		....	....	---x	----	x---	x---	----		
						Svalaskardshraun	T **-0650***	....		....	....	---x	----	x---	x---	----		
						Langviuhraun	T **-0250**z	....		....	....	---x	----	x---	x---	----		
						Kringluhraun	T **-0150***	....		....	....	---x	----	x---	x---	----		
						Saudleysuhraun	T **0250***	....		....	....	---x	----	----	x---	----		
						Eskihlidarhraun	T **0350***	....		....	....	---x	----	----	x---	----		
						Raudfossahraun	T **0750***	....		....	....	---x	----	x---	x---	----		
HEKLA (Iceland-S)	**63.98**	**N 19.70**	**W 1491**	**Stratovolc**	**1702-07=**	**Historical**												
						Svinholdahraun	T **-5850***	....		....	....	----	----	----	x---	----		
							G **-5050**?	....		....	....	----	----	x---	----	----	**5**	**-/9**
						Gunnarsholtshraun	T **-4650**z	....		....	....	----	----	----	x---	----		
						Krokahraun	T **-4550**z	....		....	....	----	----	----	x---	----		
						Knafaholdahraun	T **-4250**z	....		....	....	----	----	----	x---	----		
						Baejarhraun	T **-4050**z	....		....	....	----	----	----	x---	----		
						Axarhraun	T **-3950**z	....		....	....	----	----	----	x---	----		
						Raudkollar	T **-3350***	....		....	....	----	----	----	x---	----		
							G **-2310**p	....		....	....	----	----	xx--	----	--x-	**5**	**-/9**
						NE flank (Krokagilsoduhraun)	T **-1850***	....		....	....	---x	----	x---	x---	----		
							T **-1750**z	....		....	....	----	----	----	x---	----		

VOLCANO NAME (Subregion) ...... LAT LONG ELEV (m) TYPE NUMBER / ERUPTION — Area of Activity	Status	Start Year	Start M-Dy	P	Stop Year	Stop M-Dy	Central / Flank vent / Radial fiss / Regional*	Submarine / New island / Subglacial / Crater lake	Explosive / Pyro flow / Phreatic / Fumarolic	Lava flow / Lava lake / Dome / Spine	Fatal / Damage / Mudflow / Tsunami	VEI	Vol L/T
HEKLA (Iceland-S) *continued*	T	**-1550?**	....		....	....	----	----	xx--	----	--x-	4	-/8
NE flank	T	**-1250***	....		....	....	---x	----	x---	x---	----		
	G	**-0950?**	....		....	....	----	----	xx--	----	--x-	5+	-/9
NE flank (Raudkembingahraun)	T	**-0850***	....		....	....	---x	----	x---	x---	----		
NE flank	T	**-0750z**	....		....	....	---x	----	----	x---	----		
NE flank	T	**-0250z**	....		....	....	---x	----	x---	x---	----		
NE flank (Hestolduhraun)	T	**0250***	....		....	....	---x	----	----	x---	----		
	T	**0550***	....		....	....	----	----	----	x---	----		
NE flank (Helliskvislarhraun)	T	**0650z**	....		....	....	---x	----	x---	x---	----		
Taglgigahraun, Solvahraun, Stakahraun	T	**0750?**	....		....	....	---x	----	x---	x---	----		
Heklutaglahraun	T	**0800t**	....		....	....	---x	----	----	x---	----		
Austurhraun	T	**1050z**	....		....	....	----	----	----	x---	----		
		1104	1015q		....	....	---x	----	x---	----	-x--	5	-/9
		1158	0119		....	....	---x	----	x---	x---	-x--	4	8/8
		1206	1204		....	....	---x	----	x---	x---	-x--	3	-/7
		1222	....		....	....	---x	----	x---	x---	-x--	2	-/6
		1300	0711		**1301**	07	---x	----	x---	x---	xx--	4	8/8
		1341	0519		....	....	---x	----	x---	x---	-x--	3	-/7
Summit ridge, west flank (Raudoldur)		**1389**	1201p		**1390**	....	--xx	----	x---	x---	-x--	3	8/7
SE of Hekla	T	**1440?**	....		....	....	---x	----	x---	----	-x--		
		1510	0725		....	....	---x	----	x---	x---	xx?-	4	-/8
SW of Hekla (Raudubjallar)		**1554**	05		**1554**	06 ?	---x	----	x---	x---	----	2?	8/-
		1597	0103		**1597**	06 >	---x	----	x---	x---	-xx-	4	-/8
		1636	0508		**1637**	06	---x	----	x---	x---	-xx-	3	-/7
		1693	0213		**1693**	0914?	---x	----	x---	x---	-xxx	4	-/8
SW, south and east of Hekla		**1725**	0402		....	....	---x	----	x---	x---	----	1?	
Bjallagigar		**1766**	0405		**1768**	05	---x	----	x---	x---	-xx-	4	**9**/8
Summit, SW and NE flanks		**1845**	0902		**1846**	0405?	---x	----	x---	x---	-xx-	4	8/8
East of Hekla (Krakagigar)		**1878**	0227		**1878**	04	---x	----	x---	x---	----	2	8/-
E & NE of Hekla (Mundafit, Lambafit)		**1913**	0425	+	**1913**	0518	---x	----	x---	x---	----	2	
Hraungigur, Axlargigur, Toppgigur		**1947**	0329		**1948**	0421	---x	----	x---	x---	xxx-	4	8/8
Sudurgigar, Hlidargigar, Oldugigar		**1970**	0505	+	**1970**	0705	--x-	----	x---	x---	-x--	3	8/7
Summit, SW and NE flanks		**1980**	0817		**1980**	0820	---x	----	x---	x---	-x--	3	8/7
Summit and north flank (900 and 740 m		**1981**	0409		**1981**	0416	--x-	----	x---	x---	----	2	7/-
Summit, SW, SE & NE flank fissures		**1991**	0117		**1991**	0311	-xxx	----	x---	x---	----	3	8/7
ICELAND - NE													
GRIMSVOTN (Iceland-NE) **64.42 N 17.33 W 1725 Caldera 1703-01=**	**Historical**												
Laki (Botnahraun)	T	**-4550z**	....		....	....	---x	----	----	x---	----	0	
S of Thordarhyrna (Bergvatnsarhraun)	T	**-3550z**	....		....	....	---x	----	----	x---	----	0	8/-
Raudholar and Brunuholar	T	**-1950v**	....		....	....	---x	----	x---	x---	----	2	**9**/-
Halsagigur	T	**-0050?**	....		....	....	---x	----	x---	x---	----	2	
		0905?	....		....	....	----	--x-	----	----	----		
		1060?	....		....	....	----	--x-	----	----	----		
		1332	11		....	....	----	--x-	x---	----	----	2	
		1341	05		....	....	----	--x-	x---	----	----	2	
		1354?	....		....	....	----	--x-	----	----	----		
(Sidujokull eruption report not valid)	X	1389	....		X1390	....	----	----	----	----	----		
		1500?	....		....	....	----	--x-	----	----	----		
		1598	1107		....	....	----	--x-	x---	----	----	3?	-/8
(Vatnajokull, possibly Grimsvotn)	@	**1603**	1031		**@1603**	11	----	--x-	x---	----	----	2	
		1619	0729		....	....	----	--x-	x---	----	----	2	
		1629	....		....	....	----	--x-	x---	----	x-J-	2	
		1638	0224d		....	....	----	--x-	x---	----	----	2	
		1659	11		....	....	----	--x-	x---	----	----	2	
(Vatnajokull)	@	**1681**	0410		....	....	----	--x-	----	----	----		
		1684	1105d		**1685**	01	----	--x-	x---	----	xxJ-	2	
		1706	1015q		....	....	----	--x-	x---	----	----	2	
		1716	1006		....	....	----	--x-	x---	----	----	2	
		1725	02		....	....	----	--x-	x---	----	--J-	2	
NE of Palsfjall		**1753**	1015q		....	....	----	--x-	x---	----	-xJ-	2?	
(Vatnajokull)	@	**1768**	....		....	....	----	--x-	x---	----	----	2	
		1774	02		....	....	----	--x-	x---	----	--J-	2	
Lakagigar (Skaftar) and Grimsvotn		**1783**	05 ?	+	**1785**	0526?	---x	--x-	x---	x---	xxJ-	4*	**10**/8
(W-Vatnajokull)	?	**1794**	0715q		....	....	----	--?-	----	----	----		
(jokulhlaup, probably no eruption)	X	1796	06		....	....	----	----	----	----	--J-		
		1816	05		**1816**	06 ?	----	--x-	x---	----	----	2	
Grimsvotn-Thordarhyrna		**1823**	0204d		....	....	----	--x-	x---	----	----	2	
		1838	06		....	....	----	--x-	----	----	--J-	2	
		1854	....		....	....	----	--x-	x---	----	----	2	
	?	**1861**	05		....	....	----	--?-	?---	----	-xJ-	2	
		1867	0829		....	....	----	--x-	x---	----	--J-	1	
		1873	0108		**1873**	08	----	--x-	x---	----	--J-	4	-/8
		1883	0115		**1883**	0415e	----	--x-	x---	----	--J-	2	
Thordarhyrna		**1887**	0815		**1889**	....	----	--x-	x---	----	--J-	2	
		1891	11 ?		**1892**	0316	----	--x-	x---	----	--J-	2	
	@	**1897**	....		....	....	----	--x-	x---	----	----	2	
Grimsvotn and Thordarhyrna		**1902**	12	+	**1904**	0112	----	--x-	x---	----	--J-	4*	8/-
		1922	0929		**1922**	1023	----	--x-	x---	----	--J-	2	
North of Grimsvotn caldera		**1933**	1129a		**1933**	1209a	---x	--x-	x---	----	----	1	
Near south caldera wall		**1934**	0330		**1934**	0407	----	--x-	x---	----	--J-	2	
Vatnajokull	@	**1934**	1221		**@1934**	1226	----	--x-	----	----	----		
8 km north of Svartibunki		**1938**	05		....	....	----	--x-	----	----	--J-	1	
	?	**1939**	06		....	....	----	--?-	----	----	--J-	0	
	?	**1941**	04		**?1941**	08	----	--?-	----	----	--J-	0	
		1945	0925?		....	....	----	--x-	----	----	--J-	1	
	?	**1948**	02		....	....	----	--?-	----	----	--J-	0	
North and south part of caldera		**1954**	07		....	....	x---	--x-	--x-	----	--J-	1	
	?	**1972**	03		**?1972**	04	x---	--??	----	----	--J-	0	
Near south caldera wall		**1983**	0528		**1983**	0602	x---	--xx	x---	----	----	2	
	?	**1984**	0820<		....	....	x---	--?-	----	----	----	0	
LOKI-FOGRUFJOLL (Iceland-NE) **64.48 N 17.80 W 1570 Subglacial 1703-02=**	**Historical**												
Eastern Loki cauldron		**1910**	0618		**1910**	10	---x	--x-	x---	----	----	2	
Eastern Loki cauldron	?	**1986**	1129		**?1986**	1201?	---x	--?-	----	----	--J-	0	
Eastern Loki cauldron	?	**1991**	0812		....	....	---x	--?-	----	----	--J-	0	

VOLCANO NAME (Subregion) / ERUPTION — Area of Activity	LAT	LONG	ELEV (m)	TYPE	NUMBER	Status / Start Year	Start M-Dy	P	Stop Year	Stop M-Dy	Central / Flank vent / Radial fiss / Regional*	Submarine / New island / Subglacial / Crater lake	Explosive / Pyro flow / Phreatic / Fumarolic	Lava flow / Lava lake / Dome / Spine	Fatal / Damage / Mudflow / Tsunami	VEI	Vol L/T
BARDARBUNGA (Iceland-NE)	**64.63** N	**17.53** W	**2000**	**Stratovolc**	**1703-03=**	**Historical**											
Veidivotn (Haahraun, Botnahraun)						T **-7050***	....		....	....	---x	----	----	x---	----		
Veidivotn (Thjorsarhraun)						G **-6650**t	....		....	....	---x	----	----	x---	----		**10/-**
Veidivotn (Sigolduhraun, Kalfahraun)						T **-4550**?	....		....	....	---x	----	----	x---	----		
Trolladyngja						T **-4050**?	....		....	....	----	----	----	x---	----		
Veidivotn (Burfellshraun, Drekahraun)						T **-1250**?	....		....	....	---x	----	----	x---	----		**9/-**
Veidivotn (Tjorvahraun)						T **0150**v	....		....	....	---x	----	x---	x---	----	2?	8/-
Veidivotn (Vatnaoldur, Hnnausapollur)						T **0900**?	....		....	....	---x	----	xxx-	x---	----	4	**7/9**
						0940?	....		....	....	----	--x-	----	----	----		
						1080?	....		....	....	----	--x-	----	----	----		
						1159?	....		....	....	----	--x-	----	----	----		
						1410?	....		....	....	----	--x-	----	----	----		
Veidivotn (Veidivatnahraun)						**1477**	03 ?		....	....	---x	--x-	xxx-	x---	-x--	**5?**	**9/9**
						I **1697**	....		....	....	---x	--x-	x---	----	--J-	2	
Dyngjuhals ?						@ **1702**	....		....	....	---?	--x-	x---	----	----	2	
						1706	....		....	....	----	--x-	x---	----	----	2	
						1707	....		....	....	----	--x-	x---	----	----	2	
(Bardarbunga, not Kverkfjoll)						**1712**	0115q		....	....	----	--x-	x---	----	-xJ-	2	
(Bardarbunga, not Kverkfjoll)						**1716**	1005d		....	....	----	--x-	x---	----	-xJ-	2	
(Bardarbunga, not Kverkfjoll)						**1717**	0804		**1717**	0917>	----	--x-	x---	----	-xJ-	3?	
						I **1720**	....		....	....	---x	--x-	x---	----	----	2	
Dyngjujokull, Dyngjuhal ?						**1726**	0201p		**1726**	0501p	----	--x-	----	----	-xJ-	1?	
Dyngjuhals ?						@ **1729**	....		....	....	---?	--x-	x---	----	-xJ-	1	
						I **1739**	....		....	....	---x	--x-	x---	----	----	2	
						1766	07		....	....	----	--x-	x---	----	--J-	2	
(Bardarbunga, or Grimsvotn)						@ **1769**	....		....	....	----	--x-	x---	----	----	2	
						@ **1797**	....		....	....	---?	--?-	----	----	- mo		
NW-Vatnajokull						? **1807**	....		....	....	----	--?-	----	----	----		
Trollagigar						**1862**	0630		**1864**	1015q	---x	----	x---	x---	----	2	8/-
Dyngjuhals ?						@ **1872**?	....		....	....	---?	--?-	----	----	----		
Dyngjuhals ?						@ **1902**	12		@**1903**	06	---?	--x-	----	----	--J-	2?	
TUNGNAFELLSJOKULL (Iceland-NE)	**64.73** N	**17.92** W	**1535**	**Stratovolc**	**1703-04=**	**Holocene**											
KVERKFJOLL (Iceland-NE)	**64.65** N	**16.72** W	**1920**	**Stratovolc**	**1703-05=**	**Historical**											
Arnadalsoldugjoska						T **-7050**?	....		....	....	---x	----	?---	----	----		
Krepputunguhraun, Kverfjallahraun						T **-5550***	....		....	....	---x	----	----	x---	----		
						1655	0415q		....	....	----	--x-	----	----	--J-	0	
						1729	0215q		....	....	----	--x-	----	----	--J-	1	
						1729	08		....	....	----	--x-	----	----	--J-	1	
Hveradalur area						**1929**	01		**1929**	02	----	----	x---	----	----	1	
						1959	....		....	....	----	--x-	----	----	----		
						1968	0523		**1968**	06	----	--x-	----	----	----		
ASKJA (Iceland-NE)	**65.03** N	**16.75** W	**1516**	**Stratovolc**	**1703-06=**	**Historical**											
Holuhraun						**1797**?	....		....	....	---x	----	----	x---	----	0	
Oskjuvatn Caldera, Viti, Sveinagja						**1875**	0101	+	**1875**	1017	x--x	----	xxx-	x---	-x--	4*	-/8
Dyngjufjoll						**1919**	....		....	....	----	----	x---	----	----	2	
NE caldera wall, 0.6 km SE of Viti						**1921**	03		....	....	--x-	----	----	x---	----	0	
1 km southwest of Oskjuvatn Caldera						**1922**	11		....	....	----	----	----	x---	----	0	
SE corner of Oskjuvatn Caldera						**1923**	0115q		....	....	---x	----	----	x---	----	0	
South flank of Dyngjufjoll Massif						**1924**?	....		....	....	---x	----	----	x---	----	0?	8/-
South end of Oskjuvatn lake						**1926**	0715q		....	....	x---	-x-x	x---	x---	----	2?	-/7
South shore of Oskjuvatn lake						**1938**	1219?		....	....	x---	----	x---	x---	----	2	
North of Oskjuvatn lake (Vikraborgir)						**1961**	1026		**1961**	1205d	--x-	----	x---	xx--	----	2	8/6
FREMRINAMUR (Iceland-NE)	**65.43** N	**16.65** W	**939**	**Stratovolc**	**1703-07=**	**Tephrochronology**											
Sveinar (Rauduborgir) fissure						T **-5050***	....		....	....	---x	----	x---	x---	----		
Ketildyngja						T **-1850**?	....		....	....	----	----	----	x---	----		**9/-**
Kraeduborgir (Burfellshraun)						T **-0800**y	....		....	....	---x	----	----	x---	----		
(no 1823 eruption at Lierhafnarskord)						X 1823	....		....	....	----	----	----	----	----		
KRAFLA (Iceland-NE)	**65.73** N	**16.78** W	**650**	**Caldera**	**1703-08=**	**Historical**											
Gjastykkisbunga						T **-8050**?	....		....	....	x---	----	----	x---	----	0	
Ludent, Namafjall-Krofluhals						T **-7850**?	....		....	....	x--x	----	x-x-	x---	----		**9/-**
Heidarspordur						T **-7400**y	....		....	....	---x	----	----	x---	----	0	
Hraunbunga						T **-6950**?	....		....	....	x---	----	----	x---	----	0	
Bondholshraun, Hveragil						T **-6850**?	....		....	....	x---	----	x---	x---	----	2?	
Hveragil						T **-6800**?	....		....	....	x---	----	x---	----	----	2?	
Drangagrundahraun						T **-6150**?	....		....	....	---x	----	----	x---	----	0	
Fjarborg						T **-5750**?	....		....	....	---x	----	----	x---	----	0	
Ludent crater rows						T **-4050**?	....		....	....	---x	----	----	x---	----	0	
Hvannstod						C **-3050**?	....		....	....	---x	----	----	x---	----	0	
Hverfjall, Jarbadsholar						T **-0650**?	....		....	....	x---	----	x-x-	x---	----	4	-/8
North of Hverfjall						T **-0300**y	....		....	....	---x	----	----	x---	----	0	
Holseldar						T **-0050**?	....		....	....	---x	----	x---	x---	----	2	
Threngslaborgir-Ludentsborgir crater						T **0050**?	....		....	....	---x	----	x---	x---	----	2	9/-
Kerlingarholar						T **0250**y	....		....	....	---x	----	----	x---	----	0	
Daleldar, Svortuborgir						T **0850**?	....		....	....	---x	----	----	x---	----	0	7/-
Crater south of Viti						T **1300**x	....		....	....	x---	----	x---	----	----	2?	
Viti (1.5 km east of Leirhnjukur)						**1724**	0517		**1724**	0518	---x	----	x--x	----	----	2	-/6
(solfataric activity, no eruption)						X 1725	0111		....	....	----	----	---x	----	----		
North end of Leirhnjukur						**1727**	0821		....	....	---x	----	----	x---	----	2	
Leirhnjukur, Hrossadalur, Bjarnarflag						**1728**	0418		....	....	---x	----	----	x---	----	2	
Leirhnjukur crater row						**1728**	1218		....	....	---x	----	----	x---	----	2	8/-
Leirhnjukur crater row						**1729**	0630		**1729**	0925e	---x	----	----	x---	-x--	2	
Leirhnjukur crater row						**1746**	0710		**1746**	0710?	---x	----	x---	----	----	1	
1.5-2.5 km north of Leirhnjukur						**1975**	1220		**1975**	1220	---x	----	----	x---	----	0	5/-
3 km north of Leirhnjukur						**1977**	0427	+	**1977**	0908	---x	----	x-x-	x---	-x--	1	6/1
Leirhnjukur to 11 km north						**1980**	0316	+	**1980**	1023	---x	----	--x-	x---	----	0*	7/-
6-8 km north of Leirhnjukur						**1981**	0130		**1981**	0204	---x	----	----	x---	----	0	7/-
Leirhnjukur to 9 km north						**1981**	1118		**1981**	1123	---x	----	----	x---	----	0	7/-
Leirhnjukur to 8.5 km north						**1984**	0904		**1984**	0918	---x	----	----	x---	----	0	8/-
THEISTAREYKJARBUNGA (")	**65.88** N	**16.83** W	**564**	**Shield**	**1703-09=**	**Tephrochronology**											
Theistareykjabunga shield volcano						T **-8050**?	....		....	....	x---	----	----	x---	----	0	
Borgarhraun						T **-3050**?	....		....	....	---x	----	----	x---	----	0	
Storihver (Theistareykjahraun)						T **-0750**v	....		....	....	---x	----	----	x---	----	0	
TJORNES FRACTURE ZONE (")	**66.30** N	**17.10** W		**Submarine**	**1703-10=**	**Historical**											
Immediately north of Manareyjar Is.						**1867**	12		**1868**	01	----	x---	----	----	----		

VOLCANO NAME (Subregion) / ERUPTION — Area of Activity	LAT	LONG	ELEV (m)	TYPE	NUMBER	Status / Start Year	Start M-Dy	P	Stop Year	Stop M-Dy	Central / Flank vent / Radial fiss / Regional*	Submarine / New island / Subglacial / Crater lake	Explosive / Pyro flow / Phreatic / Fumarolic	Lava flow / Lava lake / Dome / Spine	Fatal / Damage / Mudflow / Tsunami	VEI	Vol L/T
ICELAND - SE																	
ORAEFAJOKULL (Iceland-SE)	64.00 N	16.65 W	2119	Stratovolc	1704-01=	Historical											
						1362	0605d		....	....	x---	--x-	x---	----	xxJ-	5	-/9
Caldera, west flank (to 1100 m)						1727	0803		1728	0501p	x--x	--x-	x---	----	xxJ-	4	-/8
ESJUFJOLL (Iceland-SE)	64.27 N	16.65 W	1760	Stratovolc	1704-02=	Historical											
						1927	0905d		....	....	?---	----	x---	----	--J-	1	
KOLBEINSEY RIDGE (Iceland-N of) ..	66.67 N	18.50 W		Submarine	1705-01=	Historical											
NW of Grimsey Island						1372	....		....	....	----	xx--	----	----	----	2?	
(eruption north of Iceland)						@ 1755	0918		....	....	----	?---	x---	----	----		
(no 1783 eruption north of Iceland)						X 1783	....		....	....	----	----	----	----	----		
(no 1838 eruption near Siglufjordur).......						X 1838	0611?		....	....	----	----	----	----	----		
ARCTIC OCEAN																	
JAN MAYEN (Atl-N-Jan Mayen)	71.08 N	8.17 W	2277	Stratovolc	1706-01=	Historical											
Beerenberg (Eggoya, SW flank)..........						T 1350v	....		....	....	-x--	xx--	x-x-	----	----		
Beerenberg..........................						? 1558<	....		....	....	----	----	----	----	----		
Beerenberg (Dagnyhaugen, SW flank)						1732	0517		1732	0518	-x--	----	x---	x---	----	3	
Beerenberg (Dagnyhaugen, SW flank)						1818	04		....	....	-x--	----	x---	x---	----	3?	
Beerenberg (Kokssletta, NE flank)........						1851r	....		....	....	-x--	----	----	x---	----		
Beerenberg (NE & SW flanks, summit)						1970	0918	+	1972?	....	xx-x	--x-	x-x-	x---	--J-	3	8/7
Beerenberg (NE flank, Skrukkelia)........						1973	0115q		....	....	-x--	----	x---	----	----	1	
Beerenberg (NE flank, 0-200 m)						1985	0106		1985	0109	-x-x	----	x---	x---	----	2	6/6
UNNAMED (Arctic Ocean)	88.27 N	65.60 W	-1500	Submarine	1707-01-	Historical											
						1475q	....		....	....	----	x---	x---	----	----	0	
						1725q	....		....	....	----	x---	x---	----	----	0	
						1957	1121		1957	1124	----	x---	----	----	----	0	

Atlantic Ocean (18)

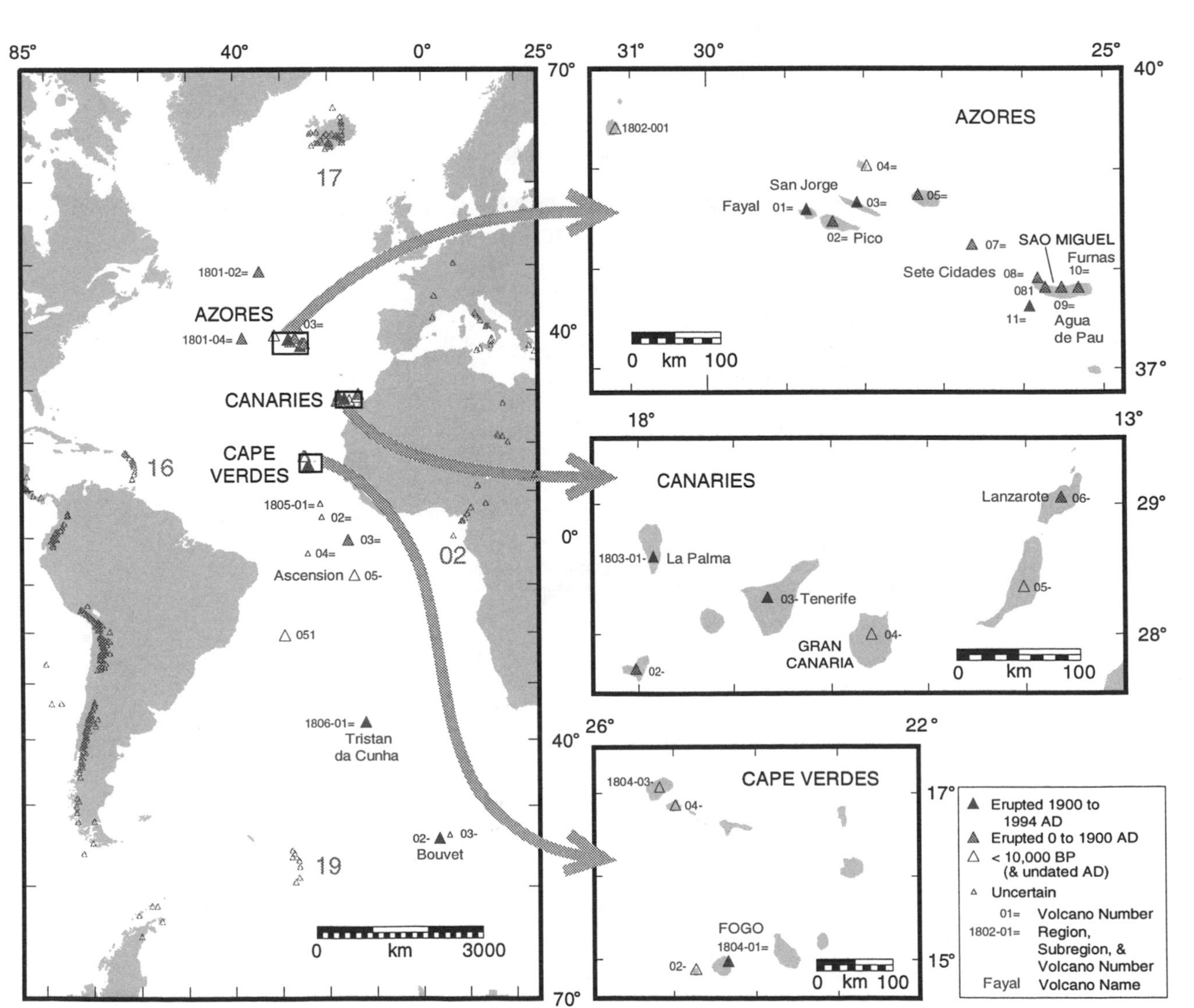

Known eruptions from this large region total 117 – only Antarctica has less – but its historical record is relatively long. The largest island group, the Canaries, is reached by favorable winds from Europe and was an important base for early voyages to the new world. In fact, Christopher Columbus recorded a 1492 eruption on Tenerife, just 7 weeks before that same logbook carried documentation of a more historic observation. The Azores were also well placed for sailors because of the predominant westerly winds used for return routes to Europe.

The Canaries were mentioned by Pliny around 40 AD, and were often rediscovered in the following centuries. They were claimed by Portugal in 1341, the year of the region's first historical eruption (a somewhat questionable report of activity somewhere on Tenerife), but were awarded to Spain by the Pope 3 years later. They were settled in 1402 and conquest of the indigenous Guanches population was complete by 1496. The Canaries now have the largest population (1.6 million) in the region and, as part of Spain, claim Pico de Teide as that nation's highest point.

A discovery date for the Azores is uncertain, but they appear on a map from 1351 AD. The Portuguese visited in 1427-31 and colonization began in 1445, a year after the first historical eruption. The 9 islands now support about 250,000 people, half of them on the island of Sao Miguel.

The Cape Verde islands were discovered by Portugal in 1456 and settled 6 years later. An eruption beginning in 1500 appears to have continued for about 260 years, with behavior similar to that of Italy's Stromboli. The islands were an important point in the trans-shipment of slaves until the 18th century. Independence from Portugal came in 1975.

Tristan de Cunha was discovered by the Portuguese in 1506 and the islands were much visited by whalers and sealers. They were first inhabited by St. Helenans in the 19th century and annexed by Britain in 1816. The residents were evacuated during the 1961 eruption, but most elected to return within two years and the 1970 population was estimated at 280.

Aside from submarine activity (most of it uncertain) the only other dated eruption in the region is from Norway's Bouvet Island, the most remote in the world. It was discovered in 1739, but its only known eruption was 2000 years ago (by magnetic dating).

Volcanism in the region is largely caused by hotspots in oceanic crust, and the region has the highest proportion of fissure vent volcanoes (as primary features). Several known volcanoes lie along or near the Mid-Atlantic Ridge that separates the Eurasian and African plates from the North and South American plates, but the Canaries and Cape Verdes lie just west of the African continental margin. The region has been unusually quiet in recent decades: Following a small eruption on La Palma (Canaries) in 1971, there has been no recorded volcanism, and only some mild unrest in 1988-90 has been reported in SEAN/GVN *Bulletins*.

VOLCANO NAME (Subregion) / ERUPTION — Area of Activity	**LAT**	**LONG**	**ELEV (m)**	**TYPE**	**NUMBER**	**Status** / Start Year	Start M-Dy	P	Stop Year	Stop M-Dy	Central / Flank vent / Radial fiss / Regional*	Submarine / New island / Subglacial / Crater lake	Explosive / Pyro flow / Phreatic / Fumarolic	Lava flow / Lava lake / Dome / Spine	Fatal / Damage / Mudflow / Tsunami	VEI	Vol L/T
ATLANTIC OCEAN - N																	
UNNAMED (Atlantic-N)	66.00 N	27.75 W	-108		1801-01=	Not a Volcano											
(incorrect eruption report)						X 1332	....		....	....	----	----	----	----	----		
(incorrect eruption report)						X 1456	....		....	....	----	----	----	----	----		
(incorrect eruption report)						X 1783	....		....	....	----	----	----	----	----		
UNNAMED (Atlantic-N)	**49.00 N**	**34.50 W**	**-1650**	**Submarine**	**1801-02=**	**Historical**											
						1884	1229		....	....	----	x---	----	----	----	0	
UNNAMED (Atlantic-N)	**39.95 N**	**25.83 W**	**-2835**	**Submarine**	**1801-03=**	**Uncertain**											
						? **1856**	1125		?**1856**	1125	----	x---	----	----	----	0	
UNNAMED (Atlantic-N)	**38.75 N**	**38.08 W**	**-4200**	**Submarine**	**1801-04=**	**Historical**											
						1865	0709		....	....	----	x---	----	----	----	0	
AZORES																	
FLORES (Azores)	**39.40 N**	**31.17 W**	**915**	**Stratovolc**	**1802-001**	**Radiocarbon**											
Caldeira Funda de Lajes						C **-1200**v	....		....	....	x---	----	x---	x---	----		
Caldeira Comprida						C **-0950**v	....		....	....	x---	----	x---	x---	----		
FAYAL (Azores)	**38.60 N**	**28.73 W**	**1043**	**Stratovolc**	**1802-01=**	**Historical**											
West flank						**1672**	0424		**1673**	0228	-x--	----	x---	x---	xx--	2	
West flank (Capelinhos) and summit						**1957**	0927		**1958**	1024	xxx-	xx--	xxx-	x---	-x--	2	7/7
PICO (Azores)	**38.47 N**	**28.40 W**	**2351**	**Stratovolc**	**1802-02=**	**Historical**											
East flank (800 m)						**1562**	0921?		**1564**?	....	-x--	----	x---	x---	-x--	2	
SE flank (200 m), NW flank (1200 m)						**1718**	0201		**1718**	1215e	-x--	?---	x---	x---	xx--	2	
SE flank (400 m)						**1720**	0710		**1720**	12 ?	-x--	----	x---	x---	-x--	2	
Off NW coast						? **1963**	1215<		....	....	----	x---	---x	----	----	0	
SAN JORGE (Azores)	**38.65 N**	**28.08 W**	**1053**	**Fissure vent**	**1802-03=**	**Historical**											
San Jorge (SW side)						**1580**	0501		**1580**	0830?	---x	----	xx--	x---	xx--	3?	
Off south coast of San Jorge						**1757**	0709		**1757**	0710	----	xx--	----	----	----	0	
Submarine vent ca. 20 km SW of Terceira						**1800**	0624		**1800**	0625	----	x---	--x-	----	----	2	
San Jorge						**1808**	0501		**1808**	0610	---x	----	xx-x	x---	xx--	1	
Submarine vent ca. 20 km SW of Terceira						**1902**	0507		**1902**	0508	----	x---	----	----	----	0	
						1907	....		....	....	----	x---	----	----	----	0	
Off SW coast						? **1964**	0218		....	....	----	?---	----	----	----	0	
GRACIOSA (Azores)	**39.02 N**	**27.97 W**	**402**	**Stratovolc**	**1802-04=**	**Holocene**											
TERCEIRA (Azores)	**38.73 N**	**27.32 W**	**1023**	**Stratovolcs**	**1802-05=**	**Historical**											
Fissure zone (south of Pico Alto)						C **-0165**?	....		....	....	---x	----	x---	x---	----		8/-
Fissure zone (east of Santa Barbara)						C **-0090**v	....		....	....	---x	----	x---	----	----		
Pico Alto domes						T **1200**y	....		....	....	----	----	----	--x-	----		
Farol I dome (Santa Barbara)						T **1400**t	....		....	....	-x--	----	----	--x-	----		
Fissure zone (east of Santa Barbara)						**1761**	0417		**1761**	0428?	---x	----	x---	x---	-x--	2	
Submarine vent west of Terceira						**1867**	0601		**1867**	0608	---x	x---	x---	----	----	3	
DON JOAO DE CASTRO BANK (")	**38.23 N**	**26.63 W**	**-14**	**Submarine**	**1802-07=**	**Historical**											
						1720	1208?		**1720**	1226e	?---	xx--	x---	----	----	3	
....	**37.87 N**	**25.78 W**	**856**	**Stratovolc**	**1802-08=**	**Historical**											
Seara Cerrado da Ladeira						T **-3050**?	....		....	....	x---	---x	x---	----	----	4	-/8
Caldeira do Alfreres and NW flank						T **-2050***	....		....	....	xx--	xx--	x---	----	----		
SE flank (Eguas)						C **-0750**y	....		....	....	-x--	----	x---	x---	----		
SE caldera floor (Lagoa de Santiago)						C **0090**v	....		....	....	x---	----	xx--	----	----	4	-/8
SE caldera floor (Lagoa Rasa)						T **0380**y	....		....	....	x---	----	x---	----	--x-	4	-/8
SE flank (Carvao)						C **0670**w	....		....	....	-xx-	----	x---	x---	----	3	7/7
SE flank (Ferraria)						C **0950**v	....		....	....	-x--	----	x---	x---	----	2	7/6
West flank (Ponta de Ferraria)						C **1110**t	....		....	....	-x--	----	x---	x---	----	2	7/6
SW side of caldera (Caldeira Seca)						**1444**?	....		....	....	x---	---x	x---	?---	--x-	4	-/8
Submarine vent west of Sete Cidades						**1638**	0703		**1638**	0728	---x	xx--	x---	----	----	2	
Submarine vent west of Sete Cidades						**1682**	1213		....	....	---x	x---	x---	----	----	2	
West flank (Pico das Camarinhas)						**1713**	....		....	....	-x--	?---	x---	x---	----	2	7/6
Submarine vent west of Sete Cidades						**1811**	0201		**1811**	0208	---x	x---	x---	----	----	2?	
Submarine vent west of Sete Cidades						**1811**	0614		**1811**	0622	---x	xx--	x---	----	----	3	

VOLCANO NAME (Subregion) / ERUPTION — Area of Activity	LAT	LONG	ELEV (m)	TYPE	NUMBER	Status / Start Year	Start M-Dy	P	Stop Year	Stop M-Dy	Central / Flank vent / Radial fiss / Regional*	Submarine / New island / Subglacial / Crater lake	Explosive / Pyro flow / Phreatic / Fumarolic	Lava flow / Lava lake / Dome / Spine	Fatal / Damage / Mudflow / Tsunami	VEI	Vol L/T
SETE CIDADES (San Miguel)																	
Submarine vent off San Miguel						@ 1861	....		....	....	----	x---	----	----	----	0	
Submarine vent off San Miguel						@ 1880	....		....	....	----	x---	----	----	----	0	
UNNAMED (San Miguel)	37.78 N*	25.67 W	350	Pyrocl cones	1802-081	Historical											
						C -4040?	....		....	....	----	----	----	x---	----		
North-central part (Aflitos)						C -0850v	....		....	....	----	----	x---	x---	----		
North-central part (Furna)						C -0510x	....		....	....	----	----	x---	x---	----		
East-central part (Caldeirao)						C 0600v	....		....	....	----	----	x---	x---	----		
East-central part (Cruz)						C 0850w	....		....	....	----	----	xx--	x---	----		
Eastern part (Mata des Feiticeiras)						C 0940v	....		....	....	----	----	x---	x---	----		
Eastern part (SW of Fogo 1 Cone)						1652	1019		1652	1026	x---	----	x---	x---	----	2	6/6
AGUA DE PAU (San Miguel)	37.77 N	25.47 W	947	Stratovolc	1802-09=	Historical											
West flank (Pico Joao Fernandes)						C -6750x	....		....	....	-x--	----	x---	x---	----		
SW flank (449 m)						C -4550v	....		....	....	-x--	----	x---	x---	----		
Lagoa do Fogo caldera and north flank						C -2985?	....		....	....	xx--	----	xx--	x---	--x-	5	-/9
East flank (East Congo maar)						C -2210w	....		....	....	-x--	----	xx--	----	----		
East flank (Lagoa do Congro)						C -1850z	....		....	....	-x--	----	xx--	--x-	----	3	6/7
Lagoa do Fogo caldera						C -1290?	....		....	....	x---	----	x---	----	----	4	-/8
NW flank (251 m)						C 0160w	....		....	....	-x--	----	x---	x---	----		
WNW flank (Mos)						C 0700w	....		....	....	-x--	----	x---	x---	----		
Caldera, NW flank (Cerro Queimado)						1563	0628	+	1563	0726e	xxx-	---x	x---	x---	-x--	4	6/8
Lagoa do Fogo caldera						1564	0210		1564	0212	x---	----	x-?-	?---	----	2	
FURNAS (San Miguel)	37.77 N	25.32 W	805	Stratovolc	1802-10=	Historical											
East rim of caldera (Pico do Canaria)						C -4570<	....		....	....	x---	----	xx--	----	----		
Central part of caldera						C -0950?	....		....	....	x---	----	xx--	----	--x-	5	-/9
Central part of caldera (Gaspar)						C 0840v	....		....	....	x---	----	xx--	--x-	----	4	7/8
Central part of caldera (Gaspar)						C 1170v	....		....	....	x---	----	x---	----	----	4	-/8
South rim of caldera (Pico da Areia)						1630	0903		1630	0910?	x---	----	xx--	--x-	xxx-	4	7/8
MONACO BANK (Azores)	37.60 N	25.88 W	-197	Submarine	1802-11=	Historical											
						1907	0401		....	....	---?	x---	----	----	----	0	
						1911	0307		....	....	---?	x---	--?-	----	----	1	
CANARY ISLANDS																	
LA PALMA (Canary Is)	28.58 N	17.83 W	2426	Stratovolc	1803-01-	Historical											
Tacande (Montana Quemada)						1435e	....		....	....	-x-x	----	x---	----	-x--	2	7/6
Tahuya						1585	0519		1585	0810	-xxx	----	x---	x---	-x--	2	
San Martin (Tigalate)						1646	1002		1646	1221	-x-BX	----	x---	x---	-x--	2	7/6
San Antonio (Fuencaliente)						1677	1117		1678	0121	-x-x	----	x---	x---	xx--	2	7/6
El Charco						1712	1009		1712	1203	--xx	----	x---	x---	-x--	2	7/-
San Juan, Llano del Banco, Hoyo Negro						1949	0624	+	1949	0730	-xxx	----	x---	x---	-x--	2?	7/5
Teneguia						1971	1026		1971	1118	-xxx	----	x---	x-x-	xx--	2	7/-
HIERRO (Canary Is)	27.73 N	18.03 W	1500	Shield	1803-02-	Historical											
East flank (Soliman)						C -0950w	....		....	....	-x--	----	x---	x---	----		
						? 1677	....		....	....	----	----	----	----	----		
						? 1692	....		....	....	----	----	----	----	----		
Volcan de Lomo Negro						1793	05		1793	06	-x--	----	----	x---	----	0	
TENERIFE (Canary Is)	28.271 N	16.641 W	3715	Stratovolc	1803-03-	Historical											
Teide-Pico Viejo complex						C -0520?	....		....	....	----	----	----	x---	----		
Teide-Pico Viejo complex						C 0040?	....		....	....	----	----	----	x---	----		
						M 1150?	....		....	....	----	----	----	----	----		
Pico del Teide						? 1341	....		....	....	x---	----	---?	----	----		
Pico del Teide						1396c	....		....	....	x---	----	?---	x---	----		
Lower Orotava Valley						1430	....		....	....	-x--	----	x---	x---	----	2	
Pico del Teide						? 1444	....		....	....	x---	----	---?	----	----		
NW flank of Pico Viejo						1492	0824<		....	....	-x--	----	?---	x---	----		
Siete Fuentes, Fasnia, Guimar						1704	1231	+	1705	0327	-x-BX	----	x---	x---	-x--	2*	
NW flank (Garachico)						1706	0505		1706	0613	-x--	----	x---	x---	-x--	2	
SW flank of Pico Viejo (Chahorra)						1798	0609		1798	0914?	---x	----	x---	x---	----	3	7/-
NW flank (Chinyero)						1909	1118		1909	1127	---x	----	x---	x---	-x--	2	7/-
GRAN CANARIA (Canary Is)	28.00 N	15.58 W	1950	Fissure vents	1803-04-	Radiocarbon											
Montagnon Negro						C -1125t	....		....	....	x---	----	x---	----	----		
FUERTEVENTURA (Canary Is)	28.358 N	14.02 W	529	Fissure vents	1803-05-	Holocene											
LANZAROTE (Canary Is)	29.03 N	13.63 W	670	Fissure vents	1803-06-	Historical											
Montana de Juan Perdomo						M 0500t	....		....	....	-x-x	----	x---	x---	----		
Mazo, Santa Catalina, Corazoncillo						M 0700t	....		....	....	-x-x	----	x---	x---	----		
Montanas del Fuego						1730	0901	+	1736	0416	-x-x	x---	x---	x---	?x--	3	9/-
Tao, Nuevo del Fuego, Tinguaton						1824	0731	+	1824	1024	---x	----	x---	x---	----	2*	7/-
CAPE VERDE ISLANDS																	
FOGO (Cape Verde Is)	14.95 N	24.35 W	2829	Stratovolc	1804-01=	Historical											
Central cone						1500	....		1761?	....	xx--	----	x---	x---	----	1	
SW side						1769	04 >		....	....	-x--	----	x---	----	----		
North flank, NW flank						1785	0124		1785	0225	?x--	----	--x-	x---	-x--	2	6/-
North flank						1799	0602		1799	0628	-x--	----	x---	x---	-x--	2	
						1816	1231y		....	....	----	----	----	----	----		
North flank						1847	0409		1847	0502?	-x--	----	x---	x---	xx--	2	
NW flank						1852	0219		1852	0330?	-x--	----	x---	x---	----	2	
SE flank						1857	0627		1857	1215	----	----	?---	----	----	2	
						1909	....		....	....	----	----	----	----	----		
South flank, NW flank						1951	0612		1951	0821	-x--	----	x---	x---	-x--	2	7/-
BRAVA (Cape Verde Is)	14.85 N	24.72 W	900	Stratovolc	1804-02-	Holocene											
SANTO ANTAO (Cape Verde Is)	17.07 N	25.17 W	1979	Stratovolc	1804-03-	Holocene											
SAN VICENTE (Cape Verde Is)	16.85 N	24.97 W	697	Stratovolc	1804-04-	Holocene											
ATLANTIC - C & S																	
UNNAMED (Atlantic-C)	7.00 N	21.83 W	-1415	Submarine	1805-01=	Uncertain											
						? 1824	0501		....	....	----	?---	----	----	----	0	
UNNAMED (Atlantic-C)	4.20 N	21.45 W	-2900	Submarine	1805-02=	Uncertain											
						? 1878	0129		....	....	----	?---	----	----	----	0	
UNNAMED (Atlantic-C)	0.58 S	15.83 W	-1528	Submarine	1805-03=	Historical											
0.38 S, 19.17 W						? 1761	0503		....	....	----	?---	----	----	----	0	
0.53 S 17.77 W						? 1816	1208		....	....	----	?---	----	----	----	0	
0.58 S 15.83 W						1836	11 <		....	....	----	?---	----	----	----	0	

VOLCANO NAME (Subregion) / ERUPTION — Area of Activity	LAT	LONG	ELEV (m)	TYPE	NUMBER	Status / Start Year	Start M-Dy	P	Stop Year	Stop M-Dy	Eruptive Characteristics	VEI
UNNAMED (Atlantic-C)	**3.50 S**	**24.50 W**	**-5300**	**Submarine**	**1805-04=**	**Uncertain**						
						? **1852**	0717		....	....	---- x--- ---- ---- ----	0
ASCENSION (Atlantic-S)	**7.95 S**	**14.37 W**	**858**	**Stratovolc**	**1805-05-**	**Holocene**						
TRINDADE (Atlantic-S)	**20.514 S**	**29.331 W**	**600**	**Stratovolc**	**1805-051**	**Holocene**						
TRISTAN DA CUNHA (Atlantic-S)	**37.092 S**	**12.28 W**	**2060**	**Stratovolc**	**1806-01=**	**Historical**						
South flank						T **1700**t	....		....	....	-x-- ---- x--- --x- ----	
North flank						**1961**	1010		**1962**	0315	-x-- ---- x--- x-x- -x--	2
BOUVET (Atlantic-S)	**54.42 S**	**3.35 E**	**780**	**Shield**	**1806-02-**	**Magnetism**						
						M **-0050**?	....		....	....	---- ---- ---- x--- ----	
(landslide deposit, not eruption)						X 1956	0715z		....	....	---- ---- ---- ---- ----	
THOMPSON ISLAND (Atlantic-S)	**53.93 S**	**5.50 E**		**Submarine ?**	**1806-03-**	**Uncertain**						
						? **1895**	1231y		....	....	---- ---- ?--- ---- ----	

Antarctica & S Sandwich Islands (19)

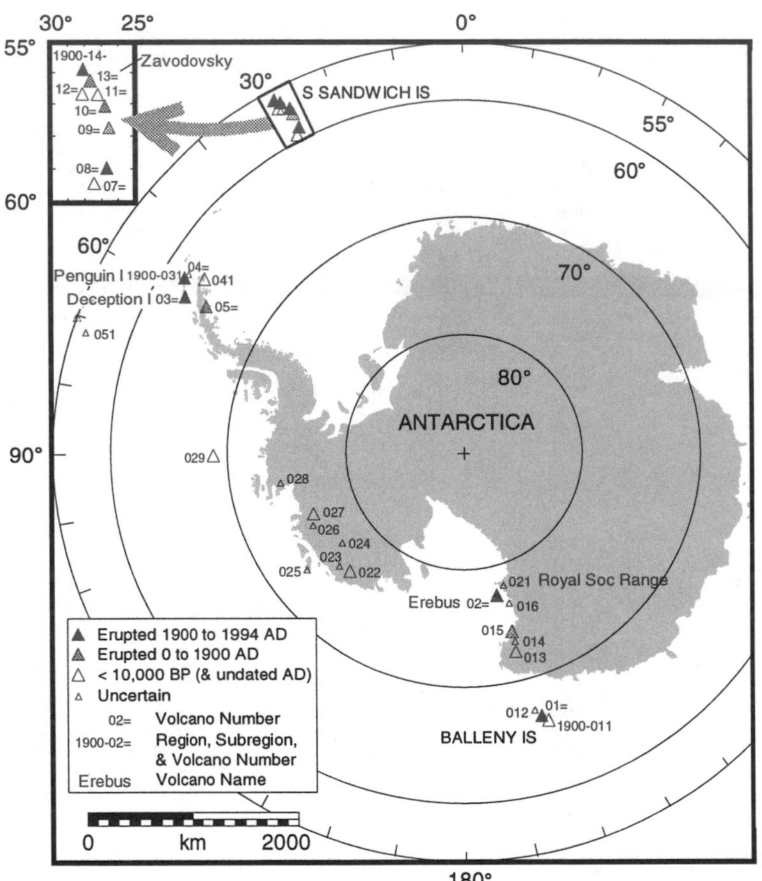

Antarctica is the largest *CAVW* region in land area and – with no permanent residents – easily the smallest in population. It is the only region unblemished by a single fatal eruption; more a reflection on its low resident population than on its hazard mitigation efforts.

Although the continent of Antarctica was not discovered until 1840 (by the Wilkes expedition, 12 hours before the French), several nearby island groups now part of region 19 were recognized earlier. The northernmost of these, the South Sandwich islands or Scotia Arc, was discovered on Captain Cook's 1772-75 voyage, and one of the group – Zavodovsky Island – was issuing a black ash cloud from its summit when discovered by Bellinghausen in 1819. Several other eruptions were reported from these islands in the following years, when fur sealing was at its peak in the region. Sometime between 1825 and 1828, sealers documented an eruption at Deception Island, a natural harbor formed by caldera collapse. And in 1839 an eruption was in progress in the Balleny Islands when they were first discovered by whalers. Two years later, Mount Erebus was erupting when this, the most active volcano in the region, was first sighted.

There followed nearly 60 years of little exploration, although whaling ships continued to work the region through the 19th century. Exploration resumed with a vengeance in 1895, with the next two decades known as the "heroic age" in Antarctica. Additional exploration between the World Wars, during the 1957-58 International Geophysical Year, and since the signing of the Antarctic Treaty in 1961 has contributed greatly to understanding this vast region, but it is clear that its historical record of volcanism is both short and very incomplete.

The Antarctic plate, largely aseismic and immobile, is broken internally by large rift structures which have produced one of the world's largest alkalic volcanic provinces. The 3200-km-long West Antarctic rift system is comparable in size to the better-known East African rift. Volcanic constructs range from large basaltic shields to small monogenetic vents; the presence of the continental icesheet has resulted in a larger volume of hyaloclastite rocks than perhaps any other subaerial volcanic region. The only subduction-related volcanoes within or adjacent to the Antarctic plate form the South Sandwich and South Shetland Islands.

Despite its size, Antarctica ranks below all other regions in number of dated eruptions, and only the Pacific and Atlantic Ocean regions have fewer historically active volcanoes. Its historical record is brief, and 75% of its known eruptions are from this century. Precise dating of past eruptions is difficult – much of the landscape is ice-covered, travel is daunting, and the wood needed for radiocarbon dating does not grow in this extreme climate – and the region has the highest proportion of volcanoes with uncertain status.

The region has produced no known large Holocene eruptions (VEI ≥4 or lava ≥1 km^3), and has the dubious distinction of leading all other regions in the proportion of its eruptions (52%) preceeded by a question mark, indicating uncertainty that the eruption took place. Antarctica also rivals Region 01 for the honor of highest proportion of discredited eruptions.

VOLCANO NAME (Subregion) / ERUPTION — Area of Activity	LAT	LONG	ELEV (m)	TYPE	NUMBER	Status / Start Year	Start M-Dy	P	Stop Year	Stop M-Dy	ERUPTIVE CHARACTERISTICS (Central, Flank vent, Radial fiss, Regional* / Submarine, New island, Subglacial, Crater lake / Explosive, Pyro flow, Phreatic, Fumarolic / Lava flow, Lava lake, Dome, Spine / Fatal, Damage, Mudflow, Tsunami)	VEI	Vol L/T
ANTARCTICA													
BUCKLE ISLAND (Balleny Is)	**66.80 S**	**163.25 E**	**1239**	**Stratovolc**	**1900-01=**	**Historical**							
						1839	0209		....	....	x--- ---- x--- ---- ----	2	
						1899	0112		....	....	---- ---- x--- ---- ----	2	
YOUNG ISLAND (Balleny Is)	**66.42 S**	**162.45 E**	**1340**	**Stratovolc**	**1900-011**	**Fumarolic**							
STURGE ISLAND (Balleny Is)	**67.40 S**	**164.83 E**	**1167**	**Stratovolc**	**1900-012**	**Uncertain**							
PLEIADES, THE (Antarctica)	**72.67 S**	**165.50 E**	**3040**	**Stratovolc**	**1900-013**	**K-Ar**							
NE of Mount Pleiones (Taygete Cone)						K **-1050***	....		....	....	x--- ---- ---- --x- ----		

VOLCANO NAME (Subregion) / ERUPTION — Area of Activity	LAT	LONG	ELEV (m)	TYPE	NUMBER	Status / Start Year	Start M-Dy	P	Stop Year	Stop M-Dy	Central / Flank vent / Radial fiss / Regional*	Submarine / New island / Subglacial / Crater lake	Explosive / Pyro flow / Phreatic / Fumarolic	Lava flow / Lava lake / Dome / Spine	Fatal / Damage / Mudflow / Tsunami	VEI	Vol L/T
UNNAMED (Antarctica)	**73.45 S***	**164.58 E**	**2987**	**Scoria cones**	**1900-014**	**Holocene?**											
MELBOURNE (Antarctica)	**74.35 S**	**164.70 E**	**2732**	**Stratovolc**	**1900-015**	**Tephrochronology**											
						T **1750v**	....		....	....	x---	----	x---	----	----		
UNNAMED (Antarctica)	**76.83 S**	**163.00 E**	**-500**	**Submarine**	**1900-016**	**Holocene?**											
EREBUS (Antarctica)	**77.53 S**	**167.17 E**	**3794**	**Stratovolc**	**1900-02=**	**Historical**											
						1841	0128?		**1841**	02	x---	----	x---	?---	----	1	
						? **1900**	02		....	....	x---	----	?--x	----	----	2	
						1903	0101*		....	....	x---	----	----	-?--	----	0	
						1908	03		**1908**	11	x---	----	x---	-?--	----	2	
						1911	04	+	**1911**	06	x---	----	x---	----	----	2	
						1911	10		....	....	x---	----	x---	----	----	2	
						1912	1212		....	....	x---	----	x--x	----	----	2	
						1915	0322		....	....	x---	----	?---	-?--	----	2	
						1915	08		....	....	x---	----	x---	----	----	2	
						1947	02		....	....	x---	----	x---	?---	----	2	
						1955	....		....	....	----	----	x---	----	----	2	
						? **1957**	....		**?1958**	....	x---	----	----	----	----		
						1963	11 <		....	....	x---	----	----	-x--	----	0	
						1972	0103?		....	....	x---	----	x---	----	----	1	
						1972	12 <		**1993>**	....	x---	----	x---	xx--	----	2*	
ROYAL SOCIETY RANGE (Antarctica)	**78.25 S***	**163.60 E**	**3000**	**Cinder cones**	**1900-021**	**Holocene?**											
BERLIN (Antarctica)	**76.05 S**	**136.00 W**	**3478**	**Shields**	**1900-022**	**Fumarolic**											
ANDRUS (Antarctica)	**75.80 S**	**132.33 W**	**2978**	**Shields**	**1900-023**	**Holocene?**											
WAESCHE (Antarctica)	**77.17 S**	**126.88 W**	**3292**	**Shields**	**1900-024**	**Holocene?**											
SIPLE (Antarctica)	**73.43 S**	**126.67 W**	**3110**	**Shield**	**1900-025**	**Holocene?**											
TONEY MOUNTAIN (Antarctica)	**75.80 S**	**115.83 W**	**3595**	**Shield**	**1900-026**	**Holocene?**											
TAKAHE (Antarctica)	**76.28 S**	**112.08 W**	**3460**	**Shield**	**1900-027**	**Ice Core**											
						I **-7050?**	....		....	....	----	----	x---	----	----		
						I **-5550?**	....		....	....	----	----	x---	----	----		
HUDSON MOUNTAINS (Antarctica)	**74.33 S**	**99.42 W**	**749**	**Stratovolcs**	**1900-028**	**Uncertain**											
Webber Nunatak						? **1985**	....		....	....	x---	----	?---	----	----		
PETER I ISLAND (Antarctica)	**68.85 S**	**90.58 W**	**1640**	**Shield**	**1900-029**	**Holocene**											
DECEPTION ISLAND (Antarctica)	**62.97 S**	**60.65 W**	**576**	**Caldera**	**1900-03=**	**Historical**											
						I **1641j**	....		....	....	----	----	x---	----	----		
N side caldera bay (near Telefon Bay)						**1800<**	....		....	....	x---	----	x---	----	----		
NE side caldera bay (Pendulum Cove)						**1827b**	....		....	....	x---	----	x---	----	----		
(vigorous steam emission only)						X 1829	....		....	....	----	----	---x	----	----		
Crater Lake--Mt. Kirkwood area						? **1839<**	....		....	....	----	----	?---	----	----		
S caldera rim (flanks of Mt Kirkwood)						**1842**	02		....	....	----	----	x---	x---	----	2	
SE side of caldera bay (Kroner Lake)						T **1871s**	....		....	....	x---	----	x---	----	----		
(fumarolic activity only)						X 1909	....		....	....	----	----	---x	----	----		
SW part of island						**1912e**	....		....	....	----	----	x---	----	----	3?	
(steam emission only)						X 1927	....		....	....	----	----	---x	----	----		
North side (Telefon Bay, Yelcho I)						**1967**	1204		**1967**	1207	----	xx--	x-x-	----	--x-	3	-/7
West side of Mount Pond						**1969**	0221		**1969**	03	----	--x-	x---	----	-xJ-	3	-/7
NE of Telefon Bay						**1970**	0812		....	....	----	x---	x-x-	----	--J-	3	
						? **1972**	0929		**?1972**	0929	----	----	----	----	----		
						? **1987**	0723		....	....	----	?---	?---	----	----		
PENGUIN ISLAND (Antarctica)	**62.10 S**	**57.93 W**	**180**	**Stratovolc**	**1900-031**	**Lichenometry**											
Deacon Peak						L **1683?**	....		....	....	x---	----	x---	----	----		
Deacon Peak						**1850?**	....		....	....	x---	----	----	x---	----		
NE flank (Petrel Crater)						L **1905?**	....		....	....	-x--	----	x---	----	----		
BRIDGEMAN ISLAND (Antarctica)	**62.05 S**	**56.75 W**	**240**	**Stratovolc**	**1900-04=**	**Uncertain**											
PAULET (Antarctica)	**63.58 S**	**55.77 W**	**353**	**Cinder cone**	**1900-041**	**Holocene**											
						? **1850**	....		....	....	----	----	----	----	----		
SEAL NUNATAKS GROUP (")	**65.03 S***	**60.05 W**	**368**	**Pyrocl cones**	**1900-05=**	**Historical**											
Lindenberg Island						**1893**	1211		....	....	xx--	----	x---	----	----	2	
Dallman, Murdoch						? **1980**	0615z		....	....	x---	----	?---	?---	----		
UNNAMED (Antarctica)	**56.25 S**	**72.17 W**		**Submarine ?**	**1900-051**	**Uncertain**											
						? **1876**	1210		....	....	----	??--	----	----	----	0	

S SANDWICH ISLANDS

VOLCANO NAME (Subregion) / ERUPTION — Area of Activity	LAT	LONG	ELEV (m)	TYPE	NUMBER	Status / Start Year	Start M-Dy	P	Stop Year	Stop M-Dy	Central / Flank vent / Radial fiss / Regional*	Submarine / New island / Subglacial / Crater lake	Explosive / Pyro flow / Phreatic / Fumarolic	Lava flow / Lava lake / Dome / Spine	Fatal / Damage / Mudflow / Tsunami	VEI	Vol L/T
THULE ISLANDS (S Sandwich Is)	**59.45 S**	**27.37 W**	**1075**	**Stratovolcs**	**1900-07=**	**Holocene**											
BRISTOL ISLAND (S Sandwich Is)	**59.03 S**	**26.58 W**	**1100**	**Stratovolc**	**1900-08=**	**Historical**											
						1823	....		....	....	----	----	?---	----	----	2	
						1935	1231		....	....	x---	----	x---	----	----	2	
						1936	1218		**1937**	0101?	x---	----	x---	x---	----	2	
						1950	0327		....	....	----	----	x---	----	----	2	
West flank						**1956**	0111		**1956**	0119?	-x--	----	x---	----	----	3	
MICHAEL (S Sandwich Is)	**57.78 S**	**26.45 W**	**990**	**Stratovolc**	**1900-09=**	**Historical**											
						1819	1229		....	....	x---	----	x---	----	----	2	
						? **1823**	....		....	....	----	----	?--?	----	----	2	
CANDLEMAS ISLAND (S Sandwich)	**57.08 S**	**26.72 W**	**550**	**Stratovolc**	**1900-10=**	**Historical**											
S Sandwich Is (probably Candlemass)						I **-1250?**	....		....	....	----	----	x---	----	----		
Lucifer Hill						**1823**	....		....	....	-x--	----	?--?	----	----	2	
Lucifer Hill						? **1911**	1106		....	....	-x--	----	?--?	----	----	2	
Lucifer Hill						? **1953**	1231y		....	....	-x--	----	----	?---	----		
HODSON (S Sandwich Is)	**56.70 S**	**27.15 W**	**1005**	**Stratovolc**	**1900-11=**	**Holocene**											
						? **1830**	0922		....	....	----	----	?--?	----	----		
						? **1930**	....		....	....	x---	----	?---	----	----		
LESKOV ISLAND (S Sandwich Is)	**56.67 S**	**28.13 W**	**190**	**Stratovolc**	**1900-12=**	**Fumarolic**											
ZAVODOVSKI (S Sandwich Is)	**56.30 S**	**27.57 W**	**551**	**Stratovolc**	**1900-13=**	**Historical**											
						1819	12		....	....	x---	----	x---	----	----	2	
						? **1823**	....		....	....	----	----	?--?	----	----	1	
						? **1830**	09		....	....	----	----	?--?	----	----	1	
						? **1908**	11		....	....	----	----	?--?	----	----	1	
PROTECTOR SHOAL (S Sandwich Is)	**55.92 S**	**28.08 W**	**-27**	**Submarine**	**1900-14-**	**Historical**											
						1962	0305?		....	....	----	x---	x---	----	----	0	-/8

Fatalities and Evacuations

- Prime instigator of, and contributor to, this table is:

  Dr. Russell Blong
  School of Earth Sciences, Macquarie University
  North Ryde 2109, NSW, Australia

  We thank him for his help and willingness to share data here.

- The **Agent** code is a single **capitalized** letter to simplify the coded information and make it easy to find all fatalities caused by each agent. We have not attempted a more detailed breakdown because the data often do not permit it, but we have included more detailed information in the **remarks** where possible. It should be easy to find all fatal eruptions with pyroclastic flows (sensu lato), for example, but readers interested in pyroclastic surge deaths as distinct from directed blast deaths must find them in the remarks. The code is to genus rather than species level. Descriptions of the various agents causing eruptive fatalities have already been described (p. 20-22). The following table identifies the code:

  A = **A**valanche (debris and landslides)
  E = **E**lectrical (lightning)
  F = **F**loods (& Jokulhlaups)
  G = **G**as (emission from eruptive craters as well as fumarolic/solfataric activity)
  I = **I**ndirect deaths (disease, starvation, exposure, desolation)
  L = **L**ava flows
  M = **M**udflows/Lahars
  m = Secondary (post-eruption) **m**udflows
  P = **P**yroclastic flows, surges, & directed blasts
  S = **S**eismic, or volcanic earthquake (tectonic earthquake deaths excluded)
  T = **T**ephra (ash, bombs, lapilli, steam blasts). Killing either by ballistic impact, or, with finer-grained ash, by suffocation, collapse of ash-covered roofs, etc.
  W = **W**aves, or Tsunami

- **Agents** with uncertain percentages are followed by a question mark. A double question mark is used when the percentages are crudely estimated from the nature of the reported eruption alone. An agent code without a percentage indicates that the agent, but not percent, of fatalities is known. An agent code followed by a question mark denotes uncertainty about the agent.

- Accurate **death** tolls are are often difficult to obtain, even today, and the historical record often fails to provide numbers. Many accounts use words like "many," "several," or "thousands," and we have not attempted to quantify the usage of the original account.

- Non-volcanic earthquake fatalities are not listed in the **deaths** column, but may be mentioned in the **remarks**. These have often been confused with volcanic fatalities, particularly on a notorious volcano like Etna, but unless we have a firm "**x**" in the fatality column of the main DIRECTORY (p. 37-161), we have resisted entering a number in the **Deaths** column here.

- Eruption-related injuries span a huge spectrum of severity, and their historical data are even less reliable than those for fatalities. We have not included entries that described injuries without evidence of clear fatalities.

- The **start date** of each eruption is included in curly brackets at the end of each eruption's remarks, using an equal sign {=} if it is the same as the date of known fatalities. This both facilitates cross-reference to other parts of the book and alerts the reader to the rather different hazard conditions that surround an eruption's first day and its second or third year.

- The following abbreviations have been used. See REFERENCES (p. 305-349) for citations.

  BVE = Bulletin of Volcanic Eruptions (Volcanological Society of Japan)
  CAVW = Catalog of Active Volcanoes of the World (IAVCEI)
  IAVCEI = International Association of Volcanology and Chemistry of Earth's Interior
  JMA = Japan Meteorological Agency
  CSLP/SEAN/GVN = Smithsonian publications of: Center for Short-Lived Phenomena (1968-75); Scientific Event Alert Network (1975-89); Global Volcanism Network (1990-present)
  VL = Volcano Letter (Hawaii Research Association, 1925-55)

Year M-Dy	Deaths	Agent	Remarks	{Start Date}
EUROPE (01)				
CAMPI FLEGREI			(0101-01=)	
1538 1006	24	$T_{100?}$	Phreatic explosion at 2200 on Monte Nuovo eruption's 8th day. Many people climbing the cone lost their footing in the dark, sliding to their deaths on loose stones.	{1538 0929}
1970	3	S_{100}	Volcanogenic earthquake: 3 killed by falling masonry and rocks in the collapse of houses.	No eruption.
VESUVIUS			(0101-02=)	
0079 0824	>3,500?	$P_{95?}$ $T_{5?}$	~2,000 skeletons found in 3/5-excavated Pompeii, recently hundreds were found in partly-excavated Herculaneum. Pyroclastic surges affected these and other towns and produced most of the fatalities (total unknown).	{=}
0787	?		Possible damage and fatalities.	{=}
1631 1216	>4,000	$P_{95?}$ $E_{?}$ $M_{?}$	Most of >4,000 fatalities caused by pyroclastic surges. Earlier accounts ascribe deaths to lava flows, mudflows and tephra falls, but lava flows are uncertain. One estimate of the total death toll reached 18,000. Hamilton reported men and beasts struck dead by lightning. 30 cm tephra in Naples.	{1631 1215}
1682 0812+	4		One fatality in Torre Annunziata, 3 in Castellammare during Aug 12-22 eruption.	{=}
1737 05	2	$T_{100?}$	Serious damage from tephra fall near end of 5-year eruption.	{1732 1225}
1779 0808	few			{1770 0215}
1794	400	$M_{?}$ $L_{?}$ $T_{?}$ $G_{?}$	60 fatalities at Torre del Greco, with 80% of the town destroyed by lava flows. Several people died from CO_2. Sapper reported 26 killed, possibly by lava flows. Hoffer described 15 deaths by lava flows and explosions when the lava reached the bay. Scandone et al. report a total of 400 fatalities, and complete destruction (by mudflows and ashfall?) of S. Guiseppe, Ottaviano, and Somma.	{1783 0818}
1805	4			{1796 0115}
1872	>9	$L_{80?}$ $G_{20?}$	Young people in Valle del Inferno failed to notice retreat cut off by lava which trapped them between precipice of Monte Somma and active flow. Nazzaro reported 9 killed and 11 injured, plus some fatalities from CO_2.	{1870 1201}
1873 Spring	9	G_{78} T_{22}	Date probably mistaken for 1872 (Vesuvius not in eruption in 1873) but Fisher reported that 2 tourists fell while fleeing a slight eruption at the summit and were covered with lava; 7 others died of suffocation.	
1905 0310	1	T_{100}	One guide killed on rim and another injured by explosion.	{1875 1218}
1906 0406	350?	$T_{99?}$ L_{1}	Nazarro suggests a total of 216 fatalities. Delme-Radcliffe indicates ~300 killed and 300 injured: 105 killed and 90 injured in fall of church roof in San Giuseppe, ~90 killed in collapse of house roofs thereabouts, ~90 killed in Ottaviano, ~20 killed in San Gennaro, and about 50 others elsewhere including 14 killed in the collapse of the Monte Oliveto Market in Naples. Lacroix indicates 3 deaths in a lava flow.	{1875 1218}
1944 03	27	$T_{88?}$ $L_{8?}$ $I_{4?}$	Roof collapses under tephra loads caused 12 deaths at Nocera and 9 at Pagani. Trees falling under tephra load or falling fragments at Terzigno killed 3. Two small boys were killed at San Sebastiano when lava exploded upon reaching a water tank. One elderly man killed himself, in sorrow at the desolation of San Sabastiano.	{1913 0705}
ISCHIA			(0101-03=)	
1302	?		People and animals reportedly killed. Many persons fled to neighboring islands and the mainland.	{1302 0118}
STROMBOLI			(0101-04=)	
1919 0522	4	T_{100}	Blocks of 30-60 tons fell on houses in S. Vicenzo (8 destroyed) & Ginostra (2 destroyed).	{=}
1930 0911	4	P_{100}	Three people killed by pyroclastic flows. A fourth died after being scalded in the sea near the point where the flows reached the coast.	{=}
1986 0724	1	T_{100}	A biologist was hit on the head by a falling block, dying instantly ~15 m from W edge of crater rim.	{1985 1206}
ETNA			(0101-06=)	
-0141 BC	40		Outburst from the volcano destroyed 40 people. Possibly 140 BC.	{-0141 1231y}
1169 02	?	S W	Violent earthquake about dawn buried many people in Catania during vigil of feast of St. Agatha, and tsunami swept away people who had gathered on shore at Messina. Earthquake (probably tectonic) occurred on 4/11/1169. Romano & Sturiale uncertain about an eruption at this time. Hyde reports 15,000 deaths during eruption in 1185 but gives no details and it is likely that this is a spurious account and/or confused with the 1169 event.	{1169 0204}
1329 0715	Many?	I	Many persons said to have died from terror. Multitudes of animals and birds perished and the fields were burned up by hot sand and ashes.	{=}
1536 0326	1	T_{100}	A physician of Lentini approached too closely (to a newly active crater?) and was killed by a volley of red-hot stones.	{1536 0322}
1669	?		Coleman indicates that 20,000 perished in this eruption, but this seems unlikely. Neither Rittmann nor Romano & Sturiale mention deaths in their accounts. Detailed report by Winchilsea mentions only a few deaths as a result of murders and executions amidst widespread destruction of towns and croplands. The Coleman account is perhaps confused with a 1693 tectonic earthquake that killed 60,000-100,000 in 50 towns in Sicily and 18,000 in Catania. Rodwell reported a 1693 eruption, but Sapper and Tanguy consider the eruption doubtful, and most others ignore it.	{1669 0311}
1832	Several	$L_{100?}$	Explosion at front of lava flow moving over ice killed several people.	{1832 1031}
1843 1124	56	$L_{100?}$	Near the end of the year, while many of the inhabitants of Bronte were watching the lava's progress, the flow front was suddenly blown out by an explosion (the lava may have entered a cistern). 36 were killed on the spot and 20 survived but a few hours. Romano & Sturiale report strong phreatic explosion on 11/24 with death and wounding of several persons.	{1843 1117}
1928 1108	5?	L_{100}	Three men who had returned to their homes in Mascali to rescue household goods were surrounded by lava flows and killed. On the same day in the same town an aged couple were also engulfed in their home.	{1928 1102}
1979 0912	9	T_{100}	Nine killed and 20 or 23 seriously injured by non-juvenile bombs ejected by violent phreatic explosion of Bocca Nuova vent. 150-200 tourists in area at time. A vehicle used for emergency accommodation was hit by a bomb, causing a gas cylinder to explode, destroying vehicle and burning several nearby tourists.	{=}
1987 0417	2	T_{100}	Phreatic explosion killed 2 tourists and injured 7 out of about 30 gathered ~500 m SSE of SE crater.	{1987 0308h}
SANTORINI			(0102-04=)	
-1650t BC	?		Deaths probably occurred here, and, as a result of tsunamis, in ports and seaside villages on Crete and elsewhere. However, no direct evidence of deaths has been found.	{=}
1650	>120?	$G_{40?}$ $W_{40?}$ $T_{20?}$	Some died of opthalmias caused by sulfurous vapor; others (~50?) were suffocated by vapors on Sept 30. The crew of a ship passing too near the volcano was suffocated on Oct 2. Others (~20 laborers) were killed by a shower of black dust on Nov 4. Fytikas attributes 50 deaths to a tsunami, and does not mention other fatalities.	{1650 0927}
1926	48	$S_{100?}$	Deaths more likely due to an earthquake than an eruption. CAVW lists no fatalities.	{1925 0811}

Year M-Dy	Deaths	Agent	Remarks	{Start Date}
AFRICA, MID-EAST, & INDIAN OCEAN (02 & 03)				
DUBBI			(0201-10=)	
1861	106		Fatalities occurred during initial explosive phase of eruption. Two villages were destroyed and large herds of cattle were killed. The agent of fatalities is not clear.	{1861 0508}
ALAYTA			(0201-112)	
1907	?		CAVW reports fatalities from Afdera, but eruption now thought to be from Alayta.	{1907 06}
DAMA ALI			(0201-141)	
1631	50	$S_{100?}$	Believed 50 deaths occurred when village of Waraba was destroyed by earthquake. Site of this eruption uncertain.	{1631 0214}
KIEYO			(0202-17=)	
1800?	?	$L_{100?}$	Oral history records an eruption about 1800 AD in which lava engulfed villages whose inhabitants were still asleep.	{=}
NYAMURAGIRA			(0203-02=)	
1912 12	20	L_{100}	20 villagers were killed when a lava flow changed directions.	{1912 1203}
NYIRAGONGO			(0203-03=)	
1977 0110	100?	$L_{100?}$	Extremely fluid, fast-moving lava flows draining from lava lake killed numbers variously estimated at none to 2,000 persons. Best estimate seems to be 50 to 100. Several villages destroyed.	{=}
OKU VOLCANIC FIELD			(0204-003)	
1984 0815	37	G_{100}	Lake Monoun. A white cloud in the vicinity of the lake at daybreak looked like typical fog, but contained CO_2. Victims suffered vomiting, paralysis, and very rapid death.	No eruption.
1986 0821	1,700	G_{100}	Lake Nyos. Deaths caused by release of large volume of CO_2 from lake. More than 300 survivors hospitalized.	{=}
HARRAT 'UWAYRID			(0301-02=)	
0640?	?	$T_{100?}$	Bedouin describe fire & stones killing herdsmen, cattle, and sheep. Location & date uncertain.	{=}
KARTHALA			(0303-01=)	
1883 03	?	L_{100}	Voluminous lava flows destroyed a village and its inhabitants.	{=}
1903	17	G_{100}	In the summer of 1903 the emanation of suffocating gases was so strong that 17 people, who stayed near the solfataras at a height of 1,600 m, were killed.	No eruption.
1904	1	L_{100}	A lava flow destroyed cultivated land and killed one person.	{1904 0225}
PITON DE LA FOURNAISE			(0303-02=)	
1972 08	3	$I_{100?}$	Three visitors died after 48 hours in cold mists on the rugged lava fields during the second phase of the eruption.	{1972 0609}
NEW ZEALAND & TONGA (04)				
WHITE ISLAND			(0401-04=)	
1914 0910	11	A_{100}	Debris avalanche from SW corner of crater wall overwhelmed party of 11 sulfur workers and two buildings.	No eruption.
OKATAINA (TARAWERA)			(0401-06=)	
1886 0610	153	$T_{98?}$	Almost all died as a result of burial by tephra. 147 Maoris and 6 Europeans. Villages affected included: Te Ariki (52 killed), Moura (39), Te Wairo (14), Rotomahana (11).	{=}
1903 0830	4	T_{100}	4 killed by eruption of Waimangu geyser.	{1900 01}
1917 0401	2	T_{100}	Steam blast at Frying Pan Flat lifted roof off Waimangu accommodation 800 m away. 3 occupants scalded by searing steam blast. Wife and child of resident guide died later.	{1917 0324}
TAUPO			(0401-07=)	
1846 0507	63	m_{100}	A lahar (mudflow) or debris avalanche from hydrothermally altered rocks along the Waihi fault destroyed fortified village of Te Heu Heu, a famous Maori chieftain. An earlier event may have occurred in 1836 but is unclear.	No eruption.
1910 0320	1	m_{100}	Lahar from collapse of hydrothermally-altered rocks at the SW end of Lake Taupo.	No eruption.
RUAPEHU			(0401-10=)	
1953 1224	151	m_{100}	Summit crater lake drained when crevassing glacier caused ash barrier holding it in to collapse. The resulting mudflow swept away one of the piers of the Tangiwai bridge just before the arrival of the Wellington-Auckland express. Locomotive, tender and 5 carriages plunged into the river.	No eruption.
NIUAFO'OU			(0403-11=)	
1853 0624	25?	$L_{100?}$	Lava flows from fissure cutting directly through village of Ahau killed 25 persons. Chief of Selusalema and 7 subjects were killed by lava flows. Estimates of fatalities range from 8 to 70-80.	{1853 0624}
1886	11?		None known to have been killed during eruption, but several missing. Several older men, including chiefs of rank, died of shock; total of dead and missing is 11.	{1886 0831}
MELANESIA (05)				
ST. ANDREW'S STRAIT (LOU ISLAND)			(0500-01=)	
-0150? BC	?		Eruption about 2,100 years ago must have killed many people on the island. Tephra covered all villages.	{-0150}
BAM			(0501-01=)	
1954	25	$I_{100?}$	The population of Bam was evacuated to Bogia on the mainland for 6 months. For a number of reasons, the people could not adapt to their new environment. 25 died while at Bogia and many more suffered from illness.	{1954 0803}
MANAM			(0501-02=)	
1898-1900?	2		Taylor writes that during "the eruption of 1902," Father Aerni was informed that two natives from Bokure village were killed. 1902 was publication date of book which may pertain to events from 1898-1900 eruption.	{=}
KARKAR			(0501-03=)	
1895	21?	$I_{95?}$ $M_{5?}$	Island covered with falls of ash and lapilli. At least one person died in a mud flow. Gardens were affected and many (20?) children and old people died of starvation. It is possible that some of these deaths resulted from smallpox.	{1895 0617}
1979 0308	2	P_{100}	Two volcanologists killed by hot high-velocity directed gas-and-ejecta blast at observation camp 800 m away on caldera rim.	{1979 0112}
LONG ISLAND			(0501-05=)	
1660?	2,000?	$T_{30??}$ $P_{15??}$ $W_{5??}$ $I_{50?}$	Impossible to give accurate estimate of deaths. Legends on Long Island report deaths in pyroclastic flows and tsunamis. On Papua New Guinea mainland widespread legends report deaths as a result of house collapse and starvation.	{=}
RITTER			(0501-07=)	
1888 0313	3,000?	W_{100}	Hundreds of people were killed on the coasts of neighboring islands (including Umboi & New Britain) by a tsunami created by the debris avalanche. Tsunami reached 12-15 m above normal sea level. Latter believes ~3,000 killed.	{=}
DAKATAUA			(0502-04=)	
1895e	?		Eruption "some years" before 1923 killed people and destroyed property on E coast. Last known eruption was in 1890s.	{=}
PAGO			(0502-08=)	
1914?	?	$I_{100?}$	People on NE coast ~13 km from volcano faced with starvation and perhaps died from it.	{1911}
RABAUL			(0502-14=)	
1850?	Many	$T_{100?}$	Many deaths caused by fall of huge blocks of pumice. Several other outbursts in ~12 yrs before 1877 report.	{=}

Year M-Dy	Deaths	Agent	Remarks	{Start Date}
1878 01	1	T_{100}	Woman supposedly killed by the first shower of stones from Tavurvur. This is the only fatality recorded, the Matupi people having fled to higher lands for safety.	{1878 0130?}
1937 0529	507	$P_{50?}$ $T_{40?}$ $W_{5?}$ $I_{5?}$	Official death toll: 505 New Guineans and 2 Europeans. Territory of Papua New Guinea medical officer at time gives 440 New Guineans killed by suffocation and/or burial with only a few dying later from exposure or shock. Subsequent investigations indicate importance of pyroclastic flows in area around Vulcan.	{=}
1990 0624+	6	G_{100}	An adult and two children died of suffocation in a vent on the east side of Tavurvur while hunting for wildfowl eggs. 3 friends and relatives died the following day trying to retrieve the bodies.	No eruption.
LAMINGTON			(0503-01=	
1951 0121	2,942	P_{100}	All killed in pyroclastic flows at N-flank villages. Of 40 survivors from inner zone of devastation who reached hospital, 22 died within 24 hours.	{1951 0117}
VICTORY			(0503-03=)	
1890j	Many	$P_{100?}$	Deaths reported by local people in 1880-1890 AD eruption.	{=}
BALBI			(0505-01=)	
1825?	Many	$P_{100?}$	Last major eruption occurred between 1800 and 1825 and produced nuees ardentes.	{1825q}
BAGANA			(0505-02=)	
1883 1231p	Several	$T_{?}$	"Great explosion" Dec1883 or Jan 1884 killed several people.	{=}
SAVO			(0505-07=)	
1840j	Many	$P_{100?}$	Between about 1830-1850 AD, ash and stones killed many people. On one occasion nuees ardentes killed all inhabitants of the island; on another occasion a few people survived.	{1835e}
TINAKULA			(0506-01=)	
1840?	Many	P_{100}	Nuees ardentes swept all sides of the island, killing all inhabitants. Heavy seas prevented escape.	{=}
AOBA			(0507-03=)	
1670?	Many	$L_{100?}$	Legend of lava flow with many fatalities about 300 years ago.	{=}
1870?	?	M_{100}	Lahars annihilated villages on SE flank about 100 years ago.	{=}
AMBRYM			(0507-04=)	
1894 1015	10	T_{60} L_{40}	Six persons were killed by volcanic bombs, 4 were overtaken by lava flows.	{=}
1913 1205	21	T_{100}	Several villages were destroyed; explosions destroyed the mission hospital at Dip Point, killing 21 persons.	{1913 1014}
KUWAE			(0507-07=)	
1425j	Many	$P_{100?}$	Pyroclastic-flow deposits on southern Tongoa associated with formation of Kuwae caldera contain human remains.	{=}

INDONESIA (06)

Year M-Dy	Deaths	Agent	Remarks	{Start Date}
SORIKMARAPI			(0601-12=)	
1892 0521	180	M_{100}	Deaths at Sibangor village, 7 km NNE of summit.	{1892 0521}
MARAPI			(0601-14=)	
1979 0430	80	M_{100}	About 300 mm of rainfall mobilized old lahar deposit and other volcanic material on N and E flanks. Landslides travelled as much as 20 km downslope and damaged 5 villages and farmland.	{1975 01}
1992 0705	1	T_{100}	One person was killed and 5 injured by volcanic bombs during climb to summit.	{1987 0115}
KABA			(0601-22=)	
1833 1124	126	M_{100}	Water ejected from crater lake. Lahars killed 36 at Talang, 90 at Klingi and Bliti villages.	{=}
KRAKATAU			(0602-00=)	
1883 0826+	36,417	$W_{<95}$ $P_{>5}$ $I_{<1}$	Although all recorded deaths have commonly been attributed to the devastating tsunamis, an estimated 2,000 were killed on southern Sumatra by "hot ashes" and there is clear evidence that pyroclastic flows reached that far. All 3,150 people in the path of these flows, on islands between Krakatau and Sumatra were killed; probably most by early tsunami but surely none survived the culminating eruption at 1000 on Aug 27. Various indirect causes killed a small number elsewhere. Unknown number of injured. 165 villages completely destroyed, 132 partly destroyed.	{1883 0520}
1993 0613	1	T_{100}	One tourist killed and 5 injured by an explosion while they were climbing on the old crater rim of Anak Krakatau.	{1992 1107}
TANKUBANPARAHU			(0603-09=)	
1846 0527	?			{=}
1923 06	3	G_{100}	End of June, 3 high school boys killed by asphyxiating gas. Carbonic acid and H_2S involved.	No eruption.
PAPANDAYAN			(0603-10=)	
1772 0812	2,957	A_{100}	Debris avalanche from collapse of NE part of mountain completely destroyed 40 villages.	{=}
1924 1218	1	G_{100}	Gas emission, believed to be H_2S caused suffocation of a volcanological observer. Death date from Jaggar.	{1923 0311}
GUNTUR			(0603-13=)	
1690	?			{=}
1800 1008+	Many	$M_{100?}$	The river became charged with white, acid, sulfurous mud, that poured down the valley carrying carcasses of men and sundry animals, and covered the countryside with a thick coat of mud. The same occurred with greater violence on the 12th.	{1800}
1829	Many?		Many killed, several wounded.	{=}
GALUNGGUNG			(0603-14=)	
1822 1008	4,011	$P_{90?}$ $M_{10?}$	114 villages destroyed. Katili & Sudrajat consider most of the fatalities to result from nuees ardentes, which extended 10 km.	{=}
1982	68?	$I_{96?}$ $T_{04?}$	Death toll estimates vary from "a few" to 72. Washington *Post* reported 3 killed by falling rocks. Koesman Aboeng reported 58 deaths at Tasikmalaya due to traffic accidents, old age, infant deaths, cold, ash, and lack of food. SEAN reported total of 27 fatalities as of late May (including deaths in refugee camps). Press reports 2 fatalities April 5, 8 on April 8. 22 villages rendered uninhabitable; damage estimates exceeded 15 million dollars.	{1982 0405}
CEREME			(0603-17=)	
1698	?			{1698 0203}
DIENG VOLCANIC COMPLEX			(0603-20=)	
1786	38	$A_{100?}$	Ground fissuring occurred and 38 persons died from a collapse that destroyed Jampang village.	{=}
1826	Several		Fatalities "low."	{1826 1011}
1847 1204	Several		Fatalities "low."	{=}
1928 0513	40?	$T_{03?}$	One person was killed by a falling rock at Simbar, 750 m from the vent near Timbang. Verstappen does not specify cause of death but reports 39 people killed at Butak. The Volcanological Survey of Indonesia (VSI) plaque near Sinila crater lists 39 fatalities in 1928.	{=}
1939 1013	10	$T_{100?}$	Lahars destroyed 50 ha of land and steam explosions caused 10 deaths and damage. Verstappen reports deaths were at Timbang.	{=}
1944 1204	117	$T_{50?}$ $T_{50?}$	VSI plaque notes 117 fatalities and 250 injuries from 1944 eruption. Van Bemmelen lists 59 dead; 55 missing; 38 hurt. Coarse gray-white ashes and blocks of old volcanic material rained on 7 villages evidently all within ~1 km of vent. Blocks reached as far as Bitingan, ~1 km from vent, where 11 people were killed and 7 hurt. Ash mud here up to 20 cm thick. At Djawera 300 m N of crater 29 were killed and 19 hurt - ash mud layer 1.5-2.0 m thick. 18 killed at Kepakisan	

Year M-Dy	Deaths	Agent	Remarks	{Start Date}
			and 1 at Pagerkandang. Wounds caused by boiling hot mud.	{=}
1964 1213	114		VSI plaque: 114 fatalities from this eruption.	{=}
1978 late	3		SEAN report mentions geothermal well blowout.	No eruption.
1979 0220	149?	G_{100}	Inhabitants of Kaputjukan, frightened by phreatic eruptions at Sinila and Sigludung Craters, fled toward Batur along trail. 149 (variously reported as 142 to 182) later found dead on the track, seeming to be asleep, in a single file as when they were walking. Killed by emission of poisonous gases from Timbang Crater; either CO_2 or CO_2 and H_2S (hydrogen sulfide).	{=}

MERAPI (0603-25=)

Year M-Dy	Deaths	Agent	Remarks	{Start Date}
0825x	Many?		The greatest part of population of central Java including King Darmawangasa was reported killed during an eruption in 1006. Later work discounts an eruption in 1006, but notes a major eruption in the 8th-10th centuries that may have produced fatalities.	{=}
1587	?			{=}
1672 0804	3,000?	$P_{100?}$	Hadikisumo gives total of 3,000 fatalities, Kusumadinata 300. Only evidence of agent is that this was a major eruption producing pyroclastic flows.	{=}
1822 1227+	100?		100 killed, many wounded, 4 villages completely destroyed, and 4 villages partly devastated. Sapper gives death toll as 20 and indicates villages were on W side. Hadikusumo gives 16 villages destroyed.	{=}
1832 1225	32?		1 village completely destroyed.	{=}
1872 0415	200	P_{85} T_{15}	3 villages completely destroyed, 8 villages partly destroyed, many cattle killed.	{=}
1904 0130	16	P_{100}	16 killed, 45 injured & 3 small villages destroyed when pyroclastic flows swept down Woro ravine.	{1902 12}
1920 1013?	33?	P_{100}	Pyroclastic flow on 10/13 killed 33 persons on flanks; another source lists 35 fatalities.	{1920 0725}
1930 1218	1,369	P_{100}	13 villages totally and 29 partially destroyed, 1,109 houses destroyed, 2,140 cattle killed. Van Bemmelen notes that deaths were caused by nuees and the volcano observer died of burns.	{1930 1125}
1954 0118	64?	P_{100}	57 wounded, 1 village totally destroyed, 2 partly destroyed, 144 houses destroyed. Pyroclastic flows reached villages of Pentjarngisor and Pentjarduwar. 30 were killed at the time of the eruption and 34 died in hospital from burns.	{1953 0302}
1961 0508	6?		8 villages totally destroyed, 2 villages partly destroyed.	{1961 0413}
1969 0107	3	$P_{100?}$		{1967 0112}
1986 1231	1	M_{100}	Driver of stalled truck swept away by rain-induced lahar.	{1972 1006}

KELUT (0603-28=)

Year M-Dy	Deaths	Agent	Remarks	{Start Date}
1311	?		Only Kusumadinata-79 lists fatalities.	{=}
1334	?		Fatalities occurred - number not known.	{=}
1376	?			{=}
1385	?		Fatalities occurred - number not known.	{=}
1586	10,000?		10,000 reported killed, cause not known. Original accounts describe violent eruption of "flaming sulfur," ejection of large stones into a city, and large amounts of ash that obscured the sun for 3 days.	{=}
1716 0720	?	$M_{?}$	Fatalities occurred- number not known.	{=}
1826 1013	?	$M_{?}$	Unknown number killed, 65 villages destroyed Kusumadinata-79 gives this as 65 wounded.	{1826 1011}
1848 0516	21	$M_{?}$	21 killed, 11 villages, & 800 houses destroyed.	{=}
1864 0104	54	M_{100}	Death toll from Natuurkundig Tijdschrift voor Nederlendisch-Indie. Kusumadinata-79 gives many killed, hundreds of houses destroyed, many cattle killed (& 0103 date).	{=}
1875 0129	?	m	Failure of W crater wall freed lakewater producing lahar that killed an unknown number and destroyed 30 villages. Kusumadinata-79 gives this as 30 wounded.	No eruption.
1901 0522	Many?			{=}
1919 0519	5,110	$M_{100?}$	5,110 killed, 9,000 houses destroyed, 104 villages destroyed. Pyroclastic flows were produced but inference is that deaths resulted from lahars. VL and some other sources give death total as 5,500. Kusumadinata-79 gives 0519-20 date.	{=}
1951 0831	7?		Volcano observer & 2 assistants killed at the crater observatory along with 4 bamboo cutters within the devastated zone.	{=}
1966 0426	215	M_{98} m_2 P	Main lahar entered R Badak attaining maximum height of 25 m and maximum distance of 31 km in SW direction. Initial reports listed 208 killed, 78 missing, 86 wounded; later official reports list 211 primary lahar, 3 secondary lahar, and 1 pyroclastic flow fatality. Other sources give death tolls ranging from 210 to 288.	{=}
1986 1231	1	m_{100}		{1972 1006}
1990 0210	32	$T_{80?}$ $P_{20?}$	30 deaths on 10 Feb with most of the damage and casualties attributed to heavy tephra falls causing house roofs to collapse. By 20 Feb official death toll had risen to 32 (GVN).	{=}
1990 1125	4	m_{100}	Lahars killed 4 about 30 km S of the volcano.	No eruption.

SEMERU (0603-30=)

Year M-Dy	Deaths	Agent	Remarks	{Start Date}
1885 0418	74	A_{100}	A debris avalanche covering 6.7 km^2 buried the Kali Bening estate with 4 administrators and some 70 Madurese workers and family members early in the morning.	{1884 1210}
1909 0829	221	m_{100}	Major, & fatal lahar was not attributed to eruptive activity, although ash & block eruptions and pyroclastic flows caused damage from Sept through Dec.	{1909 09}
1946 0507	6	F	Heavy rains caused floods in valleys below Semeru. Kusumadinata-79 gives 0304-30 dates - 6 killed, 81 houses destroyed, 8 ha rice, 1000 ha arable land destroyed (& agents T? M?).	{1946 02}
1968 0308	3	M_{100}	3 killed by mudflows, 10 ha arable land destroyed, 1,000 evacuated.	{1967 0831}
1976 1113	119?	M_{100}	BVE gives only 40 deaths, & 1111 date.	{1967 0831}
1978 0919	12	M_{100}		{1967 0831}
1981 0329	1	P_{100}	One person killed during series of pyroclastic flows down S flank.	{1967 0831}
1981 0514	372?	m_{100}	Secondary lahar due to heavy rainfall dislodged pyroclastic debris down Tunggeng and Sat rivers, killing 252 plus 120 missing, and injuring 152.	{1967 0831}
1988 0730	1	T_{100}	Climber killed by ballistic block at summit.	{1967 0831}
1994 0203	6	P_{100}	Pyroclastic flows reached Sumbersari village, killing 4 and injuring 3, of whom 2 later died.	{1967 0831}

LAMONGAN (0603-32=)

Year M-Dy	Deaths	Agent	Remarks	{Start Date}
1843 1005	4			{1843 08}
1869 0912	8	$T_{?}$ $A_{?}$	Ashfall and volcanic bombs killed 8, Neumann van Padang cites rock avalanches.	{=}

RAUNG (0603-34=)

Year M-Dy	Deaths	Agent	Remarks	{Start Date}
1593	?		A major reported eruption of Raung in 1586 that produced 10,000 fatalities is thought to have occurred in 1593, and the 10,000 fatalities in 1586 to have been from Kelut volcano.	{=}
1597 0117+?	?	$T_{?}$		{=}
1638	>1,000	M_{100}	Great flood and lahar between Stail and Klatak Rivers caused thousands of fatalities.	{=}
1730	Many	$M_{60??}$ $T_{40??}$	Explosive eruption with lahars caused damage and many fatalities.	{=}
1817	?			{1817 0116}

IJEN (0603-35=)

Year M-Dy	Deaths	Agent	Remarks	{Start Date}
1817 0115	Many	$M_{100?}$	CAVW mentions casualties but provides no further information. Kusumadinata-79 mentions 3 villages completely destroyed, 90 houses destroyed, and about	

Year M-Dy	Deaths	Agent	Remarks	{Start Date}
			400 cattle killed, but gives no human fatalities. Neall notes many casualties from lahars produced by collapse of crater lake.	{=}
BATUR			(0604-01=)	
1963	2?		2 reported killed, 3 villages partly destroyed, 18 houses destroyed, 1,600 ha arable land destroyed. VSI says there were no fatalities from this eruption.	{1963 0905}
AGUNG			(0604-02=)	
1963 0317+	1,148	P_{71} T_{14} M_{14} $A_{1?}$	Surjo gives: 820 killed, 59 injured by pyroclastic flows, 163 and 201 by pyroclastic fall, 165 and 36 by lahars. Bodies of about half victims never found. Perhaps 140 killed at Subagan village by lahar plus others swept to sea and killed crossing lahar fields during rainy season. Also, 8 killed by landslides on Batur caldera rim. 1,148 represents most recent official figure, presumably including 120 pyroclastic flow fatalities on May 16. Perhaps 200 of the lahar deaths occurred after the eruption. Keesings suggests 1,584 killed in the March eruption and 106 in the May eruption.	{1963 0219}
TAMBORA			(0604-04=)	
1815	10,000?	$P_{90?}$ $W_{10?}$	10,000 direct deaths from bomb impacts, tephra falls, and tsunamis; recent work indicates pyroclastic flows reached all but W coast and probably caused most direct fatalities on Sumbawa.	{1812}
Indirect	82,000?		An additional 38,000 on Sumbawa + 44,000 on Lombok died as a result of starvation and disease. Sapper notes 12,000 died on Sumbawa mostly from heat (?) and 44,000 died of hunger on Lombok.	
IYA			(0604-11=)	
1969 0127	2	T_{50} m_{50}	2 killed, 10 wounded, 1 village totally and 7 partly destroyed, 287 houses destroyed. VSI report houses were damaged on the island of Ende and one person was killed. Secondary lahars later caused another fatality.	{=}
PALUWEH			(0604-15=)	
1928 0804	226	$W_{70?}$ $T_{30?}$	Tsunami generated by a large landslide at two places on S and E coast of island during explosive eruption during night of Aug 4-5 killed 128 out of total 226 who perished. Latter says tsunami, consisting of 3 waves of 5-10 m in height, killed at least 160 people. 200 injured & 5 villages totally destroyed.	{=}
1964 0101	1		1 killed, 3 wounded.	{1963 1231}
LEWOTOBI			(0604-18=)	
1869 0727	2			{1869 0707}
1907 1016?	1		1 killed, several wounded.	{1907 0928}
ILIWERUNG			(0604-25=)	
1870	?			{=}
1948 0407	?		Van Bemmelen mentions no human deaths but notes nuees down E coast killed 300 cattle & destroyed 100 gardens.	{=}
1973 12?	2	W_{100}	A tsunami 50 m high generated by submarine activity swept away 2 fishermen.	{1973 1205}
1979 0718	539?	W_{100}	Massive landslide 7 km N of Ili Werung caused tsunami up to 9 m high, and devastated 4 villages. Death toll on Lomblen Island listed as 539 (175 bodies recovered and 364 missing).	No eruption.
1983 0817	?	$W_{100?}$	Some people disappeared because of tsunami associated with submarine eruption.	{=}
SIRUNG			(0604-27=)	
1953 06	5		5 killed, 1 injured.	{=}
TEON			(0605-05=)	
1660 02	3	$G_?$ $T_?$	2 or 3 choked and died.	{=}
SERUA			(0605-07=)	
1693 0604	Many?	$L_{100?}$	Many killed at Hislo on W part of the island by a stream of "burning brimstone."	{=}
BANDA API			(0605-09=)	
1598-1602?	?			{=}
1615	?		Sapper notes all settlements destroyed.	{1615 0316}
1694 1130?	Many?		The whole population at the foot of the volcano was destroyed. Neumann van Padang reports an enormous outburst on this day destroyed vegetation on the island. Some sources do not list fatalities.	{1690}
1820	?		Kusumadinata-79: unknown number killed.	{=}
1988 0509	4	T L	A lava flow overran the mosque in Batu Angus village, killing an elderly man who had sought refuge rather than flee with the evacuees. Two young men drowned when their canoe was hit by a block. SEAN gives 3 killed.	{=}
LOKON EMPUNG			(0606-10=)	
1750-1800?	?			{1775}
1991 1024	1	$T_?$ $P_?$	An amateur Swiss volcanologist was killed while observing the eruption.	{1991 0517}
MAHAWU			(0606-11=)	
1958 0712	1	$M_{100?}$	1 killed by hot mud, 10 injured.	{=}
RUANG			(0607-01=)	
1870 0827	?		Unknown number of deaths, 1 village completely destroyed, 40 houses destroyed.	{=}
1871 0303	400?	W	300-400 killed, 1 village completely destroyed, 75 houses destroyed at Bahhuas on Tagulandang Island by tsunami associated with partial collapse of lava dome.	{=}
KARANGETANG [API SIAU]			(0607-02=)	
1940 0823?	1		1 killed, 2 wounded. Date is variably given as Aug 23 or March in same source.	{1940 0620}
1974 0427	4	A_{100}	Earthquakes caused landslides.	{1972 01}
1976 1015	1	P_{100}	1 killed and 1 injured by small pyroclastic flow from collapse of lava flow front when evacuees returned at night to witness incandescent lava. 24 houses destroyed by lava.	{1976 0915}
1992 0511	6	P_{100}	7 farmers were burned by pyroclastic flows from collapsing lava flow front; 6 later died in hospitals.	{1991 0702<}
AWU			(0607-04=)	
1711 1211	~3,000	$P_{100?}$	About 3,000 killed. Sapper gives death toll as about 2030. Pyroclastic flows before morning of Dec 12 took around 3,000 lives, 2,030 of which were in the Kendhar area, 408 from Taruna, 70 from Kolongan, and the remainder from Talawid and Motane.	{1711 1210}
1812 0806	~953	$P_{75??}$ $M_{25??}$	From the number of fatalities and the amount of damage it can be concluded that the eruption also included lahars and glowing clouds. Sapper gives death toll as 953. Kusumadinata-79 gives toll as hundreds killed, 3 wounded.	{=}
1856 0302	2,806	$P_{100?}$	8 villages partly destroyed.	{=}
1892 0607	1,532	$P_{75??}$ $M_{25??}$	Fatalities all on N coast attributed to pyroclastic flows and lahars; 10-12 villages totally destroyed. Sapper gives death toll as 1,000-1,500.	{=}
1966 0812	39	$P_{72??}$ $M_{25??}$ I_3	38 killed by pyroclastic flows and lahars, one person drowned while swimming to ship. Only 1 body was found, most were covered with rocks and hot pumice flows. 1,000 were injured by the impact of ejected fragments from the lava plug. 2 villages totally destroyed, 3 partly destroyed.	{=}
DUKONO			(0608-01=)	
1550	?			{1550 1120}
GAMKONORA			(0608-04=)	
1564+	?		1564 or 1565.	{1564 1231y}
1673 0520	Many?	W_{100}	Tsunami inundated villages.	{=}
GAMALAMA			(0608-06=)	
1772 0509	35	$T_{100?}$	30-40 slaves working at NW foot of the volcano were killed by glowing ash and rock.	{1771 0828}
1773 1025	Several	$I_?$	Drownings on overloaded boats fleeing eruption.	{1773 1021}
1775	1,300?	$P_{100?}$ $I_?$	Maar-forming eruption on N coast, with widespread base surge deposition killing 141. Some	

Year M-Dy	Deaths	Agent	Remarks	{Start Date}
			drowned while escaping by boat. Bronto et al. give 1,300 fatalities.	{1775 0820}
1838 0226	4	T_{100}	Javanese sulfur collectors killed in crater.	{=}
1871 0907	1	T_{100}	1 killed & another injured by block ejection.	{1871 0807}
1962 1231	5		5 dead, 5 wounded.	{1962 0925}
MAKIAN			(0608-07=)	
1646 0719	Many		Many died. Not listed in Kusumadinata-79. VSI comments that major explosive eruption devastated villages on flanks.	{=}
1760	~2,000	$M_{100?}$	Major explosive eruption. IAVCEI attributes deaths to a lahar.	{1760 0922}
1861 1229	326	$P_{100?}$ $I_{O?}$	326 deaths, 47 injuries. Ashflows reached the coast. Some drowned while fleeing by boat. Kusumadinata-79 gives 309 killed and 15 villages totally destroyed. Wallace also mentions this eruption but places it on the same day in 1862.	{1861 1228}
1890 0629	?		Kusumadinata-79 makes no mention of human fatalities but records several villages destroyed completely, many houses destroyed, many cattle killed.	{1890 0620}

PHILIPPINES (07)

Year M-Dy	Deaths	Agent	Remarks	{Start Date}
RAGANG			(0701-06=)	
1873	?			{1873 0116}
HIBOK-HIBOK			(0701-08=)	
1871 0430	Some?		One account says nearby townspeople fled during premonitory quake activity, so there were very few victims even though destruction reached Catarman. Another says very considerable number of victims.	{=}
1950 0915	68	P_{100}	Macdonald and Alcaraz note only several killed (*Time* 12/17/51 p36 gives 68) by pyroclastic flow and that clothing was not burned.	{1948 0901}
1951 1204	>500?	P_{100}	*Time* (see above) gives 500 killed, 266 bodies found and maybe 1,500 unaccounted for. Alcaraz gives 500 killed, & 3 more on 12/06.	{1948 0901}
1954 early	2	m_{100}	2 killed by mudflows caused by typhoon rains.	{1954}
MAYON			(0703-03=)	
1766 1023	49	m_{100}	Deaths caused by mudflows from typhoon rains some months after July eruption. 30 deaths in Malinao, 16 in Albay. Death total 49 from Ramos-Villarta.	{1766 0720}
1800 10	?			{1800 1030}
1814 0201	1,200	$P_{90?}$ $M_{10?}$ $E_{?}$	COMVOL regarded most deaths as due to lahars but more recent work at Casagua suggests pyroclastic flows were dominant cause of fatalities. Town of Budiao destroyed; town of Camalig also destroyed and burned; towns of Albay, Guinobatan and Balusan partly destroyed. Some deaths from electrical discharges.	{=}
1853 0713	34?	P_{100}	33 fatalities (Sapper, Faustino) or 35 (Saderra Maso). Deaths caused by incandescent rocks rolling down from the summit, destroying many houses and their occupants (Faustino).	{=}
1858	?	$P_{?}$	Incandescent materials rolled downslope, destroying forests and plantations. Cause of fatalities not stated.	{1858 01}
1871 1208	3	P_{100}	Deaths by nuees ardentes. In the "vista" of Boctong, two persons were suffocated and in Buyuhan, one was burned.	{=}
1875	~1,500	m_{100}	Deaths due to rain-triggered lahars. Not in eruption since July 1873.	
1887 0309	15	T_{100}	20-hour ash eruption at end of 9-month eruption deposited 8 cm of ash on roofs in Guinobatan and Libog. Collapse of roofs killed 15.	{1886 0708}
1897 0625	350	$P_{90?}$ $T_{10?}$ $M_{1?}$	Large nuees burned victims or they suffocated by ash. 350 total from Saderra Maso & Sapper. Other estimates vary 250-400. 1 death at Bulawan R caused by lahar. Latter indicates 400 deaths in town of Libog. All but 56 of the 261 dead died during event - the rest during the following week.	{1897 0523}
1928 0625>	>1	P_{100}	Pyroclastic flows between June 25 and Aug 7 killed at least one (Ramos-Villarta).	{1928 0625}
1938	?			{1938 0605}
1947	?			{1947 0107}
1968	6?	$M_{80?}$ $P_{20?}$	One death by lahar in Aug or Oct, the others during the eruption. One man who was caught in a blast of hot gas died of burns to his whole body. BVE lists mudflows in SE sector; probably 3 killed.	{1968 0421}
1981 0630	>200	m_{100}	At least 200 fatalities caused by lahars initiated by typhoon. BVE gives 40 confirmed dead and 7 missing. No eruption.	
1984	1	M_{100}	1 killed by lahar. Other reports say only that unsanitary conditions led to deaths of children in evacuation centers.	{1984 0909}
1993 0202	75	P_{100}	75 killed and 100 injured by a pyroclastic flow on the SE flank.	{=}
IRIGA			(0703-041)	
1628 or 1641	?	A	Debris avalanche devastated villages at foot of volcano. Phreatic eruptions accompanied or followed avalanche. More likely date is 1628 (Taal erupted in 1641).	{1628}
TAAL			(0703-07=)	
1716	?		CAVW lists possible fatalities.	{1716 0924}
1749	?		CAVW lists possible fatalities. Arboleda et al. note casualties mentioned but it is not clear that these are deaths. Saderra Maso believes there were no deaths.	{1749 0811}
1754 0513	12	$W_{50?}$ $T_{50?}$	12 villagers killed at Taal village, some by tsunami and others by collapsing houses. As Saderra Maso refers to 4 villages around lake being completely destroyed, these fatalities may refer only to those in Taal village. Permanent abandonment of several villages on lake shore.	{=}
1874 0719	?			{=}
1911 0130	>1,335	$P_{80?}$ $W_{20?}$	~1,335 killed chiefly by pyroclastic flows. Only 732 bodies found. 12 or 13 on island survived but all badly injured. Heiser, medical officer in area at time, estimates deaths at about 2,000.	{1911 0127}
1965 0928	>200	$P_{60?}$ $W_{40?}$	Estimates range 150 to 250 including those drowned and several murdered. Many of the fatalities occurred when tsunami capsized boats filled with fleeing residents. Newspaper and other reports suggesting 3,000-5,000 deaths are very unreliable.	{=}
PINATUBO			(0703-083)	
1991 0615±	350?	P_{70} m_{30}	4 were killed and 4 injured prior to the catastrophic June 15-16 eruptions that killed several hundred. By Aug 20, mudflows had killed more than 100.	{1991 0402}
Indirect	450?	I_{100}	Disease at evacuation camps had (by Sept 20) brought the total fatalities to about 800.	{1991 0402}
1992 0712	6?	m_{100}	Secondary lahars from 1991 deposits killed 2 on July 12, 1992. Total fatalities during the 1992 rainy season were reported by one source to be 60, but the official figure was listed as 6.	{1992 0705d}
BINULUAN			(0703-088)	
1952	12	$M_{100?}$	May have been a steam eruption because sulfur melted and flowed downhill, mixing with debris and killing about a dozen people.	{=}
DIDICAS			(0704-02=)	
1969 0321	3	W_{100}	3 drowned while fishing: tsunami generated by a submarine explosion at Didicas, 70 km away.	{=}
TENGCHONG			(0705-11-)	
1609	?	E_{100}	Some shepherds and 500-600 sheep were struck by lightning.	{=}

JAPAN (08)

OKINAWA-TORI-SHIMA (0802-02=)

Year M-Dy	Deaths	Agent	Remarks	{Start Date}
1664	1	A	Landslide swept over a village, killing a woman.	{=}

KUCHINOERABU-JIMA (0802-05=)

Year M-Dy	Deaths	Agent	Remarks	{Start Date}
1841 0801	?	$T_?$	JMA reports large explosion devastating villages at volcano's foot.	{1841 0523}
1933 1224	8	T_{100}	An explosion ejected tephra to the SSE, killing 8 and injuring 26. Nanakama village, 1.5 km from the crater was burned by fire from glowing blocks. CAVW gives date as 12/23.	{1933 1223}.

KIKAI (0802-06=)

Year M-Dy	Deaths	Agent	Remarks	{Start Date}
4350 BC	?		Major ash eruption & pyroclastic flows, from Japan's largest Holocene eruption, devastated S Kyushu. Fatalities likely large, but not estimated. Kyushu not resettled for 300-800 years.	{=}

SAKURA-JIMA (0802-08=)

Year M-Dy	Deaths	Agent	Remarks	{Start Date}
0764 01	80	$T_?$ $L_?$	Deaths possibly by phreatomagmatic eruption or lava flow.	{=}
0766	Many			{0766 0720}
1471+1476	Many	$P_?$	Sakurajima's largest historical eruption caused fatalities in its first and last years. Deaths possibly resulted from pyroclastic flows.	{1471 1103}
1779 1109	153	$T_{70??}$ $W_{28??}$ $I_{2??}$	Official report dated 1780 0115 gives 79 men, 74 women killed. Kamo attributes deaths to tsunami, lava, and burial of villages by tephra. One person drowned while attempting to cross the Seto Channel which was filled with pumice. Inscription on stone monument erected in 1779 notes 148 killed and gives villages. Sapper gives 140 killed and notes that some sources say 16-17,000!. Koto notes 141 killed + 1,576 horses, 135 oxen, and that some sources report 9,600 humans killed.	{1779 1108}
1780 0209	Many	F_{100}	Water gushed from the summit and many people drowned. This account, by Milne, does not appear in other sources, and may be suspect.	{1779 1108}
1781 0411	38?	W_{100}	Tsunami upset 3 boats, drowning 14 men and 1 woman. Koto reports 23 sightseers killed in 1781 by paroxysmal outburst.	{1779 1108}
1914 0112	63?	$I_{37?}$ $S_{34?}$ $A_{19?}$ $T_{10?}$	Half or more of the deaths resulted from collapse of stone walls and cliffs, mainly in Kagoshima during the earthquake. Few (6?) deaths on island because of effective evacuation; another 12 buried in landslide that was probably earthquake-induced. Uncertain number killed in building collapses during earthquake. Two people buried by pumice at Fumato. 23 drowned attempting to swim from island. Other estimates of deaths range 23 to 140. Injuries probably totalled 121, but estimates range from 87 to 127.	{=}
1946	1			{1946 01}
1955 1013	1			{=}
1974 0617	3	M_{100}	Rain-induced mudflows killed 3.	{1955 1013}
1974 0809	5	M_{100}	Rain-induced mudflows killed 5.	{1955 1013}

KIRISHIMA (0802-09=)

Year M-Dy	Deaths	Agent	Remarks	{Start Date}
1566 1031	Many		JMA mentions fatalities, Murayama says many	{=}
1716 1109	1		1 dead and 31 injured. One source lists 6 fatalities for the 1716-1717 eruption.	{=}
1717 0207	1		1 killed and 30 injured.	{1716 1109}
1895 1016+	4	T_{100}		{1895 0716}
1896 0315	1	$T?_{100}$	One climber killed and another injured.	{1895 0716}
1900 0216	2		2 killed, 3 injured.	{1899 0728}
1923 07	1			{1923 07}

UNZEN (0802-10=)

Year M-Dy	Deaths	Agent	Remarks	{Start Date}
1664 0415q	>30	m_{100}	In the spring of 1664 water poured out of Tsukumo-jima pond at the summit of Fugen-dake, producing floods that killed >30 in the Mizunashi river valley.	{1663 1211}
1792 0521	14,524	$W_{95?}$ $A_{05?}$	Figures from Katayama indicate 9,528 fatalities along the Shimabara peninsula and an additional 4,996 fatalities in Higo and Amakusa provinces across Ariake Sea. The vast majority were killed by the tsunami, the avalanche reaching only the southern outskirts of Shimabara city.	{1792 0210}
1991 0603	43	P_{100}	A pyroclastic flow and surge killed 43, including 3 volcanologists.	{1990 1117}
1993 0623	1	P_{100}	A homeowner entered the evacuation zone to watch his house being burned by a pyroclastic flow and was killed by a second pyroclastic flow.	{1990 1117}

ASO (0802-11=)

Year M-Dy	Deaths	Agent	Remarks	{Start Date}
1331+	?		Milne says all the people of Hojo were destroyed in 19-month eruption, but other compilers list no fatalities.	{1331 12}
1485 01	1			{1485 0105}
1816 0705	1	T_{100}		{1816 06}
1827 1127	Many	$T_{100?}$	Sapper states that many people who had come to pray 2,200 m S of the crater lake died from ash suffocation. Fatalities are not mentioned in Japanese compilations.	{1827 1112}
1854 0226	3		Sapper mentions thunder, earthquakes, and eruption of muddy water, but cause of deaths not known. These were 3 pilgrims who came to crater to pray.	{=}
1872 1201	4	T?	4 sulfur miners in crater killed by explosion.	{=}
1953 0427	6	T_{100}	6 tourists killed near crater rim.	{=}
1958 0624	12	T_{100}	12 ropeway workers killed, 20 (JMA says 28) injured by nighttime explosion.	{1957 10}
1979 0906	3	T_{100}	Block ejection killed 3 tourists & injured 11, near ropeway station ~850 m NNE of crater.	{1979 0612}

HAKONE (0803-02=)

Year M-Dy	Deaths	Agent	Remarks	{Start Date}
1933 0510	1	$G_{100?}$	One killed during fumarolic activity.	No eruption.
1953 0726	10	A_{100}	Landslide killed 10.	No eruption.

ON-TAKE (0803-04=)

Year M-Dy	Deaths	Agent	Remarks	{Start Date}
1984 0914	29	A_{100}	An earthquake caused the S flank of the volcano to collapse, creating a debris avalanche which killed 10 people in a hot spa. Some deaths may be from other landslides caused by quake. First historical eruption ended in April 1980, after 6 months.	

NIIGATA-YAKE-YAMA (0803-09=)

Year M-Dy	Deaths	Agent	Remarks	{Start Date}
1974 0728	3	T_{100}	Mountain climbing students of Chiba University killed by ejecta while camped near fissure crater.	{=}

ASAMA (0803-11=)

Year M-Dy	Deaths	Agent	Remarks	{Start Date}
1596 0501+	Many	T_{100}	Many killed by tephra on May 1. One source also lists many fatalities for 8/19 eruption of same year.	{=}
1598 0513	~800	T_{100}	Religious pilgrims who had climbed the volcano were killed at the summit (where they were staying because it was not a religiously auspicious day to descend).	{=}
1721 0622	15	T_{100}	Fifteen climbers killed, some sources say 5.	{=}
1783 0805	1,491	$F_{70?}$ $P_{30?}$ I?	466 killed by Kamabara pyroclastic flow. 93 people who were able to climb up steps of small temple survived. Hot mudflows from the Kamabara nuee flowed into the Agatsuma R, causing a temporary dam. Flood downstream over a distance of 100 km washed away 1,300 houses and up to 1400 people. Suspended ash and dust decreased sunlight, and resulting cold and rainy weather caused a famine in the Kanto region. Approximately 300,000 people died in northern Japan from the Tenmei famine, which lasted from 1783-1787. Some estimates suggest up to 1 million deaths, then about 3% of Japan's population, but the eruption is considered only a contributing factor.	{1783 0509}
1803 0704/1107	?		CAVW lists fatalities but does not specify which 1803 eruption. JMA-75 and Murayama mention no fatalities for either.	{1803 0704}
1900 0715	>25?		A boulder swept through village killing 25 persons. Women and children became exhausted along road and were burned to death.	{1900 0122}
1911 0508	1		1 killed & ~60 houses destroyed.	{1909 01}
1911 0815	Many			{1909 01}
1930 0820	6	T_{100}	6 killed by projectiles near crater rim.	{1930 04}

Year M-Dy Deaths Agent Remarks {Start Date}

1931 0820 3? {1931 03}

1936 0729+ 2 $P_{50?}$ $T_{50?}$ single climbers killed on 7/29 & 10/29: the first possibly by small pyroclastic flow. {1935 01}

1941 0713 1 $T_{100?}$ Death (& 1 injury) assumed to be from ballistics because of number of explosions. Near end of >4-year eruption. {1938 03}

1947 0814 11 Eleven persons climbing volcano were killed. {1947 06}

1950 0923 1 T_{100} One climber killed, one injured from lithic ejecta. Air shock damaged houses. {=}

1961 0818 1 $T_{100?}$ A climber at the summit at the time of an eruption was killed. {=}

KUSATSU-SHIRANE (0803-12=)

1932 10 2 $M_{100?}$ 2 killed, 7 injured in lahar generated by eruption while 20 were mining native sulfur from the crater lake bottom. {1932 1001}

NASU (0803-15=)

1410 0305 180 180 persons and many cattle killed. {=}

BANDAI (0803-16=)

1888 0715 461 $A_{80??}$ $P_{20??}$ Debris avalanche buried several villages. Only ~116 bodies recovered; 70 injured, mostly burned and scarred by pyroclastic surge. {=}

ADATARA (0803-17=)

1900 0717 72 T_{100} 72 sulfur miners in crater killed, 10 injured in explosive eruption. {=}

AZUMA (0803-18=)

1893 0607 2 T_{100} 2 geologists were killed on the crater rim by falling stones. {1893 0519}

ZAO (0803-19=)

1867 1021 3 M_{100} Overflow of muddy water from Okama crater lake killed 3 hot springs bathers at E foot of Goshiki-dake. {=}

CHOKAI (0803-22=)

1801 0814 8 T_{100} Climbers killed by volcanic ejecta. {1800 12}

OSHIMA (0804-01=)

1789 ? T_{100} Heavy ashfall buried Shimotaka village, including people and animals. {=}

1953 1013 1 {1953 1005}

1957 1013 1 T_{100} One tourist killed and 53 injured by explosion. {1957 08}

1986 1115 1 I_{100} A 74-year-old man died of a heart attack while being evacuated by ship from the island, on eruption's first day. {=}

MIYAKE-JIMA (0804-04=)

1874 07 1? $T_{?}$ A person near the crater was missing and presumed dead. {1874 0703}

1940 0808 11 11 killed, 20 injured. {1940 0712}

AOGA-SHIMA (0804-06=)

1783 04 7? Eruption and earthquake; 7 persons (one source says 14) and all houses at foot of cone burned. {1780 0727}

1785 0418 ~135 CAVW-11 gives 130-140 killed by explosion in last month of 5-year eruption. Island abandoned for 50 years. {1780 0727}

BAYONNAISE ROCKS (0804-07=)

1952 0924 31 $P_{100?}$ Research ship Kaiyo-maru, while over central submarine dome Myojin-sho, sunk by explosion; all 31 on board killed. {1952 0916}

TORI-SHIMA (0804-09=)

1902 0809 125 All islanders killed; no bodies recovered. {1902 0807}

1939 2 {1939 0817}

OSHIMA-OSHIMA (0805-01=)

1741 0823 1,475 W_{100} 1467 killed on W coast of Oshima Peninsula, 729 houses washed away by tsunami following tectonic earthquake & debris avalanche from N flank of Nishi-yama. 8 more people killed & 82 houses destroyed by tsunami on coast of N Honshu. {1741 0818}

Year M-Dy Deaths Agent Remarks {Start Date}

E-SAN (0805-012)

1846 Many M_{100} Many killed by mudflows. {1846 1118}

KOMAGA-TAKE (0805-02=)

1640 0731 700 W_{100} Debris avalanche caused tsunami which killed 700. Many ships also destroyed. {=}

1856 0925 >20 $P_{100?}$ Nearly all houses at Honbetsu near Shikabe were burned. 20 fatalities produced by pumice flow. {=}

1929 2 T_{100} 2 killed and 4 injured by pyroclastic fall; VL 372 (1932) reports 1 death, probably as a result of pumice flows. {1929 0617}

USU (0805-03=)

1663 0816 5 $T_{60??}$ $P_{40??}$ Deaths by ashfall (& base surge?). {1663 0817}

1822 50 P_{100} 50 killed & 53 injured (= CAVW total of 103), all in old village of Abuta (S side of volcano). 1,437 horses also killed and old Abuta destroyed. {1822 0312}

1910 1 M_{100} Death in lahar. {1910 0725}

1944 1228 1 T_{100} Child suffocated by ash fall. {1944 0623}

1978 1024 3 m_{100} Deaths at Toyako-onsen resulted from mudflows derived from newly deposited tephra. 2 injuries also reported. {1977 0807}

SHIKOTSU [TARUMAI] (0805-04=)

1804-1817 Many? Some sources report many fatalities, but Jaggar thinks report doubtful and Katsui does not list fatalities. {1804}

TOKACHI (0805-05=)

1926 0504 146 $M_{98?}$ $T_{2?}$ Initial explosion destroyed hot spring bath house killing 3. Second explosion 4 hours later produced avalanche from cone and hot mudflows which swept down Hurano valley mixed with snowmelt reaching town 20 km W of crater in 26 minutes. 137 killed, 207 or more injured, and 5,080 houses destroyed in Hurano Valley. Finch cites newspaper reports as suggesting 400 lives lost - lava flows, floods and explosions each taking a share - with 144 bodies recovered in 2 days. {1925 1120}

1962 0629 5 T_{100} 5 killed, 11 injured by falling blocks. {=}

RUSSIA & MAINLAND ASIA (09 & 10)

RAIKOKE (0900-25=)

1778 15 T_{100} 15 persons under the command of Cpt. Cherny were killed by volcanic bombs, prompting the first volcanological investigation in the Kurile Islands. {=}

SINARKA (0900-29=)

1872 ? $P_{?}$ Ainu village destroyed, possibly by incandescent avalanches; Gorshkov considers this eruption to be from Sinarka, not Kuntomintar. {=}

HARIMKOTAN (0900-30=)

1933 0108 2 W_{100} A tsunami from the collapse of Severgin volcano reached as far as Onekotan and Paramushir Islands, where two persons were killed. Tsunami reported to be 20m high. {=}

MUTNOVSKY (1000-06=)

1991 06 1 I_{100} A geology student was killed when he fell through a snowfield crust into a thermal area mudpot. No eruption.

KLIUCHEVSKOI (1000-26=)

1762 ? Doubik writes that it is difficult to estimate the number of casualties because of lack of exact information. {=}

1978 1 T_{100} A glaciologist camped near the summit was killed by a single bomb from a strombolian eruption. {1977 0802}

1983 1 T_{100} A geophysicist was killed by a volcanic bomb 3.5-4 km from the summit. {1982 1007}

Year M-Dy Deaths Agent Remarks {Start Date}

USA & CANADA (11, 12, & 13)

CLEVELAND (1101-24-)

1944 0610 — 1 — T_{100} Large blocks ejected over island; newspaper reported one man crushed by falling rocks and later covered by lava. {=}

NOVARUPTA [KATMAI] (1102-18-)

1912 0606 — 2 — $T_{100?}$ An elderly, tuburcular Indian woman died in Kodiak during the tephra fall. One man died some weeks later after being buried for 3 hours up to his arms in wet ash. {=}

TSEAX RIVER CONE (1200-13-)

1730w — Several — G_{100} Lava flow overran village. Several people who had dug pits for shelter died of "poison smoke." {=}

ST HELENS (1201-05-)

1980 0518 — 57 — P_{96} M_2 T_2 All known direct deaths were attributable to the lateral blast, ashfall, and lahars of the May 18 eruption. Among the 25 victims who were autopsied, asphyxiation by airway constriction with ash was the cause of death in 17 and contributory in 2 others with thermal injuries. Thermal injuries alone accounted for 3 deaths; three victims died of trauma. {1980 0327}

Indirect — 4 — A pilot of a crop duster was killed when his plane hit powerlines in central Washington State during tephra fall. In Yakima, a traffic accident, attributed to poor visibility, resulted in 1 death and 2 elderly people with heart conditions died while shovelling tephra from their property. Almost certainly, other indirect deaths also occurred.

KILAUEA (1302-01-)

1790 11 — 100? — P_{100} Number of deaths variously estimated at 80 to 100. Deaths probably due to a hot, relatively ash-free base surge. Three parties of Keoua's soldiers were crossing the Kau desert, each party consisting of 80 men accompanied by their families and livestock. One party was completely exterminated, the other had a few of its members either burned to death or seriously injured, and the third party was unharmed. {=}

1823 02 — Few — $L_{100?}$ Macdonald indicates that the flow advanced so rapidly on a coastal village that a few older persons and children were killed. Stearns does not mention fatalities, but quotes the report of Ellis that the sudden inundation burned one canoe and carried others out to sea. {=}

1924 0518 — 1 — T_{100} Photographer hit by falling stones died that night from internal hemorrhage. {1924 0510}

1975 1129 — 2 — W_{100} M 7.2 earthquake created tsunami 2 hours before beginning of eruption. Extensive damage, subsidence and 2 deaths in Halape Park area when sea inundated acres of land. {1969 0524}

1993 0419 — 1 — $A?_{100}$ Man watching lava enter sea was swept away when new lava bench collapsed, sliding into the ocean near Kalapana. At the same time, steam explosions threw incandescent blocks on the lava delta, injuring 22 other spectators. {1983 0103}

MAUNA LOA (1302-02=)

1868 0402 — 77 — W_{60} M_{40} Earthquake during eruption generated tsunamis; heavy rains produced mudflows. 46 killed by tsunami, 31 by mudflows. {1868 0327}

HUALALAI (1302-04-)

1800 — 2 — L_{100} Two persons killed when lava flows surrounded hut at night. {=}

MEXICO & CENTRAL AMERICA (14)

COLIMA (1401-04=)

1576 — ? — Strong explosive eruption, great destruction of land. Deaths reported - number unknown. {=}

1818 0215 — ? — Medina lists fatalities and property damage. Servando de la Cruz suggests deaths could be due to starvation and disease after the eruption. {=}

MICHOACAN [PARICUTIN] (1401-06=)

1943 — 3 — E_{100} Lightning associated with eruptive activity. {1943 0220}

Indirect — >100 — I Deaths included killings of refugees by new neighbors, murders in land disputes after the eruption, and deaths in the refugee communities from disease and lack of will to live.

EL CHICHON (1401-12=)

1982 0329 — 1,879? — $P_{90??}$ $T_{6??}$ $M_{2??}$ $S_{2??}$ 1,755 missing and 124 dead mostly in pyroclastic flows. Other estimates range up to 2,000. Two caretakers at dam construction killed by lahar, 11 killed when dam created by pyroclastic flow broke. Government sources list 187 fatalities (including 4/04), but do not include missing persons. Most of casualties on N side were due to fires started by incandescent tephra and building collapse due to earthquakes. {1982 0328}

1982 0404 — 33 — P_{100} 32 soldiers and 1 geologist killed by pyroclastic flow that overran Francisco Leon, 5 km SW of summit. {1982 0328}

1982 0527 — 1 — m_{100} Failure of pumice dam from pyroclastic flow caused rapid drainage of lake at Francisco Leon. One worker at hydroelectric plant downstream killed. {1982 0328}

SANTA MARIA (1402-03=)

1902 1024 — 1,500? — $T_{80?}$ $G_{20?}$ Sapper says that hundreds of people were killed in collapsing houses. One source says 10 villages of 50-50,00 inhabitants each were buried beneath tons of volcanic debris. At one plantation 11 km from the volcano, 105 of 112 laborers died. At a village over 350 died, suffocated by deadly fumes. {=}

Indirect — >3,000? — Anderson suggested 2-3,000 killed and many more (i.e. >2,000) died in subsequent malaria outbreak because ashfall killed birds but not mosquitoes. Both Coleman and Wilcoxson give estimates of 6,000 killed.

1929 1102 — >200 — $P_{90??}$ $M_{10??}$ *CAVW* lists 23 fatalities for pyroclastic flow. VL gives 45 deaths, with 21 bodies found at El Palmar, 10 km from the crater but later VL details 26 more killed by hot mud at a plantation on the Rio Tambor. This source also implies that loss of life approached that in the 1902 eruption. Mercado et al. suggest 11/02 dome collapse pyroclastic flow killed from several hundred to as many as 5,000 persons. {1922 0622}

1978 0902 — 1 — M_{100} Mudflow from breakup of ash & block dams on rivers killed 1. {1922 0622}

1990 0719 — 4 — T_{100} Four hikers on a government-sponsored filming expedition were killed by explosions while on the E rim of the 1902 crater. {1922 0622}

FUEGO (1402-09=)

1963 0930 — 7 — $M_{100?}$ Renewed ashfall triggered a lahar in which 7 persons perished. {1963 0928}

1971 0914 — 10 — $M_?$ $T_?$ BVE gives 10 killed of unstated causes. CSLP gives 2 killed in San Pedro Yepocapa by about 30 cm ashfall. {1971 0914}

1974 1010 — ? — $T_?$ $M_?$ Deaths caused by a shower of bombs. 2-3 killed by "hot water and mud." Although there were few casualties, thousands abandoned their houses, many of which were destroyed by the weight of ash. {=}

AGUA (1402-10=)

1541 — >1,300 — m_{100} Draining of crater lake evidently created mudflows which destroyed former Guatemalan capital of Cuidad Vieja. Gobernadora Donna Beatrix, the first woman head of government in the American continent, was one of the dead. No eruption.

LAGUNA VERDE (1403-01=)

1990 1013 — 13 — T_{100} A minor directed phreatic explosion from a thermal area caused 13 fatalities and injured 21 persons; 13 persons later died in hospitals.

IZALCO (1403-03=)

1926 1105 — ? — P Deaths probably occurred in pyroclastic flow. {1925 1226}

SAN SALVADOR (EL BOQUERON) (1403-05=)

0590v — ? — Sheets reports bodies found in house excavated beneath Ceren tephra. Death resulted from volcanic gases, burning or suffocation from tephra. {=}

Year M-Dy	Deaths	Agent	Remarks	{Start Date}
1917 0606	325?	$S_{92?}$ $L_{8?}$	CAVW and Roy make no mention of fatalities in this eruption but Jagger reports some people caught and killed in lava flow; several hundred were killed and many wounded when 15 towns including capital destroyed by volcanogenic(?) earthquake on same day.	{1917 0607}
ILOPANGO			(1403-06=)	
0260v	Thousands?		Major Plinian eruption associated with caldera formation destroyed early Mayan cities. Sheets estimates fatalities at "thousands."	{=}
COSIGUINA			(1404-01=)	
1835 0120	Several?		Despite the magnitude of the eruption there were few fatalities in this sparsely populated region; a few cattle ranchers near the base of the volcano and some fishermen in a boat offshore. Johnston-Lavis reports deaths from "mephitic vapors." Galindo reports the death of a 7 year old girl at Union with sore throat believed to be caused by dust, and the death of 7 people in Leon on Jan 23.	{=}
CERRO NEGRO			(1404-07=)	
1992 04	2?	I_{100}	1 or 2 persons died from falls while shoveling tephra from roofs.	{1992 0409}
MOMBACHO			(1404-11=)	
1570	~400	A_{100}	Avalanche on S flank destroyed an Indian village of 400 persons.	{=}
ARENAL			(1405-033)	
1968 0729	~80	$P_{50?}$ $T_{50?}$	80 (±5) killed in first 3 days; many by pyroclastic flows, but perhaps half by ballistic blocks. Village of Tabacon nearly obliterated by impact craters. One source reports 78 killed in pyroclastic flows. Other sources give totals ranging 76 to >100.	{=}
1975 0617	2?		2 killed, many injured. Alvarado lists 1 injury, no fatalities.	{1968 0729}
1988 0706	1	T_{100}	A climber was struck on the head by tephra from an explosion while 3 m from crater rim.	{1968 0729}
IRAZU			(1405-06=)	
1963 1210+	~40	M_{95} $T_{5?}$	Waldron gives number killed in mudflows as >20. Other estimates range from "only a few" to 30. 2 killed & 10 injured by a shower of ash and stones on the crater rim in mid-April. 5 died and many wounded in April & Aug 1964. Stine & Banks report that mudflows killing 20 persons and destroying many structures along the Rio Chiquito were secondary. Over a 2-year period 46 mudflows occurred along the Rio Reventado valley; one killed at least 20 persons & destroyed 400 houses and some factories.	{1963 0313}
SOUTH AMERICA (15)				
RUIZ			(1501-02=)	
1595 0312	636	M_{100}	Lahars in the Lagunillas and Guali river valleys killed 636 persons, mostly Guali Indians.	{1595 0309}
1845 0219	~1,000	M_{100}	Mudflows, again caused by eruption melting of snow cover, buried the entire population along the Lagunillas valley.	{=}
1985 1113	23,080	M_{100}	Death tolls uncertain with most estimates in the range 23-26,000. This figure from Pierson et al., quoting office of Colombian President. Katsui et al. indicate 24,470 including 21,000 of the 29,000 inhabitants of Armero. Naranjo et al. suggest approximately 1,000 died in Chinchina. About 10,000 injured, 5,200 requiring medical attention.	{1985 0911}
PURACE			(1501-06=)	
1885 0525	Many		A catastrophic explosion accompanied by an earthquake killed many people and destroyed many houses.	{=}
1949 0526	17	$T_{100?}$	University students killed by block ejection as they attempted to reach the summit.	{1949 0526}
DONA JUANA			(1501-07=)	
1899 1113	55	$P_{100?}$	50-60 killed by burns from blocks and ash from hot avalanches. 200-300 animals also killed.	{1897 1101}
GALERAS			(1501-08=)	
1993 0114	9	T_{100}	A sudden explosion killed 9 persons, including 6 volcanologists who were in (and on the rim of) the inner crater.	{=}
GUAGUA PICHINCHA			(1502-02=)	
1993 0312	2	T_{100}	Volcanologists visiting the lava dome to investigate eruption 3 days earlier were killed by second phreatic eruption.	{1993 0309}
COTOPAXI			(1502-05=)	
-0455w BC	?	M	Giant lahar - deaths assumed?	{=}
1698	?	M	Latacunga and 3/4 of its inhabitants destroyed by lahars. Coleman also mentions other settlements destroyed.	{=}
1742 0615+	?	M	Lahars caused much destruction and fatalities: both 6/15 & 12/09 eruptions in 1742.	{=}
1768 0404	?	M	Lahars devastated the Los Chillos, Tumbaco and Cutuchi valleys. Latacunga was destroyed again.	{=}
1877 0626	>340	M_{100}	Wolf reports at Mullao the priest observed 20 people swept away by the lahar. The Latacunga district had 300 fatalities, not including outsiders and 20 Indians were killed by lahars at Napo. Coleman gives the death toll at 1,000 but the basis for this is not clear.	{1877 01}
TUNGURAHUA			(1502-08=)	
1886 0112	2	P_{100}		{1886 0111}
SANGAY			(1502-09=)	
1976 0812	2	T_{100}	2 killed and 4 seriously injured as British Vulcan Expedition neared summit of perennially active cone.	{1934 0808}
CERRO AZUL			(1503-06=)	
1943 0413b	1	$T_{100?}$	P-39 fighter pilot from WW-II Galapagos air base crashed when flying over eruption.	{=}
HUAYNAPUTINA			(1504-03=)	
1600 0219	1,400?		All or most of the inhabitants of at least 11 villages were killed. ~1,200 killed at Omate, ~200 in other villages and 30 by seismic activity.	{=}
LONQUIMAY			(1507-10=)	
1989 06	1	T_{100}	Autopsy of a 64 year old wood cutter exposed to ash for 8 hours daily, revealed lung and nervous system problems similar to that causing many livestock deaths.	{1988 1225}
LLAIMA			(1507-11=)	
1937 0209+	3	F_{100}	Castroen River swelled with ash, destroying a house and killing 1. The next day, summit lava flows melted snow to produce floods of hot water down the same river killing 2 and destroying 2 bridges.	{=}
VILLARICA			(1507-12=)	
1575	350?	S_{100}	Destruction of Villarica village during tectonic earthquake: reports of eruption are in error.	
1949 12?	36?	M?	Deaths probably in lahars.	{1948 1009}
1963 0521+	?	M_{100}	Snowmelt from lava and super-heated steam May 21-24 caused mudflows with fatalities.	{1963 0225}
1964 0302	22	M_{100}	Mudflows swept over 50% of Conripe village.	{=}
1971 11	15	M_{100}	Lahars down N, W, and S sides of volcano caused by lava flows melting ice killed 15 in Chaillupen and Turbio valleys, destroying many houses and agricultural installations. Concrete bridges across major rivers cut.	{1971 1029}
CARRAN-LOS VENADOS [NILAHUE]			(1507-14=)	
1955 0727	2	G_{100}	Two persons killed by gases.	{=}
CERRO HUDSON			(1508-057)	
1971 0818	3	M_{100}	Lahar mobilized by melting ice down Rio de Los Huemules. Adult and 2 children reported missing; houses remained intact, filling to ceiling with mud and clasts.	{1971 0812}

Year M-Dy	Deaths	Agent	Remarks	{Start Date}

CARIBBEAN, ICELAND, ATLANTIC (16, 17, & 18)

MONT PELEE (1600-12=)

1902 0505 23 M_{100} Draining of crater lake upon failure of crater rim produced mudflows that destroyed a rum distillery, killing 23. {1902 0423}

1902 0508 28,000 P_{100} CAVW gives death toll as 28,000 but accounts published at time give 30,000. More recent workers argue that normal population of 26,000 had been swollen by a few thousand refugees from outlying areas, despite the many evacuees. 28,000 is compromise figure. {1902 0423}

1902 0830 1,500 P_{100} CAVW gives estimate of 1,000, but Heilprin reports that at Morne Rouge 1,200-1,500 died, and that fatalities also occurred in Ajoupa-Bouillon, Morne Capot, Moine Balar, and Bourden. {1902 0423}

SOUFRIERE ST VINCENT (1600-15=)

1812 0430 56 $T_{100?}$ {1812 0427} Most fatalities were workers killed by falling hot stones and hut collapses. {1812 0427}

Indirect Some $m_{100?}$ Some killed in a lake burst a few months after the eruption. {1812 0427}

1902 0507 1,680 P_{100} Estimate of fatalities is that given in official documents, though most accounts give 1,565 with others ranging from 1,351 to >2,000. Of 224 in hospital after May 7, ~80 died; 221 with burns and 3 children with fractured skulls. Hovey reports only 1 killed on leeward side and 1,350 dead on windward side. {1902 0506}

VESTMANNAEYJAR [HEIMAEY] (1702-01=?)

1973 0127 1 G_{100} Sleeping man killed by pooling of CO_2 in house basement. {1973 0123}

KATLA (1702-03=)

1262 ? F? Probably some casualties. {=}

1311 0118 Many F Many farms destroyed by jokulhlaups and probably many people drowned. {=}

1755 2 E_{100} 2 killed by lightning during tephra fall. {1755 1017}

HEKLA (1702-07=)

1300 ? {1300 0711}

Indirect ~600 I_{100} Tephra-fall associated with eruption caused famine, killing 600 in the winter following the eruption.

1510 0725 1 T_{100} Man killed by block 20 km from volcano. {=}

1947 1102 1 L_{100} A scientist filming the eruption was killed by a glowing block which rolled off the front of a lava flow, killing him instantly. {1947 0329}

GRIMSVOTN (1703-01=)

1629 4? F_{100} Jokulhlaup killed a couple with children. {=}

1684 11 1 F_{100} Drowned during a jokulhlaup in the Jokulsa River. {1684 1105d}

1783 [LAKAGIGAR]

Indirect 9,350 $I_{100?}$ Widespread famine resulted from destruction of summer crops and poisoning of livestock. The human population was reduced from 48,884 in 1783 to 38,363 in 1786, a loss of 22%. When natural birth and death rates are taken into account the best estimate of the death toll becomes 9,350. Fine dust in Scotland also destroyed crops. The combined effects of the Lakagigar and Asama eruptions may have contributed to the Tenmei famine in N Japan and elsewhere. {1783 0508}

ORAEFAJOKULL (1704-01=)

1362 >220 T? F? Some deaths were from floods, but most were from tephra falls. {1362 0605d}

1727 0804 3 F_{100} 3 drowned when jokulhlaup swept chalet away. Many sheep and horses were also drowned and many horses killed by bomb fall. {1727 0803}

FAYAL (1802-01=)

1672 3? {1672 0424}

PICO (1802-02=)

1718 2? {1718 0201}

SAN JORGE (1802-03=)

1580 10 P_{100} {1580 0501}

1757 Hundreds S_{100} The submarine eruption of 1757 coincided with history's most violent earthquake in the Azores, centered in the E part of the island and causing several hundred deaths. {1757 0501}

1808 9? L_{100} People attempting to save furniture remained too long in vicinity of advancing lava. About 60 were scalded by flashes of steam. 8-10 (?) died on the spot or a few days later. {1808 0501}

FURNAS (1802-10=)

1630 09 >200 M T Violent pumice explosion, probably of vulcanian type; ejecta fell over most of island. Newhall says at least 200 persons were killed, most probably by mudflows in Ribeira Quente on the S coast. {1630 0903}

LA PALMA (1803-01-)

1677 1 G_{100} Gas killed one man and many animals. Johnston-Lavis gives date as 1678 and deaths from "mephitic vapours." {1677 1117}

1971 ? Casualties occurred but very little damage reported. {1971 1026}

LANZAROTE (1803-06=)

1730 0907 ? Johnston-Lavis reports deaths from "mephitic vapours." Other sources do not report fatalities. {1730 0901}

FOGO (1804-01=)

1847 ? S_{100} Fatalities caused by earthquake. {1847 0409}

> Relentless listing of fatal eruptions is an inescapably negative side of volcanology. A complementary positive side is the strong record of recent evacuations that have saved tens of thousands of lives from the eruptions that followed. On the next page, this record is shown for the past 19 years, the years of our monthly SEAN and GVN *Bulletins*, and includes all evacuations known to us. None can deny that the number of volcano casualties has been too high in this time period, but the rising number of successful evacuations testifies to the hard work and increased understanding of the many specialists dealing with volcano hazards on the front lines.

Year M-Dy	Volcano	Evacuees	Deaths	Causes
1976				
0708	Soufriere (Guadeloupe)	72,000	0	phreatic explosions
0812	Sangay (Ecuador)	—	2	ballistics
0903	Taal (Philippines)	several 1,000	0	explosions
0923	Sarychev (Kuril Is)	Met staff	0	explosions; lava flows
1015	Karengatang (Indonesia)	1,800	1	pyroclastic flow
11	Kadovar (PNG)	1,000?	0	thermal activity; seismicity
1202	San Miguel (El Salvador)	a few	0	explosions
1977				
0110	Nyiragongo (Zaire)	> 50,000?	100?	lava flows
0405	Karthala (Comoro Is)	4,000	0	lava flows
0408	Piton de la Fournaise	2,500	0	lava flows
0807	Usu (Japan)	27,000	3	mudflows
1003	Taal (Philippines)	Taal Is residents	0	explosions
0930	Kilauea (Hawaii)	Kalapana	0	lava flows
1978				
0204	Westdahl (Aleutian Is)	lighthouse	0	tephra fall
0507	Mayon (Philippines)	23,000	0	explosions; lava flow
0902	Santiaguito (Guatemala)	—	1	mudflows
1979				
0220	Dieng (Indonesia)	15,000	149?	CO_2
0308	Karkar (PNG)	—	2	directed blast
0413	Soufriere (St Vincent)	> 17,000	0	pyroclastic flows
0414	Carran (Chile)	125	0	explosions; lava flows
0430	Marapi (Indonesia)	—	80	landslides (rain-induced)
0707	Iliwerung (Indonesia)	—	500	tsunami (landslide-induced)
0804	Etna (Italy)	250	0	lava flows
0906	Aso (Japan)	—	3	ballistics
0912	Etna (Italy)	—	9	ballistics
1015	Llaima (Chile)	tourists/residents	0	explosions
1113	Sierra Negra (Galapagos)	30-90?	0	explosions; lava flows
1227	Bulusan (Philippines)	area residents	0	explosions; earthquakes
1980				
0518	Mt. St. Helens (USA)	< 400	57	directed blast; mudflow
0706	Bulusan (Philippines)	area residents	0	seismicity; (<4 km radius)
0904	Gamalama (Indonesia)	40,000	0	hot tephra; forest fires
1006	Ulawun (PNG)	2,000?	0	pyroclastic flows
1981				
01	Paluweh (Indonesia)	1,850	0	pyroclastic flows
0329	Semeru (Indonesia)	—	1	pyroclastic flow
0514	Semeru (Indonesia)	—	372?	mudflows (rain-induced)
0515	Pagan (Mariana Is)	53	0	explosions; lava flows
0630	Mayon (Philippines)	—	>200	mudflows (rain-induced)
0719	Gamkonora (Indonesia)	> 3,500	0	explosions
1226	Nyamuragira (Zaire)	area residents	0	lava flows
1982				
0212	Telica (Nicaragua)	>50	0	explosions
0328	El Chichon (Mexico)	> 10,000	1,879	pyroclastic flows
0405	Galunggung (Indonesia)	75,000	68?	mudflows
0825	Santiaguito (Guatemala)	hundreds	0	mudflows
0826	Soputan (Indonesia)	850	0	explosions
1983				
01	Santiaguito (Guatemala)	hundreds	0	mudflows
0718	Una Una (Indonesia)	7,000	0	pyroclastic flows
089	Gamalama (Indonesia)	> 5,000	0	explosions
1004	Miyake-jima (Japan)	1,400	0	explosions; lava flows
08	Campi Flegrei (Italy)	< 40,000	0	seismicity; uplift
1984				
0524	Soputan (Indonesia)	350	0	explosions
0615	Merapi (Indonesia)	1,000	0	pyroclastic flows
0816	L Monoun (Cameroon)	area residents	37	CO_2
0905	Karengatang (Indonesia)	20,000	0	tephra; mudflows
0909	Mayon (Philippines)	73,000	0	explosions; mudflows
1985				
01	Kilauea (Hawaii)	300	0	lava flows
0730	Sangeang Api (Indonesia)	1,242	0	lava flow; explosions
1005	Canlaon (Philippines)	area residents	0	explosions; (<4 km)
1113	Ruiz (Colombia)	—	23,080	mudflows
1986				
0104	Ruiz (Colombia)	15,000	0	explosions
0320	Piton de la Fournaise	250	0	lava flows
0507	Tacana (Mexico/Guatemala)	17,000	0	seismicity; phreatic expl
1986 (cont.)				
0528	Iliboleng (Indonesia)	570	0	hot tephra; grass fires
0724	Stromboli (Italy)	—	1	ballistics
0821	Lake Nyos (Cameroon)	5,000	1,700	CO_2
1121	Oshima (Japan)	12,200	0	explosions; lava flows
12	Kilauea (Hawaii)	100 homes	0	lava flows
1201	Santiaguito (Guate.)	many families	0	pyroclastic flow
1231	Merapi (Indonesia)	—	1	mudflow (rain-induced)
1987				
0121	Pacaya (Guatemala)	600-3,000	0	tephra fall
0417	Etna (Italy)	—	2	ballistics
0614	Pacaya (Guatemala)	600	0	tephra fall
1030	Taal (Philippines)	a few families	0	earthquake swarm
1116	Oshima (Japan)	150	0	explosions
1229	Anak Ranakah (Indonesia)	4,200	0	explosions; pyroclastic flows
1988				
0212	Gamalama (Indonesia)	3,500	0	explosions
03	Ruiz (Colombia)	several 100	0	explosions
0509	Banda Api (Indonesia)	10,000	4	ballistics and lava flow
0706	Arenal (Costa Rica)	—	1	ballistics
0717	Makian (Indonesia)	15,000	0	explosions
0730	Semeru (Indonesia)	—	1	ballistic
1224	Tokachi-dake (Japan)	800	0	mudflow hazard
1989				
01	Lonquimay (Chile)	2,000	1	tephra fall; F gas
0307	Pacaya (Guatemala)	120	0	lava flow
0422	Soputan (Indonesia)	500	0	tephra fall
0504	Galeras (Colombia)	2,000	0	tephra fall
06	Lonquimay (Chile)	4,600	0	tephra fall; F gas
0901	Ruiz (Colombia)	< 5,000	0	explosions
12	Esa 'Ala (PNG)	Dobu Is; Oiau area	0	earthquake swarm
12	Redoubt (Alaska)	15	0	explosions; mudflows
1990				
0210	Kelut (Indonesia)	60,000	32	explosions; mudflows
0404	Anatahan (Mariana Is)	23	0	seismicity; thermal activity
06	Sabancaya (Peru)	4,000?	0	explosions
0624+	Rabaul (PNG)	—	6	CO_2
0719	Santiaguito (Guatemala)	0	4	lateral blast
08	Agrigan (Mariana Is)	9	0	fumarolic activity
1013	Laguna Verde (El Salvador)	—	26	phreatic explosion
1125	Kelut (Indonesia)	350?	4	non-eruptive mudflow
1991				
0401	Taal (Philippines)	1,000	0	earthquake swarms
0402	Pinatubo (Philippines)	2,000	0	explosion, ashfall
05-08+	Unzen (Japan)	12,395	43	pyroclastic flows
0615	Pinatubo (Philippines)	250,000	800?	expl, mudflows, disease
07	Galeras (Colombia)	11	0	seismicity
0801	Pacaya (Guatemala)	1,500	0	explosions, seismicity
0812	Hudson (Chile)	11	0	explosions
1025+	Lokon-Empung (Indonesia)	10,000	1	explosions, pyroclastic flows
1992				
0119	Deception Is (Antarctica)	sci team	0	seismicity, uplift
0215	Taal (Philippines)	> 2,600	0	seismicity, deformation
0410+	Cerro Negro (Nicaragua)	6,000-9,000	2	ashfall; accidents
05	Pacaya (Guatemala)	several villages	0	explosions
0511	Karengatang (Indonesia)	—	6	pyroclastic flow
0705	Marapi (Indonesia)	—	1	explosion
07-08	Pinatubo (Philippines)	—	6?	lahars (rain-induced)
1993				
0110	Pacaya (Guatemala)	two villages	0	explosion
0114	Galeras (Colombia)	0	9	explosion
0121	Karengatang (Indonesia)	452	0	mudflows, ashfall
0202	Mayon (Philippines)	57,000	75	explosion, pyroclastic flows
0309	Raoul Is. (Kermadec)	4	0	earthquake swarm
0312	G. Pichincha (Ecuador)	0	2	phreatic explosion
0419	Kilauea (Hawaii)	0	1	lava bench collapse
0419	Lascar (Chile)	70	0	phreatic eruptions
06	Pinatubo (Philippines)	area residents	0	lahars, flooding
1994				
0203	Semeru (Indonesia)	—	6	pyroclastic flows
0517	Llaima (Chile)	> 50?	0	explosion, lahars
0721	Colima (Mexico)	some towns	0	phreatic explosion
0919	Rabaul (PNG)	>50,000	5	explosions, ashfall
1014	Pacaya (Guatemala)	142	0	explosions

Chronology of Eruptions

Engraving from photograph, Krakatau, May 1883 (see Fig. 2, Simkin and Fiske, 1983)

START YEAR	M-Dy	Duration	VOLCANO NAME (Subregion)	NUMBER	VEI	Vol L/T
G-9850 ?	....	?	**TAUPO** (New Zealand)	0401-07=	5	-/9
G-9450 ?	....	?	**TAUPO** (New Zealand)	0401-07=	4+	-/8
G-9430 ?	....	?	**TAUPO** (New Zealand)	0401-07=	4	7/8
G-9150 y	....	?	**ZUNI-BANDERA** (US-New Mexico)	1210-02-		
C-8540 >	....	?	**FUJI** (Honshu-Japan)	0803-03=		9/-
C-8300 y	....	?	**WEST EIFEL VOLC FIELD** (Germany)	0100-01-		
C-8300 *	....	?	**HIJIORI** (Honshu-Japan)	0803-191	5	
C-8055 z	....	?	**GARIBALDI, MT.** (Canada)	1200-20-	3?	9/7
T-8050 *	....	?	**CAMPI FLEGREI** (Italy)	0101-01=	4	-/8
C-8050 *	....	?	**EMURUANGOGOLAK** (Africa-E)	0202-051		
T-8050 ?	....	?	**OKATAINA [TARAWERA]** (New Zeal)	0401-05=		
T-8050 ?	....	?	**IZU-TOBU** (Honshu-Japan)	0803-01=	3	6/7
T-8050 ?	....	?	**NASU** (Honshu-Japan)	0803-15=		
T-8050 ?	....	?	**NEMO PEAK** (Kurile Is)	0900-32=		
T-8050 >	....	?	**AVACHINSKY** (Kamchatka)	1000-10=		
C-8050 ?	....	?	**KRASHENINNIKOV** (Kamchatka)	1000-19=		
T-8050 ?	....	?	**SHASTA** (US-California)	1203-01-		
C-8050 ?	....	?	**MAUNA LOA** (Hawaiian Is)	1302-02=	0	
T-8050 ?	....	?	**CHACANA** (Ecuador)	1502-022		
T-8050 ?	....	?	**KRAFLA** (Iceland-NE)	1703-08=	0	
T-8050 ?	....	?	**THEISTAREYKJARBUNGA** (Iceland)	1703-09=	0	
G-8000 ?	....	?	**TAUPO** (New Zealand)	0401-07=	5	-/9
-8000 (9950 BP)						
F-7900 *	....	?	**LIPARI** (Italy)	0101-041		
C-7850 ?	....	?	**MAUNA LOA** (Hawaiian Is)	1302-02=	0	
T-7850 ?	....	?	**KRAFLA** (Iceland-NE)	1703-08=		9/-
C-7840 x	....	?	**CHAINE DES PUYS** (France)	0100-02-		
C-7840 <	....	?	**RUAPEHU** (New Zealand)	0401-10=	4	-/8
C-7820 x	....	?	**FUJI** (Honshu-Japan)	0803-03=		
T-7800 y	....	?	**KIZIMEN** (Kamchatka)	1000-23=	5	-/9
V-7769 ?	....	?	**NEMRUT DAGI** (Turkey)	0103-02=		
C-7750 x	....	?	**TONGARIRO** (New Zealand)	0401-08=	5	-/9
T-7750 ?	....	?	**RUAPEHU** (New Zealand)	0401-10=		
C-7750 ?	....	?	**SAKURA-JIMA** (Kyushu-Japan)	0802-08=		
C-7750 ?	....	?	**SHASTA** (US-California)	1203-01-		
C-7750 ?	....	?	**ANTUCO** (Chile-C)	1507-08=		
U-7740 ?	....	?	**CHAINE DES PUYS** (France)	0100-02-		
C-7740 u	....	?	**JOCOTITLAN** (Mexico)	1401-061		
C-7720 r	....	?	**SOCHE** (Ecuador)	1502-001	5?	
T-7700 *	....	?	**MOCHO-CHOSHUENCO** (Chile-C)	1507-13=	P	
C-7690 z	....	?	**COLIMA VOLC COMPLEX** (Mexico)	1401-04=		
C-7690 z	....	?	**POPOCATEPETL** (Mexico)	1401-09=	P	
C-7650 v	....	?	**SHASTA** (US-California)	1203-01-	4	-/8
C-7590 v	....	?	**RUAPEHU** (New Zealand)	0401-10=		
V-7579 ?	....	?	**NEMRUT DAGI** (Turkey)	0103-02=		
K-7550 *	....	?	**ISCHIA** (Italy)	0101-03=		
T-7550 z	....	?	**HAKU-SAN** (Honshu-Japan)	0803-05=		
T-7550 ?	....	?	**TOWADA** (Honshu-Japan)	0803-271	5	-/9
T-7550 ?	....	?	**MUTNOVSKY** (Kamchatka)	1000-06=	2	-/6
C-7550 ?	....	?	**MALY SEMIACHIK** (Kamchatka)	1000-14=		
C-7550 ?	....	?	**MAUNA LOA** (Hawaiian Is)	1302-02=	0	
C-7550 z	....	?	**PRESTAHNUKUR** (Iceland-SW)	1701-07=	0	10/-
C-7545 t	....	?	**PAUZHETKA** (Kamchatka)	1000-022		
C-7540 x	....	?	**HUALALAI** (Hawaiian Is)	1302-04-	0	
T-7535 *	....	?	**ADAMS** (US-Washington)	1201-04-		
C-7530 y	....	?	**FUJI** (Honshu-Japan)	0803-03=		
C-7510 w	....	?	**PAGO** (New Britain-SW Pac)	0502-08=		
C-7480 t	....	?	**LVINAYA PAST** (Kurile Is)	0900-041	6+	-/10
C-7450 t	....	?	**USHISHUR** (Kurile Is)	0900-21=	C	
C-7450 y	....	?	**HALEAKALA** (Hawaiian Is)	1302-06-		
C-7450 w	....	?	**ORIZABA, PICO DE** (Mexico)	1401-10=	3	-/7
C-7420 z	....	?	**COLIMA VOLC COMPLEX** (Mexico)	1401-04=		
C-7415 y	....	?	**SHASTA** (US-California)	1203-01-		
T-7410 *	....	?	**YELLOWSTONE** (US-Wyoming)	1205-01-		
C-7410 y	....	?	**LLAIMA** (Chile-C)	1507-11=		
T-7400 y	....	?	**KRAFLA** (Iceland-NE)	1703-08=	0	
T-7350 *	....	?	**MENENGAI** (Africa-E)	0202-06=		
C-7350 ?	....	?	**ULREUNG** (Korea)	1006-03-	6	-/10
T-7350 *	....	?	**NORTH SISTER FIELD** (US-Oregon)	1202-07-	2?	
T-7350 ?	....	?	**SHASTA** (US-California)	1203-01-	0	
C-7350 ?	....	?	**MAUNA LOA** (Hawaiian Is)	1302-02=	0	
C-7345 y	....	?	**MICHOACAN-GUANAJUATO** (Mexico)	1401-06=	3	-/7
C-7305 z	....	?	**FUJI** (Honshu-Japan)	0803-03=		
C-7290 v	....	?	**UDOKAN [SINI]** (Russia-SE)	1002-03-	0	
C-7290 w	....	?	**HENGILL** (Iceland-SW)	1701-05=		8/-
T-7250 ?	....	?	**GORELY** (Kamchatka)	1000-07=	2	
C-7250 ?	....	?	**KRASHENINNIKOV** (Kamchatka)	1000-19=		
C-7225 ?	....	?	**PELEE** (W Indies)	1600-12=	P	
C-7215 w	....	?	**EDGECUMBE** (Alaska-SE)	1105-04-		
C-7200 v	....	?	**LONGONOT** (Africa-E)	0202-10=		
C-7180 y	....	?	**HENGILL** (Iceland-SW)	1701-05=	0	
C-7170 y	....	?	**FISHER** (Aleutian Is)	1101-35-	6?	-/10
C-7150 ?	....	?	**SAKURA-JIMA** (Kyushu-Japan)	0802-08=	4	
T-7150 v	....	?	**SHEVELUCH** (Kamchatka)	1000-27=		
C-7150 ?	....	?	**MAUNA LOA** (Hawaiian Is)	1302-02=	0	
C-7140 w	....	?	**KARKAR** (New Guinea-NE of)	0501-03=	C	
C-7130 v	....	?	**ITASY VOLC FIELD** (Madagascar)	0303-06-		
V-7087 ?	....	?	**NEMRUT DAGI** (Turkey)	0103-02=		
C-7050 *	....	?	**WEST EIFEL VOLC FIELD** (Germany)	0100-01-		
K-7050 ?	....	?	**PANTELLERIA** (Italy)	0101-071		
R-7050 *	....	?	**SILALI** (Africa-E)	0202-052		
T-7050 ?	....	?	**MAROA [ORAKEIKORAKO]** (N Zeal)	0401-061		
T-7050 *	....	?	**KIRISHIMA** (Kyushu-Japan)	0802-09=	3	-/7
C-7050 ?	....	?	**HAKU-SAN** (Honshu-Japan)	0803-05=		
T-7050 ?	....	?	**MEGATA** (Honshu-Japan)	0803-262		
T-7050 *	....	?	**HACHIJO-JIMA** (Izu Is-Japan)	0804-05=		
T-7050 ?	....	?	**NEMO PEAK** (Kurile Is)	0900-32=		
T-7050 *	....	?	**ZHELTOVSKY** (Kamchatka)	1000-04=	5	-/9
T-7050 *	....	?	**BEZYMIANNY** (Kamchatka)	1000-25=		
T-7050 *	....	?	**NEWBERRY VOLCANO** (US-Oregon)	1202-11-		
T-7050 ?	....	?	**SHASTA** (US-California)	1203-01-		
C-7050 ?	....	?	**LASCAR** (Chile-N)	1505-10=		
T-7050 *	....	?	**LJOSUFJOLL** (Iceland-W)	1700-03=	2	9/-
T-7050 *	....	?	**BARDARBUNGA [VEIDIVOTN]**	1703-03=		
T-7050 ?	....	?	**KVERKFJOLL** (Iceland-NE)	1703-05=		
I-7050 ?	....	?	**TAKAHE** (Antarctica)	1900-027		
C-7020 v	....	?	**CHAINE DES PUYS** (France)	0100-02-		
C-7000 ?	....	?	**GUAGUA PICHINCHA** (Ecuador)	1502-02=		
I-6955 x	....	?	**Unknown Source** (GISP2, 236 ppb sulfate)			
C-6950 ?	....	?	**LOLORU** (Bougainville-SW Pac)	0505-03=		
C-6950 ?	....	?	**HAKU-SAN** (Honshu-Japan)	0803-05=		
C-6950 ?	....	?	**SHIKOTSU [TARUMAI]** (Hokkaido-Japan)	0805-04=	5	
C-6950 ?	....	?	**MALY SEMIACHIK** (Kamchatka)	1000-14=		
C-6900 w	....	?	**USHKOVSKY** (Kamchatka)	1000-261		
C-6880 u	....	?	**LLAIMA** (Chile-C)	1507-11=	5	-/9
C-6850 ?	....	?	**HAKU-SAN** (Honshu-Japan)	0803-05=		
C-6850 t	....	?	**KSUDACH** (Kamchatka)	1000-05=	C	
T-6850 ?	....	?	**KRAFLA** (Iceland-NE)	1703-08=	2?	
C-6830 w	....	?	**ISKUT-UNUK RIVER CONES** (Canada)	1200-09-		
C-6820 x	....	?	**HUALALAI** (Hawaiian Is)	1302-04-	0	
C-6800 y	....	?	**BOLSHOI SEMIACHIK** (Kamchatka)	1000-15=		
C-6800 <	....	?	**RAINIER** (US-Washington)	1201-03-	3	-/7
T-6800 ?	....	?	**KRAFLA** (Iceland-NE)	1703-08=	2?	
I-6766 x	....	?	**Unknown Source** (GISP2, 153 ppb sulfate)			
C-6760 u	....	?	**ORIZABA, PICO DE** (Mexico)	1401-10=	4	-/8
C-6750 ?	....	?	**SHEVELUCH** (Kamchatka)	1000-27=		
C-6750 *	....	?	**BAKER** (US-Washington)	1201-01=		
H-6750 *	....	?	**MONO CRATERS** (US-California)	1203-12-		
C-6750 x	....	?	**AGUA DE PAU** (Azores)	1802-09=		
I-6721 x	....	?	**Unknown Source** (GISP2 572, 396 pp S)			
C-6700 v	....	?	**HALEAKALA** (Hawaiian Is)	1302-06-		
C-6690 ?	....	?	**VILLARRICA** (Chile-C)	1507-12=		
C-6670 w	....	?	**ORIZABA, PICO DE** (Mexico)	1401-10=	3	-/7
T-6660 <	....	?	**RUIZ** (Colombia)	1501-02=		
C-6650 y	....	?	**TOWADA** (Honshu-Japan)	0803-271	5?	-/9
T-6650 ?	....	?	**SHASTA** (US-California)	1203-01-		
C-6650 ?	....	?	**MAUNA LOA** (Hawaiian Is)	1302-02=	0	
C-6650 ?	....	?	**GUAGUA PICHINCHA** (Ecuador)	1502-02=		
G-6650 t	....	?	**BARDARBUNGA [VEIDIVOTN]**	1703-03=		10/-
I-6614 w	....	?	**Unknown Source** (GISP2, 240 ppb sulfate)			
C-6590 w	....	?	**DIENG VOLC COMPLEX** (Java)	0603-20=	0	
C-6580 j	....	?	**OKATAINA [HAROHARO]** (New Zeal)	0401-05=	6	9/10
C-6580 <	....	?	**FUJI** (Honshu-Japan)	0803-03=		
C-6560 w	....	?	**HOLOTEPEC [TETEPETL]** (Mexico)	1401-07-		
I-6555 w	....	?	**Unknown Source** (GISP2, 101 ppb sulfate)			
C-6550 ?	....	?	**CHAINE DES PUYS** (France)	0100-02-		
T-6550 *	....	?	**NAMARUNU** (Africa-E)	0202-04-		
T-6550 *	....	?	**EMURUANGOGOLAK** (Africa-E)	0202-051		
C-6550 ?	....	?	**KRASHENINNIKOV** (Kamchatka)	1000-19=		
C-6550 ?	....	?	**MAUNA LOA** (Hawaiian Is)	1302-02=	0	
C-6550 ?	....	?	**SOUFRIERE GUADELOUPE** (W Ind)	1600-06=		
T-6525 *	....	?	**BAKER** (US-Washington)	1201-01=		
C-6520 w	....	?	**ORIZABA, PICO DE** (Mexico)	1401-10=		
C-6515 x	....	?	**EDZIZA** (Canada)	1200-06-		
C-6490 >	....	?	**HOLOTEPEC [TRES CRUCES]**	1401-07-	4	-/8
C-6480 y	....	?	**MICHOACAN-GUANAJUATO** (Mexico)	1401-06=	3	-/7
I-6476 w	....	?	**Unknown Source** (GISP2, 710 ppb sulfate)			
V-6471 ?	....	?	**NEMRUT DAGI** (Turkey)	0103-02=		
I-6470 w	....	?	**Unknown Source** (GISP2, 154 ppb sulfate)			
C-6450 ?	....	?	**CAMPI FLEGREI** (Italy)	0101-01=	3	
C-6445 ?	....	?	**PELEE** (W Indies)	1600-12=		
C-6400 ?	....	?	**GUAGUA PICHINCHA** (Ecuador)	1502-02=		
I-6397 w	....	?	**Unknown Source** (GISP2 424, 130 pp S)			
I-6360 w	....	?	**Unknown Source** (GISP2, 92 ppb sulfate)			
C-6350 ?	....	?	**SAKURA-JIMA** (Kyushu-Japan)	0802-08=		
C-6350 ?	....	?	**KRASHENINNIKOV** (Kamchatka)	1000-19=		
C-6350 u	....	?	**ORIZABA, PICO DE** (Mexico)	1401-10=	3	-/7
I-6338 w	....	?	**Unknown Source** (GISP2, 222 ppb sulfate)			
C-6310 z	....	?	**OKMOK** (Aleutian Is)	1101-29-	6?	-/10
C-6300 y	....	?	**TURRIALBA** (Costa Rica)	1405-07=		
C-6300 ?	....	?	**GUAGUA PICHINCHA** (Ecuador)	1502-02=		
I-6273 w	....	?	**Unknown Source** (GISP2, 150 ppb sulfate)			
C-6270 x	....	?	**KUSATSU-SHIRANE** (Honshu-Japan)	0803-12=		
U-6250 ?	....	?	**CHAINE DES PUYS** (France)	0100-02-		
C-6250 ?	....	?	**KRASHENINNIKOV** (Kamchatka)	1000-19=		
C-6250 v	....	?	**INDIAN HEAVEN** (US-Washington)	1201-07-		8/-
C-6250 ?	....	?	**MAUNA LOA** (Hawaiian Is)	1302-02=	0	
T-6250 z	....	?	**POPOCATEPETL** (Mexico)	1401-09=		
C-6240 y	....	?	**FUJI** (Honshu-Japan)	0803-03=		
C-6220 w	....	?	**PAUZHETKA [KURILE LAKE]**	1000-022	6	-/10
C-6220 u	....	?	**ORIZABA, PICO DE** (Mexico)	1401-10=	3	-/7
V-6213 ?	....	?	**NEMRUT DAGI** (Turkey)	0103-02=		
@-6200 >	....	?	**KARAPINAR FIELD** (Turkey)	0103-001		
T-6200 *	....	?	**TOLIMA** (Colombia)	1501-03=		
C-6200 ?	....	?	**GUAGUA PICHINCHA** (Ecuador)	1502-02=		
C-6190 x	....	?	**ETNA** (Italy)	0101-06=		
G-6150 ?	....	?	**MALY SEMIACHIK** (Kamchatka)	1000-14=		
T-6150 ?	....	?	**KRAFLA** (Iceland-NE)	1703-08=	0	
C-6130 u	....	?	**PANTELLERIA** (Italy)	0101-071		
C-6100 w	....	?	**PINATUBO** (Luzon-Philippines)	0703-083		
C-6090 z	....	?	**PELEE** (W Indies)	1600-12=	P	
T-6050 ?	....	?	**CAMPI FLEGREI** (Italy)	0101-01=	3	
R-6050 *	....	?	**SILALI** (Africa-E)	0202-052		
R-6050 *	....	?	**PAKA** (Africa-E)	0202-053	C	
C-6050 <	....	?	**ITASY VOLC FIELD** (Madagascar)	0303-06-		

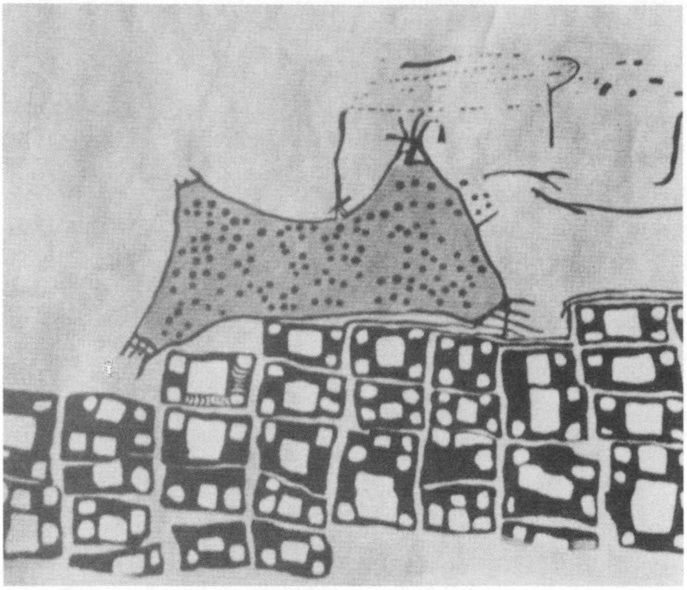

Figure 12. This 6200 BC wall mural, the earliest known eruption record, was found in excavations of Catal Hayuk, in central Turkey. Strombolian projectiles from the summit suggest a nearby low-level eruption, and the Karapinar field of young cinder cones, just 50 km to the east, seems a likely source. Reproduced from Mellaart 1967 (see REFERENCES 0102).

START YEAR	M-Dy	Duration	VOLCANO NAME (Subregion)	NUMBER	VEI	Vol L/T
C-6050 u		?	**MAYOR ISLAND** (New Zealand)	0401-021		
T-6050 ?		?	**EGMONT** (New Zealand)	0401-03=		
T-6050 ?		?	**FUJI** (Honshu-Japan)	0803-03=		
T-6050 ?		?	**ILYINSKY** (Kamchatka)	1000-03=	C	
T-6050 ?		?	**ZHELTOVSKY** (Kamchatka)	1000-04=		
T-6050 ?		?	**AVACHINSKY** (Kamchatka)	1000-10=		
C-6050 ?		?	**TOLBACHIK** (Kamchatka)	1000-24=		
C-6050 ?		?	**SHEVELUCH** (Kamchatka)	1000-27=		
C-6050 ?		?	**SHASTA** (US-California)	1203-01-		
T-6050 ?		?	**ORIZABA, PICO DE** (Mexico)	1401-10=	P	
T-6050 *		?	**BARVA** (Costa Rica)	1405-05=	P	
T-6050 *		?	**SNAEFELLSJOKULL** (Iceland-W)	1700-01=		
T-6050 ?		?	**VESTMANNAEYJAR** (Iceland-S)	1702-01=		
T-6050 *		?	**TORFAJOKULL** (Iceland-S)	1702-05=		7/-
C-6020 w		?	**CHAINE DES PUYS** (France)	0100-02-		
T-6000 ?		?	**MUTNOVSKY** (Kamchatka)	1000-06=	2	-/6
C-6000 t		?	**KRASHENINNIKOV** (Kamchatka)	1000-19=	4	9/8

-6000 (7950 BP)

START YEAR	M-Dy	Duration	VOLCANO NAME (Subregion)	NUMBER	VEI	Vol L/T
I -5995 w		?	**Unknown Source** (GISP2, 115 ppb sulfate)			
C-5990 ?		?	**QUILL, THE** (W Indies)	1600-02=	P	
C-5980 y		?	**LAMINGTON** (New Guinea)	0503-01=		
C-5960 v		?	**VESUVIUS** (Italy)	0101-02=	5	-/9
C-5950 ?		?	**SAKURA-JIMA** (Kyushu-Japan)	0802-08=		
T-5950 ?		?	**GORELY** (Kamchatka)	1000-07=	3	-/7
T-5900 ?		?	**MUTNOVSKY** (Kamchatka)	1000-06=	2	-/6
C-5890 w		?	**CRATERS OF THE MOON** (US-Idaho)	1204-02-	0	9/-
C-5860 ?		?	**QUILL, THE** (W Indies)	1600-02=		
C-5850 ?		?	**MERU** (Africa-E)	0202-16=	C	
C-5850 ?		?	**NEWER VOLCANICS PROV** (Australia)	0509-01-		
T-5850 ?		?	**KSUDACH** (Kamchatka)	1000-05=		
G-5850 ?		?	**MALY SEMIACHIK** (Kamchatka)	1000-14=		
C-5850 ?		?	**MAUNA LOA** (Hawaiian Is)	1302-02=	0	
T-5850 *		?	**HEKLA** (Iceland-S)	1702-07=		
C-5820 x		?	**MASHU** (Hokkaido-Japan)	0805-081		
T-5800 ?		?	**MUTNOVSKY** (Kamchatka)	1000-06=	2	-/6
C-5800 t		?	**TAUNSHITS** (Kamchatka)	1000-16-		
C-5800 t		?	**KRASHENINNIKOV** (Kamchatka)	1000-19=	4	7/8
M-5800 *		?	**BACHELOR** (US-Oregon)	1202-09-		
C-5795 ?		?	**PELEE** (W Indies)	1600-12=		
C-5780 w		?	**REDOUBT** (Alaska-SW)	1103-03-		
I -5676 w		?	**Unknown Source** (GISP2, 654 ppb sulfate)			
U-5760 ?		?	**CHAINE DES PUYS** (France)	0100-02-		
G-5750 ?		?	**MALY SEMIACHIK** (Kamchatka)	1000-14=		
C-5750 ?		?	**SOUFRIERE GUADELOUPE** (W Indies)	1600-06=		
T-5750 ?		?	**KRAFLA** (Iceland-NE)	1703-08=	0	
V-5745 ?		?	**NEMRUT DAGI** (Turkey)	0103-02=		
T-5700 *		?	**KIRISHIMA** (Kyushu-Japan)	0802-09=	3	-/7
C-5700 t		?	**KARYMSKY** (Kamchatka)	1000-13=	6?	-/10
C-5700 t		?	**UZON** (Kamchatka)	1000-17=		
T-5650 ?		?	**GORELY** (Kamchatka)	1000-07=	3	-/7
T-5650 ?		?	**TOLBACHIK** (Kamchatka)	1000-24=		
C-5650 ?		?	**WELLS GRAY-CLEARWATER** (Canada	1200-15-		
C-5650 ?		?	**MAUNA LOA** (Hawaiian Is)	1302-02=	0	
C-5610 v		?	**PANTELLERIA** (Italy)	0101-071		
T-5600 ?		?	**TOLBACHIK** (Kamchatka)	1000-24=		

START YEAR	M-Dy	Duration	VOLCANO NAME (Subregion)	NUMBER	VEI	Vol L/T
C-5590 v		?	**POAS** (Costa Rica)	1405-04=		
T-5550 ?		?	**OKATAINA [EDGECUMBE]** (New Zeal)	0401-05=	0	
T-5550 *		?	**RUAPEHU** (New Zealand)	0401-10=		
T-5550 z		?	**USU** (Hokkaido-Japan)	0805-03=	3?	
C-5550 u		?	**TAO-RUSYR CALDERA** (Kurile Is)	0900-31=	6	-/10
T-5550 ?		?	**NEMO PEAK** (Kurile Is)	0900-32=		
T-5550 *		?	**VILYUCHIK** (Kamchatka)	1000-083		
T-5550 *		?	**GOLDEN TROUT CREEK** (US-Calif)	1203-17-		
A-5550 *		?	**PALEI-AIKE VOLC FIELD** (Chile-S)	1508-08-		
T-5550 z		?	**HENGILL** (Iceland-SW)	1701-05=	0	
T-5550 *		?	**KVERKFJOLL** (Iceland-NE)	1703-05=		
I -5550 ?		?	**TAKAHE** (Antarctica)	1900-027		
C-5540 x		?	**FUJI** (Honshu-Japan)	0803-03=		
I -5521 w		?	**Unknown Source** (GISP2, 129 ppb sulfate)			
T-5500 ?		?	**GORELY** (Kamchatka)	1000-07=	3	-/7
C-5465 w		?	**CRATERS OF THE MOON** (US-Idaho)	1204-02-	0	9/-
T-5450 ?		?	**MUTNOVSKY** (Kamchatka)	1000-06=	2	-/6
T-5450 ?		?	**GORELY** (Kamchatka)	1000-07=	3	-/7
G-5450 ?		?	**MALY SEMIACHIK** (Kamchatka)	1000-14=		
C-5450 ?		?	**KRASHENINNIKOV** (Kamchatka)	1000-19=		
T-5450 ?		?	**TOLBACHIK** (Kamchatka)	1000-24=		
C-5440 ?		?	**PELEE** (W Indies)	1600-12=	P	
C-5400 ?		?	**SAKURA-JIMA** (Kyushu-Japan)	0802-08=		
G-5400 ?		?	**RAINIER** (US-Washington)	1201-03-	2	-/6
C-5350 z		?	**KSUDACH** (Kamchatka)	1000-05=		
T-5350 ?		?	**MUTNOVSKY** (Kamchatka)	1000-06=	2	-/6
C-5350 ?		?	**MAUNA LOA** (Hawaiian Is)	1302-02=	0	
V-5320 ?		?	**NEMRUT DAGI** (Turkey)	0103-02=		
C-5300 p		?	**OKATAINA [HAROHARO]** (New Zeal)	0401-05=	5	10/9
T-5300 ?		?	**GORELY** (Kamchatka)	1000-07=	2	
T-5300 y		?	**KIZIMEN** (Kamchatka)	1000-23=	5	-/9
G-5300 ?		?	**RAINIER** (US-Washington)	1201-03-	3	-/7
T-5300 *		?	**RATON-CLAYTON** (US-New Mexico)	1210-04-		
C-5290 <		?	**NEWER VOLCANICS PROV** (Australia)	0509-01-		
C-5290 x		?	**LLAIMA** (Chile-C)	1507-11=		
C-5290 w		?	**KRISUVIK** (Iceland-SW)	1701-03=	2	8/-
I -5278 w		?	**Unknown Source** (GISP2 404, 667 pp S)			
T-5250 ?		?	**MUTNOVSKY** (Kamchatka)	1000-06=	2	-/6
G-5250 ?		?	**KRASHENINNIKOV** (Kamchatka)	1000-19=		
T-5250 *		?	**ANIAKCHAK** (Alaska Peninsula)	1102-09-	6?	-/10
C-5250 ?		?	**SOCOMPA** (Chile-N)	1505-108		
C-5215 v		?	**NAZKO** (Canada)	1200-14-		
V-5152 ?		?	**NEMRUT DAGI** (Turkey)	0103-02=		
C-5150 w		?	**ETNA** (Italy)	0101-06=		
T-5150 ?		?	**GORELY** (Kamchatka)	1000-07=	3	-/7
C-5110 v		?	**SPURR** (Alaska-SW)	1103-04-		
G-5100 ?		?	**TAUPO** (New Zealand)	0401-07=	3	8/7
V-5085 ?		?	**NEMRUT DAGI** (Turkey)	0103-02=		
C-5070 x		?	**FUJI** (Honshu-Japan)	0803-03=		
C-5070 v		?	**ORIZABA, PICO DE** (Mexico)	1401-10=		
C-5065 t		?	**CRATER LAKE** (US-Oregon)	1202-16-	6	8/10
R-5050 *		?	**SILALI** (Africa-E)	0202-052		
C-5050 ?		?	**HARGY** (New Britain-SW Pac)	0502-10=		
T-5050 ?		?	**IBUSUKI VOLC FIELD** (Kyushu-Japan)	0802-07=		
C-5050 ?		?	**SUMIYOSHI-IKE** (Kyushu-Japan)	0802-081	2	-/6
C-5050 ?		?	**KUSATSU-SHIRANE** (Honshu-Japan)	0803-12=		
T-5050 ?		?	**TOWADA** (Honshu-Japan)	0803-271	4	-/8
C-5050 ?		?	**YOTEI** (Hokkaido-Japan)	0805-032		
T-5050 ?		?	**MUTNOVSKY** (Kamchatka)	1000-06=	3	-/7
T-5050 ?		?	**ZHUPANOVSKY** (Kamchatka)	1000-12=		
G-5050 ?		?	**MALY SEMIACHIK** (Kamchatka)	1000-14=		
C-5050 ?		?	**KRASHENINNIKOV** (Kamchatka)	1000-19=		
T-5050 ?		?	**TOLBACHIK** (Kamchatka)	1000-24=		
T-5050 ?		?	**BEZYMIANNY** (Kamchatka)	1000-25=		
T-5050 ?		?	**KLIUCHEVSKOI** (Kamchatka)	1000-26=		
T-5050 ?		?	**PIIP** (Kamchatka-E of)	1000-271		
T-5050 ?		?	**ESPENBERG** (Alaska-W)	1104-01-		
T-5050 ?		?	**COLIMA VOLC COMPLEX** (Mexico)	1401-04=	3	-/7
T-5050 ?		?	**MIRAVALLES** (Costa Rica)	1405-03=		
T-5050 *		?	**CABURGUA** (Chile-C)	1507-112		
T-5050 *		?	**REDONDO, CERRO** (Chile-C)	1507-113		
T-5050 *		?	**HUELEMOLLE** (Chile-C)	1507-114		
T-5050 ?		?	**KATLA** (Iceland-S)	1702-03=		
T-5050 *		?	**TORFAJOKULL** (Iceland-S)	1702-05=		8/-
T-5050 *		?	**VATNAFJOLL** (Iceland-S)	1702-06=		
G-5050 ?		?	**HEKLA** (Iceland-S)	1702-07=	5	-/9
T-5050 *		?	**FREMRINAMUR** (Iceland-NE)	1703-07=		
C-5040 u		?	**HANGAR** (Kamchatka)	1000-272	5	-/9
C-5020 u		?	**EGMONT** (New Zealand)	0401-03=		
C-5020 w		?	**HUDSON, CERRO** (Chile-S)	1508-057		
T-5000 ?		?	**MUTNOVSKY** (Kamchatka)	1000-06=	2	-/6
I -4988 w		?	**Unknown Source** (GISP2, 93 ppb sulfate)			
T-4950 ?		?	**GORELY** (Kamchatka)	1000-07=	2	
T-4950 *		?	**VATNAFJOLL** (Iceland-S)	1702-06=		
C-4940 w		?	**HOOD** (US-Oregon)	1202-01-	2	
G-4900 ?		?	**RAINIER** (US-Washington)	1201-03-	3	-/7
C-4895 t	1015q	?	**CRATER LAKE** (US-Oregon)	1202-16-	7	8/11
C-4875 x		?	**MASHU** (Hokkaido-Japan)	0805-081	6	-/10
C-4850 y		?	**LAMINGTON** (New Guinea)	0503-01=		
C-4850 ?		?	**HAKU-SAN** (Honshu-Japan)	0803-05=		
C-4850 ?		?	**KRASHENINNIKOV** (Kamchatka)	1000-19=		
T-4850 *		?	**GUAGUA PICHINCHA** (Ecuador)	1502-02=		
T-4850 *		?	**TORFAJOKULL** (Iceland-S)	1702-05=		7/-
V-4849 ?		?	**NEMRUT DAGI** (Turkey)	0103-02=		
I -4803 w		?	**Unknown Source** (GISP2, 141 ppb sulfate)			
C-4800 ?		?	**SAKURA-JIMA** (Kyushu-Japan)	0802-08=		
T-4750 ?		?	**GORELY** (Kamchatka)	1000-07=	3	-/7

START YEAR	M-Dy	Duration	VOLCANO NAME (Subregion)	NUMBER	VEI	Vol L/T
M-4750 ?	....	?	**CRATER LAKE** (US-Oregon)	1202-16-		
T-4750 *	....	?	**VATNAFJOLL** (Iceland-S)	1702-06=		
T-4730 z	....	?	**FUJI** (Honshu-Japan)	0803-03=		
G-4700 ?	....	?	**TAUPO** (New Zealand)	0401-07=	4	-/8
T-4700 ?	....	?	**MUTNOVSKY** (Kamchatka)	1000-06=	2	-/6
T-4700 ?	....	?	**GORELY** (Kamchatka)	1000-07=	2	
T-4700 ?	....	?	**AVACHINSKY** (Kamchatka)	1000-10=		
C-4700 y	....	?	**ISKUT-UNUK RIVER CONES** (Canada)	1200-09-		
C-4690 y	....	?	**ORIZABA, PICO DE** (Mexico)	1401-10=	3	-/7
I -4689 w	....	?	**Unknown Source** (GISP2, 310 ppb sulfate)			
C-4680 ?	....	?	**PELEE** (W Indies)	1600-12=	**P**	
T-4650 ?	....	?	**MUTNOVSKY** (Kamchatka)	1000-06=	2	-/6
T-4650 ?	....	?	**GORELY** (Kamchatka)	1000-07=	3	-/7
G-4650 ?	....	?	**MALY SEMIACHIK** (Kamchatka)	1000-14=		
C-4650 ?	....	?	**KILAUEA** (Hawaiian Is)	1302-01-	0	
T-4650 z	....	?	**HEKLA** (Iceland-S)	1702-07=		
V-4615 ?	....	?	**NEMRUT DAGI** (Turkey)	0103-02=		
T-4600 ?	....	?	**GORELY** (Kamchatka)	1000-07=	2	
C-4600 v	....	?	**CRATERS OF THE MOON** (US-Idaho)	1204-02-	0	**9/-**
I -4596 w	....	?	**Unknown Source** (GISP2, 257 ppb sulfate)			
C-4570 <	....	?	**FURNAS** (Azores)	1802-10=		
I -4564 w	....	?	**Unknown Source** (GISP2, 132 ppb sulfate)			
C-4550 ?	....	?	**SUMIYOSHI-IKE** (Kyushu-Japan)	0802-081	3	-/7
T-4550 ?	....	?	**MUTNOVSKY** (Kamchatka)	1000-06=	2	-/6
T-4550 y	....	?	**REDOUBT** (Alaska-SW)	1103-03-		
T-4550 ?	....	?	**COLIMA VOLC COMPLEX** (Mexico)	1401-04=	3	-/7
T-4550 ?	....	?	**MASAYA** (Nicaragua)	1404-10=	**5**	**-/9**
T-4550 *	....	?	**SNAEFELLSJOKULL** (Iceland-W)	1700-01=	2	
T-4550 z	....	?	**TORFAJOKULL** (Iceland-S)	1702-05=		7/-
T-4550 *	....	?	**VATNAFJOLL** (Iceland-S)	1702-06=		
T-4550 z	....	?	**HEKLA** (Iceland-S)	1702-07=		
T-4550 z	....	?	**GRIMSVOTN** (Iceland-NE)	1703-01=	0	
T-4550 ?	....	?	**BARDARBUNGA [VEIDIVOTN]**	1703-03=		
C-4550 v	....	?	**AGUA DE PAU** (Azores)	1802-09=		
T-4500 ?	....	?	**GORELY** (Kamchatka)	1000-07=	2	
G-4500 t	....	?	**MALY SEMIACHIK** (Kamchatka)	1000-14=		
V-4500 t	....	?	**JEFFERSON [FORKED BUTTE]**	1202-02-		
T-4500 ?	....	?	**GRIMSNES** (Iceland-SW)	1701-06=	0	
T-4450 ?	....	?	**GORELY** (Kamchatka)	1000-07=	2	-/6
G-4450 ?	....	?	**BOLSHOI SEMIACHIK** (Kamchatka)	1000-15=		
G-4450 ?	....	?	**KRASHENINNIKOV** (Kamchatka)	1000-19=		
H-4450 ?	....	?	**NEWBERRY VOLCANO** (US-Oregon)	1202-11-		
T-4450 ?	....	?	**GRIMSNES** (Iceland-SW)	1701-06=	2?	
I -4447 w	....	?	**Unknown Source** (GISP2, 159 ppb sulfate)			
I -4411 w	....	?	**Unknown Source** (GISP2, 183 ppb sulfate)			
C-4410 v	....	?	**HUALALAI** (Hawaiian Is)	1302-04-	0	
G-4400 ?	....	?	**AVACHINSKY** (Kamchatka)	1000-10=	**5**	**-/9**
G-4400 ?	....	?	**RAINIER** (US-Washington)	1201-03-	2	-/6
C-4390 x	....	?	**MAYOR ISLAND** (New Zealand)	0401-021	**5**	**-/9**
D-4375 ?	....	?	**Unknown Source**			
C-4350 ?	....	?	**KIKAI** (Ryukyu Is)	0802-06=	**7**	**-/11**
C-4350 ?	....	?	**KIRISHIMA** (Kyushu-Japan)	0802-09=	4	-/8
T-4350 ?	....	?	**GORELY** (Kamchatka)	1000-07=	3	-/7
T-4350 *	....	?	**VATNAFJOLL** (Iceland-S)	1702-06=		
V-4321 ?	....	?	**NEMRUT DAGI** (Turkey)	0103-02=		
C-4315 y	....	?	**NEWBERRY VOLCANO** (US-Oregon)	1202-11-	0	
C-4280 w	....	?	**BRAVO, CERRO** (Colombia)	1501-011	4	-/9
C-4270 w	....	?	**GRIMSNES** (Iceland-SW)	1701-06=	3	**9/7**
T-4250 ?	....	?	**CRATERS OF THE MOON** (US-Idaho)	1204-02-	0	8/-
C-4250 ?	....	?	**MAUNA LOA** (Hawaiian Is)	1302-02=	0	
C-4250 v	....	?	**ORIZABA, PICO DE** (Mexico)	1401-10=	3	-/7
T-4250 z	....	?	**HEKLA** (Iceland-S)	1702-07=		
C-4210 u	....	?	**NEWBERRY VOLCANO** (US-Oregon)	1202-11-	3	8/7
G-4200 ?	....	?	**RAINIER** (US-Washington)	1201-03-	3	-/7
C-4165 *	....	?	**MAKUSHIN** (Aleutian Is)	1101-31-	**5**	**-/9**
C-4150 w	....	?	**ETNA** (Italy)	0101-06=		
C-4150 ?	....	?	**LOLORU** (Bougainville-SW Pac)	0505-03=		
C-4150 ?	....	?	**HAKU-SAN** (Honshu-Japan)	0803-05=		
T-4150 ?	....	?	**GORELY** (Kamchatka)	1000-07=	2	-/6
G-4150 ?	....	?	**KARYMSKY** (Kamchatka)	1000-13=		
T-4150 *	....	?	**VATNAFJOLL** (Iceland-S)	1702-06=		
C-4135 v	....	?	**NEWBERRY VOLCANO** (US-Oregon)	1202-11-		
T-4115 y	....	?	**FUJI** (Honshu-Japan)	0803-03=		
G-4100 ?	....	?	**TAUPO** (New Zealand)	0401-07=	4	-/8
C-4100 t	....	?	**KSUDACH** (Kamchatka)	1000-05=	**C**	
C-4070 t	....	?	**CRATERS OF THE MOON** (US-Idaho)	1204-02-	0	**9/-**
K-4050 *	....	?	**ISCHIA** (Italy)	0101-03=		
C-4050 ?	....	?	**NASU** (Honshu-Japan)	0803-15=		
T-4050 ?	....	?	**TOWADA** (Honshu-Japan)	0803-271	3	-/8
T-4050 ?	....	?	**KOMAGA-TAKE** (Hokkaido-Japan)	0805-02=		
T-4050 ?	....	?	**MUTNOVSKY** (Kamchatka)	1000-06=	2	-/6
T-4050 ?	....	?	**SPURR** (Alaska-SW)	1103-04-		
C-4050 ?	....	?	**SHASTA** (US-California)	1203-01-		
H-4050 ?	....	?	**INYO CRATERS** (US-California)	1203-13-		7/-
T-4050 ?	....	?	**COLIMA VOLC COMPLEX** (Mexico)	1401-04=	3	-/7
T-4050 *	....	?	**SNAEFELLSJOKULL** (Iceland-W)	1700-01=	0	
T-4050 ?	....	?	**GRIMSNES** (Iceland-SW)	1701-06=	0	
T-4050 z	....	?	**HEKLA** (Iceland-S)	1702-07=		
T-4050 ?	....	?	**BARDARBUNGA** (Iceland-NE)	1703-03=		
T-4050 ?	....	?	**KRAFLA** (Iceland-NE)	1703-08=	0	
C-4040 w	....	?	**CHAINE DES PUYS** (France)	0100-02-		-/7
C-4040 ?	....	?	**UNNAMED** (Azores)	1802-081		
I -4037 v	....	?	**Unknown Source** (GISP2 148, 313 pp S)			
I -4010 v	....	?	**Unknown Source** (GISP2, 133 ppb sulfate)			
C-4010 v	....	?	**NEWBERRY VOLCANO** (US-Oregon)	1202-11-	0	
C-4000 t	....	?	**KASBEK** (Georgia)	0104-02-		
G-4000 ?	....	?	**TAUPO** (New Zealand)	0401-07=	3	-/7
T-4000 ?	....	?	**GRIMSNES** (Iceland-SW)	1701-06=	2?	

-4000 (5950 BP)

START YEAR	M-Dy	Duration	VOLCANO NAME (Subregion)	NUMBER	VEI	Vol L/T
I -3977 v	....	?	**Unknown Source** (GISP2, 137 ppb sulfate)			
T-3950 v	....	?	**PAUZHETKA [DIKY GREBEN]**	1000-022		
T-3950 ?	....	?	**GORELY** (Kamchatka)	1000-07=	2	-/6
T-3950 *	....	?	**VATNAFJOLL** (Iceland-S)	1702-06=		
T-3950 z	....	?	**HEKLA** (Iceland-S)	1702-07=		
C-3930 x	....	?	**MYOKO** (Honshu-Japan)	0803-10=		
C-3920 v	....	?	**NEWBERRY VOLCANO** (US-Oregon)	1202-11-		
C-3910 x	....	?	**TAMBORA** (Lesser Sunda Is)	0604-04=		
I -3905 v	....	?	**Unknown Source** (GISP2, 134 ppb sulfate)			
T-3900 ?	....	?	**GORELY** (Kamchatka)	1000-07=	2	
T-3900 ?	....	?	**GRIMSNES** (Iceland-SW)	1701-06=	0	
T-3850 ?	....	?	**KSUDACH** (Kamchatka)	1000-05=		
C-3850 w	....	?	**NEWBERRY VOLCANO** (US-Oregon)	1202-11-	0	
H-3850 *	....	?	**MONO CRATERS** (US-California)	1203-12-		
C-3820 ?	....	?	**PELEE** (W Indies)	1600-12=	**P**	
C-3810 u	....	?	**EDGECUMBE** (Alaska-SE)	1105-04-		
G-3800 ?	....	?	**RAINIER** (US-Washington)	1201-03-	3	-/7
T-3800 y	....	?	**REYKJANESHRYGGUR** (Iceland-SW)	1701-01=		
G-3800 t	....	?	**HENGILL** (Iceland-SW)	1701-05=	2	8/-
C-3750 ?	....	?	**MAUNA LOA** (Hawaiian Is)	1302-02=	0	
T-3750 ?	....	?	**GRIMSNES** (Iceland-SW)	1701-06=	0	
T-3750 *	....	?	**VATNAFJOLL** (Iceland-S)	1702-06=		
C-3730 ?	....	?	**VILLARRICA** (Chile-C)	1507-12=		
C-3700 ?	....	?	**PELEE** (W Indies)	1600-12=		
C-3690 v	....	?	**FUJI** (Honshu-Japan)	0803-03=		
C-3650 ?	....	?	**PAGO** (New Britain-SW Pac)	0502-08=		
T-3650 ?	....	?	**MUTNOVSKY** (Kamchatka)	1000-06=	2	-/6
T-3650 ?	....	?	**GRIMSNES** (Iceland-SW)	1701-06=	0	
C-3635 y	....	?	**PANTELLERIA** (Italy)	0101-071		
G-3600 ?	....	?	**RAINIER** (US-Washington)	1201-03-	2	-/6
C-3580 ?	....	?	**VESUVIUS** (Italy)	0101-02=		
K-3550 *	....	?	**VULCANO** (Italy)	0101-05=	0	
C-3550 z	....	?	**SAKURA-JIMA** (Kyushu-Japan)	0802-08=	4	
T-3550 ?	....	?	**KIRISHIMA** (Kyushu-Japan)	0802-09=	3	-/7
T-3550 >	....	?	**BARKHATNAYA SOPKA** (Kamchatka)	1000-084		
G-3550 ?	....	?	**KRASHENINNIKOV** (Kamchatka)	1000-19=		
C-3550 ?	....	?	**GLACIER PEAK** (US-Washington)	1201-02-		
T-3550 z	....	?	**HENGILL** (Iceland-SW)	1701-05=	0	
T-3550 z	....	?	**GRIMSVOTN** (Iceland-NE)	1703-01=	0	8/-
I -3541 v	....	?	**Unknown Source** (GISP2, 97 ppb sulfate)			
I -3518 v	....	?	**Unknown Source** (GISP2, 174 ppb sulfate)			
C-3510 w	....	?	**ETNA** (Italy)	0101-06=		
A-3500 ?	....	?	**ISCHIA** (Italy)	0101-03=		
G-3500 t	....	?	**MALY SEMIACHIK** (Kamchatka)	1000-14=		
C-3500 ?	....	?	**GUAGUA PICHINCHA** (Ecuador)	1502-02=		
T-3500 ?	....	?	**GRIMSNES** (Iceland-SW)	1701-06=	2?	
T-3495 x	....	?	**PELEE** (W Indies)	1600-12=	**P**	
C-3460 v	....	?	**JINGPOHU** (China-E)	1005-05-		
G-3450 ?	....	?	**TAUPO** (New Zealand)	0401-07=	3	-/7
C-3450 ?	....	?	**ASAMA** (Honshu-Japan)	0803-11=	3	
T-3450 ?	....	?	**GORELY** (Kamchatka)	1000-07=	3	-/7
G-3450 ?	....	?	**KARYMSKY** (Kamchatka)	1000-13=		
C-3450 w	....	?	**ISKUT-UNUK RIVER CONES** (Canada)	1200-09-		
C-3450 <	....	?	**VESTMANNAEYJAR [HEIMAEY]**	1702-01=	3	
T-3450 *	....	?	**VATNAFJOLL** (Iceland-S)	1702-06=		
C-3440 w	....	?	**TOWADA** (Honshu-Japan)	0803-271	**5+**	**-/9**
G-3400 ?	....	?	**TAUPO** (New Zealand)	0401-07=	4	
G-3400 ?	....	?	**RAINIER** (US-Washington)	1201-03-	3	-/7
G-3400 ?	....	?	**MAUNA KEA** (Hawaiian Is)	1302-03-		
C-3390 >	....	?	**HUDSON, CERRO** (Chile-S)	1508-057		
T-3350 ?	....	?	**TAUPO** (New Zealand)	0401-07=	3	-/7
C-3350 ?	....	?	**MAUNA LOA** (Hawaiian Is)	1302-02=	0	
T-3350 *	....	?	**VATNAFJOLL** (Iceland-S)	1702-06=		
T-3350 *	....	?	**HEKLA** (Iceland-S)	1702-07=		
G-3300 ?	....	?	**TAUPO** (New Zealand)	0401-07=	4	-/8
C-3290 ?	....	?	**PELEE** (W Indies)	1600-12=		
C-3250 >	....	?	**RISHIRI** (Hokkaido-Japan)	0805-041		
G-3250 ?	....	?	**KRASHENINNIKOV** (Kamchatka)	1000-19=		
C-3250 x	....	?	**AKUTAN** (Aleutian Is)	1101-32-	**5**	**-/9**
C-3250 ?	....	?	**SPURR** (Alaska-SW)	1103-04-		
C-3250 ?	....	?	**MAUNA LOA** (Hawaiian Is)	1302-02=	0	
C-3245 ?	....	?	**PELEE** (W Indies)	1600-12=		
I -3201 v	....	?	**Unknown Source** (GISP2, 175 ppb sulfate)			
D-3195 ?	....	?	**Unknown Source**			
C-3190 v	....	?	**ARENAL** (Costa Rica)	1405-033		
C-3190 v	....	?	**POAS** (Costa Rica)	1405-04=		
C-3150 ?	....	?	**LOLORU** (Bougainville-SW Pac)	0505-03=		
G-3150 ?	....	?	**KARYMSKY** (Kamchatka)	1000-13=	3	-/7
C-3150 ?	....	?	**GLACIER PEAK** (US-Washington)	1201-02-		
C-3150 w	....	?	**PELEE** (W Indies)	1600-12=		
A-3120 u	....	?	**CAMPI FLEGREI** (Italy)	0101-01=	3	
C-3100 y	....	?	**MAYON** (Luzon-Philippines)	0703-03=		
K-3050 *	....	?	**ISCHIA** (Italy)	0101-03=		
C-3050 w	....	?	**ETNA** (Italy)	0101-06=		
T-3050 ?	....	?	**EGMONT** (New Zealand)	0401-03=		
C-3050 ?	....	?	**TAMBORA** (Lesser Sunda Is)	0604-04=		
T-3050 ?	....	?	**KIRISHIMA** (Kyushu-Japan)	0802-09=	3	-/7
T-3050 ?	....	?	**IZU-TOBU** (Honshu-Japan)	0803-01=	4	8/8
C-3050 ?	....	?	**FUJI** (Honshu-Japan)	0803-03=		
T-3050 ?	....	?	**NEMO PEAK** (Kurile Is)	0900-32=		
T-3050 ?	....	?	**PAUZHETKA [DIKY GREBEN]**	1000-022		
C-3050 ?	....	?	**ZHELTOVSKY** (Kamchatka)	1000-04=		
T-3050 ?	....	?	**ZHUPANOVSKY** (Kamchatka)	1000-12=		
T-3050 z	....	?	**BEZYMIANNY** (Kamchatka)	1000-25=		
C-3050 ?	....	?	**WEST CRATER** (US-Washington)	1201-06-		
T-3050 *	....	?	**SHASTA** (US-California)	1203-01-	0	

START YEAR	M-Dy	Duration	VOLCANO NAME (Subregion)	NUMBER	VEI	Vol L/T
C-3050 ?	. . . .	?	**KRAFLA** (Iceland-NE)	1703-08=	0	
T-3050 ?	. . . .	?	**THEISTAREYKJARBUNGA** (Iceland)	1703-09=	0	
T-3050 ?	. . . .	?	**SETE CIDADES** (Azores)	1802-08=	4	-/8
C-3040 ?	. . . .	?	**NUMAZAWA** (Honshu-Japan)	0803-151	5?	-/9
C-3030 t	. . . .	?	**COLIMA VOLC COMPLEX** (Mexico)	1401-04=		
C-3030 t	. . . .	?	**POPOCATEPETL** (Mexico)	1401-09=		
C-3015 ?	. . . .	?	**PELEE** (W Indies)	1600-12=		
F-3000 z	. . . .	?	**NEWER VOLCANICS PROV** (Australia)	0509-01-		
T-2985 z	. . . .	?	**VILLARRICA** (Chile-C)	1507-12=	0	
C-2985 ?	. . . .	?	**AGUA DE PAU** (Azores)	1802-09=	5	-/9
C-2970 y	. . . .	?	**SNAEFELLSJOKULL** (Iceland-W)	1700-01=	0	
I -2958 v	. . . .	?	**Unknown Source** (GISP2, 124 ppb sulfate)			
T-2950 ?	. . . .	?	**CAMPI FLEGREI** (Italy)	0101-01=	4	-/8
C-2950 ?	. . . .	?	**HAKU-SAN** (Honshu-Japan)	0803-05=		
G-2950 ?	. . . .	?	**KRASHENINNIKOV** (Kamchatka)	1000-19=		
T-2950 ?	. . . .	?	**COLIMA VOLC COMPLEX** (Mexico)	1401-04=	3	-/7
T-2950 z	. . . .	?	**VATNAFJOLL** (Iceland-S)	1702-06=		
T-2920 z	. . . .	?	**BLACK PEAK** (Alaska Peninsula)	1102-08-	6	-/10
G-2900 ?	. . . .	?	**TAUPO** (New Zealand)	0401-07=	4	-/8
C-2900 w	. . . .	?	**NEWER VOLCANICS PROV** (Australia)	0509-01-		
C-2900 ?	. . . .	?	**SAKURA-JIMA** (Kyushu-Japan)	0802-08=	4	
C-2900 w	. . . .	?	**KUSATSU-SHIRANE** (Honshu-Japan)	0803-12=	2	-/6
T-2900 ?	. . . .	?	**MUTNOVSKY** (Kamchatka)	1000-06=	2	-/6
T-2900 ?	. . . .	?	**AVACHINSKY** (Kamchatka)	1000-10=		
C-2890 u	. . . .	?	**REDOUBT** (Alaska-SW)	1103-03-		
C-2880 p	. . . .	?	**OKATAINA [HAROHARO]** (New Zeal)	0401-05=	6	9/10
C-2880 ?	. . . .	?	**HUDSON, CERRO** (Chile-S)	1508-057		
T-2850 ?	. . . .	?	**CAMPI FLEGREI** (Italy)	0101-01=		
G-2850 ?	. . . .	?	**TAUPO** (New Zealand)	0401-07=	3	-/7
T-2850 y	. . . .	?	**KSUDACH** (Kamchatka)	1000-05=		
G-2850 ?	. . . .	?	**KIKHPINYCH** (Kamchatka)	1000-18=	3	-/7
C-2850 ?	. . . .	?	**KILAUEA** (Hawaiian Is)	1302-01-	0	
T-2800 ?	. . . .	?	**TAUPO** (New Zealand)	0401-07=	3	-/7
T-2800 y	. . . .	?	**FUJI** (Honshu-Japan)	0803-03=		
C-2800 v	. . . .	?	**SANTA ISABEL** (Colombia)	1501-021		
C-2790 ?	. . . .	?	**DAVIS LAKE** (US-Oregon)	1202-10-		
G-2775 q	. . . .	?	**KIKHPINYCH** (Kamchatka)	1000-18=	4	8/8
C-2770 u	. . . .	?	**HUALALAI** (Hawaiian Is)	1302-04-	0	
C-2760 w	. . . .	?	**MYOKO** (Honshu-Japan)	0803-10=		
T-2750 ?	. . . .	?	**CAMPI FLEGREI** (Italy)	0101-01=	3	
T-2750 ?	. . . .	?	**EGMONT** (New Zealand)	0401-03=		
T-2750 ?	. . . .	?	**GORELY** (Kamchatka)	1000-07=	2	-/6
C-2750 ?	. . . .	?	**MAUNA LOA** (Hawaiian Is)	1302-02=	0	
C-2750 x	. . . .	?	**MICHOACAN-GUANAJUATO** (Mexico)	1401-06=	3	-/7
T-2750 *	. . . .	?	**VATNAFJOLL** (Iceland-S)	1702-06=		
C-2710 v	. . . .	?	**ORIZABA, PICO DE** (Mexico)	1401-10=		
T-2700 *	. . . .	?	**ISCHIA** (Italy)	0101-03=		
C-2690 u	. . . .	?	**IBUSUKI [IKEDA-KO]** (Kyushu-Japan)	0802-07=	5	-/9
C-2660 t	. . . .	?	**PELEE** (W Indies)	1600-12=		
C-2660 u	. . . .	?	**BRENNISTEINSFJOLL** (Iceland-SW)	1701-04=	0	9/-
K-2650 *	. . . .	?	**VULCANO** (Italy)	0101-05=	0	
T-2650 ?	. . . .	?	**EGMONT** (New Zealand)	0401-03=		
G-2600 ?	. . . .	?	**TAUPO** (New Zealand)	0401-07=	4	-/8
T-2575 *	. . . .	?	**SAN MARTIN, VOLCAN DE** (Mexico)	1401-11=		
C-2570 u	. . . .	?	**GALERAS** (Colombia)	1501-08=	3	-/6
C-2560 v	. . . .	?	**CRATERS OF THE MOON** (US-Idaho)	1204-02-	0	9/-
C-2560 ?	. . . .	?	**PELEE** (W Indies)	1600-12=		
T-2550 ?	. . . .	?	**FUJI** (Honshu-Japan)	0803-03=		
T-2550 *	. . . .	?	**TATE-YAMA** (Honshu-Japan)	0803-08=		
A-2550 z	. . . .	?	**ASAMA** (Honshu-Japan)	0803-11=	4	
T-2550 z	. . . .	?	**HACHIJO-JIMA** (Izu Is-Japan)	0804-05=		
T-2550 z	. . . .	?	**AMAK** (Aleutian Is)	1101-39-		
C-2550 ?	. . . .	?	**SHASTA** (US-California)	1203-01-		
C-2550 y	. . . .	?	**MOMOTOMBO** (Nicaragua)	1404-09=		
C-2550 w	. . . .	?	**DONA JUANA** (Colombia)	1501-07=	C	
C-2550 ?	. . . .	?	**SOUFRIERE GUADELOUPE** (W Indies)	1600-06=		
C-2540 w	. . . .	?	**EGMONT** (New Zealand)	0401-03=		
G-2500 ?	. . . .	?	**TAUPO** (New Zealand)	0401-07=	3	-/7
C-2460 ?	. . . .	?	**PELEE** (W Indies)	1600-12=		
C-2450 ?	. . . .	?	**CAMPI FLEGREI** (Italy)	0101-01=	4	-/8
C-2450 z	. . . .	?	**FUJI** (Honshu-Japan)	0803-03=		
T-2450 ?	. . . .	?	**GORELY** (Kamchatka)	1000-07=	3	-/7
G-2450 ?	. . . .	?	**MALY SEMIACHIK** (Kamchatka)	1000-14=		
T-2450 *	. . . .	?	**VATNAFJOLL** (Iceland-S)	1702-06=		
C-2440 u	. . . .	?	**HUALALAI** (Hawaiian Is)	1302-04-	0	
C-2425 ?	. . . .	?	**PELEE** (W Indies)	1600-12=	P	
C-2405 v	. . . .	?	**MEDICINE LAKE** (US-California)	1203-02-		7/-
C-2400 x	. . . .	?	**SNAEFELLSJOKULL** (Iceland-W)	1700-01=	2?	8/-
C-2380 v	. . . .	?	**SOUFRIERE ST. VINCENT** (W Indies)	1600-15=		
C-2370 w	. . . .	?	**COLIMA VOLC COMPLEX** (Mexico)	1401-04=	4?	-/8
C-2370 u	. . . .	?	**POPOCATEPETL** (Mexico)	1401-09=		
C-2360 ?	. . . .	?	**PELEE** (W Indies)	1600-12=		
K-2350 *	. . . .	?	**ISCHIA** (Italy)	0101-03=		
G-2350 ?	. . . .	?	**KARYMSKY** (Kamchatka)	1000-13=		
C-2350 ?	. . . .	?	**MAUNA LOA** (Hawaiian Is)	1302-02=	0	
G-2335 ?	. . . .	?	**ST. HELENS** (US-Washington)	1201-05-	5	-/9
C-2330 v	. . . .	?	**ETNA** (Italy)	0101-06=		
C-2320 w	. . . .	?	**LIAMUIGA** (W Indies)	1600-03=	P	
T-2310 y	. . . .	?	**EGMONT** (New Zealand)	0401-03=		
C-2310 v	. . . .	?	**SOUFRIERE ST. VINCENT** (W Indies)	1600-15=		
G-2310 p	. . . .	?	**HEKLA** (Iceland-S)	1702-07=	5	-/9
C-2275 ?	. . . .	?	**PELEE** (W Indies)	1600-12=		
C-2270 y	. . . .	?	**SNAEFELLSJOKULL** (Iceland-W)	1700-01=	0	
C-2250 ?	. . . .	?	**HAKU-SAN** (Honshu-Japan)	0803-05=		
C-2250 ?	. . . .	?	**MENDELEEV** (Kurile Is)	0900-02=		
T-2250 ?	. . . .	?	**GORELY** (Kamchatka)	1000-07=	2	-/6
G-2250 ?	. . . .	?	**KARYMSKY** (Kamchatka)	1000-13=	4	-/8
G-2250 ?	. . . .	?	**MALY SEMIACHIK** (Kamchatka)	1000-14=		
G-2250 ?	. . . .	?	**KRASHENINNIKOV** (Kamchatka)	1000-19=		
C-2250 ?	. . . .	?	**MAUNA LOA** (Hawaiian Is)	1302-02=	0	
C-2240 ?	. . . .	?	**VILLARRICA** (Chile-C)	1507-12=		
C-2220 v	. . . .	?	**EDGECUMBE** (Alaska-SE)	1105-04-		
C-2210 w	. . . .	?	**AGUA DE PAU** (Azores)	1802-09=		
H-2200 >	. . . .	?	**MASHU** (Hokkaido-Japan)	0805-081		
T-2200 ?	. . . .	?	**GORELY** (Kamchatka)	1000-07=	2	
T-2200 ?	. . . .	?	**AVACHINSKY** (Kamchatka)	1000-10=		
C-2200 y	. . . .	?	**DOTSERO** (US-Colorado)	1208-01-	2?	
T-2200 z	. . . .	?	**KILAUEA** (Hawaiian Is)	1302-01-		
C-2200 w	. . . .	?	**SOUFRIERE ST. VINCENT** (W Indies)	1600-15=		
C-2150 ?	. . . .	?	**LOLORU** (Bougainville-SW Pac)	0505-03=		
T-2150 ?	. . . .	?	**MUTNOVSKY** (Kamchatka)	1000-06=	3	-/7
C-2150 x	. . . .	?	**HELL'S HALF ACRE** (US-Idaho)	1204-04-	0	
C-2150 ?	. . . .	?	**MAUNA LOA** (Hawaiian Is)	1302-02=	0	
C-2140 ?	. . . .	?	**VILLARRICA** (Chile-C)	1507-12=		
C-2135 t	. . . .	?	**SOUFRIERE ST. VINCENT** (W Indies)	1600-15=		
C-2120 v	. . . .	?	**HALEAKALA** (Hawaiian Is)	1302-06-		
C-2120 <	. . . .	?	**CHICHINAUTZIN** (Mexico)	1401-08=		
C-2110 v	. . . .	?	**ORIZABA, PICO DE** (Mexico)	1401-10=	P	
C-2110 v	. . . .	?	**PELEE** (W Indies)	1600-12=		
C-2095 v	. . . .	?	**AZUFRAL, VOLCAN** (Colombia)	1501-09=		
C-2075 y	. . . .	?	**GALERAS** (Colombia)	1501-08=	2	-/6
C-2050 ?	. . . .	?	**MARIVELES** (Luzon-Philippines)	0703-081		
C-2050 ?	. . . .	?	**KIRISHIMA** (Kyushu-Japan)	0802-09=	3	-/7
C-2050 ?	. . . .	?	**FUJI** (Honshu-Japan)	0803-03=		
C-2050 ?	. . . .	?	**HAKU-SAN** (Honshu-Japan)	0803-05=		
T-2050 ?	. . . .	?	**MEGATA** (Honshu-Japan)	0803-262		
T-2050 ?	. . . .	?	**HACHIJO-JIMA** (Izu Is-Japan)	0804-05=		
T-2050 ?	. . . .	?	**MUTNOVSKY** (Kamchatka)	1000-06=	2	-/6
T-2050 ?	. . . .	?	**GORELY** (Kamchatka)	1000-07=	2	-/6
G-2050 ?	. . . .	?	**KARYMSKY** (Kamchatka)	1000-13=		
T-2050 ?	. . . .	?	**TOLBACHIK** (Kamchatka)	1000-24=	3	8/7
T-2050 ?	. . . .	?	**SHEVELUCH** (Kamchatka)	1000-27=		
T-2050 ?	. . . .	?	**CRATER LAKE** (US-Oregon)	1202-16-		
C-2050 ?	. . . .	?	**SHASTA** (US-California)	1203-01-		
C-2050 ?	. . . .	?	**MAUNA LOA** (Hawaiian Is)	1302-02=	0	
A-2050 ?	. . . .	?	**MICHOACAN-GUANAJUATO** (Mexico)	1401-06=		
?-2050 ?	. . . .	?	**SOUFRIERE GUADELOUPE** (W Indies)	1600-06=		
T-2050 ?	. . . .	?	**LJOSUFJOLL** (Iceland-W)	1700-03=	3?	
T-2050 *	. . . .	?	**SETE CIDADES** (Azores)	1802-08=		
C-2040 v	. . . .	?	**LONG ISLAND** (New Guinea-NE of)	0501-05=	6	-/10
C-2040 u	. . . .	?	**HUALALAI** (Hawaiian Is)	1302-04-	0	
C-2025 ?	. . . .	?	**PELEE** (W Indies)	1600-12=		
C-2020 u	. . . .	?	**SOUFRIERE ST. VINCENT** (W Indies)	1600-15=		
T-2010 ?	. . . .	?	**IBUSUKI [KAIMON]** (Kyushu-Japan)	0802-07=	4	-/8
C-2010 v	. . . .	?	**SNAEFELLSJOKULL** (Iceland-W)	1700-01=		
G-2000 ?	. . . .	?	**MARRA, JEBEL** (Africa-N)	0205-03-	C	
C-2000 v	. . . .	?	**RAOUL ISLAND** (Kermadec Is)	0402-03=	4	-/8
T-2000 ?	. . . .	?	**GORELY** (Kamchatka)	1000-07=	2	-/6
C-2000 ?	. . . .	?	**MAUNA LOA** (Hawaiian Is)	1302-02=	0	
T-2000 *	. . . .	?	**GUAGUA PICHINCHA** (Ecuador)	1502-02=		

-2000 (3950 BP)

START YEAR	M-Dy	Duration	VOLCANO NAME (Subregion)	NUMBER	VEI	Vol L/T
T-1975 w	. . . .	?	**VILLARRICA** (Chile-C)	1507-12=	0	
K-1950 *	. . . .	?	**CAMPI FLEGREI** (Italy)	0101-01=	2	7/-
C-1950 t	. . . .	?	**HALEAKALA** (Hawaiian Is)	1302-06-		
T-1950 v	. . . .	?	**GRIMSVOTN** (Iceland-NE)	1703-01=	2	9/-
T-1900 ?	. . . .	?	**CAMPI FLEGREI** (Italy)	0101-01=	3	-/7
C-1900 ?	. . . .	?	**SAND MOUNTAIN FIELD** (US-Oregon)	1202-04-	2?	
C-1900 ?	. . . .	?	**MAUNA LOA** (Hawaiian Is)	1302-02=	0	
C-1890 ?	. . . .	?	**DANA** (Alaska Peninsula)	1102-05-	5	-/9
C-1890 u	. . . .	?	**COLIMA VOLC COMPLEX** (Mexico)	1401-04=		
C-1890 u	. . . .	?	**POPOCATEPETL** (Mexico)	1401-09=		
C-1880 w	. . . .	?	**MICHOACAN-GUANAJUATO** (Mexico)	1401-06=	3	
G-1855 ?	. . . .	?	**ST. HELENS** (US-Washington)	1201-05-	6	-/10
T-1850 ?	. . . .	?	**CAMPI FLEGREI** (Italy)	0101-01=	4	-/8
C-1850 w	. . . .	?	**FUJI** (Honshu-Japan)	0803-03=		
T-1850 ?	. . . .	?	**NEMO PEAK** (Kurile Is)	0900-32=		
T-1850 ?	. . . .	?	**HAYES** (Alaska-SW)	1103-05-		
C-1850 ?	. . . .	?	**AZUFRAL, VOLCAN** (Colombia)	1501-09=		
T-1850 z	. . . .	?	**VATNAFJOLL** (Iceland-S)	1702-06=		
T-1850 *	. . . .	?	**HEKLA** (Iceland-S)	1702-07=		
T-1850 ?	. . . .	?	**FREMRINAMUR** (Iceland-NE)	1703-07=		9/-
C-1850 z	. . . .	?	**AGUA DE PAU** (Azores)	1802-09=	3	6/7
C-1830 y	. . . .	?	**ISKUT-UNUK RIVER CONES** (Canada)	1200-09-		
T-1830 >	. . . .	?	**RECLUS** (Chile-S)	1508-063		
C-1810 x	. . . .	?	**VILLARRICA** (Chile-C)	1507-12=	5	
G-1800 t	. . . .	?	**MALY SEMIACHIK** (Kamchatka)	1000-14=		
C-1800 ?	. . . .	?	**MAUNA LOA** (Hawaiian Is)	1302-02=	0	
T-1800 y	. . . .	?	**REYKJANESHRYGGUR** (Iceland-SW)	1701-01=		
T-1800 y	. . . .	?	**REYKJANES** (Iceland-SW)	1701-02=	2	7/-
T-1780 ?	. . . .	?	**IBUSUKI [KAIMON]** (Kyushu-Japan)	0802-07=	4	-/8
C-1760 r	. . . .	?	**PELEE** (W Indies)	1600-12=		
C-1750 ?	. . . .	?	**CAMPI FLEGREI** (Italy)	0101-01=	3?	
T-1750 ?	. . . .	?	**TOLBACHIK** (Kamchatka)	1000-24=	3	
C-1750 ?	. . . .	?	**VENIAMINOF** (Alaska Peninsula)	1102-07-	6	-/10
C-1750 ?	. . . .	?	**MAUNA LOA** (Hawaiian Is)	1302-02=	0	
C-1750 w	. . . .	?	**LJOSUFJOLL** (Iceland-W)	1700-03=	2	
T-1750 z	. . . .	?	**HEKLA** (Iceland-S)	1702-07=		
C-1740 w	. . . .	?	**VESUVIUS** (Italy)	0101-02=	5	-/9
C-1710 v	. . . .	?	**LIAMUIGA** (W Indies)	1600-03=	P	
T-1700 ?	. . . .	?	**CAMPI FLEGREI** (Italy)	0101-01=	3	-/7
T-1700 ?	. . . .	?	**AVACHINSKY** (Kamchatka)	1000-10=		
C-1700 ?	. . . .	?	**MAUNA LOA** (Hawaiian Is)	1302-02=	0	
I -1695 u	. . . .	?	**Unknown Source** (GISP2, 213 ppb sulfate)			

START YEAR	M-Dy	Duration	VOLCANO NAME (Subregion)	NUMBER	VEI	Vol L/T
G-1675 ?	....	?	**ST. HELENS** (US-Washington)	1201-05-	5	-/9
C-1675 w	....	?	**CRATERS OF THE MOON** (US-Idaho)	1204-02-	0	9/-
V-1662 ?	....	?	**NEMRUT DAGI** (Turkey)	0103-02=		
G-1650 t	....	?	**SANTORINI** (Greece)	0102-04=	6	-/10
C-1650 ?	....	?	**SANBE** (Honshu-Japan)	0803-002	4?	
T-1650 ?	....	?	**KSUDACH** (Kamchatka)	1000-05=		
G-1650 ?	....	?	**KRASHENINNIKOV** (Kamchatka)	1000-19=		
T-1650 ?	....	?	**TOLBACHIK** (Kamchatka)	1000-24=		
C-1650 ?	....	?	**KILAUEA** (Hawaiian Is)	1302-01-	0	
C-1650 ?	....	?	**MAUNA LOA** (Hawaiian Is)	1302-02=	0	
V-1650 y	....	?	**MAUNA KEA** (Hawaiian Is)	1302-03-		
C-1650 x	....	?	**HUALALAI** (Hawaiian Is)	1302-04-	0	
C-1650 v	....	?	**TOLIMA** (Colombia)	1501-03=	P	
C-1650 w	....	?	**AZUFRAL, VOLCAN** (Colombia)	1501-09=		
T-1650 *	....	?	**VATNAFJOLL** (Iceland-S)	1702-06=		
D-1628 ?	....	?	**Unknown Source**			
I -1623 u	....	?	**Unknown Source** (GISP2, 145 ppb sulfate)			
T-1610 ?	....	?	**IBUSUKI [KAIMON]** (Kyushu-Japan)	0802-07=	3	-/7
G-1610 ?	....	?	**ST. HELENS** (US-Washington)	1201-05-		
G-1600 ?	....	?	**TAUPO** (New Zealand)	0401-07=	6	-/10
C-1600 u	....	?	**SOUFRIERE ST. VINCENT** (W Indies)	1600-15=		
C-1580 j	....	?	**CHACANA** (Ecuador)	1502-022		
T-1550 *	....	?	**LENGAI, OL DOINYO** (Africa-E)	0202-12=		
C-1550 u	....	?	**RABAUL** (New Britain-SW Pac)	0502-14=	5	-/9
T-1550 ?	....	?	**IBUSUKI [NABESHIMA]** (Kyushu)	0802-07=		
T-1550 z	....	?	**BEZYMIANNY** (Kamchatka)	1000-25=		
T-1550 ?	....	?	**SHEVELUCH** (Kamchatka)	1000-27=		
C-1550 w	....	?	**REDOUBT** (Alaska-SW)	1103-03-		
T-1550 ?	....	?	**HAYES** (Alaska-SW)	1103-05-	5	
C-1550 ?	....	?	**KILAUEA** (Hawaiian Is)	1302-01-	0	
C-1550 v	....	?	**ARENAL** (Costa Rica)	1405-033		
C-1550 ?	....	?	**SOUFRIERE GUADELOUPE** (W Indies)	1600-06=		
T-1550 z	....	?	**TORFAJOKULL** (Iceland-S)	1702-05=		7/-
T-1550 ?	....	?	**HEKLA** (Iceland-S)	1702-07=	4	-/8
C-1540 v	....	?	**RINCON DE LA VIEJA** (Costa Rica)	1405-02=	4	-/8
-1500 t	....	?	**ETNA** (Italy)	0101-06=	5?	
T-1500 ?	....	?	**IBUSUKI [KAIMON]** (Kyushu-Japan)	0802-07=	4	-/8
G-1500 ?	....	?	**AVACHINSKY** (Kamchatka)	1000-10=	5	-/9
C-1500 u	....	?	**ORIZABA, PICO DE** (Mexico)	1401-10=	P	
C-1490 u	....	?	**OKATAINA [HAROHARO]** (New Zeal)	0401-05=	4+	8/8
C-1490 y	....	?	**BLUE LAKE CRATER** (US-Oregon)	1202-03-		
C-1490 ?	....	?	**SAND MOUNTAIN FIELD** (US-Oregon)	1202-04-	2?	
C-1480 j	....	?	**ANIAKCHAK** (Alaska Peninsula)	1102-09-	6?	-/10
I -1459 u	....	?	**Unknown Source** (GISP2, 104 ppb sulfate)			
I -1454 u	....	?	**Unknown Source** (GISP2, 164 ppb sulfate)			
T-1450 ?	....	?	**IBUSUKI VOLC FIELD** (Kyushu-Japan)	0802-07=		
C-1450 ?	....	?	**HAKU-SAN** (Honshu-Japan)	0803-05=		
H-1450 ?	....	?	**NEWBERRY VOLCANO** (US-Oregon)	1202-11-		
C-1450 v	....	?	**ORIZABA, PICO DE** (Mexico)	1401-10=	0	8/-
C-1450 w	....	?	**MOJANDA** (Ecuador)	1502-003	2	
G-1400 ?	....	?	**KARYMSKY** (Kamchatka)	1000-13=		
V-1396 ?	....	?	**NEMRUT DAGI** (Turkey)	0103-02=		
C-1395 ?	....	?	**AGUILERA** (Chile-S)	1508-062		
G-1380 ?	....	?	**SOUFRIERE GUADELOUPE** (W Indies)	1600-06=	3?	
T-1350 w	....	?	**EGMONT** (New Zealand)	0401-03=		
C-1350 w	....	?	**RAOUL ISLAND** (Kermadec Is)	0402-03=	4	-/8
C-1350 ?	....	?	**PAGO** (New Britain-SW Pac)	0502-08=	6?	-/10
G-1350 ?	....	?	**KRASHENINNIKOV** (Kamchatka)	1000-19=	3	8/7
T-1350 ?	....	?	**BEZYMIANNY** (Kamchatka)	1000-25=		
T-1350 ?	....	?	**SHEVELUCH** (Kamchatka)	1000-27=		
T-1350 *	....	?	**VATNAFJOLL** (Iceland-S)	1702-06=		
C-1330 v	....	?	**LONGONOT** (Africa-E)	0202-10=		
C-1320 y	....	?	**SAN MARTIN, VOLCAN DE** (Mexico)	1401-11=		
C-1310 w	....	?	**BRAVO, CERRO** (Colombia)	1501-011	4	-/9
T-1300 y	....	?	**NIIGATA-YAKE-YAMA** (Honshu-Japan)	0803-09=		
T-1300 ?	....	?	**AVACHINSKY** (Kamchatka)	1000-10=		
T-1300 *	....	?	**BAKER** (US-Washington)	1201-01=	4	-/8
C-1300 ?	....	?	**MAUNA LOA** (Hawaiian Is)	1302-02=	0	
C-1290 ?	....	?	**AGUA DE PAU** (Azores)	1802-09=	4	-/8
C-1260 y	....	?	**LOLORU** (Bougainville-SW Pac)	0505-03=		
T-1250 ?	....	?	**EGMONT** (New Zealand)	0401-03=		
G-1250 ?	....	?	**TAUPO** (New Zealand)	0401-07=	3	-/7
T-1250 v	....	?	**MACHIN, CERRO** (Colombia)	1501-04=		
T-1250 *	....	?	**VATNAFJOLL** (Iceland-S)	1702-06=		
T-1250 *	....	?	**HEKLA** (Iceland-S)	1702-07=		
T-1250 ?	....	?	**BARDARBUNGA [VEIDIVOTN]**	1703-03=		9/-
I -1250 ?	....	?	**CANDLEMAS ISLAND** (Antarctica)	1900-10=		
C-1245 w	....	?	**RUIZ** (Colombia)	1501-02=		
A-1200 >	....	?	**HAYLAN, JABAL** (Arabia-S)	0301-11-	0?	
T-1200 v	....	?	**FUJI** (Honshu-Japan)	0803-03=		
C-1200 v	....	?	**FLORES** (Azores)	1802-001		
I -1192 u	....	?	**Unknown Source** (GISP2, 110 ppb sulfate)			
G-1185 ?	....	?	**ST. HELENS** (US-Washington)	1201-05-		
C-1180 p	....	?	**PELEE** (W Indies)	1600-12=		
C-1160 w	....	?	**EGMONT** (New Zealand)	0401-03=		
D-1150 ?	....	?	**Unknown Source**			
C-1150 v	....	?	**HAKONE** (Honshu-Japan)	0803-02=		
G-1150 ?	....	?	**KRASHENINNIKOV** (Kamchatka)	1000-19=		
C-1150 ?	....	?	**SHASTA** (US-California)	1203-01-		
C-1150 u	....	?	**HUALALAI** (Hawaiian Is)	1302-04-	0	
C-1150 w	....	?	**CUICOCHA** (Ecuador)	1502-002	5	-/9
T-1150 v	....	?	**TORFAJOKULL** (Iceland-S)	1702-05=		7/-
T-1150 *	....	?	**VATNAFJOLL** (Iceland-S)	1702-06=		
C-1125 t	....	?	**GRAN CANARIA** (Canary Is)	1803-04-		
C-1120 w	....	?	**KUSATSU-SHIRANE** (Honshu-Japan)	0803-12=		
T-1120 *	....	?	**BAITOUSHAN** (China-E)	1005-07-		
G-1115 y	....	?	**ZUNI-BANDERA** (US-New Mexico)	1210-02-	0	9/-
C-1100 x	....	?	**SHEVELUCH** (Kamchatka)	1000-27=		
G-1100 ?	....	?	**ST. HELENS** (US-Washington)	1201-05-		
C-1090 v	....	?	**KIKAI** (Ryukyu Is)	0802-06=	2	
C-1090 x	....	?	**IZU-TOBU** (Honshu-Japan)	0803-01=	4+	8/8
I -1084 t	....	?	**Unknown Source** (GISP2, 129 ppb sulfate)			
C-1080 y	....	?	**PANTELLERIA** (Italy)	0101-071		
C-1080 x	....	?	**HUALALAI** (Hawaiian Is)	1302-04-	0	
C-1080 ?	....	?	**VILLARRICA** (Chile-C)	1507-12=		
T-1075 w	....	?	**REDOUBT** (Alaska-SW)	1103-03-		
C-1075 t	....	?	**MEDICINE LAKE** (US-California)	1203-02-	0	6/-
C-1060 u	....	?	**KRISUVIK** (Iceland-SW)	1701-03=	0	7/-
C-1050 ?	....	?	**LOLORU** (Bougainville-SW Pac)	0505-03=		
C-1050 ?	....	?	**TINAKULA** (Santa Cruz Is-SW Pac)	0506-01=		
T-1050 ?	....	?	**KIRISHIMA** (Kyushu-Japan)	0802-09=	4	
T-1050 ?	....	?	**FUJI** (Honshu-Japan)	0803-03=	5	-/9
T-1050 ?	....	?	**TOWADA** (Honshu-Japan)	0803-271	4+	-/8
T-1050 ?	....	?	**MIYAKE-JIMA** (Izu Is-Japan)	0804-04=	C	
T-1050 ?	....	?	**KOMAGA-TAKE** (Hokkaido-Japan)	0805-02=		
T-1050 <	....	?	**KHODUTKA** (Kamchatka)	1000-053	4+	-/8
G-1050 ?	....	?	**KARYMSKY** (Kamchatka)	1000-13=		
G-1050 ?	....	?	**KRASHENINNIKOV** (Kamchatka)	1000-19=		
T-1050 ?	....	?	**KLIUCHEVSKOI** (Kamchatka)	1000-26=		
C-1050 ?	....	?	**BUZZARD CREEK** (Alaska-E)	1105-001	2	-/6
T-1050 x	....	?	**BRAVO, CERRO** (Colombia)	1501-011	4	-/8
T-1050 z	....	?	**BURNEY, MONTE** (Chile-S)	1508-07=		
K-1050 *	....	?	**PLEIADES, THE** (Antarctica)	1900-013		
C-1040 ?	....	?	**SAND MOUNTAIN FIELD** (US-Oregon)	1202-04-	2?	
C-1040 u	....	?	**BRENNISTEINSFJOLL** (Iceland-SW)	1701-04=	2	8/-
G-1010 ?	....	?	**ST. HELENS** (US-Washington)	1201-05-		
C-1005 v	....	?	**TUNGURAHUA** (Ecuador)	1502-08=		
T-1000 >	....	?	**TATE-YAMA** (Honshu-Japan)	0803-08=		
G-1000 t	....	?	**KRASHENINNIKOV** (Kamchatka)	1000-19=	3	-/7
C-1000 z	....	?	**SNAEFELLSJOKULL** (Iceland-W)	1700-01=	2	8/-
C-0980 x	....	?	**GALERAS** (Colombia)	1501-08=	2	-/6
C-0970 z	....	?	**AOGA-SHIMA** (Izu Is-Japan)	0804-06=		
C-0960 u	....	?	**TECUAMBURRO** (Guatemala)	1402-12=		
C-0950 v	....	?	**HAKONE** (Honshu-Japan)	0803-02=		
T-0950 ?	....	?	**FUJI** (Honshu-Japan)	0803-03=	4+	-/8
T-0950 ?	....	?	**KIZIMEN** (Kamchatka)	1000-23=		
C-0950 ?	....	?	**MAUNA LOA** (Hawaiian Is)	1302-02=	0	
C-0950 ?	....	?	**CUICOCHA** (Ecuador)	1502-002		
?-0950 ?	....	?	**SOUFRIERE GUADELOUPE** (W Indies)	1600-06=		
G-0950 ?	....	?	**HEKLA** (Iceland-S)	1702-07=	5+	-/9
C-0950 v	....	?	**FLORES** (Azores)	1802-001		
C-0950 ?	....	?	**FURNAS** (Azores)	1802-10=	5	-/9
C-0950 w	....	?	**HIERRO** (Canary Is)	1803-02-		
C-0935 ?	....	?	**BELKNAP** (US-Oregon)	1202-06-	0	
C-0930 >	....	?	**FUJI** (Honshu-Japan)	0803-03=	5	-/9
C-0930 ?	....	?	**AZUFRAL, VOLCAN** (Colombia)	1501-09=	P	
C-0920 u	....	?	**SOLLIPULLI** (Chile-C)	1507-111	5+	-/9
G-0900 ?	....	?	**TAUPO** (New Zealand)	0401-07=	4	-/8
C-0900 w	....	?	**ARENAL** (Costa Rica)	1405-033		
C-0870 u	....	?	**KARKAR** (New Guinea-NE of)	0501-03=		
G-0850 ?	....	?	**TAUPO** (New Zealand)	0401-07=	4+	-/8
C-0850 ?	....	?	**KHODUTKA** (Kamchatka)	1000-053		7/-
G-0850 ?	....	?	**KARYMSKY** (Kamchatka)	1000-13=		
G-0850 ?	....	?	**MALY SEMIACHIK** (Kamchatka)	1000-14=		
G-0850 ?	....	?	**KRASHENINNIKOV** (Kamchatka)	1000-19=		7/-
C-0850 ?	....	?	**GLACIER PEAK** (US-Washington)	1201-02-		
C-0850 ?	....	?	**SHASTA** (US-California)	1203-01-		
M-0850 ?	....	?	**KILAUEA** (Hawaiian Is)	1302-01-		
T-0850 ?	....	?	**RUIZ** (Colombia)	1501-02=	4	-/8
T-0850 *	....	?	**VATNAFJOLL** (Iceland-S)	1702-06=		
T-0850 *	....	?	**HEKLA** (Iceland-S)	1702-07=		
C-0850 v	....	?	**UNNAMED** (Azores)	1802-081		
A-0800 <	....	?	**VESUVIUS** (Italy)	0101-02=	3	
T-0800 ?	....	?	**TAUPO** (New Zealand)	0401-07=	2	7/6
C-0800 v	....	?	**OSHIMA-OSHIMA** (Hokkaido-Japan)	0805-01=		
C-0800 y	....	?	**SHIKOTSU [TARUMAI]** (Hokkaido)	0805-04=	5	
T-0800 ?	....	?	**TOLBACHIK** (Kamchatka)	1000-24=		
T-0800 z	....	?	**YANTARNI** (Alaska Peninsula)	1102-10-	5	8/9
G-0800 ?	....	?	**ST. HELENS** (US-Washington)	1201-05-		
T-0800 ?	....	?	**NORTH SISTER FIELD** (US-Oregon)	1202-07-	2?	
C-0800 t	....	?	**MOMOTOMBO** (Nicaragua)	1404-09=	4+	-/8
C-0800 t	....	?	**PELEE** (W Indies)	1600-12=		
T-0800 y	....	?	**FREMRINAMUR** (Iceland-NE)	1703-07=		
C-0780 v	....	?	**MEDICINE LAKE** (US-California)	1203-02-		8/-
A-0750 t	....	?	**ISCHIA** (Italy)	0101-03=		
T-0750 t	....	?	**KASBEK** (Georgia)	0104-02-		
T-0750 y	....	?	**AOGA-SHIMA** (Izu Is-Japan)	0804-06=		
T-0750 ?	....	?	**TOLBACHIK** (Kamchatka)	1000-24=		
T-0750 v	....	?	**EDZIZA** (Canada)	1200-06-		
C-0750 v	....	?	**SOUFRIERE ST. VINCENT** (W Indies)	1600-15=		
T-0750 z	....	?	**VATNAFJOLL** (Iceland-S)	1702-06=		
T-0750 z	....	?	**HEKLA** (Iceland-S)	1702-07=		
T-0750 v	....	?	**THEISTAREYKJARBUNGA** (Iceland)	1703-09=	0	
C-0750 y	....	?	**SETE CIDADES** (Azores)	1802-08=		
?-0735	....	?	**ETNA** (Italy)	0101-06=		
C-0725 u	....	?	**BRAVO, CERRO** (Colombia)	1501-011	4	-/8
C-0725 ?	....	?	**PELEE** (W Indies)	1600-12=		
C-0720 u	....	?	**HUALALAI** (Hawaiian Is)	1302-04-	0	
T-0700 u	....	?	**ISCHIA** (Italy)	0101-03=		
T-0700 ?	....	?	**IBUSUKI [KAIMON]** (Kyushu-Japan)	0802-07=	2	7/6
T-0700 ?	....	?	**TOLBACHIK** (Kamchatka)	1000-24=		
H-0700 *	....	?	**MONO CRATERS** (US-California)	1203-12-		
-0695 b	....	?	**ETNA** (Italy)	0101-06=		
C-0680 w	....	?	**PULULAGUA** (Ecuador)	1502-011		
C-0670 ?	....	?	**VILLARRICA** (Chile-C)	1507-12=		
C-0665 v	....	?	**LJOSUFJOLL** (Iceland-W)	1700-03=	2	8/-

START YEAR	M-Dy	Dura-tion	VOLCANO NAME (Subregion)	NUMBER	VEI	Vol L/T
T-0650 ?	....	?	**IBUSUKI [KAIMON]** (Kyushu-Japan)	0802-07=	4	-/8
C-0650 ?	....	?	**SAKURA-JIMA** (Kyushu-Japan)	0802-08=		
C-0650 ?	....	?	**CHOKAI** (Honshu-Japan)	0803-22=		
G-0650 ?	....	?	**MALY SEMIACHIK** (Kamchatka)	1000-14=		
G-0650 ?	....	?	**KRASHENINNIKOV** (Kamchatka)	1000-19=		
C-0650 ?	....	?	**BELKNAP** (US-Oregon)	1202-06-	2?	
C-0650 *	....	?	**SHASTA** (US-California)	1203-01-		
C-0650 ?	....	?	**SOUFRIERE GUADELOUPE** (W Indies)	1600-06=	3?	
T-0650 *	....	?	**VATNAFJOLL** (Iceland-S)	1702-06=		
T-0650 ?	....	?	**KRAFLA** (Iceland-NE)	1703-08=	4	-/8
C-0640 y	....	?	**PAGO** (New Britain-SW Pac)	0502-08=		
C-0615 w	....	?	**ISKUT-UNUK RIVER CONES** (Canada)	1200-09-		
C-0615 ?	....	?	**PELEE** (W Indies)	1600-12=		
A-0600 <	....	?	**VESUVIUS** (Italy)	0101-02=	3	
C-0600 t	....	?	**SHEVELUCH** (Kamchatka)	1000-27=		
C-0600 ?	....	?	**MAUNA LOA** (Hawaiian Is)	1302-02=	0	
C-0600 ?	....	?	**PELEE** (W Indies)	1600-12=		
I -0585 t	....	?	**Unknown Source** (GISP2, 132 ppb sulfate)			
C-0580 t	....	?	**HALEAKALA** (Hawaiian Is)	1302-06-		
C-0580 >	....	?	**SOUFRIERE GUADELOUPE** (W Indies)	1600-06=	2	
?-0565	....	?	**ETNA** (Italy)	0101-06=		
C-0550 x	....	?	**TONGARIRO [NGAURUHOE]** (New Z)	0401-08=		-/9
T-0550 ?	....	?	**KIRISHIMA** (Kyushu-Japan)	0802-09=	3	-/7
T-0550 v	....	?	**NEMO PEAK** (Kurile Is)	0900-32=		
G-0550 ?	....	?	**MALY SEMIACHIK** (Kamchatka)	1000-14=		
C-0550 ?	....	?	**TAUNSHITS** (Kamchatka)	1000-16-		
T-0550 z	....	?	**SHASTA** (US-California)	1203-01-		
C-0540 u	....	?	**FUJI** (Honshu-Japan)	0803-03=		
C-0540 j	....	?	**PELEE** (W Indies)	1600-12=		
V-0531 ?	....	?	**NEMRUT DAGI** (Turkey)	0103-02=		
G-0530 ?	....	?	**ST. HELENS** (US-Washington)	1201-05-	4?	-/8
C-0530 u	....	?	**SOUFRIERE ST. VINCENT** (W Indies)	1600-15=		
C-0520 x	....	?	**FUJI** (Honshu-Japan)	0803-03=		
G-0520 x	....	?	**RAINIER** (US-Washington)	1201-03-		
C-0520 ?	....	?	**TENERIFE** (Canary Is)	1803-03-		
C-0510 x	....	?	**UNNAMED** (Azores)	1802-081		
-0500 ?	....	?	**ISCHIA** (Italy)	0101-03=		
C-0500 u	....	?	**DIENG VOLC COMPLEX** (Java)	0603-20=		
C-0500 ?	....	?	**MAUNA LOA** (Hawaiian Is)	1302-02=	0	
C-0495 ?	....	?	**PELEE** (W Indies)	1600-12=		
-0479	08	>3yr	**ETNA** (Italy)	0101-06=		
-0478	*Cont*	....	*ETNA (Italy)*	0101-06=		
-0477	*Cont*	....	*ETNA (Italy)*	0101-06=		
-0476	*Cont*	....	*ETNA (Italy)*	0101-06=		
-0475 ?	....	?	**VULCANO** (Italy)	0101-05=		
-0470 ?	....	?	**ISCHIA** (Italy)	0101-03=		
C-0455 w	....	?	**COTOPAXI** (Ecuador)	1502-05=		
-0450 <	....	?	**STROMBOLI** (Italy)	0101-04=	2	
-0450 t	....	?	**CAMEROON, MT.** (Africa-W)	0204-01=	3	
C-0450 v	....	?	**KSUDACH** (Kamchatka)	1000-05=	4	-/8
T-0450 ?	....	?	**MUTNOVSKY** (Kamchatka)	1000-06=	2	-/6
G-0450 ?	....	?	**BEZYMIANNY** (Kamchatka)	1000-25=	4	-/8
C-0450 x	....	?	**OKMOK** (Aleutian Is)	1101-29-	**6?**	**-/10**
C-0445 w	....	?	**PULULAGUA** (Ecuador)	1502-011	**C**	
A-0442	....	?	**POPA** (SE Asia)	0705-08-		
C-0440 t	....	?	**HUALALAI** (Hawaiian Is)	1302-04-	0	
C-0440 ?	....	?	**PELEE** (W Indies)	1600-12=	**P**	
C-0430 x	....	?	**AOGA-SHIMA** (Izu Is-Japan)	0804-06=		
-0425	0315m	474w?	**ETNA** (Italy)	0101-06=		
-0424	*Cont*	....	*ETNA (Italy)*	0101-06=		
C-0420 u	....	?	**ATACAZO** (Ecuador)	1502-021	**P**	
C-0410 v	....	?	**KILAUEA** (Hawaiian Is)	1302-01-	0	
C-0410 v	....	?	**GALERAS** (Colombia)	1501-08=	2	-/6
C-0400 t	....	?	**MEAGER** (Canada)	1200-18-	**5?**	
C-0400 ?	....	?	**MAUNA LOA** (Hawaiian Is)	1302-02=	0	
C-0400 u	....	?	**HUALALAI** (Hawaiian Is)	1302-04-	0	
C-0400 v	....	?	**REYKJANES** (Iceland-SW)	1701-02=	2	8/-
-0396 ?	0715q	?	**ETNA** (Italy)	0101-06=		
C-0380 v	....	?	**PINATUBO** (Luzon-Philippines)	0703-083		
-0360 j	....	?	**VULCANO** (Italy)	0101-05=	3?	
?-0350 ?	....	?	**ISCHIA** (Italy)	0101-03=		
-0350 ?	....	?	**ETNA** (Italy)	0101-06=		
C-0350 v	....	?	**AMBITLE** (New Ireland-SW Pac)	0504-02=		
C-0350	....	?	**FUJI** (Honshu-Japan)	0803-03=		
C-0350 ?	....	?	**HAKU-SAN** (Honshu-Japan)	0803-05=		
T-0350 ?	....	?	**GORELY** (Kamchatka)	1000-07=	3	-/7
G-0350 ?	....	?	**KRASHENINNIKOV** (Kamchatka)	1000-19=		
C-0350 ?	....	?	**SOUTH SISTER** (US-Oregon)	1202-08-	4	8/8
M-0350 ?	....	?	**CRATERS OF THE MOON** (US-Idaho)	1204-02-	0	8/-
C-0350 u	....	?	**HUALALAI** (Hawaiian Is)	1302-04-	0	
C-0345 u	....	?	**BAMUS** (New Britain-SW Pac)	0502-11=		
C-0310 ?	....	?	**PELEE** (W Indies)	1600-12=		
-0300	....	?	**VULCANO** (Italy)	0101-05=	3	
T-0300 ?	....	?	**OKATAINA [EDGECUMBE]** (New Zeal)	0401-05=	0	**9/-**
T-0300 y	....	?	**KHODUTKA** (Kamchatka)	1000-053	0	
G-0300 ?	....	?	**RAINIER** (US-Washington)	1201-03-	4	-/8
T-0300 ?	....	?	**WAPI LAVA FIELD** (US-Idaho)	1204-03-	2?	**9/-**
C-0300 ?	....	?	**MAUNA LOA** (Hawaiian Is)	1302-02=	0	
T-0300 y	....	?	**KRAFLA** (Iceland-NE)	1703-08=	0	
G-0275 ?	....	?	**ST. HELENS** (US-Washington)	1201-05-		
C-0270 t	....	?	**BAMUS** (New Britain-SW Pac)	0502-11=		
T-0270 ?	....	?	**IBUSUKI [KAIMON]** (Kyushu-Japan)	0802-07=	4	-/8
C-0265 v	....	?	**TUNGURAHUA** (Ecuador)	1502-08=		
-0258 o	....	?	**METHANA** (Greece)	0102-02=	3	7/-
C-0255 q	....	?	**CRATERS OF THE MOON** (US-Idaho)	1204-02-	0	7/-
-0253 k	....	?	**CAMPI FLEGREI MAR SICILIA** (Italy)	0101-07=		
-0250 t	....	?	**ISCHIA** (Italy)	0101-03=		
G-0250 ?	....	?	**KRASHENINNIKOV** (Kamchatka)	1000-19=		
T-0250 ?	....	?	**ST. HELENS** (US-Washington)	1201-05-		
T-0250 z	....	?	**VATNAFJOLL** (Iceland-S)	1702-06=		
T-0250 z	....	?	**HEKLA** (Iceland-S)	1702-07=		
C-0240 v	....	?	**ST. ANDREW STRAIT [LOU IS.]**	0500-01=		
C-0240 ?	....	?	**TOKACHI** (Hokkaido-Japan)	0805-05=		
C-0220 t	....	?	**ZHUPANOVSKY** (Kamchatka)	1000-12=		
G-0220 ?	....	?	**ST. HELENS** (US-Washington)	1201-05-		
C-0220 u	....	?	**ARENAL** (Costa Rica)	1405-033		
-0215	....	?	**VULCANO** (Italy)	0101-05=		
C-0210 u	....	?	**RAOUL ISLAND** (Kermadec Is)	0402-03=	**6**	**-/10**
C-0210 v	....	?	**MIYAKE-JIMA** (Izu Is-Japan)	0804-04=		
D-0208 ?	....	?	**Unknown Source**			
T-0205 x	....	?	**REDOUBT** (Alaska-SW)	1103-03-		
G-0200 ?	....	?	**TAUPO** (New Zealand)	0401-07=	4+	-/8
T-0200 ?	....	?	**MUTNOVSKY** (Kamchatka)	1000-06=	2	-/6
T-0200 ?	....	?	**TOLBACHIK** (Kamchatka)	1000-24=		
C-0200 t	....	?	**KILAUEA** (Hawaiian Is)	1302-01-	0	
C-0200 ?	....	?	**MAUNA LOA** (Hawaiian Is)	1302-02=	0	
C-0200 v	....	?	**RUIZ** (Colombia)	1501-02=	4	-/8
C-0200 ?	....	?	**REYKJANES** (Iceland-SW)	1701-02=	0	
-0197	....	?	**SANTORINI** (Greece)	0102-04=	3	
C-0195 ?	....	?	**PELEE** (W Indies)	1600-12=	**P**	
C-0190 u	....	?	**KRISUVIK** (Iceland-SW)	1701-03=	2	8/-
T-0185 v	....	?	**FUJI** (Honshu-Japan)	0803-03=		
-0183	....	?	**VULCANO** (Italy)	0101-05=	4	
I -0180 s	....	?	**Unknown Source** (GISP2, 93 ppb sulfate)			
C-0165 ?	....	?	**TERCEIRA** (Azores)	1802-05=		8/-
C-0160 t	....	?	**PURACE** (Colombia)	1501-06=		
C-0150 t	....	?	**KSUDACH** (Kamchatka)	1000-05=		
G-0150 ?	....	?	**KRASHENINNIKOV** (Kamchatka)	1000-19=	**C**	
C-0150 u	....	?	**UDOKAN [CHEPE]** (Russia-SE)	1002-03-		
C-0150 ?	....	?	**SHASTA** (US-California)	1203-01-		
C-0150 ?	....	?	**KILAUEA** (Hawaiian Is)	1302-01-	4	-/8
T-0150 y	....	?	**SAN MARTIN, VOLCAN DE** (Mexico)	1401-11=		
T-0150 *	....	?	**VATNAFJOLL** (Iceland-S)	1702-06=		
-0141	1231y	?	**ETNA** (Italy)	0101-06=		
-0135	....	?	**ETNA** (Italy)	0101-06=		
-0126	06	?	**VULCANO** (Italy)	0101-05=		
-0126	06 <	?	**ETNA** (Italy)	0101-06=		
C-0126 t	....	?	**CRATERS OF THE MOON** (US-Idaho)	1204-02-	0	**9/-**
-0122	....	?	**ETNA** (Italy)	0101-06=	4?	
C-0115 v	....	?	**LIAMUIGA** (W Indies)	1600-03=		
C-0110 v	....	?	**SHIKOTSU [ENIWA]** (Hokkaido-Japan)	0805-04=	2	
-0104	....	?	**VULSINI** (Italy)	0101-003		
C-0100 w	....	?	**TAVEUNI** (Fiji Is-SW Pacific)	0405-01-	2	
T-0100 ?	....	?	**MUTNOVSKY** (Kamchatka)	1000-06=	2	-/6
T-0100 ?	....	?	**TOLBACHIK** (Kamchatka)	1000-24=		
C-0095 w	....	?	**FUJI** (Honshu-Japan)	0803-03=		
G-0095 ?	....	?	**ST. HELENS** (US-Washington)	1201-05-		
-0091	....	?	**ISCHIA** (Italy)	0101-03=		
-0091	....	?	**VULCANO** (Italy)	0101-05=	3?	
C-0090 v	....	?	**TERCEIRA** (Azores)	1802-05=		
C-0085 x	....	?	**CHICHINAUTZIN** (Mexico)	1401-08=	2?	**9/-**
T-0080 ?	....	?	**IBUSUKI [KAIMON]** (Kyushu-Japan)	0802-07=	4	-/8
C-0080 ?	....	?	**MAUNA LOA** (Hawaiian Is)	1302-02=	0	
C-0080 u	....	?	**HUALALAI** (Hawaiian Is)	1302-04-	0	8/-
C-0075 u	....	?	**HENGILL** (Iceland-SW)	1701-05=	2	8/-
C-0065 ?	....	?	**PELEE** (W Indies)	1600-12=	4	-/8
?-0061	....	?	**ETNA** (Italy)	0101-06=		
C-0060 ?	....	?	**MAUNA LOA** (Hawaiian Is)	1302-02=	0	
?-0056	....	?	**ETNA** (Italy)	0101-06=		
I -0054 s	....	?	**Unknown Source** (GISP2, 291 ppb sulfate)			
T-0050 ?	....	?	**LENGAI, OL DOINYO** (Africa-E)	0202-12=		
T-0050 ?	....	?	**RAOUL ISLAND** (Kermadec Is)	0402-03=	3?	-/7
C-0050 v	....	?	**DIENG VOLC COMPLEX** (Java)	0603-20=	0	
C-0050 ?	....	?	**MERAPI** (Java)	0603-25=		
T-0050 ?	....	?	**KIRISHIMA** (Kyushu-Japan)	0802-09=	3	
T-0050 ?	....	?	**ASO** (Kyushu-Japan)	0802-11=	4	
T-0050 ?	....	?	**IZU-TOBU** (Honshu-Japan)	0803-01=	3	8/8
C-0050 ?	....	?	**HAKU-SAN** (Honshu-Japan)	0803-05=		
T-0050 ?	....	?	**YAKE-DAKE** (Honshu-Japan)	0803-07=	4	
T-0050 ?	....	?	**NIIGATA-YAKE-YAMA** (Honshu-Japan)	0803-09=	3	
T-0050 ?	....	?	**OSHIMA** (Izu Is-Japan)	0804-01=	3	
T-0050 ?	....	?	**ZHUPANOVSKY** (Kamchatka)	1000-12=		
T-0050 ?	....	?	**KRONOTSKY** (Kamchatka)	1000-20=		
T-0050 ?	....	?	**KIZIMEN** (Kamchatka)	1000-23=		
C-0050 ?	....	?	**SOUTH SISTER** (US-Oregon)	1202-08-	3	8/7
M-0050 ?	....	?	**MEDICINE LAKE** (US-California)	1203-02-	0	7/-
T-0050 ?	....	?	**GRIMSVOTN** (Iceland-NE)	1703-01=	2	
T-0050 ?	....	?	**KRAFLA** (Iceland-NE)	1703-08=	2	
M-0050 ?	....	?	**BOUVET** (Atlantic-S)	1806-02-		
-0049	....	?	**ETNA** (Italy)	0101-06=		
-0044	03 ?	?	**ETNA** (Italy)	0101-06=	3?	
C-0040 u	....	?	**EGMONT** (New Zealand)	0401-03=		
-0036	0715q	?	**ETNA** (Italy)	0101-06=		
-0032	1231y	?	**ETNA** (Italy)	0101-06=		
C-0030 w	....	?	**NORTH SISTER FIELD** (US-Oregon)	1202-07-	2?	
C-0030 ?	....	?	**MAUNA LOA** (Hawaiian Is)	1302-02=	0	
C-0025 t	....	?	**TURRIALBA** (Costa Rica)	1405-07=		
-0024 e	....	?	**VULCANO** (Italy)	0101-05=		
-0010 j	....	?	**VULCANO** (Italy)	0101-05=		
?-0010 ?	....	?	**ETNA** (Italy)	0101-06=		
-0006 p	....	?	**ISCHIA** (Italy)	0101-03=		
↑ BC · AD ↓						
T 0000 ?	....	?	**TOLBACHIK** (Kamchatka)	1000-24=		

START YEAR	M-Dy	Duration	VOLCANO NAME (Subregion)	NUMBER	VEI	Vol L/T
C **0000** w	....	?	**SAND MOUNTAIN FIELD** (US-Oregon)	1202-04-	2?	
A **0000** v	....	?	**ACATENANGO** (Guatemala)	1402-08=		
0010 j	....	?	**ETNA** (Italy)	0101-06=		
G **0010** x	....	?	**MONO CRATERS** (US-California)	1203-12-		
T **0030** ?	....	?	**IBUSUKI [KAIMON]** (Kyushu-Japan)	0802-07=	3	-/7
0039 a	....	?	**ETNA** (Italy)	0101-06=		
C **0040** ?	....	?	**TENERIFE** (Canary Is)	1803-03-		
0046	....	365*y*	**SANTORINI** (Greece)	0102-04=	3	
0047	*Cont*	....	*SANTORINI (Greece)*	0102-04=	*2*	
0050 t	....	?	**VULCANO** (Italy)	0101-05=		
T **0050** t	....	?	**ELBRUS** (Russia-SW)	0104-01-		
C **0050** v	....	?	**AMBRYM** (Vanuatu-SW Pacific)	0507-04=	**6+**	**-/10**
T **0050** ?	....	?	**FUJI** (Honshu-Japan)	0803-03=	2	
T **0050** ?	....	?	**MUTNOVSKY** (Kamchatka)	1000-06=	2	-/6
T **0050** ?	....	?	**GORELY** (Kamchatka)	1000-07=	3	-/7
T **0050** ?	....	?	**TOLBACHIK** (Kamchatka)	1000-24=	4	8/8
T **0050** ?	....	?	**BEZYMIANNY** (Kamchatka)	1000-25=		
0050 t	....	?	**TIANSHAN VOLC GROUP** (China-W)	1004-02-		
T **0050** ?	....	?	**SHASTA** (US-California)	1203-01-	0	
C **0050** ?	....	?	**MAUNA LOA** (Hawaiian Is)	1302-02=	0	
C **0050** ?	....	?	**PELEE** (W Indies)	1600-12=	**P**	
T **0050** ?	....	?	**KRAFLA** (Iceland-NE)	1703-08=	2	**9/-**
C **0060** y	....	?	**ST. HELENS** (US-Washington)	1201-05-	0	
C **0065** x	....	?	**BONA-CHURCHILL** (Alaska-E)	1105-03-	**6**	**-/10**
0069	....	?	**ISCHIA** (Italy)	0101-03=		
C **0070** u	....	?	**HENGILL** (Iceland-SW)	1701-05=	2	
0079	0824	4*b*	**VESUVIUS** (Italy)	0101-02=	**6**	**-/10**
C **0150** ?	....	?	**SHASTA** (US-California)	1203-01-		
M **0150** y	....	?	**KILAUEA** (Hawaiian Is)	1302-01-	0	
C **0150** ?	....	?	**MAUNA LOA** (Hawaiian Is)	1302-02=	0	
C **0150** x	....	?	**LIAMUIGA** (W Indies)	1600-03=	**P**	
T **0150** v	....	?	**TORFAJOKULL** (Iceland-S)	1702-05=	3	7/7
T **0150** v	....	?	**BARDARBUNGA [VEIDIVOTN]**	1703-03=	2?	8/-
C **0155** v	....	?	**KSUDACH** (Kamchatka)	1000-05=	**6**	**-/10**
C **0160** w	....	?	**AGUA DE PAU** (Azores)	1802-09=		
0172	....	?	**VESUVIUS** (Italy)	0101-02=	2	
C **0175** v	....	?	**MASHU** (Hokkaido-Japan)	0805-081		
C **0175** ?	....	?	**BELKNAP** (US-Oregon)	1202-06-	2?	
T **0180** ?	....	?	**OKATAINA [TE KOPIA]** (New Zeal)	0401-05=		
T **0180** ?	....	?	**MAROA [ORAKAIKORAKO]** (New Z)	0401-061		
G **0180** ?	0115q	?	**TAUPO** (New Zealand)	0401-07=	**6+**	**-/10**
G **0185** ?	....	?	**ST. HELENS** (US-Washington)	1201-05-		
C **0190** x	....	?	**WRANGELL** (Alaska-E)	1105-02-	**C?**	
A **0200** >	....	?	**ARHAB, HARRA OF** (Arabia-S)	0301-09-	2?	
? **0200** ?	....	?	**PENANGGUNGAN** (Java)	0603-291		
T **0200** y	....	?	**TSURUMI** (Kyushu-Japan)	0802-13=	4	
T **0200** ?	....	?	**FUJI** (Honshu-Japan)	0803-03=	2	
T **0200** ?	....	?	**OSHIMA** (Izu Is-Japan)	0804-01=	3	
T **0200** y	....	?	**PAUZHETKA [DIKY GREBEN]**	1000-022		**10/-**
T **0200** y	....	?	**ILYINSKY** (Kamchatka)	1000-03=		
T **0200** ?	....	?	**GORELY** (Kamchatka)	1000-07=	3	-/7
C **0200** t	....	?	**GLACIER PEAK** (US-Washington)	1201-02-	4+	-/8
C **0200** ?	....	?	**MAUNA LOA** (Hawaiian Is)	1302-02=	0	

Figure 13. The famous 79 AD eruption of Vesuvius may have looked very much like this engraving of the smaller, but very similar eruption of 1631 AD. Pyroclastic flows are clearly shown sweeping down the volcano's flanks, but this violent form of volcanism did not capture the attention of the scientific community until 1902, more than 270 years after this painting. The view is from Naples, and the buried city of Pompeii is on the far side of the volcano. Artist: G. Battista Passaro. From the collection of Maurice & Katia Krafft.

START YEAR	M-Dy	Duration	VOLCANO NAME (Subregion)	NUMBER	VEI	Vol L/T
0080 a	....	?	**ISCHIA** (Italy)	0101-03=		
0080 ?	....	?	**ETNA** (Italy)	0101-06=		
C **0090** v	....	?	**ORIZABA, PICO DE** (Mexico)	1401-10=	3	7/7
C **0090** v	....	?	**HENGILL** (Iceland-SW)	1701-05=	2	8/-
C **0090** v	....	?	**SETE CIDADES** (Azores)	1802-08=	4	-/8
T **0100** z	....	?	**KIRISHIMA** (Kyushu-Japan)	0802-09=	3	-/7
T **0100** ?	....	?	**ASO** (Kyushu-Japan)	0802-11=	4	
T **0100** ?	....	?	**FUJI** (Honshu-Japan)	0803-03=	2	
T **0100** ?	....	?	**OSHIMA** (Izu Is-Japan)	0804-01=	3	
T **0100** ?	....	?	**AVACHINSKY** (Kamchatka)	1000-10=		
C **0100** ?	....	?	**MAUNA LOA** (Hawaiian Is)	1302-02=	0	
C **0110** t	....	?	**REDOUBT** (Alaska-SW)	1103-03-		
C **0110** ?	....	?	**VILLARRICA** (Chile-C)	1507-12=	0	
C **0115** x	....	?	**SAN MARTIN, VOLCAN DE** (Mexico)	1401-11=		
C **0125** ?	....	?	**PELEE** (W Indies)	1600-12=	**P**	
T **0130** ?	....	?	**IBUSUKI [KAIMON]** (Kyushu-Japan)	0802-07=	4	7/8
0144	....	?	**VULCANO** (Italy)	0101-05=		
0145 ?	....	?	**ISCHIA** (Italy)	0101-03=		
T **0150** ?	....	?	**IBUSUKI [KAIMON]** (Kyushu-Japan)	0802-07=	4	-/8
C **0150** ?	....	?	**HAKU-SAN** (Honshu-Japan)	0803-05=		
T **0150** x	....	?	**MIYAKE-JIMA** (Izu Is-Japan)	0804-04=		
T **0150** ?	....	?	**TOLBACHIK** (Kamchatka)	1000-24=		
T **0150** ?	....	?	**BEZYMIANNY** (Kamchatka)	1000-25=		
C **0200** w	....	?	**SNAEFELLSJOKULL** (Iceland-W)	1700-01=		8/-
0203	....	?	**VESUVIUS** (Italy)	0101-02=	3	
T **0210** ?	....	?	**TAUPO** (New Zealand)	0401-07=	0	8/-
T **0210** ?	....	?	**ASO** (Kyushu-Japan)	0802-11=	3	
T **0220** ?	....	?	**FUJI** (Honshu-Japan)	0803-03=	2	
C **0220** u	....	?	**PELEE** (W Indies)	1600-12=		
0222	....	>3yr	**VESUVIUS** (Italy)	0101-02=	2	
0223	*Cont*	....	*VESUVIUS (Italy)*	0101-02=	*2*	
0224	*Cont*	....	*VESUVIUS (Italy)*	0101-02=	*2*	
0225	*Cont*	....	*VESUVIUS (Italy)*	0101-02=	*2*	
0226	*Cont*	....	*VESUVIUS (Italy)*	0101-02=	*2*	
0227	*Cont*	....	*VESUVIUS (Italy)*	0101-02=	*2*	
0228	*Cont*	....	*VESUVIUS (Italy)*	0101-02=	*2*	
0229	*Cont*	....	*VESUVIUS (Italy)*	0101-02=	*2*	
0230	*Cont*	....	*VESUVIUS (Italy)*	0101-02=	*2*	
C **0230** x	....	?	**AUGUSTINE** (Alaska-SW)	1103-01-		
T **0230** ?	....	?	**ST. HELENS** (US-Washington)	1201-05-		
0231	*Cont*	....	*VESUVIUS (Italy)*	0101-02=	*2*	
0232	*Cont*	....	*VESUVIUS (Italy)*	0101-02=	*2*	
0233	*Cont*	....	*VESUVIUS (Italy)*	0101-02=	*2*	
0234	*Cont*	....	*VESUVIUS (Italy)*	0101-02=	*2*	
0235	*Cont*	....	*VESUVIUS (Italy)*	0101-02=	*2*	
C **0240** w	....	?	**FUJI** (Honshu-Japan)	0803-03=		
0250 t	....	?	**KRAKATAU** (Indonesia)	0602-00=		

START YEAR	M-Dy	Duration	VOLCANO NAME (Subregion)	NUMBER	VEI	Vol L/T
C 0250x	....	?	IRAYA (Luzon Is-N of)	0704-06-		
T 0250?	....	?	FUJI (Honshu-Japan)	0803-03=	2	
C 0250w	....	?	OSHIMA-OSHIMA (Hokkaido-Japan)	0805-01=		
T 0250?	....	?	MUTNOVSKY (Kamchatka)	1000-06=	2	-/6
T 0250?	....	?	GORELY (Kamchatka)	1000-07=	3	-/7
T 0250?	....	?	TOLBACHIK (Kamchatka)	1000-24=		
T 0250?	....	?	BEZYMIANNY (Kamchatka)	1000-25=		8/-
C 0250x	....	?	SOUFRIERE GUADELOUPE (W Indies)	1600-06=		
T 0250*	....	?	VATNAFJOLL (Iceland-S)	1702-06=		
T 0250*	....	?	HEKLA (Iceland-S)	1702-07=		
T 0250y	....	?	KRAFLA (Iceland-NE)	1703-08=	0	
0252?	0201	8*a*	ETNA (Italy)	0101-06=	3?	
? 0253<	....	?	ERCIYES DAGI (Turkey)	0103-01=		
C 0260v	....	?	ILOPANGO (El Salvador)	1403-06=	6	-/10
T 0270?	....	?	IBUSUKI [KAIMON] (Kyushu-Japan)	0802-07=	3	-/7
C 0270w	....	?	CHICHON, EL (Mexico)	1401-12=		
G 0275?	....	?	ST. HELENS (US-Washington)	1201-05-		
C 0280p	....	?	PELEE (W Indies)	1600-12=	4	-/8
0295j	....	?	ISCHIA (Italy)	0101-03=		
C 0295?	....	?	IMURUK LAKE (Alaska-W)	1104-02-		
T 0300x	....	?	RAOUL ISLAND (Kermadec Is)	0402-03=	4	-/8
T 0300?	....	?	FUJI (Honshu-Japan)	0803-03=	1	
T 0300?	....	?	OSHIMA (Izu Is-Japan)	0804-01=	3	
C 0300x	....	?	HOOD (US-Oregon)	1202-01-		
C 0300?	....	?	MAUNA LOA (Hawaiian Is)	1302-02=	0	
C 0300?	....	?	PELEE (W Indies)	1600-12=	P	
C 0315y	....	?	NEWBERRY VOLCANO (US-Oregon)	1202-11-	4	-/8
G 0315x	....	?	MONO CRATERS (US-California)	1203-12-		
C 0325?	....	?	KAGUYAK (Alaska Peninsula)	1102-25-	6	-/10
C 0330?	....	?	VILLARRICA (Chile-C)	1507-12=		
C 0350?	....	?	ST. ANDREW STRAIT [LOU IS.]	0500-01=		
C 0350y	....	?	FUJI (Honshu-Japan)	0803-03=	3	
A 0350j	1115m	?	ASAMA (Honshu-Japan)	0803-11=	4	
C 0350v	....	?	MIYAKE-JIMA (Izu Is-Japan)	0804-04=		
C 0350?	....	?	KSUDACH (Kamchatka)	1000-05=	2	-/6
T 0350?	....	?	TOLBACHIK (Kamchatka)	1000-24=		
C 0350v	....	?	NORTH SISTER FIELD (US-Oregon)	1202-07-	2?	8/-
T 0350v	....	?	MONO LAKE VOLC FIELD (US-Calif)	1203-11-		
C 0350?	....	?	MAUNA LOA (Hawaiian Is)	1302-02=	0	
C 0350y	....	?	RUIZ (Colombia)	1501-02=	3	-/7
T 0350*	....	?	VATNAFJOLL (Iceland-S)	1702-06=		
C 0360w	....	?	BELKNAP (US-Oregon)	1202-06-	0	
C 0365x	....	?	FUJI (Honshu-Japan)	0803-03=		
T 0375u	....	?	SAN MARTIN, VOLCAN DE (Mexico)	1401-11=		
0379	....	>3yr	VESUVIUS (Italy)	0101-02=	2	
0380	*Cont*	....	*VESUVIUS (Italy)*	0101-02=	*2*	
T 0380y	....	?	SETE CIDADES (Azores)	1802-08=	4	-/8
0381	*Cont*	....	*VESUVIUS (Italy)*	0101-02=	*2*	
0382	*Cont*	....	*VESUVIUS (Italy)*	0101-02=	*2*	
0383	*Cont*	....	*VESUVIUS (Italy)*	0101-02=	*2*	
0384	*Cont*	....	*VESUVIUS (Italy)*	0101-02=	*2*	
0385	*Cont*	....	*VESUVIUS (Italy)*	0101-02=	*2*	
0386	*Cont*	....	*VESUVIUS (Italy)*	0101-02=	*2*	
0387	*Cont*	....	*VESUVIUS (Italy)*	0101-02=	*2*	
0388	*Cont*	....	*VESUVIUS (Italy)*	0101-02=	*2*	
0389	*Cont*	....	*VESUVIUS (Italy)*	0101-02=	*2*	
0390	*Cont*	....	*VESUVIUS (Italy)*	0101-02=	*2*	
0391	*Cont*	....	*VESUVIUS (Italy)*	0101-02=	*2*	
0392	*Cont*	....	*VESUVIUS (Italy)*	0101-02=	*2*	
0393	*Cont*	....	*VESUVIUS (Italy)*	0101-02=	*2*	
0394	*Cont*	....	*VESUVIUS (Italy)*	0101-02=	*2*	
0395	*Cont*	....	*VESUVIUS (Italy)*	0101-02=	*2*	
C 400y	....	?	KAIKOHE-BAY OF ISLANDS (New Z)	0401-01=		
T 0400?	....	?	FUJI (Honshu-Japan)	0803-03=	2	
T 0400?	....	?	OSHIMA (Izu Is-Japan)	0804-01=	3	
T 0400?	....	?	AVACHINSKY (Kamchatka)	1000-10=		
T 0400?	....	?	TOLBACHIK (Kamchatka)	1000-24=	4	8/8
C 0400?	....	?	QUILL, THE (W Indies)	1600-02=		
0416	....	?	KRAKATAU (Indonesia)	0602-00=	C	
0417?	....	?	ETNA (Italy)	0101-06=		
C 0420v	....	?	PAGO (New Britain-SW Pac)	0502-08=		
G 0420?	....	?	ST. HELENS (US-Washington)	1201-05-		
G 0430?	....	?	OPALA (Kamchatka)	1000-08=	5+	8/9
C 0440v	....	?	MONO CRATERS (US-California)	1203-12-		
C 0445?	....	?	PELEE (W Indies)	1600-12=	P	
C 0450?	....	?	HAKU-SAN (Honshu-Japan)	0803-05=		
T 0450t	....	?	HARUNA (Honshu-Japan)	0803-122	3	-/7
T 0450?	....	?	TOLBACHIK (Kamchatka)	1000-24=	3	9/7
0450t	....	?	DATONG (China-E)	1005-01-		
M 0450<	....	?	KILAUEA (Hawaiian Is)	1302-01-	0	
C 0450?	....	?	MAUNA LOA (Hawaiian Is)	1302-02=	0	
T 0450?	....	?	COLIMA VOLC COMPLEX (Mexico)	1401-04=	3?	7/6
C 0455?	....	?	BELKNAP (US-Oregon)	1202-06-	2?	
C 0470u	....	?	MAYON (Luzon-Philippines)	0703-03=		
C 0470t	....	?	IRAYA (Luzon Is-N of)	0704-06-		
C 0470v	....	?	FUJI (Honshu-Japan)	0803-03=	3?	
0472	1105	1*a*?	VESUVIUS (Italy)	0101-02=	4	-/8
C 0480?	....	?	MAUNA LOA (Hawaiian Is)	1302-02=	0	
C 0490v	....	?	MONO CRATERS (US-California)	1203-12-		

500

START YEAR	M-Dy	Duration	VOLCANO NAME (Subregion)	NUMBER	VEI	Vol L/T
0500v	....	?	ARHAB, HARRA OF (Arabia-S)	0301-09-	0	
T 0500?	....	?	KIKAI (Ryukyu Is)	0802-06=	3	
T 0500?	....	?	OSHIMA (Izu Is-Japan)	0804-01=	3	
T 0500?	....	?	MIYAKE-JIMA (Izu Is-Japan)	0804-04=	2	
C 0500t	....	?	SHEVELUCH (Kamchatka)	1000-27=	5	-/9
T 0500t	....	?	SAN MARTIN, VOLCAN DE (Mexico)	1401-11=		
M 0500t	....	?	LANZAROTE (Canary Is)	1803-06-		
0505	1109	?	VESUVIUS (Italy)	0101-02=		
C 0505x	....	?	AUGUSTINE (Alaska-SW)	1103-01-		
C 0510w	....	?	HOOD (US-Oregon)	1202-01-		
0512	0708	?	VESUVIUS (Italy)	0101-02=	4?	
C 0520w	....	?	EGMONT (New Zealand)	0401-03=		
C 0520x	....	?	KARKAR (New Guinea-NE of)	0501-03=	C	
C 0520v	....	?	FUJI (Honshu-Japan)	0803-03=	2	
A 0520j	0601p	?	HARUNA (Honshu-Japan)	0803-122	4+	-/8
0526?	....	?	VULCANO (Italy)	0101-05=	3	
T 0530?	....	?	FUJI (Honshu-Japan)	0803-03=	3	
0536	....	?	VESUVIUS (Italy)	0101-02=	2	
C 0540v	....	?	RABAUL (New Britain-SW Pac)	0502-14=	6	-/10
C 0540u	....	?	ALAMAGAN (Mariana Is-C Pac)	0804-18=		
T 0550?	....	?	EGMONT (New Zealand)	0401-03=		
T 0550?	....	?	IBUSUKI [KAIMON] (Kyushu-Japan)	0802-07=	2	-/6
A 0550j	0601p	?	HARUNA (Honshu-Japan)	0803-122	5	8/9
T 0550?	....	?	GORELY (Kamchatka)	1000-07=	3	-/7
G 0550?	....	?	KIKHPINYCH (Kamchatka)	1000-18=	3	7/7
T 0550?	....	?	TOLBACHIK (Kamchatka)	1000-24=	3	9/7
C 0550?	....	?	KLIUCHEVSKOI (Kamchatka)	1000-26=		
C 0550?	....	?	MAUNA LOA (Hawaiian Is)	1302-02=	0	
C 0550?	....	?	GUAGUA PICHINCHA (Ecuador)	1502-02=		
T 0550*	....	?	HEKLA (Iceland-S)	1702-07=		
0553	....	?	ASO (Kyushu-Japan)	0802-11=	3↑	
0573	03 ?	?	CHOKAI (Honshu-Japan)	0803-22=		
0577	1201p	226*s*	CHOKAI (Honshu-Japan)	0803-22=		
0578	*Cont*	....	*CHOKAI (Honshu-Japan)*	0803-22=		
C 0590v	....	?	SAN SALVADOR (El Salvador)	1403-05=		
C 0595u	....	?	INYO CRATERS (US-California)	1203-13-	4?	7/7
T 0600x	....	?	RAOUL ISLAND (Kermadec Is)	0402-03=	4	-/8
T 0600?	....	?	IBUSUKI [KAIMON] (Kyushu-Japan)	0802-07=	4	8/8
T 0600?	....	?	BEZYMIANNY (Kamchatka)	1000-25=		
C 0600?	....	?	MAUNA LOA (Hawaiian Is)	1302-02=	0	
C 0600u	....	?	BARU (Panama)	1406-01-		
C 0600v	....	?	UNNAMED (Azores)	1802-081		
0605	....	?	OSHIMA (Izu Is-Japan)	0804-01=	3?	7/8
? 0610o	....	?	CHOKAI (Honshu-Japan)	0803-22=		
C 0610w	....	?	EDZIZA (Canada)	1200-06-		
C 0620?	....	?	WASHINGTON (US-Oregon)	1202-05-	1	
C 0620x	....	?	NEWBERRY VOLCANO (US-Oregon)	1202-11-	3	8/7
0630	....	?	OSHIMA (Izu Is-Japan)	0804-01=	3	
C 0630?	....	?	MAUNA LOA (Hawaiian Is)	1302-02=	0	
I 0639q	....	?	Unknown Source (GISP2, 149 ppb sulfate)			
A 0640?	....	?	'UWAYRID, HARRAT (Arabia-W)	0301-02=	2?	
0641	....	?	RAHAT, HARRAT (Arabia-W)	0301-07=	2	
? 0644	....	?	ETNA (Italy)	0101-06=		
C 0645?	....	?	PELEE (W Indies)	1600-12=		
0650t	....	?	KHAYBAR, HARRAT (Arabia-W)	0301-06=	2?	
M 0650?	....	?	RABAUL (New Britain-SW Pac)	0502-14=	0	
C 0650?	....	?	KIKHPINYCH (Kamchatka)	1000-18=		
T 0650?	....	?	KRASHENINNIKOV (Kamchatka)	1000-19=	2	-/6
0650t	....	?	TIANSHAN VOLC GROUP (China-W)	1004-02-		
T 0650z	....	?	HEKLA (Iceland-S)	1702-07=		
0654	....	?	OSHIMA (Izu Is-Japan)	0804-01=	3	8/7
T 0660?	....	?	IBUSUKI [KAIMON] (Kyushu-Japan)	0802-07=	4+	
C 0670w	....	?	SETE CIDADES (Azores)	1802-08=	3	7/7
C 0675t	....	?	RUIZ (Colombia)	1501-02=	3	-/7
? 0680	....	?	OSHIMA (Izu Is-Japan)	0804-01=		
C 0680u	....	?	KILAUEA (Hawaiian Is)	1302-01-	1?	
C 0680?	....	?	MAUNA LOA (Hawaiian Is)	1302-02=	0	
? 0681	0326	?	OSHIMA (Izu Is-Japan)	0804-01=		
0684?	1129	?	OSHIMA (Izu Is-Japan)	0804-01=		
0685	02 ?	30*p*?	VESUVIUS (Italy)	0101-02=	3	
0685	04	?	ASAMA (Honshu-Japan)	0803-11=	3	
@ 0686	....	?	YAKE-DAKE (Honshu-Japan)	0803-07=		
T 0700?	....	?	LENGAI, OL DOINYO (Africa-E)	0202-12=		
C 0700v	....	?	RAOUL ISLAND (Kermadec Is)	0402-03=	4	-/8
T 0700?	....	?	KIKAI (Ryukyu Is)	0802-06=	3	
T 0700?	....	?	AVACHINSKY (Kamchatka)	1000-10=		
T 0700t	....	?	BEZYMIANNY (Kamchatka)	1000-25=	4?	-/8
C 0700x	....	?	BONA-CHURCHILL (Alaska-E)	1105-03-	6	-/10
T 0700?	....	?	MONO CRATERS (US-California)	1203-12-		8/-
C 0700u	....	?	CHICHON, EL (Mexico)	1401-12=	P	
C 0700w	....	?	AGUA DE PAU (Azores)	1802-09=		
M 0700t	....	?	LANZAROTE (Canary Is)	1803-06-		
0706	09 ?	?	HAKU-SAN (Honshu-Japan)	0803-05=		
0708	....	?	SAKURA-JIMA (Kyushu-Japan)	0802-08=	3↑	
0711c	....	?	CHOKAI (Honshu-Japan)	0803-22=		
? 0712	....	?	SAKURA-JIMA (Kyushu-Japan)	0802-08=	3?	
0716	....	730*y*	SAKURA-JIMA (Kyushu-Japan)	0802-08=	3↑	
0717	*Cont*	....	*SAKURA-JIMA (Kyushu-Japan)*	0802-08=	*3↑*	
? 0717	07	?	CHOKAI (Honshu-Japan)	0803-22=		
0718	*Cont*	....	*SAKURA-JIMA (Kyushu-Japan)*	0802-08=	*3↑*	
T 0720?	....	?	IBUSUKI [KAIMON] (Kyushu-Japan)	0802-07=	4	-/8
C 0720v	....	?	FUJI (Honshu-Japan)	0803-03=	2	
M 0720?	....	?	MEDICINE LAKE (US-California)	1203-02-		8/-
C 0720?	....	?	PELEE (W Indies)	1600-12=		
C 0725v	....	?	COLIMA VOLC COMPLEX (Mexico)	1401-04=		
C 0725v	....	?	POPOCATEPETL (Mexico)	1401-09=		
0726	....	?	SANTORINI (Greece)	0102-04=	3	7/-
0729	....	?	LIPARI (Italy)	0101-041		
0729	....	?	VULCANO (Italy)	0101-05=		
C 0730?	....	?	KARKAR (New Guinea-NE of)	0501-03=	P	

START YEAR	M-Dy	Duration	VOLCANO NAME (Subregion)	NUMBER	VEI	Vol L/T
C **0740** w	....	?	**TAMBORA** (Lesser Sunda Is)	0604-04=		
0742	1228	?	**KIRISHIMA** (Kyushu-Japan)	0802-09=	3	
C **0750** ?	....	?	**PAGO** (New Britain-SW Pac)	0502-08=		
T **0750** ?	....	?	**NEMO PEAK** (Kurile Is)	0900-32=		
T **0750** ?	....	?	**MUTNOVSKY** (Kamchatka)	1000-06=	3	-/7
G **0750** ?	....	?	**KRASHENINNIKOV** (Kamchatka)	1000-19=	3	-/7
T **0750** *	....	?	**PACAYA** (Guatemala)	1402-11=		
C **0750** w	....	?	**BRAVO, CERRO** (Colombia)	1501-011	4	-/8
T **0750** *	....	?	**VATNAFJOLL** (Iceland-S)	1702-06=		
T **0750** ?	....	?	**HEKLA** (Iceland-S)	1702-07=		
0751	....	?	**OSHIMA** (Izu Is-Japan)	0804-01=	4	8/8
0764	01	?	**SAKURA-JIMA** (Kyushu-Japan)	0802-08=	4	
C **0765** x	....	?	**TUNGURAHUA** (Ecuador)	1502-08=	3?	-/7
0766	0720	?	**SAKURA-JIMA** (Kyushu-Japan)	0802-08=	3↑	
T **0770** ?	....	?	**IBUSUKI [KAIMON]** (Kyushu-Japan)	0802-07=	4	-/8
C **0770** x	....	?	**HUALALAI** (Hawaiian Is)	1302-04-	1	8/-
0771	....	?	**TSURUMI** (Kyushu-Japan)	0802-13=	0	
? **0773**	11 ?	?	**ZAO** (Honshu-Japan)	0803-19=		
T **0775** u	....	?	**RAOUL ISLAND** (Kermadec Is)	0402-03=	3	-/7
C **0775** y	....	?	**ST. HELENS** (US-Washington)	1201-05-		
0778	....	?	**SAKURA-JIMA** (Kyushu-Japan)	0802-08=	0?	
0781	0804	?	**FUJI** (Honshu-Japan)	0803-03=	3	
0787	....	?	**VESUVIUS** (Italy)	0101-02=	3	
0788	0418	?	**KIRISHIMA** (Kyushu-Japan)	0802-09=	4	-/8
? **0796**	08	?	**ASO** (Kyushu-Japan)	0802-11=	0?	
C **0800** t	....	?	**DAKATAUA** (New Britain-SW Pac)	0502-04=	**C**	
0800	0415	34*a*	**FUJI** (Honshu-Japan)	0803-03=	4	
M **0800** ?	....	?	**MEDICINE LAKE** (US-California)	1203-02-		8/-
G **0800** y	....	?	**LASSEN [CHAOS CRAGS]** (US-Calif)	1203-08-		
G **0800** t	....	?	**ALMOLONGA [C. QUEMADO]** (Guate)	1402-04=	3	7/7
T **0800** t	....	?	**HEKLA** (Iceland-S)	1702-07=		
0802	0206	?	**FUJI** (Honshu-Japan)	0803-03=	2?	
0804	....	730*y*	**CHOKAI** (Honshu-Japan)	0803-22=		
0805	*Cont*	....	*CHOKAI (Honshu-Japan)*	0803-22=		
0806	*Cont*	....	*CHOKAI (Honshu-Japan)*	0803-22=		
0806	....	?	**BANDAI** (Honshu-Japan)	0803-16=	3	
? **0807**	....	?	**AKITA-KOMAGA-TAKE** (Japan)	0803-23=		
? **0807**	1101	?	**AKITA-YAKE-YAMA** (Honshu-Japan)	0803-26=		
G **0810** y	....	?	**MONO CRATERS** (US-California)	1203-12-	4	-/8
C **0810** ?	....	?	**MAUNA LOA** (Hawaiian Is)	1302-02=	0	
C **0810** x	....	?	**GALERAS** (Colombia)	1501-08=	2	-/6
C **0810** p	....	?	**PELEE** (W Indies)	1600-12=	**P**	
0812 ?	....	?	**ETNA** (Italy)	0101-06=		8/5
? **0814**	....	?	**ETNA** (Italy)	0101-06=		
0817 g	....	?	**CHOKAI** (Honshu-Japan)	0803-22=		
G **0825** x	....	?	**MERAPI** (Java)	0603-25=		
T **0825** q	....	?	**KIKHPINYCH** (Kamchatka)	1000-18=		
T **0825** q	....	?	**MEDICINE LAKE** (US-California)	1203-02-		7/-
0826	....	?	**FUJI** (Honshu-Japan)	0803-03=	2?	
0829 e	....	?	**CHOKAI** (Honshu-Japan)	0803-22=		
0830	....	?	**FUJI** (Honshu-Japan)	0803-03=	2	
C **0830** ?	....	?	**MAUNA LOA** (Hawaiian Is)	1302-02=	0	
0832	....	?	**KOZU-SHIMA** (Izu Is-Japan)	0804-03=		
0837	....	730*y*?	**KIRISHIMA** (Kyushu-Japan)	0802-09=	3	
0837	0527	?	**NARUGO** (Honshu-Japan)	0803-20=	1	
0838	*Cont*	....	*KIRISHIMA (Kyushu-Japan)*	0802-09=	*2?*	
0838	0802	?	**KOZU-SHIMA** (Izu Is-Japan)	0804-03=	4	
0839	*Cont*	....	*KIRISHIMA (Kyushu-Japan)*	0802-09=	*2?*	
0839	1014	?	**CHOKAI** (Honshu-Japan)	0803-22=		
0840	....	?	**NII-JIMA** (Izu Is-Japan)	0804-02=	3	
C **0840** v	....	?	**FURNAS** (Azores)	1802-10=	4	7/8
0843	....	>3yr	**KIRISHIMA** (Kyushu-Japan)	0802-09=	2?	
0844	*Cont*	....	*KIRISHIMA (Kyushu-Japan)*	0802-09=	*2?*	
0845	*Cont*	....	*KIRISHIMA (Kyushu-Japan)*	0802-09=	*2?*	
0846	*Cont*	....	*KIRISHIMA (Kyushu-Japan)*	0802-09=	*2?*	
0847	*Cont*	....	*KIRISHIMA (Kyushu-Japan)*	0802-09=	*2?*	
0848	*Cont*	....	*KIRISHIMA (Kyushu-Japan)*	0802-09=	*2?*	
C **0850** t	....	?	**BAYUDA VOLC FIELD** (Africa-N)	0205-06-		
C **0850** y	....	?	**YASUR** (Vanuatu-SW Pacific)	0507-10=		
0850 t	....	?	**KRAKATAU** (Indonesia)	0602-00=		
G **0850** ?	....	?	**KRASHENINNIKOV** (Kamchatka)	1000-19=		
T **0850** ?	....	?	**BEZYMIANNY** (Kamchatka)	1000-25=		
C **0850** ?	....	?	**SHASTA** (US-California)	1203-01-		
M **0850** ?	....	?	**KILAUEA** (Hawaiian Is)	1302-01-	0	
T **0850** ?	....	?	**KRAFLA** (Iceland-NE)	1703-08=	0	7/-
C **0850** w	....	?	**UNNAMED** (Azores)	1802-081		
? **0853**	....	?	**HAKU-SAN** (Honshu-Japan)	0803-05=		
? **0854**	0914	?	**OSHIMA** (Izu Is-Japan)	0804-01=		
0856	....	?	**CHOKAI** (Honshu-Japan)	0803-22=		
0857	....	?	**KIRISHIMA** (Kyushu-Japan)	0802-09=	2?	
0857	05	?	**CHOKAI** (Honshu-Japan)	0803-22=		
0858	....	?	**KIRISHIMA** (Kyushu-Japan)	0802-09=	2?	
? **0859**	....	?	**ETNA** (Italy)	0101-06=		
? **0859**	....	?	**HAKU-SAN** (Honshu-Japan)	0803-05=		
D **0860** p	....	?	**Unknown Source**			
? **0860**	04	?	**IBUSUKI [KAIMON]** (Kyushu-Japan)	0802-07=	2?	
? **0860**	....	?	**UNZEN** (Kyushu-Japan)	0802-10=		
T **0860** ?	....	?	**MIYAKE-JIMA** (Izu Is-Japan)	0804-04=	3	
0861	05	?	**CHOKAI** (Honshu-Japan)	0803-22=	3	
0864	1109	?	**ASO** (Kyushu-Japan)	0802-11=	3?	
0864	06	365*p*?	**FUJI** (Honshu-Japan)	0803-03=	3	8/-
0865	*Cont*	....	*FUJI (Honshu-Japan)*	0803-03=	*3*	*8/-*
? **0866**	05	?	**IBUSUKI [KAIMON]** (Kyushu-Japan)	0802-07=	2?	
0867	0620?	?	**ASO** (Kyushu-Japan)	0802-11=	2	
0867	0304	61*m*	**TSURUMI** (Kyushu-Japan)	0802-13=	3	
0870	....	?	**FUJI** (Honshu-Japan)	0803-03=	2?	
0871	0505	?	**CHOKAI** (Honshu-Japan)	0803-22=	3	

START YEAR	M-Dy	Duration	VOLCANO NAME (Subregion)	NUMBER	VEI	Vol L/T
0874	0329	110*m*?	**IBUSUKI [KAIMON]** (Kyushu-Japan)	0802-07=	4	
C **0875** v	....	?	**ALAMAGAN** (Mariana Is-C Pac)	0804-18=		
C **0875** t	....	?	**BRENNISTEINSFJOLL** (Iceland-SW)	1701-04=	2	8/-
G **0880** y	....	?	**LASSEN [CHAOS CRAGS]** (US-Calif)	1203-08-		
? **0882**	11	?	**IBUSUKI [KAIMON]** (Kyushu-Japan)	0802-07=	2?	
0884	....	?	**ZAO** (Honshu-Japan)	0803-19=	2?	
? **0884**	0726	20*m*	**CHOKAI** (Honshu-Japan)	0803-22=		
0885	0829	30*a*	**IBUSUKI [KAIMON]** (Kyushu-Japan)	0802-07=	4	
C **0885** w	....	?	**AUGUSTINE** (Alaska-SW)	1103-01-		
C **0885** v	....	?	**MEDICINE LAKE** (US-California)	1203-02-	3	8/7
0886	0629	?	**OSHIMA** (Izu Is-Japan)	0804-01=	3	8/7
0886	0703	?	**NII-JIMA** (Izu Is-Japan)	0804-02=	4	8/-
0887	....	?	**NIIGATA-YAKE-YAMA** (Honshu-Japan)	0803-09=	4	
0887	....	?	**ASAMA** (Honshu-Japan)	0803-11=	3↑	
? **0900** ?	....	?	**HAKU-SAN** (Honshu-Japan)	0803-05=		
C **0900** t	....	?	**KSUDACH** (Kamchatka)	1000-05=	**5**	-/9
T **0900** ?	....	?	**AVACHINSKY** (Kamchatka)	1000-10=		
C **0900** t	....	?	**KIKHPINYCH** (Kamchatka)	1000-18=	3?	-/8
T **0900** ?	....	?	**TOLBACHIK** (Kamchatka)	1000-24=	4	**9/9**
C **0900** t	....	?	**GLACIER PEAK** (US-Washington)	1201-02-	3?	-/8
T **0900** ?	....	?	**KRISUVIK** (Iceland-SW)	1701-03=	2	8/-
T **0900** ?	....	?	**TORFAJOKULL** (Iceland-S)	1702-05=	3	8/7
T **0900** ?	....	?	**BARDARBUNGA [VEIDIVOTN]**	1703-03=	4	7/**9**
C **0905** u	....	?	**SOUFRIERE ST. VINCENT** (W Indies)	1600-15=		
0905 ?	....	?	**GRIMSVOTN** (Iceland-NE)	1703-01=		
C **0910** ?	....	?	**PELEE** (W Indies)	1600-12=		
C **0910** u	....	?	**BRENNISTEINSFJOLL** (Iceland-SW)	1701-04=	2	7/-
? **0911**	....	?	**ETNA** (Italy)	0101-06=		
0915	0823	9*a*	**CHOKAI** (Honshu-Japan)	0803-22=	3	
0915	0817?	?	**TOWADA** (Honshu-Japan)	0803-271	**5**	8/**9**
A **0915** n	....	?	**KATLA** (Iceland-S)	1702-03=		
C **0920** t	....	?	**HUALALAI** (Hawaiian Is)	1302-04-	0	
T **0920** ?	....	?	**REYKJANESHRYGGUR** (Iceland-SW)	1701-01=		
0925 q	....	?	**VULCANO** (Italy)	0101-05=	3?	
T **0925** q	....	?	**LANGJOKULL** (Iceland-SW)	1701-08=	0	
0932	1119	?	**FUJI** (Honshu-Japan)	0803-03=	2?	
I **0934** b	....	?	**KATLA [ELDGJA]**	1702-03=	4	**9/9**
0936	....	?	**OSHIMA** (Izu Is-Japan)	0804-01=	4	8/8
0937	12	?	**FUJI** (Honshu-Japan)	0803-03=	0	
0939	0515	?	**CHOKAI** (Honshu-Japan)	0803-22=		
C **0940** ?	....	?	**MAUNA LOA** (Hawaiian Is)	1302-02=	0	
0940 ?	....	?	**BARDARBUNGA** (Iceland-NE)	1703-03=		
C **0940** v	....	?	**UNNAMED** (Azores)	1802-081		
0945	....	?	**KIRISHIMA** (Kyushu-Japan)	0802-09=	2?	
0948	1231y	?	**CHOKAI** (Honshu-Japan)	0803-22=		
? **0950** ?	....	?	**BIR BORHUT** (Arabia-S)	0301-18-		
C **0950** ?	....	?	**HARGY** (New Britain-SW Pac)	0502-10=		
0950 t	....	?	**KRAKATAU** (Indonesia)	0602-00=		
T **0950** ?	....	?	**MUTNOVSKY** (Kamchatka)	1000-06=	2	-/6
G **0950** ?	....	?	**KARYMSKY** (Kamchatka)	1000-13=		
T **0950** ?	....	?	**TOLBACHIK** (Kamchatka)	1000-24=	4	8/8
T **0950** ?	....	?	**BEZYMIANNY** (Kamchatka)	1000-25=	4?	-/8
F **0950** *	....	?	**EDZIZA** (Canada)	1200-06-	3	-/7
V **0950** ?	....	?	**JEFFERSON [S CINDER PK]** (US-Ore)	1202-02-		
C **0950** ?	....	?	**CEBORUCO, VOLCAN** (Mexico)	1401-03=	**5**	-/**9**
0950 ?	....	?	**KATLA** (Iceland-S)	1702-03=	1	
C **0950** v	....	?	**SETE CIDADES** (Azores)	1802-08=	2	7/6
? **0952**	03 ?	?	**FUJI** (Honshu-Japan)	0803-03=		
A **0960** j	....	?	**LJOSUFJOLL** (Iceland-W)	1700-03=	2	8/-
0968	1201p	?	**VESUVIUS** (Italy)	0101-02=	3	
C **0970** v	....	?	**MASHU** (Hokkaido-Japan)	0805-081	**5**	
C **0970** ?	....	?	**GUAGUA PICHINCHA** (Ecuador)	1502-02=	**P**	
G **0980** y	....	?	**LASSEN [CHAOS CRAGS]** (US-Calif)	1203-08-		
C **0985** t	....	?	**POPOCATEPETL** (Mexico)	1401-09=		
? **0986**	0902	?	**ASO** (Kyushu-Japan)	0802-11=	2?	
? **0989**	....	?	**NIIGATA-YAKE-YAMA** (Honshu-Japan)	0803-09=		
? **0991**	....	?	**VESUVIUS** (Italy)	0101-02=	3	
? **0993**	09 ?	?	**FUJI** (Honshu-Japan)	0803-03=		
? **0999**	....	?	**VESUVIUS** (Italy)	0101-02=	3	
0999	03	?	**FUJI** (Honshu-Japan)	0803-03=	2?	
? **0999**	....	?	**CHOKAI** (Honshu-Japan)	0803-22=		

1000

START YEAR	M-Dy	Duration	VOLCANO NAME (Subregion)	NUMBER	VEI	Vol L/T
1000 <	....	?	**LUNAYYIR, HARRAT** (Arabia-W)	0301-04-		
T **1000** x	....	?	**RAOUL ISLAND** (Kermadec Is)	0402-03=	4	-/8
1000	....	?	**KELUT** (Java)	0603-28=	3	
T **1000** ?	....	?	**NIPESOTSU-UPEPESANKE** (Japan)	0805-051	2	
T **1000** ?	....	?	**KUTCHARO [ATOSANUPURI]**	0805-08=	0	
T **1000** z	....	?	**ZHUPANOVSKY** (Kamchatka)	1000-12=		
T **1000** ?	....	?	**TOLBACHIK** (Kamchatka)	1000-24=	4	**9**/8
C **1000** t	....	?	**SHEVELUCH** (Kamchatka)	1000-27=	**5**	-/**9**
H **1000** x	....	?	**MONO CRATERS** (US-California)	1203-12-		
C **1000** v	....	?	**COLIMA VOLC COMPLEX** (Mexico)	1401-04=		
T **1000** t	....	?	**POPOCATEPETL** (Mexico)	1401-09=		
T **1000** ?	....	?	**KATLA** (Iceland-S)	1702-03=	4	
1000 ?	0625d	?	**BRENNISTEINSFJOLL** (Iceland-SW)	1701-04=	0	8/-
1002	....	?	**HALLA** (Korea)	1006-04-		
? **1004**	....	?	**ETNA** (Italy)	0101-06=		
1007	....	?	**VESUVIUS** (Italy)	0101-02=	3	
1007	....	?	**HALLA** (Korea)	1006-04-		
? **1017**	....	?	**FUJI** (Honshu-Japan)	0803-03=		
T **1025** q	....	?	**GORELY** (Kamchatka)	1000-07=	3	-/7
M **1030** w	....	?	**BARRIER, THE** (Africa-E)	0202-03=	0	
C **1030** q	....	?	**BILLY MITCHELL** (Bougainville-SW Pac)	0505-011	**5+**	-/**9**
C **1030** u	....	?	**HALEAKALA** (Hawaiian Is)	1302-06-		
1033	0125	?	**FUJI** (Honshu-Japan)	0803-03=	2	
1037	0127	?	**VESUVIUS** (Italy)	0101-02=	3	

START YEAR	M-Dy	Duration	VOLCANO NAME (Subregion)	NUMBER	VEI	Vol L/T
C 1040?	....	?	**MAUNA LOA** (Hawaiian Is)	1302-02=	0	
1042	....	?	**HAKU-SAN** (Honshu-Japan)	0803-05=	3?	
? 1044	....	?	**ETNA** (Italy)	0101-06=		
1049	....	?	**VESUVIUS** (Italy)	0101-02=	1	
M 1050w	....	?	**BARRIER, THE** (Africa-E)	0202-03=	0	
1050w	....	?	**KARTHALA** (Indian O.-W)	0303-01=		
1050t	....	?	**KRAKATAU** (Indonesia)	0602-00=		
G 1050?	....	?	**KARYMSKY** (Kamchatka)	1000-13=		
T 1050?	....	?	**TOLBACHIK** (Kamchatka)	1000-24=	3	**9/7**
G 1050j	....	?	**BAITOUSHAN** (China-E)	1005-07-	**7**	**-/11**
D 1050<	....	?	**MARKAGUNT PLATEAU** (US-Utah)	1207-04-		
C 1050u	....	?	**KILAUEA** (Hawaiian Is)	1302-01-	1?	
C 1050v	....	?	**HUALALAI** (Hawaiian Is)	1302-04-	1	8/-
A 1050t	....	?	**MICHOACAN-GUANAJUATO** (Mexico)	1401-06=		
A 1050y	....	?	**SAN SALVADOR** (El Salvador)	1403-05=		
C 1050u	....	?	**BRAVO, CERRO** (Colombia)	1501-011	4	-/8
C 1050w	....	?	**QUILOTOA** (Ecuador)	1502-06=		
T 1050z	....	?	**HEKLA** (Iceland-S)	1702-07=		
C 1060w	....	?	**HALEAKALA** (Hawaiian Is)	1302-06-		
1060?	....	?	**GRIMSVOTN** (Iceland-NE)	1703-01=		
1063a	....	?	**ETNA** (Italy)	0101-06=		
C 1065x	....	?	**KARKAR** (New Guinea-NE of)	0501-03=		
D 1065	0214v	?	**SUNSET CRATER** (US-Arizona)	1209-02-		
C 1070?	....	?	**MAUNA LOA** (Hawaiian Is)	1302-02=	0	
1073e	....	?	**VESUVIUS** (Italy)	0101-02=	3	
M 1075q	....	?	**MEDICINE LAKE** (US-California)	1203-02-	3?	**9/7**
C 1075u	....	?	**KRISUVIK** (Iceland-SW)	1701-03=	0	7/-
C 1080t	....	?	**ARENAL** (Costa Rica)	1405-033		
1080?	....	?	**BARDARBUNGA** (Iceland-NE)	1703-03=		
1083	0325	?	**FUJI** (Honshu-Japan)	0803-03=	2?	
1085	....	?	**MIYAKE-JIMA** (Izu Is-Japan)	0804-04=	2	
M 1090t	....	?	**BARRIER, THE** (Africa-E)	0202-03=	0	
C 1100r	....	?	**LOLOBAU** (New Britain-SW Pac)	0502-13=	4	-/8
T 1100?	....	?	**AKITA-KOMAGA-TAKE** (Japan)	0803-23=	2	
T 1100?	....	?	**AVACHINSKY** (Kamchatka)	1000-10=		
M 1100?	....	?	**SUNSET CRATER** (US-Arizona)	1209-02-		
C 1100t	....	?	**MOMOTOMBO** (Nicaragua)	1404-09=		
T 1100t	....	?	**KRISUVIK** (Iceland-SW)	1701-03=	1	8/-
1104	1015q	?	**HEKLA** (Iceland-S)	1702-07=	**5**	-/9
1108	0905	41*m*	**ASAMA** (Honshu-Japan)	0803-11=	**5**	-/9
C 1110t	....	?	**SETE CIDADES** (Azores)	1802-08=	2	7/6
1112	0309	?	**KIRISHIMA** (Kyushu-Japan)	0802-09=	2?	
1112	1118	38*e*	**OSHIMA** (Izu Is-Japan)	0804-01=	4	8/8
1113	0227	?	**KIRISHIMA** (Kyushu-Japan)	0802-09=	2?	
M 1115w	....	?	**EMURUANGOGOLAK** (Africa-E)	0202-051	0	
1120w	....	?	**TURFAN** (China-W)	1004-01-		
C 1130?	....	?	**MAUNA LOA** (Hawaiian Is)	1302-02=	0	
1139	0601	8*a*	**VESUVIUS** (Italy)	0101-02=	3	
? 1150	....	?	**VESUVIUS** (Italy)	0101-02=		
C 1150?	....	?	**YASUR** (Vanuatu-SW Pacific)	0507-10=		
1150t	....	?	**KRAKATAU** (Indonesia)	0602-00=		
G 1150?	....	?	**KARYMSKY** (Kamchatka)	1000-13=		
H 1150x	....	?	**MONO LAKE VOLC FIELD** (US-Calif)	1203-11-		
T 1150?	....	?	**HUALALAI** (Hawaiian Is)	1302-04-	0	
M 1150?	....	?	**TENERIFE** (Canary Is)	1803-03-		
1151	....	?	**KRISUVIK** (Iceland-SW)	1701-03=	0	8/-
1154	11	?	**MIYAKE-JIMA** (Izu Is-Japan)	0804-04=	3	
1157	....	?	**ETNA** (Italy)	0101-06=	2?	
1158	0119	?	**HEKLA** (Iceland-S)	1702-07=	4	8/8
1159?	....	?	**BARDARBUNGA** (Iceland-NE)	1703-03=		
1160	....	?	**ETNA** (Italy)	0101-06=	2?	
M 1160w	....	?	**EMURUANGOGOLAK** (Africa-E)	0202-051	0	
1164	....	?	**ETNA** (Italy)	0101-06=	2?	
1167	....	?	**KIRISHIMA** (Kyushu-Japan)	0802-09=	2?	
? 1169	0204	?	**ETNA** (Italy)	0101-06=		
C 1170?	....	?	**MAUNA LOA** (Hawaiian Is)	1302-02=	0	
T 1170?	....	?	**TORFAJOKULL** (Iceland-S)	1702-05=		
C 1170v	....	?	**FURNAS** (Azores)	1802-10=	4	-/8
? 1175	01 ?	?	**KIRISHIMA** (Kyushu-Japan)	0802-09=	2?	
I 1176n	....	?	**Unknown Source** (GISP2, 148; SP, 293 S)			
1177b	....	?	**KATLA** (Iceland-S)	1702-03=	2	
1177	0518	?	**HAKU-SAN** (Honshu-Japan)	0803-05=	3?	
1179<	....	?	**REYKJANESHRYGGUR** (Iceland-SW)	1701-01=	2	
C 1180p	....	?	**OKATAINA [TARAWERA]** (New Zeal)	0401-05=	**5**	**9/9**
T 1180?	....	?	**REPOROA [WAIOTAPU]** (New Zealand)	0401-06-		
M 1180?	....	?	**SUNSET CRATER** (US-Arizona)	1209-02-		
1183	0528	?	**ZAO** (Honshu-Japan)	0803-19=	2?	
1184	0207	?	**KIRISHIMA** (Kyushu-Japan)	0802-09=	2?	
C 1185?	....	?	**PELEE** (W Indies)	1600-12=		
1188	....	?	**KRISUVIK** (Iceland-SW)	1701-03=	0	
1188?	....	?	**BRENNISTEINSFJOLL** (Iceland-SW)	1701-04=	0	8/-
C 1190?	....	?	**MAUNA LOA** (Hawaiian Is)	1302-02=	0	
1194	....	?	**ETNA** (Italy)	0101-06=	2?	
C 1195v	....	?	**DIENG VOLC COMPLEX** (Java)	0603-20=		
1198	....	?	**CAMPI FLEGREI** (Italy)	0101-01=	1	
T 1200?	....	?	**AVACHINSKY** (Kamchatka)	1000-10=		
C 1200u	....	?	**AUGUSTINE** (Alaska-SW)	1103-01-		
T 1200y	....	?	**HAYES** (Alaska-SW)	1103-05-		
C 1200?	....	?	**SHASTA** (US-California)	1203-01-		
T 1200?	....	?	**BRENNISTEINSFJOLL** (Iceland-SW)	1701-04=	2	
T 1200y	....	?	**TERCEIRA** (Azores)	1802-05=		
1206	1204	?	**HEKLA** (Iceland-S)	1702-07=	3	-/7
1211	....	?	**REYKJANES** (Iceland-SW)	1701-02=	2	7/-
1211	0831p	?	**REYKJANESHRYGGUR** (Iceland-SW)	1701-01=	2	
M 1220?	....	?	**SUNSET CRATER** (US-Arizona)	1209-02-		
1222	....	?	**ETNA** (Italy)	0101-06=	2?	
1222	....	?	**UNNAMED** (Syria)	0300-02-	0?	
1222	....	?	**HEKLA** (Iceland-S)	1702-07=	2	-/6
1223	....	?	**REYKJANESHRYGGUR** (Iceland-SW)	1701-01=	2	
1226	0715q	352*w*?	**REYKJANES** (Iceland-SW)	1701-02=	3?	8/-
1227	*Cont*	....	*REYKJANES (Iceland-SW)*	1701-02=	*3?*	*8/-*
1227	10 ?	?	**ZAO** (Honshu-Japan)	0803-19=	3	
1229	....	?	**ASO** (Kyushu-Japan)	0802-11=	2	
M 1230w	....	?	**EMURUANGOGOLAK** (Africa-E)	0202-051	0	
1230	1129	?	**ZAO** (Honshu-Japan)	0803-19=	2?	
1231	....	?	**REYKJANESHRYGGUR** (Iceland-SW)	1701-01=	3	
1235	0125	?	**KIRISHIMA** (Kyushu-Japan)	0802-09=	2?	
1238	....	?	**REYKJANESHRYGGUR** (Iceland-SW)	1701-01=	0	
1239	0208	?	**ASO** (Kyushu-Japan)	0802-11=	2	
1240	....	?	**ASO** (Kyushu-Japan)	0802-11=	2	
C 1240w	....	?	**HUALALAI** (Hawaiian Is)	1302-04-	2	8/-
C 1240t	....	?	**SOLLIPULLI** (Chile-C)	1507-111		
1240	....	?	**REYKJANESHRYGGUR** (Iceland-SW)	1701-01=	0	
1245	....	?	**KATLA** (Iceland-S)	1702-03=	2	
1250t	....	?	**VULCANO** (Italy)	0101-05=		
1250	....	?	**ETNA** (Italy)	0101-06=	2?	
1250t	....	?	**FENTALE** (Ethiopia)	0201-19=		
C 1250v	....	?	**HAKU-SAN** (Honshu-Japan)	0803-05=		
C 1250?	....	?	**SHASTA** (US-California)	1203-01-		
1251	0518	?	**AKAGI** (Honshu-Japan)	0803-13=	3?	
1253	....	?	**SAWAD, HARRA ES-** (Arabia-S)	0301-16-	3	
1256	0605	52*a*?	**RAHAT, HARRAT** (Arabia-W)	0301-07=	3	8/-
I 1259j	....	?	**Unknown Source** (GISP2, 349; SP 1220 S)			
C 1260t	....	?	**ORIZABA, PICO DE** (Mexico)	1401-10=	**P**	
C 1260p	....	?	**PELEE** (W Indies)	1600-12=		
1262	....	?	**KATLA** (Iceland-S)	1702-03=	3	
1265	1201?	?	**ASO** (Kyushu-Japan)	0802-11=	2	
1267	....	?	**OSHIMA** (Izu Is-Japan)	0804-01=	4	8/8
I 1269j	....	?	**Unknown Source** (SP, 242 ppb sulfate) .			
1269	08	?	**ASO** (Kyushu-Japan)	0802-11=	2	
? 1270	....	?	**VESUVIUS** (Italy)	0101-02=		
C 1270u	....	?	**JOCOTITLAN** (Mexico)	1401-061		
1271	0105	?	**ASO** (Kyushu-Japan)	0802-11=	2	
1272	04	?	**ASO** (Kyushu-Japan)	0802-11=	2	
1272	1129	?	**ASO** (Kyushu-Japan)	0802-11=	2	
1273	08	?	**ASO** (Kyushu-Japan)	0802-11=	2	
1274	....	?	**ASO** (Kyushu-Japan)	0802-11=	2	
I 1279j	....	?	**Unknown Source** (SP, 818 ppb sulfate) .			
1281	07	31*p*	**ASO** (Kyushu-Japan)	0802-11=	2	
1281	0703	?	**ASAMA** (Honshu-Japan)	0803-11=	3	
1282<	....	?	**LARDERELLO** (Italy)	0101-001	3?	
1284	....	198*w*?	**ETNA** (Italy)	0101-06=		
1285	*Cont*	....	*ETNA (Italy)*	0101-06=		
1286	0830	?	**ASO** (Kyushu-Japan)	0802-11=	2	
C 1290w	....	?	**BLACK ROCK DESERT** (US-Utah)	1207-05-		
? 1292	....	?	**RAHAT, HARRAT** (Arabia-W)	0301-07=		
M 1300w	....	?	**EMURUANGOGOLAK** (Africa-E)	0202-051	0	
T 1300?	....	?	**MUTNOVSKY** (Kamchatka)	1000-06=	2	-/6
? 1300y	....	?	**GLACIER PEAK** (US-Washington)	1201-02-		
C 1300w	....	?	**HALEAKALA** (Hawaiian Is)	1302-06-		
C 1300?	....	?	**SOUFRIERE GUADELOUPE** (W Indies)	1600-06=	3?	
C 1300t	....	?	**PELEE** (W Indies)	1600-12=	4	-/8
T 1300x	....	?	**KRAFLA** (Iceland-NE)	1703-08=	2?	
1300	0711	369*m*?	**HEKLA** (Iceland-S)	1702-07=	4	8/8
1301	*Cont*	....	*HEKLA (Iceland-S)*	1702-07=	*2*	*8/8*
1302	0118	59*m*	**ISCHIA** (Italy)	0101-03=		
1305	0502	?	**ASO** (Kyushu-Japan)	0802-11=	2	
C 1310?	....	?	**MAUNA LOA** (Hawaiian Is)	1302-02=	0	
1311	....	?	**KELUT** (Java)	0603-28=	3	
1311	0118	?	**KATLA** (Iceland-S)	1702-03=	4?	-/8
C 1315v	....	?	**PINATUBO** (Luzon-Philippines)	0703-083		
1324	0907	?	**ASO** (Kyushu-Japan)	0802-11=	2	
T 1325q	....	?	**GORELY** (Kamchatka)	1000-07=	2?	
C 1325u	....	?	**TSEAX RIVER CONE** (Canada)	1200-10-		
M 1325w	....	?	**KILAUEA** (Hawaiian Is)	1302-01-	0	
C 1325w	....	?	**BRAVO, CERRO** (Colombia)	1501-011	4	-/8
C 1325u	....	?	**SOUFRIERE ST. VINCENT** (W Indies)	1600-15=		
1329	0628	17*a*	**ETNA** (Italy)	0101-06=	2	
1329	0715	20*d*?	**ETNA** (Italy)	0101-06=	3?	7/6
? 1331	....	?	**AZUMA** (Honshu-Japan)	0803-18=		
? 1331	....	731*y*	**ZAO** (Honshu-Japan)	0803-19=	2?	
1331	04	15*m*	**ASO** (Kyushu-Japan)	0802-11=	2	
1331	12	548*p*	**ASO** (Kyushu-Japan)	0802-11=	2	
1332	*Cont*	....	*ASO (Kyushu-Japan)*	0802-11=	*2*	
? 1332	*Cont*	....	*ZAO (Honshu-Japan)*	0803-19=	*2?*	
1332	11	?	**GRIMSVOTN** (Iceland-NE)	1703-01=	2	
1333	*Cont*	....	*ASO (Kyushu-Japan)*	0802-11=	*2*	
? 1333	*Cont*	....	*ZAO (Honshu-Japan)*	0803-19=	*2?*	
1333	....	?	**ETNA** (Italy)	0101-06=	2	
1334	....	?	**KELUT** (Java)	0603-28=	3	
1335	0207	47*a*	**ASO** (Kyushu-Japan)	0802-11=	2	
1338	....	?	**OSHIMA** (Izu Is-Japan)	0804-01=	2	
T 1340?	....	?	**KRISUVIK** (Iceland-SW)	1701-03=	2	
1340	0203	22*a*	**ASO** (Kyushu-Japan)	0802-11=	2	
1341a	....	?	**BRENNISTEINSFJOLL** (Iceland-SW)	1701-04=	2	8/-
? 1341	....	?	**TENERIFE** (Canary Is)	1803-03-		
1341	05	?	**GRIMSVOTN** (Iceland-NE)	1703-01=	2	
1341	0519	?	**HEKLA** (Iceland-S)	1702-07=	3	-/7
1343	....	?	**ASO** (Kyushu-Japan)	0802-11=	2	
G 1345p	....	?	**MONO CRATERS** (US-California)	1203-12-	4	8/8
1345	....	730*y*	**POPOCATEPETL** (Mexico)	1401-09=	2?	

Figure 14. Sicily's Etna volcano, with the world's longest historical eruption record back to 1500 BC, is shown here in an engraving of the 1669 AD flank eruption. Lava flows from the flank vent damaged buildings in Catania while an explosive column also issued from the summit vents beyond. Artist unknown; from the collection of Maurice & Katia Krafft.

START YEAR	M-Dy	Duration	VOLCANO NAME (Subregion)	NUMBER	VEI	Vol L/T
1346	*Cont*	....	*POPOCATEPETL (Mexico)*	1401-09=	*2?*	
1346	....	?	**ASO** (Kyushu-Japan)	0802-11=	2	
1347	*Cont*	....	*POPOCATEPETL (Mexico)*	1401-09=	*2?*	
? **1347**	....	?	**VESUVIUS** (Italy)	0101-02=		
1350	....	?	**ETNA** (Italy)	0101-06=	2	
T **1350**?	....	?	**LENGAI, OL DOINYO** (Africa-E)	0202-12=		
C **1350**?	....	?	**AUCKLAND FIELD** (New Zealand)	0401-02=		**9/-**
H **1350**?	....	?	**DAWSON STRAIT GROUP** (D'Entrecas	0503-06=		
1350t	....	?	**KRAKATAU** (Indonesia)	0602-00=		
A **1350**v	....	?	**LAGUNA VOLC FIELD** (Philippines)	0703-051		
? **1350**?	....	?	**ZAO** (Honshu-Japan)	0803-19=	2?	
C **1350**v	....	?	**PAGAN** (Mariana Is-C Pac)	0804-17=		
T **1350**?	....	?	**NEMO PEAK** (Kurile Is)	0900-32=		
C **1350**?	....	?	**KIKHPINYCH** (Kamchatka)	1000-18=	4	8/8
T **1350**?	....	?	**KRASHENINNIKOV** (Kamchatka)	1000-19=	0	7/-
C **1350**t	....	?	**INYO CRATERS** (US-California)	1203-13-	4	8/8
C **1350**u	....	?	**CHICHON, EL** (Mexico)	1401-12=	**P**	
C **1350**?	....	?	**RUIZ** (Colombia)	1501-02=	4	-/8
T **1350**v	....	?	**JAN MAYEN** (Atl-N-Jan Mayen)	1706-01=		
1354	....	?	**POPOCATEPETL** (Mexico)	1401-09=	2?	
1354?	....	?	**GRIMSVOTN** (Iceland-NE)	1703-01=		
1357c	....	?	**KATLA** (Iceland-S)	1702-03=	4	-/8
C **1360**?	....	?	**MAUNA LOA** (Hawaiian Is)	1302-02=	0	
C **1360**v	....	?	**HALEAKALA** (Hawaiian Is)	1302-06-		
1361	....	?	**NIIGATA-YAKE-YAMA** (Honshu-Japan)	0803-09=	3	
1362	0605d	?	**ORAEFAJOKULL** (Iceland-SE)	1704-01=	**5**	-/9
1363	....	?	**POPOCATEPETL** (Mexico)	1401-09=	2?	
1369	....	?	**ASO** (Kyushu-Japan)	0802-11=	2	
C **1370**?	....	?	**MAUNA LOA** (Hawaiian Is)	1302-02=	0	
C **1370**?	....	?	**PELEE** (W Indies)	1600-12=		
1372	....	?	**KOLBEINSEY RIDGE** (Iceland-N of)	1705-01=	2?	
1375u	....	?	**DIENG VOLC COMPLEX** (Java)	0603-20=	3↑	
1375q	....	?	**LOKON-EMPUNG** (Sulawesi-Indonesia)	0606-10=	3↑	
1375	1220	42*a*	**ASO** (Kyushu-Japan)	0802-11=	2	
1376	....	?	**KELUT** (Java)	0603-28=	3↑	
1376	0620	?	**ASO** (Kyushu-Japan)	0802-11=	2	
1377	0506	?	**ASO** (Kyushu-Japan)	0802-11=	2	
1381	....	?	**KIRISHIMA** (Kyushu-Japan)	0802-09=	2?	
1381?	0806	?	**ETNA** (Italy)	0101-06=	2	7/6
1385	....	?	**KELUT** (Java)	0603-28=	3↑	
1387	0619	?	**ASO** (Kyushu-Japan)	0802-11=	2	
? **1388**	1016	?	**ASO** (Kyushu-Japan)	0802-11=	2	
1389	1201p	213*w*	**HEKLA** (Iceland-S)	1702-07=	3	8/7
1390	*Cont*	....	*HEKLA (Iceland-S)*	1702-07=	*2*	*8/7*
? **1390**	....	?	**ASO** (Kyushu-Japan)	0802-11=	2?	
C **1390**w	....	?	**HOOD** (US-Oregon)	1202-01-		
C **1390**?	....	?	**MAUNA LOA** (Hawaiian Is)	1302-02=	0	
1395	....	?	**KELUT** (Java)	0603-28=	3↑	
C **1395**u	....	?	**SOUFRIERE ST. VINCENT** (W Indies)	1600-15=		
1396c	....	?	**TENERIFE** (Canary Is)	1803-03-		
1397	0217	?	**NASU** (Honshu-Japan)	0803-15=	3	
C **1400**t	....	?	**EGMONT** (New Zealand)	0401-03=		
T **1400**t	....	?	**DAISETSU** (Hokkaido-Japan)	0805-06=	2	
C **1400**?	....	?	**AVACHINSKY** (Kamchatka)	1000-10=		
G **1400**t	....	?	**MALY SEMIACHIK** (Kamchatka)	1000-14=		
C **1400**?	....	?	**SOUFRIERE GUADELOUPE** (W Indies)	1600-06=	**P**	
T **1400**t	....	?	**TERCEIRA** (Azores)	1802-05=		
1400	0715q	?	**DUBBI** (Ethiopia)	0201-10=		
V **1402**?	....	?	**NEMRUT DAGI** (Turkey)	0103-02=		
1404	0211	?	**NASU** (Honshu-Japan)	0803-15=	3	
1408	0224	?	**NASU** (Honshu-Japan)	0803-15=	3	
1408	1108	12*a*?	**ETNA** (Italy)	0101-06=	3	
1410?	....	?	**BARDARBUNGA** (Iceland-NE)	1703-03=		
1410	0305	?	**NASU** (Honshu-Japan)	0803-15=	2	
1411	....	?	**KELUT** (Java)	0603-28=	3↑	
1413	....	?	**BAITOUSHAN** (China-E)	1005-07-		
1415	0521	?	**OSHIMA** (Izu Is-Japan)	0804-01=		
1416	....	?	**KATLA** (Iceland-S)	1702-03=	4?	-/8
1416	0902	104*m*	**OSHIMA** (Izu Is-Japan)	0804-01=	3?	
1421	0514	?	**OSHIMA** (Izu Is-Japan)	0804-01=	2	
? **1422**	....	?	**NISYROS** (Greece)	0102-05=	2	
1422	....	?	**REYKJANESHRYGGUR** (Iceland-SW)	1701-01=	2	
? **1427**	0707	?	**FUJI** (Honshu-Japan)	0803-03=		
? **1427**	0707	?	**ASAMA** (Honshu-Japan)	0803-11=		
1430	....	?	**TENERIFE** (Canary Is)	1803-03-	2	
1434	0510	8*a*	**ASO** (Kyushu-Japan)	0802-11=	2	
1435e	....	?	**LA PALMA** (Canary Is)	1803-01-	2	7/6
1438	0109	40*a*	**ASO** (Kyushu-Japan)	0802-11=	2	
C **1440**?	....	?	**MAUNA LOA** (Hawaiian Is)	1302-02=	0	
G **1440**v	....	?	**SOUFRIERE GUADELOUPE** (W Indies)	1600-06=	**P**	8/-
T **1440**?	....	?	**HEKLA** (Iceland-S)	1702-07=		
1441	....	?	**NEMRUT DAGI** (Turkey)	0103-02=		
1442	08	?	**OSHIMA** (Izu Is-Japan)	0804-01=	4	8/8
1444	....	?	**ETNA** (Italy)	0101-06=	2	
1444?	....	?	**SETE CIDADES** (Azores)	1802-08=	4	-/8
? **1444**	....	?	**TENERIFE** (Canary Is)	1803-03-		
1444	0204	?	**VULCANO** (Italy)	0101-05=	3	

	START YEAR	M-Dy	Duration	VOLCANO NAME (Subregion)	NUMBER	VEI	Vol L/T
	1446	0925	?	ETNA (Italy)	0101-06=	1	
	1447	0921	?	ETNA (Italy)	0101-06=	1	
?	1450t	....	?	KARS PLATEAU (Turkey)	0103-05-	2?	
	1450	....	?	KELUT (Java)	0603-28=	3↑	
G	1450?	....	?	KARYMSKY (Kamchatka)	1000-13=		
C	1450?	....	?	ANIAKCHAK (Alaska Peninsula)	1102-09-	5?	-/9
A	1450t	....	?	ACATENANGO (Guatemala)	1402-08=		
	1451	....	?	KELUT (Java)	0603-28=	3↑	
I	1452j	....	?	KUWAE (Vanuatu-SW Pacific)	0507-07=	6	-/10
	1454n	....	?	MISTI, EL (Peru)	1504-01=	3↑	
C	1460r	....	?	BARANSKY (Kurile Is)	0900-08=		
C	1460t	....	?	KILAUEA (Hawaiian Is)	1302-01-	0	
C	1460u	....	?	HALEAKALA (Hawaiian Is)	1302-06-		
C	1460p	....	?	PELEE (W Indies)	1600-12=		
	1462	....	?	KELUT (Java)	0603-28=	3↑	
	1464	....	?	IRAYA (Luzon Is-N of)	0704-06-		
	1468	....	?	SAKURA-JIMA (Kyushu-Japan)	0802-08=	2	
	1469	....	?	ATITLAN (Guatemala)	1402-06=	3↑	
?	1469	....	?	SUCHITAN VOLC FIELD (Guatemala)	1402-17-		
	1469	1224	?	MIYAKE-JIMA (Izu Is-Japan)	0804-05=	3	
C	1470x	....	?	CHYULU HILLS (Africa-E)	0202-13=		
C	1470w	....	?	KUSATSU-SHIRANE (Honshu-Japan)	0803-12=		
C	1470?	....	?	MAUNA LOA (Hawaiian Is)	1302-02=	0	
	1471	1103	>3yr	SAKURA-JIMA (Kyushu-Japan)	0802-08=	5?	8/9
	1472	*Cont*	....	*SAKURA-JIMA (Kyushu-Japan)*	0802-08=	*2?*	*8/-*
	1473	*03*	....	*SAKURA-JIMA (Kyushu-Japan)*	0802-08=	2	*8/-*
	1473	0516	334*q*	ASO (Kyushu-Japan)	0802-11=	2	
	1474	*Cont*	....	*SAKURA-JIMA (Kyushu-Japan)*	0802-08=	*2?*	*8/-*
	1474	*Cont*	....	*ASO (Kyushu-Japan)*	0802-11=	*2*	
	1475q	....	?	UNNAMED (Arctic Ocean)	1707-01-	0	
	1475	*0924*	....	*SAKURA-JIMA (Kyushu-Japan)*	0802-08=	2	*8/-*
	1476	*1008*	....	*SAKURA-JIMA (Kyushu-Japan)*	0802-08=	3	*8/-*
?	1477	....	?	CHOKAI (Honshu-Japan)	0803-22=		
	1477	03	?	TORFAJOKULL (Iceland-S)	1702-05=	2?	7/-
	1477	03 ?	?	BARDARBUNGA [VEIDIVOTN]	1703-03=	5?	9/9
	1478	0923	?	SAKURA-JIMA (Kyushu-Japan)	0802-08=	2?	
C	1480t	....	?	EGMONT (New Zealand)	0401-03=		
C	1480w	....	?	SOUFRIERE ST. VINCENT (W Indies)	1600-15=		
D	1480	0115u	?	ST. HELENS (US-Washington)	1201-05-	5+	-/9
	1481	....	?	KELUT (Java)	0603-28=	3↑	
D	1482	0115u	?	ST. HELENS (US-Washington)	1201-05-	5	
	1485	0105	?	ASO (Kyushu-Japan)	0802-11=	2	
	1487	1207	?	HACHIJO-JIMA (Izu Is-Japan)	0804-05=	2	
	1488	....	?	POPOCATEPETL (Mexico)	1401-09=	2?	
T	1490?	....	?	KATLA (Iceland-S)	1702-03=	4+	-/8
	1492	0824<	?	TENERIFE (Canary Is)	1803-03-		
	1494?	....	?	ETNA (Italy)	0101-06=	1	
	1500						
	1500	....	?	VESUVIUS (Italy)	0101-02=	2	
C	1500r	....	?	EGMONT (New Zealand)	0401-03=		
T	1500t	....	?	TONGARIRO (New Zealand)	0401-08=		
T	1500x	....	?	ANJUISKY (Russia-NE)	1001-02-	3↑	8/-
C	1500?	....	?	MAUNA LOA (Hawaiian Is)	1302-02=	0	
C	1500?	....	?	COSIGUINA (Nicaragua)	1404-01=		
C	1500v	....	?	PATATES, MORNE (W Indies)	1600-11=		
	1500?	....	?	GRIMSVOTN (Iceland-NE)	1703-01=		
	1500	....	>3yr	FOGO (Cape Verde Is)	1804-01=	1	
	1501	*Cont*	....	*FOGO (Cape Verde Is)*	1804-01=	*1*	
	1502	*Cont*	....	*FOGO (Cape Verde Is)*	1804-01=	*1*	
	1503	*Cont*	....	*FOGO (Cape Verde Is)*	1804-01=	*1*	
	1504	*Cont*	....	*FOGO (Cape Verde Is)*	1804-01=	*1*	
	1504	....	?	POPOCATEPETL (Mexico)	1401-09=	2?	
	1505	*Cont*	....	*FOGO (Cape Verde Is)*	1804-01=	*1*	
	1505?	....	?	ATITLAN (Guatemala)	1402-06=	3?	
	1505	02	?	ASO (Kyushu-Japan)	0802-11=	2	
	1506	*Cont*	....	*FOGO (Cape Verde Is)*	1804-01=	*1*	
	1506	0406	?	ASO (Kyushu-Japan)	0802-11=	2	
	1507	*Cont*	....	*FOGO (Cape Verde Is)*	1804-01=	*1*	
	1508	*Cont*	....	*FOGO (Cape Verde Is)*	1804-01=	*1*	
	1509	*Cont*	....	*FOGO (Cape Verde Is)*	1804-01=	*1*	
?	1509	....	?	POPOCATEPETL (Mexico)	1401-09=		
	1510	*Cont*	....	*FOGO (Cape Verde Is)*	1804-01=	*1*	
?	1510j	....	?	SEULAWAH AGAM (Sumatra)	0601-02=	2	
C	1510t	....	?	KILAUEA (Hawaiian Is)	1302-01-	0	
C	1510?	....	?	MAUNA LOA (Hawaiian Is)	1302-02=	0	
	1510e	....	?	SAN MIGUEL (El Salvador)	1403-10=		
	1510	0725	?	HEKLA (Iceland-S)	1702-07=	4	-/8
	1511	*Cont*	....	*FOGO (Cape Verde Is)*	1804-01=	*1*	
	1511	....	?	FUJI (Honshu-Japan)	0803-03=	2?	
	1512	*Cont*	....	*FOGO (Cape Verde Is)*	1804-01=	*1*	
	1512	....	?	SANGEANG API (Lesser Sunda Is)	0604-05=	3↑	
	1512	....	?	GUNUNGAPI WETAR (Banda Sea)	0605-03=	3↑	
?	1512	....	?	POPOCATEPETL (Mexico)	1401-09=	2?	
	1513	*Cont*	....	*FOGO (Cape Verde Is)*	1804-01=	*1*	
	1514	*Cont*	....	*FOGO (Cape Verde Is)*	1804-01=	*1*	
	1515	*Cont*	....	*FOGO (Cape Verde Is)*	1804-01=	*1*	
	1516	*Cont*	....	*FOGO (Cape Verde Is)*	1804-01=	*1*	
	1517	*Cont*	....	*FOGO (Cape Verde Is)*	1804-01=	*1*	
	1518	*Cont*	....	*FOGO (Cape Verde Is)*	1804-01=	*1*	
	1518	....	?	ASAMA (Honshu-Japan)	0803-11=		
	1518	....	?	POPOCATEPETL (Mexico)	1401-09=	2?	
	1518	02	>3yr	HACHIJO-JIMA (Izu Is-Japan)	0804-05=	2	
	1519	*Cont*	....	*HACHIJO-JIMA (Izu Is-Japan)*	0804-05=	*2*	
	1519	*Cont*	....	*FOGO (Cape Verde Is)*	1804-01=	*1*	
	1519	09	>3yr	POPOCATEPETL (Mexico)	1401-09=	3?	
	1520	*Cont*	....	*HACHIJO-JIMA (Izu Is-Japan)*	0804-05=	*2*	
	1520	*Cont*	....	*POPOCATEPETL (Mexico)*	1401-09=	*2*	
	1520	*Cont*	....	*FOGO (Cape Verde Is)*	1804-01=	*1*	
?	1520	....	?	SANTA ANA (El Salvador)	1403-02=		
	1521	*Cont*	....	*HACHIJO-JIMA (Izu Is-Japan)*	0804-05=	*2*	
	1521	*Cont*	....	*POPOCATEPETL (Mexico)*	1401-09=	*2*	
	1521	*Cont*	....	*FOGO (Cape Verde Is)*	1804-01=	*1*	
	1521	1231y	?	SANTA ANA (El Salvador)	1403-02=	3	
	1522	*Cont*	....	*HACHIJO-JIMA (Izu Is-Japan)*	0804-05=	*2*	
	1522	*Cont*	....	*POPOCATEPETL (Mexico)*	1401-09=	*2*	
	1522	*Cont*	....	*FOGO (Cape Verde Is)*	1804-01=	*1*	
	1522	0215	?	ASO (Kyushu-Japan)	0802-11=	2	
	1523	*Cont*	....	*HACHIJO-JIMA (Izu Is-Japan)*	0804-05=	*2*	
	1523	*Cont*	....	*POPOCATEPETL (Mexico)*	1401-09=	*2*	
	1523	*Cont*	....	*FOGO (Cape Verde Is)*	1804-01=	*1*	
	1524	*Cont*	....	*FOGO (Cape Verde Is)*	1804-01=	*1*	
	1524	....	?	KIRISHIMA (Kyushu-Japan)	0802-09=	2?	
	1524	....	?	MOMOTOMBO (Nicaragua)	1404-09=	3	-/7
	1524	....	>3yr	MASAYA (Nicaragua)	1404-10=	0	
	1524	0430p	77*s*	FUEGO (Guatemala)	1402-09=	2	
	1524	0430p	?	SANTA ANA (El Salvador)	1403-02=	3	
	1525	*Cont*	....	*MASAYA (Nicaragua)*	1404-10=	*0*	
	1525	*Cont*	....	*FOGO (Cape Verde Is)*	1804-01=	*1*	
D	1525q	....	?	ST. HELENS (US-Washington)	1201-05-		
C	1525p	....	?	ARENAL (Costa Rica)	1405-033	4	7/8
	1526	*Cont*	....	*MASAYA (Nicaragua)*	1404-10=	*0*	
	1526	*Cont*	....	*FOGO (Cape Verde Is)*	1804-01=	*1*	
?	1526	....	?	FUEGO (Guatemala)	1402-09=	2	
	1527	*Cont*	....	*MASAYA (Nicaragua)*	1404-10=	*0*	
	1527	*Cont*	....	*FOGO (Cape Verde Is)*	1804-01=	*1*	
	1527	....	?	OSHIMA (Izu Is-Japan)	0804-01=	3	
	1527?	....	?	TELICA (Nicaragua)	1404-04=	3?	
	1527	05	?	ASAMA (Honshu-Japan)	0803-11=	2	
	1528	*Cont*	....	*MASAYA (Nicaragua)*	1404-10=	*0*	
	1528	*Cont*	....	*FOGO (Cape Verde Is)*	1804-01=	*1*	
	1528	....	?	ASAMA (Honshu-Japan)	0803-11=	2	
	1528	....	?	POPOCATEPETL (Mexico)	1401-09=	2?	
	1528a	....	?	SAN CRISTOBAL (Nicaragua)	1404-02=	3	
@	1528	....	?	PILAS, LAS (Nicaragua)	1404-08=		
	1529	*Cont*	....	*MASAYA (Nicaragua)*	1404-10=	*0*	
	1529	*Cont*	....	*FOGO (Cape Verde Is)*	1804-01=	*1*	
	1529	....	?	TELICA (Nicaragua)	1404-04=	3	
?	1529	....	?	RINCON DE LA VIEJA (Costa Rica)	1405-02=		
	1530	*Cont*	....	*MASAYA (Nicaragua)*	1404-10=	*0*	
	1530	*Cont*	....	*FOGO (Cape Verde Is)*	1804-01=	*1*	
	1530	....	?	POPOCATEPETL (Mexico)	1401-09=	2	
	1531	*Cont*	....	*MASAYA (Nicaragua)*	1404-10=	*0*	
	1531	*Cont*	....	*FOGO (Cape Verde Is)*	1804-01=	*1*	
	1531	1231p	?	FUEGO (Guatemala)	1402-09=	2	
	1532	*Cont*	....	*MASAYA (Nicaragua)*	1404-10=	*0*	
	1532	*Cont*	....	*FOGO (Cape Verde Is)*	1804-01=	*1*	
	1532	0114	?	ASAMA (Honshu-Japan)	0803-11=	3	
?	1532	1115	?	COTOPAXI (Ecuador)	1502-05=	3	
	1533	*Cont*	....	*MASAYA (Nicaragua)*	1404-10=	*0*	
	1533	*Cont*	....	*FOGO (Cape Verde Is)*	1804-01=	*1*	
?	1533	....	?	GUAGUA PICHINCHA (Ecuador)	1502-02=	2	
	1533	0717	?	ASO (Kyushu-Japan)	0802-11=	2	
?	1533	10	30*p*	COTOPAXI (Ecuador)	1502-05=	2	
	1534	*Cont*	....	*MASAYA (Nicaragua)*	1404-10=	*0*	
	1534	*Cont*	....	*FOGO (Cape Verde Is)*	1804-01=	*1*	
?	1534	....	?	GUAGUA PICHINCHA (Ecuador)	1502-02=	2	
@	1534	02	?	TUNGURAHUA (Ecuador)	1502-08=	3↑	
	1534	06	30*p*	COTOPAXI (Ecuador)	1502-05=	4	
	1535	*Cont*	....	*MASAYA (Nicaragua)*	1404-10=	*0*	
	1535	*Cont*	....	*FOGO (Cape Verde Is)*	1804-01=	*1*	
	1535	....	?	GALERAS (Colombia)	1501-08=	3↑	
?	1535	....	?	GUAGUA PICHINCHA (Ecuador)	1502-02=	2	
	1535	03	?	MIYAKE-JIMA (Izu Is-Japan)	0804-04=	2	
	1536	*Cont*	....	*MASAYA (Nicaragua)*	1404-10=	*0*	
	1536	*Cont*	....	*FOGO (Cape Verde Is)*	1804-01=	*1*	
	1536	0322	39*a?*	ETNA (Italy)	0101-06=	3	7/5
	1537	*Cont*	....	*MASAYA (Nicaragua)*	1404-10=	*0*	
	1537	*Cont*	....	*FOGO (Cape Verde Is)*	1804-01=	*1*	
	1537	....	?	ORIZABA, PICO DE (Mexico)	1401-10=	0	
	1537	03	121*p*	ETNA (Italy)	0101-06=	2	7/6
	1538	*Cont*	....	*MASAYA (Nicaragua)*	1404-10=	*0*	
	1538	*Cont*	....	*FOGO (Cape Verde Is)*	1804-01=	*1*	
	1538	....	?	GAMALAMA (Halmahera-Indonesia)	0608-06=	3↑	
?	1538	....	?	GUAGUA PICHINCHA (Ecuador)	1502-02=	3↑	
	1538	0929	7	CAMPI FLEGREI (Italy)	0101-01=	3	-/7
	1539	*Cont*	....	*MASAYA (Nicaragua)*	1404-10=	*0*	
	1539	*Cont*	....	*FOGO (Cape Verde Is)*	1804-01=	*1*	
	1539	....	365*y*	POPOCATEPETL (Mexico)	1401-09=	2	
?	1539	....	?	GUAGUA PICHINCHA (Ecuador)	1502-02=	2	
	1540	*Cont*	....	*POPOCATEPETL (Mexico)*	1401-09=	*2*	
	1540	*Cont*	....	*MASAYA (Nicaragua)*	1404-10=	*0*	
	1540	*Cont*	....	*FOGO (Cape Verde Is)*	1804-01=	*1*	
G	1540v	....	?	AUGUSTINE (Alaska-SW)	1103-01-	4?	
C	1540?	....	?	MAUNA LOA (Hawaiian Is)	1302-02=	0	
	1540	07	?	ETNA (Italy)	0101-06=	1	
	1541	*Cont*	....	*MASAYA (Nicaragua)*	1404-10=	*0*	
	1541	*Cont*	....	*FOGO (Cape Verde Is)*	1804-01=	*1*	
@	1541	....	?	FUEGO (Guatemala)	1402-09=		
?	1541	....	?	RUIZ (Colombia)	1501-02=		
	1541	04	?	REVENTADOR (Ecuador)	1502-01=	3↑	
	1541	07 ?	?	ETNA (Italy)	0101-06=	2	
	1542	*Cont*	....	*MASAYA (Nicaragua)*	1404-10=	*0*	
	1542	*Cont*	....	*FOGO (Cape Verde Is)*	1804-01=	*1*	

	START YEAR	M-Dy	Duration	VOLCANO NAME (Subregion)	NUMBER	VEI	Vol L/T
	1542	....	?	CEBORUCO, VOLCAN (Mexico)	1401-03=		
	1542	....	?	POPOCATEPETL (Mexico)	1401-09=	2	
?	1542	....	?	MISTI, EL (Peru)	1504-01=	2	
	1542	0114	?	FUEGO (Guatemala)	1402-09=		
	1542	0429	?	ASO (Kyushu-Japan)	0802-11=	2	
	1543	Cont	....	MASAYA (Nicaragua)	1404-10=	0	
	1543	Cont	....	FOGO (Cape Verde Is)	1804-01=	1	
	1543	....	?	KAITOKU SEAMOUNT (Volcano Is)	0804-10=	0	
	1544	Cont	....	MASAYA (Nicaragua)	1404-10=	0	
	1544	Cont	....	FOGO (Cape Verde Is)	1804-01=	1	
	1545	Cont	....	FOGO (Cape Verde Is)	1804-01=	1	
	1545	....	>3yr	ORIZABA, PICO DE (Mexico)	1401-10=	2	8/-
	1546	Cont	....	ORIZABA, PICO DE (Mexico)	1401-10=	2?	8/-
	1546	Cont	....	FOGO (Cape Verde Is)	1804-01=	1	
	1547	Cont	....	ORIZABA, PICO DE (Mexico)	1401-10=	2?	8/-
	1547	Cont	....	FOGO (Cape Verde Is)	1804-01=	1	
	1547	0304	225m?	HAKU-SAN (Honshu-Japan)	0803-05=	3	
	1548	Cont	....	ORIZABA, PICO DE (Mexico)	1401-10=	2?	8/-
	1548	Cont	....	FOGO (Cape Verde Is)	1804-01=	1	
	1548	....	?	MERAPI (Java)	0603-25=	3↑	
	1548	....	?	KELUT (Java)	0603-28=	3↑	
	1548	....	?	HAKU-SAN (Honshu-Japan)	0803-05=	3?	
	1548	....	?	POPOCATEPETL (Mexico)	1401-09=	2	
	1549	Cont	....	ORIZABA, PICO DE (Mexico)	1401-10=	2?	8/-
	1549	Cont	....	FOGO (Cape Verde Is)	1804-01=	1	
	1550	Cont	....	ORIZABA, PICO DE (Mexico)	1401-10=	2?	8/-
	1550	Cont	....	FOGO (Cape Verde Is)	1804-01=	1	
	1550	....	?	VULCANO (Italy)	0101-05=	3	
G	1550v	....	?	NYAMURAGIRA (Africa-C)	0203-02=		
C	1550v	....	?	OKU VOLC FIELD [L. NYOS] (Africa)	0204-003	3	-/7
	1550t	....	?	KRAKATAU (Indonesia)	0602-00=		
	1550<	....	?	MAKIAN (Halmahera-Indonesia)	0608-07=	3↑	
C	1550?	....	?	AVACHINSKY (Kamchatka)	1000-10=		
G	1550?	....	?	MALY SEMIACHIK (Kamchatka)	1000-14=	4	-/8
T	1550?	....	?	KIKHPINYCH (Kamchatka)	1000-18=		7/-
T	1550?	....	?	KRASHENINNIKOV (Kamchatka)	1000-19=		7/-
T	1550?	....	?	TOLBACHIK (Kamchatka)	1000-24=	2	8/6
T	1550t	....	?	REDOUBT (Alaska-SW)	1103-03-		
D	1550?	....	?	WELLS GRAY-CLEARWATER	1200-15-		
T	1550y	....	?	MONO LAKE VOLC FIELD (US-Calif)	1203-11-		
	1550?	....	?	BARU (Panama)	1406-01-		
	1550t	....	?	UBINAS (Peru)	1504-02=	3?	
C	1550t	....	?	SOUFRIERE ST. VINCENT (W Indies)	1600-15=		
	1550	1120n	?	DUKONO (Halmahera-Indonesia)	0608-01=	3	-/8
	1551	Cont	....	ORIZABA, PICO DE (Mexico)	1401-10=	2?	8/-
	1551	Cont	....	FOGO (Cape Verde Is)	1804-01=	1	
	1551	....	273w>	FUEGO (Guatemala)	1402-09=	2	
	1551	....	?	MASAYA (Nicaragua)	1404-10=	0	
	1552	Cont	....	ORIZABA, PICO DE (Mexico)	1401-10=	2?	8/-
	1552	Cont	....	FUEGO (Guatemala)	1402-09=	2	
	1552	Cont	....	FOGO (Cape Verde Is)	1804-01=	1	
	1552	1007	8a	OSHIMA (Izu Is-Japan)	0804-01=	4	8/8
	1553	Cont	....	ORIZABA, PICO DE (Mexico)	1401-10=	2?	8/-
	1553	Cont	....	FOGO (Cape Verde Is)	1804-01=	1	
	1554	Cont	....	ORIZABA, PICO DE (Mexico)	1401-10=	2?	8/-
	1554	Cont	....	FOGO (Cape Verde Is)	1804-01=	1	
?	1554	....	?	ETNA (Italy)	0101-06=	2	
	1554	....	?	MERAPI (Java)	0603-25=	3↑	
	1554	....	?	KIRISHIMA (Kyushu-Japan)	0802-09=	2?	
	1554	04	808w	HAKU-SAN (Honshu-Japan)	0803-05=	3	
	1554	05	40b	HEKLA [RAUDUBJALLAR] (Iceland-S)	1702-07=	2?	8/-
	1555	Cont	....	HAKU-SAN (Honshu-Japan)	0803-05=	2	
	1555	Cont	....	ORIZABA, PICO DE (Mexico)	1401-10=	2?	8/-
	1555	Cont	....	FOGO (Cape Verde Is)	1804-01=	1	
	1555e	....	?	HUILA (Colombia)	1501-05=		
	1556	Cont	....	HAKU-SAN (Honshu-Japan)	0803-05=	2	
	1556	Cont	....	ORIZABA, PICO DE (Mexico)	1401-10=	2?	8/-
	1556	Cont	....	FOGO (Cape Verde Is)	1804-01=	1	
	1557	Cont	....	ORIZABA, PICO DE (Mexico)	1401-10=	2?	8/-
	1557	Cont	....	FOGO (Cape Verde Is)	1804-01=	1	
?	1557	....	?	TUNGURAHUA (Ecuador)	1502-08=	2	
?	1557	0115	?	FUEGO (Guatemala)	1402-09=		
	1558	Cont	....	ORIZABA, PICO DE (Mexico)	1401-10=	2?	8/-
	1558	Cont	....	FOGO (Cape Verde Is)	1804-01=	1	
	1558<	....	>3yr	STROMBOLI (Italy)	0101-04=	2	
	1558	....	365y	ASO (Kyushu-Japan)	0802-11=	2	
	1558	....	?	VILLARRICA (Chile-C)	1507-12=	2	
?	1558<	....	?	JAN MAYEN (Atl-N-Jan Mayen)	1706-01=		
	1559	Cont	....	STROMBOLI (Italy)	0101-04=	1?	
	1559	Cont	....	ASO (Kyushu-Japan)	0802-11=	2	
	1559	Cont	....	ORIZABA, PICO DE (Mexico)	1401-10=	2?	8/-
	1559	Cont	....	FOGO (Cape Verde Is)	1804-01=	1	
?	1559	0116	?	FUEGO (Guatemala)	1402-09=		
	1560	Cont	....	STROMBOLI (Italy)	0101-04=	1?	
	1560	Cont	....	ORIZABA, PICO DE (Mexico)	1401-10=	2?	8/-
	1560	Cont	....	FOGO (Cape Verde Is)	1804-01=	1	
	1560	....	?	MERBABU (Java)	0603-24=		
	1560	....	?	MERAPI (Java)	0603-25=	3↑	
	1560	....	?	FUJI (Honshu-Japan)	0803-03=	2?	
?	1560	....	?	CHOKAI (Honshu-Japan)	0803-22=		
	1560	....	?	COLIMA VOLC COMPLEX (Mexico)	1401-04=	2	
?	1560	....	?	GUAGUA PICHINCHA (Ecuador)	1502-02=	2	
	1561	Cont	....	STROMBOLI (Italy)	0101-04=	1?	
	1561	Cont	....	ORIZABA, PICO DE (Mexico)	1401-10=	2?	8/-
	1561	Cont	....	FOGO (Cape Verde Is)	1804-01=	1	
	1561	1231y	?	GAMALAMA (Halmahera-Indonesia)	0608-06=	2	
	1562	Cont	....	STROMBOLI (Italy)	0101-04=	1?	
	1562	Cont	....	ORIZABA, PICO DE (Mexico)	1401-10=	2?	8/-
	1562	Cont	....	FOGO (Cape Verde Is)	1804-01=	1	
	1562	....	?	VILLARRICA (Chile-C)	1507-12=	2	
	1562	03	?	ASO (Kyushu-Japan)	0802-11=	2	
	1562	0921?	648w?	PICO (Azores)	1802-02=	2	
	1563	Cont	....	STROMBOLI (Italy)	0101-04=	1?	
	1563	Cont	....	ORIZABA, PICO DE (Mexico)	1401-10=	2?	8/-
	1563	Cont	....	PICO (Azores)	1802-02=	2	
	1563	Cont	....	FOGO (Cape Verde Is)	1804-01=	1	
?	1563	0503	?	ASO (Kyushu-Japan)	0802-11=	2?	
	1563	0628	28e	AGUA DE PAU (Azores)	1802-09=	4	6/8
	1564	Cont	....	STROMBOLI (Italy)	0101-04=	1?	
	1564	Cont	....	ORIZABA, PICO DE (Mexico)	1401-10=	2?	8/-
	1564	Cont	....	PICO (Azores)	1802-02=	2	
	1564	Cont	....	FOGO (Cape Verde Is)	1804-01=	1	
	1564	0210	2a	AGUA DE PAU (Azores)	1802-09=	2	
	1564	12	?	ASO (Kyushu-Japan)	0802-11=	2	
	1564	1231y	?	GAMKONORA (Halmahera-Indonesia)	0608-04=	3↑	
	1565	Cont	....	STROMBOLI (Italy)	0101-04=	1?	
	1565	Cont	....	ORIZABA, PICO DE (Mexico)	1401-10=	2?	8/-
	1565	Cont	....	FOGO (Cape Verde Is)	1804-01=	1	
?	1565	....	?	FUEGO (Guatemala)	1402-09=	2	
	1565	08 ?	?	PACAYA (Guatemala)	1402-11=	3	
	1566	Cont	....	STROMBOLI (Italy)	0101-04=	1?	
	1566	Cont	....	FOGO (Cape Verde Is)	1804-01=	1	
	1566	....	?	ORIZABA, PICO DE (Mexico)	1401-10=	2	
	1566	0506	?	KIRISHIMA (Kyushu-Japan)	0802-09=	2?	
	1566	1017	30a	GUAGUA PICHINCHA (Ecuador)	1502-02=	3↑	
	1566	1031	?	KIRISHIMA (Kyushu-Japan)	0802-09=	3	
	1566	1101	?	ETNA (Italy)	0101-06=	2	7/5
	1567	Cont	....	STROMBOLI (Italy)	0101-04=	1?	
	1567	Cont	....	FOGO (Cape Verde Is)	1804-01=	1	
	1567	....	?	CEBORUCO, VOLCAN (Mexico)	1401-03=		
	1568	Cont	....	STROMBOLI (Italy)	0101-04=	1?	
	1568	Cont	....	FOGO (Cape Verde Is)	1804-01=	1	
	1568	....	?	SAVO (Solomon Is-SW Pac)	0505-07=	3	
	1569	Cont	....	STROMBOLI (Italy)	0101-04=	1?	
	1569	Cont	....	FOGO (Cape Verde Is)	1804-01=	1	
	1569	....	?	ORIZABA, PICO DE (Mexico)	1401-10=	2	
	1570	Cont	....	STROMBOLI (Italy)	0101-04=	1?	
	1570	Cont	....	FOGO (Cape Verde Is)	1804-01=	1	
	1570	....	>3yr	SANTORINI (Greece)	0102-04=	3	7/-
?	1570	....	?	MERBABU (Java)	0603-24=		
C	1570r	....	?	BARANSKY (Kurile Is)	0900-08=		
	1570?	....	?	SANTA ANA (El Salvador)	1403-02=		
	1570	....	?	MASAYA (Nicaragua)	1404-10=	0	
?	1570	....	?	MOMBACHO (Nicaragua)	1404-11=		
	1570	....	?	RUIZ (Colombia)	1501-02=		
	1571	Cont	....	STROMBOLI (Italy)	0101-04=	1?	
	1571	Cont	....	SANTORINI (Greece)	0102-04=	2?	7/-
	1571	Cont	....	FOGO (Cape Verde Is)	1804-01=	1	
	1571	....	?	POPOCATEPETL (Mexico)	1401-09=	2	
?	1571	1225	?	FUEGO (Guatemala)	1402-09=		
	1572	Cont	....	STROMBOLI (Italy)	0101-04=	1?	
	1572	Cont	....	SANTORINI (Greece)	0102-04=	2?	7/-
	1572	Cont	....	FOGO (Cape Verde Is)	1804-01=	1	
	1572	....	?	TAAL (Luzon-Philippines)	0703-07=	3	
	1572b	....	?	SAN SALVADOR (El Salvador)	1403-05=	3?	
	1573	Cont	....	STROMBOLI (Italy)	0101-04=	1?	
	1573	Cont	....	SANTORINI (Greece)	0102-04=	2?	7/-
	1573	Cont	....	FOGO (Cape Verde Is)	1804-01=	1	
	1574	Cont	....	STROMBOLI (Italy)	0101-04=	1?	
	1574	Cont	....	FOGO (Cape Verde Is)	1804-01=	1	
	1574	02	?	KIRISHIMA (Kyushu-Japan)	0802-09=	2?	
	1575	Cont	....	STROMBOLI (Italy)	0101-04=	1?	
	1575	Cont	....	FOGO (Cape Verde Is)	1804-01=	1	
?	1575	....	?	FUEGO (Guatemala)	1402-09=	2	
?	1575	....	?	OSORNO (Chile-S)	1508-01=		
	1575	0908	?	GUAGUA PICHINCHA (Ecuador)	1502-02=	2	
	1576	Cont	....	STROMBOLI (Italy)	0101-04=	1?	
	1576	Cont	....	FOGO (Cape Verde Is)	1804-01=	1	
	1576	....	730y	KIRISHIMA (Kyushu-Japan)	0802-09=	2?	
	1576	....	?	COLIMA VOLC COMPLEX (Mexico)	1401-04=	3	
?	1576	....	?	FUEGO (Guatemala)	1402-09=	2	
	1576	....	?	SANTA ANA (El Salvador)	1403-02=	3	
	1576	1115	?	ASO (Kyushu-Japan)	0802-11=	2	
	1577	Cont	....	STROMBOLI (Italy)	0101-04=	1?	
	1577	Cont	....	KIRISHIMA (Kyushu-Japan)	0802-09=	2	
	1577	Cont	....	FOGO (Cape Verde Is)	1804-01=	1	
?	1577	....	?	FUEGO (Guatemala)	1402-09=	2	
?	1577	....	?	GUAGUA PICHINCHA (Ecuador)	1502-02=	2	
	1578	Cont	....	STROMBOLI (Italy)	0101-04=	1?	
	1578	Cont	....	KIRISHIMA (Kyushu-Japan)	0802-09=	2	
	1578	Cont	....	FOGO (Cape Verde Is)	1804-01=	1	
	1578	02	?	MOMOTOMBO (Nicaragua)	1404-09=	2	
	1579	Cont	....	STROMBOLI (Italy)	0101-04=	1?	
	1579	Cont	....	FOGO (Cape Verde Is)	1804-01=	1	
	1579?	....	913w?	ATITLAN (Guatemala)	1402-06=	2	
	1579	0909?	296w?	ETNA (Italy)	0101-06=		
	1579	0927a	?	HAKU-SAN (Honshu-Japan)	0803-05=	3	
	1580	Cont	....	STROMBOLI (Italy)	0101-04=	1?	
	1580	Cont	....	ETNA (Italy)	0101-06=		
	1580	Cont	....	ATITLAN (Guatemala)	1402-06=	2	
	1580	Cont	....	FOGO (Cape Verde Is)	1804-01=	1	
C	1580p	....	?	BILLY MITCHELL (Bougainville-SW Pac)	0505-011	6	-/10
C	1580t	....	?	PAGAN (Mariana Is-C Pac)	0804-17=		
	1580	....	?	POPOCATEPETL (Mexico)	1401-09=	2?	
?	1580	....	?	GUAGUA PICHINCHA (Ecuador)	1502-02=	2	

START YEAR	M-Dy	Duration	VOLCANO NAME (Subregion)	NUMBER	VEI	Vol L/T
1580	0501	121a?	SAN JORGE (Azores)	1802-03=	3?	
1580	0811	?	KATLA (Iceland-S)	1702-03=	3	-/7
1580	1207	<1	GALERAS (Colombia)	1501-08=	4	
1581	Cont	....	STROMBOLI (Italy)	0101-04=	1?	
1581	Cont	....	ATITLAN (Guatemala)	1402-06=	2	
1581	Cont	....	FOGO (Cape Verde Is)	1804-01=	1	
1581	1205	41a	FUEGO (Guatemala)	1402-09=	2	-/8
1581	1226	....	FUEGO (Guatemala)	1402-09=	4?	-/8
1582	Cont	....	STROMBOLI (Italy)	0101-04=	1?	
1582	Cont	....	FOGO (Cape Verde Is)	1804-01=	1	
1582	....	?	HAKU-SAN (Honshu-Japan)	0803-05=	2	
1582	0114	....	FUEGO (Guatemala)	1402-09=	4?	-/8
1582	0217	?	ASO (Kyushu-Japan)	0802-11=	2	
1582	0605	>3yr	GUAGUA PICHINCHA (Ecuador)	1502-02=	2	
1583	Cont	....	STROMBOLI (Italy)	0101-04=	1?	
1583	Cont	....	GUAGUA PICHINCHA (Ecuador)	1502-02=	2	
1583	Cont	....	FOGO (Cape Verde Is)	1804-01=	1	
1583	0715q	?	REYKJANESHRYGGUR (Iceland-SW)	1701-01=	2?	
1583	1214	?	ASO (Kyushu-Japan)	0802-11=	2	
1584	Cont	....	STROMBOLI (Italy)	0101-04=	1?	
1584	Cont	....	GUAGUA PICHINCHA (Ecuador)	1502-02=	2	
1584	Cont	....	FOGO (Cape Verde Is)	1804-01=	1	
1584	....	?	MERAPI (Java)	0603-25=	3↑	
1584	08	?	ASO (Kyushu-Japan)	0802-11=	2	
1585	Cont	....	STROMBOLI (Italy)	0101-04=	1?	
1585	Cont	....	GUAGUA PICHINCHA (Ecuador)	1502-02=	2	
1585	Cont	....	FOGO (Cape Verde Is)	1804-01=	1	
1585	0110	?	COLIMA VOLC COMPLEX (Mexico)	1401-04=	4	
1585	0115	181m	FUEGO (Guatemala)	1402-09=	2	
1585	0519	83a	LA PALMA (Canary Is)	1803-01-	2	
1585	11 ?	?	KIRISHIMA (Kyushu-Japan)	0802-09=	2?	
1585	12 ?	?	YAKE-DAKE (Honshu-Japan)	0803-07=	3↑	
1586	Cont	....	STROMBOLI (Italy)	0101-04=	1?	
1586	Cont	....	GUAGUA PICHINCHA (Ecuador)	1502-02=	2	
1586	Cont	....	FOGO (Cape Verde Is)	1804-01=	1	
1586	....	?	KELUT (Java)	0603-28=	5?	-/9
? 1586	....	?	RAUNG (Java)	0603-34=	3	
? 1586	....	?	MASAYA (Nicaragua)	1404-10=	0	
1586	0417	?	BANDA API (Banda Sea)	0605-09=	3↑	
1586	0603b	196m	FUEGO (Guatemala)	1402-09=	2	
1587	Cont	....	STROMBOLI (Italy)	0101-04=	1?	
1587	Cont	....	FOGO (Cape Verde Is)	1804-01=	1	
1587	....	?	MERAPI (Java)	0603-25=	3↑	
1587	....	?	ASO (Kyushu-Japan)	0802-11=	2	
1587	0524	?	KIRISHIMA (Kyushu-Japan)	0802-09=	2?	
1587	0724	?	FUEGO (Guatemala)	1402-09=	2	
1587	0903	....	GUAGUA PICHINCHA (Ecuador)	1502-02=	3	
1588	Cont	....	STROMBOLI (Italy)	0101-04=	1?	
1588	Cont	....	GUAGUA PICHINCHA (Ecuador)	1502-02=	2	
1588	Cont	....	FOGO (Cape Verde Is)	1804-01=	1	
1588	....	?	OSHIMA (Izu Is-Japan)	0804-01=	3	
1588	0407	?	KIRISHIMA (Kyushu-Japan)	0802-09=	2?	
1589	Cont	....	STROMBOLI (Italy)	0101-04=	1?	
1589	Cont	....	GUAGUA PICHINCHA (Ecuador)	1502-02=	2	
1589	Cont	....	FOGO (Cape Verde Is)	1804-01=	1	
1590	Cont	....	STROMBOLI (Italy)	0101-04=	1?	
1590	Cont	....	GUAGUA PICHINCHA (Ecuador)	1502-02=	2	
1590	Cont	....	FOGO (Cape Verde Is)	1804-01=	1	
C 1590t	....	?	AOBA (Vanuatu-SW Pacific)	0507-03=		
C 1590t	....	?	ISKUT-UNUK RIVER CONES (Canada)	1200-09-		
1590	....	?	POPOCATEPETL (Mexico)	1401-09=	2?	
1590	....	?	REVENTADOR (Ecuador)	1502-01=	3↑	
@ 1590?	....	?	ANTISANA (Ecuador)	1502-03=	2?	
1590	0114	?	COLIMA VOLC COMPLEX (Mexico)	1401-04=	3	
1590	0415q	?	ASAMA (Honshu-Japan)	0803-11=	2?	
1591	Cont	....	STROMBOLI (Italy)	0101-04=	1?	
1591	Cont	....	GUAGUA PICHINCHA (Ecuador)	1502-02=	2	
1591	Cont	....	FOGO (Cape Verde Is)	1804-01=	1	
1591	....	?	TAAL (Luzon-Philippines)	0703-07=	3↑	
1591	0415q	228q?	ASAMA (Honshu-Japan)	0803-11=	2?	
1591	1129	....	ASAMA (Honshu-Japan)	0803-11=	3	
1592	Cont	....	STROMBOLI (Italy)	0101-04=	1?	
1592	Cont	....	GUAGUA PICHINCHA (Ecuador)	1502-02=	2	
1592	Cont	....	FOGO (Cape Verde Is)	1804-01=	1	
1592	....	?	ASO (Kyushu-Japan)	0802-11=	2	
1592	....	730y	POPOCATEPETL (Mexico)	1401-09=	2	
1593	Cont	....	STROMBOLI (Italy)	0101-04=	1?	
1593	Cont	....	POPOCATEPETL (Mexico)	1401-09=	2	
1593	Cont	....	GUAGUA PICHINCHA (Ecuador)	1502-02=	2	
1593	Cont	....	FOGO (Cape Verde Is)	1804-01=	1	
1593	....	?	RAUNG (Java)	0603-34=	5?	-/9
1594	Cont	....	STROMBOLI (Italy)	0101-04=	1?	
1594	Cont	....	POPOCATEPETL (Mexico)	1401-09=	2	
1594	Cont	....	GUAGUA PICHINCHA (Ecuador)	1502-02=	2	
1594	Cont	....	FOGO (Cape Verde Is)	1804-01=	1	
1594	....	?	VILLARRICA (Chile-C)	1507-12=	1	
1595	Cont	....	STROMBOLI (Italy)	0101-04=	1?	
1595	Cont	....	GUAGUA PICHINCHA (Ecuador)	1502-02=	2	
1595	Cont	....	FOGO (Cape Verde Is)	1804-01=	1	
1595?	....	?	ETNA (Italy)	0101-06=	3	8/7
1595	....	?	TINAKULA (Santa Cruz Is-SW Pac)	0506-01=	3↑	
1595	....	?	KIRISHIMA (Kyushu-Japan)	0802-09=	2?	
1595	0309<	?	RUIZ (Colombia)	1501-02=	2?	-/8
1595	0312	....	RUIZ (Colombia)	1501-02=	4	-/8
? 1595	0601	?	ASAMA (Honshu-Japan)	0803-11=		
1595	1122	?	MIYAKE-JIMA (Izu Is-Japan)	0804-04=	2	
1596	Cont	....	STROMBOLI (Italy)	0101-04=	1?	
1596	Cont	....	GUAGUA PICHINCHA (Ecuador)	1502-02=	2	
1596	Cont	....	FOGO (Cape Verde Is)	1804-01=	1	
? 1596	....	?	KIRISHIMA (Kyushu-Japan)	0802-09=	2?	
1596	0501	4a	ASAMA (Honshu-Japan)	0803-11=	2?	
1596	0819	?	ASAMA (Honshu-Japan)	0803-11=	2	
1597	Cont	....	STROMBOLI (Italy)	0101-04=	1?	
1597	Cont	....	GUAGUA PICHINCHA (Ecuador)	1502-02=	2	
1597	Cont	....	FOGO (Cape Verde Is)	1804-01=	1	
1597	01	?	IWAKI (Honshu-Japan)	0803-27=	2	
1597	0103	164m>	HEKLA (Iceland-S)	1702-07=	4	-/8
1597	0117	16a>	RAUNG (Java)	0603-34=	3	
1597	0417	?	ASAMA (Honshu-Japan)	0803-11=	2	
1597	0613	?	IWAKI (Honshu-Japan)	0803-27=	2	
1597	1006	?	BAITOUSHAN (China-E)	1005-07-		
1597	1008	?	XIANJINDAO (Korea)	1006-01-		
1598	Cont	....	STROMBOLI (Italy)	0101-04=	1?	
1598	Cont	....	GUAGUA PICHINCHA (Ecuador)	1502-02=	2	
1598	Cont	....	FOGO (Cape Verde Is)	1804-01=	1	
1598	....	>3yr	BANDA API (Banda Sea)	0605-09=	3	
1598	....	730y	KIRISHIMA (Kyushu-Japan)	0802-09=	2?	
1598	0513	?	ASAMA (Honshu-Japan)	0803-11=	2	
1598	1107	?	GRIMSVOTN (Iceland-NE)	1703-01=	3?	-/8
1598	12	199w	ASO (Kyushu-Japan)	0802-11=	2	
1599	Cont	....	STROMBOLI (Italy)	0101-04=	1?	
1599	Cont	....	BANDA API (Banda Sea)	0605-09=	2	
1599	Cont	....	KIRISHIMA (Kyushu-Japan)	0802-09=	2	
1599	Cont	....	ASO (Kyushu-Japan)	0802-11=	2	
1599	Cont	....	FOGO (Cape Verde Is)	1804-01=	1	
? 1599	....	?	MISTI, EL (Peru)	1504-01=	2	

1600

START YEAR	M-Dy	Duration	VOLCANO NAME (Subregion)	NUMBER	VEI	Vol L/T
1600	Cont	....	STROMBOLI (Italy)	0101-04=	1?	
1600	Cont	....	BANDA API (Banda Sea)	0605-09=	2	
1600	Cont	....	KIRISHIMA (Kyushu-Japan)	0802-09=	2	
1600	Cont	....	FOGO (Cape Verde Is)	1804-01=	1	
T 1600?	....	?	SUWANOSE-JIMA (Ryukyu Is)	0802-03=	4+	
1600	....	365y	OSHIMA (Izu Is-Japan)	0804-01=	2	
T 1600t	....	?	REDOUBT (Alaska-SW)	1103-03-		
1600	....	?	UBINAS (Peru)	1504-02=	2?	
1600	0114	14a	ASAMA (Honshu-Japan)	0803-11=	3?	
1600	0219	239m?	HUAYNAPUTINA (Peru)	1504-03=	6?	-/10
1600	0222	?	IWAKI (Honshu-Japan)	0803-27=	2	
1600	0723	2a	IWAKI (Honshu-Japan)	0803-27=	2	
1601	Cont	....	STROMBOLI (Italy)	0101-04=	1?	
1601	Cont	....	BANDA API (Banda Sea)	0605-09=	2	
1601	Cont	....	OSHIMA (Izu Is-Japan)	0804-01=	2	
1601	Cont	....	FOGO (Cape Verde Is)	1804-01=	1	
1602	Cont	....	STROMBOLI (Italy)	0101-04=	1?	
1602	Cont	....	BANDA API (Banda Sea)	0605-09=	2	
1602	Cont	....	FOGO (Cape Verde Is)	1804-01=	1	
1603	Cont	....	STROMBOLI (Italy)	0101-04=	1?	
1603	Cont	....	FOGO (Cape Verde Is)	1804-01=	1	
1603	07	>3yr	ETNA (Italy)	0101-06=	2	
@ 1603	1031	15m	GRIMSVOTN (Iceland-NE)	1703-01=	2	
1604	Cont	....	STROMBOLI (Italy)	0101-04=	1?	
1604	Cont	....	ETNA (Italy)	0101-06=	2	
1604	Cont	....	FOGO (Cape Verde Is)	1804-01=	1	
1604	....	?	ASAMA (Honshu-Japan)	0803-11=	2	
1604	0207	?	IWAKI (Honshu-Japan)	0803-27=	3?	
1605	Cont	....	STROMBOLI (Italy)	0101-04=	1?	
1605	Cont	....	ETNA (Italy)	0101-06=	2	
1605	Cont	....	FOGO (Cape Verde Is)	1804-01=	1	
1605	....	365y	MOMOTOMBO (Nicaragua)	1404-09=	4	-/8
1605	0410	?	IWAKI (Honshu-Japan)	0803-27=	2?	
1605	05	?	GAMALAMA (Halmahera-Indonesia)	0608-06=	2	
1605	1027	?	HACHIJO-JIMA (Izu Is-Japan)	0804-05=	2	
1605	12	?	ASAMA (Honshu-Japan)	0803-11=	2	
1606	Cont	....	STROMBOLI (Italy)	0101-04=	1?	
1606	Cont	....	ETNA (Italy)	0101-06=	2	
1606	Cont	....	MOMOTOMBO (Nicaragua)	1404-09=	3?	-/8
1606	Cont	....	FOGO (Cape Verde Is)	1804-01=	1	
? 1606	....	?	MERE LAVA (Vanuatu-SW Pacific)	0507-021		
1606	0123	?	HACHIJO-JIMA (Izu Is-Japan)	0804-05=	2	
1606	1125	18a>	COLIMA VOLC COMPLEX (Mexico)	1401-04=	4	
1607	Cont	....	STROMBOLI (Italy)	0101-04=	1?	
1607	Cont	....	FOGO (Cape Verde Is)	1804-01=	1	
1607	0628	?	ETNA (Italy)	0101-06=	2	7/6
1608	Cont	....	STROMBOLI (Italy)	0101-04=	1?	
1608	Cont	....	ETNA (Italy)	0101-06=	2	
1608	Cont	....	FOGO (Cape Verde Is)	1804-01=	1	
1608c	....	?	TAAL (Luzon-Philippines)	0703-07=	2?	
1608	0718	1a	GAMALAMA (Halmahera-Indonesia)	0608-06=	3	
1609	Cont	....	STROMBOLI (Italy)	0101-04=	1?	
1609	Cont	....	ETNA (Italy)	0101-06=	2	
1609	Cont	....	FOGO (Cape Verde Is)	1804-01=	1	
1609	....	?	BANDA API (Banda Sea)	0605-09=	3↑	
1609	....	?	TENGCHONG (China-S)	0705-11-		
? 1609	....	?	COSIGUINA (Nicaragua)	1404-01=		
? 1609	....	?	MOMOTOMBO (Nicaragua)	1404-09=		
1609	04	?	ASAMA (Honshu-Japan)	0803-11=	2	
1610	Cont	....	STROMBOLI (Italy)	0101-04=	1?	
1610	Cont	....	FOGO (Cape Verde Is)	1804-01=	1	
G 1610s	....	?	ST. HELENS (US-Washington)	1201-05-		8/-
C 1610t	....	?	KILAUEA (Hawaiian Is)	1302-01-	1?	
1610	0206	190a	ETNA (Italy)	0101-06=	2	7/-
1611	Cont	....	STROMBOLI (Italy)	0101-04=	1?	
1611	Cont	....	FOGO (Cape Verde Is)	1804-01=	1	

START YEAR	M-Dy	Dura-tion	VOLCANO NAME (Subregion)	NUMBER	VEI	Vol L/T
1611	....	?	**ASO** (Kyushu-Japan)	0802-11=	2	
? **1611**	....	?	**BANDAI** (Honshu-Japan)	0803-16=		
1611	0415	808*w*	**COLIMA VOLC COMPLEX** (Mexico)	1401-04=	3	
? **1611**	10	?	**USU** (Hokkaido-Japan)	0805-03=		
1612	*Cont*	....	*STROMBOLI (Italy)*	0101-04=	*1?*	
1612	*Cont*	....	*COLIMA VOLC COMPLEX (Mexico)*	1401-04=	*2*	
1612	*Cont*	....	*FOGO (Cape Verde Is)*	1804-01=	*1*	
1612	....	365*y*	**OSHIMA** (Izu Is-Japan)	0804-01=	2	
1612	0812	?	**ASO** (Kyushu-Japan)	0802-11=	2	
1612	1012	?	**KATLA** (Iceland-S)	1702-03=	2	
1613	*Cont*	....	*STROMBOLI (Italy)*	0101-04=	*1?*	
1613	*Cont*	....	*OSHIMA (Izu Is-Japan)*	0804-01=	*2*	
1613	*Cont*	....	*COLIMA VOLC COMPLEX (Mexico)*	1401-04=	*2*	
1613	*Cont*	....	*FOGO (Cape Verde Is)*	1804-01=	*1*	
1613	....	365*y*	**KIRISHIMA** (Kyushu-Japan)	0802-09=	2?	
1613	....	?	**ORIZABA, PICO DE** (Mexico)	1401-10=		
? **1613**	....	?	**SAN CRISTOBAL** (Nicaragua)	1404-02=		
1613	....	?	**TELICA** (Nicaragua)	1404-04=	2?	
? **1613**	....	?	**MASAYA** (Nicaragua)	1404-10=	0	
1613	0808	?	**ASO** (Kyushu-Japan)	0802-11=	2	
1614	*Cont*	....	*STROMBOLI (Italy)*	0101-04=	*1?*	
1614	*Cont*	....	*KIRISHIMA (Kyushu-Japan)*	0802-09=	*2?*	
1614	*Cont*	....	*FOGO (Cape Verde Is)*	1804-01=	*1*	
1614	....	?	**FUEGO** (Guatemala)	1402-09=	2	
1614	0701?	>3yr	**ETNA** (Italy)	0101-06=	2	9/6
1615	*Cont*	....	*STROMBOLI (Italy)*	0101-04=	*1?*	
1615	*Cont*	....	*ETNA (Italy)*	0101-06=	*2*	9/6
1615	*Cont*	....	*FOGO (Cape Verde Is)*	1804-01=	*1*	
1615	....	>3yr	**KIRISHIMA** (Kyushu-Japan)	0802-09=	2?	
C **1615**?	....	?	**KILAUEA** (Hawaiian Is)	1302-01-	0	
C **1615**v	....	?	**YEGUADA, LA** (Panama)	1406-02-		
1615	0316	30*m*?	**BANDA API** (Banda Sea)	0605-09=	3	
? **1615**	0807?	?	**IBUSUKI [KAIMON]** (Kyushu-Japan)	0802-07=		
1616	*Cont*	....	*STROMBOLI (Italy)*	0101-04=	*1?*	
1616	*Cont*	....	*ETNA (Italy)*	0101-06=	*2*	9/6
1616	*Cont*	....	*KIRISHIMA (Kyushu-Japan)*	0802-09=	*2?*	
1616	*Cont*	....	*FOGO (Cape Verde Is)*	1804-01=	*1*	
1616	0219	4*a*	**MAYON** (Luzon-Philippines)	0703-03=	3	
1616	0704	<1	**GALERAS** (Colombia)	1501-08=	3↑	
1616	0706	?	**MANAM** (New Guinea-NE of)	0501-02=	2?	
1617	*Cont*	....	*STROMBOLI (Italy)*	0101-04=	*1?*	
1617	*Cont*	....	*ETNA (Italy)*	0101-06=	*2*	9/6
1617	*Cont*	....	*KIRISHIMA (Kyushu-Japan)*	0802-09=	*2?*	
1617	*Cont*	....	*FOGO (Cape Verde Is)*	1804-01=	*1*	
1617	....	?	**FUEGO** (Guatemala)	1402-09=	3	
1618	*Cont*	....	*STROMBOLI (Italy)*	0101-04=	*1?*	
1618	*Cont*	....	*ETNA (Italy)*	0101-06=	*2*	9/6
1618	*Cont*	....	*KIRISHIMA (Kyushu-Japan)*	0802-09=	*2?*	
1618	*Cont*	....	*FOGO (Cape Verde Is)*	1804-01=	*1*	
1618	....	?	**VULCANO** (Italy)	0101-05=		
1618	0131	?	**IWAKI** (Honshu-Japan)	0803-27=	2	
1619	*Cont*	....	*STROMBOLI (Italy)*	0101-04=	*1?*	
1619	*Cont*	....	*ETNA (Italy)*	0101-06=	*2*	9/6
1619	*Cont*	....	*FOGO (Cape Verde Is)*	1804-01=	*1*	
1619	0729	?	**GRIMSVOTN** (Iceland-NE)	1703-01=	2	
1620	*Cont*	....	*STROMBOLI (Italy)*	0101-04=	*1?*	
1620	*Cont*	....	*ETNA (Italy)*	0101-06=	*2*	9/6
1620	*Cont*	....	*FOGO (Cape Verde Is)*	1804-01=	*1*	
1620	....	?	**KIRISHIMA** (Kyushu-Japan)	0802-09=	2?	
1620	....	?	**ZAO** (Honshu-Japan)	0803-19=	2?	
1620	....	?	**FUEGO** (Guatemala)	1402-09=	2	
1620	0603	?	**ASO** (Kyushu-Japan)	0802-11=	2	
1621	*Cont*	....	*STROMBOLI (Italy)*	0101-04=	*1?*	
1621	*Cont*	....	*ETNA (Italy)*	0101-06=	*2*	9/6
1621	*Cont*	....	*FOGO (Cape Verde Is)*	1804-01=	*1*	
? **1621**	....	?	**SANTA ANA** (El Salvador)	1403-02=		
1622	*Cont*	....	*STROMBOLI (Italy)*	0101-04=	*1?*	
1622	*Cont*	....	*ETNA (Italy)*	0101-06=	*2*	9/6
1622	*Cont*	....	*FOGO (Cape Verde Is)*	1804-01=	*1*	
1622	0608	....	**COLIMA VOLC COMPLEX** (Mexico)	1401-04=	4	
1623	*Cont*	....	*STROMBOLI (Italy)*	0101-04=	*1?*	
1623	*Cont*	....	*ETNA (Italy)*	0101-06=	*2*	9/6
1623	*Cont*	....	*FOGO (Cape Verde Is)*	1804-01=	*1*	
1623?	....	?	**PACAYA** (Guatemala)	1402-11=	3	
1623	....	?	**RUIZ** (Colombia)	1501-02=	1?	
1623	01	? 679*m*?	**ZAO** (Honshu-Japan)	0803-19=	3	
1623	01	?	**FUEGO** (Guatemala)	1402-09=	2	
1624	*Cont*	....	*STROMBOLI (Italy)*	0101-04=	*1?*	

Figure 15. A new but short-lived island formed south of Sicily during this 1831 eruption. Eight submarine eruptions are known from the Campi Flegrei del Mar Sicilia; 3 have built islands, but each has been quickly destroyed by Mediterranean waves. Phreatic eruptions are common in such settings where water gains access to the volcanic vents, and violent explosions result from the mix. The 1831 eruption is also shown on the back cover, but from a different vantage point, revealing the linear alignment of vents. Such documentation is particularly valuable for eruptions prior to the age of photography. Artist unknown; from the collection of Maurice & Katia Krafft.

START YEAR	M-Dy	Duration	VOLCANO NAME (Subregion)	NUMBER	VEI	Vol L/T
1624	Cont	....	ETNA (Italy)	0101-06=	2	9/6
1624	Cont	....	FOGO (Cape Verde Is)	1804-01=	1	
1624	0206	....	ZAO (Honshu-Japan)	0803-19=	2?	
1625	Cont	....	STROMBOLI (Italy)	0101-04=	1?	
1625	Cont	....	FOGO (Cape Verde Is)	1804-01=	1	
1625	....	?	NIKKO-SHIRANE (Honshu-Japan)	0803-14=	3	
1625	0902	12a	KATLA (Iceland-S)	1702-03=	4	-/8
1626	Cont	....	STROMBOLI (Italy)	0101-04=	1?	
1626	Cont	....	FOGO (Cape Verde Is)	1804-01=	1	
1626	03	15m	VULCANO (Italy)	0101-05=	3	
1626	0519	57m?	USU (Hokkaido-Japan)	0805-03=		
1627	Cont	....	STROMBOLI (Italy)	0101-04=	1?	
1627	Cont	....	FOGO (Cape Verde Is)	1804-01=	1	
? 1627	....	?	FUJI (Honshu-Japan)	0803-03=		
1628	Cont	....	STROMBOLI (Italy)	0101-04=	1?	
1628	Cont	....	FOGO (Cape Verde Is)	1804-01=	1	
1628?	....	?	IRIGA (Luzon-Philippines)	0703-041	2	
1628	10	?	SANGAY (Ecuador)	1502-09=	3↑	
1628	1026	?	KIRISHIMA (Kyushu-Japan)	0802-09=	2?	
1629	Cont	....	STROMBOLI (Italy)	0101-04=	1?	
1629	Cont	....	FOGO (Cape Verde Is)	1804-01=	1	
1629	....	>3yr	FUEGO (Guatemala)	1402-09=	2	
1629	....	?	GRIMSVOTN (Iceland-NE)	1703-01=	2	
1630	Cont	....	STROMBOLI (Italy)	0101-04=	1?	
1630	Cont	....	FUEGO (Guatemala)	1402-09=	2	
1630	Cont	....	FOGO (Cape Verde Is)	1804-01=	1	
C 1630t	....	?	RAOUL ISLAND (Kermadec Is)	0402-03=	4	-/8
1630	....	?	ZAO (Honshu-Japan)	0803-19=	2?	
1630	....	?	ORIZABA, PICO DE (Mexico)	1401-10=	2	
C 1630t	....	?	SOUFRIERE HILLS (W Indies)	1600-05=		
1630	0903	7a?	FURNAS (Azores)	1802-10=	4	7/8
1631	Cont	....	STROMBOLI (Italy)	0101-04=	1?	
1631	Cont	....	FUEGO (Guatemala)	1402-09=	2	
1631	Cont	....	FOGO (Cape Verde Is)	1804-01=	1	
1631	....	?	VULCANO (Italy)	0101-05=		
@ 1631	0214?	?	DAMA ALI (Ethiopia)	0201-141		
1631	12	?	ASO (Kyushu-Japan)	0802-11=	2	
1631	1215	46a?	VESUVIUS (Italy)	0101-02=	4	-/8
1632	Cont	....	VESUVIUS (Italy)	0101-02=	2	-/8
1632	Cont	....	STROMBOLI (Italy)	0101-04=	1?	
1632	Cont	....	FUEGO (Guatemala)	1402-09=	2	
1632	Cont	....	FOGO (Cape Verde Is)	1804-01=	1	
1632	....	?	CAMPI FLEGREI MAR SICILIA (Italy)	0101-07=	0	
1632	1216	?	BANDA API (Banda Sea)	0605-09=	3↑	
1633	Cont	....	STROMBOLI (Italy)	0101-04=	1?	
1633	Cont	....	FOGO (Cape Verde Is)	1804-01=	1	
? 1633	0221	?	ETNA (Italy)	0101-06=		
1634	Cont	....	STROMBOLI (Italy)	0101-04=	1?	
1634	Cont	....	FOGO (Cape Verde Is)	1804-01=	1	
1634	....	?	TAAL (Luzon-Philippines)	0703-07=	3↑	
1634	1219	>3yr	ETNA (Italy)	0101-06=	1	8/5
1635	Cont	....	STROMBOLI (Italy)	0101-04=	1?	
1635	Cont	....	ETNA (Italy)	0101-06=	1	8/5
1635	Cont	....	FOGO (Cape Verde Is)	1804-01=	1	
1635	....	?	TAAL (Luzon-Philippines)	0703-07=	3↑	
C 1635w	....	?	LASSEN [CINDER CONE] (US-Calif)	1203-08-	3?	
1635<	....	?	PELEE (W Indies)	1600-12=		
1635	0329	?	GAMALAMA (Halmahera-Indonesia)	0608-06=	2	
1635	1118	?	BANDA API (Banda Sea)	0605-09=	1?	
1636	Cont	....	STROMBOLI (Italy)	0101-04=	1?	
1636	Cont	....	ETNA (Italy)	0101-06=	1	8/5
1636	Cont	....	FOGO (Cape Verde Is)	1804-01=	1	
1636	....	653w	OSHIMA (Izu Is-Japan)	0804-01=	3	
1636<	....	?	SABA (W Indies)	1600-01=		
1636	0508	390m	HEKLA (Iceland-S)	1702-07=	3	-/7
1637	Cont	....	STROMBOLI (Italy)	0101-04=	1?	
1637	Cont	....	ETNA (Italy)	0101-06=	1	8/5
1637	Cont	....	OSHIMA (Izu Is-Japan)	0804-01=	2	
1637	Cont	....	HEKLA (Iceland-S)	1702-07=	2	-/7
1637	Cont	....	FOGO (Cape Verde Is)	1804-01=	1	
1637	....	365y	KIRISHIMA (Kyushu-Japan)	0802-09=	2?	
1637	0701	>3yr	VESUVIUS (Italy)	0101-02=	2	
1637	0929	6a	ASO (Kyushu-Japan)	0802-11=	2	
1637	10	136s	VESTMANNAEYJAR (Iceland-S)	1702-01=		
1638	Cont	....	VESUVIUS (Italy)	0101-02=	2	
1638	Cont	....	STROMBOLI (Italy)	0101-04=	1?	
1638	Cont	....	ETNA (Italy)	0101-06=	1	8/5
1638	Cont	....	KIRISHIMA (Kyushu-Japan)	0802-09=	2	
1638	Cont	....	OSHIMA (Izu Is-Japan)	0804-01=	2	
1638	Cont	....	VESTMANNAEYJAR (Iceland-S)	1702-01=		
1638	Cont	....	FOGO (Cape Verde Is)	1804-01=	1	
1638	....	?	RAUNG (Java)	0603-34=	4?	-/8
1638	0224d	?	GRIMSVOTN (Iceland-NE)	1703-01=	2	
1638	0703	25a	SETE CIDADES (Azores)	1802-08=	2	
1638	0725	?	USU (Hokkaido-Japan)	0805-03=		
1639	Cont	....	VESUVIUS (Italy)	0101-02=	2	
1639	Cont	....	STROMBOLI (Italy)	0101-04=	1?	
1639	Cont	....	FOGO (Cape Verde Is)	1804-01=	1	
1640	Cont	....	VESUVIUS (Italy)	0101-02=	2	
1640	Cont	....	STROMBOLI (Italy)	0101-04=	1?	
1640	Cont	....	FOGO (Cape Verde Is)	1804-01=	1	
1640	....	?	FOURNAISE, PITON DE LA (Indian O.)	0303-02=	2	
C 1640?	....	?	MAUNA LOA (Hawaiian Is)	1302-02=	0	
? 1640	....	?	TUNGURAHUA (Ecuador)	1502-08=	2	
? 1640	....	?	OSORNO (Chile-S)	1508-01=		
C 1640t	....	?	SOUFRIERE ST. VINCENT (W Indies)	1600-15=		
1640	02	?	LLAIMA (Chile-C)	1507-11=	4	

START YEAR	M-Dy	Duration	VOLCANO NAME (Subregion)	NUMBER	VEI	Vol L/T
1640	0203	?	VILLARRICA (Chile-C)	1507-12=	3	
1640	07	?	HAKU-SAN (Honshu-Japan)	0803-05=	3?	
1640	0731	70a	KOMAGA-TAKE (Hokkaido-Japan)	0805-02=	5	-/9
1640	12	20m	AWU (Sangihe Is-Indonesia)	0607-04=	3↑	
1641	Cont	....	VESUVIUS (Italy)	0101-02=	2	
1641	Cont	....	STROMBOLI (Italy)	0101-04=	1?	
1641	Cont	....	FOGO (Cape Verde Is)	1804-01=	1	
1641	....	?	KELUT (Java)	0603-28=	4?	-/8
1641	....	?	TAAL (Luzon-Philippines)	0703-07=	3	
1641	....	?	ZAO (Honshu-Japan)	0803-19=	2?	
1641	....	?	TUNGURAHUA (Ecuador)	1502-08=	3?	
I 1641j	....	?	DECEPTION ISLAND (Antarctica)	1900-03=		
1641	0103	....	AWU (Sangihe Is-Indonesia)	0607-04=	5?	-/9
1641	0104	?	BUD DAJO (Sulu Is-Philippines)	0700-01=	2?	
1642	Cont	....	VESUVIUS (Italy)	0101-02=	2	
1642	Cont	....	STROMBOLI (Italy)	0101-04=	1?	
1642	Cont	....	FOGO (Cape Verde Is)	1804-01=	1	
1642	....	?	POPOCATEPETL (Mexico)	1401-09=	2	
1642	0406	?	SAKURA-JIMA (Kyushu-Japan)	0802-08=	2?	
1643	Cont	....	VESUVIUS (Italy)	0101-02=	2	
1643	Cont	....	STROMBOLI (Italy)	0101-04=	1?	
1643	Cont	....	FOGO (Cape Verde Is)	1804-01=	1	
1643	0220	?	ETNA (Italy)	0101-06=	1	
1643	0331	15m	MIYAKE-JIMA (Izu Is-Japan)	0804-04=	3	
1643	0420	?	KARKAR (New Guinea-NE of)	0501-03=	3↑	
1643	0421	?	MANAM (New Guinea-NE of)	0501-02=	2	
? 1643	0615	?	GAMALAMA (Halmahera-Indonesia)	0608-06=	2	
1644	Cont	....	VESUVIUS (Italy)	0101-02=	2	
1644	Cont	....	STROMBOLI (Italy)	0101-04=	1?	
1644	Cont	....	FOGO (Cape Verde Is)	1804-01=	1	
? 1644	....	?	TUNGURAHUA (Ecuador)	1502-08=	2	
? 1644	....	?	OSORNO (Chile-S)	1508-01=		
1644	0220	?	ASAMA (Honshu-Japan)	0803-11=	2	
1645	Cont	....	VESUVIUS (Italy)	0101-02=	2	
1645	Cont	....	STROMBOLI (Italy)	0101-04=	1?	
1645	Cont	....	FOGO (Cape Verde Is)	1804-01=	1	
C 1645t	....	?	BAMUS (New Britain-SW Pac)	0502-11=		
1645	....	?	TAAL (Luzon-Philippines)	0703-07=	3↑	
1645	0224	86a	ASAMA (Honshu-Japan)	0803-11=	2	
1646	Cont	....	VESUVIUS (Italy)	0101-02=	2	
1646	Cont	....	STROMBOLI (Italy)	0101-04=	1?	
1646	Cont	....	FOGO (Cape Verde Is)	1804-01=	1	
1646e	....	?	AWU (Sangihe Is-Indonesia)	0607-04=	2?	
? 1646	....	?	TUNGURAHUA (Ecuador)	1502-08=	2	
1646	0719	2a	MAKIAN (Halmahera-Indonesia)	0608-07=	4?	-/8
1646	1002	80a	LA PALMA (Canary Is)	1803-01-	2	7/6
1646	1120	58a	ETNA (Italy)	0101-06=	2	8/7
1647	Cont	....	VESUVIUS (Italy)	0101-02=	2	
1647	Cont	....	STROMBOLI (Italy)	0101-04=	1?	
1647	Cont	....	ETNA (Italy)	0101-06=	2	8/7
1647	Cont	....	FOGO (Cape Verde Is)	1804-01=	1	
1647	0218	35a	ASAMA (Honshu-Japan)	0803-11=	2	
? 1647	0513	?	VILLARRICA (Chile-C)	1507-12=	1?	
1648	Cont	....	VESUVIUS (Italy)	0101-02=	2	
1648	Cont	....	STROMBOLI (Italy)	0101-04=	1?	
1648	Cont	....	FOGO (Cape Verde Is)	1804-01=	1	
1648	0322	?	ASAMA (Honshu-Japan)	0803-11=	2	
1648	0615	3a	GAMALAMA (Halmahera-Indonesia)	0608-06=	2	
1648	0829	?	ASAMA (Honshu-Japan)	0803-11=	2	
1649	Cont	....	STROMBOLI (Italy)	0101-04=	1?	
1649	Cont	....	FOGO (Cape Verde Is)	1804-01=	1	
1649	....	?	FOURNAISE, PITON DE LA (Indian O.)	0303-02=	2	
1649	....	?	NIKKO-SHIRANE (Honshu-Japan)	0803-14=	3	
1649	07	31p	ASO (Kyushu-Japan)	0802-11=	2	
1649	0817	1a	ASAMA (Honshu-Japan)	0803-11=	2	
1649	1128	....	VESUVIUS (Italy)	0101-02=	2	
1650	Cont	....	VESUVIUS (Italy)	0101-02=	2	
1650	Cont	....	STROMBOLI (Italy)	0101-04=	1?	
1650	Cont	....	FOGO (Cape Verde Is)	1804-01=	1	
1650t	....	?	CAMEROON, MT. (Africa-W)	0204-01=	3↑	
1650t	....	?	PALUWEH (Lesser Sunda Is)	0604-15=	3	
1650t	....	?	MUTNOVSKY (Kamchatka)	1000-06=	2	
T 1650v	....	?	AUGUSTINE (Alaska-SW)	1103-01-		
T 1650t	....	?	SPURR (Alaska-SW)	1103-04-		
? 1650?	....	?	LASSEN [CHAOS CRAGS] (US-Calif)	1203-08-		
T 1650t	....	?	KILAUEA (Hawaiian Is)	1302-01-	0	
C 1650?	....	?	MAUNA LOA (Hawaiian Is)	1302-02=	0	
C 1650t	....	?	HUALALAI (Hawaiian Is)	1302-04-	1	
? 1650t	....	?	SUMACO (Ecuador)	1502-04=	3?	
1650t	....	?	CHILLAN, NEVADOS DE (Chile-C)	1507-07=	3?	
? 1650	0702	?	ASAMA (Honshu-Japan)	0803-11=		
1650	0927	70a	SANTORINI (Greece)	0102-04=	4?	-/8
1651	Cont	....	VESUVIUS (Italy)	0101-02=	2	
1651	Cont	....	STROMBOLI (Italy)	0101-04=	1?	
1651	Cont	....	FOGO (Cape Verde Is)	1804-01=	1	
1651	....	?	VULCANO (Italy)	0101-05=		
1651	0116	897w	ETNA (Italy)	0101-06=	1	8/5
1651	0218	54a	PACAYA (Guatemala)	1402-11=	2	
1651	0412	?	ASAMA (Honshu-Japan)	0803-11=	2	
1652	Cont	....	VESUVIUS (Italy)	0101-02=	2	
1652	Cont	....	STROMBOLI (Italy)	0101-04=	1?	
1652	Cont	....	ETNA (Italy)	0101-06=	1	8/5
1652	Cont	....	FOGO (Cape Verde Is)	1804-01=	1	
1652?	....	?	BABUYAN CLARO (Luzon Is-N of)	0704-03=	3↑	
1652	....	?	AOGA-SHIMA (Izu Is-Japan)	0804-06=	3	
1652	0412	?	ASAMA (Honshu-Japan)	0803-11=	2	

	START YEAR	M-Dy	Duration	VOLCANO NAME (Subregion)	NUMBER	VEI	Vol L/T
	1652	1019	7a	**UNNAMED** (Azores)	1802-081	2	6/6
	1653	Cont	....	STROMBOLI (Italy)	0101-04=	1?	
	1653	Cont	....	ETNA (Italy)	0101-06=	1	8/5
	1653	Cont	....	FOGO (Cape Verde Is)	1804-01=	1	
	1653	1231y	?	**GAMALAMA** (Halmahera-Indonesia)	0608-06=	3↑	
	1653	1231y	?	**ASAMA** (Honshu-Japan)	0803-11=	2	
	1654	Cont	....	STROMBOLI (Italy)	0101-04=	1?	
	1654	Cont	....	FOGO (Cape Verde Is)	1804-01=	1	
	1654	....	730y?	**ETNA** (Italy)	0101-06=	1	
	1654	0225	>3yr	VESUVIUS (Italy)	0101-02=	2?	
	1655	Cont	....	VESUVIUS (Italy)	0101-02=	2?	
	1655	Cont	....	STROMBOLI (Italy)	0101-04=	1?	
	1655	Cont	....	ETNA (Italy)	0101-06=	1	
	1655	Cont	....	FOGO (Cape Verde Is)	1804-01=	1	
D	1655?	....	?	**EGMONT** (New Zealand)	0401-03=		
C	1655v	....	?	**KSUDACH** (Kamchatka)	1000-05=	4	-/8
	1655	0415q	?	**KVERKFJOLL** (Iceland-NE)	1703-05=	0	
	1655	07	?	**PACAYA** (Guatemala)	1402-11=	2	
	1655	1125	?	**ASAMA** (Honshu-Japan)	0803-11=	2	
	1656	Cont	....	VESUVIUS (Italy)	0101-02=	2?	
	1656	Cont	....	STROMBOLI (Italy)	0101-04=	1?	
	1656	Cont	....	ETNA (Italy)	0101-06=	1	
	1656	Cont	....	FOGO (Cape Verde Is)	1804-01=	1	
	1656	1210	?	**ASAMA** (Honshu-Japan)	0803-11=	2	
	1657	Cont	....	VESUVIUS (Italy)	0101-02=	2?	
	1657	Cont	....	STROMBOLI (Italy)	0101-04=	1?	
	1657	Cont	....	FOGO (Cape Verde Is)	1804-01=	1	
?	1657	0315	?	**VILLARRICA** (Chile-C)	1507-12=	1?	
	1657	1125	?	**ASAMA** (Honshu-Japan)	0803-11=	2	
	1658	Cont	....	VESUVIUS (Italy)	0101-02=	2?	
	1658	Cont	....	STROMBOLI (Italy)	0101-04=	1?	
	1658	Cont	....	FOGO (Cape Verde Is)	1804-01=	1	
	1658	....	?	**MERAPI** (Java)	0603-25=	3↑	
	1658	0724	?	**ASAMA** (Honshu-Japan)	0803-11=	2	
	1658	10 ?	?	**HAKU-SAN** (Honshu-Japan)	0803-05=	2?	
	1658	1103	?	**SAN SALVADOR** (El Salvador)	1403-05=	3	7/-
	1659	Cont	....	VESUVIUS (Italy)	0101-02=	2?	
	1659	Cont	....	STROMBOLI (Italy)	0101-04=	1?	
	1659	Cont	....	FOGO (Cape Verde Is)	1804-01=	1	
	1659	02	868w	**KIRISHIMA** (Kyushu-Japan)	0802-09=	2?	
	1659	04	>3yr	**CHOKAI** (Honshu-Japan)	0803-22=		
	1659	0421	86m?	**HAKU-SAN** (Honshu-Japan)	0803-05=	2?	
	1659	06	?	**GAMALAMA** (Halmahera-Indonesia)	0608-06=	2	
	1659	0724	?	**ASAMA** (Honshu-Japan)	0803-11=	2	
	1659	11	?	**GRIMSVOTN** (Iceland-NE)	1703-01=	2	
	1659	1111	?	**TEON** (Banda Sea)	0605-05=	3↑	
	1660	Cont	....	STROMBOLI (Italy)	0101-04=	1?	
	1660	Cont	....	KIRISHIMA (Kyushu-Japan)	0802-09=	2?	
	1660	Cont	....	CHOKAI (Honshu-Japan)	0803-22=		
	1660	Cont	....	FOGO (Cape Verde Is)	1804-01=	1	
C	1660p	....	?	**LONG ISLAND** (New Guinea-NE of)	0501-05=	6	-/10
	1660	....	?	**LEWOTOLO** (Lesser Sunda Is)	0604-23=	3↑	
	1660	....	?	**PLANCHON-PETEROA** (Chile-C)	1507-04=	3↑	
	1660	02	?	**TEON** (Banda Sea)	0605-05=	4?	-/8
	1660	0408	?	**ASAMA** (Honshu-Japan)	0803-11=	2	
	1660	0703	....	**VESUVIUS** (Italy)	0101-02=	3	
	1660	1027	32a	**GUAGUA PICHINCHA** (Ecuador)	1502-02=	4	-/8
	1660	1103	240w	**KATLA** (Iceland-S)	1702-03=	4	-/8
	1661	Cont	....	VESUVIUS (Italy)	0101-02=	2?	
	1661	Cont	....	STROMBOLI (Italy)	0101-04=	1?	
	1661	Cont	....	KIRISHIMA (Kyushu-Japan)	0802-09=	2?	
	1661	Cont	....	CHOKAI (Honshu-Japan)	0803-22=		
	1661	Cont	....	KATLA (Iceland-S)	1702-03=	2	-/8
	1661	Cont	....	FOGO (Cape Verde Is)	1804-01=	1	
	1661	0414	13a	**ASAMA** (Honshu-Japan)	0803-11=	2	
	1661	1021	?	**ASAMA** (Honshu-Japan)	0803-11=	2	
	1662	Cont	....	VESUVIUS (Italy)	0101-02=	2?	
	1662	Cont	....	STROMBOLI (Italy)	0101-04=	1?	
	1662	Cont	....	CHOKAI (Honshu-Japan)	0803-22=		
	1662	Cont	....	FOGO (Cape Verde Is)	1804-01=	1	
	1662	....	?	**UBINAS** (Peru)	1504-02=	3?	
	1662?	0126?	?	**KUJU GROUP** (Kyushu-Japan)	0802-12=	3	
	1662	09	655w	**KIRISHIMA** (Kyushu-Japan)	0802-09=	2?	
	1663	Cont	....	VESUVIUS (Italy)	0101-02=	2?	
	1663	Cont	....	STROMBOLI (Italy)	0101-04=	1?	
	1663	Cont	....	KIRISHIMA (Kyushu-Japan)	0802-09=	2	
	1663	Cont	....	CHOKAI (Honshu-Japan)	0803-22=		
	1663	Cont	....	FOGO (Cape Verde Is)	1804-01=	1	
	1663	....	>3yr	**POPOCATEPETL** (Mexico)	1401-09=	2	
	1663	....	?	**ATITLAN** (Guatemala)	1402-06=	2	
	1663	0118	?	**TEON** (Banda Sea)	0605-05=	3↑	
	1663	04	25a	**UNZEN** (Kyushu-Japan)	0802-10=	2?	
	1663	0816	20d	**USU** (Hokkaido-Japan)	0805-03=	5	7/9
	1663	1211	16a>	**UNZEN** (Kyushu-Japan)	0802-10=	2?	6/-
	1663	1231y	?	**MERAPI** (Java)	0603-25=	3↑	
	1664	Cont	....	VESUVIUS (Italy)	0101-02=	2?	
	1664	Cont	....	STROMBOLI (Italy)	0101-04=	1?	
	1664	Cont	....	KIRISHIMA (Kyushu-Japan)	0802-09=	2	
	1664	Cont	....	POPOCATEPETL (Mexico)	1401-09=	2	
	1664	Cont	....	FOGO (Cape Verde Is)	1804-01=	1	
	1664	....	?	**OKINAWA-TORI-SHIMA** (Ryukyu Is)	0802-02=		
	1664	....	?	**PACAYA** (Guatemala)	1402-11=	3	
	1664	0115?	?	**SAN MARTIN, VOLCAN DE** (Mexico)	1401-11=	3	
	1665	Cont	....	VESUVIUS (Italy)	0101-02=	2?	
	1665	Cont	....	STROMBOLI (Italy)	0101-04=	1?	
	1665	Cont	....	POPOCATEPETL (Mexico)	1401-09=	2	
	1665	Cont	....	FOGO (Cape Verde Is)	1804-01=	1	
	1666	Cont	....	VESUVIUS (Italy)	0101-02=	2?	
	1666	Cont	....	STROMBOLI (Italy)	0101-04=	1?	
	1666	Cont	....	POPOCATEPETL (Mexico)	1401-09=	2	
	1666	Cont	....	FOGO (Cape Verde Is)	1804-01=	1	
	1667	Cont	....	VESUVIUS (Italy)	0101-02=	2?	
	1667	Cont	....	STROMBOLI (Italy)	0101-04=	1?	
	1667	Cont	....	POPOCATEPETL (Mexico)	1401-09=	2	
	1667	Cont	....	FOGO (Cape Verde Is)	1804-01=	1	
?	1667	....	?	**KIRISHIMA** (Kyushu-Japan)	0802-09=		
	1667	....	?	**HUAYNAPUTINA** (Peru)	1504-03=	2?	
	1667	0923	?	**SHIKOTSU [TARUMAI]** (Hokkaido)	0805-04=	5	-/9
	1668	Cont	....	VESUVIUS (Italy)	0101-02=	2?	
	1668	Cont	....	STROMBOLI (Italy)	0101-04=	1?	
	1668	Cont	....	FOGO (Cape Verde Is)	1804-01=	1	
	1668	....	?	**ZAO** (Honshu-Japan)	0803-19=	2?	
	1668	....	?	**BAITOUSHAN** (China-E)	1005-07-		
	1668	02	?	**ASO** (Kyushu-Japan)	0802-11=	2	
	1668	08	321w	**ASO** (Kyushu-Japan)	0802-11=	2	
	1668	08	317m	**PACAYA** (Guatemala)	1402-11=	2	
	1669	Cont	....	VESUVIUS (Italy)	0101-02=	2?	
	1669	Cont	....	STROMBOLI (Italy)	0101-04=	1?	
	1669	Cont	....	ASO (Kyushu-Japan)	0802-11=	2	
	1669	Cont	....	PACAYA (Guatemala)	1402-11=	2	
	1669	Cont	....	FOGO (Cape Verde Is)	1804-01=	1	
	1669	....	?	**FOURNAISE, PITON DE LA** (Indian O.)	0303-02=	2	
	1669	....	?	**ZAO** (Honshu-Japan)	0803-19=	3	
	1669	....	?	**PAGAN** (Mariana Is-C Pac)	0804-17=		
	1669	0311	126a	ETNA (Italy)	0101-06=	2?	8/7
	1669	0325	....	**ETNA** (Italy)	0101-06=	3	8/7
	1669	0405	10a	**ASAMA** (Honshu-Japan)	0803-11=	2	
	1670	Cont	....	VESUVIUS (Italy)	0101-02=	2?	
	1670	Cont	....	STROMBOLI (Italy)	0101-04=	1?	
	1670	Cont	....	FOGO (Cape Verde Is)	1804-01=	1	
A	1670?	....	?	**AOBA** (Vanuatu-SW Pacific)	0507-03=	2?	
	1670	....	>3yr	**AOGA-SHIMA** (Izu Is-Japan)	0804-06=	2	
C	1670?	....	?	**TOKACHI** (Hokkaido-Japan)	0805-05=	2?	
	1670	....	?	**MASAYA** (Nicaragua)	1404-10=	3	
	1670	....	>3yr	**GALERAS** (Colombia)	1501-08=	2	
	1670	0426	109a>	**ZAO** (Honshu-Japan)	0803-19=	2	
?	1670	0601	?	**SAKURA-JIMA** (Kyushu-Japan)	0802-08=	2?	
	1670	0813		ZAO (Honshu-Japan)	0803-19=	2	
	1671	Cont	....	VESUVIUS (Italy)	0101-02=	2?	
	1671	Cont	....	STROMBOLI (Italy)	0101-04=	1?	
	1671	Cont	....	AOGA-SHIMA (Izu Is-Japan)	0804-06=	2	
	1671	Cont	....	GALERAS (Colombia)	1501-08=	2	
	1671	Cont	....	FOGO (Cape Verde Is)	1804-01=	1	
	1671	....	?	**FOURNAISE, PITON DE LA** (Indian O.)	0303-02=	2	
	1671?	....	?	**IYA** (Lesser Sunda Is)	0604-11=	3↑	
	1671	....	?	**ASO** (Kyushu-Japan)	0802-11=	2	
	1671	08	?	**PACAYA** (Guatemala)	1402-11=	2	
	1671	08 ?	?	**SAN SALVADOR** (El Salvador)	1403-05=	2?	
	1672	Cont	....	VESUVIUS (Italy)	0101-02=	2?	
	1672	Cont	....	STROMBOLI (Italy)	0101-04=	1?	
	1672	Cont	....	AOGA-SHIMA (Izu Is-Japan)	0804-06=	2	
	1672	Cont	....	GALERAS (Colombia)	1501-08=	2	
	1672	Cont	....	FOGO (Cape Verde Is)	1804-01=	1	
	1672	....	?	**FOURNAISE, PITON DE LA** (Indian O.)	0303-02=	2	
	1672?	....	?	**SMITH ROCK** (Izu Is-Japan)	0804-08=	0	
	1672	0424	340a	**FAYAL** (Azores)	1802-01=	2	
?	1672	0712	16a	**IWAKI** (Honshu-Japan)	0803-27=	2?	
	1672	0804	?	**MERAPI** (Java)	0603-25=	3	
	1673	Cont	....	VESUVIUS (Italy)	0101-02=	2?	
	1673	Cont	....	STROMBOLI (Italy)	0101-04=	1?	
	1673	Cont	....	AOGA-SHIMA (Izu Is-Japan)	0804-06=	2	
	1673	Cont	....	GALERAS (Colombia)	1501-08=	2	
	1673	Cont	....	FAYAL (Azores)	1802-01=	2	
	1673	Cont	....	FOGO (Cape Verde Is)	1804-01=	1	
	1673	0520	?	**GAMKONORA** (Halmahera-Indonesia)	0608-04=	5?	-/9
	1674	Cont	....	VESUVIUS (Italy)	0101-02=	2?	
	1674	Cont	....	STROMBOLI (Italy)	0101-04=	1?	
	1674	Cont	....	AOGA-SHIMA (Izu Is-Japan)	0804-06=	2	
	1674	Cont	....	GALERAS (Colombia)	1501-08=	2	
	1674	Cont	....	FOGO (Cape Verde Is)	1804-01=	1	
	1674	07	?	**PACAYA** (Guatemala)	1402-11=	2	
	1675	Cont	....	VESUVIUS (Italy)	0101-02=	2?	
	1675	Cont	....	STROMBOLI (Italy)	0101-04=	1?	
	1675	Cont	....	AOGA-SHIMA (Izu Is-Japan)	0804-06=	2	
	1675	Cont	....	GALERAS (Colombia)	1501-08=	2	
	1675	Cont	....	FOGO (Cape Verde Is)	1804-01=	1	
	1675q	....	?	**LEWOTOBI** (Lesser Sunda Is)	0604-18=	3↑	
	1675	....	?	**KARANGETANG [API SIAU]** (Sangihe	0607-02=	3↑	
	1675	0216	?	**ASO** (Kyushu-Japan)	0802-11=	2	
	1675	06 ?	?	**KUJU GROUP** (Kyushu-Japan)	0802-12=	3↑	
	1676	Cont	....	VESUVIUS (Italy)	0101-02=	2?	
	1676	Cont	....	STROMBOLI (Italy)	0101-04=	1?	
	1676	Cont	....	AOGA-SHIMA (Izu Is-Japan)	0804-06=	2	
	1676	Cont	....	GALERAS (Colombia)	1501-08=	2	
	1676	Cont	....	FOGO (Cape Verde Is)	1804-01=	1	
	1676	1231y	?	**GAMALAMA** (Halmahera-Indonesia)	0608-06=	2	
	1677	Cont	....	VESUVIUS (Italy)	0101-02=	2?	
	1677	Cont	....	STROMBOLI (Italy)	0101-04=	1?	
	1677	Cont	....	AOGA-SHIMA (Izu Is-Japan)	0804-06=	2	
	1677	Cont	....	GALERAS (Colombia)	1501-08=	2	
	1677	Cont	....	FOGO (Cape Verde Is)	1804-01=	1	
	1677	....	?	**MERAPI** (Java)	0603-25=	3↑	
	1677	....	?	**KIRISHIMA** (Kyushu-Japan)	0802-09=	2?	
	1677	....	?	**MISTI, EL** (Peru)	1504-01=	2	
	1677	....	?	**UBINAS** (Peru)	1504-02=	2	
?	1677	....	?	**HIERRO** (Canary Is)	1803-02-		

START YEAR	M-Dy	Dura-tion	VOLCANO NAME (Subregion)	NUMBER	VEI	Vol L/T
? 1677	07	?	PACAYA (Guatemala)	1402-11=		
1677	1117	65a	LA PALMA (Canary Is)	1803-01-	2	7/6
1678	Cont	....	VESUVIUS (Italy)	0101-02=	2?	
1678	Cont	....	STROMBOLI (Italy)	0101-04=	1?	
1678	Cont	....	AOGA-SHIMA (Izu Is-Japan)	0804-06=	2	
1678	Cont	....	GALERAS (Colombia)	1501-08=	2	
1678	Cont	....	LA PALMA (Canary Is)	1803-01-	2	7/6
1678	Cont	....	FOGO (Cape Verde Is)	1804-01=	1	
? 1678	0222	?	AKITA-YAKE-YAMA (Honshu-Japan)	0803-26=		
1678	0229	?	KIRISHIMA (Kyushu-Japan)	0802-09=	2?	
1678	0301	?	SAKURA-JIMA (Kyushu-Japan)	0802-08=	2?	
1678	08 ?	?	PACAYA (Guatemala)	1402-11=	2	
1678	0819	?	MERAPI (Java)	0603-25=	3↑	
1679	Cont	....	VESUVIUS (Italy)	0101-02=	2?	
1679	Cont	....	STROMBOLI (Italy)	0101-04=	1?	
1679	Cont	....	AOGA-SHIMA (Izu Is-Japan)	0804-06=	2	
1679	Cont	....	GALERAS (Colombia)	1501-08=	2	
1679	Cont	....	FOGO (Cape Verde Is)	1804-01=	1	
? 1679	....	?	FUEGO (Guatemala)	1402-09=		
1680	Cont	....	VESUVIUS (Italy)	0101-02=	2?	
1680	Cont	....	STROMBOLI (Italy)	0101-04=	1?	
1680	Cont	....	AOGA-SHIMA (Izu Is-Japan)	0804-06=	2	
1680	Cont	....	GALERAS (Colombia)	1501-08=	2	
1680	Cont	....	FOGO (Cape Verde Is)	1804-01=	1	
1680	....	?	TONGKOKO (Sulawesi-Indonesia)	0606-13=	5?	-/9
C 1680?	....	?	MAUNA LOA (Hawaiian Is)	1302-02=	0	
1680	....	?	SAN CRISTOBAL (Nicaragua)	1404-02=	2?	
1680	05	552m>	KRAKATAU (Indonesia)	0602-00=	3	-/8
1681	Cont	....	STROMBOLI (Italy)	0101-04=	1?	
1681	Cont	....	KRAKATAU (Indonesia)	0602-00=	2?	-/8
1681	Cont	....	GALERAS (Colombia)	1501-08=	2	
1681	Cont	....	FOGO (Cape Verde Is)	1804-01=	1	
@ 1681	0410	?	GRIMSVOTN (Iceland-NE)	1703-01=		
1682	Cont	....	STROMBOLI (Italy)	0101-04=	1?	
1682	Cont	....	GALERAS (Colombia)	1501-08=	2	
1682	Cont	....	FOGO (Cape Verde Is)	1804-01=	1	
1682	0812	10a	VESUVIUS (Italy)	0101-02=	3	
1682	0901	?	ETNA (Italy)	0101-06=	2	
1682	1213	?	SETE CIDADES (Azores)	1802-08=	2	
1683	Cont	....	STROMBOLI (Italy)	0101-04=	1?	
1683	Cont	....	GALERAS (Colombia)	1501-08=	2	
1683	Cont	....	FOGO (Cape Verde Is)	1804-01=	1	
1683	....	?	SERUA (Banda Sea)	0605-07=	3↑	
1683	....	?	BANDA API (Banda Sea)	0605-09=	3	
1683	....	?	TONGKOKO (Sulawesi-Indonesia)	0606-13=	3↑	
L 1683?	....	?	PENGUIN (Antarctica)	1900-031		
1683	06	?	ASO (Kyushu-Japan)	0802-11=	2	
1684	Cont	....	STROMBOLI (Italy)	0101-04=	1?	
1684	Cont	....	GALERAS (Colombia)	1501-08=	2	
1684	Cont	....	FOGO (Cape Verde Is)	1804-01=	1	
1684	0331	>3yr	OSHIMA (Izu Is-Japan)	0804-01=	3	7/8
1684	07	?	SAN CRISTOBAL (Nicaragua)	1404-02=	2	
1684	1105d	72m	GRIMSVOTN (Iceland-NE)	1703-01=	2	
1685	Cont	....	STROMBOLI (Italy)	0101-04=	1?	
1685	Cont	....	OSHIMA (Izu Is-Japan)	0804-01=	2?	7/8
1685	Cont	....	GALERAS (Colombia)	1501-08=	2	
1685	Cont	....	GRIMSVOTN (Iceland-NE)	1703-01=	2	
1685	Cont	....	FOGO (Cape Verde Is)	1804-01=	1	
C 1685?	....	?	MAUNA LOA (Hawaiian Is)	1302-02=	0	
1685	08	?	SAN CRISTOBAL (Nicaragua)	1404-02=	2	
1685	08	?	TELICA (Nicaragua)	1404-04=	2	
@ 1685	09	?	FUEGO (Guatemala)	1402-09=	2	
1685	1003	>3yr	VESUVIUS (Italy)	0101-02=	2?	
1686	Cont	....	VESUVIUS (Italy)	0101-02=	2?	
1686	Cont	....	STROMBOLI (Italy)	0101-04=	1?	
1686	Cont	....	OSHIMA (Izu Is-Japan)	0804-01=	2?	7/8
1686	Cont	....	GALERAS (Colombia)	1501-08=	2	
1686	Cont	....	FOGO (Cape Verde Is)	1804-01=	1	
1686	....	?	FUEGO (Guatemala)	1402-09=	2	
1686	0323	3a	IWATE (Honshu-Japan)	0803-24=	3?	
1686	09 ?	28m?	GAMALAMA (Halmahera-Indonesia)	0608-06=	2	
1687	Cont	....	VESUVIUS (Italy)	0101-02=	2?	
1687	Cont	....	STROMBOLI (Italy)	0101-04=	1?	
1687	Cont	....	OSHIMA (Izu Is-Japan)	0804-01=	2?	7/8
1687	Cont	....	FOGO (Cape Verde Is)	1804-01=	1	
1687	....	?	ORIZABA, PICO DE (Mexico)	1401-10=	2	
1687	....	....	GALERAS (Colombia)	1501-08=	2	
1687	0326	2a	PACAYA (Guatemala)	1402-11=	2	
1687	0414	92m	IWATE (Honshu-Japan)	0803-24=	3	
1687	0510	1a	GAMALAMA (Halmahera-Indonesia)	0608-06=	3↑	
1687	0615	?	SERUA (Banda Sea)	0605-07=	3↑	
1688	Cont	....	VESUVIUS (Italy)	0101-02=	2?	
1688	Cont	....	STROMBOLI (Italy)	0101-04=	1?	
1688	Cont	....	OSHIMA (Izu Is-Japan)	0804-01=	2?	7/8
1688	Cont	....	GALERAS (Colombia)	1501-08=	2	
1688	Cont	....	FOGO (Cape Verde Is)	1804-01=	1	
1688	....	?	VULCANO (Italy)	0101-05=		
1688	....	?	ETNA (Italy)	0101-06=	1	
1688	....	?	VILLARRICA (Chile-C)	1507-12=	2	
1689	Cont	....	VESUVIUS (Italy)	0101-02=	2?	
1689	Cont	....	STROMBOLI (Italy)	0101-04=	1?	
1689	Cont	....	OSHIMA (Izu Is-Japan)	0804-01=	2?	7/8
1689	Cont	....	GALERAS (Colombia)	1501-08=	2	
1689	Cont	....	FOGO (Cape Verde Is)	1804-01=	1	
? 1689	....	?	FUEGO (Guatemala)	1402-09=	2	
1689	0314	?	ETNA (Italy)	0101-06=	1	7/-
1689	0622	?	IWATE (Honshu-Japan)	0803-24=	3	
1690	Cont	....	VESUVIUS (Italy)	0101-02=	2?	
1690	Cont	....	STROMBOLI (Italy)	0101-04=	1?	
1690	Cont	....	OSHIMA (Izu Is-Japan)	0804-01=	2?	7/8
1690	Cont	....	FOGO (Cape Verde Is)	1804-01=	1	
1690	....	?	GUNTUR (Java)	0603-13=	3	
1690	....	>3yr	BANDA API (Banda Sea)	0605-09=	3↑	
1690	....	?	KIRISHIMA (Kyushu-Japan)	0802-09=	2?	
? 1690	....	730y	UNZEN (Kyushu-Japan)	0802-10=		
? 1690j	....	?	ASUNCION (Mariana Is-C Pac)	0804-15=		
T 1690j	....	?	CHIKURACHKI (Kurile Is)	0900-36=	4	
1690j	....	?	KOSHELEV (Kamchatka)	1000-02=	3↑	
C 1690v	....	?	KARYMSKY (Kamchatka)	1000-13=		
C 1690?	....	?	SHEVELUCH (Kamchatka)	1000-27=		
1690	....	?	COLIMA VOLC COMPLEX (Mexico)	1401-04=	3	
1690	....	?	PACAYA (Guatemala)	1402-11=	2?	
1690	....	....	GALERAS (Colombia)	1501-08=	2	
1690?	....	?	SOUFRIERE GUADELOUPE (W Indies)	1600-06=	3↑	
1691	Cont	....	VESUVIUS (Italy)	0101-02=	2?	
1691	Cont	....	STROMBOLI (Italy)	0101-04=	1?	
1691	Cont	....	BANDA API (Banda Sea)	0605-09=	2	
? 1691	Cont	....	UNZEN (Kyushu-Japan)	0802-10=		
1691	Cont	....	GALERAS (Colombia)	1501-08=	2	
1691	Cont	....	FOGO (Cape Verde Is)	1804-01=	1	
1691	....	?	REVENTADOR (Ecuador)	1502-01=	3↑	
1691	04	121p	ASO (Kyushu-Japan)	0802-11=	2	
1692	Cont	....	VESUVIUS (Italy)	0101-02=	2?	
1692	Cont	....	STROMBOLI (Italy)	0101-04=	1?	
1692	Cont	....	BANDA API (Banda Sea)	0605-09=	2	
? 1692	Cont	....	UNZEN (Kyushu-Japan)	0802-10=		
1692	Cont	....	GALERAS (Colombia)	1501-08=	2	
1692	Cont	....	FOGO (Cape Verde Is)	1804-01=	1	
? 1692	....	?	LIAMUIGA (W Indies)	1600-03=		
? 1692	....	?	HIERRO (Canary Is)	1803-02-		
? 1692	0604?	?	SERUA (Banda Sea)	0605-07=		
1693	Cont	....	VESUVIUS (Italy)	0101-02=	2?	
1693	Cont	....	STROMBOLI (Italy)	0101-04=	1?	
1693	Cont	....	BANDA API (Banda Sea)	0605-09=	2	
1693	Cont	....	GALERAS (Colombia)	1501-08=	2	
1693	Cont	....	FOGO (Cape Verde Is)	1804-01=	1	
1693	....	?	TEON (Banda Sea)	0605-05=	3↑	
1693	....	?	PACAYA (Guatemala)	1402-11=	2?	
? 1693	0109	?	ETNA (Italy)	0101-06=		
1693	0213	214a?	HEKLA (Iceland-S)	1702-07=	4	-/8
1693	0604	41m	SERUA (Banda Sea)	0605-07=	4?	-/8
1693	12	334p	ETNA (Italy)	0101-06=	2	
1694	Cont	....	STROMBOLI (Italy)	0101-04=	1?	
1694	Cont	....	GALERAS (Colombia)	1501-08=	2	
1694	Cont	....	FOGO (Cape Verde Is)	1804-01=	1	
1694	....	?	SERUA (Banda Sea)	0605-07=	3↑	
1694	....	?	TONGKOKO (Sulawesi-Indonesia)	0606-13=	3?	
1694	03	....	ETNA (Italy)	0101-06=	3?	
1694	0413	....	VESUVIUS (Italy)	0101-02=	3	
1694	0529	93a?	ZAO (Honshu-Japan)	0803-19=	2	
? 1694	0619	?	IWAKI (Honshu-Japan)	0803-27=	2?	
1694	0704	2a	KOMAGA-TAKE (Hokkaido-Japan)	0805-02=	4	-/8
1694	1130	....	BANDA API (Banda Sea)	0605-09=	3	
1695	Cont	....	STROMBOLI (Italy)	0101-04=	1?	
1695	Cont	....	BANDA API (Banda Sea)	0605-09=	2	
1695	Cont	....	GALERAS (Colombia)	1501-08=	2	
1695	Cont	....	FOGO (Cape Verde Is)	1804-01=	1	
1695	0412	?	OSHIMA (Izu Is-Japan)	0804-01=		
1696	Cont	....	STROMBOLI (Italy)	0101-04=	1?	
1696	Cont	....	BANDA API (Banda Sea)	0605-09=	2	
1696	Cont	....	FOGO (Cape Verde Is)	1804-01=	1	
1696	....	....	GALERAS (Colombia)	1501-08=	2	
1696	....	?	SOUFRIERE GUADELOUPE (W Indies)	1600-06=	3↑	
1696	0731	714a	VESUVIUS (Italy)	0101-02=	2	
1697	Cont	....	STROMBOLI (Italy)	0101-04=	1?	
1697	Cont	....	GALERAS (Colombia)	1501-08=	2	
1697	Cont	....	FOGO (Cape Verde Is)	1804-01=	1	
1697	....	365y	KLIUCHEVSKOI (Kamchatka)	1000-26=	3↑	
1697	....	?	POPOCATEPETL (Mexico)	1401-09=	2	
I 1697	....	?	BARDARBUNGA (Iceland-NE)	1703-03=	2	
1697	0918	....	VESUVIUS (Italy)	0101-02=	2	
1698	Cont	....	STROMBOLI (Italy)	0101-04=	1?	
1698	Cont	....	KLIUCHEVSKOI (Kamchatka)	1000-26=	3*	
1698	Cont	....	GALERAS (Colombia)	1501-08=	2	
1698	Cont	....	FOGO (Cape Verde Is)	1804-01=	1	
1698	....	?	COTOPAXI (Ecuador)	1502-05=	3?	
1698	0203	?	CEREME (Java)	0603-17=	3	
1698	0525	....	VESUVIUS (Italy)	0101-02=	3	
1699	Cont	....	STROMBOLI (Italy)	0101-04=	1?	
1699	Cont	....	GALERAS (Colombia)	1501-08=	2	
1699	Cont	....	FOGO (Cape Verde Is)	1804-01=	1	
1699	....	?	GUNUNGAPI WETAR (Banda Sea)	0605-03=	3↑	
? 1699a	....	?	TOLBACHIK (Kamchatka)	1000-24=	2?	
1699	....	?	FUEGO (Guatemala)	1402-09=	2	
1699	....	?	SAN MIGUEL (El Salvador)	1403-10=	2	
? 1699	0105	?	SALAK (Java)	0603-05=		
1699	0629	?	PACAYA (Guatemala)	1402-11=	2?	

1700

START YEAR	M-Dy	Dura-tion	VOLCANO NAME (Subregion)	NUMBER	VEI	Vol L/T
1700	Cont	....	STROMBOLI (Italy)	0101-04=	1?	
1700	Cont	....	GALERAS (Colombia)	1501-08=	2	
1700	Cont	....	FOGO (Cape Verde Is)	1804-01=	1	
C 1700v	....	?	EMURUANGOGOLAK (Africa-E)	0202-051	0	
1700	....	?	FUJI (Honshu-Japan)	0803-03=	2?	

START YEAR	M-Dy	Duration	VOLCANO NAME (Subregion)	NUMBER	VEI	Vol L/T
1700	....	>3yr	**AMAK** (Aleutian Is)	1101-39-		
T **1700** v	....	?	**GLACIER PEAK** (US-Washington)	1201-02-	2	
M **1700** q	....	?	**KILAUEA** (Hawaiian Is)	1302-01-	0	
T **1700** t	....	?	**TRISTAN DA CUNHA** (Atlantic-S)	1806-01=		
1700	0311	?	**ULAWUN** (New Britain-SW Pac)	0502-12=	2	
1700	0324	?	**RITTER ISLAND** (New Guinea-NE of)	0501-07=	3↑	
? **1700**	04	?	**KADOVAR** (New Guinea-NE of)	0501-002		
1700	0402	?	**MANAM** (New Guinea-NE of)	0501-02=		
1701	*Cont*	....	*STROMBOLI (Italy)*	0101-04=	*1?*	
1701	*Cont*	....	*AMAK (Aleutian Is)*	1101-39-		
1701	*Cont*	....	*GALERAS (Colombia)*	1501-08=	*2*	
1701	*Cont*	....	*FOGO (Cape Verde Is)*	1804-01=	*1*	
? **1701**	....	?	**CAMPI FLEGREI MAR SICILIA** (Italy)	0101-07=	2	
1701	0701	>3yr	**VESUVIUS** (Italy)	0101-02=	2	
1702	*Cont*	....	*VESUVIUS (Italy)*	0101-02=	*2*	
1702	*Cont*	....	*STROMBOLI (Italy)*	0101-04=	*1?*	
1702	*Cont*	....	*AMAK (Aleutian Is)*	1101-39-		
1702	*Cont*	....	*GALERAS (Colombia)*	1501-08=	*2*	
1702	*Cont*	....	*FOGO (Cape Verde Is)*	1804-01=	*1*	
1702	....	?	**BAITOUSHAN** (China-E)	1005-07-		
@ **1702**	....	?	**BARDARBUNGA** (Iceland-NE)	1703-03=	2	
1702	0308	61*a*	**ETNA** (Italy)	0101-06=	1	7/-
1702	0804	?	**FUEGO** (Guatemala)	1402-09=	2	
1703	*Cont*	....	*VESUVIUS (Italy)*	0101-02=	*2*	
1703	*Cont*	....	*STROMBOLI (Italy)*	0101-04=	*1?*	
1703	*Cont*	....	*AMAK (Aleutian Is)*	1101-39-		
1703	*Cont*	....	*GALERAS (Colombia)*	1501-08=	*2*	
1703	*Cont*	....	*FOGO (Cape Verde Is)*	1804-01=	*1*	
1703 <	....	730*y*>	**FOURNAISE, PITON DE LA** (Indian O.)	0303-02=	0	
1703	....	?	**ASAMA** (Honshu-Japan)	0803-11=	2	
1704	*Cont*	....	*VESUVIUS (Italy)*	0101-02=	*2*	
1704	*Cont*	....	*STROMBOLI (Italy)*	0101-04=	*1?*	
1704	*Cont*	....	*FOURNAISE, PITON DE LA (Indian O.)*	0303-02=	*0*	
1704	*Cont*	....	*AMAK (Aleutian Is)*	1101-39-		
1704	*Cont*	....	*GALERAS (Colombia)*	1501-08=	*2*	
1704	*Cont*	....	*FOGO (Cape Verde Is)*	1804-01=	*1*	
1704	0205	4*a*	**ASAMA** (Honshu-Japan)	0803-11=	2	
1704	1231	87*a*	**TENERIFE** (Canary Is)	1803-03-	2	
1705	*Cont*	....	*STROMBOLI (Italy)*	0101-04=	*1?*	
1705	*Cont*	....	*FOURNAISE, PITON DE LA (Indian O.)*	0303-02=	*0*	
1705	*Cont*	....	*AMAK (Aleutian Is)*	1101-39-		
1705	*Cont*	....	*GALERAS (Colombia)*	1501-08=	*2*	
1705	*Cont*	....	*FOGO (Cape Verde Is)*	1804-01=	*1*	
1705	*0105*	....	*TENERIFE (Canary Is)*	1803-03-	2	
1705	0131	2*a*	**FUEGO** (Guatemala)	1402-09=	2	
1706	*Cont*	....	*STROMBOLI (Italy)*	0101-04=	*1?*	
1706	*Cont*	....	*AMAK (Aleutian Is)*	1101-39-		
1706	*Cont*	....	*GALERAS (Colombia)*	1501-08=	*2*	
1706	*Cont*	....	*FOGO (Cape Verde Is)*	1804-01=	*1*	
1706	....	?	**BARDARBUNGA** (Iceland-NE)	1703-03=	2	
1706	01	?	**SAKURA-JIMA** (Kyushu-Japan)	0802-08=	2?	
1706	0128	?	**KIRISHIMA** (Kyushu-Japan)	0802-09=	2	
1706	0505	39*a*	**TENERIFE** (Canary Is)	1803-03-	2	
1706	*0720*	*398a*	*VESUVIUS (Italy)*	0101-02=	2?	
1706	1004	?	**FUEGO** (Guatemala)	1402-09=	2	
1706	1015q	?	**GRIMSVOTN** (Iceland-NE)	1703-01=	2	
1706	1120	?	**ASAMA** (Honshu-Japan)	0803-11=	2	
1707	*Cont*	....	*STROMBOLI (Italy)*	0101-04=	*1?*	
1707	*Cont*	....	*AMAK (Aleutian Is)*	1101-39-		
1707	*Cont*	....	*GALERAS (Colombia)*	1501-08=	*2*	
1707	*Cont*	....	*FOGO (Cape Verde Is)*	1804-01=	*1*	
1707	....	?	**TAAL** (Luzon-Philippines)	0703-07=	2	
? **1707**	....	?	**HACHIJO-JIMA** (Izu Is-Japan)	0804-05=	2	
1707	....	?	**BARDARBUNGA** (Iceland-NE)	1703-03=	2	
1707	0523	>3yr	**SANTORINI** (Greece)	0102-04=	3	8/-
1707	0729	....	**VESUVIUS** (Italy)	0101-02=	3	
1707	1216	39*a?*	**FUJI** (Honshu-Japan)	0803-03=	**5**	**-/9**
1708	*Cont*	....	*STROMBOLI (Italy)*	0101-04=	*1?*	
1708	*Cont*	....	*SANTORINI (Greece)*	0102-04=	*3*	*8/-*
1708	*Cont*	....	*FUJI (Honshu-Japan)*	0803-03=	*2?*	
1708	*Cont*	....	*AMAK (Aleutian Is)*	1101-39-		
1708	*Cont*	....	*GALERAS (Colombia)*	1501-08=	*2*	
1708	*Cont*	....	*FOGO (Cape Verde Is)*	1804-01=	*1*	
1708	04	15*m*	**FOURNAISE, PITON DE LA** (Indian O.)	0303-02=	0	7/-
? **1708**	0917	?	**ASO** (Kyushu-Japan)	0802-11=	2	
1708	1229	10*a*	**ASAMA** (Honshu-Japan)	0803-11=	2	
1709	*Cont*	....	*STROMBOLI (Italy)*	0101-04=	*1?*	
1709	*Cont*	....	*SANTORINI (Greece)*	0102-04=	*3*	*8/-*
1709	*Cont*	....	*ASAMA (Honshu-Japan)*	0803-11=	*2*	
1709	*Cont*	....	*AMAK (Aleutian Is)*	1101-39-		

Figure 16. The caldera of Santorini, on the Greek island of Thera. One of many historical new islands is shown being formed by submarine eruption. This broadly circular collapse feature, roughly 9 km in diameter, formed in part during the noted Minoan eruption about 3500 years ago. From the *Illustrated London News* of March 31, 1866.

	START YEAR	M-Dy	Duration	VOLCANO NAME (Subregion)	NUMBER	VEI	Vol L/T
	1709	Cont	....	GALERAS (Colombia)	1501-08=	2	
	1709	Cont	....	FOGO (Cape Verde Is)	1804-01=	1	
	1709	....	?	FOURNAISE, PITON DE LA (Indian O.)	0303-02=	2	
	1709	....	?	TAAL (Luzon-Philippines)	0703-07=	2	
	1709?	....	?	COSIGUINA (Nicaragua)	1404-01=		
?	1709	0116	?	FUJI (Honshu-Japan)	0803-03=		
	1709	0213	?	ASO (Kyushu-Japan)	0802-11=	2	
?	1709	0423	?	IWAKI (Honshu-Japan)	0803-27=	2?	
	1709	0423	?	MIYAKE-JIMA (Izu Is-Japan)	0804-04=		
?	1709	1014	?	FUEGO (Guatemala)	1402-09=		
	1710	Cont	....	STROMBOLI (Italy)	0101-04=	1?	
	1710	Cont	....	SANTORINI (Greece)	0102-04=	3	8/-
	1710	Cont	....	AMAK (Aleutian Is)	1101-39-		
	1710	Cont	....	FOGO (Cape Verde Is)	1804-01=	1	
	1710j	....	?	USHISHUR (Kurile Is)	0900-21=	1	
	1710j	....	?	NEMO PEAK (Kurile Is)	0900-32=	2	
	1710	....	....	GALERAS (Colombia)	1501-08=	2	
	1710	0413	?	ASAMA (Honshu-Japan)	0803-11=	2	
?	1710	0627	?	KOMAGA-TAKE (Hokkaido-Japan)	0805-02=		
	1710	1014	?	FUEGO (Guatemala)	1402-09=	2	
	1711	Cont	....	STROMBOLI (Italy)	0101-04=	1?	
	1711	Cont	....	SANTORINI (Greece)	0102-04=	3	8/-
	1711	Cont	....	GALERAS (Colombia)	1501-08=	2	
	1711	Cont	....	FOGO (Cape Verde Is)	1804-01=	1	
?	1711?	....	?	AZUMA (Honshu-Japan)	0803-18=		
	1711	0413	?	ASAMA (Honshu-Japan)	0803-11=	2	
	1711	1210	6a	AWU (Sangihe Is-Indonesia)	0607-04=	3	
	1712	Cont	....	STROMBOLI (Italy)	0101-04=	1?	
	1712	Cont	....	GALERAS (Colombia)	1501-08=	2	
	1712	Cont	....	FOGO (Cape Verde Is)	1804-01=	1	
	1712	0115q	?	BARDARBUNGA (Iceland-NE)	1703-03=	2	
	1712	0116	?	KARANGETANG [API SIAU] (Sangihe	0607-02=	2	
	1712	0204	878w	MIYAKE-JIMA (Izu Is-Japan)	0804-04=	2	-/8
	1712	0205	>3yr	VESUVIUS (Italy)	0101-02=	1	
	1712	05	214p	BANDA API (Banda Sea)	0605-09=	2	
	1712	1009	55a	LA PALMA (Canary Is)	1803-01-	2	7/-
	1712	1231y	?	CHIRPOI (Kurile Is)	0900-15=	4?	
	1713	Cont	....	STROMBOLI (Italy)	0101-04=	1?	
	1713	Cont	....	MIYAKE-JIMA (Izu Is-Japan)	0804-04=	1	-/8
	1713	Cont	....	GALERAS (Colombia)	1501-08=	2	
	1713	Cont	....	FOGO (Cape Verde Is)	1804-01=	1	
	1713	....	?	HARIMKOTAN (Kurile Is)	0900-30=	3↑	
	1713	....	?	SETE CIDADES (Azores)	1802-08=	2	7/6
	1713	0417	....	VESUVIUS (Italy)	0101-02=	2	
	1714	Cont	....	STROMBOLI (Italy)	0101-04=	1?	
	1714	Cont	....	MIYAKE-JIMA (Izu Is-Japan)	0804-04=	1	-/8
	1714	Cont	....	GALERAS (Colombia)	1501-08=	2	
	1714	Cont	....	FOGO (Cape Verde Is)	1804-01=	1	
	1714	0615	....	VESUVIUS (Italy)	0101-02=	2	
	1715	Cont	....	VESUVIUS (Italy)	0101-02=	1	
	1715	Cont	....	STROMBOLI (Italy)	0101-04=	1?	
	1715	Cont	....	GALERAS (Colombia)	1501-08=	2	
	1715	Cont	....	FOGO (Cape Verde Is)	1804-01=	1	
	1715	....	?	SANGEANG API (Lesser Sunda Is)	0604-05=	2	
	1715	....	?	TAAL (Luzon-Philippines)	0703-07=	2	
	1716	Cont	....	VESUVIUS (Italy)	0101-02=	1	
	1716	Cont	....	STROMBOLI (Italy)	0101-04=	1?	
	1716	Cont	....	GALERAS (Colombia)	1501-08=	2	
	1716	Cont	....	FOGO (Cape Verde Is)	1804-01=	1	
	1716	....	?	VILLARRICA (Chile-C)	1507-12=	1	
	1716	0311	?	KIRISHIMA (Kyushu-Japan)	0802-09=	3	-/7
	1716	0720	?	KELUT (Java)	0603-28=	2	
	1716	0924	3a	TAAL (Luzon-Philippines)	0703-07=	4?	
	1716	1005d	?	BARDARBUNGA (Iceland-NE)	1703-03=	2	
	1716	1006	?	GRIMSVOTN (Iceland-NE)	1703-01=	2	
	1716	1109	96a	KIRISHIMA (Kyushu-Japan)	0802-09=	3	-/8
	1717	Cont	....	STROMBOLI (Italy)	0101-04=	1?	
	1717	Cont	....	FOGO (Cape Verde Is)	1804-01=	1	
?	1717	....	?	PACAYA (Guatemala)	1402-11=		
	1717	....	....	GALERAS (Colombia)	1501-08=	2	
	1717	0207	....	KIRISHIMA (Kyushu-Japan)	0802-09=	3	-/8
	1717	0606	....	VESUVIUS (Italy)	0101-02=	3	
	1717	0804	44a>	BARDARBUNGA (Iceland-NE)	1703-03=	3?	
	1717	0827	121e	FUEGO (Guatemala)	1402-09=	4?	-/8
@	1717	0829	>3yr	ATITLAN (Guatemala)	1402-06=		
	1717	0919	?	KIRISHIMA (Kyushu-Japan)	0802-09=	3	-/7
	1717	0923	?	ASAMA (Honshu-Japan)	0803-11=	2	
	1718	Cont	....	VESUVIUS (Italy)	0101-02=	1	
	1718	Cont	....	STROMBOLI (Italy)	0101-04=	1?	
@	1718	Cont	....	ATITLAN (Guatemala)	1402-06=		
	1718	Cont	....	GALERAS (Colombia)	1501-08=	2	
	1718	Cont	....	FOGO (Cape Verde Is)	1804-01=	1	
	1718	0201	318e	PICO (Azores)	1802-02=	2	
	1718	0326	3a	SOUFRIERE ST. VINCENT (W Indies)	1600-15=	3?	
	1718	0926	?	ASAMA (Honshu-Japan)	0803-11=	2	
	1719	Cont	....	VESUVIUS (Italy)	0101-02=	1	
	1719	Cont	....	STROMBOLI (Italy)	0101-04=	1?	
@	1719	Cont	....	ATITLAN (Guatemala)	1402-06=		
	1719	Cont	....	GALERAS (Colombia)	1501-08=	2	
	1719	Cont	....	FOGO (Cape Verde Is)	1804-01=	1	
	1719w	....	?	DUKONO (Halmahera-Indonesia)	0608-01=		
	1719	....	?	KIRISHIMA (Kyushu-Japan)	0802-09=	2	
?	1719<	....	?	BANDAI (Honshu-Japan)	0803-16=		
	1719	....	730y	WUDALIANCHI (China-E)	1005-04-	3	9/8
	1719	....	?	OSORNO (Chile-S)	1508-01=	2	
	1719	02 ?	?	IWATE (Honshu-Japan)	0803-24=	2	7/-
@	1719	0610	1a	ASAMA (Honshu-Japan)	0803-11=		
	1720	Cont	....	VESUVIUS (Italy)	0101-02=	1	
	1720	Cont	....	STROMBOLI (Italy)	0101-04=	1?	
	1720	Cont	....	WUDALIANCHI (China-E)	1005-04-	2?	9/8
@	1720	Cont	....	ATITLAN (Guatemala)	1402-06=		
	1720	Cont	....	GALERAS (Colombia)	1501-08=	2	
	1720	Cont	....	FOGO (Cape Verde Is)	1804-01=	1	
C	1720t	....	?	RAOUL ISLAND (Kermadec Is)	0402-03=	4	-/8
	1720	....	365y	KLIUCHEVSKOI (Kamchatka)	1000-26=	2	
	1720	....	?	POPOCATEPETL (Mexico)	1401-09=	3	
T	1720w	....	?	BRAVO, CERRO (Colombia)	1501-011	4	-/8
I	1720	....	?	BARDARBUNGA (Iceland-NE)	1703-03=	2	
	1720	0606	?	ASAMA (Honshu-Japan)	0803-11=	2	
	1720	0710	159m?	PICO (Azores)	1802-02=	2	
	1720	1208?	22e?	DON JOAO DE CASTRO BANK	1802-07=	3	
	1721	Cont	....	VESUVIUS (Italy)	0101-02=	1	
	1721	Cont	....	STROMBOLI (Italy)	0101-04=	1?	
	1721	Cont	....	KLIUCHEVSKOI (Kamchatka)	1000-26=	2	
	1721	Cont	....	WUDALIANCHI (China-E)	1005-04-	2?	9/8
@	1721	Cont	....	ATITLAN (Guatemala)	1402-06=		
	1721	Cont	....	GALERAS (Colombia)	1501-08=	2	
	1721	Cont	....	FOGO (Cape Verde Is)	1804-01=	1	
	1721	0511	157q	KATLA (Iceland-S)	1702-03=	4+	-/8
	1721	06	?	FOURNAISE, PITON DE LA (Indian O.)	0303-02=	2	
	1721	0622	?	ASAMA (Honshu-Japan)	0803-11=	1	
	1722	Cont	....	VESUVIUS (Italy)	0101-02=	1	
	1722	Cont	....	STROMBOLI (Italy)	0101-04=	1?	
	1722	Cont	....	GALERAS (Colombia)	1501-08=	2	
	1722	Cont	....	FOGO (Cape Verde Is)	1804-01=	1	
	1722	....	?	BANDA API (Banda Sea)	0605-09=	2	
	1722	0312	?	SANTA ANA [SAN MARCELINO]	1403-02=	2	
	1722	1118?	16a?	ASAMA (Honshu-Japan)	0803-11=	2	
	1723	Cont	....	STROMBOLI (Italy)	0101-04=	1?	
	1723	Cont	....	GALERAS (Colombia)	1501-08=	2	
	1723	Cont	....	FOGO (Cape Verde Is)	1804-01=	1	
?	1723	....	?	TURRIALBA (Costa Rica)	1405-07=	1	
	1723	0205	?	ASAMA (Honshu-Japan)	0803-11=	2	
	1723	0216	299a	IRAZU (Costa Rica)	1405-06=	3?	
	1723	0420	....	VESUVIUS (Italy)	0101-02=	3	
	1723	0820	?	ASAMA (Honshu-Japan)	0803-11=	2	
	1723	1122	169a?	ETNA (Italy)	0101-06=	2	
	1724	Cont	....	STROMBOLI (Italy)	0101-04=	1?	
	1724	Cont	....	ETNA (Italy)	0101-06=	2	
	1724	Cont	....	GALERAS (Colombia)	1501-08=	2	
	1724	Cont	....	FOGO (Cape Verde Is)	1804-01=	1	
	1724	0517	1a	KRAFLA (Iceland-NE)	1703-08=	2	-/6
	1724	0904	>3yr	VESUVIUS (Italy)	0101-02=	2	
	1725	Cont	....	VESUVIUS (Italy)	0101-02=	2	
	1725	Cont	....	STROMBOLI (Italy)	0101-04=	1?	
	1725	Cont	....	GALERAS (Colombia)	1501-08=	2	
	1725	Cont	....	FOGO (Cape Verde Is)	1804-01=	1	
	1725s	....	?	SAVAI'I (Samoa-SW Pacific)	0404-04=	2	9/-
	1725q	....	?	SINARKA (Kurile Is)	0900-29=	2?	
?	1725	....	?	QUILOTOA (Ecuador)	1502-06=	2	
	1725q	....	?	UNNAMED (Arctic Ocean)	1707-01-	0	
	1725	02	?	GRIMSVOTN (Iceland-NE)	1703-01=	2	
	1725	0402	?	HEKLA (Iceland-S)	1702-07=	1?	
	1726	Cont	....	VESUVIUS (Italy)	0101-02=	2	
	1726	Cont	....	STROMBOLI (Italy)	0101-04=	1?	
	1726	Cont	....	GALERAS (Colombia)	1501-08=	2	
	1726	Cont	....	FOGO (Cape Verde Is)	1804-01=	1	
	1726j	....	?	KURIKOMA (Honshu-Japan)	0803-21=	1?	
	1726	0201p	90r	BARDARBUNGA (Iceland-NE)	1703-03=	1?	
	1726	05	?	IRAZU (Costa Rica)	1405-06=	2	
	1727	Cont	....	VESUVIUS (Italy)	0101-02=	2	
	1727	Cont	....	STROMBOLI (Italy)	0101-04=	1?	
	1727	Cont	....	FOGO (Cape Verde Is)	1804-01=	1	
	1727	....	?	VULCANO (Italy)	0101-05=	3	
	1727	....	>3yr	KLIUCHEVSKOI (Kamchatka)	1000-26=	2	
	1727	....	....	GALERAS (Colombia)	1501-08=	2	
	1727	0803	268p	ORAEFAJOKULL (Iceland-SE)	1704-01=	4	-/8
	1727	0821	?	KRAFLA (Iceland-NE)	1703-08=	2	
	1728	Cont	....	VESUVIUS (Italy)	0101-02=	2	
	1728	Cont	....	STROMBOLI (Italy)	0101-04=	1?	
	1728	Cont	....	KLIUCHEVSKOI (Kamchatka)	1000-26=	2	
	1728	Cont	....	GALERAS (Colombia)	1501-08=	2	
	1728	Cont	....	ORAEFAJOKULL (Iceland-SE)	1704-01=	2	-/8
	1728	Cont	....	FOGO (Cape Verde Is)	1804-01=	1	
?	1728	....	?	ANTISANA (Ecuador)	1502-03=	0	
	1728	0418	?	KRAFLA (Iceland-NE)	1703-08=	2	
	1728	0930p	>3yr	SANGAY (Ecuador)	1502-09=	3	
	1728	1110	?	ASAMA (Honshu-Japan)	0803-11=	2	
	1728	1218	?	KRAFLA (Iceland-NE)	1703-08=	2	8/-
	1729	Cont	....	VESUVIUS (Italy)	0101-02=	2	
	1729	Cont	....	STROMBOLI (Italy)	0101-04=	1?	
	1729	Cont	....	KLIUCHEVSKOI (Kamchatka)	1000-26=	2	
	1729	Cont	....	GALERAS (Colombia)	1501-08=	2	
	1729	Cont	....	SANGAY (Ecuador)	1502-09=	2	
	1729	Cont	....	FOGO (Cape Verde Is)	1804-01=	1	
	1729	....	?	TAAL (Luzon-Philippines)	0703-07=	2	
@	1729	....	?	BARDARBUNGA (Iceland-NE)	1703-03=	1	
	1729	02	?	ASAMA (Honshu-Japan)	0803-11=	2	
	1729	0215q	?	KVERKFJOLL (Iceland-NE)	1703-05=	1	
	1729	0630	87e	KRAFLA (Iceland-NE)	1703-08=	2	
	1729	08	?	KVERKFJOLL (Iceland-NE)	1703-05=	1	
	1729	11 ?	?	ASAMA (Honshu-Japan)	0803-11=	2	
	1730	Cont	....	STROMBOLI (Italy)	0101-04=	1?	
	1730	Cont	....	KLIUCHEVSKOI (Kamchatka)	1000-26=	2	

	START YEAR	M-Dy	Duration	VOLCANO NAME (Subregion)	NUMBER	VEI	Vol L/T
	1730	Cont	....	GALERAS (Colombia)	1501-08=	2	
	1730	Cont	....	SANGAY (Ecuador)	1502-09=	2	
	1730	Cont	....	FOGO (Cape Verde Is)	1804-01=	1	
	1730?	....	?	**SUMBING** (Java)	0603-22=	1	
	1730	....	?	**RAUNG** (Java)	0603-34=	3?	-/8
?	1730	....	?	**BANAHAW** (Luzon-Philippines)	0703-05=		
C	1730w	....	?	**TSEAX RIVER CONE** (Canada)	1200-10-		8/-
C	1730?	....	?	**MAUNA LOA** (Hawaiian Is)	1302-02=	0	
	1730	0227	....	**VESUVIUS** (Italy)	0101-02=	3	
	1730	0708	?	**VILLARRICA** (Chile-C)	1507-12=	2	
	1730	09	?	**FUEGO** (Guatemala)	1402-09=	2	
	1730	0901	>3yr	**LANZAROTE** (Canary Is)	1803-06-	3	9/-
	1731	Cont	....	STROMBOLI (Italy)	0101-04=	1?	
	1731	Cont	....	KLIUCHEVSKOI (Kamchatka)	1000-26=	2	
	1731	Cont	....	GALERAS (Colombia)	1501-08=	2	
	1731	Cont	....	SANGAY (Ecuador)	1502-09=	2	
	1731	Cont	....	LANZAROTE (Canary Is)	1803-06-	3	9/-
	1731	Cont	....	FOGO (Cape Verde Is)	1804-01=	1	
	1731	....	>3yr	VULCANO (Italy)	0101-05=	2?	
	1731	....	?	**TAAL** (Luzon-Philippines)	0703-07=	2	
	1731	....	?	**ASAMA** (Honshu-Japan)	0803-11=	2	
	1731	1226	293m?	**IWATE** (Honshu-Japan)	0803-24=	2	
	1732	Cont	....	STROMBOLI (Italy)	0101-04=	1?	
	1732	Cont	....	VULCANO (Italy)	0101-05=	2?	
	1732	Cont	....	IWATE (Honshu-Japan)	0803-24=	2	
	1732	Cont	....	GALERAS (Colombia)	1501-08=	2	
	1732	Cont	....	SANGAY (Ecuador)	1502-09=	2	
	1732	Cont	....	LANZAROTE (Canary Is)	1803-06-	3	9/-
	1732	Cont	....	FOGO (Cape Verde Is)	1804-01=	1	
	1732	05	?	**FUEGO** (Guatemala)	1402-09=	2	
	1732	0517	1a	**JAN MAYEN** (Atl-N-Jan Mayen)	1706-01=	3	
	1732	0730	?	**ASAMA** (Honshu-Japan)	0803-11=	2	
	1732	1209	48e	**ETNA** (Italy)	0101-06=	2	
	1732	1225	>3yr	VESUVIUS (Italy)	0101-02=	2	
	1733	Cont	....	VESUVIUS (Italy)	0101-02=	2	
	1733	Cont	....	STROMBOLI (Italy)	0101-04=	1?	
	1733	Cont	....	VULCANO (Italy)	0101-05=	2?	
	1733	Cont	....	ETNA (Italy)	0101-06=	2	
	1733	Cont	....	GALERAS (Colombia)	1501-08=	2	
	1733	Cont	....	SANGAY (Ecuador)	1502-09=	2	
	1733	Cont	....	LANZAROTE (Canary Is)	1803-06-	3	9/-
	1733	Cont	....	FOGO (Cape Verde Is)	1804-01=	1	
	1733?	....	?	**FOURNAISE, PITON DE LA** (Indian O.)	0303-02=	0	
	1733	0730	?	**ASAMA** (Honshu-Japan)	0803-11=	2	
	1734	Cont	....	VESUVIUS (Italy)	0101-02=	2	
	1734	Cont	....	STROMBOLI (Italy)	0101-04=	1?	
	1734	Cont	....	VULCANO (Italy)	0101-05=	2?	
	1734	Cont	....	GALERAS (Colombia)	1501-08=	2	
	1734	Cont	....	SANGAY (Ecuador)	1502-09=	2	
	1734	Cont	....	LANZAROTE (Canary Is)	1803-06-	3	9/-
	1734	Cont	....	FOGO (Cape Verde Is)	1804-01=	1	
	1734	0101	64a	**FOURNAISE, PITON DE LA** (Indian O.)	0303-02=	2	
	1734	06 <	?	**SANTA ANA** (El Salvador)	1403-02=	2?	
	1734	12	16m	**FOURNAISE, PITON DE LA** (Indian O.)	0303-02=	2	
	1735	Cont	....	VESUVIUS (Italy)	0101-02=	2	
	1735	Cont	....	STROMBOLI (Italy)	0101-04=	1?	
	1735	Cont	....	VULCANO (Italy)	0101-05=	2?	
	1735	Cont	....	GALERAS (Colombia)	1501-08=	2	
	1735	Cont	....	SANGAY (Ecuador)	1502-09=	2	
	1735	Cont	....	LANZAROTE (Canary Is)	1803-06-	3	9/-
	1735	Cont	....	FOGO (Cape Verde Is)	1804-01=	1	
	1735	....	?	**CHOKAI** (Honshu-Japan)	0803-22=	2	
	1735	1004	346m	**ETNA** (Italy)	0101-06=	2	
	1736	Cont	....	VESUVIUS (Italy)	0101-02=	2	
	1736	Cont	....	STROMBOLI (Italy)	0101-04=	1?	
	1736	Cont	....	VULCANO (Italy)	0101-05=	2?	
	1736	Cont	....	ETNA (Italy)	0101-06=	2	
	1736	Cont	....	SANGAY (Ecuador)	1502-09=	2	
	1736	Cont	....	LANZAROTE (Canary Is)	1803-06-	3	9/-
	1736	Cont	....	FOGO (Cape Verde Is)	1804-01=	1	
	1736	....	?	**MOMOTOMBO** (Nicaragua)	1404-09=	2?	
	1736	....	....	GALERAS (Colombia)	1501-08=	2	
	1737	Cont	....	STROMBOLI (Italy)	0101-04=	1?	
	1737	Cont	....	VULCANO (Italy)	0101-05=	2?	
	1737	Cont	....	SANGAY (Ecuador)	1502-09=	2	
	1737	Cont	....	FOGO (Cape Verde Is)	1804-01=	1	
	1737	0310	3a	**GAMALAMA** (Halmahera-Indonesia)	0608-06=	2	
	1737	0514	....	**VESUVIUS** (Italy)	0101-02=	3	
	1737	08	62m>	**AVACHINSKY** (Kamchatka)	1000-10=	3	-/7
	1737	0827	28a	**FUEGO** (Guatemala)	1402-09=	4?	-/8
	1737	0925?	40a?	**KLIUCHEVSKOI** (Kamchatka)	1000-26=	2	
	1737	1224	?	**VILLARRICA** (Chile-C)	1507-12=	2	
	1738	Cont	....	STROMBOLI (Italy)	0101-04=	1?	
	1738	Cont	....	VULCANO (Italy)	0101-05=	2?	
	1738	Cont	....	FOGO (Cape Verde Is)	1804-01=	1	
	1738	....	?	**COTOPAXI** (Ecuador)	1502-05=	2	
	1738	03	....	SANGAY (Ecuador)	1502-09=	2	
	1738	1231y	?	**CHOKAI** (Honshu-Japan)	0803-22=	2	
	1739	Cont	....	STROMBOLI (Italy)	0101-04=	1?	
	1739	Cont	....	FOGO (Cape Verde Is)	1804-01=	1	
	1739	....	....	**VULCANO** (Italy)	0101-05=	3	
	1739	....	?	**GAMALAMA** (Halmahera-Indonesia)	0608-06=	2	
	1739	....	....	SANGAY (Ecuador)	1502-09=	3	
I	1739	....	?	**BARDARBUNGA** (Iceland-NE)	1703-03=	2	
	1739	0201p	?	**TOLBACHIK** (Kamchatka)	1000-24=	2?	
	1739	0819	12a	**SHIKOTSU [TARUMAI]** (Hokkaido)	0805-04=	5	
	1740	Cont	....	STROMBOLI (Italy)	0101-04=	1?	
	1740	Cont	....	SANGAY (Ecuador)	1502-09=	2	
	1740	Cont	....	FOGO (Cape Verde Is)	1804-01=	1	
	1740	....	?	**KLIUCHEVSKOI** (Kamchatka)	1000-26=		
	1740	....	365y	**COTOPAXI** (Ecuador)	1502-05=	2	
	1740	06 ?	487p?	**CHOKAI** (Honshu-Japan)	0803-22=	2?	
	1740	12	?	**TOLBACHIK** (Kamchatka)	1000-24=	2	
?	1740	12	?	**QUILOTOA** (Ecuador)	1502-06=	2	
	1741	Cont	....	STROMBOLI (Italy)	0101-04=	1?	
	1741	Cont	....	CHOKAI (Honshu-Japan)	0803-22=	2?	
	1741	Cont	....	COTOPAXI (Ecuador)	1502-05=	2	
	1741	Cont	....	SANGAY (Ecuador)	1502-09=	2	
	1741	Cont	....	FOGO (Cape Verde Is)	1804-01=	1	
	1741	0818?	270p	OSHIMA-OSHIMA (Hokkaido-Japan)	0805-01=	3	
	1741	0829	....	**OSHIMA-OSHIMA** (Hokkaido-Japan)	0805-01=	4	
	1742	Cont	....	STROMBOLI (Italy)	0101-04=	1?	
	1742	Cont	....	OSHIMA-OSHIMA (Hokkaido-Japan)	0805-01=	3	
	1742	Cont	....	SANGAY (Ecuador)	1502-09=	2	
	1742	Cont	....	FOGO (Cape Verde Is)	1804-01=	1	
?	1742	....	?	**SANGANGUEY** (Mexico)	1401-023		
	1742	....	?	**VILLARRICA** (Chile-C)	1507-12=	2	
	1742	....	?	**MINCHINMAVIDA** (Chile-S)	1508-04=	2	
	1742	0406	?	**SAKURA-JIMA** (Kyushu-Japan)	0802-08=	2?	
	1742	0615	31m	**COTOPAXI** (Ecuador)	1502-05=	3?	
	1742	1209	?	**COTOPAXI** (Ecuador)	1502-05=	3?	
	1743	Cont	....	STROMBOLI (Italy)	0101-04=	1?	
	1743	Cont	....	SANGAY (Ecuador)	1502-09=	2	
	1743	Cont	....	FOGO (Cape Verde Is)	1804-01=	1	
?	1743	....	?	**ROBINSON CRUSOE** (Chile-Is)	1506-02=		
?	1743	04	?	**TELICA** (Nicaragua)	1404-04=	2?	
	1743	04	?	**COTOPAXI** (Ecuador)	1502-05=	2	
	1743	0927	8a	**COTOPAXI** (Ecuador)	1502-05=	2	
	1743	1022	?	**COLIMA VOLC COMPLEX** (Mexico)	1401-04=	2	
	1744	Cont	....	STROMBOLI (Italy)	0101-04=	1?	
	1744	Cont	....	SANGAY (Ecuador)	1502-09=	2	
	1744	Cont	....	FOGO (Cape Verde Is)	1804-01=	1	
	1744	0203	?	**KURIKOMA** (Honshu-Japan)	0803-21=	2	
	1744	05	214p	COTOPAXI (Ecuador)	1502-05=	2	7/8
	1744	07	427p	**ETNA** (Italy)	0101-06=	2	
	1744	1101	>3yr	VESUVIUS (Italy)	0101-02=	2	
	1744	1130	....	**COTOPAXI** (Ecuador)	1502-05=	4	7/8
	1745	Cont	....	VESUVIUS (Italy)	0101-02=	2	
	1745	Cont	....	STROMBOLI (Italy)	0101-04=	1?	
	1745	Cont	....	ETNA (Italy)	0101-06=	2	
	1745	Cont	....	SANGAY (Ecuador)	1502-09=	2	
	1745	Cont	....	FOGO (Cape Verde Is)	1804-01=	1	
	1745	....	?	**MERAPI** (Java)	0603-25=	2	
	1745	....	?	**VILLARRICA** (Chile-C)	1507-12=	2	
	1746	Cont	....	VESUVIUS (Italy)	0101-02=	2	
	1746	Cont	....	STROMBOLI (Italy)	0101-04=	1?	
	1746	Cont	....	SANGAY (Ecuador)	1502-09=	2	
	1746	Cont	....	FOGO (Cape Verde Is)	1804-01=	1	
	1746	02	?	**COTOPAXI** (Ecuador)	1502-05=	2	
	1746	0525m	?	**TRES VIRGENES** (Mexico)	1401-01=		
	1746	0710	<1	**KRAFLA** (Iceland-NE)	1703-08=	1	
	1747	Cont	....	VESUVIUS (Italy)	0101-02=	2	
	1747	Cont	....	STROMBOLI (Italy)	0101-04=	1?	
	1747	Cont	....	SANGAY (Ecuador)	1502-09=	2	
	1747	Cont	....	FOGO (Cape Verde Is)	1804-01=	1	
	1747	....	365y	**GEDE** (Java)	0603-06=	3	
	1747	....	731y	**COTOPAXI** (Ecuador)	1502-05=	2	
	1747	09	548p	**ETNA** (Italy)	0101-06=	2	
	1748	Cont	....	VESUVIUS (Italy)	0101-02=	2	
	1748	Cont	....	STROMBOLI (Italy)	0101-04=	1?	
	1748	Cont	....	ETNA (Italy)	0101-06=	2	
	1748	Cont	....	GEDE (Java)	0603-06=	2	
	1748	Cont	....	COTOPAXI (Ecuador)	1502-05=	2	
	1748	Cont	....	SANGAY (Ecuador)	1502-09=	2	
	1748	Cont	....	FOGO (Cape Verde Is)	1804-01=	1	
@	1748<	....	?	**REVENTADOR** (Ecuador)	1502-01=	2?	
	1749	Cont	....	VESUVIUS (Italy)	0101-02=	2	
	1749	Cont	....	STROMBOLI (Italy)	0101-04=	1?	
	1749	Cont	....	ETNA (Italy)	0101-06=	2	
	1749	Cont	....	COTOPAXI (Ecuador)	1502-05=	2	
	1749	Cont	....	SANGAY (Ecuador)	1502-09=	2	
	1749	Cont	....	FOGO (Cape Verde Is)	1804-01=	1	
	1749	....	?	**BANDA API** (Banda Sea)	0605-09=	2	
	1749	....	?	**COLIMA VOLC COMPLEX** (Mexico)	1401-04=	2	
	1749	0811?	35m?	**TAAL** (Luzon-Philippines)	0703-07=	3	-/8
	1749	09	?	**SAKURA-JIMA** (Kyushu-Japan)	0802-08=	2	
	1750	Cont	....	VESUVIUS (Italy)	0101-02=	2	
	1750	Cont	....	STROMBOLI (Italy)	0101-04=	1?	
	1750	Cont	....	SANGAY (Ecuador)	1502-09=	2	
	1750	Cont	....	FOGO (Cape Verde Is)	1804-01=	1	
	1750t	....	?	**TEYR, DJEBEL** (Red Sea)	0201-01=	2	
	1750t	....	?	**MUTNOVSKY** (Kamchatka)	1000-06=	2	
T	1750t	....	?	**GORELY** (Kamchatka)	1000-07=	2?	
C	1750?	....	?	**LONGGANG GROUP** (China-E)	1005-06-		
	1750?	....	?	**KILAUEA** (Hawaiian Is)	1302-01-	0	7/-
	1750?	....	?	**MAUNA LOA** (Hawaiian Is)	1302-02=	0	
T	1750t	....	?	**ARENAL** (Costa Rica)	1405-033		
	1750	....	?	**SABANCAYA** (Peru)	1504-003		
	1750	....	365y	**CHILLAN, NEVADOS DE** (Chile-C)	1507-07=	3↑	
	1750j	....	?	**ANTUCO** (Chile-C)	1507-08=	2	
	1750?	....	?	**COPAHUE** (Chile-C)	1507-09=	2	
T	1750v	....	?	**MELBOURNE** (Antarctica)	1900-015		
	1750	0902a	2a	**COTOPAXI** (Ecuador)	1502-05=	2	
	1751	Cont	....	STROMBOLI (Italy)	0101-04=	1?	
	1751	Cont	....	SANGAY (Ecuador)	1502-09=	2	

Figure 17. Pumice cone on the Italian island of Lipari, just north of Vulcano. After explosively building a cone of tephra fragments, eruptions often turn effusive, issuing a gentle lava flow like the obsidian shown here. From the 1903 textbook *Volcanoes*, by J.W. Judd, p.125 (New York: D. Appleton & Co).

	START YEAR	M-Dy	Duration	VOLCANO NAME (Subregion)	NUMBER	VEI	Vol L/T
	1751	Cont	....	CHILLAN, NEVADOS DE (Chile-C)	1507-07=	2?	
	1751	Cont	....	FOGO (Cape Verde Is)	1804-01=	1	
?	1751	....	?	FUEGO (Guatemala)	1402-09=	2	
	1751	06	15m	FOURNAISE, PITON DE LA (Indian O.)	0303-02=	2	
	1751	1025	....	VESUVIUS (Italy)	0101-02=	2	
	1751	1214	?	VILLARRICA (Chile-C)	1507-12=	1	
	1751	1218	195w	LLAIMA (Chile-C)	1507-11=	2	
	1751	1231	?	CALLAQUI (Chile-C)	1507-091	2	
	1752	Cont	....	VESUVIUS (Italy)	0101-02=	2	
	1752	Cont	....	STROMBOLI (Italy)	0101-04=	1?	
	1752	Cont	....	SANGAY (Ecuador)	1502-09=	2	
	1752	Cont	....	LLAIMA (Chile-C)	1507-11=	2	
	1752	Cont	....	FOGO (Cape Verde Is)	1804-01=	1	
	1752	....	>3yr	ETNA (Italy)	0101-06=	2	
	1752	....	?	MERAPI (Java)	0603-25=	2	
@	1752	0130	?	CHILLAN, NEVADOS DE (Chile-C)	1507-07=	2?	
	1752	0131	1a	ANTUCO (Chile-C)	1507-08=	3?	
	1752	0501	?	KELUT (Java)	0603-28=	2	
	1753	Cont	....	VESUVIUS (Italy)	0101-02=	2	
	1753	Cont	....	STROMBOLI (Italy)	0101-04=	1?	
	1753	Cont	....	ETNA (Italy)	0101-06=	2	
	1753	Cont	....	SANGAY (Ecuador)	1502-09=	2	
	1753	Cont	....	FOGO (Cape Verde Is)	1804-01=	1	
	1753	....	?	FOURNAISE, PITON DE LA (Indian O.)	0303-02=	2	
?	1753	....	365y	ASO (Kyushu-Japan)	0802-11=	2?	
	1753	1015q	....	GRIMSVOTN [PALSFJALL] (Iceland)	1703-01=	2?	
	1754	Cont	....	STROMBOLI (Italy)	0101-04=	1?	
	1754	Cont	....	ETNA (Italy)	0101-06=	2	
?	1754	Cont	....	ASO (Kyushu-Japan)	0802-11=	2?	
	1754	Cont	....	SANGAY (Ecuador)	1502-09=	2	
	1754	Cont	....	FOGO (Cape Verde Is)	1804-01=	1	
	1754	....	730y	GALERAS (Colombia)	1501-08=	2	
	1754	0515	203a	TAAL (Luzon-Philippines)	0703-07=	3	-/8
	1754	0807	12a	ASAMA (Honshu-Japan)	0803-11=	2	
	1754	1128	....	TAAL (Luzon-Philippines)	0703-07=	4	-/8
	1754	1202	....	VESUVIUS (Italy)	0101-02=	2	
	1755	Cont	....	VESUVIUS (Italy)	0101-02=	2	
	1755	Cont	....	STROMBOLI (Italy)	0101-04=	1?	
	1755	Cont	....	GALERAS (Colombia)	1501-08=	2	
	1755	Cont	....	SANGAY (Ecuador)	1502-09=	2	
	1755	Cont	....	FOGO (Cape Verde Is)	1804-01=	1	
D	1755?	....	?	EGMONT (New Zealand)	0401-03=		
	1755	....	?	MERAPI (Java)	0603-25=	2	
	1755	0309	6a	ETNA (Italy)	0101-06=	3	6/-
	1755	0705	32a	ASAMA (Honshu-Japan)	0803-11=	2	
@	1755	0918	?	KOLBEINSEY RIDGE (Iceland-N of)	1705-01=		
	1755	1017	119a	KATLA (Iceland-S)	1702-03=	4+	-/8
	1756	Cont	....	VESUVIUS (Italy)	0101-02=	2	
	1756	Cont	....	STROMBOLI (Italy)	0101-04=	1?	
	1756	Cont	....	ETNA (Italy)	0101-06=	2	
	1756	Cont	....	GALERAS (Colombia)	1501-08=	2	
	1756	Cont	....	SANGAY (Ecuador)	1502-09=	2	
	1756	Cont	....	KATLA (Iceland-S)	1702-03=	2	-/8
	1756	Cont	....	FOGO (Cape Verde Is)	1804-01=	1	
	1756	0909	?	SAKURA-JIMA (Kyushu-Japan)	0802-08=	2	
	1757	Cont	....	VESUVIUS (Italy)	0101-02=	2	
	1757	Cont	....	STROMBOLI (Italy)	0101-04=	1?	
	1757	Cont	....	ETNA (Italy)	0101-06=	2	
	1757	Cont	....	SANGAY (Ecuador)	1502-09=	2	
	1757	Cont	....	FOGO (Cape Verde Is)	1804-01=	1	
?	1757	....	?	UNNAMED (Indian O.-E)	0305-01=	0	
?	1757	....	?	TUNGURAHUA (Ecuador)	1502-08=	2	
	1757	0709	1a	SAN JORGE (Azores)	1802-03=	0	
	1758	Cont	....	VESUVIUS (Italy)	0101-02=	2	
	1758	Cont	....	STROMBOLI (Italy)	0101-04=	1?	
	1758	Cont	....	SANGAY (Ecuador)	1502-09=	2	
	1758	Cont	....	FOGO (Cape Verde Is)	1804-01=	1	
	1758	1103?	103m	ETNA (Italy)	0101-06=	2	
	1759	Cont	....	VESUVIUS (Italy)	0101-02=	2	
	1759	Cont	....	STROMBOLI (Italy)	0101-04=	1?	
	1759	Cont	....	SANGAY (Ecuador)	1502-09=	2	
	1759	Cont	....	FOGO (Cape Verde Is)	1804-01=	1	
	1759	....	?	FOURNAISE, PITON DE LA (Indian O.)	0303-02=		
?	1759	....	?	QUILOTOA (Ecuador)	1502-06=	2	
A	1759u	....	?	SANTIAGO (Galapagos)	1503-09=		
?	1759?	....	?	COPAHUE (Chile-C)	1507-09=		
	1759	0419	....	ETNA (Italy)	0101-06=	2	
	1759	0819	?	OSHIMA-OSHIMA (Hokkaido-Japan)	0805-01=	2	
	1759	0929	>3yr	MICHOACAN [JORULLO] (Mexico)	1401-06=	4	8/9
	1759	12	?	LLAIMA (Chile-C)	1507-11=	2	
	1759	12	?	VILLARRICA (Chile-C)	1507-12=	1	
	1760	Cont	....	STROMBOLI (Italy)	0101-04=	1?	
	1760	Cont	....	MICHOACAN [JORULLO] (Mexico)	1401-06=	2	8/9
	1760	Cont	....	SANGAY (Ecuador)	1502-09=	2	
	1760	Cont	....	FOGO (Cape Verde Is)	1804-01=	1	
?	1760?	....	?	CHIRINKOTAN (Kurile Is)	0900-26=	2	
?	1760	....	?	GARELOI (Aleutian Is)	1101-07-		
?	1760	....	?	GREAT SITKIN (Aleutian Is)	1101-12-		
	1760	....	?	KASATOCHI (Aleutian Is)	1101-13-	0	
?	1760	....	?	PACAYA (Guatemala)	1402-11=		
	1760	....	?	CHACANA (Ecuador)	1502-022	0	9/-
	1760	0922	220a>	MAKIAN (Halmahera-Indonesia)	0608-07=	4?	-/8
	1760	1215	14a	FOURNAISE, PITON DE LA (Indian O.)	0303-02=	2	
	1760	1223	....	VESUVIUS (Italy)	0101-02=	3	
	1761	Cont	....	VESUVIUS (Italy)	0101-02=	2	
	1761	Cont	....	STROMBOLI (Italy)	0101-04=	1?	
	1761	Cont	....	MAKIAN (Halmahera-Indonesia)	0608-07=	4?	-/8
	1761	Cont	....	MICHOACAN [JORULLO] (Mexico)	1401-06=	2	8/9
	1761	Cont	....	SANGAY (Ecuador)	1502-09=	2	
	1761	Cont	....	FOGO (Cape Verde Is)	1804-01=	1	
	1761	....	?	GEDE (Java)	0603-06=	2	
	1761	0417	11a	TERCEIRA (Azores)	1802-05=	2	
?	1761	0503	?	UNNAMED (Atlantic-C)	1805-03=	0	
	1762	Cont	....	STROMBOLI (Italy)	0101-04=	1?	
	1762	Cont	....	MICHOACAN [JORULLO] (Mexico)	1401-06=	2	8/9
	1762	Cont	....	SANGAY (Ecuador)	1502-09=	2	
	1762	....	?	BANDA API (Banda Sea)	0605-09=	2	
	1762	....	?	KLIUCHEVSKOI (Kamchatka)	1000-26=	2	
	1762	....	>3yr	PAVLOF SISTER (Alaska Peninsula)	1102-04-		-/8
	1762	....	?	SAN MIGUEL (El Salvador)	1403-10=	2	
	1762	04	?	ASAMA (Honshu-Japan)	0803-11=	2	
	1762	1203	?	PLANCHON-PETEROA (Chile-C)	1507-04=	4	
	1763	Cont	....	STROMBOLI (Italy)	0101-04=	1?	
	1763	Cont	....	PAVLOF SISTER (Alaska Peninsula)	1102-04-		-/8
	1763	Cont	....	MICHOACAN [JORULLO] (Mexico)	1401-06=	2	8/9
	1763	Cont	....	SANGAY (Ecuador)	1502-09=	2	
	1763	....	?	GAMALAMA (Halmahera-Indonesia)	0608-06=	2	7/-
	1763	....	>3yr	TANAGA (Aleutian Is)	1101-08-		
	1763	....	?	KANAGA (Aleutian Is)	1101-11-		
	1763	0206	32a?	ETNA (Italy)	0101-06=	2	7/7
	1763	0618	84a	ETNA (Italy)	0101-06=	3	8/7
	1763	0817	>3yr	MIYAKE-JIMA (Izu Is-Japan)	0804-04=	2	
	1764	Cont	....	STROMBOLI (Italy)	0101-04=	1?	
	1764	Cont	....	MIYAKE-JIMA (Izu Is-Japan)	0804-04=	2	
	1764	Cont	....	TANAGA (Aleutian Is)	1101-08-		
	1764	Cont	....	PAVLOF SISTER (Alaska Peninsula)	1102-04-		-/8
	1764	Cont	....	SANGAY (Ecuador)	1502-09=	2	
	1764	....	548m	ETNA (Italy)	0101-06=	0	
	1764	....	?	CHOKAI (Honshu-Japan)	0803-22=	2	
	1764	.... O	....	MICHOACAN [JORULLO] (Mexico)	1401-06=	4	8/9
	1764	....	?	MOMOTOMBO (Nicaragua)	1404-09=	2	
	1764	0701?	>3yr	VESUVIUS (Italy)	0101-02=	2	7/-
	1765	Cont	....	VESUVIUS (Italy)	0101-02=	2	7/-
	1765	Cont	....	STROMBOLI (Italy)	0101-04=	1?	
	1765	Cont	....	ETNA (Italy)	0101-06=	0	
	1765	Cont	....	MIYAKE-JIMA (Izu Is-Japan)	0804-04=	2	
	1765	Cont	....	TANAGA (Aleutian Is)	1101-08-		
	1765	Cont	....	PAVLOF SISTER (Alaska Peninsula)	1102-04-		-/8
	1765	Cont	....	MICHOACAN [JORULLO] (Mexico)	1401-06=	2	8/9
	1765	Cont	....	SANGAY (Ecuador)	1502-09=	2	
	1765	....	?	RAGANG (Mindanao-Philippines)	0701-06=	2	
	1765	....	?	KOMAGA-TAKE (Hokkaido-Japan)	0805-02=	2	
	1765e	....	?	PREVO PEAK (Kurile Is)	0900-19=	3↑	
	1765e	....	?	SARYCHEV PEAK (Kurile Is)	0900-24=	2?	
	1765e	....	?	RAIKOKE (Kurile Is)	0900-25=	2	
D	1765e	....	?	HOOD (US-Oregon)	1202-01-		
?	1765	....	?	FUEGO (Guatemala)	1402-09=	2	
	1765	....	?	TELICA (Nicaragua)	1404-04=	2	
	1765	....	?	RINCON DE LA VIEJA (Costa Rica)	1405-02=		
	1765m	....	?	OSORNO (Chile-S)	1508-01=	1	
	1765	01 ?	274p?	ASO (Kyushu-Japan)	0802-11=	3?	
	1765	0419	545m	BANDA API (Banda Sea)	0605-09=	2	
	1765	1024	1a	ALMOLONGA [C. QUEMADO] (Guate)	1402-04=	2	
	1766	Cont	....	STROMBOLI (Italy)	0101-04=	1?	
	1766	Cont	....	BANDA API (Banda Sea)	0605-09=	2	
	1766	Cont	....	MIYAKE-JIMA (Izu Is-Japan)	0804-04=	2	
	1766	Cont	....	TANAGA (Aleutian Is)	1101-08-		
	1766	Cont	....	PAVLOF SISTER (Alaska Peninsula)	1102-04-		-/8
	1766	Cont	....	MICHOACAN [JORULLO] (Mexico)	1401-06=	2	8/9
	1766	Cont	....	SANGAY (Ecuador)	1502-09=	2	
	1766	....	?	QUALIBOU (W Indies)	1600-14=	1	
	1766	0210	?	COTOPAXI (Ecuador)	1502-05=	3	
	1766	03	72n	FOURNAISE, PITON DE LA (Indian O.)	0303-02=	2	
	1766	0328	....	VESUVIUS (Italy)	0101-02=	2	7/-
	1766	0405	770m	HEKLA (Iceland-S)	1702-07=	4	9/8
	1766	0427	193a	ETNA (Italy)	0101-06=	2	7/6
	1766	07	?	BARDARBUNGA (Iceland-NE)	1703-03=	2	

START YEAR	M-Dy	Duration	VOLCANO NAME (Subregion)	NUMBER	VEI	Vol L/T
1767	Cont	....	STROMBOLI (Italy)	0101-04=	1?	
1767	Cont	....	MIYAKE-JIMA (Izu Is-Japan)	0804-04=	2	
1767	Cont	....	TANAGA (Aleutian Is)	1101-08-		
1767	Cont	....	PAVLOF SISTER (Alaska Peninsula)	1102-04-		-/8
1767	Cont	....	MICHOACAN [JORULLO] (Mexico)	1401-06=	2	8/9
1767	Cont	....	SANGAY (Ecuador)	1502-09=	2	
1767	Cont	....	HEKLA (Iceland-S)	1702-07=	2	9/8
? 1767	....	?	TENGGER CALDERA [BROMO]	0603-31=		
? 1767n	....	?	BANDAI (Honshu-Japan)	0803-16=		
1767	....	731y	EKARMA (Kurile Is)	0900-27=	2	
1767	....	?	KLIUCHEVSKOI (Kamchatka)	1000-26=	2	
1767	0502	?	ETNA (Italy)	0101-06=		
1767	0910	?	RABAUL (New Britain-SW Pac)	0502-14=	2	
1767	1019	....	VESUVIUS (Italy)	0101-02=	3	7/-
1768	Cont	....	MIYAKE-JIMA (Izu Is-Japan)	0804-04=	2	
1768	Cont	....	EKARMA (Kurile Is)	0900-27=	2	
1768	Cont	....	TANAGA (Aleutian Is)	1101-08-		
1768	Cont	....	PAVLOF SISTER (Alaska Peninsula)	1102-04-		-/8
1768	Cont	....	MICHOACAN [JORULLO] (Mexico)	1401-06=	2	8/9
1768	Cont	....	SANGAY (Ecuador)	1502-09=	2	
1768	Cont	....	HEKLA (Iceland-S)	1702-07=	2	9/8
1768	....	?	STROMBOLI (Italy)	0101-04=	2	
1768	....	?	FOURNAISE, PITON DE LA (Indian O.)	0303-02=	2	
1768	....	?	KIRISHIMA (Kyushu-Japan)	0802-09=	0	
1768	....	?	KANAGA (Aleutian Is)	1101-11-		
1768	....	365y	MAKUSHIN (Aleutian Is)	1101-31-	2	
? 1768	....	?	ILIAMNA (Alaska-SW)	1103-02-		
@ 1768	....	?	GRIMSVOTN (Iceland-NE)	1703-01=	2	
1768	0404	?	COTOPAXI (Ecuador)	1502-05=	4	7/8
1768	08	?	TINAKULA (Santa Cruz Is-SW Pac)	0506-01=	2	
1768	0819	?	MERAPI (Java)	0603-25=	2	
1769	Cont	....	STROMBOLI (Italy)	0101-04=	1?	
1769	Cont	....	MIYAKE-JIMA (Izu Is-Japan)	0804-04=	2	
1769	Cont	....	EKARMA (Kurile Is)	0900-27=	2	
1769	Cont	....	TANAGA (Aleutian Is)	1101-08-		
1769	Cont	....	PAVLOF SISTER (Alaska Peninsula)	1102-04-		-/8
1769	Cont	....	MICHOACAN [JORULLO] (Mexico)	1401-06=	2	8/9
1769	Cont	....	SANGAY (Ecuador)	1502-09=	2	
1769	....	?	KIRISHIMA (Kyushu-Japan)	0802-09=	2	
? 1769	....	?	IWAKI (Honshu-Japan)	0803-27=		
1769>	....	?	USHISHUR (Kurile Is)	0900-21=		7/-
1769	....	....	MAKUSHIN (Aleutian Is)	1101-31-	3↑	
1769	....	?	SAN MIGUEL (El Salvador)	1403-10=	2	
@ 1769	....	?	BARDARBUNGA (Iceland-NE)	1703-03=	2	
1769	0123	?	USU (Hokkaido-Japan)	0805-03=	4	-/8
1769	0215q	243t	TOLBACHIK (Kamchatka)	1000-24=	2	
1769	04 >	?	FOGO (Cape Verde Is)	1804-01=		
@ 1769	0806	?	ASAMA (Honshu-Japan)	0803-11=		
1770	Cont	....	TANAGA (Aleutian Is)	1101-08-		
1770	Cont	....	PAVLOF SISTER (Alaska Peninsula)	1102-04-		-/8
1770	Cont	....	MICHOACAN [JORULLO] (Mexico)	1401-06=	2	8/9
1770	Cont	....	SANGAY (Ecuador)	1502-09=	2	
1770	....	?	STROMBOLI (Italy)	0101-04=	2	
C 1770t	....	?	OLKARIA (Africa-E)	0202-09=		
1770	....	?	MARAPI (Sumatra)	0601-14=	2	
? 1770	....	?	AMUKTA (Aleutian Is)	1101-19-		
1770	....	?	COLIMA VOLC COMPLEX (Mexico)	1401-04=	2	
1770	0215	>3yr	VESUVIUS (Italy)	0101-02=	2	7/-
1770	0223	?	IZALCO (El Salvador)	1403-03=	2	
1770	05	?	KLIUCHEVSKOI (Kamchatka)	1000-26=	2	
? 1770	0528a	?	ETNA (Italy)	0101-06=		
1770	0706	156a	GAMALAMA (Halmahera-Indonesia)	0608-06=	3	
1771	Cont	....	STROMBOLI (Italy)	0101-04=	1?	
1771	Cont	....	PAVLOF SISTER (Alaska Peninsula)	1102-04-		-/8
1771	Cont	....	MICHOACAN [JORULLO] (Mexico)	1401-06=	2	8/9
1771	Cont	....	SANGAY (Ecuador)	1502-09=	2	
1771	....	?	FOURNAISE, PITON DE LA (Indian O.)	0303-02=		
1771	....	365y	KIRISHIMA (Kyushu-Japan)	0802-09=	2	-/6
1771	....	?	KARYMSKY (Kamchatka)	1000-13=	2	
1771	....	?	COLIMA VOLC COMPLEX (Mexico)	1401-04=	3	
1771	0110	?	KELUT (Java)	0603-28=	2	
1771	0217	87m	VULCANO (Italy)	0101-05=	3	
1771	0501	....	VESUVIUS (Italy)	0101-02=	2	7/-
1771	0828	407a	GAMALAMA (Halmahera-Indonesia)	0608-06=	3	
1772	Cont	....	VESUVIUS (Italy)	0101-02=	2	7/-
1772	Cont	....	STROMBOLI (Italy)	0101-04=	1?	
1772	Cont	....	GAMALAMA (Halmahera-Indonesia)	0608-06=	3	
1772	Cont	....	KIRISHIMA (Kyushu-Japan)	0802-09=	2	-/6
1772	Cont	....	PAVLOF SISTER (Alaska Peninsula)	1102-04-		-/8
1772	Cont	....	MICHOACAN [JORULLO] (Mexico)	1401-06=	2	8/9
1772	Cont	....	SANGAY (Ecuador)	1502-09=	2	
1772	....	>3yr	ASO (Kyushu-Japan)	0802-11=	2	
1772	....	?	AVACHINSKY (Kamchatka)	1000-10=	2	
1772	....	?	KLIUCHEVSKOI (Kamchatka)	1000-26=	2	
? 1772	....	?	SEMISOPOCHNOI (Aleutian Is)	1101-06-		
1772?	....	?	IZALCO (El Salvador)	1403-03=	2	
1772	02	?	FOURNAISE, PITON DE LA (Indian O.)	0303-02=	2	
1772	0316	9a?	MASAYA (Nicaragua)	1404-10=	2	
1772	0811	1a	CEREME (Java)	0603-17=	2	
1772	0811	1a	SLAMET (Java)	0603-18=	2	
1772	0812	<1	PAPANDAYAN (Java)	0603-10=	3	
1772	1118	?	FOURNAISE, PITON DE LA (Indian O.)	0303-02=	2	
1773	Cont	....	VESUVIUS (Italy)	0101-02=	2	7/-
1773	Cont	....	STROMBOLI (Italy)	0101-04=	1?	
1773	Cont	....	ASO (Kyushu-Japan)	0802-11=	2	
1773	Cont	....	PAVLOF SISTER (Alaska Peninsula)	1102-04-		-/8
1773	Cont	....	MICHOACAN [JORULLO] (Mexico)	1401-06=	2	8/9
1773	Cont	....	SANGAY (Ecuador)	1502-09=	2	
1773	....	?	NIIGATA-YAKE-YAMA (Honshu-Japan)	0803-09=	3	
? 1773	....	?	FUEGO (Guatemala)	1402-09=	2	
1773	....	?	CHACANA (Ecuador)	1502-022	0	8/-
1773	0202	5a	GAMALAMA (Halmahera-Indonesia)	0608-06=	2	
1773	0204	127m?	TUNGURAHUA (Ecuador)	1502-08=	2	
1773	0206	?	BANDA API (Banda Sea)	0605-09=	2	
1773	0423	....	TUNGURAHUA (Ecuador)	1502-08=	3	
1773	10	?	DIDICAS (Luzon Is-N of)	0704-02=	0?	
1773	10	?	UNNAMED (Luzon Is-N of)	0704-05=	0	
1773	1021	92a	GAMALAMA (Halmahera-Indonesia)	0608-06=	2	
1774	Cont	....	VESUVIUS (Italy)	0101-02=	2	7/-
1774	Cont	....	STROMBOLI (Italy)	0101-04=	1?	
1774	Cont	....	GAMALAMA (Halmahera-Indonesia)	0608-06=	2	
1774	Cont	....	ASO (Kyushu-Japan)	0802-11=	2	
1774	Cont	....	PAVLOF SISTER (Alaska Peninsula)	1102-04-		-/8
1774	Cont	....	MICHOACAN [JORULLO] (Mexico)	1401-06=	2	8/9
1774	Cont	....	SANGAY (Ecuador)	1502-09=	2	
1774	....	?	FOURNAISE, PITON DE LA (Indian O.)	0303-02=	0	7/-
1774	....	?	AMBRYM (Vanuatu-SW Pacific)	0507-04=	2	
1774	....	>3yr	YASUR (Vanuatu-SW Pacific)	0507-10=	2	
1774	....	?	CARLISLE (Aleutian Is)	1101-23-		
1774	02	?	GRIMSVOTN (Iceland-NE)	1703-01=	2	
1774	06	?	TOFUA (Tonga-SW Pacific)	0403-06=	2	
1775	Cont	....	VESUVIUS (Italy)	0101-02=	2	7/-
1775	Cont	....	STROMBOLI (Italy)	0101-04=	1?	
1775	Cont	....	YASUR (Vanuatu-SW Pacific)	0507-10=	2	
1775	Cont	....	ASO (Kyushu-Japan)	0802-11=	2	
1775	Cont	....	PAVLOF SISTER (Alaska Peninsula)	1102-04-		-/8
1775	Cont	....	SANGAY (Ecuador)	1502-09=	2	
? 1775	....	?	VULCANO (Italy)	0101-05=		
A 1775q	....	?	TULLU MOJE (Ethiopia)	0201-25-		
1775	....	?	FOURNAISE, PITON DE LA (Indian O.)	0303-02=	2	
? 1775	....	?	TENGGER CALDERA [BROMO]	0603-31=		
1775	....	?	BANDA API (Banda Sea)	0605-09=	2	
1775q	....	?	LOKON-EMPUNG (Sulawesi-Indonesia)	0606-10=	3	
? 1775j	....	?	ASUNCION (Mariana Is-C Pac)	0804-15=	2	
1775e	....	?	BALAGAN-TAS (Russia-NE)	1001-03-	2	
? 1775	....	>3yr	SHISHALDIN (Aleutian Is)	1101-36-		
1775?	....	?	IRAZU (Costa Rica)	1405-06=	2?	
1775	0104	?	CEREME (Java)	0603-17=	2	
1775	0701	22a>	PACAYA (Guatemala)	1402-11=	3	7/7
1775	0820	78a	GAMALAMA (Halmahera-Indonesia)	0608-06=	2	
1775	0906	....	GAMALAMA (Halmahera-Indonesia)	0608-06=	3	
1776	Cont	....	STROMBOLI (Italy)	0101-04=	1?	
1776	Cont	....	YASUR (Vanuatu-SW Pacific)	0507-10=	2	
1776	Cont	....	ASO (Kyushu-Japan)	0802-11=	2	
? 1776	Cont	....	SHISHALDIN (Aleutian Is)	1101-36-		
1776	Cont	....	PAVLOF SISTER (Alaska Peninsula)	1102-04-		-/8
1776	Cont	....	SANGAY (Ecuador)	1502-09=	2	
1776	....	?	ETNA (Italy)	0101-06=		
1776	....	?	FOURNAISE, PITON DE LA (Indian O.)	0303-02=	0	6/-
? 1776	....	?	DIENG VOLC COMPLEX (Java)	0603-20=		
1776	....	?	KELUT (Java)	0603-28=	2	
1776	....	?	LITTLE SITKIN (Aleutian Is)	1101-05-	1?	
1776	0103	?	TUNGURAHUA (Ecuador)	1502-08=	2	
1776	0328	....	VESUVIUS (Italy)	0101-02=	2	7/-
1776	0905	?	ASAMA (Honshu-Japan)	0803-11=	2	
1776	10	?	ZHUPANOVSKY (Kamchatka)	1000-12=	2	
1777	Cont	....	VESUVIUS (Italy)	0101-02=	2	7/-
1777	Cont	....	STROMBOLI (Italy)	0101-04=	1?	
1777	Cont	....	YASUR (Vanuatu-SW Pacific)	0507-10=	2	
1777	Cont	....	ASO (Kyushu-Japan)	0802-11=	2	
? 1777	Cont	....	SHISHALDIN (Aleutian Is)	1101-36-		
1777	Cont	....	PAVLOF SISTER (Alaska Peninsula)	1102-04-		-/8
1777	Cont	....	SANGAY (Ecuador)	1502-09=	2	
1777	....	?	GUNTUR (Java)	0603-13=	2?	
1777	....	?	ASAMA (Honshu-Japan)	0803-11=	2	
? 1777	....	?	TUNGURAHUA (Ecuador)	1502-08=	2	
1777	....	?	VILLARRICA (Chile-C)	1507-12=	1	
1777	0831	670w	OSHIMA (Izu Is-Japan)	0804-01=	3	8/8
1778	Cont	....	VESUVIUS (Italy)	0101-02=	2	7/-
1778	Cont	....	YASUR (Vanuatu-SW Pacific)	0507-10=	2	
1778	Cont	....	ASO (Kyushu-Japan)	0802-11=	2	
1778	Cont	....	OSHIMA (Izu Is-Japan)	0804-01=	2	8/8
? 1778	Cont	....	SHISHALDIN (Aleutian Is)	1101-36-		
1778	Cont	....	PAVLOF SISTER (Alaska Peninsula)	1102-04-		-/8
1778	Cont	....	SANGAY (Ecuador)	1502-09=	2	
1778	....	?	BANDA API (Banda Sea)	0605-09=	2	
1778	....	?	RAIKOKE (Kurile Is)	0900-25=	4↑	
1778	....	365y	ILIAMNA (Alaska-SW)	1103-02-		
? 1778	....	?	REDOUBT (Alaska-SW)	1103-03-		
1778	0301	1a	STROMBOLI (Italy)	0101-04=	2	
1778	1231y	?	MEDVEZHIA (Kurile Is)	0900-10=	2	
1779	Cont	....	STROMBOLI (Italy)	0101-04=	1?	
1779	Cont	....	YASUR (Vanuatu-SW Pacific)	0507-10=	2	
1779	Cont	....	ASO (Kyushu-Japan)	0802-11=	2	
1779	Cont	....	PAVLOF SISTER (Alaska Peninsula)	1102-04-		-/8
1779	Cont	....	ILIAMNA (Alaska-SW)	1103-02-		
1779	Cont	....	SANGAY (Ecuador)	1502-09=	2	
1779	0104	....	OSHIMA (Izu Is-Japan)	0804-01=	3	8/8
1779	0615	1a	AVACHINSKY (Kamchatka)	1000-10=	3	-/7
1779	0808	....	VESUVIUS (Italy)	0101-02=	3	7/-
? 1779	09 ?	?	ASAMA (Honshu-Japan)	0803-11=		
1779	1108	554m	SAKURA-JIMA (Kyushu-Japan)	0802-08=	4	9/8
1780	Cont	....	STROMBOLI (Italy)	0101-04=	1?	
1780	Cont	....	YASUR (Vanuatu-SW Pacific)	0507-10=	2	

START YEAR	M-Dy	Duration	VOLCANO NAME (Subregion)	NUMBER	VEI	Vol L/T
1780	Cont	....	ASO (Kyushu-Japan)	0802-11=	2	
1780	Cont	....	PAVLOF SISTER (Alaska Peninsula)	1102-04-		-/8
1780	Cont	....	SANGAY (Ecuador)	1502-09=	2	
1780	....	?	VULCANO (Italy)	0101-05=	2	
1780	....	?	SALAK (Java)	0603-05=	2	
1780	....	?	GUNTUR (Java)	0603-13=	2	
1780	....	?	KITA-IWO-JIMA (Volcano Is-Japan	0804-11=	0	
1780j	....	?	KOLOKOL GROUP (Kurile Is)	0900-12=	2?	
1780	....	?	TUTUPACA (Peru)	1504-04=	2	
1780	....	?	VILLARRICA (Chile-C)	1507-12=	2?	
1780	0420	56m	ETNA (Italy)	0101-06=	2	7/3
1780	0518	....	ETNA (Italy)	0101-06=	2	7/3
1780	0727	>3yr	AOGA-SHIMA (Izu Is-Japan)	0804-06=	2	6/7
1780	09	....	SAKURA-JIMA (Kyushu-Japan)	0802-08=	2?	9/8
1781	Cont	....	STROMBOLI (Italy)	0101-04=	1?	
1781	Cont	....	YASUR (Vanuatu-SW Pacific)	0507-10=	2	
1781	Cont	....	AOGA-SHIMA (Izu Is-Japan)	0804-06=	2	6/7
1781	Cont	....	PAVLOF SISTER (Alaska Peninsula)	1102-04-		-/8
1781	Cont	....	SANGAY (Ecuador)	1502-09=	2	
? 1781	....	?	FALCON ISLAND (Tonga-SW Pacific)	0403-05=	0	
1781	....	>3yr	ASO (Kyushu-Japan)	0802-11=	1	
? 1781	....	?	TUNGURAHUA (Ecuador)	1502-08=	2	
1781	0331p	40p	ETNA (Italy)	0101-06=	2	
1781	04	....	SAKURA-JIMA (Kyushu-Japan)	0802-08=	2	9/8
1782	Cont	....	STROMBOLI (Italy)	0101-04=	1?	
1782	Cont	....	YASUR (Vanuatu-SW Pacific)	0507-10=	2	
1782	Cont	....	ASO (Kyushu-Japan)	0802-11=	1	
1782	Cont	....	AOGA-SHIMA (Izu Is-Japan)	0804-06=	2	6/7
1782	Cont	....	PAVLOF SISTER (Alaska Peninsula)	1102-04-		-/8
1782	Cont	....	SANGAY (Ecuador)	1502-09=	2	
1782	0118	?	SAKURA-JIMA (Kyushu-Japan)	0802-08=	2?	
? 1782	0412	?	IWAKI (Honshu-Japan)	0803-27=		
1782	1201p	101p	IWAKI (Honshu-Japan)	0803-27=	2	
1783	Cont	....	STROMBOLI (Italy)	0101-04=	1?	
1783	Cont	....	YASUR (Vanuatu-SW Pacific)	0507-10=	2	
1783	Cont	....	ASO (Kyushu-Japan)	0802-11=	1	
1783	Cont	....	IWAKI (Honshu-Japan)	0803-27=	2	
1783	Cont	....	PAVLOF SISTER (Alaska Peninsula)	1102-04-		-/8
1783	Cont	....	SANGAY (Ecuador)	1502-09=	2	
? 1783	....	?	KURIKOMA (Honshu-Japan)	0803-21=		
1783	....	1096y	OSHIMA (Izu Is-Japan)	0804-01=	2	
1783	....	>3yr	KANAGA (Aleutian Is)	1101-11-		
1783	0410	....	AOGA-SHIMA (Izu Is-Japan)	0804-06=	3	6/7
1783	05 ?	741m?	GRIMSVOTN [LAKAGIGAR] (Iceland)	1703-01=	2	
1783	0501<	106r	REYKJANESHRYGGUR (Iceland-SW)	1701-01=	3↑	
1783	0509	88a	ASAMA (Honshu-Japan)	0803-11=	2	8/8
1783	0608A	....	GRIMSVOTN [LAKAGIGAR] (Iceland)	1703-01=	4	10/8
1783	07 ?	?	IZALCO (El Salvador)	1403-03=	0	
1783	0803	....	ASAMA (Honshu-Japan)	0803-11=	4	8/8
1783	0818	>3yr	VESUVIUS (Italy)	0101-02=	2	7/8
1783	0903	?	SAKURA-JIMA (Kyushu-Japan)	0802-08=	3	
? 1783	1203	?	IWAKI (Honshu-Japan)	0803-27=		
1784	Cont	....	VESUVIUS (Italy)	0101-02=	2	7/8
1784	Cont	....	STROMBOLI (Italy)	0101-04=	1?	
1784	Cont	....	YASUR (Vanuatu-SW Pacific)	0507-10=	2	
1784	Cont	....	ASO (Kyushu-Japan)	0802-11=	1	
1784	Cont	....	OSHIMA (Izu Is-Japan)	0804-01=	2	
1784	Cont	....	AOGA-SHIMA (Izu Is-Japan)	0804-06=	2	6/7
1784	Cont	....	KANAGA (Aleutian Is)	1101-11-		
1784	Cont	....	PAVLOF SISTER (Alaska Peninsula)	1102-04-		-/8
1784	Cont	....	SANGAY (Ecuador)	1502-09=	2	
1784	Cont	....	GRIMSVOTN [LAKAGIGAR] (Iceland)	1703-01=	2	
1784	....	365y	FOURNAISE, PITON DE LA (Indian O.)	0303-02=	2	
? 1784	....	?	GREAT SITKIN (Aleutian Is)	1101-12-		
? 1784	....	?	VSEVIDOF (Aleutian Is)	1101-27-		
1784	....	?	MISTI, EL (Peru)	1504-01=	2	
1784	....	?	UBINAS (Peru)	1504-02=	2	
1784	0208	?	KOMAGA-TAKE (Hokkaido-Japan)	0805-02=	2	
1784	03 <	?	SOUFRIERE ST. VINCENT (W Indies)	1600-15=	0	
1784	07	?	SABANCAYA (Peru)	1504-003		
1785	Cont	....	STROMBOLI (Italy)	0101-04=	1?	
1785	Cont	....	FOURNAISE, PITON DE LA (Indian O.)	0303-02=	2	
1785	Cont	....	YASUR (Vanuatu-SW Pacific)	0507-10=	2	
1785	Cont	....	ASO (Kyushu-Japan)	0802-11=	1	
1785	Cont	....	OSHIMA (Izu Is-Japan)	0804-01=	2	
1785	Cont	....	KANAGA (Aleutian Is)	1101-11-		
1785	Cont	....	PAVLOF SISTER (Alaska Peninsula)	1102-04-		-/8
1785	Cont	....	SANGAY (Ecuador)	1502-09=	2	
1785	Cont	....	GRIMSVOTN [LAKAGIGAR] (Iceland)	1703-01=	2	
1785	....	?	KELUT (Java)	0603-28=	2	
T 1785u	....	?	MONO LAKE VOLC FIELD (US-Calif)	1203-11-		
1785	0124	32a	FOGO (Cape Verde Is)	1804-01=	2	6/-
1785	0418	....	AOGA-SHIMA (Izu Is-Japan)	0804-06=	3	6/7
1785	0701	....	VESUVIUS (Italy)	0101-02=	1	7/8
1785	11	?	KLIUCHEVSKOI (Kamchatka)	1000-26=	2	
1785	1120	?	SAKURA-JIMA (Kyushu-Japan)	0802-08=	2	
1785	1231y	?	SOPUTAN (Sulawesi-Indonesia)	0606-03=	2	
1786	Cont	....	VESUVIUS (Italy)	0101-02=	2	7/8
1786	Cont	....	STROMBOLI (Italy)	0101-04=	1?	
1786	Cont	....	YASUR (Vanuatu-SW Pacific)	0507-10=	2	
1786	Cont	....	ASO (Kyushu-Japan)	0802-11=	1	
1786	Cont	....	OSHIMA (Izu Is-Japan)	0804-01=	2	
1786	Cont	....	KANAGA (Aleutian Is)	1101-11-		
1786	Cont	....	SANGAY (Ecuador)	1502-09=	2	
? 1786	....	?	VULCANO (Italy)	0101-05=	3	
1786	....	?	DIENG VOLC COMPLEX (Java)	0603-20=	2	
? 1786	....	?	OSHIMA-OSHIMA (Hokkaido-Japan)	0805-01=	2?	
1786	....	>3yr	SEGUAM (Aleutian Is)	1101-18-		
1786	....	....	PAVLOF SISTER (Alaska Peninsula	1102-04-	4?	-/8
? 1786	....	?	ILIAMNA (Alaska-SW)	1103-02-		
1786	....	?	SHASTA (US-California)	1203-01-	3	
1786	06	>3yr	AMUKTA (Aleutian Is)	1101-19-	3↑	-/8
1786	0605?	60a>	FOURNAISE, PITON DE LA (Indian O.)	0303-02=	2	
1786	0717	?	MERAPI (Java)	0603-25=	1	
1787	Cont	....	VESUVIUS (Italy)	0101-02=	2	7/8
1787	Cont	....	STROMBOLI (Italy)	0101-04=	1?	
1787	Cont	....	YASUR (Vanuatu-SW Pacific)	0507-10=	2	
1787	Cont	....	ASO (Kyushu-Japan)	0802-11=	1	
1787	Cont	....	KANAGA (Aleutian Is)	1101-11-		
1787	Cont	....	SEGUAM (Aleutian Is)	1101-18-		
1787	Cont	....	AMUKTA (Aleutian Is)	1101-19-	2?	-/8
1787	Cont	....	SANGAY (Ecuador)	1502-09=	2	
1787<	....	?	BANDAI (Honshu-Japan)	0803-16=	2?	
1787<	....	?	OSORE-YAMA (Honshu-Japan)	0803-29=		
1787	....	?	MISTI, EL (Peru)	1504-01=	2	
1787	....	?	YUCAMANE (Peru)	1504-05-		
1787	....	?	VILLARRICA (Chile-C)	1507-12=	1	
1787	0512	?	BARREN ISLAND (Andaman Is-Ind O.-E)	0600-01=	2	
1787	0604d	68e>	ETNA (Italy)	0101-06=	2	
1787	0614	48a	FOURNAISE, PITON DE LA (Indian O.)	0303-02=	2	7/-
1787	0718	....	ETNA (Italy)	0101-06=	4	
1787	09	?	KLIUCHEVSKOI (Kamchatka)	1000-26=	2?	
1787	0921	2a	SAN MIGUEL (El Salvador)	1403-10=	2	
1788	Cont	....	VESUVIUS (Italy)	0101-02=	2	7/8
1788	Cont	....	STROMBOLI (Italy)	0101-04=	1?	
1788	Cont	....	YASUR (Vanuatu-SW Pacific)	0507-10=	2	
1788	Cont	....	ASO (Kyushu-Japan)	0802-11=	1	
1788	Cont	....	SEGUAM (Aleutian Is)	1101-18-		
1788	Cont	....	AMUKTA (Aleutian Is)	1101-19-	2?	-/8
1788	Cont	....	SANGAY (Ecuador)	1502-09=	2	
1788<	....	?	MAHAWU (Sulawesi-Indonesia)	0606-11=		
1788	....	?	TOLBACHIK (Kamchatka)	1000-24=	2	
1788	02	?	KLIUCHEVSKOI (Kamchatka)	1000-26=	2	
1788	08	?	KLIUCHEVSKOI (Kamchatka)	1000-26=	2	
1789	Cont	....	VESUVIUS (Italy)	0101-02=	2	7/8
1789	Cont	....	STROMBOLI (Italy)	0101-04=	1?	
1789	Cont	....	YASUR (Vanuatu-SW Pacific)	0507-10=	2	
1789	Cont	....	SEGUAM (Aleutian Is)	1101-18-		
1789	Cont	....	AMUKTA (Aleutian Is)	1101-19-	2?	-/8
1789	Cont	....	SANGAY (Ecuador)	1502-09=	2	
1789	....	?	MAHAWU (Sulawesi-Indonesia)	0606-11=	2	
1789	....	?	OSHIMA (Izu Is-Japan)	0804-01=	2	
? 1789	....	?	AVACHINSKY (Kamchatka)	1000-10=		
1789	....	?	TOLBACHIK (Kamchatka)	1000-24=	2	
1789	0324	?	BARREN ISLAND (Andaman Is-Ind O.-E)	0600-01=	2	
1789	06	31p	FOURNAISE, PITON DE LA (Indian O.)	0303-02=	2	
1789	1201	76m	KLIUCHEVSKOI (Kamchatka)	1000-26=	2	
1790	Cont	....	STROMBOLI (Italy)	0101-04=	1?	
1790	Cont	....	YASUR (Vanuatu-SW Pacific)	0507-10=	2	
1790	Cont	....	KLIUCHEVSKOI (Kamchatka)	1000-26=	2	
1790	Cont	....	SEGUAM (Aleutian Is)	1101-18-		
1790	Cont	....	AMUKTA (Aleutian Is)	1101-19-	2?	-/8
1790	Cont	....	SANGAY (Ecuador)	1502-09=	2	
1790	....	?	LATE (Tonga-SW Pacific)	0403-09=	2	
1790	....	?	TAAL (Luzon-Philippines)	0703-07=	2	
1790p	....	?	CHIRPOI (Kurile Is)	0900-15=		
1790	....	>3yr	ALAID (Kurile Is)	0900-39=	2	
1790	....	?	TOLBACHIK (Kamchatka)	1000-24=	2	
? 1790	....	?	SEMISOPOCHNOI (Aleutian Is)	1101-06-		
1790	....	?	GARELOI (Aleutian Is)	1101-07-	2	
? 1790	....	?	KANAGA (Aleutian Is)	1101-11-		
? 1790	....	?	AKUTAN (Aleutian Is)	1101-32-		
? 1790	....	?	SHISHALDIN (Aleutian Is)	1101-36-		
1790	....	?	PAVLOF (Alaska Peninsula)	1102-03-	2	
1790?	....	?	KILAUEA (Hawaiian Is)	1302-01-	0	7/-
1790d	....	?	HALEAKALA (Hawaiian Is)	1302-06-	0	8/-
1790	....	?	VILLARRICA (Chile-C)	1507-12=	2	
1790	01 ?	?	OSHIMA-OSHIMA (Hokkaido-Japan)	0805-01=	2	
1790	0309	657e	OSORNO (Chile-S)	1508-01=	2	
1790	05	....	VESUVIUS (Italy)	0101-02=	1	7/8
? 1790	0530	?	VSEVIDOF (Aleutian Is)	1101-27-		
? 1790	0607	?	MAKUSHIN (Aleutian Is)	1101-31-		
1790	0729	?	SAKURA-JIMA (Kyushu-Japan)	0802-08=	2	
1790	1009	?	IWAKI (Honshu-Japan)	0803-27=	2	
1790	11 ?	?	KILAUEA (Hawaiian Is)	1302-01-	4	-/8
1791	Cont	....	VESUVIUS (Italy)	0101-02=	2	7/8
1791	Cont	....	STROMBOLI (Italy)	0101-04=	1?	
1791	Cont	....	YASUR (Vanuatu-SW Pacific)	0507-10=	2	
1791	Cont	....	ALAID (Kurile Is)	0900-39=	2	
1791	Cont	....	AMUKTA (Aleutian Is)	1101-19-	2?	-/8
1791	Cont	....	SANGAY (Ecuador)	1502-09=	2	
1791	Cont	....	OSORNO (Chile-S)	1508-01=	2	
1791	....	?	FONUALEI (Tonga-SW Pacific)	0403-10=	2	
1791	....	?	GARELOI (Aleutian Is)	1101-07-	2	
? 1791	....	?	KANAGA (Aleutian Is)	1101-11-		
1791	0124	?	TELICA (Nicaragua)	1404-04=		
1791	02	213p	ETNA (Italy)	0101-06=	2	
1791	04	?	KLIUCHEVSKOI (Kamchatka)	1000-26=	2	
1791	0522	?	RABAUL (New Britain-SW Pac)	0502-14=	2?	
1791	0605d	52d?	FOURNAISE, PITON DE LA (Indian O.)	0303-02=	0	7/-
? 1791	0607	?	TANAGA (Aleutian Is)	1101-08-		
1791	0717	....	FOURNAISE, PITON DE LA (Indian O.)	0303-02=	2	7/-
1791	08	?	KLIUCHEVSKOI (Kamchatka)	1000-26=	2	

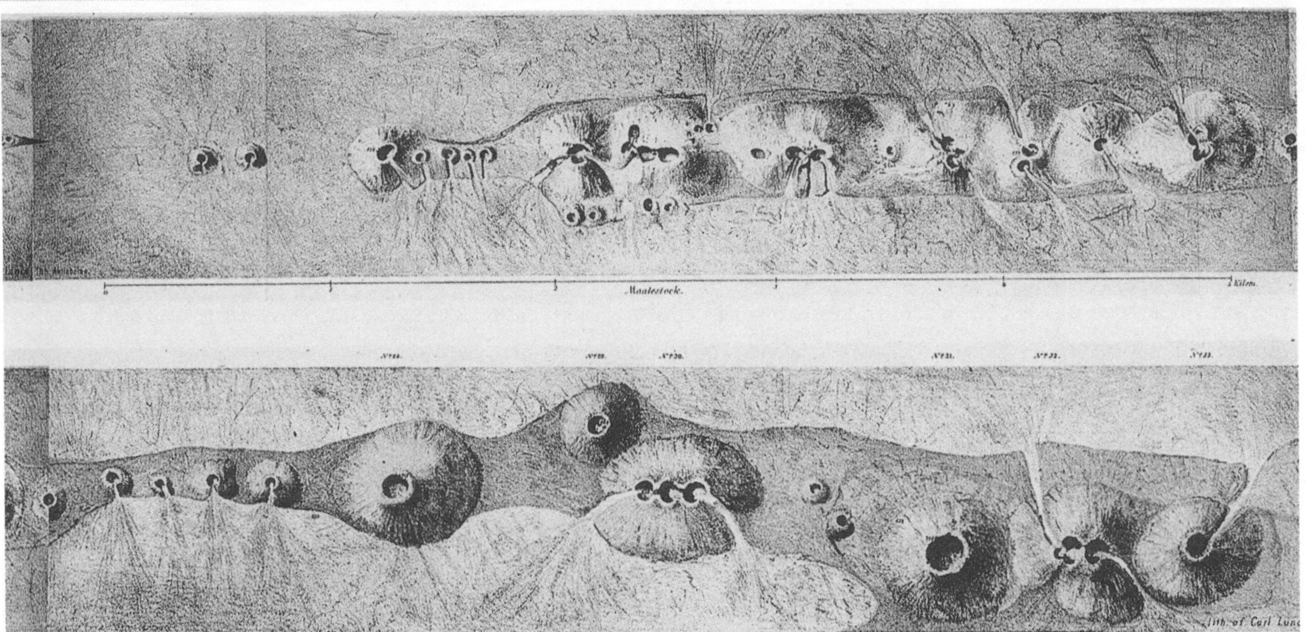

Figure 18. Crater row of Lakagigar, Iceland. This 1783-85 fissure eruption, from the Grimsvotn system, produced over 10 km^3 of lava, the largest flow in historical time. Aerial map view by A. Helland, in 1886 (16 years before the first airplane flight). Upper panel continues from left of lower panel. Reproduced from Gunnlaugsson et al, 1984 (see REFERENCES 1700).

START YEAR	M-Dy	Duration	VOLCANO NAME (Subregion)	NUMBER	VEI	Vol L/T
1791	0911	?	SAKURA-JIMA (Kyushu-Japan)	0802-08=	2	
1792	Cont	....	VESUVIUS (Italy)	0101-02=	2	7/8
1792	Cont	....	STROMBOLI (Italy)	0101-04=	1?	
1792	Cont	....	YASUR (Vanuatu-SW Pacific)	0507-10=	2	
1792	Cont	....	ALAID (Kurile Is)	0900-39=	2	
1792	Cont	....	SANGAY (Ecuador)	1502-09=	2	
1792	....	?	TOFUA (Tonga-SW Pacific)	0403-06=	0	
1792	....	?	SAKURA-JIMA (Kyushu-Japan)	0802-08=	2?	
1792	....	?	OSHIMA (Izu Is-Japan)	0804-01=	2	
? 1792	....	?	SEMISOPOCHNOI (Aleutian Is)	1101-06-		
1792	....	?	GARELOI (Aleutian Is)	1101-07-	2	
1792	....	?	BAKER (US-Washington)	1201-01=	2	
1792	....	?	VILLARRICA (Chile-C)	1507-12=	2	
1792	0122	?	PELEE (W Indies)	1600-12=	2	
1792	0210	163a	UNZEN (Kyushu-Japan)	0802-10=	2	8/-
? 1792	0214	?	MAKUSHIN (Aleutian Is)	1101-31-		
1792	03	69m	ETNA (Italy)	0101-06=	2	
1792	0525	367e	ETNA (Italy)	0101-06=	3	7/5
1792	0526e	?	GREAT SITKIN (Aleutian Is)	1101-12-		
1792	1219?	?	FOURNAISE, PITON DE LA (Indian O.)	0303-02=	0	
1793	Cont	....	VESUVIUS (Italy)	0101-02=	2	7/8
1793	Cont	....	STROMBOLI (Italy)	0101-04=	1?	
1793	Cont	....	ETNA (Italy)	0101-06=	2	7/5
1793	Cont	....	YASUR (Vanuatu-SW Pacific)	0507-10=	2	
1793	Cont	....	SANGAY (Ecuador)	1502-09=	2	
1793	....	?	ST. PAUL (Indian O.-S)	0304-03=	2	
1793f	....	?	RAUNG (Java)	0603-34=	2	
1793	....	?	EBEKO (Kurile Is)	0900-38=	2	
1793	....	?	TOLBACHIK (Kamchatka)	1000-24=	2	
? 1793	....	?	ILIAMNA (Alaska-SW)	1103-02-		
1793	02	....	ALAID (Kurile Is)	0900-39=	4↑	
1793	0302	289m	SAN MARTIN, VOLCAN DE (Mexico)	1401-11=	4	-/8
1793	0329	170m	IZALCO (El Salvador)	1403-03=	2	
1793	0402	?	IWAKI (Honshu-Japan)	0803-27=	2	
1793	05	31p	HIERRO (Canary Is)	1803-02-	0	
1793	0629	?	RITTER ISLAND (New Guinea-NE of)	0501-07=	2	
1794	Cont	....	STROMBOLI (Italy)	0101-04=	1?	
1794	Cont	....	YASUR (Vanuatu-SW Pacific)	0507-10=	2	
1794	Cont	....	SANGAY (Ecuador)	1502-09=	2	
1794	....	?	SAKURA-JIMA (Kyushu-Japan)	0802-08=	2	
1794	01	16m	FOURNAISE, PITON DE LA (Indian O.)	0303-02=	0	
1794	0403	?	IWAKI (Honshu-Japan)	0803-27=	2	
1794	05	765w	SAN MARTIN, VOLCAN DE (Mexico)	1401-11=	2?	
1794	0616	....	VESUVIUS (Italy)	0101-02=	3	7/8
? 1794	0715q	?	GRIMSVOTN (Iceland-NE)	1703-01=		
1794	0922	84m>	ZAO (Honshu-Japan)	0803-19=	2	
1795	Cont	....	STROMBOLI (Italy)	0101-04=	1?	
1795	Cont	....	YASUR (Vanuatu-SW Pacific)	0507-10=	2	
1795	Cont	....	SAN MARTIN, VOLCAN DE (Mexico)	1401-11=	2?	
1795	Cont	....	SANGAY (Ecuador)	1502-09=	2	
1795	....	?	FOURNAISE, PITON DE LA (Indian O.)	0303-02=		
1795	....	?	WESTDAHL [POGROMNI ?] (Aleutian	1101-34-	4	-/9
1795<	....	?	FISHER (Aleutian Is)	1101-35-		
@ 1795	....	?	ISANOTSKI (Aleutian Is)	1101-37-	3↑	
D 1795e	....	?	HOOD (US-Oregon)	1202-01-		
1795	....	?	COLIMA VOLC COMPLEX (Mexico)	1401-04=	2	
1795	1220	1a>	BARREN ISLAND (Andaman Is-Ind O.-E)	0600-01=	2	
1796	Cont	....	STROMBOLI (Italy)	0101-04=	1?	
1796	Cont	....	YASUR (Vanuatu-SW Pacific)	0507-10=	2	
1796	Cont	....	SAN MARTIN, VOLCAN DE (Mexico)	1401-11=	2?	
1796	Cont	....	SANGAY (Ecuador)	1502-09=	2	
1796	....	?	IJEN (Java)	0603-35=	2	
1796	....	?	WESTDAHL [POGROMNI ?] (Aleutian	1101-34-	0	
1796	....	?	AMAK (Aleutian Is)	1101-39-		
1796	....	?	VILLARRICA (Chile-C)	1507-12=	2	
1796	0115	>3yr	VESUVIUS (Italy)	0101-02=	1	-/8
1796	0324	?	ZAO (Honshu-Japan)	0803-19=	2	
1796	05	>3yr	BOGOSLOF (Aleutian Is)	1101-30-	3?	7/8
1796	11	?	OKINAWA-TORI-SHIMA (Ryukyu Is)	0802-02=	2	
1796	11	>3yr	GALERAS (Colombia)	1501-08=	2	
1797	Cont	....	VESUVIUS (Italy)	0101-02=	2	-/8
1797	Cont	....	STROMBOLI (Italy)	0101-04=	1?	
1797	Cont	....	YASUR (Vanuatu-SW Pacific)	0507-10=	2	
1797	Cont	....	BOGOSLOF (Aleutian Is)	1101-30-	0	7/8
1797	Cont	....	GALERAS (Colombia)	1501-08=	2	
1797	Cont	....	SANGAY (Ecuador)	1502-09=	2	
1797	....	>3yr	ETNA (Italy)	0101-06=	2	
1797?	....	?	FOURNAISE, PITON DE LA (Indian O.)	0303-02=	0	
1797	....	?	TINAKULA (Santa Cruz Is-SW Pac)	0506-01=	1?	
? 1797	....	?	HUNTER ISLAND (SW Pacific)	0508-02=		
1797	....	?	MERBABU (Java)	0603-24=	2	
1797	....	?	MERAPI (Java)	0603-25=	1	
1797	....	?	SAKURA-JIMA (Kyushu-Japan)	0802-08=	2	
? 1797	....	>3yr	SAN MARTIN, VOLCAN DE (Mexico)	1401-11=	2?	
@ 1797	....	?	BARDARBUNGA (Iceland-NE)	1703-03=		
1797?	....	?	ASKJA (Iceland-NE)	1703-06=	0	
1797	01	?	REVENTADOR (Ecuador)	1502-01=	3	
? 1797	0204	?	QUILOTOA (Ecuador)	1502-06=		
1797	08	?	WOLF, VOLCAN (Galapagos)	1503-02=		
1797	0929	3a	SOUFRIERE GUADELOUPE (W Indies)	1600-06=	2	
1798	Cont	....	VESUVIUS (Italy)	0101-02=	2	-/8
1798	Cont	....	STROMBOLI (Italy)	0101-04=	1?	
1798	Cont	....	ETNA (Italy)	0101-06=	2	
1798	Cont	....	YASUR (Vanuatu-SW Pacific)	0507-10=	2	
1798	Cont	....	BOGOSLOF (Aleutian Is)	1101-30-	0	7/8
? 1798	Cont	....	SAN MARTIN, VOLCAN DE (Mexico)	1401-11=	2?	
1798	Cont	....	GALERAS (Colombia)	1501-08=	2	
1798	Cont	....	SANGAY (Ecuador)	1502-09=	2	
? 1798?	....	?	SAN MIGUEL (El Salvador)	1403-10=	2	
1798	04	?	IZALCO (El Salvador)	1403-03=	2	
1798	0426	265m	SOUFRIERE GUADELOUPE (W Indies)	1600-06=	2	
1798	0609	97a	TENERIFE (Canary Is)	1803-03-	3	7/-
? 1798	1113	33m	UNZEN (Kyushu-Japan)	0802-10=		
1799	Cont	....	VESUVIUS (Italy)	0101-02=	2	-/8
1799	Cont	....	STROMBOLI (Italy)	0101-04=	1?	
1799	Cont	....	ETNA (Italy)	0101-06=	2	
1799	Cont	....	YASUR (Vanuatu-SW Pacific)	0507-10=	2	
1799	Cont	....	BOGOSLOF (Aleutian Is)	1101-30-	0	7/8
? 1799	Cont	....	SAN MARTIN, VOLCAN DE (Mexico)	1401-11=	2?	
1799	Cont	....	GALERAS (Colombia)	1501-08=	2	
1799	Cont	....	SANGAY (Ecuador)	1502-09=	2	
1799	Cont	....	SOUFRIERE GUADELOUPE (W Ind)	1600-06=	2	
1799	....	?	LAMONGAN (Java)	0603-32=	2	
1799	....	?	FUEGO (Guatemala)	1402-09=	3	-/7

	START YEAR	M-Dy	Duration	VOLCANO NAME (Subregion)	NUMBER	VEI	Vol L/T
	1799	....	?	VILLARRICA (Chile-C)	1507-12=	2	
	1799	0327	?	SAKURA-JIMA (Kyushu-Japan)	0802-08=	2	
	1799	0602	26a	FOGO (Cape Verde Is)	1804-01=	2	

1800

	START YEAR	M-Dy	Duration	VOLCANO NAME (Subregion)	NUMBER	VEI	Vol L/T
	1800	Cont	....	VESUVIUS (Italy)	0101-02=	2	-/8
	1800	Cont	....	STROMBOLI (Italy)	0101-04=	1?	
	1800	Cont	....	ETNA (Italy)	0101-06=	2	
	1800	Cont	....	YASUR (Vanuatu-SW Pacific)	0507-10=	2	
	1800	Cont	....	BOGOSLOF (Aleutian Is)	1101-30-	0	7/8
?	1800	Cont	....	SAN MARTIN, VOLCAN DE (Mexico)	1401-11=	2?	
	1800	Cont	....	GALERAS (Colombia)	1501-08=	2	
	1800	Cont	....	SANGAY (Ecuador)	1502-09=	2	
	1800?	....	?	KIEYO (Africa-E)	0202-17=	2	
	1800	....	?	GUNTUR (Java)	0603-13=		
	1800?	....	?	AZUMA (Honshu-Japan)	0803-18=		
C	1800t	....	?	PAGAN (Mariana Is-C Pac)	0804-17=		
	1800<	....	?	AKAN (Hokkaido-Japan)	0805-07=	1	
C	1800?	....	?	ISKUT-UNUK RIVER CONES (Canada)	1200-09-		
D	1800?	....	?	HOOD (US-Oregon)	1202-01-		
	1800	....	365y	HUALALAI (Hawaiian Is)	1302-04-	0	8/-
?	1800t	....	?	CONCEPCION (Nicaragua)	1404-12=	2	
	1800<	....	?	DECEPTION ISLAND (Antarctica)	1900-03=		
D	1800	0115u	?	ST. HELENS (US-Washington)	1201-05-	5	-/9
	1800	0511	?	IWAKI (Honshu-Japan)	0803-27=	2	
	1800	0624	1a	SAN JORGE (Azores)	1802-03=	2	
	1800	0821	<1	WOLF, VOLCAN (Galapagos)	1503-02=	2?	
	1800	1030	1a	MAYON (Luzon-Philippines)	0703-03=	2	
	1800	1102	6a	FOURNAISE, PITON DE LA (Indian O.)	0303-02=	0	7/-
	1800	12	>3yr	CHOKAI (Honshu-Japan)	0803-22=	1?	7/-
	1801	Cont	....	VESUVIUS (Italy)	0101-02=	2	-/8
	1801	Cont	....	STROMBOLI (Italy)	0101-04=	1?	
	1801	Cont	....	ETNA (Italy)	0101-06=	2	
	1801	Cont	....	YASUR (Vanuatu-SW Pacific)	0507-10=	2	
	1801	Cont	....	BOGOSLOF (Aleutian Is)	1101-30-	0	7/8
	1801	Cont	....	HUALALAI (Hawaiian Is)	1302-04-	0	8/-
?	1801	Cont	....	SAN MARTIN, VOLCAN DE (Mexico)	1401-11=	2?	
	1801	Cont	....	GALERAS (Colombia)	1501-08=	2	
	1801	Cont	....	SANGAY (Ecuador)	1502-09=	2	
	1801	....	?	TONGKOKO (Sulawesi-Indonesia)	0606-13=	2	6/-
	1801	....	318w>	ANTISANA (Ecuador)	1502-03=	2	
	1801	....	?	VILLARRICA (Chile-C)	1507-12=	2	
	1801	0810	....	CHOKAI (Honshu-Japan)	0803-22=	2	7/-
	1801	1027	153g	FOURNAISE, PITON DE LA (Indian O.)	0303-02=	2	
	1802	Cont	....	VESUVIUS (Italy)	0101-02=	2	-/8
	1802	Cont	....	STROMBOLI (Italy)	0101-04=	1?	
	1802	Cont	....	YASUR (Vanuatu-SW Pacific)	0507-10=	2	
	1802	Cont	....	CHOKAI (Honshu-Japan)	0803-22=	1?	7/-
	1802	Cont	....	BOGOSLOF (Aleutian Is)	1101-30-	0	7/8
?	1802	Cont	....	SAN MARTIN, VOLCAN DE (Mexico)	1401-11=	2?	
	1802	Cont	....	ANTISANA (Ecuador)	1502-03=	2	
	1802	Cont	....	SANGAY (Ecuador)	1502-09=	2	
	1802	....	?	MAKUSHIN (Aleutian Is)	1101-31-	3	
	1802	....	730y	POPOCATEPETL (Mexico)	1401-09=	1	
	1802	....	365y	IZALCO (El Salvador)	1403-03=	2	
	1802	0330	108m	TUTUPACA (Peru)	1504-04=	3	
@	1802	04 ?	31p?	REVENTADOR (Ecuador)	1502-01=	2	
	1802	1115	2	ETNA (Italy)	0101-06=	2	6/-
	1802	12	?	FOURNAISE, PITON DE LA (Indian O.)	0303-02=	2	
	1803	Cont	....	VESUVIUS (Italy)	0101-02=	2	-/8
	1803	Cont	....	STROMBOLI (Italy)	0101-04=	1?	
	1803	Cont	....	YASUR (Vanuatu-SW Pacific)	0507-10=	2	
	1803	Cont	....	CHOKAI (Honshu-Japan)	0803-22=	1?	7/-
	1803	Cont	....	BOGOSLOF (Aleutian Is)	1101-30-	0	7/8
	1803	Cont	....	POPOCATEPETL (Mexico)	1401-09=	1	
?	1803	Cont	....	SAN MARTIN, VOLCAN DE (Mexico)	1401-11=	2?	
	1803	Cont	....	IZALCO (El Salvador)	1403-03=	2	
	1803	Cont	....	SANGAY (Ecuador)	1502-09=	2	
	1803	....	>3yr	ETNA (Italy)	0101-06=	2	
	1803	0104	1a	COTOPAXI (Ecuador)	1502-05=	3	
	1803	0403	12a	GUNTUR (Java)	0603-13=	2	
	1803	0704	?	ASAMA (Honshu-Japan)	0803-11=	2	
	1803	0926	49a>	OSHIMA (Izu Is-Japan)	0804-01=	2	
	1803	11	77a>	BARREN ISLAND (Andaman Is-Ind O.-E)	0600-01=	2	
	1803	1107	14a	ASAMA (Honshu-Japan)	0803-11=	2	
	1804	Cont	....	STROMBOLI (Italy)	0101-04=	1?	
	1804	Cont	....	ETNA (Italy)	0101-06=	2	
	1804	Cont	....	YASUR (Vanuatu-SW Pacific)	0507-10=	2	
	1804	Cont	....	BARREN ISLAND (Andaman Is-Ind O.)	0600-01=	2	
	1804	Cont	....	CHOKAI (Honshu-Japan)	0803-22=	1?	7/-
	1804	Cont	....	POPOCATEPETL (Mexico)	1401-09=	1	
?	1804	Cont	....	SAN MARTIN, VOLCAN DE (Mexico)	1401-11=	2?	
	1804	Cont	....	SANGAY (Ecuador)	1502-09=	2	
	1804d	....	?	RAUNG (Java)	0603-34=	2	
	1804	....	?	BATUR (Lesser Sunda Is)	0604-01=	2	
	1804	....	>3yr	SHIKOTSU [TARUMAI] (Hokkaido)	0805-04=	3	-/7
	1804	....	?	MALY SEMIACHIK (Kamchatka)	1000-14=	3	
	1804	....	....	BOGOSLOF (Aleutian Is)	1101-30-	2	7/8
	1804	....	?	COLIMA VOLC COMPLEX (Mexico)	1401-04=	2	
	1804	05 ?	?	ZAO (Honshu-Japan)	0803-19=	2	
	1804	0812	....	VESUVIUS (Italy)	0101-02=	2	-/8
	1804	09	?	TENGGER CALDERA [BROMO]	0603-31=	2	
	1804	0905	?	ASO (Kyushu-Japan)	0802-11=	2	
	1805	Cont	....	STROMBOLI (Italy)	0101-04=	1?	
	1805	Cont	....	ETNA (Italy)	0101-06=	2	
	1805	Cont	....	YASUR (Vanuatu-SW Pacific)	0507-10=	2	
	1805	Cont	....	SHIKOTSU [TARUMAI] (Hokkaido)	0805-04=	2	-/7
?	1805	Cont	....	SAN MARTIN, VOLCAN DE (Mexico)	1401-11=	2?	
	1805	Cont	....	SANGAY (Ecuador)	1502-09=	2	
	1805	....	?	KUSATSU-SHIRANE (Honshu-Japan)	0803-12=	2	
	1805	....	?	SARYCHEV PEAK (Kurile Is)	0900-24=		
	1805	....	?	OKMOK (Aleutian Is)	1101-29-		
	1805	....	?	PACAYA (Guatemala)	1402-11=	2	
	1805	....	730y	IZALCO (El Salvador)	1403-03=	2	
	1805	0314	?	RUIZ (Colombia)	1501-02=	2	
	1805	04	?	CEREME (Java)	0603-17=	2	
	1805	0812	....	VESUVIUS (Italy)	0101-02=	2	-/8
	1806	Cont	....	STROMBOLI (Italy)	0101-04=	1?	
	1806	Cont	....	ETNA (Italy)	0101-06=	2	
	1806	Cont	....	YASUR (Vanuatu-SW Pacific)	0507-10=	2	
	1806	Cont	....	SHIKOTSU [TARUMAI] (Hokkaido)	0805-04=	2	-/7
	1806	Cont	....	IZALCO (El Salvador)	1403-03=	2	
	1806	Cont	....	SANGAY (Ecuador)	1502-09=	2	
	1806?	....	?	SUNDORO (Java)	0603-21=	2	
	1806	....	>3yr	BOGOSLOF (Aleutian Is)	1101-30-	1	7/-
?	1806	....	?	SAN SALVADOR (El Salvador)	1403-05=	0	
	1806	....	?	ANTUCO (Chile-C)	1507-08=		
	1806	....	?	VILLARRICA (Chile-C)	1507-12=	2?	
	1806	0325>	>3yr	COLIMA VOLC COMPLEX (Mexico)	1401-04=	2?	
	1806	05	?	LAMONGAN (Java)	0603-32=	2	
	1806	0531	....	VESUVIUS (Italy)	0101-02=	2	-/8
	1806	06 ?	123p?	ASO (Kyushu-Japan)	0802-11=	2	
	1806	0712	?	ZAO (Honshu-Japan)	0803-19=	2	
	1807	Cont	....	VESUVIUS (Italy)	0101-02=	2	-/8
	1807	Cont	....	STROMBOLI (Italy)	0101-04=	1?	
	1807	Cont	....	ETNA (Italy)	0101-06=	2	
	1807	Cont	....	YASUR (Vanuatu-SW Pacific)	0507-10=	2	
	1807	Cont	....	SHIKOTSU [TARUMAI] (Hokkaido)	0805-04=	2	-/7
	1807	Cont	....	BOGOSLOF (Aleutian Is)	1101-30-	1	7/-
	1807	Cont	....	COLIMA VOLC COMPLEX (Mexico)	1401-04=	1	
	1807	Cont	....	IZALCO (El Salvador)	1403-03=	2	
	1807	Cont	....	SANGAY (Ecuador)	1502-09=	2	
	1807h	....	?	CAMEROON, MT. (Africa-W)	0204-01=	3	
	1807	....	?	MARAPI (Sumatra)	0601-14=	2	
	1807	....	?	MERAPI (Java)	0603-25=	2	
?	1807	....	?	BARDARBUNGA (Iceland-NE)	1703-03=		
	1807	0201p	?	KLIUCHEVSKOI (Kamchatka)	1000-26=	2	
	1807	0323	82a	FOURNAISE, PITON DE LA (Indian O.)	0303-02=	2	
	1807	0331	?	IWAKI (Honshu-Japan)	0803-27=	2	
	1807	0901	5a	GUNTUR (Java)	0603-13=	2	
	1808	Cont	....	VESUVIUS (Italy)	0101-02=	2	-/8
	1808	Cont	....	STROMBOLI (Italy)	0101-04=	1?	
	1808	Cont	....	ETNA (Italy)	0101-06=	2	
	1808	Cont	....	YASUR (Vanuatu-SW Pacific)	0507-10=	2	
	1808	Cont	....	SHIKOTSU [TARUMAI] (Hokkaido)	0805-04=	2	-/7
	1808	Cont	....	BOGOSLOF (Aleutian Is)	1101-30-	1	7/-
	1808	Cont	....	COLIMA VOLC COMPLEX (Mexico)	1401-04=	1	
	1808	Cont	....	SANGAY (Ecuador)	1502-09=	2	
	1808	....	?	KARTHALA (Indian O.-W)	0303-01=		
	1808	....	?	AGUNG (Lesser Sunda Is)	0604-02=	2	
	1808	....	?	RUANG (Sangihe Is-Indonesia)	0607-01=	2	
	1808?	....	?	BANDAI (Honshu-Japan)	0803-16=	2	
	1808?	....	?	AKAN (Hokkaido-Japan)	0805-07=		
	1808	02	59p	TAAL (Luzon-Philippines)	0703-07=	2	
	1808	0501	40a	SAN JORGE (Azores)	1802-03=	1	
	1808	1208	?	LAMONGAN (Java)	0603-32=	2	
	1809	Cont	....	VESUVIUS (Italy)	0101-02=	2	-/8
	1809	Cont	....	STROMBOLI (Italy)	0101-04=	1?	
	1809	Cont	....	YASUR (Vanuatu-SW Pacific)	0507-10=	2	
	1809	Cont	....	SHIKOTSU [TARUMAI] (Hokkaido)	0805-04=	2	-/7
	1809	Cont	....	BOGOSLOF (Aleutian Is)	1101-30-	1	7/-
	1809	Cont	....	COLIMA VOLC COMPLEX (Mexico)	1401-04=	1	
	1809	Cont	....	SANGAY (Ecuador)	1502-09=	2	
I	1809b	....	?	Unknown Source (SP, 365 ppb sulfate)	.		
	1809	0327	13a	ETNA (Italy)	0101-06=	2	7/6
	1809	0328	3a	COSIGUINA (Nicaragua)	1404-01=	2?	
	1809	0509	?	GUNTUR (Java)	0603-13=	2	
	1809	06	>3yr	SOUFRIERE GUADELOUPE (W Indies)	1600-06=	1	
	1809	0612	200a	ZAO (Honshu-Japan)	0803-19=	2	
	1809	0717	22a	FOURNAISE, PITON DE LA (Indian O.)	0303-02=	2	
	1810	Cont	....	STROMBOLI (Italy)	0101-04=	1?	
	1810	Cont	....	YASUR (Vanuatu-SW Pacific)	0507-10=	2	
	1810	Cont	....	SHIKOTSU [TARUMAI] (Hokkaido)	0805-04=	2	-/7
	1810	Cont	....	BOGOSLOF (Aleutian Is)	1101-30-	1	7/-
	1810	Cont	....	SANGAY (Ecuador)	1502-09=	2	
	1810	Cont	....	SOUFRIERE GUADELOUPE (W Ind)	1600-06=	1	
	1810j	....	?	YAR, JABAL (Arabia-W)	0301-08-	2	
?	1810j	....	?	VICTORY (New Guinea)	0503-03=	2?	
	1810	....	?	MERAPI (Java)	0603-25=	1	
	1810j	....	?	PUTANA (Chile-N)	1505-09=		
	1810	0911	....	VESUVIUS (Italy)	0101-02=	1	-/8
?	1810	0914	12a	KANPU (Honshu-Japan)	0803-261	1?	
	1810	1120	8a	FOURNAISE, PITON DE LA (Indian O.)	0303-02=	2	
	1810	1226e	?	ETNA (Italy)	0101-06=	1	
	1811	Cont	....	VESUVIUS (Italy)	0101-02=	2	-/8
	1811	Cont	....	STROMBOLI (Italy)	0101-04=	1?	
	1811	Cont	....	YASUR (Vanuatu-SW Pacific)	0507-10=	2	
	1811	Cont	....	SHIKOTSU [TARUMAI] (Hokkaido)	0805-04=	2	-/7
	1811	Cont	....	BOGOSLOF (Aleutian Is)	1101-30-	1	7/-
	1811	Cont	....	SANGAY (Ecuador)	1502-09=	2	
	1811	Cont	....	SOUFRIERE GUADELOUPE (W Ind)	1600-06=	1	
?	1811	....	?	SAN MIGUEL (El Salvador)	1403-10=	2	
	1811	0127	1a	MIYAKE-JIMA (Izu Is-Japan)	0804-04=	2	

	START YEAR	M-Dy	Duration	VOLCANO NAME (Subregion)	NUMBER	VEI	Vol L/T
	1811	0201	104m	GAMALAMA (Halmahera-Indonesia)	0608-06=	2	
	1811	0201	7a	SETE CIDADES (Azores)	1802-08=	2?	
	1811	0605	?	KELUT (Java)	0603-28=	2	
	1811	0611	?	CHIRPOI (Kurile Is)	0900-15=	2	
	1811	0614	8a	SETE CIDADES (Azores)	1802-08=	3	
?	1811	1005	....	MAYON (Luzon-Philippines)	0703-03=	2	
	1811	1027	200m	ETNA (Italy)	0101-06=	2	7/6
	1812	Cont	....	STROMBOLI (Italy)	0101-04=	1?	
	1812	Cont	....	ETNA (Italy)	0101-06=	2	7/6
	1812	Cont	....	YASUR (Vanuatu-SW Pacific)	0507-10=	2	
	1812	Cont	....	SHIKOTSU [TARUMAI] (Hokkaido)	0805-04=	2	-/7
	1812	Cont	....	BOGOSLOF (Aleutian Is)	1101-30-	1	7/-
	1812	Cont	....	SANGAY (Ecuador)	1502-09=	2	
	1812	Cont	....	SOUFRIERE GUADELOUPE (W Ind)	1600-06=	1	
?	1812	....	?	VULCANO (Italy)	0101-05=	1?	
	1812	....	365y	MERAPI (Java)	0603-25=	1	
	1812	....	730y?	RAUNG (Java)	0603-34=	2	
	1812	....	>3yr	TAMBORA (Lesser Sunda Is)	0604-04=	2	
?	1812	....	?	BERUTARUBE (Kurile Is)	0900-04=	1	
	1812	....	?	ATKA [KLIUCHEV] (Aleutian Is)	1101-16-	3?	
	1812	....	?	AUGUSTINE (Alaska-SW)	1103-01-	3?	
	1812	0101	....	VESUVIUS (Italy)	0101-02=	1	-/8
	1812	0427	43a?	SOUFRIERE ST. VINCENT (W Indies)	1600-15=	4	-/8
	1812	08	?	TIATIA (Kurile Is)	0900-03=	2	
	1812	0805d	132n	FOURNAISE, PITON DE LA (Indian O.)	0303-02=	2	
	1812	0806	2a	AWU (Sangihe Is-Indonesia)	0607-04=	4?	-/8
	1812	09	?	KLIUCHEVSKOI (Kamchatka)	1000-26=	2	
	1812	0905d	?	ATSONUPURI (Kurile Is)	0900-05=	1	
	1812	0907	<1	GAMALAMA (Halmahera-Indonesia)	0608-06=	2	
	1813	Cont	....	STROMBOLI (Italy)	0101-04=	1?	
	1813	Cont	....	YASUR (Vanuatu-SW Pacific)	0507-10=	2	
	1813	Cont	....	MERAPI (Java)	0603-25=	1	
	1813	Cont	....	RAUNG (Java)	0603-34=	2	
	1813	Cont	....	TAMBORA (Lesser Sunda Is)	0604-04=	2	
	1813	Cont	....	SHIKOTSU [TARUMAI] (Hokkaido)	0805-04=	2	-/7
	1813	Cont	....	BOGOSLOF (Aleutian Is)	1101 30	1	7/-
	1813	Cont	....	SANGAY (Ecuador)	1502-09=	2	
	1813	....	?	SUWANOSE-JIMA (Ryukyu Is)	0802-03=	4	
?	1813	0110	?	ADATARA (Honshu-Japan)	0803-17=		
	1813	02	?	KLIUCHEVSKOI (Kamchatka)	1000-26=	2	
@	1813	0606	1a	DARWIN, VOLCAN (Galapagos)	1503-03=	2?	
@	1813	0713	?	NEGRA, SIERRA (Galapagos)	1503-05=	2?	
	1813	0714<	?	FERNANDINA (Galapagos)	1503-01=	2	
	1813	0926	61a	FOURNAISE, PITON DE LA (Indian O.)	0303-02=	2	
	1813	1029	....	VESUVIUS (Italy)	0101-02=	2	-/8
	1814	Cont	....	VESUVIUS (Italy)	0101-02=	2	-/8
	1814	Cont	....	STROMBOLI (Italy)	0101-04=	1?	
	1814	Cont	....	YASUR (Vanuatu-SW Pacific)	0507-10=	2	
	1814	Cont	....	RAUNG (Java)	0603-34=	2	
	1814	Cont	....	TAMBORA (Lesser Sunda Is)	0604-04=	2	
	1814	Cont	....	SHIKOTSU [TARUMAI] (Hokkaido)	0805-04=	2	-/7
	1814	Cont	....	SANGAY (Ecuador)	1502-09=	2	
	1814	....	?	NIUAFO'OU (Tonga-SW Pacific)	0403-11=	2	
	1814	....	?	ASO (Kyushu-Japan)	0802-11=	2	
	1814	....	....	BOGOSLOF (Aleutian Is)	1101-30-	2	7/-
	1814	....	?	UGASHIK-PEULIK (Alaska Peninsula)	1102-13A	3	
	1814	0109	<1	SOUFRIERE ST. VINCENT (W Indies)	1600-15=	1?	
	1814	0201	14a>	MAYON (Luzon-Philippines)	0703-03=	4	-/8
	1814	0309	?	RAOUL ISLAND (Kermadec Is)	0402-03=	3	-/7
	1814	07	31p	FERNANDINA (Galapagos)	1503-01=	2	
	1814	0910	33a	FOURNAISE, PITON DE LA (Indian O.)	0303-02=	2	
	1814	1127	<1	GAMALAMA (Halmahera-Indonesia)	0608-06=	2	
	1814	1231y	?	KARTHALA (Indian O.-W)	0303-01=		
	1815	Cont	....	VESUVIUS (Italy)	0101-02=	2	-/8
	1815	Cont	....	STROMBOLI (Italy)	0101-04=	1?	
	1815	Cont	....	YASUR (Vanuatu-SW Pacific)	0507-10=	2	
	1815	Cont	....	SHIKOTSU [TARUMAI] (Hokkaido)	0805-04=	2	-/7
	1815	Cont	....	BOGOSLOF (Aleutian Is)	1101-30-	1	7/-
	1815	Cont	....	SANGAY (Ecuador)	1502-09=	2	
	1815	....	>3yr	VILLARRICA (Chile-C)	1507-12=	2	
	1815	0121	6a	FOURNAISE, PITON DE LA (Indian O.)	0303-02=	2	
	1815	0210	247m	ASO (Kyushu-Japan)	0802-11=	2	
	1815	0228	?	ASAMA (Honshu-Japan)	0803-11=	3	
	1815	0405	12a>	TENGGER CALDERA [BROMO]	0603-31=	2	
	1815	0410	....	TAMBORA (Lesser Sunda Is)	0604-04=	7	-/11
	1815	0815	1a	FOURNAISE, PITON DE LA (Indian O.)	0303-02=	2	
	1815	0815	?	GUNTUR (Java)	0603-13=	2	
	1815	1231y	?	RAUNG (Java)	0603-34=	2	
	1816	Cont	....	VESUVIUS (Italy)	0101-02=	2	-/8
	1816	Cont	....	STROMBOLI (Italy)	0101-04=	1?	
	1816	Cont	....	YASUR (Vanuatu-SW Pacific)	0507-10=	2	
	1816	Cont	....	SHIKOTSU [TARUMAI] (Hokkaido)	0805 04=	2	-/7
	1816	Cont	....	BOGOSLOF (Aleutian Is)	1101-30-	1	7/-
	1816	Cont	....	SANGAY (Ecuador)	1502-09=	2	
	1816	Cont	....	VILLARRICA (Chile-C)	1507-12=	2	
	1816	....	?	PURACE (Colombia)	1501-06=		
?	1816	0306	?	ETNA (Italy)	0101-06=	0	
	1816	05	30p?	GRIMSVOTN (Iceland-NE)	1703-01=	2	
	1816	0609	27a	ASO (Kyushu-Japan)	0802-11=	2	
	1816	0921	?	GUNTUR (Java)	0603-13=	2	
	1816	1011	65m	BANDA API (Banda Sea)	0605-09=	2	
?	1816	1208	?	UNNAMED (Atlantic-C)	1805-03=	0	
	1816	1215	?	FOURNAISE, PITON DE LA (Indian O.)	0303-02=	0	
	1816	1231y	?	FOGO (Cape Verde Is)	1804-01=		
	1817	Cont	....	STROMBOLI (Italy)	0101-04=	1?	
	1817	Cont	....	YASUR (Vanuatu-SW Pacific)	0507-10=	2	
	1817	Cont	....	SHIKOTSU [TARUMAI] (Hokkaido)	0805-04=	2	-/7
	1817	Cont	....	BOGOSLOF (Aleutian Is)	1101-30-	1	7/-
	1817	Cont	....	SANGAY (Ecuador)	1502-09=	2	
	1817	Cont	....	VILLARRICA (Chile-C)	1507-12=	2	
	1817	....	?	LAMONGAN (Java)	0603-32=	2	
?	1817	....	?	YUNASKA (Aleutian Is)	1101-21-		
	1817	....	?	VSEVIDOF (Aleutian Is)	1101-27-	3?	
	1817	....	?	PAVLOF (Alaska Peninsula)	1102-03-	2	
	1817	....	?	IZALCO (El Salvador)	1403-03=	2	
@	1817<	....	?	FERNANDINA (Galapagos)	1503-01=	2	
@	1817	....	?	NEGRA, SIERRA (Galapagos)	1503-05=		
	1817	01	89p	FOURNAISE, PITON DE LA (Indian O.)	0303-02=	0	
	1817	0115e	34e?	IJEN (Java)	0603-35=	1?	
	1817	0116	25a?	RAUNG (Java)	0603-34=	4?	-/8
	1817	0124	....	IJEN (Java)	0603-35=	2	
	1817	0301	>3yr	OKMOK (Aleutian Is)	1101-29-	3	
	1817	1222	....	VESUVIUS (Italy)	0101-02=	1	-/8
	1817	1231y	?	DEMPO (Sumatra)	0601-23=	2	
	1818	Cont	....	VESUVIUS (Italy)	0101-02=	2	-/8
	1818	Cont	....	STROMBOLI (Italy)	0101-04=	1?	
	1818	Cont	....	YASUR (Vanuatu-SW Pacific)	0507-10=	2	
	1818	Cont	....	OKMOK (Aleutian Is)	1101-29-	2	
	1818	Cont	....	BOGOSLOF (Aleutian Is)	1101-30-	1	7/-
	1818	Cont	....	SANGAY (Ecuador)	1502-09=	2	
	1818	Cont	....	VILLARRICA (Chile-C)	1507-12=	2	
	1818	....	?	SUNDORO (Java)	0603-21=	2	
?	1818	....	?	MAKUSHIN (Aleutian Is)	1101-31-		
	1818	0116	154a>	ALMOLONGA [C. QUEMADO] (Guate)	1402-04=	2	
	1818	0215	74a	COLIMA VOLC COMPLEX (Mexico)	1401-04=	4	
	1818	04	?	JAN MAYEN (Atl-N-Jan Mayen)	1706-01=	3?	
	1818	1008	?	LAMONGAN (Java)	0603-32=	2	
	1818	1021	2	GUNTUR (Java)	0603-13=	2	
	1818	1108	?	SEMERU (Java)	0603-30=	2	
	1819	Cont	....	VESUVIUS (Italy)	0101-02=	2	-/8
	1819	Cont	....	STROMBOLI (Italy)	0101-04=	1?	
	1819	Cont	....	YASUR (Vanuatu-SW Pacific)	0507-10=	2	
	1819	Cont	....	OKMOK (Aleutian Is)	1101-29-	2	
	1819	Cont	....	BOGOSLOF (Aleutian Is)	1101-30-	1	7/-
	1819	Cont	....	SANGAY (Ecuador)	1502-09=	2	
	1819	....	?	LEWOTOLO (Lesser Sunda Is)	0604-23=	2	
	1819	....	?	SOPUTAN (Sulawesi-Indonesia)	0606-03=	2	
?	1819	....	?	SEMPU (Sulawesi-Indonesia)	0606-04=		
	1819	....	1096y	KLIUCHEVSKOI (Kamchatka)	1000-26=	2	
?	1819	....	?	REDOUBT (Alaska-SW)	1103-03-		
	1819	....	?	WRANGELL (Alaska-E)	1105-02-	2	
	1819	....	?	COLIMA VOLC COMPLEX (Mexico)	1401-04=	1	
	1819	....	?	FERNANDINA (Galapagos)	1503-01=	2	
	1819	0527	66a	ETNA (Italy)	0101-06=	3	7/7
	1819	0718	?	SAN MIGUEL (El Salvador)	1403-10=	2	
	1819	08	?	TAMBORA (Lesser Sunda Is)	0604-04=	2	
	1819	12	?	ZAVODOVSKI (Antarctica)	1900-13=	2	
	1819	1229	?	MICHAEL (Antarctica)	1900-09=	2	
	1820	Cont	....	STROMBOLI (Italy)	0101-04=	1?	
	1820	Cont	....	YASUR (Vanuatu-SW Pacific)	0507-10=	2	
	1820	Cont	....	KLIUCHEVSKOI (Kamchatka)	1000-26=	2	
	1820	Cont	....	OKMOK (Aleutian Is)	1101-29-	2	
	1820	Cont	....	BOGOSLOF (Aleutian Is)	1101-30-	1	7/-
	1820	Cont	....	SANGAY (Ecuador)	1502-09=	2	
	1820?	....	?	FENTALE (Ethiopia)	0201-19=	0	
	1820j	....	?	KONE (Ethiopia)	0201-20-	1	
	1820?	....	?	AMBRYM (Vanuatu-SW Pacific)	0507-04=		
	1820	....	730y	MERAPI (Java)	0603-25=	1	7/-
	1820	....	?	TENGGER CALDERA [BROMO]	0603-31=	2	
T	1820v	....	?	KUTTARA (Hokkaido-Japan)	0805-034	1	-/5
	1820	....	?	WESTDAHL [POGROMNI ?] (Aleutians)	1101-34-	2	
	1820?	....	?	BAKER (US-Washington)	1201-01=	2	
	1820?	....	?	KILAUEA (Hawaiian Is)	1302-01-	2	
	1820	....	?	ANTUCO (Chile-C)	1507-08=	2	
	1820	01	....	VESUVIUS (Italy)	0101-02=	1	-/8
	1820	01	30p	FOURNAISE, PITON DE LA (Indian O.)	0303-02=	2	
	1820	0611	58a	BANDA API (Banda Sea)	0605-09=	2	
	1821	Cont	....	VESUVIUS (Italy)	0101-02=	2	-/8
	1821	Cont	....	STROMBOLI (Italy)	0101-04=	1?	
	1821	Cont	....	YASUR (Vanuatu-SW Pacific)	0507-10=	2	
	1821	Cont	....	MERAPI (Java)	0603-25=	1	7/-
	1821	Cont	....	BOGOSLOF (Aleutian Is)	1101-30-	1	7/-
	1821	Cont	....	SANGAY (Ecuador)	1502-09=	2	
	1821	....	?	TONGKOKO (Sulawesi-Indonesia)	0606-13=	0	
?	1821	....	?	GORELY (Kamchatka)	1000-07=		
?	1821	....	?	TAJUMULCO (Guatemala)	1402-02=	2	
	1821	0127	94a	ZAO (Honshu-Japan)	0803-19=	2	
	1821	02	....	KLIUCHEVSKOI (Kamchatka)	1000-26=	2	
	1821	0227	42a	FOURNAISE, PITON DE LA (Indian O.)	0303-02=	2	
	1821	0316	?	BATUR (Lesser Sunda Is)	0604-01=	2	
?	1821	0316	?	AGUNG (Lesser Sunda Is)	0604-02=	2	
	1821	0323	?	SANGEANG API (Lesser Sunda Is)	0604-05=	2	
	1821	05	?	IRAZU (Costa Rica)	1405-06=	2	
	1821	0501	....	ZAO (Honshu-Japan)	0803-19=	2	
	1821	0523	?	CHOKAI (Honshu-Japan)	0803-22=	2?	
?	1821	0822	?	GAMALAMA (Halmahera-Indonesia)	0608-06=	1	
	1821	1215e	21e	LAMONGAN (Java)	0603-32=	2	
	1821	1219	378a	EYJAFJOLL (Iceland-S)	1702-02=	3?	-/8
	1821	1231y	?	KARTHALA (Indian O.-W)	0303-01=		
	1822	Cont	....	YASUR (Vanuatu-SW Pacific)	0507-10=	2	
	1822	Cont	....	LAMONGAN (Java)	0603-32=	2	
	1822	Cont	....	KLIUCHEVSKOI (Kamchatka)	1000-26=	2	
	1822	Cont	....	BOGOSLOF (Aleutian Is)	1101-30-	1	7/-
	1822	Cont	....	SANGAY (Ecuador)	1502-09=	2	
?	1822	....	365y	VULCANO (Italy)	0101-05=	2?	

START YEAR	M-Dy	Duration	VOLCANO NAME (Subregion)	NUMBER	VEI	Vol L/T
1822	....	730y	**OSHIMA** (Izu Is-Japan)	0804-01=	2	
? 1822	....	?	**MAIPO** (Chile-C)	1507-021		
? 1822	....	?	**TROMEN** (Argentina)	1507-071		
1822	....	?	**LLAIMA** (Chile-C)	1507-11=	2	
1822	0112	?	**KIRISHIMA** (Kyushu-Japan)	0802-09=	2	-/6
1822	*0228*	....	*EYJAFJOLL (Iceland-S)*	1702-02=	1	-/8
1822	0312	124m	**USU** (Hokkaido-Japan)	0805-03=	4	-/8
1822	0507	?	**IRAZU** (Costa Rica)	1405-06=	2	
1822	0621	?	**ETNA** (Italy)	0101-06=	1?	
1822	0723	8a	**MARAPI** (Sumatra)	0601-14=	2	
1822	1008	54p	**GALUNGGUNG** (Java)	0603-14=	5	-/9
1822	1022	....	**VESUVIUS** (Italy)	0101-02=	3	-/8
1822	1022	?	**STROMBOLI** (Italy)	0101-04=	3	
1822	11	?	**TOLIMA** (Colombia)	1501-03=	2	
1822	1119	>3yr	**SAN JOSE** (Chile-C)	1507-02=	2	
1822	1119	?	**VILLARRICA** (Chile-C)	1507-12=	2	
1822	1227	100a	**MERAPI** (Java)	0603-25=	3	8/7
1822	1228	8d	**TENGGER CALDERA [BROMO]**	0603-31=	2	
1823	*Cont*	....	*STROMBOLI (Italy)*	0101-04=	*1?*	
? *1823*	*Cont*	....	*VULCANO (Italy)*	0101-05=	*2?*	
1823	*Cont*	....	*YASUR (Vanuatu-SW Pacific)*	0507-10=	*2*	
1823	*Cont*	....	*MERAPI (Java)*	0603-25=	*2*	*8/7*
1823	*Cont*	....	*TENGGER CALDERA [BROMO]*	0603-31=	*2*	
1823	*Cont*	....	*OSHIMA (Izu Is-Japan)*	0804-01=	*2*	
1823	*Cont*	....	*BOGOSLOF (Aleutian Is)*	1101-30-	*1*	*7/-*
1823	*Cont*	....	*SANGAY (Ecuador)*	1502-09=	*2*	
1823	*Cont*	....	*SAN JOSE (Chile-C)*	1507-02=	*2*	
1823	*Cont*	....	*EYJAFJOLL (Iceland-S)*	1702-02=	*1*	*-/8*
? 1823e	....	?	**ZHELTOVSKY** (Kamchatka)	1000-04=		
1823	....	?	**IRAZU** (Costa Rica)	1405-06=	2?	
1823	....	?	**BRISTOL ISLAND** (Antarctica)	1900-08=	2	
? 1823	....	?	**MICHAEL** (Antarctica)	1900-09=	2	
1823	....	?	**CANDLEMAS ISLAND** (Antarctica)	1900-10=	2	
? 1823	....	?	**ZAVODOVSKI** (Antarctica)	1900-13=	1	
1823	02	151p	**KILAUEA** (Hawaiian Is)	1302-01-	0	7/-
1823	0204d	?	**GRIMSVOTN** (Iceland-NE)	1703-01=	2	
1823	0617	7a	**GALERAS** (Colombia)	1501-08=	2	
1823	0626	27a	**KATLA** (Iceland-S)	1702-03=	3	-/7
1823	08 <	>3yr	**KILAUEA** (Hawaiian Is)	1302-01-	0	
1824	*Cont*	....	*STROMBOLI (Italy)*	0101-04=	*1?*	
1824	*Cont*	....	*YASUR (Vanuatu-SW Pacific)*	0507-10=	*2*	
1824	*Cont*	....	*OSHIMA (Izu Is-Japan)*	0804-01=	*2*	
1824	*Cont*	....	*KILAUEA (Hawaiian Is)*	1302-01-	*0*	
1824	*Cont*	....	*SANGAY (Ecuador)*	1502-09=	*2*	
1824	*Cont*	....	*SAN JOSE (Chile-C)*	1507-02=	*2*	
1824	....	?	**ZUBAYR, JEBEL** (Red Sea)	0201-02=	2	
1824	....	?	**YUNASKA** (Aleutian Is)	1101-21-	3	
1824	....	>3yr	**OKMOK** (Aleutian Is)	1101-29-		
1824	....	?	**SHISHALDIN** (Aleutian Is)	1101-36-	3	
1824	0101?	30a?	**LAMONGAN** (Java)	0603-32=	2	
1824	02	?	**FOURNAISE, PITON DE LA** (Indian O.)	0303-02=	0	
1824	0422	67a	**BANDA API** (Banda Sea)	0605-09=	2	
? 1824	0501	?	**UNNAMED** (Atlantic-C)	1805-01=	0	
1824	*0702*	*>3yr*	*VESUVIUS (Italy)*	0101-02=	2	
1824	*0731*	*85a*	*LANZAROTE (Canary Is)*	1803-06-	1	7/-
1824	0929	....	**LANZAROTE** (Canary Is)	1803-06-	2	7/-
1824	*1016*	....	*LANZAROTE (Canary Is)*	1803-06-	2	7/-
1824	12	....	**FOURNAISE, PITON DE LA** (Indian O.)	0303-02=	0	
1825	*Cont*	....	*VESUVIUS (Italy)*	0101-02=	*2*	
1825	*Cont*	....	*STROMBOLI (Italy)*	0101-04=	*1?*	
1825	*Cont*	....	*YASUR (Vanuatu-SW Pacific)*	0507-10=	*2*	
1825	*Cont*	....	*OKMOK (Aleutian Is)*	1101-29-		
1825	*Cont*	....	*KILAUEA (Hawaiian Is)*	1302-01-	*0*	
1825	*Cont*	....	*SANGAY (Ecuador)*	1502-09=	*2*	
1825	*Cont*	....	*SAN JOSE (Chile-C)*	1507-02=	*2*	
1825j	....	?	**CAMEROON, MT.** (Africa-W)	0204-01=	2	
? 1825q	....	?	**BALBI** (Bougainville-SW Pac)	0505-01=		
1825	....	?	**DIENG VOLC COMPLEX** (Java)	0603-20=	2	
1825	....	?	**KELUT** (Java)	0603-28=	2	
1825?	....	>3yr	**BANDA API** (Banda Sea)	0605-09=	1	
1825	....	?	**KARANGETANG [API SIAU]** (Sangihe	0607-02=	2	
1825	....	?	**TAAL** (Luzon-Philippines)	0703-07=	2	
1825e	....	?	**PAGAN** (Mariana Is-C Pac)	0804-17=	2?	
1825q	....	?	**PREVO PEAK** (Kurile Is)	0900-19=	2	
1825	....	?	**SHISHALDIN** (Aleutian Is)	1101-36-	2	
1825	....	?	**PAVLOF** (Alaska Peninsula)	1102-03-	2?	
D 1825?	....	?	**RAINIER** (US-Washington)	1201-03-	2	-/6
1825	....	?	**IZALCO** (El Salvador)	1403-03=	2	
1825q	....	?	**GUALLATIRI** (Chile-N)	1505-02=	2?	
1825	0214	244m>	**FERNANDINA** (Galapagos)	1503-01=	3	
1825	0302	?	**TOLIMA** (Colombia)	1501-03=	2	
@ 1825	0310	?	**ISANOTSKI** (Aleutian Is)	1101-37-	4	-/8
1825	0614	<1	**GUNTUR** (Java)	0603-13=	2	
? 1825	0906	?	**BRIMSTONE ISLAND** (Kermadec Is)	0402-02=		
1825	10	?	**SLAMET** (Java)	0603-18=	2	
1825	1105	3a	**TENGGER CALDERA [BROMO]**	0603-31=	2	
1826	*Cont*	....	*VESUVIUS (Italy)*	0101-02=	*2*	
1826	*Cont*	....	*STROMBOLI (Italy)*	0101-04=	*1?*	
1826	*Cont*	....	*YASUR (Vanuatu-SW Pacific)*	0507-10=	*2*	
1826	*Cont*	....	*BANDA API (Banda Sea)*	0605-09=	*1*	
1826	*Cont*	....	*OKMOK (Aleutian Is)*	1101-29-		
1826	*Cont*	....	*KILAUEA (Hawaiian Is)*	1302-01-	*0*	
1826	*Cont*	....	*SANGAY (Ecuador)*	1502-09=	*2*	
1826	*Cont*	....	*SAN JOSE (Chile-C)*	1507-02=	*2*	
1826	....	?	**LAMONGAN** (Java)	0603-32=	2	
1826	....	?	**SHISHALDIN** (Aleutian Is)	1101-36-	0	
1826	....	?	**FUEGO** (Guatemala)	1402-09=	2	
? 1826	....	?	**IRAZU** (Costa Rica)	1405-06=		
? 1826	....	?	**RUIZ** (Colombia)	1501-02=	2?	
? 1826	....	?	**MISTI, EL** (Peru)	1504-01=	2	
? 1826	....	?	**UBINAS** (Peru)	1504-02=		
1826	0301	?	**MAIPO** (Chile-C)	1507-021		
1826	05	32m>	**TOLIMA** (Colombia)	1501-03=	2	
1826	06	>3yr	**MAKUSHIN** (Aleutian Is)	1101-31-	3	
1826	1003	50a	**ASO** (Kyushu-Japan)	0802-11=	2	
1826	1011	<1	**TANGKUBANPARAHU** (Java)	0603-09=	2	
1826	1011	4a	**DIENG VOLC COMPLEX** (Java)	0603-20=	2	
1826	1011	14a	**KELUT** (Java)	0603-28=	4?	-/8
1826	1011	96m?	**FISHER** (Aleutian Is)	1101-35-	3	
1826	11	?	**ATITLAN** (Guatemala)	1402-06=	2	
1826	1201	?	**WHITE ISLAND** (New Zealand)	0401-04=	2	
1827	*Cont*	....	*VESUVIUS (Italy)*	0101-02=	*2*	
1827	*Cont*	....	*STROMBOLI (Italy)*	0101-04=	*1?*	
1827	*Cont*	....	*YASUR (Vanuatu-SW Pacific)*	0507-10=	*2*	
1827	*Cont*	....	*BANDA API (Banda Sea)*	0605-09=	*1*	
1827	*Cont*	....	*OKMOK (Aleutian Is)*	1101-29-		
1827	*Cont*	....	*MAKUSHIN (Aleutian Is)*	1101-31-	*2?*	
1827	*Cont*	....	*FISHER (Aleutian Is)*	1101-35-	*2?*	
1827	*Cont*	....	*KILAUEA (Hawaiian Is)*	1302-01-	*0*	
1827	*Cont*	....	*SANGAY (Ecuador)*	1502-09=	*2*	
1827	*Cont*	....	*SAN JOSE (Chile-C)*	1507-02=	*2*	
1827	....	?	**HIBOK-HIBOK** (Mindanao-Philippines)	0701-08=	2	
1827	....	?	**OSHIMA** (Izu Is-Japan)	0804-01=		
? 1827	....	?	**KANAGA** (Aleutian Is)	1101-11-		
? 1827	....	?	**KASATOCHI** (Aleutian Is)	1101-13-		
? 1827	....	?	**SEGUAM** (Aleutian Is)	1101-18-		
1827	....	>3yr	**WESTDAHL [POGROMNI ?]** (Aleutian	1101-34-	2	
1827	....	731y	**SHISHALDIN** (Aleutian Is)	1101-36-	2	
1827	....	>3yr	**POPOCATEPETL** (Mexico)	1401-09=	1?	
1827b	....	?	**DECEPTION ISLAND** (Antarctica)	1900-03=		
1827	0327	?	**ATITLAN** (Guatemala)	1402-06=	2	
1827	05	?	**ASO** (Kyushu-Japan)	0802-11=	2	
1827	0513	?	**GUNTUR** (Java)	0603-13=	2	
1827	0627	246a	**MAYON** (Luzon-Philippines)	0703-03=	2	
1827	0627	2a	**AVACHINSKY** (Kamchatka)	1000-10=	2	
1827	0901	141m?	**ATITLAN** (Guatemala)	1402-06=	3	
1827	1010	4a	**ETNA** (Italy)	0101-06=	1?	
1827	1112	65m	**ASO** (Kyushu-Japan)	0802-11=	2	
1827	1118	?	**PURACE** (Colombia)	1501-06=	2	
1828	*Cont*	....	*VESUVIUS (Italy)*	0101-02=	*2*	
1828	*Cont*	....	*STROMBOLI (Italy)*	0101-04=	*1?*	
1828	*Cont*	....	*YASUR (Vanuatu-SW Pacific)*	0507-10=	*2*	
1828	*Cont*	....	*BANDA API (Banda Sea)*	0605-09=	*1*	
1828	*Cont*	....	*MAYON (Luzon-Philippines)*	0703-03=	*2*	
1828	*Cont*	....	*OKMOK (Aleutian Is)*	1101-29-		
1828	*Cont*	....	*MAKUSHIN (Aleutian Is)*	1101-31-	*2?*	
1828	*Cont*	....	*WESTDAHL [POGROMNI ?] (Aleutian*	1101-34-	*2*	
1828	*Cont*	....	*SHISHALDIN (Aleutian Is)*	1101-36-	*2*	
1828	*Cont*	....	*KILAUEA (Hawaiian Is)*	1302-01-	*0*	
1828	*Cont*	....	*POPOCATEPETL (Mexico)*	1401-09=	*1?*	
1828	*Cont*	....	*ATITLAN (Guatemala)*	1402-06=	*3*	
1828	*Cont*	....	*SANGAY (Ecuador)*	1502-09=	*2*	
1828	*Cont*	....	*SAN JOSE (Chile-C)*	1507-02=	*2*	
? 1828	....	?	**ADWA** (Ethiopia)	0201-17=	2	
1828	....	730y	**LITTLE SITKIN** (Aleutian Is)	1101-05-		
? 1828	....	365y?	**GARELOI** (Aleutian Is)	1101-07-	2?	
? 1828	....	?	**GREAT SITKIN** (Aleutian Is)	1101-12-		
? 1828	....	?	**KASATOCHI** (Aleutian Is)	1101-13-		
1828	....	?	**CARLISLE** (Aleutian Is)	1101-23-		
? 1828	....	?	**AKUTAN** (Aleutian Is)	1101-32-		
1828	....	?	**POAS** (Costa Rica)	1405-04=	1	
1828	....	?	**ANTUCO** (Chile-C)	1507-08=	1	
? 1828	01	?	**MATTHEW ISLAND** (SW Pacific)	0508-01=		
1828	0417	?	**AVACHINSKY** (Kamchatka)	1000-10=	2	
1828	05	?	**KARTHALA** (Indian O.-W)	0303-01=	2?	
1828	0514	55a	**GUNTUR** (Java)	0603-13=	2	
1828	06 <	?	**ASO** (Kyushu-Japan)	0802-11=	2	
1828	06	?	**GORELY** (Kamchatka)	1000-07=	3	-/7
1828	06	?	**RUIZ** (Colombia)	1501-02=	2	
1828	*0802*	*>3yr*	*ETNA (Italy)*	0101-06=	1?	
1828	*1024*	*>3yr*	*GALERAS (Colombia)*	1501-08=	2	
1828	1218	1a	**MERAPI** (Java)	0603-25=	2	
1829	*Cont*	....	*VESUVIUS (Italy)*	0101-02=	*2*	
1829	*Cont*	....	*STROMBOLI (Italy)*	0101-04=	*1?*	
1829	*Cont*	....	*ETNA (Italy)*	0101-06=	*1?*	
1829	*Cont*	....	*YASUR (Vanuatu-SW Pacific)*	0507-10=	*2*	
1829	*Cont*	....	*BANDA API (Banda Sea)*	0605-09=	*1*	
1829	*Cont*	....	*LITTLE SITKIN (Aleutian Is)*	1101-05-		
? *1829*	*Cont*	....	*GARELOI (Aleutian Is)*	1101-07-	*2?*	
1829	*Cont*	....	*OKMOK (Aleutian Is)*	1101-29-		
1829	*Cont*	....	*MAKUSHIN (Aleutian Is)*	1101-31-	*2?*	
1829	*Cont*	....	*WESTDAHL [POGROMNI ?] (Aleutian*	1101-34-	*2*	
1829	*Cont*	....	*SHISHALDIN (Aleutian Is)*	1101-36-	*2*	
1829	*Cont*	....	*KILAUEA (Hawaiian Is)*	1302-01-	*0*	
1829	*Cont*	....	*POPOCATEPETL (Mexico)*	1401-09=	*1?*	
1829	*Cont*	....	*GALERAS (Colombia)*	1501-08=	*2*	
1829	*Cont*	....	*SANGAY (Ecuador)*	1502-09=	*2*	
1829	*Cont*	....	*SAN JOSE (Chile-C)*	1507-02=	*2*	
1829?	....	?	**SORIKMARAPI** (Sumatra)	0601-12=	2	
1829	....	?	**GUNTUR** (Java)	0603-13=	2	
1829	....	?	**TANAGA** (Aleutian Is)	1101-08-		
? 1829	....	?	**KANAGA** (Aleutian Is)	1101-11-		
? 1829	....	?	**GREAT SITKIN** (Aleutian Is)	1101-12-		
? 1829	....	365y	**ATKA [KOROVIN]** (Aleutian Is)	1101-16-		

START YEAR	START M-Dy	Duration	VOLCANO NAME (Subregion)	NUMBER	VEI	Vol L/T
1829	....	?	**FUEGO** (Guatemala)	1402-09=	2	
@ 1829	....	?	**TUPUNGATITO** (Chile-C)	1507-01=	2	
1829	01	30p	**LAMONGAN** (Java)	0603-32=	2	
1829	02	?	**SEMERU** (Java)	0603-30=	2	
1829	03	?	**LOKON-EMPUNG** (Sulawesi-Indonesia)	0606-10=	2	
1829	0401	3a?	**TANGKUBANPARAHU** (Java)	0603-09=	2	
1829	06	?	**ASO** (Kyushu-Japan)	0802-11=	2	
1829	0618	?	**RUIZ** (Colombia)	1501-02=	2	
1829	0909	?	**KLIUCHEVSKOI** (Kamchatka)	1000-26=	4?	7/8
1829	1105	6a	**TENGGER CALDERA [BROMO]**	0603-31=	2	
1829	1201	15a	**OKINAWA-TORI-SHIMA** (Ryukyu Is)	0802-02=	1?	
1830	*Cont*	....	*VESUVIUS (Italy)*	0101-02=	*2*	
1830	*Cont*	....	*STROMBOLI (Italy)*	0101-04=	*1?*	
1830	*Cont*	....	*ETNA (Italy)*	0101-06=	*1?*	
1830	*Cont*	....	*YASUR (Vanuatu-SW Pacific)*	0507-10=	*2*	
1830	*Cont*	....	*BANDA API (Banda Sea)*	0605-09=	*1*	
1830	*Cont*	....	*LITTLE SITKIN (Aleutian Is)*	1101-05-		
? *1830*	*Cont*	....	*ATKA [KOROVIN] (Aleutian Is)*	1101-16-		
1830	*Cont*	....	*OKMOK (Aleutian Is)*	1101-29-		
1830	*Cont*	....	*MAKUSHIN (Aleutian Is)*	1101-31-	*2?*	
1830	*Cont*	....	*WESTDAHL [POGROMNI ?] (Aleutian*	1101-34-	*2*	
1830	*Cont*	....	*KILAUEA (Hawaiian Is)*	1302-01-	*0*	
1830	*Cont*	....	*POPOCATEPETL (Mexico)*	1401-09=	*1?*	
1830	*Cont*	....	*GALERAS (Colombia)*	1501-08=	*2*	
1830	*Cont*	....	*SANGAY (Ecuador)*	1502-09=	*2*	
1830	*Cont*	....	*SAN JOSE (Chile-C)*	1507-02=	*2*	
1830	....	?	**KARTHALA** (Indian O.-W)	0303-01=	2?	
1830	....	?	**MANAM** (New Guinea-NE of)	0501-02=	2	
? 1830	....	?	**KARKAR** (New Guinea-NE of)	0501-03=		
1830	....	?	**EBULOBO** (Lesser Sunda Is)	0604-10=	2	
1830	....	?	**ZAO** (Honshu-Japan)	0803-19=	2	
1830	....	?	**KARYMSKY** (Kamchatka)	1000-13=	2	
? 1830	....	?	**SEMISOPOCHNOI** (Aleutian Is)	1101-06-		
1830	....	?	**YUNASKA** (Aleutian Is)	1101-21-	2	
1830	....	?	**VSEVIDOF** (Aleutian Is)	1101-27-		
? 1830	....	>3yr	**VENIAMINOF** (Alaska Peninsula)	1102-07-	2	
? 1830	....	?	**PACAYA** (Guatemala)	1402-11=		
1830	....	?	**GUAGUA PICHINCHA** (Ecuador)	1502-02=	2	
1830	....	?	**UBINAS** (Peru)	1504-02=	2	
1830	02	30p	**LAMONGAN** (Java)	0603-32=	2	
1830	0216	28m	**ASO** (Kyushu-Japan)	0802-11=	2	
1830	0303	?	**TENGGER CALDERA [BROMO]**	0603-31=	2	
1830	0313?	365p?	**REYKJANESHRYGGUR** (Iceland-SW)	1701-01=	3	
1830	08	?	**FISHER** (Aleutian Is)	1101-35-	2	
? 1830	08	?	**MISTI, EL** (Peru)	1504-01=	2	
1830	0811	735m	**ASO** (Kyushu-Japan)	0802-11=	2	
? 1830	09	?	**ZAVODOVSKI** (Antarctica)	1900-13=	1	
? 1830	0922	?	**HODSON** (Antarctica)	1900-11=		
1830	10	?	**FOURNAISE, PITON DE LA** (Indian O.)	0303-02=	0	
1830	11	31p	**SHISHALDIN** (Aleutian Is)	1101-36-	3	
1830	11	?	**ISANOTSKI** (Aleutian Is)	1101-37-	2?	
1830	1215	1a	**SEMERU** (Java)	0603-30=	2	
1830	1215	1a	**TENGGER CALDERA [BROMO]**	0603-31=	2	
1831	*Cont*	....	*STROMBOLI (Italy)*	0101-04=	*1?*	
1831	*Cont*	....	*YASUR (Vanuatu-SW Pacific)*	0507-10=	*2*	
1831	*Cont*	....	*BANDA API (Banda Sea)*	0605-09=	*1*	
1831	*Cont*	....	*ASO (Kyushu-Japan)*	0802-11=	*2*	
1831	*Cont*	....	*MAKUSHIN (Aleutian Is)*	1101-31-	*2?*	
? *1831*	*Cont*	....	*VENIAMINOF (Alaska Peninsula)*	1102-07-	*2*	
1831	*Cont*	....	*KILAUEA (Hawaiian Is)*	1302-01-	*0*	
1831	*Cont*	....	*POPOCATEPETL (Mexico)*	1401-09=	*1?*	
1831	*Cont*	....	*SANGAY (Ecuador)*	1502-09=	*2*	
1831	*Cont*	....	*SAN JOSE (Chile-C)*	1507-02=	*2*	
1831	*Cont*	....	*REYKJANESHRYGGUR (Iceland-SW)*	1701-01=	*2*	
? 1831	....	?	**VULCANO** (Italy)	0101-05=	1?	
1831	....	?	**BABUYAN CLARO** (Luzon Is-N of)	0704-03=	4?	-/8
1831	....	?	**RUIZ** (Colombia)	1501-02=	2	
1831	....	?	**GUAGUA PICHINCHA** (Ecuador)	1502-02=	3	
@ 1831	03	51m	**ISANOTSKI** (Aleutian Is)	1101-37-		
1831	0304	....	**ETNA** (Italy)	0101-06=	2	
1831	05	....	**GALERAS** (Colombia)	1501-08=	3	
1831	0527	31a	**GAMALAMA** (Halmahera-Indonesia)	0608-06=	2	
1831	*0628>*	*48m<*	*CAMPI FLEGREI MAR SICILIA (Italy)*	0101-07=	2	-/8
1831	0710	....	**CAMPI FLEGREI MAR SICILIA** (Italy)	0101-07=	3	-/8
1831	08	?	**ST. HELENS** (US-Washington)	1201-05-	3	
? 1831	08	?	**MISTI, EL** (Peru)	1504-01=		
1831	*0814*	....	*VESUVIUS (Italy)*	0101-02=	1	
1831	1122	?	**ZAO** (Honshu-Japan)	0803-19=	2	
1832	*Cont*	....	*VESUVIUS (Italy)*	0101-02=	*2*	
1832	*Cont*	....	*STROMBOLI (Italy)*	0101-04=	*1?*	
1832	*Cont*	....	*YASUR (Vanuatu-SW Pacific)*	0507-10=	*2*	
1832	*Cont*	....	*ASO (Kyushu-Japan)*	0802-11=	*2*	
1832	*Cont*	....	*MAKUSHIN (Aleutian Is)*	1101-31-	*2?*	
? *1832*	*Cont*	....	*VENIAMINOF (Alaska Peninsula)*	1102-07-	*2*	
1832	*Cont*	....	*POPOCATEPETL (Mexico)*	1401-09=	*1?*	
1832	*Cont*	....	*GALERAS (Colombia)*	1501-08=	*2*	
1832	*Cont*	....	*SANGAY (Ecuador)*	1502-09=	*2*	
1832	*Cont*	....	*SAN JOSE (Chile-C)*	1507-02=	*2*	
1832	0114	?	**KILAUEA** (Hawaiian Is)	1302-01-	0	
1832	0116	?	**GUNTUR** (Java)	0603-13=	2	
1832	02	?	**GORELY** (Kamchatka)	1000-07=	3	-/7
1832	03	?	**FOURNAISE, PITON DE LA** (Indian O.)	0303-02=	0	
1832	0418	?	**SEMERU** (Java)	0603-30=	2	
1832	0420	?	**KIRISHIMA** (Kyushu-Japan)	0802-09=	2	
1832	0620	25g	**MAUNA LOA** (Hawaiian Is)	1302-02=	0	7/-
1832	0808	5a	**GUNTUR** (Java)	0603-13=	2	
1832	0829	<1	**GEDE** (Java)	0603-06=	3	
1832	1031	22a	**ETNA** (Italy)	0101-06=	2	7/6
1832	1224	?	**VILLARRICA** (Chile-C)	1507-12=	2	
1832	1225	553w	**MERAPI** (Java)	0603-25=	3	7/7
1833	*Cont*	....	*VESUVIUS (Italy)*	0101-02=	*2*	
1833	*Cont*	....	*YASUR (Vanuatu-SW Pacific)*	0507-10=	*2*	
1833	*Cont*	....	*MERAPI (Java)*	0603-25=	*2*	*7/7*
1833	*Cont*	....	*MAKUSHIN (Aleutian Is)*	1101-31-	*2?*	
? *1833*	*Cont*	....	*VENIAMINOF (Alaska Peninsula)*	1102-07-	*2*	
1833	*Cont*	....	*KILAUEA (Hawaiian Is)*	1302-01-	*0*	
1833	*Cont*	....	*POPOCATEPETL (Mexico)*	1401-09=	*1?*	
1833	*Cont*	....	*GALERAS (Colombia)*	1501-08=	*2*	
1833	*Cont*	....	*SANGAY (Ecuador)*	1502-09=	*2*	
1833	*Cont*	....	*SAN JOSE (Chile-C)*	1507-02=	*2*	
1833	....	?	**STROMBOLI** (Italy)	0101-04=	2	
1833	....	?	**KARTHALA** (Indian O.-W)	0303-01=		
1833	....	365y	**MARAPI** (Sumatra)	0601-14=	2?	
1833?	....	?	**SOPUTAN** (Sulawesi-Indonesia)	0606-03=	2	
1833	....	?	**ZAO** (Honshu-Japan)	0803-19=	2	
1833	....	?	**ATITLAN** (Guatemala)	1402-06=	2	
? 1833	....	?	**RUIZ** (Colombia)	1501-02=	2?	
1833	03	?	**ETNA** (Italy)	0101-06=	2	
1833	0411	?	**IWAKI** (Honshu-Japan)	0803-27=	2	
1833	0615	?	**GAMALAMA** (Halmahera-Indonesia)	0608-06=	2	
1833	0901	?	**GUNTUR** (Java)	0603-13=	2	
1833	10	?	**TALANG** (Sumatra)	0601-16=	2	
1833	1124	1a	**KABA** (Sumatra)	0601-22=	2	
1833	1231y	?	**TEYR, DJEBEL** (Red Sea)	0201-01=	2	
1834	*Cont*	....	*STROMBOLI (Italy)*	0101-04=	*1?*	
1834	*Cont*	....	*YASUR (Vanuatu-SW Pacific)*	0507-10=	*2*	
1834	*Cont*	....	*MARAPI (Sumatra)*	0601-14=	*2?*	
1834	*Cont*	....	*MERAPI (Java)*	0603-25=	*2*	*7/7*
1834	*Cont*	....	*MAKUSHIN (Aleutian Is)*	1101-31-	*2?*	
? *1834*	*Cont*	....	*VENIAMINOF (Alaska Peninsula)*	1102-07-	*2*	
1834	*Cont*	....	*KILAUEA (Hawaiian Is)*	1302-01-	*0*	
1834	*Cont*	....	*POPOCATEPETL (Mexico)*	1401-09=	*1?*	
1834	*Cont*	....	*SANGAY (Ecuador)*	1502-09=	*2*	
1834	*Cont*	....	*SAN JOSE (Chile-C)*	1507-02=	*2*	
1834	....	?	**RAGANG** (Mindanao-Philippines)	0701-06=	2	
1834	....	*317w*	*MAYON (Luzon-Philippines)*	0703-03=	2	
1834	....	?	**POAS** (Costa Rica)	1405-04=	2	
1834	*0301*	....	*GALERAS (Colombia)*	1501-08=	3	
1834	0709	11k	**CHOKAI** (Honshu-Japan)	0803-22=	2?	
1834	0822	....	**VESUVIUS** (Italy)	0101-02=	3	
1834	11	?	**KABA** (Sumatra)	0601-22=	2	
1834	11	?	**MINCHINMAVIDA** (Chile-S)	1508-04=		
1834	11	?	**CORCOVADO** (Chile-S)	1508-05=	2	
1834	1129	86d	**OSORNO** (Chile-S)	1508-01=	3?	
1834	12	31p	**GUNTUR** (Java)	0603-13=	2	
1835	*Cont*	....	*STROMBOLI (Italy)*	0101-04=	*1?*	
1835	*Cont*	....	*YASUR (Vanuatu-SW Pacific)*	0507-10=	*2*	
1835	*Cont*	....	*GUNTUR (Java)*	0603-13=	*2*	
1835	*Cont*	....	*MERAPI (Java)*	0603-25=	*2*	*7/7*
1835	*Cont*	....	*MAKUSHIN (Aleutian Is)*	1101-31-	*2?*	
? *1835*	*Cont*	....	*VENIAMINOF (Alaska Peninsula)*	1102-07-	*2*	
1835	*Cont*	....	*KILAUEA (Hawaiian Is)*	1302-01-	*0*	
1835	*Cont*	....	*SANGAY (Ecuador)*	1502-09=	*2*	
1835	*Cont*	....	*SAN JOSE (Chile-C)*	1507-02=	*2*	
1835	*Cont*	....	*OSORNO (Chile-S)*	1508-01=	*0*	
1835e	....	4383*	**SAVO** (Solomon Is-SW Pac)	0505-07=	3?	
1835	....	?	**HUNTER ISLAND** (SW Pacific)	0508-02=		
1835	....	?	**KELUT** (Java)	0603-28=	2	
1835	....	?	**TENGGER CALDERA [BROMO]**	0603-31=	2	
? 1835	....	?	**TUPUNGATITO** (Chile-C)	1507-01=	2	
1835	....	?	**PLANCHON-PETEROA** (Chile-C)	1507-04=	2	
1835	*0101*	*>3yr*	*VESUVIUS (Italy)*	0101-02=	1	7/-
1835	0104	?	**GAMALAMA** (Halmahera-Indonesia)	0608-06=	2	
1835	0120	5a?	**COSIGUINA** (Nicaragua)	1404-01=	**5**	**-/9**
1835	0123	?	**PURACE** (Colombia)	1501-06=	2	
1835	0220	1a	**ROBINSON CRUSOE** (Chile-Is)	1506-02=	1?	
1835	0220	23e	**MINCHINMAVIDA** (Chile-S)	1508-04=	2	
1835	0220	?	**YANTELES, CERRO** (Chile-S)	1508-051	2	
1835	03 ?	?	**ST. HELENS** (US-Washington)	1201-05-	2	
1835	0423	3a	**BANUA WUHU** (Sangihe Is-Indonesia)	0607-03=	2	6/-
1835	05	....	**MAYON** (Luzon-Philippines)	0703-03=	3	
1835	0501	?	**ASO** (Kyushu-Japan)	0802-11=	2	
1835	09	2a	**SLAMET** (Java)	0603-18=	2	
? 1835	10	?	**BANDA API** (Banda Sea)	0605-09=		
1835	1111	?	**MIYAKE-JIMA** (Izu Is-Japan)	0804-04=	2	
1835	1111	?	**CORCOVADO** (Chile-S)	1508-05=	2	
1836	*Cont*	....	*VESUVIUS (Italy)*	0101-02=	*1*	*7/-*
1836	*Cont*	....	*STROMBOLI (Italy)*	0101-04=	*1?*	
1836	*Cont*	....	*SAVO (Solomon Is-SW Pac)*	0505-07=	*2?*	
1836	*Cont*	....	*YASUR (Vanuatu-SW Pacific)*	0507-10=	*2*	
1836	*Cont*	....	*MAKUSHIN (Aleutian Is)*	1101-31-	*2?*	
? *1836*	*Cont*	....	*VENIAMINOF (Alaska Peninsula)*	1102-07-	*2*	
1836	*Cont*	....	*KILAUEA (Hawaiian Is)*	1302-01-	*0*	
1836	*Cont*	....	*SANGAY (Ecuador)*	1502-09=	*2*	
1836	*Cont*	....	*SAN JOSE (Chile-C)*	1507-02=	*2*	
1836b	....	?	**WHITE ISLAND** (New Zealand)	0401-04=	2	
1836	....	?	**IZALCO** (El Salvador)	1403-03=	2	
1836	....	?	**GALERAS** (Colombia)	1501-08=	2	
1836?	0422	2a	**RUANG** (Sangihe Is-Indonesia)	0607-01=	2	
1836	0803	2a	**SEMERU** (Java)	0603-30=	2	
1836	1011	?	**GUNTUR** (Java)	0603-13=	2	
1836	11 <	?	**UNNAMED** (Atlantic-C)	1805-03=	0	
1837	*Cont*	....	*VESUVIUS (Italy)*	0101-02=	*1*	*7/-*
1837	*Cont*	....	*STROMBOLI (Italy)*	0101-04=	*1?*	
1837	*Cont*	....	*SAVO (Solomon Is-SW Pac)*	0505-07=	*2?*	

START YEAR	M-Dy	Duration	VOLCANO NAME (Subregion)	NUMBER	VEI	Vol L/T
1837	Cont	....	YASUR (Vanuatu-SW Pacific)	0507-10=	2	
1837	Cont	....	MAKUSHIN (Aleutian Is)	1101-31-	2?	
? 1837	Cont	....	VENIAMINOF (Alaska Peninsula)	1102-07-	2	
1837	Cont	....	KILAUEA (Hawaiian Is)	1302-01-	0	
1837	Cont	....	SANGAY (Ecuador)	1502-09=	2	
1837	Cont	....	SAN JOSE (Chile-C)	1507-02=	2	
1837	....	365y	OSHIMA (Izu Is-Japan)	0804-01=	3	
? 1837	....	?	AVACHINSKY (Kamchatka)	1000-10=		
1837	02	?	PLANCHON-PETEROA (Chile-C)	1507-04=	2	
1837	06	?	ATITLAN (Guatemala)	1402-06=	2	
1837	0810	309m	MERAPI (Java)	0603-25=	3	7/7
1837	0925e	?	TELONG, BUR NI (Sumatra)	0601-05=	2	
1837	1008	?	ASO (Kyushu-Japan)	0802-11=	2	
1837	1107	14a	VILLARRICA (Chile-C)	1507-12=	2	
1837	1107	?	OSORNO (Chile-S)	1508-01=	2	
1837	1203	71a	SOUFRIERE GUADELOUPE (W Indies)	1600-06=	2	
1838	Cont	....	VESUVIUS (Italy)	0101-02=	1	7/-
1838	Cont	....	STROMBOLI (Italy)	0101-04=	1?	
1838	Cont	....	SAVO (Solomon Is-SW Pac)	0505-07=	2?	
1838	Cont	....	YASUR (Vanuatu-SW Pacific)	0507-10=	2	
1838	Cont	....	MERAPI (Java)	0603-25=	2	7/7
1838	Cont	....	OSHIMA (Izu Is-Japan)	0804-01=	2	
1838	Cont	....	MAKUSHIN (Aleutian Is)	1101-31-	2?	
1838	Cont	....	KILAUEA (Hawaiian Is)	1302-01-	0	
1838	Cont	....	SANGAY (Ecuador)	1502-09=	2	
1838	Cont	....	SAN JOSE (Chile-C)	1507-02=	2	
1838	Cont	....	SOUFRIERE GUADELOUPE (W Ind)	1600-06=	2	
1838	....	?	KERINCI (Sumatra)	0601-17=	2	
1838	....	?	RAUNG (Java)	0603-34=	2	
? 1838	....	?	CARLISLE (Aleutian Is)	1101-23-		
? 1838	....	?	AKUTAN (Aleutian Is)	1101-32-		
1838	....	?	SHISHALDIN (Aleutian Is)	1101-36-	2	
? 1838	....	?	PAVLOF (Alaska Peninsula)	1102-03-		
? 1838	....	?	SAN MARTIN, VOLCAN DE (Mexico)	1401-11=		
1838	....	730y	IZALCO (El Salvador)	1403-03=	2	
? 1838	....	?	POAS (Costa Rica)	1405-04=	2?	
1838	0226	79m	GAMALAMA (Halmahera-Indonesia)	0608-06=	2	
1838	0304	?	ASO (Kyushu-Japan)	0802-11=	2	
1838	06	?	GRIMSVOTN (Iceland-NE)	1703-01=	2	
1838	07	94m	SEMERU (Java)	0603-30=	2	
1838	0704	2a	LAMONGAN (Java)	0603-32=	2	
1838	0708	221m	ETNA (Italy)	0101-06=	2	
1838	0804	254m	VENIAMINOF (Alaska Peninsula)	1102-07-	3	
1838	1018	?	LAMONGAN (Java)	0603-32=	2	
1838	1231y	?	CAMEROON, MT. (Africa-W)	0204-01=	2	
1839	Cont	....	STROMBOLI (Italy)	0101-04=	1?	
1839	Cont	....	ETNA (Italy)	0101-06=	2	
1839	Cont	....	SAVO (Solomon Is-SW Pac)	0505-07=	2?	
1839	Cont	....	YASUR (Vanuatu-SW Pacific)	0507-10=	2	
1839	Cont	....	VENIAMINOF (Alaska Peninsula)	1102-07-	2	
1839	Cont	....	KILAUEA (Hawaiian Is)	1302-01-	0	
1839	Cont	....	IZALCO (El Salvador)	1403-03=	2	
1839	Cont	....	SANGAY (Ecuador)	1502-09=	2	
1839?	....	?	DEMPO (Sumatra)	0601-23=	2	
1839	....	?	MAYON (Luzon-Philippines)	0703-03=	2	
1839	....	?	ANTUCO (Chile-C)	1507-08=	2	
? 1839<	....	?	DECEPTION ISLAND (Antarctica)	1900-03=		
1839	0101	....	VESUVIUS (Italy)	0101-02=	3	7/-
? 1839	0112	1a	SEULAWAH AGAM (Sumatra)	0601-02=	2	
1839	0112	1a	TELONG, BUR NI (Sumatra)	0601-05=	2	
1839	0129	56a	GAMALAMA (Halmahera-Indonesia)	0608-06=	1	
1839	02	30p	TONGARIRO [NGAURUHOE] (New Z)	0401-08=	1?	
1839	0209	?	BUCKLE ISLAND (Antarctica)	1900-01=	2	
? 1839	0212	1a?	UNNAMED (Chile-Is)	1506-04=		
1839	0325	....	GAMALAMA (Halmahera-Indonesia)	0608-06=	2	
1839	0610	?	TATE-YAMA (Honshu-Japan)	0803-08=	2	
1840	Cont	....	STROMBOLI (Italy)	0101-04=	1?	
1840	Cont	....	SAVO (Solomon Is-SW Pac)	0505-07=	2?	
1840	Cont	....	YASUR (Vanuatu-SW Pacific)	0507-10=	2	
1840	Cont	....	IZALCO (El Salvador)	1403-03=	2	
1840	Cont	....	SANGAY (Ecuador)	1502-09=	2	
1840?	....	?	TINAKULA (Santa Cruz Is-SW Pac)	0506-01=	3?	
1840	....	?	RUANG (Sangihe Is-Indonesia)	0607-01=	2	
1840<	....	?	KUCHINOERABU-JIMA (Ryukyu Is)	0802-05=	2?	
1840	....	?	KLIUCHEVSKOI (Kamchatka)	1000-26=	2	
1840	....	?	PURACE (Colombia)	1501-06=	2?	
1840	01	?	MERAPI (Java)	0603-25=	2	
1840	0120	76a	RAGANG (Mindanao-Philippines)	0701-06=	2	
1840	0202	240a	GAMALAMA (Halmahera-Indonesia)	0608-06=	3	
1840	0520	4a	GUNTUR (Java)	0603-13=	2	
1840	0530	26a	KILAUEA (Hawaiian Is)	1302-01-	0	8/-
1840	1112	29a	GEDE (Java)	0603-06=	2	
1840	1201	....	GEDE (Java)	0603-06=	3	
1841	Cont	....	STROMBOLI (Italy)	0101-04=	1?	
1841	Cont	....	SAVO (Solomon Is-SW Pac)	0505-07=	2?	
1841	Cont	....	YASUR (Vanuatu-SW Pacific)	0507-10=	2	
1841	Cont	....	KILAUEA (Hawaiian Is)	1302-01-	0	
1841	Cont	....	SANGAY (Ecuador)	1502-09=	2	
1841	....	?	TONGARIRO [NGAURUHOE] (New Z)	0401-08=	2	
1841	0128?	17m?	EREBUS (Antarctica)	1900-02=	1	
1841	0315	?	HUNTER ISLAND (SW Pacific)	0508-02=		
? 1841	0330	235a	GAMALAMA (Halmahera-Indonesia)	0608-06=	1	
1841	0523	100a	KUCHINOERABU-JIMA (Ryukyu Is)	0802-05=	2	
1841	0716	396m	LAMONGAN (Java)	0603-32=	2	
1841	0801	....	KUCHINOERABU-JIMA (Ryukyu Is)	0802-05=	2	
1841	0920	>3yr	VESUVIUS (Italy)	0101-02=	2	
1841	1114	<1	GUNTUR (Java)	0603-13=	2	
1842	Cont	....	VESUVIUS (Italy)	0101-02=	2	
1842	Cont	....	STROMBOLI (Italy)	0101-04=	1?	
1842	Cont	....	SAVO (Solomon Is-SW Pac)	0505-07=	2?	
1842	Cont	....	YASUR (Vanuatu-SW Pacific)	0507-10=	2	
1842	Cont	....	LAMONGAN (Java)	0603-32=	2	
1842	Cont	....	KILAUEA (Hawaiian Is)	1302-01-	0	
1842	....	?	KERINCI (Sumatra)	0601-17=	2	
1842	....	?	TANGKUBANPARAHU (Java)	0603-09=		
1842	....	?	TAAL (Luzon-Philippines)	0703-07=	2	
1842	....	?	SHISHALDIN (Aleutian Is)	1101-36-	2	
1842	....	?	IZALCO (El Salvador)	1403-03=	2	
1842	....	?	IRAZU (Costa Rica)	1405-06=	2	
1842	....	....	SANGAY (Ecuador)	1502-09=	3	
? 1842	....	?	PLANCHON-PETEROA (Chile-C)	1507-04=		
1842	01	59p	SEMERU (Java)	0603-30=	2	
1842	0124	142m	TENGGER CALDERA [BROMO]	0603-31=	2	
1842	02	?	DECEPTION ISLAND (Antarctica)	1900-03=	2	
1842	0315	?	BAGANA (Bougainville-SW Pac)	0505-02=	1	
1842	04	?	FOURNAISE, PITON DE LA (Indian O.)	0303-02=	0	
1842	06	?	GORIASCHAIA SOPKA (Kurile Is)	0900-17B	3?	
1842	1006	87	GAMALAMA (Halmahera-Indonesia)	0608-06=	1	
1842	1118	41a?	ETNA (Italy)	0101-06=	2	
1842	1122	>3yr	ST. HELENS (US-Washington)	1201-05-	3	-/7
1843	Cont	....	VESUVIUS (Italy)	0101-02=	2	
1843	Cont	....	STROMBOLI (Italy)	0101-04=	1?	
1843	Cont	....	SAVO (Solomon Is-SW Pac)	0505-07=	2?	
1843	Cont	....	YASUR (Vanuatu-SW Pacific)	0507-10=	2	
1843	Cont	....	ST. HELENS (US-Washington)	1201-05-	2	-/7
1843	Cont	....	KILAUEA (Hawaiian Is)	1302-01-	0	
1843	....	?	FOURNAISE, PITON DE LA (Indian O.)	0303-02=	0	
1843	....	?	AGUNG (Lesser Sunda Is)	0604-02=	2	
1843	....	>3yr	TONGKOKO (Sulawesi-Indonesia)	0606-13=	2	
1843	....	?	CHIRIP (Kurile Is)	0900-09=	2?	
? 1843	....	?	ILIAMNA (Alaska-SW)	1103-02-		
1843	....	?	BAKER (US-Washington)	1201-01=	2	
? 1843	....	?	RAINIER (US-Washington)	1201-03-	2	
1843<	....	?	REVENTADOR (Ecuador)	1502-01=		
1843	....	....	SANGAY (Ecuador)	1502-09=	3	
1843	01	?	TENGGER CALDERA [BROMO]	0603-31=	2	
1843	0104	<1	GUNTUR (Java)	0603-13=	3	-/6
1843	0109	90a?	MAUNA LOA (Hawaiian Is)	1302-02=	0	8/-
? 1843	0208	?	LIAMUIGA (W Indies)	1600-03=		
1843	0410	47a	GAMALAMA (Halmahera-Indonesia)	0608-06=	2	
1843	07	>3yr	KETOI (Kurile Is)	0900-20=	2	
1843	07	?	ATITLAN (Guatemala)	1402-06=	2	
1843	0728	?	GEDE (Java)	0603-06=	2	
1843	08	411p	LAMONGAN (Java)	0603-32=	2	
1843	1021	?	TALANG (Sumatra)	0601-16=	2	
1843	1117	11a	ETNA (Italy)	0101-06=	2	7/6
1843	1126	<1	GUNTUR (Java)	0603-13=	2?	
1843	1207	?	REVENTADOR (Ecuador)	1502-01=	3	
1844	Cont	....	VESUVIUS (Italy)	0101-02=	2	
1844	Cont	....	STROMBOLI (Italy)	0101-04=	1?	
1844	Cont	....	SAVO (Solomon Is-SW Pac)	0505-07=	2?	
1844	Cont	....	YASUR (Vanuatu-SW Pacific)	0507-10=	2	
1844	Cont	....	LAMONGAN (Java)	0603-32=	2	
1844	Cont	....	TONGKOKO (Sulawesi-Indonesia)	0606-13=	2	
1844	Cont	....	KETOI (Kurile Is)	0900-20=	2	
1844	Cont	....	ST. HELENS (US-Washington)	1201-05-	2	-/7
1844	Cont	....	KILAUEA (Hawaiian Is)	1302-01-	0	
1844	Cont	....	SANGAY (Ecuador)	1502-09=	2	
? 1844	....	?	AZUMA (Honshu-Japan)	0803-18=	1?	
? 1844	....	?	ATKA [KOROVIN] (Aleutian Is)	1101-16-		
? 1844a	....	?	MAKUSHIN (Aleutian Is)	1101-31-		
1844	....	?	REVENTADOR (Ecuador)	1502-01=	3	
1844	....	?	COTOPAXI (Ecuador)	1502-05=	2	
@ 1844	....	?	NEGRA, SIERRA (Galapagos)	1503-05=	0	
1844	0319	53a	FOURNAISE, PITON DE LA (Indian O.)	0303-02=	2	
? 1844	0324	235a	GAMALAMA (Halmahera-Indonesia)	0608-06=	1	
1844	0407	?	IWAKI (Honshu-Japan)	0803-27=	2	
1844	05	?	IYA (Lesser Sunda Is)	0604-11=	2	
@ 1844	05	?	RINCON DE LA VIEJA (Costa Rica)	1405-02=	2	
1844	05	?	IRAZU (Costa Rica)	1405-06=	2	
1844	06	122p	IZALCO (El Salvador)	1403-03=	2	
1844	0725	>3yr	SAN MIGUEL (El Salvador)	1403-10=	2	
1844	08	31p	SERUA (Banda Sea)	0605-07=	2	
1844	0925	2a	SEMERU (Java)	0603-30=	2	
1844	10	92p	TONGARIRO [NGAURUHOE] (New Z)	0401-08=	2	
1844	1109	?	TENGGER CALDERA [BROMO]	0603-31=	2	
1844	12	?	FOURNAISE, PITON DE LA (Indian O.)	0303-02=	2	
1845	Cont	....	VESUVIUS (Italy)	0101-02=	2	
1845	Cont	....	STROMBOLI (Italy)	0101-04=	1?	
1845	Cont	....	TONGARIRO [NGAURUHOE] (New Z)	0401-08=	2	
1845	Cont	....	SAVO (Solomon Is-SW Pac)	0505-07=	2?	
1845	Cont	....	YASUR (Vanuatu-SW Pacific)	0507-10=	2	
1845	Cont	....	TONGKOKO (Sulawesi-Indonesia)	0606-13=	2	
1845	Cont	....	KETOI (Kurile Is)	0900-20=	2	
1845	Cont	....	ST. HELENS (US-Washington)	1201-05-	2	-/7
1845	Cont	....	KILAUEA (Hawaiian Is)	1302-01-	0	
1845	Cont	....	SAN MIGUEL (El Salvador)	1403-10=	2	
1845	Cont	....	SANGAY (Ecuador)	1502-09=	2	
1845	....	?	FOURNAISE, PITON DE LA (Indian O.)	0303-02=	0	
? 1845	....	?	SERUA (Banda Sea)	0605-07=	2	
1845e	....	?	AMBANG (Sulawesi-Indonesia)	0606-02=		
1845	....	365y	KOLOKOL GROUP (Kurile Is)	0900-12=	2	
? 1845	....	?	AKUTAN (Aleutian Is)	1101-32-		

START YEAR	M-Dy	Duration	VOLCANO NAME (Subregion)	NUMBER	VEI	Vol L/T
? **1845**	....	?	**ISANOTSKI** (Aleutian Is)	1101-37-		
1845	....	?	**ANTUCO** (Chile-C)	1507-08=	2	
1845	01	184*p*	**SEMERU** (Java)	0603-30=	2	
1845	0120a	10*b*	**MAYON** (Luzon-Philippines)	0703-03=	3	
1845	0123	41*a*	**GEDE** (Java)	0603-06=	2	
1845	0208	?	**SOPUTAN** (Sulawesi-Indonesia)	0606-03=	2	
1845	0219	?	**RUIZ** (Colombia)	1501-02=	3	-/7
1845	04	?	**COTOPAXI** (Ecuador)	1502-05=	2	
1845	0404	?	**IWAKI** (Honshu-Japan)	0803-27=	2	
1845	0422	?	**TALANG** (Sumatra)	0601-16=	2	
? **1845**	0423	133*a*	**GAMALAMA** (Halmahera-Indonesia)	0608-06=	1	
1845	0812	?	**PAVLOF** (Alaska Peninsula)	1102-03-	2	
1845	0902	215*a*?	**HEKLA** (Iceland-S)	1702-07=	4	8/8
1845	1116	2*a*	**MARAPI** (Sumatra)	0601-14=	2?	
1846	*Cont*	....	*VESUVIUS (Italy)*	0101-02=	*2*	
1846	*Cont*	....	*STROMBOLI (Italy)*	0101-04=	*1?*	
1846	*Cont*	....	*SAVO (Solomon Is-SW Pac)*	0505-07=	*2?*	
1846	*Cont*	....	*YASUR (Vanuatu-SW Pacific)*	0507-10=	*2*	
1846	*Cont*	....	*TONGKOKO (Sulawesi-Indonesia)*	0606-13=	*2*	
1846	*Cont*	....	*KOLOKOL GROUP (Kurile Is)*	0900-12=	*2*	
1846	*Cont*	....	*KETOI (Kurile Is)*	0900-20=	*2*	
1846	*Cont*	....	*KILAUEA (Hawaiian Is)*	1302-01-	*0*	
1846	*Cont*	....	*SAN MIGUEL (El Salvador)*	1403-10=	*2*	
1846	*Cont*	....	*SANGAY (Ecuador)*	1502-09=	*2*	
1846	*Cont*	....	*HEKLA (Iceland-S)*	1702-07=	*3*	*8/8*
1846	....	?	**FOURNAISE, PITON DE LA** (Indian O.)	0303-02=	0	
1846	....	?	**MAHAWU** (Sulawesi-Indonesia)	0606-11=	2	
1846	....	?	**OSHIMA** (Izu Is-Japan)	0804-01=	2	
1846	....	?	**RASSHUA** (Kurile Is)	0900-22=	3	
1846	....	?	**SINARKA** (Kurile Is)	0900-29=	3	
1846	....	?	**HARIMKOTAN** (Kurile Is)	0900-30=	2	
? **1846**	....	?	**BAKER** (US-Washington)	1201-01=		
1846	02	?	**PACAYA** (Guatemala)	1402-11=	2	
1846	0406	?	**MERAPI** (Java)	0603-25=	2	
1846	0511	?	**MAYON** (Luzon-Philippines)	0703-03=	3	
1846	0519	<1	**GAMALAMA** (Halmahera-Indonesia)	0608-06=	2	
1846	0527	?	**TANGKUBANPARAHU** (Java)	0603-09=	2	
1846	08	?	**NASU** (Honshu-Japan)	0803-15=	2	
1846	08	1*a*	**PAVLOF** (Alaska Peninsula)	1102-03-	2	
? **1846**	0814	?	**ZUBAYR, JEBEL** (Red Sea)	0201-02=	2	
1846	09 ?	?	**SERUA** (Banda Sea)	0605-07=	2	
1846	0902	409*m*	**MERAPI** (Java)	0603-25=	3	
1846	10	?	**FONUALEI** (Tonga-SW Pacific)	0403-10=	4?	7/8
1846	1004	1*a*	**CAMPI FLEGREI MAR SICILIA** (Italy)	0101-07=	2	
1846	11	?	**FERNANDINA** (Galapagos)	1503-01=	0	
1846	1118	?	**E-SAN** (Hokkaido-Japan)	0805-011	1	
1846	1126	>3yr	**AZUL, CERRO [QUIZAPU]** (Chile-C)	1507-06=	2	9/-
1847	*Cont*	....	*VESUVIUS (Italy)*	0101-02=	*2*	
1847	*Cont*	....	*STROMBOLI (Italy)*	0101-04=	*1?*	
1847	*Cont*	....	*SAVO (Solomon Is-SW Pac)*	0505-07=	*2?*	
1847	*Cont*	....	*YASUR (Vanuatu-SW Pacific)*	0507-10=	*2*	
1847	*Cont*	....	*MERAPI (Java)*	0603-25=	*2*	
1847	*Cont*	....	*KILAUEA (Hawaiian Is)*	1302-01-	*0*	
1847	*Cont*	....	*SAN MIGUEL (El Salvador)*	1403-10=	*2*	
1847	*Cont*	....	*SANGAY (Ecuador)*	1502-09=	*2*	
1847	*Cont*	....	*AZUL, CERRO [QUIZAPU] (Chile-C)*	1507-06=	*0*	9/-
1847	....	?	**FOURNAISE, PITON DE LA** (Indian O.)	0303-02=	0	
1847	....	>3yr	**TARA, BATU** (Lesser Sunda Is)	0604-26=	2	
? **1847**	....	?	**TURRIALBA** (Costa Rica)	1405-07=		
1847	0207	<1	**GAMALAMA** (Halmahera-Indonesia)	0608-06=	2	
1847	0326	92*a*	**LAMONGAN** (Java)	0603-32=	2	
1847	0326	4*a*	**ST. HELENS** (US-Washington)	1201-05-	2	
1847	0409	23*a*?	**FOGO** (Cape Verde Is)	1804-01=	2	
1847	0518	?	**IRAZU** (Costa Rica)	1405-06=	2	
1847	0709	4*a*?	**FONUALEI** (Tonga-SW Pacific)	0403-10=	3?	
1847	0907	<1	**GAMALAMA** (Halmahera-Indonesia)	0608-06=		
1847	0910	2*a*	**RINJANI** (Lesser Sunda Is)	0604-03=	2	
1847	0925	?	**LAMONGAN** (Java)	0603-32=	2	
1847	1016	12*a*	**GUNTUR** (Java)	0603-13=	2	
1847	1017	1*a*	**GEDE** (Java)	0603-06=	2	
1847	*1027*	*>3yr*	*PURACE (Colombia)*	1501-06=	2	
1847	1204	?	**DIENG VOLC COMPLEX** (Java)	0603-20=	2	
1848	*Cont*	....	*VESUVIUS (Italy)*	0101-02=	*2*	
1848	*Cont*	....	*STROMBOLI (Italy)*	0101-04=	*1?*	
1848	*Cont*	....	*YASUR (Vanuatu-SW Pacific)*	0507-10=	*2*	
1848	*Cont*	....	*TARA, BATU (Lesser Sunda Is)*	0604-26=	*2*	
1848	*Cont*	....	*KILAUEA (Hawaiian Is)*	1302-01-	*0*	
1848	*Cont*	....	*SAN MIGUEL (El Salvador)*	1403-10=	*2*	
1848	*Cont*	....	*PURACE (Colombia)*	1501-06=	*2*	
1848	*Cont*	....	*SANGAY (Ecuador)*	1502-09=	*2*	
1848	*Cont*	....	*AZUL, CERRO [QUIZAPU] (Chile-C)*	1507-06=	*0*	9/-
1848	....	?	**KARTHALA** (Indian O.-W)	0303-01=	0	
1848	....	?	**FOURNAISE, PITON DE LA** (Indian O.)	0303-02=	0	
1848	....	?	**GOLOVNIN** (Kurile Is)	0900-01=	1	
1848	....	?	**HARIMKOTAN** (Kurile Is)	0900-30=	2	
1848	....	?	**MUTNOVSKY** (Kamchatka)	1000-06=	3	-/7
1848	....	?	**KLIUCHEVSKOI** (Kamchatka)	1000-26=	2	
? **1848**	....	?	**SOCORRO** (Mexico-Is)	1401-021	2?	
1848	....	?	**LASCAR** (Chile-N)	1505-10=	2	
1848	....	?	**ANTUCO** (Chile-C)	1507-08=	2	
? **1848**	0108	?	**MERAPI** (Java)	0603-25=		
1848	0118	?	**IWAKI** (Honshu-Japan)	0803-27=	2	
1848	02	?	**SEMERU** (Java)	0603-30=	2	
1848	0305d	?	**AKUTAN** (Aleutian Is)	1101-32-	2	
1848	0401<	?	**ST. HELENS** (US-Washington)	1201-05-	2?	
? **1848**	0413	88*a*?	**RITTER ISLAND** (New Guinea-NE of)	0501-07=		
1848	0508	?	**GEDE** (Java)	0603-06=	2	
1848	0516	?	**KELUT** (Java)	0603-28=	3	
1848	0804	?	**SEMERU** (Java)	0603-30=	2	
1849	*Cont*	....	*VESUVIUS (Italy)*	0101-02=	*2*	
1849	*Cont*	....	*STROMBOLI (Italy)*	0101-04=	*1?*	
1849	*Cont*	....	*YASUR (Vanuatu-SW Pacific)*	0507-10=	*2*	
1849	*Cont*	....	*TARA, BATU (Lesser Sunda Is)*	0604-26=	*2*	
1849	*Cont*	....	*KILAUEA (Hawaiian Is)*	1302-01-	*0*	
1849	*Cont*	....	*AZUL, CERRO [QUIZAPU] (Chile-C)*	1507-06=	*0*	9/-
1849	....	?	**FOURNAISE, PITON DE LA** (Indian O.)	0303-02=	0	
1849	....	?	**BATUR** (Lesser Sunda Is)	0604-01=	2	
1849	....	?	**GORIASCHAIA SOPKA** (Kurile Is)	0900-17B	2	
? **1849**	....	?	**ST. HELENS** (US-Washington)	1201-05-	2?	
1849	....	?	**MOMOTOMBO** (Nicaragua)	1404-09=	2	

Figure 19. Perspective sketch of the Bay of Naples area, Italy. Vesuvius is on the right, with its classic somma volcano shape formed by cone growth after caldera collapse 17,000 years ago. Campi Flegrei (Phlegrean Fields) is on the left, and the city of Naples lies between. A variety of cinder cones, low-rimmed maars, and other small volcanic features fill the pre-historic caldera of Campi Flegrei. Sketch by Hans Cloos, 1946, from the Cloos memorial volume (*Bulletin of the IAEG*, No. 13-16, 1976-77).

	START YEAR	M-Dy	Duration	VOLCANO NAME (Subregion)	NUMBER	VEI	Vol L/T
@	1849	....	?	RINCON DE LA VIEJA (Costa Rica)	1405-02=	2	
	1849	0426	?	MERAPI (Java)	0603-25=	2	-/6
	1849	05	?	MAUNA LOA (Hawaiian Is)	1302-02=	0	7/-
	1849	06	92p	LAMONGAN (Java)	0603-32=	2	
	1849	0914	10a	MERAPI (Java)	0603-25=	3	-/7
	1849	1006	?	LEWOTOLO (Lesser Sunda Is)	0604-23=	2	
	1849	1127	357a	GAMALAMA (Halmahera-Indonesia)	0608-06=	2	
	1849	12	....	PURACE (Colombia)	1501-06=	3?	
	1849	12	....	SANGAY (Ecuador)	1502-09=	3	
	1849	1201	?	SLAMET (Java)	0603-18=	2	
	1849	1201p	?	RAUNG (Java)	0603-34=		
	1850	Cont	....	YASUR (Vanuatu-SW Pacific)	0507-10=	2	
	1850	Cont	....	TARA, BATU (Lesser Sunda Is)	0604-26=	2	
	1850	Cont	....	GAMALAMA (Halmahera-Indonesia)	0608-06=	2	
	1850	Cont	....	KILAUEA (Hawaiian Is)	1302-01-	0	
	1850	Cont	....	PURACE (Colombia)	1501-06=	2	
	1850	Cont	....	SANGAY (Ecuador)	1502-09=	2	
	1850	Cont	....	AZUL, CERRO [QUIZAPU] (Chile-C)	1507-06=	0	9/-
	1850	....	?	STROMBOLI (Italy)	0101-04=	2	
	1850j	....	?	ES SAFA (Syria)	0300-05-	0	
	1850?	....	?	KARTHALA (Indian O.-W)	0303-01=	0	
	1850?	....	?	RABAUL (New Britain-SW Pac)	0502-14=	2	
	1850	....	?	UNNAMED (Luzon Is-N of)	0704-05=	0	
?	1850	....	?	UNNAMED (Taiwan-E of)	0801-01=	0	
A	1850?	....	?	CHICHON, EL (Mexico)	1401-12=		
?	1850	....	?	FUEGO (Guatemala)	1402-09=	2	
	1850	....	?	IZALCO (El Salvador)	1403-03=	2	
	1850	....	?	COTOPAXI (Ecuador)	1502-05=	2	
	1850	....	?	PUNTIGUIDO-CORDON CENIZOS	1507-16-		
	1850?	....	?	PENGUIN (Antarctica)	1900-031		
?	1850	....	?	PAULET (Antarctica)	1900-041		
	1850	0205	....	VESUVIUS (Italy)	0101-02=	2	
?	1850	03	?	BAKER (US-Washington)	1201-01=		
	1850	03	61p?	ST. HELENS (US-Washington)	1201-05-	2?	
	1850	0413	44a>	NEGRO, CERRO (Nicaragua)	1404-07=	2	
	1850	1103	9a	FOURNAISE, PITON DE LA (Indian O.)	0303-02=	0	
	1851	Cont	....	STROMBOLI (Italy)	0101-04=	1?	
	1851	Cont	....	YASUR (Vanuatu-SW Pacific)	0507-10=	2	
	1851	Cont	....	TARA, BATU (Lesser Sunda Is)	0604-26=	2	
	1851	Cont	....	PURACE (Colombia)	1501-06=	2	
	1851	Cont	....	SANGAY (Ecuador)	1502-09=	2	
	1851	Cont	....	AZUL, CERRO [QUIZAPU] (Chile-C)	1507-06=	0	9/-
	1851	....	?	FOURNAISE, PITON DE LA (Indian O.)	0303-02=	0	
	1851	....	?	METIS SHOAL (Tonga-SW Pacific)	0403-07=	0	
?	1851	....	?	RINCON DE LA VIEJA (Costa Rica)	1405-02=		
	1851	....	?	OSORNO (Chile-S)	1508-01=	2?	
	1851 r	....	?	JAN MAYEN (Atl-N-Jan Mayen)	1706-01=		
	1851	01	?	SEMERU (Java)	0603-30=	2	
	1851	01	....	KILAUEA (Hawaiian Is)	1302-01-	0	
	1851	0124	?	KELUT (Java)	0603-28=	2	
	1851	0526	20m	MAYON (Luzon-Philippines)	0703-03=	1	
	1851	06	?	COTOPAXI (Ecuador)	1502-05=	2	
	1851	0805	330w	PELEE (W Indies)	1600-12=	2	
	1851	0808	3a	MAUNA LOA (Hawaiian Is)	1302-02=	0	7/-
	1851	09	?	MALY SEMIACHIK (Kamchatka)	1000-14=	2	
	1852	Cont	....	STROMBOLI (Italy)	0101-04=	1?	
	1852	Cont	....	YASUR (Vanuatu-SW Pacific)	0507-10=	2	
	1852	Cont	....	TARA, BATU (Lesser Sunda Is)	0604-26=	2	
	1852	Cont	....	KILAUEA (Hawaiian Is)	1302-01-	0	
	1852	Cont	....	PURACE (Colombia)	1501-06=	2	
	1852	Cont	....	SANGAY (Ecuador)	1502-09=	2	
	1852	Cont	....	AZUL, CERRO [QUIZAPU] (Chile-C)	1507-06=	0	9/-
	1852	Cont	....	PELEE (W Indies)	1600-12=	2	
	1852	....	?	CAMEROON, MT. (Africa-W)	0204-01=	2	
	1852	....	?	FOURNAISE, PITON DE LA (Indian O.)	0303-02=	0	
	1852	....	?	METIS SHOAL (Tonga-SW Pacific)	0403-07=	0	
	1852	....	?	HOME REEF (Tonga-SW Pacific)	0403-08=	2	
?	1852	....	?	BARREN ISLAND (Andaman Is-Ind O	0600-01=	2	
?	1852	....	?	SIRUNG (Lesser Sunda Is)	0604-27=	2	
?	1852	....	?	BULUSAN (Luzon-Philippines)	0703-01=		
	1852	....	?	KARYMSKY (Kamchatka)	1000-13=	2	
	1852	....	?	AKUTAN (Aleutian Is)	1101-32-		
?	1852	....	?	PAVLOF (Alaska Peninsula)	1102-03-		
?	1852	....	?	VENIAMINOF (Alaska Peninsula)	1102-07-		
?	1852	....	?	CHIGINAGAK (Alaska Peninsula)	1102-11-		
?	1852	....	?	UGASHIK-PEULIK (Alaska Peninsula)	1102-13A		
	1852	....	?	POPOCATEPETL (Mexico)	1401-09=	1?	
?	1852	....	?	ATITLAN (Guatemala)	1402-06=	2?	
?	1852	....	?	FUEGO (Guatemala)	1402-09=	2	
	1852	....	?	MOMOTOMBO (Nicaragua)	1404-09=	2	
	1852	....	?	COTOPAXI (Ecuador)	1502-05=	2	
	1852	....	365y	LLAIMA (Chile-C)	1507-11=	2	
?	1852	....	?	VILLARRICA (Chile-C)	1507-12=		
	1852	02	30p	KLIUCHEVSKOI (Kamchatka)	1000-26=	2	
	1852	0217	23a?	MAUNA LOA (Hawaiian Is)	1302-02=	2	8/-
	1852	0219	40a?	FOGO (Cape Verde Is)	1804-01=	2	
	1852	03	?	MUTNOVSKY (Kamchatka)	1000-06=	2	
	1852	0415q	91r	MALY SEMIACHIK (Kamchatka)	1000-14=	2	
	1852	0528	<1	GEDE (Java)	0603-06=	2	
	1852	07	?	MASAYA (Nicaragua)	1404-10=	2	
?	1852	0717	?	UNNAMED (Atlantic-C)	1805-04=	0	
	1852	08	?	KLIUCHEVSKOI (Kamchatka)	1000-26=	2	
	1852	0820	290a	ETNA (Italy)	0101-06=	2	8/6
	1852	1005	1a	LEWOTOLO (Lesser Sunda Is)	0604-23=	2	
	1852	11	62p	ANTUCO (Chile-C)	1507-08=	0	7/-
	1852	1101	?	NIIGATA-YAKE-YAMA (Honshu-Japan)	0803-09=	2	
	1852	12	?	COSIGUINA (Nicaragua)	1404-01=	2?	
	1852	1201p	45q?	BAKER (US-Washington)	1201-01=	2	
	1853	Cont	....	STROMBOLI (Italy)	0101-04=	1?	
	1853	Cont	....	ETNA (Italy)	0101-06=	2	8/6
	1853	Cont	....	YASUR (Vanuatu-SW Pacific)	0507-10=	2	
	1853	Cont	....	BAKER (US-Washington)	1201-01=	2	
	1853	Cont	....	KILAUEA (Hawaiian Is)	1302-01-	0	
	1853	Cont	....	SANGAY (Ecuador)	1502-09=	2	
	1853	Cont	....	AZUL, CERRO [QUIZAPU] (Chile-C)	1507-06=	0	9/-
	1853	Cont	....	LLAIMA (Chile-C)	1507-11=	2	
?	1853	....	?	HOOD (US-Oregon)	1202-01-		
	1853	....	365y	RINCON DE LA VIEJA (Costa Rica)	1405-02=	2	
	1853	....	?	TURRIALBA (Costa Rica)	1405-07=	2	
?	1853	....	?	LASCAR (Chile-N)	1505-10=	2?	
	1853	01	?	MUTNOVSKY (Kamchatka)	1000-06=	2	
	1853	01	....	ANTUCO (Chile-C)	1507-08=	3	7/-
	1853	0101	?	DEMPO (Sumatra)	0601-23=	2	
	1853	02	?	LONQUIMAY (Chile-C)	1507-10=	3	
	1853	0314	<1	GEDE (Java)	0603-06=	3?	
	1853	0315e	153n?	ST. HELENS (US-Washington)	1201-05-	2?	
	1853	0409?	159a>	MASAYA (Nicaragua)	1404-10=	1?	
	1853	0422	23m>	USU (Hokkaido-Japan)	0805-03=	4	8/8
	1853	0503	?	ATITLAN (Guatemala)	1402-06=	3	
	1853	0624	<1	NIUAFO'OU (Tonga-SW Pacific)	0403-11=	0	
?	1853	07	?	SOUTH SISTER (US-Oregon)	1202-08-		
	1853	0713	44	MAYON (Luzon-Philippines)	0703-03=	3	
	1853	0913	2a	COTOPAXI (Ecuador)	1502-05=	3	7/-
	1853	10	124m	KLIUCHEVSKOI (Kamchatka)	1000-26=	2	
	1853	1029	79m	UNNAMED (Taiwan-E of)	0801-03=	2?	
	1853	11	?	KABA (Sumatra)	0601-22=	2	
	1853	11	?	VILLARRICA (Chile-C)	1507-12=	2	
	1853	12	>3yr	CHIKURACHKI (Kurile Is)	0900-36=	5?	-/9
	1853	1218	87m	MUTNOVSKY (Kamchatka)	1000-06=	2	
	1854	Cont	....	STROMBOLI (Italy)	0101-04=	1?	
	1854	Cont	....	YASUR (Vanuatu-SW Pacific)	0507-10=	2	
	1854	Cont	....	UNNAMED (Taiwan-E of)	0801-03=	2	
	1854	Cont	....	CHIKURACHKI (Kurile Is)	0900-36=	2	
	1854	Cont	....	MUTNOVSKY (Kamchatka)	1000-06=	2	
	1854	Cont	....	KLIUCHEVSKOI (Kamchatka)	1000-26=	2	
	1854	Cont	....	KILAUEA (Hawaiian Is)	1302-01-	0	
	1854	Cont	....	RINCON DE LA VIEJA (Costa Rica)	1405-02=	2	
	1854	....	?	TOFUA (Tonga-SW Pacific)	0403-06=	2	
	1854	....	?	LATE (Tonga-SW Pacific)	0403-09=	2	
	1854	....	?	NIIGATA-YAKE-YAMA (Honshu-Japan)	0803-09=		
	1854	....	?	BAKER (US-Washington)	1201-01=	2	
?	1854	....	?	RAINIER (US-Washington)	1201-03-	2	
?	1854	....	?	SAN MIGUEL (El Salvador)	1403-10=	2?	
	1854	....	?	GRIMSVOTN (Iceland-NE)	1703-01=	2	
	1854	0115	?	UNNAMED (Luzon Is-N of)	0704-05=	0	
	1854	0115	?	UNNAMED (Taiwan-E of)	0801-02=	0	
	1854	0120	10a	LASCAR (Chile-N)	1505-10=	1	
	1854	02	61p	ST. HELENS (US-Washington)	1201-05-	2	
	1854	02	30p	MOMOTOMBO (Nicaragua)	1404-09=	2	
	1854	0210	?	LLULLAILLACO (Chile-N)	1505-11=	2	
	1854	0218	?	SHEVELUCH (Kamchatka)	1000-27=	5	-/9
	1854	0226	?	ASO (Kyushu-Japan)	0802-11=	2	
	1854	0403	?	COTOPAXI (Ecuador)	1502-05=	2	
	1854	0428	?	BATUR (Lesser Sunda Is)	0604-01=	1?	
	1854	0513	26a	IZALCO (El Salvador)	1403-03=	2	
?	1854	0618	<1	MAKIAN (Halmahera-Indonesia)	0608-07=	1	
	1854	0624	?	CHIRPOI (Kurile Is)	0900-15=	2	
	1854	0627	?	ALAID (Kurile Is)	0900-39=	3	
	1854	0705	?	FUSS PEAK (Kurile Is)	0900-34=	3	
?	1854	08	?	HOOD (US-Oregon)	1202-01-		
	1854	08	....	SANGAY (Ecuador)	1502-09=	2	
	1854	0829>	?	MARAPI (Sumatra)	0601-14=	2	
?	1854	09	?	MERAPI (Java)	0603-25=		
	1854	09	?	KARYMSKY (Kamchatka)	1000-13=	2	
	1854	0914	?	COTOPAXI (Ecuador)	1502-05=	2	
	1854	1214	164a	VESUVIUS (Italy)	0101-02=	2	7/-
	1855	Cont	....	YASUR (Vanuatu-SW Pacific)	0507-10=	2	
	1855	Cont	....	CHIKURACHKI (Kurile Is)	0900-36=	2	
	1855	Cont	....	KILAUEA (Hawaiian Is)	1302-01-	0	
	1855	Cont	....	SANGAY (Ecuador)	1502-09=	2	
A	1855 e	....	?	CHYULU HILLS (Africa-E)	0202-13=	2	
	1855	....	?	TONGARIRO (New Zealand)	0401-08=	2	
	1855	....	?	SINARKA (Kurile Is)	0900-29=	2	
	1855	....	?	OSORNO (Chile-S)	1508-01=	2?	
?	1855	0112	?	TACANA (Mexico)	1401-13=	1	
	1855	0228m	?	OKINAWA-TORI-SHIMA (Ryukyu Is)	0802-02=	2	
	1855	0322	?	MAYON (Luzon-Philippines)	0703-03=	2	
?	1855	04	?	GORELY (Kamchatka)	1000-07=	2?	
	1855	05	?	TURRIALBA (Costa Rica)	1405-07=	2	
	1855	0501	?	VESUVIUS (Italy)	0101-02=	3	7/-
	1855	0528	109m	AVACHINSKY (Kamchatka)	1000-10=	2	
	1855	0701p	?	KARTHALA (Indian O.-W)	0303-01=	2	
	1855	08	?	TINAKULA (Santa Cruz Is-SW Pac)	0506-01=	2	
	1855	0811	462m	MAUNA LOA (Hawaiian Is)	1302-02=	1	8/-
	1855	0929	1a	FUEGO (Guatemala)	1402-09=	2	
	1855	1002	105m	MARAPI (Sumatra)	0601-14=	2	
	1855	1003	?	STROMBOLI (Italy)	0101-04=	2	
	1855	11	?	COTOPAXI (Ecuador)	1502-05=	2	
	1855	12	?	SAN MIGUEL (El Salvador)	1403-10=	2	
	1855	1219	>3yr	VESUVIUS (Italy)	0101-02=	2	7/-
?	1855	1229	1a	BANDA API (Banda Sea)	0605-09=		
	1856	Cont	....	VESUVIUS (Italy)	0101-02=	2	7/-
	1856	Cont	....	YASUR (Vanuatu-SW Pacific)	0507-10=	2	

	START YEAR	M-Dy	Duration	VOLCANO NAME (Subregion)	NUMBER	VEI	Vol L/T
	1856	Cont	....	MARAPI (Sumatra)	0601-14=	1	
	1856	Cont	....	CHIKURACHKI (Kurile Is)	0900-36=	2	
	1856	Cont	....	KILAUEA (Hawaiian Is)	1302-01-	0	
	1856	Cont	....	MAUNA LOA (Hawaiian Is)	1302-02=	1	8/-
?	1856h	....	?	WHITE ISLAND (New Zealand)	0401-04=	2	
	1856	....	?	VEER (Kamchatka)	1000-102	0?	
?	1856	....	?	BAKER (US-Washington)	1201-01=		
?	1856	....	?	ATITLAN (Guatemala)	1402-06=	2	
	1856	0109	57a	FUEGO (Guatemala)	1402-09=	2	
	1856	0212	....	SANGAY (Ecuador)	1502-09=	3	
	1856	0301	105a	LAMONGAN (Java)	0603-32=	2	
	1856	0302	15a	AWU (Sangihe Is-Indonesia)	0607-04=	3?	-/8
	1856	0318	97a	ASO (Kyushu-Japan)	0802-11=	2	
	1856	0414	?	TELONG, BUR NI (Sumatra)	0601-05=	2	
	1856	05	?	COTOPAXI (Ecuador)	1502-05=	2	
	1856	0520	?	IWAKI (Honshu-Japan)	0803-27=	2	
	1856	0524	100a	IZALCO (El Salvador)	1403-03=	2	
	1856	07	?	STROMBOLI (Italy)	0101-04=	2	
	1856	09	?	RUANG (Sangihe Is-Indonesia)	0607-01=	1	
	1856	0910	?	SEMERU (Java)	0603-30=	2	
@	1856	0910	?	TENGGER CALDERA [BROMO]	0603-31=	2	
	1856	0925	?	KOMAGA-TAKE (Hokkaido-Japan)	0805-02=	4	-/8
	1856	0929	1a	FUEGO (Guatemala)	1402-09=	2	
	1856	0930p	>3yr	DIDICAS (Luzon Is-N of)	0704-02=	0	8/-
	1856	10	61p	COTOPAXI (Ecuador)	1502-05=	2	
	1856	1101	?	RAGANG (Mindanao-Philippines)	0701-06=	2	
?	1856	1125	<1	UNNAMED (Atlantic-N)	1801-03=	0	
	1856	12	31p	MASAYA (Nicaragua)	1404-10=	2	
	1856	1212	1a	REVENTADOR (Ecuador)	1502-01=	3	
	1857	Cont	....	VESUVIUS (Italy)	0101-02=	2	7/-
	1857	Cont	....	STROMBOLI (Italy)	0101-04=	1?	
	1857	Cont	....	YASUR (Vanuatu-SW Pacific)	0507-10=	2	
	1857	Cont	....	DIDICAS (Luzon Is-N of)	0704-02=	0	8/-
	1857	Cont	....	CHIKURACHKI (Kurile Is)	0900-36=	2	
	1857	Cont	....	KILAUEA (Hawaiian Is)	1302-01-	0	
	1857	Cont	....	MASAYA (Nicaragua)	1404-10=	2	
	1857	Cont	....	SANGAY (Ecuador)	1502-09=	2	
	1857	....	?	KARTHALA (Indian O.-W)	0303-01=	2	
?	1857	....	?	HOME REEF (Tonga-SW Pacific)	0403-08=	2	
	1857	....	?	TENGGER CALDERA [BROMO] (Java)	0603-31=	2	
	1857	....	?	MAYON (Luzon-Philippines)	0703-03=	2	
	1857<	....	?	CAMIGUIN DE BABUYANES (Luzon-N	0704-01=	2	
	1857	....	?	TOKACHI (Hokkaido-Japan)	0805-05=	2	
?	1857?	....	?	SHIRETOKO-IWO-ZAN (Hokkaido)	0805-09=		
?	1857	....	?	TRES VIRGENES (Mexico)	1401-01=		
	1857	....	?	COTOPAXI (Ecuador)	1502-05=	2	
	1857	0115	33a	FUEGO (Guatemala)	1402-09=	4?	-/8
	1857	02	18c	TONGARIRO [NGAURUHOE] (New Z)	0401-08=	2	
	1857	0215	4a>	IZALCO (El Salvador)	1403-03=	2	
	1857	04	?	ST. HELENS (US-Washington)	1201-05-	2	
	1857	0627	171a	FOGO (Cape Verde Is)	1804-01=	2	
	1857	07	?	CHIRPOI (Kurile Is)	0900-15=	3	
	1857	08	?	TINAKULA (Santa Cruz Is-SW Pac)	0506-01=	2	
	1857	0813	33m	SEMERU (Java)	0603-30=	2	
	1857	0906	?	ETNA (Italy)	0101-06=	1?	
	1857	0910	?	TUNGURAHUA (Ecuador)	1502-08=	2?	
	1857	0917	?	FUEGO (Guatemala)	1402-09=	2	
	1857	11	?	SAN MIGUEL (El Salvador)	1403-10=	2?	
	1858	Cont	....	STROMBOLI (Italy)	0101-04=	1?	
	1858	Cont	....	YASUR (Vanuatu-SW Pacific)	0507-10=	2	
	1858	Cont	....	DIDICAS (Luzon Is-N of)	0704-02=	0	8/-
	1858	Cont	....	CHIKURACHKI (Kurile Is)	0900-36=	2	
	1858	Cont	....	KILAUEA (Hawaiian Is)	1302-01-	0	
	1858	....	?	KARTHALA (Indian O.-W)	0303-01=	2	
	1858	....	?	METIS SHOAL (Tonga-SW Pacific)	0403-07=	2	
	1858	....	?	SERUA (Banda Sea)	0605-07=	2	
	1858	....	?	BAKER (US-Washington)	1201-01=	2	
?	1858	....	?	RAINIER (US-Washington)	1201-03-	2	
	1858	....	>3yr	MOMOTOMBO (Nicaragua)	1404-09=	2	
	1858	01	334p	MAYON (Luzon-Philippines)	0703-03=	2	
	1858	0206	524m	IZALCO (El Salvador)	1403-03=	2	
	1858	0218	?	RAGANG (Mindanao-Philippines)	0701-06=	2	
	1858	0304	?	TENGGER CALDERA [BROMO]	0603-31=	2	
?	1858	04	?	MASAYA (Nicaragua)	1404-10=		
	1858	04	245p	LASCAR (Chile-N)	1505-10=	2?	
?	1858	0408	?	TATE-YAMA (Honshu-Japan)	0803-08=		
	1858	0527	....	VESUVIUS (Italy)	0101-02=	2	7/-
	1858	1018	?	TENGGER CALDERA [BROMO]	0603-31=	2	
?	1858	11	302p	GAMALAMA (Halmahera-Indonesia)	0608-06=	1	
	1858	11	30p	COTOPAXI (Ecuador)	1502-05=	2	
	1858	1103	74m	FOURNAISE, PITON DE LA (Indian O.)	0303-02=	2	7/-
	1858	1110	137a	MASAYA (Nicaragua)	1404-10=	2	
	1858	12	....	SANGAY (Ecuador)	1502-09=	2	
	1859	Cont	....	VESUVIUS (Italy)	0101-02=	2	7/-
	1859	Cont	....	STROMBOLI (Italy)	0101-04=	1?	
	1859	Cont	....	YASUR (Vanuatu-SW Pacific)	0507-10=	2	
?	1859	Cont	....	GAMALAMA (Halmahera-Indonesia)	0608-06=	1	
	1859	Cont	....	DIDICAS (Luzon Is-N of)	0704-02=	0	8/-
	1859	Cont	....	CHIKURACHKI (Kurile Is)	0900-36=	2	
	1859	Cont	....	KILAUEA (Hawaiian Is)	1302-01-	0	
	1859	Cont	....	MOMOTOMBO (Nicaragua)	1404-09=	2	
	1859	Cont	....	MASAYA (Nicaragua)	1404-10=	2	
	1859	....	?	KARTHALA (Indian O.-W)	0303-01=	2	
	1859	....	?	SERUA (Banda Sea)	0605-07=	2	
	1859	....	?	MAYON (Luzon-Philippines)	0703-03=		
	1859	....	?	COTOPAXI (Ecuador)	1502-05=	2	
	1859	0123	306a	MAUNA LOA (Hawaiian Is)	1302-02=	1	8/-
	1859	0130	33d	TENGGER CALDERA [BROMO]	0603-31=	2	
	1859	0227	16m	LAMONGAN (Java)	0603-32=	2	
	1859	0421	?	TONGARIRO (New Zealand)	0401-08=	1?	
	1859	05	....	SANGAY (Ecuador)	1502-09=	2	
	1859	0508	15a>	FOURNAISE, PITON DE LA (Indian O.)	0303-02=	2	
	1859	0519	327a	VILLARRICA (Chile-C)	1507-12=	2	
?	1859	07	?	LEWOTOBI (Lesser Sunda Is)	0604-18=		
	1859	0815	2a	HOOD (US-Oregon)	1202-01-	2	
	1859	0825	?	COSIGUINA (Nicaragua)	1404-01=		
	1859	0927	?	EBEKO (Kurile Is)	0900-38=	3	
	1859	11	163m?	BAKER (US-Washington)	1201-01=	2	
	1859	1208	45a	IZALCO (El Salvador)	1403-03=	0	
	1859	1214	?	RAUNG (Java)	0603-34=	2	
	1860	Cont	....	VESUVIUS (Italy)	0101-02=	2	7/-
	1860	Cont	....	STROMBOLI (Italy)	0101-04=	1?	
	1860	Cont	....	YASUR (Vanuatu-SW Pacific)	0507-10=	2	
	1860	Cont	....	BAKER (US-Washington)	1201-01=	2	
	1860	Cont	....	KILAUEA (Hawaiian Is)	1302-01-	0	
	1860	Cont	....	IZALCO (El Salvador)	1403-03=	0	
	1860	Cont	....	MOMOTOMBO (Nicaragua)	1404-09=	2	
	1860	Cont	....	SANGAY (Ecuador)	1502-09=	2	
	1860	Cont	....	VILLARRICA (Chile-C)	1507-12=	2	
	1860?	....	?	SORETIMEAT (Vanuatu-SW Pacific)	0507-01=	2?	
?	1860	....	?	MAKIAN (Halmahera-Indonesia)	0608-07=		
	1860	....	?	MAYON (Luzon-Philippines)	0703-03=		
	1860	....	....	DIDICAS (Luzon Is-N of)	0704-02=	2	8/-
	1860	....	?	BABUYAN CLARO (Luzon Is-N of)	0704-03=	2	
	1860	....	?	SAKURA-JIMA (Kyushu-Japan)	0802-08=	1	
	1860?	....	?	CHIRIP (Kurile Is)	0900-09=	1	
	1860	....	?	RINCON DE LA VIEJA (Costa Rica)	1405-02=	2	
	1860	....	?	POAS (Costa Rica)	1405-04=	1	
	1860i	....	?	PURACE (Colombia)	1501-06=	2?	
	1860	....	730y	COTOPAXI (Ecuador)	1502-05=	2	
@	1860	....	?	NEGRA, SIERRA (Galapagos)	1503-05=	2	
	1860	....	?	PLANCHON-PETEROA (Chile-C)	1507-04=	2	
	1860	0122	58a	FOURNAISE, PITON DE LA (Indian O.)	0303-02=	2	-/5
	1860	0319	23a	SLAMET (Java)	0603-18=	2	
	1860	04	60p?	SEMERU (Java)	0603-30=	2	
	1860	0508	19a	KATLA (Iceland-S)	1702-03=	3	-/7
?	1860	06	?	GAMALAMA (Halmahera-Indonesia)	0608-06=	1	
	1860	0612	2a	TENGGER CALDERA [BROMO]	0603-31=	2	
	1860	0707	2a	ALAID (Kurile Is)	0900-39=	3	
	1860	0818	36a	FUEGO (Guatemala)	1402-09=	2	
	1860	09 <	?	RAUNG (Java)	0603-34=	2	
	1860	0911	34m	SANGEANG API (Lesser Sunda Is)	0604-05=	2	
?	1860	10	?	CAGUA (Luzon-Philippines)	0703-09=	2	
?	1860	12	?	BAKER (US-Washington)	1201-01=		
	1860	1229	?	KARTHALA (Indian O.-W)	0303-01=	0	
	1861	Cont	....	STROMBOLI (Italy)	0101-04=	1?	
	1861	Cont	....	YASUR (Vanuatu-SW Pacific)	0507-10=	2	
	1861	Cont	....	KILAUEA (Hawaiian Is)	1302-01-	0	
	1861	Cont	....	MOMOTOMBO (Nicaragua)	1404-09=	2	
	1861	Cont	....	COTOPAXI (Ecuador)	1502-05=	2	
	1861	Cont	....	SANGAY (Ecuador)	1502-09=	2	
	1861	....	?	LAMONGAN (Java)	0603-32=	2	
	1861	....	?	MAYON (Luzon-Philippines)	0703-03=	1	
	1861	....	775w	RINCON DE LA VIEJA (Costa Rica)	1405-02=	2	
?	1861	....	?	TURRIALBA (Costa Rica)	1405-07=		
	1861	....	?	TUPUNGATITO (Chile-C)	1507-01=	2	
	1861	....	?	ANTUCO (Chile-C)	1507-08=	0	
@	1861	....	?	SETE CIDADES (Azores)	1802-08=	0	
	1861	0213	92a>	RUAPEHU (New Zealand)	0401-10=	2	
	1861	0319	<1	FOURNAISE, PITON DE LA (Indian O.)	0303-02=	2	
	1861	04	?	MARAPI (Sumatra)	0601-14=	2?	
?	1861	05	?	KAWAHKARAHA (Java)	0603-16=		
?	1861	05	?	GRIMSVOTN (Iceland-NE)	1703-01=	2	
	1861	0504	14a	LEWOTOBI (Lesser Sunda Is)	0604-18=	2	
	1861	0508	130m?	DUBBI (Ethiopia)	0201-10=	3	
	1861	06	548p	CHILLAN, NEVADOS DE (Chile-C)	1507-07=	3	
?	1861	1121	?	FUEGO (Guatemala)	1402-09=	2	
	1861	1208	....	VESUVIUS (Italy)	0101-02=	3	7/-
	1861	1228	292m	MAKIAN (Halmahera-Indonesia)	0608-07=	4?	-/8
	1862	Cont	....	STROMBOLI (Italy)	0101-04=	1?	
	1862	Cont	....	YASUR (Vanuatu-SW Pacific)	0507-10=	2	
	1862	Cont	....	MAKIAN (Halmahera-Indonesia)	0608-07=	4?	-/8
	1862	Cont	....	KILAUEA (Hawaiian Is)	1302-01-	0	
	1862	Cont	....	MOMOTOMBO (Nicaragua)	1404-09=	2	
	1862	Cont	....	RINCON DE LA VIEJA (Costa Rica)	1405-02=	2	
	1862	Cont	....	COTOPAXI (Ecuador)	1502-05=	2	
	1862	Cont	....	SANGAY (Ecuador)	1502-09=	2	
	1862	Cont	....	CHILLAN, NEVADOS DE (Chile-C)	1507-07=	2	
?	1862	....	?	KARTHALA (Indian O.-W)	0303-01=	2	
	1862	....	693w	MERAPI (Java)	0603-25=	2	7/6
	1862	....	?	HIBOK-HIBOK (Mindanao-Philippines)	0701-08=	2	
	1862	....	?	MAYON (Luzon-Philippines)	0703-03=	2	
	1862	....	?	UBINAS (Peru)	1504-02=	2	
	1862	....	?	ANTUCO (Chile-C)	1507-08=		
	1862	....	?	LLAIMA (Chile-C)	1507-11=	2	
	1862	01	?	TONGARIRO [NGAURUHOE] (New Z)	0401-08=	2	
	1862	01	?	SAN MIGUEL (El Salvador)	1403-10=	2	
	1862	04	31p	TUTUPACA (Peru)	1504-04=	2	
	1862	0630	837q	BARDARBUNGA [TROLLAGIGAR]	1703-03=	2	8/-
	1862	0715	91m	GAMALAMA (Halmahera-Indonesia)	0608-06=	2	
	1863	Cont	....	STROMBOLI (Italy)	0101-04=	1?	
	1863	Cont	....	YASUR (Vanuatu-SW Pacific)	0507-10=	2	
	1863	Cont	....	KILAUEA (Hawaiian Is)	1302-01-	0	
	1863	Cont	....	MOMOTOMBO (Nicaragua)	1404-09=	2	
	1863	Cont	....	RINCON DE LA VIEJA (Costa Rica)	1405-02=	2	

START YEAR	M-Dy	Dura-tion	VOLCANO NAME (Subregion)	NUMBER	VEI	Vol L/T
1863	Cont	....	SANGAY (Ecuador)	1502-09=	2	
1863	Cont	....	BARDARBUNGA [TROLLAGIGAR]	1703-03=	2	8/-
1863	....	?	TEYR, DJEBEL (Red Sea)	0201-01=	2	
? 1863	....	?	DUBBI (Ethiopia)	0201-10=	2	
A 1863 e	....	?	LONGONOT (Africa-E)	0202-10=	0	7/-
1863	....	303w	TONGARIRO [NGAURUHOE] (New Z)	0401-08=	2	
1863	....	....	AMBRYM (Vanuatu-SW Pacific)	0507-04=	2	
1863	....	?	LOPEVI (Vanuatu-SW Pacific)	0507-05=	2	
? 1863	....	?	TAJUMULCO (Guatemala)	1402-02=	2	
1863	....	?	IZALCO (El Salvador)	1403-03=	0	
1863	....	?	COTOPAXI (Ecuador)	1502-05=	2	
1863	....	?	ANTUCO (Chile-C)	1507-08=	2	
1863	0323	?	IWAKI (Honshu-Japan)	0803-27=	1	
1863	0501	88c	ETNA (Italy)	0101-06=	2	
? 1863	0501?	45m?	GAMALAMA (Halmahera-Indonesia)	0608-06=	2	
1863	0523	?	MARAPI (Sumatra)	0601-14=	2?	
1863	0523	....	MERAPI (Java)	0603-25=	2	7/6
? 1863	0530	?	MAYON (Luzon-Philippines)	0703-03=		
1863	07	?	BAKER (US-Washington)	1201-01=	2	
1863	08	?	ISLUGA (Chile-N)	1505-03=	1?	
1863	0812	?	CAMPI FLEGREI MAR SICILIA (Italy)	0101-07=	2	
1863	0825	6a	MAKIAN (Halmahera-Indonesia)	0608-07=	1	
1863	1220	40a	FOURNAISE, PITON DE LA (Indian O.)	0303-02=	0	
1864	Cont	....	STROMBOLI (Italy)	0101-04=	1?	
1864	Cont	....	FOURNAISE, PITON DE LA (Indian O.)	0303-02=	0	
1864	Cont	....	AMBRYM (Vanuatu-SW Pacific)	0507-04=	2	
1864	Cont	....	YASUR (Vanuatu-SW Pacific)	0507-10=	2	
1864	Cont	....	MERAPI (Java)	0603-25=	2	7/6
1864	Cont	....	KILAUEA (Hawaiian Is)	1302-01-	0	
1864	Cont	....	MOMOTOMBO (Nicaragua)	1404-09=	2	
1864	Cont	....	SANGAY (Ecuador)	1502-09=	2	
1864	Cont	....	BARDARBUNGA [TROLLAGIGAR]	1703-03=	2	8/-
1864	....	?	LEWOTOLO (Lesser Sunda Is)	0604-23=	2	
1864	....	?	PAGAN (Mariana Is-C Pac)	0804-17=	1?	
1864	....	365y	CHILLAN, NEVADOS DE (Chile-C)	1507-07=	3	
1864	....	?	LLAIMA (Chile-C)	1507-11=	3	
? 1864	01	?	ALAMAGAN (Mariana Is-C Pac)	0804-18=		
1864	0104	<1	KELUT (Java)	0603-28=	2	
1864	0107	?	FARALLON DE PAJAROS (Mariana Is)	0804-14=	2	
1864	0120	28a	GAMALAMA (Halmahera-Indonesia)	0608-06=	2	
1864	0210	>3yr	VESUVIUS (Italy)	0101-02=	2	6/-
1864	0515b	396g	IZALCO (El Salvador)	1403-03=	2	
? 1864	0604d	21d	GAMALAMA (Halmahera-Indonesia)	0608-06=	1	
1864	0606	?	KARANGETANG [API SIAU] (Sangihe	0607-02=	2	
1864	0609	?	LOPEVI (Vanuatu-SW Pacific)	0507-05=	3	
1864	0609	36m	LAMONGAN (Java)	0603-32=	2	
1864	0702	166m	RAUNG (Java)	0603-34=	2	
1864	0805d	45d	ETNA (Italy)	0101-06=	2	
1864	0916	180m	TURRIALBA (Costa Rica)	1405-07=	2	
1864	10	16m	MAKIAN (Halmahera-Indonesia)	0608-07=	1	
? 1864	10	?	CALLAQUI (Chile-C)	1507-091		
1864	10	?	VILLARRICA (Chile-C)	1507-12=	2	
1864	1101	2a	MOCHO-CHOSHUENCO (Chile-C)	1507-13=	2	
1864	12	31p	TONGARIRO [NGAURUHOE] (New Z)	0401-08=	2	
1864	1227	6a	GAMALAMA (Halmahera-Indonesia)	0608-06=	2	
1865	Cont	....	VESUVIUS (Italy)	0101-02=	2	6/-
1865	Cont	....	TONGARIRO [NGAURUHOE] (New Z)	0401-08=	2	
1865	Cont	....	YASUR (Vanuatu-SW Pacific)	0507-10=	2	
1865	Cont	....	GAMALAMA (Halmahera-Indonesia)	0608-06=	2	
1865	Cont	....	KILAUEA (Hawaiian Is)	1302-01-	0	
1865	Cont	....	IZALCO (El Salvador)	1403-03=	2	
1865	Cont	....	MOMOTOMBO (Nicaragua)	1404-09=	2	
1865	Cont	....	SANGAY (Ecuador)	1502-09=	2	
1865	Cont	....	CHILLAN, NEVADOS DE (Chile-C)	1507-07=	2?	
1865	....	?	NYAMURAGIRA (Africa-C)	0203-02=		
1865	....	?	CAMEROON, MT. (Africa-W)	0204-01=	2	
1865	....	?	KARTHALA (Indian O.-W)	0303-01=	2?	
? 1865	....	?	FALCON ISLAND (Tonga-SW Pacific)	0403-05=	0	
1865 c	....	>3yr	BAGANA (Bougainville-SW Pac)	0505-02=	2	
1865?	....	?	SORETIMEAT (Vanuatu-SW Pacific)	0507-01=	2	
1865 e	....	?	KELIMUTU (Lesser Sunda Is)	0604-14=	2	
1865	....	?	RAGANG (Mindanao-Philippines)	0701-06=	2	
1865	....	?	MAKUSHIN (Aleutian Is)	1101-31-		
1865	....	?	AKUTAN (Aleutian Is)	1101-32-		
? 1865	....	?	SHISHALDIN (Aleutian Is)	1101-36-		
? 1865	....	?	BAKER (US-Washington)	1201-01=		
1865	....	?	UBINAS (Peru)	1504-02=	2	
1865	....	730y	OLCA-PARUMA (Chile-N)	1505-05=		
1865	0124	....	TURRIALBA (Costa Rica)	1405-07=	2	
1865	0126e	10j	STROMBOLI (Italy)	0101-04=	2	
1865	0130	149a	ETNA (Italy)	0101-06=	2	8/6
1865	0205	5a	FOURNAISE, PITON DE LA (Indian O.)	0303-02=	2	
1865	04	31p	TENGGER CALDERA [BROMO]	0603-31=	2	
1865	0415e	?	SEMERU (Java)	0603-30=	2	
1865	0504	?	LEWOTOBI (Lesser Sunda Is)	0604-18=	2	
1865	0709	?	UNNAMED (Atlantic-N)	1801-04=	0	
1865	09	?	KLIUCHEVSKOI (Kamchatka)	1000-26=	2	
1865	0921	117m?	HOOD (US-Oregon)	1202-01-	2	
1865	1002	>3yr	GALERAS (Colombia)	1501-08=	3	7/6
1865	1024	614w	MERAPI (Java)	0603-25=	2	7/7
1865	1201	17a	TENGGER CALDERA [BROMO]	0603-31=	2	
1865	1230	120a?	MAUNA LOA (Hawaiian Is)	1302-02=	0	7/-
1866	Cont	....	VESUVIUS (Italy)	0101-02=	2	6/-
1866	Cont	....	STROMBOLI (Italy)	0101-04=	1?	
1866	Cont	....	BAGANA (Bougainville-SW Pac)	0505-02=	2?	
1866	Cont	....	YASUR (Vanuatu-SW Pacific)	0507-10=	2	
1866	Cont	....	MERAPI (Java)	0603-25=	2	7/7
1866	Cont	....	HOOD (US-Oregon)	1202-01-	2	
1866	Cont	....	MAUNA LOA (Hawaiian Is)	1302-02=	0	7/-
1866	Cont	....	MOMOTOMBO (Nicaragua)	1404-09=	2	
1866	Cont	....	GALERAS (Colombia)	1501-08=	2	7/6
1866	Cont	....	SANGAY (Ecuador)	1502-09=	2	
1866	Cont	....	OLCA-PARUMA (Chile-N)	1505-05=		
1866	....	?	CANLAON (Philippines-C)	0702-02=	2	
1866	....	....	KILAUEA (Hawaiian Is)	1302-01-	0	
1866	....	?	LLAIMA (Chile-C)	1507-11=	2	
1866	01 ?	?	CAMEROON, MT. (Africa-W)	0204-01=	2	
1866	01	113m	TURRIALBA (Costa Rica)	1405-07=	3	-/7
1866	0126	>3yr	SANTORINI (Greece)	0102-04=	2	8/-
1866	0304	850w	COLIMA VOLC COMPLEX (Mexico)	1401-04=	0	
@ 1866	0314	?	PAVLOF (Alaska Peninsula)	1102-03-	2	
1866	0427	110e	IZALCO (El Salvador)	1403-03=	2	
1866	07	?	TENGGER CALDERA [BROMO]	0603-31=	2	
1866	0912	64e	OFU-OLOSEGA (Samoa-SW Pacific)	0404-01=	2	
1866	0918	?	GEDE (Java)	0603-06=	2	
1866	0921	5a	COTOPAXI (Ecuador)	1502-05=	2	
1867	Cont	....	STROMBOLI (Italy)	0101-04=	1?	
1867	Cont	....	SANTORINI (Greece)	0102-04=	2	8/-
1867	Cont	....	BAGANA (Bougainville-SW Pac)	0505-02=	2?	
1867	Cont	....	YASUR (Vanuatu-SW Pacific)	0507-10=	2	
1867	Cont	....	MERAPI (Java)	0603-25=	2	7/7
1867	Cont	....	KILAUEA (Hawaiian Is)	1302-01-	0	
1867	Cont	....	COLIMA VOLC COMPLEX (Mexico)	1401-04=	0	
1867	Cont	....	GALERAS (Colombia)	1501-08=	2	7/6
1867	Cont	....	SANGAY (Ecuador)	1502-09=	2	
1867	Cont	....	OLCA-PARUMA (Chile-N)	1505-05=		
1867	....	?	CAMPI FLEGREI MAR SICILIA (Italy)	0101-07=	0	
1867	....	?	UNNAMED (Taiwan-N of)	0801-04=	0	
1867	....	?	AKITA-YAKE-YAMA (Honshu-Japan)	0803-26=		
? 1867	....	?	MAKUSHIN (Aleutian Is)	1101-31-		
1867	....	?	AKUTAN (Aleutian Is)	1101-32-		
1867	....	?	ILIAMNA (Alaska-SW)	1103-02-	2	
? 1867	....	?	FUEGO (Guatemala)	1402-09=	2	
1867	....	?	COTOPAXI (Ecuador)	1502-05=	2	
1867?	....	?	COPAHUE (Chile-C)	1507-09=	2?	
? 1867	....	365y	VILLARRICA (Chile-C)	1507-12=		
1867	01	?	IYA (Lesser Sunda Is)	0604-11=	2	
? 1867	03	?	BAKER (US-Washington)	1201-01=		
? 1867	03	?	BARVA (Costa Rica)	1405-05=		
1867	04	138m	IZALCO (El Salvador)	1403-03=	2	
1867	0412	?	NIUAFO'OU (Tonga-SW Pacific)	0403-11=	1	
1867	0415e	30m	SEMERU (Java)	0603-30=	2	
1867	0524	4a	UBINAS (Peru)	1504-02=	2	
1867	0601	7a	TERCEIRA (Azores)	1802-05=	3	
1867	0829	?	GRIMSVOTN (Iceland-NE)	1703-01=	1	
1867	0908	?	SHIKOTSU [TARUMAI] (Hokkaido)	0805-04=	2	
1867	1021	?	ZAO (Honshu-Japan)	0803-19=	2	
1867	1114	16a	NEGRO, CERRO (Nicaragua)	1404-07=	2	
1867	1115	....	VESUVIUS (Italy)	0101-02=	1	6/-
1867	12	31p	TJORNES [MANAREYJAR]	1703-10=		
1867	1213	30a	TENGGER CALDERA [BROMO]	0603-31=	2	
1867	1214	64a>	SAN MIGUEL (El Salvador)	1403-10=	2	
1868	Cont	....	STROMBOLI (Italy)	0101-04=	1?	
1868	Cont	....	SANTORINI (Greece)	0102-04=	2	8/-
1868	Cont	....	BAGANA (Bougainville-SW Pac)	0505-02=	2?	
1868	Cont	....	YASUR (Vanuatu-SW Pacific)	0507-10=	2	
1868	Cont	....	TENGGER CALDERA [BROMO]	0603-31=	2	
1868	Cont	....	COLIMA VOLC COMPLEX (Mexico)	1401-04=	0	
1868	Cont	....	SAN MIGUEL (El Salvador)	1403-10=	2	
1868	Cont	....	GALERAS (Colombia)	1501-08=	2	7/6
1868	Cont	....	SANGAY (Ecuador)	1502-09=	2	
? 1868	Cont	....	VILLARRICA (Chile-C)	1507-12=		
1868	Cont	....	TJORNES [MANAREYJAR]	1703-10=		
1868	....	?	CAMEROON, MT. (Africa-W)	0204-01=	2	
1868?	....	?	DUKONO (Halmahera-Indonesia)	0608-01=	2	
1868	....	?	ISLUGA (Chile-N)	1505-03=	2?	
1868	0216	1a	IZALCO (El Salvador)	1403-03=	2	
1868	0228m	?	OKINAWA-TORI-SHIMA (Ryukyu Is)	0802-02=	1	
1868	03	?	FOURNAISE, PITON DE LA (Indian O.)	0303-02=	0	
1868	0313	<1	GAMALAMA (Halmahera-Indonesia)	0608-06=	1	
1868	0319	3a	GUAGUA PICHINCHA (Ecuador)	1502-02=	2	
1868	0327	26a	MAUNA LOA (Hawaiian Is)	1302-02=	0	8/-
1868	0402?	?	KILAUEA (Hawaiian Is)	1302-01-	1?	5/-
1868	0407	....	MAUNA LOA (Hawaiian Is)	1302-02=	2	8/-
1868	0504	?	IYA (Lesser Sunda Is)	0604-11=	2	
1868	0713<	?	LEWOTOBI (Lesser Sunda Is)	0604-18=	2	
1868	08	?	GUAGUA PICHINCHA (Ecuador)	1502-02=	2	
1868	0815	3a	COTOPAXI (Ecuador)	1502-05=	2	
1868	09	?	LLULLAILLACO (Chile-N)	1505-11=	0	
1868	10	260w	KABA (Sumatra)	0601-22=	2	
1868	1113	90a	GAMALAMA (Halmahera-Indonesia)	0608-06=	2	
1868	1115	....	VESUVIUS (Italy)	0101-02=	2	6/-
1868	1126	12a	ETNA (Italy)	0101-06=	3	
1868	1215	?	LEWOTOBI (Lesser Sunda Is)	0604-18=	2	
1868	1217	?	MAYON (Luzon-Philippines)	0703-03=	2	
? 1868	1231y	?	OSHIMA (Izu Is-Japan)	0804-01=		
1869	Cont	....	STROMBOLI (Italy)	0101-04=	1?	
1869	Cont	....	SANTORINI (Greece)	0102-04=	2	8/-
1869	Cont	....	BAGANA (Bougainville-SW Pac)	0505 02=	2?	
1869	Cont	....	YASUR (Vanuatu-SW Pacific)	0507-10=	2	
1869	Cont	....	KABA (Sumatra)	0601-22=	2	
1869	Cont	....	GAMALAMA (Halmahera-Indonesia)	0608-06=	2	
1869	Cont	....	KILAUEA (Hawaiian Is)	1302-01-	0	
1869?	....	?	FOURNAISE, PITON DE LA (Indian O.)	0303-02=	2?	

	START YEAR	M-Dy	Duration	VOLCANO NAME (Subregion)	NUMBER	VEI	Vol L/T
	1869	....	?	TONGARIRO (New Zealand)	0401-08=	2	
	1869	....	?	GORELY (Kamchatka)	1000-07=	2	
?	1869	....	?	HOOD (US-Oregon)	1202-01-		
	1869	....	....	SANGAY (Ecuador)	1502-09=	3	
?	1869	....	?	PLANCHON-PETEROA (Chile-C)	1507-04=		
	1869	....	?	ANTUCO (Chile-C)	1507-08=	2	
	1869	....	?	OSORNO (Chile-S)	1508-01=	2	
	1869	0204	....	VILLARRICA (Chile-C)	1507-12=	2	
	1869	03	?	TINAKULA (Santa Cruz Is-SW Pac)	0506-01=	2	
	1869	03	?	GUAGUA PICHINCHA (Ecuador)	1502-02=	2	
	1869	0301?	109a>	IZALCO (El Salvador)	1403-03=	2	
	1869	04	?	LLAIMA (Chile-C)	1507-11=	2?	
	1869	0406	28a	LAMONGAN (Java)	0603-32=	2	
	1869	05	153p	ASAMA (Honshu-Japan)	0803-11=	2	
@	1869	0506	?	SMITH ROCK (Izu Is-Japan)	0804-08=	0	
	1869	0528	201m?	MERAPI (Java)	0603-25=	2	7/-
?	1869	06	?	BAKER (US-Washington)	1201-01=		
	1869	0612	?	COLIMA VOLC COMPLEX (Mexico)	1401-04=	3	8/-
	1869	0615	....	GALERAS (Colombia)	1501-08=	3	7/6
	1869	07	31p	COTOPAXI (Ecuador)	1502-05=	3	
	1869	0707	20a	LEWOTOBI (Lesser Sunda Is)	0604-18=	2	
	1869	0722	33a	GUAGUA PICHINCHA (Ecuador)	1502-02=	2	
	1869	08	?	TONGARIRO [NGAURUHOE] (New Z)	0401-08=	2	
	1869	08	?	ISLUGA (Chile-N)	1505-03=	2	
?	1869	09	?	MISTI, EL (Peru)	1504-01=	2	
	1869	0912	?	LAMONGAN (Java)	0603-32=	2	
	1869	0926	<1	ETNA (Italy)	0101-06=	0	6/-
	1869	10	?	UBINAS (Peru)	1504-02=	2	
	1869	1004	43m	PURACE (Colombia)	1501-06=	3?	
	1870	Cont	....	STROMBOLI (Italy)	0101-04=	1?	
	1870	Cont	....	SANTORINI (Greece)	0102-04=	2	8/-
	1870	Cont	....	BAGANA (Bougainville-SW Pac)	0505-02=	2?	
	1870	Cont	....	YASUR (Vanuatu-SW Pacific)	0507-10=	2	
	1870	Cont	....	KILAUEA (Hawaiian Is)	1302-01-	0	
	1870	Cont	....	GALERAS (Colombia)	1501-08=	2	7/6
	1870	Cont	....	SANGAY (Ecuador)	1502-09=	2	
A	1870?	....	?	AOBA (Vanuatu-SW Pacific)	0507-03=	2?	
?	1870	....	?	AMBRYM (Vanuatu-SW Pacific)	0507-04=		
	1870	....	?	ILIWERUNG (Lesser Sunda Is)	0604-25-	3	
	1870	....	?	OSHIMA (Izu Is-Japan)	0804-01=	2	
	1870	....	?	SMITH ROCK (Izu Is-Japan)	0804-08=	1?	
	1870	....	?	BAKER (US-Washington)	1201-01=	2	
?	1870	....	?	RAINIER (US-Washington)	1201-03=	2	
	1870	....	365y	COLIMA VOLC COMPLEX (Mexico)	1401-04=	0	
	1870	....	?	MOMOTOMBO (Nicaragua)	1404-09=	2?	
	1870	....	>3yr	COTOPAXI (Ecuador)	1502-05=	2	
?	1870	....	?	SAN PEDRO (Chile-N)	1505-07=		
?	1870	0101?	14a	MAUNA LOA (Hawaiian Is)	1302-02=	0	
?	1870	0201p	?	FOURNAISE, PITON DE LA (Indian O.)	0303-02=	0	
	1870	0221	>3yr	CEBORUCO, VOLCAN (Mexico)	1401-03=	3	9/8
?	1870	03	?	MISTI, EL (Peru)	1504-01=	2	
	1870	0302	3a	LAMONGAN (Java)	0603-32=	2	
	1870	04	123m	TONGARIRO [NGAURUHOE] (New Z)	0401-08=	2	
	1870	05	?	SMITH ROCK (Izu Is-Japan)	0804-08=	2	
?	1870	0519	?	IZALCO (El Salvador)	1403-03=	2?	
	1870	0620d	105d	RAOUL ISLAND (Kermadec Is)	0402-03=	3	-/7
	1870	08	48m	GEDE (Java)	0603-06=	2	
	1870	0818	171b	LAMONGAN (Java)	0603-32=	2	
	1870	0827	1a	RUANG (Sangihe Is-Indonesia)	0607-01=	3?	
	1870	10	?	PURACE (Colombia)	1501-06=	2	
	1870	1201	563m	VESUVIUS (Italy)	0101-02=	2	7/7
	1871	Cont	....	VESUVIUS (Italy)	0101-02=	2	7/7
	1871	Cont	....	STROMBOLI (Italy)	0101-04=	1?	
	1871	Cont	....	BAGANA (Bougainville-SW Pac)	0505-02=	2?	
	1871	Cont	....	YASUR (Vanuatu-SW Pacific)	0507-10=	2	
	1871	Cont	....	LAMONGAN (Java)	0603-32=	2	
	1871	Cont	....	KILAUEA (Hawaiian Is)	1302-01-	0	
	1871	Cont	....	CEBORUCO, VOLCAN (Mexico)	1401-03=	2	9/8
	1871	Cont	....	COLIMA VOLC COMPLEX (Mexico)	1401-04=	0	
	1871	Cont	....	COTOPAXI (Ecuador)	1502-05=	2	
	1871	Cont	....	SANGAY (Ecuador)	1502-09=	2	
	1871	....	?	NISYROS (Greece)	0102-05=	2	
	1871c	....	?	BARRIER, THE (Africa-E)	0202-03=	2	
	1871	....	?	CAMEROON, MT. (Africa-W)	0204-01=	2	
	1871	....	?	TINAKULA (Santa Cruz Is-SW Pac)	0506-01=	2?	
	1871	....	?	AMBRYM (Vanuatu-SW Pacific)	0507-04=	2	
@	1871	....	?	SMITH ROCK (Izu Is-Japan)	0804-08=	0	
T	1871s	....	?	DECEPTION ISLAND (Antarctica)	1900-03=		
	1871	0130	?	REVENTADOR (Ecuador)	1502-01=	2	
	1871	0302	12a	RUANG (Sangihe Is-Indonesia)	0607-01=	2	
?	1871	04	?	NIKKO-SHIRANE (Honshu-Japan)	0803-14=		
	1871	04	?	TORI-SHIMA (Izu Is-Japan)	0804-09=	0	
	1871	0424	?	MARAPI (Sumatra)	0601-14=	2?	
	1871	0430	>3yr	HIBOK-HIBOK (Mindanao-Philippines)	0701-08=	2	8/-
	1871	0621	14a	FOURNAISE, PITON DE LA (Indian O.)	0303-02=	0	
	1871	0807	49a	GAMALAMA (Halmahera-Indonesia)	0608-06=	2	
	1871	0810	20a?	MAUNA LOA (Hawaiian Is)	1302-02=	0	7/-
	1871	0901	?	IYA (Lesser Sunda Is)	0604-11=	2	
	1871	0924	?	MARAPI (Sumatra)	0601-14=	2?	
	1871	1208<	?	RAGANG (Mindanao-Philippines)	0701-06=	2	
	1871	1208	39m	MAYON (Luzon-Philippines)	0703-03=	3	
?	1871	1225	3a	SHIKOTSU [TARUMAI] (Hokkaido)	0805-04=	2	
	1872	Cont	....	STROMBOLI (Italy)	0101-04=	1?	
	1872	Cont	....	BAGANA (Bougainville-SW Pac)	0505-02=	2?	
	1872	Cont	....	YASUR (Vanuatu-SW Pacific)	0507-10=	2	
	1872	Cont	....	HIBOK-HIBOK (Mindanao-Philippines)	0701-08=	2	8/-
	1872	Cont	....	KILAUEA (Hawaiian Is)	1302-01-	0	

	START YEAR	M-Dy	Duration	VOLCANO NAME (Subregion)	NUMBER	VEI	Vol L/T
	1872	Cont	....	CEBORUCO, VOLCAN (Mexico)	1401-03=	2	9/8
	1872	Cont	....	COTOPAXI (Ecuador)	1502-05=	2	
	1872	....	?	KARTHALA (Indian O.-W)	0303-01=	2	
	1872d	....	?	BAM (New Guinea-NE of)	0501-01=	3	
	1872	....	>3yr	SINARKA (Kurile Is)	0900-29=	4	7/-
?	1872	....	?	PLANCHON-PETEROA (Chile-C)	1507-04=		
	1872	....	?	CHILLAN, NEVADOS DE (Chile-C)	1507-07=		
@	1872?	....	?	BARDARBUNGA (Iceland-NE)	1703-03=		
?	1872	0201p	?	FOURNAISE, PITON DE LA (Indian O.)	0303-02=	0	
	1872	0226	....	COLIMA VOLC COMPLEX (Mexico)	1401-04=	3	
	1872	0415	5	MERAPI (Java)	0603-25=	4	-/8
	1872	0424	....	VESUVIUS (Italy)	0101-02=	3	7/7
	1872	05	....	SANGAY (Ecuador)	1502-09=	2	
	1872	0514	?	NIKKO-SHIRANE (Honshu-Japan)	0803-14=	2	
	1872	0606	?	LLAIMA (Chile-C)	1507-11=	2	
	1872	0606	?	QUETRUPILLAN (Chile-C)	1507-121	2?	
	1872	0809	37m?	MAUNA LOA (Hawaiian Is)	1302-02=	1	
	1872	0815	34a	LAMONGAN (Java)	0603-32=	2	
	1872	0905	4a	MAYON (Luzon-Philippines)	0703-03=	1	
	1872	1023	<1	SEMERU (Java)	0603-30=	2	
	1872	1103	74m?	MERAPI (Java)	0603-25=	2	
	1872	12	92m>	IZALCO (El Salvador)	1403-03=	2	
	1872	12	....	SANGAY (Ecuador)	1502-09=	2	
	1872	1201	189a	ASO (Kyushu-Japan)	0802-11=	2	
	1873	Cont	....	STROMBOLI (Italy)	0101-04=	1?	
	1873	Cont	....	BAGANA (Bougainville-SW Pac)	0505-02=	2?	
	1873	Cont	....	YASUR (Vanuatu-SW Pacific)	0507-10=	2	
	1873	Cont	....	MERAPI (Java)	0603-25=	2	
	1873	Cont	....	HIBOK-HIBOK (Mindanao-Philippines)	0701-08=	2	8/-
	1873	Cont	....	SINARKA (Kurile Is)	0900-29=	1	7/-
	1873	Cont	....	KILAUEA (Hawaiian Is)	1302-01-	0	
	1873	Cont	....	CEBORUCO, VOLCAN (Mexico)	1401-03=	2	9/8
	1873	Cont	....	COLIMA VOLC COMPLEX (Mexico)	1401-04=	1	
	1873	Cont	....	IZALCO (El Salvador)	1403-03=	2	
	1873	Cont	....	COTOPAXI (Ecuador)	1502-05=	2	
?	1873	....	?	ERTA ALE (Ethiopia)	0201-08=	2	
	1873	....	>3yr	KABA (Sumatra)	0601-22=	2	
	1873	....	?	LEREBOLENG (Lesser Sunda Is)	0604-20=	2	
	1873	....	?	TAAL (Luzon-Philippines)	0703-07=	2	
?	1873	....	?	SMITH ROCK (Izu Is-Japan)	0804-08=	0	
	1873?	....	?	PAGAN (Mariana Is-C Pac)	0804-17=	3?	
	1873	....	?	SEMISOPOCHNOI (Aleutian Is)	1101-06-		
	1873	....	?	GARELOI (Aleutian Is)	1101-07-	2?	
?	1873	....	?	YUNASKA (Aleutian Is)	1101-21-	2?	
	1873	0106	1a?	MAUNA LOA (Hawaiian Is)	1302-02=	0	
	1873	0108	219m	GRIMSVOTN (Iceland-NE)	1703-01=	4	-/8
	1873	0116	89m	RAGANG (Mindanao-Philippines)	0701-06=	2	
	1873	0301	....	ASO (Kyushu-Japan)	0802-11=	3	
	1873	0312	?	NIKKO-SHIRANE (Honshu-Japan)	0803-14=	2	
	1873	0420	547a?	MAUNA LOA (Hawaiian Is)	1302-02=	1	
	1873	0620	32a	MAYON (Luzon-Philippines)	0703-03=	2	
	1873	08	30p	ZAO (Honshu-Japan)	0803-19=	1?	
	1873	09	>3yr	VULCANO (Italy)	0101-05=	3	
	1873	0911	15a	NISYROS (Greece)	0102-05=	2	
	1873	11	....	SANGAY (Ecuador)	1502-09=	2	
	1874	Cont	....	VULCANO (Italy)	0101-05=	2	
	1874	Cont	....	BAGANA (Bougainville-SW Pac)	0505-02=	2?	
	1874	Cont	....	YASUR (Vanuatu-SW Pacific)	0507-10=	2	
	1874	Cont	....	KABA (Sumatra)	0601-22=	2	
	1874	Cont	....	HIBOK-HIBOK (Mindanao-Philippines)	0701-08=	2	8/-
	1874	Cont	....	SINARKA (Kurile Is)	0900-29=	1	7/-
	1874	Cont	....	KILAUEA (Hawaiian Is)	1302-01-	0	
	1874	Cont	....	MAUNA LOA (Hawaiian Is)	1302-02=	1	
	1874	Cont	....	CEBORUCO, VOLCAN (Mexico)	1401-03=	2	9/8
	1874	Cont	....	COTOPAXI (Ecuador)	1502-05=	2	
	1874	Cont	....	SANGAY (Ecuador)	1502-09=	2	
	1874	....	?	LOPEVI (Vanuatu-SW Pacific)	0507-05=	2	
	1874?	....	?	KERINCI (Sumatra)	0601-17=	2?	
	1874?	....	551w?	FARALLON DE PAJAROS (Mariana Is)	0804-14=	2	
	1874	....	?	E-SAN (Hokkaido-Japan)	0805-011		
	1874	....	?	SANTA ANA (El Salvador)	1403-02=	3	
?	1874	....	365y	IZALCO (El Salvador)	1403-03=		
?	1874	....	?	LLAIMA (Chile-C)	1507-11=		
	1874	0201p	?	FOURNAISE, PITON DE LA (Indian O.)	0303-02=		
	1874	0207	?	ASO (Kyushu-Japan)	0802-11=	2	
	1874	0208	8a	SHIKOTSU [TARUMAI] (Hokkaido)	0805-04=	2	-/7
	1874	0216R	....	SHIKOTSU [TARUMAI] (Hokkaido)	0805-04=	3	-/7
	1874	04	?	VILLARRICA (Chile-C)	1507-12=	1?	
	1874	05	106m	ETNA (Italy)	0101-06=	2	
	1874	0520	?	BAM (New Guinea-NE of)	0501-01=	2	
	1874	0520	93a	LAMONGAN (Java)	0603-32=	2	
	1874	06	?	STROMBOLI (Italy)	0101-04=	2	
	1874	0612	?	COLIMA VOLC COMPLEX (Mexico)	1401-04=	1	
	1874	0629	131a>	FOURNAISE, PITON DE LA (Indian O.)	0303-02=	2	
	1874	0703	14a?	MIYAKE-JIMA (Izu Is-Japan)	0804-04=	3	
	1874	0715q	?	VENIAMINOF (Alaska Peninsula)	1102-07-	2?	
	1874	0719	?	TAAL (Luzon-Philippines)	0703-07=	2	
	1874	0829	2a	ETNA (Italy)	0101-06=	2	6/6
	1874	1115	?	RUANG (Sangihe Is-Indonesia)	0607-01=	2	
	1875	Cont	....	STROMBOLI (Italy)	0101-04=	1?	
	1875	Cont	....	VULCANO (Italy)	0101-05=	2	
	1875	Cont	....	BAGANA (Bougainville-SW Pac)	0505-02=	2?	
	1875	Cont	....	YASUR (Vanuatu-SW Pacific)	0507-10=	2	
	1875	Cont	....	KABA (Sumatra)	0601-22=	2	
	1875	Cont	....	HIBOK-HIBOK (Mindanao-Philippin	0701-08=	2	8/-
	1875	Cont	....	FARALLON DE PAJAROS (Mariana Is)	0804-14=	2	
	1875	Cont	....	SINARKA (Kurile Is)	0900-29=	1	7/-
	1875	Cont	....	KILAUEA (Hawaiian Is)	1302-01-	0	

START YEAR	START M-Dy	Duration	VOLCANO NAME (Subregion)	NUMBER	VEI	Vol L/T
1875	Cont	....	CEBORUCO, VOLCAN (Mexico)	1401-03=	2	9/8
? 1875	Cont	....	IZALCO (El Salvador)	1403-03=		
1875	Cont	....	COTOPAXI (Ecuador)	1502-05=	2	
1875	Cont	....	SANGAY (Ecuador)	1502-09=	2	
1875	....	>3yr	COLIMA VOLC COMPLEX (Mexico)	1401-04=	1	
1875e	....	?	IRAZU (Costa Rica)	1405-06=	2	
1875	....	?	LASCAR (Chile-N)	1505-10=	2	
1875	....	365y	LLAIMA (Chile-C)	1507-11=	2	
1875	0101	289a	ASKJA (Iceland-NE)	1703-06=	2	-/8
1875	0110	30a?	MAUNA LOA (Hawaiian Is)	1302-02=	0	
1875	0329	....	ASKJA (Iceland-NE)	1703-06=	4	-/8
1875	0529<	6d>	SLAMET (Java)	0603-18=	2	
1875	0614	?	ASAMA (Honshu-Japan)	0803-11=	2	
1875	08	16m	AWU (Sangihe Is-Indonesia)	0607-04=	2	
1875	0811	7a?	MAUNA LOA (Hawaiian Is)	1302-02=	0	
? 1875	1001t	?	TONGARIRO [NGAURUHOE] (New Z)	0401-08=	2	
1875	1102b	54f	SLAMET (Java)	0603-18=	2	
1875	1117	365y	VILLARRICA (Chile-C)	1507-12=	2?	
1875	1126	15a	FOURNAISE, PITON DE LA (Indian O.)	0303-02=	0	
1875	1218	>3yr	VESUVIUS (Italy)	0101-02=	2	8/8
1876	Cont	....	VESUVIUS (Italy)	0101-02=	2	8/8
1876	Cont	....	STROMBOLI (Italy)	0101-04=	1?	
1876	Cont	....	BAGANA (Bougainville-SW Pac)	0505-02=	2?	
1876	Cont	....	YASUR (Vanuatu-SW Pacific)	0507-10=	2	
1876	Cont	....	KABA (Sumatra)	0601-22=	2	
1876	Cont	....	FARALLON DE PAJAROS (Mariana Is)	0804-14=	2	
1876	Cont	....	SINARKA (Kurile Is)	0900-29=	1	7/-
1876	Cont	....	KILAUEA (Hawaiian Is)	1302-01-	0	
1876	Cont	....	COLIMA VOLC COMPLEX (Mexico)	1401-04=	1	
1876	Cont	....	COTOPAXI (Ecuador)	1502-05=	2	
1876	Cont	....	SANGAY (Ecuador)	1502-09=	2	
1876	Cont	....	LLAIMA (Chile-C)	1507-11=	2	
1876	Cont	....	VILLARRICA (Chile-C)	1507-12=	2?	
1876	....	....	VULCANO (Italy)	0101-05=	3	
1876	....	?	KARTHALA (Indian O.-W)	0303-01=	0	
1876?	....	?	TALANG (Sumatra)	0601-16=	2	
1876	....	?	LEREBOLENG (Lesser Sunda Is)	0604-20=	2	
? 1876	....	?	AMUKTA (Aleutian Is)	1101-19-		
1876	....	?	ILIAMNA (Alaska-SW)	1103-02-	3	
1876	0213	1a	MAUNA LOA (Hawaiian Is)	1302-02=	0	
1876	04 ?	?	MAYON (Luzon-Philippines)	0703-03=		
1876	0404	?	MARAPI (Sumatra)	0601-14=	2?	
1876	08	303p	MARAPI (Sumatra)	0601-14=	2?	
1876	0923	3a	SHIRETOKO-IWO-ZAN (Hokkaido)	0805-09=	2	
1876	1126	<1	MAYON (Luzon-Philippines)	0703-03=	1	
? 1876	1210	?	UNNAMED (Antarctica)	1900-051	0	
1876	1211	<1	FOURNAISE, PITON DE LA (Indian O.)	0303-02=		
1876	1227	40a	OSHIMA (Izu Is-Japan)	0804-01=	2	6/6
1877	Cont	....	VESUVIUS (Italy)	0101-02=	2	8/8
1877	Cont	....	STROMBOLI (Italy)	0101-04=	1?	
1877	Cont	....	VULCANO (Italy)	0101-05=	2	
1877	Cont	....	BAGANA (Bougainville-SW Pac)	0505-02=	2?	
1877	Cont	....	YASUR (Vanuatu-SW Pacific)	0507-10=	2	
1877	Cont	....	MARAPI (Sumatra)	0601-14=	2?	
1877	Cont	....	KABA (Sumatra)	0601-22=	2	
1877	Cont	....	OSHIMA (Izu Is-Japan)	0804-01=	2	6/6
1877	Cont	....	SINARKA (Kurile Is)	0900-29=	1	7/-
1877	Cont	....	KILAUEA (Hawaiian Is)	1302-01-	0	
1877	Cont	....	COLIMA VOLC COMPLEX (Mexico)	1401-04=	1	
1877	Cont	....	SANGAY (Ecuador)	1502-09=	2	
1877	....	?	FALCON ISLAND (Tonga-SW Pacific)	0403-05=	2	
1877	....	?	SUWANOSE-JIMA (Ryukyu Is)	0802-03=	4	
1877	....	?	KLIUCHEVSKOI (Kamchatka)	1000-26=	2	
1877	....	?	ISLUGA (Chile-N)	1505-03=	2?	
1877?	....	?	SAN PEDRO (Chile-N)	1505-07=	2	
1877	....	?	CHILLAN, NEVADOS DE (Chile-C)	1507-07=		
1877	01	230m	COTOPAXI (Ecuador)	1502-05=	2	7/8
1877	0116	159a	LLAIMA (Chile-C)	1507-11=	2	
1877	0214	10a	MAUNA LOA (Hawaiian Is)	1302-02=	0	6/-
1877	04	?	SEMERU (Java)	0603-30=	2	
1877	0424?	?	TENGGER CALDERA [BROMO]	0603-31=	2	
1877	0424?	18a?	LAMONGAN (Java)	0603-32=	2	
1877	05	?	LLULLAILLACO (Chile-N)	1505-11=	2	
1877	0511	....	LAMONGAN (Java)	0603-32=	3?	
1877	0511	....	COTOPAXI (Ecuador)	1502-05=	2	7/8
1877	0512	?	VILLARRICA (Chile-C)	1507-12=	2	
1877	0531	....	COTOPAXI (Ecuador)	1502-05=	2	7/8
1877	0626	....	COTOPAXI (Ecuador)	1502-05=	4	7/8
1877	09	?	SEMERU (Java)	0603-30=	2	
1877	1029	15a>	MANAM (New Guinea-NE of)	0501-02=	2	
1877	1113	?	BAM (New Guinea-NE of)	0501-01=	3	
1877	12	?	CUMBAL (Colombia)	1501-10=	2	
1878	Cont	....	VESUVIUS (Italy)	0101-02=	2	8/8
1878	Cont	....	STROMBOLI (Italy)	0101-04=	1?	
1878	Cont	....	VULCANO (Italy)	0101-05=	2	
1878	Cont	....	BAGANA (Bougainville-SW Pac)	0505-02=	2?	
1878	Cont	....	KABA (Sumatra)	0601-22=	2	
1878	Cont	....	SINARKA (Kurile Is)	0900-29=	1	7/-
1878	Cont	....	KILAUEA (Hawaiian Is)	1302-01-	0	
1878	Cont	....	COLIMA VOLC COMPLEX (Mexico)	1401-04=	1	
1878	Cont	....	SANGAY (Ecuador)	1502-09=	2	
1878a	....	?	MERU (Africa-E)	0202-16=	2	
1878	....	?	METIS SHOAL (Tonga-SW Pacific)	0403-07=	2	
1878	....	?	LANGILA (New Britain-SW Pac)	0502-01=	2	
1878	....	?	ULAWUN (New Britain-SW Pac)	0502-12=	2	
1878<	....	....	YASUR (Vanuatu-SW Pacific)	0507-10=	3	
1878	....	355w	MERAPI (Java)	0603-25=	2	
1878	....	?	SEMERU (Java)	0603-30=	2	
? 1878	....	?	ASAMA (Honshu-Japan)	0803-11=	2	
1878	....	?	AVACHINSKY (Kamchatka)	1000-10=	2	
1878	....	?	AMUKTA (Aleutian Is)	1101-19-		
1878	....	?	VSEVIDOF (Aleutian Is)	1101-27-	2	
1878	....	?	OKMOK (Aleutian Is)	1101-29-	2?	
1878	....	?	TACANA (Mexico)	1401-13=	1	
? 1878	....	?	SANTA ANA (El Salvador)	1403-02=	2	
1878	....	?	IZALCO (El Salvador)	1403-03=		
1878	....	?	PLANCHON-PETEROA (Chile-C)	1507-04=	2	
? 1878	0118	?	LAUTARO (Chile-S)	1508-06=	1	
? 1878	0129	?	UNNAMED (Atlantic-C)	1805-02=	0	
1878	0130?	27b?	RABAUL (New Britain-SW Pac)	0502-14=	3	-/8
1878	02	?	ISLUGA (Chile-N)	1505-03=	2	
1878	0227	47m	HEKLA [KRAKAGIGAR] (Iceland-S)	1702-07=	2	8/-
1878	0314	16a	FOURNAISE, PITON DE LA (Indian O.)	0303-02=	0	
1878	0823	1a	COTOPAXI (Ecuador)	1502-05=	2	
1878	0831	?	PURACE (Colombia)	1501-06=	2	
1878	09	?	KLIUCHEVSKOI (Kamchatka)	1000-26=	2	
1878	0901u	?	TONGARIRO [NGAURUHOE] (New Z)	0401-08=	2	
? 1878	1002	?	TECAPA (El Salvador)	1403-08=		
1878	1014?	?	MOMOTOMBO (Nicaragua)	1404-09=	2	
1878	1112	3a	TAAL (Luzon-Philippines)	0703-07=	2	
1878	1211	?	KERINCI (Sumatra)	0601-17=	2	
1878	1223	>3yr	ETNA (Italy)	0101-06=	2	
? 1878	1231p	?	RITTER ISLAND (New Guinea-NE of)	0501-07=		
1879	Cont	....	VESUVIUS (Italy)	0101-02=	2	8/8
1879	Cont	....	VULCANO (Italy)	0101-05=	2	
1879	Cont	....	BAGANA (Bougainville-SW Pac)	0505-02=	2?	
1879	Cont	....	YASUR (Vanuatu-SW Pacific)	0507-10=	2	
1879	Cont	....	KABA (Sumatra)	0601-22=	2	
1879	Cont	....	MERAPI (Java)	0603-25=	2	
1879	....	?	SORIKMARAPI (Sumatra)	0601-12=	2	
1879	....	?	SEMERU (Java)	0603-30=	2	
1879	....	?	KLIUCHEVSKOI (Kamchatka)	1000-26=	2	
1879	....	>3yr	SHEVELUCH (Kamchatka)	1000-27=	2	
? 1879	....	?	RAINIER (US-Washington)	1201-03-	2	
? 1879	....	?	POAS (Costa Rica)	1405-04=	1	
@ 1879	....	?	LAUTARO (Chile-S)	1508-06=		
1879	0115q	?	SARYCHEV PEAK (Kurile Is)	0900-24=	0	
1879	0201p	?	SANTA ANA (El Salvador)	1403-02=	2	
1879	0202	?	VILLARRICA (Chile-C)	1507-12=	2	
1879	0205	?	STROMBOLI (Italy)	0101-04=	2	
1879	0226	113a	COTOPAXI (Ecuador)	1502-05=	2	
1879	0309	<1	MAUNA LOA (Hawaiian Is)	1302-02=	0	6/-
1879	05	31p	CHIRPOI (Kurile Is)	0900-15=	2	
1879	0518	?	DEMPO (Sumatra)	0601-23=	2	
1879	0526	12a	ETNA (Italy)	0101-06=	3	7/7
1879	0530?	16e?	REYKJANESHRYGGUR (Iceland-SW)	1701-01=	1	
1879	0603	5a	STROMBOLI (Italy)	0101-04=	2	
1879	0714	....	KILAUEA (Hawaiian Is)	1302-01-	0	
1879	0927	1a	ASAMA (Honshu-Japan)	0803-11=	2	
1879	12	....	SANGAY (Ecuador)	1502-09=	2	
1879	1223	129a	COLIMA VOLC COMPLEX (Mexico)	1401-04=	1	
1879	1225	80m	IZALCO (El Salvador)	1403-03=	2	
1879	1231	87e	ILOPANGO (El Salvador)	1403-06=	0	8/-
1880	Cont	....	VESUVIUS (Italy)	0101-02=	2	8/8
1880	Cont	....	STROMBOLI (Italy)	0101-04=	1?	
1880	Cont	....	ETNA (Italy)	0101-06=	2	
1880	Cont	....	BAGANA (Bougainville-SW Pac)	0505-02=	2?	
1880	Cont	....	YASUR (Vanuatu-SW Pacific)	0507-10=	2	
1880	Cont	....	KABA (Sumatra)	0601-22=	2	
1880	Cont	....	SHEVELUCH (Kamchatka)	1000-27=	2	
1880	Cont	....	KILAUEA (Hawaiian Is)	1302-01-	0	
1880	Cont	....	COLIMA VOLC COMPLEX (Mexico)	1401-04=	1	
1880	Cont	....	IZALCO (El Salvador)	1403-03=	2	
1880	....	?	KARTHALA (Indian O.-W)	0303-01=	2	
1880r	....	?	TAMBORA (Lesser Sunda Is)	0604-04=	2	
1880	....	?	TONGKOKO (Sulawesi-Indonesia)	0606-13=	1	
? 1880?	....	?	VETERAN (SE Asia)	0705-07-	0	
1880	....	>3yr	KITA-IWO-JIMA (Volcano Is-Japan)	0804-11=	0	
1880	....	?	MENDELEEV (Kurile Is)	0900-02=	1	
? 1880	....	?	VSEVIDOF (Aleutian Is)	1101-27-		
? 1880	....	365y	SHISHALDIN (Aleutian Is)	1101-36-		
1880	....	?	PAVLOF (Alaska Peninsula)	1102-03-		
1880	....	?	POAS (Costa Rica)	1405-04=	1	
? 1880	....	?	SOUFRIERE ST. VINCENT (W Indies)	1600-15=	0	
@ 1880	....	?	SETE CIDADES (Azores)	1802-08=	0	
1880	01	....	SANGAY (Ecuador)	1502-09=	3	
1880	0104	<1	MICOTRIN (W Indies)	1600-10=	2?	
1880	0120	....	ILOPANGO (El Salvador)	1403-06=	3	8/-
1880	02	151p	COTOPAXI (Ecuador)	1502-05=	2	
1880	03	?	SANTA ANA (El Salvador)	1403-02=	3	
1880	05	?	DEMPO (Sumatra)	0601-23=	2	
1880	0501	5a	MAUNA LOA (Hawaiian Is)	1302-02=	1	7/-
1880	0628	53a	FUEGO (Guatemala)	1402-09=	4?	-/8
1880	0703	....	COTOPAXI (Ecuador)	1502-05=	3	
? 1880?	0712	<1	SREDNII (Kurile Is)	0900-211	0	
1880	09	?	KIRISHIMA (Kyushu-Japan)	0802-09=	2	
1880	0907	81a	BAKER (US-Washington)	1201-01=	2	
1880	1105	278a	MAUNA LOA (Hawaiian Is)	1302-02=	1	8/-
? 1880	1124	2a	SHIRETOKO-IWO-ZAN (Hokkaido)	0805-09=		
1880	12	?	LENGAI, OL DOINYO (Africa-E)	0202-12=	2	
1881	Cont	....	ETNA (Italy)	0101-06=	2	
1881	Cont	....	BAGANA (Bougainville-SW Pac)	0505-02=	2?	
1881	Cont	....	YASUR (Vanuatu-SW Pacific)	0507-10=	2	

START YEAR	M-Dy	Duration	VOLCANO NAME (Subregion)	NUMBER	VEI	Vol L/T
1881	*Cont*	....	*KABA (Sumatra)*	0601-22=	*2*	
1881	*Cont*	....	*KITA-IWO-JIMA (Volcano Is-Japan)*	0804-11=	*0*	
1881	*Cont*	....	*SHEVELUCH (Kamchatka)*	1000-27=	*2*	
? *1881*	*Cont*	....	*SHISHALDIN (Aleutian Is)*	1101-36-		
1881	*Cont*	....	*KILAUEA (Hawaiian Is)*	1302-01-	*0*	
1881	*Cont*	....	*MAUNA LOA (Hawaiian Is)*	1302-02=	*0*	*8/-*
1881	*Cont*	....	*SANGAY (Ecuador)*	1502-09=	*2*	
1881	....	?	**TRAITOR'S HEAD** (Vanuatu-SW Pacific)	0507-09=	0	
1881	....	?	**SIBAYAK** (Sumatra)	0601-07=		
? **1881**	....	?	**SINABUNG** (Sumatra)	0601-08=		
1881	....	?	**RAUNG** (Java)	0603-34=		
1881	....	?	**AVACHINSKY** (Kamchatka)	1000-10=	2	
1881	....	?	**PURACE** (Colombia)	1501-06=	2	
? **1881**	....	?	**TUPUNGATITO** (Chile-C)	1507-01=		
1881	....	?	**SAN JOSE** (Chile-C)	1507-02=	2	
1881	0101	?	**IZALCO** (El Salvador)	1403-03=	0	
1881	0216	?	**DEMPO** (Sumatra)	0601-23=	2	
1881	0310	?	**GUAGUA PICHINCHA** (Ecuador)	1502-02=	2	
1881	0316	?	**LEREBOLENG** (Lesser Sunda Is)	0604-20=	2	
1881	0323?	20*a*?	**COLIMA VOLC COMPLEX** (Mexico)	1401-04=	2	
? **1881**	0602	?	**HEARD** (Indian O.-S)	0304-01=	2	
1881	0701	?	**NASU** (Honshu-Japan)	0803-15=	2?	
1881	0706	?	**TONGARIRO [NGAURUHOE]** (New Z)	0401-08=	2	
1881	0706	406*m*	**MAYON** (Luzon-Philippines)	0703-03=	3	
1881	09	?	**GORIASCHAIA SOPKA** (Kurile Is)	0900-17B	2	
1881	1015	3*a*	**STROMBOLI** (Italy)	0101-04=	2	
1881	12	16*m*	**DEMPO** (Sumatra)	0601-23=	2	
1881	*1216*	....	*VESUVIUS (Italy)*	0101-02=	1	*8/8*
1882	*Cont*	....	*VESUVIUS (Italy)*	0101-02=	*2*	*8/8*
1882	*Cont*	....	*ETNA (Italy)*	0101-06=	*2*	
1882	*Cont*	....	*BAGANA (Bougainville-SW Pac)*	0505-02=	*2?*	
1882	*Cont*	....	*YASUR (Vanuatu-SW Pacific)*	0507-10=	*2*	
1882	*Cont*	....	*KABA (Sumatra)*	0601-22=	*2*	
1882	*Cont*	....	*MAYON (Luzon-Philippines)*	0703-03=	*3*	
1882	*Cont*	....	*KITA-IWO-JIMA (Volcano Is-Japan)*	0804-11=	*0*	
1882	*Cont*	....	*SHEVELUCH (Kamchatka)*	1000-27=	*2*	
1882	*Cont*	....	*SANGAY (Ecuador)*	1502-09=	*2*	
1882	....	365*y*	**LENGAI, OL DOINYO** (Africa-E)	0202-12=	2	
1882	....	?	**NYAMURAGIRA** (Africa-C)	0203-02=		
? **1882**	....	?	**FOURNAISE, PITON DE LA** (Indian O.)	0303-02=	0	
1882	....	?	**IYA** (Lesser Sunda Is)	0604-11=	2	
1882	....	?	**ZHUPANOVSKY** (Kamchatka)	1000-12=	2	
? **1882**	....	?	**RAINIER** (US-Washington)	1201-03-	2	
1882	....	730*y*	**COLIMA VOLC COMPLEX** (Mexico)	1401-04=	1	
? **1882**	....	?	**SANTA ANA** (El Salvador)	1403-02=		
? **1882**	....	?	**IRAZU** (Costa Rica)	1405-06=	2	
1882	01	59*p*	**COTOPAXI** (Ecuador)	1502-05=	2	
1882	0401	6*a*	**SUNDORO** (Java)	0603-21=	2	
1882	0712	?	**IZALCO** (El Salvador)	1403-03=	2	
1882	0806	10*a*>	**KUSATSU-SHIRANE** (Honshu-Japan)	0803-12=	2	
1882	09	?	**KLIUCHEVSKOI** (Kamchatka)	1000-26=	2	
1882	*09*	....	*KILAUEA (Hawaiian Is)*	1302-01-	0	
1882	0909	?	**MOMOTOMBO** (Nicaragua)	1404-09=	2?	
1882	1117	13*a*	**STROMBOLI** (Italy)	0101-04=	3	
1882	1205d	?	**SAN MIGUEL** (El Salvador)	1403-10=	2	
1883	*Cont*	....	*VESUVIUS (Italy)*	0101-02=	*2*	*8/8*
1883	*Cont*	....	*STROMBOLI (Italy)*	0101-04=	*1?*	
1883	*Cont*	....	*LENGAI, OL DOINYO (Africa-E)*	0202-12=	*2*	
1883	*Cont*	....	*YASUR (Vanuatu-SW Pacific)*	0507-10=	*2*	
1883	*Cont*	....	*KABA (Sumatra)*	0601-22=	*2*	
1883	*Cont*	....	*KITA-IWO-JIMA (Volcano Is-Japan)*	0804-11=	*0*	
1883	*Cont*	....	*SHEVELUCH (Kamchatka)*	1000-27=	*2*	
1883	*Cont*	....	*KILAUEA (Hawaiian Is)*	1302-01-	*0*	
1883	*Cont*	....	*COLIMA VOLC COMPLEX (Mexico)*	1401-04=	*1*	
1883	*Cont*	....	*SANGAY (Ecuador)*	1502-09=	*2*	
1883	....	?	**TEYR, DJEBEL** (Red Sea)	0201-01=	2	
1883	....	?	**AMBRYM** (Vanuatu-SW Pacific)	0507-04=	2	
1883 a	....	?	**GUGUAN** (Mariana Is-C Pac)	0804-19=	2?	
1883	....	?	**HARIMKOTAN** (Kurile Is)	0900-30=	3	
1883	....	?	**MAKUSHIN** (Aleutian Is)	1101-31-	2	
1883	....	?	**AKUTAN** (Aleutian Is)	1101-32-	2	
1883	....	?	**SHISHALDIN** (Aleutian Is)	1101-36-	2	
1883	....	731*y*	**LASCAR** (Chile-N)	1505-10=	2	
1883	....	?	**CHILLAN, NEVADOS DE** (Chile-C)	1507-07=	2?	
1883	....	?	**LLAIMA** (Chile-C)	1507-11=	2	
1883	....	?	**VILLARRICA** (Chile-C)	1507-12=	2	
1883	0103	?	**IRAZU** (Costa Rica)	1405-06=	2	
1883	0115	90*e*	**GRIMSVOTN** (Iceland-NE)	1703-01=	2	
1883	03	473*w*	**KARTHALA** (Indian O.-W)	0303-01=	2	
? **1883**	03	?	**BAM** (New Guinea-NE of)	0501-01=		
1883	0322	2*a*	**ETNA** (Italy)	0101-06=	2	4/5
1883	0328	?	**ST. ANDREW STRAIT [TULUMAN]**	0500-01=	2	
1883	0405d	86*d*	**CONCEPCION** (Nicaragua)	1404-12=	2	
1883	0413	21*a*	**LAMONGAN** (Java)	0603-32=	2	7/-
1883	0415q	?	**GORIASCHAIA SOPKA** (Kurile Is)	0900-17B	1	7/-
1883	0425e	?	**TONGARIRO [NGAURUHOE]** (New Z)	0401-08=	2	
1883	05	31*p*	**MEDVEZHIA** (Kurile Is)	0900-10=	2	
1883	*0520*	*154a?*	*KRAKATAU (Indonesia)*	0602-00=	3	
1883	0625	....	**MARAPI** (Sumatra)	0601-14=	1	
1883	07	31*p*	**KLIUCHEVSKOI** (Kamchatka)	1000-26=	2	
1883	0725	478*m*	**MERAPI** (Java)	0603-25=	1	
1883	08 ?	?	**SUNDORO** (Java)	0603-21=	2	
1883	08	?	**COTOPAXI** (Ecuador)	1502-05=	2	
1883	0825	1*a*	**KARANGETANG [API SIAU]** (Sangihe	0607-02=	2	
1883	0825	1*a*	**AWU** (Sangihe Is-Indonesia)	0607-04=	2	
1883	0827	....	**KRAKATAU** (Indonesia)	0602-00=	**6**	**-/10**
1883	0905d	69*n*	**IZALCO** (El Salvador)	1403-03=	2	
1883	*0927<*	*>3yr*	*BOGOSLOF (Aleutian Is)*	1101-30-	1	*7/-*
1883	1006	269*w*?	**AUGUSTINE** (Alaska-SW)	1103-01-	4	8/8
1883	1007	29*a*	**SHIKOTSU [TARUMAI]** (Hokkaido)	0805-04=	2	
1883	*1020*	....	*BOGOSLOF (Aleutian Is)*	1101-30-	2?	*7/-*
1883	12	15*m*	**MARAPI** (Sumatra)	0601-14=	1	
1883	12	?	**COTOPAXI** (Ecuador)	1502-05=	2	
1883	1226e	83*e*	**DIENG VOLC COMPLEX** (Java)	0603-20=	1	
1883	1231p	?	**BAGANA** (Bougainville-SW Pac)	0505-02=	3	
1884	*Cont*	....	*VESUVIUS (Italy)*	0101-02=	*2*	*8/8*

Figure 20. Tsunami, or giant sea wave, generated by the historic 1883 eruption of Krakatau, Indonesia. The largest wave, which reached heights of 40 m above sealevel and killed over 34,000 people, stranded this ship 2½ km inland. From a March 1900 sketch reproduced in Simkin & Fiske, 1983 (see REFERENCES 0601).

START YEAR	M-Dy	Duration	VOLCANO NAME (Subregion)	NUMBER	VEI	Vol L/T
1884	Cont	....	STROMBOLI (Italy)	0101-04=	1?	
1884	Cont	....	KARTHALA (Indian O.-W)	0303-01=	2	
1884	Cont	....	YASUR (Vanuatu-SW Pacific)	0507-10=	2	
1884	Cont	....	KABA (Sumatra)	0601-22=	2	
1884	Cont	....	MERAPI (Java)	0603-25=	1	
1884	Cont	....	KITA-IWO-JIMA (Volcano Is-Japan)	0804-11=	0	
1884	Cont	....	BOGOSLOF (Aleutian Is)	1101-30-	1	7/-
1884	Cont	....	AUGUSTINE (Alaska-SW)	1103-01-	2	8/8
1884	Cont	....	COLIMA VOLC COMPLEX (Mexico)	1401-04=	1	
1884	Cont	....	SANGAY (Ecuador)	1502-09=	2	
1884	Cont	....	LASCAR (Chile-N)	1505-10=	2	
1884	....	365y	ETNA (Italy)	0101-06=	1	
1884	....	?	NYIRAGONGO (Africa-C)	0203-03=	1	
? 1884	....	?	MANAM (New Guinea-NE of)	0501-02=		
1884	....	?	LANGILA (New Britain-SW Pac)	0502-01=	2	
1884	....	?	AMBRYM (Vanuatu-SW Pacific)	0507-04=	2?	
1884	....	?	LOPEVI (Vanuatu-SW Pacific)	0507-05=		
1884	....	?	SUWANOSE-JIMA (Ryukyu Is)	0802-03=	1	
1884f	....	?	CHIRINKOTAN (Kurile Is)	0900-26=	0	
1884	....	365y	WRANGELL (Alaska-E)	1105-02-	2	
? 1884	....	?	BAKER (US-Washington)	1201-01=		
1884	....	730y	CONCEPCION (Nicaragua)	1404-12=	2	
1884	0106	168a	LAMONGAN (Java)	0603-32=	2	
1884	0122	<1	KILAUEA (Hawaiian Is)	1302-01-	0	
1884	0125	3a	SAN MIGUEL (El Salvador)	1403-10=	2	
1884	0204	1a	FOURNAISE, PITON DE LA (Indian O.)	0303-02=	0	
1884	0309	1a	SANTA ANA (El Salvador)	1403-02=	2	
1884	0309	1a	IZALCO (El Salvador)	1403-03=	2	
1884	0311	....	DIENG VOLC COMPLEX (Java)	0603-20=	1	
1884	0321	86m	ASO (Kyushu-Japan)	0802-11=	2	
1884	05	15m	GAMALAMA (Halmahera-Indonesia)	0608-06=	2	
1884	06	31p	DEMPO (Sumatra)	0601-23=	2	
1884	07	?	USHISHUR (Kurile Is)	0900-21=	1	
? 1884	0726	?	REYKJANESHRYGGUR (Iceland-SW)	1701-01=	2?	
1884	0808	2a	RINJANI (Lesser Sunda Is)	0604-03=	2	
? 1884	1208	<1	GAMALAMA (Halmahera-Indonesia)	0608-06=	1	
1884	1210?	279m?	SEMERU (Java)	0603-30=	2	
1884	1229	?	UNNAMED (Atlantic-N)	1801-02=	0	
1885	Cont	....	ETNA (Italy)	0101-06=	1	
1885	Cont	....	YASUR (Vanuatu-SW Pacific)	0507-10=	2	
1885	Cont	....	KABA (Sumatra)	0601-22=	2	
1885	Cont	....	SEMERU (Java)	0603-30=	2	
1885	Cont	....	KITA-IWO-JIMA (Volcano Is-Japan)	0804-11=	0	
1885	Cont	....	BOGOSLOF (Aleutian Is)	1101-30-	1	7/-
1885	Cont	....	WRANGELL (Alaska-E)	1105-02-	2	
1885	Cont	....	CONCEPCION (Nicaragua)	1404-12=	2	
1885	Cont	....	SANGAY (Ecuador)	1502-09=	2	
1885	Cont	....	LASCAR (Chile-N)	1505-10=	2	
1885a	....	730y	TONGARIRO (New Zealand)	0401-08=	1	
1885	....	?	KARKAR (New Guinea-NE of)	0501-03=	2?	
1885e	....	?	GAMKONORA (Halmahera-Indonesia)	0608-04=	2	
? 1885	....	?	TAAL (Luzon-Philippines)	0703-07=		
1885	....	?	IZALCO (El Salvador)	1403-03=	2	
1885	....	?	ISLUGA (Chile-N)	1505-03=	1?	
? 1885	01	?	WHITE ISLAND (New Zealand)	0401-04=	2	
1885	01	130p	SUWANOSE-JIMA (Ryukyu Is)	0802-03=	2?	
? 1885	01	274m	TUNGURAHUA (Ecuador)	1502-08=	2?	
1885	0104	?	SHIKOTSU [TARUMAI] (Hokkaido)	0805-04=	2	
? 1885	0113?	?	RITTER ISLAND (New Guinea-NE of)	0501-07=		
? 1885	0118	?	GUNTUR (Java)	0603-13=		
? 1885	0224d	?	MERAPI (Java)	0603-25=	1	
1885	03	....	KILAUEA (Hawaiian Is)	1302-01-	0	
1885	0301	9a	STROMBOLI (Italy)	0101-04=	2	
1885	0311	583e	LAMONGAN (Java)	0603-32=	2	
1885	0321	9a	SLAMET (Java)	0603-18=	2	
1885	05	?	MANAM (New Guinea-NE of)	0501-02=		
1885	0502	....	VESUVIUS (Italy)	0101-02=	1	8/8
? 1885	0520	?	BAM (New Guinea-NE of)	0501-01=		
1885	0525	?	PURACE (Colombia)	1501-06=	3	
1885	06 ?	?	TENGGER CALDERA [BROMO]	0603-31=	2	
1885	0621	1a	RAUNG (Java)	0603-34=	2	
1885	0723	?	COTOPAXI (Ecuador)	1502-05=	2	
1885	0818	?	AWU (Sangihe Is-Indonesia)	0607-04=	2	
1885	09	31m	ILIBOLENG (Lesser Sunda Is)	0604-22=	2	
1885	10	?	WHITE ISLAND (New Zealand)	0401-04=	2	
1885	10 <	?	TOFUA (Tonga-SW Pacific)	0403-06=	2	
1885	1011?	252w?	FALCON ISLAND (Tonga-SW Pacific)	0403-05=	3	-/8
1885	1031	71a	TENGGER CALDERA [BROMO]	0603-31=	2	
1885	1112	?	MARAPI (Sumatra)	0601-14=	2?	
1885	1121	11a	MAYON (Luzon-Philippines)	0703-03=	2	
1885	12	?	PACAYA (Guatemala)	1402-11=	2	
1885	1226	293m	COLIMA VOLC COMPLEX (Mexico)	1401-04=	2	
1886	Cont	....	VESUVIUS (Italy)	0101-02=	2	8/8
1886	Cont	....	STROMBOLI (Italy)	0101-04=	1?	
1886	Cont	....	FALCON ISLAND (Tonga-SW Pacific)	0403-05=	2	-/8
1886	Cont	....	YASUR (Vanuatu-SW Pacific)	0507-10=	2	
1886	Cont	....	KABA (Sumatra)	0601-22=	2	
1886	Cont	....	LAMONGAN (Java)	0603-32=	2	
1886	Cont	....	KITA-IWO-JIMA (Volcano Is-Japan)	0804-11=	0	
1886	Cont	....	BOGOSLOF (Aleutian Is)	1101-30-	1	7/-
1886	Cont	....	KILAUEA (Hawaiian Is)	1302-01-	0	
1886	Cont	....	CONCEPCION (Nicaragua)	1404-12=	2	
1886	Cont	....	SANGAY (Ecuador)	1502-09=	2	
1886?	....	?	MERU (Africa-E)	0202-16=	0	
1886	....	?	METIS SHOAL (Tonga-SW Pacific)	0403-07=	2	
1886h	....	?	BAMUS (New Britain-SW Pac)	0502-11=	3?	
1886	....	?	TINAKULA (Santa Cruz Is-SW Pac)	0506-01=		
1886	....	?	BULUSAN (Luzon-Philippines)	0703-01=	2	
1886	....	?	PAVLOF (Alaska Peninsula)	1102-03-	2?	
1886	01	?	COTOPAXI (Ecuador)	1502-05=	2	
1886	0105d	?	VULCANO (Italy)	0101-05=	3	
1886	0106	....	COLIMA VOLC COMPLEX (Mexico)	1401-04=	3	
1886	0111	902y?	TUNGURAHUA (Ecuador)	1502-08=	4	
1886	0125	213e	SEMERU (Java)	0603-30=	2	
1886	03	?	UNNAMED (Kermadec Is)	0402-04=	0	
1886	0331	33a	MARAPI (Sumatra)	0601-14=	2	
1886	0413	15a	SHIKOTSU [TARUMAI] (Hokkaido)	0805-04=	2	
1886	0415	11a	TENGGER CALDERA [BROMO]	0603-31=	2	
1886	0425	51a>	KARANGETANG [API SIAU] (Sangihe	0607-02=	2	
1886	0518	20a	ETNA (Italy)	0101-06=	3	7/6
1886	0519	409w?	MOMOTOMBO (Nicaragua)	1404-09=	2	
1886	06	?	TONGARIRO (New Zealand)	0401-08=	2	
? 1886	0610	5a?	WHITE ISLAND (New Zealand)	0401-04=	2	
1886	0610	65m	OKATAINA [TARAWERA] (New Zeal)	0401-05=	5	-/9
1886	0610	67a	GEDE (Java)	0603-06=	2	
1886	07	?	AMBRYM (Vanuatu-SW Pacific)	0507-04=	2	
1886	0708	246a	MAYON (Luzon-Philippines)	0703-03=	2	
1886	0831	18a?	NIUAFO'OU (Tonga-SW Pacific)	0403-11=	4?	-/8
1886	0916	91m?	WHITE ISLAND (New Zealand)	0401-04=	2	
1886	1111	76a	TENGGER CALDERA [BROMO]	0603-31=	2	
1886	1231y	?	CALAYO (Mindanao-Philippines)	0701-07=	2	
1887	Cont	....	VESUVIUS (Italy)	0101-02=	2	8/8
1887	Cont	....	STROMBOLI (Italy)	0101-04=	1?	
1887	Cont	....	TONGARIRO (New Zealand)	0401-08=	1	
1887	Cont	....	YASUR (Vanuatu-SW Pacific)	0507-10=	2	
1887	Cont	....	KABA (Sumatra)	0601-22=	2	
1887	Cont	....	TENGGER CALDERA [BROMO]	0603-31=	2	
1887	Cont	....	KITA-IWO-JIMA (Volcano Is-Japan)	0804-11=	0	
1887	Cont	....	BOGOSLOF (Aleutian Is)	1101-30-	1	7/-
1887	Cont	....	KILAUEA (Hawaiian Is)	1302-01-	0	
1887	Cont	....	MOMOTOMBO (Nicaragua)	1404-09=	2	
1887	Cont	....	TUNGURAHUA (Ecuador)	1502-08=	2	
1887	Cont	....	SANGAY (Ecuador)	1502-09=	2	
1887	....	?	NIUAFO'OU (Tonga-SW Pacific)	0403-11=	2	
? 1887	....	?	GUNTUR (Java)	0603-13=		
1887	....	?	AKITA-YAKE-YAMA (Honshu-Japan)	0803-26=	2	
1887	....	?	AKUTAN (Aleutian Is)	1101-32-	0	
1887	....	731y	IZALCO (El Salvador)	1403-03=	2	
1887	0116	12a?	MAUNA LOA (Hawaiian Is)	1302-02=	0	8/-
1887	0116	159a	LLAIMA (Chile-C)	1507-11=	2	
1887	02	30p	SEMERU (Java)	0603-30=	2	
@ 1887	0202	3a	RITTER ISLAND (New Guinea-NE of)	0501-07=	2	
1887	0309	....	MAYON (Luzon-Philippines)	0703-03=	3	
1887	0323	7a	KERINCI (Sumatra)	0601-17=	2?	
1887	05	?	KIRISHIMA (Kyushu-Japan)	0802-09=	2?	
1887	0527	<1	KARANGETANG [API SIAU] (Sangihe	0607-02=	2	
1887	06	>3yr	MANAM (New Guinea-NE of)	0501-02=	2	
1887	06	?	TOKACHI (Hokkaido-Japan)	0805-05=	2	
1887	0602	958m	LONQUIMAY (Chile-C)	1507-10=	2	8/-
1887	0703a	6a	LAMONGAN (Java)	0603-32=	2	
1887	0815	686w	GRIMSVOTN [THORDARHYRNA]	1703-01=	2	
1887	0903	35a	SHIKOTSU [TARUMAI] (Hokkaido)	0805-04=	2	
1887	0910	31a	SEMERU (Java)	0603-30=	2	
? 1887	1007	105a	RANAU (Sumatra)	0601-251		
1887	1022	<1	GEDE (Java)	0603-06=	2	
1887	11	103m	LAMONGAN (Java)	0603-32=	2	
1887	1113	1a	SUNDORO (Java)	0603-21=	2	
? 1887	1129	?	ALAMAGAN (Mariana Is-C Pac)	0804-18=		
1888	Cont	....	VESUVIUS (Italy)	0101-02=	2	8/8
1888	Cont	....	MANAM (New Guinea-NE of)	0501-02=	2	
1888	Cont	....	YASUR (Vanuatu-SW Pacific)	0507-10=	2	
1888	Cont	....	KABA (Sumatra)	0601-22=	2	
? 1888	Cont	....	RANAU (Sumatra)	0601-251		
1888	Cont	....	KITA-IWO-JIMA (Volcano Is-Japan)	0804-11=	0	
1888	Cont	....	BOGOSLOF (Aleutian Is)	1101-30-	1	7/-
1888	Cont	....	IZALCO (El Salvador)	1403-03=	2	
1888	Cont	....	TUNGURAHUA (Ecuador)	1502-08=	2	
1888	Cont	....	SANGAY (Ecuador)	1502-09=	2	
1888	Cont	....	LONQUIMAY (Chile-C)	1507-10=	2	8/-
1888	Cont	....	GRIMSVOTN [THORDARHYRNA]	1703-01=	2	
1888	....	?	SOUTH ISLAND (Africa-E)	0202-02=		
1888	....	?	BARRIER, THE (Africa-E)	0202-03=	0	
? 1888	....	?	BAM (New Guinea-NE of)	0501-01=		
1888	....	?	EBULOBO (Lesser Sunda Is)	0604-10=	2	
? 1888	....	>3yr	EGON (Lesser Sunda Is)	0604-16=	2	
1888	....	?	ILIBOLENG (Lesser Sunda Is)	0604-22=	2	
1888	....	?	FERNANDINA (Galapagos)	1503-01=	1	
1888	01	>3yr	POAS (Costa Rica)	1405-04=	1	
1888	02	243p	SEMERU (Java)	0603-30=	2	
1888	0219	29a	MARAPI (Sumatra)	0601-14=	2?	
1888	0221	78a	KIRISHIMA (Kyushu-Japan)	0802-09=	2	
1888	0224d	50m?	AMBRYM (Vanuatu-SW Pacific)	0507-04=	2	
? 1888	0227	?	TENGGER CALDERA [BROMO]	0603-31=	2	
1888	0313	<1	RITTER ISLAND (New Guinea-NE of)	0501-07=	2?	
1888	0414	?	KOMAGA-TAKE (Hokkaido-Japan)	0805-02=	2	
1888	0530	1a	BATUR (Lesser Sunda Is)	0604-01=	2	
1888	0715	<1	BANDAI (Honshu-Japan)	0803-16=	4	-/8
1888	08	....	KILAUEA (Hawaiian Is)	1302-01-	0	
1888	0802	806d	VULCANO (Italy)	0101-05=	3	
1888	0818	124a	MERAPI (Java)	0603-25=	3	
1888	09	21m	LAMONGAN (Java)	0603-32=	2	
1888	0925d	?	NISYROS (Greece)	0102-05=	2	
1888	1024	245a	STROMBOLI (Italy)	0101-04=	2	4/-
? 1888	12	?	IYA (Lesser Sunda Is)	0604-11=		

START YEAR	M-Dy	Duration	VOLCANO NAME (Subregion)	NUMBER	VEI	Vol L/T
1888	1215	?	MAYON (Luzon-Philippines)	0703-03=	1	
1889	Cont	....	VESUVIUS (Italy)	0101-02=	2	8/8
1889	Cont	....	STROMBOLI (Italy)	0101-04=	2	4/-
1889	Cont	....	MANAM (New Guinea-NE of)	0501-02=	2	
1889	Cont	....	YASUR (Vanuatu-SW Pacific)	0507-10=	2	
1889	Cont	....	KABA (Sumatra)	0601-22=	2	
? 1889	Cont	....	EGON (Lesser Sunda Is)	0604-16=	2	
1889	Cont	....	KITA-IWO-JIMA (Volcano Is-Japan)	0804-11=	0	
1889	Cont	....	BOGOSLOF (Aleutian Is)	1101-30-	1	7/-
1889	Cont	....	KILAUEA (Hawaiian Is)	1302-01-	0	
1889	Cont	....	IZALCO (El Salvador)	1403-03=	2	
1889	Cont	....	POAS (Costa Rica)	1405-04=	1	
1889	Cont	....	SANGAY (Ecuador)	1502-09=	2	
1889	Cont	....	GRIMSVOTN [THORDARHYRNA]	1703-01=	2	
1889	....	?	LEWOTOBI (Lesser Sunda Is)	0604-18=	2	
1889	....	?	BULUSAN (Luzon-Philippines)	0703-01=		
1889	....	?	TOKACHI (Hokkaido-Japan)	0805-05=	2	
1889	....	365y	TUPUNGATITO (Chile-C)	1507-01=	2	
1889	....	365y	SAN JOSE (Chile-C)	1507-02=	2	
1889	01	869m>	SEMERU (Java)	0603-30=	2	
1889	0219	288a	TANDIKAT (Sumatra)	0601-15=	1	
1889	0228	?	IRAZU (Costa Rica)	1405-06=	2	
1889	0327	21a?	MARAPI (Sumatra)	0601-14=	2?	
1889	0420	96m	LLAIMA (Chile-C)	1507-11=	2	
1889	0501	?	RUAPEHU (New Zealand)	0401-10=	2	
? 1889	0508<	?	GEDE (Java)	0603-06=	1	
1889	06	57m>	FOURNAISE, PITON DE LA (Indian O.)	0303-02=	2	
1889	06	?	RUANG (Sangihe Is-Indonesia)	0607-01=	1	
1889	07	?	MERAPI (Java)	0603-25=	1	
1889	0703	?	GALERAS (Colombia)	1501-08=	2	
1889	0809	14a	SHIRETOKO-IWO-ZAN (Hokkaido)	0805-09=	2?	
1889	0809	191a	COLIMA VOLC COMPLEX (Mexico)	1401-04=	2?	
1889	09	>3yr	PLANCHON-PETEROA (Chile-C)	1507-04=	2	
1889	0906	3a	BANUA WUHU (Sangihe Is-Indonesia)	0607-03=	2	
1889	0907	69m	LAMONGAN (Java)	0603-32=	2	
1889	1002	11a	SUWANOSE-JIMA (Ryukyu Is)	0802-03=	4	
1889	1026	....	COLIMA VOLC COMPLEX (Mexico)	1401-04=	3	
1889	1204	?	NIKKO-SHIRANE (Honshu-Japan)	0803-14=	2	
1889	1210	8a	KIRISHIMA (Kyushu-Japan)	0802-09=	2	
1889	1222	....	LONQUIMAY (Chile-C)	1507-10=	3	8/-
1889	1224	?	ASAMA (Honshu-Japan)	0803-11=	2	
1889	1226	....	VULCANO (Italy)	0101-05=	3	
1890	Cont	....	VESUVIUS (Italy)	0101-02=	2	8/8
1890	Cont	....	STROMBOLI (Italy)	0101-04=	1?	
1890	Cont	....	MANAM (New Guinea-NE of)	0501-02=	2	
1890	Cont	....	YASUR (Vanuatu-SW Pacific)	0507-10=	2	
1890	Cont	....	KABA (Sumatra)	0601-22=	2	
1890	Cont	....	SEMERU (Java)	0603-30=	2	
? 1890	Cont	....	EGON (Lesser Sunda Is)	0604-16=	2	
1890	Cont	....	BANUA WUHU (Sangihe Is-Indonesia)	0607-03=	2	
1890	Cont	....	KILAUEA (Hawaiian Is)	1302-01-	0	
1890	Cont	....	POAS (Costa Rica)	1405-04=	1	
1890	Cont	....	SANGAY (Ecuador)	1502-09=	2	
1890	Cont	....	TUPUNGATITO (Chile-C)	1507-01=	2	
1890	Cont	....	SAN JOSE (Chile-C)	1507-02=	2	
1890	Cont	....	PLANCHON-PETEROA (Chile-C)	1507-04=	2	
1890	Cont	....	LONQUIMAY (Chile-C)	1507-10=	2	8/-
1890	....	?	LANGILA (New Britain-SW Pac)	0502-01=	0	
1890?	....	>3yr	VICTORY (New Guinea)	0503-03=	2	
1890	....	?	SOPUTAN (Sulawesi-Indonesia)	0606-03=	2	
? 1890	....	?	ZAO (Honshu-Japan)	0803-19=	1?	
1890	....	365y	SAN MIGUEL (El Salvador)	1403-10=	2	
1890	....	?	HUEQUI (Chile-S)	1508-03=	2	
1890	02	355m	FOURNAISE, PITON DE LA (Indian O.)	0303-02=	2	
1890	02	....	BOGOSLOF (Aleutian Is)	1101-30-	2	7/-
1890	0216	....	COLIMA VOLC COMPLEX (Mexico)	1401-04=	4	
? 1890	03	?	TONGARIRO (New Zealand)	0401-08=	1	
1890	0315	....	VULCANO (Italy)	0101-05=	3	
1890	0323h	53o	LAMONGAN (Java)	0603-32=	2	
1890	0326e	25e	IZALCO (El Salvador)	1403-03=	0	
1890	04	?	USHKOVSKY (Kamchatka)	1000-261	2?	
1890	04	?	KLIUCHEVSKOI (Kamchatka)	1000-26=	2	
1890	05	123p	TENGGER CALDERA [BROMO]	0603-31=	2	
1890	0615	?	SHIRETOKO-IWO-ZAN (Hokkaido)	0805-09=	1	
1890	0620	10a	MAKIAN (Halmahera-Indonesia)	0608-07=	2	
1890	07	61m	RAUNG (Java)	0603-34=	2	
1890	0806	23a	SLAMET (Java)	0603-18=	2	
? 1890	0823?	<1	MONO LAKE VOLC FIELD (US-Calif)	1203-11-		
1890	0905d	132o>	LAMONGAN (Java)	0603-32=	2	
1890	0910	20a	MAYON (Luzon-Philippines)	0703-03=	2	
1890	0923	?	AKITA-YAKE-YAMA (Honshu-Japan)	0803-26=	2	
1890	1118	?	COLIMA VOLC COMPLEX (Mexico)	1401-04=	3	
1890	1123	<1	BANDA API (Banda Sea)	0605-09=	2	
1890	12	30p	AKITA-KOMAGA-TAKE (Japan)	0803-23=	2	
1891	Cont	....	FOURNAISE, PITON DE LA (Indian O.)	0303-02=	2	
1891	Cont	....	MANAM (New Guinea-NE of)	0501-02=	2	
1891	Cont	....	VICTORY (New Guinea)	0503-03=	1?	
1891	Cont	....	YASUR (Vanuatu-SW Pacific)	0507-10=	2	
1891	Cont	....	KABA (Sumatra)	0601-22=	2	
? 1891	Cont	....	EGON (Lesser Sunda Is)	0604-16=	2	
1891	Cont	....	BANUA WUHU (Sangihe Is-Indonesia)	0607-03=	2	
1891	Cont	....	AKITA-KOMAGA-TAKE (Japan)	0803-23=	2	
1891	Cont	....	KILAUEA (Hawaiian Is)	1302-01-	0	
1891	Cont	....	SAN MIGUEL (El Salvador)	1403-10=	2	
1891	Cont	....	POAS (Costa Rica)	1405-04=	1	
1891	Cont	....	SANGAY (Ecuador)	1502-09=	2	
1891	Cont	....	PLANCHON-PETEROA (Chile-C)	1507-04=	2	

START YEAR	M-Dy	Duration	VOLCANO NAME (Subregion)	NUMBER	VEI	Vol L/T
@ 1891<	....	?	NYIRAGONGO (Africa-C)	0203-03=		
@ 1891	....	?	VISOKE (Africa-C)	0203-05-		
1891	....	?	GEDE (Java)	0603-06=	2	
1891	....	....	BOGOSLOF (Aleutian Is)	1101-30-	3	7/-
1891	....	>3yr	IZALCO (El Salvador)	1403-03=	2	
1891	....	?	GALERAS (Colombia)	1501-08=	2	
1891?	....	?	SAN PEDRO (Chile-N)	1505-07=	2	
1891	....	?	CHILLAN, NEVADOS DE (Chile-C)	1507-07=	2	
1891	....	?	HUDSON, CERRO (Chile-S)	1508-057		
1891	02	....	SEMERU (Java)	0603-30=	2	
1891	04	15m	CONCEPCION (Nicaragua)	1404-12=	2	
1891	0607	....	VESUVIUS (Italy)	0101-02=	2	8/8
1891	0619?	?	KIRISHIMA (Kyushu-Japan)	0802-09=	2?	
1891	0624	68a	STROMBOLI (Italy)	0101-04=	3	4/-
1891	07	334p	COLIMA VOLC COMPLEX (Mexico)	1401-04=	2	
1891	0823	?	ETNA (Italy)	0101-06=	1?	
1891	0825	112m?	MERAPI (Java)	0603-25=	1	
1891	0925e	10i	LAMONGAN (Java)	0603-32=	2	
1891	1003	149a	MAYON (Luzon-Philippines)	0703-03=	2	
1891	1017	8a	PANTELLERIA (Italy)	0101-071	1	
1891	11 ?	121m?	GRIMSVOTN (Iceland-NE)	1703-01=	2	
1891	1110	10a?	KIRISHIMA (Kyushu-Japan)	0802-09=	2	
? 1891	12	?	PANTELLERIA (Italy)	0101-071		
1891	12	?	SEGUAM (Aleutian Is)	1101-18-	2	
1892	Cont	....	VESUVIUS (Italy)	0101-02=	2	8/8
1892	Cont	....	MANAM (New Guinea-NE of)	0501-02=	2	
1892	Cont	....	VICTORY (New Guinea)	0503-03=	1?	
1892	Cont	....	YASUR (Vanuatu-SW Pacific)	0507-10=	2	
1892	Cont	....	KABA (Sumatra)	0601-22=	2	
? 1892	Cont	....	EGON (Lesser Sunda Is)	0604-16=	2	
1892	Cont	....	BANUA WUHU (Sangihe Is-Indonesia)	0607-03=	2	
1892	Cont	....	MAYON (Luzon-Philippines)	0703-03=	2	
1892	Cont	....	BOGOSLOF (Aleutian Is)	1101-30-	1	7/-
1892	Cont	....	COLIMA VOLC COMPLEX (Mexico)	1401-04=	2	
1892	Cont	....	IZALCO (El Salvador)	1403-03=	2	
1892	Cont	....	SANGAY (Ecuador)	1502-09=	2	
1892	Cont	....	PLANCHON-PETEROA (Chile-C)	1507-04=	2	
1892	Cont	....	GRIMSVOTN (Iceland-NE)	1703-01=	2	
? 1892	....	?	HUNTER ISLAND (SW Pacific)	0508-02=		
1892	....	?	BULUSAN (Luzon-Philippines)	0703-01=	2	
1892	....	?	PAVLOF (Alaska Peninsula)	1102-03-	2?	
1892	....	....	KILAUEA (Hawaiian Is)	1302-01-	0	
1892	....	?	LLAIMA (Chile-C)	1507-11=	2	
1892	02	30p	TONGARIRO [NGAURUHOE] (New Z)	0401-08=	2	
1892	03	30p	SEMERU (Java)	0603-30=	2	
1892	0415q	?	SEGUAM (Aleutian Is)	1101-18-	3	
1892	0521	?	SORIKMARAPI (Sumatra)	0601-12=	2	
1892	0603	2a	WURLALI (Banda Sea)	0605-04=	2	
1892	0607	5a?	AWU (Sangihe Is-Indonesia)	0607-04=	3	
1892	0614?	?	KARANGETANG [API SIAU] (Sangihe	0607-02=	2	
1892	0620	10a	ETNA (Italy)	0101-06=	1	
1892	0708	174a	ETNA (Italy)	0101-06=	2	8/6
1892	0828	2	VENIAMINOF (Alaska Peninsula)	1102-07-	3	
1892	0923	?	AKUTAN (Aleutian Is)	1101-32-	1	
? 1892	10	?	LOPEVI (Vanuatu-SW Pacific)	0507-05=		
1892	1012?	19a?	CONCHAGUITA (El Salvador)	1403-12=	1?	
1892	11	31p	TONGARIRO [NGAURUHOE] (New Z)	0401-08=	2	
1892	1105	?	STROMBOLI (Italy)	0101-04=	2	
1892	1130	?	TONGARIRO (New Zealand)	0401-08=	2	
1892	1130	3a	MAUNA LOA (Hawaiian Is)	1302-02=	0	7/-
? 1892	1214	?	VULCANO (Italy)	0101-05=	0	
1893	Cont	....	VESUVIUS (Italy)	0101-02=	2	8/8
1893	Cont	....	MANAM (New Guinea-NE of)	0501-02=	2	
1893	Cont	....	VICTORY (New Guinea)	0503-03=	1?	
1893	Cont	....	YASUR (Vanuatu-SW Pacific)	0507-10=	2	
1893	Cont	....	BANUA WUHU (Sangihe Is-Indonesia)	0607-03=	2	
1893	Cont	....	BOGOSLOF (Aleutian Is)	1101-30-	1	7/-
1893	Cont	....	KILAUEA (Hawaiian Is)	1302-01-	0	
1893	Cont	....	IZALCO (El Salvador)	1403-03=	2	
1893	Cont	....	SANGAY (Ecuador)	1502-09=	2	
1893	Cont	....	PLANCHON-PETEROA (Chile-C)	1507-04=	2	
1893	....	?	LOPEVI (Vanuatu-SW Pacific)	0507-05=	2	
? 1893<	....	?	EMPEROR OF CHINA (Banda Sea)	0605-01=	1?	
? 1893<	....	?	NIEUWERKERK (Banda Sea)	0605-02=	1?	
1893	....	?	AWU (Sangihe Is-Indonesia)	0607-04=	2	
1893	....	?	CLEVELAND (Aleutian Is)	1101-24-		
1893	....	365y?	VILLARRICA (Chile-C)	1507-12=	2	
1893?	....	?	CORDON CAULLE (Chile-C)	1507-141		
1893	....	?	HUEQUI (Chile-S)	1508-03=	0	
1893	01	120p	SEMERU (Java)	0603-30=	2	
1893	0104	<1	SORIKMARAPI (Sumatra)	0601-12=	2	
1893	0107	374a>	CALBUCO (Chile-S)	1508-02=	4	
1893	0113	73a	TENGGER CALDERA [BROMO]	0603-31=	2	
1893	0130	?	STROMBOLI (Italy)	0101-04=	2	
1893	0329	503a>	LOKON-EMPUNG (Sulawesi-Indonesia)	0606-10=	2	
1893	0426	>3yr	ETNA (Italy)	0101-06=	2	
1893	0519	55a	AZUMA (Honshu-Japan)	0803-18=	2	
1893	07	?	CANLAON (Philippines-C)	0702-02=	2	
1893	10	?	MERAPI (Java)	0603-25=	1	
1893	1003	28a	MAYON (Luzon-Philippines)	0703-03=	1	
1893	1111	?	STROMBOLI (Italy)	0101-04=	2	
1893	1118	?	LAMONGAN (Java)	0603-32=	2	
1893	12	365y	LLAIMA (Chile-C)	1507-11=	2	
1893	1204	>3yr	COLIMA VOLC COMPLEX (Mexico)	1401-04=	2	
1893	1211	64m	SEMERU (Java)	0603-30=	2	
1893	1211	?	SEAL NUNATAKS GROUP (Antarctica)	1900-05=	2	
1894	Cont	....	STROMBOLI (Italy)	0101-04=	1?	
1894	Cont	....	ETNA (Italy)	0101-06=	2	

START YEAR	M-Dy	Dura-tion	VOLCANO NAME (Subregion)	NUMBER	VEI	Vol L/T
1894	*Cont*	....	*MANAM (New Guinea-NE of)*	0501-02=	*2*	
1894	*Cont*	....	*VICTORY (New Guinea)*	0503-03=	*1?*	
1894	*Cont*	....	*YASUR (Vanuatu-SW Pacific)*	0507-10=	*2*	
1894	*Cont*	....	*LOKON-EMPUNG (Sulawesi-Indonesia)*	0606-10=	*2*	
1894	*Cont*	....	*BANUA WUHU (Sangihe Is-Indonesia)*	0607-03=	*2*	
1894	*Cont*	....	*BOGOSLOF (Aleutian Is)*	1101-30-	*1*	*7/-*
1894	*Cont*	....	*COLIMA VOLC COMPLEX (Mexico)*	1401-04=	*2*	
1894	*Cont*	....	*IZALCO (El Salvador)*	1403-03=	*2*	
1894	*Cont*	....	*SANGAY (Ecuador)*	1502-09=	*2*	
1894	*Cont*	....	*PLANCHON-PETEROA (Chile-C)*	1507-04=	*2*	
1894	*Cont*	....	*LLAIMA (Chile-C)*	1507-11=	*2*	
1894	*Cont*	....	*VILLARRICA (Chile-C)*	1507-12=	*2*	
1894	*Cont*	....	*CALBUCO (Chile-S)*	1508-02=	*2*	
1894	....	....	*VESUVIUS (Italy)*	0101-02=	1	*8/8*
1894	....	?	**NYIRAGONGO** (Africa-C)	0203-03=	1	
1894	....	?	**METIS SHOAL** (Tonga-SW Pacific)	0403-07=	2	
1894	....	365*y*	**BAGANA** (Bougainville-SW Pac)	0505-02=	2	
1894	....	?	**BULUSAN** (Luzon-Philippines)	0703-01=	2	
1894	....	?	**ALAID** (Kurile Is)	0900-39=	2	
1894	....	?	**PAVLOF** (Alaska Peninsula)	1102-03-	2?	
1894	....	?	**IRAZU** (Costa Rica)	1405-06=		
1894	....	?	**REVENTADOR** (Ecuador)	1502-01=	3	
1894	0127	6*a*	**MERAPI** (Java)	0603-25=	2	-/6
1894	*02*	....	*SEMERU (Java)*	0603-30=	1	
1894	0208	<1	**SHIKOTSU [TARUMAI]** (Hokkaido)	0805-04=	2	
1894	0225	3*a?*	**KIRISHIMA** (Kyushu-Japan)	0802-09=	2	
1894	0306	177*a*	**ASO** (Kyushu-Japan)	0802-11=	2	
1894	0316	27*a*	**AZUMA** (Honshu-Japan)	0803-18=	2	
1894	*0321*	....	*KILAUEA (Hawaiian Is)*	1302-01-	0	
1894	0406	69*a*	**ASAMA** (Honshu-Japan)	0803-11=	2	
1894	05	31*p*	**CANLAON** (Philippines-C)	0702-02=	2	
1894	06	?	**NYAMURAGIRA** (Africa-C)	0203-02=	2	
1894	0703	<1	**ZAO** (Honshu-Japan)	0803-19=	2?	
1894	*0707*	....	*KILAUEA (Hawaiian Is)*	1302-01-	0	
1894	0725	1*a*	**KOLOKOL GROUP** (Kurile Is)	0900-12=	2	
1894	08	?	**FOURNAISE, PITON DE LA** (Indian O.)	0303-02=	2	
1894	0817	<1	**SHIKOTSU [TARUMAI]** (Hokkaido)	0805-04=	2	
1894	10	121*p*	**AVACHINSKY** (Kamchatka)	1000-10=	2	
1894	1015	118*a*>	**AMBRYM** (Vanuatu-SW Pacific)	0507-04=	3	
1894	1017	59*m*	**GALUNGGUNG** (Java)	0603-14=	3	-/7
? **1894**	1121	33*a*	**RAINIER** (US-Washington)	1201-03-		
1894	12	?	**FALCON ISLAND** (Tonga-SW Pacific)	0403-05=	2	
1895	*Cont*	....	*ETNA (Italy)*	0101-06=	*2*	
1895	*Cont*	....	*MANAM (New Guinea-NE of)*	0501-02=	*2*	
1895	*Cont*	....	*VICTORY (New Guinea)*	0503-03=	*1?*	
1895	*Cont*	....	*BAGANA (Bougainville-SW Pac)*	0505-02=	*2*	
1895	*Cont*	....	*AMBRYM (Vanuatu-SW Pacific)*	0507-04=	*2*	
1895	*Cont*	....	*YASUR (Vanuatu-SW Pacific)*	0507-10=	*2*	
1895	*Cont*	....	*AVACHINSKY (Kamchatka)*	1000-10=	*2*	
1895	*Cont*	....	*BOGOSLOF (Aleutian Is)*	1101-30-	*1*	*7/-*
1895	*Cont*	....	*COLIMA VOLC COMPLEX (Mexico)*	1401-04=	*2*	
1895	*Cont*	....	*IZALCO (El Salvador)*	1403-03=	*2*	
1895	*Cont*	....	*SANGAY (Ecuador)*	1502-09=	*2*	
1895	....	?	**BARRIER, THE** (Africa-E)	0202-03=	2	
A **1895** e	....	?	**DAKATAUA [MT. MAKALIA]** (New Brit	0502-04=	2	
? **1895**	....	?	**MAHAGNOA** (Philippines-C)	0702-07=		
1895	....	?	**POAS** (Costa Rica)	1405-04=	1	
1895 r	....	?	**SUMACO** (Ecuador)	1502-04=	2?	
1895	....	?	**COTOPAXI** (Ecuador)	1502-05=	2	
1895	....	731*y*	**SAN JOSE** (Chile-C)	1507-02=	2	
1895	....	365*y*	**LLAIMA** (Chile-C)	1507-11=	2	
1895	....	?	**CALBUCO** (Chile-S)	1508-02=		
1895	0215	35*a*	**ZAO** (Honshu-Japan)	0803-19=	2	
1895	0308	195*a*	**AZUMA** (Honshu-Japan)	0803-18=	2	
1895	0310	4*a*>	**RUAPEHU** (New Zealand)	0401-10=	2	
1895	0329	?	**STROMBOLI** (Italy)	0101-04=	2	
1895	0522	132*a*>	**SEMERU** (Java)	0603-30=	2	
1895	0617	59*m*	**KARKAR** (New Guinea-NE of)	0501-03=	2	7/-
1895	07	164*n*	**BANUA WUHU** (Sangihe Is-Indonesia)	0607-03=	2	
1895	0702	90*a*	**DEMPO** (Sumatra)	0601-23=	2	
1895	*0703*	....	*VESUVIUS (Italy)*	0101-02=	2	*8/8*
1895	0716	345*a*	**KIRISHIMA** (Kyushu-Japan)	0802-09=	2	
1895	0720	129*a*	**MAYON** (Luzon-Philippines)	0703-03=	2	
1895	0822	36*a*	**ZAO** (Honshu-Japan)	0803-19=	2	
1895	1015q	258*y*	**KORYAKSKY** (Kamchatka)	1000-09=	2	
1895	1124	?	**HUNTER ISLAND** (SW Pacific)	0508-02=		
1895	1219	<1	**GAMALAMA** (Halmahera-Indonesia)	0608-06=	1	
? **1895**	1231y	?	**THOMPSON ISLAND** (Atlantic-S)	1806-03-		
1896	*Cont*	....	*VESUVIUS (Italy)*	0101-02=	*2*	*8/8*
1896	*Cont*	....	*ETNA (Italy)*	0101-06=	*2*	
1896	*Cont*	....	*VICTORY (New Guinea)*	0503-03=	*1?*	
1896	*Cont*	....	*YASUR (Vanuatu-SW Pacific)*	0507-10=	*2*	
1896	*Cont*	....	*BANUA WUHU (Sangihe Is-Indonesia)*	0607-03=	*2*	
1896	*Cont*	....	*KORYAKSKY (Kamchatka)*	1000-09=	*2*	
1896	*Cont*	....	*COLIMA VOLC COMPLEX (Mexico)*	1401-04=	*2*	
1896	*Cont*	....	*IZALCO (El Salvador)*	1403-03=	*2*	
1896	*Cont*	....	*SANGAY (Ecuador)*	1502-09=	*2*	
1896	*Cont*	....	*SAN JOSE (Chile-C)*	1507-02=	*2*	
1896	*Cont*	....	*LLAIMA (Chile-C)*	1507-11=	*2*	
1896	....	?	**NYAMURAGIRA** (Africa-C)	0203-02=	1	
1896	....	?	**OKATAINA [WAIMANGU]** (New Zeal)	0401-05=	1?	
1896	....	?	**TENGGER CALDERA [BROMO]**	0603-31=	2	
1896	....	?	**BAYONNAISE ROCKS** (Izu Is-Japan)	0804-07=	2	
1896	....	?	**AKUTAN** (Aleutian Is)	1101-32-		
? **1896**	....	?	**SOCORRO** (Mexico-Is)	1401-021	2?	
1896	....	?	**HUEQUI** (Chile-S)	1508-03=	2	
1896	0103	25	**KILAUEA** (Hawaiian Is)	1302-01-	0	
1896	0110	?	**FUEGO** (Guatemala)	1402-09=	2?	
1896	0308	<1	**ZAO** (Honshu-Japan)	0803-19=	1	
1896	0421	15*a*	**MAUNA LOA** (Hawaiian Is)	1302-02=	0	7/-
1896	05	31*p*	**SEMERU** (Java)	0603-30=	2	
1896	0522	<1	**TANGKUBANPARAHU** (Java)	0603-09=	2	
1896	0711	76*e*	**KILAUEA** (Hawaiian Is)	1302-01-	0	
1896	0713	?	**STROMBOLI** (Italy)	0101-04=	2	
1896	08	?	**RAUNG** (Java)	0603-34=	2	
? **1896**	0803	1*a?*	**GAMALAMA** (Halmahera-Indonesia)	0608-06=	1	
1896	0831	27*a*	**MAYON** (Luzon-Philippines)	0703-03=	2	
1896	09	?	**VESTMANNAEYJAR** (Iceland-S)	1702-01=		
1896	0901?	?	**ZAO** (Honshu-Japan)	0803-19=	1?	
1896	0905	14*a*>	**LAMONGAN** (Java)	0603-32=	2	
? **1896**	0905	14*a*	**AZUMA** (Honshu-Japan)	0803-18=	2	
1896	11	44*m*	**TONGARIRO** (New Zealand)	0401-08=	2	
1896	12	334*p*	**KLIUCHEVSKOI** (Kamchatka)	1000-26=	2	
1896	1221	?	**KIRISHIMA** (Kyushu-Japan)	0802-09=	2	
1897	*Cont*	....	*VESUVIUS (Italy)*	0101-02=	*2*	*8/8*
1897	*Cont*	....	*ETNA (Italy)*	0101-06=	*2*	
1897	*Cont*	....	*VICTORY (New Guinea)*	0503-03=	*1?*	
1897	*Cont*	....	*YASUR (Vanuatu-SW Pacific)*	0507-10=	*2*	
1897	*Cont*	....	*BANUA WUHU (Sangihe Is-Indonesia)*	0607-03=	*2*	
1897	*Cont*	....	*KLIUCHEVSKOI (Kamchatka)*	1000-26=	*2*	
1897	*Cont*	....	*COLIMA VOLC COMPLEX (Mexico)*	1401-04=	*2*	
1897	*Cont*	....	*IZALCO (El Salvador)*	1403-03=	*2*	
1897	*Cont*	....	*SANGAY (Ecuador)*	1502-09=	*2*	
1897	*Cont*	....	*SAN JOSE (Chile-C)*	1507-02=	*2*	
1897	....	?	**TONGARIRO [NGAURUHOE]** (New Z)	0401-08=	2	
? **1897**	....	365*y*	**BAM** (New Guinea-NE of)	0501-01=		
1897	....	>3yr	**KUWAE [KARUA]** (Vanuatu-SW Pac)	0507-07=	2	
1897	....	?	**MERAPI** (Java)	0603-25=	3	
1897	....	?	**BATUR** (Lesser Sunda Is)	0604-01=	2	
1897	....	365*y*	**SHEVELUCH** (Kamchatka)	1000-27=	2	
1897	....	?	**CLEVELAND** (Aleutian Is)	1101-24-		
? **1897**	....	?	**SHISHALDIN** (Aleutian Is)	1101-36-		
1897	....	?	**SANTIAGO** (Galapagos)	1503-09=	0	
1897	....	365*y?*	**VILLARRICA** (Chile-C)	1507-12=	2	
@ **1897**	....	?	**GRIMSVOTN** (Iceland-NE)	1703-01=	2	
1897	01	86*m*>	**TUPUNGATITO** (Chile-C)	1507-01=	2	
1897	0101	2*a*	**SEMERU** (Java)	0603-30=	2	
1897	0105d	19*d*	**FOURNAISE, PITON DE LA** (Indian O.)	0303-02=	0	
? **1897**	0114	<1	**ZAO** (Honshu-Japan)	0803-19=	1?	
1897	0224d	?	**ASO** (Kyushu-Japan)	0802-11=	2	
1897	04	?	**RAUNG** (Java)	0603-34=	2	
1897	05 <	?	**BARRIER, THE** (Africa-E)	0202-03=	2?	
1897	0503	124*a*	**KIRISHIMA** (Kyushu-Japan)	0802-09=	2	
1897	0516?	?	**BAGANA** (Bougainville-SW Pac)	0505-02=	2	
1897	0523<	61*a*>	**MAYON** (Luzon-Philippines)	0703-03=	4	-/7
1897	0624	3*a*	**KILAUEA** (Hawaiian Is)	1302-01-	0	
1897	*0625*	....	*MAYON (Luzon-Philippines)*	0703-03=	3	-/7
1897	0708	39*a*	**KUSATSU-SHIRANE** (Honshu-Japan)	0803-12=	2	
1897	0717	?	**STROMBOLI** (Italy)	0101-04=	2	
1897	0907	17*a*	**GAMALAMA** (Halmahera-Indonesia)	0608-06=	1	
1897	0921	?	**BUD DAJO** (Sulu Is-Philippines)	0700-01=	0	
1897	*1101*	*>3yr*	*DONA JUANA (Colombia)*	1501-07=	2	
1898	*Cont*	....	*VESUVIUS (Italy)*	0101-02=	*2*	*8/8*
1898	*Cont*	....	*ETNA (Italy)*	0101-06=	*2*	
? *1898*	*Cont*	....	*BAM (New Guinea-NE of)*	0501-01=		
1898	*Cont*	....	*VICTORY (New Guinea)*	0503-03=	*1?*	
1898	*Cont*	....	*KUWAE [KARUA] (Vanuatu-SW Pac)*	0507-07=	*2*	
1898	*Cont*	....	*YASUR (Vanuatu-SW Pacific)*	0507-10=	*2*	
1898	*Cont*	....	*BANUA WUHU (Sangihe Is-Indonesia)*	0607-03=	*2*	
1898	*Cont*	....	*SHEVELUCH (Kamchatka)*	1000-27=	*2*	
1898	*Cont*	....	*COLIMA VOLC COMPLEX (Mexico)*	1401-04=	*2*	
1898	*Cont*	....	*IZALCO (El Salvador)*	1403-03=	*2*	
1898	*Cont*	....	*SANGAY (Ecuador)*	1502-09=	*2*	
1898	*Cont*	....	*VILLARRICA (Chile-C)*	1507-12=	*2*	
1898	....	?	**NYIRAGONGO** (Africa-C)	0203-03=	1	
1898 ?	....	?	**SANTA ISABEL** (Africa-W)	0204-02-		
1898	....	?	**ULAWUN** (New Britain-SW Pac)	0502-12=	3	
? **1898**	....	?	**LOPEVI** (Vanuatu-SW Pacific)	0507-05=		
1898	....	?	**NIPESOTSU-UPEPESANKE** (Japan)	0805-061	2	
1898	....	?	**SHISHALDIN** (Aleutian Is)	1101-36-	2	
1898	....	?	**LASCAR** (Chile-N)	1505-10=	2	
1898	....	?	**CHILLAN, NEVADOS DE** (Chile-C)	1507-07=	2	
1898	01	?	**TONGARIRO [NGAURUHOE]** (New Z)	0401-08=	2	
1898	0114	6*a*	**FOURNAISE, PITON DE LA** (Indian O.)	0303-02=	2	
1898	0205	10*a*	**LAMONGAN** (Java)	0603-32=	2	
1898	0208	31	**KIRISHIMA** (Kyushu-Japan)	0802-09=	2	
1898	0220	?	**KLIUCHEVSKOI** (Kamchatka)	1000-26=	2	
1898	0223	?	**SEMERU** (Java)	0603-30=	2	
1898	0326	?	**AMBRYM** (Vanuatu-SW Pacific)	0507-04=	1?	
1898	04	91*q*	**MUTNOVSKY** (Kamchatka)	1000-06=	2	-/6
? **1898**	0405	?	**ST. HELENS** (US-Washington)	1201-05-		
1898	0408	>3yr	**REVENTADOR** (Ecuador)	1502-01=	3	
1898	0502	791*w?*	**COLO [UNA UNA]** (Sulawesi-Indonesia)	0606-01=	3?	-/7
1898	0514	14*a?*	**GAMALAMA** (Halmahera-Indonesia)	0608-06=	2	
1898	08 ?	320*w*	**ASO** (Kyushu-Japan)	0802-11=	2	
1898	0824	?	**STROMBOLI** (Italy)	0101-04=	2	
1898	*0906*	....	*DONA JUANA (Colombia)*	1501-07=	2	
1898	1108	?	**RUBY MOUNTAIN** (Canada)	1200-03-	2?	
1898	1126	?	**FOURNAISE, PITON DE LA** (Indian O.)	0303-02=	2	
1898	1226	4*a*	**KIRISHIMA** (Kyushu-Japan)	0802-09=	2	
1898	1229	>3yr	**POAS** (Costa Rica)	1405-04=	1	
1899	*Cont*	....	*VESUVIUS (Italy)*	0101-02=	*2*	*8/8*
1899	*Cont*	....	*STROMBOLI (Italy)*	0101-04=	*1?*	
1899	*Cont*	....	*VICTORY (New Guinea)*	0503-03=	*1?*	

START YEAR	M-Dy	Duration	VOLCANO NAME (Subregion)	NUMBER	VEI	Vol L/T
1899	*Cont*	....	*KUWAE [KARUA] (Vanuatu-SW Pac)*	0507-07=	*2*	
1899	*Cont*	....	*YASUR (Vanuatu-SW Pacific)*	0507-10=	*2*	
1899	*Cont*	....	*COLO [UNA UNA] (Sulawesi-Indonesia)*	0606-01=	*2?*	*-/7*
1899	*Cont*	....	*BANUA WUHU (Sangihe Is-Indonesia)*	0607-03=	*2*	
1899	*Cont*	....	*ASO (Kyushu-Japan)*	0802-11=	*2*	
1899	*Cont*	....	*COLIMA VOLC COMPLEX (Mexico)*	1401-04=	*2*	
1899	*Cont*	....	*POAS (Costa Rica)*	1405-04=	*1*	
1899	*Cont*	....	*REVENTADOR (Ecuador)*	1502-01=	*2*	
1899	*Cont*	....	*SANGAY (Ecuador)*	1502-09=	*2*	
1899	....	?	**NYIRAGONGO** (Africa-C)	0203-03=	1	
1899 a	....	?	**MANAM** (New Guinea-NE of)	0501-02=	2?	
1899	....	?	**BAGANA** (Bougainville-SW Pac)	0505-02=		
1899	....	?	**KARANGETANG [API SIAU]** (Sangihe	0607-02=	2	
? **1899** ?	....	?	**KASATOCHI** (Aleutian Is)	1101-13-		
1899	....	?	**OKMOK** (Aleutian Is)	1101-29-	3	
? **1899**	....	?	**SHISHALDIN** (Aleutian Is)	1101-36-		
1899	....	?	**IRAZU** (Costa Rica)	1405-06=		
1899	....	?	**PURACE** (Colombia)	1501-06=	2	
1899	0112	?	**BUCKLE ISLAND** (Antarctica)	1900-01=	2	
1899	0117	73*a*?	**SEMERU** (Java)	0603-30=	2	
1899	02	?	**NYAMURAGIRA** (Africa-C)	0203-02=	1	
1899	0213	155*a*>	**FOURNAISE, PITON DE LA** (Indian O.)	0303-02=	2	
? **1899**	03	30*p*	**SIRUNG** (Lesser Sunda Is)	0604-27=	2	
1899	0311	?	**ASAMA** (Honshu-Japan)	0803-11=	2	
1899	0501	13*a*	**GEDE** (Java)	0603-06=	2	
1899	0602	?	**LEWOTOLO** (Lesser Sunda Is)	0604-23=	2	
1899	0701	22*a*	**MAUNA LOA** (Hawaiian Is)	1302-02=	1	7/-
1899	0710	28*a*	**ASAMA** (Honshu-Japan)	0803-11=	2	
1899	0719	17	**ETNA** (Italy)	0101-06=	3	
1899	0728	203*a*	**KIRISHIMA** (Kyushu-Japan)	0802-09=	2	
1899	0811	?	**SEMERU** (Java)	0603-30=	2	
1899	0824	80*a*	**ADATARA** (Honshu-Japan)	0803-17=	2	
1899	0903	?	**WRANGELL** (Alaska-E)	1105-02-	2	
? **1899**	0924	1*a*	**SAKURA-JIMA** (Kyushu-Japan)	0802-08=	1?	
1899	1113	....	**DONA JUANA** (Colombia)	1501-07=	4	
1899	1115	>3yr	**ETNA** (Italy)	0101-06=	1	
1899	1122	7*a*	**NEGRO, CERRO** (Nicaragua)	1404-07=	2	
1899	12	?	**SEMERU** (Java)	0603-30=	2	
1899	1231	75*m*	**IZALCO** (El Salvador)	1403-03=	2	

1900

START YEAR	M-Dy	Duration	VOLCANO NAME (Subregion)	NUMBER	VEI	Vol L/T
1900	*Cont*	....	*ETNA (Italy)*	0101-06=	*1*	
1900	*Cont*	....	*VICTORY (New Guinea)*	0503-03=	*1?*	
1900	*Cont*	....	*KUWAE [KARUA] (Vanuatu-SW Pac)*	0507-07=	*2*	
1900	*Cont*	....	*YASUR (Vanuatu-SW Pacific)*	0507-10=	*2*	
1900	*Cont*	....	*COLO [UNA UNA] (Sulawesi-Indonesia)*	0606-01=	*2?*	*-/7*
1900	*Cont*	....	*KIRISHIMA (Kyushu-Japan)*	0802-09=	*2*	
1900	*Cont*	....	*COLIMA VOLC COMPLEX (Mexico)*	1401-04=	*2*	
1900	*Cont*	....	*IZALCO (El Salvador)*	1403-03=	*2*	
1900	*Cont*	....	*POAS (Costa Rica)*	1405-04=	*1*	
1900	*Cont*	....	*DONA JUANA (Colombia)*	1501-07=	*2*	
1900	*Cont*	....	*REVENTADOR (Ecuador)*	1502-01=	*2*	
1900	*Cont*	....	*SANGAY (Ecuador)*	1502-09=	*2*	
? **1900** ?	....	?	**DUBBI** (Ethiopia)	0201-10=		
1900 ?	....	?	**TULLU MOJE** (Ethiopia)	0201-25-		
1900	....	?	**NYIRAGONGO** (Africa-C)	0203-03=	1	
1900	....	?	**LANGILA** (New Britain-SW Pac)	0502-01=	2	
1900	....	?	**KARANGETANG [API SIAU]** (Sangihe	0607-02=	2	
? **1900**	....	?	**DIDICAS** (Luzon Is-N of)	0704-02=		
1900 ?	....	325*w*?	**FARALLON DE PAJAROS** (Mariana Is	0804-14=	2	
? **1900**	....	?	**MENDELEEV** (Kurile Is)	0900-02=	2?	
1900 j	....	?	**CHIRINKOTAN** (Kurile Is)	0900-26=		
? **1900**	....	?	**TUNGURAHUA** (Ecuador)	1502-08=	2?	
1900	01	>3yr	**TARAWERA [WAIMANGU]** (New Zeal)	0401-05=	1	
1900	0122	631*m*	**ASAMA** (Honshu-Japan)	0803-11=	2	
? **1900**	02	?	**EREBUS** (Antarctica)	1900-02=	2	
1900	0301	5*a*	**MAYON** (Luzon-Philippines)	0703-03=	2	
1900	0329	13*a*>	**SEMERU** (Java)	0603-30=	2	
? **1900**	05	20*m*	**GAMALAMA** (Halmahera-Indonesia)	0608-06=	1	
1900	*0509*	....	*VESUVIUS (Italy)*	0101-02=	2	*8/8*
1900	0511	19*a*	**FOURNAISE, PITON DE LA** (Indian O.)	0303-02=	0	
1900	0604	<1	**DEMPO** (Sumatra)	0601-23=	2	
1900	0717	<1	**ADATARA** (Honshu-Japan)	0803-17=	2	-/6
1900	0804	18*a*	**STROMBOLI** (Italy)	0101-04=	2	
1900	1001	<1	**KUSATSU-SHIRANE** (Honshu-Japan)	0803-12=	1	
1900	1019	?	**STROMBOLI** (Italy)	0101-04=	2	
1900	1026	1*a*	**DEMPO** (Sumatra)	0601-23=	2	
1900	1130	1	**RINJANI** (Lesser Sunda Is)	0604-03=	2	
1901	*Cont*	....	*VESUVIUS (Italy)*	0101-02=	*2*	*8/8*
1901	*Cont*	....	*STROMBOLI (Italy)*	0101-04=	*1?*	
1901	*Cont*	....	*ETNA (Italy)*	0101-06=	*1*	
1901	*Cont*	....	*TARAWERA [WAIMANGU] (New Zeal)*	0401-05=	*2*	
1901	*Cont*	....	*VICTORY (New Guinea)*	0503-03=	*1?*	
1901	*Cont*	....	*KUWAE [KARUA] (Vanuatu-SW Pac)*	0507-07=	*2*	
1901	*Cont*	....	*YASUR (Vanuatu-SW Pacific)*	0507-10=	*2*	
1901	*Cont*	....	*ASAMA (Honshu-Japan)*	0803-11=	*2*	
1901	*Cont*	....	*FARALLON DE PAJAROS (Mariana Is)*	0804-14=	*2*	
1901	*Cont*	....	*POAS (Costa Rica)*	1405-04=	*1*	
1901	*Cont*	....	*DONA JUANA (Colombia)*	1501-07=	*2*	
1901	*Cont*	....	*REVENTADOR (Ecuador)*	1502-01=	*2*	
1901	*Cont*	....	*SANGAY (Ecuador)*	1502-09=	*2*	
1901	....	?	**NYAMURAGIRA** (Africa-C)	0203-02=	2	7/6
1901	....	?	**NYIRAGONGO** (Africa-C)	0203-03=	1	
? **1901**	....	365*y*?	**MANAM** (New Guinea-NE of)	0501-02=		
1901	....	?	**DUKONO** (Halmahera-Indonesia)	0608-01=	2	
1901	....	?	**ILYINSKY** (Kamchatka)	1000-03=	3	
1901	....	?	**SHISHALDIN** (Aleutian Is)	1101-36-		
1901	....	?	**PAVLOF** (Alaska Peninsula)	1102-03-	2?	
1901	....	....	*COLIMA VOLC COMPLEX (Mexico)*	1401-04=	1	
? **1901**	....	?	**ANTOFALLA, VOLCAN** (Argentina)	1505-123		
1901	0129	1*a*>	**SEMERU** (Java)	0603-30=	2	
1901	0204	?	**SOPUTAN** (Sulawesi-Indonesia)	0606-03=	2	
1901	0221	4*a*	**FOURNAISE, PITON DE LA** (Indian O.)	0303-02=	2	
1901	04	?	**TUPUNGATITO** (Chile-C)	1507-01=	2	
1901	0518	?	**BANDA API** (Banda Sea)	0605-09=	2	
1901	0522	1*a*	**KELUT** (Java)	0603-28=	3	-/6
1901	0525	114*m*	**SAN PEDRO** (Chile-N)	1505-07=	2	
1901	0601	<1	**RINJANI** (Lesser Sunda Is)	0604-03=	2	
1901	0704	2*a*	**FOURNAISE, PITON DE LA** (Indian O.)	0303-02=	2	
1901	0707	6*a*	**AVACHINSKY** (Kamchatka)	1000-10=	2	
1902	*Cont*	....	*VESUVIUS (Italy)*	0101-02=	*2*	*8/8*
1902	*Cont*	....	*STROMBOLI (Italy)*	0101-04=	*1?*	
1902	*Cont*	....	*ETNA (Italy)*	0101-06=	*1*	
1902	*Cont*	....	*TARAWERA [WAIMANGU] (New Zeal)*	0401-05=	*2*	
? *1902*	*Cont*	....	*MANAM (New Guinea-NE of)*	0501-02=		
1902	*Cont*	....	*VICTORY (New Guinea)*	0503-03=	*1?*	
1902	*Cont*	....	*YASUR (Vanuatu-SW Pacific)*	0507-10=	*2*	
1902	*Cont*	....	*POAS (Costa Rica)*	1405-04=	*1*	
1902	*Cont*	....	*DONA JUANA (Colombia)*	1501-07=	*2*	
1902	*Cont*	....	*REVENTADOR (Ecuador)*	1502-01=	*2*	
1902	*Cont*	....	*SANGAY (Ecuador)*	1502-09=	*2*	
1902	....	?	**NYIRAGONGO** (Africa-C)	0203-03=	1	
1902	....	365*y*	**SALAK** (Java)	0603-05=	2	
? **1902**	....	?	**MAYON** (Luzon-Philippines)	0703-03=	1	
? **1902**	....	?	**AKITA-KOMAGA-TAKE** (Japan)	0803-23=		
1902	....	?	**SEGUAM** (Aleutian Is)	1101-18-	3	
1902	....	?	**WRANGELL** (Alaska-E)	1105-02-	2	
1902	....	....	*COLIMA VOLC COMPLEX (Mexico)*	1401-04=	1	
1902	....	?	**CONCEPCION** (Nicaragua)	1404-12=	2	
1902 ?	....	?	**PURACE** (Colombia)	1501-06=	2	
1902	....	?	**LASCAR** (Chile-N)	1505-10=	2?	
1902	0118	?	**REDOUBT** (Alaska-SW)	1103-03-	3	
1902	0131	?	**CANLAON** (Philippines-C)	0702-02=	2	
1902	0203	<1	**MERAPI** (Java)	0603-25=	1	
1902	0207	<1	**ASAMA** (Honshu-Japan)	0803-11=	2	
1902	0214<	7*g*?	**KILAUEA** (Hawaiian Is)	1302-01-	0	
1902	0216	11*a*>	**RAUNG** (Java)	0603-34=	2	
? **1902**	0320	?	**BANDA API** (Banda Sea)	0605-09=		
1902	0331p	?	**MOMOTOMBO** (Nicaragua)	1404-09=	2?	
1902	0422?	?	**NYAMURAGIRA** (Africa-C)	0203-02=	0	
1902	*0423*	*>3yr*	*PELEE (W Indies)*	1600-12=	2	*8/8*
1902	0501	24*a*	**SUNDORO** (Java)	0603-21=	1	
1902	0502	....	**PELEE** (W Indies)	1600-12=	4	8/8
1902	0506	298*a*	**SOUFRIERE ST. VINCENT** (W Indies)	1600-15=	4?	-/8
1902	0507	1*a*	**SAN JORGE** (Azores)	1802-03=	0	
1902	*0508*	....	*PELEE (W Indies)*	1600-12=	4	*8/8*
1902	0510	233*a*	**IZALCO** (El Salvador)	1403-03=	2	
1902	06	153*p*	**TUTUPACA** (Peru)	1504-04=	2	
1902	0603	275*e*	**KILAUEA** (Hawaiian Is)	1302-01-	0	
? **1902**	0622	?	**RINCON DE LA VIEJA** (Costa Rica)	1405-02=	2?	
1902	0715	154*m*	**KUSATSU-SHIRANE** (Honshu-Japan)	0803-12=	2	
1902	0715	488*m*	**MASAYA** (Nicaragua)	1404-10=	2	
1902	0805	<1	**ASAMA** (Honshu-Japan)	0803-11=	2	
1902	0807	14*a*	**TORI-SHIMA** (Izu Is-Japan)	0804-09=	3	-/7
1902	0813	5*a*	**FOURNAISE, PITON DE LA** (Indian O.)	0303-02=	2	
1902	*1013*	....	*SOUFRIERE ST. VINCENT (W Indies)*	1600-15=	3?	*-/8*
1902	1024	19*a*	**SANTA MARIA** (Guatemala)	1402-03=	**6?**	**-/10**
1902	1030	18*d*	**SAVAI'I** (Samoa-SW Pacific)	0404-04=	1	
1902	12	551*n*	**MERAPI** (Java)	0603-25=	2	-/6
1902	*12*	*393m*	*GRIMSVOTN [THORDARHYRNA]*	1703-01=	2?	*8/-*
@ **1902**	12	182*p*	**BARDARBUNGA** (Iceland-NE)	1703-03=	2?	
1903	*Cont*	....	*ETNA (Italy)*	0101-06=	*1*	
1903	*Cont*	....	*TARAWERA [WAIMANGU] (New Zeal)*	0401-05=	*2*	
1903	*Cont*	....	*VICTORY (New Guinea)*	0503-03=	*1?*	
1903	*Cont*	....	*YASUR (Vanuatu-SW Pacific)*	0507-10=	*2*	
1903	*Cont*	....	*SALAK (Java)*	0603-05=	*2*	
1903	*Cont*	....	*MERAPI (Java)*	0603-25=	*2*	*-/6*
1903	*Cont*	....	*MASAYA (Nicaragua)*	1404-10=	*2*	
1903	*Cont*	....	*POAS (Costa Rica)*	1405-04=	*1*	
1903	*Cont*	....	*DONA JUANA (Colombia)*	1501-07=	*2*	
1903	*Cont*	....	*REVENTADOR (Ecuador)*	1502-01=	*2*	
1903	*Cont*	....	*PELEE (W Indies)*	1600-12=	*2*	*8/8*
@ *1903*	*Cont*	....	*BARDARBUNGA (Iceland-NE)*	1703-03=	*2?*	
? **1903**	....	?	**ERTA ALE** (Ethiopia)	0201-08=	2	
1903	....	?	**SANTA ISABEL** (Africa-W)	0204-02-		
1903 ?	....	?	**FOURNAISE, PITON DE LA** (Indian O.)	0303-02=	0	
1903	....	?	**RUAPEHU** (New Zealand)	0401-10=	2	
1903	....	?	**HUNTER ISLAND** (SW Pacific)	0508-02=		
? **1903**	....	?	**KUSATSU-SHIRANE** (Honshu-Japan)	0803-12=		
1903	....	>3yr	**SANTA MARIA** (Guatemala)	1402-03=	2	
1903	....	?	**SOUFRIERE GUADELOUPE** (W Indies)	1600-06=	2	
? **1903**	01	?	**AZUL, CERRO [QUIZAPU]** (Chile-C)	1507-06=	2?	
1903	0101	165*m*	**STROMBOLI** (Italy)	0101-04=	2	4/-
1903	0101*	?	**EREBUS** (Antarctica)	1900-02=	0	
1903	0215	27*a*	**COLIMA VOLC COMPLEX** (Mexico)	1401-04=	3	
1903	0315e	164*j*	**OKINAWA-TORI-SHIMA** (Ryukyu Is)	0802-02=	2	
1903	*0321*	....	*SOUFRIERE ST. VINCENT (W Indies)*	1600-15=	3?	*-/8*
1903	0326	81*m*	**SEMERU** (Java)	0603-30=	2	
1903	04	?	**TAAL** (Luzon-Philippines)	0703-07=	2	
1903	0512	2*a*	**LLAIMA** (Chile-C)	1507-11=	2	
1903	0528	33*a*	**ASAMA** (Honshu-Japan)	0803-11=	2	
1903	0528H	....	**GRIMSVOTN [THORDARHYRNA]**	1703-01=	4	8/-
1903	*06*	....	*SANGAY (Ecuador)*	1502-09=	3	
1903	*0713*	....	*SANGAY (Ecuador)*	1502-09=	3	
1903	*0827*	....	*VESUVIUS (Italy)*	0101-02=	2	*8/8*
1903	0829	88*a*	**KIRISHIMA** (Kyushu-Japan)	0802-09=	2	

Figure 21. Devastation of St. Pierre, Martinique, in 1902, with spine of Mont Pelee in background. In this century's worst volcanic disaster, pyroclastic flows killed 28,000 in minutes. Later development of a summit dome resulted in vertical thrusting of a dramatic lava spine that rose over 300 m before collapsing. Photo by A. Lacroix (in Lacroix, 1904, *La Montagne Pelee et ses eruptions*, Paris: Masson et Cie, 662 p).

START YEAR	START M-Dy	Duration	VOLCANO NAME (Subregion)	NUMBER	VEI	Vol L/T
1903	0901	97a?	**MAUNA LOA** (Hawaiian Is)	1302-02=	0	7/-
? **1903**	0915	?	**ST. HELENS** (US-Washington)	1201-05-		
1903	*0926*	*446m*	*COTOPAXI (Ecuador)*	1502-05=	2	
1903	1017	5a	**SUNDORO** (Java)	0603-21=	2	
1903	11	475m	**IZALCO** (El Salvador)	1403-03=	2	
1903	1111	7a	**STROMBOLI** (Italy)	0101-04=	2	
1903	1125	46a	**KILAUEA** (Hawaiian Is)	1302-01-	0	
1903	1128	48m	**RAUNG** (Java)	0603-34=	2	
1903	1208	?	**NILA** (Banda Sea)	0605-06=	2	
? **1903**	1208	?	**OLLAGUE** (Chile-N)	1505-06=		
? **1903**	1209	<1	**RANAU** (Sumatra)	0601-251		
1904	*Cont*	....	*VESUVIUS (Italy)*	0101-02=	*2*	*8/8*
1904	*Cont*	....	*STROMBOLI (Italy)*	0101-04=	*1?*	
1904	*Cont*	....	*ETNA (Italy)*	0101-06=	*1*	
1904	*Cont*	....	*TARAWERA [WAIMANGU] (New Zeal)*	0401-05=	*2*	
1904	*Cont*	....	*VICTORY (New Guinea)*	0503-03=	*1?*	
1904	*Cont*	....	*YASUR (Vanuatu-SW Pacific)*	0507-10=	*2*	
1904	*Cont*	....	*RAUNG (Java)*	0603-34=	*2*	
1904	*Cont*	....	*KILAUEA (Hawaiian Is)*	1302-01-	*0*	
1904	*Cont*	....	*SANTA MARIA (Guatemala)*	1402-03=	*2*	
1904	*Cont*	....	*IZALCO (El Salvador)*	1403-03=	*2*	
1904	*Cont*	....	*DONA JUANA (Colombia)*	1501-07=	*2*	
1904	*Cont*	....	*REVENTADOR (Ecuador)*	1502-01=	*2*	
1904	*Cont*	....	*SANGAY (Ecuador)*	1502-09=	*2*	
1904	*Cont*	....	*PELEE (W Indies)*	1600-12=	*2*	*8/8*
1904	*Cont*	....	*GRIMSVOTN [THORDARHYRNA]*	1703-01=	*2*	*8/-*
1904	....	?	**BATUR** (Lesser Sunda Is)	0604-01=	2	
1904	....	?	**ILIBOLENG** (Lesser Sunda Is)	0604-22=	2	
1904	....	?	**CANLAON** (Philippines-C)	0702-02=	2	
1904	....	?	**TOLBACHIK** (Kamchatka)	1000-24=	2	
1904	....	?	**KANAGA** (Aleutian Is)	1101-11-	0	
? **1904**	....	?	**GREAT SITKIN** (Aleutian Is)	1101-12-		
? **1904**	....	?	**ISKUT-UNUK RIVER CONES** (Canada)	1200-09-		
1904	....	730y	**COLIMA VOLC COMPLEX** (Mexico)	1401-04=	1?	
1904	....	881w	**SANTIAGO** (Galapagos)	1503-09=	0	
1904	....	?	**VILLARRICA** (Chile-C)	1507-12=	2	
1904	0102	14a	**SEMERU** (Java)	0603-30=	2	
1904	0112	14a?	**SANTA ANA** (El Salvador)	1403-02=	2	
1904	*0130*	....	*MERAPI (Java)*	0603-25=	2	-/6
1904	0131p	134p>	**KLIUCHEVSKOI** (Kamchatka)	1000-26=	2	
1904	0225	50m	**KARTHALA** (Indian O.-W)	0303-01=	2	
1904	04	31m?	**NYAMURAGIRA** (Africa-C)	0203-02=	2	7/7
1904	04	91n	**TAAL** (Luzon-Philippines)	0703-07=	1	
1904	0402	85a>	**MUTNOVSKY** (Kamchatka)	1000-06=	2	
1904	0417	<1	**BANUA WUHU** (Sangihe Is-Indonesia)	0607-03=	2	
1904	0418	<1	**MARAPI** (Sumatra)	0601-14=	1	
1904	0422	395a	**RUANG** (Sangihe Is-Indonesia)	0607-01=	3?	6/-
1904	0430p	?	**MANAM** (New Guinea-NE of)	0501-02=		
1904	05	31p	**MASAYA** (Nicaragua)	1404-10=	2	
1904	0603	?	**TEON** (Banda Sea)	0605-05=	2	
1904	*07*	....	*POAS (Costa Rica)*	1405-04=	1	
1904	0714	26a	**SLAMET** (Java)	0603-18=	2	
1904	0804	<1	**ASAMA** (Honshu-Japan)	0803-11=	2	
1904	*0809*	*435a>*	*LOLOBAU (New Britain-SW Pac)*	0502-13=	2	
1904	0819	59a	**FOURNAISE, PITON DE LA** (Indian O.)	0303-02=	2	
1904	0827	?	**BANUA WUHU** (Sangihe Is-Indonesia)	0607-03=	2	
1904	1004<	?	**MAHAWU** (Sulawesi-Indonesia)	0606-11=	2	
1904	1026	<1	**MANAM** (New Guinea-NE of)	0501-02=	3?	
? **1904**	1101r	?	**ERTA ALE** (Ethiopia)	0201-08=	2	
1904	1114	183a	**SHIN-IWO-JIMA** (Volcano Is-Japan)	0804-13=	3	8/8
1904	1114	....	**COTOPAXI** (Ecuador)	1502-05=	3	
1904	1122	?	**TONGARIRO [NGAURUHOE]** (New Z)	0401-08=	2	
1905	*Cont*	....	*VESUVIUS (Italy)*	0101-02=	*2*	*8/8*
1905	*Cont*	....	*ETNA (Italy)*	0101-06=	*1*	
1905	*Cont*	....	*VICTORY (New Guinea)*	0503-03=	*1?*	
1905	*Cont*	....	*YASUR (Vanuatu-SW Pacific)*	0507-10=	*2*	
1905	*Cont*	....	*RUANG (Sangihe Is-Indonesia)*	0607-01=	*2*	*6/-*
1905	*Cont*	....	*SHIN-IWO-JIMA (Volcano Is-Japan)*	0804-13=	*2*	*8/8*
1905	*Cont*	....	*COLIMA VOLC COMPLEX (Mexico)*	1401-04=	*1*	
1905	*Cont*	....	*SANTA MARIA (Guatemala)*	1402-03=	*2*	
1905	*Cont*	....	*IZALCO (El Salvador)*	1403-03=	*2*	
1905	*Cont*	....	*DONA JUANA (Colombia)*	1501-07=	*2*	
1905	*Cont*	....	*REVENTADOR (Ecuador)*	1502-01=	*2*	
1905	*Cont*	....	*SANGAY (Ecuador)*	1502-09=	*2*	
1905	*Cont*	....	*SANTIAGO (Galapagos)*	1503-09=	*0*	
1905	*Cont*	....	*PELEE (W Indies)*	1600-12=	*2*	*8/8*
1905	....	?	**NYIRAGONGO** (Africa-C)	0203-03=	1	
1905	....	?	**TONGARIRO [NGAURUHOE]** (New Z)	0401-08=	2	
1905	....	....	**LOLOBAU** (New Britain-SW Pac)	0502-13=	P	
1905	....	?	**DEMPO** (Sumatra)	0601-23=	0	
1905	....	?	**BATUR** (Lesser Sunda Is)	0604-01=	2	
? **1905**	....	?	**ASAMA** (Honshu-Japan)	0803-11=		
1905	....	?	**ZAO** (Honshu-Japan)	0803-19=	1?	
1905	....	?	**SHEVELUCH** (Kamchatka)	1000-27=		
1905	....	?	**SOCORRO** (Mexico-Is)	1401-021	2?	
1905	....	?	**COTOPAXI** (Ecuador)	1502-05=	2	

START YEAR	M-Dy	Duration	VOLCANO NAME (Subregion)	NUMBER	VEI	Vol L/T
? 1905	....	?	CORDON CAULLE (Chile-C)	1507-141		
L 1905?	....	?	PENGUIN (Antarctica)	1900-031		
1905	01	137m	MERAPI (Java)	0603-25=	2	-/6
1905	0116	5a	MOMOTOMBO (Nicaragua)	1404-09=	2	-/6
1905	0215	1a	FOURNAISE, PITON DE LA (Indian O.)	0303-02=	2	
1905	0218	5a	OKATAINA [WAIMANGU] (New Zeal)	0401-05=	1	
1905	0222	417m	KILAUEA (Hawaiian Is)	1302-01-	0	
1905	0407	9a	STROMBOLI (Italy)	0101-04=	2	
1905	0521	<1	KARANGETANG [API SIAU] (Sangihe	0607-02=	2	
1905	0608	....	POAS (Costa Rica)	1405-04=	1	
1905	0617	<1	OKATAINA [WAIMANGU] (New Zeal)	0401-05=	1	
1905	0722	65a>	NYAMURAGIRA (Africa-C)	0203-02=	2	7/7
1905	0804	>3yr	SAVAI'I (Samoa-SW Pacific)	0404-04=	2	9/6
1905	0804	?	SEMERU (Java)	0603-30=	2	
1905	0819	42a	KOMAGA-TAKE (Hokkaido-Japan)	0805-02=	2	
1905	10	16m	KUSATSU-SHIRANE (Honshu-Japan)	0803-12=	2	
1905	1028?	?	MAIPO (Chile-C)	1507-021		
1905	11	<1	INIELIKA (Lesser Sunda Is)	0604-09=	2	
1905	1101	?	MARAPI (Sumatra)	0601-14=	2?	
1905	1106	71a>	CANLAON (Philippines-C)	0702-02=	2	
1906	Cont	....	ETNA (Italy)	0101-06=	1	
1906	Cont	....	SAVAI'I (Samoa-SW Pacific)	0404-04=	1	9/6
1906	Cont	....	VICTORY (New Guinea)	0503-03=	1?	
1906	Cont	....	YASUR (Vanuatu-SW Pacific)	0507-10=	2	
1906	Cont	....	CANLAON (Philippines-C)	0702-02=	2	
1906	Cont	....	COLIMA VOLC COMPLEX (Mexico)	1401-04=	1	
1906	Cont	....	SANTA MARIA (Guatemala)	1402-03=	2	
1906	Cont	....	POAS (Costa Rica)	1405-04=	1	
1906	Cont	....	DONA JUANA (Colombia)	1501-07=	2	
1906	Cont	....	REVENTADOR (Ecuador)	1502-01=	2	
1906	Cont	....	SANGAY (Ecuador)	1502-09=	2	
1906	Cont	....	SANTIAGO (Galapagos)	1503-09=	0	
? 1906	....	?	BARRIER, THE (Africa-E)	0202-03=		
? 1906	....	?	NYAMURAGIRA (Africa-C)	0203-02=	1	
1906	....	?	NYIRAGONGO (Africa-C)	0203-03=	1	
? 1906	....	365y	KUCHINOERABU-JIMA (Ryukyu Is)	0802-05=		
1906	....	?	ASUNCION (Mariana Is-C Pac)	0804-15=	2	
1906	....	?	NEMO PEAK (Kurile Is)	0900-32=	2	
1906	....	>3yr	PAVLOF (Alaska Peninsula)	1102-03-	2?	
1906	....	?	PURACE (Colombia)	1501-06=	2	
1906	....	?	AZUL, CERRO [QUIZAPU] (Chile-C)	1507-06=	2	
1906	....	?	CALBUCO (Chile-S)	1508-02=	2	
1906	....	365y	HUEQUI (Chile-S)	1508-03=	2	
1906	01	30p	TOFUA (Tonga-SW Pacific)	0403-06=	2	
1906	0102	7a>	MASAYA (Nicaragua)	1404-10=	2	
1906	0201e	381e	MERAPI (Java)	0603-25=	1	-/6
1906	0221	<1	OKATAINA [WAIMANGU] (New Zeal)	0401-05=	1	
1906	0228	....	MERAPI (Java)	0603-25=	2	-/6
1906	03	?	TONGARIRO [NGAURUHOE] (New Z)	0401-08=	2	
1906	03	?	FONUALEI (Tonga-SW Pacific)	0403-10=		
1906	0301p	550p	BOGOSLOF (Aleutian Is)	1101-30-	1	6/8
1906	0315	?	RUAPEHU (New Zealand)	0401-10=	2	
1906	0404	....	VESUVIUS (Italy)	0101-02=	4	8/8
1906	0406	<1	ASAMA (Honshu-Japan)	0803-11=	2	
1906	0407	7a	BAYONNAISE ROCKS (Izu Is-Japan)	0804-07=	1	
1906	0411	?	STROMBOLI (Italy)	0101-04=	2	
1906	0422	?	VILLARRICA (Chile-C)	1507-12=	1?	
1906	0429	?	RINJANI (Lesser Sunda Is)	0604-03=	1?	
1906	05	?	ERTA ALE (Ethiopia)	0201-08=	0	
1906	05	?	KANAGA (Aleutian Is)	1101-11-		
1906	0607	?	ASO (Kyushu-Japan)	0802-11=	3	
1906	0617	90m	SOPUTAN (Sulawesi-Indonesia)	0606-03=	2	
1906	0715	?	STROMBOLI (Italy)	0101-04=	2	
1906	0806	131m	CHILLAN, NEVADOS DE (Chile-C)	1507-07=	2	
1906	0821	29a	COTOPAXI (Ecuador)	1502-05=	2	
1906	0922	89a	SUNDORO (Java)	0603-21=	2	
1906	0925	235a	TENGGER CALDERA [BROMO]	0603-31=	2	
1906	10	?	UBINAS (Peru)	1504-02=	2	
1906	12	?	TOFUA (Tonga-SW Pacific)	0403-06=	2	
1906	1202	>3yr	KILAUEA (Hawaiian Is)	1302-01-	0	
1907	Cont	....	ETNA (Italy)	0101-06=	1	
1907	Cont	....	SAVAI'I (Samoa-SW Pacific)	0404-04=	1	9/6
1907	Cont	....	VICTORY (New Guinea)	0503-03=	1?	
1907	Cont	....	YASUR (Vanuatu-SW Pacific)	0507-10=	2	
1907	Cont	....	MERAPI (Java)	0603-25=	2	-/6
? 1907	Cont	....	KUCHINOERABU-JIMA (Ryukyu Is)	0802-05=		
1907	Cont	....	PAVLOF (Alaska Peninsula)	1102-03-	2?	
1907	Cont	....	KILAUEA (Hawaiian Is)	1302-01-	0	
1907	Cont	....	SANTA MARIA (Guatemala)	1402-03=	2	
1907	Cont	....	SANGAY (Ecuador)	1502-09=	2	
1907	Cont	....	HUEQUI (Chile-S)	1508-03=	2	
? 1907	....	?	MANAM (New Guinea-NE of)	0501-02=		
1907	....	?	LANGILA (New Britain-SW Pac)	0502-01=	2	
1907	....	?	KABA (Sumatra)	0601-22=	2	
1907	....	?	BABUYAN CLARO (Luzon Is-N of)	0704-03=	2	
? 1907	....	?	KISKA (Aleutian Is)	1101-02-	2?	
1907	....	?	ATKA [KOROVIN] (Aleutian Is)	1101-16-		
1907	....	?	MAKUSHIN (Aleutian Is)	1101-31-		
1907	....	?	AKUTAN (Aleutian Is)	1101-32-		
1907	....	?	UBINAS (Peru)	1504-02=	2	
1907	....	257m	LLAIMA (Chile-C)	1507-11=	2	
1907	....	?	SAN JORGE (Azores)	1802-03=	0	
1907	0107	3a	SEMERU (Java)	0603-30=	2	
1907	0109	15a>	MAUNA LOA (Hawaiian Is)	1302-02=	0	8/-
1907	0111	138a	STROMBOLI (Italy)	0101-04=	2	
1907	0118	69a	ASAMA (Honshu-Japan)	0803-11=	2	
1907	02	91p	TONGARIRO [NGAURUHOE] (New Z)	0401-08=	2	
1907	0215	?	TUPUNGATITO (Chile-C)	1507-01=	2	
1907	0328?	?	KSUDACH (Kamchatka)	1000-05=	5	-/9
1907	04	31m	NYAMURAGIRA (Africa-C)	0203-02=	1	
? 1907	0401<	?	WRANGELL (Alaska-E)	1105-02-		
1907	0401	?	MONACO BANK (Azores)	1802-11=	0	
1907	0409	14a>	CARRAN-LOS VENADOS (Chile-C)	1507-14=	3	
1907	0422	?	CALBUCO (Chile-S)	1508-02=	2?	
1907	0427	....	STROMBOLI (Italy)	0101-04=	3	
1907	0510	16a	VILLARRICA (Chile-C)	1507-12=	2	
1907	06	50m>	ALAYTA (Ethiopia)	0201-112	2	
1907	06	?	COTOPAXI (Ecuador)	1502-05=	2	
1907	0605	20a?	SOPUTAN (Sulawesi-Indonesia)	0606-03=	2	
1907	07	?	UNNAMED (Tonga-SW Pacific)	0403-01=	0	
1907	0709<	?	SEMERU (Java)	0603-30=	2	
1907	0728	?	AZUL, CERRO [QUIZAPU] (Chile-C)	1507-06=	2	
1907	08	?	KLIUCHEVSKOI (Kamchatka)	1000-26=	2	
1907	0824	<1	ASAMA (Honshu-Japan)	0803-11=	2	
1907	0828	?	TENGGER CALDERA [BROMO]	0603-31=	2	
? 1907	0828	?	HOOD (US-Oregon)	1202-01-		
1907	09	>3yr	CONCEPCION (Nicaragua)	1404-12=	2	
1907	0901	....	BOGOSLOF (Aleutian Is)	1101-30-	3	6/8
1907	0928	?	EGON (Lesser Sunda Is)	0604-16=	2	
1907	0928	32a	LEWOTOBI (Lesser Sunda Is)	0604-18=	3	
1907	11	?	TONGARIRO [NGAURUHOE] (New Z)	0401-08=	2	
1907	11	?	BAM (New Guinea-NE of)	0501-01=	2	
1907	11	?	TELICA (Nicaragua)	1404-04=	2	
1907	1107	28a	NYAMURAGIRA (Africa-C)	0203-02=	3	
1907	1117	3a	GAMALAMA (Halmahera-Indonesia)	0608-06=	2	
1907	1129	6d	FOURNAISE, PITON DE LA (Indian O.)	0303-02=	0	
1907	1208	541a	YAKE-DAKE (Honshu-Japan)	0803-07=	2	
1907	1212	?	ASO (Kyushu-Japan)	0802-11=	2	
1907	1214	61a	TENGGER CALDERA [BROMO]	0603-31=	2	
1907	1217	272m	MARAPI (Sumatra)	0601-14=	2?	
1907	1231y	?	POAS (Costa Rica)	1405-04=	1	
1908	Cont	....	STROMBOLI (Italy)	0101-04=	1?	
1908	Cont	....	SAVAI'I (Samoa-SW Pacific)	0404-04=	1	9/6
1908	Cont	....	VICTORY (New Guinea)	0503-03=	1?	
1908	Cont	....	YASUR (Vanuatu-SW Pacific)	0507-10=	2	
1908	Cont	....	MARAPI (Sumatra)	0601-14=	2?	
1908	Cont	....	TENGGER CALDERA [BROMO]	0603-31=	2	
1908	Cont	....	YAKE-DAKE (Honshu-Japan)	0803-07=	2	
1908	Cont	....	PAVLOF (Alaska Peninsula)	1102-03-	2?	
1908	Cont	....	KILAUEA (Hawaiian Is)	1302-01-	0	
1908	Cont	....	SANTA MARIA (Guatemala)	1402-03=	2	
1908	Cont	....	CONCEPCION (Nicaragua)	1404-12=	2	
1908	Cont	....	SANGAY (Ecuador)	1502-09=	2	
1908	Cont	....	LLAIMA (Chile-C)	1507-11=	2	
1908	....	?	NYAMURAGIRA (Africa-C)	0203-02=		
? 1908	....	?	FOURNAISE, PITON DE LA (Indian O.)	0303-02=	0	
? 1908	....	?	LOLOBAU (New Britain-SW Pac)	0502-13=		
1908	....	?	AMBRYM (Vanuatu-SW Pacific)	0507-04=	2?	
1908	....	?	LOPEVI (Vanuatu-SW Pacific)	0507-05=	2	
1908	....	?	MERAPI (Java)	0603-25=	1?	
1908	....	?	KARYMSKY (Kamchatka)	1000-13=	2	
? 1908	....	?	AUGUSTINE (Alaska-SW)	1103-01-		
1908	....	>3yr	COTOPAXI (Ecuador)	1502-05=	1	
? 1908	....	?	GUALLATIRI (Chile-N)	1505-02=		
1908	01	335p	SEMERU (Java)	0603-30=	2	
? 1908	0115q	?	BOGOSLOF (Aleutian Is)	1101-30-		
1908	0117	12a?	ASO (Kyushu-Japan)	0802-11=	2	
1908	0213	6a	ASAMA (Honshu-Japan)	0803-11=	2	
1908	0216	1a	DEMPO (Sumatra)	0601-23=	2	
1908	0222	?	AKUTAN (Aleutian Is)	1101-32-	0	
1908	03	245p	EREBUS (Antarctica)	1900-02=	2	
1908	0429	1a	ETNA (Italy)	0101-06=	2	6/5
1908	0520	496a	ETNA (Italy)	0101-06=	1	
1908	06	365p	SOPUTAN (Sulawesi-Indonesia)	0606-03=	2	
1908	0712	?	BAM (New Guinea-NE of)	0501-01=	2	
1908	0715	?	BAGANA (Bougainville-SW Pac)	0505-02=	2?	
1908	0805	49a	ASAMA (Honshu-Japan)	0803-11=	2	
1908	10	259w?	KERINCI (Sumatra)	0601-17=	2	
1908	1001	<1	OKATAINA [WAIMANGU] (New Zeal)	0401-05=	1	
1908	1031	51a?	VILLARRICA (Chile-C)	1507-12=	2	
? 1908	11	?	ZAVODOVSKI (Antarctica)	1900-13=	1	
? 1908	1128	8a?	WHITE ISLAND (New Zealand)	0401-04=	2	
? 1908	1201p	?	NYIRAGONGO (Africa-C)	0203-03=		
1908	1218	78a	COLIMA VOLC COMPLEX (Mexico)	1401-04=	3	
1909	Cont	....	STROMBOLI (Italy)	0101-04=	1?	
1909	Cont	....	ETNA (Italy)	0101-06=	1	
1909	Cont	....	SAVAI'I (Samoa-SW Pacific)	0404-04=	1	9/6
1909	Cont	....	VICTORY (New Guinea)	0503-03=	1?	
1909	Cont	....	YASUR (Vanuatu-SW Pacific)	0507-10=	2	
1909	Cont	....	KERINCI (Sumatra)	0601-17=	2	
1909	Cont	....	SOPUTAN (Sulawesi-Indonesia)	0606-03=	2	
1909	Cont	....	YAKE-DAKE (Honshu-Japan)	0803-07=	2	
1909	Cont	....	PAVLOF (Alaska Peninsula)	1102-03-	2?	
1909	Cont	....	KILAUEA (Hawaiian Is)	1302-01-	0	
1909	Cont	....	COLIMA VOLC COMPLEX (Mexico)	1401-04=	2	
1909	Cont	....	SANTA MARIA (Guatemala)	1402-03=	2	
1909	Cont	....	CONCEPCION (Nicaragua)	1404-12=	2	
1909	Cont	....	COTOPAXI (Ecuador)	1502-05=	1	
1909	Cont	....	SANGAY (Ecuador)	1502-09=	2	
1909	....	>3yr	MANAM (New Guinea-NE of)	0501-02=	2	
1909	....	?	PAGAN (Mariana Is-C Pac)	0804-17=	2	
1909	....	?	IRAZU (Costa Rica)	1405-06=	2	
1909	....	?	FOGO (Cape Verde Is)	1804-01=		
1909	0108	503a	LEWOTOBI (Lesser Sunda Is)	0604-18=	2	
1909	0111	101a	SHIKOTSU [TARUMAI] (Hokkaido)	0805-04=	2	7/-
1909	0112	2a	TENGGER CALDERA [BROMO]	0603-31=	2	

START YEAR	START M-Dy	Duration	VOLCANO NAME (Subregion)	NUMBER	VEI	Vol L/T
1909	0129	>3yr	ASAMA (Honshu-Japan)	0803-11=	2	
1909	0201	>3yr	MERAPI (Java)	0603-25=	2	7/-
1909	03	123p	TONGARIRO [NGAURUHOE] (New Z)	0401-08=	2	
1909	03	?	CALBUCO (Chile-S)	1508-02=	2	
1909	0330R	....	SHIKOTSU [TARUMAI] (Hokkaido)	0805-04=	3	7/-
1909	04	?	FOURNAISE, PITON DE LA (Indian O.)	0303-02=	2	
1909	04	?	ASO (Kyushu-Japan)	0802-11=	2	
1909	0412	....	SHIKOTSU [TARUMAI] (Hokkaido)	0805-04=	3	7/-
1909	0419	147a	BAM (New Guinea-NE of)	0501-01=	2	
1909	0428	48m?	CAMEROON, MT. (Africa-W)	0204-01=	2	
1909	05	15a	NYAMURAGIRA (Africa-C)	0203-02=	1?	
1909	0502	<1	GEDE (Java)	0603-06=	1	
1909	0513	?	WHITE ISLAND (New Zealand)	0401-04=	2	
1909	06	?	KLIUCHEVSKOI (Kamchatka)	1000-26=	2	
1909	0603	43m	SUMBING (Sumatra)	0601-18=	2	
? 1909	0628	?	AMBRYM (Vanuatu-SW Pacific)	0507-04=		
? 1909	07	?	BAGANA (Bougainville-SW Pac)	0505-02=		
1909	08	?	TINAKULA (Santa Cruz Is-SW Pac)	0506-01=	2	
1909	08	?	AVACHINSKY (Kamchatka)	1000-10=	2	
1909	0819	?	VILLARRICA (Chile-C)	1507-12=	2	
1909	09	187m	SEMERU (Java)	0603-30=	2	
1909	09	369m	BOGOSLOF (Aleutian Is)	1101-30-	1	
1909	1109	?	ILIBOLENG (Lesser Sunda Is)	0604-22=	2	
1909	1118	9a	TENERIFE (Canary Is)	1803-03-	2	7/-
1909	1130	2a	RINJANI (Lesser Sunda Is)	0604-03=	2	
1910	Cont	....	STROMBOLI (Italy)	0101-04=	1?	
1910	Cont	....	SAVAI'I (Samoa-SW Pacific)	0404-04=	1	9/6
1910	Cont	....	MANAM (New Guinea-NE of)	0501-02=	2	
1910	Cont	....	VICTORY (New Guinea)	0503-03=	1?	
1910	Cont	....	YASUR (Vanuatu-SW Pacific)	0507-10=	2	
1910	Cont	....	MERAPI (Java)	0603-25=	2	7/-
1910	Cont	....	LEWOTOBI (Lesser Sunda Is)	0604-18=	2	
1910	Cont	....	ASAMA (Honshu-Japan)	0803-11=	2	
1910	Cont	....	PAVLOF (Alaska Peninsula)	1102-03-	2?	
1910	Cont	....	KILAUEA (Hawaiian Is)	1302-01-	0	
1910	Cont	....	SANTA MARIA (Guatemala)	1402-03=	2	
1910	Cont	....	CONCEPCION (Nicaragua)	1404-12=	2	
1910	Cont	....	COTOPAXI (Ecuador)	1502-05=	1	
1910	Cont	....	SANGAY (Ecuador)	1502-09=	2	
M 1910t	....	?	EMURUANGOGOLAK (Africa-E)	0202-051	0	
1910	....	?	AMBRYM (Vanuatu-SW Pacific)	0507-04=	0?	
1910	....	?	MARAPI (Sumatra)	0601-14=	2?	
1910	....	?	ILIWERUNG (Lesser Sunda Is)	0604-25=	2	
? 1910	....	?	AVACHINSKY (Kamchatka)	1000-10=		
1910	....	?	IRAZU (Costa Rica)	1405-06=		
? 1910	....	?	VILLARRICA (Chile-C)	1507-12=		
1910	01	?	TONGARIRO [NGAURUHOE] (New Z)	0401-08=	2	
? 1910	01	?	MEDICINE LAKE (US-California)	1203-02-	1?	
1910	0118	3a	TENGGER CALDERA [BROMO]	0603-31=	2	
1910	0120	....	SEMERU (Java)	0603-30=	2	
1910	0125	20m	POAS (Costa Rica)	1405-04=	2	-/5
1910	03	16m	KARTHALA (Indian O.-W)	0303-01=	1	
1910	03	16m	HEARD (Indian O.-S)	0304-01=	2	
1910	03	?	BURNEY, MONTE (Chile-S)	1508-07=	2	
1910	0323	26a	ETNA (Italy)	0101-06=	2	7/5
1910	0403	?	ASO (Kyushu-Japan)	0802-11=	2	
1910	0407	39m	TANGKUBANPARAHU (Java)	0603-09=	2	
1910	0410	?	EBULOBO (Lesser Sunda Is)	0604-10=	2	
1910	0618	120m	LOKI-FOGRUFJOLL (Iceland-NE)	1703-02=	2	
1910	0724	1a	OKATAINA [WAIMANGU] (New Zeal)	0401-05=	1	
1910	0725	113m	USU (Hokkaido-Japan)	0805-03=	2	-/6
1910	08	?	KLIUCHEVSKOI (Kamchatka)	1000-26=	2	
1910	0912	32a	POAS (Costa Rica)	1405-04=	1	
1910	0918	....	BOGOSLOF (Aleutian Is)	1101-30-	2	
1910	10	91p	TONGARIRO [NGAURUHOE] (New Z)	0401-08=	2	
1910	1026	57a	MERU (Africa-E)	0202-16=	2	
1910	1111	19a	YAKE-DAKE (Honshu-Japan)	0803-07=	2	
1910	1115q	?	SOPUTAN (Sulawesi-Indonesia)	0606-03=	2	
1910	1116	26a	FOURNAISE, PITON DE LA (Indian O.)	0303-02=	2	
1910	1116	90m	SEMERU (Java)	0603-30=	2	
1910	12	?	OSHIMA (Izu Is-Japan)	0804-01=	1	-/4
1910	1227	52a	ETNA (Italy)	0101-06=	2	
1911	Cont	....	STROMBOLI (Italy)	0101-04=	1?	
1911	Cont	....	TONGARIRO [NGAURUHOE] (New Z)	0401-08=	2	
1911	Cont	....	SAVAI'I (Samoa-SW Pacific)	0404-04=	1	9/6
1911	Cont	....	MANAM (New Guinea-NE of)	0501-02=	2	
1911	Cont	....	VICTORY (New Guinea)	0503-03=	1?	
1911	Cont	....	YASUR (Vanuatu-SW Pacific)	0507-10=	2	
1911	Cont	....	MERAPI (Java)	0603-25=	2	7/-
1911	Cont	....	ASAMA (Honshu-Japan)	0803-11=	2	
1911	Cont	....	KILAUEA (Hawaiian Is)	1302-01-	0	
1911	Cont	....	SANTA MARIA (Guatemala)	1402-03=	2	
1911	Cont	....	COTOPAXI (Ecuador)	1502-05=	1	
1911	Cont	....	SANGAY (Ecuador)	1502-09=	2	
1911	....	>3yr	PAGO (New Britain-SW Pac)	0502-08=	3	
1911	....	365y	LOLOBAU (New Britain-SW Pac)	0502-13=	4	8/8
1911	....	?	GAMKONORA (Halmahera-Indonesia)	0608-04=	2?	
1911	....	365y	ASO (Kyushu-Japan)	0802-11=	2	
1911	....	?	KARYMSKY (Kamchatka)	1000-13=	2	
1911	....	?	AKUTAN (Aleutian Is)	1101-32-	2	
? 1911	....	?	ANTOFALLA, VOLCAN (Argentina)	1505-123		
1911	....	365y	CALBUCO (Chile-S)	1508-02=	2	
1911	0127	12a	TAAL (Luzon-Philippines)	0703-07=	2	-/8
1911	0130	....	TAAL (Luzon-Philippines)	0703-07=	4	-/8
1911	0213	17a	SANGEANG API (Lesser Sunda Is)	0604-05=	2	
1911	0307	?	MONACO BANK (Azores)	1802-11=	1	
1911	04	60p	EREBUS (Antarctica)	1900-02=	2	
1911	0506	108a	YAKE-DAKE (Honshu-Japan)	0803-07=	2	
1911	08	?	ETNA (Italy)	0101-06=	1	
1911	08	61p	NYIRAGONGO (Africa-C)	0203-03=	1	
1911	08	?	UNNAMED (Tonga-SW Pacific)	0403-03=	0	
1911	0830	2a	IBU (Halmahera-Indonesia)	0608-03=	2	
1911	09	?	SAN PEDRO (Chile-N)	1505-07=	2	
1911	0902	4a	GAMALAMA (Halmahera-Indonesia)	0608-06=	1	
1911	0910	12a	ETNA (Italy)	0101-06=	1	7/6
1911	0930	?	CAMPI FLEGREI MAR SICILIA (Italy)	0101-07=	2	
1911	10	?	EREBUS (Antarctica)	1900-02=	2	
1911	11	166p	SOPUTAN (Sulawesi-Indonesia)	0606-03=	2	
1911	11	?	KLIUCHEVSKOI (Kamchatka)	1000-26=	2	
1911	1102	?	MARAPI (Sumatra)	0601-14=	2?	
? 1911	1106	?	CANDLEMAS ISLAND (Antarctica)	1900-10=	2	
1911	1108	37m	SEMERU (Java)	0603-30=	2	
1911	1115	....	SEMERU (Java)	0603-30=	3	
1911	1206	....	PAVLOF (Alaska Peninsula)	1102-03-	3	
1911	1231y	?	NEGRA, SIERRA (Galapagos)	1503-05=		
1912	Cont	....	MANAM (New Guinea-NE of)	0501-02=	2	
1912	Cont	....	PAGO (New Britain-SW Pac)	0502-08=	2	
1912	Cont	....	LOLOBAU (New Britain-SW Pac)	0502-13=	4	8/8
1912	Cont	....	VICTORY (New Guinea)	0503-03=	1?	
1912	Cont	....	YASUR (Vanuatu-SW Pacific)	0507-10=	2	
1912	Cont	....	MERAPI (Java)	0603-25=	2	7/-
1912	Cont	....	SOPUTAN (Sulawesi-Indonesia)	0606-03=	2	
1912	Cont	....	ASO (Kyushu-Japan)	0802-11=	2	
1912	Cont	....	ASAMA (Honshu-Japan)	0803-11=	2	
1912	Cont	....	KILAUEA (Hawaiian Is)	1302-01-	0	
1912	Cont	....	SANTA MARIA (Guatemala)	1402-03=	2	
1912	Cont	....	COTOPAXI (Ecuador)	1502-05=	1	
1912	Cont	....	SANGAY (Ecuador)	1502-09=	2	
1912	Cont	....	CALBUCO (Chile-S)	1508-02=	2	
1912	....	?	AMBRYM (Vanuatu-SW Pacific)	0507-04=		
1912	....	?	FARALLON DE PAJAROS (Mariana Is)	0804-14=	2	
? 1912	....	?	MAKUSHIN (Aleutian Is)	1101-31-		
1912	....	?	AKUTAN (Aleutian Is)	1101-32-		
? 1912	....	?	SHISHALDIN (Aleutian Is)	1101-36-		
1912	....	?	MAIPO (Chile-C)	1507-021		
1912	....	?	LLAIMA (Chile-C)	1507-11=	2	
1912e	....	?	DECEPTION ISLAND (Antarctica)	1900-03=	3?	
1912	01	?	KARYMSKY (Kamchatka)	1000-13=	2	
1912	0116	>3yr	IZALCO (El Salvador)	1403-03=	2	
1912	02	30p	REVENTADOR (Ecuador)	1502-01=	3	
1912	02	?	AZUL, CERRO [QUIZAPU] (Chile-C)	1507-06=	2	
1912	0211	87a	YAKE-DAKE (Honshu-Japan)	0803-07=	2	
1912	0223	340a	OSHIMA (Izu Is-Japan)	0804-01=	1	7/5
1912	04	?	OKATAINA [WAIMANGU] (New Zeal)	0401-05=	1	
1912	04	?	SANGEANG API (Lesser Sunda Is)	0604-05=	2	
1912	0429	?	UNNAMED (Tonga-SW Pacific)	0403-04=	2	
1912	0606	45a>	KATMAI (Alaska Peninsula)	1102-17-	3	-/7
1912	0606	131m?	NOVARUPTA (Alaska Peninsula)	1102-18-	6	7/10
1912	0614	?	RINCON DE LA VIEJA (Costa Rica)	1405-02=	2	
1912	0722	34a	STROMBOLI (Italy)	0101-04=	2	
1912	0804	14k	ETNA (Italy)	0101-06=	3	
1912	0828	?	SEMERU (Java)	0603-30=	2	
1912	1015e	?	NIUAFO'OU (Tonga-SW Pacific)	0403-11=	2	
1912	1203	132m	NYAMURAGIRA (Africa-C)	0203-02=	3	7/7
1912	1212	?	EREBUS (Antarctica)	1900-02=	2	
1913	Cont	....	STROMBOLI (Italy)	0101-04=	1?	
1913	Cont	....	NYAMURAGIRA (Africa-C)	0203-02=	2	7/7
1913	Cont	....	MANAM (New Guinea-NE of)	0501-02=	2	
1913	Cont	....	PAGO (New Britain-SW Pac)	0502-08=	2	
1913	Cont	....	VICTORY (New Guinea)	0503-03=	1?	
1913	Cont	....	YASUR (Vanuatu-SW Pacific)	0507-10=	2	
1913	Cont	....	MERAPI (Java)	0603-25=	2	7/-
1913	Cont	....	ASAMA (Honshu-Japan)	0803-11=	2	
1913	Cont	....	OSHIMA (Izu Is-Japan)	0804-01=	1	7/5
1913	Cont	....	KILAUEA (Hawaiian Is)	1302-01-	0	
1913	Cont	....	SANTA MARIA (Guatemala)	1402-03=	2	
1913	Cont	....	IZALCO (El Salvador)	1403-03=	2	
1913	Cont	....	COTOPAXI (Ecuador)	1502-05=	1	
1913	Cont	....	SANGAY (Ecuador)	1502-09=	2	
1913	....	?	BAM (New Guinea-NE of)	0501-01=		
? 1913	....	?	BABUYAN CLARO (Luzon Is-N of)	0704-03=	2	
1913	....	?	GUALLATIRI (Chile-N)	1505-02=	2	
1913	....	?	ISLUGA (Chile-N)	1505-03=	1?	
1913	01	?	TONGARIRO [NGAURUHOE] (New Z)	0401-08=	2	
1913	01	?	KLIUCHEVSKOI (Kamchatka)	1000-26=	2	
? 1913	0115q	?	AZUL, CERRO [QUIZAPU] (Chile-C)	1507-06=	2?	
1913	0120	>3yr	COLIMA VOLC COMPLEX (Mexico)	1401-04=	4?	-/8
1913	0127	<1	OKATAINA [WAIMANGU] (New Zeal)	0401-05=	1	
? 1913	0306	?	ANDAHUA VALLEY (Peru)	1504-002		
1913	0314	<1	AWU (Sangihe Is-Indonesia)	0607-04=	2	
1913	04	107p	SOPUTAN (Sulawesi-Indonesia)	0606-03=	2	
1913	0425	23a	HEKLA [MUNDAFIT, LAMBAFIT]	1702-07=	2	
1913	05	?	TONGARIRO [NGAURUHOE] (New Z)	0401-08=	2	
1913	0510	219m	RAUNG (Java)	0603-34=	2	
1913	0623	38a	MARAPI (Sumatra)	0601-14=	2?	
1913	0623	3a?	SEMERU (Java)	0603-30=	2	
? 1913	07	?	BOGOSLOF (Aleutian Is)	1101-30-		
1913	0705	>3yr	VESUVIUS (Italy)	0101-02=	2	8/7
1913	0710	24a	FOURNAISE, PITON DE LA (Indian O.)	0303-02=	2	
1913	0712	?	MASAYA (Nicaragua)	1404-10=	1?	
1913	09	?	TRIDENT (Alaska Peninsula)	1102-16-	1	
1913	0901	?	YAKE-DAKE (Honshu-Japan)	0803-07=	2	
1913	1014	261w	AMBRYM (Vanuatu-SW Pacific)	0507-04=	2	

START YEAR	M-Dy	Dura-tion	VOLCANO NAME (Subregion)	NUMBER	VEI	Vol L/T
1913	1108	61*a*	**KIRISHIMA** (Kyushu-Japan)	0802-09=	2	
1913	1113	>3yr	**ETNA** (Italy)	0101-06=	2	
1913	1206	....	**AMBRYM** (Vanuatu-SW Pacific)	0507-04=	3	
1914	*Cont*	....	*VESUVIUS (Italy)*	0101-02=	*2*	*8/7*
1914	*Cont*	....	*STROMBOLI (Italy)*	0101-04=	*1?*	
1914	*Cont*	....	*ETNA (Italy)*	0101-06=	*2*	
1914	*Cont*	....	*MANAM (New Guinea-NE of)*	0501-02=	*2*	
1914	*Cont*	....	*PAGO (New Britain-SW Pac)*	0502-08=	*2*	
1914	*Cont*	....	*VICTORY (New Guinea)*	0503-03=	*1?*	
1914	*Cont*	....	*AMBRYM (Vanuatu-SW Pacific)*	0507-04=	*2*	
1914	*Cont*	....	*YASUR (Vanuatu-SW Pacific)*	0507-10=	*2*	
1914	*Cont*	....	*KILAUEA (Hawaiian Is)*	1302-01-	*0*	
1914	*Cont*	....	*COLIMA VOLC COMPLEX (Mexico)*	1401-04=	*1*	*-/8*
1914	*Cont*	....	*IZALCO (El Salvador)*	1403-03=	*2*	
1914	*Cont*	....	*COTOPAXI (Ecuador)*	1502-05=	*1*	
1914	*Cont*	....	*SANGAY (Ecuador)*	1502-09=	*2*	
1914	....	?	**AZUMA** (Honshu-Japan)	0803-18=	1	
1914	....	?	**TANAGA** (Aleutian Is)	1101-08-	0	
1914	01	?	**NAKANO-SHIMA** (Ryukyu Is)	0802-04=	1	
1914	0105	?	**KUCHINOERABU-JIMA** (Ryukyu Is)	0802-05=	2?	
1914	0112	488*m*	**SAKURA-JIMA** (Kyushu-Japan)	0802-08=	4	**9/8**
1914	0113	?	**ASO** (Kyushu-Japan)	0802-11=	2	
1914	0113	220*a*>	**SHIN-IWO-JIMA** (Volcano Is-Japan)	0804-13=	3	**-/9**
1914	0128	17*m*	**OKATAINA [WAIMANGU]** (New Zeal)	0401-05=	1	
? **1914**	0213	?	**KIKAI** (Ryukyu Is)	0802-06=		
1914	0221	?	**IRAZU** (Costa Rica)	1405-06=	2	
? **1914**	0321	?	**SUWANOSE-JIMA** (Ryukyu Is)	0802-03=		
1914	0515	11*a*	**OSHIMA** (Izu Is-Japan)	0804-01=	2	7/6
1914	0529	255*p*	**RUANG** (Sangihe Is-Indonesia)	0607-01=	2	
1914	*0530*	*>3yr*	*LASSEN VOLC CENTER (US-Calif)*	1203-08-	2	
1914	0530	?	**POAS** (Costa Rica)	1405-04=	2	
1914	0531	?	**TANDIKAT** (Sumatra)	0601-15=	1	
1914	0604	<1	**GORIASCHAIA SOPKA** (Kurile Is)	0900-17B	2	
1914	0629	?	**LEWOTOBI** (Lesser Sunda Is)	0604-18=	2	
1914	0701	?	**MARAPI** (Sumatra)	0601-14=	2?	
1914	0703	?	**LLAIMA** (Chile-C)	1507-11=	2	
1914	0706	?	**PAVLOF** (Alaska Peninsula)	1102-03-	2	
1914	0815x	319*x*	**LENGAI, OL DOINYO** (Africa-E)	0202-12=	0	
1914	09	31*p*	**TONGARIRO [NGAURUHOE]** (New Z)	0401-08=	2	
1914	0908	?	**AZUL, CERRO [QUIZAPU]** (Chile-C)	1507-06=	3	
1914	10	31*p*	**NEGRO, CERRO** (Nicaragua)	1404-07=	2	
1914	1008	219*a*>	**POAS** (Costa Rica)	1405-04=	2	
1914	1108	?	**KIRISHIMA** (Kyushu-Japan)	0802-09=		
1914	1112	34*a*	**ASAMA** (Honshu-Japan)	0803-11=	2	
1914	1125	47*a*	**MAUNA LOA** (Hawaiian Is)	1302-02=	0	7/-
1915	*Cont*	....	*VESUVIUS (Italy)*	0101-02=	*2*	*8/7*
1915	*Cont*	....	*ETNA (Italy)*	0101-06=	*2*	
1915	*Cont*	....	*LENGAI, OL DOINYO (Africa-E)*	0202-12=	*0*	
1915	*Cont*	....	*PAGO (New Britain-SW Pac)*	0502-08=	*2*	
1915	*Cont*	....	*VICTORY (New Guinea)*	0503-03=	*1?*	
1915	*Cont*	....	*YASUR (Vanuatu-SW Pacific)*	0507-10=	*2*	
1915	*Cont*	....	*RUANG (Sangihe Is-Indonesia)*	0607-01=	*2*	
1915	*Cont*	....	*SAKURA-JIMA (Kyushu-Japan)*	0802-08=	*2*	**9/8**
1915	*Cont*	....	*KILAUEA (Hawaiian Is)*	1302-01-	*0*	
1915	*Cont*	....	*MAUNA LOA (Hawaiian Is)*	1302-02=	*0*	*7/-*
1915	*Cont*	....	*COLIMA VOLC COMPLEX (Mexico)*	1401-04=	*1*	*-/8*
1915	*Cont*	....	*IZALCO (El Salvador)*	1403-03=	*2*	
1915	*Cont*	....	*POAS (Costa Rica)*	1405-04=	*2*	
1915	*Cont*	....	*SANGAY (Ecuador)*	1502-09=	*2*	
1915	....	?	**ALAYTA** (Ethiopia)	0201-112		
1915	....	?	**RAGANG** (Mindanao-Philippines)	0701-06=	2	
1915	....	?	**KARYMSKY** (Kamchatka)	1000-13=	2	
1915	....	>3yr	**VILLARRICA** (Chile-C)	1507-12=	1?	
1915	01	?	**KLIUCHEVSKOI** (Kamchatka)	1000-26=	2	
1915	02	151*p*	**BAYONNAISE ROCKS** (Izu Is-Japan)	0804-07=	0	
1915	0204	68*a*	**OKATAINA [WAIMANGU]** (New Zeal)	0401-05=	1	
1915	0322	?	**EREBUS** (Antarctica)	1900-02=	2	
1915	0328	48*a*	**MERAPI** (Java)	0603-25=	2	
1915	04	?	**ULAWUN** (New Britain-SW Pac)	0502-12=	3	
1915	04	76*p*	**SOPUTAN** (Sulawesi-Indonesia)	0606-03=	2	6/-
1915	05	?	**RAUNG** (Java)	0603-34=	2	
1915	0513	106*a*	**ASAMA** (Honshu-Japan)	0803-11=	1	
1915	0522	....	**LASSEN VOLC CENTER** (US-Calif)	1203-08-	3	
1915	0606	40*a*	**YAKE-DAKE** (Honshu-Japan)	0803-07=	2	
1915	0618	162*a*	**STROMBOLI** (Italy)	0101-04=	2	5/-
? **1915**	07	61*p*	**SUWANOSE-JIMA** (Ryukyu Is)	0802-03=	2?	
1915	0722	122*a*	**FOURNAISE, PITON DE LA** (Indian O.)	0303-02=	2	
1915	08	?	**EREBUS** (Antarctica)	1900-02=	2	
1915	1010	15*a*?	**OSHIMA** (Izu Is-Japan)	0804-01=	2	
1915	1020	?	**AMBRYM** (Vanuatu-SW Pacific)	0507-04=	2	
1915	11	212*p*	**TENGGER CALDERA [BROMO]**	0603-31=	3	
1915	1104	?	**RINJANI** (Lesser Sunda Is)	0604-03=	2	
1915	1105	4*a*	**OKATAINA [WAIMANGU]** (New Zeal)	0401-05=	1	
1915	12	?	**MARAPI** (Sumatra)	0601-14=	2?	
1916	*Cont*	....	*VESUVIUS (Italy)*	0101-02=	*2*	*8/7*
1916	*Cont*	....	*ETNA (Italy)*	0101-06=	*2*	
1916	*Cont*	....	*PAGO (New Britain-SW Pac)*	0502-08=	*2*	
1916	*Cont*	....	*VICTORY (New Guinea)*	0503-03=	*1?*	
1916	*Cont*	....	*YASUR (Vanuatu-SW Pacific)*	0507-10=	*2*	
1916	*Cont*	....	*TENGGER CALDERA [BROMO]*	0603-31=	*2*	
1916	*Cont*	....	*LASSEN VOLC CENTER (US-Calif)*	1203-08-	*2*	
1916	*Cont*	....	*KILAUEA (Hawaiian Is)*	1302-01-	*0*	
1916	*Cont*	....	*COLIMA VOLC COMPLEX (Mexico)*	1401-04=	*1*	*-/8*
1916	*Cont*	....	*IZALCO (El Salvador)*	1403-03=	*2*	
1916	*Cont*	....	*SANGAY (Ecuador)*	1502-09=	*2*	
1916	*Cont*	....	*VILLARRICA (Chile-C)*	1507-12=	*1?*	
1916	....	?	**RUIZ** (Colombia)	1501-02=	2	
? **1916**	....	?	**SAN PEDRO** (Chile-N)	1505-07=		
1916	....	*>3yr*	*AZUL, CERRO [QUIZAPU] (Chile-C)*	1507-06=	2	
1916	0118	4*a*	**BULUSAN** (Luzon-Philippines)	0703-01=	2	
1916	*0303*	*>3yr*	*TUNGURAHUA (Ecuador)*	1502-08=	2	
1916	0317	26*a*	**YAKE-DAKE** (Honshu-Japan)	0803-07=	2	

Figure 22. Crater lake and dome of Soufriere St. Vincent, West Indies. This dome grew without explosions, heating the crater lake and breaking the surface in October of 1971. Dome growth ended after 5 months. It was destroyed by explosions in 1979, but another dome grew at the end of that eruption. Photo courtesy of Seismic Research Unit, University of West Indies, Trinidad.

START YEAR	M-Dy	Dura-tion	VOLCANO NAME (Subregion)	NUMBER	VEI	Vol L/T
1916	0413	....	TUNGURAHUA (Ecuador)	1502-08=	3	
1916	0418	>3yr	ZENGYU (Taiwan-N of)	0801-05=	0	
1916	0419	?	ASO (Kyushu-Japan)	0802-11=	2	
1916	0505	63a	MARAPI (Sumatra)	0601-14=	1	
1916	0512	143a	ASAMA (Honshu-Japan)	0803-11=	1	
1916	0519	11a	MAUNA LOA (Hawaiian Is)	1302-02=	0	7/-
1916	0620	14a	STROMBOLI (Italy)	0101-04=	2	4/-
1916	0621	?	SMITH ROCK (Izu Is-Japan)	0804-08=	0	
1916	0715e	?	MUTNOVSKY (Kamchatka)	1000-06=	2	
1916	11	31p	RAUNG (Java)	0603-34=	2	
1916	12	?	MUTNOVSKY (Kamchatka)	1000-06=	2	
1916	1201p	182p	LENGAI, OL DOINYO (Africa-E)	0202-12=	2?	
1917	Cont	....	VESUVIUS (Italy)	0101-02=	2	8/7
1917	Cont	....	STROMBOLI (Italy)	0101-04=	1?	
1917	Cont	....	PAGO (New Britain-SW Pac)	0502-08=	2	
1917	Cont	....	VICTORY (New Guinea)	0503-03=	1?	
1917	Cont	....	YASUR (Vanuatu-SW Pacific)	0507-10=	2	
1917	Cont	....	ZENGYU (Taiwan-N of)	0801-05=	0	
1917	Cont	....	LASSEN VOLC CENTER (US-Calif)	1203-08-	2	
1917	Cont	....	KILAUEA (Hawaiian Is)	1302-01-	0	
1917	Cont	....	COLIMA VOLC COMPLEX (Mexico)	1401-04=	1	-/8
1917	Cont	....	TUNGURAHUA (Ecuador)	1502-08=	2	
1917	Cont	....	AZUL, CERRO [QUIZAPU] (Chile-C)	1507-06=	2	
1917	Cont	....	VILLARRICA (Chile-C)	1507-12=	1?	
1917	....	?	BARRIER, THE (Africa-E)	0202-03=	2	
1917	....	?	MANAM (New Guinea-NE of)	0501-02=	2	
1917	....	?	BABUYAN CLARO (Luzon Is-N of)	0704-03=	2	
1917	....	?	YAKE-DAKE (Honshu-Japan)	0803-07=	1	
1917	....	?	PAGAN (Mariana Is-C Pac)	0804-17=	2	
? 1917	....	?	RINCON DE LA VIEJA (Costa Rica)	1405-02=		
? 1917	....	?	SAN PEDRO (Chile-N)	1505-07=		
1917	....	?	TINGUIRIRICA (Chile-C)	1507-03=	1?	
1917	01	....	LENGAI, OL DOINYO (Africa-E)	0202-12=	3	
1917	0204	?	LLAIMA (Chile-C)	1507-11=	2	
1917	0222	?	RAUNG (Java)	0603-34=	2	
1917	0225	17a	IJEN (Java)	0603-35=	1	
1917	0324	11a	OKATAINA [WAIMANGU] (New Zeal)	0401-05=	1	
1917	04	?	CALBUCO (Chile-S)	1508-02=	3?	
1917	0409	?	AGRIGAN (Mariana Is-C Pac)	0804-16=	4	
1917	0429	<1	FOURNAISE, PITON DE LA (Indian O.)	0303-02=	0	
1917	0430	12a	SHIKOTSU [TARUMAI] (Hokkaido)	0805-04=	2	
1917	0503	89a	ASAMA (Honshu-Japan)	0803-11=	1	
1917	0520	<1	SORIKMARAPI (Sumatra)	0601-12=	2	
1917	0607	161m	SAN SALVADOR (El Salvador)	1403-05=	3	
1917	0616	92a	MARAPI (Sumatra)	0601-14=	2?	
1917	0624	9d	ETNA (Italy)	0101-06=	2	
1917	0705d	?	MUTNOVSKY (Kamchatka)	1000-06=	3?	
1917	0927	>3yr	IRAZU (Costa Rica)	1405-06=	2	
1917	10	31p	TONGARIRO [NGAURUHOE] (New Z)	0401-08=	2	
1917	10	?	PAVLOF (Alaska Peninsula)	1102-03-	2	
1917	1018	<1	GAMKONORA (Halmahera-Indonesia)	0608-04=	2	
1917	11	?	SOPUTAN (Sulawesi-Indonesia)	0606-03=	2	
1918	Cont	....	VESUVIUS (Italy)	0101-02=	2	8/7
1918	Cont	....	STROMBOLI (Italy)	0101-04=	1?	
1918	Cont	....	PAGO (New Britain-SW Pac)	0502-08=	2	
1918	Cont	....	VICTORY (New Guinea)	0503-03=	1?	
1918	Cont	....	YASUR (Vanuatu-SW Pacific)	0507-10=	2	
1918	Cont	....	ZENGYU (Taiwan-N of)	0801-05=	0	
1918	Cont	....	COLIMA VOLC COMPLEX (Mexico)	1401-04=	1	-/8
1918	Cont	....	AZUL, CERRO [QUIZAPU] (Chile-C)	1507-06=	2	
1918	Cont	....	VILLARRICA (Chile-C)	1507-12=	1?	
1918	....	?	NYIRAGONGO (Africa-C)	0203-03=	1	
1918	....	730y	OKATAINA [WAIMANGU] (New Zeal)	0401-05=	1	
1918	....	>3yr	PEUET SAGUE (Sumatra)	0601-03=	2	
1918	....	?	MERAPI (Java)	0603-25=		
1918	....	?	YAKE-DAKE (Honshu-Japan)	0803-07=	1	
? 1918	....	?	ASAMA (Honshu-Japan)	0803-11=		
? 1918	....	?	TELICA (Nicaragua)	1404-04=		
1918	01	546p	CONCEPCION (Nicaragua)	1404-12=	2	
1918	0105	....	TUNGURAHUA (Ecuador)	1502-08=	3	
1918	0116	?	ASO (Kyushu-Japan)	0802-11=	2	
1918	0120	....	IRAZU (Costa Rica)	1405-06=	3	
1918	0223	14a	KILAUEA (Hawaiian Is)	1302-01-	0	5/-
1918	03	244p	ETNA (Italy)	0101-06=	1	
1918	0308	2a	MARAPI (Sumatra)	0601-14=	2?	
1918	0405	....	TUNGURAHUA (Ecuador)	1502-08=	4	
1918	0517	2a	BABUYAN CLARO (Luzon Is-N of)	0704-03=	2	
1918	0613	48a	SHIKOTSU [TARUMAI] (Hokkaido)	0805-04=	1	
1918	0629	?	RUAPEHU (New Zealand)	0401-10=	2	
1918	0717	13a	GALUNGGUNG (Java)	0603-14=	1	7/-
1918	0718	500p	BANUA WUHU (Sangihe Is-Indonesia)	0607-03=	2	
1918	0721?	?	ULAWUN (New Britain-SW Pac)	0502-12=	2	
1918	08	19m	GAMALAMA (Halmahera-Indonesia)	0608-06=	1	
? 1918	0809	?	KABA (Sumatra)	0601-22=	2?	
1918	0811	14	KARTHALA (Indian O.-W)	0303-01=	2	
1918	0815e	<1	MARAPI (Sumatra)	0601-14=	2?	
1918	0825	....	KARTHALA (Indian O.-W)	0303-01=	3	
1918	10	>3yr	BULUSAN (Luzon-Philippines)	0703-01=	2	
1918	1012	23a	KATLA (Iceland-S)	1702-03=	4	-/8
1918	1116	....	TUNGURAHUA (Ecuador)	1502-08=	3?	
1918	1129?	1a	ETNA (Italy)	0101-06=	1?	6/-
1918	1130	....	IRAZU (Costa Rica)	1405-06=	3	
1919	Cont	....	VESUVIUS (Italy)	0101-02=	2	8/7
1919	Cont	....	OKATAINA [WAIMANGU] (New Zeal)	0401-05=	1	
1919	Cont	....	VICTORY (New Guinea)	0503-03=	1?	
1919	Cont	....	YASUR (Vanuatu-SW Pacific)	0507-10=	2	
1919	Cont	....	PEUET SAGUE (Sumatra)	0601-03=	2	
1919	Cont	....	BULUSAN (Luzon-Philippines)	0703-01=	2	
1919	Cont	....	ZENGYU (Taiwan-N of)	0801-05=	0	
1919	Cont	....	COLIMA VOLC COMPLEX (Mexico)	1401-04=	1	-/8
1919	Cont	....	CONCEPCION (Nicaragua)	1404-12=	2	
1919	Cont	....	IRAZU (Costa Rica)	1405-06=	2	
1919	Cont	....	TUNGURAHUA (Ecuador)	1502-08=	2	
1919	Cont	....	AZUL, CERRO [QUIZAPU] (Chile-C)	1507-06=	2	
1919	....	?	SALAK (Java)	0603-05=	2	
1919	....	>3yr	MASAYA (Nicaragua)	1404-10=	2	
? 1919	....	?	VILLARRICA (Chile-C)	1507-12=		
1919	....	?	ASKJA (Iceland-NE)	1703-06=	2	
1919	0207	294a	KILAUEA (Hawaiian Is)	1302-01-	0	7/-
1919	0228	1a	MARAPI (Sumatra)	0601-14=	2?	
1919	0314	166a	ASAMA (Honshu-Japan)	0803-11=	2	
1919	0315	>3yr	ETNA (Italy)	0101-06=	2	
1919	04	....	BANUA WUHU (Sangihe Is-Indonesia)	0607-03=	3	
1919	04	31p	ASO (Kyushu-Japan)	0802-11=	2	
1919	05	?	BABUYAN CLARO (Luzon Is-N of)	0704-03=	2	
1919	0504	<1	SHIKOTSU [TARUMAI] (Hokkaido)	0805-04=	2	
1919	0518	219a	OSHIMA (Izu Is-Japan)	0804-01=	0	
1919	0519	1a	KELUT (Java)	0603-28=	4	-/8
1919	0522	?	STROMBOLI (Italy)	0101-04=	3	
1919	0528?	?	ULAWUN (New Britain-SW Pac)	0502-12=	2	
1919	0617	39a	KOMAGA-TAKE (Hokkaido-Japan)	0805-02=	2	
1919	0620	10a	NEGRO, CERRO (Nicaragua)	1404-07=	2	
1919	07	....	IWATE (Honshu-Japan)	0803-24=	1	
1919	0811	?	MANAM (New Guinea-NE of)	0501-02=	4	
1919	0926	40a?	MAUNA LOA (Hawaiian Is)	1302-02=	0	8/-
1919	11	?	SERUA (Banda Sea)	0605-07=	2	
1919	11	?	YAKE-DAKE (Honshu-Japan)	0803-07=	2	
1919	12	?	TELONG, BUR NI (Sumatra)	0601-05=	2	
1919	1210	37m	SAN MIGUEL (El Salvador)	1403-10=	2	
1919	1221	221a	KILAUEA (Hawaiian Is)	1302-01-	0	7/-
1920	Cont	....	VESUVIUS (Italy)	0101-02=	2	8/7
1920	Cont	....	STROMBOLI (Italy)	0101-04=	1?	
1920	Cont	....	ETNA (Italy)	0101-06=	2	
1920	Cont	....	OKATAINA [WAIMANGU] (New Zeal)	0401-05=	1	
1920	Cont	....	VICTORY (New Guinea)	0503-03=	1?	
1920	Cont	....	YASUR (Vanuatu-SW Pacific)	0507-10=	2	
1920	Cont	....	PEUET SAGUE (Sumatra)	0601-03=	2	
1920	Cont	....	BULUSAN (Luzon-Philippines)	0703-01=	2	
1920	Cont	....	ZENGYU (Taiwan-N of)	0801-05=	0	
1920	Cont	....	KILAUEA (Hawaiian Is)	1302-01-	0	7/-
1920	Cont	....	COLIMA VOLC COMPLEX (Mexico)	1401-04=	1	-/8
1920	Cont	....	MASAYA (Nicaragua)	1404-10=	2	
1920	Cont	....	IRAZU (Costa Rica)	1405-06=	2	
1920	Cont	....	TUNGURAHUA (Ecuador)	1502-08=	2	
1920	Cont	....	AZUL, CERRO [QUIZAPU] (Chile-C)	1507-06=	2	
? 1920 c	....	?	BARRIER, THE (Africa-E)	0202-03=		
1920	....	?	NYAMURAGIRA (Africa-C)	0203-02=	0	
1920	....	365y	NYIRAGONGO (Africa-C)	0203-03=	1	
? 1920 b	....	?	BAM (New Guinea-NE of)	0501-01=		
1920 b	....	?	PAGO (New Britain-SW Pac)	0502-08=	0	8/-
1920	....	?	LEWOTOLO (Lesser Sunda Is)	0604-23=	2	
1920	....	?	ASO (Kyushu-Japan)	0802-11=	2	
1920	....	?	YAKE-DAKE (Honshu-Japan)	0803-07=		
? 1920	....	?	OSHIMA (Izu Is-Japan)	0804-01=		
1920?	....	?	HUEQUI (Chile-S)	1508-03=	2	
1920	0122	?	EAST EPI (Vanuatu-SW Pacific)	0507-06=	2	
1920	06	? 760w?	POPOCATEPETL (Mexico)	1401-09=	1	
1920	0628	112a	FOURNAISE, PITON DE LA (Indian O.)	0303-02=	0	
1920	0717	5	SHIKOTSU [TARUMAI] (Hokkaido)	0805-04=	1	
1920	0725	204m	MERAPI (Java)	0603-25=	2	-/6
1920	0814	>3yr	SAN MIGUEL (El Salvador)	1403-10=	2	
1920	1013	....	MERAPI (Java)	0603-25=	3	-/6
1920	1029	163a	IZALCO (El Salvador)	1403-03=	2	
1920	11	?	SANTA ANA (El Salvador)	1403-02=	2	
1920	1205?	103m?	MANAM (New Guinea-NE of)	0501-02=	2	
1920	1206	6a	KELUT (Java)	0603-28=	2	5/-
1920	1210	201a	ASAMA (Honshu-Japan)	0803-11=	2	
1920	1210	3a	VILLARRICA (Chile-C)	1507-12=	2	
1921	Cont	....	VESUVIUS (Italy)	0101-02=	2	8/7
1921	Cont	....	ETNA (Italy)	0101-06=	2	
1921	Cont	....	NYIRAGONGO (Africa-C)	0203-03=	1	
1921	Cont	....	MANAM (New Guinea-NE of)	0501-02=	2	
1921	Cont	....	VICTORY (New Guinea)	0503-03=	1?	
1921	Cont	....	YASUR (Vanuatu-SW Pacific)	0507-10=	2	
1921	Cont	....	PEUET SAGUE (Sumatra)	0601-03=	2	
1921	Cont	....	MERAPI (Java)	0603-25=	2	-/6
1921	Cont	....	BULUSAN (Luzon-Philippines)	0703-01=	2	
1921	Cont	....	ZENGYU (Taiwan-N of)	0801-05=	0	
1921	Cont	....	ASAMA (Honshu-Japan)	0803-11=	2	
1921	Cont	....	COLIMA VOLC COMPLEX (Mexico)	1401-04=	1	-/8
1921	Cont	....	POPOCATEPETL (Mexico)	1401-09=	1	
1921	Cont	....	IZALCO (El Salvador)	1403-03=	2	
1921	Cont	....	SAN MIGUEL (El Salvador)	1403-10=	2	
1921	Cont	....	MASAYA (Nicaragua)	1404-10=	2	
1921	Cont	....	IRAZU (Costa Rica)	1405-06=	2	
1921	Cont	....	TUNGURAHUA (Ecuador)	1502-08=	2	
1921	Cont	....	AZUL, CERRO [QUIZAPU] (Chile-C)	1507-06=	2	
1921	....	>3yr	NYAMURAGIRA (Africa-C)	0203-02=	0	8/-
1921	....	?	YAKE-DAKE (Honshu-Japan)	0803-07=		
1921	....	>3yr	CONCEPCION (Nicaragua)	1404-12=	2	
1921	0101	354a	LEWOTOBI (Lesser Sunda Is)	0604-18=	2	5/-
1921	0129	78a	BATUR (Lesser Sunda Is)	0604-01=	2	
1921	02	?	LENGAI, OL DOINYO (Africa-E)	0202-12=	2	

	START YEAR	START M-Dy	Duration	VOLCANO NAME (Subregion)	NUMBER	VEI	Vol L/T
	1921	02	229t	AWU (Sangihe Is-Indonesia)	0607-04=	0	
	1921	0214d	60p	RAUNG (Java)	0603-34=	2	
	1921	03	?	KARANGETANG [API SIAU] (Sangihe	0607-02=	2	
	1921	03	?	ASKJA (Iceland-NE)	1703-06=	0	
?	1921	0318	?	ST. HELENS (US-Washington)	1201-05-		
	1921	0318	7a	KILAUEA (Hawaiian Is)	1302-01-	0	6/-
	1921	04	15m	DEMPO (Sumatra)	0601-23=	1	
	1921	05	31p	KERINCI (Sumatra)	0601-17=	2	
	1921	0523	11a	SUMBING (Sumatra)	0601-18=	2	
	1921	06	124m	TENGGER CALDERA [BROMO]	0603-31=	2	
	1921	0604	18a	STROMBOLI (Italy)	0101-04=	2	3/-
	1921	0706	<1	SHIKOTSU [TARUMAI] (Hokkaido)	0805-04=	1	
	1921	09	?	KARYMSKY (Kamchatka)	1000-13=	2	
	1921	0918	?	SERUA (Banda Sea)	0605-07=	2	
	1921	10	?	RUAPEHU (New Zealand)	0401-10=	2	
	1921	11	?	FALCON ISLAND (Tonga-SW Pacific)	0403-05=	2	
	1921	1127	6a	FOURNAISE, PITON DE LA (Indian O.)	0303-02=	2	
	1921	1208	49a	SUWANOSE-JIMA (Ryukyu Is)	0802-03=	2?	
	1921	1210	?	VILLARRICA (Chile-C)	1507-12=	2	
	1921	1213	62m	CORDON CAULLE (Chile-C)	1507-141	3?	8/-
	1921	1231y	?	BARRIER, THE (Africa-E)	0202-03=	2	
	1922	Cont	....	VESUVIUS (Italy)	0101-02=	2	8/7
	1922	Cont	....	STROMBOLI (Italy)	0101-04=	1?	
	1922	Cont	....	ETNA (Italy)	0101-06=	2	
	1922	Cont	....	NYAMURAGIRA (Africa-C)	0203-02=	0	8/-
	1922	Cont	....	VICTORY (New Guinea)	0503-03=	1?	
	1922	Cont	....	YASUR (Vanuatu-SW Pacific)	0507-10=	2	
	1922	Cont	....	BULUSAN (Luzon-Philippines)	0703-01=	2	
	1922	Cont	....	ZENGYU (Taiwan-N of)	0801-05=	0	
	1922	Cont	....	SUWANOSE-JIMA (Ryukyu Is)	0802-03=	2?	
	1922	Cont	....	COLIMA VOLC COMPLEX (Mexico)	1401-04=	1	-/8
	1922	Cont	....	POPOCATEPETL (Mexico)	1401-09=	1	
	1922	Cont	....	SAN MIGUEL (El Salvador)	1403-10=	2	
	1922	Cont	....	MASAYA (Nicaragua)	1404-10=	2	
	1922	Cont	....	CONCEPCION (Nicaragua)	1404-12=	2	
	1922	Cont	....	TUNGURAHUA (Ecuador)	1502-08=	2	
	1922	Cont	....	AZUL, CERRO [QUIZAPU] (Chile-C)	1507-06=	2	
	1922	Cont	....	VILLARRICA (Chile-C)	1507-12=	2	
	1922	Cont	....	CORDON CAULLE (Chile-C)	1507-141	3?	8/-
	1922	....	?	WHITE ISLAND (New Zealand)	0401-04=	2	
	1922	....	?	MANAM (New Guinea-NE of)	0501-02=	3?	
	1922	....	?	YAKE-DAKE (Honshu-Japan)	0803-07=		
	1922	....	?	GARELOI (Aleutian Is)	1101-07-	3	
	1922	....	?	COTOPAXI (Ecuador)	1502-05=	2	
	1922	0114	91m	ASAMA (Honshu-Japan)	0803-11=	2	
?	1922	0201p	?	UNNAMED (Sangihe Is-Indonesia)	0607-05=	0	
	1922	0203	202a	CAMEROON, MT. (Africa-W)	0204-01=	2	7/-
	1922	0205	135a	TENGGER CALDERA [BROMO]	0603-31=	2	
	1922	0218	171a	MERAPI (Java)	0603-25=	2	6/-
	1922	0411<	54a>	RINCON DE LA VIEJA (Costa Rica)	1405-02=	2?	
	1922	05	?	KLIUCHEVSKOI (Kamchatka)	1000-26=	2	
	1922	0504	222a	KARANGETANG [API SIAU] (Sangihe	0607-02=	2	
	1922	0522	?	KOMAGA-TAKE (Hokkaido-Japan)	0805-02=	2	
	1922	0528	2a	KILAUEA (Hawaiian Is)	1302-01-	0	6/-
	1922	0620	97m	AWU (Sangihe Is-Indonesia)	0607-04=	0	
	1922	0622	>3yr	SANTA MARIA (Guatemala)	1402-03=	3	8/8
	1922	0628	3a	LOPEVI (Vanuatu-SW Pacific)	0507-05=	2	
	1922	07	?	IWO-JIMA (Volcano Is-Japan)	0804-12=	1	
?	1922	08	?	METHANA (Greece)	0102-02=		
	1922	0830	?	BATUR (Lesser Sunda Is)	0604-01=	2	
	1922	0929	24a	GRIMSVOTN (Iceland-NE)	1703-01=	2	
	1922	1015q	?	SHISHALDIN (Aleutian Is)	1101-36-	2	
	1922	1024	?	LLAIMA (Chile-C)	1507-11=	2	
	1922	11	?	KRONOTSKY (Kamchatka)	1000-20=	2	
	1922	11	?	ASKJA (Iceland-NE)	1703-06=	0	
	1922	1208	53a	OSHIMA (Izu Is-Japan)	0804-01=	1	6/5
	1922	1224	66r	PAVLOF (Alaska Peninsula)	1102-03-	2	
	1923	Cont	....	VESUVIUS (Italy)	0101-02=	2	8/7
	1923	Cont	....	STROMBOLI (Italy)	0101-04=	1?	
	1923	Cont	....	NYAMURAGIRA (Africa-C)	0203-02=	0	8/-
	1923	Cont	....	VICTORY (New Guinea)	0503-03=	1?	
	1923	Cont	....	YASUR (Vanuatu-SW Pacific)	0507-10=	2	
	1923	Cont	....	ZENGYU (Taiwan-N of)	0801-05=	0	
	1923	Cont	....	OSHIMA (Izu Is-Japan)	0804-01=	1	6/5
	1923	Cont	....	PAVLOF (Alaska Peninsula)	1102-03-	2	
	1923	Cont	....	COLIMA VOLC COMPLEX (Mexico)	1401-04=	1	-/8
	1923	Cont	....	SAN MIGUEL (El Salvador)	1403-10=	2	
	1923	Cont	....	MASAYA (Nicaragua)	1404-10=	2	
	1923	Cont	....	CONCEPCION (Nicaragua)	1404-12=	2	
	1923	Cont	....	TUNGURAHUA (Ecuador)	1502-08=	2	
	1923	Cont	....	AZUL, CERRO [QUIZAPU] (Chile-C)	1507-06=	2	
	1923	Cont	....	VILLARRICA (Chile-C)	1507-12=	2	
	1923	....	?	SANTA ISABEL (Africa-W)	0204-02-		
?	1923	....	?	MANAM (New Guinea-NE of)	0501-02=	2?	
	1923	....	730y	KUWAE [KARUA] (Vanuatu-SW Pac)	0507-07=	2?	
	1923	....	?	MERAPI (Java)	0603-25=		
	1923	....	?	BATUR (Lesser Sunda Is)	0604-01=	2	
	1923h	....	?	ZAVARITZKI CALDERA (Kurile Is)	0900-18=	1	
	1923	....	....	SANTA MARIA (Guatemala)	1402-03=	2	8/8
?	1923	....	?	SAN PEDRO (Chile-N)	1505-07=		
	1923	....	?	CHILLAN, NEVADOS DE (Chile-C)	1507-07=		
	1923	01	244m	ASO (Kyushu-Japan)	0802-11=	2	
	1923	0115q	?	ASKJA (Iceland-NE)	1703-06=	0	
	1923	0117	5a	SARYCHEV PEAK (Kurile Is)	0900-24=	2	
	1923	02	? 840m?	PAGAN (Mariana Is-C Pac)	0804-17=	2	
	1923	02	190m	SHIKOTSU [TARUMAI] (Hokkaido)	0805-04=	1	
	1923	02	?	KARYMSKY (Kamchatka)	1000-13=	2	
	1923	02	?	KRONOTSKY (Kamchatka)	1000-20=	2	
	1923	0211	63m	ZHELTOVSKY (Kamchatka)	1000-04=	3	
	1923	0227	16a	KOMAGA-TAKE (Hokkaido-Japan)	0805-02=	2	
	1923	0302	72a	CENDRES, ILE DES (SE Asia)	0705-06-	2	-/8
	1923	0303	....	PAGAN (Mariana Is-C Pac)	0804-17=	3	
	1923	0311	728a	PAPANDAYAN (Java)	0603-10=	1	
	1923	0413	23a	GAMALAMA (Halmahera-Indonesia)	0608-06=	2	
	1923	0519?	<1	DEMPO (Sumatra)	0601-23=	1	
	1923	06	?	KIARABERES-GAGAK (Java)	0603-03=	1	
	1923	0602	<1	SLAMET (Java)	0603-18=	2	
	1923	0617	31a	ETNA (Italy)	0101-06=	2	7/5
	1923	0626	?	YAKE-DAKE (Honshu-Japan)	0803-07=	2	
	1923	07	16m	KIRISHIMA (Kyushu-Japan)	0802-09=	2	
	1923	0701	?	UNNAMED (Tonga-SW Pacific)	0403-03=	0	
	1923	08	30p	KLIUCHEVSKOI (Kamchatka)	1000-26=	2	
	1923	0825	<1	KILAUEA (Hawaiian Is)	1302-01-	0	5/-
	1923	09	<1	KERINCI (Sumatra)	0601-17=	1	
	1923	1009	266w	ETNA (Italy)	0101-06=	1	
	1923	1023	54m	NEGRO, CERRO (Nicaragua)	1404-07=	2	
	1923	1127	53a	SOPUTAN (Sulawesi-Indonesia)	0606-03=	2	7/-
	1923	1127	121p	POPOCATEPETL (Mexico)	1401-09=	1	
	1923	1208	?	GALERAS (Colombia)	1501-08=	2	
	1924	Cont	....	VESUVIUS (Italy)	0101-02=	2	8/7
	1924	Cont	....	STROMBOLI (Italy)	0101-04=	1?	
	1924	Cont	....	NYAMURAGIRA (Africa-C)	0203-02=	0	8/-
	1924	Cont	....	VICTORY (New Guinea)	0503-03=	1?	
	1924	Cont	....	KUWAE [KARUA] (Vanuatu-SW Pac)	0507-07=	2?	
	1924	Cont	....	YASUR (Vanuatu-SW Pacific)	0507-10=	2	
	1924	Cont	....	PAPANDAYAN (Java)	0603-10=	1	
	1924	Cont	....	ZENGYU (Taiwan-N of)	0801-05=	0	
	1924	Cont	....	COLIMA VOLC COMPLEX (Mexico)	1401-04=	1	-/8
	1924	Cont	....	POPOCATEPETL (Mexico)	1401-09=	1	
	1924	Cont	....	SAN MIGUEL (El Salvador)	1403-10=	2	
	1924	Cont	....	MASAYA (Nicaragua)	1404-10=	2	
	1924	Cont	....	CONCEPCION (Nicaragua)	1404-12=	2	
	1924	Cont	....	TUNGURAHUA (Ecuador)	1502-08=	2	
	1924	Cont	....	AZUL, CERRO [QUIZAPU] (Chile-C)	1507-06=	2	
	1924	Cont	....	VILLARRICA (Chile-C)	1507-12=	2	
	1924	....	?	WHITE ISLAND (New Zealand)	0401-04=	2	
	1924	....	?	OKATAINA [WAIMANGU] (New Zeal)	0401-05=	1	
	1924	....	?	BAM (New Guinea-NE of)	0501-01=	2	
?	1924	....	?	MANAM (New Guinea-NE of)	0501-02=	2?	
	1924	....	?	BABUYAN CLARO (Luzon Is-N of)	0704-03=	2	
?	1924	....	?	ASUNCION (Mariana Is-C Pac)	0804-15=	2?	
	1924	....	?	KETOI (Kurile Is)	0900-20=	2	
	1924	....	....	SANTA MARIA (Guatemala)	1402-03=	2	8/8
	1924	....	?	PURACE (Colombia)	1501-06=	2	
	1924?	....	?	ASKJA (Iceland-NE)	1703-06=	0?	8/-
	1924	0109	21a	TONGARIRO [NGAURUHOE] (New Z)	0401-08=	2	
	1924	0114	....	SOPUTAN (Sulawesi-Indonesia)	0606-03=	2	7/-
	1924	0117	?	PAVLOF (Alaska Peninsula)	1102-03-	2	
	1924	02 <	?	RAUNG (Java)	0603-34=	2	
	1924	0215	?	UNNAMED (Kurile Is)	0900-23=	0	
	1924	0215	?	RAIKOKE (Kurile Is)	0900-25=	4	
	1924	03	2a	BATUR (Lesser Sunda Is)	0604-01=	2	
	1924	03	?	IZALCO (El Salvador)	1403-03=	2	
	1924	03	30m	IRAZU (Costa Rica)	1405-06=	2	
	1924	0313	?	KOLOKOL GROUP (Kurile Is)	0900-12=	2?	
	1924	04	15m?	TANDIKAT (Sumatra)	0601-15=	1	
	1924	05	?	KARANGETANG [API SIAU] (Sangihe	0607-02=	2	
	1924	0510	17	KILAUEA (Hawaiian Is)	1302-01-	2	-/5
	1924	0519	4a>	FOURNAISE, PITON DE LA (Indian O.)	0303-02=	0	
	1924	0522	?	TONGARIRO [NGAURUHOE] (New Z)	0401-08=	2	
	1924	0719	10a	KILAUEA (Hawaiian Is)	1302-01-	0	5/-
	1924	0731	?	KOMAGA-TAKE (Hokkaido-Japan)	0805-02=	2	
?	1924	0820	?	RAUNG (Java)	0603-34=	2?	
	1924	0903	10a	FOURNAISE, PITON DE LA (Indian O.)	0303-02=	2	
	1924	0907	22a	ASAMA (Honshu-Japan)	0803-11=	2	
	1924	0911	2a	MERAPI (Java)	0603-25=	1	
	1924	10	31p	TONGARIRO [NGAURUHOE] (New Z)	0401-08=	2	
	1924	10	988w	GALERAS (Colombia)	1501-08=	2	
	1924	1031	?	IRIOMOTE-JIMA (Ryukyu Is)	0802-01=	4?	-/9
	1924	11	?	EBULOBO (Lesser Sunda Is)	0604-10=	2	
	1924	1116	739a	YAKE-DAKE (Honshu-Japan)	0803-07=	2	
	1924	1207	?	TELONG, BUR NI (Sumatra)	0601-05=	2	
	1924	1218	171a	ACATENANGO (Guatemala)	1402-08=	2	
	1924	1227	49m	ETNA (Italy)	0101-06=	1	
	1925	Cont	....	VESUVIUS (Italy)	0101-02=	2	8/7
	1925	Cont	....	STROMBOLI (Italy)	0101-04=	1?	
	1925	Cont	....	ETNA (Italy)	0101-06=	1	
	1925	Cont	....	NYAMURAGIRA (Africa-C)	0203-02=	0	8/-
	1925	Cont	....	VICTORY (New Guinea)	0503-03=	1?	
	1925	Cont	....	KUWAE [KARUA] (Vanuatu-SW Pac)	0507-07=	2?	
	1925	Cont	....	YASUR (Vanuatu-SW Pacific)	0507-10=	2	
	1925	Cont	....	PAPANDAYAN (Java)	0603-10=	1	
	1925	Cont	....	ZENGYU (Taiwan-N of)	0801-05=	0	
	1925	Cont	....	YAKE-DAKE (Honshu-Japan)	0803-07=	2	
	1925	Cont	....	COLIMA VOLC COMPLEX (Mexico)	1401-04=	1	-/8
	1925	Cont	....	SAN MIGUEL (El Salvador)	1403-10=	2	
	1925	Cont	....	CONCEPCION (Nicaragua)	1404-12=	2	
	1925	Cont	....	TUNGURAHUA (Ecuador)	1502-08=	2	
	1925	Cont	....	AZUL, CERRO [QUIZAPU] (Chile-C)	1507-06=	2	
	1925	Cont	....	VILLARRICA (Chile-C)	1507-12=	2	
	1925	....	?	CAMEROON, MT. (Africa-W)	0204-01=		
	1925	....	?	MANAM (New Guinea-NE of)	0501-02=	2?	
	1925	....	?	ILIBOLENG (Lesser Sunda Is)	0604-22=	2	
	1925	....	?	FARALLON DE PAJAROS (Mariana Is)	0804-14=	2	
	1925	....	?	ZHUPANOVSKY (Kamchatka)	1000-12=	2	
	1925	....	?	SHISHALDIN (Aleutian Is)	1101-36-		

	START YEAR	START M-Dy	Duration	VOLCANO NAME (Subregion)	NUMBER	VEI	Vol L/T
	1925	....	....	SANTA MARIA (Guatemala)	1402-03=	2	8/8
	1925	....	....	ACATENANGO (Guatemala)	1402-08=	3	
	1925	....	?	POAS (Costa Rica)	1405-04=	1	
	1925	....	?	TUPUNGATITO (Chile-C)	1507-01=	2	
	1925	0105d	<1	BATUR (Lesser Sunda Is)	0604-01=	2	
	1925	0106	?	ASO (Kyushu-Japan)	0802-11=	2	
	1925	0122	?	RUAPEHU (New Zealand)	0401-10=	2	
	1925	0122?	8a?	KUSATSU-SHIRANE (Honshu-Japan)	0803-12=	2	
	1925	02	80m	PAGAN (Mariana Is-C Pac)	0804-17=	2	
	1925	0215	....	GALERAS (Colombia)	1501-08=	3	
	1925	04 ?	?	MARAPI (Sumatra)	0601-14=	0	
	1925	0404	189a	KLIUCHEVSKOI (Kamchatka)	1000-26=	2	
	1925	0411	349a>	WOLF, VOLCAN (Galapagos)	1503-02=	1	
	1925	0513	?	SUWANOSE-JIMA (Ryukyu Is)	0802-03=	2?	
	1925	0525	....	GALERAS (Colombia)	1501-08=	3	
	1925	07	?	KARYMSKY (Kamchatka)	1000-13=	2	
	1925	0701	....	GALERAS (Colombia)	1501-08=	3	
	1925	0811	948a	SANTORINI (Greece)	0102-04=	2	8/-
?	1925	0924	?	NIEUWERKERK (Banda Sea)	0605-02=	2	
	1925	1012	24a	PURACE (Colombia)	1501-06=	2	
	1925	11	31p	TONGARIRO [NGAURUHOE] (New Z)	0401-08=	2	
	1925	1120	664m	TOKACHI (Hokkaido-Japan)	0805-05=	2	
	1925	1226	371m	IZALCO (El Salvador)	1403-03=	2	
	1925	1230	111a	FOURNAISE, PITON DE LA (Indian O.)	0303-02=	2	
	1926	Cont	....	VESUVIUS (Italy)	0101-02=	2	8/7
	1926	Cont	....	STROMBOLI (Italy)	0101-04=	1?	
	1926	Cont	....	NYAMURAGIRA (Africa-C)	0203-02=	0	8/-
	1926	Cont	....	VICTORY (New Guinea)	0503-03=	1?	
	1926	Cont	....	YASUR (Vanuatu-SW Pacific)	0507-10=	2	
	1926	Cont	....	ZENGYU (Taiwan-N of)	0801-05=	0	
	1926	Cont	....	YAKE-DAKE (Honshu-Japan)	0803-07=	2	
	1926	Cont	....	COLIMA VOLC COMPLEX (Mexico)	1401-04=	1	-/8
	1926	Cont	....	SANTA MARIA (Guatemala)	1402-03=	1	8/8
	1926	Cont	....	CONCEPCION (Nicaragua)	1404-12=	2	
	1926	Cont	....	GALERAS (Colombia)	1501-08=	2	
	1926	Cont	....	WOLF, VOLCAN (Galapagos)	1503-02=	1	
	1926	Cont	....	AZUL, CERRO [QUIZAPU] (Chile-C)	1507-06=	2	
	1926	Cont	....	VILLARRICA (Chile-C)	1507-12=	2	
	1926	....	?	DALLOL (Ethiopia)	0201-041	1	
	1926	....	?	LENGAI, OL DOINYO (Africa-E)	0202-12=	2	
	1926	....	?	COTOPAXI (Ecuador)	1502-05=	2	
	1926	....	?	FERNANDINA (Galapagos)	1503-01=		
	1926	0102	164a	ETNA (Italy)	0101-06=	1	
	1926	0105d	120p	REVENTADOR (Ecuador)	1502-01=	3	
	1926	0203	?	WHITE ISLAND (New Zealand)	0401-04=	2	
	1926	03	714q	MANAM (New Guinea-NE of)	0501-02=	2	
	1926	03 ?	?	KORYAKSKY (Kamchatka)	1000-09=	1?	
	1926	0301	130a	TANGKUBANPARAHU (Java)	0603-09=	1?	
	1926	0323	15a	KLIUCHEVSKOI (Kamchatka)	1000-26=	2	
	1926	0328	8a	AVACHINSKY (Kamchatka)	1000-10=	2	
	1926	0410	18a?	MAUNA LOA (Hawaiian Is)	1302-02=	0	8/-
	1926	0416	61m	TONGARIRO [NGAURUHOE] (New Z)	0401-08=	2	
	1926	0422	2a	DEMPO (Sumatra)	0601-23=	2	
	1926	05	....	SANTORINI (Greece)	0102-04=	2	8/-
	1926	0524	....	TOKACHI (Hokkaido-Japan)	0805-05=	3	
	1926	06	?	GAMKONORA (Halmahera-Indonesia)	0608-04=	1?	
	1926	0605d	?	REYKJANESHRYGGUR (Iceland-SW)	1701-01=	0	
	1926	07	715w	BOGOSLOF (Aleutian Is)	1101-30-	2	6/-
	1926	0715q	?	ASKJA (Iceland-NE)	1703-06=	2?	-/7
	1926	08	276m	ACATENANGO (Guatemala)	1402-08=	2	
	1926	08	31p	PURACE (Colombia)	1501-06=	2	
	1926	0802	50a	BATUR (Lesser Sunda Is)	0604-01=	2	7/6
	1926	0918	270a	FOURNAISE, PITON DE LA (Indian O.)	0303-02=	2	
	1926	0921	479a	ASO (Kyushu-Japan)	0802-11=	2	
	1926	10	?	KARANGETANG [API SIAU] (Sangihe	0607-02=	2	
	1926	1019	11a	SHIKOTSU [TARUMAI] (Hokkaido)	0805-04=	2	
	1926	1105	....	IZALCO (El Salvador)	1403-03=	3?	
	1926	1117	1a	OKATAINA [WAIMANGU] (New Zeal	0401-05=	1	
	1926	1123a	7b	SLAMET (Java)	0603-18=	2	
	1926	1220	1a	CUMBAL (Colombia)	1501-10=	2	
	1926	1221	9a?	TONGARIRO [NGAURUHOE] (New Z)	0401-08=	2	
	1926	1230	?	MAKUSHIN (Aleutian Is)	1101-31=	2	
	1927	Cont	....	VESUVIUS (Italy)	0101-02=	2	8/7
	1927	Cont	....	STROMBOLI (Italy)	0101-04=	1?	
	1927	Cont	....	NYAMURAGIRA (Africa-C)	0203-02=	0	8/-
	1927	Cont	....	FOURNAISE, PITON DE LA (Indian O.)	0303-02=	0	
	1927	Cont	....	MANAM (New Guinea-NE of)	0501-02=	2	
	1927	Cont	....	VICTORY (New Guinea)	0503-03=	1?	
	1927	Cont	....	YASUR (Vanuatu-SW Pacific)	0507-10=	2	
	1927	Cont	....	ZENGYU (Taiwan-N of)	0801-05=	0	
	1927	Cont	....	ASO (Kyushu-Japan)	0802-11=	2	
	1927	Cont	....	TOKACHI (Hokkaido-Japan)	0805-05=	2	
	1927	Cont	....	BOGOSLOF (Aleutian Is)	1101-30-	1	6/-
	1927	Cont	....	COLIMA VOLC COMPLEX (Mexico)	1401-04=	1	-/8
	1927	Cont	....	SANTA MARIA (Guatemala)	1402-03=	1	8/8
	1927	Cont	....	GALERAS (Colombia)	1501-08=	2	
	1927	Cont	....	AZUL, CERRO [QUIZAPU] (Chile-C)	1507-06=	2	
	1927	Cont	....	VILLARRICA (Chile-C)	1507-12=	2	
	1927	....	....	SANTORINI (Greece)	0102-04=	1	8/-
?	1927	....	?	TONGARIRO (New Zealand)	0401-08=	1?	
	1927	....	?	SANGEANG API (Lesser Sunda Is)	0604-05=	2	
	1927	....	?	ILIBOLENG (Lesser Sunda Is)	0604-22=	2	
?	1927	....	?	SIRUNG (Lesser Sunda Is)	0604-27=	2	
	1927	....	?	CANLAON (Philippines-C)	0702-02=		
?	1927	....	?	ZAO (Honshu-Japan)	0803-19=	1?	
	1927	....	?	SARYCHEV PEAK (Kurile Is)	0900-24=	2?	
?	1927	....	?	AVACHINSKY (Kamchatka)	1000-10=		
?	1927	....	?	KISKA (Aleutian Is)	1101-02-	2?	
?	1927	....	?	GARELOI (Aleutian Is)	1101-07-		
?	1927	....	?	SEGUAM (Aleutian Is)	1101-18-		
	1927	....	365y	AKUTAN (Aleutian Is)	1101-32-	2	
	1927	....	?	SHISHALDIN (Aleutian Is)	1101-36-		
	1927	....	365y?	IZALCO (El Salvador)	1403-03=	2	
	1927	....	?	PURACE (Colombia)	1501-06=	2	
	1927	01	30p	MUTNOVSKY (Kamchatka)	1000-06=	2	
	1927	0123	96	YAKE-DAKE (Honshu-Japan)	0803-07=	2	
	1927	0205	179m	MARAPI (Sumatra)	0601-14=	2	
	1927	0227	<1	SLAMET (Java)	0603-18=	2	
	1927	03	>3yr	NYIRAGONGO (Africa-C)	0203-03=	1	
	1927	03	497m	ASAMA (Honshu-Japan)	0803-11=	2	
?	1927	0301p	?	EMPEROR OF CHINA (Banda Sea)	0605-01=	2	
?	1927	0301p	?	NIEUWERKERK (Banda Sea)	0605-02=	2	
	1927	0330	....	ACATENANGO (Guatemala)	1402-08=	2	
?	1927	04	30p	AKAN (Hokkaido-Japan)	0805-07=	1	
	1927	07	63m>	ULAWUN (New Britain-SW Pac)	0502-12=	2	
	1927	0707	13a	KILAUEA (Hawaiian Is)	1302-01-	0	6/-
	1927	08	91p	TELICA (Nicaragua)	1404-04=	2	
	1927	0802	225m?	RAUNG (Java)	0603-34=	2	
	1927	0826e	?	MAGEIK (Alaska Peninsula)	1102-15-	2	
	1927	0905d	?	ESJUFJOLL (Iceland-SE)	1704-02=	1	
	1927	1004	?	FALCON ISLAND (Tonga-SW Pacific)	0403-05=	2	
	1927	1005	61a	LLAIMA (Chile-C)	1507-11=	2	
	1927	12	31p	KIZIMEN (Kamchatka)	1000-23=	2	
	1927	1213<	?	FERNANDINA (Galapagos)	1503-01=	0	
	1927	1215	<1	YAKE-DAKE (Honshu-Japan)	0803-07=	2	
	1927	1229	960a	KRAKATAU (Indonesia)	0602-00=	2	
	1927	1229	2a	KUSATSU-SHIRANE (Honshu-Japan)	0803-12=	2	
	1928	Cont	....	VESUVIUS (Italy)	0101-02=	2	8/7
	1928	Cont	....	STROMBOLI (Italy)	0101-04=	1?	
	1928	Cont	....	NYAMURAGIRA (Africa-C)	0203-02=	0	8/-
	1928	Cont	....	NYIRAGONGO (Africa-C)	0203-03=	0	
	1928	Cont	....	MANAM (New Guinea-NE of)	0501-02=	2	
	1928	Cont	....	VICTORY (New Guinea)	0503-03=	1?	
	1928	Cont	....	YASUR (Vanuatu-SW Pacific)	0507-10=	2	
	1928	Cont	....	ASAMA (Honshu-Japan)	0803-11=	2	
	1928	Cont	....	KIZIMEN (Kamchatka)	1000-23=	2	
	1928	Cont	....	BOGOSLOF (Aleutian Is)	1101-30-	1	6/-
	1928	Cont	....	AKUTAN (Aleutian Is)	1101-32-	2	
	1928	Cont	....	COLIMA VOLC COMPLEX (Mexico)	1401-04=	1	-/8
	1928	Cont	....	IZALCO (El Salvador)	1403-03=	2	
	1928	Cont	....	AZUL, CERRO [QUIZAPU] (Chile-C)	1507-06=	2	
	1928	Cont	....	VILLARRICA (Chile-C)	1507-12=	2	
?	1928	....	?	AYELU (Ethiopia)	0201-16=	2	
?	1928	....	?	ADWA (Ethiopia)	0201-17=	2	
	1928b	....	?	KARTHALA (Indian O.-W)	0303-01=	1?	
	1928	....	?	ILIWERUNG (Lesser Sunda Is)	0604-25=	2	7/-
?	1928	....	?	VETERAN (SE Asia)	0705-07-	0	
@	1928	....	?	MACDONALD (Austral Is-C Pac)	1303-07-	0?	
	1928	....	....	SANTA MARIA (Guatemala)	1402-03=	2	8/8
	1928	....	?	TELICA (Nicaragua)	1404-04=	2	
	1928	....	?	PINTA (Galapagos)	1503-07=		
	1928	01 ?	212m?	MAYON (Luzon-Philippines)	0703-03=	2	7/7
	1928	01	127m	TOKACHI (Hokkaido-Japan)	0805-05=	1	
	1928	01	16m	CONCEPCION (Nicaragua)	1404-12=	2	
	1928	0107	<1	SHIKOTSU [TARUMAI] (Hokkaido)	0805-04=	2	
	1928	0123	....	SANTORINI (Greece)	0102-04=	2	8/-
	1928	0125	40m	MUTNOVSKY (Kamchatka)	1000-06=	2	
	1928	0127	443q	SHEVELUCH (Kamchatka)	1000-27=	1	
	1928	0205	....	KRAKATAU (Indonesia)	0602-00=	2	
	1928	0214	?	SARYCHEV PEAK (Kurile Is)	0900-24=	2	
	1928	0214	102e	IRAZU (Costa Rica)	1405-06=	2	
	1928	0303	?	TONGARIRO [NGAURUHOE] (New Z)	0401-08=	2	
	1928	0315e	122m	TENGGER CALDERA [BROMO]	0603-31=	2	
	1928	0320	49a	SLAMET (Java)	0603-18=	2	
?	1928	0328	?	KOMAGA-TAKE (Hokkaido-Japan)	0805-02=		
	1928	05	?	FALCON ISLAND (Tonga-SW Pacific	0403-05=	2?	
	1928	0513	?	DIENG VOLC COMPLEX (Java)	0603-20=	2	
	1928	06	?	BULUSAN (Luzon-Philippines)	0703-01=	2	
	1928	0609	?	PINACATE PEAKS (Mexico)	1401-001	2?	
	1928	0625	....	MAYON (Luzon-Philippines)	0703-03=	3	7/7
	1928	07	?	TONGARIRO [NGAURUHOE] (New Z)	0401-08=	2	
	1928	0731	21a	ETNA (Italy)	0101-06=	1	
	1928	08	?	SHISHALDIN (Aleutian Is)	1101-36-	2	
	1928	0804	52a	PALUWEH (Lesser Sunda Is)	0604-15=	3	6/7
	1928	0807	1a	OSHIMA (Izu Is-Japan)	0804-01=	2	
	1928	0901	3a	WHITE ISLAND (New Zealand)	0401-04=	1	
	1928	0906	413a	ASO (Kyushu-Japan)	0802-11=	2	
	1928	0906	157a	SHIKOTSU [TARUMAI] (Hokkaido)	0805-04=	1	
	1928	11	?	RAUNG (Java)	0603-34=	2	
	1928	1102	16a	ETNA (Italy)	0101-06=	1	7/6
	1928	1204	21a	TOKACHI (Hokkaido-Japan)	0805-05=	1	
	1928	1215e	?	FARALLON DE PAJAROS (Mariana Is	0804-14=	2?	
	1928	1216	?	TENGGER CALDERA [BROMO]	0603-31=	2	
	1928	1231y	?	MANDA-INAKIR (Ethiopia)	0201-122		
	1929	Cont	....	STROMBOLI (Italy)	0101-04=	1?	
	1929	Cont	....	NYAMURAGIRA (Africa-C)	0203-02=	0	8/-
	1929	Cont	....	NYIRAGONGO (Africa-C)	0203-03=	0	
	1929	Cont	....	VICTORY (New Guinea)	0503-03=	1?	
	1929	Cont	....	YASUR (Vanuatu-SW Pacific)	0507-10=	2	
	1929	Cont	....	ASO (Kyushu-Japan)	0802-11=	2	
	1929	Cont	....	SHIKOTSU [TARUMAI] (Hokkaido)	0805-04=	1	
	1929	Cont	....	SHEVELUCH (Kamchatka)	1000-27=	1	
	1929	Cont	....	COLIMA VOLC COMPLEX (Mexico)	1401-04=	1	-/8
	1929	Cont	....	AZUL, CERRO [QUIZAPU] (Chile-C)	1507-06=	2	

Figure 23. Explosive eruption with airfall at Africa's Nyamuragira volcano, Zaire. Main vent at left feeds ejecta vertically that then falls downwind to form cone at right. Hot tephra steams in the foreground. This otherwise unremarkable eruption produced a large aerosol blanket; It was monitored by atmospheric scientists around the world and caused brilliant sunsets in the following months. Photo by Katia Krafft, January 1982.

START YEAR	M-Dy	Duration	VOLCANO NAME (Subregion)	NUMBER	VEI	Vol L/T
1929	....	?	**KIARABERES-GAGAK** (Java)	0603-03=	1	
? **1929**	....	365*y*?	**PAGAN** (Mariana Is-C Pac)	0804-17=		
1929	....	?	**ZHUPANOVSKY** (Kamchatka)	1000-12=	2	
1929	....	?	**KARYMSKY** (Kamchatka)	1000-13=	2	
? **1929**	....	?	**YUNASKA** (Aleutian Is)	1101-21-		
1929	....	?	**POAS** (Costa Rica)	1405-04=	1	
1929	....	?	**REVENTADOR** (Ecuador)	1502-01=	3	
1929	....	?	**CHILLAN, NEVADOS DE** (Chile-C)	1507-07=	2?	
1929	01	15*m*	**TELICA** (Nicaragua)	1404-04=	1?	
1929	01	30*p*	**KVERKFJOLL** (Iceland-NE)	1703-05=	1	
1929	0106	<1	**CALBUCO** (Chile-S)	1508-02=	3?	
1929	0107	?	**CORDON CAULLE** (Chile-C)	1507-141	2?	
1929	*0112*	....	*KRAKATAU (Indonesia)*	0602-00=	2	
1929	0122	73*a*	**ASAMA** (Honshu-Japan)	0803-11=	2	
1929	02	?	**MUTNOVSKY** (Kamchatka)	1000-06=	2	
1929	0210	33*m*	**NEGRO, CERRO** (Nicaragua)	1404-07=	2	
1929	0220	1	**KILAUEA** (Hawaiian Is)	1302-01-	0	6/-
? **1929**	03	?	**CLEVELAND** (Aleutian Is)	1101-24-		
1929	03	883*p*	**PAVLOF** (Alaska Peninsula)	1102-03-	2	
1929	04	443*w*	**GARELOI** (Aleutian Is)	1101-07-	3	
1929	0417	2*a*	**YAKE-DAKE** (Honshu-Japan)	0803-07=	2	
1929	0427r	?	**RAUNG** (Java)	0603-34=	2	
1929	05 ?	?	**AKUTAN** (Aleutian Is)	1101-32-	2	
1929	0520	<1	**TANGKUBANPARAHU** (Java)	0603-09=	0	
1929	0528	26*a*>	**SHISHALDIN** (Aleutian Is)	1101-36-	2	
1929	06	61*p*	**KLIUCHEVSKOI** (Kamchatka)	1000-26=	2	
1929	0603	....	**VESUVIUS** (Italy)	0101-02=	3	8/7
1929	0606	9*a*	**SLAMET** (Java)	0603-18=	2	
1929	0617	81*a*	**KOMAGA-TAKE** (Hokkaido-Japan)	0805-02=	4	-/8
1929	0622	<1	**MARAPI** (Sumatra)	0601-14=	2	
1929	0628	3*a*	**AMBRYM** (Vanuatu-SW Pacific)	0507-04=	2	
1929	0725	1*a*	**NIUAFO'OU** (Tonga-SW Pacific)	0403-11=	2	
1929	0725	3	**KILAUEA** (Hawaiian Is)	1302-01-	0	6/-
1929	08	?	**SAN MIGUEL** (El Salvador)	1403-10=	2	
1929	08	61*p*	**CONCEPCION** (Nicaragua)	1404-12=	2	
1929	0802	?	**ETNA** (Italy)	0101-06=	1	
1929	0807	32*a*	**TENGGER CALDERA [BROMO]**	0603-31=	2	
? **1929**	0819	118*m*	**MAGEIK** (Alaska Peninsula)	1102-15-	2	
1929	09	?	**AKITA-YAKE-YAMA** (Honshu-Japan)	0803-26=	2	
1929	0901	226*m*	**GORELY** (Kamchatka)	1000-07=	3	-/7
1929	*0916*	*>3yr*	*PELEE (W Indies)*	1600-12=	2	
1929	0918	58*a*	**ASAMA** (Honshu-Japan)	0803-11=	2	
1929	*1102*	....	*SANTA MARIA (Guatemala)*	1402-03=	3	*8/8*
1929	12	?	**KAGAMIL** (Aleutian Is)	1101-26-		
? **1929**	12	?	**CHIGINAGAK** (Alaska Peninsula)	1102-11-		
1929	12	?	**LLAIMA** (Chile-C)	1507-11=	2	
1929	1215	....	**PELEE** (W Indies)	1600-12=	3	
1929	1223	8*a*	**FOURNAISE, PITON DE LA** (Indian O.)	0303-02=	2	
1929	1227	?	**VILLARRICA** (Chile-C)	1507-12=	1	
1930	*Cont*	....	*VESUVIUS (Italy)*	0101-02=	*2*	*8/7*
1930	*Cont*	....	*NYAMURAGIRA (Africa-C)*	0203-02=	*0*	*8/-*
1930	*Cont*	....	*NYIRAGONGO (Africa-C)*	0203-03=	*0*	
1930	*Cont*	....	*VICTORY (New Guinea)*	0503-03=	*1?*	
1930	*Cont*	....	*YASUR (Vanuatu-SW Pacific)*	0507-10=	*2*	
? *1930*	*Cont*	....	*PAGAN (Mariana Is-C Pac)*	0804-17=		
1930	*Cont*	....	*GARELOI (Aleutian Is)*	1101-07-	*3*	
1930	*Cont*	....	*COLIMA VOLC COMPLEX (Mexico)*	1401-04=	*1*	*-/8*
1930	*Cont*	....	*AZUL, CERRO [QUIZAPU] (Chile-C)*	1507-06=	*2*	
1930	....	>3yr	**KITA-IWO-JIMA** (Volcano Is-Japan)	0804-11=	2?	
1930?	....	?	**IWO-JIMA** (Volcano Is-Japan)	0804-12=	1	
1930	....	....	*SANTA MARIA (Guatemala)*	1402-03=	2	*8/8*
? **1930**	....	?	**TACORA** (Chile-N)	1505-01=		
? **1930**	....	?	**PUNTIGUIDO-CORDON CENIZOS**	1507-16-		
? **1930**	....	?	**HODSON** (Antarctica)	1900-11=		
1930	*0114*	....	*KRAKATAU (Indonesia)*	0602-00=	2	
1930	0126e	?	**SAN MIGUEL** (El Salvador)	1403-10=	2	
1930	0201p	?	**SHEVELUCH** (Kamchatka)	1000-27=	1	
1930	0203	3*a*	**STROMBOLI** (Italy)	0101-04=	2	
1930	*0203*	....	*PELEE (W Indies)*	1600-12=	2	
1930	0204	2*a*	**KARANGETANG [API SIAU]** (Sangihe	0607-02=	2	
1930	0213	<1	**SARYCHEV PEAK** (Kurile Is)	0900-24=	3	
? **1930**	0301p	?	**IZU-TOBU** (Honshu-Japan)	0803-01=		
1930	0313	59*a*	**YAKE-DAKE** (Honshu-Japan)	0803-07=	2	
1930	0316	?	**WHITE ISLAND** (New Zealand)	0401-04=	2	
1930	*0330*	....	*PAVLOF (Alaska Peninsula)*	1102-03-	2	
1930	04	?	**IZALCO** (El Salvador)	1403-03=	0	
1930	0402	11*a*	**SLAMET** (Java)	0603-18=	2	
1930	*0409<*	*242a>*	*MARAPI (Sumatra)*	0601-14=	0	
? **1930**	0417	?	**GALERAS** (Colombia)	1501-08=		
1930	0418	181*m*	**ASAMA** (Honshu-Japan)	0803-11=	2	
1930	05	....	**MARAPI** (Sumatra)	0601-14=	2?	
1930	0523	1*a*	**FOURNAISE, PITON DE LA** (Indian O.)	0303-02=	0	
1930	0530	45*m*	**TENGGER CALDERA [BROMO]**	0603-31=	2	
1930	06	?	**VENIAMINOF** (Alaska Peninsula)	1102-07-	2	
1930	0706	45*a*	**LLAIMA** (Chile-C)	1507-11=	2	
1930	08	?	**LOKON-EMPUNG** (Sulawesi-Indonesia)	0606-10=	2	
1930	09	124*m*	**GORELY** (Kamchatka)	1000-07=	3	-/7
1930	0903	....	**ASO** (Kyushu-Japan)	0802-11=	2	
1930	0911	83*a*	**STROMBOLI** (Italy)	0101-04=	3	3/-
1930	10	?	**IRAZU** (Costa Rica)	1405-06=	2	
1930	*1022*	....	*STROMBOLI (Italy)*	0101-04=	2	*3/-*
1930	11 ?	?	**KARANGETANG [API SIAU]** (Sangihe	0607-02=	2	
1930	1101	?	**ETNA** (Italy)	0101-06=	1	

START YEAR	M-Dy	Duration	VOLCANO NAME (Subregion)	NUMBER	VEI	Vol L/T
1930	1119	18a	KILAUEA (Hawaiian Is)	1302-01-	0	6/-
1931	Cont	....	VESUVIUS (Italy)	0101-02=	2	8/7
1931	Cont	....	STROMBOLI (Italy)	0101-04=	1?	
1931	Cont	....	NYAMURAGIRA (Africa-C)	0203-02=	0	8/-
1931	Cont	....	NYIRAGONGO (Africa-C)	0203-03=	0	
1931	Cont	....	VICTORY (New Guinea)	0503-03=	1?	
1931	Cont	....	YASUR (Vanuatu-SW Pacific)	0507-10=	2	
1931	Cont	....	MERAPI (Java)	0603-25=	2	7/6
1931	Cont	....	KITA-IWO-JIMA (Volcano Is-Japan)	0804-11=	0	
1931	Cont	....	PAVLOF (Alaska Peninsula)	1102-03-	2	
1931	Cont	....	COLIMA VOLC COMPLEX (Mexico)	1401-04=	1	-/8
1931	Cont	....	AZUL, CERRO [QUIZAPU] (Chile-C)	1507-06=	2	
1931	Cont	....	PELEE (W Indies)	1600-12=	2	
? 1931	....	?	BALUAN (Admiralty Is-SW Pac)	0500-02-	0	
1931	....	?	COTOPAXI (Ecuador)	1502-05=	2	
1931	0122	216e	FOURNAISE, PITON DE LA (Indian O.)	0303-02=	2	8/-
1931	02	90p	TONGARIRO [NGAURUHOE] (New Z)	0401-08=	2	
1931	03	537m	ASAMA (Honshu-Japan)	0803-11=	2	
1931	03	....	SANTA MARIA (Guatemala)	1402-03=	2	8/8
1931	03	92p	SAN MIGUEL (El Salvador)	1403-10=	2	
1931	0304	485w	TOLBACHIK (Kamchatka)	1000-24=	2	
1931	0315	....	AWU (Sangihe Is-Indonesia)	0607-04=	2	6/-
1931	0321	53a>	OKMOK (Aleutian Is)	1101-29-	2	
1931	0325	2a	KLIUCHEVSKOI (Kamchatka)	1000-26=	4	
1931	0326	90a	YAKE-DAKE (Honshu-Japan)	0803-07=	2	
1931	0331t	?	IZALCO (El Salvador)	1403-03=	2	
1931	0402	81a	KUCHINOERABU-JIMA (Ryukyu Is)	0802-05=	3?	
1931	05	60r	GORELY (Kamchatka)	1000-07=	2	
1931	05	91p	AKUTAN (Aleutian Is)	1101-32-	2	
1931	0501	19a>	ANIAKCHAK (Alaska Peninsula)	1102-09-	3	
1931	0516	<1	TOKACHI (Hokkaido-Japan)	0805-05=	1	
1931	0520	....	ANIAKCHAK (Alaska Peninsula)	1102-09-	3	
1931	0726e	781n	ETNA (Italy)	0101-06=	2	
1931	08	31p	KLIUCHEVSKOI (Kamchatka)	1000-26=	2	
1931	0820	....	ASAMA (Honshu-Japan)	0803-11=	3	
1931	09	?	HARIMKOTAN (Kurile Is)	0900-30=	1	
1931	0923	147a	KRAKATAU (Indonesia)	0602-00=	2	
1931	1011	13a	SHIKOTSU [TARUMAI] (Hokkaido)	0805-04=	1	
? 1931	1018	?	ASO (Kyushu-Japan)	0802-11=	1?	
1931	1031	?	BOGOSLOF (Aleutian Is)	1101-30-	1	
1931	1208	....	ASAMA (Honshu-Japan)	0803-11=	3	
1931	1223	13a	KILAUEA (Hawaiian Is)	1302-01-	0	6/-
1932	Cont	....	VESUVIUS (Italy)	0101-02=	2	8/7
1932	Cont	....	STROMBOLI (Italy)	0101-04=	1?	
1932	Cont	....	ETNA (Italy)	0101-06=	2	
1932	Cont	....	NYAMURAGIRA (Africa-C)	0203-02=	0	8/-
1932	Cont	....	NYIRAGONGO (Africa-C)	0203-03=	0	
1932	Cont	....	VICTORY (New Guinea)	0503-03=	1?	
1932	Cont	....	YASUR (Vanuatu-SW Pacific)	0507-10=	2	
1932	Cont	....	ASAMA (Honshu-Japan)	0803-11=	2	
1932	Cont	....	KITA-IWO-JIMA (Volcano Is-Japan)	0804-11=	0	
1932	Cont	....	TOLBACHIK (Kamchatka)	1000-24=	2	
1932	Cont	....	KILAUEA (Hawaiian Is)	1302-01-	0	6/-
1932	Cont	....	PELEE (W Indies)	1600-12=	2	
1932	....	730y	MANAM (New Guinea-NE of)	0501-02=	2	
1932	....	?	MARAPI (Sumatra)	0601-14=	2?	
1932	....	?	ATSONUPURI (Kurile Is)	0900-05=	2	
? 1932?	....	?	SARYCHEV PEAK (Kurile Is)	0900-24=		
? 1932?	....	?	NEMO PEAK (Kurile Is)	0900-32=		
? 1932	....	?	GORELY (Kamchatka)	1000-07=		
1932	....	?	AZUL, CERRO (Galapagos)	1503-06=	1?	
1932	0101	?	CLEVELAND (Aleutian Is)	1101-24-		
1932	0121	1a	FUEGO (Guatemala)	1402-09=	4	-/8
1932	0125	335e	KLIUCHEVSKOI (Kamchatka)	1000-26=	2	7/6
1932	0201	110a	SHISHALDIN (Aleutian Is)	1101-36-	2	
1932	0206	?	YAKE-DAKE (Honshu-Japan)	0803-07=	2	
1932	0302	<1	LLAIMA (Chile-C)	1507-11=	2?	
1932	0313	?	NILA (Banda Sea)	0605-06=	2	
1932	0410	....	AZUL, CERRO [QUIZAPU] (Chile-C)	1507-06=	5+	-/9
1932	0523	583f	LEWOTOBI (Lesser Sunda Is)	0604-18=	3	5/-
1932	06	470m	ASO (Kyushu-Japan)	0802-11=	2	
1932	06	?	KARYMSKY (Kamchatka)	1000-13=	2	
1932	0605e	392w	DESCABEZADO GRANDE (Chile-C)	1507-05=	3	
1932	0701	71a	SLAMET (Java)	0603-18=	2	
1932	0702	22a	AKITA-KOMAGA-TAKE (Japan)	0803-23=	2	
? 1932	0723	<1	KUCHINOERABU-JIMA (Ryukyu Is)	0802-05=	1?	
1932	0907	30a	FARALLON DE PAJAROS (Mariana Is)	0804-14=	2	
1932	1001	45m	KUSATSU-SHIRANE (Honshu-Japan)	0803-12=	2	-/4
1932	1010	?	GALERAS (Colombia)	1501-08=	2	
1932	1023	....	KUSATSU-SHIRANE (Honshu-Japan)	0803-12=	3	-/4
1932	11	2a	FOURNAISE, PITON DE LA (Indian O.)	0303-02=		
1932	1110	3a	GAMALAMA (Halmahera-Indonesia)	0608-06=	2	
1932	1114	572a	KRAKATAU (Indonesia)	0602-00=	2	
1932	12	31p	CANLAON (Philippines-C)	0702-02=		
1932	12	....	SANTA MARIA (Guatemala)	1402-03=	2	8/8
1932	1201p	?	UNNAMED (Tonga-SW Pacific)	0403-01=	0	
? 1932	1231y	?	SAN MARTIN, VOLCAN DE (Mexico)	1401-11=		
1932	1231	6a	LLAIMA (Chile-C)	1507-11=	3	
1933	Cont	....	VESUVIUS (Italy)	0101-02=	2	8/7
1933	Cont	....	STROMBOLI (Italy)	0101-04=	1?	
1933	Cont	....	ETNA (Italy)	0101-06=	2	
1933	Cont	....	NYAMURAGIRA (Africa-C)	0203-02=	0	8/-
1933	Cont	....	NYIRAGONGO (Africa-C)	0203-03=	0	
1933	Cont	....	MANAM (New Guinea-NE of)	0501-02=	2	
1933	Cont	....	VICTORY (New Guinea)	0503-03=	1?	
1933	Cont	....	YASUR (Vanuatu-SW Pacific)	0507-10=	2	
1933	Cont	....	LEWOTOBI (Lesser Sunda Is)	0604-18=	3	5/-
1933	Cont	....	CANLAON (Philippines-C)	0702-02=		
1933	Cont	....	ASO (Kyushu-Japan)	0802-11=	2	
1933	Cont	....	KITA-IWO-JIMA (Volcano Is-Japan)	0804-11=	0	
1933	Cont	....	SANTA MARIA (Guatemala)	1402-03=	1	8/8
1933	Cont	....	DESCABEZADO GRANDE (Chile-C)	1507-05=	2	
1933	Cont	....	LLAIMA (Chile-C)	1507-11=	2	
1933	....	?	LONG ISLAND (New Guinea-NE of)	0501-05=		
1933	....	?	LOPEVI (Vanuatu-SW Pacific)	0507-05=		
? 1933	....	?	KUSATSU-SHIRANE (Honshu-Japan)	0803-12=		
1933	....	?	KANAGA (Aleutian Is)	1101-11-		
? 1933	....	?	GALERAS (Colombia)	1501-08=		
1933	....	?	WOLF, VOLCAN (Galapagos)	1503-02=	0	
1933	....	>3yr	AZUL, CERRO [QUIZAPU] (Chile-C)	1507-06=	2	
1933	0104	?	LONQUIMAY (Chile-C)	1507-10=	2	
1933	0105	?	VILLARRICA (Chile-C)	1507-12=	2	
1933	0108	96a>	HARIMKOTAN (Kurile Is)	0900-30=	3	8/-
1933	0109	206a	ASAMA (Honshu-Japan)	0803-11=	2	
1933	0123	?	POPOCATEPETL (Mexico)	1401-09=	1	
? 1933	02	?	SUMACO (Ecuador)	1502-04=	2	
1933	0322?	125a?	IRAZU (Costa Rica)	1405-06=	1	-/6
1933	04	?	FALCON ISLAND (Tonga-SW Pacific)	0403-05=	2	
1933	0402	?	WHITE ISLAND (New Zealand)	0401-04=	3	
? 1933	0415q	?	CHIKURACHKI (Kurile Is)	0900-36=		
1933	0501	....	KRAKATAU (Indonesia)	0602-00=	3	
? 1933	0505	?	ILIAMNA (Alaska-SW)	1103-02-		
1933	0512	<1	SLAMET (Java)	0603-18=	1?	
? 1933	0525	?	REDOUBT (Alaska-SW)	1103-03-		
1933	0607	298a	FOURNAISE, PITON DE LA (Indian O.)	0303-02=	2	
1933	0616	....	IRAZU (Costa Rica)	1405-06=	2	-/6
1933	07 ?	31p?	PAGO (New Britain-SW Pac)	0502-08=	2	
1933	0710	26a	SUOH [PEMATANG BATA] (Sumatra)	0601-27=	4	-/8
1933	0813	>3yr	DUKONO (Halmahera-Indonesia)	0608-01=	2	
1933	09	31p	KARYMSKY (Kamchatka)	1000-13=	2	
1933	1001	561m	MERAPI (Java)	0603-25=	3	7/6
1933	1009	67a	LASCAR (Chile-N)	1505-10=	2	
1933	1014	47m	OSHIMA (Izu Is-Japan)	0804-01=	0	5/-
1933	11	?	GREAT SITKIN (Aleutian Is)	1101-12-	2	
1933	1112	?	GAMALAMA (Halmahera-Indonesia)	0608-06=	2	
1933	1113	214m	ALAID (Kurile Is)	0900-39=	2	
1933	1121	15a	RAUNG (Java)	0603-34=	2	
1933	1129a	10b	GRIMSVOTN (Iceland-NE)	1703-01=	1	
1933	1130	43a>	IZALCO (El Salvador)	1403-03=	2	
1933	12	....	DUKONO (Halmahera-Indonesia)	0608-01=	3	
1933	1201	13a	SHIKOTSU [TARUMAI] (Hokkaido)	0805-04=	2	
1933	1202	16a	MAUNA LOA (Hawaiian Is)	1302-02=	0	8/-
1933	1223	20a	KUCHINOERABU-JIMA (Ryukyu Is)	0802-05=	2	
1933	1224	....	KUCHINOERABU-JIMA (Ryukyu Is)	0802-05=	4?	
1933	1225	?	BULUSAN (Luzon-Philippines)	0703-01=	2	
1934	Cont	....	VESUVIUS (Italy)	0101-02=	2	8/7
1934	Cont	....	NYAMURAGIRA (Africa-C)	0203-02=	0	8/-
1934	Cont	....	NYIRAGONGO (Africa-C)	0203-03=	0	
1934	Cont	....	FOURNAISE, PITON DE LA (Indian O.)	0303-02=	2	
1934	Cont	....	MANAM (New Guinea-NE of)	0501-02=	2	
1934	Cont	....	VICTORY (New Guinea)	0503-03=	1?	
1934	Cont	....	YASUR (Vanuatu-SW Pacific)	0507-10=	2	
1934	Cont	....	MERAPI (Java)	0603-25=	2	7/6
1934	Cont	....	DUKONO (Halmahera-Indonesia)	0608-01=	2	
1934	Cont	....	KITA-IWO-JIMA (Volcano Is-Japan	0804-11=	0	
1934	Cont	....	ALAID (Kurile Is)	0900-39=	2	
1934	Cont	....	IZALCO (El Salvador)	1403-03=	2	
1934	Cont	....	AZUL, CERRO [QUIZAPU] (Chile-C)	1507-06=	2	
? 1934	....	?	SLAMET (Java)	0603-18=		
1934	....	?	KUSATSU-SHIRANE (Honshu-Japan)	0803-12=	2	
1934	01	?	TELICA (Nicaragua)	1404-04=	2	
1934	0105	2a	ETNA (Italy)	0101-06=	1	
1934	0106	....	KRAKATAU (Indonesia)	0602-00=	2	
1934	0109	33	ASAMA (Honshu-Japan)	0803-11=	2	
1934	0111	?	SUWANOSE-JIMA (Ryukyu Is)	0802-03=	2?	
1934	0111	....	KUCHINOERABU-JIMA (Ryukyu Is)	0802-05=	2	
1934	0117	?	CHILLAN, NEVADOS DE (Chile-C)	1507-07=	2?	
1934	0124	91a	DEMPO (Sumatra)	0601-23=	2	
1934	0202	<1	STROMBOLI (Italy)	0101-04=	2	
1934	0306	?	CORDON CAULLE (Chile-C)	1507-141	2?	
1934	0330	8a	GRIMSVOTN (Iceland-NE)	1703-01=	2	
1934	0415	10a?	OSHIMA (Izu Is-Japan)	0804-01=	0	
1934	05	?	BAYONNAISE ROCKS (Izu Is-Japan)	0804-07=	0	
1934	06	?	TONGARIRO [NGAURUHOE] (New Z)	0401-08=	2	
1934	06	15m	ASAMA (Honshu-Japan)	0803-11=	2	
1934	0614	32e	SIRUNG (Lesser Sunda Is)	0604-27=	2	
1934	0715q	?	FARALLON DE PAJAROS (Mariana Is)	0804-14=	0	
1934	0716	?	ASO (Kyushu-Japan)	0802-11=	2	
1934	0808	>3yr	SANGAY (Ecuador)	1502-09=	3	
1934	0811	?	RUAPEHU (New Zealand)	0401-10=	2	
1934	0821	?	STROMBOLI (Italy)	0101-04=	2	
? 1934	09	?	OSHIMA (Izu Is-Japan)	0804-01=		
1934	0906	32a	KILAUEA (Hawaiian Is)	1302-01-	0	6/-
1934	0919	331m	KIKAI (Ryukyu Is)	0802-06=	2	
1934	1004	376q	EBEKO (Kurile Is)	0900-38=	2	-/5
1934	11	120p	KARYMSKY (Kamchatka)	1000-13=	2	8/-
1934	12	90p	TONGARIRO [NGAURUHOE] (New Z)	0401-08=	2	
1934	12	90p	RUAPEHU (New Zealand)	0401-10=	2	
1934	1214	....	SANTA MARIA (Guatemala)	1402-03=	2	8/8
@ 1934	1221	5a	GRIMSVOTN (Iceland-NE)	1703-01=		
1934	1231	2a?	PINACATE PEAKS (Mexico)	1401-001	2?	
1935	Cont	....	VESUVIUS (Italy)	0101-02=	2	8/7
1935	Cont	....	NYAMURAGIRA (Africa-C)	0203-02=	0	8/-
1935	Cont	....	NYIRAGONGO (Africa-C)	0203-03=	0	

START YEAR	M-Dy	Duration	VOLCANO NAME (Subregion)	NUMBER	VEI	Vol L/T
1935	Cont	....	TONGARIRO [NGAURUHOE] (New Z)	0401-08=	2	
1935	Cont	....	RUAPEHU (New Zealand)	0401-10=	2	
1935	Cont	....	VICTORY (New Guinea)	0503-03=	1?	
1935	Cont	....	YASUR (Vanuatu-SW Pacific)	0507-10=	2	
1935	Cont	....	MERAPI (Java)	0603-25=	2	7/6
1935	Cont	....	DUKONO (Halmahera-Indonesia)	0608-01=	2	
1935	Cont	....	KITA-IWO-JIMA (Volcano Is-Japan)	0804-11=	0	
1935	Cont	....	EBEKO (Kurile Is)	0900-38=	2	-/5
1935	Cont	....	KARYMSKY (Kamchatka)	1000-13=	2	8/-
1935	Cont	....	PINACATE PEAKS (Mexico)	1401-001	2?	
1935	Cont	....	AZUL, CERRO [QUIZAPU] (Chile-C)	1507-06=	2	
1935 ?	....	?	FOURNAISE, PITON DE LA (Indian O.)	0303-02=	2	
1935	....	?	VILLARRICA (Chile-C)	1507-12=	1?	
1935	01	911p	ASAMA (Honshu-Japan)	0803-11=	3	
1935	0104	189a	KRAKATAU (Indonesia)	0602-00=	2	
1935	0107	274a	ASO (Kyushu-Japan)	0802-11=	2	
1935	0108	....	KIKAI (Ryukyu Is)	0802-06=	2	
1935	02	?	SALAK (Java)	0603-05=	2	
1935	02	14m	CONCEPCION (Nicaragua)	1404-12=	2	
1935	02	?	WOLF, VOLCAN (Galapagos)	1503-02=		
1935	0225	2a	STROMBOLI (Italy)	0101-04=	1	3/-
1935	03	....	SANTA MARIA (Guatemala)	1402-03=	2	8/8
1935	0313	158a	AUGUSTINE (Alaska-SW)	1103-01-	2	
1935	0421	563a>	KLIUCHEVSKOI (Kamchatka)	1000-26=	2	
1935	0426	10a?	OSHIMA (Izu Is-Japan)	0804-01=	0	
1935	0531p	?	KIARABERES-GAGAK (Java)	0603-03=	1	
1935	0618	....	AUGUSTINE (Alaska-SW)	1103-01-	3	
1935	07	?	TENGGER CALDERA [BROMO]	0603-31=	2	
1935	07	....	SANGAY (Ecuador)	1502-09=	3	
1935	0707	>3yr	ETNA (Italy)	0101-06=	2	
1935	0721	?	STROMBOLI (Italy)	0101-04=	0	
1935	0831	?	KARANGETANG [API SIAU] (Sangihe	0607-02=	2	
1935	09	123p	AMBRYM (Vanuatu-SW Pacific)	0507-04=	2	
1935	0911	1a	YAKE-DAKE (Honshu-Japan)	0803-07=	2	
1935	0920	4a	SAKURA-JIMA (Kyushu-Japan)	0802-08=	1	
? 1935	1015	<1	KOMAGA-TAKE (Hokkaido-Japan)	0805-02=		
1935	1121	42a	MAUNA LOA (Hawaiian Is)	1302-02=	0	7/-
1935	12	15m	LEWOTOBI (Lesser Sunda Is)	0604-18=	2	
1935	1207	69m?	NIUAFO'OU (Tonga-SW Pacific)	0403-11=	2	
1935	1231	?	BRISTOL ISLAND (Antarctica)	1900-08=	2	
1936	Cont	....	VESUVIUS (Italy)	0101-02=	2	8/7
1936	Cont	....	ETNA (Italy)	0101-06=	2	
1936	Cont	....	NYAMURAGIRA (Africa-C)	0203-02=	0	8/-
1936	Cont	....	NYIRAGONGO (Africa-C)	0203-03=	0	
1936	Cont	....	NIUAFO'OU (Tonga-SW Pacific)	0403-11=	2	
1936	Cont	....	AMBRYM (Vanuatu-SW Pacific)	0507-04=	2	
1936	Cont	....	YASUR (Vanuatu-SW Pacific)	0507-10=	2	
1936	Cont	....	DUKONO (Halmahera-Indonesia)	0608-01=	2	
1936	Cont	....	KITA-IWO-JIMA (Volcano Is-Japan)	0804-11=	0	
1936	Cont	....	MAUNA LOA (Hawaiian Is)	1302-02=	0	7/-
1936	Cont	....	SANTA MARIA (Guatemala)	1402-03=	1	8/8
1936	Cont	....	AZUL, CERRO [QUIZAPU] (Chile-C)	1507-06=	2	
? 1936	....	?	OKMOK (Aleutian Is)	1101-29-		
1936	....	>3yr	PAVLOF (Alaska Peninsula)	1102-03-	2	
@ 1936	....	?	MACDONALD (Austral Is-C Pac)	1303-07-	0?	
? 1936 ?	....	?	SAN MIGUEL (El Salvador)	1403-10=	2	
1936	0131	?	STROMBOLI (Italy)	0101-04=	2	
1936	02	....	ASAMA (Honshu-Japan)	0803-11=	3	
1936	0201	243a	SHIRETOKO-IWO-ZAN (Hokkaido)	0805-09=	1	
1936	0205	<1	ASO (Kyushu-Japan)	0802-11=	2	
1936	0209	200a?	GALERAS (Colombia)	1501-08=	2	
1936	0218	....	KLIUCHEVSKOI (Kamchatka)	1000-26=	3	
1936	0415q	?	FARALLON DE PAJAROS (Mariana Is)	0804-14=	2	
1936	0419	<1	SHIKOTSU [TARUMAI] (Hokkaido)	0805-04=	1	
1936	0429	<1	KERINCI (Sumatra)	0601-17=	2	
1936	0509?	4a?	RUAPEHU (New Zealand)	0401-10=	2	
1936	06	?	FALCON ISLAND (Tonga-SW Pacific)	0403-05=	2	
? 1936	0618	180m	CURTIS ISLAND (Kermadec Is)	0402-01=		
? 1936	07	>3yr	BAM (New Guinea-NE of)	0501-01=		
1936	0704	1a	MAGEIK (Alaska Peninsula)	1102-15-	3	
@ 1936	0717	?	NEGRO DE MAYASQUER, CERRO	1501-11=	2	
1936	08	....	SANGAY (Ecuador)	1502-09=	2	
1936	0808	6a	ASO (Kyushu-Japan)	0802-11=	2	
1936	0813<	201a>	TOLBACHIK (Kamchatka)	1000-24=	2	
1936	0822	111a	RAUNG (Java)	0603-34=	2	
1936	0827	?	REVENTADOR (Ecuador)	1502-01=	3	
1936	0830	<1	KERINCI (Sumatra)	0601-17=	2	
1936	09	?	FOURNAISE, PITON DE LA (Indian O.)	0303-02=	0	
1936	09	>3yr	MANAM (New Guinea-NE of)	0501-02=	3	
1936	1013	34m	KRAKATAU (Indonesia)	0602-00=	1	
1936	1026	2a	KIARABERES-GAGAK (Java)	0603-03=	1	
1936	1105	20a	IJEN (Java)	0603-35=	2	
1936	1115	11a	SHIKOTSU [TARUMAI] (Hokkaido)	0805-04=	1	
1936	1126	1a	DEMPO (Sumatra)	0601-23=	2	
1936	1218	14a?	BRISTOL ISLAND (Antarctica)	1900-08=	2	
1937	Cont	....	VESUVIUS (Italy)	0101-02=	2	8/7
1937	Cont	....	ETNA (Italy)	0101-06=	2	
1937	Cont	....	NYAMURAGIRA (Africa-C)	0203-02=	0	8/-
1937	Cont	....	NYIRAGONGO (Africa-C)	0203-03=	0	
? 1937	Cont	....	BAM (New Guinea-NE of)	0501-01=		
1937	Cont	....	YASUR (Vanuatu-SW Pacific)	0507-10=	2	
1937	Cont	....	DUKONO (Halmahera-Indonesia)	0608-01=	2	
1937	Cont	....	ASAMA (Honshu-Japan)	0803-11=	2	
1937	Cont	....	KITA-IWO-JIMA (Volcano Is-Japan	0804-11=	0	
1937	Cont	....	SANTA MARIA (Guatemala)	1402-03=	1	8/8
1937	Cont	....	AZUL, CERRO [QUIZAPU] (Chile-C)	1507-06=	2	
1937	Cont	....	BRISTOL ISLAND (Antarctica)	1900-08=	2	
1937	....	?	DHAMAR, HARRAS OF (Arabia-S)	0301-12-	2	
1937	....	?	UNNAMED (Tonga-SW Pacific)	0403-04=	2	
1937	....	?	TELONG, BUR NI (Sumatra)	0601-05=		
1937	....	?	SLAMET (Java)	0603-18=		
1937 ?	....	365y?	IZALCO (El Salvador)	1403-03=	2?	
1937	....	?	COPAHUE (Chile-C)	1507-09=	2?	
1937	01	?	TONGARIRO [NGAURUHOE] (New Z)	0401-08=	2	
1937	0106	15a	STROMBOLI (Italy)	0101-04=	2	
1937	0110	....	TOLBACHIK (Kamchatka)	1000-24=	2	
1937	0113	<1	ASO (Kyushu-Japan)	0802-11=	2	
1937	0209?	266a?	LLAIMA (Chile-C)	1507-11=	2	
1937	03	31p	FERNANDINA (Galapagos)	1503-01=	0	
1937	0315	....	MANAM (New Guinea-NE of)	0501-02=	3	
1937	0317	2a	KOMAGA-TAKE (Hokkaido-Japan)	0805-02=	1	
1937	0327	19m	AMBRYM (Vanuatu-SW Pacific)	0507-04=	2	
1937	04	....	SANGAY (Ecuador)	1502-09=	3	
1937	04	20m	PLANCHON-PETEROA (Chile-C)	1507-04=	2	
1937	0403	712m	KLIUCHEVSKOI (Kamchatka)	1000-26=	3	8/7
? 1937	05	?	ULAWUN (New Britain-SW Pac)	0502-12=		
1937	0507	6a	ASO (Kyushu-Japan)	0802-11=	2	
1937	0529	4a	RABAUL (New Britain-SW Pac)	0502-14=	4?	-/8
1937	06	?	UBINAS (Peru)	1504-02=	2	
1937	0616	?	MOCHO-CHOSHUENCO (Chile-C)	1507-13=		
1937	0624	197a	CEREME (Java)	0603-17=	2	
1937	07	....	PAVLOF (Alaska Peninsula)	1102-03-	2	
1937	0717	30m	OSHIMA (Izu Is-Japan)	0804-01=	0	
? 1937	0805	?	TACORA (Chile-N)	1505-01=		
1937	0806	109a	KRAKATAU (Indonesia)	0602-00=	2	
1937	0813	104a	FOURNAISE, PITON DE LA (Indian O.)	0303-02=	2	6/-
1937	0907	?	BAGANA (Bougainville-SW Pac)	0505-02=	3	
? 1937	0908	?	TALAKMAU (Sumatra)	0601-13=	1	
1937	0908	?	KERINCI (Sumatra)	0601-17=	2	
? 1937	0918	?	CALLAQUI (Chile-C)	1507-091		
1937	1027	31a	RAUNG (Java)	0603-34=	2	
1937	11	274p	TELICA (Nicaragua)	1404-04=	2	
1937	1103	1a	YUNASKA (Aleutian Is)	1101-21-	3	
1937	1114?	?	STROMBOLI (Italy)	0101-04=	2	2/-
1937	1127	....	KUSATSU-SHIRANE (Honshu-Japan)	0803-12=	2	
1938	Cont	....	VESUVIUS (Italy)	0101-02=	2	8/7
1938	Cont	....	ETNA (Italy)	0101-06=	2	
1938	Cont	....	NYIRAGONGO (Africa-C)	0203-03=	0	
? 1938	Cont	....	BAM (New Guinea-NE of)	0501-01=		
1938	Cont	....	MANAM (New Guinea-NE of)	0501-02=	0	
1938	Cont	....	YASUR (Vanuatu-SW Pacific)	0507-10=	2	
1938	Cont	....	CEREME (Java)	0603-17=	2	
1938	Cont	....	DUKONO (Halmahera-Indonesia)	0608-01=	2	
1938	Cont	....	KITA-IWO-JIMA (Volcano Is-Japan)	0804-11=	0	
1938	Cont	....	PAVLOF (Alaska Peninsula)	1102-03-	2	
1938	Cont	....	SANTA MARIA (Guatemala)	1402-03=	1	8/8
1938	Cont	....	IZALCO (El Salvador)	1403-03=	2?	
1938	Cont	....	TELICA (Nicaragua)	1404-04=	2	
1938	Cont	....	AZUL, CERRO [QUIZAPU] (Chile-C)	1507-06=	2	
1938	....	?	LONG ISLAND (New Guinea-NE of)	0501-05=		
1938	....	?	AMBRYM (Vanuatu-SW Pacific)	0507-04=	2	
1938 j	....	?	COLO [UNA UNA] (Sulawesi-Indonesia)	0606-01=	1	
1938	....	406w	ASO (Kyushu-Japan)	0802-11=	2	
1938	....	?	CLEVELAND (Aleutian Is)	1101-24-		
1938	....	?	OKMOK (Aleutian Is)	1101-29-		
1938	....	?	WOLF, VOLCAN (Galapagos)	1503-02=		
1938	0111	16a	STROMBOLI (Italy)	0101-04=	1	4/-
1938	0119	58a	KERINCI (Sumatra)	0601-17=	2	
1938	0128	878e	NYAMURAGIRA (Africa-C)	0203-02=	1	8/-
1938	0131e	?	SALAK (Java)	0603-05=	2	
1938	02	?	SAN PEDRO (Chile-N)	1505-07=	2	
1938	0207	....	KLIUCHEVSKOI (Kamchatka)	1000-26=	3	8/7
1938	0211	?	VILLARRICA (Chile-C)	1507-12=	1?	
1938	0225	33	SAKURA-JIMA (Kyushu-Japan)	0802-08=	2	
1938	03	>3yr	ASAMA (Honshu-Japan)	0803-11=	2	
1938	0306	22a>	AVACHINSKY (Kamchatka)	1000-10=	2	
1938	0311	<1	SUWANOSE-JIMA (Ryukyu Is)	0802-03=	2?	
1938	05	31p	EBULOBO (Lesser Sunda Is)	0604-10=		
1938	05	31p	KELIMUTU (Lesser Sunda Is)	0604-14=	2	
1938	05	?	GRIMSVOTN (Iceland-NE)	1703-01=	1	
1938	0505	13a	STROMBOLI (Italy)	0101-04=	1	
1938	0515	?	BAGANA (Bougainville-SW Pac)	0505-02=	3	
1938	0605	?	MAYON (Luzon-Philippines)	0703-03=	2	-/6
1938	0704	729a	KRAKATAU (Indonesia)	0602-00=	2	
? 1938	0716<	?	AKAGI (Honshu-Japan)	0803-13=		
? 1938	0717	?	KUSATSU-SHIRANE (Honshu-Japan)	0803-12=		
1938	0725	4a	FOURNAISE, PITON DE LA (Indian O.)	0303-02=	1	
1938	0811	<1	OSHIMA (Izu Is-Japan)	0804-01=	1	5/-
1938	0812	?	NEMO PEAK (Kurile Is)	0900-32=	2	
1938	0813	110a>	RAUNG (Java)	0603-34=	2	
1938	09	....	SANGAY (Ecuador)	1502-09=	2	
1938	09	31p	PLANCHON-PETEROA (Chile-C)	1507-04=	2	
1938	0904	89a>	AVACHINSKY (Kamchatka)	1000-10=	2	
1938	0908	<1	GAMALAMA (Halmahera-Indonesia)	0608-06=	2	
1938	10	?	KARYMSKY (Kamchatka)	1000-13=	2	
1938	10	?	MAKUSHIN (Aleutian Is)	1101-31-	2	
1938	11	?	MUTNOVSKY (Kamchatka)	1000-06=	2	
1938	1105	208a	STROMBOLI (Italy)	0101-04=	1	4/-
1938	12	?	KIARABERES-GAGAK (Java)	0603-03=	1	
1938	12	?	LLAIMA (Chile-C)	1507-11=	1	
1938	1207	39a	FOURNAISE, PITON DE LA (Indian O.)	0303-02=	2	7/-
1938	1219?	?	ASKJA (Iceland-NE)	1703-06=	2	
1939	Cont	....	VESUVIUS (Italy)	0101-02=	2	8/7
1939	Cont	....	ETNA (Italy)	0101-06=	2	
1939	Cont	....	NYAMURAGIRA (Africa-C)	0203-02=	1	8/-
1939	Cont	....	NYIRAGONGO (Africa-C)	0203-03=	0	

	START YEAR	M-Dy	Duration	VOLCANO NAME (Subregion)	NUMBER	VEI	Vol L/T
	1939	Cont	....	FOURNAISE, PITON DE LA (Indian O.)	0303-02=	2	7/-
?	1939	Cont	....	BAM (New Guinea-NE of)	0501-01=		
	1939	Cont	....	MANAM (New Guinea-NE of)	0501-02=	0	
	1939	Cont	....	YASUR (Vanuatu-SW Pacific)	0507-10=	2	
	1939	Cont	....	RAUNG (Java)	0603-34=	2	
	1939	Cont	....	DUKONO (Halmahera-Indonesia)	0608-01=	2	
	1939	Cont	....	ASO (Kyushu-Japan)	0802-11=	2	
	1939	Cont	....	ASAMA (Honshu-Japan)	0803-11=	2	
	1939	Cont	....	KITA-IWO-JIMA (Volcano Is-Japan)	0804-11=	0	
	1939	Cont	....	KLIUCHEVSKOI (Kamchatka)	1000-26=	2	8/7
	1939	Cont	....	PAVLOF (Alaska Peninsula)	1102-03-	2	
	1939	Cont	....	SANTA MARIA (Guatemala)	1402-03=	1	8/8
	1939	Cont	....	SANGAY (Ecuador)	1502-09=	2	
	1939	....	?	MAYON (Luzon-Philippines)	0703-03=	1	
	1939	....	?	FARALLON DE PAJAROS (Mariana Is)	0804-14=	2	
	1939	01	151p	TELICA (Nicaragua)	1404-04=	2	
	1939	0110	....	STROMBOLI (Italy)	0101-04=	2	4/-
	1939	0130?	?	BAGANA (Bougainville-SW Pac)	0505-02=	2	
	1939	02	76m	KUSATSU-SHIRANE (Honshu-Japan)	0803-12=	2	
	1939	02	14m	OSHIMA (Izu Is-Japan)	0804-01=	1?	
	1939	02	>3yr	IZALCO (El Salvador)	1403-03=	2	
	1939	0202	?	LOPEVI (Vanuatu-SW Pacific)	0507-05=	2	
	1939	0202	?	COTOPAXI (Ecuador)	1502-05=	2	
	1939	0329	108a	SLAMET (Java)	0603-18=	2	
	1939	0406<	?	KIARABERES-GAGAK (Java)	0603-03=	1	
	1939	0430?	?	KAVACHI (Solomon Is-SW Pac)	0505-06=	2	
	1939	05	?	MUTNOVSKY (Kamchatka)	1000-06=	2	
	1939	05	61p	SAN MIGUEL (El Salvador)	1403-10=	2	
	1939	0523	34a?	VENIAMINOF (Alaska Peninsula)	1102-07-	3	
	1939	06	?	FONUALEI (Tonga-SW Pacific)	0403-10=	2	
?	1939	06	?	GRIMSVOTN (Iceland-NE)	1703-01=	0	
	1939	0604	?	YAKE-DAKE (Honshu-Japan)	0803-07=	2	
	1939	0617	....	KRAKATAU (Indonesia)	0602-00=	3	
	1939	0618	378w	IRAZU (Costa Rica)	1405-06=	2	
	1939	0624	25m	TENGGER CALDERA [BROMO]	0603-31=	2	
?	1939	07	?	ZAO (Honshu-Japan)	0803-19=	1?	
	1939	0718	12a	DEMPO (Sumatra)	0601-23=	2	
	1939	0724	<1	KICK-'EM-JENNY (W Indies)	1600-16=	1	
	1939	08	?	TONGARIRO [NGAURUHOE] (New Z)	0401-08=	2	
	1939	0817	131e	TORI-SHIMA (Izu Is-Japan)	0804-09=	2	7/-
	1939	0820	682b	SANTORINI (Greece)	0102-04=	2	7/-
	1939	0901	15a	OSHIMA (Izu Is-Japan)	0804-01=	1	5/-
	1939	0904	?	BILIRAN (Philippines-C)	0702-08=		
	1939	0925	2a	TOLBACHIK (Kamchatka)	1000-24=	2	
	1939	1013	2a	DIENG VOLC COMPLEX (Java)	0603-20=	1?	
	1939	1026	17a?	SAKURA-JIMA (Kyushu-Japan)	0802-08=	2	-/5
	1939	11	?	VENIAMINOF (Alaska Peninsula)	1102-07-	2	
	1939	11	15m	TELICA (Nicaragua)	1404-04=	2	
	1939	1101	?	LOPEVI (Vanuatu-SW Pacific)	0507-05=	2	
	1939	1119	481a	KABA (Sumatra)	0601-22=	2	
	1939	1204	<1	SLAMET (Java)	0603-18=	2	
	1939	1213	276m	MERAPI (Java)	0603-25=	2	6/-
	1939	1217	125a	LEWOTOBI (Lesser Sunda Is)	0604-18=	2	
	1939	1219	64a	DEMPO (Sumatra)	0601-23=	2	
	1940	Cont	....	VESUVIUS (Italy)	0101-02=	2	8/7
	1940	Cont	....	STROMBOLI (Italy)	0101-04=	1?	
	1940	Cont	....	SANTORINI (Greece)	0102-04=	2	7/-
	1940	Cont	....	NYAMURAGIRA (Africa-C)	0203-02=	1	8/-
	1940	Cont	....	NYIRAGONGO (Africa-C)	0203-03=	0	
	1940	Cont	....	YASUR (Vanuatu-SW Pacific)	0507-10=	2	
	1940	Cont	....	KABA (Sumatra)	0601-22=	2	
	1940	Cont	....	KRAKATAU (Indonesia)	0602-00=	2	
	1940	Cont	....	LEWOTOBI (Lesser Sunda Is)	0604-18=	2	
	1940	Cont	....	DUKONO (Halmahera-Indonesia)	0608-01=	2	
	1940	Cont	....	ASAMA (Honshu-Japan)	0803-11=	2	
	1940	Cont	....	KITA-IWO-JIMA (Volcano Is-Japan)	0804-11=	0	
	1940	Cont	....	PAVLOF (Alaska Peninsula)	1102-03-	2	
	1940	Cont	....	SANTA MARIA (Guatemala)	1402-03=	1	8/8
	1940	Cont	....	IZALCO (El Salvador)	1403-03=	2	
	1940	Cont	....	IRAZU (Costa Rica)	1405-06=	2	
	1940	Cont	....	SANGAY (Ecuador)	1502-09=	2	
	1940	....	?	ERTA ALE (Ethiopia)	0201-08=	0	
	1940	....	?	RAUNG (Java)	0603-34=	2	
	1940f	....	?	KOLOKOL GROUP (Kurile Is)	0900-12=		7/-
	1940	....	?	KARYMSKY (Kamchatka)	1000-13=	2	
	1940	....	?	COTOPAXI (Ecuador)	1502-05=	2	
	1940	....	?	AZUL, CERRO (Galapagos)	1503-06=	0	
	1940	....	?	LASCAR (Chile-N)	1505-10=	2	
	1940	01	30p	ZHUPANOVSKY (Kamchatka)	1000-12=	2	
	1940	0124	....	MERAPI (Java)	0603-25=	2	6/-
	1940	0130	....	DEMPO (Sumatra)	0601-23=	2	
	1940	02	60p	TOLBACHIK (Kamchatka)	1000-24=	2	
?	1940	02	?	LONQUIMAY (Chile-C)	1507-10=		
	1940	0204d	103d	RABAUL (New Britain-SW Pac)	0502-14=	1	
	1940	0301	8a	KARANGETANG [API SIAU] (Sangihe	0607-02=	2	
	1940	0315	31a	SLAMET (Java)	0603-18=	2	
	1940	0316	834a?	ETNA (Italy)	0101-06=	3	
	1940	04	?	RUAPEHU (New Zealand)	0401-10=	2	
	1940	04	?	BESAR, GUNUNG (Sumatra)	0601-25=	1	
	1940	0407	133a	MAUNA LOA (Hawaiian Is)	1302-02=	0	8/-
	1940	0420	....	ASO (Kyushu-Japan)	0802-11=	2	
	1940	0424	76a	SAKURA-JIMA (Kyushu-Japan)	0802-08=	2	
	1940	0425	69a>	TENGGER CALDERA [BROMO]	0603-31=	2	
	1940	0518	<1	ZAO (Honshu-Japan)	0803-19=	1	
	1940	06	123p	TELICA (Nicaragua)	1404-04=	2	
	1940	0620	64a	KARANGETANG [API SIAU] (Sangihe	0607-02=	2	
	1940	07		DEMPO (Sumatra)	0601-23=	2	
	1940	0712	24a	MIYAKE-JIMA (Izu Is-Japan)	0804-04=	2	6/6
	1940	0724	205m	LENGAI, OL DOINYO (Africa-E)	0202-12=	2	
	1940	0731	....	LENGAI, OL DOINYO (Africa-E)	0202-12=	3	
	1940	0818	1a	OSHIMA (Izu Is-Japan)	0804-01=	1	5/5
	1940	09	31p	TONGARIRO [NGAURUHOE] (New Z)	0401-08=	2	
	1940	11	242q	TOLBACHIK (Kamchatka)	1000-24=	2	7/7
	1940	1129	?	SUWANOSE-JIMA (Ryukyu Is)	0802-03=	2?	
	1941	Cont	....	ETNA (Italy)	0101-06=	2	
	1941	Cont	....	SANTORINI (Greece)	0102-04=	2	7/-
	1941	Cont	....	LENGAI, OL DOINYO (Africa-E)	0202-12=	2	
	1941	Cont	....	NYIRAGONGO (Africa-C)	0203-03=	0	
	1941	Cont	....	YASUR (Vanuatu-SW Pacific)	0507-10=	2	
	1941	Cont	....	KABA (Sumatra)	0601-22=	2	
	1941	Cont	....	DUKONO (Halmahera-Indonesia)	0608-01=	2	
	1941	Cont	....	ASO (Kyushu-Japan)	0802-11=	2	
	1941	Cont	....	ASAMA (Honshu-Japan)	0803-11=	2	
	1941	Cont	....	KITA-IWO-JIMA (Volcano Is-Japan	0804-11=	0	
	1941	Cont	....	PAVLOF (Alaska Peninsula)	1102-03-	2	
	1941	Cont	....	SANTA MARIA (Guatemala)	1402-03=	1	8/8
	1941	Cont	....	IZALCO (El Salvador)	1403-03=	2	
	1941	Cont	....	SANGAY (Ecuador)	1502-09=	2	
	1941?	....	?	FOURNAISE, PITON DE LA (Indian O.)	0303-02=	1	
?	1941	....	?	TELICA (Nicaragua)	1404-04=		
	1941	....	>3yr	POAS (Costa Rica)	1405-04=	1	
	1941	0126	<1	ULAWUN (New Britain-SW Pac)	0502-12=	2	
	1941	0128	15a	KRAKATAU (Indonesia)	0602-00=	2	
	1941	0328	?	FARALLON DE PAJAROS (Mariana Is)	0804-14=		
?	1941	04	122p	GRIMSVOTN (Iceland-NE)	1703-01=	0	
?	1941	0415	8h	COLIMA VOLC COMPLEX (Mexico)	1401-04=	3?	
	1941	0428	120a	SAKURA-JIMA (Kyushu-Japan)	0802-08=	2	
	1941	0507	....	TOLBACHIK (Kamchatka)	1000-24=	3	7/7
?	1941	0530	?	RINJANI (Lesser Sunda Is)	0604-03=		
?	1941	0605	?	ILIWERUNG (Lesser Sunda Is)	0604-25=		
	1941	0606	298p	RABAUL (New Britain-SW Pac)	0502-14=	2	
	1941	0623	?	LLAIMA (Chile-C)	1507-11=	2	
	1941	0822	?	STROMBOLI (Italy)	0101-04=	2	3/-
	1941	0823h	?	EBULOBO (Lesser Sunda Is)	0604-10=	0?	
	1941	0913	?	MAYON (Luzon-Philippines)	0703-03=	1	
	1941	0921	145m	SEMERU (Java)	0603-30=	2	7/-
	1941	1022	....	VESUVIUS (Italy)	0101-02=	2	8/7
	1941	1030	<1	KARANGETANG [API SIAU] (Sangihe	0607-02=	2	
	1941	1213	?	RAUNG (Java)	0603-34=	2	
	1942	Cont	....	VESUVIUS (Italy)	0101-02=	2	8/7
	1942	Cont	....	STROMBOLI (Italy)	0101-04=	1?	
	1942	Cont	....	NYIRAGONGO (Africa-C)	0203-03=	0	
	1942	Cont	....	RABAUL (New Britain-SW Pac)	0502-14=	2	
	1942	Cont	....	YASUR (Vanuatu-SW Pacific)	0507-10=	2	
	1942	Cont	....	SEMERU (Java)	0603-30=	2	7/-
	1942	Cont	....	DUKONO (Halmahera-Indonesia)	0608-01=	2	
	1942	Cont	....	ASAMA (Honshu-Japan)	0803-11=	2	
	1942	Cont	....	KITA-IWO-JIMA (Volcano Is-Japan)	0804-11=	0	
	1942	Cont	....	SANTA MARIA (Guatemala)	1402-03=	1	8/8
	1942	Cont	....	IZALCO (El Salvador)	1403-03=	2	
	1942	Cont	....	POAS (Costa Rica)	1405-04=	1	
	1942	Cont	....	SANGAY (Ecuador)	1502-09=	2	
?	1942e	....	?	LANGILA (New Britain-SW Pac)	0502-01=	1?	
	1942?	....	?	KAVACHI (Solomon Is-SW Pac)	0505-06=	1	
	1942	....	?	KANAGA (Aleutian Is)	1101-11-	1	
	1942	....	....	PAVLOF (Alaska Peninsula)	1102-03-	3	
?	1942	....	?	ANIAKCHAK (Alaska Peninsula)	1102-09-		
	1942	....	365y	POPOCATEPETL (Mexico)	1401-09=	1	
	1942	0129	1a	KRAKATAU (Indonesia)	0602-00=	2	
	1942	0202	?	KUSATSU-SHIRANE (Honshu-Japan)	0803-12=	1	
?	1942	0217	2a	COTOPAXI (Ecuador)	1502-05=	3?	
	1942	0426	14a	MAUNA LOA (Hawaiian Is)	1302-02=	0	8/-
	1942	0530	514e	MERAPI (Java)	0603-25=	2	6/6
	1942	0606	?	AMBRYM (Vanuatu-SW Pacific)	0507-04=	2	
?	1942	0608	14a	ASO (Kyushu-Japan)	0802-11=	1?	
	1942	0609	159m	LLAIMA (Chile-C)	1507-11=	2	
	1942	0630	5	ETNA (Italy)	0101-06=	2	6/5
	1942	0716	<1	SAKURA-JIMA (Kyushu-Japan)	0802-08=	1	
	1942	0810	?	RUAPEHU (New Zealand)	0401-10=	2	
	1942	0815	1a	PAPANDAYAN (Java)	0603-10=	1?	
	1942	0903	?	LOKON-EMPUNG (Sulawesi-Indonesia)	0606-10=	2	
	1942	0919	726a	ETNA (Italy)	0101-06=	1	
	1942	1005	20a	FOURNAISE, PITON DE LA (Indian O.)	0303-02=	2	6/-
	1942	1116	2a	KOMAGA-TAKE (Hokkaido-Japan)	0805-02=	3	-/6
	1943	Cont	....	VESUVIUS (Italy)	0101-02=	2	8/7
	1943	Cont	....	ETNA (Italy)	0101-06=	1	
	1943	Cont	....	NYIRAGONGO (Africa-C)	0203-03=	0	
	1943	Cont	....	YASUR (Vanuatu-SW Pacific)	0507-10=	2	
	1943	Cont	....	DUKONO (Halmahera-Indonesia)	0608-01=	2	
	1943	Cont	....	KITA-IWO-JIMA (Volcano Is-Japan)	0804-11=	0	
	1943	Cont	....	PAVLOF (Alaska Peninsula)	1102-03-	2	
	1943	Cont	....	POPOCATEPETL (Mexico)	1401-09=	1	
	1943	Cont	....	SANTA MARIA (Guatemala)	1402-03=	1	8/8
	1943	Cont	....	IZALCO (El Salvador)	1403-03=	2	
	1943	Cont	....	POAS (Costa Rica)	1405-04=	1	
	1943	Cont	....	SANGAY (Ecuador)	1502-09=	2	
	1943	....	?	LONG ISLAND (New Guinea-NE of)	0501-05=		
	1943e	....	?	MARAPI (Sumatra)	0601-14=		
	1943	....	?	KRAKATAU (Indonesia)	0602-00=	2	
	1943	....	?	MAYON (Luzon-Philippines)	0703-03=	1	
	1943a	....	?	IWO-JIMA (Volcano Is-Japan)	0804-12=	1	
	1943	....	?	FARALLON DE PAJAROS (Mariana Is)	0804-14=	2	
	1943	0201p	?	KARYMSKY (Kamchatka)	1000-13=	2	

	START YEAR	M-Dy	Duration	VOLCANO NAME (Subregion)	NUMBER	VEI	Vol L/T
	1943	0220	>3yr	**MICHOACAN [PARICUTIN]** (Mexico)	1401-06=	4	8/9
	1943	03	?	**TOLIMA** (Colombia)	1501-03=	2	
	1943	0317	93*a*	**RAUNG** (Java)	0603-34=	2	
?	**1943**	0318	?	**SLAMET** (Java)	0603-18=		
	1943	0320	....	**MERAPI** (Java)	0603-25=	3	6/6
	1943	0330?	56*e?*	**FOURNAISE, PITON DE LA** (Indian O.)	0303-02=	2	7/-
	1943	0407<	?	**BAGANA** (Bougainville-SW Pac)	0505-02=	1	
	1943	0413b	28*c?*	**AZUL, CERRO** (Galapagos)	1503-06=	3	
	1943	06	?	**OKMOK** (Aleutian Is)	1101-29-	1	
	1943	0621	3*a*	**ASO** (Kyushu-Japan)	0802-11=	2	
	1943	*0918*	*347a*	*WAIOWA (New Guinea)*	0503-04=	2	
	1943	0926	20*p*	**NIUAFO'OU** (Tonga-SW Pacific)	0403-11=	2	
	1943	1002	95*a*	**SLAMET** (Java)	0603-18=	2	
S	**1943**	1005	1*a*	**KICK-'EM-JENNY** (W Indies)	1600-16=	0	
	1943	1103	?	**DIENG VOLC COMPLEX** (Java)	0603-20=	1	
	1943	1124	29*a*>	**RABAUL** (New Britain-SW Pac)	0502-14=	2	
	1943	12	121*p*	**TELICA** (Nicaragua)	1404-04=	2	
	1943	1203	73*a*	**STROMBOLI** (Italy)	0101-04=	2	
	1943	1209	67*m*	**ASO** (Kyushu-Japan)	0802-11=	2	
	1943	1227	....	**WAIOWA** (New Guinea)	0503-04=	3	
	1944	*Cont*	....	*ETNA (Italy)*	0101-06=	*1*	
	1944	*Cont*	....	*NYIRAGONGO (Africa-C)*	0203-03=	*0*	
	1944	*Cont*	....	*YASUR (Vanuatu-SW Pacific)*	0507-10=	*2*	
	1944	*Cont*	....	*DUKONO (Halmahera-Indonesia)*	0608-01=	*2*	
	1944	*Cont*	....	*ASO (Kyushu-Japan)*	0802-11=	*2*	
	1944	*Cont*	....	*KITA-IWO-JIMA (Volcano Is-Japan)*	0804-11=	*0*	
	1944	*Cont*	....	*PAVLOF (Alaska Peninsula)*	1102-03-	*2*	
	1944	*Cont*	....	*MICHOACAN [PARICUTIN] (Mexico)*	1401-06=	*3*	*8/9*
	1944	*Cont*	....	*SANTA MARIA (Guatemala)*	1402-03=	*1*	*8/8*
	1944	*Cont*	....	*IZALCO (El Salvador)*	1403-03=	*2*	
	1944	*Cont*	....	*TELICA (Nicaragua)*	1404-04=	*2*	
	1944	*Cont*	....	*POAS (Costa Rica)*	1405-04=	*1*	
	1944	*Cont*	....	*SANGAY (Ecuador)*	1502-09=	*2*	

	START YEAR	M-Dy	Duration	VOLCANO NAME (Subregion)	NUMBER	VEI	Vol L/T
	1944	04	611*p*	**CONCEPCION** (Nicaragua)	1404-12=	2	
	1944	0411	20*a*	**FOURNAISE, PITON DE LA** (Indian O.)	0303-02=	2	
	1944	0509	173*a*	**SLAMET** (Java)	0603-18=	2	
	1944	06	518*p*	**ASAMA** (Honshu-Japan)	0803-11=	2	
	1944	0610	2*a*	**CLEVELAND** (Aleutian Is)	1101-24-	3	
	1944	0623	448*m*	**USU** (Hokkaido-Japan)	0805-03=	2	7/6
	1944	0630	292*a*	**RAUNG** (Java)	0603-34=	2	
	1944	0702	<1	**SHIKOTSU [TARUMAI]** (Hokkaido)	0805-04=	1	
	1944	*0723*	....	*WAIOWA (New Guinea)*	0503-04=	3	
	1944	08	61*p*	**ILIBOLENG** (Lesser Sunda Is)	0604-22=	2	
	1944	0820	67*e*	**STROMBOLI** (Italy)	0101-04=	2	2/-
?	**1944**	0820j	?	**ESMERALDA BANK** (Mariana Is-C Pac)	0804-21=	0	
	1944	*0912*	....	*STROMBOLI (Italy)*	0101-04=	2	*2/-*
	1944	10	?	**RUAPEHU** (New Zealand)	0401-10=	2	
	1944	1105	>3yr	**SHEVELUCH** (Kamchatka)	1000-27=	2	8/-
	1944	1120	26*m*	**KURIKOMA** (Honshu-Japan)	0803-21=	1	
	1944	1201p	?	**FUEGO** (Guatemala)	1402-09=	2	
	1944	1204	?	**DIENG VOLC COMPLEX** (Java)	0603-20=	2	
	1944	*1209*	*41a>*	*KLIUCHEVSKOI (Kamchatka)*	1000-26=	2	*-/8*
	1944	1225	7*a?*	**RINJANI** (Lesser Sunda Is)	0604-03=	2	7/-
	1945	*Cont*	....	*STROMBOLI (Italy)*	0101-04=	*1?*	
	1945	*Cont*	....	*NYIRAGONGO (Africa-C)*	0203-03=	*0*	
	1945	*Cont*	....	*YASUR (Vanuatu-SW Pacific)*	0507-10=	*2*	
	1945	*Cont*	....	*MERAPI (Java)*	0603-25=	*2*	
	1945	*Cont*	....	*RAUNG (Java)*	0603-34=	*2*	
	1945	*Cont*	....	*RINJANI (Lesser Sunda Is)*	0604-03=	*2*	*7/-*
	1945	*Cont*	....	*DUKONO (Halmahera-Indonesia)*	0608-01=	*2*	
	1945	*Cont*	....	*ASAMA (Honshu-Japan)*	0803-11=	*2*	
	1945	*Cont*	....	*KITA-IWO-JIMA (Volcano Is-Japan)*	0804-11=	*0*	
	1945	*Cont*	....	*USU (Hokkaido-Japan)*	0805-03=	*2*	*7/6*
	1945	*Cont*	....	*SHEVELUCH (Kamchatka)*	1000-27=	*2*	*8/-*
	1945	*Cont*	....	*PAVLOF (Alaska Peninsula)*	1102-03-	*2*	
	1945	*Cont*	....	*MICHOACAN [PARICUTIN] (Mexico)*	1401-06=	*3*	*8/9*

Figure 24. Cinder cone of Paricutin, in Michoacan, Mexico. March 1944 photo, 14 months after the eruption began in a cornfield. The cone had grown over 340 m high by then, and the eruption continued for a total of 9 years. Photo by Arno Brehme, and reproduced in Luhr & Simkin, 1993 (see REFERENCES 1400).

	START YEAR	M-Dy	Duration	VOLCANO NAME (Subregion)	NUMBER	VEI	Vol L/T
?	**1944**	....	?	**MONOWAI SEAMOUNT** (Kermadec Is)	0402-05-	0	
	1944	....	?	**BAM** (New Guinea-NE of)	0501-01=	2	
?	**1944**	....	?	**UNNAMED** (New Guinea-NE of)	0501-04=	0	
	1944	....	?	**KRAKATAU** (Indonesia)	0602-00=	2	
	1944	....	365*y*	**MERAPI** (Java)	0603-25=	2	
?	**1944**	....	?	**GORIASCHAIA SOPKA** (Kurile Is)	0900-17B	2	
	1944	....	?	**TUNGURAHUA** (Ecuador)	1502-08=	2	
	1944	....	?	**LLAIMA** (Chile-C)	1507-11=	2	
	1944	*0125*	....	*STROMBOLI (Italy)*	0101-04=	2	
	1944	0224	6*a*	**REVENTADOR** (Ecuador)	1502-01=	3	
	1944	*0318*	....	*VESUVIUS (Italy)*	0101-02=	3	*8/7*
	1944	0328	?	**VENIAMINOF** (Alaska Peninsula)	1102-07-	2	

	START YEAR	M-Dy	Duration	VOLCANO NAME (Subregion)	NUMBER	VEI	Vol L/T
	1945	*Cont*	....	*SANTA MARIA (Guatemala)*	1402-03=	*1*	*8/8*
	1945	*Cont*	....	*IZALCO (El Salvador)*	1403-03=	*2*	
	1945	*Cont*	....	*CONCEPCION (Nicaragua)*	1404-12=	*2*	
	1945	*Cont*	....	*POAS (Costa Rica)*	1405-04=	*1*	
	1945	*Cont*	....	*SANGAY (Ecuador)*	1502-09=	*2*	
	1945	....	730*y*	**BAGANA** (Bougainville-SW Pac)	0505-02=	2	
	1945	....	?	**KRAKATAU** (Indonesia)	0602-00=	2	
	1945	....	?	**CHILLAN, NEVADOS DE** (Chile-C)	1507-07=		
	1945	0101	....	**KLIUCHEVSKOI** (Kamchatka)	1000-26=	4	-/8
	1945	0115q	?	**LAUTARO** (Chile-S)	1508-06=	1	
	1945	0225	1*a*	**AVACHINSKY** (Kamchatka)	1000-10=	4	-/8
	1945	03	?	**GREAT SITKIN** (Aleutian Is)	1101-12-	2	7/-

	START YEAR	M-Dy	Duration	VOLCANO NAME (Subregion)	NUMBER	VEI	Vol L/T
	1945	0308	313m	RUAPEHU (New Zealand)	0401-10=	2	7/-
	1945	0331	4a	LLAIMA (Chile-C)	1507-11=	3	
	1945	0415	21a	FOURNAISE, PITON DE LA (Indian O.)	0303-02=	2	6/-
	1945	0604	210m	OKMOK (Aleutian Is)	1101-29-	2	7/-
	1945	0605d	132m	ETNA (Italy)	0101-06=	1	
	1945	0612	6a	SEMERU (Java)	0603-30=	2	
	1945	0619	18a	KLIUCHEVSKOI (Kamchatka)	1000-26=	3	7/7
	1945	0623	?	MUTNOVSKY (Kamchatka)	1000-06=	2	
	1945	0822	....	RUAPEHU (New Zealand)	0401-10=	3	7/-
	1945	09	?	KARYMSKY (Kamchatka)	1000-13=	2	
	1945	09 ?	212t	MALY SEMIACHIK (Kamchatka)	1000-14=	2	
	1945	0916	3a	ASO (Kyushu-Japan)	0802-11=	2	
	1945	0925?	?	GRIMSVOTN (Iceland-NE)	1703-01=	1	
	1945	1103	<1	KUCHINOERABU-JIMA (Ryukyu Is)	0802-05=	2	
	1946	Cont	....	STROMBOLI (Italy)	0101-04=	1?	
	1946	Cont	....	NYIRAGONGO (Africa-C)	0203-03=	0	
	1946	Cont	....	BAGANA (Bougainville-SW Pac)	0505-02=	2	
	1946	Cont	....	YASUR (Vanuatu-SW Pacific)	0507-10=	2	
	1946	Cont	....	DUKONO (Halmahera-Indonesia)	0608-01=	2	
	1946	Cont	....	MALY SEMIACHIK (Kamchatka)	1000-14=	2	
	1946	Cont	....	SHEVELUCH (Kamchatka)	1000-27=	2	8/-
	1946	Cont	....	PAVLOF (Alaska Peninsula)	1102-03-	2	
	1946	Cont	....	MICHOACAN [PARICUTIN] (Mexico)	1401-06=	3	8/9
	1946	Cont	....	SANTA MARIA (Guatemala)	1402-03=	1	8/8
	1946	Cont	....	IZALCO (El Salvador)	1403-03=	2	
?	1946	....	?	MEDVEZHIA (Kurile Is)	0900-10=	2	
?	1946	....	?	MAGEIK (Alaska Peninsula)	1102-15-	3	
	1946	....	365y	TUPUNGATITO (Chile-C)	1507-01=	2	
	1946	....	365y	CHILLAN, NEVADOS DE (Chile-C)	1507-07=	2?	
	1946	01	304p	SAKURA-JIMA (Kyushu-Japan)	0802-08=	2	8/7
	1946	02	243p	ETNA (Italy)	0101-06=	1	
	1946	02	91p	SEMERU (Java)	0603-30=	2	
	1946	0204d	?	BAYONNAISE ROCKS (Izu Is-Japan)	0804-07=	2	7/-
	1946	03	31p	PURACE (Colombia)	1501-06=	2	
	1946	04	91p	RUAPEHU (New Zealand)	0401-10=	2	
?	1946	04	?	KIRISHIMA (Kyushu-Japan)	0802-09=	2	
	1946	04	?	KARYMSKY (Kamchatka)	1000-13=	2	
	1946	04	123p	TELICA (Nicaragua)	1404-04=	2	
	1946	0415q	?	KOLOKOL GROUP (Kurile Is)	0900-12=	2	
	1946	0429	56a	ASO (Kyushu-Japan)	0802-11=	2	
	1946	06	384w?	MASAYA (Nicaragua)	1404-10=	0	
	1946	0618	17a	FOURNAISE, PITON DE LA (Indian O.)	0303-02=	2	6/-
	1946	0723	?	LLAIMA (Chile-C)	1507-11=	2	
	1946	0725	<1	KRAKATAU (Indonesia)	0602-00=	1	
	1946	08	152p	SHISHALDIN (Aleutian Is)	1101-36-	2	
?	1946	0814	?	GREAT SITKIN (Aleutian Is)	1101-12-		
	1946	09	31p	KARYMSKY (Kamchatka)	1000-13=	2	
	1946	09	....	SANGAY (Ecuador)	1502-09=	2	
	1946	0909	8a	NIUAFO'OU (Tonga-SW Pacific)	0403-11=	2	
	1946	0914	<1	MIRAVALLES (Costa Rica)	1405-03=	1	
	1946	10	16m	ASAMA (Honshu-Japan)	0803-11=	2	
	1946	1023	31a?	KLIUCHEVSKOI (Kamchatka)	1000-26=	2	7/5
	1946	1029	228m	SEMERU (Java)	0603-30=	2	
	1946	1104d	?	POAS (Costa Rica)	1405-04=	1	
	1946	1109	2a	SARYCHEV PEAK (Kurile Is)	0900-24=	4	
	1946	1121	192a	RUAPEHU (New Zealand)	0401-10=	1	
	1946	1124	?	KURIKOMA (Honshu-Japan)	0803-21=	2	
	1946	12	31p	AKUTAN (Aleutian Is)	1101-32-	2	
	1946	1201p	289q	MANAM (New Guinea-NE of)	0501-02=	3	7/-
	1946	1226e	224j>	KRAKATAU (Indonesia)	0602-00=	2	
	1946	1230	<1	ASO (Kyushu-Japan)	0802-11=	2	
	1947	Cont	....	STROMBOLI (Italy)	0101-04=	1?	
	1947	Cont	....	NYIRAGONGO (Africa-C)	0203-03=	0	
	1947	Cont	....	RUAPEHU (New Zealand)	0401-10=	1	
	1947	Cont	....	MANAM (New Guinea-NE of)	0501-02=	2	7/-
	1947	Cont	....	BAGANA (Bougainville-SW Pac)	0505-02=	2	
	1947	Cont	....	YASUR (Vanuatu-SW Pacific)	0507-10=	2	
	1947	Cont	....	KRAKATAU (Indonesia)	0602-00=	2	
	1947	Cont	....	SEMERU (Java)	0603-30=	2	
	1947	Cont	....	DUKONO (Halmahera-Indonesia)	0608-01=	2	
	1947	Cont	....	SHEVELUCH (Kamchatka)	1000-27=	2	8/-
	1947	Cont	....	AKUTAN (Aleutian Is)	1101-32-	2	
	1947	Cont	....	SHISHALDIN (Aleutian Is)	1101-36-	2	
	1947	Cont	....	PAVLOF (Alaska Peninsula)	1102-03-	2	
	1947	Cont	....	MICHOACAN [PARICUTIN] (Mexico)	1401-06=	3	8/9
	1947	Cont	....	SANTA MARIA (Guatemala)	1402-03=	1	8/8
	1947	Cont	....	IZALCO (El Salvador)	1403-03=	2	
	1947	Cont	....	SANGAY (Ecuador)	1502-09=	2	
	1947	Cont	....	TUPUNGATITO (Chile-C)	1507-01=	2	
	1947	Cont	....	CHILLAN, NEVADOS DE (Chile-C)	1507-07=	2?	
	1947?	....	?	FOURNAISE, PITON DE LA (Indian O.)	0303-02=	2	
	1947	....	?	FUEGO (Guatemala)	1402-09=	2	
	1947	....	....	MASAYA (Nicaragua)	1404-10=	1	
	1947	01 <	?	WHITE ISLAND (New Zealand)	0401-04=	2	
?	1947	01	?	NIUAFO'OU (Tonga-SW Pacific)	0403-11=		
	1947	01 ?	?	FARALLON DE PAJAROS (Mariana Is)	0804-14=	0?	
	1947	01	?	TOLBACHIK (Kamchatka)	1000-24=	2?	
	1947	01	30p	POPOCATEPETL (Mexico)	1401-09=	1	
	1947	0107	38m	MAYON (Luzon-Philippines)	0703-03=	2	
	1947	0129	26a	ETNA (Italy)	0101-06=	2	
	1947	02	?	EREBUS (Antarctica)	1900-02=	2	
	1947	0209	<1	KARANGETANG [API SIAU] (Sangihe	0607-02=	2	
	1947	0224	17a	ETNA (Italy)	0101-06=	1	6/4
	1947	0313s	?	BAM (New Guinea-NE of)	0501-01=	2	
	1947	0329	388a	HEKLA (Iceland-S)	1702-07=	4	8/8
	1947	04	31p	SIRUNG (Lesser Sunda Is)	0604-27=	2	
	1947	04	?	KARYMSKY (Kamchatka)	1000-13=	2	
	1947	0427	?	PURACE (Colombia)	1501-06=	2	
	1947	0526	112m	ASO (Kyushu-Japan)	0802-11=	2	
	1947	06	39a	ASAMA (Honshu-Japan)	0803-11=	2	
?	1947	06	?	ILIAMNA (Alaska-SW)	1103-02-		
	1947	0712	15a	NEGRO, CERRO (Nicaragua)	1404-07=	2	
?	1947	0715	?	GALERAS (Colombia)	1501-08=	2?	
	1947	0822	5a	SOPUTAN (Sulawesi-Indonesia)	0606-03=	2	
	1947	0902	148a	GEDE (Java)	0603-06=	2	-/5
	1947	12	?	GORELY (Kamchatka)	1000-07=	2	
	1947	1201	20a	KARANGETANG [API SIAU] (Sangihe	0607-02=	2	
	1948	Cont	....	STROMBOLI (Italy)	0101-04=	1?	
	1948	Cont	....	NYIRAGONGO (Africa-C)	0203-03=	0	
	1948	Cont	....	YASUR (Vanuatu-SW Pacific)	0507-10=	2	
	1948	Cont	....	DUKONO (Halmahera-Indonesia)	0608-01=	2	
	1948	Cont	....	SHEVELUCH (Kamchatka)	1000-27=	2	8/-
	1948	Cont	....	MICHOACAN [PARICUTIN] (Mexico)	1401-06=	3	8/9
	1948	Cont	....	SANTA MARIA (Guatemala)	1402-03=	1	8/8
	1948	Cont	....	SANGAY (Ecuador)	1502-09=	2	
	1948	Cont	....	HEKLA (Iceland-S)	1702-07=	0	8/8
	1948	....	?	AKITA-YAKE-YAMA (Honshu-Japan)	0803-26=	1?	
	1948	....	?	SHISHALDIN (Aleutian Is)	1101-36-	2	
	1948	....	502w	TELICA (Nicaragua)	1404-04=	2	
	1948	....	730y	CONCEPCION (Nicaragua)	1404-12=	2	
	1948	....	>3yr	POAS (Costa Rica)	1405-04=	1	
	1948	0124	7a>	WOLF, VOLCAN (Galapagos)	1503-02=	2	
?	1948	02	?	GRIMSVOTN (Iceland-NE)	1703-01=	0	
	1948	0214	23a	FOURNAISE, PITON DE LA (Indian O.)	0303-02=	2	6/-
	1948	0215	69a	TENGGER CALDERA [BROMO]	0603-31=	3	
	1948	0301	137e	NYAMURAGIRA (Africa-C)	0203-02=	2	7/7
	1948	0331	?	NEGRO, CERRO (Nicaragua)	1404-07=	2	
	1948	0407	233a	ILIWERUNG (Lesser Sunda Is)	0604-25=	2	6/6
	1948	0409	251m	ASO (Kyushu-Japan)	0802-11=	1	
	1948	0422	55a	KARTHALA (Indian O.-W)	0303-01=	2	
	1948	0429	?	ILIBOLENG (Lesser Sunda Is)	0604-22=	2	
	1948	0429	100a>	AKUTAN (Aleutian Is)	1101-32-	2	
	1948	0430	16m	TONGARIRO [NGAURUHOE] (New Z)	0401-08=	2	
	1948	05	....	PAVLOF (Alaska Peninsula)	1102-03-	2	
	1948	0501	?	RUAPEHU (New Zealand)	0401-10=	1	
	1948	0630p	?	AZUL, CERRO (Galapagos)	1503-06=	0	
	1948	0727	<1	SAKURA-JIMA (Kyushu-Japan)	0802-08=	1	
	1948	08	?	KLIUCHEVSKOI (Kamchatka)	1000-26=	2?	
	1948	08	182p?	NEGRA, SIERRA (Galapagos)	1503-05=	2	
	1948	09	?	TONGARIRO [NGAURUHOE] (New Z)	0401-08=	2	
	1948	0901	>3yr	HIBOK-HIBOK (Mindanao-Philippines)	0701-08=	2	
	1948	0922	7a	KUWAE [KARUA] (Vanuatu-SW Pac)	0507-07=	2	
	1948	0929	275w	MERAPI (Java)	0603-25=	2	
	1948	1009	117a	VILLARRICA (Chile-C)	1507-12=	2	
	1948	1018	....	VILLARRICA (Chile-C)	1507-12=	3	
	1948	1104	>3yr	IZALCO (El Salvador)	1403-03=	2	
	1948	1114	31a	SLAMET (Java)	0603-18=	2	
	1948	1115	82a	GEDE (Java)	0603-06=	2	-/5
	1948	12	?	KARANGETANG [API SIAU] (Sangihe	0607-02=	2	
	1948	1201p	>3yr	BAGANA (Bougainville-SW Pac)	0505-02=	2	
	1949	Cont	....	NYIRAGONGO (Africa-C)	0203-03=	0	
	1949	Cont	....	BAGANA (Bougainville-SW Pac)	0505-02=	2	
	1949	Cont	....	YASUR (Vanuatu-SW Pacific)	0507-10=	2	
	1949	Cont	....	GEDE (Java)	0603-06=	2	-/5
	1949	Cont	....	MERAPI (Java)	0603-25=	2	
	1949	Cont	....	DUKONO (Halmahera-Indonesia)	0608-01=	2	
	1949	Cont	....	HIBOK-HIBOK (Mindanao-Philippines)	0701-08=	2	
	1949	Cont	....	SHEVELUCH (Kamchatka)	1000-27=	2	8/-
	1949	Cont	....	MICHOACAN [PARICUTIN] (Mexico)	1401-06=	3	8/9
	1949	Cont	....	SANTA MARIA (Guatemala)	1402-03=	1	8/8
	1949	Cont	....	IZALCO (El Salvador)	1403-03=	2	
	1949	Cont	....	TELICA (Nicaragua)	1404-04=	2	
	1949	Cont	....	CONCEPCION (Nicaragua)	1404-12=	2	
	1949	Cont	....	POAS (Costa Rica)	1405-04=	1	
	1949	Cont	....	SANGAY (Ecuador)	1502-09=	2	
	1949	Cont	....	NEGRA, SIERRA (Galapagos)	1503-05=	2	
	1949<	....	?	MATTHEW ISLAND (SW Pacific)	0508-01=	2	
	1949	....	365y	RINJANI (Lesser Sunda Is)	0604-03=	0	
	1949	....	?	GAMKONORA (Halmahera-Indonesia)	0608-04=	2	
	1949?	....	?	AZUL, CERRO (Galapagos)	1503-06=	0	
	1949	0101	....	VILLARRICA (Chile-C)	1507-12=	3	
	1949	0105	14a>	RUANG (Sangihe Is-Indonesia)	0607-01=	2	
	1949	0106	145a	MAUNA LOA (Hawaiian Is)	1302-02=	0	8/-
	1949	0204	?	ILIBOLENG (Lesser Sunda Is)	0604-22=	2	
	1949	0205	220a	NIIGATA-YAKE-YAMA (Honshu-Japan)	0803-09=	2	
	1949	0209	22a	TONGARIRO [NGAURUHOE] (New Z)	0401-08=	2	5/-
	1949	03	214p	ASAMA (Honshu-Japan)	0803-11=	2	
	1949	04	?	KUWAE [KARUA] (Vanuatu-SW Pac)	0507-07=	3	
	1949	0409	20a	ILIWERUNG (Lesser Sunda Is)	0604-25=	2	
	1949	0415e	?	AZUL, CERRO [QUIZAPU] (Chile-C)	1507-06=	2?	
	1949	0429	1a	MARAPI (Sumatra)	0601-14=	2	
	1949	05	?	KLIUCHEVSKOI (Kamchatka)	1000-26=	2	
	1949	0512	?	KRAKATAU (Indonesia)	0602-00=	2	
	1949	0526	16a	PURACE (Colombia)	1501-06=	2	
	1949	06	?	TRIDENT (Alaska Peninsula)	1102-16-		
	1949	06	15m	NEGRO, CERRO (Nicaragua)	1404-07=	2	
	1949	0606	3a	STROMBOLI (Italy)	0101-04=	2	3/-
	1949	0612	?	ILIBOLENG (Lesser Sunda Is)	0604-22=	2	
	1949	0624	36	LA PALMA (Canary Is)	1803-01-	2?	7/5
	1949	0830	1a	AKITA-YAKE-YAMA (Honshu-Japan)	0803-26=	2	
	1949	09	?	LLAIMA (Chile-C)	1507-11=	2	
	1949	0914	?	LOKON-EMPUNG (Sulawesi-Indonesia)	0606-10=	1	
	1949	0914	?	KARANGETANG [API SIAU] (Sangihe	0607-02=	2	
?	1949	10	?	FOURNAISE, PITON DE LA (Indian O.)	0303-02=	2	

START YEAR	M-Dy	Duration	VOLCANO NAME (Subregion)	NUMBER	VEI	Vol L/T
1949	10	61p	**KUWAE [KARUA]** (Vanuatu-SW Pac)	0507-07=	3	
1949	10	>3yr	**SUWANOSE-JIMA** (Ryukyu Is)	0802-03=	2	
? 1949	10	?	**NAKANO-SHIMA** (Ryukyu Is)	0802-04=	1?	
1949	1015e	7c	**MARAPI** (Sumatra)	0601-14=	2	
1949	11	?	**FUEGO** (Guatemala)	1402-09=	2	
1949	1202	44m	**ETNA** (Italy)	0101-06=	2	6/5
1949	1222	24m	**TACANA** (Mexico)	1401-13=	1	
1949	1226	110a	**ASO** (Kyushu-Japan)	0802-11=	2	
1949	1230	8a	**GREAT SITKIN** (Aleutian Is)	1101-12-	1	-/4
1950	*Cont*	....	*NYIRAGONGO (Africa-C)*	0203-03=	*0*	
1950	*Cont*	....	*YASUR (Vanuatu-SW Pacific)*	0507-10=	*2*	
1950	*Cont*	....	*RINJANI (Lesser Sunda Is)*	0604-03=	*0*	
1950	*Cont*	....	*DUKONO (Halmahera-Indonesia)*	0608-01=	*2*	
1950	*Cont*	....	*SUWANOSE-JIMA (Ryukyu Is)*	0802-03=	*2*	
1950	*Cont*	....	*SHEVELUCH (Kamchatka)*	1000-27=	*2*	*8/-*
1950	*Cont*	....	*MICHOACAN [PARICUTIN] (Mexico)*	1401-06=	*3*	*8/9*
1950	*Cont*	....	*TACANA (Mexico)*	1401-13=	*1*	
1950	*Cont*	....	*SANTA MARIA (Guatemala)*	1402-03=	*1*	*8/8*
1950	*Cont*	....	*IZALCO (El Salvador)*	1403-03=	*2*	
1950	*Cont*	....	*CONCEPCION (Nicaragua)*	1404-12=	*2*	
1950	*Cont*	....	*POAS (Costa Rica)*	1405-04=	*1*	
1950	*Cont*	....	*SANGAY (Ecuador)*	1502-09=	*2*	
1950	....	365y	**GARELOI** (Aleutian Is)	1101-07-	1	
? 1950	....	?	**VILLARRICA** (Chile-C)	1507-12=		
1950	0110	23a	**SANTORINI** (Greece)	0102-04=	2	6/-
1950	0112	236a	**GALERAS** (Colombia)	1501-08=	2	
1950	0115	?	**KURIKOMA** (Honshu-Japan)	0803-21=	2	
1950	0124	777a?	**HEARD** (Indian O.-S)	0304-01=	2	
? 1950	02	14m	**SHIN-IWO-JIMA** (Volcano Is-Japan)	0804-13=	0	
1950	0210	9a	**AZUMA** (Honshu-Japan)	0803-18=	1	
1950	0225	36a	**FOURNAISE, PITON DE LA** (Indian O.)	0303-02=	2	6/-
1950	03	395p	**KABA** (Sumatra)	0601-22=	1	
1950	03	153p?	**ILIBOLENG** (Lesser Sunda Is)	0604-22=	2	
1950	0327	?	**BRISTOL ISLAND** (Antarctica)	1900-08=	2	
1950	0527	80m	**TENGGER CALDERA [BROMO]**	0603-31=	2	
1950	0601	22a	**MAUNA LOA** (Hawaiian Is)	1302-02=	0	8/-
1950	0616	?	**TONGARIRO [NGAURUHOE]** (New Z)	0401-08=	2	
1950	0626	<1	**RUAPEHU** (New Zealand)	0401-10=	1	
1950	0629	72a	**SAKURA-JIMA** (Kyushu-Japan)	0802-08=	1	
@ 1950	0702	47a?	**TRIDENT** (Alaska Peninsula)	1102-16-	2?	
1950	0703	4a	**KRAKATAU** (Indonesia)	0602-00=	2	
1950	0716	347a	**OSHIMA** (Izu Is-Japan)	0804-01=	2	7/6
1950	0731	289m	**PAVLOF** (Alaska Peninsula)	1102-03-	2	
1950	*0828*	>3yr	*SEMERU (Java)*	0603-30=	1	
1950	0830	6a	**FOURNAISE, PITON DE LA** (Indian O.)	0303-02=	2	
1950	0910	21	**ILIWERUNG** (Lesser Sunda Is)	0604-25=	2	
1950	*0915*		*HIBOK-HIBOK (Mindanao-Philippines)*	0701-08=	2	
1950	0923	265m	**ASAMA** (Honshu-Japan)	0803-11=	2	
1950	0926	....	**BAGANA** (Bougainville-SW Pac)	0505-02=	3	
1950	0927	626a	**MARAPI** (Sumatra)	0601-14=	2?	
1950	10	?	**GAMKONORA** (Halmahera-Indonesia)	0608-04=	2	
1950	1020	3a	**STROMBOLI** (Italy)	0101-04=	2	3/-
1950	11	61p	**ASO** (Kyushu-Japan)	0802-11=	2	
1950	1105	24a	**GREAT SITKIN** (Aleutian Is)	1101-12-		
1950	1121	391m	**NEGRO, CERRO** (Nicaragua)	1404-07=	2	
1950	1125	373a	**ETNA** (Italy)	0101-06=	2	8/6
1950	1201p	?	**KAVACHI** (Solomon Is-SW Pac)	0505-06=	2	
1950	*1206*	*354e*	*AMBRYM (Vanuatu-SW Pacific)*	0507-04=	*3*	*-/8*
1951	*Cont*	....	*NYIRAGONGO (Africa-C)*	0203-03=	*0*	
1951	*Cont*	....	*HEARD (Indian O.-S)*	0304-01=	*2*	
1951	*Cont*	....	*BAGANA (Bougainville-SW Pac)*	0505-02=	*2*	
1951	*Cont*	....	*YASUR (Vanuatu-SW Pacific)*	0507-10=	*2*	
1951	*Cont*	....	*MARAPI (Sumatra)*	0601-14=	*2?*	
1951	*Cont*	....	*SEMERU (Java)*	0603-30=	*1*	
1951	*Cont*	....	*DUKONO (Halmahera-Indonesia)*	0608-01=	*2*	
1951	*Cont*	....	*SUWANOSE-JIMA (Ryukyu Is)*	0802-03=	*2*	
1951	*Cont*	....	*ASAMA (Honshu-Japan)*	0803-11=	*2*	
1951	*Cont*	....	*OSHIMA (Izu Is-Japan)*	0804-01=	*2*	*7/6*
1951	*Cont*	....	*GARELOI (Aleutian Is)*	1101-07-	*1*	
1951	*Cont*	....	*MICHOACAN [PARICUTIN] (Mexico)*	1401-06=	*3*	*8/9*
1951	*Cont*	....	*SANTA MARIA (Guatemala)*	1402-03=	*1*	*8/8*
1951	*Cont*	....	*IZALCO (El Salvador)*	1403-03=	*2*	
1951	*Cont*	....	*NEGRO, CERRO (Nicaragua)*	1404-07=	*2*	
1951	*Cont*	....	*POAS (Costa Rica)*	1405-04=	*1*	
1951	*Cont*	....	*SANGAY (Ecuador)*	1502-09=	*2*	
? 1951	....	?	**ULAWUN** (New Britain-SW Pac)	0502-12=		
? 1951	....	?	**UNNAMED** (New Britain-SW Pac)	0502-131	0	
1951	....	....	**AMBRYM** (Vanuatu-SW Pacific)	0507-04=	4+	-/8
1951	....	?	**ILIBOLENG** (Lesser Sunda Is)	0604-22=	2?	
1951	....	?	**GAMKONORA** (Halmahera-Indonesia)	0608-04=	2	
? 1951	....	?	**ATKA [KOROVIN]** (Aleutian Is)	1101-16-		
1951	....	?	**AZUL, CERRO** (Galapagos)	1503-06=		
1951	*0117*	*>3yr*	*LAMINGTON (New Guinea)*	0503-01=	*3*	*8/-*
1951	0121	....	**LAMINGTON** (New Guinea)	0503-01=	4	8/-
1951	0129	<1	**SHIKOTSU [TARUMAI]** (Hokkaido)	0805-04=	2	
1951	02	?	**AKITA-YAKE-YAMA** (Honshu-Japan)	0803-26=	1?	
1951	0211	?	**SLAMET** (Java)	0603-18=	2	
1951	0301	<1	**CEREME** (Java)	0603-17=	2?	
1951	*0307*	....	*KABA (Sumatra)*	0601-22=	1	
1951	0319	?	**RUAPEHU** (New Zealand)	0401-10=	1	
1951	04	173d	**SHISHALDIN** (Aleutian Is)	1101-36-	2	
1951	0411	?	**STROMBOLI** (Italy)	0101-04=	2	
1951	05	?	**TONGARIRO [NGAURUHOE]** (New Z)	0401-08=	2	
1951	0504	92p?	**ASO** (Kyushu-Japan)	0802-11=	2	
1951	0522	<1	**SOCORRO** (Mexico-Is)	1401-021	2?	
1951	0527	?	**KUNLUN VOLC GROUP** (China-W)	1004-03-	2	
? 1951	06	?	**FOURNAISE, PITON DE LA** (Indian O.)	0303-02=	0	
1951	06	?	**OKATAINA [ROTOMAHANA]** (New Z)	0401-05=	1	
1951	0612	70a	**FOGO** (Cape Verde Is)	1804-01=	2	7/-
? 1951	0625	<1	**ANIAKCHAK** (Alaska Peninsula)	1102-09-		
1951	0626	185a	**SLAMET** (Java)	0603-18=	2	
1951	07	>3yr	**CONCEPCION** (Nicaragua)	1404-12=	2	
1951	*0702*	*623m*	*LOKON-EMPUNG (Sulawesi-Indonesia)*	0606-10=	2	
1951	0715q	91q	**FUKUJIN** (Volcano Is-Japan)	0804-133	0	
1951	0715q	?	**BARANSKY** (Kurile Is)	0900-08=	1	
1951	0715q	92q	**TELICA** (Nicaragua)	1404-04=	2	
@ 1951	0722	?	**MARTIN** (Alaska Peninsula)	1102-14-		
1951	0723h	8h	**UBINAS** (Peru)	1504-02=	2	
1951	0725	3a	**NYAMURAGIRA** (Africa-C)	0203-02=	1	-/4
1951	0728	<1	**SHIKOTSU [TARUMAI]** (Hokkaido)	0805-04=	2	
? 1951	0731	227m	**AKAN** (Hokkaido-Japan)	0805-07=	1	
1951	08	?	**FARALLON DE PAJAROS** (Mariana Is)	0804-14=	2	
1951	0821	?	**FONUALEI** (Tonga-SW Pacific)	0403-10=	2	
1951	0831	<1	**KELUT** (Java)	0603-28=	3	
1951	0910	10a	**FOURNAISE, PITON DE LA** (Indian O.)	0303-02=	1	
1951	0921	251a	**ETNA** (Italy)	0101-06=	1	
? 1951	0921	?	**BOGOSLOF** (Aleutian Is)	1101-30-	0	
1951	10	?	**AKUTAN** (Aleutian Is)	1101-32-	2	
1951	10	151p?	**PAVLOF** (Alaska Peninsula)	1102-03-	2	
1951	1023	34p	**TINAKULA** (Santa Cruz Is-SW Pac)	0506-01=	3	
1951	11	96m	**LASCAR** (Chile-N)	1505-10=	2?	
? 1951	1101	45m?	**CLEVELAND** (Aleutian Is)	1101-24-		
1951	1112	4a	**ILIWERUNG** (Lesser Sunda Is)	0604-25=	2	
1951	1116	61a	**NYAMURAGIRA** (Africa-C)	0203-02=	2	7/5
1951	1119	11a	**KLIUCHEVSKOI** (Kamchatka)	1000-26=	2	7/6
? 1951	1124	?	**UNNAMED** (New Guinea-NE of)	0501-04=	0	
1951	1201p	?	**KAVACHI** (Solomon Is-SW Pac)	0505-06=	2	
1951	1204	....	**HIBOK-HIBOK** (Mindanao-Philippines)	0701-08=	3	
1951	1215	?	**LEWOTOLO** (Lesser Sunda Is)	0604-23=	2	
1951	1220	?	**MAKUSHIN** (Aleutian Is)	1101-31-	1	
1952	*Cont*	....	*ETNA (Italy)*	0101-06=	*1*	
1952	*Cont*	....	*NYAMURAGIRA (Africa-C)*	0203-02=	*2*	*7/5*
1952	*Cont*	....	*NYIRAGONGO (Africa-C)*	0203-03=	*0*	
1952	*Cont*	....	*HEARD (Indian O.-S)*	0304-01=	*2*	
1952	*Cont*	....	*LAMINGTON (New Guinea)*	0503-01=	*3*	*8/-*
1952	*Cont*	....	*YASUR (Vanuatu-SW Pacific)*	0507-10=	*2*	
1952	*Cont*	....	*SLAMET (Java)*	0603-18=	*2*	
1952	*Cont*	....	*SEMERU (Java)*	0603-30=	*1*	
1952	*Cont*	....	*DUKONO (Halmahera-Indonesia)*	0608-01=	*2*	
1952	*Cont*	....	*HIBOK-HIBOK (Mindanao-Philippines)*	0701-08=	*2*	
1952	*Cont*	....	*SUWANOSE-JIMA (Ryukyu Is)*	0802-03=	*2*	
? *1952*	*Cont*	....	*AKAN (Hokkaido-Japan)*	0805-07=	*1*	
1952	*Cont*	....	*PAVLOF (Alaska Peninsula)*	1102-03-	*2*	
1952	*Cont*	....	*MICHOACAN [PARICUTIN] (Mexico)*	1401-06=	*3*	*8/9*
1952	*Cont*	....	*SANTA MARIA (Guatemala)*	1402-03=	*1*	*8/8*
1952	*Cont*	....	*IZALCO (El Salvador)*	1403-03=	*2*	
1952	*Cont*	....	*CONCEPCION (Nicaragua)*	1404-12=	*2*	
1952	*Cont*	....	*SANGAY (Ecuador)*	1502-09=	*2*	
1952	*Cont*	....	*LASCAR (Chile-N)*	1505-10=	*2?*	
1952	....	?	**MAHAWU** (Sulawesi-Indonesia)	0606-11=	2?	
? 1952	....	?	**BINULUAN** (Luzon-Philippines)	0703-088	1?	
? 1952	....	?	**ASO** (Kyushu-Japan)	0802-11=		
? 1952	....	?	**FUKUJIN** (Volcano Is-Japan)	0804-133	0	
? 1952	....	?	**MAKUSHIN** (Aleutian Is)	1101-31-		
? 1952	....	?	**ILIAMNA** (Alaska-SW)	1103-02-		
1952	01	151p	**KERINCI** (Sumatra)	0601-17=	2	
1952	01	16m	**ASAMA** (Honshu-Japan)	0803-11=	2	
1952	0115q	?	**KOLOKOL GROUP** (Kurile Is)	0900-12=	2	
1952	0117	?	**GARELOI** (Aleutian Is)	1101-07-	2?	
1952	02	137m	**KARANGETANG [API SIAU]** (Sangihe	0607-02=	2	
1952	0210?	2a?	**KARTHALA** (Indian O.-W)	0303-01=	2	
1952	0229	229m	**BAGANA** (Bougainville-SW Pac)	0505-02=	4	
1952	0316<	472w>	**DIDICAS** (Luzon Is-N of)	0704-02=	2	8/-
1952	*0323*	*>3yr*	*POAS (Costa Rica)*	1405-04=	1	
1952	0324	?	**ILIWERUNG** (Lesser Sunda Is)	0604-25=	1	
1952	0401	27a	**KABA** (Sumatra)	0601-22=	2	
1952	0416	290a?	**KAVACHI** (Solomon Is-SW Pac)	0505-06=	2	
1952	0422	2a	**IJEN** (Java)	0603-35=	1	
1952	0519	62a	**FOURNAISE, PITON DE LA** (Indian O.)	0303-02=	2	6/-
1952	*0529*	....	*MARAPI (Sumatra)*	0601-14=	2	
? 1952	06	15m	**SHIN-IWO-JIMA** (Volcano Is-Japan)	0804-13=	0	
1952	0607	10a	**STROMBOLI** (Italy)	0101-04=	2	3/-
1952	0609	<1	**ASAMA** (Honshu-Japan)	0803-11=	2	
1952	0618	?	**AZUMA** (Honshu-Japan)	0803-18=	1	
1952	0626	....	**LOKON-EMPUNG** (Sulawesi-Indonesia)	0606-10=	3	
1952	0627	136a	**KILAUEA** (Hawaiian Is)	1302-01-	0	7/-
1952	07	?	**RUAPEHU** (New Zealand)	0401-10=	1	
? 1952	07	?	**DIENG VOLC COMPLEX** (Java)	0603-20=	1?	
1952	0704?	7a?	**TANGKUBANPARAHU** (Java)	0603-09=	1	
1952	0716	51e	**GAMKONORA** (Halmahera-Indonesia)	0608-04=	2	
1952	0801	207d	**BARCENA** (Mexico-Is)	1401-02=	3	7/8
1952	0810	138e	**AMBRYM** (Vanuatu-SW Pacific)	0507-04=	2	
1952	0815e	?	**ARJUNO-WELIRANG** (Java)	0603-29=	0	
1952	0817	?	**TOKACHI** (Hokkaido-Japan)	0805-05=		
1952	0916	395m	**BAYONNAISE ROCKS** (Izu Is-Japan)	0804-07=	2	7/-
1952	1003	?	**KUWAE [KARUA]** (Vanuatu-SW Pac)	0507-07=	1	
1952	1010	1a	**KRAKATAU** (Indonesia)	0602-00=	2	
1952	1023	54m	**PILAS, LAS** (Nicaragua)	1404-08=	1	
1952	1026e	171e	**FARALLON DE PAJAROS** (Mariana Is)	0804-14=	2	
1952	11	?	**KARYMSKY** (Kamchatka)	1000-13=	2	
1952	1105	?	**KARPINSKY GROUP** (Kurile Is)	0900-35=	1	
1952	1112	7a	**TAO-RUSYR CALDERA** (Kurile Is)	0900-31=	3	7/-
1952	1129	228m	**TONGARIRO [NGAURUHOE]** (New Z)	0401-08=	2	
1952	1205d	?	**MALY SEMIACHIK** (Kamchatka)	1000-14=	2	
1953	*Cont*	....	*STROMBOLI (Italy)*	0101-04=	*1?*	

START YEAR	M-Dy	Dura-tion	VOLCANO NAME (Subregion)	NUMBER	VEI	Vol L/T
1953	Cont	....	NYIRAGONGO (Africa-C)	0203-03=	0	
1953	Cont	....	TONGARIRO [NGAURUHOE] (New Z)	0401-08=	2	
1953	Cont	....	LAMINGTON (New Guinea)	0503-01=	3	8/-
1953	Cont	....	KAVACHI (Solomon Is-SW Pac)	0505-06=	2	
1953	Cont	....	YASUR (Vanuatu-SW Pacific)	0507-10=	2	
1953	Cont	....	SEMERU (Java)	0603-30=	1	
1953	Cont	....	LOKON-EMPUNG (Sulawesi-Indonesia)	0606-10=	2	
1953	Cont	....	DUKONO (Halmahera-Indonesia)	0608-01=	2	
1953	Cont	....	HIBOK-HIBOK (Mindanao-Philippines)	0701-08=	2	
1953	Cont	....	DIDICAS (Luzon Is-N of)	0704-02=	2	8/-
1953	Cont	....	SUWANOSE-JIMA (Ryukyu Is)	0802-03=	2	
1953	Cont	....	BAYONNAISE ROCKS (Izu Is-Japan)	0804-07=	2	7/-
1953	Cont	....	FARALLON DE PAJAROS (Mariana Is)	0804-14=	2	
1953	Cont	....	BARCENA (Mexico-Is)	1401-02=	2	7/8
1953	Cont	....	SANTA MARIA (Guatemala)	1402-03=	1	8/8
1953	Cont	....	IZALCO (El Salvador)	1403-03=	2	
1953	Cont	....	CONCEPCION (Nicaragua)	1404-12=	2	
1953	Cont	....	SANGAY (Ecuador)	1502-09=	2	
1953	....	?	KARANGETANG [API SIAU] (Sangihe	0607-02=	2	
1953	....	?	KARYMSKY (Kamchatka)	1000-13=	2	
? 1953	....	365y	ATKA [KOROVIN] (Aleutian Is)	1101-16-		
1953	....	?	AKUTAN (Aleutian Is)	1101-32-		
1953g	....	?	ALCEDO, VOLCAN (Galapagos)	1503-04=	0	
1953	0131	75e	RAUNG (Java)	0603-34=	3	8/-
1953	0212	7a	EAST EPI (Vanuatu-SW Pacific)	0507-06=	3	
1953	0212	?	KUWAE [KARUA] (Vanuatu-SW Pac)	0507-07=	1?	
1953	0215	597a?	TRIDENT (Alaska Peninsula)	1102-16-	3	8/7
@ 1953	0217	?	MARTIN (Alaska Peninsula)	1102-14-		
1953	0301	?	ILIAMNA (Alaska-SW)	1103-02-	2	
1953	0302	>3yr	MERAPI (Java)	0603-25=	1	
1953	0313	117a	FOURNAISE, PITON DE LA (Indian O.)	0303-02=	2	7/-
1953	0317	48a?	KRAKATAU (Indonesia)	0602-00=	2	
1953	0319	57a>	SANGEANG API (Lesser Sunda Is)	0604-05=	3	
1953	0324	1a	DIENG VOLC COMPLEX (Java)	0603-20=	2	
1953	04	121p	MANAM (New Guinea-NE of)	0501-02=	2	
? 1953	0404	72m	LAMONGAN (Java)	0603-32=	2?	
1953	0409	4a	FUEGO (Guatemala)	1402-09=	3	
1953	0427	95a	ASO (Kyushu-Japan)	0802-11=	2	
1953	05	151m?	AMBRYM (Vanuatu-SW Pacific)	0507-04=	2	
? 1953	05	?	KITA-IWO-JIMA (Volcano Is-Japan)	0804-11=	0	
1953	05	....	POAS (Costa Rica)	1405-04=	2	
1953	0508	244a	LONG ISLAND (New Guinea-NE of)	0501-05=	3	
? 1953	0511	3a?	GREAT SITKIN (Aleutian Is)	1101-12-	2	
1953	06	92p	BAGANA (Bougainville-SW Pac)	0505-02=	2	
1953	06	?	SIRUNG (Lesser Sunda Is)	0604-27=		
1953	0607	18a	KLIUCHEVSKOI (Kamchatka)	1000-26=	2	7/6
? 1953	0625	?	CLEVELAND (Aleutian Is)	1101-24-		
1953	0627	>3yr	ST. ANDREW STRAIT [TULUMAN]	0500-01=	0	8/-
1953	0709	7a	SPURR (Alaska-SW)	1103-04-	4	
1953	0710	....	BAGANA (Bougainville-SW Pac)	0505-02=	3	
? 1953	0720	?	UNNAMED (Mexico)	1401-008	0	
? 1953	0730	?	ETNA (Italy)	0101-06=	2	
1953	08	61p	SLAMET (Java)	0603-18=	2	
1953	0820	90a	HEARD (Indian O.-S)	0304-01=	2	
1953	0827	142m	NEGRA, SIERRA (Galapagos)	1503-05=	3?	
1953	0904	1a	IYA (Lesser Sunda Is)	0604-11=	2?	
1953	0914?	<1	SHIKOTSU [TARUMAI] (Hokkaido)	0805-04=	1	
1953	0921	65a	KRAKATAU (Indonesia)	0602-00=	2	
1953	1004c	?	SHISHALDIN (Aleutian Is)	1101-36-	2	
1953	1005	126a	OSHIMA (Izu Is-Japan)	0804-01=	1	5/4
1953	1015q	?	RINJANI (Lesser Sunda Is)	0604-03=	0?	
1953	1024	5a	NASU (Honshu-Japan)	0803-15=	1	
S 1953	1030	<1	KICK-'EM-JENNY (W Indies)	1600-16=	0	
? 1953	11	?	EAST EPI (Vanuatu-SW Pacific)	0507-06=	0	
1953	11	?	SOPUTAN (Sulawesi-Indonesia)	0606-03=	2	
1953	1125	?	PAVLOF (Alaska Peninsula)	1102-03-		
1953	12	16m	ASO (Kyushu-Japan)	0802-11=	1	
? 1953	12	15m	SHIN-IWO-JIMA (Volcano Is-Japan)	0804-13=	0	
1953	1227	583a	ASAMA (Honshu-Japan)	0803-11=	2	
? 1953	1231y	?	CANDLEMAS ISLAND (Antarctica)	1900-10=		
1954	Cont	....	NYIRAGONGO (Africa-C)	0203-03=	0	
1954	Cont	....	LONG ISLAND (New Guinea-NE of)	0501-05=	2	
1954	Cont	....	LAMINGTON (New Guinea)	0503-01=	3	8/-
1954	Cont	....	YASUR (Vanuatu-SW Pacific)	0507-10=	2	
1954	Cont	....	SEMERU (Java)	0603-30=	1	
1954	Cont	....	DUKONO (Halmahera-Indonesia)	0608-01=	2	
1954	Cont	....	SUWANOSE-JIMA (Ryukyu Is)	0802-03=	2	
1954	Cont	....	ASAMA (Honshu-Japan)	0803-11=	2	
1954	Cont	....	OSHIMA (Izu Is-Japan)	0804-01=	1	5/4
? 1954	Cont	....	ATKA [KOROVIN] (Aleutian Is)	1101-16-		
1954	Cont	....	TRIDENT (Alaska Peninsula)	1102-16-	2	8/7
1954	Cont	....	SANTA MARIA (Guatemala)	1402-03=	1	8/8
1954	Cont	....	IZALCO (El Salvador)	1403-03=	2	
1954	Cont	....	CONCEPCION (Nicaragua)	1404-12=	2	
1954	Cont	....	POAS (Costa Rica)	1405-04=	2	
1954	Cont	....	SANGAY (Ecuador)	1502-09=	2	
1954	....	?	AMBRYM (Vanuatu-SW Pacific)	0507-04=	2	
1954	01	334p	FOURNAISE, PITON DE LA (Indian O.)	0303-02=		
1954	0107?	87m	AKAN (Hokkaido-Japan)	0805-07=	1?	
1954	0118	....	MERAPI (Java)	0603-25=	3	
1954	02	14m	NEGRO, CERRO (Nicaragua)	1404-07=	2?	
1954	0201	40a	STROMBOLI (Italy)	0101-04=	2	4/-
? 1954	0204d	?	SHIN-IWO-JIMA (Volcano Is-Japan)	0804-13=	0	
1954	0218T	....	ST. ANDREW STRAIT [TULUMAN]	0500-01=	2	8/-
1954	0221	96	NYAMURAGIRA (Africa-C)	0203-02=	1	7/6
1954	0221	112a	TOLBACHIK (Kamchatka)	1000-24=	2	
1954	0408	....	AKAN (Hokkaido-Japan)	0805-07=	1	
1954	0413?	61a?	HEARD (Indian O.-S)	0304-01=	2	
1954	0426	?	SANGEANG API (Lesser Sunda Is)	0604-05=	2	
1954	05	30p	MANAM (New Guinea-NE of)	0501-02=	2	
1954	0502	<1	SHIKOTSU [TARUMAI] (Hokkaido)	0805-04=	1	
1954	0513	404a	TONGARIRO [NGAURUHOE] (New Z)	0401-08=	3	6/-
1954	0518	179a	LANGILA (New Britain-SW Pac)	0502-01=	3	
1954	0526	<1	ASO (Kyushu-Japan)	0802-11=	1	
1954	0528	110m	KLIUCHEVSKOI (Kamchatka)	1000-26=	2	
1954	0531	3a	KILAUEA (Hawaiian Is)	1302-01-	0	6/-
1954	06	31p	LASCAR (Chile-N)	1505-10=	2?	
1954	0628	28a	CAMEROON, MT. (Africa-W)	0204-01=	2	
1954	07	?	GRIMSVOTN (Iceland-NE)	1703-01=	1	
1954	0726e	51n	LENGAI, OL DOINYO (Africa-E)	0202-12=	2	
1954	08	>3yr	MARAPI (Sumatra)	0601-14=	2?	
1954	08	61p	SARYCHEV PEAK (Kurile Is)	0900-24=	2	
1954	0803	883a	BAM (New Guinea-NE of)	0501-01=	2	
1954	09	15m	TOKACHI (Hokkaido-Japan)	0805-05=	1	
1954	10 ?	?	MATTHEW ISLAND (SW Pacific)	0508-01=	2	
1954	1021	<1	SAN MIGUEL (El Salvador)	1403-10=	2	
1954	1029	2a	PILAS, LAS (Nicaragua)	1404-08=	2	
? 1954	11	31p	SAKURA-JIMA (Kyushu-Japan)	0802-08=	1?	
1954	1104	?	SANGEANG API (Lesser Sunda Is)	0604-05=	2	
1954	1104	1a	BAYONNAISE ROCKS (Izu Is-Japan)	0804-07=	0	
@ 1954	1109	?	NEGRA, SIERRA (Galapagos)	1503-05=	2	
1954	1119	86	SHIKOTSU [TARUMAI] (Hokkaido)	0805-04=	1	
1954	1206	161m?	STROMBOLI (Italy)	0101-04=	2	4/-
1954	1206	<1	DIENG VOLC COMPLEX (Java)	0603-20=	0	
1955	Cont	....	NYIRAGONGO (Africa-C)	0203-03=	0	
1955	Cont	....	TONGARIRO [NGAURUHOE] (New Z)	0401-08=	2	6/-
1955	Cont	....	LAMINGTON (New Guinea)	0503-01=	3	8/-
1955	Cont	....	YASUR (Vanuatu-SW Pacific)	0507-10=	2	
1955	Cont	....	MARAPI (Sumatra)	0601-14=	2?	
1955	Cont	....	MERAPI (Java)	0603-25=	1	
1955	Cont	....	SEMERU (Java)	0603-30=	1	
1955	Cont	....	DUKONO (Halmahera-Indonesia)	0608-01=	2	
1955	Cont	....	SUWANOSE-JIMA (Ryukyu Is)	0802-03=	2	
1955	Cont	....	SHIKOTSU [TARUMAI] (Hokkaido)	0805-04=	1	
1955	Cont	....	SANTA MARIA (Guatemala)	1402-03=	1	8/8
1955	Cont	....	CONCEPCION (Nicaragua)	1404-12=	2	
1955	Cont	....	POAS (Costa Rica)	1405-04=	2	
1955	Cont	....	SANGAY (Ecuador)	1502-09=	2	
1955	....	?	AMBRYM (Vanuatu-SW Pacific)	0507-04=	2	
1955	....	?	SANGEANG API (Lesser Sunda Is)	0604-05=	1	
1955?	....	?	CHIRINKOTAN (Kurile Is)	0900-26=	2?	
1955	....	?	KARYMSKY (Kamchatka)	1000-13=	2	
1955	....	?	SHISHALDIN (Aleutian Is)	1101-36-		
1955	....	?	REVENTADOR (Ecuador)	1502-01=	2	
1955	....	?	EREBUS (Antarctica)	1900-02=	2	
1955	01	?	WHITE ISLAND (New Zealand)	0401-04=	2	
1955	0107	33a	TOLBACHIK (Kamchatka)	1000-24=	2	
1955	0118	<1	RAUNG (Java)	0603-34=	2?	
1955	0119	1a	LENGAI, OL DOINYO (Africa-E)	0202-12=	2	
1955	0210	....	ST. ANDREW STRAIT [TULUMAN]	0500-01=	2	8/-
1955	0211	?	KRAKATAU (Indonesia)	0602-00=	2	
? 1955	0213	?	UNNAMED (Sangihe Is-Indonesia)	0607-05=	0	
1955	0215	2a	LANGILA (New Britain-SW Pac)	0502-01=	2	
1955	0228	....	STROMBOLI (Italy)	0101-04=	0	4/-
1955	0228	87	KILAUEA (Hawaiian Is)	1302-01-	0	7/-
1955	0228	....	IZALCO (El Salvador)	1403-03=	3	
? 1955	04	15m	SHIN-IWO-JIMA (Volcano Is-Japan)	0804-13=	0	
1955	0405	366	ETNA (Italy)	0101-06=	1	6/-
1955	0601	15a	LANGILA (New Britain-SW Pac)	0502-01=	2	
1955	0603	....	BAM (New Guinea-NE of)	0501-01=	2	
1955	0605	8a	LONG ISLAND (New Guinea-NE of)	0501-05=	3	
1955	0611	....	ASAMA (Honshu-Japan)	0803-11=	3	
1955	0625	?	BAYONNAISE ROCKS (Izu Is-Japan)	0804-07=	0	
? 1955	0625	?	KATLA (Iceland-S)	1702-03=	1	
1955	0706	618a	FOURNAISE, PITON DE LA (Indian O.)	0303-02=	2	7/-
? 1955	0721	12a	GEDE (Java)	0603-06=	1	
1955	0725	3a	ASO (Kyushu-Japan)	0802-11=	1	
1955	0726e	?	FUEGO (Guatemala)	1402-09=	1	
1955	0727	108a	CARRAN-LOS VENADOS (Chile-C)	1507-14=	4	-/8
? 1955	08	61t	TINAKULA (Santa Cruz Is-SW Pac)	0506-01=	2?	
1955	0820	2a?	UNNAMED (Hawaiian Is)	1302-09-	0	
? 1955	10	?	UNNAMED (Taiwan-E of)	0801-011	0	
1955	1006	63a	TOLBACHIK (Kamchatka)	1000-24=	2	
1955	1013	>3yr	SAKURA-JIMA (Kyushu-Japan)	0802-08=	2	
1955	1022	496a	BEZYMIANNY (Kamchatka)	1000-25=	3	-/9
1955	1022	755m	LLAIMA (Chile-C)	1507-11=	2	
1955	1112	38a?	SLAMET (Java)	0603-18=	2	
1955	1119	<1	AKAN (Hokkaido-Japan)	0805-07=	1	-/4
1955	1229	1a	TENGGER CALDERA [BROMO]	0603-31=	2	
1956	Cont	....	NYIRAGONGO (Africa-C)	0203-03=	0	
1956	Cont	....	BAM (New Guinea-NE of)	0501-01=	2	
1956	Cont	....	LAMINGTON (New Guinea)	0503-01=	3	8/-
1956	Cont	....	YASUR (Vanuatu-SW Pacific)	0507-10=	2	
1956	Cont	....	MARAPI (Sumatra)	0601-14=	2?	
1956	Cont	....	SEMERU (Java)	0603-30=	1	
1956	Cont	....	DUKONO (Halmahera-Indonesia)	0608-01=	2	
1956	Cont	....	SUWANOSE-JIMA (Ryukyu Is)	0802-03=	2	
1956	Cont	....	SAKURA-JIMA (Kyushu-Japan)	0802-08=	2	
1956	Cont	....	IZALCO (El Salvador)	1403-03=	2	
1956	Cont	....	POAS (Costa Rica)	1405-04=	2	
1956	Cont	....	SANGAY (Ecuador)	1502-09=	2	
1956	Cont	....	LLAIMA (Chile-C)	1507-11=	2	
1956	....	?	BAGANA (Bougainville-SW Pac)	0505-02=	2	
1956b	....	?	MATTHEW ISLAND (SW Pacific)	0508-01=	0?	

Figure 25. Pyroclastic flows sweep down the flanks of Mayon volcano, Philippines, as the eruptive cloud climbs vertically. These hot, ground-hugging flows move at speeds to 100 km/hr, and are among the most dangerous of volcanic hazards. USAF photo in April 1968, from Camalig church, courtesy of William Melson.

	START YEAR	M-Dy	Dura-tion	VOLCANO NAME (Subregion)	NUMBER	VEI	Vol L/T
	1956<	....	?	PURACE (Colombia)	1501-06=	2	
	1956	01	199m	KLIUCHEVSKOI (Kamchatka)	1000-26=	2	6/-
	1956	0101	76a	STROMBOLI (Italy)	0101-04=	0	4/-
	1956	0103	....	MERAPI (Java)	0603-25=	3	
	1956	0103?	10a?	ASO (Kyushu-Japan)	0802-11=	2	
	1956	0103	2	OSHIMA (Izu Is-Japan)	0804-01=	1	
	1956	0111	32a	TONGARIRO [NGAURUHOE] (New Z)	0401-08=	2	
	1956	0111	8a?	BRISTOL ISLAND (Antarctica)	1900-08=	3	
	1956	0213	40a	RAUNG (Java)	0603-34=	2	
	1956	0219	....	RAUNG (Java)	0603-34=	3	
	1956	0228	....	ETNA (Italy)	0101-06=	2	6/-
	1956	03	335p	KARYMSKY (Kamchatka)	1000-13=	1	
	1956	03	69m	VENIAMINOF (Alaska Peninsula)	1102-07-	2	
	1956	0318	226a	AKAN (Hokkaido-Japan)	0805-07=	1	-/5
	1956	0322	6	KABA (Sumatra)	0601-22=	2	
	1956	0325	6a	LANGILA (New Britain-SW Pac)	0502-01=	2	
	1956	0329	....	ST. ANDREW STRAIT [TULUMAN]	0500-01=	2	8/-
	1956	0330	....	BEZYMIANNY (Kamchatka)	1000-25=	5	-/9
?	1956	04	30p	SHIN-IWO-JIMA (Volcano Is-Japan)	0804-13=	0	
	1956	0414	....	SANTA MARIA (Guatemala)	1402-03=	3	8/8
	1956	0428	<1	GEDE (Java)	0603-06=	2?	
	1956	05	158m	UBINAS (Peru)	1504-02=	2	
	1956	0519	....	VENIAMINOF (Alaska Peninsula)	1102-07-	3	
?	1956	0522	1a	UNNAMED (Hawaiian Is)	1302-08-	0	
	1956	06	31p?	TENGGER CALDERA [BROMO]	0603-31=	2	
	1956	06 ?	15m	TOKACHI (Hokkaido-Japan)	0805-05=	1	
	1956	0601?	?	KARTHALA (Indian O.-W)	0303-01=	2?	
	1956	0602	<1	DIENG VOLC COMPLEX (Java)	0603-20=	1	
	1956	0727	....	KLIUCHEVSKOI (Kamchatka)	1000-26=	2	6/-
	1956	08	?	ASO (Kyushu-Japan)	0802-11=	2	
?	1956	0825	1a	OSHIMA (Izu Is-Japan)	0804-01=	1?	
@	1956	0908	1a	TRIDENT (Alaska Peninsula)	1102-16-	2	
	1956	0928	428a	TOLBACHIK (Kamchatka)	1000-24=	2	
	1956	1020	4a	SOUFRIERE GUADELOUPE (W Indies)	1600-06=	1	-/4
	1956	1117	1a	NYAMURAGIRA (Africa-C)	0203-02=	1	5/4
	1956	1118	<1	RUAPEHU (New Zealand)	0401-10=	1	
	1956	12	?	SANGEANG API (Lesser Sunda Is)	0604-05=	1	
	1956	12	180p	KORYAKSKY (Kamchatka)	1000-09=	2	
	1956	1208	615m	MANAM (New Guinea-NE of)	0501-02=	2	7/7
	1956	1221	<1	ASO (Kyushu-Japan)	0802-11=	1	
	1956	1227	170m	ZHUPANOVSKY (Kamchatka)	1000-12=	2	
	1956	1230	....	FOURNAISE, PITON DE LA (Indian O.)	0303-02=	2	7/-
	1957	Cont	....	STROMBOLI (Italy)	0101-04=	1?	
	1957	Cont	....	NYIRAGONGO (Africa-C)	0203-03=	0	
	1957	Cont	....	YASUR (Vanuatu-SW Pacific)	0507-10=	2	
	1957	Cont	....	MARAPI (Sumatra)	0601-14=	2?	
	1957	Cont	....	MERAPI (Java)	0603-25=	1	
	1957	Cont	....	SEMERU (Java)	0603-30=	1	
	1957	Cont	....	DUKONO (Halmahera-Indonesia)	0608-01=	2	
	1957	Cont	....	SUWANOSE-JIMA (Ryukyu Is)	0802-03=	2	
	1957	Cont	....	SAKURA-JIMA (Kyushu-Japan)	0802-08=	2	
	1957	Cont	....	ZHUPANOVSKY (Kamchatka)	1000-12=	2	
	1957	Cont	....	KARYMSKY (Kamchatka)	1000-13=	1	
	1957	Cont	....	TOLBACHIK (Kamchatka)	1000-24=	2	
	1957	Cont	....	POAS (Costa Rica)	1405-04=	2	
	1957	Cont	....	SANGAY (Ecuador)	1502-09=	2	
	1957	....	?	SANGEANG API (Lesser Sunda Is)	0604-05=	1	
	1957	....	?	AKITA-YAKE-YAMA (Honshu-Japan)	0803-26=	1	
	1957	....	?	KLIUCHEVSKOI (Kamchatka)	1000-26=	1	
	1957	....	>3yr	TRIDENT (Alaska Peninsula)	1102-16-	2	
	1957	....	....	SANTA MARIA (Guatemala)	1402-03=	2	8/8
	1957	....	?	PURACE (Colombia)	1501-06=	2?	
@	1957	....	?	NEGRA, SIERRA (Galapagos)	1503-05=		
?	1957	....	365y	EREBUS (Antarctica)	1900-02=		
	1957	01	....	ST. ANDREW STRAIT [TULUMAN]	0500-01=	2	8/-
	1957	01	16m	TANGKUBANPARAHU (Java)	0603-09=	1	
	1957	0117	....	KORYAKSKY (Kamchatka)	1000-09=	3	
	1957	0118	....	IZALCO (El Salvador)	1403-03=	3	
	1957	0205	91a	ETNA (Italy)	0101-06=	2	6/7
	1957	0208	?	KAVACHI (Solomon Is-SW Pac)	0505-06=	0	
	1957	0208	<1	SLAMET (Java)	0603-18=	2	
	1957	0219	2a>	FUEGO (Guatemala)	1402-09=	3	-/7
	1957	0219	....	LLAIMA (Chile-C)	1507-11=	3	
	1957	0226	203a	AKAN (Hokkaido-Japan)	0805-07=	1	
?	1957	0311	1a	VSEVIDOF (Aleutian Is)	1101-27-	2	
	1957	0313	<1	GEDE (Java)	0603-06=	2	
	1957	0327	12a	CONCEPCION (Nicaragua)	1404-12=	2	
	1957	0328	<1	IWO-JIMA (Volcano Is-Japan)	0804-12=	1	
	1957	0412	<1	ASO (Kyushu-Japan)	0802-11=	1	
	1957	05	?	CHIKURACHKI (Kurile Is)	0900-36=	2	
	1957	0502	?	BAYONNAISE ROCKS (Izu Is-Japan)	0804-07=	0	
	1957	0514	779w	COLIMA VOLC COMPLEX (Mexico)	1401-04=	1	
	1957	06	?	FONUALEI (Tonga-SW Pacific)	0403-10=		
	1957	0731	<1	BEZYMIANNY (Kamchatka)	1000-25=	2	
	1957	08	122p	OSHIMA (Izu Is-Japan)	0804-01=	2	
	1957	0801	1	VISOKE (Africa-C)	0203-05-	1	5/5
?	1957	0808	1a	GILIBANTA (Lesser Sunda Is)	0604-051		
	1957	0820	<1	TOKACHI (Hokkaido-Japan)	0805-05=	1	
	1957	0825	251a	ETNA (Italy)	0101-06=	2	
	1957	0826e	50n	AMBRYM (Vanuatu-SW Pacific)	0507-04=	1?	
	1957	0902	75a	FOURNAISE, PITON DE LA (Indian O.)	0303-02=	2	6/-
	1957	0904	20a	NEGRO, CERRO (Nicaragua)	1404-07=	2	
	1957	0927	392a	FAYAL (Azores)	1802-01=	2	7/7
	1957	10	425p	ASO (Kyushu-Japan)	0802-11=	1	-/5
	1957	10	?	RASSHUA (Kurile Is)	0900-22=	1	
	1957	1026	<1	BAM (New Guinea-NE of)	0501-01=	1	
	1957	1112	19a	ZAVARITZKI CALDERA (Kurile Is)	0900-18=	2	
	1957	1121	3a	UNNAMED (Arctic Ocean)	1707-01-	0	
	1957	1128	....	ZAVARITZKI CALDERA (Kurile Is)	0900-18=	3	
	1957	1210	....	MANAM (New Guinea-NE of)	0501-02=	3	7/7
	1957	1211	?	WHITE ISLAND (New Zealand)	0401-04=	2	
	1957	1228	?	NYAMURAGIRA (Africa-C)	0203-02=	0	6/-
	1958	Cont	....	STROMBOLI (Italy)	0101-04=	1?	
	1958	Cont	....	NYIRAGONGO (Africa-C)	0203-03=	0	
	1958	Cont	....	YASUR (Vanuatu-SW Pacific)	0507-10=	2	
	1958	Cont	....	MERAPI (Java)	0603-25=	1	
	1958	Cont	....	SEMERU (Java)	0603-30=	1	
	1958	Cont	....	DUKONO (Halmahera-Indonesia)	0608-01=	2	
	1958	Cont	....	SUWANOSE-JIMA (Ryukyu Is)	0802-03=	2	
	1958	Cont	....	SAKURA-JIMA (Kyushu-Japan)	0802-08=	2	
	1958	Cont	....	TRIDENT (Alaska Peninsula)	1102-16-	2	
	1958	Cont	....	COLIMA VOLC COMPLEX (Mexico)	1401-04=	1	
	1958	Cont	....	SANGAY (Ecuador)	1502-09=	2	
	1958	Cont	....	FAYAL (Azores)	1802-01=	2	7/7
?	1958	Cont	....	EREBUS (Antarctica)	1900-02=		
	1958	....	?	SANGEANG API (Lesser Sunda Is)	0604-05=	1?	
	1958	....	?	KUSATSU-SHIRANE (Honshu-Japan)	0803-12=	1	
	1958	....	?	BAYONNAISE ROCKS (Izu Is-Japan)	0804-07=	0	
	1958	....	?	MEDVEZHIA (Kurile Is)	0900-10=	1	
	1958	....	....	SANTA MARIA (Guatemala)	1402-03=	2	8/8
	1958	....	>3yr	POAS (Costa Rica)	1405-04=	1	
	1958	01	29m	BEZYMIANNY (Kamchatka)	1000-25=	1	
	1958	01	?	TUPUNGATITO (Chile-C)	1507-01=	2	
	1958	0110	....	MANAM (New Guinea-NE of)	0501-02=	3	7/7
	1958	0201r	?	ULAWUN (New Britain-SW Pac)	0502-12=	2	
	1958	0206<	?	LENGAI, OL DOINYO (Africa-E)	0202-12=	1	
	1958	0219	672a	LOKON-EMPUNG (Sulawesi-Indonesia)	0606-10=	2	
	1958	0223	<1	AKAN (Hokkaido-Japan)	0805-07=	1	
	1958	0311j	39j?	BAM (New Guinea-NE of)	0501-01=	2	
	1958	0417	20a	SLAMET (Java)	0603-18=	2	
	1958	0417	57a	OSHIMA (Izu Is-Japan)	0804-01=	2	
	1958	0421	44d	LANGILA (New Britain-SW Pac)	0502-01=	2	
	1958	0517	103a	PAVLOF (Alaska Peninsula)	1102-03-	2	
	1958	0518	92a>	KLIUCHEVSKOI (Kamchatka)	1000-26=	1	
	1958	0521	?	BEZYMIANNY (Kamchatka)	1000-25=	1	
	1958	0526	1a	CHIKURACHKI (Kurile Is)	0900-36=	2	
	1958	0530	113a	FOURNAISE, PITON DE LA (Indian O.)	0303-02=	2	
	1958	0623	....	MARAPI (Sumatra)	0601-14=	1	
	1958	0624	....	ASO (Kyushu-Japan)	0802-11=	2	-/5
?	1958	07	91p	SHIN-IWO-JIMA (Volcano Is-Japan)	0804-13=	0	
S	1958	0709	>3yr	RUMBLE III (New Zealand)	0401-13-	0	
	1958	0712	17a	MAHAWU (Sulawesi-Indonesia)	0606-11=	2?	
	1958	0713<	?	TOLBACHIK (Kamchatka)	1000-24=	2?	
?	1958	08	31p	FUKUJIN (Volcano Is-Japan)	0804-133	0	
	1958	0807	107a	NYAMURAGIRA (Africa-C)	0203-02=	2	7/6
	1958	0814	12j	OKMOK (Aleutian Is)	1101-29-	3	8/-
	1958	09 ?	61p?	EAST EPI (Vanuatu-SW Pacific)	0507-06=	2?	
	1958	09 ?	106m>	FERNANDINA (Galapagos)	1503-01=	2	7/-
	1958	0905	5a	BAM (New Guinea-NE of)	0501-01=	2	
	1958	0913	53d	SLAMET (Java)	0603-18=	2	
	1958	1002	266d	KRAKATAU (Indonesia)	0602-00=	2	
	1958	1003	327e	ASAMA (Honshu-Japan)	0803-11=	1	-/5
	1958	1004	<1	TOKACHI (Hokkaido-Japan)	0805-05=	1	
	1958	1007?	72a?	KUWAE [KARUA] (Vanuatu-SW Pac)	0507-07=	0	
	1958	1017	8a	MARAPI (Sumatra)	0601-14=	1	
	1958	11	31p	ETNA (Italy)	0101-06=	1	
	1958	11	?	REVENTADOR (Ecuador)	1502-01=	3	
	1958	1105	13a?	TONGARIRO [NGAURUHOE] (New Z)	0401-08=	2	
	1958	1106	410a	VILLARRICA (Chile-C)	1507-12=	1	
	1958	1110	....	ASAMA (Honshu-Japan)	0803-11=	2	-/5
	1958	1118	?	AMBRYM (Vanuatu-SW Pacific)	0507-04=	2?	
	1958	1121	11a?	KAVACHI (Solomon Is-SW Pac)	0505-06=	0	
	1958	12	?	WHITE ISLAND (New Zealand)	0401-04=	1	
	1958	1218]	....	KUWAE [KARUA] (Vanuatu-SW Pac)	0507-07=	2?	
	1958	1228	92a	BEZYMIANNY (Kamchatka)	1000-25=	1	
	1958	1231u	?	TOFUA (Tonga-SW Pacific)	0403-06=	2	
	1959	Cont	....	NYIRAGONGO (Africa-C)	0203-03=	0	
S	1959	Cont	....	RUMBLE III (New Zealand)	0401-13-	0	
	1959	Cont	....	YASUR (Vanuatu-SW Pacific)	0507-10=	2	
	1959	Cont	....	SEMERU (Java)	0603-30=	1	
	1959	Cont	....	LOKON-EMPUNG (Sulawesi-Indonesia)	0606-10=	2	
	1959	Cont	....	DUKONO (Halmahera-Indonesia)	0608-01=	2	
	1959	Cont	....	SUWANOSE-JIMA (Ryukyu Is)	0802-03=	2	
	1959	Cont	....	SAKURA-JIMA (Kyushu-Japan)	0802-08=	2	
	1959	Cont	....	TRIDENT (Alaska Peninsula)	1102-16-	2	
	1959	Cont	....	COLIMA VOLC COMPLEX (Mexico)	1401-04=	1	
	1959	Cont	....	POAS (Costa Rica)	1405-04=	1	
	1959	Cont	....	VILLARRICA (Chile-C)	1507-12=	1	
?	1959	....	?	NIUAFO'OU (Tonga-SW Pacific)	0403-11=		
	1959?	....	318w?	BAGANA (Bougainville-SW Pac)	0505-02=	2	
?	1959	....	?	TRAITOR'S HEAD (Vanuatu-SW Pacific)	0507-09=		
	1959	....	?	BAYONNAISE ROCKS (Izu Is-Japan)	0804-07=	0	
	1959	....	?	ZHUPANOVSKY (Kamchatka)	1000-12=	2	
	1959	....	365y	TOLBACHIK (Kamchatka)	1000-24=	2	
	1959	....	....	SANTA MARIA (Guatemala)	1402-03=	2	8/8
	1959	....	?	SAN JOSE (Chile-C)	1507-02=	2	
	1959	....	?	KVERKFJOLL (Iceland-NE)	1703-05=		
	1959	01	16m	OSHIMA (Izu Is-Japan)	0804-01=	1	
	1959	0103	?	KLIUCHEVSKOI (Kamchatka)	1000-26=	1	
	1959	0123	55a	CAMEROON, MT. (Africa-W)	0204-01=	2	
	1959	0213	4a	KIRISHIMA (Kyushu-Japan)	0802-09=	2	-/6
	1959	0228	....	BEZYMIANNY (Kamchatka)	1000-25=	2	
	1959	0311	148a	FOURNAISE, PITON DE LA (Indian O.)	0303-02=	2	6/-
	1959	0323	33e	ETNA (Italy)	0101-06=	1	

	START YEAR	M-Dy	Dura-tion	VOLCANO NAME (Subregion)	NUMBER	VEI	Vol L/T
	1959	0326e	?	TUPUNGATITO (Chile-C)	1507-01=	2	
	1959	04	?	AMBRYM (Vanuatu-SW Pacific)	0507-04=	2	
	1959	0402	212a	BAM (New Guinea-NE of)	0501-01=	2	
	1959	0414	....	ASAMA (Honshu-Japan)	0803-11=	2	-/5
	1959	0515e	153m	AKAN (Hokkaido-Japan)	0805-07=	1	
	1959	0519	?	STROMBOLI (Italy)	0101-04=	2	
	1959	0521	72a	RUAPEHU (New Zealand)	0401-10=	1	
	1959	06	30p	MANAM (New Guinea-NE of)	0501-02=	2	
	1959	0601	?	TONGARIRO [NGAURUHOE] (New Z)	0401-08=	2	
	1959	0608	37m	OKINAWA-TORI-SHIMA (Ryukyu Is)	0802-02=	2	
	1959	0629	32a?	AZUL, CERRO (Galapagos)	1503-06=	2?	
?	1959	07	?	KARS PLATEAU (Turkey)	0103-05-	2	
	1959	07	79m	ASO (Kyushu-Japan)	0802-11=	1	
?	1959	07	91p	SHIN-IWO-JIMA (Volcano Is-Japan)	0804-13=	0	
	1959	0715e	?	GUALLATIRI (Chile-N)	1505-02=	2	
?	1959	08	61p	FUKUJIN (Volcano Is-Japan)	0804-133	0	
	1959	0815e	102e	TOKACHI (Hokkaido-Japan)	0805-05=	1	
	1959	0918?	3a	KUWAE [KARUA] (Vanuatu-SW Pac)	0507-07=	2	
	1959	10	396p	OSHIMA (Izu Is-Japan)	0804-01=	1	
	1959	1015	20a?	BEZYMIANNY (Kamchatka)	1000-25=	1	-/4
	1959	1016	?	TUPUNGATITO (Chile-C)	1507-01=	2	
	1959	1017	>3yr	ETNA (Italy)	0101-06=	1	
	1959	11	>3yr	LASCAR (Chile-N)	1505-10=	2	
	1959	1106	?	PLANCHON-PETEROA (Chile-C)	1507-04=	1	
	1959	1114	36a	KILAUEA (Hawaiian Is)	1302-01-	2	7/6
	1959	12	365p>	MANAM (New Guinea-NE of)	0501-02=	2	6/-
	1959	12	>3yr	KRAKATAU (Indonesia)	0602-00=	2	6/-
	1959	12	....	SANGAY (Ecuador)	1502-09=	3	
	1959	1214	6a	WHITE ISLAND (New Zealand)	0401-04=	2	
	1960	Cont	....	STROMBOLI (Italy)	0101-04=	1?	
	1960	Cont	....	NYIRAGONGO (Africa-C)	0203-03=	0	
S	1960	Cont	....	RUMBLE III (New Zealand)	0401-13-	0	
	1960	Cont	....	MANAM (New Guinea-NE of)	0501-02=	2	6/-
	1960	Cont	....	BAGANA (Bougainville-SW Pac)	0505-02=	2	
	1960	Cont	....	YASUR (Vanuatu-SW Pacific)	0507-10=	2	
	1960	Cont	....	KRAKATAU (Indonesia)	0602-00=	2	6/-
	1960	Cont	....	SEMERU (Java)	0603-30=	1	
	1960	Cont	....	DUKONO (Halmahera-Indonesia)	0608-01=	2	
	1960	Cont	....	SUWANOSE-JIMA (Ryukyu Is)	0802-03=	2	
	1960	Cont	....	SAKURA-JIMA (Kyushu-Japan)	0802-08=	2	
	1960	Cont	....	OSHIMA (Izu Is-Japan)	0804-01=	1	
	1960	Cont	....	TOLBACHIK (Kamchatka)	1000-24=	2	
	1960	Cont	....	TRIDENT (Alaska Peninsula)	1102-16-	2	
	1960	Cont	....	POAS (Costa Rica)	1405-04=	1	
	1960	Cont	....	SANGAY (Ecuador)	1502-09=	2	
	1960?	....	>3yr	PAVLOF (Alaska Peninsula)	1102-03-	2	
	1960	....	730y	COLIMA VOLC COMPLEX (Mexico)	1401-04=	1	7/-
	1960	....	....	SANTA MARIA (Guatemala)	1402-03=	2	8/8
?	1960	....	?	ISLUGA (Chile-N)	1505-03=	2?	
	1960	....	?	SAN JOSE (Chile-C)	1507-02=	2	
?	1960	....	?	LLAIMA (Chile-C)	1507-11=		
?	1960	....	731y	VILLARRICA (Chile-C)	1507-12=	2?	
	1960	01	?	ERTA ALE (Ethiopia)	0201-08=	0	
	1960	01	84m	ASO (Kyushu-Japan)	0802-11=	2	
	1960	0111	59a	FOURNAISE, PITON DE LA (Indian O.)	0303-02=	2	6/-
	1960	0113	37a	KILAUEA (Hawaiian Is)	1302-01-	2	8/-
	1960	0120	?	LAUTARO (Chile-S)	1508-06=	1	
	1960	03 <	>3yr	LENGAI, OL DOINYO (Africa-E)	0202-12=	1	
	1960	0313	?	SIRUNG (Lesser Sunda Is)	0604-27=	2?	
	1960	0328	....	LASCAR (Chile-N)	1505-10=	2?	
	1960	04	>3yr	KARYMSKY (Kamchatka)	1000-13=	2	6/7
	1960	0413	1	BEZYMIANNY (Kamchatka)	1000-25=	2	-/6
	1960	0428	69a	BAM (New Guinea-NE of)	0501-01=	2	
	1960	0524	32e	CORDON CAULLE (Chile-C)	1507-141	3	8/7
	1960	06	?	REVENTADOR (Ecuador)	1502-01=	3	
	1960	07 ?	?	EAST EPI (Vanuatu-SW Pacific)	0507-06=	0	
	1960	07	?	KERINCI (Sumatra)	0601-17=	2	
?	1960	07	61p	SHIN-IWO-JIMA (Volcano Is-Japan)	0804-13=	0	
	1960	0710	67m	LOPEVI (Vanuatu-SW Pacific)	0507-05=	3	
	1960	0710	?	PLANCHON-PETEROA (Chile-C)	1507-04=	1	
	1960	0715e	?	TUPUNGATITO (Chile-C)	1507-01=	2	
	1960	0717	....	ETNA (Italy)	0101-06=	3	
	1960	0721	?	BAYONNAISE ROCKS (Izu Is-Japan)	0804-07=	2	
	1960	0729c	838m	ULAWUN (New Britain-SW Pac)	0502-12=	2	
	1960	0830	<1	SARYCHEV PEAK (Kurile Is)	0900-24=	3	
	1960	09	791p	ASO (Kyushu-Japan)	0802-11=	1	
	1960	09	15m	AKAN (Hokkaido-Japan)	0805-07=	1	
	1960	0917	?	AMBRYM (Vanuatu-SW Pacific)	0507-04=	1?	
	1960	0927	?	KETOI (Kurile Is)	0900-20=	2	
	1960	0928	89e?	NEGRO, CERRO (Nicaragua)	1404-07=	2	
	1960	1010?	?	NASU (Honshu-Japan)	0803-15=	1	
	1960	1015q	183w	OKMOK (Aleutian Is)	1101-29-	3	-/7
	1960	1020	?	CHIRPOI (Kurile Is)	0900-15=	2?	
	1960	12	31p	SLAMET (Java)	0603-18=	2	
	1960	12	31p	MUTNOVSKY (Kamchatka)	1000-06=	2	-/6
	1960	12	826m>	KLIUCHEVSKOI (Kamchatka)	1000-26=	2	-/6
	1960	1202	?	GUALLATIRI (Chile-N)	1505-02=	2	
?	1960	1202	?	SAN PEDRO (Chile-N)	1505-07=	2	
	1960	1219	279e	LANGILA (New Britain-SW Pac)	0502-01=	2	4/-
	1961	Cont	....	STROMBOLI (Italy)	0101-04=	1?	
	1961	Cont	....	ETNA (Italy)	0101-06=	2	
	1961	Cont	....	LENGAI, OL DOINYO (Africa-E)	0202-12=	1	
	1961	Cont	....	NYIRAGONGO (Africa-C)	0203-03=	0	
S	1961	Cont	....	RUMBLE III (New Zealand)	0401-13-	0	
	1961	Cont	....	LANGILA (New Britain-SW Pac)	0502-01=	2	4/-
	1961	Cont	....	ULAWUN (New Britain-SW Pac)	0502-12=	2	
	1961	Cont	....	YASUR (Vanuatu-SW Pacific)	0507-10=	2	
	1961	Cont	....	KRAKATAU (Indonesia)	0602-00=	2	6/-
	1961	Cont	....	SLAMET (Java)	0603-18=	2	
	1961	Cont	....	SEMERU (Java)	0603-30=	1	
	1961	Cont	....	DUKONO (Halmahera-Indonesia)	0608-01=	2	
	1961	Cont	....	SUWANOSE-JIMA (Ryukyu Is)	0802-03=	2	
	1961	Cont	....	ASO (Kyushu-Japan)	0802-11=	1	
	1961	Cont	....	MUTNOVSKY (Kamchatka)	1000-06=	2	-/6
	1961	Cont	....	KARYMSKY (Kamchatka)	1000-13=	2	6/7
	1961	Cont	....	KLIUCHEVSKOI (Kamchatka)	1000-26=	2	-/6
	1961	Cont	....	OKMOK (Aleutian Is)	1101-29-	2	-/7
	1961	Cont	....	PAVLOF (Alaska Peninsula)	1102-03-	2	
	1961	Cont	....	COLIMA VOLC COMPLEX (Mexico)	1401-04=	1	7/-
	1961	Cont	....	SANTA MARIA (Guatemala)	1402-03=	1	8/8
	1961	Cont	....	SANGAY (Ecuador)	1502-09=	2	
	1961	Cont	....	LASCAR (Chile-N)	1505-10=	2	
?	1961	Cont	....	VILLARRICA (Chile-C)	1507-12=	2?	
?	1961	....	?	LONG ISLAND (New Guinea-NE of)	0501-05=		
?	1961	....	?	OSHIMA (Izu Is-Japan)	0804-01=		
	1961	....	?	COPAHUE (Chile-C)	1507-09=	2	
	1961	01	?	GORELY (Kamchatka)	1000-07=	2	
	1961	0201	42e	CALBUCO (Chile-S)	1508-02=	3	
	1961	0224	<1	KILAUEA (Hawaiian Is)	1302-01-	1	5/-
	1961	0228	18m	KARANGETANG [API SIAU] (Sangihe	0607-02=	2	-/6
	1961	0303	22a	KILAUEA (Hawaiian Is)	1302-01-	1	5/-
	1961	0311	35a?	PACAYA (Guatemala)	1402-11=	2	6/-
	1961	0321a	193m	FERNANDINA (Galapagos)	1503-01=	2	
	1961	0324	269a>	TOLBACHIK (Kamchatka)	1000-24=	2	
	1961	0325	1a	BEZYMIANNY (Kamchatka)	1000-25=	3	-/6
	1961	0328<	?	KAVACHI (Solomon Is-SW Pac)	0505-06=	2	
	1961	0405	20a	FOURNAISE, PITON DE LA (Indian O.)	0303-02=	0	7/-
	1961	0413	35a	MERAPI (Java)	0603-25=	2	
	1961	0502	99a	CHIKURACHKI (Kurile Is)	0900-36=	1	
	1961	0505d	101n>	TUPUNGATITO (Chile-C)	1507-01=	2	
	1961	0519	210m	LOKON-EMPUNG (Sulawesi-Indonesia)	0606-10=	2	
	1961	0521	16a	BEZYMIANNY (Kamchatka)	1000-25=	2	
	1961	0625	....	POAS (Costa Rica)	1405-04=	2	
	1961	0630?	?	TRIDENT (Alaska Peninsula)	1102-16-	2	
	1961	07	61p	MANAM (New Guinea-NE of)	0501-02=	2	
	1961	0710	7a	KILAUEA (Hawaiian Is)	1302-01-	1	7/-
	1961	0716	16a	TANGKUBANPARAHU (Java)	0603-09=	1	
	1961	0726	?	BAGANA (Bougainville-SW Pac)	0505-02=	2	
	1961	08	16m	TOKACHI (Hokkaido-Japan)	0805-05=	1	
	1961	0815	596a	AMBRYM (Vanuatu-SW Pacific)	0507-04=	1	
	1961	0818	89a	ASAMA (Honshu-Japan)	0803-11=	2	-/4
	1961	0922	1	KILAUEA (Hawaiian Is)	1302-01-	1	6/-
@	1961	10	?	LAUTARO (Chile-S)	1508-06=	2	
	1961	1009	10a>	KARANGETANG [API SIAU] (Sangihe	0607-02=	2	-/6
	1961	1010	156a	TRISTAN DA CUNHA (Atlantic-S)	1806-01=	2	
	1961	1018	58a	BEZYMIANNY (Kamchatka)	1000-25=	3	
	1961	1025	?	NEGRO, CERRO (Nicaragua)	1404-07=	2	
	1961	1026	40d	ASKJA (Iceland-NE)	1703-06=	2	8/6
	1961	1128	18m	CONCEPCION (Nicaragua)	1404-12=	2	
	1961	12	....	SAKURA-JIMA (Kyushu-Japan)	0802-08=	3	
	1962	Cont	....	STROMBOLI (Italy)	0101-04=	1?	
	1962	Cont	....	ETNA (Italy)	0101-06=	2	
	1962	Cont	....	LENGAI, OL DOINYO (Africa-E)	0202-12=	1	
	1962	Cont	....	NYIRAGONGO (Africa-C)	0203-03=	0	
S	1962	Cont	....	RUMBLE III (New Zealand)	0401-13-	0	
	1962	Cont	....	ULAWUN (New Britain-SW Pac)	0502-12=	2	
	1962	Cont	....	YASUR (Vanuatu-SW Pacific)	0507-10=	2	
	1962	Cont	....	KRAKATAU (Indonesia)	0602-00=	2	6/-
	1962	Cont	....	SEMERU (Java)	0603-30=	1	
	1962	Cont	....	DUKONO (Halmahera-Indonesia)	0608-01=	2	
	1962	Cont	....	SUWANOSE-JIMA (Ryukyu Is)	0802-03=	2	
	1962	Cont	....	SAKURA-JIMA (Kyushu-Japan)	0802-08=	2	
	1962	Cont	....	ASO (Kyushu-Japan)	0802-11=	1	
	1962	Cont	....	PAVLOF (Alaska Peninsula)	1102-03-	2	
	1962	Cont	....	COLIMA VOLC COMPLEX (Mexico)	1401-04=	1	7/-
	1962	Cont	....	SANTA MARIA (Guatemala)	1402-03=	1	8/8
	1962	Cont	....	SANGAY (Ecuador)	1502-09=	2	
	1962	Cont	....	LASCAR (Chile-N)	1505-10=	2	
	1962	Cont	....	TRISTAN DA CUNHA (Atlantic-S)	1806-01=	2	
?	1962?	....	?	KARKAR (New Guinea-NE of)	0501-03=	2?	
	1962	01	30p	KAVACHI (Solomon Is-SW Pac)	0505-06=	2	
	1962	01	>3yr	OSHIMA (Izu Is-Japan)	0804-01=	1	
	1962	01	16m	TELICA (Nicaragua)	1404-04=	1	
	1962	01	?	PLANCHON-PETEROA (Chile-C)	1507-04=	1	
	1962	0109	....	AMBRYM (Vanuatu-SW Pacific)	0507-04=	3	
	1962	0124	?	KISKA (Aleutian Is)	1101-02-	3	
	1962	0129	701m	KARANGETANG [API SIAU] (Sangihe	0607-02=	2	
	1962	0215	502w	BAGANA (Bougainville-SW Pac)	0505-02=	2	
	1962	03	513m	LANGILA (New Britain-SW Pac)	0502-01=	2	
	1962	0305?	?	PROTECTOR SHOAL (Antarctica)	1900-14-	0	-/8
	1962	0314	?	NIIGATA-YAKE-YAMA (Honshu-Japan)	0803-09=	1	
	1962	0321	24m?	NEGRO, CERRO (Nicaragua)	1404-07=	2	
	1962	04	?	MANAM (New Guinea-NE of)	0501-02=	2	
	1962	04	214p	LOKON-EMPUNG (Sulawesi-Indonesia)	0606-10=	1	
	1962	0428	<1	AKAN (Hokkaido-Japan)	0805-07=	1	
	1962	0524	?	TONGARIRO [NGAURUHOE] (New Z)	0401-08=	2	
	1962	06	15m	CONCEPCION (Nicaragua)	1404-12=	2	
	1962	0609	<1	TRIDENT (Alaska Peninsula)	1102-16-	3	
	1962	0617	377a	YAKE-DAKE (Honshu-Japan)	0803-07=	1	-/5
	1962	0629	78m	TOKACHI (Hokkaido-Japan)	0805-05=	3	-/7
?	1962	07 <	?	GAUA (Vanuatu-SW Pacific)	0507-02=		
	1962	07	?	LOPEVI (Vanuatu-SW Pacific)	0507-05=	0	
?	1962	07	152p	SHIN-IWO-JIMA (Volcano Is-Japan)	0804-13=	0	
	1962	08	320w	TOLBACHIK (Kamchatka)	1000-24=	1	
	1962	0804	97a	FUEGO (Guatemala)	1402-09=	2	6/7

	START YEAR	M-Dy	Dura-tion	VOLCANO NAME (Subregion)	NUMBER	VEI	Vol L/T
	1962	0824	2 ?	**MIYAKE-JIMA** (Izu Is-Japan)	0804-04=	2	6/6
	1962	1017	....	**KARYMSKY** (Kamchatka)	1000-13=	3	6/7
	1962	1021	16*a*	**BEZYMIANNY** (Kamchatka)	1000-25=	2	
	1962	1105d	?	**AKUTAN** (Aleutian Is)	1101-32-	2	
	1962	*1107*	....	*AMBRYM (Vanuatu-SW Pacific)*	0507-04=	3	
	1962	1109	....	**FUEGO** (Guatemala)	1402-09=	3	6/7
	1962	1113	....	**KLIUCHEVSKOI** (Kamchatka)	1000-26=	3	-/6
	1962	1207	2	**KILAUEA** (Hawaiian Is)	1302-01-	0	5/-
	1962	1215	?	**WHITE ISLAND** (New Zealand)	0401-04=	3	
	1962	1231	2*a*?	**GAMALAMA** (Halmahera-Indonesia)	0608-06=	2	
	1963	*Cont*	....	*STROMBOLI (Italy)*	0101-04=	*1?*	
	1963	*Cont*	....	*ETNA (Italy)*	0101-06=	*2*	
	1963	*Cont*	....	*LENGAI, OL DOINYO (Africa-E)*	0202-12=	*1*	
	1963	*Cont*	....	*NYIRAGONGO (Africa-C)*	0203-03=	*0*	
	1963	*Cont*	....	*LANGILA (New Britain-SW Pac)*	0502-01=	*2*	
	1963	*Cont*	....	*BAGANA (Bougainville-SW Pac)*	0505-02=	*2*	
	1963	*Cont*	....	*YASUR (Vanuatu-SW Pacific)*	0507-10=	*2*	
	1963	*Cont*	....	*KRAKATAU (Indonesia)*	0602-00=	*2*	*6/-*
	1963	*Cont*	....	*KARANGETANG [API SIAU] (Sangihe*	0607-02=	*2*	
	1963	*Cont*	....	*DUKONO (Halmahera-Indonesia)*	0608-01=	*2*	
	1963	*Cont*	....	*GAMALAMA (Halmahera-Indonesia)*	0608-06=	*2*	
	1963	*Cont*	....	*SUWANOSE-JIMA (Ryukyu Is)*	0802-03=	*2*	
	1963	*Cont*	....	*SAKURA-JIMA (Kyushu-Japan)*	0802-08=	*2*	
	1963	*Cont*	....	*YAKE-DAKE (Honshu-Japan)*	0803-07=	*1*	*-/5*
	1963	*Cont*	....	*OSHIMA (Izu Is-Japan)*	0804-01=	*1*	
	1963	*Cont*	....	*TOLBACHIK (Kamchatka)*	1000-24=	*1*	
	1963	*Cont*	....	*PAVLOF (Alaska Peninsula)*	1102-03-	*2*	
	1963	*Cont*	....	*SANTA MARIA (Guatemala)*	1402-03=	*1*	*8/8*
	1963	*Cont*	....	*SANGAY (Ecuador)*	1502-09=	*2*	
	1963	*Cont*	....	*LASCAR (Chile-N)*	1505-10=	*2*	
	1963	....	?	**TALANG** (Sumatra)	0601-16=	2	
	1963	....	365*y*	**COLIMA VOLC COMPLEX** (Mexico)	1401-04=	1	
S	**1963**	01	>3yr	**RUMBLE III** (New Zealand)	0401-13-	0	
	1963	02	91*p*>	**MANAM** (New Guinea-NE of)	0501-02=	2	
	1963	0213	?	**AMUKTA** (Aleutian Is)	1101-19-	3	
	1963	*0219*	*342a*	*AGUNG (Lesser Sunda Is)*	0604-02=	3	*8/8*
	1963	0225?	208*a*>	**VILLARRICA** (Chile-C)	1507-12=	2	
	1963	03	?	**EBEKO** (Kurile Is)	0900-38=	1	
	1963	03	?	**NEGRO, CERRO** (Nicaragua)	1404-07=	1	
	1963	0304	12*a*>	**WOLF, VOLCAN** (Galapagos)	1503-02=	0	
	1963	0313	702*a*	**IRAZU** (Costa Rica)	1405-06=	3	
	1963	0317	49*a*?	**ULAWUN** (New Britain-SW Pac)	0502-12=	2	
	1963	0317	....	**AGUNG** (Lesser Sunda Is)	0604-02=	4	8/8
	1963	*0322*	....	*KLIUCHEVSKOI (Kamchatka)*	1000-26=	2	*-/6*
	1963	0401	2*a*>	**TRIDENT** (Alaska Peninsula)	1102-16-	3	
	1963	0413	30*c*?	**NEGRA, SIERRA** (Galapagos)	1503-05=	2	
	1963	0421	86*m*	**ASO** (Kyushu-Japan)	0802-11=	1	
	1963	05	122*p*?	**BEZYMIANNY** (Kamchatka)	1000-25=	1	
	1963	0505	....	**SEMERU** (Java)	0603-30=	2	
	1963	0509	?	**CONCEPCION** (Nicaragua)	1404-12=	2	
	1963	*0511*	....	*KARYMSKY (Kamchatka)*	1000-13=	3	*6/7*
	1963	*0516*	....	*AGUNG (Lesser Sunda Is)*	0604-02=	3	*8/8*
	1963	0523	40*a*>	**POAS** (Costa Rica)	1405-04=	2	
	1963	07	?	**KERINCI** (Sumatra)	0601-17=	2	
	1963	*0703*	....	*IRAZU (Costa Rica)*	1405-06=	3	
	1963	*0707*	*724w*	*LOPEVI (Vanuatu-SW Pacific)*	0507-05=	2	
	1963	0710	82*a*	**NIIGATA-YAKE-YAMA** (Honshu-Japan)	0803-09=	1	
?	**1963**	0710	1*a*	**NASU** (Honshu-Japan)	0803-15=	1	
	1963	0821	1	**KILAUEA** (Hawaiian Is)	1302-01-	0	4/-
	1963	0830	24*a*>	**AMBRYM** (Vanuatu-SW Pacific)	0507-04=	2	
	1963	0905	247*a*	**BATUR** (Lesser Sunda Is)	0604-01=	2	7/5
S	**1963**	0911	294*w*	**UNNAMED** (SW Pacific)	0508-03-	0	
	1963	0915e	55*e*>	**GAUA** (Vanuatu-SW Pacific)	0507-02=	2	
	1963	0928	3*a*	**FUEGO** (Guatemala)	1402-09=	3	-/6
	1963	1005	1	**KILAUEA** (Hawaiian Is)	1302-01-	0	6/-
	1963	1011	313*a*	**AUGUSTINE** (Alaska-SW)	1103-01-	2	7/6
	1963	1017	31*a*?	**TRIDENT** (Alaska Peninsula)	1102-16-	3	
?	**1963**	1027	?	**SHIN-IWO-JIMA** (Volcano Is-Japan)	0804-13=	0	
	1963	11 <	?	**EREBUS** (Antarctica)	1900-02=	0	
	1963	1107	14*a*	**FOURNAISE, PITON DE LA** (Indian O.)	0303-02=	2	-/7
	1963	*1108*	*>3yr*	*VESTMANNAEYJAR [SURTSEY]*	1702-01=	0	*8/8*
	1963	1110	66*m*?	**ASO** (Kyushu-Japan)	0802-11=	2	
	1963	1113	397*m*?	**KLIUCHEVSKOI** (Kamchatka)	1000-26=	1	
	1963	1114A	....	**VESTMANNAEYJAR [SURTSEY]**	1702-01=	3	8/8
	1963	1120	1*a*	**NASU** (Honshu-Japan)	0803-15=	1	
	1963	1126	142*m*	**MANAM** (New Guinea-NE of)	0501-02=	2	6/-
	1963	*1214*	*48a?*	*KAVACHI (Solomon Is-SW Pac)*	0505-06=	0	
?	**1963**	1215<	?	**PICO** (Azores)	1802-02=	0	
	1963	1217	120*m*	**LOKON-EMPUNG** (Sulawesi-Indonesia)	0606-10=	2	
	1963	1228	?	**SHISHALDIN** (Aleutian Is)	1101-36-	2	
	1963	1231	807*a*	**PALUWEH** (Lesser Sunda Is)	0604-15=	2	7/-
	1964	*Cont*	....	*STROMBOLI (Italy)*	0101-04=	*1?*	
	1964	*Cont*	....	*LENGAI, OL DOINYO (Africa-E)*	0202-12=	*1*	
	1964	*Cont*	....	*NYIRAGONGO (Africa-C)*	0203-03=	*0*	
S	*1964*	*Cont*	....	*RUMBLE III (New Zealand)*	0401-13-	*0*	
	1964	*Cont*	....	*YASUR (Vanuatu-SW Pacific)*	0507-10=	*2*	
S	*1964*	*Cont*	....	*UNNAMED (SW Pacific)*	0508-03-	*0*	
	1964	*Cont*	....	*SEMERU (Java)*	0603-30=	*1*	
	1964	*Cont*	....	*BATUR (Lesser Sunda Is)*	0604-01=	*2*	*7/5*
	1964	*Cont*	....	*AGUNG (Lesser Sunda Is)*	0604-02=	*2*	*8/8*
	1964	*Cont*	....	*LOKON-EMPUNG (Sulawesi-Indonesia)*	0606-10=	*2*	
	1964	*Cont*	....	*DUKONO (Halmahera-Indonesia)*	0608-01=	*2*	
	1964	*Cont*	....	*SAKURA-JIMA (Kyushu-Japan)*	0802-08=	*2*	
	1964	*Cont*	....	*OSHIMA (Izu Is-Japan)*	0804-01=	*1*	
	1964	*Cont*	....	*KARYMSKY (Kamchatka)*	1000-13=	*2*	*6/7*
	1964	*Cont*	....	*KLIUCHEVSKOI (Kamchatka)*	1000-26=	*1*	
	1964	*Cont*	....	*COLIMA VOLC COMPLEX (Mexico)*	1401-04=	*1*	
	1964	*Cont*	....	*SANTA MARIA (Guatemala)*	1402-03=	*1*	*8/8*

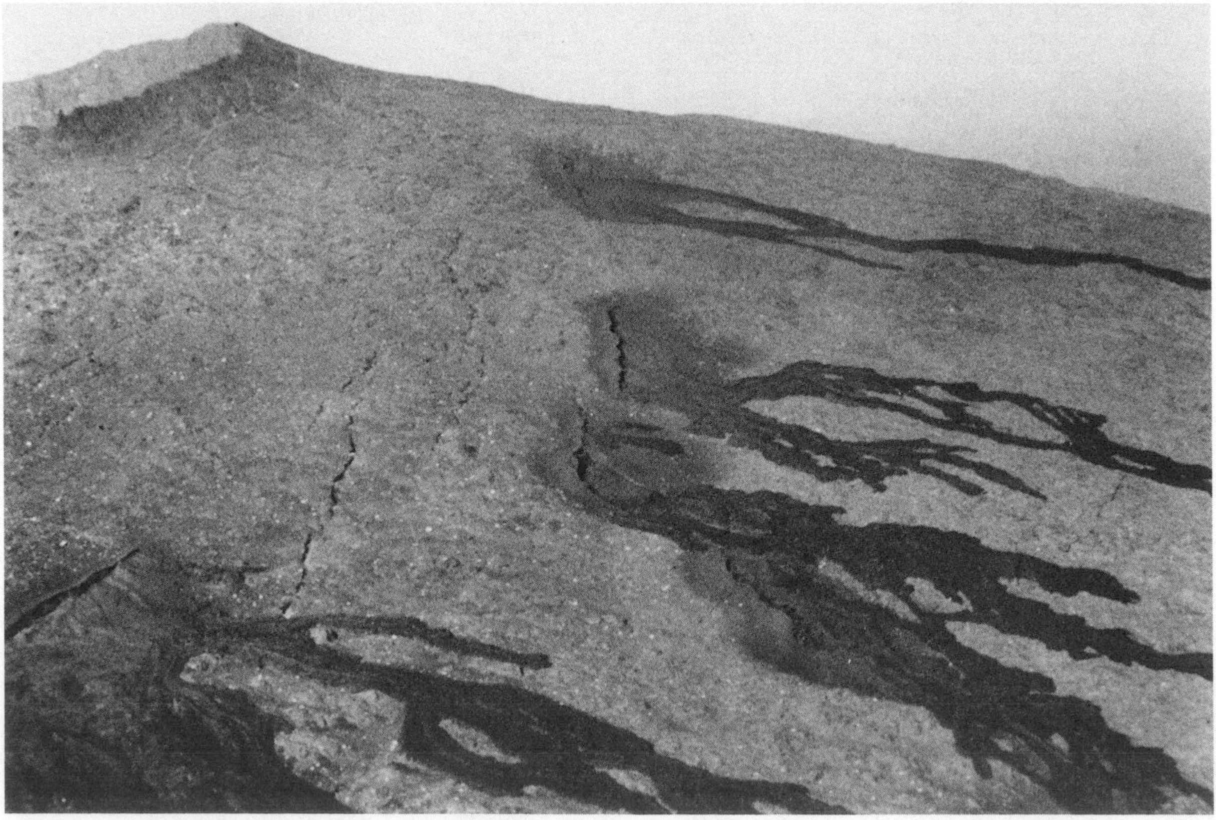

Figure 26. Fissure vents and lava flows from Piton de la Fournaise, one of the world's most active volcanoes, on the Indian Ocean island of Reunion. Summit crater rim of this oceanic shield volcano is at upper left. Aerial Photo by Katia & Maurice Krafft.

	START YEAR	START M-Dy	Duration	VOLCANO NAME (Subregion)	NUMBER	VEI	Vol L/T
	1964	Cont	....	SANGAY (Ecuador)	1502-09=	2	
	1964	....	....	SUWANOSE-JIMA (Ryukyu Is)	0802-03=	1	
	1964	....	?	NEGRO, CERRO (Nicaragua)	1404-07=	2?	
	1964	....	?	LLAIMA (Chile-C)	1507-11=	2	
	1964	01	....	MANAM (New Guinea-NE of)	0501-02=	2	6/-
	1964	0102	....	KAVACHI (Solomon Is-SW Pac)	0505-06=	2	
	1964	0114	....	IRAZU (Costa Rica)	1405-06=	3	
	1964	0129	670p?	SANGEANG API (Lesser Sunda Is)	0604-05=	2	6/-
	1964	02 ?	943p>	AMBRYM (Vanuatu-SW Pacific)	0507-04=	2	
	1964	02	....	PALUWEH (Lesser Sunda Is)	0604-15=	2	7/-
	1964	0201	....	ETNA (Italy)	0101-06=	2	
	1964	0201	12k	CHIKURACHKI (Kurile Is)	0900-36=	2	
	1964	0208	240a>	SIRUNG (Lesser Sunda Is)	0604-27=	1	
	1964	0214	<1	DEMPO (Sumatra)	0601-23=	2	
?	1964	0218	?	SAN JORGE (Azores)	1802-03=	0	
	1964	03	16m	NILA (Banda Sea)	0605-06=	1?	
	1964	03	39m>	TOLBACHIK (Kamchatka)	1000-24=	2	
	1964	0302	1a	VILLARRICA (Chile-C)	1507-12=	2	
	1964	0310	37a	WESTDAHL (Aleutian Is)	1101-34-	2	
	1964	0318	?	KISKA (Aleutian Is)	1101-02-	0	
	1964	0404	....	VESTMANNAEYJAR [SURTSEY]	1702-01=	3	8/8
	1964	0408	....	LOPEVI (Vanuatu-SW Pacific)	0507-05=	3	
?	1964	0414	?	ESMERALDA BANK (Mariana Is-C Pac)	0804-21=	2	
	1964	0414	....	IRAZU (Costa Rica)	1405-06=	3	
	1964	0424	434w	BAGANA (Bougainville-SW Pac)	0505-02=	2	
	1964	0430	8a	FOURNAISE, PITON DE LA (Indian O.)	0303-02=	2	
	1964	0514	<1	ASO (Kyushu-Japan)	0802-11=	1	
	1964	0531	?	TRIDENT (Alaska Peninsula)	1102-16-	3?	
	1964	0618?	16a?	AKAN (Hokkaido-Japan)	0805-07=	1	
	1964	0625	87a	BEZYMIANNY (Kamchatka)	1000-25=	2	6/-
	1964	0706	....	IRAZU (Costa Rica)	1405-06=	3	
	1964	0708	<1	KERINCI (Sumatra)	0601-17=	2	
	1964	0803	47a>	TUPUNGATITO (Chile-C)	1507-01=	2	
	1964	0819	....	AUGUSTINE (Alaska-SW)	1103-01-	1	7/6
	1964	0917	....	LASCAR (Chile-N)	1505-10=	2	
	1964	10	792m	ASO (Kyushu-Japan)	0802-11=	2	
	1964	1023	24m	SAN MIGUEL (El Salvador)	1403-10=	2	
	1964	1112	<1	SHEVELUCH (Kamchatka)	1000-27=	4+	-/8
	1964	1121	155a?	RAOUL ISLAND (Kermadec Is)	0402-03=	2	
	1964	1204d	658g	LANGILA (New Britain-SW Pac)	0502-01=	2	
	1964	1213	<1	DIENG VOLC COMPLEX (Java)	0603-20=	1	
	1964	1221	56a	FOURNAISE, PITON DE LA (Indian O.)	0303-02=	2?	7/-
	1964	1225	1a	BEZYMIANNY (Kamchatka)	1000-25=	1	
	1964	1225	80m	POAS (Costa Rica)	1405-04=	2	
	1965	Cont	....	STROMBOLI (Italy)	0101-04=	1?	
	1965	Cont	....	LENGAI, OL DOINYO (Africa-E)	0202-12=	1	
	1965	Cont	....	NYIRAGONGO (Africa-C)	0203-03=	0	
	1965	Cont	....	FOURNAISE, PITON DE LA (Indian O.)	0303-02=	2?	7/-
S	1965	Cont	....	RUMBLE III (New Zealand)	0401-13-	0	
	1965	Cont	....	RAOUL ISLAND (Kermadec Is)	0402-03=	1	
	1965	Cont	....	LANGILA (New Britain-SW Pac)	0502-01=	2	
	1965	Cont	....	BAGANA (Bougainville-SW Pac)	0505-02=	2	
	1965	Cont	....	AMBRYM (Vanuatu-SW Pacific)	0507-04=	2	
	1965	Cont	....	LOPEVI (Vanuatu-SW Pacific)	0507-05=	2	
	1965	Cont	....	YASUR (Vanuatu-SW Pacific)	0507-10=	2	
	1965	Cont	....	SANGEANG API (Lesser Sunda Is)	0604-05=	2	6/-
	1965	Cont	....	DUKONO (Halmahera-Indonesia)	0608-01=	2	
	1965	Cont	....	SAKURA-JIMA (Kyushu-Japan)	0802-08=	2	
	1965	Cont	....	SANTA MARIA (Guatemala)	1402-03=	1	8/8
	1965	Cont	....	POAS (Costa Rica)	1405-04=	2	
	1965	Cont	....	SANGAY (Ecuador)	1502-09=	2	
	1965	Cont	....	LASCAR (Chile-N)	1505-10=	2	
	1965	Cont	....	VESTMANNAEYJAR [SURTSEY]	1702-01=	3	8/8
	1965	....	208w>	MANAM (New Guinea-NE of)	0501-02=	2	6/-
	1965?	....	?	KRAKATAU (Indonesia)	0602-00=	1?	
	1965	....	....	SUWANOSE-JIMA (Ryukyu Is)	0802-03=	1	
	1965	....	410w	EBEKO (Kurile Is)	0900-38=	1	
	1965	....	?	TOLBACHIK (Kamchatka)	1000-24=	1	
	1965	....	?	CHILLAN, NEVADOS DE (Chile-C)	1507-07=		
	1965	0116	12a	TELICA (Nicaragua)	1404-04=	1	
?	1965	0129	16m	REDOUBT (Alaska-SW)	1103-03-		
	1965	0131	....	IRAZU (Costa Rica)	1405-06=	3	
	1965	02	30m	TANGKUBANPARAHU (Java)	0603-09=	1	
	1965	0211	....	PALUWEH (Lesser Sunda Is)	0604-15=	2	7/-
	1965	0305	10	KILAUEA (Hawaiian Is)	1302-01-	0	7/-
	1965	0309	>3yr	BEZYMIANNY (Kamchatka)	1000-25=	3	7/7
	1965	0405d	801n	KARANGETANG [API SIAU] (Sangihe	0607-02=	2	
	1965	0507	11a	SIRUNG (Lesser Sunda Is)	0604-27=	1	
	1965	0515e	<1	AKAN (Hokkaido-Japan)	0805-07=	1	
	1965	0515e	639n	KARYMSKY (Kamchatka)	1000-13=	3	
	1965	0523	<1	ASAMA (Honshu-Japan)	0803-11=	2	
	1965	0704	>3yr	PACAYA (Guatemala)	1402-11=	2	
	1965	0710	<1	LOKON-EMPUNG (Sulawesi-Indonesia)	0606-10=	1	
	1965	0712	<1	KARTHALA (Indian O.-W)	0303-01=	2?	5/-
	1965	08	498m	KLIUCHEVSKOI (Kamchatka)	1000-26=	2	8/7
	1965	0809	327w	SORETIMEAT (Vanuatu-SW Pacific)	0507-01=	2	
	1965	0818	119m	BATUR (Lesser Sunda Is)	0604-01=	1	
	1965	09	?	RINJANI (Lesser Sunda Is)	0604-03=	0	
	1965	0927	3a>	GAUA (Vanuatu-SW Pacific)	0507-02=	3	
	1965	0928	2	TAAL (Luzon-Philippines)	0703-07=	4	-/7
	1965	10	16m	TANGKUBANPARAHU (Java)	0603-09=	1	
	1965	1010?	>3yr	MASAYA (Nicaragua)	1404-10=	0	
	1965	1019	....	PACAYA (Guatemala)	1402-11=	3	
	1965	1021	....	ASO (Kyushu-Japan)	0802-11=	2	
S	1965	1025	<1	KICK-'EM-JENNY (W Indies)	1600-16=	0	
	1965	11	>3yr	COLIMA VOLC COMPLEX (Mexico)	1401-04=	1	
	1965	1102	<1	SIRUNG (Lesser Sunda Is)	0604-27=	1	
S	1965	1113	22d	TORI-SHIMA (Izu Is-Japan)	0804-09=	0	
	1965	1123	200a	TINAKULA (Santa Cruz Is-SW Pac)	0506-01=	3	
	1965	1125	201a	OSHIMA (Izu Is-Japan)	0804-01=	1	
	1965	1209	<1	SARYCHEV PEAK (Kurile Is)	0900-24=	2	
	1965	1209	....	PACAYA (Guatemala)	1402-11=	3	
	1965	1211	2a	KAVACHI (Solomon Is-SW Pac)	0505-06=	2	
	1965	1224	<1	KILAUEA (Hawaiian Is)	1302-01-	0	5/-
	1966	Cont	....	NYIRAGONGO (Africa-C)	0203-03=	0	
S	1966	Cont	....	RUMBLE III (New Zealand)	0401-13-	0	
	1966	Cont	....	MANAM (New Guinea-NE of)	0501-02=	2	6/-
	1966	Cont	....	LANGILA (New Britain-SW Pac)	0502-01=	2	
	1966	Cont	....	SORETIMEAT (Vanuatu-SW Pacific)	0507-01=	2	
	1966	Cont	....	AMBRYM (Vanuatu-SW Pacific)	0507-04=	2	
	1966	Cont	....	YASUR (Vanuatu-SW Pacific)	0507-10=	2	
	1966	Cont	....	KARANGETANG [API SIAU] (Sangihe	0607-02=	2	
	1966	Cont	....	DUKONO (Halmahera-Indonesia)	0608-01=	2	
	1966	Cont	....	SUWANOSE-JIMA (Ryukyu Is)	0802-03=	2	
	1966	Cont	....	SAKURA-JIMA (Kyushu-Japan)	0802-08=	2	
	1966	Cont	....	ASO (Kyushu-Japan)	0802-11=	2	
	1966	Cont	....	OSHIMA (Izu Is-Japan)	0804-01=	1	
	1966	Cont	....	EBEKO (Kurile Is)	0900-38=	1	
	1966	Cont	....	KARYMSKY (Kamchatka)	1000-13=	1	
	1966	Cont	....	BEZYMIANNY (Kamchatka)	1000-25=	1	7/7
	1966	Cont	....	COLIMA VOLC COMPLEX (Mexico)	1401-04=	1	
	1966	Cont	....	SANTA MARIA (Guatemala)	1402-03=	1	8/8
	1966	Cont	....	PACAYA (Guatemala)	1402-11=	1	
	1966	Cont	....	MASAYA (Nicaragua)	1404-10=	0	
	1966	Cont	....	SANGAY (Ecuador)	1502-09=	2	
	1966	Cont	....	LASCAR (Chile-N)	1505-10=	2	
	1966	Cont	....	VESTMANNAEYJAR [SURTSEY]	1702-01=	3	8/8
	1966	....	?	GAUA (Vanuatu-SW Pacific)	0507-02=	2	
	1966	....	?	SLAMET (Java)	0603-18=	2	
	1966?	....	?	TRIDENT (Alaska Peninsula)	1102-16-		
	1966	....	?	REYKJANESHRYGGUR (Iceland-SW)	1701-01=	0	
	1966	0110	>3yr	ETNA (Italy)	0101-06=	2	
	1966	0113	....	TINAKULA (Santa Cruz Is-SW Pac)	0506-01=	2	
	1966	0124	27a	REDOUBT (Alaska-SW)	1103-03-	3	
	1966	02	....	KLIUCHEVSKOI (Kamchatka)	1000-26=	3	8/7
	1966	0204	....	REDOUBT (Alaska-SW)	1103-03-	3	
	1966	0207	72a	FUEGO (Guatemala)	1402-09=	2	
	1966	0211	....	REDOUBT (Alaska-SW)	1103-03-	3	
	1966	0222	?	SAN MIGUEL (El Salvador)	1403-10=	2	
	1966	0228	260m	SANGEANG API (Lesser Sunda Is)	0604-05=	2	
	1966	03	92p	MARAPI (Sumatra)	0601-14=	1	
?	1966	0309	11a?	ROCARD (Society Is-C Pac)	1303-04-	0	
	1966	0310	....	PALUWEH (Lesser Sunda Is)	0604-15=	2	7/-
	1966	0315	61a	FOURNAISE, PITON DE LA (Indian O.)	0303-02=	2?	7/-
	1966	0315	?	PAVLOF (Alaska Peninsula)	1102-03-	2	
	1966	0319	3a>	KAVACHI (Solomon Is-SW Pac)	0505-06=	2	
	1966	0320	619a	BAGANA (Bougainville-SW Pac)	0505-02=	1	
	1966	0328	133a	RINJANI (Lesser Sunda Is)	0604-03=	1	6/4
	1966	0404	176a	RUAPEHU (New Zealand)	0401-10=	1	
	1966	0409	3	STROMBOLI (Italy)	0101-04=	2	
	1966	0415q	?	TOLBACHIK (Kamchatka)	1000-24=	2	
	1966	0420	....	FUEGO (Guatemala)	1402-09=	3	
S	1966	0421g	23n	RUBY (Mariana Is-C Pac)	0804-201	0	
	1966	0426	<1	KELUT (Java)	0603-28=	4	-/7
	1966	0428	?	BATUR (Lesser Sunda Is)	0604-01=	1	
S	1966	0505	93a	KICK-'EM-JENNY (W Indies)	1600-16=	0	
	1966	0521	543m	SOPUTAN (Sulawesi-Indonesia)	0606-03=	3	7/-
	1966	0530	....	BAGANA (Bougainville-SW Pac)	0505-02=	3	
	1966	06	15m	TELICA (Nicaragua)	1404-04=	1	
	1966	0609	21a>	KERINCI (Sumatra)	0601-17=	2	
	1966	0615e	<1	AKAN (Hokkaido-Japan)	0805-07=	1	
	1966	07	?	SAN MIGUEL (El Salvador)	1403-10=	2	
	1966	0705	30	TAAL (Luzon-Philippines)	0703-07=	2	
?	1966	08	?	MATTHEW ISLAND (SW Pacific)	0508-01=		
	1966	0804	....	TAAL (Luzon-Philippines)	0703-07=	3	
	1966	0812	64m	AWU (Sangihe Is-Indonesia)	0607-04=	4	
	1966	0812	1a	FUEGO (Guatemala)	1402-09=	3	-/6
	1966	0822	....	LENGAI, OL DOINYO (Africa-E)	0202-12=	3	
	1966	0924	6a?	LOKON-EMPUNG (Sulawesi-Indonesia)	0606-10=	2	
	1966	1006	....	KLIUCHEVSKOI (Kamchatka)	1000-26=	2	8/7
	1966	1007	100a	REDOUBT (Alaska-SW)	1103-03-	3	
	1966	1028	18m	IZALCO (El Salvador)	1403-03=	0	5/-
	1966	1113	122m	WHITE ISLAND (New Zealand)	0401-04=	3	
	1966	1122	<1	KUCHINOERABU-JIMA (Ryukyu Is)	0802-05=	2	
	1966	1129	382m	RINCON DE LA VIEJA (Costa Rica)	1405-02=	2	
	1967	Cont	....	ETNA (Italy)	0101-06=	2	
	1967	Cont	....	NYIRAGONGO (Africa-C)	0203-03=	0	
	1967	Cont	....	WHITE ISLAND (New Zealand)	0401-04=	2	
	1967	Cont	....	BAGANA (Bougainville-SW Pac)	0505-02=	2	
	1967	Cont	....	YASUR (Vanuatu-SW Pacific)	0507-10=	2	
	1967	Cont	....	DUKONO (Halmahera-Indonesia)	0608-01=	2	
	1967	Cont	....	SUWANOSE-JIMA (Ryukyu Is)	0802-03=	2	
	1967	Cont	....	SAKURA-JIMA (Kyushu-Japan)	0802-08=	2	
	1967	Cont	....	BEZYMIANNY (Kamchatka)	1000-25=	1	7/7
	1967	Cont	....	COLIMA VOLC COMPLEX (Mexico)	1401-04=	1	
	1967	Cont	....	SANTA MARIA (Guatemala)	1402-03=	1	8/8
	1967	Cont	....	PACAYA (Guatemala)	1402-11=	1	
	1967	Cont	....	MASAYA (Nicaragua)	1404-10=	0	
	1967	Cont	....	SANGAY (Ecuador)	1502-09=	2	
	1967	Cont	....	LASCAR (Chile-N)	1505-10=	2	
	1967<	....	>3yr	ERTA ALE (Ethiopia)	0201-08=	0	
	1967p	....	?	TAMBORA (Lesser Sunda Is)	0604-04=	0	
	1967	....	?	KLIUCHEVSKOI (Kamchatka)	1000-26=	1	
	1967	....	?	PLANCHON-PETEROA (Chile-C)	1507-04=		
	1967	....	?	AZUL, CERRO [QUIZAPU] (Chile-C)	1507-06=	2?	
	1967	0101	....	REDOUBT (Alaska-SW)	1103-03-	2	

	START YEAR	M-Dy	Duration	VOLCANO NAME (Subregion)	NUMBER	VEI	Vol L/T
	1967	0101	....	RINCON DE LA VIEJA (Costa Rica)	1405-02=	3	
	1967	0101	?	POAS (Costa Rica)	1405-04=	1	
	1967	0105	?	SAN MIGUEL (El Salvador)	1403-10=	2	
	1967	0112	884m	MERAPI (Java)	0603-25=	2	7/7
	1967	0119	512m	LANGILA (New Britain-SW Pac)	0502-01=	2	4/-
	1967	0122	340a	ULAWUN (New Britain-SW Pac)	0502-12=	2	
	1967	0127	794a	LOPEVI (Vanuatu-SW Pacific)	0507-05=	2	
	1967	0128	?	SHISHALDIN (Aleutian Is)	1101-36-	2	
	1967	0208	65m	EBEKO (Kurile Is)	0900-38=	1	-/4
	1967	0218	<1	KELUT (Java)	0603-28=	1	
	1967	03	61p	TOLBACHIK (Kamchatka)	1000-24=	2	
	1967	0301	....	LOPEVI (Vanuatu-SW Pacific)	0507-05=	3	
	1967	0311	....	SOPUTAN (Sulawesi-Indonesia)	0606-03=	3	7/-
S	1967	0327	13	FARALLON DE PAJAROS (Mariana Is)	0804-14=	0	
	1967	04	92p	MARAPI (Sumatra)	0601-14=	1	
	1967	0419	116a	STROMBOLI (Italy)	0101-04=	0	3/-
	1967	0422	2a	FUEGO (Guatemala)	1402-09=	2	-/6
	1967	0423	16a	NYAMURAGIRA (Africa-C)	0203-02=	2	7/7
?	1967	0426	?	UNNAMED (Kurile Is)	0900-061		
	1967	05	944p	ASO (Kyushu-Japan)	0802-11=	1	
	1967	05	92p	OSHIMA (Izu Is-Japan)	0804-01=	1	
	1967	0505	....	VESTMANNAEYJAR [SURTSEY]	1702-01=	0	8/8
	1967	0507	70m	SLAMET (Java)	0603-18=	2	
S	1967	0529	<1	MACDONALD (Austral Is-C Pac)	1303-07-	0	
	1967	0610	....	RINCON DE LA VIEJA (Costa Rica)	1405-02=	3	
	1967	07	?	GAUA (Vanuatu-SW Pacific)	0507-02=	2	
	1967	07	>3yr	AMBRYM (Vanuatu-SW Pacific)	0507-04=	2	
	1967	07	16m	TANGKUBANPARAHU (Java)	0603-09=	1	
?	1967	07	15m	SHIN-IWO-JIMA (Volcano Is-Japan)	0804-13=	0	
	1967	0708	58a	LENGAI, OL DOINYO (Africa-E)	0202-12=	3	
	1967	0722	74a?	RUAPEHU (New Zealand)	0401-10=	1	
	1967	0816	2	TAAL (Luzon-Philippines)	0703-07=	1	
	1967	0831	>3yr	SEMERU (Java)	0603-30=	2	
	1967	0905	172a	TRIDENT (Alaska Peninsula)	1102-16-	2	
	1967	0906	14a	CHIKURACHKI (Kurile Is)	0900-36=	2	
	1967	10	30p	TOLBACHIK (Kamchatka)	1000-24=	2	
	1967	1010	<1	TALANG (Sumatra)	0601-16=	1	
	1967	11	15m	KARYMSKY (Kamchatka)	1000-13=	1	
	1967	1102	?	KERINCI (Sumatra)	0601-17=	2	
	1967	1105	250a	KILAUEA (Hawaiian Is)	1302-01-	0	7/-
	1967	1125e	?	OKINAWA-TORI-SHIMA (Ryukyu Is)	0802-02=	1	
	1967	1129	3a	KARANGETANG [API SIAU] (Sangihe	0607-02=	2	
	1967	1204	3a	DECEPTION ISLAND (Antarctica)	1900-03=	3	-/7
	1967	1206	144a>	REDOUBT (Alaska-SW)	1103-03-	2	
	1967	1211<	35m>	METIS SHOAL (Tonga-SW Pacific)	0403-07=	2	
	1967	1211	<1	KELUT (Java)	0603-28=	1	
	1967	1218	....	TRIDENT (Alaska Peninsula)	1102-16-	3	
	1967	1223	<1	IWO-JIMA (Volcano Is-Japan)	0804-12=	1	
	1968	Cont	....	STROMBOLI (Italy)	0101-04=	1?	
	1968	Cont	....	ERTA ALE (Ethiopia)	0201-08=	0	
	1968	Cont	....	NYIRAGONGO (Africa-C)	0203-03=	0	
	1968	Cont	....	METIS SHOAL (Tonga-SW Pacific)	0403-07=	2?	
	1968	Cont	....	LANGILA (New Britain-SW Pac)	0502-01=	2	4/-
	1968	Cont	....	AMBRYM (Vanuatu-SW Pacific)	0507-04=	2	
	1968	Cont	....	LOPEVI (Vanuatu-SW Pacific)	0507-05=	2	
	1968	Cont	....	YASUR (Vanuatu-SW Pacific)	0507-10=	2	
	1968	Cont	....	DUKONO (Halmahera-Indonesia)	0608-01=	2	
	1968	Cont	....	SUWANOSE-JIMA (Ryukyu Is)	0802-03=	2	
	1968	Cont	....	SAKURA-JIMA (Kyushu-Japan)	0802-08=	2	
	1968	Cont	....	ASO (Kyushu-Japan)	0802-11=	1	
	1968	Cont	....	BEZYMIANNY (Kamchatka)	1000-25=	1	7/7
	1968	Cont	....	COLIMA VOLC COMPLEX (Mexico)	1401-04=	1	
	1968	Cont	....	SANTA MARIA (Guatemala)	1402-03=	1	8/8
	1968	Cont	....	MASAYA (Nicaragua)	1404-10=	0	
	1968	Cont	....	SANGAY (Ecuador)	1502-09=	2	
	1968	....	152u	GAUA (Vanuatu-SW Pacific)	0507-02=	2	
	1968	....	365y	TOLBACHIK (Kamchatka)	1000-24=	1	
	1968	....	?	TUPUNGATITO (Chile-C)	1507-01=		
	1968	01	....	SEMERU (Java)	0603-30=	2	
	1968	0103	....	PACAYA (Guatemala)	1402-11=	2	
	1968	0107	118a	ETNA (Italy)	0101-06=	0	
	1968	0114	<1	TALANG (Sumatra)	0601-16=	1	
	1968	0119	<1	OSHIMA (Izu Is-Japan)	0804-01=	1	
	1968	0123	23	BATUR (Lesser Sunda Is)	0604-01=	2	6/-
	1968	0127	382m	WHITE ISLAND (New Zealand)	0401-04=	2	
	1968	0131	61a	TAAL (Luzon-Philippines)	0703-07=	2	
	1968	0131	....	LASCAR (Chile-N)	1505-10=	2	
?	1968	02	15m	SHIN-IWO-JIMA (Volcano Is-Japan)	0804-13=	0	
	1968	02	14m	GROZNY GROUP (Kurile Is)	0900-07=	1	
	1968	0203	44a	KERINCI (Sumatra)	0601-17=	2	
	1968	0214	....	REDOUBT (Alaska-SW)	1103-03-	3	
	1968	0225	....	WHITE ISLAND (New Zealand)	0401-04=	3	
	1968	0316	88a	LONG ISLAND (New Guinea-NE of)	0501-05=	2	
	1968	0407	64a	RUAPEHU (New Zealand)	0401-10=	1	
	1968	0421	29a	MAYON (Luzon-Philippines)	0703-03=	3	7/7
	1968	0426	....	RUAPEHU (New Zealand)	0401-10=	2	
	1968	0507	39m	NILA (Banda Sea)	0605-06=	1	
	1968	0521	2a?	FERNANDINA (Galapagos)	1503-01=	2	
	1968	0523	23m	KVERKFJOLL (Iceland-NE)	1703-05=		
	1968	0603	55	KELIMUTU (Lesser Sunda Is)	0604-14=	1	
	1968	0611	23a<	FERNANDINA (Galapagos)	1503-01=	4	-/8
?	1968	0612	?	AZUL, CERRO (Galapagos)	1503-06=		
	1968	07	31p	SOPUTAN (Sulawesi-Indonesia)	0606-03=	1	
	1968	0703	<1	KLIUCHEVSKOI (Kamchatka)	1000-26=	3	
	1968	0718	<1	OKINAWA-TORI-SHIMA (Ryukyu Is)	0802-02=	1	
	1968	0728	<1	OSHIMA (Izu Is-Japan)	0804-01=	1	
	1968	0729	>3yr	ARENAL (Costa Rica)	1405-033	3	7/7
	1968	08	16m	BAGANA (Bougainville-SW Pac)	0505-02=	2	
?	1968	08	....	AWU (Sangihe Is-Indonesia)	0607-04=	2	
?	1968	0814	?	SHIN-IWO-JIMA (Volcano Is-Japan)	0804-13=	0	
	1968	0818	?	TONGARIRO [NGAURUHOE] (New Z)	0401-08=	2	
	1968	0822	4a	KILAUEA (Hawaiian Is)	1302-01-	0	4/-
	1968	09	31p	TALANG (Sumatra)	0601-16=	2	
	1968	09	?	FUKUJIN (Volcano Is-Japan)	0804-133	0	
?	1968	0905	4d	BANUA WUHU (Sangihe Is-Indonesia)	0607-03=	0	
	1968	1007	15a	KILAUEA (Hawaiian Is)	1302-01-	0	6/-
	1968	1008	....	MERAPI (Java)	0603-25=	2	7/7
	1968	1023	61a	NEGRO, CERRO (Nicaragua)	1404-07=	3	-/7
	1968	1113	<1	TRIDENT (Alaska Peninsula)	1102-16-	3	
	1968	1128	65	LEWOTOBI (Lesser Sunda Is)	0604-18=	2	
?	1968	12	16m	MARAPI (Sumatra)	0601-14=	1	
	1968	1221	79a	KUCHINOERABU-JIMA (Ryukyu Is)	0802-05=	2	
	1968	1229	....	KUCHINOERABU-JIMA (Ryukyu Is)	0802-05=	3	
	1969	Cont	....	STROMBOLI (Italy)	0101-04=	1?	
	1969	Cont	....	ETNA (Italy)	0101-06=	2	
	1969	Cont	....	ERTA ALE (Ethiopia)	0201-08=	0	
	1969	Cont	....	NYIRAGONGO (Africa-C)	0203-03=	0	
	1969	Cont	....	AMBRYM (Vanuatu-SW Pacific)	0507-04=	2	
	1969	Cont	....	LOPEVI (Vanuatu-SW Pacific)	0507-05=	2	
	1969	Cont	....	YASUR (Vanuatu-SW Pacific)	0507-10=	2	
	1969	Cont	....	SEMERU (Java)	0603-30=	2	
	1969	Cont	....	LEWOTOBI (Lesser Sunda Is)	0604-18=	2	
	1969	Cont	....	DUKONO (Halmahera-Indonesia)	0608-01=	2	
	1969	Cont	....	SUWANOSE-JIMA (Ryukyu Is)	0802-03=	2	
	1969	Cont	....	SAKURA-JIMA (Kyushu-Japan)	0802-08=	2	
	1969	Cont	....	ASO (Kyushu-Japan)	0802-11=	1	
	1969	Cont	....	TOLBACHIK (Kamchatka)	1000-24=	1	
	1969	Cont	....	COLIMA VOLC COMPLEX (Mexico)	1401-04=	1	
	1969	Cont	....	SANTA MARIA (Guatemala)	1402-03=	1	8/8
	1969	Cont	....	MASAYA (Nicaragua)	1404-10=	0	
	1969	Cont	....	SANGAY (Ecuador)	1502-09=	2	
	1969	....	365y	KERINCI (Sumatra)	0601-17=	2	
?	1969	....	?	KRAKATAU (Indonesia)	0602-00=	2?	
	1969	....	?	EBEKO (Kurile Is)	0900-38=	1	
	1969	0107	....	MERAPI (Java)	0603-25=	3	7/7
?	1969	0112	9a	IWO-JIMA (Volcano Is-Japan)	0804-12=	1	
	1969	0119	177m	OSHIMA (Izu Is-Japan)	0804-01=	1	
	1969	0121	?	TONGARIRO [NGAURUHOE] (New Z)	0401-08=	2	
	1969	0127	3a	IYA (Lesser Sunda Is)	0604-11=	3	
	1969	0205	....	KUCHINOERABU-JIMA (Ryukyu Is)	0802-05=	2	
	1969	0211	>3yr	TELICA (Nicaragua)	1404-04=	2	
	1969	0221	23m	DECEPTION ISLAND (Antarctica)	1900-03=	3	-/7
	1969	0222	6a	KILAUEA (Hawaiian Is)	1302-01-	0	7/-
	1969	0227	?	EBULOBO (Lesser Sunda Is)	0604-10=	2?	
S	1969	0311	1	SUPPLY REEF (Mariana Is-C Pac)	0804-142	0	
	1969	0321	86m	DIDICAS (Luzon Is-N of)	0704-02=	2	
?	1969	0422	7a?	MOUA PIHAA (Society Is-C Pac)	1303-05-	0	
	1969	0422	23m	RINCON DE LA VIEJA (Costa Rica)	1405-02=	2	
	1969	0503	....	ARENAL (Costa Rica)	1405-033	3	7/7
	1969	0503	31	POAS (Costa Rica)	1405-04=	2	
	1969	0516	?	LASCAR (Chile-N)	1505-10=		
	1969	0524	>3yr	KILAUEA (Hawaiian Is)	1302-01-	0	8/-
	1969	06	?	UBINAS (Peru)	1504-02=	2?	
	1969	0607	....	PACAYA (Guatemala)	1402-11=	2	
	1969	0622	<1	RUAPEHU (New Zealand)	0401-10=	2	
	1969	0623	53m	SLAMET (Java)	0603-18=	2	
?	1969	07 ?	?	LENGAI, OL DOINYO (Africa-E)	0202-12=		
	1969	0720	93a	TANGKUBANPARAHU (Java)	0603-09=	1	
	1969	08	30p	WHITE ISLAND (New Zealand)	0401-04=	2	
	1969	09	91p	KLIUCHEVSKOI (Kamchatka)	1000-26=	2	
	1969	0911	4a	KISKA (Aleutian Is)	1101-02-	2?	
	1969	0920	26a	RINCON DE LA VIEJA (Costa Rica)	1405-02=	2	
	1969	0922	?	GAUA (Vanuatu-SW Pacific)	0507-02=	2	
	1969	0929	<1	LANGILA (New Britain-SW Pac)	0502-01=	2	
	1969	1010	18	CANLAON (Philippines-C)	0702-02=	2	
	1969	1011	....	BEZYMIANNY (Kamchatka)	1000-25=	2	7/7
	1969	1028	101a	KAVACHI (Solomon Is-SW Pac)	0505-06=	2	
	1969	1029	43a	TAAL (Luzon-Philippines)	0703-07=	2	6/6
	1969	1127	394e	LOKON-EMPUNG (Sulawesi-Indonesia)	0606-10=	2	
	1969	1219	10a	NEGRO, CERRO (Nicaragua)	1404-07=	1	
	1970	Cont	....	STROMBOLI (Italy)	0101-04=	1?	
	1970	Cont	....	ETNA (Italy)	0101-06=	2	
	1970	Cont	....	ERTA ALE (Ethiopia)	0201-08=	0	
	1970	Cont	....	NYIRAGONGO (Africa-C)	0203-03=	0	
	1970	Cont	....	KAVACHI (Solomon Is-SW Pac)	0505-06=	2	
	1970	Cont	....	AMBRYM (Vanuatu-SW Pacific)	0507-04=	2	
	1970	Cont	....	YASUR (Vanuatu-SW Pacific)	0507-10=	2	
	1970	Cont	....	KERINCI (Sumatra)	0601-17=	2	
	1970	Cont	....	SEMERU (Java)	0603-30=	2	
	1970	Cont	....	LOKON-EMPUNG (Sulawesi-Indonesia)	0606-10=	2	
	1970	Cont	....	DUKONO (Halmahera-Indonesia)	0608-01=	2	
	1970	Cont	....	SUWANOSE-JIMA (Ryukyu Is)	0802-03=	2	
	1970	Cont	....	SAKURA-JIMA (Kyushu-Japan)	0802-08=	2	
	1970	Cont	....	KILAUEA (Hawaiian Is)	1302-01-	0	8/-
	1970	Cont	....	COLIMA VOLC COMPLEX (Mexico)	1401-04=	1	
	1970	Cont	....	TELICA (Nicaragua)	1404-04=	2	
	1970	Cont	....	SANGAY (Ecuador)	1502-09=	2	
S	1970	....	?	RUMBLE III (New Zealand)	0401-13-	0	
	1970	....	?	SORIKMARAPI (Sumatra)	0601-12=	2	
	1970	....	?	LEWOTOBI (Lesser Sunda Is)	0604-18=	2	
	1970	....	?	SIRUNG (Lesser Sunda Is)	0604-27=	2?	
?	1970 a	....	?	ESMERALDA BANK (Mariana Is-C Pac)	0804-21=	0	
	1970	....	?	GROZNY GROUP (Kurile Is)	0900-07=	1	

Figure 27. Lava lake of Halemaumau, on Hawaii's Kilauea volcano. Steam obscures some of the crater wall in the background, while lava flows spilling from the active lake move toward the foreground. Photo by Richard Fiske in January 1968.

START YEAR	M-Dy	Duration	VOLCANO NAME (Subregion)	NUMBER	VEI	Vol L/T
1970	....	....	*SANTA MARIA (Guatemala)*	1402-03=	2	*8/8*
1970	....	....	*ARENAL (Costa Rica)*	1405-033	2	*7/7*
1970?	....	?	**REYKJANESHRYGGUR** (Iceland-SW)	1701-01=	0	
1970	01	89*p*	**TOLBACHIK** (Kamchatka)	1000-24=	1	
@ **1970**	0103	?	**FALCON ISLAND** (Tonga-SW Pacific)	0403-05=	0	
1970	0105d	10*d*	**BATUR** (Lesser Sunda Is)	0604-01=	1	
1970	0115	27*a*	**ULAWUN** (New Britain-SW Pac)	0502-12=	3	6/6
1970	0126	5*a*	**OSHIMA** (Izu Is-Japan)	0804-01=	1	
1970	0129	137*m*	**BAYONNAISE ROCKS** (Izu Is-Japan)	0804-07=	2	
1970	02	101*n*	**SOPUTAN** (Sulawesi-Indonesia)	0606-03=	2	
1970	02	29*p*	**KOLOKOL GROUP** (Kurile Is)	0900-12=	3	
1970	*02*	....	*BEZYMIANNY (Kamchatka)*	1000-25=	2	*7/7*
1970	0330	6*a*	**SAN MIGUEL** (El Salvador)	1403-10=	1	-/4
1970	0404	....	**MASAYA** (Nicaragua)	1404-10=	1	
1970	0421	877*m*	**ASO** (Kyushu-Japan)	0802-11=	2	
1970	0505	61*a*	**HEKLA** (Iceland-S)	1702-07=	3	8/7
1970	0509	821*a*	**LOPEVI** (Vanuatu-SW Pacific)	0507-05=	2	
1970	0511	>3yr	**KARYMSKY** (Kamchatka)	1000-13=	3	7/7
1970	0520	125*a*	**LANGILA** (New Britain-SW Pac)	0502-01=	2	
1970	0521m	451*p*>	**BAGANA** (Bougainville-SW Pac)	0505-02=	2	
1970	0526	215*a*	**KLIUCHEVSKOI** (Kamchatka)	1000-26=	2	
? **1970**	0602	11*a*	**UNNAMED** (New Britain-SW Pac)	0502-131	0	
? **1970**	0621	2*a?*	**MOUA PIHAA** (Society Is-C Pac)	1303-05-	0	
1970	0630p	?	**WHITE ISLAND** (New Zealand)	0401-04=	2	
1970	0630	132*a*	**OSHIMA** (Izu Is-Japan)	0804-01=	1	
1970	07	?	**POAS** (Costa Rica)	1405-04=	1	
1970	0726e	390*e*	**MARAPI** (Sumatra)	0601-14=	2	
1970	0812	?	**DECEPTION ISLAND** (Antarctica)	1900-03=	3	
1970	0814	1*a*	**RINCON DE LA VIEJA** (Costa Rica)	1405-02=	1	
? **1970**	0912	8*a*	**KUWAE [KARUA]** (Vanuatu-SW Pac)	0507-07=	0	
1970	0916	<1	**RUAPEHU** (New Zealand)	0401-10=	1	
1970	0918	130*a*	**AKITA-KOMAGA-TAKE** (Japan)	0803-23=	1	6/5
1970	0918	652*w?*	**JAN MAYEN** (Atl-N-Jan Mayen)	1706-01=	3	8/7
1970	1109	4*a*	**TAAL** (Luzon-Philippines)	0703-07=	1	
1970	1127	78*m*	**KARANGETANG [API SIAU]** (Sangihe	0607-02=	2	
1970	1201p	?	**TOLBACHIK** (Kamchatka)	1000-24=	2	
1970	*1212*	....	*PACAYA (Guatemala)*	1402-11=	2	
1971	*Cont*	....	*ERTA ALE (Ethiopia)*	0201-08=	*0*	
1971	*Cont*	....	*NYIRAGONGO (Africa-C)*	0203-03=	*0*	
1971	*Cont*	....	*BAGANA (Bougainville-SW Pac)*	0505-02=	*2*	
1971	*Cont*	....	*YASUR (Vanuatu-SW Pacific)*	0507-10=	*2*	
1971	*Cont*	....	*MARAPI (Sumatra)*	0601-14=	*2*	
1971	*Cont*	....	*SEMERU (Java)*	0603-30=	*2*	
1971	*Cont*	....	*KARANGETANG [API SIAU] (Sangihe*	0607-02=	*2*	
1971	*Cont*	....	*DUKONO (Halmahera-Indonesia)*	0608-01=	*2*	
1971	*Cont*	....	*SUWANOSE-JIMA (Ryukyu Is)*	0802-03=	*2*	
1971	*Cont*	....	*SAKURA-JIMA (Kyushu-Japan)*	0802-08=	*2*	
1971	*Cont*	....	*ASO (Kyushu-Japan)*	0802-11=	*2*	
1971	*Cont*	....	*AKITA-KOMAGA-TAKE (Japan)*	0803-23=	*1*	*6/5*
1971	*Cont*	....	*KARYMSKY (Kamchatka)*	1000-13=	*2*	*7/7*
1971	*Cont*	....	*SANTA MARIA (Guatemala)*	1402-03=	*1*	*8/8*
1971	*Cont*	....	*PACAYA (Guatemala)*	1402-11=	*1*	
1971	*Cont*	....	*TELICA (Nicaragua)*	1404-04=	*2*	
1971	*Cont*	....	*MASAYA (Nicaragua)*	1404-10=	*0*	
1971	*Cont*	....	*SANGAY (Ecuador)*	1502-09=	*2*	
1971	*Cont*	....	*JAN MAYEN (Atl-N-Jan Mayen)*	1706-01=	*1*	*8/7*

	START YEAR	M-Dy	Dura-tion	VOLCANO NAME (Subregion)	NUMBER	VEI	Vol L/T
	1971	....	?	**EBEKO** (Kurile Is)	0900-38=	1	
	1971	01	195m	**MERAPI** (Java)	0603-25=	1	
	1971	01	?	**LEWOTOBI** (Lesser Sunda Is)	0604-18=	2	
?	1971	01	>3yr	**TOLBACHIK** (Kamchatka)	1000-24=	1?	
	1971	0126e	....	**LANGILA** (New Britain-SW Pac)	0502-01=	2	
	1971	0203	275a	**AMBRYM** (Vanuatu-SW Pacific)	0507-04=	2	
	1971	0203	11a	**NEGRO, CERRO** (Nicaragua)	1404-07=	3	-/7
	1971	0222	<1	**KUWAE [KARUA]** (Vanuatu-SW Pac)	0507-07=	2	
	1971	*03*	....	*LOPEVI (Vanuatu-SW Pacific)*	0507-05=	2	
	1971	*03*	*>3yr*	*BEZYMIANNY (Kamchatka)*	1000-25=	2?	
	1971	0311	96m	**BATUR** (Lesser Sunda Is)	0604-01=	1	
?	1971	0318	?	**BAYONNAISE ROCKS** (Izu Is-Japan)	0804-07=	0	
	1971	0324	42d	**NYAMURAGIRA** (Africa-C)	0203-02=	3	7/7
	1971	0331	31a	**STROMBOLI** (Italy)	0101-04=	2	
	1971	*04*	....	*ARENAL (Costa Rica)*	1405-033	2	7/7
	1971	*0403*	*226m*	*RUAPEHU (New Zealand)*	0401-10=	1	-/6
	1971	0405	68a	**ETNA** (Italy)	0101-06=	2	7/6
	1971	0405	<1	**OSHIMA** (Izu Is-Japan)	0804-01=	1	
	1971	0409c	?	**WHITE ISLAND** (New Zealand)	0401-04=	2	
	1971	0503	63e	**SAN CRISTOBAL** (Nicaragua)	1404-02=	1	
	1971	0508	....	**RUAPEHU** (New Zealand)	0401-10=	2	-/6
	1971	0511	168e	**LOKON-EMPUNG** (Sulawesi-Indonesia)	0606-10=	2	2/-
	1971	0512	1a	**GAUA** (Vanuatu-SW Pacific)	0507-02=	2	
	1971	0519	<1	**SOPUTAN** (Sulawesi-Indonesia)	0606-03=	1	
?	1971	06	15m	**KERINCI** (Sumatra)	0601-17=	1?	
?	1971	06	15m	**IYA** (Lesser Sunda Is)	0604-11=	1	
	1971	06	31p	**KLIUCHEVSKOI** (Kamchatka)	1000-26=	1	
	1971	07	<1	**CHIGINAGAK** (Alaska Peninsula)	1102-11-		
	1971	0719	1a	**WHITE ISLAND** (New Zealand)	0401-04=	2	
	1971	0805	<1	**KIRISHIMA** (Kyushu-Japan)	0802-09=	1	
	1971	0812	37a>	**HUDSON, CERRO** (Chile-S)	1508-057	3	
	1971	0814	<1	**KILAUEA** (Hawaiian Is)	1302-01-	0	7/-
	1971	0906	96a	**TINAKULA** (Santa Cruz Is-SW Pac)	0506-01=	2	
?	1971	0906	?	**ROCARD** (Society Is-C Pac)	1303-04-	0	
	1971	0914	<1	**RAUNG** (Java)	0603-34=	1	
	1971	0914	<1	**FUEGO** (Guatemala)	1402-09=	3	-/7
?	1971	0917	363m	**LOIHI SEAMOUNT** (Hawaiian Is)	1302-00-	0	
	1971	0919	>3yr	**ETNA** (Italy)	0101-06=	2	
	1971	0924	5a	**KILAUEA** (Hawaiian Is)	1302-01-	0	6/-
	1971	1004f	168f	**SOUFRIERE ST. VINCENT** (W Indies)	1600-15=	0	7/-
	1971	1007	<1	**AUGUSTINE** (Alaska-SW)	1103-01-	1	
	1971	1026	22	**LA PALMA** (Canary Is)	1803-01-	2	7/-
?	1971	1028	18a?	**EAST EPI** (Vanuatu-SW Pacific)	0507-06=	0	
	1971	1029	11a	**SUNDORO** (Java)	0603-21=	2	
	1971	1029	73a	**VILLARRICA** (Chile-C)	1507-12=	2	7/-
	1971	11	761p	**KLIUCHEVSKOI** (Kamchatka)	1000-26=	1	
	1971	1201p	101m	**LLAIMA** (Chile-C)	1507-11=	2	
	1972	*Cont*	....	*STROMBOLI (Italy)*	0101-04=	1?	
	1972	*Cont*	....	*ETNA (Italy)*	0101-06=	2	
	1972	*Cont*	....	*ERTA ALE (Ethiopia)*	0201-08=	0	
	1972	*Cont*	....	*NYIRAGONGO (Africa-C)*	0203-03=	0	
	1972	*Cont*	....	*LANGILA (New Britain-SW Pac)*	0502-01=	2	
	1972	*Cont*	....	*SEMERU (Java)*	0603-30=	2	
	1972	*Cont*	....	*DUKONO (Halmahera-Indonesia)*	0608-01=	2	
	1972	*Cont*	....	*SUWANOSE-JIMA (Ryukyu Is)*	0802-03=	2	
	1972	*Cont*	....	*SAKURA-JIMA (Kyushu-Japan)*	0802-08=	2	
	1972	*Cont*	....	*ASO (Kyushu-Japan)*	0802-11=	2	
	1972	*Cont*	....	*KARYMSKY (Kamchatka)*	1000-13=	2	7/7
?	*1972*	*Cont*	....	*TOLBACHIK (Kamchatka)*	1000-24=	1?	
	1972	*Cont*	....	*KLIUCHEVSKOI (Kamchatka)*	1000-26=	2	
?	*1972*	*Cont*	....	*LOIHI SEAMOUNT (Hawaiian Is)*	1302-00-	0	
	1972	*Cont*	....	*KILAUEA (Hawaiian Is)*	1302-01-	0	8/-
	1972	*Cont*	....	*SANTA MARIA (Guatemala)*	1402-03=	1	8/8
	1972	*Cont*	....	*MASAYA (Nicaragua)*	1404-10=	0	
	1972	*Cont*	....	*ARENAL (Costa Rica)*	1405-033	1	7/7
	1972	*Cont*	....	*SANGAY (Ecuador)*	1502-09=	2	
	1972	*Cont*	....	*LLAIMA (Chile-C)*	1507-11=	2	
	1972	*Cont*	....	*VILLARRICA (Chile-C)*	1507-12=	2	7/-
	1972	*Cont*	....	*SOUFRIERE ST. VINCENT (W Indies)*	1600-15=	0	7/-
	1972	*Cont*	....	*JAN MAYEN (Atl-N-Jan Mayen)*	1706-01=	1	8/7
	1972	....	*>3yr*	*BAGANA (Bougainville-SW Pac)*	0505-02=	1	6/-
	1972	....	?	**PUTANA** (Chile-N)	1505-09=		
	1972	....	?	**LASCAR** (Chile-N)	1505-10=	2?	
	1972	....	?	**CHILLAN, NEVADOS DE** (Chile-C)	1507-07=		
	1972	*01*	*>3yr*	*KARANGETANG [API SIAU] (Sangihe*	0607-02=	2	
	1972	0103?	?	**EREBUS** (Antarctica)	1900-02=	1	
S	1972	0108	4a	**UNNAMED** (Admiralty Is-SW Pac)	0500-03-	0	
	1972	0119	55m	**BATUR** (Lesser Sunda Is)	0604-01=	2	
	1972	0126	49m	**TENGGER CALDERA [BROMO]**	0603-31=	2	
	1972	*0202*	....	*PACAYA (Guatemala)*	1402-11=	2	
	1972	*0209*	*577a*	*POAS (Costa Rica)*	1405-04=	1	
	1972	03	?	**ZHELTOVSKY** (Kamchatka)	1000-04=		
	1972	03	....	**BEZYMIANNY** (Kamchatka)	1000-25=	3	
?	1972	03	31p	**GRIMSVOTN** (Iceland-NE)	1703-01=	0	
?	1972	0305e	71j?	**KUWAE [KARUA]** (Vanuatu-SW Pac)	0507-07=	0	
	1972	0319	79a	**TONGARIRO [NGAURUHOE]** (New Z)	0401-08=	2	
	1972	*04*	....	*YASUR (Vanuatu-SW Pacific)*	0507-10=	3	
	1972	*0415*	*122a*	*AMBRYM (Vanuatu-SW Pacific)*	0507-04=	2	
	1972	*0424*	....	*LOPEVI (Vanuatu-SW Pacific)*	0507-05=	1	
S	1972	0429	<1	**UNNAMED** (Kurile Is)	0900-16-	0	
?	1972	0515e	55j?	**EAST EPI** (Vanuatu-SW Pacific)	0507-06=	0	
?	1972	0604q	?	**FERNANDINA** (Galapagos)	1503-01=	0	
	1972	0609	184a	**FOURNAISE, PITON DE LA** (Indian O.)	0303-02=	2	7/5
	1972	0610c	386p	**KRAKATAU** (Indonesia)	0602-00=	2	6/-
	1972	0618	85a	**ALAID** (Kurile Is)	0900-39=	3	7/8
?	1972	0629a	?	**GALAPAGOS RIFT** (Pacific-E)	1303-02-		
	1972	07	61p	**REVENTADOR** (Ecuador)	1502-01=	2	7/-
?	1972	0704	15a?	**ROCARD** (Society Is-C Pac)	1303-04-	0	
S	1972	0705	<1	**KICK-'EM-JENNY** (W Indies)	1600-16=	0	
	1972	0728	....	**AMBRYM** (Vanuatu-SW Pacific)	0507-04=	3	
	1972	09	? 242p>	**AKUTAN** (Aleutian Is)	1101-32-	2?	
	1972	0902	<1	**KUCHINOERABU-JIMA** (Ryukyu Is)	0802-05=	2	
	1972	0908	27a	**KARTHALA** (Indian O.-W)	0303-01=	1	6/-
?	1972	0929	<1	**DECEPTION ISLAND** (Antarctica)	1900-03=		
?	1972	10	15m	**SHIN-IWO-JIMA** (Volcano Is-Japan)	0804-13=	0	
	1972	1006	>3yr	**MERAPI** (Java)	0603-25=	3	
?	1972	1007	?	**UNNAMED** (Pacific-NE)	1301-03-	0	
	1972	1009	<1	**RITTER ISLAND** (New Guinea-NE of)	0501-07=	1	
	1972	1022	74a	**RUAPEHU** (New Zealand)	0401-10=	1	
	1972	*1022*	*86a*	*PALUWEH (Lesser Sunda Is)*	0604-15=	2?	
	1972	1024	?	**KAVACHI** (Solomon Is-SW Pac)	0505-06=	0	
	1972	1112	33m	**ACATENANGO** (Guatemala)	1402-08=	1	
	1972	*1122*	*635a*	*TONGARIRO [NGAURUHOE] (New Z)*	0401-08=	2	
	1972	12 <	>3yr	**EREBUS** (Antarctica)	1900-02=	2	
	1973	*Cont*	....	*STROMBOLI (Italy)*	0101-04=	1?	
	1973	*Cont*	....	*ETNA (Italy)*	0101-06=	2	
	1973	*Cont*	....	*ERTA ALE (Ethiopia)*	0201-08=	0	
	1973	*Cont*	....	*NYIRAGONGO (Africa-C)*	0203-03=	0	
	1973	*Cont*	....	*BAGANA (Bougainville-SW Pac)*	0505-02=	1	6/-
	1973	*Cont*	....	*YASUR (Vanuatu-SW Pacific)*	0507-10=	2	
	1973	*Cont*	....	*KRAKATAU (Indonesia)*	0602-00=	2	6/-
	1973	*Cont*	....	*KARANGETANG [API SIAU] (Sangihe*	0607-02=	2	
	1973	*Cont*	....	*DUKONO (Halmahera-Indonesia)*	0608-01=	2	
	1973	*Cont*	....	*SUWANOSE-JIMA (Ryukyu Is)*	0802-03=	2	
	1973	*Cont*	....	*KARYMSKY (Kamchatka)*	1000-13=	2	7/7
?	*1973*	*Cont*	....	*TOLBACHIK (Kamchatka)*	1000-24=	1?	
	1973	*Cont*	....	*BEZYMIANNY (Kamchatka)*	1000-25=	2?	
	1973	*Cont*	....	*KLIUCHEVSKOI (Kamchatka)*	1000-26=	2	
	1973	*Cont*	....	*AKUTAN (Aleutian Is)*	1101-32-	2	
	1973	*Cont*	....	*PACAYA (Guatemala)*	1402-11=	1	
	1973	*Cont*	....	*MASAYA (Nicaragua)*	1404-10=	0	
	1973	*Cont*	....	*ARENAL (Costa Rica)*	1405-033	1	7/7
	1973	*Cont*	....	*SANGAY (Ecuador)*	1502-09=	2	
	1973	....	?	**BATUR** (Lesser Sunda Is)	0604-01=		
?	1973	....	?	**ALAID** (Kurile Is)	0900-39=		
	1973	....	....	*SANTA MARIA (Guatemala)*	1402-03=	2	8/8
	1973	01	....	**SEMERU** (Java)	0603-30=	3	
	1973	01	881p	**ASO** (Kyushu-Japan)	0802-11=	2	
	1973	01	<1	**GROZNY GROUP** (Kurile Is)	0900-07=	1	
	1973	0102G	....	**TONGARIRO [NGAURUHOE]** (New Z)	0401-08=	3	
	1973	0106	141a	**SOPUTAN** (Sulawesi-Indonesia)	0606-03=	2	
	1973	0108	8a	**FOURNAISE, PITON DE LA** (Indian O.)	0303-02=	0	
	1973	0109	....	**PALUWEH** (Lesser Sunda Is)	0604-15=	3	
	1973	0115q	?	**JAN MAYEN** (Atl-N-Jan Mayen)	1706-01=	1	
	1973	0123	156a	**VESTMANNAEYJAR [HEIMAEY]**	1702-01=	3	8/7
	1973	0124	1a	**DEMPO** (Sumatra)	0601-23=	2	
	1973	0125	....	**POAS** (Costa Rica)	1405-04=	2	
?	1973	0130	?	**COLIMA VOLC COMPLEX** (Mexico)	1401-04=	1	
	1973	0201	111a	**ASAMA** (Honshu-Japan)	0803-11=	2	
	1973	0222	<1	**OKATAINA [WAIMANGU]** (New Zeal)	0401-05=	1	-/3
	1973	0223	40a	**FUEGO** (Guatemala)	1402-09=	2	-/6
	1973	*0224d*	*>3yr*	*LANGILA (New Britain-SW Pac)*	0502-01=	2	7/-
	1973	*0228*	....	*MERAPI (Java)*	0603-25=	2	
	1973	04	319m	**LONG ISLAND** (New Guinea-NE of)	0501-05=	2	3/-
	1973	04	365p	**ILIBOLENG** (Lesser Sunda Is)	0604-22=	2	
	1973	0412	388d	**NISHINO-SHIMA** (Volcano Is-Japan)	0804-092	2	
	1973	*0415e*	*>3yr*	*AMBRYM (Vanuatu-SW Pacific)*	0507-04=	2	
	1973	05	153p	**RAUNG** (Java)	0603-34=	1	
?	1973	05	?	**GALERAS** (Colombia)	1501-08=	2	
?	1973	0505d	173i?	**EAST EPI** (Vanuatu-SW Pacific)	0507-06=	0	
?	1973	0505d	163m	**KUWAE [KARUA]** (Vanuatu-SW Pac)	0507-07=	0	
	1973	0505	<1	**KILAUEA** (Hawaiian Is)	1302-01-	0	6/-
	1973	0510	118a	**FOURNAISE, PITON DE LA** (Indian O.)	0303-02=	2	5/-
	1973	0516	1a	**GROZNY GROUP** (Kurile Is)	0900-07=	2?	
	1973	*0601*	....	*SAKURA-JIMA (Kyushu-Japan)*	0802-08=	3	
?	1973	07	?	**UNNAMED** (Samoa-SW Pacific)	0404-00-		
	1973	07	>3yr	**CHILLAN, NEVADOS DE** (Chile-C)	1507-07=	2	5/-
	1973	0711	5a	**CURACOA** (Tonga-SW Pacific)	0403-101	3	
	1973	0714	14a	**TIATIA** (Kurile Is)	0900-03=	4	-/8
	1973	0724	<1	**MARAPI** (Sumatra)	0601-14=	2	
	1973	0725	1a	**KOLOKOL GROUP** (Kurile Is)	0900-12=	1	
	1973	08	?	**SLAMET** (Java)	0603-18=	1?	
	1973	0810	49a	**CHIKURACHKI** (Kurile Is)	0900-36=	2	-/6
	1973	0825b	?	**ATKA [KOROVIN]** (Aleutian Is)	1101-16-	0	
	1973	0915	456m	**LOKON-EMPUNG** (Sulawesi-Indonesia)	0606-10=	1	
	1973	0927	148a	**FUKUJIN** (Volcano Is-Japan)	0804-133	1	
	1973	1004	15a	**ULAWUN** (New Britain-SW Pac)	0502-12=	2	7/6
	1973	1009	104a	**GAUA** (Vanuatu-SW Pacific)	0507-02=	2	
S	1973	1015	1	**RUMBLE III** (New Zealand)	0401-13-	0	
?	1973	1025	4a?	**WOLF, VOLCAN** (Galapagos)	1503-02=		
	1973	1027	1a	**PALUWEH** (Lesser Sunda Is)	0604-15=	2	
	1973	1031	383o	**RUAPEHU** (New Zealand)	0401-10=	1	
	1973	11	242p	**REVENTADOR** (Ecuador)	1502-01=	3	6/-
	1973	1105	14	**KUCHINOERABU-JIMA** (Ryukyu Is)	0802-05=	2	
	1973	1110	29a	**KILAUEA** (Hawaiian Is)	1302-01-	0	6/-
	1973	*1111*	....	*EREBUS (Antarctica)*	1900-02=	1	
	1973	1112	1a	**PAVLOF** (Alaska Peninsula)	1102-03-	2	-/6
	1973	12	....	**AMBRYM** (Vanuatu-SW Pacific)	0507-04=	3	
	1973	*1205*	*260a*	*ILIWERUNG (Lesser Sunda Is)*	0604-25=	0	
	1973	*1207*	....	*TONGARIRO [NGAURUHOE] (New Z)*	0401-08=	2	
	1973	1209	6a	**FERNANDINA** (Galapagos)	1503-01=	2	
	1973	*1218*	*60a*	*SHIN-IWO-JIMA (Volcano Is-Japan)*	0804-13=	0	
	1973	1224	19a	**CONCEPCION** (Nicaragua)	1404-12=	2	
	1974	*Cont*	....	*STROMBOLI (Italy)*	0101-04=	1?	

	START YEAR	M-Dy	Duration	VOLCANO NAME (Subregion)	NUMBER	VEI	Vol L/T
	1974	Cont	....	ERTA ALE (Ethiopia)	0201-08=	0	
	1974	Cont	....	NYIRAGONGO (Africa-C)	0203-03=	0	
	1974	Cont	....	RUAPEHU (New Zealand)	0401-10=	1	
	1974	Cont	....	LONG ISLAND (New Guinea-NE of)	0501-05=	2	3/-
	1974	Cont	....	BAGANA (Bougainville-SW Pac)	0505-02=	1	6/-
	1974	Cont	....	YASUR (Vanuatu-SW Pacific)	0507-10=	2	
	1974	Cont	....	MERAPI (Java)	0603-25=	1	
	1974	Cont	....	ILIBOLENG (Lesser Sunda Is)	0604-22=	2	
	1974	Cont	....	LOKON-EMPUNG (Sulawesi-Indonesia)	0606-10=	1	
	1974	Cont	....	DUKONO (Halmahera-Indonesia)	0608-01=	2	
	1974	Cont	....	SUWANOSE-JIMA (Ryukyu Is)	0802-03=	2	
	1974	Cont	....	SAKURA-JIMA (Kyushu-Japan)	0802-08=	2	
	1974	Cont	....	ASO (Kyushu-Japan)	0802-11=	2	
	1974	Cont	....	NISHINO-SHIMA (Volcano Is-Japan)	0804-092	2	
	1974	Cont	....	FUKUJIN (Volcano Is-Japan)	0804-133	1	
	1974	Cont	....	KARYMSKY (Kamchatka)	1000-13=	2	7/7
?	1974	Cont	....	TOLBACHIK (Kamchatka)	1000-24=	1?	
	1974	Cont	....	BEZYMIANNY (Kamchatka)	1000-25=	2?	
	1974	Cont	....	SANTA MARIA (Guatemala)	1402-03=	1	8/8
	1974	Cont	....	PACAYA (Guatemala)	1402-11=	1	
	1974	Cont	....	MASAYA (Nicaragua)	1404-10=	0	
	1974	Cont	....	CONCEPCION (Nicaragua)	1404-12=	2	
	1974	Cont	....	SANGAY (Ecuador)	1502-09=	2	
	1974	....	....	LANGILA (New Britain-SW Pac)	0502-01=	2	7/-
	1974	....	....	SEMERU (Java)	0603-30=	3	
	1974	....	>3yr	GALERAS (Colombia)	1501-08=	1?	
	1974	01	264m	LOPEVI (Vanuatu-SW Pacific)	0507-05=	2	
?	1974	01	?	IWO-JIMA (Volcano Is-Japan)	0804-12=	0	
	1974	0111	....	GAUA (Vanuatu-SW Pacific)	0507-02=	2	
	1974	0122	....	TONGARIRO [NGAURUHOE] (New Z)	0401-08=	3	
	1974	0130	58a	ETNA (Italy)	0101-06=	2	6/6
	1974	0204d	223m?	KUWAE [KARUA] (Vanuatu-SW Pac)	0507-07=	0	
	1974	0211	....	KARANGETANG [API SIAU] (Sangihe	0607-02=	3	
	1974	0211<	?	AKUTAN (Aleutian Is)	1101-32-	2	
	1974	0214	175a	KARKAR (New Guinea-NE of)	0501-03=	2	7/-
?	1974	0216	?	FONUALEI (Tonga-SW Pacific)	0403-10=	2	
	1974	0216	....	SHIN-IWO-JIMA (Volcano Is-Japan)	0804-13=	2	
	1974	0219	208m	GREAT SITKIN (Aleutian Is)	1101-12-	2	7/-
	1974	0226	236a	DEMPO (Sumatra)	0601-23=	2	
	1974	0228	114a	OSHIMA (Izu Is-Japan)	0804-01=	2	
?	1974	03	?	UNNAMED (Volcano Is-Japan)	0804-093	0	
	1974	0301	60a	CHOKAI (Honshu-Japan)	0803-22=	1	-/5
	1974	0303	....	CHILLAN, NEVADOS DE (Chile-C)	1507-07=	2	5/-
	1974	0304?	>3yr	MANAM (New Guinea-NE of)	0501-02=	3	7/-
	1974	0312	34m	BATUR (Lesser Sunda Is)	0604-01=	2	
S	1974	0312?	2a	PAVLOF (Alaska Peninsula)	1102-03-	2?	
	1974	0328	....	TONGARIRO [NGAURUHOE] (New Z)	0401-08=	3	
	1974	0401	....	ARENAL (Costa Rica)	1405-033	2	7/7
	1974	0408	251m?	KLIUCHEVSKOI (Kamchatka)	1000-26=	3	7/6
?	1974	0529	<1	SLAMET (Java)	0603-18=	2	
	1974	0603	<1	KUCHINOERABU-JIMA (Ryukyu Is)	0802-05=	1	
	1974	0615	32a?	RAUNG (Java)	0603-34=	2	
	1974	07	....	ILIWERUNG (Lesser Sunda Is)	0604-25=	2	
	1974	07	....	REVENTADOR (Ecuador)	1502-01=	2	6/-
	1974	07	61p	LASCAR (Chile-N)	1505-10=	1	
	1974	0715q	183w	TRIDENT (Alaska Peninsula)	1102-16-	3	
	1974	0719	2	KILAUEA (Hawaiian Is)	1302-01-	0	7/-
?	1974	0722?	5a?	CENTRAL ISLAND (Africa-E)	0202-01=		
	1974	0728	<1	NIIGATA-YAKE-YAMA (Honshu-Japan)	0803-09=	2	-/5
	1974	0823	....	KLIUCHEVSKOI (Kamchatka)	1000-26=	2	7/6
	1974	0901<	69a	PAVLOF (Alaska Peninsula)	1102-03-	2?	
	1974	0905	<1	KICK-'EM-JENNY (W Indies)	1600-16=	0	
	1974	0908j	?	WHITE ISLAND (New Zealand)	0401-04=	2	
	1974	0911	156m	POAS (Costa Rica)	1405-04=	2	
	1974	0919	<1	KILAUEA (Hawaiian Is)	1302-01-	0	7/-
	1974	0929	>3yr	ETNA (Italy)	0101-06=	2	7/-
	1974	1010	55a	FUEGO (Guatemala)	1402-09=	1	-/8
	1974	1017	<1	RITTER ISLAND (New Guinea-NE of)	0501-07=	1	
	1974	1029	....	PAVLOF (Alaska Peninsula)	1102-03-	3	
?	1974	11	15m?	EAST EPI (Vanuatu-SW Pacific)	0507-06=	0	
	1974	11	....	EREBUS (Antarctica)	1900-02=	1	
	1974	1112	30a?	KAVACHI (Solomon Is-SW Pac)	0505-06=	1	
	1974	1220	....	AMBRYM (Vanuatu-SW Pacific)	0507-04=	2	
	1974	1224	324a	SHIN-IWO-JIMA (Volcano Is-Japan)	0804-13=	2	
	1974	1230?	188a?	KARKAR (New Guinea-NE of)	0501-03=	2	6/-
	1974	1231	<1	KILAUEA (Hawaiian Is)	1302-01-	0	7/-
	1975	Cont	....	ERTA ALE (Ethiopia)	0201-08=	0	
	1975	Cont	....	NYIRAGONGO (Africa-C)	0203-03=	0	
	1975	Cont	....	MANAM (New Guinea-NE of)	0501-02=	2	7/-
	1975	Cont	....	KARKAR (New Guinea-NE of)	0501-03=	2	6/-
	1975	Cont	....	LANGILA (New Britain-SW Pac)	0502-01=	2	7/-
	1975	Cont		AMBRYM (Vanuatu-SW Pacific)	0507-04=	2	
	1975	Cont	....	YASUR (Vanuatu-SW Pacific)	0507-10=	2	
	1975	Cont	....	MERAPI (Java)	0603-25=	1	
	1975	Cont	....	SEMERU (Java)	0603-30=	2	
	1975	Cont	....	KARANGETANG [API SIAU] (Sangihe	0607-02=	2	
	1975	Cont	....	DUKONO (Halmahera-Indonesia)	0608-01=	2	
	1975	Cont	....	SUWANOSE-JIMA (Ryukyu Is)	0802-03=	2	
	1975	Cont	....	SAKURA-JIMA (Kyushu-Japan)	0802-08=	2	
	1975	Cont	....	SHIN-IWO-JIMA (Volcano Is-Japan)	0804-13=	2	
	1975	Cont	....	KARYMSKY (Kamchatka)	1000-13=	2	7/7
	1975	Cont	....	TRIDENT (Alaska Peninsula)	1102-16-	3	
	1975	Cont	....	PACAYA (Guatemala)	1402-11=	1	
	1975	Cont	....	MASAYA (Nicaragua)	1404-10=	0	
	1975	Cont	....	POAS (Costa Rica)	1405-04=	2	
	1975	Cont	....	GALERAS (Colombia)	1501-08=	1?	
	1975	Cont	....	SANGAY (Ecuador)	1502-09=	2	
	1975	Cont	....	CHILLAN, NEVADOS DE (Chile-C)	1507-07=	2	5/-
?	1975	....	?	NISHINO-SHIMA (Volcano Is-Japan)	0804-092	0	
	1975	....	....	EREBUS (Antarctica)	1900-02=	2	
	1975	01	>3yr	MARAPI (Sumatra)	0601-14=	2	
	1975	0212	11a	TONGARIRO [NGAURUHOE] (New Z)	0401-08=	3	-/6
	1975	0224	186a	ETNA (Italy)	0101-06=	1	6/-
	1975	03	60p	RAUNG (Java)	0603-34=	1	
	1975	0306c	109c	LOPEVI (Vanuatu-SW Pacific)	0507-05=	2	
	1975	0327	213e	KRAKATAU (Indonesia)	0602-00=	2	6/-
	1975	04	....	BAGANA (Bougainville-SW Pac)	0505-02=	2	6/-
	1975	04	....	SANTA MARIA (Guatemala)	1402-03=	2	8/8
	1975	0424	3	RUAPEHU (New Zealand)	0401-10=	2	
?	1975	0426	3a	ESMERALDA BANK (Mariana Is-C Pac)	0804-21=	0	
	1975	05	304p	TELICA (Nicaragua)	1404-04=	0	
	1975	0528	166a	FUEGO (Guatemala)	1402-09=	2	
	1975	0617	....	ARENAL (Costa Rica)	1405-033	2	7/7
	1975	0628	530a	TOLBACHIK (Kamchatka)	1000-24=	1	9/8
	1975	0705	<1	MAUNA LOA (Hawaiian Is)	1302-02=	0	7/-
	1975	0706	....	TOLBACHIK (Kamchatka)	1000-24=	4	9/8
	1975	08	?	KAVACHI (Solomon Is-SW Pac)	0505-06=	1	
?	1975	0824?	83m	LOIHI SEAMOUNT (Hawaiian Is)	1302-00-	0	
	1975	0825	?	MINAMI-HIYOSHI (Volcano Is-Japan)	0804-131	0	
?	1975	09	?	CLEVELAND (Aleutian Is)	1101-24-		
?	1975	0910	?	OMACHI SEAMOUNT (Izu Is-Japan)	0804-091	0	
?	1975	0910	?	UNNAMED (Mariana Is-C Pac)	0804-135	0	
?	1975	0910	?	UNNAMED (Mariana Is-C Pac)	0804-136	0	
	1975	0913	43e	SHISHALDIN (Aleutian Is)	1101-36-	2	
	1975	0913	549m>	PAVLOF (Alaska Peninsula)	1102-03-	2	-/7
	1975	10	89m	ASO (Kyushu-Japan)	0802-11=	1	
	1975	1002	?	TORI-SHIMA (Izu Is-Japan)	0804-09=	2	
	1975	1017<	<1	RUAPEHU (New Zealand)	0401-10=	1	
	1975	11 <	>3yr	LOKON-EMPUNG (Sulawesi-Indonesia)	0606-10=	1	4/-
?	1975	11	?	KASUGA SEAMOUNT (Volcano Is)	0804-134	0	
	1975	11	218m	COLIMA VOLC COMPLEX (Mexico)	1401-04=	2	8/-
	1975	1104	20a	STROMBOLI (Italy)	0101-04=	1	4/5
	1975	1104	154a	FOURNAISE, PITON DE LA (Indian O.)	0303-02=	1	7/5
	1975	1129	<1	KILAUEA (Hawaiian Is)	1302-01-	0	5/-
	1975	1220	<1	KRAFLA (Iceland-NE)	1703-08=	0	5/-
	1976	Cont	....	STROMBOLI (Italy)	0101-04=	1?	
	1976	Cont	....	ETNA (Italy)	0101-06=	2	7/-
	1976	Cont	....	ERTA ALE (Ethiopia)	0201-08=	0	
	1976	Cont	....	NYIRAGONGO (Africa-C)	0203-03=	0	
	1976	Cont	....	MANAM (New Guinea-NE of)	0501-02=	2	7/-
	1976	Cont	....	LANGILA (New Britain-SW Pac)	0502-01=	2	7/-
	1976	Cont	....	BAGANA (Bougainville-SW Pac)	0505-02=	1	6/-
	1976	Cont	....	YASUR (Vanuatu-SW Pacific)	0507-10=	2	
	1976	Cont	....	MARAPI (Sumatra)	0601-14=	1	
	1976	Cont	....	LOKON-EMPUNG (Sulawesi-Indonesia)	0606-10=	1	4/-
	1976	Cont	....	DUKONO (Halmahera-Indonesia)	0608-01=	2	
	1976	Cont	....	SUWANOSE-JIMA (Ryukyu Is)	0802-03=	2	
	1976	Cont	....	SAKURA-JIMA (Kyushu-Japan)	0802-08=	2	
	1976	Cont	....	ASO (Kyushu-Japan)	0802-11=	1	
	1976	Cont	....	KARYMSKY (Kamchatka)	1000-13=	2	7/7
	1976	Cont	....	TOLBACHIK (Kamchatka)	1000-24=	1	9/8
	1976	Cont	....	COLIMA VOLC COMPLEX (Mexico)	1401-04=	2	8/-
	1976	Cont	....	PACAYA (Guatemala)	1402-11=	1	
	1976	Cont	....	MASAYA (Nicaragua)	1404-10=	0	
	1976	Cont	....	GALERAS (Colombia)	1501-08=	1?	
	1976	Cont	....	SANGAY (Ecuador)	1502-09=	2	
	1976	Cont	....	CHILLAN, NEVADOS DE (Chile-C)	1507-07=	2	5/-
	1976	Cont	....	EREBUS (Antarctica)	1900-02=	1	
	1976	....	?	IWO-JIMA (Volcano Is-Japan)	0804-12=	1	
?	1976	....	?	ATKA [KOROVIN] (Aleutian Is)	1101-16-		
	1976	0102u	?	LONG ISLAND (New Guinea-NE of)	0501-05=	1	
	1976	0104	133m	REVENTADOR (Ecuador)	1502-01=	2	7/-
	1976	0115e	?	GAUA (Vanuatu-SW Pacific)	0507-02=	2	
	1976	0122?	477a?	AUGUSTINE (Alaska-SW)	1103-01-	4	7/8
?	1976	02	?	MINAMI-HIYOSHI (Volcano Is-Japan)	0804-131	0	
	1976	0204	....	MERAPI (Java)	0603-25=	2	
	1976	0302	<1	KUSATSU-SHIRANE (Honshu-Japan)	0803-12=	2	
	1976	0309	7a	SAN CRISTOBAL (Nicaragua)	1404-02=	1	
	1976	0325	?	BEZYMIANNY (Kamchatka)	1000-25=	2	
	1976	0402	<1	KUCHINOERABU-JIMA (Ryukyu Is)	0802-05=	2	
	1976	0406	<1	RUAPEHU (New Zealand)	0401-10=	1	
	1976	0406	175a?	SHISHALDIN (Aleutian Is)	1101-36-	2	
	1976	0501	126a	LOPEVI (Vanuatu-SW Pacific)	0507-05=	1	
	1976	0507	....	SANTA MARIA (Guatemala)	1402-03=	3	8/8
	1976	0524	....	AMBRYM (Vanuatu-SW Pacific)	0507-04=	2	
	1976	0607	167a	RAUNG (Java)	0603-34=	2	
	1976	0621	147m	POAS (Costa Rica)	1405-04=	2	
	1976	0708	236a	SOUFRIERE GUADELOUPE (W Indies)	1600-06=	2	-/5
?	1976	08	>3yr	SHIN-IWO-JIMA (Volcano Is-Japan	0804-13=	0	
?	1976	0802	262a	FUKUJIN (Volcano Is-Japan)	0804-133	0	
	1976	0823	5a	TONGARIRO [NGAURUHOE] (New Z)	0401-08=	1	
	1976	0824	50a?	KAVACHI (Solomon Is-SW Pac)	0505-06=	1	
	1976	0829	<1	SAN CRISTOBAL (Nicaragua)	1404-02=	1	
	1976	0831	....	SEMERU (Java)	0603-30=	2	
	1976	0903	44a	TAAL (Luzon-Philippines)	0703-07=	2	-/6
	1976	0915	365m	KARANGETANG [API SIAU] (Sangihe	0607-02=	2	7/-
	1976	0923	9a	SARYCHEV PEAK (Kurile Is)	0900-24=	2	6/-
	1976	0927	....	SHISHALDIN (Aleutian Is)	1101-36-	2	
	1976	1012	....	ARENAL (Costa Rica)	1405-033	2	7/7
	1976	1015q	205q>	AKUTAN (Aleutian Is)	1101-32-	2	
	1976	11	17d	RUAPEHU (New Zealand)	0401-10=	1	
	1976	1102	2a	FOURNAISE, PITON DE LA (Indian O.)	0303-02=	1	5/4
	1976	1103	438m>	TELICA (Nicaragua)	1404-04=	1	
	1976	1110	....	PAVLOF (Alaska Peninsula)	1102-03-	2	-/7
?	1976	1127	?	MATTHEW ISLAND (SW Pacific)	0508-01=	1?	
?	1976	12	102a	MINAMI-HIYOSHI (Volcano Is-Japan)	0804-131	0	

	START YEAR	M-Dy	Duration	VOLCANO NAME (Subregion)	NUMBER	VEI	Vol L/T
	1976	1202	77a	**SAN MIGUEL** (El Salvador)	1403-10=	1	6/-
	1976	*1218*	>3yr	*WHITE ISLAND (New Zealand)*	0401-04=	2	-/7
	1976	1223	174e	**NYAMURAGIRA** (Africa-C)	0203-02=	1	7/7
	1977	*Cont*	....	*STROMBOLI (Italy)*	0101-04=	1?	
	1977	*Cont*	....	*ETNA (Italy)*	0101-06=	2	7/-
	1977	*Cont*	....	*ERTA ALE (Ethiopia)*	0201-08=	0	
	1977	*Cont*	....	*NYAMURAGIRA (Africa-C)*	0203-02=	1	7/7
	1977	*Cont*	....	*MANAM (New Guinea-NE of)*	0501-02=	2	7/-
	1977	*Cont*	....	*LANGILA (New Britain-SW Pac)*	0502-01=	2	7/-
	1977	*Cont*	....	*BAGANA (Bougainville-SW Pac)*	0505-02=	1	6/-
	1977	*Cont*	....	*MARAPI (Sumatra)*	0601-14=	1	
	1977	*Cont*	....	*MERAPI (Java)*	0603-25=	1	
	1977	*Cont*	....	*SEMERU (Java)*	0603-30=	2	
	1977	*Cont*	....	*KARANGETANG [API SIAU] (Sangihe*	0607-02=	1	7/-
	1977	*Cont*	....	*DUKONO (Halmahera-Indonesia)*	0608-01=	2	
	1977	*Cont*	....	*SUWANOSE-JIMA (Ryukyu Is)*	0802-03=	2	
	1977	*Cont*	....	*SAKURA-JIMA (Kyushu-Japan)*	0802-08=	2	
?	*1977*	*Cont*	....	*MINAMI-HIYOSHI (Volcano Is-Japan)*	0804-131	0	
?	*1977*	*Cont*	....	*SHIN-IWO-JIMA (Volcano Is-Japan)*	0804-13=	0	
	1977	*Cont*	....	*KARYMSKY (Kamchatka)*	1000-13=	2	7/7
	1977	*Cont*	....	*AKUTAN (Aleutian Is)*	1101-32-	2	
	1977	*Cont*	....	*PAVLOF (Alaska Peninsula)*	1102-03-	2	-/7
	1977	*Cont*	....	*SAN MIGUEL (El Salvador)*	1403-10=	1	6/-
	1977	*Cont*	....	*TELICA (Nicaragua)*	1404-04=	1	
	1977	*Cont*	....	*MASAYA (Nicaragua)*	1404-10=	0	
	1977	*Cont*	....	*ARENAL (Costa Rica)*	1405-033	1	7/7
	1977	*Cont*	....	*GALERAS (Colombia)*	1501-08=	1?	
	1977	*Cont*	....	*SANGAY (Ecuador)*	1502-09=	2	
	1977	*Cont*	....	*CHILLAN, NEVADOS DE (Chile-C)*	1507-07=	2	5/-
	1977	*Cont*	....	*SOUFRIERE GUADELOUPE (W Ind)*	1600-06=	1	-/5
	1977	*Cont*	....	*EREBUS (Antarctica)*	1900-02=	1	
	1977	0110	<1	**NYIRAGONGO** (Africa-C)	0203-03=	1	7/4
S	**1977**	0114	<1	**KICK-'EM-JENNY** (W Indies)	1600-16=	0	
	1977	0120e	8e?	**AMBRYM** (Vanuatu-SW Pacific)	0507-04=	2	
	1977	0126	4a	**VILLARRICA** (Chile-C)	1507-12=	1	
?	**1977**	0201	?	**KUWAE [KARUA]** (Vanuatu-SW Pac)	0507-07=	0	
	1977	*0209*	....	*SANTA MARIA (Guatemala)*	1402-03=	3	8/8
	1977	0222	?	**KAVACHI** (Solomon Is-SW Pac)	0505-06=	1	
	1977	0303	47a	**FUEGO** (Guatemala)	1402-09=	1	-/4
	1977	0306	2a?	**SEGUAM** (Aleutian Is)	1101-18-	1	
	1977	*0311*	....	*WHITE ISLAND (New Zealand)*	0401-04=	2	-/7
	1977	0319	9a?	**PURACE** (Colombia)	1501-06=	2	
	1977	0323	4a	**FERNANDINA** (Galapagos)	1503-01=	1	
	1977	0324	23a	**FOURNAISE, PITON DE LA** (Indian O.)	0303-02=	0	6/-
	1977	0325	?	**BEZYMIANNY** (Kamchatka)	1000-25=	3	5/7
	1977	0328	<1	**LOKON-EMPUNG** (Sulawesi-Indonesia)	0606-10=	2	4/-
	1977	0330	10a	**UKINREK MAARS** (Alaska Peninsula)	1102-13B	3	5/7
S	**1977**	04	15m	**MONOWAI SEAMOUNT** (Kermadec Is)	0402-05-	0	
	1977	0404	29a	**CONCEPCION** (Nicaragua)	1404-12=	2	
	1977	0405	5a	**KARTHALA** (Indian O.-W)	0303-01=	1	6/5
	1977	0411	492m	**ASO** (Kyushu-Japan)	0802-11=	2	
	1977	*0411*	....	*AUGUSTINE (Alaska-SW)*	1103-01-	1	7/8
	1977	0413	<1	**GAUA** (Vanuatu-SW Pacific)	0507-02=	2	
	1977	0427	134	**KRAFLA** (Iceland-NE)	1703-08=	1	6/1
	1977	05	60p?	**POAS** (Costa Rica)	1405-04=	1	
	1977	0609	21a	**RAUNG** (Java)	0603-34=	2	
	1977	*07*	550m	*RUAPEHU (New Zealand)*	0401-10=	1	-/5
	1977	0704	<1	**TONGARIRO [NGAURUHOE]** (New Z)	0401-08=	1	
	1977	0717?	5a?	**KAVACHI** (Solomon Is-SW Pac)	0505-06=	1	
	1977	08	45m	**AMBRYM** (Vanuatu-SW Pacific)	0507-04=	2	
	1977	*0802*	952a	*KLIUCHEVSKOI (Kamchatka)*	1000-26=	2	5/7
	1977	0807	>3yr	**USU** (Hokkaido-Japan)	0805-03=	3	-/7
	1977	*0819*	....	*PACAYA (Guatemala)*	1402-11=	2	
	1977	0825	....	**WHITE ISLAND** (New Zealand)	0401-04=	3	-/7
	1977	0911	696a	**FUEGO** (Guatemala)	1402-09=	2	-/6
	1977	0913	17	**KILAUEA** (Hawaiian Is)	1302-01-	0	7/-
	1977	*10*	....	*YASUR (Vanuatu-SW Pacific)*	0507-10=	3	
	1977	1003	39a?	**TAAL** (Luzon-Philippines)	0703-07=	2	
?	**1977**	1014	161a	**FUKUJIN** (Volcano Is-Japan)	0804-133	0	
	1977	1016	<1	**SAN CRISTOBAL** (Nicaragua)	1404-02=	2	
	1977	1017	549a>	**MONOWAI SEAMOUNT** (Kermadec Is)	0402-05-	0	
	1977	1024	24	**FOURNAISE, PITON DE LA** (Indian O.)	0303-02=	1	7/-
	1977	1102	....	**RUAPEHU** (New Zealand)	0401-10=	2	-/5
	1977	1116	?	**MAHAWU** (Sulawesi-Indonesia)	0606-11=	0	
	1977	12	>3yr	**COLIMA VOLC COMPLEX** (Mexico)	1401-04=	1	5/-
	1977	1207	<1	**AZUMA** (Honshu-Japan)	0803-18=	1	
S	**1977**	1210	5	**MACDONALD** (Austral Is-C Pac)	1303-07-	0	
	1977	1218	159e	**POAS** (Costa Rica)	1405-04=	2	
	1978	*Cont*	....	*STROMBOLI (Italy)*	0101-04=	1?	
	1978	*Cont*	....	*ERTA ALE (Ethiopia)*	0201-08=	0	
	1978	*Cont*	....	*WHITE ISLAND (New Zealand)*	0401-04=	2	-/7
	1978	*Cont*	....	*RUAPEHU (New Zealand)*	0401-10=	1	-/5
	1978	*Cont*	....	*MONOWAI SEAMOUNT (Kermadec Is)*	0402-05-	0	
	1978	*Cont*	....	*MANAM (New Guinea-NE of)*	0501-02=	2	7/-
	1978	*Cont*	....	*LANGILA (New Britain-SW Pac)*	0502-01=	2	7/-
	1978	*Cont*	....	*BAGANA (Bougainville-SW Pac)*	0505-02=	1	6/-
	1978	*Cont*	....	*YASUR (Vanuatu-SW Pacific)*	0507-10=	2	
	1978	*Cont*	....	*MERAPI (Java)*	0603-25=	1	
	1978	*Cont*	....	*SUWANOSE-JIMA (Ryukyu Is)*	0802-03=	2	
	1978	*Cont*	....	*SAKURA-JIMA (Kyushu-Japan)*	0802-08=	2	
	1978	*Cont*	....	*ASO (Kyushu-Japan)*	0802-11=	1	
?	*1978*	*Cont*	....	*SHIN-IWO-JIMA (Volcano Is-Japan)*	0804-13=	0	
	1978	*Cont*	....	*KARYMSKY (Kamchatka)*	1000-13=	2	7/7
	1978	*Cont*	....	*KLIUCHEVSKOI (Kamchatka)*	1000-26=	2	5/7
	1978	*Cont*	....	*COLIMA VOLC COMPLEX (Mexico)*	1401-04=	1	5/-
	1978	*Cont*	....	*SANTA MARIA (Guatemala)*	1402-03=	1	8/8
	1978	*Cont*	....	*FUEGO (Guatemala)*	1402-09=	2	-/6
	1978	*Cont*	....	*PACAYA (Guatemala)*	1402-11=	1	

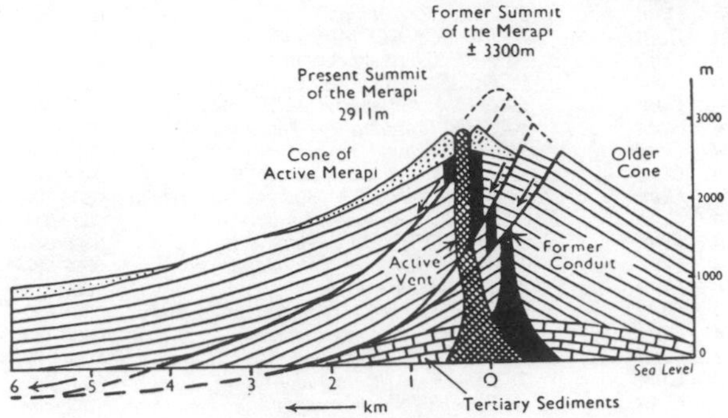

Figure 28. Cross-section of Merapi, central Java, shows the structural complexity of some volcanoes, in contrast to the apparent simplicity of symmetrical stratovolcanoes like Kliuchevskoi (opposite). Holmes, 1965, after van Bemmelen, 1949 (see note 51, p. 33 and REFERENCES 0601).

	START YEAR	M-Dy	Duration	VOLCANO NAME (Subregion)	NUMBER	VEI	Vol L/T
	1978	*Cont*	....	*TELICA (Nicaragua)*	1404-04=	1	
	1978	*Cont*	....	*MASAYA (Nicaragua)*	1404-10=	0	
	1978	*Cont*	....	*ARENAL (Costa Rica)*	1405-033	1	7/7
	1978	*Cont*	....	*GALERAS (Colombia)*	1501-08=	1?	
	1978	*Cont*	....	*SANGAY (Ecuador)*	1502-09=	2	
	1978	*Cont*	....	*CHILLAN, NEVADOS DE (Chile-C)*	1507-07=	2	5/-
	1978	*Cont*	....	*EREBUS (Antarctica)*	1900-02=	1	
	1978	*01*	....	*SEMERU (Java)*	0603-30=	1	
	1978	01	700p>	**RAUNG** (Java)	0603-34=	1	
	1978	*01*	....	*LOKON-EMPUNG (Sulawesi-Indonesia)*	0606-10=	1	4/-
	1978	0106	3a	**DIDICAS** (Luzon Is-N of)	0704-02=	2	
	1978	*0113*	....	*USU (Hokkaido-Japan)*	0805-03=	2	-/7
?	**1978**	0126?	57a?	**MINAMI-HIYOSHI** (Volcano Is-Japan)	0804-131	0	
	1978	0204	5a	**WESTDAHL** (Aleutian Is)	1101-34-	3	
	1978	0208	<1	**SHISHALDIN** (Aleutian Is)	1101-36-	2	
	1978	0222	299a	**KARANGETANG [API SIAU]** (Sangihe	0607-02=	1	
	1978	*0307*	193m?	*MAYON (Luzon-Philippines)*	0703-03=	1	7/-
	1978	0330<	35d>	**CONCEPCION** (Nicaragua)	1404-12=	2	
?	**1978**	0331	?	**UNNAMED** (Kurile Is)	0900-13-	0	
	1978	0429	36	**ETNA** (Italy)	0101-06=	2	7/-
	1978	0507	7a	**ULAWUN** (New Britain-SW Pac)	0502-12=	3	6/7
	1978	0507	....	**MAYON** (Luzon-Philippines)	0703-03=	2	7/-
	1978	0514	3a	**SHIKOTSU [TARUMAI]** (Hokkaido)	0805-04=	1	-/4
	1978	0621	31f	**KAVACHI** (Solomon Is-SW Pac)	0505-06=	2	
	1978	0627	67a	**CANLAON** (Philippines-C)	0702-02=	2	
	1978	*07*	....	*DUKONO (Halmahera-Indonesia)*	0608-01=	3	
	1978	0710	127m	**KRAKATAU** (Indonesia)	0602-00=	1	-/4
	1978	0720	?	**TIATIA** (Kurile Is)	0900-03=	2	
	1978	0729	16a	**BULUSAN** (Luzon-Philippines)	0703-01=	2	-/5
	1978	0808	18a	**FERNANDINA** (Galapagos)	1503-01=	2	6/-
	1978	0824	5	**ETNA** (Italy)	0101-06=	2	6/-
?	**1978**	0824	1a	**FUKUJIN** (Volcano Is-Japan)	0804-133	0	
	1978	*0908*	....	*MARAPI (Sumatra)*	0601-14=	2	
	1978	0908p	?	**BEZYMIANNY** (Kamchatka)	1000-25=	2	
	1978	0922	84m	**POAS** (Costa Rica)	1405-04=	1	
	1978	0925e	21m	**AKUTAN** (Aleutian Is)	1101-32-	2	
	1978	1107	7a	**ARDOUKOBA** (Djibouti)	0201-126	1	7/-
?	**1978**	1116	?	**NISHINO-SHIMA** (Volcano Is-Japan)	0804-092	0	
	1978	1118	11a	**ETNA** (Italy)	0101-06=	2	6/-
	1978	*1122*	113m	*LOPEVI (Vanuatu-SW Pacific)*	0507-05=	0	
	1978	1211	<1	**IWO-JIMA** (Volcano Is-Japan)	0804-12=	1	
	1978	1212	150a	**SHIKOTSU [TARUMAI]** (Hokkaido)	0805-04=	1	
	1979	*Cont*	....	*STROMBOLI (Italy)*	0101-04=	1?	
	1979	*Cont*	....	*ERTA ALE (Ethiopia)*	0201-08=	0	
	1979	*Cont*	....	*WHITE ISLAND (New Zealand)*	0401-04=	2	-/7
	1979	*Cont*	....	*MONOWAI SEAMOUNT (Kermadec Is)*	0402-05-	0	
	1979	*Cont*	....	*MANAM (New Guinea-NE of)*	0501-02=	2	7/-
	1979	*Cont*	....	*LANGILA (New Britain-SW Pac)*	0502-01=	2	7/-
	1979	*Cont*	....	*BAGANA (Bougainville-SW Pac)*	0505-02=	1	6/-
	1979	*Cont*	....	*YASUR (Vanuatu-SW Pacific)*	0507-10=	2	
	1979	*Cont*	....	*MARAPI (Sumatra)*	0601-14=	1	
	1979	*Cont*	....	*MERAPI (Java)*	0603-25=	1	
	1979	*Cont*	....	*SEMERU (Java)*	0603-30=	2	
	1979	*Cont*	....	*RAUNG (Java)*	0603-34=	1	
	1979	*Cont*	....	*LOKON-EMPUNG (Sulawesi-Indonesia)*	0606-10=	1	4/-
	1979	*Cont*	....	*DUKONO (Halmahera-Indonesia)*	0608-01=	2	
	1979	*Cont*	....	*SUWANOSE-JIMA (Ryukyu Is)*	0802-03=	2	
	1979	*Cont*	....	*SAKURA-JIMA (Kyushu-Japan)*	0802-08=	2	
?	*1979*	*Cont*	....	*SHIN-IWO-JIMA (Volcano Is-Japan)*	0804-13=	0	
	1979	*Cont*	....	*USU (Hokkaido-Japan)*	0805-03=	0	-/7
	1979	*Cont*	....	*SHIKOTSU [TARUMAI] (Hokkaido)*	0805-04=	1	
	1979	*Cont*	....	*KARYMSKY (Kamchatka)*	1000-13=	2	7/7
	1979	*Cont*	....	*KLIUCHEVSKOI (Kamchatka)*	1000-26=	2	5/7
	1979	*Cont*	....	*COLIMA VOLC COMPLEX (Mexico)*	1401-04=	1	5/-
	1979	*Cont*	....	*FUEGO (Guatemala)*	1402-09=	2	-/6
	1979	*Cont*	....	*PACAYA (Guatemala)*	1402-11=	1	
	1979	*Cont*	....	*MASAYA (Nicaragua)*	1404-10=	0	
	1979	*Cont*	....	*ARENAL (Costa Rica)*	1405-033	1	7/7
	1979	*Cont*	....	*GALERAS (Colombia)*	1501-08=	1?	
	1979	*Cont*	....	*SANGAY (Ecuador)*	1502-09=	2	
	1979	*Cont*	....	*CHILLAN, NEVADOS DE (Chile-C)*	1507-07=	2	5/-

Figure 29. Snow-clad stratovolcano of Kliuchevskoi, in Kamchatka, one of the most vigorous volcanoes in the Pacific's "Ring of Fire". Steam cloud in background is from Bezymianny, and a variety of flank cones are shown in the foreground. Photo by V. Podtabachny.

	START YEAR	START M-Dy	Duration	VOLCANO NAME (Subregion)	NUMBER	VEI	Vol L/T
	1979	*Cont*	....	*EREBUS (Antarctica)*	1900-02=	*1*	
	1979 e	....	?	**EAST EPI** (Vanuatu-SW Pacific)	0507-06=	0	
	1979	0112?	209*a?*	**KARKAR** (New Guinea-NE of)	0501-03=	2	-/7
	1979	0126e	23*e?*	**AMBRYM** (Vanuatu-SW Pacific)	0507-04=	2	
	1979	0129	36*a*>	**AZUL, CERRO** (Galapagos)	1503-06=	2?	
	1979	*02*	*286e*	*ASO (Kyushu-Japan)*	0802-11=	1	
	1979	02	?	**SHISHALDIN** (Aleutian Is)	1101-36-	2	
?	**1979**	0208	....	**WESTDAHL** (Aleutian Is)	1101-34-	3?	
	1979	0211	?	**BEZYMIANNY** (Kamchatka)	1000-25=	3	5/7
	1979	0216r	?	**KIRISHIMA** (Kyushu-Japan)	0802-09=	1	
	1979	0220	<1	**DIENG VOLC COMPLEX** (Java)	0603-20=	1	-/5
	1979	0224	....	**LOPEVI** (Vanuatu-SW Pacific)	0507-05=	2	
	1979	*0308*	....	*KARKAR (New Guinea-NE of)*	0501-03=	2?	*-/7*
	1979	04	543*m*	**CHIRINKOTAN** (Kurile Is)	0900-26=	2	
	1979	0413	196*e*	**SOUFRIERE ST. VINCENT** (W Indies)	1600-15=	3	7/7
	1979	0414	36*a*	**CARRAN-LOS VENADOS** (Chile-C)	1507-14=	2	6/6
?	**1979**	0426	382*a*	**FUKUJIN** (Volcano Is-Japan)	0804-133	0	
	1979	0510<	72*a*>	**METIS SHOAL** (Tonga-SW Pacific)	0403-07=	2	
	1979	0514	?	**CURACOA** (Tonga-SW Pacific)	0403-101	1	
	1979	0528	47*a*	**FOURNAISE, PITON DE LA** (Indian O.)	0303-02=	1	5/-
	1979	0531	<1	**KARANGETANG [API SIAU]** (Sangihe	0607-02=	1	
	1979	0606	101*m?*	**AMBRYM** (Vanuatu-SW Pacific)	0507-04=	2	
	1979	0613	....	**ASO** (Kyushu-Japan)	0802-11=	2	
	1979	0630	15*a*	**RUAPEHU** (New Zealand)	0401-10=	1	
	1979	0702	72*a*	**LOPEVI** (Vanuatu-SW Pacific)	0507-05=	2	
	1979	*0705d*	*>3yr*	*ETNA (Italy)*	0101-06=	1	
?	**1979**	0712	?	**NIKKO** (Volcano Is-Japan)	0804-132	0	
?	**1979**	0713	?	**BAYONNAISE ROCKS** (Izu Is-Japan)	0804-07=	0	
	1979	0715e	111*m*	**KRAKATAU** (Indonesia)	0602-00=	2	4/-
	1979	0716	24*a*	**ETNA** (Italy)	0101-06=	2	6/-
	1979	*0823*	....	*SANTA MARIA (Guatemala)*	1402-03=	2	*8/8*
?	**1979**	09	?	**KUWAE [KARUA]** (Vanuatu-SW Pac)	0507-07=	0	
	1979	0908	129*m*	**POAS** (Costa Rica)	1405-04=	1	
	1979	0912	....	**ETNA** (Italy)	0101-06=	2	
	1979	0918	?	**BEZYMIANNY** (Kamchatka)	1000-25=	2	5/6
S	**1979**	0930	<1	**MACDONALD** (Austral Is-C Pac)	1303-07-	0	
	1979	1015	44*a*	**LLAIMA** (Chile-C)	1507-11=	2	
	1979	1028	179*a*	**ON-TAKE** (Honshu-Japan)	0803-04=	1	
	1979	1113	62*a*>	**NEGRA, SIERRA** (Galapagos)	1503-05=	3	
?	**1979**	1115	?	**AHYI** (Mariana Is-C Pac)	0804-141	0	
	1979	1116	<1	**KILAUEA** (Hawaiian Is)	1302-01-	0	5/-
	1979	1205	132*a*	**RUAPEHU** (New Zealand)	0401-10=	1	
	1979	*1227*	*275a*	*BULUSAN (Luzon-Philippines)*	0703-01=	2	

	START YEAR	START M-Dy	Duration	VOLCANO NAME (Subregion)	NUMBER	VEI	Vol L/T
	1980	*Cont*	....	*STROMBOLI (Italy)*	0101-04=	*1?*	
	1980	*Cont*	....	*ERTA ALE (Ethiopia)*	0201-08=	*0*	
	1980	*Cont*	....	*WHITE ISLAND (New Zealand)*	0401-04=	*2*	*-/7*
	1980	*Cont*	....	*MANAM (New Guinea-NE of)*	0501-02=	*2*	*7/-*
	1980	*Cont*	....	*BAGANA (Bougainville-SW Pac)*	0505-02=	*1*	*6/-*
	1980	*Cont*	....	*YASUR (Vanuatu-SW Pacific)*	0507-10=	*2*	
	1980	*Cont*	....	*MERAPI (Java)*	0603-25=	*1*	
	1980	*Cont*	....	*SEMERU (Java)*	0603-30=	*2*	
	1980	*Cont*	....	*LOKON-EMPUNG (Sulawesi-Indonesia)*	0606-10=	*1*	*4/-*
	1980	*Cont*	....	*DUKONO (Halmahera-Indonesia)*	0608-01=	*2*	
	1980	*Cont*	....	*SUWANOSE-JIMA (Ryukyu Is)*	0802-03=	*2*	
	1980	*Cont*	....	*SAKURA-JIMA (Kyushu-Japan)*	0802-08=	*2*	
	1980	*Cont*	....	*ON-TAKE (Honshu-Japan)*	0803-04=	*1*	
?	*1980*	*Cont*	....	*FUKUJIN (Volcano Is-Japan)*	0804-133	*0*	
?	*1980*	*Cont*	....	*SHIN-IWO-JIMA (Volcano Is-Japan)*	0804-13=	*0*	
	1980	*Cont*	....	*USU (Hokkaido-Japan)*	0805-03=	*0*	*-/7*
	1980	*Cont*	....	*CHIRINKOTAN (Kurile Is)*	0900-26=	*2*	
	1980	*Cont*	....	*KARYMSKY (Kamchatka)*	1000-13=	*2*	*7/7*
	1980	*Cont*	....	*COLIMA VOLC COMPLEX (Mexico)*	1401-04=	*1*	*5/-*
	1980	*Cont*	....	*PACAYA (Guatemala)*	1402-11=	*1*	
	1980	*Cont*	....	*MASAYA (Nicaragua)*	1404-10=	*0*	
	1980	*Cont*	....	*ARENAL (Costa Rica)*	1405-033	*1*	*7/7*
	1980	*Cont*	....	*GALERAS (Colombia)*	1501-08=	*1?*	
	1980	*Cont*	....	*SANGAY (Ecuador)*	1502-09=	*2*	
	1980	*Cont*	....	*NEGRA, SIERRA (Galapagos)*	1503-05=	*0*	
	1980	*Cont*	....	*CHILLAN, NEVADOS DE (Chile-C)*	1507-07=	*2*	*5/-*
	1980	*Cont*	....	*EREBUS (Antarctica)*	1900-02=	*1*	
	1980	....	....	**LANGILA** (New Britain-SW Pac)	0502-01=	3	7/-
	1980	....	?	**GAUA** (Vanuatu-SW Pacific)	0507-02=	1?	
S	**1980**	01	16*m*	**MONOWAI SEAMOUNT** (Kermadec Is)	0402-05-	0	
	1980	01	....	**KLIUCHEVSKOI** (Kamchatka)	1000-26=	3	5/7
?	**1980**	0107	10*a?*	**KARKAR** (New Guinea-NE of)	0501-03=	1	
	1980	0110	1*a*	**TUPUNGATITO** (Chile-C)	1507-01=	2	
	1980	0111	248*m*	**ETNA** (Italy)	0101-06=	2	
	1980	*0122*	....	*SANTA MARIA (Guatemala)*	1402-03=	2	*8/8*
	1980	0130	25	**NYAMURAGIRA** (Africa-C)	0203-02=	3	7/7
	1980	0207	....	**BULUSAN** (Luzon-Philippines)	0703-01=	3	
S	**1980**	0212	<1	**MACDONALD** (Austral Is-C Pac)	1303-07-	0	
	1980	0311	<1	**KILAUEA** (Hawaiian Is)	1302-01-	0	
	1980	0313	<1	**IWO-JIMA** (Volcano Is-Japan)	0804-12=	1	
	1980	0315e	276*e*	**KRAKATAU** (Indonesia)	0602-00=	2	5/-
	1980	0316	221	**KRAFLA** (Iceland-NE)	1703-08=	0	7/-

START YEAR	M-Dy	Duration	VOLCANO NAME (Subregion)	NUMBER	VEI	Vol L/T
1980	0324	173a	**KARANGETANG [API SIAU]** (Sangihe	0607-02=	1	
1980	*0327*	*>3yr*	*ST. HELENS (US-Washington)*	1201-05-	2	
1980	0329	?	**MARAPI** (Sumatra)	0601-14=	1	
1980	0415	127a	**LOPEVI** (Vanuatu-SW Pacific)	0507-05=	3	
1980	0418	1a	**BEZYMIANNY** (Kamchatka)	1000-25=	3	5/7
1980	0501s	?	**MAKUSHIN** (Aleutian Is)	1101-31-	1	
1980	*0516*	*94a*	*AMBRYM (Vanuatu-SW Pacific)*	0507-04=	2	
1980	0518	....	**ST. HELENS** (US-Washington)	1201-05-	5	7/9
1980	0524	?	**EKARMA** (Kurile Is)	0900-27=	1	
1980	*0525*	....	*ST. HELENS (US-Washington)*	1201-05-	3	-/7
1980	0605a	107b	**TENGGER CALDERA [BROMO]**	0603-31=	2	
1980	*0612*	....	*ST. HELENS (US-Washington)*	1201-05-	3	6/7
1980	*0615e*	*383e*	*GORELY (Kamchatka)*	1000-07=	2	-/7
? 1980	0615z	?	**SEAL NUNATAKS GROUP** (Antarctica)	1900-05=		
1980	0620<	96a>	**VILLARRICA** (Chile-C)	1507-12=	1	
1980	0703<	5a?	**AKUTAN** (Aleutian Is)	1101-32-	2	
1980	0706a	?	**PAVLOF** (Alaska Peninsula)	1102-03-	1	
? 1980	0707	?	**NISHINO-SHIMA** (Volcano Is-Japa)n	0804-092	0	
1980	*0708*	*80a*	*ETNA (Italy)*	0101-06=	2	6/-
1980	*0710*	....	*KRAFLA (Iceland-NE)*	1703-08=	0	7/-
1980	*0722*	....	*ST. HELENS (US-Washington)*	1201-05-	3	-/7
1980	0723	....	**AMBRYM** (Vanuatu-SW Pacific)	0507-04=	3	
1980	0729	<1	**MALINAO** (Luzon-Philippines)	0703-04=	1	
1980	0731	....	**GORELY** (Kamchatka)	1000-07=	3	-/7
1980	0807	41a	**GARELOI** (Aleutian Is)	1101-07-	3?	
1980	*0807*	....	*ST. HELENS (US-Washington)*	1201-05-	3	6/6
1980	0817	3a	**HEKLA** (Iceland-S)	1702-07=	3	8/7
? 1980	0820	?	**KUWAE [KARUA]** (Vanuatu-SW Pac)	0507-07=	0	
1980	0821	5d	**BEZYMIANNY** (Kamchatka)	1000-25=	2	5/-
1980	0823	465p	**SHEVELUCH** (Kamchatka)	1000-27=	1	7/-
1980	09 ?	?	**MARION ISLAND** (Indian O.-S)	0304-08-	1	6/-
1980	0901	....	**ETNA** (Italy)	0101-06=	3	6/-
1980	0904	19a	**GAMALAMA** (Halmahera-Indonesia)	0608-06=	2	-/6
1980	0911	<1	**POAS** (Costa Rica)	1405-04=	1	
1980	0924	<1	**ASO** (Kyushu-Japan)	0802-11=	1	
1980	0928	<1	**KUCHINOERABU-JIMA** (Ryukyu Is)	0802-05=	2	-/6
1980	10	<1	**CALLAQUI** (Chile-C)	1507-091	1	
1980	1006	<1	**ULAWUN** (New Britain-SW Pac)	0502-12=	3	-/7
1980	1007	141a	**KAVACHI** (Solomon Is-SW Pac)	0505-06=	1	
1980	*1016*	....	*ST. HELENS (US-Washington)*	1201-05-	3	6/6
1980	1018	15a	**RUAPEHU** (New Zealand)	0401-10=	1	
1980	*1018*	....	*KRAFLA (Iceland-NE)*	1703-08=	0	7/-
1980	1105	314m	**PALUWEH** (Lesser Sunda Is)	0604-15=	2	6/-
1980	*1108*	*4*	*PAVLOF (Alaska Peninsula)*	1102-03-	1	-/6
S 1980	1110	97	**MACDONALD** (Austral Is-C Pac)	1303-07-	0	
1980	1111	....	**PAVLOF** (Alaska Peninsula)	1102-03-	3	-/6
? 1980	1115	41a>	**BAYONNAISE ROCKS** (Izu Is-Japan)	0804-07=	0	
1980	1226	<1	**POAS** (Costa Rica)	1405-04=	1	
1981	*Cont*	....	*STROMBOLI (Italy)*	0101-04=	*1?*	
1981	*Cont*	....	*ERTA ALE (Ethiopia)*	0201-08=	*0*	
1981	*Cont*	....	*WHITE ISLAND (New Zealand)*	0401-04=	*2*	-/7
1981	*Cont*	....	*MANAM (New Guinea-NE of)*	0501-02=	*2*	7/-
1981	*Cont*	....	*LANGILA (New Britain-SW Pac)*	0502-01=	*2*	7/-
1981	*Cont*	....	*BAGANA (Bougainville-SW Pac)*	0505-02=	*1*	6/-
1981	*Cont*	....	*KAVACHI (Solomon Is-SW Pac)*	0505-06=	*0*	
1981	*Cont*	....	*YASUR (Vanuatu-SW Pacific)*	0507-10=	*2*	
1981	*Cont*	....	*MERAPI (Java)*	0603-25=	*1*	
1981	*Cont*	....	*SEMERU (Java)*	0603-30=	*2*	
1981	*Cont*	....	*PALUWEH (Lesser Sunda Is)*	0604-15=	*2*	6/-
1981	*Cont*	....	*DUKONO (Halmahera-Indonesia)*	0608-01=	*2*	
1981	*Cont*	....	*SUWANOSE-JIMA (Ryukyu Is)*	0802-03=	*2*	
1981	*Cont*	....	*SAKURA-JIMA (Kyushu-Japan)*	0802-08=	*2*	
? *1981*	*Cont*	....	*SHIN-IWO-JIMA (Volcano Is-Japan)*	0804-13=	*0*	
1981	*Cont*	....	*USU (Hokkaido-Japan)*	0805-03=	*0*	-/7
1981	*Cont*	....	*GORELY (Kamchatka)*	1000-07=	*2*	-/7
1981	*Cont*	....	*KARYMSKY (Kamchatka)*	1000-13=	*2*	7/7
1981	*Cont*	....	*SHEVELUCH (Kamchatka)*	1000-27=	*1*	7/-
1981	*Cont*	....	*ST. HELENS (US-Washington)*	1201-05-	*1*	
S *1981*	*Cont*	....	*MACDONALD (Austral Is-C Pac)*	1303-07-	*0*	
1981	*Cont*	....	*COLIMA VOLC COMPLEX (Mexico)*	1401-04=	*1*	5/-
1981	*Cont*	....	*PACAYA (Guatemala)*	1402-11=	*1*	
1981	*Cont*	....	*ARENAL (Costa Rica)*	1405-033	*1*	7/7
1981	*Cont*	....	*GALERAS (Colombia)*	1501-08=	*1?*	
1981	*Cont*	....	*SANGAY (Ecuador)*	1502-09=	*2*	
1981	*Cont*	....	*CHILLAN, NEVADOS DE (Chile-C)*	1507-07=	*2*	5/-
1981	*Cont*	....	*EREBUS (Antarctica)*	1900-02=	*1*	
1981	....	?	**DIENG VOLC COMPLEX** (Java)	0603-20=	1?	
? 1981	0107	1a	**FUKUJIN** (Volcano Is-Japan)	0804-133	0	
1981	0125	187a?	**KLIUCHEVSKOI** (Kamchatka)	1000-26=	1	
1981	0126e	41j	**ETNA** (Italy)	0101-06=	2	6/-
1981	0130	4	**KRAFLA** (Iceland-NE)	1703-08=	0	7/-
1981	*02*	....	*SANTA MARIA (Guatemala)*	1402-03=	2	8/8
1981	02 ?	?	**TELICA** (Nicaragua)	1404-04=	1	
1981	0203	91a	**FOURNAISE, PITON DE LA** (Indian O.)	0303-02=	2	7/-
1981	0220	222a	**AMBRYM** (Vanuatu-SW Pacific)	0507-04=	2	
1981	0227<	?	**SHIKOTSU [TARUMAI]** (Hokkaido)	0805-04=	0	-/2
1981	03	61p	**POAS** (Costa Rica)	1405-04=	1	
1981	0304	143a	**GAMKONORA** (Halmahera-Indonesia)	0608-04=	1	-/5
? 1981	0305	286m	**MEHETIA** (Society Is-C Pac)	1303-06-	0	
1981	0317	6	**ETNA** (Italy)	0101-06=	1	7/5
1981	0324	<1	**OKMOK** (Aleutian Is)	1101-29-	3?	
1981	0330	59a	**PAVLOF** (Alaska Peninsula)	1102-03-	1	
1981	0409	18a	**BULUSAN** (Luzon-Philippines)	0703-01=	3	
1981	0409	7	**HEKLA** (Iceland-S)	1702-07=	2	7/-
1981	0424	178	**KRAKATAU** (Indonesia)	0602-00=	1	
1981	*0427*	*39a*	*ALAID (Kurile Is)*	0900-39=	3	-/8
1981	0430	....	**ALAID** (Kurile Is)	0900-39=	4	-/8
1981	0515	>3yr	**PAGAN** (Mariana Is-C Pac)	0804-17=	4	7/8
1981	0610	15a	**TIATIA** (Kurile Is)	0900-03=	2?	
1981	0612	724a	**BEZYMIANNY** (Kamchatka)	1000-25=	3	6/7
1981	0615	<1	**ASO** (Kyushu-Japan)	0802-11=	1	
1981	0709	<1	**GAUA** (Vanuatu-SW Pacific)	0507-02=	1?	
1981	0801x	?	**FERNANDINA** (Galapagos)	1503-01=	0	
1981	0831e	442n?	**GUAGUA PICHINCHA** (Ecuador)	1502-02=	1	-/4
? 1981	0915e	?	**KAVACHI** (Solomon Is-SW Pac)	0505-06=	0	
? 1981	0925	?	**SHISHALDIN** (Aleutian Is)	1101-36-		
1981	0925	2a	**PAVLOF** (Alaska Peninsula)	1102-03-	3	6/7
1981	1025?	171m	**RUAPEHU** (New Zealand)	0401-10=	1	
1981	1118	5	**KRAFLA** (Iceland-NE)	1703-08=	0	7/-
1981	1125	?	**ALAID** (Kurile Is)	0900-39=	2	
1981	*1125e*	*97e*	*TELICA (Nicaragua)*	1404-04=	1	
1981	1126	<1	**ETNA** (Italy)	0101-06=	2	
1981	*1216*	....	*MASAYA (Nicaragua)*	1404-10=	1	
? 1981	1221	?	**KLIUCHEVSKOI** (Kamchatka)	1000-26=		
1981	1225	20a	**NYAMURAGIRA** (Africa-C)	0203-02=	3	7/7
1982	*Cont*	....	*STROMBOLI (Italy)*	0101-04=	*1?*	
1982	*Cont*	....	*ETNA (Italy)*	0101-06=	*1*	
1982	*Cont*	....	*ERTA ALE (Ethiopia)*	0201-08=	*0*	
1982	*Cont*	....	*NYAMURAGIRA (Africa-C)*	0203-02=	*3*	7/7
1982	*Cont*	....	*RUAPEHU (New Zealand)*	0401-10=	*1*	
1982	*Cont*	....	*BAGANA (Bougainville-SW Pac)*	0505-02=	*1*	6/-
1982	*Cont*	....	*YASUR (Vanuatu-SW Pacific)*	0507-10=	*2*	
1982	*Cont*	....	*MERAPI (Java)*	0603-25=	*1*	
1982	*Cont*	....	*SEMERU (Java)*	0603-30=	*2*	
1982	*Cont*	....	*DUKONO (Halmahera-Indonesia)*	0608-01=	*2*	
1982	*Cont*	....	*SUWANOSE-JIMA (Ryukyu Is)*	0802-03=	*2*	
1982	*Cont*	....	*SAKURA-JIMA (Kyushu-Japan)*	0802-08=	*2*	
? *1982*	*Cont*	....	*SHIN-IWO-JIMA (Volcano Is-Japan)*	0804-13=	*0*	
1982	*Cont*	....	*USU (Hokkaido-Japan)*	0805-03=	*0*	-/7
1982	*Cont*	....	*KARYMSKY (Kamchatka)*	1000-13=	*2*	7/7
1982	*Cont*	....	*COLIMA VOLC COMPLEX (Mexico)*	1401-04=	*1*	5/-
1982	*Cont*	....	*SANTA MARIA (Guatemala)*	1402-03=	*1*	8/8
1982	*Cont*	....	*PACAYA (Guatemala)*	1402-11=	*1*	
1982	*Cont*	....	*ARENAL (Costa Rica)*	1405-033	*1*	7/7
1982	*Cont*	....	*GALERAS (Colombia)*	1501-08=	*1?*	
1982	*Cont*	....	*SANGAY (Ecuador)*	1502-09=	*2*	
1982	*Cont*	....	*CHILLAN, NEVADOS DE (Chile-C)*	1507-07=	*2*	5/-
1982	*Cont*	....	*EREBUS (Antarctica)*	1900-02=	*1*	
1982	....	?	**KARANGETANG [API SIAU]** (Sangihe	0607-02=	1	
? 1982	0112	64a	**FUKUJIN** (Volcano Is-Japan)	0804-133	0	
1982	0115	<1	**GARELOI** (Aleutian Is)	1101-07-	3	
1982	0115e	....	**CONCEPCION** (Nicaragua)	1404-12=	2	
? 1982	0210	4a	**TIATIA** (Kurile Is)	0900-03=	1	
1982	0212	....	**TELICA** (Nicaragua)	1404-04=	2	
1982	*0213*	....	*LANGILA (New Britain-SW Pac)*	0502-01=	3	7/-
S 1982	0301	84	**MACDONALD** (Austral Is-C Pac)	1303-07-	0	
1982	0309	1	**IWO-JIMA** (Volcano Is-Japan)	0804-12=	1	
1982	0310<	66m>	**MARAPI** (Sumatra)	0601-14=	1	
? 1982	0316	64a	**TEAHITIA** (Society Is-C Pac)	1303-03-	0	
1982	*0319*	....	*ST. HELENS (US-Washington)*	1201-05-	3	6/-
1982	0324	39a	**KLIUCHEVSKOI** (Kamchatka)	1000-26=	1	
1982	*0327*	....	*MANAM (New Guinea-NE of)*	0501-02=	3	7/-
1982	*0328*	*167a*	*CHICHON, EL (Mexico)*	1401-12=	4+	-/9
1982	0329	<1	**ALAID** (Kurile Is)	0900-39=	2	
? 1982	04	15m	**NISHINO-SHIMA** (Volcano Is-Japan)	0804-092	0	
1982	0403	....	**CHICHON, EL** (Mexico)	1401-12=	5	-/9
1982	*0405*	*278a*	*GALUNGGUNG (Java)*	0603-14=	3	-/8
? 1982	0406	?	**ESMERALDA BANK** (Mariana Is-C Pac)	0804-21=	0	
1982	0407	56b	**KAVACHI** (Solomon Is-SW Pac)	0505-06=	2	
1982	0418	<1	**GAUA** (Vanuatu-SW Pacific)	0507-02=	2	
1982	0426	<1	**ASAMA** (Honshu-Japan)	0803-11=	2	
1982	0430	<1	**KILAUEA** (Hawaiian Is)	1302-01-	0	5/-
S 1982	05	16m	**MONOWAI SEAMOUNT** (Kermadec Is)	0402-05-	0	
1982	0517	....	**GALUNGGUNG** (Java)	0603-14=	4	-/8
1982	*0528*	....	*GUAGUA PICHINCHA (Ecuador)*	1502-02=	1	-/4
1982	*0610*	....	*BEZYMIANNY (Kamchatka)*	1000-25=	2	6/7
1982	0621	118m	**NYIRAGONGO** (Africa-C)	0203-03=	1	7/-
? 1982	0715q	?	**PAVLOF** (Alaska Peninsula)	1102-03-		
1982	0718	2a	**RAUNG** (Java)	0603-34=	3	
1982	0826	76a	**SOPUTAN** (Sulawesi-Indonesia)	0606-03=	3	-/6
1982	0828	9a?	**WOLF, VOLCAN** (Galapagos)	1503-02=	1	
1982	0925	<1	**KILAUEA** (Hawaiian Is)	1302-01-	0	6/-
1982	*0930*	....	*PAGAN (Mariana Is-C Pac)*	0804-17=	3?	7/8
1982	1002	<1	**ASAMA** (Honshu-Japan)	0803-11=	1	
1982	1005d	221n	**AKUTAN** (Aleutian Is)	1101-32-	2	
1982	1007	263a	**KLIUCHEVSKOI** (Kamchatka)	1000-26=	2	7/-
1982	*1007*	....	*MASAYA (Nicaragua)*	1404-10=	1	
1982	1016	27a	**CAMEROON, MT.** (Africa-W)	0204-01=	2	7/5
1982	1024	1a	**LOPEVI** (Vanuatu-SW Pacific)	0507-05=	2	
1982	1026	64	**KUSATSU-SHIRANE** (Honshu-Japan)	0803-12=	1	
1982	1117	<1	**ILIBOLENG** (Lesser Sunda Is)	0604-22=	2	
1982	1122	?	**CHIRPOI** (Kurile Is)	0900-15=	2	
1982	1128	....	**IWO-JIMA** (Volcano Is-Japan)	0804-12=	1	
1982	12	15m	**MARAPI** (Sumatra)	0601-14=	1	
? 1982	1215	?	**FUKUJIN** (Volcano Is-Japan)	0804-133	0	
1983	*Cont*	....	*STROMBOLI (Italy)*	0101-04=	*1?*	
1983	*Cont*	....	*ERTA ALE (Ethiopia)*	0201-08=	*0*	
1983	*Cont*	....	*MANAM (New Guinea-NE of)*	0501-02=	*2*	7/-
1983	*Cont*	....	*BAGANA (Bougainville-SW Pac)*	0505-02=	*1*	6/-
1983	*Cont*	....	*YASUR (Vanuatu-SW Pacific)*	0507-10=	*2*	
1983	*Cont*	....	*GALUNGGUNG (Java)*	0603-14=	*1*	-/8
1983	*Cont*	....	*MERAPI (Java)*	0603-25=	*1*	
1983	*Cont*	....	*SEMERU (Java)*	0603-30=	*2*	
1983	*Cont*	....	*DUKONO (Halmahera-Indonesia)*	0608-01=	*2*	

START YEAR	M-Dy	Duration	VOLCANO NAME (Subregion)	NUMBER	VEI	Vol L/T
1983	Cont	....	SUWANOSE-JIMA (Ryukyu Is)	0802-03=	2	
1983	Cont	....	SAKURA-JIMA (Kyushu-Japan)	0802-08=	2	
? 1983	Cont	....	SHIN-IWO-JIMA (Volcano Is-Japan)	0804-13=	0	
1983	Cont	....	PAGAN (Mariana Is-C Pac)	0804-17=	2	7/8
1983	Cont	....	AKUTAN (Aleutian Is)	1101-32-	2	
1983	Cont	....	PACAYA (Guatemala)	1402-11=	1	
1983	Cont	....	MASAYA (Nicaragua)	1404-10=	0	
1983	Cont	....	ARENAL (Costa Rica)	1405-033	1	7/7
1983	Cont	....	GALERAS (Colombia)	1501-08=	1?	
1983	Cont	....	SANGAY (Ecuador)	1502-09=	2	
1983	Cont	....	CHILLAN, NEVADOS DE (Chile-C)	1507-07=	2	5/-
1983	Cont	....	EREBUS (Antarctica)	1900-02=	1	
1983	....	?	AMBRYM (Vanuatu-SW Pacific)	0507-04=	2	
1983	....	?	MARAPI (Sumatra)	0601-14=	1	
1983	0101	>3yr	LENGAI, OL DOINYO (Africa-E)	0202-12=	2	
1983	0103	>3yr	KILAUEA (Hawaiian Is)	1302-01-	0	8/-
1983	0129	....	SANTA MARIA (Guatemala)	1402-03=	2	8/8
1983	0202	....	ST. HELENS (US-Washington)	1201-05-	2	7/-
1983	0206	15a	RINCON DE LA VIEJA (Costa Rica)	1405-02=	1	
? 1983	0211	4a	COLIMA VOLC COMPLEX (Mexico)	1401-04=	1?	
1983	0308	....	KLIUCHEVSKOI (Kamchatka)	1000-26=	1	7/-
S 1983	0314	68a	MACDONALD (Austral Is-C Pac)	1303-07-	0	
1983	1221	<1	TENGGER CALDERA [BROMO] (	0603-31=	1	
1983	1226e	48e	WHITE ISLAND (New Zealand)	0401-04=	2	
1984	Cont	....	STROMBOLI (Italy)	0101-04=	1?	
1984	Cont	....	ERTA ALE (Ethiopia)	0201-08=	0	
1984	Cont	....	LENGAI, OL DOINYO (Africa-E)	0202-12=	1	
1984	Cont	....	FOURNAISE, PITON DE LA (Indian O.)	0303-02=	2	7/-
1984	Cont	....	WHITE ISLAND (New Zealand)	0401-04=	2	
1984	Cont	....	BAGANA (Bougainville-SW Pac)	0505-02=	1	6/-
1984	Cont	....	YASUR (Vanuatu-SW Pacific)	0507-10=	2	
1984	Cont	....	SEMERU (Java)	0603-30=	2	
1984	Cont	....	DUKONO (Halmahera-Indonesia)	0608-01=	2	
1984	Cont	....	SUWANOSE-JIMA (Ryukyu Is)	0802-03=	2	
1984	Cont	....	SAKURA-JIMA (Kyushu-Japan)	0802-08=	2	
? 1984	Cont	....	SHIN-IWO-JIMA (Volcano Is-Japan)	0804-13=	0	
1984	Cont	....	PAGAN (Mariana Is-C Pac)	0804-17=	2	7/8
1984	Cont	....	ST. HELENS (US-Washington)	1201-05-	1	
? 1984	Cont	....	TEAHITIA (Society Is-C Pac)	1303-03-	0	
S 1984	Cont	....	MACDONALD (Austral Is-C Pac)	1303-07-	0	
1984	Cont	....	SANTA MARIA (Guatemala)	1402-03=	1	8/8
1984	Cont	....	SANGAY (Ecuador)	1502-09=	2	
1984	Cont	....	CHILLAN, NEVADOS DE (Chile-C)	1507-07=	2	5/-
1984	....	616w>	AMBRYM (Vanuatu-SW Pacific)	0507-04=	2	

Figure 30. Fumaroles at the summit of Medvezhia, Kurile Islands. Such vigorous steaming can be easily mistaken for an eruption, and many historical reports may in fact have been nothing more than fumarolic activity. No emission of dark ash is visible with this steam. Photo courtesy of Genrich Steinberg.

START YEAR	M-Dy	Duration	VOLCANO NAME (Subregion)	NUMBER	VEI	Vol L/T
1983	0316	9a	CONCEPCION (Nicaragua)	1404-12=	2	
1983	0328	131a	ETNA (Italy)	0101-06=	1	8/5
1983	0408	<1	ASAMA (Honshu-Japan)	0803-11=	2	
? 1983	0415e	74f	TENGGER CALDERA [BROMO]	0603-31=	1	
1983	0415	<1	NIIGATA-YAKE-YAMA (Honshu-Japan)	0803-09=	1	
1983	0418	....	LANGILA (New Britain-SW Pac)	0502-01=	3	7/-
1983	05	>3yr	KARANGETANG [API SIAU] (Sangihe	0607-02=	1	4/-
1983	0511	337a	ILIBOLENG (Lesser Sunda Is)	0604-22=	1	
? 1983	0512	?	BAYONNAISE ROCKS (Izu Is-Japan)	0804-07=	0	
1983	0517	....	LANGILA (New Britain-SW Pac)	0502-01=	3	7/-
1983	0522	....	BEZYMIANNY (Kamchatka)	1000-25=	3	6/7
1983	0528	4	GRIMSVOTN (Iceland-NE)	1703-01=	2	
1983	0602	319a	VENIAMINOF (Alaska Peninsula)	1102-07-	3	7/-
? 1983	0615	1a	UNNAMED (New Britain-SW Pac)	0502-001		
1983	0625	4	BULUSAN (Luzon-Philippines)	0703-01=	2	
1983	07	92p	ASO (Kyushu-Japan)	0802-11=	1	
1983	0708	<1	OKMOK (Aleutian Is)	1101-29-	2	
1983	0711	7a	PAVLOF (Alaska Peninsula)	1102-03-		
? 1983	0712	14a	TEAHITIA (Society Is-C Pac)	1303-03-	0	
1983	0718	150m	COLO [UNA UNA] (Sulawesi-Indonesia)	0606-01=	2	
1983	0723	....	COLO [UNA UNA] (Sulawesi-Indonesia)	0606-01=	4	
1983	0726	147	KUSATSU-SHIRANE (Honshu-Japan)	0803-12=	1	
1983	0809	2	GAMALAMA (Halmahera-Indonesia)	0608-06=	3	
1983	0817	<1	ILIWERUNG (Lesser Sunda Is)	0604-25=	1	
1983	0914	?	TANGKUBANPARAHU (Java)	0603-09=	1	
1983	1003	<1	MIYAKE-JIMA (Izu Is-Japan)	0804-04=	3	6/6
1983	1014	....	VILLARRICA (Chile-C)	1507-12=	1	
S 1983	1027	68a	MACDONALD (Austral Is-C Pac)	1303-07-	0	
1983	1106	128a	ULAWUN (New Britain-SW Pac)	0502-12=	1	
1983	1114	34a	PAVLOF (Alaska Peninsula)	1102-03-	3	-/7
1983	1204	76a	FOURNAISE, PITON DE LA (Indian O.)	0303-02=	2	7/-
? 1983	1218	208a	TEAHITIA (Society Is-C Pac)	1303-03-	0	
1984	0103	....	ILIBOLENG (Lesser Sunda Is)	0604-22=	2	
1984	0107	....	LANGILA (New Britain-SW Pac)	0502-01=	3	7/-
1984	0109	22a?	GALUNGGUNG (Java)	0603-14=	1	
1984	02	....	MANAM (New Guinea-NE of)	0501-02=	3	7/-
1984	0205	313m	BEZYMIANNY (Kamchatka)	1000-25=	2	-/7
1984	0223	20a	NYAMURAGIRA (Africa-C)	0203-02=	2	7/7
1984	0301	4a	HOME REEF (Tonga-SW Pacific)	0403-08=	3?	
1984	0308	18a	KAITOKU SEAMOUNT (Volcano Is)	0804-10=	0	
1984	0310	324a	KLIUCHEVSKOI (Kamchatka)	1000-26=	1	
1984	0317	173a	SHEVELUCH (Kamchatka)	1000-27=	2?	
1984	0325	21a	MAUNA LOA (Hawaiian Is)	1302-02=	0	8/-
1984	0330	?	FERNANDINA (Galapagos)	1503-01=	1	
1984	0331	16m	RINCON DE LA VIEJA (Costa Rica)	1405-02=	1	
1984	0405	....	MASAYA (Nicaragua)	1404-10=	1	
1984	0413c	437d	ASO (Kyushu-Japan)	0802-11=	1	
1984	0420	220a	LLAIMA (Chile-C)	1507-11=	2	
1984	0427?	174	ETNA (Italy)	0101-06=	2	7/-
1984	0509	12a	PALUWEH (Lesser Sunda Is)	0604-15=	2	
1984	0515	....	PACAYA (Guatemala)	1402-11=	2	
1984	0521	10a	TENGGER CALDERA [BROMO]	0603-31=	1	
1984	0524	99	SOPUTAN (Sulawesi-Indonesia)	0606-03=	3	-/7
1984	0603<	375a>	TINAKULA (Santa Cruz Is-SW Pac)	0506-01=	2	
1984	0603	....	ARENAL (Costa Rica)	1405-033	2	7/7
? 1984	0605d	163n	LOKON-EMPUNG (Sulawesi-Indonesia)	0606-10=	1	
1984	0615	....	MERAPI (Java)	0603-25=	3	
1984	0712	<1	CLEVELAND (Aleutian Is)	1101-24-	1	
1984	0720	796	ETNA (Italy)	0101-06=	2	5/6
1984	0804	779a?	GORELY (Kamchatka)	1000-07=	2	
1984	0811	464a	VILLARRICA (Chile-C)	1507-12=	2	6/-
? 1984	0820<	?	GRIMSVOTN (Iceland-NE)	1703-01=	0	
1984	0823	19a	ULAWUN (New Britain-SW Pac)	0502-12=	1	
1984	0831	....	SOPUTAN (Sulawesi-Indonesia)	0606-03=	3	-/7

	START YEAR	M-Dy	Duration	VOLCANO NAME (Subregion)	NUMBER	VEI	Vol L/T
	1984	0904	14	KRAFLA (Iceland-NE)	1703-08=	0	8/-
	1984	0905	....	KARANGETANG [API SIAU] (Sangihe	0607-02=	3	4/-
	1984	0909	27	MAYON (Luzon-Philippines)	0703-03=	3	7/7
	1984	0913	....	MAYON (Luzon-Philippines)	0703-03=	3?	7/7
	1984	0913	....	EREBUS (Antarctica)	1900-02=	2	
	1984	0919	....	KILAUEA (Hawaiian Is)	1302-01-	1	8/-
	1984	1013	....	BEZYMIANNY (Kamchatka)	1000-25=	3	-/7
?	1984	1111	71a	LOIHI SEAMOUNT (Hawaiian Is)	1302-00-	0	
	1984	1113	....	KLIUCHEVSKOI (Kamchatka)	1000-26=	3	
	1984	1115	<1	MARAPI (Sumatra)	0601-14=	1	
	1984	1129	7a?	VENIAMINOF (Alaska Peninsula)	1102-07-	2	
	1984	12	17m	CONCEPCION (Nicaragua)	1404-12=	1	
	1984	1222	87a?	RUIZ (Colombia)	1501-02=	1	
	1984	1230	28a	ULAWUN (New Britain-SW Pac)	0502-12=	1	5/-
	1985	Cont	....	ERTA ALE (Ethiopia)	0201-08=	0	
	1985	Cont	....	LENGAI, OL DOINYO (Africa-E)	0202-12=	1	
	1985	Cont	....	MANAM (New Guinea-NE of)	0501-02=	2	7/-
	1985	Cont	....	BAGANA (Bougainville-SW Pac)	0505-02=	1	6/-
	1985	Cont	....	TINAKULA (Santa Cruz Is-SW Pac)	0506-01=	2	
	1985	Cont	....	AMBRYM (Vanuatu-SW Pacific)	0507-04=	2	
	1985	Cont	....	YASUR (Vanuatu-SW Pacific)	0507-10=	2	
	1985	Cont	....	MERAPI (Java)	0603-25=	1	
	1985	Cont	....	SEMERU (Java)	0603-30=	2	
	1985	Cont	....	KARANGETANG [API SIAU] (Sangihe	0607-02=	2	4/-
	1985	Cont	....	DUKONO (Halmahera-Indonesia)	0608-01=	2	
	1985	Cont	....	SUWANOSE-JIMA (Ryukyu Is)	0802-03=	2	
	1985	Cont	....	SAKURA-JIMA (Kyushu-Japan)	0802-08=	2	
	1985	Cont	....	ASO (Kyushu-Japan)	0802-11=	1	
?	1985	Cont	....	SHIN-IWO-JIMA (Volcano Is-Japan)	0804-13=	0	
	1985	Cont	....	PAGAN (Mariana Is-C Pac)	0804-17=	2	7/8
	1985	Cont	....	GORELY (Kamchatka)	1000-07=	2	
	1985	Cont	....	ST. HELENS (US-Washington)	1201-05-	1	
?	1985	Cont	....	LOIHI SEAMOUNT (Hawaiian Is)	1302-00-	0	
	1985	Cont	....	PACAYA (Guatemala)	1402-11=	1	
	1985	Cont	....	SANGAY (Ecuador)	1502-09=	2	
	1985	Cont	....	CHILLAN, NEVADOS DE (Chile-C)	1507-07=	2	5/-
	1985	Cont	....	VILLARRICA (Chile-C)	1507-12=	2	6/-
	1985	Cont	....	EREBUS (Antarctica)	1900-02=	1	
	1985	....	188w	COLIMA VOLC COMPLEX (Mexico)	1401-04=	1	
	1985	....	....	ARENAL (Costa Rica)	1405-033	2	7/7
?	1985	....	?	HUDSON MOUNTAINS (Antarctica)	1900-028		
	1985	0102	....	CONCEPCION (Nicaragua)	1404-12=	2	
	1985	0103	....	KILAUEA (Hawaiian Is)	1302-01-	1	8/-
	1985	0106	3a	JAN MAYEN (Atl-N-Jan Mayen)	1706-01=	2	6/6
?	1985	0110	15a	TEAHITIA (Society Is-C Pac)	1303-03-	0	
	1985	0114	732m?	HEARD (Indian O.-S)	0304-01=	2?	
	1985	0124	....	SANTA MARIA (Guatemala)	1402-03=	2	8/8
	1985	0129	....	LANGILA (New Britain-SW Pac)	0502-01=	3	7/-
	1985	0203	<1	PALUWEH (Lesser Sunda Is)	0604-15=	1	
?	1985	03 ?	122p?	LASCAR (Chile-N)	1505-10=	0	
	1985	0308	127a	ETNA (Italy)	0101-06=	2	7/-
	1985	0313	<1	CANLAON (Philippines-C)	0702-02=	1	
	1985	0321	<1	NIUAFO'OU (Tonga-SW Pacific)	0403-11=	0	-/2
	1985	04	....	MASAYA (Nicaragua)	1404-10=	1	
	1985	05	31p	GUAGUA PICHINCHA (Ecuador)	1502-02=	1	
	1985	0519	<1	SOPUTAN (Sulawesi-Indonesia)	0606-03=	2	-/6
	1985	0521<	19a>	RUAPEHU (New Zealand)	0401-10=	1	
	1985	0526	152a	SHEVELUCH (Kamchatka)	1000-27=	2	
	1985	0612	185a	BEZYMIANNY (Kamchatka)	1000-25=	1	-/7
	1985	0614	>3yr	FOURNAISE, PITON DE LA (Indian O.)	0303-02=	1	8/-
	1985	0619	1	TOKACHI (Hokkaido-Japan)	0805-05=	1	
	1985	0629	....	BEZYMIANNY (Kamchatka)	1000-25=	3	-/7
	1985	0730	929a	SANGEANG API (Lesser Sunda Is)	0604-05=	3	7/-
	1985	0816	158a	KLIUCHEVSKOI (Kamchatka)	1000-26=	2	
	1985	0823	127a	RAUNG (Java)	0603-34=	2	
?	1985	0902	?	SUPPLY REEF (Mariana Is-C Pac)	0804-142	0	
?	1985	0902	?	SAN CRISTOBAL (Nicaragua)	1404-02=		
	1985	0911	>3yr	RUIZ (Colombia)	1501-02=	2	-/7
	1985	1005	2a?	CANLAON (Philippines-C)	0702-02=	1	
	1985	1015q	109t	RINCON DE LA VIEJA (Costa Rica)	1405-02=	1	
	1985	11	91p>	SAN MIGUEL (El Salvador)	1403-10=	1	
	1985	1113	....	RUIZ (Colombia)	1501-02=	3	-/7
?	1985	1115	<1	TANGKUBANPARAHU (Java)	0603-09=	1	
	1985	1117	4	ULAWUN (New Britain-SW Pac)	0502-12=	2	6/6
	1985	1120	....	ULAWUN (New Britain-SW Pac)	0502-12=	3	6/6
?	1985	1201	?	GUALLATIRI (Chile-N)	1505-02=		
?	1985	1202	<1	NISHINO-SHIMA (Volcano Is-Japan)	0804-092	0	
	1985	1202	....	KLIUCHEVSKOI (Kamchatka)	1000-26=	3	
	1985	1202a	139b?	CONCEPCION (Nicaragua)	1404-12=	1	
	1985	1206	112a	STROMBOLI (Italy)	0101-04=	2	6/4
	1985	1209	81c	KAVACHI (Solomon Is-SW Pac)	0505-06=	1	
?	1985	1210	?	CLEVELAND (Aleutian Is)	1101-24-	1	
	1985	1219	13a	ETNA (Italy)	0101-06=	2	6/-
	1986	Cont	....	STROMBOLI (Italy)	0101-04=	2	6/4
	1986	Cont	....	ERTA ALE (Ethiopia)	0201-08=	0	
	1986	Cont	....	LENGAI, OL DOINYO (Africa-E)	0202-12=	1	
	1986	Cont	....	FOURNAISE, PITON DE LA (Indian O.)	0303-02=	1	8/-
	1986	Cont	....	HEARD (Indian O.-S)	0304-01=	1	
	1986	Cont	....	MANAM (New Guinea-NE of)	0501-02=	2	7/-
	1986	Cont	....	LANGILA (New Britain-SW Pac)	0502-01=	2	7/-
	1986	Cont	....	BAGANA (Bougainville-SW Pac)	0505-02=	1	6/-
	1986	Cont	....	YASUR (Vanuatu-SW Pacific)	0507-10=	2	
	1986	Cont	....	MERAPI (Java)	0603-25=	1	
	1986	Cont	....	SEMERU (Java)	0603-30=	2	
	1986	Cont	....	SANGEANG API (Lesser Sunda Is)	0604-05=	3	7/-
	1986	Cont	....	KARANGETANG [API SIAU] (Sangihe	0607-02=	2	4/-
	1986	Cont	....	DUKONO (Halmahera-Indonesia)	0608-01=	2	
	1986	Cont	....	SUWANOSE-JIMA (Ryukyu Is)	0802-03=	2	
	1986	Cont	....	SAKURA-JIMA (Kyushu-Japan)	0802-08=	2	
	1986	Cont	....	GORELY (Kamchatka)	1000-07=	2	
	1986	Cont	....	KILAUEA (Hawaiian Is)	1302-01-	0	8/-
	1986	Cont	....	COLIMA VOLC COMPLEX (Mexico)	1401-04=	1	
	1986	Cont	....	SANTA MARIA (Guatemala)	1402-03=	1	8/8
	1986	Cont	....	PACAYA (Guatemala)	1402-11=	1	
	1986	Cont	....	SAN MIGUEL (El Salvador)	1403-10=	1	
	1986	Cont	....	CONCEPCION (Nicaragua)	1404-12=	1	
	1986	Cont	....	ARENAL (Costa Rica)	1405-033	1	7/7
	1986	Cont	....	RUIZ (Colombia)	1501-02=	2	-/7
	1986	Cont	....	SANGAY (Ecuador)	1502-09=	2	
	1986	Cont	....	CHILLAN, NEVADOS DE (Chile-C)	1507-07=	2	5/-
	1986	Cont	....	EREBUS (Antarctica)	1900-02=	1	
	1986	0118	3a	SHIN-IWO-JIMA (Volcano Is-Japan)	0804-13=	2	
	1986	0120	<1	TUPUNGATITO (Chile-C)	1507-01=	1	
	1986	0201?	>3yr	WHITE ISLAND (New Zealand)	0401-04=	1	
	1986	0208	1a?	RUAPEHU (New Zealand)	0401-10=	1	
	1986	0318	104a	AKUTAN (Aleutian Is)	1101-32-	2	
	1986	0319	333a?	SHISHALDIN (Aleutian Is)	1101-36-	2	
	1986	0322	417a	LOKON-EMPUNG (Sulawesi-Indonesia)	0606-10=	2	
	1986	0326e	95e	BEZYMIANNY (Kamchatka)	1000-25=	1	6/5
	1986	0327	157a	AUGUSTINE (Alaska-SW)	1103-01-	4?	-/8
	1986	0328	701a	SHEVELUCH (Kamchatka)	1000-27=	2	
	1986	0416	850a	PAVLOF (Alaska Peninsula)	1102-03-	2	6/-
	1986	0416	....	ST. HELENS (US-Washington)	1201-05-	2	
	1986	0418	....	PAVLOF (Alaska Peninsula)	1102-03-	3	6/-
	1986	0428	29a>	CLEVELAND (Aleutian Is)	1101-24-	2	
	1986	0508	<1	TACANA (Mexico)	1401-13=	1	
S	1986	0516	78a	MACDONALD (Austral Is-C Pac)	1303-07-	0	
?	1986	0523	?	ATKA [KOROVIN] (Aleutian Is)	1101-16-	1	
	1986	0525	3c	ALAID (Kurile Is)	0900-39=	2?	
	1986	0528	179	ILIBOLENG (Lesser Sunda Is)	0604-22=	1	
S	1986	06	15m	MONOWAI SEAMOUNT (Kermadec Is)	0402-05-	0	
	1986	0603	76a	CANLAON (Philippines-C)	0702-02=	2	-/5
	1986	0608	33a	KLIUCHEVSKOI (Kamchatka)	1000-26=	2	
S	1986	0615	51a?	RUMBLE III (New Zealand)	0401-13-	0	
	1986	0622	....	BEZYMIANNY (Kamchatka)	1000-25=	2	6/5
	1986	0705	18a	KAVACHI (Solomon Is-SW Pac)	0505-06=	1	
	1986	0705	9a	SORIKMARAPI (Sumatra)	0601-12=	1	-/2
	1986	0716	35a	NYAMURAGIRA (Africa-C)	0203-02=	2	7/7
?	1986	0716	89a	TALANG (Sumatra)	0601-16=	1	
	1986	08 ?	?	UNNAMED (Pacific-NE)	1301-02-	0	7/-
	1986	0804	....	SHEVELUCH (Kamchatka)	1000-27=	3	
	1986	0806	<1	DIENG VOLC COMPLEX (Java)	0603-20=	1	
?	1986	0821	131a?	OKU VOLC FIELD [L. NYOS] (Afica-W)	0204-003		
	1986	09 ?	?	SARYCHEV PEAK (Kurile Is)	0900-24=		
	1986	0914	2a	LASCAR (Chile-N)	1505-10=	1	-/7
	1986	0916	....	LASCAR (Chile-N)	1505-10=	3	-/7
?	1986	0920	<1	LOIHI SEAMOUNT (Hawaiian Is)	1302-00-	0	
	1986	0924	....	ETNA (Italy)	0101-06=	2	5/6
	1986	1011	1a	CHIRINKOTAN (Kurile Is)	0900-26=	1	
?	1986	1024	<1	BAYONNAISE ROCKS (Izu Is-Japan)	0804-07=	0	
	1986	1030	120a	ETNA (Italy)	0101-06=	2	7/6
	1986	1113	6a?	AMBRYM (Vanuatu-SW Pacific)	0507-04=	2	
	1986	1115	32	OSHIMA (Izu Is-Japan)	0804-01=	2	7/7
	1986	1118	19a	CHIKURACHKI (Kurile Is)	0900-36=	2	7/8
	1986	1118	467a	OKMOK (Aleutian Is)	1101-29-	1	
	1986	1120	....	CHIKURACHKI (Kurile Is)	0900-36=	4?	7/8
	1986	1121	....	OSHIMA (Izu Is-Japan)	0804-01=	3	7/7
	1986	1127	>3yr	KLIUCHEVSKOI (Kamchatka)	1000-26=	2	7/-
?	1986	1129	2a?	LOKI-FOGRUFJOLL (Iceland-NE)	1703-02=	0	
	1986	12	?	SABANCAYA (Peru)	1504-003	1	
	1986	1209	594e	BEZYMIANNY (Kamchatka)	1000-25=	0	
	1986	1216	....	BEZYMIANNY (Kamchatka)	1000-25=	3	
	1986	1231	<1	RINCON DE LA VIEJA (Costa Rica)	1405-02=	1	
	1987	Cont	....	STROMBOLI (Italy)	0101-04=	1?	
	1987	Cont	....	ERTA ALE (Ethiopia)	0201-08=	0	
	1987	Cont	....	LENGAI, OL DOINYO (Africa-E)	0202-12=	1	
	1987	Cont	....	FOURNAISE, PITON DE LA (Indian O.)	0303-02=	1	8/-
	1987	Cont	....	HEARD (Indian O.-S)	0304-01=	1	
	1987	Cont	....	MANAM (New Guinea-NE of)	0501-02=	2	7/-
	1987	Cont	....	LANGILA (New Britain-SW Pac)	0502-01=	2	7/-
	1987	Cont	....	BAGANA (Bougainville-SW Pac)	0505-02=	1	6/-
	1987	Cont	....	YASUR (Vanuatu-SW Pacific)	0507-10=	2	
	1987	Cont	....	MERAPI (Java)	0603-25=	1	
	1987	Cont	....	SEMERU (Java)	0603-30=	2	
	1987	Cont	....	LOKON-EMPUNG (Sulawesi-Indonesia)	0606-10=	2	
	1987	Cont	....	DUKONO (Halmahera-Indonesia)	0608-01=	2	
	1987	Cont	....	SUWANOSE-JIMA (Ryukyu Is)	0802-03=	2	
	1987	Cont	....	SAKURA-JIMA (Kyushu-Japan)	0802-08=	2	
	1987	Cont	....	SHISHALDIN (Aleutian Is)	1101-36-	2	
	1987	Cont	....	PAVLOF (Alaska Peninsula)	1102-03-	2	6/-
	1987	Cont	....	KILAUEA (Hawaiian Is)	1302-01-	0	8/-
	1987	Cont	....	SANTA MARIA (Guatemala)	1402-03=	1	8/8
	1987	Cont	....	RUIZ (Colombia)	1501-02=	2	-/7
	1987	Cont	....	SANGAY (Ecuador)	1502-09=	2	
	1987	Cont	....	CHILLAN, NEVADOS DE (Chile-C)	1507-07=	2	5/-
	1987	Cont	....	EREBUS (Antarctica)	1900-02=	1	
	1987	....	756w	RAUNG (Java)	0603-34=	1	
	1987	01	....	SANGEANG API (Lesser Sunda Is)	0604-05=	1	7/-
	1987	0105d	41m?	FUEGO (Guatemala)	1402-09=	1	
	1987	0115	>3yr	MARAPI (Sumatra)	0601-14=	2	6/-
	1987	0121	....	PACAYA (Guatemala)	1402-11=	3	
	1987	0125	....	WHITE ISLAND (New Zealand)	0401-04=	2	
	1987	0131	....	OKMOK (Aleutian Is)	1101-29-	2	
	1987	0131	144a	AKUTAN (Aleutian Is)	1101-32-	2	

	START YEAR	M-Dy	Duration	VOLCANO NAME (Subregion)	NUMBER	VEI	Vol L/T
	1987	0206	....	KARANGETANG [API SIAU] (Sangihe	0607-02=	3	4/-
	1987	0215	<1	MASAYA (Nicaragua)	1404-10=	1	
	1987	0219	....	KLIUCHEVSKOI (Kamchatka)	1000-26=	3	7/-
	1987	0302	<1	MAKUSHIN (Aleutian Is)	1101-31-	1	
	1987	0304?	14a?	ATKA [KOROVIN] (Aleutian Is)	1101-16-	1	
	1987	0308h	69h	ETNA (Italy)	0101-06=	1	
	1987	0310	<1	KUPREANOF (Alaska Peninsula)	1102-06-	1	
?	1987	0318	?	GREAT SITKIN (Aleutian Is)	1101-12-		
	1987	0318N	....	ATKA [KOROVIN] (Aleutian Is)	1101-16-	2?	
	1987	0318	....	ARENAL (Costa Rica)	1405-033	2	7/7
	1987	0319	<1	VENIAMINOF (Alaska Peninsula)	1102-07-	1	
?	1987	0325	<1	UNNAMED (Kermadec Is)	0402-04=	0	
	1987	0330?	38a?	CANLAON (Philippines-C)	0702-02=	1	
	1987	0401	<1	RINCON DE LA VIEJA (Costa Rica)	1405-02=	1	
	1987	0413	13a	GAMKONORA (Halmahera-Indonesia)	0608-04=	1	
	1987	0413	?	SEMISOPOCHNOI (Aleutian Is)	1101-06-	2?	
?	1987	0415	?	KISKA (Aleutian Is)	1101-02-		
	1987	0417	....	ETNA (Italy)	0101-06=	2	
	1987	0425e	?	NIIGATA-YAKE-YAMA (Honshu-Japan)	0803-09=	1?	
?	1987	0526	?	ESMERALDA BANK (Mariana Is-C Pac)	0804-21=	0	
	1987	06	>3yr	POAS (Costa Rica)	1405-04=	1	
	1987	0604	603a>	MACDONALD (Austral Is-C Pac)	1303-07-	0	
	1987	0610	....	PACAYA (Guatemala)	1402-11=	3	
	1987	0619	70a	CLEVELAND (Aleutian Is)	1101-24-	2	
	1987	0702	<1	COLIMA VOLC COMPLEX (Mexico)	1401-04=	1	
	1987	0714	34a?	SHIN-IWO-JIMA (Volcano Is-Japan	0804-13=	0	
	1987	0719	....	SHEVELUCH (Kamchatka)	1000-27=	3	
?	1987	0723	?	DECEPTION ISLAND (Antarctica)	1900-03=		
	1987	0824	6a	RUAPEHU (New Zealand)	0401-10=	1	
	1987	0828	....	CLEVELAND (Aleutian Is)	1101-24-	3	
?	1987	09	>3yr	SHIN-IWO-JIMA (Volcano Is-Japan)	0804-13=	0	
	1987	0904	<1	PAGAN (Mariana Is-C Pac)	0804-17=	1	
	1987	0904	?	GARELOI (Aleutian Is)	1101-07-	1?	
	1987	0904?	?	AMUKTA (Aleutian Is)	1101-19-	1	
	1987	1002	....	ILIBOLENG (Lesser Sunda Is)	0604-22=	2	
	1987	1011	....	BEZYMIANNY (Kamchatka)	1000-25=	1	
	1987	1014	93m	EBEKO (Kurile Is)	0900-38=	1	-/4
?	1987	1021	<1	BAYONNAISE ROCKS (Izu Is-Japan)	0804-07=	0	
?	1987	11	?	SAN CRISTOBAL (Nicaragua)	1404-02=		
	1987	11	....	TELICA (Nicaragua)	1404-04=	1	
	1987	11 ?	731p?	LASCAR (Chile-N)	1505-10=	0	6/-
	1987	1116	72	OSHIMA (Izu Is-Japan)	0804-01=	3	-/4
?	1987	1116	?	CARLISLE (Aleutian Is)	1101-23-		
	1987	1228	473m>	RANAKAH, GUNUNG (Lesser Sunda I)	0604-071	2	7/6
	1987	1230	4	NYAMURAGIRA (Africa-C)	0203-02=	1	6/6
	1988	Cont	....	STROMBOLI (Italy)	0101-04=	1?	
	1988	Cont	....	ERTA ALE (Ethiopia)	0201-08=	0	
	1988	Cont	....	LENGAI, OL DOINYO (Africa-E)	0202-12=	1	
	1988	Cont	....	NYAMURAGIRA (Africa-C)	0203-02=	1	6/6
	1988	Cont	....	FOURNAISE, PITON DE LA (Indian O.)	0303-02=	1	8/-
	1988	Cont	....	MANAM (New Guinea-NE of)	0501-02=	2	7/-
	1988	Cont	....	LANGILA (New Britain-SW Pac)	0502-01=	2	7/-
	1988	Cont	....	BAGANA (Bougainville-SW Pac)	0505-02=	1	6/-
	1988	Cont	....	YASUR (Vanuatu-SW Pacific)	0507-10=	2	
	1988	Cont	....	MARAPI (Sumatra)	0601-14=	2	6/-
	1988	Cont	....	MERAPI (Java)	0603-25=	1	
	1988	Cont	....	SEMERU (Java)	0603-30=	2	
	1988	Cont	....	RAUNG (Java)	0603-34=	1	
	1988	Cont	....	SANGEANG API (Lesser Sunda Is)	0604-05=	3	7/-
	1988	Cont	....	KARANGETANG [API SIAU] (Sangihe	0607-02=	2	4/-
	1988	Cont	....	DUKONO (Halmahera-Indonesia)	0608-01=	2	
	1988	Cont	....	SUWANOSE-JIMA (Ryukyu Is)	0802-03=	2	
	1988	Cont	....	SAKURA-JIMA (Kyushu-Japan)	0802-08=	2	
?	1988	Cont	....	SHIN-IWO-JIMA (Volcano Is-Japan)	0804-13=	0	
	1988	Cont	....	EBEKO (Kurile Is)	0900-38=	1	-/4
	1988	Cont	....	BEZYMIANNY (Kamchatka)	1000-25=	0	
	1988	Cont	....	KLIUCHEVSKOI (Kamchatka)	1000-26=	2	7/-
	1988	Cont	....	OKMOK (Aleutian Is)	1101-29-	2	
	1988	Cont	....	PAVLOF (Alaska Peninsula)	1102-03-	2	6/-
	1988	Cont	....	KILAUEA (Hawaiian Is)	1302-01-	0	8/-
	1988	Cont	....	MACDONALD (Austral Is-C Pac)	1303-07-	0	
	1988	Cont	....	SANTA MARIA (Guatemala)	1402-03=	1	8/8
	1988	Cont	....	PACAYA (Guatemala)	1402-11=	1	
	1988	Cont	....	RUIZ (Colombia)	1501-02=	2	-/7
	1988	Cont	....	SANGAY (Ecuador)	1502-09=	2	
	1988	Cont	....	EREBUS (Antarctica)	1900-02=	1	
	1988	01	....	LASCAR (Chile-N)	1505-10=	2	6/-
	1988	0103	....	RANAKAH, GUNUNG (Lesser Sunda Is)	0604-071	3	7/6
	1988	0105?	44a	AKAN (Hokkaido-Japan)	0805-07=	1	
	1988	0118	<1	KIKAI (Ryukyu Is)	0802-06=	1	
	1988	0125	....	OSHIMA (Izu Is-Japan)	0804-01=	1	-/4
	1988	02	....	ARENAL (Costa Rica)	1405-033	2	7/7
	1988	0212?	192a?	AMBRYM (Vanuatu-SW Pacific)	0507-04=	3	6/-
	1988	0212	33m?	GAMALATAU (Halmahera-Indonesia)	0608-06=	2	
	1988	0214e	60n?	KRAKATAU (Indonesia)	0602-00=	2	5/-
?	1988	0216	?	PAGAN (Mariana Is-C Pac)	0804-17=		
	1988	0220	16	BULUSAN (Luzon-Philippines)	0703-01=	2	-/4
	1988	0314	....	WHITE ISLAND (New Zealand)	0401-04=	3	
?	1988	0318	1a	BAYONNAISE ROCKS (Izu Is-Japan)	0804-07=	0	
	1988	0320	66c	RUAPEHU (New Zealand)	0401-10=	1	
	1988	0326	116a	AKUTAN (Aleutian Is)	1101-32-	2	
	1988	0409	....	POAS (Costa Rica)	1405-04=	2	
	1988	0421	10a	LOKON-EMPUNG (Sulawesi-Indonesia)	0606-10=	1	
	1988	0509	8a	BANDA API (Banda Sea)	0605-09=	3?	6/-
	1988	0526e	5e	ASO (Kyushu-Japan)	0802-11=	1	
	1988	0601	2a>	UNNAMED (Tonga-SW Pacific)	0403-04=	0	
	1988	0621	10	CANLAON (Philippines-C)	0702-02=	1	
	1988	0622	?	SABANCAYA (Peru)	1504-003	1	
	1988	0712	<1	SLAMET (Java)	0603-18=	1	
	1988	0729	7a	MAKIAN (Halmahera-Indonesia)	0608-07=	3	
?	1988	08	?	EAST EPI (Vanuatu-SW Pacific)	0507-06=	0	
	1988	0824	49a	PAGAN (Mariana Is-C Pac)	0804-17=	2	
S	1988	0908	<1	MONOWAI SEAMOUNT (Kermadec Is)	0402-05-	0	
	1988	0914	2	FERNANDINA (Galapagos)	1503-01=	2?	6/-
	1988	1004	269a	ETNA (Italy)	0101-06=	1	
	1988	11	< 594w>	COLIMA VOLC COMPLEX (Mexico)	1401-04=	1	
	1988	1115q	?	VIEDMA, VOLCAN (Argentina)	1508-061		
	1988	1207	<1	SHEVELUCH (Kamchatka)	1000-27=	2?	
	1988	1208	87a?	RUAPEHU (New Zealand)	0401-10=	1	
	1988	1216	150m	TOKACHI (Hokkaido-Japan)	0805-05=	2	-/5
	1988	1225	395b	LONQUIMAY (Chile-C)	1507-10=	2	8/8
	1988	1227	....	LONQUIMAY (Chile-C)	1507-10=	3	8/8
	1988	1228	<1	ASO (Kyushu-Japan)	0802-11=	1	
S	1988	1229	<1	KICK-'EM-JENNY (W Indies)	1600-16=	0	
	1989	Cont	....	STROMBOLI (Italy)	0101-04=	1?	
	1989	Cont	....	ERTA ALE (Ethiopia)	0201-08=	0	
	1989	Cont	....	LENGAI, OL DOINYO (Africa-E)	0202-12=	1	
	1989	Cont	....	MANAM (New Guinea-NE of)	0501-02=	2	7/-
	1989	Cont	....	LANGILA (New Britain-SW Pac)	0502-01=	2	7/-
	1989	Cont	....	BAGANA (Bougainville-SW Pac)	0505-02=	1	6/-
	1989	Cont	....	YASUR (Vanuatu-SW Pacific)	0507-10=	2	
	1989	Cont	....	MARAPI (Sumatra)	0601-14=	2	6/-
	1989	Cont	....	MERAPI (Java)	0603-25=	1	
	1989	Cont	....	SEMERU (Java)	0603-30=	2	
	1989	Cont	....	RAUNG (Java)	0603-34=	1	
	1989	Cont	....	RANAKAH, GUNUNG (Lesser Sunda I)	0604-071	0	7/6
	1989	Cont	....	DUKONO (Halmahera-Indonesia)	0608-01=	2	
	1989	Cont	....	SUWANOSE-JIMA (Ryukyu Is)	0802-03=	2	
	1989	Cont	....	SAKURA-JIMA (Kyushu-Japan)	0802-08=	2	
?	1989	Cont	....	SHIN-IWO-JIMA (Volcano Is-Japan)	0804-13=	0	
	1989	Cont	....	TOKACHI (Hokkaido-Japan)	0805-05=	2	-/5
	1989	Cont	....	KLIUCHEVSKOI (Kamchatka)	1000-26=	2	7/-
	1989	Cont	....	KILAUEA (Hawaiian Is)	1302-01-	0	8/-
	1989	Cont	....	MACDONALD (Austral Is-C Pac)	1303-07-	0	
	1989	Cont	....	COLIMA VOLC COMPLEX (Mexico)	1401-04=	0	
	1989	Cont	....	RUIZ (Colombia)	1501-02=	2	-/7
	1989	Cont	....	SANGAY (Ecuador)	1502-09=	2	
	1989	Cont	....	LASCAR (Chile-N)	1505-10=	0	6/-
	1989	Cont	....	LONQUIMAY (Chile-C)	1507-10=	2	8/8
	1989	Cont	....	EREBUS (Antarctica)	1900-02=	1	
	1989	....	....	ARENAL (Costa Rica)	1405-033	2	7/7
	1989	0101	349m?	ULAWUN (New Britain-SW Pac)	0502-12=	2	
?	1989	0106	<1	KUSATSU-SHIRANE (Honshu-Japan)	0803-12=	1	
	1989	0113	1a	SARYCHEV PEAK (Kurile Is)	0900-24=	1?	
	1989	0202	232a?	EBEKO (Kurile Is)	0900-38=	2	-/6
	1989	0219	79a	GALERAS (Colombia)	1501-08=	2	-/5
	1989	0220	102a?	MASAYA (Nicaragua)	1404-10=	1	
	1989	0227	29a<	AKUTAN (Aleutian Is)	1101-32-	2	
	1989	0307	....	PACAYA (Guatemala)	1402-11=	3	
	1989	0314	....	WHITE ISLAND (New Zealand)	0401-04=	2	
	1989	0405	675a	ASO (Kyushu-Japan)	0802-11=	0	
	1989	0407	80	SHEVELUCH (Kamchatka)	1000-27=	2	
	1989	0419	7a	NIIGATA-YAKE-YAMA (Honshu-Japan)	0803-09=	1	
	1989	0422	<1	SOPUTAN (Sulawesi-Indonesia)	0606-03=	2	
	1989	0424	113e	NYAMURAGIRA (Africa-C)	0203-02=	3	7/7
	1989	0424	243a	AMBRYM (Vanuatu-SW Pacific)	0507-04=	2	
	1989	05	....	POAS (Costa Rica)	1405-04=	2	
	1989	0503	95d	GROZNY GROUP (Kurile Is)	0900-07=	2	
	1989	07	16m	KARANGETANG [API SIAU] (Sangihe	0607-02=	1	
	1989	0701	81a?	RUAPEHU (New Zealand)	0401-10=	1	
	1989	0712	1	SLAMET (Java)	0603-18=	1	
	1989	0713	<1	IZU-TOBU (Honshu-Japan)	0803-01=	1	-/5
	1989	0716	....	ASO (Kyushu-Japan)	0802-11=	2	
	1989	0719	....	SANTA MARIA (Guatemala)	1402-03=	3	8/8
	1989	0801	3a	BEZYMIANNY (Kamchatka)	1000-25=	2	
	1989	0817	?	GARELOI (Aleutian Is)	1101-07-	1	
	1989	0911	28a	ETNA (Italy)	0101-06=	2	7/-
S	1989	0921	97	SUPPLY REEF (Mariana Is-C Pac)	0804-142	0	
	1989	1025	49a>	CANLAON (Philippines-C)	0702-02=	2	
?	1989	1025c	?	CLEVELAND (Aleutian Is)	1101-24-	0	
?	1989	12	?	IRRUPUTUNCU (Chile-N)	1505-04=		
	1989	1207	30a	ST. HELENS (US-Washington)	1201-05-	1	
	1989	1214	173d	REDOUBT (Alaska-SW)	1103-03-	3	7/-
	1989	1216	120m	ETNA (Italy)	0101-06=	1	
	1990	Cont	....	STROMBOLI (Italy)	0101-04=	1?	
	1990	Cont	....	ERTA ALE (Ethiopia)	0201-08=	0	
	1990	Cont	....	LENGAI, OL DOINYO (Africa-E)	0202-12=	1	
	1990	Cont	....	WHITE ISLAND (New Zealand)	0401-04=	1	
	1990	Cont	....	MANAM (New Guinea-NE of)	0501-02=	2	7/-
	1990	Cont	....	LANGILA (New Britain-SW Pac)	0502-01=	2	7/-
	1990	Cont	....	BAGANA (Bougainville-SW Pac)	0505-02=	1	6/-
	1990	Cont	....	YASUR (Vanuatu-SW Pacific)	0507-10=	2	
	1990	Cont	....	MARAPI (Sumatra)	0601-14=	2	6/-
	1990	Cont	....	MERAPI (Java)	0603-25=	1	
	1990	Cont	....	SEMERU (Java)	0603-30=	2	
	1990	Cont	....	DUKONO (Halmahera-Indonesia)	0608-01=	2	
	1990	Cont	....	SUWANOSE-JIMA (Ryukyu Is)	0802-03=	2	
	1990	Cont	....	SAKURA-JIMA (Kyushu-Japan)	0802-08=	2	
	1990	Cont	....	ASO (Kyushu-Japan)	0802-11=	0	
?	1990	Cont	....	SHIN-IWO-JIMA (Volcano Is-Japan)	0804-13=	0	
	1990	Cont	....	EBEKO (Kurile Is)	0900-38=	2	-/6
	1990	Cont	....	KILAUEA (Hawaiian Is)	1302-01-	0	8/-
	1990	Cont	....	COLIMA VOLC COMPLEX (Mexico)	1401-04=	0	
	1990	Cont	....	POAS (Costa Rica)	1405-04=	1	
	1990	Cont	....	RUIZ (Colombia)	1501-02=	2	-/7

	START YEAR	START M-Dy	Duration	VOLCANO NAME (Subregion)	NUMBER	VEI	Vol L/T
	1990	Cont	....	SANGAY (Ecuador)	1502-09=	2	
	1990	Cont	....	LONQUIMAY (Chile-C)	1507-10=	2	8/8
	1990	Cont	....	EREBUS (Antarctica)	1900-02=	1	
	1990	....	....	ARENAL (Costa Rica)	1405-033	2	7/7
	1990	01 <	334p>	RAUNG (Java)	0603-34=	2	
	1990	0102	....	REDOUBT (Alaska-SW)	1103-03-	3	7/-
	1990	0104?	>3yr	PACAYA (Guatemala)	1402-11=	1	
	1990	0106	....	ST. HELENS (US-Washington)	1201-05-	2	
	1990	0107	24a	RUAPEHU (New Zealand)	0401-10=	1	
	1990	0107	921a	GALERAS (Colombia)	1501-08=	1	
	1990	0118	110a	FOURNAISE, PITON DE LA (Indian O.)	0303-02=	0	6/-
	1990	0126e	3a	AKUTAN (Aleutian Is)	1101-32-	2	
	1990	0128	138m	LEWOTOBI (Lesser Sunda Is)	0604-18=	1	
	1990	0129	308a>	BEZYMIANNY (Kamchatka)	1000-25=	2	
	1990	0129	156a	SHEVELUCH (Kamchatka)	1000-27=	2	
	1990	0201	....	KLIUCHEVSKOI (Kamchatka)	1000-26=	3	7/-
	1990	0210	6a	KELUT (Java)	0603-28=	4	-/8
	1990	0220	45	LASCAR (Chile-N)	1505-10=	3	
	1990	0225	273a	LLAIMA (Chile-C)	1507-11=	1	
	1990	0305	<1	PAVLOF (Alaska Peninsula)	1102-03-	2?	
	1990	0310	....	BEZYMIANNY (Kamchatka)	1000-25=	3	
S	1990	0326	1	KICK-'EM-JENNY (W Indies)	1600-16=	0	
	1990	0416	24a	GUAGUA PICHINCHA (Ecuador)	1502-02=	1	
?	1990	0424	<1	PULAR (Chile-N)	1505-105	1?	
	1990	0425	1a	GAMALAMA (Halmahera-Indonesia)	0608-06=	3?	
	1990	0528	627m>	SABANCAYA (Peru)	1504-003	2	
S	1990	0530	299a	MONOWAI SEAMOUNT (Kermadec Is)	0402-05-	0	
	1990	0601	<1	KISKA (Aleutian Is)	1101-02-	2	
	1990	0605	....	SABANCAYA (Peru)	1504-003	3	
	1990	0617	83a<	RUAPEHU (New Zealand)	0401-10=	0	
	1990	0713	....	SANTA MARIA (Guatemala)	1402-03=	3	8/8
	1990	0714	....	PACAYA (Guatemala)	1402-11=	2	
	1990	0720	<1	ASAMA (Honshu-Japan)	0803-11=	2	
	1990	0804	....	SHEVELUCH (Kamchatka)	1000-27=	3	
	1990	09 <	304p>	AMBRYM (Vanuatu-SW Pacific)	0507-04=	2	
	1990	0906	25a	AKUTAN (Aleutian Is)	1101-32-	2	
	1990	10	554m	ETNA (Italy)	0101-06=	1	
	1990	1004	<1	OSHIMA (Izu Is-Japan)	0804-01=	2	
?	1990	1029	21a	UNNAMED (Pacific-S)	1304-03-	0	
	1990	1105	101a	ST. HELENS (US-Washington)	1201-05-	3?	
	1990	1117	>3yr	UNZEN (Kyushu-Japan)	0802-10=	1	8/6
	1990	1124	?	LASCAR (Chile-N)	1505-10=	1	
	1991	Cont	....	STROMBOLI (Italy)	0101-04=	1?	
	1991	Cont	....	ERTA ALE (Ethiopia)	0201-08=	0	
	1991	Cont	....	LENGAI, OL DOINYO (Africa-E)	0202-12=	1	
S	1991	Cont	....	MONOWAI SEAMOUNT (Kermadec Is)	0402-05-	0	
	1991	Cont	....	MANAM (New Guinea-NE of)	0501-02=	2	7/-
	1991	Cont	....	LANGILA (New Britain-SW Pac)	0502-01=	2	7/-
	1991	Cont	....	BAGANA (Bougainville-SW Pac)	0505-02=	1	6/-
	1991	Cont	....	AMBRYM (Vanuatu-SW Pacific)	0507-04=	2	
	1991	Cont	....	YASUR (Vanuatu-SW Pacific)	0507-10=	2	
	1991	Cont	....	MARAPI (Sumatra)	0601-14=	2	6/-
	1991	Cont	....	SEMERU (Java)	0603-30=	2	
	1991	Cont	....	DUKONO (Halmahera-Indonesia)	0608-01=	2	
	1991	Cont	....	SUWANOSE-JIMA (Ryukyu Is)	0802-03=	2	
	1991	Cont	....	SAKURA-JIMA (Kyushu-Japan)	0802-08=	2	
	1991	Cont	....	UNZEN (Kyushu-Japan)	0802-10=	2	8/6
	1991	Cont	....	ASO (Kyushu-Japan)	0802-11=	0	
	1991	Cont	....	ST. HELENS (US-Washington)	1201-05-	3?	
	1991	Cont	....	KILAUEA (Hawaiian Is)	1302-01-	0	8/-
	1991	Cont	....	RUIZ (Colombia)	1501-02=	2	-/7
	1991	Cont	....	GALERAS (Colombia)	1501-08=	1	
	1991	Cont	....	SANGAY (Ecuador)	1502-09=	2	
	1991	Cont	....	SABANCAYA (Peru)	1504-003	2	
	1991	Cont	....	EREBUS (Antarctica)	1900-02=	1	
	1991	....	....	ARENAL (Costa Rica)	1405-033	2	7/7
	1991	01	3a	EBEKO (Kurile Is)	0900-38=	1	
	1991	0113	17a	AVACHINSKY (Kamchatka)	1000-10=	3	
	1991	0117	52	HEKLA (Iceland-S)	1702-07=	3	8/7
	1991	0209	21b	PLANCHON-PETEROA (Chile-C)	1507-04=	2	
	1991	03 <	?	RANAKAH, GUNUNG (Lesser Sunda I	0604-071	1	
	1991	03 <	?	UNNAMED (Pacific-E)	1303-01-	0	
	1991	0301	228m	COLIMA VOLC COMPLEX (Mexico)	1401-04=	2	
	1991	0306	81e	POAS (Costa Rica)	1405-04=	1	
?	1991	0311	8a	UNNAMED (Pacific-S)	1304-02-	0	
	1991	04	228p	BEZYMIANNY (Kamchatka)	1000-25=	0	
	1991	0402	153a	PINATUBO (Luzon-Philippines)	0703-083	2?	
	1991	0406<	208g>	BARREN ISLAND (Andaman Is-Ind O	0600-01=	2	
	1991	0408	77a?	KLIUCHEVSKOI (Kamchatka)	1000-26=	2	
	1991	0408	31a?	SHEVELUCH (Kamchatka)	1000-27=	3	
	1991	0410	....	SANTA MARIA (Guatemala)	1402-03=	2	8/8
	1991	0419	4	FERNANDINA (Galapagos)	1503-01=	2?	
	1991	0504<	44c>	KAVACHI (Solomon Is-SW Pac)	0505-06=	2	
	1991	0506	2a	RINCON DE LA VIEJA (Costa Rica)	1405-02=	1	
	1991	0508	53a>	ILIBOLENG (Lesser Sunda Is)	0604-22=	1	
	1991	0511	218m?	LEWOTOBI (Lesser Sunda Is)	0604-18=	1	
	1991	0517	243m	LOKON-EMPUNG (Sulawesi-Indonesia)	0606-10=	1	5/-
	1991	0522	24m	SOPUTAN (Sulawesi-Indonesia)	0606-03=	1	6/-
?	1991	0615	<1	GAMALAMA (Halmahera-Indonesia)	0608-06=	1?	
	1991	0615	....	PINATUBO (Luzon-Philippines)	0703-083	6	-/10
	1991	0702<	776m>	KARANGETANG [API SIAU] (Sangihe	0607-02=	1	6/6
?	1991	0705?	9a?	RUAPEHU (New Zealand)	0401-10=	1	
	1991	0711	<1	KARTHALA (Indian O.-W)	0303-01=	2	
	1991	0719	1	FOURNAISE, PITON DE LA (Indian O.)	0303-02=	0	
	1991	0727	...	PACAYA (Guatemala)	1402-11=	3	
	1991	0808	80	HUDSON, CERRO (Chile-S)	1508-057	3	
	1991	0812	....	HUDSON, CERRO (Chile-S)	1508-057	5	-/9
?	1991	0812	?	LOKI-FOGRUFJOLL (Iceland-NE)	1703-02=	0	
	1991	0829	<1	RINCON DE LA VIEJA (Costa Rica)	1405-02=	1	
	1991	0830	18a	VILLARRICA (Chile-C)	1507-12=	2	
	1991	09	16m	POAS (Costa Rica)	1405-04=	0	
	1991	0910	23a>	RAUNG (Java)	0603-34=	2	
?	1991	0913	?	ARJUNO-WELIRANG (Java)	0603-29=		
	1991	0915	44a	AKUTAN (Aleutian Is)	1101-32-	2	
	1991	0916	....	WHITE ISLAND (New Zealand)	0401-04=	3	
	1991	0920	507a	NYAMURAGIRA (Africa-C)	0203-02=	2	
	1991	0925	51m?	MARCHENA (Galapagos)	1503-08=	2	
?	1991	0930	18a	SHIN-IWO-JIMA (Volcano Is-Japan)	0804-13=	0	
	1991	1012	612m>	SOPUTAN (Sulawesi-Indonesia)	0606-03=	1?	7/-
	1991	1015	....	NYAMURAGIRA (Africa-C)	0203-02=	3	
	1991	1021	215a?	LASCAR (Chile-N)	1505-10=	2	-/6
	1991	1025	....	LOKON-EMPUNG (Sulawesi-Indonesia)	0606-10=	2	5/-
	1991	1103	12a	ILIBOLENG (Lesser Sunda Is)	0604-22=	1	
	1991	1127	....	BEZYMIANNY (Kamchatka)	1000-25=	2	
	1991	1129	47a?	WESTDAHL (Aleutian Is)	1101-34-	3	
	1991	1214	472a	ETNA (Italy)	0101-06=	2	8/-
	1992	Cont	....	STROMBOLI (Italy)	0101-04=	1?	
	1992	Cont	....	ETNA (Italy)	0101-06=	2	8/-
	1992	Cont	....	ERTA ALE (Ethiopia)	0201-08=	0	
	1992	Cont	....	LENGAI, OL DOINYO (Africa-E)	0202-12=	1	
	1992	Cont	....	NYAMURAGIRA (Africa-C)	0203-02=	2	
	1992	Cont	....	WHITE ISLAND (New Zealand)	0401-04=	1	
	1992	Cont	....	LANGILA (New Britain-SW Pac)	0502-01=	2	7/-
	1992	Cont	....	BAGANA (Bougainville-SW Pac)	0505-02=	1	6/-
	1992	Cont	....	YASUR (Vanuatu-SW Pacific)	0507-10=	2	
	1992	Cont	....	MARAPI (Sumatra)	0601-14=	2	6/-
	1992	Cont	....	SEMERU (Java)	0603-30=	2	
	1992	Cont	....	SOPUTAN (Sulawesi-Indonesia)	0606-03=	1?	7/-
	1992	Cont	....	LOKON-EMPUNG (Sulawesi-Indonesia)	0606-10=	1	5/-
	1992	Cont	....	KARANGETANG [API SIAU] (Sangihe	0607-02=	1	6/6
	1992	Cont	....	DUKONO (Halmahera-Indonesia)	0608-01=	2	
	1992	Cont	....	SUWANOSE-JIMA (Ryukyu Is)	0802-03=	2	
	1992	Cont	....	SAKURA-JIMA (Kyushu-Japan)	0802-08=	2	
	1992	Cont	....	UNZEN (Kyushu-Japan)	0802-10=	2	8/6
	1992	Cont	....	WESTDAHL (Aleutian Is)	1101-34-	3	
	1992	Cont	....	KILAUEA (Hawaiian Is)	1302-01-	0	8/-
	1992	Cont	....	SANTA MARIA (Guatemala)	1402-03=	1	8/8
	1992	Cont	....	PACAYA (Guatemala)	1402-11=	1	
	1992	Cont	....	SANGAY (Ecuador)	1502-09=	2	
	1992	Cont	....	SABANCAYA (Peru)	1504-003	2	
	1992	Cont	....	LASCAR (Chile-N)	1505-10=	2	-/6
	1992	Cont	....	EREBUS (Antarctica)	1900-02=	1	
	1992	....	....	ARENAL (Costa Rica)	1405-033	2	7/7
	1992	01 ?	70m?	RINCON DE LA VIEJA (Costa Rica)	1405-02=	1	
	1992	0108	....	CANLAON (Philippines-C)	0702-02=	1	
?	1992	0117	1a	HEARD (Indian O.-S)	0304-01=		
	1992	0120	695m>	MERAPI (Java)	0603-25=	2	7/-
	1992	0125	110a?	KLIUCHEVSKOI (Kamchatka)	1000-26=	2	
	1992	0128	<1	KIRISHIMA (Kyushu-Japan)	0802-09=	1	-/2
	1992	02	31p	POAS (Costa Rica)	1405-04=	1	
	1992	0208	27a	RUAPEHU (New Zealand)	0401-10=	1	
?	1992	0212	21a	MINAMI-HIYOSHI (Volcano Is-Japan)	0804-131	0	
	1992	0308	74a	AKUTAN (Aleutian Is)	1101-32-	2	
	1992	0312	4a	BEZYMIANNY (Kamchatka)	1000-25=	2	
	1992	0407i	?	AWU (Sangihe Is-Indonesia)	0607-04=	1	
	1992	0409	5a	NEGRO, CERRO (Nicaragua)	1404-07=	3	-/7
	1992	0413	<1	PAGAN (Mariana Is-C Pac)	0804-17=	1?	
	1992	0423	326m?	ASO (Kyushu-Japan)	0802-11=	0	
	1992	0529?	?	HEARD (Indian O.-S)	0304-01=	0	
	1992	0610	<1	CANLAON (Philippines-C)	0702-02=	2	
	1992	0627	81	SPURR (Alaska-SW)	1103-04-	4	-/7
	1992	0705d	117a	PINATUBO (Luzon-Philippines)	0703-083	1	
	1992	0706	20e	BOGOSLOF (Aleutian Is)	1101-30-	3	
	1992	0716	....	GALERAS (Colombia)	1501-08=	2	
	1992	0722	71a	COPAHUE (Chile-C)	1507-09=	2	
?	1992	08	16m	RINCON DE LA VIEJA (Costa Rica)	1405-02=		
	1992	0818	....	SPURR (Alaska-SW)	1103-04-	3	-/7
	1992	0823	10a	LLAIMA (Chile-C)	1507-11=	1	
	1992	0827	27a	FOURNAISE, PITON DE LA (Indian O.)	0303-02=	1	
	1992	0831	....	MANAM (New Guinea-NE of)	0501-02=	3	7/-
	1992	0911	96m>	VILLARRICA (Chile-C)	1507-12=	1	
	1992	0917	....	SPURR (Alaska-SW)	1103-04-	3	-/7
	1992	10	365p	POAS (Costa Rica)	1405-04=	0	
	1992	1026	....	ASO (Kyushu-Japan)	0802-11=	2	
	1992	1107	341m	KRAKATAU (Indonesia)	0602-00=	1	6/-
	1992	1110	8a?	SHIN-IWO-JIMA (Volcano Is-Japan)	0804-13=	1	
	1992	1218	?	AKUTAN (Aleutian Is)	1101-32-	1	
	1992	1227	3a	SEGUAM (Aleutian Is)	1101-18-	1	
	1993	Cont	....	STROMBOLI (Italy)	0101-04=	1?	
	1993	Cont	....	ERTA ALE (Ethiopia)	0201-08=	0	
	1993	Cont	....	NYAMURAGIRA (Africa-C)	0203-02=	2	
	1993	Cont	....	WHITE ISLAND (New Zealand)	0401-04=	1	
	1993	Cont	....	LANGILA (New Britain-SW Pac)	0502-01=	2	7/-
	1993	Cont	....	BAGANA (Bougainville-SW Pac)	0505-02=	1	6/-
	1993	Cont	....	YASUR (Vanuatu-SW Pacific)	0507-10=	2	
	1993	Cont	....	MARAPI (Sumatra)	0601-14=	2	6/-
	1993	Cont	....	KRAKATAU (Indonesia)	0602-00=	1	6/-
	1993	Cont	....	MERAPI (Java)	0603-25=	2	7/-
	1993	Cont	....	SEMERU (Java)	0603-30=	2	
	1993	Cont	....	SOPUTAN (Sulawesi-Indonesia)	0606-03=	1?	7/-
	1993	Cont	....	KARANGETANG [API SIAU] (Sangihe	0607-02=	1	6/6
	1993	Cont	....	DUKONO (Halmahera-Indonesia)	0608-01=	2	
	1993	Cont	....	SUWANOSE-JIMA (Ryukyu Is)	0802-03=	2	
	1993	Cont	....	SAKURA-JIMA (Kyushu-Japan)	0802-08=	2	

START YEAR	M-Dy	Duration	VOLCANO NAME (Subregion)	NUMBER	VEI	Vol L/T
1993	*Cont*	....	*UNZEN (Kyushu-Japan)*	0802-10=	*2*	*8/6*
1993	*Cont*	....	*ASO (Kyushu-Japan)*	0802-11=	*0*	
1993	*Cont*	....	*KILAUEA (Hawaiian Is)*	1302-01-	*0*	*8/-*
1993	*Cont*	....	*SANTA MARIA (Guatemala)*	1402-03=	*1*	*8/8*
1993	*Cont*	....	*POAS (Costa Rica)*	1405-04=	*0*	
1993	*Cont*	....	*SANGAY (Ecuador)*	1502-09=	*2*	
1993	*Cont*	....	*EREBUS (Antarctica)*	1900-02=	*1*	
1993	....	....	*ARENAL (Costa Rica)*	1405-033	2	*7/7*
1993	0102m	?	**HEARD** (Indian O.-S)	0304-01=	2?	
1993	*0110*	....	*PACAYA (Guatemala)*	1402-11=	2	
1993	0112	19*a*	**ULAWUN** (New Britain-SW Pac)	0502-12=	2	
1993	0114	144*a*>	**GALERAS** (Colombia)	1501-08=	2	-/6
1993	0115e	181*m*>	**PAGAN** (Mariana Is-C Pac)	0804-17=	2	
1993	0123	<1	**DIENG VOLC COMPLEX** (Java)	0603-20=	1	
1993	0129	19*a?*	**SOCORRO** (Mexico-Is)	1401-021	0	
1993	*0130*	*98a*	*LASCAR (Chile-N)*	1505-10=	2	*6/8*
? **1993**	02	213*p*	**SHIN-IWO-JIMA** (Volcano Is-Japan	0804-13=	0	
1993	0202	59*a?*	**MAYON** (Luzon-Philippines)	0703-03=	2?	7/6
1993	0203	<1	**ETNA** (Italy)	0101-06=	1	
1993	0309	3*a*	**GUAGUA PICHINCHA** (Ecuador)	1502-02=	1	
1993	0315e	220*m?*	**KLIUCHEVSKOI** (Kamchatka)	1000-26=	2	
1993	*0318*	*211m?*	*SHEVELUCH (Kamchatka)*	1000-27=	2	
1993	0328	?	**ARACAR** (Argentina)	1505-107	2	
1993	0401t	?	**RAUNG** (Java)	0603-34=	1	
1993	0419	....	**LASCAR** (Chile-N)	1505-10=	4	6/8
1993	0422	....	**SHEVELUCH** (Kamchatka)	1000-27=	3?	
? **1993**	0425	?	**TAFTAN** (Iran)	0302-05-		
1993	0506	25*a*	**GAMALAMA** (Halmahera-Indonesia)	0608-06=	2	
1993	0528	95*a*>	**SEGUAM** (Aleutian Is)	1101-18-	2	
1993	06 ?	31*p?*	**ILIBOLENG** (Lesser Sunda Is)	0604-22=	1?	
1993	*0614*	....	*LENGAI, OL DOINYO (Africa-E)*	0202-12=	2	
1993	0616	121*m*>	**MASAYA** (Nicaragua)	1404-10=	1	
1993	0626	8*a?*	**UNNAMED** (Pacific-NE)	1301-01-	0	
1993	0703	29*a*	**IJEN** (Java)	0603-35=	1	
1993	*0714*	....	*MYANAM (New Guinea-NE of)*	0501-02=	3	*7/-*
1993	0730	154*a*>	**VENIAMINOF** (Alaska Peninsula)	1102-07-	2	
1993	0803	63*d*	**ETNA** (Italy)	0101-06=	1	
1993	0825	9	**CANLAON** (Philippines-C)	0702-02=	2	
1993	0915	3	**ILIWERUNG** (Lesser Sunda Is)	0604-25=	2	
1993	1021	28*a?*	**BEZYMIANNY** (Kamchatka)	1000-25=	3	
1993	1028	?	**SHISHALDIN** (Aleutian Is)	1101-36-	2	
1993	1105d	?	**LONG ISLAND** (New Guinea-NE of)	0501-05=	0	
1993	1217	?	**LASCAR** (Chile-N)	1505-10=	2	

Figure 31. Mudflow at Mt. Pinatubo, Philippines, 4 months after its major eruption in 1991. These devastating, thick, and highly erosive flows may reoccur long after an eruption has ended. They need nothing more than abundant rains to combine with fresh ash on a volcano's steep and barren slopes. By 1994, the channel shown here had filled, and mudflow deposits had buried a 3-km-wide swath of homes by as much as 15 m. Photo by Chris Newhall.

Gazetteer

The gazetteer lists volcano names, synonyms, and subsidiary feature names (with their synonyms). For each volcano, we also list type, number of eruptions, and date of the last eruption (these eruptions do not include uncertain events, and neither dating method codes nor uncertainties are listed). Some frequently encountered spelling variations of names have been eliminated from the gazetteer for reasons of space and redundancy.

- The Japanese word for island is transliterated *shima* or *jima* in the officially-approved style; the older Hepburn-style transliteration of *sima* or *zima* is often not listed. *Chokai* is similarly preferred over *Tyokai*, and *Fuji* over *Huzi*. However, synonyms with distinct spelling differences are listed separately in the gazetteer.
- The Dutch "oe" spelling of the Indonesian "u" (*Keloed*, *Kelud*) is not listed where it would have resulted in adjacent entries in the gazetteer. However, other spelling variations, such as the Dutch "Tj" for the Indonesian "C", and "Dj" for "J" appear separately in the gazetteer; both *Cereme* and its synonym *Tjereme* are listed.
- Variations of Cyrillic transliterations such as Karymsky, Karymskiy, Karymiskii, Karymskaya, and Karymskaia, are not listed separately.

A synonym of a volcano name is sometimes followed by one or more additional synonyms that would otherwise have appeared in an adjacent line. When synonyms of a volcano subsidiary feature name are so similar as to result in adjacent entries in the gazetteer, one of the entries has been removed, and the preferred name is shown in brackets following the synonym.

NAME (Subregion)	Type (Eruption Total, Most Recent) Status . . . Relation to NAMED VOLCANO	NUMBER

A

NAME (Subregion)	Type (Eruption Total, Most Recent) Status . . . Relation to NAMED VOLCANO	NUMBER
ABANG, GUNUNG (Lesser Sunda Is)	Stratovolc of BATUR	0604-01=
ABARO (Ethiopia)	Cone of CORBETTI CALDERA	0201-29-
ABAS TEPE (Turkey)	Cone of ERCIYES DAGI	0103-01=
ABBOTT PEAK (Antarctica)	Cone of EREBUS	1900-02=
ABEJERA, MONTANA (Canary Is)	Cone of TENERIFE	1803-03-
ABIDA (Ethiopia)	Synonym of ADWA	0201-17=
ABILI AGITUK [WARGESS] (Africa-E)	Tuff cone of BARRIER, THE	0202-03=
ABINGDON (Galapagos)	Synonym of PINTA	1503-07=
ABOA (Vanuatu-SW Pacific)	Synonym of AOBA	0507-03=
ABOUR, JEBEL EL (Africa-N)	Cone of BAYUDA VOLC FIELD	0205-06-
ABRIGO, CERRO DEL (US-New Mexico)	Dome of VALLES CALDERA	1210-03-
ABU (Honshu-Japan)	Shields (None) Holocene	**0803-001**
ABU HARIS, JABAL (Arabia-W)	Dome of KISHB, HARRAT	0301-071
ABYAD, JABAL (Arabia-W)	Dome of KHAYBAR, HARRAT	0301-06=
ACAMARCHI (Chile-N)	Stratovolc (None) Holocene?	**1505-096**
ACATENANGO (Guatemala)	Stratovolc (5, 1972) Historical	**1402-08=**
ACCADEMIA [MT. OLIBANO] (Italy)	Dome of CAMPI FLEGREI	0101-01=
ACHACARA, LOMA (Peru)	Cone of ANDAHUA VALLEY	1504-002
ACHELONE (Greece)	Vent of NISYROS	0102-05=
ACHI-YAMA (Izu Is-Japan)	Dome of NII-JIMA	0804-02=
ACHLAN (Kamchatka)	Synonym of ICHINSKY	1000-28=
ACIGOL (Turkey)	Crater of KARAPINAR FIELD	0103-001
ACIGOL-NEVSEHIR (Turkey)	Maars (None) Holocene	**0103-004**
ACIGOL-NEYSEHIR (Turkey)	Synonym of ACIGOL-NEVSEHIR	0103-004
ACOTANGO (Chile-N)	Stratovolcs (None) Holocene	**1505-017**
ACROPOLI (Italy)	Cone of PANTELLERIA	0101-071
ADAGDAK (Aleutian Is)	Stratovolc (None) Holocene	**1101-112**
ADAMS (US-Washington)	Stratovolc (1, -7535) Tephrochronology	**1201-04-**
ADAS TEPE [ABAS TEPE] (Turkey)	Cone of ERCIYES DAGI	0103-01=
ADATARA (Honshu-Japan)	Stratovolcs (2, 1900) Historical	**0803-17=**
ADATARA-YAMA (Honshu-Japan)	Dome of ADATARA	0803-17=
ADHAMAS (Greece)	Thermal Feature of MILOS	0102-03=
ADIKA-WILIS (Java)	Synonym of WILIS	0603-27=
ADO ALE (Ethiopia)	Synonym of ASSAB VOLC FIELD	0201-125
ADO WADJUNG [ADO WAJUNG] (Lesser Su	Crater of ILIWERUNG	0604-25=
ADWA (Ethiopia)	Stratovolc (None) Holocene	**0201-17=**
AEK AMDURANA [AEK MADURANA]	Thermal Feature of BUAL BUALI	0601-11=
AEK WALIRAN (Sumatra)	Thermal Feature of BUAL BUALI	0601-11=
AER PANAS (Sumatra)	Thermal Feature of GAYOLESTEN	0601-06=
AESEPUT (Sulawesi-Indonesia)	Cone of SOPUTAN	0606-03=
AESEPUT WERO (Sulawesi-Indonesia)	Dome of SOPUTAN	0606-03=
AESUPUT (Java)	Stratovolc of DANAU COMPLEX	0603-01=
AETNA (Italy)	Synonym of ETNA	0101-06=
AFANA (SW Pacific)	Crater of WALLIS ISLANDS	0404-05-
AFATE, CERRO [APALE] (El Salvador)	Dome of COATEPEQUE CALDERA	1403-041
AFDERA (Ethiopia)	Stratovolc (None) Holocene?	**0201-11=**
AFLITOS (Azores)	Cone of UNNAMED	1802-081
AFOLAU (Samoa-SW Pacific)	Cone of UPOLU	0404-03-
AFONO (Samoa-SW Pacific)	Dome of TUTUILA	0404-02-
AFOSA, MONTANA DE (Canary Is)	Cone of HIERRO	1803-02-
AFRERA (Ethiopia)	Synonym of AFDERA	0201-11=
AFUTINA (Samoa-SW Pacific)	Cone of SAVAI'I	0404-04=
AGAJEDAN (Aleutian Is)	Synonym of SHISHALDIN	1101-36-
AGASCHAGOCH (Aleutian Is)	Synonym of BOGOSLOF	1101-30-
AGELU (Ethiopia)	Synonym of AYELU	0201-16=
AGHIE [PECHAN] (China-W)	Cone of TIANSHAN VOLC GROUP	1004-02-
AGIN-COURT (Taiwan-N of)	Synonym of PENG-CHIA-HSU	0801-041
AGIOS JOANNIS (Greece)	Vent of NISYROS	0102-05=
AGMAGAN-KARADAG (Armenia)	Volc field (None) Holocene	**0104-07-**
AGNANO (Italy)	Caldera of CAMPI FLEGREI	0101-01=
AGNANO MONTE SPINA (Italy)	Crater of CAMPI FLEGREI	0101-01=
AGOENG (Lesser Sunda Is)	Synonym of AGUNG	0604-02=
AGONIA, PUIG S' (Spain)	Cone of OLOT VOLC FIELD	0100-03-
AGOTU VALLEY (New Guinea)	Cone of CRATER MOUNTAIN	0503-001
AGRI DAGI (Turkey)	Synonym of ARARAT, MT.	0103-04-
AGRIGAN (Mariana Is-C Pac)	Stratovolc (1, 1917) Historical	**0804-16=**
AGRIHAN (Mariana Is-C Pac)	Synonym of AGRIGAN	0804-16=
AGRITAS, VOLCAN LAS (Mexico)	Cone of MASCOTA VOLC FIELD	1401-031
AGUA (Guatemala)	Stratovolc (None) Holocene	**1402-10=**
AGUA AMARGA, CERRO (Chile-N)	Dome of PURICO COMPLEX	1505-094
AGUA CALIENTE DEL TUZGLE (Argentina)	Thermal Feature of TUZGLE, CERRO	1505-111
AGUA, CERRO DEL (Mexico)	Cone of CHICHINAUTZIN	1401-08=
AGUA DE PAU (Azores)	Stratovolc (10, 1564) Historical	**1802-09=**
AGUA FRIA, LAGUNA DE (Costa Rica)	Synonym of POAS	1405-04=
AGUA, LAGUNA DE (Nicaragua)	Crater of SAN CRISTOBAL	1404-02=
AGUA SHUCA (El Salvador)	Thermal Feature of VERDE, LAGUNA	1403-01=
AGUALVA (Azores)	Dome of TERCEIRA	1802-05=
AGUAS CALIENTES (Chile-N)	Stratovolc of LASCAR	1505-10=
AGUAS PERDIDAS (Chile-N)	Synonym of NEGRILLAR, LA	1505-109
AGUAS TERMALES (Costa Rica)	Thermal Feature of RINCON DE LA VIEJA	1405-02=
AGUAS ZARCAS GROUP (Costa Rica)	Pyrocl cones (None) Holocene	**1405-035**
AGUERO, CERRO DE (Nicaragua)	Cone of TELICA	1404-04=
AGUILA, CERRO EL (El Salvador)	Stratovolc of VERDE, LAGUNA	1403-01=
AGUILA, EL (Mexico)	Stratovolc of TACANA	1401-13=
AGUILERA (Chile-S)	Stratovolc ? (1, -1395) Radiocarbon	**1508-062**
AGUNG (Java)	Crater of GUNTUR	0603-13=
AGUNG (Lesser Sunda Is)	Stratovolc (3, 1964) Historical	**0604-02=**
AGUROSHI-YAMA (Honshu-Japan)	Cone of KURIKOMA	0803-21=
AHALAPAM CINDER FIELD (US-Oregon)	Synonym of NORTH SISTER FIELD	1202-07-
AHDING INGRID MOUNTAIN (Alaska-W)	Cone of NUNIVAK ISLAND	1104-06-
AHKIWIKSNUK (Alaska-W)	Maar of NUNIVAK ISLAND	1104-06-
AHOLO, VOLCAN (Mexico)	Cone of TENAYO GROUP	1401-081
AHRUP (New Guinea-NE of)	Synonym of LONG ISLAND	0501-05=
AHUACATLAN, VOLCAN DE (Mexico)	Synonym of CEBORUCO, VOLCAN	1401-03=
AHUACHAPAN (El Salvador)	Thermal Feature of VERDE, LAGUNA	1403-01=
AHUAZATEPEL, VOLCAN (Mexico)	Cone of TENAYO GROUP	1401-081
AHYI (Mariana Is-C Pac)	Submarine (None) Uncertain	**0804-141**
AI-LAAU (Hawaiian Is)	Shield of KILAUEA	1302-01-
AIELU (Ethiopia)	Synonym of AYELU	0201-16=
AIGAGIN (Aleutian Is)	Synonym of MAKUSHIN	1101-31-
AIGUANEGRA, VOLCA (Spain)	Cone of OLOT VOLC FIELD	0100-03-
AIGUILLE NOIRE (Indian O.-S)	Cone of KERGUELEN ISLANDS	0304-02=
AILERON (W Indies)	Dome of PELEE	1600-12=
AINO-MINE (Honshu-Japan)	Cone of KUSATSU-SHIRANE	0803-12=
AIRA (Kyushu-Japan)	Pleistocene caldera of SAKURA-JIMA	0802-08=
AIRE, CERRO DEL (Mexico)	Cone of MICHOACAN-GUANAJUATO	1401-06=
AISEPOET [AESEPUT] (Sulawesi-Indonesia)	Cone of SOPUTAN	0606-03=
AIYANSH VOLCANO (Canada)	Synonym of TSEAX RIVER CONE	1200-10-
AIZU-FUJI (AIZU-YAMA) (Honshu-Japan)	Synonym of BANDAI	0803-16=
AJAGIN (AJAGISCH) (Aleutian Is)	Synonym of MAKUSHIN	1101-31-
AJAKAN [AYAKAN] (Java)	Crater of GUNTUR	0603-13=
AJATA, VOLCANES DE (Chile-N)	Cone of PARINACOTA	1505-016
AJEL (Ethiopia)	Synonym of AYELU	0201-16=
AJELOU (Ethiopia)	Synonym of AYELU	0201-16=
AJER PANAS [AYER PANAS] (Sumatra)	Thermal Feature of LUMUT BALAI, BUKIT	0601-24=
AJUSCO, VOLCAN (Mexico)	Shield of CHICHINAUTZIN	1401-08=
AKA (Kurile Is)	Synonym of SINARKA	0900-29=
AKA-DAKE (Hokkaido-Japan)	Stratovolc of DAISETSU	0805-06=
AKA DAKE (Kurile Is)	Synonym of SINARKA	0900-29=
AKADEMIA NAUK (Kamchatka)	Stratovolcs (None) Holocene	**1000-123**
AKAGI (Honshu-Japan)	Stratovolc (1, 1251) Historical	**0803-13=**
AKAHANI-YAMA (Honshu-Japan)	Stratovolc of BANDAI	0803-16=
AKAI (Kyushu-Japan)	Cone of ASO	0802-11=
AKAKUBO (Honshu-Japan)	Cone of IZU-TOBU	0803-01=
AKAKURA (Honshu-Japan)	Thermal Feature of MYOKO	0803-10=
AKAKURA-DAKE (Honshu-Japan)	Cone of HAKKODA GROUP	0803-28=
AKAMIZU (Kyushu-Japan)	Thermal Feature of ASO	0802-11=
AKAN (Hokkaido-Japan)	Caldera (14, 1988) Historical	**0805-07=**
AKAN-HUZI [AKAN-FUJI] (Hokkaido-Japan)	Stratovolc of AKAN	0805-07=
AKAN-KOHAN (Hokkaido-Japan)	Thermal Feature of AKAN	0805-07=
AKASAKA-MINAMI (Honshu-Japan)	Cone of IZU-TOBU	0803-01=
AKATSUKA (Honshu-Japan)	Cone of FUJI	0803-03=
AKAZAKI-NO-MINE (Izu Is-Japan)	Dome of NII-JIMA	0804-02=
AKAZAWA-KAIKYU (Honshu-Japan)	Submarine vent of IZU-TOBU	0803-01=
AKERLUNDH (Antarctica)	Cone of SEAL NUNATAKS GROUP	1900-05=
AKHAT (Mongolia)	Cone of DARIGANGA VOLC FIELD	1003-04-
AKHLAN (Kamchatka)	Synonym of ICHINSKY	1000-28=
AKHOMTEN (Kamchatka)	Cone of MUTNOVSKY	1000-06=
AKHTANG (Kamchatka)	Shield (None) Holocene	**1000-32-**
AKHUACHAPAN [AHUACHAPAN] (El Salvad	Thermal Feature of VERDE, LAGUNA	1403-01=
AKITA-FUJI (Honshu-Japan)	Synonym of CHOKAI	0803-22=
AKITA-KOMAGA-TAKE (Honshu-Japan)	Stratovolcs (4, 1971) Historical	**0803-23=**
AKITA-YAKE-YAMA (Honshu-Japan)	Complx volc (8, 1957) Historical	**0803-26=**
AKKKTIVNAYA VORONKA (Kamchatka)	Crater of MUTNOVSKY	1000-06=
AKOMA, TAVANI (Vanuatu-SW Pacific)	Cone of KUWAE	0507-07=
AKU (Russia-SE)	Stratovolc of UDOKAN VOLC FIELD	1002-03-
AKUSEKI-JIMA (Ryukyu Is)	Stratovolc (None) Holocene	**0802-021**
AKUTAN (Aleutian Is)	Stratovolc (36, 1992) Historical	**1101-32-**
AL-DJABAL AL-ASWAD (Arabia-S)	Synonym of SAWAD, HARRA ES-	0301-16-
AL-KHURDJ BAL DJILD [KHURDJ EL-AISA	Tuff cone of HAYLAN, JABAL	0301-11-
AL WAHBAH (Arabia-W)	Maar of KISHB, HARRAT	0301-071
ALA DAG (Turkey)	Cone of KARS PLATEAU	0103-05-
ALAE (Hawaiian Is)	Former pit crater of KILAUEA	1302-01-
ALAEMBAKEO, VUTI (Vanuatu-SW Pacific)	Cone of AOBA	0507-03=
ALAGEY (Armenia)	Synonym of ARAGATS	0104-06-
ALAID (Kamchatka)	Cone of TOLBACHIK	1000-24=
ALAID (Kurile Is)	Stratovolc (10, 1986) Historical	**0900-39=**
ALAMAGAN (Mariana Is-C Pac)	Stratovolc (2, 0875) Radiocarbon	**0804-18=**
ALANG (Java)	Stratovolc of DIENG VOLC COMPLEX	0603-20=
ALAUAWA, PUU (Hawaiian Is)	Cone of HUALALAI	1302-04-
ALAYTA (Ethiopia)	Shield (2, 1915) Historical	**0201-112**
ALBAINS, MONTS (Italy)	Synonym of ALBANO, MONTE	0101-004
ALBAN HILLS (Italy)	Synonym of ALBANO, MONTE	0101-004
ALBANO (Italy)	Crater of ALBANO, MONTE	0101-004
ALBANO, MONTE (Italy)	Caldera (None) Holocene?	**0101-004**
ALBANO, MONTE (Italy)	Cone of ETNA	0101-06=
ALBANY ISLAND (Galapagos)	Cone of SANTIAGO	1503-09=
ALBAY VOLCANO (Luzon-Philippines)	Synonym of MAYON	0703-03=
ALBERCA, CERRO DE LA (Mexico)	Cone of MICHOACAN-GUANAJUATO	1401-06=
ALBERCA, LA (Mexico)	Maar of MICHOACAN-GUANAJUATO	1401-06=
ALBERT, MT. (New Zealand)	Cone of AUCKLAND FIELD	0401-02=
ALBERT PARK (New Zealand)	Cone of AUCKLAND FIELD	0401-02=
ALBIT HUT (Arabia-S)	Synonym of BIR BORHUT	0301-18-
ALCEDO, VOLCAN (Galapagos)	Shield (1, 1953) Historical	**1503-04=**
ALE BAGU (Ethiopia)	Stratovolc (None) Holocene	**0201-09=**
ALEBBAGU (Ethiopia)	Synonym of ALE BAGU	0201-09=
ALEGRIA, CERRO (El Salvador)	Cone of TECAPA	1403-08=
ALEGRIA, LAGUNA DE (El Salvador)	Thermal Feature of TECAPA	1403-08=
ALESSI, DJEBEL [JABAL EL-ESI] (Arabia)	Stratovolc of DHAMAR, HARRAS OF	0301-12-
ALEXANDROS (Greece)	Crater of NISYROS	0102-05=
ALEYONE (Antarctica)	Cone of PLEIADES, THE	1900-013
ALFERES, CALDEIRA DO (Azores)	Cone of SETE CIDADES	1802-08=
ALFERES, CALDEIRA DO (Azores)	Pumice ring of SETE CIDADES	1802-08=
ALFRED PICARD, CRATERE (Indian O.-W)	Crater of FOURNAISE, PITON DE LA	0303-02=
ALFTAKVISLARHRAUN (Iceland-S)	Fissure vent of KATLA	1702-03=
ALFTARHOLL (Iceland-SW)	Crater of GRIMSNES	1701-06=
ALI BOGO (Ethiopia)	Synonym of ERTA ALE	0201-08=
ALI DAG (Turkey)	Dome of ERCIYES DAGI	0103-01=
ALIANNGEI (Kamchatka)	Synonym of ICHINSKY	1000-28=
ALIANTE (Chile-C)	Synonym of LLAIMA	1507-11=
ALID (Ethiopia)	Stratovolc (None) Holocene	**0201-04=**
ALIT (Ethiopia)	Synonym of ALID	0201-04=
ALJANNGEJ (Kamchatka)	Synonym of ICHINSKY	1000-28=
ALLIGATOR LAKE (Canada)	Volc field (None) Holocene	**1200-02-**
ALLIGATOR LAKE (Luzon-Philippines)	Maar of MAQUILING	0703-06=
ALMARCHIGA [VOLCAN DE FASNIA]	Cone of TENERIFE	1803-03-
ALMENNINGAHRAUN (Iceland-S)	Fissure vent of KATLA	1702-03=
ALMOLONGA (Guatemala)	Stratovolc (3, 1818) Historical	**1402-04=**
ALMOLONGA, BANOS (Guatemala)	Thermal Feature of ALMOLONGA	1402-04=
ALMONZA (Italy)	Vent of PANTELLERIA	0101-071
ALNEI (Kamchatka)	Synonym of ICHINSKY	1000-28=
ALNEY (Kamchatka)	Stratovolc of ALNEY-CHASHAKONDZHA	1000-45-
ALNEY-CHASHAKONDZHA (Kamchatka)	Stratovolc (None) Holocene	**1000-45-**
ALNGEI (Kamchatka)	Synonym of ALNGEY	1000-60-
ALNGEY (Kamchatka)	Stratovolc (None) Holocene	**1000-60-**
ALOFAU (Samoa-SW Pacific)	Pleistocene caldera of TUTUILA	0404-02-
ALOI (Hawaiian Is)	Former pit crater of KILAUEA	1302-01-
ALON, MT. (Halmahera-Indonesia)	Cone of GAMKONORA	0608-04=
ALPEHUE (Chile-C)	Crater of SOLLIPULLI	1507-111
ALPHA (Russia-NE)	Cone of ALUCHIN GROUP	1001-01-
ALSEY (Iceland-S)	Cone of VESTMANNAEYJAR	1702-01=
ALTA, MONTANA (Canary Is)	Cone of GRAN CANARIA	1803-04-
ALTER VOSS (Germany)	Cone of WEST EIFEL VOLC FIELD	0100-01-
ALTINETES, PICO (Azores)	Dome of AGUA DE PAU	1802-09=
ALTO (Spanish for PEAK) see proper name (e.g. SANTANO, ALTO LA)		
ALTO, CERRO (El Salvador)	Cone of COATEPEQUE CALDERA	1403-041
ALTO, CERRO (Guatemala)	Cone of CUILAPA-BARBARENA	1402-111
ALTO GRANDE, CERRO (Costa Rica)	Cone of IRAZU	1405-06=
ALTO, PICO (Azores)	Stratovolc of TERCEIRA	1802-05=
ALU (Ethiopia)	Fissure vents (None) Holocene	**0201-06=**
ALUCHIN GROUP (Russia-NE)	Cones (None) Holocene	**1001-01-**

NAME (Subregion)	Type (Eruption Total, Most Recent) Status / Relation to NAMED VOLCANO	NUMBER
ALUNALUN (Java)	Crater of PAPANDAYAN	0603-10=
ALUTU (Ethiopia)	Stratovolc (None) Holocene	**0201-27-**
ALZATATE, VOLCAN (El Salvador)	Cone of SAN DIEGO	1403-012
AMADO (Ethiopia)	Dome of BORAWLI COMPLEX	0201-121
AMAGASE (Kyushu-Japan)	Thermal Feature of KUJU GROUP	0802-12=
AMAGI (Honshu-Japan)	Stratovolc of IZU-TOBU	0803-01=
AMAK (Aleutian Is)	Stratovolc (3, 1796) Historical	**1101-39-**
AM'AM, JABAL (Arabia-W)	Dome of KHAYBAR, HARRAT	0301-06=
AMARCHTA (Aleutian Is)	Synonym of AMUKTA	1101-19-
AMARGURA (Tonga-SW Pacific)	Synonym of FONUALEI	0403-10=
AMARILLA, MONTANA (Canary Is)	Cone of LANZAROTE	1803-06-
AMARILLO, CERRO (Chile-Is)	Tuff cone of SAN FELIX	1506-01=
AMARTI (Ethiopia)	Synonym of BORAWLI	0201-107
AMATEPEQUE [JABALI] (El Salvador)	Stratovolc of SAN SALVADOR	1403-05=
AMATITLAN (Guatemala)	Pleistocene caldera of PACAYA	1402-11=
AMATOFUA (Tonga-SW Pacific)	Synonym of TOFUA	0403-06=
AMAYA, AUSOL DE (El Salvador)	Thermal Feature of VERDE, LAGUNA	1403-01=
AMAYO, VOLCAN (Guatemala)	Cone of SANTIAGO, CERRO	1402-16-
AMAYTOLI (Ethiopia)	Synonym of ALE BAGU	0201-09=
AMBAE (Vanuatu-SW Pacific)	Synonym of AOBA	0507-03=
AMBALATUNGAN GROUP (Luzon-Philippine	Compnd volc (None) Fumarolic	**0703-089**
AMBANG (Sulawesi-Indonesia)	Complx volc (1, 1845) Historical	**0606-02=**
AMBATO [AMPATO] (Peru)	Stratovolc of SABANCAYA	1504-003
AMBITLE (New Ireland-SW Pac)	Stratovolc (1, -0350) Radiocarbon	**0504-02=**
AMBOELOMBO (Lesser Sunda Is)	Synonym of EBULOBO	0604-10=
AMBOHIBE (Madagascar)	Dome of ITASY VOLC FIELD	0303-06-
AMBOHIMALALA (Madagascar)	Cone of ITASY VOLC FIELD	0303-06-
AMBOHITRITAINERINA (Madagascar)	Cone of ITASY VOLC FIELD	0303-06-
AMBOHITRONDRY (Madagascar)	Cone of ITASY VOLC FIELD	0303-06-
AMBOY (US-California)	Cinder cone (None) Holocene	**1203-20-**
AMBRE-BOBAOMBY (Madagascar)	Volc field (None) Holocene	**0303-03-**
AMBRIM (Vanuatu-SW Pacific)	Synonym of AMBRYM	0507-04=
AMBRYM (Vanuatu-SW Pacific)	Stratovolc (49, 1991) Historical	**0507-04=**
AMBUREMBU (AMBUROMBU) (Indonesia)	Synonym of EBULOBO	0604-10=
AMES RANGE (Antarctica)	Synonym of ANDRUS	1900-023
AMGAI HIGHLANDS-HIGASHI (Honshu)	Vent of IZU-TOBU	0803-01=
AMIAK (Aleutian Is)	Synonym of AMAK	1101-39-
AMIATA (Italy)	Lava domes (None) Pleistocene-Fumarolic	**0101-002**
AMIC (W Indies)	Crater of SOUFRIERE GUADELOUPE	1600-06=
AMIC, MORNE (W Indies)	Dome of SOUFRIERE GUADELOUPE	1600-06=
AMIKAKE SPA (Honshu-Japan)	Thermal Feature of IWATE	0803-24=
AMKA-USYR (Kurile Is)	Synonym of NEMO PEAK	0900-32=
AMOISSA (Ethiopia)	Synonym of ADWA	0201-17=
AMOLOC, VOLCAN (Mexico)	Cone of TENAYO GROUP	1401-081
AMOR (Vanuatu-SW Pacific)	Stratovolc of SORETIMEAT	0507-01=
AMORONG (Luzon-Philippines)	Unknown (None) Fumarolic	**0703-085**
AMPARY (Madagascar)	Dome of ITASY VOLC FIELD	0303-06-
AMPATO (Peru)	Stratovolc of SABANCAYA	1504-003
AMSTERDAM ISLAND (Indian O.-S)	Stratovolc (None) Holocene	**0304-04-**
AMUCHTA (Aleutian Is)	Synonym of AMUKTA	1101-19-
AMUKTA (Aleutian Is)	Stratovolc (4, 1987) Historical	**1101-19-**
ANAGI-YAMA (Izu Is-Japan)	Dome of KOZU-SHIMA	0804-03=
ANAGONA (Vanuatu-SW Pacific)	Cone of AOBA	0507-03=
ANAK KRAKATAU (Indonesia)	Cone of KRAKATAU	0602-00=
ANAK RANAKAH (Lesser Sunda Is)	Dome of RANAKAH, GUNUNG	0604-071
ANALLAJSI, NEVADO (Bolivia)	Stratovolc (None) Holocene?	**1505-013**
ANAMARAMA, MAUNGA (Pacific-C)	Cone of EASTER ISLAND	1303-08-
ANANGUSIK (Aleutian Is)	Synonym of GARELOI	1101-07-
ANANO-YAMA (Honshu-Japan)	Dome of IZU-TOBU	0803-01=
ANANOKUBO (Honshu-Japan)	Tuff ring of IZU-TOBU	0803-01=
ANAOTA (Samoa-SW Pacific)	Cone of SAVAI'I	0404-04=
ANATAHAN (Mariana Is-C Pac)	Stratovolc (None) Holocene	**0804-20=**
ANATOM (Vanuatu-SW Pacific)	Synonym of ANEITYUM	0507-11-
ANAUN (Kamchatka)	Stratovolc (None) Holocene	**1000-39-**
ANCHAL, MAAR D' (France)	Maar of CHAINE DES PUYS	0100-02-
ANDAGUA VALLEY (Peru)	Synonym of ANDAHUA VALLEY	1504-002
ANDAHUA VALLEY (Peru)	Cinder cones (None) Holocene	**1504-002**
ANDES, CERRO LOS (Peru)	Cone of CHACHANI, NEVADO	1504-005
ANDIKLI-AYIRTMEKE TEPE (Turkey)	Cone of KARAPINAR FIELD	0103-001
ANDIKLI TEPE (Turkey)	Cone of KARAPINAR FIELD	0103-001
ANDJASMORO (Java)	Stratovolc of ARJUNO-WELIRANG	0603-29=
ANDRAIKIBA (Madagascar)	Crater of ANKARATRA FIELD	0303-07-
ANDRANOJAVATRA (Madagascar)	Cone of ITASY VOLC FIELD	0303-06-
ANDRANORATSY (Madagascar)	Crater of ITASY VOLC FIELD	0303-06-
ANDRANOTORAHA (Madagascar)	Crater of ITASY VOLC FIELD	0303-06-
ANDRES (Chile-C)	Cone of PALOMO	1507-022
ANDREW BAY (Aleutian Is)	Caldera of ADAGDAK	1101-112
ANDREW'S VOLCANO (Africa-E)	Stratovolc of BARRIER, THE	0202-03=
ANDROMEDA CONE (Alaska-W)	Cone of IMURUK LAKE	1104-02-
ANDRUS (Antarctica)	Shields (None) Holocene?	**1900-023**
ANEITYUM (Vanuatu-SW Pacific)	Stratovolcs (None) Holocene?	**0507-11-**
ANGALAFIB (Africa-N)	Cone of BAYUDA VOLC FIELD	0205-06-
ANGAR, GOF (Africa-E)	Maar of MARSABIT	0202-021
ANGAVO (Madagascar)	Dome of ITASY VOLC FIELD	0303-06-
ANGET (Sumatra)	Crater of LUMUT BALAI, BUKIT	0601-24=
ANGILA (New Britain-SW Pac)	Cone of LANGILA	0502-01=
ANGLAIS, MORNE (W Indies)	Cone of MICOTRIN	1600-10=
ANGNJIOMAN [ANGNYIOMAN] (Lesser Sund	Thermal Feature of ILIMUDA	0604-17=
ANGOES, BATOE [BATU ANGUS] (Sulawesi)	Dome of TONGKOKO	0606-13=
ANGOSTURA, LA (Argentina)	Tuff ring of HUANQUIHUE GROUP	1507-123
ANGUS BARU, BATU (Sulawesi-Indonesia)	Dome of TONGKOKO	0606-13=
ANGUS, BATU (Banda Sea)	Crater of BANDA API	0605-09=
ANGUS, BATU (Sulawesi-Indonesia)	Dome of TONGKOKO	0606-13=
ANIAKCHAK (Alaska Peninsula)	Caldera (4, 1931) Historical	**1102-09-**
ANILLO, CERRO DEL (Mexico)	Cone of MICHOACAN-GUANAJUATO	1401-06=
ANIMAS, CERRO DE LAS (Galapagos)	Cone of AZUL, CERRO	1503-06=
ANIR (New Ireland-SW Pac)	Synonym of AMBITLE	0504-02=
ANIUSK (Russia-NE)	Cone of ANJUISKY	1001-02-
ANJAR, GUNUNG (Java)	Cone of IJEN	0603-35=
ANJAR, KAWAH (Java)	Thermal Feature of KAWAHKAMOJANG	0603-12=
ANJUISKY (Russia-NE)	Complx volc (1, 1500) Tephrochronology	**1001-02-**
ANKAIZINA VOLC FIELD (Madagascar)	Cinder cones (None) Holocene	**0303-05-**
ANKARATRA VOLC FIELD (Madagascar)	Cinder cones (None) Holocene	**0303-07-**
ANOENGOLA [ANUNGGOLA] (Lesser Sunda	Crater of SIRUNG	0604-27=
ANONIMO (Chile-C)	Synonym of LLAIMA	1507-11=
ANSEI (Hokkaido-Japan)	Crater of KOMAGA-TAKE	0805-02=
ANTECJOSO (El Salvador)	Dome of COATEPEQUE CALDERA	1403-041
ANTI, GUNUNG (Lesser Sunda Is)	Cone of BATUR	0604-01=
ANTICURA (Chile-C)	Cone of ANTILLANCA GROUP	1507-153
ANTILLANCA GROUP (Chile-C)	Stratovolcs (None) Holocene	**1507-153**
ANTIMILOS (Greece)	Cone of MILOS	0102-03=
ANTIPODES ISLAND (Pacific-S)	Pyrocl cones (None) Holocene?	**1304-01-**

NAME (Subregion)	Type (Eruption Total, Most Recent) Status / Relation to NAMED VOLCANO	NUMBER
ANTISANA (Ecuador)	Stratovolc (2, 1802) Historical	**1502-03=**
ANTIZANA (Ecuador)	Synonym of ANTISANA	1502-03=
ANTOCO (Chile-C)	Synonym of ANTUCO	1507-08=
ANTOFAGASTA DE LA SIERRA (Argentina)	Scoria cones (None) Holocene	**1505-124**
ANTOFALLA, VOLCAN (Argentina)	Stratovolc (None) Fumarolic	**1505-123**
ANTOINE, LAKE (W Indies)	Crater of ST. CATHERINE	1600-17=
ANTOJO (Chile-C)	Synonym of ANTUCO	1507-08=
ANTONELLI (Indian O.-S)	Cone of AMSTERDAM ISLAND	0304-04-
ANTONIA PEAK (Kurile Is)	Synonym of TIATIA	0900-03=
ANTSIFEROVA (Kurile Is)	Synonym of SHIRINKI	0900-331
ANTSIRABE (Madagascar)	Cone of ANKARATRA FIELD	0303-07-
ANTSIRABLE (Madagascar)	Synonym of ANKARATRA FIELD	0303-07-
ANTUCO (Chile-C)	Stratovolc (14, 1869) Historical	**1507-08=**
ANUNCIACION, CERRO (Costa Rica)	Pyrocl cone (None) Holocene?	**1405-032**
ANUNGGOLA (Lesser Sunda Is)	Crater of SIRUNG	0604-27=
ANVIL PEAK (Aleutian Is)	Cone of SEMISOPOCHNOI	1101-06-
ANVIL, THE [EL YUNQUE] (Chile-Is)	Stratovolc of ROBINSON CRUSOE	1506-02=
ANYUY GROUP (Russia-NE)	Synonym of ANJUISKY	1001-02-
AOBA (Vanuatu-SW Pacific)	Shield (3, 1870) Anthropology	**0507-03=**
AOBUNA (Honshu-Japan)	Stratovolc of TOWADA	0803-271
A'OFA (Samoa-SW Pacific)	Shield of OFU-OLOSEGA	0404-01=
AOGA-SHIMA (Izu Is-Japan)	Stratovolc (6, 1785) Historical	**0804-06=**
AOPO [MAUGA MU] (Samoa-SW Pacific)	Cone of SAVAI'I	0404-04=
AOSO-YAMA (Honshu-Japan)	Stratovolc of ZAO	0803-19=
AP-SAN (Korea)	Shield of CH'UGA-RYONG	1006-02-
APACAGUA (Guatemala)	Synonym of PACAYA	1402-11=
APACHETA, CERRO (Chile-N)	Dome of AZUFRE, CERRO DEL	1505-065
APACHINSKAIA SOPKA (Kamchatka)	Synonym of OPALA	1000-08=
APAGADO, EL [ESCALANTE] (Chile-N)	Stratovolc of SAIRECABUR	1505-091
APAKHONCHICH (Kamchatka)	Crater of KLIUCHEVSKOI	1000-26=
APALE (El Salvador)	Dome of COATEPEQUE CALDERA	1403-041
APALONG (New Guinea-NE of)	Crater of UMBOI	0501-06=
APALSKAIA SOPKA (Kamchatka)	Synonym of OPALA	1000-08=
APANECA, CERRO DE (El Salvador)	Stratovolc of VERDE, LAGUNA	1403-01=
APANTES, CERRO DE (Guatemala)	Cone of SANTIAGO, CERRO	1402-16-
APASTEPE, LOMA (Nicaragua)	Dome of SAN CRISTOBAL	1404-02=
APASTEPEQUE, CERRO DE (El Salvador)	Dome of APASTEPEQUE FIELD	1403-071
APASTEPEQUE, LAGUNA (El Salvador)	Pit crater of APASTEPEQUE FIELD	1403-071
APASTEPEQUE VOLC FIELD (El Salvador)	Volc field (None) Holocene	**1403-071**
APAXTEPEC (Mexico)	Cone of COLIMA VOLC COMPLEX	1401-04=
API (Banda Sea)	Synonym of GUNUNGAPI WETAR	0605-03=
API SIAU (Sangihe)	Synonym of KARANGETANG [API SIAU]	0607-02=
APO (Mindanao-Philippines)	Stratovolc (None) Fumarolic	**0701-03=**
APOLIMA (Samoa-SW Pacific)	Tuff cone of UPOLU	0404-03-
APOYEQUE (Nicaragua)	Stratovolc (None) Anthropology	**1404-091**
APOYO (Africa-E)	Cone of HOMA MOUNTAIN	0202-07=
APOYO (Nicaragua)	Caldera (None) Uncertain	**1404-101**
APOYOITO (Nicaragua)	Dome of APOYO	1404-101
APSIAN (Luzon-Philippines)	Cone of NATIB	0703-082
APUAHOE [ROLLES PEAK] (New Zealand)	Stratovolc of MAROA	0401-061
ARA-KHANGAY VOLC FIELD (Mongolia)	Synonym of TARYATU-CHULUTU	1003-01-
ARA-YAMA (Honshu-Japan)	Synonym of NIKKO-SHIRANE	0803-14=
ARA-YAMA (Honshu-Japan)	Cone of IZU-TOBU	0803-01=
ARACAR (Argentina)	Stratovolc (1, 1993) Historical	**1505-107**
ARADES, CERRO LAS (Guatemala)	Cone of SANTIAGO, CERRO	1402-16-
ARAFO, VOLCAN DE [VOLCAN DE GUIMAR]	Cone of TENERIFE	1803-03-
ARAGATS (Armenia)	Stratovolc (None) Holocene	**0104-06-**
ARAGATZ (ARAGAY) (Armenia)	Synonym of ARAGATS	0104-06-
ARAISA (Kurile Is)	Synonym of ATSONUPURI	0900-05=
ARAITO (ARAITO-FUJI) (Kurile Is)	Synonym of ALAID	0900-39=
ARANGUADI (Ethiopia)	Tuff ring of BISHOFTU FIELD	0201-22-
ARARAT, MT. (Turkey)	Stratovolc (None) Holocene	**0103-04-**
ARAUMAKUTAN (Kurile Is)	Synonym of HARIMKOTAN	0900-30=
ARAYAT (Luzon-Philippines)	Stratovolc (None) Holocene	**0703-084**
ARBRE (Africa-C)	Cone of KARISIMBI	0203-04-
ARCHIAVERNO (Italy)	Crater of CAMPI FLEGREI	0101-01=
ARCOTANGO (Chile-N)	Synonym of ACOTANGO	1505-017
ARCTOWSKY (Antarctica)	Cone of SEAL NUNATAKS GROUP	1900-05=
ARDJOENO [ARJUNO] (Java)	Stratovolc of ARJUNO-WELIRANG	0603-29=
ARDOUKOBA (Djibouti)	Fissure vents (1, 1978) Historical	**0201-126**
ARDSCHICH DAGH (Turkey)	Synonym of ERCIYES DAGI	0103-01=
AREIA, PICO DA (Azores)	Dome of FURNAS	1802-10=
AREKIKAPAKAPA (New Zealand)	Thermal Feature of ROTORUA	0401-042
ARENA, MONTANA DE LA (Canary Is)	Cone of FUERTEVENTURA	1803-05-
ARENAL (Costa Rica)	Stratovolc (8, 1993) Historical	**1405-033**
ARENAL (Ecuador)	Dome of ATACAZO	1502-021
ARENAL, VOLCAN (Chile-C)	Tuff ring of LANIN	1507-122
ARENAS (Colombia)	Crater of RUIZ	1501-02=
ARENAS, MONTANA DE LAS [VOL. GUIMAR	Cone of TENERIFE	1803-03-
AREQUIPA, VOLCAN DE (Peru)	Synonym of MISTI, EL	1504-01=
'ARES, DJEBEL EL- [JABAL 'URAIS] (Arabia)	Cone of SAWAD, HARRA ES-	0301-16-
ARFAT (Halmahera-Indonesia)	Synonym of GAMALAMA	0608-06=
ARGAEUS MONS (ARGAIOS) (Turkey)	Synonym of ERCIYES DAGI	0103-01=
ARGAPURA (Java)	Stratovolc of IYANG-ARGAPURA	0603-33=
ARGELIA, CERRO DE (Guatemala)	Cone of FLORES, VOLCAN DE	1402-14-
ARGOPEORO [ARGAPURA] (Java)	Stratovolc of IYANG-ARGAPURA	0603-33=
ARHAB, HARRA OF (Arabia-S)	Volc field (2, 0500) Historical	**0301-09-**
ARICCIA (Italy)	Crater of ALBANO, MONTE	0101-004
ARINTICA, VOLCAN (Chile-N)	Stratovolc (None) Holocene	**1505-023**
ARIS ISLAND (New Guinea-NE of)	Synonym of BOISA	0501-011
ARJUNO-WELIRANG (Java)	Stratovolc (1, 1952) Historical	**0603-29=**
ARMADILLO PEAK (Canada)	Stratovolc of EDZIZA	1200-06-
ARMADO, EL (Costa Rica)	Cone of TURRIALBA	1405-07=
ARMADO, ISLA EL (Nicaragua)	Cone of ZAPATERA ISLAND	1404-111
ARNARDALSOLDUGJOSKA YNGRI (Iceland)	Crater row of KVERKFJOLL	1703-05=
ARNARSETUR (Iceland-SW)	Crater row of REYKJANES	1701-02=
AROOMA (Ethiopia)	Crater of DUBBI	0201-10=
AROP (New Guinea-NE of)	Synonym of LONG ISLAND	0501-05=
ARPONG (Korea)	Cone of ULREUNG	1006-03-
ARRABALES, CALDERA DE LOS (Canary Is)	Crater of FUERTEVENTURA	1803-05-
ARRAYANES (Chile-C)	Cone of ANTILLANCA GROUP	1507-153
ARROYO SAN JOSE (Mexico)	Synonym of JARAQUAY VOLC FIELD	1401-004
ARSO (Italy)	Cone of ISCHIA	0101-03=
ARSO, MONTE (Italy)	Cone of ETNA	0101-06=
ARTALI (Ethiopia)	Synonym of ERTA ALE	0201-08=
ARTEMISIO (Italy)	Synonym of ALBANO, MONTE	0101-004
ARUCAS, MONTANA DE (Canary Is)	Cone of GRAN CANARIA	1803-04-
ARUFAT (Halmahera-Indonesia)	Synonym of GAMALAMA	0608-06=
ARUFTA (Ethiopia)	Stratovolc of GABILLEMA	0201-15=
ARUICAS, MONTANA (Canary Is)	Cone of GRAN CANARIA	1803-04-
ARUM (Java)	Crater of SUNDORO	0603-21=
ARUSI (Ethiopia)	Cone of MEGA BASALT FIELD	0201-33-

NAME (Subregion)	Type (Eruption Total, Most Recent) Status / Relation to NAMED VOLCANO	NUMBER
AS SUMTH [ET-TADAWIN] (Arabia-S)	Tuff cone of HAYLAN, JABAL	0301-11-
ASACHA (Kamchatka)	Complx volc (None) Holocene	**1000-062**
ASACHA (Kamchatka)	Synonym of MUTNOVSKY	1000-06=
ASACHA (Kamchatka)	Synonym of GORELY	1000-07=
ASAHI-DAKE (Hokkaido-Japan)	Stratovolc of DAISETSU	0805-06=
ASAHINA-DAKE (Honshu-Japan)	Dome of OSORE-YAMA	0803-29=
ASAKIZUKA (Honshu-Japan)	Cone of FUJI	0803-03=
ASAM, WAI (Sumatra)	Thermal Feature of HULUBELU	0601-28=
ASAMA (Honshu-Japan)	Complx volc (121, 1990) Historical	**0803-11=**
ASAR (Iceland-SW)	Shield of HENGILL	1701-05=
ASASE (Ryukyu Is)	Cone of KIKAI	0802-06=
ASAVIO (Ethiopia)	Synonym of ASAVYO	0201-104
ASAVYO (Ethiopia)	Shield (None) Holocene	**0201-104**
ASAY KNOLL (US-Utah)	Cone of MARKAGUNT PLATEAU	1207-04-
ASBORU (Ethiopia)	Stratovolc of GABILLEMA	0201-15=
ASCENSION (Atlantic-S)	Stratovolc (None) Holocene	**1805-05-**
ASDAGA (Ethiopia)	Synonym of SORKALE	0201-103
ASEBA, OL DOINYO (Africa-E)	Cone of CHYULU HILLS	0202-13=
ASH CONE (Africa-E)	Cone of MERU	0202-16=
ASH HILL (New Zealand)	Tuff cone of AUCKLAND FIELD	0401-02=
ASH PIT, THE (Canada)	Cone of SPECTRUM RANGE	1200-07-
ASHEN HILLS (Antarctica)	Cone of MICHAEL	1900-09=
ASHIKULEI [KA-ER-DAXI] (China-W)	Cone of KUNLUN VOLC GROUP	1004-03-
'ASI, HALA-'L- (Arabia-W)	Tuff cone of 'UWAYRID, HARRAT	0301-02=
ASI, MT. (Samoa-SW Pacific)	Cone of SAVAI'I	0404-04=
ASIN HOT SPRING (Luzon-Philippines)	Thermal Feature of NATIB	0703-082
ASKAHRAUN (Iceland-NE)	Fissure vent of BARDARBUNGA	1703-03=
ASKJA (Iceland-NE)	Stratovolc (10, 1961) Historical	**1703-06=**
ASLAJ, JABAL (Arabia-W)	Cone of KISHB, HARRAT	0301-071
ASMARA (Ethiopia)	Pyrocl cone (None) Holocene	**0201-142**
ASO (Kyushu-Japan)	Caldera (155, 1993) Historical	**0802-11=**
ASO-SAN (Kyushu-Japan)	Synonym of ASO	0802-11=
ASO-UCHINOMAKI (Kyushu-Japan)	Thermal Feature of ASO	0802-11=
ASOBENOMORI (Honshu-Japan)	Synonym of IWAKI	0803-27=
ASOG (Luzon-Philippines)	Synonym of IRIGA	0703-041
ASOMADA, MONTANA DE (Canary Is)	Cone of HIERRO	1803-02-
ASOMADAS NEGRAS, MONTANA (Canary Is	Cone of HIERRO	1803-02-
ASOSOSCA, CERRO (Nicaragua)	Cone of PILAS, LAS	1404-08=
ASOSOSCA, LAGUNA DE (Nicaragua)	Maar of NEJAPA-TICOMO	1404-092
ASOSOSCA, LAGUNA DE (Nicaragua)	Maar of PILAS, LAS	1404-08=
ASPERO, CERRO (Chile-N)	Dome of PURICO COMPLEX	1505-094
ASSAB VOLC FIELD (Ethiopia)	Volc field (None) Holocene	**0201-125**
ASSALO (Ethiopia)	Synonym of AYELU	0201-16=
ASSIRMATSKY (Kurile Is)	Synonym of EBEKO	0900-38=
ASSONGSONG (Mariana Is-C Pac)	Synonym of ASUNCION	0804-15=
ASTILLERO, CERRITO EL (Guatemala)	Cone of CHIQUIMULA FIELD	1402-20-
ASTILLERO, CERRO EL (El Salvador)	Cone of SANTA ANA	1403-02=
ASTROL, PUIG (Spain)	Cone of OLOT VOLC FIELD	0100-03-
ASTRONI (Italy)	Tuff ring of CAMPI FLEGREI	0101-01=
ASUNCION (Mariana Is-C Pac)	Stratovolc (1, 1906) Historical	**0804-15=**
ASUNCION, LA (Guatemala)	Cone of SUCHITAN VOLC FIELD	1402-17-
ASUR (Vanuatu-SW Pacific)	Synonym of YASUR	0507-10=
ASYRMINTAR (Kurile Is)	(None) Not a Volcano	0900-33=
AT-TABAB (Arabia-S)	Cone of BAL HAF, HARRA OF	0301-17-
ATACAMA, VOLCAN DE (Chile-N)	Synonym of LASTARRIA	1505-12=
ATACAMA, VOLCAN DE (Chile-N)	Synonym of LICANCABUR	1505-092
ATACAZO (Ecuador)	Stratovolc (1, -0420) Radiocarbon	**1502-021**
ATAGAWA-KAIKYU (Honshu-Japan)	Submarine vent of IZU-TOBU	0803-01=
ATALAYA, LA (Canary Is)	Cone of TENERIFE	1803-03-
ATIMBIA, MT. (Luzon-Philippines)	Cone of LAGUNA VOLC FIELD	0703-051
ATITLAN (Guatemala)	Stratovolc (12, 1853) Historical	**1402-06=**
ATKA (Aleutian Is)	Stratovolcs (4, 1987) Historical	**1101-16-**
ATLACORRA, VOLCAN (Mexico)	Cone of TENAYO GROUP	1401-081
ATLAS, MT. [MT. PLEIONES] (Antarctica)	Stratovolc of PLEIADES, THE	1900-013
ATLASOVA (Kamchatka)	Shields (None) Holocene	**1000-65-**
ATOSA (ATOSANOBORI) (Kurile Is)	Synonym of ATSONUPURI	0900-05=
ATOSANUPURI (Hokkaido-Japan)	Dome of KUTCHARO	0805-08=
ATOSANUPURI (Kurile Is)	Synonym of ATSONUPURI	0900-05=
ATSONUPURI (Kurile Is)	Stratovolc (2, 1932) Historical	**0900-05=**
ATTALORA, CUDDIA (Italy)	Cone of PANTELLERIA	0101-071
ATTI-YAMA [ACHI-YAMA] (Izu Is-Japan)	Dome of NII-JIMA	0804-02=
ATUG (Vanuatu-SW Pacific)	Cone of MOTLAV	0507-001
ATUK MOUNTAIN (Alaska-W)	Cone of KOOKOOLIGIT MOUNTAINS	1104-03-
ATUNAPARA (D'Entrecasteaux Is)	Thermal Feature of DAWSON STRAIT GP	0503-06=
ATWELL PEAK (Canada)	Dome of GARIBALDI, MT.	1200-20-
AUCANQUILCHA, CERRO (Chile-N)	Stratovolc (None) Holocene	**1505-051**
AUCKLAND FIELD (New Zealand)	Volc field (1, 1350) Radiocarbon	**0401-02=**
AUEL (Germany)	Maar of WEST EIFEL VOLC FIELD	0100-01-
AUGUSTINE (Alaska-SW)	Lava domes (13, 1986) Historical	**1103-01-**
AUNUU ISLAND (Samoa-SW Pacific)	Tuff cone of TUTUILA	0404-02-
AURUHOE [NGAURUHOE] (New Zealand)	Stratovolc of TONGARIRO	0401-08=
AUSOLES (Spanish for FUMAROLE FIELD)	see proper name (e.g. SAN VICENTE, AUSOLES DE)	
AUSTURHRAUN (Iceland-S)	Fissure vent of HEKLA	1702-07=
AUVERGNE, MONTS D' (France)	Synonym of CHAINE DES PUYS	0100-02-
AVACHA (Kamchatka)	Synonym of AVACHINSKY	1000-10=
AVACHI (Kamchatka)	Cone of AVACHINSKY	1000-10=
AVACHINSKAIA, SOPKA (Kamchatka)	Synonym of AVACHINSKY	1000-10=
AVACHINSKY (Kamchatka)	Stratovolc (33, 1991) Historical	**1000-10=**
AVDALSMOYA (Atl-N-Jan Mayen)	Dome of JAN MAYEN	1706-01=
AVERNO (Italy)	Tuff ring of CAMPI FLEGREI	0101-01=
AVLHAUGENE (Atl-N-Jan Mayen)	Tuff ring of JAN MAYEN	1706-01=
AWAATUA BAY (New Zealand)	Crater of OKATAINA	0401-05=
AWARU RIVER (New Guinea)	Synonym of MUSA RIVER	0503-02=
AWASA (Ethiopia)	Pleistocene caldera of CORBETTI	0201-29-
AWATSCHA (AWATSCHINSKIJ) (Kamchatka	Synonym of AVACHINSKY	1000-10=
'AWAYRIDH, HARRAT EL- (Arabia-W)	Synonym of 'UWAYRID, HARRAT	0301-02=
AWOE (Sangihe Is-Indonesia)	Synonym of AWU	0607-04=
AWOEH (Sangihe)	Synonym of KARANGETANG [API SIAU]	0607-02=
AWU (Sangihe Is-Indonesia)	Stratovolc (16, 1992) Historical	**0607-04=**
AXLARGIGUR (Iceland-S)	Fissure vent of HEKLA	1702-07=
AXUSCO [LAGUNA DE ASOSOSCA] (Nicara	Maar of PILAS, LAS	1404-08=
AY-ALU (Ethiopia)	Synonym of AYELU	0201-16=
AYAGSH (Aleutian Is)	Synonym of MAKUSHIN	1101-31-
AYAKAN (Java)	Crater of GUNTUR	0603-13=
AYAKTAS TEPE (Turkey)	Cone of ACIGOL-NEVSEHIR	0103-004
AYALU (Ethiopia)	Synonym of AYELU	0201-16=
AYAQUEME, CERRO (Mexico)	Cone of TENAYO GROUP	1401-081
AYECO [MALA CARA] (El Salvador)	Cone of SANTA ANA	1403-02=
AYELU (Ethiopia)	Stratovolc (None) Holocene	**0201-16=**
AYER PANAS (Sumatra)	Thermal Feature of LUMUT BALAI, BUKIT	0601-24=
AYGORGOLU (Turkey)	Maar of SUPHAN DAGI	0103-021
AYMOND (Chile-S)	Cone of PALEI-AIKE VOLC FIELD	1508-08-
AYYALU (Ethiopia)	Synonym of ADWA	0201-17=
AZEITONA, PICO DA (Azores)	Cone of FURNAS	1802-10=
AZUCAR, PITON DE [PICO DEL TEIDE]	Stratovolc of TENERIFE	1803-03-
AZUFRADO (Costa Rica)	Stratovolc of PLATANAR, CERRO	1405-036
AZUFRADOS, BANOS (Guatemala)	Thermal Feature of ALMOLONGA	1402-04=
AZUFRAL (Guatemala)	Thermal Feature of TECUAMBURRO	1402-12=
AZUFRAL DE TUQUERRES (Colombia)	Synonym of AZUFRAL, VOLCAN	1501-09=
AZUFRAL, EL (Chile-C)	Crater of CORDON CAULLE	1507-141
AZUFRAL, VOLCAN (Colombia)	Stratovolc (4, -0930) Radiocarbon	**1501-09=**
AZUFRALES (Costa Rica)	Thermal Feature of RINCON DE LA VIEJA	1405-02=
AZUFRE (Chile-C)	Caldera of PLANCHON-PETEROA	1507-04=
AZUFRE, BANOS (Chile-C)	Thermal Feature of PLANCHON-PETERO	1507-04=
AZUFRE, CERRO DE (Chile-N)	Synonym of LASTARRIA	1505-12=
AZUFRE, CERRO DE (Chile-N)	Synonym of COPIAPO	1505-14-
AZUFRE, CERRO DEL (Chile-N)	Stratovolc (None) Holocene	**1505-065**
AZUFRE, MT. (Philippines-C)	Thermal Feature of MANDALAGAN	0702-03=
AZUFRE-PLACHON-PETEROA (Chile-C)	Synonym of PLANCHON-PETEROA	1507-04=
AZUFRE, VOLCAN DE (Galapagos)	Thermal Feature of NEGRA, SIERRA	1503-05=
AZUFRE, VOLCAN EL (Mexico)	Stratovolc of TRES VIRGENES	1401-01=
AZUFRERA AGUAS CALIENTES, CERRO	Cone of CORDON DE PUNTAS NEGRAS	1505-102
AZUFRERA PERRO MUERTO, CERRO	Cone of CORDON DE PUNTAS NEGRAS	1505-102
AZUFRERA YACIMIENTO, CERRO (Chile-N)	Cone of CORDON DE PUNTAS NEGRAS	1505-102
AZUFRERAS TUYAJTO (Chile-N)	Cone of CORDON CHALVIRI	1505-103
AZUFRERES, LAS [LOS AZUFRES] (Chile-C)	Thermal Feature of CORDON CAULLE	1507-141
AZUL, CERRO (Galapagos)	Cone of SAN CRISTOBAL	1503-12-
AZUL, CERRO (Galapagos)	Shield (8, 1979) Historical	**1503-06=**
AZUL, CERRO [QUIZAPU] (Chile-C)	Stratovolc (9, 1967) Historical	**1507-06=**
AZUMA (Honshu-Japan)	Stratovolcs (8, 1977) Historical	**0803-18=**
AZUMA-KOHUZI [AZUMA-KOFUJI] (Honshu)	Cone of AZUMA	0803-18=
AZUMA-YAMA (Honshu-Japan)	Synonym of FUJI	0803-03=
AZUMA-YAMA (Kyushu-Japan)	Dome of UNZEN	0802-10=

B

NAME (Subregion)	Type (Eruption Total, Most Recent) Status / Relation to NAMED VOLCANO	NUMBER
BABASE (New Ireland-SW Pac)	Stratovolc of AMBITLE	0504-02=
BABBINGTONS HILL (Australia)	Dome of NEWER VOLCANICS PROV	0509-01-
BABILONIA, CERRO (Honduras)	Cone of YOJOA, LAKE	1403-15-
BABIY KAMEN (Kamchatka)	Dome of BARKHATNAYA SOPKA	1000-084
BABUYAN CLARO (Luzon Is-N of)	Stratovolcs (8, 1924) Historical	**0704-03=**
BABUYAN, MT. [SMITH VOLCANO] (Luzon)	Stratovolc of BABUYAN CLARO	0704-03=
BABY CAPULIN (US-New Mexico)	Cone of RATON-CLAYTON	1210-04-
BACHELOR (US-Oregon)	Stratovolc (1, -5800) Tephrochronology	**1202-09-**
BACHELOR BUTTE (US-Oregon)	Synonym of BACHELOR	1202-09-
BACKLOCKDAM (Korea)	Crater of HALLA	1006-04-
BACOLI (Italy)	Crater of CAMPI FLEGREI	0101-01=
BACON (Luzon-Philippines)	Synonym of POCDOL MOUNTAINS	0703-02=
BADAK, KAWAH (Java)	Crater of TANGKUBANPARAHU	0603-09=
BADGER PEAK (US-California)	Cone of MEDICINE LAKE	1203-02-
BADJINI (Indian O.-W)	Cone of KARTHALA	0303-01=
BADLANDS (Africa-E)	Synonym of ELMENTEITA BADLANDS	0202-071
BADSVALLAGIGIR (Iceland-SW)	Crater row of REYKJANES	1701-02=
BAEGDU (China-E)	Synonym of BAITOUSHAN	1005-07-
BAEJARHRAUN (Iceland-S)	Fissure vent of HEKLA	1702-07=
BAEKDOOSAN (China-E)	Synonym of BAITOUSHAN	1005-07-
BAGAGAURE (D'Entrecasteaux Is)	Thermal Feature of DAWSON STRAIT GP	0503-06=
BAGANA (Bougainville-SW Pac)	Lava cone (24, 1993) Historical	**0505-02=**
BAGIAI (New Guinea-NE of)	Cone of KARKAR	0501-03=
BAGUSA (Africa-C)	Crater of BUNYARUGURU FIELD	0203-005
BAIA (Italy)	Crater of CAMPI FLEGREI	0101-01=
BAISHAN [PECHAN] (China-W)	Cone of TIANSHAN VOLC GROUP	1004-02-
BAITOUSHAN (China-E)	Stratovolc (6, 1702) Historical	**1005-07-**
BAIYUDA VOLC FIELD (Africa-N)	Synonym of BAYUDA VOLC FIELD	0205-06-
BAKAL (Java)	Cone of ARJUNO-WELIRANG	0603-29=
BAKANG (BAKANGIN) (Kamchatka)	Synonym of BAKENIN	1000-122
BAKENIN (Kamchatka)	Caldera (None) Holocene	**1000-122**
BAKENING (Kamchatka)	Synonym of BAKENIN	1000-122
BAKER (US-Washington)	Stratovolc (13, 1880) Historical	**1201-01=**
BAKER HOT SPRINGS (US-Washington)	Thermal Feature of BAKER	1201-01=
BAKKENIN (Kamchatka)	Synonym of BAKENIN	1000-122
BAL HAF, HARRA OF (Arabia-S)	Volc field (None) Holocene	**0301-17-**
BALAGAN-TAS (Russia-NE)	Cinder cone (1, 1775) Historical	**1001-03-**
BALAI, BUKIT (Sumatra)	Stratovolc of LUMUT BALAI, BUKIT	0601-24=
BALANTOK (Luzon-Philippines)	Cone of TAAL	0703-07=
BALASTRERA, EL CERRITO (El Salvador)	Cone of SAN SALVADOR	1403-05=
BALATOCAN (Mindanao-Philippines)	Compnd volc (None) Fumarolic	**0701-072**
BALBI (Bougainville-SW Pac)	Stratovolc (None) Holocene	**0505-01=**
BALD CRATER (US-Oregon)	Cone of CRATER LAKE	1202-16-
BALD KNOLL (US-Utah)	Cinder cones (None) Holocene?	**1207-03-**
BALENG (Africa-W)	Maar of OKU VOLC FIELD	0204-003
BALI, PEAK OF (Lesser Sunda Is)	Synonym of AGUNG	0604-02=
BALILE (Lesser Sunda Is)	Cone of ILIBOLENG	0604-22=
BALJANE (Atl-N-Jan Mayen)	Cone of JAN MAYEN	1706-01=
BALMANN, PITON DE (Indian O.-W)	Cone of FOURNAISE, PITON DE LA	0303-02=
BALMET, PUY (France)	Cone of CHAINE DES PUYS	0100-02-
BALONG ANITO (Luzon-Philippines)	Thermal Feature of MARIVELES	0703-081
BALUAN (Admiralty Is-SW Pac)	Stratovolc (None) Holocene?	**0500-02-**
BALURAN (Java)	Stratovolc (None) Holocene?	**0603-351**
BALUSAN (Luzon-Philippines)	Synonym of BULUSAN	0703-01=
BALUT (Mindanao-Philippines)	Stratovolc (None) Holocene	**0701-01=**
BAM (New Guinea-NE of)	Stratovolc (16, 1960) Historical	**0501-01=**
BAMAOQIONGZHONG (China-W)	Shield of UNNAMED	1004-04-
BAMBULUWE, LAKE (Africa-W)	Maar of OKU VOLC FIELD	0204-003
BAMUS (New Britain-SW Pac)	Stratovolc (4, 1886) Anthropology	**0502-11=**
BANAHAO (Luzon-Philippines)	Synonym of BANAHAW	0703-05=
BANAHAW (Luzon-Philippines)	Complx volc (None) Holocene	**0703-05=**
BANAHAW DE LUCBAN (Luzon-Philippines)	Stratovolc of BANAHAW	0703-05=
BANAJAO (Luzon-Philippines)	Synonym of BANAHAW	0703-05=
BANBANLONGWAN (China-E)	Crater of LONGGANG GROUP	1005-06-
BANCAH CALDERA (Sumatra)	Caldera of MARAPI	0601-14=
BANCEN (Java)	Thermal Feature of MERBABU	0603-24=
BANCO DI NISIDA (Italy)	Cone of CAMPI FLEGREI	0101-01=
BANCO MISENO (Italy)	Cone of CAMPI FLEGREI	0101-01=
BANDA API (Banda Sea)	Caldera (23, 1988) Historical	**0605-09=**
BANDAI (Honshu-Japan)	Stratovolc (4, 1888) Historical	**0803-16=**
BANDAI-SAN (Honshu-Japan)	Synonym of BANDAI	0803-16=
BANDAIKO HOT SPRINGS (Honshu-Japan)	Thermal Feature of KUSATSU-SHIRANE	0803-12=
BANDAMA, CALDERA DE (Canary Is)	Maar of GRAN CANARIA	1803-04-
BANDERA, CERRO (US-New Mexico)	Cone of ZUNI-BANDERA	1210-02-
BANDERA, CERRO DE LA (El Salvador)	Synonym of CONCHAGUA	1403-11=
BANDERA CRATER (US-New Mexico)	Cone of ZUNI-BANDERA	1210-02-
BANDERA LAVA FIELD (US-New Mexico)	Synonym of ZUNI-BANDERA	1210-02-
BANDERAS, CERRO LAS (Nicaragua)	Cone of ZAPATERA ISLAND	1404-111

NAME (Subregion)	Type (Eruption Total, Most Recent) Status . . . Relation to NAMED VOLCANO	NUMBER
BANGESHAN (China-S)	Cone of TENGCHONG	0705-11-
BANGO (New Britain-SW Pac)	Synonym of PAGO	0502-08=
BANGULA BAY (New Britain-SW Pac)	Synonym of WALO	0502-09=
BANI ABDULLAH, HARRAT (Arabia-W)	Blank of RAHAT, HARRAT	0301-07=
BANNIERES, PUY DES (France)	Cone of CHAINE DES PUYS	0100-02-
BANOEA WOEHOE (Sangihe Is-Indonesia)	Synonym of BANUA WUHU	0607-03=
BANOS (Spanish for SPA) see proper name (e.g. AZUFRADOS, BANOS)		
BANOS, LOS (Argentina)	Thermal Feature of TROMEN	1507-071
BANOS, NEVADO DE LOS (Chile-C)	Synonym of PLANCHON-PETEROA	1507-04=
BANTJAH CALDERA [BANCAH CALDERA]	Caldera of MARAPI	0601-14=
BANUA BAUJA (BANUA BAUYA) (Sangihe Is)	Synonym of BANUA WUHU	0607-03=
BANUA WUHU (Sangihe Is-Indonesia)	Submarine (6, 1919) Historical	**0607-03=**
BAR-ALI (Ethiopia)	Cone of DABBAYRA	0201-114
BARACHUMA, GOF (Africa-E)	Maar of MARSABIT	0202-021
BARANSKII (Kurile Is)	Synonym of BARANSKY	0900-08=
BARANSKY (Kurile Is)	Stratovolc (3, 1951) Historical	**0900-08=**
BARANY (Kamchatka)	Stratovolc of GAMCHEN	1000-21=
BARANY AMPHITHEATER (Kamchatka)	Crater of OPALA	1000-08=
BARARUMBO (Africa-N)	Cone of BAYUDA VOLC FIELD	0205-06-
BARBA (Costa Rica)	Synonym of BARVA	1405-05=
BARBERENA, CERRITO DE (Guatemala)	Cone of CUILAPA-BARBARENA	1402-111
BARCENA (Mexico-Is)	Cinder cones (1, 1953) Historical	**1401-02=**
BARDARBUNGA (Iceland-NE)	Stratovolc (29, 1903) Historical	**1703-03=**
BARDARLAUG (Iceland-W)	Cone of SNAEFELLSJOKULL	1700-01=
BARICHA [BERICHA] (Ethiopia)	Stratovolc of BOSET-BERICHA	0201-21-
BARIK (New Guinea-NE of)	Stratovolc of UMBOI	0501-06=
BARKHATNAYA (Kamchatka)	Cone of VILYUCHIK	1000-083
BARKHATNAYA SOPKA (Kamchatka)	Lava domes (1, -3550) Tephrochronology	**1000-084**
BARME, PUY DE (France)	Cone of CHAINE DES PUYS	0100-02-
BARNABE, PICO (Azores)	Dome of AGUA DE PAU	1802-09=
BARNABORG (Iceland-W)	Cone of LJOSUFJOLL	1700-03=
BAROMBE MBO, LAKE (Africa-W)	Maar of MANENGOUBA	0204-004
BARRANCAS. CERRO (Chile-C)	Cone of MAULE, LAGUNA DEL	1507-062
BARRANCO, EL (Nicaragua)	Maar of COSIGUINA	1404-01=
BARRANES COLORADO (Chile-S)	Cone of HUEQUI	1508-03=
BARRANTES, LOMA (Costa Rica)	Cone of AGUAS ZARCAS GROUP	1405-035
BARREN ISLAND (Andaman Is-Ind O)	Stratovolc (5, 1991) Historical	**0600-01=**
BARRIER, THE (Africa-E)	Shield (9, 1921) Historical	**0202-03=**
BARTHOLOME, PIC (Africa-C)	Stratovolc of KARISIMBI	0203-04-
BARTHOLOMEW ISLAND (Galapagos)	Crater of SANTIAGO	1503-09=
BARU (Java)	Crater of GEDE	0603-06=
BARU (Panama)	Complx volc (2, 1550) Historical	**1406-01-**
BARU, KABA (Sumatra)	Crater of KABA	0601-22=
BARU, KAWAH (Java)	Crater of TANGKUBANPARAHU	0603-09=
BARU, KAWAH (Java)	Crater of PAPANDAYAN	0603-10=
BARU [GUNUNG BARUJARI] (Lesser Sunda)	Cone of RINJANI	0604-03=
BARUN-NERTE-ULA (Mongolia)	Cone of DARIGANGA VOLC FIELD	1003-04-
BARUTA (Africa-C)	Cone of NYIRAGONGO	0203-03=
BARVA (Costa Rica)	Complx volc (1, -6050) Tephrochronology	**1405-05=**
BAS DONG NAI (SE Asia)	Volc field (None) Holocene?	**0705-05=**
BASANJO (Africa-E)	Synonym of LENGAI, OL DOINYO	0202-12=
BASAR (Sumatra)	Synonym of BESAR, GUNUNG	0601-25=
BASEN (Atl-N-Jan Mayen)	Cone of JAN MAYEN	1706-01=
BASILE, PICO DE (Africa-W)	Synonym of SANTA ISABEL	0204-02-
BASS MARLE (Africa-E)	Synonym of CENTRAL ISLAND	0202-01=
BASSO NAROK (Africa-E)	Synonym of CENTRAL ISLAND	0202-01=
BASTIONI HILL (Africa-E)	Dome of MERU	0202-16=
BATANG (Java)	Dome of MERAPI	0603-25=
BATAPONA MOUNTAIN (Admiralty Is)	Cone of BALUAN	0500-02-
BATEA, LA (Mexico)	Cone of MICHOACAN-GUANAJUATO	1401-06=
BATHHOUSE SPRING (US-New Mexico)	Thermal Feature of VALLES CALDERA	1210-03-
BATIDORAS, LAS (Nicaragua)	Thermal Feature of COSIGUINA	1404-01=
BATOE, BATU (Dutch spelling of, and Indonesian word for MT.) see proper name (e.g. ANGUS, BATU)		
BATOER (Lesser Sunda Is)	Synonym of BATUR	0604-01=
BATOK (Java)	Cone of TENGGER CALDERA	0603-31=
BATOR (Lesser Sunda Is)	Synonym of BATUR	0604-01=
BATSHRAUN (Iceland-NE)	Fissure vent of ASKJA	1703-06=
BATU FIELD (Sumatra)	Thermal Feature of GAYOLESTEN	0601-06=
BATUHARANG, DOLOK (Sumatra)	Cone of TOBA	0601-09=
BATUKAU (Lesser Sunda Is)	Stratovolc of BRATAN	0604-001
BATUKOLOK (Sulawesi-Indonesia)	Thermal Feature of TONDANO CALDERA	0606-07-
BATUR (Lesser Sunda Is)	Caldera (23, 1974) Historical	**0604-01=**
BATUWALANG MERAPI (Java)	Stratovolc of MERAPI	0603-25=
BAUL, EL [CERRO TECUN UMAN] (Guatem	Dome of ALMOLONGA	1402-04=
BAY OF ISLANDS (New Zealand)	Synonym of KAIKOHE-BAY OF ISLANDS	0401-01=
BAYAN-TSAGAN (Mongolia)	Cone of DARIGANGA VOLC FIELD	1003-04-
BAYAQUITOS, MT. (Luzon-Philippines)	Cone of LAGUNA VOLC FIELD	0703-051
BAYDA, JABAL (Arabia-W)	Tuff cone of KHAYBAR, HARRAT	0301-06=
BAYO, CERRO (Argentina)	Cone of TROMEN	1507-071
BAYO, CERRO (Chile-N)	Complx volc (None) Holocene	**1505-122**
BAYONESU-GANSHO (Izu Is-Japan)	Synonym of BAYONNAISE ROCKS	0804-07=
BAYONNAISE REEF (Izu Is-Japan)	Synonym of BAYONNAISE ROCKS	0804-07=
BAYONNAISE ROCKS (Izu Is-Japan)	Submarine (13, 1970) Historical	**0804-07=**
BAYUDA VOLC FIELD (Africa-N)	Cinder cones (1, 0850) Radiocarbon	**0205-06-**
BAYUYO (Canary Is)	Vent of FUERTEVENTURA	1803-05-
BAZMAN (Iran)	Stratovolc (None) Fumarolic	**0302-03-**
BEAGLE (Galapagos)	Tuff cone of DARWIN, VOLCAN	1503-03=
BEAR BUTTE (US-Oregon)	Cone of CRATER LAKE	1202-16-
BEAR WALLOW BUTTE (US-California)	Cone of TUMBLE BUTTES	1203-06-
BEARHEAD PEAK (US-New Mexico)	Dome of VALLES CALDERA	1210-03-
BEARPAW BUTTE (US-California)	Cone of MEDICINE LAKE	1203-02-
BEAULOUP, MAAR DE (France)	Maar of CHAINE DES PUYS	0100-02-
BEAUNIT, CRATERE DE (France)	Maar of CHAINE DES PUYS	0100-02-
BEAVER RIDGE (US-Utah)	Vent of BLACK ROCK DESERT	1207-05-
BECCO, MT. (Italy)	Cone of VULSINI	0101-003
BEDR, HALA-'L- (Arabia-W)	Cone of 'UWAYRID, HARRAT	0301-02=
BEDUL (Admiralty Is-SW Pac)	Cone of ST. ANDREW STRAIT	0500-01=
BEEHIVES, THE (New Zealand)	Dome of EGMONT	0401-03=
BEEHIVES, THE [DAVAPIA ROCKS] (New Z)	Cone of RABAUL	0502-14=
BEERENBERG (Atl-N-Jan Mayen)	Stratovolc of JAN MAYEN	1706-01=
BEGOUR (Africa-N)	Maar of TOH, TARSO	0205-001
BEIGELAQIUSHAN (China-E)	Cone of WUDALIANCHI	1005-04-
BEIHUOKOU (China-W)	Cone of KUNLUN VOLC GROUP	1004-03-
BEKEL, GUNUNG (Java)	Dome of PENANGGUNGAN	0603-291
BELAIA SOPKA (Kamchatka)	Synonym of ICHINSKY	1000-28=
BELAYA (Aleutian Is)	Synonym of GREAT SITKIN	1101-12-
BELEN'KAYA (Kamchatka)	Stratovolc (None) Holocene	**1000-042**
BELERANG, GUNUNG (Sulawesi-Indonesia)	Synonym of COLO [UNA UNA]	0606-01=
BELESME (Turkey)	Cone of ERCIYES DAGI	0103-01=
BELFOND (W Indies)	Dome of QUALIBOU	1600-14=
BELIANKIN (Kamchatka)	Stratovolc of AKADEMIA NAUK	1000-123
BELIANKIN [BELYANKIN] (Kamchatka)	Crater of KLIUCHEVSKOI	1000-26=

NAME (Subregion)	Type (Eruption Total, Most Recent) Status . . . Relation to NAMED VOLCANO	NUMBER
BELIRANG (Sumatra)	Crater of SUMBING	0601-18=
BELIRANG (Sumatra)	Thermal Feature of HULUBELU	0601-28=
BELIRANG-BERITI (Sumatra)	Compnd volc (None) Fumarolic	**0601-20=**
BELIRANG, GUNUNG (Sumatra)	Synonym of KUNYIT	0601-19=
BELKNAP (US-Oregon)	Shields (5, 0455) Radiocarbon	**1202-06-**
BELLAIRE, VOLCA (Spain)	Cone of OLOT VOLC FIELD	0100-03-
BELLAVISTA (Ecuador)	Cone of TULABUG	1502-081
BELLAVISTA, CERRO (Chile-C)	Cone of CARRAN-LOS VENADOS	1507-14=
BELLEVUE MOUNTAIN (W Indies)	Dome of DIABLE, MORNE AU	1600-08=
BELLINGSHAUSEN ISLAND (Antarctica)	Submarine vent of THULE ISLANDS	1900-07=
BELLISLE MOUNTAIN (US-New Mexico)	Cone of RATON-CLAYTON	1210-04-
BELLIZZI, CUDDIE (Italy)	Vent of PANTELLERIA	0101-071
BELOW, MT. [MT. TALAWE] (New Britain)	Stratovolc of LANGILA	0502-01=
BELU, WAI (Sumatra)	Thermal Feature of HULUBELU	0601-28=
BELVEDERE (Italy)	Crater of CAMPI FLEGREI	0101-01=
BELY (Kamchatka)	Shields (None) Holocene	**1000-64-**
BELYANKIN (Kamchatka)	Crater of KLIUCHEVSKOI	1000-26=
BELYI (Kamchatka)	Synonym of BELY	1000-64-
BEN LOMOND (New Zealand)	Dome of MAROA	0401-061
BENBOW (Vanuatu-SW Pacific)	Crater of AMBRYM	0507-04=
BENDA (New Britain-SW Pac)	Synonym of DAKATAUA	0502-04=
BENGO, CERRO (El Salvador)	Cone of APASTEPEQUE FIELD	1403-071
BENI MAIMUN (Arabia-S)	Crater of ARHAB, HARRA OF	0301-09-
BENI ZUBEIR (Arabia-S)	Crater of ARHAB, HARRA OF	0301-09-
BEPPU (Kyushu-Japan)	Thermal Feature of TSURUMI	0802-13=
BERAPI (Sumatra)	Synonym of KERINCI	0601-17=
BERAPI (Sumatra)	Synonym of MARAPI	0601-14=
BERAPI-ELOK (Sumatra)	Crater of KERINCI	0601-17=
BERCEK, KAWAH (Java)	Thermal Feature of KAWAHKAMOJANG	0603-12=
BERESOWSKAJA (Kamchatka)	Synonym of KARYMSKY	1000-13=
BEREZOVAIA SOPKA (Kamchatka)	Synonym of KARYMSKY	1000-13=
BEREZOVY (Kamchatka)	Stratovolc of MALY SEMIACHIK	1000-14=
BERG (Kurile Is)	Somma volcano of KOLOKOL GROUP	0900-12=
BERG ISI [JABAL EL-ESI] (Arabia-S)	Stratovolc of DHAMAR, HARRAS OF	0301-12-
BERGHOLL (Iceland-SW)	Shield of REYKJANES	1701-02=
BERGVATNSARHRAUN (Iceland-NE)	Crater row of GRIMSVOTN	1703-01=
BERICCIO (Ethiopia)	Pit crater of BORA-BERICCIO COMPLEX	0201-24-
BERICHA (Ethiopia)	Stratovolc of BOSET-BERICHA	0201-21-
BERICHA (Ethiopia)	Synonym of BORA-BERICCIO COMPLEX	0201-24-
BERITARIBI (Kurile Is)	Synonym of BERUTARUBE	0900-04=
BERLIN (Antarctica)	Shields (None) Fumarolic	**1900-022**
BERLIN (El Salvador)	Cone of TECAPA	1403-08=
BERMEJA, MONTANA (Canary Is)	Cone of LANZAROTE	1803-06-
BERMEJA, MONTANA (Canary Is)	Cone of FUERTEVENTURA	1803-05-
BERNA (Atl-N-Jan Mayen)	Cone of JAN MAYEN	1706-01=
BERNADSKOGO [VERNADSKIY] (Kamchatk	Crater of KLIUCHEVSKOI	1000-26=
BERRAZALES (Canary Is)	Thermal Feature of GRAN CANARIA	1803-04-
BERRITARABENOBORI (Kurile Is)	Synonym of BERUTARUBE	0900-04=
BERTJEK, KAWAH [KAWAH BERCEK] (Java	Thermal Feature of KAWAHKAMOJANG	0603-12=
BERU (Ethiopia)	Unknown (None) Holocene	**0201-191**
BERUTARUBE (Kurile Is)	Stratovolc (None) Holocene	**0900-04=**
BESAR, GUNUNG (Sumatra)	Stratovolc ? (1, 1940) Historical	**0601-25=**
BESAR, KABA [LAMA, KABA] (Sumatra)	Crater of KABA	0601-22=
BESSIE BUTTE (US-Oregon)	Cone of NEWBERRY VOLCANO	1202-11-
BESYMYANNAYA (Kamchatka)	Synonym of BEZYMIANNY	1000-25=
BETA (Russia-NE)	Cone of ALUCHIN GROUP	1001-01-
BETAFO (Madagascar)	Cone of ANKARATRA FIELD	0303-07-
BEYONESU-RETUGAN (Izu Is-Japan)	Synonym of BAYONNAISE ROCKS	0804-07=
BEZYMIANNY (Kamchatka)	Stratovolc (46, 1993) Historical	**1000-25=**
BEZYMJANNAJA SOPKA (Kamchatka)	Synonym of BEZYMIANNY	1000-25=
BEZYMYANNAYA (Kamchatka)	Dome of UZON	1000-17=
BIAM (New Guinea-NE of)	Synonym of BAM	0501-01=
BIAO, PICO (Africa-W)	Synonym of SAN JOAQUIN	0204-03-
BICHBALICK [PECHAN] (China-W)	Cone of TIANSHAN VOLC GROUP	1004-02-
BIEI-DAKE (Hokkaido-Japan)	Stratovolc of TOKACHI	0805-05=
BIEI-FUJI (Hokkaido-Japan)	Stratovolc of TOKACHI	0805-05=
BIEM (New Guinea-NE of)	Synonym of BAM	0501-01=
BIETE MENGEST (Ethiopia)	Tuff ring of BISHOFTU FIELD	0201-22-
BIG BEN (Indian O.-S)	Stratovolc of HEARD	0304-01=
BIG BUNCHGRASS (US-Oregon)	Pyrocl cone (None) Holocene	**1202-162**
BIG CAVE (US-California)	Shield (None) Holocene?	**1203-04-**
BIG CINDER BUTTE (US-Idaho)	Cone of CRATERS OF THE MOON	1204-02-
BIG CRATERS (US-Idaho)	Cone of CRATERS OF THE MOON	1204-02-
BIG GLASS MOUNTAIN [GLASS MTN.]	Dome of MEDICINE LAKE	1203-02-
BIG HILL (Australia)	Cone of NEWER VOLCANICS PROV	0509-01-
BIG JOHN (New Zealand)	Former crater of WHITE ISLAND	0401-04=
BIG LAVA BED CONE (US-Washington)	Cone of INDIAN HEAVEN	1201-07-
BIG MT. WORRI (New Britain-SW Pac)	Cone of GARUA HARBOUR	0502-06=
BIG OBSIDIAN FLOW (US-Oregon)	Vent of NEWBERRY VOLCANO	1202-11-
BIG SAND BUTTE (US-California)	Cone of MEDICINE LAKE	1203-02-
BIHADI (Africa-N)	Crater of BAYUDA VOLC FIELD	0205-06-
BIHIRAM (Africa-C)	Cone of KARISIMBI	0203-04-
BIHUNDE (Africa-C)	Cone of NYAMURAGIRA	0203-02=
BIJAGUA (Costa Rica)	Cone of TENORIO GROUP	1405-031
BIJIASHAN (China-E)	Cone of WUDALIANCHI	1005-04-
BIL TEPE (Turkey)	Dome of ERCIYES DAGI	0103-01=
BILATE RIVER FIELD (Ethiopia)	Volc field (None) Holocene	**0201-291**
BILIBIN (Kurile Is)	Cone of VERNADSKII RIDGE	0900-37-
BILIRAN (Philippines-C)	Compnd volc (1, 1939) Historical	**0702-08=**
BILIUKAYA [BILYUKAI] (Kamchatka)	Crater of KLIUCHEVSKOI	1000-26=
BILLY MITCHELL (Bougainville-SW)	Pyrocl shield (2, 1580) Radiocarbon	**0505-011**
BILMA, MONTANA (Canary Is)	Cone of TENERIFE	1803-03-
BILYUKAI (Kamchatka)	Crater of KLIUCHEVSKOI	1000-26=
BINALIK (Alaska-W)	Maar of NUNIVAK ISLAND	1104-06-
BINANGUNAN, MT. (Sulawesi-Indonesia)	Stratovolc of AMBANG	0606-02=
BINDLOE (Galapagos)	Synonym of MARCHENA	1503-08=
BINEM (Java)	Cone of DIENG VOLC COMPLEX	0603-20=
BINGA (Mindanao-Philippines)	Dome of PACO	0701-09-
BININTIANG MALAKI (Luzon-Philippines)	Cone of TAAL	0703-07=
BININTIANG MALAQUI [BININTIANG MALA	Cone of TAAL	0703-07=
BININTIANG MUNTI (Luzon-Philippines)	Cone of TAAL	0703-07=
BINNA (Atl-N-Jan Mayen)	Dome of JAN MAYEN	1706-01=
BINULUAN (Luzon-Philippines)	Compnd volc (None) Fumarolic	**0703-088**
BIOKOS' (Kamchatka)	Crater of KLIUCHEVSKOI	1000-26=
BIR ALI (Arabia-S)	Synonym of BAL HAF, HARRA OF	0301-17-
BIR BAHRAHUT (BIR BAHUT) (Arabia-S)	Synonym of BIR BORHUT	0301-18-
BIR BARHOUT (BIR BARHUT) (Arabia-S)	Synonym of BIR BORHUT	0301-18-
BIR BORHUT (Arabia-S)	Volc field (None) Holocene?	**0301-18-**
BIRD MOUNTAIN (US-Washington)	Cone of INDIAN HEAVEN	1201-07-
BIRD NEST ISLAND (Africa-E)	Crater of CENTRAL ISLAND	0202-01=
BIRUA (Africa-C)	Cone of VISOKE	0203-05-
BISAROQUES, VOLCA LES (Spain)	Cone of OLOT VOLC FIELD	0100-03-

NAME (Subregion)	Type (Eruption Total, Most Recent) Status . . . Relation to NAMED VOLCANO	NUMBER
BISATI NDUBI (Africa-C)	Cone of VISOKE	0203-05-
BISENTINA, ISOLA (Italy)	Cone of VULSINI	0101-003
BISHAN WAKA (Ethiopia)	Pit crater of TEPI	0201-292
BISHOFTU FIELD (Ethiopia)	Fissure vents (None) Holocene	**0201-22-**
BISHOFTU HAYK (Ethiopia)	Tuff ring of BISHOFTU FIELD	0201-22-
BISHUSHA (Africa-C)	Cone of NYAMURAGIRA	0203-02=
BISMO [BISMA] (Java)	Cone of DIENG VOLC COMPLEX	0603-20=
BISOKE (BISOKO) (Africa-C)	Synonym of VISOKE	0203-05-
BITINGAN, KAWAH (Java)	Crater of DIENG VOLC COMPLEX	0603-20=
BITIVOGALA (Solomon Is-SW Pac)	Crater of SAVO	0505-07=
BITJARA, LAKE (Halmahera-Indonesia)	Maar of IBU	0608-03=
BIU PLATEAU (Africa-W)	Volc field (None) Holocene?	**0204-001**
BIWA-IKE (Kyushu-Japan)	Crater of KIRISHIMA	0802-09=
BIWANOKUBA (Kyushu-Japan)	Vent of UNZEN	0802-10=
BJALLAGIGAR (Iceland-S)	Fissure vent of HEKLA	1702-07=
BJARNAREY (Iceland-S)	Cone of VESTMANNAEYJAR	1702-01=
BJARNARGIGAR [BJARNARFLAG] (Iceland)	Crater row of KRAFLA	1703-08=
BLACK BUTTE (US-California)	Dome of SHASTA	1203-01-
BLACK BUTTE CRATER (US-Idaho)	Shield of SHOSHONE LAVA FIELD	1204-01-
BLACK BUTTE [CINDER CONE] (US-Calif)	Cone of LASSEN VOLC CENTER	1203-08-
BLACK BUTTES (US-Washington)	Stratovolc of BAKER	1201-01=
BLACK CONE (US-Nevada)	Cone of CRATER FLAT	1206-03-
BLACK CRATER (El Salvador)	Dome of TECAPA	1403-08=
BLACK HILL (Australia)	Cone of NEWER VOLCANICS PROV	0509-01-
BLACK KNOLL (US-Utah)	Cone of BALD KNOLL	1207-03-
BLACK MOUNTAIN (Africa-E)	Synonym of MERU	0202-16=
BLACK MOUNTAIN (US-California)	Cone of MEDICINE LAKE	1203-02-
BLACK PEAK (Alaska Peninsula)	Stratovolc (1, -2920) Radiocarbon	**1102-08-**
BLACK PEAK (Alaska Peninsula)	Synonym of VENIAMINOF	1102-07-
BLACK POINT (Hawaiian Is)	Cone of KOOLAU	1302-07-
BLACK POINT (US-Calif)	Cone of MONO LAKE VOLC FIELD	1203-11-
BLACK ROCK DESERT (US-Utah)	Volc field (1, 1290) Radiocarbon	**1207-05-**
BLACK ROCK VOLCANO (US-Utah)	Cone of BLACK ROCK DESERT	1207-05-
BLACK TOP BUTTE (US-Idaho)	Cone of CRATERS OF THE MOON	1204-02-
BLACK TUSK, THE (Canada)	Stratovolc of GARIBALDI LAKE	1200-19-
BLACKWOOD, MT. (Australia)	Cone of NEWER VOLCANICS PROV	0509-01-
BLAKISTON (Kurile Is)	Synonym of TAO-RUSYR CALDERA	0900-31=
BLANCA (Mexico)	Maar of MICHOACAN-GUANAJUATO	1401-06=
BLANCA, CALDERA (Canary Is)	Crater of LANZAROTE	1803-06-
BLANCA, LOMA (Chile-C)	Stratovolc (None) Holocene	**1507-065**
BLANCA, MONTANA (Canary Is)	Cone of LANZAROTE	1803-06-
BLANCA, MONTANA (Canary Is)	Fissure vent of TENERIFE	1803-03-
BLANCAS, CALDERAS (Canary Is)	Cone of FUERTEVENTURA	1803-05-
BLANCHE BAY (New Britain-SW Pac)	Synonym of RABAUL	0502-14=
BLANCHE CRATER (US-Idaho)	Cone of SHOSHONE LAVA FIELD	1204-01-
BLANCO, CERRO (Argentina)	Dome of ROBLEDO	1505-128
BLANCO, CERRO (Chile-C)	Stratovolc of CHILLAN, NEVADOS DE	1507-07=
BLANCO, CERRO (El Salvador)	Thermal Feature of VERDE, LAGUNA	1403-01=
BLAUFDEL [BURFELL I OLFUSI] (Iceland)	Shield of HENGILL	1701-05=
BLERANG-BERITI (Sumatra)	Synonym of BELIRANG-BERITI	0601-20=
BLIZHNAYA PLOSKAYA [KRESTOVSKY]	Stratovolc of USHKOVSKY	1000-261
BLIZHNY PLOSKI [KRESTOVSKY] (Kamcha	Stratovolc of USHKOVSKY	1000-261
BLIZNETS (Kamchatka)	Stratovolc (None) Holocene	**1000-49-**
BLOSSEVILLE ISLAND (New Guinea-NE of)	Synonym of KADOVAR	0501-002
BLOWOUTS, THE (US-Oregon)	Vent of DEVILS GARDEN	1202-12-
BLUE LAKE (Australia)	Tuff ring of NEWER VOLCANICS PROV	0509-01-
BLUE LAKE (Kermadec Is)	Crater of RAOUL ISLAND	0402-03=
BLUE LAKE (New Zealand)	Crater of TONGARIRO	0401-08=
BLUE LAKE CRATER (US-Oregon)	Maar (1, -1490) Radiocarbon	**1202-03-**
BLUE MOUNTAIN (Australia)	Dome of NEWER VOLCANICS PROV	0509-01-
BLUE, VOLCAN (Nicaragua)	Cinder cones (None) Holocene	**1404-14-**
BLUFF, THE (Australia)	Cone of NEWER VOLCANICS PROV	0509-01-
BLUP BLUP (New Guinea-NE of)	Stratovolc (None) Holocene	**0501-001**
BO-SHAN (China-E)	Synonym of WUDALIANCHI	1005-04-
BOAT COVE (Kermadec Is)	Synonym of RAOUL ISLAND	0402-03=
BOBADILLA, CRATER (Chile-C)	Cone of MAULE, LAGUNA DEL	1507-062
BOBAOMBY (Madagascar)	Cone of AMBRE-BOBAOMBY	0303-03-
BOBOPAJO (Halmahera-Indonesia)	Caldera of JAILOLO	0608-051
BOBROF (Aleutian Is)	Stratovolc (None) Holocene?	**1101-10-**
BOCAS DE FOGO (Azores)	Vent of PICO	1802-02=
BOCCA DEL FOSSAMONACA (Italy)	Cone of VESUVIUS	0101-02=
BOCCA DEL VIULO (Italy)	Cone of VESUVIUS	0101-02=
BOCCA GRANDE (Colombia)	Crater of CUMBAL	1501-10=
BOCCA NUOVA (Italy)	Crater of ETNA	0101-06=
BOCHAROVA ? (Alaska Peninsula)	Synonym of UGASHIK-PEULIK	1102-13A
BODE AMEDA HAYK (Ethiopia)	Crater of BILATE RIVER FIELD	0201-291
BOEAL BOEALI (Sumatra)	Synonym of BUAL BUALI	0601-11=
BOEKIT, BOER (Dutch: of Indonesian word for HILL, MT.) see proper name (e.g. MOETELONG, BOER)		
BOEKITDAOEN (Sumatra)	Synonym of LUMUTDAUN, BUKIT	0601-21=
BOELIRAN, KAWAH [KAWAH BULIRAN]	Thermal Feature of KAWAHKAMOJANG	0603-12=
BOENDER [BUNDER] (Lesser Sunda Is)	Cone of BATUR	0604-01=
BOETAK PETARANGAN [BUTAK PETARAN	Cone of DIENG VOLC COMPLEX	0603-20=
BOETAK [BUTAK] (Java)	Cone of DIENG VOLC COMPLEX	0603-20=
BOGANA (Bougainville-SW Pac)	Synonym of BAGANA	0505-02=
BOGATYR RIDGE (Kurile Is)	Stratovolc (None) Holocene	**0900-06-**
BOGDAN KHMELNITSKII (Kurile Is)	Stratovolc of CHIRIP	0900-09=
BOGDANOVICH (Kamchatka)	Shield of KOLKHOZHNY	1000-221
BOGDANOVICH (Kurile Is)	Crater of VERNADSKII RIDGE	0900-37-
BOGGEL (Indian O.-S)	Cone of PRINCE EDWARD ISLAND	0304-07-
BOGOSLOF (Aleutian Is)	Submarine (8, 1992) Historical	**1101-30-**
BOGOSLOF HILL (Alaska-W)	Cone of ST. PAUL ISLAND	1104-07-
BOI (Africa-E)	Synonym of CENTRAL ISLAND	0202-01=
BOI, PICO DO (Azores)	Cone of SETE CIDADES	1802-08=
BOILING LAKE (W Indies)	Thermal Feature of MICOTRIN	1600-10=
BOINA (Djibouti)	Fumarole fld (None) Pleistocene-Fumarolic	**0201-14=**
BOINA (Ethiopia)	Cone of DABBAHU	0201-113
BOIS D'INDE FRANCIOU (W Indies)	Dome of QUALIBOU	1600-14=
BOISA (New Guinea-NE of)	Stratovolc (None) Holocene?	**0501-011**
BOKKI (Iceland-NE)	Crater row of TUNGNAFELLSJOKULL	1703-04=
BOKLUCA (Turkey)	Cone of ERCIYES DAGI	0103-01=
BOLA (New Britain-SW Pac)	Stratovolc (None) Holocene	**0502-05=**
BOLETAS, CERRO (US-New Mexico)	Dome of VALLES CALDERA	1210-03-
BOLICHE (Ecuador)	Dome of CHACANA	1502-022
BOLIN (Lesser Sunda Is)	Synonym of ILIBOLENG	0604-22=
BOLJSHAIA UDINA [BOLSHAYA UDINA]	Stratovolc of UDINA	1000-241
BOLJSHOY [BOLSHOY] (Kamchatka)	Shield of BOLSHOY-KEKUKNAYSKY	1000-36-
BOLLONS ISLAND (Pacific-S)	Cone of ANTIPODES ISLAND	1304-01-
BOLSENA (Italy)	Pleistocene caldera of VULSINI	0101-003
BOLSHAYA PLOSKY [DALJNY PLOSKY]	Shield of USHKOVSKY	1000-261
BOLSHAYA UDINA (Kamchatka)	Stratovolc of UDINA	1000-241
BOLSHE-BANNAYA (Kamchatka)	Lava domes (None) Holocene	**1000-087**
BOLSHOI SEMIACHIK (Kamchatka)	Stratovolcs (2, -4450) Radiocarbon	**1000-15=**
BOLSHOI SEMIACHIK (Kamchatka)	Synonym of MALY SEMIACHIK	1000-14=
BOLSHOI SITKIN (Aleutian Is)	Synonym of GREAT SITKIN	1101-12-
BOLSHOY (Kamchatka)	Shield of BOLSHOY-KEKUKNAYSKY	1000-36-
BOLSHOY-KEKUKNAYSKY (Kamchatka)	Shields (None) Holocene	**1000-36-**
BOLSHOY PAYALPAN (Kamchatka)	Shields (None) Holocene	**1000-30-**
BOL'SHOY SEMIACHIK (Kamchatka)	Synonym of BOLSHOI SEMIACHIK	1000-15=
BOLUDO (Mexico)	Cone of HOLOTEPEC	1401-07-
BOMB PEAK (Antarctica)	Cone of EREBUS	1900-02=
BOMBALAI (Borneo)	Cone (None) Holocene?	**0610-01-**
BOMBARDIA (Greece)	Dome of MILOS	0102-03=
BOMBELLESTOPPEN (Atl-N-Jan Mayen)	Dome of JAN MAYEN	1706-01=
BOMBON, LAKE (Luzon-Philippines)	Synonym of TAAL	0703-07=
BONA-CHURCHILL (Alaska-E)	Stratovolcs (2, 0700) Radiocarbon	**1105-03-**
BONDE (Africa-C)	Cone of KARISIMBI	0203-04-
BONDHOLSHRAUN (Iceland-NE)	Shield of KRAFLA	1703-08=
BONETE, CERRO EL (Guatemala)	Cone of MOYUTA	1402-13-
BONGKOK, BUKIT (Lesser Sunda Is)	Cone of BATUR	0604-01=
BONGOLE, GOF (Africa-E)	Maar of MARSABIT	0202-021
BONGSU, KEPUNDAN (Sumatra)	Crater of MARAPI	0601-14=
BONIN, MORNE (W Indies)	Dome of QUALIBOU	1600-14=
BONITA BUTTE (US-California)	Cone of MEDICINE LAKE	1203-02-
BONNET, LE (Indian O.-W)	Crater of FOURNAISE, PITON DE LA	0303-02=
BONO (New Guinea-NE of)	Crater of UMBOI	0501-06=
BONSULTON, CUDDIE (Italy)	Vent of PANTELLERIA	0101-071
BOOBY HILL (W Indies)	Dome of SABA	1600-01=
BOOSER (Germany)	Maar of WEST EIFEL VOLC FIELD	0100-01-
BOOT ROCK (Indian O.-S)	Tuff cone of MARION ISLAND	0304-08-
BOQUERON, AUSOL EL (El Salvador)	Thermal Feature of CHINAMECA	1403-09=
BOQUERON, EL (El Salvador)	Stratovolc of SAN SALVADOR	1403-05=
BOQUERON, EL (Mexico-Is)	Synonym of BARCENA	1401-02=
BOQUERONCITOS (El Salvador)	Fissure vent of SAN SALVADOR	1403-05=
BOR-ELI (Ethiopia)	Synonym of BORALE ALE	0201-071
BOR GHELEBA (Africa-E)	Synonym of CENTRAL ISLAND	0202-01=
BORA (Ethiopia)	Pit crater of BORA-BERICCIO COMPLEX	0201-24-
BORA-BERICCIO COMPLEX (Ethiopia)	Pumice cones (None) Holocene	**0201-24-**
BORALE ALE (Ethiopia)	Stratovolc (None) Holocene	**0201-071**
BORAULE (Ethiopia)	Synonym of BORAWLI COMPLEX	0201-121
BORAWLI (Ethiopia)	Stratovolc (None) Holocene	**0201-107**
BORAWLI COMPLEX (Ethiopia)	Lava domes (None) Holocene	**0201-121**
BORDER MOUNTAIN (US-California)	Cone of MEDICINE LAKE	1203-02-
BORELE-ALI (Ethiopia)	Synonym of BORALE ALE	0201-071
BORGAHRAUN (Iceland)	Fissure vent of THEISTAREYKJARBUNGA	1703-09=
BORGARHOLAR (Iceland-SW)	Cone of GRIMSNES	1701-06=
BORGARHRAUN (Iceland-SW)	Crater row of REYKJANES	1701-02=
BORIATIKO VOUNO (Greece)	Dome of NISYROS	0102-05=
BORIQUEN (Costa Rica)	Thermal Feature of RINCON DE LA VIEJA	1405-02=
BORISYAK, MT. (Kurile Is)	Cone of LOMONOSOV GROUP	0900-351
BORO, GOF (Africa-E)	Maar of MARSABIT	0202-021
BORT (Kamchatka)	Stratovolc of BOLSHOI SEMIACHIK	1000-15=
BORTOVAYA (Kamchatka)	Dome of UZON	1000-17=
BORY (Indian O.-W)	Crater of FOURNAISE, PITON DE LA	0303-02=
BORZOV (Kurile Is)	Cone of KOLOKOL GROUP	0900-12=
BOSCHAN [PECHAN] (China-W)	Cone of TIANSHAN VOLC GROUP	1004-02-
BOSCO DEI CONTI (Italy)	Cone of ISCHIA	0101-03=
BOSCO DELLA MADDALENA (Italy)	Stratovolc of ISCHIA	0101-03=
BOSET (Ethiopia)	Stratovolc of BOSET-BERICHA	0201-21-
BOSET-BERICHA (Ethiopia)	Stratovolcs (None) Holocene	**0201-21-**
BOSETI-BARICCIA (Ethiopia)	Synonym of BOSET-BERICHA	0201-21-
BOSETI-BERICCIA [BERICHA] (Ethiopia)	Stratovolc of BOSET-BERICHA	0201-21-
BOSETI-GUDDA [BOSET] (Ethiopia)	Stratovolc of BOSET-BERICHA	0201-21-
BOSOTLAN (El Salvador)	Synonym of SAN MIGUEL	1403-10=
BOSQUE ALEGRE (Costa Rica)	Maar of POAS	1405-04=
BOSQUE ALEGRE, LAGUNA (Costa Rica)	Stratovolc of POAS	1405-04=
BOTNA-SKYRTUNNA (Iceland-W)	Cone of LJOSUFJOLL	1700-03=
BOTNAHRAUN (Iceland-NE)	Fissure vent of GRIMSVOTN	1703-01=
BOTNAHRAUN (Iceland-NE)	Fissure vent of ASKJA	1703-06=
BOTOS (Costa Rica)	Cone of POAS	1405-04=
BOTTOM HILL (W Indies)	Dome of SABA	1600-01=
BOUVET (Atlantic-S)	Shield (1, -0050) Magnetism	**1806-02-**
BOUVETOYA (Atlantic-S)	Synonym of BOUVET	1806-02-
BOVE, VALLE DEL (Italy)	Caldera of ETNA	0101-06=
BOWDEN CRATER (US-Oregon)	Synonym of JACKIES BUTTE	1202-20-
BOWERS KNOLL (US-Utah)	Cone of MARKAGUNT PLATEAU	1207-04-
BOYNA (Ethiopia)	Synonym of DABBAHU	0201-113
BOZ DAG (Turkey)	Cone of ERCIYES DAGI	0103-01=
BOZ DAG (Turkey)	Dome of ERCIYES DAGI	0103-01=
BOZU-JIGOKU (Kyushu-Japan)	Thermal Feature of TSURUMI	0802-13=
BRAMA [BROMO] (Java)	Cone of TENGGER CALDERA	0603-31=
BRANCA, CALDEIRA (Azores)	Maar of FLORES	1802-001
BRANCA, CALDERA (Africa-C)	Pleistocene caldera of KARISIMBI	0203-04-
BRANCA, MONT (Indian O.-S)	Cone of POSSESSION, ILE DE LA	0304-05-
BRANCO, PICO (Atlantic-S)	Dome of TRINDADE	1805-051
BRANDUR (Iceland-S)	Cone of VESTMANNAEYJAR	1702-01=
BRASIL, CERRO (Guatemala)	Cone of CUILAPA-BARBARENA	1402-111
BRAT CHIRPOEV (Kurile Is)	Cone of CHIRPOI	0900-15=
BRATAN (Lesser Sunda Is)	Caldera (None) Holocene	**0604-001**
BRAUN [VON SEEBACH] (Costa Rica)	Cone of RINCON DE LA VIEJA	1405-02=
BRAVA (Cape Verde Is)	Stratovolc (None) Holocene	**1804-02-**
BRAVARD (Chile-C)	Synonym of TUPUNGATITO	1507-01=
BRAVAS, LAGUNAS (Chile)	Synonym of NEVADA, SIERRA	1505-125
BRAVO, CERRO (Colombia)	Stratovolc (8, 1720) Radiocarbon	**1501-011**
BREDES, PITON (Indian O.-W)	Cone of FOURNAISE, PITON DE LA	0303-02=
BRENA, LA (Mexico)	Maar of DURANGO VOLC FIELD	1401-022
BRENAL (Mexico)	Synonym of DURANGO VOLC FIELD	1401-022
BRENNISTEINSFJOLL (Iceland-SW)	Crater rows (8, 1341) Historical	**1701-04=**
BRENNISTEINSGIGAR (Iceland-SW)	Synonym of BRENNISTEINSFJOLL	1701-04=
BREW, MT. (Canada)	Vent of GARIBALDI LAKE	1200-19-
BRIDGE RIVER CONES (Canada)	Volc field (None) Holocene	**1200-17-**
BRIDGE RIVER VENT (Canada)	Vent of MEAGER	1200-18-
BRIDGEMAN ISLAND (Antarctica)	Stratovolc (None) Uncertain	**1900-04=**
BRIDGMAN ISLAND (Antarctica)	Synonym of BRIDGEMAN ISLAND	1900-04=
BRILLANTES, MONTAGNAS (Alaska-SW)	Synonym of ILIAMNA	1103-02-
BRIMSTONE HILL (W Indies)	Dome of LIAMUIGA	1600-03=
BRIMSTONE ISLAND (Kermadec Is)	Submarine ? (None) Uncertain	**0402-02=**
BRISTOL ISLAND (Antarctica)	Stratovolc (5, 1956) Historical	**1900-08=**
BRITO, CERRO DE (Guatemala)	Cone of CUILAPA-BARBARENA	1402-111
BROADLANDS (New Zealand)	Thermal Feature of REPOROA	0401-06-
BROCKMAN FLAT (US-California)	Synonym of EAGLE LAKE FIELD	1203-09-
BROKEN BACK (US-New Mexico)	Crater of CARRIZOZO	1210-01-
BROKEN ISLAND (Africa-E)	Crater of CENTRAL ISLAND	0202-01=
BROKEN TOP (US-Idaho)	Cone of CRATERS OF THE MOON	1204-02-
BROKEOFF MOUNTAIN (US-Calif)	Stratovolc of LASSEN VOLC CENTER	1203-08-

NAME (Subregion)	Type (Eruption Total, Most Recent) Status . . . Relation to NAMED VOLCANO	NUMBER
BROMO (Java)	Cone of TENGGER CALDERA	0603-31=
BROWN PEAK (Antarctica)	Synonym of STURGE ISLAND	1900-012
BROWN'S ISLAND [MOTUKOREA] (New Z)	Cone of AUCKLAND FIELD	0401-02=
BRUCE (Antarctica)	Cone of SEAL NUNATAKS GROUP	1900-05=
BRUCIATA, CUDDIA (Italy)	Cone of PANTELLERIA	0101-071
BRUCK (Germany)	Crater of WEST EIFEL VOLC FIELD	0100-01-
BRUJA, LOMA LA (Nicaragua)	Cone of SAN CRISTOBAL	1404-02=
BRUJILLO, CERRO (Guatemala)	Cone of IXTEPEQUE, VOLCAN	1402-18-
BRUJO, CERRO (Galapagos)	Tuff cone of SAN CRISTOBAL	1503-12-
BRUJO, EL (Guatemala)	Vent of SANTA MARIA	1402-03=
BRULANT (Indian O.-W)	Crater of FOURNAISE, PITON DE LA	0303-02=
BRULOT (Indian O.-S)	Cone of AMSTERDAM ISLAND	0304-04-
BRUNABORG [HROSSADALIUR] (Iceland-N)	Crater row of KRAFLA	1703-08=
BRUNAGIGIR (Iceland-SW)	Crater row of BRENNISTEINSFJOLL	1701-04=
BRUSHY BUTTE (US-California)	Shield (None) Holocene?	**1203-03-**
BRYDJUHRAUN (Iceland-NE)	Fissure vent of BARDARBUNGA	1703-03=
BRYTALAEKIR (Iceland-S)	Fissure vent of KATLA	1702-03=
BU JERMAN (SE Asia)	Shield of HAUT DONG NAI	0705-04-
BU KONG RONG (SE Asia)	Caldera of HAUT DONG NAI	0705-04-
BUAL BUALI (Sumatra)	Stratovolc (None) Fumarolic	**0601-11=**
BUBAY, MT. (Luzon-Philippines)	Cone of LAGUNA VOLC FIELD	0703-051
BUBOCHKA (Kamchatka)	Cone of TOLBACHIK	1000-24=
BUCK BUTTE (US-California)	Cone of MEDICINE LAKE	1203-02-
BUCK HILL (Canada)	Cone of WELLS GRAY-CLEARWATER	1200-15-
BUCK KNOLL (US-Utah)	Cone of BALD KNOLL	1207-03-
BUCKLE ISLAND (Antarctica)	Stratovolc (2, 1899) Historical	**1900-01=**
BUCU, GUNUNG (Java)	Cone of DIENG VOLC COMPLEX	0603-20=
BUD DAJO (Sulu Is-Philippines)	Pyrocl cones (2, 1897) Historical	**0700-01=**
BUDAKLETTUR (Iceland-W)	Cone of SNAEFELLSJOKULL	1700-01=
BUDAMADO HAYK (Ethiopia)	Crater of BILATE RIVER FIELD	0201-291
BUENA VISTA, CERRO (El Salvador)	Dome of ILOPANGO	1403-06=
BUENA VISTA, CERRO (Guatemala)	Cone of MOYUTA	1402-13-
BUENAVISTA (Mexico)	Vent of IZTACCIHUATL	1401-086
BUENOS AIRES (Costa Rica)	Cone of AGUAS ZARCAS GROUP	1405-035
BUEY, LAGUNA LA (Colombia)	Crater of PURACE	1501-06=
BUEYES, CERRO DE LOS (Guatemala)	Cone of CUILAPA-BARBARENA	1402-111
BUG ISLAND (Africa-E)	Crater of CENTRAL ISLAND	0202-01=
BUGESHI (Africa-C)	Cone of KARISIMBI	0203-04-
BUGOGO (Africa-C)	Cone of NYIRAGONGO	0203-03=
BUGUMBA (Africa-C)	Tuff cone of FORT PORTAL FIELD	0203-002
BUGWAYE (Africa-C)	Crater of BUNYARUGURU FIELD	0203-005
BUHANGIN (Mindanao-Philippines)	Dome of PACO	0701-09-
BUHARA (Africa-C)	Tuff cone of RUSEKERE	0203-001
BUHI (Luzon-Philippines)	Synonym of MALINAO	0703-04=
BUHUBIE (Africa-C)	Cone of NYAMURAGIRA	0203-02=
BUHUMA (Africa-C)	Cone of NYIRAGONGO	0203-03=
BUJISHAN (China-E)	Cone of DATONG	1005-01-
BUKIT, BUR (Indonesian for HILL, MT.) see proper name (e.g. DAUN, BUKIT)		
BUKOLI (Africa-C)	Cone of NYAMURAGIRA	0203-02=
BULA (New Britain-SW Pac)	Synonym of BOLA	0502-05=
BULAL VOLC FIELD (Ethiopia)	Synonym of MEGA BASALT FIELD	0201-33-
BULALO, MT. (Luzon-Philippines)	Cone of LAGUNA VOLC FIELD	0703-051
BULDIR (Aleutian Is)	Stratovolc (None) Holocene	**1101-01-**
BULENGIRA (Africa-C)	Cone of KARISIMBI	0203-04-
BULENGO (Africa-C)	Cone of NYIRAGONGO	0203-03=
BULGAN VOLC FIELD (Mongolia)	Synonym of KHANUY GOL	1003-02-
BULIENMERRI, LAKE (Australia)	Tuff ring of NEWER VOLCANICS PROV	0509-01-
BULIRAN, KAWAH (Java)	Thermal Feature of KAWAHKAMOJANG	0603-12=
BULKA (Kamchatka)	Dome of AVACHINSKY	1000-10=
BULL (Antarctica)	Cone of SEAL NUNATAKS GROUP	1900-05=
BULLAROOK HILL (Australia)	Cone of NEWER VOLCANICS PROV	0509-01-
BULLENGAROOK, MT. (Australia)	Cone of NEWER VOLCANICS PROV	0509-01-
BULU (New Britain-SW Pac)	Synonym of BOLA	0502-05=
BULU [GULU] (New Britain-SW Pac)	Cone of LANGILA	0502-01=
BULUMORSUM (Admiralty Is-SW Pac)	Cone of ST. ANDREW STRAIT	0500-01=
BULUSAN (Luzon-Philippines)	Stratovolc (13, 1988) Historical	**0703-01=**
BUMABAG (Luzon-Philippines)	Cone of AMBALATUNGAN GROUP	0703-089
BUMPASS HELL (US-Calif)	Thermal Feature of LASSEN VOLC CENT	1203-08-
BUMPASS MOUNTAIN (US-Calif)	Dome of LASSEN VOLC CENTER	1203-08-
BUNAGA [CERISY PEAK] (New Guinea-NE)	Stratovolc of LONG ISLAND	0501-05=
BUNANYA (Kamchatka)	Shield of KEKURNY	1000-41-
BUNANYA (Kamchatka)	Shield of UKSICHAN	1000-35-
BUNBULAN (Lesser Sunda Is)	Crater of BATUR	0604-01=
BUNDER (Lesser Sunda Is)	Cone of BATUR	0604-01=
BUNDJULI (Africa-C)	Cone of KARISIMBI	0203-04-
BUNGBRUNG (Java)	Crater of PAPANDAYAN	0603-10=
BUNGSU, KAPUNDAN [KEPUNDAN BUNGS	Crater of MARAPI	0601-14=
BUNINYONG, MT. (Australia)	Cone of NEWER VOLCANICS PROV	0509-01-
BUNKER HILL (W Indies)	Dome of SABA	1600-01=
BUNNELL BUTTE (US-Washington)	Cone of ADAMS	1201-04-
BUNOT, LAKE (Luzon-Philippines)	Maar of LAGUNA VOLC FIELD	0703-051
BUNUHOLAR (Iceland-NE)	Fissure vent of GRIMSVOTN	1703-01=
BUNYAMPAKA [KASENYI] (Africa-C)	Tuff cone of KATWE-KIKORONGO FIELD	0203-004
BUNYARO (Africa-C)	Cone of VISOKE	0203-05-
BUNYARUGURU VOLC FIELD (Africa-C)	Expl craters (None) Holocene	**0203-005**
BUNYOGWE (Africa-C)	Cone of KARISIMBI	0203-04-
BUNYOKE (Africa-C)	Cone of VISOKE	0203-05-
BURACO, PICO DO (Azores)	Dome of FURNAS	1802-10=
BURAK (Lesser Sunda Is)	Crater of LEREBOLENG	0604-20=
BURAUEN (Philippines-C)	Synonym of MAHAGNOA	0702-07=
BURAYA (Kamchatka)	Cone of TOLBACHIK	1000-24=
BUREVESTNIK (Kurile Is)	Cone of BOGATYR RIDGE	0900-06-
BURFELL (Iceland-SW)	Crater row of KRISUVIK	1701-03=
BURFELL I OLFUSI (Iceland-SW)	Shield of HENGILL	1701-05=
BURFELLSHRAUN (Iceland-NE)	Fissure vent of BARDARBUNGA	1703-03=
BURILAN (Vanuatu-SW Pacific)	Cone of GAUA	0507-02=
BURLIASTCHY [BURLYASHCHY] (Kamchatk	Stratovolc of BOLSHOI SEMIACHIK	1000-15=
BURLICH (Germany)	Tuff cone of WEST EIFEL VOLC FIELD	0100-01-
BURLOW HILL (Africa-E)	Dome of MERU	0202-16=
BURLYASHCHY (Kamchatka)	Stratovolc of BOLSHOI SEMIACHIK	1000-15=
BURNEY, MONTE (Chile-S)	Stratovolc (2, 1910) Historical	**1508-07=**
BURNING MOUNTAIN (Alaska-SW)	Synonym of ILIAMNA	1103-02-
BURNING VOLCANO (Aleutian Is)	Synonym of GARELOI	1101-07-
BURNT LAVA FLOW (US-California)	Fissure vent of MEDICINE LAKE	1203-02-
BURNT MOUNTAIN (Alaska-SW)	Synonym of REDOUBT	1103-03-
BURR, MT. (Australia)	Cone of NEWER VOLCANICS PROV	0509-01-
BURRU, DOINYO (Africa-E)	Synonym of EBURRU, OL DOINYO	0202-08=
BURU (New Britain-SW Pac)	Caldera of PAGO	0502-08=
BURU, DOINYO (Africa-E)	Synonym of EBURRU, OL DOINYO	0202-08=
BUS-OBO (Mongolia)	Cinder cone (None) Holocene?	**1003-03-**
BUSHENYE (Africa-C)	Cone of NYIRAGONGO	0203-03=
BUSHWAGA (Africa-C)	Cone of NYIRAGONGO	0203-03=

NAME (Subregion)	Type (Eruption Total, Most Recent) Status . . . Relation to NAMED VOLCANO	NUMBER
BUTAJIRI-SILTI FIELD (Ethiopia)	Fissure vents (None) Holocene	**0201-26-**
BUTAK (Java)	Cone of DIENG VOLC COMPLEX	0603-20=
BUTAK PETARANGAN (Java)	Cone of DIENG VOLC COMPLEX	0603-20=
BUTAKA (Africa-C)	Cone of KARISIMBI	0203-04-
BUTLER'S MOUNTAIN (W Indies)	Cone of NEVIS PEAK	1600-04=
BUTTON HILL (Africa-E)	Dome of MERU	0202-16=
BUTUBUT, MT. (Vanuatu-SW Pacific)	Cone of KUWAE	0507-07=
BUTUS, GUNUNG (Lesser Sunda Is)	Cone of BATUR	0604-01=
BUYUK AGRI DAGI (Turkey)	Synonym of ARARAT, MT.	0103-04-
BUYUK KIZIL TEPE (Turkey)	Cone of ERCIYES DAGI	0103-01=
BUYUKKALE TEPE (Turkey)	Dome of ERCIYES DAGI	0103-01=
BUZZ (Africa-E)	Synonym of CENTRAL ISLAND	0202-01=
BUZZARD CREEK (Alaska-E)	Tuff rings (1, -1050) Radiocarbon	**1105-001**
BWASI-IAI-IAI (D'Entrecasteaux Is)	Thermal Feature of DAWSON STRAIT GP	0503-06=
BYAKUSHI-IKE [BYAKUSHI-IKE] (Kyushu)	Crater of KIRISHIMA	0802-09=
BYLANDT RHEYT (Atl-N-Jan Mayen)	Cone of JAN MAYEN	1706-01=
BYLINKINOY [BYLINKINA] (Kamchatka)	Crater of KLIUCHEVSKOI	1000-26=
BYOBU-DAKE (Honshu-Japan)	Stratovolc of ZAO	0803-19=

C

NAME (Subregion)	Type (Eruption Total, Most Recent) Status . . . Relation to NAMED VOLCANO	NUMBER
CAANOAN (Luzon-N of)	Cone of CAMIGUIN DE BABUYANES	0704-01=
CABALIAN (Philippines-C)	Stratovolc (None) Holocene	**0702-05=**
CABALLITO (Mexico)	Cone of CHICHINAUTZIN	1401-08=
CABEZA DE VACA (Chile-S)	Cone of CAYUTE-LA VIGUERIA	1508-021
CABEZA DE VACA, CERRO (Costa Rica)	Cone of IRAZU	1405-06=
CABEZA DE VACA, CERRO (Nicaragua)	Cone of PILAS, LAS	1404-08=
CABEZA, LA (Mexico)	Cone of IZTACCIHUATL	1401-086
CABO COWAN (Galapagos)	Cone of SANTIAGO	1503-09=
CABRA, ISLA DE [CERRO GRANDE] (El Salv	Dome of COATEPEQUE CALDERA	1403-041
CABRAS, CERRO LAS (Mexico)	Cone of MICHOACAN-GUANAJUATO	1401-06=
CABRAS, MONTANA DE LAS [SAN ANTONI	Cone of LA PALMA	1803-01-
CABRAS, PICO (Canary Is)	Cone of TENERIFE	1803-03-
CABRET, DJEBEL (Red Sea)	Synonym of TEYR, DJEBEL	0201-01=
CABRIOLER, VOLCANS DE (Spain)	Cone of OLOT VOLC FIELD	0100-03-
CABRIS, PITON DES (Indian O.-W)	Cone of FOURNAISE, PITON DE LA	0303-02=
CABURGUA (Chile-C)	Cinder cones (1, -5050) Tephrochronology	**1507-112**
CABUT, BUKIT (Sumatra)	Cone of BESAR, GUNUNG	0601-25=
CACAO (Costa Rica)	Cone of OROSI	1405-01=
CACHANI (Peru)	Synonym of CHACHANI, NEVADO	1504-005
CACHE HILL (Canada)	Shield of EDZIZA	1200-06-
CACHE MOUNTAIN (US-Oregon)	Cone of WASHINGTON	1202-05-
CACHIO, CERRO (El Salvador)	Stratovolc of VERDE, LAGUNA	1403-01=
CACHO NEGRO, VOLCAN (Costa Rica)	Stratovolc of BARVA	1405-05=
CACTUS PEAK (US-California)	Dome of COSO VOLC FIELD	1203-18-
CADENITA (Mexico)	Cone of CHICHINAUTZIN	1401-08=
CAFIERI (Italy)	Crater of ISCHIA	0101-03=
CAGUA (Luzon-Philippines)	Stratovolc (None) Holocene	**0703-09=**
CAILLE, ISLE DE (W Indies)	Crater of ST. CATHERINE	1600-17=
CAIMAN, MONTANA (Canary Is)	Cone of FUERTEVENTURA	1803-05-
CAIRAT, VOLCA (Spain)	Cone of OLOT VOLC FIELD	0100-03-
CAJETE, EL (US-New Mexico)	Crater of VALLES CALDERA	1210-03-
CAJON LOS CALABOZOS (Chile-C)	Thermal Feature of CALABOZOS	1507-042
CALA DELL'ALCA (Italy)	Cone of PANTELLERIA	0101-071
CALA DELL'ALTURA (Italy)	Shield of PANTELLERIA	0101-071
CALABOZOS (Chile-C)	Caldera (None) Holocene	**1507-042**
CALAJALATA, CERRO (Chile-N)	Stratovolc of ARINTICA, VOLCAN	1505-023
CALAYO (Mindanao-Philippines)	Tuff cone (1, 1886) Historical	**0701-07=**
CALBUCO (Chile-S)	Stratovolc (9, 1961) Historical	**1508-02=**
CALDEIRA (Azores)	Crater of UNNAMED	1802-081
CALDERA, CALDERAS, CALDIERA see proper name (e.g. CUERVOS, CALDERA DE LOS)		
CALDERA, CERRO DE LA (Mexico)	Cone of SANTA CATARINA RANGE	1401-082
CALDERA, LA (Canary Is)	Crater of LANZAROTE	1803-06-
CALDERA, LAGUNA (El Salvador)	Cone of SAN SALVADOR	1403-05=
CALDERAS, LAS (Canary Is)	Crater of FUERTEVENTURA	1803-05-
CALDERETA, LA (Canary Is)	Crater of TENERIFE	1803-03-
CALDERETA, MONTANA DE LA (Canary Is)	Cone of FUERTEVENTURA	1803-05-
CALDERITA, LA (Canary Is)	Vent of FUERTEVENTURA	1803-05-
CALDERON, EL (US-New Mexico)	Crater of ZUNI-BANDERA	1210-02-
CALDERON, VOLCAN (Galapagos)	Synonym of ALCEDO, VOLCAN	1503-04=
CALDIERA (Azores)	Caldera of FAYAL	1802-01=
CALDWELL BUTTE (US-California)	Cone of MEDICINE LAKE	1203-02-
CALDWELL ISLAND (Galapagos)	Tuff cone of FLOREANA	1503-10=
CALIBATO, LAKE (Luzon-Philippines)	Maar of LAGUNA VOLC FIELD	0703-051
CALIENTE (Guatemala)	Vent of SANTA MARIA	1402-03=
CALIENTE, CERRO (Peru)	Twin volcano of YUCAMANE	1504-05-
CALLAQUEN (Chile-C)	Synonym of CALLAQUI	1507-091
CALLAQUI (Chile-C)	Stratovolc (2, 1980) Historical	**1507-091**
CALLO, CERRITO DEL (Ecuador)	Cone of COTOPAXI	1502-05=
CALLVUCO (CALLUNETO) (Chile-S)	Synonym of OSORNO	1508-01=
CALOMETS, PITON (Indian O.-W)	Cone of FOURNAISE, PITON DE LA	0303-02=
CALVARIO, EL (Mexico)	Cone of HOLOTEPEC	1401-07-
CAM TIEM MT. (SE Asia)	Cone of BAS DONG NAI	0705-05-
CAMALDOLI DELLA TORRE (Italy)	Cone of VESUVIUS	0101-02=
CAMARINHAS, PICO DAS (Azores)	Cone of SETE CIDADES	1802-08=
CAMBADO, PICO DO (Azores)	Cone of UNNAMED	1802-081
CAMBRIA, MT. (New Zealand)	Cone of AUCKLAND FIELD	0401-02=
CAMELS HUMP, THE (Australia)	Dome of NEWER VOLCANICS PROV	0509-01-
CAMERON, MT. (Australia)	Cone of NEWER VOLCANICS PROV	0509-01-
CAMEROON, MT. (Africa-W)	Stratovolc (16, 1982) Historical	**0204-01=**
CAMEROUN, MONT (Africa-W)	Synonym of CAMEROON, MT.	0204-01=
CAMIGUIN DE BABUYANES (Luzon-N of)	Stratovolc (1, 1857) Historical	**0704-01=**
CAMIGUIN DE MINDANAO [MT. VULCAN]	Dome of HIBOK-HIBOK	0701-08=
CAMIGUIN DE MISAMIS [MT. VULCAN]	Dome of HIBOK-HIBOK	0701-08=
CAMIGUIN DEL SUR [MT. VULCAN]	Dome of HIBOK-HIBOK	0701-08=
CAMILLE CONE (Alaska-W)	Cone of IMURUK LAKE	1104-02-
CAMP HILL (Canada)	Shield of EDZIZA	1200-06-
CAMPAGNANO, MT. (Italy)	Crater of ISCHIA	0101-03=
CAMPANARIO, EL (Canary Is)	Cone of HIERRO	1803-02-
CAMPI FLEGREI (Italy)	Caldera (15, 1538) Historical	**0101-01=**
CAMPI FLEGREI MAR SICILIA (Italy)	Subm volcs (7, 1911) Historical	0101-07=
CAMPOSANTO, CERRO (Guatemala)	Cone of IXTEPEQUE, VOLCAN	1402-18-
CAMPOTESE (Italy)	Crater of ISCHIA	0101-03=
CAMPRIDA, CALDEIRA (Azores)	Tuff ring of FLORES	1802-001
CAN SIMO, VOLCA (Spain)	Cone of OLOT VOLC FIELD	0100-03-
CAN TIA, VOLCA (Spain)	Cone of OLOT VOLC FIELD	0100-03-
CANADAS, LAS (Canary Is)	Pleistocene caldera of TENERIFE	1803-03-
CANALAON (Philippines-C)	Synonym of CANLAON	0702-02=
CANAR (Java)	Crater of TALAGABODAS	0603-15=
CANARIO, LAGOA DO (Azores)	Maar of SETE CIDADES	1802-08=
CANARIO, PICO DO (Azores)	Pumice cone of FURNAS	1802-10=
CANASTO (Chile-C)	Crater of LONQUIMAY	1507-10=

NAME (Subregion)	Type (Eruption Total, Most Recent) Status . . . Relation to NAMED VOLCANO	NUMBER
CANDADO, EL (Chile-C)	Cone of MAULE, LAGUNA DEL	1507-062
CANDLEMAS ISLAND (Antarctica)	Stratovolc (2, 1823) Historical	**1900-10=**
CANGKUANG (Java)	Crater of SALAK	0603-05=
CANLAON (Philippines-C)	Stratovolc (19, 1993) Historical	**0702-02=**
CANTARIELLO (Italy)	Cone of ISCHIA	0101-03=
CANTARO (Mexico)	Stratovolc of COLIMA VOLC COMPLEX	1401-04=
CANYA, VOLCA LA (Spain)	Cone of OLOT VOLC FIELD	0100-03-
CANYE (Chile-C)	Synonym of CORDON CAULLE	1507-141
CANYON CREEK [SECOND CANYON]	Cone of ISKUT-UNUK RIVER CONES	1200-09-
CAOLANGOJAN [KASIBOI] (Philippines)	Cone of MAHAGNOA	0702-07=
CAOPO (China-S)	Cone of TENGCHONG	0705-11-
CAPACUARO, CERROS DE (Mexico)	Cone of MICHOACAN-GUANAJUATO	1401-06=
CAPARINA (Ecuador)	Dome of CHACANA	1502-022
CAPARRA, LOMA (Nicaragua)	Dome of SAN CRISTOBAL	1404-02=
CAPATACUTIRO, CERRO DE (Mexico)	Cone of MICHOACAN-GUANAJUATO	1401-06=
CAPE BERKELEY VOLCANO (Galapagos)	Synonym of ECUADOR, VOLCAN	1503-011
CAPE BIDLINGMAIER (Indian O.-S)	Cone of HEARD	0304-01=
CAPE BRIDGEWATER (Australia)	Cone of NEWER VOLCANICS PROV	0509-01-
CAPE CARTWRIGHT (Indian O.-S)	Cone of HEARD	0304-01=
CAPE ESPENBERG (Alaska-W)	Synonym of ESPENBERG	1104-01-
CAPE RIVER (Greece)	Pleistocene caldera of SANTORINI	0102-04=
CAPE VALDIVIA (Atlantic-S)	Dome of BOUVET	1806-02-
CAPELINHOS (Azores)	Cone of FAYAL	1802-01=
CAPRARA (Italy)	Dome of CAMPI FLEGREI	0101-01=
CAPRICORN, MT. (Canada)	Cone of MEAGER	1200-18-
CAPULIN (Mexico)	Cone of CHICHINAUTZIN	1401-08=
CAPULIN MOUNTAIN (US-New Mexico)	Cone of RATON-CLAYTON	1210-04-
CAPURATA [ELENA CAPURATA] (Chile-N)	Stratovolc of ACOTANGO	1505-017
CARABAO KILLER (Philippines-C)	Thermal Feature of CANLAON	0702-02=
CARACOL (Chile-C)	Crater of AZUL, CERRO [QUIZAPU]	1507-06=
CARACOL, VOLCAN (Chile-C)	Cone of TOLGUACA	1507-092
CARBET, FUMEROLLES DU (W Indies)	Thermal Feature of SOUFR. GUADELOUPE	1600-06=
CARCABULLO O PEDREGAL (Canary Is)	Crater of LANZAROTE	1803-06-
CARDAKH (Turkey)	Crater of ERCIYES DAGI	0103-01=
CARDOS, LOS (Mexico)	Cone of CHICHINAUTZIN	1401-08=
CAREME (Java)	Synonym of CEREME	0603-17=
CARIBALD HILL [GARIBALDI HILL] (W Ind)	Cone of SOUFRIERE HILLS	1600-05=
CARIK TEPE (Turkey)	Cone of ERCIYES DAGI	0103-01=
CARLISLE (Aleutian Is)	Stratovolc (2, 1828) Historical	**1101-23-**
CARMELO, LA MONTANA DEL (US-Wash)	Synonym of BAKER	1201-01=
CARMICHAEL (W Indies)	Stratovolc of SOUFRIERE GUADELOUPE	1600-06=
CARNERO, CERRO EL (Guatemala)	Cone of FLORES, VOLCAN DE	1402-14-
CAROLI ? (Aleutian Is)	Synonym of SHISHALDIN	1101-36-
CARPINTERO NORTE, EL (Mexico)	Cone of COLIMA VOLC COMPLEX	1401-04=
CARPINTERO SUR, EL (Mexico)	Cone of COLIMA VOLC COMPLEX	1401-04=
CARR MOUNTAIN (US-New Mexico)	Cone of RATON-CLAYTON	1210-04-
CARRAN (Chile-C)	Maar of CARRAN-LOS VENADOS	1507-14=
CARRAN, CERRO [LOS GUINDOS] (Chile-C)	Stratovolc of CARRAN-LOS VENADOS	1507-14=
CARRAN-LOS VENADOS (Chile-C)	Pyrocl cones (3, 1979) Historical	**1507-14=**
CARRIZOZO (US-New Mexico)	Cinder cone (None) Holocene	**1210-01-**
CARTAGO, VOLCAN DE (Costa Rica)	Synonym of IRAZU	1405-06=
CARVAO (Azores)	Cone of SETE CIDADES	1802-08=
CASA DIABLO HOT SPRINGS (US-California	Thermal Feature of LONG VALLEY	1203-14-
CASA, LA (Costa Rica)	Thermal Feature of TENORIO GROUP	1405-031
CASABLANCA (Chile-C)	Stratovolc of ANTILLANCA GROUP	1507-153
CASIBOY [KASIBOI] (Philippines-C)	Cone of MAHAGNOA	0702-07=
CASIMIRO (Chile-C)	Crater of MAIPO	1507-021
CASIRI, NEVADOS (Peru)	Stratovolc (None) Holocene	**1504-06-**
CASITA (Nicaragua)	Stratovolc of SAN CRISTOBAL	1404-02=
CASITAS, VOLCAN (Chile-C)	Fissure vent of AZUL, CERRO [QUIZAPU]	1507-06=
CASSIEN, CRATERE (Indian O.-W)	Crater of FOURNAISE, PITON DE LA	0303-02=
CASSIOPE CONE (Alaska-W)	Cone of IMURUK LAKE	1104-02-
CASTEIHANO, PICO DO (Azores)	Cone of UNNAMED	1802-081
CASTELGANDOLFO [ALBANO] (Italy)	Crater of ALBANO, MONTE	0101-004
CASTELLARO (Italy)	Pleistocene caldera of LIPARI	0101-041
CASTELLO D'ISCHIA (Italy)	Dome of ISCHIA	0101-03=
CASTELO BRANCO (Azores)	Dome of FAYAL	1802-01=
CASTIGLIONE (Italy)	Crater of ALBANO, MONTE	0101-004
CASTIGLIONE (Italy)	Dome of ISCHIA	0101-03=
CASTILLO, CERRO DE LOS (Guatemala)	Cone of CHINGO VOLC FIELD	1402-15-
CASTLE OF ISCHIA [CASTELLO D'ISCHIA	Dome of ISCHIA	0101-03=
CASTLE PEAK (W Indies)	Dome of SOUFRIERE HILLS	1600-05=
CASTLE ROCK (Aleutian Is)	Dome of BOGOSLOF	1101-30-
CASTOR (Antarctica)	Cone of SEAL NUNATAKS GROUP	1900-05=
CASUELA JUYU (Guatemala)	Synonym of TOLIMAN	1402-07=
CATACU, CERRO DE (Mexico)	Cone of MICHOACAN-GUANAJUATO	1401-06=
CATANIA, MONTE DI (Italy)	Synonym of ETNA	0101-06=
CATARMAN (Mindanao-Philippines)	Synonym of HIBOK-HIBOK	0701-08=
CATHEDRAL ROCK [NAPERITO] (Africa-E)	Tuff cone of BARRIER, THE	0202-03=
CATHERINE (Ethiopia)	Tuff ring (None) Holocene	**0201-051**
CATINOCJUYUP [CERRO QUEMADO] (Guat	Dome of ALMOLONGA	1402-04=
CATU (Lesser Sunda Is)	Crater of BATUR	0604-01=
CATUR CALDERA (Lesser Sunda Is)	Synonym of BRATAN	0604-001
CAUA (Luzon-Philippines)	Synonym of CAGUA	0703-09=
CAUBET, CRATERE (Indian O.-W)	Crater of FOURNAISE, PITON DE LA	0303-02=
CAULLE (Chile-C)	Synonym of CORDON CAULLE	1507-141
CAULLE CHICO [PICHI CAULLE] (Chile-C)	Cone of PUYEHUE	1507-15=
CAULLE GRANDE (Chile-C)	Synonym of PUYEHUE	1507-15=
CAUYE (Chile-C)	Synonym of CORDON CAULLE	1507-141
CAVA NOCELLE (Italy)	Crater of ISCHIA	0101-03=
CAVA PETRELLA (Italy)	Cone of ISCHIA	0101-03=
CAVAGNARO (Galapagos)	Crater of SANTA CRUZ	1503-091
CAVALO, PICO DO (Azores)	Cone of SETE CIDADES	1802-08=
CAVERNE, ILE DE LA (Indian O.-S)	Synonym of PRINCE EDWARD ISLAND	0304-07-
CAVERNE POMME DE TERRE, PITON	Cone of FOURNAISE, PITON DE LA	0303-02=
CAVO, MONTE (Italy)	Synonym of ALBANO, MONTE	0101-004
CAVO, MT. (Italy)	Cone of ALBANO, MONTE	0101-004
CAWALO (Lesser Sunda Is)	Thermal Feature of PALUWEH	0604-15=
CAWS ROAD (New Zealand)	Dome of MAROA	0401-061
CAYAMBE (Ecuador)	Compnd volc (None) Holocene	**1502-004**
CAYAPIREN (Chile-S)	Synonym of MINCHINMAVIDA	1508-04=
CAYONAN (Luzon Is-N of)	Cone of BABUYAN CLARO	0704-03=
CAYUSE CONE (US-Oregon)	Cone of SOUTH SISTER	1202-08-
CAYUTE-LA VIGUERIA (Chile-S)	Pyrocl cones (None) Holocene	**1508-021**
CEBOROQUITO (Mexico)	Cone of CEBORUCO, VOLCAN	1401-03=
CEBORUCO, VOLCAN (Mexico)	Stratovolc (4, 1875) Historical	**1401-03=**
CEDAR HILL (Africa-E)	Dome of EBURRU, OL DOINYO	0202-08=
CEDRO, PICO DO (Azores)	Cone of SETE CIDADES	1802-08=
CEHENNEM TEPE (Turkey)	Crater of TENDURUK DAGI	0103-03=
CEILLE, PITON (Indian O.-W)	Cone of FOURNAISE, PITON DE LA	0303-02=
CEKOK, KAWAH (Java)	Thermal Feature of GALUNGGUNG	0603-14=
CELLE (Italy)	Crater of CAMPI FLEGREI	0101-01=
CELOSA, CERRO LA (Chile-N)	Cone of OLLAGUE	1505-06=
CEMARA, GUNUNG (Java)	Cone of IJEN	0603-35=
CEMEL TEPE (Turkey)	Maar of KULA	0103-00-
CEMENTARIO BRITO, CERRO DEL (Guatem	Cone of CUILAPA-BARBARENA	1402-111
CEMENTERIO CERRO REDONDO, CERRO	Cone of CUILAPA-BARBARENA	1402-111
CEMETARY CRATER (New Zealand)	Maar of AUCKLAND FIELD	0401-02=
CEMRKOPRU BARAJ GOLU (Turkey)	Cone of KULA	0103-00-
CENDRES, ILE DES (SE Asia)	Subm volcs (1, 1923) Historical	0705-06-
CENGYU (Taiwan-N of)	Synonym of ZENGYU	0801-05=
CENIZA, VOLCAN (Mexico)	Cone of SAN QUINTIN VOLC FIELD	1401-002
CENIZAS, CERRO (Chile-C)	Synonym of CORDON CENIZOS	1507-16-
CENIZAS, CERRO (Chile-N)	Cone of CORDON DE PUNTAS NEGRAS	1505-102
CENO-SEMIACHIK (Kamchatka)	Stratovolc of MALY SEMIACHIK	1000-14=
CENTENARI, MONTE (Italy)	Cone of ETNA	0101-06=
CENTRAL ATITLAN (Guatemala)	Cone of TOLIMAN	1402-07=
CENTRAL GROUP (US-Oregon)	Cone of SAND MOUNTAIN FIELD	1202-04-
CENTRAL ISLAND (Africa-E)	Stratovolc (None) Holocene	**0202-01=**
CENTRAL, PICO (Guatemala)	Synonym of ACATENANGO	1402-08=
CENTRAL PUMICE CONE (US-Oregon)	Cone of NEWBERRY VOLCANO	1202-11-
CENTRALNY (Kamchatka)	Shield of POGRANYCHNY	1000-47-
CENTRO, EL (Mexico)	Dome of CEBORUCO, VOLCAN	1401-03=
CERBERUS, MT. (Alaska Peninsula)	Dome of NOVARUPTA	1102-18-
CEREBUS (Aleutian Is)	Stratovolc of SEMISOPOCHNOI	1101-06-
CEREME (Java)	Stratovolc (6, 1951) Historical	**0603-17=**
CERIMAI (Java)	Synonym of CEREME	0603-17=
CERISY PEAK (New Guinea-NE of)	Stratovolc of LONG ISLAND	0501-05=
CERME (Java)	Synonym of CEREME	0603-17=
CERRA, LA (Guatemala)	Cone of PACAYA	1402-11=
CERRADO NOVO (Azores)	Dome of AGUA DE PAU	1802-09=
CERRILLO CHAJNANTOR, CERRO EL (Chile	Cone of PURICO COMPLEX	1505-094
CERRITITO (Nicaragua)	Dome of APOYO	1404-101
CERRITO, EL (El Salvador)	Cone of VERDE, LAGUNA	1403-01=
CERRITO, EL (Nicaragua)	Dome of APOYO	1404-101
CERRITOS, LOS (Guatemala)	Cone of SANTIAGO, CERRO	1402-16-
CERRITOS, VOLCAN LOS (Mexico)	Cone of MASCOTA VOLC FIELD	1401-031
CERRO, CERRITO (Spanish for PEAK) see proper name (e.g. MESA, CERRO DE LA)		
CERRON, CERRO EL (Guatemala)	Cone of IXTEPEQUE, VOLCAN	1402-18-
CERRON, EL (El Salvador)	Synonym of SINGUIL, CERRO	1403-011
CEYSSAT, MAAR DE (France)	Maar of CHAINE DES PUYS	0100-02-
CHA (Cape Verde Is)	Caldera of FOGO	1804-01=
CHA DE MORTE (Cape Verde Is)	Caldera of SANTO ANTAO	1804-03-
CHABBI [CHEBBI] (Ethiopia)	Stratovolc of CORBETTI CALDERA	0201-29-
CHAC-INCA, CERRO (Chile-N)	Dome of AZUFRE, CERRO DEL	1505-065
CHACANA (Ecuador)	Caldera (4, 1773) Historical	**1502-022**
CHACHA (Kurile Is)	Synonym of TIATIA	0900-03=
CHACHANI, NEVADO (Peru)	Stratovolc (None) Holocene	**1504-005**
CHACHANOBORI (CHACHANUPURI) (Kurile	Synonym of TIATIA	0900-03=
CHACHANUPURI (Kurile Is)	Synonym of ALAID	0900-39=
CHADUTKA (Kamchatka)	Synonym of KHODUTKA	1000-053
CHAGUITILLO, CERRO (Guatemala)	Dome of IXTEPEQUE, VOLCAN	1402-18-
CHAGULAK (Aleutian Is)	Stratovolc (None) Holocene	**1101-20-**
CHAHALE (Indian O.-W)	Pit crater of KARTHALA	0303-01=
CHAHOLO (Africa-E)	Dome of SW USANGU BASIN	0202-163
CHAHORRA (Canary Is)	Cone of TENERIFE	1803-03-
CHAIKUTES (Greece)	Thermal Feature of KOS	0102-06=
CHAIMU (Africa-E)	Cone of CHYULU HILLS	0202-13=
CHAIN OF CRATERS (Africa-E)	Crater of CENTRAL ISLAND	0202-01=
CHAINE DES PUYS (France)	Cinder cones (8, -4040) Radiocarbon	**0100-02-**
CHAISANDUKU (Africa-C)	Crater of BUNYARUGURU FIELD	0203-005
CHAITEN (Chile-S)	Caldera (None) Holocene	**1508-041**
CHALA (Africa-E)	Cone of KILIMANJARO	0202-15=
CHALARD, PUY (France)	Cone of CHAINE DES PUYS	0100-02-
CHALCHIHUITES (Mexico)	Cone of CHICHINAUTZIN	1401-08=
CHALCHUAPA, CERRITO DE (El Salvador)	Cone of APASTEPEQUE FIELD	1403-071
CHALCHUAPA, LAGUNA DE (El Salvador)	Pit crater of APASTEPEQUE FIELD	1403-071
CHALLAPIREN (Chile-S)	Synonym of MINCHINMAVIDA	1508-04=
CHALLHUE MAURAS, VOLCAN (Peru)	Cone of ANDAHUA VALLEY	1504-002
CHAMBAGUNGURU (Africa-E)	Cone of KIEYO	0202-17=
CHAMBAJI (Africa-E)	Dome of SW USANGU BASIN	0202-163
CHAMBASEGERA (Africa-E)	Cone of KIEYO	0202-17=
CHAMBUGA [MBUGA] (Africa-C)	Tuff cone of KATWE-KIKORONGO FIELD	0203-004
CHAMENGO (Africa-C)	Crater of BUNYARUGURU FIELD	0203-005
CHAMONGERA (Africa-E)	Dome of SW USANGU BASIN	0202-163
CHAMPALALA (Africa-E)	Dome of SW USANGU BASIN	0202-163
CHAMPES PHLEGRAIS (Italy)	Synonym of CAMPI FLEGREI	0101-01=
CHAMPION ISLAND (Galapagos)	Tuff cone of FLOREANA	1503-10=
CHANA (Chile-S)	Synonym of MINCHINMAVIDA	1508-04=
CHANAL, CERRO EL (Nicaragua)	Cone of APOYO	1404-101
CHANCE'S MOUNTAIN (W Indies)	Synonym of SOUFRIERE HILLS	1600-05=
CHANCE'S PEAK (W Indies)	Dome of SOUFRIERE HILLS	1600-05=
CHANCHANI (Peru)	Synonym of CHACHANI, NEVADO	1504-005
CHANCHOCO, TERMAS DE (Chile-C)	Thermal Feature of COPAHUE	1507-09=
CHANCHOS, LOS (Nicaragua)	Dome of COSIGUINA	1404-01=
CHANEL (Chile-C)	Synonym of LLAIMA	1507-11=
CHANG-PAI (China-E)	Thermal Feature of BAITOUSHAN	1005-07-
CHANG-PAI-SHAN [CHANGBAISHAN]	Shield of BAITOUSHAN	1005-07-
CHANG PEAK (Antarctica)	Shield of WAESCHE	1900-024
CHANGAR (Kamchatka)	Synonym of HANGAR	1000-272
CHANGBAISHAN (China-E)	Shield of BAITOUSHAN	1005-07-
CHANGOMENI (Indian O.-W)	Pit crater of KARTHALA	0303-01=
CHANGOU-CHAHALE (Indian O.-W)	Crater of KARTHALA	0303-01=
CHANGPO (China-S)	Cone of TENGCHONG	0705-11-
CHANKA (Chile-N)	Dome of AZUFRE, CERRO DEL	1505-065
CHANKOROGO (Africa-E)	Dome of SW USANGU BASIN	0202-163
CHANMICO, LAGUNA DE (El Salvador)	Maar of SAN SALVADOR	1403-05=
CHANUJ GOL (Mongolia)	Synonym of KHANUY GOL	1003-02-
CHAO (Chile-N)	Lava dome (None) Holocene	**1505-072**
CHAOKHCH (Kamchatka)	Synonym of KOSHELEV	1000-02=
CHAOS CRAGS (US-Calif)	Dome of LASSEN VOLC CENTER	1203-08-
CHAPARRASTIQUE (El Salvador)	Synonym of SAN MIGUEL	1403-10=
CHAPCHAP (Africa-W)	Cone of OKU VOLC FIELD	0204-003
CHAPULTEPEC (Mexico)	Cone of HOLOTEPEC	1401-07-
CHAPULTEPEC, CERRO (Mexico)	Cone of SANTA CATARINA RANGE	1401-082
CHAPULUL, CERRO (Chile-C)	Cinder cone (None) Holocene	**1507-101**
CHARCO, EL (Canary Is)	Cone of LA PALMA	1803-01-
CHARLES (Galapagos)	Synonym of FLOREANA	1503-10=
CHARMONT, PUY DE (France)	Cone of CHAINE DES PUYS	0100-02-
CHAROS (Greece)	Thermal Feature of MILOS	0102-03=
CHASCON, CERRO (Bolivia)	Lava dome (None) Holocene	**1505-071**
CHASCON, CERRO (Chile-C)	Cone of CARRAN-LOS VENADOS	1507-14=
CHASCON, CERRO (Chile-N)	Dome of GUAYAQUES	1505-093
CHASCON, CERRO EL (Chile-N)	Dome of PURICO COMPLEX	1505-094

NAME (Subregion)	Type (Eruption Total, Most Recent) Status . . . Relation to NAMED VOLCANO	NUMBER
CHASCON DE PURICO [EL CHASCON]	Dome of PURICO COMPLEX	1505-094
CHASHAKONDZHA (Kamchatka)	Stratovolc of ALNEY-CHASHAKONDZHA	1000-45-
CHASM, THE [LA VORAGINE] (Italy)	Crater of ETNA	0101-06=
CHASM, THE [WAHANGA-WAIMANGU] (N Z)	Fissure vent of OKATAINA	0401-05=
CHAT, PITON DE (Indian O.-W)	Cone of FOURNAISE, PITON DE LA	0303-02=
CHATEAU FORT, LE (Indian O.-W)	Crater of FOURNAISE, PITON DE LA	0303-02=
CHATHAM (Galapagos)	Synonym of SAN CRISTOBAL	1503-12-
CHATITO (Costa Rica)	Cone of ARENAL	1405-033
CHATO, CERRITO (US-New Mexico)	Dome of VALLES CALDERA	1210-03-
CHATO, CERRO (Costa Rica)	Cone of ARENAL	1405-033
CHATO, CERRO (Costa Rica)	Cone of RINCON DE LA VIEJA	1405-02=
CHAUDIERES, LES (W Indies)	Thermal Feature of SOUFRIERE GUADEL	1600-06=
CHAUDRON (Indian O.-S)	Cone of AMSTERDAM ISLAND	0304-04-
CHAUMONT, PUY DE (France)	Cone of CHAINE DES PUYS	0100-02-
CHAUSU-DAKE (Honshu-Japan)	Dome of NASU	0803-15=
CHAUSU-YAMA (Honshu-Japan)	Synonym of NIIGATA-YAKE-YAMA	0803-09=
CHAYLL (Chile-C)	Synonym of LLAIMA	1507-11=
CHEBBI (Ethiopia)	Stratovolc of CORBETTI CALDERA	0201-29-
CHEBRIT ALE (Ethiopia)	Synonym of GADA ALE	0201-05=
CHECHITNO PEAK (Alaska-E)	Synonym of WRANGELL	1105-02-
CHEIMU [CHAIMU] (Africa-E)	Cone of CHYULU HILLS	0202-13=
CHEJU-DO (Korea)	Synonym of HALLA	1006-04-
CHEMINEE NORD [CHANGOMENI] (Indian O.	Pit crater of KARTHALA	0303-01=
CHEMINEE SUD [CHAHALE] (Indian O.-W)	Pit crater of KARTHALA	0303-01=
CHENGZILOU (China-S)	Cone of TENGCHONG	0705-11-
CHEPE (Russia-SE)	Shield of UDOKAN VOLC FIELD	1002-03-
CHEPTOMAS (Africa-E)	Dome of PAKA	0202-053
CHEQUEPUQUINA (Peru)	Synonym of HUAYNAPUTINA	1504-03=
CHERINGERAN, CERRO DE (Mexico)	Cone of MICHOACAN-GUANAJUATO	1401-06=
CHERINKUTAN (Kurile Is)	Synonym of CHIRINKOTAN	0900-26=
CHERNABURA (Alaska-SW)	Synonym of AUGUSTINE	1103-01-
CHERNIYE SKALY (Kamchatka)	Stratovolc of PAUZHETKA	1000-022
CHERNOYE LAKE (Kamchatka)	Thermal Feature of BOLSHOI SEMIACHIK	1000-15=
CHERNY (Kamchatka)	Stratovolc (None) Holocene	**1000-46-**
CHERNY (Kamchatka)	Dome of BOLSHOI SEMIACHIK	1000-15=
CHERNY (Kurile Is)	Stratovolc of CHIRPOI	0900-15=
CHERNYI UTES (Kamchatka)	Dome of KSUDACH	1000-05=
CHESORO (Africa-E)	Vent of KOROSI	0202-054
CHETKIN (Aleutian Is)	Synonym of GREAT SITKIN	1101-12-
CHEYU (Africa-E)	Dome of SW USANGU BASIN	0202-163
CHFEALIN (Kamchatka)	Synonym of ICHINSKY	1000-28=
CHIAUS (Banda Sea)	Synonym of TEON	0605-05=
CHICHALDINSKOI (Aleutian Is)	Synonym of SHISHALDIN	1101-36-
CHICHICASTEPEC [CERRO DE APANECA]	Stratovolc of VERDE, LAGUNA	1403-01=
CHICHIGALPA [CASITA] (Nicaragua)	Stratovolc of SAN CRISTOBAL	1404-02=
CHICHINAUTZIN (Mexico)	Volc field (2, -0085) Radiocarbon	**1401-08=**
CHICHINAUTZIN, CERRO (Mexico)	Shield of CHICHINAUTZIN	1401-08=
CHICHINTOR, CERRITO (Guatemala)	Cone of IPALA VOLC FIELD	1402-19-
CHICHON, EL (Mexico)	Lava domes (5, 1982) Historical	**1401-12=**
CHICHONAL, EL (Mexico)	Synonym of CHICHON, EL	1401-12=
CHICHONTEPEQUE (El Salvador)	Synonym of SAN VICENTE	1403-07=
CHICKEN KILLER (Philippines-C)	Thermal Feature of CANLAON	0702-02=
CHICO, PICO [YEPOCAPA] (Guatemala)	Cone of ACATENANGO	1402-08=
CHICO VOLC FIELD (US-New Mexico)	Synonym of RATON-CLAYTON	1210-04-
CHICO, VOLCAN (Galapagos)	Crater of NEGRA, SIERRA	1503-05=
CHIEN-SHUI-TING-TZU [JIANSHUIDINGZI]	Cone of LONGGANG GROUP	1005-06-
CHIESA VECCHIA (Italy)	Stratovolc of LIPARI	0101-041
CHIEWO (Africa-E)	Cone of HOMA MOUNTAIN	0202-07=
CHIGIGNAGAK (Alaska Peninsula)	Synonym of CHIGINAGAK	1102-11-
CHIGINAGAK (Alaska Peninsula)	Stratovolc (1, 1971) Historical	**1102-11-**
CHIGOWE (Africa-E)	Dome of SW USANGU BASIN	0202-163
CHIKOSE (Africa-E)	Dome of SW USANGU BASIN	0202-163
CHIKUBO (Honshu-Japan)	Cone of IZU-TOBU	0803-01=
CHIKURA-DAKE (Kurile Is)	Synonym of CHIKURACHKI	0900-36=
CHIKURACHKI (Kurile Is)	Stratovolcs (9, 1986) Historical	**0900-36=**
CHILCAS, CERRO LAS (Peru)	Dome of HUAYNAPUTINA	1504-03=
CHILCAYOC GRANDE, VOLCAN (Peru)	Cone of ANDAHUA VALLEY	1504-002
CHILCAYOC, VOLCANES (Peru)	Cone of ANDAHUA VALLEY	1504-002
CHILCOTIN CREEK (Canada)	Cone of SATAH MOUNTAIN	1200-13-
CHILES (Colombia)	Stratovolc of NEGRO DE MAYASQUER	1501-11=
CHILES, LOS (Costa Rica)	Cone of AGUAS ZARCAS GROUP	1405-035
CHILIQUES (Chile-N)	Stratovolc (None) Holocene	**1505-101**
CHILLAHUITA, CERRO (Chile-N)	Dome of TOCONCE, CERRO	1505-073
CHILLAN, NEVADOS DE (Chile-C)	Stratovolc (19, 1987) Historical	**1507-07=**
CHILLAN VIEJO [VOLCAN VIEJO] (Chile-C)	Stratovolc of CHILLAN, NEVADOS DE	1507-07=
CHILLING ISLAND [SILENGE ISLAND]	Cone of MUNDUA	0502-021
CHILOE, VOLCAN DE? (Chile-S)	Synonym of CORCOVADO	1508-05=
CHILTEPE (Nicaragua)	Synonym of APOYEQUE	1404-091
CHILTEPE, VOLCAN (Nicaragua)	Dome of APOYEQUE	1404-091
CHIMNEY CRATER (New Britain-SW Pac)	Crater of LANGILA	0502-01=
CHIMNEY MOUNTAIN (Galapagos)	Cone of SANTA CRUZ	1503-091
CHINA HAT (US-Oregon)	Dome of NEWBERRY VOLCANO	1202-11-
CHINABORA, MT. (Alaska-SW)	Synonym of AUGUSTINE	1103-01-
CHINAL (Chile-C)	Synonym of LLAIMA	1507-11=
CHINAMECA (El Salvador)	Stratovolc (None) Fumarolic	**1403-09=**
CHINANDEGA (Nicaragua)	Synonym of SAN CRISTOBAL	1404-02=
CHINCILLAS, CERRO LAS (Chile-N)	Cone of CORDON DE PUNTAS NEGRAS	1505-102
CHINCONQUIAT, CERRO (Mexico)	Cone of TENAYO GROUP	1401-081
CHINENDEGA (Nicaragua)	Synonym of SAN CRISTOBAL	1404-02=
CHING-PE (China-E)	Synonym of JINGPOHU	1005-05-
CHINGANA, CERRO LA (Peru)	Dome of CHACHANI, NEVADO	1504-005
CHINGEINGEIN (Kamchatka)	Shield of UKSICHAN	1000-35-
CHINGO VOLC FIELD (Guatemala)	Stratovolc (None) Holocene	**1402-15-**
CHINGO, VOLCAN (Guatemala)	Cone of CHINGO VOLC FIELD	1402-15-
CHINGPOHU (China-E)	Synonym of JINGPOHU	1005-05-
CHINGYU (China-E)	Synonym of LONGGANG GROUP	1005-06-
CHINITOS, LOS (El Salvador)	Fissure vent of SAN SALVADOR	1403-05=
CHINO, CERRO (El Salvador)	Cone of SANTA ANA	1403-02=
CHINO, CERRO (Guatemala)	Cone of PACAYA	1402-11=
CHINO, CERRO DEL (Mexico)	Cone of MICHOACAN-GUANAJUATO	1401-06=
CHINOIKE-JIGOKU (Kyushu-Japan)	Thermal Feature of TSURUMI	0802-13=
CHINYERO (Canary Is)	Cone of TENERIFE	1803-03-
CHIQUIMULA VOLC FIELD (Guatemala)	Cinder cones (None) Holocene	**1402-20-**
CHIQUIOMATE (Peru)	Synonym of HUAYNAPUTINA	1504-03=
CHIQUITO, CERRO (Guatemala)	Dome of PACAYA	1402-11=
CHIRACHA (Ethiopia)	Stratovolc (None) Holocene	**0201-30-**
CHIRI-YAMA (Honshu-Japan)	Synonym of FUJI	0803-03=
CHIRICA (Italy)	Stratovolc of LIPARI	0101-041
CHIRIHOI [BRAT CHIRPOEV] (Kurile Is)	Cone of CHIRPOI	0900-15=
CHIRIHOIGAKU [BRAT CHIRPOEV] (Kurile Is	Cone of CHIRPOI	0900-15=
CHIRINKOTAN (Kurile Is)	Stratovolc (5, 1986) Historical	**0900-26=**
CHIRINKUTAN (Kurile Is)	Synonym of CHIRINKOTAN	0900-26=
CHIRIP (Kurile Is)	Stratovolcs (2, 1860) Historical	**0900-09=**
CHIRIPNAPUI (CHIRIPNUPURI) (Kurile Is)	Synonym of CHIRIP	0900-09=
CHIRIPORUPURI (CHIRIPPU-DAKE) (Kurile	Synonym of CHIRIP	0900-09=
CHIRIQUI (Panama)	Synonym of BARU	1406-01-
CHIRPOI (Kurile Is)	Caldera (8, 1982) Historical	**0900-15=**
CHIRRIQUI (Panama)	Synonym of BARU	1406-01-
CHISHIMA-IWO-ZAN (Kurile Is)	Synonym of EBEKO	0900-38=
CHISNY, PITON (Indian O.-W)	Cone of FOURNAISE, PITON DE LA	0303-02=
CHITU (Ethiopia)	Maar of SHALA	0201-28-
CHIUCHAM, CERRO (Guatemala)	Dome of TZANJUYUB, VOLCAN DE	1402-05=
CHIVO, CERRO (Galapagos)	Cone of SAN CRISTOBAL	1503-12-
CHIVO, CERRO EL (Mexico)	Cone of PINACATE PEAKS	1401-001
CHIVO, LOMA EL (Ecuador)	Dome of PULULAGUA	1502-011
CHOASCHEN (Kamchatka)	Synonym of ICHINSKY	1000-28=
CHOCOSUELA (Costa Rica)	Caldera of PLATANAR, CERRO	1405-036
CHODUECO (CHODUANPIRE) (Chile-S)	Synonym of OSORNO	1508-01=
CHOJOCHONGEN (Kamchatka)	Synonym of KHODUTKA	1000-053
CHOKAI (Honshu-Japan)	Stratovolcs (24, 1974) Historical	**0803-22=**
CHOKAI-SAN (Honshu-Japan)	Synonym of CHOKAI	0803-22=
CHOLCANI, CERRO DE (Bolivia)	Cone of MACIZO DE PACUNI	1505-015
CHOME (Chile-C)	Crater of LLAIMA	1507-11=
CHOMPIPE, CERRO (Costa Rica)	Stratovolc of BARVA	1405-05=
CH'ON-JI [TIANCHI] (China-E)	Caldera of BAITOUSHAN	1005-07-
CHONAJTAJUYUB, CERRO (Guatemala)	Dome of TZANJUYUB, VOLCAN DE	1402-05=
CHONCLE [EL CHONCE] (Nicaragua)	Stratovolc of SAN CRISTOBAL	1404-02=
CHONI (Greece)	Dome of METHANA	0102-02=
CHOPINE, PUY (France)	Dome of CHAINE DES PUYS	0100-02-
CHOPO, CERRO (Costa Rica)	Synonym of ANUNCIACION, CERRO	1405-032
CHORNY (Kamchatka)	Synonym of CHERNY	1000-46-
CHOSHICHIRO-YAMA (Honshu-Japan)	Dome of AKAGI	0803-13=
CHOSHUENCO (Chile-C)	Stratovolc of MOCHO-CHOSHUENCO	1507-13=
CHOSHUENCO-PILLAN (Chile-C)	Synonym of MOCHO-CHOSHUENCO	1507-13=
CHOUPANOV (Kamchatka)	Synonym of ZHUPANOVSKY	1000-12=
CHRISTENSEN NUNATAK (Antarctica)	Cone of SEAL NUNATAKS GROUP	1900-05=
CHRISTMAS (New Zealand)	Former crater of WHITE ISLAND	0401-04=
CHUBBE, JABAL (Arabia-S)	Crater of ARHAB, HARRA OF	0301-09-
CHUFQUEN, VOLCAN (Chile-C)	Cone of SOLLIPULLI	1507-111
CH'UGA-RYONG (Korea)	Shield (None) Holocene?	**1006-02-**
CHUGUL (Aleutian Is)	Synonym of SEGULA	1101-03-
CHULLCANI, CERRO [CERRO DE CHOLCA	Stratovolc of MACIZO DE PACUNI	1505-015
CHULUUT (Mongolia)	Synonym of TARYATU-CHULUTU	1003-01-
CHUN-PO (China-S)	Synonym of TENGCHONG	0705-11-
CHUNGURURU (Africa-E)	Maar of KIEYO	0202-17=
CHUO-KAKOKYU (Hokkaido-Japan)	Cone of TOKACHI	0805-05=
CHUPADERO (Guatemala)	Crater of TECUAMBURRO	1402-12=
CHUPIQUINA, NEVADO (Chile-N)	Stratovolc of TACORA	1505-01=
CHURCHILL (Alaska-E)	Caldera of BONA-CHURCHILL	1105-03-
CHUWERA (Africa-C)	Crater of BUNYARUGURU FIELD	0203-005
CHYORNOGO (Kurile Is)	Synonym of CHIRPOI	0900-15=
CHYULU HILLS (Africa-E)	Volc field (2, 1855) Anthropology	**0202-13=**
CIAMPINO (Italy)	Crater of ALBANO, MONTE	0101-004
CIATUR (Java)	Thermal Feature of TANGKUBANPARAHU	0603-09=
CIBEUREUM (Java)	Thermal Feature of KIARABERES-GAGAK	0603-03=
CIBEUREUM (Java)	Thermal Feature of KAWAHKAMOJANG	0603-12=
CIBEUREUM PALASARI (Java)	Thermal Feature of KIARABERES-GAGAK	0603-03=
CIBODAS, CIPANAS (Java)	Thermal Feature of KIARABERES-GAGAK	0603-03=
CIBODAS, KAWAH (Java)	Thermal Feature of SALAK	0603-05=
CIBODAS, KAWAH (Java)	Thermal Feature of KIARABERES-GAGAK	0603-03=
CIBOLANG, KAWAH (Java)	Thermal Feature of WAYANG-WINDU	0603-08=
CIBUNI, KAWAH (Java)	Thermal Feature of PATUHA	0603-07=
CIBURIAL (Java)	Thermal Feature of KAWAHKAMOJANG	0603-12=
CIGAMEA, KAWAH (Java)	Thermal Feature of SALAK	0603-05=
CIGLIANO (Italy)	Crater of CAMPI FLEGREI	0101-01=
CIGLIO (Italy)	Cone of ISCHIA	0101-03=
CIGUPAKAN (Java)	Thermal Feature of KAWAHMANUK	0603-11=
CIHIDEUNG, CIPANAS (Java)	Thermal Feature of SALAK	0603-05=
CIKALUWUNG, CIPANAS (Java)	Thermal Feature of KIARABERES-GAGAK	0603-03=
CIKALUWUNG PUTRI, KAWAH (Java)	Thermal Feature of SALAK	0603-05=
CIKALUWUNGHERANG, KAWAH (Java)	Thermal Feature of PERBAKTI	0603-04=
CILIK, GUNUNG (Java)	Cone of IJEN	0603-35=
CINCO PICOS (Azores)	Shield of TERCEIRA	1802-05=
CINDER BUTTE (US-California)	Cone of MEDICINE LAKE	1203-02-
CINDER CLIFF (Canada)	Cone of EDZIZA	1200-06-
CINDER CONE (US-Calif)	Cone of LASSEN VOLC CENTER	1203-08-
CINDER CONE (US-California)	Cone of MEDICINE LAKE	1203-02-
CINDER CONE (US-California)	Cone of SHASTA	1203-01-
CINDER CONE, THE (Canada)	Cone of GARIBALDI LAKE	1200-19-
CINDER HILL (US-Oregon)	Cone of NEWBERRY VOLCANO	1202-11-
CINDER HILLS (Hawaiian Is)	Cone of KILAUEA	1302-01-
CINDER MOUNTAIN (Canada)	Cone of ISKUT-UNUK RIVER CONES	1200-09-
CINNAMON BUTTE (US-Oregon)	Cinder cones (None) Holocene?	**1202-15-**
CINQUE DENTI (Italy)	Pleistocene caldera of PANTELLERIA	0101-071
CINTRAO (Azores)	Dome of AGUA DE PAU	1802-09=
CIOTHIRAI (Africa-E)	Cone of NYAMBENI HILLS	0202-056
CIPAMATUTAN (Java)	Thermal Feature of PERBAKTI	0603-04=
CIPANAS (Indonesian for HOT SPRINGS)	see proper name (e.g. CIBODAS, CIPANAS)	
CIPANAS, KAWAH (Java)	Thermal Feature of SALAK	0603-05=
CIPENGASAHAN, KAWAH (Java)	Thermal Feature of KAWAHKAMOJANG	0603-12=
CIREMAI (Java)	Synonym of CEREME	0603-17=
CIS, MT. (Antarctica)	Cone of EREBUS	1900-02=
CISALADA, CIPANAS (Java)	Thermal Feature of SALAK	0603-05=
CISALADA, KAWAH (Java)	Thermal Feature of SALAK	0603-05=
CISEKATI, CIPANAS (Java)	Thermal Feature of KIARABERES-GAGAK	0603-03=
CISEUPAN, CIPANAS (Java)	Thermal Feature of PERBAKTI	0603-04=
CISNE, NEVADO EL (Colombia)	Dome of RUIZ	1501-02=
CISTERNAZZA (Italy)	Crater of ETNA	0101-06=
CITERNE, CRATERE (Indian O.-W)	Crater of KARTHALA	0303-01=
CITERNE, LA (W Indies)	Cone of SOUFRIERE GUADELOUPE	1600-06=
CITLALTEPETL (Mexico)	Synonym of ORIZABA, PICO DE	1401-10=
CITRONS GALETS, PITON (Indian O.-W)	Cone of FOURNAISE, PITON DE LA	0303-02=
CIWIDEI, KAWAH (Java)	Thermal Feature of PATUHA	0603-07=
CLAPEROLS, VOLCA (Spain)	Cone of OLOT VOLC FIELD	0100-03-
CLARA, MONTANA (Canary Is)	Cone of LANZAROTE	1803-06-
CLARA PEAK (US-New Mexico)	Shield of VALLES CALDERA	1210-03-
CLARKS BUTTE (US-Oregon)	Shield of JORDAN CRATERS	1202-19-
CLAY, MT. (Australia)	Cone of NEWER VOLCANICS PROV	0509-01-
CLEAR LAKE (US-California)	Volc field (None) Holocene	**1203-10-**
CLEARWATER CONE GROUP (Canada)	Synonym of WELLS GRAY-CLEARWATER	1200-15-
CLEETWOOD (US-Oregon)	Vent of CRATER LAKE	1202-16-
CLERIGO DUARTE, MONTANA DEL	Cone of LANZAROTE	1803-06-
CLERMONT CHAMALIERES (France)	Maar of CHAINE DES PUYS	0100-02-
CLEVELAND (Aleutian Is)	Stratovolc (8, 1987) Historical	**1101-24-**

NAME (Subregion)	Type (Eruption Total, Most Recent) Status . . . Relation to NAMED VOLCANO	NUMBER
CLIERZOU (France)	Dome of CHAINE DES PUYS	0100-02-
CLINKER PEAK (Canada)	Stratovolc of GARIBALDI LAKE	1200-19-
COATEPEQUE CALDERA (El Salvador)	Caldera (None) Holocene	**1403-041**
COATS CALDERA (Aleutian Is)	Caldera of YUNASKA	1101-21-
COAXUSCO (Mexico)	Cone of HOLOTEPEC	1401-07-
COBB MOUNTAIN (US-California)	Cone of CLEAR LAKE	1203-10-
COCHONS, ILE AUX (Indian O.-S)	Stratovolc (None) Holocene	**0304-06-**
COCHONS, PITON DES (Indian O.-W)	Cone of FOURNAISE, PITON DE LA	0303-02=
COCO, PITON DE (Indian O.-W)	Cone of FOURNAISE, PITON DE LA	0303-02=
COCOA (Canada)	Crater of EDZIZA	1200-06-
COCONUCOS, LOS (Colombia)	Cone of PURACE	1501-06=
COCONUSCOS-AGUAS HERVIENDO	Thermal Feature of PURACE	1501-06=
COCONUSCOS-AGUAS TIBIAS (Colombia)	Thermal Feature of PURACE	1501-06=
COFFEE (Canada)	Crater of EDZIZA	1200-06-
COFFEEPOT CRATER (US-Oregon)	Crater of JORDAN CRATERS	1202-19-
COHUAZALO, VOLCAN (Mexico)	Cone of TENAYO GROUP	1401-081
COIGUE (Chile-C)	Crater of LLAIMA	1507-11=
COJUTEPEQUE (El Salvador)	Synonym of ILOPANGO	1403-06=
COLACHI (Chile-N)	Stratovolc (None) Holocene	**1505-095**
COLANGAL, CERRO (Ecuador)	Dome of MOJANDA	1502-003
COLARDEAU, FUMEROLLES (W Indies)	Thermal Feature of SOUFR. GUADELOUPE	1600-06=
COLD BAY VOLC CENTER (Alaska Pen.)	Synonym of FROSTY	1102-01-
COLEMAN SEAMOUNT (Solomon Is-SW)	Submarine (None) Holocene	**0505-053**
COLIMA, NEVADO DE (Mexico)	Stratovolc of COLIMA VOLC COMPLEX	1401-04=
COLIMA VOLC COMPLEX (Mexico)	Stratovolc (57, 1991) Historical	**1401-04=**
COLLAQUI (Chile-C)	Synonym of CALLAQUI	1507-091
COLLE MARGHERITA (Italy)	Cone of VESUVIUS	0101-02=
COLLE UMBERTO (Italy)	Cone of VESUVIUS	0101-02=
COLLI ALBANI (Italy)	Synonym of ALBANO, MONTE	0101-004
COLLI EUGANEI GROUP (Italy)	(None) Not a Volcano	0101-00-
COLLI LAZIALE (Italy)	Synonym of ALBANO, MONTE	0101-004
COLLIER CONE (US-Oregon)	Cone of NORTH SISTER FIELD	1202-07-
COLLUMA, CERRO (Bolivia)	Maar (None) Holocene?	**1505-021**
COLO [UNA UNA] (Sulawesi-Indonesia)	Stratovolc (3, 1983) Historical	**0606-01=**
COLOCI [TAULEVU] (Fiji Is-SW Pacific)	Cone of TAVEUNI	0405-01-
COLOMBO BANK (Greece)	Maar of SANTORINI	0102-04=
COLOOT (Java)	Synonym of KELUT	0603-28=
COLORADA, CALDERA (Canary Is)	Crater of LANZAROTE	1803-06-
COLORADA, MONTANA [RODEOS]	Crater of LANZAROTE	1803-06-
COLORADAS, LOMAS (Mexico-Is)	Cone of SOCORRO	1401-021
COLORADO (Chile-C)	Crater of LLAIMA	1507-11=
COLORADO (Chile-C)	Cone of ANTILLANCA GROUP	1507-153
COLORADO (Chile-S)	Cone of PALEI-AIKE VOLC FIELD	1508-08-
COLORADO, CERRO (Chile-C)	Cone of CALABOZOS	1507-042
COLORADO, CERRO (Chile-C)	Cone of CHILLAN, NEVADOS DE	1507-07=
COLORADO, CERRO (Chile-N)	Cone of PUTANA	1505-09=
COLORADO, CERRO (Mexico)	Tuff ring of PINACATE PEAKS	1401-001
COLORADO, CERRO (Nicaragua)	Cone of MOMOTOMBO	1404-09=
COLORADO, CERRO (US-New Mexico)	Cone of ZUNI-BANDERA	1210-02-
COLUMBIA CREST (US-Washington)	Crater of RAINIER	1201-03-
COLUMBO BANK [COLOMBO BANK]	Maar of SANTORINI	0102-04=
COLUMNAR PEAK (Canada)	Dome of GARIBALDI, MT.	1200-20-
COMAL CHICO (Mexico)	Cone of COLIMA VOLC COMPLEX	1401-04=
COMAL GRANDE (Mexico)	Cone of COLIMA VOLC COMPLEX	1401-04=
COMALITO (Nicaragua)	Cone of MASAYA	1404-10=
COMBEGRASSE, PUY DE (France)	Cone of CHAINE DES PUYS	0100-02-
COME, PUY DE (France)	Cone of CHAINE DES PUYS	0100-02-
COMMERSON, CRATERE (Indian O.-W)	Cone of FOURNAISE, PITON DE LA	0303-02=
COMPANIA, CERRO (Guatemala)	Cone of CHINGO VOLC FIELD	1402-15-
COMPANY BUTTE (US-Oregon)	Cone of NEWBERRY VOLCANO	1202-11-
COMPETRI, MONTE (Italy)	Cone of ALBANO, MONTE	0101-004
CONCEPCION (Costa Rica)	Cone of BARVA	1405-05=
CONCEPCION (Nicaragua)	Stratovolc (24, 1986) Historical	**1404-12=**
CONCHAGUA (El Salvador)	Stratovolc (None) Uncertain	**1403-11=**
CONCHAGUA ISLAND (El Salvador)	Synonym of CONCHAGUITA	1403-12=
CONCHAGUITA (El Salvador)	Stratovolc (1, 1892) Historical	**1403-12=**
CONCOLA (Italy)	Crater of CAMPI FLEGREI	0101-01=
CONCORDIA, CERRO LA (Costa Rica)	Stratovolc of BARVA	1405-05=
CONDON BUTTE (US-Oregon)	Cone of NORTH SISTER FIELD	1202-07-
CONDOR, CERRO EL (Argentina)	Stratovolc (None) Holocene	**1505-126**
CONDRODIMUKO (Java)	Thermal Feature of DIENG VOLC COMP	0603-20=
CONDRODIMUKO, KAWAH (Java)	Thermal Feature of MERBABU	0603-24=
CONE CRATER (Hawaiian Is)	Cone of KILAUEA	1302-01-
CONE GLACIER (Canada)	Cone of ISKUT-UNUK RIVER CONES	1200-09-
CONE PEAK (Hawaiian Is)	Cone of KILAUEA	1302-01-
CONE PLACE (Africa-E)	Cone of KILIMANJARO	0202-15=
CONEJAL, CERRO EL (El Salvador)	Cone of SANTA ANA	1403-02=
CONGO, CERRO (Costa Rica)	Stratovolc of POAS	1405-04=
CONGRESS (New Zealand)	Former crater of WHITE ISLAND	0401-04=
CONGRO, LAGOA DO (Azores)	Maar of AGUA DE PAU	1802-09=
CONGUACO, CERRO (Guatemala)	Crater of MOYUTA	1402-13-
CONGUILLIO GROUP (Chile-C)	Crater of LLAIMA	1507-11=
CONIL, MONT (W Indies)	Stratovolc of PELEE	1600-12=
CONTE, LE (US-Oregon)	Cone of SOUTH SISTER	1202-08-
CONTE VIDUA SOLFATARA FIELD (Sulawe	Thermal Feature of TONDANO CALDERA	0606-07-
CONTRADA CAFFEFI, CUDDIOLI DI (Italy)	Vent of PANTELLERIA	0101-071
COOK (Solomon Is-SW Pac)	(None) Not a Volcano	0505-051
COOK, ISLA (Chile-S)	Lava domes (None) Holocene	**1508-09-**
COOK ISLAND (Antarctica)	Submarine vent of THULE ISLANDS	1900-07=
COOPER KNOLL (US-Utah)	Cone of MARKAGUNT PLATEAU	1207-04-
COPACOYA, GEISERS DE (Chile-N)	Synonym of TATIO	1505-08=
COPAHUE (Chile-C)	Stratovolc (5, 1992) Historical	**1507-09=**
COPAHUES, LOS (Chile-C)	Synonym of COPAHUE	1507-09=
COPETE, EL (Ecuador)	Dome of REVENTADOR	1502-01=
COPIAPO (Chile-N)	Stratovolc (None) Uncertain	**1505-14-**
COPITIRO, CERRO DE (Mexico)	Cone of MICHOACAN-GUANAJUATO	1401-06=
COQUILLE, PUY DE LA (France)	Cone of CHAINE DES PUYS	0100-02-
CORA (Turkey)	Crater of ERCIYES DAGI	0103-01=
CORAGULAC, LAKE (Australia)	Tuff ring of NEWER VOLCANICS PROV	0509-01-
CORAZONCILLO, CALDERA DEL (Canary Is)	Crater of LANZAROTE	1803-06-
CORBETTI CALDERA (Ethiopia)	Caldera (None) Holocene	**0201-29-**
CORCOBADO (Chile-S)	Synonym of CORCOVADO	1508-05=
CORCOVADO (Chile-S)	Stratovolc (2, 1835) Historical	**1508-05=**
CORDEMOY, CRATERE DE (Indian O.-W)	Crater of FOURNAISE, PITON DE LA	0303-02=
CORDILLERA BLANCA (Chile-C)	Synonym of CALLAQUI	1507-091
CORDILLERA DEL PEDREGAL (Chile-C)	Synonym of CORDON CAULLE	1507-141
CORDILLERA DORSAL (Canary Is)	Fissure vent of TENERIFE	1803-03-
CORDILLERA NEVADA (Chile-C)	Caldera of CORDON CAULLE	1507-141
CORDILLERA PELADA (Chile-C)	Synonym of CORDON CAULLE	1507-141
CORDON CAULLE (Chile-C)	Fissure vents (5, 1960) Historical	**1507-141**
CORDON CENIZOS (Chile-C)	Cone of PUNTIGUIDO-CORDON CENIZOS	1507-16-
CORDON CHALVIRI (Chile-N)	Stratovolcs (None) Holocene	**1505-103**

NAME (Subregion)	Type (Eruption Total, Most Recent) Status . . . Relation to NAMED VOLCANO	NUMBER
CORDON DE PUNTAS NEGRAS (Chile-N)	Stratovolcs (None) Holocene	**1505-102**
CORDON DEL AZUFRE (Chile-N)	Complx volc (None) Holocene	**1505-121**
CORDON EL CAUYE (Chile-C)	Synonym of PUNTIGUIDO-CORDON CENI	1507-16-
CORINTH HEAD (Indian O.-S)	Cone of HEARD	0304-01=
CORMORANT POINT (Galapagos)	Tuff cone of FLOREANA	1503-10=
CORONA, LA [LA CALDERETA] (Canary Is)	Crater of TENERIFE	1803-03-
CORONA, MONTE (Canary Is)	Cone of LANZAROTE	1803-06-
CORONADO (Mexico)	Stratovolc (None) Fumarolic	**1401-005**
COROPUNA (Peru)	Stratovolc (None) Holocene	**1504-001**
COROZAL VIEJO, EL (Nicaragua)	Cone of MADERA, LA	1404-13-
CORRAL KNOLL [BLACK KNOLL] (US-Utah)	Cone of BALD KNOLL	1207-03-
CORRAL QUEMADO [RININAHUE] (Chile-C)	Maar of CARRAN-LOS VENADOS	1507-14=
CORRAO [GUILA FERDINANDEO] (Italy)	Submarine vent of CAMPI FLEGREI MAR	0101-07=
CORTADERAL, CERRO EL (Peru)	Fissure vent of CHACHANI, NEVADO	1504-005
CORTADERAS, LAS [PAMPA DE PALACIO]	Shield of CHACHANI, NEVADO	1504-005
COS (Greece)	Synonym of KOS	0102-06=
COSEGUINA (Nicaragua)	Synonym of COSIGUINA	1404-01=
COSIGUINA (Nicaragua)	Stratovolc (6, 1859) Historical	**1404-01=**
COSO HOT SPRINGS (US-California)	Thermal Feature of COSO VOLC FIELD	1203-18-
COSO RANGE (US-California)	Synonym of COSO VOLC FIELD	1203-18-
COSO VOLC FIELD (US-California)	Lava domes (None) Pleistocene-Hot Springs	**1203-18-**
COSTA D'AGOSTO (Italy)	Stratovolc of LIPARI	0101-041
COSTA DE LENZUOLA (Italy)	Crater of ISCHIA	0101-03=
COSTA, PUIG DE LA (Spain)	Cone of OLOT VOLC FIELD	0100-03-
COSTA SPARAINA (Italy)	Dome of ISCHIA	0101-03=
COTJI, CERRO (Mexico)	Cone of MICHOACAN-GUANAJUATO	1401-06=
COTOPAXI (Ecuador)	Stratovolc (57, 1940) Historical	**1502-05=**
COTTERIL, MT. (Australia)	Cone of NEWER VOLCANICS PROV	0509-01-
COTTO BARANO, MT. (Italy)	Cone of ISCHIA	0101-03=
COTTO, MONTE (Italy)	Cone of ISCHIA	0101-03=
COUGAR BUTTE (US-California)	Cone of MEDICINE LAKE	1203-02-
COVA DA BURRA [PICO DA AREIA] (Azores)	Dome of FURNAS	1802-10=
COVA, PICO DO (Azores)	Cone of UNNAMED	1802-081
COW HILL SOUFRIERE [TAR RIVER SOUFR	Thermal Feature of SOUFRIERE HILLS	1600-05=
COYOLTEPEC (Mexico)	Cone of HOLOTEPEC	1401-07-
COYOTE BUTTE (US-Idaho)	Cone of CRATERS OF THE MOON	1204-02-
COYOTEPE, CERRO EL (Nicaragua)	Cone of MASAYA	1404-10=
COYOTES, CERRO LOS (El Salvador)	Cone of SAN DIEGO	1403-012
CRABIER, MORNE (W Indies)	Dome of PATATES, MORNE	1600-11=
CRAC, PITON DE (Indian O.-W)	Cone of FOURNAISE, PITON DE LA	0303-02=
CRACATOA (Indonesia)	Synonym of KRAKATAU	0602-00=
CRACKER CREEK CONE (Canada)	Synonym of RUBY MOUNTAIN	1200-03-
CRATER, CRATERE see proper name (e.g. CITERNE, CRATER)		
CRATER BUTTES (US-Oregon)	Cone of NEWBERRY VOLCANO	1202-11-
CRATER DOME (New Zealand)	Dome of OKATAINA	0401-05=
CRATER FLAT (US-Nevada)	Volc field (None) Holocene?	**1206-03-**
CRATER HILL (New Zealand)	Tuff cone of AUCKLAND FIELD	0401-02=
CRATER HILL (US-Utah)	Cone of KOLOB	1207-02-
CRATER LAKE (Antarctica)	Crater of DECEPTION ISLAND	1900-03=
CRATER LAKE (New Zealand)	Crater of RUAPEHU	0401-10=
CRATER LAKE (US-Oregon)	Caldera (4, -2050) Radiocarbon	**1202-16-**
CRATER MOUNTAIN (Alaska-W)	Cone of ST. MICHAEL	1104-04-
CRATER MOUNTAIN (New Guinea)	Stratovolc (None) Holocene?	**0503-001**
CRATER MOUNTAIN (US-California)	Dome of MONO CRATERS	1203-12-
CRATER PEAK (Alaska-SW)	Stratovolc of SPURR	1103-04-
CRATER PEAK (US-Oregon)	Cone of CRATER LAKE	1202-16-
CRATER RIDGE (Alaska-SE)	Stratovolc of EDGECUMBE	1105-04-
CRATER ROCK (US-Oregon)	Dome of HOOD	1202-01-
CRATER TOP (Kamchatka)	Dome of SHEVELUCH	1000-27=
CRATERED DOME (US-California)	Dome of MONO CRATERS	1203-12-
CRATERES, MONTE DE (Indian O.-S)	Cone of POSSESSION, ILE DE LA	0304-05-
CRATERS OF THE MOON (US-Idaho)	Cinder cones (10, -0126) Radiocarbon	**1204-02-**
CRATERS OF THE MOON (New Zealand)	Thermal Feature of MAROA	0401-061
CRAVEN, MT. (W Indies)	Dome of ST. CATHERINE	1600-17=
CRAWFORD BAY (Indian O.-S)	Tuff cone of MARION ISLAND	0304-08-
CRESCENT (US-Utah)	Crater of BLACK ROCK DESERT	1207-05-
CRESCENT BUTTE (US-California)	Cone of MEDICINE LAKE	1203-02-
CRESCENT BUTTE (US-Idaho)	Cone of CRATERS OF THE MOON	1204-02-
CRESCENT CRATER (US-Calif)	Crater of LASSEN VOLC CENTER	1203-08-
CRESPO, CERRO [CERRO QUEMADO]	Dome of ALMOLONGA	1402-04=
CRISTO REY (Nicaragua)	Cone of NEGRO, CERRO	1404-07=
CROCKER, MT. (Galapagos)	Cone of SANTA CRUZ	1503-091
CROCODILE ISLAND (Africa-E)	Synonym of CENTRAL ISLAND	0202-01=
CROCODILE LAKE (Africa-E)	Crater of CENTRAL ISLAND	0202-01=
CROCODRILOS, LAGUNA (Mexico)	Maar of SAN MARTIN, VOLCAN DE	1401-11=
CROMMYONIA (Greece)	Synonym of SUSAKI	0102-01=
CROSCAT, VOLCA (Spain)	Cone of OLOT VOLC FIELD	0100-03-
CROSS HILL (Antarctica)	Crater of DECEPTION ISLAND	1900-03=
CROW LAGOON (Canada)	Pyrocl cone (None) Holocene	**1200-11-**
CRUCES, CERRO LAS (El Salvador)	Cone of SANTA ANA	1403-02=
CRUZ, PICO DA (Azores)	Cone of SETE CIDADES	1802-08=
CRUZ, PICO DO (Azores)	Cone of UNNAMED	1802-081
CRYDER BUTTE (US-Oregon)	Cone of DAVIS LAKE	1202-10-
CU-LAO BO BAI (SE Asia)	Cone of CU-LAO RE GROUP	0705-02-
CU-LAO RE GROUP (SE Asia)	Cones (None) Holocene	**0705-02-**
CUATEPEL, VOLCAN (Mexico)	Cone of TENAYO GROUP	1401-081
CUATES, CERRO LOS (Mexico)	Crater of PINACATE PEAKS	1401-001
CUAUATL (Mexico)	Cone of HOLOTEPEC	1401-07-
CUAUHTEMOC (Mexico)	Cone of COLIMA VOLC COMPLEX	1401-04=
CUAUTZIN (Mexico)	Shield of CHICHINAUTZIN	1401-08=
CUCHUCAVI (Chile-S)	Synonym of MINCHINMAVIDA	1508-04=
CUDDIA, CUDDIE (Italian for HILL) see proper name (e.g. ROSSE, CUDDIA DEL)		
CUERNOS DE NEGROS (Philippines-C)	Synonym of MAGASO	0702-01=
CUERVO, THE [CALDERA DE LOS LAPAS]	Crater of LANZAROTE	1803-06-
CUERVOS, CALDERA DE LOS	Crater of LANZAROTE	1803-06-
CUERVOS, MONTANA DE LOS	Crater of LANZAROTE	1803-06-
CUESTA DEL GUAYABO (Guatemala)	Cone of SUCHITAN VOLC FIELD	1402-17-
CUEVAS, MONTANA DE LAS (Canary Is)	Cone of HIERRO	1803-02-
CUGNO DI MANDRA (Italy)	Stratovolc of LIPARI	0101-041
CUICOCHA (Ecuador)	Caldera (2, -0950) Radiocarbon	**1502-002**
CUIDAD ARCE, CERRITO (El Salvador)	Dome of COATEPEQUE CALDERA	1403-041
CUILAPA-BARBARENA (Guatemala)	Volc field (None) Holocene	**1402-111**
CUILAPA SUR, CERRO (Guatemala)	Cone of CUILAPA-BARBARENA	1402-111
CUILAPA, VOLCAN (Guatemala)	Cone of CUILAPA-BARBARENA	1402-111
CULEBRAS BANK ? (Tonga-SW Pacific)	Synonym of FALCON ISLAND	0403-05=
CULIACAN (Mexico)	Maar of MICHOACAN-GUANAJUATO	1401-06=
CULLOMA, CERRO (Bolivia)	Synonym of COLLUMA, CERRO	1505-021
CULMA, VOLCAN (Guatemala)	Cone of SANTIAGO, CERRO	1402-16-
CUMA (Italy)	Dome of CAMPI FLEGREI	0101-01=
CUMBAL (Colombia)	Stratovolc (2, 1926) Historical	**1501-10=**
CUMBAL, NEVADO DE (Colombia)	Synonym of CUMBAL	1501-10=
CUMBRE, CERRO LA (El Salvador)	Cone of VERDE, LAGUNA	1403-01=

NAME (Subregion)	Type (Eruption Total, Most Recent) Status . . . Relation to NAMED VOLCANO	NUMBER
CUMBRE DE LA LINEA (Chile-N)	Cone of FALSO AZUFRE	1505-129
CUMBRE DEL LAUDO (Chile)	Stratovolc of NEVADA, SIERRA	1505-125
CUMBRE, LA (Galapagos)	Synonym of FERNANDINA	1503-01=
CUNISTEPEQUE, CERRO (Guatemala)	Cone of CHINGO VOLC FIELD	1402-15-
CUPAHUE (Chile-C)	Synonym of COPAHUE	1507-09=
CURA, BANOS DEL (Guatemala)	Thermal Feature of ALMOLONGA	1402-04=
CURACOA (Tonga-SW Pacific)	Submarine (2, 1979) Historical	**0403-101**
CURIQUINCA, CERRO (Chile-N)	Stratovolc of SAIRECABUR	1505-091
CURITZERAN, CERRO DE (Mexico)	Cone of MICHOACAN-GUANAJUATO	1401-06=
CURRY, MT. (Antarctica)	Submarine vent of ZAVODOVSKI	1900-13=
CURTIS ISLAND (Kermadec Is)	Submarine (None) Uncertain	**0402-01=**
CURUB (Ethiopia)	Synonym of KURUB	0201-12=
CUSCACHAPA, LAGUNA DE (El Salvador)	Pit crater of SANTA ANA	1403-02=
CUTZATO, CERRO DE (Mexico)	Cone of MICHOACAN-GUANAJUATO	1401-06=
CUYANAUSOL, AUSOLES DE (El Salvador)	Thermal Feature of VERDE, LAGUNA	1403-01=
CUYOTEPE (El Salvador)	Cone of VERDE, LAGUNA	1403-01=
CUYUFA (Ecuador)	Synonym of SUMACO	1502-04=
CWEAJAIN (Kamchatka)	Synonym of ICHINSKY	1000-28=

D

NAME (Subregion)	Type (Eruption Total, Most Recent) Status . . . Relation to NAMED VOLCANO	NUMBER
DA ORE (Ethiopia)	Tuff ring of HARARO MANDA	0201-115
DAAM (Banda Sea)	Synonym of WURLALI	0605-04=
DABAYRA (Ethiopia)	Synonym of DABBAYRA	0201-114
DABBAHU (Ethiopia)	Stratovolc (None) Holocene	**0201-113**
DABBAIRA [BOINA] (Ethiopia)	Cone of DABBAHU	0201-113
DABBAYRA (Ethiopia)	Shield (None) Holocene	**0201-114**
DABITA (Ethiopia)	Synonym of ADWA	0201-17=
DABITA ALE (Ethiopia)	Synonym of HERTALI	0201-171
DACHT-I-NAVAR GROUP (Afghanistan)	Lava domes (None) Holocene	**0302-06-**
DA'ENKEI (Hokkaido-Japan)	Crater of KOMAGA-TAKE	0805-02=
DAFNI (Greece)	Dome of SANTORINI	0102-04=
DAGAN, JABAL (Arabia-S)	Crater of ARHAB, HARRA OF	0301-09-
DAGIT-DAGITAN (Luzon-Philippines)	Stratovolc (None) Pleistocene-Fumarolic	**0703-045**
DAGNYHAUGEN (Atl-N-Jan Mayen)	Cone of JAN MAYEN	1706-01=
DAGONGJIE (China-S)	Cone of TENGCHONG	0705-11-
DAGUSHANZI [DAYISHAN] (China-E)	Cone of LONGGANG GROUP	1005-06-
DAI-IO-SAN [TATARINOV] (Kurile Is)	Stratovolc of CHIKURACHKI	0900-36=
DAICHIMORI (Honshu-Japan)	Cone of KURIKOMA	0803-21=
DAINICHI-DAKE (Honshu-Japan)	Synonym of KURIKOMA	0803-21=
DAINO-YAMA (Honshu-Japan)	Dome of IZU-TOBU	0803-01=
DAISEN (Honshu-Japan)	Stratovolc (None) Holocene	**0803-004**
DAISETSU (Hokkaido-Japan)	Stratovolcs (1, 1400) Tephrochronology	**0805-06=**
DAISETU-ZAN (Hokkaido-Japan)	Synonym of DAISETSU	0805-06=
DAITIMORI [DAICHIMORI] (Honshu-Japan)	Cone of KURIKOMA	0803-21=
DAITON GEOTHERMAL AREA (Taiwan)	Synonym of DATUN GROUP	0801-032
DAKARA, GOF (Africa-E)	Maar of MARSABIT	0202-021
DAKATAUA (New Britain-SW Pac)	Caldera (2, 1895) Anthropology	**0502-04=**
DAKELABAI (DAKELABALAI) (Luzon-N of)	Synonym of CAMIGUIN DE BABUYANES	0704-01=
DAKONGSHAN (China-S)	Cone of TENGCHONG	0705-11-
DAKULA, MT. (Sulu Is-Philippines)	Cone of BUD DAJO	0700-01=
DALA FILLA (Ethiopia)	Synonym of DALAFFILLA	0201-07=
DALAFFILLA (Ethiopia)	Stratovolc (None) Holocene	**0201-07=**
DALAHRAUN (Iceland-SW)	Crater row of REYKJANES	1701-02=
DALAHUM (Vanuatu-SW Pacific)	Cone of AMBRYM	0507-04=
DALELDAR (Iceland-NE)	Crater row of KRAFLA	1703-08=
DALFJALL (Iceland-NE)	Fissure vent of KRAFLA	1703-08=
DALIUCHONG (China-S)	Cone of TENGCHONG	0705-11-
DALJNY PLOSKY (Kamchatka)	Shield of USHKOVSKY	1000-261
DALLOL (Ethiopia)	Expl crater (1, 1926) Historical	**0201-041**
DALMAN (Antarctica)	Cone of SEAL NUNATAKS GROUP	1900-05=
DAL'NEE, LAKE [LAKE DALNY] (Kamchatka)	Maar of UZON	1000-17=
DAL'NII PLOSKY [DALJNY PLOSKY]	Shield of USHKOVSKY	1000-261
DALNY (Kamchatka)	Cone of BOLSHOI SEMIACHIK	1000-15=
DALNY (Kamchatka)	Cone of TOLBACHIK	1000-24=
DALNY, LAKE (Kamchatka)	Maar of UZON	1000-17=
DALNYAYA PLOSKY [DALJNY PLOSKY]	Shield of USHKOVSKY	1000-261
DAL'NYEYE, LAKE [LAKE DALNY] (Kamchat	Maar of UZON	1000-17=
DALONGWAN (China-E)	Crater of LONGGANG GROUP	1005-06-
DALTON DOME (Canada)	Dome of GARIBALDI, MT.	1200-20-
DALY-TAPA (Armenia)	Synonym of DAR-ALAGES	0104-08-
DAMA ALE (Ethiopia)	Synonym of DAMA ALI	0201-141
DAMA ALI (Ethiopia)	Shield (1, 1631) Holocene	**0201-141**
DAMA HALI (DAMAHALE) (Ethiopia)	Synonym of DAMA ALI	0201-141
DAMAR (Banda Sea)	Synonym of WURLALI	0605-04=
DAMAVAND (Iran)	Stratovolc (None) Holocene	**0302-01-**
DAMMER (Banda Sea)	Synonym of WURLALI	0605-04=
DAMPIER ISLAND (New Guinea-NE of)	Synonym of KARKAR	0501-03=
DANA (Alaska Peninsula)	Stratovolc (1, -1890) Radiocarbon	**1102-05-**
DANAN (Philippines-C)	Thermal Feature of MAHAGNOA	0702-07=
DANAU (Indonesian for LAKE) see proper name (e.g. TALANG, DANAU)		
DANAU COMPLEX (Java)	Caldera (None) Holocene	**0603-01=**
DANBARU (Kyushu-Japan)	Crater of KUJU GROUP	0802-12=
DANGER BAY (US-Oregon)	Stratovolc of CRATER LAKE	1202-16-
D'ANGO, PITON (Indian O.-W)	Cone of FOURNAISE, PITON DE LA	0303-02=
DANKOLE (Ethiopia)	Cone of BISHOFTU FIELD	0201-22-
DAR-ALAGES (Armenia)	Unknown (None) Holocene	**0104-08-**
DARALAGES KETTE (Armenia)	Synonym of DAR-ALAGES	0104-08-
DARALAGEZSKIY KHREBET (Armenia)	Synonym of DAR-ALAGES	0104-08-
DARIGANGA VOLC FIELD (Mongolia)	Cinder cones (None) Holocene	**1003-04-**
DARNLEY, MT. (Antarctica)	Cone of BRISTOL ISLAND	1900-08=
DARWIN BAY (Galapagos)	Caldera of GENOVESA	1503-081
DARWIN, VOLCAN (Galapagos)	Shield (1, 1813) Holocene	**1503-03=**
DATONG (China-E)	Cinder cones (1, 0450) Historical	**1005-01-**
DATUN GROUP (Taiwan)	Stratovolc (None) Pleistocene-Fumarolic	**0801-032**
DAUN, BUKIT (DAUN, BOEKIT) (Sumatra)	Synonym of LUMUTDAUN, BUKIT	0601-21=
DAUNER (Germany)	Maar of WEST EIFEL VOLC FIELD	0100-01-
DAUPHINE ESTATE, LA (W Indies)	Crater of QUALIBOU	1600-14=
DAVAO VOLCANO (Mindanao-Philippines)	Synonym of APO	0701-03=
DAVAPIA ROCKS (New Britain-SW Pac)	Cone of RABAUL	0502-14=
DAVEY PEAK (Antarctica)	Cone of TONEY MOUNTAIN	1900-026
DAVIDOF (Aleutian Is)	Stratovolc (None) Holocene?	**1101-04-**
DAVIS LAKE (US-Oregon)	Volc field (1, -2790) Radiocarbon	**1202-10-**
DAVIS MOUNTAIN (US-Oregon)	Shield of DAVIS LAKE	1202-10-
DAWON, BOEKIT (Sumatra)	Synonym of LUMUTDAUN, BUKIT	0601-21=
DAWSON STRAIT GROUP (D'Entrecasteaux	Volc field (1, 1350) Hydration Rind	**0503-06=**
DAYANZHIFENG (China-E)	Cone of BAITOUSHAN	1005-07-
DAYINGSHAN (China-S)	Stratovolc of TENGCHONG	0705-11-
DAYISHAN (China-E)	Cone of LONGGANG GROUP	1005-06-
DEACON PEAK (Antarctica)	Cone of PENGUIN ISLAND	1900-031
DEADEA [DEIDEI] (D'Entrecasteaux Is)	Thermal Feature of DAWSON STRAIT GP	0503-06=
DEADMAN CREEK (US-California)	Dome of INYO CRATERS	1203-13-

NAME (Subregion)	Type (Eruption Total, Most Recent) Status . . . Relation to NAMED VOLCANO	NUMBER
DEBADO GERA HAYK (Ethiopia)	Maar of LIADO HAYK FIELD	0201-172
DEBAWALA (D'Entrecasteaux Is)	Thermal Feature of IAMELELE	0503-05=
DEBAWALA (D'Entrecasteaux Is)	Synonym of IAMELELE	0503-05=
DEBRE ZEIT (Ethiopia)	Synonym of BISHOFTU FIELD	0201-22-
DEBUNSCHA (Africa-W)	Cone of CAMEROON, MT.	0204-01=
DECEPTION ISLAND (Antarctica)	Caldera (8, 1970) Historical	**1900-03=**
DEDICA (DEDICAS) (Luzon Is-N of)	Synonym of DIDICAS	0704-02=
DEEP CRATER (Galapagos)	Crater of SANTA CRUZ	1503-091
DEEP CRATER (US-California)	Crater of MEDICINE LAKE	1203-02-
DEER MOUNTAIN (US-California)	Dome of LONG VALLEY	1203-14-
DEER MOUNTAIN [CERRO HUECO]	Shield of ZUNI-BANDERA	1210-02-
DEIDEI (D'Entrecasteaux Is)	Thermal Feature of DAWSON STRAIT GP	0503-06=
DEL AGRIO (Chile-C)	Crater of COPAHUE	1507-09=
DELAIRE, VOLCAN (Mexico)	Cone of TENAYO GROUP	1401-081
DELAKI, GUNUNG (Lesser Sunda Is)	Synonym of SIRUNG	0604-27=
DELICIAS, CERRO LAS (El Salvador)	Dome of ILOPANGO	1403-06=
DELIRIO, EL (Nicaragua)	Cone of MADERA, LA	1404-13-
DEMA ALI (Ethiopia)	Synonym of DAMA ALI	0201-141
DEMAVEND (DEMAWEND) (Iran)	Synonym of DAMAVAND	0302-01-
DEMENEGAK (Greece)	Dome of MILOS	0102-03=
DEMON (Kurile Is)	Stratovolc (None) Holocene	**0900-11-**
DEMPO (Sumatra)	Stratovolc (24, 1974) Historical	**0601-23=**
DENHAM BAY (Kermadec Is)	Caldera of RAOUL ISLAND	0402-03=
DENISON (Alaska Peninsula)	Stratovolc (None) Uncertain	**1102-21-**
DENT BICORNE (Indian O.-S)	Cone of KERGUELEN ISLANDS	0304-02=
DENT BLANCHES (Indian O.-S)	Cone of KERGUELEN ISLANDS	0304-02=
DERIBA (Africa-N)	Caldera of MARRA, JEBEL	0205-03-
DES VOEUX PEAK (Fiji Is-SW Pacific)	Cone of TAVEUNI	0405-01-
DESCABEZADO CHICO (Chile-C)	Cone of CALABOZOS	1507-042
DESCABEZADO DEL MAULE (Chile-C)	Synonym of DESCABEZADO GRANDE	1507-05=
DESCABEZADO GRANDE (Chile-C)	Stratovolc (1, 1933) Historical	**1507-05=**
DESEJADO, PICO (Atlantic-S)	Dome of TRINDADE	1805-051
DESERET (US-Utah)	Vent of BLACK ROCK DESERT	1207-05-
DESERT CONE (US-Oregon)	Cone of CRATER LAKE	1202-16-
DESLACS ISLAND (New Britain-SW Pac)	Synonym of GAROVE	0502-03=
DESMONTE, VOLCAN (Mexico)	Cone of MASCOTA VOLC FIELD	1401-031
DESOLATION LAVA FIELD (Canada)	Vent of EDZIZA	1200-06-
DESOLATION, VALLEY OF (W Indies)	Thermal Feature of MICOTRIN	1600-10=
DEUXIEME FORMICA LEO (Indian O.-W)	Crater of FOURNAISE, PITON DE LA	0303-02=
DEVASTATION (Canada)	Vent of MEAGER	1200-18-
DEVASTATION VOLCANO [POGROMNI]	Stratovolc of WESTDAHL	1101-34-
DEVASTATOR, THE (Canada)	Cone of MEAGER	1200-18-
DEVIL MOUNTAIN (Alaska-W)	Shield of ESPENBERG	1104-01-
DEVIL MOUNTAIN LAKES (Alaska-W)	Maar of ESPENBERG	1104-01-
DEVIL ROCK [NGWALA ROCK] (Vanuatu)	Tuff cone of AOBA	0507-03=
DEVILS CAULDRON (US-Idaho)	Cone of CRATERS OF THE MOON	1204-02-
DEVILS DESK (Alaska Peninsula)	Stratovolc (None) Uncertain	**1102-24-**
DEVILS GARDEN (US-Oregon)	Volc field (None) Holocene?	**1202-12-**
DEVILS HILL (US-Oregon)	Dome of SOUTH SISTER	1202-08-
DEVILS THROAT (Hawaiian Is)	Pit crater of KILAUEA	1302-01-
DEWA-FUJI (Honshu-Japan)	Synonym of CHOKAI	0803-22=
DGIDA BASIN (Russia-SE)	Cinder cones (None) Holocene	**1002-04-**
DHAMAR, HARRAS OF (Arabia-S)	Volc field (1, 1937) Historical	**0301-12-**
DHIN, JABAL (Arabia-S)	Crater of ARHAB, HARRA OF	0301-09-
DHU RAKHAM, JABAL (Arabia-S)	Cone of DHAMAR, HARRAS OF	0301-12-
DI BARUH, DANAU (Sumatra)	Crater of TALANG	0601-16=
DIABLE, MORNE AU (W Indies)	Stratovolc (None) Fumarolic	**1600-08=**
DIABLOTINS, MORNE (W Indies)	Stratovolc (None) Fumarolic	**1600-09=**
DIAMANTE (Chile-C)	Pleistocene caldera of MAIPO	1507-021
DIAMOND CRATERS (US-Oregon)	Volc field (None) Holocene?	**1202-17-**
DIAU [MT. OIAU] (D'Entrecasteaux Is)	Stratovolc of DAWSON STRAIT GROUP	0503-06=
DIBA' AL HURUS, JIBAL (Arabia-W)	Dome of RAHAT, HARRAT	0301-07=
DIDICA (DIDACAS) (Luzon Is-N of)	Synonym of DIDICAS	0704-02=
DIDICAS (Luzon Is-N of)	Compnd volc (5, 1978) Historical	**0704-02=**
DIDIKAS ROCKS (Luzon Is-N of)	Synonym of DIDICAS	0704-02=
DIDIMTU (Ethiopia)	Cone of MEGA BASALT FIELD	0201-33-
DIEGO DEL HAYA (Costa Rica)	Crater of IRAZU	1405-06=
DIENG VOLC COMPLEX (Java)	Complx volc (22, 1993) Historical	**0603-20=**
DIETRO ISOLA, CUDDIOLI DI (Italy)	Shield of PANTELLERIA	0101-071
DIKKARTINI (Turkey)	Dome of ERCIYES DAGI	0103-01=
DIKY KHREBET [DIKY GREBEN] (Kamchat	Dome of PAUZHETKA	1000-022
DIKYE GREBEN [DIKY GREBEN] (Kamchat	Dome of PAUZHETKA	1000-022
DILEKENE (Halmahera-Indonesia)	Crater of DUKONO	0608-01=
DILLER CONE [MAKLAKS CRATER] (US-Or	Cone of CRATER LAKE	1202-16-
DIMA (Kamchatka)	Cone of KRASHENINNIKOV	1000-19=
DIMMADALSHAEDH (Iceland-SW)	Shield of HENGILL	1701-05=
DINERO (Chile-S)	Cone of PALEI-AIKE VOLC FIELD	1508-08-
DIODIO (D'Entrecasteaux Is)	Maar of GOODENOUGH	0503-041
DIOGENEAS, MT. [HANGING ROCK] (Austr	Dome of NEWER VOLCANICS PROV	0509-01-
DIONISIO (Luzon Is-N of)	Cone of BABUYAN CLARO	0704-03=
DISAPPOINTMENT PEAK (US-Washington)	Dome of GLACIER PEAK	1201-02-
DISHPAN GAP (US-Washington)	Cone of GLACIER PEAK	1201-02-
DIVES, MONT DE LA (Indian O.-S)	Stratovolc of AMSTERDAM ISLAND	0304-04-
DIXON, MT. (Indian O.-S)	Stratovolc of HEARD	0304-01=
DJABI (Ethiopia)	Synonym of CORBETTI CALDERA	0201-29-
DJAILOLO (Halmahera-Indonesia)	Synonym of JAILOLO	0608-051
DJAMBANGAN [JAMBANGAN] (Java)	Crater of IYANG-ARGAPURA	0603-33=
DJAPATI [JAPATI] (Java)	Crater of GUNTUR	0603-13=
DJAR'A, DJEBEL (Arabia-W)	Synonym of YAR, JABAL	0301-08-
DJAR'ATAIN, HARRA OF [JAR'ATAIN]	Cone of YAR, JABAL	0301-08-
DJARIAN, KAWAH [KAWAH JARIAN] (Java)	Crater of TANGKUBANPARAHU	0603-09=
DJARRA (Arabia-W)	Synonym of YAR, JABAL	0301-08-
DJAWALO [JAWALO] (Lesser Sunda Is)	Crater of PALUWEH	0604-15=
DJEBEL (French: of Arabic word for MT.) see proper name (e.g. DHIN, DJEBEL)		
DJEMBANGAN [JEMBANGAN] (Java)	Caldera of SEMERU	0603-30=
DJERBAN (Arabia-S)	Crater of ARHAB, HARRA OF	0301-09-
DJERO [JERO] (Java)	Crater of ARJUNO-WELIRANG	0603-29=
DJINGGO, KAPUNDAN [KEPUNDAN JINGG	Crater of MARAPI	0601-14=
DJIRING PLATEAU (SE Asia)	Synonym of HAUT DONG NAI	0705-04-
DJONGGRING SELOKO [JONGGRING SELO	Crater of SEMERU	0603-30=
DJOUGOUDJA DSAHA (Indian O.-W)	Crater of KARTHALA	0303-01=
DJUNGO, LE (Africa-W)	Cone of MANENGOUBA	0204-004
DJURIG, KAWAH [KAWAH JURIG] (Java)	Crater of TANGKUBANPARAHU	0603-09=
DOBU (D'Entrecasteaux Is)	Stratovolc of DAWSON STRAIT GROUP	0503-06=
DODOEKKO (Halmahera-Indonesia)	Synonym of DUKONO	0608-01=
DOE PEAK (US-California)	Cone of MEDICINE LAKE	1203-02-
DOEANG (Sangihe Is-Indonesia)	Synonym of RUANG	0607-01=
DOEKONO (Halmahera-Indonesia)	Synonym of DUKONO	0608-01=
DOEWANG (Sangihe Is-Indonesia)	Synonym of RUANG	0607-01=
DOFAN (DOFANE, DOFANI) (Ethiopia)	Synonym of DOFEN	0201-18=
DOFEN (Ethiopia)	Stratovolc (None) Holocene	**0201-18=**
DOGANA, LA (Italy)	Cone of VULSINI	0101-003

NAME (Subregion)	Type (Eruption Total, Most Recent) Status Relation to NAMED VOLCANO	NUMBER
DOGS HEAD (US-Washington)	Dome of ST. HELENS	1201-05-
DOHMBERG (Germany)	Cone of WEST EIFEL VOLC FIELD	0100-01-
DOINYO, DONYO (Masai for MT.) see proper name (e.g. BURU, DOINYO)		
DOLINNIY (Russia-SE)	Cone of UDOKAN VOLC FIELD	1002-03-
DOLOK (Indonesian for MOUNTAIN) see proper name (e.g. SINGGALANG, DOLOK)		
DOLOMIEU (Indian O.-W)	Crater of FOURNAISE, PITON DE LA	0303-02=
DOMA ALE (Ethiopia)	Synonym of DAMA ALI	0201-141
DOMA PEAKS (New Guinea)	Stratovolc (None) Holocene?	**0503-00-**
DOMADALSHRAUN (Iceland-S)	Fissure vent of TORFAJOKULL	1702-05=
DOMAIN (New Zealand)	Tuff ring of AUCKLAND FIELD	0401-02=
DOMAS, KAWAH (Java)	Crater of TANGKUBANPARAHU	0603-09=
DOME, PUY DE (France)	Dome of CHAINE DES PUYS	0100-02-
DOME, THE (New Zealand)	Dome of EGMONT	0401-03=
DOME, THE (US-Oregon)	Cone of NEWBERRY VOLCANO	1202-11-
DOMESHNYAYA (Kamchatka)	Dome of KSUDACH	1000-05=
DOMO DEL AZUFRE (Chile-C)	Dome of CORDON CAULLE	1507-141
DOMUYO, VOLCAN (Argentina)	Stratovolc (None) Holocene?	**1507-068**
DON GREGORIO [CERRO DON CHANA]	Cone of CUILAPA-BARBARENA	1402-111
DON JOAO DE CASTRO BANK (Azores)	Submarine (1, 1720) Historical	**1802-07=**
DONA JUANA (Colombia)	Stratovolc (2, 1906) Historical	**1501-07=**
DONALD (Antarctica)	Cone of SEAL NUNATAKS GROUP	1900-05=
DONALD DUCK (New Zealand)	Crater of WHITE ISLAND	0401-04=
DONGDAPOTOU (China-S)	Cone of TENGCHONG	0705-11-
DONGHENGDAOSHAN (China-E)	Cone of LONGGANG GROUP	1005-06-
DONGHUOKOU (China-W)	Cone of KUNLUN VOLC GROUP	1004-03-
DONGJIAODEBUSHAN (China-E)	Cone of WUDALIANCHI	1005-04-
DONGLONGMENSHAN (China-E)	Cone of WUDALIANCHI	1005-04-
DONGLONGWAN (China-E)	Crater of LONGGANG GROUP	1005-06-
DONGO, MORNE (W Indies)	Dome of SOUFRIERE GUADELOUPE	1600-06=
DONKORO-YAMA (Hokkaido-Japan)	Cone of USU	0805-03=
DONNOYE (Kamchatka)	Thermal Feature of MUTNOVSKY	1000-06=
DOON KINIMI [DOON KIDIMI] (Africa-N)	Crater of TOUSSIDE, TARSO	0205-01=
DOON OREI [TROU AU NATRON] (Africa-N)	Pleistocene caldera of TOUSSIDE, TARSO	0205-01=
DOON [TROU AU NATRON] (Africa-N)	Crater of VOON, TARSO	0205-02=
DOON [TROU AU NATRON] (Africa-N)	Pleistocene caldera of TOUSSIDE, TARSO	0205-01=
DORA, MT. (US-New Mexico)	Shield of RATON-CLAYTON	1210-04-
DORO AFI TOI (Lesser Sunda Is)	Dome of TAMBORA	0604-04=
DORO API (Lesser Sunda Is)	Cone of SANGEANG API	0604-05=
DORO MANTOI [DORO MANTAI] (Lesser S	Cone of SANGEANG API	0604-05=
DORR FUMAROLE FIELD (US-Washington)	Thermal Feature of BAKER	1201-01=
DOS EQUIS (Mexico)	Dome of CEBORUCO, VOLCAN	1401-03=
DOS NOVILLOS, VOLCAN (Costa Rica)	Stratovolc of TURRIALBA	1405-07=
DOTSERO (US-Colorado)	Expl crater (1, -2200) Radiocarbon	**1208-01-**
DOUBLE CRATER (Alaska Peninsula)	Stratovolc of EMMONS LAKE	1102-02-
DOUBLE HOLE CRATER (US-California)	Crater of MEDICINE LAKE	1203-02-
DOUGLAS (Alaska Peninsula)	Stratovolc (None) Fumarolic	**1102-27-**
DOUKKHAN, DJEBEL (Red Sea)	Synonym of TEYR, DJEBEL	0201-01=
DOUSSAINTS (Costa Rica)	Cone of IRAZU	1405-06=
DOWI [MT. REAMUR] (New Guinea-NE of)	Stratovolc of LONG ISLAND	0501-05=
DOWNS CONE (Antarctica)	Cone of TONEY MOUNTAIN	1900-026
DR. FERREIRA, PICO (Azores)	Cone of UNNAMED	1802-081
DRAGON (Canada)	Cone of WELLS GRAY-CLEARWATER	1200-15-
DRAKON (Kurile Is)	Dome of GROZNY GROUP	0900-07=
DRANGAGRUNDIR (Iceland-NE)	Fissure vent of KRAFLA	1703-08=
DREISER WEIHER (Germany)	Maar of WEST EIFEL VOLC FIELD	0100-01-
DREKAGIGAROD (Iceland-NE)	Fissure vent of BARDARBUNGA	1703-03=
DRINGO (Java)	Crater of DIENG VOLC COMPLEX	0603-20=
DRUSE, JABAL (Syria)	Cone of ES SAFA	0300-05-
DRY BUTTE (US-Oregon)	Cone of BACHELOR	1202-09-
DRY CRATER (Africa-E)	Crater of CENTRAL ISLAND	0202-01=
DRY CREEK DOME (US-California)	Dome of LONG VALLEY	1203-14-
DRYDEN'S ROCK [HANGING ROCK] (Austr	Dome of NEWER VOLCANICS PROV	0509-01-
DUA SAUDARA (Sulawesi-Indonesia)	Stratovolc of TONGKOKO	0606-13=
DUANG (Sangihe Is-Indonesia)	Synonym of RUANG	0607-01=
DUANI (Africa-E)	Cone of CHYULU HILLS	0202-13=
DUANZISHAN [TUANZISHAN] (China-E)	Cone of KELUO GROUP	1005-03-
DUBBEH, DJEBEL (Ethiopia)	Synonym of DUBBI	0201-10=
DUBBEY, GEBEL (Ethiopia)	Synonym of DUBBI	0201-10=
DUBBI (Ethiopia)	Stratovolc (2, 1861) Historical	**0201-10=**
DUCHAN, DJEBEL (Red Sea)	Cone of TEYR, DJEBEL	0201-01=
DUCK LAKE (US-Wyoming)	Crater of YELLOWSTONE	1205-01-
DUCROT (Indian O.-W)	Crater of FOURNAISE, PITON DE LA	0303-02=
DUDERS HILL (New Zealand)	Cone of AUCKLAND FIELD	0401-02=
DUENJO (Masai for MT.) see proper name (e.g. NGAI, DUENJO)		
DUFFERINBREEN (Atl-N-Jan Mayen)	Cone of JAN MAYEN	1706-01=
DUFFRIN ISLAND (Canada)	Cone of MILBANKE SOUND GROUP	1200-12-
DUGA (Kamchatka)	Cone of KRASHENINNIKOV	1000-19=
DUJIANSHAN (China-W)	Cone of KUNLUN VOLC GROUP	1004-03-
DUKO MA TALA (Halmahera-Indonesia)	Synonym of DUKONO	0608-01=
DUKONO (Halmahera-Indonesia)	Complx volc (5, 1993) Historical	**0608-01=**
DUMAS (Indian O.-S)	Cone of AMSTERDAM ISLAND	0304-04-
DUMILAH (Java)	Crater of LAWU	0603-26=
DUNCAN CANAL (Alaska-SE)	Unknown (None) Holocene	**1105-05-**
DUNDOLI (Africa-E)	Cone of NGOZI	0202-164
DUPORTAIL (New Britain-SW Pac)	Synonym of LOLOBAU	0502-13=
DUPPACHER WEIHER (Germany)	Maar of WEST EIFEL VOLC FIELD	0100-01-
DURANDAL (Indian O.-W)	Cone of FOURNAISE, PITON DE LA	0303-02=
DURANGO VOLC FIELD (Mexico)	Cinder cones (None) Holocene	**1401-022**
DURAZNERO [SAN JUAN] (Canary Is)	Fissure vent of LA PALMA	1803-01-
DURAZNILLO, CERRO (El Salvador)	Stratovolc of SANTA ANA	1403-02=
DURKANA VOLC FIELD (Ethiopia)	Synonym of MEGA BASALT FIELD	0201-33-
DURRES (Germany)	Maar of WEST EIFEL VOLC FIELD	0100-01-
DUSY (Mongolia)	Cone of DARIGANGA VOLC FIELD	1003-04-
DUTTON (Alaska Peninsula)	Stratovolc (None) Holocene	**1102-011**
DUTTON CLIFF (US-Oregon)	Stratovolc of CRATER LAKE	1202-16-
DUUFDUGA (Kamchatka)	Cone of KRASHENINNIKOV	1000-19=
DUWANG (Sangihe Is-Indonesia)	Synonym of RUANG	0607-01=
DVEGGAR (Iceland-NE)	Crater row of TUNGNAFELLSJOKULL	1703-04=
DVERGAHRAUN (Iceland-NE)	Crater row of BARDARBUNGA	1703-03=
DVOINOI (Russia-SE)	Dome of NE UDOKAN PLATEAU	1002-02-
DVOINOY (Kamchatka)	Cone of TOLBACHIK	1000-24=
DVOR (Kamchatka)	Stratovolc of KARYMSKY	1000-13=
DVUKHGLAVY (Kamchatka)	Dome of BEZYMIANNY	1000-25=
DYNFJURJOLL (DYNGJUFJALL) (Iceland-NE	Synonym of ASKJA	1703-06=
DYNGJUFJALLAHRAUN (Iceland-NE)	Crater row of ASKJA	1703-06=
DYNGJUFJOLL (Iceland-NE)	Crater row of ASKJA	1703-06=
DYNGJUHALS (Iceland-NE)	Fissure vent of BARDARBUNGA	1703-03=
DYNGNAHRAUN (Iceland-SW)	Crater row of KRISUVIK	1701-03=
DZAN TOLOGAI (Mongolia)	Cone of TARYATU-CHULUTU	1003-01-
DZENZURSKAIA, SOPKA (Kamchatka)	Synonym of DZENZURSKY	1000-11=
DZENZURSKY (Kamchatka)	Compnd volc (None) Holocene	**1000-11=**
DZHANGA-TAPA (Armenia)	Cone of ARAGATS	0104-06-
DZHIDA BASIN (Russia-SE)	Synonym of DGIDA BASIN	1002-04-
DZIGOKU [TREZUBETZ] (Kurile Is)	Somma volcano of KOLOKOL GROUP	0900-12=
DZUN-NERETTE (Mongolia)	Cone of DARIGANGA VOLC FIELD	1003-04-

E

NAME (Subregion)	Type (Eruption Total, Most Recent) Status Relation to NAMED VOLCANO	NUMBER
E-SAN (Hokkaido-Japan)	Stratovolc (2, 1874) Historical	**0805-011**
EAGLE LAKE FIELD (US-California)	Fissure vents (None) Holocene?	**1203-09-**
EAGLE PEAK (US-Calif)	Dome of LASSEN VOLC CENTER	1203-08-
EAGLE TAIL MOUNTAIN (US-New Mexico)	Cone of RATON-CLAYTON	1210-04-
EANASTICK MEADOW (Canada)	Vent of GARIBALDI, MT.	1200-20-
EARTHQUAKE DOME (US-California)	Dome of LONG VALLEY	1203-14-
EAST BUTTE (US-Oregon)	Dome of NEWBERRY VOLCANO	1202-11-
EAST CAPE VOLCANO (Aleutian Is)	Stratovolc of BULDIR	1101-01-
EAST CRATER (New Zealand)	Crater of RUAPEHU	0401-10=
EAST CRATER (New Zealand)	Crater of WHITE ISLAND	0401-04=
EAST CRATER (US-Washington)	Cone of INDIAN HEAVEN	1201-07-
EAST DOME (US-Washington)	Dome of ST. HELENS	1201-05-
EAST EPI (Vanuatu-SW Pacific)	Caldera (5, 1979) Historical	**0507-06=**
EAST LAKE FISSURE (US-Oregon)	Fissure vent of NEWBERRY VOLCANO	1202-11-
EAST LAVA FIELD (US-Oregon)	Synonym of SQUAW RIDGE FIELD	1202-13-
EAST MAAR (Alaska Peninsula)	Maar of UKINREK MAARS	1102-13B
EAST-MATTHEW (SW Pacific)	Cone of MATTHEW ISLAND	0508-01=
EAST MAUI VOLCANO (Hawaiian Is)	Synonym of HALEAKALA	1302-06-
EAST RIFT ZONE (Hawaiian Is)	Fissure vent of KILAUEA	1302-01-
EAST SAND BUTTE (US-California)	Cone of MEDICINE LAKE	1203-02-
EASTER ISLAND (Pacific-C)	Shields (None) Holocene	**1303-08-**
EASTERN DOME (New Zealand)	Dome of OKATAINA	0401-05=
EASTERN HILL (Australia)	Cone of NEWER VOLCANICS PROV	0509-01-
EBEKO (Kurile Is)	Somma volc (11, 1991) Historical	**0900-38=**
EBINO-DAKE (Kyushu-Japan)	Stratovolc of KIRISHIMA	0802-09=
EBO LOBO (EBOELOBA) (Lesser Sunda Is)	Synonym of EBULOBO	0604-10=
EBOGA (Africa-W)	Caldera of MANENGOUBA	0204-004
EBOSHI-DAKE (Hokkaido-Japan)	Stratovolc of DAISETSU	0805-06=
EBOSHI-DAKE (Honshu-Japan)	Cone of NORIKURA	0803-06=
EBOSHI-DAKE (Kyushu-Japan)	Stratovolc of ASO	0802-11=
EBOSHI-DAKE (Kyushu-Japan)	Cone of KIRISHIMA	0802-09=
EBOSI-DAKE [EBOSHI-DAKE] (Hokkaido)	Stratovolc of DAISETSU	0805-06=
EBOSI-DAKE [EBOSHI-DAKE] (Kyushu)	Cone of KIRISHIMA	0802-09=
EBU LOBO (Lesser Sunda Is)	Synonym of EBULOBO	0604-10=
EBULOBO (Lesser Sunda Is)	Stratovolc (7, 1969) Historical	**0604-10=**
EBURRU (Africa-E)	Synonym of EBURRU, OL DOINYO	0202-08=
EBURRU, OL DOINYO (Africa-E)	Complx volc (None) Holocene	**0202-08=**
ECCLES, MT. (Australia)	Cone of NEWER VOLCANICS PROV	0509-01-
ECHO CRATER BUTTE (US-Idaho)	Cone of CRATERS OF THE MOON	1204-02-
ECKERSLEY, MT. (Australia)	Cone of NEWER VOLCANICS PROV	0509-01-
ECOMA, KAWAH (Java)	Crater of TANGKUBANPARAHU	0603-09=
ECUADOR, VOLCAN (Galapagos)	Shield (None) Holocene	**1503-011**
EDD, VOLCANO OF (Ethiopia)	Synonym of DUBBI	0201-10=
EDDYSTONE ISLAND (Solomon Is-SW Pac)	Synonym of SIMBO	0505-05=
EDEN, MT. (New Zealand)	Cone of AUCKLAND FIELD	0401-02=
EDGECUMBE (Alaska-SE)	Stratovolcs (3, -2220) Radiocarbon	**1105-04-**
EDGECUMBE, MT. (New Zealand)	Dome of OKATAINA	0401-05=
EDZIZA (Canada)	Stratovolc (4, 0950) Radiocarbon	**1200-06-**
EEK (Alaska Peninsula)	Synonym of VENIAMINOF	1102-07-
EGAN (US-Oregon)	Cone of BACHELOR	1202-09-
EGGELLA (Kamchatka)	Shield (None) Holocene	**1000-42-**
EGGOYA (Atl-N-Jan Mayen)	Tuff cone of JAN MAYEN	1706-01=
EGMONT (New Zealand)	Stratovolc (18, 1755) Radiocarbon	**0401-03=**
EGON (Lesser Sunda Is)	Stratovolc (1, 1907) Historical	**0604-16=**
EGUAS (Azores)	Cone of SETE CIDADES	1802-08=
EHI (Chad term for MOUNTAIN) see proper name (e.g. SOSSO, EHI)		
EIFEL VOLC FIELD (Germany)	Synonym of WEST EIFEL VOLC FIELD	0100-01-
EIGO-ZAN (Honshu-Japan)	Synonym of FUJI	0803-03=
EILER BUTTE (US-California)	Cone of TUMBLE BUTTES	1203-06-
EININDRANGUR (Iceland-S)	Submarine vent of VESTMANNAEYJAR	1702-01=
EKARMA (Kurile Is)	Stratovolc (2, 1980) Historical	**0900-27=**
EKARUMA (Kurile Is)	Synonym of EKARMA	0900-27=
EKSTRUSIVNY GREBEN (Kamchatka)	Dome of BEZYMIANNY	1000-25=
EKUNDO (Africa-W)	Cone of CAMEROON, MT.	0204-01=
EL see proper name (e.g. NUEVO, EL)		
ELAHO VALLEY (Canada)	Vent of MEAGER	1200-18-
ELBRUS (Russia-SW)	Stratovolc (1, 0050) Tephrochronology	**0104-01-**
ELDBORG (Iceland-W)	Cone of LJOSUFJOLL	1700-03=
ELDBORG A BRENNISTEINSFJOLLUM	Crater row of BRENNISTEINSFJOLL	1701-04=
ELDBORG-DROTTNINGU (Iceland-SW)	Crater row of BRENNISTEINSFJOLL	1701-04=
ELDBORG NYRDRI AT LAMBAFELL (Iceland	Crater row of BRENNISTEINSFJOLL	1701-04=
ELDBORG SYDRI AT LAMBAFELL (Iceland)	Crater row of BRENNISTEINSFJOLL	1701-04=
ELDBORG-THINGVALLAVATN (Iceland-SW)	Crater row of HENGILL	1701-05=
ELDBORG-TROLLADYNGJA (Iceland-SW)	Crater row of KRISUVIK	1701-03=
ELDBORG UNDIR MEITLUM (Iceland-SW)	Crater row of HENGILL	1701-05=
ELDBORGIR (Iceland-SW)	Crater row of HENGILL	1701-05=
ELDBORGIR-TINDASKAGA (Iceland-SW)	Crater row of HENGILL	1701-05=
ELDEYJAR (Iceland-SW)	Submarine vent of REYKJANESHRYGGUR	1701-01=
ELDEYJARBODI (Iceland-SW)	Submarine vent of REYKJANESHRYGGUR	1701-01=
ELDFELL (Iceland-S)	Fissure vent of VESTMANNAEYJAR	1702-01=
ELDGIGUR (Iceland-NE)	Fissure vent of GRIMSVOTN	1703-01=
ELDGJA (Iceland-S)	Fissure vent of KATLA	1702-03=
ELDIVIDARHRAUN (Iceland-S)	Fissure vent of HEKLA	1702-07=
ELDOERNE [ELDEYJAR] (Iceland-SW)	Submarine vent of REYKJANESHRYGGUR	1701-01=
ELDVORP (Iceland-SW)	Crater row of REYKJANES	1701-02=
ELECTRA, MT. (Antarctica)	Synonym of PLEIADES, THE	1900-013
ELEGANTE, VOLCAN EL (Mexico)	Maar of PINACATE PEAKS	1401-001
ELEITOGA (Samoa-SW Pacific)	Cone of SAVAI'I	0404-04=
ELELAU (Ethiopia)	Synonym of JALUA	0201-03=
ELENA CAPURATA (Chile-N)	Stratovolc of ACOTANGO	1505-017
ELENGOUM (Africa-W)	Caldera of MANENGOUBA	0204-004
ELEPHANT, MT. (Australia)	Cone of NEWER VOLCANICS PROV	0509-01-
ELIZA, MT. (Australia)	Dome of NEWER VOLCANICS PROV	0509-01-
ELLIDAEY (Iceland-S)	Cone of VESTMANNAEYJAR	1702-01=
ELLIS CONE (Antarctica)	Cone of TONEY MOUNTAIN	1900-026
ELLITTICO (Italy)	Caldera of ETNA	0101-06=
ELMAU (Africa-E)	Cone of CHYULU HILLS	0202-13=
ELMENTEITA BADLANDS (Africa-E)	Pyrocl cones (None) Holocene	**0202-071**
ELOVSKY (Kamchatka)	Shields (None) Holocene	**1000-59-**
ELWYN HOT SPRINGS (Canada)	Thermal Feature of EDZIZA	1200-06-
EMAO [LOBOA] (Vanuatu-SW Pacific)	Stratovolc of NORTH VATE	0507-081
EMBOCADERO, VOLCAN (Mexico)	Cone of MASCOTA VOLC FIELD	1401-031
EMBORIO (Greece)	Thermal Feature of NISYROS	0102-05=
EMI (Chad term for MOUNTAIN) see proper name (e.g. KOUSSI, EMI)		
EMMONS LAKE (Alaska Peninsula)	Caldera (None) Holocene	**1102-02-**
EMMONS, MT. (Alaska Peninsula)	Stratovolc of EMMONS LAKE	1102-02-

NAME (Subregion)	Type (Eruption Total, Most Recent) Status Relation to NAMED VOLCANO	NUMBER
EMPEROR OF CHINA (Banda Sea)	Submarine ? (None) Uncertain	**0605-01=**
EMPOENG (Sulawesi-Indonesia)	Synonym of LOKON-EMPUNG	0606-10=
EMPONG [EMPUNG] (Sulawesi-Indonesia)	Crater of LOKON-EMPUNG	0606-10=
EMSTRUHRUAN (Iceland-S)	Fissure vent of KATLA	1702-03=
EMURUANGOGOLAK (Africa-E)	Shield (8, 1910) Radiocarbon	**0202-051**
EMURUEPOLI (Africa-E)	Cone of EMURUANGOGOLAK	0202-051
ENAMBABA (Africa-E)	Cone of EMURUANGOGOLAK	0202-051
'ENAZ, HALA-'L- (Arabia-W)	Cone of 'UWAYRID, HARRAT	0301-02=
ENCANTADA, CALDERA (Canary Is)	Crater of FUERTEVENTURA	1803-05-
ENCANTADA, LA (Mexico)	Dome of SAN LUIS GONZAGA, ISLA	1401-003
ENCANTADA, LAGUNA (Mexico)	Maar of SAN MARTIN, VOLCAN DE	1401-11=
ENCIERRO, CERRO (US-New Mexico)	Vent of ZUNI-BANDERA	1210-02-
ENCLOS VELAIN [VELAIN] (Indian O.-W)	Crater of FOURNAISE, PITON DE LA	0303-02=
ENDEH API (Lesser Sunda Is)	Synonym of IYA	0604-11=
ENDERBY ISLAND (Galapagos)	Tuff cone of FLOREANA	1503-10=
ENDUT (Java)	Stratovolc of KIARABERES-GAGAK	0603-03=
ENFORCADO, PICO DO (Azores)	Cone of SETE CIDADES	1802-08=
ENGARE SUKUTA [SUGUTA-LOGKIPI]	Thermal Feature of BARRIER, THE	0202-03=
ENGELORETI, OL DOINYO (Africa-E)	Cone of CHYULU HILLS	0202-13=
ENGLISH'S CRATER (W Indies)	Crater of SOUFRIERE HILLS	1600-05=
ENIWA (Hokkaido-Japan)	Stratovolc of SHIKOTSU	0805-04=
ENKO-DAKE (Honshu-Japan)	Cone of NORIKURA	0803-06=
ENOSTUCK MEADOW [EANASTICK MEADO	Vent of GARIBALDI, MT.	1200-20-
ENSENADA DEL VIEJO (Nicaragua)	Cone of ZAPATERA ISLAND	1404-111
ENSENADA LOS CHIQUEROS (Nicaragua)	Cone of ZAPATERA ISLAND	1404-111
ENSENADAS DE PUNTA GORDA (Nicaragua	Cone of ZAPATERA ISLAND	1404-111
ENVAL, MAAR D' (France)	Maar of CHAINE DES PUYS	0100-02-
EONOSTUCK MEADOW [EANASTICK MEAD	Vent of GARIBALDI, MT.	1200-20-
EPI CALDERA (Vanuatu-SW Pacific)	Synonym of EAST EPI	0507-06=
EPIA (Vanuatu-SW Pacific)	Cone of EAST EPI	0507-06=
EPIB (Vanuatu-SW Pacific)	Cone of EAST EPI	0507-06=
EPIC (Vanuatu-SW Pacific)	Cone of EAST EPI	0507-06=
EPOMEO (Italy)	Synonym of ISCHIA	0101-03=
EPSOM AVENUE (New Zealand)	Cone of AUCKLAND FIELD	0401-02=
EPUN (Chile-C)	Crater of CALLAQUI	1507-091
ER-BAL HAF (Arabia-S)	Synonym of BAL HAF, HARRA OF	0301-17-
ERA KOHOR (Africa-N)	Crater of KOUSSI, EMI	0205-021
ERBENSCHELL (Germany)	Cone of WEST EIFEL VOLC FIELD	0100-01-
ERCIYAS DAGI (Turkey)	Synonym of ERCIYES DAGI	0103-01=
ERCIYES DAGI (Turkey)	Stratovolc (None) Holocene	**0103-01=**
ERDJAS (ERDSCHIAS, ERDZHIAS) (Turkey)	Synonym of ERCIYES DAGI	0103-01=
EREBUS (Antarctica)	Stratovolc (13, 1993) Historical	**1900-02=**
EREBUS (Indian O.-S)	Cone of KERGUELEN ISLANDS	0304-02=
ERH-LUNG-WAN [ERLONGWAN] (China-E)	Crater of LONGGANG GROUP	1005-06-
ERITA, LA (Mexico)	Cone of COLIMA VOLC COMPLEX	1401-04=
ERLONGWAN (China-E)	Crater of LONGGANG GROUP	1005-06-
ERMAK (Kurile Is)	Dome of GROZNY GROUP	0900-07=
ERRANT CONE (Nicaragua)	Cone of MASAYA	1404-10=
ERTA ALE (Ethiopia)	Shield (4, 1993) Historical	**0201-08=**
ERTA ALI (ERTAHALE, ERTO ALE) (Ethiopia	Synonym of ERTA ALE	0201-08=
ES SAFA (Syria)	Volc field (1, 1850) Historical	**0300-05-**
ES-SAWAD, DJEBEL (Arabia-S)	Synonym of MARHA, JABAL EL-	0301-10-
ESA 'ALA (D'Entrecasteaux Is)	Synonym of DAWSON STRAIT GROUP	0503-06=
ESAN (Hokkaido-Japan)	Synonym of E-SAN	0805-011
ESCALA (Bolivia)	Lava dome (None) Holocene	**1505-062**
ESCALANTE (Chile-N)	Stratovolc of SAIRECABUR	1505-091
ESCANGRAGA, MONTANA DE (Canary Is)	Cone of FUERTEVENTURA	1803-05-
ESCHELLE (W Indies)	Cone of SOUFRIERE GUADELOUPE	1600-06=
ESCLAVOS, CERRITO LOS (Guatemala)	Cone of CUILAPA-BARBARENA	1402-111
ESCOBETA, CERRO (Mexico)	Cone of TENAYO GROUP	1401-081
ESCONDIDA, CERRO LAGUNA (Chile-N)	Cone of CORDON DE PUNTAS NEGRAS	1505-102
ESCONDIDA, LAGUNA (Argentina)	Synonym of CONDOR, CERRO EL	1505-126
ESCORIAL, CERRO (Chile-N)	Stratovolc (None) Holocene	**1505-112**
ESCURO, MONTE (Azores)	Cone of AGUA DE PAU	1802-09=
ESH-SHAMIT, DJEBEL (Arabia-W)	Cone of KHAYBAR, HARRAT	0301-06=
ESHOUGEDASHAN (China-E)	Cone of DATONG	1005-01-
ESI, JABAL EL- (Arabia-S)	Stratovolc of DHAMAR, HARRAS OF	0301-12-
ESJUFJOLL (Iceland-SE)	Stratovolc (1, 1927) Historical	**1704-02=**
ESKIHLIDARFJOLL (Iceland-S)	Crater row of VATNAFJOLL	1702-06=
ESKKRATERET (Atl-N-Jan Mayen)	Cone of JAN MAYEN	1706-01=
ESMERALDA BANK (Mariana Is-C Pac)	Submarine (None) Fumarolic	**0804-21=**
ESPANA, CERRO (Colombia)	Dome of SANTA ISABEL	1501-021
ESPEJOS, LOMA DE LOS (Chile-C)	Dome of MAULE, LAGUNA DEL	1507-062
ESPENBERG (Alaska-W)	Volc field (1, -5050) Tephrochronology	**1104-01-**
ESPERANCE, MT. (Solomon Is-SW Pac)	Cone of GALLEGO	0505-062
ESPINASSE, PUY D' (France)	Cone of CHAINE DES PUYS	0100-02-
ESPINO, CERRITO EL (El Salvador)	Dome of ILOPANGO	1403-06=
ESPIRITU SANTO (Chile-C)	Stratovolc of SAN JOSE	1507-02=
ESSA (Atl-N-Jan Mayen)	Cone of JAN MAYEN	1706-01=
ESSI, DJEBEL AL [JABAL EL-ESI] (Arabia)	Stratovolc of DHAMAR, HARRAS OF	0301-12-
ESSINGEN (Germany)	Maar of WEST EIFEL VOLC FIELD	0100-01-
ESSINO (Greece)	Thermal Feature of KOS	0102-06=
ESTANY, VOLCA L' (Spain)	Cone of OLOT VOLC FIELD	0100-03-
ESTIVADOUX, MAAR D' (France)	Maar of CHAINE DES PUYS	0100-02-
ESTRADA (Mexico)	Maar of MICHOACAN-GUANAJUATO	1401-06=
ESTRELLA, CERRO DE LA (Mexico)	Cone of SANTA CATARINA RANGE	1401-082
ET-TADAWIN (Arabia-S)	Tuff cone of HAYLAN, JABAL	0301-11-
ETHNEIN, HALA-'L- (Arabia-W)	Synonym of ITHNAYN, HARRAT	0301-05=
ETINDE (Africa-W)	Stratovolc of CAMEROON, MT.	0204-01=
ETNA (Italy)	Shield (191, 1993) Historical	**0101-06=**
ETNEA (Italy)	Synonym of ETNA	0101-06=
ETOILE, PIC DE L' (Vanuatu-SW Pacific)	Synonym of MERE LAVA	0507-021
ETOROFU-ATOSANUPURI (Kurile Is)	Synonym of ATSONUPURI	0900-05=
EURH, JABAL EL (Arabia-S)	Cone of DHAMAR, HARRAS OF	0301-12-
EVANGELISTA, MT. (Italy)	Cone of VULSINI	0101-003
EVANS KNOLL (Antarctica)	Cone of HUDSON MOUNTAINS	1900-028
EVE (Canada)	Cone of EDZIZA	1200-06-
EVE [GALLOSEULO] (New Britain-SW Pac)	Stratovolc of HARGY	0502-10=
EVENSEN (Antarctica)	Cone of SEAL NUNATAKS GROUP	1900-05=
EVERITT HILL (US-California)	Shield of SHASTA	1203-01-
EVERMANN, CERRO (Mexico-Is)	Cone of SOCORRO	1401-021
EVLIYA TEPE (Turkey)	Dome of ERCIYES DAGI	0103-01=
EWEN, MT. (Australia)	Cone of NEWER VOLCANICS PROV	0509-01-
EXILE HILL (Canada)	Cone of SPECTRUM RANGE	1200-07-
EXPEDITION CRATER (Kermadec Is)	Crater of RAOUL ISLAND	0402-03=
EXPEDITSII (Kamchatka)	Dome of BEZYMIANNY	1000-25=
EYAFJALLA (Iceland-S)	Synonym of EYJAFJOLL	1702-02=
EYJAFJOLL (Iceland-S)	Stratovolc (1, 1823) Historical	**1702-02=**
EYRA (Iceland-SW)	Fissure vent of BRENNISTEINSFJOLL	1701-04=
EZH [YEZH] (Kamchatka)	Dome of BOLSHOI SEMIACHIK	1000-15=

F

NAME (Subregion)	Type (Eruption Total, Most Recent) Status Relation to NAMED VOLCANO	NUMBER
FAAMOTU (Tonga-SW Pacific)	Cone of NIUAFO'OU	0403-11=
FA'ANI (Samoa-SW Pacific)	Cone of SAVAI'I	0404-04=
FA'ASEMENE (Samoa-SW Pacific)	Tuff cone of TA'U	0404-001
FAGALO (Samoa-SW Pacific)	Cone of SAVAI'I	0404-04=
FAGAMAA (Samoa-SW Pacific)	Tuff cone of TUTUILA	0404-02-
FAGATELE (Samoa-SW Pacific)	Tuff cone of TUTUILA	0404-02-
FAGRADALSHRAUN (Iceland-SW)	Shield of KRISUVIK	1701-03=
FAGULULU (D'Entrecasteaux Is)	Synonym of IAMELELE	0503-05=
FAIAL (Azores)	Synonym of FAYAL	1802-01=
FAINA (Kamchatka)	Crater of KLIUCHEVSKOI	1000-26=
FAKO (Africa-W)	Crater of CAMEROON, MT.	0204-01=
FALCON ISLAND (Tonga-SW Pacific)	Submarine (9, 1970) Historical	**0403-05=**
FALEASAO (Samoa-SW Pacific)	Tuff cone of TA'U	0404-001
FALLING MOUNTAIN (Alaska Peninsula)	Dome of NOVARUPTA	1102-18-
FALLS CREEK [DRAGON CONE] (Canada)	Cone of WELLS GRAY-CLEARWATER	1200-15-
FALSO AZUFRE (Chile-N)	Complx volc (None) Holocene	**1505-129**
FANG (Antarctica)	Stratovolc of EREBUS	1900-02=
FANTALE (FANTALI, FANTALLE) (Ethiopia)	Synonym of FENTALE	0201-19=
FANTHAMS PEAK (New Zealand)	Cone of EGMONT	0401-03=
FANUA LAI (Tonga-SW Pacific)	Synonym of FONUALEI	0403-10=
FANUATAPU (Samoa-SW Pacific)	Tuff ring of UPOLU	0404-03-
FARAGLIONE (Italy)	Cone of VULCANO	0101-05=
FARALLON A FORTUNA (Volcano Is-Japan)	Synonym of IWO-JIMA	0804-12=
FARALLON DE PAJAROS (Mariana Is)	Stratovolc (16, 1967) Historical	**0804-14=**
FARIS (Aleutian Is)	Cone of WESTDAHL	1101-34-
FARM FLAT (W Indies)	Dome of LIAMUIGA	1600-03=
FAROL (Azores)	Dome of TERCEIRA	1802-05=
FASNIA, VOLCAN DE (Canary Is)	Cone of TENERIFE	1803-03-
FATHER, THE (New Britain-SW Pac)	Synonym of ULAWUN	0502-12=
FATOULEO-KAKOULO (Vanuatu-SW Pacific)	Stratovolc of NORTH VATE	0507-081
FATUAGA POINT (Samoa-SW Pacific)	Cone of OFU-OLOSEGA	0404-01=
FAUJAS, CRATERE (Indian O.-W)	Crater of FOURNAISE, PITON DE LA	0303-02=
FAYAL (Azores)	Stratovolc (2, 1958) Historical	**1802-01=**
FEARN ISLAND (SW Pacific)	Synonym of HUNTER ISLAND	0508-02=
FEDON'S CAMP (W Indies)	Cone of ST. CATHERINE	1600-17=
FEDOTYCH (Kamchatka)	Shield (None) Holocene	**1000-51-**
FEFINA (Tonga-SW Pacific)	Synonym of FALCON ISLAND	0403-05=
FELL (Chile-S)	Cone of PALEI-AIKE VOLC FIELD	1508-08-
FELLSHRAUN (Iceland-SW)	Crater row of REYKJANES	1701-02=
FENI (New Ireland-SW Pac)	Synonym of AMBITLE	0504-02=
FENTALE (Ethiopia)	Stratovolc (2, 1820) Historical	**0201-19=**
FENTE DU NORD, FUMEROLLE DE LA (W I)	Thermal Feature of SOUFR. GUADELOUPE	1600-06=
FERLE (Italy)	Cone of PANTELLERIA	0101-071
FERN LAKE (US-Wyoming)	Crater of YELLOWSTONE	1205-01-
FERNAND (Indian O.-S)	Stratovolc of AMSTERDAM ISLAND	0304-04-
FERNANDEZ, VOLCANO DE (Aleutian Is)	Synonym of SHISHALDIN	1101-36-
FERNANDINA (Galapagos)	Shield (22, 1991) Historical	**1503-01=**
FERRARIAS (Azores)	Cone of SETE CIDADES	1802-08=
FERRO (Canary Is)	Synonym of HIERRO	1803-02-
FERRO, PICO DO (Azores)	Dome of FURNAS	1802-10=
FEUERBERG (Germany)	Cone of WEST EIFEL VOLC FIELD	0100-01-
FIAMOE (Samoa-SW Pacific)	Cone of UPOLU	0404-03-
FIFTYTWO RIDGE (Canada)	Tuya of WELLS GRAY-CLEARWATER	1200-15-
FILAKOPI (Greece)	Dome of MILOS	0102-03=
FILETE CRESTA MONTOSA (Nicaragua)	Caldera of COSIGUINA	1404-01=
FILETE EL YANKEE (Nicaragua)	Cone of COSIGUINA	1404-01=
FILETE LA SALVIA (Nicaragua)	Cone of COSIGUINA	1404-01=
FILO DELLO ZOLFO (Italy)	Vent of STROMBOLI	0101-04=
FIMERICH (Germany)	Cone of WEST EIFEL VOLC FIELD	0100-01-
FINCA LIEBRES, VOLCAN (Costa Rica)	Stratovolc of TURRIALBA	1405-07=
FINCH, MT. (Aleutian Is)	Cone of FISHER	1101-35-
FINLEY BUTTE (US-Oregon)	Cone of NEWBERRY VOLCANO	1202-11-
FIREPIT KNOLL (US-Utah)	Cone of KOLOB	1207-02-
FIRESTONE BUTTE (US-Oregon)	Cone of NEWBERRY VOLCANO	1202-11-
FIRGAS, MONTANA DE (Canary Is)	Cone of GRAN CANARIA	1803-04-
FIRST (Kamchatka)	Dome of UZON	1000-17=
FIRURA, NEVADOS (Peru)	Stratovolcs (None) Holocene	**1504-00-**
FISCHBACH (Germany)	Cone of WEST EIFEL VOLC FIELD	0100-01-
FISHER (Aleutian Is)	Stratovolc (4, 1830) Historical	**1101-35-**
FISSURE BUTTE (US-Idaho)	Cone of CRATERS OF THE MOON	1204-02-
FISSURE CRATER (New Britain-SW Pac)	Crater of LANGILA	0502-01=
FITEKO (Africa-E)	Cone of KIEYO	0202-17=
FITO (Samoa-SW Pacific)	Cone of UPOLU	0404-03-
FIUCHA (Chile-C)	Stratovolc of ANTILLANCA GROUP	1507-153
FIUMICELLO (Italy)	Tuff ring of CAMPI FLEGREI	0101-01=
FJARBORG (Iceland-NE)	Fissure vent of KRAFLA	1703-08=
FJARHOLADYDYNGJA (Iceland-NE)	Shield of ASKJA	1703-06=
FLAGDAHRAUN (Iceland-NE)	Fissure vent of BARDARBUNGA	1703-03=
FLAMINGO LAKE (Africa-E)	Crater of CENTRAL ISLAND	0202-01=
FLATADYNGJA (Iceland-NE)	Shield of ASKJA	1703-06=
FLATIRON (Canada)	Cone of WELLS GRAY-CLEARWATER	1200-15-
FLEALLIN (Kamchatka)	Synonym of ICHINSKY	1000-28=
FLJOTAHRAUN (Iceland-S)	Fissure vent of KATLA	1702-03=
FLJOTSODDAHRAUN (Iceland-NE)	Crater row of GRIMSVOTN	1703-01=
FLOREANA (Galapagos)	Shield (None) Holocene	**1503-10=**
FLORES (Azores)	Stratovolc (2, -0950) Radiocarbon	**1802-001**
FLORES, CERRO LAS (Nicaragua)	Cone of NEGRO, CERRO	1404-07=
FLORES, VOLCAN DE (Guatemala)	Volc field (None) Holocene	**1402-14-**
FLOTUDYNGJUHRAUN (Iceland-NE)	Shield of ASKJA	1703-06=
FLOURMILL (Canada)	Cone of WELLS GRAY-CLEARWATER	1200-15-
FOERSTNER (Italy)	Submarine vent of PANTELLERIA	0101-071
FOGALEPULU (Samoa-SW Pacific)	Cone of UPOLU	0404-03-
FOGAPOA (Samoa-SW Pacific)	Cone of SAVAI'I	0404-04=
FOGO (Azores)	Synonym of AGUA DE PAU	1802-09=
FOGO (Cape Verde Is)	Stratovolc (10, 1951) Historical	**1804-01=**
FOGO, LAGOA DO (Azores)	Pleistocene caldera of AGUA DE PAU	1802-09=
FOGRUFJOLL (Iceland-NE)	Fissure vent of LOKI-FOGRUFJOLL	1703-02=
FOND DOUX (W Indies)	Cone of QUALIBOU	1600-14=
FONDI DI BAIA (Italy)	Crater of CAMPI FLEGREI	0101-01=
FONDO FERRARO (Italy)	Dome of ISCHIA	0101-03=
FONDO RICCIO (Italy)	Cone of CAMPI FLEGREI	0101-01=
FONTAIPE, CRATERE (Indian O.-W)	Crater of FOURNAISE, PITON DE LA	0303-02=
FONTPOBRA, VOLCA (Spain)	Cone of OLOT VOLC FIELD	0100-03-
FONTUR (Iceland-NE)	Fissure vent of BARDARBUNGA	1703-03=
FONUA FO'OU (Tonga-SW Pacific)	Synonym of FALCON ISLAND	0403-05=
FONUAFOOA (Tonga-SW Pacific)	Synonym of METIS SHOAL	0403-07=
FONUALEI (Tonga-SW Pacific)	Stratovolc (7, 1957) Historical	**0403-10=**
FOREST HILL (Australia)	Cone of NEWER VOLCANICS PROV	0509-01-
FORGIA VECCHIA (Italy)	Crater of VULCANO	0101-05=

NAME (Subregion)	Type (Eruption Total, Most Recent) Status / Relation to NAMED VOLCANO	NUMBER
FORGIA VECCHIA (Italy)	Vent of LIPARI	0101-041
FORGOTTEN CONE (US-Oregon)	Cone of CRATER LAKE	1202-16-
FORGOTTEN CRATER [WILLIAMS CRATER	Crater of CRATER LAKE	1202-16-
FORKED BUTTE (US-Oregon)	Cone of JEFFERSON	1202-02-
FORMICA LEO (Indian O.-W)	Crater of FOURNAISE, PITON DE LA	0303-02=
FORNEAU (Indian O.-S)	Cone of AMSTERDAM ISLAND	0304-04-
FORT DE KOCK (Sumatra)	Synonym of MARAPI	0601-14=
FORT PORTAL VOLC FIELD (Africa-C)	Tuff cones (None) Holocene	**0203-002**
FORT SELKIRK (Canada)	Volc field (None) Holocene	**1200-01-**
FOSSA (Italy)	Tuff cone of VULCANO	0101-05=
FOSSA, CALDERA DELLA (Italy)	Caldera of VULCANO	0101-05=
FOSSA CARBONARA (Italy)	Dome of PANTELLERIA	0101-071
FOSSA DEL RUSSO (Italy)	Dome of PANTELLERIA	0101-071
FOSSA LUPARA (Italy)	Crater of CAMPI FLEGREI	0101-01=
FOSTER CRATER (Antarctica)	Cone of ROYAL SOCIETY RANGE	1900-021
FOUMBOT VOLC FIELD (Africa-W)	Synonym of OKU VOLC FIELD	0204-003
FOUNDLAND (W Indies)	Cone of MICOTRIN	1600-10=
FOUQUE (Greece)	Dome of SANTORINI	0102-04=
FOUR CRATERS LAVA FIELD (US-Oregon)	Volc field (None) Holocene?	**1202-14-**
FOUR-IN-ONE CONE (US-Oregon)	Cone of NORTH SISTER FIELD	1202-07-
FOUR PEAKS, ISLAND OF THE (Alaska Pen)	Synonym of FOURPEAKED	1102-26-
FOURCHE, PITON DE (Indian O.-W)	Cone of FOURNAISE, PITON DE LA	0303-02=
FOURMILE HILL (US-California)	Cone of MEDICINE LAKE	1203-02-
FOURNAISE, PITON DE LA (Indian O.-W)	Shield (153, 1992) Historical	**0303-02=**
FOURPEAKED (Alaska Peninsula)	Stratovolc (None) Uncertain	**1102-26-**
FOURTH TOP (Kamchatka)	Dome of SHEVELUCH	1000-27=
FOUS, MORNE (W Indies)	Dome of PATATES, MORNE	1600-11=
FOX HILL CONE (Alaska-W)	Cone of ST. PAUL ISLAND	1104-07-
FRAILE, MONTANA (Canary Is)	Cone of TENERIFE	1803-03-
FRAILE, VOLCAN EL (Mexico)	Stratovolc of POPOCATEPETL	1401-09=
FRAILES, LOS [CERRO NOCARNE] (Peru)	Dome of CHACHANI, NEVADO	1504-005
FRAILES, MONTANA DE LOS (Canary Is)	Cone of HIERRO	1803-02-
FRAISSE, PUY DE (France)	Cone of CHAINE DES PUYS	0100-02-
FRANKLIN, MT. (Australia)	Cone of NEWER VOLCANICS PROV	0509-01-
FRASCATI (Italy)	Crater of ALBANO, MONTE	0101-004
FRAY CARLOS, CERRO (Chile-C)	Cone of TINGUIRIRICA	1507-03=
FRAZER, MT. (Australia)	Cone of NEWER VOLCANICS PROV	0509-01-
FRED'S HILL (Indian O.-S)	Cone of MARION ISLAND	0304-08-
FREEMAN PEAK (Antarctica)	Synonym of YOUNG ISLAND	1900-011
FREMRINAMUR (Iceland-NE)	Stratovolc (3, -0800) Tephrochronology	**1703-07=**
FRENCHMEN'S SOLFATARA (Vanuatu)	Thermal Feature of SORETIMEAT	0507-01=
FROSTY (Alaska Peninsula)	Stratovolcs (None) Holocene	**1102-01-**
FRUMENTO DELLA CONCAZZE, MONTE	Cone of ETNA	0101-06=
FRUMENTO, MONTE (Italy)	Cone of ETNA	0101-06=
FRUMENTO SUPINO, MONTE (Italy)	Cone of ETNA	0101-06=
FRUTILLA, CERRO (Chile-C)	Cone of ANTILLANCA GROUP	1507-153
FUALUA (Samoa-SW Pacific)	Cone of SAVAI'I	0404-04=
FUBO-ZAN (Honshu-Japan)	Stratovolc of ZAO	0803-19=
FUCHICH (Africa-E)	Synonym of CENTRAL ISLAND	0202-01=
FUDESHIMA (Izu Is-Japan)	Stratovolc of OSHIMA	0804-01=
FUDO-IKE (Kyushu-Japan)	Crater of KIRISHIMA	0802-09=
FUE SAN (Kurile Is)	Synonym of SARYCHEV PEAK	0900-24=
FUEGO (Guatemala)	Stratovolc (55, 1987) Historical	**1402-09=**
FUEGO DE TIMANFAYA, MONTANAS DEL	Crater of LANZAROTE	1803-06-
FUEGO, MONTANAS DEL (Canary Is)	Cone of LANZAROTE	1803-06-
FUEGO, VOLCAN DE (Mexico)	Synonym of COLIMA VOLC COMPLEX	1401-04=
FUENCALIENTE, CALDERA DE [CORAZON	Crater of LANZAROTE	1803-06-
FUENCALIETNE [SAN ANTONIO] (Canary Is	Cone of LA PALMA	1803-01-
FUERTEVENTURA (Canary Is)	Fissure vents (None) Holocene	**1803-05-**
FUGEN-DAKE (Kyushu-Japan)	Stratovolc of UNZEN	0802-10=
FUI (Chile-C)	Cone of MOCHO-CHOSHUENCO	1507-13=
FUI'AVEA (Samoa-SW Pacific)	Cone of SAVAI'I	0404-04=
FUJI (Honshu-Japan)	Stratovolc (57, 1708) Historical	**0803-03=**
FUJI-SAN (FUJIGA-DAKE) (Honshu-Japan)	Synonym of FUJI	0803-03=
FUJIMIKUBO (Honshu-Japan)	Tuff ring of IZU-TOBU	0803-01=
FUKENO-YU (Honshu-Japan)	Thermal Feature of HACHIMANTAI	0803-25=
FUKUJIN (Volcano Is-Japan)	Submarine (3, 1974) Historical	**0804-133**
FUKUJIN-KAIZAN (Volcano Is-Japan)	Synonym of FUKUJIN	0804-133
FUKUJIN-OKANOBA (Volcano Is-Japan)	Synonym of FUKUJIN	0804-133
FUKUKAZEANA-YAMA (Honshu-Japan)	Synonym of FUJI	0803-03=
FUKUTOKU-OKANOBA (Volcano Is-Japan)	Synonym of SHIN-IWO-JIMA	0804-13=
FUMAROLE, FUMEROLLE see proper name (e.g. GAMBOULI, FUMAROLE FIELD OF)		
FUMAROLE VALLEY (US-California)	Thermal Feature of LONG VALLEY	1203-14-
FUMAROLLES, MONT DES (Indian O.-S)	Thermal Feature of KERGUELEN ISLAND	0304-02=
FUNABARA (Honshu-Japan)	Cone of IZU-TOBU	0803-01=
FUNDA DE LAJES, CALDEIRA (Azores)	Tuff ring of FLORES	1802-001
FUNDA, LAGOA (Azores)	Stratovolc of FLORES	1802-001
FUNDERA (Italy)	Crater of ISCHIA	0101-03=
FUNKA-ASANE (Volcano Is-Japan)	Crater of KITA-IWO-JIMA	0804-11=
FUPPUSHI (Hokkaido-Japan)	Stratovolc of AKAN	0805-07=
FUPPUSHI-DAKE (Hokkaido-Japan)	Stratovolc of SHIKOTSU	0805-04=
FUREBETSU (Hokkaido-Japan)	Stratovolc of AKAN	0805-07=
FURIHATA-YAMA (Kyushu-Japan)	Dome of SAKURA-JIMA	0802-08=
FURNA (Azores)	Cone of UNNAMED	1802-081
FURNAS (Azores)	Stratovolc (5, 1630) Historical	**1802-10=**
FURO-SEN (Kyushu-Japan)	Thermal Feature of TSURUMI	0802-13=
FURU-DAKE (Ryukyu Is)	Cone of KUCHINOERABU-JIMA	0802-05=
FUSS PEAK (Kurile Is)	Stratovolc (1, 1854) Historical	**0900-34=**
FUTAGO-YAMA (Honshu-Japan)	Dome of HAKONE	0803-02=
FUTAGO-YAMA (Honshu-Japan)	Dome of KUSATSU-SHIRANE	0803-12=
FUTAGO-YAMA (Honshu-Japan)	Cone of FUJI	0803-03=
FUTAGO-YAMA (Izu Is-Japan)	Cone of OSHIMA	0804-01=
FUTAGOISHI (Kyushu-Japan)	Stratovolc of KIRISHIMA	0802-09=
FUTATSU-DAKE (Honshu-Japan)	Dome of HARUNA	0803-122
FUTATSU-ISHI (Kyushu-Japan)	Stratovolc of KIRISHIMA	0802-09=
FUTATSU-YAMA (Honshu-Japan)	Cone of FUJI	0803-03=
FUTATSUZUKA (Honshu-Japan)	Cone of FUJI	0803-03=
FUTIGA (Samoa-SW Pacific)	Cone of TUTUILA	0404-02-
FUYOGA-MINE (Honshu-Japan)	Synonym of FUJI	0803-03=
FUZZTAIL BUTTE (US-Oregon)	Cone of NEWBERRY VOLCANO	1202-11-
FYRIPLAKA (Greece)	Cone of MILOS	0102-03=

G

NAME (Subregion)	Type (Eruption Total, Most Recent) Status / Relation to NAMED VOLCANO	NUMBER
GABII [CASTIGLIONE] (Italy)	Crater of ALBANO, MONTE	0101-004
GABILLEMA (Ethiopia)	Stratovolc (None) Holocene	**0201-15=**
GABRIEL, MT. [WAITOMOKIA] (New Zealand	Cone of AUCKLAND FIELD	0401-02=
GABULI (Ethiopia)	Synonym of DALAFFILLA	0201-07=
GADA ALE (Ethiopia)	Stratovolc (None) Holocene	**0201-05=**
GADAMSA CALDERA (Ethiopia)	Synonym of GEDAMSA CALDERA	0201-23-
GADANG, GUNUNG (Sumatra)	Synonym of KERINCI	0601-17=
GADIR, CUDDIA DEL (Italy)	Shield of PANTELLERIA	0101-071
GADJAH [GAJAH] (Java)	Crater of GUNTUR	0603-13=
GADJAHMOENGKOER [GAJAMUNKUR]	Dome of KELUT	0603-28=
GAFANHOTO (Azores)	Cone of FURNAS	1802-10=
GAFURANINDI (Africa-C)	Cone of NYAMURAGIRA	0203-02=
GAGAK, MT. (Java)	Synonym of KIARABERES-GAGAK	0603-03=
GAGE HILL (Canada)	Tuya of WELLS GRAY-CLEARWATER	1200-15-
GAGES LOWER SOUFRIERE (W Indies)	Thermal Feature of SOUFRIERE HILLS	1600-05=
GAGE'S MT. (W Indies)	Dome of SOUFRIERE HILLS	1600-05=
GAGES UPPER SOUFRIERE (W Indies)	Thermal Feature of SOUFRIERE HILLS	1600-05=
GAGUA (Luzon-Philippines)	Synonym of CAGUA	0703-09=
GAGXANUL (Guatemala)	Synonym of SANTA MARIA	1402-03=
GAHI (SW Pacific)	Tuff cone of WALLIS ISLANDS	0404-05-
GAHINGA (Africa-C)	Cone of MUHAVURA	0203-06-
GAIA [TAVURVUR] (New Britain-SW Pac)	Stratovolc of RABAUL	0502-14=
GAIRIA, CALDERA DE (Canary Is)	Crater of FUERTEVENTURA	1803-05-
GAJAH (Java)	Crater of GUNTUR	0603-13=
GAJAMUNGKUR (Java)	Dome of KELUT	0603-28=
GAJOLESTEN (Sumatra)	Synonym of GAYOLESTEN	0601-06=
GAKARARANGA (Africa-C)	Cone of NYAMURAGIRA	0203-02=
GALAN, MONTE (Nicaragua)	Caldera of MOMOTOMBO	1404-09=
GALAPAGO, CERRO [LAS MAJADAS] (Guat	Cone of SANTA MARIA	1402-03=
GALAPAGOS RIFT (Pacific-E)	Submarine (None) Holocene	**1303-02-**
GALERA, LA (Colombia)	Synonym of GALERAS	1501-08=
GALERAS (Colombia)	Complx volc (26, 1993) Historical	**1501-08=**
GALION (W Indies)	Thermal Feature of PATATES, MORNE	1600-11=
GALLEGO (Solomon Is-SW Pac)	Volc field (None) Holocene?	**0505-062**
GALLO (Italy)	Vent of PANTELLERIA	0101-071
GALLO, CERRO (Costa Rica)	Cone of RINCON DE LA VIEJA	1405-02=
GALLO, CUDDIA DEL (Italy)	Dome of PANTELLERIA	0101-071
GALLOP (Africa-E)	Synonym of CENTRAL ISLAND	0202-01=
GALLOSEULO (New Britain-SW Pac)	Stratovolc of HARGY	0502-10=
GALLOWAY, MT. (Pacific-S)	Cone of ANTIPODES ISLAND	1304-01-
GALOENGGOENG (Java)	Synonym of GALUNGGUNG	0603-14=
GALUNGGUNG (Java)	Stratovolc (5, 1984) Historical	**0603-14=**
GALWAY'S MT. (W Indies)	Dome of SOUFRIERE HILLS	1600-05=
GALWAY'S SOUFRIERE (W Indies)	Thermal Feature of SOUFRIERE HILLS	1600-05=
GAM ITJI, LAKE (Halmahera-Indonesia)	Maar of IBU	0608-03=
GAMALAMA (Halmahera-Indonesia)	Stratovolcs (57, 1993) Historical	**0608-06=**
GAMBIER, MT. (Australia)	Maar of NEWER VOLCANICS PROV	0509-01-
GAMBOULI, FUMAROLE FIELD OF (Djibouti)	Synonym of BOINA	0201-14=
GAMCHEN (Kamchatka)	Complx volc (None) Holocene	**1000-21=**
GAMKANORA (Halmahera-Indonesia)	Synonym of GAMKONORA	0608-04=
GAMKONORA (Halmahera-Indonesia)	Stratovolc (12, 1987) Historical	**0608-04=**
GAMKUNORA (Halmahera-Indonesia)	Synonym of GAMKONORA	0608-04=
GAMMA (Russia-NE)	Cone of ALUCHIN GROUP	1001-01-
GAMMA HOT SPRINGS (US-Washington)	Thermal Feature of GLACIER PEAK	1201-02-
GAMMACANORE (Halmahera-Indonesia)	Synonym of GAMKONORA	0608-04=
GAMMAKUNOWA (Halmahera-Indonesia)	Synonym of GAMKONORA	0608-04=
GAMPING (Java)	Crater of LAWU	0603-26=
GAMTSCHEN (Kamchatka)	Synonym of GAMCHEN	1000-21=
GAN-ANA (Honshu-Japan)	Vent of FUJI	0803-03=
GANANIAS, MONTANA (Canary Is)	Cone of TENERIFE	1803-03-
GANAYA (Africa-C)	Cone of NYIRAGONGO	0203-03=
GANDO-SAN (Honshu-Japan)	Stratovolc of ZAO	0803-19=
GANJU-SAN (GANZYU-SAN) (Honshu-Japan	Synonym of IWATE	0803-24=
GAOLULE (Ethiopia)	Synonym of DALAFFILLA	0201-07=
GAOZHI (China-S)	Cone of TENGCHONG	0705-11-
GAR-ULI (Ethiopia)	Synonym of MA ALALTA	0201-111
GARACHICO, VOLCAN DE (Canary Is)	Cone of TENERIFE	1803-03-
GARAN-DAKE (Kyushu-Japan)	Dome of TSURUMI	0802-13=
GARAT, MT. (Vanuatu-SW Pacific)	Cone of GAUA	0507-02=
GARBES (Djibouti)	Fumarole fld (None) Pleistocene-Fumarolic	**0201-13=**
GARBUNA GROUP (New Britain-SW Pac)	Stratovolcs (None) Holocene	**0502-07=**
GARCA, PUIG DE LA (Spain)	Cone of OLOT VOLC FIELD	0100-03-
GARDA, MONTANA (Canary Is)	Cone of TENERIFE	1803-03-
GARDNERS ISLAND (Tonga-SW Pacific)	Synonym of FONUALEI	0403-10=
GARELOI (Aleutian Is)	Stratovolc (12, 1989) Historical	**1101-07-**
GARIBALDI HILL (W Indies)	Cone of SOUFRIERE HILLS	1600-05=
GARIBALDI LAKE (Canada)	Volc field (None) Holocene	**1200-19-**
GARIBALDI, MT. (Canada)	Stratovolc (1, -8055) Radiocarbon	**1200-20-**
GARIBOLDI (Ethiopia)	Synonym of KONE	0201-20-
GARNOT ISLAND (New Guinea-NE of)	Synonym of BLUP BLUP	0501-001
GAROU, MORNE (W Indies)	Synonym of SOUFRIERE ST. VINCENT	1600-15=
GAROVE (New Britain-SW Pac)	Stratovolc (None) Holocene	**0502-03=**
GARRINADA, VOLCA LA (Spain)	Cone of OLOT VOLC FIELD	0100-03-
GARU, MORNE (W Indies)	Synonym of SOUFRIERE ST. VINCENT	1600-15=
GARUA HARBOUR (New Britain-SW Pac)	Volc field (None) Holocene?	**0502-06=**
GASENYI (Africa-C)	Cone of NYAMURAGIRA	0203-02=
GASHOVU (Africa-C)	Cone of NYAMURAGIRA	0203-02=
GASPAR, PICO DO (Azores)	Dome of FURNAS	1802-10=
GAUA (Vanuatu-SW Pacific)	Stratovolc (13, 1982) Historical	**0507-02=**
GAURO (Italy)	Crater of CAMPI FLEGREI	0101-01=
GAVRILOVA (Kamchatka)	Stratovolc of KOLKHOZHNY	1000-221
GAYOLESTEN (Sumatra)	Fumarole fld (None) Fumarolic	**0601-06=**
GEBEL (Italian: of Arabic word for MT.) see proper name (e.g. TEER, GEBEL)		
GEDAMSA CALDERA (Ethiopia)	Caldera (None) Holocene	**0201-23-**
GEDE (Java)	Stratovolc (21, 1957) Historical	**0603-06=**
GEDE (Java)	Stratovolc of DANAU COMPLEX	0603-01=
GEDEH (Java)	Synonym of GEDE	0603-06=
GEDRITS, MT. (Kurile Is)	Dome of SMIRNOV	0900-031
GEGER HALANG (Java)	Pleistocene caldera of CEREME	0603-17=
GEIRFUGLADRANGUR (Iceland-SW)	Submarine vent of REYKJANESHRYGGUR	1701-01=
GEIRFUGLASKER (Iceland-S)	Cone of VESTMANNAEYJAR	1702-01=
GEISERS, GEYSERS see proper name (e.g. COPACOYA, GEISERS DE)		
GEITLANDSHRAUN (Iceland-SW)	Fissure vent of PRESTAHNUKUR	1701-07=
GEIZERNAYA (Kamchatka)	Dome of UZON	1000-17=
GELAMAN, GUNUNG (Java)	Cone of IJEN	0603-35=
GELFISER, MONTE (Italy)	Cone of PANTELLERIA	0101-071
GELI MUTU (GELI MOETOE) (Lesser Sunda	Synonym of KELIMUTU	0604-14=
GELIMOEN [GELIMUN] (Lesser Sunda Is)	Crater of LEREBOLENG	0604-20=
GELKHAMAR, MONTE (Italy)	Cone of PANTELLERIA	0101-071
GELLIBRAND, MT. (Australia)	Cone of NEWER VOLCANICS PROV	0509-01-
GEMELKERET (Vanuatu-SW Pacific)	Crater of SORETIMEAT	0507-01=
GEMELLARO, MONTE (Italy)	Cone of ETNA	0101-06=
GEMELOS, CERRO DE LOS (Galapagos)	Cone of FLOREANA	1503-10=
GEMOLONG (Java)	Crater of LAWU	0603-26=
GEMUNDEN (Germany)	Maar of WEST EIFEL VOLC FIELD	0100-01-
GEMURAH BADAS (Sumatra)	Thermal Feature of BESAR, GUNUNG	0601-25=
GEMURAH BUBUR (Sumatra)	Thermal Feature of BESAR, GUNUNG	0601-25=
GEMURAH ILAHAN (Sumatra)	Thermal Feature of BESAR, GUNUNG	0601-25=
GEMURAH KENININGAN (Sumatra)	Thermal Feature of BESAR, GUNUNG	0601-25=
GENDAL, KAWAH (Java)	Thermal Feature of MERAPI	0603-25=

NAME (Subregion)	Type (Eruption Total, Most Recent) Status Relation to NAMED VOLCANO	NUMBER
GENDINGWALUH, GUNUNG (Java)	Cone of IJEN	0603-35=
GENDOL, KAWAH (Java)	Thermal Feature of MERBABU	0603-24=
GENGI, VOLCA (Spain)	Cone of OLOT VOLC FIELD	0100-03-
GENOVESA (Galapagos)	Shield (None) Holocene	**1503-081**
GENTA-ANA (Hokkaido-Japan)	Crater of USU	0805-03=
GENTENG, GUNUNG (Java)	Cone of IJEN	0603-35=
GEODESISTOY (Kamchatka)	Shield (None) Holocene	**1000-38-**
GEORGIOS (Greece)	Dome of SANTORINI	0102-04=
GERALDINO (Galapagos)	Synonym of PINTA	1503-07=
GERENTE, LE (Indian O.-W)	Crater of FOURNAISE, PITON DE LA	0303-02=
GERMAV TEPE (Turkey)	Dome of NEMRUT DAGI	0103-02=
GESI (Java)	Crater of LAWU	0603-26=
GESTSSTADAVATN (Iceland-SW)	Maar of KRISUVIK	1701-03=
GETENG (Africa-E)	Crater of KOROSI	0202-054
GETLANDSHRAUN [GEITLANDSHRAUN]	Fissure vent of PRESTAHNUKUR	1701-07=
GEULIS (Java)	Crater of GUNTUR	0603-13=
GEUREUDONG, BOER NI (Sumatra)	Synonym of GEUREUDONG, BUR NI	0601-04=
GEUREUDONG, BUR NI (Sumatra)	Stratovolc (None) Fumarolic	**0601-04=**
GEYSER VALLEY (New Zealand)	Thermal Feature of MAROA	0401-061
GEYSERNAYA [GEYZERNAYA] (Kamchatka)	Pleistocene caldera of UZON	1000-17=
GEYSERS, THE (US-California)	Thermal Feature of CLEAR LAKE	1203-10-
GEYSERS, VALLEY OF (Kamchatka)	Thermal Feature of UZON	1000-17=
GEYSIR (Iceland-SW)	Thermal Feature of LANGJOKULL	1701-08=
GEYZERNAYA (Kamchatka)	Pleistocene caldera of UZON	1000-17=
GHAIE [TAVURVUR] (New Britain-SW Pac)	Stratovolc of RABAUL	0502-14=
GHARAT, MT. [MT. GARAT] (Vanuatu)	Cone of GAUA	0507-02=
GHENTOLUG (Vanuatu-SW Pacific)	Stratovolc of SORETIMEAT	0507-01=
GHOST (SW Pacific)	Crater of WALLIS ISLANDS	0404-05-
GIANO (Ethiopia)	Dome of TULLU MOJE	0201-25-
GIANT CRATER (US-California)	Crater of MEDICINE LAKE	1203-02-
GIARDINA, MONTE (Italy)	Dome of LIPARI	0101-041
GIBILLE, MONTI (Italy)	Dome of PANTELLERIA	0101-071
GIBRUS (New Zealand)	Crater of WHITE ISLAND	0401-04=
GIGANTE, CERRO (Guatemala)	Cone of MOYUTA	1402-13-
GIGIR AT STORKONUGJA (Iceland-SW)	Crater row of BRENNISTEINSFJOLL	1701-04=
GIGOLDUGJOSKA (Iceland-NE)	Crater row of ASKJA	1703-06=
GIGUAN (Aleutian Is)	Synonym of SEGUAM	1101-18-
GIL (Galapagos)	Synonym of SANTIAGO	1503-09=
GILBERT DOME (US-California)	Dome of LONG VALLEY	1203-14-
GILIBANTA (Lesser Sunda Is)	Submarine ? (None) Uncertain	**0604-051**
GILLETT NUNATAKS (Antarctica)	Cone of TONEY MOUNTAIN	1900-026
GILLIVER (New Zealand)	Former crater of WHITE ISLAND	0401-04=
GILOLO (Halmahera-Indonesia)	Synonym of JAILOLO	0608-051
GIMBALA, JEBEL (Africa-N)	Synonym of MARRA, JEBEL	0205-03-
GIMIE, MT. (W Indies)	Stratovolc of QUALIBOU	1600-14=
GIN-NUMA (Hokkaido-Japan)	Crater of USU	0805-03=
GINNA ALE (Ethiopia)	Synonym of ERTA ALE	0201-08=
GIPPS ISLAND (New Britain-SW Pac)	Synonym of NARAGE	0502-02=
GIRA-LE-KOMA (Djibouti)	Cone of ARDOUKOBA	0201-126
GIRDLESTONE (New Zealand)	Crater of RUAPEHU	0401-10=
GIREKOL (Turkey)	Unknown (None) Holocene	**0103-022**
GIRUNGO-NAMLAGIRA (Africa-C)	Synonym of NYAMURAGIRA	0203-02=
GISBORNE, MT. (Australia)	Cone of NEWER VOLCANICS PROV	0509-01-
GISI (Africa-C)	Cone of NYIRAGONGO	0203-03=
GITEBE (Africa-C)	Cone of NYAMURAGIRA	0203-02=
GITURO (Africa-C)	Cone of NYAMURAGIRA	0203-02=
GIUTURNA (Italy)	Crater of ALBANO, MONTE	0101-004
GIWU PEAK (New Britain-SW Pac)	Cone of LOLOBAU	0502-13=
GJASTYKKISBUNGA (Iceland-NE)	Shield of KRAFLA	1703-08=
GLACE, PITON (Indian O.-W)	Cone of FOURNAISE, PITON DE LA	0303-02=
GLACIER (Canada)	Dome of EDZIZA	1200-06-
GLACIER PEAK (US-Washington)	Stratovolc (6, 1700) Tephrochronology	**1201-02-**
GLACIER PIKES (Canada)	Dome of GARIBALDI, MT.	1200-20-
GLADKY (Kamchatka)	Dome of BEZYMIANNY	1000-25=
GLASS CREEK (US-California)	Dome of INYO CRATERS	1203-13-
GLASS MOUNTAIN (US-California)	Dome of LONG VALLEY	1203-14-
GLASS MOUNTAIN (US-California)	Dome of MEDICINE LAKE	1203-02-
GLENBERVIE [MARUATA] (New Zealand)	Cone of WHANGAREI	0401-011
GLI MOETOE (Lesser Sunda Is)	Synonym of KELIMUTU	0604-14=
GLINDO (Italy)	Vent of PANTELLERIA	0101-071
GLORIA, CERRO LA (El Salvador)	Dome of COATEPEQUE CALDERA	1403-041
GOAN (Africa-N)	Cone of BAYUDA VOLC FIELD	0205-06-
GOAT BUTTE (US-Washington)	Cone of ADAMS	1201-04-
GOAT ROCKS (US-Washington)	Former dome of ST. HELENS	1201-05-
GOAT'S PEAK (US-Oregon)	Dome of JEFFERSON	1202-02-
GOD, MOUNTAIN OF (Africa-E)	Synonym of LENGAI, OL DOINYO	0202-12=
GODAGI (New Guinea-NE of)	Cone of MANAM	0501-02=
GOEHA SONGGADIKIT (Lesser Sunda Is)	Crater of BATUR	0604-01=
GOENOENG (Sumatra)	Synonym of GEUREUDONG, BUR NI	0601-04=
GOENTOER (Java)	Synonym of GUNTUR	0603-13=
GOF (Kenyan term for HILL) see proper name (e.g. DAKARA, GOF)		
GOG (Vanuatu-SW Pacific)	Synonym of GAUA	0507-02=
GOK DAG (Turkey)	Dome of ERCIYES DAGI	0103-01=
GOLAN (Ethiopia)	Cone of MEGA BASALT FIELD	0201-33-
GOLAYA (Kamchatka)	Stratovolc (None) Holocene	**1000-061**
GOLDEN GATE (Indian O.-S)	Tuff cone of PRINCE EDWARD ISLAND	0304-07-
GOLDEN TROUT CREEK (US-Calif)	Volc field (1, -5550) Tephrochronology	**1203-17-**
GOLETS-TORNYI GROUP (Kurile Is)	Pyrocl cones (None) Holocene?	**0900-091**
GOLGAT (Armenia)	Cone of ARAGATS	0104-06-
GOLLU DAG (Turkey)	Lava dome (None) Holocene	**0103-003**
GOLOVNIN (Kurile Is)	Caldera (1, 1848) Historical	**0900-01=**
GOLYGINA (GOLYGINSKI) (Kamchatka)	Synonym of KHODUTKA	1000-053
GOLYI (Kamchatka)	Shield of VISOKIY	1000-063
GOMA, MONT (Africa-C)	Cone of NYIRAGONGO	0203-03=
GOMON-ISHI (Honshu-Japan)	Dome of TOWADA	0803-271
GOMULION [KOMOLION] (Africa-E)	Vent of KOROSI	0202-054
GOMWA BAY-SALAMO AREA (D'Entrecaste	Thermal Feature of DAWSON STRAIT GP	0503-06=
GONGEN-YAMA (Kyushu-Japan)	Dome of SAKURA-JIMA	0802-08=
GONGORA (Costa Rica)	Cone of OROSI	1405-01=
GONNARD, PUY (France)	Cone of CHAINE DES PUYS	0100-02-
GONO-IKE (Honshu-Japan)	Crater of ON-TAKE	0803-04=
GONZALES, ISLOTA (Chile-Is)	Tuff cone of SAN FELIX	1506-01=
GOOD HOPE ISLAND (Tonga-SW Pacific)	Synonym of NIUAFO'OU	0403-11=
GOODENOUGH ISLAND (D'Entrecasteaux)	Volc field (None) Holocene	**0503-041**
GOODHOPE BAY (Indian O.-S)	Tuff cone of MARION ISLAND	0304-08-
GOOSE CREEK KNOLL (US-Utah)	Cone of KOLOB	1207-02-
GOOSENEST (US-Oregon)	Shield (None) Holocene	**1202-161**
GORA CHETIEREK GLAVAIA (Alaska Pen.)	Synonym of FOURPEAKED	1102-26-
GORA EDGKOM (Alaska-SE)	Synonym of EDGECUMBE	1105-04-
GORDA (Nicaragua)	Cone of MADERA, LA	1404-13-
GORDO, CERRITO (Guatemala)	Cone of CUILAPA-BARBARENA	1402-111
GORDO, CERRO (Guatemala)	Cone of MOYUTA	1402-13-

NAME (Subregion)	Type (Eruption Total, Most Recent) Status Relation to NAMED VOLCANO	NUMBER
GORDO, CERRO (Mexico)	Cinder cone (None) Holocene	**1401-083**
GORDO DE JUTIAPA, CERRO (Guatemala)	Cone of FLORES, VOLCAN DE	1402-14-
GORDON (Alaska-E)	Cinder cones (None) Holocene	**1105-021**
GORDON'S HILL (Australia)	Cone of NEWER VOLCANICS PROV	0509-01-
GORDON'S HILL (Indian O.-S)	Cone of MARION ISLAND	0304-08-
GORELAIA SOPKA (Kamchatka)	Synonym of GORELY	1000-07=
GORELAIA SOPKA (Kamchatka)	Synonym of AVACHINSKY	1000-10=
GORELI (Aleutian Is)	Synonym of SEGUAM	1101-18-
GORELOI (Alaska-SW)	Synonym of REDOUBT	1103-03-
GORELY (Kamchatka)	Caldera (43, 1986) Historical	**1000-07=**
GORELY KHREBET (GORELY KUREBET)	Synonym of GORELY	1000-07=
GORIACHY PLIAZH (Kurile Is)	Thermal Feature of MENDELEEV	0900-02=
GORIASCHAIA SOPKA (Kurile Is)	Stratovolc (5, 1914) Historical	**0900-17B**
GORIASCHI DOL (Kamchatka)	Synonym of UZON	1000-17=
GORNA, MONTE (Italy)	Cone of ETNA	0101-06=
GORNOE PLATEAU (Kamchatka)	Dome of UZON	1000-17=
GORNOGO INSTITUTA (Kamchatka)	Synonym of GORNY INSTITUTE	1000-53-
GORNY INSTITUTE (Kamchatka)	Stratovolc (None) Holocene	**1000-53-**
GORODONG (Sumatra)	Synonym of GEUREUDONG, BUR NI	0601-04=
GOROPU (New Guinea)	Synonym of WAIOWA	0503-04=
GORSHKOV (Kamchatka)	Cone of USHKOVSKY	1000-261
GORU (New Britain-SW Pac)	Crater of MUNDUA	0502-021
GORUPU (New Guinea)	Synonym of WAIOWA	0503-04=
GORYACHY (Kamchatka)	Dome of BOLSHOI SEMIACHIK	1000-15=
GORYASHCHAYA SOPKA (Kurile Is)	Synonym of GORIASCHAIA SOPKA	0900-17B
GORYASHCHIY DOL (Kamchatka)	Synonym of UZON	1000-17=
GOSEI-DAKE (Honshu-Japan)	Synonym of ZAO	0803-19=
GOSHIKI-DAKE (Honshu-Japan)	Tuff cone of ZAO	0803-19=
GOSHIKI-NUMA (Honshu-Japan)	Crater of AZUMA	0803-18=
GOSHIKI-NUMA [OKAMA] (Honshu-Japan)	Crater of ZAO	0803-19=
GOSHIKIIWA (Honshu-Japan)	Stratovolc of TOWADA	0803-271
GOSHOGAKE (Honshu-Japan)	Thermal Feature of AKITA-YAKE-YAMA	0803-26=
GOSIKI-DAKE [GOSHIKI-DAKE] (Honshu)	Tuff cone of ZAO	0803-19=
GOSIKI-NUMA [GOSHIKI-NUMA] (Honshu)	Crater of AZUMA	0803-18=
GOSLING CONE (Alaska-W)	Cone of IMURUK LAKE	1104-02-
GOSYOGAKE [GOSHOGAKE] (Honshu)	Thermal Feature of AKITA-YAKE-YAMA	0803-26=
GOT OJAWA (Africa-E)	Cone of HOMA MOUNTAIN	0202-07=
GOT OLOO (Africa-E)	Cone of HOMA MOUNTAIN	0202-07=
GOTTERBERG (Africa-W)	Synonym of CAMEROON, MT.	0204-01=
GOUDBERG (Sumatra)	Synonym of SEULAWAH AGAM	0601-02=
GOUFFRE DUPUIS (W Indies)	Crater of SOUFRIERE GUADELOUPE	1600-06=
GOUFFRE TARISSAN (W Indies)	Crater of SOUFRIERE GUADELOUPE	1600-06=
GOULES, PUY DE (France)	Cone of CHAINE DES PUYS	0100-02-
GOULIE, PUY DE LA (France)	Cone of CHAINE DES PUYS	0100-02-
GOULVAIN [DOBU] (D'Entrecasteaux Is)	Stratovolc of DAWSON STRAIT GROUP	0503-06=
GOUTTES, PUY DE (France)	Cone of CHAINE DES PUYS	0100-02-
GOVERNMENT GARDENS (New Zealand)	Thermal Feature of ROTORUA	0401-042
GOZYACHAYA SOPKA (Kamchatka)	Dome of BARKHATNAYA SOPKA	1000-084
GRAAKULA (Iceland-W)	Cone of LJOSUFJOLL	1700-03=
GRACIOSA (Azores)	Stratovolc (None) Holocene	**1802-04=**
GRAENAVATN (Iceland-SW)	Maar of KRISUVIK	1701-03=
GRAF GOTZEN KRATER (Africa-C)	Synonym of NYIRAGONGO	0203-03=
GRAFELDUR (Iceland-SW)	Crater row of BRENNISTEINSFJOLL	1701-04=
GRAFELLSHRAUN (Iceland-S)	Crater row of VATNAFJOLL	1702-06=
GRAHAHRAUN (Iceland-NE)	Fissure vent of BARDARBUNGA	1703-03=
GRAHAM ISLAND [GUILA FERDINANDEO]	Submarine vent of CAMPI FLEGREI MAR	0101-07=
GRAHAM, MT. (Australia)	Cone of NEWER VOLCANICS PROV	0509-01-
GRAKOLLUHRAUN (Iceland-S)	Fissure vent of TORFAJOKULL	1702-05=
GRAMELUR (Iceland-SW)	Crater row of HENGILL	1701-05=
GRAN CANARIA (Canary Is)	Fissure vents (1, -1125) Radiocarbon	**1803-04-**
GRAN CONO (Italy)	Stratovolc of VESUVIUS	0101-02=
GRAN CRATERE (Italy)	Crater of VULCANO	0101-05=
GRANADA CONES (Nicaragua)	Cone of APOYO	1404-101
GRANADITO (Nicaragua)	Cone of APOYO	1404-101
GRANBY, MT. (W Indies)	Cone of ST. CATHERINE	1600-17=
GRAND BOTOUM (Africa-N)	Cone of TOUSSIDE, TARSO	0205-01=
GRAND DADOI (Africa-N)	Cone of TOUSSIDE, TARSO	0205-01=
GRAND ETANG (W Indies)	Crater of ST. CATHERINE	1600-17=
GRAND PAYS BRULE (Indian O.-W)	Synonym of FOURNAISE, PITON DE LA	0303-02=
GRAND SARCOUI (France)	Dome of CHAINE DES PUYS	0100-02-
GRAND SOUFRIERE HILLS (W Indies)	Cone of MICOTRIN	1600-10=
GRAND SOUFRIERE [VALLEY OF DESOLA	Thermal Feature of MICOTRIN	1600-10=
GRAND SUCHET, LE (France)	Cone of CHAINE DES PUYS	0100-02-
GRANDE, CERRO (El Salvador)	Dome of APASTEPEQUE FIELD	1403-071
GRANDE, CERRO (El Salvador)	Dome of COATEPEQUE CALDERA	1403-041
GRANDE, CERRO (Guatemala)	Dome of PACAYA	1402-11=
GRANDE, CERRO (Nicaragua)	Cone of PILAS, LAS	1404-08=
GRANDE DE GUIMAR, MONTANA (Canary Is	Cone of TENERIFE	1803-03-
GRANDE DECOUVERTE, LA (W Indies)	Stratovolc of SOUFRIERE GUADELOUPE	1600-06=
GRANDE MARMITE (Indian O.-S)	Crater of AMSTERDAM ISLAND	0304-04-
GRANDE, PICO (Azores)	Cone of UNNAMED	1802-081
GRANDE, PICO (Cape Verde Is)	Synonym of FOGO	1804-01=
GRANDE, SIERRA (US-New Mexico)	Shield of RATON-CLAYTON	1210-04-
GRANDE, VOLCAN (Galapagos)	Synonym of NEGRA, SIERRA	1503-05=
GRANDES PENTES (Indian O.-W)	Synonym of FOURNAISE, PITON DE LA	0303-02=
GRANDFATHER'S CHAIR (US-Nevada)	Maar of LUNAR CRATER FIELD	1206-02-
GRANDS BOIS, PITON DES (Indian O.-W)	Cone of FOURNAISE, PITON DE LA	0303-02=
GRANGE KOP, LA (Indian O.-S)	Tuff cone of MARION ISLAND	0304-08-
GRANTS MALPAIS (US-New Mexico)	Synonym of ZUNI-BANDERA	1210-02-
GRASLEYSUFJOLL (Iceland-S)	Crater row of VATNAFJOLL	1702-06=
GRASSY (US-Idaho)	Cone of CRATERS OF THE MOON	1204-02-
GRATI (Java)	Maar of TENGGER CALDERA	0603-31=
GRAY (Antarctica)	Cone of SEAL NUNATAKS GROUP	1900-05=
GRAY BUTTE (US-California)	Dome of SHASTA	1203-01-
GRAZINAS, PICO (Atlantic-S)	Dome of TRINDADE	1805-051
GREAT CRACK (Hawaiian Is)	Fissure vent of KILAUEA	1302-01-
GREAT CRATER (Iran)	Maar of QAL'EH HASAN ALI	0302-02-
GREAT DOMBERG HILL (Africa-E)	Cone of MERU	0202-16=
GREAT HILL (W Indies)	Dome of SABA	1600-01=
GREAT RIFT ZONE (US-Idaho)	Fissure vent of CRATERS OF THE MOON	1204-02-
GREAT SITCHIN (Aleutian Is)	Synonym of GREAT SITKIN	1101-12-
GREAT SITKIN (Aleutian Is)	Stratovolc (6, 1974) Historical	**1101-12-**
GREBEN' (Kamchatka)	Dome of UZON	1000-17=
GRECHISHKINA (Kamchatka)	Shield of SNEZHNIY	1000-66-
GREEN BUTTE (US-Oregon)	Cone of NEWBERRY VOLCANO	1202-11-
GREEN HILL (New Zealand)	Cone of AUCKLAND FIELD	0401-02=
GREEN ISLAND (W Indies)	Crater of ST. CATHERINE	1600-17=
GREEN LAKE PLUG (New Zealand)	Dome of OKATAINA	0401-05=
GREEN LAKE PUMICE CRATER (Kermadec	Crater of RAOUL ISLAND	0402-03=
GREENOCK, MT. (Australia)	Cone of NEWER VOLCANICS PROV	0509-01-
GREWINGK [NEW BOGOSLOF] (Aleutian Is)	Former dome of BOGOSLOF	1101-30-
GRIGGS (Alaska Peninsula)	Stratovolc (None) Holocene	**1102-19-**

NAME (Subregion)	Type (Eruption Total, Most Recent) Status Relation to NAMED VOLCANO	NUMBER
GRILLE, LA (Indian O.-W)	Shield (None) Holocene	**0303-001**
GRIMSNES (Iceland-SW)	Crater rows (9, -3500) Tephrochronology	**1701-06=**
GRIMSVOTN (Iceland-NE)	Caldera (44, 1983) Historical	**1703-01=**
GRIS (Chile-C)	Crater of CORDON CAULLE	1507-141
GROPPO (Ethiopia)	Stratovolc (None) Holocene	**0201-116**
GROS BENARD, LE (Indian O.-W)	Crater of FOURNAISE, PITON DE LA	0303-02=
GROS FOUGAS (W Indies)	Cone of SOUFRIERE GUADELOUPE	1600-06=
GROS HASAN DAG (Turkey)	Dome of HASAN DAGI	0103-002
GROS PITON (Indian O.-W)	Cone of FOURNAISE, PITON DE LA	0303-02=
GROS PITON (W Indies)	Dome of QUALIBOU	1600-14=
GROSSE SSEMJATSCHIK (Kamchatka)	Synonym of MALY SEMIACHIK	1000-14=
GROTTA DEL CANE (Italy)	Crater of CAMPI FLEGREI	0101-01=
GROUND CRATER (Hokkaido-Japan)	Crater of TOKACHI	0805-05=
GROUNDHOG (US-Calif)	Cone of GOLDEN TROUT CREEK	1203-17-
GROUSE HILL (US-Oregon)	Dome of CRATER LAKE	1202-16-
GROZNY (Kurile Is)	Dome of GROZNY GROUP	0900-07=
GROZNY GROUP (Kurile Is)	Complx vols (5, 1989) Historical	**0900-07=**
GUA WALED [GUA WALET] (Java)	Crater of CEREME	0603-17=
GUACAMAYAS, CERRO DE LAS (Guatemala	Cone of CHINGO VOLC FIELD	1402-15-
GUACAMAYERO, CERRO (El Salvador)	Dome of COATEPEQUE CALDERA	1403-041
GUACAMAYO (Ecuador)	Synonym of SUMACO	1502-04=
GUADALUPE, CERRO DE (El Salvador)	Cone of SAN VICENTE	1403-07=
GUADELUPE (Mexico)	Shield (None) Holocene	**1401-006**
GUAGUA PICHINCHA (Ecuador)	Stratovolc (25, 1993) Historical	**1502-02=**
GUAGUA-PUTINA (Peru)	Synonym of MISTI, EL	1504-01=
GUAGUA SUMACO (Ecuador)	Cone of SUMACO	1502-04=
GUAILLANE, CERRO (Chile-N)	Stratovolc of PUCHULDIZA	1505-031
GUALLATIRI (Chile-N)	Stratovolc (4, 1960) Historical	**1505-02=**
GUARARI (Costa Rica)	Cone of BARVA	1405-05=
GUARDA, CERRO EL (Mexico)	Cone of TENAYO GROUP	1401-081
GUARDIA, MONTE (Italy)	Dome of LIPARI	0101-041
GUARDIAN, CERRO (Costa Rica)	Cone of IRAZU	1405-06=
GUARDIOLA, LA (Italy)	Cone of ISCHIA	0101-03=
GUATISEA, MONTANA (Canary Is)	Cone of LANZAROTE	1803-06-
GUATOJON, CERRO (Guatemala)	Cone of CHIQUIMULA FIELD	1402-20-
GUATUSA, LOMA LA (Nicaragua)	Dome of MOMOTOMBO	1404-09=
GUAYABO (Costa Rica)	Caldera of MIRAVALLES	1405-03=
GUAYAQUES (Chile-N)	Lava domes (None) Holocene	**1505-093**
GUAYTA (Peru)	Synonym of HUAYNAPUTINA	1504-03=
GUAZAPA (El Salvador)	Stratovolc (None) Holocene	**1403-051**
GUBERABIA (Africa-C)	Cone of NYIRAGONGO	0203-03=
GUDUACK (Korea)	Cone of HALLA	1006-04-
GUEUIE RONDE, PITON (Indian O.-W)	Cone of FOURNAISE, PITON DE LA	0303-02=
GUFA (Ethiopia)	Volc field (None) Holocene	**0201-124**
GUGUAN (Mariana Is-C Pac)	Stratovolc (1, 1883) Historical	**0804-19=**
GUIANASON, MT (Philippines-C)	Thermal Feature of BILIRAN	0702-08=
GUIJA VOLC FIELD (El Salvador)	Synonym of SAN DIEGO	1403-012
GUILA FERDINANDEO (Italy)	Submarine vent of CAMPI FLEGREI MAR	0101-07=
GUILHERME MONIZ (Azores)	Stratovolc of TERCEIRA	1802-05=
GUIMAR, VOLCAN DE (Canary Is)	Cone of TENERIFE	1803-03-
GUINDOS, LOS (Chile-C)	Stratovolc of CARRAN-LOS VENADOS	1507-14=
GUISO DEL MONTE PANAMAO (Philippines)	Thermal Feature of BILIRAN	0702-08=
GULIZAR (Turkey)	Crater of TENDURUK DAGI	0103-03=
GULLBORG (Iceland-W)	Cone of LJOSUFJOLL	1700-03=
GULU (New Britain-SW Pac)	Cone of LANGILA	0502-01=
GUMANSAN (Philippines-C)	Dome of BILIRAN	0702-08=
GUMAWANG (Java)	Crater of LAWU	0603-26=
GUMURUH (Java)	Crater of GEDE	0603-06=
GUN CREEK (Canada)	Synonym of BRIDGE RIVER CONES	1200-17-
GUNGPO (China-S)	Synonym of TENGCHONG	0705-11-
GUNNARSHOLTSHRAUN (Iceland-S)	Fissure vent of HEKLA	1702-07=
GUNTUR (Java)	Crater of GALUNGGUNG	0603-14=
GUNTUR (Java)	Complx volc (24, 1847) Historical	**0603-13=**
GUNUNG (Indonesian for MT.) see proper name (e.g. TARUB, GUNUNG)		
GUNUNGAPI NORTH OF WETAR (Banda	Synonym of GUNUNGAPI WETAR	0605-03=
GUNUNGAPI (Lesser Sunda Is)	Synonym of LEWOTOLO	0604-23=
GUNUNGAPI (Lesser Sunda Is)	Synonym of AGUNG	0604-02=
GUNUNGAPI (Lesser Sunda Is)	Synonym of IYA	0604-11=
GUNUNGAPI BIMA (Lesser Sunda Is)	Synonym of SANGEANG API	0604-05=
GUNUNGAPI WETAR (Banda Sea)	Stratovolc (2, 1699) Historical	**0605-03=**
GURAUNDO-KAKO [GROUND CRATER]	Crater of TOKACHI	0805-05=
GUSHAN (China-E)	Cone of KELUO GROUP	1005-03-
GUYNEMER, MASSIF (Indian O.-S)	Stratovolc of KERGUELEN ISLANDS	0304-02=
GVENDARSELSGIGAR (Iceland-SW)	Crater row of KRISUVIK	1701-03=
GWANGUOA (Africa-C)	Cone of KARISIMBI	0203-04-
GYOJA-NO-IWAYA (Izu Is-Japan)	Stratovolc of OSHIMA	0804-01=
GYP (US-Arizona)	Crater of SUNSET CRATER	1209-02-

H

NAME (Subregion)	Type (Eruption Total, Most Recent) Status Relation to NAMED VOLCANO	NUMBER
HAABUNGA (Iceland-NE)	Cone of GRIMSVOTN	1703-01=
HAAHRAUN (Iceland-NE)	Fissure vent of BARDARBUNGA	1703-03=
HAAHRAUN (Iceland-S)	Fissure vent of HEKLA	1702-07=
HABUMINATO (Izu Is-Japan)	Crater of OSHIMA	0804-01=
HACCHO-RINDO (Honshu-Japan)	Vent of IZU-TOBU	0803-01=
HACHI-YAMA (Honshu-Japan)	Cone of IZU-TOBU	0803-01=
HACHIGAKUBO GROUP (Honshu-Japan)	Cone of IZU-TOBU	0803-01=
HACHIJO-FUJI (Izu Is-Japan)	Synonym of HACHIJO-JIMA	0804-05=
HACHIJO-JIMA (Izu Is-Japan)	Stratovolcs (7, 1606) Historical	**0804-05=**
HACHIJO-JIMA NISHI-YAMA (Izu Is-Japan)	Synonym of HACHIJO-JIMA	0804-05=
HACHIKUBO-YAMA (Honshu-Japan)	Cone of IZU-TOBU	0803-01=
HACHIMAKI-YAMA (Kyushu-Japan)	Dome of UNZEN	0802-10=
HACHIMAN-JIGOKU (Kyushu-Japan)	Thermal Feature of TSURUMI	0802-13=
HACHIMAN-YAMA (Izu Is-Japan)	Cone of HACHIJO-JIMA	0804-05=
HACHIMANTAI (Honshu-Japan)	Stratovolc (None) Holocene	**0803-25=**
HACHINOKUBO (Kyushu-Japan)	Vent of UNZEN	0802-10=
HACHIYAMA-HIGASHIOKU (Honshu-Japan)	Cone of IZU-TOBU	0803-01=
HACHIYO-TAKE (Honshu-Japan)	Synonym of FUJI	0803-03=
HACIENDA DE JARIDEO GROUP (Mexico)	Thermal Feature of MICHOACAN-GUANAJ	1401-06=
HACIENDA DEL AGUA FRIA GROUP	Thermal Feature of MICHOACAN-GUANAJ	1401-06=
HADJI, KAWAH [KAWAH HAJI] (Java)	Crater of KARANG	0603-02=
HADJI, KAWAH [KAWAH HAJI] (Java)	Crater of DANAU COMPLEX	0603-01=
HAGAFELL (Iceland-SW)	Shield of KRISUVIK	1701-03=
HAGAVIKURHRAUN (Iceland-SW)	Fissure vent of HENGILL	1701-05=
HAGONGUHRAUN (Iceland-NE)	Fissure vent of BARDARBUNGA	1703-03=
HAGOROMO-YAMA (Honshu-Japan)	Synonym of FUJI	0803-03=
HAGUE (Alaska Peninsula)	Stratovolc of EMMONS LAKE	1102-02-
HAID AL-ISI [JABAL EL-ESI] (Arabia-S)	Stratovolc of DHAMAR, HARRAS OF	0301-12-
HAID EL-'ARQUB (Arabia-S)	Cone of SAWAD, HARRA ES-	0301-16-
HAID EL-ESI [JABAL EL-ESI] (Arabia-S)	Stratovolc of DHAMAR, HARRAS OF	0301-12-
HAIMON-DAKE [KAIMON] (Kyushu-Japan)	Stratovolc of IBUSUKI VOLC FIELD	0802-07=
HAININI (New Zealand)	Dome of OKATAINA	0401-05=

NAME (Subregion)	Type (Eruption Total, Most Recent) Status Relation to NAMED VOLCANO	NUMBER
HAINOA CRATER (Hawaiian Is)	Crater of HUALALAI	1302-04-
HAIQUE (Chile-C)	Cone of ANTILLANCA GROUP	1507-153
HAIWAHINE, PUU (Hawaiian Is)	Cone of MAUNA KEA	1302-03-
HAJI, KAWAH (Java)	Crater of DANAU COMPLEX	0603-01=
HAJI, KAWAH (Java)	Crater of KARANG	0603-02=
HAKKA (Honshu-Japan)	Stratovolc of TOWADA	0803-271
HAKKEN-YAMA (Honshu-Japan)	Cone of FUJI	0803-03=
HAKKODA GROUP (Honshu-Japan)	Stratovolcs (None) Holocene	**0803-28=**
HAKKODA-ODAKE (Honshu-Japan)	Cone of HAKKODA GROUP	0803-28=
HAKONE (Honshu-Japan)	Complx volc (2, -0950) Radiocarbon	**0803-02=**
HAKU-SAN (Honshu-Japan)	Stratovolc (26, 1659) Historical	**0803-05=**
HAKUDAIRYUO (Honshu-Japan)	Cone of FUJI	0803-03=
HAKUEN (HAKUEN-ZAN) (Kurile Is)	Synonym of KARPINSKY GROUP	0900-35=
HAKUTO (China-E)	Synonym of BAITOUSHAN	1005-07-
HAKUUN-DAKE (Hokkaido-Japan)	Dome of DAISETSU	0805-06=
HALA- (Arabic for VOLCANIC CONE) see proper name (e.g. 'ASI, HALA-'L-)		
HALALII (Hawaiian Is)	Cone of HALEAKALA	1302-06-
HALEAKALA (Hawaiian Is)	Shield (11, 1790) Historical	**1302-06-**
HALEKAMAHINA (Hawaiian Is)	Cone of KILAUEA	1302-01-
HALEMAUMAU (Hawaiian Is)	Pit crater of KILAUEA	1302-01-
HALEPA (Greece)	Dome of MILOS	0102-03=
HALEYJABUNGA (Iceland-SW)	Shield of REYKJANES	1701-02=
HALF CONE (Alaska Peninsula)	Cone of ANIAKCHAK	1102-09-
HALF CONE (Indian O.-S)	Tuff cone of PRINCE EDWARD ISLAND	0304-07-
HALF CONE (US-Idaho)	Cone of CRATERS OF THE MOON	1204-02-
HALL BUTTE (US-California)	Cone of TUMBLE BUTTES	1203-06-
HALLA (Korea)	Shield (2, 1007) Historical	**1006-04-**
HALLMUNDARHRAUN (Iceland-SW)	Shield of LANGJOKULL	1701-08=
HALSAGIGIR (Iceland-NE)	Fissure vent of GRIMSVOTN	1703-01=
HALYKI (Greece)	Thermal Feature of MILOS	0102-03=
HAMARINN (Iceland-NE)	Stratovolc of LOKI-FOGRUFJOLL	1703-02=
HAMILTON, MT. (Australia)	Cone of NEWER VOLCANICS PROV	0509-01-
HAMMA AL-HAMDANI [JABAL EL-ESI]	Stratovolc of DHAMAR, HARRAS OF	0301-12-
HAMMAM EL-ZEBIB (Arabia-S)	Thermal Feature of DHAMAR, HARRAS	0301-12-
HAMMAN ALESSI, DJEBEL [JABAL EL-ESI]	Stratovolc of DHAMAR, HARRAS OF	0301-12-
HAMMAN DEMT, JABAL (Arabia-S)	Cone (None) Anthropology	**0301-13-**
HAMMAT ES-SA'TAR (Arabia-S)	Cone of DHAMAR, HARRAS OF	0301-12-
HAMNER BUTTE (US-Oregon)	Shield of DAVIS LAKE	1202-10-
HAMRAGARDARHRAUN (Iceland-S)	Fissure vent of EYJAFJOLL	1702-02=
HAMUGOMA (Africa-C)	Tuff cone of FORT PORTAL FIELD	0203-002
HANARE-YAMA (Honshu-Japan)	Dome of ASAMA	0803-11=
HANAUMA BAY (Hawaiian Is)	Tuff cone of KOOLAU	1302-07-
HANDO-IWA (Kyushu-Japan)	Vent of UNZEN	0802-10=
HANGAR (Kamchatka)	Stratovolc (1, -5040) Radiocarbon	**1000-272**
HANGELBERG (Germany)	Cone of WEST EIFEL VOLC FIELD	0100-01-
HANGING ROCK (Australia)	Dome of NEWER VOLCANICS PROV	0509-01-
HANJALE, GOF (Africa-E)	Maar of MARSABIT	0202-021
HANKOW REEF (New Guinea-NE of)	Synonym of YOMBA	0501-041
HANNAH, MT. (US-California)	Dome of CLEAR LAKE	1203-10-
HANS MEYER CRATER [MUNTANGO]	Pit crater of KARISIMBI	0203-04-
HANSA ISLAND (New Guinea-NE of)	Synonym of MANAM	0501-02=
HANTSONGOMA (Indian O.-W)	Crater of KARTHALA	0303-01=
HANUY GOL (Mongolia)	Synonym of KHANUY GOL	1003-02-
HAOFA (SW Pacific)	Tuff cone of WALLIS ISLANDS	0404-05-
HAOLDUHRAUN (Iceland-S)	Fissure vent of TORFAJOKULL	1702-05=
HAOLDUHRAUN (Iceland-SW)	Fissure vent of HOFSJOKULL	1701-09=
HAOTIANSI (China-E)	Cone of DATONG	1005-01-
HAPBERG [KAPBERG] (New Britain-SW Pac	Stratovolc of LOLO	0502-071
HARAI (Honshu-Japan)	Vent of IZU-TOBU	0803-01=
HARAKANDI (Africa-C)	Cone of NYAMURAGIRA	0203-02=
HARANGGAOL (Sumatra)	Caldera of TOBA	0601-09=
HARARO MANDA (Ethiopia)	Fissure vents (None) Holocene	**0201-115**
HARARU (Ethiopia)	Synonym of HARARO MANDA	0201-115
HARDIN BUTTE (US-California)	Cone of MEDICINE LAKE	1203-02-
HARDT-MAAR (Germany)	Maar of WEST EIFEL VOLC FIELD	0100-01-
HARGY (New Britain-SW Pac)	Stratovolc (2, 0950) Radiocarbon	**0502-10=**
HARIMKOTAN (Kurile Is)	Stratovolc (6, 1933) Historical	**0900-30=**
HARO MAJA (Ethiopia)	Tuff ring of BISHOFTU FIELD	0201-22-
HARO MAJA (Ethiopia)	Maar of BUTAJIRI-SILTI FIELD	0201-26-
HAROHARO (New Zealand)	Fissure vent of OKATAINA	0401-05=
HAROSU (Izu Is-Japan)	Synonym of BAYONNAISE ROCKS	0804-07=
HAROTSIATSIANOPORI (Kurile Is)	Synonym of RASSHUA	0900-22=
HAROUDJ (Africa-N)	Synonym of HARUJ	0205-00-
HARRA, HARRAS, HARRAT, HARRET (Arabic for LAVA FIELD) see proper name (e.g. ER-RAHA, HARRAT)		
HARUJ (Africa-N)	Scoria cones (None) Holocene	**0205-00-**
HARUMUKOTAN (Kurile Is)	Synonym of HARIMKOTAN	0900-30=
HARUNA (Honshu-Japan)	Stratovolc (3, 0550) Anthropology	**0803-122**
HARUNA-FUJI (Honshu-Japan)	Cone of HARUNA	0803-122
HARUTA-YAMA (Kyushu-Japan)	Dome of SAKURA-JIMA	0802-08=
HASAN DAGI (Turkey)	Stratovolc (1, -6200) Holocene	**0103-002**
HASAN DAGI (Turkey)	Cone of ERCIYES DAGI	0103-01=
HAT CREEK (US-California)	Fissure vent of POTATO BUTTE	1203-07-
HAT MOUNTAIN (US-Calif)	Cone of LASSEN VOLC CENTER	1203-08-
HATACHI-YAMA (Honshu-Japan)	Synonym of FUJI	0803-03=
HATCHOBARU (Kyushu-Japan)	Thermal Feature of KUJU GROUP	0802-12=
HATENJI (Africa-E)	Cone of NGOZI	0202-164
HATIMAKI-YAMA [HACHIMAKI-YAMA]	Dome of UNZEN	0802-10=
HATIMANTAI (Honshu-Japan)	Synonym of HACHIMANTAI	0803-25=
HATIZYO-HUZI (Izu Is-Japan)	Synonym of HACHIJO-JIMA	0804-05=
HATIZYO-ZIMA NISI-YAMA (Izu Is-Japan)	Synonym of HACHIJO-JIMA	0804-05=
HATTAB, JABAL [KAULET HATTAB] (Arabia)	Tuff cone of ARHAB, HARRA OF	0301-09-
HATTUR (Iceland-NE)	Fissure vent of BARDARBUNGA	1703-03=
HA'U EPA, MAUNGA (Pacific-C)	Cone of EASTER ISLAND	1303-08-
HAUG, CRATERE (Indian O.-W)	Crater of FOURNAISE, PITON DE LA	0303-02=
HAUGUR (Iceland-SW)	Crater row of REYKJANES	1701-02=
HAUHUNGATAHI (New Zealand)	Cone of RUAPEHU	0401-10=
HAUKADALUR (Iceland-SW)	Thermal Feature of LANGJOKULL	1701-08=
HAUT DONG NAI (SE Asia)	Volc field (None) Holocene?	**0705-04-**
HAUY, PITON (Indian O.-W)	Cone of FOURNAISE, PITON DE LA	0303-02=
HAVFUEN PEAK (Antarctica)	Cone of BRISTOL ISLAND	1900-08=
HAWSHUENSHAN [MAANSHAN] (China-S)	Cone of TENGCHONG	0705-11-
HAYES (Alaska-SW)	Stratovolc (3, 1200) Radiocarbon	**1103-05-**
HAYLAN, JABAL (Arabia-S)	Volc field (1, -1200) Anthropology	**0301-11-**
HAYLI GUB (Ethiopia)	Synonym of HAYLI GUBBI	0201-091
HAYLI GUBBI (Ethiopia)	Shield (None) Holocene	**0201-091**
HAYRICK BUTTE (US-Oregon)	Cone of WASHINGTON	1202-05-
HAZAM KHADRA', JABAL (Arabia-W)	Cone of ITHNAYN, HARRAT	0301-05=
HEARD (Indian O.-S)	Stratovolc (7, 1993) Historical	**0304-01=**
HEART LAKE (US-Wyoming)	Thermal Feature of YELLOWSTONE	1205-01-
HEART PEAKS (Canada)	Shield (None) Holocene	**1200-04-**
HEBERT (Indian O.-S)	Cone of AMSTERDAM ISLAND	0304-04-

NAME (Subregion)	Type (Eruption Total, Most Recent) Status Relation to NAMED VOLCANO	NUMBER
HEHU (Africa-C)	Cone of KARISIMBI	0203-04-
HEIDARSPORDUR (Iceland-NE)	Shield of KRAFLA	1703-08=
HEIDIN HA (Iceland-SW)	Shield of BRENNISTEINSFJOLL	1701-04=
HEIENLIGLAR [MARUMLIGLAR] (Vanuatu)	Crater of AMBRYM	0507-04=
HEIGUOTOU (China-W)	Cone of UNNAMED	1004-04-
HEIHEIAHULU (Hawaiian Is)	Shield of KILAUEA	1302-01-
HEIJI-DAKE (Kyushu-Japan)	Stratovolc of KUJU GROUP	0802-12=
HEIKONGSHAN (China-S)	Cone of TENGCHONG	0705-11-
HEIMAEY (Iceland-S)	Cone of VESTMANNAEYJAR	1702-01=
HEISHAN (China-E)	Cone of DATONG	1005-01-
HEISHAN (China-E)	Cone of KELUO GROUP	1005-03-
HEISHAN (China-S)	Cone of TENGCHONG	0705-11-
HEISHIBEIHU (China-W)	Cone of KUNLUN VOLC GROUP	1004-03-
HEIZI-DAKE [HEIJI-DAKE] (Kyushu-Japan)	Stratovolc of KUJU GROUP	0802-12=
HEJO, KAWAH (Java)	Thermal Feature of GALUNGGUNG	0603-14=
HEKLA (Iceland-S)	Stratovolc (46, 1991) Historical	**1702-07=**
HEKLUFELL (HEKLUFJALL) (Iceland-S)	Synonym of HEKLA	1702-07=
HEKLUGJA (Iceland-S)	Fissure vent of HEKLA	1702-07=
HELATOBA-TAROETOENG (Sumatra)	Synonym of HELATOBA-TARUTUNG	0601-10=
HELATOBA-TARUTUNG (Sumatra)	Fumarole fld (None) Fumarolic	**0601-10=**
HELECHOS, LOS (Canary Is)	Cone of LANZAROTE	1803-06-
HELEN, MT. (US-Calif)	Dome of LASSEN VOLC CENTER	1203-08-
HELENA (Africa-W)	Cone of CAMEROON, MT.	0204-01=
HELGADALSHRAUN (Iceland-SW)	Crater row of BRENNISTEINSFJOLL	1701-04=
HELGAFELL (Iceland-S)	Cone of VESTMANNAEYJAR	1702-01=
HELGAFELLSGIGIR (Iceland-SW)	Crater row of KRISUVIK	1701-03=
HELLISEY (Iceland-S)	Cone of VESTMANNAEYJAR	1702-01=
HELLISKVISLARHRAUN (Iceland-S)	Fissure vent of HEKLA	1702-07=
HELL'S GATE (New Zealand)	Thermal Feature of ROTORUA	0401-042
HELL'S HALF ACRE (US-Idaho)	Shield (1, -2150) Radiocarbon	**1204-04-**
HELMET PEAK (Canada)	Cone of MILBANKE SOUND GROUP	1200-12-
HELVITI [VITI] (Iceland-NE)	Maar of KRAFLA	1703-08=
HEMBE (Africa-C)	Cone of NYAMURAGIRA	0203-02=
HENEDURA, LA (Chile-C)	Crater of ANTUCO	1507-08=
HENEOWARA (Halmahera-Indonesia)	Crater of DUKONO	0608-01=
HENGILL (Iceland-SW)	Crater rows (8, 0090) Radiocarbon	**1701-05=**
HENGSTWEILER (Germany)	Maar of WEST EIFEL VOLC FIELD	0100-01-
HENRI RALLIER DU BATY, MONT (Indian O.	Cone of KERGUELEN ISLANDS	0304-02=
HENRIE KNOLLS (US-Utah)	Cone of MARKAGUNT PLATEAU	1207-04-
HENWOSHAN (China-E)	Cone of DATONG	1005-01-
HERAI-DAKE (Honshu-Japan)	Stratovolc of TOWADA	0803-271
HERALD ISLETS (Kermadec Is)	Crater of RAOUL ISLAND	0402-03=
HERBERT (Aleutian Is)	Stratovolc (None) Holocene	**1101-22-**
HERDISARVIKURHRAUN (Iceland-SW)	Shield of BRENNISTEINSFJOLL	1701-04=
HERDUBREIDARTAGLAGJOSKA (Iceland)	Crater of ASKJA	1703-06=
HERMOSO, VALLE (Costa Rica)	Cone of AGUAS ZARCAS GROUP	1405-035
HERRADURA (Mexico)	Cone of SANTA CATARINA RANGE	1401-082
HERRERA, CRATER (Mexico-Is)	Cone of BARCENA	1401-02=
HERTALE (Ethiopia)	Synonym of ERTA ALE	0201-08=
HERTALI (Ethiopia)	Fissure vent (None) Holocene	**0201-171**
HERTHA (Antarctica)	Cone of SEAL NUNATAKS GROUP	1900-05=
HERVIDEROS (Spanish for HOT SPRINGS)	see proper name (e.g. SAN JACINTO, HERVIDEROS DE)	
HERZ (Kamchatka)	Cone of USHKOVSKY	1000-261
HESTOLDUHRAUN (Iceland-S)	Fissure vent of HEKLA	1702-07=
HFEALIN (Kamchatka)	Synonym of ICHINSKY	1000-28=
HIBOK-HIBOK (Mindanao-Philippines)	Stratovolc (4, 1953) Historical	**0701-08=**
HIERRO (Canary Is)	Shield (2, 1793) Historical	**1803-02-**
HIGASHI-AZUMA (Honshu-Japan)	Cone of AZUMA	0803-18=
HIGASHI-DAITEN (Honshu-Japan)	Cone of AZUMA	0803-18=
HIGASHI-DAKE (Hokkaido-Japan)	Cone of AKAN	0805-07=
HIGASHI-HAKUUNZAN (Izu Is-Japan)	Cone of HACHIJO-JIMA	0804-05=
HIGASHI-IZU-OKI GROUP (Honshu-Japan)	Synonym of IZU-TOBU	0803-01=
HIGASHI-MARUYAMA (Hokkaido-Japan)	Dome of USU	0805-03=
HIGASHI-OIKE (Honshu-Japan)	Maar of IZU-TOBU	0803-01=
HIGASHI-ONSEN (Kyushu-Japan)	Thermal Feature of TSURUMI	0802-13=
HIGASHI-TSURUGI (Honshu-Japan)	Cone of FUJI	0803-03=
HIGASHI-USUZUKA (Honshu-Japan)	Cone of FUJI	0803-03=
HIGASHI-YAMA (Hokkaido-Japan)	Stratovolc of OSHIMA-OSHIMA	0805-01=
HIGASHI-YAMA (Izu Is-Japan)	Stratovolc of HACHIJO-JIMA	0804-05=
HIGASI-DAKE [HIGASHI-DAKE] (Hokkaido)	Cone of AKAN	0805-07=
HIGASI-YAMA [HIGASHI-YAMA] (Izu Is-Japan	Stratovolc of HACHIJO-JIMA	0804-05=
HIGATURU (New Guinea)	Synonym of LAMINGTON	0503-01=
HIGH HOLE CRATER (US-California)	Crater of MEDICINE LAKE	1203-02-
HIIAKA (Hawaiian Is)	Pit crater of KILAUEA	1302-01-
HIJANG (Java)	Synonym of IYANG-ARGAPURA	0603-33=
HIJIORI (Honshu-Japan)	Caldera (1, -8300) Radiocarbon	**0803-191**
HIJIRI-YU (Kyushu-Japan)	Thermal Feature of TSURUMI	0802-13=
HIJO DEL VOLCANO [SANTIAGUITO]	Dome of SANTA MARIA	1402-03=
HIKINOHIRA (Kyushu-Japan)	Dome of SAKURA-JIMA	0802-08=
HIKUBO (Izu Is-Japan)	Crater of OSHIMA	0804-01=
HIKUTEMOTU (Tonga-SW Pacific)	Cone of NIUAFO'OU	0403-11=
HIL, JABAL (Arabia-W)	Crater of KISHB, HARRAT	0301-071
HILAS, CERRO DE LAS (Guatemala)	Cone of MOYUTA	1402-13-
HILDARHRAUN (Iceland-SW)	Shield of HENGILL	1701-05=
HILL PIECE (Atlantic-S)	Tuff cone of TRISTAN DA CUNHA	1806-01=
HILLA ETHNAN (Arabia-W)	Synonym of ITHNAYN, HARRAT	0301-05=
HILLMAN PEAK (US-Oregon)	Stratovolc of CRATER LAKE	1202-16-
HIMAICAGAN [KASIBOI] (Philippines-C)	Cone of MAHAGNOA	0702-07=
HIMO (Africa-E)	Cone of KILIMANJARO	0202-15=
HINAMORI-DAKE (Kyushu-Japan)	Stratovolc of KIRISHIMA	0802-09=
HINEMOA POINT (New Zealand)	Dome of ROTORUA	0401-042
HINKELSMAAR (Germany)	Maar of WEST EIFEL VOLC FIELD	0100-01-
HINOKIZUKA (Honshu-Japan)	Cone of FUJI	0803-03=
HIPAUA (New Zealand)	Thermal Feature of TAUPO	0401-07=
HIPPERSBACH (Germany)	Tuff ring of WEST EIFEL VOLC FIELD	0100-01-
HIPPO BUTTE (US-California)	Cone of MEDICINE LAKE	1203-02-
HIRABE-YAMA (Izu Is-Japan)	Crater of MIYAKE-JIMA	0804-04=
HIRAKIKI-DAKE [KAIMON] (Kyushu-Japan)	Stratovolc of IBUSUKI VOLC FIELD	0802-07=
HIRASE (Kyushu-Japan)	Cone of SAKURA-JIMA	0802-08=
HIRATSUKA (Honshu-Japan)	Cone of FUJI	0803-03=
HIRO (Lesser Sunda Is)	Synonym of ILIWERUNG	0604-25=
HIRUP, KAWAH (Java)	Thermal Feature of SALAK	0603-05=
HISAGO-GATA (Hokkaido-Japan)	Crater of KOMAGA-TAKE	0805-02=
HITIM (Sumatra)	Stratovolc of KABA	0601-22=
HITOKAPPU VOLCANO GROUP (Kurile Is)	Synonym of BOGATYR RIDGE	0900-06-
HIUCHI (Honshu-Japan)	Stratovolc (None) Holocene	**0803-131**
HIUKAU, PUU (Hawaiian Is)	Cone of MAUNA KEA	1302-03-
HIVA HIVA, MAUNGA (Pacific-C)	Cone of EASTER ISLAND	1303-08-
HIWAISH ABU SIBA (Africa-N)	Cone of BAYUDA VOLC FIELD	0205-06-
HIYANG (Java)	Synonym of IYANG-ARGAPURA	0603-33=
HIYORI-YAMA (Hokkaido-Japan)	Dome of KUTTARA	0805-034
HIYOSHI-OKINOBA (Volcano Is-Japan)	Synonym of MINAMI-HIYOSHI	0804-131
HIYOSI-OKINOBA (Volcano Is-Japan)	Synonym of MINAMI-HIYOSHI	0804-131
HIZIORI (Honshu-Japan)	Synonym of HIJIORI	0803-191
HLASCAR (Chile-N)	Synonym of LASCAR	1505-10=
HLIDARGIGAR (Iceland-S)	Fissure vent of HEKLA	1702-07=
HLIDARHRAUN (Iceland-SW)	Shield of BRENNISTEINSFJOLL	1701-04=
HLIDARSEL [DALFJALL] (Iceland-NE)	Fissure vent of KRAFLA	1703-08=
HNAPPAFELLSJOKULL (Iceland-SE)	Synonym of ORAEFAJOKULL	1704-01=
HNAUSAGIGAROD (Iceland-NE)	Fissure vent of BARDARBUNGA	1703-03=
HNAUSAPOLLUR (Iceland-NE)	Crater of BARDARBUNGA	1703-03=
HOASHEN (Kamchatka)	Synonym of ICHINSKY	1000-28=
HOBICHA CALDERA (Ethiopia)	Caldera (None) Holocene?	**0201-293**
HOBLEY VOLCANO (Africa-E)	Synonym of OLKARIA	0202-09=
HOBSON, MT. (New Zealand)	Cone of AUCKLAND FIELD	0401-02=
HOCHAN [PECHAN] (China-W)	Cone of TIANSHAN VOLC GROUP	1004-02-
HOCHSETTER (Atl-N-Jan Mayen)	Cone of JAN MAYEN	1706-01=
HODDER'S VOLCANO (W Indies)	(None) Not a Volcano	1600-13=
HODGSON NUNATAK (Antarctica)	Cone of HUDSON MOUNTAINS	1900-028
HODO (Korea)	Dome of HALLA	1006-04-
HODSON (Antarctica)	Stratovolc (None) Holocene	**1900-11=**
HOEDBERG (Indian O.-S)	Cone of PRINCE EDWARD ISLAND	0304-07-
HOEFDHAJOKULL (Iceland-S)	Synonym of KATLA	1702-03=
HOEI CRATERS (Honshu-Japan)	Crater of FUJI	0803-03=
HOELOEBELOE (Sumatra)	Synonym of HULUBELU	0601-28=
HOFDAHRAUN (Iceland-S)	Fissure vent of EYJAFJOLL	1702-02=
HOFDARHRAUN (Iceland-SW)	Crater row of KRISUVIK	1701-03=
HOFENFELS (Germany)	Maar of WEST EIFEL VOLC FIELD	0100-01-
HOFFMAN, MT. (US-California)	Dome of MEDICINE LAKE	1203-02-
HOFSFJALL (Iceland-SE)	Cone of ORAEFAJOKULL	1704-01=
HOFSJOKULL (Iceland-SW)	Subglacial (None) Holocene	**1701-09=**
HOG KILLER (Philippines-C)	Thermal Feature of CANLAON	0702-02=
HOHEN LIST (Germany)	Maar of WEST EIFEL VOLC FIELD	0100-01-
HOHENLOHOE (Atl-N-Jan Mayen)	Cone of JAN MAYEN	1706-01=
HOHNEL ISLAND (Africa-E)	Synonym of SOUTH ISLAND	0202-02=
HOHONU, LUA (Hawaiian Is)	Pit crater of MAUNA LOA	1302-02=
HOKIBARA-HIGASHI (Honshu-Japan)	Maar of IZU-TOBU	0803-01=
HOKKAIDO-KOMAGATAKE (Hokkaido-Japan	Synonym of KOMAGA-TAKE	0805-02=
HOKUTIN-DAKE [HOKUCHIN-DAKE]	Dome of DAISETSU	0805-06=
HOLAHOLAR (Iceland-W)	Cone of SNAEFELLSJOKULL	1700-01=
HOLANDESA (Chile-C)	Crater of LONQUIMAY	1507-10=
HOLANDESA, VOLCAN LA (Chile-C)	Cone of TOLGUACA	1507-092
HOLANTINDUR (Iceland-W)	Cone of SNAEFELLSJOKULL	1700-01=
HOLLOWBACK, MT. (Australia)	Cone of NEWER VOLCANICS PROV	0509-01-
HOLMSHRAUN (Iceland-SW)	Crater row of BRENNISTEINSFJOLL	1701-04=
HOLOTEPEC (Mexico)	Volc field (2, -6490) Radiocarbon	**1401-07-**
HOLSELDAR (Iceland-NE)	Crater row of KRAFLA	1703-08=
HOLTE CREEK (Canada)	Cone of SATAH MOUNTAIN	1200-13-
HOLUHRAUN (Iceland-NE)	Crater row of ASKJA	1703-06=
HOLZMAAR (Germany)	Maar of WEST EIFEL VOLC FIELD	0100-01-
HOMA MOUNTAIN (Africa-E)	Complx volc (None) Holocene	**0202-07=**
HOMBRE MUERTO, MONTANA DEL	Cone of HIERRO	1803-02-
HOME REEF (Tonga-SW Pacific)	Submarine (2, 1984) Historical	**0403-08=**
HOME VALLEY KNOLL (US-Utah)	Cone of KOLOB	1207-02-
HONDO, CALDERON (Canary Is)	Crater of FUERTEVENTURA	1803-05-
HONGGEERTU (China-E)	Cinder cones (None) Holocene	**1005-02-**
HONOKAHUA (Hawaiian Is)	Cone of HALEAKALA	1302-06-
HONOR, MT. (Halmahera-Indonesia)	Cone of TODOKO-RANU	0608-05=
HONTANIGAWA-SHIRYU (Honshu-Japan)	Vent of IZU-TOBU	0803-01=
HONTSUKA (Kyushu-Japan)	Cone of ASO	0802-11=
HOOD (US-Oregon)	Stratovolc (9, 1866) Historical	**1202-01-**
HOODOO BUTTE (US-Oregon)	Cone of WASHINGTON	1202-05-
HOODOO MOUNTAIN (Canada)	Subglacial (None) Holocene	**1200-08-**
HOOKOMO, PUU (Hawaiian Is)	Cone of MAUNA KEA	1302-03-
HOOPER CRAGS (Antarctica)	Cone of ROYAL SOCIETY RANGE	1900-021
HOOPERS SHOULDER (Antarctica)	Cone of EREBUS	1900-02=
HOPUA (New Zealand)	Tuff ring of AUCKLAND FIELD	0401-02=
HORA ARSEDI HAYK (Ethiopia)	Tuff ring of BISHOFTU FIELD	0201-22-
HORARO HAYK (Ethiopia)	Tuff ring of BISHOFTU FIELD	0201-22-
HORCONES, CERRO DE (Guatemala)	Cone of SUCHITAN VOLC FIELD	1402-17-
HORNILLAS, LAS (Costa Rica)	Thermal Feature of MIRAVALLES	1405-03=
HORNITOS, LOS (Chile-C)	Cinder cones (None) Holocene	**1507-061**
HORNOPIREN, VOLCAN (Chile-S)	Stratovolc (None) Holocene?	**1508-023**
HOROKA (Japan)	Thermal Feature of NIPESOTSU-UPEPES	0805-061
HOROMATANGI REEF (New Zealand)	Vent of TAUPO	0401-07=
HOROSSADAL [HROSSADALIUR] (Iceland)	Crater row of KRAFLA	1703-08=
HORQUETA, CERRO (Peru)	Cone of CHACHANI, NEVADO	1504-005
HORSE BUTTE (US-Oregon)	Cone of NEWBERRY VOLCANO	1202-11-
HORSESHOE CONE (US-Oregon)	Cone of JEFFERSON	1202-02-
HORSESHOE CRATER (US-New Mexico)	Cone of RATON-CLAYTON	1210-04-
HOSH ED DALAN (Africa-N)	Crater of BAYUDA VOLC FIELD	0205-06-
HOSH ES SIDDIG (Africa-N)	Crater of BAYUDA VOLC FIELD	0205-06-
HOSH UMM ARAYSH, JEBEL (Africa-N)	Cone of BAYUDA VOLC FIELD	0205-06-
HOSYO-ZAN [HOSHO-ZAN] (Kyushu-Japan)	Dome of KUJU GROUP	0802-12=
HOT CREEK (US-California)	Thermal Feature of LONG VALLEY	1203-14-
HOT LAGOON (Solomon Is-SW Pac)	Thermal Feature of SIMBO	0505-05=
HOT SPRINGS BAY (Aleutian Is)	Thermal Feature of AKUTAN	1101-32-
HOT SPRINGS CONE (Aleutian Is)	Thermal Feature of OKMOK	1101-29-
HOTCHEOU (China-W)	Synonym of TURFAN	1004-01-
HOTHAM [GUILA FERDINANDEO] (Italy)	Submarine vent of CAMPI FLEGREI MAR	0101-07=
HOTTA (Kyushu-Japan)	Thermal Feature of TSURUMI	0802-13=
HOU, LUA (Hawaiian Is)	Pit crater of MAUNA LOA	1302-02=
HOYA DE FILEBA (Canary Is)	Crater of HIERRO	1803-02-
HOYA, LA (Nicaragua)	Crater of SAN CRISTOBAL	1404-02=
HOYADA DE LOS GEISERS DEL TATIO	Synonym of TATIO	1505-08=
HOYADA, LA (Nicaragua)	Crater of SAN CRISTOBAL	1404-02=
HOYBERG (Atl-N-Jan Mayen)	Cone of JAN MAYEN	1706-01=
HOYO, CERRO EL (Honduras)	Cone of YOJOA, LAKE	1403-15-
HOYO DE CIBOLA (US-New Mexico)	Vent of ZUNI-BANDERA	1210-02-
HOYO DE CUAJUSTE (El Salvador)	Crater of VERDE, LAGUNA	1403-01=
HOYO, EL (Nicaragua)	Synonym of PILAS, LAS	1404-08=
HOYO EL HUANILLO (Mexico)	Cone of MICHOACAN-GUANAJUATO	1401-06=
HOYO, LAGUNA DE (Guatemala)	Maar of SUCHITAN VOLC FIELD	1402-17-
HOYO NEGRO (Canary Is)	Crater of LA PALMA	1803-01-
HRAFNSHILDARGIGIR (Iceland-SW)	Crater row of KRISUVIK	1701-03=
HRAFTINNUHRAUN (Iceland-S)	Crater row of TORFAJOKULL	1702-05=
HRAFTINNUSKER (Iceland-S)	Dome of TORFAJOKULL	1702-05=
HRAUNBUNGA (Iceland-NE)	Shield of KRAFLA	1703-08=
HRAUNGIGUR (Iceland-S)	Fissure vent of HEKLA	1702-07=
HRAUNHALSHRAUN (Iceland-S)	Crater row of VATNAFJOLL	1702-06=
HRAUNHOLL (Iceland-SW)	Crater row of KRISUVIK	1701-03=
HRAUNSELS-VATNSFELL (Iceland-SW)	Shield of KRISUVIK	1701-03=
HREIDHUR (Iceland-SW)	Crater row of REYKJANES	1701-02=
HROLFSVIKURHRAUN (Iceland-SW)	Shield of REYKJANES	1701-02=

NAME (Subregion)	Type (Eruption Total, Most Recent) Status / Relation to NAMED VOLCANO	NUMBER
HROSSABORG (Iceland-NE)	Tuff ring of ASKJA	1703-06=
HROSSAGIGAR [HROSSADALIUR] (Iceland	Crater row of KRAFLA	1703-08=
HRUTAGJARDYNGJA (Iceland-SW)	Shield of KRISUVIK	1701-03=
HRUTSHALSAR (Iceland-NE)	Fissure vent of ASKJA	1703-06=
HSI-CHIAO-TE-PU-SHAN [XIJIAODEBUSHA	Cone of WUDALIANCHI	1005-04-
HSI-HENG-TAO-SHAN [XIHENGDAOSHAN]	Cone of LONGGANG GROUP	1005-06-
HSI-PAI-TZU-LUNG-WAN [XIBAIZILONGWA	Crater of LONGGANG GROUP	1005-06-
HSIAO-I-SHAN [XIAOYISHAN] (China-E)	Cone of LONGGANG GROUP	1005-06-
HSIAO-KU-SHAN [XIAOKUSHAN] (China-E)	Cone of LONGGANG GROUP	1005-06-
HSIAO-LUNG-WAN [XIAOLONGWAN] (China	Crater of LONGGANG GROUP	1005-06-
HSIAO-WENG-CHUAN [XIAOWENGJUAN]	Cone of LONGGANG GROUP	1005-06-
HSIAO-YEN-CHIH-FENG [XIAOYANZHIFEN	Cone of BAITOUSHAN	1005-07-
HSING-AN-NAN-SHAN [XINGANNANSHAN]	Cone of LONGGANG GROUP	1005-06-
HUACHANGUERAN, CERRO DE (Mexico)	Cone of MICHOACAN-GUANAJUATO	1401-06=
HUALALAI (Hawaiian Is)	Shield (21, 1801) Historical	**1302-04-**
HUALALAI, PUU (Hawaiian Is)	Synonym of HUALALAI	1302-04-
HUALCA HUALCA (Peru)	Stratovolc of SABANCAYA	1504-003
HUALLATIRE (HUALLATIRI) (Chile-N)	Synonym of GUALLATIRI	1505-02=
HUANGYANGLING (China-W)	Cone of KUNLUN VOLC GROUP	1004-03-
HUANQUIHUE GROUP (Argentina)	Pyrocl cone (None) Holocene	**1507-123**
HUAPO (China-S)	Cone of TENGCHONG	0705-11-
HUAYNAPUTINA (Peru)	Stratovolc ? (2, 1667) Historical	**1504-03=**
HUAYPUNA [AMPATO] (Peru)	Stratovolc of SABANCAYA	1504-003
HUBERT, PITON (Indian O.-W)	Cone of FOURNAISE, PITON DE LA	0303-02=
HUCKACK (Korea)	Cone of HALLA	1006-04-
HUDO-IKE [FUDO-IKE] (Kyushu-Japan)	Crater of KIRISHIMA	0802-09=
HUDSON, CERRO (Chile-S)	Stratovolc (6, 1991) Historical	**1508-057**
HUDSON MOUNTAINS (Antarctica)	Stratovolcs (None) Uncertain	**1900-028**
HUECHULEPUN, VOLCAN (Chile-C)	Cone of SOLLIPULLI	1507-111
HUECO, CERRO (US-New Mexico)	Shield of ZUNI-BANDERA	1210-02-
HUEHUEL, VOLCAN (Mexico)	Cone of TENAYO GROUP	1401-081
HUEHUELCON, VOLCAN (Mexico)	Cone of TENAYO GROUP	1401-081
HUELEMOLLE (Chile-C)	Cinder cones (1, -5050) Tephrochronology	**1507-114**
HUENUAUCA (Chile-S)	Synonym of OSORNO	1508-01=
HUEQUE (HUEQUEN) (Chile-S)	Synonym of HUEQUI	1508-03=
HUEQUI (Chile-S)	Stratovolc (5, 1920) Historical	**1508-03=**
HUGEN-DAKE [FUGEN-DAKE] (Kyushu)	Stratovolc of UNZEN	0802-10=
HUGOLIN, CRATERES (Indian O.-W)	Crater of FOURNAISE, PITON DE LA	0303-02=
HUIHUILANCO, LOMAS (Mexico)	Cone of TENAYO GROUP	1401-081
HUILA (Colombia)	Stratovolc (1, 1555) Historical	**1501-05=**
HUILILCO (Chile-C)	Cone of QUETRUPILLAN	1507-121
HUILOTE (Mexico)	Cone of CHICHINAUTZIN	1401-08=
HUILOTITO (Mexico)	Cone of CHICHINAUTZIN	1401-08=
HUIPILO, VOLCAN (Mexico)	Cone of TENAYO GROUP	1401-081
HUITAN, CERRO (Guatemala)	Dome of ALMOLONGA	1402-04=
HUIZTOMAYO, CERRO (Mexico)	Cone of TENAYO GROUP	1401-081
HUKENO-YU [FUKENO-YU] (Honshu-Japan)	Thermal Feature of HACHIMANTAI	0803-25=
HUKUTOKU-OKANOBA (Volcano Is-Japan)	Synonym of SHIN-IWO-JIMA	0804-13=
HUKUZIN-KAIZAN (Volcano Is-Japan)	Synonym of FUKUJIN	0804-133
HUKUZIN-OKANOBA (Volcano Is-Japan)	Synonym of FUKUJIN	0804-133
HULE, LAGUNA [BOSQUE ALEGRE] (Costa	Maar of POAS	1405-04=
HULU (New Britain-SW Pac)	Dome of LOLOBAU	0502-13=
HULUBELU (Sumatra)	Caldera (None) Fumarolic	**0601-28=**
HULUHULU, PUU (Hawaiian Is)	Cone of KILAUEA	1302-01-
HULULONGWAN (China-E)	Crater of LONGGANG GROUP	1005-06-
HULUMAJANG (Sumatra)	Synonym of HUTAPANJANG	0601-171
HUMARATA (Chile-N)	Stratovolc of ACOTANGO	1505-017
HUMILLADEROS, MONTANA DE LOS	Cone of HIERRO	1803-02-
HUMINGBIRD FUMAROLE (US-New Mexico)	Thermal Feature of VALLES CALDERA	1210-03-
HUNAHPU (Guatemala)	Synonym of AGUA	1402-10=
HUNAHPU (Guatemala)	Synonym of FUEGO	1402-09=
HUNIHO (New Ireland-SW Pac)	Stratovolc of LIHIR	0504-01=
HUNTER ISLAND (SW Pacific)	Stratovolc (4, 1903) Historical	**0508-02=**
HUOSHAN [HEISHAN] (China-S)	Cone of TENGCHONG	0705-11-
HUOSHAOSHAN (China-E)	Cone of WUDALIANCHI	1005-04-
HUPPUSI-DAKE [FUPPUSHI-DAKE] (Hokka	Stratovolc of SHIKOTSU	0805-04=
HUPPUSI [FUPPUSHI] (Hokkaido-Japan)	Stratovolc of AKAN	0805-07=
HURANO-DAKE (Hokkaido-Japan)	Stratovolc of TOKACHI	0805-05=
HURATA, TAVANI (Vanuatu-SW Pacific)	Cone of KUWAE	0507-07=
HUREBETU [FUREBETSU] (Hokkaido-Japan)	Stratovolc of AKAN	0805-07=
HURU-DAKE [FURU-DAKE] (Ryukyu Is)	Cone of KUCHINOERABU-JIMA	0802-05=
HURUS, JABAL AL (Arabia-W)	Cone of RAHAT, HARRAT	0301-07=
HUTAPANJANG (Sumatra)	Stratovolc (None) Holocene	**0601-171**
HUTAYM, HARRAT (Arabia-W)	Synonym of ITHNAYN, HARRAT	0301-05=
HUZI (Honshu-Japan)	Synonym of FUJI	0803-03=
HVANNSTOD (Iceland-NE)	Crater row of KRAFLA	1703-08=
HVERADALAHRAUN (Iceland-SW)	Crater row of HENGILL	1701-05=
HVERADALUR (Iceland-NE)	Thermal Feature of KVERKFJOLL	1703-05=
HVERAGERDI (Iceland-SW)	Thermal Feature of HENGILL	1701-05=
HVERAGIL (Iceland-NE)	Crater of KRAFLA	1703-08=
HVERFJALL (Iceland-NE)	Tuff ring of KRAFLA	1703-08=
HWEIAIN (Kamchatka)	Synonym of ICHINSKY	1000-28=
HYALO RIDGE (Canada)	Tuya of WELLS GRAY-CLEARWATER	1200-15-
HYDEWELL, MT. (Australia)	Shield of NEWER VOLCANICS PROV	0509-01-
HYDROGRAPHERS RANGE (New Guinea)	Stratovolc (None) Holocene	**0503-011**
HYOGOWAN (Izu Is-Japan)	Crater of TORI-SHIMA	0804-09=
HYOTAN-YAMA (Izu Is-Japan)	Cone of MIYAKE-JIMA	0804-04=
HYUUGA-DAKE (Kyushu-Japan)	Dome of TSURUMI	0802-13=

I

NAME (Subregion)	Type (Eruption Total, Most Recent) Status / Relation to NAMED VOLCANO	NUMBER
IAHU (IAHUE, IAHUL) (Vanuatu-SW Pacific)	Synonym of YASUR	0507-10=
IAMELELE (D'Entrecasteaux Is)	Lava domes (None) Holocene	**0503-05=**
IASUR (Vanuatu-SW Pacific)	Synonym of YASUR	0507-10=
IBAYL, JABAL (Arabia-W)	Dome of KHAYBAR, HARRAT	0301-06=
IBEX MOUNTAIN CONE (Canada)	Cone of ALLIGATOR LAKE	1200-02-
IBI [GALLOSEULO] (New Britain-SW Pac)	Stratovolc of HARGY	0502-10=
IBOE (Halmahera-Indonesia)	Synonym of IBU	0608-03=
IBU (Halmahera-Indonesia)	Stratovolc (1, 1911) Historical	**0608-03=**
IBUNGU HILLS (Africa-E)	Cone of KIEYO	0202-17=
IBUSUKI VOLC FIELD (Kyushu-Japan)	Calderas (23, 0885) Historical	**0802-07=**
ICE PEAK (Canada)	Stratovolc of EDZIZA	1200-06-
ICE SPRING (US-Utah)	Crater of BLACK ROCK DESERT	1207-05-
ICEFALL (Canada)	Cone of EDZIZA	1200-06-
ICHA (Kamchatka)	Synonym of ICHINSKY	1000-28=
ICHINO-IKE (Honshu-Japan)	Crater of NORIKURA	0803-06=
ICHINO-IKE (Honshu-Japan)	Crater of ON-TAKE	0803-04=
ICHINOMEGATA (Honshu-Japan)	Maar of MEGATA	0803-262
ICHINSKY (Kamchatka)	Stratovolc (None) Holocene	**1000-28=**
IDA RIDGE (Canada)	Cone of WELLS GRAY-CLEARWATER	1200-15-
IDAK, MT. (Aleutian Is)	Cone of OKMOK	1101-29-
IDAMDEHE (Halmahera-Indonesia)	Caldera of JAILOLO	0608-051
IDJEN, KAWAH (Java)	Synonym of IJEN	0603-35=
IDO-DAKE (Honshu-Japan)	Cone of HAKKODA GROUP	0803-28=
IDUP, KAWAH (Java)	Thermal Feature of SALAK	0603-05=
IDWA, JEBEL (Africa-N)	Cone of MARRA, JEBEL	0205-03-
IEGATA-YAMA (Honshu-Japan)	Cone of AZUMA	0803-18=
IETTUNUP (Kamchatka)	Shields (None) Holocene	**1000-71-**
IFAGAO (Luzon-Philippines)	Thermal Feature of POCDOL MOUNTAIN	0703-02=
IFWOKA (Africa-E)	Cone of NGOZI	0202-164
IGATONO-YAMA (Honshu-Japan)	Cone of FUJI	0803-03=
IGEK (Alaska Peninsula)	Synonym of VENIAMINOF	1102-07-
IGIR BINEM [BINEM] (Java)	Cone of DIENG VOLC COMPLEX	0603-20=
IGLA MOUNTAIN (Kurile Is)	Stratovolc of GORIASCHAIA SOPKA	0900-17B
IGOREVSKY VOLCANO (Kamchatka)	Synonym of DZENZURSKY	1000-11=
IGOREWSKIY (Kamchatka)	Synonym of DZENZURSKY	1000-11=
IGUANERO, CERRO (Guatemala)	Cone of IXTEPEQUE, VOLCAN	1402-18-
IGWISI HILLS (Africa-E)	Tuff cones (None) Holocene	**0202-161**
IHUMATAO [MAUNGATAKETAKE] (New Zeal	Cone of AUCKLAND FIELD	0401-02=
IILEWA (Hawaiian Is)	Cone of KILAUEA	1302-01-
IIMORI-YAMA (Kyushu-Japan)	Stratovolc of KIRISHIMA	0802-09=
IIUSU (Kurile Is)	Synonym of BARANSKY	0900-08=
IIZUNA (Honshu-Japan)	Stratovolc (None) Holocene	**0803-102**
IJA (Lesser Sunda Is)	Synonym of IYA	0604-11=
IJANG-ARGAPURA (Java)	Synonym of IYANG-ARGAPURA	0603-33=
IJEN (Java)	Stratovolcs (6, 1993) Historical	**0603-35=**
IJEN, KAWAH (Java)	Synonym of IJEN	0603-35=
IKAPO (Africa-E)	Maar of KIEYO	0202-17=
IKARMA (Kurile Is)	Synonym of EKARMA	0900-27=
IKATHIWIK CRATER (Alaska-W)	Cone of NUNIVAK ISLAND	1104-06-
IKEDA-HIGASHI (Honshu-Japan)	Cone of IZU-TOBU	0803-01=
IKEDA-KO (Kyushu-Japan)	Caldera of IBUSUKI VOLC FIELD	0802-07=
IKENOSAWA (Izu Is-Japan)	Caldera of AOGA-SHIMA	0804-06=
IKEZOKO (Kyushu-Japan)	Maar of IBUSUKI VOLC FIELD	0802-07=
IKINCILGOL TEPE (Turkey)	Cone of NEMRUT DAGI	0103-02=
IKTUNUP (Kamchatka)	Shields (None) Holocene	**1000-67-**
ILAEMAEN (ILAEMANSCHEN) (Alaska-SW)	Synonym of ILIAMNA	1103-02-
ILAMATEPEC (El Salvador)	Synonym of SANTA ANA	1403-02=
ILDBORG [ELDBORG] (Iceland-W)	Cone of LJOSUFJOLL	1700-03=
ILE (French for ISLAND) see proper name (e.g. CENDRES, ILE DES)		
ILHEU DOS MOSTEIROS (Azores)	Cone of SETE CIDADES	1802-08=
ILIAMNA (Alaska-SW)	Stratovolc (4, 1953) Historical	**1103-02-**
ILIBOLENG (Lesser Sunda Is)	Stratovolc (20, 1993) Historical	**0604-22=**
ILIBOTONG (Lesser Sunda Is)	Cone of ILIMUDA	0604-17=
ILIBURAK (Lesser Sunda Is)	Synonym of LEREBOLENG	0604-20=
ILIGRIPE (Lesser Sunda Is)	Dome of ILIWERUNG	0604-25=
ILIINSKAIA, SOPKA (Kamchatka)	Synonym of ILYINSKY	1000-03=
ILIINSKAYA (ILIINSKY) (Kamchatka)	Synonym of ILYINSKY	1000-03=
ILILABALEKAN (Lesser Sunda Is)	Stratovolc (None) Fumarolic	**0604-24=**
ILILAMARAP (ILILAMARARAP) (Lesser Sund	Synonym of ILILABALEKAN	0604-24=
ILILEWOTO (ILILEWOTOLO) (Lesser Sunda	Synonym of LEWOTOLO	0604-23=
ILIMOEDA (Lesser Sunda Is)	Synonym of ILIMUDA	0604-17=
ILIMONJET (Lesser Sunda Is)	Dome of ILIWERUNG	0604-25=
ILIMUDA (Lesser Sunda Is)	Stratovolc (None) Fumarolic	**0604-17=**
ILINA (Kamchatka)	Synonym of ILYINSKY	1000-03=
ILINITZA (Ecuador)	Synonym of ILINIZA	1502-041
ILINIZA (Ecuador)	Stratovolc (None) Holocene	**1502-041**
ILINSKY (Kamchatka)	Synonym of ILYINSKY	1000-03=
ILIPENUTUN (Lesser Sunda Is)	Dome of ILIWERUNG	0604-25=
ILIPETRUS [ILIGRIPE] (Lesser Sunda Is)	Dome of ILIWERUNG	0604-25=
ILIPOEGORA (Lesser Sunda Is)	Synonym of ILIWERUNG	0604-25=
ILITEBULELE (Lesser Sunda Is)	Cone of ILILABALEKAN	0604-24=
ILIWEROENG (Lesser Sunda Is)	Synonym of ILIWERUNG	0604-25=
ILIWERUNG (Lesser Sunda Is)	Complx volc (11, 1993) Historical	**0604-25=**
ILIWOKAR (Lesser Sunda Is)	Cone of LEWOTOBI	0604-18=
ILIYIN SOPKA (Kamchatka)	Synonym of ILYINSKY	1000-03=
ILLAHRAUN (Iceland-SW)	Crater row of REYKJANES	1701-02=
ILLAHRAUN (Iceland-SW)	Crater row of KERLINGARFJOLL	1701-10=
ILLANO (Mindanao-Philippines)	Synonym of RAGANG	0701-06=
ILLANO (Mindanao-Philippines)	Synonym of MAKATURING	0701-04=
ILLASCAR (Chile-N)	Synonym of LASCAR	1505-10=
ILLI, PUU O (Hawaiian Is)	Cone of HALEAKALA	1302-06-
ILLNIZA (Ecuador)	Synonym of ILINIZA	1502-041
ILLVIDRAHNJUKAHRAUN (Iceland-SW)	Fissure vent of HOFSJOKULL	1701-09=
ILONGO (Africa-E)	Dome of SW USANGU BASIN	0202-163
ILOPANGO (El Salvador)	Caldera (2, 1880) Historical	**1403-06=**
ILYAMINSKAYA (Alaska-SW)	Synonym of ILIAMNA	1103-02-
ILYINSKY (Kamchatka)	Stratovolc (3, 1901) Historical	**1000-03=**
IMAC HILL (Luzon-Philippines)	Cone of LAGUNA VOLC FIELD	0703-051
IMAGINATION PEAK (US-Oregon)	Pyrocl cone (None) Holocene	**1202-163**
IMORIGASHIRO (Kyushu-Japan)	Dome of TSURUMI	0802-13=
IMPERIAL (Chile-C)	Synonym of LLAIMA	1507-11=
IMURUK LAKE (Alaska-W)	Shields (1, 0295) Radiocarbon	**1104-02-**
INABOSHI-YAMA (Kyushu-Japan)	Dome of KUJU GROUP	0802-12=
INAMURA-DAKE (Ryukyu Is)	Cone of KIKAI	0802-06=
INATORI GROUP (Honshu-Japan)	Crater of IZU-TOBU	0803-01=
INCEKAYA (Turkey)	Stratovolc of NEMRUT DAGI	0103-02=
INDE (SE Asia)	Crater of LOWER CHINDWIN	0705-09-
INDEFATIGABLE (Galapagos)	Synonym of SANTA CRUZ	1503-091
INDIAN BUTTE (US-California)	Cone of MEDICINE LAKE	1203-02-
INDIAN BUTTE (US-Oregon)	Dome of NEWBERRY VOLCANO	1202-11-
INDIAN BUTTE (US-Oregon)	Cone of NEWBERRY VOLCANO	1202-11-
INDIAN HEAVEN (US-Washington)	Shields (1, -6250) Radiocarbon	**1201-07-**
INDIAN PASS (US-Washington)	Cone of GLACIER PEAK	1201-02-
INDIGIRSKY (INDIGHIRSKY) (Russia-NE)	Synonym of BALAGAN-TAS	1001-03-
INDOOLI MOUNTAIN (Alaska-W)	Cone of NUNIVAK ISLAND	1104-06-
INDRAPURA, PEAK OF (Sumatra)	Synonym of KERINCI	0601-17=
INE RUA (Lesser Sunda Is)	Thermal Feature of POCO LEOK	0604-07=
INERI (Lesser Sunda Is)	Synonym of INIERIE	0604-08=
INFANTES, LOS [SIETE FUENTES] (Canary	Cone of TENERIFE	1803-03-
INFERNO (US-Idaho)	Cone of CRATERS OF THE MOON	1204-02-
INFIERNILLOS DE CHINAMECA (El Salvador	Thermal Feature of CHINAMECA	1403-09=
INFIERNILLOS DE SAN VICENTE	Thermal Feature of SAN VICENTE	1403-07=
INGAKSLUGWAT HILLS (Alaska-W)	Cinder cones (None) Holocene	**1104-05-**
INGENIO, EL [CERRO LA CELOSA] (Chile-C)	Cone of OLLAGUE	1505-06=
INGILOFOTSY (Madagascar)	Dome of ITASY VOLC FIELD	0303-06-
INGO (Africa-C)	Cone of KARISIMBI	0203-04-
INGRI BUTTE (Alaska-W)	Cone of NUNIVAK ISLAND	1104-06-
INGRIJOAK HILLS (Alaska-W)	Cone of NUNIVAK ISLAND	1104-06-
INGRILUKAT-NASKORAT HILL (Alaska-W)	Cone of NUNIVAK ISLAND	1104-06-
INGRIRUK HILL (Alaska-W)	Cone of NUNIVAK ISLAND	1104-06-
INIE LIKA (Lesser Sunda Is)	Synonym of INIELIKA	0604-09=
INIE RIE (Lesser Sunda Is)	Synonym of INIERIE	0604-08=
INIELIKA (Lesser Sunda Is)	Complx volc (1, 1905) Historical	**0604-09=**

NAME (Subregion)	Type (Eruption Total, Most Recent) Status . . . Relation to NAMED VOLCANO	NUMBER
INIELIKA, WOLO (Lesser Sunda Is)	Crater of INIELIKA	0604-09=
INIERIE (Lesser Sunda Is)	Stratovolc (None) Fumarolic	**0604-08=**
INMAN NUNATAK (Antarctica)	Cone of HUDSON MOUNTAINS	1900-028
INN, CERRO (Galapagos)	Cone of SANTIAGO	1503-09=
INNACCESIBLE CONES (US-Oregon)	Cone of BELKNAP	1202-06-
INNDALSMOYA-STAKKEN (Atl-N-Jan Mayen)	Dome of JAN MAYEN	1706-01=
INREROW ATAMWAN (Vanuatu-SW Pacific)	Stratovolc of ANEITYUM	0507-11-
INUKURA-YAMA (Honshu-Japan)	Stratovolc of IWATE	0803-24=
INUNUMURI (New Britain-SW Pac)	Cone of DAKATAUA	0502-04=
INUSUZUMI-YAMA (Honshu-Japan)	Cone of FUJI	0803-03=
INYENYESE (Africa-E)	Cone of KIEYO	0202-17=
INYO CRATERS (US-California)	Lava domes (3, 1350) Radiocarbon	**1203-13-**
IO SAN [CHERNY] (Kurile Is)	Stratovolc of CHIRPOI	0900-15=
IO-SIMA (Volcano Is-Japan)	Synonym of IWO-JIMA	0804-12=
IO-YAMA (Kurile Is)	Synonym of EBEKO	0900-38=
IO [KUDRIAVY] (Kurile Is)	Cone of MEDVEZHIA	0900-10=
IOZIMA-SINTO [SHOWA-IWO-JIMA] (Ryukyu)	Dome of KIKAI	0802-06=
IPALA VOLC FIELD (Guatemala)	Stratovolc (None) Holocene	**1402-19-**
IPPEKI-KO (Honshu-Japan)	Maar of IZU-TOBU	0803-01=
IPSWOOT BUTTE (US-Oregon)	Cone of NEWBERRY VOLCANO	1202-11-
IRADA (Luzon Is-N of)	Synonym of IRAYA	0704-06-
IRAMBA (Africa-E)	Maar of KIEYO	0202-17=
IRARHRAUN (Iceland-S)	Fissure vent of EYJAFJOLL	1702-02=
IRAYA (Luzon Is-N of)	Stratovolc (3, 1464) Historical	**0704-06-**
IRAZU (Costa Rica)	Stratovolc (24, 1965) Historical	**1405-06=**
IRIGA (Luzon-Philippines)	Stratovolc (1, 1628) Historical	**0703-041**
IRIOMOTE-JIMA (Ryukyu Is)	Submarine (1, 1924) Historical	**0802-01=**
IRIOMOTEZIMA (Ryukyu Is)	Synonym of IRIOMOTE-JIMA	0802-01=
IROSIN (Luzon-Philippines)	Pleistocene caldera of BULUSAN	0703-01=
IRRUPUTUNCO (Chile-N)	Synonym of IRRUPUTUNCU	1505-04=
IRRUPUTUNCU (Chile-N)	Stratovolc (None) Holocene	**1505-04=**
IRTA ALE (Ethiopia)	Synonym of ERTA ALE	0201-08=
ISABELLA (Africa-W)	Cone of CAMEROON, MT.	0204-01=
ISANNACH (ISANNACHOTSKI) (Aleutian Is)	Synonym of ISANOTSKI	1101-37-
ISANOTSKI (Aleutian Is)	Stratovolc (4, 1831) Historical	**1101-37-**
ISAROG (Luzon-Philippines)	Stratovolc (None) Holocene	**0703-042**
ISBIL, JABAL (Arabia-S)	Stratovolc of DHAMAR, HARRAS OF	0301-12-
ISCHDSCHEA, HARRET [HALA-'L-'ISHQUA]	Tuff cone of 'UWAYRID, HARRAT	0301-02=
ISCHIA (Italy)	Complx volc (18, 1302) Historical	**0101-03=**
ISCHIA, ISOLA DELL' (Italy)	Synonym of ISCHIA	0101-03=
ISHI-MINE (Kyushu-Japan)	Dome of IBUSUKI VOLC FIELD	0802-07=
ISHIBORA (Japan)	Fissure vent of AKITA-KOMAGA-TAKE	0803-23=
'ISHQUA, HALA-'L- (Arabia-W)	Tuff cone of 'UWAYRID, HARRAT	0301-02=
ISKUT CANYON [ISKUT RIVER] (Canada)	Cone of ISKUT-UNUK RIVER CONES	1200-09-
ISKUT-UNUK RIVER CONES (Canada)	Cinder cones (7, 1800) Radiocarbon	**1200-09-**
ISLA DEL CERRO [CERRO GRANDE]	Dome of COATEPEQUE CALDERA	1403-041
ISLA, ISLOTA, ISOLA (Spanish and Italian for ISLAND) see proper name (e.g. ZAPATERA, ISLA)		
ISLAND PARK (US-Wyoming)	Caldera of YELLOWSTONE	1205-01-
ISLETA, LA (Canary Is)	Fissure vent of GRAN CANARIA	1803-04-
ISLETA, LA (Canary Is)	Cone of GRAN CANARIA	1803-04-
ISLONGA (ISLUCA) (Chile-N)	Synonym of ISLUGA	1505-03=
ISLUGA (Chile-N)	Stratovolc (7, 1913) Historical	**1505-03=**
ISOTOCHNIKY (Kamchatka)	Cone of TOLBACHIK	1000-24=
ISSAIKYO (Honshu-Japan)	Cone of AZUMA	0803-18=
ISSANAKSKI (Aleutian Is)	Synonym of ISANOTSKI	1101-37-
ISTHMUS (Greece)	Synonym of SUSAKI	0102-01=
ISUAN (Luzon-Philippines)	Synonym of MAQUILING	0703-06=
ITAM (Java)	Thermal Feature of UNGARAN	0603-23=
ITAMBA (Africa-E)	Maar of KIEYO	0202-17=
ITANKIOI (Kurile Is)	Synonym of PREVO PEAK	0900-19=
ITASHIBEONI-IWO-ZAN (Hokkaido)	Synonym of SHIRETOKO-IWO-ZAN	0805-09=
ITASIBEONI-IWO-ZAN (Hokkaido)	Synonym of SHIRETOKO-IWO-ZAN	0805-09=
ITASY VOLC FIELD (Madagascar)	Scoria cones (2, -6050) Radiocarbon	**0303-06-**
ITENDE (Africa-E)	Maar of KIEYO	0202-17=
ITETE (Africa-E)	Cone of KIEYO	0202-17=
ITHNAIN (Arabia-W)	Synonym of ITHNAYN, HARRAT	0301-05=
ITHNAYN, HARRAT (Arabia-W)	Volc field (None) Holocene	**0301-05=**
ITHUNDU (Africa-E)	Cone of CHYULU HILLS	0202-13=
ITIBISINAI (Kurile Is)	Synonym of GOLOVNIN	0900-01=
ITINO-IKE [ICHINO-IKE] (Honshu-Japan)	Crater of NORIKURA	0803-06=
ITINO-IKE [ICHINO-IKE] (Honshu-Japan)	Crater of ON-TAKE	0803-04=
ITINOMEGATA [ICHINOMEGATA] (Honshu)	Maar of MEGATA	0803-262
ITSCHINSKIJ (Kamchatka)	Synonym of ICHINSKY	1000-28=
ITTISA (Ethiopia)	Cone of GEDAMSA CALDERA	0201-23-
IULT (Kamchatka)	Stratovolc (None) Holocene	**1000-231**
IVAN GROZNY (Kurile Is)	Somma volcano of GROZNY GROUP	0900-07=
IVANOV (Kamchatka)	Dome of BOLSHOI SEMIACHIK	1000-15=
IVAO GROUP (Kurile Is)	Cinder cones (None) Holocene	**0900-111**
IVTH NATIONAL VOLC CONGRESS (Kamch	Crater of KLIUCHEVSKOI	1000-26=
IWA-YAMA (Kurile Is)	Synonym of SMIRNOV	0900-031
IWAKI (Honshu-Japan)	Stratovolc (19, 1863) Historical	**0803-27=**
IWAKI-SAN (Honshu-Japan)	Dome of IWAKI	0803-27=
IWALE (Africa-E)	Crater of KIEYO	0202-17=
IWANO-YAMA (Honshu-Japan)	Dome of IZU-TOBU	0803-01=
IWANOKUBO (Honshu-Japan)	Cone of IZU-TOBU	0803-01=
IWANOKUBO (Honshu-Japan)	Tuff ring of IZU-TOBU	0803-01=
IWAONUPURI (Hokkaido-Japan)	Stratovolcs (None) Holocene	**0805-031**
IWATE (Honshu-Japan)	Complx volc (6, 1919) Historical	**0803-24=**
IWATE-FUJI (IWATE-HUZI) (Honshu-Japan)	Synonym of IWATE	0803-24=
IWIKAU (New Zealand)	Vent of RUAPEHU	0401-10=
IWO-DAKE (Honshu-Japan)	Synonym of YAKE-DAKE	0803-07=
IWO-DAKE (Ryukyu Is)	Stratovolc of KIKAI	0802-06=
IWO-JIMA (Volcano Is-Japan)	Caldera (10, 1982) Historical	**0804-12=**
IWO-TORI-SHIMA (Ryukyu Is)	Synonym of OKINAWA-TORI-SHIMA	0802-02=
IWO-YAMA (Honshu-Japan)	Synonym of ADATARA	0803-17=
IWO-YAMA (Izu Is-Japan)	Cone of TORI-SHIMA	0804-09=
IWO-YAMA (Kyushu-Japan)	Dome of KIRISHIMA	0802-09=
IWO-ZAN (Kurile Is)	Synonym of EBEKO	0900-38=
IWO-ZIMA (Volcano Is-Japan)	Synonym of IWO-JIMA	0804-12=
IWODAKE (Ryukyu Is)	Cone of OKINAWA-TORI-SHIMA	0802-02=
IXPACO, LAGUNA (Guatemala)	Tuff ring of TECUAMBURRO	1402-12=
IXTACCIHUATL (Mexico)	Synonym of IZTACCIHUATL	1401-086
IXTEPECE (Guatemala)	Synonym of IXTEPEQUE, VOLCAN	1402-18-
IXTEPEQUE, VOLCAN (Guatemala)	Lava domes (None) Holocene	**1402-18-**
IXTLAN, GEYSERS DE (Mexico)	Thermal Feature of MICHOACAN-GUANAJ	1401-06=
IYA (Lesser Sunda Is)	Stratovolc (8, 1969) Historical	**0604-11=**
IYANG-ARGAPURA (Java)	Complx volc (None) Holocene	**0603-33=**
IYU-ZAN (Honshu-Japan)	Cone of IZU-TOBU	0803-01=
IZALCO (El Salvador)	Stratovolc (51, 1966) Historical	**1403-03=**
IZTACCIHUATL (Mexico)	Stratovolc (None) Holocene	**1401-086**
IZTALTETLAC, CERRO (Mexico)	Cone of PAPAYO	1401-085
IZU-OSHIMA (Izu Is-Japan)	Synonym of OSHIMA	0804-01=
IZU-TOBU (Honshu-Japan)	Pyrocl cones (5, 1989) Historical	**0803-01=**
IZU-TORI-SHIMA (Izu Is-Japan)	Synonym of TORI-SHIMA	0804-09=
IZUMBWE-MPOLI (Africa-E)	Pyrocl cones (None) Holocene	**0202-165**

J

NAME (Subregion)	Type (Eruption Total, Most Recent) Status . . . Relation to NAMED VOLCANO	NUMBER
JABAL (Arabic for MT.) see proper name (e.g. HAYLAN, JABAL)		
JABALI (El Salvador)	Stratovolc of SAN SALVADOR	1403-05=
JABALI, CERROS DEL (Mexico)	Cone of MICHOACAN-GUANAJUATO	1401-06=
JABALINCITO, EL [SITIO GRANDE] (El Salv	Crater of SAN SALVADOR	1403-05=
JABLE, MONTANA DEL (Canary Is)	Cone of HIERRO	1803-02-
JABUT, BUKIT [BUKIT CABUT] (Sumatra)	Cone of BESAR, GUNUNG	0601-25=
JACKIES BUTTE (US-Oregon)	Volc field (None) Holocene?	**1202-20-**
JACKMOSKY (Kurile Is)	Synonym of CHIKURACHKI	0900-36=
JACK'S JUMP (Canada)	Cone of WELLS GRAY-CLEARWATER	1200-15-
JADI, GUNUNG (Java)	Former dome of GALUNGGUNG	0603-14=
JAG PEAK (Aleutian Is)	Cone of OKMOK	1101-29-
JAHSAYA, CERRO (Peru)	Stratovolc of FIRURA, NEVADOS	1504-00-
JAILOLO (Halmahera-Indonesia)	Stratovolc (None) Holocene	**0608-051**
JAJARANA, CERRO (Peru)	Cone of ANDAHUA VALLEY	1504-002
JALAJALA (Luzon-Philippines)	Fumarole fld (None) Fumarolic	**0703-08=**
JALI (Greece)	Synonym of YALI	0102-051
JALUA (Ethiopia)	Stratovolc (None) Holocene	**0201-03=**
JAMAKATAN (Africa-E)	Cone of PAKA	0202-053
JAMBANGAN (Java)	Crater of IYANG-ARGAPURA	0603-33=
JAMES (Galapagos)	Synonym of SANTIAGO	1503-09=
JAN MAYEN (Atl-N-Jan Mayen)	Stratovolc (7, 1985) Historical	**1706-01=**
JANG (Java)	Synonym of IYANG-ARGAPURA	0603-33=
JANGHUDI (JANGUDI) (Ethiopia)	Synonym of YANGUDI	0201-151
JANOO (Kyushu-Japan)	Cone of ASO	0802-11=
JAPATI (Java)	Crater of GUNTUR	0603-13=
JAPONES (Chile-C)	Crater of LLAIMA	1507-11=
JAQUEY, EL (Mexico)	Maar of DURANGO VOLC FIELD	1401-022
JARA, CERRO LA (US-New Mexico)	Dome of VALLES CALDERA	1210-03-
JARAPENA, VOLCAN LA (Mexico)	Crater of PINACATE PEAKS	1401-001
JARAQUAY VOLC FIELD (Mexico)	Cinder cones (None) Holocene	**1401-004**
JAR'ATAIN, HARRA OF (Arabia-W)	Cone of YAR, JABAL	0301-08-
JARDBADSHOLAR [BJARNARFLAG]	Crater row of KRAFLA	1703-08=
JARIAN, KAWAH (Java)	Crater of TANGKUBANPARAHU	0603-09=
JARRA (Arabia-W)	Synonym of YAR, JABAL	0301-08-
JAWALO (Lesser Sunda Is)	Crater of PALUWEH	0604-15=
JEAN (Indian O.-W)	Crater of FOURNAISE, PITON DE LA	0303-02=
JEBEL, JIBAL, JIBBEL (Arabic for MT.) see proper name (e.g. MARRA, JEBEL)		
JECHAPITA, VOLCAN (Peru)	Cone of ANDAHUA VALLEY	1504-002
JEFFERSON (US-Oregon)	Stratovolc (2, 0950) Varve Count	**1202-02-**
JEJU (Korea)	Synonym of HALLA	1006-04-
JELLICOE PARK (New Zealand)	Cone of AUCKLAND FIELD	0401-02=
JEMBANGAN (Java)	Caldera of SEMERU	0603-30=
JEMEZ SPRINGS (US-New Mexico)	Thermal Feature of VALLES CALDERA	1210-03-
JEMEZ VOLC FIELD (US-New Mexico)	Synonym of VALLES CALDERA	1210-03-
JENCHANA, VOLCAN (Peru)	Cone of ANDAHUA VALLEY	1504-002
JEREMINE (Indian O.-W)	Crater of FOURNAISE, PITON DE LA	0303-02=
JERO (Java)	Crater of ARJUNO-WELIRANG	0603-29=
JESUS GRANDE, ISLA DE (Nicaragua)	Cone of ZAPATERA ISLAND	1404-111
JGOREWSKIJ (Kamchatka)	Synonym of DZENZURSKY	1000-11=
JIANSHUIDINGZI (China-E)	Cone of LONGGANG GROUP	1005-06-
JIAOSHAN (China-S)	Cone of TENGCHONG	0705-11-
JICALAN, CERRO DE (Mexico)	Cone of MICHOACAN-GUANAJUATO	1401-06=
JIGABO (Luzon-Philippines)	Thermal Feature of MALINAO	0703-04=
JIGOKU (Honshu-Japan)	Thermal Feature of OSORE-YAMA	0803-29=
JIGOKU (Honshu-Japan)	Crater of ON-TAKE	0803-04=
JIGOKU (Kyushu-Japan)	Thermal Feature of ASO	0802-11=
JIGOKU-ATO (Kyushu-Japan)	Crater of UNZEN	0802-10=
JIGOKU-DANI (Hokkaido-Japan)	Crater of KUTTARA	0805-034
JIGOKU-DANI (Honshu-Japan)	Crater of TATE-YAMA	0803-08=
JIGOKU-NO-OANA (Honshu-Japan)	Crater of HAKU-SAN	0803-05=
JIGOKU YAMA [TREZUBETZ] (Kurile Is)	Somma volcano of KOLOKOL GROUP	0900-12=
JILOA, LAGUNA (Nicaragua)	Maar of APOYEQUE	1404-091
JIM JIM, THE (Australia)	Cone of NEWER VOLCANICS PROV	0509-01-
JIMAT (Java)	Cone of DIENG VOLC COMPLEX	0603-20=
JINAKA-YAMA (Izu Is-Japan)	Dome of NII-JIMA	0804-02=
JINAMAR, MONTANA (Canary Is)	Cone of GRAN CANARIA	1803-04-
JINETSU HOT SPRINGS (Honshu-Japan)	Thermal Feature of KUSATSU-SHIRANE	0803-12=
JING-BEI (JINGBO, JINGBOHU) (China-E)	Synonym of JINGPOHU	1005-05-
JINGGO, KEPUNDAN (Sumatra)	Crater of MARAPI	0601-14=
JINGLONGDINGZI (China-E)	Cone of LONGGANG GROUP	1005-06-
JINGPOHU (China-E)	Volc field (1, -3460) Radiocarbon	**1005-05-**
JINJINSHANSI (China-E)	Cone of DATONG	1005-01-
JINSHAN (China-E)	Cone of DATONG	1005-01-
JIROU-UEMONTSUKA (Honshu-Japan)	Cone of FUJI	0803-03=
JISKOOKSNUK HILL (Alaska-W)	Cone of NUNIVAK ISLAND	1104-06-
JIYUNLING (SE Asia)	Cone of LEIZHOU BANDAO	0705-01-
JIZO-DAKE (Honshu-Japan)	Dome of AKAGI	0803-13=
JIZO HOT SPRINGS (Honshu-Japan)	Thermal Feature of KUSATSU-SHIRANE	0803-12=
JIZO-SAN (Honshu-Japan)	Stratovolc of ZAO	0803-19=
JIZODO GROUP (Honshu-Japan)	Vent of IZU-TOBU	0803-01=
JIZONO-YU (Kyushu-Japan)	Thermal Feature of TSURUMI	0802-13=
JLIAMNA (Alaska-SW)	Synonym of ILIAMNA	1103-02-
JOAO FERNANDES, PICO (Azores)	Cone of AGUA DE PAU	1802-09=
JOB, MT. (Canada)	Cone of MEAGER	1200-18-
JOBOSHI (Honshu-Japan)	Cone of IZU-TOBU	0803-01=
JOCOTILLO, CERRO EL (Guatemala)	Cone of CUILAPA-BARBARENA	1402-111
JOCOTITLAN (Mexico)	Stratovolc (2, 1270) Radiocarbon	**1401-061**
JOGORO-YAMA (Izu Is-Japan)	Dome of KOZU-SHIMA	0804-03=
JOHANN ALBRECHT HAFEN (New Britain)	Caldera of GAROVE	0502-03=
JOLO (Sulu Is-Philippines)	Synonym of BUD DAJO	0700-01=
JOLOM, CERRO (Guatemala)	Dome of TZANJUYUB, VOLCAN DE	1402-05=
JONGGRING SELOKO (Java)	Crater of SEMERU	0603-30=
JORDA, PUIG (Spain)	Cone of OLOT VOLC FIELD	0100-03-
JORDAN CRATERS (US-Oregon)	Volc field (None) Holocene	**1202-19-**
JORGENCAL (JORJENCAL) (Chile-N)	Synonym of PUTANA	1505-09=
JORMAJAN, MT. (Luzon-Philippines)	Cone of BULUSAN	0703-01=
JOROBADO (Chile-S)	Synonym of CORCOVADO	1508-05=
JORULLO (Mexico)	Cone of MICHOACAN-GUANAJUATO	1401-06=
JOSE BUTTE (US-New Mexico)	Cone of RATON-CLAYTON	1210-04-
JOYA, CERRO LA (Mexico)	Cone of TENAYO GROUP	1401-081
JOYA DE LIMON, CERRITO (Guatemala)	Cone of CUILAPA-BARBARENA	1402-111
JOYA, LA (El Salvador)	Cone of SAN SALVADOR	1403-05=
JOYA, LA (Nicaragua)	Crater of APOYO	1404-101
JOYA, LA (Nicaragua)	Maar of PILAS, LAS	1404-08=
JUAN MURILLO (Costa Rica)	Cone of AGUAS ZARCAS GROUP	1405-035
JUAN PERDOMO, MONTANA DE (Canary Is)	Cone of LANZAROTE	1803-06-

NAME (Subregion)	Type (Eruption Total, Most Recent) Status Relation to NAMED VOLCANO	NUMBER
JUBILEE [YUBILEINOYE] (Kamchatka)	Crater of KLIUCHEVSKOI	1000-26=
JUEOCKACK (Korea)	Cone of HALLA	1006-04-
JULAN, MONTANAS DE (Canary Is)	Cone of HIERRO	1803-02-
JULIEN, MORNE (W Indies)	Cone of PELEE	1600-12=
JUMENTOS (Mexico)	Cone of CHICHINAUTZIN	1401-08=
JUMES, PUY DE (France)	Cone of CHAINE DES PUYS	0100-02-
JUNGA-IKE (Honshu-Japan)	Crater of YAKE-DAKE	0803-07=
JUNQUILLO, CERRO EL (El Salvador)	Cone of SAN DIEGO	1403-012
JUNQUILLO NORTE, CERRO EL (Guatemala	Cone of CUILAPA-BARBARENA	1402-111
JUNQUILLO SUR, CERRO EL (Guatemala)	Cone of CUILAPA-BARBARENA	1402-111
JURANG SIUNIK (Sumatra)	Crater of SORIKMARAPI	0601-12=
JURIG, KAWAH (Java)	Crater of TANGKUBANPARAHU	0603-09=
JURIQUES, VOLCAN (Chile-N)	Stratovolc of LICANCABUR	1505-092
JUTE, CERRO DEL (Guatemala)	Cone of MOYUTA	1402-13-
JUTIAPA GROUP (Guatemala)	Synonym of SANTIAGO, CERRO	1402-16-
JYOBU HOT SPRINGS (Honshu-Japan)	Thermal Feature of KUSATSU-SHIRANE	0803-12=

K

NAME (Subregion)	Type (Eruption Total, Most Recent) Status Relation to NAMED VOLCANO	NUMBER
KA-ER-DAXI (China-W)	Cone of KUNLUN VOLC GROUP	1004-03-
KA MOA O PELE (Hawaiian Is)	Cone of HALEAKALA	1302-06-
KAABA (Sumatra)	Synonym of KABA	0601-22=
KAALKOPPIE (Indian O.-S)	Tuff cone of MARION ISLAND	0304-08-
KABA (Indonesian for CRATER) see proper name (e.g. BARU, KABA)		
KABA (Sumatra)	Stratovolc (10, 1956) Historical	**0601-22=**
KABARGIN OTH GROUP (Georgia)	Cinder cones (None) Holocene	**0104-03-**
KABARUGI (Africa-C)	Crater of BUNYARUGURU FIELD	0203-005
KABIRANJUMA (Africa-C)	Crater of MUHAVURA	0203-06-
KABIU [KOMBIU] (New Britain-SW Pac)	Stratovolc of RABAUL	0502-14=
KABUJUTAN [KABUYUTAN] (Java)	Crater of GUNTUR	0603-13=
KABUN BUNGO [KEBUN BUNGO] (Sumatra)	Crater of MARAPI	0601-14=
KABUTO-YAMA (Honshu-Japan)	Cone of AZUMA	0803-18=
KABUYUTAN (Java)	Crater of GUNTUR	0603-13=
KADIENDI NAE (Lesser Sunda Is)	Dome of TAMBORA	0604-04=
KADJOR [KAJOR] (Java)	Fissure vent of MERBABU	0603-24=
KADONO (Honshu-Japan)	Cone of IZU-TOBU	0803-01=
KADOVAR (New Guinea-NE of)	Stratovolc (None) Holocene	**0501-002**
KADOWAKI-KAIKYU (Honshu-Japan)	Submarine vent of IZU-TOBU	0803-01=
KAGAMIL (Aleutian Is)	Stratovolc (1, 1929) Historical	**1101-26-**
KAGO-YAMA (Honshu-Japan)	Dome of ADATARA	0803-17=
KAGODE (Africa-C)	Tuff cone of FORT PORTAL FIELD	0203-002
KAGUSA HOT SPRINGS (Honshu-Japan)	Thermal Feature of KUSATSU-SHIRANE	0803-12=
KAGUYAK (Alaska Peninsula)	Stratovolc (1, 0325) Holocene	**1102-25-**
KAHAUALEA, PUU (Hawaiian Is)	Cone of KILAUEA	1302-01-
KAHE KAHE (Tonga-SW Pacific)	Synonym of FALCON ISLAND	0403-05=
KAHEKAHE TANGATA (Tonga-SW Pacific)	Synonym of METIS SHOAL	0403-07=
KAHOLUA O KAHAWALI (Hawaiian Is)	Cone of KILAUEA	1302-01-
KAHONGOLE (Africa-C)	Cone of NYAMURAGIRA	0203-02=
KAHOOLAWE (Hawaiian Is)	Shield (None) Holocene?	**1302-05-**
KAHUALOA (Hawaiian Is)	Tuff cone of KOOLAU	1302-07-
KAHUWAI (Hawaiian Is)	Pit crater of KILAUEA	1302-01-
KAIA [TAVURVUR] (New Britain-SW Pac)	Stratovolc of RABAUL	0502-14=
KAIBUN [KAIMON] (Kyushu-Japan)	Stratovolc of IBUSUKI VOLC FIELD	0802-07=
KAIKOHE (New Zealand)	Cone of KAIKOHE-BAY OF ISLANDS	0401-01=
KAIKOHE-BAY OF ISLANDS (New Zealand)	Volc field (1, 0400) Radiocarbon	**0401-01=**
KAILENEY (Kamchatka)	Shield (None) Holocene	**1000-62-**
KAILIA (Greece)	Thermal Feature of NISYROS	0102-05=
KAILUPA (Halmahera-Indonesia)	Cone of JAILOLO	0608-051
KAIMALOO (Hawaiian Is)	Cone of HALEAKALA	1302-06-
KAIMANAWA (New Zealand)	Dome of MAROA	0401-061
KAIMENI [KAMENO VOUNO] (Greece)	Dome of METHANA	0102-02=
KAIMON (Kyushu-Japan)	Stratovolc of IBUSUKI VOLC FIELD	0802-07=
KAINO-SEMIACHIK [CENO-SEMIACHIK]	Stratovolc of MALY SEMIACHIK	1000-14=
KAIRURU (New Zealand)	Dome of REPOROA	0401-06-
KAISER WILHELM MOUNTAIN (Indian O.-S)	Synonym of HEARD	0304-01=
KAITOKU KAIZAN (Volcano Is-Japan)	Synonym of KAITOKU SEAMOUNT	0804-10=
KAITOKU-OKANOBA (Volcano Is-Japan)	Synonym of KAITOKU SEAMOUNT	0804-10=
KAITOKU SEAMOUNT (Volcano Is-Japan)	Submarine (2, 1984) Historical	**0804-10=**
KAJONGO (Africa-C)	Tuff cone of RUSEKERE	0203-001
KAJOR (Java)	Fissure vent of MERBABU	0603-24=
KAKAMBUI (Africa-E)	Cone of CHYULU HILLS	0202-13=
KAKHTANA (Kamchatka)	Shield of VOYAMPOLSKY	1000-72-
KAKO (Africa-C)	Crater of BUNYARUGURU FIELD	0203-005
KAKORINYA (Africa-E)	Shield of BARRIER, THE	0202-03=
KALAIEHA, PUU (Hawaiian Is)	Cone of MAUNA KEA	1302-03-
KALALUA (Hawaiian Is)	Cone of KILAUEA	1302-01-
KALAMA (Hawaiian Is)	Cone of KOOLAU	1302-07-
KALAMOS (Greece)	Thermal Feature of MILOS	0102-03=
KALANG (Java)	Synonym of KARANG	0603-02=
KALANG [KARANG] (Java)	Stratovolc of DANAU COMPLEX	0603-01=
KALATUNGAN (Mindanao-Philippines)	Stratovolc (None) Holocene	**0701-061**
KALE TEPE (Turkey)	Dome of NEMRUT DAGI	0103-02=
KALEM (Germany)	Cone of WEST EIFEL VOLC FIELD	0100-01-
KALEPEAMOA, PUU (Hawaiian Is)	Cone of MAUNA KEA	1302-03-
KALFADALSHRAUN (Iceland-SW)	Crater row of BRENNISTEINSFJOLL	1701-04=
KALFELLSHRAUN (Iceland-SW)	Crater row of REYKJANES	1701-02=
KALFSHOLAR (Iceland-SW)	Crater row of GRIMSNES	1701-06=
KALGNITUNUP (Kamchatka)	Stratovolc of KEBENEY	1000-50-
KALIKIIR (Lesser Sunda Is)	Crater of SIRUNG	0604-27=
KALIU (Hawaiian Is)	Cone of KILAUEA	1302-01-
KALOLENYANG (Africa-E)	Shield of BARRIER, THE	0202-03=
KALUAIKI (Hawaiian Is)	Cone of HALEAKALA	1302-06-
KALUBU CRATER [DORO API] (Lesser Sund	Cone of SANGEANG API	0604-05=
KALUU O KA OO (Hawaiian Is)	Cone of HALEAKALA	1302-06-
KALYANGO (Africa-C)	Tuff cone of FORT PORTAL FIELD	0203-002
KAMA-YAMA (Honshu-Japan)	Cone of ASAMA	0803-11=
KAMABUSE-YAMA (Honshu-Japan)	Dome of OSORE-YAMA	0803-29=
KAMADO-JIGOKU (Kyushu-Japan)	Thermal Feature of TSURUMI	0802-13=
KAMAKAIA (Hawaiian Is)	Shield of KILAUEA	1302-01-
KAMAKAIAUKA (Hawaiian Is)	Cone of KILAUEA	1302-01-
KAMAKAIAWAENA (Hawaiian Is)	Cone of KILAUEA	1302-01-
KAMAOLI (Hawaiian Is)	Cone of HALEAKALA	1302-06-
KAMARI (Greece)	Pleistocene caldera of KOS	0102-06=
KAMBALNAIA, SOPKA (Kamchatka)	Synonym of KAMBALNY	1000-01=
KAMBALNY (Kamchatka)	Stratovolc (None) Holocene	**1000-01=**
KAMCHATKA PEAK (Kamchatka)	Synonym of BAKENIN	1000-122
KAMCHATSKAIA GORA (Kamchatka)	Synonym of KLIUCHEVSKOI	1000-26=
KAMCHATSKY VULKAN (Kamchatka)	Synonym of KLIUCHEVSKOI	1000-26=
KAMEGA-IKE (Honshu-Japan)	Crater of NORIKURA	0803-06=
KAMEGAWA (Kyushu-Japan)	Thermal Feature of TSURUMI	0802-13=
KAMEHAME HILL (Hawaiian Is)	Cone of KILAUEA	1302-01-
KAMEN (Kamchatka)	Stratovolc (None) Holocene	**1000-251**
KAMENAE (Greece)	Dome of SANTORINI	0102-04=
KAMENI [KAMENO VOUNO] (Greece)	Dome of METHANA	0102-02=
KAMENISTAYA (Kamchatka)	Cone of KSUDACH	1000-05=
KAMENISTAYA (Kamchatka)	Cone of TOLBACHIK	1000-24=
KAMENO VOUNO (Greece)	Dome of METHANA	0102-02=
KAMERUNGEBIRGE (Africa-W)	Synonym of CAMEROON, MT.	0204-01=
KAMI-HOROKAMETTOKU-YAMA (Hokkaido)	Stratovolc of TOKACHI	0805-05=
KAMI-YAMA (Honshu-Japan)	Dome of HAKONE	0803-02=
KAMI-YUZAWA (Kyushu-Japan)	Dome of KUJU GROUP	0802-12=
KAMIBORI (Honshu-Japan)	Crater of YAKE-DAKE	0803-07=
KAMIJI-YAMA (Honshu-Japan)	Synonym of FUJI	0803-03=
KAMINAKIA (Greece)	Thermal Feature of NISYROS	0102-05=
KAMMOURTA (Ethiopia)	Cone of MANDA-INAKIR	0201-122
KAMOAMOA, PUU (Hawaiian Is)	Cone of KILAUEA	1302-01-
KAMODJAN (KAMOJAN) (Java)	Synonym of KAWAHKAMOJANG	0603-12=
KAMOJANG, KAWAH (Java)	Synonym of KAWAHKAMOJANG	0603-12=
KAMTSCHATSKAJA (Kamchatka)	Synonym of KLIUCHEVSKOI	1000-26=
KAMUI (Kurile Is)	Cone of DEMON	0900-11-
KAMUINUPURI (Hokkaido-Japan)	Stratovolc of MASHU	0805-081
KAMUISHUTO [KAMUISHI] (Hokkaido-Japan)	Dome of MASHU	0805-081
KAMUISSYUTO [KAMUISHI] (Hokkaido)	Dome of MASHU	0805-081
KAMUNZUKWA (Africa-C)	Crater of BUNYARUGURU FIELD	0203-005
KANA (Canada)	Cone of EDZIZA	1200-06-
KANA KEOKI (Solomon Is-SW Pac)	Submarine (None) Holocene	**0505-052**
KANAGA (Aleutian Is)	Stratovolc (7, 1942) Historical	**1101-11-**
KANAGIOI (New Guinea-NE of)	Stratovolc of KARKAR	0501-03=
KANAKANA (New Zealand)	Dome of OKATAINA	0401-05=
KANAMHARAGI (Africa-C)	Cone of NYAMURAGIRA	0203-02=
KANATON (Aleutian Is)	Pleistocene caldera of KANAGA	1101-11-
KANAVA (Greece)	Thermal Feature of MILOS	0102-03=
KANDO-YAMA (Izu Is-Japan)	Crater of HACHIJO-JIMA	0804-05=
KANE NUI O HAMO (Hawaiian Is)	Shield of KILAUEA	1302-01-
KANEDA (Honshu-Japan)	Dome of OMANAGO GROUP	0803-142
KANGAROO HILL (Australia)	Cone of NEWER VOLCANICS PROV	0509-01-
KANI-NUMA (Honshu-Japan)	Crater of AKITA-YAKE-YAMA	0803-26=
KANLAON (Philippines-C)	Synonym of CANLAON	0702-02=
KANNABE (Honshu-Japan)	Shield (None) Holocene	**0803-005**
KANNAWA-JIGOKU (Kyushu-Japan)	Thermal Feature of TSURUMI	0802-13=
KANNON-MORI (Honshu-Japan)	Cone of CHOKAI	0803-22=
KANNONYAMA-HIGASHI (Honshu-Japan)	Cone of IZU-TOBU	0803-01=
KANPU (Honshu-Japan)	Lava dome (None) Holocene	**0803-261**
KANSU-YAMA (Honshu-Japan)	Cone of FUJI	0803-03=
KANYAMBUZI (Africa-C)	Cone of NYIRAGONGO	0203-03=
KANYMAGASHU (Africa-C)	Cone of NYIRAGONGO	0203-03=
KAOHIKAIPU (Hawaiian Is)	Cone of KOOLAU	1302-07-
KAOLKHON (Kamchatka)	Synonym of ICHINSKY	1000-28=
KAPAYAHAN (Mindanao-Philippines)	Crater of PACO	0701-09-
KAPBERG (New Britain-SW Pac)	Stratovolc of LOLO	0502-071
KAPELLUGIGAR (Iceland-SW)	Crater row of KRISUVIK	1701-03=
KAPI FUMAROLE FIELD (Sumatra)	Thermal Feature of GAYOLESTEN	0601-06=
KAPOHO (Hawaiian Is)	Tuff cone of KILAUEA	1302-01-
KAPUNDAN (Indonesian for CRATER) see proper name (e.g. BONGSU, KAPUNDAN)		
KAPUSIKEJU (Africa-E)	Cone of EMURUANGOGOLAK	0202-051
KAR, LAS (Chile-N)	Synonym of LASCAR	1505-10=
KARA-GAMA (Honshu-Japan)	Crater of KUSATSU-SHIRANE	0803-12=
KARA-YAMA (Kyushu-Japan)	Stratovolc of IBUSUKI VOLC FIELD	0802-07=
KARABUKI (Honshu-Japan)	Thermal Feature of KUSATSU-SHIRANE	0803-12=
KARACADAG (Turkey)	Synonym of KARACALIDAG	0103-011
KARACALIDAG (Turkey)	Shield (None) Holocene	**0103-011**
KARADIVLIT TEPE (Turkey)	Cone of KULA	0103-00-
KARAHA, KAWAH (Java)	Synonym of KAWAHKARAHA	0603-16=
KARAKULI (Kamchatka)	Dome of PAUZHETKA	1000-022
KARAKUNI-DAKE (Kyushu-Japan)	Stratovolc of KIRISHIMA	0802-09=
KARAMA (Africa-E)	Cone of NYAMBENI HILLS	0202-056
KARAN (Kamchatka)	Dome of SHEVELUCH	1000-27=
KARANG (Java)	Stratovolc of DANAU COMPLEX	0603-01=
KARANG (Java)	Stratovolc (None) Fumarolic	**0603-02=**
KARANGETANG (Sangihe Is-Indonesia)	Stratovolc (42, 1993) Historical	**0607-02=**
KARAPINAR FIELD (Turkey)	Cinder cones (1, -6200) Holocene	**0103-001**
KARAPITI [CRATERS OF THE MOON] (N Z)	Thermal Feature of MAROA	0401-061
KARASIVRI TEPE (Turkey)	Cone of ERCIYES DAGI	0103-01=
KARATALA (Indian O.-W)	Synonym of KARTHALA	0303-01=
KARAVIA BAY (New Britain-SW Pac)	Stratovolc of RABAUL	0502-14=
KARE-NUMA (Honshu-Japan)	Crater of AKITA-YAKE-YAMA	0803-26=
KARIANG (Halmahera-Indonesia)	Cone of DUKONO	0608-01=
KARIMKOTAN (Kurile Is)	Synonym of HARIMKOTAN	0900-30=
KARIMSKY (Kamchatka)	Synonym of KARYMSKY	1000-13=
KARISIMBI (Africa-C)	Stratovolc (None) Holocene	**0203-04-**
KARITA-DAKE (Honshu-Japan)	Synonym of ZAO	0803-19=
KARIYA (Africa-C)	Crater of BUNYARUGURU FIELD	0203-005
KARKAR (New Guinea-NE of)	Stratovolc (11, 1979) Historical	**0501-03=**
KARNIYARIK (Turkey)	Cone of ARARAT, MT.	0103-04-
KARNIYARIK TEPELER (Turkey)	Cone of ERCIYES DAGI	0103-01=
KAROET, BATOE [BATU KARUT] (Java)	Stratovolc of DANAU COMPLEX	0603-01=
KAROLERO (Africa-C)	Crater of BUNYARUGURU FIELD	0203-005
KARPINSKII (Kurile Is)	Synonym of KARPINSKY GROUP	0900-35=
KARPINSKY GROUP (Kurile Is)	Cones (1, 1952) Historical	**0900-35=**
KARS PLATEAU (Turkey)	Volc field (None) Holocene?	**0103-05-**
KARSA KILE (Africa-E)	Maar of MARSABIT	0202-021
KARSO, KAWAH (Java)	Thermal Feature of GALUNGGUNG	0603-14=
KARTALA (Indian O.-W)	Synonym of KARTHALA	0303-01=
KARTHALA (Indian O.-W)	Shield (30, 1991) Historical	**0303-01=**
KARTIN DAG (Turkey)	Dome of ERCIYES DAGI	0103-01=
KARTOLA (Indian O.-W)	Synonym of KARTHALA	0303-01=
KARUA (Vanuatu-SW Pacific)	Submarine cone of KUWAE	0507-07=
KARUT, BATU (Java)	Stratovolc of DANAU COMPLEX	0603-01=
KARYMSKAIA SOPKA (Kamchatka)	Synonym of KARYMSKY	1000-13=
KARYMSKY (Kamchatka)	Stratovolc (45, 1982) Historical	**1000-13=**
KARYMSKY LAKE (Kamchatka)	Pleistocene caldera of AKADEMIA NAUK	1000-123
KASA-YAMA (Honshu-Japan)	Dome of IIZUNA	0803-102
KASAKAT HILL (Africa-E)	Cone of PAKA	0202-053
KASATOCHI (Aleutian Is)	Stratovolc (1, 1760) Historical	**1101-13-**
KASBEK (Georgia)	Stratovolc (2, -0750) Tephrochronology	**0104-02-**
KASEGA-DAKE (Kyushu-Japan)	Dome of IBUSUKI VOLC FIELD	0802-07=
KASEKERE (Africa-C)	Synonym of RUSEKERE	0203-001
KASENYI (Africa-C)	Tuff cone of KATWE-KIKORONGO FIELD	0203-004
KASHAKA (Africa-C)	Cone of NYIRAGONGO	0203-03=
KASIBOI (Philippines-C)	Cone of MAHAGNOA	0702-07=
KASIDIA (Africa-C)	Crater of BUNYARUGURU FIELD	0203-005
KASOLALI (New Britain-SW Pac)	Thermal Feature of PAGO	0502-08=
KASSIGIE [KASSIJIE] (Madagascar)	Cone of ITASY VOLC FIELD	0303-06-
KASTANAS (Greece)	Thermal Feature of MILOS	0102-03=

NAME (Subregion)	Type (Eruption Total, Most Recent) Status . . . Relation to NAMED VOLCANO	NUMBER
KASTRIULYA (Kamchatka)	Shield of ZAOZERNY	1000-48-
KASUGA-KAIZAN (Volcano Is-Japan)	Synonym of KASUGA SEAMOUNT	0804-134
KASUGA SEAMOUNT (Volcano Is-Japan)	Submarine (None) Uncertain	**0804-134**
KATABUTA-YAMA N & S (Honshu-Japan)	Cones of FUJI	0803-03=
KATAKURA-YAMA (Japan)	Cone of AKITA-KOMAGA-TAKE	0803-23=
KATALIM (Africa-E)	Cone of PAKA	0202-053
KATANUMA (Honshu-Japan)	Crater of NARUGO	0803-20=
KATASU HILL (Canada)	Cone of MILBANKE SOUND GROUP	1200-12-
KATINDA (Africa-C)	Crater of BUNYARUGURU FIELD	0203-005
KATKATKONO (Africa-N)	Crater of MEIDOB VOLC FIELD	0205-05-
KATLA (Iceland-S)	Subglacial (21, 1918) Historical	**1702-03=**
KATLAR (Iceland-SW)	Crater row of KRISUVIK	1701-03=
KATLOGIAA (Iceland-S)	Synonym of KATLA	1702-03=
KATMAI (Alaska Peninsula)	Stratovolc (1, 1912) Historical	**1102-17-**
KATT, CUDDIA DEL (Italy)	Cone of PANTELLERIA	0101-071
KATTA-DAKE (Honshu-Japan)	Stratovolc of ZAO	0803-19=
KATUBA (Africa-C)	Crater of BUNYARUGURU FIELD	0203-005
KATUBUI (Africa-E)	Crater of KIEYO	0202-17=
KATUNGA (Africa-C)	Tuff cone (None) Holocene	**0203-006**
KATWE (Africa-C)	Tuff cone of KATWE-KIKORONGO FIELD	0203-004
KATWE-KIKORONGO FIELD (Africa-C)	Tuff cones (None) Holocene	**0203-004**
KAUFFMAN VOLCANO (Antarctica)	Shield of ANDRUS	1900-023
KAUKA, PUU (Hawaiian Is)	Cone of KILAUEA	1302-01-
KAULET EL-HAURI (Arabia-S)	Crater of ARHAB, HARRA OF	0301-09-
KAULET HATTAB (Arabia-S)	Tuff cone of ARHAB, HARRA OF	0301-09-
KAUMUKI (Hawaiian Is)	Cone of KILAUEA	1302-01-
KAUPO (Hawaiian Is)	Cone of KOOLAU	1302-07-
KAUPULEHU (Hawaiian Is)	Cone of HUALALAI	1302-04-
KAVACHI (Solomon Is-SW Pac)	Submarine (25, 1991) Historical	**0505-06=**
KAVAKLIDAG (Turkey)	Dome of ERCIYES DAGI	0103-01=
KAWA (Luzon-Philippines)	Synonym of CAGUA	0703-09=
KAWAGODAIRA (Honshu-Japan)	Maar of IZU-TOBU	0803-01=
KAWAH (Indonesian for CRATER) see proper name (e.g. BARU, KAWAH)		
KAWAHKAMOJANG (Java)	Fumarole fld (None) Fumarolic	**0603-12=**
KAWAHKARAHA (Java)	Fumarole fld (None) Fumarolic	**0603-16=**
KAWAHMANUK (Java)	Fumarole fld (None) Fumarolic	**0603-11=**
KAWAK BUTTE (US-Oregon)	Cone of NEWBERRY VOLCANO	1202-11-
KAWAL KARAHA (Java)	Synonym of KAWAHKARAHA	0603-16=
KAWANA-MINAMI (Honshu-Japan)	Cone of IZU-TOBU	0803-01=
KAWAYU-IWO-ZAN [ATOSANUPURI]	Dome of KUTCHARO	0805-08=
KAWERAU (New Zealand)	Thermal Feature of OKATAINA	0401-05=
KAWI-BUTAK (Java)	Stratovolcs (None) Holocene	**0603-281**
KAWITI (New Zealand)	Cone of KAIKOHE-BAY OF ISLANDS	0401-01=
KAYABENOBORI (Hokkaido-Japan)	Synonym of KOMAGA-TAKE	0805-02=
KAZBEK (Georgia)	Synonym of KASBEK	0104-02-
KEALAALEA HILLS (Hawaiian Is)	Shield of KILAUEA	1302-01-
KEANAKAKOI (Hawaiian Is)	Pit crater of KILAUEA	1302-01-
KEBENEI (Kamchatka)	Synonym of KEBENEY	1000-50-
KEBENEY (Kamchatka)	Shield (None) Holocene	**1000-50-**
KEBONGO (Africa-E)	Cone of KOROSI	0202-054
KEBRIT ALE (Ethiopia)	Synonym of GADA ALE	0201-05=
KEBUN BUNGO (Sumatra)	Crater of MARAPI	0601-14=
KECHII [KURAISWA] (Africa-E)	Vent of KOROSI	0202-054
KECHUCAVI OF MOLINA (Chile-S)	Synonym of MINCHINMAVIDA	1508-04=
KECIL, DANAU (Sumatra)	Crater of TALANG	0601-16=
KECIL, KABA [BARU, KABA] (Sumatra)	Crater of KABA	0601-22=
KEFELI (Turkey)	Cone of ERCIYES DAGI	0103-01=
KEFENLI TEPE (Turkey)	Cone of ERCIYES DAGI	0103-01=
KEIGETSU-DAKE (Hokkaido-Japan)	Dome of DAISETSU	0805-06=
KEIGETU-DAKE [KEIGETSU-DAKE]	Dome of DAISETSU	0805-06=
KEILAMBETE, LAKE (Australia)	Maar of NEWER VOLCANICS PROV	0509-01-
KEIZUKA-YAMA (Honshu-Japan)	Shield of NIKKO-SHIRANE	0803-14=
KEKAU, GUNUNG [BUKIT MELAYU]	Cone of GAMALAMA	0608-06=
KEKEP (Java)	Crater of SUNDORO	0603-21=
KEKEXILI (China-W)	Caldera of UNNAMED	1004-04-
KEKUKNAYSKY (Kamchatka)	Shield of BOLSHOY-KEKUKNAYSKY	1000-36-
KEKURNY (Kamchatka)	Shields (None) Holocene	**1000-41-**
KELAKIRANA TEPE (Turkey)	Cone of NEMRUT DAGI	0103-02=
KELANG, MT. (Sulawesi-Indonesia)	Cone of KLABAT	0606-12=
KELBEY'S RIDGE (W Indies)	Dome of SABA	1600-01=
KELI MUTU (Lesser Sunda Is)	Synonym of KELIMUTU	0604-14=
KELIBARA (Lesser Sunda Is)	Cone of KELIMUTU	0604-14=
KELIDO (Lesser Sunda Is)	Cone of KELIMUTU	0604-14=
KELIMUTU (Lesser Sunda Is)	Complx volc (3, 1968) Historical	**0604-14=**
KELL (Kamchatka)	Stratovolc (None) Holocene	**1000-041**
KELLY BUTTE (US-Oregon)	Cone of NEWBERRY VOLCANO	1202-11-
KELLYA (Kamchatka)	Synonym of KELL	1000-041
KELOET (KELUIT) (Java)	Synonym of KELUT	0603-28=
KELSAY POINT (US-Oregon)	Cone of CINNAMON BUTTE	1202-15-
KELUD (KELOED) (Java)	Synonym of KELUT	0603-28=
KELUO GROUP (China-E)	Pyrocl cones (None) Holocene	**1005-03-**
KELUONANSHAN [NANSHAN] (China-E)	Cone of KELUO GROUP	1005-03-
KELUT (Java)	Stratovolc (34, 1990) Historical	**0603-28=**
KEMBANG (Java)	Crater of SUNDORO	0603-21=
KEMBAR N & S (Java)	Cones of ARJUNO-WELIRANG	0603-29=
KEMMERLING (Java)	Crater of SEMERU	0603-30=
KEMOENTJOEP, GUNUNG [KEMUNCUP]	Dome of PENANGGUNGAN	0603-291
KEMULAN (Java)	Stratovolc of DIENG VOLC COMPLEX	0603-20=
KEMUNCUP, GUNUNG (Java)	Dome of PENANGGUNGAN	0603-291
KENA (Canada)	Cone of EDZIZA	1200-06-
KENASHI-YAMA (Honshu-Japan)	Dome of IIZUNA	0803-102
KENDANG CRATER (Java)	Synonym of KAWAHMANUK	0603-11=
KENDENG (Java)	Caldera of IJEN	0603-35=
KENDIL (Java)	Cone of DIENG VOLC COMPLEX	0603-20=
KENDIL, GUNUNG (Java)	Cone of TELOMOYO	0603-231
KENFIELD NUNATAK (Antarctica)	Cone of HUDSON MOUNTAINS	1900-028
KENGA-MINE (Hokkaido-Japan)	Cone of AKAN	0805-07=
KENGAMINE (Honshu-Japan)	Dome of HAKU-SAN	0803-05=
KENNEDY HOT SPRINGS (US-Washington)	Thermal Feature of GLACIER PEAK	1201-02-
KENT CRATER (Indian O.-S)	Tuff cone of PRINCE EDWARD ISLAND	0304-07-
KENTON, CERRO (Mexico)	Cone of SAN QUINTIN VOLC FIELD	1401-002
KENZE (Africa-E)	Cone of CHYULU HILLS	0202-13=
KEO PEAK (Lesser Sunda Is)	Synonym of EBULOBO	0604-10=
KEONEHUNEHUNE (Hawaiian Is)	Cone of HALEAKALA	1302-06-
KEONENELU (Hawaiian Is)	Cone of HALEAKALA	1302-06-
KEPALA, GUNUNG (Java)	Stratovolc of SEMERU	0603-30=
KEPEZ TEPE (Turkey)	Dome of ERCIYES DAGI	0103-01=
KEPOLO, GUNUNG [GUNUNG KEPALA]	Stratovolc of SEMERU	0603-30=
KEPUNDAN (Indonesian word for CRATER) see proper name (e.g. TUO, KEPUNDAN)		
KERAMAT, BUKIT (Halmahera-Indonesia)	Cone of GAMALAMA	0608-06=
KERAROA (New Guinea)	Synonym of VICTORY	0503-03=
KERAVIA [VULCAN] (New Britain-SW Pac)	Pumice cone of RABAUL	0502-14=

NAME (Subregion)	Type (Eruption Total, Most Recent) Status . . . Relation to NAMED VOLCANO	NUMBER
KEREKERE, VUTI (Vanuatu-SW Pacific)	Cone of AOBA	0507-03=
KEREM (Turkey)	Cone of ERCIYES DAGI	0103-01=
KERGUELEN ISLANDS (Indian O.-S)	Stratovolcs (None) Holocene	**0304-02=**
KERHOLL (Iceland-SW)	Crater of GRIMSNES	1701-06=
KERI (New Zealand)	Cone of KAIKOHE-BAY OF ISLANDS	0401-01=
KERID (Iceland-SW)	Maar of GRIMSNES	1701-06=
KERINCI (Sumatra)	Stratovolc (20, 1970) Historical	**0601-17=**
KERINTJI (Sumatra)	Synonym of KERINCI	0601-17=
KERKORUMIKSI TEPE (Turkey)	Cone of NEMRUT DAGI	0103-02=
KERKUR (Turkey)	Dome of NEMRUT DAGI	0103-02=
KERLINGARDYNGA (Iceland-NE)	Shield of FREMRINAMUR	1703-07=
KERLINGARFJOLL (Iceland-SW)	Stratovolc (None) Holocene	**1701-10=**
KERLINGARHOLAR (Iceland-NE)	Fissure vent of KRAFLA	1703-08=
KERLINGARHOLL (Iceland-SW)	Crater row of GRIMSNES	1701-06=
KERUAR (New Guinea-NE of)	Synonym of KADOVAR	0501-002
KETEN (Halmahera-Indonesia)	Synonym of MOTIR	0608-061
KETETAHI (New Zealand)	Thermal Feature of TONGARIRO	0401-08=
KETIL [KETILDYNGJA] (Iceland-NE)	Shield of FREMRINAMUR	1703-07=
KETJIL, DANAU [DANAU KECIL] (Sumatra)	Crater of TALANG	0601-16=
KETJIL, KABA [BARU, KABA] (Sumatra)	Crater of KABA	0601-22=
KETO KETO, MAUNGA (Pacific-C)	Cone of EASTER ISLAND	1303-08-
KETOI (Kurile Is)	Stratovolc (3, 1960) Historical	**0900-20=**
KETOI-JIMA (KETOY) (Kurile Is)	Synonym of KETOI	0900-20=
KETREDEGUIN (Chile-C)	Synonym of LONQUIMAY	1507-10=
KETRUDEHUIN (Chile-C)	Synonym of CALLAQUI	1507-091
KEVENEYTUNUP (Kamchatka)	Shield of BELY	1000-64-
KHADUTKA (Kamchatka)	Synonym of KHODUTKA	1000-053
KHAGINAK ? (Aleutian Is)	Synonym of ROUNDTOP	1101-38-
KHAIBAR, HARRAT EL- (Arabia-W)	Synonym of KHAYBAR, HARRAT	0301-06=
KHAIBER, HARRAT EL- (Arabia-W)	Synonym of KHAYBAR, HARRAT	0301-06=
KHALA [PECHAN] (China-W)	Cone of TIANSHAN VOLC GROUP	1004-02-
KHAMCHENSKAYA, SOPKA (Kamchatka)	Synonym of GAMCHEN	1000-21=
KHAMMA, CUDDIA (Italy)	Shield of PANTELLERIA	0101-071
KHANGAR (Kamchatka)	Synonym of HANGAR	1000-272
KHANUY GOL (Mongolia)	Volc field (None) Holocene	**1003-02-**
KHARA-BOLDOK (Russia-SE)	Cone of TUNKIN DEPRESSION	1002-05-
KHARA LAGUNA (Bolivia)	Synonym of CHASCON, CERRO	1505-071
KHARIMKOTAN (Kurile Is)	Synonym of HARIMKOTAN	0900-30=
KHARTIBUCALE (Italy)	Cone of PANTELLERIA	0101-071
KHAYBAR, HARRAT (Arabia-W)	Volc field (1, 0650) Historical	**0301-06=**
KHEBRIT, DJEBEL (Red Sea)	Synonym of TEYR, DJEBEL	0201-01=
KHETIK (Kamchatka)	Shield of OSTANETS	1000-056
KHOASHEN (Kamchatka)	Synonym of ICHINSKY	1000-28=
KHOBOK GROUP (Russia-SE)	Cone of TUNKIN DEPRESSION	1002-05-
KHODUKTA SPRINGS (Kamchatka)	Thermal Feature of KHODUTKA	1000-053
KHODUTKA (Kamchatka)	Stratovolcs (3, -0300) Radiocarbon	**1000-053**
KHODUTKINSKY (Kamchatka)	Maar of KHODUTKA	1000-053
KHOIOKHONGEN (Kamchatka)	Synonym of KHODUTKA	1000-053
KHOROG (Mongolia)	Cone of TARYATU-CHULUTU	1003-01-
KHURDJ EL-AISAR (Arabia-S)	Tuff cone of HAYLAN, JABAL	0301-11-
KHUTSI (Honshu-Japan)	Synonym of FUJI	0803-03=
KIALAGVIK (Alaska Peninsula)	Stratovolc (None) Holocene	**1102-12-**
KIAPU (Hawaiian Is)	Cone of KILAUEA	1302-01-
KIARABERES (Java)	Synonym of KIARABERES-GAGAK	0603-03=
KIARABERES-GAGAK (Java)	Stratovolc (6, 1939) Historical	**0603-03=**
KIBATI (Africa-C)	Cone of NYIRAGONGO	0203-03=
KIBITHEWA (Africa-E)	Pit crater of NYAMBENI HILLS	0202-056
KIBO (Africa-E)	Stratovolc of KILIMANJARO	0202-15=
KIBONGOTO (Africa-E)	Cone of KILIMANJARO	0202-15=
KIBREALE (Ethiopia)	Synonym of GADA ALE	0201-05=
KICHPINITSCH (Kamchatka)	Synonym of KIKHPINYCH	1000-18=
KICHWAMBE VOLC FIELD (Africa-C)	Synonym of BUNYARUGURU FIELD	0203-005
KICK-'EM-JENNY (W Indies)	Submarine (10, 1990) Historical	**1600-16=**
KICKER ROCK (Galapagos)	Tuff cone of SAN CRISTOBAL	1503-12-
KIE BESI (Halmahera-Indonesia)	Synonym of MAKIAN	0608-07=
KIEYO (Africa-E)	Stratovolc (1, 1800) Historical	**0202-17=**
KIGALGIN (Aleutian Is)	Synonym of CARLISLE	1101-23-
KIGAMIL (KIGAMILJACH) (Aleutian Is)	Synonym of KAGAMIL	1101-26-
KIGERE (Africa-C)	Tuff cone of FORT PORTAL FIELD	0203-002
KIGEZI (Africa-C)	Crater of BUNYARUGURU FIELD	0203-005
KIJONGO KALEMA (Africa-C)	Tuff cone of FORT PORTAL FIELD	0203-002
KIJONGO KATABYIRE (Africa-C)	Tuff cone of FORT PORTAL FIELD	0203-002
KIKAI (Ryukyu Is)	Caldera (6, 1988) Historical	**0802-06=**
KIKAIGA-SHIMA (Ryukyu Is)	Synonym of KIKAI	0802-06=
KIKDOOLI BUTTE (Alaska-W)	Cone of NUNIVAK ISLAND	1104-06-
KIKHPINYCH (Kamchatka)	Stratovolcs (8, 1550) Radiocarbon	**1000-18=**
KIKHPINYCH (Kamchatka)	Synonym of BOLSHOI SEMIACHIK	1000-15=
KIKIKYAK HILL (Alaska-W)	Cone of NUNIVAK ISLAND	1104-06-
KIKOMBE (Africa-C)	Cone of KARISIMBI	0203-04-
KIKORONGO (Africa-C)	Tuff cone of KATWE-KIKORONGO FIELD	0203-004
KILAUEA (Hawaiian Is)	Shield (86, 1993) Historical	**1302-01-**
KILAUEA (Hawaiian Is)	Caldera of KILAUEA	1302-01-
KILAUEA IKI (Hawaiian Is)	Pit crater of KILAUEA	1302-01-
KILEMA (Africa-E)	Cone of KILIMANJARO	0202-15=
KILEO (Africa-E)	Cone of KILIMANJARO	0202-15=
KILIAN CRATERE (France)	Dome of CHAINE DES PUYS	0100-02-
KILIMA DSCHARO (KILIMA NJARO) (Africa-E	Synonym of KILIMANJARO	0202-15=
KILIMANDJARO (Africa-E)	Synonym of KILIMANJARO	0202-15=
KILIMANJARO (Africa-E)	Stratovolc (None) Holocene	**0202-15=**
KILLEAK LAKES (Alaska-W)	Maar of ESPENBERG	1104-01-
KILLIS VOLC REGION (Syria)	Synonym of UNNAMED	0300-02-
KILOLE (Ethiopia)	Tuff ring of BISHOFTU FIELD	0201-22-
KIMANURA (Africa-C)	Cone of NYAMURAGIRA	0203-02=
KIMEN-ZAN (Honshu-Japan)	Dome of ADATARA	0803-17=
KIMIJOOKSUK BUTTE (Alaska-W)	Cone of NUNIVAK ISLAND	1104-06-
KIMIKSTHEK HILL (Alaska-W)	Cone of NUNIVAK ISLAND	1104-06-
KIMIKTHAK HILLS (Alaska-W)	Cone of NUNIVAK ISLAND	1104-06-
KIMILOS (Greece)	Cone of MILOS	0102-03=
KINAMI (New Ireland-SW Pac)	Stratovolc of LIHIR	0504-01=
KINANGA (Africa-E)	Cone of KILIMANJARO	0202-15=
KING CREEK (Canada)	Cone of ISKUT-UNUK RIVER CONES	1200-09-
KING MOUNTAIN FISSURE (US-Washington)	Fissure vent of ADAMS	1201-04-
KINGIRI (Africa-E)	Maar of KIEYO	0202-17=
KING'S BOWL RIFT (US-Idaho)	Fissure vent of WAPI LAVA FIELD	1204-03-
KINIHA (Africa-C)	Cone of NYIRAGONGO	0203-03=
KINUGASA (Kyushu-Japan)	Stratovolc of UNZEN	0802-10=
KINYAMBATSHA (Africa-C)	Cone of NYIRAGONGO	0203-03=
KINYAMUAGA (Africa-C)	Cone of NYAMURAGIRA	0203-02=
KINYANGAKI (Africa-C)	Cone of KARISIMBI	0203-04-
KIOGA (Africa-E)	Cone of KIEYO	0202-17=
KIOLIK HILL (Alaska-W)	Cone of NUNIVAK ISLAND	1104-06-
KIRARO (Africa-E)	Cone of NYAMBENI HILLS	0202-056

NAME (Subregion)	Type (Eruption Total, Most Recent) Status . . . Relation to NAMED VOLCANO	NUMBER
KIRAUEA (Hawaiian Is)	Synonym of KILAUEA	1302-01-
KIRCHWEILER (Germany)	Maar of WEST EIFEL VOLC FIELD	0100-01-
KIREREMA (Africa-C)	Cone of KARISIMBI	0203-04-
KIRGURICH (Kamchatka)	Crater of KLIUCHEVSKOI	1000-26=
KIRIFUKI (Kurile Is)	Synonym of ASYRMINTAR	0900-33=
KIRIMA-ITUNE (Africa-E)	Cone of NYAMBENI HILLS	0202-056
KIRISHIMA (Kyushu-Japan)	Shield (75, 1992) Historical	**0802-09=**
KIRISIMA (Kyushu-Japan)	Synonym of KIRISHIMA	0802-09=
KIRKJUFELL [ELDFELL] (Iceland-S)	Fissure vent of VESTMANNAEYJAR	1702-01=
KIRKOR DAGI [KERKUR] (Turkey)	Dome of NEMRUT DAGI	0103-02=
KIRMIZI TEPE (Turkey)	Cone of ERCIYES DAGI	0103-01=
KIRUNGA CHA NINA GONGO (Africa-C)	Synonym of NYIRAGONGO	0203-03=
KIRUNGA I (Africa-C)	Cone of NYIRAGONGO	0203-03=
KIRUNGA VISOKE (Africa-C)	Synonym of VISOKE	0203-05-
KIRUNGE CHA NIRAGONGO (Africa-C)	Synonym of NYIRAGONGO	0203-03=
KIRUNGE YA GONGO (Africa-C)	Synonym of NYIRAGONGO	0203-03=
KIRUNGO CHA GONGO (Africa-C)	Synonym of NYIRAGONGO	0203-03=
KIRUNGU TSCHA GONGO (Africa-C)	Synonym of NYIRAGONGO	0203-03=
KIRUNGU TSCHA GONGWE (Africa-C)	Synonym of NYIRAGONGO	0203-03=
KIRUTALE [KITUHARU] (Africa-C)	Cone of NYAMURAGIRA	0203-02=
KISHB, HARRAT (Arabia-W)	Volc field (None) Holocene	**0301-071**
KISHIMA-DAKE (Kyushu-Japan)	Stratovolc of ASO	0802-11=
KISKA (Aleutian Is)	Stratovolc (4, 1990) Historical	**1101-02-**
KISO-ONTAKE (Honshu-Japan)	Synonym of ON-TAKE	0803-04=
KISSOBA (Africa-E)	Crater of KIEYO	0202-17=
KISTA (Iceland-SW)	Crater row of BRENNISTEINSFJOLL	1701-04=
KISTUFELL (Iceland-SW)	Fissure vent of BRENNISTEINSFJOLL	1701-04=
KISTUFELLSGJOSKA (Iceland-NE)	Fissure vent of ASKJA	1703-06=
KISTUFELLSHRAUN (Iceland-NE)	Crater row of ASKJA	1703-06=
KITA-DAKE (Hokkaido)	Crater of SHIRETOKO-IWO-ZAN	0805-09=
KITA-DAKE (Kyushu-Japan)	Stratovolc of SAKURA-JIMA	0802-08=
KITA-HIYOSHI (Volcano Is-Japan)	Submarine vent of MINAMI-HIYOSHI	0804-131
KITA IWO DAKE (Kurile Is)	Synonym of KUNTOMINTAR	0900-28=
KITA-IWO-JIMA (Volcano Is-Japan)	Stratovolc (3, 1945) Historical	**0804-11=**
KITA-KANSU-YAMA (Honshu-Japan)	Cone of FUJI	0803-03=
KITA-KORI-IKE (Honshu-Japan)	Vent of FUJI	0803-03=
KITA-SENRIGAHAMA (Kyushu-Japan)	Crater of KUJU GROUP	0802-12=
KITA TIRIPPU (Kurile Is)	Synonym of CHIRIP	0900-09=
KITA-YAMA (Hokkaido-Japan)	Stratovolc of SHIKOTSU	0805-04=
KITA-YAMA (Hokkaido-Japan)	Cone of AKAN	0805-07=
KITAGAWA (Honshu-Japan)	Thermal Feature of KUSATSU-SHIRANE	0803-12=
KITAIO (Kurile Is)	Synonym of KUNTOMINTAR	0900-28=
KITANOHARA-HIGASHI (Honshu-Japan)	Maar of IZU-TOBU	0803-01=
KITAYATSUGA-TAKE (Honshu-Japan)	Synonym of TATESHINA	0803-031
KITAYATUGA-TAKE (Honshu-Japan)	Synonym of TATESHINA	0803-031
KITAZUNGURWA (Africa-C)	Cone of NYAMURAGIRA	0203-02=
KITEMA (Africa-E)	Cone of KIEYO	0202-17=
KITHETU HILL (Africa-E)	Pit crater of NYAMBENI HILLS	0202-056
KITIA (Madagascar)	Dome of ITASY VOLC FIELD	0303-06-
KITOMBOLD (Madagascar)	Cone of ITASY VOLC FIELD	0303-06-
KITSHIMBANY [KITSIMBANYI] (Africa-C)	Cone of NYAMURAGIRA	0203-02=
KITTIWAKE POND (Aleutian Is)	Maar of BULDIR	1101-01-
KITUHARU (Africa-C)	Cone of NYAMURAGIRA	0203-02=
KITURO [GITURO] (Africa-C)	Cone of NYAMURAGIRA	0203-02=
KIVANDIMWE (Africa-C)	Cone of NYAMURAGIRA	0203-02=
KIYOMI-DAKE (Kyushu-Japan)	Dome of IBUSUKI VOLC FIELD	0802-07=
KIZIL TEPE (Turkey)	Cone of ACIGOL-NEVSEHIR	0103-004
KIZILKUYU TEPE (Turkey)	Cone of ERCIYES DAGI	0103-01=
KIZIMA-DAKE [KISHIMA-DAKE] (Kyushu)	Stratovolc of ASO	0802-11=
KIZIMEN (Kamchatka)	Stratovolc (5, 1928) Historical	**1000-23=**
KIZINEN (Kamchatka)	Synonym of KIZIMEN	1000-23=
KJALHRAUN (Iceland-SW)	Shield of LANGJOKULL	1701-08=
KLABAT (Sulawesi-Indonesia)	Stratovolc (None) Fumarolic	**0606-12=**
KLAK BUTTE (US-Oregon)	Cone of BACHELOR	1202-09-
KLASTLINE (Canada)	Cone of EDZIZA	1200-06-
KLAWHOP BUTTE (US-Oregon)	Cone of NEWBERRY VOLCANO	1202-11-
KLEINE SSEMJATSCHIK (Kamchatka)	Synonym of KARYMSKY	1000-13=
KLESHNYA (Kamchatka)	Cone of TOLBACHIK	1000-24=
KLIUCHEF (Aleutian Is)	Stratovolc of ATKA	1101-16-
KLIUCHEVSKAIA SOPKA (Kamchatka)	Synonym of KLIUCHEVSKOI	1000-26=
KLIUCHEVSKOI (Kamchatka)	Stratovolc (88, 1993) Historical	**1000-26=**
KLIUCHEVSKOY [KLIUCHEF] (Aleutian Is)	Stratovolc of ATKA	1101-16-
KLJUTSCHEW (Kamchatka)	Synonym of KLIUCHEVSKOI	1000-26=
KLJUTSCHEWSKAJA SOPKA (Kamchatka)	Synonym of KLIUCHEVSKOI	1000-26=
KLOET (Java)	Synonym of KELUT	0603-28=
KLOFNINGAHRAUN (Iceland-SW)	Crater row of REYKJANES	1701-02=
KLONE BUTTE (US-Oregon)	Cone of NEWBERRY VOLCANO	1202-11-
KLUCHEV (Kamchatka)	Synonym of KLIUCHEVSKOI	1000-26=
KLUTLAN GLACIER (Alaska-E)	Synonym of BONA-CHURCHILL	1105-03-
KLYUCHGVSKAYA (Kamchatka)	Synonym of KLIUCHEVSKOI	1000-26=
KNAPPAFELLSJOKULL (Iceland-SE)	Synonym of ORAEFAJOKULL	1704-01=
KNIFE PEAK (Alaska Peninsula)	Synonym of GRIGGS	1102-19-
KO-ASAMA-YAMA (Honshu-Japan)	Dome of ASAMA	0803-11=
KO-ATOSANUPURI (Hokkaido-Japan)	Stratovolc of KUTCHARO	0805-08=
KO-FUJI (Honshu-Japan)	Stratovolc of FUJI	0803-03=
KO-HIYOSHI (Volcano Is-Japan)	Submarine vent of MINAMI-HIYOSHI	0804-131
KO-JIMA (Izu Is-Japan)	Stratovolc of HACHIJO-JIMA	0804-05=
K'O-LO-NAN-SHAN (China-E)	Synonym of KELUO GROUP	1005-03-
KO-TOKACHI-DAKE (Hokkaido-Japan)	Stratovolc of TOKACHI	0805-05=
KO-USU (Hokkaido-Japan)	Dome of USU	0805-03=
KO-YAMA (Honshu-Japan)	Cone of AZUMA	0803-18=
KO-ZIMA [KO-JIMA] (Izu Is-Japan)	Stratovolc of HACHIJO-JIMA	0804-05=
KOA (Lesser Sunda Is)	Thermal Feature of PALUWEH	0604-15=
KOA [SOUTHERN DOME] (New Zealand)	Dome of OKATAINA	0401-05=
KOAE, PUU (Hawaiian Is)	Cone of KILAUEA	1302-01-
KOANG, MT. (Australia)	Cone of NEWER VOLCANICS PROV	0509-01-
KOBANDAI (Honshu-Japan)	Stratovolc of BANDAI	0803-16=
KOBE-YAMA (Izu Is-Japan)	Dome of KOZU-SHIMA	0804-03=
KOBU-YAMA (Hokkaido-Japan)	Cone of AKAN	0805-07=
KOCATEPE (Turkey)	Cone of ACIGOL-NEVSEHIR	0103-004
KOCDAGI (Turkey)	Cone of ERCIYES DAGI	0103-01=
KOCHER [HUOSHAOSHAN] (China-E)	Cone of WUDALIANCHI	1005-04-
KODAKE (Japan)	Cone of AKITA-KOMAGA-TAKE	0803-23=
KODDA GINNI KOMA (Djibouti)	Tuff cone of ARDOUKOBA	0201-126
KOEKOESAN [KUKUSAN] (Java)	Cone of IJEN	0603-35=
KOENJIT (Sumatra)	Synonym of KUNYIT	0601-19=
KOERINCI (KOERINTJI) (Sumatra)	Synonym of KERINCI	0601-17=
KOERSI, GUNUNG [GUNUNG KURSI] (Java)	Cone of TENGGER CALDERA	0603-31=
KOETLEGIAA (Iceland-S)	Synonym of KATLA	1702-03=
KOH-I BAZMAN (Iran)	Synonym of BAZMAN	0302-03-
KOH-I TAFTAN (Iran)	Synonym of TAFTAN	0302-05-
KOHUORA (New Zealand)	Tuff cone of AUCKLAND FIELD	0401-02=

NAME (Subregion)	Type (Eruption Total, Most Recent) Status . . . Relation to NAMED VOLCANO	NUMBER
KOIKE (Honshu-Japan)	Vent of IZU-TOBU	0803-01=
KOINAKA-YAMA (Honshu-Japan)	Synonym of FUJI	0803-03=
KOIZUMI-DAKE (Hokkaido-Japan)	Stratovolc of DAISETSU	0805-06=
KOJIN-YAMA (Honshu-Japan)	Cone of CHOKAI	0803-22=
KOKHERA (China-E)	Synonym of WUDALIANCHI	1005-04-
KOKKINO VOUNO (Greece)	Cone of SANTORINI	0102-04=
KOKO (Hawaiian Is)	Tuff cone of KOOLAU	1302-07-
KOKO HEAD (Hawaiian Is)	Tuff cone of KOOLAU	1302-07-
KOKON (Banda Sea)	Synonym of NILA	0605-06=
KOKON-EMPUNG (Sulawesi-Indonesia)	Synonym of LOKON-EMPUNG	0606-10=
KOKOOLAU (Hawaiian Is)	Cone of KILAUEA	1302-01-
KOKOR, WAI (Lesser Sunda Is)	Thermal Feature of POCO LEOK	0604-07=
KOLANH DAG (Turkey)	Cone of ERCIYES DAGI	0103-01=
KOLANLI DAG (Turkey)	Dome of ERCIYES DAGI	0103-01=
KOLBEINSEY RIDGE (Iceland-N of)	Submarine (2, 1755) Historical	**1705-01=**
KOLBO, GOF (Africa-E)	Maar of MARSABIT	0202-021
KOLCHON (Kamchatka)	Synonym of ICHINSKY	1000-28=
KOLDUKVISLARHRAUN (Iceland-NE)	Fissure vent of BARDARBUNGA	1703-03=
KOLE, PUU (Hawaiian Is)	Cone of MAUNA KEA	1302-03-
KOLEKOLE (Hawaiian Is)	Cone of HALEAKALA	1302-06-
KOLEKOLE, PUU (Hawaiian Is)	Cone of KILAUEA	1302-01-
KOLGRAFARHOLL (Iceland-SW)	Cone of GRIMSNES	1701-06=
KOLKHOZHNY (Kamchatka)	Stratovolc (None) Holocene	**1000-221**
KOLLATTADYNGJA (Iceland-NE)	Shield of ASKJA	1703-06=
KOLOB (US-Utah)	Volc field (None) Holocene?	**1207-02-**
KOLOB PEAK (US-Utah)	Cone of KOLOB	1207-02-
KOLOKOL (Kurile Is)	Stratovolc of KOLOKOL GROUP	0900-12=
KOLOKOL GROUP (Kurile Is)	Somma volcs (9, 1973) Historical	**0900-12=**
KOMA-DAKE (Japan)	Synonym of AKITA-KOMAGA-TAKE	0803-23=
KOMA KULSHAN (US-Washington)	Synonym of BAKER	1201-01=
KOMAGA-TAKE (Hokkaido-Japan)	Stratovolc (16, 1942) Historical	**0805-02=**
KOMAGA-TAKE (Honshu-Japan)	Synonym of KURIKOMA	0803-21=
KOMAGA-TAKE (Honshu-Japan)	Dome of HAKONE	0803-02=
KOMAKATA-YAMA (Japan)	Synonym of AKITA-KOMAGA-TAKE	0803-23=
KOMANAGO (Honshu-Japan)	Dome of OMANAGO GROUP	0803-142
KOMAROV (Kamchatka)	Stratovolc (None) Holocene	**1000-22=**
KOMAROVA (Kamchatka)	Synonym of KOMAROV	1000-22=
KOMBIU (New Britain-SW Pac)	Stratovolc of RABAUL	0502-14=
KOMBUNG (Admiralty Is-SW Pac)	Cone of ST. ANDREW STRAIT	0500-01=
KOMETSUKA (Kyushu-Japan)	Cone of ASO	0802-11=
KOMIA (Greece)	Thermal Feature of MILOS	0102-03=
KOMIKASA-YAMA (Honshu-Japan)	Cone of ON-TAKE	0803-04=
KOMITAKE (Honshu-Japan)	Stratovolc of FUJI	0803-03=
KOMOCHI-YAMA (Izu Is-Japan)	Cone of TORI-SHIMA	0804-09=
KOMOLION (Africa-E)	Vent of KOROSI	0202-054
KOMOTI-YAMA [KOMOCHI-YAMA] (Izu Is)	Cone of TORI-SHIMA	0804-09=
KOMPIRA-YAMA (Hokkaido-Japan)	Dome of USU	0805-03=
KOMURO-YAMA (Honshu-Japan)	Cone of IZU-TOBU	0803-01=
KONE (Ethiopia)	Calderas (1, 1820) Historical	**0201-20-**
KONGOLO (Africa-E)	Dome of SW USANGU BASIN	0202-163
KONGSFELL (Iceland-SW)	Crater row of BRENNISTEINSFJOLL	1701-04=
KONI (Ethiopia)	Synonym of KONE	0201-20-
KONIA (Aleutian Is)	Stratovolc of ATKA	1101-16-
KONIUJI (Aleutian Is)	Stratovolc (None) Uncertain	**1101-14-**
KONIUSHI (Aleutian Is)	Synonym of KONIUJI	1101-14-
KONO (Honshu-Japan)	Crater of AKAGI	0803-13=
KONOCTI, MT. (US-California)	Dome of CLEAR LAKE	1203-10-
KONSEI-ZAN (Honshu-Japan)	Dome of NIKKO-SHIRANE	0803-14=
KONWONSAVARO (Vanuatu-SW Pacific)	Crater of SORETIMEAT	0507-01=
KOOKOOLIGIT MOUNTAINS (Alaska-W)	Shield (None) Holocene	**1104-03-**
KOOKOOLIT HILL (Alaska-W)	Cone of KOOKOOLIGIT MOUNTAINS	1104-03-
KOOLAU (Hawaiian Is)	Shield (None) Holocene?	**1302-07-**
KOPENG (Java)	Fissure vent of MERBABU	0603-24=
KORANGA (New Guinea)	Expl crater (None) Holocene	**0503-003**
KORATH RANGE (Ethiopia)	Tuff cones (None) Holocene?	**0201-32-**
KORI-IKE (Honshu-Japan)	Vent of FUJI	0803-03=
KORIAKA (KORIAKSKY) (Kamchatka)	Synonym of KORYAKSKY	1000-09=
KORIANA (Honshu-Japan)	Vent of FUJI	0803-03=
KORIATZKAIA, SOPKA (Kamchatka)	Synonym of KORYAKSKY	1000-09=
KORINCI (KORINTJI) (Sumatra)	Synonym of KERINCI	0601-17=
KORJAKA (KORJAZKIJ) (Kamchatka)	Synonym of KORYAKSKY	1000-09=
KORO (Fiji Is-SW Pacific)	Cinder cones (None) Holocene?	**0405-02-**
KORONA (Kamchatka)	Dome of BOLSHOI SEMIACHIK	1000-15=
KOROSI (Africa-E)	Shield (None) Holocene	**0202-054**
KOROWINSKY [KOROVIN] (Aleutian Is)	Stratovolc of ATKA	1101-16-
KORYAKA (KORYAKSKAYA SOPKA)	Synonym of KORYAKSKY	1000-09=
KORYAKSKY (Kamchatka)	Stratovolc (3, 1957) Historical	**1000-09=**
KOS (Greece)	Fumarole flds (None) Pleistocene-Fumarolic	**0102-06=**
KOSCHELEWA (Kamchatka)	Synonym of KOSHELEV	1000-02=
KOSCHELEWA PEAK (Kamchatka)	Synonym of OPALA	1000-08=
KOSCIUSKO (Antarctica)	Shield of ANDRUS	1900-023
KOSEKUMARU (Honshu-Japan)	Cone of FUJI	0803-03=
KOSHELEV (Kamchatka)	Stratovolc (1, 1690) Historical	**1000-02=**
KOSHELEVA, SOPKA (Kamchatka)	Synonym of KOSHELEV	1000-02=
KOSHELEVSKY (Kamchatka)	Synonym of KOSHELEV	1000-02=
KOSHIKI-DAKE (Kyushu-Japan)	Cone of KIRISHIMA	0802-09=
KOSHIKIRIZUKA (Honshu-Japan)	Cone of FUJI	0803-03=
KOSIKI-DAKE [KOSHIKI-DAKE] (Kyushu)	Cone of KIRISHIMA	0802-09=
KOSINGE REEF (Solomon Is-SW Pac)	Thermal Feature of SIMBO	0505-05=
KOSTAL (Canada)	Cone of WELLS GRAY-CLEARWATER	1200-15-
KOTAMOI [TEBENKOV] (Kurile Is)	Stratovolc of GROZNY GROUP	0900-07=
KOTCHLONGA (Kamchatka)	Synonym of ICHINSKY	1000-28=
KOTHRAUNSKULA (Iceland-W)	Cone of LJOSUFJOLL	1700-03=
KOTIATO SAN (Kurile Is)	Synonym of RASSHUA	0900-22=
KOTKHLONGA (Kamchatka)	Synonym of ICHINSKY	1000-28=
KOTLUGJA (Iceland-S)	Synonym of KATLA	1702-03=
KOU, PUU (Hawaiian Is)	Shield of KILAUEA	1302-01-
KOU'A, MAUNGA (Pacific-C)	Cone of EASTER ISLAND	1303-08-
KOUSSI, EMI (Africa-N)	Stratovolc (None) Holocene	**0205-021**
KOVACHI (Solomon Is-SW Pac)	Synonym of KAVACHI	0505-06=
KOVRIZHKA (Russia-SE)	Cone of TUNKIN DEPRESSION	1002-05-
KOYA-JIGOKU (Kyushu-Japan)	Thermal Feature of TSURUMI	0802-13=
KOZEI (Kamchatka)	Crater of KLIUCHEVSKOI	1000-26=
KOZEL [KOZELSKIY] (Kamchatka)	Stratovolc of AVACHINSKY	1000-10=
KOZIN-YAMA [KOJIN-YAMA] (Honshu-Japan)	Cone of CHOKAI	0803-22=
KOZU-SHIMA (Izu Is-Japan)	Lava domes (2, 0838) Historical	**0804-03=**
KOZU-SIMA (Izu Is-Japan)	Synonym of KOZU-SHIMA	0804-03=
KOZUKA-YAMA (Honshu-Japan)	Dome of HAKONE	0803-02=
KOZUKUSI-YAMA [KOZUKUSHI-YAMA]	Dome of OSORE-YAMA	0803-29=
KOZYREVSKII (Kurile Is)	Cone of VERNADSKII RIDGE	0900-37-
KOZYREVSKY (Kamchatka)	Shield (None) Holocene	**1000-33-**
KRAB (Kamchatka)	Cone of KIKHPINYCH	1000-18=

NAME (Subregion)	Type (Eruption Total, Most Recent) Status / Relation to NAMED VOLCANO	NUMBER
KRAEDUBORGIR (Iceland-NE)	Fissure vent of FREMRINAMUR	1703-07=
KRAEVEDCHESKY (Kamchatka)	Thermal Feature of DZENZURSKY	1000-11=
KRAFAKHOLAHRAUN (Iceland-S)	Fissure vent of HEKLA	1702-07=
KRAFLA (Iceland-NE)	Caldera (29, 1984) Historical	**1703-08=**
KRAINY (Kamchatka)	Shield (None) Holocene	**1000-40-**
KRAKAGIGAR (Iceland-S)	Fissure vent of HEKLA	1702-07=
KRAKAR (New Guinea-NE of)	Synonym of KARKAR	0501-03=
KRAKATAO (Indonesia)	Synonym of KRAKATAU	0602-00=
KRAKATAU (Indonesia)	Caldera (41, 1993) Historical	**0602-00=**
KRAKATOA (Indonesia)	Synonym of KRAKATAU	0602-00=
KRAKSHRAUN (Iceland-SW)	Fissure vent of LANGJOKULL	1701-08=
KRASHENINNIKOV (Kamchatka)	Crater of KLIUCHEVSKOI	1000-26=
KRASHENINNIKOV (Kamchatka)	Caldera (31, 1550) Radiocarbon	**1000-19=**
KRASHENINNIKOV (Kurile Is)	Crater of VERNADSKII RIDGE	0900-37-
KRASNAYA (Kamchatka)	Dome of SHEVELUCH	1000-27=
KRASNUKH, MT. (Kurile Is)	Cone of VERNADSKII RIDGE	0900-37-
KRATIOTI (Greece)	Dome of NISYROS	0102-05=
KRAYNIY (Kamchatka)	Synonym of KRAINY	1000-40-
KRENITZYN PEAK (Kurile Is)	Stratovolc of TAO-RUSYR CALDERA	0900-31=
KREPPUHRAUN (Iceland-NE)	Fissure vent of KVERKFJOLL	1703-05=
KREPPUTUNGUHRAUN (Iceland-NE)	Fissure vent of KVERKFJOLL	1703-05=
KRESTOVSKAYA [KRESTOVSKY] (Kamchat	Stratovolc of USHKOVSKY	1000-261
KRESTOVSKII [KRESTOVSKY] (Kamchatka)	Stratovolc of USHKOVSKY	1000-261
KRIKAHRAUN (Iceland-S)	Fissure vent of KATLA	1702-03=
KRINGLUHRAUN (Iceland-S)	Crater row of VATNAFJOLL	1702-06=
KRISUVIK (Iceland-SW)	Crater rows (9, 1340) Historical	**1701-03=**
KROFLUELDAR (Iceland-NE)	Crater row of KRAFLA	1703-08=
KROKAGILSOLDUHRAUN (Iceland-S)	Fissure vent of HEKLA	1702-07=
KROKAHRAUN (Iceland-S)	Fissure vent of HEKLA	1702-07=
KROKUR (Kamchatka)	Maar of KRASHENINNIKOV	1000-19=
KROMYONIA (Greece)	Synonym of SUSAKI	0102-01=
KRONER LAKE (Antarctica)	Crater of DECEPTION ISLAND	1900-03=
KRONOTSKY (Kamchatka)	Stratovolc (3, 1923) Historical	**1000-20=**
KRONOTZKAIA SOPKA (Kamchatka)	Synonym of KRONOTSKY	1000-20=
KRONOTZKY (KRONOZKY) (Kamchatka)	Synonym of KRONOTSKY	1000-20=
KROPOTKIN (Russia-SE)	Cone of OKA VOLC FIELD	1002-06-
KRUGLAYA (Kamchatka)	Dome of UZON	1000-17=
KRUGLENKY (Kamchatka)	Cone of TOLBACHIK	1000-24=
KRUMMEL (Germany)	Cone of WEST EIFEL VOLC FIELD	0100-01-
KRUMMEL (New Britain-SW Pac)	Stratovolc of GARBUNA GROUP	0502-07=
KRUTAYA MOUNTAIN (Kurile Is)	Cone of IVAO GROUP	0900-111
KRUTOI (Kamchatka)	Dome of BOLSHOI SEMIACHIK	1000-15=
KRUTOI (Kurile Is)	Dome of GOLOVNIN	0900-01=
KRYSHANOVSKOGO [KRYZHANOVSKIY]	Crater of KLIUCHEVSKOI	1000-26=
KRYSUVIK (Iceland-SW)	Thermal Feature of KRISUVIK	1701-03=
KRYZHANOVSKII (Kurile Is)	Caldera of TAO-RUSYR CALDERA	0900-31=
KRYZHANOVSKIY (Kamchatka)	Crater of KLIUCHEVSKOI	1000-26=
KSKHUDACH (Kamchatka)	Synonym of KSUDACH	1000-05=
KSUDACH (Kamchatka)	Shield (14, 1907) Historical	**1000-05=**
KSUDATSCH (Kamchatka)	Synonym of KSUDACH	1000-05=
KTENAS (Greece)	Dome of SANTORINI	0102-04=
KU-LAO-RHE (SE Asia)	Synonym of CU-LAO RE GROUP	0705-02-
KUAN-TZO-LING (China-E)	Cone of LONGGANG GROUP	1005-06-
KUANI HILL (Africa-E)	Cone of NYAMBENI HILLS	0202-056
KUCHIERABU-JIMA (Ryukyu Is)	Synonym of KUCHINOERABU-JIMA	0802-05=
KUCHINO-SHIMA (Ryukyu Is)	Stratovolcs (None) Holocene	**0802-041**
KUCHINOERABU-JIMA (Ryukyu Is)	Stratovolcs (13, 1980) Historical	**0802-05=**
KUCUK ARARAT (Turkey)	Cone of ARARAT, MT.	0103-04-
KUCUK KEFELI (Turkey)	Cone of ERCIYES DAGI	0103-01=
KUCUKMEDET TEPE (Turkey)	Cone of KARAPINAR FIELD	0103-001
KUDRIAVY (Kurile Is)	Cone of MEDVEZHIA	0900-10=
KUEI-SHAN-TAO (Taiwan)	Stratovolc (None) Pleistocene-Fumarolic	**0801-031**
KUGAK (KUGAT) (Alaska Peninsula)	Synonym of KUKAK	1102-23-
KUGIDACH-JAGUTSCHA [POGROMNI]	Stratovolc of WESTDAHL	1101-34-
KUH-E BAZMAN (Iran)	Synonym of BAZMAN	0302-03-
KUH-E TAFTAN (Iran)	Synonym of TAFTAN	0302-05-
KUHARUA (New Zealand)	Dome of TAUPO	0401-07=
KUIRAU PARK (New Zealand)	Thermal Feature of ROTORUA	0401-042
KUJU GROUP (Kyushu-Japan)	Stratovolcs (2, 1675) Historical	**0802-12=**
KUJYU GROUP (Kyushu-Japan)	Synonym of KUJU GROUP	0802-12=
KUKAI, PUU (Hawaiian Is)	Cone of KILAUEA	1302-01-
KUKAK (Alaska Peninsula)	Stratovolc (None) Fumarolic	**1102-23-**
KUKII, PUU [PUU KUKAI] (Hawaiian Is)	Cone of KILAUEA	1302-01-
KUKUSAN (Java)	Cone of IJEN	0603-35=
KUKUSAN (Java)	Cone of SEMERU	0603-30=
KULA (Turkey)	Cinder cones (None) Holocene	**0103-00-**
KULABU (Sumatra)	Cone of SORIKMARAPI	0601-12=
KULADIVLIT (Turkey)	Cone of KULA	0103-00-
KULAKOV (Kamchatka)	Dome of BOLSHOI SEMIACHIK	1000-15=
KULANAPAHU (Hawaiian Is)	Cone of HALEAKALA	1302-06-
KULICH (Kamchatka)	Dome of BEZYMIANNY	1000-25=
KULKEV (Kamchatka)	Shield (None) Holocene	**1000-37-**
KULKUL (New Guinea-NE of)	Synonym of RITTER ISLAND	0501-07=
KULSHAN (US-Washington)	Synonym of BAKER	1201-01=
KULUA, PUU (Hawaiian Is)	Cone of MAUNA LOA	1302-02=
KUMA-DAKE (Hokkaido-Japan)	Stratovolc of DAISETSU	0805-06=
KUMA, MAUNGA (Pacific-C)	Cone of EASTER ISLAND	1303-08-
KUMA-OTOSI [KUMA-OTOSHI] (Hokkaido)	Crater of KUTCHARO	0805-08=
KUMANO-DAKE (Honshu-Japan)	Synonym of ZAO	0803-19=
KUMANO-DAKE (Honshu-Japan)	Stratovolc of ZAO	0803-19=
KUMBANG (Java)	Thermal Feature of DIENG VOLC COMP	0603-20=
KUMMEN (Atl-N-Jan Mayen)	Cone of JAN MAYEN	1706-01=
KUMU, PUU (Hawaiian Is)	Cone of HALEAKALA	1302-06-
KUNASHIRI-RAUSU (Kurile Is)	Synonym of MENDELEEV	0900-02=
KUNG-PO (China-S)	Synonym of TENGCHONG	0705-11-
KUNIANG, KAPUNDAN [KEPUNDAN KUNIA	Crater of MARAPI	0601-14=
KUNIANG, KEPUNDAN (Sumatra)	Crater of MARAPI	0601-14=
KUNII [KUNIR] (Java)	Cone of DIENG VOLC COMPLEX	0603-20=
KUNINOFUKA-YAMA (Honshu-Japan)	Synonym of FUJI	0803-03=
KUNJIT (Sumatra)	Synonym of KUNYIT	0601-19=
KUNLUN VOLCANO GROUP (China-W)	Pyrocl cones (1, 1951) Historical	**1004-03-**
KUNTOMINTAR (Kurile Is)	Hydrothrm fld (None) Pleistocene-Fumarolic	**0900-28=**
KUNUMI-DAKE (Kyushu-Japan)	Dome of UNZEN	0802-10=
KUNUWERI (Banda Sea)	Synonym of TEON	0605-05=
KUNYIT (Sumatra)	Stratovolc (None) Fumarolic	**0601-19=**
KUPAIANAHA (Hawaiian Is)	Shield of KILAUEA	1302-01-
KUPENUI (New Zealand)	Cone of WHANGAREI	0401-011
KUPOL SKALISTY (Kamchatka)	Dome of BOLSHOI SEMIACHIK	1000-15=
KUPREANOF (Alaska Peninsula)	Stratovolc (1, 1987) Historical	**1102-06-**
KURAISHI-DAKE (Honshu-Japan)	Synonym of ZAO	0803-19=
KURAISWA (Africa-E)	Vent of KOROSI	0202-054
KURASAKI (Izu Is-Japan)	Stratovolc of AOGA-SHIMA	0804-06=

NAME (Subregion)	Type (Eruption Total, Most Recent) Status / Relation to NAMED VOLCANO	NUMBER
KURDJ AYMAN (Arabia-S)	Cone of HAYLAN, JABAL	0301-11-
KURIKOMA (Honshu-Japan)	Stratovolc (5, 1950) Historical	**0803-21=**
KURILE LAKE (Kamchatka)	Caldera of PAUZHETKA	1000-022
KURINO-DAKE (Kyushu-Japan)	Stratovolc of KIRISHIMA	0802-09=
KURO (Kurile Is)	Synonym of SINARKA	0900-29=
KURO-DAKE (Hokkaido-Japan)	Dome of DAISETSU	0805-06=
KURO DAKE (Kurile Is)	Synonym of SINARKA	0900-29=
KURO-DAKE (Kyushu-Japan)	Dome of KUJU GROUP	0802-12=
KURODANI (Honshu-Japan)	Crater of YAKE-DAKE	0803-07=
KUROFU-YAMA (Honshu-Japan)	Stratovolc of ASAMA	0803-11=
KUROHIME (Honshu-Japan)	Stratovolc (None) Holocene	**0803-101**
KUROI (KUROISI) (Kurile Is)	Synonym of TAO-RUSYR CALDERA	0900-31=
KUROISHI-DAKE (Kurile Is)	Synonym of TAO-RUSYR CALDERA	0900-31=
KUROISHIMORI (Honshu-Japan)	Dome of AKITA-YAKE-YAMA	0803-26=
KUROIWA-YAMA (Kyushu-Japan)	Cone of KUJU GROUP	0802-12=
KUROKAWA (Kyushu-Japan)	Thermal Feature of KUJU GROUP	0802-12=
KUROSE HOLE (Izu Is-Japan)	Submarine (None) Holocene	**0804-041**
KUROTSUKA (Honshu-Japan)	Cone of FUJI	0803-03=
KURSI, GUNUNG (Java)	Cone of TENGGER CALDERA	0603-31=
KURUB (Ethiopia)	Stratovolc (None) Holocene	**0201-12=**
KURUM (New Guinea-NE of)	Crater of KARKAR	0501-03=
KURUMI-DAKE (Honshu-Japan)	Dome of NARUGO	0803-20=
KURURI (New Guinea)	Cone of MANAGLASE PLATEAU	0503-021
KURWEETON, MT. (Australia)	Cone of NEWER VOLCANICS PROV	0509-01-
KUSATSU-SHIRANE (Honshu-Japan)	Stratovolcs (22, 1983) Historical	**0803-12=**
KUSATU-SIRANE (Honshu-Japan)	Synonym of KUSATSU-SHIRANE	0803-12=
KUSENBU (Kyushu-Japan)	Stratovolc of UNZEN	0802-10=
KUSENRI-GAHAMA (Kyushu-Japan)	Pit crater of ASO	0802-11=
KUSHIGA-MINE (Honshu-Japan)	Stratovolc of BANDAI	0803-16=
KUSHUIHUAN-BEISHAN (China-W)	Cone of UNNAMED	1004-04-
KUSIGA-MINE [KUSHIGA-MINE] (Honshu)	Stratovolc of BANDAI	0803-16=
KUSKA (Aleutian Is)	Synonym of KISKA	1101-02-
KUST (Kamchatka)	Cone of TOLBACHIK	1000-24=
KUSUKU (Ryukyu Is)	Dome of OKINAWA-TORI-SHIMA	0802-02=
KUTALI, TAVANI (Vanuatu-SW Pacific)	Stratovolcs (None) Holocene?	**0507-061**
KUTCHARO (Hokkaido-Japan)	Caldera (1, 1000) Tephrochronology	**0805-08=**
KUTIERABU-ZIMA (Ryukyu Is)	Synonym of KUCHINOERABU-JIMA	0802-05=
KUTINA (Kamchatka)	Stratovolc of OSTRY	1000-68-
KUTINO-SIMA (Ryukyu Is)	Synonym of KUCHINO-SHIMA	0802-041
KUTINOERABU-ZIMA (Ryukyu Is)	Synonym of KUCHINOERABU-JIMA	0802-05=
KUTINSKY GROUP (Russia-SE)	Cone of TUNKIN DEPRESSION	1002-05-
KUTLYUKHAT (Alaska Peninsula)	Synonym of KUKAK	1102-23-
KUTTARA (Hokkaido-Japan)	Stratovolc (1, 1820) Tephrochronology	**0805-034**
KUTTYARO CALDERA (Hokkaido-Japan)	Synonym of KUTCHARO	0805-08=
KUTUM VOLC FIELD (Africa-N)	Scoria cones (None) Holocene?	**0205-04-**
KUWAE (Vanuatu-SW Pacific)	Caldera (12, 1974) Historical	**0507-07=**
KUWANOKI-DAIRA (Izu Is-Japan)	Cone of MIYAKE-JIMA	0804-04=
KUYUP (Kamchatka)	Shield of UKSICHAN	1000-35-
KUZYU VOLCANO GROUP (Kyushu-Japan)	Synonym of KUJU GROUP	0802-12=
KVERKFJALLARANAMYNDUN (Iceland-NE)	Crater row of KVERKFJOLL	1703-05=
KVERKFJOLL (Iceland-NE)	Stratovolc (8, 1968) Historical	**1703-05=**
KVIAHNJUKUR (Iceland-W)	Cone of SNAEFELLSJOKULL	1700-01=
KVOSTOF ISLAND (Aleutian Is)	Synonym of DAVIDOF	1101-04-
KWA MIKUNGU (Africa-E)	Cone of KILIMANJARO	0202-15=
KWADISHA (Africa-E)	Cone of CHYULU HILLS	0202-13=
KWAMWIGA (Africa-C)	Crater of BUNYARUGURU FIELD	0203-005
KWANKAIJI-ONSEN (Kyushu-Japan)	Thermal Feature of TSURUMI	0802-13=
KWEO BUTTE (US-Oregon)	Cone of NEWBERRY VOLCANO	1202-11-
KWETEON (Vanuatu-SW Pacific)	Cone of GAUA	0507-02=
KWINNUM BUTTE (US-Oregon)	Cone of NEWBERRY VOLCANO	1202-11-
KWITINTOG (Vanuatu-SW Pacific)	Stratovolc of SORETIMEAT	0507-01=
KWOHL BUTTE (US-Oregon)	Shield of BACHELOR	1202-09-
KYAMWERU (Africa-C)	Crater of BUNYARUGURU FIELD	0203-005
KYATWA VOLC FIELD (Africa-C)	Tuff cones (None) Holocene	**0203-003**
KYAUKKA (SE Asia)	Vent of LOWER CHINDWIN	0705-09-
KYAUKMYET (SE Asia)	Vent of LOWER CHINDWIN	0705-09-
KYEGANYWA (Africa-C)	Tuff cone of FORT PORTAL FIELD	0203-002
KYEMA (Africa-C)	Crater of BUNYARUGURU FIELD	0203-005
KYIWIN TAUNG (SE Asia)	Vent of LOWER CHINDWIN	0705-09-
KYOGA (Africa-C)	Crater of BUNYARUGURU FIELD	0203-005
KYOWA-YAMA (Honshu-Japan)	Dome of CHOKAI	0803-22=

L

LA see proper name (e.g. CORONA, LA)

NAME (Subregion)	Type (Eruption Total, Most Recent) Status / Relation to NAMED VOLCANO	NUMBER
LA PALMA (Canary Is)	Stratovolc (7, 1971) Historical	**1803-01-**
LABO (Luzon-Philippines)	Compnd volc (None) Holocene	**0703-043**
LABOR, AUSOL LA (El Salvador)	Thermal Feature of VERDE, LAGUNA	1403-01=
LACONA (Vanuatu-SW Pacific)	Synonym of GAUA	0507-02=
LACROIX, FUMEROLLE (W Indies)	Thermal Feature of SOUFR. GUADELOUPE	1600-06=
LACROIX, PITON (Indian O.-W)	Cone of FOURNAISE, PITON DE LA	0303-02=
LAGAFELL (Iceland-SW)	Shield of REYKJANES	1701-02=
LAGENDA (New Britain-SW Pac)	Synonym of GARUA HARBOUR	0502-06=
LAGERNY (Kamchatka)	Dome of KARYMSKY	1000-13=
LAGERNY (Kamchatka)	Cone of TOLBACHIK	1000-24=
LAGERNY (Kamchatka)	Shield of BELY	1000-64-

LAGO, LAGOA, LAGUNA (Portuguese and Spanish for LAKE) see proper name (e.g. CHANMICO, LAGUNA)

NAME (Subregion)	Type (Eruption Total, Most Recent) Status / Relation to NAMED VOLCANO	NUMBER
LAGULA, MT. (Luzon-Philippines)	Cone of LAGUNA VOLC FIELD	0703-051
LAGUMISHERA (Africa-E)	Cone of KILIMANJARO	0202-15=
LAGUNA (Halmahera-Indonesia)	Crater of GAMALAMA	0608-06=
LAGUNA (US-New Mexico)	Fissure vent of ZUNI-BANDERA	1210-02-
LAGUNA, ALTO DE LA (Colombia)	Dome of RUIZ	1501-02=
LAGUNA, CALDERA DE (Canary Is)	Crater of FUERTEVENTURA	1803-05-
LAGUNA VOLC FIELD (Luzon-Philippines)	Scoria cones (1, 1350) Anthropology	**0703-051**
LAGUNITA, LA [LAGUNA LAS NINFAS]	Crater of VERDE, LAGUNA	1403-01=
LAHENDONG (Sulawesi-Indonesia)	Maar of TONDANO CALDERA	0606-07-
LAHER, KAWAH (Java)	Thermal Feature of KAWAHMANUK	0603-11=
LAIFENGSHAN (China-S)	Cone of TENGCHONG	0705-11-
LAIKA (Vanuatu-SW Pacific)	Cone of KUWAE	0507-07=
LAIKA BANK [KARUA] (Vanuatu-SW Pacific)	Submarine cone of KUWAE	0507-07=
LAIMANA, PUU (Hawaiian Is)	Cone of KILAUEA	1302-01-
LAJA (Chile-C)	Synonym of ANTUCO	1507-08=
LAJA, LOS CERRITOS DE LA (Mexico)	Shield of MASCOTA VOLC FIELD	1401-031
LAJARA (Chile-C)	Synonym of MOCHO-CHOSHUENCO	1507-13=
LAKAGIGAR [LAKI] (Iceland-NE)	Crater row of GRIMSVOTN	1703-01=

LAKE see proper name (e.g. WISDOM, LAKE)

NAME (Subregion)	Type (Eruption Total, Most Recent) Status / Relation to NAMED VOLCANO	NUMBER
LAKE HILL (Alaska-W)	Cone of ST. PAUL ISLAND	1104-07-
LAKESHORE CONE (Aleutian Is)	Cone of SEMISOPOCHNOI	1101-06-
LAKI (Iceland-NE)	Crater row of GRIMSVOTN	1703-01=
LAKONA (Vanuatu-SW Pacific)	Synonym of GAUA	0507-02=
LAKWA, VUTI (Vanuatu-SW Pacific)	Cone of AOBA	0507-03=

NAME (Subregion)	Type (Eruption Total, Most Recent) Status Relation to NAMED VOLCANO	NUMBER
LALALA (New Britain-SW Pac)	Cone of DAKATAUA	0502-04=
LALASHO, OL DOINYO (Africa-E)	Cone of CHYULU HILLS	0202-13=
LALOANEA (Samoa-SW Pacific)	Cone of UPOLU	0404-03-
LALOLALO (SW Pacific)	Crater of WALLIS ISLANDS	0404-05-
LALUAI (Bougainville-SW Pac)	Pleistocene caldera of LOLORU	0505-03=
LAM TEUBA (Sumatra)	Pleistocene caldera of SEULAWAH AGAM	0601-02=
LAMA HERU (Lesser Sunda Is)	Synonym of ILIWERUNG	0604-25=
LAMA, KABA (Sumatra)	Crater of KABA	0601-22=
LAMATELANG (Lesser Sunda Is)	Synonym of ILIBOLENG	0604-22=
LAMBADALSHRAUN (Iceland-S)	Crater row of VATNAFJOLL	1702-06=
LAMBAFIT (Iceland-S)	Fissure vent of HEKLA	1702-07=
LAMBAGAI, OL DOINYO (Africa-E)	Cone of CHYULU HILLS	0202-13=
LAMBAGIGAR [LAMBAFIT] (Iceland-S)	Fissure vent of HEKLA	1702-07=
LAMBAHRAUN (Iceland-SW)	Shield of LANGJOKULL	1701-08=
LAMBAHRAUN (Iceland-SW)	Fissure vent of HOFSJOKULL	1701-09=
LAMBAVATNSGIGAR (Iceland-NE)	Fissure vent of GRIMSVOTN	1703-01=
LAMINGTON (New Guinea)	Stratovolc (3, 1956) Historical	**0503-01=**
LAMONA [LAMONAI] (D'Entrecasteaux Is)	Stratovolc of DAWSON STRAIT GROUP	0503-06=
LAMONAI-OIAU GROUP (D'Entrecasteaux)	Synonym of DAWSON STRAIT GROUP	0503-06=
LAMONGAN (Java)	Stratovolc (41, 1898) Historical	**0603-32=**
LAMUTSKY (Kamchatka)	Shield of IETTUNUP	1000-71-
LANANG (Java)	Crater of GEDE	0603-06=
LANANG, KAWAH [KAWAH UPAS] (Java)	Crater of TANGKUBANPARAHU	0603-09=
LANGALANGA, MT. (New Britain-SW Pac)	Cone of DAKATAUA	0502-04=
LANGE, CRATER (New Britain-SW Pac)	Crater of GAROVE	0502-03=
LANGFOIS, LE (Indian O.-W)	Crater of FOURNAISE, PITON DE LA	0303-02=
LANGHOLL (Iceland-SW)	Shield of REYKJANES	1701-02=
LANGILA (New Britain-SW Pac)	Complx volc (18, 1993) Historical	**0502-01=**
LANGJOKULL (Iceland-SW)	Stratovolc (1, 0925) Radiocarbon	**1701-08=**
LANGLA (New Britain-SW Pac)	Synonym of LANGILA	0502-01=
LANGOAN (Sulawesi-Indonesia)	Thermal Feature of TONDANO CALDERA	0606-07-
LANGUDI (Ethiopia)	Synonym of YANGUDI	0201-151
LANGUISHAN (China-E)	Cone of DATONG	1005-01-
LANGVIUHRAUN (Iceland-S)	Crater row of VATNAFJOLL	1702-06=
LANIN (Chile-C)	Stratovolc (None) Holocene	**1507-122**
LANITULI (SW Pacific)	Crater of WALLIS ISLANDS	0404-05-
LANO (SW Pacific)	Cone of WALLIS ISLANDS	0404-05-
LANO-O-LEPA (Samoa-SW Pacific)	Cone of UPOLU	0404-03-
LANO-O-MOA (Samoa-SW Pacific)	Cone of UPOLU	0404-03-
LANQUIMAY (Chile-C)	Synonym of LONQUIMAY	1507-10=
LANTEGY, PUY DE (France)	Cone of CHAINE DES PUYS	0100-02-
LANUATA'ATA (Samoa-SW Pacific)	Cone of UPOLU	0404-03-
LANUMAHU (SW Pacific)	Crater of WALLIS ISLANDS	0404-05-
LANUTAVAKE (SW Pacific)	Crater of WALLIS ISLANDS	0404-05-
LANUTO'O, LAKE (Samoa-SW Pacific)	Cone of UPOLU	0404-03-
LANZAROTE (Canary Is)	Fissure vents (4, 1824) Historical	**1803-06-**
LAO-HEI-TING-TZU [LAOHEIDINGZI] (China)	Shield of BAITOUSHAN	1005-07-
LAOGUIPO (China-S)	Cone of TENGCHONG	0705-11-
LAOHEIDINGZI (China-E)	Shield of BAITOUSHAN	1005-07-
LAOHEISHAN (China-E)	Cone of WUDALIANCHI	1005-04-
LAPAS, CALDERA DE LAS (Canary Is)	Crater of LANZAROTE	1803-06-
LARDARELLO (Italy)	Synonym of LARDERELLO	0101-001
LARDERELLO (Italy)	Expl craters (1, 1282) Historical	**0101-001**
LARGA, LOMA (Mexico)	Cone of MICHOACAN-GUANAJUATO	1401-06=
LARGO, CERRO (El Salvador)	Cone of SAN DIEGO	1403-012
LARSEN (Antarctica)	Cone of SEAL NUNATAKS GROUP	1900-05=
LAS see proper name (e.g. PILAS, LAS)		
LASCAR (Chile-N)	Stratovolcs (23, 1993) Historical	**1505-10=**
LASCHAMP, PUY DE (France)	Cone of CHAINE DES PUYS	0100-02-
LASKAR (Chile-N)	Synonym of LASCAR	1505-10=
LASO (Africa-E)	Cone of KILIMANJARO	0202-15=
LASSEN PEAK (US-Calif)	Dome of LASSEN VOLC CENTER	1203-08-
LASSEN VOLC CENTER (US-California)	Stratovolc (5, 1917) Historical	**1203-08-**
LASSOLAS, PUY DE (France)	Cone of CHAINE DES PUYS	0100-02-
LASTARRIA (Chile-N)	Synonym of COPIAPO	1505-14-
LASTARRIA (Chile-N)	Stratovolc (None) Holocene	**1505-12=**
LATA (Samoa-SW Pacific)	Pleistocene caldera of TA'U	0404-001
LATE (Tonga-SW Pacific)	Stratovolc (2, 1854) Historical	**0403-09=**
LATERA (Italy)	Pleistocene caldera of VULSINI	0101-003
LATHROP WELLS (US-Nevada)	Cone of CRATER FLAT	1206-03-
LATIAL (Italy)	Synonym of ALBANO, MONTE	0101-004
LATTE (Tonga-SW Pacific)	Synonym of LATE	0403-09=
LATUKAN (Mindanao-Philippines)	Stratovolc (None) Holocene	**0701-05=**
LAUAAN (Philippines-C)	Dome of BILIRAN	0702-08=
LAUFAFELL (Iceland-S)	Dome of TORFAJOKULL	1702-05=
LAUFAHRAUN (Iceland-S)	Fissure vent of TORFAJOKULL	1702-05=
LAUGAHRAUN (Iceland-S)	Crater row of TORFAJOKULL	1702-05=
LAUGHLIN PEAK (US-New Mexico)	Cone of RATON-CLAYTON	1210-04-
L'AUMONE, PUY DE (France)	Dome of CHAINE DES PUYS	0100-02-
LAUTARO (Chile-S)	Stratovolc ? (4, 1961) Historical	**1508-06=**
LAUTI (Samoa-SW Pacific)	Cone of UPOLU	0404-03-
LAVA BUTTE (US-Oregon)	Cone of NEWBERRY VOLCANO	1202-11-
LAVA BUTTE [ROCKY BUTTE] (US-Oregon)	Cone of JORDAN CRATERS	1202-19-
LAVA FORK (Canada)	Cone of ISKUT-UNUK RIVER CONES	1200-09-
LAVA MOUNTAIN (US-Oregon)	Cone of SQUAW RIDGE FIELD	1202-13-
LAVA PEAK (Aleutian Is)	Cone of AKUTAN	1101-32-
LAVA PLASTERED CONES (Hawaiian Is)	Cone of KILAUEA	1302-01-
LAVA POINT (Aleutian Is)	Cone of AKUTAN	1101-32-
LAVA TOP BUTTE (US-Oregon)	Cone of NEWBERRY VOLCANO	1202-11-
LAVIC LAKE (US-California)	Volc field (None) Holocene	**1203-19-**
LAVOVY SHISH (Kamchatka)	Cone of USHKOVSKY	1000-261
LAWALACLOUGH (US-Washington)	Synonym of ST. HELENS	1201-05-
LAWALUK (Australia)	Vent of NEWER VOLCANICS PROV	0509-01-
LAWOE (Java)	Synonym of LAWU	0603-26=
LAWORKAWRA (Banda Sea)	Synonym of NILA	0605-06=
LAWU (Java)	Stratovolc (None) Holocene	**0603-26=**
LAXA (Chile-C)	Synonym of ANTUCO	1507-08=
LAZIALE, VULCANO (Italy)	Synonym of ALBANO, MONTE	0101-004
LE see proper name (e.g. TOUO, LE)		
LEAL (Chile-C)	Synonym of RESAGO, VOLCAN	1507-066
L'EAU, PITON DE (Indian O.-W)	Cone of FOURNAISE, PITON DE LA	0303-02=
LEBAKDJERO [LEBAKJERO] (Java)	Crater of TALAGABODAS	0603-15=
LEBETOBI (Lesser Sunda Is)	Synonym of LEWOTOBI	0604-18=
LEFULUFULUA (Samoa-SW Pacific)	Dome of TUTUILA	0404-02-
LEGA, WOLO (Lesser Sunda Is)	Crater of INIELIKA	0604-09=
LEGATALA (LEGELALA, LEGETALA) (Banda	Synonym of SERUA	0605-07=
LEGGJARBRJOTUR [SOLKATLA] (Iceland)	Shield of LANGJOKULL	1701-08=
LEHNSESSEL (El Salvador)	Synonym of TABURETE	1403-072
LEHUA, PUU (Hawaiian Is)	Cone of HUALALAI	1302-04-
LEILA (Samoa-SW Pacific)	Dome of TUTUILA	0404-02-
LEIRHAFNARSKORD (Iceland-NE)	Vent of FREMRINAMUR	1703-07=
LEIRHNUKAGIGAR [LEIRHNJUKUR] (Iceland	Crater row of KRAFLA	1703-08=

NAME (Subregion)	Type (Eruption Total, Most Recent) Status Relation to NAMED VOLCANO	NUMBER
LEIRHNUKUR [LEIRHNJUKUR] (Iceland-NE)	Crater row of KRAFLA	1703-08=
LEITIN (Iceland-SW)	Shield of BRENNISTEINSFJOLL	1701-04=
LEIZHOU BANDAO (SE Asia)	Volc field (None) Holocene	**0705-01-**
LEJAS, MONTANA (Canary Is)	Cone of TENERIFE	1803-03-
LEKER (Java)	Cone of SEMERU	0603-30=
LEMA (New Guinea)	Synonym of DOMA PEAKS	0503-00-
LEMEI ROCK (US-Washington)	Cone of INDIAN HEAVEN	1201-07-
LEMONGAN (Java)	Synonym of LAMONGAN	0603-32=
LEMONGO (Africa-E)	Cone of KILIMANJARO	0202-15=
LEMRIKA (Africa-E)	Cone of KILIMANJARO	0202-15=
LENGAI, OL DOINYO (Africa-E)	Stratovolc (17, 1993) Historical	**0202-12=**
L'ENGAI, OLDONYO (Africa-E)	Synonym of LENGAI, OL DOINYO	0202-12=
LENGKOAN (Sulawesi-Indonesia)	Cone of TONDANO CALDERA	0606-07-
LENGLET, MORNE (W Indies)	Cone of SOUFRIERE GUADELOUPE	1600-06=
LENGUA DE VULCANO (Chile-C)	Synonym of MONDACA	1507-041
LENINGRADETS [KEKIKNAYSKY] (Kamchat	Shield of BOLSHOY-KEKUKNAYSKY	1000-36-
LENTIA (Italy)	Dome of VULCANO	0101-05=
LENTISCAL, MONTANA (Canary Is)	Cone of GRAN CANARIA	1803-04-
LEON DORMIENTE, EL (Galapagos)	Tuff cone of SAN CRISTOBAL	1503-12-
LEONA, CERRO LA (El Salvador)	Cone of COATEPEQUE CALDERA	1403-041
LEONARD RANGE (Mindanao-Philippines)	Stratovolc (None) Holocene	**0701-031**
LEONE, VALLE DEL (Italy)	Caldera of ETNA	0101-06=
LEPER'S ISLAND (Vanuatu-SW Pacific)	Synonym of AOBA	0507-03=
LEPRE, MONTE (Italy)	Cone of ETNA	0101-06=
LEPTADAUNG (SE Asia)	Cone of LOWER CHINDWIN	0705-09-
LEPU'E (Samoa-SW Pacific)	Cone of TA'U	0404-001
LEREBOLENG (Lesser Sunda Is)	Complx volc (3, 1881) Historical	**0604-20=**
LEREK (Lesser Sunda Is)	Caldera of ILIWERUNG	0604-25=
LEROBOLENG (Lesser Sunda Is)	Synonym of LEREBOLENG	0604-20=
LERONGO (Africa-E)	Cone of KILIMANJARO	0202-15=
LESHE (SE Asia)	Crater of LOWER CHINDWIN	0705-09-
LESHNAYA (Kamchatka)	Cone of TOLBACHIK	1000-24=
LESKOV ISLAND (Antarctica)	Stratovolc (None) Fumarolic	**1900-12=**
LESONG (Lesser Sunda Is)	Stratovolc of BRATAN	0604-001
LESSON ISLAND (New Guinea-NE of)	Synonym of BAM	0501-01=
L'ETANG SEC, CALDEIRA DE (W Indies)	Crater of PELEE	1600-12=
LETHA TAUNG (SE Asia)	Synonym of SINGU PLATEAU	0705-10-
LETTE (Tonga-SW Pacific)	Synonym of LATE	0403-09=
LEURA, MT. (Australia)	Tuff ring of NEWER VOLCANICS PROV	0509-01-
LEUTAK, KAWAH (Java)	Thermal Feature of KAWAHKAMOJANG	0603-12=
LEUTIK, KAWAH (Java)	Crater of GEDE	0603-06=
LEUTONGEY (Kamchatka)	Shield (None) Holocene	**1000-54-**
LEVEL MOUNTAIN (Canada)	Shield (None) Holocene	**1200-05-**
LEVEL, THE (W Indies)	Dome of SABA	1600-01=
LEVERA HILL (W Indies)	Dome of ST. CATHERINE	1600-17=
LEVERA POND (W Indies)	Crater of ST. CATHERINE	1600-17=
LEWENO (LEWERO, LEWEROH) (Lesser Su	Synonym of LEREBOLENG	0604-20=
LEWETOBI (Lesser Sunda Is)	Synonym of LEWOTOBI	0604-18=
LEWETOBI PERAMPUAN [L. PEREMPUAN]	Stratovolc of LEWOTOBI	0604-18=
LEWOLEMBWI (Vanuatu-SW Pacific)	Maar of AMBRYM	0507-04=
LEWONO (LEWOROH) (Lesser Sunda Is)	Synonym of LEREBOLENG	0604-20=
LEWOTOBI (Lesser Sunda Is)	Stratovolcs (19, 1991) Historical	**0604-18=**
LEWOTOBI LAKILAKI (Lesser Sunda Is)	Stratovolc of LEWOTOBI	0604-18=
LEWOTOLO (Lesser Sunda Is)	Stratovolc (8, 1951) Historical	**0604-23=**
LEXONE (Chile-N)	Lava domes (None) Holocene	**1505-011**
LHO BALOHAN CEUNOKOT (Sumatra)	Thermal Feature of PULAU WEH	0601-01=
LHO BALOHAN TJEUNOKOT [LHO BAL. CE	Thermal Feature of PULAU WEH	0601-01=
LIADO HAYK FIELD (Ethiopia)	Maars (None) Holocene?	**0201-172**
LIAMUIGA (W Indies)	Stratovolc (4, 0150) Radiocarbon	**1600-03=**
LIANBANSHAN [HUOSHAOSHAN] (China-E)	Cone of WUDALIANCHI	1005-04-
LIATSIKAS (Greece)	Dome of SANTORINI	0102-04=
LICANCABUR (Chile-N)	Stratovolc (None) Holocene	**1505-092**
LICANCAUR (Chile-N)	Synonym of LICANCABUR	1505-092
LICHTMESS INSEL (Antarctica)	Synonym of CANDLEMAS ISLAND	1900-10=
LIDHOGDA (Atl-N-Jan Mayen)	Cone of JAN MAYEN	1706-01=
LIEN KHANG MT. (SE Asia)	Caldera of HAUT DONG NAI	0705-04-
LIERWEISEN (Germany)	Maar of WEST EIFEL VOLC FIELD	0100-01-
LIESKOW ISLAND (Antarctica)	Synonym of LESKOW ISLAND	1900-12=
LIFOS TEPE (Turkey)	Cone of ERCIYES DAGI	0103-01=
LIHIR (New Ireland-SW Pac)	Volc complx (None) Holocene	**0504-01=**
L'IIET, PITON DE (Indian O.-W)	Cone of FOURNAISE, PITON DE LA	0303-02=
LIJSKOW ISLAND (Antarctica)	Synonym of LESKOW ISLAND	1900-12=
LIKAIU E & W (Africa-E)	Shields of BARRIER, THE	0202-03=
LIKAYU [LIKAIU] (Africa-E)	Shield of BARRIER, THE	0202-03=
LILEY (Germany)	Cone of WEST EIFEL VOLC FIELD	0100-01-
LILLOOET CONES (Canada)	Synonym of BRIDGE RIVER CONES	1200-17-
LIMAS (Java)	Cone of WILIS	0603-27=
LIMAY, MT. (Luzon-Philippines)	Cone of MARIVELES	0703-081
LIMBO, CERRO EL (El Salvador)	Cone of CHINAMECA	1403-09=
LINA (Banda Sea)	Synonym of NILA	0605-06=
LINDAHRAUN (Iceland-NE)	Fissure vent of ASKJA	1703-06=
LINDAHRAUN (Iceland-NE)	Fissure vent of KVERKFJOLL	1703-05=
LINDENBERG ISLAND (Antarctica)	Cone of SEAL NUNATAKS GROUP	1900-05=
LINEINYI CRATER (Kurile Is)	Cone of VERNADSKII RIDGE	0900-37-
LINGKER, GUNUNG (Java)	Cone of IJEN	0603-35=
LINGSHI (SE Asia)	Cone of LEIZHOU BANDAO	0705-01-
LINOW LAHENDONG [LAHENDONG]	Maar of TONDANO CALDERA	0606-07-
LIPARI (Italy)	Stratovolc (2, 0729) Historical	**0101-041**
LIR (New Ireland-SW Pac)	Synonym of LIHIR	0504-01=
LIRIA, CALDERA DE (Canary Is)	Crater of FUERTEVENTURA	1803-05-
LISERSER (Vanuatu-SW Pacific)	Stratovolc of SORETIMEAT	0507-01=
LISTON, EL (Nicaragua)	Stratovolc of TELICA	1404-04=
LITLA ELDBORG UNDIR GEITLAHLID	Crater row of BRENNISTEINSFJOLL	1701-04=
LITLADYNGJA (Iceland-NE)	Shield of ASKJA	1703-06=
LITLAHRAUN (Iceland-SW)	Crater row of HENGILL	1701-05=
LITTLE BEAR MOUNTAIN (Canada)	Tuya of HOODOO MOUNTAIN	1200-08-
LITTLE BELKNAP (US-Oregon)	Shield of BELKNAP	1202-06-
LITTLE BLACK PEAK (US-New Mexico)	Cone of CARRIZOZO	1210-01-
LITTLE BROTHER (US-Oregon)	Shield of NORTH SISTER FIELD	1202-07-
LITTLE CACHE MOUNTAIN (US-Oregon)	Cone of WASHINGTON	1202-05-
LITTLE CONES (US-Nevada)	Cone of CRATER FLAT	1206-03-
LITTLE DONALD (New Zealand)	Crater of WHITE ISLAND	0401-04=
LITTLE GLASS MOUNTAIN (US-California)	Dome of MEDICINE LAKE	1203-02-
LITTLE HEBE (US-Calif)	Crater of UBEHEBE CRATERS	1203-16-
LITTLE HILL (Australia)	Cone of NEWER VOLCANICS PROV	0509-01-
LITTLE HOT CREEK (US-California)	Thermal Feature of LONG VALLEY	1203-14-
LITTLE ISKUT (Canada)	Shield of SPECTRUM RANGE	1200-07-
LITTLE MERU (Africa-E)	Stratovolc of MERU	0202-16=
LITTLE MORNE, THE (Vanuatu-SW Pacific)	Cone of KUTALI, TAVANI	0507-061
LITTLE MT. ADAMS (US-Washington)	Cone of ADAMS	1201-04-
LITTLE MT. HOFFMAN (US-California)	Cone of MEDICINE LAKE	1203-02-
LITTLE MT. WORRI (New Britain-SW Pac)	Cone of GARUA HARBOUR	0502-06=

NAME (Subregion)	Type (Eruption Total, Most Recent) Status Relation to NAMED VOLCANO	NUMBER
LITTLE NASH CRATER (US-Oregon)	Cone of SAND MOUNTAIN FIELD	1202-04-
LITTLE POTATO BUTTE (US-California)	Cone of POTATO BUTTE	1203-07-
LITTLE RANGITOTO (New Zealand)	Cone of AUCKLAND FIELD	0401-02=
LITTLE SAND BUTTE (US-California)	Cone of MEDICINE LAKE	1203-02-
LITTLE SITCHIN (Aleutian Is)	Synonym of LITTLE SITKIN	1101-05-
LITTLE SITKIN (Aleutian Is)	Stratovolc (2, 1830) Historical	**1101-05-**
LITTLE WHITNEY (US-Calif)	Cone of GOLDEN TROUT CREEK	1203-17-
LIUCHOW PENINSULA (SE Asia)	Synonym of LEIZHOU BANDAO	0705-01-
LIUHUANGDABAN (China-W)	Cone of KUNLUN VOLC GROUP	1004-03-
LIWOWO (Africa-W)	Cone of CAMEROON, MT.	0204-01=
LJOSAKRIDHA (Iceland-W)	Cone of SNAEFELLSJOKULL	1700-01=
LJOSUFJALLAHRAUN (Iceland-NE)	Crater row of BARDARBUNGA	1703-03=
LJOSUFJOLL (Iceland-W)	Fissure vents (5, 0960) Anthropology	**1700-03=**
LJOTIPOLLUR (Iceland-NE)	Crater of BARDARBUNGA	1703-03=
LLAFENCO GROUP (Chile-C)	Crater of VILLARRICA	1507-12=
LLAGDEGUIN (Chile-C)	Synonym of CALLAQUI	1507-091
LLAIMA (Chile-C)	Stratovolc (47, 1992) Historical	**1507-11=**
LLALLICUPE (Chile-C)	Synonym of SOLLIPULLI	1507-111
LLANGANATE (Ecuador)	(None) Not a Volcano	1502-07=
LLANILLOS, LOS (Canary Is)	Cone of HIERRO	1803-02-
LLANO, CERRO EL (Nicaragua)	Cone of ZAPATERA ISLAND	1404-111
LLANO DEL BANCO (Canary Is)	Fissure vent of LA PALMA	1803-01-
LLANO GRANDE (Mexico)	Pleistocene caldera of IZTACCIHUATL	1401-086
LLANOS, LOS [TACANDE] (Canary Is)	Cone of LA PALMA	1803-01-
LLANQUIHUE (Chile-S)	Synonym of OSORNO	1508-01=
LLAO BAY (US-Oregon)	Shield of CRATER LAKE	1202-16-
LLAO ROCK (US-Oregon)	Vent of CRATER LAKE	1202-16-
LLAYMAS (Chile-C)	Synonym of LLAIMA	1507-11=
LLOLLI, BANOS DE (Chile-C)	Thermal Feature of CALABOZOS	1507-042
LLULLAILLACO (Chile-N)	Stratovolc (3, 1877) Historical	**1505-11=**
LOA, MT. (Hawaiian Is)	Synonym of MAUNA LOA	1302-02=
LOALOA, PUU (Hawaiian Is)	Cone of MAUNA KEA	1302-03-
LOBETOBI (Lesser Sunda Is)	Synonym of LEWOTOBI	0604-18=
LOBO RADJA (LOBO RAJA) (Sumatra)	Synonym of RAJABASA	0601-29=
LOBOA (Vanuatu-SW Pacific)	Stratovolc of NORTH VATE	0507-081
LOBOBUTU (Lesser Sunda Is)	Pleistocene caldera of INIELIKA	0604-09=
LOBOS, ISLA DE (Canary Is)	Crater of FUERTEVENTURA	1803-05-
LOBOS, MONTANA (Canary Is)	Cone of LANZAROTE	1803-06-
LOCKIT BUTTE (US-Oregon)	Cone of NEWBERRY VOLCANO	1202-11-
LODHMUNDUR (Iceland-SW)	Dome of KERLINGARFJOLL	1701-10=
LOEMOET BALAI, BOEKIT (Sumatra)	Synonym of LUMUT BALAI, BUKIT	0601-24=
LOEROES (Java)	Synonym of LURUS	0603-321
LOEWINSSON-LESSIN (Kamchatka)	Crater of KLIUCHEVSKOI	1000-26=
LOFIA (Tonga-SW Pacific)	Cone of TOFUA	0403-06=
LOGKIPI GEYSER (Africa-E)	Thermal Feature of BARRIER, THE	0202-03=
LOIHI SEAMOUNT (Hawaiian Is)	Submarine (None) Seismicity	**1302-00-**
LOKHMATY (Kamchatka)	Dome of BEZYMIANNY	1000-25=
LOKI (Iceland-NE)	Fissure vent of LOKI-FOGRUFJOLL	1703-02=
LOKI-FOGRUFJOLL (Iceland-NE)	Subglacial (1, 1910) Historical	**1703-02=**
LOKIPPI [SUGUTA-LOGKIPI] (Africa-E)	Thermal Feature of BARRIER, THE	0202-03=
LOKON (Sulawesi-Indonesia)	Cone of LOKON-EMPUNG	0606-10=
LOKON-EMPOENG (Sulawesi-Indonesia)	Synonym of LOKON-EMPUNG	0606-10=
LOKON-EMPUNG (Sulawesi-Indonesia)	Stratovolc (21, 1992) Historical	**0606-10=**
LOKON WALLENAURE [TOMPALUAN]	Crater of LOKON-EMPUNG	0606-10=
LOKUKUS (Africa-E)	Vent of PAKA	0202-053
LOLAH BUTTE (US-Oregon)	Cone of BACHELOR	1202-09-
LOLARU (Bougainville-SW Pac)	Synonym of LOLORU	0505-03=
LOLATOLO [KASOLALI] (New Britain)	Thermal Feature of PAGO	0502-08=
LOLCO, VOLCAN (Chile-C)	Cone of TOLGUACA	1507-092
LOLLO (New Britain-SW Pac)	Synonym of LOLO	0502-071
LOLO (New Britain-SW Pac)	Stratovolc (None) Holocene?	**0502-071**
LOLO BUTTE (US-Oregon)	Cone of BACHELOR	1202-09-
LOLOBAU (New Britain-SW Pac)	Caldera (3, 1912) Historical	**0502-13=**
LOLORU (Bougainville-SW Pac)	Pyrocl shield (6, -1050) Radiocarbon	**0505-03=**
LOLRUPANDE, OL DOINYO (Africa-E)	Cone of CHYULU HILLS	0202-13=
LOLWAI (Vanuatu-SW Pacific)	Tuff cone of AOBA	0507-03=
LOMA (Spanish for HILL) see proper name (e.g. ACHACARA, LOMA)		
LOMBOK (Lesser Sunda Is)	Synonym of RINJANI	0604-03=
LOMO NEGRO, VOLCAN DE (Canary Is)	Cone of HIERRO	1803-02-
LOMONOSOV GROUP (Kurile Is)	Cinder cones (None) Holocene	**0900-351**
LONDOLOVIT (New Ireland-SW Pac)	Stratovolc of LIHIR	0504-01=
LONDON, ISLA (Chile-S)	Synonym of COOK, ISLA	1508-09-
LONE BUTTE (US-Washington)	Cone of INDIAN HEAVEN	1201-07-
LONG ISLAND (New Guinea-NE of)	Complx volc (11, 1993) Historical	**0501-05=**
LONG VALLEY (US-California)	Caldera (None) Pleistocene-Fumarolic	**1203-14-**
LONGAVI, NEVADO DE (Chile-C)	Stratovolc (None) Holocene	**1507-064**
LONGGANG GROUP (China-E)	Cinder cones (1, 1750) Radiocarbon	**1005-06-**
LONGHUSHAN (China-S)	Cone of TENGCHONG	0705-11-
LONGHUXIAOSHAN (China-S)	Cone of TENGCHONG	0705-11-
LONGONOT (Africa-E)	Shield (3, 1863) Anthropology	**0202-10=**
LONGTAN (China-S)	Cone of TENGCHONG	0705-11-
LONGUEN, NEVADO DE (Chile-C)	Synonym of LONGAVI, NEVADO DE	1507-064
LONGWAN GROUP (China-E)	Synonym of LONGGANG GROUP	1005-06-
LONPUIMAY (Chile-C)	Synonym of LONQUIMAY	1507-10=
LONQUEN, NEVADO DE (Chile-C)	Synonym of LONGAVI, NEVADO DE	1507-064
LONQUIMAY (Chile-C)	Stratovolc (4, 1990) Historical	**1507-10=**
LOOKOUT BUTTE (US-California)	Cone of MEDICINE LAKE	1203-02-
LOOKOUT BUTTE (US-Oregon)	Cone of CRATER LAKE	1202-16-
LOOKOUT MOUNTAIN (US-California)	Dome of LONG VALLEY	1203-14-
LOOLSUNI (Banda Sea)	Synonym of WURLALI	0605-04=
LOPEVI (Vanuatu-SW Pacific)	Stratovolc (22, 1982) Historical	**0507-05=**
LOPEX DE VILLALOBOS, CERRO (Mexico)	Dome of BARCENA	1401-02=
LORETO, CERRO (Mexico)	Cone of TENAYO GROUP	1401-081
LOS see proper name (e.g. VOTOS, LOS)		
LOSETOM (Africa-E)	Tuff cone of EMURUANGOGOLAK	0202-051
LOSOLAVA-TARASAG (Vanuatu-SW Pacific)	Cone of GAUA	0507-02=
LOST JIM (Alaska-W)	Cone of IMURUK LAKE	1104-02-
LOST LAKE GROUP (US-Oregon)	Cone of SAND MOUNTAIN FIELD	1202-04-
LOST WOMAN (US-New Mexico)	Cone of ZUNI-BANDERA	1210-02-
LOTIGELLI (Africa-E)	Cone of KILIMANJARO	0202-15=
LOT'S WIFE (New Zealand)	Former crater of WHITE ISLAND	0401-04=
LOU (Admiralty Is-SW Pac)	Synonym of ST. ANDREW STRAIT	0500-01=
LOUCHADIERE, PUY DE (France)	Cone of CHAINE DES PUYS	0100-02-
LOUSE (Kurile Is)	Synonym of MENDELEEV	0900-02=
LOWER CHINDWIN (SE Asia)	Volc field (None) Holocene?	**0705-09-**
LOWER GEYSER BASIN (US-Wyoming)	Thermal Feature of YELLOWSTONE	1205-01-
LOWETOBI (Lesser Sunda Is)	Synonym of LEWOTOBI	0604-18=
LOWULLO BUTTE (US-Oregon)	Cone of NEWBERRY VOLCANO	1202-11-
LQUILLA, CERRO (Chile-N)	Dome of LEXONE	1505-011
LUA (Hawaiian for CRATER) see proper name (e.g. HOHONU, LUA)		
LUA-O-FAFINE (Samoa-SW Pacific)	Cone of UPOLU	0404-03-
LUA-O-TANE (Samoa-SW Pacific)	Cone of UPOLU	0404-03-
LUALAITITI (Samoa-SW Pacific)	Pit crater of TA'U	0404-001
LUAMAKAMI (Hawaiian Is)	Cone of HUALALAI	1302-04-
LUATELE (Samoa-SW Pacific)	Shield of TA'U	0404-001
LUBWA (Africa-E)	Dome of NYAMBENI HILLS	0202-056
LUCIFER HILL (Antarctica)	Cone of CANDLEMAS ISLAND	1900-10=
LUDENT (Iceland-NE)	Tuff ring of KRAFLA	1703-08=
LUDENTSBORGIR (Iceland-NE)	Crater row of KRAFLA	1703-08=
LUGUGUGUT [ANDREW'S VOLCANO]	Stratovolc of BARRIER, THE	0202-03=
LUISE (New Ireland-SW Pac)	Stratovolc of LIHIR	0504-01=
LUJONGO (Africa-C)	Crater of BUNYARUGURU FIELD	0203-005
LUKOVITSA (Kamchatka)	Dome of GAMCHEN	1000-21=
LUKUKA (Africa-C)	Cone of KARISIMBI	0203-04-
LULUKAN (Mindanao-Philippines)	Synonym of LATUKAN	0701-05=
LUMANTO, CERRO (Chile-C)	Cone of CARRAN-LOS VENADOS	1507-14=
LUMBUNG SELAJUR [LUMBUNG SELAYUR]	Crater of LAWU	0603-26=
LUMRUN BUTTE (US-Oregon)	Cone of BACHELOR	1202-09-
LUMUT BALAI, BUKIT (Sumatra)	Stratovolc ? (None) Fumarolic	**0601-24=**
LUMUT, BUKIT (Sumatra)	Stratovolc of LUMUT BALAI, BUKIT	0601-24=
LUMUTDAUN, BUKIT (Sumatra)	Stratovolc (None) Fumarolic	**0601-21=**
LUN-ULA (Mongolia)	Cone of DARIGANGA VOLC FIELD	1003-04-
LUNA BUTTE (US-Oregon)	Cone of NEWBERRY VOLCANO	1202-11-
LUNA, LA (Nicaragua)	Cone of MASAYA	1404-10=
LUNA, VOLCAN LA (Mexico)	Crater of PINACATE PEAKS	1401-001
LUNAIYIR, HARRAT (Arabia-W)	Synonym of LUNAYYIR, HARRAT	0301-04-
LUNAR CRATER FIELD (US-Nevada)	Cinder cones (None) Holocene?	**1206-02-**
LUNAYYIR, HARRAT (Arabia-W)	Volc field (1, 1000) Historical	**0301-04-**
LUNG-WAN GROUP (China-E)	Synonym of LONGGANG GROUP	1005-06-
LUOGANGLING (SE Asia)	Cone of LEIZHOU BANDAO	0705-01-
LURUS (Java)	Complx volc (None) Holocene?	**0603-321**
LUSIBA (Africa-E)	Crater of RUNGWE	0202-166
LUSITOBE N & S (Lesser Sunda Is)	Craters of ILIWERUNG	0604-25=
LUXSAR, CERRO (Bolivia)	Stratovolc of PAMPA LUXSAR	1505-042
LVINAYA PAST (Kurile Is)	Stratovolc (1, -7480) Radiocarbon	**0900-041**
L'VINAYA PASTI (Kurile Is)	Synonym of LVINAYA PAST	0900-041
LYESKOV ISLAND (Antarctica)	Synonym of LESKOV ISLAND	1900-12=
LYONS PEAK (US-California)	Cone of MEDICINE LAKE	1203-02-
LYSUHOLL (Iceland-W)	Pyrocl cones (None) Holocene	**1700-02=**
LYSUHYRNA (Iceland-W)	Vent of LYSUHOLL	1700-02=

M

NAME (Subregion)	Type (Eruption Total, Most Recent) Status Relation to NAMED VOLCANO	NUMBER
MA ALALTA (Ethiopia)	Stratovolc (None) Holocene	**0201-111**
MAANSHAN (China-S)	Cone of TENGCHONG	0705-11-
MAAR (see proper name (e.g. ESTIVADOUX, MAAR D')		
MABILOG, MT. (Luzon-Philippines)	Cone of LAGUNA VOLC FIELD	0703-051
MABUANI (Africa-E)	Cone of CHYULU HILLS	0202-13=
MACA (Chile-S)	Stratovolc (None) Holocene	**1508-056**
MACANZE, CERRO (El Salvador)	Cone of GUAZAPA	1403-051
MACAQUE, MORNE (W Indies)	Synonym of MICOTRIN	1600-10=
MACAS, VOLCAN DE (Ecuador)	Synonym of SANGAY	1502-09=
MACAULEY ISLAND (Kermadec Is)	Caldera (1, -0050) Holocene	**0402-021**
MACCOTTA, CUDDIA (Italy)	Shield of PANTELLERIA	0101-071
MACDONALD (Austral Is-C Pac)	Submarine (12, 1989) Hydrophonic	**1303-07-**
MACEY CONE (Indian O.-S)	Cone of HEARD	0304-01=
MACHEKHA [MACHEKH] (Kurile Is)	Crater of GROZNY GROUP	0900-07=
MACHIN, CERRO (Colombia)	Stratovolc (1, -1250) Tephrochronology	**1501-04=**
MACHIOTO (Africa-E)	Dome of SW USANGU BASIN	0202-163
MACHMEL RIVER (Canada)	Cone of SILVERTHRONE	1200-16-
MACHUCA (Chile-N)	Synonym of PUTANA	1505-09=
MACICO DA AGUALVA [GUILHERME MONIZ]	Stratovolc of TERCEIRA	1802-05=
MACIZO DE LARANCAGUA (Bolivia)	Stratovolc (None) Holocene?	**1505-014**
MACIZO DE PACUNI (Bolivia)	Stratovolc (None) Holocene?	**1505-015**
MACKENNEY (Guatemala)	Cone of PACAYA	1402-11=
MACOLOD (Luzon-Philippines)	Cone of TAAL	0703-07=
MACON, CERROS DE (Chile-N)	Stratovolc of PURICO COMPLEX	1505-094
MACOUBA, MORNE (W Indies)	Crater of PELEE	1600-12=
MACUTURIN (MACUTUSING) (Mindanao)	Synonym of MAKATURING	0701-04=
MADAHRAUN (Iceland-NE)	Fissure vent of BARDARBUNGA	1703-03=
MADDEN'S MT. (W Indies)	Cone of NEVIS PEAK	1600-04=
MADELEINE (W Indies)	Dome of SOUFRIERE GUADELOUPE	1600-06=
MADERA, LA (Nicaragua)	Stratovolc (None) Holocene?	**1404-13-**
MADERAS (Nicaragua)	Synonym of MADERA, LA	1404-13-
MADIENA, BUKIT [BUKIT KERAMAT]	Cone of GAMALAMA	0608-06=
MADILOGO (New Guinea)	Pyrocl cone (None) Holocene	**0503-004**
MADINAH, HARRAT [HARRAT RASHID]	Blank of RAHAT, HARRAT	0301-07=
MADREPORE (Italy)	Submarine vent of CAMPI FLEGREI MAR	0101-07=
MAE-DAKE (Ryukyu Is)	Cone of KUCHINO-SHIMA	0802-041
MAE-DAKE [MAYU-YAMA] (Kyushu-Japan)	Dome of UNZEN	0802-10=
MAE-TOKACHI-DAKE (Hokkaido-Japan)	Stratovolc of TOKACHI	0805-05=
MAEEBOSHI-DAKE (Honshu-Japan)	Stratovolc of ZAO	0803-19=
MAEKAKE-YAMA (Honshu-Japan)	Stratovolc of ASAMA	0803-11=
MAELIFELLSHRAUN (Iceland-S)	Fissure vent of KATLA	1702-03=
MAENIR (Iceland-SW)	Dome of KERLINGARFJOLL	1701-10=
MAFANE (Samoa-SW Pacific)	Cone of SAVAI'I	0404-04=
MAFRA, PICO DE (Azores)	Cone of SETE CIDADES	1802-08=
MAFURA CRATERS (Africa-C)	Crater of BUNYARUGURU FIELD	0203-005
MAGA (Samoa-SW Pacific)	Cone of SAVAI'I	0404-04=
MAGA POINT (Samoa-SW Pacific)	Cone of OFU-OLOSEGA	0404-01=
MAGADINI (Africa-E)	Cone of KILIMANJARO	0202-15=
MAGASO (Philippines-C)	Stratovolc (None) Holocene	**0702-01=**
MAGASU (Mindanao-Philippines)	Synonym of RAGANG	0701-06=
MAGASU (Philippines-C)	Synonym of MAGASO	0702-01=
MAGDGO (Africa-C)	Crater of BUNYARUGURU FIELD	0203-005
MAGEIK (Alaska Peninsula)	Stratovolc (2, 1936) Historical	**1102-15-**
MAGNE, CRATERE (Indian O.-W)	Crater of FOURNAISE, PITON DE LA	0303-02=
MAGNETO, EL (Chile-S)	Cone of CAYUTE-LA VIGUERIA	1508-021
MAGSUYUAN (Mindanao-Philippines)	Dome of PACO	0701-09-
MAGUSKIN (Kamchatka)	Cone of TOLBACHIK	1000-24=
MAHAGNAW (Philippines-C)	Synonym of MAHAGNOA	0702-07=
MAHAGNOA (Philippines-C)	Stratovolc (None) Fumarolic	**0702-07=**
MAHAMERU (Java)	Synonym of SEMERU	0603-30=
MAHAWOE (Sulawesi-Indonesia)	Synonym of MAHAWU	0606-11=
MAHAWU (Sulawesi-Indonesia)	Stratovolc (7, 1977) Historical	**0606-11=**
MAHENGETANG (Sangihe Is-Indonesia)	Synonym of BANUA WUHU	0607-03=
MAHOE, PUU (Hawaiian Is)	Cone of HALEAKALA	1302-06-
MAHOKDUM (Mindanao-Philippines)	Crater of PACO	0701-09-
MAIDEN HILL (Australia)	Cone of NEWER VOLCANICS PROV	0509-01-
MAILE (Samoa-SW Pacific)	Cone of SAVAI'I	0404-04=
MAILE, PUU (Hawaiian Is)	Cone of HALEAKALA	1302-06-
MAILLARD (Indian O.-W)	Crater of FOURNAISE, PITON DE LA	0303-02=
MAINIT (Luzon-Philippines)	Synonym of MAQUILING	0703-06=
MAIORO (Kurile Is)	Synonym of MEDVEZHIA	0900-10=

NAME (Subregion)	Type (Eruption Total, Most Recent) Status . . . Relation to NAMED VOLCANO	NUMBER
MAIPO (Chile-C)	Caldera (3, 1912) Historical	**1507-021**
MAIPO (Chile-C)	Synonym of SAN JOSE	1507-02=
MAIPU (Chile-C)	Synonym of SAN JOSE	1507-02=
MAIPU (Chile-C)	Synonym of MAIPO	1507-021
MAISH NUNATAK (Antarctica)	Cone of HUDSON MOUNTAINS	1900-028
MAITEI (Africa-E)	Cone of NYAMBENI HILLS	0202-056
MAITLAND, MT. (W Indies)	Cone of ST. CATHERINE	1600-17=
MAJADAS, LAS (Guatemala)	Cone of SANTA MARIA	1402-03=
MAJAIJAI (Luzon-Philippines)	Synonym of BANAHAW	0703-05=
MAJAK (Russia-NE)	Dome of BALAGAN-TAS	1001-03-
MAJI JA MOTO (Africa-C)	Synonym of MAY-YA-MOTO	0203-01=
MAJUA, MONTANA (Canary Is)	Cone of TENERIFE	1803-03-
MAKALIA, MT. (New Britain-SW Pac)	Shield of DAKATAUA	0502-04=
MAKATITI (New Zealand)	Dome of OKATAINA	0401-05=
MAKATURING (Mindanao-Philippines)	Stratovolc (None) Holocene	**0701-04=**
MAKHAHNAS (Mariana Is-C Pac)	Submar. vent of FARALLON DE PAJAROS	0804-14=
MAKIAN (Halmahera-Indonesia)	Stratovolc (8, 1988) Historical	**0608-07=**
MAKILING (Luzon-Philippines)	Synonym of MAQUILING	0703-06=
MAKINKU [MWAILO] (Africa-E)	Cone of CHYULU HILLS	0202-13=
MAKINOTO (Kyushu-Japan)	Thermal Feature of KUJU GROUP	0802-12=
MAKJAN (Halmahera-Indonesia)	Synonym of MAKIAN	0608-07=
MAKKO-DAI (Ryukyu Is)	Stratovolc of SUWANOSE-JIMA	0802-03=
MAKLAKS CRATER (US-Oregon)	Cone of CRATER LAKE	1202-16-
MAKOME (Africa-C)	Tuff cone of FORT PORTAL FIELD	0203-002
MAKOUCHINE (Aleutian Is)	Synonym of MAKUSHIN	1101-31-
MAKUA, PUU (Hawaiian Is)	Cone of HALEAKALA	1302-06-
MAKULOT [MACOLOD] (Luzon-Philippines)	Cone of TAAL	0703-07=
MAKUOPUHI (Hawaiian Is)	Pit crater of KILAUEA	1302-01-
MAKUSHIN (Aleutian Is)	Stratovolc (12, 1987) Historical	**1101-31-**
MAKUWAN-CHISAPPU (Hokkaido-Japan)	Dome of KUTCHARO	0805-08=
MAKUWAN-TISAPPU [MAKUWAN-CHISAPP	Dome of KUTCHARO	0805-08=
MAKWET (Africa-W)	Cone of OKU VOLC FIELD	0204-003
MAKYAN (Halmahera-Indonesia)	Synonym of MAKIAN	0608-07=
MALA CARA (El Salvador)	Cone of SANTA ANA	1403-02=
MALACARA I, CERRO (El Salvador)	Cone of SINGUIL, CERRO	1403-011
MALAIA SEMIACHIK (Kamchatka)	Synonym of MALY SEMIACHIK	1000-14=
MALAIA UDINA [MALAYA UDINA] (Kamchatk	Stratovolc of UDINA	1000-241
MALALA, MT. [MT. MAKALIA] (New Britain)	Shield of DAKATAUA	0502-04=
MALANG (Java)	Crater of TANGKUBANPARAHU	0603-09=
MALANG, MT. (Java)	Cone of SLAMET	0603-18=
MALANG PLAIN (Java)	Maars (None) Holocene	**0603-292**
MALASPINA (Philippines-C)	Synonym of CANLAON	0702-02=
MALAYA PLOSKAYA [KRESTOVSKY]	Stratovolc of USHKOVSKY	1000-261
MALAYA UDINA (Kamchatka)	Stratovolc of UDINA	1000-241
MALENKY (Kamchatka)	Cone of TOLBACHIK	1000-24=
MALEN'KY (Kamchatka)	Cone of BOLSHOI SEMIACHIK	1000-15=
MALESPINA (Philippines-C)	Synonym of CANLAON	0702-02=
MALETTO, MONTE (Italy)	Cone of ETNA	0101-06=
MALGRETOUTE (W Indies)	Dome of QUALIBOU	1600-14=
MALHA (Africa-N)	Crater of MEIDOB VOLC FIELD	0205-05-
MALINAO (Luzon-Philippines)	Stratovolc (none) Fumarolic	**0703-04=**
MALINCHE, CERRO DE LA (Mexico)	Cone of SAN BORJA VOLC FIELD	1401-007
MALINCHE, LA (Mexico)	Stratovolc (None) Holocene?	**1401-091**
MALINDANG (Mindanao-Philippines)	Stratovolc (None) Holocene	**0701-071**
MALINDIG (Luzon-Philippines)	Stratovolc ? (None) Hot Springs	**0703-044**
MALIOTA (Samoa-SW Pacific)	Cone of UPOLU	0404-03-
MALISBOG (Philippines-C)	Thermal Feature of SILAY	0702-04=
MALISHI (Kamchatka)	Cone of TOLBACHIK	1000-24=
MALJA GLAT (Greece)	Dome of METHANA	0102-02=
MALJA SKURTI (Greece)	Dome of METHANA	0102-02=
MALJSA (Greece)	Dome of METHANA	0102-02=
MALLAHLE (Ethiopia)	Stratovolc (None) Holocene?	**0201-102**
MALLALI (Ethiopia)	Synonym of MALLAHLE	0201-102
MALLARD LAKE (US-Wyoming)	Dome of YELLOWSTONE	1205-01-
MALLOLA, VOLCA (Spain)	Cone of OLOT VOLC FIELD	0100-03-
MALO (New Britain-SW Pac)	Cone of LOLOBAU	0502-13=
MALOEPANG MAGIWE [MALUPANG MAGI	Crater of DUKONO	0608-01=
MALOEPANG WARIANG [MALUPANG WAR	Stratovolc of DUKONO	0608-01=
MALPAIS (Mexico)	Synonym of MICHOACAN-GUANAJUATO	1401-06=
MALPAIS, CERRO EL (Mexico)	Cone of MASCOTA VOLC FIELD	1401-031
MALPAIS, THE (US-New Mexico)	Synonym of CARRIZOZO	1210-01-
MALPAIS VOLC FIELD (US-New Mexico)	Synonym of ZUNI-BANDERA	1210-02-
MALPAIS, VOLCAN (Mexico)	Cone of MASCOTA VOLC FIELD	1401-031
MALPASO (Canary Is)	Cone of HIERRO	1803-02-
MALUATIA (Samoa-SW Pacific)	Cone of TA'U	0404-001
MALUPANG MAGIWE (Halmahera-Indonesia)	Crater of DUKONO	0608-01=
MALUPANG WARIANG (Halmahera)	Stratovolc of DUKONO	0608-01=
MALY PAYALPAN (Kamchatka)	Shields (None) Holocene	**1000-29-**
MALY SEMIACHIK (Kamchatka)	Synonym of KARYMSKY	1000-13=
MALY SEMIACHIK (Kamchatka)	Caldera (23, 1952) Historical	**1000-14=**
MALY SEMYACHIK (Kamchatka)	Synonym of MALY SEMIACHIK	1000-14=
MALYI SITKIN (Aleutian Is)	Synonym of LITTLE SITKIN	1101-05-
MALYJ SEMJATSCHIK (Kamchatka)	Synonym of MALY SEMIACHIK	1000-14=
MALYSH (Kurile Is)	Cone of GROZNY GROUP	0900-07=
MAMANE, PUU (Hawaiian Is)	Cone of HALEAKALA	1302-06-
MAMBACHO (Nicaragua)	Synonym of MOMBACHO	1404-11=
MAMBAJAO (Mindanao-Philippines)	Stratovolc of HIBOK-HIBOK	0701-08=
MAMELON CENTRAL (Indian O.-W)	Dome of FOURNAISE, PITON DE LA	0303-02=
MAMMAMUR (New Guinea-NE of)	Synonym of MANAM	0501-02=
MAMMOTH CRATER (US-California)	Crater of MEDICINE LAKE	1203-02-
MAMMOTH HOT SPRINGS (US-Wyoming)	Thermal Feature of YELLOWSTONE	1205-01-
MAMMOTH KNOLLS (US-California)	Dome of LONG VALLEY	1203-14-
MAMMOTH MOUNTAIN (US-California)	Dome of LONG VALLEY	1203-14-
MAMRUT DAGH (Turkey)	Synonym of NEMRUT DAGI	0103-02=
MANA [MANNA] (New Guinea)	Dome of MANAGLASE PLATEAU	0503-021
MANACAGAN [KASIBOI] (Philippines-C)	Cone of MAHAGNOA	0702-07=
MANAGLASE PLATEAU (New Guinea)	Volc field (None) Anthropology	**0503-021**
MANAM (New Guinea-NE of)	Stratovolc (31, 1993) Historical	**0501-02=**
MANAMUR (New Guinea-NE of)	Synonym of MANAM	0501-02=
MANANA (Hawaiian Is)	Tuff cone of KOOLAU	1302-07-
MANANTIAL, VOLCAN DEL (Argentina)	Synonym of PEINADO	1505-127
MANA'OMIA (Samoa-SW Pacific)	Cone of SAVAI'I	0404-04=
MANAREYJAR (Iceland-N of)	Submarine vent of TJORNES FRACTURE	1703-10=
MANARO NGORU (Vanuatu-SW Pacific)	Crater of AOBA	0507-03=
MANCHAS, LAS [LLANO DEL BANCO]	Fissure vent of LA PALMA	1803-01-
MANDA-INAKIR (Ethiopia)	Fissure vents (1, 1928) Historical	**0201-122**
MANDALAGAN (Philippines-C)	Stratovolc (None) Holocene	**0702-03=**
MANDANJI (Africa-E)	Dome of KIEYO	0202-17=
MANDASOWU, GUNUNG (Lesser Sunda Is)	Cone of RANAKAH, GUNUNG	0604-071
MANDEGUGUSU (Solomon Is-SW Pac)	Synonym of SIMBO	0505-05=
MANENGOUBA (Africa-W)	Stratovolc (None) Holocene	**0204-004**
MANENGUBA (Africa-W)	Synonym of MANENGOUBA	0204-004

NAME (Subregion)	Type (Eruption Total, Most Recent) Status . . . Relation to NAMED VOLCANO	NUMBER
MANGA AFI [MAUGA AFI] (Samoa-SW Pac)	Cone of SAVAI'I	0404-04=
MANGA-MA-LOBA (Africa-W)	Synonym of CAMEROON, MT.	0204-01=
MANGANAMU (New Zealand)	Dome of TAUPO	0401-07=
MANGATOETOE (New Zealand)	Dome of MAROA	0401-061
MANGATUTU (New Zealand)	Dome of MAROA	0401-061
MANGAWHAKAMANA (New Zealand)	Dome of OKATAINA	0401-05=
MANGERE LAGOON (New Zealand)	Tuff ring of AUCKLAND FIELD	0401-02=
MANGERE MOUNTAIN (New Zealand)	Cone of AUCKLAND FIELD	0401-02=
MANGINANGINA (New Zealand)	Cone of KAIKOHE-BAY OF ISLANDS	0401-01=
MANGUF (Ethiopia)	Cone of MEGA BASALT FIELD	0201-33-
MANITO (Luzon-Philippines)	Thermal Feature of POCDOL MOUNTAIN	0703-02=
MANNA (New Guinea)	Dome of MANAGLASE PLATEAU	0503-021
MANO DE DIABLO (Chile-S)	Cone of RECLUS	1508-063
MANOEK (Banda Sea)	Synonym of MANUK	0605-08=
MANOEK, KAWAH (Java)	Synonym of KAWAHMANUK	0603-11=
MANOKAMI-DAKE (Honshu-Japan)	Stratovolc of ZAO	0803-19=
MANTECA (Mexico)	Cone of CHICHINAUTZIN	1401-08=
MANTHE, MT. (Antarctica)	Stratovolc of HUDSON MOUNTAINS	1900-028
MANU, LUA (Hawaiian Is)	Pit crater of KILAUEA	1302-01-
MANUK (Banda Sea)	Stratovolc (None) Fumarolic	**0605-08=**
MANUK, KAWAH (Java)	Thermal Feature of WAYANG-WINDU	0603-08=
MANUK, KAWAH (Java)	Thermal Feature of KAWAHKAMOJANG	0603-12=
MANUK, KAWAH (Java)	Thermal Feature of PAPANDAYAN	0603-10=
MANUK, KAWAH (Java)	Synonym of KAWAHMANUK	0603-11=
MANUKA (Fiji Is-SW Pacific)	Cone of TAVEUNI	0405-01-
MANUM (MANUN) (New Guinea-NE of)	Synonym of MANAM	0501-02=
MANUMUDAR (New Guinea-NE of)	Synonym of MANAM	0501-02=
MANUPIRUA SPRINGS (New Zealand)	Thermal Feature of ROTORUA	0401-042
MANUREWA (New Zealand)	Cone of AUCKLAND FIELD	0401-02=
MANYATTA (Africa-E)	Cone of SUSWA	0202-11=
MANZA HOT SPRINGS (Honshu-Japan)	Thermal Feature of KUSATSU-SHIRANE	0803-12=
MAQUILAN (Luzon-Philippines)	Synonym of MAQUILING	0703-06=
MAQUILING (Luzon-Philippines)	Stratovolc (None) Holocene	**0703-06=**
MAR, PUIG DE (Spain)	Cone of OLOT VOLC FIELD	0100-03-
MARAEMANUKA (New Zealand)	Dome of MAROA	0401-061
MARAGONG-ONG (Mindanao-Philippines)	Dome of PACO	0701-09-
MARAPI (Sumatra)	Complx volc (55, 1993) Historical	**0601-14=**
MARCA, LOMA LA (Ecuador)	Dome of PULULAGUA	1502-011
MARCHENA (Galapagos)	Shield (1, 1991) Historical	**1503-08=**
MARCO, CRATERE (Indian O.-W)	Crater of FOURNAISE, PITON DE LA	0303-02=
MARCONDAS, PICA DAS [MURCONDAS]	Dome of FURNAS	1802-10=
MARDJA (Africa-W)	Crater of NGAOUNDERE PLATEAU	0204-002
MARE (Halmahera-Indonesia)	Cone of MOTIR	0608-061
MARECOCCO (Italy)	Dome of ISCHIA	0101-03=
MAREOROA SPRINGS (New Zealand)	Thermal Feature of ROTORUA	0401-042
MARETA, CALDERA DE LA (Canary Is)	Crater of HIERRO	1803-02-
MARETA, LA (Canary Is)	Cone of TENERIFE	1803-03-
MARGA BAJUR [MARGA BAYUR] (Sumatra)	Thermal Feature of BESAR, GUNUNG	0601-25=
MARGARITAS, VOLCANCITO (Guatemala)	Cone of MOYUTA	1402-13-
MARHA, JABAL EL- (Arabia-S)	Tuff cone (None) Holocene	**0301-10-**
MARIANA, PICO DA (Azores)	Cone of AGUA DE PAU	1802-09=
MARIBAYA (Java)	Thermal Feature of TANGKUBANPARAHU	0603-09=
MARIKANGEN (Java)	Stratovolc of DANAU COMPLEX	0603-01=
MARION ISLAND (Indian O.-S)	Shields (1, 1980) Historical	**0304-08-**
MARISHITEN (Honshu-Japan)	Crater of NORIKURA	0803-06=
MARISHITEN (Honshu-Japan)	Crater of ON-TAKE	0803-04=
MARIVELES (Luzon-Philippines)	Stratovolc (1, -2050) Radiocarbon	**0703-081**
MARKAGUNT PLATEAU (US-Utah)	Volc field (1, 1050) Dendrochronology	**1207-04-**
MARKARFLJOT (Iceland-S)	Dome of TORFAJOKULL	1702-05=
MARLANGA (Luzon-Philippines)	Synonym of MALINDIG	0703-044
MARMOLEJO (Chile-C)	Stratovolc of SAN JOSE	1507-02=
MAROA (New Zealand)	Calderas (2, 0180) Tephrochronology	**0401-061**
MAROA N, S & W (New Zealand)	Domes of MAROA	0401-061
MAROANUI (New Zealand)	Dome of MAROA	0401-061
MAROTIRI (New Zealand)	Dome of TAUPO	0401-07=
MAROUM [MARUM] (Vanuatu-SW Pacific)	Crater of AMBRYM	0507-04=
MARQUEZ, CERRO DEL (Mexico)	Cone of SANTA CATARINA RANGE	1401-082
MARRA, JEBEL (Africa-N)	Volc field (1, -2000) Radiocarbon	**0205-03-**
MARSABIT (Africa-E)	Shield (None) Holocene?	**0202-021**
MARTANA, ISOLA (Italy)	Cone of VULSINI	0101-003
MARTELES, CALDERA DE (Canary Is)	Maar of GRAN CANARIA	1803-04-
MARTIN (Alaska Peninsula)	Stratovolc (2, 1953) Historical	**1102-14-**
MARTIN [SAN MARTIN] (Canary Is)	Cone of LA PALMA	1803-01-
MARTINYA, PUIG DE (Spain)	Cone of OLOT VOLC FIELD	0100-03-
MARU-YAMA (Hokkaido-Japan)	Dome of KUTCHARO	0805-08=
MARU-YAMA (Hokkaido-Japan)	Cone of TOKACHI	0805-05=
MARU-YAMA (Honshu-Japan)	Dome of OSORE-YAMA	0803-29=
MARU-YAMA (Honshu-Japan)	Cone of FUJI	0803-03=
MARU-YAMA (Honshu-Japan)	Cone of IZU-TOBU	0803-01=
MARU-YAMA (Izu Is-Japan)	Cone of AOGA-SHIMA	0804-06=
MARU-YAMA (Japan)	Dome of NIPESOTSU-UPEPESANKE	0805-061
MARU-YAMA (Kyushu-Japan)	Stratovolc of ASO	0802-11=
MARUATA (New Zealand)	Cone of WHANGAREI	0401-011
MARUM (Vanuatu-SW Pacific)	Crater of AMBRYM	0507-04=
MARUMLIGLAR (Vanuatu-SW Pacific)	Crater of AMBRYM	0507-04=
MARUNO-YAMA (Honshu-Japan)	Cone of IZU-TOBU	0803-01=
MARUOKA-YAMA (Kyushu-Japan)	Cone of KIRISHIMA	0802-09=
MARUSHIMA-YAMA (Izu Is-Japan)	Dome of NII-JIMA	0804-02=
MARUSIMA-YAMA [MARUSHIMA-YAMA]	Dome of NII-JIMA	0804-02=
MARUYAMA (Honshu-Japan)	Cone of BANDAI	0803-16=
MARY BAY (US-Wyoming)	Crater of YELLOWSTONE	1205-01-
MARY'S POINT MOUNTAIN (W Indies)	Dome of SABA	1600-01=
MAS, KAWAH (Java)	Thermal Feature of PAPANDAYAN	0603-10=
MASA (Samoa-SW Pacific)	Cone of SAVAI'I	0404-04=
MASAKARI-YAMA (Kurile Is)	Synonym of EBEKO	0900-38=
MASARAGA (Luzon-Philippines)	Stratovolc (None) Holocene	**0703-031**
MASARANG (Sulawesi-Indonesia)	Cone of MAHAWU	0606-11=
MASATIERRA (Chile-Is)	Synonym of ROBINSON CRUSOE	1506-02=
MASAYA (Nicaragua)	Caldera (20, 1993) Historical	**1404-10=**
MASCOTA VOLC FIELD (Mexico)	Shields (None) Holocene	**1401-031**
MASECHA (Africa-C)	Crater of BUNYARUGURU FIELD	0203-005
MASEM, KAWAH (Sulawesi-Indonesia)	Crater of SEMPU	0606-04=
MASHIGA (Africa-C)	Cone of NYAMURAGIRA	0203-02=
MASHKOVTSEV (Kamchatka)	Stratovolc (None) Holocene	**1000-001**
MASHU (Hokkaido-Japan)	Caldera (5, 0970) Radiocarbon	**0805-081**
MASHUMANGABO (Africa-C)	Cone of NYAMURAGIRA	0203-02=
MASIGIT (Java)	Crater of TALAGABODAS	0603-15=
MASIGIT (Java)	Crater of GUNTUR	0603-13=
MASIPELID (Mindanao-Philippines)	Dome of PACO	0701-09-
MASSAKO (Africa-E)	Maar of KIEYO	0202-17=
MASSIF (French for MOUNTAIN RANGE) see proper name (e.g. GUEYNEMER, MASSIF)		
MASTEIRO, CALDEIRA (Azores)	Crater of FLORES	1802-001

NAME (Subregion)	Type (Eruption Total, Most Recent) Status / Relation to NAMED VOLCANO	NUMBER
MASUAN (Mindanao-Philippines)	Synonym of CALAYO	0701-07=
MASYU (Hokkaido-Japan)	Synonym of MASHU	0805-081
MAT ALA (Ethiopia)	Crater of BORAWLI	0201-107
MAT ALA (Ethiopia)	Shield (None) Holocene	**0201-105**
MATA DAS FEITICEIRAS (Azores)	Cone of UNNAMED	1802-081
MATA OLE AFI (Samoa-SW Pacific)	Crater of SAVAI'I	0404-04=
MATA UTA (SW Pacific)	Tuff cone of WALLIS ISLANDS	0404-05-
MATA'AGA (Samoa-SW Pacific)	Cone of SAVAI'I	0404-04=
MATAFA (Samoa-SW Pacific)	Cone of SAVAI'I	0404-04=
MATAFAO (Samoa-SW Pacific)	Dome of TUTUILA	0404-02-
MATAHAWRA (New Zealand)	Dome of OKATAINA	0401-05=
MATALTEPE, CERRO (Guatemala)	Cone of SUCHITAN VOLC FIELD	1402-17-
MA'TAN, JABAL (Arabia-W)	Cone of RAHAT, HARRAT	0301-07=
MATAULANO (Samoa-SW Pacific)	Cone of SAVAI'I	0404-04=
MATAVANU (Samoa-SW Pacific)	Cone of SAVAI'I	0404-04=
MATEER (Africa-W)	Crater of CAMEROON, MT.	0204-01=
MATHAIONI (Africa-E)	Cone of CHYULU HILLS	0202-13=
MATHEU (MATHEW) (SW Pacific)	Synonym of MATTHEW ISLAND	0508-01=
MATI (Java)	Crater of ARJUNO-WELIRANG	0603-29=
MATI, LAKE (Halmahera-Indonesia)	Maar of IBU	0608-03=
MATIANKANINA (Madagascar)	Cone of ITASY VOLC FIELD	0303-06-
MATSUGA-KUBO (Kyushu-Japan)	Maar of IBUSUKI VOLC FIELD	0802-07=
MATSUGA-MINE (Honshu-Japan)	Dome of NARUGO	0803-20=
MATSUKAWA (Honshu-Japan)	Thermal Feature of HACHIMANTAI	0803-25=
MATSUKAWA SPA (Honshu-Japan)	Thermal Feature of IWATE	0803-24=
MATSUWA JIMA (Kurile Is)	Synonym of SARYCHEV PEAK	0900-24=
MATTHEW ISLAND (SW Pacific)	Stratovolc (3, 1956) Historical	**0508-01=**
MATUA JIMA (Kurile Is)	Synonym of SARYCHEV PEAK	0900-24=
MATUFFA CRATER (Africa-E)	Cone of MERU	0202-16=
MATUGA-MINE [MATSUGA-MINE] (Honshu)	Dome of NARUGO	0803-20=
MATUKURUA (New Zealand)	Cone of AUCKLAND FIELD	0401-02=
MATUPI [TAVURVUR] (New Britain-SW Pac)	Stratovolc of RABAUL	0502-14=
MATUPIT ISLAND (New Britain-SW Pac)	Cone of RABAUL	0502-14=
MATUTAN (Mindanao-Philippines)	Synonym of MATUTUM	0701-02=
MATUTUM (Mindanao-Philippines)	Stratovolc (None) Holocene	**0701-02=**
MAU [LOBOA] (Vanuatu-SW Pacific)	Stratovolc of NORTH VATE	0507-081
MAUGA AFI (Samoa-SW Pacific)	Cone of SAVAI'I	0404-04=
MAUGA ALI'I (Samoa-SW Pacific)	Cone of UPOLU	0404-03-
MAUGA MU (Samoa-SW Pacific)	Cone of SAVAI'I	0404-04=
MAUGA-O-SAVAI'I (Samoa-SW Pacific)	Cone of UPOLU	0404-03-
MAUGALOA (Samoa-SW Pacific)	Cone of SAVAI'I	0404-04=
MAUGASILISILI (Samoa-SW Pacific)	Cone of SAVAI'I	0404-04=
MAUI, PUU O (Hawaiian Is)	Cone of HALEAKALA	1302-06-
MAULE (Chile-C)	Dome of MAULE, LAGUNA DEL	1507-062
MAULE, LAGUNA DEL (Chile-C)	Stratovolcs (None) Holocene	**1507-062**
MAUNA HALEAKALA (Hawaiian Is)	Synonym of HALEAKALA	1302-06-
MAUNA HINA (Hawaiian Is)	Cone of HALEAKALA	1302-06-
MAUNA IKI (Hawaiian Is)	Shield of KILAUEA	1302-01-
MAUNA KEA (Hawaiian Is)	Shield (2, -1650) Radiocarbon	**1302-03-**
MAUNA LOA (Hawaiian Is)	Shield (109, 1984) Historical	**1302-02=**
MAUNA ULU (Hawaiian Is)	Shield of KILAUEA	1302-01-
MAUNGA (Polynesian for MT.) see proper name (e.g. KUMA, MAUNGA)		
MAUNGAITI (New Zealand)	Dome of MAROA	0401-061
MAUNGAKAKARAMEA (New Zealand)	Cone of OKATAINA	0401-05=
MAUNGAKARAMEA (New Zealand)	Cone of WHANGAREI	0401-011
MAUNGAKAWAKAWA (New Zealand)	Cone of KAIKOHE-BAY OF ISLANDS	0401-01=
MAUNGANAMU (New Zealand)	Dome of TAUPO	0401-07=
MAUNGAONGAONGA (New Zealand)	Cone of OKATAINA	0401-05=
MAUNGATAKETAKE (New Zealand)	Cone of AUCKLAND FIELD	0401-02=
MAUNGATAPERE (New Zealand)	Cone of WHANGAREI	0401-011
MAUNGATUROTO (New Zealand)	Cone of KAIKOHE-BAY OF ISLANDS	0401-01=
MAUNU (New Zealand)	Cone of WHANGAREI	0401-011
MAURAS, CERRO (Peru)	Cone of ANDAHUA VALLEY	1504-002
MAURELLE ISLAND OF 1781 ? (Tonga)	Synonym of METIS SHOAL	0403-07=
MAVAHLIDARGIGIR (Iceland-SW)	Crater row of KRISUVIK	1701-03=
MAWENZI (Africa-E)	Stratovolc of KILIMANJARO	0202-15=
MAWRA CREMNA (Greece)	Thermal Feature of MILOS	0102-03=
MAY-YA-MOTO (Africa-C)	Fumarole fld (None) Fumarolic	**0203-01=**
MAYE-YAMA [MAYU-YAMA] (Kyushu-Japan)	Dome of UNZEN	0802-10=
MAYON (Luzon-Philippines)	Stratovolc (47, 1993) Historical	**0703-03=**
MAYONDON POINT (Luzon-Philippines)	Cone of MAQUILING	0703-06=
MAYOR ISLAND (New Zealand)	Shield (2, -4390) Radiocarbon	**0401-021**
MAYOR, PICO (Guatemala)	Synonym of ACATENANGO	1402-08=
MAYOTEPE, CERRO [CERRO MOYOTEPE]	Stratovolc of SAN CRISTOBAL	1404-02=
MAYU-GATA (Hokkaido-Japan)	Crater of KOMAGA-TAKE	0805-02=
MAYU-YAMA (Kyushu-Japan)	Dome of UNZEN	0802-10=
MAZAMA, MT. (US-Oregon)	Synonym of CRATER LAKE	1202-16-
MAZATEPEC (Mexico)	Cone of SANTA CATARINA RANGE	1401-082
MAZHANG (SE Asia)	Cone of LEIZHOU BANDAO	0705-01-
MAZIK DAGI (Turkey)	Dome of NEMRUT DAGI	0103-02=
MAZO, MT. (Mexico)	Cone of SAN QUINTIN VOLC FIELD	1401-002
MAZO, VOLCAN DE [ROJA DE MAZO]	Crater of LANZAROTE	1803-06-
MAZRUB, JEBEL (Africa-N)	Cone of BAYUDA VOLC FIELD	0205-06-
MAZZACARUSO, MONTE (Italy)	Stratovolc of LIPARI	0101-041
MBATI (Africa-C)	Cone of NYIRAGONGO	0203-03=
MBATNOU (Africa-W)	Cone of OKU VOLC FIELD	0204-003
MBENUMBENU (Fiji Is-SW Pacific)	Cone of TAVEUNI	0405-01-
MBUELESU [MBWELESU] (Vanuatu-SW Pac	Crater of AMBRYM	0507-04=
MBUGA (Africa-C)	Tuff cone of KATWE-KIKORONGO FIELD	0203-004
MBUYUNI (Africa-E)	Cone of KILIMANJARO	0202-15=
MBUZI (Africa-C)	Tuff cone of FORT PORTAL FIELD	0203-002
MBWELESU (Vanuatu-SW Pacific)	Crater of AMBRYM	0507-04=
MCALL KOP (Indian O.-S)	Cone of PRINCE EDWARD ISLAND	0304-07-
MCCARTYS (US-New Mexico)	Fissure vent of ZUNI-BANDERA	1210-02-
MCCAULEY SPRING (US-New Mexico)	Thermal Feature of VALLES CALDERA	1210-03-
MCCULLOCH PEAK (Aleutian Is)	Former dome of BOGOSLOF	1101-30-
MCINTYRE, MT. (Australia)	Cone of NEWER VOLCANICS PROV	0509-01-
MCKAY BUTTE (US-Oregon)	Dome of NEWBERRY VOLCANO	1202-11-
MCKEE (SW Pacific)	Cone of WALLIS ISLANDS	0404-05-
MCKENZIE BUTTE (US-California)	Dome of SHASTA	1203-01-
MCKENZIE HIGHWAY LAVA FIELD (US-Ore)	Synonym of BELKNAP	1202-06-
MCKINNEY BUTTE (US-Idaho)	Cone of SHOSHONE LAVA FIELD	1204-01-
MCLENNAN'S HILL (New Zealand)	Cone of AUCKLAND FIELD	0401-02=
MCLEOD HILL (Canada)	Tuya of WELLS GRAY-CLEARWATER	1200-15-
MCLOUGHLIN'S HILL [MATUKURUA]	Cone of AUCKLAND FIELD	0401-02=
MCNISH BAY CONE (Indian O.-S)	Tuff cone of PRINCE EDWARD ISLAND	0304-07-
ME-AKAN (Hokkaido-Japan)	Stratovolc of AKAN	0805-07=
MEAGER (Canada)	Complx volc (1, -0400) Radiocarbon	**1200-18-**
MEAGER CREEK HOT SPRING (Canada)	Thermal Feature of MEAGER	1200-18-
MEAGER CREEK VOLC FIELD (Canada)	Synonym of MEAGER	1200-18-
MEDAKE (Japan)	Cone of AKITA-KOMAGA-TAKE	0803-23=
MEDAM, JABAL (Arabia-S)	Crater of ARHAB, HARRA OF	0301-09-
MEDIA LUNA, VOLCAN (Chile-C)	Cone of CARRAN-LOS VENADOS	1507-14=
MEDIA MONTANA (Canary Is)	Cone of TENERIFE	1803-03-
MEDICINE LAKE (US-California)	Shield (9, 1075) Radiocarbon	**1203-02-**
MEDICINE LAKE HIGHLAND (US-California)	Synonym of MEDICINE LAKE	1203-02-
MEDINA, HARRAT EL- [HARRAT RASHID]	Blank of RAHAT, HARRAT	0301-07=
MEDIO, CERRO DEL [QUIZAPU] (Chile-C)	Crater of AZUL, CERRO [QUIZAPU]	1507-06=
MEDIO, CERRO EL (Chile-C)	Cone of CALABOZOS	1507-042
MEDIO, CERRO EL (US-New Mexico)	Dome of VALLES CALDERA	1210-03-
MEDJA [PUI] (Lesser Sunda Is)	Cone of IYA	0604-11=
MEDNYI (Kurile Is)	Stratovolc of TAO-RUSYR CALDERA	0900-31=
MEDVEVEZHY (Kamchatka)	Stratovolc of LEUTONGEY	1000-54-
MEDVEZHIA (Kurile Is)	Somma volc (3, 1958) Historical	**0900-10=**
MEDVEZHII (Kurile Is)	Synonym of MEDVEZHIA	0900-10=
MEERFELD (Germany)	Maar of WEST EIFEL VOLC FIELD	0100-01-
MEGA BASALT FIELD (Ethiopia)	Pyrocl cones (None) Holocene	**0201-33-**
MEGALO VOUNO (Greece)	Shield of SANTORINI	0102-04=
MEGALOS POLYBOTES (Greece)	Vent of NISYROS	0102-05=
MEGATA (Honshu-Japan)	Maars (2, -2050) Tephrochronology	**0803-262**
MEHETIA (Society Is-C Pac)	Stratovolc (None) Anthropology	**1303-06-**
MEIDOB VOLC FIELD (Africa-N)	Scoria cones (None) Holocene	**0205-05-**
MEIZI-SINZAN [MEIJI SHINZAN] (Hokkaido)	Dome of USU	0805-03=
MEJA [PUI] (Lesser Sunda Is)	Cone of IYA	0604-11=
MEKE DAG (Turkey)	Cone of KARAPINAR FIELD	0103-001
MEKEGOLU (Turkey)	Crater of KARAPINAR FIELD	0103-001
MEKEOBRUK (Turkey)	Crater of KARAPINAR FIELD	0103-001
MELAMETE (Africa-W)	Cone of CAMEROON, MT.	0204-01=
MELAN OROS (Arabia-S)	Synonym of SAWAD, HARRA ES-	0301-16-
MELATEN, GUNUNG (Java)	Cone of IJEN	0603-35=
MELAYU, BUKIT (Halmahera-Indonesia)	Cone of GAMALAMA	0608-06=
MELBOURNE (Antarctica)	Stratovolc (1, 1750) Tephrochronology	**1900-015**
MELHOLL (Iceland-SW)	Crater row of REYKJANES	1701-02=
MELHOLL (Iceland-SW)	Crater row of KRISUVIK	1701-03=
MELIMOTO (MELIMOYA) (Chile-S)	Synonym of MELIMOYU	1508-053
MELIMOYU (Chile-S)	Stratovolc (None) Holocene	**1508-053**
MELON, VOLCAN (Mexico)	Cone of MASCOTA VOLC FIELD	1401-031
MELRAKKAHRAUN (Iceland-SW)	Crater row of KRISUVIK	1701-03=
MENCHECA (Chile-C)	Stratovolc (None) Holocene	**1507-151**
MENCO, CERRO EL (Nicaragua)	Cone of ZAPATERA ISLAND	1404-111
MENDANA (Santa Cruz Is-SW Pac)	Cone of TINAKULA	0506-01=
MENDELEEV (Kurile Is)	Stratovolc (2, 1880) Historical	**0900-02=**
MENDELEYEV (Kurile Is)	Synonym of MENDELEEV	0900-02=
MENENGAI (Africa-E)	Shield (1, -7350) Tephrochronology	**0202-06=**
MENJER (Java)	Crater of DIENG VOLC COMPLEX	0603-20=
MENMARUBI (Honshu-Japan)	Vent of FUJI	0803-03=
MENNER (Kamchatka)	Shield of GAMCHEN	1000-21=
MENSHOI BRAT (Kurile Is)	Dome of MEDVEZHIA	0900-10=
MENTOLAT (Chile-S)	Stratovolc (None) Holocene?	**1508-055**
MERA LAVA (Vanuatu-SW Pacific)	Synonym of MERE LAVA	0507-021
MERAH, DANAU (Sumatra)	Crater of SORIKMARAPI	0601-12=
MERALAB (Vanuatu-SW Pacific)	Synonym of MERE LAVA	0507-021
MERAPI (Java)	Stratovolc of IJEN	0603-35=
MERAPI (Java)	Stratovolc (68, 1993) Historical	**0603-25=**
MERAPI (Sumatra)	Synonym of MARAPI	0601-14=
MERBABOE (Java)	Synonym of MERBABU	0603-24=
MERBABU (Java)	Stratovolc (2, 1797) Historical	**0603-24=**
MERCADEL, MONTANA DE (Canary Is)	Cone of HIERRO	1803-02-
MERCIMEK TEPE (Turkey)	Cone of ACIGOL-NEVSEHIR	0103-004
MERCOEUR, PUY DE (France)	Cone of CHAINE DES PUYS	0100-02-
MERDODO [MERDADA] (Java)	Cone of DIENG VOLC COMPLEX	0603-20=
MERE LAVA (Vanuatu-SW Pacific)	Stratovolc (None) Holocene	**0507-021**
MERKER KEGEL [ASH CONE] (Africa-E)	Cone of MERU	0202-16=
MERKURHRAUN (Iceland-S)	Fissure vent of TORFAJOKULL	1702-05=
MERREM PEAK (Antarctica)	Caldera of BERLIN	1900-022
MERRIAM CONE (US-Oregon)	Cone of CRATER LAKE	1202-16-
MERRIAM POINT (US-Oregon)	Dome of CRATER LAKE	1202-16-
MERSIDAT (Africa-N)	Cone of BAYUDA VOLC FIELD	0205-06-
MERU (Africa-E)	Stratovolc (4, 1910) Historical	**0202-16=**
MESA, CERRO DE LA (Luzon-Philippines)	Tuff cone of MAQUILING	0703-06=
MESA, LA (Mexico)	Cone of TENAYO GROUP	1401-081
MESA NEVADA DE HERVEO (Colombia)	(None) Not a Volcano	1501-01=
MESAH (Banda Sea)	Synonym of TEON	0605-05=
MESAS, VOLCAN LAS (Mexico)	Cone of MASCOTA VOLC FIELD	1401-031
MESETA (Guatemala)	Cone of FUEGO	1402-09=
MESO-SEMIACHIK (Kamchatka)	Stratovolc of MALY SEMIACHIK	1000-14=
MESS CREEK HOT SPRING (Canada)	Thermal Feature of SPECTRUM RANGE	1200-07-
MESS LAKE HOT SPRINGS (Canada)	Thermal Feature of SPECTRUM RANGE	1200-07-
MESS LAKE LAVA FIELD (Canada)	Vent of SPECTRUM RANGE	1200-07-
MESZAH PEAK (Canada)	Cone of LEVEL MOUNTAIN	1200-05-
METATE, CERRO EL (Mexico)	Cone of MICHOACAN-GUANAJUATO	1401-06=
METCALF DOMES (Aleutian Is)	Former dome of BOGOSLOF	1101-30-
METEPEC (Mexico)	Cone of HOLOTEPEC	1401-07-
METHANA (Greece)	Lava domes (1, -0258) Historical	**0102-02=**
METIS SHOAL (Tonga-SW Pacific)	Submarine (8, 1979) Historical	**0403-07=**
METLALCUEYATLE (Mexico)	Synonym of MALINCHE, LA	1401-091
METROGOON LAKE (Aleutian Is)	Synonym of FISHER	1101-35-
MEY, PUY DE (France)	Cone of CHAINE DES PUYS	0100-02-
MEYERS NUNATAK (Antarctica)	Cone of HUDSON MOUNTAINS	1900-028
MEZHDUSOPOCHNY (Kamchatka)	Shield (None) Holocene	**1000-57-**
MFOMBEN (Africa-W)	Cone of OKU VOLC FIELD	0204-003
MGAHINGA [GAHINGA] (Africa-C)	Cone of MUHAVURA	0203-06-
MI-IKE (Kyushu-Japan)	Maar of KIRISHIMA	0802-09=
MI-TAKE [KITA-DAKE] (Kyushu-Japan)	Stratovolc of SAKURA-JIMA	0802-08=
MICHAEL (Antarctica)	Stratovolc (1, 1819) Historical	**1900-09=**
MICHICO, CERRO (Argentina)	Cone of TROMEN	1507-071
MICHINCHA, CERRO (Chile-N)	Stratovolc of OLCA-PARUMA	1505-05=
MICHINMAHUIDA (MICHINMAVIDA) (Chile-S	Synonym of MINCHINMAVIDA	1508-04=
MICHOACAN-GUANAJUATO (Mexico)	Cinder cones (8, 1952) Historical	**1401-06=**
MICOS, CERRO DE LOS (El Salvador)	Dome of ILOPANGO	1403-06=
MICOTRIN (W Indies)	Lava domes (1, 1880) Historical	**1600-10=**
MIDA, CUDDIA (Italy)	Vent of PANTELLERIA	0101-071
MIDAGAHARA (Honshu-Japan)	Synonym of TATE-YAMA	0803-08=
MIDASHI-YAMA (Honshu-Japan)	Synonym of FUJI	0803-03=
MIDDLE GOBI (Mongolia)	Cinder cones (None) Holocene?	**1003-05-**
MIDDLE HILL [MT. PATUKIO] (Solomon Is)	Cone of SIMBO	0505-05=
MIDDLE SISTER (US-Oregon)	Stratovolc of NORTH SISTER FIELD	1202-07-
MIDHDALSJOKULL (Iceland-S)	Synonym of KATLA	1702-03=
MIDKVISLARHRAUN (Iceland-S)	Fissure vent of KATLA	1702-03=
MIDORI (Kurile Is)	Synonym of ZAVARITZKI CALDERA	0900-18=
MIDORIGA-IKE (Honshu-Japan)	Crater of HAKU-SAN	0803-05=
MIDORIIKO (Kurile Is)	Synonym of ZAVARITZKI CALDERA	0900-18=
MIDSKALARHEIDARHRAUN (Iceland-S)	Fissure vent of EYJAFJOLL	1702-02=
MIE-YAMA (Honshu-Japan)	Synonym of FUJI	0803-03=

NAME (Subregion)	Type (Eruption Total, Most Recent) Status . . . Relation to NAMED VOLCANO	NUMBER
MIGULULU (Africa-E)	Cone of CHYULU HILLS	0202-13=
MIHAGA (Africa-C)	Cone of NYAMURAGIRA	0203-02=
MIHARA (Izu Is-Japan)	Pleistocene caldera of HACHIJO-JIMA	0804-05=
MIHARA-YAMA (Izu Is-Japan)	Cone of OSHIMA	0804-01=
MIHARASHI-YAMA (Honshu-Japan)	Dome of AKAGI	0803-13=
MIHONGA (Africa-C)	Cone of NYAMURAGIRA	0203-02=
MIKAGE-SAN (Honshu-Japan)	Synonym of FUJI	0803-03=
MIKAMI-YAMA (Honshu-Japan)	Synonym of FUJI	0803-03=
MIKASA-YAMA (Honshu-Japan)	Cone of ON-TAKE	0803-04=
MIKOMBE (Africa-C)	Cone of NYAMURAGIRA	0203-02=
MIKRO PROFITAS ILIAS (Greece)	Shield of SANTORINI	0102-04=
MIKROS POLYBOTES (Greece)	Vent of NISYROS	0102-05=
MIKURIGAIKE (Honshu-Japan)	Crater of TATE-YAMA	0803-08=
MILBANKE SOUND GROUP (Canada)	Cinder cones (None) Holocene	**1200-12-**
MILLER KNOLL (US-Utah)	Cone of MARKAGUNT PLATEAU	1207-04-
MILNE (Kurile Is)	Somma volc (None) Holocene	**0900-17A**
MILOS (Greece)	Stratovolcs (None) Holocene	**0102-03=**
MILU TATU (Africa-E)	Cone of NYAMBENI HILLS	0202-056
MIMATA-YAMA (Kyushu-Japan)	Dome of KUJU GROUP	0802-12=
MINA, VOLCAN LA (Mexico)	Cone of MICHOACAN-GUANAJUATO	1401-06=
MINABUL (Luzon-N of)	Cone of CAMIGUIN DE BABUYANES	0704-01=
MINAMI-DAKE (Hokkaido-Japan)	Stratovolc of AKAN	0805-07=
MINAMI-DAKE (Hokkaido)	Crater of SHIRETOKO-IWO-ZAN	0805-09=
MINAMI-DAKE (Kyushu-Japan)	Stratovolc of SAKURA-JIMA	0802-08=
MINAMI-HIYOSHI (Volcano Is-Japan	Submarine (1, 1975) Historical	**0804-131**
MINAMI-HIYOSHI KAIZAN (Volcano Is-Japan)	Synonym of MINAMI-HIYOSHI	0804-131
MINAMI IWO DAKE (Kurile Is)	Synonym of KUNTOMINTAR	0900-28=
MINAMI-IWO-JIMA (Volcano Is-Japan)	Synonym of SHIN-IWO-JIMA	0804-13=
MINARDO, MONTE (Italy)	Cone of ETNA	0101-06=
MINASGUILCA CHICO [NINAHUILCA]	Dome of ATACAZO	1502-021
MINCHENMADON (MINCHINMADON) (Chile	Synonym of MINCHINMAVIDA	1508-04=
MINCHINMAVIDA (Chile-S)	Stratovolc (3, 1835) Historical	**1508-04=**
MINEZI [MINEJI] (Izu Is-Japan)	Dome of NII-JIMA	0804-02=
MINIAYAO (Mindanao-Philippines)	Dome of PACO	0701-09-
MINMA (SE Asia)	Cone of LOWER CHINDWIN	0705-09-
MINNEI (Vanuatu-SW Pacific)	Crater of AMBRYM	0507-04=
MINOPOLI (Italy)	Crater of CAMPI FLEGREI	0101-01=
MINOWA-YAMA (Honshu-Japan)	Stratovolc of ADATARA	0803-17=
MIPPANA (Izu Is-Japan)	Crater of MIYAKE-JIMA	0804-04=
MIRADOR (Chile-C)	Crater of LLAIMA	1507-11=
MIRADOR (Chile-C)	Cone of CARRAN-LOS VENADOS	1507-14=
MIRAFLORES (Guatemala)	Stratovolc of TECUAMBURRO	1402-12=
MIRAFLORES (Nicaragua)	Dome of APOYEQUE	1404-091
MIRAIBTA, JEBEL EL (Africa-N)	Cone of BAYUDA VOLC FIELD	0205-06-
MIRANDA (Alaska-SW)	Synonym of ILIAMNA	1103-02-
MIRANDO (Alaska-SW)	Synonym of REDOUBT	1103-03-
MIRAVALLES (Costa Rica)	Stratovolc (2, 1946) Historical	**1405-03=**
MISAHUANA MAURAS, VOLCAN (Peru)	Cone of ANDAHUA VALLEY	1504-002
MISAKI (Honshu-Japan)	Synonym of OKI-DOGO	0803-003
MISENO (Italy)	Crater of CAMPI FLEGREI	0101-01=
MISERY PEAK, MT. (W Indies)	Dome of LIAMUIGA	1600-03=
MISTI, EL (Peru)	Stratovolc (4, 1787) Historical	**1504-01=**
MITAD, EL (Guatemala)	Vent of SANTA MARIA	1402-03=
MITAN, MORNE (W Indies)	Thermal Feature of SOUFR. GUADELOUPE	1600-06=
MITCHELL, MT. (Australia)	Cone of NEWER VOLCANICS PROV	0509-01-
MITER (US-Utah)	Crater of BLACK ROCK DESERT	1207-05-
MITSU-DAKE (Honshu-Japan)	Dome of OMANAGO GROUP	0803-142
MITSUGO-JIMA (MITUGO-ZIMA) (Izu Is)	Synonym of TORI-SHIMA	0804-09=
MITUISI-YAMA [MITSUISHI-YAMA] (Honshu)	Stratovolc of IWATE	0803-24=
MIYAKE-JIMA (Izu Is-Japan)	Stratovolc (21, 1983) Historical	**0804-04=**
MIYAZUKA-YAMA (Izu Is-Japan)	Dome of NII-JIMA	0804-02=
MIZU-GAMA (Honshu-Japan)	Crater of KUSATSU-SHIRANE	0803-12=
MIZUNASHI (Kyushu-Japan)	Maar of IBUSUKI VOLC FIELD	0802-07=
MOCHO-CHOSHUENCO (Chile-C)	Stratovolc (3, 1937) Historical	**1507-13=**
MOCHO, EL (Chile-C)	Stratovolc of MOCHO-CHOSHUENCO	1507-13=
MODENDA (Africa-C)	Cone of KARISIMBI	0203-04-
MODOC-MEDICINE LAKE FIELD (US-Calif)	Synonym of MEDICINE LAKE	1203-02-
MOE-SHIMA (Ryukyu Is)	Synonym of SUWANOSE-JIMA	0802-03=
MOEDER-EN-KIND (Indian O.-S)	Cone of PRINCE EDWARD ISLAND	0304-07-
MOETELONG, BOER (Sumatra)	Synonym of TELONG, BUR NI	0601-05=
MOFETE (Italy)	Crater of CAMPI FLEGREI	0101-01=
MOFFETT (Aleutian Is)	Stratovolc (None) Holocene	**1101-111**
MOGOTE DE LAS PILAS, CERRO EL	Cone of CONCEPCION	1404-12=
MOGOTE, LOMA EL (Nicaragua)	Cone of CONCEPCION	1404-12=
MOIKESHI (Kurile Is)	Synonym of LVINAYA PAST	0900-041
MOINA (Ethiopia)	Synonym of DABBAHU	0201-113
MOIRO, CERRO (Bolivia)	Scoria cone (None) Holocene?	**1505-064**
MOJANDA (Ecuador)	Stratovolc (1, -1450) Radiocarbon	**1502-003**
MOJON, MONTANA DEL (Canary Is)	Cone of LANZAROTE	1803-06-
MOKA, PICO DO (Africa-W)	Synonym of SAN JOAQUIN	0204-03-
MOKA, PITON (Indian O.-W)	Cone of FOURNAISE, PITON DE LA	0303-02=
MOKAI (New Zealand)	Dome of MAROA	0401-061
MOKHNATAYA (Kamchatka)	Cone of TOLBACHIK	1000-24=
MOKOIA (New Zealand)	Dome of ROTORUA	0401-042
MOKOL (Java)	Stratovolc of DANAU COMPLEX	0603-01=
MOKST BUTTE (US-Oregon)	Cone of NEWBERRY VOLCANO	1202-11-
MOKUAWEOWEO (Hawaiian Is)	Caldera of MAUNA LOA	1302-02=
MOKUNDO (Africa-W)	Cone of CAMEROON, MT.	0204-01=
MOLABUSHAN (China-E)	Cone of WUDALIANCHI	1005-04-
MOLARA (Italy)	Crater of ISCHIA	0101-03=
MOLCAJETE, EL (Mexico)	Cone of HOLOTEPEC	1401-07-
MOLCAJETE, VOLCAN (Mexico)	Cone of MASCOTA VOLC FIELD	1401-031
MOLCAJETE, VOLCAN EL (Mexico)	Cone of MASCOTA VOLC FIELD	1401-031
MOLENGRAAFF CALDERA (Lesser Sunda Is	Synonym of BATUR	0604-01=
MOLINO (Italy)	Cone of VULSINI	0101-003
MOLO (Lesser Sunda Is)	Cone of TAMBORA	0604-04=
MOLODOI KIKHPINYCH (Kamchatka)	Synonym of KIKHPINYCH	1000-18=
MOLODOY (Kamchatka)	Vent of KRASHENINNIKOV	1000-19=
MOLODOY SHEVELUCH (Kamchatka)	Dome of SHEVELUCH	1000-27=
MOLOKINI ISLET (Hawaiian Is)	Tuff cone of HALEAKALA	1302-06-
MOMBACHO (Nicaragua)	Stratovolc (None) Fumarolic	**1404-11=**
MOMOTOMBITO, VOLCAN (Nicaragua)	Cone of MOMOTOMBO	1404-09=
MOMOTOMBO (Nicaragua)	Stratovolc (18, 1905) Historical	**1404-09=**
MONACO BANK (Azores)	Submarine (2, 1911) Historical	**1802-11=**
MONASTERO (Italy)	Shield of PANTELLERIA	0101-071
MONASTERO [CINQUE DENTI] (Italy)	Pleistocene caldera of PANTELLERIA	0101-071
MONASTYR (Kamchatka)	Synonym of AVACHINSKY	1000-10=
MONASTYR (Kamchatka)	Cone of AVACHINSKY	1000-10=
MONDACA (Chile-C)	Lava dome (None) Holocene	**1507-041**
MONDILIBI (Australia)	Vent of NEWER VOLCANICS PROV	0509-01-
MONGIBELLO (Italy)	Shield of ETNA	0101-06=
MONGIBELLO (Italy)	Synonym of ETNA	0101-06=

NAME (Subregion)	Type (Eruption Total, Most Recent) Status . . . Relation to NAMED VOLCANO	NUMBER
MONGO-MA-LOBA (Africa-W)	Synonym of CAMEROON, MT.	0204-01=
MONGOGOGURA (Africa-E)	Synonym of LENGAI, OL DOINYO	0202-12=
MONGOMANE (Africa-C)	Cone of KARISIMBI	0203-04-
MONGOY, CERRO (Guatemala)	Cone of CHINGO VOLC FIELD	1402-15-
MONI RIVER (New Guinea)	Synonym of MUSA RIVER	0503-02=
MONJE, EL (Guatemala)	Vent of SANTA MARIA	1402-03=
MONKUL (Admiralty Is-SW Pac)	Cone of ST. ANDREW STRAIT	0500-01=
MONO BLANCO, CERRO (Mexico)	Cone of SAN MARTIN, VOLCAN DE	1401-11=
MONO CRATERS (US-California)	Lava domes (11, 1345) Radiocarbon	**1203-12-**
MONO LAKE ISLANDS (US-Calif)	Synonym of MONO LAKE VOLC FIELD	1203-11-
MONO LAKE VOLC FIELD (US-Calif)	Cinder cones (4, 1785) Tephrochronology	**1203-11-**
MONOUN, LAKE (Africa-W)	Maar of OKU VOLC FIELD	0204-003
MONOWAI SEAMOUNT (Kermadec Is)	Submarine (7, 1991) Historical	**0402-05-**
MONPELOSO (Italy)	Cone of ETNA	0101-06=
MONPILIERI, MONTE (Italy)	Cone of ETNA	0101-06=
MONS GIBEL UTLAMAT (Italy)	Synonym of ETNA	0101-06=
MONSERRAT, CERRO (Chile-C)	Cone of TINGUIRIRICA	1507-03=
MONT, MONTAGNE, MONTANA, MONTE, MORNE, MOUNT, MT. see proper name (e.g. FUEGO, MONTANAS DEL)		
MONTAGNOLA, LA (Italy)	Cone of ETNA	0101-06=
MONTAGNONE-MASCHIATA (Italy)	Dome of ISCHIA	0101-03=
MONTCHAL, PUY DE (France)	Cone of CHAINE DES PUYS	0100-02-
MONTCHATRE, MAAR DE (France)	Maar of CHAINE DES PUYS	0100-02-
MONTCHIER, PUY (France)	Cone of CHAINE DES PUYS	0100-02-
MONTCINEYRE, PUY DE (France)	Cone of CHAINE DES PUYS	0100-02-
MONTE, CUDDIA DEL (Italy)	Cone of PANTELLERIA	0101-071
MONTEFIASCONE (Italy)	Cone of VULSINI	0101-003
MONTENARD, PUY DE (France)	Cone of CHAINE DES PUYS	0100-02-
MONTEZUMA, CERRO (Costa Rica)	Stratovolc of TENORIO GROUP	1405-031
MONTGY, PUY DE (France)	Cone of CHAINE DES PUYS	0100-02-
MONTICELLI (Italy)	Crater of CAMPI FLEGREI	0101-01=
MONTICULO CINERITICO (Mexico-Is)	Cone of BARCENA	1401-02=
MONTIONE, MT. (Italy)	Cone of VULSINI	0101-003
MONTJUGEAT, PUY DE (France)	Cone of CHAINE DES PUYS	0100-02-
MONTOLIVET, VOLCA (Spain)	Cone of OLOT VOLC FIELD	0100-03-
MONTON DE TRIGO (Chile-S)	Crater of OSORNO	1508-01=
MONTOSO, CERRO (Nicaragua)	Cone of TELICA	1404-04=
MONTOSO, CERRO (Nicaragua)	Cone of MOMOTOMBO	1404-09=
MONTSACOPA, VOLCA (Spain)	Cone of OLOT VOLC FIELD	0100-03-
MONUMENTO (Atlantic-S)	Dome of TRINDADE	1805-051
MOOLORT, MT. (Australia)	Cone of NEWER VOLCANICS PROV	0509-01-
MOOROOKYLE, MT. (Australia)	Cone of NEWER VOLCANICS PROV	0509-01-
MORABU (Africa-C)	Crater of BUNYARUGURU FIELD	0203-005
MORAINE (Canada)	Cone of EDZIZA	1200-06-
MORE, CRATER (New Britain-SW Pac)	Crater of GAROVE	0502-03=
MORERA, LOMA (Costa Rica)	Cone of AGUAS ZARCAS GROUP	1405-035
MORHOVOI (Alaska Peninsula)	Stratovolc of FROSTY	1102-01-
MORO (Halmahera-Indonesia)	Crater of IBU	0608-03=
MORO, CUDDIA DEL (Italy)	Shield of PANTELLERIA	0101-071
MORRO (Chile-C)	Thermal Feature of CORDON CAULLE	1507-141
MORRO DE AZUFRE (Chile-C)	Synonym of TINGUIRIRICA	1507-03=
MORRO DE LAS ATALAYAS (Canary Is)	Cone of LANZAROTE	1803-06-
MORRO DESCONHECIDO (Atlantic-S)	Dome of TRINDADE	1805-051
MORRO, EL (Chile-S)	Crater of OSORNO	1508-01=
MORRO VERMELHO (Atlantic-S)	Cone of TRINDADE	1805-051
MOS (Azores)	Cone of AGUA DE PAU	1802-09=
MOSAKIRI-YAMA (Kurile Is)	Synonym of EBEKO	0900-38=
MOSBRUCH (Germany)	Maar of WEST EIFEL VOLC FIELD	0100-01-
MOSENBERG (Germany)	Cone of WEST EIFEL VOLC FIELD	0100-01-
MOSES (Aleutian Is)	Synonym of SHISHALDIN	1101-36-
MOSES, MT. (Antarctica)	Stratovolc of HUDSON MOUNTAINS	1900-028
MOSHKOVSKAYA (Kamchatka)	Synonym of MASHKOVTSEV	1000-001
MOSIMUS, MT. (Luzon-Philippines)	Twin volcano of BINULUAN	0703-088
MOSQUITO MOUND (Canada)	Tuya of WELLS GRAY-CLEARWATER	1200-15-
MOTA LAVA (Vanuatu-SW Pacific)	Synonym of MOTLAV	0507-001
MOTASTEPE, CERRO (Nicaragua)	Cone of NEJAPA-TICOMO	1404-092
MOTHER, THE [KOMBIU] (New Britain)	Stratovolc of RABAUL	0502-14=
MOTI (Halmahera-Indonesia)	Synonym of MOTIR	0608-061
MOTIR (Halmahera-Indonesia)	Stratovolc (None) Uncertain	**0608-061**
MOTLAV (Vanuatu-SW Pacific)	Stratovolc (None) Holocene	**0507-001**
MOTMOT (New Guinea-NE of)	Cone of LONG ISLAND	0501-05=
MOTO-SHIRANE (Honshu-Japan)	Cone of KUSATSU-SHIRANE	0803-12=
MOTONUPURI (Kurile Is)	Cone of GROZNY GROUP	0900-07=
MOTU LAHI (Tonga-SW Pacific)	Cone of NIUAFO'OU	0403-11=
MOTU MOLIMOLI (Tonga-SW Pacific)	Cone of NIUAFO'OU	0403-11=
MOTUAPU (New Zealand)	Dome of TAUPO	0401-07=
MOTUHORA ISLAND (New Zealand)	Synonym of WHALE ISLAND	0401-041
MOTUKAIKO (New Zealand)	Dome of TAUPO	0401-07=
MOTUKOREA (New Zealand)	Cone of AUCKLAND FIELD	0401-02=
MOTUMA (New Zealand)	Dome of TAUPO	0401-07=
MOUA PIHAA (Society Is-C Pac)	Submarine (None) Seismicity	**1303-05-**
MOUMOUKAI (Kermadec Is)	Stratovolc of RAOUL ISLAND	0402-03=
MOUNA HUARARAI (Hawaiian Is)	Synonym of HUALALAI	1302-04-
MOUSA ALLI (Ethiopia)	Stratovolc (None) Holocene	**0201-123**
MOUSGOU, EHI (Africa-N)	Stratovolc of VOON, TARSO	0205-02=
MOUSSA ALLI (Ethiopia)	Synonym of MOUSA ALLI	0201-123
MOUSTABISMEN, PITON DE (Indian O.-W)	Cone of FOURNAISE, PITON DE LA	0303-02=
MOWNA ROA (Hawaiian Is)	Synonym of MAUNA LOA	1302-02=
MOWNA WORRARAR (Hawaiian Is)	Synonym of HUALALAI	1302-04-
MOYE (Ethiopia)	Synonym of TULLU MOJE	0201-25-
MOYORO-DAKE [KUDRIAVY] (Kurile Is)	Cone of MEDVEZHIA	0900-10=
MOYOTEPE, CERRO (Nicaragua)	Stratovolc of SAN CRISTOBAL	1404-02=
MOYUTA (Guatemala)	Stratovolc (None) Hot Springs	**1402-13-**
MPOLI (Africa-E)	Cone of IZUMBWE-MPOLI	0202-165
MUAGA MUA [MAUGA AFI] (Samoa-SW Pac)	Cone of SAVAI'I	0404-04=
MUBONYAKYA (Africa-E)	Cone of CHYULU HILLS	0202-13=
MUCU (Lesser Sunda Is)	Thermal Feature of POCO LEOK	0604-07=
MUD BAY (D'Entrecasteaux Is)	Cone of GOODENOUGH	0503-041
MUD HILL (US-New Mexico)	Cone of RATON-CLAYTON	1210-04-
MUE (Africa-E)	Cone of KILIMANJARO	0202-15=
MUEGGEN, CUDDIA (Italy)	Shield of PANTELLERIA	0101-071
MUERTO, ISLA EL (Nicaragua)	Cone of ZAPATERA ISLAND	1404-111
MUGARA (Africa-C)	Cone of NYIRAGONGO	0203-03=
MUGOGO (Africa-C)	Cone of VISOKE	0203-05-
MUHABURA (Africa-C)	Synonym of MUHAVURA	0203-06-
MUHAVURA (Africa-C)	Stratovolc (None) Holocene	**0203-06-**
MUHAVURU (Africa-C)	Synonym of MUHAVURA	0203-06-
MUHLENBERG (Germany)	Cone of WEST EIFEL VOLC FIELD	0100-01-
MUHOTI (Africa-C)	Tuff cone of FORT PORTAL FIELD	0203-002
MUHUBOLI (Africa-C)	Vent of NYAMURAGIRA	0203-02=
MUIRHEAD, MT. (Australia)	Cone of NEWER VOLCANICS PROV	0509-01-
MUJA (Africa-C)	Cone of NYIRAGONGO	0203-03=

NAME (Subregion)	Type (Eruption Total, Most Recent) Status / Relation to NAMED VOLCANO	NUMBER
MUKO-YAMA [MUKAI-YAMA] (Izu Is-Japan)	Dome of NII-JIMA	0804-02=
MUKUANI HILL (Africa-E)	Dome of NYAMBENI HILLS	0202-056
MULAS, ALTO DE LAS (Chile-C)	Fissure vent of DESCABEZADO GRANDE	1507-05=
MULATA (Azores)	Cone of SETE CIDADES	1802-08=
MULCARES SOUFRIERE (W Indies)	Thermal Feature of SOUFRIERE HILLS	1600-05=
MULDERI (Africa-C)	Crater of KARISIMBI	0203-04-
MULE, CERRO LA (Nicaragua)	Cone of NEGRO, CERRO	1404-07=
MULIMAUGA (Samoa-SW Pacific)	Cone of SAVAI'I	0404-04=
MULINO DE VALENTANO (Italy)	Cone of VULSINI	0101-003
MULUKROKO [ILITEBULELE] (Lesser Sunda)	Cone of ILILABALEKAN	0604-24=
MUNDACA (Chile-C)	Synonym of MONDACA	1507-041
MUNDAGIGAR [MUNDAFELL] (Iceland-S)	Fissure vent of HEKLA	1702-07=
MUNDI (Africa-E)	Cone of PAKA	0202-053
MUNDING, KAWAH (Java)	Thermal Feature of KAWAHKAMOJANG	0603-12=
MUNDO, CERRO (Galapagos)	Cone of SAN CRISTOBAL	1503-12-
MUNDO NUEVA (Colombia)	Crater of CUMBAL	1501-10=
MUNDUA (New Britain-SW Pac)	Complx volc (None) Holocene	**0502-021**
MUNGO-MA-LOBA (Africa-W)	Synonym of CAMEROON, MT.	0204-01=
MUNGOGO WA BOGWE (Africa-E)	Synonym of LENGAI, OL DOINYO	0202-12=
MUNLULU (New Britain-SW Pac)	Crater of LANGILA	0502-01=
MUNLULU, MT. (New Britain-SW Pac)	Cone of LANGILA	0502-01=
MUNTANGO (Africa-C)	Pit crater of KARISIMBI	0203-04-
MUNYINYA (Africa-C)	Crater of KARISIMBI	0203-04-
MURAMBE (Africa-C)	Crater of BUNYARUGURU FIELD	0203-005
MURARA (Africa-C)	Cone of NYAMURAGIRA	0203-02=
MURCONDAS, PICA DAS (Azores)	Dome of FURNAS	1802-10=
MURDOCH (Antarctica)	Cone of SEAL NUNATAKS GROUP	1900-05=
MURNIAU (Africa-E)	Tuff cone of BARRIER, THE	0202-03=
MURUESE (Africa-E)	Cone of PAKA	0202-053
MUSA ALI (Ethiopia)	Synonym of MOUSA ALLI	0201-123
MUSA RIVER (New Guinea)	Hydrothrm fld (None) Hot Springs	**0503-02=**
MUSANULA (Africa-C)	Cone of KARISIMBI	0203-04-
MUSEAU DE TANCHE (Indian O.-S)	Cone of AMSTERDAM ISLAND	0304-04-
MUSHUSHWE (Africa-C)	Cone of NYIRAGONGO	0203-03=
MUSIDE (Africa-C)	Cone of VISOKE	0203-05-
MUSONGE (Africa-W)	Cone of CAMEROON, MT.	0204-01=
MUSSA-ALI (Ethiopia)	Synonym of MOUSA ALLI	0201-123
MUSUAN (Mindanao-Philippines)	Synonym of CALAYO	0701-07=
MUTA DO LEAL (Azores)	Cone of UNNAMED	1802-081
MUTELONG, BUR (Sumatra)	Synonym of TELONG, BUR NI	0601-05=
MUTI (Africa-C)	Cone of NYIRAGONGO	0203-03=
MUTJU [MUCU] (Lesser Sunda Is)	Thermal Feature of POCO LEOK	0604-07=
MUTNAIA, SOPKA [MUTNAJA] (Kamchatka)	Synonym of MUTNOVSKY	1000-06=
MUTNOVSKAIA, SOPKA (Kamchatka)	Synonym of MUTNOVSKY	1000-06=
MUTNOVSKY (Kamchatka)	Complx volc (43, 1961) Historical	**1000-06=**
MUTNOWSKIJ (Kamchatka)	Synonym of MUTNOVSKY	1000-06=
MUTONAJU (Africa-E)	Cone of CHYULU HILLS	0202-13=
MUTSA [MUJA] (Africa-C)	Cone of NYIRAGONGO	0203-03=
MUTSU-HIUCHI-DAKE (Honshu-Japan)	Stratovolc (None) Fumarolic	**0803-30-**
MUVO (Africa-C)	Cone of NYAMURAGIRA	0203-02=
MUWEILIH (Africa-N)	Crater of BAYUDA VOLC FIELD	0205-06-
MWAILO (Africa-E)	Cone of CHYULU HILLS	0202-13=
MYAYEIK (SE Asia)	Cone of LOWER CHINDWIN	0705-09-
MYOBAN (Kyushu-Japan)	Thermal Feature of TSURUMI	0802-13=
MYOE [NYEY] (Iceland-SW)	Submarine vent of REYKJANESHRYGGUR	1701-01=
MYOGA-TAKE (Honshu-Japan)	Cone of FUJI	0803-03=
MYOHOJI (Izu Is-Japan)	Cone of HACHIJO-JIMA	0804-05=
MYOJIN-SHO (Izu Is-Japan)	Dome of BAYONNAISE ROCKS	0804-07=
MYOKEN-DAKE (Kyushu-Japan)	Dome of UNZEN	0802-10=
MYOKO (Honshu-Japan)	Stratovolc (2, -2760) Radiocarbon	**0803-10=**
MYOKO-DAKE (Honshu-Japan)	Stratovolc of IWATE	0803-24=
MYOKO-SAN (Honshu-Japan)	Synonym of FUJI	0803-03=
MYOKO-SAN (Honshu-Japan)	Dome of MYOKO	0803-10=
MYORO-DAKE [KUDRIAVY] (Kurile Is)	Cone of MEDVEZHIA	0900-10=
MYOZIN-SYO [MYOJIN-SHO] (Izu Is-Japan)	Dome of BAYONNAISE ROCKS	0804-07=
MYRDALSJOKULL (Iceland-S)	Synonym of KATLA	1702-03=
MYRIAM, VOLCAN (Guatemala)	Stratovolc of MOYUTA	1402-13-
MYVATNSELDAR (Iceland-NE)	Crater row of KRAFLA	1703-08=
MYVETNINGAHRAUN (Iceland-NE)	Fissure vent of ASKJA	1703-06=

N

NAME (Subregion)	Type (Eruption Total, Most Recent) Status / Relation to NAMED VOLCANO	NUMBER
NA PUU O NA ELEMAKULE (Hawaiian Is)	Cone of KILAUEA	1302-01-
NABBEO (Ethiopia)	Synonym of NABRO	0201-101
NABE-MORI (Honshu-Japan)	Stratovolc of CHOKAI	0803-22=
NABE-YAMA (Kyushu-Japan)	Cone of SAKURA-JIMA	0802-08=
NABELBERG [PUSUKBUKIT] (Sumatra)	Stratovolc of TOBA	0601-09=
NABESHIMA-DAKE (Kyushu-Japan)	Dome of IBUSUKI VOLC FIELD	0802-07=
NABOIYOTON [NABUYATOM] (Africa-E)	Tuff cone of BARRIER, THE	0202-03=
NABRO (Ethiopia)	Stratovolc (None) Holocene?	**0201-101**
NABUGANDO (Africa-C)	Tuff cone of KATWE-KIKORONGO FIELD	0203-004
NABUYATOM (Africa-E)	Tuff cone of BARRIER, THE	0202-03=
NADUG-KHOLDONGER (China-E)	Synonym of WUDALIANCHI	1005-04-
NAFTILOS (Greece)	Dome of SANTORINI	0102-04=
NAGA-YAMA (Honshu-Japan)	Cone of FUJI	0803-03=
NAGANO (Honshu-Japan)	Vent of IZU-TOBU	0803-01=
NAGANO-HIGASHI (Honshu-Japan)	Vent of IZU-TOBU	0803-01=
NAGAO-YAMA (Honshu-Japan)	Cone of FUJI	0803-03=
NAGARAMASAINA (Africa-E)	Synonym of BARRIER, THE	0202-03=
NAGAT (Vanuatu-SW Pacific)	Cone of TRAITOR'S HEAD	0507-09=
NAGAYAMA-DAKE (Hokkaido-Japan)	Stratovolc of DAISETSU	0805-06=
NAGCARLANG, MT. (Luzon-Philippines)	Cone of LAGUNA VOLC FIELD	0703-051
NAGIRA MWAITEN (Africa-E)	Cone of BARRIER, THE	0202-03=
NAGLEGBENG [NAGLAGBONG] (Luzon-Phil	Thermal Feature of MALINAO	0703-04=
NAHAHA, PUU (Hawaiian Is)	Cone of HUALALAI	1302-04-
NAHIMBI (Africa-C)	Cone of NYAMURAGIRA	0203-02=
NAHTO (Canada)	Cone of SPECTRUM RANGE	1200-07-
NAIGONESOIT (Africa-E)	Dome of MERU	0202-16=
NAIO, PUU (Hawaiian Is)	Cone of HALEAKALA	1302-06-
NAKA-AZUMA (Honshu-Japan)	Cone of AZUMA	0803-18=
NAKA-DAKE (Hokkaido)	Cone of SHIRETOKO-IWO-ZAN	0805-09=
NAKA-DAKE (Kyushu-Japan)	Stratovolc of SAKURA-JIMA	0802-08=
NAKA-DAKE (Kyushu-Japan)	Cone of ASO	0802-11=
NAKA-DAKE (Kyushu-Japan)	Stratovolc of KIRISHIMA	0802-09=
NAKA-HIYOSHI (Volcano Is-Japan)	Submarine vent of MINAMI-HIYOSHI	0804-131
NAKA-IWO-ZIMA (Volcano Is-Japan)	Synonym of IWO-JIMA	0804-12=
NAKA-JIMA (Hokkaido-Japan)	Dome of USU	0805-03=
NAKA-JIMA (Hokkaido-Japan)	Cone of KUTCHARO	0805-08=
NAKAMACHINESHIRI (Hokkaido-Japan)	Crater of AKAN	0805-07=
NAKAMARU-YAMA (Honshu-Japan)	Stratovolc of ZAO	0803-19=
NAKAMATINESHIRI [NAKAMACHINESHIRI]	Crater of AKAN	0805-07=
NAKANO-SHIMA (Ryukyu Is)	Stratovolcs (1, 1914) Historical	**0802-04=**
NAKANO-SIMA (Ryukyu Is)	Synonym of NAKANO-SHIMA	0802-04=
NAKANOGO (Izu Is-Japan)	Cone of HACHIJO-JIMA	0804-05=
NAKANOUMI (Honshu-Japan)	Caldera of TOWADA	0803-271
NAKAO-TOGE (Honshu-Japan)	Crater of YAKE-DAKE	0803-07=
NAKONOMINE (Honshu-Japan)	Dome of IIZUNA	0803-102
NAKOT (Africa-E)	Cone of EMURUANGOGOLAK	0202-051
NAKWA, MT. (Ethiopia)	Cone of KORATH RANGE	0201-32-
NAMAFJALL (Iceland-NE)	Thermal Feature of KRAFLA	1703-08=
NAMAFJALL-KROFLUHALS (Iceland-NE)	Crater row of KRAFLA	1703-08=
NAMAGURA (New Britain-SW Pac)	Thermal Feature of PAGO	0502-08=
NAMAKO-YAMA (Hokkaido)	Dome of SHIRETOKO-IWO-ZAN	0805-09=
NAMANA O KE AKUA (Hawaiian Is)	Cone of HALEAKALA	1302-06-
NAMANG (Lesser Sunda Is)	Synonym of EGON	0604-16=
NAMARUNU (Africa-E)	Shield (1, -6550) Tephrochronology	**0202-04-**
NAMBROQUE, PICO DEL (Canary Is)	Synonym of LA PALMA	1803-01-
NAMBROQUE [SAN JUAN] (Canary Is)	Fissure vent of LA PALMA	1803-01-
NAMBU-FUJI (NAMBU-HUZI) (Honshu-Japan	Synonym of IWATE	0803-24=
NAMLAGIRA (Africa-C)	Synonym of NYAMURAGIRA	0203-02=
NAMSHRAUN (Iceland-S)	Crater row of TORFAJOKULL	1702-05=
NAMU'A (Samoa-SW Pacific)	Tuff ring of UPOLU	0404-03-
NAMUI, VUSI (Vanuatu-SW Pacific)	Cone of AOBA	0507-03=
NAMURINYANG (Africa-E)	Tuff cone of BARRIER, THE	0202-03=
NAN-KO-LA-SHAN [NANGELAQIUSHAN]	Cone of WUDALIANCHI	1005-04-
NANAWAREZ (Vanuatu-SW Pacific)	Stratovolc of ANEITYUM	0507-11-
NANGELAQIUSHAN (China-E)	Cone of WUDALIANCHI	1005-04-
NANGETSU-YAMA (Honshu-Japan)	Stratovolc of NASU	0803-15=
NANGILA (New Britain-SW Pac)	Synonym of LANGILA	0502-01=
NANGKLAK, KAWAH (Java)	Crater of PAPANDAYAN	0603-10=
NANGOENA (Sulawesi-Indonesia)	Synonym of COLO [UNA UNA]	0606-01=
NANI [MOTMOT] (New Guinea-NE of)	Cone of LONG ISLAND	0501-05=
NANLA (New Britain-SW Pac)	Synonym of LANGILA	0502-01=
NANLONGWAN (China-E)	Crater of LONGGANG GROUP	1005-06-
NANOOK (Canada)	Dome of EDZIZA	1200-06-
NANSHAN (China-E)	Cone of KELUO GROUP	1005-03-
NANTAI (Honshu-Japan)	Stratovolc (None) Holocene	**0803-141**
NANWAKSJIAK (Alaska-W)	Maar of NUNIVAK ISLAND	1104-06-
NANXING (SE Asia)	Cone of LEIZHOU BANDAO	0705-01-
NAPAU (Hawaiian Is)	Pit crater of KILAUEA	1302-01-
NAPERITO (Africa-E)	Tuff cone of BARRIER, THE	0202-03=
NAPIER, MT. (Australia)	Cone of NEWER VOLCANICS PROV	0509-01-
NAPOLEON, CRATERE (W Indies)	Crater of SOUFRIERE GUADELOUPE	1600-06=
NAPPE DE LAVE DE DAMAR (Arabia-S)	Synonym of DHAMAR, HARRAS OF	0301-12-
NAR, DJEBEL EN- (Arabia-S)	Synonym of NAR, JABAL AN	0301-14-
NAR, HARRAT EN- (Arabia-W)	Synonym of 'UWAYRID, HARRAT	0301-02=
NAR, JABAL AN (Arabia-S)	(None) Not a Volcano	0301-14-
NARAGE (New Britain-SW Pac)	Stratovolc (None) Pleistocene-Geysers	**0502-02=**
NARANJOS, CERRO LOS (El Salvador)	Stratovolc of SANTA ANA	1403-02=
NARAO-DAKE (Kyushu-Japan)	Stratovolc of ASO	0802-11=
NARATA (Fiji Is-SW Pacific)	Cone of TAVEUNI	0405-01-
NARBOROUGH (Galapagos)	Synonym of FERNANDINA	1503-01=
NARCONDAM (Andaman Is-Ind O)	Synonym of NARCONDUM	0600-001
NARCONDUM (Andaman Is-Ind O)	Stratovolc (None) Holocene	**0600-001**
NAREGA (New Britain-SW Pac)	Synonym of NARAGE	0502-02=
NARI COL (Korea)	Caldera of ULREUNG	1006-03-
NARIKAWA (Kyushu-Japan)	Maar of IBUSUKI VOLC FIELD	0802-07=
NAROVE ISLAND (Solomon Is-SW Pac)	Synonym of SIMBO	0505-05=
NARRAGA (NARRAGE) (New Britain-SW Pac	Synonym of NARAGE	0502-02=
NARSE D'AMPOIX (France)	Maar of CHAINE DES PUYS	0100-02-
NARSE D'ESPINSASSE (France)	Maar of CHAINE DES PUYS	0100-02-
NARUGO (Honshu-Japan)	Lava domes (1, 0837) Historical	**0803-20=**
NARUKO (Honshu-Japan)	Synonym of NARUGO	0803-20=
NARUSAWATAKANE (Honshu-Japan)	Synonym of FUJI	0803-03=
NASH CRATER (US-Oregon)	Cone of SAND MOUNTAIN FIELD	1202-04-
NASO (Honshu-Japan)	Synonym of NASU	0803-15=
NASU (Honshu-Japan)	Stratovolcs (11, 1963) Historical	**0803-15=**
NASU-YAMA (Honshu-Japan)	Synonym of NASU	0803-15=
NASUYUMOTO SPA (Honshu-Japan)	Thermal Feature of NASU	0803-15=
NATIB (Luzon-Philippines)	Stratovolc (None) Holocene?	**0703-082**
NATOROTORO (Vanuatu-SW Pacific)	Thermal Feature of KUWAE	0507-07=
NATUGNOS (Luzon-Philippines)	Thermal Feature of MAQUILING	0703-06=
NATYIN TAUNG (SE Asia)	Cone of LOWER CHINDWIN	0705-09-
NAUE, PUU (Hawaiian Is)	Cone of HALEAKALA	1302-06-
NAUGA (Chile-S)	Synonym of CALBUCO	1508-02=
NAUTHUNILAWE (Fiji Is-SW Pacific)	Cone of TAVEUNI	0405-01-
NAVIDAD (Chile-C)	Cone of LONQUIMAY	1507-10=
NAVOLIVOLI (Fiji Is-SW Pacific)	Cone of TAVEUNI	0405-01-
NAYAVULOA (Fiji Is-SW Pacific)	Cone of TAVEUNI	0405-01-
NAYDI (Luzon Is-N of)	Cone of BABUYAN CLARO	0704-03=
NAZKO (Canada)	Cinder cones (1, -5215) Radiocarbon	**1200-14-**
NDAKAZA (Africa-C)	Crater of NYAMURAGIRA	0203-02=
NDALE (Africa-C)	Synonym of KYATWA VOLC FIELD	0203-003
NDAMUKORO (Africa-C)	Cone of NYIRAGONGO	0203-03=
NDANA (Fiji Is-SW Pacific)	Cone of TAVEUNI	0405-01-
NDEKE (Africa-C)	Tuff cone of FORT PORTAL FIELD	0203-002
NDETE NAPU (Lesser Sunda Is)	Fumarole fld (None) Fumarolic	**0604-13=**
NDETU NAPU (NDETOE NAPOE) (Lesser S	Synonym of NDETE NAPU	0604-13=
NDIRU (Africa-E)	Cone of HOMA MOUNTAIN	0202-07=
NDOBWA (Africa-E)	Dome of NYAMBENI HILLS	0202-056
NDONYU YUKI HILL (Africa-E)	Pit crater of NYAMBENI HILLS	0202-056
NDWATI (Africa-E)	Crater of RUNGWE	0202-166
NE CH'E DDHAWA (Canada)	Cone of FORT SELKIRK	1200-01-
NE UDOKAN PLATEAU (Russia-SE)	Volc field (None) Holocene	**1002-02-**
NECK, THE (Canada)	Cone of EDZIZA	1200-06-
NEDOSTUPNY (Kamchatka)	Cone of TOLBACHIK	1000-24=
NEGAMI-DAKE (Ryukyu Is)	Stratovolc of SUWANOSE-JIMA	0802-03=
NEGIT ISLAND (US-Calif)	Cone of MONO LAKE VOLC FIELD	1203-11-
NEGOP-GHANG (Africa-W)	Maar of OKU VOLC FIELD	0204-003
NEGRA, MONTANA [SIETE FUENTES]	Cone of TENERIFE	1803-03-
NEGRA, MONTANA [GARACHICO]	Cone of TENERIFE	1803-03-
NEGRA, MONTANA [NUEVO DEL FUEGO]	Crater of LANZAROTE	1803-06-
NEGRA, SIERRA (Chile-C)	Synonym of BLANCA, LOMA	1507-065
NEGRA, SIERRA (Galapagos)	Shield (11, 1980) Historical	**1503-05=**
NEGRILLAR, EL (Chile-N)	Pyrocl cones (None) Holocene?	**1505-106**
NEGRILLAR, LA (Chile-N)	Pyrocl cones (None) Holocene?	**1505-109**
NEGRITAS, LAS (Mexico)	Thermal Feature of MICHOACAN-GUANAJ	1401-06=
NEGRO (Chile-S)	Cone of PALEI-AIKE VOLC FIELD	1508-08-
NEGRO, CERRO (Bolivia)	Maar of PAMPA LUXSAR	1505-042
NEGRO, CERRO (Bolivia)	Synonym of MOIRO, CERRO	1505-064
NEGRO, CERRO (Chile-C)	Cone of CARRAN-LOS VENADOS	1507-14=
NEGRO, CERRO (Chile-C)	Cone of CHILLAN, NEVADOS DE	1507-07=
NEGRO, CERRO (Chile-N)	Dome of PURICO COMPLEX	1505-094
NEGRO, CERRO (Nicaragua)	Cinder cones (22, 1992) Historical	**1404-07=**

NAME (Subregion)	Type (Eruption Total, Most Recent) Status . . . Relation to NAMED VOLCANO	NUMBER
NEGRO, CRATER (Chile-C)	Crater of MAULE, LAGUNA DEL	1507-062
NEGRO DE MAYASQUER, CERRO (Colom	Stratovolc (1, 1936) Holocene?	**1501-11=**
NEGRO, EL (Mexico)	Cone of HOLOTEPEC	1401-07-
NEGRO, LAGUNA (Chile-C)	Maar of CARRAN-LOS VENADOS	1507-14=
NEGRO, MONTAGNON (Canary Is)	Cone of GRAN CANARIA	1803-04-
NEJAPA PIT (Nicaragua)	Maar of NEJAPA-TICOMO	1404-092
NEJAPA-TICOMO (Nicaragua)	Fissure vent (None) Holocene	**1404-092**
NEKO-DAKE (Kyushu-Japan)	Stratovolc of ASO	0802-11=
NELRUNA [VOLCANO MOUNTAIN] (Canada)	Cone of FORT SELKIRK	1200-01-
NELSON, PITON (Indian O.-W)	Cone of FOURNAISE, PITON DE LA	0303-02=
NEMASHI (Africa-E)	Cone of CHYULU HILLS	0202-13=
NEMI (Italy)	Crater of ALBANO, MONTE	0101-004
NEMO PEAK (Kurile Is)	Caldera (11, 1938) Historical	**0900-32=**
NEMO-SAN (Kurile Is)	Synonym of NEMO PEAK	0900-32=
NEMRUT BOYNU (Turkey)	Fissure vent of NEMRUT DAGI	0103-02=
NEMRUT DAGI (Turkey)	Stratovolc (17, 1441) Historical	**0103-02=**
NEMRUT KALE [NEMRUTBASI] (Turkey)	Cone of NEMRUT DAGI	0103-02=
NEOZHIDANNYI (Kurile Is)	Cone of EBEKO	0900-38=
NEPRIYATNAYA (Kamchatka)	Dome of PAUZHETKA	1000-022
NEREUANTOP (Vanuatu-SW Pacific)	Thermal Feature of SORETIMEAT	0507-01=
NERITA BANK (Italy)	Submarine vent of CAMPI FLEGREI MAR	0101-07=
NERITA [GUILA FERDINANDEO] (Italy)	Submarine vent of CAMPI FLEGREI MAR	0101-07=
NERO, MONTE (Italy)	Cone of ETNA	0101-06=
NESIGE (Kurile Is)	Synonym of NEMO PEAK	0900-32=
NESJAHRAUN (Iceland-SW)	Fissure vent of HENGILL	1701-05=
NEVADA DE LAGUNAS BRAVAS, SIERRA	Synonym of NEVADA, SIERRA	1505-125
NEVADA, SIERRA (Argentina)	Volc field (None) Holocene	**1505-125**
NEVADO (Spanish for MT.) see proper name (e.g. CUMBAL, NEVADO DE)		
NEVADO [CERRO BLANCO] (Chile-C)	Stratovolc of CHILLAN, NEVADOS DE	1507-07=
NEVIS PEAK (W Indies)	Stratovolc (None) Holocene	**1600-04=**
NEW AMSTERDAM (Indian O.-S)	Synonym of ST. PAUL	0304-03=
NEW BOGOSLOF (Aleutian Is)	Former dome of BOGOSLOF	1101-30-
NEW CRATER, THE (W Indies)	Crater of SOUFRIERE ST. VINCENT	1600-15=
NEWBERRY (US-Oregon)	Dome of SOUTH SISTER	1202-08-
NEWBERRY VOLCANO (US-Oregon)	Shield (11, 0620) Radiocarbon	**1202-11-**
NEWER VOLCANICS PROV (Australia)	Shields (4, -2900) Radiocarbon	**0509-01-**
NEXPAYANTLA (Mexico)	Stratovolc of POPOCATEPETL	1401-09=
NEZAMETNAYA (Kamchatka)	Dome of KSUDACH	1000-05=
NEZAMETNYI (Kurile Is)	Cone of EBEKO	0900-38=
NFOU, LAKE (Africa-W)	Maar of OKU VOLC FIELD	0204-003
NFOUET, LAKE (Africa-W)	Maar of OKU VOLC FIELD	0204-003
NGADISARI (Java)	Caldera of TENGGER CALDERA	0603-31=
NGAHEWA, LAKE (New Zealand)	Crater of REPOROA	0401-06-
NGAHUHA (New Zealand)	Cone of KAIKOHE-BAY OF ISLANDS	0401-01=
NGAI, DUENJO (Africa-E)	Synonym of LENGAI, OL DOINYO	0202-12=
NGAI, DONYO (Africa-E)	Synonym of LENGAI, OL DOINYO	0202-12=
NGALATA (Africa-E)	Cone of CHYULU HILLS	0202-13=
NGALUPALA (Africa-E)	Dome of SW USANGU BASIN	0202-163
NGANGIHO (New Zealand)	Dome of MAROA	0401-061
NGANHA (Africa-W)	Stratovolc of NGAOUNDERE PLATEAU	0204-002
NGAOUNDERE PLATEAU (Africa-W)	Volc field (None) Holocene?	**0204-002**
NGAPI (Lesser Sunda Is)	Synonym of LEWOTOLO	0604-23=
NGAPOURI, LAKE (New Zealand)	Crater of REPOROA	0401-06-
NGAPUNA (New Zealand)	Thermal Feature of ROTORUA	0401-042
NGARAMO (Africa-E)	Crater of KIEYO	0202-17=
NGATAMARIKI (New Zealand)	Thermal Feature of MAROA	0401-061
NGAURUHOE (New Zealand)	Stratovolc of TONGARIRO	0401-08=
NGAUTUKU (New Zealand)	Dome of MAROA	0401-061
NGAWHA HOT SPRINGS (New Zealand)	Thermal Feature of KAIKOHE-BAY OF	0401-01=
NGAWKASOLI [PARASO] (Solomon Is)	Thermal Feature of NONDA	0505-04=
NGAZANI (Africa-E)	Cone of CHYULU HILLS	0202-13=
NGERE KWON (Vanuatu-SW Pacific)	Stratovolc of SORETIMEAT	0507-01=
NGESONG (Java)	Stratovolc of DIENG VOLC COMPLEX	0603-20=
NGEZI (Africa-C)	Cone of VISOKE	0203-05-
NGONGOTAHA (New Zealand)	Dome of ROTORUA	0401-042
NGOZI (Africa-E)	Caldera (None) Holocene	**0202-164**
NGULIA HILLS [CHAIMU] (Africa-E)	Cone of CHYULU HILLS	0202-13=
NGUNA [TABUTERA] (Vanuatu-SW Pacific)	Stratovolc of NORTH VATE	0507-081
NGURDOTO CRATER (Africa-E)	Cone of MERU	0202-16=
NGUSUNA (Solomon Is-SW Pac)	Crater of SIMBO	0505-05=
NGWALA ROCK (Vanuatu-SW Pacific)	Tuff cone of AOBA	0507-03=
NGWANGU (Africa-E)	Cone of NGOZI	0202-164
NIAFU (Tonga-SW Pacific)	Synonym of NIUAFO'OU	0403-11=
NIANIAU, PUU (Hawaiian Is)	Cone of HALEAKALA	1302-06-
NIAWUAN (Sulawesi-Indonesia)	Crater of MAHAWU	0606-11=
NIBUSI-OYAKOTU [NIBUSHI-OYAKOTSU]	Dome of KUTCHARO	0805-08=
NICKENS, MT. (Antarctica)	Cone of HUDSON MOUNTAINS	1900-028
NICOLSON ROCK (Antarctica)	Cone of TONEY MOUNTAIN	1900-026
NIEUWERKERK (Banda Sea)	Submarine ? (None) Uncertain	**0605-02=**
NIGORIGAWA (Hokkaido-Japan)	Hydrothrm fld (None) Pleistocene-Fumarolic	**0805-021**
NIGORIKAWA (Hokkaido-Japan)	Synonym of NIGORIGAWA	0805-021
NIHONMATSUREI (Honshu-Japan)	Synonym of ADATARA	0803-17=
NII-JIMA (Izu Is-Japan)	Lava domes (2, 0886) Historical	**0804-02=**
NII-YAMA (Honshu-Japan)	Synonym of FUJI	0803-03=
NIIGATA-YAKE-YAMA (Honshu-Japan)	Lava dome (14, 1989) Historical	**0803-09=**
NIIJIMA-YAMA (Izu Is-Japan)	Dome of NII-JIMA	0804-02=
NIIYAMA-ZAWA (Honshu-Japan)	Thermal Feature of HACHIMANTAI	0803-25=
NIIZIMA-YAMA [NIIJIMA-YAMA] (Izu Is-Japan	Dome of NII-JIMA	0804-02=
NIKA (Banda Sea)	Synonym of NILA	0605-06=
NIKI (Greece)	Dome of SANTORINI	0102-04=
NIKIA (Greece)	Thermal Feature of NISYROS	0102-05=
NIKKO (Volcano Is-Japan)	Submarine (None) Uncertain	**0804-132**
NIKKO-BA (NIKKO-KAIZAN) (Volcano Is)	Synonym of NIKKO	0804-132
NIKKO-SHIRANE (Honshu-Japan)	Shield (5, 1889) Historical	**0803-14=**
NIKKO-SIRANE (Honshu-Japan)	Synonym of NIKKO-SHIRANE	0803-14=
NILA (Banda Sea)	Stratovolc (4, 1968) Historical	**0605-06=**
NILAHUE (Chile-C)	Synonym of CARRAN-LOS VENADOS	1507-14=
NILAM, MT. (Sumatra)	Cone of TALAKMAU	0601-13=
NIMRUD DAGH (Turkey)	Synonym of NEMRUT DAGI	0103-02=
NINAGONGO (Africa-C)	Synonym of NYIRAGONGO	0203-03=
NINAHUILCA (Ecuador)	Dome of ATACAZO	1502-021
NINDIRI (Nicaragua)	Crater of MASAYA	1404-10=
NINEPIN ROCK (Indian O.-S)	Synonym of ST. PAUL	0304-03=
NINFAS, CERRO DE LAS (El Salvador)	Stratovolc of VERDE, LAGUNA	1403-01=
NINFAS, LAGUNA LAS (El Salvador)	Crater of VERDE, LAGUNA	1403-01=
NINO DE JESUS [SANTIAGUITO] (Guatemal	Dome of SANTA MARIA	1402-03=
NINO-IKE (Honshu-Japan)	Crater of ON-TAKE	0803-04=
NINOMEGATA (Honshu-Japan)	Maar of MEGATA	0803-262
NIPESOTSU-UPEPESANKE (Hokkaido)	Lava domes (2, 1898) Historical	**0805-061**
NIRAGONGO (NIRAGONGWE) (Africa-C)	Synonym of NYIRAGONGO	0203-03=
NIRECO (Chile-C)	Crater of CALLAQUI	1507-091
NIRI MBWELESU (Vanuatu-SW Pacific)	Crater of AMBRYM	0507-04=

NAME (Subregion)	Type (Eruption Total, Most Recent) Status . . . Relation to NAMED VOLCANO	NUMBER
NIRI MBWELESU TATEN (Vanuatu-SW Pac)	Crater of AMBRYM	0507-04=
NIRI TATEN (Vanuatu-SW Pacific)	Crater of AMBRYM	0507-04=
NIRRES, LOS (Chile-C)	Crater of MENCHECA	1507-151
NISEKO (Hokkaido-Japan)	Synonym of IWAONUPURI	0805-031
NISHI-ASAKIZUKA (Honshu-Japan)	Cone of FUJI	0803-03=
NISHI-AZUMA (Honshu-Japan)	Cone of AZUMA	0803-18=
NISHI-CHIGASAKI-KAIKYU (Honshu-Japan)	Submarine vent of IZU-TOBU	0803-01=
NISHI-DAITEN (Honshu-Japan)	Cone of AZUMA	0803-18=
NISHI-DAKE (Honshu-Japan)	Synonym of ADATARA	0803-17=
NISHI-FUTATSUSUKA (Honshu-Japan)	Cone of FUJI	0803-03=
NISHI-HAKUUNZAN (Izu Is-Japan)	Pleistocene caldera of HACHIJO-JIMA	0804-05=
NISHI-HITOKAPPU [STOKAP] (Kurile Is)	Stratovolc of BOGATYR RIDGE	0900-06-
NISHI-KOSEKUMARU (Honshu-Japan)	Cone of FUJI	0803-03=
NISHI-KUROTSUKA (Honshu-Japan)	Cone of FUJI	0803-03=
NISHI-MARUYAMA (Hokkaido-Japan)	Dome of USU	0805-03=
NISHI-OKUNIWA (Honshu-Japan)	Cone of FUJI	0803-03=
NISHI-TSURUGI (Honshu-Japan)	Cone of FUJI	0803-03=
NISHI-USUZUKA (Honshu-Japan)	Cone of FUJI	0803-03=
NISHI-YAMA (Hokkaido-Japan)	Cone of AKAN	0805-07=
NISHI-YAMA (Hokkaido-Japan)	Stratovolc of OSHIMA-OSHIMA	0805-01=
NISHI-YAMA (Hokkaido-Japan)	Dome of USU	0805-03=
NISHI-YAMA (Izu Is-Japan)	Stratovolc of HACHIJO-JIMA	0804-05=
NISHIBETSU (Hokkaido-Japan)	Stratovolc of MASHU	0805-081
NISHINO-SHIMA (Volcano Is-Japan)	Caldera (1, 1974) Historical	**0804-092**
NISI-AZUMA [NISHI-AZUMA] (Honshu-Japan)	Cone of AZUMA	0803-18=
NISI-DAITEN [NISHI-DAITEN] (Honshu)	Cone of AZUMA	0803-18=
NISI-YAMA [NISHI-YAMA] (Hokkaido-Japan)	Cone of AKAN	0805-07=
NISI-YAMA [NISHI-YAMA] (Izu Is-Japan)	Stratovolc of HACHIJO-JIMA	0804-05=
NISIBETU [NISHIBETSU] (Hokkaido-Japan)	Stratovolc of MASHU	0805-081
NISIDA (Italy)	Crater of CAMPI FLEGREI	0101-01=
NISINO-SIMA (Volcano Is-Japan)	Synonym of NISHINO-SHIMA	0804-092
NISYROS (Greece)	Stratovolc (3, 1888) Historical	**0102-05=**
NITUNG (Lesser Sunda Is)	Thermal Feature of PALUWEH	0604-15=
NIU-AFU (NIUA FO'OU, NIAU'FOU) (Tonga Is	Synonym of NIUAFO'OU	0403-11=
NIUAFO'OU (Tonga-SW Pacific)	Shield (11, 1985) Historical	**0403-11=**
NIULLIHUELCO (Chile-C)	Synonym of CALLAQUI	1507-091
NIXTAMALAPAN, LAGUNA (Mexico)	Maar of SAN MARTIN, VOLCAN DE	1401-11=
NIZHNE-KOSHELEVSKIE (Kamchatka)	Thermal Feature of KOSHELEV	1000-02=
NJALE, GOF (Africa-E)	Maar of MARSABIT	0202-021
NJOGOINE (Africa-E)	Dome of NYAMBENI HILLS	0202-056
NJOLIMWANYA (Africa-E)	Cone of NGOZI	0202-164
NKUGUTI (Africa-C)	Crater of BUNYARUGURU FIELD	0203-005
NKUNGA, LAKE (Africa-E)	Crater of NYAMBENI HILLS	0202-056
NO-DAKE (Kyushu-Japan)	Dome of UNZEN	0802-10=
NOBO, MT. (Lesser Sunda Is)	Synonym of LEWOTOBI	0604-18=
NOBO, MT. [LEWOTOBI LAKILAKI]	Stratovolc of LEWOTOBI	0604-18=
NOBORIBETU [NOBORIBETSU] (Hokkaido)	Thermal Feature of KUTTARA	0805-034
NOBORIO-MINAMI (Honshu-Japan)	Vent of IZU-TOBU	0803-01=
NOCARANE, CERRO (Peru)	Dome of CHACHANI, NEVADO	1504-005
NOCHE BUENO, CERRO (Costa Rica)	Cone of IRAZU	1405-06=
NOISY NELLIE (New Zealand)	Crater of WHITE ISLAND	0401-04=
NOKOGIRI-DAKE (Hokkaido-Japan)	Stratovolc of TOKACHI	0805-05=
NOLE, PUU (Hawaiian Is)	Cone of HALEAKALA	1302-06-
NOMOER (China-E)	Cone of WUDALIANCHI	1005-04-
NONDA (Solomon Is-SW Pac)	Stratovolc (None) Pleistocene-Fumarolic	**0505-04=**
NONOMORI-YAMA (Honshu-Japan)	Stratovolc of ZAO	0803-19=
NOORAT, MT. (Australia)	Tuff ring of NEWER VOLCANICS PROV	0509-01-
NORD ISLAND (New Britain-SW Pac)	Synonym of NARAGE	0502-02=
NORD-JAN [BEERENBERG] (Atl-N)	Stratovolc of JAN MAYEN	1706-01=
NORDESTE (Azores)	Shield of FURNAS	1802-10=
NORIKURA (Honshu-Japan)	Stratovolcs (None) Holocene	**0803-06=**
NORRIS GEYSER BASIN (US-Wyoming)	Thermal Feature of YELLOWSTONE	1205-01-
NORTH BROTHER [CHERNY] (Kurile Is)	Stratovolc of CHIRPOI	0900-15=
NORTH COULEE (US-California)	Dome of MONO CRATERS	1203-12-
NORTH CRATER (New Zealand)	Crater of TONGARIRO	0401-08=
NORTH CRATER (New Zealand)	Crater of RUAPEHU	0401-10=
NORTH CRATER (US-Idaho)	Crater of CRATERS OF THE MOON	1204-02-
NORTH DAUGHTER [TOVANUMBATIR]	Stratovolc of RABAUL	0502-14=
NORTH DEADMAN CREEK (US-California)	Dome of INYO CRATERS	1203-13-
NORTH HEAD (New Zealand)	Cone of AUCKLAND FIELD	0401-02=
NORTH ISLAND (Africa-E)	Tuff cones (None) Holocene	**0202-001**
NORTH ISLAND (New Britain-SW Pac)	Synonym of NARAGE	0502-02=
NORTH MAKEON (Vanuatu-SW Pacific)	Cone of GAUA	0507-02=
NORTH PAGAN (Mariana Is-C Pac)	Stratovolc of PAGAN	0804-17=
NORTH PAULINA PEAK (US-Oregon)	Cone of NEWBERRY VOLCANO	1202-11-
NORTH SISTER FIELD (US-Oregon)	Complx volc (4, 0350) Radiocarbon	**1202-07-**
NORTH VATE (Vanuatu-SW Pacific)	Stratovolcs (None) Holocene	**0507-081**
NORTHEAST CRATER (Italy)	Crater of ETNA	0101-06=
NORTHEAST RIFT ZONE (Hawaiian Is)	Fissure vent of MAUNA LOA	1302-02=
NORTHERN ATITLAN (Guatemala)	Synonym of TOLIMAN	1402-07=
NORTHERN CONE (US-Nevada)	Cone of CRATER FLAT	1206-03-
NORTHERN CRATER (Lesser Sunda Is)	Crater of SIRUNG	0604-27=
NORTHERN CRATER (Mindanao-Philippines)	Crater of APO	0701-03=
NORTHERN CRATER (Philippines-C)	Crater of CANLAON	0702-02=
NORTHERN LAKE ABAYA FIELD (Ethiopia)	Synonym of HOBICHA CALDERA	0201-293
NORTHWEST DOME (US-Washington)	Dome of ST. HELENS	1201-05-
NORTHWEST RIFT ZONE (US-Oregon)	Fissure vent of NEWBERRY VOLCANO	1202-11-
NOSOWSKOJ [POGROMNI] (Aleutian Is)	Stratovolc of WESTDAHL	1101-34-
NOSSA SENHORA DE LOURDES, PICO	Dome of TRINDADE	1805-051
NOSSI BE (Madagascar)	Synonym of NOSY-BE	0303-04-
NOSY-BE (Madagascar)	Cinder cones (None) Holocene	**0303-04-**
NOTCH BUTTE (US-Idaho)	Cone of SHOSHONE LAVA FIELD	1204-01-
NOTUCO (Chile-C)	Synonym of COPAHUE	1507-09=
NOUVEAU (Indian O.-W)	Crater of FOURNAISE, PITON DE LA	0303-02=
NOVAGRABLENOVA (Kamchatka)	Shield of ATLASOVA	1000-65-
NOVARUPTA (Alaska Peninsula)	Caldera (1, 1912) Historical	**1102-18-**
NOVILLERO, VOLCAN (Mexico)	Cone of MASCOTA VOLC FIELD	1401-031
NOVY (Kamchatka)	Dome of BEZYMIANNY	1000-25=
NOYA (Kyushu-Japan)	Thermal Feature of KUJU GROUP	0802-12=
NSHENYI (Africa-C)	Crater of BUNYARUGURU FIELD	0203-005
NTOBE (Africa-C)	Cone of KARISIMBI	0203-04-
NTUMBI (Africa-E)	Dome of SW USANGU BASIN	0202-163
NUAKAJU (Lesser Sunda Is)	Thermal Feature of PALUWEH	0604-15=
NUBALYKICH (Kamchatka)	Shield of UKSICHAN	1000-35-
NUDO DE COROPUNA (Peru)	Synonym of COROPUNA	1504-001
NUEVO DEL FUEGO, VOLCAN (Canary Is)	Crater of LANZAROTE	1803-06-
NUEVO, EL (Mexico)	Synonym of NEGRO, CERRO	1404-07=
NUEVO MUNDO (Bolivia)	Lava domes (None) Holocene	**1505-033**
NUEVO, VOLCAN (Chile-C)	Cone of CHILLAN, NEVADOS DE	1507-07=
NUEVO, VOLCAN (Chile-C)	Crater of AZUL, CERRO [QUIZAPU]	1507-06=
NUEVO, VOLCAN [TINGUATON] (Canary Is)	Crater of LANZAROTE	1803-06-
NUGERE, PUY DE LA (France)	Cone of CHAINE DES PUYS	0100-02-

NAME (Subregion)	Type (Eruption Total, Most Recent) Status Relation to NAMED VOLCANO	NUMBER
NUHA LUA (Lesser Sunda Is)	Synonym of PALUWEH	0604-15=
NUI DAT (SE Asia)	Cone of BAS DONG NAI	0705-05-
NUKABIRA (Japan)	Thermal Feature of NIPESOTSU-UPEPES	0805-061
NUKUAFO (SW Pacific)	Tuff cone of WALLIS ISLANDS	0404-05-
NUKUATEA (SW Pacific)	Tuff cone of WALLIS ISLANDS	0404-05-
NUKUFUTU (SW Pacific)	Tuff cone of WALLIS ISLANDS	0404-05-
NUKUTAAKIMUA (SW Pacific)	Tuff cone of WALLIS ISLANDS	0404-05-
NUKUTAPU (SW Pacific)	Tuff cone of WALLIS ISLANDS	0404-05-
NUM RIVER (New Ireland-SW Pac)	Thermal Feature of AMBITLE	0504-02=
NUMAJIRI (Honshu-Japan)	Thermal Feature of ADATARA	0803-17=
NUMAJIRI-YAMA (Honshu-Japan)	Synonym of ADATARA	0803-17=
NUMANO-TAIRA (Honshu-Japan)	Crater of BANDAI	0803-16=
NUMANO-TAIRA (Honshu-Japan)	Crater of ADATARA	0803-17=
NUMANOTAIRA GROUP (Honshu-Japan)	Vent of IZU-TOBU	0803-01=
NUMANUMA (D'Entrecasteaux Is)	Synonym of DAWSON STRAIT GROUP	0503-06=
NUMAZAWA (Honshu-Japan)	Shield (1, -3040) Radiocarbon	**0803-151**
NUNIVAK ISLAND (Alaska-W)	Shield (None) Holocene	**1104-06-**
NUNURCO (Ecuador)	Dome of CHACANA	1502-022
NUNZIATA, MONTE (Italy)	Cone of ETNA	0101-06=
NUOVO, MONTE (Italy)	Cone of CAMPI FLEGREI	0101-01=
NUOVO, MONTE (Italy)	Cone of ETNA	0101-06=
NUPURI-ONDO (Hokkaido-Japan)	Dome of KUTCHARO	0805-08=
NURETO, CERRO DE (Mexico)	Cone of MICHOACAN-GUANAJUATO	1401-06=
NUSA KUA (Lesser Sunda Is)	Synonym of PALUWEH	0604-15=
NUTAKU KAMUSHUPE (Hokkaido-Japan)	Synonym of DAISETSU	0805-06=
NUTAKU KAMUSYUPE (Hokkaido-Japan)	Synonym of DAISETSU	0805-06=
NU'U (Samoa-SW Pacific)	Tuff cone of OFU-OLOSEGA	0404-01=
NU'ULUA (Samoa-SW Pacific)	Tuff ring of UPOLU	0404-03-
NU'UTELE (Samoa-SW Pacific)	Tuff ring of UPOLU	0404-03-
NYABUSA (Africa-C)	Cone of NYIRAGONGO	0203-03=
NYABUSOZI (Africa-C)	Tuff cone of FORT PORTAL FIELD	0203-002
NYAGASHOLE (Africa-C)	Cone of NYAMURAGIRA	0203-02=
NYAMATOTO (Africa-E)	Cone of HOMA MOUNTAIN	0202-07=
NYAMBARAMO (Africa-C)	Cone of NYAMURAGIRA	0203-02=
NYAMBENI HILLS (Africa-E)	Shield (None) Holocene	**0202-056**
NYAMERSINGERI (Africa-C)	Crater of BUNYARUGURU FIELD	0203-005
NYAMLAGIRA (Africa-C)	Synonym of NYAMURAGIRA	0203-02=
NYAMUNUKA (Africa-C)	Tuff cone of KATWE-KIKORONGO FIELD	0203-004
NYAMURAGIRA (Africa-C)	Shield (35, 1993) Historical	**0203-02=**
NYAMUSHWA (Africa-C)	Cone of NYIRAGONGO	0203-03=
NYAMUTSIBU (Africa-C)	Cone of NYIRAGONGO	0203-03=
NYARUTSHIRU (Africa-C)	Cone of NYIRAGONGO	0203-03=
NYASANJA (Africa-E)	Cone of HOMA MOUNTAIN	0202-07=
NYASHEKE 1 & 2 (Africa-C)	Cones of NYAMURAGIRA	0203-02=
NYEY (Iceland-SW)	Submarine vent of REYKJANESHRYGGUR	1701-01=
NYHAHRAUN (Iceland-S)	Submarine vent of VESTMANNAEYJAR	1702-01=
NYI, LAKE (Africa-W)	Maar of OKU VOLC FIELD	0204-003
NYIRAGONGO (Africa-C)	Stratovolc (16, 1982) Historical	**0203-03=**
NYODO-SAN (Honshu-Japan)	Stratovolc of ZAO	0803-19=
NYOS, LAKE (Africa-W)	Maar of OKU VOLC FIELD	0204-003
NYOTAI-SAN (Honshu-Japan)	Synonym of NIKKO-SHIRANE	0803-14=
NYUDO-SAN (Honshu-Japan)	Cone of ZAO	0803-19=
NYUKI, DOINYA LA [OL DOINYO NYUKIE]	Stratovolc of SUSWA	0202-11=
NYUNGU (Africa-C)	Crater of BUNYARUGURU FIELD	0203-005
NZONGWE (Africa-E)	Cone of NGOZI	0202-164
NZURU (Africa-C)	Cone of NYAMURAGIRA	0203-02=

O

NAME (Subregion)	Type (Eruption Total, Most Recent) Status Relation to NAMED VOLCANO	NUMBER
O-AKAN (Hokkaido-Japan)	Stratovolc of AKAN	0805-07=
O KORO, MAUNGA (Pacific-C)	Cone of EASTER ISLAND	1303-08-
O-MINE (Izu Is-Japan)	Pit crater of NII-JIMA	0804-02=
O-SIMA (Hokkaido-Japan)	Synonym of OSHIMA-OSHIMA	0805-01=
O-SIMA (Izu Is-Japan)	Synonym of OSHIMA	0804-01=
O-USU (Hokkaido-Japan)	Dome of USU	0805-03=
O-YUNUMA (Hokkaido-Japan)	Crater of KUTTARA	0805-034
O'A CALDERA (Ethiopia)	Synonym of SHALA	0201-28=
OANA (Honshu-Japan)	Crater of AZUMA	0803-18=
OANA (Izu Is-Japan)	Crater of HACHIJO-JIMA	0804-05=
OANA (Izu Is-Japan)	Crater of MIYAKE-JIMA	0804-04=
OBA (Vanuatu-SW Pacific)	Synonym of AOBA	0507-03=
OBAMA (Kyushu-Japan)	Thermal Feature of UNZEN	0802-10=
OBANDAI (Honshu-Japan)	Stratovolc of BANDAI	0803-16=
OBERWINKEL (Germany)	Maar of WEST EIFEL VOLC FIELD	0100-01-
OBMANUVSHY (Kamchatka)	Cone of MALY SEMIACHIK	1000-14=
OBRAJUELO, LAGUNA (Guatemala)	Cone of IXTEPEQUE, VOLCAN	1402-18-
OBRINNISHOLAR (Iceland-SW)	Crater row of KRISUVIK	1701-03=
OBRUK (Turkey)	Cone of HASAN DAGI	0103-002
OBRUK (Turkey)	Crater of ERCIYES DAGI	0103-01=
OBSERVATORY VENT (Hawaiian Is)	Shield of KILAUEA	1302-01-
OBSIDIAN (US-California)	Dome of INYO CRATERS	1203-13-
OBUCHI (Honshu-Japan)	Crater of FUJI	0803-03=
OCCIDENTALES, CALDERAS [QUEMADAS]	Crater of LANZAROTE	1803-06-
OCEANA (Antarctica)	Cone of SEAL NUNATAKS GROUP	1900-05=
OCOTE, CERRO DEL (El Salvador)	Synonym of CONCHAGUA	1403-11=
OCOTES, CERRO LOS (Mexico)	Dome of TEPETILTIC, VOLCAN	1401-024
OCOXUSCO, VOLCAN (Mexico)	Cone of TENAYO GROUP	1401-081
OCUSACAYO (Mexico)	Cone of CHICHINAUTZIN	1401-08=
ODAIRA (Honshu-Japan)	Vent of IZU-TOBU	0803-01=
ODAMOI-SAN [TEBENKOV] (Kurile Is)	Cone of GROZNY GROUP	0900-07=
ODIAWO (Africa-E)	Cone of HOMA MOUNTAIN	0202-07=
ODINOKAIA (Kamchatka)	Dome of AVACHINSKY	1000-10=
ODNOBOKY (Kamchatka)	Pleistocene caldera of AKADEMIA NAUK	1000-123
OELOEBELOE (Sumatra)	Synonym of HULUBELU	0601-28=
OEMSINI (OEMTJINA) (New Guinea-W)	Synonym of UMSINI	0609-01=
OENA OENA (Sulawesi-Indonesia)	Synonym of COLO [UNA UNA]	0606-01=
OENGARAN (Java)	Synonym of UNGARAN	0603-23=
OEPAS, GUNUNG [UPAS] (Java)	Thermal Feature of DIENG VOLC COMP	0603-20=
OERTEALE (Ethiopia)	Synonym of ERTA ALE	0201-08=
OFU-OLOSEGA (Samoa-SW Pacific)	Shields (1, 1866) Historical	**0404-01=**
OGA-TAKE (Honshu-Japan)	Dome of NARUGO	0803-20=
OGARI-YAMA (Hokkaido-Japan)	Dome of USU	0805-03=
OGI (Honshu-Japan)	Cone of IZU-TOBU	0803-01=
OGIGAHANA (Kyushu-Japan)	Dome of KUJU GROUP	0802-12=
OGMUNDARGIGAR (Iceland-SW)	Crater row of KRISUVIK	1701-03=
OGMUNDUR (Iceland-SW)	Dome of KERLINGARFJOLL	1701-10=
OGNEDIESHUTSHAI GORA (Aleutian Is)	Synonym of MAKUSHIN	1101-31-
OGURA-YAMA (Honshu-Japan)	Dome of TOWADA	0803-271
OHAAKI [BROADLANDS] (New Zealand)	Thermal Feature of REPOROA	0401-06-
OHACHI (Honshu-Japan)	Crater of NIIGATA-YAKE-YAMA	0803-09=
OHACHI (Honshu-Japan)	Crater of IWATE	0803-24=
OHACHI (Kyushu-Japan)	Crater of KIRISHIMA	0802-09=
OHACHIDAIRA (Hokkaido-Japan)	Pleistocene caldera of DAISETSU	0805-06=
OHAKI [BROADLANDS] (New Zealand)	Thermal Feature of REPOROA	0401-06-
OHAKUNE (New Zealand)	Tuff ring of RUAPEHU	0401-10=
OHALAHOUM [DALAHUM] (Vanuatu-SW Pac	Cone of AMBRYM	0507-04=
OHANABE-YAMA (Honshu-Japan)	Stratovolc of TOWADA	0803-271
OHATA-IKE (Kyushu-Japan)	Crater of KIRISHIMA	0802-09=
OHATA-YAMA (Kyushu-Japan)	Stratovolc of KIRISHIMA	0802-09=
OHATANO (Honshu-Japan)	Maar of IZU-TOBU	0803-01=
OHATI [OHACHI] (Honshu-Japan)	Crater of NIIGATA-YAKE-YAMA	0803-09=
OHATI [OHACHI] (Honshu-Japan)	Crater of IWATE	0803-24=
OHATI [OHACHI] (Kyushu-Japan)	Crater of KIRISHIMA	0802-09=
OHEINUI (New Zealand)	Dome of MAROA	0401-061
OHINEMUTU (New Zealand)	Thermal Feature of ROTORUA	0401-042
OHIRA-YAMA (Honshu-Japan)	Cone of FUJI	0803-03=
OHMACHI SEAMOUNT (Izu Is-Japan)	Synonym of OMACHI SEAMOUNT	0804-091
OIAKOBA (Kurile Is)	Synonym of ALAID	0900-39=
OIAU, MT. (D'Entrecasteaux Is)	Stratovolc of DAWSON STRAIT GROUP	0503-06=
OIAVA-AI, MT. (D'Entrecasteaux Is)	Cone of GOODENOUGH	0503-041
OIBOR, OLDOINYO (Africa-E)	Synonym of KILIMANJARO	0202-15=
OIKE (Honshu-Japan)	Vent of IZU-TOBU	0803-01=
OIKE-MINAMI (Honshu-Japan)	Vent of IZU-TOBU	0803-01=
OILE, PUU (Hawaiian Is)	Cone of HALEAKALA	1302-06-
OIRA (New Zealand)	Pumice cone of MAYOR ISLAND	0401-021
OIRASE (Honshu-Japan)	Cone of TOWADA	0803-271
OJIGOKU (Honshu-Japan)	Thermal Feature of IWATE	0803-24=
OJO-DAKE (Kyushu-Japan)	Stratovolc of ASO	0802-11=
OJO DE AGUA, CERRO (Nicaragua)	Cone of PILAS, LAS	1404-08=
OJO DE AGUA DE LA VIRGEN, CERRO EL	Stratovolc of VERDE, LAGUNA	1403-01=
OJO DE AGUA, LOMA (Nicaragua)	Cone of SAN CRISTOBAL	1404-02=
OJO DEL MAR (El Salvador)	Synonym of COATEPEQUE CALDERA	1403-041
OJO DEL SALADO (Chile-N)	Synonym of OJOS DEL SALADO, NEVADO	1505-13=
OJOCHAL, EL (Nicaragua)	Cone of TELICA	1404-04=
OJOS DEL SALADO, NEVADOS (Chile-N)	Stratovolc (None) Holocene	**1505-13=**
OKA VOLC FIELD (Russia-SE)	Cinder cones (None) Holocene	**1002-06-**
OKAIHAU (New Zealand)	Cone of KAIKOHE-BAY OF ISLANDS	0401-01=
OKAMA (Honshu-Japan)	Crater of IWATE	0803-24=
OKAMA (Honshu-Japan)	Crater of ZAO	0803-19=
OKAMA (Honshu-Japan)	Crater of ASAMA	0803-11=
OKAMADO-YAMA (Kyushu-Japan)	Stratovolc of ASO	0802-11=
OKARO, LAKE (New Zealand)	Crater of REPOROA	0401-06-
OKATA (Izu Is-Japan)	Stratovolc of OSHIMA	0804-01=
OKATAINA (New Zealand)	Lava domes (28, 1973) Historical	**0401-05=**
OKATTA-DAKE [AOSO-YAMA] (Honshu)	Stratovolc of ZAO	0803-19=
OKE-NUMA (Honshu-Japan)	Crater of AZUMA	0803-18=
OKI-DOGO (Honshu-Japan)	Shield (None) Anthropology	**0803-003**
OKINAWA-TORI-SHIMA (Ryukyu Is)	Complx volc (9, 1968) Historical	**0802-02=**
OKISE (Kyushu-Japan)	Cone of SAKURA-JIMA	0802-08=
OKMOK (Aleutian Is)	Stratovolc (16, 1988) Historical	**1101-29-**
OKOLI (Africa-W)	Crater of CAMEROON, MT.	0204-01=
OKOMA-YAMA (Honshu-Japan)	Synonym of KURIKOMA	0803-21=
OKPO HILL (SE Asia)	Cone of LOWER CHINDWIN	0705-09-
OKU VOLC FIELD (Africa-W)	Maars (1, 1550) Radiocarbon	**0204-003**
OKUNO-FUJI (Honshu-Japan)	Synonym of IWAKI	0803-27=
OL BURU, DOINYO (Africa-E)	Synonym of EBURRU, OL DOINYO	0202-08=
OL KOKWE (Africa-E)	Shield (None) Holocene	**0202-055**
OL MOROUK (Africa-E)	Cone of KILIMANJARO	0202-15=
OL OLONGOT (Africa-E)	Synonym of LONGONOT	0202-10=
OLAF (Atlantic-S)	Cone of TRISTAN DA CUNHA	1806-01=
OLAI, PUU (Hawaiian Is)	Cone of HALEAKALA	1302-06-
OLAKKRAN (Turkey)	Cone of ERCIYES DAGI	0103-01=
OLCA-PARUMA (Chile-N)	Stratovolcs (1, 1867) Historical	**1505-05=**
OLCA SUR, CERRO (Chile-N)	Stratovolc of OLCA-PARUMA	1505-05=
OLD BOGOSLOF (Aleutian Is)	Former dome of BOGOSLOF	1101-30-
OLD BOOBY HILL (W Indies)	Dome of SABA	1600-01=
OLD CRATER (Java)	Thermal Feature of PERBAKTI	0603-04=
OLD CRATER, THE (W Indies)	Crater of SOUFRIERE ST. VINCENT	1600-15=
OLDOINYO, OLDONYO, OL DOINYO (Masai for MT.) see proper name (e.g. LENGAI, OL DOINYO)		
OLDUGIGAR (Iceland-S)	Fissure vent of HEKLA	1702-07=
OLENGURUONI (Africa-E)	Synonym of OLKARIA	0202-09=
OLENIY [OLENY] (Kamchatka)	Shield of ZAOZERNY	1000-48-
OLGARIA (Africa-E)	Synonym of OLKARIA	0202-09=
OLGORETI, OL DOINYO (Africa-E)	Cone of CHYULU HILLS	0202-13=
OLGURTAM (Africa-E)	Cone of CHYULU HILLS	0202-13=
OLIBANO, MT. (Italy)	Dome of CAMPI FLEGREI	0101-01=
OLILA, MT. (Luzon-Philippines)	Cone of LAGUNA VOLC FIELD	0703-051
OLIVAS, CERRO LOS (Guatemala)	Cone of SUCHITAN VOLC FIELD	1402-17-
OLIVE, MT. (Aleutian Is)	Cone of SHISHALDIN	1101-36-
OLKARIA (Africa-E)	Pumice cones (1, 1770) Radiocarbon	**0202-09=**
OLKOVIY (Kamchatka)	Shield (None) Holocene	**1000-055**
OLLA, CERRO LA (El Salvador)	Cone of SINGUIL, CERRO	1403-011
OLLA DE CARNE (Costa Rica)	Cone of TENORIO GROUP	1405-031
OLLA DE FLORES (Mexico)	Maar of MICHOACAN-GUANAJUATO	1401-06=
OLLA DE ZINTORA (Mexico)	Maar of MICHOACAN-GUANAJUATO	1401-06=
OLLADA DE LOS GEISERS DEL TATIO	Synonym of TATIO	1505-08=
OLLADA, LA (Nicaragua)	Crater of SAN CRISTOBAL	1404-02=
OLLAGUA (Chile-N)	Synonym of OLLAGUE	1505-06=
OLLAGUE (Chile-N)	Stratovolc (None) Holocene	**1505-06=**
OLLETA, LA (Colombia)	Dome of RUIZ	1501-02=
OLMEDO (Galapagos)	Synonym of SANTIAGO	1503-09=
OLMOTI (Africa-E)	Cone of CHYULU HILLS	0202-13=
OLOLICA (Mexico)	Cone of CHICHINAUTZIN	1401-08=
OLOMANU (Samoa-SW Pacific)	Cone of TA'U	0404-001
OLOMANU TAI (Samoa-SW Pacific)	Cone of SAVAI'I	0404-04=
OLOMANU UTA (Samoa-SW Pacific)	Cone of SAVAI'I	0404-04=
OLOMATIMU (Samoa-SW Pacific)	Cone of TA'U	0404-001
OLOMOANA (Samoa-SW Pacific)	Shield of TUTUILA	0404-02-
OLONONGOT (Africa-E)	Synonym of LONGONOT	0202-10=
OLORERER (Africa-E)	Cone of CHYULU HILLS	0202-13=
OLOT VOLC FIELD (Spain)	Pyrocl cones (None) Holocene?	**0100-03-**
OLOTANIA (Samoa-SW Pacific)	Cone of TA'U	0404-001
OLOTELE (Samoa-SW Pacific)	Cone of TUTUILA	0404-02-
OLYMPE (Indian O.-S)	Cone of AMSTERDAM ISLAND	0304-04-
OLYMPUS, MT. (Galapagos)	Cone of FLOREANA	1503-10=
OMACHI SEAMOUNT (Izu Is-Japan)	Submarine (None) Uncertain	**0804-091**
OMANAGO GROUP (Honshu-Japan)	Lava domes (None) Holocene	**0803-142**
OMAPERE (New Zealand)	Cone of KAIKOHE-BAY OF ISLANDS	0401-01=
OMATE (OMATO) (Peru)	Synonym of HUAYNAPUTINA	1504-03=
OMBA (Vanuatu-SW Pacific)	Synonym of AOBA	0507-03=
OMBUS (Vanuatu-SW Pacific)	Cone of YASUR	0507-10=
OMETEPE (Nicaragua)	Synonym of CONCEPCION	1404-12=
OMINE (Kyushu-Japan)	Cone of ASO	0802-11=
OMO ANGA, MAUNGA (Pacific-C)	Cone of EASTER ISLAND	1303-08-

NAME (Subregion)	Type (Eruption Total, Most Recent) Status . . . Relation to NAMED VOLCANO	NUMBER
OMORI-YAMA (Honshu-Japan)	Cone of ZAO	0803-19=
OMOTURCO (Ecuador)	Dome of ATACAZO	1502-021
OMSINI (New Guinea-W)	Synonym of UMSINI	0609-01=
OMURO (Honshu-Japan)	Crater of IWATE	0803-24=
OMURO-YAMA (Honshu-Japan)	Cone of FUJI	0803-03=
OMURO-YAMA (Honshu-Japan)	Cone of IZU-TOBU	0803-01=
OMUROYAMA-AMAGI GROUP (Honshu)	Synonym of IZU-TOBU	0803-01=
ON-TAKE (Honshu-Japan)	Complx volc (1, 1980) Historical	**0803-04=**
ON-TAKE (Ryukyu Is)	Stratovolc of NAKANO-SHIMA	0802-04=
ON-TAKE (Ryukyu Is)	Cone of AKUSEKI-JIMA	0802-021
ON-TAKE (Ryukyu Is)	Stratovolc of SUWANOSE-JIMA	0802-03=
ONAGAREMARU-YAMA (Honshu-Japan)	Cone of FUJI	0803-03=
ONAMEDAKE (Japan)	Cone of AKITA-KOMAGA-TAKE	0803-23=
ONAMI-IKE (Kyushu-Japan)	Crater of KIRISHIMA	0802-09=
ONASHIROKO (Honshu-Japan)	Crater of IWATE	0803-24=
ONDVERDARNESHOLAR (Iceland-W)	Shield of SNAEFELLSJOKULL	1700-01=
ONE TREE HILL (New Zealand)	Cone of AUCKLAND FIELD	0401-02=
ONE, VUSI (Vanuatu-SW Pacific)	Cone of AOBA	0507-03=
ONEPOTO (New Zealand)	Tuff ring of AUCKLAND FIELD	0401-02=
ONEPU (New Zealand)	Cone of OKATAINA	0401-05=
ONEPU SPRINGS (New Zealand)	Thermal Feature of OKATAINA	0401-05=
ONIGAJO (Honshu-Japan)	Dome of AKITA-YAKE-YAMA	0803-26=
ONIGAJO (Honshu-Japan)	Stratovolc of IWATE	0803-24=
ONIGAZYO [ONIGAJO] (Honshu-Japan)	Dome of AKITA-YAKE-YAMA	0803-26=
ONIGAZYO [ONIGAJO] (Honshu-Japan)	Stratovolc of IWATE	0803-24=
ONIWA-OKUNIWA (Honshu-Japan)	Cone of FUJI	0803-03=
ONMAE-DAKE (Honshu-Japan)	Stratovolc of ZAO	0803-19=
ONSEN-DAKE (Kyushu-Japan)	Synonym of UNZEN	0802-10=
ONTAR (Vanuatu-SW Pacific)	Cone of GAUA	0507-02=
ONU (Halmahera-Indonesia)	Cone of TODOKO-RANU	0608-05=
ONYOKE, OL DOINYO [OL DOINYO NYUKIE	Stratovolc of SUSWA	0202-11=
O'O, PUU (Hawaiian Is)	Cone of KILAUEA	1302-01-
OO-SIMA (Izu Is-Japan)	Synonym of OSHIMA	0804-01=
OOJINI (Africa-E)	Cone of CHYULU HILLS	0202-13=
OONAMI-IKE [ONAMI-IKE] (Kyushu-Japan)	Crater of KIRISHIMA	0802-09=
OOSHIMA (Izu Is-Japan)	Synonym of OSHIMA	0804-01=
OPAL CONE (Canada)	Cone of GARIBALDI, MT.	1200-20-
OPALA (Kamchatka)	Caldera (1, 0430) Radiocarbon	**1000-08=**
OPALINSKAJA (OPALNAJA) (Kamchatka)	Synonym of OPALA	1000-08=
OPALNY (Kamchatka)	Dome of BOLSHOI SEMIACHIK	1000-15=
OPALSKAIA SOPKA (Kamchatka)	Synonym of OPALA	1000-08=
OPHIR (Sumatra)	Synonym of TALAKMAU	0601-13=
OPO BAY (New Zealand)	Tuff cone of MAYOR ISLAND	0401-021
OPOURI, LAKE [LAKE NGAPOURI] (New Z)	Crater of REPOROA	0401-06-
OPUTATESIKE [OPUTATESHIKE] (Hokkaido	Dome of KUTCHARO	0805-08=
ORAEFAJOKULL (Iceland-SE)	Stratovolc (2, 1728) Historical	**1704-01=**
ORAKEI BASIN (New Zealand)	Tuff ring of AUCKLAND FIELD	0401-02=
ORAKEIKORAKO (New Zealand)	Thermal Feature of MAROA	0401-061
ORCA (New Zealand)	Crater of WHITE ISLAND	0401-04=
ORCHILLA, MONTANA DE (Canary Is)	Cone of HIERRO	1803-02-
OREJA, CERRO DE LA (Colombia)	Synonym of NEGRO DE MAYASQUER,	1501-11=
ORENGINGNAI (Africa-E)	Synonym of OLKARIA	0202-09=
ORFIALDSJOKULL (Iceland-SE)	Synonym of ORAEFAJOKULL	1704-01=
ORI, MAUNGA (Pacific-C)	Cone of EASTER ISLAND	1303-08-
ORION SEAMOUNT (Kermadec Is)	Synonym of MONOWAI SEAMOUNT	0402-05-
ORIR (Vanuatu-SW Pacific)	Crater of SORETIMEAT	0507-01=
ORITO, MAUNGA (Pacific-C)	Cone of EASTER ISLAND	1303-08-
ORIZABA, PICO DE (Mexico)	Stratovolc (23, 1687) Historical	**1401-10=**
ORMUS ISLANDS (Arabia-E)	(None) Not a Volcano	0301-19-
ORO, CERRO DE (Guatemala)	Dome of TOLIMAN	1402-07=
OROK, OLDOINYO (Africa-E)	Synonym of MERU	0202-16=
OROKURA [KANEDA] (Honshu-Japan)	Dome of OMANAGO GROUP	0803-142
ORONGATEA (New Zealand)	Pumice cone of MAYOR ISLAND	0401-021
OROSI (Costa Rica)	Stratovolcs (None) Uncertain	**1405-01=**
OROTA (Nicaragua)	Synonym of ROTA	1404-06-
ORPHAN BUTTE (US-Oregon)	Cone of NEWBERRY VOLCANO	1202-11-
ORUAHINAWE (New Zealand)	Dome of MAROA	0401-061
ORUANUI (New Zealand)	Dome of MAROA	0401-061
ORUKA [TATARINOV] (Kurile Is)	Stratovolc of CHIKURACHKI	0900-36=
OS, PUIG DE L' (Spain)	Cone of OLOT VOLC FIELD	0100-03-
OSHIDASHIZAWA (Hokkaido-Japan)	Crater of KOMAGA-TAKE	0805-02=
OSHIMA (Izu Is-Japan)	Stratovolc (74, 1990) Historical	**0804-01=**
OSHIMA-FUJI (Hokkaido-Japan)	Synonym of KOMAGA-TAKE	0805-02=
OSHIMA-OSHIMA (Hokkaido-Japan)	Stratovolc (5, 1790) Historical	**0805-01=**
OSHO-YAMA (Honshu-Japan)	Stratovolc of ADATARA	0803-17=
OSIMA-O-SIMA (Hokkaido-Japan)	Synonym of OSHIMA-OSHIMA	0805-01=
OSOBAYA PEAK (Kurile Is)	Cone of ALAID	0900-39=
OSOGOT (Africa-E)	Cone of CHYULU HILLS	0202-13=
OSORE-YAMA (Honshu-Japan)	Stratovolc (1, 1787) Historical	**0803-29=**
OSORNO (Chile-S)	Stratovolc (8, 1869) Historical	**1508-01=**
OSTANETS (Kamchatka)	Dome of UZON	1000-17=
OSTANETS (Kamchatka)	Shields (None) Holocene	**1000-056**
OSTRAYA ZIMINA (Kamchatka)	Stratovolc of ZIMINA	1000-242
OSTRIY (Kamchatka)	Synonym of OSTRY	1000-68-
OSTRY (Kamchatka)	Stratovolcs (None) Holocene	**1000-68-**
OSTRY TOLBACHIK (Kamchatka)	Stratovolc of TOLBACHIK	1000-24=
OSYO-YAMA [OSHO-YAMA] (Honshu-Japan)	Stratovolc of ADATARA	0803-17=
OTAKE (Kyushu-Japan)	Thermal Feature of KUJU GROUP	0802-12=
OTARA HILL (New Zealand)	Cone of AUCKLAND FIELD	0401-02=
OTDELNIY (Kamchatka)	Shields (None) Holocene	**1000-057**
OTEI SPRINGS (New Zealand)	Thermal Feature of OKATAINA	0401-05=
OTKHODYASHCHY (Kamchatka)	Cone of MUTNOVSKY	1000-06=
OTKRYTAYA (Kamchatka)	Cone of UZON	1000-17=
OTOMEKO-YAMA (Honshu-Japan)	Synonym of FUJI	0803-03=
OTOROA (New Zealand)	Cone of KAIKOHE-BAY OF ISLANDS	0401-01=
OTRO LADO, CERRO EL (Guatemala)	Cone of CHIQUIMULA FIELD	1402-20-
OTSUBO-NO-IKE (Japan)	Crater of AKITA-KOMAGA-TAKE	0803-23=
OTTOMOI (Kurile Is)	Synonym of EBEKO	0900-38=
OTUATAUA (New Zealand)	Cone of AUCKLAND FIELD	0401-02=
OTUBO-NO-IKE [OTSUBO-NO-IKE] (Japan)	Crater of AKITA-KOMAGA-TAKE	0803-23=
OTURU (New Zealand)	Pumice cone of MAYOR ISLAND	0401-021
OTUTARARA SPRINGS (New Zealand)	Thermal Feature of ROTORUA	0401-042
OTU'U, MAUNGA (Pacific-C)	Cone of EASTER ISLAND	1303-08-
OUAHA (New Zealand)	Dome of TAUPO	0401-07=
OULENOU (Vanuatu-SW Pacific)	Cone of TRAITOR'S HEAD	0507-09=
OULIABOUNE [MORNE ANGLAIS] (W Indies)	Cone of MICOTRIN	1600-10=
OUNDA GINNA KOMA (Djibouti)	Tuff cone of ARDOUKOBA	0201-126
OUSON (Kamchatka)	Synonym of UZON	1000-17=
OUTCAST HILL (Canada)	Cone of SPECTRUM RANGE	1200-07-
OUTHWAITE PARK (New Zealand)	Cone of AUCKLAND FIELD	0401-02=
OVALNAYA ZIMINA (Kamchatka)	Stratovolc of ZIMINA	1000-242
OVALNYE (Kamchatka)	Dome of BOLSHOI SEMIACHIK	1000-15=
OVE (Solomon Is-SW Pac)	Synonym of SIMBO	0505-05=
OVE, LAKE (Solomon Is-SW Pac)	Crater of SIMBO	0505-05=
OVEJERO, CERRO EL (Guatemala)	Cone of SUCHITAN VOLC FIELD	1402-17-
OVERO, CERRO (Chile-N)	Maar (None) Holocene	**1505-097**
OW RIG (Vanuatu-SW Pacific)	Stratovolc of SORETIMEAT	0507-01=
OW SORLAV-OW PLANMEN (Vanuatu)	Stratovolc of SORETIMEAT	0507-01=
OWAKUDANI (Honshu-Japan)	Thermal Feature of HAKONE	0803-02=
OXI (Iceland-S)	Fissure vent of HEKLA	1702-07=
OYAGUA (OYAHUE) (Chile-N)	Synonym of OLLAGUE	1505-06=
OYAKOBA-YAMA (OYAKOBATSKA) (Kurile	Synonym of ALAID	0900-39=
OYAMA (Izu Is-Japan)	Crater of MIYAKE-JIMA	0804-04=
OZERNAIA (Kamchatka)	Synonym of ILYINSKY	1000-03=
OZERNAYA (Kamchatka)	Synonym of OZERNOY	1000-051
OZERNOVSKY POTOK (Kamchatka)	Vent of ELOVSKY	1000-59-
OZERNOY (Kamchatka)	Shield of ELOVSKY	1000-59-
OZERNOY (Kamchatka)	Cone of KRASHENINNIKOV	1000-19=
OZERNOY (Kamchatka)	Shield (None) Holocene	**1000-051**
OZIGOKU [OJIGOKU] (Honshu-Japan)	Thermal Feature of IWATE	0803-24=
OZUKUSI-YAMA [OZUKUSHI-YAMA]	Dome of OSORE-YAMA	0803-29=
OZYO-DAKE [OJO-DAKE] (Kyushu-Japan)	Stratovolc of ASO	0802-11=

P

NAME (Subregion)	Type (Eruption Total, Most Recent) Status . . . Relation to NAMED VOLCANO	NUMBER
PABELLON, CERRO (Chile-N)	Dome of AZUFRE, CERRO DEL	1505-065
PABELLON MAURAS, VOLCAN (Peru)	Cone of ANDAHUA VALLEY	1504-002
PACAYA (Guatemala)	Complx volc (21, 1993) Historical	**1402-11=**
PACAYAL, LAGUNA SECA EL (El Salvador)	Crater of CHINAMECA	1403-09=
PACHO, CERRO (El Salvador)	Dome of COATEPEQUE CALDERA	1403-041
PACO (Mindanao-Philippines)	Compnd volc (None) Fumarolic	**0701-09-**
PADDO (US-Washington)	Synonym of ADAMS	1201-04-
PAEH, KAWAH (Java)	Thermal Feature of SALAK	0603-05=
P'AEKTU-SAN (China-E)	Synonym of BAITOUSHAN	1005-07-
PAGAN (Mariana Is-C Pac)	Stratovolcs (16, 1993) Historical	**0804-17=**
PAGERKANDANG (Java)	Cone of DIENG VOLC COMPLEX	0603-20=
PAGERKANDANG, KAWAH (Java)	Thermal Feature of DIENG VOLC COMP	0603-20=
PAGO (New Britain-SW Pac)	Caldera (9, 1933) Historical	**0502-08=**
PAGO (Samoa-SW Pacific)	Pleistocene caldera of TUTUILA	0404-02-
PAHANGAHANGA (New Zealand)	Cone of KAIKOHE-BAY OF ISLANDS	0401-01=
PAHTO (US-Washington)	Synonym of ADAMS	1201-04-
PAILOUSHAN (China-E)	Cone of DATONG	1005-01-
PAINT POT CRATER (US-California)	Crater of MEDICINE LAKE	1203-02-
PAISLEY (US-Idaho)	Cone of CRATERS OF THE MOON	1204-02-
PAJANALES, CERRO (Chile-N)	Stratovolc of PULAR	1505-105
PAJANG (Lesser Sunda Is)	Crater of BATUR	0604-01=
PAJARITA, CERRO LA (Guatemala)	Cone of FLORES, VOLCAN DE	1402-14-
PAJARITOS (Chile-C)	Cone of ANTILLANCA GROUP	1507-153
PAJAROS (Mariana Is-C Pac)	Synonym of FARALLON DE PAJAROS	0804-14=
PAJAS, CERRO DE (Galapagos)	Cone of FLOREANA	1503-10=
PAJOENG [PAJUNG] (Java)	Stratovolc of DANAU COMPLEX	0603-01=
PAJONALES, CERRO (Chile-N)	Stratovolc of PULAR	1505-105
PAJUNG (Java)	Stratovolc of DANAU COMPLEX	0603-01=
PAKA (Africa-E)	Shield (1, -6050) Ar/Ar	**0202-053**
PAKKA (Africa-E)	Synonym of PAKA	0202-053
PAKUSHIN (Aleutian Is)	Cone of MAKUSHIN	1101-31-
PAKUWOJO [PAKUWAJA] (Java)	Cone of DIENG VOLC COMPLEX	0603-20=
PALACPAQUEN, LAKE (Luzon-Philippines)	Maar of LAGUNA VOLC FIELD	0703-051
PALAMITO (Mexico)	Cone of CHICHINAUTZIN	1401-08=
PALANGIAGIA (New Britain-SW Pac)	Stratovolc of RABAUL	0502-14=
PALAO RAGANG (Mindanao-Philippines)	Synonym of RAGANG	0701-06=
PALAR (Chile-N)	Synonym of PULAR	1505-105
PALEI-AIKE VOLC FIELD (Chile-S)	Cinder cones (1, -5550) Anthropology	**1508-08-**
PALENA VOLC GROUP (Chile-S)	Cinder cones (None) Holocene	**1508-052**
PALEO-SEMIACHIK (Kamchatka)	Stratovolc of MALY SEMIACHIK	1000-14=
PALETERA (Colombia)	Cone of PURACE	1501-06=
PALFFY (Atl-N-Jan Mayen)	Cone of JAN MAYEN	1706-01=
PALIOREWMA (Greece)	Thermal Feature of MILOS	0102-03=
PALIRON (Mindanao-Philippines)	Dome of PACO	0701-09-
PALLAS PEAK (Kurile Is)	Stratovolc of KETOI	0900-20=
PALMA SUR, CERRITO LA (El Salvador)	Dome of ILOPANGO	1403-06=
PALMAS, MONTANA DE LAS (Canary Is)	Cone of GRAN CANARIA	1803-04-
PALMIRA, CERROS (Costa Rica)	Stratovolc of PLATANAR, CERRO	1405-036
PALO BLANCO (US-New Mexico)	Cone of RATON-CLAYTON	1210-04-
PALOE (Lesser Sunda Is)	Synonym of PALUWEH	0604-15=
PALOMO (Chile-C)	Stratovolc (None) Holocene	**1507-022**
PALOMOS, CERRO LAS (Nicaragua)	Cone of MOMOTOMBO	1404-09=
PALOWE (Lesser Sunda Is)	Synonym of PALUWEH	0604-15=
PALSFJALL (Iceland-NE)	Cone of GRIMSVOTN	1703-01=
PALUWEH (Lesser Sunda Is)	Stratovolc (8, 1985) Historical	**0604-15=**
PAM LIN (Admiralty Is-SW Pac)	Cone of ST. ANDREW STRAIT	0500-01=
PAM MANDIAN (Admiralty Is-SW Pac)	Cone of ST. ANDREW STRAIT	0500-01=
PAMPA DE PALACIO (Peru)	Shield of CHACHANI, NEVADO	1504-005
PAMPA LUXSAR (Bolivia)	Volc field (None) Holocene	**1505-042**
PAN DE AZUCAR (Alaska-SW)	Synonym of AUGUSTINE	1103-01-
PAN DE AZUCAR (Colombia)	Stratovolc of PURACE	1501-06=
PAN DE AZUCAR (Ecuador)	Stratovolc (None) Holocene	**1502-031**
PAN DE AZUCAR [PICO DEL TEIDE] (Canary	Stratovolc of TENERIFE	1803-03-
PAN-PAN-LUNG-WAN [BANBANLONGWAN]	Crater of LONGGANG GROUP	1005-06-
PANALVIA, CERRO (Guatemala)	Dome of IPALA VOLC FIELD	1402-19-
PANAMAO (Philippines-C)	Dome of BILIRAN	0702-08=
PANAMAO, MT. (Sulu Is-Philippines)	Crater of BUD DAJO	0700-01=
PANANDJAKAN [PANANJAKAN] (Java)	Cone of TENGGER CALDERA	0603-31=
PANANJAKAN (Java)	Cone of TENGGER CALDERA	0603-31=
PANAY (Luzon-Philippines)	Stratovolc (None) Pleistocene-Fumarolic	**0703-046**
PANDAN (Sumatra)	Synonym of PENDAN	0601-191
PANDAN, GUNUNG (Lesser Sunda Is)	Cone of BATUR	0604-01=
PANDERE HILL (Africa-E)	Cone of KIEYO	0202-17=
PANDI, LAKE (Luzon-Philippines)	Maar of LAGUNA VOLC FIELD	0703-051
PANECILLO, CERRO EL (Ecuador)	Dome of MOJANDA	1502-003
PANGALU (New Britain-SW Pac)	Thermal Feature of GARUA HARBOUR	0502-06=
PANGASAHAN, KAWAH (Java)	Thermal Feature of KAWAHKAMOJANG	0603-12=
PANGASUN, MT. (Luzon Is-N of)	Crater of BABUYAN CLARO	0704-03=
PANGGILINGAN, KAWAH (Java)	Thermal Feature of KAWAHKAMOJANG	0603-12=
PANGGUJANGAN BADAK (Java)	Crater of TANGKUBANPARAHU	0603-09=
PANGGUNGAN (Java)	Crater of LAWU	0603-26=
PANGGUYANGAN BADAK (Java)	Crater of TANGKUBANPARAHU	0603-09=
PANGO (New Britain-SW Pac)	Synonym of PAGO	0502-08=
PANGONAN (Java)	Cone of DIENG VOLC COMPLEX	0603-20=
PANGRANGO (Java)	Twin volcano of GEDE	0603-06=
PANGUES, LOS (Chile-C)	Cone of ANTUCO	1507-08=
PANGUIPULLI (Chile-C)	Synonym of MOCHO-CHOSHUENCO	1507-13=
PANGUJAAN [DANAN] (Philippines-C)	Thermal Feature of MAHAGNOA	0702-07=
PANIER, MT. (Australia)	Shield of NEWER VOLCANICS PROV	0509-01-

NAME (Subregion)	Type (Eruption Total, Most Recent) Status . . . Relation to NAMED VOLCANO	NUMBER
PANMURE BASIN (New Zealand)	Tuff ring of AUCKLAND FIELD	0401-02=
PANSO [PANSOL] (Luzon-Philippines)	Cone of MAQUILING	0703-06=
PANTANO SECCO (Italy)	Crater of ALBANO, MONTE	0101-004
PANTAR API (Lesser Sunda Is)	Synonym of SIRUNG	0604-27=
PANTELLERIA (Italy)	Shield (6, 1891) Historical	**0101-071**
PANTELLERIA BANK (Italy)	Submarine vent of CAMPI FLEGREI MAR	0101-07=
PANTOJA, CERRO (Chile-C)	Stratovolc (None) Holocene	**1507-152**
PANUM (US-California)	Dome of MONO CRATERS	1203-12-
PAO DE ACUCAR (Atlantic-S)	Dome of TRINDADE	1805-051
PAOHA ISLAND (US-Calif)	Cone of MONO LAKE VOLC FIELD	1203-11-
PAPAK, GUNUNG (Java)	Cone of IJEN	0603-35=
PAPAK, GUNUNG (Java)	Cone of SEMERU	0603-30=
PAPANDAJAN (Java)	Synonym of PAPANDAYAN	0603-10=
PAPANDAYAN (Java)	Stratovolc (3, 1942) Historical	**0603-10=**
PAPATELE (Samoa-SW Pacific)	Cone of TUTUILA	0404-02-
PAPAYO (Mexico)	Lava dome (None) Holocene	**1401-085**
PAPOOSE HILL (US-California)	Cone of MEDICINE LAKE	1203-02-
PARABAKTI, CIPANAS (Java)	Thermal Feature of KIARABERES-GAGAK	0603-03=
PARABAKTI, KAWAH (Java)	Thermal Feature of KIARABERES-GAGAK	0603-03=
PARABAKTI, TJIPANAS [CIPANAS PARABA	Thermal Feature of KIARABERES-GAGAK	0603-03=
PARACHO, CERROS DE (Mexico)	Cone of MICHOACAN-GUANAJUATO	1401-06=
PARADA, CERRITO LA (Guatemala)	Cone of IPALA VOLC FIELD	1402-19-
PARADA NORTE, CERRO LA (Guatemala)	Cone of IPALA VOLC FIELD	1402-19-
PARAKASAK (Java)	Cone of DANAU COMPLEX	0603-01=
PARAMASAM (Java)	Thermal Feature of UNGARAN	0603-23=
PARAMO DE RUIZ (Colombia)	Synonym of RUIZ	1501-02=
PARAMO DE TAJUMBINA (Colombia)	Synonym of DONA JUANA	1501-07=
PARANGUEO, EL (Mexico)	Maar of MICHOACAN-GUANAJUATO	1401-06=
PARAROA (New Zealand)	Dome of OKATAINA	0401-05=
PARASA [PARASO] (Solomon Is-SW Pac)	Thermal Feature of NONDA	0505-04=
PARATUN (Chile-S)	Synonym of OSORNO	1508-01=
PARAZIT (Kurile Is)	Cone of ALAID	0900-39=
PAREHE, MAUNGA (Easter Island)	Dome of EASTER ISLAND	1303-08-
PAREWHAITI (New Zealand)	Dome of OKATAINA	0401-05=
PARICUTIN (Mexico)	Cone of MICHOACAN-GUANAJUATO	1401-06=
PARINACOTA (Chile-N)	Stratovolc (None) Holocene	**1505-016**
PARIO, CERRO DE (Mexico)	Cone of MICHOACAN-GUANAJUATO	1401-06=
PARIOU, PUY DE (France)	Cone of CHAINE DES PUYS	0100-02-
PARISH HILL (W Indies)	Dome of SABA	1600-01=
PARTIDO, PICO (Canary Is)	Cone of LANZAROTE	1803-06-
PARU, MT. (Solomon Is-SW Pac)	Cone of GALLEGO	0505-062
PARUGPUG (Java)	Crater of PAPANDAYAN	0603-10=
PARUMA, VOLCAN (Chile-N)	Stratovolc of OLCA-PARUMA	1505-05=
PARUPUJAN [PARUPUYAN] (Java)	Crater of GUNTUR	0603-13=
PARUSNAYA MOUNTAIN (Kurile Is)	Cone of GOLETS-TORNYI GROUP	0900-091
PARYASHCHAYA DOLINA (Kamchatka)	Thermal Feature of BOLSHOI SEMIACHIK	1000-15=
PARYASHCHYI GREBEN (Kamchatka)	Dome of KSUDACH	1000-05=
PARYASHCHYI USTUP (Kamchatka)	Dome of KSUDACH	1000-05=
PAS DES SABLES, PUY (Indian O.-W)	Cone of FOURNAISE, PITON DE LA	0303-02=
PASAMAN (Sumatra)	Stratovolc of TALAKMAU	0601-13=
PASAR ARBAA (Sumatra)	Stratovolc of TALANG	0601-16=
PASCUA, ISLA DE (Pacific-C)	Synonym of EASTER ISLAND	1303-08-
PASIR BESAR (Banda Sea)	Crater of BANDA API	0605-09=
PASIRLEBAR, KAWAH [KAPI FUMAROLE FI	Thermal Feature of GAYOLESTEN	0601-06=
PASQUI, CERRO (Costa Rica)	Cone of IRAZU	1405-06=
PASSAGE, CRATERE DU (Indian O.-W)	Crater of FOURNAISE, PITON DE LA	0303-02=
PASTO, VOLCAN DE (Colombia)	Synonym of GALERAS	1501-08=
PASTORIA, CERRO LA (Mexico)	Crater of PINACATE PEAKS	1401-001
PATA (Chile-S)	Synonym of OSORNO	1508-01=
PATAH (Sumatra)	Unknown (None) Uncertain	**0601-231**
PATAHUILLE (Chile-S)	Synonym of OSORNO	1508-01=
PATAMBAN, CERRO (Mexico)	Cone of MICHOACAN-GUANAJUATO	1401-06=
PATATE, MORNE (W Indies)	Synonym of PATATES, MORNE	1600-11=
PATATES, MORNE (W Indies)	Stratovolc (1, 1500) Radiocarbon	**1600-11=**
PATILLA PATA (Bolivia)	Stratovolc (None) Holocene?	**1505-012**
PATILO (New Guinea-NE of)	Crater of KARKAR	0501-03=
PATITE, CUDDIE (Italy)	Shield of PANTELLERIA	0101-071
PATOC (Luzon-Philippines)	Stratovolc (None) Fumarolic	**0703-087**
PATOEHA (Java)	Synonym of PATUHA	0603-07=
PATOS, ISLAS DE LOS (El Salvador)	Dome of ILOPANGO	1403-06=
PATRICIO, CERRO (Galapagos)	Cone of SAN CRISTOBAL	1503-12-
PATUHA (Java)	Stratovolc (None) Holocene	**0603-07=**
PATUHA KALER (Java)	Crater of PATUHA	0603-07=
PATUKIO, MT. (Solomon Is-SW Pac)	Cone of SIMBO	0505-05=
PATULUL (Guatemala)	Synonym of ATITLAN	1402-06=
PAUAHI (Hawaiian Is)	Pit crater of KILAUEA	1302-01-
PAUGARANI (Peru)	Synonym of CASIRI, NEVADOS	1504-06-
PAUGNAT, PUY DE (France)	Cone of CHAINE DES PUYS	0100-02-
PAUK (Kamchatka)	Cone of KRASHENINNIKOV	1000-19=
PAUKOHUREA (New Zealand)	Thermal Feature of OKATAINA	0401-05=
PAULET (Antarctica)	Cinder cone (None) Holocene	**1900-041**
PAULINA PEAK (US-Oregon)	Dome of NEWBERRY VOLCANO	1202-11-
PAULOWSKY (Alaska Peninsula)	Synonym of PAVLOF	1102-03-
PAUZHETKA (Kamchatka)	Calderas (5, 0200) Radiocarbon	**1000-022**
PAVANT BUTTE (US-Utah)	Tuff cone of BLACK ROCK DESERT	1207-05-
PAVAS, CERRO LAS (El Salvador)	Cone of ILOPANGO	1403-06=
PAVIN (France)	Maar of CHAINE DES PUYS	0100-02-
PAVLOF (Alaska Peninsula)	Stratovolc (36, 1990) Historical	**1102-03-**
PAVLOF SISTER (Alaska Peninsula)	Stratovolc (1, 1786) Historical	**1102-04-**
PAWAI (Hawaiian Is)	Pit crater of KILAUEA	1302-01-
PAWENEN, GUNUNG (Java)	Cone of IJEN	0603-35=
PAWON (Lesser Sunda Is)	Cone of AGUNG	0604-02=
PAXAPA, CERRO (Guatemala)	Cone of CHIQUIMULA FIELD	1402-20-
PAXTE, CERRO EL (Guatemala)	Cone of IPALA VOLC FIELD	1402-19-
PAXTON SPRINGS (US-New Mexico)	Cone of ZUNI-BANDERA	1210-02-
PAYACHATA, NEVADOS DE (Chile-N)	Synonym of PARINACOTA	1505-016
PAYALPAN (Kamchatka)	Shield of BOLSHOY PAYALPAN	1000-30-
PAYUN MATRU, CERRO (Argentina)	Shield (None) Holocene	**1507-067**
PEAK HILL (W Indies)	Dome of SABA	1600-01=
PEBBLE CREEK HOT SPRING (Canada)	Thermal Feature of MEAGER	1200-18-
PECHAN (China-W)	Cone of TIANSHAN VOLC GROUP	1004-02-
PECHO, EL (Mexico)	Cone of IZTACCIHUATL	1401-086
PECUL (Guatemala)	Synonym of PACAYA	1402-11=
PEDRE BARBA, MONTANA DE (Canary Is)	Cone of LANZAROTE	1803-06-
PEDREGOSO, CERRO (Mexico)	Dome of CEBORUCO, VOLCAN	1401-03=
PEDRERA, CERRO LA (Guatemala)	Dome of ALMOLONGA	1402-04=
PEGGY'S WHIM (W Indies)	Thermal Feature of ST. CATHERINE	1600-17=
PEGUNUNGAN DIENG (Java)	Synonym of DIENG VOLC COMPLEX	0603-20=
PEHUALTEPEC (Mexico)	Cone of HOLOTEPEC	1401-07-
PEINADO (Argentina)	Stratovolc (None) Holocene	**1505-127**
PEISHAN [PECHAN] (China-W)	Cone of TIANSHAN VOLC GROUP	1004-02-
PELADO, CERRO (Chile-S)	Cone of MINCHINMAVIDA	1508-04=
PELADO, VOLCAN (Mexico)	Shield of CHICHINAUTZIN	1401-08=
PELAGATOS, CERRO (Mexico)	Cone of TENAYO GROUP	1401-081
PELAT, PUY (France)	Cone of CHAINE DES PUYS	0100-02-
PELATO, MONTE (Italy)	Cone of LIPARI	0101-041
PELE, MONT [LE DJUNGO] (Africa-W)	Cone of MANENGOUBA	0204-004
PELE, MONTAGNE (W Indies)	Synonym of PELEE	1600-12=
PELE, PUU O (Hawaiian Is)	Cone of HALEAKALA	1302-06-
PELE [FATOULEO-KAKOULO] (Vanuatu)	Stratovolc of NORTH VATE	0507-081
PELEE (W Indies)	Stratovolc (53, 1932) Historical	**1600-12=**
PELLADO (Chile-C)	Stratovolc of SAN PEDRO-PELLADO	1507-063
PELMEN (Kamchatka)	Cone of TOLBACHIK	1000-24=
PELON (El Salvador)	Stratovolc of TECAPA	1403-08=
PELON, CERRO (Costa Rica)	Stratovolc of PLATANAR, CERRO	1405-036
PELON, CERRO (Mexico)	Cone of MICHOACAN-GUANAJUATO	1401-06=
PELON, CERRO (Mexico)	Cone of DURANGO VOLC FIELD	1401-022
PELON, CERRO (US-New Mexico)	Dome of VALLES CALDERA	1210-03-
PELON, EL (Nicaragua)	Cone of MASAYA	1404-10=
PELONA, LOMA LA (Nicaragua)	Caldera of SAN CRISTOBAL	1404-02=
PEMATANG BATA (Sumatra)	Crater of SUOH	0601-27=
PENA BLANCA, CERRO (Guatemala)	Dome of TECUAMBURRO	1402-12=
PENA BLANCA [OJO DE AGUA DE LA VIRG	Stratovolc of VERDE, LAGUNA	1403-01=
PENANGGUNGAN (Java)	Stratovolc (None) Holocene	**0603-291**
PENAVALLELS, ALTOS DE LOS (Canary Is)	Cone of GRAN CANARIA	1803-04-
PENCELUT, KAWAH (Java)	Thermal Feature of KAWAHKAMOJANG	0603-12=
PENDAN (Sumatra)	Unknown (None) Holocene	**0601-191**
PENDAPURAN, KABA [KABA VOGELSANG]	Crater of KABA	0601-22=
PENDIL, GUNUNG (Java)	Cone of IJEN	0603-35=
PENG-CHIA-HSU (Taiwan-N of)	Stratovolc (None) Pleistocene-Fumarolic	**0801-041**
PENGUIN (Antarctica)	Stratovolc (3, 1905) Lichenometry	**1900-031**
PENJELUANG, KABA [KABA VOGELSANG]	Crater of KABA	0601-22=
PENOETOEN (Lesser Sunda Is)	Synonym of ILIWERUNG	0604-25=
PENON DE LOS BANOS (Mexico)	Cone of SANTA CATARINA RANGE	1401-082
PENON DEL MARQUES (Mexico)	Cone of SANTA CATARINA RANGE	1401-082
PENONES, CERRO LOS (Peru)	Dome of CHACHANI, NEVADO	1504-005
PENTA PALUMMO (Italy)	Cone of CAMPI FLEGREI	0101-01=
PENTJELUT, KAWAH [KAWAH PENCELUT]	Thermal Feature of KAWAHKAMOJANG	0603-12=
PENYELUANG, KABA [KABA VOGELSANG]	Crater of KABA	0601-22=
PERBAKTI (Java)	Stratovolc (None) Fumarolic	**0603-04=**
PERBOEWATAN [PERBUWATAN] (Indonesia	Former cone of KRAKATAU	0602-00=
PERCHE'S MT. (W Indies)	Dome of SOUFRIERE HILLS	1600-05=
PERDIDOS, CERRO LOS (Costa Rica)	Cone of ARENAL	1405-033
PEREMYCHKA (Kamchatka)	Dome of BOLSHOI SEMIACHIK	1000-15=
PERETOLCHIN (Russia-SE)	Cone of OKA VOLC FIELD	1002-06-
PEREZA, CERRO LA (Guatemala)	Cone of IXTEPEQUE, VOLCAN	1402-18-
PERFAIT, PITON (Indian O.-W)	Crater of FOURNAISE, PITON DE LA	0303-02=
PERIKARTINI (Turkey)	Cone of ERCIYES DAGI	0103-01=
PERLA, LA (Guatemala)	Stratovolc of TECUAMBURRO	1402-12=
PEROL, EL (El Salvador)	Crater of SANTA ANA	1403-02=
PEROLITOS, LOS (El Salvador)	Synonym of SAN MIGUEL	1403-10=
PERTOLICHINA (Russia-SE)	Cone of OKA VOLC FIELD	1002-06-
PERURU (Mariana Is-C Pac)	Cone of PAGAN	0804-17=
PERUTARUBE-SAN (Kurile Is)	Synonym of BERUTARUBE	0900-04=
PERVAYA (Kamchatka)	Dome of UZON	1000-17=
PERVAYA (Kamchatka)	Cone of UZON	1000-17=
PESCHANAYA, SOPKA (Kamchatka)	Synonym of ZAVARITSKY	1000-121
PESCHANIE GORKY (Kamchatka)	Cone of TOLBACHIK	1000-24=
PETACAS (Colombia)	Lava dome (None) Holocene?	**1501-062**
PETER HAFEN (New Britain-SW Pac)	Crater of GAROVE	0502-03=
PETER I ISLAND (Antarctica)	Shield (None) Holocene	**1900-029**
PETEROA (Chile-C)	Submarine vent of PLANCHON-PETEROA	1507-04=
PETIT BOTOUM (Africa-N)	Cone of TOUSSIDE, TARSO	0205-01=
PETIT CHEMINEE EXTERIEURE (Indian O.)	Crater of KARTHALA	0303-01=
PETIT DADOI (Africa-N)	Cone of TOUSSIDE, TARSO	0205-01=
PETIT HASAN DAG (Turkey)	Dome of HASAN DAGI	0103-002
PETIT PITON (W Indies)	Dome of QUALIBOU	1600-14=
PETIT PUY DE DOME (France)	Cone of CHAINE DES PUYS	0100-02-
PETIT SARCOUI (France)	Cone of CHAINE DES PUYS	0100-02-
PETIT SUCHET [PUY DE L'AUMONE]	Dome of CHAINE DES PUYS	0100-02-
PETIT TROU AU NATRON [DOON KIDIMI]	Crater of TOUSSIDE, TARSO	0205-01=
PETREL CRATER (Antarctica)	Maar of PENGUIN ISLAND	1900-031
PEUET SAGOEE (Sumatra)	Synonym of PEUET SAGUE	0601-03=
PEUET SAGUE (Sumatra)	Complx volc (1, 1921) Historical	**0601-03=**
PEULIK (Alaska Peninsula)	Stratovolc of UGASHIK-PEULIK	1102-13A
PEUT SAGUE (Sumatra)	Synonym of PEUET SAGUE	0601-03=
PHANTOM CONE (US-Oregon)	Stratovolc of CRATER LAKE	1202-16-
PHARAOH (Canada)	Dome of EDZIZA	1200-06-
PHLEGRAEAN FIELDS (Italy)	Synonym of CAMPI FLEGREI	0101-01=
PHLEGRAEAN FIELDS OF THE SICILY SEA	Synonym of CAMPI FLEGREI MAR SICILIA	0101-07=
PHLEGRAEISHE FELDER (Italy)	Synonym of CAMPI FLEGREI	0101-01=
PHYRIPLAKA [FYRIPLAKA] (Greece)	Cone of MILOS	0102-03=
PI-CHIA-SHAN [BIJIASHAN] (China-E)	Cone of WUDALIANCHI	1005-04-
PIANO, CALDERA DEL (Italy)	Caldera of ETNA	0101-06=
PIANO, CALDERA DEL (Italy)	Caldera of VULCANO	0101-05=
PIANO DEL LAGO (Italy)	Caldera of ETNA	0101-06=
PIC, PICA, PICO, PIEK (Portuguese, Spanish and Dutch for PEAK) see proper name (e.g. CHICO, PICO)		
PICACHO (El Salvador)	Stratovolc of SAN SALVADOR	1403-05=
PICACHO (Mexico)	Cone of SAN QUINTIN VOLC FIELD	1401-002
PICACHO, CERRO (US-New Mexico)	Dome of VALLES CALDERA	1210-03-
PICACHO, EL (Nicaragua)	Blank of PILAS, LAS	1404-08=
PICADA, LA (Chile-S)	Stratovolc of OSORNO	1508-01=
PICHANCHA, LA (Mexico)	Cone of CEBORUCO, VOLCAN	1401-03=
PICHARES (Chile-C)	Cone of REDONDO, CERRO	1507-113
PICHI (Chile-C)	Cone of CARRAN-LOS VENADOS	1507-14=
PICHI CAULLE (Chile-C)	Cone of PUYEHUE	1507-15=
PICHI LAGUNA (Chile-S)	Maar of CAYUTE-LA VIGUERIA	1508-021
PICHIGOLGOL (Chile-C)	Crater of MENCHECA	1507-151
PICHIHUA, CERRO (Peru)	Cone of ANDAHUA VALLEY	1504-002
PICHIMALLA (Chile-C)	Crater of CALLAQUI	1507-091
PICO (Azores)	Stratovolc (3, 1720) Historical	**1802-02=**
PICO (Mexico)	Stratovolc of ORIZABA, PICO DE	1401-10=
PICO, PICO DO (Azores)	Synonym of PICO	1802-02=
PICUNG (Java)	Crater of GUNTUR	0603-13=
PIEDMONTE (Italy)	Dome of ISCHIA	0101-03=
PIEDRA DE AGUA, CERRO (Nicaragua)	Cone of CONCEPCION	1404-12=
PIEDRA DEL SAL, MONTANA (Canary Is)	Cone of FUERTEVENTURA	1803-05-
PIEDRAS, CERRO LAS (Guatemala)	Shield of IXTEPEQUE, VOLCAN	1402-18-
PIERRE PRUVOST (Ethiopia)	Synonym of MA ALALTA	0201-111
PIES, EL (Mexico)	Cone of IZTACCIHUATL	1401-086
PIETRA, LA (Italy)	Crater of CAMPI FLEGREI	0101-01=
PIGEON MOUNTAIN (New Zealand)	Cone of AUCKLAND FIELD	0401-02=
PIGNA SAN NICOLA (Italy)	Crater of CAMPI FLEGREI	0101-01=
PIIP (Kamchatka-E of)	Submarine (1, -5050) Tephrochronology	**1000-271**

NAME (Subregion)	Type (Eruption Total, Most Recent) Status . . . Relation to NAMED VOLCANO	NUMBER
PIIP (Kamchatka)	Crater of KLIUCHEVSKOI	1000-26=
PIIPA (Kamchatka-E of)	Synonym of PIIP	1000-271
PIK (Kamchatka)	Stratovolc of KIKHPINYCH	1000-18=
PIKESA (Greece)	Dome of METHANA	0102-02=
PILAR, LAGOA DO (Azores)	Cone of SETE CIDADES	1802-08=
PILAS, LAS (Costa Rica)	Thermal Feature of RINCON DE LA VIEJA	1405-02=
PILAS, LAS (Nicaragua)	Synonym of NEGRO, CERRO	1404-07=
PILAS, LAS (Nicaragua)	Complx volc (3, 1954) Historical	**1404-08=**
PILATO, MONTE [MONTE PELATO] (Italy)	Crater of LIPARI	0101-041
PILATO, MT. (Italy)	Cone of VULSINI	0101-003
PILI, CERRO (Chile-N)	Synonym of ACAMARCHI	1505-096
PILIMBALA (Colombia)	Thermal Feature of PURACE	1501-06=
PILLAN (Chile-S)	Synonym of OSORNO	1508-01=
PILLAN [EL MOCHO] (Chile-C)	Stratovolc of MOCHO-CHOSHUENCO	1507-13=
PILLANILAHUE [CARRAN] (Chile-C)	Maar of CARRAN-LOS VENADOS	1507-14=
PILLAR BUTTE (US-Idaho)	Shield of WAPI LAVA FIELD	1204-03-
PILLOW CREEK (Canada)	Cone of WELLS GRAY-CLEARWATER	1200-15-
PILLOW RIDGE (Canada)	Vent of EDZIZA	1200-06-
PILON, CERRO EL (Nicaragua)	Cone of ZAPATERA ISLAND	1404-111
PILON D'AZUCAR (Alaska-SW)	Synonym of AUGUSTINE	1103-01-
PILON, EL [CERRO LOS NARANJOS]	Stratovolc of SANTA ANA	1403-02=
PILPIL BUTTE (US-Oregon)	Cone of NEWBERRY VOLCANO	1202-11-
PIMENTON (Chile-C)	Crater of VILLARRICA	1507-12=
PIMOE (Hawaiian Is)	Cone of HALEAKALA	1302-06-
PINA, CERRO (Chile-N)	Unknown (None) Holocene?	**1505-032**
PINACATE PEAKS (Mexico)	Cinder cones (2, 1935) Historical	**1401-001**
PINAGDALAN (Luzon-Philippines)	Thermal Feature of MAQUILING	0703-06=
PINANG (Java)	Cone of DANAU COMPLEX	0603-01=
PINATUBO (Luzon-Philippines)	Stratovolc (5, 1992) Historical	**0703-083**
PINE BUTTE (US-Oregon)	Cone of DAVIS LAKE	1202-10-
PINGGANG (Java)	Cone of IYANG-ARGAPURA	0603-33=
PINGUIN BAY (Indian O.-S)	Synonym of ST. PAUL	0304-03=
PINNACLE PEAK (US-New Mexico)	Dome of VALLES CALDERA	1210-03-
PINNACLE RIDGE (New Zealand)	Vent of RUAPEHU	0401-10=
PINNACLE, THE (US-Oregon)	Vent of HOOD	1202-01-
PINNACLES (Alaska-SW)	Vent of AUGUSTINE	1103-01-
PINNE MARINE [PINNE] (Italy)	Submarine vent of CAMPI FLEGREI MAR	0101-07=
PINO, CERRITO EL (Guatemala)	Cone of CUILAPA-BARBARENA	1402-111
PINO, CERRO DEL (Mexico)	Cone of SANTA CATARINA RANGE	1401-082
PINO REDONDO, CERRO (Guatemala)	Dome of IXTEPEQUE, VOLCAN	1402-18-
PINOONAN (Luzon-Philippines)	Cone of NATIB	0703-082
PINOS DE GALDAR, CALDERA DE LOS	Maar of GRAN CANARIA	1803-04-
PINTA (Galapagos)	Shield (1, 1928) Historical	**1503-07=**
PINTO, MT. (Sumatra)	Twin volcano of SIBAYAK	0601-07=
PINTOS, CERRO LOS (Guatemala)	Cone of IPALA VOLC FIELD	1402-19-
PINTU KECIL (Banda Sea)	Crater of BANDA API	0605-09=
PIOA (Samoa-SW Pacific)	Dome of TUTUILA	0404-02-
PIOAO (Samoa-SW Pacific)	Cone of TUTUILA	0404-02-
PIPE, MT. [SURIBACHI-YAMA] (Volcano Is)	Cone of IWO-JIMA	0804-12=
PIRANA, ALTO LA (Colombia)	Dome of RUIZ	1501-02=
PIRATKOVSKY (Kamchatka)	Stratovolc (None) Holocene	**1000-054**
PIRE (PIREPILLAN) (Chile-S)	Synonym of OSORNO	1508-01=
PIRIA (Greece)	Thermal Feature of NISYROS	0102-05=
PIRO-PIRASO (Luzon-Philippines)	Cone of TAAL	0703-07=
PISAMBILLA (Ecuador)	Synonym of REVENTADOR	1502-01=
PISANI (Italy)	Crater of CAMPI FLEGREI	0101-01=
PISE (Chile-S)	Synonym of OSORNO	1508-01=
PISGAH CRATER (US-California)	Cone of LAVIC LAKE	1203-19-
PISGAH, MT. (Australia)	Cone of NEWER VOLCANICS PROV	0509-01-
PISTOL BUTTE (US-Oregon)	Cone of BACHELOR	1202-09-
PITAL, LOMA (Costa Rica)	Cone of AGUAS ZARCAS GROUP	1405-035
PITJUNG [PICUNG] (Java)	Crater of GUNTUR	0603-13=
PITON (Spanish for PEAK) see proper name (e.g. FOURNAISE, PITON DE LA)		
PITOS, SIERRA DE LAS (Mexico)	Unknown (None) Holocene	**1401-084**
PIUQUENES (Chile-C)	Cone of ANTILLANCA GROUP	1507-153
PLAISANCE (W Indies)	Dome of QUALIBOU	1600-14=
PLAKES (Greece)	Dome of MILOS	0102-03=
PLAN DEL HOYO (El Salvador)	Crater of SANTA ANA	1403-02=
PLANCHON (Chile-C)	Caldera of PLANCHON-PETEROA	1507-04=
PLANCHON-PETEROA (Chile-C)	Calderas (14, 1991) Historical	**1507-04=**
PLAT PAYS, MORNE (W Indies)	Stratovolc of PATATES, MORNE	1600-11=
PLATA (Galapagos)	Synonym of FERNANDINA	1503-01=
PLATANAR, CERRO (Costa Rica)	Stratovolcs (None) Holocene	**1405-036**
PLATEAU DOME [KANAKANA] (New Zeal)	Dome of OKATAINA	0401-05=
PLAYA HERMOSA (Costa Rica)	Crater of IRAZU	1405-06=
PLAYON DE AHUACHAPAN (El Salvador)	Thermal Feature of VERDE, LAGUNA	1403-01=
PLAYON, EL (El Salvador)	Cone of SAN SALVADOR	1403-05=
PLEIADES, THE (Antarctica)	Stratovolc (1, -1050) K-Ar	**1900-013**
PLEIONES, MT. (Antarctica)	Stratovolc of PLEIADES, THE	1900-013
PLINTH MOUNTAIN (Canada)	Cone of MEAGER	1200-18-
PLOSKAYA (Kamchatka)	Synonym of PLOSKY	1000-63-
PLOSKAYA (PLOSKI) (Kamchatka)	Synonym of USHKOVSKY	1000-261
PLOSKII (Kurile Is)	Crater of VERNADSKII RIDGE	0900-37-
PLOSKO-KRUGLEN'KY (Kamchatka)	Cone of BOLSHOI SEMIACHIK	1000-15=
PLOSKY (Kamchatka)	Shield (None) Holocene	**1000-63-**
PLOSKY (Kamchatka)	Shield (None) Holocene	**1000-31-**
PLOSKY (Kamchatka)	Stratovolc of BOLSHOI SEMIACHIK	1000-15=
PLOSKY (Kamchatka)	Synonym of USHKOVSKY	1000-261
PLOSKY TOLBACHIK (Kamchatka)	Shield of TOLBACHIK	1000-24=
PLOSKYE SOPKI (Kamchatka)	Synonym of USHKOVSKY	1000-261
PLOTINA (Kamchatka)	Dome of BEZYMIANNY	1000-25=
PLUPUH, KAWAH (Java)	Crater of ARJUNO-WELIRANG	0603-29=
POA (Lesser Sunda Is)	Crater of PALUWEH	0604-15=
POAS (Costa Rica)	Stratovolc (41, 1993) Historical	**1405-04=**
POCDOL MOUNTAINS (Luzon-Philippines)	Compnd volc (None) Holocene	**0703-02=**
POCHETERO, CERRO (Mexico)	Dome of CEBORUCO, VOLCAN	1401-03=
POCHNOI (Aleutian Is)	Shield of SEMISOPOCHNOI	1101-06-
POCO LEOK (Lesser Sunda Is)	Unknown (None) Fumarolic	**0604-07=**
POCO MANASAWU [G. MANDASOWU]	Cone of RANAKAH, GUNUNG	0604-071
POCO SOL, LAGUNA (Costa Rica)	Expl crater ? (None) Uncertain	**1405-034**
POCOIHUEN (Chile-S)	Cone of CAYUTE-LA VIGUERIA	1508-021
POCURA, LAGUNA (Chile-C)	Maar of CARRAN-LOS VENADOS	1507-14=
PODAKAN (Luzon-Philippines)	Cone of AMBALATUNGAN GROUP	0703-089
PODGORNY (Russia-SE)	Cone of TUNKIN DEPRESSION	1002-05-
PODIOK, KAWAH [KAWAH PONDOK] (Java)	Thermal Feature of KAWAHKAMOJANG	0603-12=
PODKOVA (Kamchatka)	Crater of KLIUCHEVSKOI	1000-26=
PODUSHECHNY (Kurile Is)	Dome of GOLOVNIN	0900-01=
POEI [PUI] (Lesser Sunda Is)	Cone of IYA	0604-11=
POELASARI [PULOSARI] (Java)	Stratovolc of DANAU COMPLEX	0603-01=
POELOE WE (Sumatra)	Synonym of PULAU WEH	0601-01=
POERAKNJA, BUKIT [BUKIT PURAKNJA]	Cone of BATUR	0604-01=
POERUA (New Zealand)	Cone of KAIKOHE-BAY OF ISLANDS	0401-01=
POESOEK BOEKIT [PUSIKBUKIT] (Sumatra)	Stratovolc of TOBA	0601-09=
POGRANYCHNY (Kamchatka)	Shields (None) Holocene	**1000-47-**
POGROMNI (Aleutian Is)	Stratovolc of WESTDAHL	1101-34-
POGROMNI'S SISTER (Aleutian Is)	Stratovolc of WESTDAHL	1101-34-
POGRUMNOY [POGROMNI] (Aleutian Is)	Stratovolc of WESTDAHL	1101-34-
POHATUROA (New Zealand)	Dome of MAROA	0401-061
POHATUROA (New Zealand)	Dome of ROTORUA	0401-042
POHOLO, LUA (Hawaiian Is)	Pit crater of MAUNA LOA	1302-02=
POIKE (Pacific-C)	Shield of EASTER ISLAND	1303-08-
POINT KADIN (Aleutian Is)	Vent of MAKUSHIN	1101-31-
POINTED STICK (Canada)	Cone of WELLS GRAY-CLEARWATER	1200-15-
POISENTEPE, LOMA (Nicaragua)	Dome of APOYO	1404-101
POKURU (New Zealand)	Dome of MAROA	0401-061
POLIPOLI (Hawaiian Is)	Cone of HALEAKALA	1302-06-
POLLOK (Mindanao-Philippines)	Synonym of MAKATURING	0701-04=
POLLOK (Mindanao-Philippines)	Synonym of RAGANG	0701-06=
POLLUX (Antarctica)	Cone of SEAL NUNATAKS GROUP	1900-05=
POLOVINA HILL (Alaska-W)	Cone of ST. PAUL ISLAND	1104-07-
POLOVINKA (Kamchatka)	Pleistocene caldera of AKADEMIA NAUK	1000-123
POLUKUPOL (Kamchatka)	Dome of BOLSHOI SEMIACHIK	1000-15=
POLVADERA PEAK (US-New Mexico)	Dome of VALLES CALDERA	1210-03-
POLYEGOS (Greece)	Cone of MILOS	0102-03=
POLYTOP BUTTE (US-Oregon)	Cone of NEWBERRY VOLCANO	1202-11-
POMARE, MT. (Vanuatu-SW Pacific)	Synonym of KUTALI, TAVANI	0507-061
POMERAPE (Chile-N)	Stratovolc of PARINACOTA	1505-016
POMICIARI, MONTE (Italy)	Cone of ETNA	0101-06=
PONAFIDIN (Izu Is-Japan)	Synonym of TORI-SHIMA	0804-09=
POND, MT. (W Indies)	Cone of ST. CATHERINE	1600-17=
PONDOK, KAWAH (Java)	Thermal Feature of KAWAHKAMOJANG	0603-12=
PONDONA, LOMA (Ecuador)	Dome of PULULAGUA	1502-011
PONMATINESIRI [PONMACHINESHIRI]	Crater of AKAN	0805-07=
PONOHOHOA CHASMS (Hawaiian Is)	Shield of KILAUEA	1302-01-
POPA (SE Asia)	Stratovolc (1, -0442) Anthropology	**0705-08-**
POPKOV (Kamchatka)	Stratovolc of BOLSHOI SEMIACHIK	1000-15=
POPLOVAYA (Kurile Is)	Vent of EBEKO	0900-38=
POPOCATEPETL (Mexico)	Stratovolcs (36, 1947) Historical	**1401-09=**
POPOLODJO, MT. (Halmahera-Indonesia)	Cone of GAMKONORA	0608-04=
POPORI, MT. (Solomon Is-SW Pac)	Cone of GALLEGO	0505-062
PORA, MT. (Halmahera-Indonesia)	Cone of TODOKO-RANU	0608-05=
PORCELANA (Chile-S)	Cone of HUEQUI	1508-03=
PORDON, MT. (Australia)	Cone of NEWER VOLCANICS PROV	0509-01-
POROTO RIDGE (Africa-E)	Synonym of NGOZI	0202-164
PORSEA (Sumatra)	Caldera of TOBA	0601-09=
PORT FOSTER (Antarctica)	Caldera of DECEPTION ISLAND	1900-03=
PORT RESOLUTION (Vanuatu-SW Pacific)	Synonym of YASUR	0507-10=
PORTERILLOS (Ecuador)	Dome of CHACANA	1502-022
PORTO D'ISCHIA (Italy)	Vent of ISCHIA	0101-03=
PORTO MISENO (Italy)	Crater of CAMPI FLEGREI	0101-01=
PORTRILLO, LOS (Nicaragua)	Cone of TELICA	1404-04=
PORUNA, LA (Chile-N)	Cone of SAN PEDRO	1505-07=
PORUNITA, LA (Chile-N)	Cone of OLLAGUE	1505-06=
PORVENIR, CERRO (Costa Rica)	Stratovolc of PLATANAR, CERRO	1405-036
PORVENIR, CERRO EL (Guatemala)	Cone of CUILAPA-BARBARENA	1402-111
POSINTEPE, CERRO (Nicaragua)	Cone of MOMBACHO	1404-11=
POSOS, CERROS DE LOS (US-New Mexico)	Dome of VALLES CALDERA	1210-03-
POSSESSION, ILE DE LA (Indian O.-S)	Stratovolc (None) Holocene	**0304-05-**
POSTA LUBRANO (Italy)	Dome of ISCHIA	0101-03=
POT HILL (Alaska-W)	Cone of ST. PAUL ISLAND	1104-07-
POTATO BUTTE (US-California)	Shields (None) Holocene?	**1203-07-**
POTATO HILL (US-Washington)	Cone of ADAMS	1201-04-
POTATO MOUNTAIN (W Indies)	Synonym of PATATES, MORNE	1600-11=
POTERYANNY (Kamchatka)	Cone of TOLBACHIK	1000-24=
POTHOLE BUTTE (US-Oregon)	Cone of CRATER LAKE	1202-16-
POTJO DEDEHG (Lesser Sunda Is)	Cone of SANO, WAI	0604-06=
POTJO LEOK (Lesser Sunda Is)	Synonym of POCO LEOK	0604-07=
POTJO MANASAWU [G. MANDASOWU]	Cone of RANAKAH, GUNUNG	0604-071
POTJOK LEOK (Lesser Sunda Is)	Synonym of POCO LEOK	0604-07=
POTTA (Atl-N-Jan Mayen)	Cone of JAN MAYEN	1706-01=
POUCHARET, PUY DE (France)	Cone of CHAINE DES PUYS	0100-02-
POVOACAO (Azores)	Pleistocene caldera of FURNAS	1802-10=
POVOROTNAIA SOPKA (Kamchatka)	Synonym of MUTNOVSKY	1000-06=
POWDER HILL (US-California)	Cone of MEDICINE LAKE	1203-02-
POWERS CALDERA (Hawaiian Is)	Caldera of KILAUEA	1302-01-
POWOROTNAJA ASSATSCHA (Kamchatka)	Synonym of MUTNOVSKY	1000-06=
POZAS, CERRO LAS (Guatemala)	Cone of IXTEPEQUE, VOLCAN	1402-18-
POZO, EL (Argentina)	Crater of TROMEN	1507-071
POZO, EL (El Salvador)	Pit crater of SANTA ANA	1403-02=
PRA-KARYMSKY (Kamchatka)	Stratovolc of KARYMSKY	1000-13=
PRA-VISOKAYA (Kamchatka)	Cone of TOLBACHIK	1000-24=
PRAHU (Java)	Stratovolc of DIENG VOLC COMPLEX	0603-20=
PRAMBANAN (Java)	Cone of DIENG VOLC COMPLEX	0603-20=
PRARAUQUE (Chile-S)	Synonym of OSORNO	1508-01=
PRATA PORCI (Italy)	Crater of ALBANO, MONTE	0101-004
PRAVAIA MUTNOVSKAIA SOPKA (Kamchatk	Synonym of GORELY	1000-07=
PRAVILNY (Kamchatka)	Dome of BEZYMIANNY	1000-25=
PRAWAJA MUTNOWSKAJA (Kamchatka)	Synonym of GORELY	1000-07=
PREDSKANZANNYI (Kamchatka)	Crater of KLIUCHEVSKOI	1000-26=
PREDVIDENNOYE (Kamchatka)	Crater of KLIUCHEVSKOI	1000-26=
PRESTAHNUKUR (Iceland-SW)	Subglacial (1, -7550) Radiocarbon	**1701-07=**
PRETO, PICO (Atlantic-S)	Dome of TRINDADE	1805-051
PREVO PEAK (Kurile Is)	Stratovolc (2, 1825) Historical	**0900-19=**
PREVOSTE (Kurile Is)	Synonym of PREVO PEAK	0900-19=
PRICE BAY (Canada)	Cone of GARIBALDI LAKE	1200-19-
PRICE ISLAND (Canada)	Cone of MILBANKE SOUND GROUP	1200-12-
PRICE, MT. (Canada)	Stratovolc of GARIBALDI LAKE	1200-19-
PRIEMYSH (Kamchatka)	Stratovolc of KHODUTKA	1000-053
PRIETO, CERRO (Mexico)	Cone of MICHOACAN-GUANAJUATO	1401-06=
PRIETO, CERRO (Mexico)	Cinder cone (None) Holocene	**1401-00-**
PRINCE EDWARD ISLAND (Indian O.-S)	Shield (None) Holocene	**0304-07-**
PRINCE ISLAND (Antarctica)	Synonym of ZAVODOVSKI	1900-13=
PRINCESS (New Zealand)	Crater of WHITE ISLAND	0401-04=
PRINCESS PEAK (Alaska Peninsula)	Synonym of SNOWY	1102-20-
PRIYEMYSH [PRIEMYSH] (Kamchatka)	Stratovolc of KHODUTKA	1000-053
PRIZRAK (Kamchatka)	Pleistocene caldera of KELL	1000-041
PROBLEMATICHNY (Kamchatka)	Cone of BOLSHOI SEMIACHIK	1000-15=
PROFIT ELIAS (Greece)	Dome of NISYROS	0102-05=
PROPUSHCHENNYI (Kamchatka)	Crater of KLIUCHEVSKOI	1000-26=
PROSPECT PEAK (US-California)	Shield of POTATO BUTTE	1203-07-
PROTECTOR SHOAL (Antarctica)	Submarine (1, 1962) Historical	**1900-14-**
PROVATAS (Greece)	Thermal Feature of MILOS	0102-03=
PROVIDENCIA, CERRO LA (Guatemala)	Cone of CUILAPA-BARBARENA	1402-111
PRYOR CLIFF (Antarctica)	Cone of HUDSON MOUNTAINS	1900-028

NAME (Subregion)	Type (Eruption Total, Most Recent) Status . . . Relation to NAMED VOLCANO	NUMBER
PSOROCHOMA (Greece)	Synonym of SUSAKI	0102-01=
PUAI, PUU (Hawaiian Is)	Cone of KILAUEA	1302-01-
PUAIALUA (Hawaiian Is)	Pit crater of KILAUEA	1302-01-
PUCANU (Chile-C)	Synonym of VILLARRICA	1507-12=
PUCHULDIZA (Chile-N)	Hydrothrm fld (None) Pleistocene-Geysers	**1505-031**
PUCON (Chile-C)	Synonym of VILLARRICA	1507-12=
PUCU MAURAS, CERRO (Peru)	Cone of ANDAHUA VALLEY	1504-002
PUE, LE (Samoa-SW Pacific)	Cone of UPOLU	0404-03-
PUEBLITO, EL (Mexico)	Cone of MICHOACAN-GUANAJUATO	1401-06=
PUEBLO VIEJO, CERRO DEL (Mexico)	Cone of MICHOACAN-GUANAJUATO	1401-06=
PUELAMARUM [MARUM] (Vanuatu-SW Pac)	Crater of AMBRYM	0507-04=
PUERTA, VOLCAN EL (Mexico)	Cone of MASCOTA VOLC FIELD	1401-031
PUERTO, CERRO DEL (Mexico)	Cone of MICHOACAN-GUANAJUATO	1401-06=
PUERTO DE LA LAGUNA (El Salvador)	Maar of SAN SALVADOR	1403-05=
PUERTO, VOLCAN EL (Mexico)	Cone of MASCOTA VOLC FIELD	1401-031
PUESTO CORTADERAS (Argentina)	Pyrocl cone (None) Holocene	**1507-072**
PUET SAGU (Sumatra)	Synonym of PEUET SAGUE	0601-03=
PUHIMAU (Hawaiian Is)	Pit crater of KILAUEA	1302-01-
PUHIPUHI (New Zealand)	Dome of OKATAINA	0401-05=
PUHUAHUEN (Chile-S)	Synonym of OSORNO	1508-01=
PUI (Lesser Sunda Is)	Cone of IYA	0604-11=
PU'I, MAUNGA (Pacific-C)	Cone of EASTER ISLAND	1303-08-
PUIA HOU [TE MARI] (New Zealand)	Crater of TONGARIRO	0401-08=
PUIG (Spanish for HILL) see proper name (e.g. SUBIA, PUIG)		
PUJAJAUCO (PUJAJEN) (Chile-S)	Synonym of OSORNO	1508-01=
PUJALOS, VOLCA (Spain)	Cone of OLOT VOLC FIELD	0100-03-
PUKAKI (New Zealand)	Tuff cone of AUCKLAND FIELD	0401-02=
PUKEAHUA (New Zealand)	Dome of MAROA	0401-061
PUKEITI (New Zealand)	Cone of AUCKLAND FIELD	0401-02=
PUKEKAHU (New Zealand)	Dome of REPOROA	0401-06-
PUKEKAIKIONE (New Zealand)	Cone of TONGARIRO	0401-08=
PUKEKAIKIORE (New Zealand)	Dome of TAUPO	0401-07=
PUKEKIWIRIKI (New Zealand)	Tuff ring of AUCKLAND FIELD	0401-02=
PUKEKOHU (Kermadec Is)	Crater of RAOUL ISLAND	0402-03=
PUKEMOREMORE (New Zealand)	Dome of MAROA	0401-061
PUKEONAKE (New Zealand)	Cone of RUAPEHU	0401-10=
PUKEONAKE (New Zealand)	Cone of TONGARIRO	0401-08=
PUKEPOTO (New Zealand)	Dome of OKATAINA	0401-05=
PUKEPOTO (New Zealand)	Cone of WHANGAREI	0401-011
PUKEROA (New Zealand)	Dome of ROTORUA	0401-042
PUKETARATA (New Zealand)	Dome of MAROA	0401-061
PUKETUTU (New Zealand)	Cone of KAIKOHE-BAY OF ISLANDS	0401-01=
PUKETUTU ISLAND (New Zealand)	Cone of AUCKLAND FIELD	0401-02=
PUK'H'KOWITZ (US-Washington)	Synonym of BAKER	1201-01=
PUKOPUHI, MAUNGA (Pacific-C)	Cone of EASTER ISLAND	1303-08-
PUKU NGAAHAAHA (Pacific-C)	Cone of EASTER ISLAND	1303-08-
PULALI [PARASO] (Solomon Is-SW Pac)	Thermal Feature of NONDA	0505-04=
PULAR (Chile-N)	Stratovolcs (None) Holocene	**1505-105**
PULASARI [PULOSARI] (Java)	Stratovolc of DANAU COMPLEX	0603-01=
PULAU WEH (Sumatra)	Stratovolc (None) Fumarolic	**0601-01=**
PULE (Samoa-SW Pacific)	Cone of SAVAI'I	0404-04=
PULEA (Samoa-SW Pacific)	Cone of SAVAI'I	0404-04=
PULO (Luzon-Philippines)	Synonym of TAAL	0703-07=
PULO WEH (Sumatra)	Synonym of PULAU WEH	0601-01=
PULOSARI (Java)	Stratovolc of DANAU COMPLEX	0603-01=
PULU BETAH (Lesser Sunda Is)	Synonym of TARA, BATU	0604-26=
PULU KAMBING II (PULU KOMBA) (Lesser	Synonym of TARA, BATU	0604-26=
PULU WEH (Sumatra)	Synonym of PULAU WEH	0601-01=
PULULAGUA (Ecuador)	Caldera (2, -0445) Radiocarbon	**1502-011**
PULULAHUA (Ecuador)	Synonym of PULULAGUA	1502-011
PULVERMAAR (Germany)	Maar of WEST EIFEL VOLC FIELD	0100-01-
PUMA RANGA, CERRO (Peru)	Cone of ANDAHUA VALLEY	1504-002
PUMAS, LOS (Chile-S)	Crater of OSORNO	1508-01=
PUMICE PIT DOME (US-California)	Dome of MONO CRATERS	1203-12-
PUMICE STONE MOUNTAIN (US-California)	Cone of MEDICINE LAKE	1203-02-
PUMPKIN HILL (Honduras)	Cone of UTILA ISLAND	1403-16-
PUNA (Samoa-SW Pacific)	Cone of SAVAI'I	0404-04=
PUNATA (Chile-N)	Synonym of GUALLATIRI	1505-02=
PUNCHBOWL (US-California)	Dome of MONO CRATERS	1203-12-
PUNCHBOWL, THE (W Indies)	Crater of ST. CATHERINE	1600-17=
PUNDUTAN N & S (Java)	Craters of LAWU	0603-26=
PUNG (New Guinea-NE of)	Crater of UMBOI	0501-06=
PUNTA DEL'ARCO (Italy)	Vent of PANTELLERIA	0101-071
PUNTA DELLA CANNUCCIA (Italy)	Cone of ISCHIA	0101-03=
PUNTA GORDA (Nicaragua)	Cone of CONCEPCION	1404-12=
PUNTA IMPERATORE (Italy)	Crater of ISCHIA	0101-03=
PUNTA LA SCROFA (Italy)	Cone of ISCHIA	0101-03=
PUNTA MARMOLITE (Italy)	Dome of CAMPI FLEGREI	0101-01=
PUNTA OAXACA (Mexico-Is)	Dome of BARCENA	1401-02=
PUNTA SERRA (Italy)	Tuff ring of CAMPI FLEGREI	0101-01=
PUNTA TOSCA (Mexico-Is)	Dome of SOCORRO	1401-021
PUNTA TRACINO (Italy)	Vent of PANTELLERIA	0101-071
PUNTA VINCENTE ROCA (Galapagos)	Tuff cone of ECUADOR, VOLCAN	1503-011
PUNTA ZACATEPEQUE (El Salvador)	Dome of ILOPANGO	1403-06=
PUNTAS NEGRAS, VOLCAN (Chile-N)	Stratovolc of CORDON DE PUNTAS NEG	1505-102
PUNTEAGUDO, CERRO (Chile-C)	Synonym of PUNTIGUIDO-CORDON CENI	1507-16-
PUNTIAGUDO, CERRO (Mexico)	Cone of SAN MARTIN, VOLCAN DE	1401-11=
PUNTIGUIDO-CORDON CENIZOS (Chile-C)	Stratovolc (1, 1850) Historical	**1507-16-**
PUPANDJI [PUPANJI] (Sumatra)	Cone of GEUREUDONG, BUR NI	0601-04=
PUPUKE, LAKE (New Zealand)	Tuff ring of AUCKLAND FIELD	0401-02=
PUQUINTICA, CERRO (Chile-N)	Stratovolc of ARINTICA, VOLCAN	1505-023
PURACE (Colombia)	Stratovolcs (25, 1977) Historical	**1501-06=**
PURAHILLA (PURAHUILLE) (Chile-S)	Synonym of OSORNO	1508-01=
PURAKKANGINAN (Lesser Sunda Is)	Crater of BATUR	0604-01=
PURAKKAUHAN (Lesser Sunda Is)	Crater of BATUR	0604-01=
PURAKNJA, BUKIT (Lesser Sunda Is)	Cone of BATUR	0604-01=
PURARRAHUE (Chile-S)	Synonym of OSORNO	1508-01=
PURAU (Vanuatu-SW Pacific)	Cone of KUWAE	0507-07=
PURCHAS HILL (New Zealand)	Cone of AUCKLAND FIELD	0401-02=
PUREORA (New Zealand)	Dome of MAROA	0401-061
PURERUA (New Zealand)	Cone of KAIKOHE-BAY OF ISLANDS	0401-01=
PURICO COMPLEX (Chile-N)	Stratovolcs (None) Holocene	**1505-094**
PURKHOLAR (Iceland-W)	Cone of SNAEFELLSJOKULL	1700-01=
PURPLE (Alaska Peninsula)	Synonym of BLACK PEAK	1102-08-
PURRUMBETE, LAKE (Australia)	Maar of NEWER VOLCANICS PROV	0509-01-
PURVINE MESA (US-New Mexico)	Fissure vent of RATON-CLAYTON	1210-04-
PUSUKBUKIT (Sumatra)	Stratovolc of TOBA	0601-09=
PUTAHI (New Zealand)	Dome of KAIKOHE-BAY OF ISLANDS	0401-01=
PUTANA (Chile-N)	Stratovolc (2, 1972) Historical	**1505-09=**
PUTAS, CERRO (Chile-N)	Dome of PURICO COMPLEX	1505-094
PUTIH, KAWAH (Java)	Crater of PATUHA	0603-07=
PUTING LUPA E & SE (Luzon-Philippines)	Thermal Features of MAQUILING	0703-06=
PUTRI, GUNUNG (Java)	Cone of GUNTUR	0603-13=
PUU, PUY (Hawaiian and French for HILL) see proper name (e.g. HUALALAI, PUU)		
PUULENA (Hawaiian Is)	Pit crater of KILAUEA	1302-01-
PUYEHUE (Chile-C)	Stratovolc (None) Holocene	**1507-15=**
PUYUHUAPI (Chile-S)	Cinder cones (None) Holocene	**1508-054**
PUYULEK (Alaska Peninsula)	Synonym of UGASHIK-PEULIK	1102-13A
PYRAMID (Canada)	Dome of EDZIZA	1200-06-
PYRAMID MOUNTAIN (Canada)	Cone of WELLS GRAY-CLEARWATER	1200-15-
PYRE PEAK (Aleutian Is)	Stratovolc of SEGUAM	1101-18-

Q

NAME (Subregion)	Type (Eruption Total, Most Recent) Status . . . Relation to NAMED VOLCANO	NUMBER
QAL'EH HASAN ALI (Iran)	Maars (None) Holocene?	**0302-02-**
QIANGBAQIAN (China-W)	Shield of UNNAMED	1004-04-
QIDR, JABAL (Arabia-W)	Stratovolc of KHAYBAR, HARRAT	0301-06=
QIXINGLING (SE Asia)	Cone of LEIZHOU BANDAO	0705-01-
QIXINGSHAN (Taiwan)	Cone of DATUN GROUP	0801-032
QOL, JABAL (Arabia-S)	Crater of ARHAB, HARRA OF	0301-09-
QUALIBOU (W Indies)	Caldera (1, 1766) Historical	**1600-14=**
QUANSHUIGOU (China-W)	Cone of KUNLUN VOLC GROUP	1004-03-
QUATRE GUEULES (Indian O.-W)	Crater of FOURNAISE, PITON DE LA	0303-02=
QUEBRADA DEL AZUFRE GRANDE	Thermal Feature of ANTISANA	1502-03=
QUEBRADA SECA (Colombia)	Caldera of BRAVO, CERRO	1501-011
QUECHUCABI OF OVALLE (Chile-S)	Synonym of MINCHINMAVIDA	1508-04=
QUEEN MARY (Atlantic-S)	Cone of TRISTAN DA CUNHA	1806-01=
QUEEN'S PARK (W Indies)	Crater of ST. CATHERINE	1600-17=
QUEIMADO, CERRO (Azores)	Dome of AGUA DE PAU	1802-09=
QUELLAIPE (QUELLAYPE) (Chile-S)	Synonym of CALBUCO	1508-02=
QUEMADA DE ORZOLA, LA (Canary Is)	Crater of LANZAROTE	1803-06-
QUEMADA, MONTANA (Canary Is)	Cone of FUERTEVENTURA	1803-05-
QUEMADA, MONTANA [CALDERA RAJADA]	Crater of LANZAROTE	1803-06-
QUEMADA, MONTANA [TACANDE] (Canary	Cone of LA PALMA	1803-01-
QUEMADAS, ISLAS (El Salvador)	Dome of ILOPANGO	1403-06=
QUEMADAS, LAS CALDERAS (Canary Is)	Crater of LANZAROTE	1803-06-
QUEMADAS, LOS (Costa Rica)	Thermal Feature of TENORIO GROUP	1405-031
QUEMADO, CERRO (Bolivia)	Synonym of SACABAYA, VOLCAN DE	1505-022
QUEMADO, CERRO (Guatemala)	Dome of ALMOLONGA	1402-04=
QUEMADO, VOLCAN DE EL (Canary Is)	Crater of LANZAROTE	1803-06-
QUEMADO [RININAHUE] (Chile-C)	Maar of CARRAN-LOS VENADOS	1507-14=
QUEMADOS, CERRO DE (Costa Rica)	Cone of IRAZU	1405-06=
QUEMADOS, CERROS [ISLAS QUEMADAS]	Dome of ILOPANGO	1403-06=
QUESTRODUGUN (Chile-C)	Synonym of SOLLIPULLI	1507-111
QUETENA (Bolivia)	Fissure vent (None) Holocene?	**1505-074**
QUETRODUGON (Chile-C)	Synonym of SOLLIPULLI	1507-111
QUETRUPE (Chile-S)	Synonym of OSORNO	1508-01=
QUETRUPILLAN (Chile-C)	Caldera (1, 1872) Historical	**1507-121**
QUETZALTENANGO, VOLCAN DE [C. QUEM	Dome of ALMOLONGA	1402-04=
QUEZALTEPEQUE (Guatemala)	Unknown (None) Holocene	**1402-21-**
QUEZALTEPEQUE [BOQUERON, EL]	Stratovolc of SAN SALVADOR	1403-05=
QUICK-SMAN-IK (US-Washington)	Synonym of BAKER	1201-01=
QUILATOA (Ecuador)	Synonym of QUILOTOA	1502-06=
QUILL, THE (W Indies)	Stratovolc (3, 0400) Radiocarbon	**1600-02=**
QUILLAICAHUE (Chile-C)	Crater of CALLAQUI	1507-091
QUILOTOA (Ecuador)	Caldera (1, 1050) Radiocarbon	**1502-06=**
QUIMSACHATA (Peru)	Lava dome (None) Holocene	**1504-004**
QUINCEO (Mexico)	Cone of MICHOACAN-GUANAJUATO	1401-06=
QUINISTAQUILLAS (Peru)	Synonym of HUAYNAPUTINA	1504-03=
QUIROTOA (Ecuador)	Synonym of QUILOTOA	1502-06=
QUITRALPILLAN (Chile-C)	Synonym of VILLARRICA	1507-12=
QUIZAPU (Chile-C)	Crater of AZUL, CERRO [QUIZAPU]	1507-06=
QUMMATAIN (Arabia-W)	Cone of YAR, JABAL	0301-08-

R

NAME (Subregion)	Type (Eruption Total, Most Recent) Status . . . Relation to NAMED VOLCANO	NUMBER
RABATANA [RABALANAKAIA] (New Britain)	Cone of RABAUL	0502-14=
RABAUL (New Britain-SW Pac)	Pyrocl shield (11, 1943) Historical	**0502-14=**
RABBIT EARS (US-New Mexico)	Cone of RATON-CLAYTON	1210-04-
RABBIT MOUNTAIN (US-New Mexico)	Dome of VALLES CALDERA	1210-03-
RABOT (W Indies)	Dome of QUALIBOU	1600-14=
RACO, VOLCA (Spain)	Cone of OLOT VOLC FIELD	0100-03-
RADERSBERG (Germany)	Cone of WEST EIFEL VOLC FIELD	0100-01-
RADJABASA (RADJOBASO) (Sumatra)	Synonym of RAJABASA	0601-29=
RAGANG (Mindanao-Philippines)	Stratovolc (9, 1915) Historical	**0701-06=**
RAGGED JACK (Aleutian Is)	Synonym of ISANOTSKI	1101-37-
RAGGED TOP (Aleutian Is)	Cone of SEMISOPOCHNOI	1101-06-
RAHA, HARRAT ER- (Arabia-W)	Synonym of RAHAT, HARRAT	0301-07=
RAHA, HARRAT ER- (Arabia-W)	Synonym of RAHAH, HARRAT AR	0301-01=
RAHAH, HARRAT AR (Arabia-W)	Volc field (None) Anthropology	**0301-01=**
RAHAT, HARRAT (Arabia-W)	Volc field (2, 1256) Historical	**0301-07=**
RAHOUM [DALAHUM] (Vanuatu-SW Pacific)	Cone of AMBRYM	0507-04=
RAIKOKE (Kurile Is)	Stratovolc (3, 1924) Historical	**0900-25=**
RAIKOKETO (RAIKOKU) (Kurile Is)	Synonym of RAIKOKE	0900-25=
RAINBOW MTN [MAUNGAKAKARAMEA]	Cone of OKATAINA	0401-05=
RAINIER (US-Washington)	Stratovolc (12, 1825) Dendrochronology	**1201-03-**
RAIRAINDREKETI (Fiji Is-SW Pacific)	Cone of TAVEUNI	0405-01-
RAJABASA (Sumatra)	Stratovolc (None) Fumarolic	**0601-29=**
RAJADA, CALDERA (Canary Is)	Crater of LANZAROTE	1803-06-
RAJADA, MONTANA (Canary Is)	Cone of TENERIFE	1803-03-
RAJADA, MONTANA [CALDERA RAJADA]	Crater of LANZAROTE	1803-06-
RAJOBASO (Sumatra)	Synonym of RAJABASA	0601-29=
RAKATA (Indonesia)	Stratovolc of KRAKATAU	0602-00=
RAKER PEAK (US-Calif)	Cone of LASSEN VOLC CENTER	1203-08-
RAKHOHKKO (Kurile Is)	Synonym of RAIKOKE	0900-25=
RAKIHAN (Sumatra)	Cone of BESAR, GUNUNG	0601-25=
RALKOKESHIMA (Kurile Is)	Synonym of RAIKOKE	0900-25=
RALUAN [VULCAN] (New Britain-SW Pac)	Pumice cone of RABAUL	0502-14=
RAMIREZ, CERRO (El Salvador)	Cone of SAN VICENTE	1403-07=
RANA, LAGUNA SECA DE LA (El Salvador)	Crater of VERDE, LAGUNA	1403-01=
RANAKAH, GUNUNG (Lesser Sunda Is)	Lava domes (2, 1991) Historical	**0604-071**
RANAS, CERRO LAS (El Salvador)	Stratovolc of VERDE, LAGUNA	1403-01=
RANAU (Sumatra)	Caldera (None) Holocene?	**0601-251**
RANAU PAKIS (Java)	Cone of SEMERU	0603-30=
RANCAGUA (Chile-C)	Synonym of TINGUIRIRICA	1507-03=
RANCO (Chile-C)	Synonym of PUYEHUE	1507-15=
RANDAZZO, CUDDIA (Italy)	Cone of PANTELLERIA	0101-071
RANGATAUA LAKES (New Zealand)	Maar of RUAPEHU	0401-10=
RANGITAHUA (Kermadec Is)	Crater of RAOUL ISLAND	0402-03=
RANGITOTO (New Zealand)	Cone of AUCKLAND FIELD	0401-02=
RANGITUKUA (New Zealand)	Dome of TAUPO	0401-07=
RANGKONG (Java)	Dome of DANAU COMPLEX	0603-01=
RANO AROI (Pacific-C)	Cone of EASTER ISLAND	1303-08-
RANO KAU (Pacific-C)	Shield of EASTER ISLAND	1303-08-

NAME (Subregion)	Type (Eruption Total, Most Recent) Status / Relation to NAMED VOLCANO	NUMBER
RANO KULO (Sulawesi-Indonesia)	Thermal Feature of TONDANO CALDERA	0606-07-
RANO RANDANG (Sulawesi-Indonesia)	Thermal Feature of TONDANO CALDERA	0606-07-
RANO RARAKU (Pacific-C)	Cone of EASTER ISLAND	1303-08-
RANO SAPET (Sulawesi-Indonesia)	Thermal Feature of TONDANO CALDERA	0606-07-
RANOE DAROENGAN [RANU DARUNGAN]	Cone of SEMERU	0603-30=
RANTE (Java)	Stratovolc of IJEN	0603-35=
RANTOP, MT. (Vanuatu-SW Pacific)	Cone of TRAITOR'S HEAD	0507-09=
RANU (Halmahera-Indonesia)	Caldera of TODOKO-RANU	0608-05=
RANU DARUNGAN (Java)	Cone of SEMERU	0603-30=
RAOENG (Java)	Synonym of RAUNG	0603-34=
RAOUL ISLAND (Kermadec Is)	Stratovolc (14, 1965) Historical	**0402-03=**
RAPA NUI (Pacific-C)	Synonym of EASTER ISLAND	1303-08-
RAPANUI (New Zealand)	Dome of MAROA	0401-061
RAPOGI (Africa-E)	Cone of HOMA MOUNTAIN	0202-07=
RASA, CALDEIRA (Azores)	Crater of FLORES	1802-001
RASA, LAGOA (Azores)	Pumice ring of SETE CIDADES	1802-08=
RASBERRY HILLS (W Indies)	Dome of SOUFRIERE HILLS	1600-05=
RASCHLENENNY (Kamchatka)	Dome of BEZYMIANNY	1000-25=
RASHID, HARRAT (Arabia-W)	Blank of RAHAT, HARRAT	0301-07=
RASHOWA (Kurile Is)	Synonym of RASSHUA	0900-22=
RASSHUA (Kurile Is)	Stratovolc (2, 1957) Historical	**0900-22=**
RASSOSHINA (Kamchatka)	Shield of TITILA	1000-56-
RASUYACU (Ecuador)	Dome of ILINIZA	1502-041
RASYOVA (Kurile Is)	Synonym of RASSHUA	0900-22=
RATAS, LAS (Mexico)	Cone of HOLOTEPEC	1401-07-
RATASCHENNY (Kamchatka)	Cone of TOLBACHIK	1000-24=
RATIENG (Africa-E)	Cone of HOMA MOUNTAIN	0202-07=
RATON-CLAYTON (US-New Mexico)	Volc field (1, -5300) Tephrochronology	**1210-04-**
RATON MESA VOLC FIELD (US-New Mexico	Synonym of RATON-CLAYTON	1210-04-
RATU (Java)	Crater of GEDE	0603-06=
RATU, KAWAH (Java)	Thermal Feature of SALAK	0603-05=
RATU, KAWAH (Java)	Crater of TANGKUBANPARAHU	0603-09=
RAUDAHALSAR (Iceland-W)	Cone of LJOSUFJOLL	1700-03=
RAUDAHRAUN (Iceland-S)	Fissure vent of EYJAFJOLL	1702-02=
RAUDAKULA (Iceland-W)	Cone of LJOSUFJOLL	1700-03=
RAUDAKULA-HORGSHOLTSHRAUN	Cone of LJOSUFJOLL	1700-03=
RAUDAKULA-SVELGARHRAUN (Iceland-W)	Cone of LJOSUFJOLL	1700-03=
RAUDAKULAR (Iceland-W)	Cone of LYSUHOLL	1700-02=
RAUDFOSSAHRAUN (Iceland-S)	Crater row of VATNAFJOLL	1702-06=
RAUDHALSAR (Iceland-W)	Cone of LJOSUFJOLL	1700-03=
RAUDHOLAR (Iceland-NE)	Fissure vent of GRIMSVOTN	1703-01=
RAUDHOLAR (Iceland-NE)	Fissure vent of FREMRINAMUR	1703-07=
RAUDHOLAR (Iceland-SW)	Crater row of REYKJANES	1701-02=
RAUDHOLAR (Iceland-SW)	Crater of GRIMSNES	1701-06=
RAUDHOLAR (Iceland-W)	Cone of SNAEFELLSJOKULL	1700-01=
RAUDHOLL (Iceland-NE)	Crater row of GRIMSVOTN	1703-01=
RAUDHOLL-HAFNARFJORDUR (Iceland)	Crater row of KRISUVIK	1701-03=
RAUDIBOTN (Iceland-S)	Crater of KATLA	1702-03=
RAUDIMELUR (Iceland-SW)	Crater row of KRISUVIK	1701-03=
RAUDKEMBINGUR (Iceland-S)	Fissure vent of HEKLA	1702-07=
RAUDKOLLAR (Iceland-S)	Fissure vent of HEKLA	1702-07=
RAUDOLDUHRAUN (Iceland-S)	Crater row of VATNAFJOLL	1702-06=
RAUDOLDUR (Iceland-S)	Crater of HEKLA	1702-07=
RAUDUBJALLAR (Iceland-S)	Fissure vent of HEKLA	1702-07=
RAUDUBORGIR (Iceland-NE)	Fissure vent of FREMRINAMUR	1703-07=
RAUDUHNUKAGIGIR (Iceland-SW)	Crater row of BRENNISTEINSFJOLL	1701-04=
RAUKOKE (Kurile Is)	Synonym of RAIKOKE	0900-25=
RAUNG (Java)	Stratovolc (54, 1993) Historical	**0603-34=**
RAUSU (Hokkaido-Japan)	Stratovolc (None) Holocene	**0805-082**
RAUSU-DAKE (Kurile Is)	Synonym of MENDELEEV	0900-02=
RAWON (Java)	Synonym of RAUNG	0603-34=
RAY MOUNTAIN (Canada)	Fissure vent of WELLS GRAY-CLEARWAT	1200-15-
RAYHUEN (Chile-C)	Cone of ANTILLANCA GROUP	1507-153
RAYKOKE (Kurile Is)	Synonym of RAIKOKE	0900-25=
RAYMOND, PUYS (Indian O.-W)	Cone of FOURNAISE, PITON DE LA	0303-02=
RAZLATY (Kamchatka)	Dome of BEZYMIANNY	1000-25=
RAZRUSHENNYI [RASCHLENENNY]	Dome of BEZYMIANNY	1000-25=
RAZVAL, MT. (Kurile Is)	Cone of RASSHUA	0900-22=
RAZVALENNY (Kamchatka)	Stratovolc of PAUZHETKA	1000-022
READING PEAK (US-Calif)	Dome of LASSEN VOLC CENTER	1203-08-
REALENCO, EL [CERRITO BALASTRERA]	Cone of SAN SALVADOR	1403-05=
REAMUR, MT. (New Guinea-NE of)	Stratovolc of LONG ISLAND	0501-05=
REBANADA, CALDERA DE (Canary Is)	Crater of FUERTEVENTURA	1803-05-
REBEKE, JEBEL (Arabia-S)	Tuff cone of HAYLAN, JABAL	0301-11-
REBUNSHIRI (Kurile Is)	Cone of GROZNY GROUP	0900-07=
RECHERCHE, LA (Kermadec Is)	Synonym of RAOUL ISLAND	0402-03=
RECHESCHNOI (Aleutian Is)	Stratovolc (None) Holocene	**1101-28-**
RECK (Greece)	Dome of SANTORINI	0102-04=
RECLUS (Chile-S)	Stratovolc ? (1, -1830) Radiocarbon	**1508-063**
RED BUTTE (US-Washington)	Cone of ADAMS	1201-04-
RED CAP MOUNTAIN (US-California)	Cone of MEDICINE LAKE	1203-02-
RED CINDER BUTTE (US-Oregon)	Cone of CINNAMON BUTTE	1202-15-
RED CONE (US-Nevada)	Cone of CRATER FLAT	1206-03-
RED CONE (US-Oregon)	Vent of CRATER LAKE	1202-16-
RED CONES (Hawaiian Is)	Cone of KILAUEA	1302-01-
RED CONES (US-California)	Cinder cones (None) Holocene	**1203-15-**
RED CRATER (New Zealand)	Crater of TONGARIRO	0401-08=
RED CRATER (US-Oregon)	Cone of BACHELOR	1202-09-
RED HILL (Galapagos)	Cone of SANTA CRUZ	1503-091
RED HILL (Hawaiian Is)	Cone of HALEAKALA	1302-06-
RED HILL (US-Calif)	Cone of GOLDEN TROUT CREEK	1203-17-
RED HILL (US-California)	Cone of MEDICINE LAKE	1203-02-
RED ISLAND (Indian O.-S)	Cone of HEARD	0304-01=
RED MOUNTAIN (US-New Mexico)	Cone of RATON-CLAYTON	1210-04-
RED MOUNTAIN (US-Washington)	Cone of INDIAN HEAVEN	1201-07-
RED MOUNTAIN-BIG LAVA BED (US-Wash)	Synonym of INDIAN HEAVEN	1201-07-
RED MOUNTAIN [MT. PRICE] (Canada)	Stratovolc of GARIBALDI LAKE	1200-19-
RED MOUNTAIN [OL DOINYO NYUKIE]	Stratovolc of SUSWA	0202-11=
RED ROCK (Australia)	Maar of NEWER VOLCANICS PROV	0509-01-
RED ROCK HILL (US-California)	Cone of TWIN BUTTES	1203-05-
RED SHALE BUTTE (US-California)	Cone of MEDICINE LAKE	1203-02-
REDCLOUD (US-Oregon)	Vent of CRATER LAKE	1202-16-
REDONDO, CERRO (Chile-C)	Cinder cones (1, -5050) Tephrochronology	**1507-113**
REDONDO, CERRO (Guatemala)	Cone of CHINGO VOLC FIELD	1402-15-
REDONDO, CERRO (Guatemala)	Cone of CUILAPA-BARBARENA	1402-111
REDONDO DE LA CRUZ, CERRO (Costa Ri	Cone of BARVA	1405-05=
REDONDO PEAK (US-New Mexico)	Dome of VALLES CALDERA	1210-03-
REDONDO, VOLCAN (Chile-C)	Cone of SOLLIPULLI	1507-111
REDOUBT (Alaska-SW)	Stratovolc (14, 1990) Historical	**1103-03-**
REICHO-SEN (Kyushu-Japan)	Thermal Feature of TSURUMI	0802-13=
REINI (Bougainville-SW Pac)	Stratovolc of BILLY MITCHELL	0505-011
REJO TE KAVACHI (Solomon Is-SW Pac)	Synonym of KAVACHI	0505-06=
RELIBUENTU (Chile-S)	Synonym of HUEQUI	1508-03=
RENDIJA, CERRO (US-New Mexico)	Cone of ZUNI-BANDERA	1210-02-
RENIHUE (Chile-C)	Synonym of MOCHO-CHOSHUENCO	1507-13=
RENON, EL (Nicaragua)	Cone of MASAYA	1404-10=
REPARO, CERRO EL (Guatemala)	Cone of SUCHITAN VOLC FIELD	1402-17-
REPAS, VOLCA (Spain)	Cone of OLOT VOLC FIELD	0100-03-
REPOROA (New Zealand)	Caldera (1, 1180) Tephrochronology	**0401-06-**
REREWHAKAAITU (New Zealand)	Tuff cone of OKATAINA	0401-05=
REREWHAKAAITU (New Zealand)	Fissure vent of OKATAINA	0401-05=
RESAGO, VOLCAN (Chile-C)	Cinder cone (None) Holocene	**1507-066**
RESCHUELOS, EL (US-New Mexico)	Dome of VALLES CALDERA	1210-03-
RESOLANA, LA (Chile-C)	Cone of AZUL, CERRO [QUIZAPU]	1507-06=
RESTINGA (Canary Is)	Cone of HIERRO	1803-02-
RETANA CALDERA (Guatemala)	Caldera of SUCHITAN VOLC FIELD	1402-17-
RETCHECHNOI (Aleutian Is)	Synonym of RECHESCHNOI	1101-28-
RETES, CERRO (Costa Rica)	Cone of IRAZU	1405-06=
RETIRO, CERRO EL (El Salvador)	Cone of SANTA ANA	1403-02=
RETU, MAUNGA (Pacific-C)	Cone of EASTER ISLAND	1303-08-
REUNION, VOLCAN DE LA (Indian O.-W)	Synonym of FOURNAISE, PITON DE LA	0303-02=
REUSCH PIT (Africa-E)	Crater of KILIMANJARO	0202-15=
REVENTADOR (Ecuador)	Stratovolc (24, 1976) Historical	**1502-01=**
REVENTADOR, EL (Ecuador)	Synonym of REVENTADOR	1502-01=
REVILLAGIGEDO ISLAND (Alaska-SE)	Cinder cones (None) Holocene?	**1105-07-**
REVIRE NGANGA (Africa-C)	Synonym of NYIRAGONGO	0203-03=
REYDARVATNSHRAUN (Iceland-S)	Fissure vent of HEKLA	1702-07=
REYKJAFELLSGIGIR (Iceland-SW)	Crater row of HENGILL	1701-05=
REYKJANES (Iceland-SW)	Crater rows (5, 1227) Historical	**1701-02=**
REYKJANESHRYGGUR (Iceland-SW)	Subm volcs (17, 1970) Historical	1701-01=
REYNIFELLSHRAUN (Iceland-S)	Crater row of VATNAFJOLL	1702-06=
RF CRATER (New Zealand)	Former crater of WHITE ISLAND	0401-04=
RHODODENDRON CONE (Alaska-W)	Cone of IMURUK LAKE	1104-02-
RIANG KOTANG (Lesser Sunda Is)	Fumarole fld (None) Fumarolic	**0604-21=**
RICCO, MONTE (Italy)	Cone of ETNA	0101-06=
RICHARD-FOY, MT. (Indian O.-S)	Cone of COCHONS, ILE AUX	0304-06-
RICHMOND, MT. (New Zealand)	Cone of AUCKLAND FIELD	0401-02=
RICHTHOFEN [GALLOSEULO] (New Britain)	Stratovolc of HARGY	0502-10=
RICO, CERRO DE MONTE (Guatemala)	Cone of IPALA VOLC FIELD	1402-19-
RIDGE (Canada)	Cone of EDZIZA	1200-06-
RIDGE DOME (New Zealand)	Dome of OKATAINA	0401-05=
RIDUBIDUBINA, LAKE (New Guinea)	Cone of VICTORY	0503-03=
RIMDO (Korea)	Dome of HALLA	1006-04-
RINATU, MONTE (Italy)	Cone of ETNA	0101-06=
RINCON DE LA CERCA, EL (Canary Is)	Cone of HIERRO	1803-02-
RINCON DE LA VIEJA (Costa Rica)	Complx volc (21, 1992) Historical	**1405-02=**
RINCON, EL (Mexico)	Maar of MICHOACAN-GUANAJUATO	1401-06=
RINCONADA CERRO BAYO (Chile-N)	Cone of BAYO, CERRO	1505-122
RINDJANI (Lesser Sunda Is)	Synonym of RINJANI	0604-03=
RINGGIT (Java)	Synonym of RAUNG	0603-34=
RINGGIT, GUNUNG (Java)	Cone of IJEN	0603-35=
RINGGIT, GUNUNG (Java)	Stratovolc of ARJUNO-WELIRANG	0603-29=
RINGO BUTTE (US-Oregon)	Shield of DAVIS LAKE	1202-10-
RINIHUE (Chile-C)	Synonym of MOCHO-CHOSHUENCO	1507-13=
RININAHUE (Chile-C)	Maar of CARRAN-LOS VENADOS	1507-14=
RINJANI (Lesser Sunda Is)	Stratovolc (12, 1966) Historical	**0604-03=**
RIO COLORADO (Chile-C)	Pleistocene caldera of SAN PEDRO	1507-063
RIO CORBORE (Italy)	Crater of ISCHIA	0101-03=
RIO CUARTO, LAGUNA (Costa Rica)	Maar of POAS	1405-04=
RIO CURINHAUS (Nicaragua)	Synonym of BLUE, VOLCAN	1404-14-
RIONE DELLE MOFETE [MOFETE] (Italy)	Crater of CAMPI FLEGREI	0101-01=
RISHIRI (Hokkaido-Japan)	Dome of KUTCHARO	0805-08=
RISHIRI (Hokkaido-Japan)	Stratovolc (1, -3250) Radiocarbon	**0805-041**
RISIRI (Hokkaido-Japan)	Synonym of RISHIRI	0805-041
RISIRI [RISHIRI] (Hokkaido-Japan)	Dome of KUTCHARO	0805-08=
RITTER (Galapagos)	Cone of FLOREANA	1503-10=
RITTER ISLAND (New Guinea-NE of)	Stratovolc (6, 1974) Historical	**0501-07=**
RITTMANN, MONTE (Italy)	Cone of ETNA	0101-06=
RIVEROLL, CERRO (Mexico)	Cone of SAN QUINTIN VOLC FIELD	1401-002
RJUPNADYNGJUR (Iceland-SW)	Shield of BRENNISTEINSFJOLL	1701-04=
ROA (Tonga-SW Pacific)	Synonym of LATE	0403-09=
ROBERT MEYER (Africa-W)	Crater of CAMEROON, MT.	0204-01=
ROBERTS MOUNTAIN (Alaska-W)	Cone of NUNIVAK ISLAND	1104-06-
ROBERTSON, MT. (New Zealand)	Cone of AUCKLAND FIELD	0401-02=
ROBERTSON'S HILL (Australia)	Cone of NEWER VOLCANICS PROV	0509-01-
ROBINSON CRUSOE (Chile-Is)	Shields (1, 1835) Historical	**1506-02=**
ROBINSON MOUNTAIN (US-New Mexico)	Cone of RATON-CLAYTON	1210-04-
ROBLEDO (Argentina)	Caldera (None) Holocene	**1505-128**
ROCA CHALLENGER (Mexico-Is)	Dome of BARCENA	1401-02=
ROCA NEGRA, VOLCA (Spain)	Cone of OLOT VOLC FIELD	0100-03-
ROCARD (Society Is-C Pac)	Submarine (None) Seismicity	**1303-04-**
ROCAS TRINIDAD (Mexico-Is)	Dome of BARCENA	1401-02=
ROCCA DE PAPA (Italy)	Cone of ALBANO, MONTE	0101-004
ROCCHE ROSSE (Italy)	Vent of LIPARI	0101-041
ROCHE'S BLUFF (W Indies)	Dome of SOUFRIERE HILLS	1600-05=
ROCHE'S MOUNTAIN [PERCHE'S MTN.]	Dome of SOUFRIERE HILLS	1600-05=
ROCK MESA (US-Oregon)	Dome of SOUTH SISTER	1202-08-
ROCKESKYLL-SW (Germany)	Tuff ring of WEST EIFEL VOLC FIELD	0100-01-
ROCKY BUTTE (US-Oregon)	Cone of JORDAN CRATERS	1202-19-
RODDE, PUY DE LA (France)	Cone of CHAINE DES PUYS	0100-02-
RODEOS, MONTANA (Canary Is)	Crater of LANZAROTE	1803-06-
RODNEY, MT. (W Indies)	Dome of ST. CATHERINE	1600-17=
ROEANG (Sangihe Is-Indonesia)	Synonym of RUANG	0607-01=
ROEMENGAN (Sulawesi-Indonesia)	Synonym of MAHAWU	0606-11=
ROEWANG (Sangihe Is-Indonesia)	Synonym of RUANG	0607-01=
ROFUBODI (Iceland-S)	Submarine vent of VESTMANNAEYJAR	1702-01=
ROGERS HEAD (Indian O.-S)	Cone of HEARD	0304-01=
ROJA, CALDERILLA DE (Canary Is)	Crater of FUERTEVENTURA	1803-05-
ROJA DE MAZO, CALDERA (Canary Is)	Crater of LANZAROTE	1803-06-
ROKA PIEK (Lesser Sunda Is)	Synonym of INIERIE	0604-08=
ROKATINDA [ROKATENDA] (Lesser Sunda)	Crater of PALUWEH	0604-15=
ROKKA PEAK (Lesser Sunda Is)	Synonym of INIERIE	0604-08=
ROKKANNON-MI-IKE (Kyushu-Japan)	Crater of KIRISHIMA	0802-09=
ROLLES PEAK (New Zealand)	Stratovolc of MAROA	0401-061
ROLLIZOS (Chile-S)	Cone of CAYUTE-LA VIGUERIA	1508-021
ROMANI HILL (Africa-E)	Dome of NYAMBENI HILLS	0202-056
ROMANO (Italy)	Crater of CAMPI FLEGREI	0101-01=
ROMANOVKA (Kamchatka)	Stratovolc (None) Holocene	**1000-34-**
ROMBONGAN, GUNUNG (Lesser Sunda Is)	Dome of RINJANI	0604-03=
ROMO, VOLCAN (Mexico)	Maar of PINACATE PEAKS	1401-001
ROND, PITON (Indian O.-W)	Cone of FOURNAISE, PITON DE LA	0303-02=
RONGO (Africa-E)	Cone of HOMA MOUNTAIN	0202-07=
ROODJA [ROOJA] (Lesser Sunda Is)	Cone of IYA	0604-11=
ROOKE ISLAND (New Guinea-NE of)	Synonym of UMBOI	0501-06=

NAME (Subregion)	Type (Eruption Total, Most Recent) Status . . . Relation to NAMED VOLCANO	NUMBER
ROOK'S BAY (Indian O.-S)	Tuff cone of MARION ISLAND	0304-08-
ROQUE DE INFIERNO (Canary Is)	Cone of LANZAROTE	1803-06-
ROQUE GRANDE (Canary Is)	Cone of HIERRO	1803-02-
ROQUILLO, MONTANA DEL	Cone of TENERIFE	1803-03-
ROSARIO, BANOS DEL (Guatemala)	Thermal Feature of ALMOLONGA	1402-04=
ROSARITO VOLC FIELD, EL (Mexico)	Synonym of SAN BORJA VOLC FIELD	1401-007
ROSAS, MONTANA DE LAS (Canary Is)	Cone of HIERRO	1803-02-
ROSKILL, MT. (New Zealand)	Cone of AUCKLAND FIELD	0401-02=
ROSS, MT. (Indian O.-S)	Stratovolc of KERGUELEN ISLANDS	0304-02=
ROSS ROCKS (Indian O.-S)	Tuff cone of PRINCE EDWARD ISLAND	0304-07-
ROSSE, CUDDIE (Italy)	Cone of PANTELLERIA	0101-071
ROSSO, MONTE (Italy)	Cone of VULCANO	0101-05=
ROSSO, MONTE (Italy)	Cone of ETNA	0101-06=
ROSSO, MT. (Italy)	Cone of VULSINI	0101-003
ROSTO DE CAO (Azores)	Tuff cone of UNNAMED	1802-081
ROTA (Nicaragua)	Shield (None) Holocene	**1404-06-**
ROTARO (Italy)	Dome of ISCHIA	0101-03=
ROTOATUA, LAKE (New Zealand)	Crater of OKATAINA	0401-05=
ROTOEHU, LAKE [ROTOMA GEOTHERMAL	Thermal Feature of OKATAINA	0401-05=
ROTOKAKAHI (New Zealand)	Dome of OKATAINA	0401-05=
ROTOKAUA (New Zealand)	Thermal Feature of MAROA	0401-061
ROTOKAWA, LAKE (New Zealand)	Thermal Feature of ROTORUA	0401-042
ROTOKAWA [ROTOKAUA] (New Zealand)	Thermal Feature of MAROA	0401-061
ROTOKAWAU, LAKE (New Zealand)	Crater of OKATAINA	0401-05=
ROTOKOHU (New Zealand)	Dome of OKATAINA	0401-05=
ROTOMA (New Zealand)	Pleistocene caldera of OKATAINA	0401-05=
ROTOMA GEOTHERMAL FIELD (New Zeal)	Thermal Feature of OKATAINA	0401-05=
ROTOMAHANA (New Zealand)	Thermal Feature of OKATAINA	0401-05=
ROTOMAHANA (New Zealand)	Dome of OKATAINA	0401-05=
ROTORUA (New Zealand)	Caldera (None) Pleistocene-Geysers	**0401-042**
ROTORUA GEOTHERMAL FIELD (New Zeal)	Thermal Feature of ROTORUA	0401-042
ROUGE, MORNE (Indian O.-S)	Cone of COCHONS, ILE AUX	0304-06-
ROUGE, MORNE (W Indies)	Cone of PATATES, MORNE	1600-11=
ROUGE, PITON (Indian O.-W)	Cone of FOURNAISE, PITON DE LA	0303-02=
ROUND HEAD (Aleutian Is)	Cone of KANAGA	1101-11-
ROUND HILL (W Indies)	Synonym of QUILL, THE	1600-02=
ROUND MOUNTAIN (Canada)	Vent of GARIBALDI, MT.	1200-20-
ROUND MOUNTAIN (US-California)	Cone of CLEAR LAKE	1203-10-
ROUND TOP (Hawaiian Is)	Cone of KOOLAU	1302-07-
ROUNDHEAD, MT. (Solomon Is-SW Pac)	Cone of GALLEGO	0505-062
ROUNDTOP (Aleutian Is)	Stratovolc (None) Holocene	**1101-38-**
ROUNDTOP MOUNTAIN (US-California)	Cone of CLEAR LAKE	1203-10-
ROUNG (Java)	Synonym of RAUNG	0603-34=
ROUSE (Kurile Is)	Synonym of MENDELEEV	0900-02=
ROYAL SOCIETY RANGE (Antarctica)	Cinder cones (None) Holocene?	**1900-021**
ROYCE (New Zealand)	Crater of WHITE ISLAND	0401-04=
RUAGARE (Africa-C)	Cone of KARISIMBI	0203-04-
RUAHINE SPRINGS (New Zealand)	Thermal Feature of ROTORUA	0401-042
RUAMATA (New Zealand)	Pumice cone of MAYOR ISLAND	0401-021
RUANG (Sangihe Is-Indonesia)	Stratovolc (11, 1949) Historical	**0607-01=**
RUAPAHU (New Zealand)	Synonym of RUAPEHU	0401-10=
RUAPEHU (New Zealand)	Stratovolc (53, 1992) Historical	**0401-10=**
RUAWAHIA (New Zealand)	Dome of OKATAINA	0401-05=
RUBIO, CERRO (US-New Mexico)	Dome of VALLES CALDERA	1210-03-
RUBONA (Africa-C)	Cone of NYIRAGONGO	0203-03=
RUBY (Mariana Is-C Pac)	Submarine (1, 1966) Hydrophonic	**0804-201**
RUBY MOUNTAIN (Canada)	Cinder cones (1, 1898) Historical	**1200-03-**
RUCU PICHINCHA (Ecuador)	Stratovolc of GUAGUA PICHINCHA	1502-02=
RUDAKOV (Kurile Is)	Stratovolc (None) Holocene?	**0900-112**
RUDERBUSCH (Germany)	Cone of WEST EIFEL VOLC FIELD	0100-01-
RUDICH'S CONE (Kamchatka)	Dome of UZON	1000-17=
RUDOLF (New Zealand)	Former crater of WHITE ISLAND	0401-04=
RUEDAS, CERRO LAS (Guatemala)	Cone of IPALA VOLC FIELD	1402-19-
RUGARAMA (Africa-C)	Cone of NYAMURAGIRA	0203-02=
RUGARAMBIRO (Africa-C)	Cone of NYAMURAGIRA	0203-02=
RUHARA (Africa-C)	Cone of KARISIMBI	0203-04-
RUIZ (Colombia)	Stratovolc (18, 1991) Historical	**1501-02=**
RUIZ, NEVADO (Colombia)	Synonym of RUIZ	1501-02=
RUK ISLAND (New Guinea-NE of)	Synonym of UMBOI	0501-06=
RUKO (Kurile Is)	Synonym of EBEKO	0900-38=
RUKONDJA (Africa-C)	Cone of KARISIMBI	0203-04-
RUMBLE I (New Zealand)	Submarine (None) Uncertain	**0401-11-**
RUMBLE II (New Zealand)	Submarine (None) Uncertain	**0401-12-**
RUMBLE III (New Zealand)	Submarine (5, 1986) Hydrophonic	**0401-13-**
RUMBLE IV (New Zealand)	Submarine (None) Fumarolic	**0401-14-**
RUMBLE V (New Zealand)	Submarine (None) Fumarolic	**0401-15-**
RUMENGAN (Sulawesi-Indonesia)	Synonym of MAHAWU	0606-11=
RUMOKA (Africa-C)	Cone of NYAMURAGIRA	0203-02=
RUNGU (Africa-C)	Cone of KARISIMBI	0203-04-
RUNGWE (Africa-E)	Stratovolc (None) Holocene	**0202-166**
RUNU, WOLO (Lesser Sunda Is)	Crater of INIELIKA	0604-09=
RURUI (Kurile Is)	Stratovolc of SMIRNOV	0900-031
RUSA RAJA (RUSA RADJA) (Lesser Sunda	Synonym of PALUWEH	0604-15=
RUSCIELLO, MONTE (Italy)	Crater of CAMPI FLEGREI	0101-01=
RUSEKERE (Africa-C)	Tuff cones (None) Holocene	**0203-001**
RUSH HILL (Alaska-W)	Cone of ST. PAUL ISLAND	1104-07-
RUSHASHU (Africa-C)	Cone of KARISIMBI	0203-04-
RUSHAYO (Africa-C)	Cone of NYIRAGONGO	0203-03=
RUSSEL PEAK (Antarctica)	Synonym of STURGE ISLAND	1900-012
RUTOKE (Africa-C)	Cone of NYIRAGONGO	0203-03=
RWAMISEGA (Africa-C)	Cone of KARISIMBI	0203-04-
RWENKUBA (Africa-C)	Tuff cone of FORT PORTAL FIELD	0203-002
RYOSHI-DAKE (Kyushu-Japan)	Cone of KUJU GROUP	0802-12=
RYOUN-DAKE (Hokkaido-Japan)	Dome of DAISETSU	0805-06=
RYPONKICHA (Kurile Is)	Synonym of USHISHUR	0900-21=
RYUZAN (Honshu-Japan)	Stratovolc of ZAO	0803-19=

S

NAME (Subregion)	Type (Eruption Total, Most Recent) Status . . . Relation to NAMED VOLCANO	NUMBER
SAAR, KAWAH (Java)	Thermal Feature of KAWAHKAMOJANG	0603-12=
SAAT, KAWAH (Java)	Thermal Feature of TALAGABODAS	0603-15=
SABA (W Indies)	Stratovolc (1, 1636) Historical	**1600-01=**
SABANA REDONDA (Costa Rica)	Cone of POAS	1405-04=
SABANCAYA (Peru)	Stratovolcs (5, 1992) Historical	**1504-003**
SABANETAS, LAS [LAGUNA SECA] (Nicarag	Maar of PILAS, LAS	1404-08=
SABINOSA (Canary Is)	Cone of HIERRO	1803-02-
SABOBER (Ethiopia)	Tuff ring of FENTALE	0201-19=
SABOMA (Admiralty Is-SW Pac)	Crater of BALUAN	0500-02-
SABRANA, LA [CERRO ALEGRIA] (El Salv)	Cone of TECAPA	1403-08=
SABU, OL DOINYO (Africa-E)	Cone of NYAMBENI HILLS	0202-056
SACABAYA, VOLCAN DE (Bolivia)	Cinder cone (None) Holocene	**1505-022**
SACHIUSU-DAKE (Kurile Is)	Synonym of BARANSKY	0900-08=
SADDLE BUTTE (US-Oregon)	Volc field (None) Holocene?	**1202-18-**
SADDLE ISLAND (Red Sea)	Shield of ZUBAYR, JEBEL	0201-02=
SADDLE POINT (Indian O.-S)	Cone of HEARD	0304-01=
SAEFELL (Iceland-S)	Tuff ring of VESTMANNAEYJAR	1702-01=
SAFONT, PUIG (Spain)	Cone of OLOT VOLC FIELD	0100-03-
SAGUTA SWAMP [SUGUTA-LOGKIPI] (Africa	Thermal Feature of BARRIER, THE	0202-03=
SAHO BRANI (Halmahera-Indonesia)	Crater of DUKONO	0608-01=
SAHU (Halmahera-Indonesia)	Cone of TODOKO-RANU	0608-05=
SAING (Java)	Cone of IYANG-ARGAPURA	0603-33=
SAINOKAWARA HOT SPRINGS (Honshu)	Thermal Feature of KUSATSU-SHIRANE	0803-12=
ST. ALLOURAN (Indian O.-S)	Cone of KERGUELEN ISLANDS	0304-02=
ST. ANDREW STRAIT (Admiralty Is-SW Pac)	Complx volc (4, 1957) Historical	**0500-01=**
ST. ANTONY PEAK (Kurile Is)	Synonym of TIATIA	0900-03=
ST. AUGUSTINE (Alaska-SW)	Synonym of AUGUSTINE	1103-01-
ST. CATHERINE (W Indies)	Stratovolc (None) Holocene	**1600-17=**
ST. DOLMAT (Alaska Peninsula)	Synonym of FOURPEAKED	1102-26-
ST. GEORGE'S HARBOR (W Indies)	Crater of ST. CATHERINE	1600-17=
ST. GEORGE'S HILL (W Indies)	Cone of SOUFRIERE HILLS	1600-05=
ST. HELENS (US-Washington)	Stratovolc (36, 1991) Historical	**1201-05-**
ST. HELIERS (New Zealand)	Tuff ring of AUCKLAND FIELD	0401-02=
ST. HIPPOLYTE, CRATERE DE (France)	Maar of CHAINE DES PUYS	0100-02-
ST. HYACINTHE, MT. (Alaska-SE)	Synonym of EDGECUMBE	1105-04-
ST. JOHN, MT. (New Zealand)	Cone of AUCKLAND FIELD	0401-02=
ST. JOHN'S FLAT (W Indies)	Dome of SABA	1600-01=
ST. JOSEPH'S MT. [LASSEN PEAK]	Dome of LASSEN VOLC CENTER	1203-08-
ST. MARYS CRATER (New Zealand)	Maar of AUCKLAND FIELD	0401-02=
ST. MICHAEL (Alaska-W)	Cinder cones (None) Anthropology	**1104-04-**
ST. MICHAEL MOUNTAIN (Alaska-W)	Cone of ST. MICHAEL	1104-04-
ST. PAUL (Indian O.-S)	Stratovolc (1, 1793) Historical	**0304-03=**
ST. PAUL ISLAND (Alaska-W)	Cinder cones (None) Holocene	**1104-07-**
ST. PAULO (Indian O.-S)	Synonym of ST. PAUL	0304-03=
ST. PETER'S DOME (US-New Mexico)	Dome of VALLES CALDERA	1210-03-
ST. THOMAS (Africa-W)	Synonym of SAO TOME	0204-05-
SAIRECABUR (Chile-N)	Stratovolcs (None) Holocene	**1505-091**
SAJAKA (Aleutian Is)	Stratovolc of TANAGA	1101-08-
SAJIKI-YAMA (Honshu-Japan)	Cone of FUJI	0803-03=
SAKA (Africa-C)	Tuff cone of FORT PORTAL FIELD	0203-002
SAKAR (New Guinea-NE of)	Stratovolc (None) Holocene?	**0501-08=**
SAKARAT, KAWAH (Java)	Thermal Feature of KAWAHKAMOJANG	0603-12=
SAKURA-JIMA (Kyushu-Japan)	Stratovolc (45, 1993) Historical	**0802-08=**
SAKURA-ZIMA (Kyushu-Japan)	Synonym of SAKURA-JIMA	0802-08=
SALAITA (Africa-E)	Cone of KILIMANJARO	0202-15=
SALAK (Java)	Stratovolc (5, 1938) Historical	**0603-05=**
SALAL CREEK (Canada)	Synonym of BRIDGE RIVER CONES	1200-17-
SALAL GLACIER (Canada)	Cone of BRIDGE RIVER CONES	1200-17-
SALASI (Sumatra)	Synonym of TALANG	0601-16=
SALELELOGA (Samoa-SW Pacific)	Cone of SAVAI'I	0404-04=
SALT LAKE (D'Entrecasteaux Is)	Thermal Feature of IAMELELE	0503-05=
SALT LAKE (Galapagos)	Crater of SANTIAGO	1503-09=
SALTOS, MONTANA DE LOS (Canary Is)	Cone of FUERTEVENTURA	1803-05-
SAMA (Africa-E)	Crater of RUNGWE	0202-166
SAMAT, MT. (Luzon-Philippines)	Cone of MARIVELES	0703-081
SAMAU (Samoa-SW Pacific)	Cone of SAVAI'I	0404-04=
SAMBE (Honshu-Japan)	Synonym of SANBE	0803-002
SAMBU, OL DOINYO (Africa-E)	Cone of CHYULU HILLS	0202-13=
SAMBU, OLDONYO (Africa-E)	Cone of MERU	0202-16=
SAMPALOC LAKE (Luzon-Philippines)	Maar of LAGUNA VOLC FIELD	0703-051
SAMPEANWANI, BUKIT (Lesser Sunda Is)	Cone of BATUR	0604-01=
SAN AGUSTIN, CERRO (Bolivia)	Stratovolc (None) Holocene?	**1505-052**
SAN ALESSANDRO (Volcano Is-Japan)	Synonym of KITA-IWO-JIMA	0804-11=
SAN ANDRES, MONTANA DE (Canary Is)	Cone of FUERTEVENTURA	1803-05-
SAN ANDRES, SIERRA DE (Mexico)	Thermal Feature of MICHOACAN-GUANAJ	1401-06=
SAN ANGELO, MONTE (Italy)	Stratovolc of LIPARI	0101-041
SAN ANTONIO (Canary Is)	Cone of LA PALMA	1803-01-
SAN ANTONIO (Philippines-C)	Thermal Feature of BILIRAN	0702-08=
SAN ANTONIO HOT SPRINGS (US-New Mex	Thermal Feature of VALLES CALDERA	1210-03-
SAN ANTONIO I, CERRO (Guatemala)	Cone of SANTIAGO, CERRO	1402-16-
SAN ANTONIO MOUNTAIN (US-New Mexico	Dome of VALLES CALDERA	1210-03-
SAN BARTOLO, CERRO (Guatemala)	Cone of CHINGO VOLC FIELD	1402-15-
SAN BENEDICTO ISLAND (Mexico-Is)	Synonym of BARCENA	1401-02=
SAN BORJA VOLC FIELD (Mexico)	Cinder cones (None) Holocene	**1401-007**
SAN BRAS, LAGOA DE (Azores)	Maar of AGUA DE PAU	1802-09=
SAN CARLOS (Africa-W)	Shield (None) Holocene	**0204-04-**
SAN CARLOS (El Salvador)	Thermal Feature of VERDE, LAGUNA	1403-01=
SAN CRISTOBAL (Galapagos)	Shield (None) Holocene	**1503-12-**
SAN CRISTOBAL (Luzon-Philippines)	Stratovolc of BANAHAW	0703-05=
SAN CRISTOBAL (Nicaragua)	Stratovolc (8, 1977) Historical	**1404-02=**
SAN DIEGO (El Salvador)	Volc field (None) Holocene	**1403-012**
SAN FELIX (Chile-Is)	Shield (None) Holocene	**1506-01=**
SAN FERNANDO [MASAYA] (Nicaragua)	Crater of MASAYA	1404-10=
SAN FRANCISCO (Guatemala)	Dome of TECUAMBURRO	1402-12=
SAN FRANSISCO (Peru)	Synonym of MISTI, EL	1504-01=
SAN GASPAR, CERRO (Guatemala)	Cone of IXTEPEQUE, VOLCAN	1402-18-
SAN GERONIMO (Mexico)	Maar of MICHOACAN-GUANAJUATO	1401-06=
SAN GIACOMO (Italy)	Crater of CAMPI FLEGREI	0101-01=
SAN ISIDRO (Mexico)	Cone of COLIMA VOLC COMPLEX	1401-04=
SAN ISIDRO, LOMA (Nicaragua)	Cone of SAN CRISTOBAL	1404-02=
SAN JACINTO [SANTA CLARA] (Nicaragua)	Stratovolc of TELICA	1404-04=
SAN JACINTO, CERRO (El Salvador)	Dome of ILOPANGO	1403-06=
SAN JACINTO, HERVIDEROS DE (Nicaragua	Thermal Feature of TELICA	1404-04=
SAN JOAQUIN (Africa-W)	Shield (None) Holocene	**0204-03-**
SAN JORGE (Azores)	Fissure vent (6, 1907) Historical	**1802-03=**
SAN JOSE (Chile-C)	Stratovolc (6, 1960) Historical	**1507-02=**
SAN JOSE (El Salvador)	Thermal Feature of VERDE, LAGUNA	1403-01=
SAN JOSE DE MAIPO (Chile-C)	Synonym of SAN JOSE	1507-02=
SAN JUAN (Canary Is)	Fissure vent of LA PALMA	1803-01-
SAN JUAN (Nicaragua)	Crater of MASAYA	1404-10=
SAN JUAN, CERRO (Guatemala)	Cone of SANTIAGO, CERRO	1402-16-
SAN JUAN DE AMATITLAN (Guatemala)	Synonym of PACAYA	1402-11=
SAN JUAN, LOMA (Nicaragua)	Cone of COSIGUINA	1404-01=
SAN LAZARO, CERRO (El Salvador)	Dome of VERDE, LAGUNA	1403-01=
SAN LORENZO (El Salvador)	Pit crater of APASTEPEQUE FIELD	1403-071
SAN LUCAS (Guatemala)	Synonym of TOLIMAN	1402-07=
SAN LUCAS, LOMA (Nicaragua)	Cone of SAN CRISTOBAL	1404-02=
SAN LUIS, CERRO (US-New Mexico)	Dome of VALLES CALDERA	1210-03-
SAN LUIS GONZAGA, ISLA (Mexico)	Expl craters (None) Holocene	**1401-003**
SAN LUIS, ISLA (Mexico)	Synonym of SAN LUIS GONZAGA, ISLA	1401-003
SAN MARCELINO (El Salvador)	Cone of SANTA ANA	1403-02=
SAN MARTIN (Canary Is)	Cone of LA PALMA	1803-01-
SAN MARTIN (Mexico)	Cone of SAN QUINTIN VOLC FIELD	1401-002
SAN MARTIN, VOLCAN DE (Mexico)	Shield (9, 1796) Historical	**1401-11=**
SAN MARTINO (Italy)	Crater of CAMPI FLEGREI	0101-01=

NAME (Subregion)	Type (Eruption Total, Most Recent) Status / Relation to NAMED VOLCANO	NUMBER
SAN MARTINO, ISOLOTTO DI (Italy)	Dome of CAMPI FLEGREI	0101-01=
SAN MIGUEL (El Salvador)	Stratovolc (28, 1986) Historical	**1403-10=**
SAN MIGUEL (Nicaragua)	Cone of NEGRO, CERRO	1404-07=
SAN NICOLAS (Mexico)	Cone of SANTA CATARINA RANGE	1401-082
SAN PABLO (Chile-N)	Twin volcano of SAN PEDRO	1505-07=
SAN PEDRO (Chile-C)	Stratovolc of SAN PEDRO-PELLADO	1507-063
SAN PEDRO (Chile-N)	Stratovolcs (5, 1938) Historical	**1505-07=**
SAN PEDRO (Nicaragua)	Crater of MASAYA	1404-10=
SAN PEDRO, LAGUNA DE (Guatemala)	Maar of SUCHITAN VOLC FIELD	1402-17-
SAN PEDRO, LOMAS DE (El Salvador)	Dome of ILOPANGO	1403-06=
SAN PEDRO-PELLADO (Chile-C)	Stratovolcs (None) Holocene	**1507-063**
SAN QUINTIN VOLC FIELD (Mexico)	Cinder cones (None) Holocene	**1401-002**
SAN RAFAEL, CERRO (Guatemala)	Cone of MOYUTA	1402-13-
SAN SALVADOR (El Salvador)	Stratovolc (6, 1917) Historical	**1403-05=**
SAN SALVADOR (Galapagos)	Synonym of SANTIAGO	1503-09=
SAN SEBASTION, CERRO DE (El Salvador)	Cone of APASTEPEQUE FIELD	1403-071
SAN VICENTE (Cape Verde Is)	Stratovolc (None) Holocene	**1804-04-**
SAN VICENTE (El Salvador)	Stratovolc (None) Fumarolic	**1403-07=**
SAN VICENTE, AUSOLES DE (El Salvador)	Thermal Feature of SAN VICENTE	1403-07=
SAN VITO (Italy)	Vent of PANTELLERIA	0101-071
SANAGAY (Ecuador)	Synonym of SANGAY	1502-09=
SANAROA ISLAND (D'Entrecasteaux Is)	Cone of DAWSON STRAIT GROUP	0503-06=
SANBANG-SAN (Korea)	Dome of HALLA	1006-04-
SANBE (Honshu-Japan)	Caldera (1, -1650) Radiocarbon	**0803-002**
SANBONYARI (Honshu-Japan)	Stratovolc of NASU	0803-15=
SAND BUTTE (US-Oregon)	Cone of NEWBERRY VOLCANO	1202-11-
SAND MOUNTAIN CONES (US-Oregon)	Cone of SAND MOUNTAIN FIELD	1202-04-
SAND MOUNTAIN FIELD (US-Oregon)	Cinder cones (4, 0000) Radiocarbon	**1202-04-**
SANDEY (Iceland-SW)	Tuff cone of HENGILL	1701-05=
SANDFELL (Iceland-W)	Cone of SNAEFELLSJOKULL	1700-01=
SANDFELLSGIGIR (Iceland-SW)	Crater row of HENGILL	1701-05=
SANDFELLSHAED (Iceland-SW)	Shield of REYKJANES	1701-02=
SANDFELLSKLOFAGIGIR (Iceland-SW)	Crater row of KRISUVIK	1701-03=
SANDIAGO VOLCANIC BELT (Canary Is)	Cone of TENERIFE	1803-03-
SANDSEA (Java)	Synonym of TENGGER CALDERA	0603-31=
SANDY POINT HILL (W Indies)	Dome of LIAMUIGA	1600-03=
SANFORD (Alaska-E)	Shield (None) Holocene?	**1105-01-**
SANGAI (Ecuador)	Synonym of SANGAY	1502-09=
SANGANGUEY (Mexico)	Stratovolc (None) Holocene	**1401-023**
SANGAY (Ecuador)	Stratovolc (3, 1993) Historical	**1502-09=**
SANGEAN API (Lesser Sunda Is)	Synonym of SANGEANG API	0604-05=
SANGEANG API (Lesser Sunda Is)	Complx volc (17, 1988) Historical	**0604-05=**
SANGIANG BURUAN (Java)	Crater of GUNTUR	0603-13=
SANGIANG DJARIAN [SANGIANG JARIAN]	Crater of GUNTUR	0603-13=
SANGIRAN (Java)	Crater of LAWU	0603-26=
SANGUIL (SANGUILI) (Mindanao-Philipines)	Synonym of BALUT	0701-01=
SANGULA (Africa-E)	Dome of SW USANGU BASIN	0202-163
SANGUMBURI (Korea)	Cone of HALLA	1006-04-
SANJIANSHAN [BIJIASHAN] (China-E)	Cone of WUDALIANCHI	1005-04-
SANKAKUTEN-YAMA (Ryukyu Is)	Cone of KUCHINOERABU-JIMA	0802-05=
SANNAK (Aleutian Is)	Synonym of ISANOTSKI	1101-37-
SANNO-BOSHI (Honshu-Japan)	Dome of OMANAGO GROUP	0803-142
SANNO-IKE (Honshu-Japan)	Crater of ON-TAKE	0803-04=
SANNOHARA-KITA (Honshu-Japan)	Cone of IZU-TOBU	0803-01=
SANNOMEGATA (Honshu-Japan)	Maar of MEGATA	0803-262
SANO, WAI (Lesser Sunda Is)	Caldera (None) Fumarolic	**0604-06=**
SANPOKOJIN-SAN (Honshu-Japan)	Stratovolc of ZAO	0803-19=
SANTA ANA (El Salvador)	Stratovolc (12, 1920) Historical	**1403-02=**
SANTA ANGELO (Italy)	Dome of ISCHIA	0101-03=
SANTA BARBARA (Azores)	Stratovolc of TERCEIRA	1802-05=
SANTA CATALINA, CALDERA DE (Canary Is	Crater of LANZAROTE	1803-06-
SANTA CATARINA MITA (Guatemala)	Synonym of SUCHITAN VOLC FIELD	1402-17-
SANTA CATARINA RANGE (Mexico)	Volc field (None) Anthropology	**1401-082**
SANTA CLARA (Mexico)	Synonym of PINACATE PEAKS	1401-001
SANTA CLARA (Nicaragua)	Stratovolc of TELICA	1404-04=
SANTA CLARA (US-Utah)	Volc field (None) Holocene	**1207-01-**
SANTA CLARA, CERRITO DE (El Salvador)	Cone of APASTEPEQUE FIELD	1403-071
SANTA CLARA [CASITA] (Nicaragua)	Stratovolc of SAN CRISTOBAL	1404-02=
SANTA CRUZ (Galapagos)	Shield (None) Holocene	**1503-091**
SANTA ELENA (El Salvador)	Cone of USULUTAN	1403-081
SANTA ELENA, CERRITO DE (Guatemala)	Cone of CUILAPA-BARBARENA	1402-111
SANTA ISABEL (Africa-W)	Shield (3, 1923) Historical	**0204-02-**
SANTA ISABEL (Colombia)	Shield (1, -2800) Radiocarbon	**1501-021**
SANTA ISABEL, CERRO (Bolivia)	Stratovolc (None) Holocene?	**1505-063**
SANTA JULIA, SIERRA (Nicaragua)	Cone of ZAPATERA ISLAND	1404-111
SANTA LUCE (Italy)	Cone of VULSINI	0101-003
SANTA MARGARIDA, VOLCA (Spain)	Cone of OLOT VOLC FIELD	0100-03-
SANTA MARIA (Argentina)	Cone of PAYUN MATRU, CERRO	1507-067
SANTA MARIA (Costa Rica)	Cone of RINCON DE LA VIEJA	1405-02=
SANTA MARIA (Galapagos)	Synonym of FLOREANA	1503-10=
SANTA MARIA (Guatemala)	Stratovolc (3, 1993) Historical	**1402-03=**
SANTA MARIA (Vanuatu-SW Pacific)	Synonym of GAUA	0507-02=
SANTA MARIA DI SALA (Italy)	Cone of VULSINI	0101-003
SANTA MICHELE (Italy)	Crater of ISCHIA	0101-03=
SANTA PANCRAZIO (Italy)	Dome of ISCHIA	0101-03=
SANTA RITA, CERRO (El Salvador)	Dome of APASTEPEQUE FIELD	1403-071
SANTA RITA, MT. (Luzon-Philippines)	Cone of NATIB	0703-082
SANTA ROSA (Mexico)	Maar of MICHOACAN-GUANAJUATO	1401-06=
SANTA ROSA, CERRO (US-New Mexico)	Dome of VALLES CALDERA	1210-03-
SANTA ROSA HILL (Indian O.-S)	Cone of MARION ISLAND	0304-08-
SANTA ROSALINA (Philippines-C)	Thermal Feature of BILIRAN	0702-08=
SANTA TERESA (Mexico)	Cone of MICHOACAN-GUANAJUATO	1401-06=
SANTA TERESA, MONTE (Italy)	Crater of CAMPI FLEGREI	0101-01=
SANTA URSULA (El Salvador)	Pit crater of APASTEPEQUE FIELD	1403-071
SANT'ANGELO (Italy)	Dome of ISCHIA	0101-03=
SANTANO, ALTO DE (Colombia)	Dome of RUIZ	1501-02=
SANT'ELMO, MONTE (Italy)	Cone of PANTELLERIA	0101-071
SANTIAGO (Galapagos)	Shield (3, 1906) Historical	**1503-09=**
SANTIAGO (Nicaragua)	Crater of MASAYA	1404-10=
SANTIAGO, CERRO (Guatemala)	Volc field (None) Holocene	**1402-16-**
SANTIAGO, CERRO EL (Mexico)	Cone of SANTA CATARINA RANGE	1401-082
SANTIAGO, EL CERRO DE (Mexico)	Dome of SANTA CATARINA RANGE	1401-082
SANTIAGO, LAGOA DE (Azores)	Pumice ring of SETE CIDADES	1802-08=
SANTIAGO [SANTIAGUITO] (Guatemala)	Dome of SANTA MARIA	1402-03=
SANTIAGO VOLC FIELD, VALLE DE (Mexico)	Maar of MICHOACAN-GUANAJUATO	1401-06=
SANTIAGUITO (Guatemala)	Dome of SANTA MARIA	1402-03=
SANTIDAD, MONTANA DE (Canary Is)	Cone of GRAN CANARIA	1803-04-
SANTO ANTAO (Cape Verde Is)	Stratovolc (None) Holocene	**1804-03-**
SANTO DOMINGO, CERRO (Chile-N)	Dome of GUAYAQUES	1505-093
SANTO TOMAS (Luzon-Philippines)	Stratovolc (None) Uncertain	**0703-086**
SANTO TOMAS, VOLCAN (Galapagos)	Synonym of NEGRA, SIERRA	1503-05=
SANTORINI (Greece)	Shields (11, 1950) Historical	**0102-04=**
SAO BONIFACIO, PICO (Atlantic-S)	Dome of TRINDADE	1805-051
SAO JORGE (Azores)	Synonym of SAN JORGE	1802-03=
SAO THOME (Africa-W)	Synonym of SAO TOME	0204-05-
SAO TIAGO, LAGOA DE [LAGOA SANTIAGO	Pumice ring of SETE CIDADES	1802-08=
SAO TOME (Africa-W)	Shield (None) Holocene?	**0204-05-**
SAPICHU (Mexico)	Cone of MICHOACAN-GUANAJUATO	1401-06=
SAP'O [BORA] (Ethiopia)	Pit crater of BORA-BERICCIO COMPLEX	0201-24-
SARABWE (Africa-E)	Cone of KIEYO	0202-17=
SARACENO, MONTE (Italy)	Cone of VULCANO	0101-05=
SARANGAN (Java)	Crater of LAWU	0603-26=
SARANGANI (Mindanao-Philippines)	Synonym of BALUT	0701-01=
SARANGSONG (Sulawesi-Indonesia)	Thermal Feature of TONDANO CALDERA	0606-07-
SARI GOL (Turkey)	Crater of ERCIYES DAGI	0103-01=
SARIA (Kamchatka)	Synonym of AVACHINSKY	1000-10=
SARICHEF (Aleutian Is)	Stratovolc of ATKA	1101-16-
SARIDAG (Turkey)	Cone of ERCIYES DAGI	0103-01=
SARIGAN (Mariana Is-C Pac)	Stratovolc (None) Holocene	**0804-191**
SARNICHEFF (Kurile Is)	Synonym of SARYCHEV PEAK	0900-24=
SARNOSO (Chile-C)	Stratovolc of ANTILLANCA GROUP	1507-153
SARSKRATERET (Atl-N-Jan Mayen)	Cone of JAN MAYEN	1706-01=
SARUANA (Honshu-Japan)	Crater of CHOKAI	0803-22=
SARUHA-YAMA (Kyushu-Japan)	Dome of UNZEN	0802-10=
SARUKURA-YAMA (Honshu-Japan)	Stratovolc of ZAO	0803-19=
SARUTSCHEW-SERGIEF (Aleutian Is)	Synonym of SERGIEF	1101-15-
SARUTSCHEW [SARICHEF] (Aleutian Is)	Stratovolc of ATKA	1101-16-
SARYCHEV PEAK (Kurile Is)	Stratovolc (14, 1989) Historical	**0900-24=**
SARYTCHEV [SARICHEF] (Aleutian Is)	Stratovolc of ATKA	1101-16-
SASHIUSU-DAKE (Kurile Is)	Synonym of BARANSKY	0900-08=
SASO (Chile-C)	Cone of SAN PEDRO-PELLADO	1507-063
SASTRES, LAS (Nicaragua)	Cone of MASAYA	1404-10=
SAT AGOMARA (Ethiopia)	Synonym of ERTA ALE	0201-08=
SATAH MOUNTAIN (Canada)	Volc field (None) Holocene	**1200-13-**
SATAK (Java)	Synonym of SALAK	0603-05=
SATSUMA-FUJI [KAIMON] (Kyushu-Japan)	Stratovolc of IBUSUKI VOLC FIELD	0802-07=
SATSUMA-IWO-JIMA (Ryukyu Is)	Synonym of KIKAI	0802-06=
SATUMA-HUZI [KAIMON] (Kyushu-Japan)	Stratovolc of IBUSUKI VOLC FIELD	0802-07=
SAUCE, EL (El Salvador)	Thermal Feature of VERDE, LAGUNA	1403-01=
SAUCER, THE (Canada)	Cone of EDZIZA	1200-06-
SAUDA, HARRA ES- (Arabia-S)	Synonym of SAWAD, HARRA ES-	0301-16-
SAUDLEYSUHRAUN (Iceland-S)	Crater row of VATNAFJOLL	1702-06=
SA'UMANE (Samoa-SW Pacific)	Cone of TA'U	0404-001
SAUNDERS ISLAND VOLCANO (Antarctica)	Synonym of MICHAEL	1900-09-
SAUVETAGE, PITON (Indian O.-W)	Cone of FOURNAISE, PITON DE LA	0303-02=
SAVAI'I (Samoa-SW Pacific)	Shield (3, 1911) Historical	**0404-04=**
SAVANA, VOLCAN DE LA [CUYOTEPE]	Cone of VERDE, LAGUNA	1403-01=
SAVICH (Kamchatka)	Cone of KIKHPINYCH	1000-18=
SAVIGAN (Mariana Is-C Pac)	Synonym of SARIGAN	0804-191
SAVO (Solomon Is-SW Pac)	Stratovolc (2, 1847) Historical	**0505-07=**
SAWAD, HARRA ES- (Arabia-S)	Volc field (1, 1253) Historical	**0301-16-**
SAWADOWSKY (Antarctica)	Synonym of ZAVODOVSKI	1900-13=
SAWAN-TISAPPU [SAWAN-CHISAPPU]	Dome of KUTCHARO	0805-08=
SAWARA-DAKE (Hokkaido-Japan)	Synonym of KOMAGA-TAKE	0805-02=
SAWARA-YAMA (Honshu-Japan)	Cone of FUJI	0803-03=
SAWTOOTH MOUNTAIN (US-Washington)	Cone of INDIAN HEAVEN	1201-07-
SAXHOLAR (Iceland-W)	Cone of SNAEFELLSJOKULL	1700-01=
SAYHUA, CERRO (Peru)	Cone of ANDAHUA VALLEY	1504-002
SCARA (Azores)	Pit crater of SETE CIDADES	1802-08=
SCARLET HILL (Indian O.-S)	Cone of HEARD	0304-01=
SCARRUPO (Italy)	Cone of ISCHIA	0101-03=
SCAURI, CUDDIA DI (Italy)	Shield of PANTELLERIA	0101-071
SCENERY, MT. (W Indies)	Dome of SABA	1600-01=
SCHALKENMEHREN (Germany)	Maar of WEST EIFEL VOLC FIELD	0100-01-
SCHANK, MT. (Australia)	Cone of NEWER VOLCANICS PROV	0509-01-
SCHAPINSKAIA SOPKA (Kamchatka)	Synonym of KIZIMEN	1000-23=
SCHILDKROTE [SKJALDBAKA] (Iceland-NE)	Shield of FREMRINAMUR	1703-07=
SCHINOPI (Greece)	Thermal Feature of MILOS	0102-03=
SCHISCHEL (Kamchatka)	Synonym of SHISHEL	1000-58-
SCHIWELUTSCH (Kamchatka)	Synonym of SHEVELUCH	1000-27=
SCHLEUTHER, MT. (New Britain-SW Pac)	Cone of GARUA HARBOUR	0502-06=
SCHONCHIN BUTTE (US-California)	Cone of MEDICINE LAKE	1203-02-
SCHREIBERS MEADOW CONE (US-Wash)	Cone of BAKER	1201-01=
SCHTJUBELJA [STUBEL] (Kamchatka)	Maar of KSUDACH	1000-05=
SCHTSCHAPINSKIJ (Kamchatka)	Synonym of KIZIMEN	1000-23=
SCHUBERTS FAIRY (New Zealand)	Former crater of WHITE ISLAND	0401-04=
SCHUVELUTSCH (Kamchatka)	Synonym of SHEVELUCH	1000-27=
SCIARA (Italy)	Vent of STROMBOLI	0101-04=
SCIRCCA [GUILA FERDINANDEO] (Italy)	Submarine vent of CAMPI FLEGREI MAR	0101-07=
SCIUVECHI, CUDDIA (Italy)	Shield of PANTELLERIA	0101-071
SCOTT (Atl-N-Jan Mayen)	Cone of JAN MAYEN	1706-01=
SCOTT CONE (Antarctica)	Cone of BUCKLE ISLAND	1900-01=
SCOTT, MT. (US-Oregon)	Stratovolc of CRATER LAKE	1202-16-
SCOUT HILL (US-Oregon)	Cone of CRATER LAKE	1202-16-
SE, PICO DA (Azores)	Stratovolc of FLORES	1802-001
SEAL NUNATAKS GROUP (Antarctica)	Pyrocl cones (1, 1893) Historical	**1900-05=**
SEARA CERRADO DE LADEIRA (Azores)	Pumice cone of SETE CIDADES	1802-08=
SEBAIN, DJEBEL (Red Sea)	Synonym of TEYR, DJEBEL	0201-01=
SECA, CALDEIRA (Azores)	Crater of FLORES	1802-001
SECA, CALDEIRA (Azores)	Pumice ring of SETE CIDADES	1802-08=
SECA, LAGUNA (El Salvador)	Pit crater of APASTEPEQUE FIELD	1403-071
SECA, LAGUNA (El Salvador)	Pit crater of SANTA ANA	1403-02=
SECA, LAGUNA (Nicaragua)	Crater of SAN CRISTOBAL	1404-02=
SECA, LAGUNA (Nicaragua)	Maar of PILAS, LAS	1404-08=
SECCA D'ISCHIA (Italy)	Cone of ISCHIA	0101-03=
SECO, CERRO (US-New Mexico)	Dome of VALLES CALDERA	1210-03-
SECOND CANYON (Canada)	Cone of ISKUT-UNUK RIVER CONES	1200-09-
SEDANKINSKY (Kamchatka)	Shield (None) Holocene	**1000-52-**
SEEMALIK BUTTE (Alaska-W)	Cone of NUNIVAK ISLAND	1104-06-
SEENG, KAWAH (Java)	Thermal Feature of WAYANG-WINDU	0603-08=
SEGARA ANAK (Lesser Sunda Is)	Caldera of RINJANI	0604-03=
SEGARA MUNJAK (Lesser Sunda Is)	Crater of RINJANI	0604-03=
SEGARA MUNTJAR [SEGARA MUNJAR]	Crater of RINJANI	0604-03=
SEGARAWEDI KEDUL (Java)	Crater of TENGGER CALDERA	0603-31=
SEGARAWEDI LOR (Java)	Crater of TENGGER CALDERA	0603-31=
SEGEHIKI (Honshu-Japan)	Vent of IZU-TOBU	0803-01=
SEGERERUA PLATEAU (Africa-E)	Pyrocl cones (None) Holocene	**0202-05-**
SEGORO BANDJARAN [SEGORO BANJAR	Crater of SUNDORO	0603-21=
SEGORO BANJARAN (Java)	Crater of SUNDORO	0603-21=
SEGORO WEDI (Java)	Crater of SUNDORO	0603-21=
SEGUAM (Aleutian Is)	Stratovolcs (7, 1993) Historical	**1101-18-**
SEGULA (Aleutian Is)	Stratovolc (None) Holocene	**1101-03-**
SEKIGUCHI GROUP (Honshu-Japan)	Crater of IZU-TOBU	0803-01=
SEKIGUCHIGAWA-JORYU (Honshu-Japan)	Vent of IZU-TOBU	0803-01=

NAME (Subregion)	Type (Eruption Total, Most Recent) Status / Relation to NAMED VOLCANO	NUMBER
SEKINCAU BELIRANG (Sumatra)	Caldera (None) Fumarolic	**0601-26=**
SEKINTJAU BELIRANG (Sumatra)	Synonym of SEKINCAU BELIRANG	0601-26=
SEKISON-ZAN (Honshu-Japan)	Dome of ASAMA	0803-11=
SELA (Java)	Crater of GEDE	0603-06=
SELAWAJAN (Sumatra)	Synonym of SEULAWAH AGAM	0601-02=
SELAWAJANTEN (SELAWAJANTEN)	Synonym of SEULAWAH AGAM	0601-02=
SELHOLL N & S (Iceland-SW)	Crater rows of GRIMSNES	1701-06=
SELHRAUNSGIGIR (Iceland-SW)	Crater row of KRISUVIK	1701-03=
SELIMKARTINI (Turkey)	Cone of ERCIYES DAGI	0103-01=
SELLA, MONTI (Italy)	Cone of ETNA	0101-06=
SELLA [SADDLE ISLAND] (Red Sea)	Shield of ZUBAYR, JEBEL	0201-02=
SELSUNDSHRAUN N & S (Iceland-S)	Fissure vents of HEKLA	1702-07=
SELVA DEL LAMONE (Italy)	Cone of VULSINI	0101-003
SELVA DEL NAPOLITANO (Italy)	Dome of ISCHIA	0101-03=
SELVOGSHEIDI (Iceland-SW)	Shield of HENGILL	1701-05=
SEMEROE (Java)	Synonym of SEMERU	0603-30=
SEMERU (Java)	Crater of IYANG-ARGAPURA	0603-33=
SEMERU (Java)	Stratovolc (57, 1993) Historical	**0603-30=**
SEMI CRATER (US-California)	Crater of MEDICINE LAKE	1203-02-
SEMINUNG, GUNUNG (Sumatra)	Stratovolc of RANAU	0601-251
SEMISOPOCHNOI (Aleutian Is)	Stratovolc (2, 1987) Historical	**1101-06-**
SEMKAROK (Kamchatka)	Dome of SHEVELUCH	1000-27=
SEMONGKRONG, GUNUNG (Java)	Cone of TENGGER CALDERA	0603-31=
SEMONTE, MT. (Italy)	Cone of VULSINI	0101-003
SEMPOE (Sulawesi-Indonesia)	Synonym of SEMPU	0606-04=
SEMPU (Sulawesi-Indonesia)	Caldera (None) Fumarolic	**0606-04=**
SENDA-YAMA (Kyushu-Japan)	Dome of IBUSUKI VOLC FIELD	0802-07=
SENDORO (Java)	Synonym of SUNDORO	0603-21=
SENGA, MONTE (Italy)	Cone of CAMPI FLEGREI	0101-01=
SENGERETI (Africa-E)	Cone of KIEYO	0202-17=
SENHORA, PICA DA (Azores)	Cone of FURNAS	1802-10=
SENNIN-ZAN (Honshu-Japan)	Synonym of FUJI	0803-03=
SENTINEL ROCK (US-Oregon)	Stratovolc of CRATER LAKE	1202-16-
SENTINEL, THE (US-Idaho)	Cone of CRATERS OF THE MOON	1204-02-
SEONGINBONG (Korea)	Synonym of ULREUNG	1006-03-
SEPANAS (Sumatra)	Crater of LUMUT BALAI, BUKIT	0601-24=
SERANGANI (SERANGANO) (Mindanao)	Synonym of BALUT	0701-01=
SERAWERNA (Banda Sea)	Synonym of TEON	0605-05=
SEREH, GUNUNG (Lesser Sunda Is)	Synonym of SIRUNG	0604-27=
SERET BERAPI (Sumatra)	Synonym of SORIKMARAPI	0601-12=
SERETMAT (Vanuatu-SW Pacific)	Synonym of SORETIMEAT	0507-01=
SERGA (Kamchatka)	Cone of TOLBACHIK	1000-24=
SERGEEVA (Kamchatka)	Shield of BELY	1000-64-
SERGEIN (Africa-N)	Cone of BAYUDA VOLC FIELD	0205-06-
SERGIEF (Aleutian Is)	Stratovolc (None) Uncertain	**1101-15-**
SERGUEJEYSKI (Aleutian Is)	Synonym of SERGIEF	1101-15-
SEROEA (Banda Sea)	Synonym of SERUA	0605-07=
SERRA DO MORIAO [GUILHERME MONIZ]	Stratovolc of TERCEIRA	1802-05=
SERRA GORDA (Azores)	Cone of UNNAMED	1802-081
SERRA PIZZUTA CALVARINA, MONTE (Italy	Cone of ETNA	0101-06=
SERRA PIZZUTA, MONTE (Italy)	Cone of ETNA	0101-06=
SERUA (Banda Sea)	Stratovolc (10, 1921) Historical	**0605-07=**
SERY, CRATERE (Indian O.-W)	Crater of FOURNAISE, PITON DE LA	0303-02=
SESARGA (Solomon Is-SW Pac)	Synonym of SAVO	0505-07=
SESEGARA HILLS (New Guinea)	Synonym of SESSAGARA	0503-031
SESSAGARA (New Guinea)	Unknown (None) Holocene	**0503-031**
SESSHOGAWARA (Honshu-Japan)	Thermal Feature of KUSATSU-SHIRANE	0803-12=
SESSYO-ISI [SESSHO-ISHI] (Honshu-Japan)	Thermal Feature of NASU	0803-15=
SESTRENKA (Kamchatka)	Dome of UZON	1000-17=
SETE CIDADES (Azores)	Stratovolc (16, 1880) Historical	**1802-08=**
SETO-YAMA (Izu Is-Japan)	Dome of NII-JIMA	0804-02=
SETUPA (Java)	Crater of LAWU	0603-26=
SEUGA (Samoa-SW Pacific)	Cone of UPOLU	0404-03-
SEULAWAH AGAM (Sumatra)	Stratovolc (None) Holocene	**0601-02=**
SEULAWAIH AGAM (SEULAWAIN AGAM)	Synonym of SEULAWAH AGAM	0601-02=
SEVERGIN (Kurile Is)	Cone of HARIMKOTAN	0900-30=
SEVERNO-KOSHELEVSKIE [VERKNE-KOS	Thermal Feature of KOSHELEV	1000-02=
SEVERNY (Kamchatka)	Shield (None) Holocene	**1000-70-**
SEVERNY CHERPUK (Kamchatka)	Cone of ICHINSKY	1000-28=
SEVERNY GAMCHEN (Kamchatka)	Stratovolc of GAMCHEN	1000-21=
SEYDISHOLAR (Iceland-SW)	Crater row of GRIMSNES	1701-06=
SFINKS (Kamchatka)	Dome of KSUDACH	1000-05=
SHABUBEMBE (Africa-C)	Crater of NYAMURAGIRA	0203-02=
SHACHI (Tonga-SW Pacific)	Synonym of CURACOA	0403-101
SHADWELL, MT. (Australia)	Cone of NEWER VOLCANICS PROV	0509-01-
SHAHERU (Africa-C)	Cone of NYIRAGONGO	0203-03=
SHAITANI (Africa-E)	Cone of CHYULU HILLS	0202-13=
SHAKUNAGE HOT SPRINGS (Honshu-Japan	Thermal Feature of KUSATSU-SHIRANE	0803-12=
SHALA (Ethiopia)	Stratovolc (None) Holocene	**0201-28-**
SHALMAN, JABAL (Arabia-W)	Dome of KISHB, HARRAT	0301-071
SHAM HILL (Canada)	Cone of BRIDGE RIVER CONES	1200-17-
SHAMROCK HILL (Antarctica)	Cone of HODSON	1900-11=
SHAMUHIRO (Africa-C)	Cone of NYAMURAGIRA	0203-02=
SHANDUN (SE Asia)	Synonym of LEIZHOU BANDAO	0705-01-
SHANGRI-LA (Chile-C)	Cone of CHILLAN, NEVADOS DE	1507-07=
SHARAT KOVAKAB (Syria)	Volc field (None) Holocene	**0300-01-**
SHARP PEAK (Luzon-Philippines)	Cone of BULUSAN	0703-01=
SHARP PEAK (US-Oregon)	Dome of CRATER LAKE	1202-16-
SHASTA (US-California)	Stratovolc (23, 1786) Historical	**1203-01-**
SHASTA BUTTE (US-California)	Synonym of SHASTA	1203-01-
SHASTINA (US-California)	Dome of SHASTA	1203-01-
SHAVARYN-TSARAM (Mongolia)	Cone of TARYATU-CHULUTU	1003-01-
SHCHAPINSKAYA (Kamchatka)	Synonym of KIZIMEN	1000-23=
SHE-TOE-SHAN [MAANSHAN] (China-S)	Cone of TENGCHONG	0705-11-
SHEEP TRAIL BUTTE (US-Idaho)	Cone of CRATERS OF THE MOON	1204-02-
SHEJIUSHAN [MAANSHAN] (China-S)	Cone of TENGCHONG	0705-11-
SHELL MOUNTAIN (Alaska-SE)	Stratovolc of EDGECUMBE	1105-04-
SHELTOWSKIJ (Kamchatka)	Synonym of ZHELTOVSKY	1000-04=
SHENGLIDABAN (China-W)	Cone of KUNLUN VOLC GROUP	1004-03-
SHEPHERD DOME (Antarctica)	Cone of HUDSON MOUNTAINS	1900-028
SHERIDAN MOUNTAIN (US-Oregon)	Shield of BACHELOR	1202-09-
SHERMAN CRATER (US-Washington)	Crater of BAKER	1201-01=
SHEROKHOVATAYA (Kamchatka)	Dome of SHEVELUCH	1000-27=
SHEVELUCH (Kamchatka)	Stratovolc (28, 1993) Historical	**1000-27=**
SHIBASEKI (Kyushu-Japan)	Thermal Feature of TSURUMI	0802-13=
SHIBUNO-YU (Kyushu-Japan)	Thermal Feature of TSURUMI	0802-13=
SHICHIHO-YAMA (Honshu-Japan)	Synonym of FUJI	0803-03=
SHIELD NUNATAK (Antarctica)	Cone of MELBOURNE	1900-015
SHIGA (Honshu-Japan)	Shields (None) Holocene	**0803-121**
SHIGA-KOGEN (Honshu-Japan)	Synonym of SHIGA	0803-121
SHIH-MEN=TZU-SHAN [SHIMENZISHAN]	Cone of LONGGANG GROUP	1005-06-
SHIKANOKASHIRA (Honshu-Japan)	Cone of FUJI	0803-03=
SHIKARIBETSU GROUP (Hokkaido-Japan)	Lava domes (None) Holocene	**0805-062**
SHIKINE-JIMA (Izu Is-Japan)	Dome of NII-JIMA	0804-02=
SHIKINONARU-YAMA (Honshu-Japan)	Synonym of FUJI	0803-03=
SHIKOTSU (Hokkaido-Japan)	Caldera (37, 1981) Historical	**0805-04=**
SHILIN-BOGDO (Mongolia)	Cone of DARIGANGA VOLC FIELD	1003-04-
SHIMENZISHAN (China-E)	Cone of LONGGANG GROUP	1005-06-
SHIMOBORI (Honshu-Japan)	Crater of YAKE-DAKE	0803-07=
SHIMOKITA-HIUCHI (Honshu-Japan)	Synonym of MUTSU-HIUCHI-DAKE	0803-30-
SHIN-BEPPU (Kyushu-Japan)	Thermal Feature of TSURUMI	0802-13=
SHIN-DAKE (Ryukyu Is)	Cone of KUCHINOERABU-JIMA	0802-05=
SHIN-FUNKAKO (Hokkaido-Japan)	Crater of TOKACHI	0805-05=
SHIN-IO-JIMA (Volcano Is-Japan)	Synonym of SHIN-IWO-JIMA	0804-13=
SHIN-IWO-JIMA (Volcano Is-Japan)	Submarine (7, 1992) Historical	**0804-13=**
SHIN-IWO-JIMA [SHOWA-IWO-JIMA]	Dome of KIKAI	0802-06=
SHIN-YAMA [MYOKO-SAN] (Honshu-Japan)	Dome of MYOKO	0803-10=
SHIN-ZAN (Honshu-Japan)	Dome of CHOKAI	0803-22=
SHINING MOUNTAIN (Africa-E)	Synonym of KILIMANJARO	0202-15=
SHINMIYO-IKE (Izu Is-Japan)	Crater of MIYAKE-JIMA	0804-04=
SHINMOE-DAKE (Kyushu-Japan)	Stratovolc of KIRISHIMA	0802-09=
SHINMYO (Izu Is-Japan)	Crater of MIYAKE-JIMA	0804-04=
SHINO-IKE (Honshu-Japan)	Crater of ON-TAKE	0803-04=
SHINO-YU (Kyushu-Japan)	Thermal Feature of TSURUMI	0802-13=
SHINSHERIDAKE (Kurile Is)	Synonym of PREVO PEAK	0900-19=
SHINSHIRU-DAKE (Kurile Is)	Synonym of GORIASCHAIA SOPKA	0900-17B
SHINSHIRU FUJI (Kurile Is)	Synonym of PREVO PEAK	0900-19=
SHIP ROCK (Aleutian Is)	Former dome of BOGOSLOF	1101-30-
SHIP ROCK (Indian O.-S)	Tuff cone of PRINCE EDWARD ISLAND	0304-07-
SHIRA (Africa-E)	Stratovolc of KILIMANJARO	0202-15=
SHIRAHATA HOT SPRINGS (Honshu-Japan)	Thermal Feature of KUSATSU-SHIRANE	0803-12=
SHIRAISHI-DAKE (Honshu-Japan)	Synonym of ZAO	0803-19=
SHIRAMIZU (Honshu-Japan)	Crater of YAKE-DAKE	0803-07=
SHIRANE-SAN (Honshu-Japan)	Dome of NIKKO-SHIRANE	0803-14=
SHIRANE-SAN (Honshu-Japan)	Cone of KUSATSU-SHIRANE	0803-12=
SHIRANEZAWA (Honshu-Japan)	Thermal Feature of KUSATSU-SHIRANE	0803-12=
SHIRANUTANOIKE (Honshu-Japan)	Maar of IZU-TOBU	0803-01=
SHIRATORI-YAMA (Kyushu-Japan)	Stratovolc of KIRISHIMA	0802-09=
SHIRETOKO-IO-ZAN (Hokkaido)	Synonym of SHIRETOKO-IWO-ZAN	0805-09=
SHIRETOKO-IWO-ZAN (Hokkaido-Japan)	Stratovolc (4, 1936) Historical	**0805-09=**
SHIRIBETSU (Hokkaido-Japan)	Stratovolc ? (None) Holocene	**0805-033**
SHIRINKI (Kurile Is)	Stratovolc (None) Holocene	**0900-331**
SHIRIYAZIRI-DAKE (SHIRIYAZIRI) (Kurile Is)	Synonym of FUSS PEAK	0900-34=
SHIROGANE (Hokkaido-Japan)	Thermal Feature of TOKACHI	0805-05=
SHIROKOE PLATEAU (Kamchatka)	Dome of UZON	1000-17=
SHIROTSUKA (Honshu-Japan)	Cone of FUJI	0803-03=
SHISHALDIN (Aleutian Is)	Stratovolc (29, 1993) Historical	**1101-36-**
SHISHEL (Kamchatka)	Shield (None) Holocene	**1000-58-**
SHISHIDO-DAKE (Kyushu-Japan)	Stratovolc of KIRISHIMA	0802-09=
SHIVELUCH (Kamchatka)	Synonym of SHEVELUCH	1000-27=
SHIWANSHAN (SE Asia)	Cone of LEIZHOU BANDAO	0705-01-
SHIYINLING (SE Asia)	Cone of LEIZHOU BANDAO	0705-01-
SHO-CHIRIPPU [IVAN GROZNY] (Kurile Is)	Cone of GROZNY GROUP	0900-07=
SHO-FUJI [KAIMON] (Kyushu-Japan)	Stratovolc of IBUSUKI VOLC FIELD	0802-07=
SHOAL BAY (New Zealand)	Tuff cone of AUCKLAND FIELD	0401-02=
SHOHAPINSKY (Kamchatka)	Synonym of KIZIMEN	1000-23=
SHOJI-YAMA (Honshu-Japan)	Dome of OSORE-YAMA	0803-29=
SHOKUROHIME (Honshu-Japan)	Cone of KUROHIME	0803-101
SHOSHONE GEYSER BASIN (US-Wyoming)	Thermal Feature of YELLOWSTONE	1205-01-
SHOSHONE LAVA FIELD (US-Idaho)	Cinder cones (None) Holocene?	**1204-01-**
SHOSHUENCO [CHOSHUENCO] (Chile-C)	Stratovolc of MOCHO-CHOSHUENCO	1507-13=
SHOTGUN PEAK (US-California)	Cone of MEDICINE LAKE	1203-02-
SHOVE (Africa-C)	Cone of NYAMURAGIRA	0203-02=
SHOWA (Hokkaido-Japan)	Crater of TOKACHI	0805-05=
SHOWA-IWO-JIMA (Ryukyu Is)	Dome of KIKAI	0802-06=
SHOWA-SHINZAN (Hokkaido-Japan)	Dome of USU	0805-03=
SHTYUBEL [STUBEL] (Kamchatka)	Maar of KSUDACH	1000-05=
SHUANGSHAN (China-E)	Cone of DATONG	1005-01-
SHULI (Africa-C)	Cone of NYAMURAGIRA	0203-02=
SHUPANOWSKIJ (Kamchatka)	Synonym of ZHUPANOVSKY	1000-12=
SHUQURA VOLC FIELD (Arabia-S)	Synonym of SAWAD, HARRA ES-	0301-16-
SHURADO (Honshu-Japan)	Crater of NARUGO	0803-20=
SHUSHALDINSKAYA (Aleutian Is)	Synonym of SHISHALDIN	1101-36-
SI NABUN (Sumatra)	Synonym of SINABUNG	0601-08=
SIAH BUTTE (US-Oregon)	Cone of BACHELOR	1202-09-
SIANG (Java)	Crater of GALUNGGUNG	0603-14=
SIASSI ISLAND (New Guinea-NE of)	Synonym of UMBOI	0501-06=
SIBAJAK (Sumatra)	Synonym of SIBAYAK	0601-07=
SIBANDUNG (Sumatra)	Caldera of TOBA	0601-09=
SIBANGGOR DJULU [SIBANGOR JULU]	Thermal Feature of SORIKMARAPI	0601-12=
SIBANTENG (Java)	Thermal Feature of DIENG VOLC COMP	0603-20=
SIBAYAK (Sumatra)	Stratovolc (1, 1881) Historical	**0601-07=**
SIBUAL BOALIE (SIBULABOALIE) (Sumatra)	Synonym of BUAL BUALI	0601-11=
SICUIN, CERRO DE (Mexico)	Cone of MICHOACAN-GUANAJUATO	1401-06=
SIDAS (Canada)	Cone of EDZIZA	1200-06-
SIERRA (Spanish for MOUNTAIN RANGE)	see proper name (e.g. SAN ANDRES, SIERRA DE)	
SIETE, CERRO EL (Costa Rica)	Stratovolc of PLATANAR, CERRO	1405-036
SIETE FUENTES (Canary Is)	Cone of TENERIFE	1803-03-
SIGA (Honshu-Japan)	Synonym of SHIGA	0803-121
SIGADJAH [SIGAJAH] (Java)	Thermal Feature of DIENG VOLC COMP	0603-20=
SIGA'ELE (Samoa-SW Pacific)	Cone of UPOLU	0404-03-
SIGALA, BATU (Sumatra)	Crater of SINABUNG	0601-08=
SIGLAGAH (Java)	Thermal Feature of DIENG VOLC COMP	0603-20=
SIGLUDUK (Java)	Cone of DIENG VOLC COMPLEX	0603-20=
SIGNAL BUTTE (US-California)	Cone of SHASTA	1203-01-
SIGNAL DE L'ENCLOS (Indian O.-W)	Crater of FOURNAISE, PITON DE LA	0303-02=
SIGOLDUHRAUN (Iceland-NE)	Fissure vent of BARDARBUNGA	1703-03=
SIGUAM (Aleutian Is)	Synonym of SEGUAM	1101-18-
SIGURDBREEN (Atl-N-Jan Mayen)	Cone of JAN MAYEN	1706-01=
SIHARSLAN TEPE (Turkey)	Cone of ERCIYES DAGI	0103-01=
SIHMIRAN TEPE (Turkey)	Cone of NEMRUT DAGI	0103-02=
SIKIDANG (Java)	Thermal Feature of DIENG VOLC COMP	0603-20=
SIKINE-ZIMA [SHIKINE-JIMA] (Izu Is-Japan)	Dome of NII-JIMA	0804-02=
SIKOTU (Hokkaido-Japan)	Synonym of SHIKOTSU	0805-04=
SIKUNANG (Java)	Cone of DIENG VOLC COMPLEX	0603-20=
SIL (Africa-E)	Synonym of BARRIER, THE	0202-03=
SILALI (Africa-E)	Shield (3, -5050) Ar/Ar	**0202-052**
SILANGAN (Luzon-Philippines)	Cone of NATIB	0703-082
SILAUNG (SE Asia)	Vent of LOWER CHINDWIN	0705-09-
SILAWAIH AGAM (Sumatra)	Synonym of SEULAWAH AGAM	0601-02=
SILAY (Philippines-C)	Stratovolc (None) Holocene	**0702-04=**
SILE [SILI] (New Britain-SW Pac)	Cone of LOLOBAU	0502-13=
SILENGE ISLAND (New Britain-SW Pac)	Cone of MUNDUA	0502-021
SILENT CONE (US-Idaho)	Cone of CRATERS OF THE MOON	1204-02-

NAME (Subregion)	Type (Eruption Total, Most Recent) Status . . . Relation to NAMED VOLCANO	NUMBER
SILERI (Java)	Cone of DIENG VOLC COMPLEX	0603-20=
SILI (New Britain-SW Pac)	Cone of LOLOBAU	0502-13=
SILI (Samoa-SW Pacific)	Shield of OFU-OLOSEGA	0404-01=
SILLON ABAJO, CERRITO EL (Guatemala)	Cone of CHIQUIMULA FIELD	1402-20-
SILLON, CERRITO EL (Guatemala)	Cone of CHIQUIMULA FIELD	1402-20-
SILUMAN, KAWAH (Java)	Crater of TANGKUBANPARAHU	0603-09=
SILVA, LA (Mexico)	Cone of HOLOTEPEC	1401-07-
SILVERTHRONE (Canada)	Caldera (None) Holocene	**1200-16-**
SIMABARA (Kyushu-Japan)	Synonym of UNZEN	0802-10=
SIMAGH, JABAL (Arabia-W)	Maar of KISHB, HARRAT	0301-071
SIMANOBORI (Kurile Is)	Synonym of MENDELEEV	0900-02=
SIMBA, VOLCAN [AGUAS CALIENTES]	Stratovolc of LASCAR	1505-10=
SIMBI, LAKE (Africa-E)	Maar of HOMA MOUNTAIN	0202-07=
SIMBO (Solomon Is-SW Pac)	Stratovolc (None) Uncertain	**0505-05=**
SIMINYNG [GUNUNG SEMINUNG] (Sumatra	Stratovolc of RANAU	0601-251
SIMOKITA-HIUTI (Honshu-Japan)	Synonym of MUTSU-HIUCHI-DAKE	0803-30-
SIMONE, MONTE (Italy)	Cone of ETNA	0101-06=
SIMS BUTTE (US-Oregon)	Cone of NORTH SISTER FIELD	1202-07-
SIMUSIRU FUDZI (Kurile Is)	Synonym of PREVO PEAK	0900-19=
SIN-DAKE [SHIN-DAKE] (Ryukyu Is)	Cone of KUCHINOERABU-JIMA	0802-05=
SIN-HUNKAKO [SHIN-FUNKAKO] (Hokkaido)	Crater of TOKACHI	0805-05=
SIN-IO-JIMA (SIN-IWO-ZIMA) (Volcano Is)	Synonym of SHIN-IWO-JIMA	0804-13=
SIN NOMBRE (Chile-S)	Cone of CAYUTE-LA VIGUERIA	1508-021
SIN NOMBRE, NEVADO (Chile-C)	Stratovolc of TUPUNGATITO	1507-01=
SIN-ZAN [SHIN-ZAN] (Honshu-Japan)	Dome of CHOKAI	0803-22=
SINABOENG (Sumatra)	Synonym of SINABUNG	0601-08=
SINABUNG (Sumatra)	Stratovolc (None) Fumarolic	**0601-08=**
SINAI, MT. (W Indies)	Cone of ST. CATHERINE	1600-17=
SINARKA (Kurile Is)	Stratovolc (4, 1878) Historical	**0900-29=**
SINARKO (Kurile Is)	Synonym of SINARKA	0900-29=
SINDORO (Java)	Synonym of SUNDORO	0603-21=
SINGGALANG (Sumatra)	Twin volcano of TANDIKAT	0601-15=
SINGGALANG, DOLOK (Sumatra)	Cone of TOBA	0601-09=
SINGIRO (Africa-C)	Cone of NYAMURAGIRA	0203-02=
SINGU PLATEAU (SE Asia)	Fissure vents (None) Holocene	**0705-10-**
SINGUIL, CERRO (El Salvador)	Cinder cone (None) Holocene	**1403-011**
SINI (Russia-SE)	Cone of UDOKAN VOLC FIELD	1002-03-
SINILA (Java)	Cone of DIENG VOLC COMPLEX	0603-20=
SINITIOPE, LOMA DE (Nicaragua)	Cone of CONCEPCION	1404-12=
SINMIYO [SHINMYO] (Izu Is-Japan)	Crater of MIYAKE-JIMA	0804-04=
SINMOE-DAKE [SHINMOE-DAKE] (Kyushu)	Stratovolc of KIRISHIMA	0802-09=
SINO-IKE [SHINO-IKE] (Honshu-Japan)	Crater of ON-TAKE	0803-04=
SINTUMBI (Africa-E)	Cone of NGOZI	0202-164
SIO TSIRARIPPU [IVAN GROZNY] (Kurile Is)	Somma volcano of GROZNY GROUP	0900-07=
SIOPE (Samoa-SW Pacific)	Cone of SAVAI'I	0404-04=
SIOSIORENA (D'Entrecasteaux Is)	Thermal Feature of DAWSON STRAIT GP	0503-06=
SIPANDU (Java)	Thermal Feature of DIENG VOLC COMP	0603-20=
SIPLE (Antarctica)	Shield (None) Holocene?	**1900-025**
SIRAHATA (Kurile Is)	Synonym of KETOI	0900-20=
SIRANE-SAN [SHIRANE-SAN] (Honshu)	Dome of NIKKO-SHIRANE	0803-14=
SIRATORI-YAMA [SHIRATORI-YAMA]	Cone of KIRISHIMA	0802-09=
SIREN ROCK (Antarctica)	Cone of HUDSON MOUNTAINS	1900-028
SIRENEVY (Kamchatka)	Cone of DZENZURSKY	1000-11=
SIRETOKO-IO-ZAN (Hokkaido)	Synonym of SHIRETOKO-IWO-ZAN	0805-09=
SIRIADZIRI (Kurile Is)	Synonym of FUSS PEAK	0900-34=
SIROENG (Lesser Sunda Is)	Synonym of SIRUNG	0604-27=
SIRONEMURI (Kurile Is)	Synonym of KETOI	0900-20=
SIRUNG (Lesser Sunda Is)	Complx volc (8, 1970) Historical	**0604-27=**
SISAGUK (Aleutian Is)	Synonym of SHISHALDIN	1101-36-
SISEL (Kamchatka)	Synonym of SHISHEL	1000-58-
SISIDO-DAKE [SHISHIDO-DAKE] (Kyushu)	Stratovolc of KIRISHIMA	0802-09=
SISQUK (SISSAGJUK) (Aleutian Is)	Synonym of SHISHALDIN	1101-36-
SISTERS, THE (Alaska-W)	Cone of ST. MICHAEL	1104-04-
SITCHIN (Aleutian Is)	Synonym of GREAT SITKIN	1101-12-
SITCHIN (SITIGNAK?) (Aleutian Is)	Synonym of LITTLE SITKIN	1101-05-
SITIO GRANDE (El Salvador)	Crater of SAN SALVADOR	1403-05=
SITIO HORNILLAS (Costa Rica)	Thermal Feature of RINCON DE LA VIEJA	1405-02=
SITKUM BUTTE (US-Oregon)	Cone of BACHELOR	1202-09-
SIX SHOOTER BUTTE (US-California)	Cone of MEDICINE LAKE	1203-02-
SIYUT (Mindanao-Philippines)	Synonym of MAKATURING	0701-04=
SIYUT (Mindanao-Philippines)	Synonym of RAGANG	0701-06=
SJADUKTA (Kamchatka)	Synonym of KSUDACH	1000-05=
SJONARHOLL (Iceland-W)	Cone of SNAEFELLSJOKULL	1700-01=
SKAFTA [LAKI] (Iceland-NE)	Crater row of GRIMSVOTN	1703-01=
SKALAFELL (Iceland-SW)	Shield of REYKJANES	1701-02=
SKALARALDA (Iceland-NE)	Crater of ASKJA	1703-06=
SKALISTAYA (Kamchatka)	Dome of OPALA	1000-08=
SKAPTARJOKULL [LAKI] (Iceland-NE)	Crater row of GRIMSVOTN	1703-01=
SKARDSMYRARHRAUN (Iceland-SW)	Crater row of HENGILL	1701-05=
SKAROS (Greece)	Shield of SANTORINI	0102-04=
SKEIFUHRAUN (Iceland-NE)	Fissure vent of BARDARBUNGA	1703-03=
SKERJAHRAUN (Iceland-S)	Fissure vent of EYJAFJOLL	1702-02=
SKI HEIL PEAK (US-Calif)	Dome of LASSEN VOLC CENTER	1203-08-
SKINNER HILL (New Zealand)	Dome of EGMONT	0401-03=
SKJALDBAKA (Iceland-NE)	Shield of FREMRINAMUR	1703-07=
SKJALDBREIDUR (Iceland-SW)	Shield of PRESTAHNUKUR	1701-07=
SKOFLUNGER (Iceland-SW)	Shield of PRESTAHNUKUR	1701-07=
SKOTUHRYGGUR (Iceland-S)	Submarine vent of VESTMANNAEYJAR	1702-01=
SKRUKKEFJELLET (Atl-N-Jan Mayen)	Dome of JAN MAYEN	1706-01=
SKRUKKELIA (Atl-N-Jan Mayen)	Cone of JAN MAYEN	1706-01=
SKUGGADYNGJA (Iceland-NE)	Shield of FREMRINAMUR	1703-07=
SKYRTUNNA (Iceland-W)	Crater of LJOSUFJOLL	1700-03=
SLADEN BOILING SPRINGS (Vanuatu)	Thermal Feature of GAUA	0507-02=
SLAMAT (Java)	Synonym of SLAMET	0603-18=
SLAMET (Java)	Stratovolc (39, 1989) Historical	**0603-18=**
SLATTUDALSHRAUN (Iceland-SW)	Crater row of BRENNISTEINSFJOLL	1701-04=
SLEET (Canada)	Cone of EDZIZA	1200-06-
SLETTAHRAUN (Iceland-S)	Fissure vent of TORFAJOKULL	1702-05=
SLUSHER NUNATAK (Antarctica)	Cone of HUDSON MOUNTAINS	1900-028
SMAHRAUNAKULA (Iceland-W)	Cone of LJOSUFJOLL	1700-03=
SMALES HILL [OTARA HILL] (New Zealand)	Cone of AUCKLAND FIELD	0401-02=
SMART, MT (New Zealand)	Cone of AUCKLAND FIELD	0401-02=
SMEATON HILL (Australia)	Cone of NEWER VOLCANICS PROV	0509-01-
SMEROE (SMERU) (Java)	Synonym of SEMERU	0603-30=
SMIRNOV (Kurile Is)	Stratovolc (None) Holocene	**0900-021**
SMIROE (Java)	Synonym of SEMERU	0603-30=
SMITH (Greece)	Dome of SANTORINI	0102-04=
SMITH BUTTE (US-Washington)	Cone of ADAMS	1201-04-
SMITH CRATER (Kermadec Is)	Crater of RAOUL ISLAND	0402-03=
SMITH ROCK (Izu Is-Japan)	Submarine (6, 1916) Historical	**0804-08=**
SMITH VOLCANO (Luzon Is-N of)	Stratovolc of BABUYAN CLARO	0704-03=
SMOKING MOSES (Aleutian Is)	Synonym of SHISHALDIN	1101-36-
SMOKY MOUNTAIN (Alaska Peninsula)	Synonym of UGASHIK-PEULIK	1102-13A
SMYT BANK I & II (Italy)	Submarine vents of CAMPI FLEGREI MAR	0101-07=
SNAEFELLSJOKULL (Iceland-W)	Stratovolc (9, 0200) Radiocarbon	**1700-01=**
SNAEKOLLUR (Iceland-SW)	Dome of KERLINGARFJOLL	1701-10=
SNAG HILL (US-California)	Cone of MEDICINE LAKE	1203-02-
SNEGOVOY (Kamchatka)	Shield (None) Holocene	**1000-69-**
SNEZHNAYA (Kamchatka)	Synonym of SNEZHNIY	1000-66-
SNEZHNIY (Kamchatka)	Shield (None) Holocene	**1000-66-**
SNIPES MOUNTAIN (US-Washington)	Cone of ADAMS	1201-04-
SNIPPAKER CREEK (Canada)	Cone of ISKUT-UNUK RIVER CONES	1200-09-
SNOU [SNOW] (Kurile Is)	Stratovolc of CHIRPOI	0900-15=
SNOWSHOE LAVA FIELD (Canada)	Vent of EDZIZA	1200-06-
SNOWY (Alaska Peninsula)	Stratovolc (None) Fumarolic	**1102-20-**
SOAL (New Guinea-NE of)	Stratovolc of UMBOI	0501-06=
SOBOLINY (Kamchatka)	Stratovolc of MALY SEMIACHIK	1000-14=
SOBOR (Africa-N)	Synonym of VOON, TARSO	0205-02=
SOBOROM (Africa-N)	Thermal Feature of VOON, TARSO	0205-02=
SOBOUROUN (Africa-N)	Synonym of VOON, TARSO	0205-02=
SOCHE (Ecuador)	Stratovolc (1, -7720) Radiocarbon	**1502-001**
SOCHOL, CERRO (Mexico)	Cone of TENAYO GROUP	1401-081
SOCOMPA (Chile-N)	Stratovolc (1, -5250) Radiocarbon	**1505-108**
SOCONUSCO (Mexico)	Synonym of TACANA	1401-13=
SOCORRO (Mexico-Is)	Shield (3, 1993) Historical	**1401-021**
SODA DAM (US-New Mexico)	Thermal Feature of VALLES CALDERA	1210-03-
SODA PEAK (US-Washington)	Cone of WEST CRATER	1201-06-
SODORE (Ethiopia)	Pyrocl cones (None) Holocene	**0201-222**
SOEKARIA CALDERA (Lesser Sunda Is)	Synonym of SUKARIA CALDERA	0604-12=
SOEKET [SUKET] (Java)	Stratovolc of RAUNG	0603-34=
SOELASIH (Sumatra)	Synonym of TALANG	0601-16=
SOELHEIMAJOKULL (Iceland-S)	Synonym of KATLA	1702-03=
SOEMBING (Java)	Synonym of SUMBING	0603-22=
SOEMBING (Sumatra)	Synonym of SUMBING	0601-18=
SOENDA CALDERA [SUNDA CALDERA]	Pleistocene caldera of TANGKUBANPARA	0603-09=
SOENDORO (Java)	Synonym of SUNDORO	0603-21=
SOENGPANACK (Korea)	Vent of HALLA	1006-04-
SOEOH-SENKE (Sumatra)	Synonym of SUOH	0601-27=
SOFUNOBORI (Kurile Is)	Synonym of TIATIA	0900-03=
SOGAGIGIR (Iceland-SW)	Crater row of KRISUVIK	1701-03=
SOLCHIARO (Italy)	Tuff ring of CAMPI FLEGREI	0101-01=
SOLEDAD, CERRO LA (Guatemala)	Dome of TECUAMBURRO	1402-12=
SOLFATARA (Italy)	Crater of CAMPI FLEGREI	0101-01=
SOLIMAN (Canary Is)	Cone of HIERRO	1803-02-
SOLIS (Mexico)	Maar of MICHOACAN-GUANAJUATO	1401-06=
SOLITARIO, EL (Mexico)	Cone of IZTACCIHUATL	1401-086
SOLITARIO, EL (Mexico)	Dome of IZTACCIHUATL	1401-086
SOLKATLA (Iceland-SW)	Shield of LANGJOKULL	1701-08=
SOLLIPULLI (Chile-C)	Caldera (2, 1240) Radiocarbon	**1507-111**
SOLO (Sulu Is-Philippines)	Synonym of BUD DAJO	0700-01=
SOLOWA AGAM (SOLAWAIK AGAM) (Sumat	Synonym of SEULAWAH AGAM	0601-02=
SOMBUTANG (Lesser Sunda Is)	Crater of SIRUNG	0604-27=
SOMMA CRATER (W Indies)	Crater of SOUFRIERE ST. VINCENT	1600-15=
SOMMA, MONTE (Italy)	Stratovolc of VESUVIUS	0101-02=
SOMMA-VESUVIANA (Italy)	Synonym of VESUVIUS	0101-02=
SOMMATA, LA (Italy)	Cone of VULCANO	0101-05=
SONA, MONTE (Italy)	Cone of ETNA	0101-06=
SONCCO ORCCO, CERRO (Peru)	Stratovolc of FIRURA, NEVADOS	1504-00-
SONGAK-SAN (Korea)	Tuff ring of HALLA	1006-04-
SONGAN (Lesser Sunda Is)	Dome of BATUR	0604-01=
SONGE (Africa-E)	Dome of MERU	0202-16=
SONGYAUNG (SE Asia)	Crater of LOWER CHINDWIN	0705-09-
SOPAS, LAS (Chile-C)	Thermal Feature of CORDON CAULLE	1507-141
SOPKA (Russian for VOLCANO) see proper name (e.g. ILIINA, SOPKA)		
SOPOCHNAIA (Kamchatka)	Synonym of ICHINSKY	1000-28=
SOPOETAN (Sulawesi-Indonesia)	Synonym of SOPUTAN	0606-03=
SOPOTSCHNAJA (Kamchatka)	Synonym of ICHINSKY	1000-28=
SOPUTAN (Sulawesi-Indonesia)	Stratovolc (28, 1993) Historical	**0606-03=**
SOR-JAN (Atl-N-Jan Mayen)	Cone of JAN MAYEN	1706-01=
SORC-ALI (SORC-ALLI) (Ethiopia)	Synonym of MALLAHLE	0201-102
SORCALI (Ethiopia)	Synonym of SORKALE	0201-103
SOREA (Banda Sea)	Synonym of SERUA	0605-07=
SORETIMEAT (Vanuatu-SW Pacific)	Complx volc (3, 1966) Historical	**0507-01=**
SORIEQ BERAPI (Sumatra)	Synonym of SORIKMARAPI	0601-12=
SORIKMARAPI (Sumatra)	Stratovolc (7, 1986) Historical	**0601-12=**
SORIKMERAPI (Sumatra)	Synonym of SORIKMARAPI	0601-12=
SORKALE (Ethiopia)	Stratovolc (None) Holocene?	**0201-103**
SOROPATI (Java)	Stratovolc of TELOMOYO	0603-231
SOSED (Kamchatka)	Cone of TOLBACHIK	1000-24=
SOSSO, EHI (Africa-N)	Cone of TOUSSIDE, TARSO	0205-01=
SOTARA (Colombia)	Stratovolc ? (None) Holocene	**1501-061**
SOUFRIERE GUADELOUPE (W Indies)	Stratovolc (20, 1977) Historical	**1600-06=**
SOUFRIERE HILLS (W Indies)	Stratovolc (1, 1630) Radiocarbon	**1600-05=**
SOUFRIERE, LA (W Indies)	Dome of SOUFRIERE GUADELOUPE	1600-06=
SOUFRIERE ST. VINCENT (W Indies)	Stratovolc (21, 1979) Historical	**1600-15=**
SOUNKYO (Hokkaido-Japan)	Thermal Feature of DAISETSU	0805-06=
SOUNZAN (Honshu-Japan)	Thermal Feature of HAKONE	0803-02=
SOUR CREEK (US-Wyoming)	Dome of YELLOWSTONE	1205-01-
SOURCE HILL (Canada)	Fissure vent of SPECTRUM RANGE	1200-07-
SOURETAMATI (Vanuatu-SW Pacific)	Synonym of SORETIMEAT	0507-01=
SOUSAKI (Greece)	Synonym of SUSAKI	0102-01=
SOUTH BELKNAP (US-Oregon)	Cone of BELKNAP	1202-06-
SOUTH BUTTE (US-Washington)	Cone of ADAMS	1201-04-
SOUTH CINDER PEAK (US-Oregon)	Cone of JEFFERSON	1202-02-
SOUTH COULEE (US-California)	Dome of MONO CRATERS	1203-12-
SOUTH DAUGHTER [TURANGUNAN]	Stratovolc of RABAUL	0502-14=
SOUTH EAST MOUNTAIN (W Indies)	Cone of ST. CATHERINE	1600-17=
SOUTH FORK [RED HILL] (US-Calif)	Cone of GOLDEN TROUT CREEK	1203-17-
SOUTH GROUP (US-Oregon)	Cone of SAND MOUNTAIN FIELD	1202-04-
SOUTH ISLAND (Africa-E)	Stratovolc (1, 1888) Historical	**0202-02=**
SOUTH MOUNTAIN (US-New Mexico)	Dome of VALLES CALDERA	1210-03-
SOUTH PAGAN (Mariana Is-C Pac)	Stratovolc of PAGAN	0804-17=
SOUTH PIT (Hawaiian Is)	Pit crater of MAUNA LOA	1302-02=
SOUTH RIFT ZONE (Hawaiian Is)	Fissure vent of MAUNA KEA	1302-03-
SOUTH SISTER (US-Oregon)	Complx volc (2, -0050) Radiocarbon	**1202-08-**
SOUTH SON (New Britain-SW Pac)	Synonym of BAMUS	0502-11=
SOUTH SOUFRIERE HILLS (W Indies)	Stratovolc of SOUFRIERE HILLS	1600-05=
SOUTHEAST CRATER (Italy)	Crater of ETNA	0101-06=
SOUTHERN CRATER (Mindanao-Philippines)	Crater of APO	0701-03=
SOUTHERN CRATER (Philippines-C)	Crater of CANLAON	0702-02=
SOUTHERN DOME (New Zealand)	Dome of OKATAINA	0401-05=
SOUTHERN SIKHOTE-ALIN (Russia-SE)	Volc field (None) Holocene	**1002-01-**
SOUTHWEST HILL [VOLCAN SUDOESTE]	Cone of SAN QUINTIN VOLC FIELD	1401-002
SOUTHWEST RIFT ZONE (Hawaiian Is)	Fissure vent of MAUNA LOA	1302-02=

NAME (Subregion)	Type (Eruption Total, Most Recent) Status Relation to NAMED VOLCANO	NUMBER
SOUTHWEST RIFT ZONE (Hawaiian Is)	Fissure vent of KILAUEA	1302-01-
SPACCATA, MONTAGNA (Italy)	Crater of CAMPI FLEGREI	0101-01=
SPANISH BONK (Canada)	Cone of WELLS GRAY-CLEARWATER	1200-15-
SPANISH CREEK [SPANISH LAKE] (Canada)	Cone of WELLS GRAY-CLEARWATER	1200-15-
SPANISH LAKE (Canada)	Cone of WELLS GRAY-CLEARWATER	1200-15-
SPANISH MUMP (Canada)	Cone of WELLS GRAY-CLEARWATER	1200-15-
SPECTRUM RANGE (Canada)	Shield (None) Holocene	**1200-07-**
SPENCE HOT SPRING (US-New Mexico)	Thermal Feature of VALLES CALDERA	1210-03-
SPENDLOVE KNOLL (US-Utah)	Cone of KOLOB	1207-02-
SPHINX (Canada)	Dome of EDZIZA	1200-06-
SPHINX MORAINE (Canada)	Vent of GARIBALDI LAKE	1200-19-
SPINAIO, MT. (Italy)	Cone of VULSINI	0101-003
SPLIT BUTTE (US-Idaho)	Maar of WAPI LAVA FIELD	1204-03-
SPLIT BUTTE (US-Idaho)	Cone of CRATERS OF THE MOON	1204-02-
SPRING BUTTE (US-Oregon)	Cone of NEWBERRY VOLCANO	1202-11-
SPRING GHAUT SOUFRIERE (W Indies)	Thermal Feature of SOUFRIERE HILLS	1600-05=
SPRING HILL (Australia)	Cone of NEWER VOLCANICS PROV	0509-01-
SPRING HILL (US-California)	Cone of SHASTA	1203-01-
SPRINKER (Germany)	Maar of WEST EIFEL VOLC FIELD	0100-01-
SPURR (Alaska-SW)	Stratovolc (6, 1992) Historical	**1103-04-**
SQUAW LAKE (US-Wyoming)	Crater of YELLOWSTONE	1205-01-
SQUAW RIDGE FIELD (US-Oregon)	Volc field (None) Holocene?	**1202-13-**
SREDNI (Kurile Is)	Cone of MEDVEZHIA	0900-10=
SREDNII (Kurile Is)	Submarine (None) Holocene	**0900-211**
SREDNIY (Kurile Is)	Crater of EBEKO	0900-38=
SREDNY (Kamchatka)	Shield of TUZOVSKY	1000-55-
SREDNYAYA [SREDNY] (Kamchatka)	Stratovolc of USHKOVSKY	1000-261
SREZANNAIA MOUNTAIN (Kamchatka)	Synonym of MALY SEMIACHIK	1000-14=
SRODJO [SROJA] (Java)	Cone of DIENG VOLC COMPLEX	0603-20=
SRONGGA, BUKIT (Lesser Sunda Is)	Cone of BATUR	0604-01=
SSAWADOWSKI (Antarctica)	Synonym of ZAVODOVSKI	1900-13=
STAKAHRAUN (Iceland-S)	Fissure vent of HEKLA	1702-07=
STAMPAR (Iceland-SW)	Crater row of REYKJANES	1701-02=
STANGARHALS (Iceland-SW)	Fissure vent of HENGILL	1701-05=
STAR PEAK (Vanuatu-SW Pacific)	Synonym of MERE LAVA	0507-021
STARICHKY (Kamchatka)	Cone of TOLBACHIK	1000-24=
STARY KIKHPINYCH [PIK] (Kamchatka)	Stratovolc of KIKHPINYCH	1000-18=
STARY SHEVELUCH (Kamchatka)	Stratovolc of SHEVELUCH	1000-27=
STATE PRESIDENT SWART PEAK (Indian	Cone of MARION ISLAND	0304-08-
STAUGHTONS HILL (Australia)	Maar of NEWER VOLCANICS PROV	0509-01-
STE-ROSE, PITON (Indian O.-W)	Cone of FOURNAISE, PITON DE LA	0303-02=
STEAMBOAT SPRINGS (US-Nevada)	Lava domes (None) Pleistocene-Fumarolic	**1206-01-**
STEAMING HILL LAKE (Vanuatu-SW Pacific)	Synonym of GAUA	0507-02=
STEFANOS (Greece)	Vent of NISYROS	0102-05=
STELLER (Alaska Peninsula)	Unknown (None) Uncertain	**1102-22-**
STENA (Kamchatka)	Stratovolc of MALY SEMIACHIK	1000-14=
STENA (Kamchatka)	Dome of KSUDACH	1000-05=
STEPHANOS [STEFANOS] (Greece)	Vent of NISYROS	0102-05=
STEPHENS HILL (Alaska-W)	Cone of ST. MICHAEL	1104-04-
STERNA GAMBRU (Greece)	Dome of METHANA	0102-02=
STOCKYARD HILL (Australia)	Tuff ring of NEWER VOLCANICS PROV	0509-01-
STOKAP (Kurile Is)	Stratovolc of BOGATYR RIDGE	0900-06-
STOLOVAYA (Kamchatka)	Dome of OPALA	1000-08=
STONE MOUNTAIN [LITTLE GLASS MTN.]	Dome of MEDICINE LAKE	1203-02-
STONY HILL (Atlantic-S)	Dome of TRISTAN DA CUNHA	1806-01=
STORA ELDBORG UNDIR GEITLAHLID	Crater row of BRENNISTEINSFJOLL	1701-04=
STORA-VITI (Iceland)	Shield of THEISTAREYKJARBUNGA	1703-09=
STORAHVERSMOR (Iceland)	Shield of THEISTAREYKJARBUNGA	1703-09=
STORHOFDI (Iceland-S)	Crater of VESTMANNAEYJAR	1702-01=
STORHOFDI (Iceland-SE)	Cone of ORAEFAJOKULL	1704-01=
STORI BOLLI (Iceland-SW)	Crater row of BRENNISTEINSFJOLL	1701-04=
STORM (Canada)	Cone of EDZIZA	1200-06-
STOVES OF NERO (Italy)	Crater of CAMPI FLEGREI	0101-01=
STRARIY (Russia-SE)	Cone of OKA VOLC FIELD	1002-06-
STRAWBERRY KNOLLS (US-Utah)	Cone of MARKAGUNT PLATEAU	1207-04-
STRELOSHNAIA SOPKA (Kamchatka)	Synonym of KORYAKSKY	1000-09=
STRELOTSCHNAJA (Kamchatka)	Synonym of KORYAKSKY	1000-09=
STROHN (Germany)	Maar of WEST EIFEL VOLC FIELD	0100-01-
STROMBOLI (Italy)	Stratovolc (67, 1986) Historical	**0101-04=**
STROMBOLICCHIO (Italy)	Cone of STROMBOLI	0101-04=
STROMPAR (Iceland-SW)	Shield of BRENNISTEINSFJOLL	1701-04=
STRONGYLE (Italy)	Synonym of STROMBOLI	0101-04=
STUART HILL (Alaska-W)	Shield of ST. MICHAEL	1104-04-
STUART HILL (Honduras)	Cone of UTILA ISLAND	1403-16-
STUBEL CRATER (Kamchatka)	Maar of KSUDACH	1000-05=
STUFE DI KAZEN (Italy)	Cone of PANTELLERIA	0101-071
STUPENCHATY (Kamchatka)	Dome of BEZYMIANNY	1000-25=
STUPENCHATY BASTION (Kamchatka)	Stratovolc of MALY SEMIACHIK	1000-14=
STURGE ISLAND (Antarctica)	Stratovolc (None) Uncertain	**1900-012**
STYAKS SWAMP (New Zealand)	Cone of AUCKLAND FIELD	0401-02=
SUACHU (Kamchatka)	Synonym of AVACHINSKY	1000-10=
SUBAI [KUDRIAVY] (Kurile Is)	Cone of MEDVEZHIA	0900-10=
SUBIA, PUIG (Spain)	Cone of OLOT VOLC FIELD	0100-03-
SUCHILTEPEQUEZ (Guatemala)	Synonym of ATITLAN	1402-06=
SUCHIOC CHICO (Mexico)	Cone of CHICHINAUTZIN	1401-08=
SUCHIOC GRANDE (Mexico)	Cone of CHICHINAUTZIN	1401-08=
SUCHITAN VOLC FIELD (Guatemala)	Stratovolcs (None) Holocene	**1402-17-**
SUCHITEPEQUEZ (Guatemala)	Synonym of ATITLAN	1402-06=
SUDOESTE, VOLCAN (Mexico)	Cone of SAN QUINTIN VOLC FIELD	1401-002
SUDSOHN (New Britain-SW Pac)	Synonym of BAMUS	0502-11=
SUDUREY (Iceland-S)	Cone of VESTMANNAEYJAR	1702-01=
SUDURGIGAR (Iceland-S)	Fissure vent of HEKLA	1702-07=
SUELICH (Kamchatka)	Former dome of SHEVELUCH	1000-27=
SUEMEZ STRAIT (Alaska-SE)	Vent of TLEVAK STRAIT-SUEMEZ IS.	1105-06-
SUGAR BOWL (US-Washington)	Dome of ST. HELENS	1201-05-
SUGAR LOAF (Hawaiian Is)	Tuff cone of KOOLAU	1302-07-
SUGARLOAF (Aleutian Is)	Cone of MAKUSHIN	1101-31-
SUGARLOAF MOUNTAIN (US-California)	Dome of COSO VOLC FIELD	1203-18-
SUGARLOAF PEAK (Aleutian Is)	Stratovolc of SEMISOPOCHNOI	1101-06-
SUGARLOAF PEAK (US-California)	Shield of POTATO BUTTE	1203-07-
SUGARPINE BUTTE (US-Oregon)	Cone of NEWBERRY VOLCANO	1202-11-
SUGATAMI-NO-IKE (Hokkaido-Japan)	Crater of DAISETSU	0805-06=
SUGIGAMINE (Honshu-Japan)	Stratovolc of ZAO	0803-19=
SUGOBO [ANDREW'S VOLCANO] (Africa-E)	Cone of BARRIER, THE	0202-03=
SUGUTA-LOGKIPI (Africa-E)	Thermal Feature of BARRIER, THE	0202-03=
SUIRO (Philippines-C)	Dome of BILIRAN	0702-08=
SUJUT (Mindanao-Philippines)	Synonym of RAGANG	0701-06=
SUJUT (Mindanao-Philippines)	Synonym of MAKATURING	0701-04=
SUKARIA CALDERA (Lesser Sunda Is)	Caldera (None) Fumarolic	**0604-12=**
SUKAWA-DAKE (Honshu-Japan)	Synonym of KURIKOMA	0803-21=
SUKET (Java)	Stratovolc of RAUNG	0603-34=
SUKHOI (Kamchatka)	Stratovolc of MALY SEMIACHIK	1000-14=

NAME (Subregion)	Type (Eruption Total, Most Recent) Status Relation to NAMED VOLCANO	NUMBER
SUKUMO-YAMA (Honshu-Japan)	Cone of IZU-TOBU	0803-01=
SUKUTA SEE [SUGUTA-LOGKIPI] (Africa-E)	Thermal Feature of BARRIER, THE	0202-03=
SULFUR HILL (Luzon-Philippines)	Synonym of JALAJALA	0703-08=
SULFUR WORKS (US-Calif)	Thermal Feature of LASSEN VOLC CENT	1203-08-
SULFUREO, LAGO [LAGO VECCIENNA]	Crater of LARDERELLO	0101-001
SULLA TACOMI [TOLIRE JAHA] (Halmahera)	Crater of GAMALAMA	0608-06=
SULNASKER (Iceland-S)	Cone of VESTMANNAEYJAR	1702-01=
SULPHUR BANK (Hawaiian Is)	Thermal Feature of KILAUEA	1302-01-
SULPHUR CONE (Hawaiian Is)	Cone of MAUNA LOA	1302-02=
SULPHUR CREEK (New Britain-SW Pac)	Crater row of RABAUL	0502-14=
SULPHUR HOT SPRINGS (US-Washington)	Thermal Feature of GLACIER PEAK	1201-02-
SULPHUR ISLAND (Volcano Is-Japan)	Synonym of IWO-JIMA	0804-12=
SULPHUR LAGOON [LOWER TE MARI]	Crater of TONGARIRO	0401-08=
SULPHUR LAKE (D'Entrecasteaux Is)	Thermal Feature of IAMELELE	0503-05=
SULPHUR SPRINGS (US-New Mexico)	Thermal Feature of VALLES CALDERA	1210-03-
SULPHUR SPRINGS (W Indies)	Vent of QUALIBOU	1600-14=
SULPHUR VALLEY (New Zealand)	Thermal Feature of WHALE ISLAND	0401-041
SULU (Sulu Is-Philippines)	Synonym of BUD DAJO	0700-01=
SUMACO (Ecuador)	Stratovolc (1, 1895) Historical	**1502-04=**
SUMBER PANAS (Java)	Thermal Feature of KIARABERES-GAGAK	0603-03=
SUMBING (Java)	Dome of KELUT	0603-28=
SUMBING (Java)	Stratovolc (1, 1730) Historical	**0603-22=**
SUMBING (Sumatra)	Stratovolc (2, 1921) Historical	**0601-18=**
SUMISU-JIMA (SUMISU-SHO) (Izu Is-Japan)	Synonym of SMITH ROCK	0804-08=
SUMIYOSHI-IKE (Kyushu-Japan)	Maars (2, -4550) Radiocarbon	**0802-081**
SUMUR (Java)	Crater of DIENG VOLC COMPLEX	0603-20=
SUMUR BANDUNG (Java)	Crater of ARJUNO-WELIRANG	0603-29=
SUNDA CALDERA (Java)	Pleistocene caldera of TANGKUBANPARA	0603-09=
SUNDAY ISLAND (Kermadec Is)	Synonym of RAOUL ISLAND	0402-03=
SUNDHNUKAR (Iceland-SW)	Crater row of REYKJANES	1701-02=
SUNDORO (Java)	Stratovolc (9, 1971) Historical	**0603-21=**
SUNFLOWER FLAT (US-Calif)	Dome of LASSEN VOLC CENTER	1203-08-
SUNSET (US-Idaho)	Cone of CRATERS OF THE MOON	1204-02-
SUNSET CRATER (US-Arizona)	Cinder cone (4, 1220) Dendrochronology	**1209-02-**
SUOH (Sumatra)	Maars (1, 1933) Historical	**0601-27=**
SUPHAN DAGI (Turkey)	Stratovolc (None) Holocene	**0103-021**
SUPPLY REEF (Mariana Is-C Pac)	Submarine (2, 1989) Hydrophonic	**0804-142**
SURETAMATI (Vanuatu-SW Pacific)	Synonym of SORETIMEAT	0507-01=
SURETAMETAI (Vanuatu-SW Pacific)	Synonym of SORETIMEAT	0507-01=
SURIBACHI-KAKOKYU (Hokkaido-Japan)	Cone of TOKACHI	0805-05=
SURIBATI-YAMA [SURIBACHI-YAMA]	Cone of IWO-JIMA	0804-12=
SURTSEY (Iceland-S)	Cone of VESTMANNAEYJAR	1702-01=
SURUNDARO, CERRO DE (Mexico)	Cone of MICHOACAN-GUANAJUATO	1401-06=
SUSAH, KAWAH (Java)	Thermal Feature of SALAK	0603-05=
SUSAKI (Greece)	(None) Not a Volcano	0102-01=
SUSAKI (Ryukyu Is)	Cone of SUWANOSE-JIMA	0802-03=
SUSUA (Africa-E)	Synonym of SUSWA	0202-11=
SUSWA (Africa-E)	Shield (None) Holocene	**0202-11=**
SUTDONDURAN (Turkey)	Cone of ERCIYES DAGI	0103-01=
SUWANOSE-JIMA (Ryukyu Is)	Stratovolc (12, 1993) Historical	**0802-03=**
SUWANOSE-ZIMA (Ryukyu Is)	Synonym of SUWANOSE-JIMA	0802-03=
SUWOLBONG (Korea)	Tuff ring of HALLA	1006-04-
SUYAMA-DAKE (Honshu-Japan)	Synonym of KURIKOMA	0803-21=
SUYELICH [SUELICH] (Kamchatka)	Former dome of SHEVELUCH	1000-27=
SUZANNA MOUNT (SE Asia)	Cone of BAS DONG NAI	0705-05-
SUZUGA-TAKE (Honshu-Japan)	Dome of AKAGI	0803-13=
SVALASKARDSHRAUN (Iceland-S)	Crater row of VATNAFJOLL	1702-06=
SVALTHUFA (Iceland-W)	Cone of SNAEFELLSJOKULL	1700-01=
SVARTADYNGJA (Iceland-NE)	Shield of ASKJA	1703-06=
SVARTAHRAUN (Iceland-SW)	Crater row of LANGJOKULL	1701-08=
SVARTIHRYGGUR (Iceland-SW)	Crater row of BRENNISTEINSFJOLL	1701-04=
SVARTIKROKUR (Iceland-NE)	Crater row of BARDARBUNGA	1703-03=
SVEIFLUGIGIR (Iceland-SW)	Crater row of KRISUVIK	1701-03=
SVEINAGJA (Iceland-NE)	Fissure vent of ASKJA	1703-06=
SVEINAR (Iceland-NE)	Fissure vent of FREMRINAMUR	1703-07=
SVIAGIGUR (Iceland-NE)	Synonym of GRIMSVOTN	1703-01=
SVINHOFDARHRAUN (Iceland-S)	Fissure vent of HEKLA	1702-07=
SVORTUBORGIR (Iceland-NE)	Crater row of KRAFLA	1703-08=
SVORTUTINDAR (Iceland-W)	Cone of SNAEFELLSJOKULL	1700-01=
SVYASHCHENNAYA (Russia-SE)	Cone of TUNKIN DEPRESSION	1002-05-
SW USANGU BASIN (Africa-E)	Volc field (None) Holocene	**0202-163**
SWAMP WELLS BUTTE (US-Oregon)	Cone of NEWBERRY VOLCANO	1202-11-
SWARTKOP POINT (Indian O.-S)	Tuff cone of MARION ISLAND	0304-08-
SYKES (Mexico)	Crater of PINACATE PEAKS	1401-001
SYMONDS STREET (New Zealand)	Cone of AUCKLAND FIELD	0401-02=
SYOWA-IWO-ZIMA [SHOWA-IWO-JIMA]	Dome of KIKAI	0802-06=
SYOWA-SINZAN [SHOWA-SHINZAN]	Dome of USU	0805-03=
SYOZI-YAMA [SHOJI-YAMA] (Honshu-Japan)	Dome of OSORE-YAMA	0803-29=
SYRDRI RAUDAMELSKULA (Iceland-W)	Cone of LJOSUFJOLL	1700-03=
SYRFELLSHRAUN (Iceland-SW)	Crater row of REYKJANES	1701-02=
SYRKHISSAR (Georgia)	Dome of KASBEK	0104-02-
SYURADO [SHURADO] (Honshu-Japan)	Crater of NARUGO	0803-20=
SZIWAN, DJEBEL (Red Sea)	Synonym of TEYR, DJEBEL	0201-01=

T

NAME (Subregion)	Type (Eruption Total, Most Recent) Status Relation to NAMED VOLCANO	NUMBER
TA-I-SHAN [DAYISHAN] (China-E)	Cone of LONGGANG GROUP	1005-06-
TA-KU-SHAN-TZU [DAYISHAN] (China-E)	Cone of LONGGANG GROUP	1005-06-
TA-LUNG-WAN [DALONGWAN] (China-E)	Crater of LONGGANG GROUP	1005-06-
TA-T'UNG (China-E)	Synonym of DATONG	1005-01-
TA-TUNG (Taiwan)	Synonym of DATUN GROUP	0801-032
TA-YEN-CHIH-FENG [DAYANZHIFENG]	Cone of BAITOUSHAN	1005-07-
TAAL (Luzon-Philippines)	Stratovolc (33, 1977) Historical	**0703-07=**
TABAC, MT. (W Indies)	Stratovolc of QUALIBOU	1600-14=
TABAQUILLO (Mexico)	Cone of CHICHINAUTZIN	1401-08=
TABARO, MT. (Luzon-Philippines)	Vent of TAAL	0703-07=
TABASHINE-YAMA (Honshu-Japan)	Synonym of ZAO	0803-19=
TABERNACLE HILL (US-Utah)	Tuff cone of BLACK ROCK DESERT	1207-05-
TABLAS (El Salvador)	Stratovolc of SINGUIL, CERRO	1403-011
TABLE MT. CRATER (Galapagos)	Crater of SANTA CRUZ	1503-091
TABLE, THE (Canada)	Tuya of GARIBALDI LAKE	1200-19-
TABLE TOP-WIDE BAY (Aleutian Is)	Cinder cones (None) Holocene?	**1101-311**
TABLON, LOMA DEL (El Salvador)	Cone of SAN DIEGO	1403-012
TABONAL, EL (Canary Is)	Cone of TENERIFE	1803-03-
TABOR, MONTE (Italy)	Dome of ISCHIA	0101-03=
TABURETE (El Salvador)	Stratovolc (None) Holocene	**1403-072**
TABURIENTE, CALDERA DE (Canary Is)	Stratovolc of LA PALMA	1803-01-
TABUTERA (Vanuatu-SW Pacific)	Stratovolc of NORTH VATE	0507-081
TACANA (Mexico)	Stratovolc (3, 1986) Historical	**1401-13=**
TACANDE (Canary Is)	Cone of LA PALMA	1803-01-
TACATICES, CERRO (Nicaragua)	Cone of PILAS, LAS	1404-08=
TACHIBANA HOT SPRINGS (Honshu-Japan	Thermal Feature of KUSATSU-SHIRANE	0803-12=

NAME (Subregion)	Type (Eruption Total, Most Recent) Status . . . Relation to NAMED VOLCANO	NUMBER
TACO ARRIBA, CERRITO DE (Guatemala)	Cone of CHIQUIMULA FIELD	1402-20-
TACO, MONTANA DE (Canary Is)	Cone of TENERIFE	1803-03-
TACOMA, MT. (TACOMAN) (US-Washington)	Synonym of RAINIER	1201-03-
TACORA (Chile-N)	Stratovolc (None) Fumarolic	**1505-01=**
TADEKHO HILL (Canada)	Cone of SPECTRUM RANGE	1200-07-
TAFIRA, MONTANA (Canary Is)	Cone of GRAN CANARIA	1803-04-
TAFTAN (Iran)	Stratovolc (None) Holocene	**0302-05-**
TAFUA SAVAI'I (Samoa-SW Pacific)	Cone of SAVAI'I	0404-04=
TAFUA UPOLU (Samoa-SW Pacific)	Cone of UPOLU	0404-03-
TAGABO HILLS (Africa-N)	Synonym of KUTUM VOLC FIELD	0205-04-
TAGHUM BUTTE (US-Oregon)	Cone of NEWBERRY VOLCANO	1202-11-
TAGIRI (Kyushu-Japan)	Cone of SAKURA-JIMA	0802-08=
TAGLABUNGA [TALABUNGA] (Iceland-NE)	Shield of FREMRINAMUR	1703-07=
TAGLGIGAHRAUN (Iceland-S)	Fissure vent of HEKLA	1702-07=
TAGOTALA (Samoa-SW Pacific)	Cone of SAVAI'I	0404-04=
TAGUS (Galapagos)	Tuff cone of DARWIN, VOLCAN	1503-03=
TAHE (Lesser Sunda Is)	Cone of TAMBORA	0604-04=
TAHEKE (New Zealand)	Thermal Feature of ROTORUA	0401-042
TAHOMA PEAK (Aleutian Is)	Former dome of BOGOSLOF	1101-30-
TAHONELATCLAH (US-Washington)	Synonym of ST. HELENS	1201-05-
TAHORANUI (New Zealand)	Cone of KAIKOHE-BAY OF ISLANDS	0401-01=
TAHUAL, VOLCAN (Guatemala)	Stratovolc of SUCHITAN VOLC FIELD	1402-17-
TAHUNATARA (New Zealand)	Dome of TAUPO	0401-07=
TAHUYA (Canary Is)	Cone of LA PALMA	1803-01-
TAIHEI-ZAN (Kyushu-Japan)	Dome of TSURUMI	0802-13=
TAIR, DJEBEL (Red Sea)	Synonym of TEYR, DJEBEL	0201-01=
TAIRAGA-DAKE (Hokkaido-Japan)	Stratovolc of TOKACHI	0805-05=
TAIROIKE (Izu Is-Japan)	Crater of MIYAKE-JIMA	0804-04=
TAISEN-ZAN (Kyushu-Japan)	Cone of KUJU GROUP	0802-12=
TAISHO (Honshu-Japan)	Crater of YAKE-DAKE	0803-07=
TAISYO-KAKO [TAISHO-KAKO] (Hokkaido)	Crater of TOKACHI	0805-05=
TAITO'ELAU (Samoa-SW Pacific)	Cone of UPOLU	0404-03-
TAJUMULCO (Guatemala)	Stratovolc (None) Holocene	**1402-02=**
TAKA-DAKE (Kyushu-Japan)	Stratovolc of ASO	0802-11=
TAKA-YAMA (Honshu-Japan)	Cone of FUJI	0803-03=
TAKA-YAMA (Honshu-Japan)	Synonym of ZAO	0803-19=
TAKACHIHO-MINE (Kyushu-Japan)	Stratovolc of KIRISHIMA	0802-09=
TAKADEKKI (Honshu-Japan)	Dome of IIZUNA	0803-102
TAKAHACHI-YAMA (Honshu-Japan)	Cone of FUJI	0803-03=
TAKAHARA (Hokkaido-Japan)	Thermal Feature of DAISETSU	0805-06=
TAKAHARA (Honshu-Japan)	Stratovolc (None) Holocene	**0803-143**
TAKAHE (Antarctica)	Shield (2, -6550) Ice Core	**1900-027**
TAKAHIRA-YAMA (Kyushu-Japan)	Cone of TSURUMI	0802-13=
TAKAIWA-YAMA (Kyushu-Japan)	Dome of UNZEN	0802-10=
TAKAMAKA, PITON (Indian O.-W)	Cone of FOURNAISE, PITON DE LA	0303-02=
TAKAMURO-YAMA (Honshu-Japan)	Cone of IZU-TOBU	0803-01=
TAKANOSU (Kyushu-Japan)	Dome of KUJU GROUP	0802-12=
TAKASHI-YAMA (Honshu-Japan)	Synonym of FUJI	0803-03=
TAKATIHO-MINE [TAKACHIHO-MINE]	Stratovolc of KIRISHIMA	0802-09=
TAKATSUKA-YAMA (Honshu-Japan)	Cone of IZU-TOBU	0803-01=
TAKAWANGHA (Aleutian Is)	Stratovolc (None) Holocene	**1101-09-**
TAKE-YAMA (Kyushu-Japan)	Dome of IBUSUKI VOLC FIELD	0802-07=
TAKEFJELLET (Atl-N-Jan Mayen)	Dome of JAN MAYEN	1706-01=
TAKENOHIRA (Izu Is-Japan)	Cone of OSHIMA	0804-01=
TAKENOYU (Kyushu-Japan)	Thermal Feature of KUJU GROUP	0802-12=
TAKETOMI (Kurile Is)	Crater of ALAID	0900-39=
TAKETORI-YAMA (Honshu-Japan)	Synonym of FUJI	0803-03=
TAKIT (Luzon-Philippines)	Synonym of MALINAO	0703-04=
TAKODO-YAMA (Izu Is-Japan)	Dome of KOZU-SHIMA	0804-03=
TAKOU (New Zealand)	Cone of KAIKOHE-BAY OF ISLANDS	0401-01=
TAKUAN GROUP (Bougainville-SW Pacific)	Volc complx (None) Holocene	**0505-021**
TAKUMI-YAMA (Honshu-Japan)	Cone of OKI-DOGO	0803-003
TALA (Halmahera-Indonesia)	Synonym of DUKONO	0608-01=
TALA (Luzon-Philippines)	Dome of NATIB	0703-082
TALABUNGA (Iceland-NE)	Shield of FREMRINAMUR	1703-07=
TALAGABODAS (Java)	Stratovolc (None) Fumarolic	**0603-15=**
TALAKMAU (Sumatra)	Complx volc (None) Holocene	**0601-13=**
TALAMAU (Sumatra)	Synonym of TALAKMAU	0601-13=
TALANG (Sumatra)	Stratovolc (8, 1968) Historical	**0601-16=**
TALANG, DANAU (Sumatra)	Crater of TALANG	0601-16=
TALAO, VUTI (Vanuatu-SW Pacific)	Cone of AOBA	0507-03=
TALASEA GOVERNMENT STATION	Thermal Feature of GARUA HARBOUR	0502-06=
TALASEA HARBOUR (New Britain-SW Pac)	Synonym of GARUA HARBOUR	0502-06=
TALAWE, MT. (New Britain-SW Pac)	Stratovolc of LANGILA	0502-01=
TALAYA GROUP (Russia-SE)	Cone of TUNKIN DEPRESSION	1002-05-
TALBOT BANK (Italy)	Submarine vent of CAMPI FLEGREI MAR	0101-07=
TALGUIAN (Mexico)	Stratovolc of TACANA	1401-13=
TALIPAO, MT. (Sulu Is-Philippines)	Cone of BUD DAJO	0700-01=
TALLANG (Sumatra)	Synonym of TALANG	0601-16=
TALO (New Guinea-NE of)	Stratovolc of UMBOI	0501-06=
TALOLINGA, LOMA (Nicaragua)	Cone of SAN CRISTOBAL	1404-02=
TALPETATE, CERRO (Nicaragua)	Dome of APOYEQUE	1404-091
TAMA LAKES (New Zealand)	Crater of RUAPEHU	0401-10=
TAMACITE, MONTANA (Canary Is)	Cone of FUERTEVENTURA	1803-05-
TAMAGASTEPEC [TAMAGES] (El Salvador)	Cone of SANTA ANA	1403-02=
TAMAGAWA SPA (Honshu-Japan)	Thermal Feature of AKITA-YAKE-YAMA	0803-26=
TAMAGES (El Salvador)	Cone of SANTA ANA	1403-02=
TAMAMI (Santa Cruz Is-SW Pac)	Synonym of TINAKULA	0506-01=
TAMAN GEDANG (Sumatra)	Crater of KUNYIT	0601-19=
TAMAN, KAWAH (Java)	Thermal Feature of PERBAKTI	0603-04=
TAMAN SAAT (Java)	Crater of PATUHA	0603-07=
TAMANHIDUP (Java)	Crater of IYANG-ARGAPURA	0603-33=
TAMANKERING (Java)	Crater of IYANG-ARGAPURA	0603-33=
TAMANO-IKE (Honshu-Japan)	Crater of CHOKAI	0803-22=
TAMANSARI GROUP (Lesser Sunda Is)	Crater of BATUR	0604-01=
TAMBORA (Lesser Sunda Is)	Stratovolc (7, 1967) Historical	**0604-04=**
TAMBUNARAKWE, VITI (Vanuatu-SW Pacific	Cone of AOBA	0507-03=
TAMERTIOU, TARSO (Africa-N)	Cone of TOUSSIDE, TARSO	0205-01=
TAMIA, MONTANA (Canary Is)	Cone of LANZAROTE	1803-06-
TAMLANG, MT. (Luzon-Philippines)	Cone of LAGUNA VOLC FIELD	0703-051
TAMOJANG [TAMOYANG] (Lesser Sunda Is)	Crater of SIRUNG	0604-27=
TAMPOMAS (Java)	Stratovolc (None) Holocene	**0603-131**
TAMPUSU [TOMPUSU] (Sulawesi-Indonesia)	Cone of TONDANO CALDERA	0606-07-
TANA (Vanuatu-SW Pacific)	Synonym of YASUR	0507-10=
TANAGA (Aleutian Is)	Stratovolcs (3, 1914) Historical	**1101-08-**
TANAH LAPANG (Halmahera-Indonesia)	Crater of DUKONO	0608-01=
TANAK-ANGUNAK (Aleutian Is)	Synonym of CARLISLE	1101-23-
TANDIKAI (Sumatra)	Synonym of TANDIKAT	0601-15=
TANDIKAT (Sumatra)	Stratovolc (3, 1924) Historical	**0601-15=**
TANDUKBENUA, DOLOK (Sumatra)	Cone of TOBA	0601-09=
TANDUREK (Turkey)	Synonym of TENDURUK DAGI	0103-03=
TANEMAKISHIRO (Honshu-Japan)	Crater of IWAKI	0803-27=
TANEMAKISIRO [TANEMAKISHIRO]	Crater of IWAKI	0803-27=
TANG-SHUI-CHANG (China-E)	Thermal Feature of BAITOUSHAN	1005-07-
TANGANASOGA (Canary Is)	Cone of HIERRO	1803-02-
TANGANO (Africa-E)	Shield of NGOZI	0202-164
TANGAROA, MAUNGA (Pacific-C)	Cone of EASTER ISLAND	1303-08-
TANGKOEBAN PRAHOE (Java)	Synonym of TANGKUBANPARAHU	0603-09=
TANGKUBAN PERAHU (Java)	Synonym of TANGKUBANPARAHU	0603-09=
TANGKUBANPARAHU (Java)	Stratovolc (16, 1983) Historical	**0603-09=**
TANGLUP, MT. (New Guinea-NE of)	Cone of UMBOI	0501-06=
TANGUERRES (Colombia)	Synonym of AZUFRAL, VOLCAN	1501-09=
TANGUES, PITON (Indian O.-W)	Cone of FOURNAISE, PITON DE LA	0303-02=
TANGWANGI, VUTI (Vanuatu-SW Pacific)	Cone of AOBA	0507-03=
TANJUNG TIRAMANA (Lesser Sunda Is)	Thermal Feature of PALUWEH	0604-15=
TANK FARM (New Zealand)	Tuff ring of AUCKLAND FIELD	0401-02=
TANNA (Vanuatu-SW Pacific)	Synonym of YASUR	0507-10=
TANODOUREK (Turkey)	Synonym of TENDURUK DAGI	0103-03=
TANSEI (Honshu-Japan)	Dome of NANTAI	0803-141
TANTALUS (Hawaiian Is)	Tuff cone of KOOLAU	1302-07-
TAO-RUSYR CALDERA (Kurile Is)	Stratovolc (2, 1952) Historical	**0900-31=**
TAO, VOLCAN DE (Canary Is)	Cone of LANZAROTE	1803-06-
TAPAHORO (New Zealand)	Dome of OKATAINA	0401-05=
TAPAK (Lesser Sunda Is)	Stratovolc of BRATAN	0604-001
TAPEIXTE, CERRO (Mexico)	Cone of TENAYO GROUP	1401-081
TAPIRAG, MT. (Alaska Peninsula)	Synonym of FOURPEAKED	1102-26-
TAPU'ELE'ELE (Samoa-SW Pacific)	Cone of SAVAI'I	0404-04=
TAPUNIKANDI, VUTI (Vanuatu-SW Pacific)	Cone of AOBA	0507-03=
TAPUTAPU (Samoa-SW Pacific)	Shield of TUTUILA	0404-02-
TAR, DJEBEL (Red Sea)	Synonym of TEYR, DJEBEL	0201-01=
TAR RIVER SOUFRIERE (W Indies)	Thermal Feature of SOUFRIERE HILLS	1600-05=
TARA, BATOE (Lesser Sunda Is)	Synonym of TARA, BATU	0604-26=
TARA, BATU (Lesser Sunda Is)	Stratovolc (1, 1852) Historical	**0604-26=**
TARANAKI (New Zealand)	Synonym of EGMONT	0401-03=
TARASCAN VOLC FIELD (Mexico)	Synonym of MICHOACAN-GUANAJUATO	1401-06=
TARATIMI (New Zealand)	Tuff ring of MAYOR ISLAND	0401-021
TARAWERA (New Zealand)	Fissure vent of OKATAINA	0401-05=
TARDARFJOLL (Iceland-SW)	Crater row of KRISUVIK	1701-03=
TAREWAKOURA (New Zealand)	Dome of MAYOR ISLAND	0401-021
TARI (Pacific-C)	Cone of EASTER ISLAND	1303-08-
TARIAT-CHOLOOT (Mongolia)	Synonym of TARYATU-CHULUTU	1003-01-
TARO (Honshu-Japan)	Dome of OMANAGO GROUP	0803-142
TAROEB [TARUB] (Java)	Stratovolc of LAMONGAN	0603-32=
TAROKA GROUP (Bougainville-SW Pac)	Cone of LOLORU	0505-03=
TARSO (Chad term for MOUNTAIN) see proper name (e.g. VOON, TARSO)		
TARTARET (France)	Cone of CHAINE DES PUYS	0100-02-
TARUB (Java)	Stratovolc of LAMONGAN	0603-32=
TARUMAI (Hokkaido-Japan)	Stratovolc of SHIKOTSU	0805-04=
TARUTAMA (Kyushu-Japan)	Thermal Feature of ASO	0802-11=
TARYATU-CHULUTU (Mongolia)	Volc field (None) Holocene	**1003-01-**
TASOVI, VUSI (Vanuatu-SW Pacific)	Cone of AOBA	0507-03=
TAT ALI (Ethiopia)	Shield (None) Holocene	**0201-106**
TATA SABAYA (Bolivia)	Stratovolc (None) Holocene	**1505-024**
TATARA-SAN PEDRO [SAN PEDRO] (Chile)	Stratovolc of SAN PEDRO-PELLADO	1507-063
TATARINOV (Kurile Is)	Stratovolc of CHIKURACHKI	0900-36=
TATARIWAN (Sulawesi-Indonesia)	Cone of LOKON-EMPUNG	0606-10=
TATE-YAMA (Honshu-Japan)	Stratovolc (3, 1839) Historical	**0803-08=**
TATESHINA (Honshu-Japan)	Stratovolcs (None) Holocene	**0803-031**
TATIO (Chile-N)	Hydrothrm fld (None) Pleistocene-Geysers	**1505-08=**
TATODOMJI (Africa-N)	Cone of TOUSSIDE, TARSO	0205-01=
TATUN GEOTHERMAL AREA (Taiwan)	Synonym of DATUN GROUP	0801-032
TA'U (Samoa-SW Pacific)	Shield (None) Holocene	**0404-001**
TAU (Samoa-SW Pacific)	Dome of TUTUILA	0404-02-
TAUANUI (New Zealand)	Cone of KAIKOHE-BAY OF ISLANDS	0401-01=
TAUGA POINT (Samoa-SW Pacific)	Tuff cone of OFU-OLOSEGA	0404-01=
TAUHARA (New Zealand)	Dome of TAUPO	0401-07=
TAUHARA-TAUPO (New Zealand)	Thermal Feature of TAUPO	0401-07=
TAULEVU (Fiji Is-SW Pacific)	Cone of TAVEUNI	0405-01-
TAUNGBYAUK (SE Asia)	Crater of LOWER CHINDWIN	0705-09-
TAUNGGALA (SE Asia)	Cone of POPA	0705-08-
TAUNSHITS (Kamchatka)	Stratovolc (2, -0550) Radiocarbon	**1000-16-**
TAUPE, PUY DE LA (France)	Cone of CHAINE DES PUYS	0100-02-
TAUPO (New Zealand)	Caldera (25, 0210) Radiocarbon	**0401-07=**
TAVAI RURO (Vanuatu-SW Pacific)	Stratovolc (None) Holocene?	**0507-062**
TAVALAPA (Vanuatu-SW Pacific)	Cone of KUWAE	0507-07=
TAVANI (Melanesian word for MOUNTAIN) see proper name (e.g. KUTALI, TAVANI)		
TAVEUNI (Fiji Is-SW Pacific)	Shield (1, -0100) Radiocarbon	**0405-01-**
TAVOKA (Solomon Is-SW Pac)	Thermal Feature of SAVO	0505-07=
TAVURVUR (New Britain-SW Pac)	Stratovolc of RABAUL	0502-14=
TAVUYANGA (Fiji Is-SW Pacific)	Cone of TAVEUNI	0405-01-
TAWEH HOT SPRINGS (Canada)	Thermal Feature of EDZIZA	1200-06-
TAY-IN-SHAN [DAYINGSHAN] (China-S)	Stratovolc of TENGCHONG	0705-11-
TAYGETE CONE (Antarctica)	Dome of PLEIADES, THE	1900-013
TAYIR, DJEBEL (Red Sea)	Synonym of TEYR, DJEBEL	0201-01=
TAYLORS HILL (New Zealand)	Cone of AUCKLAND FIELD	0401-02=
TAZA, CERRO LA (Chile-C)	Cone of CARRAN-LOS VENADOS	1507-14=
TAZA, CERRO LA (Mexico)	Cone of MICHOACAN-GUANAJUATO	1401-06=
TAZA, LA (Chile-C)	Cone of ANTILLANCA GROUP	1507-153
TAZENAT (France)	Maar of CHAINE DES PUYS	0100-02-
TCHEGULACH (Aleutian Is)	Synonym of CHAGULAK	1101-20-
TCHOBBE (Ethiopia)	Synonym of CORBETTI CALDERA	0201-29-
TE AHUAHU (New Zealand)	Cone of KAIKOHE-BAY OF ISLANDS	0401-01=
TE ANANUI (New Zealand)	Tuff ring of MAYOR ISLAND	0401-021
TE ARAAKA (New Zealand)	Tuff ring of MAYOR ISLAND	0401-021
TE HAEHAENGA (New Zealand)	Thermal Feature of OKATAINA	0401-05=
TE HAPEOTOROA (New Zealand)	Dome of OKATAINA	0401-05=
TE HORO (New Zealand)	Tuff ring of MAYOR ISLAND	0401-021
TE HOROA (New Zealand)	Dome of OKATAINA	0401-05=
TE KAHU REA, MAUNGA (Pacific-C)	Cone of EASTER ISLAND	1303-08-
TE KAUHANGA O VARU, MAUNGA (Pacific	Cone of EASTER ISLAND	1303-08-
TE KOPIA (New Zealand)	Thermal Feature of OKATAINA	0401-05=
TE KUKUTA (New Zealand)	Vent of MAYOR ISLAND	0401-021
TE KUMETE (New Zealand)	Dome of OKATAINA	0401-05=
TE MAARI [TE MARI] (New Zealand)	Crater of TONGARIRO	0401-08=
TE PARITU (New Zealand)	Vent of MAYOR ISLAND	0401-021
TE PENE (New Zealand)	Cone of KAIKOHE-BAY OF ISLANDS	0401-01=
TE PUHA ROA, MAUNGA (Pacific-C)	Cone of EASTER ISLAND	1303-08-
TE PUKE (New Zealand)	Cone of KAIKOHE-BAY OF ISLANDS	0401-01=
TE TERATA (New Zealand)	Dome of MAROA	0401-061
TE WHAU (New Zealand)	Cone of KAIKOHE-BAY OF ISLANDS	0401-01=
TE WHEKAU (New Zealand)	Crater of OKATAINA	0401-05=
TEA-TEA, MAUNGA (Pacific-C)	Dome of EASTER ISLAND	1303-08-
TEAHITIA (Society Is-C Pac)	Submarine (None) Seismicity	**1303-03-**
TEAU (Banda Sea)	Synonym of TEON	0605-05=

NAME (Subregion)	Type (Eruption Total, Most Recent) Status / Relation to NAMED VOLCANO	NUMBER
TEBEL HEBEISH (Africa-N)	Crater of BAYUDA VOLC FIELD	0205-06-
TEBEL QUREIN (Africa-N)	Cone of BAYUDA VOLC FIELD	0205-06-
TEBENKOV (Kurile Is)	Stratovolc of GROZNY GROUP	0900-07=
TECAPA (El Salvador)	Stratovolc (None) Fumarolic	**1403-08=**
TECOLOTE, CERRO (Guatemala)	Cone of MOYUTA	1402-13-
TECOLUCA, CERRO (El Salvador)	Dome of ILOPANGO	1403-06=
TECOMATEPE, CERRO (El Salvador)	Stratovolc of GUAZAPA	1403-051
TECONTO (Mexico)	Cone of HOLOTEPEC	1401-07-
TECUAMBURRO (Guatemala)	Stratovolc (1, -0960) Radiocarbon	**1402-12=**
TECUN UMAN, CERRO (Guatemala)	Dome of ALMOLONGA	1402-04=
TE'ELAGI (Samoa-SW Pacific)	Cone of SAVAI'I	0404-04=
TEER, GEBEL (Red Sea)	Synonym of TEYR, DJEBEL	0201-01=
TEETERS NUNATAK (Antarctica)	Stratovolc of HUDSON MOUNTAINS	1900-028
TEEUW (Banda Sea)	Synonym of TEON	0605-05=
TEIDE, PICO DEL (Canary Is)	Stratovolc of TENERIFE	1803-03-
TEIR, DJEBEL (Red Sea)	Synonym of TEYR, DJEBEL	0201-01=
TEISHI KNOLL [TEISHI KAIKYU] (Honshu)	Submarine vent of IZU-TOBU	0803-01=
TEIXCAL [SAN MARCELINO] (El Salvador)	Cone of SANTA ANA	1403-02=
TEKAI (Honshu-Japan)	Synonym of CHOKAI	0803-22=
TELAGABODAS (Java)	Synonym of TALAGABODAS	0603-15=
TELAGAKUNING (Java)	Crater of LAWU	0603-26=
TELAGARANU (Halmahera-Indonesia)	Synonym of TODOKO-RANU	0608-05=
TELAGAWARU (Java)	Crater of IJEN	0603-35=
TELCAMPANA (Mexico)	Cone of COLIMA VOLC COMPLEX	1401-04=
TELEKI'S VOLCANO (Africa-E)	Cone of BARRIER, THE	0202-03=
TELICA (Nicaragua)	Stratovolcs (28, 1987) Historical	**1404-04=**
TELOGO KETJIL [TELOGOKECIL] (Sumatra)	Crater of LUMUTDAUN, BUKIT	0601-21=
TELOGOPASIR (Java)	Crater of DIENG VOLC COMPLEX	0603-20=
TELOGOTERUS (Java)	Thermal Feature of DIENG VOLC COMP	0603-20=
TELOGOWURO (Java)	Crater of LAWU	0603-26=
TELOMOJO (Java)	Synonym of TELOMOYO	0603-231
TELOMOYO (Java)	Stratovolc (None) Holocene	**0603-231**
TELONG, BUR NI (Sumatra)	Stratovolc (6, 1937) Historical	**0601-05=**
TELORI (Halmahera-Indonesia)	Crater of DUKONO	0608-01=
TEMBARGENA, MONTANA (Canary Is)	Cone of HIERRO	1803-02-
TEMBERGENA (Canary Is)	Cone of HIERRO	1803-02-
TEMEREJEQUE, MONTANA (Canary Is)	Cone of FUERTEVENTURA	1803-05-
TEMPASO [TEMPANG] (Sulawesi-Indonesia)	Cone of TONDANO CALDERA	0606-07-
TEMPISQUE, CERRO (Guatemala)	Dome of IPALA VOLC FIELD	1402-19-
TEMPOEROENG [TEMPURUNG] (Java)	Dome of DANAU COMPLEX	0603-01=
TENACA, MONTANA (Canary Is)	Cone of HIERRO	1803-02-
TENANGO [CERRO TETEPETL] (Mexico)	Cone of HOLOTEPEC	1401-07-
TENAYO, CERRO (Mexico)	Cone of TENAYO GROUP	1401-081
TENAYO GROUP (Mexico)	Cinder cones (None) Holocene	**1401-081**
TENCHUN (China-S)	Synonym of TENGCHONG	0705-11-
TENDUREK DAG (Turkey)	Synonym of TENDURUK DAGI	0103-03=
TENDURUK DAGI (Turkey)	Shield (None) Holocene	**0103-03=**
TENDURUK GOLU (Turkey)	Crater of TENDURUK DAGI	0103-03=
TENEGUIA (Canary Is)	Cone of LA PALMA	1803-01-
TENERIFE (Canary Is)	Stratovolc (10, 1909) Historical	**1803-03-**
TENERIFE, MONTANA (Canary Is)	Cone of HIERRO	1803-02-
TENESEDRA, MONTANA (Canary Is)	Cone of HIERRO	1803-02-
TENG-CHIA-WANG [TENGJIAWANGSHAN]	Cone of LONGGANG GROUP	1005-06-
TENG-YUEH (China-S)	Synonym of TENGCHONG	0705-11-
TENGA, KEPUNDAN [VERBEEK] (Sumatra)	Crater of MARAPI	0601-14=
TENGCHONG (China-S)	Pyrocl cones (1, 1609) Historical	**0705-11-**
TENGGER CALDERA (Java)	Stratovolc (53, 1984) Historical	**0603-31=**
TENGJIAWANGSHAN (China-E)	Cone of LONGGANG GROUP	1005-06-
TENGU-DAKE (Honshu-Japan)	Dome of IIZUNA	0803-102
TENGU-YAMA (Honshu-Japan)	Dome of TATE-YAMA	0803-08=
TENJIN-YAMA (Honshu-Japan)	Cone of FUJI	0803-03=
TENJO-SAN (Izu Is-Japan)	Dome of KOZU-SHIMA	0804-03=
TENNENA (Canada)	Cone of EDZIZA	1200-06-
TENORIO GROUP (Costa Rica)	Stratovolcs (None) Holocene	**1405-031**
TENSHI (Honshu-Japan)	Stratovolc of IZU-TOBU	0803-01=
TENUSSET, PUY DE (France)	Cone of CHAINE DES PUYS	0100-02-
TENZYO-SAN [TENJO-SAN] (Izu Is-Japan)	Dome of KOZU-SHIMA	0804-03=
TEODORO WOLF, ISLA (Ecuador)	Dome of CUICOCHA	1502-002
TEON (Banda Sea)	Stratovolc (5, 1904) Historical	**0605-05=**
TEOU (Banda Sea)	Synonym of TEON	0605-05=
TEPECIK TEPE (Turkey)	Cone of ERCIYES DAGI	0103-01=
TEPECINGO (Mexico)	Cone of HOLOTEPEC	1401-07-
TEPESIDELIK DAMLARU (Turkey)	Vent of ERCIYES DAGI	0103-01=
TEPETILTIC, VOLCAN (Mexico)	Stratovolc (None) Holocene	**1401-024**
TEPETL (Mexico)	Cone of CHICHINAUTZIN	1401-08=
TEPETLAPAN (Mexico)	Cone of CHICHINAUTZIN	1401-08=
TEPEZINGO (Mexico)	Cone of HOLOTEPEC	1401-07-
TEPI (Ethiopia)	Shield (None) Holocene	**0201-292**
TER, DJEBEL (Red Sea)	Synonym of TEYR, DJEBEL	0201-01=
TERBANG-GEDOR (Java)	Dome of DANAU COMPLEX	0603-01=
TERCEIRA (Azores)	Stratovolcs (6, 1867) Historical	**1802-05=**
TEREVAKA, MAUNGA (Pacific-C)	Shield of EASTER ISLAND	1303-08-
TERMALNY (Kamchatka)	Stratovolc of PAUZHETKA	1000-022
TERMAS (Spanish for SPA) see proper name (e.g. COPAHUE, TERMAS DE)		
TERMOPILES, LAS (El Salvador)	Thermal Feature of VERDE, LAGUNA	1403-01=
TERNATE, PEAK OF (Halmahera-Indonesia)	Synonym of GAMALAMA	0608-06=
TERNATE, PIEK VAN (Halmahera-Indonesia)	Synonym of GAMALAMA	0608-06=
TERRA MURATA (Italy)	Tuff ring of CAMPI FLEGREI	0101-01=
TERRACE (US-Utah)	Crater of BLACK ROCK DESERT	1207-05-
TERRANG, LAKE (Australia)	Tuff ring of NEWER VOLCANICS PROV	0509-01-
TERRE BLANCHE (W Indies)	Dome of QUALIBOU	1600-14=
TERRE ELM (W Indies)	Thermal Feature of PATATES, MORNE	1600-11=
TERRIBILE BANK (Italy)	Submarine vent of CAMPI FLEGREI MAR	0101-07=
TESKI GROUP (Chile-S)	Crater of OSORNO	1508-01=
TESORO (Canary Is)	Cone of HIERRO	1803-02-
TESTACCIO (Italy)	Crater of ISCHIA	0101-03=
TETA, LA (Nicaragua)	Dome of SAN CRISTOBAL	1404-02=
TETECON (Mexico)	Cone of SANTA CATARINA RANGE	1401-082
TETEPETL, CERRO (Mexico)	Cone of HOLOTEPEC	1401-07-
TETEQUILLO (Mexico)	Cone of CHICHINAUTZIN	1401-08=
TETERA, CERRO [LA TETRA] (US-New Mex)	Cone of ZUNI-BANDERA	1210-02-
TETU-ZAN [TETSU-ZAN] (Honshu-Japan)	Stratovolc of ADATARA	0803-17=
TETYAEV (Kamchatka)	Cone of DZENZURSKY	1000-11=
TEUHTLI, VOLCAN (Mexico)	Shield of CHICHINAUTZIN	1401-08=
TEUN (Banda Sea)	Synonym of TEON	0605-05=
TEUPIN IBOIH (Sumatra)	Thermal Feature of PULAU WEH	0601-01=
TEUPIN KRUENG MADUN (Sumatra)	Thermal Feature of PULAU WEH	0601-01=
TEXONTEPEC (Mexico)	Cone of HOLOTEPEC	1401-07-
TEYOTL PEAK (Mexico)	Cone of IZTACCIHUATL	1401-086
TEYR, DJEBEL (Red Sea)	Stratovolc (4, 1883) Historical	**0201-01=**
TEZIOLO, CERRO EL (Mexico)	Cone of TENAYO GROUP	1401-081
TEZONTAL (Mexico)	Cone of COLIMA VOLC COMPLEX	1401-04=
TEZONTLE (Mexico)	Cone of HOLOTEPEC	1401-07-
TEZOYO, CERRO EL (Mexico)	Cone of TENAYO GROUP	1401-081
TEZTONTLE, VOLCAN (Mexico)	Cone of TEPETILTIC, VOLCAN	1401-024
THAIS HILL (W Indies)	Dome of SABA	1600-01=
THAW HILL (Canada)	Cone of SPECTRUM RANGE	1200-07-
THAZI (SE Asia)	Vent of LOWER CHINDWIN	0705-09-
THE see proper name (e.g. FATHER, THE)		
THEISTAREVKIR (Iceland)	Synonym of THEISTAREYKJARBUNGA	1703-09=
THEISTAREYKJAHRAUN (Iceland)	Fissure vent of THEISTAREYKJARBUNGA	1703-09=
THEISTAREYKJARBUNGA (Iceland-NE)	Shield (3, -0750) Tephrochronology	**1703-09=**
THERA (Greece)	Synonym of SANTORINI	0102-04=
THIERRY (Indian O.-W)	Crater of FOURNAISE, PITON DE LA	0303-02=
THIOLET, PUY (France)	Cone of CHAINE DES PUYS	0100-02-
THIRA (Greece)	Synonym of SANTORINI	0102-04=
THIRASIA (Greece)	Shield of SANTORINI	0102-04=
THIRSTY POINT (US-Oregon)	Cone of CINNAMON BUTTE	1202-15-
THJOFAHRAUN (Iceland-SW)	Fissure vent of HENGILL	1701-05=
THOLOTHI (Fiji Is-SW Pacific)	Cone of TAVEUNI	0405-01-
THOMPSON ISLAND (Atlantic-S)	Submarine ? (None) Uncertain	**1806-03-**
THORDARHYRNA (Iceland-NE)	Stratovolc of GRIMSVOTN	1703-01=
THORSARHRAUN (Iceland-NE)	Fissure vent of BARDARBUNGA	1703-03=
THRAINSSKJOLDUR (Iceland-SW)	Shield of REYKJANES	1701-02=
THREE KINGS (New Zealand)	Tuff ring of AUCKLAND FIELD	0401-02=
THREE-QUARTER CONE (Aleutian Is)	Cone of SEMISOPOCHNOI	1101-06-
THREE SISTERS (US-California)	Cone of MEDICINE LAKE	1203-02-
THREE SISTERS CONES (Antarctica)	Cone of EREBUS	1900-02=
THREE TRAPPERS (US-Oregon)	Cone of BACHELOR	1202-09-
THRENGSLABORGIR (Iceland-NE)	Crater row of KRAFLA	1703-08=
THRIDRANGAR (Iceland-S)	Submarine vent of VESTMANNAEYJAR	1702-01=
THRIHNUKAR (Iceland-SW)	Fissure vent of BRENNISTEINSFJOLL	1701-04=
THROSKULDSHRAUN (Iceland-NE)	Crater row of BARDARBUNGA	1703-03=
THULE ISLAND (Antarctica)	Submarine vent of THULE ISLANDS	1900-07=
THULE ISLANDS (Antarctica)	Stratovolcs (None) Holocene	**1900-07=**
THUMB, THE (New Guinea)	Dome of VICTORY	0503-03=
TIANCHI (China-E)	Caldera of BAITOUSHAN	1005-07-
TIANSHAN VOLCANO GROUP (China-W)	Volc field (2, 0650) Historical	**1004-02-**
TIANTISHAN (China-S)	Cone of TENGCHONG	0705-11-
TIATALA (Samoa-SW Pacific)	Cone of UPOLU	0404-03-
TIATIA (Kurile Is)	Stratovolc (4, 1981) Historical	**0900-03=**
TIAU (TIAUW) (Banda Sea)	Synonym of TEON	0605-05=
TIAWIR (Luzon-Philippines)	Dome of NATIB	0703-082
TIBAS (Costa Rica)	Stratovolc of BARVA	1405-05=
TICOMA [TICOMO PIT] (Nicaragua)	Maar of NEJAPA-TICOMO	1404-092
TICSANI (Peru)	Stratovolc (None) Holocene	**1504-031**
TIDICHI, EHI (Africa-N)	Synonym of TOUSSIDE, TARSO	0205-01=
T'IDO HAYK (Ethiopia)	Crater of BILATE RIVER FIELD	0201-291
TIEGUOSHAN (China-S)	Cone of TENGCHONG	0705-11-
TIEN-CHI [TIANCHI] (China-E)	Caldera of BAITOUSHAN	1005-07-
TIENDILLA (Costa Rica)	Cone of TURRIALBA	1405-07=
TIERRA COLORADO, CERRO (Guatemala)	Cone of SUCHITAN VOLC FIELD	1402-17-
TIGALATE [SAN MARTIN] (Canary Is)	Cone of LA PALMA	1803-01-
TIGHE ROCK (Antarctica)	Cone of HUDSON MOUNTAINS	1900-028
TIGRE, ISLA EL (Honduras)	Stratovolc (None) Holocene	**1403-13-**
TIHO (Djibouti)	Fumarole fld (None) Pleistocene-Fumarolic	**0201-127**
TIHUYA [TAHUYA] (Canary Is)	Cone of LA PALMA	1803-01-
TIIS, KAWAH (Java)	Thermal Feature of PATUHA	0603-07=
TIJAW (Banda Sea)	Synonym of TEON	0605-05=
TIKITERE (New Zealand)	Thermal Feature of ROTORUA	0401-042
TIKORANGI (New Zealand)	Dome of OKATAINA	0401-05=
TIKURA (Kurile Is)	Synonym of CHIKURACHKI	0900-36=
TILAPA (Mexico)	Cone of HOLOTEPEC	1401-07-
TILAPIA LAKE (Africa-E)	Crater of CENTRAL ISLAND	0202-01=
TILING (Java)	Crater of LAWU	0603-26=
TILLMAN, MT. (Alaska-E)	Synonym of WRANGELL	1105-02-
TILMBEG (Vanuatu-SW Pacific)	Cone of MOTLAV	0507-001
TIMANFAYA ANTIGUA (Canary Is)	Cone of LANZAROTE	1803-06-
TIMANFAYA, MONTANAS DEL (Canary Is)	Synonym of LANZAROTE	1803-06-
TIMBANG (Java)	Cone of DIENG VOLC COMPLEX	0603-20=
TIMBER CRATER (US-Oregon)	Shield of CRATER LAKE	1202-16-
TIMBERED CRATER (US-California)	Tuff ring of BRUSHY BUTTE	1203-03-
TIMBERED PEAK (US-Washington)	Cone of WEST CRATER	1201-06-
TIMBOROMBO, MONTANA DE (Canary Is)	Cone of HIERRO	1803-02-
TIMI, EHI (Africa-N)	Stratovolc of TOUSSIDE, TARSO	0205-01=
TIMPONE CARRUBBO (Italy)	Stratovolc of LIPARI	0101-041
TIMPONE DEL FUOCO (Italy)	Cone of STROMBOLI	0101-04=
TIMPONE OSPEDALE (Italy)	Stratovolc of LIPARI	0101-041
TIMPONE PATASO (Italy)	Stratovolc of LIPARI	0101-041
TIMPOONG [MAMBAJAO] (Mindanao)	Stratovolc of HIBOK-HIBOK	0701-08=
TIN CAN ISLAND (Tonga-SW Pacific)	Synonym of NIUAFO'OU	0403-11=
TINAJA DE LOS PAPAGOS [ROMO]	Maar of PINACATE PEAKS	1401-001
TINAJITA, VOLCAN EL (Mexico)	Maar of PINACATE PEAKS	1401-001
TINAKORO (Santa Cruz Is-SW Pac)	Synonym of TINAKULA	0506-01=
TINAKULA (Santa Cruz Is-SW Pac)	Stratovolc (15, 1985) Historical	**0506-01=**
TINDAYA, MONTANA (Canary Is)	Cone of FUERTEVENTURA	1803-05-
TINDFJALLAJOKULL (Iceland-S)	Stratovolc (None) Holocene	**1702-04=**
TINDFJOLL (Iceland-S)	Synonym of TINDFJALLAJOKULL	1702-04=
TINDIMA (Africa-E)	Cone of CHYULU HILLS	0202-13=
TINDUR (Iceland-SW)	Dome of KERLINGARFJOLL	1701-10=
TINGA, MONTANA DE (Canary Is)	Cone of LANZAROTE	1803-06-
TINGUATON (Canary Is)	Crater of LANZAROTE	1803-06-
TINGUIRIRICA (Chile-C)	Stratovolc (1, 1917) Historical	**1507-03=**
TIOCA (Mexico)	Cone of CHICHINAUTZIN	1401-08=
TIOQUITAS (Mexico)	Cone of CHICHINAUTZIN	1401-08=
TIPAS (Argentina)	Complx volc (None) Holocene	**1505-131**
TIPT PON (Sulu Is-Philippines)	Synonym of BUD DAJO	0700-01=
TIR, JIBBEL (Red Sea)	Synonym of TEYR, DJEBEL	0201-01=
TIRAC (Luzon-Philippines)	Dome of NATIB	0703-082
TIRANUS (Kamchatka)	Crater of KLIUCHEVSKOI	1000-26=
TIRBA, MONTANA (Canary Is)	Cone of FUERTEVENTURA	1803-05-
TIRIHOI [BRAT CHIRPOEV] (Kurile Is)	Cone of CHIRPOI	0900-15=
TIRIHOIGAKU [BRAT CHIRPOEV] (Kurile Is)	Cone of CHIRPOI	0900-15=
TIRINKOTAN (Kurile Is)	Synonym of CHIRINKOTAN	0900-26=
TIROHANGA (New Zealand)	Dome of MAROA	0401-061
TISATE, HERVIDEROS DE (Nicaragua)	Thermal Feature of TELICA	1404-04=
TISCAPA, LAGUNA DE (Nicaragua)	Maar of NEJAPA-TICOMO	1404-092
TISCHO, CERRO (Peru)	Cone of ANDAHUA VALLEY	1504-002
TISON LAKE [MARDJA] (Africa-W)	Crater of NGAOUNDERE PLATEAU	0204-002
TITILA (Kamchatka)	Shield (None) Holocene	**1000-56-**
TIWI (Luzon-Philippines)	Thermal Feature of MALINAO	0703-04=
TIWONGO (New Britain-SW Pac)	Cone of LOLOBAU	0502-13=
TIWU ATA MBUPU (Lesser Sunda Is)	Crater of KELIMUTU	0604-14=
TIWU ATA POLO (Lesser Sunda Is)	Crater of KELIMUTU	0604-14=

NAME (Subregion)	Type (Eruption Total, Most Recent) Status Relation to NAMED VOLCANO	NUMBER
TIWU NUA MURI KOOH TAI (Lesser Sunda	Crater of KELIMUTU	0604-14=
TIYAW (Banda Sea)	Synonym of TEON	0605-05=
TJALDSTADAGJA (Iceland-SW)	Crater row of REYKJANES	1701-02=
TJANAR [CANAR] (Java)	Crater of TALAGABODAS	0603-15=
TJAREME (Java)	Synonym of CEREME	0603-17=
TJARNAHNUKUR (Iceland-SW)	Crater row of HENGILL	1701-05=
TJARNARHOLAR (Iceland-SW)	Crater row of GRIMSNES	1701-06=
TJATOE [CATU] (Lesser Sunda Is)	Crater of BATUR	0604-01=
TJATUR CALDERA (Lesser Sunda Is)	Synonym of BRATAN	0604-001
TJEMARA, GUNUNG [GUNUNG CEMERA]	Cone of IJEN	0603-35=
TJEREME (TJEREMAI, TJERME) (Java)	Synonym of CEREME	0603-17=
TJIANGKUANG [CANGKUANG] (Java)	Crater of SALAK	0603-05=
TJIAW (Banda Sea)	Synonym of TEON	0605-05=
TJIBEUREUM PALASARI [CIBEUREUM PAL	Thermal Feature of KIARABERES-GAGAK	0603-03=
TJIBEUREUM [CIBEUREUM] (Java)	Thermal Feature of KIARABERES-GAGAK	0603-03=
TJIBEUREUM [CIBEUREUM] (Java)	Thermal Feature of KAWAHKAMOJANG	0603-12=
TJIBODAS, KAWAH [KAWAH CIBODAS]	Thermal Feature of KIARABERES-GAGAK	0603-03=
TJIBODAS, KAWAH [KAWAH CIBODAS]	Thermal Feature of SALAK	0603-05=
TJIBODAS, TJIPANAS [CIPANAS CIBODAS	Thermal Feature of KIARABERES-GAGAK	0603-03=
TJIBOERIAL [CIBURIAL] (Java)	Thermal Feature of KAWAHKAMOJANG	0603-12=
TJIBOLANG, KAWAH [KAWAH CIBOLANG]	Thermal Feature of WAYANG-WINDU	0603-08=
TJIBULIRAN [CIBURIAL] (Java)	Thermal Feature of KAWAHKAMOJANG	0603-12=
TJIBUNI, KAWAH [KAWAH CIBUNI] (Java	Thermal Feature of PATUHA	0603-07=
TJIGAMEA, KAWAH [KAWAH CIGAMEA]	Thermal Feature of SALAK	0603-05=
TJIGUPAKAN [CIGUPAKAN] (Java)	Thermal Feature of KAWAHMANUK	0603-11=
TJIHIDEUNG, TJIPANAS [CIPANAS CIHIDE	Thermal Feature of SALAK	0603-05=
TJIKALUWUNG PUTRI, KAWAH [CIKALUWU	Thermal Feature of SALAK	0603-05=
TJIKALUWUNG, TJIPANAS [CIPANAS CIKA	Thermal Feature of KIARABERES-GAGAK	0603-03=
TJIKALUWUNGHERANG, KAWAH [CIKALUW	Thermal Feature of PERBAKTI	0603-04=
TJILIK, GUNUNG [GUNUNG CILIK] (Java)	Cone of IJEN	0603-35=
TJIPAMATUTAN [CIPAMATUTAN] (Java)	Thermal Feature of PERBAKTI	0603-04=
TJIPANAS (Dutch: of Indonesian word for HOT SPRING) see proper name (e.g. TJIBODAS, TJIPANAS)		
TJIPANAS, KAWAH [KAWAH CIPANAS]	Thermal Feature of SALAK	0603-05=
TJIPENGASAHAN, KAWAH [KAWAH CIPEN	Thermal Feature of KAWAHKAMOJANG	0603-12=
TJIREMAI (Java)	Synonym of CEREME	0603-17=
TJISALADA, KAWAH [KAWAH CISALADA]	Thermal Feature of SALAK	0603-05=
TJISALADA, TJIPANAS [CIPANAS CISALA	Thermal Feature of SALAK	0603-05=
TJISEKATI, TJIPANAS [CIPANAS CISEKA	Thermal Feature of KIARABERES-GAGAK	0603-03=
TJISEUPAN, TJIPANAS [CIPANAS CISEUP	Thermal Feature of PERBAKTI	0603-04=
TJIWIDEI, KAWAH [KAWAH CIWIDEI] (Java)	Thermal Feature of PATUHA	0603-07=
TJOLO, GUNUNG (Sulawesi-Indonesia)	Synonym of COLO [UNA UNA]	0606-01=
TJONDRODIMUKO, KAWAH [KAWAH COND	Thermal Feature of MERBABU	0603-24=
TJONDRODIMUKO [CONDRODIMUKO]	Thermal Feature of DIENG VOLC COMP	0603-20=
TJONDROKEMUKO, KAWAH [KAWAH CON	Thermal Feature of MERBABU	0603-24=
TJORNES FRACTURE ZONE (Iceland-NE)	Submarine (1, 1868) Historical	**1703-10=**
TLACOTEPEC (Mexico)	Cone of HOLOTEPEC	1401-07-
TLACUALLCLI (Mexico)	Cone of CHICHINAUTZIN	1401-08=
TLACUAYOL, CERRO (Mexico)	Cone of TENAYO GROUP	1401-081
TLALOC, VOLCAN (Mexico)	Shield of CHICHINAUTZIN	1401-08=
TLAMACASCO (Mexico)	Cone of CHICHINAUTZIN	1401-08=
TLAPEXCUA, VOLCAN (Mexico)	Cone of TENAYO GROUP	1401-081
TLEVAK STRAIT-SUEMEZ ISLAND (Alaska)	Volc field (None) Holocene	**1105-06-**
TO-OD GRANDE (Philippines-C)	Thermal Feature of MAHAGNOA	0702-07=
TO-OD PEQUENA (Philippines-C)	Thermal Feature of MAHAGNOA	0702-07=
TO-SHIMA (Izu Is-Japan)	Stratovolc (None) Holocene?	**0804-011**
TO'A (Samoa-SW Pacific)	Tuff cone of TA'U	0404-001
TOA TOA, MAUNGA (Pacific-C)	Cone of EASTER ISLAND	1303-08-
TO'AGA (Samoa-SW Pacific)	Cone of OFU-OLOSEGA	0404-01=
TOBA (Sumatra)	Caldera (None) Holocene	**0601-09=**
TOBAL (New Britain-SW Pac)	Cone of LOLOBAU	0502-13=
TOBARU (Halmahera-Indonesia)	Synonym of IBU	0608-03=
TOCO, CERRO (Chile-N)	Stratovolc of PURICO COMPLEX	1505-094
TOCONADO (TOCONAO) (Chile-N)	Synonym of LASCAR	1505-10=
TOCONCE, CERRO (Chile-N)	Stratovolc (None) Holocene	**1505-073**
TOCOPURI, CERRO DE (Chile-N)	Synonym of TOCORPURI, CERROS DE	1505-081
TOCORPURI, CERROS DE (Chile-N)	Stratovolc (None) Holocene	**1505-081**
TODAKO (TODOEKOE, TODOKE)	Synonym of TODOKO-RANU	0608-05=
TODOKE, LAKE (Halmahera-Indonesia)	Maar of IBU	0608-03=
TODOKO (Halmahera-Indonesia)	Caldera of TODOKO-RANU	0608-05=
TODOKO-RANU (Halmahera-Indonesia	Calderas (None) Fumarolic	**0608-05=**
TODUOKO, LAKE (Halmahera-Indonesia)	Maar of IBU	0608-03=
TOEBAROE (Halmahera-Indonesia)	Synonym of IBU	0608-03=
TOEDOE [TUDU] (Lesser Sunda Is)	Crater of PALUWEH	0604-15=
TOFOOA (Tonga-SW Pacific)	Synonym of TOFUA	0403-06=
TOFUA (Tonga-SW Pacific)	Caldera (7, 1958) Historical	**0403-06=**
TOGASA-YAMA (Honshu-Japan)	Stratovolc of IZU-TOBU	0803-01=
TOGO (Mongolia)	Cone of KHANUY GOL	1003-02-
TOH, TARSO (Africa-N)	Volc field (None) Holocene	**0205-001**
TO'IAVEA (Samoa-SW Pacific)	Cone of SAVAI'I	0404-04=
TOKACHI (Hokkaido-Japan)	Stratovolcs (19, 1989) Historical	**0805-05=**
TOKACHI-DAKE (Hokkaido-Japan)	Synonym of TOKACHI	0805-05=
TOKAJAIN (Lesser Sunda Is)	Synonym of LEWOTOLO	0604-23=
TOKARA-IWO-JIMA (Ryukyu Is)	Synonym of KIKAI	0802-06=
TOKATI (Hokkaido-Japan)	Synonym of TOKACHI	0805-05=
TOKISHIRAZU-YAMA (Honshu-Japan)	Synonym of FUJI	0803-03=
TOKIWA-YAMA (Honshu-Japan)	Synonym of FUJI	0803-03=
TOKOKO (Sulawesi-Indonesia)	Synonym of TONGKOKO	0606-13=
TOKOLOTAI, VITI (Vanuatu-SW Pacific)	Cone of AOBA	0507-03=
TOKUOKO (Halmahera-Indonesia)	Synonym of TODOKO-RANU	0608-05=
TOLAV [TOW LAV] (Vanuatu-SW Pacific)	Stratovolc of SORETIMEAT	0507-01=
TOLBACHIK (Kamchatka)	Shield (57, 1976) Historical	**1000-24=**
TOLBACHINSKAIA SOPKA (Kamchatka)	Synonym of TOLBACHIK	1000-24=
TOLBATSCHINSKAJA SSOPKA (Kamchatka)	Synonym of TOLBACHIK	1000-24=
TOLEDO (US-New Mexico)	Caldera of VALLES CALDERA	1210-03-
TOLEDO, CERRO (US-New Mexico)	Dome of VALLES CALDERA	1210-03-
TOLGUACA (Chile-C)	Stratovolc (None) Holocene	**1507-092**
TOLHUACA (Chile-C)	Synonym of TOLGUACA	1507-092
TOLIMA (Colombia)	Stratovolc (6, 1943) Historical	**1501-03=**
TOLIMAN (Guatemala)	Stratovolc (None) Holocene	**1402-07=**
TOLIRE DJAHA [TOLIRE JAHA] (Halmahera)	Crater of GAMALAMA	0608-06=
TOLIRE KETJIL [TOLIRE KECIL] (Halmahera	Crater of GAMALAMA	0608-06=
TOLLNERODDEN (Atl-N-Jan Mayen)	Cone of JAN MAYEN	1706-01=
TOLMACHEV DOL (Kamchatka)	Cinder cones (None) Holocene	**1000-082**
TOLMACHEV VALLEY (Kamchatka)	Synonym of TOLMACHEV DOL	1000-082
TOLO (Halmahera-Indonesia)	Synonym of DUKONO	0608-01=
TOLUACH (Kamchatka)	Synonym of TOLBACHIK	1000-24=
TOM MACKAY CREEK (Canada)	Cone of ISKUT-UNUK RIVER CONES	1200-09-
TOMARI-YAMA (Kurile Is)	Synonym of GOLOVNIN	0900-01=
TOMASQUILLO (Mexico)	Cone of HOLOTEPEC	1401-07-
TOMBEL PLAIN (Africa-W)	Synonym of MANENGOUBA	0204-004
TOMBORO (Lesser Sunda Is)	Synonym of TAMBORA	0604-04=
TOMBULUAN (Sulawesi-Indonesia)	Cone of MAHAWU	0606-11=

NAME (Subregion)	Type (Eruption Total, Most Recent) Status Relation to NAMED VOLCANO	NUMBER
TOMPALUAN (Sulawesi-Indonesia)	Crater of LOKON-EMPUNG	0606-10=
TOMPASSO (Sulawesi-Indonesia)	Thermal Feature of TONDANO CALDERA	0606-07-
TOMPO-MALANG (Java)	Stratovolc of DANAU COMPLEX	0603-01=
TOMPUSU (Sulawesi-Indonesia)	Cone of TONDANO CALDERA	0606-07-
TOMU (Lesser Sunda Is)	Thermal Feature of PALUWEH	0604-15=
TONDACHI (Ryukyu Is)	Cone of SUWANOSE-JIMA	0802-03=
TONDANO CALDERA (Sulawesi-Indonesia)	Caldera (None) Fumarolic	**0606-07-**
TONDATI [TONDACHI] (Ryukyu Is)	Cone of SUWANOSE-JIMA	0802-03=
TONEY MOUNTAIN (Antarctica)	Shield (None) Holocene?	**1900-026**
TONGARIRO (New Zealand)	Stratovolcs (70, 1977) Historical	**0401-08=**
TONGKOKO (Sulawesi-Indonesia)	Stratovolc (7, 1880) Historical	**0606-13=**
TONGLON (Luzon-Philippines)	Synonym of SANTO TOMAS	0703-086
TONKAYA (Kamchatka)	Dome of KSUDACH	1000-05=
TONKOKO (Sulawesi-Indonesia)	Synonym of TONGKOKO	0606-13=
TONTOG (Vanuatu-SW Pacific)	Cone of MOTLAV	0507-001
TONY MOUNTAIN (Antarctica)	Synonym of TONEY MOUNTAIN	1900-026
TOOWA VALLEY (US-Calif)	Synonym of GOLDEN TROUT CREEK	1203-17-
TOPILEJO-XICOMULCO VOLC FIELD	Synonym of CHICHINAUTZIN	1401-08=
TOPOLNIKA (Kamchatka)	Synonym of VEER	1000-102
TOPPGIG (Iceland-W)	Cone of SNAEFELLSJOKULL	1700-01=
TOPPGIGUR (Iceland-S)	Fissure vent of HEKLA	1702-07=
TOPSO BUTTE (US-Oregon)	Cone of NEWBERRY VOLCANO	1202-11-
TORE (Bougainville-SW Pac)	Lava cone (None) Holocene	**0505-00-**
TORFAJOKULL (Iceland-S)	Stratovolc (10, 1477) Historical	**1702-05=**
TORI-SHIMA (Izu Is-Japan)	Stratovolc (5, 1975) Historical	**0804-09=**
TORI-SIMA (Izu Is-Japan)	Synonym of TORI-SHIMA	0804-09=
TORIKABUTO-YAMA (Honshu-Japan)	Stratovolc of ZAO	0803-19=
TORIKABUTO-YAMA (Kyushu-Japan)	Dome of UNZEN	0802-10=
TORINO-UMI (Honshu-Japan)	Crater of CHOKAI	0803-22=
TORINOKO-YAMA (Honshu-Japan)	Synonym of FUJI	0803-03=
TORINOUMI (Honshu-Japan)	Crater of IWAKI	0803-27=
TORN, VOLCA EL (Spain)	Cone of OLOT VOLC FIELD	0100-03-
TORNYI (Kurile Is)	Cone of GOLETS-TORNYI GROUP	0900-091
TORO PUGRO (Ecuador)	Dome of CHACANA	1502-022
TOROENG PRONG (SE Asia)	Unknown (None) Holocene?	**0705-03-**
TORRE CAPPELLA (Italy)	Crater of CAMPI FLEGREI	0101-01=
TORRE GAVETA (Italy)	Cone of CAMPI FLEGREI	0101-01=
TORRENT, VOLCA EL (Spain)	Cone of OLOT VOLC FIELD	0100-03-
TORRES (Galapagos)	Synonym of MARCHENA	1503-08=
TORRIONE (Italy)	Vent of STROMBOLI	0101-04=
TORTA, CERRO LA (Chile-N)	Dome of TOCORPURI, CERROS DE	1505-081
TORTIK (Kamchatka)	Dome of UZON	1000-17=
TORTUGA, ISLA (Mexico)	Shield (None) Holocene	**1401-011**
TOSA SUCHA (Ethiopia)	Cinder cones (None) Holocene	**0201-31-**
TOSAMOSIBE [TOSAMOSHIBE] (Hokkaido)	Dome of KUTCHARO	0805-08=
TOSITI SPA [TOSHICHI SPA] (Honshu-Japan	Thermal Feature of HACHIMANTAI	0803-25=
TOT MOUNTAIN (US-Oregon)	Cone of BACHELOR	1202-09-
TOTOGAN MALANG (Java)	Cone of SEMERU	0603-30=
TOUO, LE [WOOSANTAPALIPLIP] (Vanuatu)	Cone of AMBRYM	0507-04=
TOUPE, PUY DE LA (France)	Cone of CHAINE DES PUYS	0100-02-
TOUR, LA [WOOSANTAPALIPLIP] (Vanuatu)	Cone of AMBRYM	0507-04=
TOUSSIDE, TARSO (Africa-N)	Stratovolc (None) Holocene	**0205-01=**
TOVANUMBATIR (New Britain-SW Pac)	Stratovolc of RABAUL	0502-14=
TOW ALESERE (Vanuatu-SW Pacific)	Stratovolc of SORETIMEAT	0507-01=
TOW LAV (Vanuatu-SW Pacific)	Stratovolc of SORETIMEAT	0507-01=
TOW MARAVRIG (Vanuatu-SW Pacific)	Crater of SORETIMEAT	0507-01=
TOW MARKONG (Vanuatu-SW Pacific)	Crater of SORETIMEAT	0507-01=
TOW MEAR (Vanuatu-SW Pacific)	Crater of SORETIMEAT	0507-01=
TOW VETAM (Vanuatu-SW Pacific)	Stratovolc of SORETIMEAT	0507-01=
TOWADA (Honshu-Japan)	Stratovolc (7, 0915) Historical	**0803-271**
TOWADA-KO (Honshu-Japan)	Caldera of TOWADA	0803-271
TOWADA-YAMA (Honshu-Japan)	Stratovolc of TOWADA	0803-271
TOWARI-YAMA (Honshu-Japan)	Stratovolc of TOWADA	0803-271
TOWAWASAG (Vanuatu-SW Pacific)	Stratovolc of SORETIMEAT	0507-01=
TOWER (Galapagos)	Synonym of GENOVESA	1503-081
TOWER HILL (Australia)	Maar of NEWER VOLCANICS PROV	0509-01-
TOWER PEAK [WOOSANTAPALIPLIP]	Cone of AMBRYM	0507-04=
TOWNDROW PEAK (US-New Mexico)	Cone of RATON-CLAYTON	1210-04-
TOWON GAR (Vanuatu-SW Pacific)	Stratovolc of SORETIMEAT	0507-01=
TOYA (Hokkaido-Japan)	Pleistocene caldera of USU	0805-03=
TOYAGA-MORI (Honshu-Japan)	Dome of NARUGO	0803-20=
TOYATSUKA (Honshu-Japan)	Cone of FUJI	0803-03=
TRACHYLAS [TRACHILAS] (Greece)	Cone of MILOS	0102-03=
TRAHUILES (Chile-C)	Thermal Feature of CORDON CAULLE	1507-141
TRAITOR'S HEAD (Vanuatu-SW Pacific)	Stratovolc (1, 1881) Historical	**0507-09=**
TRAPA-TRAPA (Chile-C)	Caldera of COPAHUE	1507-09=
TRAPA-TRAPA (Chile-C)	Synonym of COPAHUE	1507-09=
TRAPEZINA (Greece)	Dome of NISYROS	0102-05=
TRAPICHITO, CERRO (Guatemala)	Cone of CUILAPA-BARBARENA	1402-111
TRAUTZBERGER (Germany)	Maar of WEST EIFEL VOLC FIELD	0100-01-
TRAVERSA CAMPANA (Italy)	Crater of CAMPI FLEGREI	0101-01=
TREBOL, VOLCAN EL (Mexico)	Crater of PINACATE PEAKS	1401-001
TRENTAREMI (Italy)	Crater of CAMPI FLEGREI	0101-01=
TRES CRUCES (Mexico)	Cone of HOLOTEPEC	1401-07-
TRES CRUCES, CERRO (Mexico)	Cone of CHICHINAUTZIN	1401-08=
TRES CUMBRES, CERRO (Mexico)	Cone of TENAYO GROUP	1401-081
TRES HERMANAS [YEPOCAPA] (Guatemala	Cone of ACATENANGO	1402-08=
TRES MARIAS [YEPOCAPA] (Guatemala)	Cone of ACATENANGO	1402-08=
TRES VIRGENES (Mexico)	Stratovolc (1, 1746) Historical	**1401-01=**
TRESCHINA (Kamchatka)	Cone of TOLBACHIK	1000-24=
TRESSOUS, PUY DE (France)	Cone of CHAINE DES PUYS	0100-02-
TRETIY (Kamchatka)	Crater of KLIUCHEVSKOI	1000-26=
TREUGOLNY ZUB (Kamchatka)	Dome of BEZYMIANNY	1000-25=
TREZUBETZ (Kurile Is)	Somma volcano of KOLOKOL GROUP	0900-12=
TRI SESTRY (Kurile Is)	Stratovolc (None) Holocene?	**0900-113**
TRIANGLE (Canada)	Dome of EDZIZA	1200-06-
TRIDENT (Alaska Peninsula)	Stratovolc (15, 1975) Historical	**1102-16-**
TRIFOGLIETTO (Italy)	Shield of ETNA	0101-06=
TRILOPE (Chile-C)	Synonym of COPAHUE	1507-09=
TRINDADE (Atlantic-S)	Stratovolc (None) Holocene	**1805-051**
TRINDADE, PICO (Atlantic-S)	Dome of TRINDADE	1805-051
TRINITYBERGET (Atl-N-Jan Mayen)	Cone of JAN MAYEN	1706-01=
TRIPLEX (Canada)	Cone of EDZIZA	1200-06-
TRIPPAFJOLL [TRIPPABJALLAR] (Iceland-S)	Fissure vent of HEKLA	1702-07=
TRIPPODI, MONTE (Italy)	Dome of ISCHIA	0101-03=
TRISTAN DA CUNHA (Atlantic-S)	Stratovolc (2, 1962) Historical	**1806-01=**
TRITON (Greece)	Dome of SANTORINI	0102-04=
TRITRIVA (Madagascar)	Cone of ANKARATRA FIELD	0303-07-
TROIS PITONS, MORNE (W Indies)	Dome of MICOTRIN	1600-10=
TROIS SOLS, PUY DES [PUY DE TRESSOU	Cone of CHAINE DES PUYS	0100-02-
TROIS TETES, PITON (Indian O.-W)	Cone of FOURNAISE, PITON DE LA	0303-02=
TROITZKY [TROITSKY] (Kamchatka)	Crater of MALY SEMIACHIK	1000-14=

NAME (Subregion)	Type (Eruption Total, Most Recent) Status . . . Relation to NAMED VOLCANO	NUMBER
TROLLADYNGJA (Iceland-NE)	Synonym of ASKJA	1703-06=
TROLLADYNGJA (Iceland-NE)	Shield of BARDARBUNGA	1703-03=
TROLLADYNGJA (Iceland-SW)	Crater row of KRISUVIK	1701-03=
TROLLADYNGJUKERFID (Iceland-SW)	Synonym of KRISUVIK	1701-03=
TROLLAGIGAR (Iceland-NE)	Crater row of BARDARBUNGA	1703-03=
TROLLASKOGAHRAUN (Iceland-S)	Crater row of VATNAFJOLL	1702-06=
TROLOPE (Chile-C)	Synonym of COPAHUE	1507-09=
TROMEN (Argentina)	Stratovolc (None) Holocene	**1507-071**
TRONADOR, EL (El Salvador)	Thermal Feature of TECAPA	1403-08=
TROPHY MOUNTAIN (Canada)	Cone of WELLS GRAY-CLEARWATER	1200-15-
TROU AU NATRON (Africa-N)	Crater of VOON, TARSO	0205-02=
TROU AU NATRON (Africa-N)	Pleistocene caldera of TOUSSIDE, TARSO	0205-01=
TROU AU NATRON AU KOUSSI [ERA KOHO	Crater of KOUSSI, EMI	0205-021
TROUT CREEK HILL (US-Washington)	Shield of WEST CRATER	1201-06-
TROY (W Indies)	Dome of SABA	1600-01=
TSANZERGWE (Africa-C)	Cone of KARISIMBI	0203-04-
TSCHAOCHTSCH (Kamchatka)	Synonym of KOSHELEV	1000-02=
TSCHERNIYE SKALY [CHERNIYE SKALY]	Stratovolc of PAUZHETKA	1000-022
TSEAX RIVER CONE (Canada)	Pyrocl cone (2, 1730) Radiocarbon	**1200-10-**
TSEKONE RIDGE (Canada)	Vent of EDZIZA	1200-06-
TSENTRALNY [CENTRALNY] (Kamchatka)	Shield of POGRANYCHNY	1000-47-
TSENTRALNYY SEMIACHIK [ZENTRALNY	Stratovolc of BOLSHOI SEMIACHIK	1000-15=
TSEPOCHKA (Kamchatka)	Cone of TOLBACHIK	1000-24=
TSERBER (Aleutian Is)	Synonym of SEMISOPOCHNOI	1101-06-
TSHABWATO (Africa-C)	Cone of NYIRAGONGO	0203-03=
TSHAMBENE (Africa-C)	Vent of NYAMURAGIRA	0203-02=
TSHANIA (Africa-C)	Cone of VISOKE	0203-05-
TSHEGERE, ILE (Africa-C)	Cone of NYIRAGONGO	0203-03=
TSHIBINDA (Africa-C)	Cinder cones (None) Holocene	**0203-08-**
TSHOVE [SHOVE] (Africa-C)	Cone of NYAMURAGIRA	0203-02=
TSIATSIA (Kurile Is)	Synonym of TIATIA	0900-03=
TSIFAJAVONA (Madagascar)	Cone of ITASY VOLC FIELD	0303-06-
TSIKURA (Kurile Is)	Synonym of CHIKURACHKI	0900-36=
TSUBAME (Honshu-Japan)	Thermal Feature of MYOKO	0803-10=
TSUETATE (Kyushu-Japan)	Thermal Feature of KUJU GROUP	0802-12=
TSUGAMORI (Honshu-Japan)	Stratovolc of AKITA-YAKE-YAMA	0803-26=
TSUGAO-YAMA (Honshu-Japan)	Cone of FUJI	0803-03=
TSUGARU-FUJI (Honshu-Japan)	Synonym of IWAKI	0803-27=
TSUJINO-DAKE (Kyushu-Japan)	Dome of IBUSUKI VOLC FIELD	0802-07=
TSUKAHARA (Kyushu-Japan)	Thermal Feature of TSURUMI	0802-13=
TSUKUMO-JIMA (Kyushu-Japan)	Crater of UNZEN	0802-10=
TSUKUSHI-FUJI [KAIMON] (Kyushu-Japan)	Stratovolc of IBUSUKI VOLC FIELD	0802-07=
TSURUGA-IKE (Honshu-Japan)	Crater of NORIKURA	0803-06=
TSURUGI-DAKE (Honshu-Japan)	Cone of HAKKODA GROUP	0803-28=
TSURUGI-DAKE (Honshu-Japan)	Cone of KURIKOMA	0803-21=
TSURUGI-YAMA (Honshu-Japan)	Dome of OSORE-YAMA	0803-29=
TSURUMI (Kyushu-Japan)	Lava domes (3, 0867) Historical	**0802-13=**
TSURUMI-DAKE (Kyushu-Japan)	Dome of TSURUMI	0802-13=
TUAHU (New Zealand)	Tuff cone of OKATAINA	0401-05=
TUAHU (New Zealand)	Dome of MAROA	0401-061
TUANSHAN (China-S)	Cone of TENGCHONG	0705-11-
TUANZISHAN (China-E)	Cone of KELUO GROUP	1005-03-
TUBARU (Halmahera-Indonesia)	Synonym of IBU	0608-03=
TUBER HILL (Canada)	Stratovolc of BRIDGE RIVER CONES	1200-17-
TUCHOV CRATER (Kamchatka)	Synonym of ZARECHNY	1000-262
TUCLE, CERRO (Chile-N)	Synonym of TUJLE, CERRO	1505-104
TUDDAHRAUN (Iceland-S)	Fissure vent of KATLA	1702-03=
TUDU (Lesser Sunda Is)	Crater of PALUWEH	0604-15=
TUDU (Lesser Sunda Is)	Thermal Feature of PALUWEH	0604-15=
TUFTON HALL (W Indies)	Thermal Feature of ST. CATHERINE	1600-17=
TUGAMORI [TSUGAMORI] (Honshu-Japan)	Stratovolc of AKITA-YAKE-YAMA	0803-26=
TUGARU-HUZI (Honshu-Japan)	Synonym of IWAKI	0803-27=
TUHINGAMATA (New Zealand)	Dome of TAUPO	0401-07=
TUHUA (New Zealand)	Synonym of MAYOR ISLAND	0401-021
TUI LAKE (Kermadec Is)	Crater of RAOUL ISLAND	0402-03=
TUILA [TUYLA] (Kamchatka)	Crater of KLIUCHEVSKOI	1000-26=
TUJLE, CERRO (Chile-N)	Maar (None) Holocene	**1505-104**
TUKULLUM (US-Washington)	Synonym of BAKER	1201-01=
TULABUG (Ecuador)	Scoria cones (None) Holocene	**1502-081**
TULAMAN [TULUMAN] (Admiralty Is-SW Pac	Cone of ST. ANDREW STRAIT	0500-01=
TULIK (Aleutian Is)	Cone of OKMOK	1101-29-
TULLU MOJE (Ethiopia)	Pumice cone (2, 1900) Anthropology	**0201-25-**
TULU BILLA (Ethiopia)	Cone of SHALA	0201-28-
TULU FIKE (Ethiopia)	Cone of SHALA	0201-28-
TULU MOJE (Ethiopia)	Synonym of TULLU MOJE	0201-25-
TULUACH (Kamchatka)	Synonym of TOLBACHIK	1000-24=
TULULUSIA (Africa-E)	Dome of MERU	0202-16=
TULUMAN (Admiralty Is-SW Pac)	Cone of ST. ANDREW STRAIT	0500-01=
TUMANOV (Kamchatka)	Stratovolc of ASACHA	1000-062
TUMBA DEL BUEY, LA (Chile-C)	Crater of MOCHO-CHOSHUENCO	1507-13=
TUMBLE BUTTES (US-California)	Cinder cones (None) Holocene?	**1203-06-**
TUNAS, CERRO LAS (Mexico)	Cone of DURANGO VOLC FIELD	1401-022
TUNAUMURI (New Britain-SW Pac)	Maar of DAKATAUA	0502-04=
TUNDROVIY (Kamchatka)	Shields (None) Holocene	**1000-059**
TUNG-CHIAO-TE-PU-SHAN [DONGJIAODE	Cone of WUDALIANCHI	1005-04-
TUNG-HENG-TAO-SHAN [DONGHENGDAO	Cone of LONGGANG GROUP	1005-06-
TUNG-LUNG-MEN-SHAN [DONGLONGMEN	Cone of WUDALIANCHI	1005-04-
TUNG-LUNG-WAN [DONGLONGWAN]	Crater of LONGGANG GROUP	1005-06-
TUNGGUL, BUKIT (Java)	Stratovolc of TANGKUBANPARAHU	0603-09=
TUNGNAFELLSJOKULL (Iceland-NE)	Stratovolc (None) Holocene	**1703-04=**
TUNGNARBOTNAHRAUN (Iceland-NE)	Fissure vent of BARDARBUNGA	1703-03=
TUNGURAGUA (Ecuador)	Synonym of TUNGURAHUA	1502-08=
TUNGURAHUA (Ecuador)	Stratovolc (11, 1944) Historical	**1502-08=**
TUNIPILYAKUM (Kamchatka)	Shield of IKTUNUP	1000-67-
TUNISSET, PUY DE [PUY DE TENUSSET]	Cone of CHAINE DES PUYS	0100-02-
TUNKIN DEPRESSION (Russia-SE)	Volc field (None) Holocene	**1002-05-**
TUNNEL CONE (US-Calif)	Cone of GOLDEN TROUT CREEK	1203-17-
TUNOA (Samoa-SW Pacific)	Shield of TA'U	0404-001
TUO, KAPUNDAN [KEPUNDAN TUO] (Sumat	Crater of MARAPI	0601-14=
TUPINIER (New Guinea-NE of)	Synonym of SAKAR	0501-08=
TUPUNGATITO (Chile-C)	Stratovolc (17, 1986) Historical	**1507-01=**
TURANGUNAN (New Britain-SW Pac)	Stratovolc of RABAUL	0502-14=
TURBID LAKE (US-Wyoming)	Crater of YELLOWSTONE	1205-01-
TURCHIO, MONTE (Italy)	Cone of ETNA	0101-06=
TURFAN (China-W)	Cone (1, 1120) Historical	**1004-01-**
TURKEY RIDGE (US-New Mexico)	Dome of VALLES CALDERA	1210-03-
TURRAH, HARRAT (Arabia-W)	Blank of RAHAT, HARRAT	0301-07=
TURRIALBA (Costa Rica)	Stratovolc (6, 1866) Historical	**1405-07=**
TURU (Costa Rica)	Stratovolc of BARVA	1405-05=
TURUGA-IKE [TSURUGA-IKE] (Honshu)	Crater of NORIKURA	0803-06=
TURUGI-DAKE [TSURUGI-DAKE] (Honshu)	Cone of HAKKODA GROUP	0803-28=
TURUGI-YAMA [TSURUGI-DAKE] (Honshu)	Cone of KURIKOMA	0803-21=
TURUGI-YAMA [TSURUGI-YAMA] (Honshu)	Dome of OSORE-YAMA	0803-29=
TURUMI (Kyushu-Japan)	Synonym of TSURUMI	0802-13=
TURUMI-DAKE [TSURUMI-DAKE] (Kyushu)	Dome of TSURUMI	0802-13=
TUTAEHEKA (New Zealand)	Dome of OKATAINA	0401-05=
TUTE, CERRO EL (El Salvador)	Dome of APASTEPEQUE FIELD	1403-071
TUTONG, GUNUNG (Sumatra)	Synonym of TELONG, BUR NI	0601-05=
TUTUILA (Samoa-SW Pacific)	Tuff cones (None) Holocene	**0404-02-**
TUTUKAU (New Zealand)	Dome of MAROA	0401-061
TUTUPACA (Peru)	Stratovolc (4, 1902) Historical	**1504-04=**
TUVIO, MONT (Vanuatu-SW Pacific)	Cone of AMBRYM	0507-04=
TUVURVUR [TAVURVUR] (New Britain)	Stratovolc of RABAUL	0502-14=
TUXTEPEC (Mexico)	Cone of HOLOTEPEC	1401-07-
TUXTLA, VOLCAN DE (Mexico)	Synonym of SAN MARTIN, VOLCAN DE	1401-11=
TUYAJTO, CERRO (Chile-N)	Stratovolc of CORDON CHALVIRI	1505-103
TUYIO [MONT TUVIO] (Vanuatu-SW Pacific)	Cone of AMBRYM	0507-04=
TUYLA (Kamchatka)	Crater of KLIUCHEVSKOI	1000-26=
TUZGLE, CERRO (Argentina)	Stratovolc (None) Holocene?	**1505-111**
TUZOVSKY (Kamchatka)	Shields (None) Holocene	**1000-55-**
TV1 (New Zealand)	Crater of WHITE ISLAND	0401-04=
TVIBOLLAR (Iceland-SW)	Crater row of BRENNISTEINSFJOLL	1701-04=
TVILLING (Atl-N-Jan Mayen)	Cone of JAN MAYEN	1706-01=
TVITUNUP (Kamchatka)	Shield of TUZOVSKY	1000-55-
TWIN (Canada)	Cone of EDZIZA	1200-06-
TWIN BUTTES (US-California)	Cinder cones (None) Holocene?	**1203-05-**
TWIN BUTTES (US-Oregon)	Cone of SQUAW RIDGE FIELD	1202-13-
TWIN CALDERAS (Alaska-W)	Shield of IMURUK LAKE	1104-02-
TWIN CRATER (New Britain-SW Pac)	Crater of LANGILA	0502-01=
TWIN CRATERS (US-New Mexico)	Crater of ZUNI-BANDERA	1210-02-
TWIN CRATERS (US-Oregon)	Cone of BELKNAP	1202-06-
TWIN MOUNTAIN (Alaska-W)	Cone of NUNIVAK ISLAND	1104-06-
TWIN MOUNTAIN (US-New Mexico)	Cone of RATON-CLAYTON	1210-04-
TWINDAUNG (SE Asia)	Crater of LOWER CHINDWIN	0705-09-
TWINYWA (SE Asia)	Crater of LOWER CHINDWIN	0705-09-
TWO POINT BUTTE (US-Idaho)	Cone of CRATERS OF THE MOON	1204-02-
TWUNAMURI (New Britain-SW Pac)	Maar of DAKATAUA	0502-04=
TYATYA (Kurile Is)	Synonym of TIATIA	0900-03=
TYAUSU-DAKE [CHAUSU-DAKE] (Honshu)	Dome of NASU	0803-15=
TYAUSU-YAMA (Honshu-Japan)	Synonym of NIIGATA-YAKE-YAMA	0803-09=
TYOKAI (Honshu-Japan)	Synonym of CHOKAI	0803-22=
TYOSITIRO-YAMA [CHOSHICHIRO-YAMA]	Dome of AKAGI	0803-13=
TYUO-KAKOKYU [CHUO-KAKOKYU]	Cone of TOKACHI	0805-05=
TZANJUYUB, VOLCAN DE (Guatemala)	Stratovolc (None) Pleistocene-Fumarolic	**1402-05=**
TZEMPOLI (Mexico)	Cone of CHICHINAUTZIN	1401-08=
TZINTZUNGO, CERRO DE (Mexico)	Cone of MICHOACAN-GUANAJUATO	1401-06=

U

NAME (Subregion)	Type (Eruption Total, Most Recent) Status . . . Relation to NAMED VOLCANO	NUMBER
UACHLAR (UAKHLAR) (Kamchatka)	Synonym of ICHINSKY	1000-28=
UBAKURA-YAMA (Honshu-Japan)	Stratovolc of IWATE	0803-24=
UBAYU (Honshu-Japan)	Thermal Feature of AZUMA	0803-18=
UBEHEBE CRATERS (US-Calif)	Maars (None) Holocene	**1203-16-**
UBINAS (Peru)	Stratovolc (16, 1969) Historical	**1504-02=**
UCHI-YAMA (Kyushu-Japan)	Dome of TSURUMI	0802-13=
UCHINO (Honshu-Japan)	Cone of IZU-TOBU	0803-01=
UCHIURA-DAKE (Hokkaido-Japan)	Synonym of KOMAGA-TAKE	0805-02=
UCHTAPOLIAR (Armenia)	Cone of AGMAGAN-KARADAG	0104-07-
UCTEPELER (Turkey)	Cone of ERCIYES DAGI	0103-01=
UCUK DAGI (Turkey)	Cone of ERCIYES DAGI	0103-01=
UD'ALE (Ethiopia)	Synonym of ASSAB VOLC FIELD	0201-125
UDINA (Kamchatka)	Stratovolcs (None) Holocene	**1000-241**
UDOKAN VOLC FIELD (Russia-SE)	Shields (2, -0150) Radiocarbon	**1002-03-**
UEA ISLAND (SW Pacific)	Synonym of WALLIS ISLANDS	0404-05-
UGASHIK (Alaska Peninsula)	Pleistocene caldera of UGASHIK-PEULIK	1102-13A
UGASHIK-PEULIK (Alaska Peninsula)	Stratovolc (1, 1814) Historical	**1102-13A**
UHAMBULE (Africa-E)	Dome of SW USANGU BASIN	0202-163
UINKARET FIELD (US-Arizona)	Volc field (None) Holocene	**1209-01-**
UIUN-KHOLDONGI (China-E)	Synonym of WUDALIANCHI	1005-04-
UJAKUSHATSCH (Alaska-SW)	Synonym of REDOUBT	1103-03-
UJUN-HOLDONGI (China-E)	Synonym of WUDALIANCHI	1005-04-
UKA (Kamchatka)	Shield (None) Holocene	**1000-61-**
UK'ELEDI (Alaska-E)	Synonym of WRANGELL	1105-02-
UKINREK MAARS (Alaska Peninsula)	Maars (1, 1977) Historical	**1102-13B**
UKSICHAN (Kamchatka)	Shield (None) Holocene	**1000-35-**
'UKWATAIN (Arabia-W)	Cone of YAR, JABAL	0301-08-
ULAULA, PUU (Hawaiian Is)	Cone of MAUNA LOA	1302-02=
ULAULA, PUU (Hawaiian Is)	Cone of KILAUEA	1302-01-
ULAWON (New Britain-SW Pac)	Synonym of ULAWUN	0502-12=
ULAWUN (New Britain-SW Pac)	Stratovolc (22, 1993) Historical	**0502-12=**
ULE'EG (Vanuatu-SW Pacific)	Stratovolc of SORETIMEAT	0507-01=
ULIAEGAN (Aleutian Is)	Synonym of ULIAGA	1101-25-
ULIAGA (Aleutian Is)	Stratovolc (None) Holocene?	**1101-25-**
ULIAGA (Aleutian Is)	Synonym of CARLISLE	1101-23-
ULLUNG-DO (Korea)	Synonym of ULREUNG	1006-03-
ULMENER (Germany)	Maar of WEST EIFEL VOLC FIELD	0100-01-
ULO [PARASO] (Solomon Is-SW Pac)	Thermal Feature of NONDA	0505-04=
ULREUNG (Korea)	Stratovolc (1, -7350) Radiocarbon	**1006-03-**
ULREUNG IS. (ULREUNGDO) (Korea)	Synonym of ULREUNG	1006-03-
ULTIMO PUESTO (Chile-C)	Cone of ANTILLANCA GROUP	1507-153
ULUG-ARGINSKY (Russia-SE)	Cinder cone (None) Holocene	**1002-07-**
ULUINGGALAU (Fiji Is-SW Pacific)	Cone of TAVEUNI	0405-01-
ULUMAM (New Guinea-NE of)	Cone of KARKAR	0501-03=
ULUMAN, MT. (New Guinea-NE of)	Synonym of KARKAR	0501-03=
ULUWUN (New Britain-SW Pac)	Synonym of ULAWUN	0502-12=
ULYABORSKIY [KHARA-BOLDOK] (Russia)	Cone of TUNKIN DEPRESSION	1002-05-
UMANI (Africa-E)	Cone of CHYULU HILLS	0202-13=
UMBOI (New Guinea-NE of)	Complx volc (None) Holocene	**0501-06=**
UMCEN (UMCINA) (New Guinea-W)	Synonym of UMSINI	0609-01=
UMI-JIGOKU (Kyushu-Japan)	Thermal Feature of TSURUMI	0802-13=
UMM AD DULU, JABAL (Arabia-W)	Maar of KISHB, HARRAT	0301-071
UMM KHANDAG, JEBEL (Africa-N)	Cone of BAYUDA VOLC FIELD	0205-06-
UMM MARAFIEB, JEBEL (Africa-N)	Scoria cones (None) Holocene?	**0205-07-**
UMM QUREINAT (Africa-N)	Cone of BAYUDA VOLC FIELD	0205-06-
UMM RUQUBAH, JABAL (Arabia-W)	Dome of RAHAT, HARRAT	0301-07=
UMMUNA (Ethiopia)	Synonym of ALE BAGU	0201-09=
UMSINI (New Guinea-W)	(None) Not a Volcano	0609-01=
UNA UNA (Sulawesi-Indonesia)	Synonym of COLO [UNA UNA]	0606-01=
UNAGI (Kyushu-Japan)	Maar of IBUSUKI VOLC FIELD	0802-07=
UNALAVQUEN (Chile-C)	Synonym of CALLAQUI	1507-091
UNDAKA ISLAND [UNDAGA ISLAND]	Cone of MUNDUA	0502-021
UNGARAN (Java)	Stratovolc (None) Holocene	**0603-23=**
UNION PEAK (US-Oregon)	Cone of CRATER LAKE	1202-16-
UNNAMED (Admiralty Is-SW Pac)	Submarine (1, 1972) Hydrophonic	**0500-03-**

NAME (Subregion)	Type (Eruption Total, Most Recent) Status / Relation to NAMED VOLCANO	NUMBER
UNNAMED (Africa-C)	Cinder cones (None) Holocene	**0203-07-**
UNNAMED (Africa-E)	Pyrocl cone (None) Holocene	**0202-162**
UNNAMED (Alaska Peninsula)	Cinder cones (None) Holocene	**1102-051**
UNNAMED (Alaska Peninsula)	Lava dome (None) Holocene	**1102-131**
UNNAMED (Aleutian Is)	(None) Not a Volcano	1101-17-
UNNAMED (Antarctica)	Submarine (None) Holocene?	**1900-016**
UNNAMED (Antarctica)	Scoria cones (None) Holocene?	**1900-014**
UNNAMED (Antarctica)	Submarine ? (None) Uncertain	**1900-051**
UNNAMED (Arabia-S)	Submarine (None) Uncertain	**0301-15-**
UNNAMED (Arctic Ocean)	Submarine (3, 1957) Historical	**1707-01-**
UNNAMED (Atlantic-C)	Submarine (None) Uncertain	**1805-01=**
UNNAMED (Atlantic-C)	Submarine (1, 1836) Historical	**1805-03=**
UNNAMED (Atlantic-C)	Submarine (None) Uncertain	**1805-04=**
UNNAMED (Atlantic-C)	Submarine (None) Uncertain	**1805-02=**
UNNAMED (Atlantic-N)	(None) Not a Volcano	1801-01=
UNNAMED (Atlantic-N)	Submarine (1, 1865) Historical	**1801-04=**
UNNAMED (Atlantic-N)	Submarine (None) Uncertain	**1801-03=**
UNNAMED (Atlantic-N)	Submarine (1, 1884) Historical	**1801-02=**
UNNAMED (Azores)	Pyrocl cones (7, 1652) Historical	**1802-081**
UNNAMED (Chile-Is)	Submarine (None) Uncertain	**1506-04=**
UNNAMED (Chile-N)	Pumice cone (None) Holocene?	**1505-041**
UNNAMED (China-W)	Volc field (None) Holocene	**1004-04-**
UNNAMED (Ethiopia)	Fissure vents (None) Holocene	**0201-252**
UNNAMED (Ethiopia)	Cinder cones (None) Holocene	**0201-311**
UNNAMED (Ethiopia)	Fissure vents (None) Holocene	**0201-251**
UNNAMED (Ethiopia)	Pyrocl cones (None) Holocene	**0201-201**
UNNAMED (Ethiopia)	Fissure vents (None) Holocene	**0201-221**
UNNAMED (Georgia)	Cones (None) Holocene	**0104-05-**
UNNAMED (Georgia)	Cinder cones (None) Holocene	**0104-04-**
UNNAMED (Hawaiian Is)	Submarine (1, 1955) Historical	**1302-09-**
UNNAMED (Hawaiian Is)	Submarine (None) Uncertain	**1302-08-**
UNNAMED (Indian O.-E)	Submarine ? (None) Uncertain	**0305-01=**
UNNAMED (Iran)	Volc field (None) Holocene?	**0302-04-**
UNNAMED (Kamchatka)	Shields (None) Holocene	**1000-086**
UNNAMED (Kamchatka)	Cinder cones (None) Holocene	**1000-263**
UNNAMED (Kamchatka)	Cinder cones (None) Holocene?	**1000-232**
UNNAMED (Kamchatka)	Shield (None) Holocene	**1000-43-**
UNNAMED (Kamchatka)	Cinder cone (None) Holocene	**1000-081**
UNNAMED (Kamchatka)	Cinder cones (None) Holocene	**1000-101**
UNNAMED (Kamchatka)	Pyrocl cones (None) Holocene	**1000-058**
UNNAMED (Kamchatka)	Volc field (None) Holocene	**1000-052**
UNNAMED (Kamchatka)	Cinder cone (None) Holocene	**1000-021**
UNNAMED (Kamchatka)	Shields (None) Holocene	**1000-085**
UNNAMED (Kermadec Is)	Submarine (1, 1886) Historical	**0402-04=**
UNNAMED (Kurile Is)	Submarine (1, 1972) Hydrophonic	**0900-16-**
UNNAMED (Kurile Is)	Submarine (1, 1924) Historical	**0900-23=**
UNNAMED (Kurile Is)	Submarine (None) Uncertain	**0900-061**
UNNAMED (Kurile Is)	Submarine ? (None) Uncertain	**0900-13-**
UNNAMED (Luzon Is-N of)	Submarine (3, 1854) Historical	**0704-05=**
UNNAMED (Mariana Is-C Pac)	Submarine ? (None) Uncertain	**0804-136**
UNNAMED (Mariana Is-C Pac)	Submarine ? (None) Uncertain	**0804-135**
UNNAMED (Mexico)	Submarine ? (None) Uncertain	**1401-008**
UNNAMED (Mindanao-Philippines)	Unknown (None) Hot Springs	**0701-032**
UNNAMED (New Britain-SW Pac)	Submarine ? (None) Uncertain	**0502-131**
UNNAMED (New Britain-SW Pac)	Submarine ? (None) Uncertain	**0502-001**
UNNAMED (New Guinea-NE of)	Submarine ? (None) Uncertain	**0501-04=**
UNNAMED (Pacific-E)	Submarine (1, 1991) Historical	**1303-01-**
UNNAMED (Pacific-NE)	Submarine (1, 1993) Historical	**1301-01-**
UNNAMED (Pacific-NE)	Submarine (1, 1986) Historical	**1301-02-**
UNNAMED (Pacific-NE)	Submarine ? (None) Uncertain	**1301-03-**
UNNAMED (Pacific-S)	Submarine (None) Uncertain	**1304-03-**
UNNAMED (Pacific-S)	Submarine (None) Uncertain	**1304-02-**
UNNAMED (Samoa-SW Pacific)	Submarine (None) Uncertain	**0404-00-**
UNNAMED (Sangihe Is-Indonesia)	Submarine ? (None) Uncertain	**0607-05=**
UNNAMED (Solomon Is-SW Pac)	Submarine (None) Holocene	**0505-061**
UNNAMED (SW Pacific)	Submarine (1, 1964) Hydrophonic	**0508-03-**
UNNAMED (Syria)	Volc field (None) Holocene	**0300-04-**
UNNAMED (Syria)	Volc field (None) Holocene	**0300-06-**
UNNAMED (Syria)	Volc field (None) Holocene	**0300-03-**
UNNAMED (Syria)	Unknown (1, 1222) Historical	**0300-02-**
UNNAMED (Taiwan-E of)	Submarine (None) Uncertain	**0801-011**
UNNAMED (Taiwan-E of)	Submarine (1, 1854) Historical	**0801-02=**
UNNAMED (Taiwan-E of)	Submarine ? (None) Uncertain	**0801-01=**
UNNAMED (Taiwan-E of)	Submarine (1, 1854) Historical	**0801-03=**
UNNAMED (Taiwan-N of)	Submarine (1, 1867) Historical	**0801-04=**
UNNAMED (Tonga-SW Pacific)	Submarine (2, 1932) Historical	**0403-01=**
UNNAMED (Tonga-SW Pacific)	Submarine (3, 1988) Historical	**0403-04=**
UNNAMED (Tonga-SW Pacific)	Submarine (2, 1923) Historical	**0403-03=**
UNNAMED (Tonga-SW Pacific)	(None) Not a Volcano	0403-02=
UNNAMED (US-Calif)	(None) Not a Volcano	1203-21-
UNNAMED (Vanuatu-SW Pacific)	Stratovolcs (None) Holocene	**0507-08-**
UNNAMED (Volcano Is-Japan)	Submarine ? (None) Uncertain	**0804-093**
UNNAMED (W Indies)	Submarine (None) Pleistocene	**1600-07=**
UNSEN-DAKE (Kyushu-Japan)	Synonym of UNZEN	0802-10=
UNUK RIVER [SECOND CANYON] (Canada)	Cone of ISKUT-UNUK RIVER CONES	1200-09-
UNZEN (Kyushu-Japan)	Complx volc (4, 1993) Historical	**0802-10=**
UOIVE GROUP (UOIVI) (New Guinea)	Synonym of MANAGLASE PLATEAU	0503-021
UPAS (Java)	Thermal Feature of DIENG VOLC COMP	0603-20=
UPAS, KAWAH (Java)	Crater of TANGKUBANPARAHU	0603-09=
UPEPESANKE (Japan)	Dome of NIPESOTSU-UPEPESANKE	0805-061
UPEPESANKE (Japan)	Cone of NIPESOTSU-UPEPESANKE	0805-061
UPOLU (Samoa-SW Pacific)	Shield (None) Holocene	**0404-03-**
UPPER ATIAMURI (New Zealand)	Dome of MAROA	0401-061
UPPER BOL'SHOY YENISEY (Russia-SE)	Synonym of ULUG-ARGINSKY	1002-07-
UPPER DOME (US-California)	Dome of MONO CRATERS	1203-12-
UPPER GEYSER BASIN (US-Wyoming)	Thermal Feature of YELLOWSTONE	1205-01-
UQUILA, CERRO (Bolivia)	Stratovolc of PAMPA LUXSAR	1505-042
URACAS (URACCAS) (Mariana Is-C Pac)	Synonym of FARALLON DE PAJAROS	0804-14=
'URAIS, JABAL (Arabia-S)	Cone of SAWAD, HARRA ES-	0301-16-
URATAMAN (Kurile Is)	Somma volc (None) Holocene	**0900-191**
URDALSHRAUN EYSTRI (Iceland-NE)	Crater row of KVERKFJOLL	1703-05=
URDALSHRAUN VESTARI (Iceland-NE)	Crater row of KVERKFJOLL	1703-05=
URIKOMAM (Ethiopia)	Synonym of ALAYTA	0201-112
URJI (Ethiopia)	Cone of CORBETTI CALDERA	0201-29-
'URR, JABAL EL- (Arabia-S)	Cone of DHAMAR, HARRAS OF	0301-12-
URUF, JEBEL (Africa-N)	Cone of BAYUDA VOLC FIELD	0205-06-
URUP-FUJI [KOLOKOL] (Kurile Is)	Stratovolc of KOLOKOL GROUP	0900-12=
URUPPU FUDZI [KOLOKOL] (Kurile Is)	Stratovolc of KOLOKOL GROUP	0900-12=
USAMI (Honshu-Japan)	Stratovolc of IZU-TOBU	0803-01=
USASYR (Kurile Is)	Synonym of USHISHUR	0900-21=
USHIGAKUBO (Honshu-Japan)	Vent of FUJI	0803-03=
USHIRO-ASAHI-DAKE (Hokkaido-Japan)	Stratovolc of DAISETSU	0805-06=

NAME (Subregion)	Type (Eruption Total, Most Recent) Status / Relation to NAMED VOLCANO	NUMBER
USHIROEBOSHI-DAKE (Honshu-Japan)	Stratovolc of ZAO	0803-19=
USHISHIRU (Kurile Is)	Synonym of USHISHUR	0900-21=
USHISHUR (Kurile Is)	Caldera (4, 1884) Historical	**0900-21=**
USHKINSKAYA (USHKOVSKAYA) (Kamchatk	Synonym of USHKOVSKY	1000-261
USHKOVSKY (Kamchatka)	Compnd volc (2, 1890) Historical	**1000-261**
USIRO-ASAHI-DAKE [USHIRO-ASAHI-DAKE	Stratovolc of DAISETSU	0805-06=
USISIRU (Kurile Is)	Synonym of USHISHUR	0900-21=
USKOVSKII (Kamchatka)	Synonym of USHKOVSKY	1000-261
USMAJAC (Mexico)	Cone of COLIMA VOLC COMPLEX	1401-04=
USON (Kamchatka)	Synonym of UZON	1000-17=
USORI-YAMA (Honshu-Japan)	Synonym of OSORE-YAMA	0803-29=
USTUP (Kamchatka)	Cone of OPALA	1000-08=
USU (Hokkaido-Japan)	Stratovolc (10, 1982) Historical	**0805-03=**
USU-SHINZAN (Hokkaido-Japan)	Dome of USU	0805-03=
USU-YAMA (Honshu-Japan)	Cone of FUJI	0803-03=
USULUTAN (El Salvador)	Stratovolc (None) Holocene	**1403-081**
UTAL, CERRO DEL (El Salvador)	Cone of SINGUIL, CERRO	1403-011
UTAMA, KAWAH (Lesser Sunda Is)	Crater of PALUWEH	0604-15=
UTASCHUT (UTASHUT) (Kamchatka)	Synonym of ZHELTOVSKY	1000-04=
UTESIKI U SUKHOGO (Kamchatka)	Synonym of VEER	1000-102
UTI-YAMA [UCHI-YAMA] (Kyushu-Japan)	Dome of TSURUMI	0802-13=
UTILA ISLAND (Honduras)	Pyrocl cones (None) Holocene	**1403-16-**
UTIURA-DAKE (Hokkaido-Japan)	Synonym of KOMAGA-TAKE	0805-02=
UTSUBO-SHIMA [KAIMON] (Kyushu-Japan)	Stratovolc of IBUSUKI VOLC FIELD	0802-07=
UTSURYO-TO (Korea)	Synonym of ULREUNG	1006-03-
UTULOKA POINT (SW Pacific)	Cone of WALLIS ISLANDS	0404-05-
UTURUNCO (Bolivia)	Stratovolc (None) Holocene	**1505-075**
UVEA ISLAND (SW Pacific)	Synonym of WALLIS ISLANDS	0404-05-
UVERA'A (Vanuatu-SW Pacific)	Stratovolc of SORETIMEAT	0507-01=
UVILLAS (UVINAS) (Peru)	Synonym of UBINAS	1504-02=
'UWAYRID, HARRAT (Arabia-W)	Volc field (1, 0640) Anthropology	**0301-02=**
'UWEIRIZH, HARRAT EL- (Arabia-W)	Synonym of 'UWAYRID, HARRAT	0301-02=
UYAKUZHACH (Kurile Is)	Synonym of ALAID	0900-39=
UYUN-KHOLDONGI (China-E)	Synonym of WUDALIANCHI	1005-04-
UYUNHORDONGI (China-E)	Synonym of WUDALIANCHI	1005-04-
UZON (Kamchatka)	Calderas (1, -5700) Radiocarbon	**1000-17=**

V

NAME (Subregion)	Type (Eruption Total, Most Recent) Status / Relation to NAMED VOLCANO	NUMBER
VAALKOP (Indian O.-S)	Tuff cone of PRINCE EDWARD ISLAND	0304-07-
VACHE, PUY DE LA (France)	Cone of CHAINE DES PUYS	0100-02-
VAHILSKAIA, SOPKA (Kamchatka)	Synonym of ZHUPANOVSKY	1000-12=
VAI A HEVA, MAUNGA (Pacific-C)	Dome of EASTER ISLAND	1303-08-
VAI FO (Tonga-SW Pacific)	Cone of NIUAFO'OU	0403-11=
VAIALA (Samoa-SW Pacific)	Cone of SAVAI'I	0404-04=
VAILOATAI (Samoa-SW Pacific)	Tuff cone of TUTUILA	0404-02-
VAIOLO (Samoa-SW Pacific)	Cone of SAVAI'I	0404-04=
VAKA, MAUNGA (Pacific-C)	Cone of EASTER ISLAND	1303-08-
VAKAK VOLCANO GROUP (Afghanistan)	Volc field (None) Holocene	**0302-07-**
VAKHILSKAYA (Kamchatka)	Synonym of ZHUPANOVSKY	1000-12=
VAKHUL'SKAYA SOPKA (Kamchatka)	Synonym of ZHUPANOVSKY	1000-12=
VALAGJA (Iceland-S)	Fissure vent of HEKLA	1702-07=
VALDIVIA (Chile-C)	Synonym of MOCHO-CHOSHUENCO	1507-13=
VALENTANO (Italy)	Cone of VULSINI	0101-003
VALENTIN (Kamchatka)	Cone of KOSHELEV	1000-02=
VALLE, VALLEY see proper name (e.g. LEONE, VALLE DEL)		
VALLE, VOLCAN DEL (Guatemala)	Cone of SANTA MARIA	1402-03=
VALLES CALDERA (US-New Mexico)	Caldera (None) Pleistocene-Fumarolic	**1210-03-**
VALLETTA, CUDDIA (Italy)	Shield of PANTELLERIA	0101-071
VAMBU ISLAND (New Britain-SW Pac)	Cone of MUNDUA	0502-021
VAN HEUTSZ CRATER (Sumatra)	Crater of SEULAWAH AGAM	0601-02=
VAN ZINDEREN BAKKER PEAK (Indian O.-S	Cone of PRINCE EDWARD ISLAND	0304-07-
VANA KEI VUNA (Fiji Is-SW Pacific)	Cone of TAVEUNI	0405-01-
VANGORI (New Britain-SW Pac)	Synonym of BOLA	0502-05=
VANUA LAVA (Vanuatu-SW Pacific)	Synonym of SORETIMEAT	0507-01=
VAO O HAO, MAUNGA (Pacific-C)	Cone of EASTER ISLAND	1303-08-
VARADOURO (Azores)	Thermal Feature of FAYAL	1802-01=
VARZEA, PICO DO (Azores)	Cone of SETE CIDADES	1802-08=
VARZIN, MT. (New Britain-SW Pac)	Stratovolc of RABAUL	0502-14=
VASSET, PUY (France)	Dome of CHAINE DES PUYS	0100-02-
VATELIERO (Italy)	Crater of ISCHIA	0101-03=
VATIA (Samoa-SW Pacific)	Dome of TUTUILA	0404-02-
VATNAFJOLL (Iceland-S)	Fissure vents (26, 0750) Tephrochronology	**1702-06=**
VATNAOLDUR (Iceland-NE)	Crater row of BARDARBUNGA	1703-03=
VATNSHEIDI (Iceland-SW)	Shield of REYKJANES	1701-02=
VATR (New Britain-SW Pac)	Synonym of ULAWUN	0502-12=
VE'A (Samoa-SW Pacific)	Cone of SAVAI'I	0404-04=
VECCHIA, LA (Italy)	Pleistocene caldera of PANTELLERIA	0101-071
VECCHIENNA, LAGO (Italy)	Crater of LARDERELLO	0101-001
VEDURHALSHRAUN (Iceland-S)	Fissure vent of KATLA	1702-03=
VEER (Kamchatka)	Cinder cones (1, 1856) Historical	**1000-102**
VEGA, CERRITO LA (Guatemala)	Cone of CUILAPA-BARBARENA	1402-111
VEGA, CERRO LOS (Guatemala)	Cone of CUILAPA-BARBARENA	1402-111
VEGGJABUNGA (Iceland-NE)	Shield of ASKJA	1703-06=
VEIDIVOTN (Iceland-NE)	Crater row of BARDARBUNGA	1703-03=
VEKHNE-INGAMAKITSKY II (Russia-SE)	Cone of NE UDOKAN PLATEAU	1002-02-
VELAIN (Indian O.-W)	Crater of FOURNAISE, PITON DE LA	0303-02=
VELHA, CALDEIRA (Azores)	Thermal Feature of AGUA DE PAU	1802-09=
VELIE NUNATAK (Antarctica)	Cone of HUDSON MOUNTAINS	1900-028
VELLA LAVELLA SULFUR FIELD [PARASO]	Thermal Feature of NONDA	0505-04=
VELLUDA, SIERRA (Chile-C)	Stratovolc of ANTUCO	1507-08=
VENADOS, LOS (Chile-C)	Maar of CARRAN-LOS VENADOS	1507-14=
VENIAMINOF (Alaska Peninsula)	Stratovolc (13, 1993) Historical	**1102-07-**
VENT MOUNTAIN (Alaska Peninsula)	Cone of ANIAKCHAK	1102-09-
VENTANITA (El Salvador)	Pit crater of APASTEPEQUE FIELD	1403-071
VENTARRON, EL (Nicaragua)	Caldera of MASAYA	1404-10=
VENTISQUEROS, CERRO DE LOS (Chile-S)	Synonym of HUDSON, CERRO	1508-057
VENUS (Indian O.-S)	Cone of AMSTERDAM ISLAND	0304-04-
VERBEEK, KAWAH (Sumatra)	Crater of MARAPI	0601-14=
VERDE, CERRO (El Salvador)	Cone of TABURETE	1403-072
VERDE, CERRO (El Salvador)	Cone of SANTA ANA	1403-02=
VERDE, LAGUNA (El Salvador)	Stratovolcs (1, 1990) Holocene	**1403-01=**
VERDE, VOLCAN LAGUNA (Chile-C)	Cone of TOLGUACA	1507-092
VERDELOMA (Ecuador)	Stratovolc of SANGAY	1502-09=
VERDUGO, VOLCAN EL (Mexico)	Maar of PINACATE PEAKS	1401-001
VERKHNE-KOSHELEVSKIE (Kamchatka)	Thermal Feature of KOSHELEV	1000-02=
VERKHNEYE (Kamchatka)	Thermal Feature of MUTNOVSKY	1000-06=
VERKHNEYE THERMAL FIELD (Kamchatka)	Thermal Feature of BOLSHOI SEMIACHIK	1000-15=
VERKHOVOY (Kamchatka)	Shield (None) Holocene	**1000-44-**
VERMELHO, PICO (Azores)	Cone of AGUA DE PAU	1802-09=
VERMILLION CHASM (US-Idaho)	Fissure vent of CRATERS OF THE MOON	1204-02-
VERNADSKII CRATER (Kurile Is)	Cone of VERNADSKII RIDGE	0900-37-

NAME (Subregion)	Type (Eruption Total, Most Recent) Status . . . Relation to NAMED VOLCANO	NUMBER
VERNADSKII RIDGE (Kurile Is)	Cinder cones (None) Holocene	**0900-37-**
VERNADSKIY (Kamchatka)	Crater of KLIUCHEVSKOI	1000-26=
VERRIERES, PUY DE [PUY THIOLET]	Cone of CHAINE DES PUYS	0100-02-
VESLESSA (Atl-N-Jan Mayen)	Cone of JAN MAYEN	1706-01=
VESTASTI URDARHALSGIGUR (Iceland-NE)	Crater row of KVERKFJOLL	1703-05=
VESTISNUTEN (Atl-N-Jan Mayen)	Cone of JAN MAYEN	1706-01=
VESTMANNAEYJAR (Iceland-S)	Submarine (6, 1973) Historical	**1702-01=**
VESUVIO (VESUVE) (Italy)	Synonym of VESUVIUS	0101-02=
VESUVIUS (Italy)	Complx volc (48, 1944) Historical	**0101-02=**
VETERAN (SE Asia)	Submarine (None) Fumarolic	**0705-07-**
VETLAM (Vanuatu-SW Pacific)	Cone of AMBRYM	0507-04=
VETMWAN (Vanuatu-SW Pacific)	Cone of MOTLAV	0507-001
VETORE, MONTE (Italy)	Cone of ETNA	0101-06=
VEYER (Kamchatka)	Synonym of VEER	1000-102
VEYO VOLCANO (US-Utah)	Cone of SANTA CLARA	1207-01-
VEZZI, MONTE DI (Italy)	Dome of ISCHIA	0101-03=
VIATOA (Samoa-SW Pacific)	Cone of UPOLU	0404-03-
VIBORAS, VOLCAN LAS (Guatemala)	Cone of CHINGO VOLC FIELD	1402-15-
VICA, MONTANA LA (Canary Is)	Cone of TENERIFE	1803-03-
VICHATEL, PUY DE (France)	Cone of CHAINE DES PUYS	0100-02-
VICO, MONTE (Italy)	Dome of ISCHIA	0101-03=
VICTORIA, MT. (New Zealand)	Cone of AUCKLAND FIELD	0401-02=
VICTORIA VOLC FIELD (Australia)	Synonym of NEWER VOLCANICS PROV	0509-01-
VICTORIABERG (Africa-W)	Synonym of CAMEROON, MT.	0204-01=
VICTORY (New Guinea)	Stratovolc (1, 1935) Historical	**0503-03=**
VIDAL, CERRITO DE LOS (Guatemala)	Cone of CHIQUIMULA FIELD	1402-20-
VIDRIOS, VOLCAN LOS (Mexico)	Maar of PINACATE PEAKS	1401-001
VIEDMA, VOLCAN (Argentina)	Subglacial (1, 1988) Historical	**1508-061**
VIEJO, EL (Nicaragua)	Synonym of SAN CRISTOBAL	1404-02=
VIEJO, PICO (Canary Is)	Stratovolc of TENERIFE	1803-03-
VIEJO, VOLCAN (Chile-C)	Stratovolc of CHILLAN, NEVADOS DE	1507-07=
VIEJONA, AUSOLES DE LA [VOLCANCITO]	Thermal Feature of CHINAMECA	1403-09=
VIENTO, MONTANA DEL (Canary Is)	Cone of GRAN CANARIA	1803-04-
VIESOKAIA (Alaska-SW)	Synonym of REDOUBT	1103-03-
VIETLAM [VETLAM] (Vanuatu-SW Pacific)	Cone of AMBRYM	0507-04=
VIGIA, CERRO (Mexico)	Cone of SAN MARTIN, VOLCAN DE	1401-11=
VIGIA, EL (Honduras)	Cone of TIGRE, ISLA EL	1403-13-
VIGIA, PICO DO (Atlantic-S)	Dome of TRINDADE	1805-051
VIGNA VECCHIA (Italy)	Cone of STROMBOLI	0101-04=
VIGUERIA, LA (Chile-S)	Cone of CAYUTE-LA VIGUERIA	1508-021
VIKAHRAUN (Iceland-NE)	Fissure vent of ASKJA	1703-06=
VIKRABORGIR (Iceland-NE)	Crater of ASKJA	1703-06=
VILFILFELLSHRAUN (Iceland-SW)	Crater row of BRENNISTEINSFJOLL	1701-04=
VILIUCHINSKAYA (Kamchatka)	Synonym of VILYUCHIK	1000-083
VILLA RICA (Chile-C)	Synonym of VILLARRICA	1507-12=
VILLARRICA (Chile-C)	Stratovolc (70, 1992) Historical	**1507-12=**
VILLARS, MAAR DE (France)	Maar of CHAINE DES PUYS	0100-02-
VILLELE, CRATERE DE (Indian O.-W)	Crater of FOURNAISE, PITON DE LA	0303-02=
VILYAMS, MT. (Kurile Is)	Cone of SMIRNOV	0900-031
VILYUCHIK (Kamchatka)	Stratovolc (1, -5550) Tephrochronology	**1000-083**
VILYUCHINSKAYA (Kamchatka)	Synonym of VILYUCHIK	1000-083
VILYUCHINSKIY (Kamchatka)	Synonym of VILYUCHIK	1000-083
VINA, LA (Canary Is)	Cone of HIERRO	1803-02-
VINAS, CERRITO LAS (Guatemala)	Cone of CUILAPA-BARBARENA	1402-111
VINDICATION ISLAND (Antarctica)	Cone of CANDLEMAS ISLAND	1900-10=
VINE (Kamchatka)	Synonym of ILYINSKY	1000-03=
VINI [NU'UTELE] (Samoa-SW Pacific)	Tuff ring of UPOLU	0404-03-
VIRGEN, MONTANA DE LA (Canary Is)	Cone of HIERRO	1803-02-
VIRGENES, VOLCAN LAS (Mexico)	Synonym of TRES VIRGENES	1401-01=
VISOKAYA (Kamchatka)	Cone of TOLBACHIK	1000-24=
VISOKE (Africa-C)	Stratovolc (2, 1957) Historical	**0203-05-**
VISOKIY (Kamchatka)	Stratovolc (None) Holocene	**1000-063**
VISOKOI VOLCANO (Antarctica)	Synonym of HODSON	1900-11=
VITA FUMO (Italy)	Dome of CAMPI FLEGREI	0101-01=
VITI (Iceland-NE)	Maar of KRAFLA	1703-08=
VITI (Iceland-NE)	Crater of ASKJA	1703-06=
VITU (New Britain-SW Pac)	Synonym of GAROVE	0502-03=
VIUDITA, LA (Ecuador)	Dome of ATACAZO	1502-021
VIVARA (Italy)	Tuff ring of CAMPI FLEGREI	0101-01=
VNESHNII (Kurile Is)	Dome of GOLOVNIN	0900-01=
VODORAZDELNY (Kamchatka)	Shield of POGRANYCHNY	1000-47-
VOGALA (Solomon Is-SW Pac)	Thermal Feature of SAVO	0505-07=
VOGELENZANG [KABA VOGELSANG]	Crater of KABA	0601-22=
VOGELSANG, KABA (Sumatra)	Crater of KABA	0601-22=
VOHITRA (Madagascar)	Cone of ANKARATRA FIELD	0303-07-
VOHON, TARSO (Africa-N)	Synonym of VOON, TARSO	0205-02=
VOLADERO I, CERRO EL (Guatemala)	Cone of IXTEPEQUE, VOLCAN	1402-18-
VOLCAN, VOLCA, VOLCANCITO, VOLCANO	see proper name (e.g. FUEGO, VOLCAN DE)	
VOLCAN (Mindanao-Philippines)	Synonym of CALAYO	0701-07=
VOLCAN (Nicaragua)	Synonym of MADERA, LA	1404-13-
VOLCAN, EL (Honduras)	Cone of YOJOA, LAKE	1403-15-
VOLCAN, EL (Peru)	Synonym of MISTI, EL	1504-01=
VOLCAN ISLAND (New Guinea-NE of)	Synonym of MANAM	0501-02=
VOLCAN, MONTANA DEL [SIETE FUENTES]	Cone of TENERIFE	1803-03-
VOLCANCILLO, CERRO EL (Peru)	Cone of CHACHANI, NEVADO	1504-005
VOLCANCITO (Guatemala)	Cone of PACAYA	1402-11=
VOLCANCITO, AUSOLES DEL (El Salvador)	Thermal Feature of CHINAMECA	1403-09=
VOLCANCITO, EL (Mexico)	Cone of COLIMA VOLC COMPLEX	1401-04=
VOLCANCITOS (Costa Rica)	Thermal Feature of RINCON DE LA VIEJA	1405-02=
VOLCANES DEL TATIO, GEISERS DE LOS	Synonym of TATIO	1505-08=
VOLCANIA (Greece)	Thermal Feature of KOS	0102-06=
VOLCANIC CREEK CONE (Canada)	Cone of RUBY MOUNTAIN	1200-03-
VOLCANICO, CERRO (Argentina)	Cinder cone (None) Holocene	**1508-024**
VOLCANO BUTTE (US-California)	Cone of COSO VOLC FIELD	1203-18-
VOLCANO ISLAND (Luzon-Philippines)	Synonym of TAAL	0703-07=
VOLCANO MOUNTAIN (Canada)	Cone of FORT SELKIRK	1200-01-
VOLCANO PEAK (US-California)	Cone of COSO VOLC FIELD	1203-18-
VOLSINI (Italy)	Synonym of VULSINI	0101-003
VOLVIC, MAAR DE (France)	Maar of CHAINE DES PUYS	0100-02-
VON DRASCHE, CRATERE (Indian O.-W)	Crater of FOURNAISE, PITON DE LA	0303-02=
VON FRANTZIUS (Costa Rica)	Stratovolc of POAS	1405-04=
VON HOHNEL ISLAND (Africa-E)	Synonym of SOUTH ISLAND	0202-02=
VON SEEBACH (Costa Rica)	Cone of RINCON DE LA VIEJA	1405-02=
VONIUCHI KHREBET (Kamchatka)	Synonym of KSUDACH	1000-05=
VONYUCHI KHREBET (Kamchatka)	Synonym of KSUDACH	1000-05=
VOON, TARSO (Africa-N)	Stratovolc (None) Fumarolic	**0205-02=**
VORAGINE, LA (Italy)	Crater of ETNA	0101-06=
VORDUFELLSBORGIR (Iceland-SW)	Fissure vent of BRENNISTEINSFJOLL	1701-04=
VORDUFELLSHRAUN (Iceland-S)	Fissure vent of TINDFJALLAJOKULL	1702-04=
VOSMYORKA (Kamchatka)	Crater of KLIUCHEVSKOI	1000-26=
VOSTOCHNOYE THERMAL FIELD (Kamchat	Thermal Feature of UZON	1000-17=
VOSTOCHNY BARANY (Kamchatka)	Stratovolc of BOLSHOI SEMIACHIK	1000-15=
VOTOS, LOS (Costa Rica)	Synonym of POAS	1405-04=
VOURKA (Greece)	Thermal Feature of KOS	0102-06=
VOYAMPOLSKY (Kamchatka)	Shields (None) Holocene	**1000-72-**
VROMOTOPOS (Greece)	Thermal Feature of KOS	0102-06=
VSEVIDOF (Aleutian Is)	Stratovolc (3, 1878) Historical	**1101-27-**
VTORAIA MUTNOVSKAIA SOPKA (Kamchat	Synonym of GORELY	1000-07=
VUELTA KOPPER (Costa Rica)	Cone of AGUAS ZARCAS GROUP	1405-035
VUI, LAKE (Vanuatu-SW Pacific)	Crater of AOBA	0507-03=
VUITAVOA, VUSI (Vanuatu-SW Pacific)	Cone of AOBA	0507-03=
VULCAIN (Indian O.-S)	Cone of AMSTERDAM ISLAND	0304-04-
VULCAN (New Britain-SW Pac)	Pumice cone of RABAUL	0502-14=
VULCAN ISLAND (New Britain-SW Pac)	Cone of RABAUL	0502-14=
VULCAN, MT. (Mindanao-Philippines)	Dome of HIBOK-HIBOK	0701-08=
VULCANELLO (Italy)	Cone of VULCANO	0101-05=
VULCANO (Italy)	Stratovolc (31, 1890) Historical	**0101-05=**
VULCANO ISLAND (New Guinea-NE of)	Synonym of RITTER ISLAND	0501-07=
VULCANS CASTLE (US-Calif)	Dome of LASSEN VOLC CENTER	1203-08-
VULCAN'S THRONE (US-Arizona)	Cone of UINKARET FIELD	1209-01-
VULCAO (Cape Verde Is)	Synonym of FOGO	1804-01=
VULCAO DE LAGOA DO FOGO (Azores)	Synonym of AGUA DE PAU	1802-09=
VULCAO PAREDAO (Atlantic-S)	Cone of TRINDADE	1805-051
VULKAN [KA-ER-DAXI] (China-W)	Cone of KUNLUN VOLC GROUP	1004-03-
VULSINI (Italy)	Caldera (1, -0104) Historical	**0101-003**
VUNAKOKOR [VARZIN, MT.] (New Britain)	Stratovolc of RABAUL	0502-14=
VUNUWERI (Banda Sea)	Synonym of TEON	0605-05=
VUSI, VUTI (Melanesian term for HILL)	see proper name (e.g. NAMUI, VUSI)	
VUTUSUALA (Solomon Is-SW Pac)	Thermal Feature of SAVO	0505-07=
VUVUNGANA, VUTI (Vanuatu-SW Pacific)	Cone of AOBA	0507-03=
VYSOKAYA (Kamchatka)	Cone of GORELY	1000-07=
VYSOKII (Kamchatka)	Synonym of VISOKIY	1000-063

W

NAME (Subregion)	Type (Eruption Total, Most Recent) Status . . . Relation to NAMED VOLCANO	NUMBER
WAAWAA, PUU (Hawaiian Is)	Cone of HUALALAI	1302-04-
WADE (New Zealand)	Crater of WHITE ISLAND	0401-04=
WADON (Java)	Crater of GEDE	0603-06=
WAESCHE (Antarctica)	Shields (None) Holocene?	**1900-024**
WAGIFA ISLAND [WAGIPA ISLAND]	Cone of GOODENOUGH	0503-041
WAGIO (Sulawesi-Indonesia)	Crater of MAHAWU	0606-11=
WAGIPA ISLAND (D'Entrecasteaux Is)	Cone of GOODENOUGH	0503-041
WAGO-ZAN (Honshu-Japan)	Synonym of FUJI	0803-03=
WAHA PELE (Hawaiian Is)	Cone of HUALALAI	1302-04-
WAHANGA (New Zealand)	Dome of OKATAINA	0401-05=
WAHANGA-WAIMANGU (New Zealand)	Fissure vent of OKATAINA	0401-05=
WAHI, GUNUNG [TEMPANG] (Sulawesi)	Cone of TONDANO CALDERA	0606-07-
WAI (Indonesian for STREAM)	see proper name (e.g. ASAM, WAI)	
WAIHI-TOKAANU (New Zealand)	Thermal Feature of TAUPO	0401-07=
WAIKITE (New Zealand)	Thermal Feature of OKATAINA	0401-05=
WAIKORO (Lesser Sunda Is)	Thermal Feature of PALUWEH	0604-15=
WAIKORO (Lesser Sunda Is)	Crater of PALUWEH	0604-15=
WAILAGI CONES (D'Entrecasteaux Is)	Cone of GOODENOUGH	0503-041
WAIMANGU (New Zealand)	Thermal Feature of OKATAINA	0401-05=
WAIMATE (New Zealand)	Cone of KAIKOHE-BAY OF ISLANDS	0401-01=
WAIMIMITI (New Zealand)	Cone of KAIKOHE-BAY OF ISLANDS	0401-01=
WAI'OA (New Guinea)	Synonym of WAIOWA	0503-04=
WAIORA VALLEY (New Zealand)	Thermal Feature of MAROA	0401-061
WAIOTAPU (New Zealand)	Thermal Feature of REPOROA	0401-06-
WAIOWA (New Guinea)	Pyrocl cone (1, 1944) Historical	**0503-04=**
WAIPA (New Zealand)	Thermal Feature of ROTORUA	0401-042
WAIRAKEI (New Zealand)	Thermal Feature of MAROA	0401-061
WAITA-YAMA (Kyushu-Japan)	Cone of KUJU GROUP	0802-12=
WAITANGI SODA SPRINGS (New Zealand)	Thermal Feature of OKATAINA	0401-05=
WAITOMOKIA (New Zealand)	Cone of AUCKLAND FIELD	0401-02=
WAIWHAKAPA [RIDGE DOME] (New Zealand	Dome of OKATAINA	0401-05=
WAJANG-WINDU (Java)	Synonym of WAYANG-WINDU	0603-08=
WAKALA HILL (D'Entrecasteaux Is)	Cone of GOODENOUGH	0503-041
WAKAMIKO (Kyushu-Japan)	Pleistocene caldera of SAKURA-JIMA	0802-08=
WAKE BUTTE (US-Oregon)	Cone of BACHELOR	1202-09-
WAKIONG (Halmahera-Indonesia)	Synonym of MAKIAN	0608-07=
WAKKA (Lesser Sunda Is)	Synonym of ILIBOLENG	0604-22=
WAKOTO-OYAKOTU (Hokkaido-Japan)	Dome of KUTCHARO	0805-08=
WALANG (Java)	Synonym of WAYANG-WINDU	0603-08=
WALDAU (Africa-W)	Crater of CAMEROON, MT.	0204-01=
WALDSDORFER (Germany)	Maar of WEST EIFEL VOLC FIELD	0100-01-
WALELANG (Sulawesi-Indonesia)	Crater of SEMPU	0606-04=
WALKOUT CREEK (Canada)	Cone of EDZIZA	1200-06-
WALLENAURE [TOMPALUAN] (Sulawesi)	Crater of LOKON-EMPUNG	0606-10=
WALLIS ISLANDS (SW Pacific)	Shields (None) Holocene	**0404-05-**
WALO (New Britain-SW Pac)	Hydrothrm fld (None) Hot Springs	**0502-09=**
WALTER PENK, CERRO (Argentina)	Synonym of TIPAS	1505-131
WAMBU ISLAND [VANBU ISLAND]	Cone of MUNDUA	0502-021
WANGI, GUNUNG (Java)	Dome of PENANGGUNGAN	0603-291
WANGORE (New Britain-SW Pac)	Synonym of BOLA	0502-05=
WAPI LAVA FIELD (US-Idaho)	Shield (1, -0300) Radiocarbon	**1204-03-**
WARA, WAI (Lesser Sunda Is)	Thermal Feature of POCO LEOK	0604-07=
WARAMUNG PLANTATION (New Ireland)	Thermal Feature of AMBITLE	0504-02=
WARGESS (Africa-E)	Tuff cone of BARRIER, THE	0202-03=
WARIRANG (Java)	Crater of GALUNGGUNG	0603-14=
WARM SPRINGS DOME (US-New Mexico)	Dome of VALLES CALDERA	1210-03-
WARRENHELP, MT. (Australia)	Cone of NEWER VOLCANICS PROV	0509-01-
WARRNAMBOOL, MT. (Australia)	Tuff ring of NEWER VOLCANICS PROV	0509-01-
WARTGESBERG (Germany)	Cone of WEST EIFEL VOLC FIELD	0100-01-
WASHIGA-MINE (Kyushu-Japan)	Stratovolc of ASO	0802-11=
WASHINGTON (US-Oregon)	Shield (1, 0620) Radiocarbon	**1202-05-**
WASHIO-DAKE (Kyushu-Japan)	Cone of IBUSUKI VOLC FIELD	0802-07=
WASHUNGWE (Africa-C)	Cone of NYIRAGONGO	0203-03=
WASSILJEW [LAOHEISHAN] (China-E)	Cone of WUDALIANCHI	1005-04-
WASUREZUNO-YAMA (Honshu-Japan)	Synonym of ZAO	0803-19=
WATALUMA HILL (D'Entrecasteaux Is)	Cone of GOODENOUGH	0503-041
WATANGAN, GUNUNG (Java)	Cone of TENGGER CALDERA	0603-31=
WATCHMAN, THE (US-Idaho)	Cone of CRATERS OF THE MOON	1204-02-
WATERHOUSE, MT. (Pacific-S)	Cone of ANTIPODES ISLAND	1304-01-
WATOM ISLAND (New Britain-SW Pac)	Cone of RABAUL	0502-14=
WATT MOUNTAIN (W Indies)	Cone of MICOTRIN	1600-10=
WATTEN WAVEN [WOTTEN WAVEN] (W Ind	Thermal Feature of MICOTRIN	1600-10=
WATU (Java)	Crater of SUNDORO	0603-21=
WAYANG-WINDU (Java)	Stratovolc (None) Fumarolic	**0603-08=**
WAZIN TAUNG (SE Asia)	Cone of LOWER CHINDWIN	0705-09-
WEAMBI (Africa-W)	Cone of CAMEROON, MT.	0204-01=
WEATHERBOARD HILL (Australia)	Cone of NEWER VOLCANICS PROV	0509-01-
WEBBER NUNATAK (Antarctica)	Cone of HUDSON MOUNTAINS	1900-028
WEINFELDER (Germany)	Maar of WEST EIFEL VOLC FIELD	0100-01-

NAME (Subregion)	Type (Eruption Total, Most Recent) Status / Relation to NAMED VOLCANO	NUMBER
WEISHAN (China-E)	Cone of WUDALIANCHI	1005-04-
WEJER (Kamchatka)	Synonym of VEER	1000-102
WELCKER (New Britain-SW Pac)	Stratovolc of GARBUNA GROUP	0502-07=
WELIRANG (Java)	Stratovolc of ARJUNO-WELIRANG	0603-29=
WELIRANG, KAWAH (Java)	Crater of KARANG	0603-02=
WELIRANG, KAWAH (Java)	Crater of DANAU COMPLEX	0603-01=
WELLEYS ISLAND (Antarctica)	Synonym of HODSON	1900-11=
WELLINGTON, MT (New Zealand)	Cone of AUCKLAND FIELD	0401-02=
WELLS GRAY-CLEARWATER (Canada)	Cinder cones (2, 1550) Dendrochronology	**1200-15-**
WENG-CHUAN [WENGJUAN] (China-E)	Cone of LONGGANG GROUP	1005-06-
WENJAMINOW (Alaska Peninsula)	Synonym of VENIAMINOF	1102-07-
WENSAORO (Vanuatu-SW Pacific)	Crater of SORETIMEAT	0507-01=
WESLEY ROCK (Tonga-SW Pacific)	Synonym of METIS SHOAL	0403-07=
WESSELOW (Aleutian Is)	Synonym of MAKUSHIN	1101-31-
WEST CRATER (New Zealand)	Crater of WHITE ISLAND	0401-04=
WEST CRATER (US-Washington)	Volc field (1, -3050) Radiocarbon	**1201-06-**
WEST CRATER [CRATER LAKE] (New Zeal)	Crater of RUAPEHU	0401-10=
WEST EIFEL VOLC FIELD (Germany)	Maars (2, -7050) Radiocarbon	**0100-01-**
WEST HILL (Alaska-W)	Cone of ST. MICHAEL	1104-04-
WEST LOSOLAVA (Vanuatu-SW Pacific)	Cone of GAUA	0507-02=
WEST MAAR (Alaska Peninsula)	Maar of UKINREK MAARS	1102-13B
WEST-MATTHEW (SW Pacific)	Cone of MATTHEW ISLAND	0508-01=
WEST PROSPECT PEAK (US-California)	Shield of POTATO BUTTE	1203-07-
WEST SAKUKAN (Russia-SE)	Cone of NE UDOKAN PLATEAU	1002-02-
WEST UMBOI ISLAND (New Guinea-NE of)	Synonym of UMBOI	0501-06=
WESTDAHL (Aleutian Is)	Stratovolc (7, 1992) Historical	**1101-34-**
WESTERN DOME (New Zealand)	Dome of OKATAINA	0401-05=
WESTERN VICTORIA VOLC FIELD (Australia	Synonym of NEWER VOLCANICS PROV	0509-01-
WETALTH RIDGE (Canada)	Cone of SPECTRUM RANGE	1200-07-
WHAKAARI (New Zealand)	Synonym of WHITE ISLAND	0401-04=
WHAKAMARU (New Zealand)	Pleistocene caldera of MAROA	0401-061
WHAKAPAKA (New Zealand)	Cone of RUAPEHU	0401-10=
WHAKAPAPATARINGA (New Zealand)	Dome of MAROA	0401-061
WHAKAPOUNGAKAU (New Zealand)	Dome of OKATAINA	0401-05=
WHAKAREWAREWA (New Zealand)	Thermal Feature of ROTORUA	0401-042
WHALE ISLAND (New Zealand)	Complx volc (None) Pleistocene-Fumarolic	**0401-041**
WHANGAREI (New Zealand)	Cinder cones (None) Holocene?	**0401-011**
WHATITIRI (New Zealand)	Shield of WHANGAREI	0401-011
WHITE CHUCK (US-Washington)	Cone of GLACIER PEAK	1201-02-
WHITE CREEK (Canada)	Cone of SATAH MOUNTAIN	1200-13-
WHITE FISH LAKE (Alaska-W)	Maar of ESPENBERG	1104-01-
WHITE ISLAND (New Zealand)	Stratovolcs (27, 1993) Historical	**0401-04=**
WHITE MOUNTAIN (Africa-E)	Synonym of KILIMANJARO	0202-15=
WHITE MOUNTAIN (US-Utah)	Dome of BLACK ROCK DESERT	1207-05-
WHITE MOUNTAIN HOT SPRINGS	Thermal Feature of YELLOWSTONE	1205-01-
WHITE RIVER (Alaska-E)	Synonym of BONA-CHURCHILL	1105-03-
WHITEHORSE BLUFFS (Canada)	Cone of WELLS GRAY-CLEARWATER	1200-15-
WHITFORD'S SOLFATARA (Vanuatu)	Thermal Feature of SORETIMEAT	0507-01=
WHITMORE HOT SPRINGS (US-California)	Thermal Feature of LONG VALLEY	1203-14-
WHITNEY BUTTE (US-California)	Cone of MEDICINE LAKE	1203-02-
WHITON, MT. (Galapagos)	Synonym of WOLF, VOLCAN	1503-02=
WIDADAREN (Java)	Cone of IJEN	0603-35=
WIDE BAY (Aleutian Is)	Cone of TABLE TOP-WIDE BAY	1101-311
WIDODAREN, GUNUNG (Java)	Cone of TENGGER CALDERA	0603-31=
WIDODAREN [ARJUNO] (Java)	Stratovolc of ARJUNO-WELIRANG	0603-29=
WIDU (New Britain-SW Pac)	Synonym of GAROVE	0502-03=
WILHELMPLATAET (Atlantic-S)	Caldera of BOUVET	1806-02-
WILIS (Java)	Stratovolc (None) Holocene	**0603-27=**
WILLIAMS (Canada)	Cone of EDZIZA	1200-06-
WILLIAMS CRATER (US-Oregon)	Crater of CRATER LAKE	1202-16-
WILLIAMS, MT. (Galapagos)	Synonym of DARWIN, VOLCAN	1503-03=
WILLOW BUTTE (US-Oregon)	Cone of NEWBERRY VOLCANO	1202-11-
WILSON BUTTE (US-California)	Dome of INYO CRATERS	1203-13-
WINDU (Java)	Twin volcano of WAYANG-WINDU	0603-08=
WINDWARD ISLAND (Pacific-S)	Cone of ANTIPODES ISLAND	1304-01-
WINE (Kamchatka)	Synonym of ILYINSKY	1000-03=
WINGOL (Vanuatu-SW Pacific)	Stratovolc of MOTLAV	0507-001
WINGORU [GORU] (New Britain-SW Pac)	Crater of MUNDUA	0502-021
WIRI MOUNTAIN [MANUREWA] (New Zeal)	Cone of AUCKLAND FIELD	0401-02=
WISDOM, LAKE (New Guinea-NE of)	Caldera of LONG ISLAND	0501-05=
WISSOKE (Africa-C)	Synonym of VISOKE	0203-05-
WITORI (New Britain-SW Pac)	Caldera of PAGO	0502-08=
WITTMERBERG [MT. OLYMPUS] (Galapagos	Cone of FLOREANA	1503-10=
WITU (New Britain-SW Pac)	Synonym of GAROVE	0502-03=
WIZARD ISLAND (US-Oregon)	Cone of CRATER LAKE	1202-16-
WOEARLILI (WOELOER, WOELOER) (Banda	Synonym of WURLALI	0605-04=
WOEROENG, KAWAH [KAWAH WURUNG]	Crater of IJEN	0603-35=
WOHUSHAN (China-E)	Cone of WUDALIANCHI	1005-04-
WOLF, VOLCAN (Galapagos)	Shield (9, 1982) Historical	**1503-02=**
WOLFSBEUEL (Germany)	Cone of WEST EIFEL VOLC FIELD	0100-01-
WOLKBERG (Indian O.-S)	Cone of PRINCE EDWARD ISLAND	0304-07-
WOLO (Indonesian for MT.) see proper name (e.g. LEGA, WOLO)		
WOLOKROKO [ILITEBULELE] (Lesser Sunda	Cone of ILILABALEKAN	0604-24=
WONJUTSCHIJ CHREBET (Kamchatka)	Synonym of KSUDACH	1000-05=
WOOSANTAPALIPLIP (Vanuatu-SW Pacific)	Cone of AMBRYM	0507-04=
WOOSANTAPALIPLIP (Vanuatu-SW Pacific)	Vent of AMBRYM	0507-04=
WOOTTEN'S CONE [NE CH'E DDHAWA]	Cone of FORT SELKIRK	1200-01-
WORO, KAWAH (Java)	Thermal Feature of MERAPI	0603-25=
WORRI [KRUMMEL] (New Britain-SW Pac)	Stratovolc of GARBUNA GROUP	0502-07=
WOTTEN WAVEN (W Indies)	Thermal Feature of MICOTRIN	1600-10=
WRANGELL (Alaska-E)	Shield (5, 1902) Historical	**1105-02-**
WU-TA-LIEN-CH'IH (China-E)	Synonym of WUDALIANCHI	1005-04-
WUDALIANCHI (China-E)	Volc field (1, 1721) Historical	**1005-04-**
WUISOKIJ ISLAND (Antarctica)	Synonym of HODSON	1900-11=
WULU WOLOR FIELD (Lesser Sunda Is)	Thermal Feature of RIANG KOTANG	0604-21=
WUM, LAKE (Africa-W)	Maar of OKU VOLC FIELD	0204-003
WURLALI (Banda Sea)	Stratovolc (1, 1892) Historical	**0605-04=**
WURUNG, KAWAH (Java)	Crater of IJEN	0603-35=
WUZI (Africa-E)	Dome of SW USANGU BASIN	0202-163
WYEAST (US-Oregon)	Synonym of HOOD	1202-01-

X

NAME (Subregion)	Type (Eruption Total, Most Recent) Status / Relation to NAMED VOLCANO	NUMBER
XACALTEPEC, CERRO [XALTEPEC] (Mexico	Cone of IZTACCIHUATL	1401-086
XALLIQUEHUAC (Mexico)	Synonym of POPOCATEPETL	1401-09=
XALTEPEC (Mexico)	Cone of IZTACCIHUATL	1401-086
XALTEPEC (Mexico)	Cone of SANTA CATARINA RANGE	1401-082
XIANJINDAO (Korea)	Unknown (1, 1597) Historical	**1006-01-**
XIAO-KU-SHAN [XIAOGUSHAN] (China-E)	Cone of LONGGANG GROUP	1005-06-
XIAOGUSHAN (China-E)	Cone of WUDALIANCHI	1005-04-
XIAOKONGSHAN (China-S)	Cone of TENGCHONG	0705-11-
XIAOKUSHAN (China-E)	Cone of LONGGANG GROUP	1005-06-
XIAOLIUCHONG (China-S)	Cone of TENGCHONG	0705-11-
XIAOLONGWAN (China-E)	Crater of LONGGANG GROUP	1005-06-
XIAOMIPO (China-S)	Cone of TENGCHONG	0705-11-
XIAOTUANSHAN (China-S)	Cone of TENGCHONG	0705-11-
XIAOWENGJUAN (China-E)	Cone of LONGGANG GROUP	1005-06-
XIAOYANZHIFENG (China-E)	Cone of BAITOUSHAN	1005-07-
XIAOYISHAN (China-E)	Cone of LONGGANG GROUP	1005-06-
XIAOYISHAN (China-E)	Cone of KELUO GROUP	1005-03-
XIAYILUO (China-S)	Cone of TENGCHONG	0705-11-
XIBAIZILONGWAN (China-E)	Crater of LONGGANG GROUP	1005-06-
XICO (Mexico)	Cone of SANTA CATARINA RANGE	1401-082
XICOMULCO (Mexico)	Cone of CHICHINAUTZIN	1401-08=
XICONTLE (Mexico)	Cone of CHICHINAUTZIN	1401-08=
XIHENGDAOSHAN (China-E)	Cone of LONGGANG GROUP	1005-06-
XIHUOKOU (China-W)	Cone of KUNLUN VOLC GROUP	1004-03-
XIJIAODEBUSHAN (China-E)	Cone of WUDALIANCHI	1005-04-
XILONGMENSHAN (China-E)	Cone of WUDALIANCHI	1005-04-
XINGANNANSHAN (China-E)	Cone of LONGGANG GROUP	1005-06-
XIPING (China-E)	Cone of DATONG	1005-01-
XISHAN (China-E)	Cone of KELUO GROUP	1005-03-
XITLI [XITLE] (Mexico)	Cone of CHICHINAUTZIN	1401-08=
XIZIJULEBAC (China-E)	Cone of DATONG	1005-01-
XOXOCOL (Mexico)	Cone of CHICHINAUTZIN	1401-08=
XOYACAN, CERRO (Mexico)	Cone of TENAYO GROUP	1401-081
XUAN LOC (SE Asia)	Synonym of BAS DONG NAI	0705-05-

Y

NAME (Subregion)	Type (Eruption Total, Most Recent) Status / Relation to NAMED VOLCANO	NUMBER
YA-DAKE (Kyushu-Japan)	Dome of UNZEN	0802-10=
YA-PA-KANG [YABAGANG] (China-E)	Cone of LONGGANG GROUP	1005-06-
YAEMA (Izu Is-Japan)	Crater of MIYAKE-JIMA	0804-04=
YAGLICA DAG (Turkey)	Cone of KARS PLATEAU	0103-05-
YAHAZU-YAMA (Honshu-Japan)	Dome of IZU-TOBU	0803-01=
YAHI, JABAL (Arabia-W)	Dome of KISHB, HARRAT	0301-071
YAIMA (YAIMAS) (Chile-C)	Synonym of LLAIMA	1507-11=
YAKE-DAKE (Honshu-Japan)	Stratovolc (27, 1963) Historical	**0803-07=**
YAKE-YAMA (Honshu-Japan)	Synonym of AKITA-YAKE-YAMA	0803-26=
YAKE-YAMA (Honshu-Japan)	Synonym of NIIGATA-YAKE-YAMA	0803-09=
YAKE-YAMA (Honshu-Japan)	Synonym of OSORE-YAMA	0803-29=
YAKE-YAMA [IVAN GROZNY] (Kurile Is)	Cone of GROZNY GROUP	0900-07=
YAKI (Kurile Is)	Synonym of GORIASCHAIA SOPKA	0900-17B
YAKI [MENSHOI BRAT] (Kurile Is)	Dome of MEDVEZHIA	0900-10=
YAKUSHI-DAKE (Honshu-Japan)	Stratovolc of IWATE	0803-24=
YAKUTSK (Russia-SE)	Dome of NE UDOKAN PLATEAU	1002-02-
YALI (Greece)	Lava domes (None) Holocene	**0102-051**
YALWA ? (Ethiopia)	Synonym of JALUA	0201-03=
YAMAKAWA (Kyushu-Japan)	Maar of IBUSUKI VOLC FIELD	0802-07=
YAMBO, LAKE (Luzon-Philippines)	Maar of LAGUNA VOLC FIELD	0703-051
YANA MAURAS, VOLCAN (Peru)	Cone of ANDAHUA VALLEY	1504-002
YANAMAURAS, CERRO (Peru)	Cone of ANDAHUA VALLEY	1504-002
YANG (Java)	Synonym of IYANG-ARGAPURA	0603-33=
YANGUDI (Ethiopia)	Complx volc (None) Holocene	**0201-151**
YANKEE VOLCANO (US-New Mexico)	Cone of RATON-CLAYTON	1210-04-
YANKICHA (Kurile Is)	Synonym of USHISHUR	0900-21=
YANTALES (Chile-S)	Synonym of YANTELES, CERRO	1508-051
YANTARNI (Alaska Peninsula)	Stratovolc (1, -0800) Tephrochronology	**1102-10-**
YANTELES, CERRO (Chile-S)	Stratovolc (1, 1835) Historical	**1508-051**
YAO-CHUAN-SHAN [YAOQUANSHAN]	Cone of WUDALIANCHI	1005-04-
YAPOAH CRATER (US-Oregon)	Cone of NORTH SISTER FIELD	1202-07-
YAPONCHA (US-Arizona)	Crater of SUNSET CRATER	1209-02-
YAR, JABAL (Arabia-W)	Volc field (1, 1810) Historical	**0301-08-**
YARANGALU (Ecuador)	Dome of CHACANA	1502-022
YASOUR (YASOWA) (Vanuatu-SW Pacific)	Synonym of YASUR	0507-10=
YASUR (Vanuatu-SW Pacific)	Stratovolc (3, 1993) Historical	**0507-10=**
YATAKE (Kyushu-Japan)	Stratovolc of KIRISHIMA	0802-09=
YATE, MT. (Chile-S)	Stratovolc (None) Holocene	**1508-022**
YAUTEPEMES, LOS (Mexico)	Dome of IZTACCIHUATL	1401-086
YAUTEPEMES, LOS (Mexico)	Cone of IZTACCIHUATL	1401-086
YAWUSHAN (China-S)	Cone of TENGCHONG	0705-11-
YEDO PEAK (Canada)	Cone of SPECTRUM RANGE	1200-07-
YEGUADA, LA (Panama)	Stratovolc (1, 1615) Radiocarbon	**1406-02-**
YEGUAS, LAS [SAN PEDRO] (Chile-C)	Stratovolc of SAN PEDRO-PELLADO	1507-063
YELIA (New Guinea)	Stratovolc (None) Holocene?	**0503-002**
YELLOW CONE (Hawaiian Is)	Cone of KILAUEA	1302-01-
YELLOWSTONE (US-Wyoming)	Calderas (1, -7410) Tephrochronology	**1205-01-**
YELLOWSTONE PLATEAU (US-Wyoming)	Synonym of YELLOWSTONE	1205-01-
YEN-PEI-SHAN [XIAOGUSHAN] (China-E)	Cone of WUDALIANCHI	1005-04-
YENKAHE (Vanuatu-SW Pacific)	Caldera of YASUR	0507-10=
YENKAHE MAIN CONE (Vanuatu-SW Pacific)	Stratovolc of YASUR	0507-10=
YEPOCAPA (Guatemala)	Cone of ACATENANGO	1402-08=
YERAKH, JABAL (Arabia-S)	Dome of DHAMAR, HARRAS OF	0301-12-
YEROVI, ISLA (Ecuador)	Cone of CUICOCHA	1502-002
YERSEY (Lesser Sunda Is)	Submarine ? (None) Uncertain	**0604-28=**
YEZH (Kamchatka)	Dome of BOLSHOI SEMIACHIK	1000-15=
YIALI (Greece)	Synonym of YALI	0102-051
YILANLI DAG (Turkey)	Cone of ERCIYES DAGI	0103-01=
YILANLI DAGI (Turkey)	Cone of HASAN DAGI	0103-002
YILANOBRUGU (Turkey)	Crater of KARAPINAR FIELD	0103-001
YILBAT (Turkey)	Cone of ERCIYES DAGI	0103-01=
YINGBEISHAN [XIAOGUSHAN] (China-E)	Cone of WUDALIANCHI	1005-04-
YIRRIGUE (Africa-N)	Pleistocene caldera of TOUSSIDE, TARSO	0205-01=
YJAKUSHATSCH (Alaska-SW)	Synonym of REDOUBT	1103-03-
YOICHIZAKA (Honshu-Japan)	Vent of IZU-TOBU	0803-01=
YOJOA, LAKE (Honduras)	Volc field (None) Holocene	**1403-15-**
YOKOKURA-YAMA (Honshu-Japan)	Stratovolc of ZAO	0803-19=
YOMBA (New Guinea-NE of)	Unknown (None) Uncertain	**0501-041**
YOMINE-YAMA (Kyushu-Japan)	Stratovolc of ASO	0802-11=
YONEKUBO (Kyushu-Japan)	Crater of KUJU GROUP	0802-12=
YONEMARU (Kyushu-Japan)	Maar of SUMIYOSHI-IKE	0802-081
YONGBOCUO (China-W)	Shield of UNNAMED	1004-04-
YORIDAI-ZAWA (Izu Is-Japan)	Crater of MIYAKE-JIMA	0804-04=
YORK (Galapagos)	Synonym of SANTIAGO	1503-09=
YORO-YAMA (Honshu-Japan)	Synonym of FUJI	0803-03=
YOSUA (YOSUR) (Vanuatu-SW Pacific)	Synonym of YASUR	0507-10=
YOTEI (Hokkaido-Japan)	Stratovolc (1, -5050) Radiocarbon	**0805-032**
YOTUGA-TAKE [YOTSUGA-TAKE] (Honshu	Dome of NORIKURA	0803-06=
YOUKOU (Africa-W)	Crater of NGAOUNDERE PLATEAU	0204-002
YOUNG ISLAND (Antarctica)	Stratovolc (None) Fumarolic	**1900-011**
YOUTLKUT BUTTE (US-Oregon)	Cone of NEWBERRY VOLCANO	1202-11-
YRTRI RAUDAMELSKULA (Iceland-W)	Cone of LJOSUFJOLL	1700-03=
YU-GAMA (Honshu-Japan)	Crater of KUSATSU-SHIRANE	0803-12=
YUBATAKE HOT SPRINGS (Honshu-Japan)	Thermal Feature of KUSATSU-SHIRANE	0803-12=

NAME (Subregion)	Type (Eruption Total, Most Recent) Status Relation to NAMED VOLCANO	NUMBER
YUBI-YAMA (Kyushu-Japan)	Dome of KUJU GROUP	0802-12=
YUBILEINOYE (Kamchatka)	Crater of KLIUCHEVSKOI	1000-26=
YUCAMANE (Peru)	Stratovolc (1, 1787) Historical	**1504-05-**
YUCAMANE (YUCAMANI) (Peru)	Synonym of YUCAMANE	1504-05-
YUFU-DAKE (Kyushu-Japan)	Dome of TSURUMI	0802-13=
YUFUIN (Kyushu-Japan)	Thermal Feature of TSURUMI	0802-13=
YUGAOKA (Honshu-Japan)	Vent of IZU-TOBU	0803-01=
YUHU-DAKE [YUFU-DAKE] (Kyushu-Japan)	Dome of TSURUMI	0802-13=
YUJIADASHAN (China-S)	Cone of TENGCHONG	0705-11-
YUMI-IKE (Honshu-Japan)	Maar of KUSATSU-SHIRANE	0803-12=
YUMI-ITSUKA (Honshu-Japan)	Cone of FUJI	0803-03=
YUMIA, CERRO (Bolivia)	Cone (None) Holocene?	**1505-061**
YUMURTADAG (Turkey)	Cone of NEMRUT DAGI	0103-02=
YUNASKA (Aleutian Is)	Shield (3, 1937) Historical	**1101-21-**
YUNOHIRA (Kyushu-Japan)	Dome of SAKURA-JIMA	0802-08=
YUNOTANI (Kyushu-Japan)	Dome of ASO	0802-11=
YUNOTANI (Kyushu-Japan)	Thermal Feature of ASO	0802-11=
YUNOTANI-DAKE (Kyushu-Japan)	Stratovolc of KIRISHIMA	0802-09=
YUNQUE, EL (Chile-Is)	Stratovolc of ROBINSON CRUSOE	1506-02=
YUNUMA (Hokkaido-Japan)	Crater of TOKACHI	0805-05=
YUPILTEPEQUE, CERRO DE (Guatemala)	Cone of CHINGO VOLC FIELD	1402-15-
YUPITER (Kamchatka)	Cone of TOLBACHIK	1000-24=
YURIEVSKY (Kamchatka)	Cone of DZENZURSKY	1000-11=
YUSHNY (Kamchatka)	Cone of MALY SEMIACHIK	1000-14=
YUYIEHU (China-W)	Cone of UNNAMED	1004-04-
YUZHNY (Kamchatka)	Vent of KRASHENINNIKOV	1000-19=
YUZHNY CHERPUK (Kamchatka)	Cone of ICHINSKY	1000-28=
YUZHNY GAMCHEN (Kamchatka)	Stratovolc of GAMCHEN	1000-21=
YUZHNY [YUSHNY] (Kamchatka)	Cone of MALY SEMIACHIK	1000-14=
YVES ROCARD (Society Is-C Pac)	Synonym of ROCARD	1303-04-
YWATHA (SE Asia)	Vent of LOWER CHINDWIN	0705-09-

Z

NAME (Subregion)	Type (Eruption Total, Most Recent) Status Relation to NAMED VOLCANO	NUMBER
ZACAPU, VOLCANES DE (Mexico)	Cone of MICHOACAN-GUANAJUATO	1401-06=
ZACARIAS, CERRO (Guatemala)	Cone of IPALA VOLC FIELD	1402-19-
ZACATE GRANDE, ISLA (Honduras)	Stratovolc (None) Holocene	**1403-14-**
ZAKURA MISAKA (Honshu-Japan)	Stratovolc of TOWADA	0803-271
ZAMETNY (Kamchatka)	Cone of KRASHENINNIKOV	1000-19=
ZAMOK (Kamchatka)	Dome of KSUDACH	1000-05=
ZANETTI, MT. (Alaska-E)	Cone of WRANGELL	1105-02-
ZAO (Honshu-Japan)	Complx volc (30, 1940) Historical	**0803-19=**
ZAO-NUMA [OKAMA] (Honshu-Japan)	Crater of ZAO	0803-19=
ZAOZERNY (Kamchatka)	Shields (None) Holocene	**1000-48-**
ZAPADNY (Kamchatka)	Cone of KIKHPINYCH	1000-18=
ZAPADNY BARANY (Kamchatka)	Stratovolc of BOLSHOI SEMIACHIK	1000-15=
ZAPATERA ISLAND (Nicaragua)	Stratovolc (None) Holocene	**1404-111**
ZAPATERA, LAGUNA DE (Nicaragua)	Cone of ZAPATERA ISLAND	1404-111
ZAPETON (ZAPATERO) (Nicaragua)	Synonym of ZAPATERA ISLAND	1404-111
ZAPOTITLAN (Guatemala)	Synonym of ATITLAN	1402-06=
ZAPOVEDNY (Kamchatka)	Synonym of KOMAROV	1000-22=
ZAPOVEDNY [SEVERNY GAMCHEN]	Stratovolc of GAMCHEN	1000-21=
ZAPRETNY (Kamchatka)	Cone of TOLBACHIK	1000-24=
ZARA (Italy)	Dome of ISCHIA	0101-03=
ZARECHNY (Kamchatka)	Somma volc (None) Holocene	**1000-262**
ZARZONA, CERRO DE (Guatemala)	Cone of IPALA VOLC FIELD	1402-19-
ZASIPANNIE (Kamchatka)	Cone of TOLBACHIK	1000-24=
ZAVARITSKY (Kamchatka)	Crater of KLIUCHEVSKOI	1000-26=
ZAVARITSKY (Kamchatka)	Stratovolc (None) Holocene	**1000-121**
ZAVARITZKI CALDERA (Kurile Is)	Caldera (2, 1957) Historical	**0900-18=**
ZAVODOVSKI (Antarctica)	Stratovolc (1, 1819) Historical	**1900-13=**
ZAWADOWSKI (Antarctica)	Synonym of ZAVODOVSKI	1900-13=
ZAZEN-YAMA (Honshu-Japan)	Dome of NIKKO-SHIRANE	0803-14=
ZBEV-BUNANYA (Kamchatka)	Shield of UKSICHAN	1000-35-
ZEBAYIR ISLAND, JEBEL (Red Sea)	Synonym of ZUBAYR, JEBEL	0201-02=
ZEBIB, JABAL (Arabia-S)	Tuff cone of ARHAB, HARRA OF	0301-09-
ZEIN UMM ARAYSH, JEBEL (Africa-N)	Cone of BAYUDA VOLC FIELD	0205-06-
ZENGYU (Taiwan-N of)	Submarine (1, 1927) Historical	**0801-05=**
ZENTRALNY SEMIACHIK (Kamchatka)	Stratovolc of BOLSHOI SEMIACHIK	1000-15=
ZENZUR (Kamchatka)	Synonym of DZENZURSKY	1000-11=
ZEUTONGEI (Kamchatka)	Synonym of LEUTONGEY	1000-54-
ZHANJIANG (SE Asia)	Cone of LEIZHOU BANDAO	0705-01-
ZHELTAYA (Kamchatka)	Dome of UZON	1000-17=
ZHELTAYA SOPKA (Kamchatka)	Cone of KIKHPINYCH	1000-18=
ZHELTOVSKAIA, SOPKA (Kamchatka)	Synonym of ZHELTOVSKY	1000-04=
ZHELTOVSKY (Kamchatka)	Stratovolc (5, 1972) Historical	**1000-04=**
ZHELTYI (Kamchatka)	Stratovolc of ASACHA	1000-062
ZHUPANOVSKAIA, SOPKA (Kamchatka)	Synonym of ZHUPANOVSKY	1000-12=
ZHUPANOVSKY (Kamchatka)	Compnd volc (12, 1959) Historical	**1000-12=**
ZIGOKU-NO-OANA [JIGOKU-NO-OANA]	Crater of HAKU-SAN	0803-05=
ZIGOKU [JIGOKU] (Honshu-Japan)	Thermal Feature of OSORE-YAMA	0803-29=
ZIGOKU [JIGOKU] (Honshu-Japan)	Crater of ON-TAKE	0803-04=
ZIGOKU [TREZUBETZ] (Kurile Is)	Somma volcano of KOLOKOL GROUP	0900-12=
ZIMINA (Kamchatka)	Stratovolcs (None) Holocene	**1000-242**
ZINAKA-YAMA [JINAKA-YAMA] (Izu Is-Japan)	Dome of NII-JIMA	0804-02=
ZINI (Greece)	Dome of KOS	0102-06=
ZIZO-DAKE [JIZO-DAKE] (Honshu-Japan)	Dome of AKAGI	0803-13=
ZOCEYUCA, CERRO (Mexico)	Cone of TENAYO GROUP	1401-081
ZOE (Indian O.-W)	Cone of FOURNAISE, PITON DE LA	0303-02=
ZOO-DAKE (Honshu-Japan)	Synonym of ZAO	0803-19=
ZOOMIE (Aleutian Is)	Synonym of OKMOK	1101-29-
ZOYAZAL, VOLCAN (Mexico)	Cone of TENAYO GROUP	1401-081
ZUBAYR, JEBEL (Red Sea)	Shield (1, 1824) Historical	**0201-02=**
ZUBCHATKA (Kamchatka)	Stratovolc of BOLSHOI SEMIACHIK	1000-15=
ZUNI-BANDERA (US-New Mexico)	Volc field (2, -1115) Anthropology	**1210-02-**
ZUNIL (Guatemala)	Dome of TZANJUYUB, VOLCAN DE	1402-05=
ZURN PEAK (Antarctica)	Cone of TONEY MOUNTAIN	1900-026
ZURQUI (Costa Rica)	Stratovolc of BARVA	1405-05=
ZUWAYR, JABAL (Arabia-W)	Vent of KISHB, HARRAT	0301-071
ZVEZDA (Kamchatka)	Cone of TOLBACHIK	1000-24=
ZWAVELBERG (Lesser Sunda Is)	Synonym of LEWOTOLO	0604-23=
ZYANOO [JANOO] (Kyushu-Japan)	Cone of ASO	0802-11=
ZYOGORO-YAMA [JOGORO-YAMA] (Izu Is)	Dome of KOZU-SHIMA	0804-03=

References

Abbreviations Used In Citations

Abs	-	Abstract
Acad	-	Academy
Akad	-	Akademiia
Amer	-	America, American
Ann	-	Annual
Arch	-	Archaeology
Ariz	-	Arizona
Assoc	-	Association
Astron	-	Astronomy, Astronomical
Aust	-	Australia
Auth	-	Authorlty
Bol	-	Boletin
Boll	-	Bolletino
Brit	-	Britain, British
Bull	-	Bulletin
Bur	-	Bureau
Calif	-	California
Can	-	Canada, Canadian
Chpt	-	Chapter
Circ	-	Circular
Comm	-	Commission
Conf	-	Conference
Cong	-	Congress
Contr	-	Contribution(s)
Dept	-	Department, Departmento
Deut	-	Deutsche
Devel	-	Development
Div	-	Division
Earthq	-	Earthquake
Econ	-	Economic
Ed(s)	-	Editor(s)
Envir	-	Environmental
Excur	-	Excursion
Expl	-	Exploration
Fac	-	Faculty
Geochem	-	Geochemical, Geochemistry
Geodynam	-	Geodynamics
Geog	-	Geography, Geographic, Geograficos
Geol	-	Geology, Geologic, Geological, Geologique, Geologische, Geologie, Geologia, Geologico
Geophys	-	Geophysics, Geophysical, Geophysique, Geofisica
Geosurv	-	Geosurvey
Geotherm	-	Geothermal
Ges	-	Gesellschaft
His	-	History, Historical
IAVCEI	-	International Association of Volcanology and Chemistry of the Earth's Interior
Ind	-	Industry, Industrial
Info	-	Information
Inst	-	Institute, Institution
Internac	-	Internacional
Internatl	-	International
Invest	-	Investigation
Is	-	Islands
IUGG	-	International Union of Geodesy and Geophysics
IUGS	-	International Union of Geological Sciences
Jahrb	-	Jarhbuch
Jour	-	Journal
Lett	-	Letter(s)
MA	-	Master of Arts
Mag	-	Magazine
Mech	-	Mechanical
Mem	-	Memoir, Memorie
Min	-	Mines
Mineral	-	Mineral, Mineralogist, Mineralogical, Mineralogy, Mineria
MSci	-	Master of Science
Mtg	-	Meeting
N	-	North, Northern
Nac	-	Nacional
Nat	-	Natural
Natl	-	National
New Zeal	-	New Zealand
Newsl	-	Newsletter
No	-	Number
NOAA	-	National Oceanic and Atmospheric Administration
Observ	-	Observatory
Occ Pap	-	Occasional Paper
P	-	Page
Paleont	-	Paleontology
Pap	-	Paper
Petr	-	Petrology, Petrologist, Petrological
Petrol	-	Petroleum
PhD	-	Doctor of Philosophy
Phil	-	Philosophical
Phys	-	Physical, Physique
Planet	-	Planetary
Proc	-	Proceedings
Prof Pap	-	Professional Paper
Prog	-	Program
Proj	-	Project
Pub	-	Publication, Publishers
Quart	-	Quarterly
Rec	-	Record
Reg	-	Regional
Res	-	Research
Resour	-	Resource(s)
Rev	-	Review
Roy	-	Royal
Rpt	-	Report
S	-	South, Southern
Sci	-	Science, Scientific
Sec	-	Section
Seism	-	Seismological
Ser	-	Series
Serv	-	Service, Servicio
Sess	-	Session
Soc	-	Society, Sociedad, Societa
Spec	-	Special
Sta	-	Station
Suppl	-	Supplement
Surv	-	Survey
Symp	-	Symposium
Tech	-	Technology
Trans	-	Transaction(s)
U S	-	United States
Univ	-	University, Universidad
Unpub	-	Unpublished
V	-	Volume
Volc	-	Volcanological, Volcanologie, Volcanology, Volcanism
Vulkanol	-	Vulkanologicheskikh
Wash	-	Washington
Zeit	-	Zeitschrift

GLOBAL REFERENCES

Scrope G P
1825 *Considerations on Volcanos.* London: W Phillips, 270 p

1862 *Volcanoes: The Character of Their Phenomena, Their Share in the Structure and Composition of the Surface of the Globe and Their Relation to its Internal Forces.* London: Longman, Green, Longmans & Roberts (2nd edition), 490 p

Humboldt A von
1869 [& 1872] *Cosmos: A Sketch of a Physical Description of the Universe, V [& I].* New York: Harper Brothers, 462 p [& 375 p]

Anonymous
1879 Volcanic phenomena and earthquakes during 1878. *Nature*, 20: 378-379

Sapper K
1917 *Katalog der Geschichtlichen Vulkanausbruche.* Strasbourg: Karl J Trubner, 358 p

1927 *Vulkankunde.* Stuttgart: J Engelhorns Nachf, 424 p

Wolff F von
1929 *Der Volcanismus II Band: Spezieller Teil 1 Teil Die Neue Welt (Pazifische Erdhalfte) der Pazifische Ozean und Seine Randgebiete.* Stuttgart: Ferdinand Enke, 828 p

Neumann van Padang M
1938 Uber die Unterseevulkane der Erde. *Ingenieur Nederlandsch-Indie*, 4(5&6): 69-83 & 85-104

Hantke G
1939a Ubersicht uber die Vulkanische Tatigkeit vom Januar 1937 bis Marz 1938. *Zeit Deut Geol Ges*, 91: 160-168

1939b Ubersicht uber die Vulkanische Tatigkeit vom April bis Dezember 1938. *Zeit Deut Geol Ges*, 91: 757-765

Kennedy W Q, Richey J E
1947 Catalogue of the Active Volcanoes of the World. *Bull Volc*, 7: 1-11

Hantke G
1951 Ubersicht uber die Vulkanische Tatigkeit 1941-1947. *Bull Volc*, 11: 161-208

1953 Ubersicht uber die Vulkanische Tatigkeit 1948-1950. *Bull Volc*, 14: 151-180

Gutenberg B, Richter C F
1954 *Seismicity of the Earth and Related Phenomena.* Princeton, New Jersey: Princeton Univ Press, 310 p

Fiske R S, Simkin T, Nielsen E A (eds)
1987 *The Volcano Letter.* Washington, DC: Smithsonian Inst Press, 1536 p [Reprinting of 1925-1955 issues, with index]

Hantke G
1955 Ubersicht uber die Vulkanische Tatigkeit 1951-1953. *Bull Volc*, 16: 71-114

1959 Ubersicht uber die Vulkanische Tatigkeit 1954-1956. *Bull Volc*, 20: 3-36

Volcanological Society of Japan
1960-93 [Annual reports, issued 1 to 3 years after event year. Published since 1986 in *Bull Volc*]. *Bull Volc Eruptions*, no 1-30.

Hantke G
1962 Ubersicht uber die Vulkanische Tatigkeit 1957-1959. *Bull Volc*, 24: 321-348

Rittmann A
1962 *Volcanoes and Their Activity.* New York: John Wiley, 305 p

Hedervari P
1963 On the energy and magnitude of volcanic eruptions. *Bull Volc*, 25: 373-386

Moore J G
1967 Base surge in recent volcanic eruptions. *Bull Volc*, 30: 337-363

Hedervari P
1968 Volcanophysical investigations on the energetics of the Minoan eruption of volcano Santorin. *Bull Volc*, 32: 435-468

Smithsonian Institution-CSLP
1968-75 [Event cards] Center for Short-Lived Phenomena (CSLP), Cambridge, Mass.

Lamb H H
1970 Volcanic dust in the atmosphere; with a chronology and assessment of its meteorological significance. *Phil Trans Roy Soc London*, Ser A, 266: 425-533

Decker R W
1971 *Table of Active Volcanoes of the World.* [Unpublished 41 page table, compiled primarily from IAVCEI catalogs with revisions by many volcanologists]

Green J, Short N M
1971 *Volcanic Landforms and Surface Features: a Photographic Atlas and Glossary.* New York: Springer-Verlag, 519 p

Katsui Y (ed)
1971 *List of the World Active Volcanoes.* [Volc Soc Japan draft ms, limited circulation], 160 p

Macdonald G A
1972 *Volcanoes.* Englewood Cliffs, New Jersey: Prentice-Hall, 510 p

IAVCEI
1973-80 Post-Miocene Volcanoes of the World. *IAVCEI Data Sheets, Internatl Assoc Volc & Chem of Earth's Interior, Rome*

Shimozuru D (ed)
1974 Compiled list of dangerous volcanoes and associated information. *Bull Volc*, 38: 1-81

Latter J H
1975 The history and geography of active and dormant volcanoes. A worldwide catalogue and index of active and potentially active volcanoes, with an outline of their eruptions. [Ms submitted to a yet unpublished *Encyclopedia of Volcanology*]

Smithsonian Institution-SEAN
1975-89 [Monthly event reports]. *Scientific Event Alert Netweork (SEAN) Bull*, v 1-14, Washington DC

Lamb H H
1977 Supplementary Dust Veil Index assessments. *Climate Monitor*, 6: 57-67

Gushchenko I I
1979 *Eruptions of Volcanoes of the World: A Catalog.* Moscow: Nauka Pub, *Acad Sci USSR Far Eastern Sci Center*, 474 p (in Russian)

Rampino M R, Self S, Fairbridge R W
1979 Can rapid climatic change cause volcanic eruptions? *Science*, 206: 826-829

Latter J H
1981 Tsunamis of volcanic origin: summary of causes, with particular reference to Krakatoa, 1883. *Bull Volc*, 44: 467-490

Hedervari P
1983 Catalog of submarine volcanoes and hydrological phenomena associated with volcanic events 1500 B.C. to Dec 31, 1899. *NOAA World Data Center A Rpt*, SE-36: 1-75

Newhall C G, Melson W G
1983 Explosive activity associated with the growth of volcanic domes. *Jour Volc Geotherm Res*, 17: 111-132

Blong R J
1984 *Volcanic Hazards.* Sydney: Academic Press, 427 p

Hedervari P
1986 Catalog of submarine volcanoes and hydrological phenomena associated with volcanic events, 1900-1959. *NOAA World Data Center A Rpt*, 35 p

Siebert L, Glicken H, Ui T
1987 Volcanic hazards from Bezymianny- and Bandai-type eruptions. *Bull Volc*, 49: 435-459

Newhall C G, Dzurisin D
1988 Historical unrest at large calderas of the world. *U S Geol Surv Bull*, 1855: 1108 p, 2 vol

Latter J H (ed)
1989 *Volcanic Hazards - Assessment and Monitoring.* Berlin: Springer-Verlag, 625 p

McClelland L, Simkin T, Summers M, Nielsen E, Stein T C (eds)
1989 *Global Volcanism 1975-1985.* Englewood Cliffs, New Jersey: Prentice Hall & Washington, DC: Amer Geophys Union, 655 p

Pyle D M
1989 The thickness, volume and grainsize of tephra fall deposits. *Bull Volc*, 51: 1-15

Smithsonian Institution-GVN
1990-93 [Monthy event reports]. *Global Volc Network (GVN) Bull*, v 15-18, Washington DC

Fierstein J, Nathenson M
1992 Another look at the calculation of fallout tephra volumes. *Bull Volc*, 54: 156-167

ITALY (0101)

Rodwell G F
1878 *Etna: A History of the Mountain and of its Eruptions.* London: C Kegan Paul, 146 p

Lacroix A
1907 Eruption of Vesuvius April 1906. *Smithsonian Inst Rpt*, 1754: 223-248

Washington H S
1909 The submarine eruptions of 1831 and 1891 near Pantelleria. *Amer Jour Sci*, 27: 130-150

Alfano G B, Friedlander I
1929 *La Storia del Vesuvio.* Naples: K Holm, 71 p, 107 Plates

Keller W D
1946 The natural steam at Larderello, Italy. *Jour Geol*, 54: 327-334

Blanc A C
1953 Excursion au Mont Circe. *Internatl Quaternary Assoc (INQUA) Guidebook*, p 5-19

Cumin G
1954 L'eruzione laterale Etnea del Novembre 1950-Dicembre 1951. *Bull Volc*, 15: 3-70

Marinelli G
1963 Some geological data on the geothermal areas of Tuscany. *Bull Volc*, 33: 319-333

Rittmann A
1964 Vulkanismus und Tektonik des Aetna. *Geol Rundschau*, 53: 788-800

Imbo G
1965 ★ Italy. *Catalog of Active Volcanoes of the World*, Rome: IAVCEI, 18: 1-72

Imbo G, Luongo G
1968 Contribution to the knowledge of the magmatic evolution by the study of the variation of the coefficient of viscosity [Vesuvius]. *Bull Volc*, 32: 365-376

Walker G P L
1968 Mount Etna. *Geog Mag*, 11: 929-935

Pichler H
1970 Volcanism in eastern Sicily and the Aeolian Islands. *In*: Alvarez W and Gohbrandt K H A (eds) *Geol and Hist of Sicily*, Petrol Expl Soc Libya, p 261-281

Keller J
1970a Datierung der Obsidiane und Bimstuffe von Lipari. *Neues Jahrb Geol Palaont Monatsh*, 1970(2): 90-101

1970b Die Historischen Eruptionen von Vulcano und Lipari. *Zeit Deut Geol Ges*, 121: 179-185

Lirer L, Pescatore T, Booth B, Walker G P L
1973 Two Plinian pumice-fall deposits from Somma-Vesuvius, Italy. *Geol Soc Amer Bull*, 84: 759-772

Guest J E, Huntingdon A T, Wadge G, Brander J L, Booth B, Carter S, Duncan A
1974 Recent eruption of Mount Etna. *Nature*, 250: 385-387

Krafft M
1974 ★ Guide des Volcans d'Europe. Neuchatel: Delachaux & Niestle, 412 p

Sparks R S J
1975 Stratigraphy and geology of the ignimbrites of Vulsini volcano, central Italy. *Geol Rundschau*, 64: 497-523

Bullard F M
1976 *Volcanoes of the Earth*. Austin: Univ Texas Press, 579 p

Capaldi C, Civetta L, Gasparini P
1976-77 Volcanic history of the island of Ischia (south Italy). *Bull Volc*, 40: 11-22

Grindley G W
1976 Relation of volcanism to earth movements, Bay of Naples, Italy. *In*: Gonzalez-Ferran O (ed) *Proc Symp Andean & Antarctic Volcanology Problems (Santiago, Chile, Sept 1974)*, Rome: IAVCEI, p 598-612

Nappi G
1976 Recent activity of Stromboli. *Nature*, 261: 119-120

Pinkerton H, Sparks R S J
1976 Formation of the 1975 subterminal compound lava flow, Mount Etna. *Jour Volc Geotherm Res*, 1: 167-182

Tanguy J C, Kieffer G
1976-77 The 1974 eruption of Mount Etna. *Bull Volc*, 40: 239-252

Nappi G
1977 Rischio vulcanico e sorveglianza nei Campi Flegrei e nell'Isola di Stromboli. *Boll Serv Geol Italia*, 98: 141-156

Wadge G
1977 The storage and release of magma on Mount Etna. *Jour Volc Geotherm Res*, 2: 361-384

Capaldi G, Guerra I, Lo Bascio A, Luongo G, Pece R, Rapolla A, Scarpa R, Del Pezzo E, Martini M, Ghiara M R,
1978 Stromboli and its 1975 eruption. *Bull Volc*, 41: 259-285

Keller J, Ryan W B F, Ninkovich D, Altherr R
1978 Explosive volcanic activity in the Mediterranean over the past 200,000 years as recorded in deep-sea sediments. *Geol Soc Amer Bull*, 89: 591-604

Delibrias G, Di Paola G M, Rosi M, Santacroce R
1979 La storia eruttiva del complesso vulcanico Somma Vesuvio ricostruita dalle successioni piroclastiche del Monte Somma. *Rendiconti Soc Italiana Min Petr*, 35: 411-438

Kieffer G
1979 L'activite de l'Etna pendant les derniers 20,000 ans. *Comptes Rendus Acad Sci Paris*, Ser-D, 288: 1023-1026

Romano R, Sturiale C, Lentini F
1979 *Geological Map of Mount Enta*. CNR Istituto Internat Vulcanologia, Catania, 1:50,000 geol map

Wadge G
1979 The storage and release of magma on Mount Etna: a reply to a discussion by J. C. Tanguy. *Jour Volc Geotherm Res*, 6: 189-195

Tanguy J C
1979a The storage and release of magma on Mount Etna: a discussion. *Jour Volc Geotherm Res*, 6: 179-188

1979b Sur l'eruption de l'Etna en 1879 (Mont Umberto-Margherita). *Comptes Rendus Acad Sci Paris*, 288: 1453-1456

Guest J E, Murray J, Kilburn C, Lopes R
1980 Eruptions on Mount Etna during 1979. *Earthq Info Bull*, 12: 155-160

Keller J
1980 The island of Vulcano. *Soc Italiana Min Petr*, 36: 368-413

Pichler H
1980 The island of Lipari. *Rendiconti Soc Italiana Min Petr*, 36: 415-440

Rosi M
1980 Isola Stromboli. *Rendicotti Soc Italiana Min Petr*, 36: 345-368

Varekamp J C
1980 The geology of the Vulsinian area, Lazio, Italy. *Bull Volc*, 43: 487-504

Rosi M, Santacroce R, Sheridan M
1981 Volcanic hazards of Vesuvius (Italy). *Bull BRGM*, 4: 169-179

Tanguy J C
1981 Les eruptions historiques de l'Etna: chronologie et localisation. *Bull Volc*, 44: 585-640

Guest J E
1982 Styles of eruptions and flow morphology on Mt. Etna. *Mem Soc Geol Italiana*, 23: 49-67

Kieffer G
1982 L'eruption du 17 au 22 Mars 1981 de l'Etna; sa signification dans l'evolution actuelle du volcan. *Geol Mediterraneenne*, 9: 59-67

Romano R (ed)
1982 Mount Etna volcano. *Mem Soc Geol Italiana*, 23: 1-205

Sigurdsson H, Cashdollar S, Sparks S R J
1982 The eruption of Vesuvius in AD 79: reconstruction from historical and volcanological evidence. *Amer Jour Arch*, 86: 39-51

Clover F M
1983 Olympiodorus of Thebes and the Historia Augusta [Etna]. *Antiquitas Beitrage Historia-Augusta-Forschung*, 15: 127-156

Cornette Y, Crisci G M, Gillot P Y, Orsi G
1983 Recent volcanic history of Pantelleria: a new interpretation. *Jour Volc Geotherm Res*, 17: 361-374

Frazzetta G, La Volpe L, Sheridan M F
1983 Evolution of the Fossa cone, Vulcano. *Jour Volc Geotherm Res*, 17: 329-360

Rosi M, Santacroce R
1983 The AD 472 "Pollena" eruption: volcanological and petrological data for this poorly-known, Plinian-type event at Vesuvius. *Jour Volc Geotherm Res*, 17: 249-271

Rosi M, Sbrana A, Principe C
1983 The Phlegrean Fields: structural evolution, volcanic history and eruptive mechanisms. *Jour Volc Geotherm Res*, 17: 273-288

Santacroce R
1983 A general model for the behavior of the Somma-Vesuvio volcanic complex. *Jour Volc Geotherm Res*, 17: 237-248

Scott S C
1983 Variations in lava composition during the March 1981 eruption of Mount Etna and the implications of a compositional comparison with earlier historic eruptions. *Bull Volc*, 46: 393-412

Stothers R B, Rampino M R
1983 Volcanic eruptions in the Mediterranean before AD 630 from written and archaeological sources. *Jour Geophys Res*, 88: 6357-6371

Barberi F, Innocenti F, Landi P, Rossi U, Saitta M, Santacroce R, Villa I M
1984 The evolution of Latera caldera (Central Italy) in the light of subsurface data. *Bull Volc*, 47: 125-143

Di Girolama P, Ghiara M R, Lirer L, Munno R, Rolandi G, Stanzione D
1984 Vulcanologia e petrologia dei Campi Flegrei. *Boll Soc Geol Italia*, 103: 394-413

Frazzetta G, Gillot P Y, La Volpe L, Sheridan M F
1984 Volcanic hazards at Fossa of Vulcano: data from the last 6000 years. *Bull Volc*, 47: 105-125

Rosi M, Santacroce R
1984 Volcanic hazard assessment in the Phlegraean Fields: a contribution based on stratigraphic and historical data. *Bull Volc*, 47: 359-371

Capaldi G, Civetta L, Gillot P Y
1985 Geochronology of Plio-Pleistocene volcanic rocks form southern Italy. *Rendiconti Soc Italiana Min Petr*, 40: 25-44

Krautschick S
1985 An eruption of the Vesuvius not noticed up to now. *Mitteilschen Geograph Gesell*, 31/32: 581-582

Mulargia F, Tinti S, Boschi E
1985 A statistical analysis of flank eruptions on Mount Etna volcano. *Jour Volc Geotherm Res*, 23: 263-272

Sigurdsson H, Carey S N, Cornell W, Pescatore T
1985 The eruption of Vesuvius in AD 79. *Natl Geog Res*, 1: 332-387

Albore Livadie C (ed)
1986 *Tremblements de Terre, Eruptions Volcaniques et Vie des Hommes dan la Campanie Antique*. Naples: Centre Jean Berard, 232 p

Albore Livadie C
1986 Considerations sur l'homme prehistorique et son environment dans le territoire Phlegreen. *In*: Albore Livadie C (ed), p 189-205 (see above)

Albore Livadie C, D'Alessio G, Mastrolorenzo G, Rolandi G
1986 Le eruzioni del Somma-Vesuvio in epoca protohistorica. *In*: Albore Livadie C (ed), p 55-66 (see above)

Buchner G
1986 Eruzione vulcaniche fenomeni vulcano-tettonica di eta prehistorica e storica nell'Isola s'Ischia. *In*: Albore Livadie C (ed), p 145-188 (see above)

Colucci Pescatori G
1986 Fonti antiche relative alle eruzioni Vesuviane ed altri fenomeni vulcanici successivi 79 DC. *In*: Albore Livadie C (ed), p 134-141 (see above)

Cortese M, Frazzetta G, La Volpe L
1986 Volcanic history of Lipari (Aeolian Islands, Italy) during the last 10,000 years. *Jour Volc Geotherm Res*, 27: 117-135

Luongo G, Coppola G, Cubellis E, Ferri M, Forgione G, Orbrizzo F, Ricciardi G P, Romano R
1986 Richio vulcanico - Vesuvio, Campi Flegrei, Ischia, Etna, Stromboli, Vulcano. *Rivista dell'Amministrazione Provinciale Napoli*, 8: 34-61

Mahood G A, Hildreth W
1986 Geology of the peralkaline volcano at Pantelleria, Strait of Sicily. *Bull Volc*, 48: 143-172

Nazzaro A
1986 Il Vesuvio: storia naturale dal 1631 al 1944. *Boll Soc Nat Napoli*, 94: 1-26

Vezzoli L
1986 *Geologic Map of the Island of Ischia*. CNR Progetto Finalizzato Geodinamica, Rome

Di Vito M, Lirer L, Mastrolorenzo G, Rolandi G
1987 The 1538 Monte Nuovo eruption (Campi Flegrei, Italy). *Bull Volc*, 49: 608-615

Lirer L, Luongo G, Scandone R
1987 On the volcanological evolution of Campi Flegrei. *Eos, Trans Amer Geophys Union*, 68: 226-227, 229, 231, 233-234

Rosi M, Santacroce R, Sbrana A
1987 *Geological Map of Somma-Vesuvius Volcanic Complex*. CNR Progetto Finalizzato Geodinamica, Rome

Rosi M, Sbrana A
1987 *Consigliio Nazionale delle Ricerche Quaderni de "la Ricerca Scientifica"*. CNR Progetto Finalizzato Geodinamica, Rome, v 9

Civetta L, Cornette Y, Gillot P Y, Orsi G
1988 The eruptive history of Pantelleria (Sicily Channel) in the last 50 ka. *Bull Volc*, 50: 47-57

Mastrolorenzo G, Lirer L, Di Vito M, Rolandi G, Scandone R
1988 The eruptive dynamic in Campi Flegrei and Roccamonfina volcanic areas (southern Italy) (abs). *Kagoshima Internatl Conf Volc Abs*, p 330

Barberi F, Cioni R, Rosi M, Santacroce R, Sbrana A, Vecci R
1989 Magmatic and phreatomagmatic phases in explosive eruptions of Vesuvius as deduced by grain-size and component analysis of the pyroclastic deposits. *Jour Volc Geotherm Res*, 38: 287-307

Forgione G, Luongo G, Romano R
1989 Mt. Etna (Sicily): volcanic hazard assessment. *In*: Latter J H (ed), p 137-150 (see global reference)

Barberi F, Bertagnini A, Landi P (eds)
1990 Mt. Etna: the 1989 eruption. CNR-Gruppo Nazionale Vulcanologia Italy, 75 p

Uchrin G
1990 Olympiodorus's eruption of Mount Etna. *Eos, Trans Amer Geophys Union*, 71: 329 & 334

Rolandi G, Barrella A M, Borrelli A
1993 The 1631 eruption of Vesuvius. *Jour Volc Geotherm Res*, 58: 183-202

Rosi M, Principe C, Vecci R
1993 The 1631 Vesuvius eruption. A reconstruction based on historical and stratigraphical data. *Jour Volc Geotherm Res*, 58: 151-182

Scandone R, Giacomelli L, Gasparini P
1993 Mount Vesuvius: 2000 years of volcanological observations. *Jour Volc Geotherm Res*, 58: 5-26

EUROPE TO CAUCASUS (0100, 0102-04)

Washington H S
1924 Notes on the Solfatara of Sousaki (Greece), a recent eruption at Methana (Greece), and recent Maccalube at Vulcano. *Jour Geol*, 32: 460-462

Pelletier H, Delibrias G, Labeyrie J, Perquis M T, Rudel A
1959 Mesure de l'age d'une des coulees volcaniques issues du Puy de la Vache (Puy de Dome) par la methode du carbone 14. *Compte Rendus Acad Sci Paris*, Series-D, 214: 2221

Sviatlovsky A E
1959 ★ Atlas of Volcanoes of the Soviet Union. Moscow: Akad Nauk SSSR, 170 p (in Russian with English summary)

Georgalas G C
1962 ★ Greece. *Catalog of Active Volcanoes of the World*, Rome: IAVCEI, 12: 1-40

Blumenthal M M, van der Kaaden G, Vlodavetz V I
1964 ★ Turkey & Caucasus. *Catalog of Active Volcanoes of the World*, Rome: IAVCEI, 17: 1-23

Gorshkov G S
1966 The structure of Aragatz volcano and its ignimbrites. *In*: Cook E F (ed) *Tuff Lavas and Ignimbrites, a Survey of Soviet Studies*, New York: Elsevier, 212 p

Mellaart J
1967 *Catal Huyuk a Neolithic Town in Anatolia*. New York: McGraw Hill, 232 p

Pasquare G
1968 Geology of the Cenozoic volcanic area of Central Anatolia. *Roma Accad Nazionale Lincei Mem*, 9: 55-204

Brousse R, Delibrias G, Labeyrie J, Rudel A
1969 Elements de chronologie des eruptions de la Chaine des Puys. *Bull Soc Geol France*, 7: 770-793

Rutten M G
1969 *The Geology of Western Europe*. Amsterdam: Elsevier, 520 p

Hedervari P
1971 Energetical calculations concerning the Minoan eruption of Santorini. *In*: Kaloyeropoyloy A (ed), p 257-276 (see below)

Kaloyeropoyloy A (ed)
1971 *Acta of the 1st International Science Congress on the Volcano of Thera, held in Greece, 15th-23rd September, 1969*. Athens: Arch Serv Greece, 436 p

Keller J
1971 The major volcanic events in recent eastern Mediterranean volcanism and their bearing on the problem of Santorini ash layers. *In*: Kaloyeropoyloy A (ed), p 152-169 (see above)

Neumann van Padang M
1971 Two catastrophic eruptions in Indonesia, comparable with the Plinian outburst of the volcano of Thera (Santorini) in Minoan time. *In*: Kaloyeropoyloy A (ed), p 51-63 (see above)

Vink B W, Schuilling R D
1971 Estimates of the various types of energy released bythe eruption of Thera, Greece, at about 1400 B.C. *In*: Kaloyeropoyloy A (ed), p 288-292 (see above)

Borsi S, Ferrara G, Innocenti F, Mazzuoli R
1972 Geochronology and petrology of recent volcanics in the eastern Aegean Sea (west Anatolia and Lesvos Island). *Bull Volc*, 36: 473-496

Brousse R
1973 Le volcanisme Quaternaire en France-chronologie des differentes phase eruptives de la Chaine des Puys au Quaternaire recent. *Internatl Quaternary Assoc (INQUA) Cong*, 9: 105-109

Ozpeker I
1973 Volcanological evolution of Nemrut Dagi. *4th Symp Mech Sci Res Center Turkey*, p 1-17 (in Turkish)

Di Paola G M
1974 Volcanology and Petrology of Nisyros Island (Dodecanese, Greece). *Bull Volc*, 38: 944-987

Keller J
1974 Quaternary maar volcanism near Karapinar in central Anatolia. *Bull Volc*, 38: 378-396

Krafft M
1974 ★ Guide des Volcans d'Europe. Neuchatel: Delachaux & Niestle, 412 p

Lambert R S J, Holland J G, Owen P F
1974 Chemical petrology of a suite of calc-alkaline lavas from Mount Ararat, Turkey. *Jour Geol*, 82: 419-438

Djanelidze C P
1975 On the middle Holocene age of the last eruption of Kazbek volcano. *Geomorphologia*, 2: 75-77

Innocenti F, Mazzuoli R, Pasquare G, Radicati di Brozolo F, Villari L
1975 The Neogene calcalkaline volcanism of central Anatolia: geochronological data on the Kayseri-Nigde area. *Geol Mag*, 112: 349-360

Bond A, Sparks R S J
1976 The Minoan eruption of Santorini, Greece. *Jour Geol Soc London*, 132: 1-16

Brinkmann R
1976 *Geology of Turkey*. Amsterdam: Elsevier, 158 p

Tchalenko J S
1977 A reconnaissance of the seismicity and tectonics at the northern border of the Arabian Plate (Lake Van region). *Rev Geog Phys Geol Dynamique*, 19: 189-208

Lorenz V, Buchel G
1978 Phreatomagmatische Vulkane in der Sudlichen Westeifel, Ihr Alter und Ihre Beziehung zum Talnetz (abs). *Nachrichten Deut Geol Gesellschaft*, 19: 30

Watkins N D, Sparks R S J, Sigurdsson H, Huang T C, Federman A, Carey S, Ninkovich D
1978 Volume and extent of the Minoan tephra from Santorini volcano: new evidence from deep-sea sediment cores. *Nature*, 271: 122-126

Keller J
1980 The island of Vulcano [Nisyros, Yali, Turkey]. *Soc Italiana Min Petr*, 36: 368-413

Buchel G, Lorenz V
1982 Zum Alter des Maarvulkanismus der Westeifel. *Neues Jahrb Geol Palaont Abh*, 163: 1-22

Ercan T, Oztunali O
1982 Characteristic features and "base surges" bed forms of Kula volcanics. *Bull Geol Soc Turkey*, 25: 117-125 (in Turkish with English abs)

Innocenti F, Mazzuoli R, Pasquare G, Radicati di Brozolo F, Villari L
1982 Tertiary and Quaternary volcanism of the Erzurum-Kars area (eastern Turkey): geochronological data and geodynamic evolution. *Jour Volc Geotherm Res*, 13: 223-240

Keller J
1982 Mediterranean Island Arcs. *In*: Thorpe R S (ed) *Andesites*, New York: John Wiley Sons, p 307-326

Arana V, Aparicio A, Martin Escorza C, Garcia Cacho L, Ortiz R, Vaquer R, Barberi F, Ferrara G, Albert J, Gassiot X
1983 El volcanismo Neogeno-Cuaternario de Catalunya: caracteres estructurales, petrologicos y geodinamicos. *Acta Geol Hispanica*, 18: 1-17

Guerin G
1983 La thermoluminescence des plagioclases, methode de datation du volcanisme. Application au domaine volcanique Francais: Chaine des Puys, Monts-Dore, Cezallier, Bas-Vivarais. *Unpublished PhD thesis*, Univ Pierre et Marie Curie, 253 p

Hetier J M, Guillet B, Brousse R, Delibrias G, Maury R C
1983 ^{14}C dating of buried soils in the volcanic Chaine des Puys (France). *Bull Volc*, 46: 193-202

Mertes H, Schmincke H-U
1983 Age distribution of volcanoes in the West-Eifel. *Neues Jahrb Geol Palaont Monatsh*, 166: 260-293

Stothers R B, Rampino M R
1983 Volcanic eruptions in the Mediterranean before AD 630 from written and archaeological sources. *Jour Geophys Res*, 88: 6357-6371

Degens E T, Wong H K, Kempe S, Kurtman F
1984 A geological study of Lake Van, eastern Turkey. *Geol Rundschau*, 73: 701-734

Fytikas M, Innocenti F, Manetti P, Mazzuoli R, Peccerillo A, Villari L
1984 Tertiary to Quaternary evolution of volcanism in the Aegean region. *In*: Dixon J E and Robertson A H F (eds) *The Geological Evolution of the Eastern Mediterranean*, Geol Soc London Spec Pub 17: 687-701

Guner Y
1984 Geology, geomorphology and evolution of the Nemrut volcano. *Jeomorfoloji Dergisi*, 12: 23-65 (in Turkish with English abs)

Heiken G, McCoy F
1984 Caldera development during the Minoan eruption, Thira, Cyclades Greece. *Jour Geophys Res*, 89: 8441-8462

Mallarach J M
1985 Geologic map of the Olot volcanic zone--lithology and geomorphology. *Realitacio Cartografica*, 1:250,000 geol map

Fytikas M, Innocenti F, Kolios N, Manetti P, Mazzuoli R, Poli G, Rita F, Villari L
1986 Volcanology and petrology of volcanic products from the island of Milos and neighbouring islets. *Jour Volc Geotherm Res*, 28: 297-318

Guenet P
1986 Datation par l'analyse pollinique de l'explosion des volcans du groupe du Pavin (Besse-en-Chandesse, Puy-de-Dome, France). *11eme Reunion Sci Terre, Clermont-Ferrand, Soc Geol France*, p 85

Fytikas M, Kolios N, Vougioukalakis G
1990 Post-Minoan volcanic activity of the Santorini volcano: volcanic hazard and risk, forecasting possibilities. *In*: Hardy D (ed), p 183-198 (see below)

Hardy D (ed)
1990 *Thera and the Aegean World III*. London: Thera Foundation

Juvigne E, Bastin B, Beaulieu J L de, Etlicher M, Gewelt M, Gilot E, Goeury C, Janssen C R, Milcamps V, Van Leeuwen J
1990 Tephrostratigraphy of the late glacial and the Holocene of the French Massif Central based on investigations in peat-bogs (abs). *IAVCEI Internatl Volc Cong, Mainz, Abs Vol* (unpaginated)

Keller J, Rehren T, Stadlbauer E
1990 Explosive volcanism in the Hellenic arc: a summary and review. *In*: Hardy D (ed), p 13-26 (see above)

Pearce J A, Bender J F, de Long S E, Kidd W S F, Low P J, Guner Y, Saroglu F, Yilmaz Y, Moorbath S, Mitchell J G
1990 Genesis of collision volcanism in eastern Anatolia, Turkey. *Jour Volc Geotherm Res*, 44: 184-229

Pyle D M
1990 New estimates for the volume of the Minoan eruption. *In*: Hardy D (ed), p 113-121 (see above)

Sigurdsson H, Carey S, Devine J D
1990 Assessment of mass, dynamics and environmental effects of the Minoan eruption of Santorini volcano. *In*: Hardy D (ed), p 100-112 (see above)

Yilmaz Y
1990 Comparison of young volcanic associations of western and eastern Anatolia formed under a compressional regime: a review. *Jour Volc Geotherm Res*, 44: 69-87

de Goer A, Boivin P, Camus G, Gourgaud A, Kieffer G, Mergoil J, Vincent P M
1991 Volcanologie de la Chaine des Puys. *Paris: Inst Geog Natl*, 127 p and 1:25,000 geol map

Limburg E, Varekamp J C
1991 Young pumice deposits on Nisyros, Greece. *Bull Volc*, 54: 68-77

Aydar E, Gourgaud A
1992 A multi-caldera strato-volcano: Hasan Dag (Central Anatolia, Turkiye). *29th Internatl Geol Cong, Kyoto, abs*, 2: 484

Druitt T H, Francaviglia V
1992 Caldera formation on Santorini and the physiography of the islands in the late Bronze age. *Bull Volc*, 54: 484-493

Feraud J
1992 Volcans actifs de Turquie. *Mem l'Assoc Volc Europeenne (L.A.V.E.)*, 2: 1-82

Kuniholm P I
1994 Long tree-ring chronologies for the Eastern Mediterranean [Santorini]. *Theme Volume 29th Internatl Symp Archaeometry*, in press

AFRICA: EAST & CENTRAL (0201-03)

Cavendish H S H
1898 Through Somaliland and around and south of Lake Rudolf. *Geog Jour*, 11: 372-293

Hobley C W
1906 Notes on the geography and people of the Baringo district of the East Africa Protectorate. *Geog Jour*, 28: 471-481

Jack E M
1913 The Bufumbiro Mountains. *Geog Jour*, 41: 532-550

Hobley C W
1918 A volcanic eruption in East Africa [Ol Doinyo Lengai]. *Jour East Africa & Uganda Nat Hist Soc*, 3: 339-342

Holmes A, Harwood H F
1932 Petrology of the volcanic fields east and south-east of Ruwenzori, Uganda. *Quart Jour Geol Soc London*, 88: 370-442

Champion A M
1935 Teleki's volcano and the lava fields at the southern end of Lake Rudolf. *Geog Jour*, 85: 322-341

Combe A D
1937 The Katunga volcano, southwest Uganda. *Geol Mag*, 74: 190-200

Campbell Smith W
1938 Petrographic description of volcanic rocks from Turkana, Kenya Colony, with notes on their field occurrence from the manscript of Mr. A.M. Champion. *Quart Jour Geol Soc London*, 94: 528-531

Richard J J
1942 Oldoinyo Lengai-the 1940-41 eruption volcanological observations in East Africa. *Jour East Africa & Uganda Nat Hist Soc*, 16: 89-108

Holmes A
1950 Petrogenesis of katungite [Fort Portal Volc Field]. *Amer Mineral*, 35: 772-792

Guest N J, Leedal G P
1953 The volcanic activity of Mt. Meru. *Tanganyika Geol Surv Div Rec*, 3: 40-47

Reece A W
1955 The Bunyaruguru volcanic field. *Rec Geol Surv Dept Uganda (1953)*, p 29-47

Guest N J
1956 The volcanic activity of Oldonyo l'Engai, 1954. *Rec Geol Surv Tanganyika*, 4: 56-59

Sampson D N
1956 The volcanic hills at Igwisi. *Rec Geol Surv Tanganyika 1953*, p 48-53

Richard J J, Neumann van Padang M
1957 ★ Africa and the Red Sea. *Catalog of Active Volcanoes of the World*, Rome: IAVCEI 4: 1-118

Verhaeghe M
1958 L'eruption du Volcan Mugogo an Kivu. *Comptes Rendus Acad Sci Paris*, Ser-D, 246: 2917-2920

Berg E
1959 Volcanic eruption in Belgian Congo. *Jour Geophys Res*, 64: 580

Harkin D A
1960 The Rungwe volcanics at the northern end of Lake Nyasa. *Geol Surv Tanganyika Mem*, 2: 1-172

Mohr P A
1961 The geology, structure, and origin of the Bishoftu explosion craters. *Bull Geophys Observ Addis Ababa*, 2: 65-101

Dawson J B
1962 The geology of Oldoinyo Lengai. *Bull Volc*, 24: 349-387

Dodson R G
1963 Geology of the South Horr area. *Geol Surv Kenya Rpt*, 60: 1-53

Saggerson E P
1963 Geology of the Simba-Kibwezi area. *Geol Surv Kenya Rpt*, 58: 1-70

Thompson A O, Dodson R G
1963 Geology of the Naivasha area. *Geol Surv Kenya Rpt*, 55: 1-80

McCall G J H, Bristow C M
1965 An introductory account of Suswa volcano, Kenya. *Bull Volc*, 28: 333-367

Gibson I L
1967 Preliminary account of the volcanic geology of Fantale, Shoa, Ethiopia. *Bull Geophys Observ Addis Ababa*, 10: 59-68

Dawson J B, Bowden P, Clark G C
1968 Activity of the carbonatite volcano Oldoinyo Lengai, 1966. *Geol Rundschau*, 57: 865-879

Brown F H, Carmichael I S E
1969 Quaternary volcanics of the Lake Rudolf Region, 1. The Korath Range. *Lithos*, 2: 239-260

Cole J W
1969 Gariboldi volcanic complex, Ethiopia. *Bull Volc*, 33: 566-578

Denaeyer M E
1969 Nouvelles donnees lithologiques sur les volcans actifs des Virunga (Afrique centrale). *Bull Volc*, 33: 1128-1144

Gibson I L
1969 The structure and volcanic geology of an axial portion of the main Ethiopian Rift. *Tectonophysics*, 8: 561-565

Barberi F, Varet J
1970 The Erta Ale volcanic range (Danakill depression, Northern Afar , Ethiopia). *Bull Volc*, 34: 848-917

Williams L A J
1970 The volcanics of the Gregory Rift Valley, East Africa. *Bull Volc*, 34: 439-465

Di Paola G M
1971 Geology of the Corbetti Caldera (main Ethiopian rift valley). *Bull Volc*, 35: 497-506

Tinkler K J
1971 Statistical analysis of tectonic patterns in areal volcanism: the Bunyaruguru volcanic field in West Uganda. *Mathematical Geol*, 3: 335-355

Varet M J
1971 Sur l'activite recente de l'Erta Ale (Dankalie, Ethiopie). *Comptes Rendus Acad Sci Paris*, Ser-D, 272: 1964-1967

Di Paola G M
1972 The Ethiopian Rift Valley (between 7° 00' and 8° 40' lat north). *Bull Volc*, 36: 517-560

Downie C, Wilkinson P
1972 *The Geology of Kilimanjaro*. England: Univ Sheffield Dept Geol, 253 p

Pouclet A, Villeneuve M
1972 L'eruption du Rugarama (Mars-Mai 1971) au Volcan Nyamuragira (rep. Zaire). *Bull Volc*, 36: 200-221

CNR-CNRS Afar Team
1973 Geology of northern Afar (Ethiopia). *Rev Geog Phys Geol Dynamique*, 15: 443-490

De Fino M, La Volpe L, Lirer L, Varet J
1973 Geology and petrology of Manda-Inakir range and Moussa Alli volcano, central eastern Afar (Ethiopia and TFAI). *Rev Geog Phys Geol Dynamique*, 15: 373-386

Nixon P H
1973 Kimberlitic volcanoes in East Africa. *Overseas Geol Min Res*, 41: 119-138

Nixon P H, Hornung G
1973 The carbonatite lavas and tuffs near Fort Portal, western Uganda. *Overseas Geol Min Res*, 41: 168-179

United Nations
1973 Geology, geochemistry and hydrology of hot springs of the East African Rift system within Ethiopia. *United Nations Tech Rpt*, New York, DP/SF/UN 116: 1-220

Stieltjes L
1974 Geologic map of the Asal Rift. *Bur Recherches Geol Minieres France*, 1:50,000

CNR-CNRS
1975 *Geological Maps of Afar: 1, Northern Afar (1971); 2, Central and Southern Afar* (1975). La Celle St Cloud, France: Geotechnip

Delibrias G, Marinelli G, Stieltjes L
1975 Spreading rate of the Asal Rift: A geological approach. *In*: Pilger A and Rosler A (eds) *Afar Depression of Ethiopia*, Inter-Union Comm Geodynam Sci Rpt, 14: 214-221, Stuttgart: E Schweizerbart'sche

Pouclet A
1975 Activites du Volcan Nyamuragira (rift ouest de l'Afrique centrale), evaluation des volumes de materiaux emis. *Bull Volc*, 39: 466-478

Skinner N J, Iles W, Brock A
1975 The recent secular variation of declination and inclination in Kenya. *Earth Planet Sci Lett*, 25: 338-346

Emilia D A, Last B J, Wood C A, Dakin F M
1976-77 Geophysics and geology of an explosion crater in the Ethiopian Rift Valley [Bishoftu]. *Bull Volc*, 40: 133-140

Mohr P A, Wood C A
1976 Volcano Spacings and Lithospheric Attenuation in the Eastern Rift of Africa. *Earth Planet Sci Lett*, 33: 126-144

Tazieff H
1976-77 An exceptional eruption: Mt. Niragongo, Jan 10th, 1977. *Bull Volc*, 40: 189-200

Weaver S D
1976-77 The Quaternary caldera volcano Emuruangogolak, Kenya Rift, and the petrology of a bimodal ferrobasalt pantelleritic trachyte association. *Bull Volc*, 40: 209-230

Le Bas M J
1977 *Carbonatite-Nephelinite Volcanism*. New York: John Wiley, 347 p

Pouclet A
1977 Contribution l'etude structurale de l'aire volcanique des Virunga, rift de l'Afrique centrale. *Rev Geog Phys Geol Dynamique*, 19: 115-124

Berhe S M
1978 Geological map of the Nazret area. (Ethiopian Mapping Agency}, 1:250,000

Bizouard H, Di Paola G M
1978 Minerology of the Tullu Mose active volcano area (Arussi: Ethiopian Rift Valley). *In*: Neuman E-R and Ramberg I B (eds) *Petrology and Geochemistry of Continental Rifts*, Dordrecht, Holland: D Reidel, p 87-92

Gouin P
1979 Earthquake history of Ethiopia and the Horn of Africa. *Internatl Devel Res Centre (Canada)*, 118E: 259

Tazieff H
1979 *Nyiragongo: the Forbidden Volcano*. Woodbury, New York: Barrons Educational Ser, 287 p

Mohr P A, Mitchell J G, Raynolds R G H
1980 Quaternary volcanism and faulting at O'a caldera, central Ethiopian Rift. *Bull Volc*, 43: 173-190

Scott S C
1980 The geology of Longonot volcano, Central Kenya: a question of volumes. *Phil Trans Roy Soc London*, Ser A, 296: 438-466

Brousse R, Caron J-P, Kampunzu A B, Lubala R T, Musengie M K, Vellutini P-J
1981 Eruption et nature de la lave du Gasenyi: un nouveau volcan (Janvier-Fevrier 1980) au flanc nord du Nyamulagira (Kivu, Zaire). *Comptes Rendus Acad Sci Paris*, Ser-II, 292: 1413-1416

Cattermole P
1982 Meru - A rift valley giant. *Volcano News*, 11: 1-3

Ferguson A J D, Harbott B J
1982 Geographical, physical and chemical aspects of Lake Turkana. *In*: Hopson A J (ed) *Lake Turkana: a Report on the Findings of the Lake Turkana Project 1972-75*, London: Rpt Overseas Devel Admin, p 1-107

Davidson A
1983 The Omo River project - reconnaissance geology and geochemistry of parts of Ilubabor, Kefa, Gemu Gofa, and Sidamo, Ethiopia. *Ethiopian Inst Geol Surv Bull*, 2: 1-89

Hamaguchi H (ed)
1983 *Volcanoes Nyiragongo and Nyamuragira: Geophysical Aspects.* Sendai: Tohoku Univ Fac Sci, 130 p

Ueki S
1983 Recent volcanism of Nyamuragira and Nyiragongo. *In*: Hamaguchi H (ed) *Volcanoes Nyamuragira and Nyiragongo: Geophys Aspects*, Japan: Tohoku Univ, Sendai, p 7-18

Kampunzu A B, Lubala R T, Brousse R, Caron J P-H, Cluzel D, Lenoble L, Vellutini P J
1984 Sur l'eruption du Nyamulagira de Decembre 1981 a Janvier 1982: cone et coulee du Rugarambiro (Kivu, Zaire). *Bull Volc*, 47: 79-105

Leat P T, Macdonald R, Smith R L
1984 Geochemical evolution of the Menengai Caldera volcano, Kenya. *Jour Geophys Res*, 89: 8571-8592

Tazieff H
1984 Mt Niragongo: renewed activty of the lava lake. *Jour Volc Geotherm Res*, 20: 267-280

Williams L A J, Macdonald R, Chapman G R
1984 Late Quaternary caldera volcanoes of the Kenya Rift Valley. *Jour Geophys Res*, 89: 8553-8570

de Mulder M
1985 The Karisimbi volcano. *Annales Musee Roy Afrique Central Ser 8 Sci Geol*, 90: 1-101

Wilkinson P, Mitchell J G, Cattermole P J, Downie C
1986 Volcanic chronology of the Meru-Kilimanjaro region, northern Tanzania. *Jour Geol Soc London*, 143: 601-605

WoldeGabriel G
1986 The Awasa caldera in the main Ethiopian Rift (MER) (abs). *IAVCEI Cong, New Zeal, Abs*, p 351

Charsley T J
1987a Geology of the Laisamis area. *Rpt Mines Geol Dept Kenya*, 106: 1-70
1987b Geology of the North Horr area. *Rpt Mines Geol Dept Kenya*, 110: 1-40

Francis P W, Rothery D A
1987 Using the Landsat Thematic Mapper to detect and monitor active volcanoes: an example from Lascar volcano, northern Chile [Erta Ale]. *Geology*, 15: 614-617

Key R M
1987a Geology of the Maralal area. *Rpt Mines Geol Dept Kenya*, 105: 1-93
1987b Geology of the Marsabit area. *Rpt Mines Geol Dept Kenya*, 108: 1-42

Key R M, Rop B P, Rundle C C
1987 The development of the late Cenozoic alkali basaltic Marsabit shield volcano, northern Kenya. *Jour African Earth Sci*, 6: 475-491

Hackman B D
1988 Geology of the Baringo-Laikipia area. *Rpt Mines Geol Dept Kenya*, 104: 1-79

Kasahara M, Zana N
1988 Recent volcanism of Nyiragongo and Nyamuragira. *In*: Tanaka K (ed), p 4-15 (in Japanese with English abs, see below)

Key R M, Watkins R T
1988 Geology of the Sabarei area. *Rpt Mines Geol Dept Kenya*, 111: 1-57

Nyamweru C
1988 Activity of Ol Doinyo Lengai volcano, Tanzania, 1983-1987. *Jour African Earth Sci*, 7: 603-610

Ochieng' J O, Wilkinson A F, Kagasi J, Kimomo S
1988 Geology of the Loiyangalani area. *Rpt Mines Geol Dept Kenya*, 107: 1-53

Tanaka K (ed)
1988 *Geophysical Studies of Volcanoes Nyiragongo and Nyamuragira.* Hirosaki: Hirosaki Univ Fac Sci, 78 p (in Japanese with English abs)

Wilkinson A F
1988 Geology of the Allia Bay area. *Rpt Mines Geol Dept Kenya*, 109: 1-54

Ebinger C J, Deino A L, Drake R E, Tesha A L
1989 Chronology of volcanism and rift basin propagation: Rungwe volcanic province, East Africa. *Jour Geophys Res*, 94: 15,785-15,803

Hackman B D, Charsley T J, Kagasi J, Key R M, Siambi W S, Wilkinson A F
1989 Geology of the Isiolo area. *Rpt Mines Geol Dept Kenya*, 103: 1-88

Hay R L
1989 Holocene carbonatite nephelinite tephra deposits of Oldoinyo Lengai, Tanzania. *Jour Volc Geotherm Res*, 37: 77-91

Audin J, Vellutini P J, Coulon C, Piguet P, Vincent J
1990 The 1928-1929 eruption of Kammourta volcano - evidence of tectono-magmatic activity in the Manda-Inakir rift and comparison with the Asal Rift, Afar depression, Republic of Djibuti. *Bull Volc*, 52: 551-561

Krafft M
1990 *Fuhrer zu den Virunga-Vulkanen.* Stuttgart: Ferdinand Enke, 187 p

Dunkley P N, Smith M. Allen D A, Darling W G
1993 The geothermal activity and geology of the northern sector of the Kenya Rift Valley. *Brit Geol Res Rpt* SD/93/1

Ebinger C J, Yemane T, WoldeGabriel G, Aronson J L, Walter R C
1993 Late Eocene-Recent volcanism and faulting the southern main Ethiopian rift. *Jour Geol Soc London*, 150: 99-108

Zana N, Kasahara M, Kasereka M, Azangi M, Wafula M
1993 Surface formations and seismic activities related to the 1991-1992 Nyamuragira eruption (abs). *IAVCEI, Canberra Mtg Abs*, p 127

Karson J A, Curtis P C
1994 Axial Quaternary volcanic centers in the Turkana rift, N. Kenya. *Jour African Earth Sci*, 18: 15-35

AFRICA: WEST & NORTH (0204-05)

Geze B
1953 Les volcans du Cameroun occidental. *Bull Volc*, 13: 63-92

Richard J J, Neumann van Padang M
1957 ★ Africa and the Red Sea. *Catalog of Active Volcanoes of the World*, Rome: IAVCEI 4: 1-118

Geze B, Hudeley H, Vincent P, Wacrenier P
1959 Les volcacans du Tibesti (Sahara du Tchard). *Bull Volc*, 22: 135-172

Hasselo H N, Swarbrick J T
1960 The eruption of the Cameroon Mountain in 1959. *Jour West African Sci Assoc*, 6: 96-101

Vincent P M
1963 Les volcans Tertiares et Quaternaires de Tibesti occidental et central (Sahara du Tchad). *Mem Bur Recherche Geol Min*, 23: 1-307

Bederman S H
1966 Mount Cameroon: West Africa's active volcano. *Nigerian Geog Jour*, 9: 115-128

Burton A N, Wickens G E
1966 Jebel Marra volcano, Sudan. *Nature*, 210: 1146-1147

Hinchingbrooke J
1968 Trek to the Tibesti Range. *Geog Mag*, 11: 1024-1033

Klitzsch E
1968 Der Basaltvulkanismus des Djebel Haroudj Ostfezzan/Libyen. *Geol Rundschau*, 57: 585-601

Almond D C, Ahmed F, Khalil B E
1969 An excursion to the Bayuda volcanic field of northern Sudan. *Bull Volc*, 33: 549-565

Tchoua F M
1971 Le volcanisme Strombolien de la plaine de Tombel (Cameroun). *Annales Fac Sci, Yaounde, Cameroun*, 7-8: 53-78

Vail J R
1972 Jebel Marra, a dormant volcano in Darfur Province, western Sudan. *Bull Volc*, 36: 251-268

Francis P W, Thorpe R S, Ahmed F
1973 Setting and significance of Tertiary-Recent volcanism in the Darfur Province of western Sudan. *Nature*, 243: 30-31

Almond D C
1974 The composition of basaltic lavas from Bayuda, Sudan and their place in the Cainozoic volcanic history of north-east Africa. *Bull Volc*, 38: 345-360

Tchoua F M
1983 Les explosions magmatophreatiques de Monoun. *Rev Sci Tech*, 3: 87-97

Almond D C, Kheir O M, Poole S
1984 Alkaline basalt volcanism in northeastern Sudan: a comparison of the Bayuda and Gedaref areas. *Jour African Earth Sci*, 2: 233-245

Fitton G
1984 Mt. Cameroon, W. Africa. *Volcano News*, 18: 2-3

Fitton J G, Dunlop H M
1985 The Cameroon line, West Africa, and its bearing on the origin of oceanic and continental alkali basalt. *Earth Planet Sci Lett*, 72: 23-38

Deruelle B, N'ni J, Kambou R
1987 Mount Cameroon: an active volcano of the Cameroon Line. *Jour African Earth Sci*, 6: 197-214

Fitton J G
1987 The Cameroon line, West Africa: a comparison between oceanic and continental alkaline volcanism. *In*: Fitton J G and Upton B G J (eds) *Alkaline Igneous Rocks*, Geol Soc Amer Spec Pub 30: 273-291

Sigurdsson H, Devine J D, Tchoua F M, Presser T S, Pringle M K W, Evans W C
1987 Origin of the lethal gas burst from Lake Monoun Cameroun. *Jour Volc Geotherm Res*, 31: 1-16

Liniger-Goumaz M
1988 *Historical Dictionary of Equatorial Guinea*. Metuchen, New Jersey: Scarecrow Press, African Historical Dictionaries, no 21

Lockwood J P, Costa J E, Tuttle M L, Nni J, Tebor S G
1988 The potential for catastrophic dam failure at Lake Nyos maar, Cameroon. *Bull Volc*, 50: 340-349

Barberi F, Chelini W, Marinelli G, Martini M
1989 The gas cloud of Lake Nyos (Cameroon, 1986): results of the Italian technical mission. *Jour Volc Geotherm Res*, 39: 125-134

Kling G W, Tuttle M L, Evans W C
1989 The evolution of thermal structure and water chemistry in Lake Nyos. *Jour Volc Geotherm Res*, 39: 151-165

Lockwood J P, Rubin M
1989 Origin and age of the Lake Nyos maar, Cameroon. *Jour Volc Geotherm Res*, 39: 117-124

Tazieff H
1989 Mechanisms of the Nyos carbon dioxide disaster and of so-called phreatic stream eruptions. *Jour Volc Geotherm Res*, 39: 109-116

Deruelle B, Kambou R, Joron J-L
1990 New petrological data on volcanic rocks of Bioko Island (Equatorial Guinea) (abs). *IAVCEI Internatl Volc Cong, Mainz, Abs*, (unpaginated)

Paulick H, Franz G, Urlacher G
1993 The alkaline Meidob volcanic field, Pliocene to Holocene, W Sudan (abs). *IAVCEI, Canberra Mtg Abs*, p 84

MIDDLE EAST (0300-02)

Sondhi V P
1947 The Makran earthquake, 28th November 1945, the birth of new islands. *Indian Min*, 1: 147-154

Neumann van Padang M
1963 ★ Arabia and the Indian Ocean. *Catalog of Active Volcanoes of the World*, Rome: IAVCEI, 16: 1-64

Gansser A
1966 ★ Iran. *Catalog of Active Volcanoes of the World*, Rome: IAVCEI, 17: 1-20

Baker P E, Brosset R, Gass I G, Neary C R
1973 Jebel al Abyad: a recent alkalic volcanic complex in western Saudi Arabia. *Lithos*, 6: 291-314

Milton D J
1976-77 Qal'eh Hasan Ali maars, Central Iran. *Bull Volc*, 40: 201-208

Cox K G, Gass I G, Mallick D I J
1977 Western Part of Shuqura volcanic field, South Yemen. *Lithos*, 10: 185-192

White R S, Ross D A
1979 Tectonics of the western Gulf of Oman. *Jour Geophys Res*, 84: 3479-3489

Poirier J P, Taher M A
1980 Historical seismicity in the Near and Middle East, North Africa, and Spain from Arabic documents (7th-18th century). *Bull Seism Soc Amer*, 70: 2185-2202

Camp V E, Hooper P R, Roobol M J, White D L
1987 The Madinah eruption, Saudi Arabia: magma mixing and simultaneous extrusion of the three basaltic chemical types. *Bull Volc*, 49: 489-508

Capaldi G, Chiesa S, Conticelli S, Manetti P
1987 Jabal an Nar : an upper Miocene volcanic center near Al Mukha. *Jour Volc Geotherm Res*, 31: 345-352

Camp V E, Roobol M J
1989 The Arabian continental alkali basalt province: Part I. Evolution of Harrat Rahat, Kingdom of Saudi Arabia. *Geol Soc Amer Bull*, 101: 71-95

1991 Geologic map of the Cenozoic lava field of Harrat Rahat, Kingdom of Saudi Arabia. *Saudi Arabia Directorate Gen Min Res*, Map GM-123, 1:250,000 geol map and text

Camp V E, Roobol M J, Hooper P R
1991 The Arabia continental alkali basalt province: Part II. Evolution of Harrats Khaybar, Ithnayn, and Kura, Kingdom of Saudi Arabia. *Geol Soc Amer Bull*, 103: 363-391

Roobol M J, Camp V E
1991 Geologic map of the Cenozoic lava field of Harrat Kishb, Kingdom of Saudi Arabia. *Saudi Arabia Directorate Gen Min Res*, Map GM-132, 1:250,000 Geol map and text

Camp V E, Roobol M J, Hooper P R
1992 The Arabian continental alkali basalt province: Part III. Evolution of Harrat Kishb, Kingdom of Saudia Arabia. *Geol Soc Amer Bull*, 104: 379-396

INDIAN OCEAN (0303-05)

Bory de St. Vincent J B G M
1805 *Voyage to, and Travels Through the Four Principal Islands of the African Seas*. London: Richard Phillips, 71 St Paul's Church

Battistini R
1962 Le massif volcanique de l'Itasy (Madagascar). *Annales Geog*, 384: 167-178

Neumann van Padang M
1963 ★ Arabia and the Indian Ocean. *Catalog of Active Volcanoes of the World*, Rome: IAVCEI, 16: 1-64

Bellair P
1964 Recent data on the geology of Isles Crozet. *In*: Adie R J (ed) *Antarctic Geol, Proc 1st Internatl Symp Antarctic Geol*, Amsterdam: Elsevier, p3-7

Verwoerd W J, Langenegger O
1967 Marion and Prince Edward Islands geological studies. *Nature*, 213: 231-232

Esson J, Flower M F J, Strong D F, Upton B G J,, Wadsworth W J
1970 Geology of the Comores Archipelago. *Geol Mag*, 107: 549-557

Strong D F, Jacquot C
1970 The Karthala caldera, Grande Comore. *Bull Volc*, 34: 663-680

Gunn B M, Abranson C E, Nougier J, Watkins N, Hajash A
1971 Amsterdam Island, an isolated volcano in the southern Indian Ocean. *Contr Mineral Petr*, 32: 79-92

Verwoerd W J
1971 Geology of Marion and Prince Edward Islands. *In*: Bakker E M, et al (eds) *Marion and Prince Edward Islands*, Cape Town, South Africa: A A Balkema, p 40-62

Gunn B M, Abranson E C, Watkins N D, Nougier J
1972 Petrology and geochemistry of Iles Crozet: a summary. *In*: Adie R J (ed) *Antarctic Geol and Geophys*, IUGS Ser-B(1): 825-829

Montaggioni L, Nativel P, Billard G
1972 L'activite actuelle du Piton de la Fournaise (Ile de la Reunion, Ocean Indien). *Comptes Rendus Acad Sci Paris*, Ser-D, 275: 2615-2618

Nougier J
1972 Geochronology of the volcanic activity in Iles Kerguelen. *In*: Adie R J (ed) *Antarctic Geol and Geophys*, IUGS Ser-B(1): 803-808

Besairie H J
1973 Precis de geologie Malgache. *Annales Geol Madagascar*, 36: 1-141

Upton B G J, Wadsworth W J, Latrille E
1974 The 1972 eruption of Kartala volcano, Grand Comore. *Bull Volc*, 38: 136-148

Benard R, Krafft M
1977 *La Fournaise, Volcan Actif de l'Ile de la Reunion*. Strasbourg: Istra, 121 p

Kieffer G, Tricot B, Vincent P M
1977 An unusual eruption (April 1977) at Piton de la Fournaise (Reunion Island): its volcanological and structural consequence. *Comptes Rendus Acad Sci Paris*, Ser-D, 285: 957-960

Krafft M, Gerente A
1977 Volcanic activity of "Piton de la Fournaise" between October 1972 and May 1973 [& between November 1975 and April 1976] (Reunion Island, Indian Ocean). *Comptes Rendus Acad Sci Paris*, Ser-D, 284: 607-610 [& 2091-2094]

Ludden J N
1977 Eruptive patterns for the volcano Piton de la Fournaise, Reunion Island. *Jour Volc Geotherm Res*, 2: 385-396

Verwoerd W J, Russell S, Berruti A
1981 1980 volcanic eruption reported on Marion Island. *Earth Planet Sci Lett*, 54: 153-156

Bachelery P, Blum P A, Cheminee J, Chevallier L, Gaulon R, Girardin N, Juapart C, Lalanne F, Le Mouel J L, Ruegg J C, Vincent P
1982 Eruption at Le Piton de la Fournaise volcano on 3 February 1981. *Nature*, 297: 395-397

Duffield W A, Stieltjes L, Varet J
1982 Huge landslide blocks in the growth of Piton de la Fournaise, Reunion, and Kilauea volcano, Hawaii. *Jour Volc Geotherm Res*, 12: 147-160

Krafft M
1982 L'eruption volcanique du Kartala en Avril 1977 (Grande Comore, Ocean Indien). *Comptes Rendus Acad Sci Paris*, Ser-II, 294: 753-758

Nougier J
1982 Volcanism of Saint Paul and Amsterdam Islands (TAAF): some aspects of volcanism along plate margins. *In*: Craddock C (ed) *Antarctic Geoscience*, Madison: Univ Wisconsin Press, p 755-765

Krafft M
1983 Guide des volcans de la Grande Comore. *Unpublished ms*, 101 p

Ballestracci R, Nougier J
1984 Detection by infrared thermography and modelling of an ice-capped geothermal system in Kerguelen Archipelago. *Jour Volc Geotherm Res*, 20: 85-100

Stieltjes L
1985 Carte des coulees historiques du volcan de la Fournaise. *Bur Recherches Geol Minieres France*, 1:50,000

Benard R, Krafft M
1986 *Au Cour de la Fournaise*. Mahe, Seychelle Islands: Editions Nourault/Benard (& Air France), 220 p

Verwoerd W J, Chevallier L
1987 Contrasting types of surtseyan tuff cones on Marion and Prince Edward islands, southwest Indian Ocean. *Bull Volc*, 49: 399-413

Delorme H, Bachelery P, Blum P A, Cheminee J L, Delarue J F, Delmond J, Hirn A, Lepine J C, Vincent P M, Zlotnicki J
1989 March 1986 eruptive episodes at Piton de la Fournaise volcano (Reunion Island). *Jour Volc Geotherm Res*, 36: 189-208

Gillot P-Y, Nativel P
1989 Eruptive history of the Piton de la Fournaise volcano, Reunion Island, Indian Ocean. *Jour Volc Geotherm Res*, 36: 53-65

Lenat J-F, Bachelery P, Bonneville A, Tarits P, Cheminee J-L, Delorme H
1989 The December 4, 1983 to February 18, 1984 eruption of Piton de la Fournaise (la Reunion, Indian Ocean); description and interpretation. *Jour Volc Geotherm Res*, 36: 87-112

Lenat J-F, Bachelery P, Bonneville A, Hirn A
1989 The beginning of the 1985-1987 eruptive cycle at Piton de la Fournaise (la Reunion); new insights in the magmatic and volcano-tectonic systems. *Jour Volc Geotherm Res*, 36: 209-232

Lenat J-F, Vincent P, Bachelery P
1989 The off-shore continuation of an active basaltic volcano: Piton de la Fournaise (Reunion Island, Indian Ocean); structural and geomorphological interpretation from SEABEAM mapping. *Jour Volc Geotherm Res*, 36: 1-36

Stieltjes L, Moutou P
1989 A statistical and probabilistic study of the historic activity of Piton de la Fournaise, Reunion Island, Indian Ocean. *Jour Volc Geotherm Res*, 36: 67-86

LeMasurier W E, Thomson J W (eds)
1990 ★ Volcanoes of the Antarctic Plate and Southern Oceans. Washington, DC: Amer Geophys Union, 487 p

NEW ZEALAND & KERMADEC IS (0401-02)

Ward G A
1922 White Island. *New Zeal Jour Sci Tech*, 5: 220-226

Thomson J A
1926 ★ Volcanoes of the New Zealand-Tonga volcanic zone--a record of eruptions. *New Zeal Jour Sci Tech*, B8: 354-371

Jaggar T A
1928 Recent activities in New Zealand. *Volcano Lett*, 200: 1

Allen L R
1948 Activity at Ngauruhoe, April - May, 1948. *New Zeal Jour Sci Tech*, 30: 187-193

Healy J
1956 New Zealand: report of the standing committee on volcanology. *Proc 8th Pacific Sci Cong*, 2: 27-30

Hamilton W M, Baumgart I L
1959 White Island. *New Zeal Dept Sci Ind Res Bull*, 127: 1-84

Gregg D R
1960 Volcanoes of Tongariro National Park. *New Zeal Geol Soc Handbook Info Ser*, 28: 1-82

Thompson B N
1961 Geological map of New Zealand Sheet 2A--Whangarei. *New Zeal Geol Surv* 1:250,000 geol map and text

Richard J J
1962 ★ Kermadec, Tonga and Samoa. *Catalog of Active Volcanoes of the World*, Rome: IAVCEI, 13: 1-38

Kear D, Thompson B N
1964 Volcanic risk in Northland. *New Zeal Jour Geol Geophys*, 7: 87-93

Thompson B N, Kermode L O, Ewart A
1965 New Zealand volcanology-central volcanic region. *New Zeal Geol Surv Handbook Info Ser*, no 50

Kibblewhite A C
1966 The acoustic detection and location of an underwater volcano. *New Zeal Jour Sci*, 9: 178-199

Adams R D, Dibble R R
1967 Seismological studies of the Raoul Island eruption, 1964. *New Zeal Jour Geol Geophys*, 19: 1948-1961

Kibblewhite A C
1967 Note on another active seamount in the south Kermadec Ridge group. *New Zeal Jour Sci*, 10: 68-70

Kibblewhite A C, Denham R N
1967 The bathymetry and total magnetic field of the south Kermadec ridge seamounts. *New Zeal Jour Sci*, 10: 52-67

Ewart A, Taylor S R, Capp A C
1968 Geochemistry of the pantellerites of Mayor Island, New Zealand. *Contr Mineral Petr*, 17: 116-140

Brothers R N, Searle E J
1970 The geology of Raoul Island, Kermadec Group, southwest Pacific. *Bull Volc*, 34: 7-37

Clark R H
1970 Volcanic activity on White Island, Bay of Plenty, 1966-69 Part 1. Chronology and crater floor level changes. *New Zeal Jour Geol Geophys*, 13: 565-574

Neall V E
1971 Volcanic domes and lineations in Egmont National Park. *New Zeal Jour Geol Geophys*, 14: 71-81

1972 Tephrochronology and tephrostratigraphy of western Taranaki (N108-109), New Zealand. *New Zeal Jour Geol Geophys*, 15: 507-557

Clark R H
1973 Surveillance of White Island volcano, 1968-1972. Part 1 - Volcanic events and deformation of the crater floor. *New Zeal Jour Geol Geophys*, 16: 949-957

Healy J
1973 Volcano observations, 1971. *New Zeal Volc Rec*, 1: 10-18

Topping W W
1973 Tephrostratigraphy and chronology of late Quaternary eruptives from the Tongariro volcanic centre, New Zealand. *New Zeal Jour Geol Geophys*, 16: 397-423

Topping W W, Kohn B P
1973 Rhyolitic tephra marker beds in the Tongariro area, North Island, New Zealand. *New Zeal Jour Geol Geophys*, 16: 375-395

Vucetich C G, Pullar W A
1973 Holocene tephra formations erupted in the Taupo Area, and interbedded tephras from other volcanic sources. *New Zeal Jour Geol Geophys*, 16: 745-780

Hewson C A Y, Nairn I A
1974 Ngauruhoe: observed activity and seismic data. *New Zeal Volc Rec*, 2: 32-34

Nairn I A
1974 Volcanological observations, individual volcanoes, Raupehu, observations and inspections. *New Zeal Volc Rec*, 2: 11-15

Neall V E
1974 *The Volcanic History of Taranaki*. Egmont National Park, 14 p

Latter J H
1975 Note on inferred submarine eruption, Rumble No. 3 volcano. *New Zeal Volc Rec*, 3: 58

Nairn I A
1975 Volcanological observations: individual volcanoes, Ruapehu, observations and inspections. *New Zeal Volc Rec*, 4: 27-30

Nairn I A, Cole J W
1975 ★ New Zealand. *Catalog of Active Volcanoes of the World*, Rome: IAVCEI, 22: 1-156

Latter J H
1977 Volcanic tremor, and A- and B-type earthquakes at Ruapehu and Ngauruhoe during 1976. *New Zeal Volc Rec*, 6: 24-31

1978 Submarine eruption south of Tonga. *New Zeal Volc Rec*, 7: 61

Nairn I A, Self S
1978 Explosive eruptions and pyroclastic avalanches from Ngauruhoe in February 1975. *Jour Volc Geotherm Res*, 3: 39-60

Scott B J
1978 Observed activity at Ngauruhoe. *New Zeal Volc Rec*, 7: 44

Doyle A C, Singleton R J, Yaldwyn J C
1979 Volcanic activity and recent uplift on Curtis and Cheeseman Islands, Kermadec group, southwest Pacific. *Jour Roy Soc New Zeal*, 9: 123-140

Nairn I A, Wood C P, Hewson C A Y
1979 Phreatic eruptions of Ruapehu: April 1975. *New Zeal Jour Geol Geophys*, 22: 155-169

Neall V E
1979 New Plymouth, Egmont North, Egmont South and Manaia. *New Zeal Dept Sci Ind Res*, 1:50,000 geol map, 3 sheets and notes

Beetham R D, Nairn I A, Otway P M
1980 Ruapehu Crater Lake outflow investigations, 27 June 1980. *New Zeal Geol Surv Preliminary Rpt*

Davey F J
1980 The Monowai Seamount: an active submarine volcanic centre on the Tonga-Kermadec Ridge (note). *New Zeal Jour Geol Geophys*, 23: 533-536

Latter J H
1980 Volcano-seismic activity at Ruapehu volcano during 1979. *New Zeal Volc Rec*, 9: 23-29

Walker G P L
1980 The Taupo pumice: product of the most powerful known (ultraplinian) eruption? *Jour Volc Geotherm Res*, 8: 69-94

Wilson C J N, Ambraseys N N, Bradley J, Walker G P L
1980 A new date for the Taupo eruption, New Zealand. *Nature*, 288: 252-253

Buck M D, Briggs R M, Nelson C S
1981 Pyroclastic deposits and volcanic history of Mayor Island. *New Zeal Jour Geol Geophys*, 24: 449-468

Froggatt P C
1981a Karapiti tephra formation: a 10,000 years B.P. rhyolitic tephra from Taupo. *New Zeal Jour Geol Geophys*, 24: 95-98

1981b Motutere tephra formation and redefinition of Hinemaiaia tephra formation, Taupo volcanic centre, New Zealand. *New Zeal Jour Geol Geophys*, 24: 99-106

1981c Stratigraphy and nature of Taupo pumice formation. *New Zeal Jour Geol Geophys*, 24: 231-248

Lloyd E F, Nathan S
1981 Geology and tephrochronology of Raoul Island, Kermadec Group, New Zealand. *New Zeal Geol Surv Bull*, 95: 1-102

Latter J H
1981 Volcano-seismic activity at Ruapehu during 1980. *New Zeal Volc Rec*, 10: 23-29

Walker G P L
1981 The ground layer of the Taupo ignimbrite: a striking example of sedimentation from a pyroclastic flow. *Jour Volc Geotherm Res*, 10: 1-12

Allis R G
1984 The 9 April 1983 steam eruption at Craters of the Moon thermal area, Wairakei. *New Zeal Dept Sci Ind Res Rpt*, 196: 1-25

Walker G P L, Self S, Wilson L
1984 Tarawera 1886, New Zealand - A basaltic Plinian fissure eruption. *Jour Volc Geotherm Res*, 21: 61-78

Wilson C J N, Rogan A M, Smith I E M, Northey D J, Nairn I A, Houghton B F
1984 Caldera volcanoes of the Taupo volcanic zone, New Zealand. *Jour Geophys Res*, 89: 8463-8484

Buck M D
1985 An assessment of volcanic risk on and from Mayor Island, New Zealand. *New Zeal Jour Geol Geophys*, 28: 283-298

Hall L H
1985 Rumble IV Seamount - no rumble? *New Zeal Jour Geol Geophys*, 28: 569

Wilson C J N, Walker G P L
1985 The Taupo eruption, New Zealand. I. General aspects. *Phil Trans Roy Soc London*, Ser A, 314: 199-228

Clark R H, Cole J W
1986 White Island. *In*: Smith I E M (ed) *Late Cenozoic Volcanism in New Zealand*, Roy Soc New Zeal Bull, 23: 169-178

Cole J W, Graham I J, Hackett W R, Houghton B F
1986 Volcanology and petrology of the Quaternary composite volcanoes of the Tongariro volcanic centre, Taupo volcanic zone. *Roy Soc New Zeal Bull*, 23: 224-250

Cole J W, Hochstein M P, Skinner D N B, Briggs R M
1986 Tectonic setting of North Island Cenozoic volcanism (Tour Guide C1). *New Zeal Geol Surv Rec*, 11: 5-60

Hackett W R, Houghton B F
1986 Active composite volcanoes of Taupo volcanic zone (Tour Guide C4). *New Zeal Geol Surv Rec*, 11: 61-114

Heming R F, Barnet P R
1986 The petrology and petrochemistry of the Auckland volcanic field. *Roy Soc New Zeal Bull*, 23: 64-75

Houghton B F, Wilson C J N
1986 Explosive rhyolite volcanism: the case studies of Mayor Island and Taupo volcanoes (Tour Guide A1). *New Zeal Geol Surv Rec*, 12: 33-100

Lowe D J
1986 Revision of the age and stratigraphic relationships of Hinemaiaia tephra and Whakatane ash, North Island, New Zealand, using distal occurrences in organic deposits. *New Zeal Jour Geol Geophys*, 29: 61-73

Nairn I A, Cole J W, Houghton B F, Wilson C J N
1986 Tarawera 1886 eruption. *New Zeal Internatl Volc Cong Handbook*, p 111-121

Neall V E, Alloway B V
1986 Quaternary volcaniclastics and volcanic hazards of Taranaki (Tour Guide C3). *New Zeal Geol Surv Rec*, 12: 101-137

Smith I E, Day R A, Ashcroft J
1986 Volcanic associations of Northland (Tour Guide A4). *New Zeal Geol Surv Rec*, 12: 5-32

Wilson C J N, Houghton B F, Lloyd E F
1986 Volcanic history and evolution of Maroa-Taupo area, central North Island. *In*: Smith I E M (ed) *Late Cenozoic Volcanism in New Zealand*, Roy Soc New Zeal Bull, 23: 194-223

Houghton B F, Latter J H, Hackett W R
1987 Volcanic hazard assessment for Ruapehu composite volcano, Taupo volcanic zone, New Zealand. *Bull Volc*, 49: 737-751

Hackett W R, Houghton B F
1989 A facies model for a Quaternary andesitic composite volcano: Ruapehu, New Zealand. *Bull Volc*, 51: 51-68

Johnson R W, Knutson J, Taylor S R (eds)
1989 ★ Intraplate Volcanism in Eastern Australia and New Zealand. Cambridge, England: Cambridge Univ Press, 408 p

Nairn I A
1989 Mount Tarawera. *New Zeal Geol Surv* 1:50,000 geol map sheet V16 AC and 55 p text

Froggatt P C, Lowe D J
1990 A review of late Quaternary silicic and some other tephra formations from New Zealand: their stratigraphy, nomenclature, distribution, volume, and age. *New Zeal Jour Geol Geophys*, 33: 89-109

Lloyd E F
1991 Curtis volcano, Kermadec Group, a review and reinterpretation. *Volc Seism*, 1991(1): 117-121 (English translation 1992, 13: 128-134)

Nairn I A
1991 Volcanic hazards at Okataina Volcanic Centre. *New Zeal Ministry Civil Defense, Volc Hazards Info Ser*, 2: 1-29<

Houghton B F, Weaver S D, Wilson C J N, Lanphere M A
1992 Evolution of a Quaternary peralkaline volcano: Mayor Island, New Zealand. *Jour Volc Geotherm Res*, 51: 217-236

Latter J H, Lloyd E F, Smith I E M, Nathan S
1992 Volcanic hazards in the Kermadec Islands, and at submarine volcanoes between southern Tonga and New Zealand. *New Zeal Ministry Civil Defense, Volc Hazards Info Ser*, 4: 1-45

Smith I E M, Allen S R
1993 Volcanic hazards at the Auckland Volcanic Field. *New Zeal Ministry Civil Defense, Volc Hazards Info Ser*, 5: 1-34

Wilson C J N
1993 Stratigraphy, chronology, styles and dynamics of late Quaternary eruptions from Taupo volcano, New Zealand. *Phil Trans Roy Soc London*, Ser A, 343: 205-306

TONGA, SAMOA, & FIJI (0403-05)

Phillips C
1899 The volcanoes of the Pacific. *Trans New Zeal Inst*, 31: 510-551

Jensen H I
1907 The geology of Samoa, and the eruptions in Savaii. *Proc Linnean Soc New South Wales*, 31: 641-672

Anderson T
1910 The volcano of Matavanu in Savaii. *Quart Jour Geol Soc London*, 66: 621-639

Jaggar T A
1930 The island volcano of Niuafoou. *Volcano Lett*, 312: 1-3

1931 Geology and geography of Niuafoou volcano. *Volcano Lett*, 318: 1-3

Stearns H T
1944 Geology of the Samoan Islands. *Geol Soc Amer Bull*, 55: 1279-1332

1945 Geology of the Wallis Islands. *Geol Soc Amer Bull*, 56: 849-860

Macdonald G A
1948 Notes on Niuafo'ou. *Amer Jour Sci*, 246: 65-77

Pacific Islands Pilot
1956 [Unnamed Tonga submarine volcano]. *Pacific Islands Pilot*, 2: 396

Kear D, Wood B L
1959 The geology and hydrology of western Samoa. *New Zeal Geol Surv Bull*, 63: 1-92

Richard J J
1962 ★ Kermadec, Tonga and Samoa. *Catalog of Active Volcanoes of the World*, Rome: IAVCEI, 13: 1-38

Macdonald G A
1968 A contribution to the petrology of Tutuila, American Samoa. *Geol Rundschau*, 57: 821-837

Stice G D, McCoy F W
1968 The geology of the Manu'a Islands, Samoa. *Pacific Sci*, 22: 427-457

Bauer G R
1970 The geology of Tofua Island, Tonga. *Pacific Sci*, 24: 333-350

Brodie J W
1970 Notes on the volcanic activity at Fonualei Tonga. *New Zeal Jour Geol Geophys*, 13: 30-38

Frost E L
1974 Taveuni, Fiji. *Asian Pacific Arch Ser*, 6: 1-175

Coulson F I E
1976 Geology of the Lomaiviti and Moala Island Groups. *Fiji Min Res Div Bull*, 2: 1-162

Latter J H
1976 Variations in stress release preceding and accompanying a submarine eruption in northern Tonga. *In*: Johnson R W (ed) *Volcanism in Australasia*, Amsterdam: Elsevier, p 355-374

Woodhall D
1985 Geology of Taveuni, Qamea, Laucala, Cikobia and adjacent islands. *Mineral Resour Dept Fiji*, 1:50,000 geol map

Price R C, Maillet P, McDougall I, Dupont J
1991 The geochemistry of basalts from the Wallis Islands, northern Melanesian borderland: evidence for a lithospheric origin for Samoan-type basaltic magmas? *Jour Volc Geotherm Res*, 45: 267-288

Taylor P W
1991 The geology and petrology of Niuafo'ou Island, Tonga: subaerial volcanism in an active back-arc basin. *MSci thesis*, Maquarie Univ

NEW GUINEA, NEW BRITAIN, & SOLOMONS (0500-06)

Jaggar T A
1937 Eruptions at Rabaul, New Guinea. *Volcano Lett*, 448: 1-6

Fisher N H
1939a Geology and volcanology of Blanche Bay and the surrounding area, New Britain. *New Guinea Geol Bull*, 1: 1-53

1939b Report on the volcanoes of the Territory of New Guinea. *New Guinea Geol Bull*, 2: 1-16

Baker G
1946 Preliminary note on volcanic eruptions in the Goropu Mountains, south-eastern Papua, during the period December, 1943 to August 1944. *Jour Geol*, 54: 19-31

Taylor G A
1953 Notes on Ritter, Sakar, Umboi and Long Island volcanoes. *Aust Bur Min Resour Geol Geophys Rec*, 1953/43: 1-5

Reche O
1954 *Ergebnisse der Sudsee Expedition 1908-1910.* Hamburg: Appel, II Ethnographie: A Melanesien, 4: 94

Grover J C
1955 Geology, mineral deposits and prospects of mining development in the British Solomon Islands Protectorate. *Interim Geol Surv Brit Solomon Is Mem*, 1: 1-151

Taylor G A
1955 Report on Bam Island volcano and an inspection of Kadovar and Blup Blup. *Aust Bur Min Resour Geol Geophys Rec*, 1955/73: 1-9

Fisher N H
1957 ★ Melanesia. *Catalog of Active Volcanoes of the World*, Rome: IAVCEI, 5: 1-105

Grover J C
1958 The Solomon Islands--geological exploration and research 1953-1956. *Geol Surv Brit Solomon Is Mem*, 2: 1-150

Taylor G A
1958a The 1951 eruption of Mount Lamington, Papua. *Aust Bur Min Resour Geol Geophys Bull*, 38: 1-117

1958b The eruptive trend of Manam volcano. *Aust Bur Min Resour Geol Geophys Rec*, 1958/73: 1-11

1960 An experiment in volcanic prediction [Manam]. *Aust Bur Min Resour Geol Geophys Rec*, 1960/74: 1-17

1963 Seismic and tilt phenomena preceding a Pelean type eruption from a basaltic volcano [Manam]. *Bull Volc*, 26: 5-11

Branch C D
1965 Volcanic activity at Lake Dakataua caldera, New Britain. *Aust Bur Min Resour Geol Geophys Rec*, 1965/67: 1-8

Ruxton B P
1966a A late Pleistocene to Recent rhyodacite-trachybasalt-basaltic latite volcanic association in north-east Papua. *Bull Volc*, 29: 347-374

1966b Correlation and stratigraphy of dacitic ash-fall layers in northeastern Papua. *Jour Geol Soc Aust*, 13: 41-67

Blake D H, Miezitis Y
1967 Geology of Bougainville and Buka Islands, New Guinea. *Aust Bur Min Resour Geol Geophys Bull*, 93: 1-56

Branch C D
1967 Short papers from the Vulcanological Observatory, Rabual, New Britain. *Aust Bur Min Resour Geol Geophys Rpt*, 107: 1-42

Blake D H
1968 Post Miocene volcanoes on Bougainville Island, Territory of Papua and New Guinea. *Bull Volc*, 32: 121-140

Grover J C
1968 Submarine volcanoes and oceanographic observations in the New Georgia Group, 1963-64. *Brit Solomon Is Geol Rec, 1963-67 Rpt*, 96: 116-125

Smith I E
1969 Notes on the volcanoes Mount Bagana and Mount Victory, Territory of Papua and New Guinea. *Aust Bur Min Resour Geol Geophys Rec*, 1968/12: 1-21

Blake D H, Bleeker P
1970 Volcanoes of the Cape Hoskins area, New Britain, Territory of Papua and New Guinea. *Bull Volc*, 34: 385-405

Lowder G G, Carmichael I S E
1970 The volcanoes and caldera of Talasea, New Britain: geology and petrology. *Geol Soc Amer Bull*, 81: 17-38

Johnson R W
1971 Bamus volcano, Lake Hargy area, and Sulu Range, New Britain: volcanic geology and petrology. *Aust Bur Min Resour Geol Geophys Rec*, 1971/55: 1-36

Johnson R W, Davies R A, Palfreyman W D
1971 Cape Gloucester Area, New Britain' volcanic geology, petrology, and eruptive history of Langila Craters up to 1970. *Aust Bur Min Resour Geol Geophys Rec*, 1971/14: 1-34

Johnson R W, Blake D H
1972 The Cape Hoskins area, southern Willaumez Peninsula, the Witu Islands, and associated volcanic centres, New Britain: volcanic geology and petrology. *Aust Bur Min Resour Geol Geophys Rec*, 1972/133: 1-102

Johnson R W, Davies R A, White A J R
1972 Ulawun volcano, New Britain. *Aust Bur Min Resour Geol Geophys Bull*, 142: 1-42

Johnson R W, Davies R A
1972 Volcanic geology of the St. Andrew Strait Islands, Bismarck Sea, Papua New Guinea. *Geol Surv Papua New Guinea, Note on Invest*, 72-002: 1-29

Johnson R W, Taylor G A M, Davies R A
1972 Geology and petrology of Quaternary volcanic islands off the north coast of New Guinea. *Aust Bur Min Resour Geol Geophys Rec*, 1972/21: 1-127

Blake D H, McDougall I
1973 Ages of the Cape Hoskins volcanoes, New Britain, Papua New Guinea. *Jour Geol Soc Aust*, 20: 199-204

Heming R F
1974 Geology and petrology of Rabaul Caldra, Papua New Guinea. *Geol Soc Amer Bull*, 85: 1253-1264

Ball E E, Johnson R W
1976 Volcanic history of Long Island, Papua New Guinea. *In*: Johnson R W (ed), p 133-148 (see below)

Blake D H
1976 Madilogo, late Quaternary volcano near Port Moresby, Papua New Guinea. *In*: Johnson R W (ed), p 253-258 (see below)

Bultitude R J
1976 Eruptive history of Bagana volcano, Papua New Guinea, between 1882 and 1975. *In*: Johnson R W (ed), p 317-336 (see below)

Cooke R J S, Baldwin J T, Sprod T J
1976 Recent volcanoes and mineralization in Papua New Guinea. *25th Internatl Geol Cong, Sydney, Excur Guide* 53: 1-30 p

Cooke R J S, McKee C O, Dent V F, Wallace D A
1976 Striking sequence of volcanic eruptions in the Bismarck volcanic arc, Papua New Guinea, in 1972-75. *In*: Johnson R W (ed), p 149-172 (see below)

Fisher N H
1976 1941-42 eruption of Tavurvur volcano, Rabaul, Papua New Guinea. *In*: Johnson R W (ed), p 201-210 (see below)

Johnson R W (ed)
1976 *Volcanism in Australasia*. Amsterdam: Elsevier, 405 p

McKee C O
1976 Investigations at Mount Lamington 1960-75. *Geol Surv Papua New Guinea Rpt*, 76/21

McKee C O, Cooke R J S, Wallace D A
1976 1974-75 eruptions of Karkar volcano, Papua New Guinea. *In*: Johnson R W (ed), p 173-196 (see above)

Palfreyman W D, Cooke R J S
1976 Eruptive history of Manam volcano, Papua New Guinea. *In*: Johnson R W (ed), p 117-132 (see above)

Reynolds M A, Best J G
1976 Summary of the 1953-57 eruption of Tuluman volcano, Papua New Guinea. *In*: Johnson R W (ed), p 287-296 (see above)

Smith I E M
1976 Peralkaline rhyolites from the d'Entrecasteaux Islands, Papua New Guinea. *In*: Johnson R W (ed), p 275-285 (see above)

Taylor G R
1976 Residual volcanic emanations from the British Solomon Islands. *In*: Johnson R W (ed), p 343-345 (see above)

Cooke R J S
1977 Rabaul Volcanological Observatory and Geophysical Surveillance of the Rabaul volcano. *Aust Physicist*, Feb, p 27-30

Pigram C J, Johnson R W, Taylor G A M
1977 Investigation of hot gas emissions from Koranga volcano, Papua New Guinea, in 1967. *Aust Bur Min Resour Geol Geophys Jour*, 2: 59-62

Cooke R J S, Johnson R W
1978 ★ Volcanoes and volcanology in Papua New Guinea. *Geol Surv Papua New Guinea Rpt*, 78/2: 1-46

Blong R J
1979 Huli legends and volcanic eruptions, Papua New Guinea [Long I.]. *Search*, 10: 93-94

Bultitude R J
1979 Bagana volcano, Bouganiville Island geology, petrology and summary of eruptive history between 1875 and 1975. *Geol Surv Papua New Guinea Mem*, 6: 1-35

Hackman B D
1980 The geology of Guadalcanal, Solomon Islands. *Brit Inst Geol Sci Overseas Mem*, no 6

Reynolds M A, Best J G, Johnson R W
1980 1953-57 eruption of Tuluman volcano: rhyolitic volcanic activity in the northern Bismarck Sea. *Geol Surv Papua New Guinea Mem*, 7: 1-44

Bultitude R J
1981 Literature search for pre-1945 sightings of volcanoes and their activity on Bougainville Island. *Geol Surv Papua New Guinea Mem*, 10: 227-242

Bultitude R J, Cooke R J S
1981 Note on activity from Bagana volcano from 1975 to 1980. *Geol Surv Papua New Guinea Mem*, 10: 243-248

Cooke R J S, Johnson R W
1981 Bam volcano: morphology, geology, and reported eruptive history. *Geol Surv Papua New Guinea Mem*, 10: 13-22

Emeleus T G
1981 Palaeomagnetic directions in lava flows of the Rabaul volcanic complex: preliminary application to dating. *Geol Surv Papua New Guinea Mem*, 10: 201-207

Fisher N H, Branch C D
1981 Late Cainozoic volcanic deposits of the Morobe goldfield. *Geol Surv Papua New Guinea Mem*, 10: 249-256

Gust D A, Johnson R W
1981 Amphibole-bearing inclusions from Boisa Island, Papua New Guinea: evaluation of the role of fractional crystallization in an andesitic volcano. *Jour Geol*, 89: 219-232

Hughes G W, Craig P M, Dennis R A
1981 Geology of the eastern Outer Islands. *Solomon Is Geol Surv Bull*, 4: 1-33

Johnson R W, Everingham I B, Cooke R J S
1981 Submarine volcanic eruptions in Papua New Guinea: 1878 activity of Vulcan (Rabaul) and other examples. *Geol Surv Papua New Guinea Mem*, 10: 167-180

McKee C O
1981 Geomorphology, geology, and petrology of Manam volcano. *Geol Surv Papua New Guinea Mem*, 10: 23-38

McKee C O, Almond R A, Cooke R J S, Talai B
1981 Basaltic pyroclastic avalanches and flank effusion from Ulawun volcano in 1978. *Geol Surv Papua New Guinea Mem*, 10: 153-166

McKee C O, Wallace D A, Almond R A, Talai B
1981 Fatal hydro-eruption of Karkar volcano in 1979: development of maar-like crater. *Geol Surv Papua New Guinea Mem*, 10: 63-84

McKee C O, Wallace D A
1981 Lava fields in the inner caldera of Karkar volcano. *Geol Surv Papua New Guinea Mem*, 10: 49-62

Mennis M R
1981 Yomba Island: real or mythical volcano? *Geol Surv Papua New Guinea Mem*, 10: 95-100

Pain C F
1981 Stratigraphy and chronology of volcanic-ash beds on Lou Island. *Geol Surv Papua New Guinea Mem*, 10: 221-226

Pain C F, Blong R J, McKee C O
1981 Pyroclastic deposits and eruptive sequences of Long Island. Part 1: Lithology, stratigraphy, and volcanology. *Geol Surv Papua New Guinea Mem*, 10: 101-107

Pain C F, McKee C O
1981 Late Quaternary eruptive history of Karkar Island. *Geol Surv Papua New Guinea Mem*, 10: 39-48

Palfreyman W D, Wallace D A, Cooke R J S
1981 Langila volcano: summary of reported eruptive history, and eruption periodicity from 1961 to 1972. *Geol Surv Papua New Guinea Mem*, 10: 125-134

Smith I E M
1981 Young volcanoes in eastern Papua. *Geol Surv Papua New Guinea Mem*, 10: 257-265

Walker G P L, Heming R F, Sprod T J, Walker H R
1981 Latest major eruptions of Rabaul volcano. *Geol Surv Papua New Guinea Mem*, 10: 181-194

Wallace D A, Cooke R J S, Dent V F, Norris D, Johnson R W
1981 Kadovar volcano and investigations of an outbreak of thermal activity in 1976. *Geol Surv Papua New Guinea Mem*, 10: 1-12

Cooke R J S
1981a Eruptive history of the volcano at Ritter Island. *Geol Surv Papua New Guinea Mem*, 10: 115-124

1981b Eruptions at Pago volcano, 1911-1933. *Geol Surv Papua New Guinea Mem*, 10: 135-146

1981c Notes on the activity of Ulawun volcano, 1700-1958: results of literature search. *Geol Surv Papua New Guinea Mem*, 10: 147-152

Blong R J
1982 *The Time of Darkness: Local Legends and Volcanic Reality in Papua New Guinea* [Long I.]. Canberra: Aust Nat Univ Press, 257 p

Lowenstein P L
1982 ★ Problems of volcanic hazards in Papua New Guinea. *Geol Surv Papua New Guinea Rpt*, 82/7: 1-62

Saint Ours P de
1982 Potential volcanic hazards at Manam Island. *Geol Surv Papua New Guinea Rpt*, 82/22: 1-19

Solomon Islands Geol Surv
1982 Vella Lavella Island. *New Georgia Geol Map*, sheet no 1, 1:100,000

Taylor B
1982 Active submarine volcano sampled [Kavachi]. *Eos, Trans Amer Geophys Union*, 63: 609

Johnson R W, Macnab R P, Arculus R J, Ryburn R J, Cooke R J S
1983 Bamus volcano, New Guinea: dormant neighbour of Ulawun, and magnesian-andesite locality. *Geol Rundschau*, 72: 207-237

McKee C O
1983 Volcanic hazards at Ulawun volcano. *Geol Surv Papua New Guinea Rpt*, 83/13: 1-20

Wallace D A, Johnson R W, Chappell B W, Arculus R J, Perfit M R, Crick I H
1983 Cainozoic volcanism of the Tabar, Lihir, Tanga, and Feni Islands, Papua New Guinea: geology, whole-rock analyses, and rock-forming mineral compositions. *Aust Bur Min Resour Geol Geophys Rpt*, 243: 1-62

Mackenzie D E, Johnson R W
1984 Pleistocene volcanoes of the western Papua New Guinea Highlands: morphology, geology, petrography, and modal and chemical analyses. *Aust Bur Min Resour Geol Geophys Rpt*, 246: 1-271

Sillitoe R H, Baker E M, Brook W A
1984 Gold deposits and hydrothermal eruption breccias associated with a maar volcano at Wau, Papua New Guinea. *Econ Geol*, 79: 638-655

Johnson R W, Threlfall N A
1985 *Volcano Town: the 1937-43 Rabaul Eruptions.* Bathurst, Australia: Robert Brown & Assoc, 151 p

McKee C O, Johnson R W, Lowenstein P L, Riley S, Blong R J, de Saint Ours P, Talai B
1985 Rabaul Caldera, Papua New Guinea: volcanic hazards, surveillance, and eruption contingency planning. *Jour Volc Geotherm Res,* 23: 195-238

Okrugin V M
1985 Information note on the results of the 7th cruise of the R/V 'Vulcanolog' in the vicinity of the Solomon Islands. *Solomon Is Geol Div File Rpt,* unpublished

Exon N F, Johnson R W
1986 The elusive Cook volcano and other submarine forearc volcanoes in the Solomon Islands. *Aust Bur Min Resour Geol Geophys Jour,* 10: 77-83

Tiffin D L, Taylor B, Crook K A W, Sinton J, Frankel E
1986 *Surveys in the Solomon Islands and Papua New Guinea using SEAMARC II--A Cruise Report of the R/V Moana Wave, November 29, 1985 - January 9, 1986.* CCOP/SOPAC Cruise Rpt 117 (unpublished)

Johnson R W
1987 Large-scale volcanic cone collapse: the 1888 slope failure of Ritter volcano, and other examples from Papua New Guinea. *Bull Volc,* 49: 669-679

Johnson R W, Tuni D
1987 Kavachi, an active forearc voclano in the western Solomon Islands: reported eruptions between 1950 and 1982. *In:* Taylor B and Exon N F (eds) *Marine Geology, Geophysics, and Geochemistry of the Woodlark Basin, Solomon Islands,* Circum-Pacific Council Energy Min Resour Earth Sci Ser, 7: 89-112

Licence P S, Terrill J E, Fergusson L J
1987 Epithermal gold mineralization, Ambitle Island, Papua New Guinea. *Proc Pacific Rim Cong 1987,* 1: 273-278

Taylor B
1987 A geophysical survey of the Woodlark-Solomons region. *In:* Taylor B and Exon N F (eds) *Marine Geology, Geophysics, and Geochemistry of the Woodlark Basin, Solomon Islands,* Circum-Pacific Council Energy Min Resour Earth Sci Ser, 7: 25-48

Blong R, Aislabie C
1988 The impact of volcanic hazards at Rabaul Papua New Guinea. *Papua New Guinea Inst Natl Affairs, Discussion Pap,* no 33

McKee C O, Patia H, Johnson R W
1988 Contrasting eruptive styles at the adjacent volcanoes Bagana and Billy Mitchell on Bouganville Island, Papua New Guinea. *Proc Kagoshima Internatl Conf Volc,* p 131-134

Crook K A W, Musgrave R J
1989 Triple-junction tectonics, NE Woodlark Basin: construction of "near-trench" of island arc volcanoes on Indo-Australian plate and their transfer to the Pacific plate (abs). *Eos, Trans Amer Geophys Union,* 70: 1319

Hall L H [& Exon N F, Johnson R W]
1989 Discussion [& Reply]: The elusive Cook volcano and other submarine forearc volcanoes in the Solomon Islands. *Aust Bur Min Resour Geol Geophys Jour,* 11: 119-120 [& 121]

McKee C O, Johnson R W, Patia H
1989 Assessment of volcanic hazards on Bougainville Island, Papua New Guinea (abs). *New Mexico Bur Mines Min Resour Bull,* 131: 182

Mori J, McKee C, Talai B, Itikarai I
1989 A summary of precursors to volcanic eruptions in Papua New Guinea. *In:* Latter J H (ed), p 260-291 (see global reference)

Nairn I A, Talai B, Wood C P, McKee C O
1989 Rabaul Caldera, Papua New Guinea - 1:25,000 reconnaissance geological map and eruption history. *New Zeal Geol Surv Dept Sci Ind Res,* geol map

Rogerson R J, Hilyard D B, Finlayson E J, Johnson R W, Mckee C O
1989 The geology and mineral resources of Bougainville and Buka Islands, Papua New Guinea. *Geol Surv Papua New Guinea Mem,* no 16

McKee C O, Johnson R W, Rogerson R
1990 Explosive volcanism on Bougainville Island: ignimbrites, calderas, and volcanic hazards. *Proc Pacific Rim Cong 1990,* 2: 237-245

Machida H, Blong R, Moriwaki H, Hayakawa Y, Talai B, Sprecht J, Torrence R, Pain C
1992 Holocene explosive eruptions of Witori and Dakataua volcanoes in west New Britain, Papua New Guinea and their possible impact of human environment. *29th Internatl Geol Cong, Kyoto, abs,* 2: 506

Lolok D, McKee C O
1993 Eruption history, stratigraphy and petrology of the pyroclastic sequence at Hargy volcano, Papua New Guinea (abs). *IAVCEI, Canberra Mtg Abs,* p 63

Patia H, McKee C O
1993 Lolobau volcano, Papua New Guinea - cyclic basaltic to rhyodacitic eruptions and phreatomagmantic activity (abs). *IAVCEI Canberra Conf Abs* (revised abs)

VANUATU AREA (0507-08)

Atkin J
1868 On volcanoes in the New Hebrides and Bank's Islands. *Proc Geol Soc London,* 24: 305-307

Purey-Cust H E
1896 The eruption of Ambrym Island, New Hebrides, south-west Pacific, 1894. *Geog Jour,* 8: 585-602

Phillips C
1899 The volcanoes of the Pacific. *Trans New Zeal Inst,* 31: 510-551

Gregory J W
1917 The Ambrym eruptions of 1913-14. *Geol Mag,* 4: 529-540

Taylor G A
1956 Australian National Committee on Geodesy and Geophysics. Report of the Sub-Committee on Vulcanology, 1953 Review of volcanic activity in the Territory of Papua-New Guinea, the Solomon and New Hebrides Islands, 1951-53. *Bull Volc,* 18: 25-38

Fisher N H
1957 ★ Melanesia. *Catalog of Active Volcanoes of the World,* Rome: IAVCEI, 5: 1-105

Blot C, Priam R
1963 Volcanisme et seismicite dans l'Archipel des Nouvelles-Hebrides. *Bull Volc,* 26: 167-180

New Hebrides Geological Survey
1964-74 Annual report of the Geological Survey. New Hebrides Geol. Survey

Williams C E F, Warden A J
1964 *Progress Report of the Geological Survey for the Period 1959-1962.* New Hebrides: British Service, 75 p

Priam R
1964a Contribution a la connaissance du Volcan de l'Ilot Matthew (sud des Nouvelles-Hebrides). *Bull Volc,* 27: 331-340

1964b Une nouvelle eruption du Volcan de Lopevi (Nouvelle-Hebrides) et son analogie sismique avec les eruptions precedentes. *Bull Volc,* 27: 341-346

Kibblewhite A C
1966 The acoustic detection and location of an underwater volcano [unnamed SW Pacific volcano]. *New Zeal Jour Sci,* 9: 178-199

Warden A J
1967a The 1963-65 eruption of Lopevi volcano (New Hebrides). *Bull Volc,* 30: 277-318

1967b Distribution and development of the volcanoes of the Central Islands. *New Hebrides Geol Surv Ann Rpt 1965,* p 27-33

1967c The geology of the Central Islands. *New Hebrides Condominium Geol Surv Reg Rpt,* 5: 1-108

Stephenson P J, McCall G J H, LeMaitre R W, Robinson G P
1968 The Ambrym Island Research Project. *New Hebrides Geol Surv Ann Rpt 1966,* p 9-15

Mallick D I J, Ash R P
1970 Gaua. *New Hebrides Geol Surv Ann Rpt 1968,* p 27-29

McCall G J H, LeMaitre R W, Malahoff A, Robinson G P, Stephenson P J
1970 The geology and geophysics of the Ambrym Caldera, New Hebrides. *Bull Volc,* 34: 681-696

Warden A J
1970 Evolution of Aoba Caldera volcano, New Hebrides. *Bull Volc,* 34: 107-140

Ash R P
1971 Vanua Lava. *New Hebrides Geol Surv Ann Rpt 1970,* p 7-12

Colley H, Ash R P
1971 The geology of Erromango. *New Hebrides Condominium Geol Surv Reg Rpt,* 112 p

Mallick D I J
1971 Southern Banks Islands. *New Hebrides Geol Surv Ann Rpt 1970,* p 12-16

New Hebrides Geological Survey
1972 Geology of the Central Islands. *New Hebrides Geol Surv,* 1:100,000 geol map sheet 8

1973 Geology of Efate and offshore islands. *New Hebrides Geol Surv,* 1:100,000 geol map sheet 9

1974 Geology of Erromango. *New Hebrides Geol Surv,* 1:100,000 geol map sheet 10

Mallick D I J, Ash R P
1975 Geology of the southern Banks Islands. *New Hebrides Condominium Geol Surv Reg Rpt,* 33 p

New Hebrides Geological Survey
1976 Geology of Pentecost and Ambrym. *New Hebrides Geol Surv*, 1:100,000 geol map sheet 6

New Hebrides Geological Survey
1978a Geology of the Banks Islands. *New Hebrides Geol Surv*, 1:100,000 geol map sheet 2

1978b Geology of Tanna, Aneityum, Futuna and Aniwa. *New Hebrides Geol Surv*, 1:100,000 geol map sheet 11

Carney J N, Macfarlane A
1979 Geology of Tanna, Aneityum, Futuna and Aniwa. *New Hebrides Geol Surv Reg Rpt*, 81 p

New Hebrides Geological Survey
1979 Geology of Aoba and Maewo. *New Hebrides Geol Surv*, 1:100,000 geol map sheet 5

Ash R P, Carney J N, Macfarlane A
1980 Geology of the northern Banks Islands. *New Hebrides Geol Surv Reg Rpt*, 49 p

Maillet P, Monzier M, Lefevre C
1986 Petrology of Matthew and Hunter volcanoes, south New Hebrides island arc (southwest Pacific). *Jour Volc Geotherm Res*, 30: 1-27

Crawford A J, Greene H G, Exon N F
1988 Geology, petrology and geochemistry of submarine volcanoes around Epi Island, New Hebrides island arc. *In*: Greene H G and Wong F L (eds), 8: 301-327 (see below)

Macfarlane A, Carney J N, Crawford A J, Greene H G
1988 Vanuatu--A review of the onshore geology. *In*: Greene H G and Wong F L (eds), 8: 45-91 (see below)

Greene H G, Wong F L (eds)
1988 *Geology and Offshore Resources of Pacific Island Arcs--Vanuatu Region*, Circum-Pacific Council Energy Min Resour Earth Sci Ser, 8: 1-442

Wong F L, Greene H G
1988 Geologic hazards in the central basin region, Vanuatu. *In*: Greene H G and Wong F L (eds), 8: 225-251 (see above)

Eissen J-P, Monzier M, Robin C, Picard C, Douglas C
1990 Report on the volcanological field work on Ambrym and Tanna Islands (Vanuatu) from 2 to 25 September 1990. *Orstom (Noumea) Rapport Missions Sci Terre Geol-Geophys*, 22: 1-22

Eissen J-P, Blot C, Louat R
1991 Chronologie de l'activite volcanique historique de l'arc insulaire des Nouvelles-Hebrides de 1595 a 1991. *ORSTOM Rapports Sci Tech Sci Terre Geol-Geophys*, 2: 1-69

Monzier M, Robin C, Eissen J-P
1993 Kuwae (1425 A.D.): the forgotten caldera. *Jour Volc Geotherm Res*, 59: 207-218

Robin C, Eissen J-P, Monzier M
1993 Giant tuff cone and 12-km-wide associated caldera at Ambrym volcano (Vanuatu, New Hebrides arc). *Jour Volc Geotherm Res*, 55: 225-238

Robin C, Monzier M, Eissen J-P
1994 Formation of the mid-fifteenth century Kuwae caldera (Vanuatu) by an initial hydroclastic and subsequent ignimbritic eruption. *Bull Volc*, 56: 170-183

AUSTRALIA (0509)

Gill E D
1964 Rocks contiguous with the basaltic cuirass of western Victoria. *Proc Roy Soc Victoria*, 77: 331-355

Singleton O P, Joyce E B
1969 Cainozoic volcanicity in Victoria. *Geol Soc Aust Spec Pub*, 2: 145-154

Gill E D
1971 Applications of radiocarbon dating in Victoria, Australia. *Proc Roy Soc Victoria*, 84: 71-85

Thomas L
1976 Geothermal resources in Australia. *In*: *Proc 2nd United Nations Symp Devel Use Geotherm Resour, San Francisco* Washington D C: U S Government Printing Office, 1: 273-274

Sheard M J
1978 The volcanic history of the Mount Gambier volcanic complex, southeast South Australia. *Trans Roy Soc S Aust*, 102: 125-139

Selby J, Sheard M J
1979 Volcanoes of the Mount Gambier area. *South Aust Dept Mines Energy Min Info Ser*, 12 p

Blackburn G, Allison G B, Leaney F W J
1982 Further evidence on the age of tuff at Mt. Gambier, South Australia. *Trans Roy Soc S Aust*, 106: 163-167 (plus vol 108: 130 errata)

Sheard M J
1986 Some volcanological observations at Mount Schank, southeast South Australia. *South Aust Geol Surv, Quart Geol Notes*, 100: 14-20

Smith B W, Prescott J R
1987 Thermoluminescence dating of the eruption at Mt. Schank, South Australia. *Aust Jour Earth Sci*, 34: 335-342

Johnson R W, Knutson J, Taylor S R (eds)
1989 ★ Intraplate Volcanism in Eastern Australia and New Zealand. Cambridge, England: Cambridge Univ Press, 408 p

ANDAMAN IS (0600)

Mallet F R
1885 The volcanoes of Barren Island and Narcondam, in the Bay of Bengal. *Geol Surv India Mem*, 21(4): 251-286

1895 Some early allusions to Barren Island; with a few remarks thereon. *Geol Surv India Mem*, 28(1): 22-34

Neumann van Padang M
1951 ★ Indonesia. *Catalog of Active Volcanoes of the World*, Rome: IAVCEI, 1: 1-271

Krishnan M S
1957 Volcanic episodes in Indian geology. *Jour Madras Univ*, 27: 193-209

Haldar D, Laskar T, Bandyopadhyay P C, Sarkar N K, Biswas J K
1992 Volcanic eruption of the Barren Island volcano, Andaman Sea. *Jour Geol Soc India*, 39: 411-419

Volc Surv Indonesia
1993 *Journal of volcanic activity in Indonesia*, v 1

INDONESIA: SUMATRA & JAVA (0601-03)

Verbeek R D M
1885 *Krakatau*. Batavia: Landsdrukkerij, 495 p

Judd J W
1888 On the volcanic phenomena of the eruption, and on the nature and distribution of the ejected materials. *In*: Symons G J (ed) *The Eruption of Krakatoa and Subsequent Phenomena*, London: Tribner, Roy Soc London Rpt: 1-56

1889 The earlier eruptions of Krakatoa. *Nature*, 40:365-366

Van Gestel J T
1895 The Krakatoa eruption: described for the first time by an eye-witness of its horrors. *The Cosmopolitan*, 18: 719-727

Stehn C E
1927 Die Vulkanicshen Ereignisse in Niederlandisch-Indien in den Jahren 1924-1926. *Zeit Vulk*, 11: 41-52

Jaggar T A
1928 Poisonous gases in Java. *Volcano Lett*, 201: 1

Stehn C E
1928 Volcanological work in the Dutch East Indies during 1923-1926. *Proc 3rd Pacific Sci Cong*, 1: 718-734

Stehn C E
1929a Kawah Komodjang. *4th Pacific Sci Cong Java*, Excur C2, 13 p

1929b Keloet. *4th Pacific Sci Cong Java*, Excur 2A, p 3-23

1929c Tangkoeban Prahoe. *4th Pacific Sci Cong Java*, Excur B3, 22 p

Miyake R A
1930 The eruption of Krakatoa, 1883. *Volcano Lett*, 306: 1-2

Jaggar T A
1932 Eruption of Merapi (Java) 1930. *Volcano Lett*, 387: 1

Hartmann M
1934 The volcanic activity of Merapi volcano (central Java) in its eastern summit area between 1902 and 1908. *Ingenieur Nederlandsch-Indie*, 1: 61-73

Neumann van Padang M
1934 Haben Bei den Ausbruchen des Slametvulkans Eruptionsregen Stattgefunden? *Leidsche Geol Mededel*, 6: 79-97

Kuenen P H
1935 Contributions to the geology of the East Indies from the Snellius expedition, part 1, volcanoes. *Leidsche Geol Mededel*, 7: 273-283

Bemmelen R W van
1937 The volcano-tectonic structure of the residency of Malang (eastern Java). *Ingenieur Nederlandsch-Indie*, 4: 159-172

Neumann van Padang M
1937a Bestaat er Verband Tusschen den Regenval op den de Vulkanen Semeroe en Lamongan en Hunne Uitbarstingen. *Ingenieur Nederlandsch-Indie*, 4: 1-7

1937b De uitbarsting van den Tjerimai in 1937. *Ingenieur Nederlandsch-Indie*, 4: 211-227

Bemmelen R W van
1941 Bulletin of the East Indian Volcanology Survey for the year 1941. *East Indian Volc Surv Bull*, 95-98: 1-110

1949a Report on the volcanic activity and volcanological research in Indonesia during the period 1936-1948. *Bull Volc*, 9: 3-30

1949b ★ The Geology of Indonesia. The Hague: Government Printing Office, v 1, 732 p

Neumann van Padang M
1951 ★ Indonesia. *Catalog of Active Volcanoes of the World*, Rome: IAVCEI, 1: 1-271

Petroeschevsky W A, Klompe T H F
1951 ★ Vulcanological Investigations in Indonesia. *Organization Sci Res Indonesia Pub*, 23: 187-204

de Waard D, Klompe H F
1952 The recent activity of G. Marapi in central Sumatra. *Natuurkundig Tijdschrift Voor Nederlandsch-Indie*, 108: 131-140

Petroeschevsky W A
1952 The volcanic activity in Indonesia during the period 1942-1948. *Berita Gunung Berapi*, 1(1-2): 17-30; (3-4): 9-31

Bemmelen R W van
1956 The influence of geologic events on human history (an example from central Java). *Verh Kon Ned Geol Mijnb Genoot Geol*, 16: 20-36

Decker R W, Hadikusumo D
1961 Results of the 1960 expedition to Krakatau. *Jour Geophys Res*, 66: 3497-3511

Hadikusumo D
1961 Report on the volcanological research and volcanic activity in Indonesia for the period 1950-1957. *Bull Volc Surv Indonesia*, 100: 1-122

Suryo I
1961a Report on the volcanic activity in Indonesia for the year 1958. *Bull Volc Surv Indonesia*, 101: 1-27

1961b Report on the volcanic activity in Indonesia for the year 1959. *Bull Volc Surv Indonesia*, 102: 1-31

Neumann van Padang M
1963 The temperatures in the crater region of some Indonesian volcanoes before the eruption. *Bull Volc*, 26: 319-336

Zen M T, Hadikusumo D
1964 Recent changes in the Anak-Krakatau volcano. *Bull Volc*, 27: 259-268

Zen M T
1970 Growth and state of Anak Krakatau in September 1968. *Bull Volc*, 34: 205-215

Bemmelen R W van
1971 Four volcanic outbursts that influenced human history. Toba, Sunda, Merapi, and Thera. *In*: Kaloyeropoyloy A (ed) *Acta 1st International Science Congress on the Volcano of Thera*, Athens: Arch Serv Greece, p 5-50

Posavec M, Taylor D, Van Leeuwen T, Spector A
1973 Tectonic controls of volcanism and complex movements along the Sumatran fault system. *Geol Soc Malaysia Bull*, 6: 43-60

Suryo I
1978 Volcanic phenomena during the year 1960. *Bull Volc Surv Indonesia*, 103: 1-42

Kusumadinata K
1979 ★ Data Dasar Gunungapi Indonesia. Bandung: Volc Surv Indonesia, 820 p (in Indonesian)

Bennett J D, Bridge D M, Cameron N R, Djuneddin A, Ghazali S A, Jeffery D H, Keats W, Rock N M S, Thompson S J, Whandoyo R
1981 Geologic map of the Banda Aceh quadrangle, North Sumatra. *Geol Res Devel Centre Indonesia*, 1:250,000 scale

Latter J H
1981 Tsunamis of volcanic origin: summary of causes, with particular reference to Krakatoa, 1883. *Bull Volc*, 44: 467-490

Self S, Rampino M R
1981 The 1883 eruption of Krakatau. *Nature*, 294: 699-704

Le Guern F, Tazieff H, Faivre Pierret R
1982 An example of health hazard: people killed by gas during a phreatic eruption: Dieng Plateau (Java Indonesia), Feb 20th 1979. *Bull Volc*, 45: 153-156

Rock N M S, Syah H H, Davis A E, Hutchison D, Styles M T, Lena R
1982 Permian to Recent volcanism in northern Sumatra, Indonesia: a preliminary study of its distribution, chemistry, and peculiarities. *Bull Volc*, 45: 127-152

Neumann van Padang M
1983 History of volcanology in the former Netherlands East Indies. *Scripta Geol*, 71: 1-76

Simkin T, Fiske R S
1983 *Krakatau 1883: The Volcanic Eruption and its Effects*. Washington, D C: Smithsonian Inst Press, 464 p

Katili J A, Sudradjat A
1984a *Galunggung: the 1982-1983 eruption*. Bandung: Volc Surv Indon, 102 p

1984b The devastating 1983 eruption of Colo volcano, Una-Una Island, central Sulawesi, Indonesia [also Galunggung]. *Geol Jahrb*, 75: 27-47

Volc Surv Indonesia
1984 Tangkubanparahu excursion. *Unpublished ms*, 14 p

Alzwar M
1985 Gunung Kelut. *Bull Volc Surv Indonesia*, 108: 1-60 (in Indonesian)

de Neve G A
1985 Earlier eruptive activities of Krakatau in historic time and during the Quaternary. *In*: Sastrapradja D et al (eds) *Proc Symp on 100 Years Devel of Krakatau and its Surroundings*, Jakarta: Lembaga Ilmu Pengetahuan Indonesia, 1: 35-46

Siswowidjoyo S
1985 The renewed activity of Krakatau volcano after its catastrophic eruption in 1883. *In*: Sastraptradja D et al (eds) *Proc Symp on 100 Years Devel of Krakatau and its Surroundings*, Jakarta: Lembaga Ilmu Pengetahuan Indonesia, 1: 192-198

Suryo I
1985 Report on the volcanic activity in Indonesia during the period 1964-1970. *Bull Volc Surv Indonesia*, 106: 1-150

Djumarma A, Bronto S, Bahar I, Suparban F, Sukihar R, Newhall C, Holcomb R T, Banks N G, Torley R, Lockwood J P, Tilling R I, Rubin M, del Marmol M A
1986 Did Merapi volcano (central Java) erupt catastrophically in 1006 A.D.? (abs). *IAVCEI Cong, New Zeal, Abs*, p 236

Knight M D, Walker G P L, Ellwood B B, Diehl J F
1986 Stratigraphy, paleomagnetism, and magnetic fabric of the Toba Tuffs: constraints on the sources and eruptive styles. *Jour Geophys Res*, 91: 10,355-10,382

Sukhyar R, Sumartadipura N S, Effendi W
1986 Geologic map of Dieng volcano complex, central Java. *Volc Surv Indonesia*, geol map

Suryo I
1986 G Semeru. *Bull Volc Surv Indonesia*, 111: 1-52 (in Indonesian)

Casadevall T J, de Neve G, Kaswanda O, MacLeod N S
1989 The 1988 eruption of Anak Krakatau, Indonesia: a return to the pre-1981 compositions (abs). *New Mexico Bur Mines Min Resour Bull*, 131: 46

Dvorak J, Matahelumual J, Okamura A T, Said H, Casadevall T J, Mulyadi D
1990 Recent uplift and hydrothermal activity at Tangkuban Parahu volcano, west Java, Indonesia. *Bull Volc*, 53: 20-28

Chesner C A, Rose W I
1991 Stratigraphy of the Toba tuffs and the evolution of the Toba caldera complex, Sumatra, Indonesia. *Bull Volc*, 53: 343-356

Volc Surv Indonesia
1993 *Journal of volcanic activity in Indonesia, v 1*

INDONESIA: EAST & NORTH (0604-10)

Ross J T
1816 Narrative of the effects of the eruption from the Tomboro Mountain in the Island of Sumbawa on the 11th and 12th of April, 1815. *Lembaga Kebudajaan Indonesia Vehandelingen*, 8: 343-460

Wichmann A
1902 Der Vulkan der Insel Una-Una (Nanguna) in Busen von Tomini, Celebes. *Jour German Geol Soc*, 54: 144-158

Gogarten E
1918 Die Vulkane der Nordlichen Molukken. *Zeit Vulk*, 2: 1-298

Kemmerling G L L
1923 De vulkanen van de Sangi-Archipel en van de Minahassa. *Vulkanol Seism Mededeelingen Dienst Mijnw Ned-Indie*, 5: 1-157

Stehn C E
1927 Die Vulkanicshen Ereignisse in Niederlandisch-Indien in den Jahren 1924-1926. *Zeit Vulk*, 11: 41-52

1928 Volcanological work in the Dutch East Indies during 1923-1926. *Proc 3rd Pacific Sci Cong*, 1: 718-734

Jaggar T A
1928 The Rokatinda eruption. *Volcano Lett*, 207: 1

Boerema J
1929 A new undersea volcano. *Proc 4th Pacific Sci Cong*, 2B: 919-920

Jaggar T A
1929 The Bali eruption 1926. *Volcano Lett*, 215: 1

Neumann van Padang M
1930 Padoweh. *Vulkanol Seism Mededeelingen Dienst Mijnw Ned-Indie*, 11: 1-141

Bemmelen R W van
1949 Report on the volcanic activity and volcanological research in Indonesia during the period 1936-1948. *Bull Volc*, 9: 3-30

Neumann van Padang M
1951 ★ Indonesia. *Catalog of Active Volcanoes of the World*, Rome: IAVCEI, 1: 1-271

Petroeschevsky W A, Klompe T H F
1951 ★ Vulcanological Investigations in Indonesia. *Organization Sci Res Indonesia Pub*, 23: 187-204

Petroeschevsky W A
1952 The volcanic activity in Indonesia during the period 1942-1948. *Berita Gunung Berapi*, 1(1-2): 17-30; (3-4): 9-31

Neumann van Padang M
1959 Changes in the top of Mount Ruang (Indonesia). *Geol En Mijnbouw*, 21: 113-118

Hadikusumo D
1961 Report on the volcanological research and volcanic activity in Indonesia for the period 1950-1957. *Bull Volc Surv Indonesia*, 100: 1-122

Suryo I
1961a Report on the volcanic activity in Indonesia for the year 1958. *Bull Volc Surv Indonesia*, 101: 1-27
1961b Report on the volcanic activity in Indonesia for the year 1959. *Bull Volc Surv Indonesia*, 102: 1-31

Katili J A, Kartaadiputra L, Surio
1963 Magma type and tectonic position of the Una-Una Island, Indonesia. *Bull Volc*, 26: 431-454

Verstappen H Th
1964 Some volcanoes of Halmahera (Moluccas) and their geomorphological setting. *Ned Aardr Gen*, 81: 297-316

Zelenov K K
1964 The submarine volcano Banua Wuhu, Indonesia. *Bandung Inst Tech Dept Geol Contr*, 55: 19-34

Zen M T, Hadikusumo D
1964 Recent changes in the Anak-Krakatau volcano. *Bull Volc*, 27: 259-268

Kirk H J C
1968 The igneous rocks of Sarawak and Sabah. *Geol Surv Borneo Region Malasia Bull*, 5: 1-220

Effendi A C
1976 Geologic map of the Manado quadrangle, north Sulawesi. *Volc Surv Indonesia*, geol map

Kusumadinata K
1977 Data on the Dukono volcano. *Berita Direktorat Geol Geosurv Newsl*, 9: 185

Sumartadipura A S
1977 Photo interpretation of Umsini volcano. *Geosurv Newsl*, 9: 99-101

Suryo I
1978 Volcanic phenomena during the year 1960. *Bull Volc Surv Indonesia*, 103: 1-42

Jezek P
1979 Volcano resume--Ibu. *Volcano News*, 1: 7

Kusumadinata K
1979 ★ Data Dasar Gunungapi Indonesia. Bandung: Volc Surv Indonesia, 820 p (in Indonesian)

Tjia H D, Hadian R, Sumailani A R, Martono A
1980 The nature of Umsini volcano, Irian Jaya, Indonesia. *Bull Volc*, 43: 595-600

Lockwood J P, Melson W G, Lanphere M A, Bronto S
1981 Petrology and eruptive characteristics of Gamalama volcano, Ternate Island, Indonesia (abs). *IAVCEI, Tokyo Mtg Abs*, p 207

Bronto S, Hadisantono R D, Lockwood J P
1982 Geologic map of Gamalama volcano, Ternate, North Maluku. *Volc Surv Indonesia*, 1:25,000 geol map and text

Davis T A
1982 Report on visits of volcano affected areas of Mt. Soputan of Minahasa District, North Sulawesi Province. *Unpublished ms*, 5 p

Neumann van Padang M
1983 History of volcanology in the former Netherlands East Indies. *Scripta Geol*, 71: 1-76

Katili J A, Sudradjat A
1984a *Galunggung: the 1982-1983 eruption* [also Colo]. Bandung: Volc Surv Indonesia, 102 p
1984b The devastating 1983 eruption of Colo volcano, Una-Una Island, central Sulawesi, Indonesia. *Geol Jahrb*, 75: 27-47

Self S, Rampino M R, Newton M S, Wolff J A
1984 Volcanological Study of the Great Tambora eruption of 1815. *Geology*, 12: 659-663

Stothers R B
1984 The great Tambora eruption in 1815 and its aftermath. *Science*, 224: 1191-1198

Varekamp J C, Snellius II Shipboard Party
1984 The Banda arc volcanoes, eastern Indonesia (abs). *Eos, Trans Amer Geophys Union*, 65: 1135

Matahelumual J
1985 G Awu. *Bull Volc Surv Indonesia*, 107: 1-51 (in Indonesian)

Suryo I
1985 Report on the volcanic activity in Indonesia during the period 1964-1970. *Bull Volc Surv Indonesia*, 106: 1-150

Manalu L
1986 G Karangetang. *Bull Volc Surv Indonesia*, 109: 1-48 (in Indonesian)

Wheller G E
1986 Petrogenesis of Batur caldera, Bali, and the geochemistry of Sunda-Banda arc basalts. *PhD thesis*, Univ Tasmania

Matahelumual J
1986a G Makian. *Bull Volc Surv Indonesia*, 110: 1-37 (in Indonesian)

Matahelumual J
1986b G Lokon-Empung. *Bull Volc Surv Indonesia*, 114: 1-52 (in Indonesian)

Casadevall T J, Pardyanto L, Abas H, Tulus
1989 The 1988 eruption of Banda Api volcano, Maluku, Indonesia. *Geol Indonesia*, 12: 603-635

Sigurdsson H, Carey S
1989 Plinian and co-ignimbrite tephra fall from the 1815 eruption of Tambora volcano. *Bull Volc*, 51: 243-270
1992 Eruptive history of Tambora volcano, Indonesia. *In*: Degens E T, Wong H K, Zen M T (eds) *The Sea off Mount Tambora*, Mittelschen Geol-Palaont Inst Univ Hamburg, 70: 187-206

Volc Surv Indonesia
1993 *Journal of volcanic activity in Indonesia, v 1*

PHILIPPINES (0700-04)

Packard R L
1900 Remarkable volcanic eruptions in the Philippines. *Popular Sci Monthly*, 56: 374-379

Worcester D C
1912 Taal volcano and its recent destructive eruption. *Natl Geog*, 23: 313-368

Faustino L A
1934 Taal volcano and its eruptions. *Proc 5th Pacific Sci Cong*, 3: 2377-2378

Selga M
1937 Las erupciones de Mayon en 1853. *Boll Soc Sismologica Italiana*, 35(3-4): 165-167

Alcaraz A, Abad L F, Quema J C
1952 Hibok-Hibok volcano, Philippine Islands, and activity since 1948. *Volcano Lett*, 516: 1-6 & 517: 1-4

Neumann van Padang M
1953 ★ Philippine Islands and Cochin China. *Catalog of Active Volcanoes of the World*, Rome: IAVCEI, 2: 1-49

Macdonald G A, Alcaraz A
1954 Philippine volcanoes during 1953 and 1954. *Volcano Lett*, 523: 1-5

Alcaraz A, Abad L F, Tupas M H
1956 The Didicas submarine volcano. *Proc 8th Pacific Sci Cong*, 2: 139-156

Alvir A D
1956 A cluster of little known Phillipine volcanoes. *Proc 8th Pacific Sci Cong*, 2: 205-206

Nakamura K
1966 The magmatophreatic eruption of Taal volcano in 1965, Phillippines. *Jour Geog Tokyo Geog Soc*, 75: 33-44 (in Japanese with English abs)

Moore J G, Melson W G
1969 Nuees ardentes of the 1968 eruption of Mayon volcano, Philippines. *Bull Volc*, 33: 600-620

Santos G G, Wainerdi R E
1969 Notes on the 1965 Taal volcanic eruptions. *Bull Volc*, 33: 503-529

Ebasco Services
1977 Preliminary safety analysis report, Philippine Nuclear Power Plant #1 [Pinatubo]. *Philippine Atomic Energy Comm Open-File Rpt and response to questions*

Newhall C G
1977 Geology and petrology of Mayon volcano, southeastern Luzon, Philippines. *MSci thesis*, Univ Calif (Davis), 292 p
1979 Temporal variation in the lavas of Mayon volcano, Philippines. *Jour Volc Geotherm Res*, 5: 61-84

Nuclear Regulatory Commission
1979 *Initial Site Examination Information Review, Philippine Nuclear Power Plant, National Power Corporation, Napot Point Site* [Mariveles]. Washington, D C: Nuclear Regulatory Commission

COMVOL
1981 H Catalogue of Philippine volcanoes and solfataric areas. *Philippine Comm Volc*, 87 p

Ruelo H B
1983 Morphological and crater development of Mt. Tabaro eruption site, Taal volcano, Philippines. *Philippine Jour Volc*, 1: 19-68

Wolfe J A, Self S
1983 Structural lineaments and Neogene volcanism in southwestern Luzon. *In:* Hayes D E (ed) *The Tectonic and Geological Evolution of Southeast Asian Seas and Islands: Part 2*, Amer Geophys Union Monograph 27

Corpuz E G
1985 Chronology of the September-October 1984 eruption of Mayon volcano, Philippines. *Philippine Jour Volc*, 2: 36-51

Magalit C T, Ruelo H B
1985 Features and characteristics of the 1984 Mayon lava flows. *Philippine Jour Volc*, 2: 52-67

Punongbayan R S
1985 An approach for estimating ages of active volcanoes [Mayon]. *Philippine Jour Volc*, 2: 191-205

Ramos-Villarta S C, Corpuz E G, Newhall C G
1985 Eruptive history of Mayon volcano, Philippines. *Philippine Jour Volc*, 2: 1-35

Aguila L G, Newhall C G, Miller C D, Listanco E L
1986 Reconnaissance geology of a large debris avalanche from Iriga volcano, Philippines. *Philippine Jour Volc*, 3: 54-72

PHIVOLCS
1986 Close monitoring and surveillance of Canlaon volcano. *Nat Sci Tech Auth Ann Rpt*, p 2

Richard M, Maury R C, Bellon H, Stephan J F, Boirat J M, Calderon A
1986 Geology of Mt. Iraya volcano and Batan Island, northern Philippines. *Philippine Jour Volc*, 3: 1-27

Bautista L P
1988 The 1988 Bulusan volcano activity. *Phivolcs Observer*, 4(1)

Sincioco J
1988 The 1988 eruptive activity of Canlaon volcano. *Phivolcs Observer*, 3: 3

Defant M J, Jacques D, Maury R C, de Boer J, Joron J-L
1989 Geochemistry and tectonic setting of the Luzon arc, Philippines. *Geol Soc Amer Bull*, 101: 663-672

PHIVOLCS
1991 H Volcanoes of the Philippines. Manila: PHIVOLCS Press, 41 p

Pinatubo Volcano Observatory Team
1991 Lessons from a major eruption: Mt. Pinatubo, Philippines. *Eos, Trans Amer Geophys Union*, 72: 545, 552-553, 555

Ruaya J R, Panem C C
1991 Mt. Natib, Philippines: a geochemical model of a caldera-hosted geothermal system. *Jour Volc Geotherm Res*, 45: 255-265

Salise P C, Manzano J A, Sierra J, Barela H
1991 Geo-environmental hazard investigation of Malindang Range volcanic complex and risk assessment of town centres, Misamis Occidental (abs). *Geol Soc Philippines 4th Ann Geol Conv Abs*, p 16-17

SOUTHEAST ASIA (0705)

Anonymous
1923 Two new volcanic islands in the China Sea. *Geog Jour*, 62: 135-138

Patte E
1925 Etude de l'Ile des Cendres, volcan apparu au large de la Cote d'Annam. *Bull Serv Geol Indochina*, 13: 5-19

Neumann van Padang M
1953 H Philippine Islands and Cochin China. *Catalog of Active Volcanoes of the World*, Rome: IAVCEI, 2: 1-49

Saurin E
1967 La neotectonique de l'Indochine. *Rev Geog Phys Geol Dynamique*, 9: 143-152

Stephenson D, Marshall T R
1984 The petrology and mineralogy of Mt. Popa volcano and the nature of the late-Cenozoic Burma volcanic area. *Jour Geol Soc London*, 141: 747-762

Bondarenko V I, Nadezhnyi A M
1985 Main structural features and morphology of the volcanic zone and individual submarine volcanoes in the vicinity of the Catwic-Phu Quy islands on the Vietnamese shelf as revealed by continuous seismic profiling data. *Volc Seism*, 1985(5): 34-43 (English translation 1989, 7: 701-716)

Chen S (ed)
1986 *Atlas of Geo-Science, Analysis of Landsat Imagery in China*. Beijing: Chinese Acad Sci Press, 228 p

Whitford-Stark J L
1987 H A survey of Cenozoic volcanism on mainland Asia. *Geol Soc Amer Spec Pap*, 213: 74

TAIWAN & SW JAPAN (0801-02)

Milne J
1886 H The volcanoes of Japan. *Trans Seism Soc Japan*, 9: 1-184

Jaggar T A
1924 Sakurajima, Japan's greatest volcanic eruption: a convulsion of nature whose ravages were minimized by scientific knowledge, compared with the terrors and destruction of the recent Tokyo earthquake. *Natl Geog*, 65: 441-470

Honma F
1926 Beppu, the Hot-Spring City. *Pan-Pacific Sci Cong Guidebook Excur*, E-1.5: 1-16

Iki T
1926 Geological notes on the Aso volcano. *Pan-Pacific Sci Cong Guidebook Excur*, E-4: 1-14

Iki T, Tsuboi S
1926 Notes on the great eruption of Sakura-jima volcano in 1914. *Pan-Pacific Sci Cong Guidebook Excur*, E-4.5: 1-12

Onishi K
1930 Eruption of Sakurajima 1914. *Volcano Lett*, 308: 1-3

Jaggar T A
1931 Japanese volcanoes arranged in series. *Volcano Lett*, 323: 1-3

Tanakadate H
1931 Volcanic activity in Japan and vicinity during the period between 1924 and 1931. *Japan Jour Astron Geophys*, 9: 47-64

1934 Volcanic activity in Japan during the period between June 1931 and June 1934. *Japan Jour Astron Geophys*, 12: 89-108

Tsuya H, Minakami T
1940 Minor activity of volcano Sakura-zima in October, 1939. *Bull Earthq Res Inst, Univ Tokyo*, 18: 319-339 (in Japanese with English abs)

Minakami T
1950 Report on the volcanic activities in Japan during 1939-1947. *Bull Volc*, 10: 45-58

Minakami T, Sakuma S
1953 Report on volcanic activities and volcanological studies concerning them in Japan during 1948-1951. *Bull Volc*, 14: 79-132

Kuno H
1962 H Japan, Taiwan and Marianas. *Catalog of Active Volcanoes of the World*, Rome: IAVCEI, 11: 1-332

Minakami T
1962 Report on volcanic activity in Japan for the period from 1957 to 1959. *Bull Volc*, 24: 7-22

Aramaki S, Yamasaki M
1963 Pyroclastic flows in Japan. *Bull Volc*, 26: 89-99

Tsuya H, Morimoto R
1963 Types of volcanic eruptions in Japan. *Bull Volc*, 26: 209-222

Nakamura M
1967 On the volcanic products and history of Kaimon-dake volcano. *Bull Volc Soc Japan*, 12: 119-131

Minakami T, Shimozuru D, Miyazaki T, Hiraga S, Yamaguti M
1968 The 1959 eruption of Simmoe-dake and the 1961 Iimori-yama earthquake swarm. *Bull Earthq Res Inst, Univ Tokyo*, 46: 965-992

Katayama N
1974 Old records of natural phenomena concerning the Shimabara catastrophe. *Sci Rpt Shimabara Volc Observ, Fac Sci Kyushu Univ*, 9: 1-45 (in Japanese with English abs)

Machida H
1976 Stratigraphy and chronology of late Quaternary marker-tephras in Japan. *Tokyo Metropolitan Univ Geog Rpt*, 11: 109-132

Sumi K, Takashima I
1976 Absolute ages of the hydrothermal alteration halos and associated volcanic rocks in some Japanese geothermal fields. *In: Proc 2nd United Nations Symp Devel Use Geotherm Resour, San Francisco* Washington D C: U S Government Printing Office 1: 625-634

Yamasaki T, Hayashi M
1976 Geologic background of Otake and other geothermal areas in north-central Kyushu, southwestern Japan. *In: Proc 2nd United Nations Symp Devel Use Geotherm Resour, San Francisco* Washington D C: U S Government Printing Office, 1: 673-684

Chen C
1978 Petrochemistry and origin of Pleistocene volcanic rocks from northern Taiwan. *Bull Volc*, 41: 513-528

Suwa A
1978 The surveillance of volcanic activities in Japan. *Bull Volc Soc Japan*, 23: 83-89 (in Japanese with English abs)

Nakamura M
1980 Possibility of new volcanic activity at Ibusuki volcanic field, Kyushu, Japan. *Bull Volc Soc Japan*, 25: 195-205 (in Japanese with English abs)

Aramaki S, Fukuyama H, Kamo K, Kamada M
1981 Sakurajima volcano. *In*: Kubotera A (ed), p 1-17 (see below)

Chen C H
1981 Petrochemical aspects and tectonic implication of Pleistocene andesitic rocks of northern Taiwan and off-shore islets (abs). *IAVCEI, Tokyo Mtg Abs*, p 50-51

Kobayashi T, Aramaki S, Watanabe T, Kamada M
1981 Kirishima volcano. *In*: Kubotera A (ed), p 18-32 (see below)

Kubotera A (ed)
1981 *Sym Arc Volc Field Excursion Guide to Sakurajima, Kirishima and Aso Volcanoes*. Tokyo: Volc Soc Japan, 52 p

Ono K, Kubotera A, Ota K
1981 Aso volcano. *In*: Kubotera A (ed), p 33-52 (see above)

Kato Y
1982 Position and amount of erupted pumice from the Iriomote submarine volcano, Ryukyu Islands. *Ryukyu Is Geol Studies*, 6: 41-47

Kobayashi T
1982 Geology of Sakurajima volcano: a review. *Bull Volc Soc Japan*, 27: 277-292 (in Japanese with English abs)

Ono K, Soya T, Hosono T
1982 Geology of the Satsuma-Io-Jima district. *Geol Surv Japan*, 1:50,000 geol map and text (in Japanese)

Aramaki S
1984 Formation of the Aira caldera, southern Kyushu, 22,000 years ago. *Jour Geophys Res*, 89: 8485-8501

Ota K
1984 Unzen volcano. *Nagasaki Prefecture*, 98 p (in Japanese)

Ono K, Watanabe K
1985 Geologic map of Aso volcano. *Geol Surv Japan*, 1:50,000 geol map and text (in Japanese with English summary)

Chen S (ed)
1986 *Atlas of Geo-Science, Analysis of Landsat Imagery in China*. Beijing: Chinese Acad Sci Press, 228 p

Moriwaki H, Machida H, Hatsumi Y, Matsushima Y
1986 Phreatomagmatic eruptions affected by postglacial transgression in the northern coastal area of Kagoshima Bay, southern Kyushu, Japan. *Chigaku Zasshi (Jour Geog)*, 95: 24-43 (in Japanese with English abs)

Japan Assoc Quaternary Research
1987 *Quaternary Maps of Japan: Landforms, Geology, and Tectonics*. Tokyo: Univ Tokyo Press

Kyoto Univ. Disaster Prevention Institute
1987 *Research on Eruptions--Prediction of Volcanic Eruptions and the Role of Universities*. Kyoto Univ Disaster Prevention Inst and Nat Univ Res Group for Volcanoes

Inoue K
1988 The growth history of Takachiho composite volcano in the Kirishima volcano group. *Ganko (Petr Min)*, 83: 26-41 (in Japanese with English abs)

Kagoshima Prefectural Museum
1988 *The 1914 eruption of Sakurajima, Japan*. Kagoshima, Japan: Kagoshima Prefectural Museum, 64 p

Kobayashi T, Ishihara K
1988 Historic eruptions and recent activities. *In*: Aramaki S, Kamo K, Kamada M (eds) *A Guide Book for Sakurajima Volcano*, Kagoshima Internatl Conf on Volcanoes, p 7-11

Naruo H
1988 The influence of the earliest eruption of Kaimon Dake volcano on a society of the latter term of the Jomon era (ca 4000 BP) in southern Kyushu (abs). *Kagoshima Internatl Conf Volc Abs*, p 562

Ui T, Kobayashi T
1988 Catastrophic pyroclastic flow eruption at Kikai caldera, 6300 years ago (abs). *Kagoshima Internatl Conf Volc Abs*, p 396

Machida H
1990 Frequency and magnitude of catastrophic explosive volcanism in the Japan region during the past 130 ka: implications for human occupance of volcanic regions. *Geol Soc Aust Symp Proc*, 1: 27-36

Murayama I
1990 ★ Volcanoes of Japan (III). Tokyo: Daimedo, 259 p (in Japanese)

Ohta T, Hasenaka T, Fujimaki H
1990 Geology and petrography of Yufu-Tsurumi volcano group, Oita Prefecture. *Jour Min Petr Econ Geol*, 85: 113-129 (in Japanese with English abs)

Imura R, Kobayashi T
1991 Eruptions of Shinmoedake volcano, Kirishima volcano group, in the last 300 years. *Bull Volc Soc Japan*, 36: 135-148 (in Japanese)

Imura R
1992 Minor phreatic activity of Shinmoedake, Kirishima volcano, in 1991-92. *Bull Volc Soc Japan*, 37: 281-283 (in Japanese)

Machida H, Arai F
1992 ★ Atlas of tephra in and around Japan. Tokyo: Univ Tokyo Press, 276 p (in Japanese)

Hayakawa Y
1994 ★ A catalog of the volcanic eruptions during the last 2000 years in Japan. *Sci Rpt Fac Education Gumma Univ*, in press (in Japanese with English abs)

JAPAN: HONSHU (0803)

Milne J
1886 ★ The volcanoes of Japan. *Trans Seism Soc Japan*, 9: 1-184

Sekiya S, Kikuchi Y
1889 The eruption of Bandai-San. *Jour College Sci Imperial Univ Japan*, 3: 91-172

Powers S
1915 The eruption of Yake-dake, central Japan, 1915. *Zeit Vulk*, 3: 34-35

Tsuboi S, Sugi K
1926 Geological guide to the Nikko district. *Pan-Pacific Sci Cong Guidebook Excur*, B-1: 4-25

Tanakadate H
1931 Volcanic activity in Japan and vicinity during the period between 1924 and 1931. *Japan Jour Astron Geophys*, 9: 47-64

Jaggar T A
1931 Japanese volcanoes arranged in series. *Volcano Lett*, 323: 1-3

Tanakadate H
1934 Volcanic activity in Japan during the period between June 1931 and June 1934. *Japan Jour Astron Geophys*, 12: 89-108

Minakami T
1938 Magnetic surveys of volcano Kusatu-Sirane. *Bull Earthq Res Inst, Univ Tokyo*, 16: 117-124

1950 Report on the volcanic activities in Japan during 1939-1947. *Bull Volc*, 10: 45-58

Ichimura T
1951 Geological investigations on the Zao volcanoes. 1. Goshikidake, a central cone of the Zao proper. *Bull Earthq Res Inst, Univ Tokyo*, 39: 327-339

Minakami T, Hiraga S
1951 The minor activity of volcano Azuma in February 1950. *Bull Earthq Res Inst, Univ Tokyo*, 39: 383-391

Tsuya H
1955 Geological and petrological studies of volcano Fuji. Part 5: on the 1707 eruption of volcano Fuji. *Bull Earthq Res Inst, Univ Tokyo*, 33: 341-383

Aramaki S
1956 The 1783 activity of Asama volcano, part 1. *Japan Jour Geol Geog*, 27: 189-229

Minakami T
1956 Report on volcanic activities and volcanological studies in Japan for the period from 1951 to 1954. *Bull Volc*, 18: 39-76

Aramaki S
1957 The 1783 activity of Asama volcano, part 2. *Japan Jour Geol Geog*, 28: 11-33

Ishikawa T, Minato M, Kuno H, Matsumoto T, Yagi K
1957 Welded tuffs and deposits of pumice flow and nuee ardente in Japan. *20th Internatl Geol Cong, Mexico City*, Sec 1: 137-150

Minakami T, Mogi K
1959 Report on volcanic activities in Japan for the period from 1954 to 1957. *Bull Volc*, 21: 127-152

Kuno H
1962 ★ Japan, Taiwan and Marianas. *Catalog of Active Volcanoes of the World*, Rome: IAVCEI, 11: 1-332

Murai I
1962 A brief note on the eruption of the Yake-dake volcano of June 17, 1962. *Bull Earthq Res Inst, Univ Tokyo*, 40: 805-814

Aramaki S
1963 Geology of Asama volcano. *Univ Tokyo Fac Sci Jour*, 14: 229-443

Aramaki S, Yamasaki M
1963 Pyroclastic flows in Japan. *Bull Volc*, 26: 89-99

Tsuya H, Morimoto R
1963 Types of volcanic eruptions in Japan. *Bull Volc*, 26: 209-222

Machida H
1964 Tephrochronological study of volcano Fuji and adjacent areas. *Chigaku Zasshi (Jour Geog)*, 73: 293-308, 337-350 (in Japanese with English abs)

Murai I, Hosoya Y
1964 The eruptive activity of Mt. Asama from 1958 to 1961 and the associated minor pyroclastic flows. *Bull Earthq Res Inst, Univ Tokyo*, 42: 203-236

Yamasaki M, Nakanishi N, Kaseno Y
1964 Nuee ardente deposit of Hakusan volcano. *Sci Rpt Kanazawa Univ*, 9: 189-201

Yamasaki M, Nakanishii N, Miyata K
1966 History of Tateyama volcano. *Sci Rpt Kanazawa Univ*, 11: 73-92

Machida H
1967 The recent development of the Fuji volcano, Japan. *Tokyo Metropolitan Univ Geog Rpt*, 2: 11-20

Tomita T
1969 Volcanic geology of the Cenozoic alkaline petrographic province of eastern Asia. *In*: Ogura T (ed) *Geology and Minerals of the Far East*, Tokyo: Univ Tokyo Press, p 139-179

Kuno H, Oki Y, Ogino K, Hirota S
1970 Structure of the Hakone caldera as revealed by drilling. *Bull Volc*, 34: 713-725

Moriya I
1970 History of Akagi volcano. *Bull Volc Soc Japan*, 15: 120-131 (in Japanese with English abs)

Yagi K
1971 Some genetic problems of the calderas in Japan. *In*: Kaloyeropoyloy A (ed) *Acta 1st International Science Congress on the Volcano of Thera*, Athens: Arch Serv Greece, p 73-87

Nakagawa H, Chuman N, Ishida T, Matsuyama T, Nanasaki O, Oide K, Oike S, Takahashi H
1972 Historical development of Towada volcano-an outline. *Tohoku Univ Inst Geol Paleont Contr*, 73: 7-18 (in Japanese with English abs)

Yagi K, Takeshita H, Oba Y
1972 Petrological study on the 1970 eruption of Akita-Komagatake volcano, Japan. *Hokkaido Univ Fac Sci Jour*, 15: 109-138

Japan Meteorological Agency
1975 ★ National Catalogue of the Active Volcanoes in Japan. Tokyo: Japan Meteorological Agency, 119 p (in Japanese)

Hayatsu K
1976 Geologic study on the Myoko volcanoes, central Japan - Part 1. Stratigraphy. *Kyoto Univ Ser Geol Min*, 42: 131-170

Machida H
1976 Stratigraphy and chronology of late Quaternary marker-tephras in Japan. *Tokyo Metropolitan Univ Geog Rpt*, 11: 109-132

Sumi K, Takashima I
1976 Absolute ages of the hydrothermal alteration halos and associated volcanic rocks in some Japanese geothermal fields. *In: Proc 2nd United Nations Symp Devel Use Geotherm Resour, San Francisco* Washington D C: U S Government Printing Office 1: 625-634

Ui T, Nakamura K, Shibahashi K
1976-77 1974 activity of Chokai volcano, Japan. *Bull Volc*, 40: 231-238

Aramaki S, Hamuro K
1977 Geology of the Higashi-Izu monogenetic volcano group. *Bull Earthq Res Inst, Univ Tokyo*, 52: 235-278 (in Japanese with English abs)

Hamuro K
1977 ^{14}C ages of Chikubo Central Cone scoria fall, Kawagodaira pyroclastic flow, Omuroyama-Amagi lateral volcano groups, Izu Peninsula. *Bull Volc Soc Japan*, 22: 277-278 (in Japanese)

Katsui Y, Oba Y, Soya T
1978 Records of volcanic eruptions in historic times and estimation of future eruptions. *Bull Volc Soc Japan*, 23: 41-52 (in Japanese with English abs)

Nakamura Y
1978 Geology and petrology of Bandai and Nekoma volcanoes. *Tokyo Univ Sci Rpt*, 14: 67-119

Oki Y, Aramaki S, Nakamura K, Hakamata K
1978 *Volcanoes of Hakone, Izu and Oshima*. Hakone: Hakone Town Office, 59 p

Shimozuru D, Kagiyama T
1978 A newly devised infra-red ground scanner and its application to geothermal research in volcanoes [Kusatsu-Shirane]. *Jour Volc Geotherm Res*, 4: 251-264

Suwa A
1978 The surveillance of volcanic activities in Japan. *Bull Volc Soc Japan*, 23: 83-89 (in Japanese with English abs)

Takahashi E
1978 Petrologic model of the crust and upper mantle of the Japanese island arcs. *Bull Volc*, 41: 529-547

Hayatsu K, Arai F
1980 Tephrochronological study on the Myoko volcano tephra layers an their relation to activity of the volcano. *Jour Geol Soc Japan*, 86: 243-263 (in Japanese with English abs)

Aramaki S (ed)
1981 *Symp Arc Volc Field Excursion Guide to Fuji, Asama, Kusatsu-Shirane and Nantai Volcanoes.* Tokyo: Volc Soc Japan, 75 p

Aramaki S, Shimozuru D, Ossaka J
1981 Asama volcano. *In*: Aramaki S (ed), p 23-48 (see above)

Hayakawa Y, Aramaki S, Shimozuru D, Ossaka J
1981 Kusatsu-Shirane volcano. *In*: Aramaki S (ed), p 49-63 (see above)

Ono K, Soya T, Mimura K
1981 Volcanoes of Japan. *Geol Surv Japan Map Ser*, no 11, 2nd edition, 1:2,000,000

Oshima O
1981 The latest dacitic eruption of Haruna volcano, Japan: compositional varation of minerals (abs). *IAVCEI, Tokyo Mtg Abs*, p 283

Ueki S, Aoki K
1981 Chokai-San. *Nat Disaster Res Rpt*, Japan Ministry Education, A-56-1: 33-41 (in Japanese)

Yamasaki M
1981 Nantai and adjacent volcanoes in the Nikko region. *In*: Aramaki S (ed), p 64-75 (see above)

Yokoyama S
1981 Base surge deposits in Japan. *In*: Self S and Sparks R (eds) *Tephra Studies*, Dordrecht, Holland: Reidel, p 427-432

Hayakawa Y
1983 Chuseri tephra formation from Towada volcano, Japan. *Bull Volc Soc Japan*, 28: 263-273 (in Japanese with English abs)

Kusakabe M, Hayashi N, Kobayashi T
1983 Genesis of banded sulfur sediments at Jigokudani valley, Tateyama volcano, Japan. *Bull Volc Soc Japan*, 28: 245-261 (in Japanese with English abs)

Uto K, Hayakawa Y, Aramaki S, Ossaka J
1983 Geologic map of Kusatsu-Shirane volcano. *Geol Surv Japan*, 1:25,000 geol map

Moriya I, Togashi S
1984 Eruptions of Kusatsu volcano in the last 10,000 years. *Bull Volc Soc Japan*, 29: 330 (in Japanese)

Endo K
1985 Peat deposits and volcanic ashes on Haku-san volcano. *Hakusan Nature Conservation Center, Rpt of Sci Res on the Alpine Zone of Mt Hakusan*, p 11-30 (in Japanese)

Hamuro K
1985 Petrology of the Higashi-Izu monogenetic volcano group. *Bull Earthq Res Inst, Univ Tokyo*, 60: 335-400

Hayakawa Y
1985 Pyroclastic geology of Towada volcano. *Bull Earthq Res Inst, Univ Tokyo*, 60: 507-592

Hayatsu K
1987 Pyroclastic flows erupted in medieval time at Niigata-Yakeyama volcano, Japan. *Bull Volc Soc Japan*, 32: 77-80 (in Japanese)

Japan Assoc Quaternary Research
1987 *Quaternary Maps of Japan: Landforms, Geology, and Tectonics.* Tokyo: Univ Tokyo Press

Kyoto Univ. Disaster Prevention Institute
1987 *Research on Eruptions--Prediction of Volcanic Eruptions and the Role of Universities.* Kyoto Univ Disaster Prevention Inst and Nat Univ Res Group for Volcanoes

Murayama I
1987 ★ Volcanoes of Japan (I). Tokyo: Daimedo, 315 p (2nd edition, in Japanese)

Ishii T, Watanabe M, Ishizuka T, Ohta S, Sakai H, Haramura H, Shikazono N, Togashi K, Minai Y, Tominaga T, Chinzei K, Horikoshi M, Matsumoto E
1988 Geological study with the "Shinkai 2000" in the West Sagami Bay including Calyptogena colonies. *In*: *Technical Reports of the Japan Marine Science and Technology Center*, p. 189-218

Matsumoto A, Uto K, Togashi S
1988 Measuring ages of volcanoes (radiometric dating), II. Application to active volcanoes (abs) [Nasu]. *Kagoshima Internatl Conf Volc Abs*, p 406

Miki K, Fujiwara A, Hashimoto Y
1988 Debris-flow generation and its counter measures near by Yakeyama volcano in Niigata Japan (abs). *Kagoshima Internatl Conf Volc Abs*, p 540

Miyaji N
1988 History of Younger Fuji volcano. *Jour Geol Soc Japan*, 94: 433-452 (in Japanese with English abs)

Tsuya H, Machida H, Shimozuru D
1988 Geologic map of Mt. Fuji. *Geol Surv Japan*, geol map and 24 p text, 2nd printing

Yamasaki M, Shimizu S, Moriya I, Togashi S, Endo K, Higashino T
1988 Evolution of Hakusan volcano, Central Japan, during the last 10000 years and the volcanic disasters in future. *Proc Kagoshima Internatl Conf Volc*, p 445-447

Hayakawa Y, Yui M
1989 Eruptive history of the Kusatsu Shirane volcano. *Quaternary Res*, 28: 1-17 (in Japanese with English abs)

Higashino T
1989 *The Documented Record of the Historic Activity of Mt. Hakusan*. Ishikawa Prefecture: Hakusan Nature Conservation Center, 8 p

Ida Y, Osada N, Sawada M, Koyama E, Kagiyama T
1989 Seismological study based on recently installed permanent stations and a small eruptive event on January 6, 1989 at Kusatsu-Shirane volcano. *Bull Earthq Res Inst, Univ Tokyo*, 64: 325-345 (in Japanese with English abs)

Murayama I
1989 ★ Volcanoes of Japan (II and III). Tokyo: Daimedo, 285 and 259 p (in Japanese)

Suzuki T
1990 Tephrochronological study on the 200,000 years eruptive history of Akagi volcano in north Kanto, central Japan. *Chigaku Zasshi (Jour Geog)*, 99: 60-75 (in Japanese with English abs)

Yamamoto T, Soya T, Suto S, Uto K, Takada A, Sakaguchi K, Ono K
1991 The 1989 submarine eruption off eastern Izu Peninsula, Japan: ejecta and eruption mechanisms. *Bull Volc*, 53: 301-308

Hayakawa Y, Koyama M
1992 Eruptive history of the Higashi Izu monogenetic volcano field 1: 0-32 ka. *Bull Volc Soc Japan*, 37: 167-181 (in Japanese with English abs)

Machida H, Arai F
1992 ★ Atlas of tephra in and around Japan. Tokyo: Univ Tokyo Press, 276 p (in Japanese)

Miyaji N, Endo K, Togashi S, Uesugi Y
1992 Tephrochronological history of Mt. Fuji. *29th Internatl Geol Cong, Kyoto, Field Trip*, C12: 75-109

Suzuki T
1992 Tephrochronological study on Nasu volcano. *Bull Volc Soc Japan*, 37: 251-263 (in Japanese with English abs)

Aramaki S
1993 Geological map of Asama volcano. *Geol Surv Japan*, 1:50,000 geol map and text (in Japanese with English summary)

Hayakawa Y, Soda T, Arai F
1993 Asama and Haruna volcanoes: recent eruptions and hazards. *Climatic impact of explosive volc conf, Tokyo, Dec 3-4, 1993*, 28 p guidebook

Hayakawa Y
1994 ★ A catalog of the volcanic eruptions during the last 2000 years in Japan. *Sci Rpt Fac Education Gumma Univ*, in press (in Japanese with English abs)

IZU IS, VOLCANO IS, & MARIANA IS (0804)

Milne J
1886 ★ The volcanoes of Japan. *Trans Seism Soc Japan*, 9: 1-184

Tanakadate H
1931 Volcanic activity in Japan and vicinity during the period between 1924 and 1931. *Japan Jour Astron Geophys*, 9: 47-64

Nagata T
1938 Geophysical studies of Mihara volcano, Oosima Island, IV, a minor activity of volcano Mihara, August 11, 1938. *Bull Earthq Res Inst, Univ Tokyo*, 16: 702-720

Minakami T
1950 Report on the volcanic activities in Japan during 1939-1947. *Bull Volc*, 10: 45-58

Johnson C G
1953 Activity in the Marianas and Volcano Islands. *Volcano Lett*, 520: 7

Minakami T, Sakuma S
1953 Report on volcanic activities and volcanological studies concerning them in Japan during 1948-1951. *Bull Volc*, 14: 79-132

Foster H L
1954 Volcanic activity in Japan. *Volcano Lett*, 526: 7

Corwin G, Foster H L
1959 The 1957 explosive eruption on Iwo Jima, Volcano Islands. *Amer Jour Sci*, 257: 161-171

Kuno H
1962 ★ Japan, Taiwan and Marianas. *Catalog of Active Volcanoes of the World*, Rome: IAVCEI, 11: 1-332

Minakami T
1962 Report on volcanic activity in Japan for the period from 1957 to 1959. *Bull Volc*, 24: 7-22

Isshiki N
1964 Mode of eruption of Miyake-jima volcano in historic times. *Bull Volc*, 27: 29-48

Minakami T
1964 The 1962 eruption of Miyake-Sima, one of the seven Izu Islands, Japan. *Bull Volc*, 27: 225-236

Nakamura K
1964 Volcano-stratigraphic study of Oshima volcano, Izu. *Bull Earthq Res Inst, Univ Tokyo*, 42: 649-728

Norris R A, Johnson R H
1969 Submarine volcanic eruptions recently located in the Pacific by SOFAR hydrophones. *Jour Geophys Res*, 74: 650-664

Corwin G
1971 Quaternary volcanics of the Marianas Islands. *Unpublished ms*, 137 p

Zobin V M
1972 Focal mechanism of volcanic earthquakes [Tori-shima]. *Bull Volc*, 36: 561-571

Johnson R H
1973 Acoustic observations of nonexplosive submarine volcanism. *Jour Geophys Res*, 78: 6093-6096

Japan Meteorological Agency
1975 ★ National Catalogue of the Active Volcanoes in Japan. Tokyo: Japan Meteorological Agency, 119 p (in Japanese)

Yokoyama S, Arai T
1976 ^{14}C ages of Tairoike and Yaema lateral explosion craters, Miyake-Jima volcano, Izu. *Bull Volc Soc Japan*, 21: 57-58 (in Japanese)

Stern R J
1978 Agrigan: an introduction to the geology of an active volcano in the Northern Mariana Island Arc. *Bull Volc*, 41: 43-55

Suwa A
1978 The surveillance of volcanic activities in Japan. *Bull Volc Soc Japan*, 23: 83-89 (in Japanese with English abs)

Yokoyama S, Tokunaga T
1978 Base surge deposits of Mukaiyama volcano, Nii-Jima, Izu Islands. *Bull Volc Soc Japan*, 23: 249-262 (in Japanese with English abs)

Meijer A, Reagan M
1981 Petrology and geochemistry of the island of Sarigan in the Mariana arc: calc-alkaline volcanism in an oceanic setting. *Contr Mineral Petr*, 77: 337-354

Ono K, Soya T, Mimura K
1981 Volcanoes of Japan. *Geol Surv Japan Map Ser*, no 11, 2nd edition, 1:2,000,000

Yokoyama S
1981 Base surge deposits in Japan. *In*: Self S and Sparks R (eds) *Tephra Studies*, Dordrecht, Holland: Reidel, p 427-432

Gorshkov A P, Gavrilenko G M, Seliverstov N I, Scripko K A
1982 Geologic structure and fumarolic activity of the Esmeralda submarine volcano. *In*: Schmincke H-U, Baker P E, Forjaz V H (eds) *Proc Symp Activity Oceanic Volcanoes*, Arquipelago, Revista Univ dos Acores, 3: 271-298

Japan Meteorological Agency
1982 List of the Active Volcanoes in Japan. *Volc Bull Japan Meteorological Agency*, 20: 2

Banks N G, Koyanagi R Y, Sinton J M, Honma K T
1984 The eruption of Mount Pagan volcano, Mariana Islands, 15 May 1981. *Jour Volc Geotherm Res*, 22: 225-270

Togashi S
1984 ^{14}C ages of charcoal from pyroclastics of Tenjosan volcano, Kozushima, the Izu Islands, Japan. *Bull Volc Soc Japan*, 29: 277-283 (in Japanese with English abs)

Sumita M
1985 Ring-shaped cone formed during the 1983 Miyake-jima eruption. *Bull Volc Soc Japan*, 30: 11-32 (in Japanese with English abs)

Aramaki S, Hayakawa Y, Fujii T, Nakamura K, Fukuoka T
1986 The October 1983 eruption of Miyakejima volcano. *Jour Volc Geotherm Res*, 29: 203-230

Koyaguchi T
1986 Evidence for two-stage mixing in magmatic inclusions and rhyolitic lava domes on Niijima Island, Japan. *Jour Volc Geotherm Res*, 29: 71-98

Japan Assoc Quaternary Research
1987 *Quaternary Maps of Japan: Landforms, Geology, and Tectonics.* Tokyo: Univ Tokyo Press

Soya T, Sakaguchi K, Uto K, Nakano S, Hoshizumi H, Kamata H, Sumii T, Kaneko N, Yamamoto T, Tsuchiya N, Suto S, Yamazaki H, Yamaguchi Y, Okumura K, Togashi S
1987 The 1986 eruption and products of Isu-Oshima volcano. *Geol Surv Japan Bull*, 38: 609-630 (in Japanese with English abs)

Earthquake Research Institute
1988 The 1986-1987 eruption of Izu-Oshima volcano. *Earthq Res Inst, Univ Tokyo*, 62 p

Bloomer S H, Stern R J, Smoot N C
1989 Physical volcanology of the submarine Mariana and Volcano arcs. *Bull Volc*, 51: 210-224

Murayama I
1990 ★ Volcanoes of Japan (II and III). Tokyo: Daimedo, 285 and 259 p (in Japanese)

Tsukui M, Moriizumi M, Suzuki M
1991 Eruptive history of the Higashiyama volcano, Hachijo Island during the last 22,000 years. *Bull Volc Soc Japan*, 36: 345-356 (in Japanese with English abs)

Machida H, Arai F
1992 ★ Atlas of tephra in and around Japan. Tokyo: Univ Tokyo Press, 276 p (in Japanese)

Takada A, Oshima O, Aramaki S, Ono K, Yoshida T, Kajima K
1992 Geology of Aogashima volcano, Izu Islands, Japan. *Bull Volc Soc Japan*, 37: 233-250

Hayakawa Y
1994 ★ A catalog of the volcanic eruptions during the last 2000 years in Japan. *Sci Rpt Fac Education Gumma Univ*, in press (in Japanese with English abs)

JAPAN: HOKKAIDO (0805)

Milne J
1886 ★ The volcanoes of Japan. *Trans Seism Soc Japan*, 9: 1-184

Oinouye Y
1917 A few interesting phenomena on the eruption of Usu. *Jour Geol*, 25: 258

Tsuya H
1930 The volcano Komagatake, Hokkaido: its geology, activity, and petrography. *Bull Earthq Res Inst, Univ Tokyo*, 8: 238-270

Tanakadate H
1931 Volcanic activity in Japan and vicinity during the period between 1924 and 1931. *Japan Jour Astron Geophys*, 9: 47-64

Jaggar T A
1931 The lava dome eruption of Tarumai. *Volcano Lett*, 317: 1-3

Tanakadate H
1934 Volcanic activity in Japan during the period between June 1931 and June 1934. *Japan Jour Astron Geophys*, 12: 89-108

Ishikawa T
1950 New eruption of Usu volcano, Hokkaido, Japan, during 1943-1945. *Hokkaido Univ Fac Sci Jour*, 7: 237-260

Minakami T, Ishikawa T, Yagi K
1951 The 1944 eruption of volcano Usu in Hokkaido, Japan. *Bull Volc*, 11: 46-157

Minakami T
1956 Report on volcanic activities and volcanological studies in Japan for the period from 1951 to 1954. *Bull Volc*, 18: 39-76

Kuno H
1962 ★ Japan, Taiwan and Marianas. *Catalog of Active Volcanoes of the World*, Rome: IAVCEI, 11: 1-332

Minakami T
1962 Report on volcanic activity in Japan for the period from 1957 to 1959. *Bull Volc*, 24: 7-22

Tsuya H, Morimoto R
1963 Types of volcanic eruptions in Japan. *Bull Volc*, 26: 209-222

Oba Y
1966 Geology and petrology of Usu volcano, Hokkaido, Japan. *Hokkaido Univ Fac Sci Jour*, 13: 185-236

Ishikawa T, Katsui Y, Oba Y, Satoh H
1969 Some problems of the calderas in Hokkaido. *Bull Volc Soc Japan*, 14: 97-108

Yagi K
1971 Some genetic problems of the calderas in Japan. *In*: Kaloyeropoyloy A (ed) *Acta 1st International Science Congress on the Volcano of Thera*, Athens: Arch Serv Greece, p 73-87

Japan Meteorological Agency
1975 ★ National Catalogue of the Active Volcanoes in Japan. Tokyo: Japan Meteorological Agency, 119 p (in Japanese)

Katsui Y, Ando S, Inaba K
1975 Formation and magmatic evolution of Mashu volcano, east Hokkaido, Japan. *Hokkaido Univ Fac Sci Jour*, 16: 533-552

Katsui Y, Yokoyama I, Fujita T, Ehara S
1975 *Komagatake. Report of the Volcanoes in Hokkaido, Part 4.* Sapporo: Committee Prevention Natural Disasters Hokkaido, 194 p (in Japanese)

Machida H
1976 Stratigraphy and chronology of late Quaternary marker-tephras in Japan. *Tokyo Metropolitan Univ Geog Rpt*, 11: 109-132

Sumi K, Takashima I
1976 Absolute ages of the hydrothermal alteration halos and associated volcanic rocks in some Japanese geothermal fields. *In*: *Proc 2nd United Nations Symp Devel Use Geotherm Resour, San Francisco* Washington D C: U S Government Printing Office 1: 625-634

Katsui Y, Oba Y, Onuma K, Suzuki T, Kondo Y, Watanabe T, Niida K, Uda T, Hagiwara S, Nagao T, Nishikawa K,, Yamamoto M, Ikeda Y, Katagawa H, Tsuchiya N, Shrahase M,, Nemoto S, Yokoyama S, Soya T, Fujita T, Inaba K, Koide K
1978 Preliminary report of the 1977 eruption of Usu volcano. *Hokkaido Univ Fac Sci Jour*, 18: 385-408

Katsui Y, Oba Y, Soya T
1978 Records of volcanic eruptions in historic times and estimation of future eruptions. *Bull Volc Soc Japan*, 23: 41-52 (in Japanese with English abs)

Suwa A
1978 The surveillance of volcanic activities in Japan. *Bull Volc Soc Japan*, 23: 83-89 (in Japanese with English abs)

Niida K, Katsui Y, Suzuki T, Kondo Y
1980 The 1977-1978 eruption of Usu volcano. *Hokkaido Univ Fac Sci Jour*, 19: 357-394

Katsui Y (ed)
1981 *Symp Arc Volc Field Excursion Guide to Usu and Tarumai Volcanoes and Noboribetsu Spa.* Tokyo: Volc Soc Japan, 64 p

Katsui Y, Yamamoto M
1981 The 1741-1742 activity of Oshima-Oshima volcano, north Japan. *Hokkaido Univ Fac Sci Jour*, 19: 527-536

Katsui Y, Yokoyama I, Watanabe H, Murozumi M
1981 Usu volcano. *In*: Katsui Y (ed), p 1-37 (see above)

Ono K, Soya T, Mimura K
1981 Volcanoes of Japan. *Geol Surv Japan Map Ser*, no 11, 2nd edition, 1:2,000,000

Soya T, Katsui Y
1981 The Zenkoji debris avalanche of Usu volcano, Hokkaido, Japan (abs). *IAVCEI, Tokyo Mtg Abs*, p 347

Katsui Y, Yokoyama I, Murozumi M
1981a Tarumai volcano. *In*: Katsui Y (ed), p 38-54 (see above)

1981b Noboribetsu Spa. *In*: Katsui Y (ed), p 55-64 (see above)

Yokoyama I, Katsui Y, Abiko T
1983 The 1979-1982 activities of Usu volcano. *In*: *Report on Volcanic Activities and Volcanological Studies in Japan for the Period 1979-1982*, Bull Volc Soc Japan, 28: 15-19

Katsui Y, Komuro H
1984 Formation of fractures in Komagatake volcano, Hokkaido. *Hokkaido Univ Fac Sci Jour*, 21: 183-195

Okumura K, Sangawa A
1984 Age and distribution of Toya pyroclastic flow. *Bull Volc Soc Japan*, 29: 338 (in Japanese)

Katsui Y, Komuro H, Uda T
1985 Development of faults and growth of Usu-Shinzan cryptodome in 1977-1982 at Usu volcano, north Japan. *Hokkaido Univ Fac Sci Jour*, 21: 339-362

Japan Assoc Quaternary Research
1987 *Quaternary Maps of Japan: Landforms, Geology, and Tectonics.* Tokyo: Univ Tokyo Press

Kyoto Univ. Disaster Prevention Institute
1987 *Research on Eruptions--Prediction of Volcanic Eruptions and the Role of Universities.* Kyoto Univ Disaster Prevention Inst and Nat Univ Res Group for Volcanoes

Murayama I
1987 ★ Volcanoes of Japan (I). Tokyo: Daimedo, 315 p (2nd edition, in Japanese)

Katsui Y
1988 Historic eruptions in Hokkaido and associated volcanic disasters (abs). *Kagoshima Internatl Conf Volc Abs*, p 334

Katsui Y, Kawachi S, Aramaki S, Kondo Y
1989 The 1988-89 eruption of Tokachi-dake, its sequence and mechanisms. *Rpt Nat Disaster Sci Res*, no B-63-5 (in Japanese with English abs)

Katsui Y, Suzuki T, Soya T, Yoshihisa Y
1989 Geological map of Hokkaido-Komagatake volcano. *Geol Surv Japan*, 1:50,000 geol map

Sawada Y, Tanaka Y, Seino M
1989 Volcanic activity in Japan monitored by the Japan Meteorological Agency using detected precursory phenomena. *In*: Latter J H (ed), *Volcanic Hazards - Assessment and Monitoring*, Berlin: Springer-Verlag, p 246-259

Katsui Y, Kawachi S, Kondo Y, Ikeda Y, Nakagawa M, Gotoh Y, Yamagishi H, Yamazaki T, Sumita M
1990 The 1988-1989 explosive eruption of Tokachi-dake, central Hokkaido, its sequence and mode. *Bull Volc Soc Japan*, 35: 111-129

Machida H, Arai F
1992 ★ Atlas of tephra in and around Japan. Tokyo: Univ Tokyo Press, 276 p (in Japanese)

Hayakawa Y
1994 ★ A catalog of the volcanic eruptions during the last 2000 years in Japan. *Sci Rpt Fac Education Gumma Univ*, in press (in Japanese with English abs)

KURILE IS (0900)

Tanakadate H
1931 Volcanic activity in Japan and vicinity during the period between 1924 and 1931. *Japan Jour Astron Geophys*, 9: 47-64

1934 Volcanic activity in Japan during the period between June 1931 and June 1934. *Japan Jour Astron Geophys*, 12: 89-108

Gorshkov G S
1958 ★ Kurile Islands. *Catalog of Active Volcanoes of the World*, Rome: IAVCEI, 7: 1-99

1967 ★ Volcanism and the Upper Mantle; Investigations in the Kurile Island Arc. Moscow: Nauka, 286 p (in Russian, 1970 translation, New York: Plenum Publishing Corp, 385 p)

Vlasov G M
1967 Kamchatka, Kuril, and Komandorskiye Islands: geological description. *In*: *Geol of the USSR*, Moscow, 31: 1-827

Erlich E N, Melekestev I V
1972 Evolution of Quaternary volcanism and tectonics in the western part of the Pacific Ring. *Pacific Geol*, 4: 1-22

Abdurakhmanov A I, Fedorchenko V I
1976 On volcanic activity in the Kurile Islands in 1973 and some previously undescribed eruptions. *Trudy Sakhalin Complex Res Inst*, 48: 114-118 (in Russian)

Suwa A
1978 The surveillance of volcanic activities in Japan. *Bull Volc Soc Japan*, 23: 83-89 (in Japanese with English abs)

Firstov P P, Ivanov B V, Karpukhina Y V
1979 Temporal and energetical regularities of volcanic eruptions of Kurile-Kamchatka region in 1956-1976. *Akad Nauk SSSR, Sibirsk Otdeleniye Byull Vulkanol Stantsii*, 57: 3-11 (in Russian)

Fedotov S A, Ivanov B V, Avdeyko G P, Flerov G, Andreyev V N, Dvigalo V N, Dubik Y M, Cherkov A M
1981 1981 eruption of the Alaid volcano. *Volc Seism*, 1981(5): 82-87 (in Russian)

Ivanov B V, Chirkov A M, Dubik Y M, Gavrilov V A, Stepanov V V, Rulenko O P, Firstov P P
1981 The state of volcanoes in Kamchatka and Kurile Islands in 1980. *Volc Seism*, 1981(3): 99-103 (in Russian)

Menyailov I A, Nikitina L P, Shapar V N
1981 Possibility of forecasting phreatic eruptions of island-arc andesitic volcanoes (abs). *IAVCEI, Tokyo Mtg Abs*, p 234

Ono K, Soya T, Mimura K
1981 Volcanoes of Japan. *Geol Surv Japan Map Ser*, no 11, 2nd edition, 1:2,000,000

Ivanov B V, Andreev V N, Bogoyavlenskaya G E, Doubik Y M, Kirsanov I T, Rulenko O P, Firstov P P, Chirkov A M
1982 The activity of volcanoes of Kamchatka and Kurile Islands in 1981. *Volc Seism*, 1982(4): 103-108 (in Russian)

Markhinin E K
1983 On the state of Kunashir Island volcanoes (March, 1974-May, 1982). *Volc Seism*, 1983(1): 43-51 (English translation 1984, 5: 45-52)

Ivanov B V, Chirkov A M, Dubik Y M, Khrenov A P, Dvigalo V N, Razina A A, Stepanov V V, Chubarova O S
1984 Active volcanoes of Kamchatka and Kuril Islands: status in 1982. *Volc Seism*, 1984(4): 104-110 (English translation 1988, 6: 623-634)

Melekestsev I V, Braitseva O A
1984 Gigantic rockslide avalanches on volcanoes. *Volc Seism*, 1984(4): 14-23 (English translation 1988, 4: 495-508)

Erlich E N
1986 ★ Geology of the calderas of Kamchatka and Kurile Islands with comparison to calderas of Japan and the Aleutians, Alaska. *U S Geol Surv Open-File Rpt*, 86-291: 1-300

Kirianov V Y, Egorova I A, Litasova S N
1986 Volcanic ash on Bering Island (Commander Islands) and Kamchatka Holocene eruptions. *Volc Seism*, 1986(6): 18-28 (English translation 1990, 8: 850-868)

Murayama I
1987 *Volcanoes of Japan (I)*. Tokyo: Daimedo, 315 p (2nd edition, in Japanese)

Dvigalo V N, Andreev V I, Gavrilenko G M, Ovsyannikov A A, Razina A, Chirkov M
1988 Activity of the southeast Kamchatka and north Kuriles volcanoes in 1985-1986. *Volc Seism*, 1988(3): 13-20 (English translation 1990, 10: 347-359)

Melekestsev I V, Braitseva O A, Sulerzhitskiy L D
1988 Catastrophic explosive volcanic eruptions in Kamchatka and the Kurile Islands in late Pleistocene-early Holocene time. *Trans (Doklady) USSR Acad Sci Earth Sci Sec*, 300: 55-59

Menyailov I A, Ovsyannikov A A, Shirokov V A
1988 Eruption of Ebeko volcano in October-December 1987. *Volc Seism*, 1988(3): 105-108 (English translation 1990, 10: 493-498)

Melekestsev I V, Braitseva O A, Kirianov V Y
1990 History of eruptive activity and predicting impending eruptions of the peak Nemo volcano on the Onekotan Island, Kuriles (abs). *IAVCEI Internatl Volc Cong, Mainz, Abs*, (unpaginated)

Menyailov I A, Nikitina L P, Budnikov V A
1992 Activity of Ebeko volcano in 1987-1991: character of eruptions, composition of erupted material, volcanic hazard for Severo-Kurilsk. *Volc Seism*, 1992(5-6): 21-33 (English translation 1993, 14: 515-531)

Ovsyannikov A A, Muraviev Y D
1992 The 1986 eruption of Chikurachki volcano. *Volc Seism*, 1992(5-6): 3-20 (English tranlation 1993, 14: 493-514)

Hayakawa Y
1994 A catalog of the volcanic eruptions during the last 2000 years in Japan. *Sci Rpt Fac Education Gumma Univ*, in press (in Japanese with English abs)

KAMCHATKA (1000)

Krasheninnikov S P
1755 *Explorations of Kamchatka*. Portland: Oregon Hist Soc, English translation by E A P Crownhart-Vaughan, 371 p

Jaggar T A
1931 Kamchatka volcanoes in 1931. *Volcano Lett*, 353: 1-3

Krijanovsky N
1934 ★ Volcanoes of Kamchatka. *Geol Soc Amer Bull*, 45: 529-549

Vlodavetz V I
1947 The volcanoes of the Karymsky Group. *Acad Sci USSR Trans Kamchatka Volc Station*, 3: 47 (in Russian with English abs)

Tomkeieff S I
1949 The volcanoes of Kamchatka. *Bull Volc*, 8: 87-114

Gorshkov G S
1959 Gigantic eruption of the volcano Bezymianny. *Bull Volc*, 20: 77-109

Sviatlovsky A E
1959 ★ Atlas of Volcanoes of the Soviet Union. Moscow: Akad Nauk SSSR, 170 p (in Russian with English summary)

Vlodavetz V I, Piip B I
1959 ★ Kamchatka and Continental Areas of Asia. *Catalog of Active Volcanoes of the World*, Rome: IAVCEI, 8: 1-110

Basharina L A
1965 Gases of Kamchatka volcanoes. *Bull Volc*, 28: 95-106

Polak B G
1967 An energy appraisal of volcanic and hydrothermal phenomena (on the example of Kamchatka). *Bull Volc*, 30: 129-138

Vlasov G M
1967 Kamchatka, Kuril, and Komandorskiye Islands: geological description. *In*: *Geol of the USSR*, Moscow, 31: 1-827

Gorshkov G S, Kirsanov I T
1968 Eruption of Piip Crater (Kamchatka). *Bull Volc*, 32: 269-282

Kirsanov I T
1968 Eruption of Klyuchevskoi volcano in 1966 and the outbreak of the lateral Piip craters. *Akad Nauk SSSR, Sibirsk Otdeleniye Byull Vulkanol Stantsii*, 44: 11-29 (Thornton translation)

Lotze F, Niedermeier G
1969 Notizen zur Aktuo-Geologie: 205 Bericht Endogene Dynamik April bis Juni 1967. *Neues Jahrb Geol Palaont Monatsh*, 31: 54-56

Gorshkov G S, Dubik Y M
1970 Gigantic directed blast at Shiveluch volcano (Kamchatka). *Bull Volc*, 34: 261-288

Erlich E N, Melekestsev I V, Tarakanovsky A A, Zubin M I
1972 Quaternary calderas of Kamchatka. *Bull Volc*, 36: 222-237

Ogorodov N V, Kozhemyaka N N, Vazheevskaya A A, Ogorodov A S
1972 *Volcanoes and the Quaternary Volcanism of the Sredinny Ridge in Kamchatka.* Moscow: Nauka Pub, 190 p (in Russian)

Luchitsky I V (ed)
1974 *History of the Development of Relief of Siberia and the Far East. Kamchatka, Kurile and Komander Islands.* Moscow: Nauka Press, 439 p (in Russian)

Fedotov S A, Gorel'chik V I, Stepnov V V
1977 Seismologic data on magma chambers, mechanisms, and evolution of the 1975 Tolbachik basalt fissure eruption on Kamchatka. *Trans (Doklady) USSR Acad Sci Earth Sci Sec*, 228: 93-96

Fedotov S A, Khrenov A P, Chirkov A M
1977 The great fissure eruption at Tolbachik, Kamchatka. *Trans (Doklady) USSR Acad Sci Earth Sci Sec*, 228: 87-89

Ogorodov N V, Volynets O N, Koloskov A V, Polytov E Y
1978 Dikiy Greben'. *Akad Nauk SSSR, Sibirsk Otdeleniye Byull Vulkanol Stantsii*, 54: 75-88 (in Russian)

Tokarev P I
1978 Prediction and characteristics of the 1975 eruption of Tolbachik volcano, Kamchatka. *Bull Volc*, 41: 251-258

Braitseva O A, Egorova I A, Sulerzhitsky L D
1979 Tephrochronological investigations of the Karymsky volcano. *Volc Seism*, 1979(1): 48-58 (in Russian)

Erlich E N, Gorshkov G S (eds)
1979 Quaternary volcanism and tectonics in Kamchatka. *Bull Volc*, 42(1-4)

Firstov P P, Ivanov B V, Karpukhina Y V
1979 Temporal and energetical regularities of volcanic eruptions of Kurile-Kamchatka region in 1956-1976. *Akad Nauk SSSR, Sibirsk Otdeleniye Byull Vulkanol Stantsii*, 57: 3-11 (in Russian)

Kozhemyaka N N
1979 Quaternary pumice, tuff-ignimbrite fields and centers of eruption in southern Kamchatka. *Akad Nauk SSSR, Sibirsk Otdeleniye Byull Vulkanol Stantsii*, 57: 26-38 (in Russian)

Masurenkov Y P (ed)
1980 *Volcanic Center: Structure, Dynamics and Products.* Moscow: Nauka Pub, 299 p (in Russian)

Braitseva O A, Melekestsev I V, Ponomareva V V, Litasova S N, Sulerzhitsky L D
1981 Tephrochronological and geochronological studies of Tolbachik regional zone of scoria cones. *Volc Seism*, 1981(3): 14-28 (in Russian)

Ivanov B V, Chirkov A M, Dubik Y M, Gavrilov V A, Stepanov V V, Rulenko O P, Firstov P P
1981 The state of volcanoes in Kamchatka and Kurile Islands in 1980. *Volc Seism*, 1981(3): 99-103 (in Russian)

Steinberg G S
1981 Kliuchevskoy volcano eruption of 1980 and eruption cyclicity. *Volcano News*, 8: 2-3

Braitseva O A, Kirianov V Y
1982 On the past activity of Bezymianny volcano as shown by data of tephrochronological studies. *Volc Seism*, 1982(6): 44-55 (in Russian)

Ivanov B V, Andreev V N, Bogoyavlenskaya G E, Doubik Y M, Kirsanov I T, Rulenko O P, Firstov P P, Chirkov A M
1982 The activity of volcanoes of Kamchatka and Kurile Islands in 1981. *Volc Seism*, 1982(4): 103-108 (in Russian)

Khrenov A P, Doubik, Y M, Ovsyannikov A A, Pilipenko V P, Taran Y A, Firstov P, Chirkov A M
1982 Eruptive activity of Karymsky volcano over the period of 10 years (1970-1980). *Volc Seism*, 1982(4): 29-48 (in Russian)

Belousov V I, Grib E N, Leonov V L
1983 The geological setting of the hydrothermal systems in the geysers valley of Uzon caldera. *Volc Seism*, 1983(1): 65-79 (English translation 1984, 5: 67-82)

Fedotov S A, Markhinin Y K (eds)
1983 *The Great Tolbachik Fissure Eruption.* Cambridge, England: Cambridge Univ Press, 341 p (English translation)

Kirsanov I T, Ozerov A Y
1983 Composition of products and energy yield of the 1980-1981 Gorelyi volcano eruption. *Volc Seism*, 1983(1): 25-42 (English translation 1984, 5: 23-44)

Seleznev B V, Dvigalo V N, Gusev N A
1983 Evolution of Bezymyannai volcano from stereoscopic plotting of aerial photographs of 1950, 1967 and 1976-1981. *Volc Seism*, 1983(1): 52-64 (English translation 1984, 5: 53-66)

Shirokov V A
1983 The influence of the 19-year tidal cycle on large-scale eruptions and earthquakes in Kamchatka, and their long-term prediction. *In*: Fedotov S A and Markhinin Y K (eds) *The Great Tolbachik Fissure Eruption, Geol and Geophys Data 1975-1976*, p 232-242

Braitseva O A, Sulerzhitskii L D, Litasova S N, Grebzdy E I
1984 Radiocarbon dating of soils and pyroclastic deposits in Klyuchevskoi group of volcanoes. *Volc Seism*, 1984(2): 110-115 (English translation 1988, 6: 317-325)

Dvigalo V N
1984 Growth of a dome in the crater of Shiveluch volcano in 1980-1981 from photogrammetry data. *Volc Seism*, 1984(2): 104-109 (English translation 1988, 6: 307-315)

Florenskii I V
1984 On the age of Uzon and Krasheninnikov calderas. *Volc Seism*, 1984(1): 102-106 (English translation 1988, 6: 147-154)

Gavrilov V A, Gordeev E I, Ivanov V V, Ivshin V M, Stepanov V V, Farberov A I, Shirokov V A, Yashchuk V V
1984 Volcanic tremor and earthquakes associated with the 1980-1981 eruption of Gorelyi volcano. *Volc Seism*, 1984(6): 3-17 (English translation 1988, 6: 795-813)

Ivanov B V, Chirkov A M, Dubik Y M, Khrenov A P, Dvigalo V N, Razina A A, Stepanov V V, Chubarova O S
1984 Active volcanoes of Kamchatka and Kuril Islands: status in 1982. *Volc Seism*, 1984(4): 104-110 (English translation 1988, 6: 623-634)

Ivanov B V, Gavrilenko G M, Dvigalo V N, Ovsyannikov A A, Ozerov A, Razina A, Tokarev P I, Khrenov A P, Chirkov A M
1984 Activity of volcanoes in Kamchatka and the Kuril Islands in 1983. *Volc Seism*, 1984(6): 114-121 (English translation 1988, 6: 959-972)

Kirsanov T P, Melekestsev I V
1984 On the origin and age of Khodutka thermal springs. *Volc Seism*, 1984(5): 49-59 (English translation 1988, 6: 711-725)

Kozhemyaka N N, Litasov N E, Vazheevskaya A A
1984 The Asacha group of volcanoes in Kamchatka. *Volc Seism*, 1984(3): 14-24 (English translation 1988, 6: 365-378)

Melekestsev I V, Kiryanov V Y
1984 When will Avacha volcano in Kamchatka erupt? *Volc Seism*, 1984(6): 107-110 (English translation 1988, 6: 943-951)

Popruzhenko S V
1984 On the formation of the Opala caldera. *Volc Seism*, 1984(6): 111-113 (English translation 1988, 6: 953-958)

Bogoyavlenskaya G E, Braitseva O A, Melekestsev I V, Kiriyanov V Y, Miller C D
1985 Catastrophic eruptions of the directed-blast type at Mount St. Helens, Bezymianny and Shiveluch volcanoes. *Jour Geodynam*, 3: 189-218

Braitseva O A, Florenskii I V, Ponomareva V V, Litasova S N
1985 The history of the activity of Kikhpinych volcano in the Holocene. *Volc Seism*, 1985(6): 3-19 (English translation 1989, 7: 845-872)

Braitseva O A, Kirianov V Y, Sulerzhitskiy L D
1985 Marker intercalations of Holocene tephra in the eastern volcanic zone of Kamchatka. *Volc Seism*, 1985(5): 80-96 (English translation 1989, 7: 785-814)

Fedotov S A, Ivanov B V, Dvigalo V N, Kirsanov I T, Murav'ev Y, Ovsyannikov A, Razina A A, Seliversov N I, Stepanov V V, Khrenov A P, Chirkov A M
1985 Activity of the volcanoes of Kamchatka and the Kuril Islands in 1984. *Volc Seism*, 1985(5): 3-23 (English translation 1989, 7: 647-682)

Khrenov A P, Ozerov A Y, Litasov N E, Slezin Y B, Murav'ev Y D, Zharinov N A
1985 Parasitic eruption of Klyuchevskoi volcano (Preskazannyi eruption, 1983). *Volc Seism*, 1985(1): 3-20 (English translation 1988, 7: 1-24)

Ponomareva V V, Tsyurupa A A
1985 Extended liquid acidic lava flows at Krasheninnikov volcano. *Volc Seism*, 1985(3): 85-92 (English translation 1988, 7: 447-458)

Tokarev P I
1985 Prediction of lateral eruption of Klyuchevskoy volcano in March 1983. *Jour Volc Geotherm Res*, 25: 173-180

1985 The March-June 1984 eruption of Klyuchevskoi and its present state as estimated from ongoing observations. *Volc Seism*, 1985(1): 106-108 (English translation 1988, 7: 143-148)

Erlich E N
1986 Geology of the calderas of Kamchatka and Kurile Islands with comparison to calderas of Japan and the Aleutians, Alaska. *U S Geol Surv Open-File Rpt*, 86-291: 1-300

Gavrilov V A, Ivanov V V, Trukhin Y P, Shuvalov R A, Yashchuk V V
1986 The activation of Gorelyi volcano in August-September 1984. *Volc Seism*, 1986(5): 90-92 (English translation 1990, 8: 794-799)

Kirianov V Y, Egorova I A, Litasova S N
1986 Volcanic ash on Bering Island (Commander Islands) and Kamchatka Holocene eruptions. *Volc Seism*, 1986(6): 18-28 (English translation 1990, 8: 850-868)

Seliverstov N I, Avdeiko G P, Ivanenko A N, Shkira V A, Khubunaya S A
1986 A new submarine volcano in the west of the Aleutian island arc. *Volc Seism*, 1986(4): 3-16 (English translation 1990, 8: 473-495)

Fedotov S A, Khrenov A P, Zharinov N A
1987 The activity of Klyuchevskoi volcano in the years 1932-1986 and the prospects for the future.. *Volc Seism*, 1987(4): 1-16 (English translation 1990, 9: 501-521)

Melekestsev I V, Braitseva O A, Ponomareva V V
1987 Holocene activity dynamics of Mutnovskii and Gorelyi volcanoes and the volcanic risk for adjacent areas (as indicated by tephrochronological studies). *Volc Seism*, 1987(3): 3-18 (English translation 1990, 9: 337-362)

Melekestsev I V, Sulerzhitsky L D
1987 Ksudach volcano (Kamchatka) over the last ten thousand years. *Volc Seism*, 1987(4): 28-39 (English translation 1990, 9: 537-556)

Ponomareva V V
1987 The history of Krasheninnikov volcano and the dynamics of its activity. *Volc Seism*, 1987(5): 28-44 (English translation 1990, 9: 714-741)

Selyangin O B
1987 Geological structure and evolution of the calderas of Ksudach volcano. *Volc Seism*, 1987(5): p 16-27 (English translation 1990, 9: 690-713)

Alidibirov M A, Bogoyavlenskaya G E, Kirsanov I T, Kirsanov I T, Firstov P P, Girina O A, Belousov A B, Zhkanova E Y, Malyshev A I
1988 The 1985 eruption of Bezymianny. *Volc Seism*, 1988(6): 3-17 (English translation 1990, 10: 839-863)

Belousov A B, Bogoyavlenskaya G E
1988 Debris avalanche of the 1956 Bezymianny eruption. *Proc Kagoshima Internatl Conf Volc*, p 460-462

Budnikov V A
1988 The eruption of Gorelyi volcano in April 1986. *Volc Seism*, 1988(4): 99-103 (English translation 1990, 10: 650-658)

Dvigalo V N, Andreev V I, Gavrilenko G M, Ovsyannikov A A, Razina A, Chirkov M
1988 Activity of the southeast Kamchatka and north Kuriles volcanoes in 1985-1986. *Volc Seism*, 1988(3): 13-20 (English translation 1990, 10: 347-359)

Melekestsev I V, Braitseva O A, Sulerzhitskiy L D
1988 Catastrophic explosive volcanic eruptions in Kamchatka and the Kurile Islands in late Pleistocene-early Holocene time. *Trans (Doklady) USSR Acad Sci Earth Sci Sec*, 300: 55-59

Zharinov N A, Zhdanova E Y, Belousov A B, Belousova M G, Ivanov A P, Malyshev A I, Khanzutin V P
1988 Activity of north Kamchatka volcanoes in 1985. *Volc Seism*, 1988(3): 3-12 (English translation 1990, 10: 331-346)

Melekestsev I V, Braitseva O A, Ponomareva V V
1989 Prediction of volcanic hazards on the basis of the study of dynamics of volcanic activity, Kamchatka. *In*: Latter J H (ed), p 10-35 (see global reference)

Seliverstov N I, Gavrilenko G M, Kirianov V Y
1989 Modern activity of Piip submarine volcano, Komandorsky Basin. *Volc Seism*, 1989(6): 3-18 (English translation 1990, 11: 757-779)

Braitseva O A, Melekestsev I V, Bogoyavlenskaya G E, Maksimov A P
1990 Bezymiannyi volcano: eruptive history and dynamics. *Volc Seism*, 1990(2): 3-22 (English translation 1991, 12: 165-194)

Fedotov S A, Andreev V N, Bogoyavlenskaya G E, Dvigalo V N, Khrenov A P, Zharinov N A
1990 Main eruptions of Kamchatka volcanoes in 1985-1990 (abs). *IAVCEI Internatl Volc Cong, Mainz, Abs*, (unpaginated)

Melekestsev I V, Braitseva O A, Ponomareva V V, Sulerzhitsky L D
1990 Ages and dynamics of development of the active volcanoes of the Kurile-Kamchatka region. *Internatl Geol Rev*, 32: 436-448

Ponomareva V V, Braitseva O A
1990 Volcanic hazards for the area of the Kronotsky Lake - Uzon, Geizerny Valley. *Volc Seism*, 1990(1) p 27-44 (English translation 1991, 12: 42-69)

Bursik M I, Melekestsev I V, Braitseva O A
1991 Preliminary stratigraphic and grain size data for most recent fall deposits of Ksudach volcano, Kamchatka (abs). *Eos, Trans Amer Geophys Union*, 72: 569

Doubik Y M, Sheridan M F, Macias J L
1991 Deposits of the giant 1907 blast of Ksudach volcano, Kamchatka (abs). *Eos, Trans Amer Geophys Union*, 72: 569

Fedotov S A, Masurenkov Y P (eds)
1991 H Active Volcanoes of Kamchatka. Moscow: Nauka Publ, 2 volumes, 302 & 415 p

Maksimov A P, Firstov P P, Girina O A, Malyshev A P
1991 The June 1986 eruption of Bezymiannyi. *Volc Seism*, 1991(1): 3-20 (English translation 1992, 13: 1-20)

Melekestsev I V, Felitsyn S B, Kirianov V Y
1991 The eruption of Opala in A.D. 500 -- the largest explosive eruption in Kamchatka in the Christian era. *Volc Seism*, 1991(1): 21-34 (English translation 1992, 13: 21-36)

Bindeman I N
1992 Petrology of Dikiy Greben volcano, southern Kamchatka. *Volc Seism*, 1992(4): 33-55 (English translation 1993, 14: 386-410)

Selyangin O B
1993 Mutnovskiy volcano, Kamchatka: new evidence on structure, evolution, and future activity. *Volc Seism*, 1993(1): 17-35 (English translation 1993, 15: 17-38)

MAINLAND ASIA (1001-06)

Ustiev E K
1959 Aniusky volcano and localization problems of Quaternary volcanism in north-eastern Asia. *Bull Volc*, 20: 155-172

Vlodavetz V I, Piip B I
1959 H Kamchatka and Continental Areas of Asia. *Catalog of Active Volcanoes of the World*, Rome: IAVCEI, 8: 1-110

Gorodinskiy M Y, Dovgal' Y M, Sterligova V Y
1967 The Aluchin group of late Quaternary volcanoes in western Chukotka. *Internatl Geol Rev*, 10: 1045-1054

Ogura T
1969 Volcanoes in Manchuria. *In*: Ogura T (ed) *Geology and Mineral Resources of the Far East*, Tokyo: Univ Tokyo Press, 2: 373-413

Tomita T
1969 Volcanic geology of the Cenozoic alkaline petrographic province of eastern Asia. *In*: Ogura T (ed) *Geology and Minerals of the Far East*, Tokyo: Univ Tokyo Press, p 139-179

Devyatkin Y V, Smelov S B
1979 Position of basalts in the Cenozoic sedimentary sequence of Mongolia. *Internatl Geol Rev*, 22: 307-317

Feng M, Guo K, Wang F
1979 *Wudalianchi Volcanoes in China*. Shanghai: Shanghai Sci Tech Publishers, 85 p

Lee D S
1981 Volcanic activity in the southwest part of Choogaryong Rift Valley, Korea (abs). *IAVCEI, Tokyo Mtg Abs*, p 200-202

Feng M
1982 The eruptions of Wudalianchi volcanoes of China. *Volcano News*, 10: 4-5

Lee M W
1982 Petrology and geochemistry of Jeju volcanic island, Korea. *Sci Rpt Tohoku Univ*, Ser 3, 15: 177-256

Machida H, Arai F
1983 Extensive ash falls in and around the Sea of Japan from large, late Quaternary eruptions. *Jour Volc Geotherm Res*, 18: 151-164

Shen Y, Wang X
1983 Volcanic rocks in Jingbo Lake and its tectonic setting. *IUGG, 18th General Assembly, Hamburg*, 2: 573

Chen S (ed)
1986 *Atlas of Geo-Science, Analysis of Landsat Imagery in China*. Beijing: Chinese Acad Sci Press, 228 p

Feng M, Whitford-Stark J L
1986 The 1719-1721 eruptions of potassium-rich lavas at Wudalianchi, China. *Jour Volc Geotherm Res*, 30: 130-148

Shi Z, Lee Q, Wu H, Yang Y
1986 A possible historical slow earthquake in eastern China. *Roy Soc New Zeal Bull*, 24: 547-552

Whitford-Stark J L
1987 H A survey of Cenozoic volcanism on mainland Asia. *Geol Soc Amer Spec Pap*, 213: 1-74

Liu J
1988 The volcanoes in the Kunlun Mountain, west China (abs). *Kagoshima Internatl Conf Volc Abs*, p 392

Moriwaki H, Machida H, Zhao D, Arai F
1988 Great eruption of Baegdu (Changbai) volcano occurred around a thousand years ago (abs). *Kagoshima Internatl Conf Volc Abs*, p 400

Tong W, Mu Z, Liu S, Zhang M
1988 Late Cenozoic volcanoes and active geothermal systems in China. *Proc Kagoshima Internatl Conf Volc*, p 847-850

Sohn Y K, Chough S K
1989 Depositional processes of the Suwolbong tuff ring, Cheju Island (Korea). *Sedimentology*, 36: 837-855

Chough S K, Sohn Y
1990 Depostional mechanics and sequences of base surges, Songaksan tuff ring, Cheju Island, Korea. *Sedimentology*, 37: 1115-1135

Machida H
1990 Frequency and magnitude of catastrophic explosive volcanism in the Japan region during the past 130 ka: implications for human occupance of volcanic regions. *Geol Soc Aust Symp Proc*, 1: 27-36

Machida H, Moriwaki H, Zhao D
1990 The recent major eruption of Changbai volcano and its environmental effects. *Geog Rpt Tokyo Metropolitan Univ*, 25: 1-25

Dunlap C E, Gill J B, Palacz Z A
1992 U/Th disequilibria in the large-volume chemically-zoned eruption of Baitoushan, 1010 AD (abs). *Eos, Trans Amer Geophys Union*, 73: 611

Liu R, Wei H, Li J
1992 Volcano at Tianci Lake, Changbaishan Mt.--the potentially most dangerous volcano in Chinese mainland. *29th Internatl Geol Cong, Kyoto, abs*, 2: 501

ALASKA: ALEUTIAN ARC (1101-03)

Doroshin P
1870 ★ Some volcanoes, their eruptions, and earthquakes in the former Russian holdings in America. *Verh Russ Kais Mineral Ges St Petersberg, Zweite Ser*, p 25-44, (in Russian)

Becker G F
1898 ★ Reconnaissance of the gold fields of southern Alaska, with some notes on general geology. *U S Geol Surv 18th Ann Rpt*, Part 3: 13-14

Holden E S
1898 A catalogue of earthquakes on the Pacific Coast 1769 to 1897. *Smithsonian Inst Misc Coll*, no 1087

Smith W R, Baker A A
1922 The Cold Bay-Chignik district, Alaska. *U S Geol Surv Bull*, 755-D: 156-157 & 191-192

Smith W R
1925 Aniakchak Crater, Alaska Peninsula. *U S Geol Surv Prof Pap*, 132-J: 139-149

Jaggar T A
1927a Three press reports. *Volcano Lett*, 108: 1
1927b The Aleutian Islands. *Volcano Lett*, 116: 1
1927c Eruption of Mageik in Alaska. *Volc Lett*, 147: 1

Fenner C N
1930 Mount Katmai and Mount Mageik. *Zeit Vulk*, 13: 1-24

Jaggar T A
1930 Recent activity of Bogoslof volcano. *Volcano Lett*, 275: 1-3

Okimura H
1930 The eruption of Katmai, Alaska, 1912. *Volcano Lett*, 305: 1-3

Hubbard B R
1931 World inside a mountain: Aniakchak, the new volcanic wonderland of the Alaska Peninsula, is explored. *Natl Geog*, 60: 319-345

Jaggar T A
1932 Aleutian eruptions 1930-1932. *Volcano Lett*, 375: 1-3

Finch R H
1934 Shishaldin volcano. *Proc 5th Pacific Sci Cong*, 3: 2369-2376

Bradley C C
1948 Geologic notes on Adak Island and the Aleutian chain, Alaska. *Amer Jour Sci*, 246: 214-240

Robinson G D
1948 Exploring Aleutian volcanoes. *Natl Geog*, 94: 509-528

Coats R R
1950 Volcanic activity in the Aleutian Arc. *U S Geol Surv Bull*, 974-B: 35-47

Sumner L
1951 Magnificent Katmai. *Sierra Club Bull*, 37: 29-51

Coats R R
1951 Geology of Buldir Island, Aleutian Islands, Alaska. *U S Geol Surv Bull*, 989-A: 1-26

Jones A E
1952 Aleutian volcanoes. *Volcano Lett*, 516: 8-9

Byers F M, Barth T F W
1953 Volcanic activity on Akun and Akutan Islands, Alaska. *Proc 7th Pacific Sci Congr*, 2: 382-397

Keller F, Meuschke J L, Alldredge L R
1954 Aeromagnetic surveys in the Aleutian, Marshall, and Bermuda Islands. *Eos, Trans Amer Geophys Union*, 35: 558-572

Muller E, Juhle W, Coulter H
1954 Current volcanic activity in Katmai National Monument, Alaska. *Science*, 119: 319-321

Snyder G L
1954 Eruption of Trident volcano, Katmai National Monument, Alaska, February-June 1953. *U S Geol Surv Circ*, 318: 1-7

Kennedy G C, Waldron H H
1955 Geology of Pavlof volcano and vicinity Alaska. *U S Geol Surv Bull*, 1028-A: 1-18

Simons F S, Mathewson D E
1955 Geology of Great Sitkin Island, Alaska.. *U S Geol Surv Bull*, 1028-B: 29-32

Coats R R
1956a Geology of northern Adak Island, Alaska. *U S Geol Surv Bull*, 1028-C: 47-66
1956b Geology of northern Kanaga Island, Alaska. *U S Geol Surv Bull*, 1028-D: 69-81
1956c Reconnaissance geology of some western Aleutian islands, Alaska. *U S Geol Surv Bull*, 1023-E: 83-100

Powers H A
1958 Alaska Peninsula-Aleutian Islands. *In*: Williams H (ed) *Landscapes of Alaska*, Los Angeles: Univ Calif Press, p 62-75

Byers F M
1959 Geology of Umnak and Bogoslof Islands, Aleutian Islands, Alaska. *U S Geol Surv Bull*, 1028-L: 267-365

Keller A S, Reiser H N
1959 Geology of the Mt. Katmai Area, Alaska. *U S Geol Surv Bull*, 1058-G: 264-268

Nelson W H
1959 Geology of Segula, Davidof, and Khvostof Islands, Alaska. *U S Geol Surv Bull*, 1028-K: 257-266

Snyder G L
1959 Geology of Little Sitkin Island, Alaska. *U S Geol Surv Bull*, 1028-H: 169-210

Wilcox R E
1959 Some effects of recent volcanic ash falls with special reference to Alaska. *U S Geol Surv Bull*, 1028-N: 409-476

Coats R R
1959a Geologic reconnaissance of Semisopochnoi Island western Aleutian Islands Alaska. *U S Geol Surv Bull*, 1028-O: 477-519
1959b Geologic reconnaissance of Gareloi Island, Aleutian Islands, Alaska. *U S Geol Surv Bull*, 1028-J: 249-256

Byers F M
1961 Petrology of three volcanic suites, Umnak and Bogoslof Islands, Aleutian Island, Alaska. *Geol Soc Amer Bull*, 72: 93-128

Coats R R, Nelson W H, Lewis R Q, Powers H A
1961 Geologic reconnaissance of Kiska Island, Aleutian Islands, Alaska. *U S Geol Surv Bull*, 1028-R: 563-581

Drewes H, Fraser G D, Snyder G L, Barnett H F
1961 Geology of Unalaska Island and adjacent insular shelf, Aleutian Islands, Alaska. *U S Geol Surv Bull*, 1028-S: 583-676

Waldron H H
1961 Geological reconnaissance of Frosty Peak volcano and vicinity, Alaska. *U S Geol Surv Bull*, 1028-T: 677-708

Burk C A
1965 Geology of the Alaska Peninsula-island arc and continental margin (Part 1). *Geol Soc Amer Mem*, 99: 1-250

Decker R W
1967 Investigations at active volcanoes. *Eos, Trans Amer Geophys Union*, 48: 639-647

Ward P L, Matumoto T
1967 A summary of volcanic and seismic activity in Katmai National Monument, Alaska. *Bull Volc*, 31: 107-130

Curtis G H
1968 The stratigraphy of the ejecta from the 1912 eruption of Mount Katmai and Novarupta, Alaska. *Geol Soc Amer Mem*, 116: 153-210

Detterman R L
1968 Recent volcanic activity on Augustine Island, Alaska. *U S Geol Surv Prof Pap*, 600-C: 126-129

Norris R A, Johnson R H
1969 Submarine volcanic eruptions recently located in the Pacific by SOFAR hydrophones. *Jour Geophys Res*, 74: 650-664

Wilson C R, Forbes R B
1969 Infrasonic waves from Alaskan volcanic eruptions. *Jour Geophys Res*, 74: 4511-4522

Wright T L
1971 Chemistry of Kilauea and Mauna Loa in space and time [Trident, Redoubt]. *U S Geol Surv Prof Pap*, 735: 1-40

Mauk F J, Kienle J
1973 Microearthquakes at St. Augustine volcano, Alaska, triggered by Earth tides. *Science*, 182: 386-389

Miller T P, Smith R L
1975 Ash flows on the Alaska Peninsula: a preliminary report on their distribution, composition and age (abs). *Geol Soc Amer Abs Prog*, 7: 1201

Smith R L, Shaw H R
1975 Igneous-related geothermal systems. *U S Geol Surv Circ*, 726: 58-83

Henning R A, Rosenthal C H, Olds B (eds)
1976 Alaska's volcanoes. *Alaska Geog*, 4: 1-88

Kienle J, Forbes R B
1976 Augustine: evolution of a volcano. *Alaska Univ Geophys Inst 1975-76 Ann Rpt*, p 26-48

Rymer M J, Sims J D
1976 Preliminary survey of modern glaciolacustrine sediments for earthquake-induced deformational structures, south-central Alaska. *U S Geol Surv Open-File Rpt*, 76-373: 1-31

Miller T P, Smith R L
1977 Spectacular mobility of ash flows around Aniakchak and Fisher Calderas, Alaska. *Geology*, 5: 173-176

Nakamura K, Jacob K H, Davies J N
1977 Volcanoes as possible indicators of tectonic stress orientation Aleutians and Alaska. *Pure Applied Geophys*, 115: 87-112

Smith R L, Shaw H R, Luedke R G, Russell S L
1978 Comprehensive tables giving physical data and thermal energy estimates for young igneous systems of the United States. *U S Geol Surv Open-File Rpt*, 78-925: 1-25

Johnston D A
1979 Volcanic gas studies at Alaskan volcanoes [Augustine]. *U S Geol Surv Circ*, 804-B: 83-84

Johnston D A, Detterman R L
1979 Revision of the recent eruption history of Augustine volcano - elimination of the "1902 eruption". *U S Geol Surv Circ*, 804-B: 80-83

Marsh B D, Leitz R E
1979 Geology of Amak Island, Aleutian Islands, Alaska. *Jour Geol*, 87: 715-723

Kienle J, Kyle P R, Self S, Motyka R J, Lorenz V
1980 Ukinrek Maars, Alaska, I. April 1977 eruption sequence, petrology and tectonic setting. *Jour Volc Geotherm Res*, 7: 11-37

Kienle J, Swanson S E
1980 Volcanic hazards from future eruptions of Augustine volcano, Alaska. *Univ Alaska Geophys Inst*, UAG R-275, 122 p

Riehle J R, Kienle J, Emmel K S
1981 Lahars in Crescent River valley, lower Cook Inlet, Alaska. *Alaskan Geol Geophys Surv Geol Rpt*, 53: 1-10

Hildreth W
1983 The compositionally zoned eruption of 1912 in the Valley of Ten Thousand Smokes, Katmai National Park, Alaska. *Jour Volc Geotherm Res*, 18: 1-56

Kienle J, Swanson S E
1983 Volcanism in the eastern Aleutian Arc: late Quaternary and Holocene centers, tectonic setting and petrology. *Jour Volc Geotherm Res*, 17: 393-432

Reeder J W
1983a Caption to cover photo [Okmok and Akutan]. *Eos, Trans Amer Geophys Union*, 64: 50 & 451

1983b Preliminary dating of the caldera-forming Holocene volcanic events for the eastern Aleutian Islands (abs). *Geol Soc Amer Abs Prog*, 15: 638

Yount E M, Miller T P, Emanuel R P, Wilson F H
1983 Eruption in an ice-filled caldera, Mount Veniaminof, Alaska Peninsula. *U S Geol Surv Circ*, 945: 59-60

Miller T P
1984 Two-stage volcanism at the Ugashik-Peulik volcanic center, Alaska Peninsula (abs). *Geol Soc Amer Abs Prog*, 16: 322

Reeder J W
1985 Hydrothermal manifestations of the northern part of Atka Island of the Aleutian arc, and their geologic and tectonic setting (abs). *IAVCEI 1985, Scientific Assembly Potassic Volc Mt Etna Volcano, Abs*, p 195-196

Riehle J R
1985 A reconnaissance of the major Holocene tephra deposits in the Upper Cook Inlet Region, Alaska. *Jour Volc Geotherm Res*, 26: 37-74

Brophy J G
1987 The Cold Bay volcanic center, Aleutian volcanic arc. II. Implications for fractionation and mixing mechanism in calc-alkaline andesite genesis. *Contr Mineral Petr*, 97: 378-388

Detterman R L, Wilson F H, Yount M E, Miller T P
1987 Quaternary geologic map of the Ugashik, Bristol Bay, and western part of Karluk quadrangles, Alaska. *U S Geol Surv Map*, I-1801

Hildreth W
1987 New perspectives on the eruption of 1912 in the Valley of Ten Tousand Smokes, Katmai National Park, Alaska. *Bull Volc*, 49: 680-693

McNutt S R
1987 Eruption characteristics and cycles at Pavlof volcano, Alaska, and their relation to regional earthquake activity. *Jour Volc Geotherm Res*, 31: 239-267

McNutt S R, Beavan R J
1987 Eruptions of Pavlof volcano and their possible modulation by ocean load and tectonic stresses. *Jour Geophys Res*, 92: 11,509-11,523

Miller T P, Smith R L
1987 Late Quaternary caldera-forming eruptions in the eastern Aleutian arc, Alaska. *Geology*, 15: 434-438

Riehle J R, Yount M E, Miller T P
1987 Petrography, chemistry, and geologic history of Yantarni volcano, Aleutian volcanic arc, Alaska. *U S Geol Surv Bull*, 1761: 1-27

Yount M E, Miller T P, Gamble B M
1987 The 1986 eruptions of Augustine volcano, Alaska: hazards and effects. *U S Geol Surv Circ*, 998: 4-13

Fournelle J H
1988 The geology and petrology of Shishaldin volcano, Unimak Island, Aleutian arc, Alaska. *Unpublished PhD thesis*, John Hopkins Univ, 507 p

Swanson S E, Kienle J
1988 The 1986 eruption of Mount St. Augustine: field test of a hazard evaluation. *Jour Geophys Res*, 93: 4500-4520

Siebert L, Glicken H, Kienle J
1989 Debris avalanches and lateral blasts at Mount St. Augustine volcano, Alaska. *Natl Geog Res*, 5: 232-249

Wilson F H
1989 Geologic setting, petrology, and age of Pliocene to Holocene volcanoes of the Stepovak Bay Area, Western Alaska Peninsula. *U S Geol Surv Bull*, 1903: 84-95

Alaska Volcano Observatory Staff
1990 The 1989-1990 eruption of Redoubt volcano. *Eos, Trans Amer Geophys Union*, 71: 265-275

Brantley S R (ed)
1990 The eruptions of Redoubt volcano, Alaska December 14, 1989 - August 31, 1990. *U S Geol Surv Circ*, 1061: 1-33

Nye C J, Turner D L
1990 Petrology, geochemistry, and age of the Spurr volcanic complex, eastern Aleutian arc. *Bull Volc*, 52: 205-226

Wood C A, Kienle J (eds)
1990 ★ Volcanoes of North America. Cambridge, England: Cambridge Univ Press, 354 p

Hildreth W
1991 The timing of caldera collapse at Mount Katmai in response to magma withdrawal toward Novarupta. *Geophys Res Lett*, 18: 1541-1544

McNutt S R, Miller T P, Taber J J
1991 Geological and seismological evidence of increased explosivity during the 1986 eruptions of Pavlof volcano, Alaska. *Bull Volc*, 53: 86-98

Beget J E, Kienle J
1992 Cyclic formation of debris avalanches at Mount St. Augustine volcano. *Nature*, 356: 701-704

Fierstein J, Hildreth W
1992 The Plinian eruptions of 1912 at Novarupta, Katmai National Park, Alaska. *Bull Volc*, 54: 646-684

Lamb D, Linneman S R, Myers J D, Nicolaysen K E
1992 Caldera formation on Yumaska Island, central Aleutian arc (abs). *Eos, Trans Amer Geophys Union*, 73(43): 645

Neal C A, McGimsey R G, Braitseva O, Miller T P, Eichelberger J C, Nye C
1992 Post-caldera eruptive history of Aniakchak caldera, Alaska (abs). *Eos, Trans Amer Geophys Union*, 73(43): 645

Nicolaysen K E, Myers J D, Linneman S R, Lamb D
1992 Geologic relations of the Yunaska volcanic complex, central Aleutian arc (abs). *Eos, Trans Amer Geophys Union*, 73(43): 645

Nye C J, Beget J E, Motyka R J, Layer P W
1992 Geology and geochemistry of Mt. Douglas volcano, eastern Aleutian arc, Alaska (abs). *Eos, Trans Amer Geophys Union*, 73(43): 645

Beget J E, Nye C J
1994 Postglacial eruption history of Mt. Redoubt, Alaska. *Jour Volc Geotherm Res*, 62: 31-54

Beget J E, Stihler S D, Stone D B
1994 A 500-year-long record of tephra falls from Mt. Redoubt and other volcanoes in upper Cook Inlet, Alaska. *Jour Volc Geotherm Res*, 62: 55-67

Miller T P, McGimsey R G, Riehle J R, Richter D H, Yount M E

1994 ★ Catalogue of the active volcanoes of Alaska. *U S Geol Surv Bull* (in review)

Myers J D

1994 ★ *The Geology, Geochemistry and Petrology of the Recent Magmatic Phase of the Central and Western Aleutian Arc.* Baltimore : John Hopkins Univ Press (in preparation)

Siebert L, Beget J E, Glicken H

1994 The 1883 and late-prehistoric eruptions of Augustine volcano, Alaska. *Jour Volc Geotherm Res*, in press

ALASKA: W, E, & SE (1104-05)

Becker G F

1898 ★ Reconnaissance of the gold fields of southern Alaska, with some notes on general geology. *U S Geol Surv 18th Ann Rpt*, Part 3: 13-14

Mendenhall W C

1903 The Wrangell Mountains, Alaska. *Natl Geog*, 14: 395-407

1905 Geology of the central Copper River region, Alaska. *U S Geol Surv Prof Pap*, 41: 54-62

Moffit F H

1905 The Fairhaven gold placers, Seward, Alaska [St. Michael]. *U S Geol Surv Bull*, 247: 34

Crosby W O

1907 Volcanic activity in Alaska [Wrangell]. *Science*, 24: 78

Collier A J, Hess F L, Smith P S, Brooks A H

1908 The gold placer of parts of Seward Peninsula. *U S Geol Surv Bull*, 328: 103

Buddington A F, Chapin T

1929 Geology and mineral deposits of southeastern Alaska. *U S Geol Surv Bull*, 800: 278-279

Jaggar T A

1931 St. Paul Island in the Pribilof Group. *Volcano Lett*, 335: 1-4

Barth T F W

1956 Geology and petrology of the Pribilof Islands, Alaska. *U S Geol Surv Bull*, 1028-F: 101-160

Coonrad W L

1957 Geologic reconnaissance in the Yukon Kuskokwim Delta region, Alaska. *U S Geol Surv Map*, I-223, 1:500,000

Cox A, Hopkins D M, Dalrymple G B

1966 Geomagnetic polarity epochs: Pribilof Islands, Alaska. *Geol Soc Amer Bull*, 77: 883-910

Hoare J M, Condon W H, Cox A, Dalrymple G B

1968 Geology, paleomagnetism and potassium-argon ages of basalts [Nunivak Island]. *Geol Soc Amer Mem*, 116: 377-414

Brew D A, Muffler L J P, Loney R A

1969 Reconnaissance geology of the Mount Edgecumbe volcanic field, Kruzof Island, southeastern Alaska. *U S Geol Surv Prof Pap*, 650-D: 1-18

Lerbekmo J F, Campbell F A

1969 Distribution, Composition, and Source of the White River Ash, Yukon Territory. *Can Jour Earth Sci*, 6: 109-116

Wanek A A, Callahan J E

1971 Geologic reconnaissance of a proposed powersite at Lake Grace, Revillagigedo Island southeastern Alaska. *U S Geol Surv Bull*, 1211-E: 1-24

Lerbekmo J F, Westgate J A, Smith D G W, Denton G H

1975 New data on the character and history of the White River volcanic eruption, Alaska. *In*: Suggate R P and Cresswell M M (eds) *Quaternary Studies*, Wellington: Roy Soc New Zeal, p 203-209

Smith R L, Shaw H R

1975 Igneous-related geothermal systems. *U S Geol Surv Circ*, 726: 58-83

Henning R A, Rosenthal C H, Olds B (eds)

1976 Alaska's volcanoes. *Alaska Geog*, 4: 1-88

Smith R L, Shaw H R, Luedke R G, Russell S L

1978 Comprehensive tables giving physical data and thermal energy estimates for young igneous systems of the United States. *U S Geol Surv Open-File Rpt*, 78-925: 1-25

Benson C S, Motyka R J

1979 Glacier - volcano interactions on Mt. Wrangell, Alaska. *Univ Alaska Geophys Inst Ann Rpt*, 1977-78: 1-25

Kosco D G

1981 The Mt. Edgecumbe volcanic field, Alaska: an example of tholeiitic and calc-alkaline volcanism. *Jour Geol*, 89: 459-478

Riehle J R, Brew D A

1984 Explosive Holocene activity of the Mount Edgecumbe volcanic field, Alaska. *U S Geol Surv Circ*, 939: 111-115

Riehle J R, Brew D A, Lanphere M A

1989 Geologic map of the Mount Edgecumbe volcanic field, Kruzof Island, southeastern Alaska. *U S Geol Surv Map*, I-1983

Wood C A, Kienle J (eds)

1990 ★ Volcanoes of North America. Cambridge, England: Cambridge Univ Press, 354 p

McGimsey R G, Richter D H, DuBois G D, Miller T P

1992 A postulated new source for the White River Ash, Alaska. *U S Geol Surv Bull*, 1999: 212-218

Riehle J R, Champion D E, Brew D A, Lanphere M A

1992 Pyroclastic deposits of the Mount Edgecumbe volcanic field, southeast Alaska: eruptions of a stratified magma chamber. *Jour Volc Geotherm Res*, 53: 117-143

Miller T P, McGimsey R G, Riehle J R, Richter D H, Yount M E

1994 ★ Catalogue of the active volcanoes of Alaska. *U S Geol Surv Bull* (in review)

CANADA (1200)

Dolmage V

1921 Coast and islands of British Columbia between Burke and Douglas Channels. *Geol Surv Canada Summary Rpt*, no 29

1924 Post-Pleistocene volcanics of the British Columbia coast. *Jour Geol*, 32: 36-48

1928 Gun Creek map-area, British Columbia. *Geol Surv Canada Summary Rpt*, Part A: 78-93

Davis N F G

1930 Clearwater Lake area, British Columbia. *Geol Surv Canada Summary Rpt*, Part A: 274-293

Bostock H S

1936 Carmacks District, Yukon. *Geol Surv Canada Mem*, 189

Kerr F A

1948 Lower Stikine and western Iskut River areas, British Columbia. *Geol Surv Canada Mem*, 246: 1-94

Lord C S

1948 McConnell Creek map area, Cassiar District, British Columbia. *Geol Surv Canada Mem*, 251: 1-72

Mathews W H

1958 Geology of the Mt. Garibaldi map-area, S.W. British Columbia. *Geol Soc Amer Bull*, 69: 186

Aitken J D

1959 Atlin map-area, British Columbia. *Geol Surv Canada Mem*, 307<: 1-89

Tipper H W

1959 Quesnel Cariboo District, British Columbia. *Geol Surv Canada Map*, 12-1959

Campbell R B

1961 Quesnel Lake, west half, British Columbia. *Geol Surv Canada Map*, 3-1961

Gabrielse H, Souther J G

1962 Dease Lake, British Columbia. *Geol Surv Canada Map*, 21-1962

Campbell R B

1963 Quesnel Lake, east half, British Columbia. *Geol Surv Canada Map*, 1-1963

Souther J G

1966 Cordilleran volcanic study. *Geol Surv Canada Pap*, 66-1: 87-89

Campbell R B

1967 Canoe River, west half, British Columbia. *Geol Surv Canada Map*, 15-1967

Nasmith H, Mathews W H, Rouse G E

1967 Bridge River ash and some other Recent ash beds in British Columbia. *Can Jour Earth Sci*, 4: 163-170

Gabrielse H

1969 Geology of Jenning River map-area. *Geol Surv Canada Pap*, 68-55: 1-37

Sutherland-Brown A

1969 Aiyansh lava flow, British Columbia. *Can Jour Earth Sci*, 6: 1460-1468

Souther J G

1970 Volcanism and its relationship to recent crustal movements in the Canadian Cordillera. *Can Jour Earth Sci*, 7: 553-568

Campbell R B, Tipper H W

1971 Geology of Bonaparte Lake map-area, British Columbia. *Geol Surv Canada Mem*, 363: 1-100

Fulton F J

1971 Radiocarbon geochronology of southern British Columbia. *Geol Surv Canada Pap*, 71-37: 1-28

Souther J G

1972 Telegraph Creek map-area British Columbia. *Geol Surv Canada Pap*, 71-44: 1-38

Souther J G, Lambert M B
1972 Volcanic rocks of the northern Canadian Cordillera. *24th Internatl Geol Cong, Montreal, Guidebook*, Sec 2: 1-54

Aumento F, Souther J G
1973 Fission track dating of Late Tertiary and Quaternary volcanic glass from the Mount Edziza volcano, British Columbia. *Can Jour Earth Sci*, 10: 1156-1163

Baer A J
1973 Bella Coola-Laredo Sound map areas, British Columbia. *Geol Surv Canada Mem*, 372: 1-122

Souther J G
1973 Cordilleran volcanic project Spectrum Range. *Geol Surv Canada Pap*, 73-1: 46-48

Souther J G, Symons D T A
1974 Stratigraphy and paleomagnetism of Mount Edziza volcanic complex, northwestern British Columbia. *Geol Surv Canada Pap*, 73-32: 1-48

Grove E W
1976 Deglaciation a possible triggering mechanism for recent volcanism. *In*: Gonzalez-Ferran O (ed) *Proc Symp Andean & Antarctic Volcanology Problems (Santiago, Chile, Sept 1974)*, Rome: IAVCEI, p 88-97

Holland S S
1976 Landforms of British Columbia, a physiographic outline. *Brit Columbia Dept Mines Petrol Resour Bull*, 48: 1-138 (2nd printing)

Souther J G
1976 Geothermal potential of western Canada. *In*: *Proc 2nd United Nations Symp Devel Use Geotherm Resour, San Francisco* Washington D C: U S Government Printing Office, 1: 259-267

Hamilton T S, Scarfe C M
1977 Preliminary report on the petrology of the Level Mountain Volcanic Centre, northwest British Columbia. *Geol Surv Canada Pap*, 77-1A: 429-433

Read P B
1977 Meager Creek volcanic complex, southwestern British Columbia. *Geol Surv Canada Pap*, 77-1A: 277-285

Westgate J A
1977 Identification and significance of late Holocene tephra from Otter Creek, southern British Columbia, and localities in west-central Alberta. *Can Jour Earth Sci*, 14: 2593-2600

Souther J G
1977a Volcanism and tectonic environments in the Canadian Cordillera, a second look. *Geol Assoc Canada Spec Pap*, 16: 3-24

1977b Volcano fly-by. *Geol Assoc Canada 1977 Ann Mtg, Vancouver, Fieldtrip Guidebook 16*, 15 p

Lewis T J, Souther J G
1978 Meager Mountain, B.C.- A possible geothermal energy resource. *Energy Mines Resour Canada, Geotherm Ser*, 9: 1-17

Read P B
1978 Meager Creek geothermal area. *Geol Surv Canada, Open-File 603*, 1:20,000 geol map and text

Wuorinen V
1978 Age of Aiyansh volcano, British Columbia. *Can Jour Earth Sci*, 15: 1037-1038

Clague J J
1981 Late Quaternary geology and geochronology of British Columbia. Part 2: Summary and discussion of radiocarbon-dated Quaternary history. *Geol Surv Canada Pap*, 80-35: 1-41

Elliott R L, Koch R D, Robinson S W
1981 Age of basalt flows in the Blue River valley, Bradfield Canal quadrangle. *U S Geol Surv Circ* 823-B: 115-116

Green N L
1981 Geology and petrology of Quaternary volcanic rocks, Garibaldi Lake area, southwestern British Columbia summary. *Geol Soc Amer Bull*, 92: 697-702

Allen C C, Jercinovic M J, Allen J S B
1982 Subglacial volcanism in north-central British Columbia and Iceland. *Jour Geol*, 90: 699-715

Hickson C J, Souther J G
1984 Late Cenozoic volcanic rocks of the Clearwater-Wells Gray area, British Columbia. *Can Jour Earth Sci*, 21: 267-277

Lawrence R B, Armstrong R L, Berman R G
1984 Garibaldi Group volcanic rocks of the Salal Creek area, southwestern British Columbia: alkaline lavasw on the fringe of the predominately calc-alkaline Garibaldi (Cascade) volcanic arc. *Jour Volc Geotherm Res*, 21: 255-276

Blake W
1985 Geological Survey of Canada radiocarbon dates XXV. *Geol Surv Canada Pap*, 85: 19

Hickson C J
1986 Quaternary volcanism in the Wells Grey-Clearwater area, east central British Columbia. *Unpublished PhD thesis*, Univ British Columbia

Eiche G E, Francis D M, Ludden J N
1987 Primary alkaline magmas associated with the Quaternary Alligator Lake volcanic complex, Yukon Territory, Canada. *Contr Mineral Petr*, 95: 191-201

Metcalf P M
1987 Petrogenesis of Quaternary alkaline lavas in Wells Gray Provincial Park, B.C. and constraints on the petrology of the subcordilleran mantle. *Unpublished PhD thesis*, Univ Alberta, 395 p

Souther J G, Clague J J, Mathewes R W
1987 Nazko cone: a Quaternary volcano in the eastern Anahim belt. *Can Jour Earth Sci*, 24: 2477-2485

Green N L, Armstrong R L, Harakal J E, Souther J G, Read P B
1988 Eruptive history and K-Ar geochronology of the late Cenozoic Garibaldi volcanic belt, southwestern British Columbia. *Geol Soc Amer Bull*, 100: 563-579

Jackson L E
1989 Pleistocene subglacial volcanism near Fort Selkirk, Yukon Territory. *Geol Surv Canada Pap*, 89-1E: 251-256

Read P B, Brown R L, Psutka J F, Moore J M, Journeay M, Lane L S, Orchard M J
1989 Geology of parts of Snippaker Creek (104B/10), Forrest Kerr Creek (104B/15), Bob Quinn Lake (104B/16), Iskut River (104G/1) and More Creek (104G/2). *Geol Surv Canada Open File* no 2094, map and text, 2 sheets

Green N L
1990 Late Cenozoic volcanism in the Mount Garibaldi and Garibaldi Lake volcanic fields, Garibaldi volcanic belt, southwestern British Columbia. *Geoscience Canada*, 17: 171-174

Read P B
1990 Mount Meager complex, Garibaldi belt, southwestern British Columbia. *Geoscience Canada*, 17: 167-170

Stasiuk M V, Russell J K
1990 Quaternary volcanic rocks of the Iskut River region, northwestern British Columbia. *Geol Surv Canada Pap*, 90-1E: 153-157

Wood C A, Kienle J (eds)
1990 ★Volcanoes of North America. Cambridge, England: Cambridge Univ Press, 354 p

Brooks G R, Friele P A
1992 Bracketing ages for the formation of the Ring Creek lava flow, Mount Garibaldi volcanic field, southwestern British Columbia. *Can Jour Earth Sci*, 29: 2425-2428

Jackson L E, Stevens W
1992 A recent eruptive history of Volcano Mountain, Yukon Territory. *Geol Surv Canada Pap*, 92-1A: 33-39

Souther J G
1992 The late Cenozoic Mount Edziza volcanic complex, British Columbia. *Geol Surv Canada Mem*, 420: 1-320

Charland A, Francis D, Ludden J
1993 Stratigraphy and geochemistry of the Itcha Volcanic Complex, central British Columbia. *Can Jour Earth Sci*, 30: 132-144

Souther J G, Weiland I
1993 Crow Lagoon tephra--new evidence of recent volcanism in west-central British Columbia. *Geol Surv Canada Pap*, 93-1A: 57-62

Edwards B R, Russell J K
1994 Preliminary stratigraphy of Hoodoo Mountain volcanic centre, northwestern British Columbia. *Geol Surv Canada Pap*, 94-1A: 69-76

Hauksdottir S, Enegren E G, Russell J K
1994 Recent basaltic volcanism in the Iskut-Unuk rivers area, northwestern British Columbia. *Geol Surv Canada Pap*, 94-1A: 57-67

Hickson C J, Soos A, Wright R
1994 ★Volcanic features of the Canadian Cordillera. *Geol Surv Canada Open-File*, in press

Stasiuk M V, Russell J K, Hickson C J
1994 Influence of magma chemistry on eruption behavior from the distribution and nature of the 2400 B.P. eruption products of Mount Meager, British Columbia. *Geol Surv Canada Open-File*, 2843: 1-38 and 1:50,000 geol map

USA: PACIFIC NW (1201-02)

Jillson W R
1917 The volcanic activity of Mount St. Helens and Mt. Hood in historical times. *Geol Rev*, 3: 481-485

Smith W D
1927 Contribution to the geology of southeastern Oregon (Steens and Pueblo Mountains). *Jour Geol*, 35: 421-440

Coombs H A
1939 Mount Baker, a Cascade volcano. *Geol Soc Amer Bull*, 50: 1493-1510

Williams H
1942 The geology of Crater Lake National Park, Oregon. *Carnegie Inst Wash Pub*, 540: 1-162
1944 Volcanoes of the Three Sisters region, Oregon Cascades. *Univ Calif Pub Geol Sci*, 27: 37-84

Holmes K L
1955 Mount St. Helens' recent eruptions. *Ore Hist Quart*, 56: 197-210

Williams H
1957 A geologic map of the Bend Quadrangle, Oregon and a reconnaissance geologic map of the central portion of the High Cascade Mountains. *Oregon Dept Geol Min Ind*, 1:125,000 and 1:250,000

Coombs H A, Howard A D
1960 ★United States of America. *Catalog of Active Volcanoes of the World*, Rome: IAVCEI, 9: 1-68

Hopson C A, Waters A C, Bender V R, Rubin M
1962 The latest eruptions from Mount Rainier volcano. *Jour Geol*, 70: 635-647

Fiske R S, Hopson C A, Waters A C
1963 Geology of Mount Rainier National Park, Washington. *U S Geol Surv Prof Pap*, 444: 1-93

Peterson N V, Groh E A
1963 Recent volcanic landforms in central Oregon. *Ore Bin*, 25: 1-15

Benson G T
1965 The age of Clear Lake, Oregon. *Ore Bin*, 27: 1-4

Moxham R M, Crandell D R, Marlatt W E
1965 Thermal features at Mount Rainier, Washington, as revealed by infrared surveys. *U S Geol Surv Prof Pap*, 525-D: 93-100

Taylor E M
1965 Recent volcanism between Three Fingered Jack and North Sister Oregon Cascade Range. *Ore Bin*, 27: 121-148

Peterson N V, Groh E A
1966 Lunar Geological Field Conference guidebook. *Oregon Dept Geol Min Ind*, 51 p

Walker G W, Greene R C, Pattee E C
1966 Mineral resources of the Mount Jefferson primitive area, Oregon. *U S Geol Surv Bull*, 1230-D: 1-32

Taylor E M
1968 Roadside geology, Santiam and McKenzie Pass Highways, Oregon. *Oregon Dept Geol Min Ind Bull*, 62: 3-34

Williams H, Goles G
1968 Volume of the Mazama ash-fall and origin of Crater Lake caldera. *Oregon Dept Geol Min Ind Bull*, 62: 37-41

Wise W S
1968 Geology of the Mount Hood volcano. *Oregon Dept Geol Min Ind Bull*, 62: 81-98

Crandell D R
1969 The geologic story of Mount Rainier. *U S Geol Surv Bull*, 1292: 1-43

Higgins M W
1969 Airfall ash and pumice lapilli deposits from Central Pumice Cone, Newberry Caldera, Oregon. *U S Geol Surv Prof Pap*, 650-D: 26-32

Mullineaux D R, Sigafoos R S, Hendricks E L
1969 A historic eruption of Mt. Rainier, Wash. *U S Geol Surv Prof Pap*, 650-B: 15-18

Peterson N V, Groh E A
1969 The ages of some Holocene volcanic eruptions in the Newberry volcano area, Oregon. *Ore Bin*, 31: 73-87

Tabor R W, Crowder D F
1969 On batholiths and volcanoes: intrusion and eruption of late Cenozoic magmas in the Glacier Peak area, North Cascades, Washington. *U S Geol Surv Prof Pap*, 604: 1-67

Folsom M M
1970 Volcanic eruptions: the pioneers' attitude on the Pacific Coast from 1800 to 1875. *Ore Bin*, 32: 61-80

Wise W S
1970 Cenozoic volcanism in the Cascade Mountains of southern Washington. *Wash Dept Nat Resour Bull*, 60: 1-45

Crandell D R
1971 Postglacial lahars from Mount Rainier volcano, Washington. *U S Geol Surv Prof Pap*, 677: 1-75

Friedman I
1971 Obsidian hydration dates in the Newberry volcano area, Oregon. *U S Geol Surv Prof Pap*, 750-A: A-117

Greeley R, Hyde J H
1972 Lava tubes of the Cave basalt, Mount St. Helens, Washington. *Geol Soc Amer Bull*, 83: 2397-2418

Crandell D R, Mullineaux D R
1973 Pine Creek volcanic assemblage at Mount St. Helens, Washington. *U S Geol Surv Bull*, 1383-A: 1-23

Higgins M W
1973 Petrology of Newberry volcano, central Oregon. *Geol Soc Amer Bull*, 84: 455-488

Mullineaux D R
1974 Pumice and other pyroclastic deposits in Mount Rainier National Park, Washington. *U S Geol Surv Bull*, 1326: 1-83

Crandell D R, Mullineaux D R, Rubin M
1975 Mount St. Helens volcano: recent and future behavior. *Science*, 187: 438-441

Mullineaux D R, Hyde J H, Rubin M
1975 Widespread late glacial and postglacial tephra deposits from Mount St. Helens volcano, Washington. *U S Geol Surv Jour Res*, 3: 329-336

Smith R L, Shaw H R
1975 Igneous-related geothermal systems. *U S Geol Surv Circ*, 726: 58-83

Hammond P E, Pedersen S A, Hopkins K D, Aiken D, Harle D S, Danes Z F, Konicek D L, Stricklin C R
1976 Geology and gravimetry of the Quaternary basaltic volcanic field, southern Cascade Range, Washington. *In*: *Proc 2nd United Nations Symp Devel Use Geotherm Resour, San Francisco* Washington D C: U S Government Printing Office, 1: 397-405

Harris S L
1976 Fire and Ice, the Cascade Volcanoes. Seattle: The Mountaineers, 320 p

Hopkins K D
1976 Geology of the south and east slopes of Mount Adams volcano, Cascade Range, Washington. *PhD thesis*, Univ Washington, 143 p

Peterson N V, Groh E A, Taylor E M, Stensland D E
1976 Geology and mineral resources of Deschutes County Oregon. *Oregon Dept Geol Min Ind Bull*, 89: 1-62

Chitwood L A, Jensen R A, Groh E A
1977 The age of Lava Butte. *Ore Bin*, 39: 157-164

Friedman I
1977 Hydration dating of volcanism at Newberry Crater Oregon. *U S Geol Surv Jour Res*, 5: 337-342

Mehringer P J, Blinman E, Petersen K L
1977 Pollen influx and volcanic ash [Glacier Peak, Mazama]. *Science*, 198: 257-261

Otto B R, Hutchison D A
1977 The geology of the Jordan Craters, Malhuer County, Oregon. *Ore Bin*, 39: 125-140

Scott W E
1977 Quaternary glaciation and volcanism, Metolius River area, Oregon. *Geol Soc Amer Bull*, 88: 113-124

Crandell D R, Mullineaux D R
1978 Potential hazards from future eruptions of Mount St. Helens volcano, Washington. *U S Geol Surv Bull*, 1383-C: 1-26

Hyde J H, Crandell D R
1978 Postglacial volcanic deposits at Mount Baker, Washington, and potential hazards from future eruptions. *U S Geol Surv Prof Pap*, 1022-C: 1-17

Majors H M (ed)
1978 *Mount Baker: a Chronicle of its Historic Eruptions and First Ascent*. Seattle: Northwest Press, 221 p

Smith R L, Shaw H R, Luedke R G, Russell S L
1978 Comprehensive tables giving physical data and thermal energy estimates for young igneous systems of the United States. *U S Geol Surv Open-File Rpt*, 78-925: 1-25

Blinman E, Mehringer P J, Shephard J C
1979 Pollen influx and the depositon of Mazama and Glacier Peak tephra. *In*: Sheets P D and Grayson D K (eds) *Volcanic Activity and Human Ecology*, New York: Academic Press, p 393-425

Crandell D R, Mullineaux D R, Miller C D
1979 Volcanic-hazards studies in the Cascade Range of the western United States. *In*: Sheets P D and Grayson D K (eds) *Volcanic Activity and Human Ecology*, New York: Academic Press, p 195-219

Mack R N, Okazaki R, Valastro S
1979 Bracketing dates for two ash falls from Mount Mazama. *Nature*, 279: 228-229

Sherrod D R, MacLeod N S
1979 The last eruptions at Newberry volcano, central Oregon (abs). *Geol Soc Amer Abs Prog*, 11: 127

Christiansen R L
1980 Eruption of Mt. St. Helens: volcanology. *Nature*, 285: 531-533

Crandell D R
1980 Recent eruptive history of Mount Hood, Oregon, and potential hazards from future eruptions. *U S Geol Surv Bull*, 1492: 1-81

Hammond P E, Anderson J L, Manning K J
1980 Guide to the geology of the Upper Clackamas and North Santiam Rivers area, northern Oregon Cascade Range. *Oregon Dept Geol Min Ind Bull*, 101: 133-167

Hoblitt R P, Crandell D R, Mullineaux D R
1980 Mount St. Helens eruptive behavior during the past 1500 years. *Geology*, 8: 555-559

Majors H M
1980 Three newly discovered accounts of activity on Mount St. Helens. *Northwest Discovery*, 1: 36-41

Beget J E
1981 Early Holocene glacier advance in the north Cascade Range, Washington. *Geology*, 9: 409-413

Friedman I, Obradovich J
1981 Obsidian hydration dating of volcanic events. *Quaternary Res*, 16: 37-47

Lipman P W, Mullineaux D R (eds)
1981 The 1980 eruptions of Mount St. Helens, Washington. *U S Geol Surv Prof Pap*, 1250: 1-844

MacLeod N S, Sherrod D R, Chitwood L A, McKee E H
1981 Newberry volcano, Oregon. *U S Geol Surv Circ*, 838: 85-91

Majors H M, McCollum R C
1981a Mount St. Helens the 1844-1857 eruptions. *Northwest Discovery*, 2: 541-550

1981b Mount Rainier: the tephra eruption of 1894. *Northwest Discovery*, 2: 334-381

Taylor E M
1981 Roadlog for central High Cascade geology, Bend, Sisters, McKenzie Pass, and Santiam Pass, Oregon. *U S Geol Surv Circ*, 838: 59-83

Wozniak K C, Taylor E M
1981 Late Pleistocene summit construction and Holocene flank eruptions of South Sister volcano, Oregon (abs). *Eos, Trans Amer Geophys Union*, 62: 61

Beget J E
1982 Recent volcanic activity at Glacier Peak. *Science*, 215: 1389-1390

Luedke R G, Smith R L
1982 Map showing distribution, composition, and age of late Cenozoic volcanic centers in Oregon and Washington. *U S Geol Surv Map*, I-1091-D

MacLeod N S, Sherrod D R, Chitwood L A
1982 Geologic map of Newberry volcano, Deschutes, Klamath, and Lake Counties, Oregon. *U S Geol Surv Open-File Rpt*, 82-847: map and 27 p text

Bacon C R
1983 Eruptive history of Mount Mazama and Crater Lake caldera, Cascade Range, U S A. *Jour Volc Geotherm Res*, 18: 57-116

Beget J E
1983 Glacier Peak, Washington: a potentially hazardous Cascade volcano. *Envir Geol*, 5: 83-92

Champion D E
1983 Paleomagnetic "dating" of Holocene volcanic activity at Mount Mazama, Crater Lake, Oregon (abs). *Geol Soc Amer Abs Prog*, 15: 331

Frank D
1983 Origin, distribution, and rapid removal of hydrothermally formed clay at Mount Baker, Washington. *U S Geol Surv Prof Pap*, 1022-E: 1-31

Harris S L
1983 In the shadow of the mountains. *Pacific Northwest*, 17: 24-33

Hart W K, Mertzman S A
1983 Late Cenozoic stratigraphy of the Jordan Valley area, southeastern Oregon. *Oregon Geol*, 45: 15-19

Priest G R
1983 A field trip guide to the central Oregon Cascades. *Oregon Geol*, 45: 133-141

Sarna-Wojcicki A M, Champion D E, Davis J O
1983 Holocene volcanism in the conterminous United States and the role of silicic volcanic ash layers in correlation of latest Pleistocene and Holocene deposits. *In*: Wright H E (ed) *Late-Quaternary Environments of the United States*, Minneapolis: Univ Minnesota Press, 2: 52-77

Swanson D A, Casadevall T J, Dzurisin D, Malone S D Newhall C G, Weaver C S
1983 Predicting eruptions at Mount St. Helens, June 1980 through Dec 1982. *Science*, 221: 1369-1376

Wozniak K C
1983 Geology of the northern part of the south-east Three Sisters Quadrangle, Oregon. *Oregon Geol*, 45: 88

Yamaguchi D
1983 New tree-ring dates for recent eruptions of Mount St. Helens. *Quaternary Res*, 20: 246-250

Hammond P E
1984 Indian Heaven, S. Washington Cascade Range a basaltic volcanic field supplied by a central magma system? (abs). *Geol Soc Amer Abs Prog*, 16: 528

Barnett B, Korosec M A
1986 Geothermal exploratory drilling by the State of Washington in 1985. *Wash Geol Newsl*, 14: 21-28

Cameron K A, Pringle P
1986 Post-glacial lahars of the Sandy River basin, Mount Hood, Oregon. *Northwest Sci*, 60: 255-237

Mullineaux D R
1986 Summary of pre-1980 tephra-fall deposits erupted from Mount St. Helens, Washington State, USA. *Bull Volc*, 48: 17-27

Cameron K A, Pringle P T
1987 A detailed chronology of the most recent major eruptive period at Mount Hood, Oregon. *Geol Soc Amer Bull*, 99: 845-851

Crandell D R
1987 Deposits of pre-1980 pyroclastic flows and lahars from Mount St. Helens volcano, Washington. *U S Geol Surv Prof Pap*, 1444: 1-93

Korosec M A
1987 Geologic map of Mount Adams. *Wash Div Geol Earth Sci*, 1:100,000 geol map

Scott W E
1987 Holocene rhyodacite eruptions on the flanks of South Sister volcano, Oregon. *Geol Soc Amer Spec Pap*, 212: 35-53

Swanson D A, Dzurisin D, Holcomb R T, Iwatsubo E Y, Chadwick W W, Casadevall T J, Ewert J W, Heliker C C
1987 Growth of the lava dome at Mount St. Helens, Washington, (USA), 1981-1983. *Geol Soc Amer Spec Pap*, 212: 1-16

Bacon C R, Druitt T H
1988 Compositional evolution of the zoned calcalkaline magma chamber of Mount Mazama, Crater Lake, Oregon. *Contr Mineral Petr*, 98: 224-256

Harris S L
1988 ★ *Fire Mountains of the West: the Cascade and Mono Lake Volcanoes.* Missoula Montana: Mountain Press, 379 p

MacLeod N S, Sherrod D R
1988 Geologic evidence for a magma chamber beneath Newberry volcano, Oregon. *Jour Geophys Res*, 93: 10,067-10,079

Scott W E, Gardner C A, Sarna-Wojcicki A M
1989 Guidebook for field trip to the Mount Bachelor-South Sister-Bend area, central Oregon High Cascades. *U S Geol Surv Open-File Rpt*, 89-645: 1-68

Swanson D A, Cameron K A, Evarts R C, Pringle P T, Vance J A
1989 Excursion 1A: Cenozoic volcanism in the Cascade Range and Columbia Plateau, southern Washington. *New Mexico Bur Mines Min Resour Mem*, 47: 1-50

Hopson C A, Melson W G
1990 Compositional trends and eruptive cycles at Mount St. Helens. *Geoscience Canada*, 17: 131-141

Wood C A, Kienle J (eds)
1990 ★ Volcanoes of North America. Cambridge, England: Cambridge Univ Press, 354 p

Yamaguchi D K, Hoblitt R P, Lawrence D B
1990 A new tree-ring date for the "floating island" lava flow, Mount St. Helens, Washington. *Bull Volc*, 52: 545-550

Myers B
1992 Small explosions interrupt 3-year quiescence of Mount St. Helens, Washington. *Earthq Volcanoes*, 23: 58-7

Scott W E, Gardner C A
1992 Geologic map of the Mount Bachelor volcanic chain and surrounding area, Cascade Range, Oregon. *U S Geol Surv Misc Invest Map, I-1967*, 1:50,000 geol map

Yamaguchi D K, Lawrence D B
1993 Tree-ring evidence for 1842-1843 eruptive activity at the Goat Rocks dome, Mount St. Helens, Washington. *Bull Volc*, 55: 264-272

Carey S, Gardner J, Sigurdsson H
1994 The intensity and magnitude of Holocene plinian eruptions from Mount St. Helens volcano. *Jour Volc Geotherm Res*, in press

USA: CALIFORNIA (1203)

Harkness H W
1875 A recent volcano in Plumas County. *Calif Acad Sci Proc*, 5: 408-412

Finch R H
1928 Possible 1851 lava flow at Lassen Cinder Cone. *Volcano Lett*, 199: 1

Williams H
1932 Geology of the Lassen Volcanic National Park, California. *Univ Calif Pub Geol Sci*, 21: 195-385

Anderson C A
1936 Volcanic history of the Clear Lake area, Calif. *Geol Soc Amer Bull*, 47: 629-664

Finch R H
1937 A tree ring calendar for dating volcanic events at Cinder Cone, Lassen National Park, California. *Amer Jour Sci*, 33: 140-146

Townley S D, Maxwell W A
1939 Descriptive catalog of earthquakes of the Pacific Coast of the United States 1769 to 1928. *Bull Seism Soc Amer*, 29: 83

Anderson C A
1940 Hat Creek lava flow. *Amer Jour Sci*, 238: 477-492
1941 Volcanoes of the Medicine Lake Highland California. *Univ Calif Pub Geol Sci*, 25: 347-422

Williams H
1942 The geology of Crater Lake National Park, Oregon. *Carnegie Inst Wash Pub*, 540: 1-162
1949 Geology of the Macdoel quadrangle (California). *Calif Div Mines Geol Bull*, 151: 7-60

Chesterman C W
1955 Age of the obsidian flow at Glass Mountain, Siskiyou County, California. *Amer Jour Sci*, 253: 418-424

Sharp R P
1957 Geomorphology of Cima Dome, Mojave Desert, California. *Geol Soc Amer Bull*, 68: 273-290

California Div. Mines and Geology
1958-69 Geologic atlas of California, 1:250,0000 scale. *Calif Div Mines Geol*

Coombs H A, Howard A D
1960 ★ United States of America. *Catalog of Active Volcanoes of the World*, Rome: IAVCEI, 9: 1-68

Parker R B
1963 Recent volcanism at Amboy Crater, San Bernardino County, California. *Calif Div Mines Geol Spec Rpt*, 76: 7-21

Bassett A M, Kupfer D H
1964 A geologic reconnaissance in the southeastern Mojave Desert, California. *Calif Div Mines Geol Spec Rpt*, 83: 1-43

Rinehart C D, Ross D C
1964 Geology and mineral deposits of the Mount Morrison quadrangle Sierra Nevada, California. *U S Geol Surv Prof Pap*, 385: 1-106

Rinehart C D, Huber N K
1965 The Inyo Crater Lakes-a blast in the past. *Calif Div Mines Geol Min Info Serv*, 18: 169-172

Bateman P C, Wahrhaftig C
1966 Geology of the Sierra Nevada. *Calif Div Mines Geol Bull*, 190: 107-172

James D E
1966 Geology and rock magnetism of Cinder Cone lava flows, Lassen Volcanic National Park, California. *Geol Soc Amer Bull*, 77: 303-312

Macdonald G A
1966 Geology of the Cascade Range and Modoc Plateau. *Calif Div Mines Geol Bull*, 190: 65-95

Huber N K, Rinehart C D
1967 Cenozoic volcanic rocks of the Devils Postpile quadrangle, eastern Sierra Nevada California. *U S Geol Surv Prof Pap*, 554-D: 1-21

Friedman I
1968 Hydration rind dates rhyolite flows. *Science*, 159: 878-880

Chesterman C W
1971 Volcanism in California. *Calif Geol*, 24: 139-147

Garrison L E
1972 Geothermal steam in the Geysers-Clear Lake region, California. *Geol Soc Amer Bull*, 83: 1449-1468

Crowe B M, Fisher R V
1973 Sedimentary structures in base-surge deposits with special reference to cross-bedding, Ubehebe Craters, Death Valley, California. *Geol Soc Amer Bull*, 84: 663-682

Crandell D R, Mullineaux D R, Sigafoos R S, Rubin M
1974 Chaos Crags eruptions and rockfall-avalanches, Lassen Volcanic National Park, California. *U S Geol Surv Jour Res*, 2: 49-59

Smith R L, Shaw H R
1975 Igneous-related geothermal systems. *U S Geol Surv Circ*, 726: 58-83

Bailey R A, Dalrymple G B, Lanphere M A
1976 Volcanism, structure, and geochronology of Long Valley Caldera, Mono County, California. *Jour Geophys Res*, 81: 725-744

Christiansen R L, Miller C D
1976 Volcanic evolution of Mt. Shasta, California (abs). *Geol Soc Amer Abs Prog*, 8: 360-361

Harris S L
1976 ★ Fire and Ice, the Cascade Volcanoes. Seattle: The Mountaineers, 320 p

Robinson P T, Elders W A, Muffler L J P
1976 Quaternary volcanism in the Salton Sea geothermal field, Imperial Valley, California. *Geol Soc Amer Bull*, 87: 347-360

Wood S H
1977 Distribution, correlation, and radiocarbon dating of late Holocene tephra, Mono and Inyo Craters, eastern California. *Geol Soc Amer Bull*, 88: 89-95

Heiken G
1978a Characteristics of tephra from Cinder Cone, Lassen Volcanic National Park, California. *Bull Volc*, 41: 119-130
1978b Plinian-type eruptions in the Medicine Lake Highland, California, and the nature of the underlying magma. *Jour Volc Geotherm Res*, 4: 375-402

Miller C D
1978 Holocene pyroclastic-flow deposits from Shastina and Black Butte, west of Mount Shasta, California. *U S Geol Surv Jour Res*, 6: 611-624

Smith R L, Shaw H R, Luedke R G, Russell S L
1978 Comprehensive tables giving physical data and thermal energy estimates for young igneous systems of the United States. *U S Geol Surv Open-File Rpt*, 78-925: 1-25

Crandell D R, Mullineaux D R, Miller C D
1979 Volcanic-hazards studies in the Cascade Range of the western United States. *In*: Sheets P D and Grayson D K (eds) *Volcanic Activity and Human Ecology*, New York: Academic Press, p 195-219

Wood S H, Brooks R
1979 Panum crater tephra dated 640 ± 40 radiocarbon Y.B.P., Mono Craters, California (abs). *Geol Soc Amer Abs Prog*, 11: 543

Duffield W A, Bacon C R, Dalrymple G B
1980 Late Cenozoic volcanism, geochronology, and structure of the Coso Range, Inyo County, California. *Jour Geophys Res*, 85: 2381-2404

Kilbourne R T, Chesterman C W, Wood S H
1980 Recent volcanism in the Mono Basin-Long Valley Region of Mono County, California. *Calif Div Mines Geol Spec Rpt*, 150: 7-22

Miller C D
1980 Potential hazards from future eruptions in the vicinity of Mount Shasta volcano, northern California. *U S Geol Surv Bull*, 1503: 1-43

Peterson J A, Martin L M
1980 Geologic map of the Baker-Cypress BLM roadless area and Timbered Crater RARE II Areas, Modoc, Shasta, and Siskiyou Counties, California. *U S Geol Surv Map*, MF-1214-A, 1:62,500 geol map

Fink J H
1981 Structure and emplacement of a rhyolite obsidian flow: Little Glass Mountain, Medicine Lake Highland, northern California. *Geol Soc Amer Bull*, 94: 362-380

Friedman I, Obradovich J
1981 Obsidian hydration dating of volcanic events. *Quaternary Res*, 16: 37-47

Kilbourne R T, Anderson C L
1981 Volcanic history and "active" volcanism in California. *Calif Geol*, 34: 159-168

Luedke R G, Smith R L
1981 Map showing distribution, composition, and age of late Cenozoic volcanic centers in California and Nevada. *U S Geol Surv Map*, I-1091-C

Chesterman C W
1982 Potentially active volcanic zones in California. *Calif Dept Conservation Div Mines Geol Spec Pub*, 63: 9-16

Kilbourne R T
1982 Chronology of eruptions in California during the last 2,000 years. *Calif Dept Conservation Div Mines Geol Spec Pub*, 63: 29-40

Moore J G, Lanphere M
1983 Age of the Golden Trout Creek volcanic field, Sierra Nevada, California (abs). *Eos, Trans Amer Geophys Union*, 64: 895

Rundle J B, Eichelberger J C
1983 Caption to cover photo [Inyo Craters]. *Eos, Trans Amer Geophys Union*, 64: 11

Sarna-Wojcicki A M, Champion D E, Davis J O
1983 Holocene volcanism in the conterminous United States and the role of silicic volcanic ash layers in correlation of latest Pleistocene and Holocene deposits. *In*: Wright H E (ed) *Late-Quaternary Environments of the United States*, Minneapolis: Univ Minnesota Press, 2: 52-77

Crandell D R, Miller C D, Glicken H X, Christiansen R L, Newhall C G
1984 Catastrophic debris avalanche from ancestral Mount Shasta volcano, California. *Geology*, 12: 143-146

Hill D P, Bailey R A, Ryall A S
1985 Active tectonic and magmatic processes beneath Long Valley caldera, eastern California: an overview. *Jour Geophys Res*, 90: 11,111-11,120

Miller C D
1985 Holocene eruptions at the Inyo volcanic chain, California: implications for possible eruptions in Long Valley caldera. *Geology*, 13: 14-17

Sieh K, Bursik M
1986 Most recent eruption of the Mono Craters, eastern central California. *Jour Geophys Res*, 91: 12,539-12,571

Donnelly-Nolan J M, Champion D E
1987 Geologic map of Lava Beds National Monument, northern California. *U S Geol Surv Map*, I-1804

Bailey R A
1989 Geologic map of Long Valley caldera, Mono-Inyo Craters volcanic chain, and vicinity, eastern California. *U S Geol Surv Map*, I-1933, 11 p text

Bailey R A, Miller C D, Sieh K
1989 Excursion 13B: Long Valley caldera and Mono-Inyo Craters volcanic chain. *New Mexico Bur Mines Min Resour Mem*, 47: 227-254

Donnelly-Nolan J M, Champion D E, Miller C D, Trimble D A
1989 Implications of post-11,000-year volcanism at Medicine Lake volcano, northern California Cascade Range. *In*: Muffler L J P and Weaver C S (eds) *Geology, Geophysics and Tectonic Setting of the Cascade Range*, U S Geol Surv, Open-File Rpt 89-178: 556-580

Miller C D
1989 Potential hazards from future volcanic eruptions in California. *U S Geol Surv Bull*, 1847: 1-17

Clynne M A
1990 Stratigraphic, lithologic, and major element geochemical constraints on magmatic evolution at Lassen Volcanic Center, California. *Jour Geophys Res*, 95: 19,651-19,669

Donnelly-Nolan J M, Champion D E, Miller C D, Grove T L, Trimble D A
1990 Post-11,000-year volcanism at Medicine Lake volcano, Cascade Range, northern California. *Jour Geophys Res*, 95: 19,693-19,704

Wood C A, Kienle J (eds)
1990 ★ Volcanoes of North America. Cambridge, England: Cambridge Univ Press, 354 p

USA: WESTERN INTERIOR (1204-10)

Stearns H T, Crandall L, Steward W G
1938 Geology and ground-water resources of the Snake River Plain in southeastern Idaho. *U S Geol Surv Water Supply Pap*, 774: 1-268

Nichols R L
1946 McCartys basalt flow, Valencia County, New Mexico. *Geol Soc Amer Bull*, 57: 1049-1086

Gregory H E
1949 Geologic and geographic reconnaissance of Eastern Markagunt Plateau, Utah. *Geol Soc Amer Bull*, 60: 969-998

1950 Geology and geography of the Zion Park region Utah and Arizona. *U S Geol Surv Prof Pap*, 220: 1-200

Smiley T L
1958 The geology and dating of Sunset Crater, Flagstaff, Arizona. *New Mexico Geol Soc Guidebook*, 9th Field Conf, p 186-190

Coombs H A, Howard A D
1960 ★ United States of America. *Catalog of Active Volcanoes of the World*, Rome: IAVCEI, 9: 1-68

Bass N W, Northrop S A
1963 Geology of Glenwood Springs quadrangle and vicinty, northwestern Colorado. *U S Geol Surv Bull*, 1142-J: 1-74

Malde H E, Powers H A, Marshall C H
1963 Reconnaissance geologic map of west-central Snake River Plain, Idaho. *U S Geol Surv Map*, I-373, 1:125,000

White D E, Thompson G A, Sandberg C H
1964 Rocks structure and geologic history of Steamboat Spring thermal area Washoe County Nevada. *U S Geol Surv Prof Pap*, 458-B: 1-62

Waring G A, Blankenship R R, Bentall R
1965 Thermal springs of the United States and other countries of the world, a summary. *U S Geol Surv Prof Pap*, 492: 1-383

Robinson P T, McKee E H, Moiola R J
1968 Cenozoic volcanism and sedimentation, Silver Peak region western Nevada and adjacent California. *Geol Soc Amer Mem*, 116: 577-612

Smith R L, Bailey R A
1968 Resurgent cauldrons. *Geol Soc Amer Mem*, 116: 613-662

Prinz M
1970 Idaho rift system, Snake River Plain, Idaho. *Geol Soc Amer Bull*, 81: 941-948

Scott D H, Trask N J
1971 Geology of the Lunar Crater volcanic field, Nye County, Nevada. *U S Geol Surv Prof Pap*, 599-I: 11-122

Condie K C, Barsky C K
1972 Origin of Quaternary basalts from the Black Rock Desert region, Utah. *Geol Soc Amer Bull*, 83: 333-352

Laughlin A W, Brookins D G, Causey J D
1972 Late Cenozoic basalts from the Bandera lava field, Valencia County, New Mexico. *Geol Soc Amer Bull*, 83: 1543-1552

Lipman P W, Moench R H
1972 Basalts of the Mount Taylor volcanic field, New Mexico. *Geol Soc Amer Bull*, 83: 1335-1344

Stormer J C
1972 Mineralogy and petrology of the Raton-Clayton volcanic field, northeastern New Mexico. *Geol Soc Amer Bull*, 83: 3299-3322

Best M G, Brimhall W H
1974 Late Cenozoic alkalic basaltic magmas in the western Colorado Plateaus and the Basin and Range transition zone, U.S.A., and their bearing on mantle dynamics. *Geol Soc Amer Bull*, 85: 1677-1690

Hamblin W K
1974 Late Cenozoic volcanism in the western Grand Canyon. *In*: Breed W J and Roat E C (eds) *Geol of the Grand Canyon*, Flagstaff: Museum of Northern Arizona, p 142-185

Nielson R L
1974 The geomorphic evolution of the Crater Hill volcanic field of Zion National Park. *Brigham Young Univ Geol Studies*, 24: 55-70

Larson E E, Ozima M, Bradley W C
1975 Late Cenozoic basic volcanism in northwestern Colorado and its implications concerning tectonism and the origin of the Colorado River system. *Geol Soc Amer Mem*, 144: 115-178

Smith R L, Shaw H R
1975 Igneous-related geothermal systems. *U S Geol Surv Circ*, 726: 58-83

Greeley R, Black D (eds)
1977 Abstracts for the Planetary Geology Field Conference on the Snake River Plain, Idaho. *NASA TM-78, 436, Abs Snake River Conf*, 39 p

Greeley R, King J S (eds)
1977 Volcanism of the eastern Snake River Plain, Idaho: a comparative planetary geology guidebook. *NASA (Washington, DC)*, CR-154621: 1-308

Bailey R A, Smith R L
1978 Volcanic geology of the Jemez Mountains, New Mexico. *New Mexico Bur Mines Socorro Circ*, 163: 184-196

Crumpler L S
1982 Volcanism in the Mount Taylor region. *New Mexico Geol Soc Guidebook*, 33rd Field Conf, p 291-297

Kuntz M A, Champion D E, Spiker E C, Lefebvre R H, McBroome L A
1982 The Great Rift and the evolution of the Craters of the Moon lava field, Idaho. *In*: Bonnichsen B, Breckenridge R M (eds), *The Great Rift and the Evolution of the Craters of the Moon Lava Field, Idaho*, Idaho Bur Mines Geol Bull, 26: 423-437

Maxwell C H
1982 El Malpais. *New Mexico Geol Soc Guidebook*, 33rd Field Conf, p 299-301

Self S, Amos R C
1982 Large magnitude strombolian eruptions: the example of Sunset Crater, Arizona (abs). *Workshop in Explosive Volcanism (Prog & Abs)*, Consig Naziona Delle Ricerche & Nat Sci Foundation

Christiansen R L
1984 Yellowstone magmatic evolution: its bearing on understanding large-volume explosive volcanism. *In*: *Explosive Volcanism: Inception, Evolution, and Hazards*, Washington, D C: Nat Acad Press, p 84-95

Smith R B, Braile L W
1984 Crustal structure and evolution of an explosive silicic volcanic system at Yellowstone National Park. *In*: *Explosive Volcanism: Inception, Evolution, and Hazards*, Washington D C: Nat Acad Press, p 96-109

Heiken G, Goff F, Stix J, Tamanyu S, Shafiqullah M, Garcia S, Hagan R
1986 Intracaldera volcanic activity, Toledo caldera and embayment, Jemez Mountains, New Mexico. *Jour Geophys Res*, 91: 1799-1816

Kuntz M A, Champion D E, Spiker E C, Lefebvre R H
1986 Contrasting magma types and steady-state, volume predictable, basaltic volcanism along the Great Rift, Idaho. *Geol Soc Amer Bull*, 97: 579-594

Maxwell C H
1986 Geologic map of El Malpais lava field and surrounding areas, Cibola County, New Mexico. *U S Geol Surv Map*, I-1595

Hamblin W K
1987 Late Cenozoic volcanism in the St. George basin, Utah. *Geol Soc Amer Centennial Field Guide, Rocky Mountain Section*, 2: 291-294

Holm R F, Moore R B
1987 Holocene scoria cone and lava flows at Sunset Crater, northern Arizona. *In*: Bues S S (ed) *Geol Soc Amer Centennial Field Guide, Rocky Mountain Sec*, 2: 1-475

Moore R B, Wolfe E W
1987 Geologic map of the east part of the San Fransisco volcanic field, north-Central Arizona. *U S Geol Surv Map*, MF-1960, 46 p text

Dungan M A, Thompson R A, Stormer J S, O'Neill J M
1989 Rio Grande Rift volcanism: northeastern Jemez zone, New Mexico. *New Mexico Bur Mines Min Resour Mem*, 46: 435-486

Goff F, Gardner J N, Baldridge W S, Hulen J B, Neilsen L, Vaniman D, Heiken G, Dungan M A, Brixton D
1989 Excursion 17B: volcanic and hydrothermal evolution of Valles caldera and Jemez volcanic field. *New Mexico Bur Mines Min Resour Mem*, 46: 381-434

Leat P T, Thompson R N, Dickin A P, Morrison M A, Hendry G L
1989 Quaternary volcanism in northwestern Colorado: implications for the roles of asthenosphere and lithosphere in the genesis of continental basalts. *Jour Volc Geotherm Res*, 37: 291-310

Stoeser D B, Senterfit M K, Zelten J E
1989 Mineral resources of the Little Black Peak and Carrizozo Lava Flow wilderness study areas, Lincoln County, New Mexico. *U S Geol Surv Bull*, 1734-4: 1-20

Wells S G, McFadden L D, Renault C E, Crowe B M
1990 Geomorphic assessment of late Quaternary volcanism in the Yucca Mountain area, southern Nevada: implications for the proposed high-level radioactive waste repository. *Geology*, 18: 549-553

Wood C A, Kienle J (eds)
1990 ★ Volcanoes of North America. Cambridge, England: Cambridge Univ Press, 354 p

Oviatt C G
1991 Quaternary geology of the Black Rock Desert, Millard County, Utah. *Utah Geol Min Surv Spec Studies*, 73: 1-23

Hamilton W L, Bailey A L, Minor D R
1992 Holocene Yellowstone tephras: progress in locating possible source vent and dating (abs). *Eos, Trans Amer Geophys Union*, 73: 637

Minor D R, Hamilton W L
1992 Deposits and landforms produced by the Mary Bay and Turbid Lake hydrothermal explosions, Yellowstone National Park, Wyoming (abs). *Eos, Trans Amer Geophys Union*, 73: 637

Laughlin A W, Poths J, Healey H A, Reneau S, WoldeGabriel G
1994 Dating of Quaternary basalts using the cosmogenic ^{3}He and ^{14}C methods with implications for excess ^{40}Ar. *Geology*, 22: 135-138

USA: HAWAII (1302)

Brigham W T
1868 Eruption at Mauna Loa on the Hawaiian Islands. *Boston Soc Nat Hist Proc*, 12: 82-83

Green W L
1887 *Vestiges of the Molten Globe*. Honolulu: Hawaiian Gazette, 337 p

Brigham W T
1909 The volcanoes of Kilauea and Mauna Loa. *Mem B P Bishop Museum*, 2: 1-222

Hitchcock C H
1909 *Hawaii and its Volcanoes*. Honolulu: Hawaiian Gazette, 306 p

Wood H O
1917 On cyclical variations in eruption at Kilauea. *Rep Hawaiian Volcano Observ*, 2: 1-59

Stearns H T
1926 The Keaina or 1823 lava flow from Kilauea volcano, Hawaii. *Jour Geol*, 34: 336-351

Macdonald G A
1944 The 1840 eruption and crystal differentiation in the Kilauean magma column. *Amer Jour Sci*, 242: 177-189

Stearns H T
1946 Geology of the Hawaiian Islands. *Hawaii Div Hydrography Bull*, 8: 1-105

Jaggar T A
1947 Origin and developement of craters. *Geol Soc Amer Mem*, 21: 1-508

Macdonald G A
1954 The 1942 eruption of Mauna Loa, Hawaii. *Amer Jour Sci*, 241: 241-256
1955 ★ Hawaiian Islands. *Catalog of Active Volcanoes of the World*, Rome: IAVCEI, 3: 1-37
1959 The activity of Hawaiian volcanoes during the years 1951-1956. *Bull Volc*, 22: 3-70

Reber G
1959 Age of lava flows on Haleakala, Hawaii. *Geol Soc Amer Bull*, 70: 1245-1246

Macdonald G A
1962 The 1959 and 1960 eruptions of Kilauea volcano, Hawaii, and the construction of walls to restrict the spread of the lava flows. *Bull Volc*, 24: 249-294

Moore J G, Krivoy H L
1964 The 1962 flank eruption of Kilauea volcano and structure of the East Rift Zone. *Jour Geophys Res*, 69: 2033-2045

Stearns H T
1966 *Geology of the State of Hawaii*. Palo Alto, California: Pacific Books Pub, 266 p

Fiske R S, Koyanagi R Y
1968 The December 1965 eruption of Kilauea volcano, Hawaii. *U S Geol Surv Prof Pap*, 607: 1-21

Wright T L, Kinoshita W T, Peck D L
1968 March 1965 eruption of Kilauea volcano and the formation of Makaopuhi lava lake. *Jour Geophys Res*, 73: 3181-3205

Moore J G, Koyanagi R Y
1969 The October 1963 eruption of Kilauea volcano, Hawaii. *U S Geol Surv Prof Pap*, 614-C: 1-13

Macdonald G A, Abbott A T
1970 ★ Volcanoes in the Sea. Honolulu: Univ Hawaii Press, 441 p

Wright T L
1971 Chemistry of Kilauea and Mauna Loa in space and time. *U S Geol Surv Prof Pap*, 735: 1-40

Porter S C
1973 Stratigraphy and chronology of late Quaternary tephra along the South Rift Zone of Mauna Kea volcano, Hawaii. *Geol Soc Amer Bull*, 84: 1923-1940

Swanson D A, Christiansen R L
1973 Tragic base surge in 1790 at Kilauea volcano. *Geology*, 1: 83-86

Macdonald G A, Hubbard D H
1975 Volcanoes of the National Parks in Hawaii. *Hawaii Nat Hist Assoc*, 60 p

Macdonald G A
1978 Geologic map of the crater section of Haleakala National Park, Maui, Hawaii. *U S Geol Surv Map*, I-1088, 8 p text

Klein F W, Koyanagi R Y
1979 Seismicity of Kilauea and Loihi volcanoes, Hawaii (abs). *Hawaii Symp Intraplate Volc & Submarine Volc, Abs Vol, Hilo, Hawaii*, p 124

Moore J G, Normark W R, Lipman P W
1979 Loihi seamount-a young submarine Hawaiian volcano (abs). *Hawaii Symp Intraplate Volc & Submarine Volc, Abs Vol, Hilo, Hawaii*, p 127

Swanson D A, Duffield W A, Jackson D B, Peterson D W
1979 Chronological narrative of the 1969-71 Mauna Ulu eruption of Kilauea volcano, Hawaii. *U S Geol Surv Prof Pap*, 1056: 1-55

Moore R B, Helz R T, Dzurisin D, Eaton G P, Koyanagi R Y, Lipman P W, Lockwood J P, Puniwai G S
1980 The 1977 eruption of Kilauea volcano, Hawaii. *Jour Volc Geotherm Res*, 7: 189-210

Duffield W A, Christiansen R L, Koyanagi R Y, Peterson D W
1982 Storage, migration, and eruption of magma at Kilauea volcano, Hawaii, 1971-1972. *Jour Volc Geotherm Res*, 13: 273-307

Klein F W
1982 Earthquakes at Loihi submarine volcano and the Hawaiian hot spot. *Jour Geophys Res*, 87: 7719-7726

Crandell D R
1983 Potential hazards from future volcanic eruptions on the island of Maui, Hawaii. *U S Geol Surv Map*, I-1442

Decker R W, Christiansen R L
1984 Explosive eruptions of Kilauea volcano, Hawaii. *In*: *Explosive Volcanism: Inception, Evolution, and Hazards*, Washington, D C: Nat Acad Press, p 122-132

Heliker C, Griggs J D, Takahashi T J, Wright T L
1986 Volcano Monitoring at the U.S. Geological Survey's Hawaiian Volcano Observatory. *Earthq Volcanoes*, 18: 3-71

Lockwood J P, Rubin M
1986 Distribution and age of the Uwekahuna Ash, Kilauea volcano, Hawaii (abs). *IAVCEI Cong, New Zeal, Abs*, p 112

Casadevall T J, Dzurisin D
1987 Stratigraphy and petrology of the Uwekahuna Bluff section, Kilauea Caldera, Hawaii. *U S Geol Surv Prof Pap*, 1350: 351-375

Decker R W, Wright T L, Stauffer P H (eds)
1987 ★ Volcanism in Hawaii. *US Geol Surv Prof Pap*, 1350:1-1667

Holcomb R T
1987 Eruptive history and long-term behavior of Kilauea volcano, Hawaii. *U S Geol Surv Prof Pap*, 1350: 261-350

Langenheim V A M, Clague D A
1987 The Hawaiian-Emperor volcanic chain, Part II: Stratigraphic framework of volcanic rocks of the Hawaiian Islands. *U S Geol Surv Prof Pap*, 1350: 55-84

Lockwood J P, Dvorak J J, English T T, Koyanagi R Y, Okamura A T, Summers L, Tanigawa W R
1987 Mauna Loa 1974-1984: A decade of intrusive and extrusive activity. *U S Geol Surv Prof Pap*, 1350: 537-570

Lockwood J P, Lipman P W
1987 Holocene eruptive history of Mauna Loa volcano. *U S Geol Surv Prof Pap*, 1350: 509-535

Moore R B, Clague D A, Rubin M, Bohrson W A
1987 Hualalai volcano: a preliminary summary of geologic, petrologic, and geophysical data. *U S Geol Surv Prof Pap*, 1350: 571-585

Mullineaux D R, Peterson D W, Crandell D R
1987 Volcanic hazards in the Hawaiian Islands. *U S Geol Surv Prof Pap*, 1350: 599-621

Peterson D W, Moore R B
1987 Geologic history and evolution of geologic concepts, island of Hawaii. *U S Geol Surv Prof Pap*, 1350: 149-189

Sharp R P, Dzurisin D, Malin M C
1987 An early nineteenth century reticulite pumice from Kilauea volcano. *U S Geol Surv Prof Pap*, 1350: 395-404

Fornari D J, Garcia M O, Tyce R C, Gallo D G
1988 Morphology and structure of Loihi seamount based on SEABEAM sonar mapping. *Jour Geophys Res*, 93: 15,227-15,238

Moore J G, Clague D A, Holcomb R T, Lipman P W, Normark W R, Torresan M E
1989 Prodigous submarine landslides on the Hawaiian Ridge. *Jour Geophys Res*, 94: 17,465-17,484

Moore R B, Trusdell F A
1991 Geologic map of the lower east rift zone of Kilauea volcano, Hawaii. *U S Geol Surv Misc Invest Map* I-2225, 1:24,000 geol map

Wright T L, Takahashi T J, Griggs J D
1992 ★ Hawai'i Volcano Watch: a Pictorial History, 1779-1991. Honolulu: Univ Hawaii Press, 162 p

PACIFIC OCEAN (1301, 1303-04)

Cullen D J
1969 Quaternary volcanism at the Antipodes Islands: its bearing on structural interpretation of the southwest Pacific. *Jour Geophys Res*, 74: 4213-4220

Johnson R H
1970 Active submarine volcanism in the Austral Islands [Macdonald]. *Science*, 167: 977-979

Baker P E, Buckley F, Holland J G
1974 Petrology and geochemistry of Easter Island. *Contr Mineral Petr*, 44: 85-100

Macdonald K C, Mudie J D
1974 Microearthquakes on the Galapagos spreading centre and the seismicity of fast-spreading ridges. *Geophys Jour Roy Astron Soc*, 36: 245-257

Warham J, Johns P M
1975 The University of Canterbury Antipodes Island Expedition 1969. *Jour Roy Soc New Zeal*, 5: 103-131

Duncan R A, McDougall I
1976 Linear volcanism in French Polynesia. *Jour Volc Geotherm Res*, 1: 197-227

Johnson R H
1976 Possible submarine volcanic eruption off southern California. *Deep Sea Res*, 23: 265-267

Talandier J, Kuster G T
1976 Seismicity and submarine volcanic activity in French Polynesia. *Jour Geophys Res*, 81: 936-948

Clark J G, Dymond J
1977 Geochronology and petrochemistry of Easter and Sala y Gomez Islands: implications for the origin of the Sala y Gomez ridge. *Jour Volc Geotherm Res*, 2: 29-48

Baker P E
1979 Geological aspects of volcano prediction [Easter Island]. *Jour Geol Soc London*, 136: 341-345

Corliss J B, Dymond J, Gordon L I, Edmond J M, Von Herzen R P, Ballard R D, Green K, Williams D, Bainbridge A,
1979 Submarine thermal springs on the Galapagos rift. *Science*, 203: 1073-1083

Talandier J, Okal E A
1984a The volcanoseismic swarms of 1981-1983 in the Tahiti-Mehetia area, French Polynesia. *Jour Geophys Res*, 89: 11,216-11,234

1984b New surveys of Macdonald Seamount, southcentral Pacific, following volcanoseismic activity, 1977-1983. *Geophys Res Lett*, 1: 813-816

Baker E T
1991 Megaplumes [Juan de Fuca Ridge]. *Oceanus*, 34: 84-91

Chadwick W W, Embley R W, Fox C G
1991 Evidence for volcanic eruption on the southern Juan de Fuca Ridge between 1981 and 1987. *Nature*, 350: 416-418

Embley R W, Chadwick W, Perfit M R, Baker E T
1991 Geology of the northern Cleft Segment, Juan de Fuca Ridge: recent lava flows, sea-floor spreading, and the formation of megplumes. *Geology*, 19: 771-775

Haymon R M, Fornari D J, Edwards M H, Carbotte S, Wright D, Macdonald K C
1991 Hydrothermal vent distribution along the East Pacific Rise crest (9° 9'-54' N) and its relationship to magmatic and tectonic processes on fast-spreading mid-ocean ridges. *Earth Planet Sci Lett*, 104: 513-534

Binard N, Maury R C, Guille G, Talandier J, Gillot P Y, Cotten J
1993 Mehetia Island, South Pacific: geology and petrology of the emerged part of the Society hot spot. *Jour Volc Geotherm Res*, 55: 239-260

MEXICO (1401)

Ordonez M E
1906 De Mexico a Jalapa. *10th Internatl Geol Cong, Mexico, Excur Guide* 1: 1-11

Waitz P
1906 Les geysers d'Ixtlan. *10th Internatl Geol Cong, Mexico, Excur*, 12: 1-22

Atl Dr
1921 L'attivita del Popocatepetl. *Zeit Vulk*, 6: 183-191

Waitz P
1921 Popocatepetl again in activity. *Amer Jour Sci*, 5: 81-87

Friedlander I, Sonder R A
1923 Ueber das Vulkangebeit von San Martin Tuxtla in Mexico. *Zeit Vulk*, 7: 162-187

Mullerried F K G, Scheuble H
1925-26 Uber die Tatigkelt des Popocatepetl (Mexico) vom November 1923 bis Marz 1924. *Zeit Vulk*, 9: 52-55

Woodford A O
1928 The San Quintin volcanic field, lower California. *Amer Jour Sci*, 15: 337-345

Gadow H
1930 *Jorullo*. London: Cambridge Univ Press, 100 p

Beal C H
1948 Reconnaissance of the geology and oil possibilities of Baja California, Mexico. *Geol Soc Amer Mem*, 31: 1-138

Williams H
1950 Volcanoes of the Paricutin region Mexico. *U S Geol Surv Bull*, 965-B: 165-279

McBirney A R
1955 Thoughts on the eruption of the Nicaraguan volcano Las Pilas. *Bull Volc*, 17: 113-118

Foshag W F, Gonzalez-Reyna J
1956 Birth and development of Paricutin volcano. *U S Geol Surv Bull*, 965-D: 355-489

Gonzalez-Reyna J
1956 A new volcano [possible Baha Peninsula submarine volcano]. *Proc 8th Pacific Sci Cong*, 2: 25

Ives R L
1956 Age of Cerro Colorado Crater, Pinacate, Sonora, Mexico. *Eos, Trans Amer Geophys Union*, 37: 221-223

Mooser F, Meyer-Abich H, McBirney A R
1958 ★ Central America. *Catalog of Active Volcanoes of the World*, Rome: IAVCEI, 6: 1-146

Galbraith F W
1959 Craters of the Pinacates. *Ariz Geol Soc, Southern Ariz Guidebook*, 2: 161-164

Richards A F
1959 Geology of the Islas Revillagigedo, Mexico 1. Birth and development of Volcan Barcena, Isla San Benedicto. *Bull Volc*, 22: 73-124

Mooser F, Maldonado-Koerdell M
1961 Pene-contemporaneous tectonics along the Mexican Pacific Ocean coast. *Geofisica Internac*, 1: 3-20

Ives R L
1962 Dating of the 1746 eruption of Tres Virgines volcano, Baja California del Sur, Mexico. *Geol Soc Amer Bull*, 73: 647-648

Bryan W B
1966 History and mechanism of eruption of soda-rhyolite and alkali basalt Socorro Island, Mexico. *Bull Volc*, 29: 453-480

Richards A F
1966 Geology of the Islas Revillagigego, Mexico, 2. Geology and petrography of Isla San Benedicto. *Proc Calif Acad Sci*, 33: 361-414

Yarza de De La Torre E
1971 ★ Volcanes de Mexico. Mexico City: Aguilar, 237 p

Bloomfield K
1973 The age and significance of the Tenango basalt, central Mexico. *Bull Volc*, 37: 586-595

1975 A late-Quaternary monogenetic volcano field in central Mexico. *Geol Rundschau*, 64: 476-496

Gastil R G, Phillips R P, Allison E C
1975 Reconnaissance geology of the State of Baja California. *Geol Soc Amer Mem*, 140: 1-170

Alonso H
1976 Geothermal potential of Mexico. *In: Proc 2nd United Nations Symp Devel Use Geotherm Resour, San Francisco* Washington D C: U S Government Printing Office 1: 621-624

Reed M J
1976 Geology and hydrothermal metamorphism in the Cerro Prieto geothermal field, Mexico. *In: Proc 2nd United Nations Symp Devel Use Geotherm Resour, San Francisco* Washington D C: U S Government Printing Office, 1: 539-547

Thorpe R S, Gibson I L, Vizcaino J S
1977 Andesitic pyroclastic flows from Colima volcano. *Nature*, 265: 724-725

Batiza R
1978 Geology, petrology, and geochemistry of Isla Tortuga, a recently formed tholeiitic island in the Gulf of California. *Geol Soc Amer Bull*, 89: 1309-1324

Gastil R G, Krummenacher D, Minch J
1979 The record of Cenozoic volcanism around the Gulf of California. *Geol Soc Amer Bull*, 90: 839-857

Luhr J F, Carmichael I S E
1980 The Colima volcanic complex, Mexico I. Post caldera andesites from Volcan Colima (and unpub list : History of eruptions of Volcan Colima). *Contr Mineral Petr*, 71: 343-372

Nelson S A
1980 Geology and petrology of Volcan Ceboruco, Nayarit, Mexico - Summary. *Geol Soc Amer Bull*, 91: 639-643

Luhr J F
1981 Colima: history and cyclicity of eruptions. *Volcano News*, 7: 1-3

Luhr J F, Carmichael I S E
1981 The Colima volcanic complex, Mexico: part II Late Quaternary cinder cones. *Contr Mineral Petr*, 76: 127-147

Martin del Pozzo A L
1982 Monogentic volcanism in Sierra Chichinautzin, Mexico. *Bull Volc*, 45: 9-24

Robin C, Cantagrel J M
1982 Le Pico de Orizaba (Mexique): structure et evolution d'un grand volcan andesitique complexe. *Bull Volc*, 45: 299-315

Gutierrez-Coutino R, Moreno-Corzo M, Cruz-Borraz C
1983 Determinacion del volumen del material arrojado y grado de explosivadad alcanzado por el Volcan Chichonal, Estado De Chipas. *In: El Volcan Chichonal*, Mexico City: Univ Nac Autonoma Mexico Inst Geol, p 68-80

Medina Martinez F
1983 Analysis of the eruptive history of the Volcan de Colima, Mexico (1560-1980). *Geofisica Internac*, 22: 157-178

Cantagrel J-M, Gourgaud A, Robin C
1984 Repetitive mixing events and Holocene pyroclastic activity at Pico de Orizaba and Popocatepetl (Mexico). *Bull Volc*, 47: 735-748

Casadevall T J, de la Cruz-Reyna S, Rose W I, Bagley S, Finnegan D L, Zoller W
1984 Crater Lake and post-eruption hydrothermal activity, El Chichon volcano, Mexico. *Jour Volc Geotherm Res*, 23: 169-191

Duffield W A, Tilling R I, Canul R
1984 Geology of El Chichon volcano, Chiapas, Mexico. *Jour Volc Geotherm Res*, 20: 117-132

Nelson S A, Carmichael I S E
1984 Pleistocene to Recent alkalic volcanism in the region of Sanganguey volcano, Nayarit, Mexico. *Contr Mineral Petr*, 85: 321-335

Robin C
1984 Le Volcan Popocatepetl (Mexique): structure, evolution petrologique et risques. *Bull Volc*, 47: 1-25

Rose W I, Bornhorst T J, Halsor S P, Capaul W A, Plumley P J, Cruz-Reyna S, Mena M, Mota R
1984 Volcan El Chichon, Mexico: pre-1982 S-rich eruptive activity. *Jour Volc Geotherm Res*, 23: 147-168

Sigurdsson H, Carey S N, Espindola J M
1984 The 1982 eruptions of El Chichon volcano, Mexico: stratigraphy of pyroclastic deposits. *Jour Volc Geotherm Res*, 23: 11-38

Tilling R I, Rubin M, Sigurdsson H, Carey S, Duffield W A, Rose W I
1984 Holocene eruptive activity of El Chichon volcano, Chiapas, Mexico. *Science*, 224: 747-749

Varekamp J C, Luhr J F, Prestegaard K L
1984 The 1982 eruptions of El Chichon volcano (Chiapas, Mexico): character of the eruptions, ash-fall deposits, and gas phase. *Jour Volc Geotherm Res*, 23: 39-68

White S E
1984 Popocatepetl - the ever-burning torch. *Volcano News*, 17: 1-3

Carmichael I S E, Luhr J F
1985 Minettes and related lavas near Mascota, Jalisco, Mexico (abs). *Geol Soc Amer Abs Prog*, 17: 539

Hasenaka T, Carmichael I S E
1985 The cinder cones of Michoacan-Guanajuato, central Mexico: their age, volume and distribution, and magma discharge rate. *Jour Volc Geotherm Res*, 25: 105-124

Luhr J F, Carmichael I S E
1985 Jorullo volcano, Michoacan, Mexico (1759-1774): the earliest stages of fractionation in calc-alkaline magmas. *Contr Mineral Petr*, 90: 142-161

Rogers G, Saunders A D, Terrell D J, Verma S P, Marriner G F
1985 Geochemistry of Holocene volcanic rocks associated with ridge subduction in Baja California, Mexico. *Nature*, 315: 389-392

Carey S, Sigurdsson H
1986 The 1982 eruptions of El Chichon volcano, Mexico (2): Observations and numerical modelling of tephra-fall distribution. *Bull Volc*, 48: 127-142

Nelson S A, Livieres R A
1986 Contemporaneous calc-alkaline and alkaline volcanism at Sanganguey volcano, Nayarit, Mexico. *Geol Soc Amer Bull*, 97: 798-808

Nelson S A, Sanchez-Rubio G
1986 ★ Trans Mexican volcanic belt field guide. *Geol Assoc Canada*, 108 p

White S E
1986 Iztaccihuatl, Mexico. *Volcano News*, 23: 1-3

Robin C, Boudal C
1987 A gigantic Bezymianny-type event at the beginning of modern Volcan Popocatepetl. *Jour Volc Geotherm Res*, 31: 115-130

Robin C, Mossand P, Camus G, Cantagrel J-M, Gourgaud A, Vincent P M
1987 Eruptive history of the Colima Volcanic Complex (Mexico). *Jour Volc Geotherm Res*, 31: 99-113

Saunders A D, Rogers G, Marriner G F, Terrell D J, Verma S P
1987 Geochemistry of Cenozoic volcanic rocks, Baja California, Mexico: implications for the petrogenesis of post-subduction magmas. *Jour Volc Geotherm Res*, 32: 223-245

de Cserna Z, Aranda-Gomez J J, Mitre-Salazar L M
1988 Mapa fotogeologico preliminar: secciones estructurales y resumen de la historia eruptiva del Volcan Tacana, Mexico y Guatemala. *Inst Geol Univ Nac Autonoma Mexico*, Cartas Geolgicas Mineras no 7

de la Cruz-Reyna S
1988 Magnitude-characterized poisson patterns of explosive activity in Colima volcano (abs). *Kagoshima Internatl Conf Volc Abs*, p 384

Delgado G H, Carrasco N G, Urrutia F J, Casanova B M
1988 Analysis of the eruptive records of the Popocatepetl volcano, Mexico. *Proc Kagoshima Internatl Conf Volc*, p 510-517

Luhr J F, Prestegaard K L
1988 Caldera formation at Volcan Colima, Mexico, by a large Holocene volcanic debris avalanche. *Jour Volc Geotherm Res*, 35: 335-348

Wallace P J, Johnson T M, Carmichael I S E 1988
1988 Temporal, spacial and chemical distribution of late Cenozoic lavas along the volcanic front of the western Mexican volcanic belt (abs). *Eos, Trans Amer Geophys Union*, 69: 1493

Boudal C, Robin C
1989 Volcan Popocatepetl: recent eruptive history, and potential hazards and risks in future eruptions. *In*: Latter J H (ed), p 110-128 (see global reference)

Medina F, Suarez F, Espindola J M
1989 Historic and Holocene volcanic centers in NW Mexico. *Bull Volc Eruptions*, 26: 91-93

Nixon G T
1989 The geology of Iztaccihuatl volcano and adjacent areas of the Sierra Nevada and Valley of Mexico. *Geol Soc Amer Spec Pap*, 219: 1-58

Kirianov V Y, Koloskov A V, de la Cruz-Reyna S, Martin del Pozo A L
1990 Main stages of the most recent volcanism in the Chichinautzin zone, Mexico volcanic belt. *Trans (Doklady) USSR Acad Sci Earth Sci Sec*, 311: 81-83

Nelson S A
1990 Volcanic hazards in Mexico--a summary. *Univ Nac Auton Mexico Inst Geol, Revista*, 9: 71-81

Reinhardt B K
1991 Volcanology of the younger volcanic sequence and volcanic hazards study of the Tuxtla volcanic field, Veracruz, Mexico. *MSci thesis*, Tulane Univ, 147 p

Aranda-Gomez J J, Luhr J F, Pier J G
1992 The La Brena - El Jaguey maar complex, Durango, Mexico: I. Geological evolution. *Bull Volc*, 54: 393-404

Mercado R, Rose W I
1992 Reconocimiento geologico y evaluacion preliminar de peligrosidad del volcan Tacana, Guatemala/Mexico. *Geofisica Internac*, 31: 205-237

Siebe C, Komorowski J-C, Sheridan M F
1992 Morphology and emplacement of an unusual debris-avalanche deposit at Jocotitlan volcano, central Mexico. *Bull Volc*, 54: 573-589

Hoskuldsson A, Robin C
1993 Late Pleistocene to Holocene eruptive activity of Pico de Orizaba, Eastern Mexico. *Bull Volc*, 55: 571-587

Luhr J F, Simkin, T (eds)
1993 *Paricutin: The Volcano Born in a Mexican Cornfield.* Phoenix: Geoscience Press, 427 p

Martin del Pozzo A L
1993 Potential hazards from Popocatepetl and Chichinautzin monogenetic volcanoes near Mexico City (abs). *IAVCEI, Canberra Mtg Abs*, p 68

Nelson S A, Gonzalez-Caver E
1993 Geology and K-Ar dating of the Tuxtla volcanic field, Veracruz, Mexico. *Bull Volc*, 55: 85-96

Siebe C, Abrams M, Sheridan M F
1993 Major Holocene block-and-ash fan at the western slope of ice-capped Pico de Orizaba volcano, Mexico: Implications for future hazards. *Jour Volc Geotherm Res*, 59: 1-33

CENTRAL AMERICA: NORTHERN (1402-03)

Dunn H
1828 *Guatemala in 1827-28.* New York: G & C Carvill, 318 p

Squier E G
1851 On the volcanoes of Central America and the geographical and topographical features, as connected with the proposed interoceanic canal. *Amer Assoc Adv Sci Proc*, 4: 101-122

Montessus de Ballore F
1884 ★Temblores y Erupciones Volcanicas en Centro-America. San Salvador: F Sagrini, 246 p

Anderson T
1908 The volcanoes of Guatemala. *Roy Geog Soc*, p 473-489

Schneider K
1911 *Die Vulkanischen Erscheinungen der Erde* [C. Querado, Santa Ana]. Berlin: Gebruder Borntraeger, 272 p

Powers S
1918 Letter concerning San Salvador eruption. *Zeit Vulk*, 4: 201

Jaggar T A
1925 Izalco volcano. *Volcano Lett*, 19: 1

Sapper K
1925 *The Volcanoes of Central America.* Halle: Verlag Max Niemeyer, 144 p

Jaggar T A
1931 Volcano activity of Central America. *Volcano Lett*, 355: 1-3

Vazquez de Espinosa A
1942 Compendum and description of the West Indies [Fuego, Pacaya]. *Smithsonian Inst Misc Coll*, 862 p

Marden L
1944 Coffee is king in El Salvador. *Natl Geog*, 84: 575-616

Dozy J J
1949 Some notes on the volcanoes of Guatemala. *Bull Volc*, 8: 47-68

Weyl R
1952 *Estudios Geologicos de la Region del Rio Comalapa, El Salvador.* Communic Itic Ano I, San Salvador

Williams H, Meyer-Abich H
1954 Historia volcanica del de Coatepeque (El Salvador) y sus alrededores. *El Salvador Univ Inst Tropical Invest Cient Comun*, 3: 107-120
1955 Volcanism in the southern part of El Salvador with particular reference to the collapse basins of Lakes Coatepeque and Ilopango. *Univ Calif Pub Geol Sci*, 32: 1-64

Meyer-Abich H
1956 Los volcanes activos de Guatemala y El Salvador. *Anales Serv Geol Nac El Salvador*

Bullard F M
1957 Active volcanoes of Central America. *20th Internatl Geol Cong, Mexico City*, Sec 1: 351-371

Pough F H, Mulford J W
1957 The Cranbook Central American volcano expedition. *Cranbook Inst Sci Newsl*, 27: 10-29

Mooser F, Meyer-Abich H, McBirney A R
1958 ★Central America. *Catalog of Active Volcanoes of the World*, Rome: IAVCEI, 6: 1-146

Williams H
1960 Volcanic history of the Guatemalan Highlands. *Univ Calif Pub Geol Sci*, 38: 1-86

Williams H, McBirney A R, Dengo G
1964 Geologic reconnaissance of southeastern Guatemala. *Univ Calif Pub Geol Sci*, 50: 1-62

Gall F
1966 *Cerro Quemado Volcan de Quezaltenango.* Guatemala: Ministerio De Educacion, 115 p

McBirney A R, Bass M N
1969 Geology of Bay Islands, Gulf of Honduras. *Amer Assoc Petrol Geol Mem*, 11: 229-243

Rose W I, Stoiber R E
1969 The 1966 eruption of Izalco volcano, El Salvador. *Jour Geophys Res*, 74: 3119-3130

Williams H, McBirney A R
1969 Volcanic history of Honduras. *Univ Calif Pub Geol Sci*, 85: 1-101

Stoiber R E, Rose W I
1970 The geochemistry of Central American volcanic gas condensates. *Geol Soc Amer Bull*, 81: 2891-2912

Rose W I
1972 Notes on the 1902 eruption of Santa Maria volcano, Guatemala. *Bull Volc*, 36: 29-45

Bonis S, Salazar O
1973 The 1971 and 1973 eruptions of volcano Fuego, Guatemala, and some socio-economic considerations for the volcanologist. *Bull Volc*, 37: 394-400

Rose W I
1973 Pattern and mechanism of volcanic activity at the Santiaguito volcanic dome, Guatemala. *Bull Volc*, 37: 73-94

Rose W I, Bonis S, Stoiber R E, Keller M, Bickford T
1973 Studies of volcanic ash from two recent Central American eruptions. *Bull Volc*, 37: 338-364

Stoiber R E, Carr M J
1973 Quaternary volcanic and tectonic segmentation of Central America. *Bull Volc*, 37: 304-325

Romagnoli P, Cuellar G, Jimenez M, Ghezzi G
1976 Hydrogeological characteristics of the geothermal field of Ahuachapan, El Salvador. *In: Proc 2nd United Nations Symp Devel and Use Geotherm Resour, San Francisco*, Washington, D C: U S Government Printing Office, 1: 571-574

Martinez-H M A
1977 The eruption of 2 December 1976 of San Miguel volcano, Republic of El Salvador, Central America. *Center Geotech Invest, El Salvador Ministry Public Works*, unpublished rpt, 4 p

Golombek M P, Carr M J
1978 Tidal triggering of seismic and volcanic phenomena during the 1879-1880 eruption of Islas Quemadas volcano in El Salvador, Central America. *Jour Volc Geotherm Res*, 3: 299-308

Rose W I, Anderson A T, Woodruff L G, Bonis S
1978 The October 1974 basaltic tephra from Fuego volcano Guatemala: description and history of the magma body. *Jour Volc Geotherm Res*, 4: 3-53

Eggers A A, Chavez D
1979 Temporal gravity variations at Pacaya volcano, Guatemala. *Jour Volc Geotherm Res*, 6: 391-402

Hughes J M, Stoiber R E, Ide G M, Maynard S R, Mackay A
1979 Quaternary volcanism east of the Zunil Fault Zone, west Guatemala (abs). *Eos, Trans Amer Geophys Union*, 61: 69

Martin D P
1979 The historic activity of Fuego volcano, Guatemala: constraints on the subsurface magma bodies and processes therein. *MSci thesis*, Michigan Tech Univ, 87 p

Sheets P D
1979 Environmental and cultural effects of the Ilopango eruption in Central America. *In*: Sheets P D and Grayson D K (eds) *Volcanic Activity and Human Ecology*, New York: Academic Press, p 525-564

Rose W I, Penfield G T, Drexler J W, Larson P B
1980 Geochemistry of the andesite flank lavas of three composite cones within the Atitlan Cauldron, Guatemala. *Bull Volc*, 43: 131-154

Martin D P, Rose W I
1981 Behavioral patterns of Fuego volcano, Guatemala. *Jour Volc Geotherm Res*, 10: 67-81

Hart W J E
1983 Classic to postclassic tephra layers exposed in archeological sites, eastern Zapotitan Valley. *In*: Sheets P D (ed) *Archeology and Volcanism in Central America*, Austin: Univ Texas Press, p 44-51

Hart W J E, Steen-Mcintyre V
1983 Tierra Blanca Joven tephra from the AD 260 eruption of Ilopango caldera. *In*: Sheets P D (ed), *Archeology and Volcanism in Central America*, Austin: Univ Texas Press, p 14-34

Williams S N, Self S
1983 The October 1902 Plinian eruptions of Santa Maria volcano, Guatemala. *Jour Volc Geotherm Res*, 16: 33-56

Chesner C A, Rose W I
1984 Geochemistry and evolution of the Fuego volcanic complex, Guatemala. *Jour Volc Geotherm Res*, 21: 25-44

Jordan J N, Martinez M
1984 Seismic history of El Salvador. *Unpublished ms*, 25 p

Wunderman R L, Rose W I
1984 Amatitlan, an actively resurging cauldron 10 km south of Guatemala City. *Jour Geophys Res*, 89: 8525-8539

Feldman L H
1986 Master list of historic (pre-1804) earthquakes and volcanic eruptions in Central America. *In*: Claxton R H (ed) *Investigating Natural Hazards in Latin American History*, West Georgia College: Studies in the Social Sciences, 25: 63-105

Newhall C G
1987 Geology of the Lake Atitlan region, western Guatemala. *Jour Volc Geotherm Res*, 33: 23-55

Reynolds J H
1987 Timing and sources of Neogene and Quaternary volcanism in south-central Guatemala. *Jour Volc Geotherm Res*, 33: 9-22

Rose W I
1987a Santa Maria, Guatemala: biomodal soda-rich calc-alkalic stratovolcano. *Jour Volc Geotherm Res*, 33: 109-129

1987b Volcanic activity at Santiaguito volcano, 1976-1984. *Geol Soc Amer Spec Pap*, 212: 17-27

Incer J
1988 Central American volcanic events (1524-1924). *Unpublished ms*, 52 p

Mercado R, Rose W I, Matias O
1988 Eruptive history and volcanic hazard assessment of Fuego, Guatemala (abs). *Eos, Trans Amer Geophys Union*, 69: 506

Mercado R, Rose W I, Matias O, Giron J
1988 November 1929 dome collapse and pyroclastic flow at Santiaguito dome, Guatemala (abs). *Eos, Trans Amer Geophys Union*, 69: 1487

Duffield W A, Heiken G H, Wohletz K H, Maassen L W, Dengo G, Mckee E H
1989 Geology and geothermal potential of the Tecamburro volcano area of Guatemala. *Geotherm Res Council Trans*, 13: 125-131

Duffield W A, Heiken G H, Wohletz K H, Maassen L W, Dengo G, Pinzon O
1991 Geologic map of Tecuamburro volcano and surrounding area, Guatemala. *U S Geol Surv Map*, I-2197, 1:50,000 geol map

Conway F M, Vallance J W, Rose W I, Johns G W, Paniagua S
1992 Cerro Quemado, Guatemala: the volcanic history and hazards of an exogenous volcanic dome complex. *Jour Volc Geotherm Res*, 52: 303-323

Feldman L H
1993 *Mountains of Fire, Lands that Shake: Earthquakes and Volcanic Eruptions In the Historic Past of Central America (1505-1899)*. Culven City, Calif: Labyrinthos, 295 p

Vallance J W, Siebert L, Rose W I, Giron J R, Banks N G
1994 Edifice collapse and related hazards in Guatemala. *Jour Volc Geotherm Res*, in press

CENTRAL AMERICA: SOUTHERN (1404-06)

Caldcleugh A
1836 Some account of the volcanic eruption of Coseguina. *Phil Trans Roy Soc London*, Part I: 27-36

Squier E G
1851 ★ On the volcanoes of Central America and the geographical and topographical features, as connected with the proposed interoceanic canal. *Amer Assoc Adv Sci Proc*, 4: 101-122

Montessus de Ballore F
1884 ★ Temblores y Erupciones Volcanicas en Centro-America. San Salvador: F Sagrini, 246 p

Chamberlain P W
1903 The volcanoes of Nicaragua. *U S 57th Cong 2nd Sess, Senate Document*, 131: 27-33

Sapper K
1925 ★ The Volcanoes of Central America. Halle: Verlag Max Niemeyer, 144 p

Jaggar T A
1931 Volcano activity of Central America. *Volcano Lett*, 355: 1-3

Vazquez de Espinosa A
1942 Compendum and description of the West Indies. *Smithsonian Inst Misc Coll*, 862 p

Williams H
1952 The great eruption of Coseguina, Nicaragua in 1835. *Univ Calif Pub Geol Sci*, 29: 21-45

McBirney A R
1955 Thoughts on the eruption of the Nicaraguan volcano Las Pilas. *Bull Volc*, 17: 113-118

Bullard F M
1956 Volcanic activity in Costa Rica and Nicaragua in 1954. *Eos, Trans Amer Geophys Union*, 37: 75-82

McBirney A R
1956 The Nicaraguan volcano Masaya and its caldera. *Eos, Trans Amer Geophys Union*, 37: 83-96

Bullard F M
1957 Active volcanoes of Central America. *20th Internatl Geol Cong, Mexico City*, Sec 1: 351-371

Mooser F, Meyer-Abich H, McBirney A R
1958 ★ Central America. *Catalog of Active Volcanoes of the World*, Rome: IAVCEI, 6: 1-146

McBirney A R, Williams H
1965 Volcanic history of Nicaragua. *Univ Calif Pub Geol Sci*, 55: 1-65

Murata K J, Dondoli C, Saenz R
1966 The 1963-65 eruption of Irazu volcano, Costa Rica. *Bull Volc*, 29: 765-793

Krushensky R D, Escalante G
1967 Activity of Irazu and Poas volcanoes, Costa Rica, November 1964-July 1965. *Bull Volc*, 31: 75-84

Incer J
1970 *Nuevo Geografia de Nicaragua*. Mangua: Talere S de Editorial Recalde, 582 p

Oppenheim V
1970 Eruption of Arenal, Costa Rica. *Texas Jour Sci*, 22: 88-90

Stoiber R E, Rose W I
1970 The geochemistry of Central American volcanic gas condensates. *Geol Soc Amer Bull*, 81: 2891-2912

Viramonte J G, Ubeda E, Martinez M
1971 The 1971 eruption of Cerro Negro volcano, Nicaragua. *Smithsonian Inst Center Short-Lived Phenomena*, 28 p

Rose W I
1972 Notes on the 1902 eruption of Santa Maria volcano, Guatemala [Cerro Negro]. *Bull Volc*, 36: 29-45

Ui T
1972 Recent volcanism in Masaya-Granada area, Nicaragua. *Bull Volc*, 36: 174-190

Williams R L (ed)
1972 The geology of western Nicaragua. *Parsons Corp Final Technical Rpt*, 4:1-221

Carr M J, Stoiber R E
1973 Intermediate depth earthquakes and volcanic eruptions in Central America 1961-1972. *Bull Volc*, 37: 326-337

Melson W G, Saenz R
1973 Volume, energy and cyclicity of eruptions of Arenal volcano, Costa Rica. *Bull Volc*, 37: 416-437

Stoiber R E, Carr M J
1973 Quaternary volcanic and tectonic segmentation of Central America. *Bull Volc*, 37: 304-325

Linares O F, Sheets P D, Rosenthal E J
1975 Prehistoric agriculture in tropical highlands [Volcan Baru, Panama]. *Science*, 187: 137-145

Barquero Hernandez J
1976 *El Volcan Irazu y su Actividad*. San Jose, Costa Rica: Escula de Ciencias Geograficas, 63 p

Raccichini S, Bennett F D
1977 Nuevos aspectos de las erupciones del Volcan Poas. *Revista Geografica America Central*, 5-6: 37-53

Francis P W, Thorpe R S, Brown G C, Glasscock J
1980 Pyroclastic sulphur eruption at Poas volcano, Costa Rica. *Nature*, 283: 754-756

Thorpe R S, Locke C A, Brown G C, Francis P W, Randall M
1981 Magma chamber below Poas volcano, Costa Rica. *Jour Geol Soc London*, 138: 367-373

Melson W G
1982 Alternation Between Acidic and Basic Magmas in major explosive eruptions of Arenal volcano, Costa Rica. *Bol Vulcanologia Univ Nac Costa Rica*, p 1-9

Barquero J, De Dios Segura J
1983 La actividad del Volcan Rincon de la Vieja. *Univ Nac Bol Vulcanologia*, 13: 5-10

Casertano L, Borgia A, Cigolini C
1983 El Volcan Poas, Costa Rica: cronologia y caracteristicas de la actividad. *Geofisica Internac*, 22: 215-236

Prosser J T
1983 The geology of Poas volcano, Costa Rica. *Unpublished MA thesis*, Dartmouth College

Williams S N
1983 Plinian airfall deposits of basaltic composition. *Geology*, 11: 211-214

Saenz R, Barquero J, Malavassi E
1984 Excursion al Volcan Irazu. *Bol Vulcanologia Univ Nac Costa Rica*, 14: 109-116

Prosser J T
1985 Geology and medium-term temporal magmatic variation found at the summit region of Poas volcano, Costa Rica. *Bol Vulcanologia Univ Nac Costa Rica*, 15: 21-39

Sussman D
1985 Apoyo Caldera, Nicaragua: a major Quaternary silicic eruptive center. *Jour Volc Geotherm Res*, 24: 249-282

Thorpe R S, Brown G, Rymer H, Barritt S, Randal M
1985 Recent volcano monitoring in Costa Rica. *Earthq Info Bull*, 17: 44-49

Carr M J, Chesner C A, Gemmell J B
1986 Nuevos analisis de lavas y bombas del volcan Rincon de la Vieja, Costa Rica. *Bol Vulcanologia Univ Nac Costa Rica*, 16: 23-26

Feldman L H
1986 Master list of historic (pre-1804) earthquakes and volcanic eruptions in Central America. *In*: Claxton R H (ed) *Investigating Natural Hazards in Latin American History*, West Georgia College: Studies in the Social Sciences, 25: 63-105

Melson W G, Barquero-H J, Saenz-R R, Fernandez E
1986 Erupciones explosivas de importancia en volcanes de Costa Rica. *Bol Vulcanologia Univ Nac Costa Rica*, 16: 15-20

Paniagua-P S, Soto-B G
1986 Reconocimiento de los riesgos volcanicos potenciales de la Cordillera Central de Costa Rica, America Central. *Unpublished ms, Simposio Internac sobre Neotectonica y Riesgos Volcanicos*, Bogota, 1986, 29 p

Barquero-H J, Saenz-R R
1987 Aparatos volcanicos de Costa Rica. *Heredia, Costa Rica: OVSICORI-UNA*, 1:750,000 map and volcano list

Hazlett R W
1987 Geology of the San Cristobal volcanic complex, Nicaragua. *Jour Volc Geotherm Res*, 33: 223-230

Borgia A, Poore C, Carr M J, Melson W G, Alvarado G E
1988 Structural, stratigraphic, and petrologic aspects of Arenal-Chato volcanic system, Costa Rica: evolution of a young stratovolcanic complex. *Bull Volc*, 50: 86-105

de Boer J Z, Defant M J, Stewart R H, Restrepo J F, Clark L F, Ramirez A H
1988 Quaternary calc-alkaline volcanism in western Panama: regional variation and implication for the plate tectonic framework. *Jour South Amer Earth Sci*, 1: 275-293

Incer J
1988 Central American volcanic events (1524-1924). *Unpublished ms*, 52 p

Kirianov V Y, Melekstsev I V, Ovsyannikov A A, Andreev V N
1988 Reconstruction of the eruptive activity of Momotombo volcano (Nicaragua) to assess volcanic hazards. *Proc Kagoshima Internatl Conf Volc*, p 495-498

Melson W G
1988 Major explosive eruptions of Costa Rican volcanoes: update for Costa Rican volcanism workshop. *Costa Rica Volc Workshop, Smithsonian Inst*, Nov 1988, 6 p

Melson W G, Saenz-R R, Barquero-H J, Fernandez-S E
1988 Edad relativa de las erupciones del Cerro Congo y Laguna Hule. *Bol Vulcanologia Univ Nac Costa Rica*, 19: 8-10

Reagan M
1988 An outline of the recent eruptive history of Turrialba volcano, Costa Rica. *Costa Rica Volc Workshop, Smithsonian Inst*, Nov 1988, 33 p

Soto-B G J
1988 Geologia y volcanologia del Volcan Turrialba, Costa Rica. *Costa Rica Volc Workshop, Smithsonian Inst*, Nov 1988, 13 p

Alvarado-I G E
1989 *Los Volcanes de Costa Rica*. San Jose, Costa Rica: Universidad Estatal a Distancia, 175 p

Kempter K A, Benner S G
1989 Rincon de la Vieja volcano, northwestern Costa Rica: evolution of a compound stratovolcano (abs). *New Mexico Bur Mines Min Resour Bull*, 131: 150

Self S, Rampino M R, Carr M J
1989 A reappraisal of the 1835 eruption of Cosiguina and its atmospheric impact. *Bull Volc*, 52: 57-65

Stine C M, Banks N G
1991 Costa Rica volcano profile. *U S Geol Surv Open-File Rpt*, 67 p

Feldman L H
1993 *Mountains of Fire, Lands that Shake: Earthquakes and Volcanic Eruptions In the Historic Past of Central America (1505-1899)*. Culven City, Calif: Labyrinthos, 295 p

COLOMBIA & ECUADOR (1501-02)

Hulbert C
1827 *Volcanic Wonders, and Scenes of Astonishment* [Cotopaxi]. Shrewsbury: C Hulbert, Second Edition, 68 p

Friedlander I
1927 Uber Einige Vulkane Columbiens (I & II Teil). *Zeit Vulk*, 10: 159-172, 223-231

Lewis G E
1950 El Sangay, fire-breathing giant of the Andes. *Natl Geog*, 98: 117-138

Oppenheim V
1950 The volcano Purace. *Amer Jour Sci*, 248: 171-179

Lewis G E, Tschopp H J, Marks J G
1956 Ecuador. *In*: Jenks W F (ed) *Handbook of South American Geol*, Geol Soc Amer Mem 65: 249-292

Hantke G, Parodi I
1966 ★ Colombia, Ecuador and Peru. *Catalog of Active Volcanoes of the World*, Rome: IAVCEI, 19: 1-73

Hall M L
1977 ★ El Volcanismo en El Ecuador. Quito: Biblioteca Ecuador, 120 p

Miller C D, Mullineaux D R, Hall M L
1978 Reconnaissance map of potential volcanic hazards from Cotopaxi volcano, Ecuador. *U S Geol Surv Map*, I-1072

Hall M L
1980 El Reventador, Ecuador, un volcan activo de los Andes septentrionales. *Revista Politecnica, Quito*, 5: 123-136

INECEL
1980 Estudio de reconocimiento de los recursos geotermicos de la Republica del Ecuador. *Informe Geovulcanologico Realirado por Aquater/BRGM/OLADE*, unpublished rpt

Herd D G
1982 Glacial and volcanic geology of the Ruiz - Tolima volcanic complex Cordillera Central, Colombia. *Pub Geol Especiales INGEOMINAS*, Bogata, 8: 1-48

Hall M L, Vera R
1985 La actividad volcanica del volcan Tungurahua: sus peligros y sus riesgos volcanicos. *Revista Politecnica, Quito*, 10: 91-144

Thouret J-C, Vatin-Perignon N, Cantagrel J M, Salinas R, Murcia A
1985 Le Nevado El Ruiz (Cordillere Centrale des Andes de Colombie): stratigraphie, structures et dynamisme d'un appareil volcanique andesitique, compose et polygenique. *Rev Geog Phys Geol Dynamique*, 26: 257-271

Almeida E, Cruz M
1986 Estudio geologico del Volcan Reventador. *Inst Ecuatoriano Electrificacion (INECEL), Quito*, unpublished rpt, 43 p

Herd D G, Comite de Estudios Vulcanologicos
1986 The 1985 Ruiz volcano disaster. *Eos, Trans Amer Geophys Union*, 67: 457-460

Cuellar Rodriguez J V, Ramirez Lopez C
1987 ★ Descripcion de los volcanes Colombianos. *Revista CIAF, Bogota*, p 189-222

Hall M L
1987 Peligros potenciales de las erupciones futuras del volcan Cotopaxi. *Revista Politecnica, Quito*, 12: 41-80

INECEL
1987 Estudio de prefactibilidad del "Projecto Geotermico Binacional Tufino-Chiles-Cerro Negro". *Informe Geovulcanologico Realirado por Aquater/BRGM/OLADE*, unpublished rpt

Cepeda H, Munoz F, Acevedo A P, Gil F, Pulgarin B, Nieto A, Londono A, Mejia I, Calvache M L, Mora H, Carvajal C A, Banks N
1989 Reactivacion del Volcan Galeras, Colombia, Suramerica. *Unpublished ms*, 6 p

Hillebrandt-M C G von
1989 The evolution of Cuicocha volcano and the volcanic hazards associated with it (abs). *New Mexico Bur Mines Min Resour Bull*, 131: 283

Steimle U
1989 The Dona Juana volcano, Departamento de Narino, southern Colombia. *MSci thesis*, Eberhard Karls Univ, 97 p

Thouret J-C, Cantagrel J-M, Cepeda H, Murcia A
1989 Geomorphology, stratigraphy, and hazard mapping at Nevado del Tolima, Cordillera Central, Colombia (abs). *New Mexico Bur Mines Min Resour Bull*, 131: 270

Calvache-V M L
1990 Geology and volcanology of the recent evolution of Galeras volcano, Colombia. *MSci thesis*, Louisiana State Univ, 172 p

Espinosa-B A
1990 *Datos Preliminares Sobre la Actividad Historica del Volcan Nevado del Huila*. Popoyan, Colombia: INGEOMINAS, 5 p

Lescinsky D T
1990 Geology, volcanology, and petrology of Cerro Bravo, a young, dacitic stratovolcano in west-central Colombia. *MSci thesis*, Lousiana State Univ, 244 p

Parra E, Cepeda H
1990 Volcanic hazard maps of the Nevado del Ruiz volcano, Colombia. *Jour Volc Geotherm Res*, 42: 117-127

Pierson T C, Janda R J, Thouret J-C, Borrero C A
1990 Perturbation and melting of snow and ice by the 13 November 1985 eruption of Nevado del Ruiz, Colombia, and consequent mobilization, flow and deposition of lahars. *Jour Volc Geotherm Res*, 41: 17-66

Thouret J-C, Cantagrel J M, Salinas R, Murcia A
1990 Quaternary eruptive history of Nevado del Ruiz (Colombia). *Jour Volc Geotherm Res*, 41: 225-251

Thouret J-C, Salinas R, Murcia A
1990 Eruption and mass-wasting-induced processes during the late Holocene destructive phase of Nevado del Ruiz volcano, Colombia. *Jour Volc Geotherm Res*, 41: 203-224

Voight B
1990 The 1985 Nevado del Ruiz volcano catastrophe: anatomy and retrospection. *Jour Volc Geotherm Res*, 44: 349-386

Almeida E, Ramon P
1991 Las erupciones historicas del Volcan Tungurahua. *Bol Geol Ecuatoriano*, 2: 89-138

Cepeda H, Monsalve M L, Pulgarin B
1991 Origen y mecanismo eruptivo del flujo piroclastico de Agua Blanca, Volcan Purace. *Simposio Magmatismo Andino Marco Tectonico, Univ Caldas, Memorias*, 2: 40-57

Fontaine E
1991 Evolution petrologique et geochimique du complexe de domes du volcan Azufral Colombie (Amerique du Sud). *Undergraduate proj*, Univ Montreal, 58 p

Monsalve M L
1991 Caracteristicas geoquimicas y dataciones en episodios tipo San Vincente en el Volcano Purace. *Bol Geol INGEOMINAS, Colombia*, 33: 3-17

Young R H
1991 Eruption dynamics and petrology of the most recent eruptions of Nevado del Ruiz volcano, Colombia, South America. *MSci thesis*, Louisiana State Univ, 121 p

Barberi F, Ghigliotti M, Macedonio G, Orellana H, Pareschi M T, Rosi M
1992 Volcanic hazard assessment of Guagua Pichincha (Ecuador) based on past behavior and numerical models. *Jour Volc Geotherm Res*, 49: 53-68

GALAPAGOS (1503)

Martinez N G
1934 *Impressions de un Viaje a Galapagos*. Quito: Talleres Geog Nac, 182 p

Richards A F
1957 Volcanism in Eastern Pacific Ocean Basin: 1945-1955. *20th Internatl Geol Cong, Mexico City*, Sec 1: 19-31

Slevin J R
1959 The Galapagos Islands, a history of their exploration. *Calif Acad Sci Occ Pap*, 25: 1-150

Richards A F
1962 ★ Archipelago de Colon, Isla San Felix and Islas Juan Fernandez. *Catalog of Active Volcanoes of the World*, Rome: IAVCEI, 14: 1-50

Heyerdahl T
1963 Archaeology in the Galapagos Islands. *Calif Acad Sci Occ Pap*, 44: 45-51

McBirney A R, Williams H
1969 ★ Geology and petrology of the Galapagos Islands. *Geol Soc Amer Mem*, 118: 1-197

Simkin T, Howard K A
1970 Caldera collapse in the Galapagos Islands, 1968. *Science*, 169: 429-437

Cox A
1971 Paleomagnetism of San Cristobal Island, Galapagos. *Earth Planet Sci Lett*, 11: 152-160

Delaney J R, Colony W E, Gerlach T M, Nordlie B E
1973 Geology of the Volcan Chico area on Sierra Negra volcano, Galapagos Islands. *Geol Soc Amer Bull*, 84: 2455-2470

Simkin T
1984 Geology of Galapagos Islands. *In*: Perry R (ed) *Galapagos*, Oxford: Pergamon, p 15-41

Geist D J, McBirney A R, Duncan R A
1986 Geology and petrogenesis of lavas from San Cristobal Island, Galapagos archipelago. *Geol Soc Amer Bull*, 97: 555-566

Vicenzi E P, McBirney A R, White W M, Hamilton M
1990 The geology and geochemistry of Isla Marchena, Galapagos Archipelago: an ocean island adjacent to a mid-ocean ridge. *Jour Volc Geotherm Res*, 40: 291-315

Chadwick W W, De Roy T, Carrasco A
1991 The September 1988 intracaldera avalanche and eruption at Fernandina volcano, Galapagos Islands. *Bull Volc*, 53: 276-286

Rowland S K, Munro D C
1992 The caldera of Volcan Fernandina: a remote sensing study of its structure and recent activity. *Bull Volc*, 55: 97-109

PERU, N CHILE & BOLIVIA (1504-06)

Willis B, Washington H
1924 San Felix and San Ambrosio: their geology and petrology. *Geol Soc Amer Bull*, 35: 365-384

Jaggar T A
1925 Chilean volcanoes. *Volcano Lett*, 1: 1

Shippee R
1932 Lost valleys of Peru: results of the Shippee-Johnson Peruvian expedition. *Geog Rev*, 22: 562-581

Vazquez de Espinosa A
1942 Compendum and description of the West Indies [Huaynaputina]. *Smithsonian Inst Misc Coll*, 862 p

Bruggen J
1950 ★ Fundamentals of the Geology of Chile. Santiago: Editado por el Instituto Geografico Militar, p 1-374

Rudolph W E
1955 Licancabur: mountain of the Atacamenos. *Geog Rev*, 45: 151-171

Jenks W F (ed)
1956 Handbook of South American geology, an evaluation of the geologic map of South America. *Geol Soc Amer Mem*, 65: 1-378

Spann H
1956 El Volcan Ubinas. *Proc 8th Pacific Sci Cong*, 2: 56-59

Bullard F M
1962 Volcanoes of Southern Peru. *Bull Volc*, 24: 443-453

Richards A F
1962 ★ Archipelago de Colon, Isla San Felix and Islas Juan Fernandez. *Catalog of Active Volcanoes of the World*, Rome: IAVCEI, 14: 1-50

Casertano L
1963a ★ Chilean Continent. *Catalog of Active Volcanoes of the World*, Rome: IAVCEI, 15: 1-55

1963b General characteristics of active Andean volcanoes and a summary of their activities during recent centuries. *Bull Seism Soc Amer*, 53: 1415-1433

Hantke G, Parodi-I A
1966 ★ Colombia, Ecuador and Peru. *Catalog of Active Volcanoes of the World*, Rome: IAVCEI, 19: 1-73

Katsui Y, Gonzalez-Ferran O
1968 Geologia del area neovolcanica de los Nevados de Payachata. *Chile Univ Inst Geol Pub*, 29: 1-161

Guest J E, Sanchez-R J
1969 A large dacitic lava flow in northern Chile. *Bull Volc*, 33: 778-790

Pichler H, Zeil W
1971 The Cenozoic rhyolite-andesite association of the Chilean Andes. *Bull Volc*, 35: 424-452

Gonzalez-Ferran O
1972 ★ Distribucion del volcanismo activo de Chile y la reciente erupcion del Volcan Villarrica. *Instituto Geog Militar Chile*, O/T 3491

Fernandez C A, Hormann P K, Kussmaul S, Meave J, Pichler H, Subieta T
1973 First petrologic data on young volcanic rocks of SW-Bolivia. *Tschermaks Min Petr Mitt*, 19: 149-172

Hormann P K, Pichler H, Zeil W
1973 New data on the young volcanism in the Puna of NW-Argentina. *Geol Rundschau*, 62: 397-405

Parodi-I A
1975 Volcanes del Peru. *Soc Geog Lima Bull*, 94: 20-23

Gonzalez-Ferran O (ed)
1976 ★ *Proceedings of the Symposiom on Andean and Antarctic Volcanology Problems, Santiago, Chile, Sept 1974.* Rome: IAVCEI, 765 p

Roobal M J, Francis P W, Ridley W I, Rhodes M, Walker G P
1976 Physio-chemical characteristics of the Andean volcanic chain between latitudes 21° and 22° south. *In*: Gonzalez-Ferran O (ed), p 450-464 (see above)

Schwab K, Lippolt H
1976 K-Ar mineral ages and late Cenozoic history of the Salar de Cauchari area (Argentine Puna). *In*: Gonzalez-Ferran O (ed), p 698-714 (see above)

Kussmaul S, Hormann P K, Ploskonka E, Subieta T
1977 Volcanism and structure of southwestern Bolivia. *Jour Volc Geotherm Res*, 2: 73-111

Francis P W, Hammill M, Kretzschmar G, Thorpe R S
1978 The Cerro Galan caldera, north-west Argentina and its tectonic setting. *Nature*, 274: 749-751

Baker P E, Keyvan-Scocouhi F A
1982 Petrology and geochemistry of the Juan Fernandez Islands, south east Pacific. *In*: Schmincke H-U, Baker P E, Forjaz V H (eds) *Proc Symp Activity Oceanic Volcanoes*, Arquipelago, Revista Univ dos Acores, 3: 255-264

Francis P W
1982 The Cerro Galan caldera, Argentina. *Earthq Info Bull*, 14: 124-133

Hawkesworth C J, Hammill M, Gledhill A R, van Calsteren P, Rogers G
1982 Isotope and trace element evidence for late-stage intra-crustal melting in the High Andes. *Earth Planet Sci Lett*, 58: 240-254

Francis P W, McDonough W F, Hammill M, O'Callaghan L J, Thorpe R S
1984 The Cerro Purico shield complex, north Chile. *In*: Harmon R S and Barreiro B A (eds) *Andean Magmatism - Chemical and Isotopic Constraints*, Cheshire, UK: Shiva Pub, p 106-123

Stuessy T F, Foland K A, Sutter J F, Sanders R W, Mario Silva O
1984 Botanical and geological significance of potassium-argon dates from the Juan Fernandez Islands. *Science*, 225: 49-51

Francis P W, Gardeweg M, Ramirez C F, Rothery D A
1985 Catastrophic debris avalanche deposit of Socompa volcano, northern Chile. *Geology*, 13: 600-603

Naranjo J A
1985 Sulphur flows at Lastarria volcano in the north Chilean Andes. *Nature*, 313: 778-780

Klinck B A, Ellison R A, Hawkins M P
1986 The geology of the Cordillera Occidental and Altiplano west of Lake Titicaca southern Peru. *Brit Geol Surv Open-File Rpt*, 353 p

O'Callaghan L J, Francis P W
1986 Volcanological and petrological evolution of San Pedro volcano, Provincia El Loa, north Chile. *Jour Geol Soc London*, 143: 275-286

Francis P W, Rothery D A
1987 Using the Landsat Thematic Mapper to detect and monitor active volcanoes: an example from Lascar volcano, northern Chile. *Geology*, 15: 614-617

Francis P W, Wells G L
1988 Landsat thematic mapper observations of debris avalanche deposits in the central Andes. *Bull Volc*, 50: 258-278

Worner G, Harmon R S, Davidson J, Moorbath S, Turner D L, McMillan N, Nye C, Lopez-Escobar L, Moreno H
1988 The Nevados de Payachata volcanic region, I: geological, geochemical, and isotopic observations. *Bull Volc*, 50: 287-303

Glaze L S, Francis P W, Self S, Rothery D A
1989 The 16 September 1986 eruption of Lascar volcano, north Chile: satellite investigations. *Bull Volc*, 51: 149-160

de Silva S L, Francis P W
1990 Potentially active volcanoes of Peru - observations using Landsat Thematic Mapper and Space Shuttle imagery. *Bull Volc*, 52: 286-301

Gonzalez-Ferran O
1990 Huaynaputina volcano: the biggest historical dacitic eruption in the central Andes of South America, on February 19, 1600 (abs). *IAVCEI Internatl Volc Cong, Mainz, Abs*, (unpaginated)

de Silva S L, Francis P W
1991 ★ Volcanoes of the Central Andes. Berlin: Springer-Verlag, 216 p

Coira B, Kay S M
1993 Implications of Quaternary volcanism at Cerro Tuzgle for crustal and mantle evolution of the Puna Plateau, Central Andes, Argentina. *Contr Mineral Petr*, 113: 40-58

de Silva S L, Davidson J P, Croudace I W, Escobar A
1993 Volcanological and petrological evolution of Volcan Tata Sabaya, SW Bolivia. *Jour Volc Geotherm Res*, 55: 305-335

Gardeweg M C
1993 Evolution of Lascar volcano, North Chile (abs). *IAVCEI, Canberra Mtg Abs*, p 37

Petit-Breuilh M E
1994 Tabla resumen de la actividad eruptiva del Volcan Lascar. *Serv Nac Geol Min Chile*, unpublished rpt

CHILE & ARGENTINA (1507-08)

Jaggar T A
1925 Chilean volcanoes. *Volcano Lett*, 1: 1

Stone J B
1930 Two active volcanoes of Chile. *Volcano Lett*, 284: 1-3

Stone J B, Ingerson E
1934 Some volcanoes of Southern Chile. *Amer Jour Sci*, 28: 269-287

Stone J B
1935 The volcanoes of southern Chile. *Zeit Vulk*, 16: 81-97

Bruggen J
1950 ★ Fundamentals of the Geology of Chile. Santiago: Editado por el Instituto Geografico Militar, p 1-374

Muller G, Veyl G
1957 The birth of Nilahue, a new maar type volcano at Rininahue, Chile. *20th Internatl Geol Cong, Mexico City*, Sec 1: 375-396

Auer V
1959 The Pleistocene of Fuego-Patagonia Part 3: Shoreline displacements. *Suomalainen Tiedeakatemia Helsingfors Toimituksia*, Ser A-3, 60: 1-247

Shipton E
1960 Volcanic activity on the Patagonian ice cap. *Geog Jour*, 126: 389-396

Gonzalez-Ferran O, Vergara M
1962 Reconocimiento geologico de la Cordillera de los Andes entre los paralelos 35° y 38° latitud sur. *Chile Univ Inst Geol Pub*, 24: 1-121

Klohn E
1963 The February 1961 eruption of Calbuco volcano. *Bull Seism Soc Amer*, 53: 1435-1436

Casertano L
1963a ★ Chilean Continent. *Catalog of Active Volcanoes of the World*, Rome: IAVCEI, 15: 1-55

1963b General characteristics of active Andean volcanoes and a summary of their activities during recent centuries. *Bull Seism Soc Amer*, 53: 1415-1433

Auer V
1965 The Pleistocene of Fuego-Patagonia Part 4: bog profiles. *Suomalainen Tiedeakatemia Helsingfors Toimituksia*, Ser A-3, 80: 1-160

Katsui Y, Katz H R
1967 Lateral fissure eruptions in the southern Andes of Chile. *Hokkaido Univ Fac Sci Jour*, 13: 443-448

Pichler H, Zeil W
1971 The Cenozoic rhyolite-andesite association of the Chilean Andes. *Bull Volc*, 35: 424-452

Gonzalez-Ferran O
1972 Distribucion del volcanismo activo de Chile y la reciente erupcion del Volcan Villarrica. *Instituto Geog Militar Chile*, O/T 3491

Zollner W, Amos A J
1973 Descripcion geologica de la Hoja 32b, Chos Malal. *Servicio Geol Nac Argentina Bol*, 143: 1-91

Moreno H
1974 ★ Airplane flight over active volcanoes of central-south Chile. *Internatl Symp Volc Andean & Antarctic Volc Problems Guidebook*, Excur D-3, 56 p

Deruelle B, Deruelle J
1975 Geologie des volcans Quaternaires des Nevados de Chillan (Chili). *Bull Volc*, 38: 425-444

Drake R E
1976a Chronology of Cenozoic igneous and tectonic events in the central Chilean Andes-latitudes 35.5° to 36° S. *Jour Volc Geotherm Res*, 1: 265-284
1976b The chronology of Cenozoic igneous and tectonic events in the central Chilean Andes. *In*: Gonzalez-Ferran O (ed), p 670-697 (see below)

Fuenzalida-Ponce R
1976 The Hudson volcano. *In*: Gonzalez-Ferran O (ed), p 78-87 (see below)

Fuenzalida R, Etchart H
1976 Evidencias de migracion volcanica reciente desde la linea de volcanes de la Patagonia Chilena. *In*: Gonzalez-Ferran O (ed), p 392-397 (see below)

Gonzalez-Ferran O (ed)
1976 ★ *Proceedings of the Symposium on Andean and Antarctic Volcanology Problems, Santiago, Chile, Sept 1974*. Rome: IAVCEI, 765 p

Holmberg E
1976 Descripcion geologica de la Hoja 32c, Buta Ranquil. *Servicio Geol Nac Argentina Bol*, 152: 1-86

Moreno H
1976 The upper Cenozoic volcanism in the Andes of southern Chile (from 40° 00' to 41° 30' lat S). *In*: Gonzalez-Ferran O (ed), p 143-171 (see above)

Skewes M A, Stern C R
1979 Petrology and geochemistry of alkali basalts and ultramafic inclusions from the Palei-Aike volcanic field in southern Chile and the origin of the Patagonian plateau lavas. *Jour Volc Geotherm Res*, 6: 3-25

Moreno H
1980 La erupcion del Volcan Mirador en Abril-Mayo de 1979, Lago Ranco-Rininahue, Andes del Sur. *Communicaciones Univ Chile*, 28: 1-23

Ramos V A
1981 Descripcion geologica de la Hoja 33c, Los Chihuidos Norte. *Servicio Geol Nac Argentina Bol*, 182: 1-103

Frey F A, Gerlach D C, Hickey R L, Lopez-Escobar L, Munizaga-Villavicencio F
1984 Petrogenesis of the Laguna del Maule volcanic complex, Chile (36°). *Contr Mineral Petr*, 88: 133-149

Harrington R, Amini H, Stern C R, Charrier R
1984 The Maipo stratovolcano-caldera complex in the southern Andes of central Chile (abs). *Eos, Trans Amer Geophys Union*, 65: 1136

Hildreth W, Grunder A L, Drake R E
1984 The Loma Seca tuff and the Calabozos caldera: a major ash-flow and caldera complex in the southern Andes of Chile. *Geol Soc Amer Bull*, 95: 45-54

Puig A, Herve M, Suarez M, Saunders A D
1984 Calc-alkaline and alkaline Miocene and calc-alkaline recent volcanism in the southernmost Patagonian Cordillera, Chile. *Jour Volc Geotherm Res*, 21: 149-163

Corbella H, Susana Alonso M
1987 Post-glacial hydroclastic and pyroclastic deposits in the Lanin National Park, north Patagonian cordillera, Nequen, Argentina. *Andean Volc Internatl Symp, Tucaman, Argentina*, 9 p

Riffo P, Fuentealba G, Urra L H
1987 Sintesis historica de als erupciones del Volcan Villarrica, Chile. *Bol Vulcanologia Univ Nac Costa Rica*, 18: 8-11

Gerlach D C, Frey F A, Moreno H, Lopez-Escobar L
1988 Recent volcanism in the Puyehue-Cordon Caulle region, southern Andes, Chile (40.5° S): petrogenesis of evolved lavas. *Jour Petr*, 29: 333-382

Hildreth W, Moorbath S
1988 Crustal contribution to arc magmatism in the Andes of central Chile. *Contr Mineral Petr*, 98: 455-489

Hickey-Vargas R, Moreno H, Lopez-Escobar L, Frey F A
1989 Geochemical variations in Andean basaltic and silicic lavas from the Villarrica-Lanin volcanic chain (39.5° S): an evaluation of source heterogeneity, fractional crystallization and crustal assimilation. *Contr Mineral Petr*, 103: 361-386

Moreno H, Gardeweg M C
1989 La erupcion reciente en el complejo volcanico Lonquimay (Diciembre 1988-), Andes del Sur. *Revista Geol Chile*, 16: 93-117

Tormey D R, Frey F A, Lopez Escobar L
1989 Geologic history of the active Azufre-Planchon-Peteroa volcanic center (35° 15' S, southern Andes), with implications for the development of compositional gaps. *Asociacion Geol Argentina Rev*, 44: 420-430

Stern C R
1990 Tephrochronology of southernmost Patagonia. *Natl Geog Res*, 6: 110-126

Moreno H, Naranjo J A
1991 The southern Andes volcanoes (33°-41° 30' S), Chile. *6th Geol Cong Chile, Excur PC-3*, 26 p

Naranjo J A, Moreno H
1991 Actividad explosiva postglacial en el volcan Llaima, Andes del Sur (38° 45' S). *Revista Geol Chile*, 18: 69-80

Anonymous
1992 Hudson volcanic eruption of August 12-15, 1991: ash fall characteristics and natural disaster assessment in Patagonia, Argentina. *Episodes*, 15: 280

Hildreth W, Drake R E
1992 Volcan Quizapu, Chilean Andes. *Bull Volc*, 54: 93-125

Moreno H
1992 Estudio preliminar del riesgo volcanico del area de Ralco. *Proyecto Ralco, INGENDESA, Chile*, unpublished rpt

Narranjo J A
1992 Chemistry and petrological evolution of the Lastarria volcanic complex in the northern Chilean Andes. *Geol Mag*, 129: 723-740

Narranjo J A, Sparks R S J, Stasiuk M V, Moreno H, Ablay G J
1992 Morphological, structural and textural variations in the 1988-1990 andesite lava of Lonquimay volcano, Chile. *Geol Mag*, 129: 657-678

Moreno H
1993 Volcan Villarica, geologia y evaluacion del riesgo volcanico, regiones IX y X, 39° 25' S. *Serv Nac Geol Min Chile*, 1:50,000 geol map and 112 p text

Naranjo J A, Moreno H, Emparan C, Murphy M
1993 Volcanismo explosivo reciente en la caldera del volcan Sollipulli, Andes del Sur (39° S). *Revista Geol Chile*, 20: 167-191

Naranjo J A, Moreno R, Banks N G
1993 La erupcion del volcan Hudson en 1991 (46° S), region XI, Aisen, Chile. *Bol Serv Nac Geol Min Chile*, 44: 1-50

Petit-Breuilh M E
1993 Chronologia eruptiva historica del volcan Llaima. *Serv Nac Geol Min Chile*, unpublished rpt

WEST INDIES (1600)

Nicholls H A A
1880 The volcanic eruption in Dominica. *Nature*, 21: 372-373

Anderson T, Flett J S
1903 Report on the eruptions of the Soufriere, in St. Vincent, in 1902, and on a visit to Montagne Pelee, Martinique. - Part I.. *Phil Tran Roy Soc London*, Ser A, 200: 353-553

Anderson T
1908 The volcanoes of Guatemala [Soufriene St. Vincent]. *Roy Geog Soc*, p 473-489

Perret F A
1937 The eruption of Mt. Pelee 1929-1932. *Carnegie Inst Wash Pub*, 458: 1-126

Barrabe L, Jolivet J
1958 Les recentes manifestations d'activite de la Guadeloupe (Petites Antilles). *Bull Volc*, 19: 143-158

Hay R L
1959 Formation of the crystal-rich glowing avalanche deposits of St. Vincent B W I. *Jour Geol*, 67: 540-562

Robson G R, Tomblin J
1966 ★ West Indies. *Catalog of Active Volcanoes of the World*, Rome: IAVCEI, 20: 1-56

Shepherd J B, Tomblin J F, Woo D A
1971 Volcano-seismic crisis in Montserrat, West Indies. *Bull Volc*, 35: 143-163

Dorel J, Eschenbrenner S, Feuillard M
1972 Les volcans actifs de la Guadeloupe et de la Martinique, Petites Antilles. *Bull Volc*, 36: 359-381

Aspinall W P, Sigurdsson H, Shepherd J B
1973 Eruption of Soufriere volcano on St. Vincent Island, 1971-1972. *Science*, 181: 117-124

Sigurdsson H, Shepherd J B
1974 Amphibole-bearing basalts from the submarine volcano Kick-'em-Jenny in the Lesser Antilles Island Arc. *Bull Volc*, 38: 891-910

Roobol M J, Smith A L
1975 A comparison of the recent eruptions of Mt. Pelee, Martinique and Soufriere, St Vincent. *Bull Volc*, 39: 14-20

Tomblin J F
1975 The Lesser Antilles and Aves Ridge. *In*: Nairn A E M, Stehli F G (eds) *The Ocean Basins and Margins*, New York: Plenum Publishing Corp, 3: 467-500

Arculus R J
1976 Geology and geochemistry of the alkali basalt-andesite association of Grenada, Lesser Antilles island arc. *Geol Soc Amer Bull*, 87: 612-624

Roobol M J, Smith A L
1976 A pattern of alternating eruptive styles [Pelee]. *Geology*, 4: 521-524

Rowley K C
1978 Stratigraphy and geochemistry of the Soufriere volcano, St. Vincent, West Indies. *PhD thesis*, Univ West Indies, 282 p

Shepherd J B, Aspinall W P, Rowley K C, Pereire J, Sigurdsson H, Fiske R S, Tomblin J F
1979 The eruption of Soufriere volcano, St. Vincent April-June 1979. *Nature*, 282: 24-28

Sigurdsson H, Sparks R S J
1979 An active submarine volcano [Kick-'em-Jenny]. *Nat Hist*, 88: 38-43

Baker P E
1980 Geology and geochemistry of the Mansion pyroclast fall succession, St. Kitts. *Bull Volc*, 43: 303-310

Baker P E, Buckley F, Padfield T
1980 Petrology of the volcanic rocks of Saba, West Indies. *Bull Volc*, 43: 337-346

Bouysse P
1980 Sur l'existence d'un volcan sous-marin dans l'archipel de la Guadeloupe. *Bull BRGM*, Ser 2: 3-14

Le Guern F, Bernard A, Chevrier R M
1980 Soufriere of Guadeloupe, 1976-1977 eruption mass and energy transfer and volcanic health hazards. *Bull Volc*, 43: 577-594

Westercamp D
1980 Une methode d'evaluation et de zonation des risques volcaniques a la Soufriere de Guadeloupe, Antilles Francaises. *Bull Volc*, 43: 431-452

Roobol M J, Smith A L, Wright J V
1981 Revisions in the pyroclastic stratigraphy of Mt. Misery volcano, St. Kitts, Lesser Antilles: ^{14}C ages and recognition of pyroclastic flow deposits. *Jour Geol Soc London*, 138: 713-718

Bouysse P, Sigurdsson H
1982 The "Hodder" phenomenon of 1902: no submarine volcano off St. Lucia (Lesser Antilles). *Marine Geol*, 50: M29-M36

Shepherd J B, Sigurdsson H
1982 Mechanism of the 1979 explosive eruption of Soufriere volcano, St. Vincent. *Jour Volc Geotherm Res*, 13: 119-130

Sigurdsson H
1982 Tephra from the 1979 Soufriere explosive eruption. *Science*, 216: 1106-1108

Feuillard M, Allegre C J, Brandeis G, Gaulon R, Le Mouel J L, Mercier C, Pozzo P, Semet M P
1983 The 1975-1977 crisis of La Soufriere de Guadeloupe (FWI): a still-born magmatic eruption. *Jour Volc Geotherm Res*, 16: 317-334

Roobol M J, Wright J V, Smith A L
1983 Calderas of gravity-slide structures in the Lesser Antilles Island Arc? *Jour Volc Geotherm Res*, 19: 121-134

Westercamp D, Traineau H
1983 The past 5,000 Years of volcanic activity at Mt. Pelee, Martinique, (FWI): implications for assessment of volcanic hazards. *Jour Volc Geotherm Res*, 17: 159-186

Baker P E
1985 Volcanic hazards on St. Kitts and Montserrat, West Indies. *Jour Geol Soc London*, 142: 279-295

Roobol M J, Smith A L, Wright J V
1985 Dispersal and characteristics of pyroclastic fall deposits from Mt. Misery volcano, West Indies. *Geol Rundschau*, 74: 321-335

Wadge G
1985 Morne Patates volcano, southern Dominica, Lesser Antilles. *Geol Mag*, 122: 253-260

Wohletz K, Heiken G, Ander M, Goff F, Vuataz F-D, Wadge G
1986 The Qualibu caldera, St. Lucia, West Indies. *Jour Volc Geotherm Res*, 27: 77-117

Boudon G, Semet M P, Vincent P M
1987 Magma and hydrothermally driven sector collapses: The 3,100 and 11,500 y.b.p. eruptions of la Grande Decouverte (la Soufriere) volcano, Guadaloupe, French West Indies. *Jour Volc Geotherm Res*, 33: 317-323

Wadge G, Isaacs M C
1988 Mapping the volcanic hazards from Soufriere Hills volcano, Montserrat, West Indies using an image processor. *Jour Geol Soc London*, 145: 541-551

Boudon G, Semet M P, Vincent P M
1989 The evolution of la Grande Devouverte (la Soufriere) volcano, Guadalope (FWI). *In*: Latter J H (ed), p 86-109 (see global reference)

Bourdier J L, Boudon G, Gourgaud A
1989 Stratigraphy of the 1902 and 1929 nuee-ardente deposits, Mt. Pelee, Martinique. *Jour Volc Geotherm Res*, 38: 77-96

Chretien S, Brousse R
1989 Events preceeding the great eruption of 8 May, 1902 at Mount Pelee, Martinique. *Jour Volc Geotherm Res*, 38: 67-75

Roobol M J, Smith A L
1989 Volcanic and associated hazards in the Lesser Antilles. *In*: Latter J H (ed), p 57-85 (see global reference)

Shepherd J B
1989 Eruptions, eruption precursors and related phenomena in the Lesser Antilles. *In*: Latter J H (ed), p 292-311 (see global reference)

Traineau H, Westercamp D, Bardintzeff J-M, Mickovsky J-C
1989 The recent pumice eruptions of Mt. Pelee volcano, Martinique, Part I: depositional sequences, description of pumiceous deposits. *Jour Volc Geotherm Res*, 38: 17-32

Vincent P M, Bourdier J L, Boudon G
1989 The primitive volcano of Mount Pelee: Its construction and partial destruction by flank collapse. *Jour Volc Geotherm Res*, 38: 1-15

Smith A L, Roobol M J
1990 Mont Pelee, Martinique--A study of an active island arc volcano. *Geol Soc Amer Mem*, 175: 114 p

ICELAND (1700-05)

Russell W S C
1917 Askja, a volcano in the interior of Iceland. *Geog Rev*, 3: 212-221

Askelsson J
1946 A contribution to the geology of the Kerlingarfjoll. *Acta Naturalia Islandica*, 1: 1-15

Barth T F W
1950 Volcanic geology, hot springs, and geysers of Iceland. *Carnegie Inst Wash Pub*, 587: 1-126

Thorarinsson S
1958 The Oraefajokull eruption of 1362. *Acta Naturalia Islandica*, 2: 1-102

Johannsson M
1959 An autumn excursion to Vatnajokull 1959. *Jokull*, 9: 41-42 (in Icelandic)

Einarsson T
1960 The geology of Hellisheidi. *Natturufraedingurinn*, 30: 151-175 (in Icelandic)

Thorarinsson S (ed)
1960 On the geology and geophysics of Iceland. *21st Internatl Geol Cong, Copenhagen, Guidebook* A2: 1-73 p

Thorarinsson S, Sigvaldason G E
1962 The eruption in Askja, 1961, a preliminary report. *Amer Jour Sci*, 260: 641-651

Berninghausen W H
1964 A checklist of Icelandic volcanic activity. *Bull Seism Soc Amer*, 54: 443-450

Kjartansson G
1965 *Geological Map of Iceland, Sheet 5, Central Iceland.* Reykjavik: Museum Nat Hist Dept Geol Geog, 1:250,000 geol map

Saemundsson K
1965 On the geologic history of Thingvallavatn. *Natturufraedingurinn*, 35: 103-144 (in Icelandic with German summary)

Thorarinsson S
1965 Submarine eruptions near Iceland. *Natturufraedingurinn*, 35: 49-74 (in Icelandic with English summary)

Jakobsson S P
1966 The Grimsnes lavas SW-Iceland. *Acta Naturalia Islandica*, 2: 6-30

Kjartansson G
1966 The volume of shield volcano lavas. *Natturufraedingurinn*, 36: 125 (in Icelandic)

Saemundsson K
1967 Vulkanismus und Tektonik des Hengill-Gebietes in Sudwest-Island. *Acta Naturalia Islandica*, 2: 1-105

Steinthorsson S
1967 Two new ^{14}C datings on tephra from Snaefellsjokull. *Natturufraedingurinn*, 37: 236-238 (in Icelandic with English abs)

Thorarinsson S
1967a *The Eruptions of Hekla in Historical Times.* Reykjavik: Societas Scientiarum Islandica, p 1-183

1967b *Surtsey - The New Island in the North Atlantic.* New York: Viking Press, p 1-47

Kjartansson G
1968 Geological map of Iceland, sheet 2, west-central Iceland. *Icelandic Museum Nat Hist*, 1:250,000 geol map

Thorarinsson S
1968 Roadlog: Scandinavian geological excursion. *Unpublished Field Trip Guide*

1969 The Lakagigar eruption of 1783. *Bull Volc*, 33: 910-929

1970 *Hekla, a Notorious Volcano*. Reykjavik: Almenna Bokafelagid, 62 p

Jakobsson S P
1972 Chemistry and distribution pattern of recent basaltic rocks in Iceland. *Lithos*, 5: 365-386

Jonsson J
1972 Eldborgir undir Geitahlid. *Natturufraedingurinn*, 42: 59-66 (in Icelandic)

Kjartansson G
1972 The Burfellshraun lava flow and its age. *Natturufraedingurinn*, 42: 159-183 (in Icelandic with English summary)

Saemundsson K
1972 Notes on the geology of the Torfajokull central volcano. *Natturufraedingurinn*, 42: 81-89 (in Icelandic with English summary)

Thorarinsson S, Sigvaldason G E
1972 The Hekla eruption of 1970. *Bull Volc*, 36: 269-288

Piper J D A
1973 Volcanic history and tectonics of the North Langjokull region central Iceland. *Can Jour Earth Sci*, 10: 164-179

Einarsson T
1974 *The Heimaey Eruption in Words and Pictures*. Reykjavik: Heimskringla, 88 p

Jakobsson S P
1974 Eruption at Eldeyjarbodi. *Natturufraedingurinn*, 44: 22-40 (in Icelandic with English summary)

Jonsson J
1974 Obrinnisholar. *Natturufraedingurinn*, 44: 109-119 (in Icelandic)

Krafft M
1974 ★ Guide des Volcans d'Europe. Neuchatel: Delachaux & Niestle, 412 p

Thorarinsson S
1974 *The History of Grimsvotn Eruptions and Skeidara Floods*. Reykjavik: Bokautgafa Menningarsjods, 254 p (in Icelandic)

Jonsson J
1975 A few datings. *Natturufraedingurinn*, 45: 27-20 (in Icelandic)

Thorarinsson S
1975 Katla and the annal of Katla eruptions. *Arbok Ferdafelags Islands 1975*, p 125-149

Jakobsson S P
1976 The age of the Grimsnes lavas. *Natturufraedingurinn*, 46: 153-162 (in Icelandic)

Bjornsson A, Saemundsson K, Einarsson P, Tryggvason E, Gronvold K
1977 Current rifting episode in North Iceland. *Nature*, 266: 318-323

Johannesson H
1977 There is not the farm, where now is the Eldborg crater. *Natturufraedingurinn*, 47: 129-141 (in Icelandic with English summary)

Larsen G, Thorarinsson S
1977 H4 and other acid Hekla tephra layers. *Jokull*, 27: 1-19

Steinthorsson S
1977 Tephra layers in a drill core from the Vatnajokull ice cap. *Jokull*, 27: 2-27

Jonsson J
1977a Reykjafellsgigir and Skardsmnyrihraun on Hellisheidi. *Natturufraedingurinn*, 47: 17-26 (in Icelandic)

1977b Tvi-Bollar and Tvibollahraun. *Natturufraedingurinn*, 47: 103-109 (in Icelandic)

Jakobsson S P, Jonsson J, Shido F
1978 Petrology of the western Reykjanes Peninsula, Iceland. *Jour Petr*, 19: 669-705

Jonsson J
1978 Geology of the Reykjanes Peninsula. *Orkustofnun Jardhitadeild*, OS-JHD-7831, Geol maps and 303 p text (in Icelandic)

Sigurdsson H, Sparks R S J
1978 Rifting episode in North Iceland in 1874-1875 and the eruptions of Askja and Sveinagja. *Bull Volc*, 41: 149-167

Eliasson S
1979 Kerlingarholar, old eruptive fissures on the Krafla fault swarm. *Natturufraedingurinn*, 49: 51-63 (in Icelandic with English summary)

Jakobsson S P
1979 Petrology of recent basalts of the eastern volcanic zone, Iceland. *Acta Naturalia Islandica*, 26: 1-103

Larsen G
1979 The age of Eldgja lavas. *Natturufraedingurinn*, 49: 1-26 (in Icelandic with English summary)

Larsen G, Gronvold K, Thorarinsson S
1979 Volcanic eruption through a geothermal borehole at Namafjall, Iceland. *Nature*, 278: 707-710

Sigvaldason G E
1979 Rifting, magmatic activity, and interaction between acid and basic liquids. *Nordic Volc Inst Univ Iceland*, no 7903, 43p

Thorarinsson S
1979 The postglacial history of the Myvatn area. *Oikos*, 32: 17-28

Jonsson J
1979a On the age of the Svinahraun lava flow. *Natturufraedingurinn*, 49: 46-50 (in Icelandic with English summary)

1979b Volcanoes and lava flows in Skaftafellssysla. *Natturufraedingurinn*, 48: 196-232 (in Icelandic with English summary)

Einarsson E H, Larsen G, Thorarinsson S
1980 The Solheimar tephra layer and the Katla eruption of ca. 1357. *Acta Naturalia Islandica*, 3: 1-24

Gudmundsson G, Saemundsson K
1980 Statistical analysis of damaging earthquakes and volcanic eruptions in Iceland from 1550-1978. *Jour Geophys Res*, 47: 99-109

Saemundsson K, Einarsson S
1980 Geological map of Iceland, sheet 3, south-west Iceland. *Icelandic Museum Nat Hist & Iceland Geodetic Surv*, 1:250,000 geol map

Benjaminsson J
1981 Tephra layer-A. *In*: Self S and Sparks R (eds) *Tephra Studies*, Dordrecht, Holland: Reidel, p 331-336

Johannesson H, Flores R M, Jonsson J
1981 A short account of the Holocene tephrochronology of the Snaefellsjokull central volcano, western Iceland. *Jokull*, 9: 23-30

Johannesson H
1982 Summary of the geology of Snaefellsnes. *Arbok Ferdafelags Islands 1982*, p 151-172 (in Icelandic)

Johannesson H, Jakobsson S P, Saemundsson K
1982 Geological map of Iceland, sheet 6, south Iceland. *Icelandic Museum Nat Hist & Iceland Geodetic Surv*, 1:250,000 geol map, 2nd edition

Saemundsson K
1982 Excursion guide and road log for field trips A and B. *IAVCEI/IAGC Sci Assembly, Reykjavik, Generation of Major Basalt Types*

Gronvold K, Larsen G, Einarsson P, Thorarinsson, Saemundsson K
1983 The Hekla eruption of 1980-1981. *Bull Volc*, 46: 349-364

Johannesson H
1983 Submarine eruption off the Vestmannaeyjar Islands in 1637-38. *Natturufraedingurinn*, 52: 33-36 (in Icelandic with English summary)

Jonsson J
1983 Volcanic eruptions in historical time on the Reykjanes Peninsula, southwest Iceland. *Natturufraedingurinn*, 52: 127-139 (in Icelandic with English summary)

Leys C A
1983 Volcanic and sedimentary processes during formation of the Saefell tuff-ring, Iceland. *Trans Roy Soc Edinburgh: Earth Sci*, 74: 15-22

Steinthorsson S, Oskarsson N
1983 Chemical monitoring of jokulhlaup water in Skeidara and the geothermal system in Grimsvotn, Iceland. *Jokull*, 33: 73-86

Bjornsson H, Kristmannsdottir H
1984 The Grimsvotn geothermal area, Vatnajokull, Iceland. *Jokull*, 34: 25-50

Brandsdottir B
1984 Seismic activity in Vatnajokull in 1900-1982 with special reference to Skeidararhlaups, Skaftarhlaups and Vatnajokull eruptions. *Jokull*, 34: 141-150

Gronvold K
1984 Myvatn fires 1724-1729, chemical composition of the lava. *Nordic Volc Inst Univ Iceland*, no 8401, 24p

Gronvold K, Johannesson H
1984 Eruption in Grimsvotn 1983; course of events and chemical studies of tephra. *Jokull*, 34: 1-11

Gunnlaugsson G A, Gudbergsson G M, Thorarinsson S, Rafnsson S, Einarsson T (eds)
1984 *Skaftareldar 1783-1784*. Reykjavik: Mal og Menning, 442 p (in Icelandic, with English summaries)

Hammer C U
1984 Traces of Icelandic eruptions in the Greenland ice sheet. *Jokull*, 34: 51-65

Johannesson H
1984 The Grimsvotn eruption 1933 and more from that year. *Jokull*, 34: 151-158 (in Icelandic with English summary)

Larsen G
1984 Recent volcanic history of the Veidivotn fissure swarm, southern Iceland - an approach to volcanic risk assessment. *Jour Volc Geotherm Res*, 22: 33-58

Tryggvason E
1984 Widening of the Krafla fissure swarm during the 1975-1981 volcano-tectonic episode. *Bull Volc*, 47: 47-71

Johannesson H
1985 The endless lavas at the foot of Eyjafjoll and glaciers of the last glaciation. *Jokull*, 35: 83-95 (in Icelandic with English summary)

Vilmundardottir E G, Gudmundsson A, Snorrason S P
1985 Geology of the Burfell area. *Natturufraedingurinn*, 54: 97-113 (in Icelandic with English summary)

Vilmundardottir E G, Hjartarson A
1985 Pumice flows during Hekla eruptions. *Natturufraedingurinn*, 54: 17-30 (in Icelandic with English summary)

Jonsson J
1986 The lava flow at Lanbagja. *Nattururfraedingurinn*, 56: 209-212 (in Icelandic with English summary)

Larsen G
1986 Phreatomagmatic eruptions in Iceland: two case histories (abs). *IAVCEI Cong, New Zeal, Abs*, p 110

Gudmundsson A T
1986a Eruptions at Dyngjuhals in the 18th century. *Natturufraedingurinn*, 56: 43-48 (in Icelandic with English summary)

1986b ★ Iceland-fires. Reykjavik: Vaka-Helgafell, 168 p (in Icelandic)

Johannesson H
1987 Grimsvotn eruption in 1816. *Natturufraedingurinn*, 57: 157-159 (in Icelandic with English summary)

Jonsson J
1987 The Eldgjar eruption and the Landbrot lava. *Natturufraedingurinn*, 57: 1-20 (in Icelandic with English summary)

Hjartarson A
1988 The Thorsa lava--the largest Holocene lava flow on earth. *Natturufraedingurinn*, 58: 1-16 (in Icelandic with English summary)

Saemundsson K
1988 The geology of the Torfajokull region. *Arbok Ferdafelags Islands 1988*, p 164-180

Sigbjarnarson G
1988 *Krepputunga and Bruardalir--Explanatory Text to Geologic Map.* Reykjavik: Orkustofnun OS-88038/VOD-06, 44 p (in Icelandic with English summary)

Vilmundardottir E G, Snorrason S P, Larsen G, Gudmundsson A
1988 *Geological Map, Sigalda-Veidivotn 3340 B, 1:50,000.* Reykjavik: National Energy Authority, Hydro Power Div and National Power Company

Johannesson H, Einarsson S
1988a Krisuvik eruptions 1. Age of the Ogmundarhraun lava flow and the medieval tephra layer, Reykjanes Peninsula, southwest Iceland. *Jokull*, 38: 71-87 (in Icelandic with English summary)

1988b The age of Illahraun at Svartsengi. *Fjolrit Natturufraedistofnunar*, 7: 1-11 (in Icelandic with English summary)

Einarsson S, Johannesson H
1989 The age of Arnarsetur lava on the Reykjanes Peninsula. *Fjolrit Natturufraedistofnunar*, no 8 (in Icelandic with English summary)

Johannesson H
1989 Age of the Hallmundarhraun lava flow in Borgarfjordur. *Fjolrit Natturufraedistofnunar*, 9: 1-12 (in Icelandic with English summary)

Miller J
1989 The 10th century eruption of Eldgja, southern Iceland. *Nordic Volc Inst Univ Iceland*, no 8903, 29p

Bardason T
1990 Lava flows near Snaefellsjokull. *Rannsoknarverkefni Hakoli Islands*, 17 p (in Icelandic)

Bjornsson H, Einarsson P
1990 Volcanoes beneath Vatnajokull, Iceland: evidence from radio echo-sounding, earthquakes and jokulhlaups. *Jokull*, 40: 147-168

Vilmundardottir E G, Gudmundsson A, Snorrason S P, Larsen G
1990 Geological map, Botnafjoll, 1913 IV, 1:50,000. *Iceland Geodetic Surv, Natl Energy Authority and Natl Power Company, Reykjavik*

Gudmundsson A, Backstrom K
1991 Structure and development of the Sveinagja graben, northeast Iceland. *Tectonophysics*, 200: 111-125

Saemundsson K
1991 The geology of the Krafla area. *In*: Gardarsson A and Einarsson A (eds) *Natural History of Lake Myvatn*, Reykjavik: Hid Islenska Natturufraedifelag, p 25-95 (in Icelandic)

Gudmundsson A, Oskarsson N, Gronvold K, Saemundsson K, Sigurdsson O, Stefansson R, Gislason R, Einarsson P, Brandsdottir B, Larsen G, Johannesson H, Thordarson T
1992 The 1991 eruption of Hekla, Iceland. *Bull Volc*, 54: 238-246

Saemundsson K
1992 Geology of the Thingvallavatn area. *Oikos*, 64: 40-68

Sigurgeirsson M A
1992 Tephra fall formations on the Reykjanes Peninsula. *MSci thesis*, Univ Iceland, 114 p

Thordarson T, Self S
1993 The Laki (Skaftar Fires) and Grimsvotn eruptions in 1783-1785. *Bull Volc*, 55: 233-263

Pilcher J R, Hall V A, McCormac F G
1994 Dates of Holocene Icelandic volcanic eruptions from tephra layers in Irish peats. *The Holocene*, in press

Steinthorsson S, et al.
1994 ★ Catalog of Active Volcanoes--Iceland, in preparation

JAN MAYEN & ARCTIC OCEAN (1706-07)

Hantke G
1962 Ubersicht uber die Vulkanische Tatigkeit 1957-1959. *Bull Volc*, 24: 321-348

Fitch F J
1964 The development of the Beerenberg volcano, Jan Mayen. *Proc Geol Assoc London*, 75: 133-165

Birkenmajer K
1972 Geotectonic aspects of the Beerenberg volcanic eruption 1970 Jan Mayen Island. *Acta Geol Polon*, 22: 1-15

Siggerud T
1972 The volcanic eruption on Jan Mayen 1970. *Norsk Polarinstitutt Arbok 1970*, p 5-18

Sylvester A G
1975 History and surveillance of volcanic activity on Jan Mayen Island. *Bull Volc*, 39: 313-335

Imsland P
1984 Petrology, mineralogy and evolution of the Jan Mayen magma system. *Visindafelag Islendinga, Reykjavik, Pub* no 43, 332 p

Imsland P
1986 The volcanic eruption on Jan Mayen, January 1985: interaction between a volcanic island and a fracture zone. *Jour Volc Geotherm Res*, 28: 45-54

AZORES & N ATLANTIC OCEAN (1801-02)

Weston F S
1964 List of recorded volcanic eruptions in the Azores with brief reports. *Bol Mus Lab Miner, Geol Fac Ciencas Lisboa*, 10: 3-18

Neumann van Padang M, Richards A F, Machado F Bravo T, Baker E, Le Maitre W
1967 ★ Atlantic Ocean. *Catalog of Active Volcanoes of the World*, Rome: IAVCEI, 21: 1-128

Walker G P L, Croasdale R
1970 Two Plinian-type eruptions in the Azores. *Jour Geol Soc London*, 127: 17-55

Shotton F W, Williams R E G, Johnson A S
1974 [Radiocarbon dates on Terceira volcano]. *Radiocarbon*, 16: 293

Mitchell-Thome R C
1976 ★ Geology of the Middle Atlantic Islands. Berlin: Gebruder Borntraeger, 382 p

Self S
1976 The recent volcanology of Terceira, Azores. *Jour Geol Soc London*, 132: 645-666

Booth B, Croasdale R, Walker G P L
1978 A quantitative study of five thousand years of volcanism on Sao Miguel, Azores. *Phil Trans Roy Soc London*, Ser A, 288: 271-319

Mitchell-Thome R C
1981 Vulcanicity of Historic Times in the Middle Atlantic Islands. *Bull Volc*, 44: 57-70

Machado F
1982 Excursion guide for field trip V3, Islands of Fayal and Pico. *Proc Internatl Symp Activity Oceanic Volc, Archipelago Univ Azores*, 3: 343-349

Martins J A
1982 Excursion guide for field trip V1, Island of Sao Miguel. *Proc Internatl Symp Activity Oceanic Volc, Archipelago Univ Azores*, 3: 315-328

Moore R B
1983a Preliminary geologic map of Sete Cidades volcano, Sao Miguel, Azores (1:18,000). *U S Geol Surv Open-File Rpt*, 83-742

1983b Preliminary geologic map of Furnas volcano, Sao Miguel, Azores (1:15,000). *U S Geol Surv Open-File Rpt*, 83-395

Morisseau M, Traineau H
1985 Mise en evidence d'une activite hydromagmatique Holocene sur l'Ile de Flores (Acores). *Comptes Rendus Acad Sci Paris*, 301: 1309-1314

Moore R B
1986 Preliminary geologic map of Agua de Pau volcano, Sao Miguel, Azores. *U S Geol Surv Open-File Rpt*, 86-192
1990 Volcanic geology and eruption frequency, Sao Miguel, Azores. *Bull Volc*, 52: 602-614
1991 Geologic map of Sao Miguel, Azores. *U S Geol Surv Map*, I-2007

Moore R B, Rubin M
1991 Radiocarbon dates for lava flows and pyroclastic deposits on Sao Miguel, Azores. *Radiocarbon*, 33: 151-164

CANARY IS & ATLANTIC: CENTRAL & S (1803-06)

Almeida F F M
1961 Geologia e petrologia da Ilha da Trindade. *Dept Nac Producao Min, Rio de Janeiro*, Monografia 17

Machado F
1963 Erupcoes da Ilha de la Palma (Canarias). *Bolivia Museum Laboratory Min Geol Fac Ciencas Lisbon*, 9: 143-157

Baker P E
1967 Historical and geological notes on Bouvetoya. *Brit Antarctic Surv Bull*, 13: 71-84

Lamb H H
1967 The problem of "Thompson Island" volcanic eruptions and meteorological evidence. *Brit Antarctic Surv Bull*, 13: 85-88

Neumann van Padang M, Richards A F, Machado F Bravo T, Baker E, Le Maitre W
1967 ★ Atlantic Ocean. *Catalog of Active Volcanoes of the World*, Rome: IAVCEI, 21: 1-128

Fuster J M, Arana V, Brandle J L, Navarro M, Alonso U, Aparicio A
1968 *Geology and Volcanology of the Canary Islands - Tenerife.* Madrid: Inst "Lucas Mallada", 218 p

Fuster J M, Cendrero A, Gastesi P, Ibarrola E, Lopez Ruiz J
1968 *Geology and Volcanology of the Canary Islands - Fuerteventura.* Madrid: Inst "Lucas Mallada", 239 p

Fuster J M, Fernandez Santin S, Sagredo J
1968 *Geology and Volcanology of the Canary Islands - Lanzarote.* Madrid: Inst "Lucas Mallada", 177 p

Fuster M, Hernandez-Pacheco A, Munoz M, Rodriguez Badiola E, Garcia Cacho L
1968 *Geology and Volcanology of the Canary Islands - Gran Canaria.* Madrid: Inst "Lucas Mallada", 243 p

Nogales J, Schminke H-U
1968 El pino enterrado de la Canada de las Arenas (Gran Canaria). *Cuadernos Botanica Canario*, 5: 23-25

Ridley W I
1971 The field relations of the Canadas volcanoes, Tenerife, Canary Islands. *Bull Volc*, 35: 318-334

Bell J D, Atkins F B, Baker P E, Smith D G W
1972 Notes on the petrology and age of Ascension Island, south Atlantic (abs). *Eos, Trans Amer Geophys Union*, 53: 168

Hausen H
1972 Outlines of the geology of Hierro (Canary Islands). *Finska Vetenskapssocietan Helsingfors, Commentationes Physico-Mathematicae*, 43: 65-148

Afonso A
1974 Geological sketch and historic volcanoes in La Palma, Canary Islands. *Estudios Geol, V Teneguia*, p 7-13

Mitchell-Thome R C
1976 ★ Geology of the Middle Atlantic Islands. Berlin: Gebruder Borntraeger, 382 p

Verwoerd W J, Erlank A J, Kable E J D
1976 Geology and geochemistry of Bouvet Island. *In*: Gonzalez-Ferran O (ed), p 203-237 (see Antarctica reference)

Arana V, Carracedo J C
1979 *Los Volcanes de las Islas Canarias. II. Lanzarote-Fuerteventura.* Madrid: Rueda, 176 p

Mitchell-Thome R C
1981 Vulcanicity of Historic Times in the Middle Atlantic Islands. *Bull Volc*, 44: 57-70

Hernandez-Pacheco A, Valls M C
1982 The historic eruptions of La Palma Island (Canaries). *Proc Internatl Symp Activity Oceanic Volc, Archipelago Univ Azores*, 3: 83-94

Prestvik T
1982 The geology, volcanic activity, and age of Bouvetoya, south Atlantic. *Proc Internatl Symp Activity Oceanic Volc, Archipelago Univ Azores*, 3: 115-123

Soler V, Carracedo J C, Heller F
1984 Geomagnetic secular variation in historical lavas from the Canary Islands. *Geophys Jour Roy Astron Soc*, 78: 313-318

Wolff J A, Turbeville B N
1985 Recent pyroclastic deposits on Brava, Cape Verde Islands (abs). *Eos, Trans Amer Geophys Union*, 66: 1152

Ortiz R, Arana V, Valberde C
1986 Aproximacion al conocimiento del mecanismo de la erupcion de 1730-1736 en Lanzarote. *Sociedad Espanola Fisica, Anales Fisica* Ser B, 82: 127-142

Chevallier L, Verwoerd W J
1987 A dynamic interpretation of Tristan da Cunha volcano, South Atlantic Ocean. *Jour Volc Geotherm Res*, 34: 35-49

Ancochea E, Fuster J M, Ibarrola E, Cendrero A, Coello J, Hernan F, Cantagrel M, Jamond C
1990 Volcanic evolution of the island of Tenerife (Canary Islands) in the light of new K-Ar data. *Jour Volc Geotherm Res*, 44: 231-249

LeMasurier W E, Thomson J W (eds)
1990 ★ Volcanoes of the Antarctic Plate and Southern Oceans. Washington, D C: Amer Geophys Union, 487 p

Schminke H-U
1990 Geological field guide--Gran Canaria. *IAVCEI Internatl Volc Cong, Mainz*, Excur 7BI: 1-199

Carracedo J C, Badiola E R
1991 *Lanzarote, la Erupcion Volcanica de 1730.* Lanzarote: Servicio de Publicaciones, 184 p

Romero C
1991 ★ *Las Manifestaciones Volcanicas Historicas del Archipielago Canario.* Tenerife: Gobierno de Canarias, 2 vol, 695 & 768 p

Carracedo J C, Badiola E R, Soler V
1992 The 1730-1736 eruption of Lanzarote, Canary Islands: a long, high-magnitude basaltic fissure eruption. *Jour Volc Geotherm Res*, 53: 239-250

ANTARCTICA & S SANDWICH IS (1900)

Berninghausen W H, Neumann van Padang M
1960 ★ Antarctica. *Catalog of Active Volcanoes of the World*, Rome: IAVCEI, 10: 1-32

Gass I G, Harris P G, Holdgate M W
1963 Pumice eruption in the area of the south Sandwich Islands. *Geol Mag*, 100: 321-330

Craddock C, Bastien T W, Rutford R H
1964 Geology of the Jones Mountains area. *In*: Adie R J (ed) *Antarctic Geol, Proc 1st Internatl Symp Antarctic Geol*, Amsterdam: Elsevier, p 172-187

Quartermain L B
1964 The Balleny Islands a descriptive and historical outline. *Antarctic Div Dept Sci Ind Res*, p 1-10

Coombs D S, Landis C A
1966 Pumice from the South Sandwich eruption of March 1962 reaches New Zealand. *Nature*, 209: 289-290

Baker P E
1968 Comparative volcanology and petrology of the Atlantic island arcs. *Bull Volc*, 32: 189-206

Nathan S, Schulte F J
1968 Geology and petrology of the Campbell-Aviator Divide, Northern Victoria Land, Antarctica, Part 1 Post Paleozoic rocks. *New Zeal Jour Geol Geophys*, 11: 940-975

Riddolls B W, Hancox G T
1968 The geology of the Upper Mariner Glacier region, North Victoria Land, Antarctica. *New Zeal Jour Geol Geophys*, 11: 881-899

Baker P E, Davies T G, Roobol M J
1969 Volcanic activity at Deception Island in 1967 and 1968. *Nature*, 224: 553-560

LeMasurier W E
1971 Spatial variation in Cenozoic volcanism of Marie Byrd Land and Ellsworth Land. *Antarctic Jour United States*, 6: 187-188

Adie R J (ed)
1972 *Antarctic Geology and Geophysics.* Oslo: Universitetsforlaget, 875 p

Dort W
1972 Late Cenozoic volcanism in Antarctica. *In*: Adie R J (ed) *Antarctic Geol and Geophys*, IUGS Ser-B(1): 645-652

Gonzalez-Ferran O
1972 Distribucion del volcanismo activo de Chile y la reciente erupcion del Volcan Villarrica. *Instituto Geog Militar Chile*, O/T 3491

Gonzalez-Ferran O, Gonzalez-Bonorino F
1972 The volcanic ranges of Marie Byrd land between long 100° and 140° W. *In*: Adie R J (ed), p 261-275 (see above)

LeMasurier W E
1972 Volcanic record of Cenozoic glacial history Marie Byrd Land. *In*: Adie R J (ed), p 251-260 (see above)

Orheim O
1972 Volcanic activity on Deception Island, South Shetland Islands. *In*: Adie R J (ed), p 117-120 (see above)

Shultz C H
1972 Eruption at Deception Island, Antarctica, August 1970. *Geol Soc Amer Bull*, 83: 2837-2842

Baker P E, Gonzalez-Ferran O, Vergara M
1973 Paulet Island and the James Ross Island volcanic group. *Brit Antarctic Surv Bull*, 32: 89-95

Giggenbach W F, Kyle P R, Lyon G L
1973 Present volcanic activity on Mount Erebus, Ross Island, Antarctica. *Geology*, 1: 135-136

Roobol M J
1973 Historic volcanic activity at Deception Island. *Brit Antarctic Surv Bull*, 32: 23-30

Treves S B, Kyle P R
1973 Renewed volcanic activity of Mt. Erebus, Antarctica. *Antarctic Jour United States*, 8: 156

Lyon G L, Giggenbach W F
1974 Geothermal activity in Victoria Land, Antarctica. *New Zeal Jour Geol Geophys*, 17: 511-521

Baker P E, McReath I, Harvey M R, Roobol M J, Davies T
1975 The geology of the South Shetland Islands: V. Volcanic evolution of Deception Island. *Brit Antarctic Surv Sci Rpt*, 78: 1-81

Baker P E, Gonzalez-Ferran O, Vergara M
1976 Geology and geochemistry of Paulet Island and the James Ross Island volcanic group. *In*: Gonzalez-Ferran O (ed), p 39-47 (see above)

Gonzalez-Ferran O (ed)
1976 *Proceedings of the Symposium on Andean and Antarctic Volcanology Problems, Santiago, Chile, Sept 1974*. Rome: IAVCEI, 765 p

LeMasurier W E, Wade F A
1976 Volcanic history in Marie Byrd Land: implications with regard to southern hemisphere tectonic reconstructions. *In*: Gonzalez-Ferran O (ed), p 398-424 (see above)

Kyle P R, Jezek P A
1978 Compositions of three tephra layers from the Byrd Station Ice Core, Antarctica. *Jour Volc Geotherm Res*, 4: 225-232

Kyle P R, McIntosh W
1978 Observations of volcanic activity at Mt. Erebus. *Antarctic Jour United States*, 13: 32-34

Birkenmajer K
1979 Age of the Penguin Island volcano, South Shetland Islands (West Antarctica), by the Lichenometric Method. *Bull Acad Polonaise, Sci Ser Sci Terre*, 27(1-2): 69-76

Roobol M J
1979 A model for the eruptive mechanism of Deception Island from 1820 to 1970. *Brit Antarctic Surv Bull*, 49: 137-156

Kyle P R
1982 Volcanic geology of the Pleiades, Northern Victoria Land, Antarctica. *In*: Craddock C (ed) *Antarctic Geoscience*, Madison: Univ Wisconsin Press, p 747-754

Kyle P R, Dibble R R, Giggenbach W F, Keys J
1982 Volcanic activity associated with the anorthoclase phonolite lava lake, Mount Erebus, Antarctica. *In*: Craddock C (ed) *Antarctic Geoscience*, Madison: Univ Wisconsin Press, p 735-745

Kyle P, Palais J, Delmas R
1982 The volcanic record of Antarctic ice cores: preliminary results and potential for future investigations. *Annals Glaciology*, 3: 172-177

Gonzalez-Ferran O
1983 The Seal Nunataks: an active volcanic group on the Larsen Ice Shelf, West Antarctica. *In*: Oliver R L, James P R, Jago J B (eds) *Antarctic Earth Science*, New York: Cambridge Univ Press, p 334-337

Keys J R, McIntosh W C, Kyle P R
1983 Volcanic activity of Mount Melbourne, Northern Victoria Land. *Antarctic Jour United States*, 18: 10-11

Behrendt J C, Cooper A K, Yuan A
1987 Interpretation of marine magnetic gradiometer and multichannel seismic-reflection observations over the western Ross Sea shelf, Antarctica. *In*: Cooper A K and Davey F J (eds) *The Antarctic Continental Margin: Geol and Geophys of the Western Ross Sea*, Circum-Pacific Council Energy Mineral Resour Earth Sci Ser, 5B: 155-177

Palais J M, Kyle P R, Mosley-Thompson E, Thomas E
1987 Correlation of a 3200 year old tephra in ice cores from Vostok and South Pole Stations, Antarctica. *Geophys Res Lett*, 14: 804-807

LeMasurier W E, Thomson J W (eds)
1990 H Volcanoes of the Antarctic Plate and Southern Oceans. Washington, D C: Amer Geophys Union, 487 p

Prestvik T, Barnes C G, Sundvoll B, Duncan R A
1990 Petrology of Peter I Oy (Peter I Island), west Antarctica. *Jour Volc Geotherm Res*, 44: 315-338

SOURCE VOLCANO UNKNOWN

Baillie M G L, Munro M A R
1988 Irish tree-rings, Santorini and volcanic dust veils. *Nature*, 332: 344-346

Delmas R J, Kirchner S, Palais J M, Petit J-R
1992 1000 years of explosive volcanism at the South Pole. *Tellus*, 44B: 335-350

Pilcher J R, Hall V A, McCormac F G
1994 Dates of Holocene Icelandic volcanic eruptions from tephra layers in Irish peats. *The Holocene*, in press

Zielinski G A, Mayewski P A, Meeker L D, Whitlow S, Twickler M S, Morrison M, Meese D A, Gow A J, Alley R B
1994 Record of volcanism since 7000 B.C. from the GISP2 Greenland ice core and implications for the volcano-climate system. *Science*, 264: 948-952

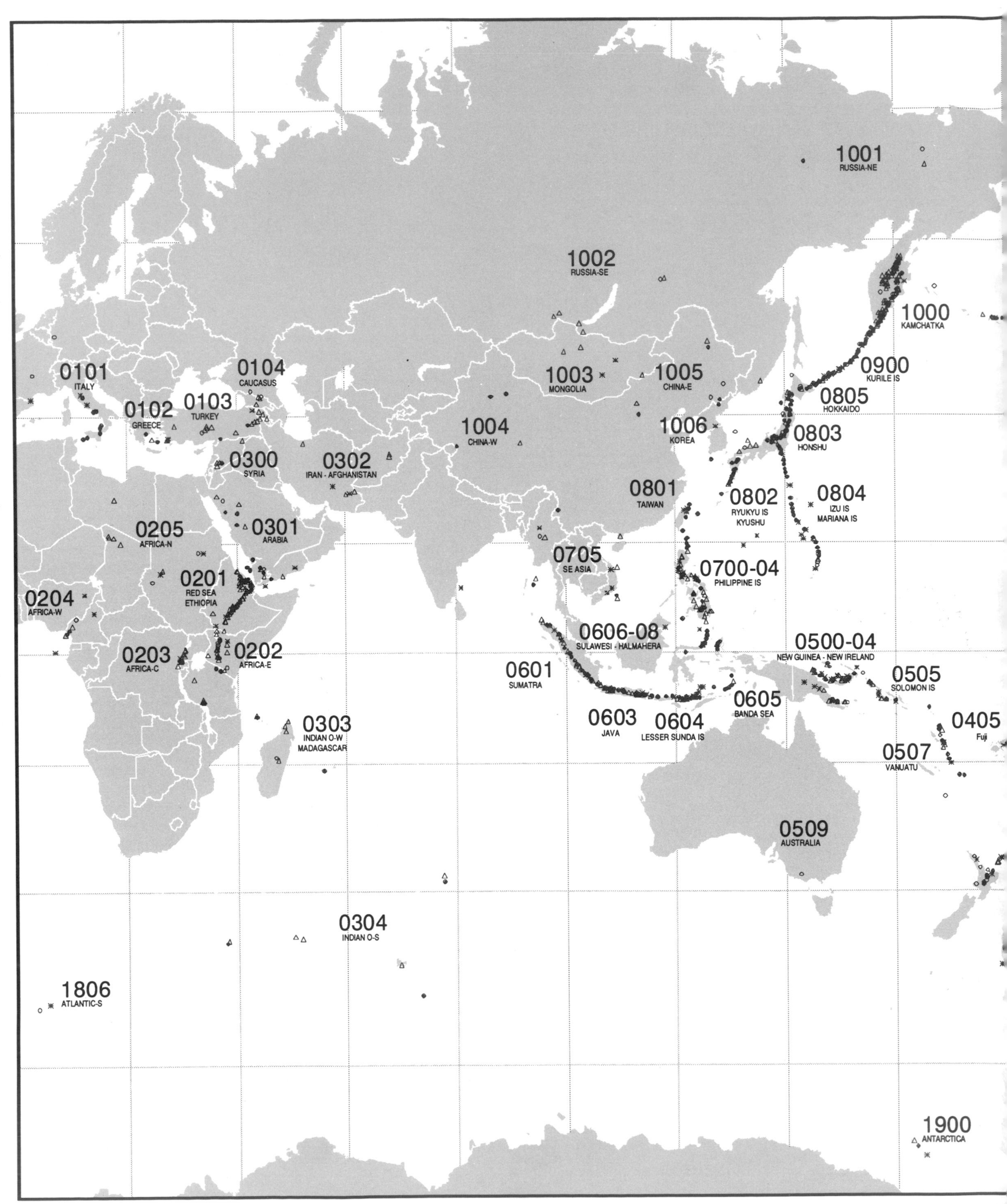

1001
RUSSIA-NE
1002
RUSSIA-SE
1000
KAMCHATKA
0101
ITALY
0104
CAUCASUS
1003
MONGOLIA
1005
CHINA-E
0900
KURILE IS
0102
GREECE
0103
TURKEY
0805
HOKKAIDO
1004
CHINA-W
1006
KOREA
0803
HONSHU
0300
SYRIA
0302
IRAN - AFGHANISTAN
0801
TAIWAN
0802
RYUKYU IS
KYUSHU
0804
IZU IS
MARIANA IS
0205
AFRICA-N
0301
ARABIA
0705
SE ASIA
0700-04
PHILIPPINE IS
0201
RED SEA
ETHIOPIA
0204
AFRICA-W
0606-08
SULAWESI - HALMAHERA
0500-04
NEW GUINEA - NEW IRELAND
0203
AFRICA-C
0202
AFRICA-E
0601
SUMATRA
0505
SOLOMON IS
0605
BANDA SEA
0303
INDIAN O-W
MADAGASCAR
0603
JAVA
0604
LESSER SUNDA IS
0405
Fuji
0507
VANUATU
0509
AUSTRALIA
0304
INDIAN O-S
1806
ATLANTIC-S
1900
ANTARCTICA